The **Rough Guide** to

Germany

written and researched by

Gordon McLachlan

NEW YORK • LONDON • DELHI

www.roughguides.com

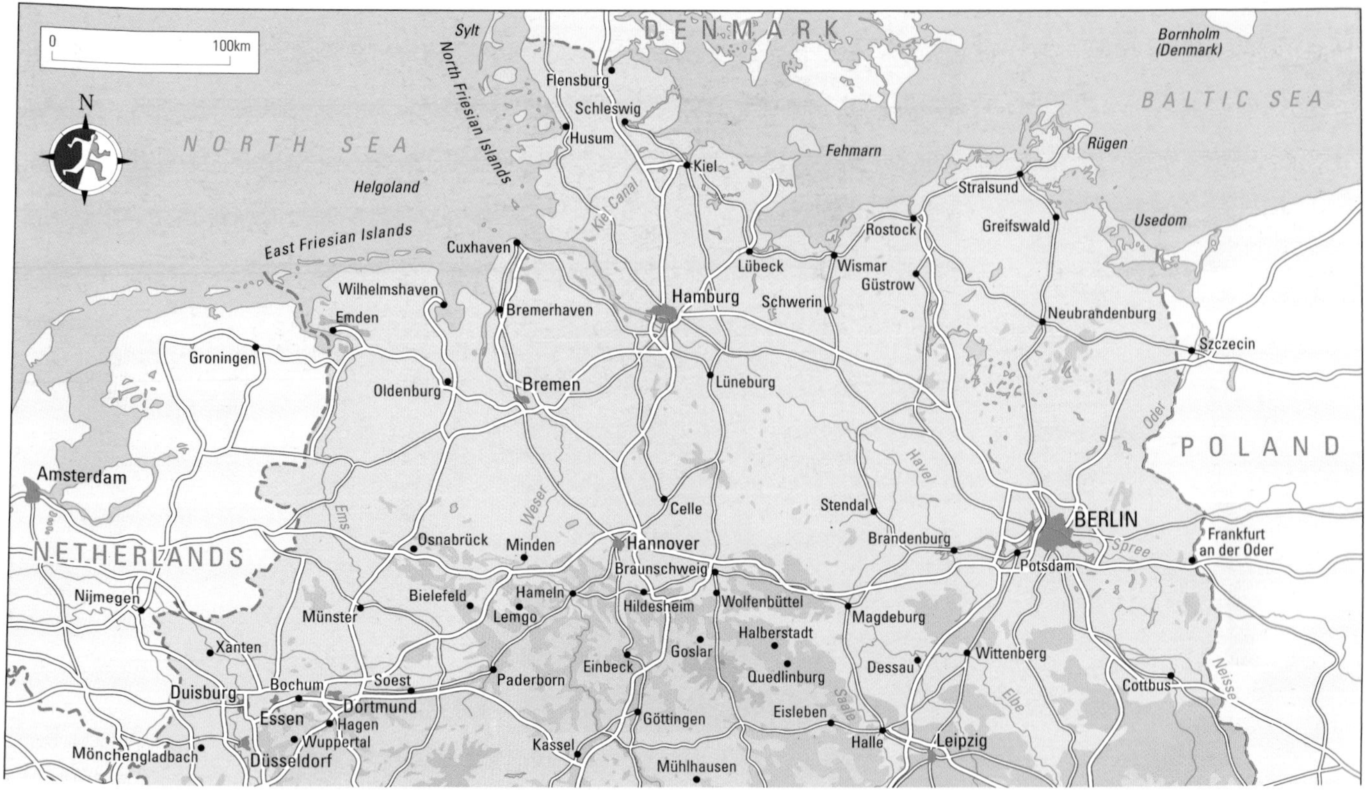

0 100km
N
NORTH SEA
BALTIC SEA
DENMARK
POLAND
NETHERLANDS
Bornholm (Denmark)
Sylt
North Friesian Islands
Helgoland
East Friesian Islands
Fehmarn
Rügen
Usedom
Flensburg
Schleswig
Husum
Kiel
Kiel Canal
Cuxhaven
Wilhelmshaven
Emden
Bremerhaven
Groningen
Oldenburg
Bremen
Hamburg
Lübeck
Wismar
Rostock
Güstrow
Schwerin
Stralsund
Greifswald
Neubrandenburg
Szczecin
Lüneburg
Amsterdam
Ems
Weser
Celle
Havel
Stendal
Oder
BERLIN
Spree
Frankfurt an der Oder
Brandenburg
Potsdam
Osnabrück
Minden
Hannover
Braunschweig
Nijmegen
Bielefeld
Hameln
Lemgo
Hildesheim
Wolfenbüttel
Magdeburg
Münster
Halberstadt
Goslar
Xanten
Einbeck
Wittenberg
Dessau
Quedlinburg
Paderborn
Soest
Bochum
Duisburg
Dortmund
Essen
Hagen
Wuppertal
Mönchengladbach
Düsseldorf
Göttingen
Eisleben
Saale
Elbe
Cottbus
Neisse
Kassel
Halle
Leipzig
Mühlhausen

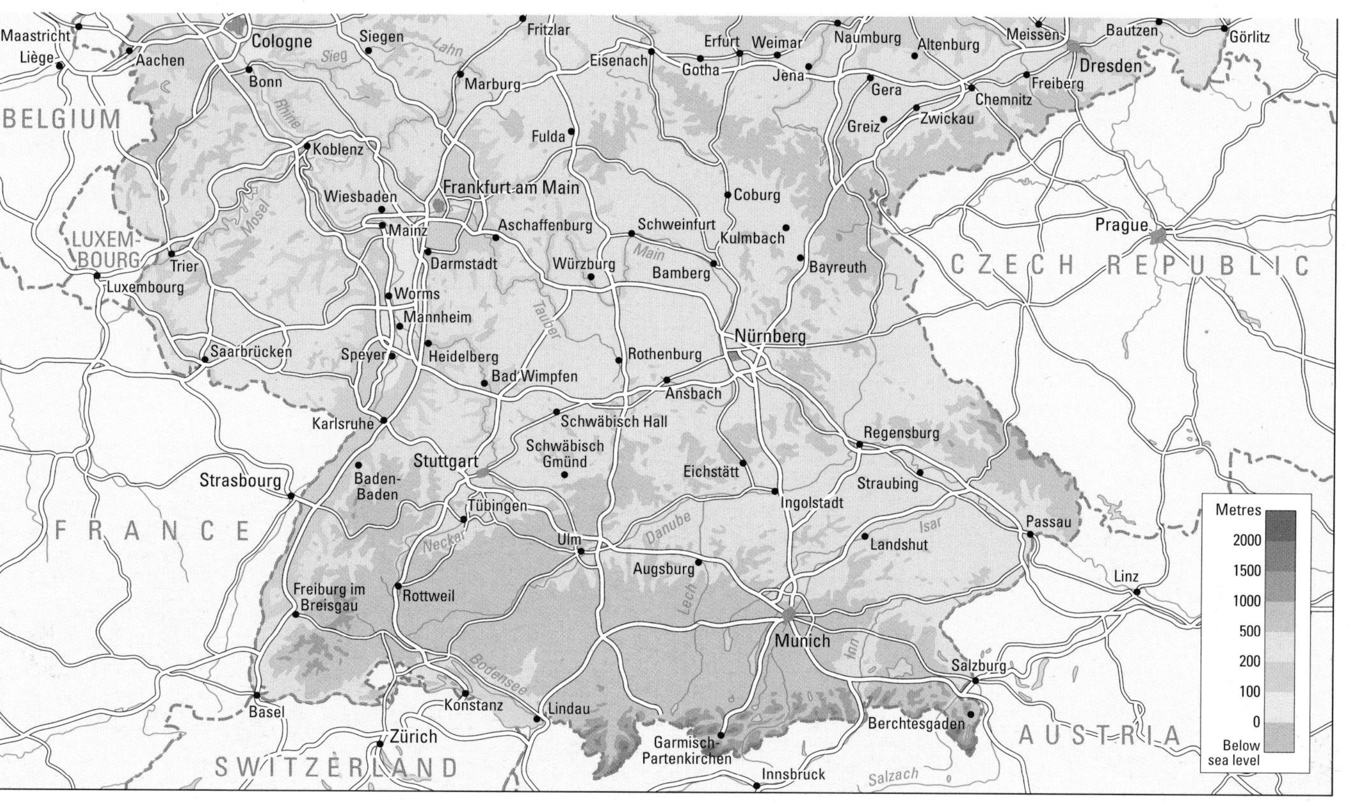
BELGIUM
LUXEMBOURG
FRANCE
SWITZERLAND
CZECH REPUBLIC
AUSTRIA
Maastricht
Liège
Aachen
Cologne
Bonn
Siegen
Fritzlar
Marburg
Koblenz
Fulda
Eisenach
Erfurt
Gotha
Weimar
Jena
Naumburg
Altenburg
Gera
Greiz
Zwickau
Chemnitz
Meissen
Freiberg
Dresden
Bautzen
Görlitz
Frankfurt am Main
Wiesbaden
Mainz
Darmstadt
Aschaffenburg
Schweinfurt
Coburg
Kulmbach
Bayreuth
Bamberg
Würzburg
Trier
Luxembourg
Worms
Mannheim
Saarbrücken
Speyer
Heidelberg
Bad Wimpfen
Rothenburg
Nürnberg
Ansbach
Karlsruhe
Schwäbisch Hall
Schwäbisch Gmünd
Regensburg
Straubing
Eichstätt
Ingolstadt
Stuttgart
Baden-Baden
Strasbourg
Tübingen
Ulm
Augsburg
Landshut
Passau
Linz
Prague
Freiburg im Breisgau
Rottweil
Munich
Salzburg
Berchtesgaden
Basel
Konstanz
Lindau
Zürich
Garmisch-Partenkirchen
Innsbruck
Rhine
Mosel
Sieg
Lahn
Main
Tauber
Neckar
Danube
Lech
Isar
Inn
Salzach
Bodensee
Metres
2000
1500
1000
500
200
100
0
Below sea level

△ Crocus field and Karwendl mountains, Upper Bavarian Alps

Introduction to Germany

Germany was for long the problem child of Europe. For over a millennium it was no more than a loose confederation of separate states and territories, whose number at times topped the thousand mark. When unification belatedly came about in 1871, it was achieved almost exclusively by military might; as a direct result of this, the new nation was consumed by a thirst for power and expansion abroad. Defeat in World War I only led to a desire for revenge, the consequence of which was the Third Reich, a regime bent on mass genocide and on European, indeed world, domination. It took another tragic global war to crush this system and its people. When the victors quarrelled over how to prevent Germany ever again becoming dominant, they divided it into two hostile states; the parts held by the Western powers were developed into the Federal Republic of Germany, while the eastern zone occupied by the Soviets became the German Democratic Republic.

The contest between the two was an unequal one – the GDR, never able to break free from being a client state of the Soviet Union and forced to adopt a Communist system at odds with the national character, had fallen so far behind its rival in living standards that in 1961 the authorities constructed the notorious electrified barbed-wire frontier, with the **Berlin Wall** as its lynchpin, to halt emigration. This was the first time

Fact file

- Germany occupies an area of 356,700 sq km and has borders with nine countries. Of the total population of just over 82 million, nearly 90 percent live in urban areas.
- The country has a fully federal structure, and is divided into sixteen Länder. Ten of these constituted the old West German state; five were formed out of the former East Germany (GDR); the last is the re-united city of Berlin.
- The Länder vary widely in size: Bremen is the smallest, with an area of 404 sq km; much the biggest is Bavaria, with 70,548 sq km. By far the most populous is North Rhine-Westphalia, with 18 million inhabitants. Each Land has its own parliament and government, which is headed by a mayor in the case of the three city-states, a minister-president in all the others.
- Berlin is the federal capital and seat of the federal parliament or Bundestag, which is elected for fixed four-year terms. Bonn, which had the status of "provisional" capital of the West German state, remains a secondary seat of government.
- The federal government is headed by the Chancellor, but the head of state is the President, who has an almost exclusively ceremonial role and is chosen by an electoral college to serve for a five-year period.

▽ Half-timbered houses, Goslar

in the history of the world that a fortification system had been erected by a regime against its own people. Thereafter, the society settled down, but the GDR was a grey, cheerless place whose much trumpeted economic success was a mirage, and bought at the price of terrible pollution problems.

On the other hand, the Federal Republic – which was seen as the natural successor to the old Reich, if only on account of its size – had not only picked itself up by the bootstraps, but developed into what many outsiders regarded as a **model modern society**. A nation with little in the way of a liberal tradition, and even less of a democratic one, quickly developed a degree of political maturity that put other countries to shame. In atonement for past sins, the new state committed itself to providing a haven for foreign refugees and dissidents. It also became a multiracial and multicultural society – even if the reason for this was less one of penance than the self-interested need to acquire extra cheap labour to fuel the economic boom. A delicate balance was struck between the old and the new. Historic town centres were immaculately restored, while the corporate skyscrapers and well-stocked department stores represented a commitment to a modern consumer society. Vast sums of money were lavished on preserving the best of the country's cultural legacy, yet equally generous budgets were allocated to encourage all kinds of contemporary expression in the arts.

While Germany has officially been one again for well over a decade, in some ways it still continues to look and feel like two separate countries

Officially, the Federal Republic was always a "provisional" state, biding its time before national reunification occurred. Yet there was a realization that nobody outside Germany was really much in favour of this. "I love Germany so much I'm glad there are two of them", scoffed the French novelist François Mauriac, articulating the unspoken gut reactions of the powers on both sides of the Iron Curtain. German division may have been cruel, but at least it had provided a lasting solution to the German "problem". Such thinking was rendered obsolete by the unstoppable momentum of events in the wake of the **Wende**, the peaceful revolution that toppled the Communist regime in the GDR in 1989, leading to the full union of the two Germanys less than a year later. Yet initial euphoria was quickly replaced by concern about the myriad problems facing the new nation as it attempted to integrate the bankrupt social and economic system of the GDR into the successful framework of the Federal Republic. While Germany has officially been one again for well over a decade, in some ways it still

△ Street café, Berlin

The Nazi legacy

Plenty of reminders of the cataclysmic twelve-year era that was the Nazis' Third Reich can be seen throughout Germany. Their preservation and upkeep present special problems, not least because there is such a fine line between maintaining an educative function and showing respect for the regime's many victims while at the same time avoiding the growth of ghoulish forms of tourism or the development of neo-Nazi shrines.

The concentration camps where the main extermination programmes of Jews and others were carried out were all set up in occupied or annexed parts of Poland. Those on German soil were relatively minor, but include Dachau, the first camp to be established, plus other notorious names such as Buchenwald (in the outskirts of Weimar), Bergen-Belsen, Oranienburg-Sachsenhausen and Mittelbau-Dora (near Nordhausen). Each of these has been preserved as a memorial.

One of the few Nazi legacies that is still regarded with pride is the Kehlsteinstrasse in the Berchtesgadener Land, which leads to the fabled "Eagle's Nest" tea house. Another is the Olympiastadion in Berlin, built for the heavily manipulated Olympic Games of 1936, which will stage the final of football's World Cup in 2006.

▽ Buildings at dusk, Potsdamer Platz, Berlin

continues to look and feel like two separate countries – a situation likely to persist for a while yet. Moreover, international pressure has ensured that, far from being a re-creation of the old Reich, the country comprises no more than the nineteenth-century concept of a *Kleines Deutschland* ("little Germany"), excluding not only Austria but also the "lost" Eastern Territories, which are now part of Poland, the Czech Republic, Lithuania and the Russian Federation.

In total contrast to Germany's intrinsic fascination as the country which played such a determining role in the history of the twentieth century, is its otherwise **romantic image**. This is the land of fairy-tale castles, of thick dark forests, of the legends collected by the Brothers Grimm, of perfectly preserved timber-framed medieval towns, and of jovial locals swilling from huge foaming mugs of beer. As always, there *is* some truth in these stereotypes, though most of them stem from the southern part of the country, particularly **Bavaria**, which, as a predominantly rural and Catholic area, stands apart from the urbanized Protestant north which engineered the unity of the nation in the nineteenth century and thereafter dominated its affairs.

△ Gartentheater of the Grosser Garten, Hannover

Regional characteristics, indeed, are a strong feature of German life, and there are many hangovers from the days when the country was a political patchwork, even though some historical provinces have vanished from the map and others have merged. More detail on each of the current Länder, as the constituent states are now known, can be found in the chapter introductions. **Hamburg** and **Bremen**, for example, retain their age-old status as free cities. The imperial capital, **Berlin**, also stands apart, as an island in the midst of the erstwhile GDR where the liberalism of the West was pushed to its extreme: sometimes decadent, always exciting. In polar opposition to it, and as a corrective to the normal view of the Germans as an essentially serious race, is the **Rhineland**, where the great river's majestic sweep has spawned a particularly rich fund of legends and folklore, and where the locals are imbued with a Mediterranean-type sense of fun. The five **new Länder** which have supplanted the GDR, and in particular the small towns and rural areas, are in many ways the ones which best encapsulate the feel and appearance of Germany as it was before the war and the onset of foreign influences which were an inevitable consequence of defeat.

△ Watzmann peaks, Berchtesgadener Land

Where to go

There's enough variety within all but the smallest Länder to fill several weeks of travel, and you may prefer to confine your trip to just one or two regions. Among the **scenic highlights** are the Bavarian Alps, the Bodensee, the Black Forest, the valleys of the Rhine and Mosel, the Baltic island of Rügen, the Harz, and Saxon Switzerland. However, you may prefer one of the many less spectacular areas of natural beauty, which can be found in every province – these are the places the Germans themselves love the most, and where they spend their holidays and weekends. Several of the cities have the air of capitals, though **Bonn** has lost the role it "temporarily" carried for fifty years. Nearby **Cologne**, on the other hand, is one of the most characterful cities in the country, and the richest in historic monuments. Bavaria's capital, **Munich**, is another obvious star and boasts of having the best the country has to offer – whether in museums, beer, fashion or sport. **Nürnberg** reflects on its bygone years of glory, while **Frankfurt** looks on itself as the "real" capital of the country, and **Stuttgart** and **Düsseldorf** compete for the title of champion of German postwar success. In the east, **Dresden** has made a comeback as one of the world's great cultural centres, while **Leipzig** has returned to its role as one of the continent's main trading centres. However, as all these cities have suffered to a considerable extent from bomb damage and ugly postwar redevelopment, the smaller places in many respects offer a more satisfying experience. Chief among these is the university city of **Heidelberg**, star and guiding light of the Romantic movement. Trier, Bamberg, Regensburg, Rothen-

▽ View of the Altstadt from the River Inn, Passau

△ Kochelsee in winter

burg and Marburg in the west, and Potsdam, Meissen and Quedlinburg in the east, are some of the many towns which deserve to be regarded among the most outstanding in Europe.

Germany's museums

Thanks in part to the impact of the Romantic movement, which nourished a passion for collecting and a great respect for the past, and in part to the nation's long history of division into a multitude of competing states, Germany has an astonishingly large number of major museums. Indeed, the country can legitimately claim to have more public collections of the first rank than any other country in the world.

Berlin has the largest and most extensive museums, thanks to the presence of the former Prussian state collections, which are particularly strong in archeological finds from the great civilizations of the ancient world. However, the Bavarian state collections in Munich are richer in art and artefacts of German origin, while the Saxon state collections in Dresden stand out for their distinctive character and consistently high quality.

Cologne can also boast several world-class collections, while Kassel and Karlsruhe have museum legacies which belie their present-day size and status. Nürnberg, Stuttgart, Frankurt, Darmstadt, Bremen, Hannover, Braunschweig, Hamburg and Leipzig all have at least one museum well worth making a special trip to see.

When to go

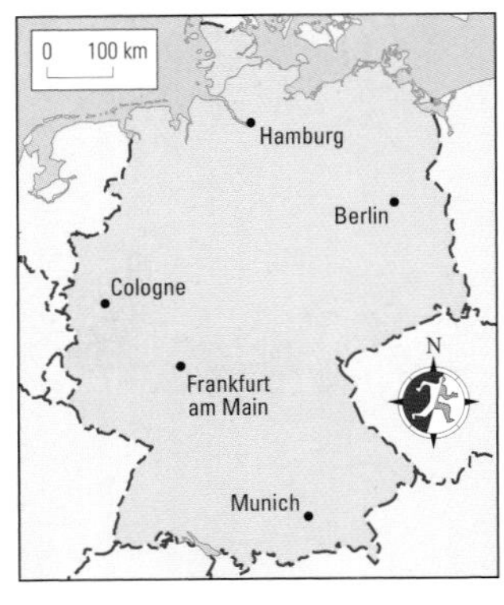

The best **times to go** are between April and October. Germany has a fairly volatile climate, not so different from that of Britain or New England. Summers are usually warm, but not overpoweringly so; good weather may come at an unexpected time, while it's not uncommon to have several abrupt changes in temperature within a single day. Rain occurs fairly regularly throughout the year. Unless you're intending to go skiing, winter travel can't really be recommended, other than for seeing the cities stripped of tourist hordes. Otherwise, there's a chance of snow at any time from November onwards. In the really popular areas, the claustrophobic effect of masses of organized tour groups is a factor to be taken into account between mid-June and mid-September: best avoid such places altogether then, and head for the many less spoiled alternatives. All things considered, however, the ideal times for visiting Germany are late spring and early autumn.

Average daily temperatures °C

	Jan	Feb	Mar	Apr	May	Jun	Jul	Aug	Sep	Oct	Nov	Dec
Berlin												
max	2	4	8	12	18	22	24	24	18	13	7	3
min	-4	-3	3	4	7	13	14	14	10	5	2	-1
Cologne												
max	5	6	10	13	18	22	23	23	19	15	8	6
min	-1	-2	3	3	7	12	13	12	10	7	3	2
Frankfurt am Main												
max	3	5	10	13	18	23	24	24	19	15	8	6
min	-2	-1	2	4	7	13	14	14	11	5	3	1
Hamburg												
max	3	4	7	12	17	20	23	23	18	13	7	5
min	-1	-2	2	3	7	11	13	12	9	7	3	0
Munich												
max	2	3	9	12	17	20	23	24	18	13	7	3
min	-4	-3	0	3	6	10	12	12	9	4	0	-3

things not to miss

It's not possible to see everything that Germany has to offer in one trip – and we don't suggest you try. What follows is a selective and subjective taste of the country's highlights: historic cities, beautiful architecture, spectacular festivals and unforgettable journeys. They're arranged in five colour-coded categories to help you find the very best things to see, do and experience. All entries have a page reference to take you straight into the guide, where you can find out more.

01 Bamberg Page **190** • Wonderfully well preserved and beautifully situated on seven hills, Bamberg has a great brewing tradition as well as a distinguished artistic legacy.

02 Park Sanssouci, Potsdam Page **806** • Frederick the Great's fabled retreat forms the heart of the extraordinary garden city of Potsdam.

03 Bavarian Rococo Page **115** • The extravagantly sumptuous Bavarian Rococo style is seen at its most resplendent in one of Germany's most popular places of pilgrimage, the Wieskirche.

04 Religious festivals Page **50** • Corpus Christi in Bamberg is a good example of the solemn but colourful celebrations of the great festivals of the Church calendar held in the Catholic parts of Germany.

05 The castles of the Rhineland Page **478** • Great feudal castles can be seen all over the Rhineland, though none is more dramatic than the isolated Burg Eltz.

06 The Grünes Gewölbe, Dresden Page **968** • One of the world's great art cities, Dresden is famous above all for the fabulous Rococo treasures in the Grünes Gewölbe, such as *Moor with a Basket of Emeralds*.

07 Frankfurt am Main Page **371** • Its skyline may have earned it the unflattering nickname of Mainhattan, but the German financial metropolis has a homely side, as manifested in its apple wine taverns.

08 Walpurgisnacht Page **847** • The witches' gathering on the Brocken on April 30 is celebrated throughout the Harz region.

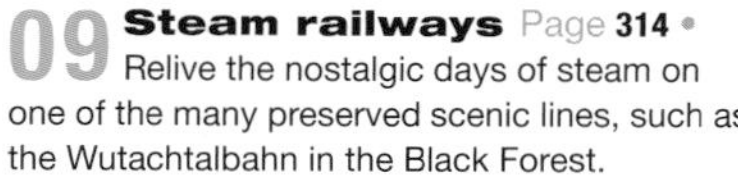

09 Steam railways Page **314** • Relive the nostalgic days of steam on one of the many preserved scenic lines, such as the Wutachtalbahn in the Black Forest.

10 Rügen Page **736** • Germany's largest island has a wonderful variety of landscapes, the best-known being the chalk cliffs in the Nationalpark Jasmund.

11 Weimar Page **885** • Never more than a modest country town, this is nonetheless Germany's literary capital, thanks to its association with the two titans of German letters, Goethe and Schiller.

12 Carnival Page **277** • Rottweil's Fastnet is a very traditional Shrovetide celebration dominated by characters in wooden masks; the Rhenish Karneval has a stronger political and satirical emphasis.

13 The Bodensee Page **290** • The Pfalbauten, reconstructions of Stone and Iron Age buildings, are among the diverse attractions of Germany's biggest lake.

14 Kaffee und Kuchen Page **40** • All over Germany there are wonderful traditional cafés specializing in coffee and home-baked cakes.

15 Historic costume festivals Page **263** • Schwäbisch Hall's Kuchen- und Brunnenfest is among the most enjoyable of the many German festivals featuring historical re-enactments.

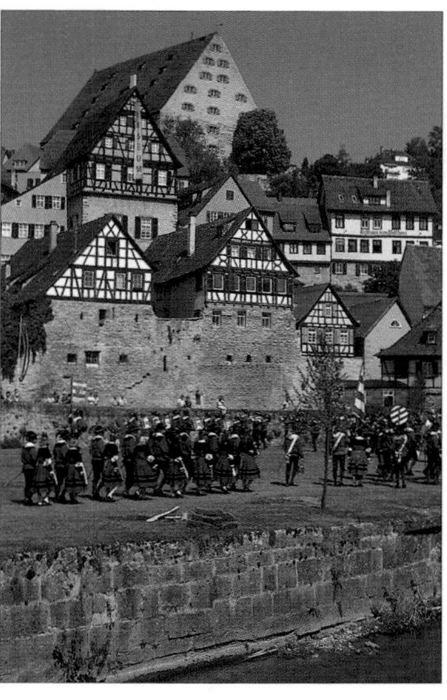

16 Beer Page **43** • The variety and quality of German beers is unmatched, and there's no more civilized place to drink them than in a beer garden, an institution especially associated with Munich.

17 Hiking in the Alps Page **118** • The Zugspitze is the highest point in the Bavarian Alps, Germany's best hiking countryside by far.

18 Heidelberg Page **347** • With its majestic ruined Schloss and its red-roofed Altstadt on the banks of the Neckar, Heidelberg has come to symbolize the romantic image of Germany.

19 Christkindlesmarkt, Nürnberg Page **168** • A great city worth visiting at any time of year, Nürnberg also hosts the Christkindlesmarkt, the most famous of the country's Advent markets.

20 Wine Page **45** • Many experts consider German white wines to be the world's best, and the most characteristic are produced in the vineyards of the Mosel.

21 The spa cure Page **328** • There's no better place to experience the full spa treatment, so beloved of the Germans, than the Friedrichbad in Baden-Baden.

22 The Residenz, Würzburg Page **206** • In the magnificence of its architecture and the sheer artistic quality of its decoration, the palace of the Würzburg prince-bishops surpasses any of Europe's royal residences.

23 The Dom, Aachen Page **494** • The kernel of Aachen's Dom, home of one of the world's richest treasuries, is Charlemagne's palace chapel, in whose gallery the emperor's elevated throne can still be seen.

24 The Black Forest Page **301** • The Murg is one of the many beautiful river valleys in Germany's most famous and extensive forest.

25 Hamburg Page **661** • There's far more to Germany's second city and largest port than its notorious nightlife: it has a highly distinctive cityscape punctuated by lakes, canals and parks.

26 The statues of the founders, Naumburg
Page **877** • The statues of Ekkehardt II and Uta in Naumburg's Dom form part of the most inventive sculptural programme to be found in any of Europe's medieval cathedrals.

27 **The half-timbered towns** Page **622** • Half-timbered houses dominate townscapes all over central Germany; the Pied Piper's town of Hameln has some particularly elaborate examples.

28 **Rhine cruises** Page **449** • Take a boat trip along the Rhine and enjoy wonderful views of its great landmarks, such as the Marksburg, in comfort.

29 **Oktoberfest** Page **86** • The world's biggest orgy of beer drinking takes place in a village of massive tents set up on Munich's Theresienwiese.

30 The Altstadt, Cologne Page **515** • The metropolis of the Rhine preserves no fewer than twelve Romanesque churches, but is dominated by its Gothic Dom, which took all of 632 years to complete.

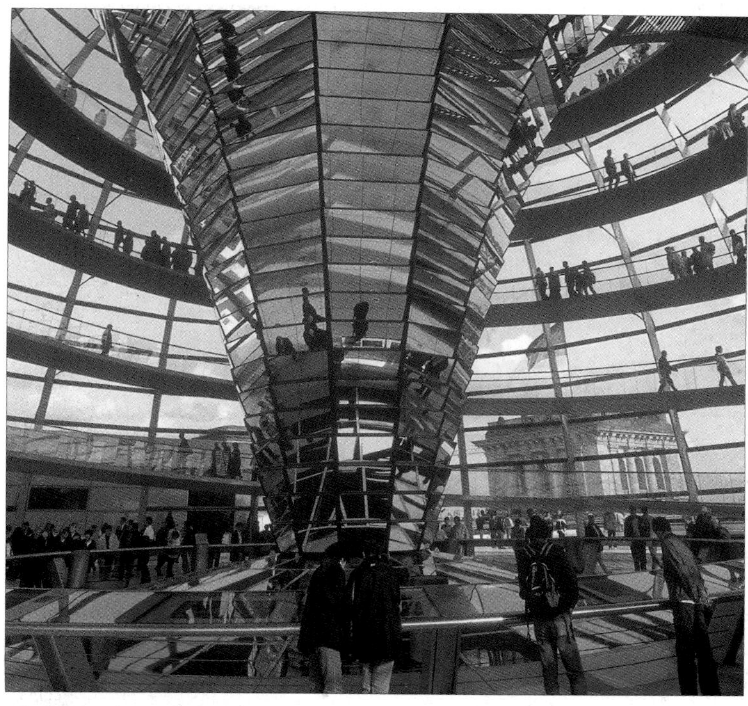

31 Contemporary architecture, Berlin Page **776** • The dynamic, thrusting character of postunification Berlin is manifested in some spectacular examples of modern architecture, such as the new dome of the Bundestag.

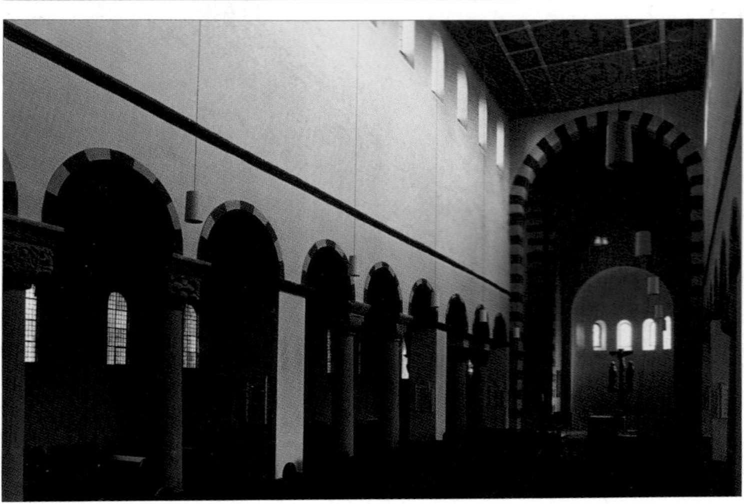

32 St Michaelis, Hildesheim Page **629** • The Romanesque, Northern Europe's first indigenous artistic style, came to fruition in Hildesheim, above all in the great church of St Michaelis.

33 Wurst Page **146** • The Historische Wurstkuche in Regensburg is the most famous of Germany's speciality sausage restaurants.

34 Porta Nigra, Trier Page **466** • Germany's oldest city, Trier, preserves the finest assemblage of Roman monuments north of the Alps, among which the Porta Nigra is the undoubted star.

35 King Ludwig II's far king's megalomanical passic Schloss Neuschwanstein in the A

Map and chapter list

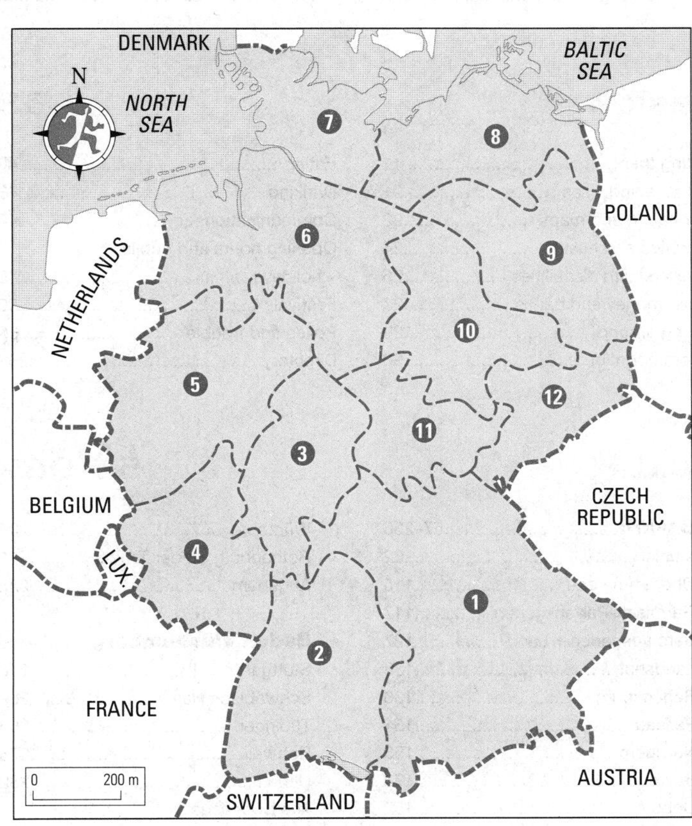

Contents

Colour section i–xxiv

Basics 9–53

Guide 55–987

Contexts 990–1051

Language 1053–1068

small print and Index 1093–1104

Map symbols

Maps are listed in the full index using coloured text.

Railway
Major road
Minor road
Pedestrianized street
Motorway
Funicular railway
Footpath
Ferry route
Coastline/river
Chapter division boundary
National boundary
International boundary
Point of interest
Peak

U-Bahn station
S-Bahn station
Synagogue
Gate
Wall
Garden
Chapel
Post office
Bridge
Tourist office
Building
Church
Cemetery
Park
Forest

Basics

Basics

Getting there

Germany can be reached from the UK by flights from numerous airports, by train or bus through the Channel Tunnel, and by a direct ferry. Choice of how to get there can accordingly be left to personal preference for a particular means of transport – or by considerations of cost. A large number of airlines offer direct flights to various German destinations from cities throughout North America and Australasia, so it's well worth shopping around for the best deal.

Booking flights online

Many discount travel websites offer you the opportunity to book flight tickets and holiday packages online, cutting out the costs of agents and middlemen; these are worth going for, as long as you don't mind the inflexibility of non-refundable, non-changeable deals. There are some bargains to be had on auction sites too, if you're prepared to bid keenly. Almost all airlines have their own websites, offering flight tickets that can sometimes be just as cheap, and are often more flexible.

Online booking agents and general travel sites

Ⓦ **www.cheapflights.co.uk** (in UK & Ireland), Ⓦ **www.cheapflights.com** (in US), Ⓦ **www.cheapflights.ca** (in Canada), Ⓦ **www.cheapflights.com.au** (in Australia). Flight deals, travel agents, plus links to other travel sites.

Ⓦ **www.cheaptickets.com** Discount flight specialists (US only). Also at Ⓣ 1-888/922-8849.

Ⓦ **www.ebookers.com** Efficient, easy to use flight finder, with competitive fares.

Ⓦ **www.etn.nl/discount.htm** A hub of consolidator and discount agent links, maintained by the nonprofit European Travel Network.

Ⓦ **www.expedia.co.uk** (in UK), Ⓦ **www.expedia.com** (in US), Ⓦ **www.expedia.ca** (in Canada). Discount airfares, all-airline search engine and daily deals.

Ⓦ **www.flyaow.com** "Airlines of the Web" – online air travel info and reservations.

Ⓦ **www.gaytravel.com** US gay travel agent, offering accommodation, cruises, tours and more. Also at Ⓣ 1-800/GAY-TRAVEL.

Ⓦ **www.geocities.com/thavery2000** An extensive list of airline websites and US toll-free numbers.

Ⓦ **www.kelkoo.co.uk** Useful UK-only price-comparison site, checking several sources of low-cost flights (and other goods & services) according to specific criteria.

Ⓦ **www.lastminute.com** (in UK), Ⓦ **www.lastminute.com.au** (in Australia), Ⓦ **www.lastminute.co.nz** (in New Zealand). Good last-minute holiday package and flight-only deals.

Ⓦ **www.opodo.co.uk** Popular and reliable source of low UK airfares. Owned by, and run in conjunction with, nine major European airlines.

Ⓦ **www.priceline.co.uk** (in UK), Ⓦ **www.priceline.com** (in US). Name-your-own-price website that has deals at around forty percent off standard fares.

Ⓦ **www.skyauction.com** Bookings from the US only. Auctions tickets and travel packages to destinations worldwide.

Ⓦ **www.travelocity.co.uk** (in UK), Ⓦ **www.travelocity.com** (in US), Ⓦ **www.travelocity.ca** (in Canada), Ⓦ **www.zuji.com.au** (in Australia). Destination guides, hot fares and great deals for car rental, accommodation and lodging.

Ⓦ **www.travelshop.com.au** Australian site offering discounted flights, packages, insurance, and online bookings. Also on Ⓣ 1800/108 108.

Ⓦ **www.travel.yahoo.com** Incorporates some Rough Guides material in its coverage of destination countries and cities across the world, with information about places to eat and sleep.

From Britain and Ireland

The most convenient and usually best-value way to get to Germany is to fly – flights from London to Frankfurt take little over an hour and to Berlin around an hour and a half. Travelling by train through the Channel Tunnel makes a pleasant alternative, and journey times have improved recently: from London to Frankfurt via Brussels and Cologne takes just under eight hours. Getting over to Germany with your car is also fairly easy with the Eurotunnel Shuttle. If you're heading for north Germany or destinations in the former GDR you can cut down on the driving by taking the ferry from Harwich to Cuxhaven.

Flights

Most major west German cities have numerous daily scheduled links with London (principally Heathrow and Gatwick), as well as with several regional UK airports. Flight times are around an hour to an hour and a half. Often you'll find that the lowest fares and the most frequent flights are to **Frankfurt**, very much at the centre of German air routes. To fly to other western German cities – such as Munich, Stuttgart, Hamburg, Düsseldorf or Cologne/Bonn – usually costs slightly more, while **Berlin** and the former GDR cities are the most expensive of all to reach.

The main airlines that fly to Germany from the UK are **British Airways** and **Lufthansa**. Their standard fares are expensive – often upwards of £200 return, and considerably more than that at peak times – but they have numerous special offers throughout the year. Usually, these tickets come with various restrictions and have to be booked well in advance. BA and Lufthansa also offer **fly-drive deals** and **open-jaw flights**, which allow you to fly into one airport and back from another. From Ireland, the only regular scheduled flights to Germany are with **Aer Lingus**.

Better deals than those offered by the airlines themselves are usually available from **discount flight agents**. The ones listed on p.13 make good starting points, and the **German Travel Centre**, which specializes in flights to Germany, is particularly worth trying. Other agents can be found on the pages of the Sunday or local evening papers, regional listings magazines and, in London, *Time Out*. If you're a student or under 26, you're best off contacting the independent travel specialist **STA Travel**, which offer discounted fares to young people. They are also worth calling even if you aren't a student, as they offer a good range of budget fares. Typical fares **from London** from discount agents tend to be in the region of £120–150, plus airport tax of between £20 and £30. Expect to pay an extra £20–30 from Birmingham, Manchester, Edinburgh or Glasgow, all of which are linked – not necessarily directly – with several major German airports. Bear in mind that tickets bought from discount agents usually come with certain **conditions**: you'll probably have to stay for a minimum of three nights, one of which will be a Saturday, and once the tickets are booked, they tend to be non-refundable and the dates non-changeable.

Although they receive rather a mixed press, and are certainly not always as cheap as they at first appear, the **low-cost airlines** have really revolutionized travel to the Continent over the past few years. Provided you can be flexible, and are able to book well in advance, it should be possible to undercut every other way of getting to Germany. The range of destinations is prone to change, but seems to be on a steady upward curve.

Ryanair currently have the largest choice of German destinations, as well as the lowest advertised fares. Indeed, they frequently promote supposedly free flights, charging only taxes and a booking fee. More common, and rather easier to obtain, if booked well in advance, are flights costing between £2 and £9 single plus the aforementioned extras. The company mostly uses rather small and/or obscure airports within Germany, some with rather misleading names: what they call Hamburg is actually Lübeck, while Frankfurt–Hahn is a former military airport which is a ninety-minute bus ride from the city. However, the services to Frankfurt–Hahn are undoubtedly attractive propositions for anyone who lives near Bournemouth or Glasgow Prestwick, which both have Ryanair links there, as do both Shannon and Kerry in Ireland. Furthermore, some of Ryanair's chosen German airports score not only for the speedy processing of passengers and luggage at both arrival and departure, but for location as well. Friedrichshafen, for example, is just a few minutes by train from the shores of the Bodensee.

Many of Ryanair's flights depart from London Stansted. Another budget carrier which uses this airport is **Air Berlin**. It flies not only to Berlin, but to many other German airports, mostly little-known, including Paderborn, Münster/Osnabrück and Dortmund. Prices start at £19 single. The Lufthansa subsidiary **Germanwings**, which started operations in 2003, has flights from both Stansted and Edinburgh (the latter during the summer half of the year only) to its main base of Cologne/Bonn. Its starting price for a single ticket is the sterling equivalent of €19 (currently around £14), and the Edinburgh flights are particularly good value, regularly coming up at £19–49 one-way. One particularly good feature of Germanwings is that the prices it quotes on its website are the ones you actually pay – there are none of the hidden extras added on by so many low-cost carriers. **Easyjet** currently only has one service to Germany – from Stansted to Munich. However, it has flights costing from £19 single from various British cities to Amsterdam, from where there are good train connections to northern Germany. Other low-cost airlines worth considering are: **bmibaby** which flies to Munich from Cardiff and East Midlands; **duo** (formerly Maersk Air) which operates from Birmingham to Berlin, Cologne/Bonn and Stuttgart; **Germania Express** has flights from Glasgow Prestwick to Berlin; and **Hapag-Lloyd Express** operates from Manchester to Cologne/Bonn.

Airlines

Aer Lingus UK ⓣ0845/084 4444, Republic of Ireland ⓣ0818/365 000, ⓦwww.aerlingus.com.
Air Berlin UK ⓣ0870/738 8880, ⓦwww.airberlin.com.
bmi UK ⓣ0870/607 0555, ⓦwww.flybmi.com.
bmibaby UK ⓣ0870/264 2229, Republic of Ireland ⓣ01/435 0011, ⓦwww.bmibaby.com.
British Airways UK ⓣ0870/850 9850, Republic of Ireland ⓣ1800/626 747, ⓦwww.ba.com.
duo UK ⓣ0871/700 0700, ⓦwww.duo.com.
easyJet UK ⓣ0871/750 0100, ⓦwww.easyjet.com.
Germania Express UK ⓣ01805/737 100, ⓦwww.gexx.de.
Germanwings UK ⓣ020/8321 7255, ⓦwww.germanwings.com.
Hapag-Lloyd Express UK ⓦwww.hlx.com.
KLM UK ⓣ0870/507 4074, ⓦwww.klm.com.
Lufthansa UK ⓣ0845/773 7747, Republic of Ireland ⓣ01/844 5544, ⓦwww.lufthansa.com.
Ryanair UK ⓣ0871/246 0000, Republic of Ireland ⓣ0818/30 30 30, ⓦwww.ryanair.com.

Travel agents

German Travel Centre UK ⓣ020/8429 2900, ⓦwww.german-travel-uk.com. Discount flight specialists who can also arrange accommodation and other services.
Joe Walsh Tours Republic of Ireland ⓣ01/676 0991, ⓦwww.joewalshtours.ie. Long-established general budget fares and holidays agent.
North South Travel UK ⓣ01245/608291, ⓦwww.northsouthtravel.co.uk. Friendly, competitive travel agency, offering discounted fares worldwide – profits are used to support projects in the developing world, especially the promotion of sustainable tourism.
STA Travel UK ⓣ0870/160 0599, ⓦwww.statravel.co.uk. Worldwide specialists in low-cost flights, overlands and holiday deals. Good discounts for students and under-26s.
Trailfinders UK ⓣ020/7938 3939, ⓦwww.trailfinders.com; Republic of Ireland ⓣ01/677 7888, ⓦwww.trailfinders.ie. One of the best-informed and most efficient agents for independent travellers.
USIT Northern Ireland ⓣ028/9032 7111, ⓦwww.usitnow.com; Republic of Ireland ⓣ0818/200 020, ⓦwww.usit.ie. Specialists in student, youth and independent travel flights, trains, study tours, TEFL, visas and more.

By train

Journey times **by train** from the UK to Germany have been greatly reduced in recent years by the high-speed Eurostar services (currently up to ten a day) direct from London Waterloo to Brussels-Midi/Zuid, where they connect with similarly fast trains onwards to Aachen and Cologne – taking five or six hours in total. Tickets can also be bought for destinations further afield, which are reached by trains operating on Germany's internal network, and unlimited stopovers can be made en route. Through ticketing from British mainline stations – including the tube journey to Waterloo – is also available from some agents. With return fares from London to Cologne starting at £110, it has to be said that taking the train very often works out as a far more expensive option than a flight, particularly if you're starting from outside London and/or continuing beyond Cologne. However, there are circumstances where it's definitely worth considering: for example you could use a through ticket to Munich to visit Frankfurt, Würzburg, Nürnberg and Regensburg on the way out, and see Augsburg, Ulm, Stuttgart and Heidelberg on the way back.

If you plan to travel extensively in Germany by train, there are more flexible and better-value options than simply buying a return ticket. You might consider investing in an **InterRail** pass, available from Rail Europe or any travel agent; the only restriction on purchase is that you must have been resident in Europe for at least six months. There are two different versions of this. The **InterRail Global** pass is valid for one month's unlimited travel in 26 European countries, including Germany, and costs £198 for children, £278 for under-26s, and £395 for over-26s. The other option is an **InterRail Zonal** pass: the 26 countries are split into zones and you choose how many you want the pass to be valid for. A one-zone card valid for 12 days costs £95 for children, £130 for under-26s, £190 for over-26s; for 22 days these rise to £106, £142 and £207 respectively. For 22 days in any two contiguous zones, the prices are £144, £204 and £288; for three zones, £168, £235 and £335. Germany is in the same zone as Austria, Switzerland and Denmark. The two adjoining zones are: France, Belgium, the Netherlands and Luxembourg; and the Czech Republic, Slovakia, Poland, Hungary, Bulgaria and Croatia. Note that InterRail passes do not include travel between Britain and the Continent, although InterRail pass-holders are eligible for discounts on rail travel in the UK, on Eurostar services and on cross-Channel ferries.

Be prepared to pay extra supplements on some German trains, especially on InterCityExpress services. There are also some private lines, including east Germany's narrow-gauge steam rail lines, on which passes are not valid. Specific **passes for travel in Germany only** (see p.31) can be bought from agents before you go.

If you're 60 or over and have a British Rail Senior Card (£18 from any train station), you can get a **Rail Europe Senior Card** for £12, which is valid for a year and gives discounts of approximately thirty percent on cross-border sea and train travel, including Eurostar, in 25 European countries.

Rail agents

Eurostar UK ⓣ0870/160 6600, ⓦwww.eurostar.com. Sells all kinds of tickets in which a Eurostar crossing forms at least portion of the journey.

German Rail UK ⓣ0870/243 5363, ⓦwww.deutschebahn.sagenet.co.uk. Can issue point-to-point tickets and passes on all train companies – including Eurostar – for travel to and within Germany and most of Europe (not Britain, France or certain Eastern European countries).

Iarnród Éireann Republic of Ireland ⓣ01/703 1885, ⓦwww.irishrail.ie. Point-to-point tickets to major western European destinations, with discounts available, plus InterRail and Eurodomino.

International Rail UK ⓣ0870/751 5000, ⓦwww.international-rail.com. Offers a wide variety of rail options, including Eurostar, all European passes and tickets, international sleepers, ferry crossings and more.

Rail Europe UK ⓣ0870/584 8848, ⓦwww.raileurope.co.uk. Offers a broad range of mainstream rail options, including Eurostar, tickets for major Eruopean destinations, national passes, InterRail and Eurodomino. Eurail (see p.19) must normally be bought outside Europe, but people resident outside the EU can go to Rail Europe's central London office and buy a Eurail pass over the counter, on production of a non-EU passport.

Trainseurope UK ⓣ0900/195 0101 (60p/min, refundable against a booking), ⓦwww.trainseurope.co.uk. Sells point-to-point tickets, passes, Eurotunnel, national passes, InterRail and Eurodomino.

By bus

Travelling to Germany **by bus** won't bring any major savings over the cheapest air fares, and the journey will be long and uncomfortable, interrupted every three to four hours by stops at highway services. The one advantage is that you can have an open return at no extra cost.

The main operator is **Eurolines**, which offers connections to all the major German cities. Summer frequencies, timings and return fares from London to the major cities are: Cologne (daily; 12hr; £70); Frankfurt (daily; 14hr 45min; £78); Hamburg (4 weekly; 20hr 30min; £78); Berlin (4 weekly; 23hr 30min; £80); Munich (daily; 23hr 30min; £84). Winter departures are only slightly fewer and fares are usually the same as during the summer. There are small reductions (£2–10) for students, youths and senior citizens, slightly more substantial ones for children. Tickets can be booked through most major travel agents; Eurolines sells tickets and through transport to London at all National Express bus terminals.

Eurolines' fares are slightly undercut by two smaller operators: Anglia Lines, which has services to Hannover and Hamburg, and Gullivers, which covers these same two cities plus Berlin.

Bus companies

Anglia Lines UK ⓣ0870/608 8806, ⓦwww.anglia-lines.co.uk.
Eurolines UK ⓣ0870/514 3219, ⓦwww.eurolines.co.uk; Republic of Ireland ⓣ01/836 6111, ⓦwww.eurolines.ie.
Gullivers International toll-free ⓣ00800/4855 4837, ⓦwww.gullivers.de.

By car

Travelling by **car**, your route across to the Continent will be largely determined by where you're starting from, and which part of Germany you're heading for. For the Rhineland and south Germany, you're best off going to France or Belgium; for northern Germany or Berlin and the former GDR, you'll save on driving time by taking a boat to Holland or direct to Cuxhaven. Once across, particularly if you drive through Holland or Belgium – less so in France – you'll rarely need to travel on anything but highways all the way to any German city. From Calais and the other Channel ports allow about three hours to Cologne or Düsseldorf, six to seven to Hamburg or Frankfurt and twelve to Munich or Berlin. For practical details on driving in Germany see p.33.

Perhaps the most convenient way of taking your car across to the Continent is to drive down to the Channel Tunnel, load your car on the **Shuttle train**, and be whisked under the Channel in 35 minutes. The tunnel entrance is off the M20 at Junction 11A, just outside Folkestone; at the other end, you emerge just outside Calais. The Shuttle train operates services round the clock, 365 days a year. Trains run up to four times an hour during the day and once hourly at night. Tickets can be bought on arrival, but advance booking (by phone or via the Internet: see the Eurotunnel entry p.16) is advised at peak times. The recommended check-in time is thirty minutes beforehand. Prices are charged per vehicle, with no extra charge for passengers. Fares vary significantly depending on the season, how far in advance you book and which day and time you choose. For example, a short-stay (2–5 days) booked seven days in advance starts at £163, while a long-stay return (more than 5 days) booked fourteen days in advance costs £283.

An alternative is the time-honoured tradition of taking a **ferry** (see list below). In addition to the numerous short Channel crossings to France, there are various much longer routes across the North Sea, which are particularly worth considering if you live outside the south of England. For example, Superfast Ferries have introduced a service from Rosyth (across the Forth Bridge from Edinburgh) to Zeebrugge in Belgium, which is also linked with Hull by P&O. From Ireland, the nearest any ferry gets to Germany is the northwest of France, which is served by both Irish Ferries and P&O Irish Sea.

The only **direct ferry** from the British Isles to Germany is with DFDS Seaways, which sails three or four times weekly from Harwich to Cuxhaven in Lower Saxony; this has replaced the former service to Hamburg. Passengers are required to book at least a reclining chair for the crossing, which takes around seventeen hours (cabins with shower and toilet are available for a supplementary price). Standard fares are dependent on the season (from £55 during July and August, from £34 rest of year). The vehicle tariff is then added on – cars under 1.85m high and 6m in length are currently £46 off-peak and £56 peak season.

Ferry and cross-channel crossings

Brittany Ferries UK ⓣ0870/366 5333, ⓦwww.brittanyferries.co.uk; Republic of Ireland

Ⓣ021/427 7801, Ⓦwww.brittanyferries.ie. Portsmouth to Caen; Portsmouth to St Malo; Portsmouth to Cherbourg; Poole to Cherbourg.
Condor Ferries UK Ⓣ0845/345 2000, Ⓦwww.condorferries.co.uk. Weymouth to St Malo via Guernsey & Jersey; Poole to Cherbourg; Portsmouth to Cherbourg. Discounts are available for train travel from all round the UK to Poole harbour for the sea crossing.
DFDS Seaways UK Ⓣ0870/533 3000, Ⓦwww.dfdsseaways.co.uk. Harwich to Cuxhaven; Newcastle/South Shields to IJmuiden near Amsterdam.
Eurotunnel UK Ⓣ0870/535 3535, Ⓦwww.eurotunnel.com. Car Shuttle services.
Hoverspeed UK Ⓣ0870/240 8070, Ⓦwww.hoverspeed.co.uk. Dover to Calais; Newhaven to Dieppe.
Irish Ferries Britain Ⓣ0870/517 1717, Northern Ireland Ⓣ0800/018 2211, Republic of Ireland Ⓣ1890/313 131, Ⓦwww.irishferries.com. Rosslare to Cherbourg; Rosslare to Roscoff.
Norfolk Line UK Ⓣ0870/870 1020, Ⓦwww.norfolkline.com. Dover to Dunkerque.
P&O Ferries UK Ⓣ0870/520 2020, Ⓦwww.poferries.com. Dover to Calais; Hull to Zeebrugge; Hull to Rotterdam; Portsmouth to Cherbourg; Portsmouth to Le Havre.
P&O Irish Sea UK Ⓣ0870/242 4777, Republic of Ireland Ⓣ1800/409 049, Ⓦwww.poirishsea.com. Dublin to Cherbourg; Rosslare to Cherbourg.
SeaFrance UK Ⓣ0870/571 1711, Ⓦwww.seafrance.com. Dover to Calais.
Stena Line Britain Ⓣ0870/570 70 70, Ⓦwww.stenaline.co.uk. Harwich to Hook of Holland.
Superfast Ferries UK Ⓣ0870/234 0870, Ⓦwww.superfast.com. Rosyth to Zeebrugge.
Transmanche Ferries Ⓣ0800/917 1201, Ⓦwww.transmancheferries.com. Newhaven to Dieppe.

Package holidays

Most travel agents have brochures detailing the many **package holidays** to Germany. The most common type of package, and also the best value, tends to be **motoring holidays**, where you drive your own car to Germany and stay in pre-arranged accommodation in hotels or guesthouses in several locations. The price also includes travel by Eurotunnel or ferry, insurance, and sometimes meals. The pick of these are operated by **DER Travel Service** (see below), which has a wide selection of packages all over Germany. The same company offers **fly-drive packages**, where you fly to a German city and pick up a rental car there.

Short **city breaks** are offered by most major travel agents. If you don't want the hassle of booking the flight and finding accommodation yourself, these can be very convenient, and, especially out of season, you can get some good bargains. Adding extra nights or upgrading your hotel is possible. The prices always include return flights, transfers and bed and breakfast in a centrally located hotel. Again, ask your travel agent for the best deal, and check the specialists below. If you want an all-inclusive trip to the **Oktoberfest** arranged for you, you're looking at upwards of £325 for three nights. Other than DER, companies with a good choice of holidays throughout Germany are Moswin's and Taber. Organized **cruises** on the Rhine and Mosel, Danube or Elbe are offered by several operators, though these are usually expensive. Several companies offer guided **walking tours**; recommended operators include Ramblers Holidays, Bents and Waymark Holidays.

Tour operators

Bents Ⓣ01568/780800, Ⓦwww.bentstours.com. Cycling and walking tours.
DER Travel Service Ⓣ020/7290 1111, Ⓦwww.dertravel.co.uk. The national German travel agency, offering a full range of tours, as well as accommodation service and rail passes.
Martin Randall Travel Ⓣ020/8742 3355, Ⓦwww.martinrandall.com. Small-group cultural tours, led by experts on art, music or archeology, and invariably expensive.
Moswin's Ⓣ0116/271 4982, Ⓦwww.moswin.com. A specialist in Germany, with a wide variety of air, rail and self-drive package holidays.
Peter Deilmann Ⓣ020/7436 2931, Ⓦwww.deilmann-cruises.co.uk. Elbe, Rhine and Mosel cruises.
Ramblers Holidays Ⓣ01707/320226, Ⓦwww.ramblersholidays.co.uk. A long-established and reputable walking holiday specialist, offering organized trips to the Black Forest.
Taber Holidays Ⓣ01274/594656, Ⓦwww.taberhols.co.uk. German specialists, offering city breaks, cruises and self-catering holidays.

Waymark Holidays 44 Windsor Rd, Slough SL1 2EJ ⓣ01753/516477, ⓦwww.waymarkholidays.com. Walking holidays in the Black Forest and winter cross-country skiing trips to Oberammergau.

From North America

Fares between North America and Germany are among the cheapest transatlantic crossings. Frankfurt, Germany's largest airport, handles most international flights, and has onward connections to all other major cities. Lufthansa, Germany's national airline, has the most direct flights to Germany from the US and Canada, flying nonstop to Frankfurt, Munich and Düsseldorf from more than a dozen North American cities.

Though it may be more interesting, it's not usually cheaper to stop over in **another European country** and make your way to Germany from there. You may find cheap flights to **Paris** or **Amsterdam**, but the most common deals available through the seat consolidators are on scheduled airlines plying long-haul routes to the Gulf states, almost all of which stop in **London**. From mainland Europe, **trains** are the cheapest and easiest way to make the final leg to Germany – a Eurail pass (see p.19) is useful, especially if you are on a longer European trip, as you can use it to get from any part of Europe to Germany. From the UK, flying is often as cheap if not cheaper than ground travel.

Flights

You can usually find **direct flights** from the major gateway cities of New York JFK, Newark, Atlanta, Boston, Washington DC, Miami, Chicago and Los Angeles to either **Frankfurt** or **Berlin**, with connections to Hamburg, Stuttgart, Munich and Düsseldorf. There are constant fare wars raging between the airlines on flights to Germany. On average, the European airlines offer some of the lowest fares and best connection possibilities, and many nonstop flights have been added in recent years. There is no great change in price between any of the German hub cities from the US and you'll find airport tax to be the main factor in price difference.

Note that fares are heavily dependent on **season**, and are highest from early June to the end of September; they drop during the "shoulder" seasons, April, May and October, and you'll get the best deals during the low season, November to the end of March (excluding Christmas). Note that flying on weekends ordinarily adds $60 to the return fare; prices quoted below assume mid-week travel.

Typical flights from the **east coast** to Germany can start as low as $350 with restrictions during low season, and rise up to $1100 during high season. From the **mid-west** flights to Germany start at around $400 low season but prices can rise to over $1400 high season. Flying direct from the **west coast** isn't that much more expensive than flying out of New York, with average fares to Germany being around $500 in low season and $1100 in high season. You can usually get direct flights from the **main gateways** of Los Angeles, San Francisco and Seattle.

It is also worth looking out for **courier flights** as these can be exceptionally good value. In return for shepherding a parcel through customs and possibly giving up your baggage allowance, you can expect to pay around $300 for a return ticket. **Travel clubs** are another option – most charge an annual membership fee, which may be worth it for their discounts on air tickets and car rental.

Flying from **Canada**, you have fewer direct options than from the US, though again European carriers such as British Airways, Lufthansa and Northwest/KLM offer the most choices with a stopover in Europe. The best selections are out of **Toronto** and **Montréal** – direct fares with Air Canada to Frankfurt range from CDN$800 (low season) to CDN$1500 (high season) – and from **Vancouver** to Frankfurt, starting at CDN$1000 and rising up to CDN$2000. In most cases you will find cheaper fares with a travel agent or by travelling to **New York** and picking up a flight from there. With reduced options, it's worth considering getting a discount fare to a city like London, Amsterdam or Paris and travelling on from there.

Airlines

Air Canada ⓣ 1-888/247-2262, ⓦ www.aircanada.com.
Air France US ⓣ 1-800/237-2747, Canada ⓣ 1-800/667-2747, ⓦ www.airfrance.com.
American Airlines ⓣ 1-800/624-6262. ⓦ www.aa.com.
bmi ⓣ 1-800/788-0555, ⓦ www.flybmi.com.
British Airways ⓣ 1-800/AIRWAYS, ⓦ www.ba.com.
Continental Airlines ⓣ 1-800/231-0856, ⓦ www.continental.com.
Delta International ⓣ 1-800/241-4141, ⓦ www.delta.com.
Lufthansa US ⓣ 1-800/645-3880, Canada ⓣ 1-800/563-5954, ⓦ www.lufthansa.com.
Northwest/KLM International ⓣ 1-800/447-4747, ⓦ www.nwa.com, ⓦ www.klm.com.
Singapore Airlines US ⓣ 1-800/742-3333, Canada ⓣ 1-800/387-8039 or 663-3046, ⓦ www.singaporeair.com.
Swiss ⓣ 1-877/FLY-SWISS, ⓦ www.swiss.com.
United Airlines ⓣ 1-800/538-2929, ⓦ www.united.com.
US Airways ⓣ 1-800/622-1015, ⓦ www.usair.com.

Courier flights

Air Courier Association ⓣ 1-800/282-1202, ⓦ www.aircourier.org. Courier flight broker. Membership (US$35 for a year) also entitles you to twenty percent discount on travel insurance and name-your-own-price non-courier flights.
International Association of Air Travel Couriers ⓣ 308/632-3273, ⓦ www.courier.org. Courier flight broker. One year's membership costing US$45 in the US or Canada (US$50 elsewhere).

Travel agents

Air Brokers International ⓣ 1-800/883-3273, ⓦ www.airbrokers.com. Consolidator and specialist in round-the-world and Circle Pacific tickets.
Educational Travel Center ⓣ 1-800/747-5551 or 608/256-5551, ⓦ www.edtrav.com. Low-cost fares worldwide, student/youth discount offers, and Eurail passes, car rental and tours.
Flightcentre US ⓣ 1-866/WORLD-51, ⓦ www.flightcentre.us, Canada ⓣ 1-888/WORLD-55, ⓦ www.flightcentre.ca. Rock-bottom fares worldwide.
New Frontiers US ⓣ 1-800/677-0720, ⓦ www.newfrontiers.com. Discount firm, specializing in travel from the US to Europe, with hotels and package deals.
STA Travel US ⓣ 1-800/329-9537, Canada ⓣ 1-888/427-5639, ⓦ www.statravel.com. Worldwide specialists in independent travel; also student IDs, travel insurance, car rental, rail passes, and more.
Student Flights ⓣ 1-800/255-8000 or 480/951-1177, ⓦ www.isecard.com/studentflights. Student/youth fares, plus student IDs and European rail and bus passes.
TFI Tours ⓣ 1-800/745-8000 or 212/736-1140, ⓦ www.lowestairprice.com. Consolidator with global fares.
Travel Avenue ⓣ 1-800/333-3335, ⓦ www.travelavenue.com. Full-service travel agent that offers discounts in the form of rebates.
Travel Cuts US ⓣ 1-800/592-CUTS, Canada ⓣ 1-888/246-9762, ⓦ www.travelcuts.com. Popular, long-established student-travel organization, with worldwide offers.
Travelers Advantage ⓣ 1-877/259-2691, ⓦ www.travelersadvantage.com. Discount travel club, with cashback deals and discounted car rental. Membership required ($1 for 3 months' trial).
Travelosophy US ⓣ 1-800/332-2687, ⓦ www.itravelosophy.com. Good range of discounted and student fares worldwide.

Package holidays

The **German National Tourist Office** (see p.22) is your best starting-off point for gathering information, and the airlines are all good sources for deals. Delta and some other airlines have city and **fly-drive packages**. Delta, for example, can arrange hotel stays in Munich, Frankfurt, Berlin, Heidelberg, Dresden, Cologne and Nürnberg. Most of the tour operators listed below arrange similar city packages and fly-drives as well as trips to the **Oktoberfest**. Other specialist companies offer skiing, cycling and river **cruises**. Cruises generally start at around US$1000.

Tour operators

Abercrombie & Kent ⓣ 1-800/323-7308 or 630/954-2944, ⓦ www.abercrombiekent.com. General tour operator with a strong reputation; offers independent and escorted tours of Germany.
Adventure Center ⓣ 1-800/228-8747 or 510/654-1879, ⓦ www.adventurecenter.com. Has ski vacation packages in the Bavarian Alps.
CBT Tours ⓣ 1-800/736-2453 or 773/871-5510, ⓦ www.cbttours.com. Offers a bike tour of Germany.
Cross-Culture ⓣ 1-800/491-1148 or 413/256-6303, ⓦ www.crosscultureinc.com. Specialist in small-group cultural tours.

Delta Vacations ⓣ1-800/654-6559, ⓦwww.deltavacations.com. Organizes package deals to various German cities.

DER Tours ⓣ1-888/337 7350, ⓦwww.dertravel.com. The American branch of Germany's national travel agency offers a full range of tours, and also books accommodation and rail passes.

Euro-Bike & Walking Tours ⓣ1-800/321-6060, ⓦwww.eurobike.com. Has both cycling and walking tours in Germany.

Europe Through the Back Door ⓣ425/771-8303 ext. 217, ⓦwww.ricksteves.com. Trips led by a well-known tour leader and guidebook writer.

Europe Train Tours ⓣ1-800/551-2085 or 845/756-3283, ⓦwww.etttours.com. Organizes luxury train trips in Germany and other European countries.

Insight International Tours ⓣ1-800/582-8380, ⓦwww.inusa.insightvacations.com. Upmarket tours by coach.

Maupintour ⓣ1-800/255-4266, ⓦwww.maupintour.com. Arranges customized city break tours and has two escorted tours of Germany.

Rail Europe ⓣ1-877/EUROVAC, ⓦwww.raileurope.com. Organizes rail passes and good airfares, bookings for hotels and rental cars, and flexible, multi-centre vacation packages.

Rail passes

A **Eurail pass** (ⓦwww.eurail.com) is not likely to pay for itself if you're travelling solely within Germany but is worth considering if planning a wider tour. The pass, which is only available to non-European residents, should be purchased before arrival in Europe, though it is possible to buy it there at a higher cost. It allows **unlimited train travel** in Germany and sixteen other countries, and is available in several different forms. The standard Eurail pass, which is for first-class travel, must be used on consecutive days, and is available for periods of fifteen days, 21 days, and one, two or three months; the respective prices are US$588, US$762, US$946, US$1338 and US$1654. Two or more people travelling together can each buy a **Eurail Saver pass** at a fifteen percent discount on these rates. The **Eurail Flexipass**, likewise for first-class travel, is available for either ten or fifteen days (from the first time you use it) within a two-month period; the respective prices are US$694 and US$914, and there are also Saver versions of these at fifteen percent less for two or more people travelling together. Those under 26 can buy a **Eurail Youth pass**, which is for second-class travel, and for the same periods as the standard pass; the respective prices are US$414, US$534, US$664, US$938 and US$1160. There's also a **Eurail Youth Flexipass**, again for ten or fifteen days within a two-month period, and costing US$488 and US$642 respectively.

Finally, you should remember that North Americans are also eligible to purchase more specific passes valid for travel in Germany only, for details of which see "Getting Around", p.31. The more common European passes can be purchased through most travel agents or try the agents listed opposite.

From Australia and New Zealand

There is a good choice of **scheduled flights** from Australia and New Zealand to German destinations, chiefly via Southeast Asian cities to Frankfurt. Some stopovers will be only a few hours, while with other flights you have to change planes or break your journey en route. Charter flights are hard to come by as there is little cargo traffic flying directly to Germany, and as there's little to be saved in terms of cost, they're not really worth considering. Similarly, while travel agents can organize fly-drive deals these rarely offer enormous savings; generally, it is cheaper to buy a scheduled flight and rent the car on arrival in Germany.

One thing that is worth considering before you leave home is a **rail pass** (see above) – these can offer substantial savings on basic rail fares, and are of particular value if your trip includes Germany as part of a wider European tour.

Flights

As destinations in Europe are "common-rated" – you pay the same fare whatever your destination – some airlines offer free flight coupons, car rental or accommodation if you arrange these extras with your ticket. Choose carefully, though, as these perks are impossible to alter later. Alternatively, you could buy the cheapest possible flight to anywhere in Europe and make your way to Germany by stand-by flight, train or bus, but this rarely works out as cheaply as buying a discounted airfare all the way.

For extended trips, a **round-the-world** (RTW) ticket can work out very good value – especially from New Zealand, where airlines offer fewer bonuses to fly with them. Currently the best deals on offer are Cathay Pacific/United's "Globetrotter", Air New Zealand/KLM/Northwest's "World Navigator", and Qantas/BA's "Global Explorer" tickets: all allow six stopovers worldwide with limited backtracking and open-jaw travel, from AUS$2500 and NZ$3200.

Fares are seasonally adjusted with high season mid-May to August (the European summer) and December to mid-January, shoulder seasons March to mid-May and September, and low season the rest of the year. Seasons vary slightly depending on the airline. Tickets purchased direct from the airlines tend to be expensive. Travel agents offer much better deals and have the latest information on limited specials and stopovers, with the best discounts being through Flight Centres and STA, who can also advise on visa regulations. Students and under-26s are usually able to get at least ten percent off published prices.

Most of the major airlines quote the same fare from all the eastern Australian cities (ie they are common-rated), with flights from Perth via Asia and Africa around $200 less and via the Americas about $400 more. The cheapest scheduled flights **via Asia** (these generally involve a transfer in the carrier's Asian hub city) are with Philippine Airlines and Garuda for around $1600 in low season and $2000 in high season. In the mid range, JAL, Malaysia Airlines, Thai Airways, and Singapore Airlines all fly to Frankfurt for around AUS$1900–2600. If you're after a bit more comfort, British Airways and Qantas both quote published fares from AUS$2400 in low season up to AUS$3200 in high season.

Flights are pricier **via North America**, with United Airlines offering the cheapest deal via LA and either New York, Washington or Chicago for AUS$2300–2900, while Air New Zealand via Auckland and LA and Canadian Airlines via Toronto or Vancouver are both around AUS$2500–3100.

From Auckland fares are all similar so it depends on which route you prefer. The lowest are to Frankfurt with Garuda NZ$1900 low season, NZ$2500 high season and Thai Airways NZ$2100–2600, while Malaysia Airlines, Singapore Airlines, Air New Zealand, Lufthansa and JAL charge around NZ$2200–3000. United Airlines fly via LA from NZ$2600.

Airlines

Aeroflot Australia ⓣ 02/9262 2233, ⓦ www.aeroflot.com.au.
Air France Australia ⓣ 1300/361 400, New Zealand ⓣ 09/308 3352, ⓦ www.airfrance.com.
Air New Zealand Australia ⓣ 13 24 76, ⓦ www.airnz.com.au, New Zealand ⓣ 0800/737 000, ⓦ www.airnz.co.nz.
Alitalia Australia ⓣ 02/9244 2445, New Zealand ⓣ 09/308 3357, ⓦ www.alitalia.com.
Austrian Airlines Australia ⓣ 1800/642 438 or 02/9251 6155, New Zealand ⓣ 09/522 5948, ⓦ www.aua.com.
British Airways Australia ⓣ 1300/767 177, New Zealand ⓣ 0800/274 847, ⓦ www.ba.com.
Garuda Indonesia Australia ⓣ 1300/365 330 or 02/9334 9944, New Zealand ⓣ 09/366 1862, ⓦ www.garuda-indonesia.com.
JAL Japan Airlines Australia ⓣ 02/9272 1111, New Zealand ⓣ 09/379 9906, ⓦ www.jal.com.
KLM Australia ⓣ 1300/303 747, New Zealand ⓣ 09/309 1782, ⓦ www.klm.com.
Lufthansa Australia ⓣ 1300/655 727, New Zealand ⓣ 0800/945 220, ⓦ www.lufthansa.com.
Malaysia Airlines Australia ⓣ 13 26 27, New Zealand ⓣ 0800/777 747, ⓦ www.malaysia-airlines.com.
Philippine Airlines Australia ⓣ 02/9279 2020, New Zealand ⓣ 09/379 8522, ⓦ www.philippineairlines.com.
Qantas Australia ⓣ 13 13 13, New Zealand ⓣ 0800/808 767 or 09/357 8900, ⓦ www.qantas.com.
Singapore Airlines Australia ⓣ 13 10 11, New Zealand ⓣ 0800/808 909, ⓦ www.singaporeair.com.
Swiss Australia ⓣ 1800/883 199, New Zealand ⓣ 09/977 2238, ⓦ www.swiss.com.
Thai Airways Australia ⓣ 1300/651 960, New Zealand ⓣ 09/377 3886, ⓦ www.thaiair.com.

Travel agents

Flight Centre Australia ⓣ 13 31 33, ⓦ www.flightcentre.com.au; New Zealand ⓣ 0800 243 544, ⓦ www.flightcentre.co.nz. Rock-bottom fares worldwide.

Holiday Shoppe New Zealand ⓣ0800/808 480, ⓦwww.holidayshoppe.co.nz. Great deals on flights, hotels and holidays.
OTC Australia ⓣ1300/855 118, ⓦwww.otctravel.com.au. Deals on flights, hotels and holidays.
STA Travel Australia ⓣ1300/733 035, New Zealand ⓣ0508/782 872, ⓦwww.statravel.com. Worldwide specialists in low-cost flights, overlands and holiday deals. Good discounts for students and under-26s.
Student Uni Travel Australia ⓣ02/9232 8444, ⓦwww.sut.com.au; New Zealand ⓣ09/379 4224, ⓦwww.sut.co.nz. Great deals for students.
Trailfinders Australia ⓣ02/9247 7666, ⓦwww.trailfinders.com.au. One of the best-informed and most efficient agents for independent travellers.
travel.com.au and **travel.co.nz** Australia ⓣ1300/130 482 or 02/9249 5444, ⓦwww.travel.com.au; New Zealand ⓣ0800/468 332, ⓦwww.travel.co.nz. Comprehensive online travel company, with discounted fares.

Tour operators

Abercrombie & Kent Australia ⓣ1300/851 800, New Zealand ⓣ0800/441 638, ⓦwww.abercrombiekent.com.au. Classy tour operator with a strong reputation; cruises on the great German rivers are among the trips it offers.
Martin Randall Travel Australia ⓣ1300/559 595, ⓦwww.martinrandall.com. British company running small-group cultural tours.
Swiss Travel Australia ⓣ02/9250 9320, ⓦwww.swisstravel.com.au. Package deals not only to Switzerland, but also other countries in Europe, Germany included.
Walkabout Gourmet Adventures Australia ⓣ03/5159 6556, ⓦwww.walkaboutgourmet.com. Classy food, wine and walking tours in Germany and elsewhere.

Red tape and visas

Citizens of most EU countries (and of Norway and Iceland) need only a valid national identity card to enter Germany for an indefinite period. Since Britain has no identity card system, however, British citizens do have to take a passport.

US, Canadian, Australian and New Zealand passport holders can also enter the country for ninety days (in any one year) for a tourist visit without a visa. However, you're strongly advised, if you know your stay will be longer than this, to apply for an extension visa from the local German embassy before you go. In order to extend a stay once in the country, all visitors should contact the *Ausländeramt* (Alien Authorities) in the nearest large town: addresses are in the phone books.

EU nationals are also entitled to **work in Germany**, but anyone else has to have secured a job before arrival in order to get a work permit, for which they should apply to their local German consulate or embassy. For casual labour jobs during harvests or in the hotel and catering trades, nobody is going to ask too many questions, but wages are accordingly low and the work tough.

German embassies abroad

Australia 119 Empire Circuit, Yarralumla, Canberra, ACT 2600 ⓣ02/6270 1911, ⓦwww.german-embassy.org.au.
Britain 23 Belgrave Square, London SW1X 8PZ ⓣ020/7824 1300, ⓦwww.german-embassy.org.uk.
Canada 1 Waverly St, Ottawa, Ont. K2P 0T8 ⓣ613/232-1101, ⓦwww.germanembassyottawa.org.
Ireland 31 Trimelston Ave, Booterstown, Blackrock, Co. Dublin ⓣ01/269 3011, ⓦwww.germany.ie.
New Zealand 90–92 Hobson St, Thordon, Wellington ⓣ04/473 6063, ⓦwww.deutschebotschaftwellington.co.nz.
US 4645 Reservoir Rd NW, Washington DC 20007 ⓣ202/298 4000, ⓦwww.germany-info.org.

Information and maps

Before you leave, it's worth contacting the German National Tourist Office (see below), which has extensive information on campsites, youth hostels, hotels, train timetables and many glossy brochures besides.

Tourist offices

In **Germany**, you'll find **tourist offices** everywhere, even in tiny villages – addresses are listed in the Guide. They're almost universally friendly and very efficient, providing large amounts of free maps and brochures in a selection of languages. Most publish an annual accommodation price list (which becomes a glossy prospectus in resort towns); many also produce a monthly programme of events. The German word for a tourist office is *Fremdenverkehrsamt* (or just *Verkehrsamt*) though many sport a sign saying "Tourist Information". Another useful facility is that they can book a room for you, for which there may or may not be a small booking fee (see "Accommodation" p.37). An increasing number of tourist offices, particularly in major cities and resorts, have an after-hours computer-based service.

Opening hours are given throughout the Guide, but beware that these are prone to change, especially in the case of resorts whose volume of tourism fluctuates according to the season. A weekend shutdown from Friday lunchtime is quite common during the off-season in many smaller towns. In major cities, offices are open virtually every day of the year from early morning until late at night.

The **German Travel Agency** is universally represented by the DER offices (Ⓦwww.der.de), generally to be found near train stations or next to tourist offices. They'll book your national and international train tickets, and provide general information about travel onwards from Germany (see p.16 & p.19).

German National Tourist Offices

Australia c/o German-Australian Chamber of Industry and Commerce, PO Box 1461, Sydney NSW 2001 Ⓣ02/8296 0488, Ⓦwww.germany.org.au

Canada 480 University Ave, Suite 1410, Toronto, Ontario M5G 102 Ⓣ416/968 1685, Ⓦwww.cometogermany.com.

UK PO Box 2695, London W1A 3TN Ⓣ020/7317 0908, Ⓦwww.germany-tourism.de.

US 122 East 42nd St, 52nd Floor, New York, NY 10168-0072 Ⓣ212/661 7200, Ⓦwww.cometogermany.com.

The Internet

The **Internet** is now a major souce for tourist information material about Germany – though it has to be said that individual websites vary enormously in extent, quality and helpfulness. Some of the most useful general sites are listed below. Inevitably, many sites are in German only, though others offer a full or partial English translation. Each tourist office has a website address, which is mentioned at the appropriate point in the Guide. Usually, this is a section of a larger site about the municipality, which also includes information about its economy, politics and local services. However, in an ever increasing number of cases such sites are supplemented or replaced by ones devoted solely to tourist information. The best sites give up-to-the-minute information about opening times and prices, and comprehensive accommodation listings complete with on-line booking facilities. Others are little more than glorified advertisements inviting an email or phone call for the dispatch of the latest brochure, though these are thankfully becoming ever rarer. Most museums, monuments and hotels also have their own individual sites, or else share a site with related institutions. Again, these are listed in the Guide, though it is fair to predict that many more will spring up over the next few years.

Other useful websites include those of the German National Tourist Office (see above) and of the individual Länder, which can be accessed by keying in www. followed by the German name, then .de. When **surfing** for German names, remember that the Internet convention is that those of two or more words are hyphenated (even when this is not the case in normal practice) or the names are run on (thus Bad Frankenhasuen becomes bad-frankenhausen and Bad Urach becomes badurach), and that the letters ä, ö and ü are rendered as ae, oe and ue respectively.

Useful websites

The following sites provide useful information and help for preparing a trip to Germany.

Ⓦ **www.bahn.de** The site of Deutsche Bahn, the national railway company, has a comprehensive timetabling service with instructions available in English, enabling train journeys to be planned in advance in the minutest detail.

Ⓦ **www.germany-info.org** The site of the German embassy in Washington DC has all sorts of official statistics about the country.

Ⓦ **www.germany-tourism.de** The German National Tourist Office's site covers all matters connected with tourism.

Ⓦ **www.goethe.de** The site of the Goethe Institut, which runs language courses and cultural institutes throughout the world.

Ⓦ **www.lodging-germany.com** Provides information on hotels throughout Germany. You can view photos and then request a reservation through the secure server.

Ⓦ **www.ltu.com** Operated by the tourist arm of Lufthansa, the German national airline, this takes the form of a practical travel guide to the country.

Ⓦ **www.museum.de** Links to most of the country's best museums.

Ⓦ **www.party.de** Nightlife and events listings.

Ⓦ **www.rhinecastles.com** Searchable information site for the castle-obsessed.

Maps

German maps set international standards, and there's no shortage of excellent regional, motoring and hiking maps in most of the country's bookshops, newsagents and tourist offices. The best general publications are Mairs' road map at 1:750,000, which combines detailed road information, star ratings for places of interest, plenty of names of geographical features, and street plans of the main cities; and Berndtson's laminated map at 1:800,000, which gives a very clear picture of Germany's Autobahn network. Mairs also covers the whole country in a series of twelve 1:200,000 sheets. Excellent A-Z city maps are published by Falk and ADAC, among others. Rough Guides publish a full-colour map of Frankfurt.

The most comprehensive selection of **walking** maps is available from Kompass Wanderkarten, whose recently expanded series at 1:50,000 now covers all the main hiking areas in the country. Specialist maps of German **alpine climbs and hikes** are published by the Deutscher Alpenverein, Prater Insel 5, Munich. For cyclists, the best mapping comes from the ADFC (Algemeinen Deutschen Fahrrad-Clubs), in a series of 27 maps at 1:150,000; or from Bikeline, who have a wide selection of atlases for all the country's most popular routes (available from bookshops in Germany).

If you want to stock up before leaving home, Stanfords in London is one of the best travel bookshops in the world, with a global catalogue and mail order service. In the States, the map wholesalers Map Link (Ⓦwww.maplink.com) has a useful list of specialist map/travel bookstores in every US state, as well as some worldwide; click on Retail Partners.

Map outlets

In the UK and Ireland

Blackwell's Map Centre 50 Broad St, Oxford Ⓣ01865/793 550, Ⓦmaps.blackwell.co.uk. Branches in Bristol, Cambridge, Cardiff, Leeds, Liverpool, Newcastle, Reading & Sheffield.

The Map Shop 30a Belvoir St, Leicester Ⓣ0116/247 1400, Ⓦwww.mapshopleicester.co.uk.

National Map Centre 22–24 Caxton St, London SW1 Ⓣ020/7222 2466, Ⓦwww.mapsnmc.co.uk.

National Map Centre Ireland 34 Aungier St, Dublin Ⓣ01/476 0471, Ⓦwww.mapcentre.ie.

Stanfords 12–14 Long Acre, London WC2 Ⓣ020/7836 1321, Ⓦwww.stanfords.co.uk. Also at 39 Spring Gardens, Manchester Ⓣ0161/831 0250, and 29 Corn St, Bristol Ⓣ0117/929 9966.

The Travel Bookshop 13–15 Blenheim Crescent, London W11 Ⓣ020/7229 5260, Ⓦwww.thetravelbookshop.co.uk.

Traveller 55 Grey St, Newcastle-upon-Tyne Ⓣ0191/261 5622, Ⓦwww.newtraveller.com.

In the US and Canada

110 North Latitude US ⓣ336/369-4171, ⓦwww.110nlatitude.com.
Book Passage 51 Tamal Vista Blvd, Corte Madera, CA 94925 ⓣ1-800/999-7909, ⓦwww.bookpassage.com.
Distant Lands 56 S Raymond Ave, Pasadena, CA 91105 ⓣ1-800/310-3220, ⓦwww.distantlands.com.
Globe Corner Bookstore 28 Church St, Cambridge, MA 02138 ⓣ1-800/358-6013, ⓦwww.globecorner.com.
Longitude Books 115 W 30th St #1206, New York, NY 10001 ⓣ1-800/342-2164, ⓦwww.longitudebooks.com.
Map Town 400 5 Ave SW #100, Calgary, AB, T2P 0L6 ⓣ1-877/921-6277, ⓦwww.maptown.com.
Travel Bug Bookstore 3065 W Broadway, Vancouver, BC, V6K 2G9 ⓣ604/737-1122, ⓦwww.travelbugbooks.ca.
World of Maps 1235 Wellington St, Ottawa, ON, K1Y 3A3 ⓣ1-800/214-8524, ⓦwww.worldofmaps.com.

In Australia and New Zealand

Map Centre ⓦwww.mapcentre.co.nz.
Mapland 372 Little Bourke St, Melbourne ⓣ03/9670 4383, ⓦwww.mapland.com.au.
Map Shop 6–10 Peel St, Adelaide ⓣ08/8231 2033, ⓦwww.mapshop.net.au.
Map World 371 Pitt St, Sydney ⓣ02/9261 3601, ⓦwww.mapworld.net.au. Also at 900 Hay St, Perth ⓣ08/9322 5733.
Map World 173 Gloucester St, Christchurch ⓣ0800/627 967, ⓦwww.mapworld.co.nz.

Insurance and health

A typical travel insurance policy usually provides cover for the loss of baggage, tickets and – up to a certain limit – cash or cheques, as well as cancellation or curtailment of your journey. Most of them exclude so-called dangerous sports unless an extra premium is paid: in Germany this can mean climbing, skiing and whitewater rafting. Read the small print and benefits tables of prospective policies carefully; coverage can vary wildly for roughly similar premiums. Many policies can be chopped and changed to exclude coverage you don't need – for example, sickness and accident benefits can often be excluded or included at will. If you do take medical coverage, ascertain whether benefits will be paid as treatment proceeds or only after return home, and whether there is a 24-hour medical emergency number. When securing baggage cover, make sure the per-article limit – typically under £500 equivalent – will cover your most valuable possession. If you need to make a claim, you should keep receipts for medicines and medical treatment, and in the event you have anything stolen, you must obtain an official statement (*Aussage*) from the police. Bank and credit cards often have certain levels of medical or other insurance included and you may automatically get travel insurance if you use a major credit card to pay for your trip.

Although covered for reciprocal health care while in Germany (see p.25), citizens of **Britain** and **Ireland** would still do well to take out an insurance policy before travelling to cover against cancellation, loss and theft – and these will generally give you some kind of health cover, too. Travel agents and tour operators are likely to require some sort of insurance when you book a package holiday, though under UK law they can't make you buy their own (other than a £1 premium for "schedule airline failure"). If you have a good all-risks home insurance policy it *may* cover your possessions against loss or theft even when overseas. Note also, that many private medical schemes such as BUPA or PPP also offer coverage plans for abroad, including baggage loss, cancellation or curtailment and cash replacement as well as sickness or accident.

Americans and **Canadians** should also check that they're not already covered. Canadian provincial health plans usually provide partial cover for medical mishaps overseas. Holders of official student/teacher/youth cards are entitled to meagre accident coverage and hospital in-patient benefits. Students will often find that their student health coverage extends during the vacations and for one term beyond the date of last enrolment. Homeowners' or renters' insurance often covers theft or loss of documents, money and valuables while overseas, though conditions and maximum amounts vary from company to company.

Health

Citizens of all EU countries are entitled to free medical care in Germany on production of a **form E111**, available over the counter from main post offices. Without this form you'll have to pay in full for all medical treatment, which is expensive – currently a minimum of €20 for a visit to the doctor. The scheme does not cover you for dental charges. Whether or not you are eligible for an E111, it's sensible to take out some form of **health insurance** and remember that to make claims you will need to keep copies of receipts and prescriptions.

In the case of an **emergency**, such as a broken leg, the fastest way (though it is not free of charge) to contact an ambulance is to call ⓣ19222; information on which doctors are on duty at night and at weekends is also available via this number. The free but slower alternative is ⓣ112, which covers rescue services as well as medical emergencies. For **minor ailments**, you'll need to visit an *Arzt für Allgemeinmedizin* (doctor for general medicine) in their surgery; these are usually open on weekday mornings, and on afternoons other than Wednesday. In major cities there's a doctor on call for out-of-hours emergencies (*Ärztlicher Notdienst*); the numbers can be found in the phone book. Most German doctors can speak English. The national **AIDS** help organization, Deutsche AIDS-Hilfe e.V (DAH), is at Dieffenbachstr. 33, Berlin (ⓣ 0 30/6 90 08 70).

To get a prescription made up, go to a pharmacy (*Apotheke*): German pharmacists are well trained and often speak English. *Apotheken* serving **international prescriptions** can be found in most large cities, and a rota of late-opening or 24-hour places in larger towns is posted on all *Apotheken* doors.

Travellers with disabilities

You'll find that ease of access and facilities are good in Germany and plenty of information is available.

All ICE, IC and EC trains (see p.29) are adapted for wheelchair access, as are all IR trains and regional double-deckers and many of the suburban S-Bahns; on the ICE, IC and EC trains there's also a mandatory right to a free seat reservation. Within cities, modern trams and U-Bahns tend to have low entrance platforms and are thus suitable for wheelchairs. Sometimes, old and modern trams alternate on the same routes, and it is common practice to identify the latter on the timetables posted beside stops: the key word to look out for is Niedrig (low), hence Niedrigeingang (low entrance) or Neidrigflur (low floor). Help within stations is available if requested in advance. Museums and public buildings are usually equipped with ramps.

The **Touristik Union International** (TUI), 3000 Hannover 61 (Ⓣ05 11/56 70), has a centralized information bank on many German hotels, pensions and resorts that cater to the needs of disabled travellers or those with specific dietary requirements – not in specially designed and separate establishments, but within the mainstream of German tourist facilities. The TUI can also book you onto a package tour or organize rooms according to individual itineraries, taking into account each customer's needs, which are gauged from a questionnaire filled out before booking arrangements commence. Their services also include such details as providing suitable wheelchairs for train travel, the transportation of travellers' own wheelchairs, and the provision of transport at airports and stations.

Contacts for travellers with disabilities

In the UK and Ireland

Access Travel 6 The Hillock, Astley, Lancashire M29 7GW Ⓣ01942/888 844, Ⓦwww.access-travel.co.uk. Tour operator that can arrange flights, transfer and accommodation. This is a small business, personally checking out places before recommendation.

Holiday Care 2nd floor, Imperial Building, Victoria Rd, Horley, Surrey RH6 7PZ Ⓣ0845/124 9971, minicom Ⓣ0845/124 9976, Ⓦwww.holidaycare.org.uk. Provides free lists of accessible accommodation abroad – European, American and long haul destinations – plus a list of accessible attractions in the UK. Information on financial help for holidays available.

Irish Wheelchair Association Blackheath Drive, Clontarf, Dublin 3 Ⓣ01/818 6400, Ⓦwww.iwa.ie. Useful information provided about travelling abroad with a wheelchair.

Tripscope Alexandra House, Albany Rd, Brentford, Middlesex TW8 0NE Ⓣ0845/7585 641, Ⓦwww.tripscope.org.uk. This registered charity provides a national telephone information service offering free advice on UK and international transport for those with a mobility problem.

In the US and Canada

Access-Able Ⓦwww.access-able.com. Online resource for travellers with disabilities.

Directions Unlimited 123 Green Lane, Bedford Hills, NY 10507 Ⓣ1-800/533-5343 or 914/241-1700. Travel agency specializing in bookings for people with disabilities.

Mobility International USA 451 Broadway, Eugene, OR 97401 Ⓣ541/343-1284, Ⓦwww.miusa.org. Information and referral services, access guides, tours and exchange programmes. Annual membership $35 (includes quarterly newsletter).

Society for the Advancement of Travelers with Handicaps (SATH) 347 5th Ave, New York, NY 10016 Ⓣ212/447-7284, Ⓦwww.sath.org. Non-profit educational organization that has actively represented travellers with disabilities since 1976.

Wheels Up! Ⓣ1-888/38-WHEELS, Ⓦwww.wheelsup.com. Provides discounted airfare, tour and cruise prices for disabled travellers, also publishes a free monthly newsletter and has a comprehensive website.

In Australia and New Zealand

ACROD (Australian Council for Rehabilitation of the Disabled) PO Box 60, Curtin ACT 2605; Suite 103, 1st floor, 1–5 Commercial Rd, Kings Grove 2208; ⓣ02/6282 4333, TTY ⓣ02/6282 4333, ⓦwww.acrod.org.au. Provides lists of travel agencies and tour operators for people with disabilities.

Disabled Persons Assembly 4/173–175 Victoria St, Wellington, New Zealand ⓣ04/801 9100 (also TTY), ⓦwww.dpa.org.nz. Resource centre with lists of travel agencies and tour operators for people with disabilities.

Costs, money and banks

Germany has the world's third largest economy and, despite the cost of unification, remains a wealthy consumer nation. Prior to the advent of the euro – a pet German project – its currency, the Deutschmark, was itself among those by which international financial standards were set. One point which catches many visitors by surprise is that it is a cash society: people carry money with them, rather than rely on credit cards. Outside the major cities, it's a surprisingly affordable country to travel in, with the reasonable price of food and accommodation in popular holiday areas helping keep costs down.

Costs

If you're prepared to cut every corner by staying in youth hostels or campsites, and never eating out, you could get by on as little as €40 (around £28/$40) per day, though €70–100 is a more realistic budget on which to enjoy yourself properly. Should you have the means to spend a bit more than that, you will be able to live really well. Bear in mind that visiting cities will cost far more than staying in the countryside – a gap that is widening – and that a trip to Berlin is guaranteed to knock a large hole in any budget. If you intend to base yourself mainly in one or two rural areas – even ones as famous as the Alps or Black Forest – as opposed to travelling around a lot, you should be able to reduce the above figures by a quarter.

Accommodation costs per person can be confined to an average of about €15–20 per day for youth hostels, around €20–25 for rooms in private houses, and €25–35 for guesthouses, pensions and the more basic hotels: double rooms cost on average a bit less than twice the above rates. **Food** prices in shops are slightly lower than in Britain, and eating out is markedly cheaper at every level – except for the relative scarcity of bargain lunches. North Americans, however, will find prices slightly higher than at home, as will Australians and New Zealanders. Snack bars abound, and for around €5–10 you can put together a very filling meal. €12–15 should buy a hearty German meal plus drink in a traditional Gaststätte, while a decent dinner in a more upmarket restaurant can be had for around €18–25. Drink is marginally more expensive than in Britain or the US, but the quality, especially of the beer, is significantly higher.

Though seldom a major expense, **admission charges** for museums vary markedly, and tend to reflect whether the relevant authority regards them as a social service or an exploitable asset, rather than their intrinsic quality. Moreover, temporary exhibitions do not always have separate entrance fees: often the normal cost of admission (which is quoted throughout the Guide) is bumped up instead. The free museum, which was quite common in western Germany prior to unification, is now a rarity. Historic monuments tend to charge around €1.50–5, comparing favourably with similar places in Britain and the US. Wherever you go, a **student card** usually brings a reduction in admission costs, often substantial. It's always worth asking about combination tickets or museum passes to several sights in the same city, which bring substantial savings.

Public transport is the one area where prices are likely to present a problem. A single fare within a city, for example, is generally around €1.50–3, while a sample single train fare from Munich to Frankfurt would be €64.80. However, these costs can be softened by the use of rail and other passes, by confining your travel to a limited area, or making use of the organized hitching alternative, the *Mitfahrzentralen* (see p.35).

Currency and the exchange rate

On January 1, 2002, Germany was one of twelve European Union countries to change over to a single currency, the **euro** (€), which is split into 100 cents. There are **coins** of 1, 2, 5, 10, 20 and 50 cents, and of 1 and 2 euros; and **notes** of 5, 10, 20, 50, 100, 200 and 500 euros. The coins feature a common EU design on the face specifying the denomination, but different country-specific designs on the other. All euro currency can be also be used in any of the other participating states (Austria, Belgium, Finland, France, Greece, Ireland, Italy, Luxembourg, the Netherlands, Portugal and Spain).

At the time of writing, the exchange rate hovered around €1.45 to the pound, €0.85 to the US dollar, €0.65 to the Canadian dollar, €0.60 to the Australian dollar and €0.50 to the New Zealand dollar. For the most up-to-date exchange rates, consult the currency converter website Ⓦ www.oanda.com.

Credit cards and travellers' cheques

Unusually, for such a consumer-oriented society, **credit cards** are little used in Germany, at least by British or American standards. Though they have grown considerably in popularity in recent years, plenty of shops and restaurants still do not accept them.

Where they do come into their own, however, is for obtaining **cash advances**, and this is now by far the quickest and most convenient means of changing money. Provided you have a Personal Identification Number (PIN), there's no longer any need to go to a bank counter to make this transaction, as ATM machines accepting a wide range of credit cards are now ubiquitous features of German shopping streets, even in quite small towns. Mostly, they are just holes-in-the-wall outside banks, though some are located in secure areas which require a swipe of the card to gain admission. The machines invariably offer the option of instructions in German or English, and sometimes other languages as well. Typically, you are offered a choice of sums of money which can be withdrawn; the upper limit is usually €250 or €300, though there is often the possibility of requesting more.

In comparison to credit cards, **travellers' cheques** now seem a cumbersome option, though they remain a safe and reliable way of carrying money. Theoretically, they can be cashed in any bank or exchange office, though banks in small towns can be very choosy about which travellers' cheques they will accept, often refusing even some of the best-known names. In contrast to the United States, very few stores accept them in lieu of cash.

Banking hours are Monday to Friday 9am–noon and 1.30–3.30pm, with late opening on Thursday until 6pm. In the cities, these hours are often extended and you'll always find at least one bank open on a Saturday morning, as well as the *Postbank* in the main post office. If you're on a tight budget, it may be worth shopping around several banks (including the savings banks or *Sparkassen*), as the amount of commission deducted varies. Commission tends to be charged at a flat rate, meaning that small-scale transactions are not cost-effective.

Exchange facilities for cash and travellers' cheques can be found in virtually all banks as well as in commercial exchange shops called *Wechselstuben*, usually located near stations and airports, though often also in city centres, on the main shopping street. The *Reisebank* has branches in the train stations and airports of most main cities; these are generally open seven days a week, and until quite late in the evening.

Getting around

While it may not necessarily be cheap, getting around Germany is spectacularly quick and easy. Barely a square kilometre of the country is untouched by an unfailingly reliable public transport system, and it's a simple matter to jump from train to bus on the integrated network. Driving is also a straightforward affair on what's probably the best road network on the continent. Costs can be offset by various discounts and passes available to visitors, and it's worth studying all the options outlined below before committing yourself.

Trains

By far the best means of public transport in Germany is the train. The **rail network**, operated by the privatized national company Deutsche Bahn (DB; ⓦwww.bahn.de) – formed in 1994 from the union of the old West and East German networks – is far denser than that of any other comparable country in the world, and also has the most frequent service levels. It is particularly comprehensive in the former GDR, where there have hardly ever been any line closures, while an encouraging recent devolopment in the west has been the re-instatement of passenger trains to a number of towns cut off from the network since the 1970s. Where natural obstacles or a sparse population make rail routes unrealistic, the DB-associated buses, Bahnbusse, take over. North–south travel is particularly straightforward, while east–west journeys may require a change along the way. Everywhere services are very efficient, but relatively expensive. Up to 100km, a series of zone tariffs apply. Above that distance, the rates are calculated per kilometre.

On all intercity routes, even from one end of the country to another, the minimum **frequency** of service from early morning till late evening is one per hour, and in many cases is several times that. Between smaller towns, it's seldom worse than every two hours, and even the most isolated lines have several trains per day, although these are liable to cease in the early evening and be much reduced at weekends.

There are several **types of train**: most luxurious is the 330km-per-hour InterCityExpress (ICE), which only operates on the most popular intercity routes, though these are gradually being extended. On top of the normal fare, there's a supplement to be paid on these trains, increasing according to the distance travelled up to a maximum of €25. Otherwise, the fastest and most comfortable trains are those designated InterCity (IC) and EuroCity (EC); the only difference between them is that the ECs cross international borders. With these you can travel from one end of the country to the other – Hamburg to Munich, for example, takes six and a half hours. The only drawback is that fares are slightly higher than on regional trains on the same routes.

Slightly downscale from the ICs and ECs are the InterRegio (IR) trains, which offer a swift cross-country service along less heavily used routes, and the relatively cumbersome D-Zug or Schnellzug, which is now used primarily on evening and overnight routes. Of the more localized services, the InterRegioExpress (IRE) and RegionalExpress (RE) cover the most ground in the shortest time; the RegionalBahn (RB) is prone to stop just about everywhere.

Around major cities, the **S-Bahn** is a commuter network on which all rail passes are valid, though these usually cannot be used on the underground **U-Bahn** system, or on municipally owned trams and buses.

The colossal national **timetable** (*Kursbuch*), which is published annually, can be bought from stations for €12.50, though it's too bulky to be easily portable. Otherwise, you can easily plan your route by picking up the many free leaflets detailing intercity services, available at any main train station; by using the computerized information service available from the credit card vending machines (*Fahrkartenautomaten*) found in most stations; or by checking the company's website: ⓦwww.bahn.de.

Ticket types

Normal **tickets** (*Fahrkarten*) permit you to break the journey as often as you wish. For distances of up to 100km, they're valid for a day; for longer distances, for four days. Return tickets are valid for one month. Prices are based on distance travelled and therefore a return will cost the same as two singles. With rare exceptions, even the smallest stations have automatic ticket **vending machines**. These come in two formats: the old-style ones for cash sales, which offer tickets to nominated destinations within the surrounding region, plus a selection of major stations a bit further afield; and the new-generation ones for credit card purchases, which can be used to buy tickets to anywhere within Germany. Although it is usually possible to buy a ticket from the conductor (or the driver on some rural routes), you should make sure that you seek him or her out immediately on boarding. Otherwise, failure to produce a valid ticket results in a doubling of the normal fare, with a minimum charge of €30.

Apart from the various passes (see p.31), DB offers a range of other options which offer savings – often substantial ones – on regular fares. Note that these are particularly prone to change: a major revamp of ticketing arrangements at the end of 2002 has resulted in a more complicated system than existed before; far more bargains are now available, but a number of long-established special deals were withdrawn. For a clear English-language summary of what is currently available, it's always worth checking the website of DB's British office: ⓦwww.deutsche-bahn.co.uk.

There are a number of bargain options for **fixed return** journeys. Depending on availability, the Sparpreis 25 and Sparpreis 50 respectively give a discount of 25 and 50 percent for journeys booked at least three days in advance. When groups of up to five people are travelling together, further reductions are available with the Gruppe & Spar system, which gives a 50 percent discount at any time, rising to 60 percent for journeys booked a minimum of seven days in advance of departure, 70 percent for bookings made at least fourteen days in advance.

Although its price has risen steeply over the past few years, the €28 **Schönes-Wochenend-Ticket** is still – potentially at least – the best bargain DB offers. It allows up to five people travelling together to use any local trains (IRE, RE, RB and S-Bahn) on either a Saturday or a Sunday. (Until 1999, it covered the entire weekend, but the old name, which now seems rather misleading, has been retained.) Even for a single traveller, this soon pays for itself, and it can make astronomical savings if used to make a long cross-country journey – which it can easily do, albeit in short and slowish stages. The introduction of this ticket has had the desired effect of filling up previously little-patronized services, though there are periodic threats to withdraw it because of widespread abuses (many people sell or give away their tickets after they have finished using them, others tag along for free with perfect strangers).

The nearest weekday equivalents are the **Ländertickets**, which likewise cover up to five people travelling together (with the alternative of one or both parents accompanied by any or all of their own children aged 17 or under) on the local trains. They are valid on Mondays to Fridays from 9am until 3am the following day; on public holidays which fall on weekdays they can be used the whole day long. A ticket bought in Thuringia, Saxony-Anhalt or Saxony can be used in all three of these Länder; the same arrangement exists in Schleswig-Holstein, Hamburg and Mecklenburg-Lower Pomerania. The Lower Saxony ticket also covers the city-states of Bremen and Hamburg, while there are combined tickets for Brandenburg and Berlin, and for Rhineland-Palatinate and Saarland. Those for Bavaria, Baden-Württemberg, Hesse and North Rhine-Westphalia are valid only within their own Land. The Hesse ticket is currently the only one which is also available on Saturdays and Sundays; at €25, it's also, together with that of North Rhine-Westphalia, the most expensive. All the other tickets cost €21, except that for Brandenburg and Berlin, which is €23.

One very confusing point about the Schönes Wochenend-Ticket and the Ländertickets is that they can be used on some trams and buses, but not others. For example, in Bavaria they are currently valid on all forms of public transport within Munich and Nürnberg, but not in any of the province's smaller cities; in Baden-Württemberg they are accepted on buses in and around Konstanz, but not those on the opposite side of the Bodensee. Always check locally for their exact validity outside the rail network.

If **travelling with kids**, note that those under six travel free, while those aged between six and fourteen travel for half the adult price. Long-distance trains generally have a special compartment, designated a *Kinderabteilung*, for mothers and toddlers.

On long journeys, such as from the North Sea coast to Bavaria, it's worth considering **travelling overnight**. If aiming to sit up, note that conditions can be very cramped on Fridays and Sundays; on other nights you should manage to find an empty or near-empty compartment. However, this can be a dangerous option, as there are professional gangs "working" such trains; their favourite technique is to spray gas into compartments through air ducts, thereby ensuring that the passengers inside remain asleep while they are robbed. Far better and safer are the new-generation night trains, NachtZug (NZ), which currently have reclining seats and couchettes only; and CityNightLine (CNL), which also has sleepers, and travels to and from Austria and Switzerland. Under the *SparNight* system, a limited number of remarkably good-value all-inclusive one-way tickets right across the country and beyond are available on these trains: reclining seats from €30, couchettes from €40, sleepers upwards of €60.

Rail passes

InterRail (see p.14) and **Eurail** (see p.19) passes are valid on all trains but you will have to pay supplements on ICE trains (and, in the former case, on IC and EC trains as well, though conductors do not always enforce this). If you're using the trains extensively in Germany, there are other passes which may make train travel cheaper.

The broadest-ranging pass is the **EuroDomino** which needs to be bought outside the country in which it is going to be used (you can book online through Ⓦwww.raileurope.co.uk), and is only available to those who have been resident in Europe for six months or more. In Germany, it entitles the holder to unlimited travel on: all trains and Bahnbusse; the buses which ply the tourist-orientated **scenic routes** such as the Burgenstrasse (Castle Road) the Romantische Strasse (Romantic Road) and the Schwarzwald-Hochstrasse (Black Forest Highway); and the K-D Linie steamers on the Mosel and on the Rhine between Cologne and Mainz (see "Boats" on p.32). With prices ranging from €185 for three days to €280 for eight days (not necessarily consecutive) within the period of a month, it can be excellent value, especially as no further supplements are payable, except on ICE trains.

Should you be staying in Germany for an extended period it's worth considering the **BahnCard**. The BahnCard 25, which costs €50 for second class, €100 for first class, brings a 25 percent reduction on all regular ticket prices, plus Sparpreis 25, over the course of a year; the BahnhCard 50 gives a 50 percent reduction for a payment of €200 in second class, €400 in first class.

Private railways

An increasing number of stretches of railway line lie outside the DB network. They have their own special ticketing arrangements, though rail passes are generally still valid on those which are normal mainline routes, such as the BOB network in Upper Bavaria. However, passes cannot be used on the famous **narrow-gauge lines** in Saxony, the Harz and the coast of Mecklenburg-Lower Pomerania which were, prior to the creation of the new DB in 1994, an integral part of the old East German system. Their privatization has brought much higher fares and led to plenty of protests, though at least their long-term future now seems totally secure. **Steam engines** are still used regularly on these lines, though modern diesels frequently take their place.

There's a much larger number of lines no longer used for regular passenger services where DB allows a local preservation society to run special excursions, usually with historic locomotives, throughout the summer. In some cases, such as the spectacular Wutachtalbahn in the Black Forest, these are quite frequent; more typically, they take place only once or twice a month, invariably at weekends or on public holidays.

The most interesting private railways are all described in the Guide. Full operational details, including the exact dates of excursion services, can be found in DB's *Kursbuch*.

Buses

At such rare times as you have to forsake the trains for **buses**, you'll find no decline in the standard of efficiency. Most buses are run in association with DB and are known as Bahnbusse. They're organized into regional associations, which offer **runabout passes** for a variety of periods; these can be quite remarkable value, particularly if you're making an extended stay in a scenic area such as the Alps or the Black Forest. There are also some privately operated routes outside this system.

You're most likely to need buses in remote rural areas – or along the designated **scenic routes** (see "Rail Passes", p.31). On these routes buses are luxury-class, often packed with tourists, and pause long enough by the major points of scenic or historic interest for passengers to hop out and take a couple of photographs. Although expensive to use without a railcard (EuroDomino and Eurail holders travel free and InterRail cards get a 50 percent reduction), these buses are usually the only way to visit certain locales if you don't have your own transport or the patience to zigzag around on the slow local buses.

A point to watch out for in the remoter country areas is **punctuality**. Unlike trains, buses are allowed to run ahead of their timetable – and often do if they have few passengers to pick up. It's therefore prudent to be at the stop at least ten minutes before the bus is due to arrive.

Finally, although there are some **long-distance** bus routes undercutting the railways, these are on a very small scale in comparison with Britain or the US. Many link major holiday resorts and the big population centres, and are clearly targeted at the latter's less affluent residents.

Boats

Travelling by **boat** is another option, though more for relaxation than covering large distances. All along the major rivers, and in particular the **Rhine** and **Mosel**, there are innumerable local boats waiting to ferry you across or around the waters. For a longer trip, K-D Linie steamers sail on the Rhine between Cologne and Mainz, and on the Mosel between Koblenz and Cochem, every day from April to October inclusive. On these routes, possession of a EuroDomino or Eurail pass will get you free passage, while InterRail brings a 50 percent reduction.

The steamers call at many riverside villages and you can get on or off wherever you want. The fare, as you'd expect, depends on how far you travel; Cologne to Koblenz, for example, costs €40.60 single, €46 for a day return. Several smaller companies also operate short-haul services along both the Rhine and Mosel, and along most other main navigable rivers as well. In the former GDR, there are particularly beautiful cruises to be had on the Elbe, particularly the stretch from Dresden south into the Czech Republic.

Germany's biggest lake, an enormous bulge in the Rhine called the **Bodensee**, is also a prime spot for water-borne travel, either for a direct journey or a lazy cruise to explore the nooks and crannies of its shoreline, which spans Austria and Switzerland as well as Germany; full details are on p.291. Cruise boats also ply many of Bavaria's Alpine and pre-Alpine lakes.

Municipal public transport

Municipal public transport in most German cities (though western Berlin and Hamburg are notable exceptions) is still centred on **trams**. Increasingly, these are sleek modern vehicles capable of moving at a fair speed between stops. They often have an underground stretch in the city centre, where they're known as the **U-Bahn**. This is often a source of confusion; it's important to remember that Berlin, Hamburg, Munich and Nürnberg have a much more extensive U-Bahn system using tube trains as distinct from trams, while in cities with trams only you may have to look both above and below ground in the central area to find the stop for the service you want. In some cities, old boneshaker trams are still the mainstay of the public transport system, though these are gradually being replaced. Wherever the trams and U-Bahns do not go, you can be sure that there will be a **bus** to fill the void.

Tickets, which can be bought from automatic vending machines or the driver, are valid on all the different forms of transport – which include the S-Bahn and mainline **trains** as well in all the major conurbations – and you can change from one to another, with no supplement for transfers. This means that, if making a train journey between two places within the same public transport authority, you are entitled to have what are in effect free rides on the local public transport systems at either end, provided these are made within the allowed time periods. Normal **single** fares are relatively expensive – €2 is the standard rate in many cities, though there's generally a special lower tariff for short journeys (*Kurzstrecke*).

If you're planning to make several journeys, it's advisable either to buy in **blocks** (usually offering a total saving of around 30 percent), or invest in a **fixed time period** (generally 24 hrs) ticket. The latter, which can be bought for the city itself or the whole of the regional network, can be a tremendous bargain – in some cities, up to two adults and two children are covered by the ticket, for an outlay of around €5 or €8 respectively. Even better value are the cards which, for a minimal extra outlay, include free or reduced admission to the main museums and monuments. Details of these are given throughout the Guide, but note that exact conditions are particularly prone to change.

Ticket purchase functions largely on the honour system, and spot checks by plainclothes inspectors are fairly rare. However, they do take place rather more frequently than was once the case, and result in an automatic €30–40 **fine** for anyone caught without a valid ticket.

Planes

While **domestic flights** with the national airline Lufthansa are numerous and quick between the major cities, they are geared squarely at businesspeople and are correspondingly expensive: expect to pay a minimum of €110 for a Frankfurt–Berlin return, €130 for a Frankfurt–Hamburg return. At periods of high demand, such as trade fairs or major events, these prices may be several times higher. More reasonable rates are now available from German Wings, Lufthansa's low cost subsidiary, though at the moment these are mostly to and from its home base of Cologne/Bonn. If you definitely want to fly between German cities and are starting and finishing your journey in the UK, it's cheaper to book all the flights together, although this usually means that dates of travel cannot be changed.

Germania Express has introduced the concept of fixed-price flights at all times, regardless of when booked, and is currently charging a flat €77 single for all its domestic services. Its main hub is Berlin-Tegel, from where it operates flights to and from Munich, Stuttgart and Frankfurt.

Driving and vehicle rental

Foreigners may drive in Germany for one year with a national or international driving licence (for more than a year non-EU citizens must have a German licence). At least third-party **insurance** is mandatory (normal third-party insurance in Britain does not cover foreign travel, although more extensive policies do). It's not necessary to carry a green card, but some other form of proof of insurance is essential.

Seatbelts are compulsory for all passengers as well as the driver, and **children under 12** years must sit in the back. Understanding **right of way** can be problematic: if nothing is indicated, priority is always with vehicles coming from the right. In cities, be aware that **trams** always have the right of way. Unfamiliarity with the traffic system means that unwary visiting drivers are prone to cut in front of turning trams at junctions – a frightening and potentially lethal error. Also, when trams halt at their designated stops it's forbidden to overtake until the tram starts moving, to allow passengers time to cross the road and board.

Germany's highways, or **Autobahnen**, are the most extensive and efficient network in Europe, though those in the north can sometimes be only two lanes. Fuel stations, roadside restaurants and motels are located every 30–40km, and every city and virtually all the towns are within simple striking distance, using equally high-quality secondary roads to link them to the Autobahnen. A huge amount of work has been done in the former GDR to bring its road system up to western standards, though many minor routes still remain in a poor state of repair.

There are no legally enforced **speed limits** on the Autobahnen although there is a recommended limit of 130kmph. The official speed limit on country roads is 100kmph, and in built-up areas 50kmph, unless a lower figure is indicated.

Note that there are **on-the-spot fines** for speeding and other offences. For speeding these are charged on a sliding scale from about €10–25; after a cut-off point of roughly 25km above the limit, you're charged and taken to court.

Car rental (*Autovermietung*) is available at all airports and major train stations, and regional tourist offices will be able to inform you of the nearest car-rental firm. Although the major companies like Avis, Budget or Hertz are easy to find, smaller local companies often offer better rates. Rates tend to be higher than in the UK and markedly higher than in the US (upwards of €300 for a small hatchback for a week). You'll need to be 21 or over to rent a car in Germany.

Fly-drive deals can be good value if you know in advance that you want to rent a car, but you'll often get a better deal through someone who deals with local agents.

Car rental agencies

In Australia

Avis ⓣ13 63 33 or 02/9353 9000, ⓦwww.avis.com.au.
Budget ⓣ1300/362 848, ⓦwww.budget.com.au.
Dollar ⓣ02/9223 1444, ⓦwww.dollarcar.com.au.
Europcar ⓣ1300/131 390, ⓦwww.deltaeuropcar.com.au.
Hertz ⓣ13 30 39 or 03/9698 2555, ⓦwww.hertz.com.au.
National ⓣ13 10 45, ⓦwww.nationalcar.com.au.
Thrifty ⓣ1300/367 227, ⓦwww.thrifty.com.au.

In Ireland

Avis ⓣ01/605 7500, ⓦwww.avis.ie.
Budget ⓣ0903/277 11, ⓦwww.budget.ie.
Europcar ⓣ01/614 2888, ⓦwww.europcar.ie.
Hertz ⓣ01/676 7476, ⓦwww.hertz.ie.
Holiday Autos ⓣ01/872 9366, ⓦwww.holidayautos.ie.
Thrifty ⓣ1800/515 800, ⓦwww.thrifty.ie.

In New Zealand

Apex ⓣ0800/93 95 97 or 03/379 6897, ⓦwww.apexrentals.co.nz.
Avis ⓣ09/526 2847 or 0800/655 111, ⓦwww.avis.co.nz.
Budget ⓣ09/976 2222, ⓦwww.budget.co.nz.
Hertz ⓣ0800/654 321, ⓦwww.hertz.co.nz.
National ⓣ0800/800 115, ⓦwww.nationalcar.co.nz.
Thrifty ⓣ09/309 0111, ⓦwww.thrifty.co.nz.

In North America

Alamo US ⓣ1-800/522-9696, ⓦwww.alamo.com.
Auto Europe US ⓣ1-800/223-5555, Canada ⓣ1-888/223-5555, ⓦwww.autoeurope.com.
Avis US ⓣ1-800/331-1084, Canada ⓣ1-800/272-5871, ⓦwww.avis.com.
Budget US ⓣ1-800/527-0700, ⓦwww.budgetrentacar.com.
Dollar US ⓣ1-800/800-4000, ⓦwww.dollar.com.
Europcar US & Canada ⓣ1-877/940 6900, ⓦwww.europcar.com.
Europe by Car US ⓣ1-800/223-1516, ⓦwww.europebycar.com.
Hertz US ⓣ1-800/654-3001, Canada ⓣ1-800/263-0600, ⓦwww.hertz.com.
National US ⓣ1-800/227-7368, ⓦwww.nationalcar.com.
Thrifty US ⓣ1-800/367-2277, ⓦwww.thrifty.com.

In the UK

Avis ⓣ0870/606 0100, ⓦwww.avis.co.uk.
Budget ⓣ0800/181 181, ⓦwww.budget.co.uk.
Europcar ⓣ0845/722 2525, ⓦwww.europcar.co.uk.
National ⓣ0870/536 5365, ⓦwww.nationalcar.co.uk.
Hertz ⓣ0870/844 8844, ⓦwww.hertz.co.uk.

Suncars ⓣ0870/500 5566, ⓦwww.suncars.com.
Thrifty ⓣ01494/751 600, ⓦwww.thrifty.co.uk.

Motoring organizations

In the UK and Ireland

AA UK ⓣ0870/600 0371, ⓦwww.theaa.com.
AA Ireland Dublin ⓣ01/617 9988, ⓦwww.aaireland.ie.
RAC UK ⓣ0800/550 055, ⓦwww.rac.co.uk.

In North America

AAA ⓣ1-800/AAA-HELP, ⓦwww.aaa.com. Each state has its own club – check the phone book for local address and phone number.
CAA ⓣ613/247-0117, ⓦwww.caa.ca. Each region has its own club – check the phone book for local address and phone number.

In Australia and New Zealand

AAA Australia ⓣ02/6247 7311, ⓦwww.aaa.asn.au.
New Zealand AA New Zealand ⓣ09/377 4660, ⓦwww.nzaa.co.nz.

Taxis

In cities and towns, taking into account the high cost of local public transport, several people sharing a cab may actually save money over using a local bus or train. Taxis (nearly all of which are Mercedes) have a sign on the roof which is illuminated if they are free. Hail one from the street, or wait at the taxi stands – alternatively there are always plenty hovering around train stations and big hotels.

Mitfahrzentralen

As in most other countries today, casual hitching in Germany is not recommended as a safe method of getting around.

However, the Germans have developed an institutionalized form of hitching called **Mitfahrzentralen**, located in most large cities. These are agencies that put drivers and travellers in touch with each other for a nominal fee, and then it's up to the participants to work out an agreeable fuel contribution, usually a simple two-way split, although the agency does suggest a reasonable sum. There's a valuable safety factor in this system, since all drivers have to notify the agencies of their addresses and car registration numbers. Both of the two main national networks have the same number – ⓣ1 94 40 and ⓣ1 94 44 – in each city. There are also a few **women-only agencies**, known as *Frauenmitfahrzentralen*.

Cycling

Cyclists are well catered for in Germany – at least in comparison with the UK or US – though sensibly they're banned from the Autobahnen. Many smaller roads have marked cycle-paths, and bike-only lanes are a common sight in cities and towns. Fairly hassle-free **long-distance cycling** is possible all over the country, but obviously you'll need a strong pair of legs and a sturdy, reliable machine to get much joy out of the Bavarian Alps. To take your own **bike on a train**, you need to purchase a *Fahrrad-Karte* (bicycle ticket), which costs €3 for up to 100km, €6 otherwise. On express services, you have to take the bike to the luggage van; on S-Bahn and regional trains, there are marked carriages where cyclists can stay with their bikes.

Between April and October, the best place to **rent a bike** is from a train station participating in the Fahrrad am Bahnhof scheme (most of the main stations), whereby a bike costs from €6–10 per day. You can return it to any other participating station and EuroDomino or InterRail card-holders get a 50 percent discount. This is obviously perfect for splitting train travel with pedalling as and when the mood, terrain or weather takes you. During the rest of the year, or in an area where there's no suitable station, simply look in the phone book under Fahrradverleih to find the address of a local bike rental outlet. Renting this way, however, means you'll have to leave a deposit, usually at least €25.

Walking and hiking

The German countryside is laced with colour-coded **hiking trails**, most of which are suitable for a Sunday afternoon stroll, though many are actually sections of much longer hikes. Very few hikes pass through remote or isolated areas and there's always a village, campsite or youth hostel fairly close by so you can make a trek of just a few hours or of several days' duration without much trouble. The best of the trails are described in the Guide and the local tourist offices have masses of **information and maps** (*Wanderkarten*) relating to the walks in their area. Because the hikes are so easy, you won't need any specialist equipment, but take a comfortable day-pack for carrying picnic provisions.

There are some **potential frustrations**, however. The prevalence of trees in all the scenic areas (with the exception of the Swabian Jura and the upper reaches of the Bavarian Alps) not only means that you're only occasionally rewarded with long-range views, but also ensures that there's seldom much chance to deviate from the regimentation of the marked paths. Don't let this rigidity fool you into skimping on proper maps: at times the trails can peter out or become confused, particularly when signs have become weather-worn or have been vandalized.

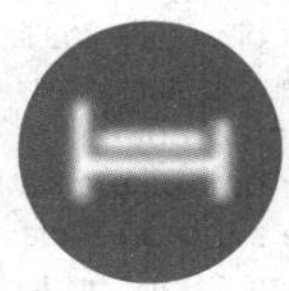

Accommodation

Be it high-rise city hotels or half-timbered guest houses in the country, accommodation of all types is easy to find in Germany and can often be good value – especially in the growing number of rooms available in private houses. For those on a really tight budget, the youth hostels and campsites which proliferate over the entire country are a sound, cost-cutting alternative.

There are wide variations in the prices charged for similar types of accommodation. Predictably, Berlin is the most expensive destination in the country, with the likes of Munich, Hannover, Stuttgart, Cologne and Düsseldorf not too far behind. Yet other major cities, including Nürnberg, Augsburg and, to a lesser extent, Hamburg, Frankfurt and Dresden, are well-endowed with good-quality budget accommodation, whereas many far smaller towns are not.

Accommodation of all types in popular holiday areas – even ones as famous as the Bavarian Alps and the Black Forest – can be remarkably good value. Note that, in spas and other health resorts, there's a hidden extra charge in the form of the *Kurtaxe*, a **tax** levied on behalf of the municipality, which can be for anything up to €4 per day. In return, the guest is given a *Kurkarte*, which gives free or reduced entry to many local sights and facilities – sometimes including municipal buses. However, some proprietors do not bother implementing the system if a guest is only staying for a night or two.

Online booking facilities for accommodation of all types are on the increase. Even when an establishment does not have an individual website or email address, it may still be possible to book online via the tourist office site.

Hotels

Accommodation in Germany is subject to a somewhat complicated categorization system. The official classification of **Hotel** is not applied as widely as in many other countries, being confined in the main to mid-range and expensive establishments which have a manned reception desk and offer a full range of services, including a restaurant. Those of similar standing which serve no meals other than breakfast are classified as **Hotel Garni**. The designation **Gasthof** signifies a uniquely German institution, one roughly equivalent to the traditional English inn. More often than not, you have to ask for a room at its bar-cum-restaurant. The latter almost invariably has a regular local clientele, and often forms the mainstay of the business, with accommodation playing a secondary role.

Despite these different categories, the bedrooms on offer tend not to vary much: they're normally clean, comfortable and functional with conveniences like TV, phone and en-suite bathroom usually taken for granted in the medium-range establishments upwards. Note that in the former GDR most hotels are either new or recently refurbished, and hence tend to be more expensive than their western counterparts. The listings in the Guide concentrate on the best options in all price categories from the points of view of convenience, character and value for money. However, it's always worth calling into the nearest **tourist office** to check any special deals which they may have with local establishments. This can result in you spending less than the figures quoted on the official **accommodation lists** which every tourist office provides. Many tourist offices charge €2–5 for finding you a room, but others perform the service free. In many of the principal cities, hotel prices are bumped up, often to double the normal rate or more, when there's a trade fair, or *Messe*, taking place. During the biggest of these, all available rooms in the city and its hinterland are booked out months in advance.

In budget and medium-priced hotels, there's rarely any great saving to be made by two people sharing as opposed to one person travelling alone. In country areas, the least you'll have to spend is about €20 for a single, €35 for a double; something similar in a city is likely to be at least €5–10 extra. Remember that any savings on accommodation costs that can be made by staying on the outskirts of a city may be offset by the price of public transport into the centre.

Pensions and private rooms

The official designation of **Pension** is applied to less formal establishments than hotels. In such places, the rooms are usually within a private house or apartment block. The term **Gästehaus** (guesthouse) is sometimes used instead, particularly in popular holiday areas such as the Bavarian Alps, where the accommodation is almost invariably in huge chalets. Prices tend to be quite a bit lower than in hotels, though this is less marked in cities than in the countryside.

In busy holiday areas, an increasingly prevalent budget option is **bed and breakfast** accommodation in a private house (look for signs saying *Fremdenzimmer* or *Zimmer frei*): prices vary but are usually around €20–25 for a single, €27.50–35 for a double. Very few west German cities have private rooms on offer other than to relieve congestion when there's a trade fair on; rates are then comparable with those of hotels. In the former GDR, on the other hand, thousands of householders have opened up their **homes** to guests, in order to earn a bit of extra cash. This helped plug the huge shortfall in accommodation for travellers that would otherwise have existed in the years immediately following the *Wende*, and nowadays provides a budget alternative to the hotel sector, which in eastern

Accommodation price codes

All the pensions and hotels in this book have been graded according to the following price categories. The codes quoted are for the cheapest available double room, except for establishments which have rooms costing widely different rates, when the most expensive price is given as well. Exact charges are given for youth hostels; in the case of the official DJH (HI) establishments, this is the lowest available rate. When two figures or ranges of figures are quoted for these hostels, the first applies to juniors (ie under 27 years of age), the second to seniors (27 and above). In Bavaria, the hostel price applies to juniors only.

- ❶ less than €30
- ❷ €30–39
- ❸ €40–49
- ❹ €50–62
- ❺ €63–74
- ❻ €75–99
- ❼ €100–124
- ❽ €125–149
- ❾ €150 and upwards

Germany is now dominated by expensive business-class ventures. In the cities, many of the rooms are in high-rise apartment blocks, and thus impossible to locate under your own steam. You therefore need to go to the local tourist office or one of the **private agencies** (*Zimmervermittlung*), which are often open until late in the evening, to book a room. Usually, there's a charge similar to that made for booking hotels, but beware of any tourist office or agency which wants to levy a daily fee: in such cases, book for one night and then try to negotiate a longer stay with your hosts.

Farmhouse holidays (*Ferien auf dem Bauernhof*) are increasingly popular in Germany, and in many ways are the best bargains of all, with full-board rates from as little as €20 per person per day. Full lists are available from local tourist offices; the major snag is that this option is really only feasible if you have your own transport.

Even more ubiquitous are **holiday homes** (*Ferienhäuser*) which you rent by the week, and these can be the cheapest option if you are travelling with a family or a group. Full lists are available from tourist offices in all main holiday areas. In major cities, it's well worth contacting one of the **flat- and room-letting agencies** (*Mitwohnzentralen*) if you intend to stay for an extended period. Some will only arrange accommodation for a minimum period of a month, but even if you leave early this may still undercut any other option.

Youth hostels

In Germany, you're never far away from an official **youth hostel** (*Jugendherberge*) – the YH movement was born here, in fact, in 1909 – and these are likely to form the backbone of genuine budget travelling. Note, however, that at any time of the year they're liable to be block-booked by school groups – this is particularly likely on weekdays during the summer, and at weekends out of season. It's therefore advisable to make a reservation by phoning or emailing the hostel as far in advance as possible to be sure of a place – and be prepared to put up with marauding adolescents. Though most **wardens** and their staff are courteous and helpful, there's an unfortunate minority who seem to be leftovers from the leadership of the Hitler Youth, insisting on rigid regimentation and pedantic enforcement of the rules. You should be wary, too, of **age restrictions** (see below) and the fact that prices are slightly cheaper if you're under 27 years of age.

More than six hundred hostels are run by the **German Youth Hostel Association** (Deutsches Jugendherbergswerk) and indicated by signs reading DJH. Full details (in English and German) of all its hostels can be found on its website Ⓦwww.jugendherberge.de, which can also be used to email bookings to any individual establishment. **Prices**, which start at around €10 in the most basic establishments, are inclusive bed-and-breakfast rates, and apply to HI members; non-members, if admitted at all, will be charged a supplement. If you're not a member and intend to use hostels for more than a couple of nights, it's wise to buy a year's HI **membership** from your own national association, before leaving home. You can buy the same thing at larger hostels in Germany but it's slightly more expensive.

German youth hostels do carry a number of other **rules** and restrictions. **Reservations** will only be held until 6pm unless you've informed the warden that you'll be arriving late. When things are busy, **priority** is given to people under 18, or hiking families travelling with children. Those **over 27**, if they've not made a reservation, are only supposed to get a place if the hostel is not fully booked at 6pm – though this is by no means strictly applied. A more serious restriction for this age group is that they can't use the hostels in **Bavaria** at all, unless they are accompanying children. Elsewhere, they have to pay a slightly higher rate (usually an extra €2.70) at all but the hostels which bear the designation of **youth guesthouse** (*Jugendgästehaus*). These are more luxurious than the others, with accommodation in two- and four-bedded dorms and a wide range of facilities. However, at upwards of €20 per head they can work out as a more expensive option than a guesthouse for two people sharing – and are almost invariably so for those travelling in a small group.

All hostels have a **curfew**, which can be as early as 10pm (and usually is in rural areas), but may be later (as is the case in all the big cities). The latest time you are able to check in is generally 10pm, too. **Length of stay** is officially limited to three days unless a longer period has been booked in advance. You can, however, stay longer – provided you're not going to deprive new arrivals from getting in. In **winter** many hostels close altogether; many more shut every other weekend. Very few German hostels offer self-catering facilities, but most do provide meals.

Privately owned hostels are, in general, far more relaxed and less regimented than their official counterparts, dispensing with the more offputting hostelling traditions such as lockouts, curfews and supplements for older guests. They are found mainly in the larger cities (Berlin and Munich both offer a wide choice of establishments) and are usually run by friendly, savvy young staff responsive to the needs of modern travellers.

Finally, the **Naturfreundehaus** association offers a variant on the hostel theme. Its establishments, often located in rural countryside close to towns and cities, are designed more for older people, with accommodation in singles, doubles or very small dorms.

Youth hostel associations

Australia Australian Youth Hostels Association ⓣ02/9261 1111, ⓦwww.yha.com.au.
Canada Hostelling International Canada ⓣ1-800/663 5777 or 613/237 7884, ⓦwww.hostellingintl.ca.
England and Wales Youth Hostel Association (YHA) ⓣ0870/770 8868, ⓦwww.yha.org.uk.
Germany Deutsches Jugendherbergswerk ⓣ0 52 31/7 40 10, ⓦwww.jugendherberge.de.
Ireland Irish Youth Hostel Association ⓣ01/830 4555, ⓦwww.irelandyha.org.
New Zealand Youth Hostelling Association New Zealand ⓣ0800/278 299 or 03/379 9970, ⓦwww.yha.co.nz.
Northern Ireland Hostelling International Northern Ireland ⓣ028/9032 4733, ⓦwww.hini.org.uk.
Scotland Scottish Youth Hostel Association ⓣ0870/155 3255, ⓦwww.syha.org.uk.
US Hostelling International-American Youth Hostels ⓣ202/783-6161, ⓦwww.hiayh.org.

Camping

Big, well-managed **campsites** are a feature of Germany, and they're located almost anywhere anybody could even think about wanting to camp. It's significant that sites are officially graded on a scale beginning at "good" and working up to "excellent". Even those in the lowest grade have toilet and washing facilities and a shop on the site, while the grandest are virtually open-air hotels with swimming pools, supermarkets and various other comforts – though it must be said that camping purists find German sites rather too regimented. **Prices** are based on facilities and location, comprising a fee per person and per tent (each around €3–6). There are extra fees for cars, caravans, etc, so you could easily spend quite a bit more than you might in other countries if there are several of you travelling in a car.

Bear in mind, too, that many sites, especially those in popular holiday areas, are nearly always full from June to September, and you should arrive early in the afternoon for a good chance of getting in. Most campsites close down in the winter, but those in popular skiing areas remain open all year; months of closure, where they exist, are indicated throughout the Guide.

All the most useful sites are listed in the Guide, and you can also pick up the highly condensed **list of sites** which is available free from German National Tourist Offices. The complete official guide is available in bookshops throughout Germany, or direct from the German Camping Club, the DDC, at Mandlstr. 28, Munich. The motoring organization, ADAC (ⓦwww.adac.de), produces a similar guide which includes Germany and much of northern and central Europe.

Rough camping on communally owned land is illegal – in the interests of protecting the environment – though a blind eye seems to be turned to camper vans: indeed stays ranging from 24 hours to three days are sometimes officially sanctioned. You can camp on private farmland by obtaining permission – which is often freely granted – from the owner.

Eating

German food is, as a rule, both good value and of high quality. However, it does help if you share the national penchant for solid, fatty food accompanied by compensatingly healthy fresh vegetables and salad. The pig is the staple element of the German menu – it's prepared in umpteen different ways, and just about every part of it is eaten. It also forms the main ingredient for sausages, which are not only the most popular snack, but are regarded as serious culinary fare – in Bavaria, there are even specialized *Wurstküchen* (sausage kitchens) which have gained Michelin ratings. German food terms are covered in Language p.1059.

Breakfast

The vast majority of German hotels and guesthouses, and all youth hostels, include breakfast in the price of their accommodation. Although some places go in for the spartan French affair of rolls, jam and coffee, the normal German breakfast lies midway between this and the elaborate Scandinavian-style cold table, but the latter is catching on, particularly in middle- and upper-range hotels. Typically, you'll be offered a small platter of **cold meats** (usually sausage-based) and **cheeses**, along with a selection of marmalades, jams and honey. Muesli or another cereal is sometimes included as well. You're generally given a variety of **breads**, which are among the most distinctive features of German cuisine. Both brown and white rolls are popular; these are often given a bit of zap by the addition of a condiment, such as caraway, coriander, poppy or sesame seeds. The rich-tasting black rye bread, known as Pumpernickel, is a particular national favourite, as is the salted Brezel, which tastes nothing like any foreign imitation. **Coffee** (which is normally freshly brewed) is the usual accompaniment. Drinking chocolate is a common alternative, as are both herbal and plain **tea**. Tea is served black, often with optional lemon, but does not blend well with German milk. Fruit juice – almost invariably orange – is sometimes included as well.

If breakfast isn't included in your accommodation costs, you can usually do quite well by going to a local **baker's shop**, which generally opens from 7am, if not before. Most chain bakeries have an area set aside for breakfast, known as a *Stehcafé* (standing café), a practice taken up by some family establishments as well. The coffee and chocolate on offer tend to be of high quality, and there's the added bonus of being able to choose from the freshly made bakery on display; €3–5 should cover an adequate breakfast.

Snacks and fast food

Just as the English have their morning and afternoon tea, so the Germans have *Kaffee und Kuchen* (coffee and cakes). Though the elegant type of **café** serving a choice of espresso, capuccino and mocha to the accompaniment of cream cakes, pastries or handmade chocolates is indelibly associated with Austria, it's every bit as popular an institution in Germany. This hardly constitutes a cheap snack but is unlikely to be a rip-off – except in the most obvious tourist traps. An almost equally ubiquitous institution is the **ice-cream parlour** (*Eiscafé*). Almost invariably, these are run by Italian émigrés and offer a huge range of flavours and concoctions to choose from, which can either be eaten on the premises or taken away.

More substantial food is available from **butcher's shops**. Even in rural areas, you can generally choose from a variety of freshly roasted meats to make up a hot sandwich. It's also worth going to the open-air **markets** which are held anything from once to six times a week in the central square of most towns. With a bit of judicious shopping round the stalls, you should be able to make up an irresistible picnic for a modest outlay. Larger cities tend to have a daily indoor version of this, known as the *Markthalle*.

The easiest option for a quick snack, however, is to head for the ubiquitous **Imbiss** stands and shops. In the latter you have the option of eating in or taking away; the price is the same. These indigenous types of snack bar tend to serve a range of sausages, plus meatballs, hamburgers and chips; the better ones have soups, schnitzels, chops and salads as well. Spit-roasted chicken is usually recommendable and very cheap, at around €3 for half a bird. Mustard is usually available at no extra cost with all dishes, whereas small supplements are often levied for mayonnaise or ketchup. Most *Imbiss* places sell beer, but as many are unlicensed you may be forbidden from consuming it on the premises.

Among the fast-food **chains**, Kochlöffel stands out for cleanliness and good food. The speciality here is spit-roast chicken; prices compare very favourably with the many American-owned hamburger joints. Another chain with decent food is Wienerwald, but its menu, set-up and price structure are more comparable to a restaurant than a snack bar. The Bavarian butcher's chain Vincenz Murr sells full main courses to be eaten on your feet, costing €3–6; many smaller concerns throughout the country offer a similar service. Virtually the only places outside northern Germany where you can regularly find salt-water **fish** are the shops of the Nordsee chain. These vary a lot in size and hence choice, and the pre-prepared dishes for consumption on the premises seldom look as appetising as the fish sold for cooking at home. Nonetheless, they are reliable choices for a quick lunch. By far the most innovative and original chain is that run by the Swiss company Mövenpick under the Restaurant Marché logo. Here, fresh market ingredients are the watchwords, whether in the enormous cold buffet selection from which you help yourself, or in the hot grill dishes cooked to order before your eyes. Because of the sheer scale of each operation, they're only to be found in the centres of major cities.

Ethnic snack bars are predominantly Italian, Greek or Turkish. The **pizzerias** are a major boon if you're on a tight budget. Either taking away or eating standing up, prices start at around €3 for a simple tomato and cheese pizza. Most pizzerias also serve pasta dishes, though these are usually less of a bargain. As always, the **kebab** houses adapt their technique to suit the national taste. The *Gyros* or *Döner* was until recently nearly always based on real lamb meat and fat, but health scares have led to an increasing number of establishments using chicken or turkey as a substitute. It's served in bread, generally with tsatziki as a sauce, and costs around €3.

Meals and restaurants

All **restaurants** display their menus and prices by the door, as well as their *Ruhetag*, the day they are closed. Hot meals are usually served throughout the day, but certainly where it says *durchgehend warme Küche*. The Gaststätte, Gasthaus, Gasthof, Brauhaus, Wirtschaft or Wirthaus establishments, which are the nearest equivalents to old-fashioned English inns, mostly belong to a brewery and function as social meeting points, drinking havens and cheap restaurants combined. Their style of cuisine is known as **gutbürgerliche Küche**; this resembles hearty German home cooking (hence the comparatively low prices), and portions are almost invariably generous. Most of these places have a hard core of regular customers who sit at tables marked *Stammtisch*; unless invited to do so, it's not the done thing to sit there. However, don't be surprised if you're expected to share your table with strangers – in all but the poshest of restaurants, customers are often asked to give up free seats at their table at busy times. The bulk of the menu is the same all day long, though some establishments offer two- or three-course lunches at a bargain price. **Standards** are amazingly high: you're far less likely to be served a dud meal in a German restaurant than in almost any other country.

Starters tend to be fairly unsophisticated – either a salad, pâté or cold meat dish. Choice for **soup** is fairly restricted, and tends to be based on an adaptation of foreign fare; prices are usually in the range of €3–5. Among the most popular are

Gulaschsuppe, a liquidized version of the staple Magyar dish (despite often being dignified as "Ungarische", it's not something a Hungarian would recognize); *Bohnensuppe*, which is often quite spicy, and derived from the Serbian model; and *Zwiebelsuppe*, which is a direct copy of the famous French brown-onion soup, usually with floating cheese and croutons. In east Germany, you'll also find *Soljanka*, a spicy Ukrainian soup with sliced sausages. More authentically German are the clear soups with dumplings, of which the Bavarian *Leberknödelsuppe* is the best known.

Main courses in all German restaurants are overwhelmingly based on **pork**. As a rule, this is of noticeably higher quality than in Britain, and the variety in taste wrought by using different sauces (it's quite common to find a choice of up to twenty different types) and unexpected parts of the animal means that the predominance of the pig is far less tedious than might be supposed. As an alternative to the ubiquitous *Schnitzel*, try *Schweinehaxe* or *Eisbein*, respectively the grilled (or roasted) and boiled versions of pig's knuckles. **Sausages** regularly feature on the menu, with distinct regional varieties.

Whereas a main-course pork-based dish is likely to cost €12 or less, one with **beef** will cost a fair bit more. As is the case with snack bars, **chicken** dishes are comparatively cheap. Many restaurants have a **game** menu, with more exotic poultry such as duck or goose, along with venison, rabbit and hare; prices then tend to be €15 or more.

Outside northern Germany, where a wide variety of newly caught salt-water **fish** is readily available, you'll probably have to be content with fresh-water varieties, except in June and July, when restaurants all over the country offer special menus featuring young herring (*Matjes*). Trout is by far the most popular fresh-water fish, though there's obviously a greater choice in places close to lakes and rivers. Where salt-water fish is generally available, the unfamiliar rosefish (*Rotbarsch*) – similar in taste to whiting – is generally the most reliable. Oddly enough, you're far more likely to encounter a choice of fresh fish in east Germany, where there are many privatized survivors from the long-established Gastmahl des Meeres chain.

The main-course price invariably includes **vegetables**. Potatoes are usually sautéed, puréed or made into a cold salad. Boiled potatoes, often garnished with parsley, are increasingly popular, but baking, mashing and oven-roasting find little favour. Dumplings made from potatoes and flour are a common alternative. Cabbage is the other popular accompaniment – the green variety is pickled as *Sauerkraut*, whereas the red is normally cooked with apple as *Apfelrotkohl*. Salads of lettuce, cucumber, beetroot, carrots and gherkins are often included as a side-dish. From April to late June, when **asparagus** is in season, many restaurants have a special menu (*Spargelkarte*) of dishes – both vegetarian and carnivore – with this vegetable as a key ingredient. The **noodles** known as *Spätzle* and *Maultaschen* are distinctive components of Swabian cuisine, occasionally adopted elsewhere.

Because so many Germans go to cafés (see p.40) for their daily helping of cakes, **desserts** in restaurants are an anticlimax, where they exist at all. The Bavarian *Dampfnudel* (steamed dumpling) is one of the few distinctive dishes; otherwise there's just the usual selection of fresh and stewed fruits, cheeses and ice creams.

Germany has a wide variety of **ethnic restaurants**. The density of these is very much in line with the general *Gastarbeiter* influx, and there's a heavy southern European bias. Of these, the Italian are generally the best recommendations; there are also plenty offering Balkan, Greek and Turkish cuisines. Chinese restaurants are also ubiquitous and usually very consistent, with most offering good-value set lunches. On the other hand, Indian and Thai food is often toned down, largely because few Germans care for hot spices.

Only a very small percentage of German restaurants aspire to genuine **gourmet** status. Those which do – unless attached to a prestigious hotel – tend to have a much higher turnover than the national norm, which is otherwise extremely stable.

Vegetarian food

In Germany, the very concept of **vegetarianism** is still tarnished by its association with Hitler, who had an extremely sanctimonious attitude about the virtues of his own meat-free diet. Vegetarians will therefore find Germany less than ideal – most menus are almost exclusively for carnivores, and even an innocent-sounding item like tomato soup might have small chunks of bacon floating around in it. However, it's usually easy enough to find such staples as salads, omelettes, pancakes, pasta and pizzas. Most cities – though not so many as a few years ago – have at least one specialist vegetarian and wholefood restaurant, and these are listed throughout the Guide. Some have self-service buffets where you pay for the items chosen according to their weight.

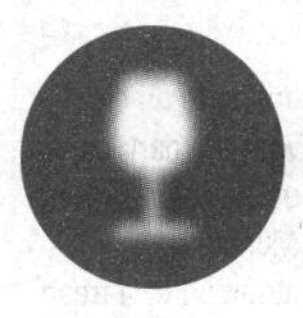

Drinking

The division between eating and drinking establishments in Germany is less demarcated than in the English-speaking world. Despite their inevitable connotations with beer and wine, the Brauhäuser and Weinstuben inevitably double as restaurants: the former usually offer a full range of *gutbürgerliche Küche*, whereas the latter tend to have shortish menus of rather lighter fare. There are also some purely drinking dens, generally known as Kneipen. Apart from beer and wine, there's nothing very distinctive about German beverages, save for Apfelwein, a variant of cider. The most popular spirits are the fiery *Korn* and after-dinner liqueurs, which are mostly fruit-based.

Beer

For serious **beer** drinkers, Germany is the ultimate paradise. Wherever you go, you can be sure of getting a product made locally, often brewed in a distinctive style. The country has well over 1200 breweries, with over half the total in Bavaria alone. By far the densest concentration is in Upper Franconia, where the traditional institution of the Hausbrauerei, a combination of a small brewery and a pub-restaurant (often offering accommodation as well) still survives in force. All German breweries voluntarily adhere to the *Reinheitsgebot* (Purity Law) of 1516, which lays down stringent standards of production, including a ban on chemical susbtitutes. Despite a growing trend towards takeovers and amalgamations, particularly among large and medium-sized brewers, the effect on consumer choice has been minimal. Often, production has been allowed to continue as before in different locations, though in others the brewing for several different labels has been consolidated in a single site. Another positive aspect has been the revival of long-forgotten techniques, often put into practice in new-generation Hausbrauereien. Often subsidiaries of larger local or regional breweries, these are springing up all the time, and are deservedly very popular, often being the trendiest spot in town.

More generally, there's an encouraging continuation of old-fashioned **top-fermented** brewing styles. Until the nineteenth century, all beers were made this way, but the interaction of the yeasts with a hot atmosphere meant that brewing had to be suspended during the summer. It was the Germans who discovered that the yeast sank to the foot of the container when stored under icy conditions; thereafter, brewing took on a more scientific nature, and yeast strains were bred so that beer could be **bottom-fermented**, thus allowing its production all year round. The top-fermentation process, on the other hand, allows for a far greater individuality in the taste (often characterized by a distinct fruitiness), and can, of course, now be used throughout the year, thanks to modern temperature controls. All wheat beers use this process.

A quick beer tour of Germany would inevitably begin in **Munich**, which occupies third place in the world production league table. The city's beer gardens and beer halls are the most famous drinking dens in the country, offering a wide variety of premier products, from dark lagers through tart *Weizens* to powerful *Bocks*. Nearby **Freising** boasts the oldest brewery in the world, dating back to the eleventh century. In Upper Franconia, distinctive traditions are found in **Bamberg** (national champion for beer consumption per resident), **Kulmbach** and **Bayreuth**.

Local brews in Baden-Württemberg are sweeter and softer, in order to appeal to palates accustomed to wine; **Stuttgart** and **Mannheim** are the main production centres. Central Germany is even more strongly wedded to wine, though there are odd pockets of resistance. Indeed, **Frankfurt**, the German cider metropolis, also has, in Binding, one of the country's largest breweries.

Further north, where it's too cold to grow grapes, the beer tradition returns with a vengeance. **Cologne** holds the world record for the number of city breweries, all of which produce the jealously guarded *Kölsch*. **Düsseldorf** again has its own distinctive brew, the dark *Alt*. **Dortmund** even manages to beat Munich for the title of European capital of beer production, and is particularly associated with *Export*. Equally good are the delicate brews of the **Sauerland**, made using the soft local spring water. One of these, the heavily promoted *Pils* produced by Warsteiner, is now Germany's best-selling beer, albeit with less than 5 percent of the total market.

Hannover, **Bremen** and **Hamburg** all have long brewing pedigrees, with many of their products widely available abroad. The most distinctive beers of the northernmost Länder, however, are those of **Einbeck** (the original home of *Bock*) and **Jever**. In contrast to these heady brews is the acidic *Weisse* of **Berlin**, which is completely transformed into a refreshing summer thirst-quencher by the addition of a dash of syrup.

East German brews are far less exciting, with the notable exception of *Köstrizer*, an outstanding black beer made in **Bad Köstritz** in the outskirts of Gera. **Leipzig** has managed a revival of its varied brewing tradition since the fall of Communism, but elsewhere there's seldom anything other than the standard fare of light beers and local variations of *Pils*, of which the best are from **Radeberg** near Dresden and those made from the soft water of the **Vogtland**.

Beer glossary

Alt Literally, any beer made according to an old formula; particularly associated with the dark brown top-fermented barley malt beer of Düsseldorf (also made in Mönchengladbach and Münster).

Altbierbowle Glass of *Alt* with addition of a fresh fruit punch.

Berliner Weisse Wheat beer from Berlin, usually served in a bowl-shaped glass, and with addition of woodruff (*mit Grün*) or raspberry essence (*mit Schuss*).

Bernstein Amber-coloured beer.

Bock Light or dark strong beer, originally from Einbeck, but particularly popular in Bavaria, containing at least 6.25 percent alcohol.

Braunbier Generic name for brown beer.

Doppelbock Extra-strong *Bock*, usually made specially for festivals.

Dunkel Generic name for any dark beer.

Eisbock "Ice beer", particularly associated with Kulmbach; the freezing process concentrates the alcohol.

Export Originally, beers made to be exported. Now used to describe a premium beer, or in association with the brewing style of Dortmund, stronger than a *Pils* and lying midway between dry and sweet in taste.

Fassbier, Schankbier Draught beer.

Flaschenbier Bottled beer.

Hausbrauerei, Gasthausbrauerei "House brewery", or pub where beer is brewed on the premises.

Hefe-Weizen Wheat beer given strong yeast boost.

Hell, Helles Generic names for light beers.

Hofbräu Brewery formerly belonging to a court; that in Munich is the most famous.

Kellerbier, Kräusen, Zwickelbier Unfiltered beers, each brewed to a slightly different formula.

Klosterbräu Brewery attached to a monastery.

Kölsch Top-fermented pale coloured beer peculiar to Cologne, invariably served in small glasses.

Kristall-Weizen Sparkling brew made from wheat: the beer answer to champagne.
Leichtbier Low-alcohol beer.
Maibock Pale, high premium *Bock*, specially made to celebrate spring.
Malz Unfermented black malt beer, similar to sweet stout.
Märzenbier Strong beer made in March, but stored for later consumption; particularly associated with Munich's Oktoberfest.
Münchener Brown-coloured lager, a style pioneered in Munich.
Ökobier Organically produced beer.
Pils Bottom-fermented golden-coloured beer with a very high hop content.
Radler, Alsterwasser Shandy.
Rauchbier Aromatic beer from Bamberg made from smoked malt.
Roggenbier Dark beer made with rye.
Schwarzbier Generic name for black beer.
Spezial Name given by breweries to their premium product, or to that made for special events.
Starkbier Generic name for strong beer.
Urquell Name used to identify the original of a particular brewing style.
Vollbier Standard medium-strong beer.
Weihnachtsbier Special strong beer made for Christmas.
Weissbier, Weisse Pale coloured wheat beer.
Weizen Light or dark wheat beer.

Wine

Many people's knowledge of German wine starts and ends with *Liebfraumilch*, the medium-sweet easy-drinking wine. Sadly, its success has obscured the quality of other German wines, especially those made from the *Riesling* grape, and it's worth noting that the *Liebfraumilch* drunk in Germany tastes nothing like the bilge swilled back abroad.

The vast majority of German wine is white since the northern climate doesn't ripen red grapes regularly. If after a week or so you're pining for a glass of red, try a *Spätburgunder* (the *Pinot Noir* of Burgundy).

First step in any exploration of German wine should be to understand what's on the label: the predilection for Gothic script and gloomy martial crests makes this an uninviting prospect, but the division of categories is intelligent and helpful – if at first a little complex.

German wines may be *trocken* (dry), *halbtrocken* (medium dry), *lieblich* (medium sweet, and generally low in alcohol content) or *süss* (sweet). The term *mild*, which denotes a low acidity, is often used as well as, or instead of, *lieblich*, while *edelsüss* (nobly sweet) signifies that the sweetness has been caused by incomplete fermentation, and is applied to high quality wines only.

Like most EU wine, German wine is divided into two broad categories. **Tafelwein** (table wine) is basically cheap plonk. It can be a blend of wines from any EU country, whereas *Deutscher Tafelwein* must be 100 percent German. *Landwein* is a superior *Tafelwein*, equivalent to the French *Vin de Pays*. However, the wines to look out for are those labelled **Qualitätswein** (quality wine), and are equivalent to the French *Appellation Contrôlée*.

Qualitätswein

There are two basic subdivisions of *Qualitätswein*: **Qba** (*Qualitätswein eines bestimmten Anbaugebietes*) and **Qmp** (*Qualitätswein mit Prädikat*). *Qba* wines come from thirteen delimited regions and must pass an official tasting and analysis. *Qmp* wines are further divided into six grades:
Kabinett The first and lightest style.
Spätlese Must come from late-picked grapes, which result in riper flavours.
Auslese Made from a selected bunch of grapes, making a concentrated medium-sweet wine. If labelled as *Trocken*, the wine will have lots of body and weight.
Beerenauslese Wine made from late-harvested, individually picked grapes. A rare wine, made only in the very best years, and extremely sweet.
Trockenbeerenauslese *Trocken* here means dry in the sense that the grapes have been left on the vine until some of the water content has evaporated. As with *Beerenauslese*, each grape will be individually picked. This is a very rare wine which is intensely sweet and concentrated.
Eiswein Literally "ice wine", this is made from Beerenauslese grapes – a hard frost freezes the water content of the grape, concentrating the juice. The flavour of an *Eiswein* is remarkably fresh tasting, due to its high acidity.

Grape varieties

These often appear on wine labels and are a handy guide to judging a wine's flavour.

Riesling Germany's best grape variety. It can have a floral aroma when young, is often "honeyed" when ripe and develops interesting bouquets after five to seven years in the bottle.
Gewürztraminer *Gewürz* means spicy, and the wine has an intense aromatic nose, likened by some people to lychees and by others to Turkish delight.
Müller-Thurgau The most widely planted grape in Germany. Its flavour is less distinguished than *Riesling* but is generally fruity, has less acidity and a grapey, *Muscat* taste.
Silvaner A fairly neutral wine, quite full-bodied and often blended with more aromatic varieties.

Wine regions

Particularly at the *Qualitätswein* level, regional variations in climate produce markedly differing styles of wine.
Ahr Small area on both sides of the Ahr valley, devoted primarily to *Spätburgunder* and *Portugieser* red wines.
Baden The most southerly wine-growing region, extending almost continuously from Heidelberg to the Swiss border, with another area around the Bodensee. Its warm climate allows French grape varieties to be grown, and the majority of the wines are dry in flavour.
Franken (Franconia) Largely based around the Main valley, this produces high-quality, full-bodied wines which are easy to identify, as they always come in a distinctively dumpy, round-shouldered bottle known as a *Bocksbeutel*.
Hessische Bergstrasse (Hessian Mountain Road) The vineyards here are mainly minute operations run on a part-time basis producing wines similar to those of the more famous Rheingau, albeit with more body and less acidity.
Mittelrhein (Middle Rhine) Although the vineyards on the steep slopes of the Rhine gorge are among Germany's most famous tourist sights, the wines, which are earthier than those of the nearby Rheingau, are mainly consumed locally.
Mosel-Saar-Ruwer The steep banks of the River Mosel and two of its tributaries enable the vines to catch long hours of sun, thus allowing grapes to ripen, despite the northerly latitude. Much *Riesling* is grown in the slatey soil, producing elegant wines in the best years. Thanks to a heavy export volume, these have come to be regarded as Germany's most characteristic wines.
Nahe Both geographically and stylistically between the Mosel-Saar-Ruwer and the Rheingau, this is a relatively small region whose acidic, fruity wines are often underrated.
Rheingau On the sloping northern bank of the Rhine as it flows between Hochheim and Assmanshausen, this is a prestigious region that produces wines slightly fuller than those from the Mosel region. The reds in particular are considered to be among the country's finest.
Rhein-Hessen (Rhine-Hesse) Germany's largest and most productive wine area is the main producer of *Liebfraumilch* from plantations of *Müller-Thurgau* and *Silvaner* grapes.
Rheinpfalz (Palatinate) A southern wine region that produces full-bodied, ripe wines, chiefly *Liebfraumilch* and *Riesling*.
Saale-Unstrut Around Naumburg is the country's most northerly wine-growing area, best known for its *Sekt*.
Sachsen (Saxony) *Sekt* is likewise a speciality of the vineyards in the vicinity of Meissen, the easternmost of the wine-growing regions.
Württemberg Centred on the Stuttgart conurbation, this is one of those regions characterized by smallholdings, which are best known for their red *Trollinger* wines.

Communications

It almost goes without saying that Germany, as one of the world's largest and most successful economies, has excellent postal and telecommunications services and a lively media, though its television coverage has to be regarded as something of a weak link.

Mail

Post offices (*Postämter*) are normally open Monday to Friday 8am to 6pm and Saturday 8am to noon. A restricted range of services is available beyond these hours at offices in or beside main train stations in large cities. Outbound mail should reach the UK within a few days, North America in one to two weeks and Australia in over two weeks.

Poste restante services are available at the main post office (*Hauptpost*) in any given town (see listings in the Guide for addresses in the major cities): collect it from the counter marked *Postlagernde Sendungen* (always remember to take your passport). It's worth asking anyone writing to you to use this designation as well as, or instead of, poste restante. Incredible as it may seem in view of the country's reputation for super-efficiency, many German post offices don't understand the international term and are likely to return a letter to the sender marked "address unknown". Bear in mind also that mail is usually only held for a couple of weeks. If you want your mail to be **registered**, ask for it to be sent *einschreiben*. **Fax** services are available at large post offices, usually at more favourable rates than in copy shops or hotels.

Telephones

Telephoning is simple and most kiosks are equipped with basic instructions in several languages, including English. You can **call abroad** from all but those clearly marked "National". Calling **rates**, other than to some long-haul international destinations, vary according to the time of day. Within Germany, the first cheap period begins at 6pm, the next at 9pm, the last at 2am; within the EU, rates are reduced between 6pm and 8am. Some boxes are equipped with a ringing symbol to indicate that you can be called back on that phone. The major international codes are given below; when using them, remember to omit the initial zero from the subscriber's number.

For **local calls**, you need to insert a minimum of €0.10, which will last for a minimum of 90 seconds at the peak daytime rate. In the Guide, local codes are included with each telephone number.

Coins of €0.10, €0.20, €0.50, €1 and €2 are accepted; only wholly unused ones are returned. However, a large percentage of pay phones in Germany accept **phone cards** only. These cost €5 or €10 from post offices or newsagents, and are well worth buying, especially if you're intending to call home. Another option is to use the cut-price services offered by the many **call shops** which have sprung up in the last few years. They are largely run by and on behalf of the *Gastarbeiter* (guest worker) communities, and are most commonly found in the vicinity of train stations.

As an alternative to calling an operator for **directory enquiries** within Germany, look up the website ⓦwww.dastelefonbuch.de, which has instructions in English as well as German. All you need to do is enter the name and town of the subscriber, press the Search/*Suchen* button, and the telephone number will come up, along with the address and any other information given in the relevant printed phone book.

International calls

From Germany dial ⓣ00 + IDD country code + area code minus first 0 + subscriber number.
From Britain and Ireland to Germany dial ⓣ00 49 + area code minus first 0 + number.

From North America to Germany dial ☎011 49 + area code minus first 0 + number.

From Australia or New Zealand dial ☎0011 49 + area code minus first 0 + number.

IDD codes

Australia ☎61
Britain ☎44
Canada ☎1
Ireland ☎353
New Zealand ☎64
USA ☎1

Useful numbers within Germany

Operator ☎03
Directory enquiries ☎11833
International directory enquiries ☎11834
Operator wake-up call ☎01141
Ambulance ☎112
Fire ☎112
Police ☎110

Email and the Internet

The Germans have enthusiastically embraced the Internet, as the continuing proliferation of websites testifies. However, the institution of the **cybercafé** – which in so many other countries has been the principal means by which travellers maintain contact with home – has failed to secure much of a foothold. Such cafés do exist, especially in the larger cities, and are listed in the Guide, but their continued existence cannot be taken for granted, as many others have come and gone. Their function has largely been subsumed by the telephone **call shops**, most of which have at least two or three computer terminals, while others are equipped with a whole roomful or more. Charges are usually very reasonable – expect to pay between €2 and €4 per hour. Oddly enough, Internet access is often available, albeit at higher rates than in the call shops, in **amusement arcades**, particularly those within stations, and **department stores**: the Karstadt chain, which has branches throughout the country, is particularly good in this respect. Most **hotels** in all price categories are now wired up to the Net, and some allow guests to surf and send emails free of charge, though others levy a fee for this facility.

Media

Germany is well supplied with **British newspapers**: in the larger cities it's relatively easy to pick up most of the London-printed editions on the same day, with the *Financial Times* having a particularly wide distribution. Some **US papers**, especially the *International Herald Tribune* and *USA Today*, are also readily obtainable.

With a few exceptions, **German newspapers** tend to be highly regionalized, mixing local and international news. Only the liberal *Frankfurter Rundschau* and Munich's *Süddeutsche Zeitung* are distributed much outside their own areas. Berlin produces two reputable organs: the *Tagesspiegel*, a good left-wing read, and the Greenish/alternative *Tageszeitung*, universally known as the *Taz*. Of the national daily papers, the two best-sellers come from the presses of the late, unlamented Axel Springer: *Die Welt* is a right-wing heavyweight, and the tabloid *Bild* a reactionary, sleazy and sensationalist rag. The *Frankfurter Allgemeine* is again conservative, appealing particularly to the business community, but follows a politically independent line.

Germany has more **magazines** than any other country in Europe. The leftish weekly news and current affairs magazine *Der Spiegel* is the most in-depth magazine for political analysis and investigative journalism. Unless your German is fluent, though, it's a heavy and often difficult read. Further to the right, *Die Zeit* is a wider-ranging (and to learners of the language, easier-to-read) alternative; *Focus* is another influential weekly with a conservative slant. *Stern* is the most popular current affairs magazine, though its prestige took a tumble following its publication of the forged Hitler diaries and, well over a decade later, has still not entirely recovered.

German **television** does not show the country at its best, though it has an undeniably varied output. Some of the more serious discussion programmes have a presentation style that is still reminiscent of the 1960s and early 1970s and might as well be broadcast on radio. Yet there are also plenty of derivatives of the banal game and chat shows characteristic of present-day American and British daytime TV, while in the late evenings pornography that leaves nothing to the imagination is often broadcast. There are two main national channels, **ARD** and **ZDF**, plus regional stations run by individual Länder and a number of commercial channels. The Austrian, Swiss, Dutch, Danish and Polish networks can be picked up in the areas they border. Many houses and hotels are equipped with **satellite** or **cable TV**; in such cases, you'll have access to a choice of British and American channels: CNN is particularly ubiquitous.

The only **English-speaking radio** channels are the BBC World Service (90.2FM), the British Forces station BFBS (98.8FM) and the dire American Armed Forces radio station AFN (87.6FM), which combines American music charts with military news. These should continue broadcasting for at least as long as the troops remain.

Opening hours and public holidays

Shopping hours in western Germany were strictly curtailed by a law passed in the 1950s in a bid to counter national workaholic tendencies. This measure remained in force, modified only by a limited reform in 1996, until 2003, when opening times were finally liberalised.

All shops are now allowed to remain open until 8pm from Monday to Saturday. Many take full advantage of this, though others still adhere to the old deadlines of 6.30pm from Monday to Friday and 2pm on Saturday, extending the latter only on the first Saturday of the month, the so-called *Langer Samstag*. A fair number of shops, mainly grocery stores run by members of the *Gastarbeiter* community, now stay open well past the authorized time, and the authorities seem to be turning a blind eye to this – something that would have been unthinkable not so long ago. All shops, except for bakers, are supposed to close on Sunday, but this is no longer honoured universally. Even when the restrictive opening hours were in force, there was a legal loophole which allowed shops attached to filling stations and in and around train stations to stay open late seven days a week, and many choose to do so. Pharmacists have always been allowed to extend their normal opening hours on a strict basis of rotation. For banking hours, see "Costs, money and banks" p.28.

It has long been the custom in Germany for **museums** and **historic monuments** to close their doors to the public on Monday, unless it is a public holiday. Traditionally, there have only been a few exceptions to this rule, some of which take another day off instead. This blanket Monday shutdown has long been a major source of frustration to visitors, a fact that has at least been recognized in Bavaria, where in 2000 the traditional day of closure was abolished for many of the state-owned castles and palaces. Mondays apart, opening times (which are detailed in the Guide) are usually more generous than in other countries, with lunchtime closures rare. Many major civic museums are additionally open on at least one evening per week.

There's rarely any difficulty gaining access to **churches**, hence opening times are only listed in the Guide for ancillary attractions such as treasuries or towers, or when set times are both limited and rigidly enforced. Bear in mind that churches used for Protestant worship (predominantly in Swabia, Hesse, northern Germany and the former GDR) tend to keep office hours, whereas those in Catholic areas usually open earlier and close later.

Finally, it is worth noting that many sites of interest are open for shorter hours in winter – which in Germany is considered to be November to February, inclusive, plus any or all of March, April and October. Where opening or closing times differ only by these distinct seasonal variations, they are indicated in the Guide with a slash: for example, Tues–Sun 10am–4/6pm.

Public holidays

New Year's Day Jan 1
Epiphany Jan 6; only honoured in Bavaria and Baden-Württemberg.
Good Friday
Easter Monday
May Day May 1
Ascension Day
Whit Monday
Corpus Christi early or mid-June; honoured only in Bavaria, Baden-Württemberg, Hesse, Rhineland-Palatinate, Saarland and North Rhine-Westphalia.
Feast of the Assumption Aug 15; honoured only in Bavaria and Saarland.
Day of German Unity Oct 3
All Saints Day Nov 1; honoured only in Bavaria, Baden-Württemberg, Rhineland-Palatinate, Saarland and North Rhine-Westphalia.
Christmas Dec 25 and 26

Festivals

Germany probably has more annual festivals than any other European country, with almost every village having its own summer fair, as well as a rich mixture of Christian and pagan festivals that have merged over the ages to fill the whole calendar.

These tend to flourish most in Bavaria, Baden-Württemberg and the Rhineland. In the former GDR, there are far fewer festivals – Communism is by no means entirely to blame for this, the roots lying in the puritanism which has long characterized the area. Since the *Wende*, a fair number of festivals have been initiated or reinstated.

The most famous German festival is undoubtedly the **Oktoberfest** in Munich, but **Carnival** and the **Christmas fairs** are other annual highlights, and take place all over the country. There's also a wealth of **music festivals**, ranging from opera seasons to open-air jazz and rock concerts. Main events are listed in the Guide, but below is a general overview.

January is a quiet month, though there are various events associated with the **Carnival season**, particularly the proclamation of the "Carnival King". Climax of the season comes in **February** or **March**, seven weeks before the date nominated for Easter. The Rhenish Karneval tends to have rather more gusto, and have a more overtly political tinge than its Bavarian counterpart, known as Fasching. Cologne has the most spectacular celebrations (detailed in the Guide on p.520), followed by those of Mainz and Düsseldorf; in each case, the Rosenmontag parade is the highpoint. Baden-Württemberg's Fastnet is a distinctive, very pagan, carnival tradition, best experienced in Rottweil. Another old pagan rite is the Schäfertanz held in Rothenburg in March and repeated on several subsequent occasions throughout the year. During Holy Week, and particularly on **Easter Day** (variable date in March/April), colourful church services are held throughout the country, particularly in rural Catholic areas. Another important **April** festival is the witches' sabbath of Walpurgisnacht, celebrated throughout the Harz region on the 30th of the month.

May marks the start of many of the **summer festivals**. Costume plays such as the Rattenfängerspiele in Hameln begin regular weekend performances, while there are classical concerts in historic buildings, such as the Schlosstheater in Schwetzingen. Every ten years (next in 2010), the famous Passionspiele in Oberammergau begins its run. On a lighter note, there's the Stabenfest in Nördlingen. **Whitsun** (variable date in May/June) sees distinctive religious festivals in many towns. On the same weekend, there are two celebrated reconstructions of historic events – the Meistertrunk drama in Rothenburg and the Kuchen- und Brunnenfest in Schwäbisch Hall. Shortly afterwards, Fronleichnam (Corpus Christi) is celebrated in Catholic areas, and is best experienced in Cologne or Bamberg.

June sees important **classical music festivals**, with the Bach-Woche during the second weekend of the month in Lüneburg, the Händel-Festspiele in Göttingen and Halle, the Schumann-Woche in Zwickau and the Europäische Wochen in Passau, while there's a big festival of all kinds of music held under canvas in Freiburg. Throughout northern Germany, the shooting season is marked by Schützenfeste, the largest being Hannover's. Bad Wimpfen's Talmarkt, which begins at the end of the month, is a fair which can trace its history back a thousand years.

July is a particularly busy festival month, with summer fairs and both **wine** and **beer festivals** opening up every week; pick of the latter is that in Kulmbach. Dinkelsbühl's Kinderzeche and Ulm's Schwörmontag are the most famous folklore events at this time. The Bayreuth Opernfest, exclusively devoted to Wagner, begins its month-long run during late July, but note that all tickets are put on sale a year in advance and immediately snapped up. A more wide-ranging Opernfest takes place in Munich around the same time.

August is the main month for colourful displays of fireworks and illuminations, such as the Schlossfest in Heidelberg and Der Rhein in Flammen in Koblenz. There are a host of Weinfeste during the month in the Rhine-Mosel area, notably those in Rüdesheim and Mainz, while Straubing's Gäubodenfest is one of the country's largest beer festivals. Other important events at this time are the Plärrer city fair in Augsburg, the Mainfest in Frankfurt and the Zissel folk festival in Kassel.

Paradoxically, Munich's renowned Oktoberfest actually takes place mostly in **September** – it usually starts on the second last Saturday, but it can be the third last (see box on p.86). This month has many of the other bacchanalian festivals, including Bad Cannstatt's Volksfest. **October** sees things quietening down, though there's still the odd Weinfest in the Rhineland, along with the Freimarkt folk festival in Bremen, while in the Alpine region there are a number of religious festivals with an equestrian component; the Colomansfest in Schwangau is the most famous of these. In **November**, there's the month-long Hamburger Dom fair in Hamburg, while the Martinsfest on the 10th/11th of the month is celebrated in northern Baden and the Rhineland, most notably in Düsseldorf.

Finally, **December** is the month of the Christmas market (variably known as Christkindelsmarkt or Weihnachtsmarkt), which features stalls selling handmade goods of all kinds, from toys and leatherware to sweets and biscuits. Practically every town in the country has one; the most enjoyable are those, such as Nürnberg and Augsburg, which are most faithful to tradition.

Trouble and the police

The German police (*Polizei*) are not renowned for their friendliness, but they usually treat foreigners with courtesy. It's important to remember that you are expected to carry ID (your passport, or at least a student card or driving licence) at all times. Failure to do so could turn a routine police check into a drawn-out and unpleasant process.

Traffic offences or any other misdemeanours will result in a rigorous checking of documentation, and on-the-spot fines are best paid without argument. The police are generally very correct, and shouldn't subject you to any unnecessary chicanery.

Reporting thefts at local police stations is straightforward, but inevitably there'll be a great deal of bureaucratic bumf to wade through. All **drugs** are illegal in Germany, and anyone caught with them will face either prison or deportation: consulates will not be sympathetic towards those on drug charges. **Jaywalking** is illegal in Germany and you can, theoretically, be fined if caught. However, in the past few years increasing numbers of German pedestrians have abandoned the once prevalent habit of standing rigidly to attention – even when no car was in sight – until the lights changed in their favour.

> Throughout Germany the number to ring for the police is ☎110.

The **GDR**'s claim that it was a crime-free state was a myth: there were always unsafe areas in the main cities, and particular problems with skinheads and football hooligans; these have, if anything, increased since unification. Bear in mind that the level of **theft** in the eastern part of Germany has – inevitably – increased dramatically in line with unemployment. However, provided you take the normal precautions, there's certainly no particular cause for alarm.

Finally, thanks to the massive *Gastarbeiter* influx, mainly from southern Europe, Germany is now firmly multicultural. However, there's no effective law against **racial discrimination**, and it's far from unknown for crankish pub landlords or nightclub proprietors to refuse entry on grounds of ethnicity. More seriously, a hardcore and sometimes violent racist element has arisen in the former GDR from the ranks of the disaffected.

Directory

Addresses The street name is always written before the number. Strasse (street) is commonly abbreviated as Str. and often joined on to the end of the previous word. Other terms include Allee (avenue), Damm (embankment), Gasse (alley), Platz (square), Ring (ring road), Ufer (quay) and Weg (way). Note that when a town or village has been incorporated into the municipality of a larger neighbour, it assumes a double-barrelled name: thus Babelsberg appears in addresses as Potsdam-Babelsberg, Bad Godesberg as Bonn-Bad Godesberg, Hohenschwangau as Schwangau-Hohenschwangau.

Electric current The supply is 220 volts. Sockets are of the two-pin variety, so a travel plug is useful.

Embassies and consulates are listed under the relevant cities. Bear in mind that the level of help, other than in Berlin or Bonn, is likely to be variable – some cities keep up a fantasy diplomatic life, in which the honorary consul is a local businessman who has bought the title for the kudos it confers on him.

Gay Germany Germany is one of the best countries in Europe in which to be gay (in German, *schwul*). The only real legal restriction is that the male age of consent is 18, and on the whole it's a tolerant place as far as attitudes go. All the big cities, and especially Berlin, Hamburg, Munich, Cologne and Frankfurt, have thriving gay scenes, as do many medium-sized towns. Germany's most widely read gay magazine is *Männer*, which comes out bi-monthly; there are also numerous local publications.

Outside the major cities, Germany's lesbian community is more muted than its male counterpart; being openly out in rural areas, particularly those where Roman Catholicism remains strong, is virtually impossible. *GAIA's Guide*, available from bookstores in Britain and Germany, lists lesbian bars and contact addresses throughout the country. Worth scanning while you're in Germany is *UKZ-Unsere Zeitung*, the monthly lesbian magazine.

Kids Travelling with youngsters shouldn't be a problem. Kids under 6 travel free on trains; those between 6 and 14 qualify for half-fare. On many municipal public transport tickets, kids travel free if accompanied by an adult. Similarly reduced rates are offered by hotels and guesthouses. Most towns have crèche facilities: contact tourist offices for details.

Laundry Laundries are not a very common sight in Germany, but they do exist – look under *Wäscherei* in the local Yellow Pages to find the nearest. Dry cleaners (*Reinigung*) are more frequent, but also quite expensive. Many youth hostels have washing machines in their basements.

Left luggage All main stations have a vast number of left-luggage lockers. The smallest and cheapest are large enough to hold all but the bulkiest rucksack or suitcase, and at €1 for 24 hours they make humping heavy luggage around town a false economy. As yet, there are only a handful of stations with new computerized lockers which operate with codes rather than keys, and the operation of these (some of which cost twice the price of the old lockers of the same size) has unfortunately been bedevilled by technical problems. Leaving bags with the station attendants costs €2 per item, but this is often the only option in small towns, where the hours of service are often very restricted.

Student cards are worth carrying for the substantial reductions on entry fees they bring.

Time Germany is one hour ahead of Britain and Ireland, six hours ahead of US Eastern Standard Time, nine hours ahead of US Pacific Standard Time, nine hours behind Sydney, and eleven hours behind Auckland. Clocks are turned an hour forward at the end of March, and an hour back in late October.

Tipping This is seldom necessary in restaurants, as prices are almost invariably inclusive, but rounding up to at least the next €0.50 or €1 (as appropriate) is expected. In taxis, add a euro or two to the total.

Guide

Guide

Bavaria

DENMARK
N
NORTH SEA
BALTIC SEA
POLAND
NETHERLANDS
BELGIUM
LUX.
CZECH REPUBLIC
FRANCE
AUSTRIA
SWITZERLAND
0 200 m
1 2 3 4 5 6 7 8 9 10 11 12

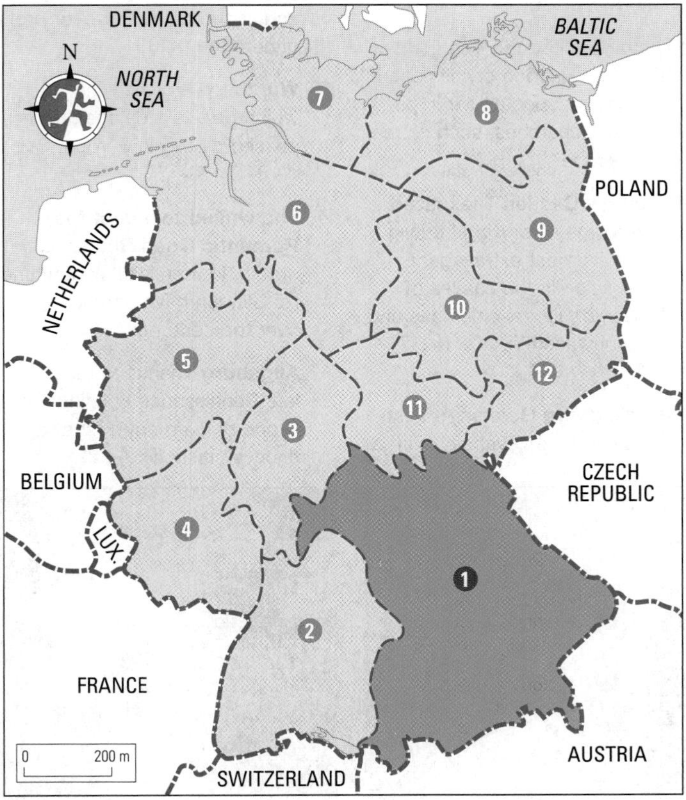

CHAPTER 1 Highlights

* **Munich** The state capital is home of the Oktoberfest, innumerable beer halls and some world-class museums. See p.62

* **The Alps** With its majestic peaks and beautiful lakes, the Bavarian Alps have Germany's most dramatic scenery. See p.118 & p.129

* **Bavarian Rococo** The florid Bavarian Rococo style is seen at its most spectacular in pilgrimage churches, such as the Wieskirche. See p.115

* **Fantasy Castles** The crazed megalomania of King Ludwig II found its most extravagant expression in the castles of Linderhof, Herrenchiemsee and Neuschwanstein. See p.117, p.125 & p.234

* **Regensburg** Germany's best-preserved medieval city, with a fine setting on the Danube. See p.136

* **Nürnberg** Some of the greatest achievements of German culture compete with the depraved legacy of the Nazis in Bavaria's second city. See p.155

* **Bamberg** This miniature Rome has a wonderful artistic legacy and is another major beer producer. See p.190

* **Würzburg** A great wine city which boasts a palace unsurpassed by any in Europe. See p.204

* **The walled towns of the Romantic Road** Rothenburg ob der Tauber, Dinkelsbühl and Nördlingen have altered little over the centuries. See p.211

* **Augsburg** Thanks to its stylish late Renaissance buildings, this is one of Germany's most distinctive cities. See p.222

△ The Plönlein, Rothenburg ob der Tauber

1

Bavaria

Bavaria (Bayern) is the original home of many of Germany's best-known clichés: beer-swilling Lederhosen-clad men, sausage dogs, cowbells and Alpine villages, Sauerkraut and Wurst and the fairy-tale castle of Neuschwanstein. Yet all this is only a small part of the Bavarian picture, and one that's restricted to the southern areas in and around the Alps.

Historically and **politically**, Bavaria has always occupied a special position within Germany. Although a wealthy duchy within the Holy Roman Empire, its rulers preferred artistic patronage to the territorial expansionism and dynastic feuding characteristic of the rest of the nation. A fundamental change in Bavaria's status occurred at the beginning of the nineteenth century, when it profited from Napoleon's decision to re-order the map of Germany: it was doubled in size, and promoted to the rank of a kingdom. Thereafter, it retained much of its independence and its own monarch, even after the union of Germany in 1871. Following the demise of the monarchy at the end of World War I, Bavaria briefly became a free state, but quickly degenerated into a hotbed of right-wing extremism where Hitler had his first successes. This reputation for reactionary politics continues to the present day: Bavaria has been ruled continuously since the end of World War II by the ultra-conservative CSU, whose stranglehold on power seems unshakeable.

Bavaria is made up of four distinct regions, each with its own identity and culture, and its cities are equally varied in character. In **Munich** the Land has a cosmopolitan, if conservative, capital that ranks as one of Germany's star attractions. The city lies at the centre of **Upper Bavaria**, the state's heartland, a region that ranges from the snow-capped peaks of the **Alps** to gentle hop-growing farmland. It's a traditional, deeply Catholic area whose rural traditions continue in spite of the inroads of mass tourism.

West of here is **Bavarian Swabia**. Detached by Napoleon from the rest of its traditional province (thereafter officially known as Württemberg), it remains stubbornly Swabian in culture – most obviously in its distinctive pasta-based cuisine. Even so, it is home to the most outrageous of the Romantic castles which form such a crucial part of the Bavarian stereotype. Outside of the mountainous **Allgäu** area in the south, this is a region of undulating agricultural country, ideal for walking and cycling holidays. The pristine local capital of **Augsburg** has been a place of importance since the days of the Romans, and its resplendent late Renaissance buildings give it a highly distinctive appearance.

To the north lies **Franconia**, which was likewise absorbed into Bavaria in 1803. The most obvious evidence of its distinctiveness can be seen in the wine-growing area around **Würzburg** in the northwest, where a culture quite at odds with the beer-loving rest of Bavaria exists. In the northeast of Franconia

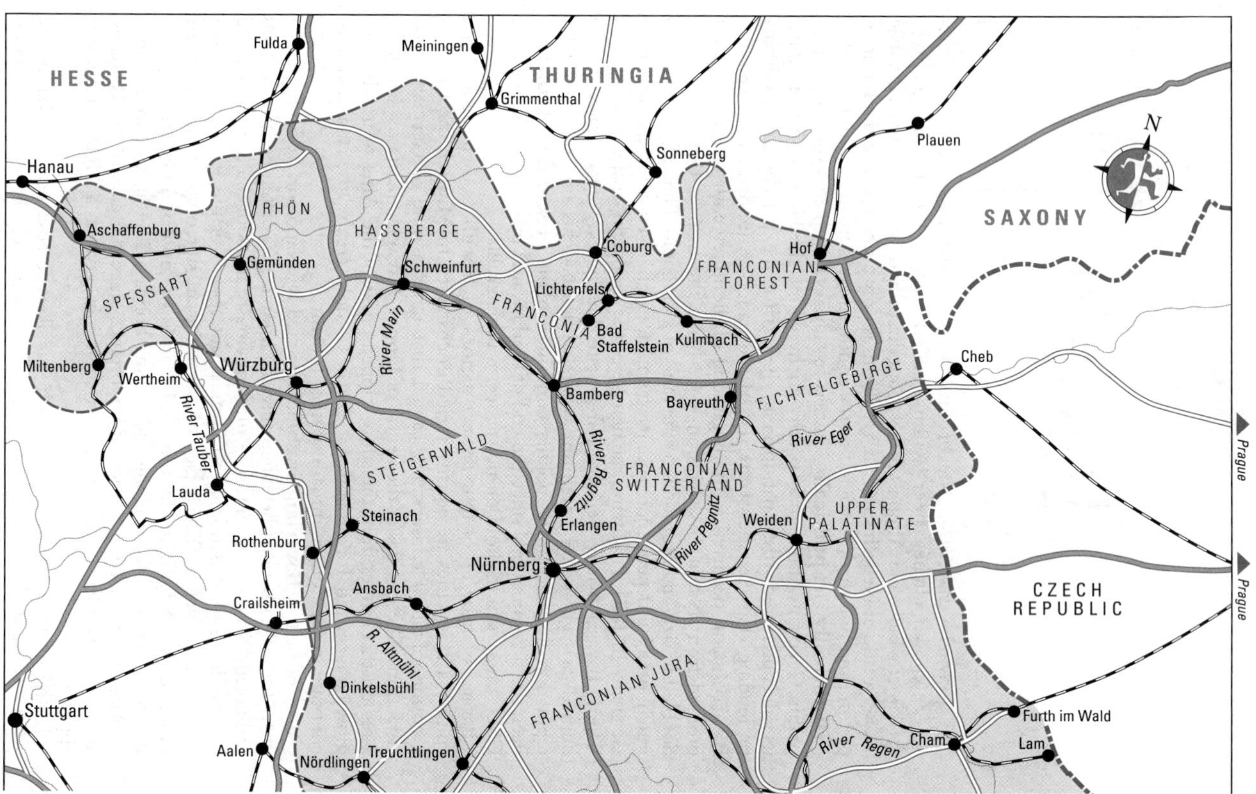
HESSE
THURINGIA
SAXONY
CZECH REPUBLIC
N
Fulda
Meiningen
Grimmenthal
Plauen
Hanau
Sonneberg
RHÖN
HASSBERGE
Aschaffenburg
Gemünden
Schweinfurt
Coburg
Hof
FRANCONIAN FOREST
SPESSART
Lichtenfels
FRANCONIA
Bad Staffelstein
Kulmbach
Miltenberg
Wertheim
Würzburg
River Main
Cheb
FICHTELGEBIRGE
Bamberg
Bayreuth
River Tauber
River Eger
Prague
STEIGERWALD
River Regnitz
FRANCONIAN SWITZERLAND
Lauda
Steinach
Erlangen
Weiden
UPPER PALATINATE
Rothenburg
River Pegnitz
Nürnberg
Prague
Ansbach
Crailsheim
R. Altmühl
FRANCONIAN JURA
Dinkelsbühl
Stuttgart
Furth im Wald
Cham
River Regen
Lam
Aalen
Treuchtlingen
Nördlingen

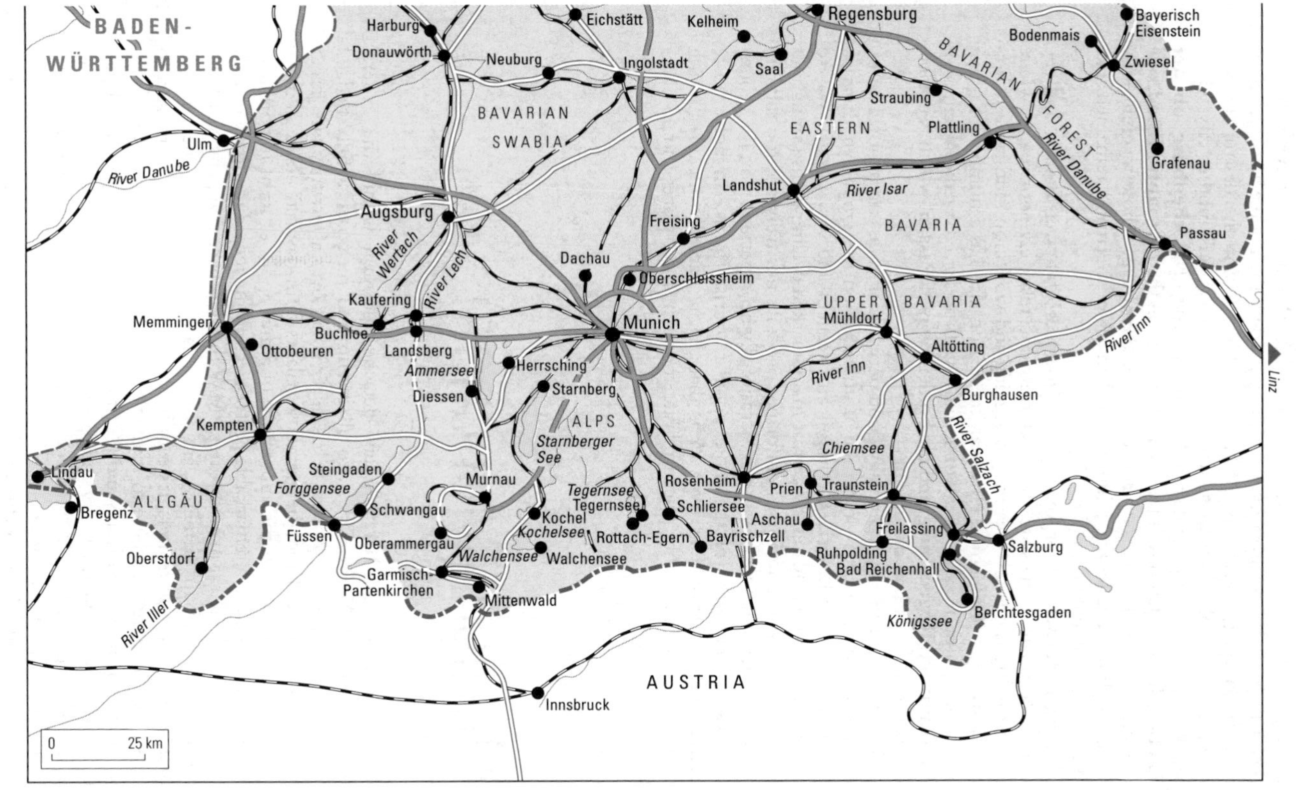
BADEN-
WÜRTTEMBERG
Harburg
Donauwörth
Neuburg
Eichstätt
Ingolstadt
Kelheim
Saal
Regensburg
Bodenmais
Bayerisch
Eisenstein
Zwiesel
Straubing
Plattling
Grafenau
BAVARIAN FOREST
River Danube
EASTERN
BAVARIA
Passau
BAVARIAN
SWABIA
Ulm
River Danube
Landshut
River Isar
Augsburg
River Wertach
River Lech
Freising
Dachau
Oberschleissheim
Kaufering
Memmingen
Buchloe
Ottobeuren
Landsberg
Munich
UPPER BAVARIA
Mühldorf
River Inn
Altötting
Ammersee
Herrsching
Diessen
Starnberg
River Inn
Burghausen
Linz
ALPS
Starnberger See
Kempten
River Salzach
Chiemsee
Lindau
Steingaden
Forggensee
Murnau
Rosenheim
Prien
Traunstein
ALLGÄU
Tegernsee
Tegernsee
Schliersee
Aschau
Bregenz
Schwangau
Kochel
Kochelsee
Rottach-Egern
Bayrischzell
Freilassing
Salzburg
Füssen
Oberammergau
Walchensee
Walchensee
Ruhpolding
Bad Reichenhall
Oberstdorf
Garmisch-
Partenkirchen
Mittenwald
Königssee
Berchtesgaden
River Iller
AUSTRIA
Innsbruck
0
25 km

the difference can be seen most obviously in the elegantly plain Baroque architecture of the Lutheran strongholds of **Ansbach** and **Bayreuth**: the Reformation left Franconia more or less split down the middle along religious lines. **Nürnberg**, a place risen from the rubble of wartime destruction and restored to the splendour of its Middle Ages heyday, was another city which quickly embraced Protestantism. The same is true of **Rothenburg ob der Tauber**, the most famous of the medieval towns on the **Romantic Road**, one of Germany's most famous tourist routes. Yet **Bamberg**, whose magnificently varied architectural legacy is unsurpassed in all of Germany, remained, like Würzburg, staunchly Catholic.

Eastern Bavaria, incorporating the provinces of Lower Bavaria and the Upper Palatinate, is the state's backwater: a rustic, relatively poor region where life in the highlands revolves around logging and workshop industries such as traditional glass production. However, the region also has a number of urban attractions, most notably the wonderfully well-preserved medieval cities of **Landshut** and **Regensburg**, and the border town of **Passau**, which is notable for its harmonious Baroque layout.

Travel is made easy by a generally good network of trains and regional buses, though public transport is sometimes a little thin on the ground in Bavarian Swabia and Eastern Bavaria. Cycling is an excellent and very popular way to get around, and is facilitated by a great many marked cycling paths throughout the state. **Accommodation** is uniformly good; it's normally not too difficult to find a bed, though problems may occasionally be experienced in the mountain resorts and some of the more popular tourist towns. An unfortunate **restriction for travellers over 27** is that they're barred from using youth hostels, though reasonably priced private rooms in most places should compensate.

Munich (München)

One consequence of Bavaria's semi-detached position within the Federal Republic is that **MUNICH** is, to all intents and purposes, a fully-fledged European capital. Even though it has never ruled over a territory any larger than the present-day Land, the grandiose palaces from Bavaria's era as an independent kingdom give it the appearance of a metropolis of great importance. When this is added to a remarkable postwar economic record (courtesy of such hi-tech giants as the car manufacturer BMW, the aerospace company MBB and the electronics group Siemens), and to its hard-won status as the national trendsetter in fashion matters, it's easy to see why Munich acts as a magnet to outsiders. Students flock here to study; the rich and jet-set like to live here, as do writers, painters, musicians and film-makers. Its visitor numbers far surpass those of any other German city and foreign nationals now make up more than a fifth of the population. Munich's other, more familiar face is of a homely city of provincially minded locals whose zest for drinking, seen at an extreme during the annual **Oktoberfest**, is kept up all year round in cavernous beer halls and spacious gardens.

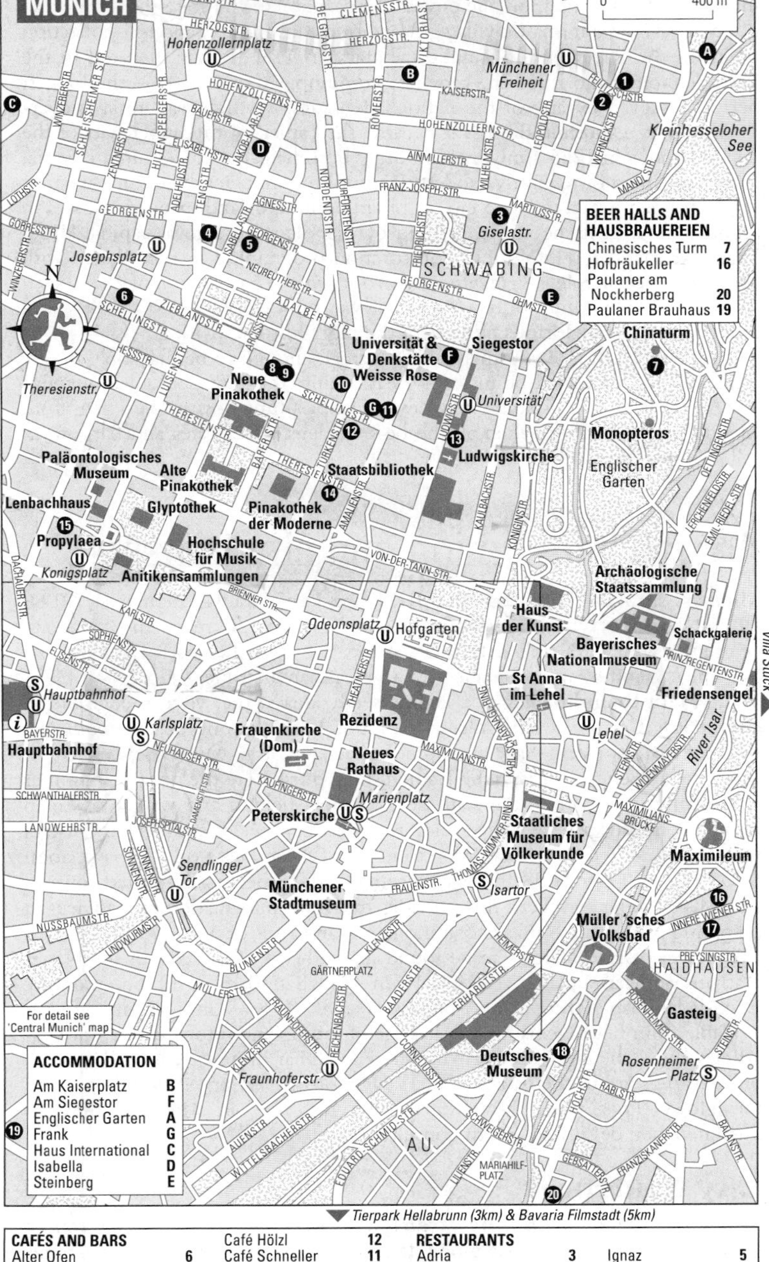

CAFÉS AND BARS				RESTAURANTS			
Alter Ofen	6	Café Hölzl	12	Adria	3	Ignaz	5
Alter Simpl	10	Café Schneller	11	Bernard & Bernard	17	Opatija	15
Café Altschwabing	8	Cyber Ice-C@fé	1	Bodega Dalí	4	Schelling-Salon	9
Café an der Universität	13	Drugstore	2	Cohen's	14		
		Wirtshaus in der Au	18				

The city is something of a late developer in German terms. It was founded in 1158 by Henry the Lion, the powerful Saxon duke who for a short time also ruled Bavaria, as a monastic village (*Mönchen* means monks) and toll-collection point on the River Isar, a Danube tributary. In 1180, it was allocated to the **Wittelsbachs**, who ruled the province continuously until 1918 – the longest period achieved by any of the nation's dynasties. Munich was initially overshadowed by Landshut, though it became the capital of the upper part of the divided duchy in 1255. Only in 1503 did it become capital of a united Bavaria, and it remained of relatively modest size until the nineteenth century, when it was expanded into a planned city of broad boulevards and spacious squares in accordance with its new role, granted by Napoleon, as a royal capital. Hitler began an even more ambitious construction programme in accordance with Munich's special role as *Hauptstadt der Bewegung* "Capital city of the (Nazi) Movement"; thankfully, only a part of it was built, surviving to this day as a reminder of this inglorious chapter in the city's history.

Despite its cosmopolitanism, Munich is small enough to be digestible in one visit, and has the added bonus of a great setting, the snow-dusted mountains and Alpine lakes just an hour's drive away. The best time of year to come is from May to early October, when all the beer gardens, street cafés and bars are in full swing.

Arrival, information and city transport

Munich's spankingly modern **airport**, Franz-Josef-Strauss-Flughafen (Ⓣ0 89 /97 52 13 13, Ⓦwww.munich-airport.de), lies some 30km north of the city centre, to which it's linked by one of the two branches of S-Bahn #1, by S-Bahn #8, and by buses operated by the Lufthansa airline.

The **Hauptbahnhof** lies in a slightly seedy area at the western edge of the city centre. On its eastern side, at Bahnhofplatz 2, is one of the municipal **tourist offices** (Mon–Sat 9am–8pm, Sun 10am–6pm; Ⓣ0 89/23 39 65 00, Ⓦwww.muenchen-tourist.de). Although long queues are the norm in summer and during Oktoberfest, the staff are extremely helpful and will always help find a room. Within the station, alongside platform 11, is another very useful information office, **EurAide** (May to end of Oktoberfest daily 7.45am–noon & 1–6pm; Ⓣ0 89/59 38 89, Ⓦwww.euraide.de). Specifically geared towards English-speaking travellers, this provides free train information and advice on preparing itineraries, books accommodation and runs excursions.

Another **tourist office** can be found in the heart of the city, in the Neues Rathaus on Marienplatz (Mon–Fri 10am–8pm, Sat 10am–4pm). The monthly English-language **magazine**, *Munich Found* (Ⓦwww.munichfound.com), available from newsagents for €3, has useful listings and information, as well as articles about the city and Germany in general. Far more extensive (German-only) listings are in the tourist office's *Offizielles Monatsprogramm* (€1.55) and the glossy *Prinz* (€1, Ⓦwww.prinz.de); the free *In München* (Ⓦwww.in-muenchen.de) is also worth consulting.

City transport

Munich's integrated **public transport system** (MVV; Ⓦwww.mvv-muenchen.de or www.mvg-mobil.de), an integrated network of buses, trams and S- and U-Bahn trains, is good, though the fare and ticketing system, despite attempts at simplification, remains by far the most complicated in

Germany. **Prices** vary according to how many zones are crossed: the city is divided up into a series of concentric circles, clearly displayed on the transport maps at any station, tram or bus stop.

If staying for a week or more, it may be worth investing in a **travel pass**; the cheapest, covering the city centre and most of Schwabing, costs €9.50 for a week or €35.50 for a month. For the whole circuit, including places such as Dachau and the Ammersee, a weekly pass is €39, its monthly equivalent €145.60. Note that weekly passes are only valid from Monday to Monday, so buying mid-week means losing out. Similarly, monthly passes are for calendar months only.

Other tickets for city transport are available from ticket machines in all S- and U-Bahn stations, at some bus and tram stops, and inside trams. If you're going to be making several journeys in the course of your stay it's not worth buying single tickets. Better value is a **strip ticket** (*Streifenkarte*), costing €9 for ten strips. You stamp two strips for every zone crossed except for journeys of up to four bus or tram stops or two S- or U-Bahn stops, when only one has to be cancelled. It's not necessary to cancel every strip: only the last needs to be punched. A child's strip ticket costs €3.80 for five strips; only one strip needs to be cancelled per journey, regardless of its length.

Various **day tickets** are also available. The *Single-Tageskarte* for individual travellers costs €4.50 for journeys within Munich, or €9 for the city and S-Bahn region. These charges rise to €8 and €16 respectively for the *Partner-Tageskarte*, which covers up to five adults or ten children. An enticing variant of this is the **München Welcome Card**, which can be purchased at the tourist offices. In addition to covering all public transport costs within Munich, this gives reductions of up to fifty percent on the entrance fees to the main museums and monuments. The *Single-Tageskarte* version of this costs €6.50 for one day, €15.50 (€26 including the airport) for three days, while the *Partner-Tageskarte* is available, in the same three formats, for €9.50, €22.50 and €38 respectively.

Accommodation

Munich has abundant **hotels** in every category from the basic to the hyper-luxury, and there are several **hostels** in which the normal Bavarian restriction on those over 27 does not apply. Beware, however, that without advance booking it can be virtually impossible to find budget accommodation during the Oktoberfest beer festival/fair that runs from the last Saturday in September to the first Sunday in October: to be in with a chance, turn up very early in the day at the tourist office, and be prepared to queue for hours. On each of the three weekends, the only places likely to have free rooms are the most expensive hotels. If planning an extended stay in Munich, contact one of the competing **Mitwohnzentralen** for a room or a flat.

Hotels and pensions

There are well over 300 **hotels** and **pensions** scattered all over Munich. By far the densest concentration is around the Hauptbahnhof, particularly its southern side. Unfortunately, although there are many good-value establishments here, this area can feel a little rough after dark, despite being well policed. There are also plenty of places – mostly homely-type pensions – in Schwabing and the area around the university just to the south; these have the advantage of proximity to many of the best bars and restaurants. Provision in the city centre is sparser, though most of the luxury establishments are located in this area.

Am Kaiserplatz Kaiserplatz 12 Ⓣ0 89/34 91 90, Ⓕ33 93 16. Very friendly pension with a good location. Wacky decor, with each room done in a different style – ranging from red satin to Bavarian rustic. ❸

Am Siegestor Akademiestr. 5 Ⓣ0 89/39 95 50, Ⓕ34 30 50. Well-regarded pension just a stone's throw from the Siegestor and the main university building. ❹

Bayerischer Hof Promenadeplatz 6 Ⓣ0 89/2 12 00, Ⓦwww.bayerischerhof.de. An internationally celebrated hotel which has been run by four generations of the same family. The public rooms are beautifully furnished, while the facilities include a roof garden swimming pool with sun terrace, sauna, solarium and massage. There are three restaurants: the moderately priced *Palais Keller*, the *Garden-Restaurant* with terrace and winter garden, and the renowned Polynesian-speciality *Trader Vic's* (evenings only). ❾

Central Bayerstr. 55 Ⓣ0 89/5 43 98 46, Ⓕ5 43 98 47. Basic but perfectly acceptable hotel whose reasonable prices make it a popular choice with young travellers from around the globe. ❹–❻

Englischer Garten Liebergesellstr. 8 Ⓣ0 89/3 83 94 10, Ⓕ38 39 41 33. This guesthouse occupies a fine old villa on the edge of the Englischer Garten, by the Kleinhesseloher See. ❻

Europäischer Hof Bayerstr. 31 Ⓣ0 89/55 15 10, Ⓦwww.heh.de. Directly facing the Hauptbahnhof, and offering a very high overall standard; it's also one of the few hotels in the area with a restaurant. ❼–❾

Excelsior Schützenstr. 11 Ⓣ0 89/55 13 70, Ⓦwww.excelsior-muenchen.de. The most upmarket hotel in the vicinity of the Hauptbahnhof, with a renowned wine bar-restaurant, *Vinothek*. ❾

Frank Schellingstr. 24 Ⓣ0 89/28 14 51, Ⓦwww.pension-frank.de. Located midway between Ludwigstrasse and the Neue Pinakothek, and mainly frequented by young travellers. It has lovely big rooms, and there's a fridge to keep food in. ❸

Helvetia Schillerstr. 6 Ⓣ0 89/5 90 68 50, Ⓦwww.hotel-helvetia.de. This presents itself as an alternative to the hostels, having multi-bed rooms as well as some of the cheapest singles and doubles in the area. ❸–❻

Isabella Isabellastr. 35 Ⓣ0 89/2 71 35 03, Ⓕ2 71 29 03. Tiny pension with just 12 beds with one bathroom on the landing. ❹

Jedermann Bayerstr. 95 Ⓣ0 89/54 32 40, Ⓦwww.hotel-jedermann.de. Located five minutes' walk from the Hauptbahnhof in the opposite direction from the centre, well away from any noise and seediness. It has a friendly English-speaking management, a wide choice of rooms of various degrees of luxury and an excellent breakfast buffet. Guests can surf the internet and send email from the hotel computer free of charge. ❸–❽

Königshof Karlsplatz 25 Ⓣ0 89/55 13 60, Ⓦwww.koenigshof-muenchen.de. Fine old privately owned hotel which has been going strong since the 1860s. Its restaurant, which boasts an outstanding wine list, is among the best in the city. ❾

Kriemhild Guntherstr. 16 Ⓣ0 89/1 71 11 70, Ⓦwww.kriemhild.de. Although far from the centre, it's only a short walk from Schloss Nymphenburg and its beautiful park, and is good value at the price asked. ❻

Mandarin Oriental Neuturmstr. 1 Ⓣ0 89/29 09 80, Ⓦwww.mandarinoriental.com. Super-luxury establishment in a neo-Renaissance building of the 1880s. The bedrooms are individually decorated with antiques; there's also a roof terrace with swimming pool and a highly exclusive restaurant. ❾

Mariandl Goethestr. 51 Ⓣ0 89/53 41 08, Ⓦwww.mariandl.com. Characterful middle-range option, which is run in tandem with the downstairs *Café am Beethovenplatz*, Munich's oldest Viennese-style coffee house. ❺–❼

Platzl Sparkassenstr. 10 Ⓣ0 89/23 70 30, Ⓦwww.platzl.de. Modernized luxury hotel in the heart of the Altstadt. Its restaurant, *Pfistermühle*, in the adjoining sixteenth-century building, serves high-quality specialities from the different regions of Bavaria, and beers from the "country" brewery of Aying. ❾

St Paul St-Paul-Str. 7 Ⓣ0 89/54 40 78 00, Ⓦwww.hotel-stpaul.de. Family-run hotel located right beside the Theresienwiese U-Bahn station. It has well-appointed bedrooms and offers fine buffet breakfasts. ❻–❾

Steinberg Ohmstr. 9 Ⓣ0 89/33 10 11, Ⓕ38 88 99 68. Pension with a nice atmosphere and a good location right by the university. ❹

Toskana Schwanthalerstr. 42 Ⓣ0 89/53 19 70, Ⓕ5 32 82 40. Apartment-block hotel whose rooms all lack en-suite facilities and are correspondingly inexpensive. ❺

Vier Jahreszeiten Maximilianstr. 17 Ⓣ0 89/2 12 50, Ⓦwww.kempinski-vierjahreszeiten.de. Grand hotel built at royal request in 1858 as an essential adornment to the latest showpiece boulevard. Now part of the Kempinski chain, and fully refurbished, it maintains its reputation as one of the world's leading hotels. The facilities include a rooftop swimming pool, nightclub and three restaurants. ❾

Mitwohnzentralen

City Mitwohnzentralen Lämmerstr. 6 ⓣ0 89/1 94 30, ⓦwww.mitwohnzentrale.de. Located conveniently close to the Hauptbahnhof.
Mit-Wohn-Börse Schulstr. 31 ⓣ0 89/1 94 45, ⓦwww.homecompany.de. Part of a national network, this can find accommodation for any period from two nights upwards.
Mitwohnzentrale an der Uni Adalbertstr. 6 ⓣ0 89/2 86 60 60, ⓦwww.mw2-munich.de. Located by the university, this is staffed by English-speakers.
Mitwohnzentrale Mr Lodge Barer Str. 32 ⓣ0 89/3 40 82 30, ⓦwww.mrlodge.de. Deals only in stays of a month or longer.

Hostels

4 you münchen ökologisches Jugendgästehaus Hirtenstr. 18 ⓣ0 89/5 52 16 60, ⓦwww.the4you.de. Modern, environmentally conscious hostel with vegetarian restaurant. Dorm beds from €16.50, singles from €43.50, doubles from €46.50.
CVJM-Jugendgästehaus Landwehrstr. 13 ⓣ0 89 /5 52 14 10, ⓦwww.cvjm-muenchen.org/hotel. The local YMCA hostel, located a couple of blocks from the Hauptbahnhof and open to everyone. Beds in dorms €25, singles from €32, doubles from €53.60.
Haus International Elisabethstr. 87 ⓣ0 89/12 00 60, ⓦwww.haus-international.de. A no-age-limit Gästehaus in Schwabing, complete with disco and swimming pool. Beds in small dorms from €23; singles from €30, doubles from €52.
IN VIA Marienherberge Goethestr. 9 ⓣ0 89/55 58 05, ⓕ55 02 82 60. Roman Catholic hostel near the Hauptbahnhof for women aged 25 or under. Beds in small dorms cost €17; there are also singles for €25, doubles for €40.
Jugendgästehaus München Miesingstr. 4 ⓣ0 89/7 23 65 50. This is the nicest and most expensive of the three HI establishments (see also the two following entries): all require a membership card, and are open only to those under 27, except for parents travelling with children. Take either U-Bahn #3 to Thalkirchen and then walk, or U-Bahn #6 or S-Bahn #7 to Harras then tram #16 to Boschetsriederstrasse. €20.10.
Jugendherberge München Wendl-Dietrich-Str. 20 ⓣ0 89/13 11 56. This is the largest and most basic hostel, with beds in large, spartan dormitories. Take U-Bahn #1 to Rotkreuzplatz, from where it's a short walk down Wendl-Dietrich-Strasse. €20.10.
Jugendherberge Pullach Burg Schwaneck, Burgweg 4–6, Pullach ⓣ0 89/74 48 66 80. Atmospherically housed in an old castle by the River Isar, but a long way south of downtown Munich. Take S-Bahn 7 to Pullach, then follow the signs. €15.50.
Kolpinghaus St Theresia Hanebergstr. 8 ⓣ0 89 /12 60 50, ⓦwww.kolpinghaus-muenchen.de. Another Catholic hostel, this time open to everyone. Beds in dorms €20, singles €28, doubles from €42. Take U-Bahn #1 to Rotkreuzplatz; it's then a five-minute walk.

Campsites

Kapuzinerhölzl Frank-Shrank-Strasse ⓣ0 89/1 41 43 00. Known as "The Tent" and municipally run, this is the cheapest place to stay during its period of operation (mid-June to early Sept), and is a fun place to be, despite the lack of privacy (it can accommodate up to 300 people). Young people only (preferably under 23) are admitted. Take tram #17 to Botanischer Garten, walk down Frank-Schrank-Strasse and turn left at the end of the road.
Langwieder See Eschenrieder Str. 119 ⓣ0 89/8 64 15 66, ⓕ8 63 23 42. Small site in a quiet lakeside setting on the western fringe of the city. Open year-round, though notification must be given in advance from Nov 1 to March 14. Being off the U- and S-Bahn routes, it's really only practical if you've got your own transport.
Obermenzing Lochhausener Str. 59 ⓣ0 89/8 11 22 35, ⓕ8 14 48 07. In a posh suburb, close to Schloss Nymphenburg, and open March 15 to Oct 31. Take S-Bahn #2 to Obermenzing, then bus #75 to Lochhausener Strasse.
Thalkirchen Zentralländstr. 49 ⓣ0 89/72 43 08 08, ⓕ7 24 31 77. Set in an attractive part of the Isar valley and open March 15 to Oct 31. Very popular during Oktoberfest because of its proximity to the fairground. Take U-Bahn #3 to Thalkirchen or U-Bahn #7 to Siemenswerke.

The City

Marienplatz is the heart of the city and its **Altstadt**; the pedestrian centre fans out from here in an approximate circle of one square kilometre. This is tourist and shopping land, with all the city's major department stores, the central market, the royal palace and the most important churches. North of Marienplatz, Ludwigstrasse and Leopoldstrasse run straight through the heart of **Schwabing**, Munich's entertainment quarter, full of *Schickies* who frequent the many bars and pose in the street cafés. It's also close to the city's main park, the **Englischer Garten**. West of the Marienplatz–Schwabing axis is the main **museum quarter**, with many of the most important of Munich's three dozen or so museums, including the world-famous Alte Pinakothek. The **Theresienwiese**, of Oktoberfest fame, is just to the southwest of the Hauptbahnhof. Running the length of the eastern part of town is the River Isar, while **Nymphenburg**, with its palace and gardens, is the most enticing of the outer districts.

The Altstadt

Relatively little is left of medieval Munich, but three of the early fourteenth-century **gateways** remain to mark the boundaries of the Altstadt. Bounded by **Odeonsplatz** and the **Sendlinger Tor** to the north and south, and the **Isartor** and **Karlstor** to the east and west, it's only a fifteen-minute walk from one end to the other. This doesn't mean you can see everything in a single day: there is enough to keep you occupied for a few days packed into this seemingly small area.

Marienplatz and around

There's something almost cosy about **Marienplatz**. Street musicians and artists entertain the crowds and local youths lounge around the **Fischbrunnen** (Fish Fountain) and the **Mariensäule**, which is topped by a gilded statue of the Virgin Mary as Queen of Heaven by **Hubert Gerhard**, a sixteenth-century Dutch-born sculptor whose work is a ubiquitous feature of the city.

At 11am and noon, the square fills with tourists as the carillon in the **Neues Rathaus** jingles into action, displaying two events that happened on this spot: the marriage of Wilhelm V to Renata von Lothringen in 1568, and the first *Schäfflertanz* (coopers' dance) of 1517, intended to cheer people up during the plague. This dance is still held every seven years, next in 2005. The Neues Rathaus itself is a late nineteenth-century neo-Gothic monstrosity, whose redeeming feature is the view from its **tower** (ascent by elevator May–Oct Mon–Fri 9am–7pm, Sat & Sun 10am–7pm; Nov–April Mon–Thurs 9am–4pm, Fri 9am–1pm; €2). To the right is the Gothic tower of the **Altes Rathaus**, which was rebuilt to its original fifteenth-century form after being destroyed by lightning. Today it houses the **Spielzeugmuseum** (daily 10am–5.30pm; €3, kids €1), a fascinating collection of historic toys.

Just to the south is the **Peterskirche** (popularly known as Alter Peter), the oldest church within the bounds of the old city walls. Its distinctive **tower** (Mon–Sat 9am–5/8pm, Sun 10am–5/7pm; €1.50) offers an even higher and better view than that from the Rathaus, and is far less busy. Originally a pillared Romanesque basilica, the church owes its present form to a fourteenth-century Gothic rebuilding following a fire. The original **high altar**, a collaboration between **Erasmus Grasser** and **Jan Polack**, respectively Munich's leading sculptor and painter in the fertile late Gothic period, is split

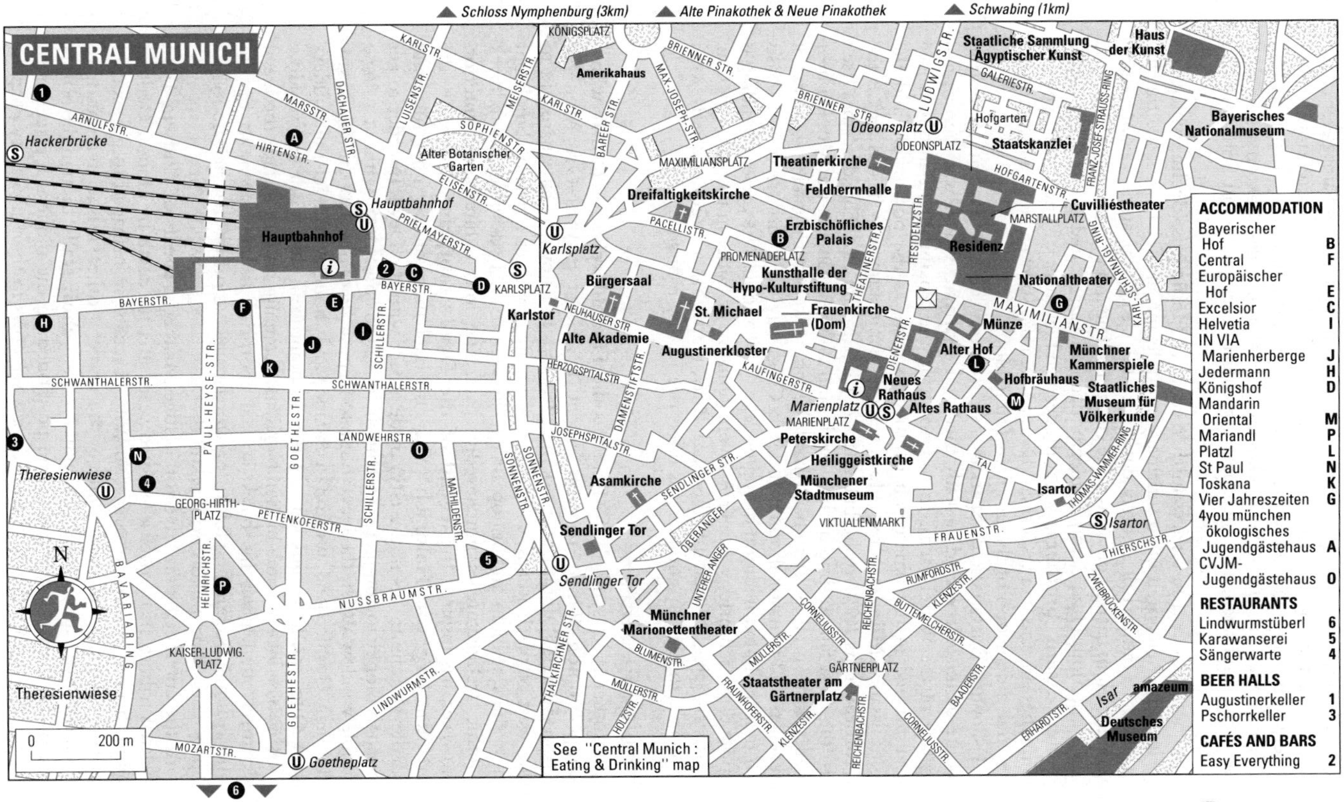

CENTRAL MUNICH

▲ Schloss Nymphenburg (3km) ▲ Alte Pinakothek & Neue Pinakothek ▲ Schwabing (1km)

Hackerbrücke
Hauptbahnhof
Alter Botanischer Garten
Karlsplatz
Karlstor
Bürgersaal
St. Michael
Alte Akademie
Augustinerkloster
Amerikahaus
Dreifaltigkeitskirche
Theatinerkirche
Feldherrnhalle
Erzbischöfliches Palais
Kunsthalle der Hypo-Kulturstiftung
Frauenkirche (Dom)
Odeonsplatz
Staatliche Sammlung Ägyptischer Kunst
Haus der Kunst
Bayerisches Nationalmuseum
Hofgarten
Staatskanzlei
Cuvilliéstheater
Residenz
Nationaltheater
Münze
Alter Hof
Münchner Kammerspiele
Hofbräuhaus
Staatliches Museum für Völkerkunde
Neues Rathaus
Altes Rathaus
Marienplatz
Peterskirche
Heiliggeistkirche
Münchener Stadtmuseum
Viktualienmarkt
Isartor
Asamkirche
Sendlinger Tor
Münchner Marionettentheater
Staatstheater am Gärtnerplatz
Gärtnerplatz
Isar
amazeum
Deutsches Museum
Theresienwiese
Goetheplatz
Georg-Hirth-Platz
Kaiser-Ludwig-Platz

Arnulfstr. Marsstr. Hirtenstr. Dachauer Str. Luisenstr. Karlstr. Meiserstr. Sophienstr. Elisenstr. Prielmayerstr. Bayerstr. Schillerstr. Schwanthalerstr. Paul-Heyse-Str. Goethestr. Landwehrstr. Pettenkoferstr. Mathildenstr. Sonnenstr. Nussbaumstr. Heinrichstr. Bavariaring Lindwurmstr. Mozartstr. Königsplatz Brienner Str. Max-Joseph-Str. Bareer Str. Maximiliansplatz Pacellistr. Promenadeplatz Neuhauser Str. Herzogspitalstr. Damenstiftstr. Josephspitalstr. Kaufingerstr. Theatinerstr. Dienerstr. Residenzstr. Ludwigstr. Galeriestr. Hofgartenstr. Franz-Josef-Strauss-Ring Marstallplatz Maximilianstr. Karl-Scharnagl-Ring Thomas-Wimmer-Ring Tal Frauenstr. Thierschstr. Zweibrückenstr. Sendlinger Str. Oberanger Unterer Anger Thalkirchner Str. Blumenstr. Müllerstr. Holzstr. Fraunhoferstr. Klenzestr. Corneliusstr. Reichenbachstr. Rumfordstr. Buttermelcherstr. Baaderstr. Erhardtstr.

N

0 — 200 m

See "Central Munich: Eating & Drinking" map

▼ 6 ▼

ACCOMMODATION

Bayerischer Hof	B
Central	F
Europäischer Hof	E
Excelsior	C
Helvetia	I
IN VIA Marienherberge	J
Jedermann	H
Königshof	D
Mandarin Oriental	M
Mariandl	P
Platzl	L
St Paul	N
Toskana	K
Vier Jahreszeiten	G
4you münchen ökologisches Jugendgästehaus	A
CVJM-Jugendgästehaus	O

RESTAURANTS

Lindwurmstüberl	6
Karawanserei	5
Sängerwarte	4

BEER HALLS

Augustinerkeller	1
Pschorrkeller	3

CAFÉS AND BARS

Easy Everything	2

up and distributed throughout the chancel, with the statue of Saint Peter centre stage in a theatrical Rococo extravaganza. However, your attention is most likely to be caught by the grizzly **shrine to Saint Munditia**, the patron saint of single women. Her skeletal relics are displayed in a glass box on a side altar, with the skull wrapped in netting and two glass eyes gazing out from a deathly face.

Although only a few paces further east, the **Heiliggeistkirche**, which was originally the church of an infirmary and pilgrims' hostel, lay outside the city walls. Its Gothic hall church design is still clearly apparent, despite many modifications carried out down the centuries. The most significant of these was the sumptuous High Baroque interior decoration executed in the 1720s by the prolific **Asam brothers**, who modernized a host of medieval Bavarian churches in this way. Cosmas Damian Asam's spectacular ceiling frescoes include a depiction of the hospice's foundation.

Following Burgstrasse or Sparkassenstrasse from the Altes Rathaus, you soon come to the **Alter Hof**, a shady medieval courtyard which was the original palace of the Wittelsbachs. To the north lie the **Postamt**, a Baroque palace transformed in the nineteenth century to serve as the post office, and the Renaissance **Münze** (Mint). However, the prime attraction in this area is the **Hofbräuhaus** (Ⓦwww.hofbraeuhaus.de) just to the east. This describes itself as "the most famous pub in the world", and is the epitome of the Munich beer hall, with spacious chambers, hard benches, well-worn tables, crowds of revellers and traditional oompah music. Originally the court brewery, it boasts an uninterrupted tradition dating back to 1589, though the present building is some three centuries younger. A favourite haunt of Hitler in the days when he was struggling to establish the Nazi Party, it still has a large hard-core local clientele, though in summer it is often overrun by tourists.

The Frauenkirche

The other great symbol of Munich is the **Frauenkirche** (or **Dom**), whose copper onion-domed **towers** (ascent by elevator April–Oct Mon–Sat 10am–5pm; €3) dominate the skyline. It stands in its own small square, just to the west of the Rathaus. Close up, the building, built as a parish church but now the seat of an archbishop, isn't really seen to best advantage: its redbrick Gothic architecture is unrelievedly spare. The lofty whitewashed interior, however, has inspired the **legend of the Devil's footprint**. Apparently the architect **Jerg von Halspach** (who also built most of the other surviving medieval monuments in the city) made a pact with the Devil. In order to get enough money to complete this church, he had to construct it without a single visible window. When the Devil came to inspect the completed church, he saw the high Gothic windows from a distance and thought he'd get the builder's soul. Once inside, he was led to a certain point from which not one window was visible, since all were hidden by pillars. Stamping his foot in rage the Devil stormed off, leaving his black hoofed footprint in the pavement by the entrance hall. Rebuilding following war damage has meant the trick no longer quite works, but the footprint is still there.

At the entrance to the nave is the huge Mannerist **tomb of Ludwig IV**, a belated tribute, made over a hundred years after his death by Hubert Gerhard and others, to the first of only two Wittelsbachs who managed to get elected as Holy Roman Emperor. Some of the church's other artistic treasures have been destroyed, among them Erasmus Grasser's **choir stalls**, though the arresting wooden statues were saved and positioned on the modern replacements. There also remain beautiful stained-glass windows in the ambulatory chapels, notably the central Sakramentskapelle, which also has a fine painted altar, *The Virgin of the Protecting Cloak*, by Jan Polack.

West of Marienplatz

The almost straight line between Marienplatz and the Hauptbahnhof is the hub of the city's commercial activity; alongside the numerous department stores some of the city's most famous beer halls are to be found, as well as a series of contrasting churches. At the point where the pedestrianized Kaufingerstrasse changes its name to Neuhauser Strasse is the deconsecrated **Augustinerkloster**, whose ornate Rococo interior now houses the **Deutsches Jagd- und Fischerei Museum** (Mon–Wed & Fri–Sun 9.30am–5pm, Thurs 9.30am–9pm; €3.50; Ⓦwww.jagd-fischerei-museum.de), an array of hunting and fishing trophies and dioramas of animals in their natural environments.

Immediately beyond, the Mannerist facade of **St Michael** stands in line with the street's other buildings. Built between 1583 and 1597 under the auspices of Wilhelm V, this Jesuit church – the first in northern Europe – was intended to symbolize the local victory of Catholicism over Lutherism. Hubert Gerhard's large bronze statue between the two entrances shows the Archangel Michael fighting for the Faith and killing Evil in the shape of a satyr. The interior, with a barrel vault second only in size to St Peter's in Rome, is decorated in elegant white stucco. A huge Neoclassical monument to Eugène de Beauharnais by Bertel Thorwaldsen can be seen in the transept. In the **crypt** (Mon–Fri 9.30am–4pm, Sat 9.30am–2.30pm; €2) are the tombs of the Wittelsbach dynasty, among them the famous castle-builder Ludwig II, whose coffin is permanently draped with flowers, a candle burning at its foot.

Alongside the church, forming a continuous architectural unit with it, is the **Alte Akademie**, the college where the Jesuits instilled their burning missionary ideals in the hearts and minds of their pupils. In front is the **Richard-Strauss-Brunnen**, a fountain in honour of the Munich-born composer. The reliefs show scenes from his opera *Salomé*, based on Oscar Wilde's play of the same name.

A few paces westwards is the **Bürgersaal**, which was built for a Marian student congregation in the early eighteenth century. Pride of the upstairs **oratory** (Mon–Fri 11am–3pm) is a set of guardian angels under the organ gallery, carved by Ignaz Günther, Bavaria's greatest Rococo sculptor. However, it's the crypt at entrance level that is most visited, since **Rupert Mayer**, one of the city's main opponents of Nazism, is buried there and his grave has become something of a pilgrims' centre, particularly since his beatification in 1987. Mayer was the parish priest during the war and became such a nuisance to the authorities that he was shipped off to Sachsenhausen concentration camp. Because of his immense popularity and the bad press his death would have caused, he was transferred to house arrest in Kloster Ettal in the Alps. He survived to return to the Bürgersaal after the war, but died later the same year.

South of Marienplatz

Immediately south of Peterskirche is the **Viktualienmarkt**, the city's main marketplace for the last 200 years. Delicious-looking fruit and vegetables, as well as all kinds of cheeses, meats and other foodstuffs can be bought there. Though not cheap, the quality is uniformly excellent. Right in the middle of all the bustle is a small beer garden, a good place to have a snack.

On St Jakobsplatz to the rear is the **Münchner Stadtmuseum** (Tues–Sun 10am–6pm; €2.50; Ⓦwww.stadtmuseum-online.de). This has fascinating permanent displays about the history of the city – including a new section on the Third Reich – supplemented by changing special exhibitions. On the ground floor are the **Waffenhalle**, containing a magnificent array of historic weapons, and the wonderfully contorted set of Morris dancers, carved as adornments for the ballroom of the Altes Rathaus by **Erasmus Grasser**. The upper floors house specialist displays on photos and films, brewing, musical instruments, and one of the largest collections of puppets in the world, from Indian and Chinese paper dolls to the large mechanical European variety.

To the west is Sendlinger Strasse, where at no. 62 is the small **Asamkirche** (officially known as **St-Johann-Nepomuk**), one of the most enchanting examples of the Bavarian Rococo style. Built between 1733 and 1746, it's the crowning effort of the partnership of the two Asam brothers, who here successfully achieved their goal of a building whose architecture was completely integrated with all aspects of its interior decoration. The younger brother, Egid Quirin Asam (who was the sculptor and stuccoist), bought the land and underwrote the cost of the whole enterprise, which was intended to serve as his private family church, and therefore one where he had the rare luxury of being able to put his artistic ideals into effect without the intervention of a patron. He added a Rococo facade to the sixteenth-century house next door and lived there for the rest of his life.

The southeastern boundary of the Altstadt is marked by the **Isartor**. This is the only one of the three gateways open to the public, its two octagonal towers being home to the **Valentin-Musäum** (Mon, Tues, Fri & Sat 11.01am–5.29pm, Sun 10.01am–5.29pm; €1.99). As its eccentric opening times and prices indicate, it's a whimsical institution, dedicated to the memory of the great local humorist Karl Valentin (1882–1948), his partner Liesl Karlstadt and the Munich folksinger tradition. On the top floor of one of the towers is a much-loved café, whose truly *gemütlich* interior features Jugendstil furniture from the famous Thonet factory.

North of Marienplatz

The smartest part of the city centre lies north of Marienplatz, where ritzy shops and expensive cafés line Theatinerstrasse, Maffeistrasse and Kardinal-Faulhaber-Strasse. At Theatinerstr. 15 is the **Kunsthalle der Hypo-Kulturstiftung** (daily 10am–8pm; €6; Ⓦwww.hypo-kunsthalle.de), which puts on a programme of international-class temporary exhibitions on artistic and archeological themes. Kardinal-Faulhaber-Strasse has the most ostentatious buildings of the lot, mostly palaces of the earlier rich which have been turned into banks and insurance houses. One which is still lived in is François Cuvilliés' **Erzbischöfliches-Palais**, the residence of the archbishop of Munich and Freising. West of here, on Parcellistrasse, a Carmelite church, the **Dreifaltigkeitskirche**, was one of the few historic buildings in Munich to come through the last war unscathed. It's a copybook example of Italianate Baroque by the Swiss architect Giovanni Antonio Viscardi (who was also responsible for the design of the Bürgersaal), with a vivacious dome fresco of *The Adoration of the Trinity* by Cosmas Damian Asam.

The Residenz

In the late fourteenth century, the Wittelsbachs moved their seat from the Alter Hof in the heart of the Altstadt to a new site at what was then the northeastern periphery of the town. Between 1570 and 1620, this fortress was replaced by a splendid Mannerist **Residenz**, constructed by a team of mostly

Netherlandish architects and designers led by **Friedrich Sustris**. It was modified and expanded in the Baroque and Rococo periods, though the most significant additions were made, in accordance with its new function as a royal palace, by **Leo von Klenze**, the architect primarily responsible for giving Munich its nineteenth-century face: he added the rusticated Königsbau facing Max-Joseph-Platz to the south and the Festsaalbau on the garden side to the north. Extensively damaged in the last war, the Residenz was reconstructed in the 1950s and 1960s – and is still the subject of restoration work.

The Residenzmuseum

About half the palace, including all the most significant historical apartments, is open to the public as the **Residenzmuseum** (daily: April to mid-Oct 9am–6pm; mid-Oct to March 10am–4pm; €5, or €8.50 combined ticket with the Schatzkammer; Ⓦwww.schloesser.bayern.de), entered from Max-Joseph-Platz. To see it all you have to go round twice, as part of it is open mornings only, with a different, albeit partially overlapping, section open in the afternoons.

On both tours, you see the **Ahnengalerie** (Ancestors' Gallery), decorated in the richest Rococo style, which looks like a Hall of Mirrors, except that the glass is replaced by 121 (mostly imaginary) portraits of the Wittelsbachs, who tried to give their line the most prestigious roots possible by including tenuously linked predecessors such as Charlemagne. The morning tour then proceeds to the Mannerist **Grottenhof** (Grotto Court), whose centrepiece is a fountain with a statue of Perseus. Under the loggia is the grotto of tufa, crystal and coloured shells, framing a statue of Mercury. Alongside is the **Antiquarium**, the oldest and most original part of the palace. This long, cavernous chamber was built in 1571 to house the family's famous collection of antiquities. A generation later, its austere architecture was sharply modified in accordance with the new Mannerist craze to serve as a festive hall, and its tunnel vault covered with humanist-inspired frescoes. In the **Kurfürstenzimmer** (Rooms of the Elector), look out for three paintings by Bernardo Bellotto, who here applied to Munich the technique his uncle Canaletto had used so successfully to immortalize the Venice of his day. Other highlights are a passageway hung with a cycle of 25 views of Italy by the Munich Romantic painter Carl Rottmann, and a suite of rooms containing extensive collections of fourteenth- to nineteenth-century Chinese, Japanese and European porcelain.

The last stage of the morning tour can also be seen in the afternoon. This includes the eight appropriately named **Reiche Zimmer** (Rich Rooms) in the sumptuous Rococo style of François Cuvilliés, and the five **Nibelungensäle** (Halls of the Nibelungs), in which medieval Germany's most famous epic is depicted in a series of paintings by the Nazarene artist Julius Schnorr von Carolsfeld. Other rooms can be seen in the afternoon only, and include further displays of ceramics, along with the silverware collection and the sumptuous early Baroque **Goldener Saal** (Golden Hall). You can also see the ecclesiastical treasury and the two chapels, which were both built in the early years of the seventeenth century. The larger **Hofkapelle**, closely modelled on the town church of St Michael, was for general use, while the more lavish **Reichekapelle** was for the private meditations of one of the most famous of the Wittelsbachs, Maximilian I. Another memento of Maximilian comes with the **Steinzimmer**, a suite of profusely furnished rooms with a complicated set of allegories illustrating the Elector's personal vision of the world and the after-life.

The rest of the complex

Sharing the same entrance but requiring a separate ticket is the **Schatzkammer** (same times; €5; Ⓦwww.schloesser.bayern.de), which houses a really fabulous collection of treasures. Among the early items, look out for the late ninth-century **miniature ciborium** that belonged to King Arnulf of Carinthia, and the early eleventh-century **cross** of Queen Gisela of Hungary. There's a spectacular array of **crowns** too, including that of Princess Blanche of England (daughter of Henry IV), but the star piece of the whole display, kept in a room of its own, is the **statuette of St George**, made in Munich around 1590 for Wilhelm V. This has a base of gold, silver and enamel, and is encrusted with diamonds, rubies, sapphires, emeralds and rock crystal. The outstanding German Renaissance tradition in the decorative arts can be seen in a host of chalices, tankards, caskets, pendants, clocks and portable altars; look out for the rock crystal dish with gold mount designed by Holbein. Faced with such competition, the Bavarian **crown jewels**, made in the early nineteenth century soon after the duchy was promoted to a kingdom, seem rather tame.

From the northern Residenzstrasse entrance, you pass through the Kapellenhof into the elongated **Brunnenhof**, in the middle of which stands a large fountain in honour of the Wittelsbachs, replete with allegorical figures of the Elements, river gods, tritons and dragons. At the far end is the entrance to the **Cuvilliéstheater** (same times; €2; Ⓦwww.schloesser.bayern.de), a perfectly intact Rococo gem, dripping in gold and bristling with intricate carvings and delicate stucco. Formerly the Wittelsbachs' private theatre, it's now the jewel in the crown of the city's performing arts venues. It's deservedly named after the man who built it, **François Cuvilliés**, a tenacious little Walloon who began his career in the debilitating role of court dwarf to the Elector Max Emanuel, but proved that he was capable of greater things by designing defensive systems for the army he was precluded from joining. As a result, he was sent to Paris to study the latest architectural theories, and on his return developed the new Rococo style to its most extravagant limits in a series of stunningly original buildings.

The northwestern part of the Residenz, entered from Hofgartenstrasse, houses the **Staatliche Sammlung Ägyptischer Kunst** (Tues 9am–5pm & 7–9pm, Wed–Fri 9am–5pm, Sat & Sun 10am–5pm; €3.50, free Sun; Ⓦwww.aegyptisches-museum-muenchen.de). As well as objects from all periods of Egyptian antiquity, this features displays of Coptic art and monumental reliefs from Assyria. Highlights include the copper statue of Amenemhet III, a masterpiece of royal portraiture from about 1800 BC; the gilded coffin mask of Queen Satdjehuti-Satibu of around 1575 BC; the gold treasure of the Queen of Meroë; and Egyptian-style statues from the palace of Emperor Hadrian at Tivoli. The **Hofgarten** to the north, formerly the royal park, is an ideal place for a quiet stroll. At the far end, the bombed-out Armeemuseum was long left as an anti-war memorial, its contents having been transferred to Ingolstadt. It has since been rebuilt with modern wings as the **Staatskanzlei**, the Bavarian State Chancellery.

The nineteenth-century city

The nineteenth-century additions to the Residenz were merely one aspect of the changing face of Munich in line with its new royal status; the city was greatly expanded, particularly to the north, with a series of broad boulevards and spacious squares lined by grandiosely self-confident Neoclassical buildings.

Odeonsplatz

In 1817, Leo von Klenze began the project to link Munich with the outlying village of Schwabing to the north by constructing the **Odeonsplatz** at the far end of the Residenz. The southwest corner of this square, however, was already occupied by the Baroque **Theatinerkirche** (or **St Catejan**), which ranks as one of Munich's most regal churches, its golden-yellow towers and green copper dome adding a welcome splash of colour to the city skyline. It was designed in the 1660s by the Bolognese Agostino Barelli, on the model of St Andrea della Valle in Rome, though many alterations to the original plan were made by Enrico Zuccalli, his successor as court architect, and it was only completed by Cuvilliés over a century later – hence the Rococo bravura of the facade.

Although other buildings in the square, including the **Odeon** itself (originally a music college, now a government office), are by Klenze, the building which finished it off, the **Feldherrnhalle** on the southern side, is by his rival **Friedrich von Gärtner**. The hall, closely modelled on the Loggia dei Lanzi in Florence, shelters statues of Bavaria's two greatest military heroes: Johann Tilly, the imperial field marshal in the Thirty Years' War, and Karl Philipp von Wrede, the commander of the Bavarian corps originally allied with Napoleon, which changed sides in time to help defeat the French at the Battle of the Nations. Between the two is a memorial to the Bavarian dead of the Franco-Prussian War. It was here on November 9, 1923 that armed police stopped Hitler's Beer Hall Putsch in its tracks, opening fire on the future dictator's band of would-be revolutionaries as they stood at the head of the narrow Residenzstrasse, in the shadow of the Feldherrnhalle.

Ludwigstrasse

From Odeonsplatz, the dead straight **Ludwigstrasse** leads to Schwabing. Its name comes from King Ludwig I, who commissioned it; though it remained unfinished when he was forced to abdicate as a result of a scandal caused by his affair with a dancer, he continued to fund it from his private resources – a decision which later proved to have been a shrewd business investment, as he was able to let the buildings at enormous rates. The most southerly palaces, up to and including the **Bayerisches Hauptstaatsarchiv**, are in a style imitating the Italian Renaissance. Immediately to the north, and in a broadly similar style, is the **Bayerische Staatsbibliothek**: it houses one of Europe's richest libraries, the most famous treasure being the original of the great monastic collection of medieval songs and poems, *Carmina Burana*. There's usually a **thematic exhibition** (Mon–Wed & Fri–Sun 10am–5pm, Thurs 10am–7pm; free; Ⓦ www.bsb-muenchen.de) on display.

Beyond stands one of the country's most significant nineteenth-century churches, the inevitably named **Ludwigskirche**. It's an example of the peculiarly German architectural style known as *Rundbogenstil*, which took its cue from any previous form of building – whether Classical, early Christian, Romanesque or Renaissance – using rounded arches; this appears to have been the invention of Ludwig as much as Gärtner. The chancel fresco of *The Last Judgment* by the Nazarene painter Peter Cornelius is one of the largest paintings in the world, and is a self-conscious (if ultimately unsuccessful) attempt to rival Michelangelo.

Further north is the main building of the **Ludwig-Maximilian-Universität**, which is now the biggest university in Germany. Although it's relatively young, only establishing itself in Munich in 1826, it has a distinguished academic record. The philosopher Friedrich Wilhelm von Schelling was an early luminary, while later professors have included such celebrated scientists as Georg Simon Ohm (discoverer of the law of magnetic resistance which bears his name), Justus von Liebig (father of scientific agriculture) and Wilhelm Conrad Röntgen (inventor of the X-ray). Linking the university with the **Priesterseminar** (Seminary) opposite is a circular plaza known as Geschwister-Scholl-Platz. This is one of a large number of places in Germany dedicated to the memory of Hans Scholl and his sister Sophie, the Munich students who launched the Weisse Rose (White Rose) resistance movement to Hitler – an act of defiance which cost them their lives. There's now a small memorial and documentation centre, the **Denkstätte Weisse Rose** (Mon–Thurs 10am–4pm, Fri 10am–3pm; free), on the ground floor of the university building.

The final building on Ludwigstrasse, before it passes into Schwabing and becomes known as Leopoldstrasse, is the **Siegestor**, a triumphal arch balancing the Feldherrnhalle, this time exclusively dedicated to commemorating the Bavarian army's part in the wars against Napoleon between 1813 and 1815.

Königsplatz

West of Ludwigstrasse, a planned town was laid out on a strict geometrical pattern of huge squares. The focus of this is **Königsplatz**, which was intended as a sort of Bavarian Acropolis, with a grassy middle surrounded by showpiece public buildings. In the Nazi period, it was paved over to serve as a parade ground, and it has only recently been returned to its original form.

On the north side of the square is the **Glyptothek** (Tues & Thurs 10am–8pm, Wed & Fri–Sun 10am–5pm; €3, free Sun), built by Klenze to house Ludwig I's collection of Greek and Roman sculptures. At the heart of the display are the surviving parts of the front of the **Aphaia temple of Aegina**, whose sculptures rank among the supreme masterpieces of Hellenistic art. As these were acquired under decidedly dubious circumstances, the Greeks would like them back: indeed they rank alongside the British Museum's Elgin Marbles at the top of Greece's shopping list in appeals for the return of the country's "looted" heritage. Other highlights of the museum are the tomb relief of Mnesarete, the daughter of Socrates; the famous **Barberini Faun**, a surpassingly beautiful carving of a sleeping satyr from about 220 BC; and a large collection of Roman busts, including one of the finest of more than 200 extant portraits of Emperor Augustus.

Across the square, a later building contains the **Staatliche Antikensammlungen** (previously Tues & Thurs–Sun 10am–5pm, Wed 10am–8pm; €3, free Sun, but closed since 2002 for structural repairs), whose displays include Greek vases from the fifth and sixth centuries BC, as well as jewellery and small statues from Greek, Etruscan and Roman antiquity.

On the west side of the square is the **Propylaeum**, a severe twin-towered structure in an unashamedly derivative Grecian style. The reliefs show the Greek War of Independence against the Turks, whose successful conclusion led to the western powers forcing Prince Otto of Bavaria on the victors as their king. This didn't prove to be a happy match: Otto's authoritarian methods went down badly with his subjects, and he was eventually forced to abdicate. Before that had happened, however, this Propylaeum had already been built in his honour.

Just off Königsplatz, facing the Glyptothek in a picturesquely manicured garden, is the **Lenbachhaus** (Tues–Sun 10am–6pm; €6; Ⓦwww.lenbachhaus.de), the villa of the nineteenth-century Bavarian painter **Franz von Lenbach**, an enormously successful high society portraitist. Many of his paintings are displayed inside, in rooms furnished as he knew them. Works by other Munich painters down the centuries are also featured, with the highlight being those by Der Blaue Reiter (see p.1035), whose members included **Kandinsky**, **Klee**, **Marc** and **Macke**; the Kandinsky collection here is particularly outstanding. In recent years the museum has also concentrated on important contemporary German art, and is worth checking for special exhibitions.

Immediately to the north, at Richard-Wagner-Str. 10, is the **Paläontologisches Museum** (Mon–Thurs 8am–4pm, Fri 8am–2pm, first Sun in month 10am–4pm; free; Ⓦwww.palaeo.de/museum-muenchen). Kids will love the display of prehistoric animal skeletons in the entrance hall, which include a sabre-toothed tiger from California, a giant deer from Ireland, and an elephant found in Upper Bavaria which is calculated to be ten million years old. However, these are mere striplings in comparison to some of the skeletons upstairs, such as a fish and a crocodile found in Baden-Württemberg, both of which date back 190 million years.

The most sinister building in Munich stands on Arcisstrasse, opposite the Glyptothek. Now serving as a music academy known as the **Hochschule für Musik**, it was formerly the local Nazi headquarters, and the place where Neville Chamberlain made the infamous agreement to force Czechoslovakia to cede Hitler the Sudetenland, thereby making the very name of Munich synonymous in the English language with treachery.

The Alte Pinakothek

The **Alte Pinakothek** (Tues & Thurs 10am–8pm, Wed & Fri–Sun 10am–5pm; €5, or €12 combined day ticket with Neue Pinakothek and Pinakothek der Moderne, free Sun; Ⓦwww.alte-pinakothek.de), a Florentine-style *palazzo* by Klenze at Barer Str. 27, is one of the largest art galleries in Europe, housing an outstanding collection of paintings spanning the period from the fourteenth to eighteenth centuries, including the finest representation of the German School to be found anywhere in the world (for more information on these artists, see Contexts p.1019). The ground floor covers fifteenth-century German painting in the left wing, and sixteenth- to seventeenth-century German, Flemish and Dutch painting in the right, while the first floor begins with fifteenth-century Netherlandish painting in the left wing, and then proceeds to German, Italian, Flemish, Dutch, French and Spanish art.

German painting of the fifteenth century has predominantly religious themes, and, in keeping with an age that believed art was for the greater glory of God, the names of many of the artists have not survived. Look out for the beautifully observed narrative cycle which has provided the nickname of **Master of the Life of the Virgin** for an unknown Cologne painter. Until recently the contemporaneous Bavarian who painted idiosyncratic trompe l'oeil scenes as if in imitation of carved retables was identified by the pseudonym of Master of the Tegernsee Altar, but he has now been unmasked as **Gabriel Angler**. From the following generation, the works of the Tyrolean **Michael Pacher** stand out. Though better known as a sculptor, his luxuriant *Altarpiece of the Four Fathers of the Church*, an early attempt at fusing the rich late Gothic style of southern Germany with the new approach of the Italian Renaissance, shows he was no less talented with the brush than the chisel.

Under the impact of the Renaissance, portraiture became increasingly popular, and **Dürer**'s *Self-Portrait* is one of the most famous paintings from this time, the artist looking out with a self-assured poise, his face framed by shoulder-length golden locks and his torso clad in a fur coat. The famous panels of *The*

Four Apostles come from the very end of Dürer's career and are generally held to be his greatest achievement. Originally, they were meant as wings of an altarpiece dedicated to the Virgin, but the project was scrapped when the city of Nürnberg – with the artist himself an enthusiastic supporter – went over to Protestantism.

Another painting with a Reformation connection is **Grünewald**'s *Disputation of SS Erasmus and Maurice*. This was commissioned by the leading member of the conciliatory Catholic party, Cardinal Albrecht von Brandenburg. The gorgeously attired Saint Erasmus, who is shown arguing for the peaceful conversion of the world against the armed struggle favoured by the black warrior Saint Maurice, represents a double allusion to the contemporary approach favoured by the Cardinal and his great friend, Erasmus of Rotterdam. As can be seen in the early *Mocking of Christ*, Grünewald himself was of a far more impassioned nature, and he became a supporter of the extreme wing of Protestantism. Strange as it seems, Cardinal Albrecht also patronized Luther's very own propagandist, **Lucas Cranach the Elder**, who took advantage of the new liberties of the age to introduce sensually explicit nudes – such as the full-lengths of *Lucretia* and *Venus and Cupid* – into German art for the first time. This approach was soon taken up and developed by **Hans Baldung**, as in the pair of allegorical female figures, perhaps representing *Prudence* and *Music*.

Albrecht Altdorfer's *Battle of Alexander*, depicting the victory of Alexander the Great over the Persian king Darius III in 333 BC, is a masterpiece of another new genre, that of history painting. Literally hundreds of soldiers are painted individually in minute detail, but at the same time represented as a heaving mass, dramatically giving the sense of a momentous battle. The artist often used identifiable landscapes in the Danube valley as backgrounds for his paintings; indeed, in *St George and the Dragon* the ostensible subject is really an excuse for a masterly nature study of the lush foliage of the beech trees which are a feature of the region.

Among the fifteenth-century Flemish works, **Rogier van der Weyden**'s *Adoration of the Magi*, which was commissioned for St Kolumba in Cologne, is regarded as one of the greatest portrayals of this classic, Christmas-card subject. It makes a fascinating contrast with the tiny house altar of the same scene (known as *The Pearl of Brabant* because of its highly polished sheen), by **Dieric Bouts**. Equally outstanding is **Memling**'s lyrical *Seven Joys of the Virgin*, which integrates all the scenes into a single dream-like fantasy of architecture and landscape. From the following century comes **Pieter Bruegel the Elder**'s *Land of Cockaigne*, depicting a seemingly utopian scene of plenty, where food cooks itself and pigs come ready-roasted; it's full of entertaining details, but, for all its humour, the real purpose of the work was actually to condemn gluttony and idleness. Very different in style is the exquisite small-scale art of his son **Jan Brueghel**, who is copiously represented here.

Centrepiece of the entire museum, and the main consideration in its architectural design, is the collection of works by the seventeenth-century Flemish painter **Rubens**. Sixty-two paintings display a wide range of the artist's prodigious output, including everything from the modellos the master made for the guidance of his large workshop to such massive finished altarpieces as *The Fall of the Rebel Angels* and *The Last Judgment* (which was commissioned for the Hofkirche in Neuburg an der Donau); from intimate portraits such as *Rubens and Isabella Brandt in the Honeysuckle Bower* (painted to celebrate his first marriage) to such boisterous mythological scenes as *Drunken Silenus*, and from the quiet beauty of *Landscape with a Rainbow* to the horrors of *The Massacre of the Innocents*.

Van Dyck, Rubens' most distinguished pupil, is also extensively represented, with portraits and religious scenes drawn from the main phases of his career. The small cabinet rooms beyond contain the largest collection of works in existence by **Adriaen Brouwer**, the most trenchant observer of the seamier side of life in seventeenth-century Flanders. There's also a haunting *Passion Cycle* by **Rembrandt**, commissioned by the House of Orange as Reformed Protestant visions of Holy Week. In both *The Raising of the Cross* and *The Deposition*, the familiar figure of Rembrandt himself appears as a leading witness to the events.

The Italian section begins with three little panels from a dispersed altarpiece by **Giotto**; other highlights include **Fra Filippo Lippi**'s classically inspired *The Annunciation*, **Botticelli**'s theatrical *Pietà*, **Raphael**'s tender *Holy Family*, and a rare authenticated example of the young **Leonardo da Vinci**, *Madonna of the Carnation*. However, works by **Titian** steal the show here, notably the *Seated Portrait of Charles V*, which perfectly captures the self-confident poise of a man of destiny, and *Christ Crowned with Thorns*, dating from the end of the artist's very long life. Among later Italian works, **Tiepolo**'s *Adoration of the Magi*, a product of his Würzburg years, stands out. The French display includes **Poussin**'s *Lamentation over the Dead Christ* and several classical landscapes by **Claude**. There's also a room of seventeenth-century Spanish painting, including a *Portrait of a Young Man* by **Velázquez**, and genre pictures by **Murillo**; the latter were to have an enormous influence on French and English art of the following century.

The Neue Pinakothek

The **Neue Pinakothek** (Mon & Fri–Sun 10am–5pm, Wed & Thurs 10am–8pm; €5, free Sun; Ⓦwww.neue-pinakothek.de) immediately to the north takes over where the Alte Pinakothek leaves off, housing the Bavarian state's collection of late eighteenth- to early twentieth-century painting and sculpture. When the previous building on the site opened to the public in 1853, it was the first public museum in Europe to be devoted solely to contemporary art.

The displays, which are arranged in a broadly chronological order, are dominated by German works, but begin with some notable canvases by Goya and the Swiss Angelika Kaufmann; an outstanding example of French Neoclassical portraiture in **David**'s cool, detached and precise *Marquise de Sourcy de Thélusson*; plus what is, by continental standards, a very respectable representation of British painting, dominated by two ravishing portraits by Gainsborough. There then follow several rooms of Romantic-era landscapes; highlights include *The Acropolis* by **Leo von Klenze**, which shows that Munich's great architect was also a highly gifted painter; and *The Watzmann* by **Ludwig Richter**, an early tribute to the stunning beauty of Bavaria's own scenery. A roomful of paintings by **Moritz von Schwind** includes a couple of exquisite decorative narratives: *The Story of Cinderella* and *A Symphony*. Equally detailed, but very different in style, are the documentary paintings of contemporary life – among which *A Procession in Hofgastein* stands out – by **Adolf Menzel**.

The wry, gentle humour of the Munich painter **Carl Spitzweg** is demonstrated in a whole group of subtly observed compositions, including *The Poor Poet*, *The Bookworm* and *The Childhood Friend*. More controversial are the heroic visions of the city's mid-nineteenth century history painters. The sketches by **Wilhelm von Kaulbach** for the frescoes of the exterior of the original Neue Pinakothek are the only reminders left of this grandiose scheme, which was, along with the building itself, completely destroyed in the war. A monumental *Destruction of Jerusalem by Titus* by the same artist is remarkable for its scale and attention to detail, though the most celebrated example of this style is the far less bombastic *Seni with the Corpse of Wallenstein* by his pupil **Karl von Piloty**.

Of the works by French Impressionists and Post-Impressionists, **Manet**'s *Breakfast in the Studio* is probably the most famous; other highlights are one of **van Gogh**'s *Sunflowers* and **Gauguin**'s *Breton Farmwomen*. The main German exponents of this phase are **Max Liebermann**, whose *Munich Beer Garden* is an accurate record of the appearance of the *Augustinerkeller* (see p.89) in the 1880s, and **Lovis Corinth**, whose *Self Portrait* shows him painting with his left hand, shortly after a stroke had paralysed the right hand he had previously used. The museum rounds off with a small selection of Symbolism and Art Nouveau. In **Franz von Stuck**'s *Sin*, the vice represented as a lascivious woman exposing herself; much more romantic and stylized is **Gustav Klimt**'s *Margarethe Stonborough-Wittgenstein*, a portrait of the sister of the philosopher Ludwig Wittgenstein.

The Pinakothek der Moderne

The long-awaited **Pinakothek der Moderne** (Tues, Wed, Sat & Sun 10am–5pm, Thurs & Fri 10am–8pm; €9, free Sun; Ⓦwww.pinakothek.de) finally opened in 2002 in what had hitherto been Munich's most notorious gap site, the block immediately east of the Alte Pinakothek. An open competition for the design of this building, which houses four separate museums, was won by the local architect Stefan Braunfels in 1992. The project was thereafter dogged by numerous delays, caused by, among other factors, ever-spiralling costs and by a legal suit between Braunfels and the construction authorities. Nonetheless, the end result has been hailed as a contemporary masterpiece. Its solutions are highly complex: the building has a central core of a vast central hall, staircase and light-emitting dome, round which the various constituent parts are wrapped like layers of skin, while dramatic use is made of the diagonal both inside and out.

Well over half the display space is allocated to the modern art collection of the **Bayerische Staatsgemäldesammlungen**, which is housed on the first floor. This continues onwards from the Neue Pinakothek, and is likewise laid out chronologically, although the design of the building allows for some unexpected cross-references to be made. The first few rooms in the west wing are devoted to Expressionism, with strong representations of Kirchner and of the artists of Der Blaue Reiter. Canvases by **Picasso** and **Beckmann** are hung in challenging juxtaposition, with several major examples of the latter artist, notably *Temptation*, a triptych inspired by Flaubert's novel *The Temptations of St Anthony*. There are some memorable examples of Surrealism, including *The Acrobat's Exercises* by **Magritte**, *The Enigma of Desire* by **Dalí**, and *Fireside Angel* by **Ernst**. In the east wing, which is devoted to the postwar period, the rooms are mostly devoted to individual artists, and photography, video art and installations are all featured in addition to painting and sculpture. Particular strengths are the work of Joseph Beuys and Georg Baselitz, and American Pop Art (especially Warhol).

The ground floor has space for major temporary exhibitions of contemporary art, plus areas for two institutions to display selections from holdings which, for conservation reasons, cannot be kept on permanent view. One of these is the **Staatliche Graphische Sammlung**, the Bavarian state's collection of works on paper, which ranges from old masters to living artists. The other is the **Architekturmuseum der Technischen Universität München**, a collection of architects' models, casts, plans and technical drawings.

In the basement, the **Neue Sammlung**, otherwise known as the **Staatliches Museum für Angewandte Kunst**, has been given the first space it has ever had for permanent displays since its foundation in 1907. It has amassed a huge archive of design items in this period, including cars, motorbikes, computers, radios, televisions, furniture and a host of utilitarian objects. There are illuminating sections on Bauhaus products and on the chairs produced by the Thonet factory, while two rotating paternosters are used for exhibiting myriad examples of favourite contemporary accessories such as mobile phones and trainers.

Maximilianstrasse

Maximilian II, who succeeded his disgraced father in 1848, also wanted to have a showpiece boulevard named in his own honour; indeed, he had begun planning for it long before he came to the throne. The resultant **Maximilianstrasse** runs east from Max-Joseph-Platz in front of the Residenz, forming Munich's answer to the Champs-Elysées.

As with Odeonsplatz, there was already an extant building at the beginning of the street, this time Klenze's **Nationaltheater**, which maintains its reputation as one of Europe's most prestigious opera houses; almost completely destroyed by bombs in World War II, it was re-created at enormous expense by 1963. In many ways, it sets the tone for the rest of the street, which is a real theatre quarter, an almost equally prestigious venue being the Jugendstil **Münchener Kammerspiele** at no. 26. Across the road is the city's most exclusive address, the **Hotel Vierjahreszeiten**, while elsewhere are some two dozen commercial galleries and a seemingly endless number of luxury shops selling the latest fashions and trendiest designer goods.

Over the hideous ring road, at no. 42 on the street, is the **Staatliches Museum für Völkerkunde** (Tues–Sun 9.30am–5.15pm; €3, free Sun, €6 including temporary exhibitions; Ⓦwww.voelkerkundemuseum-muenchen.de), which is devoted to the art and history of non-European cultures. Currently it has permanent displays on India, China, Japan, Africa and both North and South America, supplemented by changing thematic exhibitions. Further east is a huge bronze monument to Maximilian II. To the north, St-Anna-Strasse leads to the Franciscan church of **St Anna im Lehel**, designed by Johann Michael Fischer and decorated by the Asam brothers. Maximilianstrasse itself continues eastwards over the River Isar to the **Maximileum**, a grandiose palace by the Dresden architect Gottfried Semper. Intended as a cultural establishment, it's now home to the Bavarian parliament.

The Haus der Kunst and Archäologische Staatssammlung

The last of Munich's three great boulevards is **Prinzregentenstrasse**, which runs east from the Prinz-Carl-Palais at the far end of the Hofgarten. Laid out at the end of the nineteenth century and the beginning of the twentieth, its name comes from Prince Luitpold, who ruled as regent after the deposition of his nephew Ludwig II. Nowadays, it's the city's second main museum quarter. The **Haus der Kunst** (daily 10am–10pm; variable charge; Ⓦwww.hausderkunst.de), the first building on the northern side, was built by the Nazis as a showcase for the sort of art they favoured. It's now used for temporary artistic exhibitions – usually two or three at a time, with at least one of international blockbuster status.

Just to the northeast, at Lerchenfeldstr. 2, is the **Archäologische Staatssammlung** (Tues–Sun 9am–4.30pm; €2.50, free Sun; Ⓦwww.archaeologie.bayern.de). This makes a good attempt at bringing alive Bavarian prehistory, the Roman occupation and early medieval life. Look out in particular for the Roman treasure from Eining, the jewellery from tribal graves, the Carolingian choir screen and the surprising wheel-shaped Byzantine chandelier.

The Bayerisches Nationalmuseum

Directly in front, facing Prinzregentenstrasse, is the rambling pile of the **Bayerisches Nationalmuseum** (Tues, Wed & Fri–Sun 10am–5pm, Thurs 10am–8pm; €3, free Sun; Ⓦwww.bayerisches-nationalmuseum.de). For many years its magnificent collections were only partly accessible, but they can now be seen in their entirety as a result of structural repairs completed in time for the museum's jubilee in 2000. On the first floor, the exhibition halls are pastiches of the architectural style contemporary with the artefacts they display. The medieval sections feature the surviving sculptures from the original Kloster Wessobrunn (where German as a written language was born) and *Der Kleine Dom*, a gorgeous miniature cathedral made by a fourteenth-century goldsmith. This is followed by a superb display of German wood sculpture at its fifteenth- and sixteenth-century peak. There are examples of **Tilman Riemenschneider**'s art drawn from all phases of his career, ranging from the early *St Mary Magdalene Surrounded by Angels*, via a magnificently characterized set of Apostles made to adorn the Marienkapelle in Würzburg, to the serene late *St Barbara*. Many of his most talented contemporaries – Hans Multscher, Michel and Gregor Erhart, Hans Leinberger and Erasmus Grasser – are also well represented.

From the following generation is a statuette of *Judith with the Head of Holofernes* by **Conrad Meit**, one of the few major German sculptors to work in an Italianate style. There's also a miniature *Portrait of a 27-year-old Man* by **Hans Holbein the Younger**; this probably depicts Harry Maynert, a painter-colleague at the English court of Henry VIII, and is one of only a dozen or so miniatures by Holbein to have survived. The hall dedicated to Duke Albrecht V contains a spectacular **painted table top**, with an ornamental map of Bavaria in the middle, by Hans Wertinger; a far more scientific **map** of the province drawn by the great geographer Philipp Apian some thirty years later, in the 1560s; and lovingly crafted **models** of the province's five courtly capitals made in the course of the following decade by Jacob Sandtner. Despite the focus on Bavarian art, there's a decent Italian Renaissance section, which includes six magnificent bronze reliefs of *The Passion* by **Giambologna**, plus sculptures by Luca della Robbia and Antonio Rossellino. The late Renaissance section features the extraordinary costumes and jewellery retrieved from the tombs of members of the House of Pfalz-Neuburg. Bavarian Rococo art is copiously represented, notably by a number of impressive large-scale statues by **Ignaz Günther**.

Upstairs are displays of porcelain and musical instruments, plus a fascinating room devoted to **historic board games**, many of which are of great beauty. However, even these are overshadowed by the Rococo **dinner service** of the Prince-bishops of Hildesheim, arguably the most spectacular example of Augsburg's long and proud silverware tradition. The museum's basement features Bavarian folk art and a really outstanding collection of **Christmas cribs** from Bavaria, Austria and Italy.

Eastwards along Prinzregentenstrasse

Further along the street from the Bayerisches Nationalmuseum is the former Prussian embassy, now housing the **Schackgalerie** (10am–5pm, closed Tues; €2.50, free Sun). Count Schack was Munich's most important art patron during the nineteenth century, supporting struggling painters such as Franz von Lenbach, Marées, Böcklin and others until they achieved public acclaim. The museum, which preserves his collection intact, contains important examples of all those artists, plus other Romantic painters such as Moritz von Schwind, Feuerbach and Spitzweg.

Following Prinzregentenstrasse across the Isar over the Luitpoldbrücke, you come to the **Friedensengel**, a nineteenth-century monument to peace shining in gold splendour. Past Europaplatz at Prinzregentenstr. 60 is Munich's most eccentric nineteenth-century building, the **Villa Stuck** (Tues–Sun 10am–6pm; €4; Ⓦwww.villastuck.de). This was the house of Franz von Stuck, the leader of the Munich Secession, and was designed by him – using a decidedly eclectic mix of styles, though showing distinct echoes of the city's Neoclassical palaces built earlier in the century – in his only attempt at architecture. Inside is a large collection of his paintings, plus other examples of *fin-de-siècle* art, with Jugendstil predominating.

Schwabing

Just north of the city centre lies the stylish district of **Schwabing**. During the Second Reich and the Weimar Republic it gained a reputation as a centre for radical bohemian chic. Its habitués included outcast revolutionary politicians, the young Lenin and Hitler among them, the artists of Der Blaue Reiter, and writers such as Ibsen, the Mann brothers, Rilke, Brecht and Wedekind. Today, in contrast, Munich's real Latin Quarter has moved to Haidhausen, leaving Schwabing as the favourite haunt of the city's *Schickies*.

A much larger area than the city centre, Schwabing spreads untidily to the left and right of Leopoldstrasse, the northern continuation of Ludwigstrasse, with the Englischer Garten making up the eastern border. West of Leopoldstrasse, residential streets mix with wacky shops, student bars and restaurants. Along the centre line and to its right, trendy shops and café-bars ensure permanent crowds, day and night. Nightclubs are thick on the ground here too, especially around the Wedekindplatz near Münchener Freiheit. The far north of Schwabing is a tidily bourgeois residential area, uninteresting for visitors apart from the Olympiapark, which is at the terminus of U-Bahn #3. For listings of the area's bars, restaurants and clubs see pp.92–95.

The Englischer Garten

The vast **Englischer Garten** takes its name from the eighteenth-century landscaping fashion which tried to create parks resembling untouched nature. Occupying what was formerly marshland, it was created at the instigation of Bavaria's most unlikely statesman, the American-born Benjamin Thompson, who was a leading minister under the garden-loving Elector Carl Theodor.

When you've had enough of the city, the Eisbach meadow opposite the **Monopteros**, a Neoclassical temple by Klenze, is a good place to relax. People come here to sunbathe, picnic, swim in the aptly named **Eisbach** (ice stream) or ride horses. Visitors often find the large-scale nudity a little unnerving – and it certainly wouldn't be acceptable in any other German city. Even "respectable" businessmen will pop over in the lunch hour, fold their suits in a neat pile and read the paper stark naked. There are rules on where exactly nude sunbathing is allowed, but the police have given up trying to enforce them.

One of the city's most famous beer gardens is around the **Chinesischer Turm** (known locally as the Chinaturm) to the north of the Monopteros. It's at its best (or worst) on Sunday afternoons, when a Bavarian band blares across the crowd from the heights of the Chinaturm itself. Two more peaceful beer gardens are not far off by the **Kleinhesseloher See**. Heading north from here, you get the feeling of being in the countryside rather than in a city park.

The Olympiapark and around

During the summer months of July and August the **Olympiapark** (ⓦwww.olympiapark-muenchen.de) is the setting for open-air rock and pop concerts every weekend. Usually it's local bands of varying standards, but it doesn't cost anything and is worth checking out; the venue is a modern-day version of a Greek theatre, known as the **Theatron**, right next to the park's lake. The stadia all around were built for the 1972 Olympics and still have a somewhat futuristic look about them. In particular, the main **Olympiastadion** (daily 9am–6pm; €1.50) is a strange construction of steel poles and plexiglass expanses, looking rather like an overgrown tent. From the 290-metre-high tower (daily 9am–midnight; €3), there's a wonderful view over Munich and the Alps.

Just to the west rises another of Munich's most arresting modern buildings, the **BMW-Gebäude**, symbolically shaped as four tightly clustered cylindrical towers. The separate structure alongside houses the **BMW-Museum** (daily 9am–5pm; €3; ⓦwww.bmw-mobiletradition.com). This has a certain novelty value in being laid out along a gently sloping ramp which you gradually ascend on your way round. A fair number of vintage models are on view, but essentially the presentation is a flash – and often none-too-subtle – advert for the company and its products. If you'd like to see round the works, ask at the reception (or better still, call ⓣ0 89/38 95 33 06 as far in advance as possible); tours (in English as well as German) are held regularly, but are often booked up weeks in advance.

South along the River Isar

Wiener Platz, just off the east of the Maximileum, marks the beginning of **Haidhausen**. Around here it's still more or less the working-class quarter that it always was, with its own market and the large and shady beer garden of the Hofbräukeller. Until the early 1980s, Haidhausen was a run-down part of town that had become something of a Turkish ghetto. The peeling squares and prewar houses have since been rediscovered, and now trendy little health-food stores, alternative craftshops and hip bars have sprouted like mushrooms. It's become *the* place to live, and spiralling rents have forced out most of the original inhabitants.

Down towards the Isar on Rosenheimer Strasse is hidden one of Munich's real gems, the **Müller' sches Volksbad** (daily 7.30am–11pm; prices range from €2.90 for a swim to €38 for the full treatment of a Roman-Irish bath), a beautifully restored Jugendstil indoor swimming hall. High stuccoed ceilings arch over two pools, with mahogany changing cubicles surrounding each, and the sound of splashing water issuing from sculptured fountains makes the atmosphere perfect. There are a couple of saunas and a traditional Turkish bath.

On an island spanned by Ludwigsbrücke is the **Deutsches Museum** (Mon, Tues & Thurs–Sun 9am–5pm, Wed 9am–8pm; €7.50; ⓦwww.deutsches-museum.de). Covering every conceivable aspect of technical endeavour, from the first flint tools to the research labs of modern industry, this is the most compendious collection of its type in Europe. The sheer scale of the place is in itself impressive – it's well worth spending the whole day there – and some of the large-scale exhibits, such as biplanes and boats, are ranged in rooms the size of hangars. Among the mould-breaking inventions on view in the engineering section on the ground floor is the very first **diesel engine**, completed by Rudolf Diesel in 1897. The **chemistry** department on the first floor features several notable historic displays, including the monastic pharmacy from St Emmeram in Regensburg, and original equipment from Justus von Liebig's Munich laboratory. Part of the second floor has been converted into a replica of the Altamira caves while in the basement there's a convincingly gloomy mock-up of a **coalmine**. Meticulously constructed large-scale models are featured throughout, and the use of interactive displays makes them as absorbing for kids as adults. Check the noticeboards for the times of the daily demonstrations given by museum staff; that of the historical **musical instruments** on the first floor is particularly worth catching.

As a supplement, it's worth visiting the **amazeum** (daily 9am–11pm; Ⓦwww.amazeum.de) next door. This boasts an ultra-modern Planetarium (various programmes from €7) and a 400-square-metre screen for IMAX films (€4 with Deutsches Museum ticket, otherwise €7–9), shown throughout the day.

From the Reichenbachbrücke onwards, paths follow the course of the Isar all the way to the city's zoo, **Tierpark Hellabrunn** (daily: April–Sept 8am–6pm; Oct–March 9am–5pm; €7), which can be reached from the city centre by taking U-Bahn #3 to Thalkirchen. The east bank rises steeply around here and the river and canals are completely hidden by thick woodland. Europe's largest film-making centre, **Bavaria Filmstadt** (guided tours daily: March–Oct 9am–4pm; Nov–Feb 10am–3pm; €10; Ⓦwww.filmstadt.de) is 2km further south from the zoo and reached by tram #25: this can be picked up on Grünwalder Strasse a block to the east of the zoo or at the Silberhorn U-Bahn station (line #2 from the centre). The standard tour encompasses a toytown train ride through the grounds, a look round several original sets (including the submarine used in *Das Boot*), and participation in a short film sequence which is then mixed in with previously shot material and played back at the end. For a €4 supplement, you can also visit the interactive cinema, the Erlebniskino; paying €7 on top of the normal entrance also gives admission to an action show with stuntmen.

The Theresienwiese

Southwest of the Hauptbahnhof, reached by U-Bahn #4 or #5, lies a large egg-shaped fairground known as the **Theresienwiese**. For most of the year, this is an unremarkable meadow, but for sixteen days it's home to Germany's biggest annual event, the world-famous beer festival-cum-fair, the **Oktoberfest** (see box, p.86). Until recently, it was also Munich's trade fair quarter, but this has moved to the suburb of Riem. The three splendid exhibition halls from the early twentieth century have been given a new role as the home of the **Verkehrszentrum** (daily 9am–5pm; €2.50; Ⓦverkehrszentrum.deutsches-museum.de), the land transport branch of the Deutsches Museum. In 2003, the first of the halls, which features displays on key inventions and on the history of motor racing, opened to the public; the other two are due to be ready in 2005.

Overlooking the field to the west is the colonnaded **Ruhmeshalle** (Hall of Fame), a Bavarian counterpart to the earlier Walhalla near Regensburg which was likewise paid for by Ludwig I and built by Leo von Klenze. In front stands the colossal bronze statue of **Bavaria** (April to mid-Oct daily 9am–6pm; €2), a very Germanicized derivative of the art of Classical Greece. Designed by Ludwig von Schwanthaler, it took all of six years to cast.

The Oktoberfest

Munich's **Oktoberfest** (Ⓦwww.oktoberfest.de) has its origins in the marriage between the Bavarian Crown Prince Ludwig (the future King Ludwig I) and Princess Thérèse of Saxe-Hildburghausen on October 17, 1810. A massive fair was held on the fields now named after the princess, and it was such a popular event that it has been repeated annually ever since, and has spawned innumerable smaller imitations throughout Germany. Nowadays, it's quite simply an orgy of beer-drinking, with an estimated 6.1 million litres consumed, ensuring fabulous profits for the brewers – and the publicans lucky enough to be chosen as landlords. Each of the seven Munich breweries (Hacker-Pschorr counting as two for this purpose, even though Paulaner now makes all the beers which appear under the joint label) has its own huge **tent**, where in addition to beer, bretzels, chicken halves, sausages and pork knuckles are sold. Visitors sit ten to a bench, and after a few litres of beer half the hall is singing and dancing on the tables. There are also a number of smaller tents, which tend to be far less boisterous and not so overcrowded. The accompanying **fair** offers some great rides to churn your guts, some so hairy that they're banned in countries such as the US.

Despite its name, the Oktoberfest actually begins in September: it lasts for sixteen days, always ending on the first Sunday of October. The traditional **opening ceremonies** on the first Saturday revolve around the great horse-drawn brewery wagons arriving at the fairground at 11am to the sound of brass bands and much pomp and speech-making. That evening, a **folklore concert** is held in the Circus-Krone-Bau, Marsstr. 43, involving a selection of those taking part in the big **procession** the following day. It leaves from the centre of town at 10am, this time made up of hundreds of traditional folklore groups, marching bands, musicians, jesters, commercial floats and decorated horsemen that slowly converge on the fairground. A week later, a concert of all the Oktoberfest bands is held on the steps of the Bavaria statue at 11am, though this is postponed for a week if the weather is poor.

The proportions of the fair are so massive that the grounds are divided along four main **avenues**, creating a boisterous city of its own, heaving with revellers from morning till night. Ostensibly a family affair, with rides and stalls of every description jostling for customers, it attracts six to seven million visitors annually. Over seventy percent of these come from Bavaria and its immediate vicinity; the rest are drawn from all over the world, with Australians, New Zealanders and Italians forming the largest foreign contingents. Things are fairly relaxed during daylight hours, and it's advisable to visit at lunchtime if you want to eat and drink in comfort, or to avoid long queues for the rides. However, the atmosphere gets increasingly wild as the evening wears on: many of the big tents are packed to overflowing, and at closing time (around 11pm) staff have the unenviable task of trying to eject hundreds of fighting drunks.

For **information** on the opening ceremonies and pageants, look up the website, read the *Monatsmagazin* or contact the tourist office; advance **tickets** for the folklore concert are available from the organizers, Münchner Festring, Pestalozzistr. 3a (Ⓣ0 89/2 60 81 34). The next celebrations will be held from September 18 to October 3 2004 and from September 17 to October 2 2005. Even though entrance to the grounds is free, expect to spend lots of money. Accommodation during this time is often hiked up price-wise; on any of the three weekends you'll have trouble finding anything at all if you haven't booked in advance, while on weekdays only middle- and upper-range hotels are likely to have vacancies. Many Munich women choose to avoid the Oktoberfest altogether, and it's probably wise for unaccompanied women to proceed with caution after dark, avoiding the more raucous tents. The event also faces accusations of being a massive cartel. Not only are the many excellent breweries based around the fringes of the city resolutely excluded; even a man as well connected as Prince Luitpold of Bavaria found that the ploy of opening a new brewery in Munich itself does not bring access to the Oktoberfest closed shop.

Nymphenburg

Schloss Nymphenburg (daily: April to mid-Oct 9am–6pm; mid-Oct to March 10am–4pm; €3.50, or €7.50 including the Marstallmuseum and pavilions; Ⓦwww.schloesser.bayern.de), which lies some 4km northwest of central Munich on the route of tram #17, was the summer residence of the Wittelsbachs. Its kernel is a small Italianate palace begun in 1664 by Agostino Barelli for the frivolous Electress Adelaide, who dedicated it to the pastoral pleasures of the goddess Flora and her nymphs – hence the name. Her son Max Emmanuel commissioned an ingenious extension, whereby four pavilions were built to the side of the palace and connected to it by arcaded passages. Later, the palace itself was modified and much larger wings added, resulting in a remarkably unified whole, despite having been nearly a century in the making. By this time, an extensive French-style park had been laid out as an appropriate backdrop. In 1761 the famous porcelain factory was transferred to the site, but plans to establish a planned town on the model of Ludwigsburg in Württemberg came to nothing.

A resplendent Rococo festive hall, the **Grosser Saal** (or **Steinerner Saal**) forms the centrepiece of the interior. In its present form, it dates back to the 1750s, and is a late work by one of the finest decorative artists of the period, Johann Baptist Zimmermann, whose gloriously coloured ceiling fresco incorporates a number of mythological scenes, including one of Flora receiving homage from her nymphs. Otherwise, the most celebrated room is the **Schönheitengalerie**, a collection of portraits by Joseph Stieler of beauties who caught King Ludwig I's eye between 1827 and 1850. Outsiders among the predominantly aristocratic line-up include the so-called Schöne Münchnerin, the daughter of a local shoemaker, and the dancer Lola Montez, who caused the king's downfall.

There is free access to the **Schlosskapelle**, which is cunningly concealed within one of the northern pavilions, with no outward sign of its ecclesiastical function. The ceiling frescoes by the Tyrolean Joseph Mölck illustrate the life of the chapel's patroness, St Mary Magdalene, while the high altar has a gilded tabernacle-cum-reliquary designed by Cuvilliés. In the northernmost wing is the recently revamped **Museum Mensch und Natur** (Tues–Sun 9am–5pm; €2.50; Ⓦwww.musmn.de), featuring plenty of hands-on natural history displays which are popular with kids.

Housed within the Schloss' southern wing is the **Marstallmuseum** (same hours as Schloss; €2.50 for separate ticket; Ⓦwww.schloesser.bayern.de), whose ground floor halls display the elaborate **coaches** and **sleighs** of the Wittelsbachs. There are some magnificent Rococo pieces, notably the Paris-built coronation coach of Charles VII, the second and last of the Wittlesbachs to gain election as Holy Roman Emperor, and two racing sleighs carved in the workshop of the local court sculptor, Johann Baptist Straub. Even more riotously ornate are the fairytale state and gala coaches made more than a century later for the ill-fated King Ludwig II. Upstairs is a comprehensive display of Nymphenburg **porcelain**, ranging from the early years of production to the twentieth century.

The Schlosspark

For all its splendours, the Schloss is overshadowed by the wonderful **Schlosspark** to the rear. Three of its four garden **pavilions** (same hours as Schloss; combined ticket €3; Ⓦwww.schloesser.bayern.de), which are all of a markedly different character, were designed by **Joseph Effner**, the innovative court architect who was also responsible for the harmonization of the Schloss. A short walk from the northern wing is the **Magdalenenklause**, deliberately built to resemble a ruined hermitage, with a grotto and four simple cell-like rooms within. It's a very early example of the Historicism which was later to become a German obsession, borrowing elements from Roman, Gothic and even Moorish architecture. The Elector would come here when he wished to meditate – and he hadn't far to go if he tired of its peace and asceticism. Westwards through the park is the recently restored **Pagodenburg**, which was used for the most exclusive parties thrown by the court. Effner's third building, the **Badenburg**, lies on the opposite side of the canal, at the tip of the larger of the park's two lakes. It reflects contemporary interest in chinoiserie, though both the bathing room and the two-storey banqueting hall are in the richest Baroque tradition.

For all their charm, Effner's pavilions are overshadowed by the stunning **Amalienburg** (same hours as Schloss; €1.50; Ⓦwww.schloesser.bayern.de), the hunting lodge built behind the south wing of the Schloss by his successor as court architect, **François Cuvilliés**. This is among the supreme expressions of the Rococo style, marrying a cunningly thought-out design – which makes the little building seem like a full-scale palace – with extravagant decoration. The entrance chamber, with its niches for the hunting dogs, must be the most tasteful kennel ever built, and the elaborately tiled kitchen is likewise without peer. However, the showpiece is the circular **Spiegelsaal** (Hall of Mirrors), best seen on a bright day when the light casts magical reflections on the pale blue walls and the silvery rocaille console tables, panelled garlands and stuccowork nymphs and putti, creating the uncanny illusion that the chamber forms a seamless whole with the landscape outside.

To the north of the Schloss, the **Botanischer Garten** (daily 9am–4.30/7pm; €2) is primarily an institution with a serious scientific purpose, but is also a beautiful place to visit at any time of year. There are several different sections – including a showpiece floral garden, a rose garden, an arboretum, a moor and heath garden, a rhododendron grove, an Alpine garden and a complex of hothouses (closed Mon–Fri 11.45am–1pm) with over two thousand types of orchids.

Eating and drinking

Munich is awash with places to eat and drink, and you can find somewhere open at any time of the day or night. Though best known for its cavernous beer halls and leafy beer gardens, it also has a host of ethnic eateries as well as a lively café-bar culture which carries on well into the early hours. It's not difficult to eat well for relatively little money, with generous portions of heavy food being the norm in establishments which specialize in Bavarian cuisine.

If you're on a very tight budget, **mensas** are the cheapest places to get a good basic meal: you're supposed to have a valid student card to eat in them, but no one seems to check. The most central is at Leopoldstr. 13a; another is at the Technical University, Arcisstr. 17 (both 11am–2pm). Most **butchers' shops** sell bread rolls with various hot and cold fillings from as little as €2. Good places for this type of snack are the shops of the Vinzenz Murr chain, which can be found all over the city; they usually also serve hot daily specials which can be eaten within the shop.

Beer halls and beer gardens

The **beer cellar** (Bierkeller) and **beer garden** (Biergarten) are Munich's most characteristic institutions. Generally speaking the former are roomy halls (rather than cellars), serving strong, heady beer produced in a local brewery, plus hearty traditional Bavarian food. Those in the suburbs generally stand in large, leafy gardens; their city centre counterparts often have a very much smaller equivalent. Although a few have become tainted by excessive tourism, they remain essential and unmissable features of the city. The enduring image of both the halls and the gardens is of traditionally clad waitresses sailing from table to table clutching several enormous, foaming glasses in each hand while the resident brass band plays an endless succession of oompah tunes.

Altes Hackerhaus Sendlinger Str. 75. The city-centre beer hall of the Hacker-Pschorr brewery, jam-packed with bric-a-bric and with a minute beer garden.

Augustinerbräu Neuhauser Str. 27. One of Munich's most celebrated beer halls, with an unusually long menu, wonderfully evocative late nineteenth-century décor and an Italian garden to the rear.

Augustinerkeller Arnulfstr. 52. Located well away from the beaten tourist track, just to the northeast of the S-Bahn stop Hackerbrücke, this has a huge, shady garden.

Aumeister Sondermeierstr. 1. Occupying a former royal hunting lodge at the far northern end of the Englischer Garten, this serves Hofbräu beer and is a good place for a daytime break. Take U-Bahn #6 to Studentenstadt.

Ayingers Speis und Trank Platzl 1a. The principal Munich outlet of the brewery in the satellite town of Aying. At least six different beers are always available.

Chinesischer Turm Englischer Garten 3. Owing allegiance to Hofbräu, the beer garden has a lovely setting between its own beer hall and the tower from which it takes its name. It hosts a Sommerfest in August, a Weinfest in a heated tent in October, and its own Weihnachtsmarkt during Advent.

Hirschau Gysslingstr. 15. Spaten's Englischer Garten beer garden lies on the opposite side of the busy Isarring from *Seehaus* (see opposite), and is a popular refreshment stop for cyclists.

Hirschgarten Hirschgartenallee 1, Nymphenburg. A ten-minute walk south of Schloss Nymphenburg, this has the largest seating capacity – 8500 – of any of the city's beer gardens, yet it is still quite civilized. It is unusual in offering beers from different breweries – Augustiner, Hofbräu and Kaltenberg.

Hofbräuhaus Platzl 9. The most famous Bierkeller of all – which is consequently on the itinerary of just about every visitor to the city. Nonetheless, it's perfectly genuine, with plenty of regular customers, and the food and drink are fairly priced. The layout is rambling, with several huge halls, a small garden and a terrace.

Hofbräukeller Innere Wiener Str. 19, Haidhausen. The beer hall's very grand building houses Munich's most famous variety venue, the ValentinKarlstadt Theater, in its cellars. At the back is the only beer garden in the city with a cocktail bar. Take tram #18 to Wiener Platz.

Löwenbräukeller Nymphenburger Str. 2. Located a short distance west of Königsplatz, this serves excellent food and has a moderately sized beer garden.

Menterschwaige Menterschwaigstr. 4, Harlaching. Occupying an old agricultural estate in a southern suburb and serving Löwenbräu beers, this is another cyclists' favourite, being right beside the Isar valley cycle track. It lies a few minutes' walk to the west of the route of trams #15 and #25.

Münchner Haupt Zielstattstr. 6, Sendling. A short walk south of the Mittersendling S-Bahn station, on the opposite side of the tracks, this palatial beer hall with garden serves the varied products of Prinz Luitpold of Bavaria's castle brewery at Kaltenberg to the west of Munich. There are bargain menus Mon–Fri lunchtime.

Paulaner am Nockherberg Hochstr. 77, Au. Situated alongside the brewery, up on the Nockherberg in the district immediately south of Haidhausen, this is the venue for Munich's main springtime Starkbierfest and the only place where the unfiltered *Nockherberger* is served. The beer hall has recently been rebuilt following fire damage and is now the most modern and salubrious in the city, with an imaginative menu.

Pschorrkeller Theresienhöhe 7. Located on the heights above the Theresienwiese, there are two cavernous halls and a front garden.

Seehaus Kleinhesselohe 3. This Paulaner outlet has a marvellous setting on the eastern shore of the Kleinhesseloher See in the central area of the Englischer Garten. The standard of food served is a cut above that of most of the other beer gardens.

Spatenhaus Residenzstr. 12. The most upmarket of Spaten's hostelries, with an interior decked out in traditional Alpine style, complete with a frescoed ceiling.

Spatenhofkeller Neuhauser Str. 39. A rare example of a Bierkeller that actually occupies a cellar. It offers hearty Bavarian cooking at lower than average prices, with bargain midday menus which sometimes feature quite innovative dishes.

Weisses Bräuhaus Tal 10. This is the flagship of the Schneider brewery, a *Weissbier* specialist which moved its production base after the war from this site to Kelheim in Eastern Bavaria. Though it has a full menu, it's best known for its *Weisswurst*, which should preferably be eaten to the accompaniment of a *Weissbier*.

Zum Erdinger Weissbräu Heiglhofstr. 13, Grosshadern. The Munich beer hall and garden of the eponymous brewery in the small town of Erding to the northeast of the city, which is well known for its wide range of wheat beers. It's just a stone's throw from the Grosshadern station on U-Bahn line #6.

Zum Flaucher Isarauen 2, Thalkirchen. Hiding amid the tall trees of the park on an island in the Isar, it serves Löwenbrau and Franziskaner beers, and does excellent fish dishes in summer. It lies directly north of the zoo, a ten-minute walk from the Thalkirchen station on U-Bahn line #3.

Zum Franziskaner Perusastr. 5. A good choice for either a full meal or a snack: it's said to serve Munich's best *Weisswurst*, the white sausage which traditionally should only be eaten before noon.

Munich's beer culture

Munich's **beer halls** have their origins in the Middle Ages, when brewers stored barrels indoors, planting chestnut trees around their premises to shade them from the heat of the sun. Whereas the halls operate all year round, the associated **beer gardens** – many of which can seat several thousand customers – close down soon after Oktoberfest, and only reopen when the weather starts to become fine again in the spring. In the gardens, beers – other than *Weissbier*, which is always served in the traditional half-litre glass – are generally only available in litre *Mass* measures. As an alternative to the full menu available from the main kitchen indoors, many of the gardens have their own grill areas and stalls from which a wide variety of fast food – including such perennial favourites as roasted half chickens, sausages, pork knuckles, radishes and spicy cream cheese – is dispensed. In most beer gardens, it is permitted to bring your own food, but consuming any drink not bought on the premises is regarded as a very serious breach of etiquette.

Munich ranks as the third largest producer of beer in the world, and it can legitimately claim to be both the most influential and the most varied in output: it pioneered wheat-based and brown-coloured beers, and adapted the original *Bock* of Einbeck to the form in which it's generally known today. The largest of the local **breweries** is **Paulaner**, which produces a full range of styles, generally with a drier flavour than those of its competitors; the dark and extremely powerful *Salvator-Doppelbock* is its star product. Paulaner has taken over **Hacker-Pschorr** (two formerly separate breweries which later united), whose product lines include an amber-coloured *Märzen* and a very pale wheat beer. **Löwenbräu**, better known abroad through being a bigger exporter, produces a similarly wide variety of generally maltier beers, among which the *Pils* enjoys the highest reputation. Though it continues to operate as a separate entity, Löwenbräu is now owned by its erstwhile rival **Spaten**, which has the best amber and black beers – known respectively as *Ur-Märzen* and *Ludwig-Thoma-Dunkel* – but is equally known for its *Franziskaner Weissbier* (available in both light and dark versions) and *Maibock*. **Hofbräu**, the old court brewery, makes the classic *Maibock* plus a number of contrasting wheat beers, though its standard line is an *Export*. The main strength of **Augustiner** is its pale (*Hell*) beer, but it produces several prestigious dark brews as well.

Hausbrauereien

Predictably, Munich has played a pioneering role in the current craze for new Hausbrauereien, which represent a return to traditional methods by having a boutique brewery in or alongside the bar-restaurant where it is served, thereby ensuring the utmost freshness.

Braustüberl der Forschungsbrauerei Unterhachinger Str. 76, Altperlach. In a southeastern suburban setting with garden, just north of the Perlach station on S-Bahn line #2. It produces a blond *Bock* known as *St Jakobus* and an *Export* called *Pilsissimus*. Closed Mon & mid-Oct to mid-March.

Flieger-Bräu Sonnenstr. 2, Feldkirchen. In an eastern suburb, reached by S-Bahn #6, this is a sister establishment of the better-known *Isar-Bräu*.

Isar-Bräu Kreuzeckstr. 23, Grosshesselohe. Located within the Grosshesselohe Isartalbahnhof on S-Bahn line #7, it makes a *Weissbier* and a dark *Spezial*, and also serves the products of its parent, the out-of-town Hofbräuhaus Traunstein.

Paulaner Bräuhaus Kapuzinerplatz 5. Paulaner converted a defunct brewery, the Thomasbräu, into this new generation home brew establishment. It has the unlikely facility of a library, as well as a pleasant rear garden. Very trendy, particularly on Thurs, the day the new *Weissbier* is brewed.

Unionsbräu Einsteinstr. 42, Haidhausen. Löwenbräu set this Hausbrauerei up in a long vanished brewery, reviving its name in the process. The cellar has huge communal benches where you sit to sip the fine *Helles* made on the premises.

Restaurants

Munich has a wide selection of restaurants, and plenty of places offer good food at reasonable prices. As well as a wide choice of ethnic eateries (including some of the best Italian cuisine north of the Alps) and several vegetarian specialists, there are many traditional Gaststätten and Wirtshäuser which serve traditional Bavarian fare in a more intimate atmosphere than that of the beer halls listed above.

Gaststätten and Wirtshäuser

Andechser am Dom Weinstr. 7a. Despite its short menu, this restaurant is very "in"; it's also the only place in Munich serving the products of the monastic brewery at Andechs.

Asam-Schlössl Maria-Einsiedel-Str. 45, Thalkirchen. The Rococo mansion of the painter Cosmas Damian Asam has undergone a tasteful conversion into a restaurant by the Augustiner brewery. Good-value set lunches are offered, and there's a garden to the rear. It can be reached by U-Bahn #3 or bus #57.

Bamberger Haus Brunnerstr. 2, Schwabing. Occupies a lovely Rococo mansion moved stone-by-stone from Bamberg to the Luitpoldpark, just east of the Olympiapark. Since Augustiner took it over from Prince Luitpold of Bavaria, it no longer brews its own beer, but the food is excellent and the garden terrace is a good place to relax when the weather is fine. It lies due west of the Scheidplatz U-Bahn station (lines #3 and #5).

Burg Pappenheim Baaderstr. 46. Intimate old Gaststätte that's hugely popular with just about everyone. Evenings only.

Donisl Weinstr. 1. A lively yet traditional establishment, with a pedigree dating back to the early eighteenth century.

Fraunhofer Fraunhoferstr. 9. Attached to a cabaret theatre, this is a hugely popular traditional Wirtshaus with a good range of vegetarian as well as traditional dishes. Open daily from 4.30pm, it's usually packed out in the early evening.

Haxnbauer Corner of Sparkassenstrasse and Ledererstrasse. Specializes in the delicious roasted pork knuckles that are such a highpoint of German cuisine; the lamb version is no less tasty. The beers come not from Munich but from Dinkelacker in Stuttgart.

Hundskugel Hotterstr. 18. Munich's oldest surviving inn, established in 1440, has a cosy little interior. The dishes are lighter than in most rival establishments – which many will rate a positive advantage.

Lindwurmstüberl Lindwurmstr. 32. A time-warped Munich institution, located beside the southwestern entrance to the Goetheplatz U-Bahn station (lines #3 and #6). It's renowned for its spit-roast chicken, but serves a good range of dishes, including fried fish. Closed Sun.

Nürnberger Bratwurst-Glöckl Frauenplatz 9. Standing in the shadow of the Dom, this is a transplant of the famous gourmet sausage restaurants of Nürnberg, with beer served straight from wooden barrels.

Ratskeller Marienplatz 8. The cavernous cellars of the Neues Rathaus serve typically hearty meals. They also incorporate the *Fränkische Weinprobierstube*, where Franconian wines are served, as well as the informal *Frankenwein Vinothek*, where these vintages can be sampled from open bottles.

Sängerwarte Pettenkoferstr. 48. Splendidly old-fashioned Gaststätte whose menu includes bargain set lunches, good-value duck dishes, and fish from the Upper Bavarian lakes.

Schelling-Salon Schellingstr. 54, Schwabing. A true golden oldie, having been run by the same family since 1872. It serves hearty and very inexpensive meals, is also a popular choice for breakfast, and has a wide range of board and table games on offer. Closed Tues & Wed.

Schlosswirtschaft zur Schwaige Eingang 30, Schloss Nymphenburg. A highly recommendable restaurant in its own right, and an ideal place to break for a meal when visiting Nymphenburg. It has a pleasant small beer garden.

Wirtshaus zum Straubinger Blumenstr. 5. Cosy traditional hostelry with long wooden benches and a garden to the side. It offers excellent cooking, with a variety of bargain options, including set lunches.

Zum Spöckmeier Rosenstr. 9. Large and popular two-storey Gaststätte, one of the few left in Munich still adhering to the old tradition of serving as its own butcher.

Non-German cuisines

Adria Leopoldstr. 19, Schwabing. This keeps very long hours, staying open until 3am, and has excellent pizzas and other Italian food at reasonable prices.

Bangkok-House Ledererstr. 17. Munich's most popular Thai restaurant. Evenings only, except in summer when it's open Wed & Thurs for set lunches.
Bella Italia Herzog-Wilhelm-Str. 8. The most centrally sited of a small local chain of bargain-priced Italian restaurants.
Bernard & Bernard Innere Wiener Str. 32, Haidhausen. Good choice for crêpes. Evenings only.
Bodega Dalí Tengstr. 6, Schwabing. One of the best Spanish places in town, despite lower than average prices. Evenings only.
Cohen's Theresienstr. 31. This serves Jewish cuisine in its various manifestations – Middle Eastern, Eastern European and American.
Friulana Zenettistr. 43. A genuine, homely local much patronized by Italian expatriates; it's way off the tourist track, yet is just a short walk southeast of Theresienwiese.
Ganga Baaderstr. 11. Offers a wide range of classic Indian dishes at reasonable prices. On weekdays, it has bargain menus at lunchtimes; on Sat & Sun it's open evenings only.
Il Falco Falkenstr. 38, Au. Good-value Italian restaurant with changing daily specials, not far from the Deutsches Museum.
Karawanserei Pettenkoferstr. 1. This is the pick of several fine Persian restaurants in the city. It has appropriately exotic decor, a back courtyard with a fountain, and bargain menus at lunchtime.
KUK Monarchie Reichenbachstr. 22. This features dishes from throughout the old Austro-Hungarian Empire (Kaiserliche- und Königliche Monarchie), with separate Austrian, Magyar, Czech and Yugoslav menus. Evenings only.
Kyris Taverne Sebastiansplatz 8. Perpetually crowded Greek taverna offering a changing daily selection of fresh fish flown in from the Mediterranean.
Matoi Hans-Sachs-Str. 10. Japanese restaurant offering bargain lunches. Closed Sun.
Opatija Rindermarkt 2 and Brienner Str. 41. Long-established Balkan favourites; the former has the benefit of a summertime patio, the latter is handy for the Königsplatz museums.
Riva Tal 44. The deliciously crispy pizzas made here are universally regarded as the best in Munich - which is tantamount to saying the best in Germany.

Vegetarian restaurants

buxs Frauenstr. 9. Has a mouth-watering cold buffet which you pay for by weight.
Das Gollier Gollierstr. 83, Westend. Reached by tram #18 or #19, this serves excellent vegetarian food and organically produced drinks, with inexpensive lunchtime buffets on weekdays. On Sat it's only open in the evening.
Ignaz Georgenstr. 67, Schwabing. Thanks to its location, this has a large student clientele. There are breakfast and lunch buffets Mon–Fri, brunch buffets Sat & Sun.
Prinz Myshkin Hackenstr. 2. The long bar is the focal point of this otherwise minimalist restaurant, which offers creative vegetarian dishes plus wholemeal pizzas.

Bars and café-bars

Much of the city's social life revolves around its bars and café-bars. Beer, coffee and snacks are served in most places, and while the list of "in" and "out" bars is ever-changing, the ones listed below are of proven worth. *Schickies* hang out in **Schwabing** and hipsters head for **Haidhausen**, though things are pretty provincial in both areas. The city's bars suffer from limiting licensing laws (midnight closing at most places).

Alter Ofen Zieblandstr. 41, Schwabing. Although a little worn about the edges, this is still immensely popular with its student crowd.
Alter Simpl Türkenstr. 57, Schwabing. Famous literary café and bistro which spawned the satirical magazine *Simplicissimus*; after a long period in the doldrums, it has become fashionable again.
Café Altschwabing Schellingstr. 56. This Wilhelmine-era café with a fine stuccowork interior was a favourite of writers such as Mann and Wedekind, but for long lay derelict before being restored in 2000. It now has a contemporary café-bar ambience, and serves good bistro-style cooking.
Café an der Universität Ludwigstr. 24. Very popular with students from the nearby university, and nearly always packed to the gills.
Café im Hinterhof Sedanstr. 29, Haidhausen. Café-bar which also offers health food for times when the beer and schnapps become too much.

Cyber Ice-C@fé Sendlinger-Tor-Platz 5 and Feilitzschstr. 15, Schwabing. Both of these combine a cybercafé with an ice cream parlour.
Drugstore Feilitzschstr. 12, Schwabing. A hardy survivor from Schwabing's "Swinging Sixties", this offers just about everything from breakfasts to freshly made pizzas to cocktails, and also incorporates a revue theatre, Bel Etage.
Easy Everything Bahnhofplatz 1. Much the largest and most frequented of the city's cybercafés, though it only has a limited choice of drinks and snacks.
Eisbach Marstallplatz 3. This modern glass palace, which makes an unlikely pair with Leo von Klenze's dignified Neoclassical Marstall (stables) alongside, is currently one of the hottest spots in town.
Havana Club Herrnstr. 30. Great place for cocktails; so packed it's normally standing room only.
Internet Café Altheimer Eck 12. A conveniently central place in which to surf the net: it's open daily 11am–1am, and serves pizzas and other Italian food.
Jodlerwirt Altenhofstr. 4. There's a typical Gaststube on the ground floor which serves Aying beers, but the draw is the cramped little bar above, which is always jam-packed for the yodelling sessions: come along in the late evening and you'll immediately be sucked into the arm-linking singalong, a harmless piece of kitsch that's great fun.
Julep's Breisacher Str. 18, Haidhausen. A cocktail bar decked out in imitation of a New York speakeasy.
Nachtcafé Maximiliansplatz 5. Haunt of the true night owls, this is the place to see and be seen in the early hours of the morning. Open 9pm–6am.
Opern Espresso Maximilianstr. 6. Italian-style café directly opposite the side entrance to the Bayerisches Staatsoper, well patronized by performers and audience alike.
Orlando Platzl 4. This injects a modern note into the square dominated by the Hofbräuhaus.
Paris Bar Gravelottestr. 7, Haidhausen. Very trendy *Schickie* hangout.
Roma Maximilianstr. 31. Hugely chic establishment, popular with German film stars and other celebrities, and with lighting effects by the celebrated Munich-based designer Ingo Maurer.
Ruffini Orffstr. 22, Neuhausen. A long-established collective in the western part of the city; take U-Bahn #1 or #7 to Rotkreuzplatz. It's run in tandem with a shop selling organic food and wines, and has a pleasant roof terrace. Closed Mon.
Schumann's Maximilianstr. 36. Munich's movers and shakers congregate here, so this is the place to head for if you're looking to make contacts.
Tambosi Odeonsplatz 18. Something of a cross between a traditional café and a trendy café-bar, this is one of the most obvious places in the city in which to play at being seen. In summer, it spills over into Odeonsplatz and the Hofgarten.
Wirtshaus in der Au Lilienstr. 51, Au. This place manages the difficult task of combining the functions of a traditional beer hall and a modern café-bar.

Traditional cafés

Although traditional *Kaffee und Kuchen* establishments are not so obviously prominent in Munich as in most other major German cities, plenty of recommendable places can be found throughout the city.

Café Frischhut Prälat-Zeistl-Str. 8. A true original, popular with the local market traders and best-known for the *Schmalznudel*, a deep-fried doughnut which can be eaten plain or sprinkled with sugar. Open Mon–Sat 5am–5pm.
Café Hag Residenzstr. 25–26. An adjunct to Konditorei Rottenhöfer, the former court confectioners, which was founded in 1825 and makes a wonderful range of cakes and chocolate.
Café Hölzl Schellingstr. 27, Schwabing and Hirschgartenallee 48, Nymphenburg. These are two of the most convenient branches of a small local chain.
Café Kreuzkamm Maffeistr. 4. Delicious cakes, sweets and chocolates make this one of the best cafés in town. Closed Sun.
Café Luitpold Brienner Str. 11. Still an extremely elegant café, despite losing its sumptuous neo-Rococo decoration during the war, save for a couple of huge statues now in the Bayerisches Nationalmuseum. It offers all-day breakfasts and also serves light meals. Closed Sun.
Café Schneller Amalienstr. 59, Schwabing. A university location and a predilection for wholemeal cakes mean that this is popular with students rather than the antique lady contingent. It closes for the weekend at 2pm on Sat.
Café Wünsche St-Anna-Str. 13. Excellent coffee house located right by the entrance to the Lehel U-Bahn station.

Wine bars

There's a limited choice of wine bars in this beer haven, though a wide geographical choice of vintages is on offer, particularly when the *Ratskeller* (see p.92) is added to those listed below.

Café Nymphenburg Sekt Am Viktualienmarkt. Located alongside the fountain dedicated to Karl Valentin, this is a good place to sample Munich's own sparkling wine.

Pfälzer Weinprobierstuben Residenzstr. 1. Wines and food from the Rhineland are served in a pleasant atmosphere in this wine bar in the Residenz.

Rolandseck Viktoriastr. 23, Schwabing. This place has the best selection of Baden wines in town; it also serves beers from the rural Arcobräu, and has a good menu.

Weinhaus Neuner Herzogspitalstr. 8. Nineteenth-century wine bar known for its high-class food. The set lunches are reasonably priced. Closed Sun.

Weintrödler Brienner Str. 10. This is open daily 5pm–6am, and consequently tends to get packed in the early hours, when everywhere else is closed.

Nightlife and entertainment

Munich has a great deal to offer musically, whether you're into classical concerts or more modern fare. There's everything you'd expect to find in a cosmopolitan capital, and during the summer a glut of open-air music festivals takes place in or around the city. Several orchestras of international repute are based here, and the annual opera festival in July ranks with the Salzburg and Bayreuth festivals. Not that it's all highbrow: there's plenty of trash and tinsel as well, though perhaps the bars are more interesting than the discos. The various listings magazines (see p.64) are good sources of information on what's on.

Nightclubs and live music

Munich has a thriving **nightclub** scene, though in this city where money and appearances are everything, the snooty attitudes of many clubs can be rather off-putting. Most places are open 10pm–4am and entrance is about €5. During the summer there are **free rock concerts** by the lake in the Olympiapark, at the purpose-built stage known as the Theatron. There are also a few venues which have regular live music programmes throughout the year.

Crash Ainmillerstr. 10, Schwabing. Heavy metal mecca and headbanger's delight.

Jackie O Rosenkavalierplatz 12, Bogenhausen. Just about the strictest door policy in town, so unless you're loaded and look it, forget it.

Kaffee Giesing Bergstr. 5, Untergiesing Ⓦwww.kaffee-giesing.de. Run by the singer Konstantin Wecker, and usually featuring small bands or solo artists.

Kunstpark-Ost Grafinger Str. 6, Haidhausen. Though perennially under threat of closure, this mini-city of nightclubs, housed in a network of disused factories, is at the cutting edge of Munich's nightlife scene; all kinds of musical and social tastes are catered for. There's talk of it relocating to the northern suburb of Freimann (on the U-Bahn #6 line) in the near future.

Muffathalle Zellstr. 4, Haidhausen Ⓦwww.muffathalle.de. This converted waterworks is a major live music venue, often attracting well-known bands.

Nachtwerk Landsberger Str. 185, Laim. One of the city's best and most affordable nightlife possibilities. They put on occasional indie gigs here too.

Parkcafé Sophienstr. 7. Ranks among Munich's most popular nightclubs; it also serves bistro food during the daytime and has a nice beer garden.

The Atomic Café Neuturmstr. 5 Ⓦwww.atomic.de. Central venue where chart stuff, hip-hop and techno are the order of the evening.

Jazz and folk

Munich has a monthly jazz magazine called *Münchener Jazz-Zeitung*, available in music shops and jazz venues. The city is corporate headquarters of the

The gay scene

Deeply conservative Bavaria is not the best part of Germany in which to be gay. Nonetheless, Munich has gradually developed one of Germany's most active and visible gay scenes, centred on the bars in and around Gärtnerplatz. The widely available *Columbia Fun Map* shows the main gay meeting-places; there's also a glossy monthly magazine entitled *Our Munich* (despite it's name, it's in German only). The main gay **information** point, the *Schwules Kommunikations- und Kulturzentrum*, is at Müllerstr. 43 (ⓣ0 89/60 30 56).

The **Women's Centre**, *Frauenzentrum*, Güllstr. 3 (ⓣ0 89/7 25 42 71) runs a series of workshops and a café for all women, not just lesbians. On Tuesday between 1pm and 8pm, women from 13 to 20 years old meet in the café, with Friday evenings specifically for lesbians. The best-known café that caters predominantly for lesbians is *Inge's Karotte*, Baaderstr. 13; the only nightclub is *Mylord*, Ickstattstr. 2a (daily 6–9pm, 6pm–3am weekends).

Among the many **gay men's bars**, the following are the best known: *Colibri*, Utzschneiderstr. 8; *Juice*, Buttermelcherstr. 2a; *Klimperkasten*, Maistr. 28; *Nil*, Hans-Sachs-Str. 2 and *Teddybar*, Hans-Sachs-Str. 1. *Ochsengarten*, Müllerstr. 47, is a leather bar. The disco *Fortuna*, Maximiliansplatz 5, caters for both gays and lesbians. *Morizz*, Klenzestr. 43, is a recommendable gay-run **restaurant** that attracts plenty of straight customers.

avant-garde jazz record label ECM, and club dates are accordingly more exciting than the German norm, attracting many big names on tour. Predictably, the Munich folk scene is dominated by Germany's two favourite foreign imports – Irish and Country.

Alabamahalle Domagkstr. 33, Schwabing ⓦwww.alabamahalle.de. As the name suggests, this plays predominantly Dixieland fare.

Feierwerk Hansastr. 39, Sendling ⓦwww.feierwerk.de. Has jazz, blues or rock every evening from 9pm.

Jam Rosenheimer Str. 4, Haidhausen. A good bet for solid, reliable jazz, though don't expect any musical surprises. During the daytime, it's a normal café.

Max-Emanuel-Brauerei Adalbertstr. 33, Schwabing. For much of the time this is a normal Gaststätte, but it has tango evenings on Tues, salon music on Wed & Fri, 50s records on Sun. Entrance to these is upwards of €5.

Mister B's Herzog-Heinrich-Str. 38 ⓦwww.misterbs.de. Small jazz club with live music from 9.30pm. Closed Mon.

Oklahoma Schäftlarnstr. 156, Thalkirchen. Has live Country music Wed–Sun from 7pm.

Rattlesnake Saloon Schneeglöckchenstr. 91, Moosach. There's either live Country music or blues every evening Thurs–Sun from 7pm.

Shamrock Irish Pub Trautenwolfstr. 6, Schwabing. Live music, usually Irish folk, is played from 9pm each evening.

Unterfahrt Einsteinstr. 42, Haidhausen ⓦwww.unterfahrt.de. Munich's modern jazz venue. Big names and unknowns play here, and the music is nearly always excellent. Closed Mon.

Classical music and theatre

A number of resident **orchestras** and two **opera houses** cater to a very spoilt audience. The local radio orchestra, the Bayerisches-Rundfunk-Sinfonie-Orchester, (ⓦwww.br-online.de) has recently appointed the Latvian conductor Mariss Jansons. For a quarter of a century, the Münchner Philharmoniker (ⓦwww.muenchnerphilharmoniker.de) was directed by the Romanian Sergiu Celibidache, one of the great conductors of the twentieth century, a man who developed an aura by his stubborn refusal to make records. His death left a huge question mark over the orchestra's future status, which was resolved when highly regarded American, James Levine, was secured as his successor. Yet another member of the conducting jet-set, the Indian Zubin Mehta, is musical director of a third full-sized body, the Bayerischer Staatsorchester, whose primary function is to play for the opera, which is managed by Britain's Sir Peter Jonas. A smaller ensemble, the Münchener Kammerorchester (Ⓦwww.muenchener-kammerorchester.de), has gained international standing for its interpretations of Baroque music and the Viennese classics; its current musical director is Christoph Poppen. Among several distinguished **choirs**, the Münchener-Bach-Chor (Ⓦwww.muenchener-bachchor.de) has long been renowned for its performances, often accompanied by the Münchener-Bach-Orchester, of Bach's church cantatas, notwithstanding the irony of the championship of such overtly Protestant music in this stoutly Catholic city. Finally, the **Münchener Opernfest**, which takes place from the middle of July to the beginning of August, has a very high reputation. Classical concerts are also held at Schloss Nymphenburg and in the courtyard of the Residenz at this time of year.

Munich has a host of theatre venues, all of which are listed in the official programmes and the local press. Almost all productions are exclusively in German. Advance **tickets** can be bought at the relevant box offices or commercial ticket shops, such as München Ticket in the tourist office in the Neues Rathaus (Mon–Fri 10am–8pm, Sat 10am–4pm; Ⓣ0 89/54 81 81 81, Ⓦwww.muenchenticket.de).

Bayerische Staatsoper (or **Nationaltheater**) Max-Joseph-Platz 2 Ⓣ0 89/21 85 19 20, Ⓦwww.bayerische.staatsoper.de and www.bayerische.staatsballett.de. One of the world's most beautiful and distinguished opera houses, presenting both grand opera and ballet. Unsold and cheap standing tickets can be bought an hour before performance within the theatre itself.

Circus-Krone-Bau Marsstr. 43 Ⓣ0 89/55 81 66, Ⓦwww.circus-krone.de. Germany's only permanent circus tent, located close to the Hackerbrücke S-Bahn station.

Cuvilliéstheater (or **Altes Residenztheater**) Residenzstr. 1, tickets from Bayerische Staatsoper. This magnificent Rococo building (see p.74) saw the premiere of Mozart's *Idomeneo*. Nowadays it is rarely used for opera, though it does host some concerts, and is a regular drama venue.

Deutsches Theater Schwanthalerstr. 13 Ⓣ0 89/55 23 44 44, Ⓦwww.deutsches-theater.de. Features both home-grown and imported musicals.

Gasteig Rosenheimer Str. 5 Ⓣ0 89/48 09 80, Ⓦwww.gasteig.de. Modern concert hall complex in Haidhausen, built on the site of the *Bürgerbräukeller*, scene of the Beer Hall Putsch of 1923. In addition to the main Philharmonie, where symphony orchestras perform, there's the Carl-Orff-Saal for chamber orchestras, and the Kleiner Konzertsaal for soloists and small ensembles.

Hochschule für Musik Arcisstr. 12 Ⓣ0 89/5 59 15 89, Ⓦwww.musikhochschule-muenchen.de. The one-time Nazi Party headquarters, nowadays the local music academy, often stages high-quality solo instrumental and chamber music concerts, many of them free.

Münchner Kammerspiele Maximilianstr.26 Ⓣ0 89/2 33 37 00, Ⓦwww.muenchner-kammerspiele.de. An excellent venue, offering a wide variety of productions.

Münchner Marionettentheater Blumenstr. 29a Ⓣ0 89/26 57 12, Ⓦwww.muenchner-marionettentheater.de. A puppet theatre – mainly for kids, though once a week the marionettes are put to more serious use in the performance of an opera or drama classic.

Olympiahalle in the Olympiapark Ⓣ0 89/3 06 70, Ⓦwww.olympiapark-muenchen.de. The huge sports hall is frequently used for blockbuster all-star operas and concerts. High prices for even the worst seats.

Prinzregententheater Prinzregentenplatz 12 Ⓣ 0 89/21 85 28 99, Ⓦwww.prinzregententheater.de. This is used by the Bayerische Staatsoper for staging Baroque and chamber operas; small-scale ballets and concerts are also featured.

Residenz Residenzstr. 1 Ⓣ0 89/29 06 71 or 29 06 72 63. There are two concert halls within the palace – the tapestry-lined Herkulessaal for orchestral music, and the Max-Joseph-Saal for chamber performances.

Residenztheater Max-Joseph-Platz 1 Ⓣ0 89/21 85 19 40, Ⓦwww.bayerischesstaatschauspiel.de. Traditional dramatic fare in high quality productions.

Staatstheater am Gärtnerplatz Gärtnerplatz 3 Ⓣ0 89/21 85 19 60, Ⓦwww.staatstheater-am-gaertnerplatz.de. Presents operettas and the lighter fare of the operatic repertoire.

Munich's festivals

Inevitably, all local **festivals** stand in the shadow of the **Oktoberfest** (see p.86), but there are plenty of other annual events. **Fasching**, Munich's Carnival, begins in earnest immediately after Epiphany with a week-long series of costume parades. Fancy-dress balls are held regularly up to and including Carnival Week. A couple of weeks later begins **Starkbierzeit**, the period when strong beer is served in the taverns to help make the stringencies of Lent bearable. In late April and early May the Theresienwiese stages a small-scale springtime version of the Oktoberfest, the **Frühlingsfest** (www.muenchner-volksfeste.de). There are further opportunities to drink specially brewed strong beer at the **Maibock-Anstich** in May. Held in the Olympiapark during June and July, **Tollwood** (www.tollwood.de) is a world music festival which additionally features stalls selling a similarly international range of food and handicrafts. There's also a smaller wintertime version of this, held throughout December on the Theresienwiese.

The **Auer Dult** is a traditional market that takes place on the Mariahilfplatz during the last weeks of April, July and October each year. It has a combination of hardware, crafts and antiques, as well as a fairground for the kids. An annual Christmas market, the **Christkindlmarkt**, is held on the Marienplatz during Advent, though the ones at the Münchener Freiheit, and around the Pariser Platz in Haidhausen, are less commercialized, with more hand-made crafts.

Listings

American Express Promenadeplatz 6 (Mon–Fri 9am–5.30pm, Sat 9.30am–12.30pm; ⓣ0 89/22 80 14 65).
Bike rental The most convenient place is Radius Touristik, located opposite platform 31 in the Hauptbahnhof. Many of the outlying S-Bahn stations, such as Dachau, Freising, Herrsching, Starnberg and Tutzing, also offer bike rental.
Bookstores Words'worth, which has shops at Schellingstr. 3 and Schellingstr. 21, stocks a good selection of paperbacks and English-language newspapers. Geobuch, Rosental 6, has the best selection of maps and guides, and there's a women's bookstore at Barer Str. 70.
Consulates British, Bürkleinstr. 10 ⓣ0 89/21 10 90; Canadian, Tal 29 ⓣ0 89/2 19 95 70; Dutch, Nymphenburger Str. 1 ⓣ0 89/5 45 96 70; Irish, Denninger Str. 15 ⓣ0 89/20 80 59 90; US, Königinstr. 5 ⓣ0 89/2 88 80.
Cultural institutes Amerikahaus, Karolinenplatz 3 ⓣ0 89/5 52 53 70; British Council, Goethestr. 20 ⓣ0 89/20 60 33 10.
Cultural societies The following run social functions advertised in the local press: Deutsch-Britische Gesellschaft ⓣ0 89/21 10 91 11; Deutsch-Kanadische Gesellschaft ⓣ0 89/3 07 33 45 or 3 14 84 10; Munich Caledonians ⓣ0 89/7 23 72 66.
Football FC Bayern München, Germany's most consistent football club, winner of many European trophies down the years, play at the Olympiastadion in the Olympiapark, which is also the venue for major athletics meetings.
Medical emergencies ⓣ0 89/55 17 71.
Pharmacy At the Internationale Apotheke, Neuhauser Str. 11, you can get your prescription no matter which country it comes from.
Post office The main post office is at Residenzstr. 2 (Mon–Fri 8am–6.30pm, Sat 9am–12.30pm; the longest hours are kept by the branch at Bahnhofplatz 1 (Mon–Fri 7.30am–8pm, Sat 9am–4pm).
Taxis ⓣ0 89/1 94 10 or 2 16 10.
Travel agents Studiosus Reisen, Oberanger 6 ⓣ0 89/2 35 05 20; Thomas Cook, Rindermarkt 16 ⓣ0 89/2 36 63 50.

Upper Bavaria

The name of **Upper Bavaria** (Oberbayern), Munich's own traditional province, is associated above all with the Alps. Quite simply, this is the most spectacular scenery Germany has to offer: a wonderfully contrasting array of glacial lakes and peaks commanding stunning panoramic views, with many dramatic castles and churches for good measure. Amid this picture-book scenery you'll find the Bavarian folklore and customs that are the subject of so many tourist brochures – men still wear leather Lederhosen and checked shirts, and women the traditional Dirndl dresses. Superficially it can all seem very kitsch, but beyond the packaged culture lies a fascinating mixture of Catholic and pagan rites that dominate the annual calendar – events usually accompanied by large amounts of eating and drinking.

From **Oberammergau**, where the world-famous Passion Play is staged every ten years, it's only a few kilometres to the international ski resort of **Garmisch-Partenkirchen**, above which towers the **Zugspitze**, Germany's highest and most famous peak. The most dramatic heights of all are in the Berchtesgadener Land, an area that includes the town of **Berchtesgaden** as well as the marvellous peak of the **Watzmann**. The area is intensely geared towards tourism, as are the **Upper Bavarian lakes**, most of which lie in the glacial valleys of the Alpine foothills. In contrast, other parts of the province are relatively little known, yet offer plenty of varied attractions. Between the Alps and the Land capital lie some equally enticing lakes and monasteries; to the east is the pilgrimage site of **Altötting**, while north of Munich are several wonderful old towns – the old metropolitan see of **Freising**, the former university and ducal capital of **Ingolstadt**, the planned residential seat of **Neuburg**, and the little cathedral city of **Eichstätt**.

Manifold culinary delights are available in the wonderful old Gaststätten, often with beer gardens, where traditional Bavarian menus and innumerable regional beers are served. There are rail links to many destinations, and a network of connecting bus services between the Alpine towns, the only snag being that some of the latter only operate only a few times a day. **Accommodation** shouldn't be a major problem, except during July and August in the most sought-after destinations. There's a huge choice of rooms in private houses (identified by the *Zimmer frei* signs), and prices – even in major resorts such as Garmisch – are surprisingly reasonable.

North from Munich

North from Munich, making easy day-trips by the city's excellent S-Bahn network, are three sharply contrasting excursion possibilities. A visit to **Dachau** concentration camp is a harrowing experience, while **Freising** is one of Bavaria's most venerable and attractive towns and **Oberschleissheim** has three impressive palaces.

Dachau

Situated on the S-Bahn #2 line, 17km north of Munich, **DACHAU** is a picturesque provincial town. It was formerly one of the seats of the Wittelsbachs, who built a Renaissance **Schloss** (April–Sept Tues–Sun 9am–6pm; Oct–March Tues–Sun 10am–4pm; €1.50; Ⓦwww.schloesser.bayern.de) there in the sixteenth century. Three of the wings were pulled down by order of King Max I Joseph, leaving only the block with the main **Festsaal**, which features a spectacular coffered wooden vault and a frieze depicting mythological deities. It has excellent acoustics, and concerts are regularly held there in summer. The **Schlossgarten** outside is a fine formal garden, while the *Schlosscafé* serves excellent cakes.

Despite tireless promotional efforts by the authorities, virtually none of the hordes of foreign visitors who come here venture into the town centre to experience its undoubted charms. Dachau's great misfortune is that its very name is synonymous with horrors that have been indelibly stamped on the consciousness of the modern mind, having been the site of Germany's **first concentration camp**, built in the outskirts in 1933, and the model for all others. Though not itself an extermination camp, many thousands were murdered here, and the motto that greeted new arrivals at the gates has taken its own chilling place in the history of Third Reich brutality: *Arbeit Macht Frei* – "Work Brings Freedom". The camp was mainly for political prisoners, and numbered among its inmates Pastor Martin Niemöller, the former French premier Léon Blum, and Johann Elser, who tried to assassinate Hitler in 1939.

To reach the camp or **Konzentrationslager** (Tues–Sun 9am–5pm; free), take bus #724 or #726 from Dachau's Bahnhof. The rows of huts where prisoners lived were all torched by the Allies after the war, and neat windswept patches of rectangular gravel mark their former outlines. A replica of one of these huts gives some idea of the cramped conditions prisoners were cooped up in, but the only original buildings still standing are the gas chambers, which were never used, as the war ended before they could be set to work. Open ovens gape at you, and bright whitewashed walls almost distract from the ominous gas outlets set in the ceilings of the shower rooms. The stark wire perimeter fencing and watchtowers also remain. A permanent exhibition, with photographs and accompanying text in several languages including English, speaks for itself. Turn up at 11.30am or 3.30pm and you can also view the short, deeply disturbing documentary *KZ-Dachau* in English. Three small memorial churches – Catholic, Protestant and Orthodox – have been built within the complex, and the first two are normally kept open for visits.

Oberschleissheim

In the outskirts of the satellite town of **OBERSCHLEISSHEIM**, 14km north of Munich by S-Bahn #1, is the third major palace complex of the Wittelsbach dynasty (the first two being the Residenz in central Munich, see p.72, and Nymphenburg, see p.87). All three palaces are located in **Park Schleissheim**, which is a ten-minute signposted walk from the Bahnhof.

The Renaissance **Altes Schloss Schleissheim** (Tues–Sun 10am–5pm; €2.50, free Sun; Ⓦwww.bayerisches-nationalmuseum.de) was built at the beginning of the seventeenth century as a spiritual retreat for the pious Duke Wilhelm V, who used only two of its forty-four rooms, going out every day to pray in the hermitages in the nearby woods. Suitably, therefore, the building, which was almost completely destroyed in World War II, has been rebuilt to house a museum of religious folk art entitled Das Gottesjahr und seine Feste. Assembled by a single collector, Gertrud Weinhold, the exhibits come predominantly from Eastern Europe, Latin America, Africa and Asia, and are displayed thematically. Most are from the Christian tradition, though other religions are represented in the final section on Paradise. The rooms on the opposite side of the entrance hall contain displays on the former German provinces of West and East Prussia. An outbuilding houses the *Schlosswirtschaft*, the obvious place to break for a meal or a drink when visiting the park.

Directly opposite is the far larger and more significant **Neues Schloss Schleissheim** (April–Sept Tues–Sun 9am–6pm; Oct–March Tues–Sun 10am–4pm; €3, or €4.50 combined ticket with Schloss Lustheim; Ⓦ www.schloesser.bayern.de), which was commissioned by Elector Max Emmanuel in 1701. The project was initially riddled with bad luck: architect Enrico Zuccalli failed to establish sufficiently secure foundations for such an enormous building and, as a result, it had to be propped up with mounds of earth, spoiling the proportions and leaving the impression that it is built on quicksand. Work then had to be halted for ten years when the Elector was forced into exile as a result of his defeat in the War of the Spanish Succession. However, building eventually resumed under the direction of Joseph Effner. Aided by such outstanding decorators as Ignaz Günther, Cosmas Damian Asam and Johann Baptist Zimmermann, he turned the seemingly ill-fated scheme into one of Germany's finest Baroque palaces. Of particular note are the monumental double **staircase** and the richly stuccoed **Festsaal**, where concerts are held every summer weekend. Scattered throughout the chambers is a collection of 300 Baroque paintings, including works by Rubens, Van Dyck, Ribera, Poussin and Guercino. Joachim von Sandrart, who is nowadays chiefly remembered as the pioneering historian of German art, is copiously represented, and the inventive cycle of *The Months*, in particular, proves that he was himself a distinguished painter.

Prior to commissioning this extravaganza, Max Emmanuel had asked Zuccalli to build **Schloss Lustheim** (same hours; €2.50; Ⓦ www.schloesser.bayern.de), a small hunting and garden palace; this lies at the far end of the park, and is connected to the Neues Schloss by a landscaped canal. The architect created an Italianate masterpiece, which now contains an impressive collection of illustrating the entire history of Meissen porcelain, including some pieces from the famous Swan service.

Just outside the boundaries of the park, just a stone's throw to the south of the Altes Schloss, is the **Flugwerft Schleissheim** (daily 9am–5pm; €3.50, or €7 combined ticket with the Deutsches Museum in Munich; Ⓦ www.deutsches-museum.de), one of Germany's oldest airports, constructed in 1912–17. Nowadays an outstation of the Deutsches Museum, it displays a huge array of early flying machines, aeroplanes and helicopters in the original hangar and the modern exhibition hall alongside.

Freising

FREISING, the terminus of one of the branches of S-Bahn #1, lies some 35km north of Munich, about halfway towards Landshut, and only 8km from the airport, to which it's linked by bus #635. One of Bavaria's oldest towns, it was the province's spiritual capital from 739 to 1803, and its name is retained in the title of the local archbishop, who now resides in Munich. Despite its proximity to the state capital, it gives no impression of belonging to commuter-belt land, retaining instead the very distinct atmosphere of a country town, particularly in the centre, where the picturesque **Markt** and **Hauptstrasse**, overlooked by the handsome Baroque tower of the Gothic **Stadtpfarrkirche St Georg**, are lined by colourful mansions of varying dates.

The hill between the River Isar and the centre, known as the Domberg, is a self-contained episcopal quarter centred on the twin-towered Romanesque **Dom**, whose exterior is covered with a startling coat of whitewash. After this, the interior comes as another surprise, the original architecture masked by a lavish decoration scheme carried out by the Asam brothers in an idiom which belongs to the final phase of Baroque. A few older furnishings, such as the late Gothic choir stalls with busts of the local prince-bishops and the *Lamentation* group by Erasmus Grasser in the apse of the north aisle, look rather incongruous amid this theatricality. Thankfully, the Asams didn't tamper with the **crypt**, the resting place of Saint Korbinian, founder of the bishopric. Among the pillars supporting the vault of this beautiful chamber is the amazing *Bestiensäule*, which is festooned with carvings of fantastic animals. The **cloisters** built onto the east end of the Dom have Rococo decoration by Johann Baptist Zimmermann, as does François Cuvilliés' **Bibliotheksaal** (May–Oct Mon–Fri 2–3pm) alongside.

At the far end of the cloisters is the Gothic **Benediktuskirche**. A second and much larger church of the same period, the **Johanniskirche**, is built right against the front end of the Dom, and is in turn linked to the former **Residenz** of the prince-bishops, thereby creating a truly monumental complex of interconnected buildings. Occupying a former seminary at the western end of the Domberg is the **Diözesanmuseum** (Tues–Sun 10am–5pm; €2), the largest ecclesiastical museum in Germany. It features works by many of the leading Baroque and Rococo artists of Bavaria, though its most valuable treasure, gleaming in a dimly lit room, is a Byzantine icon known as the *Lukasbild*. There are also two magnificent paintings by **Rubens** of *The Adoration of the Shepherds* and *Pentecost*, which originally adorned the side altars of the Hofkirche in Neuburg an der Donau.

West of the town centre is another hill, on which stands **Kloster Weihenstephan**, a former monastery which is now home to the agricultural and brewing faculties of Munich's technical university. Its main claim to fame is the **Weihenstephan-Brauerei**, which has been in operation since 1040, and is thus generally accepted as the oldest brewery in the world. Guided tours (€2) are run through the present ultra-modern premises from Monday to Thursday, but it's necessary to phone ahead (ⓣ0 81 61/53 60, ⓦwww.brauerei-weihenstephan.de) to join a group. Otherwise, you can content yourself with sampling the products – of which the wheat beers are the best known – in the *Bräustüberl* or its beer garden.

Ingolstadt

Even by German standards, **INGOLSTADT**, 60km due north of Munich, reeks of prosperity, courtesy of its four oil refineries, fed by pipelines from France and Italy, and the Audi car factory which migrated from Zwickau when the Iron Curtain went up. At least some of the wealth generated is used wisely, for the town spends more money on the upkeep of its historic monuments than anywhere else in Bavaria.

The Town

For centuries one of Germany's most redoubtable fortresses, Ingolstadt is compact enough to be seen in a day, as all the notable historic monuments lie within the fortification system, and only one other important attraction lies further afield.

The fortifications

The Altstadt snuggles within its medieval horseshoe-shaped **Stadtmauer** on the north bank of the Danube, safely away from the industrial quarters. In the nineteenth century, an additional set of fortifications in a stern Neoclassical style was designed by Leo von Klenze to encase them, and to protect both sides of the bridgehead. Those on the south bank command a marvellous view of the whole skyline. They're centred on the **Reduit Tilly** (Tues–Sun 8.45am–4.30pm; €3, or €4 combined ticket with Bayerisches Armeemuseum; Ⓦwww.bayerisches-armeemuseum.de), which contains displays about World War I.

Crossing over Konrad-Adenauer-Brücke, the most impressive stretch of the medieval walls lies just to the left; it's made yet more picturesque by the houses which were built directly on to it. This section is pierced by the **Taschenturm** (Pocket Tower), whose tall, whitewashed and gabled silhouette has a fairy-tale look about it, for all that it's perfectly genuine. Even it is eclipsed, however, by the **Kreuztor** which now stands like a pint-sized castle in splendid isolation further north. Nowadays, it seems hard to believe that such a lovingly crafted masterpiece of brickwork was built for purely military purposes.

Beyond, a green belt has been laid out round the huge polygonal fragments of the Neoclassical fortifications. One of these, the **Kavalier Hepp** to the northwest, now contains the **Stadtmuseum** (Tues–Fri 9am–5pm, Sat & Sun 10am–5pm; €2.50), whose exhibits range from a Celtic silver hoard via sculptures from the medieval city gates and the teaching stool of Johannes Eck, the Ingolstadt theologian who provided the (none-too-successful) frontline Catholic defence against Luther, to a stuffed horse said to have been King Gustavus Adolphus's mount during the Swedish siege in the Thirty Years' War.

From here, you can continue all the way round the walls to the strongest point of the defences, the **Neues Schloss**, which sits in gleaming white splendour at the far end of the waterfront. The original structure, with its distinctive angular towers, was built in the fifteenth century during the short period when Ingolstadt was capital of an independent duchy; the imposing battlements were added a hundred years later. Built for the Francophile Duke Ludwig the Bearded, it looks completely un-German, resembling instead a French château. Part of the Schloss now houses the **Bayrisches Armeemuseum** (Tues–Sun 8.45am–4.30pm; €3; Ⓦwww.bayerisches-armeemuseum.de), the most comprehensive collection of arms and armour in Germany. On the ground floor, the **Dürnitz**, the great banqueting hall, forms an appropriately grand setting for an outstanding section on the Thirty Years' War. Highlight of the displays upstairs is the booty, including a magnificent golden helmet, captured from the Turks in 1682; here also is the finest room in the building, the **Schöner Saal**, whose vault springs from a graceful central pillar.

The Altstadt

The pedestrianized shopping streets lie west of the Neues Schloss. Along Hallstrasse, and now very much in the shadow of the huge modern Theater Ingolstadt, is the modestly sized **Altes Schloss**, built in the thirteenth century as a second residence for the Landshut dukes. Later prettified by the addition of ornate gables, it was demoted to serving as a granary when the Neues Schloss was built, but has found a new lease of life as the public library. Further along is the **Altes Rathaus**, created at the end of the nineteenth century by knocking several old burghers' houses together. Behind is the Gothic **Stadtkirche St Moritz**, one of whose towers, the **Pfeifturm**, can be ascended on Saturday mornings for a view of the town. On Ludwigstrasse, a block to the north, is the **Ickstatthaus**, the most ornate of the town's many Rococo mansions.

From the Stadtkirche, Dollstrasse and Hoher Schulstrasse lead westwards to the **Hohe Schule**, built as a prebendary, but from 1472 until 1800 the main building of the University of Bavaria, one of the most famous in Germany and a leading centre of Counter-Reformation theology. Ingolstadt's academic tradition lay dormant until 1989, when an economics faculty was opened, but several reminders of its pre-eminence survive in this quarter. One of these is the **Alte Anatomie** at the end of Griesbadgasse to the southeast, a dignified, classically inspired Baroque building which was the place where Frankenstein created his monster in Mary Shelley's Gothic novel. The courtyard once again serves as a herb garden, while the interior contains the **Deutsches Medizinhistorisches Museum** (Tues–Sun 10am–noon & 2–5pm; €2.50), which shows the evolution of medical instruments from the ancient Egyptians to the present day.

To the north, and just east of the Kreuztor, is the huge **Liebfrauenmünster**, begun by Duke Ludwig as a sacred counterbalance to the Neues Schloss at the opposite end of town. The unfinished towers, set at startlingly oblique angles, are reminiscent of those of the castle, but otherwise this is a copybook German hall church, the plain brickwork outside brilliantly offset by the sweeping elevation of the grey and white interior. As work neared completion in the early sixteenth century, the masons created for the six nave chapels the most spectacularly ornate **vaults** in the entire history of European architecture. Here the delicately coloured filigree stonework has been twisted into such shapes as a crown of thorns, a giant insect and great flowering plants, which seem to sprout from the ceiling like huge jewels. The Liebfrauenmünster served as the parish church of the university, whose centenary was commemorated by the commissioning of Hans Mielich's **high altar**: look out for the scenes on the reverse, showing cameos of the different faculties at work. On the north side of the ambulatory is the bronze epitaph to Johannes Eck; also of special note are the brilliantly coloured **stained-glass windows** of the east end, made from designs by Dürer and his followers.

A very different but equally dazzling church is the **Maria-de-Victoria-Kirche** (March–Nov Tues–Sun 9am–noon & 1–5pm; Dec–Feb Tues–Sun 10am–noon & 1–4pm; €1.50) immediately to the north on Konviktstrasse, an oratory built by the Asam brothers for the Jesuit-run Marian student congregation. Egid Quirin's simple little hall is little more than a stage-set for Cosmas Damian's colossal **ceiling fresco**, which was executed in just eight weeks. Its subject – a complicated allegory on the mystery of the Incarnation – hardly seems to matter, as you're likely to be completely mesmerized by its illusionistic tricks, in which everything appears to be in correct perspective, no matter what your vantage point. Ask the caretaker to show the **monstrance** depicting the Battle of Lepanto, another display of Rococo pyrotechnics, this time by an Augsburg goldsmith.

The Audi Forum

Audi's plush visitor centre, the **Audi Forum** (Ⓦwww.audi.com), lies within the factory grounds in the far north of the city, some 5km from the centre, and reached by bus #11. The complex was initiated in 1992, and contains a variety of attractions, including a showroom with all the current models, a shop, a kid's centre and two restaurants. However, it really only became a major tourist magnet with the construction of the **museum mobile** (daily 10am–8pm; free; Ⓦwww.museummobile.de), an imposing circular steel and glass building built in 2000 to display the historical collection. This includes examples of each of the four manufacturers – Audi, DKW, Horch and Wanderer – whose merger is celebrated in the four rings of the company logo, as well as NSU, a later addition to the group. The display techniques are innovative: fourteen of the

△ Gabled houses, Dinkelsbühl

vehicles rotate all day long on giant paternosters, while the rarest exhibits – such as the Horch 855 roadster, one of just twelve that were ever made – are symbolically treated like priceless treasures by being housed in glass cases.

Practicalities

Ingolstadt's **Hauptbahnhof** lies 2km south of the Altstadt, to which it's connected by buses #10, #11, #15, #16 and #44. The **tourist office** (Mon–Fri 8am–5pm, Sat 9am–noon; ⓣ08 41/3 05 30 30, ⓦwww.ingolstadt.de) is in the Altes Rathaus, Rathausplatz 2. There are a couple of **pensions** fairly close to the Hauptbahnhof: *Bauer*, Hölzlstr. 2 (ⓣ0841/6 60 99; ❹) is to the northeast, *Eisinger*, Dorfstr. 17a (ⓣ08 41/97 36 60; ❹) to the southwest. In the Altstadt there are several **hotels**, including *Anker*, Tränktorstr. 1 (ⓣ08 41/ 3 00 50, ⓦwww.hotel-restaurant-anker.de; ❻); *Adler*, Theresienstr. 22 (ⓣ08 41/3 51 07, ⓦwww.hotel-adler-ingolstadt.de; ❻); *Bayerischer Hof*, Münzbergstr. 12 (ⓣ08 41/93 40 60, ⓦwww.bayerischer-hof-ingolstadt.de; ❻); and *Rappensberger*, Harderstr. 3 (ⓣ08 41/31 40, ⓦwww.rappensberger.de; ❼–❾). The **youth hostel** is close to the Kreuztor at Friedhofstr. 41/2 (ⓣ08 41/3 41 77; €12.70). **Camping** facilities are available at Auwaldsee in the outskirts (April–Sept only; ⓣ08 41/9 61 16 16, ⓦwww.azur-camping.de); take bus #60. All the hotels listed above have good **restaurants**; also of special note is the flagship one of the local breweries, *Weissbrauhaus zum Herrnbräu*, Dollstr. 3, a true old Bavarian tavern. However, the top place to eat is *Im Stadttheater*, Schlossländle 1; as its name suggests, it is within the Theater Ingolstadt (ⓣ08 41/1 32 00, ⓦwww.theater.ingolstadt.de), which presents the usual mix of operatic and dramatic fare. The main **festival** is the *Bürgenfest* on the first or second weekend of July.

Neuburg an der Donau

NEUBURG AN DER DONAU, 22km upstream from Ingolstadt on the rail line to Ulm, makes an enjoyable afternoon's outing or restful overnight stop. Perched on a chalk promontory overlooking the Danube, it was a strategic trading post in Roman times, but was thereafter an insignificant village until 1505, when it became the capital of the new Wittelsbach principality of Pfalz-Neuburg. Throughout the sixteenth and seventeenth centuries, it was developed into a proud Residenzstadt of elegant buildings, leafy squares and dreamy cobblestoned streets, presenting a Renaissance, Mannerist and Baroque architectural mix which has no counterpart elsewhere in Bavaria.

Neuburg's most significant and dominant building is the **Residenzschloss** (April–Sept Tues–Sun 9am–6pm; Oct–March Tues–Sun 10am–4pm; €2.50; ⓦwww.schloesser.bayern.de). The original Renaissance palace was erected between 1527 and 1545 by order of the first ruler of Pfalz-Neuburg, Ottheinrich, who later became Elector of the Palatinate and transformed the great Schloss in Heidelberg. This structure is dwarfed by the Baroque wing added in the 1660s, whose massive cylindrical towers give the complex its highly distinctive silhouette. On the ground floor of the northern tower is the **Grottenanlage**, a spectacular suite of artificial grottoes made from shells, tufa, glass and stucco. The first floor of the Schloss is devoted to the history of Pfalz-Neuburg, and is particularly notable for the mementoes of Ottheinrich, including a sculpted portrait head, some of his clothes and two magnificent Brussels tapestries, one of which illustrates his pilgrimage to the Holy Land. On the second floor the region's pre- and early history is documented by means of the extensive archeological finds it has yielded, while the top storey features a display of religious art, including a wonderful group of Baroque embroideries woven at the local Ursuline convent. The **Schlosskapelle** by the courtyard entrance is the oldest custom-built Protestant church in Bavaria, and is adorned with a cycle of frescoes by the Salzburg artist Hans Bocksberger illustrating the Bible in line with the tenets of the new faith.

Uphill from the Residenzschloss, the central **Karlsplatz** is a particularly stylish example of town planning, despite having been built over a period of well over a hundred years. The two main buildings, the **Rathaus** on the north side and the **Hofkirche** on the east, were both begun in the first decade of the seventeenth century. At the time, the intention was that the latter should be the Protestant answer to the Jesuits' St Michael in Munich, but the House of Pfalz-Neuburg converted back to Catholicism during its construction, so it was finished off in a rather more elaborate manner than originally intended. The interior is, quite literally, covered with wonderfully ornate white stuccowork, with just a lick of gold highlighting to create a light and harmonious whole. Rubens was commissioned to paint three huge altarpieces for the church, but these were later replaced, and can now be seen in Munich's Alte Pinakothek and the Diözesanmuseum in Freising. Also on the square are mansions of noblemen and wealthy burghers, while the east side is closed by the **Provinzialbibliothek**, an early Rococo building with an imposing facade.

Practicalities

Neuburg's **Bahnhof** lies at the southern edge of town. The **tourist office** (May–Oct Mon–Fri 9am–6pm, Sat & Sun 10am–noon & 2–5pm; Nov–April Mon–Thurs 8am–noon & 2–4pm, Fri 8am–noon; ⓣ0 84 31/5 52 40, ⓦwww.neuburg-donau.de) is at Residenzstr. A65. There's a reasonable supply of rooms in **private houses** (❷–❸). The **campsite** is at Oskar-Wittmann-Str. 5 (ⓣ0 84 31/94 73). **Hotels** include *Neuwirt*, Färberstr. 88 (ⓣ0 84 31/20 78; ❸); *Kieferlbräu*, Eybstr. 239 (ⓣ0 84 31/6 73 40, ⓦwww.kieferlbraeu.de; ❹); *Bergbauer*, Fünfzehnerstr. 11 (ⓣ0 84 31/6 16 89 13, ⓦwww.hotel-gasthof-bergbauer.de; ❺); and *Am Fluss*, with a fine location by the Danube at Ingolstädter Str. 2 (ⓣ0 84 31/6 76 80, ⓦwww.neuburgdonau.com/hotel-am-fluss; ❻). All but the last of these have **restaurants**: *Kiefelbräu* offers vegetarian as well as *bürgerliche* cuisine, while *Bergbauer*, open evenings only, is probably the best in town. One **café** particularly worth visiting is *Arco-Schlösschen*, Arcostr. 78, which commands a wonderful view of the town from its riverside location 1km east of the centre

In odd-numbered years, there's a Renaissance-style folklore **festival**, the Schlossfest (ⓦwww.schlossfest.de), on the last weekend of June and the first weekend of July. There's also an annual festival of Baroque music (ⓦwww.neuburger-barockkonzerte.de) in late September or early October in the Kongregationssaal, the former Jesuit oratory beside the Residenzschloss.

Eichstätt

EICHSTÄTT, which lies 27km northwest of Ingolstadt, is the gateway to Germany's largest *Naturpark*, the **Altmühl valley**. This Jurassic region was first inhabited by humans 100,000 years ago, and its soils have produced many yields of prehistoric fossils and minerals in a quite remarkable state of preservation. The town itself was for centuries a prince-bishopric at the junction of the three historic provinces of Bavaria, Franconia and Swabia, and was sufficiently prestigious for one of its rulers, Gebhard I, to gain election as Pope Victor II. Having been almost completely destroyed in the Thirty Years' War, it was rebuilt in the eighteenth century by Italian Baroque architects, who gave it an incongruously Mediterranean appearance. Incorporated into Bavaria in the Napoleonic reforms, it thereafter sank into obscurity, but received a major boost in 1980, when its theological college was promoted to the status of a Catholic university – the only one in the German-speaking world.

Eichstätt presents an agreeable mixture of old and new: the university and its predecessor have been astute patrons of some of Germany's leading architectural practices, gaining much praise for the way they have augmented the historical heritage, which came through World War II virtually unscathed.

The Town

Inevitably, the **Dom** is the focal point of the Altstadt, which lies on the right bank of the Altmühl. Its twin towers are Romanesque, but otherwise it's a fourteenth-century Gothic structure with a distinctive German accent, being a hall church with choirs at both end of the building. Prominent among the outstanding art treasures inside is the **Pappenheim altar** in the north transept, an astonishing virtuoso carving of the Crucifixion, with each of the myriad figures carefully characterized by a late Gothic carver known as Master VW from his cryptic signature. Fronting the western choir is the extraordinarily realistic seated **statue of St Willibald**, a memorial to the first Eichstätt bishop. Though dating from just a couple of decades after the altar, it is fully Renaissance in style and is by one of the few German sculptors to master this idiom, **Loy Hering**, who also carved the *Wolfsteinaltar* on the west wall of the nave and the crucifix in the Sakramentskapelle.

Off the west side of the cloisters is the **Mortuarium**, which is anything but the grim chamber its name suggests: it's a stately Gothic hall divided by a row of differently shaped columns, one of which is known as the Schöne Säule (Beautiful Pillar) from its profuse carvings. There's also a brilliantly coloured stained-glass window of *The Last Judgment*, designed by Holbein the Elder, and a *Crucifixion* group by Hering. Stairs lead up to the **Domschatz- und Diözesanmuseum** (April–Oct Wed–Fri 10.30am–5pm, Sat & Sun 10am–5pm; €2, free Sun), whose exhibits include the Dom's treasury, the original sculptures from its north portal, the chasuble of St Willibald, and a trio of fifteenth-century tapestries illustrating the life of his sister, St Walburga.

Gabriel de Gabrieli, the most outstanding of the eighteenth-century architects who transformed Eichstätt, added a Baroque facade to the Dom in order that it could form an integral part of the new **Residenzplatz**, a truly monumental piece of urban design which is something of a hybrid between a crescent and the square its name suggests. One side is lined with the Baroque and Rococo palaces of the local knights, canons and ecclesiastical administration, while in the centre is the cheerful **Mariensäule**. The **Residenz** itself (guided tours Mon–Thurs 11am & 3pm, Fri 11am, Sat & Sun 10.15–11.45am & 2–3.30pm; €1), the former palace of the prince-bishops, is now occupied by municipal offices, but retains some splendid interiors, notably the grand staircase, the tiny **Hauskapelle** and the second-floor **Spiegelsaal**. In the last of these, stuccowork is present not only on the walls and ceiling, but on the mirrors themselves, a feature that is apparently unique.

Immediately east of Residenzplatz is a huge Jesuit church, the **Schutzengelkirche**. A short distance to the north, at the top end of Kardinal-Preysing-Platz, is the former **Kloster Notre Dame de Sacre Coeur**, whose domed church was designed by Gabrieli and frescoed by Johann Georg Bergmüller. Its conventual buildings now house the **Informationszentrum Naturpark Altmühltal** (April–Oct Mon–Sat 9am–5/6pm, Sun 10am–5/6pm; Nov–March Mon–Thurs 8am–noon & 2–4pm, Fri 8am–noon), with displays on the flora, fauna, geology, history and culture of the valley. Further east lies the **Hofgarten**, one of whose borders is taken up by the long frontage of the **Sommerresidenz**, formerly the second residence of the bishops, now the administrative headquarters of the Catholic university. Just beyond is the **Kapuzinerkirche**, which houses a twelfth-century **Holy Sepulchre**, one of the earliest and most accurate reproductions of the Jerusalem original, constructed with the help of descriptions supplied by Crusaders who had been there.

To the north of the Dom, the commercial life of the town is centred on **Marktplatz**, another Baroque square whose central fountain bears a second Renaissance statue of St Willibald. On a prominent elevated site to the north is the huge complex of the **Kloster St Walburg**, a Benedictine convent with a richly decorated Baroque church and a Gothic crypt containing the tomb of St Walburga. Its terrace commands a fine view across the valley.

Occupying a dominant position high above the left bank of the Altmühl, best reached via Burgstrasse, is the **Willibaldsburg**, the huge fortress of the prince-bishops. The earliest sections date back to the mid-fourteenth century, but the most prominent part is the sumptuous palatial wing designed in the early seventeenth century by the great Augsburg architect, Elias Holl. This now houses the **Jura-Museum** and the **Museum Für Ur- und Frühgeschichte** (both April–Sept Tues–Sun 9am–6pm; Oct–March Tues–Sun 10am–4pm; €3). In the former, hi-tech display techniques are employed in the presentation of some of the many fossil finds made in the region. The rarest object is the skeleton (one of only seven yet discovered) of a prehistoric bird known as the archeopteryx. The latter museum is mostly devoted to archeological excavations, but also includes a four-metre-high, sixty-thousand-year-old skeleton of a mammoth. One of the towers can be ascended for a view of the town and the valley, though a closer panorama of the former can be had from the **Bastionsgarten**, a recent re-creation of the Hortus Eystettensis, a famous Renaissance-era garden whose appearance had been documented in a meticulously accurate set of coloured engravings.

Practicalities

Eichstätt's **Bahnhof**, on the main line linking Ingolstadt with both Würzburg and Nürnberg, is in the middle of nowhere. Small diesels connect with all services, travelling along the 5km line to the **Stadtbahnhof**, which faces the Altstadt from the other side of the Altmühl. The **tourist office** (April–Oct Mon–Sat 9am–6pm, Sun 10am–1pm; Nov–April Mon–Thurs 10am–noon & 2–4pm, Fri 10am–noon; ⓣ0 84 21/9 88 00, ⓦwww.eichstaett.de) is at Domplatz 8.

There's a good range of central **hotels**, including *Gasthof Ratskeller*, Kardinal-Preysing-Platz 8 (ⓣ0 84 21/90 12 58; ❹); *Gasthof Sonne*, Buchtal 17 (ⓣ0 84 21/67 91, ⓦwww.sonne-eichstaett.de; ❹); *Gasthof Klosterstuben*, Pedettistr. 26 (ⓣ0 84 21/35 00, ⓦwww.klosterstuben-eichstaett.de; ❹); *Gasthof Trompete*, Ostenstr. 3 (ⓣ0 84 21/9 81 70; ❺); and *Adler*, which occupies a Baroque mansion at Marktplatz 22–24 (Ⓣ0 84 21/67 67, Ⓦwww.ei-online.de/adler; ❻). There are also plenty of **private houses** offering rooms (❷–❸): the tourist office can supply a list. The **youth hostel** is midway between the Stadtbahnhof and the Willibaldsburg at Reichenaustr. 15 (Ⓣ0 84 21/9 80 40; €14.80).

All the hotels listed above, with the exception of *Adler*, have **restaurants**, and all are good and reasonably priced; *Trompete* is the main tap of the local Hofmuhl brewery. Other enticing choices for a meal are *Zum Kavalier*, in the old theatre building at Residenzplatz 17, and *Krone*, Domplatz 3, which also has a beer garden. However, the top cuisine in town is at the pricey *Domherrenhof*, which occupies a Rococo mansion at Domplatz 5.

The Five Lakes Region (Fünf-Seen-Land)

The **Five Lakes Region** is a popular playground of the people of Munich, and it can easily be explored in day-trips from the city by S-Bahn. Three of the lakes are small and of minor interest, but the **Starnberger See** and **Ammersee** bear comparison with their Alpine counterparts.

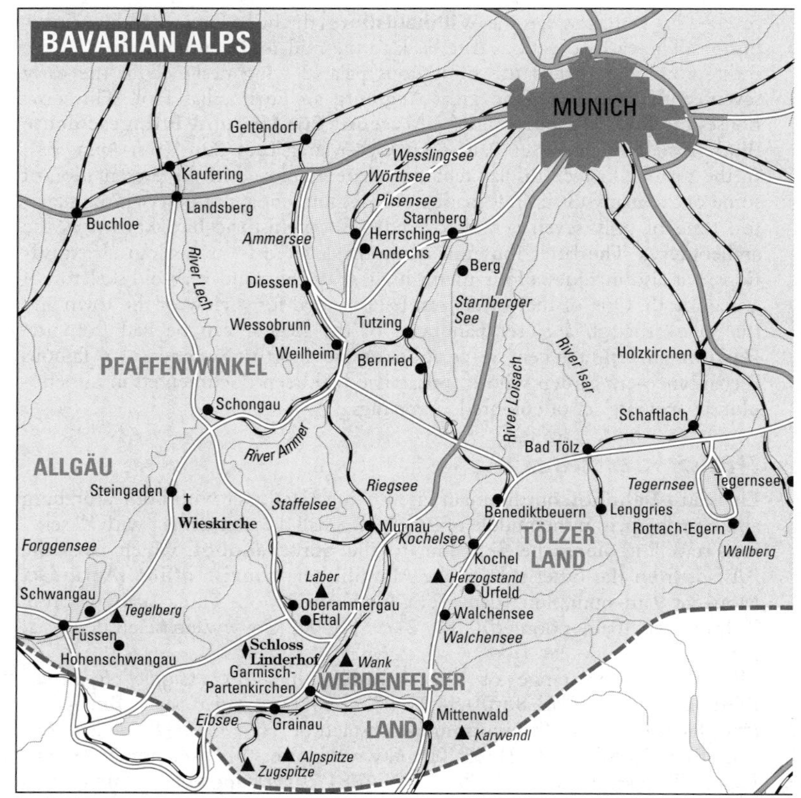

The Starnberger See

Lying just to the southwest of the city and reached by S-Bahn #6, the largest lake of the group, the **Starnberger See**, is predominantly the domain of the city's rich and their weekend villas. The main resort is **STARNBERG** at the northernmost tip, where the local **tourist office** (June–Sept Mon–Fri 8am–6pm, Sat 9am–1pm; rest of year Mon–Fri only; ⓣ0 81 51/9 06 00, ⓦwww.sta5.de) is at Wittelsbacher Str. 2c. By far the most bracing way to explore the lake is by **boat**; Staatliche Schifffahrt Starnberger See (ⓣ0 81 51/1 20 23, ⓦwww.bayerische-seenschifffahrt.de) charges €13.80 for a three-hour round trip, while journeys from one stop to the next cost upwards of €3.50.

The eastern shore of the Starnberger See is lined with private properties and it's not always possible to get at the water, though there are some small public stretches between the villages of Berg, Leoni and Ammerland. The **Schloss** of the first (still a private residence of the Wittelsbachs and not open for visits) was where the ill-starred King Ludwig II was staying at the time of his mysterious death. Just to the south, a small **Votivkapelle**, modelled on the Church of the Holy Sepulchre in Jerusalem, has been erected in his memory. Another tribute comes in the form of Germany's most popular long-distance footpath, the **King Ludwig Way** (König-Ludwig-Weg), covering the 120km between

Starnberg and Füssen. It's easy to follow, being marked by signposts showing a blue K with a crown; although the scenery is imposing, the terrain is undemanding and is easily covered in a four- or five-day hike.

The S-Bahn continues down the western side of the lake, which is far more commercialized, as far as its terminus at Tutzing. This marks the end of obvious commuter territory; the next village, **BERNRIED**, on the main rail line south to Kochel, is indubitably Alpine in character. At its northern edge, a twenty-minute walk from the Bahnhof, is the much-publicized and highly controversial new **Buchheim Museum**, otherwise known as the **Museum der Phantasie** (April–Oct Mon–Fri 10am–6pm, Sat & Sun 10am–8pm; Nov–March Tues–Fri 10am–5pm, Sat & Sun 10am–6pm; €7.80; Ⓦwww.buchheimmuseum.de), a foundation established by **Lothar-Günther Buchheim**, who is best-known internationally for his anti-war novel *Das Boot*, and for the screenplay of the film based on it. A genuine polymath, he has also been active as a painter, photographer, publisher, writer on art – and as a passionate collector of decidedly idiosyncratic tastes. He amassed a remarkable array of **Expressionist paintings** and works on paper – particularly by members of Die Brücke – in the years after World War II, when they were available at knockdown prices, and also acquired other masterpieces of twentieth-century German art, including Corinth's *Dancing Dervish* and Beckmann's *Riders on the Beach*. In the aftermath of a world tour in the 1980s, several prestigious museums offered to provide a permanent home for these works, but all baulked at Buchheim's demand that they be displayed alongside the other material he collected – which ranges from Bavarian, African and Asian folk art via a huge array of circus paraphernalia, some three thousand paperweights, large representations of Naive artists to dried leaves worked into compositions of animals and birds by his own wife, Ditti Buchheim. However, the opening of this new institution, which has received extensive funding from the Bavarian state, has fulfilled all Buchheim's wishes. The end result is egotistical in the extreme, though many will like it all the more for that. Günter Bernisch's striking museum building – incorporating a pier-like footbridge into the Starnberger See – had to be modified and turned round 90 degrees in order to fit this location, after public opposition in the intended site of Feldafing, on the other side of Tutzing, forced it to be built here instead.

The Ammersee

The S-Bahn #5 line goes from Munich to the resort of **HERRSCHING** on the **Ammersee**; its three previous stops cover the remaining lakes of the group – Wessling is by the minute lake of the same name; Steinebach is on the west side of the deep blue Wörthsee; while Seefeld lies on the peaceful Pilsensee. Herrsching is a favourite place to go swimming and sailing and can get very crowded, particularly on summer weekends. There's a footpath along the water's edge to the west, where a few public beaches are slotted in between stretches of private property. The **tourist office** (April–Oct Mon–Fri 8.30am–noon & 2–5pm, Sat 10am–12.30pm; Nov–March Mon–Fri 8.30am–noon; Ⓣ0 81 52/52 27, Ⓦwww.herrsching.de) is at Bahnhofplatz 3. **Boat trips** are run by Staatliche Schifffahrt Ammersee (Ⓣ0 81 43/2 29, Ⓦwww.bayerische-seenschifffahrt.de); three-hour cruises cost €13, though there are various cheaper options.

The village of **ANDECHS** sits atop the hill of the same name, Bavaria's "Holy Mountain". There's an attractive if strenuous walking trail from Herrsching as an alternative to the regular service by buses #951 and #956. A Benedictine **Kloster** (Ⓦwww.andechs.de) was built in the late fourteenth century to celebrate the rediscovery of some relics brought to Andechs from Jerusalem by the local count in 952. Its Gothic church still survives, though the interior was remodelled in Rococo style by Johann Baptist Zimmermann. The only part still in its original form is the elevated **Heilige Kapelle**, which contains an extraordinary cabinet of reliquaries, many of them masterpieces of the goldsmith's art; this is normally only accessible on guided tours of the church (Mon–Fri at 3pm; €3). An extensive view over the Ammersee region can be enjoyed from the **tower** (Mon–Sat 9am–5pm, Sun 12.15–5pm; €1). The Andechs monks still follow the time-honoured German tradition of brewing their own **beers**, making seven varieties in all, the most notable being a dark *Doppelbock*. These can be sampled in the *Bräustüberl* attached to the monastery; hearty local dishes and homemade cheese are also available. **Brewery tours** (June to early Oct Mon & Tues at 1.30pm; €3) have recently been introduced.

Across the lake, on a rail line beyond the S-Bahn network, lies **DIESSEN**, a village whose population includes a sizeable artistic colony, with potters pre-eminent. On the hill above is an Augustinian **Kloster**, which boasts one of Bavaria's finest Rococo churches: the design is by J.M. Fischer, the high altar by Cuvilliés, the ceiling frescoes by Johann Georg Bergmüller, while among the side altars is a theatrical *Martyrdom of St Sebastian* by Tiepolo.

Landsberg am Lech and the Pfaffenwinkel

A staging-post on the Romantic Road (see p.232), **LANDSBERG** lies less than 40km up the River Lech from Augsburg, and about 55km west of Munich. Like the latter, it was founded by Henry the Lion, and until the Napoleonic period it was Bavaria's westernmost outpost. It later became the site of a jail for high-profile political prisoners, and has the misfortune to have gone down in history as the place where Hitler, imprisoned following the botched Beer Hall Putsch, dictated to Rudolf Hess the insidious rantings of *Mein Kampf*. This connection notwithstanding, it's a highly attractive town with easy access to the pre-Alpine countryside to the south. Known as the **Pfaffenwinkel** (literally, "Clerics' Corner"), this has no major towns, but – as the name suggests – is dotted with religious foundations. Be aware that the public transport network in this area is based primarily on buses, which operate very infrequently at weekends, particularly out-of-season. However, the Pfaffenwinkel is ideal walking country, and the King Ludwig Way (see p.111) cuts all the way through it.

Landsberg am Lech

As befits its long status as a border town, Landsberg was equipped with a formidable **Stadtmauer**, and its southern, eastern and western ranges still survive. The most impressive part, situated high above the town centre, is the fifteenth-century **Bayertor** (May–Sept daily 10am–noon & 2–5pm; €1), a mighty gateway consisting of an outer barbican and a 36-metre-high tower whose outer face is adorned with a monumental carving of the Crucifixion. On a clear day, the Alps can be seen from the top, though much of the Altstadt is out of view.

In spite of being sandwiched among a row of mansions, the **Rathaus** (May–Oct Mon–Fri 8am–6pm, Sat & Sun 10am–noon; Nov–April Mon–Wed

8am–noon & 2–5pm, Thurs 8am–noon & 2–5.30pm, Fri 8am–12.30pm; €1) dominates the Hauptplatz, in large part because of its exuberant stuccowork facade. Together with the decoration of the main **Ratsstube** on the second floor, this was the only major secular commission undertaken by the great Rococo church-builder Dominikus Zimmermann, who did a stint as burgomaster of the town. He also created the **Johanniskirche** a short distance north on Vorderer Anger. Despite the minute size of the site, this is a wonderfully original design, with an oval nave preceding a horseshoe-shaped chancel filled with a theatrical high altar of the Baptism of Christ. The choir of the large Gothic **Stadtpfarrkirche Mariä Himmelfahrt** diagonally opposite contains another work by Zimmermann, a Rosary altar made to shelter a beautiful *Madonna and Child* by the fifteenth-century Ulm sculptor Hans Multscher.

On the left bank of the Lech is the curious **Mutterturm** (Mother Tower; April–Jan Tues–Sun 2–5pm; €1), built by the Anglo-German artist Hubert von Herkomer as his Landsberg studio. Although now neglected, Herkomer was a leading light of Victorian society; a successful painter, film pioneer, early racing car promoter and occasional composer who was friendly with many of the greatest musicians of the day. The tower contains examples of his graphic work; portraits, landscapes and drawings can be seen in the adjacent **Herkomer-Museum** (same times and ticket), formerly the home of his parents.

Landsberg is now a dead-end for passenger trains; the **Bahnhof** is on the west side of the Lech, not far from the Mutterturm. The **tourist office** is in the Rathaus, Hauptplatz 1 (same hours as above; Ⓣ0 81 91/12 82 46, Ⓦwww.landsberg.de). One of the biggest and most colourful **children's festivals** in Germany, the Ruethenfest, takes place over a weekend in July every four years (next in 2007), and features two big processions plus recreations of military camps, a handicrafts market, street theatre and concerts. Budget accommodation is in short supply: there are only a few **private rooms** (❷–❸) plus one small **guesthouse**, *Christine*, Galgenweg 4 (Ⓣ0 81 91/52 10, Ⓕ92 16 80, Ⓦwww.gaestehaus-christine.de; ❹). Otherwise, there are several good **hotels** to choose from, including *Landsberger Hof*, Weilheimer Str. 5 (Ⓣ0 81 91/3 20 20; ❺); *Gasthof Zum Mohren*, Hauptplatz 148 (Ⓣ0 81 91/4 22 10, Ⓦwww.zummohren.de; ❺); and *Goggl*, Herkomerstr. 19–20 (Ⓣ0 81 91/32 40, Ⓦwww.hotelgoggl.de; ❻). There's also a **campsite**, *Romantik am Lech*, in a woodland setting by the Lech to the south of the Altstadt at Am Pössinger Wald (Ⓣ0 81 91/4 75 05, Ⓕ2 14 06). All the hotels listed above have **restaurants**, though strong competition comes from *Zederbräu*, Hauptplatz 155.

Steingaden

STEINGADEN, another stop on the Romantic Road, can be reached by bus from either Landsberg (this sometimes involves a change at Schongau) or Füssen (see p.232). The little town is centred on the **Welfenmünster**, the church of a former Premonstratensian monastery. It encompasses virtually the entire history of Bavarian ecclesiastical architecture: the exterior is one of the area's rare Romanesque survivors, the entrance porch and the frescoed Brunnenkapelle in the cloisters are Gothic, the choir stalls are Renaissance, the high altar and decoration of the chancel are Mannerist, while the nave was remodelled in Rococo style to celebrate the monastery's 600th anniversary, with refined stuccowork, a showy pulpit, and an outstanding set of ceiling frescoes of the life of the order's founder, St Norbert, by Johann Georg Bergmüller.

There are three **hotels**: *Gasthof Graf*, Schongauer Str. 15 (Ⓣ0 88 62/2 46, Ⓦwww.gasthof-graf.de; ❷–❹); *Gasthof Zur Post*, Marktplatz 1 (Ⓣ0 88 62/2 03;

❸); and *Gasthof Lindenhof*, Schongauer Str. 35 (Ⓣ0 88 62/60 11; ❹). Each has a **restaurant** serving homely Bavarian fare at moderate prices.

The Wieskirche

Within Steingaden's municipality, albeit tucked away in the countryside 5km southeast, is the **Wieskirche** (Meadow Church), the best-known pilgrimage church in Germany, and a UNESCO World Heritage Site. When the Steingaden monks discarded a statue of the suffering Christ which they formerly carried in their Holy Week processions, a farmer's wife found the figure crying. So many pilgrims flocked to the simple shrine her husband built that the abbot asked **Dominikus Zimmermann** to erect a worthy temple for the image. His carefully thought-out design, based on his earlier pilgrimage church in Steinhausen (see p.289), has an almost umbilical relationship with the mountains in the background.

The plain exterior belies the extravagance of the interior, which is crammed with furnishings displaying craftsmanship of the highest class. In a symbolic reference to the contrast between earth and heaven, the plain white pillars are offset by the gold-plated stucco ornamentation of the arches above and the bravura ceiling **fresco** by Johann Baptist Zimmermann (Dominikus's elder brother). Executed in glowing, pastel-like colours, this presents a radiant vision of the afterlife: the resurrected Christ sits on a rainbow in the centre, with the still unoccupied Throne of Judgment and the as yet unopened Gate to Eternity at either end.

Dominikus Zimmermann, a deeply pious man, built a house for himself alongside the church, and lived out his retirement there. Nowadays, it's a **restaurant**, *Schweiger*, serving marvellous Bavarian cuisine; *Moser*, which is down by the car park, also offers good food. If you fancy a quiet night in the countryside, a couple of the nearby farmhouses offer **rooms** (❶–❷). Note that there are only three or four **buses** a day to and from Steingaden, though there's a very pleasant walking trail.

Oberammergau and Ettal

OBERAMMERGAU, the terminus of a branch rail line at the western edge of the Upper Bavarian Alps, is world-famous for the **Passion Play** that the local villagers have been performing since 1634; the next performances will take place in the year 2010. Without the tradition of the play, it's likely that Oberammergau would be stuck in relative obscurity, instead of being the tourist trap it has become, crammed with souvenir shops selling examples of the local **woodcarving** to the busloads of organized tour parties who roll up every summer. Nevertheless, it does preserve features genuinely characteristic of small Alpine communities. In particular, the facades of many of the houses are adorned with **frescoes**, which you can see as either quaint or kitsch. This style of decoration, known as *Lüftlmalerei*, dates back to the mid-eighteenth century, and is a uniquely Catholic art. Thus the scenes depicted are usually based on biblical stories, making a highly distinctive transfer of a sacred art form to secular buildings.

Just north of the central axis, Dorfstrasse, is the huge **Passionspielhaus**, the theatre where the Passion Play performances are held. It was custom-built in the 1890s to ensure that every member of the vast audience can see and hear all the action, and was modified in the 1930s and again in the late 1990s.

Although a decidedly curious piece of architecture – the open-air stage is loosely modelled on the theatres of ancient Rome, while the covered auditorium resembles an aircraft hangar – it fulfils its purpose admirably. The backstage areas, including the collections of historic costumes and props, can be visited by **guided tour** (daily 10am–4pm; €2.50).

The **Heimatmuseum** (closed until June 2004 for reconstruction, previously mid-May to mid-Oct Tues–Sun 2–6pm; rest of year Sat 2–6pm only; €2.50) at Dorfstr. 8 contains extensive displays of folk art, particularly woodcarvings and paintings behind glass. There's a fine collection of historic cribs made from a variety of different materials; predictably, it's the wooden examples which are the most imposing. In the **Pilatushaus** (Mon–Fri 1–6pm; free), on Verlegergasse just to the south, you can watch some of the local craftsmen at work. The building itself is of special note for having been decorated by Franz Zwinck, Oberammergau's first and most celebrated *Lüftlmaler*. Beyond the far end of Dorfstrasse is the **Pfarrkirche St-Peter-und-Paul**, a splendid example of an Upper Bavarian village church. It was designed and built in 1736–49 by Joseph Schmuzer, a member of a prolific dynasty of architects and stuccoists, and embellished by several distinguished collaborators, notably the fresco painter Matthäus Günther and the sculptor Franz Xaver Schmädl. The best view of Oberammergau and its surroundings is from the summit of the **Laber** (1683m), which can be reached from the eastern end of the village by cable car (€7.50 single, €11 return; Ⓦwww.laber-bergbahn.de).

Practicalities

Oberammergau's **Bahnhof** is on the west bank of the Ammer, just a few minutes' walk from the centre on the opposite side of the river. The **tourist office** is at Eugen-Papst-Str. 9a (Mon–Fri 8.30am–6pm, Sat 9am–noon; Ⓣ0 88 22/9 23 10, Ⓦwww.oberammergau.de). **Tickets** for the next performances of the Passion Play are unlikely to go on sale before 2008. The village is well-endowed with **private rooms** (❶–❸) and **pensions**, such as *Reiser*, In der Breitenau 6 (Ⓣ0 88 22/47 47; ❷); *Dedlerhaus*, Ettaler Str. 8 (Ⓣ0 88 22/35 93, Ⓦwww.dedlerhaus.de; ❷) and *Enzianhof*, Ettaler Str. 33 (Ⓣ0 88 22/2 15; ❷). Among several classy **hotels** are *Alte Post*, Dorfstr. 19 (Ⓣ0 88 22/91 00, Ⓦwww.altepost.ogau.de; ❺); *Wittelsbach*, Dorfstr. 21 (Ⓣ0 88 22/9 28 00, Ⓦwww.hotelwittelsbach.de; ❺); and *Turmwirt*, Ettaler Str. 2 (Ⓣ0 88 22/9 26 00, Ⓦwww.turmwirt.de; ❻). The **youth hostel** is at the southwestern edge of the village at Mahlensteinweg 10 (Ⓣ0 88 22/41 14; €12.70); the **campsite** is at the southern fringe at Ettaler Str. 54b (Ⓣ0 88 22/9 41 05, Ⓦwww.campingplatz-oberammergau.de). As usual in resorts of this kind, the best **restaurants** are attached to hotels, and those listed above are as good as any.

Ettal and Schloss Linderhof

The small health resort of **ETTAL**, 4km down the road, grew up around its Benedictine **Kloster** (Ⓦwww.kloster-ettal.de), which was founded in 1330 by Emperor Ludwig IV, and for several centuries wielded temporal (though not spiritual) jurisdiction over Oberammergau. A twelve-cornered design, based on the Church of the Holy Sepulchre in Jerusalem, was adopted for the original Gothic **Klosterkirche**, and this shape, along with much of the masonry, was preserved in the Baroque rebuilding carried out by Enrico Zuccalli and Joseph Schmuzer. Johann Straub carved the pulpit and assemblage of nave altars, while the fresco decoration of the vaults was entrusted to two Tyroleans, Johann

Jakob Zeiller and Martin Knoller. A miraculous statue of the *Madonna and Child*, which the founder brought back from a journey to Italy, is the focus of the high altar. The monastery produces a variety of wonderful fruit liqueurs and brandies, plus some fine beers. A highly recommendable **hotel** with restaurant, *Ludwig der Bayer*, occupies the old monastic guesthouse at Kaiser-Ludwig-Platz 10–12 (Ⓣ0 88 22/91 50, Ⓦwww.kloster-ettal.de/hotel; ❹).

Some 11km west of Ettal, but still within its municipal area, is **Schloss Linderhof** (guided tours daily: April–Sept 9am–6pm; €6 including pavilions; Oct–March 10am–4pm; €4.50; Ⓦwww.linderhof.de), which can be reached by several buses daily. One of King Ludwig II's more restrained fantasies – and the only one that was actually completed – it was built as a private residence rather than a statement in royal architecture. From the garden terraces its creamy white walls and square shape make it look like a sparkling wedding cake. As you enter, it's impossible to miss a large bronze statue of one of Ludwig's heroes, Louis XIV, and, although this was a private retreat, Ludwig still had a reception room with gold-painted carvings, stucco ornamentation and a throne canopy draped in ermine curtains.

However, the top attraction is the delightful **Schlosspark**. The palace forms the axis of a cross-shaped design, which was laid out on the Italian Renaissance model of terraces, cascades and pools rising up in front and behind, while the shorter gardens to the right and left have strictly manicured lawns, hedges and flowerbeds. Initially, it's hard to tell that the surrounding "wild" scenery is actually a clever English garden design that gradually blends into the forests beyond. A number of romantic little buildings (open summer only) are dotted around the park, the most remarkable of which is the **Venus-Grotte**. It's supposed to be based on the set from the first act of Wagner's opera *Tannhäuser* and has an illuminated lake with an enormous golden conch floating on it in which the king would sometimes take rides. Equally outrageous is the **Maurischer Kiosk**, a mock-Moorish pavilion in which stands a throne with a backdrop of three huge peacocks crafted out of enamel and coloured glass. Also in the grounds is the *Schlosshotel* (Ⓣ0 88 22/7 90, Ⓦwww.schlosshotel-linderhof.com; ❺), which offers **rooms** with balconies and a restaurant specializing in game dishes.

Garmisch-Partenkirchen and Mittenwald

GARMISCH-PARTENKIRCHEN, some 19km south of Oberammergau by road, is the most famous resort in the German Alps, partly because it's at the foot of the highest mountain – the **Zugspitze** – and partly because it hosted the fourth Winter Olympics back in 1936. Its location is marvellous, lying between the gentle Ammer mountains and the imposing peaks of the Wetterstein chain which form the frontier with Austria. During the winter months Garmisch is one of the foremost **skiing** bases, and it has excellent facilities for **skating** and other winter sports too. In summer, mountaineers and **hiking** enthusiasts come to explore the craggy heights, while there are cable cars for the less energetic. The 1936 games quite literally put the town on the map; previously Garmisch and Partenkirchen had been separate villages, lying west and east of the River Partnach respectively. The area between them has now been built up, so that at first the town appears as a seamless whole, but closer acquaintance reveals that each part preserves its historic core and at least something of its old identity.

Garmisch's centre is the ritzier of the two, with plenty of fashionable shops and cafés. Its **Kurpark** (daily 9am–10pm; €1) has both formal and "natural" sections, and regularly hosts open-air concerts. Within the park is the **Kurhaus**, which contains the **Stiftung Aschenbrenner** (Tues–Fri 9am–noon & 3–6.30pm, Sat & Sun 10am–noon & 3–6.30pm; free), a delightful collection of Meissen porcelain and historic toys. A short distance to the west is the **Pfarrkirche St Martin**, a typical example of the work of Joseph Schmuzer. Further south is the **Alte Kirche**, which dates back to the time of Garmisch's foundation in the late thirteenth century, although the original Romanesque structure was partially modified in Gothic style. Inside are fourteenth- to sixteenth-century fresco cycles.

Partenkirchen's centre is characterized by the presence of many traditional painted houses, and one of these, the former merchant's residence at Ludwigstr. 47, contains the **Werdenfelser Heimatmuseum** (Tues–Fri 10am–1pm & 3–6pm, Sat & Sun 10am–1pm; €2), which vividly brings the region's distinctive culture to life. Among the exhibits are sculptures by Ignaz Günther and the house's former owner, Joseph Wackerle, reconstructed interiors, Carnival masks, an eighteenth-century crib, costumes, glass paintings and furniture. Another church by Joseph Schmuzer, the Franciscan **Wallfahrtskirche St Anton**, lies in a rustic setting at the eastern edge of Partenkirchen, and is approached via a steepish path lined with ten pilgrimage chapels.

The peaks

From Garmisch, there are two possibilities for ascending the **Zugspitze** (2966m) by public transport (Ⓦwww.zugspitze.de); each costs €24.50 single, €43 return in summer, €19.50 single, €34 return in winter. The electric train, the Zugspitzbahn, travels westwards to a forest lake, the **Eibsee**. Here you can either continue by the rack rail line, the Gletscherbahn, which goes up a winding tunnel carved through the interior of the mountain, or transfer to the Eibseebahn cable car. Whereas the latter goes straight to the summit, the former deposits you at the *Schneefernhaus* (2645m), which commands a huge skiing area. You can then ascend to the summit by the Gipfelbahn cable car, or walk via the tunnel to the customs point, the Zugspitzkamm (2805m), from where yet another cable car, the Tiroler Zugspitzbahn, runs to Ehrwald in Austria. The **views** from the top are all you'd expect, stretching from the Tyrolean High Alps to the Allgäu and the Bavarian lowlands.

Closer to Garmisch, the **Alpspitze** (2628m) is the highest peak in a range popular with serious hikers. In this case, the cable car, the Alpspitzbahn (€14 single, €19 return; Ⓦwww.alpspitzbahn.de) does not go all the way to the summit, but terminates at the nearby **Osterfelderkopf** (2050m). The valley station is at the southwestern edge of Garmisch, reached by bus #2 from the centre; close by is the departure point of another cable car, which ascends to the **Kreuzeck** (1652m) for €12 single, €17 return. Two other peaks to the south of town, **Hausberg** (1350m) and **Eckbauer** (1236m) also have their own cable cars (€8 single, €11 return and €7.50 single, €10 return respectively). A short walk south of the latter's valley station is the magnificent gorge known as the **Partnachklamm** (a €2 admission is levied throughout most of the day), which can be traversed by a circular path hewn out of the rock. East of Partenkirchen, the unfortunately named **Wank** (1780m) offers the best view of the basin in which the town is set, as well as a complete panorama of the

Wetterstein chain. A cable car, whose valley station is served by buses #3, #4 and #5, goes to the summit for €11 single, €16 return.

Practicalities

Garmisch-Partenkirchen's **Bahnhof** is handily placed between the two constituent villages; immediately to its rear is the **Zugspitzbahnhof**, terminus of the mountain rail line. At the latter you can buy passes (a passport photograph is required) covering all the cable cars, except those on the Zugspitze, for periods of between three and fourteen days – something well worth considering if you're planning on doing a lot of hiking. The **tourist office** (Mon–Sat 8am–6pm, Sun 10am–noon; ⓣ0 88 21/18 06, ⓦwww.garmischpartenkirchen.de) is at Richard-Strauss-Platz 2, five minutes' walk south of the Bahnhof.

Budget accommodation options include the **youth hostel**, Jochstr. 10 (ⓣ0 88 21/29 80; €12.70) in the incorporated village of Burgrain, reached by bus #3, #4 or #5 from the Bahnhof, and a **campsite**, *Zugspitze* (ⓣ0 88 21/31 80), ideally placed for the peaks, by the village of Grainau to the west. **Private rooms** (❶–❸), while on average marginally more expensive than elsewhere in the Alps, are still wonderful value, as are the many **guesthouses**, such as *Neuner*, Kreuzstr. 21, (ⓣ0 88 21/5 62 91, ⓦwww.pension-neuner.de; ❸), *Christina*, Burgstr. 61 (ⓣ0 88 21/13 34 or 23 75, ⓕ5 42 10, ⓦwww.gaestehaus-christina.de; ❸); and *Reiter*, Burgstr. 55 (ⓣ0 88 21/22 33, ⓦwww.reiter-gap.de; ❸–❺).

Among the town's **hotels**, *Berggasthof Panorama*, up from the Wank cable car station at St Anton 3 (ⓣ0 88 21/25 15, ⓦwww.gapinfo.de/berggasthof-panorama; ❺) offers the most spectacular views. A couple of medium-range alternatives in the heart of Partenkirchen are *Gasthof Zum Rassen*, Ludwigstr. 45 (ⓣ0 88 21/20 89, ⓦwww.gasthof-rassen.de; ❹–❻); and *Gasthof Fraundorfer*, Ludwigstr. 24 (ⓣ0 88 21/92 70, ⓦwww.gasthof-fraundorfer.de; ❺–❼). There are many enticing luxury options, including *Posthotel Partenkirchen*, Ludwigstr. 49 (ⓣ0 88 21/9 36 30, ⓦwww.ph-gap.de.de; ❼), a marvellous old inn decked out in rustic style; and the top-of-the-range *Reindl's Partenkircher Hof*, Bahnhofstr. 15 (ⓣ0 88 21/5 80 25, ⓦwww.reindls.de; ❼–❾), which is furnished with antiques, has a swimming pool, fitness room, winter garden and balconies with panoramic views. All the hotels listed above have recommendable **restaurants** open to non-residents. Among Garmisch's many enticing **cafés**, *Krönner*, Am Kurpark 5, and *Pavillon*, Am Kurpark 2, stand out.

Mittenwald

Just 20km southeast of Garmisch by road or rail, **MITTENWALD** could hardly be more different. In 1786 Goethe described it as a "living picture book", and so it remains, having the feel of a community and not just a resort. This is reflected in the carved pews with their family nameplates in the **Pfarrkirche St-Peter-und-Paul**. The church, yet another of Joseph Schmuzer's designs, is also notable for frescoes by Johann Georg Bergmüller, which give a deliberately prominent role to angel musicians, in recognition of the important role of music in the life of Mittenwald. In particular, it has been an internationally renowned centre of violin-making ever since **Matthias Klotz**, who is honoured by a statue outside the church, introduced this highly specialized craft to the village in the seventeenth century, thus raising it from the status of an impoverished backwater. Some of the finest work of the local craftsmen, from Klotz to the present day, can be seen in the

Geigenbaumuseum (Tues–Fri 10am–1pm & 3–6pm, Sat & Sun 10am–1pm; €2), a short distance to the north at Ballenhausgasse 3. There's also a mock-up of Klotz's workshop, as well as a collection of festive masks and an impressive crib. To the west, on Im Gries, stand the oldest Mittenwald houses, with faded frescoes decorating their frontages.

Towering above Mittenwald is the **Karwendl** (2244m), one of the most popular climbs in Germany. The view from the top is exhilarating; a cable car (Ⓦwww.karwendlbahn.de) goes up for €12 single, €19 return. There are plenty of enticing but less demanding walks in the Isar valley below, including the **Leutaschklamm** (May–Oct daily 9.30am–5.30pm; €2) 2km south of Mittenwald. Though technically in Austria, this dramatic narrow gorge with a 23-metre-high waterfall is inaccessible from that side of the border. To the west of town, two small lakes, the **Lautersee** and the **Ferchensee**, stand in the shadow of the mighty Wetterstein mountains; there are boats for rent and a good country Gasthof at each. The path from Mittenwald, which starts just beyond the Kurpark, passes via a pretty waterfall, the **Laintalschlucht**.

Practicalities

Mittenwald's **Bahnhof** is at the eastern edge of the town centre; the **tourist office** (Mon–Fri 8am–noon & 1–5pm, Sat 10am–noon; Ⓣ0 88 23/3 39 81, Ⓦwww.mittenwald.de) is a short walk away at Dammkarstr. 3. There are many good-value **guesthouses**, such as *Sonnenheim*, Dammkarstr. 5 (Ⓣ0 88 23/9 21 60, Ⓦwww.sonnenheim-tourismus.de; ❹); *Franziska*, Innsbrucker Str. 24 (Ⓣ0 88 23/9 20 30, Ⓦwww.franziska-tourismus.de; ❹); and *Sonnenbichl*, Klausnerweg 32 (Ⓣ0 88 23/9 22 30, Ⓦwww.sonnenbichl-tourismus.de; ❹), the last of which is the place for a view. **Hotels** in the town centre include *Alpenrose*, Obermarkt 1 (Ⓣ0 88 23/9 27 00, Ⓦwww.alpenrose-mittenwald.de; ❺); and *Post*, Obermarkt 9 (Ⓣ0 88 23/10 94, Ⓦwww.posthotel-mittenwald.de; ❻). For an isolated setting, with the bonus of wonderful panoramas, there's *Alpengasthof Gröblalm* (Ⓣ0 88 23/91 10, Ⓦwww.groeblalm.de; ❹–❻), 2km north. The **youth hostel** at Buckelwiesen 7 (Ⓣ0 88 23/17 01; €12.70) is an hour's walk from the Bahnhof, so isn't a very practical option. However, the tourist office can fix you up with a room in a **private house** (❶–❸). The nearest **campsite**, the year-round *Am Isarhorn* (Ⓣ0 88 23/52 16, Ⓦwww.camping-isarhorn.de), is 3km north, on the road to Garmisch. All the hotels mentioned above have good **restaurants**. *Postkeller*, Innsbrucker Str. 13, the tap of the local brewery, is also recommendable, while *Arnspitze*, Innsbrucker Str. 68, is the best and most expensive in town.

The Tölzer Land

To the north of Mittenwald, the **Tölzer Land** offers altogether gentler scenery. Nonetheless, the area embraces two major lakes – the **Walchensee** and the **Kochelsee** – as well as **Benediktbeuern**, the oldest monastery in Upper Bavaria. It also has a rich folklore tradition of riflemen's festivals and costumed parades.

The Walchensee

Of the Tölzer Land's two lakes, the **Walchensee**, some 25km southwest of Bad Tölz, and 19km north of Mittenwald, is by far the more dramatic. Its depth is unknown and the water is so cold in the lower reaches that the many trees fallen from the mountainous shores haven't been able to sink completely; instead they've formed an impenetrable false bottom to the lake. This is a good place to come for **boating** and **windsurfing**, as it's never as crowded as the lowland lakes, and is cheaper too. A popular trip around here is the three-hour hike from **URFELD** at the northern tip of the lake to the summit of the **Herzogstand** (1731m). This commands a breathtaking panorama of the region's two lakes plus the snow-capped Austrian peaks to the south and the Bavarian plateau to the north. Alternatively, take the cable car (€7 single, €12 return; Ⓦwww.herzogstandbahn.de) from the northern end of the scattered village of **WALCHENSEE** on the western shore.

The local **youth hostel** is at Mittenwalder Str. 17 (Ⓣ0 88 51/2 30; €13.70) in Urfeld. Walchensee has several **guesthouses**, including *Seeblick,* Ringstr. 68a (Ⓣ0 88 58/2 28; ❷) and *Edeltraut*, Seestr. 90 (Ⓣ0 88 58/2 62; ❸). There are also two lakeside **hotels**: *Schwaigerhof*, Seestr. 42 (Ⓣ0 88 58/9 20 20; ❸–❺) and *Seehotel zur Post*, Seestr. 52 (Ⓣ0 88 58/4 64; ❹–❻). A full accommodation list can be had from the **tourist office** (mid-May to mid-Oct Mon–Fri 9am–noon & 1–5pm, Sat 10am–noon; mid-Oct to mid-May Mon–Thurs 9am–noon & 2–4pm, Fri 9am–noon; Ⓣ0 88 58/4 11, Ⓦwww.walchensee.de) in the Rathaus, Ringstr. 1.

The Kochelsee

A wonderful twisting nine-kilometre-long road links Urfeld with the **Kochelsee**. This lake combines lowland and highland attractions: to the north lies marshland while the craggy Benediktenwand, the first slopes in the Alpine chain, rise immediately from its southern shore. The shoreline has an agreeably empty feel to it, but a good deal of the immediate surrounding area is flat and rather dull. The village of **KOCHEL** on the northeastern side is the largest settlement; it's the terminus of a branch rail line which links up with the Munich S-Bahn network at Tutzing on the Starnberger See. **Franz Marc** lived around here from 1908 until 1916, when he was killed in action in World War I at the age of 36. Unlike his friends in Der Blaue Reiter – such as Kandinsky and Macke – he preferred country to city life, and his pictures of horses and other animals are his most famous works. The **Franz-Marc-Museum** at Herzogstandweg 43 (Tues–Sun 2–6pm; closed mid-Jan to March; €4; Ⓦwww.franz-marc-museum.de) contains a representative collection of his work, comprising about a hundred paintings, as well as examples of other members of Der Blaue Reiter.

Kochel's **tourist office** (Mon–Fri 8am–noon & 1–5pm; Ⓣ0 88 51/3 38, Ⓦwww.kochel.de) is at Kalmbachstr. 11. **Cruises**, costing €6 for a 75-minute round trip, are run between June and September by Motorschiffahrt Kochelsee (Ⓣ0 88 51/4 16). Accommodation possibilities include a **youth hostel** at Badstr. 2 (Ⓣ0 88 51/52 96; €12.70) and the **campsites** *Kesselberg*, Altjoch 2½ (Ⓣ0 88 51/4 64) and *Renken*, Mittenwalder Str. 106 (Ⓣ0 88 51/57 76). There are also numerous **hotels**, including *Gasthof Waltraud*, Bahnhofstr. 20 (Ⓣ0 88 51/3 33, Ⓦwww.gasthof-waltraud.de; ❹); the lakeside *Seehotel Grauer Bär*, Mittenwalder Str. 82–6 (Ⓣ0 88 51/9 25 00, Ⓦwww.grauer-baer.de; ❺); and *Zur Post*, Schmied-von-Kochel-Platz 6 (Ⓣ0 88 51/9 24 10, Ⓦwww.posthotel-kochel.de; ❻), all of which have excellent **restaurants**.

Benediktbeuern

BENEDKITBEUERN, 8km north of Kochel on the rail line to Munich, is a small health resort with its back to the Benediktenwand. Its **Kloster**, which dates back to 789, is indelibly associated with the famous *Carmina Burana* manuscript, which was housed in its library for several centuries prior to the Napoleonic secularization, when it was carted off to Munich. For long, it was believed that this anthology of eleventh- to thirteenth-century (mostly Latin) lyrics – moral, religious and satirical verses, ribald love laments, bucolic drinking and gaming songs – had been compiled and illuminated at Benediktbeuern, but it has now been established that it originated somewhere on the opposite side of the Alps. Nothing remains of the medieval Kloster, which was entirely rebuilt in the Baroque epoch. The **Klosterkirche** boasts a fresco cycle of the life of Christ by Hans Georg Asam (father of the famous brothers), but is rather overshadowed by the **Anastasiakapelle**, a separate chapel to the north, which is a miniature masterpiece by Johann Michael Fischer. In 1930, the monastic buildings were re-occupied by a congregation of Salesian monks, who have established a school and cultural centre. Concerts and exhibitions are regularly held there; also on the premises are a fine **restaurant** with beer garden and a **youth hostel** (Ⓣ0 88 57/8 83 50; €14.80).

The Tegernsee and beyond

The **Tegernsee**, some 15km east of Bad Tölz, is among the most beautiful lakes in Bavaria. It has long been a favourite with the rich, who have built weekend homes along its privately owned sections, and a couple of the leading Alpine resorts can be found on its banks. To the east and southeast lies countryside that is far less well known, including two more lakes and the most isolated section of the Bavarian Alps. Trains throughout this area are now operated by a private company, Bayerische Oberlandbahn (BOB), though this currently accepts all DB and international rail passes.

Tegernsee

The little town of **TEGERNSEE** is on the east bank of the lake, at the end of a branch railway from Schaftlach on the main line to Munich. By the waterside towards the southern end of the resort is the former Benedictine **Kloster**, which was founded in 746 and flourished for over a millennium. A major centre for manuscript illumination and calligraphy, it once had a library considered superior to that of the Vatican. Following the Napoleonic secularization, Leo von Klenze converted the monastic buildings into a summertime **Schloss** for the Bavarian kings. He also added a twin-towered facade to the Baroque **Klosterkirche**, whose main body was designed by Enrico Zuccalli and frescoed by Hans Georg Asam.

The **tourist office** is in the Haus des Gastes, Hauptstr. 2 (May to mid-Oct Mon–Fri 8am–6pm, Sat & Sun 10am–noon & 3–5pm; rest of year Mon–Fri 8am–noon & 1–5pm, Sat & Sun 10am–noon & 3–5pm; Ⓣ0 80 22/18 01 40, Ⓦwww.tegernsee.de). Here you can pick up a list of **private rooms** and **guesthouses** (❶–❹). There are several lakeside **hotels**, including *Fischerstüberl am See*, Seestr. 51 (Ⓣ0 80 22/91 98 90, Ⓦwww.hotel-fischerstueberl-tegernsee.de; ❹–❻); and *Bischoff am See*, Schwaighofstr. 53 (Ⓣ0 80 22/39 66, Ⓦwww.bischoff-am-see.de; ❾). Rivalling the latter for the right to be regarded as Tegernsee's top address is *Bayern*, uphill from the Bahnhof in the north of town at Neureuthstr. 23 (Ⓣ0 80 22/18 20, Ⓦwww.hotel-bayern.de; ❼–❾).

The north wing of the Schloss contains the *Bräustüberl* of the local **brewery**, the Herzogliches Bayerisches Brauhaus, which is still owned by the Wittelsbach family. This is an extraordinary sight in the evening, when it's crammed full of local farmers trying to drink each other under the table. Only basic snacks are served there; for a full meal and a quieter atmosphere, go instead to the adjacent cellar **restaurant**, the *Schlossgaststätte*. Alternative places to eat can be found in all the hotels listed on p.122; another good choice is the long-established *Café am See*, Hauptstr. 45. **Cruises** are run by Staatliche Schifffahrt Tegernsee (Ⓣ0 80 22/9 33 11, Ⓦwww.bayerische-seenschifffahrt.de), which charges €2.40 for the short sail to Rottach-Egern, €7.60 for an hour-long trip around the southern part of the lake, €11.50 for the complete circuit.

Rottach-Egern

At the southern end of the lake, reached by bus or boat from Tegernsee, is the double village of **ROTTACH-EGERN**. From there, you can take a cable car (€8 single, €13 return; Ⓦwww.wallbergbahn.de) up the **Wallberg** (1722m) for a grandstand view over the lake and the surrounding hills. There's a pleasant terrace **restaurant**, *Alpenwildpark*, at the valley station. Rottach-Egern has a few reasonably priced **hotels**, including *Café Sonnenhof*, Sonnenmoosstr. 20 (Ⓣ0 80 22/ 58 12; ❺); and *Reuther*, Salitererweg 6 (Ⓣ0 80 22/2 40 24, Ⓦwww.hotel-reuther.de; ❻). However, no matter how incongruous it may seem in this country setting, it's best known as a hangout of the chic, who favour such super-luxury establishments as *Park-Hotel Egerner Hof*, Aribostr. 19 (Ⓣ0 80 22/66 60, Ⓦwww.egernerhof.de; ❾), whose *St Florian* is one of Bavaria's leading gourmet restaurants; and *Bachmair am See*, Seestr. 47 (Ⓣ0 80 22/27 20, Ⓦwww.bachmair.de; ❾), which comes complete with a glorious park and a high-fashion boutique.

The Schliersee

The next lake to the east, the **Schliersee**, has a more distinctively Alpine feel to it. At its northeast corner is the pretty village of **SCHLIERSEE**, which can be reached by bus from Tegernsee and Rottach-Egern or by the branch rail line from Munich, which then backtracks and loops round the west side of the lake. Although a popular resort, it hasn't been annexed by the Porsche-driving set, instead preserving a traditional rural culture in which poaching was, until quite recently, an established feature. In the centre of the village stands the **Pfarrkirche St Sixtus**, which boasts frescoes and stuccowork by Johann Baptist Zimmermann and a painting of *The Madonna of Mercy* by Jan Polack. The nearby **Rathaus**, originally a courthouse, bristling with turrets and oriels, ranks among the most picturesque in the Alpine region.

From the east side of the village, cable car gondolas (€3.50 single, €6 return; Ⓦwww.schliersbergalm.de) ascend to the **Schliersbergalm** (1061m), which commands the finest view over the area; in summer, those wanting the thrill of a helter-skelter descent can do so via the chute. **Cruises** on the lake are run between June and September by Motorschiffahrt Schliersee (Ⓣ0 80 26/46 40 or 83 82), and cost €4 for 35 minutes. There's a regular bus service up to the **Spitzingsee**, a much smaller mountain lake on whose eastern shore is the village of the same name, a popular winter sports centre.

The **tourist office** (late May to early Oct Mon–Fri 8am–6pm, Sat & Sun 10am–noon; rest of year Mon–Fri 8.30am–5pm; Ⓣ0 80 26/6 06 50, Ⓦwww.schliersee.de) is at Bahnhofstr. 11a. As usual, there's a wide provision of **private rooms** and **guesthouses** (❷–❹), as well as some splendid **hotels**, notably *Terofal*, Xaver-Terofal-Platz 2 (Ⓣ0 80 26/40 45, Ⓦwww.hotel-terofal.de; ❹–❻) and *Schlierseer Hof am See*, Seestr. 21 (Ⓣ0 80 26/94 00,

Ⓦwww.schlierseerhof.de; ❻–❽). Both of these have superb **restaurants**, whose menus feature freshly-caught fish from the lake. Among several colourful annual **festivals**, pride of place goes to the Alt-Schlierseer-Kirchtag on a Sunday in August, for which the locals don traditional costumes and sail across the lake in boats adorned with floral garlands.

Bayrischzell

BAYRISCHZELL, the terminus of the branch railway, is a small health and winter sports resort in the enclosed setting of the upper valley of the River Leitzach, and has an appropriate end-of-the-line feel. Towering above is the rocky peak of the **Wendelstein** (1838m), one of the best-loved mountains in the Bavarian Alps, particularly with rock climbers. For the less energetic, there are two possible means of ascent to the summit, on which stand an eighteenth-century chapel, a meteorological station and an observatory with one of the most modern telescopes in Germany. Much the quicker of the two is the **cable car** (€9.50 single, €16.50 return; Ⓦwww.wendelsteinbahn.de) from the incorporated village of Osterhofen, 3km northwest of Bayrischzell. A far more atmospheric approach is the **rack railway** (€14 single, €22.50 return; Ⓦwww.wendelsteinbahn.de) up the eastern side of the mountain from Brannenburg, a town on the rail line between Munich and Kufstein in the Austrian Tyrol (note that the valley terminus of the rack railway is a twenty-minute walk from the mainline Bahnhof). This was laid out in 1912, though the current trains date from 1991 and have halved the old journey time to thirty minutes. It's possible to ascend by cable car and descend via the rack railway, or vice versa; this costs €21.50, or €24 including use of the Wendelstein-Ringlinie, the circular bus service round the mountain.

Bayrischzell's **tourist office** is in the Kurverwaltung, Kirchplatz 2 (Mon–Fri 8am–noon & 1–5/6pm, Sat 8am–noon; Ⓣ0 80 23/6 48, Ⓦwww.bayrischzell.de). In addition to numerous **private houses** and **guesthouses** (❶–❸), there are several fine **hotels**, including *Café Stumpp*, Scudelfeldstr. 5 (Ⓣ0 80 23/6 28; ❸); *Wendelstein*, Ursprungstr. 1 (Ⓣ0 80 23/8 08 90; ❹); and *Gasthof Zur Post*, Schulstr. 3 (Ⓣ0 80 23/81 97 10; ❺), the last two of which have **restaurants**.

The Chiemsee and Chiemgau

The **Chiemgau** is a large Alpine and pre-Alpine region, stretching eastwards from the industrial town of Rosenheim, a major railway junction, all the way to the border with Austria along the River Salzach. At its western edge is the **Chiemsee**, Bavaria's largest lake, which is usually regarded as a separate region in its own right.

Prien am Chiemsee

The Chiemsee's main resort, well placed for visiting all the local beauty spots, is **PRIEN**, at the southwestern edge of the lake: it's easily accessible, as it lies on the main Munich–Salzburg rail line. In the town centre, set back 1.5km from the lake, is the Baroque **Pfarrkirche Mariä Himmelfahrt**, which has a spectacular illusionist ceiling fresco by Johann Baptist Zimmermann depicting the Christian naval victory over the Turks at the Battle of Lepanto. Though it's a pleasant enough walk down Seestrasse to the harbour district of **Stock**, it's far more fun to take the **narrow-gauge railway**, the Chiemseebahn (Easter–Sept only; €2 single, €3 return), which has been running since 1887 from its own little terminal alongside the Bahnhof, and is pulled by a steam engine at weekends and on public holidays. Stock is the hub of the watersports activities and of the **ferry** connections to the islands and the other resorts on the lake run by the Chiemseeschifffahrt (Ⓣ0 80 51/60 90, Ⓦwww.chiemseeschifffahrt.de).

The **tourist office** is in the Kurverwaltung at Alte Rathausstr. 11 (Mon–Fri 8.30am–6pm, Sat 9am–noon; Ⓣ0 80 51/6 90 50, Ⓦwww.tourismus.prien.de). **Private houses** (❶–❸) with rooms to let can be found all over town; otherwise, the main concentration of accommodation is in and around Stock. Among the **hotels** here are *Neuer am See*, Seestr. 104 (Ⓣ0 80 51/60 99 60, Ⓦwww.neuer-am-see.de; ❺); *Seehotel Feldhütter*, Seestr. 101 (Ⓣ0 80 51/6 09 90, Ⓦwww.seehotel-feldhuetter.de; ❻); *Luitpold am See*, Seestr. 110 (Ⓣ0 80 51/60 91 00; ❻); and *Reinhart*, Seestr. 117 (Ⓣ0 80 51/69 40; ❻). There are a few other hotels in the town centre, including *Bayerischer Hof*, Bernauer Str. 3 (Ⓣ0 80 51/60 30, Ⓦwww.bayerischerhof-prien.de; ❻). Just west of Stock and north of Seestrasse, at Carl-Braun-Str. 66, is the **youth hostel** (Ⓣ0 80 51/6 87 70; €14.80). Two of the lake's many **campsites** are at the extreme southern edge of Prien: *Hofbauer* (Ⓣ0 80 51/41 36, Ⓕ6 26 57) is off the main road out of town, while *Harras* (Ⓣ0 80 51/9 04 60) is by the lakeside. All the hotels listed above have **restaurants**; another good place to eat and drink is *Weissbräu-Bräustuben*, Höhenbergstr. 6.

The Chiemsee islands

Just a few minutes by boat (€5.70 return) from Prien is the Chiemsee's largest island, **Herreninsel**, site of King Ludwig II's final monument to glorious absolutism and isolation: **Schloss Herrenchiemsee** (guided tours daily: April–Sept 9am–6pm; Oct 9.40am–5pm; Nov–March 9.40am–4pm; €6.50; Ⓦwww.herren-chiemsee.de). After saving the island from deforestation, Ludwig II set about building a complete replica of Versailles. Funds ran out in 1885 with only the central section – including a faithful copy of the Hall of the Mirrors – complete. For all the money squandered, the king only ever lived there for one week. The guided tours through the state apartments are very rushed, whereas you can see the **König-Ludwig-II-Museum** (same times and ticket) at leisure. This contains a fascinating collection of Ludwig memorabilia, including portraits, photographs, his christening and coronation robes, plans for unexecuted buildings and model backdrops for Wagner's operas. The nearby **Altes Schloss** (daily: April–Oct 9am–6pm; Oct 10am–5.45pm; Nov–March 10am–4.45pm; same ticket, otherwise €2.50), originally an Augustinian monastery, was the setting for the 1948 constitutional assembly which drew up the Federal Republic's constitution, the *Grundgesetz*. It now contains an exhibition honouring this event, and also displays around eighty paintings by the Munich Secessionist Julius Exter.

The neighbouring **Fraueninsel** (€6.80 return from Prien, which allows the journey to be broken at Herreninsel, €8.70 combined ticket with Chiemseebahn) is a much smaller island, built up with holiday homes, restaurants, cafés and an ancient, still-functioning Benedictine nunnery, the **Frauenwörth** (Ⓦwww.frauenwoerth.de), which sells a variety of home-made liqueurs and biscuits. Its **Klosterkirche** preserves its original Romanesque form save for the fancy late Gothic vault and the onion dome crowning the freestanding belfry. An even rarer survival is the Carolingian gatehouse or

Torhalle (late May to early Oct daily 8am–noon & 1–6pm; free), which features an upstairs chapel with ninth-century frescoes; reproductions of the church's Romanesque ceiling paintings – now concealed above the vaulting – are also on display.

Aschau im Chiemgau

A small railway, the Chiemgaubahn, runs from Prien up towards the Chiemgau Alps. It terminates at the mountain resort of **ASCHAU**, directly below the **Kampenwand** (1669m), one of the most popular hiking areas in the whole Alpine region. From the northern end of the village, a cable car (€8.50 single, €13 return; Ⓦwww.kampenwand.de) ascends to the summit; otherwise, it's a walk of about three and a half hours. Just east of the cable car station, the immense **Schloss Hohenaschau** (guided tours May–Sept Tues–Fri at 9.30am, 10.30am & 11.30am; April & Oct Thurs only, same times; €2.50) rises above a hilltop. The interior includes a fine Baroque **Schlosskapelle** and the **Preysingsaal**, an extraordinary reception room covered in white stuccowork, with gigantic statues of the local dynasty's ancestors.

Aschau's **tourist office** is in the Kurverwaltung, Kampenwandstr. 38 (May to mid-Oct Mon–Fri 8am–6pm, Sat 9am–noon, Sun 10am–noon; mid-Oct to April Mon–Fri 8am–noon & 1.30–5pm, Sat 9am–noon; Ⓣ0 80 52/90 49 37, Ⓦwww.aschau.de). There are plenty of **private rooms** (❶–❸) and **hotels**; *Alpengasthof Brucker*, Schlossbergstr. 12 (Ⓣ0 80 52/49 87; ❸) is a particular bargain, and also has a good restaurant. *Residenz Heinz Winkler*, Kirchplatz 1 (Ⓣ0 80 52/1 79 90, Ⓦwww.residenz-heinz-winkler.de; ❾), a supremely elegant modern hotel within a historic coaching inn, is one of the top gourmet addresses in the whole of Germany.

Bad Reichenhall

At the far eastern end of the Chiemgau, just 19km from Salzburg, the old salt-producing town of **BAD REICHENHALL** lies in a majestic mountain-framed setting in the valley of the River Saalach. Its saline springs are the most concentrated in Europe, with a salt content of 24 percent. Their curative properties led to its nineteenth-century development into one of the country's classiest spas – a status it still holds – and the town is full of grand villas from this period.

The old saltworks, the **Alte Saline** (guided tours April–Oct daily 10–11.30am & 2–4pm; Nov–March Tues & Thurs 2–4pm; €3.50), is at the southern edge of the town centre. It was established in the sixteenth century, but remodelled in the 1830s by King Ludwig I according to the mock-medieval tastes then in vogue. All the equipment – including a pair of water wheels 13 metres in diameter and 15 tonnes in weight – is in good working order and can be seen in action, but production has long since moved to larger and more practical premises a few blocks away.

Just to the north the elegant Ludwigstrasse, the town's main street, is lined with exclusive shops and spa hotels. At its far end is the **Kurpark**, a carefully tended park with mountain views and the principal spa buildings, the **Kurhaus** and the **Trinkhalle**; the latter regularly hosts concerts by the forty-strong Philharmonisches Orchester (Ⓦwww.philharmonikerreichenhall.de), the largest spa orchestra in Germany. The focal point of the park is the huge wooden **Gradierwerk**, whose function is to ensure that the air is kept as fresh and healthy as possible. Still further north, beyond Karlspark, is the basilica of **St Zeno**, built in the early thirteenth century in the Lombard Romanesque style. Although remodelled down the centuries, it preserves some of its original features, including the peaceful cloisters and the magnificent, very Italianate coloured-marble entrance portal complete with crouching lions and a tympanum showing the Madonna and Child adored by the church's patron and St Rupert, the Irish monk who became the first bishop of Salzburg.

Just south of the town centre, in the district of Kirchberg on the opposite side of the Saalach, is the valley station for the cable car (€9.50 single, €15 return; Ⓦwww.predigtstuhl-bahn.de) to the **Predigtstuhl** (1613m). From the upper station, follow the signs to the Aussichtskanzel belvedere, which gives a fine northwards view. For more extensive panoramas of the region, take the hiking trail to the nearby summits of **Hochschlegel** (1688m), **Karkopf** (1738m) and **Dreisesselberg** (1680m); a round trip will last about three hours.

Immediately north of Bad Reichenhall is a small massif whose main peak is **Hochstaufen** (1771m). The direct way up is not for the faint-hearted, as it involves ascents by fixed ladders, but there's also a normal path which swings round towards the summit from the west. For gentler walks, take bus #2, 4km west to its terminus at **Thumsee**, a pretty little lake circumnavigated by a path. It has a couple of country Gaststätten, while at the roadside immediately to the east is an even smaller and equally picturesque stretch of water, the **Seerosen-Anlage**.

Practicalities

Bad Reichenhall's **Hauptbahnhof** lies west of St Zeno on the main outer axis. A second station, **Bahnhof Kirchberg**, is at the extreme southern end of town, on the opposite side of the river from the cable car. The **tourist office** is just to the south of the Hauptbahnhof, in the Kurgastzentrum at Wittelsbacherstr. 15 (Mon–Fri 8am–5/5.30pm, Sat 9am–noon; Ⓣ0 86 51/60 63 03, Ⓦwww.bad-reichenhall.de).

There are plenty of rooms in **private houses** and **guesthouses**; among the cheapest, a short walk north of St Zeno, are *Haus Rachl*, Salzburger Str. 44 (Ⓣ0 86 51/36 41; ❷); and *Landhaus Kirchholz*, Salzburger Str. 44c (Ⓣ0 86 51/55 82; ❷). The town has **hotels** to suit all tastes: *Hofwirt*, Salzburger Str. 21 (Ⓣ0 86 51/9 83 80, Ⓦwww.hofwirt.de; ❻) is a renovated sixteenth-century inn; the environmentally conscious *Hansi*, Rinckstr. 3 (Ⓣ0 86 51/9 83 10, Ⓦwww.hotel-hansi.de; ❻) occupies a town centre villa, and has a vegetarian restaurant for guests; while *Bürgerbräu*, Waaggasse 2 (Ⓣ0 86 51/60 89; ❻) is the grand Wirtshaus of the local brewery. The two leading spa hotels are *Parkhotel Luisenbad*, Ludwigstr. 33 (Ⓣ0 86 51/60 40, Ⓦwww.parkhotel.de; ❼–❾); and *Axelmannstein*, Salzburger Str. 2–6 (Ⓣ0 86 51/77 70, Ⓦwww.holiday.steigenberger.de; ❾). There's a **campsite** (Ⓣ0 86 51/21 34; closed Nov–March) at the north end of town, by the Saalach. The hotels above all have excellent **restaurants**, though the top gourmet address is *Kirchberg-Schlössl*, Thumseestr. 11. Among the many fine **cafés**, pride of place goes to *Café Reber*, Ludwigstr. 10, whose home-made chocolates, sold in the adjoining shop, are among the best known in Germany.

The Berchtesgadener Land

Almost entirely surrounded by mountains, the area south of Bad Reichenhall, the **Berchtesgadener Land**, gives the impression of being a separate little country. In fact this is exactly what it used to be: for centuries it was one of the smallest states in the Holy Roman Empire, ruled by an Augustinian prior. There's a magical atmosphere here, especially in the mornings, when mists rise from the lakes and swirl around lush valleys and rocky mountainsides. Not surprisingly the area is steeped in legends, often featuring the spiky peaks of the **Watzmann** (2713m), Germany's second highest mountain. A popular one has it that they're really the family of a tyrant king who ruled so mercilessly that God punished him and his family by turning them to stone. The entire southern half of the region has been declared the **Nationalpark Berchtesgaden**, and is thus under stricter environmental protection than any other part of the Bavarian Alps.

Berchtesgaden

The town of **BERCHTESGADEN** itself is 18km from Bad Reichenhall by rail or by either of two magnificent scenic roads, both of which are serviced by bus. At its heart is an attractive triangular square dominated by the **Schloss** (guided tours Whit to mid-Oct 10am–noon & 2–4pm, closed Sat; rest of year Mon–Fri at 11am & 2pm; €4; Ⓦwww.haus-bayern.com), which was originally the Augustinian priory. Following the Napoleonic secularization, when Berchtesgaden was incorporated into Bavaria, the complex was transformed into a sumptuous royal residence. After World War I, the deposed King Ludwig III fled here, and it remains the property of the family. Inside you can see the art treasures collected by his son, Crown Prince Ruprecht – medieval religious wood carvings, sixteenth- and seventeenth-century Italian furniture, and a fearsome collection of weaponry. Some parts of the medieval architecture still survive, notably the Romanesque cloister with its beautiful columns, and the graceful Gothic dormitory. Alongside the Schloss is the **Stiftskirche**, another Romanesque and Gothic mix, with elaborate choir stalls inside.

In the north of town, a twenty-minute walk from the centre along the valley of the Berchtesgadener Ache, is the salt mine, the **Salzbergwerk** (guided tours May to mid-Oct daily 9am–5pm; mid-Oct to April Mon–Sat 12.30–3.30pm; €12; Ⓦwww.salzbergwerk-berchtesgaden.de), which has been the region's source of wealth since 1515. Donning the traditional protective clothing, you're taken deep into the mountain astride a wooden train. Once underground, the tour passes all the machinery and processes of salt-mining in disused shafts connected by wooden shoots, which everyone descends in groups, rather like at the fairground. There follows a raft trip across an underground salt lake, a ride back up towards the surface in the miners' elevator, before a final train journey to the exit. It's all great fun, so don't be deterred by the high entrance cost and the inevitable commercial trappings of the place. Be sure to arrive early, or else be prepared to queue.

Practicalities

Berchtesgaden's **Bahnhof** and **bus station** are at the southern end of town. The regional **tourist office** for the Berchtesgadener Land is directly opposite, in the Kurdirektion at Königsseer Str. 2 (late June to mid-Oct Mon–Fri 8am–6pm, Sat 8am–5pm, Sun 9am–3pm; rest of year Mon–Fri 8am–5pm, Sat 9am–noon; Ⓣ0 86 52/96 70, Ⓦwww.berchtesgadener-land.de). An **information centre** on the Berchtesgaden National Park is in the heart of town at Franziskanerplatz 7 (Mon–Sat 9am–5pm; Ⓣ0 86 52/6 43 43, Ⓦwww.nationalpark-berchtesgaden.de).

There are plenty of remarkably good value **guesthouses**. The very friendly *Haus am Hang*, Göllsteinbichl 3 (Ⓣ0 86 52/43 59, Ⓦwww.haus-am-hang.de;

❷) has bedrooms with balconies offering grandstand views of the surrounding mountains. Other inexpensive possibilities are *Hansererhäusl*, Hansererweg 8 (Ⓣ0 86 52/25 23; ❷); *Gästehaus Alpina*, Ramsauer Str. 6 (Ⓣ0 86 52/25 17, Ⓦwww.gaestehaus-alpina-berchtesgaden.de; ❷); and *Gästehaus Achental*, Ramsauer Str. 4 (Ⓣ0 86 52/45 49; ❷). **Hotels** include *Watzmann*, Franziskanerplatz 2 (Ⓣ0 86 52/20 55; ❸); *Vier Jahreszeiten*, Maximilianstr. 20 (Ⓣ0 86 52/95 20, Ⓦwww.berchtesgaden.com/vier-jahreszeiten; ❺–❽); and *Fischer*, Königsseer Str. 51 (Ⓣ0 86 52/95 50, Ⓦwww.hotel-fischer.de; ❻–❽). All these hotels have **restaurants**, though there are plenty of other recommendable places to eat and drink. *Da Noi*, Kälbersteinstr. 4, is an Italian restaurant in a villa built for King Maximilian II. On the way to the Salzbergwerk, at Bräuhausstr. 13, the *Bräustübl* of the adjoining brewery, the Hofbräuhaus Berchtesgaden, serves hearty Bavarian fare.

The only official **youth hostel** is in the village of Strub, 2.5km west of Berchtesgaden on the road to Ramsau, at Gebirgsjägerstr. 52 (Ⓣ0 86 52/9 43 70; €12.70). There are several **campsites** in the region, the nearest to town being Allweglehen (Ⓣ0 86 52/23 96) in Untersalzberg.

The Königssee

The focal point of the Nationalpark Berchtesgaden is the **Königssee**, Germany's highest lake, which lies 5km south of town and can be reached by bus. This bends around the foot of the Watzmann, rather like a Norwegian fjord, and the surrounding rock faces rise steeply and dramatically straight from the water. The northern tip of the lake, which is outside the park, is crammed with cafés, restaurants and snack bars; to escape the crowds, follow the marked path to the *Malerwinkel* belvedere for an overall view. For a far more extensive panorama of the lake and the surrounding peaks, take the cable car (€13.50 single, €18 return; Ⓦwww.jennerbahn.de) up the **Jenner** (1874m). This summit is also a useful starting point for an extended hike in the mountains.

Ferries, run by Motorschiffahrt Königssee, Seestr. 55 (Ⓣ0 86 52/40 26, Ⓦwww.bayerische-seenschifffahrt.de), make round trips to the far end of the Königssee and back. Although rather expensive at €13.80 return, it's money well spent; the boats have been electric-powered since 1909, so the deep green waters are refreshingly clean and healthy. The boats stop at the lakeside church of **St Bartholomä**, whose appearance is familiar from its pictures in all the tourist brochures to the region. Romanesque by origin, it was remodelled in Baroque at the end of the seventeenth century by the addition of the projecting apses and onion-domed towers. Alongside is the former **Jagdschloss** of the Bavarian kings, which was converted into a restaurant almost immediately after the fall of the monarchy. There are some wonderful mountain hikes to be made from St Bartholomä; another good starting point is Salet at the far end of the Königssee, the only other place where the boats make a scheduled stop. This lies just a few minutes' walk from another, much smaller lake, the **Obersee**.

Obersalzberg

High above Berchtesgaden to the east is the scattered village of **OBERSALZBERG**, which can be reached from the town by cable car (€5 single, €7.50 return; Ⓦwww.obersalzbergbahn.de), or by a steep winding road. Hitler rented a home here which was later enlarged into the **Berghof**, a stately retreat where he could meet foreign dignitaries. With a final dramatic sweep of steps, its setting was expressly designed to awe visitors. Here, in 1938, British Prime Minister Neville Chamberlain journeyed to dissuade Hitler from attacking

Czechoslovakia, the first in a series of meetings that ended with Chamberlain returning from Munich clutching the infamous piece of paper that would ensure "peace in our time" at the expense of Czechoslovakia. "He seemed a nice old man," smirked Hitler, "so I thought I would give him my autograph." Today the remains of the Berghof are almost entirely overgrown; what was left after wartime bombing was blown up by US troops in 1952 to avoid it becoming an object of pilgrimage for future Nazi generations. The only intact part of the complex is a **hotel**, *Zum Türken*, Hintereck 2 (Ⓣ0 86 52/24 28, Ⓦwww.hotel-zum-tuerken.de; ❹–❻), which pre-dated Hitler's appropriation of the site, and was afterwards returned to its rightful owners. Underneath it is the Nazi-era **Bunker**, which is now connected up with the new **Dokumentation Obersalzberg** (April–Oct daily 9am–5pm; Nov–March Tues–Sun 10am–3pm; €2.50; Ⓦwww.obersalzberg.de), a permanent exhibition linking the history of the site with coverage of some of the key aspects of the government of the Nazis.

One of the very few legacies of the Third Reich still looked upon with a large amount of pride is the 6.5-kilometre-long **Kehlsteinstrasse**, which rises from Obersalzberg in a series of curves before making a bold ascent up the northwest side of the **Kehlstein** (1834m). The road – generally considered the most spectacular in the country – is impassable because of snow for most of the year and permanently closed to normal traffic, but regular local buses (€13 return) make the ascent from the Hintereck stop between early May and mid-October. From the bus terminus, there's a long tunnel through the mountain to a lift (included in the ticket price), which covers the final 124m to the summit. Here is the **Kehlsteinhaus** (Ⓦwww.eagles-nest.de), nowadays a restaurant, but originally Hitler's tea house, which became known as the "Eagle's Nest". The views across the Alps are stunning, and there's an enjoyable short trail round the summit which leads to very different vantage points, one offering a close-range perspective of the mighty **Hoher Göll** (2522m) to the southeast.

Another magnificent road from Obersalzberg, again served by regular buses, though also one on which you can take your own car (€5 toll), is the 21-kilometre-long **Rossfeld-Höhen-Ringstrasse**. This circular route passes through glacier country below the Hoher Göll, climbing to a height of 1604 metres, then for a time hugs the Austrian frontier, before making a return loop to Obersalzberg through the wooded Oberau valley.

Elsewhere in the Berchtesgadener Land

Two of the finest yet least demanding walks in the region are along gorges reachable from Berchtesgaden in just a few minutes by bus. The larger and more dramatic is the **Almbachklamm** (€2 admission levied throughout most of the day) 6km to the northeast, just off the road to Marktschellenberg. At the entrance to the gorge is the **Kugelmühle**, a mill for grinding marble which has been in operation since the seventeenth century.

The **Wimbachklamm** (€1 admission), a similar distance to the southwest, has the advantage of being a jumping-off point for various longer hikes in the region. It's certainly well worth continuing as far as the refreshment hut known as the *Wimbachschloss*, as the path passes through a dramatic rocky valley, where the Wimbach follows an underground course. The northern end of the Wimbachklamm is the starting point for the main **trail up the Watzmann**. After three to four hours of walking, there's the *Watzmannhaus* refuge (Ⓣ0 86 52/96 42 22, Ⓦwww.huettenwirte.com/watzmannhaus) at 1930m, where you can break the journey for the night; note that the final push to the summit requires mountaineering skills and has claimed many lives.

Some 3km west of the Wimbachklamm is the small resort of **RAMSAU**, the most popular base after Berchtesgaden for exploring the region. Continuing westwards through the enchanted forest of the **Zauberwald** brings you to the **Hintersee**, a beautiful lake commanding views towards the rugged precipices of the **Reiteralpe** and the icy blue **Hochkalter** (2608m), the most northerly glacier in the Alps.

Altötting

North of the Alpine region, and some 65km east of Munich, lies **ALTÖTTING**, a small town of spires and domes which ranks as one of the most venerable in Germany, having been a favourite residence of both the Carolingian emperors and the early Bavarian dukes. However, for the past five hundred years it has chiefly been famous as the site of one of the most visited **shrines** in the country.

An immaculately tended square lined by dignified buildings, **Kapellplatz** forms the centre of the town. Its outsized dimensions really come into play at the time of the big pilgrimages: the most important is to celebrate the Feast of the Assumption (Aug 15); Corpus Christi (variable date in May/June) is next in order of rank, but there are many others throughout the year.

The goal of the believers is the **Gnadenkapelle** (or **Heilige-Kapelle**) in the centre of the square, a tiny octagonal chapel which offers a tantalizing reminder of Altötting's distinguished early history as it dates back to Carolingian times and may once have served as the baptistry of the imperial palace. In 1489, a 3-year-old local child who had drowned in the River Inn was brought back to life when her grief-stricken mother placed her in front of the **wooden statue** of the *Black Madonna* at the high altar. News of the miracle quickly spread, and the chapel was immediately extended by the erection of a nave and covered walkway. The sculpture seems to have been working cures relentlessly ever since, to judge from the thousands of **ex–votos** – many of them outstanding examples of folk art – which now completely cover the walls. Since the seventeenth century, it has been housed in an elaborate silver shrine and is now generally to be seen draped in gorgeous robes which stand in stark contrast to the simplicity of the original carving. Opposite the altar are appropriately shaped urns containing the hearts of many of the Bavarian dukes, who thereby commended the most precious part of themselves to the special care of the Virgin.

Across from the Gnadenkapelle is the twin-towered **Stiftskirche**, a fine late Gothic church erected in the early years of the sixteenth century in order to cater for the ever-growing influx of pilgrims. Its **Schatzkammer** (May–Oct Tues–Sun 10am–noon & 2–4pm; €2) contains an excellent collection of treasury items. Particularly outstanding is the **Goldenes Rössl** (Golden Steed), a masterpiece by a Parisian goldsmith of the turn of the fifteenth century, commissioned by Isobel of Bavaria as a present for her husband, King Charles VI of France. Another exceptional piece is the **Füllkreuz**, a late sixteenth-century crucifix adorned with nineteen miniatures of the Passion painted on lapis lazuli. From the church's cloisters you can descend to the **Tilly-Gruft** (May–Oct daily 8–10am & 2–4pm; free) and peer into the coffin containing the gruesome skeleton of Field Marshal Johann Tilly, the Catholic hero of the Thirty Years' War.

As the Stiftskirche eventually proved insufficiently large for the number of people who flocked here, a monstrous neo-Baroque **Basilika**, capable of accommodating six thousand worshippers at a time, was erected just off the square at the beginning of the twentieth century. Also from this period is the **Panorama** (March–Oct daily 9am–5pm; Nov–Feb Sat & Sun 11am–2pm; €2.50; ⓦwww.panorama-altoetting.de), a few minutes' walk to the east at Gebhard-Fugel-Weg 10. Housed in a custom-built rotunda, this monumental circular painting was a co-operative venture between Gebhard Fugel, who painted the figurative passages, notably the main scene of the Crucifixion, and Josef Krieger, who was responsible for the lovingly detailed background depiction of Jerusalem. Nearby, at Kreszentiaheimstr. 18, is the **Mechanische Krippe** (Mechanical Crib; daily 9am–5pm; €1), which was made in the 1920s by woodcarvers from Oberammergau.

Practicalities

Altötting's **Bahnhof** is just south of the centre. The **tourist office** (May–Oct Mon–Fri 8am–noon & 2–5pm, Sat 9am–noon; Nov–April Mon–Thurs 8am–noon & 2–5pm, Fri 8am–noon; ⓣ0 86 71/80 68, ⓦwww.altoetting-touristinfo.de) is in the Rathaus, Kapellplatz 2a. Here you can book to stay in one of the many **private houses** (❶–❸) with rooms to let. There are also plenty of **hotels** in the heart of town, most of them very good value for what they offer. They include *Weissbräustuben*, Kapuzinerstr. 3b (ⓣ0 86 71/55 11, ⓦwww.weissbraeustuben.de; ❸); *Altöttinger Hof*, Mühldorfer Str. 1 (ⓣ0 86 71/54 22; ❹); *Zwölf Apostel*, Bruder-Konrad-Platz 3–4 (ⓣ0 86 71/9 69 60, ⓦwww.hotel-zwoelf-apostel.de; ❺); *Plankl*, Schlotthamer Str. 4 (ⓣ0 86 71/65 22 or 92 84 80, ⓦwww.hotel-plankl.de; ❺); and *Scharnagl*, Neuöttinger Str. 2 (ⓣ0 86 71/69 83; ❺). *Zur Post*, Kapellplatz 2 (ⓣ0 86 71/50 40, ⓦwww.zurpostaltoetting.de; ❻–❽), which has wonderful bathing facilities, is the best hotel in town. These hotels all have good **restaurants**. Other places to eat and drink are the taps of the two local breweries: *Altöttinger Bräustübl* is just to the north of the centre at Herrenmühlstr. 15, while *Weisses Brauhaus* is south of the Bahnhof at Graming 79; both have beer gardens.

Eastern Bavaria

Eastern Bavaria (Ostbayern), which incorporates **Lower Bavaria** (Niederbayern) and the **Upper Palatinate** (Oberpfalz), two of the three provinces into which the medieval duchy was divided, is the least well-known region of the whole state, among Germans as well as visitors. Nonetheless, it includes both the cities that preceded Munich as capital of Bavaria: **Regensburg**, the main seat of power in the tribal days of the Dark Ages and nowadays capital of the Upper Palatinate, survived World War II with little damage, and stands today as the most complete and one of the most beautiful medieval cities in Germany; and, in the region's southwestern corner is the wonderfully preserved town of **Landshut**, the capital of Lower Bavaria, which rivalled Munich in wealth and status during the fifteenth and sixteenth centuries. Downstream along the Danube from Regensburg are two other enticing old towns, **Straubing** and **Passau**. Most of the southeastern part of the region is taken up by the Bavarian Forest, part of the largest forested area in Central Europe and one that still retains much of its primeval character.

Landshut

One of Germany's most visually striking towns, **LANDSHUT** is set below wooded hills on the banks of the Isar 70km northeast of Munich. The Wittelsbachs established it as their main seat at the beginning of the thirteenth century, and it consistently outshone Munich, even when the latter became capital of the separate duchy of Upper Bavaria. When the local dukes died out in 1503 and Bavaria became a united province again, it lost its status as a capital, but nonetheless flourished as the second residence. However, it went into decline as a result of the Thirty Years' War, never to recover. As a result, its showpiece centre was subject to few later alterations and remains wonderfully evocative of its fifteenth- and sixteenth-century heydays. Nowadays, it serves as the perfect backdrop for Germany's largest **costumed festival**, the Landshut Wedding (Landshuter Hochzeit).

Arrival, information and accommodation

Landshut's **Hauptbahnhof**, a major rail junction, is 2km northwest of the centre, which can be reached by buses #1, #2, #3, #4, #6 or #8. The **tourist office** (Mon–Fri 9am–5pm, Sat 9am–noon; ⓣ08 71/92 20 50, ⓦwww.landshut.de) is at Altstadt 315. Annual **festivals** include the Fischerfest and Altstadtfest on consecutive weekends in July, while the Hofmusiktage, featuring concerts of both old and new music, takes place in late June and early July in even-numbered years. The next enactment of the Landshut Wedding (ⓦwww.landshuter-hochzeit.de) will be from June 25 to July 17, 2005. A varied year-round **cultural** programme is presented at the Stadttheater Landshut, Landtorplatz 2–5 (ⓣ08 71/9 22 08 33, ⓦwww.suedostbayerisches-staedtetheater.de).

There's a decent choice of **hotels**, most of them good value in terms of what they offer. The **youth hostel** is just south of Burg Trausnitz at Richard-Schirrmann-Weg 6 (ⓣ08 71/2 34 49; €12.70), while the **campsite** (April–Sept only; ⓣ&ⓕ08 71/5 33 66) is on the bank of the Isar at Breslauer Str. 122 in the northeastern district of Mitterwöhr.

Hotels

Bayerwald Bayerwaldstr. 43 ⓣ08 71/1 25 36. This Alpine-style guest house to the north of the Hauptbahnhof has some of the cheapest rooms in town. ❷–❹

Fürstenhof Stethaimer Str. 3 ⓣ08 71/9 25 50, ⓦwww.romantikhotels.com/landshut. Delightful hotel in a gabled Romantic-era building just north of Abtei Seligenthal. Its two restaurants, *Herzogstüberl* and *Fürstenzimmer*, are of gourmet status. ❻

Goldene Sonne Neustadt 520 ⓣ08 71/9 25 30, ⓦwww.goldenesonne.de. Family-run hotel and restaurant in a splendid historic building which was first documented as an inn in the mid-fifteenth century. ❻

Lindner Hotel Kaiserhof Papierstr. 2 ⓣ08 71/08 71/68 70, ⓦwww.lindner.de. Luxury modern hotel with restaurant, directly overlooking the Isar at the point where it splits into two arms. ❻–❽

Park-Café Papierstr. 36 ⓣ08 71/97 40 00, ⓦwww.hotel-park-cafe.de. This hotel and café (closed Sat), midway between the Hauptbahnhof and the historic centre, offers a choice of basic and well-appointed rooms. ❸–❺

Schloss Schönbrunn Schönbrunn 1 ⓣ08 71/9 52 20, ⓦwww.hotel-schoenbrunn.de. Hotel in a historicist castle at the northeastern edge of town,

2km from the centre. It also has a beer garden and restaurant (closed Tues). ⑥

Zur Insel Badstr. 16 ⓣ08 71/92 31 60, ⓕ9 23 16 36. A high-quality Gasthof near the top of the island formed by the two arms of the Isar, offering fine views towards Burg Trausnitz. Its moderately priced restaurant, which has a riverside terrace, specializes in fish dishes. ④–⑥

The Town

Many of Landshut's sights are concentrated on its main street, whose magnificence is immediately suggested by its name – **Altstadt**, the term normally used for the entire central part of a German city. Starting from the south bank of the southern arm of the Isar, it ascends in the direction of Burg Trausnitz, the old feudal fortress dominating the town, by means of a majestically sweeping curve.

Altstadt

Of an unusual width and spaciousness, Altstadt is lined with a resplendent series of colourful high-gabled mansions of widely varying design. Two very different hall churches stand at either end of the street; both were designed by **Hans von Burghausen**, one of Europe's most brilliant late Gothic architects. Overlooking the river is the **Heiliggeistkirche** (or **Spitalkirche**), which uses the same architectural methods as its earlier counterpart at the opposite end, but with each detail cleverly modified: the tower, for example, stands over the transept. Now deconsecrated, the church serves as the town's main space for temporary exhibitions, and is only open in conjunction with these. The hospital buildings it once served are across the road, but these were rebuilt in the Baroque period.

About halfway down Altstadt is the **Rathaus**, an assemblage of several burghers' mansions. Under the patronage of King Ludwig II, this was given a neo-Gothic facelift, starting with a new facade. A team of Romantic artists was then asked to decorate the main reception hall, the **Prunksaal** (Mon–Fri 2–3pm; free). They painted it with colourful scenes showing the 1475 wedding between the last Duke of Lower Bavaria and Princess Jadwiga of Poland. Such a stir was caused by this work that the people of Landshut decided they would re-enact the event – and have continued to do so every four years (see p.133).

Across from the Rathaus is the **Stadtresidenz** (guided tours April–Sept Tues–Sun 9am–6pm, Oct–March Tues–Sun 10am–4pm; €2.50; ⓦwww.schloesser.bayern.de). The front portion, the **Deutscher Bau**, was begun in 1536 as a relatively modest Renaissance palace for Ludwig X. However, later the same year the duke travelled to Italy, where he saw Giulio Romano's recently completed Palazzo Tè in Mantua, and was so impressed by this Mannerist masterpiece that he immediately decided to commission something similar for himself. The following year, a team of craftsmen who had worked on the Mantuan palace came to Landshut to construct the triple-winged **Italienischer Bau**, which was built onto the Deutscher Bau, with its own showpiece facade on Ländgasse to the rear and a magnificent arcaded inner courtyard which immediately evokes a sunny Mediterranean atmosphere. Of the showpiece apartments on the first floor, the most imposing is the **Italienischer Saal**, with its carved medallions of the Labours of Hercules and ceiling frescoes by the Salzburg artist Hans Bocksberger depicting the great personalities of the ancient world. Also of special note is the **Sternenzimmer**, whose remarkable coffered vault is covered with painted symbols of the planets and stars. Another chamber is devoted to the gods and goddesses of Classical mythology, while Apollo, Venus and Diana each have a room in their honour.

Dominating Altstadt from the far end is Landshut's proudest adornment, the church of **St Martin**. In design alone, its **tower** (guided tours May–Nov first Sun in month at 11.15am; €1) is extraordinarily ingenious, beginning as a square shape, then narrowing and changing into an octagon. With a height of 131m, it's also the tallest brick structure in the world. The walls of the main body of the church are pierced by five portals richly decorated with terracotta sculptures, while on the south side is a memorial tablet to the architect Hans von Burghausen. The vertiginous **interior**, with slender pillars sweeping up to the lofty network vault, is hardly less impressive than the tower, the spareness of effect enhanced by the relative lack of furnishings. Nonetheless there are some notable works, such as the stone high altar and pulpit, Michel Erhart's impassioned *Triumphal Cross*; and the elaborate choir stalls. Finest of all is the larger-than-life polychrome wood *Madonna and Child* in the south aisle, carved around 1520 by the local sculptor Hans Leinberger.

The rest of the lower town

A block to the south of Altstadt is **Neustadt**, which follows a roughly parallel course and offers even more dramatic views towards Burg Trausnitz. It also preserves a picturesque array of houses, many of which were rebuilt in the Baroque epoch. Closing the southern end of the street is the **Jesuitenkirche**, a towerless early seventeenth-century church by the Augsburg architect Johannes Holl. Its barrel-vaulted interior was decorated in the middle of the same century, and is one of the earliest examples of the highly distinctive south German Baroque style, featuring lavish stuccowork and an extravagant high altar showing Christ appearing to St Ignatius Loyola.

Regierungsplatz, which lies just east of the central part of Neustadt, is dominated by the former **Dominikanerkloster**, which was founded in the late thirteenth century. Its Gothic church of **St Blasius** was completely transformed in Rococo style by Johann Baptist Zimmermann, who was responsible for both the stuccowork and the illusionistic ceiling frescoes; subsequently, it was given a Neoclassical facade. Following the secularization of 1802, the conventual buildings became the seat of the University of Bavaria on its move from Ingolstadt, but this function ended in 1826, when the institution was transferred to Munich. Thirteen years later, the premises found another lease of life as the headquarters of the government of Lower Bavaria, a role retained to this day.

A huge, still-inhabited convent of Cistercian nuns, **Abtei Seligenthal**, lies ten minutes' walk north of the city centre, across both arms of the Isar. Founded a few decades before the Dominikanerkloster, it was likewise almost totally remodelled in the Rococo era, and the **Abteikirche** contains bravura frescoes and stucco by J.B. Zimmermann, including a depiction of the Coronation of the Virgin on the dome.

Burg Trausnitz

The most direct way of approaching **Burg Trausnitz** (guided tours daily: April–Sept 9am–6pm, Thurs 9am–8pm; Oct–March 10am–4pm; €2.50; Ⓦwww.burgtrausnitz.de) is via the stone stairway from Alte Bergstrasse, which runs southeastwards from Dreifaltigkeitsplatz at the end of Altstadt. A more gentle ascent can be made via the expansive **Hofgarten**, which dates back to the mid-fifteenth century and is thus one of Bavaria's oldest landscaped gardens. The fortress itself was begun in the early thirteenth century, and much of the original castle – including the **Torbau** (entrance gateway), the keep, or **Wittelsbacher Turm**, and the **Palas** – still survives. In the fifteenth century, the defences were greatly strengthened, notably by the construction of a curtain wall with towers. The following century, work began on converting the castle into a Renaissance palace; this came to a halt when Ludwig X decided to concentrate resources on the Stadtresidenz, but was revived again a generation later, reaching a climax with the construction of a new extension, the Italienische Anbau, and the remodelling of the inner courtyard into a graceful two-storey loggia.

Among the highlights of the tour of the interior is the late Romanesque **Burgkapelle St Georg**, which is visited first at ground level, then later from the Renaissance ducal oratory directly below the vault. The chapel's original polychromed decoration, which has no counterpart in Germany, survives almost intact: its main components are a stucco frieze on the balcony showing Christ and the Apostles, and a monumental Crucifixion group of carved oak suspended directly above. Among the later furnishings are three fifteenth-century winged altars. Another survivor from the original castle is the early Gothic **Alte Dürnitz**, a low hall reminiscent of monastic refectories of the period. From the first phase of Renaissance building comes the **Söller** or balcony, which commands a marvellous panoramic view over Landshut's red-tiled roofs and church steeples, with St Martin prominent in the foreground. Sadly, many of the Mannerist interiors were stripped of their decoration by a fire in 1961, but a tantalizing reminder of what they looked like is provided by the **Narrentreppe** (Buffoons' Staircase), which is decorated with vivacious portrayals of characters from the *commedia dell'arte*.

Eating and drinking

Although most of the best restaurants are in the hotels (see pp.133–34), there are several other eateries well worth seeking out.

Bernlochner Ländtorplatz 2–5. Classy, fairly pricey theatre restaurant, which presents itself as a modern version of the traditional German tavern.

Burgschenke Burg Trausnitz. The fifteenth-century cellars of the castle's Fürstenbau have been converted into a visitors' café-restaurant. Open April–Oct only.

Kochwirt Herrngasse 388. Occupying a splendid gabled house, this is the main tap of the Wittmann brewery, which makes a variety of light, dark and wheat beers. It also serves good-value meals.

Martinsklause Kirchgasse 229. Situated to the rear of St Martin, this Gaststätte with beer garden owes allegiance to the Landshuter Brauhaus, which has a similar product range to its rival.

Residenzcafé Altstadt 79. Traditional café in the Stadtresidenz.

Stegfellner Altstadt 71. This wonderful delicatessen has a self-service snack counter in the shop itself, and a cosy daytime restaurant upstairs which serves high quality meals, including moderately priced set lunches. Closed Sun.

Regensburg

"Regensburg surpasses every German city with its outstanding and vast buildings" drooled Emperor Maximilian I in 1517. The centre of **REGENSBURG** (sometimes referred to as Ratisbon in English) has changed remarkably little since then, and gives a unique insight into the size and feel of a prosperous community of the Middle Ages. Founded as the military camp Castra Regina by the Romans, the city remained of importance during the Frankish period and was capital of the earliest Bavarian duchy. Most of the surviving architecture originates from the glory days between the thirteenth and sixteenth centuries, when it was a Free Imperial City, rich from trade with Europe, the Balkans and the Orient. Although other German cities may have individual setpieces which are more spectacular, none can match the satisfyingly integrated nature of the Regensburg townscape. When this is added to the stunning location on the banks of the Danube, and to the ample provision of Gaststätten and beer gardens – the favoured haunts of the large student population – there can be no doubt that it's a place well worth a visit of several days.

Arrival, information and accommodation

Regensburg's **Hauptbahnhof** is at the southern end of the city. The **tourist office** (Mon–Fri 9.15am–6pm, Sat 9.15am–4pm, Sun 9.30am–2.30/4pm; Ⓣ09 41/5 07 44 10, Ⓦwww.regensburg.de) is in the Altes Rathaus, Rathausplatz 3.

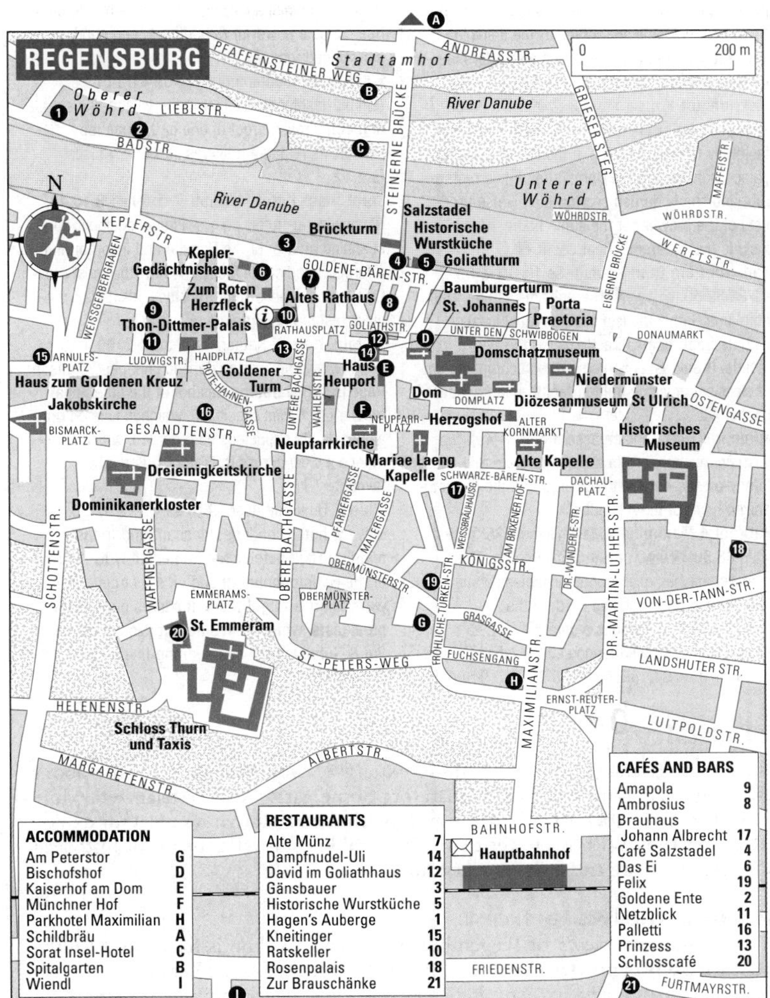

ACCOMMODATION

Am Peterstor	G
Bischofshof	D
Kaiserhof am Dom	E
Münchner Hof	F
Parkhotel Maximilian	H
Schildbräu	A
Sorat Insel-Hotel	C
Spitalgarten	B
Wiendl	I

RESTAURANTS

Alte Münz	7
Dampfnudel-Uli	14
David im Goliathhaus	12
Gänsbauer	3
Historische Wurstküche	5
Hagen's Auberge	1
Kneitinger	15
Ratskeller	10
Rosenpalais	18
Zur Brauschänke	21

CAFÉS AND BARS

Amapola	9
Ambrosius	8
Brauhaus Johann Albrecht	17
Café Salzstadel	4
Das Ei	6
Felix	19
Goldene Ente	2
Netzblick	11
Palletti	16
Prinzess	13
Schlosscafé	20

There are plenty of good choices for **accommodation**, including several atmospheric places on islands in the Danube, though most of the top hotels are in the Altstadt. The **youth hostel** is about five minutes' walk from the heart of town at Wöhrdstr. 60 (Ⓣ09 41/5 74 02; €15.80) on the island of Unterer Wöhrd, while the **campsite**, *Azur-Camping*, is about twenty minutes' walk from the centre, pleasantly situated next to the river at Weinweg 40 (Ⓣ09 41/27 00 25, Ⓦwww.azur-camping.de).

Hotels

Am Peterstor Fröhliche-Türken-Str. 12 Ⓣ09 41/5 45 45, Ⓕ5 45 42. By cutting services to a bare minimum, this hotel is able to offer modern, well-appointed bedrooms at minimal cost, though there's only a small discount for single occupancy. Optional breakfasts are served at the adjoining Italian restaurant, *L'Astice*, which also offers inexpensive set lunches and dinners. ❹

Bischofshof Krautermarkt 3 Ⓣ09 41/5 84 60, Ⓦwww.hotel-bischofshof.de. A grand hotel with tastefully furnished rooms in the former episcopal palace right beside the Dom. It has a fine restaurant and shady garden serving the diverse products of the brewery of the same name, which include five different wheat beers. ❼

Kaiserhof am Dom Kramgasse 10–12 Ⓣ09 41/58 53 50, Ⓦwww.kaiserhof-am-dom.de. This hotel in a Gothic mansion has an ideal location, with its front rooms directly facing the Dom's facade. Breakfast is served to the accompaniment of classical music in the fourteenth-century house chapel. ❻

Münchner Hof Tändlergasse 9 Ⓣ5 84 40, Ⓦwww.muenchner-hof.de. Comfortable mid-range family-owned hotel with restaurant in the pedestrianized heart of the Altstadt. ❻

Parkhotel Maximilian Maximilianstr. 28 Ⓣ09 41/5 68 50, Ⓦwww.maximilian-hotel.de. This long-established luxury hotel occupies palatial neo-Rococo premises just north of the Hauptbahnhof. It also has a café. ❽

Prösslbräu Dominikanerinnenstr. 2, Adlersberg Ⓣ09 41/0 94 04/18 22 or 8 08 36, Ⓕ0 94 04/52 33. Occupying a former convent in the north western outskirts and reached by bus #12, this is the epitome of a country Gasthof. As well as inexpensive rooms, it has a restaurant (closed Mon) with a large shady beer garden serving the products of the small adjoining brewery (light and dark beers plus a powerful *Doppelbock*) and good, sensibly priced food. ❸

Schildbräu Stadtamhof 24 Ⓣ09 41/8 57 24. A real old-fashioned Gasthof in the village-like setting of the main street of one of the Danube islands. Its restaurant serves inexpensive local fare. ❹

Sorat Insel-Hotel Müllerstr. 7 Ⓣ09 41/8 10 40, Ⓦwww.sorat-hotels.com. This new designer hotel, spanning an arm of the Danube and incorporating a former handicrafts factory, is now the most prestigious and expensive in the city. It also has a top-class restaurant, *Brandner*. ❽–❾

Spitalgarten St-Katharinen-Platz 1 Ⓣ09 41/8 47 74, Ⓦwww.spitalgarten.de. The cheapest rooms in Regensburg are at the Gasthof of the little Spital brewery (a *Helles* specialist), which is located right alongside. Its capacious beer garden, which commands a view across the Danube, is a local favourite. ❸

Wiendl Universitätsstr. 9 Ⓣ09 41/92 02 70, Ⓦwww.hotelwiendl.de. Pleasant and friendly middle-range hotel, sited immediately to the rear of the Hauptbahnhof, though it's a circuitous walk or drive to get there. It serves good buffet breakfasts, while the restaurant (closed all day Sat & Sun evening) has a strong line in fish dishes. ❺

The City

Regensburg's medieval heart is quite extensive, even though it is only about twice the size of the original Roman fort. Some parts are pedestrianized, while others are only open to public transport, with the result that it's ideal for exploration on foot. With no fewer than 1300 buildings listed as being of historical interest, there are treasures at every turn.

Around the waterfront

One of the best views of Regensburg's medieval skyline is from the twelfth-century **Steinerne Brücke** (Stone Bridge), which spans the Danube by means of fifteen (originally sixteen) arches. At the time it was built, it was the only safe and fortified crossing along the entire length of the Danube, and thus had tremendous value for the city as a major international trading centre. It's a remarkable piece of engineering for its date, and its stability (it bore the full brunt of motorized traffic until 1997, and is still used by buses) is in large part attributable to its massive pier supports. These have protected it down the centuries from damage by water and ice, albeit at the cost of creating a very fast current, as the space the river is left to pass through is a third of its natural width.

The Steinerne Brücke crosses over an island in the Danube, **Oberer Wöhrd**. Together with the other island to the east, **Unterer Wöhrd**, which stretches to the confluence with the Regen, this traditionally belonged to Regensburg, the only municipality within the original Bavarian duchy which managed to establish independence from aristocratic or episcopal control. However, the next island to the north, **Stadtamhof**, always remained under the rule of the dukes, with the exception of the **St-Katharinen-Spital** at its southern end. The village which grew up beyond did not become part of Regensburg until 1924 and even now retains a distinctive character and atmosphere of its own. It has a broad main street lined with tall nineteenth-century houses, to the east of which is the elaborate Rococo church of **St Mang**, originally part of an Augustinian collegiate foundation.

Of the Steinerne Brücke's three original watchtowers, only the **Brückturm** (April–Oct Tues–Sun 10am–5pm; €2), which guards the entrance to Regensburg's Altstadt, still survives. It was made accessible to the public a few years ago, though the views it offers are fairly restricted ones. The seven-storey building with the steeply-pitched roof which adjoins it to the east is the seventeenth-century salt depot, the **Salzstadel**. A little further along the waterfront is the **Historische Wurstküche**, which is known to be at least five hundred years old and has been run by the same family for generations. Its menu is abbreviated, essentially consisting of potato soup and Regensburger sausages. The latter, which are traditionally served with sweet mustard and sauerkraut, are regarded by many aficionados as the ultimate German Wurst – though this is not an opinion shared by the rival sausage metropolis of Nürnberg. As the watermark on the outside wall shows, the building was almost washed away in 1988.

The Dom

The Altstadt's skyline is dominated by the **Dom**, Bavaria's most magnificent Gothic building. It replaced an earlier Romanesque cathedral, of which the **Eselsturm** (Donkey Tower) on the north side is the only remaining part above ground; this takes its name from the fact that donkeys were used to carry building materials up the ramp inside. Although begun around 1250, the Dom was

The legend of the Steinerne Brücke

Legend has it that the bridge builder and the Dom's master mason laid a bet as to which of them would finish his project first. To ensure success, the former made a pact with the Devil to give him the first three souls who crossed the finished bridge. He duly completed his project in just eleven years and so won the wager. When the duke, the bishop and the leading local merchant came to lead the inspection of the newly finished bridge, the Devil turned up in the expectation of claiming them for himself, only to be foiled by the crafty builder, who shooed a dog, a cock and a hen across the bridge. Whereupon the Devil vainly tried to uproot the central arch, leaving it with a permanent hump.

still incomplete in 1525, when work was suspended as a result of the Reformation, with the city council eventually going over to the Lutheran side, while the bishopric remained Catholic. The upper parts of the twin **towers**, with their distinctively Germanic openwork spires, were belatedly erected in the mid-nineteenth century. An ambitious cleaning project, now nearing completion, has rid the exterior of its thick coat of grime, making it easy to distinguish the white limestone used by the medieval builders from the pale green sandstone of the neo-Gothic additions. The restoration has also had a revelatory effect on the small-scale **exterior sculptures**, which are iconographically highly unusual. Those on the facade include a depiction of St Peter, the Dom's patron, in his fishing boat, and representations of four of the great heathen rulers of the ancient world riding on wild beasts. Much controversy still surrounds a relief on one of the pillars on the Dom's south side, which, in a piece of calculated anti-Semitism, shows Jews suckling on a large sow.

More fine sculptures can be seen inside the Dom, the most outstanding being the expressive late thirteenth-century **Annunciation group** in the transept. Also of special note are the equestrian statues of SS Martin and George on the inner wall of the facade, and the quirky figures known as the **Devil** and the **Devil's grandmother** on either side of the main portal. The exact significance of the latter pair is disputed; they may have been placed in this position to remind the congregation that as soon as they left the safety of the church evil and temptation awaited. Other features from the medieval period are the **stained-glass windows** in the chancel; the five fifteenth-century **canopied altars**; and the sixteenth-century crucifix on the south transept wall which, according to local legend, will herald Judgment Day when its real human hair grows to knee-length. Among the few later furnishings remaining in the Dom are the **tomb** of Cardinal Philipp Wilhelm by the Munich Mannerist sculptor Hans Krumper at the western end of the nave, and the **high altar**, an elaborate Baroque creation by Augsburg silversmiths. It's well worth trying to hear a concert or sung service (generally at 9am on Sunday) featuring the **Domspatzen** (Cathedral Sparrows), the most famous Catholic choir in Germany.

The **cloisters**, which are only accessible during **guided tours** (May–Oct Mon–Sat 10am, 11am & 2pm, Sun 1pm; Nov–April Mon–Sat 11am, Sun noon; €2.50), have two interesting chapels, of which the **Allerheiligenkapelle** is a Romanesque gem, with many of the original twelfth-century frescoes surviving. Nearby, the eleventh-century **Stephanskapelle** was the bishop's private chapel, and though the frescoes have been lost, the altar is from the original building period.

The Domstadt

The dense complex of ecclesiastical buildings around the Dom is collectively known as the **Domstadt**. Much of the **Bischofshof**, the former episcopal palace, is now a hotel and restaurant (see p.138), but one of its wings, entered from the Dom's northern transept, contains the **Domschatzmuseum** (April–Oct Tues–Sat 10am–5pm, Sun noon–5pm; Dec–March Fri & Sat 10am–4pm, Sun noon–5pm; €1.50, or €2.50 joint ticket with Diözesanmuseum St Ulrich; Ⓦwww.bistumsmuseen-regensburg.de). This incorporates another chapel, the **Zwölfbotenkapelle**, which has fallen heir to a beautiful Renaissance **retable** made for the Obermünster, a convent church in the south of the Altstadt which was Regensburg's most serious loss to wartime bombs. Set in a red-and-white marble frame, its limestone reliefs were carved from designs by **Albrecht Altdorfer**, the city's greatest-ever artist.

Among the highlights of the Dom's treasury displayed in the rooms alongside and upstairs are two thirteenth-century crosses, one containing a reliquary of Saint Andrew, the other a gift to the Dom from King Ottokar II of Bohemia; the so-called chalice of Saint Wolfgang, from the same century; and a fourteenth-century reliquary chest adorned with gilded miniatures. There are also several precious textiles, notably an eleventh-century chasuble traditionally but erroneously associated with Saint Wolfgang, and the thirteenth-century antependium of Bishop Heinrich von Rotteneck.

Treasures from elsewhere in the diocese are housed in the **Diözesanmuseum St Ulrich** (April–Oct Tues–Sun 10am–5pm; €1.50; Ⓦwww.bistumsmuseen-regensburg.de) immediately to the rear of the Dom. Constructed in the Transitional style between Romanesque and Gothic, the church itself is one of the most remarkable buildings in the city, featuring an unusual interior arrangement, with galleries on all four sides. This suggests that it was originally built as a court chapel, but when Regensburg gained the status of a Free Imperial City in 1245 it became the Dom's parish church and served as such for nearly six centuries. Nowadays, it is the chapel of the Dom's chapter, notwithstanding the fact that it is fitted out as a museum. The displays begin with a number of Romanesque items, including a lion's head door knocker and a polychromed Crucified Christ, both from the Obermünster, and bishops' staffs which supposedly belonged to Saint Wolfgang and Saint Emmeram. In the Gothic section are a number of retables and the *Minnekästchen*, a beautiful painted casket used for storing documents or jewellery. Most of the gallery space is taken up by Baroque and Rococo artefacts, but pride of price is given to Altdorfer's *The Fair Virgin* altar.

A copy of the last-named can be seen in its original location, the former baptistery of **St Johannes**, at the western edge of the Domstadt. At the opposite end of the ecclesiastical complex is the **Niedermünster**, which has taken over St Ulrich's function as the Dom's parish church. Built as a collegiate foundation for noblewomen, it still preserves its Romanesque outline, including its austere twin towers, though it was remodelled internally in Baroque style.

The eastern Altstadt

On Pfauengasse, an alley leading south from Domplatz, is the tiny chapel popularly known as **Mariae-Laeng-Kapelle** after the seventeenth-century belief that the best way to get one's prayers heard was to write out prayer notes the same length (*laeng*) as the statue of Mary herself. The Church never accepted this idea, but people have come here ever since to pray to the Virgin and leave notes and gifts, examples of which can be seen the back of the chapel.

A little further east is a large square, Alter Kornmarkt, at the northwestern end of which stands the much-altered Romanesque ducal palace, the **Herzogshof**, which is nowadays a cultural centre. It is linked by a covered passageway to the so-called **Römerturm** on the other side of the road. The latter was probably a treasury tower and, despite its name, its earliest masonry is Carolingian rather than Roman. On the south side of Alter Kornmarkt stands the **Alte Kapelle**, whose sober medieval exterior hardly prepares you for the riotous fricassee of Rococo decoration inside.

Just to the southwest, on Dachauplatz the **Historisches Museum** (Tues–Sun 10am–4pm; €2.20; Ⓦwww.museen-regensburg.de) encompasses over 100 rooms spread out on four floors of the former Minorite friary, one of several well-preserved monastic complexes in the city, and charts local cultural and artistic history from the Stone Age to the present day. The medieval department features the **tapestries** which formerly adorned the Altes Rathaus, and a fine collection of Gothic retables which includes a *Passion Altar* from St Ulrich, one of the few surviving works by **Rueland Frueauf the Elder**, the founding-father of the Danube School. In the Renaissance section, the main focus is on **Albrecht Altdorfer**, who, apart from being one of Germany's greatest artists, was also a leading local politician, being involved in the decisions which saw the expulsion of the Jews and the introduction of the Reformation. The remains of the frescoes he painted for the bath house of the Bischofshof are on view, along with a panel showing *The Two St Johns*, which is set in a typically luxuriant Danube landscape. Among his etchings are two of the beautiful Romanesque-Gothic synagogue he helped destroy, which make a fascinating documentary record; these are displayed near the original wooden model (not by Altdorfer) of the huge pilgrimage church which was intended to replace it.

On the other side of the Domstadt, on the road known as Unter den Schibbögen, remains of the Roman fort are still visible at the corner of one of the houses. The **Porta Praetoria**, once the northern watchtower, was discovered during restoration work in 1887. From the end of the street, Ostengasse leads to the **Ostentor**, the only surviving gateway from the city's medieval defensive system. Overlooking the Danube in the little park to the north is the neo-Gothic **Königliche Villa**, which was built so that King Maximilian of Bavaria could have an appropriate place to stay and entertain guests on his rare visits to the city.

The merchant quarter

The streets west of the Dom were where the merchants who made Regensburg so prosperous in the Middle Ages had their homes. Unique for a German medieval town are the many **towers** built in the style of Italian fortified palaces; about twenty of these survive. Unlike their southern counterparts, however, they had no real defensive function; instead they were a statement of the competitive ethos that ruled their owners' lives: the higher the tower, the richer and more prestigious the occupier.

Directly facing the Dom is the **Haus Heuport**, a splendid patrician mansion in Venetian Gothic style, which boasts another of the city's jokey sculptures in the form of a stone relief at the left-hand corner of the courtyard staircase representing the seduction of a careless virgin. One of the most beautiful of the fortified towers with high balconies is the **Baumburgerturm** in Watmarkt, just west of here. A few paces to the east is another notable example, the **Goliathhaus**, which takes its name from the huge re-touched sixteenth-century mural of an appropriately gargantuan Goliath about to face David in combat. On Wahlenstrasse to the southwest is the **Goldener Turm**, the town's highest remaining tower.

A handsome Gothic clock tower is the dominant external feature of the **Altes Rathaus** on Kohlenmarkt. Between 1663 and 1806 it served as the home of the so-called Perpetual Imperial Diet, Germany's first permanent parliament, and in honour of this role much of the interior is now designated the **Reichstagsmuseum** (guided tours in English May–Sept Mon–Sat at 3.15pm; guided tours in German year-round Mon–Sat 9.30am–noon & 2–4pm, Sun 10am–noon; €2.80; Ⓦ www.museen-regensburg.de). Notable rooms include the **Kurfürstliches Nebenzimmer** (Electors' Ante-chamber), with its Renaissance panelling and fittings, and the **Blauer Saal** (Blue Hall), which has a glittering star-studded ceiling. Largest and most significant of all is the **Beratungszimmer der Reichsstände**, which was built as the municipal ballroom, but was later the setting for the full sessions of the Diet. The seating order was strictly defined by status: the emperor was enthroned on a dais with four steps; the Electors were placed on either side of him, two steps above the floor; the other princes sat on the benches along the walls one step lower, while the representatives of the Free Imperial Cities had to sit at the back and at floor level. Also included on the tour are the basement dungeons, which contain some gruesome instruments of torture.

Because the Altes Rathaus was allocated to the Diet, a new home was required for the municipal administration, and as a result a large Baroque building, the **Neues Rathaus**, was built on its eastern side. At the back of the Altes Rathaus is a tiny alleyway known as **Roter Herzfleck** (Red Heart Patch). It takes its name from the large Italianate mansion of **Zum Roten Herz**, which was formerly a Gasthaus, and reputedly once a brothel as well.

To the west lies the triangular-shaped **Haidplatz**. On its northern side is the **Thon-Dittmer-Palais**, whose arcaded courtyard is nowadays a regular summertime venue for plays and concerts. A little further along is the **Haus zum Goldenen Kreuz**, the town's main hotel between the sixteenth and nineteenth centuries and the site of its biggest scandal – the illicit meetings during the 1546 Diet of Emperor Charles V and a local girl named Barbara Blomberg. In the grand tradition of royal illegitimates, their son, John of Austria, became a great naval commander, winning the Battle of Lepanto against the Turks, and died Governor of the Netherlands in 1578.

To the north, at Keplerstr. 5, the **Kepler-Gedächtnishaus** (Tues–Sun 10am–noon & 2–4pm; €2.20; Ⓦwww.museen-regensburg.de) occupies the merchant residence where the great astronomer Johannes Kepler, compiler of the *Rudolphine Tables* and author of *The Mystery of the Universe*, died in 1630, during a visit to the Diet. Although forced to waste his talents dabbling in astrology in order to earn his keep from the superstitious monarchs of the day, Kepler achieved ground-breaking advances in the study of both astronomy (proving the elliptical path of planetary movements) and optics (being the first to understand how the eye works). Among the exhibits are early editions of his publications, plus globes and other scientific instruments from his time, including a stone table with a perpetual calendar. The building itself is also of note as a prosperous mercantile home preserving many of its original fittings.

The southern Altstadt

In the southern part of the Altstadt are four notable churches, each markedly different in style. Oldest is the Romanesque **St Jakob** just off Bismarckplatz; this was first settled by Irish Benedictines, but is still generally known as the Schottenkirche in honour of the Scottish community which lived there from the sixteenth century until its dissolution in 1862, and which was subsequently re-established at Fort Augustus on Loch Ness. The magnificent **north portal**, which has suffered badly from pollution and was placed under a protective glass pavilion a few years ago, features a mixture of pagan and Christian images and delicate decorative patterns. Just inside the doorway is an amusing sculpture of a monk named Rydan, who is depicted in a recumbent position with the key and the bar by which he secured the doorway every night. Other notable Romanesque carvings are the capitals of the pillars and the monumental **triumphal cross** above the beam at the entrance to the choir.

On Beraiterweg to the east stands the **Dominikanerkloster** (guided tours Easter–Oct Sat & Sun at 11am; €2.50), one of the earliest Gothic buildings in Germany. In the later stages of its construction period, its prior was Saint Albertus Magnus, who ranks among the most highly regarded scholars of medieval Europe, a man of unusually broad sympathies steeped in the works of his Jewish and Arab contemporaries. The priory church of **St Blasius** is a masterly example of the plain and pure architecture favoured by the mendicant orders: the facade portal with its statue of the patron is the sole exterior adornment. There are some notable Gothic furnishings inside, including murals, choir stalls, epitaphs and tombstones, though these are overshadowed by the majestic severity of the interior space. The guided tour also takes in the cloisters and the Albertuskapelle, which was partially remodelled in neo-Gothic style.

A few paces to the northeast, at the junction of Am Ölberg and Gesandtenstrasse, is the **Dreieinigkeitskirche** (Easter–Oct Tues–Sun noon–6pm; €1.60), a typical example of Lutheran Baroque, the only decorative note in the galleried interior being the intricate star-shaped vault. The admission ticket gives access to the treasury in the west gallery; the secluded cemetery on the north side, with its row of elaborate tombstones; and to the tower, which commands what is by far the best aerial view of Regensburg generally accessible to the public.

Further east, in the centre of the recently pedestrianized Neupfarrplatz, is the **Neupfarrkirche**. This occupies the site of the old synagogue, and was intended to be a vast pilgrimage church dedicated to the Virgin as thanksgiving for deliverance from the Jewish "peril". However, the city council's cynical attempts to foster the bogus cult met with such apathy that the project was hastily dropped. When the council decided to adopt the Reformation a few years later, the church was completed in a much reduced form to serve as the city's Protestant flagship. Notwithstanding its unfortunate history, it's a dapper little building, with an unusual hexagonal nave.

The Abtei St Emmeram and Schloss Thurn und Taxis

A Benedictine foundation from around 700, the vast complex of the **Abtei St Emmeram**, named in honour of a martyred Regensburg bishop, lies south of the original city walls. For more than six centuries it was a quasi-independent state, subject only to the Holy Roman Emperor, and not to the local bishop or the authorities of the Free Imperial City. Following the Napoleonic secularization, the main church was transferred to parish use, while the monastic buildings were eventually donated to the Thurn und Taxis family as partial compensation for the loss of the imperial postal monopoly they had held for the previous 250 years. This dual arrangement has survived to the present day.

From Emmeramsplatz, which is lined by the Neoclassical headquarters of the government of the Upper Palatinate, a mid-thirteenth-century gateway leads into a little garden, where the detached **belfry**, a Renaissance building with a distinctively Italianate appearance, can be seen to the left. Ahead is a large sunken vestibule, whose eastern doorway gives access to the church of **St Rupert**, which served the local parish prior to secularization.

The former **Abteikirche St Emmeram** is entered from the same vestibule via a **portal** adorned with outstanding Romanesque sculptures of Christ, St Emmeram and St Dionysius. Inside, the original architecture of the main body of the church is smothered by the exuberant decorative scheme created by the Asam brothers, which includes two huge **ceiling frescoes**, one illustrating St Emmeram's martyrdom, the other the glorification of St Benedict. A **pantheon** of monuments to leading figures in early Bavarian history can be found at the eastern end of the two aisles: most notable are the grief-stricken Gothic tombstone to the executed Queen Hemma and its idealized counterpart to the legendary Blessed Aurelia. The church has several **crypts**, the oldest of which dates back to the eighth century, though the only one normally accessible to the public is that below the west choir; it bears a dedication to St Wolfgang, and preserves its original Romanesque form.

Following their acquisition of the monastic buildings, the Thurn und Taxis family set about converting them into the most modern residence of the day, with hot and cold running water, flushing toilets, central heating, and most luxurious of all, electricity. The resultant **Schloss Thurn und Taxis** (guided tours April–Oct Mon–Fri at 11am, 2pm, 3pm & 4pm, Sat & Sun at 10am, 11am, 2pm, 3pm & 4pm; Nov–March Sat & Sun at 10am, 11am, 2pm & 3pm; €8; Ⓦwww.thurnundtaxis.de) is claimed as the largest aristocratic palace in Europe, surpassing all the Continent's royal residences in sheer scale. Most of it is kept firmly private, but the tour covers the main state rooms, which are still regularly used for lavish functions – whose guest lists usually feature international celebrities as well as nobility. The **Spiegelsalon**, which was transferred from one of the buildings on Emmermasplatz, and the **Grüner Salon**, which is based on designs by Leo von Klenze, are both Neoclassical in style. Other rooms are clearly modelled on those of the Rococo palaces of Bavaria; among these is the **Thronsaal**, where a beautifully crafted Parisian easy-chair of the 1730s does service as the princely throne. Hung throughout the apartments are splendid seventeenth-century Brussels **tapestries** depicting the family's illustrious history.

St Emmeram's former **cloisters** (included in the tour, otherwise €4), offer a fascinating visual record of architectural development from the Romanesque of the mid-twelfth century via the Transitional and early Gothic styles to the High Gothic of the early fourteenth century. There is a good deal of fine decorative detail to be seen, not least in the pure Gothic **portal** which now gives the family its own private access to the church. Jutting into the cloister garth is their one significant addition, the neo-Gothic **Gruftkapelle**, whose vault contains 29 sarcophagi of members of the dynasty.

In the Neoclassical Marstall or stables are two museums that can be visited at leisure. The long-established **Marstallmuseum** (April–Oct Mon–Fri 11am–5pm, Sat & Sun 10am–5pm; €4.50, or €10 joint ticket with Schloss) holds a large collection of nineteenth- and early twentieth-century travelling and ceremonial coaches and winter sleighs. Curiously, all of these were for the family's own private use, none of the vehicles from the time of the postal monopoly having been retained by them. The **Thurn und Taxis Museum** (April–Oct Mon–Fri 11am–5pm, Sat & Sun 10am–5pm; Nov–March Sat & Sun 10am–5pm; €3.50; Ⓦwww.bayerisches-nationalmuseum.de) represents a happy solution to the colossal death duties which became due when Prince Johannes, who was reckoned to be Germany's richest man, died in 1990. In lieu of a monetary payment, the family made over to the Bavarian state several hundred *objets d'art*, together with rooms in which they could be displayed to the public to the best possible advantage. The artefacts are seventeenth- to nineteenth-century in date, and are mostly quite small-scale: indeed a highlight is what is probably the world's finest collection of snuffboxes. There are also some stunning pieces of jewellery, plus dinner services, silverware, glassware, clocks, furniture and weapons.

Eating and drinking

You're spoilt for places to eat and drink in Regensburg, which has a bewildering variety of restaurants (including several of real curiosity value), bars, beer gardens and cafés, both traditional and modern. See the hotels section (p.138) for further recommendations.

Restaurants

Alte Münz Fischmarkt 7. Top-class, moderately priced traditional restaurant with a special line in delicacies of the Upper Palatinate.

Dampfnudel-Uli Watmarkt 4. Eccentric little restaurant in the former house chapel of the Baumburgerturm. It specializes in steamed dumplings with vanilla sauce, but serves a range of typically Bavarian main course dishes as well. Open Tues–Fri 10.01am–6.01pm, Sat 10.01am–3.01pm.

David im Goliathhaus Watmarkt 5. Its droll name notwithstanding, this is a serious culinary enterprise, with a wonderful location at the top of one of the city's great tower houses; it also has a roof terrace. Evenings only, closed Sun & Mon.

Gänsbauer Keplerstr. 10. Cosy and fairly pricey restaurant with a pretty inner courtyard. Evenings only.

Hagen's Auberge Badstr. 54. Upmarket restaurant commanding a fine view across the Danube to the Altstadt. Its specialities are classic Mediterranean dishes and Black Angus steaks. Evenings only, closed Sun.

Historische Wurstküche An der Steinernen Brücke. This famous sausage restaurant has become one of the essential sights of Regensburg. It has a truly *gemütlich* little dining room, though this is often closed off in summer, when tables are set up outside. Daily 8am–7pm.

Kneitinger Arnulfsplatz 3. Excellent traditional Gaststätte, dating back to the 1870s, of the eponymous local brewery, a charitable foundation which is best known for its dark beers.

Kneitinger-Keller Galgenbergstr. 18. The brewery's other main outlet is in the southern part of the city, near the university and accordingly popular with students. It also has Regensburg's largest beer garden, with some 1200 seats.

Ratskeller Rathausplatz 1. Moderately priced and typically reliable example of its kind, with a pleasant small courtyard.

Rosenpalais Minoritenweg 20. Regensburg's top gourmet address occupies an eighteenth-century palace. The upstairs restaurant is very expensive, the downstairs bistro rather less so. Both are closed Sun & Mon.

Zur Brauschänke Galgenbergstr. 3. The main Gaststätte of the princely Thurn und Taxis brewery, which makes a wide variety of beers, including a fine dark *Roggenbier*. Closed Sun.

Cafés and bars

Amapola Am Römling 1. One of a number of trendy bars in the western part of the Altstadt.

Ambrosius Brückstr. 5. A good choice for breakfast; open till 1am.

Brauhaus Johann Albrecht Schwarze-Bären-Str. 6. Hausbrauerei with a predominantly young clientele which brews both light and dark beers and serves full meals.

Café Salzstadel Weisse-Lamm-Gasse 1. Good daytime café in one of the waterfront's most prominent buildings. It also serves the products of the adjacent Historische Wurstküche.

Das Ei Keplerstr. 3. A recently revamped bar with a beer garden in a quaint medieval courtyard overgrown with vines. It serves the products of the monastic brewery of Weltenburg.

Felix Fröhliche-Türken-Str. 6. *Szene* café-bar, and another popular breakfast choice.

Goldene Ente Badstr. 32. Student Kneipe which serves a limited menu of hot dishes and has the benefit of a beer garden shaded by chestnut trees.

Netzblick Am Römling 9. Internet café-bar. Open daily 6pm–1am.

Palletti Pustet Passage, Gesandtenstr. 6. An enduring haunt of the local in-crowd.

Prinzess Rathausplatz 2. The oldest coffee house in Germany, founded in 1686, and still the best choice for hand-made chocolates (especially pralines) and cakes. These can be bought in the downstairs shop, or eaten in the café or tea salon which occupy the two floors above.

Schlosscafé Emmeramsplatz 5. Cosy little daytime café in a glass pavilion in the entrance courtyard of Schloss Thurn und Taxis. Open April–Nov only.

Schwedenkugel Lokanta Haaggasse 15. Another student favourite, with the unexpected bonus of a menu of Kurdish cuisine.

Entertainment and festivals

From Easter to late October, Regensburger Personenschiffahrt Klinger (ⓣ09 41/5 21 04 or 5 53 59, ⓦwww.schifffahrtklinger.de) runs hourly **cruises** (10am–4pm; €6.50) around the city, which include going through the rapids under the Steinerne Brücke. Throughout the same season, the company normally offers two daily trips along the Danube to Walhalla (€6.50 single, €9.50 return), plus occasional excursions to Straubing, Passau and the Altmühl valley via the Rhine–Main–Danube Canal. Tickets for all of these can be bought at the landing stage just east of the Historische Wurstküche.

Regensburg's main **theatre**, featuring a varied programme of drama, opera, musicals and concerts by the Philharmonisches Orchester der Stadt Regensburg, is the Stadttheater, Bismarckplatz 7 (Ⓣ09 41/5 07 24 24, Ⓦwww.theater-regensburg.de); there is also the marionette Figurentheater im Stadtpark, Dr-Johann-Maier-Str. 3 (Ⓣ09 41/2 83 28). The Kulturzentrum Alte Mälzerei, Galgenbergstr. 20 (Ⓣ09 41/78 88 10, Ⓦwww.alte-maelzerei.de), presents all kinds of **live music** as well as cabaret and theatre, while the main **jazz** venue is Leerer Beutel, Bertoldstr. 9 (Ⓣ09 41/56 33 75, Ⓦwww.jazz-club.com).

Two big beer **festivals**, each lasting two weeks, take place annually – the Maidult in May, and the Herbstdult at the end of August and beginning of September. Another major folklore event is the Brückenfest in July. There is also a contrasting pair of music festivals each summer: the Bach-Woche in June and the Bayerisches Jazz-Weekend in July.

The Danube country around Regensburg

Within easy reach of Regensburg are some wonderful Danube landscapes, together with several spectacular historic monuments. While all the places described in this section are readily accessible by road, the cruise ships which run in summer are a far more atmospheric way to travel.

Kelheim

At the confluence of the Altmühl and the Danube about 20km southwest of Regensburg is **KELHEIM**, a little medieval town unusual for its time in having been laid out as a planned grid. Crowning the isolated Michelsberg above is the **Befreiungshalle** (Liberation Hall; daily: mid-March to Oct 9am–6pm; Nov to mid-March 10am–4pm; €2.50; Ⓦwww.schloesser.bayern.de), one of two grandiose constructions on either side of Regensburg funded by King Ludwig I and built by Leo von Klenze. Designed in the manner of an early Christian rotunda, it commemorates the Bavarian dead in the wars against Napoleon. Its 18 sides symbolize the fact that the key victories over the French – at Leipzig in 1813 and Waterloo in 1815 – both took place on the 18th of the month, and the massive figures atop the exterior buttresses represent eighteen different German peoples who took part in the battles. Around the perimeter of the interior stand 34 Victories, one for each of the German states that existed at the time. You can also climb up to the balconies, which command wonderful views over Kelheim and the Danube and Altmühl valleys.

Kelheim does not lie on a rail line, but **buses** connect with arrivals at **Bahnhof Saal** on the Donautalbahn between Regensburg and Ingolstadt; the most convenient stop is Wöhrdplatz, which lies between the town centre and the Danube jetty. The **tourist office** (Mon–Fri 9.30am–12.30pm & 2–5pm, Sat 2–5pm; Ⓣ0 94 41/70 12 34, Ⓦwww.kelheim.de or www.altmuehltal.de) is in the Rathaus, Ludwigsplatz 14. Schneider, one of Bavaria's best-known **breweries**, decamped to Kelheim from Munich after World War II. It makes several classic wheat beers, including *Schneiderweisse Original* and *Aventinus-Starkbier*, which can be sampled in the rambling *Weisses Bräuhaus*, Emil-Ottl-Str. 3. Among the town's several **hotels**, two are attached to the other local breweries: *Gasthof Frischeisen*, which is midway between Bahnhof Saal and the town centre at Regensburger Str. 69 (Ⓣ0 94 41/5 04 90; ❸); and *Gasthof Aukoferbräu*, at the northwestern fringe of the centre at Alleestr. 27 (Ⓣ0 94 41/20 20, Ⓦwww.brauerei-aukofer.de; ❹). Other central options include *Ehrnthaller*, Donaustr. 22 (Ⓣ0 94 41/2 05 40, Ⓦwww.hotel-ehrnthaller.de; ❹); *Gasthof Weisses Lamm*, Ludwigstr. 12 (Ⓣ0 94 41/2 00 90, Ⓦwww.weisses-lamm-kelheim.de; ❹); and *Gasthof Stockhammer*, Am Oberen Zweck 2 (Ⓣ0 94 41/7 00 40, Ⓦwww.gasthof-stockhammer.com; ❺). All have recommendable **restaurants**, with the last-named's *Ratskeller* the pick of the bunch.

The Donaudurchbruch

From Easter until early October, there are between ten and twenty daily **cruises** (€3.80 single, €6.60 return) from Kelhiem's Danube jetty (Ⓣ0 94 41/58 58) through the famous **Donaudurchbruch** gorge. Here the river washes past some very attractive wooded hillsides, and then dramatically cuts through white cliffs, becoming a fast current only eighty metres wide. The Danube took an estimated four thousand years to force its way through these rocks; once past the obstacle, it widens out into a broad sweep.

Situated on a bend of the river is the goal of the excursion boats, **Kloster Weltenburg**, Bavaria's oldest monastery, founded in the early seventh century by Benedictine monks. The complex was completely rebuilt in Baroque style, and the **Klosterkirche St Georg** is an early example of the collaborative skills of the Asam brothers. Despite its small size and plain exterior, it has a truly dazzling interior whose focal point is an illusionistic **high altar** with carved figures by Egid Quirin depicting the fight between Saint George and the dragon against a painted backdrop of *The Immaculate Conception* by Cosmas Damian. The latter, who was also the church's architect, covered the nave's cupola with an allegorical fresco, *The Triumph of the Church*, and filled the large niche on the south side with a depiction of the arrival of Benedictine monks in the American continent on Columbus' *Santa Maria*. On the balustrade above, he painted a half-length vignette of himself, bewigged and holding a brush and palette. In the *Klosterschenke*, a **restaurant** with beer garden, you can sample the dark **beers** (*Barock-Dunkel* and the strong *Asam-Bock*) made in the monastery's own brewery, the oldest of its type in the world.

Walhalla

Ludwig I's **Walhalla** monument (daily: April–Sept 9am–5.45pm; Oct 9am–4.45pm; Nov–March 10–11.45am & 1–3.45pm; €2.50) stands in splendid isolation high above the Danube 11km east of Regensburg, just beyond the village of Donaustauf. Self-consciously modelled on the Parthenon in Athens, the building takes its name from the Nordic mythological resting place for warriors' souls, and contains a frieze illustrating the country's history, busts of around 130 famous Germans, and 64 plaques for older celebrities whose likenesses are unknown. The qualification adopted for being a German is a decidedly generous one, as Swiss, Austrian and even Dutch nationals are all deemed eligible; yet there are many unfathomable omissions along with others whose claim to everlasting fame now seems decidedly dubious. Busts continue to be added, normally every five to seven years, though there have been several recent additions, including St Maria Theresia and Sophie Scholl, who have boosted the miserly female tally to eleven. If the whole idea behind this project now seems slightly sinister, the view across the Danube valley is magnificent, and the surrounding park and forests are good places for picnics.

Straubing

About 30km downstream from Regensburg, **STRAUBING** is the main market town of the fertile Gäuboden region, one of the country's principal granaries. In 1353, as a result of a division of the Wittelsbach lands, it was united with the Netherlandish provinces of Holland, Zeeland, Friesland and Hainaut to form the Duchy of Straubing-Holland. Although this only survived until 1425, and although The Hague was the ducal capital, with Straubing the seat of a secondary court run by a relative of the ruling duke, it was nonetheless a true golden age for the town, and most of its finest monuments date from then. Nowadays, Straubing is best known for Bavaria's second largest **fair**, the Gäubodenvolksfest, which began in the early nineteenth century as a farmers' market but is nowadays a smaller-scale version of Munich's Oktoberfest – albeit one that attracts over a million visitors.

The Town

A peculiarity of Straubing is that its largely pedestrianized historic centre is called the **Neustadt** (new town), this being a reflection of the fact that it is not the location of the original settlement. At its heart lie two contiguous elongated market squares, Theresienplatz and Ludwigsplatz, which are lined with a mixture of medieval, Baroque, Neoclassical, Historicist and Jugendstil houses. In the middle of the former stands the early eighteenth-century **Dreifaltigkeitssäule** (Holy Trinity Column); the latter has Baroque fountains dedicated to the local patrons, Saint James and Saint Tiburtius. Separating the two squares is the town's symbol, the **Stadtturm**, a picturesque Gothic tower crowned with five steeples. Alongside is the **Rathaus**, a fourteenth-century building (originally the local trading hall) with a neo-Gothic facade.

Rising just to the north, **St Jakob** is a majestic late Gothic hall church designed by the great fifteenth-century architect Hans von Burghausen, to which a slender tower was appended in the sixteenth century. It contains an extraordinary array of works of art of various periods. In the main body of the church are the carved and painted **high altar** from Nürnberg, which features six beautifully coloured panels by Dürer's master, Michael Wolgemut, and an extravagant Rococo **pulpit**. Despite their sober and regular external appearance, the side chapels are profusely furnished and decorated. The one immediately to the left of the central apsidal chapel contains the magnificent fifteenth-century **tomb slab** of Burgomaster Ulrich Kastenmayr, which is strikingly similar in style to the famous contemporary paintings of Jan van Eyck, who for a time was the Straubing-Holland court painter in The Hague. That on the other side of the apsidal chapel preserves its dazzling original **stained glass**, while the next in line was lavishly remodelled by the Asam brothers. The fifth chapel on the north side of the nave contains a touching *Madonna and Child* by Holbein the Elder.

A couple of blocks east of here, on Fraunhoferstrasse, is the **Gäubodenmuseum** (Tues–Sun 10am–4pm; €2.50 or €3.50 combined ticket with Sammlung Rudolf Kriss), which contains one of the most important hordes of **Roman treasures** ever found on German soil. This numbers 116 different pieces, ranging from iron and bronze tools and domestic ware to ornamental statuettes and beautifully crafted armour and masks for both soldiers and horses. The decorative nature of the horse masks, in which Oriental as well as Hellenistic influence is evident, suggests they were used for parades and exhibition games rather than war. Almost equally spectacular are the

jewellery and **glassware** from a graveyard of the early Bavarian period excavated just a few years ago. The museum also has notable prehistoric displays, plus a collection of religious art ranging from Romanesque to Rococo.

A further block to the east is the **Karmelitenkirche**, another impressive design by Hans von Burghausen, albeit one given a heavy Baroque interior overlay by Wolfgang Dientzenhofer, a member of a prolific architectural dynasty active mainly in Franconia and Bohemia. It served as the pantheon of the local ducal family; appropriately enough, the most imposing tomb is that in the monks' choir to Albrecht II, who presided over the most brilliant flowering of the Straubing court. On Burggasse, the next alley to the east, is **St Ursula**, the last church the Asam brothers built and decorated together. Egid Quirin designed the building and executed the stuccowork and sculptures, including expressive statues of SS Charles Borromeo and Ignatius Loyola. Cosmas Damian, whose daughter became a member of the still-functioning Ursuline convent to which the church belongs, painted Saint Ursula's martyrdom in the vault above the organ, and filled the cupola with a fresco which combines the saint's glorification with an allegory of the continents.

Immediately to the north of here, overlooking the Danube, stands the somewhat austere fourteenth-century **Schloss**, which is guarded by formidable corner towers. Much of the complex is used as offices, but part houses an outstation of Bayerisches Nationalmuseum, the **Sammlung Rudolf Kriss** (Tues–Sun 10am–4pm; €2.50; Ⓦwww.bayerisches-nationalmuseum.de). Named in honour of its founder, this collection of seventeenth- to twentieth-century religious folk art is displayed thematically in three sections: private devotions, major church festivals, and pilgrimages and votive offerings. The entrance ticket also gives admission to the heavily restored **Rittersaal**, the only one of the historic interiors generally open to the public.

Just over 1km to the east is the somnolent **Altstadt**, the former town of Strupinga, the predecessor of Straubing. Its twin-towered parish church, **St Peter**, is a real rarity for Bavaria, a pillared Romanesque basilica untouched by Baroque or Rococo decorators. It preserves two original **portals**, whose tympana show battles between a man and a dragon and between two imaginary beasts; inside a polychrome crucifix survives from the same period.

The church stands within a walled cemetery which is unquestionably one of the most beautiful in Germany, preserving many historic tombstones, plus three Gothic chapels. A tragic story lies behind one of these, the **Agnes-Bernauer-Kapelle**. Following the extinction of the House of Straubing-Holland, Straubing passed to the Upper Bavarian duchy and became the residence of its heir, the future Albrecht III. At a tournament in Augsburg, he met and fell in love with a local barber's daughter named Agnes Bernauer; he subsequently married her in secret and took her to Straubing, where she presided over the life of the court. Scandalized by his son's union with a commoner, the reigning Duke Ernst tricked him into leaving town for a while, then had Agnes tried for witchcraft and drowned in the Danube. In expiation, he had this chapel erected in her memory, in which stands a marble epitaph with a poignant relief portrait of the deceased. Alongside is the ossuary or **Totenkapelle**, which contains a lively cycle of paintings of *The Dance of Death* by the Rococo artist Felix Hölzl.

Practicalities

Straubing's **Hauptbahnhof** lies just to the south of the Neustadt. The **tourist office** is in the Rathaus, Theresienplatz 20 (Mon–Wed & Fri 9am–5pm, Thurs

9am–6pm, Sat 9am–noon; ⓣ0 94 21/94 43 07, ⓦwww.straubing.de). There's a good range of town-centre **hotels**: *Bischofshof*, Fraunhoferstr. 16 (ⓣ0 94 21/1 29 92; ❸); *Gasthof Bayerischer Löwe*, Ludwigsplatz 24 (ⓣ0 94 21/1 05 65; ❹); *Röhrlbräu*, Theresienplatz 7 (ⓣ0 94 21/9 90 80, ⓦwww.hotel-roehrlbraeu.de; ❹); *Gäubodenhof*, Theresienplatz 8a (ⓣ0 94 21/1 22 75, ⓦwww.hotel-gaeubodenhof.de; ❹); and *Seethaler*, Theresienplatz 25 (ⓣ0 94 21/9 39 50, ⓦwww.hotel-seethaler.de; ❻). The **youth hostel** is a short walk east of the Hauptbahnhof at Friedhofstr. 12 (ⓣ0 94 21/8 04 36; €10.50), while the **campsite** (May 1 to Oct 15 only) is at the far northern edge of town at Wundermühlweg 9 (ⓣ0 94 21/8 97 94).

All of the hotels listed above have **restaurants**, of which the best is *Seethaler*. Inexpensive meals and local beers are available at the *Straubinger Weissbierhaus*, Theresienplatz 32, while *Spezerei*, Simon-Höller-Str. 8, is a daytime wholefood restaurant. The main **festivals** are the aforementioned Gäubodenvolksfest, which begins on the second Friday in August and lasts for ten days, and the Agnes-Bernauer-Festspiele, performances in the Schloss courtyard of a play about the eponymous local heroine, which are held every four years (next in July 2007).

Passau

"In all of Germany I never saw a town more beautiful" is how the marauding Napoleon Bonaparte is said to have reacted to **PASSAU**. Tucked away by the Austrian border, 90km downstream from Straubing, it's a place that the tourist brochures hail as the "Bavarian Venice". While that's a piece of hyperbole, the city does have a certain magic, and its character is very much defined by water, standing as it does at the confluence of the Danube, Inn and Ilz. For centuries, Passau was the seat of a powerful prince-bishopric, the largest in the Holy Roman Empire, and it was probably for this court that the national epic, the *Nibelungenlied* (see p.437), was written at the turn of the thirteenth century. Nowadays, it's a bustling town given a youthful edge by a university founded in 1978.

Arrival, information and accommodation

Passau's **Hauptbahnhof** is immediately west of the Altstadt. Outside, at Bahnhofstr. 36, is one of the **tourist offices** (Easter to mid-Oct Mon–Fri 9am–5pm, Sat & Sun 9am–1pm; rest of year Mon–Thurs 9am–5pm, Fri 9am–4pm; ⓣ08 51/95 59 80, ⓦwww.passau.de); the other is at Rathausplatz 3 (Easter to mid-Oct Mon–Fri 8.30am–6pm, Sat & Sun 9.30am–3pm; rest of year Mon–Thurs 8.30am–5pm, Fri 8.30am–4pm; ⓣ08 51/95 59 80).

Passau has a good choice of **hotels** in all categories. The **youth hostel** (ⓣ08 51/49 37 80; €14.80) is within the Veste Oberhaus, while there's a **campsite**, *Zeltplatz Ilzstadt*, next to the River Ilz at Halserstr. 34 (ⓣ08 51/4 14 57).

Hotels and pensions

Altstadthotel Bräugasse 23–29 ⓣ33 70, ⓦwww.altstadt-hotel.de. Hotel with a marvellous location at Dreiflusseck; less expensive rooms are available in its guesthouse, *Zum Laubenwirt*, while its restaurant, *Donaustuben*, specializes in creative regional cooking. ❺–❽

Passauer Wolf Rindermarkt 6 ⓣ08 51/93 15 10, ⓦwww.passauerwolf.de. Elegant hotel in the central part of the Altstadt. Its restaurant (closed Sat lunchtime & Sun) is among the very best in Passau. ❻–❽

Rosencafé Donaustr. 23 ⓣ08 51/4 28 11, ⓦwww.rosencafe.com. Very good value Gasthof on the north bank of the Danube, at the extreme eastern edge of the city. It can be reached from the centre by bus #1 or #3, though the walk is very pleasant. ❸

Rössner Bräugasse 19 ⓣ08 51/93 13 50, ⓦwww.pension-roessner.de. An immaculately maintained pension in a restored mansion in the eastern part of the Altstadt. All rooms have private facilities. ❸

Rotel Inn Donaulände ⓣ08 51/9 51 60, ⓦwww.rotel.de. Directly overlooking the Danube, just a stone's throw from the Hauptbahnhof, this building in the shape of a sleeping man is a patented hotel idea based on the sort of transportable accommodation used on long-haul safaris. The "rooms" are cabins measuring just 4m by 1.5m. May–Sept only. ❷

Weisser Hase Ludwigstr. 23 ⓣ08 51/9 21 10, ⓦwww.weisser-hase.de. Historic hotel and restaurant (evenings only) in the very heart of the Altstadt, completely refurbished to a very high standard a few years back. ❼

Wienerwald Grosse Klingergasse 17 ⓣ08 51/3 30 69, ⓕ3 30 60. Attached to the eponymous chain restaurant, this hotel offers good value at the price asked, particularly in view of its convenient Altstadt setting. ❸

Wilder Mann Am Rathausplatz ⓣ08 51/3 50 71, ⓦwww.wilder-mann.com. Passau's best-known hotel, occupying a former patrician mansion. Its accommodation ranges from relatively simple rooms to exquisitely furnished suites named after two former guests, King Ludwig II and Empress Susi. The latter also gives her name to the evenings-only gourmet restaurant, which draws on the world's largest collection of German-language cookery books for inspiration. The rooftop café-restaurant is open throughout the day. ❻–❽

The City

Passau's Altstadt is crammed along the peninsula between the Danube and Inn. Even in medieval times, the city spilled across the rivers to form suburbs on each bank, the most important being Oberhaus, north of the Danube and west of the Ilz, and the Innstadt south of the Inn.

Virtually the whole of the **Altstadt** burnt down in the seventeenth century, so the architectural picture features predominantly Baroque, Rococo and Neoclassical facades, which give the town a pleasingly elegant feel in spite of the tight squeeze of buildings. The enormous **Dom** is suitably enthroned at the highest point. Nearly all the original Gothic structure was destroyed by fire, to be replaced by a Baroque building designed by the Italian architect Carlo Lurago. His fellow-countrymen, the stuccoist Giovanni Battista Carlone and the fresco painter Carpoforo Tencalla, were entrusted with the interior decoration, which is sumptuous in the extreme. The side altars were entrusted to other artists; of special note are the four by Austria's leading Baroque painter, Johann Michael Rottmayr, in the end chapels at either side of the nave. However, the most notable furnishing is the world's largest church **organ**, which has no fewer than 17,300 pipes and 231 separate registers. Recitals are given every weekday from May to October at noon (€3); longer ones on Thursdays at 7.30pm (€5).

Residenzplatz, which is lined by the mansions of wealthy burgher families, is one of the very few open spaces in the tightly packed centre, and offers a fine view of the Dom's resplendent east end, the only significant section remaining from the Gothic period. It's named after the **Neue Residenz**, the Baroque town palace of the prince-bishops. Part of this houses the valuable treasures of the **Domschatz-und-Diözesanmuseum** (Easter–Oct Mon–Sat 10am–4pm; €1.50); the ticket also gives admission to the **Bibliotheksaal**, which is festooned with trompe l'oeil frescoes, and the magnificent main staircase.

Down towards the Danube is the **Rathaus**, a Gothic building with neo-Gothic accretions, notably the tall tower, where you can see the marks from the alarmingly high floods that have plagued the town. The main reception room, the **Rathaussaal** (Easter–Oct daily 10am–4pm; €3), is lined with heroic nineteenth-century paintings illustrating key events in Passau's history.

Directly opposite, the **Glasmuseum** (daily March–Oct 10am–4pm; Nov–Feb 1–4pm; €4; Ⓦwww.glasmuseum.de) in the Hotel Wilder Mann has a huge collection of glass – 30,000 exhibits in 35 rooms – ranging in style from Baroque to modern via Neoclassical, Empire, Biedermeier, Jugendstil and Art Deco. Products from the nearby glass-blowers' huts in the Bavarian and Bohemian forests feature prominently.

To the east, alleys and streets intertwine in picturesque disorder, offering a tantalizing reminder of how the medieval town must have looked. A restored patrician mansion at Bräugasse 17 contains the **Museum Moderner Kunst** (Tues–Sun 10am–6pm; €5; Ⓦwww.mmk-passau.de), which has no permanent collection, staging instead highly ambitious temporary exhibitions, often of big names in the international art world. The tip of the peninsula is known as the **Dreiflusseck** (Three Rivers Corner), being the point where the Ilz, Danube and Inn all come together. Since the days of antiquity, the great combined river which flows east from here through three European capitals to the Black Sea has been known as the Danube. However, as can be seen clearly from this vantage point, the Inn is actually the major river: it is deeper, broader and faster-flowing, and has also travelled further to reach the place of convergence.

On the peninsula on the opposite side of the Danube is the **Veste Niederhaus**, a formidable-looking medieval fortress – nowadays in private hands and inaccessible to the public – which formed the outermost part of the defensive system of the castle of the prince-bishops, the **Veste Oberhaus**, high on the hill above. The steep walk up to the latter by the path along the southern side of the ramparts is enjoyable in its own right; alternatively, take one of the buses from Rathausplatz, which run every thirty minutes from 11.30am to 5pm between Easter and October. Much of the complex is given over to the **Oberhausmuseum** (Mon–Fri 9am–5pm, Sat & Sun 10am–6pm; €4; Ⓦwww.oberhausmuseum.de), which contains displays on local and regional history, with informative sections on the medieval salt trade and on local sculptors and painters, the latter including Altdorfer's most talented follower, Wolf Huber. The museum circuit includes access to a section of the medieval fortifications, from where there's a wonderful picture-postcard view over the city and the confluence of the three rivers.

Itself a fine vantage point, the Innbrücke links the Altstadt with the **Innstadt** on the opposite side of the Inn. This suburb is dominated by the **Wallfahrtskirche Mariahilf**, a pretty twin-towered Baroque pilgrimage church approached via an extraordinary covered stairway with 321 steps. From the terrace, there's yet another wonderful panoramic view. A short walk west of the Innbrücke, at Ledergasse 43, is the **Römermuseum Kastell Boiotro** (March–Nov Tues–Sun 10am–noon & 1/2–4pm; €2). Outdoors, you can see the excavations of the eponymous Roman fort; the medieval house in the grounds contains archeological finds from the Passau region.

Eating and drinking

There's a wide range of enticing places to eat and drink in Passau, quite apart from the many fine hotel restaurants listed on pp.151–52.

Bayerischer Löwe Dr-Hans-Kupfinger-Str. 3. A traditional Gaststätte with a spacious beer garden, serving the products of the Innstadt brewery.
Bräustüberl Hacklberg Bräuhausplatz 7. A highly atmospheric beer hall, complete with Passau's biggest beer garden. It's located alongside its brewery, a handsome Baroque building on the north side of the Danube (cross by the western of the two bridges, the Schanzlbrücke) which produces around a dozen different beers. Highly innovative meals are also served.
Bräustüberl Löwenbrauerei Kleiner Exerzierplatz

17. The beer hall of Passau's Löwenbrauerei (no relation of its Munich namesake), which is located on the hill directly above and brews light, dark and wheat beers.

Café Simon Rindermarkt 10. Fine traditional café, well-known for its homemade pralines, particularly the gold-leaf *Alt Passauer Goldhauben*. There's another branch in the Donaupassage, the shopping mall opposite the Hauptbahnhof.

Goldenes Schiff Unterer Sand 8. A good old-fashioned Gaststätte, popular with students and seasoned drinkers alike. The food is tasty and cheap; the beers come from the Peschl brewery.

Heilig-Geist-Stift-Schenke Heiliggeistgasse 4. Wonderful Weinstube in a fourteenth-century hospital building, serving wines from its own vineyard and some of the best meals in Passau, including fish dishes and Austrian pastries. In addition to the main dining rooms, it has intimate candlelit cellars and a peaceful rear garden. Closed Wed.

Peschl-Terrasse Rossstränke 4. Right alongside the original Peschl brewery is its own terrace restaurant, commanding a fine view over the Danube. Closed Mon.

Ratskeller Rathausplatz 2. As well as the usual fare, this has an extensive fish menu, and a wide range of wines. In summer it spills out onto the square outside, which offers a wonderful view up to the Veste Oberhaus.

Cruises, festivals and entertainment

An excellent way to get an overall impression of the city is to take the Dreiflüsse-Rundfahrt **cruise** (€6.50 for 45 min, €9.50 for 2hr) offered by Wurm & Köck, Höllgasse 26 (Ⓣ08 51/92 92 92, Ⓦwww.wurm-koeck.de). From March to early November there are daily sailings from the quay at Rathausplatz, with departures every 30 minutes at the height of the season. Between May and mid-October, the same company also runs cruises (€21 single, €24 return) to Linz, the capital of Upper Austria, daily except Wednesdays.

The Maidult is a large and colourful market and beer **festival**, while during the Europäische Wochen in June, July and August, **concerts** are played by internationally renowned orchestras and musicians, and there's also ballet and opera. Passau's star **venue**, worth checking on throughout the year, is the eighteenth-century Fürstbischöfliches Opernhaus, Gottfried-Schäffer-Str. 2–4 (Ⓣ08 51/9 29 19 13, Ⓦwww.suedostbayerisches-staedtetheater.de). Scharfrichterhaus, Milchgasse 2 (Ⓣ08 51/3 59 00), has live music and cabaret, plus a cinema and a relaxed bar.

Franconia

Franconia (Franken) makes up the northern portion of Bavaria, bordering on Thuringia, Hesse and Baden-Württemberg. About half of it is covered by highland forest ranges, which span the entire width of the province, but the chief attractions are urban. **Nürnberg**, Bavaria's second city, is a particularly evocative place, with its heady reminders of the very best and the very worst of German culture. Within easy reach is the courtly town of **Ansbach**, while to the north lie Wagner's **Bayreuth**, **Coburg**, the town from which the British royal family originally descended, and the artistic treasure chest of **Bamberg**. Further west are the old episcopal residential cities of **Aschaffenburg** and **Würzburg**. The latter is the starting point of Germany's most popular tourist route, the **Romantic Road**, whose highlights include the magnificently well-preserved medieval towns of **Rothenburg ob der Tauber** and **Dinkelsbühl**.

Franconia takes its name from the Frankish tribes of whose territory it formed a major part. In the tenth century it was made into a duchy which stretched all the way to the Rhine, but this was later split into two and the name retained only for the eastern half. Although the prince-bishops of Würzburg styled themselves dukes of Franconia, they ruled only a small part of its traditional territory: the ambitious Hohenzollern dynasty established two principalities on Franconian soil, while several of the towns, most significantly Nürnberg, became city-states. **Political fragmentation** later spawned a religious split within the old province, as the Hohenzollerns and the Free Imperial Cities became enthusiastic supporters of the Reformation, while the prince-bishoprics remained loyal to Catholicism. This division was in turn reflected in architecture, with the plain lines and sombre colours of Lutheran Baroque standing in potent contrast to the sumptuousness favoured in the Catholic lands. In 1803, the centuries of division came to an end when most of what was historically regarded as Franconia was absorbed into the new Bavarian kingdom. It was subsequently divided into three administrative provinces, which still exist today: Middle Franconia (Mittelfranken), Upper Franconia (Oberfranken) and Lower Franconia (Unterfranken).

Even after two centuries as part of Bavaria, the people still cling to their **regional heritage** and often only grudgingly see themselves as Bavarian. Certainly their dress, food and dialect are quite different. No one wears *Lederhosen* here and Nürnberg is one of a very few cities in this conservative state with a strong Social Democratic pedigree. Old divisions within Franconia linger on, not least in drinking habits, with the central and western areas staunch beer zones, while the district around Würzburg is very much a wine area.

Nürnberg (Nuremberg)

Nothing more magnificent or splendid is to be found in the whole of Europe. When one perceives this glorious city from afar, its splendour is truly dazzling. When one enters it, one's original impression is confirmed by the beauty of the streets and the comeliness of the houses. The burghers' dwellings seem to have been built for princes. In truth, the kings of Scotland would be glad to be housed so luxuriously as the ordinary citizen of Nürnberg.

This mid-fifteenth-century eulogy, written by the future Pope Pius II, shows the esteem in which medieval **NÜRNBERG** was held. As the favourite royal residence and seat of the first Diet called by each new emperor, the city then functioned as the unofficial capital of Germany. It was a status which had been achieved with remarkable speed, as Nürnberg was only founded in the eleventh century; thereafter, its position at the intersection of the north–south and east–west trading routes led to economic prosperity, and, as a corollary, political power. The arts flourished, too, though the most brilliant period was not to come until the late fifteenth and early sixteenth centuries, when the roll-call of citizens was led by **Albrecht Dürer**, Germany's most complete personification of Renaissance Man.

Like other wealthy European cities, Nürnberg went into gradual decline once the maritime trading routes to the Americas and Far East had been estab-

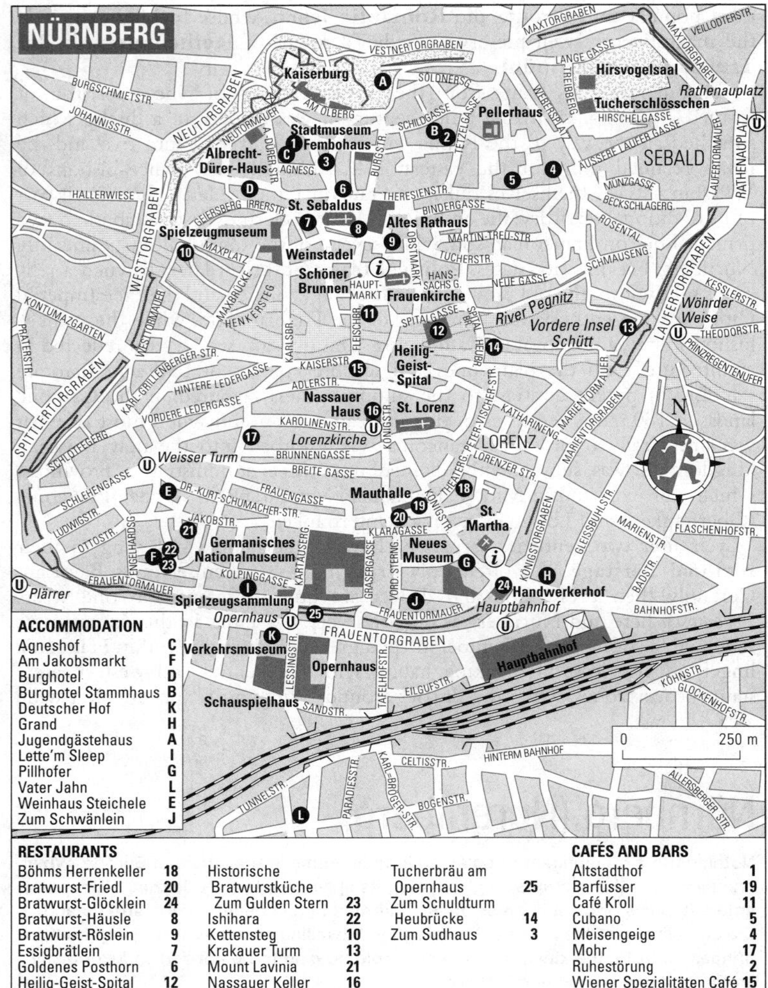

lished; moreover, the official civic adoption of the Reformation cost the city the patronage of the Catholic emperors. It made a comeback in the nineteenth century, when it became the focus for the **Pan-German movement**, and the Germanisches Nationalmuseum – the most important and extensive collection of the country's arts and crafts – was founded at this time. This symbolic status was given a horrifying twist during the Third Reich; even today the city's image is marred by its association with the regime, a tangible reminder of which survives in the weather-beaten **Nazi architecture** of suburban Luitpoldhain, site of the mass rallies.

There's so much to see in Nürnberg that two or three days are probably the minimum necessary to get to know the place. It's especially enticing in the summer, when the Altstadt is alive with street theatre and music, and there are open-air pop concerts in the parks and stadiums; but there's always a wide and varied range of nightlife. In winter, the renowned month-long **Christkindlesmarkt** (Christmas market) is held in the city's main square.

Arrival and accommodation

Arriving at the **Hauptbahnhof**, you're just outside the medieval fortifications which still enclose the Altstadt. One of the **tourist offices** (Mon–Sat 9am–7pm; during Christkindlesmarkt also Sun 10am–4pm; ⓣ09 11/2 33 61 31, ⓦwww.tourismus.nuernberg.de) is diagonally opposite, in the Kulturzentrum K4, Königstr. 93; another branch (May–Sept Mon–Sat 9am–6pm, Sun 10am–4pm; Oct–April Mon–Sat 9am–6pm; during Christkindlesmarkt Mon–Sat 9am–7pm, Sun 10am–7pm; ⓣ09 11/2 33 61 35) is at Hauptmarkt 18 in the Altstadt. The **public transport** network (ⓦwww.vgn.de) is serviced by the U-Bahn (this is the smallest conurbation in Europe with a genuine tube train network), trams and buses, and the same tickets are valid on all three. A **day-ticket** costs €3.60 for individuals, €5.80 for up to two adults and four children. For €18, the **Nürnberg Card** covers two days' travel plus entrance to most of the museums and sights. The **airport** (ⓣ09 11/9 37 00, ⓦwww.airport-nuernberg.de) in the far north of the city is the terminus of U-Bahn #2.

Hotels and pensions

There are plenty of mid-range hotels within the Altstadt and this is also where you'll find Nürnberg's many excellent upmarket addresses. The majority of budget establishments are situated in the immediate vicinity of the Hauptbahnhof. Bookings for all the city's hotels can be made a minimum of three days in advance via the tourist office website.

Agneshof Agnesgasse 10 ⓣ09 11/21 44 40, ⓦwww.agneshof-nuernberg.de. Named in honour of one-time nearby resident Agnes Dürer (wife of Albrecht), this fine hotel boasts a sauna, solarium, whirlpool and garden terrace. ❼–❾

Am Jakobsmarkt Schottengasse 5 ⓣ09 11/2 00 70, ⓦwww.hotel-am-jakobsmarkt.de. Good mid-range hotel at the southwestern edge of the Altstadt. ❻

Burghotel Lammsgasse 3 ⓣ09 11/20 44 14, ⓦwww.altstadthotels-nuernberg.de. Pleasant hotel situated just below the Kaiserburg, offering a swimming pool, sauna and solarium. ❻–❾

Burghotel Stammhaus Schildgasse 14–16 ⓣ09 11/20 30 40, ⓦwww.burghotel-stamm.de. Another good medium-range hotel in the upper part of the Altstadt, and again with bathing facilities. ❺

Deutscher Hof Frauentorgraben 29 ⓣ09 11/2 49 40, ⓕ22 76 34. Although outside the Altstadt, this has a handy enough location alongside the Opernhaus. It has a high-calibre, rustically decorated restaurant, *Weinstube Bocksbeutelkeller* (evenings only). ❺–❼

Grand Bahnhofstr. 1–3 ⓣ09 11/2 32 20, ⓦwww.grand-hotel.de. Nürnberg's leading hotel, now part of the Meridien chain, is a large and stylish Art Deco building directly opposite the Hauptbahnhof. It also has one of the city's leading restaurants, *Brasserie*. ❾

Pillhofer Königstr. 78 ⓣ09 11/22 63 22, ⓕ2 14 56 20. Reasonably priced Gasthof at the southern end of one of the main pedestrian streets, with a restaurant offering Franconian specialties. ❸–❻

Vater Jahn Jahnstr. 13 ⓣ09 11/44 45 07, ⓕ4 31 52 36. Well-maintained, very good-value pension situated just west and to the rear of the Hauptbahnhof. ❷–❺

Weinhaus Steichele Knorrstr. 2–8 ⓣ09 11/20 22 80, ⓕ22 19 14. A member of the Flair group, this is probably Nürnberg's most atmospheric hotel, occupying an old wine house. Its restaurant (closed Sun) serves good and fairly priced meals. ❻

Zum Schwänlein Hintere Sterngasse 11 ⓣ09 11/22 51 62, ⓕ2 41 90 08. In many ways this is the epitome of a traditional German Gasthof, though most of the staff are Czechs. The restaurant serves Bohemian and Franconian specialities, and has a pleasantly secluded beer garden nestling under the city wall. ❸

Campsite and hostels

Campingplatz am Stadion Hans-Kalb-Str. 56 ⓣ 09 11/81 11 22, ⓕ81 27 68. The campsite is beside the football stadium; take the U-Bahn #1 to Messezentrum. May–Sept only.
Jugendgästehaus Burg 2 ⓣ09 11/2 30 93 60. A top-class youth hostel located in the former stables of the Kaiserburg, the castle overlooking the Altstadt. It's a 20min walk from the Hauptbahnhof. €17.70.
Jugendhotel Rathsbergstr. 300 ⓣ09 11/5 21 60 92, ⓕ5 21 69 54. A privately owned hostel without age restrictions, situated to the north of the city. The journey from the Hauptbahnhof by U-Bahn #2 to Herrenhütte and then bus #21 to Felsenkeller takes 20min. Dorm beds from €18.50, singles from €26, doubles from €41.
Lette'm Sleep Frauentormauer 42 ⓣ09 11/9 92 81 28, ⓕ9 92 81 30. New independent backpackers' hostel with an excellent location by the Stadtbefestigung. Doubles €44–52.

The city centre

On January 2, 1945 a storm of bombs reduced ninety percent of Nürnberg's city centre to ash and rubble. Yet walking through the **Altstadt** today, you'd never guess this had ever happened, so loving and effective was the postwar rebuilding. Covering about four square kilometres, the reconstructed medieval core is neatly spliced by the River Pegnitz and surrounded by the **Stadtbefestigung**, which is guarded by eighty towers and pierced by four massive gateways. To walk from one end to the other takes about twenty minutes, but much of the centre, especially the area around the castle (known as the **Burgviertel**), is on a steep hill, and speedy walking is impractical, even although most of the area is pedestrianized. There's a refreshing (and deliberate) mix of old and new, with plenty of significant examples of modern architecture and open spaces amid the predominantly medieval cityscape.

The Kaiserburg

On one of the highest points of the city, and offering the best views, the **Kaiserburg** (guided tours of the interiors daily: April–Sept 9am–6pm; Oct–March 10am–4pm; €5; ⓦwww.schloesser.bayern.de) sits chunkily above all else. Scene of many imperial meetings from the eleventh to the sixteenth century, this castle was the "treasure chest of the German Empire", and, despite innumerable modifications and war damage down the centuries, it remains a key feature of the city's silhouette.

The earliest surviving part of the castle is the **Fünfeckturm** (Pentagonal Tower) on the eastern side, which dates back to the eleventh-century Salian epoch. A century later, Frederick Barbarossa decided to extend the castle to the west, using the Salian buildings as the first line of defence. From this period there remain several examples of the smooth ashlar structures characteristic of the Hohenstaufens. The **Sinwellturm** (Round Tower), built directly on the rock, can be ascended for the best of all the views. Another survivor is the two-storey **Kaiserkapelle**, a chapel whose high and airy upper level was reserved for the use of the emperor, with the courtiers confined to the squat and heavy lower tier. In a most unusual architectural arrangement, the bizarrely named **Heidenturm** (Heathens' Tower) was built over its chancel. At the extreme east end is the fourteenth-century **Luginslandturm**, which was erected by the city council to protect Nürnberg from the ambitious Hohenzollern family, who had acquired the old Salian part of the fortress and aimed to take control over local affairs. After a long war of attrition, the city emerged victorious, but most of the original castle was destroyed in the process.

Apart from the east wall, the Hohenstaufen residential quarters were demolished in the mid-fifteenth century and replaced by the late Gothic **Palais**, which retains its suite of halls. These now look rather plain and soulless, redeemed only by two eye-catching painted wooden ceilings, which were added the following century. In the western tract, the Germanisches Nationalmuseum has recently established an outstation, the **Kaiserburg-Museum**, which is visited independently; it contains models of the castle and a notable collection of historic weapons. At the end of the fifteenth century, the local authorities joined their Luginslandturm to the formerly hostile Fünfeckturm by building the vast **Kaiserstallung**, which today makes the perfect setting for a youth hostel (see p.158). During the sixteenth century the covered **Tiefer Brunnen** (Deep Well) was built and the defences strengthened by the erection of huge bastions on the north side.

The northwestern quarter

The area around the **Tiergärtner Tor** next to the Kaiserburg is one of the most attractive parts of the Altstadt, and the open space inside the city gate is the main meeting point for summertime street vendors, artists and musicians. On warm evenings the surrounding pubs spill out on to the cobblestoned piazza and the half-timbered houses form a picturesque backdrop for relaxed summer drinking.

A few minutes' walk away along Johannisstrasse lies the **Johannisfriedhof** (daily April–Sept 7am–7pm; Oct–March 8am–5pm). This medieval cemetery, set outside the confines of the old city, is one of the country's most fascinating graveyards. The tombstones lie lengthwise above the graves, like so many coffins lined side by side, each simply decorated with a bowl of red-flowering plants. Look carefully on the "lids" – some show little scenes from the deceased person's life or trade chiselled into the stone.

Among the worthies buried in the graveyard is Albrecht Dürer. The **Albrecht-Dürer-Haus** (March–Oct Tues, Wed & Fri–Sun 10am–5pm, Thurs 10am–8pm; Nov–Feb Tues–Fri 1–5pm, Sat & Sun 10am–5pm; €4; Ⓦwww.museen.nuernberg.de), where the versatile painter, engraver, scientist, writer, traveller and politician lived from 1509 to 1528, is virtually next door to the Tiergärtner Tor at Albrecht-Dürer-Str. 39. It's one of the very few original medieval houses still standing in the city, though there are many skilful reconstructions in the streets round about. Much of the furniture and decor dates back to the fifteenth century, giving a real sense of how people lived in the late Middle Ages. There's a fully-functioning workshop from Dürer's time, where printing and other artistic techniques are demonstrated. A selection of the master's own graphic work is on display in the gallery beneath the eaves.

Southeast from here runs Bergstrasse, where at no. 19 you'll find the **Altstadthof**, a late sixteenth-century courtyard. Here you can visit the **Felsengänge** (guided tours daily at 11am, 1pm, 3pm & 5pm; €4), a series of sandstone storage cellars four floors deep which were used as shelters in World War II. There's also a museum-piece brewery, the **Altstadthof-Hausbrauerei**, which makes organic light, dark, white and "red" beers. These can be bought in bottles at the end of the tour, or sampled on draught in the adjoining bar (see p.168). At no. 52 on Obere Schmiedgasse, the next street to the north, is the entrance to another subterranean attraction, the **Historischer Kunstbunker** (guided tours April–Oct daily at 3pm; Jan–March Tues, Sat & Sun at 3pm; €4). The 24-metre-deep rock cellars below the Kaiserburg were where the city's great art treasures were stored in moisture-proof cells during the war, thus saving them from the devastating effect the air raids had on the buildings where they were normally housed.

Proceeding southwards past the Weinmarkt, you come to the **Spielzeugmuseum** (Toy Museum; Tues & Thurs–Sun 10am–5pm, Wed

10am–9pm; €4, Ⓦwww.museen.nuernberg.de) at Karlstr. 15. This celebrates Nürnberg's continuing role as the European metropolis of toy production by means of a thorough historical presentation of the craft. It's a must for kids – but is just as enjoyable for adults, who can enjoy a sentimental wallow in nostalgia. Further south, the huge half-timbered **Weinstadel**, a medieval wine depot, overlooks a particularly picturesque stretch of the Pegnitz, lined with weeping willows and spanned by the covered wooden walkway known as **Henkersteg** (Hangman's Bridge).

St Sebaldus

Nürnberg's oldest and most important church, the twin-towered **St Sebaldus**, lies just to the east of the Spielzeugmuseum via the quaint Weissgerbergasse. It was erected in the thirteenth century in the Transitional style, with choirs at each end of the building. A century later, the eastern choir was replaced by a soaring hall design. The exterior of the church drips with sculpture: on the south side are early fourteenth-century portals dedicated to the Last Judgment and to the Virgin Mary, while to the north is the slightly later Bridal Doorway, with its carvings of the Wise and Foolish Virgins.

An even more astonishing array of works of art can be found inside the church. Particularly striking is the bronze **shrine of St Sebald**, an early sixteenth-century masterpiece which combines late Gothic and Renaissance decoration and is heavy with religious symbols. **Peter Vischer the Elder**, aided by his two sons, took eleven years to complete this project. The figure of the master founder at work, dressed in skullcap and apron, has traditionally been assumed to be a self-portrait, but is now thought to be the work of Peter the Younger. On the pillar behind is an expressive Crucifixion scene (whose figures are taken from two separate groups, made two decades apart) by Nürnberg's most famous sculptor, **Veit Stoss**. The same artist also made the *St Andrew* and the three stone *Passion* reliefs on the end walls of the chancel.

The northeastern quarter

Immediately to the east of St Sebaldus is the **Altes Rathaus**, a self-confident late Renaissance building in the style of a Venetian *palazzo* which incorporates two older houses. If you're into the gorier side of medieval times, visit the torture chambers of its **Lochgefängnisse** (mid-April to mid-Oct Tues–Sun 10am–4.30pm; rest of year Tues–Fri at 4.30pm; €2). On a lighter note, go through to Rathausgasse to see one of the finest of the city's many fountains, the Renaissance **Gänsemännchen Brunnen**, which shows a farmer carrying two water-spouting geese to market.

Up the road at Burgstr. 15 is the **Stadtmuseum Fembohaus** (March–Oct Tues, Wed & Fri–Sun 10am–5pm, Thurs 10am–8pm; Nov–Feb Tues–Fri 1–5pm, Sat & Sun 10am–5pm; €4; Ⓦwww.museen.nuernberg.de). Originally built at the end of the sixteenth century for a rich silk merchant, the mansion has truly startling interior decoration, featuring lurid colour schemes of pastel pink, yellow and green, with riotously ornate white stuccoed ceilings forming the icing on top. A number of interiors from other houses which failed to make it through the war have also been transferred here.

One of these comes from the **Pellerhaus** on the north side of nearby Egidienplatz. This was considered the finest patrician house in the city, but following almost total destruction by wartime bombs only the stately arcaded late Renaissance courtyard was rebuilt. Further along, in the shadow of the modern university buildings at Hirschelgasse 9–11, is the earlier **Tucherschlösschen** (Mon 10am–3pm, Thurs 1–5pm, Sun 10am–5pm; €4;

Ⓦwww.museen.nuernberg.de). This home of another Nürnberg dynasty survived in better shape, and was recently fully restored to serve as an illuminating illustration of the lifestyle enjoyed by its former owners. The exhibits include a portrait of Hans VI Tucher by Dürer's teacher Michael Wolgemut and a magnificent double goblet by Nürnberg's most distinguished silversmith of the Renaissance period, Wenzel Jamnitzer. At the northern end of the garden (not its original location), the **Hirsvogelsaal** (same times and ticket) was re-erected in 2000, having been in store since the war. Nürnberg's most spectacular patrician interior, it dates from the 1530s and is the work of two leading local artists: the sculptor Peter Flötner was responsible for the wall decoration, while Dürer's pupil Georg Pencz executed the colourful ceiling paintings.

The Hauptmarkt and around

Commercial heart of the city and main venue for the normal daily markets and the famous Christmas market, the **Hauptmarkt** lies just south of the Altes Rathaus, occupying the site of the Jewish quarter, which was razed to make way for it in a fourteenth-century pogrom. In the centre of the square stands a brightly coloured replica of the celebrated Gothic **Schöner Brunnen** (Beautiful Fountain). A tall stone pyramid chiselled out in filigree style and adorned with statues of the Electors accompanied by pagan, Jewish and Christian heroes, prophets, evangelists and Church Fathers, it has the dimensions of a great church spire rather than a mere fountain.

The Hauptmarkt's east side is bounded by the **Frauenkirche**. This little jewel of a church, commissioned by Emperor Charles IV as his court chapel, was one of the first buildings by the celebrated Parler family. Its facade, sheltering a porch with a delicately carved doorway dedicated to the Nativity, was enlivened in the early sixteenth century by the addition of a gable, an oriel and a clockwork mechanism known as the Männleinlaufen, which tinkles away each day at noon. The rather recondite story it tells is of the **Golden Bull** of 1356, whereby the church's founder established the identities of the seven Electors (here shown honouring him) on a permanent basis, as well as designating Nürnberg as the city in which every new emperor had to hold his first Imperial Diet. Among the works of art inside, pride of place goes to the *Tucher Altar* in the chancel, a late Gothic *Crucifixion* **triptych** painted by an unknown but highly expressive artist – now dubbed the Master of the Tucher Altar as a result – who was Nürnberg's finest painter of the period prior to Dürer.

Walking southwards from Hauptmarkt, you cross the River Pegnitz by Museumsbrücke, which gives a good view of the **Fleischbrücke** to the right (modelled on the Rialto Bridge in Venice) and the **Heilig-Geist-Spital** on the left. The latter – one of the largest hospitals built in the Middle Ages – stands on an islet, with two graceful arches spanning the water. Now a restaurant, it has an old-world inner courtyard with wooden galleries and a famous fountain statue of a shawm player named Hansel. The last-named is a copy, the original figure having been moved for preservation reasons to the Germanisches Nationalmuseum (see p.163).

The southern quarter

Following Königstrasse south from the river, you shortly come to the parish church of **St Lorenz**. Its shape and ground plan are nearly identical to those of St Sebaldus, but this church of the southern of the two city centre parishes is otherwise very different from its northern counterpart, with each of its constituent sections being about fifty years later in date. Thus the nave, complete with a majestic main portal and a resplendent rose window, is modelled on the High Gothic cathedrals in France, while the hall chancel, lit by a gleaming set of stained-glass windows, is in the Flamboyant style. Look out for the graceful late fifteenth-century **tabernacle** some 20m high, worked out of local sandstone by **Adam Kraft**, who depicted himself as a fiery, pensive figure crouching at the base. Equally spectacular is the larger-than-life polychrome wood *Annunciation* by **Veit Stoss** which is suspended from the ceiling above the high altar. It's set in a garland of roses and rosary beads and has seven small roundels illustrating the mysteries of this cult.

Outside the church is another wonderful fountain, the Mannerist **Tugendbrunnen**, in which water gushes from the breasts of the Seven Virtues and from the trumpets of the putti. Diagonally opposite is the oldest house in the city, the thirteenth-century **Nassauer Haus**. If you follow Karolinenstrasse west from here, you can see two notable modern additions to the city's tally of fountains. The **Peter-Henlein-Brunnen** on Hefnersplatz honours the local inventor who produced the first-ever pocket watch in the early sixteenth century. On Ludwigsplatz further west is the **Ehekarussell Brunnen**; illustrating a poem by the celebrated Mastersinger and cobbler Hans Sachs, it displays six scenes from marriage, humorously alternating between bliss and nightmare.

Returning to Nassauer Haus and continuing down Königstrasse in the direction of the Hauptbahnhof you come to the massive and austere Renaissance **Mauthalle**, whose sloping roof is pierced by six tiers of windows. Formerly a granary and later a customs house, it now houses various stores plus another Hausbrauerei (see p.168). Beyond is the Gothic church of **St Martha**, the former hall of the Mastersingers. The **Handwerkerhof** (mid-March to Dec Mon–Fri 10am–6.30pm, Sat 10am–4pm; restaurants open till 10pm) by the Königstor, is an enclosed "medieval" village that brings to life historic Nürnberg trades such as handmade tin soldiers, dolls, brass objects, and such famed local delicacies as *Lebkuchen* spice-cakes and *Nürnberger Bratwürste*.

A stone's throw to the west is the strikingly curvaceous facade of the **Neues Museum** (Tues–Fri 10am–8pm, Sat & Sun 10am–6pm; €3.50; Ⓦwww.nmn.de), whose opening in 2000 brought to an end Nürnberg's unwanted status as the only major German city without a permanent showcase for modern art. The ground floor displays a host of postwar international design classics, including many humorous items, such as Andy Warhol's *Cow Wallpaper*, Yonel Lebovici's *Safety Pin* and Guido Drocco and Franco Meilo's *Cactus Coat Stand*. Among the artworks exhibited upstairs, the iconic *Telephone* by the American Pop artist Richard Lindner, whose childhood was spent in Nürnberg, has pride of place. Gerhard Richter's *Stadtbild*, which resembles an aerial photo, is another painting of special note, while there are several eye-catching installations, such as *One Year* by George Maciunas and *Sweeping Out* by Joseph Beuys.

Just outside the Altstadt, at Lessingstr. 6, is the **Verkehrsmuseum** (Transport Museum; Tues–Sun 9am–5pm; €3). This actually contains two separate institutions – the **Museum für Post und Kommunikation** (Ⓦwww.museumsstiftung.de), which is devoted to the history of the postal services in Bavaria, and the **DB Museum** (Ⓦwww.dbmuseum.de), the national railway museum. The latter has many ancient locomotives parked in its showrooms; these include a copy of the country's first train (named the *Adler* after Germany's eagle symbol) and the original of King Ludwig II's state train – which really does look like a miniature version on wheels of one of his fantasy castles. An instructive section on the role of rail during the Third Reich is also featured.

The Germanisches Nationalmuseum

The **Germanisches Nationalmuseum** (Tues & Thurs–Sun 10am–5pm, Wed 10am–9pm; €5, free Wed 6–9pm, when the museum is only partially open; Ⓦwww.gnm.de) on Kartäusergasse is one of the largest and most varied collections in the country. Its defining characteristic is that it is devoted exclusively to the German cultural tradition, which, in accordance with the perspective of its nineteenth-century founders, is taken to embrace Austria, Switzerland and the Netherlands. The museum occupies the late fourteenth-century **Karthaus** (Charterhouse) which is itself of considerable interest as one of the most complete examples of this type of monastery in Germany, though the modern galleries which have been added to provide badly needed extra display space seriously mar the effect.

The exhibits in the archeology department on the north wing of the ground floor range from a Bronze Age **golden cone** – now believed to be a priestly hat – found at Ezelsdorf-Buch to the **eagle fibula** and seven associated pieces of jewellery made around the turn of the sixth century for the Ostrogothic royal court. Highlight of the medieval treasury in the hall beyond is the tenth-century **Echternach Gospel book**. From there, the circuit leads to the rooms around the cloisters, where the **original sculptures** from some of Nürnberg's most famous buildings (notably the Schöner Brunnen and the two parish churches) can be seen. You next enter the **Karthauskirche**, which still preserves the simple Gothic form favoured by the silent Carthusian monks. Exhibited here are the reliefs of *The Seven Stations of the Cross* by Adam Kraft, which originally lined the road to the Johannisfriedhof.

In the room beyond are carvings by **Veit Stoss**, including an anguished *Crucifixion*, a light-hearted pair of *Tobias and the Archangel Raphael*, and the *Rosenkranztafel*, a large wooden panel graphically portraying the drama of Judgment Day. A few sculptures by the other great woodcarver of the period, **Tilman Riemenschneider** – notably a noble figure of *St Elizabeth* – can be seen in the next gallery, which is chiefly devoted to fifteenth-century painting. The most important work here is *The Annunciation*, one of the best of the few surviving examples of **Konrad Witz**, who played a crucial role in moving German painting towards a greater sense of realism: the perspective attempted in this panel is a world away from the flat backgrounds found in most of the other paintings here. Next comes an outstanding collection of historical **musical instruments**, which occupies the whole of the south wing.

German painting at its Renaissance peak dominates the north wing of the first floor, where you can see some **Dürer** originals. *Hercules Slaying the Stymphalian Birds* is a fairly early work, and the only mythological painting by the artist to have survived. The pair of imaginary portraits of *The Emperor Charlemagne* and *The Emperor Sigismund* were commissioned to adorn the room in which the imperial treasury (now in Vienna) was kept during the years it was displayed in Nürnberg; the actual crown, orb and sceptre are accurately depicted in the paintings. In contrast, *The Artist's Mother*, *Emperor Maximilian I* and *Michael Wolgemut* are portraits made from life; the first of these has only recently been identified as an early autograph work, while the last-named is a touching yet unsentimental portrayal of the artist's former teacher, by then a wrinkled old man of 82. Three panels from a dispersed series of *The Life of St Florian* by **Altdorfer** use the landscapes of the Danube valley to impressive effect; this same backdrop also occurs in **Baldung**'s *Rest on the Flight into Egypt*. Most interesting of several works by **Cranach the Elder** is *King Christian II of Denmark*; the monarch had by then been deposed and had fled to Wittenberg, where he stayed as the artist's house guest. By **Cranach the Younger** is an unusual heart-shaped altar painted for Schloss Colditz.

The adjacent rooms focus on the diversity of Nürnberg's achievements during the Renaissance. There was a strong **goldsmith** tradition, shown to best effect in the superbly fashioned model of a three-masted ship which served as a table centrepiece. The city also played a leading role in the fast-developing science of geography, and among the globes is the first-ever one of the earth, which was made by **Martin Behaim** in 1491 – just before the discovery of America. An insight into the lifestyle of the patrician families is provided by objects such as the Santiago **pilgrim's outfit** of Stephan Praun, and the luxuriant **carved bed** of the Scheurl family. At the far end of the same wing is a collection of Dutch paintings, including a couple of small works by **Rembrandt**.

This floor of the south wing and the storeys directly above it are devoted to German **folklore**, in particular religious traditions which show the roots of customs still prevalent in rural areas. There's also a new presentation on nineteenth-century bourgeois culture which includes a fine collection of Romantic-era paintings centred on the monumental *Battle of the Amazons* by **Feuerbach**. The modern east wing contains displays of arms and armour, Baroque courtly art and, on the top floor, twentieth-century paintings and sculpture, including a large number of works by the Dadaist **Hannah Höch**.

In 2002, the museum opened an outpost, the **Spielzeugsammlung** (same hours and ticket) in a school building on the opposite side of Kartäusergasse, thus giving the city a second museum of historic toys. On the ground floor are some spectacular seventeenth-century **dolls' houses** made for the children of prominent local dynasties. The oldest, dating from 1611, is decorated with wall paintings of high artistic merit, and has a largely eighteenth-century inventory; the slightly later Stromsches Puppenhaus, on the other hand, preserves over a thousand objects from the time it was made. Educational and artistic toys from the eighteenth century onwards are on view upstairs, while the top floor is devoted to paper theatres and parlour games.

The Nazi city

In virtually everyone's mind the word Nürnberg conjures up thoughts of Nazi rallies and the war-crime trials: in most peoples' memories are the scratchy black-and-white newsreels of fanatical crowds roaring "Sieg Heil", and of Göring, Ribbentrop and other leaders standing in the dock a few years later. Nürnberg has the unenviable task of facing up to its historical role (see box p.165) more closely and openly than other cities, and the authorities, to their credit, have made positive moves towards helping visitors get to grips with the events of that time – though this inevitably leaves them open to the charge of exploiting the dark side of the past for commercial gain.

Luitpoldhain

The park known as the **Luitpoldhain** in the southeastern suburbs of the city, where many of the Nazi buildings still stand, has been dedicated to the memory of their victims, though it is also used for commercial and recreational purposes. If this seems a somewhat incongruous mix, it is in reality a case of history turning full circle, as the Luitpoldhain was originally laid out for the Bavarian Jubilee Exhibition of 1906, and was later a memorial for the dead of World War I before being commandeered by the Nazis.

At the northern entrance to the park, reached from the city centre by tram #9 or bus #36, is the **Luitpoldarena**, where parades of Nazi groups such as

Nürnberg under the Nazis

As the present city council is eager to point out, the Nazis' choice of Nürnberg as the backdrop for their *Reichsparteitage* had little to do with local support of the "brown" ideology. Indeed, in marked contrast to Munich, the votes cast for them here in each of the elections before their assumption of power were derisory. The crucial factor was what the medieval city represented in German history: not only had it been the de facto capital, its rapid rise to prominence was seen as showing the nation's dynamism at its very peak. Also, the local police made it very easy for the NSDAP to gain the upper hand here, since they resented centralized Bavarian control and hoped to gain more independence if the Nazis took over.

The first of the **Nürnberg rallies** was held in 1927; between 1933 and 1938 they were an annual event, Hitler using the 1938 rally to raise world tension during the Munich crisis. As the most important display of Nazi power for home and foreign consumption, they were highly organized and ritualized mass demonstrations. Hitler's speeches formed the climax of the show, the intention being to underline his own unquestioned status as *Führer* and the total unity of purpose existing between the leadership and the led. Up to 250,000 people took part in these events, which were expertly stage-managed and totally hypnotic for the mass of participants. The sheer organizational skills which had to be brought to bear were themselves a form of preparation for war – and intended as a further warning to potential enemies. Leni Riefenstahl's film *Triumph of the Will*, a lyrical hymn to Nazism, filmed at the 1934 rally is the best record of the week-long event.

There was no more fanatical proponent of the Nazis' anti-Semitic policies than the Franconian party chief, **Julius Streicher**, who strode around the city administering instant "justice" with his whip, and whose depravities reached such depths that even fellow party members felt sickened. His odious anti-Semitic newspaper *Der Stürmer* was specifically designed to stir up hysteria against the Jews, with its stories of their alleged child sacrifices and sexual perversities. The highlight of his career came with the passing of the so-called **Nürnberg Laws** in 1935, which deprived Jews of their citizenship and forbade relations between Jews and Gentiles. It was through these laws that the Nazis justified their extermination of six million Jews, ten thousand of whom came from Nürnberg – where the Jewish population was reduced to single figures by the end of the war.

So great was Nürnberg's identification with the proudest demonstrations of power of the Third Reich that it was deliberately chosen by the victorious Allies as the place for the **war-crime trials**, which are graphically recounted in Rebecca West's book *A Train of Powder*. The surviving leading players of the "Thousand Year Reich", before whom an entire nation had trembled for twelve years, now mostly appeared as broken men and were shown up publicly as the ragbag of fanatics and misfits they had in reality always been. Ten of the most important Nazis – Ribbentrop, Keitel, Kaltenbrunner, Rosenberg, Frank, Frick, Streicher, Seyss-Inquart, Sauckel and Jodl – were successively hanged here at short intervals in the early hours of October 16, 1946. Former Reichsmarschall Hermann Göring committed suicide by swallowing a concealed cyanide pill two hours before his appointed execution. Of the rest, Hess, Funk and Raeder were confined to prison for life, while Speer, Schirach, Dönitz and Neurath were all given long-term sentences. Three men were acquitted: the propaganda officer Hans Fritzsche; Franz von Papen, the bungling ex-Chancellor who was more responsible than anyone else for Hitler's initial assumption of power; and Hjalmar Schacht, the financial guru who had managed the economic affairs of the Third Reich with the same enthusiasm, shrewdness and lack of political concern as he had shown when running the national economy in the days of the Weimar Republic.

the SA and SS were held. Its grounds contained the former exhibition hall where the party conferences took place, but this was completely destroyed by bombing in 1945.

The custom-built but unfinished **Kongressbau** behind, however, remains standing, and is the most chilling surviving visual reminder of the pretensions of the Third Reich. Built in the debased Neoclassical style beloved of modern totalitarian dictators, it self-consciously tries to present an updated, upstaging version of Rome's Coliseum. For decades, all attempts to find a suitable permanent use for this monstrosity came to naught. However, a small part of it has been converted to house the **Dokumentationszentrum Reichsparteitagsgelände** (Mon–Fri 9am–6pm, Sat & Sun 10am–6pm; €5, or €6 combined ticket with Schwurgerichtsaal 600; Ⓦwww.museen.nuernberg.de). Günther Domenig, the Austrian architect entrusted with the project, has erected a dramatically symbolic 130m-long steel and glass walkway to pierce the granite facade of the original building. Inside, the full gamut of modern display techniques are used in a nineteen-room audio-visual presentation (headphones with a full English-language commentary are available) of the Nazi era, with special emphasis on Nürnberg's role within it. Familiarity and the passage of time have failed to dampen the capacity of the archive film (which is a major feature of the display) to shock the viewer.

To the rear, the **Grosse Strasse** leads over the artificial lake down to another parade ground, the **Märzfeld**. The dimensions of this road – 2km long and 60m wide – are awesome; the vista it opens up includes a distant view of the Kaiserburg, thus creating a visual reference to the symbolic union the Nazis wished to have with the medieval city. Nowadays, part of it is used as a car park by visitors to the modern trade-fair buildings nearby. You can return to the Kongressbau by taking the path to the east. This passes firstly the **Stadion**, used for meetings of the Hitler Youth but now returned to its original purpose as a sports venue as home of the football club FC Nürnberg. Further north is the **Zeppelinfeld**, which was transformed by Albert Speer (Hitler's favourite architect, and subsequently armaments minister) into a stadium for the most important parades. The colonnaded tribunes, so familiar from old films, had to be dismantled for safety reasons, but the towers and terraces remain. Nowadays, the complex is used as a sports centre and for the celebrated **Norisring car races** in late June. (Information and tickets are available from MCN Motorsport-Club Nürnberg, Spittlertorgraben 47 Ⓣ09 11/26 79 90, Ⓦwww.norisring.de).

The Landgericht Nürnberg-Fürth

In 2000, limited public access was belatedly introduced to the setting of the Nürnberg trials, the **Landgericht Nürnberg-Fürth**, a still-functioning courthouse at Fürther Str. 110 to the west of the city centre which can be reached by taking U-Bahn #1 or #11 to Bärenschanze. **Schwurgerichtsaal 600** (Courtroom 600; guided tours Sat & Sun at 1pm, 2pm, 3pm & 4pm; €2) was specially reconstructed for the trials, which were mould-breaking both in the depth of evidence presented – 240 witnesses were called and over 300,000 statements examined – and in introducing three new offences: crimes against peace, war crimes and crimes against humanity. As such, they have served as a model for all subsequent attempts at regulating international order by the force of law, though circumstances have seldom permitted repetitions of the clear-cut outcome that was achieved here. The presentation includes the showing of archive film of the trial, though this can also be viewed in the Kongressbau.

Eating, drinking and nightlife

Nürnberg is the liveliest Bavarian city next to Munich, with a wealth of watering-holes and nightspots to suit all tastes and pockets. If the Bavarian's favourite snack is a *Weisswurst*, the Franconian's is a *Bratwurst* – a slim **pork sausage** roasted over wood fires and usually served at least six at a time, with a choice of sauerkraut, potato salad, onions or radishes as accompaniment. The most curious culinary feature of Nürnberg is that these sausages have been turned into an item of serious cuisine, best sampled in the highly rated speciality restaurants to the accompaniment of a glass of one of the wide variety of beers produced by the local Tucher or Lederer breweries. Equally ubiquitous are *Nürnberger Lebkuchen*, delicious **cakes** made from flour, nuts, honey, eggs and spices. Usually they're only eaten around Christmas, but here you can buy them all year round. The best-known maker is *Lebkuchen Schmidt*, which has shops in the Handwerkerhof and by the southeastern corner of the Hauptmarkt at Plobenhofstr. 6. While many of the obviously recommendable places to eat and drink are in or near the Altstadt, it's also worth taking the U-Bahn to the grand nineteenth-century inner suburbs to the west, where there are some enticing alternatives.

Nürnberg hosts numerous festivals, as well as a predictably wide choice of entertainment all year round. For details of **what's on**, consult either the *Monatsmagazin* (€1), available from the tourist office, or *Plärrer* (Ⓦwww.plaerrer.de; €2), on sale at any kiosk.

Sausage Restaurants

Bratwurst-Friedl Hallplatz 21. Offers a full, moderately priced menu in addition to the sausage specialities. Closed Sat evening & Sun.

Bratwurst-Glöcklein Im Handwerkerhof. Despite its commercialized position in the crafts market, the food here can rival that of any of its competitors. Closed Sun.

Bratwurst-Häusle Rathausplatz 1. With its huge chimney for grilling the sausages, this is the most famous of the group: in spite of the restricted menu and frequent tourist hordes, it really shouldn't be missed. Closed Sun.

Bratwurst-Röslein Obstmarkt 1. Has a wide-ranging menu in addition to the traditional sausage fare, and actively campaigns for low restaurant prices. Closed Mon.

Historische Bratwurstküche Zum Gulden Stern Zirkelschmiedsgasse 26. Housed in a renovated fifteenth-century tavern, with a truly *gemütlich* atmosphere. Closed Sun.

Other restaurants

Barockhäusle Johannisstr. 47. A multi-functional restaurant, café and beer garden in a Baroque house between the Kaiserburg and the Johannisfriedhof.

Böhms Herrenkeller Theatergasse 19. Popular old wine bar-cum-restaurant. Closed Sun.

Essigbrätlein Weinmarkt 3. One of the city's top restaurants for both international and traditional German cuisine. Very expensive; closed Sun & Mon.

Goldenes Posthorn Glöckleinsgasse 2. A Gaststätte which has been on the go since the time of Dürer, and is still among the best in the city.

Heilig-Geist-Spital Spitalgasse 12. Occupying the medieval hospital, this is arguably the city's most atmospheric restaurant; the food is outstanding and reasonably priced too.

Ishihara Schottengasse 3. Highly rated, fairly expensive Japanese restaurant, though it does do bargain lunches. Closed Sun.

Kettensteg Maxplatz 35. Traditional Gasthaus with picturesque beer garden by the River Pegnitz.

Krakauer Turm Vordere Insel Schütt 34. Polish restaurant and cultural centre (a spin-off of Nürnberg's twinning link with Kraków) in one of the medieval towers of the Stadtbefestigung.

Lederer-Kulturbrauerei Sielstr. 12. The tap of the adjacent Lederer brewery, whose main product is an olive-coloured beer known as *Krokodil*. It has a capacious beer garden and serves very traditional Franconian fare. Take U-Bahn #1 or #11 to Bärenschanze.

Mount Lavinia Jakobsplatz 22. The first and best Sinhalese restaurant in Germany, with curries ranging from mild to very hot, and good selections of both Thai and ayurvedic vegetarian dishes. Bargain lunches are offered on weekdays; on Sun it's open evenings only.

Nassauer Keller Karolinenstr. 2. Highly rated restaurant in the cellars of Nürnberg's oldest house. Closed Sun.
Pele-Mele Grossweidenmühlstr. 17. Bistro just west of the Altstadt which presents a choice of riverside beer garden or cool vaulted cellar in which to have your meal.
Tucherbräu am Opernhaus Kartäusergasse 1. Gaststätte of the Tucher brewery, with a small beer garden perched directly over the city's ramparts.
Zum Schuldturm Heubrücke Vordere Insel Schütt 4. Gaststätte with the nicest beer garden in the Altstadt, directly overlooking the Pegnitz.
Zum Sudhaus Bergstr. 20. Well-regarded, fairly pricey restaurant with engagingly rustic decor. Closed Sun.

Bars, cafés and café-bars

Altstadthof Bergstr. 19. A small Kneipe is attached to the Altstadthof-Hausbrauerei mentioned on p.159. It also serves the products of its parent, the out-of-town Lammsbräu.
Balazzo Brozzi Hochstr. 2. Located just west of the Altstadt, this is a good place to start the day if you want a choice of cheap and decent breakfast dishes.
Barfüsser Hallplatz 2. Hausbrauerei in the cavernous cellars of the Mauthalle, whose walls are lined with pictures of film stars of the Fifties and Sixties. It brews a *Weisse* as well as light and dark beers; the food is inexpensive and typically hearty.
Café Dampfnudel-Bäcker Johannisstr. 34. Multiple award-winning café specializing in steamed dumplings; it also serves a good range of salads, pancakes and pasta dishes.
Café Kroll Hauptmarkt 6. The pick of the traditional *Kaffee und Kuchen* establishments, with a terrace overlooking the main square.
Cubano Innere-Laufer-Gasse 13. Good choice for late-night drinking (and eating).
Meisengeige Am Laufer Schlagturm 3. Tiny café-bar catering for a mixed and unpretentious crowd; there's also a small cinema attached that runs an off-beat selection of films you won't find in the commercial venues.
Mohr Färberstr. 3. Candlelit café-bar in the western Altstadt.
Palais Schaumburg Kernstr. 46. Reached by taking U-Bahn #1 or #11 to Gostenhof, this has a beer garden, and also serves inexpensive meals, including an extensive vegetarian menu.

Nürnberg's festivals

Nürnberg really comes alive in the summer when open-air music and theatre festivals abound. The season starts around Whit weekend (variable date in May/June) with **Rock im Park** (Ⓦwww.rock-im-park.de). June is also the month for **Musica Franconia**, a week-long series of concerts of old music played on period instruments; it also sees the beginning of the ten-day-long **Internationale Orgelwoche** (Ⓦwww.ion-nuernberg.de), featuring organ recitals in the city's churches and in the Meistersingerhalle. The **Bardentreffen** (Ⓦwww.bardtreffen.de) in the last week of July or first week of August is a popular annual event where singers and song writers from Europe come together in free open-air concerts all over the city. Around the same time is **Moving Cultures** (Ⓦwww.moving-cultures.de), a festival of world music and theatre. In early September, it's the turn of chamber music, with the **Internationales Kammermusikfestival** (Ⓦwww.kammermusik-festival.de), while the last week of October sees the **Ost-West Jazzfestival** (Ⓦwww.jazz-ost-west.de), which encompasses every jazz style and brings together musicians from around the world.

Prominent among **folklore festivals** is the **Altstadtfest** (Ⓦwww.altstadtfest.de) at the end of September, a local fair celebrating Franconian culture, with lots of food and drink, as well as river tournaments and a procession in traditional costumes. Finally, with a 400-year tradition, the Nürnberg **Christkindlesmarkt** (Christmas market; Ⓦwww.christkindlesmarkt.de) held on the Hauptmarkt from November 25 until December 24, is the largest and most popular in Germany, as well as being the founder of what has become very much a national institution, with derivatives found in every town of any size. It stands apart from its imitators by the wealth of handmade quality goods on sale, such as toys, brass utensils and tin soldiers, glass objects of all kinds, and, of course, the delicious *Lebkuchen*.

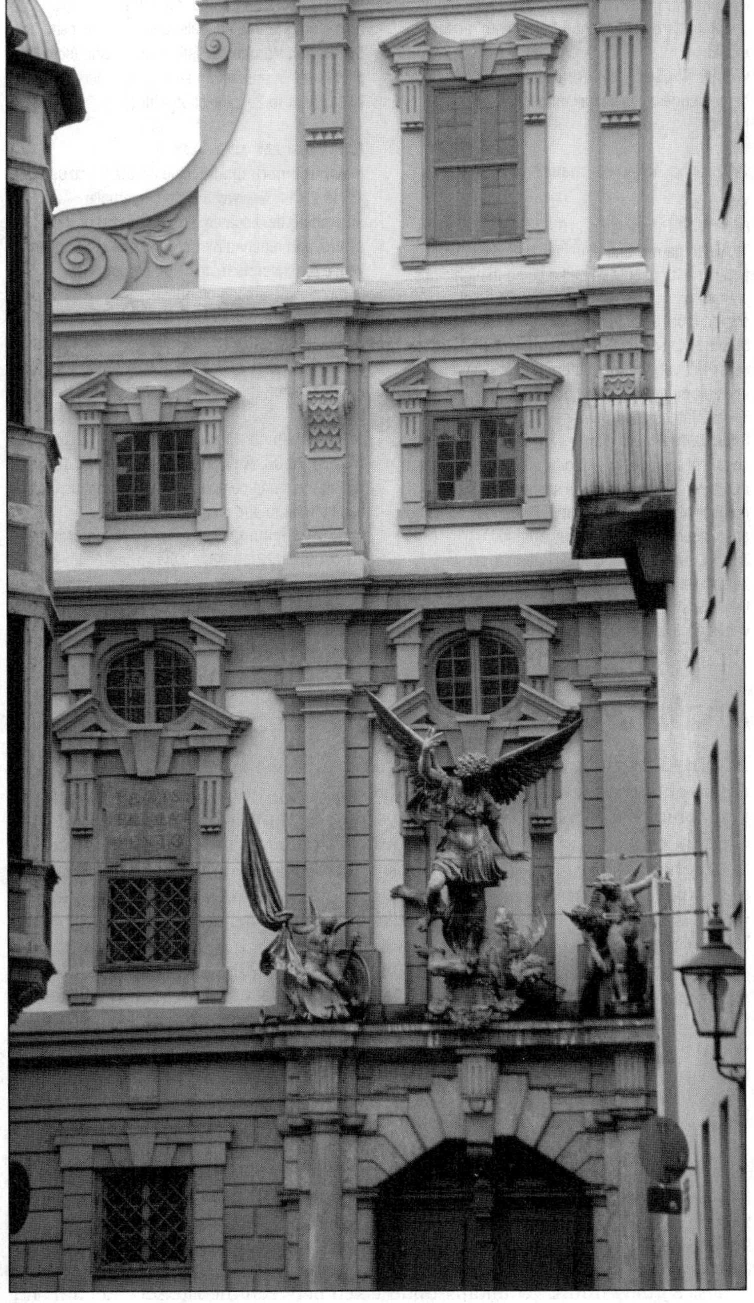

△ Zeughaus Facade, Augsburg

Ruhestörung Tetzelgasse 21. One of the main young and trendy watering-holes, with raucous music.
Wiener Spezialitäten Café Kaiserstr. 1. As its name suggests, this is a Viennese-style coffee house.

Music bars and nightclubs

Bezirk 40 Humboldstr. 116. Cosy place offering TV, video games and pinball machines, which is popular with people who like going to nightclubs without having to make too much of an effort. Also serves food. Daily 7pm–1am.
Mach 1 Kaiserstr. 1–9. Currently the city's trendiest nightspot; the four different bars ensure variety, and there are some good lighting effects. Thurs–Sat 10pm–4/5am.
Rock-Café Brown Sugar Königstorgraben 3. A couple of minutes' walk north of the Hauptbahnhof, this is the best of the city's seemingly endless number of heavy metal bars, with pinball machines and videos among the heady attractions.
Zabo-Linde Zerzabelshofer Hauptstr. 28, Zerzabelshof ⓦwww.zabo-linde.de. Both a traditional Gaststätte with beer garden and a regular venue for live music, ranging from rock to disco. Worth making the trip out for, if the evening's music programme appeals. Check the website or the *Plärrer*, Nürnberg's listings magazine (see p.167). It's in an eastern suburb, reached by bus #43 or #44 to Zerzabelshof/Mitte.

Cultural venues

Meistersingerhalle Münchener Str. 21 ⓣ09 11/49 20 11, ⓦwww.meistersingerhalle.nuernberg.de. Located 2km southeast of the centre, and reached by tram #9, this is the main venue for concerts by the Nürnberger Symphoniker, among others.
Opernhaus Richard-Wagner-Platz 2 ⓣ09 11/2 31 38 08, ⓦwww.theater.nuernberg.de. Located in a grand Historicist building just west of the Hauptbahnhof, this presents operas, operettas and dance.
Schauspielhaus Richard-Wagner-Platz 2 ⓣ09 11/2 31 38 08, ⓦwww.theater.nuernberg.de. Within the same complex as the Opernhaus, this has both large and small stages.
Theater der Puppen im KALI Frauentorgraben 73 ⓣ09 11/22 43 88, ⓦwww.theater-im-kali.de. Puppet theatre served by two separate companies, with shows for both adults and children.

Ansbach

ANSBACH, 50km southwest of Nürnberg, is less than a tenth of the size of its neighbour, but is nevertheless the capital of the province of Middle Franconia. With only a relatively short interregnum, it has had capital status ever since 1331, when it became the seat of the first principality established by the Hohenzollerns. For most of its history, this was known as the Margraviate of Brandenburg-Ansbach, though it was never the frontier district its name would suggest: the title was transferred from the dynasty's subsequent power base of Brandenburg after the latter was promoted to the rank of an Electorate of the Holy Roman Empire. The town wears a grand air which is quite disproportionate to its small size, and is well-endowed with handsome buildings from a variety of architectural periods. It has also gone down in the annals of German history as the site of the unsolved murder of **Kaspar Hauser**, the notorious foundling (see p.172).

The Town

The dominant building is the huge **Residenzschloss** (guided tours April–Sept Tues–Sun 9am–6pm; Oct–March Tues–Sun 10am–4pm; €3; ⓦwww.schloesser.bayern.de) at the southeastern edge of the Altstadt. It was originally a moated castle, and a Gothic hall which survives from this contains the ticket office and a collection of locally made porcelain. In its present form, the complex dates almost entirely from a rebuilding undertaken between the late seventeenth and mid-eighteenth centuries. Initially, the work was carried out in a classicizing form of Baroque by the Italian Gabriel de Gabrieli, and the most striking feature of this is the **inner courtyard**, with its three tiers of open arcades. The last phase of construction was entrusted to the Rococo architect and interior designer Leopold Retti, who was responsible for the magnificent suite of 27 chambers on the first floor. With a single exception, these preserve their original decoration absolutely intact: the abdication of the last margrave in 1791 spelt an end to the building's function as a residential palace, and thus it was never modernized. The only room in the grand manner is the **Festsaal**, which has elaborate stuccowork and a ceiling fresco by Carlo Carlone glorifying the wise government of the patron, Margrave Carl Wilhelm Friedrich. All the other chambers are intimate in scale, and are grouped into three separate groups of apartments – for the margrave, the margravine and guests. Each has one highly idiosyncratic room: respectively these are the **Marmorkabinett** (Marble Cabinet), the **Spiegelkabinett** (Cabinet of Mirrors), and the **Gekachelter Saal** (Tiled Room), which is covered with 2800 delicately designed tiles made in the local factory.

Right in the heart of the Altstadt is the church of **St Gumbertus**. Originally it was part of a Romanesque collegiate foundation, but the only survivor from that period is the **crypt** (Fri–Sun 11am–noon & 3–5pm), which later served as the pantheon of the local margraves. Directly above is the Gothic chancel, which was converted to serve as the **Schwannenritterordenkapelle**, and shelters the elaborate epitaphs and death shields of members of the Order of the Swan, a lay foundation of Margrave Albrecht Achilles. The **nave** was remodelled in the eighteenth century into a vast preaching hall according to the restrained Lutheran tastes of the day. It's a classic among German Protestant churches – all slate grey and cream, without paintings or side altars, it presents a cool clarity, in which the focus is placed firmly on the small marble altar and the pulpit above.

To the rear of St Gumbertus is the **Beringershof**, a sixteenth-century mansion with a beautiful galleried courtyard, complete with a stair tower. On the west side of the church lies the sixteenth-century **Stadthaus**, the seat of the mayor and town council. Beyond is the main square, Martin-Luther-Platz, which is dominated by **St Johannis**, a large Gothic hall church built for parish use and containing an altar by the Nürnberg sculptor Peter Flötner. Just to the north, down Schaitbergerstrasse, is the **Markgrafenmuseum** (Tues–Sun 10am–noon & 2–5pm; €2.50). One part of this is devoted to the history of the margraviate; the other, on the opposite side of the road, documents the life and times of Kaspar Hauser in a comprehensive fashion, though you'll need to have some German to get the most from the display. The exhibits include the bloodstained coat he was wearing when he was murdered, and it was a DNA sample taken from this which finally laid to rest the theory that he was an unwanted member of Baden's grand ducal family. For more on Hauser, see the box on p.172.

At the far southern end of the Altstadt is the **Herrieder Tor**, a medieval gateway refashioned in the Baroque period. On Rosenbadstrasse, a short distance to the northwest, is the **Synagoge**, which was built by Leopold Retti in the 1740s. It deserves to be considered as one of the most beautiful surviving Jewish temples in Germany, but its interior can unfortunately only be seen on guided tours of the town: these are held at 11am every Sunday between May and September and depart from **Anscavallo**, an avant-garde statue of a horse directly opposite the Residenzschloss.

Just to the southeast of the Altstadt is **Karlsplatz**, a monumental square planned in the late seventeenth century as the focal point of a Huguenot suburb. It was only completed in 1840, ironically enough with the building of the Neoclassical **Ludwigskirche**, the main Catholic church in this staunchly

Protestant town. Further east lies the **Hofgarten**, which contains both formal gardens and "natural" sections with centuries-old trees. Its **Orangerie** is a fine French-style Baroque building near which, at the spot where Kaspar Hauser received his fatal stab wounds, is a stone memorial with the inscription: "Here died a man unknown by means unknown".

Practicalities

Ansbach's **Bahnhof** is a few minutes' walk south of the centre. The **tourist office** (May–Oct Mon–Fri 9am–5pm, Sat 10am–1pm; Nov–April Mon–Fri 9am–12.30pm & 2–5pm; ⓣ09 81/5 12 43, ⓦwww.ansbach.de) is in the Stadthaus, Johann-Sebastian-Platz 1.

Of the centrally sited **hotels**, the lowest rates are at *Augustiner*, Karolinenstr. 30 (ⓣ09 81/24 32; ❸). There are several more upmarket options, including *Schwarzer Bock*, Pfarrstr. 31 (ⓣ09 81/42 12 40, ⓦwww.schwarzerbock.de; ❺); *Der Platengarten*, Promenade 30 (ⓣ09 81/97 14 20; ❺–❼); *Am DrechselsGarten*, Am Drechselsgarten 1 (ⓣ09 81/8 90 20, ⓦwww.drechselsgarten.bestwestern.de; ❼); and *Bürger-Palais*, Neustadt 48 (ⓣ09 81/9 51 31, ⓦwww.hotel-buergerpalais.de; ❼), a beautifully renovated Baroque mansion. All these have **restaurants**, which rank as the best in town; that of *Der Platengarten* also has the benefit of a beer garden. Another popular eatery with the same facility is *Zum Mohren*, Pfarrstr. 9.

A number of **festivals** take place in Ansbach, the best known being the Bach-Woche, which is held in the two civic churches at the end of July in even-numbered years. The Ansbacher Rokokospiele are period plays, music and dance events performed in the Residenzschloss and the local parks in late June and early July each year, while in early August various artistic events based around the story of the mysterious foundling are enacted under the title of the Kaspar-Hauser-Festspiele. Held every four years (next in 2006), the Heimatfest is a grand occasion where eighteenth-century music and dance play the most important part, but there's also a fair with plenty of regional delicacies.

The mystery of Kaspar Hauser

One day in 1828, a bewildered-looking youth turned up in the streets of Nürnberg, carrying two letters addressed to the authorities. One was from a labourer who claimed to have guarded him for the past sixteen years, albeit in conditions of close confinement; the other purported to be from his natural mother, stating that his deceased father had been a cavalry officer. The boy gave his name as **Kaspar Hauser**, but was unable to say where he came from, ate nothing but bread and water, and seemed to lack all knowledge of external objects. His appearance caused an immediate sensation locally, which soon spread across Germany and beyond. There were all kinds of wild speculations as to his origins: one theory that was particularly popular was that he was the eldest son of Grand Duke Carl Ludwig of Baden, who had been kidnapped by order of his step-mother, though this seemed to be contradicted by evidence that the child in question had died in infancy, and was conclusively disproved by DNA tests carried out in 1997. In due course Kaspar was educated and proved to be highly intelligent and creative. He moved to Ansbach in 1831, becoming clerk to the president of the court of appeal. Two years later, just as he seemed to be falling out of the limelight, he met his violent death there. His murderer was never found, adding a final unsettling mystery to his life story: many suspected that he had died by his own hand. Much has been written about him since, little of it conclusive.

Bayreuth

The capital of Upper Franconia, polished and respectable **BAYREUTH**, which lies some 80km northeast of Nürnberg, enjoys its reputation as one of the great cultural centres of Europe. Except for the five-week festival period beginning in the second half of July, it's a quiet provincial town, which was something of a late developer, only coming to prominence in 1603 when it displaced nearby Kulmbach as the seat of the second of the Hohenzollerns' Franconian principalities. Its subsequent fame is due to a series of imported creative spirits, two of whom played defining roles. The first of these was **Wilhelmine of Prussia**, Frederick the Great's elder sister, who was intended for the British royal throne, but was married off instead in 1732 to her amiable but dull kinsman, the future Margrave Friedrich of Brandenburg-Bayreuth. Instead of settling down to obscurity, Wilhelmine set about creating a vibrant courtly life, employing architects, painters, interior designers, landscape gardeners and musicians from all over Europe. The following century, **Richard Wagner** decided to settle in Bayreuth because the town offered to build him a stage large enough to put on his grand-scale opera productions, and the festival he founded, the Richard-Wagner-Festspiele, soon established itself as one of the great annual events of the

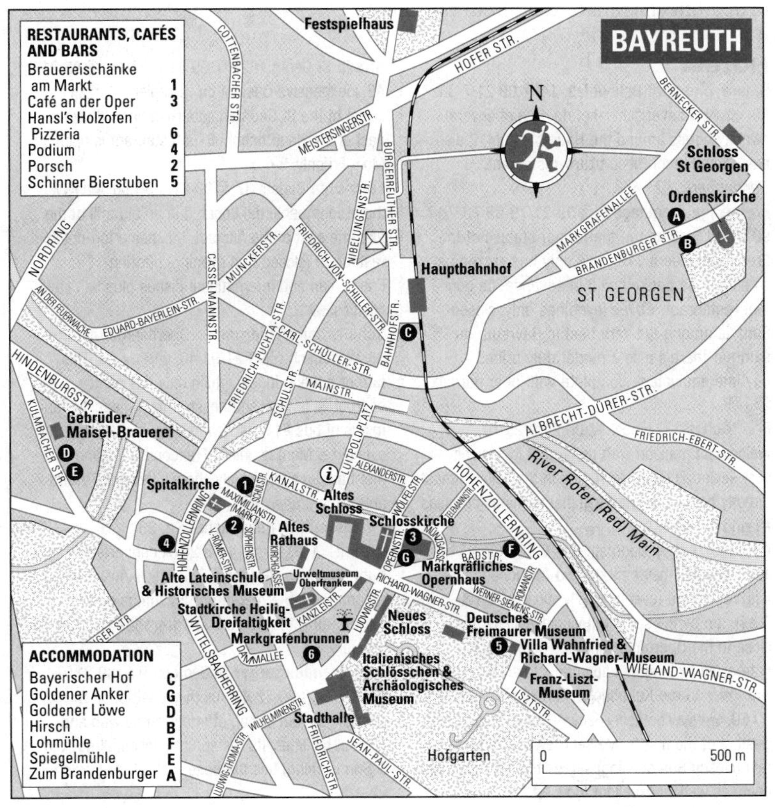

music world. In common with everything else to do with Wagner, it was tarnished by association with Hitler's patronage and exploitation for propaganda purposes, but continues to flourish, with demand for tickets always exceeding supply many times over.

Arrival, information and accommodation

Bayreuth's **Hauptbahnhof** is a short walk north of the town centre. The **tourist office** is at Luitpoldplatz 9 (during the festival Mon–Fri 9am–6pm, Sat 9.30am–4.30pm, Sun 10am–1pm; rest of year Mon–Fri 9am–6pm, Sat 9.30am–1pm; ⓣ09 21/8 85 88, ⓦwww.bayreuth-tourismus.de). At €9 for three days, the **Bayreuth Card** is a good investment: it covers travel on the local buses (beware that some of these use different numbers for opposite directions of the same route) plus entrance to the local museums (but not the palaces and opera houses).

If visiting Bayreuth for the festival, you should reserve accommodation well in advance, preferably as soon as you receive your tickets, though it's normally possible to find a room at short notice. Note that **hotels**, of which the town has a plentiful supply in all categories, jack up their prices (usually by around fifty percent) for the duration of the festival. The **youth hostel** is in the south-eastern part of town, almost next door to the University at Universitätsstr. 28 (ⓣ09 21/76 43 80; €12.70); bus #4 runs there regularly, though it's no more than a fifteen-minute walk from the centre.

Hotels

Bayerischer Hof Bahnhofstr. 14 ⓣ09 21/7 86 00, ⓦwww.bayerischer-hof.de. One of several swanky hotels around the Hauptbahnhof; it also has a fine French-style bistro-restaurant, *Gendarmerie*. ❼

Eremitage Eremitage 6 ⓣ09 21/79 99 70, ⓕ7 99 97 11. Located in the former stables of the Eremitage (see p.178), this only has six rooms, so should be booked well in advance. Its gourmet restaurant, *Cuvée* (evenings only, closed Sun), is among the very best in Bayreuth; in summer there's also a moderately priced daytime equivalent, complete with beer garden. ❻–❽

Friedrichsthal Laineck ⓣ09 21/9 25 10. Welcoming pension with restaurant in a rustic, very secluded riverside setting in the valley almost directly below the Friedrichsthal terminus of buses #1 and #3. ❹

Goldener Anker Opernstr. 6 ⓣ09 21/6 50 51, ⓦwww.anker-bayreuth.de. Old-fashioned hotel with restaurant (evenings only, closed Mon & Tues), run by the same family since 1753. It's close to the Opernhaus and has been much patronized by singers and conductors. ❻

Goldener Löwe Kulmbacher Str. 30 ⓣ09 21/74 60 60, ⓦwww.goldener-loewe-bayreuth.de. Cosy Gasthof of the nearby Maisel brewery. Its restaurant (closed Sun evening) serves the full range of beers as well as excellent food. ❺

Hirsch St Georgen 26 ⓣ09 21/2 67 14, ⓕ85 31 42. Inexpensive Gasthof on the splendid main street of the St Georgen suburb, a short distance east of the Hauptbahnhof. Its restaurant is open Mon–Fri only. ❷

Lohmühle Badstr. 37 ⓣ09 21/5 30 60, ⓦwww.hotel-lohmuehle.de. Located in an old mill at the extreme east of the Altstadt, this has a top-notch restaurant (closed Sun evening) offering Franconian and international dishes plus fish specialities. ❻

Schlosshotel Thiergarten Oberthiergärtner Str. 36, Wolfsbach ⓣ09 21/98 40, ⓕ9 84 29. This former hunting lodge, which only has eight bedrooms, is 6km southeast of town near the terminus of bus #11. Its *Kaminrestaurant* (closed Sun evening & Mon) is one of Franconia's leading gourmet haunts; alternatively, there's the more affordable *Jägerstüberl*. ❼

Spiegelmühle Kulmbacher Str. 28 ⓣ09 21/4 10 91, ⓕ4 73 20. A converted mill right alongside *Goldener Löwe*. It likewise has a recommendable restaurant (evenings only, closed Sun); the beers come from the rival Glenk brewery. ❺

Zum Brandenburger St Georgen 9 ⓣ09 21/78 90 60, ⓕ78 90 62 40. Another Gasthof on St Georgen's main street, offering rooms with and without facilities. Its restaurant (closed all day Sat & Sun evening) has the benefit of a beer garden. ❷–❻

The Town

Bayreuth is a small place with many of the sights grouped together in the compact centre and the Hofgarten just beyond. Several other key attractions lie much further afield, but all can be reached by regular bus services.

The town centre

Margravine Wilhelmine's proudest legacy is the **Markgräfliches Opernhaus** (daily: April–Sept 9am–6pm; Oct–March 10am–4pm; €4 including audio-visual presentation, €6 combined ticket with Neues Schloss; Ⓦwww.schloesser.bayern.de) on Opernstrasse in the northern part of the town centre, which was erected in four years of concentrated activity in the 1740s. The exterior by the court architect, the Frenchman Joseph Saint-Pierre, is unusual in that it forms part of a terrace of buildings. Its sobriety stands in stark contrast to the glamorous interior, which was entrusted to Giuseppe and Carlo Galli da Bibiena, a father-and-son team from the great Bolognese dynasty of theatre-designers. Made entirely of wood, it's painted sea-green highlighted with gold, white, yellow and red, with the obligatory fresco of Apollo and the Muses on the ceiling. All the seats are in boxes on either side of the margravial loge, whose baldachin, like the proscenium arch opposite, is adorned with the coat-of-arms of Brandenburg-Bayreuth and the royal crown of Prussia. The stage, which preserves beautiful illusionistic scenery, is the same size as the auditorium, and remained the largest in Germany until the advent of Wagner. Although he found it too small for his purposes, it makes an ideal venue for eighteenth-century opera and vocal recitals, and is still a regular performance venue.

Immediately to the west stands the **Schlosskirche**, a Baroque church erected by Saint-Pierre during the following decade. Painted in a delicate pink and adorned with tasteful stuccowork, it's a typical example of Lutheran Baroque, though it has been Bayreuth's main Catholic church since 1813. In a vault beneath the organ are the tombs of Wilhelmine, her husband and their only child, Elisabeth Friederike Sophie. Alongside, dominated by its octagonal Renaissance tower, is the largely Baroque **Altes Schloss**. Much of this palace was accidentally burnt down in 1753 by the unfortunate Margrave Friedrich with a misplaced candle, but it was subsequently restored, and is now used as offices. The side facing the broad Maximilianstrasse (which is also known as the Markt) is decorated with vigorous late seventeenth-century medallions of deities and heroes of Classical mythology.

Directly opposite, at the top end of Kanzleistrasse, is the **Urweltmuseum Oberfranken** (July & Aug daily 10am–5pm; Sept–June Tues–Sun 10am–5pm; €2; Ⓦwww.urwelt-museum.de). This contains some remarkable local finds, including a number of very rare dinosaur bones (notably the only extant examples of the *Pistosaurus* and *Capitosaurus*) plus a collection of 200-million-year-old fossilized plants from the time when Upper Franconia was a tropical river delta. A few paces to the west along Maximilianstrasse, the **Altes Rathaus**, a Renaissance building with prominent oriels, has been converted into a cultural centre. Its focal point is the **Kunstmuseum** (July & Aug Mon, Tues & Thurs–Sun 10am–5pm, Wed 10am–8pm; Sept–June Tues & Thurs–Sun 10am–5pm, Wed 10am–8pm; €1.60; Ⓦwww.kunstmuseum-bayreuth.de), whose holdings of twentieth-century art are displayed in rotating exhibitions. Also on Maximilianstrasse are three Baroque **fountains**, dedicated to Fame, Hercules and Neptune. At the far western end of the street is Saint-Pierre's **Spitalkirche**, which boasts a handsome sandstone facade and a galleried interior.

The narrow, twisting streets immediately south of Maximilianstrasse are medieval in origin, but lost most of their original buildings in two seventeenth-century fires. Among the casualties of the first of these, which occurred just two years after Bayreuth became a margravial residence, was the main civic church, the **Stadtkirche Heilig-Dreifaltigkeit**. It was immediately rebuilt in a, by then, totally anachronistic Gothic style, the only authentically Baroque note being the steeple-crowned turrets above the twin towers, which are linked by a covered passageway. Inside are two notable furnishings from the same period as the rebuilding: the **font**, which has eight alabaster reliefs with a baptismal theme; and the **Kuffner'sche Epitaph**, which incorporates an older relief of *The Adoration of the Magi*, below which is a predella showing a distant view of Bayreuth.

On Kirchplatz to the side of the church is the **Alte Lateinschule**, the home of the **Historisches Museum** (July & Aug daily 10am–5pm; Sept–June Tues–Sun 10am–5pm; €1.60), which presents well thought-out displays illustrating the town's past. The focus is firmly on the margravial period, with models illustrating Bayreuth's development, and an extensive collection of local porcelain, plus examples of the distinctive stoneware of the nearby village of Creussen. To its credit, the museum does not baulk at featuring the town's high-profile role during the Third Reich, and has on display an extensive photographic documentation of this period.

Friedrichstrasse, the southernmost of the central streets, is a splendid piece of eighteenth-century town planning, lined with Baroque palaces. Some were built as the homes of court officials, though others had a public function: that at no. 15 was the town's first university, while no. 14 was originally an orphanage, as the relief of a mother and child above the doorway indicates. About halfway down the street is a square, Jean-Paul-Platz, on which stands the monumental **Reiterhalle**, the former margravial riding hall, which has found a new lease of life as the Stadthalle, the town's exhibition and congress centre.

The Neues Schloss and the Hofgarten

South of the Altes Schloss is the replacement **Neues Schloss** (daily: April–Sept 9am–6pm; Oct–March 10am–4pm; €3; Ⓦwww.schloesser.bayern.de), which was completed to plans by Saint-Pierre in 1755 after just two years' work. The building served as a residence only until 1769, when the male line of the House of Brandenburg-Bayreuth died out, and the territory passed to the Ansbach Hohenzollerns. This resulted in the great state rooms being stripped of their furnishings, but the private apartments survive intact as testaments to Wilhelmine's very personal version of the Rococo style. Her own chambers, which are on the northern wing of the first floor, are hung with portraits by Antoine Pesne, court painter to Frederick the Great, plus a large number of **pastels**, including some perfectly competent works by Wilhelmine herself. However, these are outclassed by the portraits of the margravine and her daughter by one of the greatest pastellists of all time, the Swiss, Jean Étienne Liotard. Of the interiors themselves, the **Japanisches Zimmer** (Japanese Room) and the **Spiegelscherbenkabinett** (Broken Mirror Cabinet) stand out. The latter is lined from top to bottom with broken and uneven shapes, as if put together from several broken mirrors; based on a design by Wilhelmine, it's thought to be her comment on the false glamour of her age. Some highly individual examples of Rococo decoration can also be seen among the margrave's apartments in the southern wing, especially the **Palmenzimmer** (Palm Room), which is arranged as a trompe l'oeil grove of palm trees, and the **Spalierzimmer** (Trellis Room), which adopts a similar illusionistic technique. The ground floor rooms are devoted to displaying products of the local **porcelain** factory.

Adjoining the Neues Schloss to the south is the **Italienisches Schlösschen**, which was built for Margrave Friedrich's second wife, Sophie Karoline of Braunschweig-Wolfenbüttel, by Carl von Gontard, who went on to pursue a highly successful career in Berlin. It has some fine interiors, though these can only be seen in conjunction with the **Archäologisches Museum** (April–Oct Sat 10am–3pm, first Sun of month 10am–noon; €1), a collection of local excavations. In the square in front of the Neues Schloss stands the swaggering late Baroque **Markgrafenbrunnen**, which was moved from its original location beside the Altes Schloss. The equestrian statue is of Margrave Christian Ernst in his role as Imperial Field Marshal in the wars against the Turks; around him are representations of the four continents. On the other side of the palace is the **Hofgarten**, which includes a formal parterre plus a far more extensive English-style landscape garden.

From the northern side of the Hofgarten, a pathway leads to a late nineteenth-century masonic lodge which now contains the national collections and library of the German freemasons, the **Deutsches-Freimaurer-Museum** (Tues–Fri 10am–noon & 2–4pm, Sat 10am–noon; during the festival daily 10am–4pm; €1). Predictably, freemasonry is represented here as an international peace movement rather than anything sinister, though the ritual objects featured in the display are unlikely to win over any sceptics. It's revealing to see just how many well-known people were Freemasons, including Frederick the Great, Haydn, Mozart, Goethe, Dickens, Churchill, George Washington, Benjamin Franklin and Harry S. Truman.

A short walk to the east stands the sternly Neoclassical **Villa Wahnfried**, now the **Richard-Wagner-Museum** (April–Oct Mon, Wed & Fri–Sun 9am–5pm, Tues & Thurs 9am–8pm; Nov–March daily 10am–5pm; €4; Ⓦwww.wagnermuseum.de or www.wahnfried.de). Wagner had this built to his own designs as his Bayreuth home: its enigmatic name literally means "peace from delusion". The large sitting-room-cum-concert-room, which was destroyed by a bomb in 1945 but rebuilt thirty years later to serve as a recital venue, was the setting for Wagner's famed soirées, attended by intellectuals, musicians and royalty alike. His wife Cosima was the daughter of another famous composer, Franz Liszt, and the combination of the couple's backgrounds and interests made the household an important focus of German cultural life. Theirs was also one of the most famous love stories of the nineteenth century (he lured her from her first husband, the conductor Hans von Bülow, who was sufficiently stoic about the affair to maintain his role as the leading contemporary interpreter of Wagner's music), and they lie buried together in the villa's garden. Wagner's life and the history of the festival are documented in the villa's other rooms, while the basement contains a collection of models of the stage sets used in the latter's productions. Videos of his music dramas are screened in the now interconnected Siegfried-Wagner-Haus alongside.

A block to the east, at Wahnfriedstr. 9, the **Franz-Liszt-Museum** (daily: July & Aug 10am–5pm; Sept–June 10am–noon & 2–5pm; €1.60) has been set up in the forester's house where Wagner's father-in-law lodged on his visits to Bayreuth, and where he died in 1886. The displays illustrate the phases of his startlingly diverse career as a peripatetic concert virtuoso, the *Kappelmeister* of the Weimar court, and as an abbé in a monastery in Rome.

The inner suburbs

A short walk west of the town centre, at Kulmbacher Str. 40, is the **Gebrüder-Maisel-Brauerei**, a splendid late nineteenth-century redbrick tower brewery which has been mothballed as the **Brauerei- und Büttnerei-Museum** (guided tours Mon–Sat at 10am; €3.60; Ⓦwww.maisel.com), while production continues in the ultra-modern premises alongside. The brewery preserves its old equipment – including steam engines, coal-fired boilers and copper brewing kettles – in full working order, as well as its Büttnerei (coopers' workshop), where wooden beer barrels were made until the 1950s. The tour ends at the old bottling plant, now transformed into a saloon bar of the 1920s, where a half-litre glass of beer is served at no extra charge. The company is now primarily a *Weissbier* specialist, having abandoned production of the dark steam beer (*Dampfbier*) which was once its best-known line.

Bayreuth's most famous nineteenth-century building is the **Festspielhaus** (guided tours Tues–Sun at 10am, 10.45am, 2.15pm & 3pm; 10am & 10.45am only during the festival; closed Nov; €1.50), the custom-built theatre for the performance of Wagner's music dramas, which is set on a little hill in the far north of town, reached by following Bürgerreuther Strasse straight ahead from the Hauptbahnhof. Based on designs by Gottfried Semper, the leading German architect of the day and one of Wagner's comrades-in-arms on the Dresden barricades during the 1849 revolution, the theatre was inaugurated in 1876, when the *Ring* cycle was staged in its entirety for the first time. Ever since, nothing but Wagner's operas has been performed there. After the composer's death in 1882, his widow Cosima ensured that the annual festival continued, and various family members have been in charge ever since. It was during his English-born daughter-in-law Winifred's "reign" from 1931 to 1944 that the festival had the unfortunate honour of Hitler's patronage, and he stayed as her house-guest whenever he came to Bayreuth. Wagner buffs still argue over the extent to which she should be blamed for the misappropriation of Wagner's music during the Nazi era, and bitter quarrels within the Wagner family have continued to fuel the flames. Although externally prepossessing, the interior is spartan in the extreme, with the comfort of the audience (most of whom sit on hard wooden benches) and the orchestra (whose members have to endure their own high decibel sound in the cramped, sweaty conditions of a deep pit) sacrificed for the sake of achieving the best possible acoustics.

A short distance to the southeast, immediately to the rear of the Hauptbahnhof, is **St Georgen**, a planned town founded in 1701 which was not incorporated into Bayreuth until after the Bavarian takeover in 1810. Although never completed, it contains many fine Baroque buildings, including the **Schloss** of the courtly Roter-Adler-Orden (Red Eagle Order), a porcelain manufactory and two churches, the larger of which, the **Ordenskirche**, preserves an intact period-piece interior.

The Eremitage

Lying 4km east of town, and reached by bus #20 from Marktplatz, is the curious **Eremitage**, which has its origins in the eighteenth-century fad of the nobility for playing at asceticism by occasionally staying in sparse monks' cells and eating nothing but soup. When the original hermitage or **Altes Schloss** (guided tours April to mid-Oct daily 9am–6pm; €2.50; Ⓦwww.schloesser.bayern.de) was given to Wilhelmine as a birthday present in 1735, the year her husband inherited the margraviate, she proceeded to enlarge it into a glamorous summer hideaway in line with her own quirky vision of retreat as perfect indulgence. Thus some splendid Rococo chambers, notably the **Musikzimmer** and **Japanisches Kabinett**, are juxtaposed with the original bare cells. Between the two wings is the **Grotte**, featuring 200 fountains grouped in three concentric circles which could be activated in various different ways to surprise or spray unwary guests.

Wilhlemine later commissioned a brand-new palace, the **Neues Schloss**, from Saint-Pierre and Gontard, and this was built just a short distance away. It is designed in a horseshoe shape, with mosaic-encrusted arcaded wings (which lost their interior decoration as a result of an artillery bombardment in the war) flanking a central rotunda known as the **Sonnentempel** after the gilded sculptural group of Apollo and his sun chariot on its roof. In the space between the wings is the **Obere Grotte**, whose **fountains** of tritons and fantastical creatures play hourly on the hour from 10am until 5pm between May and mid-October. Ten minutes later, the jets are activated in the **Untere Grotte**, a nymphaeum with nymphs, putti, dolphins and sea-horses. Among the follies in the park is an open-air theatre built in the shape of a Roman ruin, where the margravine was wont to take to the stage, sometimes with her friend Voltaire.

Eating, drinking and entertainment

Bayreuth is awash with quality restaurants, many of the best choices being in the hotels (see p.174). As the home of several breweries, it's also a good place for a pub crawl.

Restaurants and cafés

Becher-Bräu St-Nikolaus-Str. 25. Located in a residential district to the west of the centre (take bus #5 to Freiheitsplatz), this is Bayreuth's oldest brewery-owned Gaststätte, with a tradition going back more than two centuries. These days, however, the Becher label products (a *Pils*, a *Bock* and a *Dunkel*) are made under contract by the Schinner brewery. Closed Tues.

Brauereischänke am Markt Maximilianstr. 56. A fairly genteel pub-restaurant on the main square, serving the beers of the Bayreuther brewery.

Café an der Oper Opernstr. 16. A supremely elegant café in the Redoutenhaus, the former court gardener's residence next door to the Opernhaus. Live classical music performances are sometimes featured.

Café Orangerie Neues Schloss Eremitage. This café, which has indoor seating in the Orangerie and a terrace overlooking the fountains, is an attractive place for a break during a visit to the Eremitage.

Hansl's Holzofen Pizzeria Friedrichstr. 13. This tiny place, which makes delicious pizzas in a wood-fired oven, is a favourite with local students.

Podium Gerberhaus, Gerberplatz 1. Bayreuth's jazz and blues bar; it serves Thai food and has a beer garden.

Porsch Maximilianstr. 63. A time-warped Gaststätte, offering generous portions of inexpensive local fare plus beers from the rural Stöckel brewery.

Schinner Bierstuben Richard-Wagner-Str. 38. Since 1860 this has been the main tap of the Schinner brewer, whose principal product is a brown beer. It serves typical Franconian cooking, with inexpensive lunchtime specials.

Schützenhaus Am Schiesshaus 2. Located to the northeast of the Festspielhaus, this serves inexpensive Franconian specialities and has a large beer garden. Closed Thurs.

Zur Sudpfanne Oberkonnersreuther Str. 6, Oberkonnersreuth. Situated in an incorporated village 3km southeast of town (bus #11 stops at the door), this is the Gaststätte of the small Schaller brewery alongside, which produces a fine unfiltered beer, *Storchentrunk Zwickelbier*. Exquisite food is served in the large hall and the very formal *König-Ludwig-Saal*, more basic pub grub in the *Storchenkeller* beer garden. On Sat, it's only open in the evening.

Culture and festivals

Demand for **tickets** for the Richard-Wagner-Festspiele (Ⓦwww.bayreuther-festspiele.de) is so great that you need to write the year before you wish to visit to Kartenbüro, Festspielleitung Bayreuth, 95402 Bayreuth, but this only ensures entry into the lottery, and the normal waiting time for first-time individual applicants is between three and seven years. The various Wagner societies around the world receive special allocations, but the only other way you will realistically get to see a performance is to take an expensive package tour from abroad (see p.16 & p.18 for tour operators). Formal evening dress is the normal attire, but is not *de rigeur*. Note that it is necessary to pay more than one visit to see the entire Wagner canon (six different operas are normally staged in a season), and that each festival has a fair number of non-performance days.

Advance tickets for **opera**, **concerts** and **drama** performances in the Markgräflisches Opernhaus and other local venues can be bought from the box office in the tourist office premises at Luitpoldplatz 9 (Ⓣ09 21/6 90 01). Musical **festivals** by no means begin and end with the Wagner jamboree; in addition, there's the Musica Bayreuth (Ⓦwww.musica-bayreuth.de) in early May, the Fränkische Festwoche in June, and Bayreuther Barock (Ⓦwww.bayreuther-barock.bayreuth.de) in late September. Folklore events include Maisels Weissbierfest in mid-May, the Volksfest in early June and the Bürgerfest at the beginning of July.

Kulmbach

KULMBACH, which lies 22km northwest of Bayreuth on the banks of the Weisser (White) Main, just west of the point where it joins the Roter (Red) Main to form the River Main proper, is best-known for its **beer**, holding as it does two national records – the largest output per head of population and the strongest brew in regular production (*EKU 28*). Although the town was the capital of a Hohenzollern principality from 1398 until the court moved to Bayreuth in 1603, it preserves very few reminders of its medieval origins. The blame for this lies squarely with Margrave Albrecht Alcibiades of Brandenburg-Kulmbach, a megalomaniacal and unprincipled ruler who hoped to turn the great sixteenth-century religious divide to his own advantage by establishing control over the whole of the old Franconian duchy. Instead, he succeeded in uniting the Protestant city-state of Nürnberg and the Catholic prince-bishoprics of Bamberg and Würzburg in common cause against him, and in 1553, after a long siege, their combined forces captured the town and laid it to waste. The following year, the same fate befell the huge feudal fortress high above the eastern side of Kulmbach, whereupon Albrecht was deposed and forced into exile while a largely new town arose from the ashes of the old.

The Town

The original castle, the **Plassenburg**, was replaced almost immediately by a splendid new Renaissance building of the same name, erected under the supervision of Caspar Vischer, a local architect who had recently worked on the great Schloss in Heidelberg. Within its formidable outer defences are two distinct entities. The lower castle, known as the **Niederburg** or **Kasernenhof**, has an austere silhouette of massive high walls, the only decorative note being the early seventeenth-century triumphal arch with an equestrian statue of Margrave Christian, who, ironically enough, was the man responsible for Kulmbach losing its capital status, largely because there was no room on this hill for the large residential palace he craved.

In contrast, the upper castle or **Hochburg** (guided tours of the interiors daily: April–Sept 9am–6pm; Oct–March 10am–4pm; €3; Ⓦwww.schloesser.bayern.de) ranks as one of the richest creations of the German Renaissance. Its four corner towers are evidence of its defensive status, but the arcaded courtyard, the **Schöner Hof**, has a true festive air, and makes an ideal open-air venue for concerts and theatre in the summer. On three of its four sides, virtually every square centimetre of the arches, pilasters and balustrades is festooned with carvings of foliage, mythological beasts, putti, vases, candelabra, scrollwork and medallion portraits of members of the Hohenzollern dynasty and their supposed ancient Roman ancestors. The tour takes in a suite of restored margravial chambers, which are decked out with period furniture, the most spectacular being the seventeenth-century four-poster bed, guarded by statues of Charity and Piety, of Margravine Maria. Most of the paintings on display are family portraits, but there is also a panel of *The Mysteries of the Rosary* by the town's most celebrated artist, Hans Suess von Kulmbach, a pupil of Dürer. Also included on the tour is the **Schlosskapelle**, one of the earliest custom-built Protestant chapels. Its three key focal points – the pulpit, altar and organ – are somewhat later than the structure itself, all dating from the early seventeenth century.

The same entrance ticket gives admission to the **Armeemuseum Friedrich der Grosse**, which can be visited at leisure. This contains a wide range of exhibits illustrating the history of the legendary army of Frederick the Great and his predecessors, the primary force behind the rise of the Hohenzollern heartlands of Brandenburg and Prussia from rural backwaters to the dominant power in Europe. On display are arms and uniforms representing each of the component divisions of the army – regular infantry, artillery, riflemen, hussars, cuirassiers and dragoons. Also on view are nine original banners, the most precious being a blue silk dragoon standard of 1685.

Two other museums can be found within the Hochburg. The **Landschaftsmuseum Obermain** (same times; €2) is an extensive and well-presented regional history museum. Among its exhibits are a fine nineteenth-century copy of the now-destroyed map of the world from the Lower Saxon convent of Ebstorf, which features a depiction of the original Plassenburg; a predella of *The Four Doctors of the Church*, painted by Hans Suess von Kulmbach for an altarpiece in the famous Mariacki church in the Polish city of Kraków; the Renaissance stone pulpit from Kulmbach's Petrikirche; the Pörbitsch treasure, a horde of goblets, tankards, dishes, bowls and cutlery by Nürnberg and Augsburg goldsmiths and silversmiths buried for safekeeping during the Thirty Years' War and only rediscovered in 1912; and a collection of 7000 historic cookbooks and 1000 associated samples from the foundation established by the spice company RAPS, a leading local employer.

Across the courtyard is the **Deutsches Zinnfigurenmuseum** (same times; €2; Ⓦwww.zinnfigurenmuseum.de), which contains the world's premier collection of tin figures, an art form taken very seriously in Germany. Dating from the eighteenth century onwards, there are 300,000 individual pieces on view, grouped in 150 different scenes illustrating historic and literary episodes. Among them is the largest diorama ever made, showing the 1553 siege of Kulmbach.

In comparison with the Plassenburg, the Altstadt is very low-key, with only a few historic buildings of note. Directly below the castle is the **Roter Turm**, a medieval tower with a half-timbered superstructure; nearby is the Renaissance **Kanzlei**, a gabled margravial administrative building. Further down and to the southeast, with a terrace commanding a fine view up to the Plassenburg, is the **Petrikirche**, a somewhat gaunt Gothic hall church containing the graves of members of the local margravial family. From there, Obere Stadt, an elongated former market square, swoops down to Marktplatz, on which stands the cheerful Rococo **Rathaus**.

On the opposite bank of the Main, about 2km northeast of Marktplatz, the town's brewing tradition is celebrated in the **Bayerisches Brauereimuseum Kulmbach** (Tues–Sun 10am–5pm; €2), which occupies the former

Mönchshof brewery at Hofer Str. 20. The Mönchshof label, best-known for its coal-black *Schwarzbier*, still exists, as does the Kapuziner designation used for its wheat beers, though the brewery was one of two (the other being Sandlerbräu, whose name now has a very tenuous existence) taken over in the 1980s by the rival Reichelbräu, a Pils specialist whose highly-regarded *Eisbock*, a powerful ice beer, is only available in winter. In 1996 Reichelbräu subsumed its one remaining local competitor, the better-known EKU; subsequently, it abolished its own name, adopting the new Kulmbacher label instead, and consolidated production of all the labels in one new hi-tech brewery.

Practicalities

Kulmbach's **Bahnhof**, which has regular direct services to both Bayreuth and Bamberg, is a few minutes' walk northwest of the Altstadt. The **tourist office** (May–Oct Mon–Fri 9am–1pm & 1.30–5.30pm, Sat 9.30am–1pm, Sun 11am–1pm; Nov–April same hours Mon–Fri only; ⓣ0 92 21/9 58 80, ⓦwww.stadt-kulmbach.de) is in the Stadthalle, Sutte 2. There are plenty of **hotels**, but only *Weisses Ross*, Marktplatz 12 (ⓣ0 92 21/9 56 50; ❸–❺); and *Kronprinz*, Fischergasse 4 (ⓣ0 92 21/9 21 80; ❺–❼) are in the Altstadt. However, there's a concentration around the Stadtpark to the west of the centre: *Ertl*, Hardenbergstr. 3 (ⓣ0 92 21/97 40 00, ⓦwww.hotel-ertl.com; ❸–❻); *Purucker*, Melkendorfer Str. 4 (ⓣ0 92 21/9 02 00, ⓦwww.hotel-purucker.de; ❺); *Hansa*, Weltrichstr. 2a (ⓣ0 92 21/6 00 90, ⓦwww.hansa-hotel-kulmbach.de; ❻–❽); and *Astron*, Luitpoldstr. 2 (ⓣ0 92 21/60 30, ⓦwww.astron-hotel.de; ❼).

All the hotels around the Stadtpark have high-quality **restaurants**, while *Kronprinz* has a café. Tracking down the different local **beers** can be a time-consuming process. A good selection is offered by the *Burgschänke* in the Burg, but most other restaurants remain loyal to a particular label. The *Mönchshof Bräuhaus*, in the same complex as the Brauereimuseum, has a huge beer garden and serves the full range of Mönchshof and Kapuziner products; these are also available in the town centre at the *Stadtschänke*, Holzmarkt 3, which has different themed lunch menus each day. Kulmbacher beers are served at *Anno*, a bistro at Marktplatz 4; EKU beers at *Zunftstube*, Obere Stadt 4. No local beer tour is complete without a visit to *Kulmbacher Kommunbräu*, Grünwehr 17, the town's only Hausbrauerei: it makes light and amber brews and serves hearty local dishes. Altogether different in style is a trendy French-style brasserie, *Alte Feuerwache*, Grabenstr. 4.

Special strong brews are served in litre measures in a huge tent set up beside the Stadthalle for the duration of the main local **festival**, the nine-day-long *Kulmbacher Bierfest*, which begins on the last Saturday of July. At the beginning of the same month is an annual folklore event, the *Altstadtfest*, while in the second week of August in odd-numbered years tin figure enthusiasts descend on the town for the *Zinnfiguren-Börse*.

Coburg

A hugely imposing little town with a truly illustrious history and a mixed Franconian-Thuringian pedigree, **COBURG** lies about 50km northwest of Kulmbach. Following several changes of aristocratic ownership, it came into the hands of the powerful House of Wettin in 1353, and was initially regarded by them as a Saxon outpost within Franconia. In 1586, it was raised to the status of capital of one of the dynasty's splintered Saxon-Thuringian territories, the new Duchy of Saxe-Coburg. The ruling house proved to be masterly at self-promotion, particularly in the nineteenth century, when its clever dynastic marriage policy created ties with the royal families of Belgium, Bulgaria and Portugal as well as Great Britain, the last being achieved when **Albert of Saxe-Coburg-Gotha** married his first cousin, Queen Victoria, thus establishing the present British royal house, which tactfully renamed itself Windsor during World War I. This marriage in turn led to a union with Germany's ruling dynasty, the Hohenzollerns, when the couple's eldest child, Victoria, married the future Kaiser Friedrich III. In 1920, two years after the abdication of the last duke, the locals voted to join Bavaria – which proved a fortuitous choice, as it saved Coburg from the fate of all the other old Saxon-Thuringian principalities, which were incorporated into the GDR after World War II. As a virtual dead end, the town had a tough time economically during the decades of German division, but has recovered well.

Arrival, information and accommodation

Coburg's **Hauptbahnhof** is situated on the northwestern side of town; the quickest way to the centre is by going sharp right along Lossaustrasse. The **tourist office** is just off the Marktplatz at Herrngasse 4 (April–Oct Mon–Fri 9am–6.30pm, Sat 9am–1pm; Nov–March Mon–Fri 9am–5pm, Sat 9am–1pm; ⓣ0 95 61/7 41 80, ⓦwww.coburg-tourist.de).

Coburg has plenty of recommendable **hotels**, particularly in the middle-range category. There are a few **private houses** (❷–❸) with rooms to rent, bookable via the tourist office. The **youth hostel** occupies a redbrick neo-Gothic castle, Schloss Ketschendorf, 2km south of the centre at Parkstr. 2 (ⓣ0 95 61/1 53 30; €13.70); bus #1 stops outside.

Hotels

Blankenburg Rosenauer Str. 30 ⓣ0 95 61/64 40, ⓦwww.blankenburg.bestwestern.de. This fine hotel is in the north of town, beside the municipal swimming pool, which guests can use free of charge. It has a rustic-style restaurant serving moderately priced local and international dishes, as well as the gourmet favourite, *Kräutergarten*. ❻–❽

Coburger Tor Ketschendorfer Str. 22 ⓣ0 95 61/2 50 74, ⓕ2 88 74. Located across from the Rosengarten, this hotel prides itself on its breakfasts and even more on its evenings-only restaurant, *Schaller* (closed Sun), which has a summer garden and serves what is generally considered to be the finest cuisine in Coburg. ❻–❽

Festungshof Festungsberg 1 ⓣ0 95 61/8 02 90, ⓦwww.hotel-festungshof.de. The Veste Coburg's very own hotel, occupying a century-old building outside the fortifications. It also has a good restaurant, complete with café terrace and a large beer garden. ❺–❼

Goldene Sonne Creidlitzer Str. 93, Creidlitz ⓣ0 95 61/2 90 97, ⓕ2 60 93. Inexpensive rooms with and without facilities are available at this Gasthof on the main street of an incorporated village 2km south of the Altstadt, reached by bus #1. Its own butcher's shop is the main source for the meals served in the restaurant. ❷

Goldene Traube Am Viktoriabrunnen 2 ⓣ0 95 61/87 60, ⓦwww.romantikhotels.com/coburg. Grand hotel in the heart of the Altstadt; the facilities include a sauna and a cosmetic studio. Haute cuisine and fish dishes are served in the drolly-titled *Meer & mehr*, less expensive fare in the rustic-style *Weinstüble*, which has a large selection of wines, available by the glass. ❼–❾

Grosch Oeslauer Str. 115, Rödental ⓣ0 95 63/75 00, ⓕ75 01 47. This Gasthof has a pedigree dating back to 1425, and still preserves the traditional pattern of a hotel, restaurant and brewery all grouped together. It's located right alongside Bahnhof Rödental (two stops by train from the Hauptbahnhof), not far from Schloss Rosenau. ❺

Stadt Coburg Lossaustr. 12 ⓣ0 95 61/87 40, ⓦwww.hotel-stadt-coburg.de. A member of the Ringhotel group, this lies just across from the Hauptbahnhof. It has a fine restaurant, *Backstüble* (closed Sun), which specializes in dishes cooked on its open grill. ❻

The Town

Despite Coburg's modest size, its attractions are well spaced out: the great feudal castle which gives the town its name lies high above the eastern side of the compact centre, while there are two important palaces in the far outskirts.

The Veste Coburg

Towering 167 metres above the town and visible from miles around, the **Veste Coburg**, one of the largest surviving medieval fortresses in Germany, can be reached by bus #8 from the Markt, or by a steep thirty-minute walk. The oldest part, the **Blauer Turm** (Blue Tower), was built around 1230, but most of the present massive complex, which is enclosed by two rings of defensive walls, postdates a fire in 1499 which destroyed much of the earlier structure. In the early seventeenth century, four of the outer wall's roundels were replaced by bastions, including the protruding **Bärenbastei** to the north-west which, as its name suggests, contained a bear pit. Considerable restoration work was carried out on the fortress in the nineteenth and early twentieth centuries. Latterly, this was done in a scholarly rather than a romantic manner, and although not all the details are authentic, the Veste, in contrast to so many other German castles, still has a predominantly medieval silhouette.

Within the inner walls are two courtyards. That to the right is dominated by the impressive half-timbered facade of the residential **Fürstenbau**, which until a few years ago was still in the possession of the descendants of the local dukes, with its main apartments open for guided tours. The family has now moved out, severing a link with the Veste of nearly six and a half centuries, and the building is likely to be under restoration and closed to the public for a few years yet. Adjoining it to the east is the **Lutherkapelle**, a mid-nineteenth century structure on the site of its Romanesque predecessor. Its name commemorates the great reformer's five-and-a-half-month sojourn at the Veste under the protection of Elector John the Steadfast for the duration of the 1530 Diet of Augsburg, which, as an outlaw of the Holy Roman Empire, he was unable to attend. On the south side of the left-hand courtyard is the **Hohes Haus**, a tall building with a steeply pitched roof which was formerly an arsenal, and now contains the offices of the castle administration. Alongside is an elegant Renaissance **cistern**.

The three other edifices house one of Germany's most varied and remarkable museums, the **Kunstsammlungen der Veste Coburg** (April–Oct Tues–Sun 10am–5pm; Nov–March Tues–Sun 1–4pm; €3; Ⓦwww.kunstsammlungen-coburg.de), whose exhibits are drawn predominantly but by no means exclusively from the ducal collections. Tickets are bought at the central building, the **Carl-Eduard-Bau**, the top two storeys of which house the largest department, the **Kupfestichkabinett**. Its 300,000-strong graphics collection is among the most important in the country, including as it does major examples of the work of Dürer, Cranach and Rembrandt. None of this is on permanent view, though temporary exhibitions are held at least a couple of times a year. In the same building are displays of decorative art, dominated by a fabulous **glass** section on the first floor, which includes many outstanding Venetian examples.

The **Steinerne Kemenate** (literally, "Heated Stone Chamber") on the eastern side of the courtyard contains the **Lutherstube**, where the reformer progressed with his translation of the Bible and wrote no fewer than 26 works on issues arising from the Reformation. Adjoining it is a memorial room with portraits of the Saxon Electors Frederick the Wise and John the Steadfast by Cranach the Elder, and of Luther by Cranach the Younger. Also on view is an engraved Islamic drinking glass which once belonged to Saint Elisabeth and was later given as a present to Luther. Across the corridor is the **Grosse Hofstube**, containing a huge cast-iron stove of 1501, the oldest of its type in Germany, as well some splendid pieces of tournament armour, including items made for Emperors Maximilian I and Ferdinand I.

Upstairs is the **Jagdintarsienzimmer** (Marquetry Hunting Room), a chamber unlike any other in Germany. Completed in 1632, this extraordinary masterpiece of late Renaissance joinery originally adorned Schloss Ehrenburg in the town centre. On the walls are sixty highly detailed panels of inlaid coloured woods illustrating deer, boar and bear hunts, while the coffered ceiling has ornamental intarsia patterns and 72 human and animal heads. A small but highly distinguished display of old German masters, many on permanent loan from the Schäfer collection in Schweinfurt, can be seen in the rooms opposite. Of particular note are a very Italianate *Madonna and Child in a Landscape* by the young **Dürer**; a gorgeous painting of the same title by **Burgkmair**, featuring delicate depictions of flowers, plants and birds; two little panels of *The Last Supper* and *SS Dorothy and Agnes*, the earliest surviving works of **Grünewald**; *The Capture of Christ* by **Baldung**; and a dozen or so examples of the elder **Cranach**, including the very characteristic *Lucretia* and *Lot and his Daughters*, as well as a somewhat untypical *Last Judgment*. A few sculptures are displayed alongside, including a heartbreakingly intense *Pietà* by an anonymous local woodcarver of the second half of the fourteenth century.

Each floor of the **Herzoginbau** (Duchess Building) on the western side of the courtyard is devoted to a particular theme. One level contains historic **hunting weapons**, many of high artistic merit, another the **Rüstkammer**, which ranks among Europe's richest armouries. The armour of Johann Casimir, the first Duke of Saxe-Coburg, is displayed beside that of his dwarf, the cuirass of the Veste's commandant alongside the smaller swords of his children. There are also some rarities, such as a late sixteenth-century war chest, complete with coins, and an early seventeenth-century organ-pipe canon, so called because of its arrangement of 49 barrels in seven rows, each of which could be fired separately. The basement contains contemporary porcelain plus a large array of seventeenth- and eighteenth-century **stoneware tankards** from Creussen. Most remarkable of all is the floor devoted to **coaches** and **carousels**. Among the former are both of the oldest ceremonial coaches to have survived intact anywhere in Europe, those used at Johann Casimir's weddings in 1586 and 1599. Having been made in Braunschweig for the 1561 royal wedding in Copenhagen of the duke's parents-in-law, the latter is actually the older of the two. The thirteen carousels, which are all individually carved and painted, were used at tournament games staged by the ladies of the court in the seventeenth and eighteenth centuries.

Schloss Ehrenburg

In accordance with the fashion of the time, a new Renaissance palace, known as **Schloss Ehrenburg** (guided tours Tues–Sun: April–Sept 9am–5pm; Oct–March 10am–3pm; €3, or €4.50 combined ticket with Schloss Rosenau; Ⓦwww.sgvcoburg.de), was begun in the 1540s immediately to the east of the Altstadt, and the wing facing Steingasse is a survivor of this period. It was extended under Johann Casimir, and the inner courtyard largely dates from his reign. Following a fire in 1690, the palace was transformed in Baroque style by a team of decorators from northern Italy. Externally, there is little evidence of their work: the Schloss underwent extensive modifications throughout the course of the nineteenth century, and this included the remodelling of the front courtyard according to designs by the great Berlin architect Karl Friedrich Schinkel which were clearly inspired by the Tudor architecture of England.

For all its diversity, the palace is incredibly rich and sumptuous inside, crammed with paintings, furniture and tapestries, and with intricate parquet floors made to different designs in each room. The Baroque **Riesensaal** (Hall of Giants), the setting for festive events, takes its name from the 28 candelabra-bearing atlantes supporting the entablature, above which are 56 coats-of-arms of the various territories of the House of Wettin and a magnificent white stucco ceiling with allegorical paintings of the arts and sciences. Stuccowork of even greater virtuosity can be seen in the **Gobelinsaal**, where the foliage and garlands appear to hang down into the room in a naturalistic manner. Another fine interior by the Italian craftsmen is the **Hofkirche**, which is unusually ornate for a Lutheran church of the period, with stucco-framed ceiling frescoes illustrating the Book of Revelation. Its altar is based on Bernini's famous baldachin in St Peter's in Rome, subtly modified for Protestant worship by the insertion of a swallow's nest pulpit in the centre. The nineteenth-century chambers are influenced by the French Neoclassical and Empire styles; of particular importance is the **Thronsaal**, which is directly modelled on Napoleon's throne room in the Tuileries Palace in Paris. Many rooms are equipped with modern gadgets – the flushing mahogany toilet in the bedroom used by Queen Victoria is believed to be the first of its kind on the Continent.

As a supplement to the tour, it's well worth visiting the **Landesbibliothek** (Mon–Thurs 10am–5pm, Fri & Sat 10am–1pm; free), where five more of the Schloss' historic interiors are open to the public as reading and exhibition rooms. Among these is the Neoclassical **Silbersaal**, where temporary displays of the library's rich holdings of manuscripts, books, maps and engravings are regularly held.

The Altstadt

The boundaries of Coburg's Altstadt are still easily discernible, thanks to the survival of three now disembodied gateways. Crowned with an onion dome, the **Spitaltor** at the junction of Spitalgasse and Georgengasse served as the northern entrance; the **Judentor** on Judengasse and the **Ketschentor** on Ketschengasse were its western and southern counterparts.

At the heart of the Altstadt is the **Markt**, lined with handsome Renaissance buildings erected in the early years of the duchy, and with a statue of Prince Albert, paid for by his widow, in the middle. The **Rathaus** on the southern side was extensively rebuilt in Rococo style, but retains the characteristic two-storey oriel, plus the main hall on the second floor. Opposite stands the **Stadthaus**, the former government building, still in all its original splendour. On the eastern side, at the corner of Steingasse, the **Hofapotheke** is a mixture of Gothic and Renaissance elements, with an oriel in the older style. Leading off the square are several streets of half-timbered houses, the most grandiose being the **Münzmeisterhaus** (Mint Master's House) on Ketschengasse. Just to its east is another imposing Renaissance building, the **Gymnasium Casimirianum**, founded with the intention of developing into a university, but which never rose beyond the status of a school.

Across from the Gymnasium is **St Moriz**, a fourteenth-century Gothic church with fifteenth-century towers which were intended to be identical but ended up with one much shorter than the other. Inside, the chamber under the south tower contains the only remaining medieval furnishing, the **tombstone** of a local fifteenth-century knight, Albrecht von Bach. Towards the end of the sixteenth century, Johann Casimir had the chancel converted into his family mausoleum, and on the end wall stands the massive alabaster **epitaph to Johann Friedrich II**, the duke's father, by the Thuringian sculptor Nikolaus Bergner. In the foreground are statues of the deceased, his two wives and four sons; behind is an altar-like structure with polychromed Old and New Testament scenes. The largest of these, showing Joseph and his brothers escorting the coffin of their father Jacob from Egypt to Canaan, is an allegorical reference to the repatriation of the remains of Johann Friedrich, who was deposed as Duke of Saxony and spent the last 28 years of his life imprisoned in Austria. To the right of the monument are bronze **tombplates** with relief portraits of Johann Friedrich and his second wife, Elisabeth von der Pfalz. In contrastingly light mode is the **font** alongside, carved some six decades earlier with depictions of putti at play. The church's **nave** was remodelled in Lutheran Baroque style, with double galleries, a stuccoed ceiling and an organ (now with modern pipework).

A short distance north of the church, at Rückertstr. 2–3, is a large fifteenth-century mansion which for several years was the home of the poet and orientalist Friedrich Rückert, and now contains the **Coburger Puppenmuseum** (April–Oct daily 9am–5pm; Nov–March Tues–Sun 10am–5pm; €2, kids €1; Ⓦwww.coburger-puppenmuseum.de). Exhibited in 33 rooms arranged in chronological order are some nine hundred individual dolls and toys, plus over fifty dolls' houses dating from the beginning of the nineteenth century until the 1950s.

The outskirts

The descendants of the ducal family live 4km north of the Altstadt in **Schloss Callenberg** (guided tours April–Oct daily at 10am, 11am, noon, 2pm, 3pm & 4pm; Nov 1 to Jan 6, Feb & March Tues–Sun at 2pm, 3pm & 4pm; €2.50; Ⓦwww.schloss-callenberg.de), reached by bus #5. By origin the seat of the knights of Callenberg, the medieval fortress was rebuilt in the late sixteenth century in Mannerist style and given another makeover under Dukes Ernst I and II, acquiring an extravagant mock-medieval silhouette. Inside is the family's private collection of paintings and *objets d'art*, including several paintings by Cranach, some outstanding Renaissance gold- and silverware and a valuable array of furniture. The tour ends with a visit to the **Schlosskapelle**, which still preserves much of its Mannerist outline. A live music **festival**, the Schlossfest, is held in the grounds over a weekend in August.

Seven kilometres to the northeast of the town centre lies **Schloss Rosenau** where Prince Albert was born in 1819 (guided tours Tues–Sun: April–Sept 9am–5pm; Oct–March 10am–3pm; €2.50; Ⓦwww.sgvcoburg.de); buses #8311 and #8312 stop nearby, otherwise it's a short walk from Bahnhof Rödental, two stops on an hourly service from the Hauptbahnhof. This little palace is fifteenth-century in origin, and was built as the home of the lords of Rosenau, who were Coburg's mint masters. In 1805 it was acquired by the ducal family and shortly after remodelled as their summer residence to plans by Schinkel, with the grounds fashioned into a romantic English-style park. Half of the Schloss' ground floor is occupied by the **Marmorsaal**, which takes its name from its grey marble decoration. Alongside is the tiny eleven-sided **Bibliothek**, which was built to house a collection of chivalrous novels, and is decorated with paintings of Friedrich de la Motte Fouquet's *The Travels of Thiodolf the Icelander*. It looks more like a chapel than a library, and was used as such from 1890. Upstairs, the private apartments are decked out with

Biedermeier furniture from Vienna. Among the family heirlooms is a cradle which was probably once used by Prince Albert.

Eating, drinking and entertainment

All the leading **restaurants** are in the hotels, though there are plenty of good, cheaper alternatives, as well as some extremely enticing **cafés**. The favourite local **snack** is the *Coburger*, a long sausage given a distinctively sharp taste by being grilled over pine cones rather than the usual wood or charcoal; the stands on Marktplatz sell authentic examples. Coburg is also known for its dumplings, made according to a recipe combining the Thuringian and Franconian traditions by using both raw and cooked potatoes.

A varied programme of operas, musicals, ballet and concerts is performed at the former court **theatre**, a Neoclassical building of 1840 now known as the Landestheater, Schlossplatz 6 (Ⓣ0 95 61/9 27 42, Ⓦwww.landestheater.coburg.de).

Restaurants and cafés

Bratwurstglöckle Kleine Johannisgasse 5. Inexpensive Altstadt Gaststätte, always with freshly-made dumplings on the menu, as well as beers from the local Scheidmantel brewery, whose premier product is the dark *Cortendorfer Dunkel*.

Burgschänke Veste Coburg 1b. The Veste's café-restaurant occupies a whimsical little building which was added during the early twentieth-century restorations. It also has a small beer garden.

Café Feyler Biedermeiercafé Rosengasse 6–8. A lovely daytime café and cake shop which, as its name suggests, has Biedermeier decor. Its main specialities are *Lebkuchen* and *Coburger Schmätzchen* (Coburg Kisses), the latter being gingerbread decorated with gold leaf.

Café Schubart Mohrenstr. 11. Another excellent traditional café, with a wide selection of home-made pralines.

Künstler-Klause Theaterplatz 4a. *Gemütlich* little restaurant serving Franconian specialities. Tues–Sat from 4.30pm, Sun 11.30am–2pm.

Naturkostrestaurant Tie Leopoldstr. 14. Primarily a wholefood specialist, though it also serves organic meat and fish dishes. Tues–Sun from 5pm.

Parkrestaurant Rosenau Rosenau 5, Rödental. This occupies one of the outbuildings of Schloss Rosenau, and has a pleasant garden terrace. Closed Mon.

Ratskeller Markt 1. Moderately priced restaurant in the Rathaus serving hearty Franconian and Bavarian fare.

Rosengarten Berliner Platz 1. Classy restaurant in the Kongresshaus, with an international menu. Closed Mon.

Schmittners Ahorner Str. 11. The main Gaststätte of the Sturm brewery, whose diverse products include a Pils named in honour of Prince Albert. Closed Wed.

Bad Staffelstein

About 25km south of Coburg, almost exactly halfway towards Bamberg, two of Germany's most famous ecclesiastical complexes can be seen in exhilaratingly lofty positions on either side of the Main valley. Both lie within the scattered municipality of **BAD STAFFELSTEIN**, a recuperative health resort with a pretty half-timbered town centre. The main attraction of its Kurpark is the **Obermain Therme** (daily 8am–9pm), which offers some of the best and most up-to-date bathing facilities in Bavaria.

Kloster Banz

Kloster Banz, which stands on top of a hill to the west of the Main, directly above the incorporated village of Altenbanz, is about 3km from the town centre. The only buses which go there are school services, though it's a pleasant enough walk by a paved footpath. Benedictine monks first settled on the hilltop in the eleventh century, but the present Baroque buildings all date from the eighteenth century. Work was begun under Leonhard Dientzenhofer, the court architect in Bamberg, and continued after his death by his brother Johann. It was brought to completion by Balthasar Neumann, who designed the buildings round the spacious entrance courtyard. After the Napoleonic secularisation, the abbey was taken over by the Wittelsbachs as a summer residence.

Nowadays, the monastic buildings belong to a foundation and are used for seminars and conferences; the only part generally accessible to the public is the **Petrefakten Sammlung** (March 1 to Nov 1 Tues–Sun 10am–5pm; €1) by the main entrance. This contains a collection of fossils found locally, mostly in the first half of the nineteenth century. These are around 180 million years old, and are almost exclusively of maritime creatures, which suggests that the area was covered by a sea at the time. Of special note is the largest skull of a prehistoric fish ever found in Europe: it is more than two metres long and belonged to a reptile resembling a dolphin. Also on view are the artefacts accumulated by Duke Max of Bavaria on a voyage to Egypt in 1838; these include a 3000-year-old mummy and a stuffed crocodile he himself captured in the Nile.

The former abbey church of **St-Petrus-und-St-Dionysius** is now in parish use. It's normally only open as far as the grille: to penetrate further it's necessary to ring for a **guided tour** (May–Oct Mon–Sat 9am–noon & 2–5pm, Sun 10.15am–noon & 2–5pm; Nov–April Mon–Sat 9am–noon, Sun 10.15am–noon; donation requested). Designed and built by Johann Dientzenhofer, the church is a brilliant spatial composition based on a series of ovals. The **high altar** performs a crucial architectural function: it separates the choir, which was reserved for the use of the monks, from the main body of the church, while giving the congregation a framed view through to the choir altar, with its depiction of the martyrdom of St Dionysius. Among the abundant furnishings, the walnut **choir stalls** have pride of place; their backs are adorned with small illusionistic intarsia scenes of the life of St Benedict made from several different woods plus ivory, silver and mother-of-pearl. The nave **frescoes** by the Tyrolean Melchior Steidl are also of high artistic quality; the depiction of Pentecost on the dome is flanked by the Conversion of Saul and The Last Supper. At 11.30am on summer Sundays, recitals are held on the magnificent **organ**. Although the original pipework was removed from the case a century ago, another instrument by the same Baroque master, Johann Philipp Seuffert, has now taken its place.

Vierzehnheiligen

The pilgrimage church of **Vierzehnheiligen** on the opposite side of the Main lies 5km northeast of the centre of Staffelstein, and almost exactly the same distance southeast of the railway junction of Lichtenfels, the next town to the north. Some of the buses between the two towns pass via the church (check the posted timetables); additionally, there are two return services per day from Lichtenfels' Bahnhof. By foot, the way is clearly signposted from both towns, and the latter stages of these give some wonderful views up to the church and across the valley.

Vierzehnheiligen has its origins in three apparitions of the Christ child in 1445–46 to a shepherd who worked for **Kloster Langheim**, a Cistercian monastery (nowadays occupied by Franciscans) high above Staffelstein. In the last of these, the child was accompanied by 14 smaller children who told the shepherd they were the auxiliary saints (those invoked by Roman Catholics for intercessory purposes in almost every sphere of life), and that they wished a chapel to be erected on the spot. A miraculous healing occurred shortly afterwards, and the site quickly became a popular place of pilgrimage. In 1743 **Balthasar Neumann** was commissioned to replace the dilapidated old church with a splendid new construction. Although he died ten years later with work far from complete, the result is in many ways his greatest achievement, one particularly admired by practising architects for the sheer complexity of its solutions.

The handsome twin-towered sandstone **facade** directly faces that of Banz, and is designed to appear like a great sentinel to pilgrims as they ascend the hill; the rest of the exterior consists of plain, straight walls. There could be no greater contrast with the **interior**, which is sumptuously decorated and imparts a restless sense of movement by dispensing with straight lines altogether, replacing them with curves. The groundplan is a development of that of Banz, being based on a series of intersecting oval rotundas; the fourteen piers symbolise the saints to whom the church is dedicated. In the middle of the church stands the **Gnadenaltar**, a unique shrine-cum-altar which looks like a huge yet extremely fragile piece of porcelain; it was made by a large team of stuccowork artists led by one of Germany's greatest Rococo craftsmen, Johann Michael Feichtmayr. Statues of the fourteen intercessory saints are grouped on and around the shrine; inside is a painting illustrating the shepherd's third miraculous vision. The same sculptors also made the high altar and the two large side altars; that on the north side contains the two most impressive figures of all – St Sebastian and the farmers' patron, St Wendelin. Unfortunately, the ceiling **frescoes** (which include a depiction of the fourteen saints in the company of the patrons of the Bamberg diocese, Heinrich II and Kunigunde) by the Italian Guiseppe Appiani were damaged by dampness in the nineteenth century, and their colours have faded badly.

Practicalities

Bad Staffelstein's **Bahnhof** is on the west side of town, close to the Kurpark; **taxis** can be hired at the rank outside if you don't want to walk to Banz or wait for a bus to Vierzehnheiligen. Among the town's **hotels** are *Gasthof Grüner Baum*, Bamberger Str. 33 (ⓣ0 95 73/2 93, ⓦwww.traditionsgasthof-gruener-baum.de; ❸); *Rödiger*, Zur Herrgottsmühle 2 (ⓣ0 95 73/92 60, ⓦwww.hotel-roediger.de; ❺); and *Kurhotel an der Obermaintherme*, Am Kurpark 7 (ⓣ0 95 73/33 30, ⓦwww.kurhotel-staffelstein.de; ❻). Another option is *Haus Frankenthal* (ⓣ0 95 73/92 68; ❸), which is just a few paces from Vierzehnheiligen, though it is primarily a holiday retreat rather than a regular hotel. It adjoins the fifteenth-century *Gasthof Goldener Hirsch*, nowadays a daytime **restaurant**. A short walk uphill is the *Alte Klosterbrauerei*, a traditional Hausbrauerei with a beer garden and bar, which also serves food; its main product is the dark *Nothelfer*. There are also good restaurants in each of the three hotels in town, while Kloster Banz has a daytime-only establishment, *Klosterschenke*.

Bamberg

There can be no doubt about the status of **BAMBERG** as one of the most beautiful small cities in Europe. Brought to prominence by the saintly eleventh-century Emperor Heinrich II, who wanted to turn it into a German metropolis to rival Rome, it never grew to be particularly big, but nonetheless has a sense of spacious grandeur which belies its actual size. Its relative geographical isolation, some 60km north of Nürnberg and 50km south of Coburg, has been a key factor in preserving its magnificent **artistic heritage** from the ravages of war. Every single European style from the Romanesque onwards has left its mark on the city, each bequeathing at least one outstanding building. It also has one of the most marvellously diverse arrays of sculpture to be found in the country.

Not the least of Bamberg's attractions is that, in contrast to some of Franconia's other picturesque old towns, it hasn't been mothballed into a museum-piece, being an animated city of modern industries which profits from the youthful presence of a university. It's also one of the country's great **beer** centres, holding the national record for consumption per inhabitant. Out of the 64 breweries the city had a century ago, nine still survive; all are traditional Hausbrauereien, and some have an in-house hotel as well as the

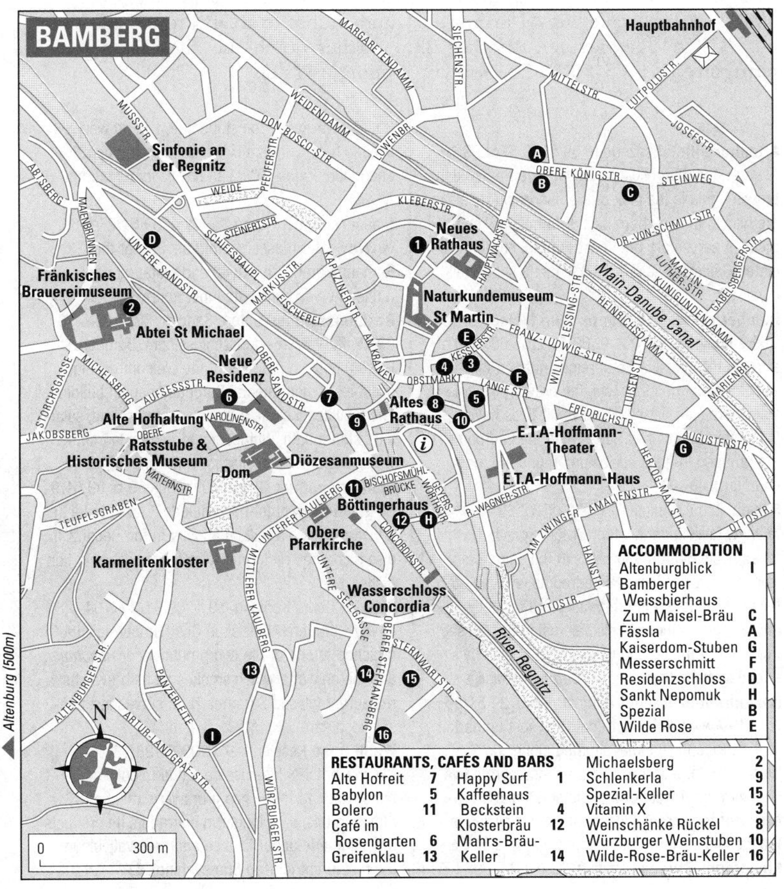

obligatory restaurant. Together they produce more than thirty different products, the most notable being the appropriately named *Rauchbier* (smoky beer): made from smoked malt according to a formula developed in the sixteenth century, it's as distinctive a local brew as you'll find in Germany, leaving its own very special lingering aftertaste.

Arrival, information and accommodation

Bamberg's **Hauptbahnhof** is about fifteen minutes' walk to the northeast of the Altstadt. The **tourist office** (April–Oct Mon–Fri 9am–6pm, Sat & Sun 9.30am–2.30pm; rest of year same hours Mon–Sat only; ⓣ09 51/87 11 61, ⓦwww.bamberg.info.de) is on an island in the River Pegnitz at Geyerswörthstr. 3. Regnitz **cruises**, run by Personenschiffahrt Bamberg (ⓣ09 51/2 66 79, ⓦwww.personenschiffahrt-bamberg.de), depart from Am Kranen and cost €5 for an 80-minute round trip.

Bamberg offers an exceptionally good choice of **hotels**, ranging from inexpensive brewery-owned inns (Brauereigasthöfe) to upmarket establishments in characterful historic buildings. The **youth hostel** is pleasantly situated on the bank of the Regnitz 2km south of the centre at Oberer Leinritt 70 (ⓣ09 51/5 60 02; €12.70); take bus #1 from the Hauptbahnhof to ZOB Promenade, then bus #18 to Regnitzufer. Another 2km further down the river is the *Insel* **campsite** (ⓣ09 51/5 63 20, ⓦwww.campinginsel.de).

Hotels

Altenburgblick Panzerleite 59 ⓣ09 51/9 53 10, ⓦwww.altenburgblick.de. Run by the Greifenklau brewery, this is the pick of the panorama hotels in the hills in the southern part of Bamberg. The only meals it serves are breakfast buffets, but the associated Gaststätte (see p.197) is just a short walk away. ❺

Bamberger Weissbierhaus Zum Maisel-Bräu Obere Königstr. 38 ⓣ & ⓕ09 51/2 55 03. One of a trio of inexpensive Brauereigasthöfe on the street; unlike the other two, the brewery itself is elsewhere (see p.198). However, it does have a bar-restaurant (closed Sun), while the bedrooms are grouped in quiet seclusion around the inner courtyard. ❷–❹

Fässla Obere Königstr. 21 ⓣ09 51/2 65 16, ⓦwww.faessla.de. Another Brauereigasthof, which recently celebrated 350 years in the same premises. It offers modernized bedrooms with private facilities, good buffet breakfasts and typically homely fare in the no-frills bar-restaurant (closed Sun after 1pm). Among its products is the city's strongest beer, the seasonal *Bambergator.* ❹

Kaiserdom Gaustadter Hauptstr. 26 ⓣ09 51/96 51 40, ⓦwww.kaiserdom.de. The most upmarket of the Brauereigasthöfe, situated alongside Bamberg's largest brewery in an incorporated village 4km northwest of the Altstadt. It has an excellent restaurant (closed Mon) specializing in Franconian cuisine plus a large beer garden. ❺

Kaiserdom-Stuben Urbanstr. 18 ⓣ09 51/98 07 30, ⓦwww.kaiserdomstuben.de. The brewery's second hotel is much closer to the town centre, and incorporates a Catalan speciality restaurant, *El Niu.* ❺

Messerschmitt Lange Str. 41 ⓣ09 51/2 78 66, ⓦwww.hotel-messerschmitt.de. Part of the Romantik group, this hotel and restaurant occupy a fine old Weinhaus with inner courtyard. ❼

Residenzschloss Untere Sandstr. 32 ⓣ09 51/6 09 10, ⓦwww.residenzschloss.com. Bamberg's leading hotel, a member of the Welcome chain, occupies a monumental Baroque hospital building. The facilities include a fitness centre, sauna, solarium, steam bath, whirlpool and two restaurants: *Orangerie* and *Fürst Bischof von Erthal.* ❾

Sankt Nepomuk Obere Mühlbrücke 9 ⓣ09 51/9 84 20, ⓦwww.hotel-nepomuk.de. Classy hotel in a picturesque old mill on an islet in the Regnitz. It also has a fine restaurant which specializes in fish dishes. ❼

Spezial Obere Königstr. 10 ⓣ09 51/2 43 04, ⓦwww.brauerei-spezial.de Cosy Brauereigasthof attached to one of the two producers of *Rauchbier*, and the only one which smokes all its brews. Its restaurant (closed Sat after 2pm) serves inexpensive local fare. ❸

Wilde Rose Kesslerstr. 7 ⓣ09 51/98 18 20, ⓦwww.hotel-wilde-rose.de. Good middle-range hotel which formerly had a brewery attached. Although this is no longer in operation, its products are still made under licence and are available in the restaurant (closed Sun evening). ❻

The City

Like Rome, on which it was very consciously modelled, Bamberg is built on seven hills, pocked with belvederes which each offer a different perspective on the city. The Dom and related structures take up the entire crown of the main hill, towering high above the town centre to form the Domstadt, the headquarters of the prince-bishopric which ruled until the Napoleonic suppression, whereupon it gave way to the purely spiritual archbishopric still based here. Clinging to the lower slopes of the valley of the River Regnitz are the residential districts, which constitute an unusually complete Baroque townscape of picturesque corners.

The Dom

Consecrated in 1012, the **Dom** (often dignified as the **Kaiserdom**) was burnt down twice in the following two centuries, and the present sandstone structure is the result of a slow rebuilding process that continued throughout the thirteenth century. During this period architectural tastes were beginning to change, but the ground plan follows the precedent of the imperial cathedrals of the Rhineland in having a choir at both ends of the building, each of which is flanked by twin towers. The east chancel is dedicated to the warrior St George, symbolizing the Empire, while its western counterpart bears a dedication to St Peter, representing the Papacy. These were the first and last parts of the Dom to be completed, and you can see that the rounded Romanesque arches and heavy vaults of the eastern choir had given way to the tall pointed windows and graceful ribs characteristic of early Gothic by the west end. In between, the nave was erected in the Transitional style, offering insight into the way the original masons were experimenting with the new techniques.

What makes the Kaiserdom one of Europe's greatest cathedrals is the astonishing array of **sculptural decoration**. As with the architecture, this was initially executed in an orthodox Romanesque style, the best example being the **Fürstenportal** on the nave's north side, facing the main slope of the square. Its tympanum warns of the Last Judgment, while the progressively receding arches are each adorned with the figure of an Apostle standing on the shoulders of an Old Testament prophet. Carvings in a similar style can be found on the **Marienportal** on the right-hand door to the east chancel, which shows the Madonna and Child adored by the Kaiserdom's patrons, founders and builders, and on the choir screen panels, also placing Apostles and prophets in juxtaposition.

Created by an unknown French-trained artist, the most famous of all this sculpture is the enigmatic **Bamberg Rider** (Bamberger Reiter) just inside the entrance doorway, one of the few equestrian statues which had been made since the days of classical antiquity. Nobody knows for sure who this noble figure is; the Romantics imagined it was an idealized portrait of a German emperor of the Hohenstaufen line. This was eagerly seized on by the Nazis, and during the Third Reich the statue was the national symbol of Germanic perfection, adorning every public hall and classroom. Two other **statues** to look out for are the female personifications of the Christian and Jewish faiths at the southeast end of the nave. The victory of Christianity over Judaism is highlighted by the women's contrasting countenances: the Christian is a beautiful woman clad in rich cloth, while the Jewess stands blindfolded holding a broken rod and wearing a plain tunic that emphasizes the outline of her fallen breasts. Even finer are the two figures of the Visitation group directly opposite. The Virgin Mary is young and bright, draped in a swirling dress; Saint Elizabeth is a haggard old crone whose expression speaks of an overwhelming sense of pathos.

As a perfect complement to the carvings associated with its construction, the Dom also contains a masterpiece by each of the two most famous sculptors of the early sixteenth century. Focus of the nave is the white limestone **tomb** of **Heinrich II and Kunigunde**, the canonized imperial couple, which stands slightly elevated as a result of the crypt built below. **Tilman Riemenschneider** laboured away for fourteen years on this sarcophagus, whose reliefs depict scenes taken from the life and times of the couple. The south transept contains **Veit Stoss**' dark limewood **Nativity altar**, made when the artist was about eighty years old, as a result of a commission from his son, who was the Carmelite prior in Nürnberg. It was meant as a sort of artistic testament, executed without the usual studio assistance. Unfortunately, it's unfinished – the younger Stoss, a virulent anti-Protestant, was kicked out of Nürnberg when the city council adopted the Reformation, and the sculptor received no payment for his retable, which was soon afterwards moved to Bamberg.

Although it's not accessible to the public, it's worth knowing that the western choir holds the only **papal grave** north of the Alps, namely that of Pope Clement II. He was the local bishop before becoming pope, but died in 1047 after having enjoyed the papacy for a mere ten months. Tomb slabs to the Dom's other bishops can be found scattered throughout the building. The most impressive, artistically speaking, is the **monument to Friedrich von Hohenlohe** in the south aisle, just before the transept. Dating from the latter half of the fourteenth century, it conveniently represents the period midway between the Bamberg Rider and the works of Riemenschneider and Stoss.

Entered from the southern aisle, the cloisters and associated buildings now house the **Diözesanmuseum** (Tues–Sun 10am–5pm; €2). On the walls of the cloister walks are lapidary fragments, most notably the six original statues from the **Adamportal**, the dogtooth doorway to the left of the east choir. Here the ubiquitous Emperor and his wife turn up in the company of the Dom's two patrons, plus Adam and Eve. The last two are unashamedly sensual; covered only by fig-leaves, they come as near to erotic art as was ever dared in the Middle Ages. Upstairs, displayed under specially dimmed lights, is a collection of early medieval **vestments** – including the cloaks of Heinrich, Kunegunde and Pope Clement II – whose vibrant colours and intricate designs are quite amazingly well preserved. There are also some valuable treasury items, such as a twelfth-century ivory Crucifix and the so-called staff of St Otto, as well as a magnificent tapestry of the Passion from around 1500.

Domplatz

Domplatz is lined with such a superb variety of buildings, which unfold like a great picture-book of architecture, and uses its spacious, sloping site to such dramatic advantage, that it has no possible rival for the title of Germany's finest square. The **Ratsstube** is a Renaissance gem, with elegantly tapering gables and an ornate oriel window. It now contains the **Historisches Museum** (Tues–Sun 9am–5pm; €2), which covers local and regional history from the Stone Age onwards, as well as Bamberg's rich artistic tradition. The exhibits include a tenth-century ivory *Madonna and Child* from Constantinople; an intricate late sixteenth-century clock; a typically idiosyncratic panel of *The Great Flood* by **Hans Baldung Grien**, who here tackled with relish a subject most painters shied away from; and Balthasar Neumann's original wooden model for Vierzehnheiligen.

Adjoining the Ratsstube is the **Reiche Tor**, in which Heinrich and Kunigunde appear once more; the model they carry is recognizably the Kaiserdom. This gate leads into the huge fifteenth-century courtyard of the **Alte Hofhaltung**, the former episcopal palace, which incorporates the remains of the eleventh-century hall of the Imperial Diet. The overhanging eaves of the huge sloping roof shelter two tiers of wooden galleries, and there's an unusual perspective on the towers of the Dom. One wing contains an annexe of the Historisches Museum.

Across the street is the building which supplanted it, the **Neue Residenz** (guided tours daily: April–Sept 9am–6pm; Oct–March 10am–4pm; €3; Ⓦwww.schloesser.bayern.de). An early example of the passion for building huge new palaces in the Baroque style that was to sweep across the German principalities, it was erected at the turn of the eighteenth century to an L-shape plan by Leonhard Dientzenhofer. Inside, a suite of rooms designed expressly for occasions when the emperor stayed as guest culminate in the huge **Kaisersaal**, which is nowadays a regular concert venue. Its walls are entirely covered with rich stuccowork and colourful frescoes by Melchior Steidl, including portraits of the emperors of ancient Rome and a ceiling with an allegorical composition extolling the benefits of wise rule. The private apartments of the prince-bishops are far more homely in feel; the most original is the **Chinesische Kabinett**, a curious hybrid in which traditional Baroque decoration is mixed with chinoiserie.

Also included in the entrance ticket, but visited independently, is the **Staatsgalerie Bamberg** (same times), which occupies two suites of apartments. The first of these contains works by Bamberg painters of the Gothic and Renaissance periods, and by some of their German contemporaries, including the Master of the Life of the Virgin, Hans Suess von Kulmbach, Baldung and Cranach. In the second gallery, which is devoted to the Baroque era, the geographical scope is widened to include Dutch and Flemish paintings. The palace also houses the **Staatsbibliothek** (Mon–Fri 9am–5pm, Sat 9am–noon; free; Ⓦwww.staatsbibliothek-bamberg.de), and it's worth having at least a quick look at the elegant Baroque hall which serves as its reading room. It usually stages a couple of exhibitions per year; facsimiles of its most valuable treasures, including some stunning illuminated manuscripts, are on permanent view in the corridor. To the rear of the complex is the **Rosengarten**, a formal rose garden with playful Rococo statues. It commands marvellous views, particularly up to the Abtei St Michael.

The lower town

Below Domplatz is the lower town (Unterstadt), which is laid out on both sides of the Regnitz. From its islet position, the **Altes Rathaus**, which seems almost too picturesque for its own good, anchors together two of the connecting bridges, the Obere Brücke and Untere Brücke. Except for the half-timbered section overhanging the rapids, the original Gothic building was transformed in Rococo style, and its walls are busily tattooed with exuberant frescoes. Inside is the **Sammlung Ludwig** (Tues–Sun 9.30am–4.30pm; €3.50), a collection of Baroque porcelain and faience from all over Europe. On a much larger island to the south stands **Schloss Geyerswörth**, the Renaissance palace of the prince-bishops. Its **tower** (key available from the tourist office – see p.192) commands a fine view of the Domstadt. The famous **Klein-Venedig** (Little Venice) of fishermen's houses is best seen from the Untere Brücke and presents one of the very few medieval scenes in the lower parts of town.

The bridges lead over to the elongated Grüner Markt, which is dominated by the facade of **St Martin**, a huge Jesuit church designed by the Dientzenhofer brothers. Within its former monastic buildings to the rear is the **Naturkundemuseum** (April–Sept Tues–Sun 9am–5pm; Oct–March Tues–Sun 10am–4pm; €1.50; Ⓦwww.uni-bamberg.de/natmus), which contains fossils found in the Franconian Jura as well as crystals and stuffed animals, including a rare quagga. However, the main attraction is what is described as a "museum within the museum", a beautiful Neoclassical exhibition hall still preserving its original display cabinets and their exhibits. The ground floor is entirely devoted to ornithology, and is divided equally between Central European and exotic species. In the upstairs galleries are small mammals, reptiles, fish, insects and shells.

Beyond Grüner Markt is the vast open space of **Maxplatz**, where daily markets are held. On its northern side is the **Neues Rathaus**, which was built by Balthasar Neumann, originally for use as a seminary. A smaller but prettier square on this side of the river is Schillerplatz to the southeast. Here, at no. 26, is the **E.T.A.-Hoffmann-Haus** (May–Oct Tues–Fri 4–6pm, Sat & Sun 10am–noon; €1; Ⓦwww.etahg.de), the home of one of the foremost figures of the Romantic movement. For the five years he lived in Bamberg, he tried to establish himself as a composer, conductor and theatre director, having previously failed as a painter; it was only later that he came to realize that his genius lay with words, becoming an unusually perspicacious music critic and an author of weird short stories reflecting his own rather schizophrenic nature. In addition to the expected memorabilia and documentation on his diverse career, it now contains contemporary artistic installations inspired by his stories.

Back on the west bank, the southern end of the lower town is dominated by the **Wasserschloss Concordia**, a riverside mansion built by Johann Dientzenhofer for the Franconian chargé d'affaires. The same patron had previously commissioned a grand Baroque palace, the **Böttingerhaus**, which lies a short walk to the north at Judenstr. 14.

The hills

On Unter Kaulberg, which sweeps uphill from Judenstrasse, is Bamberg's main parish church, the **Obere Pfarrkirche**. Architecturally, it's something of a hotchpotch, though the chancel and the **Brautportal** (bridal portal), whose carvings of the Wise and Foolish Virgins strike a suitable warning note, are distinguished productions of the famous fourteenth-century Parler family. The interior was remodelled in Baroque style, and contains a huge **high altar** of the period incorporating a much-venerated Gothic statue of the Virgin and Child. Other furnishings of special note include a highly elaborate late fourteenth-century **tabernacle**, now banished to one of the ambulatory chapels; an early sixteenth-century **font** with reliefs of the Sacraments; and a large painting of *The Assumption* by **Tintoretto**.

Further up the same hill is the **Karmelitenkloster**, whose Baroque church was designed by Leonhard Dientzenhofer. Of more interest are the surviving parts of the suppressed convent which formerly occupied the site: the Romanesque portal, guarded by lions, which is incongruously stranded in a walled-up position at the back of the present church, and the **cloister** (daily 8.30–11.30am & 2.30–5.30pm; free), the largest in Germany. The latter is now known to be late fourteenth-century in date, though it was built in the long-superseded Romanesque style. Despite this anachronism, the column capitals were carved by masons possessed of fertile imagination: in addition to the biblical scenes, there's a fabulous bestiary, ranging from fearsome dragons to weird creepy-crawlies.

Crowning the hill to the north of the Dom is the **Abtei St Michael**, an eleventh-century Benedictine foundation. The **Abteikirche** still preserves some of its Romanesque masonry from the following century, though it was badly damaged by fire in 1610 and partially rebuilt in a tardy Gothic style. Also from this period are the **vault paintings**, which depict more than six hundred plants with medicinal properties, and the **organ gallery**, which is in the late Renaissance style then fashionable. The small crypt to the rear of the high altar contains the beautifully carved thirteenth-century **tomb of St Otto**, a Bamberg bishop of the previous century; there's also a polyrchromed portrait slab of him, made around the same time. In the nineteenth century, the grand tombs of the prince-bishops who ruled between the mid-sixteenth and late eighteenth centuries were moved here from the Dom, and placed in the aisles of the nave. Among the many large-scale furnishings added during the Baroque era, the finest are the gilded **pulpit**, which is topped by a dramatic composition of St Michael overcoming Satan, and the **choir stalls**, with their backs of inlaid wood. The part-stucco, part-painted depiction of the Dance of Death on the vault of the **Heilig-Grab-Kapelle** is from the same period.

Leonhard Dietzenhofer, who added a new facade to the church, also began the monumental complex of monastic buildings around the front courtyard; his work was continued by his brother Johann and Balthasar Neumann, among others. The cellars now house the **Fränkisches Brauereimuseum** (April–Oct Wed–Sun 1–5pm; €2), which displays all the equipment used in traditional brewing, as well as memorabilia of Bamberg breweries past and present. From the terrace beyond, there's a wonderful panorama of the town and the surrounding hills.

However, the most dramatic views of Bamberg's skyline are obtained from the footpath leading up to the **Altenburg**, a heavily restored feudal fortress at the southwestern edge of town. Dating back at least as far as the early twelfth century, it became the residence of the local prince-bishops a couple of hundred years later. During daylight hours, there's normally unrestricted access to the castle, whose ramparts command an extensive view over the surrounding countryside, but a far less satisfying one of the city itself than those en route.

Eating, drinking and entertainment

Many of Bamberg's best restaurants are in the hotels (see p.192). The brewery-owned restaurants (Brauereigaststätten) and their associated beer gardens (some on site, others, usually much larger, on the hills above the town) are the obvious places for solid, good-value food accompanied by locally made beer. Note that, as well as those listed below, there are others which also offer accommodation and are therefore included in the hotel section.

Brewery restaurants and beer gardens

Greifenklau Laurenziplatz 20. Beer cellar of Bamberg's smallest brewery, which produces a *Weizen* and a golden amber *Lagerbier*. Its garden offers a view up to the Altenburg. Closes at 2pm on Sun.

Keesmann Wunderburg 5. Another small operation, this time in a right-bank inner suburb, whose premier product is Bamberg's best Pils. It occupies a handsome building with a tree-shaded inner courtyard. Closed Sat after 3pm & Sun.

Klosterbräu Obere Mühlbrücke 3. This picturesque riverside brewery, complete with inner courtyard and a medieval tithe barn where beer festivals are held in April and August, is the oldest in Bamberg, dating back to 1533. In accordance with its ecclesiastical origins, it's best-known for its dark brews, *Braunbier* and *Schwärzla*. Closed Wed.

Mahrs-Bräu Wunderburg 10. The decor of this Gaststätte has been preserved almost unaltered for more than a century; there's also a courtyard garden. The brewery alongside makes a range of predominantly pale-coloured beers.
Mahrs-Bräu-Keller Oberer Stephansberg 36. Beer garden and restaurant of the eponymous brewery; the latter occupies a half-timbered building with a Jugendstil extension. Evenings only, except on Sun; closed Mon.
Maisel-Keller Moosstr. 32. Bamberg's Maisel brewery (which is completely separate from its Bayreuth namesake) is a relative newcomer, being just over a century old, though it makes a wider variety of beers than its local rivals. Lying 1km southeast of the Hauptbahnhof, on the opposite side of the tracks, it has a large garden on site.
Schlenkerla Dominikanerstr. 6. Not to be missed: the seventeenth-century tavern of the Heller brewery, which makes what's generally regarded as the ultimate smoky beer, *Aecht Schlenkerla Rauchbier*: the standard version is a *Märzen*, though there's a smoked *Weizen* as well. It also serves hearty local cuisine.Closed Tues.
Spezial-Keller Oberer Stephansberg 47, entrance on Sternwartstrasse. Large and popular beer cellar-cum-garden, commanding a fine distant view of the city, of the other *Rauchbier* specialist. Open Tues–Sat from 3pm, Sun from 10am, closed Mon.
Wilde-Rose-Bräu-Keller Obere Stephansberg 49. Beer garden, complete with pavilions, serving the products of a label which has survived the closure of the brewery itself. May–Sept only: weekdays from 4pm, weekends from 3pm.

Other restaurants

Alte Hofreit Dominikanerstr. 10. Restaurant combining a traditional beer hall atmosphere with wholefood dishes.
Babylon Lange Str. 22. Serves good North African and Mediterranean food, including vegetarian specialities.
Burggaststätte Altenburg 1. Cosy restaurant in the Altenburg. Closed Sun evening & Mon.
Michaelsberg Michaelsberg 10e. Occupying part of the abbey complex, this has a salad bar and a large terrace offering a wonderful view over Bamberg. Closed Tues.
Weinschänke Rückel Habergasse 4. Bamberg's oldest wine bar, founded in 1826, offers a good choice of vintages plus beers from the rural Reckendorf brewery. Evenings only, closed Sun.
Würzburger Weinstuben Zinkenwörth 6. Classy wine bar-restaurant in a half-timbered building. Closed Tues evening & Wed.

Bars and cafés

Bolero Judenstr. 7. Popular tapas bar with a large beer garden.
Café im Rosengarten Domplatz 1. A daytime café in a pavilion of the rose garden of the Neues Residenz; tables are also set up on the terrace outside. April–Oct only.
Happy Surf Frauenstr. 5. Internet café which serves a good milky coffee and a range of meals and snacks. Open Mon-Fri 11am-1am, Sat 11am-2am, Sun 2pm-1am.
Kaffeehaus Beckstein Lange Str. 9. Viennese-style coffee house; also serves lunch dishes. Closed Sun.
Vitamin X Kesslerstr. 12. Located within a wholefood shop, this vegetarian café has a particularly good range of freshly pressed juices.

Music, theatre and festivals

For its size, Bamberg has an amazingly vibrant cultural centre, especially for **classical music**. The Bamberger Symphoniker was actually the old Deutsches Orchester of Prague, which fled over the border at the time the Iron Curtain was going up. Now under the musical directorship of Britain's Jonathan Nott, the orchestra ranks among Germany's very best and has a new custom-built home, the Sinfonie an der Regnitz (Ⓣ09 51/9 67 41 00, Ⓦwww.bamberger-symphoniker.de). *Jazzkeller*, Obere Sandstr. 18, has **jazz** on Tuesday and Thursday; *Live-Club*, Obere Sandstr. 7, features **live bands** on Monday and Saturday; while *Downstairs*, Lange Str. 16, is the leading **nightclub**. The principal **theatre** is the E.T.A. Hoffmann-Theater, Schillerplatz 7 (Ⓣ09 51/2 08 73 07 or 87 14 33, Ⓦwww.theater.bamberg.de); the resident company also holds an open-air season in June and July in the Alte Hofhaltung. Performances by the Marionettentheater Loose take place in a 16-seater puppet theatre of 1821 in the Staubsches Haus, Untere Sandstr. 30 (Ⓣ09 51/6 76 00).

Bamberg's most colourful religious **festival** is Corpus Christi (*Fronleichnam*; variable date in May/June), when an open-air Mass on Domplatz is followed by a procession in which devotional statues and ecclesiastical objects are carried through the streets of the town on stretchers adorned with magnificent floral garlands. In early summer, a couple of musical festivals are held in the Neues Residenz – the Residenz Festival and the Tage Alter Musik. A wine festival, the Fränkisches Weinfest, is held in Schloss Geyerswörth in late June, while the Fränkisches Brauereimuseum runs a beer festival, Brauerei Nostalgiefest, in early July. The main folklore event is the Strassenfest in late September.

Schweinfurt

The former Free Imperial City of **SCHWEINFURT** lies 55km down the Main from Bamberg on the looping rail line along the valley to Würzburg. Its Altstadt lies on the north bank of the river, a harbour and industrial district on the opposite side. For the past century, it has been known principally as a ball-bearing metropolis, and this ensured it was subject to severe aerial bombardment during World War II. Afterwards, the American forces, who established a large and still active base in the town, allowed the ball-bearing tycoon Georg Schäfer to return to his factory, and he had an enormously successful career, establishing subsidiary concerns all around the globe. Schäfer used his fortune to fund his passion for art, concentrating exclusively on the German-speaking world, and a few years after his death in 1975 his choice group of old masters was put on permanent display in Coburg. In the meantime, the nineteenth-century paintings and drawings which formed the core of his collection, rivalling and in many respects surpassing the holdings of this period in the great public galleries of Berlin, Hamburg and Munich, remained with his descendants, though selections were sometimes exhibited. The first steps towards making the works permanently accessible to the public were not taken until 1997, when a foundation was set up with the aim of giving Schweinfurt the major attraction it had hitherto lacked, yet desperately wanted in its bid to become a tourist and conference centre.

The Town

After an almost miraculously short period of planning and construction work, the **Museum Georg Schäfer** (Tues, Wed & Fri–Sun 10am–5pm, Thurs 10am–9pm; €3.50, or €6 including the themed exhibitions; Ⓦwww.museumgeorgschaefer.de) opened in 2000 at Brückenstr. 20 in the town centre. It has attracted rave reviews, not only for the quality of the exhibits, but also for the building by the Berlin architect Volker Staab (who was also responsible for the Neues Museum in Nürnberg), a satisfying blend of modernity and tradition, expertly lit and commanding fine views over the town from its top level, where about a third of the total stock of more than 1000 works is displayed in strict chronological order. The first room contains a wonderful group of canvases by **Friedrich**, ranging from a poetic nocturne, *Evening on the Baltic*, to a visionary masterpiece, *The Cathedral*. There are more than a hundred works in various media by **Menzel**, the most versatile German artist of the nineteenth century. These include historical vignettes of the court life of Frederick the

Great and documentations of the contemporary court of Kaiser Wilhlem I, topographical views and scenes of the industrial world, as well as many superb portraits, including the artist Chodowiecki (depicted sketching on Jannowitzbrücke in Berlin), the author Paul Heyse, the so-called Rabbi of Baghdad, and a young girl, Friederike Arnold, drawn in gorgeous pastel colours. The Biedermeier artist **Spitzweg**, whose fun-poking yet never cruel humour is seen at its most effective in paintings such as *The Bookworm*, *The Cactus Lover* and *The Portraitist*, is even more copiously represented, by some 160 oils and 100 drawings, by far the largest collection of his work in existence, though much of it is usually in store. Other highpoints of the collection are an oval *The Madonna and Child with St John* by **Overbeck**; the jewel-like *Sulamith and Maria* by his short-lived Nazarene colleague **Franz Pforr**; the salacious *Going for a Ride* by **Franz von Stuck**; and self-portraits by Wilhelm Busch (better-known as the father of the strip cartoon), Lenbach, Liebermann and Corinth. The first floor is devoted to themed exhibitions, which draw on the foundation's extensive collection of graphic art as well as its reserve of paintings.

Although the museum overshadows everything else in town, the Altstadt has some fine historic buildings, notably the **Rathaus**, which is at the top end of the same street. A mixture of Gothic and Renaissance elements, with a prominent tower-cum-oriel, the building was designed in the 1570s by the Saxon architect Nickel Hoffmann. It faces **Marktplatz**, where markets are held on Wednesday and Saturday mornings and Tuesday and Friday afternoons.

On Martin-Luther-Platz, the next square to the north is the church of **St Johannis**, which was built over the course of several centuries, and is thus a mixture of Romanesque and both early and late Gothic elements. It also has a fine Renaissance chapel, the **Herrenkapelle**, on its north side, which contains a valuable documentary painting illustrating the presentation of the basic Protestant creed, the Confession of Augsburg, to Emperor Charles V in 1530. Nearby are three of the constituent parts of the **Städtische Sammlungen** (all Tues–Fri 2–5pm, Sat & Sun 10am–1pm & 2–5pm; free; ⓦwww.sammlungen-schweinfurt.de). Directly facing the Herrenkapelle is another handsome Renaissance building, the **Altes Gymnasium**, which contains the local history museum, including memorabilia of Friedrich Rückert and a series of cartoons of nineteenth-century citizens, called "Schweinfurt originals", by a sugar factory owner, Jens Sattler. Across the square is the **Museum Gunnar-Wester-Haus**, which features Russian icons of the sixteenth to nineteenth centuries, and a collection of historic lamps, lights and lanterns from Roman times onwards. Modern Franconian paintings and sculptures are housed in the **Alte Reichsvogtei**, a plain Renaissance building just round the corner from the Altes Gymnasium at Obere Str. 11.

Practicalities

Schweinfurt's **Hauptbahnhof**, a junction of the Würzburg-Bamberg line with that to Erfurt, lies 2km west of the Altstadt. Much closer to the centre, albeit a bit to the east, is the **Stadtbahnhof**, one stop away in the direction of Bamberg. The **tourist office** (Mon–Fri 10am–5pm, Sat 10am–2pm, ⓣ0 97 21/5 14 98, ⓦwww.schweinfurt.de) is on the ground floor of the Museum Georg Schäfer.

Hotels with a central location include *Gasthof Erdinger Weissbräu*, Obere Str. 21 (ⓣ0 97 21/53 30 94; ❸); *Gasthof Mangold*, Kornmarkt 13–15 (ⓣ0 97 21/1 60 96, ⓦwww.gasthof-mangold.de; ❸); *Panorama*, Am Oberen Marienbach 1 (ⓣ0 97 21/20 40; ❺); and the venerable *Ross*, Postplatz 9 (ⓣ0 97 21/2 00 10,

Ⓦwww.hotel-ross.de; ❻). Top of the range is *Mercure*, Maininsel, 10–12 (Ⓣ0 97 21/7 30 60, Ⓦwww.mercure.de ❼), which forms part of the new conference centre on the island opposite the Altstadt. The **youth hostel** is about 1km north of the Hauptbahnhof at Niederwerrner Str. 17 1/2 (Ⓣ0 97 21/2 14 04; €13.70). All the hotels listed above except *Panorama* have **restaurants**, and that in *Ross* ranks as the best in town. There are also plenty of good places to eat and drink around the Markt, with outside tables in summer: *Brauhaus am Markt*, Markt 30, is the tap of one of local breweries, Schweinfurter Brauhaus; *Brauerei Roth*, Obere Str. 24, of the other. *Kunstcafé*, Markt 12, is an artists' **café** with regular exhibitions.

Main **cruises** are run by Schweinfurter Personnenschiffahrt on Gutermannpromenade (Ⓣ0 97 21/4 33 02). The main local **festivals** are the Stadtmaifeste, a series of markets held each May weekend; the two-week-long Schweinfurter Volksfest in late June and early July, and the Strassenfest in mid-September. All kinds of **music** and **theatre** are performed by visiting artistes at the Theater der Stadt, Rossbrunnstr. 2 (Ⓣ0 97 21/5 14 75, Ⓦwww.theater-schweinfurt.de).

Aschaffenburg

King Ludwig I called **ASCHAFFENBURG**, which is situated on the River Main at the extreme northwestern corner of the state, about 80km due west of Schweinfurt, his "Bavarian Nice". Although the town has lost some of its charm since those days, the characterful historic centre and pleasant parks make it an agreeable place to spend a day or two, and it's also the obvious jumping-off point for exploring the unspoiled highland countryside of the Odenwald to the south. Once the preferred (though officially only secondary) residence of the powerful Archbishop-Electors of Mainz, Aschaffenburg is now mainly a dormitory town for Frankfurt.

The Town

Aschaffenburg's compact centre is dominated by **Schloss Johannisburg** (April–Sept Tues–Sun 9am–6pm; Oct–March Tues–Sun 10am–4pm; €3, or €4.50 combined ticket with Pompejanum; Ⓦwww.schloesser.bayern.de), a very French-looking late Renaissance red sandstone pile built at the beginning of the seventeenth century for the Mainz Electors by the Strasbourg architect Georg Ridinger. It was the first purely residential princely palace ever erected in Germany, and the first to adopt symmetrical principles of a regular ground-plan of four wings, though the keep of the previous medieval castle was retained as a fifth tower, counterbalancing those at the corners. The Schloss was badly damaged in World War II, and the surviving historic interiors, a suite of Neoclassical apartments on the second floor, are quite modest. A collection of eighteenth-century **ecclesiastical vestments**, which are displayed alongside liturgical objects and relief portraits of the archbishops, offer a more vivid evocation of the Mainz Electorate. However, these are overshadowed by the delectable collection of **cork models** of the monuments of ancient Rome, the earliest of which date back to the 1790s, and were made by the court pastry cook, Carl Joseph May. Even finer are the nine large models by his son, the civil engineer Georg Heinrich May, all of which are based on accurate on-the-spot measurements and observations.

Also within the Schloss, and covered by the same ticket, are two museums. The **Bayerische Staatsgalerie** on the first floor contains paintings by old German masters, many commissioned by one of the leading Catholic figures of the Reformation era, Cardinal Albrecht von Brandenburg. They include a large group of works by **Cranach** and his followers, **Baldung**'s *Calvary*, and the *Aschaffenburg Triptych* by the **Master of the Wendelin Altar**. There are also Dutch and Flemish works, including examples of Rubens, Van Dyck and Dou, as well as ten small but arresting scenes from a *Passion* cycle by **Arent de Gelder**, who continued the tradition of his master Rembrandt well into the eighteenth century. Upstairs, the **Städtische Sammlung** contains sculptures from the time of the Schloss' construction; products of the former stoneware factory in Damm, nowadays a suburb of Aschaffenburg; memorabilia of one-time local resident Clemens Brentano, the Romantic-era writer who jointly compiled the celebrated folk poetry anthology *Des Knaben Wunderhorn*; and paintings by the Neue Sachlichkeit artist Christian Schad.

Within the palace's north wing is the **Schlosskirche**, though the only exterior clues as to its presence are the spire and the courtyard portal, above which is a relief of the Baptism of Christ. This is attributed to the early seventeenth-century court sculptor Hans Juncker, who made the church's pulpit and its alabaster and marble **high altar**, which stretches from the ceiling all the way to the vault and incorporates a dozen scenes from Jesus' life.

A few minutes' walk downstream along the Main is the **Pompejanum** (April–Sept Tues–Sun 9am–6pm; €3; Ⓦ www.schloesser.bayern.de), a replica of the house of Castor and Pollux in Pompeii, built by Friedrich Gärtner for King Ludwig I. Its luxuriant gardens of Mediterranean trees and plants and its vineyard sloping down to the River Main make for an enjoyable stroll. The interior, which was badly damaged in the war, was only restored a few years ago, and now exhibits original Roman antiquities alongside the mock-classical decoration.

A walk down Pfaffengstrasse from Schloss Johannisburg takes you through the heart of the Altstadt, with its narrow streets of half-timbered houses, and leads to Stiftsplatz and Aschaffenburg's principal church, the **Stiftskirche St-Peter-und-Alexander**. Founded in the tenth century, it combines Romanesque, Gothic and Baroque features and it's this architectural identity crisis that gives it real visual impact. The furnishings are equally diverse: they include a poignant wooden **crucifix** which was made around 980, another pulpit by Juncker, and numerous **funerary monuments**. Of particular importance is the magnificent bronze memorial in the north transept to Cardinal Albrecht von Brandenburg; this and the accompanying relief of the Madonna and Child were both cast in the famous Vischer workshop in Nürnberg. In the last chapel of the southern aisle is a small panel of *The Lamentation* by Grünewald, which appears to be truncated but is in fact complete. The same artist also painted *The Madonna of the Snows* altarpiece in the elevated **Maria-Schnee-Kapelle** (Fri–Sun 1–5pm; €1), but the original is now in Stuppach (see p.363) and has been replaced here with a copy by Christian Schad. Included in the entrance ticket to the chapel is a visit to the late Romanesque **cloisters** on the south side of the church. It's also worth asking to see the **Schatzkammer**, which contains the gilded reliquaries of the two patron saints.

The buildings around the cloisters are home to the **Stiftsmuseum** (10am–1pm & 2–5pm, closed Tues; €2.50), which has wide-ranging collections, principally of archeology and sacred art. Especially intriguing are treasury items formerly belonging to Cardinal Albrecht, including a reliquary calendar in the shape of a book and Germany's oldest surviving chessboard; the latter dates from around 1300 and is a beautiful object made from wood, enamel, jasper, rock crystal, silver and clay. Among the sculptures are a panel of *The Nativity* by Riemenschneider and Junker's imaginary portrait of Duke Otto of Swabia and Bavaria, the son of the founder of the Stiftskirche. Two remarkable mid-eighteenth-century painted panels mapping out the holdings of Kloster Himmelthal are the highlights of a room devoted to artefacts from Cistercian convents in the former Mainz Electorate. One of the museum's proudest possessions is the *Aschaffenburger Tafel*, a badly damaged but enormously powerful thirteenth-century painting of Christ as Judge which was once part of the Stiftskirche's high altar, but was later demoted to serve as a floor board and only rediscovered during restoration work in 1986.

Just beyond the eastern end of the Altstadt is **Park Schöntal**, which features a lake with a ruined monastery. About 1km further east is the **Fasanerie** (Pheasantery): to get there, walk up Lindenallee, cross the rail bridge and continue along Bismarckallee, whose restaurants and beer gardens are popular destinations in summer. **Park Schönbusch**, on the western bank of the Main (reached by bus #4 from the Hauptbahnhof) is an eighteenth-century English-style landscape park, featuring a labyrinth of paths leading through woods and gardens past miniature temples and mazes. Here also is the pretty **Schlösschen Schönbusch** (guided tours April–Sept Tues–Sun 9am–6pm; €2.50; Ⓦwww.schloesser.bayern.de), the Neoclassical summer palace of the Mainz Electors.

Finally, on the southern edge of town at Obernnauer Str. 125 (reached by bus #61 or #62 from the Hauptbahnhof), the **Rosso Bianco Collection** (April–Oct Tues–Sun 10am–6pm; Nov–March Sun 10am–6pm; €6; Ⓦwww.rosso-bianco.de) has the biggest array of racing cars in the world – some 200 gleaming Porsches, Ferraris, Alfa Romeos and the like.

Practicalities

Aschaffenburg's **Hauptbahnhof** is just north of the Altstadt. The **tourist office** is in the Stadthalle, Schlossplatz 1 (April–Sept Mon–Fri 9am–6pm, Sat 9am–1pm; Oct–March Mon–Fri 9am–5pm, Sat 10am–1pm; Ⓣ0 60 21/39 58 00, Ⓦwww.info-aschaffenburg.de). Main **cruises** are run by Aschaffenburger Personenschiffahrt Sankt Martin, Ruhlandstr. 5 (Ⓣ0 60 21/8 72 88).

Of the **hotels** with a central location, the lowest rates are at *Pape*, Würzburger Str. 16 (Ⓣ0 60 21/2 2 6 73; ❸); *Central*, Steingasse 5 (Ⓣ0 60 21/2 33 11 or 2 33 92; ❹); and *Gasthof Goldener Karpfen*, Löherstr. 20 (Ⓣ0 60 21/4 43 69 70; ❹). More upmarket options include *Wilder Mann*, Löherstr. 51 (Ⓣ0 60 21/30 20, Ⓦwww.hotel-wilder-mann.de; ❻); and *Post*, Goldbacher Str. 19-21 (Ⓣ0 60 21/33 40, Ⓦwww.post-ab.de; ❻). The **youth hostel** is in the southeastern outskirts at Beckerstr. 47 (Ⓣ0 60 21/93 07 63; €11.20) and is reached by taking bus #5 or #41 to Schroberstrasse, from where it's a ten-minute walk. **Camping** is possible at Mainparksee (Ⓣ0 60 21/27 82 22) and in the suburb of Mainaschaff (Ⓣ0 60 21/27 82 22), fifteen minutes away by bus #44 from the Hauptbahnhof.

There are **restaurants** in all but the first two hotels listed above. Among other possibilities, *Schönbusch*, in the former court gardener's house at Kleine Schönbuschallee 1, is of gourmet standard. *Zeughaus*, Bismarckallee 5, is particularly worth visiting in summer, when you can drink locally produced apple wine in the shade of chestnut trees. Within Schloss Johannisburg is a recommendable wine bar-restaurant with its own vintages, *Schlossweinstuben*; the pick of the traditional beer taverns is *Wirthaus Zum Fegerer*, Schlossgasse 14. *Aloha*, Rossmarkt 21, is a lively, friendly cocktail bar; *Engelsberg*, Dalbergstr. 66, is a traditional but arty pub. The Neoclassical Stadttheater, Schlossgasse 8 (Ⓣ0 60 21/2 70 78) hosts **drama** and **concerts**.

Würzburg

Capital of Lower Franconia, local wine metropolis and northern terminus of Germany's most famous tourist route, the Romantic Road (see box on p.232), **WÜRZBURG** straddles the River Main some 80km southeast of Aschaffenburg and 50km southwest of Schweinfurt. During the night of March 16, 1945 it got the same treatment from Allied bombers that Nürnberg had received two months earlier. The city had no important war industries but the presence of a busy rail junction provided a tenuous rationale for its destruction. Unfortunately, Würzburg has been less successful in rebuilding itself: gone is much of the Altstadt, leaving individual surprises of Baroque and Gothic beauty sandwiched between modern supermarkets and the new town. For all that, the city's location on both banks of the Main, a number of really outstanding sights and a marvellous range of places to eat and drink easily justify a visit of several days.

Würzburg has been one of Germany's most influential episcopal cities for many centuries, and some of the greatest architects and artists were employed by the prince-bishops, bequeathing an exceptionally rich legacy. Prominent among them was the sculptor **Tilman Riemenschneider**, whose hauntingly characterized carvings, executed in the heady years leading up to the Reformation, decorate so many churches throughout Franconia. Two major exhibitions of his works will be among the highlights of the city's celebrations of its 1300th birthday in 2004. The eighteenth century saw the patronage of **Balthasar Neumann**, who was then totally unknown and untried, but who duly developed here into the most inventive and accomplished architect in Europe.

Arrival and accommodation

Würzburg's **Hauptbahnhof** is at the northern end of the city centre. The headquarters of the **tourist office** (Mon–Thurs 8.30am–5pm, Fri 8.30am–noon; Ⓣ09 31/37 23 35, Ⓦwww.wuerzburg.de) are at Am Congress Centrum, though the main public branch is in the Haus zum Falken on the Markt (Jan–March Mon–Fri 10am–4pm, Sat 10am–1pm; April, Nov & Dec Mon–Fri 10am–6pm, Sat 10am–2pm; May–Oct Mon–Fri 9am–6pm, Sat & Sun 10am–2pm; Ⓣ09 31/37 23 98).

Though budget options are fairly thin on the ground, Würzburg has plenty of good middle- and upper-range **hotels**. The **youth hostel**, Burkarderstr. 44 (Ⓣ09 31/4 25 90; €16.90) is situated on the left bank of the Main below the Marienberg fortress; take tram #3 to Ludwigsbrücke from the Hauptbahnhof. There are several **campsites** in the outskirts, the most convenient being *Kalte Quelle*, Winterhäuser Str. 160 (Ⓣ09 31/6 55 98) in Heidingsfeld, about 4km south of the centre and best reached by taking bus #16 from Barbarossaplatz.

Hotels and pensions

Alter Kranen Kärrnergasse 11 Ⓣ09 31/3 51 80, Ⓦwww.hotel-alter-kranen.de. Middle-range hotel with a lovely location right by the Main. ❻

Rebstock Neubaustr. 7 Ⓣ09 31/3 09 30, Ⓦwww.rebstock.com. A splendid Rococo mansion in the university quarter, completely modernized inside. It serves wonderful buffet breakfasts, while full meals are available at either the reasonably priced *Fränkische Weinstube* (evenings only, closed Tues) or the pricey main restaurant (closed Sun evening). ❾

Russ Wolfahrtsgasse 1 Ⓣ09 31/5 00 16,

Ⓦwww.hotel-russ.de. Hotel with a well-regarded restaurant, handily located in the Altstadt. ❺

Schlosshotel Steinburg Auf dem Steinberg Ⓣ09 31/9 70 20, Ⓦwww.steinburg.com. Occupies a Romantic-era castle built on the foundations of its medieval predecessor on a hill 6km northwest of the centre. The facilities include a sauna, a swimming pool, a garden terrace commanding a grandstand view of the city, and a high-class wine restaurant. ❼–❾

Schönleber Theaterstr. 5 Ⓣ09 31/3 04 89 00, Ⓦwww.hotel-schoenleber.de. Pleasant, moderately priced hotel in the heart of the city. ❹–❻

Siegel Reisgrubengasse 7 Ⓣ09 31/5 29 41 or 5 29 64, Ⓕ5 29 67. Würzburg's cheapest pension, notable for its startling painted wallpaper and its convenient location between the Hauptbahnhof and the centre of the city. ❹

Spehnkuch Röntgenring 7 Ⓣ09 31/5 47 52, Ⓕ5 47 60. Small pension in a grand tenement directly facing the Hauptbahnhof. ❹

Till Eulenspiegel Sanderstr. 1a Ⓣ09 31/35 58 40, Ⓦwww.hotel-till-eulenspiegel.de. Non-smoking hotel in the heart of the university quarter. It has a pleasant Weinstube plus a Bierkeller which is one of the liveliest nightspots in the district. ❻–❽

Walfisch Am Pleidenturm 5 Ⓣ09 31/3 52 00, Ⓦwww.hotel-walfisch.com. Upmarket hotel with restaurant commanding a wonderful view over the Main at its most picturesque spot. ❼–❾

Zur Stadt Mainz Semmelstr. 39 Ⓣ09 31/5 31 55, Ⓦwww.hotel-stadtmainz.de. This is a real gem, a Franconian inn dating back to the fifteenth century, albeit with fully modern bedrooms. Its restaurant serves wonderful local dishes, including a couple from its own recipe book of 1850. The gargantuan breakfast buffet (also available to non-residents) must be a contender for the title of the best in Germany. ❼

The City

The heart of the old city lies between the Main and the Residenz, roughly encompassed by the Juliuspromenade to the north and Neubaustrasse to the south. Most of the sights lie within this compact area, though you need to cross over to the right bank for a couple of major attractions – and the best views.

The Residenz

The **Residenz** (daily: April–Oct 9am–6pm; Nov–March 10am–4pm; €4; Ⓦwww.schloesser.bayern.de) on the eastern edge of the town centre is a truly marvellous palace set in a park to match. It was intended to symbolize all the wealth and status of the Würzburg bishops, and to show they could hold their own with such great European courts as Versailles and Vienna – which, in artistic terms, they more than succeeded in doing. Construction was left largely in the hands of the prolific **Balthasar Neumann**, who had started off as a humble craftsman of churchbells and weapons before working his way into the fine art of architecture. The palace is built in a great U-shape made up of a central pavilion and four equally proportioned two-storey courts. Its main facade and garden front are strongly contrasted, the former grand and ceremonial, heavily laden with sculptural decoration, while the latter has a playful, festive air. However, for all their impressive monumentality, they're rather overshadowed by the overwhelming magnificence of the interior.

As you enter the palace via the central wing, you're almost immediately confronted with the famed **staircase** which is covered by a single unsupported vault of audacious design. In response to jealous rivals who claimed this was bound to collapse, Neumann offered to have a battery of artillery fired under it. This experiment was never carried out, but full vindication of Neumann's faith in his design came in 1945, when the vault held firm against aerial bombardment. Its **fresco**, the largest in the world, thus miraculously survived unscathed. An allegory extolling the fame of the prince-bishops in the most immodest way imaginable, it was painted by the greatest decorator of the age, the Venetian **Giovanni Battista Tiepolo**. The four continents then known are depicted paying their respects to the ruler of Würzburg, Carl Philipp von Greiffenklau, who is transported to Heaven in triumph in the centre of the composition. Each continent is personified as a representative female character, Europe being a Greek goddess enthroned above a globe to symbolize this continent's status as ruler of the world. To her right, sitting on an old cannon, a reference to his original trade, Neumann surveys the scene; behind him are Tiepolo and his fellow-decorators.

The **Weisser Saal**, whose plain white stucco is a tasteful contrast to the staircase, gives the visitor a break before being hit by the opulence of the **Kaisersaal**, which is the centrepiece of the palace and the room reserved for the use of the emperor whenever he happened to be in the area. The marble, the gold-leaf stucco and the sparkling chandeliers combine to produce an effect of dazzling magnificence, but finest of all are more frescoes by Tiepolo, which dovetail with the architecture to absolute perfection. This time they glorify the concept of the Holy Roman Empire and Würzburg's part within it. On the ceiling, Beatrix of Burgundy is brought to the city as Frederick Barbarossa's betrothed: on the southern wall, the couple are married by the prince-bishop, who is invested with the title of Duke of Franconia in the scene opposite. To the left and right are an array of **state rooms**, painstakingly re-created from the ashes with the help of photographs and old etchings. Look out in particular for the **Spiegelkabinett**, a unique work of its kind, the walls consisting entirely of glass panels decorated on the back.

Built discreetly into the southwest corner of the palace in order not to spoil the symmetry, the **Hofkirche** (which you visit independently) is a brilliant early example of the spatial illusionism that was to become a Neumann speciality – the interior, based on a series of ovals, appears to be much larger than is actually the case. Both the side altars of *The Fall of the Rebel Angels* and *The Assumption* are by Tiepolo. Entered from within the main courtyard is the **Martin-von-Wagner-Museum** (Tues–Sat 9.30am–12.30pm & 2–5pm, Sun 9.30am–12.30pm; free; Ⓦwww.uni-wuerzburg.de/museum). In the mornings and on alternate Sundays you see the gallery, featuring works by Riemenschneider and Tiepolo; at other times the collection of classical antiquities is on view. To the rear of the Residenz is the **Hofgarten**, a series of delightful terraced gardens enlivened by playful Rococo sculptures.

The episcopal and academic quarters

From the Residenz, it's only a short walk along Hofstrasse to the city's episcopal centre, in which the two main churches nestle side by side. The more northerly is the **Neumünster**, a Romanesque basilica partly rebuilt in the Baroque period, whose perfect symmetry is highlighted by a twin set of steps leading up to the elevated entrance from either side. In the **crypt**, a modern shrine contains the remains of Saint Kilian, an Irish missionary martyred on the spot in 689, together with his assistants St Kolonat and St Totnan, for trying to convert Franconia. The busts of the three martyrs on the church's high altar are copies of the originals by Riemenschneider, which were destroyed in 1945, but the statue of the Madonna and Child under the dome is a genuine work by the same sculptor.

Leaving the Neumünster by its northern exit, you come to the tiny **Lusamgärtchen** and the remains of the twelfth-century cloister. These days it's a romantically overgrown square, and at its centre is a commemorative block to the famous medieval minstrel **Walther von der Vogelweide**. He was the most popular poet and singer of the early thirteenth century, but also a valued political commentator of the Staufen rulers, which is why he was given a pension from the estate of this church and is assumed to have been buried in the cloister in 1230. To the northeast stand several fine old mansions, including the Renaissance **Hof Conti**, the present-day home of Würzburg's bishop.

Adjoining the Neumünster to the south is the new **Museum am Dom** (Tues–Sun 10am–5/7pm; €3, or €4 combined ticket with Domschatz; Ⓦwww.museum-am-dom.de). This collection of ecclesiastical art of the Würzburg diocese is presented in a defiantly non-traditional manner, being grouped thematically rather than chronologically. Although the emphasis is firmly on the modern, there are some notable older works, including *The Last Judgment* by an anonymous Bohemian master of the turn of the fifteeth century, several sculptures by Riemenschneider and his circle, a rare panel painting, *St Joseph and the Christ Child*, by Cosmas Damian Asam, and a large group of Romanian behind-glass paintings. There's also a generous representation of GDR-era artists, including Werner Tübke, Willi Sitte and Volker Stelzmann.

The **Dom**, again consecrated to Saint Kilian, was one of the largest Romanesque churches in Germany, but was completely burnt out in 1945, and only the exterior is true to the original. Inside, the rich stucco embellishments of the eighteenth century have only been restored in the transept and chancel, and for the rest the walls are left plain white, with surviving **tombstones** of canons and prince-bishops lining the pillars: look out for those on the seventh and eighth bays of the north side, which are both by Riemenschneider. At the end of the northern transept, Balthasar Neumann's **Schönbornkapelle** holds the remains of four bishops from the House of Schönborn, the dynasty which specialized in collecting episcopal appointments and then building great palaces as spin-offs – Bamberg, Bruchsal and Würzburg itself being among their legacies. The **crypt** is fitted out as a museum of the Dom's history, with lapidary fragments from the eighth century onwards.

Immediately to the south, on Plattnerstrasse, the former workrooms of the **Marmelsteiner Hof**, a mansion by Balthasar Neumann, have been fitted out as the home of the **Domschatz** (Tues–Sun 2–5/7pm; €2). The most intriguing exhibits are the contents of the excavated graves of two medieval bishops, Berthold von Sternburg and Gerhard von Schwarzburg. Most of the collection of ecclesiastical treasure and vestments dates from the Baroque and Rococo periods, though there are a few older pieces, including a Byzantine reliquary.

A couple of blocks further south, the eastern end of Neubaustrasse is dominated by the huge Renaissance frontage of the **Alte Universität**, built in the late sixteenth century by order of one of the city's most enlightened prince-bishops, Julius Echter. The attached church also dates from this period, but the tower was added by Antonio Petrini, the seventeenth-century Italian architect who was responsible for transforming Würzburg into one of Germany's first Baroque cities.

Marktplatz, the hospitals and the waterfront

To the west of the episcopal quarter is the city's commercial heart, centred on **Marktplatz**, whose daily food market ensures that there's always a lively bustle. Just off the northeast side is the **Haus zum Falken**, the city's prize example of a Rococo mansion, bristling with white stucco decorations and perfectly restored to the very last curl. It now houses one of the city's tourist offices and the municipal library.

Overlooking Marktplatz is the **Marienkapelle**, an exceptionally graceful Gothic church of the fourteenth century, whose most interesting feature is the tympanum of the northern portal. The scene represented is *The Annunciation*, and if you look closely, you'll see that the artist has chosen to be very literal in his interpretation. There's the usual archangel with his scripted band indicating his speech to Mary, but another band leads from God the Father above to Mary's ear, and tucked away in the folds of this band, a little baby is sliding down towards her. Riemenschneider's sculptures for the southern side of the church, including the famous figures of Adam and Eve, have been replaced by copies, but inside is an original work by the same sculptor, the touching sandstone tomb of the knight Conrad von Schaumberg.

Eichhornstrasse leads eastwards from the Markt to Theaterstrasse and the **Bürgerspital**, a charitable institution for the poor, old and sick established in the early fourteenth century by the wealthier citizens of the city. Its good works were funded from its vineyards, still among the largest in Germany; in accordance with the wishes of the founders, residents get a quarter of a litre of wine each day and double on Sundays. The Gothic chapel remains from the initial complex, though other parts were rebuilt in the Baroque period. A short walk away on Juliuspromenade is the **Juliusspital**, a second and much larger institution of the same kind. It takes its name from its benefactor, Bishop Julius Echter, but again it was rebuilt in the Baroque period, partly by Petrini, who added the beautiful little pharmacy, which survives as an intact period-piece. It's best to visit the hospitals when you're in the mood for something to eat and drink, as they each incorporate a Weinstube (see p.210) where the products of their vineyards can be sampled. While walking between the two, it's worth making a short detour down Hauger Pfarrgasse to see Petrini's strikingly Roman-looking **Stift Haug**, which contains a large painting of *The Crucifixion* by Tintoretto.

At the western end of Juliuspromenade, the eighteenth-century **Alte Kranen** (old cranes), used to unload shipping, stand guard over the Main. Beyond the Friedensbrücke to the north, a large warehouse has recently been converted to serve as a gallery known as the **Kulturspeicher** (Tues–Sun 11am–6pm; €3). One half of this serves to house temporary exhibitions and the municipal collection of art from the nineteenth century onwards, including works by Leibl, Liebermann, Slevogt and Trübner. The rest of the building displays the Peter C. Ruppert collection of European Concrete art since 1945, which represents artists from 22 different countries.

South of the Alter Kranen stands the **Alte Mainbrücke**, the oldest bridge spanning this river. Built in 1133, it was often damaged over the centuries, most recently in 1945 when the Allies toppled the eighteenth-century statues of the town's bishops and saints into the river. However, some of the originals have been reinstated, joining with a number of copies to oversee the traffic once again. Just to the east is the **Grafeneckart** or **Rathaus**, a thirteenth-century Romanesque-Gothic building with a Renaissance extension.

The Marienberg

Towering high above the left bank of the Main, the **Festung Marienberg** (Ⓦwww.schloesser.bayern.de) was home to the prince-bishops from 1253 to 1719. Over this period, it evolved from a medieval castle into a Renaissance palace, which was fortified in the Baroque period, following its sacking at the hands of the Swedes, by the addition of a ring of bastions. At the entrance to the complex, the seventeenth-century **Zeughaus** houses the large **Mainfränkisches Museum** (Tues–Sun 10am–4/5pm; €3, or €4 joint ticket with Fürstenbau; Ⓦwww.mainfraenkisches-museum.de). Pride of place among the collections is taken by a magnificent array of **Riemenschneider sculptures**, including the original stone carvings from the Marienkapelle; there's also an impressive display of old wooden wine presses.

Within the courtyard is the round **Marienkirche**, Würzburg's original cathedral. This dates back to the eighth century and is claimed to be the oldest intact church in Germany, though it has been remodelled on several occasions. Another structure of special note is the Renaissance **Brunnenhaus**, an ornate octagonal structure sheltering the 105-metre well which was chiselled through rock in the early fourteenth century to ensure self-sufficiency in water. The eastern palace wing or **Fürstenbau** (April–Oct Tues–Sun 9am–6pm; Nov–March Tues–Sun 10am–4pm; €2.50) contains a historical museum whose exhibits include the thirteenth-century battle standard, the St Kilian banner, and the treasury of the prince-bishops. On the terrace below the palace is the **Fürstengarten**, a formal Baroque garden seen at its best when the roses are in bloom in summer, but always worth visiting for the sake of the wonderful view over the city.

Elsewhere on the left bank

Returning to the waterfront and heading south towards the youth hostel, you pass **St Burkhard**, whose late Gothic choir picturesquely straddles the street, forming a covered walkway. It's also worth a look inside to see a tender polychrome *Madonna and Child* by Riemenschneider.

During work on the Residenz, Balthasar Neumann took time off to build the **Käppele**, a twin-towered pilgrimage church crowned with onion domes, imperiously perched on the heights at the southwestern end of the city. Apart from the opportunity to see the interior, lavishly covered with frescoes and stucco, it's well worth visiting for the **view** from the terrace, which offers a frontal panorama of the Marienberg surrounded by its vineyards, with the city nestling in the valley below.

Eating, drinking and entertainment

Würzburg is one of Germany's leading gourmet cities. The best places to sample the local wines and traditional Franconian cooking are the famous Weinstuben, but the city is amply endowed with a wide range of restaurants (see the hotels section on pp.204–05 for more recommendations) and bars. There are also several annual festivals, which are the undoubted highpoints of local cultural life.

Weinstuben

Bürgerspital Theaterstr. 19. The obvious place to sample the wines from the vineyards of the famous old hospital. Produces very dry *Riesling*, *Silvaner* and *Müller-Thurgau*; the food is almost equally excellent and surprisingly reasonably priced.

Haus des Frankenweins Kranenkai 1. Directly overlooking the Main, this has a shop selling the full range of Franconian wines, plus a restaurant, terrace and garden.

Juliusspital Juliuspromenade 19. Full-bodied wines, with *Silvaner* being the most common type, are characteristic of this hospital's vineyards; they're matured in old oak casks to give a particularly strong flavour. Meals are also very good value here.

Residenzgaststätten Residenzplatz 1. The Hofkeller, the former court vineyards, maintain a modern rivalry to those of the two hospitals; its wide variety of wines can be enjoyed here in an outbuilding of the Residenz. Closed Mon.

Wirtshaus Zum Lämmle Marienplatz 5. This has an evenings-only vaulted cellar, plus a ground floor dining room open at lunchtime, with tables on the square outside during summer. Closed Sun.

Zum Stachel Gressengasse 1. Founded in 1413, the city's oldest wine-drinking inn has a particularly picturesque courtyard for alfresco meals and does river fish specialities, but is a little pricier than its rivals. Closed Sun; evenings only Mon & Tues.

Other restaurants

Backöfele Ursulinergasse 2. Top-class traditional Gaststätte with a covered front courtyard. The specialities include steaks grilled in a wood-fired oven.

Burggaststätten Festung Marienberg. The restaurant complex in the Marienberg includes a Weinstube (featuring wines from the Hofkeller), a beer garden (selling the local Hofbräu beers) and a traditional café; any of these is well worth patronizing when you're visiting the fortress.

Hofbräukeller Höchberger Str. 28. In this wine stronghold, it's appropriate that the leading Bierkeller, whose garden can seat 1000 people, is way out of the centre on the western side of the city. An adventurous menu includes many vegetarian options as well as the expected Franconian dishes.

Kham Burkardstr. 2–4. Innovative restaurant serving a range of Asian cuisines. It does bargain lunch buffets (brunch on Sun) except Tues, when it's closed.

Ratskeller Langgasse 1. Serves Franconian and international dishes, and has an extensive wine list.

Schiffbäuerin Katzengasse 7. Top choice for local fish specialities, with a fine selection of wines. Closed Sun evening & Mon.

Schützenhof Gutsschänke Mainleitenweg 48. Terrace restaurant offering a beautiful view over the Main from its lofty position just south of the Käppele. Serves fruit wines and homemade cakes as well as Franconian dishes.

Bars and cafés

Brückenbäck Zeller Str. 2. Coffee house which also serves light meals, and has the benefit of wonderful riverside views.

Café Uni Neubaustr. 2. Trendy café-bar popular with local students.

Fränkisches Brauhaus Die Goldene Gans Burkarderstr. 2–4. Cellar Hausbrauerei producing an unfiltered beer; it's primarily a drinking establishment but also serves light meals. Daily except Sun 8pm–2am.

Gehrings Neubaustr. 24. Café-bistro right by the Alte Universität.

Kult Landwehrstr. 10. Student Kneipe serving a variety of breakfasts and vegetarian dishes.

Victoria Neubaustr. 8. A good choice for *Kaffee und Kuchen.*

Würzburg's festivals

Würzburg hosts several **wine festivals** throughout the year. The series begins in mid-May with the Kulturtage in the Juliusspital (ⓦwww.juliusspital.de), which features classical concerts as well as wine. Later the same month, and continuing into June, is the Würzburger Weindorf (ⓦwww.weindorf-wuerzburg.de), held in some forty little huts set up on the Markt. The Bürgerspital (ⓦwww.buergerspital.de) has its Weinfest in late June; the Hofkeller (ⓦwww.hofkeller.de) hosts a similar event in the Hofgarten soon after. In late July and early August, the Weinparade am Dom (ⓦwww.weinparade.de) is held in tents set up on Paradeplatz.

The main **musical** event is the Mozartfest (ⓦwww.mozartfest-wuerzburg.de) throughout June, in which Mozart concerts are held outdoors in the Hofgarten and indoors by candlelight in the opulent settings of the Weisser Saal and Kaisersaal of the Residenz. There's also a shorter festival devoted to Bach, the Bachtage (ⓦwww.bachchor-wuerzburg.de), in late November and early December, in which the Würzburger Bachchor and Würzburger Bachorchester play prominent roles. At the beginning of July is the most important **popular** and **religious** festival, the fortnight-long Kilianifest (ⓦwww.kiliani-bierzelt.de). This consists for the most part of a huge funfair at the Talavera, a fairground on the left bank of the Main opposite the Congress-Centrum. However, it begins on a Saturday afternoon with a costumed pageant through the city; the following morning, there's a solemn religious procession followed by High Mass in the Dom.

Entertainment

The main year-round **cultural** venue, with a varied programme of drama, opera, dance and music, is the Mainfranken Theater Würzburg, Theaterstr. 21 (ⓣ09 31/3 90 81 24, ⓦwww.theaterwuerzburg.de). From the Alter Kranen, **cruises** are run by two competing companies: Kurth und Schiebe (ⓣ09 31/5 85 73, ⓦwww.schiffstouristik.de) and Veitshöchhheimer Personenschiffahrt Heinrich Herbert (ⓣ09 31/5 56 33, ⓦwww.vpsherbert.de). By far the most popular trip (€5.50 single, €8 return) is downstream to **Schloss Veitshöchheim** (guided tours April–Oct Tues–Sun 9am–6pm; €1.50, but closed in 2003 for restoration; ⓦwww.schloesser.bayern.de), the summer residence of the Würzburg prince-bishops, which is set in beautiful formal gardens. Upstream, there are occasional sailings to the fortified towns of Ochsenfurt and Sulzfeld.

Rothenburg ob der Tauber

ROTHENBURG OB DER TAUBER, which is some 60km south of Würzburg, is the most famous and most visited medieval town in Germany, and although it's very beautiful, it has been reduced to the ultimate museum-piece, with nearly half its working population employed in the tourist trade. Nonetheless, it should still merit at least one overnight stop: the only way to get this place to yourself is to stay the night and go out, either early in the morning or in the evening, when the crowds are absent.

Perched on a promontory 90m above the River Tauber, Rothenburg was a prosperous Free Imperial City in medieval times, but later found itself cut off from the new trading routes and reduced to a very provincial market town. Without money to expand or erect new buildings, it vegetated until the nineteenth century, when its self-evident attraction for the Romantic movement led to the enforcement of preservation orders. In 1945, part of the town suffered

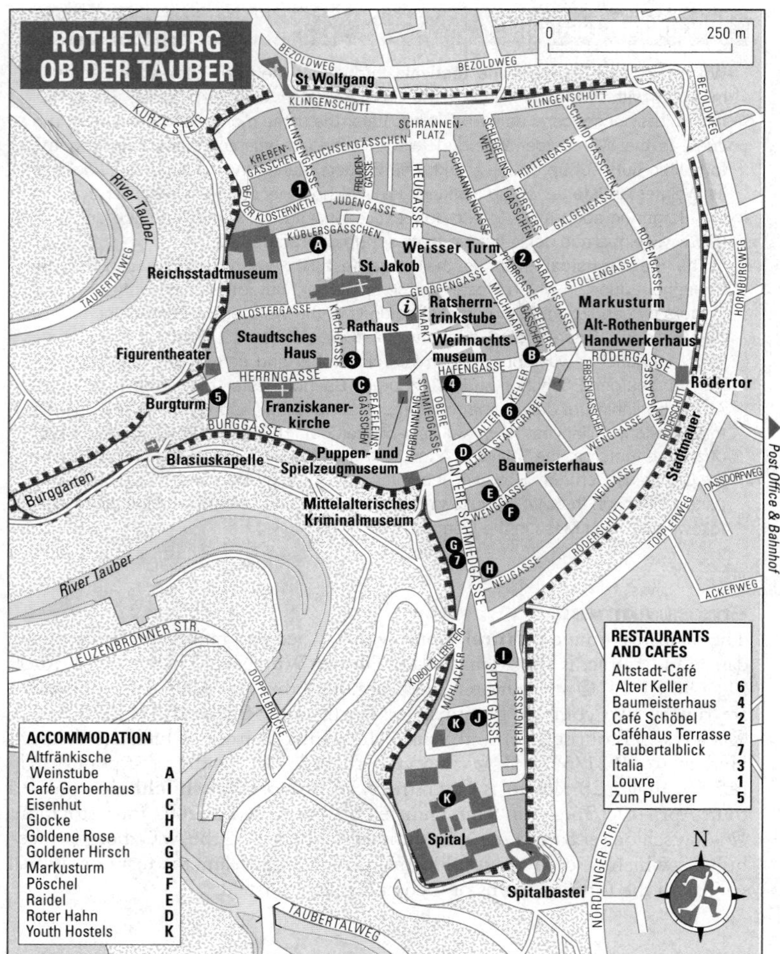

severe damage in an American air raid. Thankfully, a civilian working for the US army, J.J. McCloy (later the High Commissioner to Germany), knew and loved Rothenburg, and lobbied successfully for it to be spared from further bombing. Money to pay for its restoration subsequently poured in from abroad, and it was soon returned to its former appearance. Nowadays, its conservation policies are the strictest in Germany: even the biggest international chains are obliged to use traditional wrought-iron shop signs instead of corporate logos.

Arrival, information and accommodation

Rothenburg is the terminus of a branch rail line from Steinach on the stretch between Würzburg and Ansbach. From the **Bahnhof**, it's no more than a five-minute walk to the Rödertor. The **tourist office** (May–Oct Mon–Fri 9am–noon & 1–6pm, Sat & Sun 10am–3pm; Nov–April Mon–Fri 9am–noon

& 1–5pm, Sat 10am–1pm; ⓣ0 98 61/4 04 92, ⓦwww.rothenburg.de) is in the Ratsherrntrinkstube, Marktplatz 2.

Rothenburg offers a huge choice of accommodation, ranging from remarkably cheap **pensions** to luxurious historic **hotels**. Despite the volume of tourism, there's rarely any problem finding somewhere with vacancies. **Private rooms** (❷–❸) are also in reasonable supply – look out for *Zimmer frei* signs. The two **youth hostels** are in beautifully restored half-timbered houses off the bottom of the Spitalgasse: *Rossmühle*, Mühlacker 1 (ⓣ0 98 61/9 41 60; €15.80), is the main building; the *Spitalhof* is its rather more spartan annex. Both **campsites** are in Detwang: *Tauber-Romantik* (ⓣ0 98 61/61 91, ⓕ8 68 99) and *Tauber-Idyll* (ⓣ0 98 61/31 77, ⓕ9 28 45).

Hotels and pensions

Altfränkische Weinstube Klosterhof 7 ⓣ0 98 61/64 04, ⓕ64 10. Small hotel attached to a wine bar-restaurant. The local English Conversation Club meets in the latter every Wednesday at 8pm, and invites all English-speaking visitors to the town to join them for a chat. ❹

Café Gerberhaus Spitalgasse 25 ⓣ0 98 61/9 49 00, ⓦwww.gerberhaus.rothenburg.de. Named after the old tannery it occupies, this offers modern hotel comforts at moderate prices. The buffet breakfasts are outstanding. ❹–❻

Eisenhut Herrengasse 3–7 ⓣ0 98 61/70 50, ⓦwww.eisenhut.com. Rothenburg's leading hotel occupies four patrician mansions on its most prestigious street. It is beautifully decorated with furniture and antiques, has a garden terrace and a first-rate restaurant. ❾

Glocke Am Plönlein 1 ⓣ0 98 61/95 89 90, ⓦwww.glocke-rothenburg.de. Fine old inn, now part of the Ringhotel group, situated at one of Rothenburg's most famous corners. Its restaurant, *Wirtshaus in Franken*, has a strong line in fish dishes. ❺–❼

Goldene Rose Spitalgasse 28 ⓣ0 98 61/46 38, ⓕ8 64 17. Typical Franconian Gasthof, with a variety of rooms, including tiny singles which are among the cheapest in town. ❷

Goldener Hirsch Untere Schmiedgasse 16 ⓣ0 98 61/70 80, ⓦwww.goldenerhirsch.rothenburg.de. One of the town's most luxurious hotels, with a renowned restaurant, *Die Blaue Terrasse*, commanding a wonderful view over the Tauber valley. ❻–❾

Markusturm Rödergasse 1 ⓣ0 98 61/9 42 80, ⓦwww.romantikhotels.com/rothenburg. Tastefully furnished hotel with restaurant. Located at one of the town's most picturesque corners, it takes its name from the adjoining tower, a survivor of the original twelfth-century Stadtmauer. ❼–❾

Pöschel Wenggasse 22 ⓣ0 98 61/34 30. Small family-run pension with immaculate, comfortable bedrooms. ❷

Raidel Wenggasse 3 ⓣ0 98 61/31 15, ⓕ93 52 55. Another good-value guesthouse, located in a 600-year-old half-timbered house. ❷

Roter Hahn Obere Schmiedgasse 21 ⓣ0 98 61/97 40, ⓦwww.roterhahn.com. A famous old hotel, formerly the home of Burgomaster Nusch. It has a good and reasonably priced restaurant. ❻–❽

The Town

The best way to get your bearings and a first impression is to walk round the fourteenth-century **Stadtmauer**, most of whose sentry walk survives. Tightly packed within the walls, the town's houses get larger towards the middle where the local patricians and merchants lived. Nearer the wall, tradesfolk and peasants lived in crooked little dolls' houses, half-timbered and with steeply pointed roofs. The plan of the town is also highly distinctive, having a shape like a question mark, with an elongated southern stalk. For a more elevated view, climb the eastern gateway, the **Rödertor** (April–Oct daily 9am–6pm; €1.50).

Marktplatz

The sloping central Marktplatz is dominated by the **Rathaus**, which is in two clearly defined parts. To the rear is the surviving half of the original Gothic building, the rest of which was destroyed by fire and replaced in the 1570s by a splendid new Renaissance structure, which was adorned with Baroque arcades a century later. Access to both parts of the Rathaus is via the stair turret which leads up to the wood-beamed **Kaisersaal** on the first floor, where festive events are held. From the landing above, a narrow staircase goes up to the top of the slender 60-metre **tower** (April–Oct daily 9.30am–12.30pm & 1.30–5pm; Nov & Jan-March Sat & Sun noon–3pm; Dec daily noon–3pm; €1) of the Gothic Rathaus. It's the highest point in Rothenburg and provides the best view of the town and surrounding countryside. Back at street level, the inner courtyard between the two parts of the Rathaus gives access to the dungeons or **Historiengewölbe** (daily: April & Oct–Dec 10am–5pm; May–Sept 9am–6pm; €2) below, which were said to be more dreadful than any others of the day.

The other main tourist attraction on the Marktplatz is the pair of figures looking out from the windows on either side of the three clocks on the gable of the **Ratsherrntrinkstube** (Councillors' Tavern). Every day at 11am, noon, 1pm, 2pm, 3pm, 8pm, 9pm and 10pm, they re-enact a famous but apocryphal event. The story goes that in 1631, during the Thirty Years' War, the imperial army, led by the fearsome Johann Tilly, captured the town and intended to destroy it as a punishment for its support of the Protestant cause. In a gesture of peace, the field marshal was brought the huge civic tankard known as the Meistertrunk, which was filled with wine to its capacity of 3.25 litres, and was persuaded to accept the wager that Rothenburg should be spared if one of the councillors could down the contents in one go. The former burgomaster Georg Nusch duly obliged, taking ten minutes to accomplish the feat, after which he needed three days to sleep off the effects.

To the opposite side of the Marktplatz is Rothenburg's largest building, the Gothic parish church of **St Jakob** (daily Easter–Oct 9am–5.30pm; rest of year 10am–noon & 2–4pm; €1.50), whose main body and two towers rise above the sea of red roofs like a great ship, visible for miles around. The elevated west choir, built over an archway straddling the street, contains **Riemenschneider**'s *Holy Blood Altar*, which is exquisitely carved in limewood, with a centrepiece showing the Last Supper. Also of note is the church's high altar, the *Twelve Apostles Altar*, by the Nördlingen artist Friedrich Herlin. The outer wings illustrate *The Legend of St James*; the scene where the saint's dead body is carried to a medieval town features a depiction of fifteenth-century Rothenburg.

North of Marktplatz

Just to the northwest of St Jakob is the **Reichsstadtmuseum** (daily: April–Oct 10am–5pm; Nov–March 1–4pm; €3; Ⓦ www.reichsstadtmuseum.rothenburg.de) on Klosterhof. This occupies the former Dominican convent and is most interesting for the building's original medieval workrooms, which include the oldest surviving kitchen in Germany. Other highlights are the *Rothenburg Passion*, a cycle of twelve pictures painted at the end of the fifteenth century by Martinus Schwarz, the abbot of the Franciscan friary, and the decorated glass vessel which inspired the Meistertrunk legend. Also of note is the collection on Jewish local history. In the thirteenth century Rothenburg had a large settlement of Jews, but their synagogue and ghetto were destroyed in the fifteenth-century pogroms.

You can see one surviving feature of their heritage, however, by going eastwards from here along Judengasse. At the end, built up against the twelfth-century **Weisser Turm** (White Tower), is the former Jewish dance hall, whose walls are embedded with gravestones. A couple of blocks to the south are the only other surviving parts of the original town wall: the hip-roofed **Markusturm** and the **Röderbogen**, to which a clock turret was later appended.

At the extreme northwestern end of town stands the late Gothic church of **St Wolfgang** (April–Oct daily 10am–1pm & 2–5pm; €1.50), whose austere northern wall, pierced only by embrasures, forms part of the Stadtmauer. Now deconsecrated, it was traditionally the parish of the local shepherds, and the sentry's house above the adjoining gateway appropriately contains a display on the *Schäfertanz* (see box on p.216).You can also descend to the casemates below the church, which have dungeons and gun emplacements.

West of Marktplatz

Herrngasse, which leads west from Marktplatz, is the widest street in Rothenburg. At its eastern end is **Käthe Wohlfahrt** (Ⓦwww.wohlfahrt.com), Europe's largest all-year-round Christmas store and the most obviously over-the-top of the many tourist-orientated shops which have lumbered the town with a reputation for kitsch. It has now spawned its own museum, the **Deutsches Weihnachtsmuseum** (April–Dec daily 10am–5.30pm; Jan–March Sat 10am–5.30pm; €4; Ⓦwww.weihnachtsmuseum.de). The street also has many outstanding patrician mansions, notably the **Staudtsches Haus** at no. 18, where you can ring for a short guided tour (daily 9.30am–5pm; €1) which takes in the lobby, the kitchen, and the remarkable wooden stairwell. Opposite is the severe early Gothic **Franziskanerkirche**, which still preserves the rood screen which divided the friars from the laity. Its walls and floor are covered with funerary monuments to local families, and there's a startlingly realistic retable, believed to be an early work by Riemenschneider, showing *The Stigmatization of St Francis*.

At the far end of Herrngasse is the tiny **Figurentheater** (Ⓣ0 98 61/73 54, Ⓦwww.figurentheater.rothenburg.de), which has gained international acclaim for the gentle humour and artistic integrity of its puppet shows. These take place at 8pm from Monday to Saturday; there are also shorter performances at 3pm on Saturday all year round, and on weekdays as well from June to September. Alongside is the **Burgtor**, the tallest of the town's gateways, which gives access to the immaculately tended **Burggarten**, from where there are wonderful views of the town's skyline and the Tauber valley below. In the early Middle Ages there was a castle belonging to the Hohenstaufen emperors here, but it was destroyed by a violent earthquake in 1356. Some of its masonry was used to construct the **Blasiuskapelle**, which is now a memorial to the dead of the two World Wars.

South of Marktplatz

At no. 13 on Hofbronnengasse, which leads off the southern side of Marktplatz, is the **Puppen- und Spielzeugmuseum** (daily: Jan & Feb 11am–5pm; March–Dec 9.30am–6pm; €4; Ⓦwww.spielzeugmuseum.rothenburg.de), Germany's largest private collection of toys and dolls. The exhibits date from 1780 to 1940 and are all beautifully displayed. Facing you across Burggasse at the end of the street is the fascinating **Mittelalterisches Kriminalmuseum** (daily: April–Oct 9.30am–6pm; Nov & Jan–March 2–4pm; Dec 10am–4pm; €3.20; Ⓦwww.kriminalmuseum.rothenburg.de), which contains extensive collections of torture instruments and punishment devices – for example the beer barrels that drunks were forced to walk around in. An added attraction is that all exhibits are fully labelled and explained in English.

Schmiedgasse, which leads off the southeastern corner of Marktplatz, is lined with the most prestigious of all the mansions in town. The **Baumeisterhaus**, the finest house, was built by the same architect who designed the Rathaus, Leonhard Weidmann. The first floor is adorned with statues of the Seven Virtues; on the next level, the Seven Deadly Sins sound their warning notes. Burgomaster Nusch of Meistertrunk fame lived at no. 21, now a hotel called **Roter Hahn**. For an insight into how the medieval tradesfolk lived, it's worth making a short detour east along Alter Stadtgarten to see the **Alt-Rothenburger Handwerkerhaus** (Easter–Oct daily 9am–6pm; €2), which is believed to be the oldest surviving house in town, dating back to 1270. Its eleven rooms are decked out in the style of centuries past.

At the far end of Schmiedgasse is the **Plönlein**, an outrageously picturesque little triangular square. Beyond lies the narrow southern stem of the town, which functioned as the hospital quarter. The **Spital** itself is a complex of various dates: the chapel is Gothic, the main building is by Weidmann. One of the town's two youth hostels occupies its former bakery; another is in the nearby **Rossmühle**, a sixteenth-century mill formerly powered by sixteen horses. To the east is the **Spitalbastei**, the strongest as well as most modern part of the fortification system, dating from the turn of the seventeenth century.

Outside the walls

From either Plönlein or the Spitalbastei, you can descend to the **Doppelbrücke**, a Gothic viaduct faithfully reconstructed after the war. From here, there's a superb long-range view of Rothenburg. More fine panoramas can be had by following the S-bend in the Tauber downstream to the **Topplerschlösschen** (Fri–Sun 1–4pm; €1.50), the summer and weekend retreat of Burgomaster Heinrich Toppler. This late fourteenth-century tower house has a bizarre top-heavy effect, with the upper storeys jutting out well over the stumpy base.

From here it's a 2km walk down the Tauber to **DETWANG**, a village which is actually older than Rothenburg, but has been part of its municipality since the thirteenth century. The Romanesque **Pfarrkirche St-Peter-und-Paul** (April–Oct daily 8.30am–noon & 1.30–5/6pm; Nov–March Tues–Sun

Rothenburg's festivals and folklore

If you can stand the crowds and a certain sense of tweeness, it's worth trying to make your visit coincide with one of Rothenburg's many **festivals**. Each Whit Monday, the **Meistertrunk drama** (Ⓦwww.meistertrunk.de) is re-enacted – albeit with no more than a pretence at matching Nusch's feat. The preceding day sees one of the renditions of the historic **Schäfertanz** (Shepherds' Dance) in front of the Rathaus; this is repeated on selected Sundays in spring and summer. According to one tradition, the dance began as a thanksgiving for Rothenburg's deliverance from the plague; another theory asserts that it derives from the celebration of a discovery of hidden treasure by one of the shepherds. Also at Whitsun, and throughout July and August, there are costume performances of **plays by Hans Sachs**. The second weekend in September sees the **Freiereichstadtfest**, featuring pageants, historical tableaux and a fireworks display, as well as performances of the Meistertrunk and the *Schäfertanz*. Rothenburg, like neighbouring Dinkelsbühl and Nördlingen, is among the last towns in Europe still employing a **nightwatchman**. From April to October, he leads tours round the town, starting from the Rathaus; the 8pm tour is in English, the one at 9.30pm in German.

10am–noon & 2–4pm; €1) contains another masterpiece by Riemenschneider, the *Holy Cross Altar*, featuring a central *Crucifixion* by the master, with wing reliefs of *The Agony in the Garden* and *The Resurrection* by his assistants.

Eating and drinking

The distinctive local **snowball** (*Schneebällchen*) is Rothenburg's best-known culinary speciality; this is made of dough, twisted into shape, then dipped in any one of several different coverings. For the best selection, visit *Diller* at Hofbronnengasse 16 or Hafengasse 4. Most of the town's many excellent **restaurants** are attached to hotels (see p.213), though there are a few other eateries worth a visit.

Altstadt-Café Alter Keller Alter Keller 8. Offers Franconian food and wines, plus home-made cakes and gateaux. Closed Sun evening & Tues.

Baumeisterhaus Obere Schmiedgasse 5. Provides a strong rivalry to its hotel counterparts for traditional German dishes. It's located in one of the town's most important Renaissance buildings, with a charming covered inner courtyard.

Café Schöbel Galgengasse 6. This café is one of those offering its own range of home-made snowballs.

Caféhaus Terrasse Taubertalblick Untere Schmiedgasse 18. Coffee house which, as its name suggests, has a back terrace commanding a lovely view over the Tauber valley.

Italia Herrngasse 8. Italian café-restaurant serving the usual menu of pasta, pizzas and ice creams.

Louvre Klingengasse 15. Rothenburg's most creative restaurant, serving French-inspired cuisine and hosting changing art exhibitions. Evenings only, closed Sun & Mon.

Zum Pulverer Herrngasse 31. Weinstube located right alongside the Burgturm.

Dinkelsbühl

Some 40km southwards along the Romantic Road (see box on p.232) from Rothenburg is **DINKELSBÜHL**, which presents another immaculately preserved townscape from the Middle Ages. In contrast to its neighbour, it has managed to avoid being overrun by tourists and thus has a rather more authentic air.

The **Stadtmauer** survives almost intact, except for the sentry walk, of which only a small section remains. It's therefore best to begin your tour by walking round the outside of the walls via the pathway known as the Alte Promenade. Of the four gateways, the eastern **Wörnitz Tor** is part of the original thirteenth-century fortification system, though it was later prettified by the addition of a clock gable and a coating of orange paint. Proceeding southwards, you pass the most photogenic of the towers, the **Bäuerlinsturm**, whose projecting half-timbered upper storey was added when it passed into residential use. Beyond stands the late fourteenth-century **Nördlinger Tor**, again embellished with a Renaissance gable.

Alongside it is the **Stadtmühle**, perhaps the most formidable-looking mill ever built; because it lay outside the walls, it had to be fortified with corner towers and gun loops. It now houses the **Museum 3 Dimension** (April–Oct daily 10am–6pm; Nov–March Sat & Sun 11am–4pm; €7), an unexpected yet fascinating series of hands-on displays about three-dimensional effects. The western section of the Stadtmauer is pierced by a series of round towers, but its gateway, the **Segringer Tor**, is a decorative Baroque replacement for the one destroyed in the Thirty Years' War. However, the northern **Rothenburger Tor** still preserves most of its medieval form, including a sturdy gatehouse.

Within the walls, the dominant monument is the church of **St Georg** on Weinmarkt. From the top of its **tower** (Easter–Sept Mon–Fri 9am–noon & 1–6pm, Sat 10am–noon & 1–5pm, Sun 1–5pm; €1.50), which survives from the original Romanesque church, there's a marvellous view of the town. The rest of the building is a textbook Gothic hall church from the second half of the fifteenth century, with an airily light interior of slender pillars and elaborate network vaults. In the north walk of the ambulatory is a didactic panel of *The Ten Commandments*, which pairs each scene with the consequences of failure to obey.

Facing the church are five magnificent mansions, of which the most notable are the half-timbered **Deutsches Haus**, now a hotel-restaurant, and the resplendently gabled **Schranne**, which contains the town's main festive hall. More fine houses can be seen down Segringer Strasse to the west: nos. 3 and 5 share a single gable, while no. 7 has a lovely arcaded, flower-strewn courtyard. In the opposite direction, the Altrathausplatz in the shadow of the Wörnitz Tor is another of the most picturesque corners, with the **Löwenbrunnen** (Lion Fountain) as its focal point.

Practicalities

Dinkelsbühl lies on a rail line which used to provide a handy link with Nördlingen, the next stop on the Romantic Road some 30km south, but this has been superseded, except for occasional excursion steam trains in summer, by a **bus** service. Most departures are from the **Bahnhof**, a few minutes' walk east of the Altstadt, though the Europabus coaches travelling the Romantic Road leave from Schweinemarkt in the heart of town. The **tourist office** is on Marktplatz (May–Oct Mon–Fri 9am–6pm, Sat 10am–1pm & 2–4pm, Sun 10am–noon; Nov–April Mon–Fri 10am–noon & 2–5pm, Sat 10am–noon; ⓣ0 98 51/9 02 40, ⓦwww.dinkelsbuehl.de). Ask here if you're interested in staying in either a **private house** (❷–❸) or a neighbouring **farm** (❶–❷); provided you've got your own transport, the latter can be a tremendous bargain, particularly for stays of four days or more.

Dinkelsbühl folklore

In common with Rothenburg and Nördlingen, Dinkelsbühl still has a paid **nightwatchman**. Decked out in cloak, breeches and felt hat, and carrying a halberd, horn and lantern, he sets out from St Georg at 9pm each evening from April to October (9.30pm in July and August), and does the rounds of the town's hotels. At each, he performs his song, and is thereupon presented with a glass of wine, which is passed round the tourists accompanying him.

The most famous piece of local folklore is the **Kinderzeche** (ⓦwww.kinderzeche.de), a ten-day-long festival held each July, the pivotal date being the third Monday of the month. This commemorates an event in the Thirty Years' War which has obvious parallels with Rothenburg's Meistertrunk. This time it was the Swedes who were bent on destruction. According to legend, when the town finally capitulated after a long siege, the Swedish commander was dissuaded from ransacking it by a deputation of local children. The events are re-enacted in plays performed in the Schranne, while on the Monday and each of the two Saturdays and Sundays there are costumed pageants through the streets. Music is provided by the Knabenkapelle; perhaps the best-known boys' band in Germany, its members are kitted out like little soldiers in red-and-white eighteenth-century uniform. In line with Bavarian taste, there are side-shows of open-air theatre, fireworks and the inevitable beer tents.

Otherwise, the cheapest rooms are at a small and homely Altstadt **pension**, *Lutz*, Schäfergässlein 4 (ⓣ0 98 51/94 54; ❷). There are numerous **hotels**, all of them in characterful old buildings; they include *Gasthof Goldene Krone*, Nördlinger Str. 24 (ⓣ0 98 51/22 93, ⓦwww.goldenekrone.de; ❹); *Weib's Brauhaus*, Untere Schmiedgasse 13 (ⓣ0 98 51/57 94 90, ⓦwww.weibsbrauhaus.de; ❺); *Eisenkrug*, Dr-Martin-Luther-Str. 1 (ⓣ0 98 51/5 77 00, ⓦwww.hotel-eisenkrug.de; ❺); *Weisses Ross*, Steingasse 12 (ⓣ0 98 51/57 98 90, ⓦwww.flairhotel.com/weissesross; ❺); *Goldene Rose*, Marktplatz 4 (ⓣ0 98 51/5 77 50, ⓦwww.hotel-goldene-rose.com; ❺–❼); *Blauer Hecht*, Schweinemarkt 1 (ⓣ0 98 51/58 10, ⓦwww.hotel-blauer-hecht.de; ❻); and *Deutsches Haus*, Weinmarkt 3 (ⓣ0 98 51/60 59, ⓦwww.deutsches-haus-dkb.de; ❻). The **youth hostel** is housed in an old granary at Koppengasse 10 (ⓣ0 98 51/95 09; €12.70), while there's a **campsite** to the northeast of the old town, just off the road from Rothenburg, at Kobeltsmühle 6 (ⓣ0 98 51/78 17, ⓦwww.campingplatz-dinkelsbuehl.de). All the hotels listed above have **restaurants**, and these are generally very good value; as its name suggests, *Weib's Brauhaus* also brews its own beer.

Bavarian Swabia

Approximately bordered by the rivers Iller and Lech, the southwestern part of Bavaria presents a landscape of rolling farmland dotted with quiet villages and picturesque medieval towns. The region is called **Bavarian Swabia** (Bayerisch-Schwaben) and used to form part of the medieval Duchy of Swabia, the rest of which became the separate state of Württemberg. Its capital is **Augsburg**, one of the greatest metropolises of sixteenth-century Europe and still an elegant city full of fine Renaissance architecture, largely unspoilt by later building.

North of here is the stretch of the **Romantic Road** immediately following on from the initial Franconian section; its main draws are **Nördlingen**, a well-preserved medieval walled town in a truly extraordinary natural setting, and fortified **Harburg**. South of Augsburg is the **Allgäu** region. The hilly pre-Alpine section includes the health resort of **Ottobeuren**, whose Benedictine abbey should stun even the most jaded visitor of Baroque churches. Beyond here, everything is played against the dramatic backdrop of snow-capped mountains and sparkling lakes: highlights are the pair of fantasy castles near the adjacent towns of **Füssen** and **Schwangau**, and the island town of **Lindau** on the Bodensee.

An added pleasure of travelling through this region is the distinctive and excellent **food**: delicate handmade pasta and rich sauces quite different from the Italian kind, followed by sweets with irreverent names like *Nonnenfürzle* (Nun's Fart) and *Versoffene Jungfern* (Drunken Virgins).

Nördlingen and around

NÖRDLINGEN, together with 99 villages, lies in an enormous crater, known as the **Ries**, which was formed about 15 million years ago by a meteor which crashed to earth at a speed of about 100,000 kilometres per hour, and with a velocity 250,000 times that of the Hiroshima bomb. The initially transient crater spread to cover an almost circular area with a diameter of about 25km, in the process bringing a new type of rock, known as suevite, into existence. It's among the largest craters on earth, and presents one of the main locations for scientists to study stone formations similar to those on the moon; it also provided ideal terrain for the Apollo 14 team to prepare for their lunar mission.

The Town

Along with Rothenburg and Dinkelsbühl, Nördlingen makes up the trio of towns on the Romantic Road which have almost completely retained their fortified medieval character. Of the three, it's the one which has made the most concessions to the modern commercial world, but the illusion remains. The fourteenth-century **Stadtmauer** forms an almost perfect circle, guarded by five gates, eleven towers and one bastion. You can traverse the covered sentry walk, the only one in Germany to survive intact, all the way round the 3km circuit. There is also the opportunity of ascending the eastern gateway, the **Löpsinger Tor** (April–Oct daily 10am–4.30pm; €1).

However, the best view – which shows clearly the distinctive shape and topography of the Ries – is from the 90-metre **Danielturm** (daily: April–Oct 9am–8pm; Nov–March 9am–5.30pm; €2), the town's symbol, its highest building – and also the bull's-eye of the circular urban plan. The tower illustrates a gradual shift in architectural tastes from the late Gothic of its lower storeys to the full-blooded Renaissance of its cupola. A watchman still lives at the top of the tower, and sounds out the watch every half-hour from 10pm until midnight. The Danielturm actually forms part of the hall church of **St Georg**, the largest suevite building in the world, whose design closely resembles that of its namesake in Dinkelsbühl. At the high altar is an emotional polychrome wood *Crucifixion* by the great fifteenth-century Dutch sculptor Nicolaus Gerhaert von Leyden.

On the opposite side of the spacious Marktplatz lies the **Rathaus**, which has an entertaining little detail beside its ritzy outdoor stairway. The space underneath the steps used to hold the town's prisoners, and just by the wooden entrance is a medieval fool carved into the wall with an inscription saying *Nun sind unser zwey* – "Now there are two of us". Directly across is the half-timbered **Tanzhaus** (Dance Hall), bearing a statue of Emperor Maximilian I who had a special affinity with the town; he's depicted in the guise by which he most wanted to be remembered, that of a chivalrous knight. Walking northwards from Marktplatz, you reach the curious building known as the **Klösterle** (Little Monastery), which has had a decidedly chequered history. Once the church of the bare-footed Franciscan friars, it was converted into a grain store after the Reformation, and is now the town's main festive hall.

Beyond, on Vordere Gerbergasse, is the **Spital**, an extensive medieval hospital complex complete with its own church, mill and stores. It now houses the **Stadtmuseum** (March–Oct Tues–Sun 1.30–4.30pm; €2; Ⓦ www.stadtmuseum-noerdlingen.de), whose main treasure is a colourful cycle of paintings of *The Legend of St George* by the fifteenth-century local master Friedrich Herlin. The local history section features terrible exhibits from the torture chambers used during the sixteenth-century witch-hunts: in Nördlingen alone, 35 women were put to death. There's also a diorama of the Battle of

Nördlingen of 1634, the worst Protestant reverse in the Thirty Years' War. On nearby Hintere Gerbergasse, a fifteenth-century barn has been converted to house the snazzy **Reiskrater-Museum** (Tues–Sun: May–Oct 10am–4.30pm; Nov–April 10am–noon & 1.30–4.30pm; €3) which gives detailed information on the Ries crater's formation and geological history.

Practicalities

Nördlingen's **Bahnhof**, which lies on the slow route between Augsburg and Stuttgart via Schwäbisch Gmünd, is just to the east of the Altstadt. The **tourist office** is at Marktplatz 2 (Easter–Oct Mon–Thurs 9am–6pm, Fri 9am–4.30pm, Sat 9.30am–1pm; rest of the year Mon–Thurs 9am–5pm, Fri 9am–3.30pm; Ⓣ0 90 81/43 80 or 8 41 16, Ⓦwww.noerdlingen.de).

There are plenty of budget **hotels** within or beside the Stadtmauer, including *Gasthof Walfisch*, Hallgasse 15 (Ⓣ0 90 81/31 07; ❷–❹); *Gasthof Drei Mohren*, Reimlinger Str. 18 (Ⓣ0 90 81/31 13, Ⓦwww.gasthof-drei-mohren.de; ❸); *Gasthof Zum Engel*, Wemdinger Str. 4 (Ⓣ0 90 81/31 67; ❸); and *Café Altreuter*, Marktplatz 11 (Ⓣ0 90 81/43 19; ❹). Two good upmarket choices are *Sonne*, Marktplatz 3 (Ⓣ0 90 81/50 67, Ⓦwww.kaiserhof-hotel-sonne.de; ❻); and *Klösterle*, Beim Klösterle 1 (Ⓣ0 90 81/8 70 80, Ⓦwww.astron-hotels.com; ❼). There's also a **youth hostel**, in an old half-timbered house just to the northwest of the Stadtmauer at Kaiserwiese 1 (Ⓣ & Ⓕ0 90 81/27 18 16), but this is closed indefinitely for refurbishment. The **restaurants** of the last two hotels listed above are the best in town, while all the aforementioned Gasthöfe serve good and inexpensive Swabian cuisine. For a trendier atmosphere, try *Café Radlos*, Löpsinger Str. 8, which serves bistro-type food and has a wide range of guest beers on tap.

Harburg

From Nördlingen, it's only about 15km by road or rail to the next stop on the Romantic Road, the picturesquely sited little town of **HARBURG**. High above, dominating the valley of the River Wörnitz, is a huge **Schloss** (guided tours late March to Oct Tues–Sun 10am–5pm; €4.50), which was founded in the twelfth century by the Hohenstaufen emperors, before passing to the counts of Oettingen, whose descendants still own it. Never taken in battle, its fortifications and residential buildings – which date from a variety of periods – survive in pretty good condition. The Renaissance Fürstenbau houses the **Kunstsammlung** (late March to Oct Tues–Sun 10am–noon & 2–5pm; €3), whose prize exhibit is a poignant, almost

Nördlingen's festivals

On a Monday in mid-May, the Stabenfest (Staff Festival) celebrates the arrival of spring with a children's procession. Trumpets sound the festival's beginning from the heights of the Danielturm and boys gather holding flags and poles decorated with flowers, the girls wearing costumes and crowns of flowers around their heads. At around 9am, the procession moves off accompanied by music and song until it reaches the Kaiserwiese, the fairground just to the north of the Stadtmauer, where the usual trappings of a Bavarian fair are set up around the beer tent. Another popular annual event is the Scharlachrennen (Ⓦwww.scharlachrennen.de) in mid-July, whose origins lie in a horse race first held in 1438, with a piece of red cloth as a prize. Today, carriage events are also featured.

monumental ivory Crucifix of the eleventh-century Ottonian period, a unique work of its kind. There are also several outstanding treasury items, notably a jewelled reliquary cross bearing the figures of the donor, Count Ludwig XII of Oettingen, and his family.

Gasthof Zum Straussen, Marktplatz 2 (Ⓣ0 90 80/13 98; ❸) is one of the best-value **hotels** anywhere in Germany, and its **restaurant** serves king-sized portions of superb Swabian cuisine. The main alternative is the *Fürstliche Burgschenke* in the Schloss (Ⓣ0 90 80/15 04, Ⓦwww.ries-gastronomie.de/burgschenke-harburg; ❺).

Augsburg

Only 60km northwest of Munich, **AUGSBURG** certainly doesn't suffer from any inferiority complexes, despite being no more than a quarter of its size. Founded in 15 BC as *Augusta Vindelicorum* by two stepsons of Augustus, the city is one of the oldest in Germany. A Free Imperial City from 1276 and a frequent choice for meetings of the Diet, Augsburg had its heyday between the fifteenth and seventeenth centuries, when the **Fugger** and **Welser** dynasties made it Europe's most important centre of high finance. As a result it grew into one of the largest cities on the continent. It was the one major city in Germany to take the Renaissance style to its heart, and the highly individualistic buildings of **Elias Holl**, who served as municipal architect from 1602 until 1635, still dominate the townscape.

Local people have gone to vast expense to restore the numerous palaces and civic buildings to their original splendour. In fact civilian municipal life is the key to Augsburg's history. Trade and banking riches spawned a social conscience – in 1514 Augsburg built the world's first housing estate for the poor, the **Fuggerei**, an institution still in use today. Here too the revolutionary reforms of Martin Luther found their earliest support, as the city played a pivotal role in the Reformation and its aftermath. It became the model example of how different faiths could co-exist, making this visible by the curious practice of building new Protestant churches alongside existing Catholic ones.

Despite these associations, Augsburg is far from being a museum-piece. It has long been a leading centre for **new technologies**: here, for example, Rudolf Diesel invented the engine which has put his name into languages all round the world. There's also a lively cultural scene ranging from Mozart festivals to jazz and cabaret, and the local university means you'll find plenty of student bars and a thriving alternative culture.

Arrival, information and accommodation

The **Hauptbahnhof** lies just to the west of the Altstadt and is itself a remarkable sight, a mock *palazzo* of the 1840s which ranks as the longest-serving main station of any city in the world. Just down the road, at Bahnhofstr. 7, is the **tourist office** (Mon–Fri 9am–5pm; Ⓣ08 21/50 20 70, Ⓦwww.augsburg-tourismus.de). This has a small branch on Rathausplatz (May to mid-Oct Mon–Wed & Fri 9am–5pm, Thurs 9am–5.30pm, Sat 10am–4pm, Sun 10am–2pm; rest of year Mon–Sat only). A day ticket on the **public transport** network is a good investment; it costs €5 for the city, €10.50 for the whole circuit.

Augsburg has a wide choice of **hotels** and **pensions**, with a surprisingly large number of eminently good budget options for such a major city. The

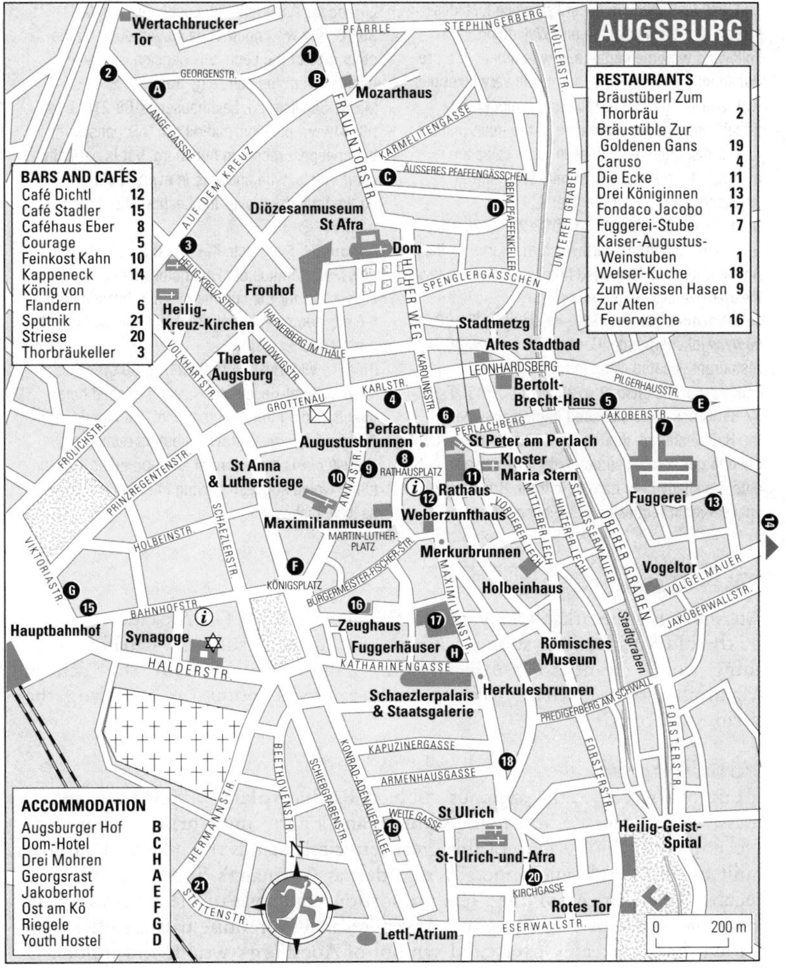

youth hostel is centrally located, three minutes' walk from the Dom, at Beim Pfaffenkeller 3 (ⓣ08 21/3 39 09; €12.70). The nearest **campsite**, *Augusta*, is at highway exit Augsburg-Ost, next to the Autobahnsee (ⓣ08 21/70 75 75, ⓦwww.campingplatz-augusta.de), and reachable by bus #75.

Hotels and pensions

Augsburger Hof Auf dem Kreuz 2 ⓣ08 21/34 30 50, ⓦwww.augsburger-hof.de. Part of the Romantik group, this classy hotel and restaurant occupies a historic building in the northern Altstadt. 6–8

Dom-Hotel Frauentorstr. 8 ⓣ08 21/34 39 30, ⓦwww.domhotel-augsburg.de. Attractive hotel occupying the former Domprobstei, the palace of the Dom's provost, in heart of the quiet episcopal quarter. It has a garden terrace and an indoor swimming pool with sauna and solarium. 5–8

Drei Mohren Maximilianstr. 40 ⓣ08 21/5 03 60, ⓦwww.augsburg.steigenberger.de. This is one of Germany's most famous hotels, founded in 1723 and with an illustrious guest list which includes Mozart, Goethe, Napoleon and Wellington. Following wartime damage, it was rebuilt in a predominantly modern style, but is still very luxurious, with a lovely garden terrace and a moderately priced bistro as an alternative to the main restaurant. Substantial reductions in room rates are available from early July to mid-Sept, and at weekends throughout the year. ❾

Georgsrast Georgenstr. 31 ⓣ08 21/50 26 10, ⓕ5 02 61 27. In the northwestern quarter of the Altstadt, this old-fashioned hotel is one of the few inexpensive places in the area. ❸

Jakoberhof Jakoberstr. 39–41 ⓣ08 21/51 00 30, ⓦwww.jakoberhof.de. Good-value hotel with restaurant, located close to the Fuggerei. ❹

Lenzhalde Thelottstr. 2 ⓣ08 21/52 07 45, ⓕ52 87 61. Greek-run hotel sited immediately behind the Hauptbahnhof, though it's a circuitous walk or drive to get here. In summer, its taverna spills out onto the shady beer garden in front. Breakfast is only served if requested in advance. ❸

Linderhof Aspernstr. 38, Lechhausen ⓣ08 21/71 30 16, ⓦwww.linderhof.de.vu. Although on the other side of the Lech, this pension is only ten minutes from the centre by tram #1. ❷

Märkl Schillstr. 20, Lechhausen ⓣ08 21/79 14 99, ⓦwww.pension-maerkl.de. This pension has the cheapest rooms in Augsburg, but is perfectly comfortable, with showers in every room. It's on the first street over the Lechbrücke; take tram #1. ❷

Ost am Kö Fuggerstr. 4–6 ⓣ08 21/50 20 40, ⓦwww.ostamkoe.de. Fine hotel which is equally convenient for the commercial and historic parts of the city centre. A buffet breakfast is included in the room price. ❺–❾

Riegele Viktoriastr. 4 ⓣ08 21/50 90 00, ⓦwww.hotel-riegele.de. Nicely furnished hotel directly facing the Hauptbahnhof. It's named after Augsburg's largest brewery, but its restaurant, *Bräustüble*, is more formal and upmarket than the name would suggest, serving international as well as local dishes. ❻

The City

Augsburg is a remarkably easy city to get to grips with. The Altstadt is defined by the old fortifications, substantial parts of which still survive. Virtually everything you'll want to see is within walking distance of the central Maximilianstrasse, which makes a ready reference point for exploring the various quarters.

Rathausplatz

Heart of the city is the spacious cobbled **Rathausplatz**, which turns into a massive open-air café during the summer and a glittering Christmas market in December. At the baseline of this great semicircle stands the massive **Rathaus** built by Elias Holl, and generally regarded as Germany's finest example of a secular Renaissance building. The proportions and style of the elegantly plain exterior topped by two octagonal towers recall a Florentine palace rather than a town hall, a likeably overstated symbol of Augsburg's wealth and influence. What stands today is a painstaking reconstruction; only the shell survived a 1944 air raid targeting the city's Messerschmidt aircraft factories. Not that you'd guess this from looking at the showpiece **Goldener Saal** (daily 10am–6pm; €2), which is once more resplendent with its gold-leaf pillars, marble floor and painted cedarwood ceiling.

Next to the Rathaus stands the **Perlachturm** (daily May–Oct 10am–6pm; €1), which was remodelled by Holl to its present height of just over 70m. A climb to the top gives a good vantage point from which to take in the whole city and get your bearings on Augsburg's main axis, neatly formed between the Dom to the north and the church of St-Ulrich-und-Afra at the far end of Maximilianstrasse to the south. The tower forms part of the Romanesque church of **St Peter am Perlach**, the oldest brick building in southern Germany, which preserves life-sized thirteenth-century murals of four saints. Opposite is the Mannerist **Augustusbrunnen**, by the Dutchman Hubert Gerhard, one of many grandiose fountains dotting the centre of the city, bearing a statue of the emperor and symbolic figures representing Augsburg's four rivers.

Maximilianstrasse

Maximilianstrasse is a true showpiece thoroughfare, lined with the headquarters of the leading corporate and municipal bodies, and the palatial residences of the richest merchant families who dominated their affairs. It's named in honour of the Habsburg Maximilian I, the last Holy Roman Emperor to preside over a unified empire and the man who set in motion his family's plans for European-wide domination. Augsburg was his favourite residence – no doubt partly because his political scheming was dependent on the backing of the city's bankers.

The first building of note is the fourteenth-century **Weberzunfthaus**, the guild hall of the linen weavers. Beyond, in the centre of the street, is the resplendent **Merkurbrunnen** by another Dutch-born Mannerist, Adrian de Vries, court sculptor to the Habsburgs. Soon after, the **Fuggerhäuser** stand proudly to the right. Built in 1515 by Jacob Fugger "the Rich", these mansions remain in family hands, but you can walk through the main door to see the arcaded **Damenhof**, designed in Italian Renaissance style and often used for plays in the summer. In 1518 this courtyard was the venue for the meeting between Martin Luther and Cardinal Tommaso Cajetan, in which the great reformer attempted to justify his 95 theses against Catholic orthodoxy.

Continuing south down Maximilianstrasse, you come to Adrian de Vries' heroic **Herkulesbrunnen**, the most arresting of all the city's fountains. To the right is the **Schaezlerpalais** (Tues–Sun 10am–5pm; €3, free first Sun of month), the town's foremost Rococo building. Its sumptuous ballroom is in its original condition – right down to the candle-lit chandeliers that are still used during the annual Mozart concerts held in June and July. There's also a collection of sixteenth- to eighteenth-century German and Austrian paintings, plus a few works by foreigners, including Veronese and Tiepolo. Through the courtyard and included on the same entrance ticket is the old Dominican nunnery, now housing the **Staatsgalerie**. This displays the work of the fifteenth- and sixteenth-century school of local painters – notably Hans Holbein the Elder and Hans Burgkmair – as well as Dürer's portrait of Jacob Fugger "the Rich", looking every bit the king-maker that he was.

Towards its end, Maximilianstrasse widens and sweeps up to the late Gothic basilica of **St-Ulrich-und-Afra**, whose Renaissance tower is crowned by the most famous of the city's characteristic onion domes. In the airily light interior are the tombs of the city's two patrons. St Afra, a Roman virgin martyr, is interred in a simple sarcophagus, whereas St Ulrich, the local prince-bishop whose army helped save the empire by turning back the rampaging Magyars at the Battle of Lechfeld in 955, is honoured by an ornate Rococo shrine. The three monumental gilded altars by Hans Degler in the choir are late Renaissance masterpieces belonging to the same brilliant artistic period as Holl's buildings. In the early eighteenth century, as a symbol of the religious tolerance of the time, the preaching hall on the north side of the basilica was rebuilt as the Lutheran church of **St Ulrich**, its cheerful Baroque facade making an effective foil to its much grander neighbour.

The eastern Altstadt

Just to the southeast of St-Ulrich-und-Afra is another distinctive landmark, the **Rotes Tor**, a fortified tower strengthened by Holl at the time of the Thirty

Years' War, whose courtyard is now used as an open-air theatre. The same architect's **Heilig-Geist-Spital** alongside is home to the celebrated Puppenkiste marionette theatre, whose history, illustrated by many original sets and figures, is celebrated in the **Augsburger Puppentheatermuseum** (Tues–Sun 10am–7pm; €4.20, or €3.20 if attending a performance; Ⓦwww.diekiste.net). Following Bäckergasse and then Dominikanergasse back towards the city centre, you come to the former Dominican priory, which now houses the **Römisches Museum** (Tues–Sun 10am–5pm; €3, free first Sun of month; Ⓦwww.roemisches-museum.de), the city's collection of prehistoric and Roman remains. The richly stuccoed interior of the church makes an excellent setting for the artefacts, including a life-sized second-century bronze horse's head, which was probably part of a statue honouring Emperor Marcus Aurelius.

East of here is the most impressive surviving part of the medieval **Stadtmauer**, dominated by the fifteenth-century **Vogeltor**. Beyond lies the picturesque old artisans' quarter, laid out along the narrow canals of the Vorderer, Mittlerer and Unterer Lech. These back streets must have looked very similar a few hundred years ago, when they were populated with the tradesfolk and craftspeople who serviced the grand houses on Maximilianstrasse. At Vorderer Lech 20 the **Holbeinhaus** (Tues–Sun 11am–5pm; free) stands on the site of the original, which was destroyed in 1944. Here Hans the Younger, portraitist of the brilliant English court of Henry VIII, spent his childhood, his father having established himself as the city's leading painter. Changing exhibitions complement documentary material on the artists' lives.

Continuing northwards, you come to Elias-Holl-Platz to the rear of the Rathaus, on which stands a convent, **Kloster Maria Stern**. Originally built in the 1570s in late Gothic style by Johannes Holl, father of Elias, it was remodelled inside in the Baroque period. The slender brick belfry is crowned by the earliest example of the Welsche Haube, the distinctive onion dome that is a recurrent feature of the Augsburg skyline. A few paces on, fronting Schachthausgasse, is one of Elias Holl's finest buildings, the **Stadtmetzg**, the former guild hall and market of the butchers. Though its rusticated facade is the most visually impressive feature, it was also a technical tour-de-force in its day, harnessing the waters of the Lech canals which lie directly underneath for the cooling of meats and disposal of waste.

At Auf dem Rain 7 just to the north is the **Bertolt-Brecht-Haus** (Tues–Sun 10am–5pm; €1.50), the birthplace of the great poet and playwright whose relationship with the city is far more problematic than that of any of its other famous sons. The embarrassing fact is that the people of Augsburg couldn't stand Brecht when he was alive – but then neither could he stomach his bourgeois home city. Today, however, all is forgiven, and the house presents a mainly photographic record of the writer, predictably concentrating on his early life in Augsburg. On Leonhardsberg immediately to the north is the luxuriant Jugendstil **Altes Stadtbad** (Mon & Tues 8am–7pm, Wed–Fri 8am–9pm, Sat 8am–8pm, Sun 8am–6pm; prices start at €4 for a swim, €11 for a full Roman-Irish bath), one of Germany's finest bathing halls.

The Fuggerei

One "Our Father", one "Hail Mary" and one "Credo" daily, plus €0.88 per annum, and good Catholics can retire to the **Fuggerei** (Ⓦwww.fugger.de) at the age of 55. It's the world's oldest housing estate for the poor and must be one of the cleverest ploys ever devised for a place in Heaven – even if it now appears that Jacob Fugger's seeming generosity was at least partly inspired by the opportunities it offered for laundering part of his fortune. Entered via a gate which, in accordance with the still-enforced original regulations, is kept locked between 10pm and 5am, it's a town within a town, with two-storey ivy-covered houses lining six pedestrian-only streets. Originally intended for families with children, it has gradually evolved into a retirement colony, though residents must still be Roman Catholic, needy, free of a criminal record, and citizens of Augsburg.

Behind the main gateway is the the Fuggerei's modest little church, the **Markuskirche**, which was built by Johannes Holl. The only other interior open to the public is that of Mittlere Gasse 13, which has been designated the **Fuggereimuseum** (March 1 to Dec 23 daily 10am–6pm; €1), with furnishings vividly illustrating the lifestyle of the community's inhabitants of the seventeenth and eighteenth centuries. Another house from the time of the first settlement is no. 14 in the same street, which is where Mozart's great-grandfather lived in the late seventeenth century.

The western Altstadt

Exactly the other side of town, on Annastrasse, stands the Gothic church of **St Anna**, whose Renaissance tower was added by Elias Holl in an unconvential position above the body of the building, rather than on its own base. The chancel contains a number of devotional paintings, notably *Christ Blessing Children* by Cranach. Alongside is the **Goldschmiedkapelle** (Goldsmiths' Chapel), which preserves its original fresco cycle. In 1509, Ulrich and Jacob Fugger endowed a memorial chapel for themselves and their deceased brother Georg. The clout they wielded is shown by the fact that, against all convention, this formed an extension of the nave, instead of taking the humbler normal position off an aisle. The sumptuous **Fuggerkapelle** which resulted marks the belated German debut of the full-blooded Italian Renaissance style. An integrated, no-expenses-spared decorative scheme – marble pavement, an organ with painted shutters, stained glass, choir stalls, balustrade with putti, a monumental sculptural group of *The Lamentation over the Dead Christ*, and memorial relief tablets made after woodcuts designed by Dürer – creates an effect of overwhelming richness. Now thought to have been the work of local rather than Italian craftsmen, its influence on Augsburg was profound, inspiring all subsequent building there for over a century.

St Anna is also celebrated for its role in the Reformation, when Luther found refuge with its Carmelite friars when he was summoned to meet the Pope's legate Cardinal Cajetan, and today part of the former friary has been turned into the **Lutherstiege** (Tues–Sun 10am–noon & 3–5pm; free), a museum of the reformer's life and times. Along with extensive documentation on the events, you can see the **Lutherkammer**, the actual room where he stayed in 1518; the *Empore*, the old gallery for the Carmelites, shows the excommunication bull which resulted from his refusal to retract his views.

Across from the friary, in a Renaissance mansion with sgraffito decoration at Philippine-Welser-Str. 24, is the **Maximilianmuseum** (Tues–Sun 10am–5pm; €3, free first Sun of month; Ⓦ www.maximilianmuseum.de). Its courtyard (free access) has been covered with a glass roof in order that **original figures** from the city's three great Mannerist fountains can be displayed in natural light conditions, while protecting them from the elements. The rest of the museum has been undergoing reconstruction for many years, but is gradually being made accessible again, with work scheduled to be completed in late 2006. Of special note is the collection of historic **wooden models** made by practising architects: that of the Gothic Rathaus makes for a fascinating comparison with the one Holl prepared in advance of his rebuilding project; there's another showing progress on the Perlachturm, which is shrounded under scaffolding. There are extensive holdings of the wonderful Baroque and Rococo creations of the goldsmiths, silversmiths and watchmakers who made Augsburg one of Europe's leading producers of luxury goods, plus displays of sculptures from Gothic to Rococo, porcelain, and historic scientific instruments.

A couple of blocks further south, dominating the square named after it, is the **Zeughaus**, the first structure designed by Holl in his capacity as municipal architect. It's a brilliantly original composition whose facade is uncannily anticipatory of the Baroque style to come. Above its doorway is a striking monumental bronze group of *St Michael overcoming Satan*, the masterpiece of Hans Reichle, one of the few native German Mannerists.

The northern Altstadt

Dominating the northern part of the Altstadt is the **Dom**. Architecturally, it's a bit of a hotchpotch: in the fourteenth century, Gothic aisles were added to the original eleventh-century structure; a hundred years later, a lofty hall choir replaced its predecessor altogether. Entry is via the **portals** on the north and south sides of the chancel, which are dedicated to the Virgin Mary, and crowded with richly decorative Gothic sculptures. On the southern side of the nave's clerestory are five **stained-glass windows** showing the Old Testament figures of Moses, David, Hosea, Daniel and Jonah. The freshness of colour and the vibrancy of the design make it hard to believe they were made in the eleventh century: they're the oldest windows remaining *in situ* in any church in the world. Another Romanesque survivor is the **bishop's throne** in the west choir, imperiously perched on crouching lions. Look out also for the eight fine **altarpieces** by Hans Holbein the Elder, fixed to the pillars of the nave, of scenes from the life of the Virgin.

Housed in the chambers off the cloisters, but entered from Kornhausgasse to the north, is the **Diözesanmuseum St Afra** (Tues–Sat 10am–5pm, Sun 2–5pm, first Fri in month 10am–9pm; €2.50). This is now home to the Dom's celebrated Romanesque **bronze doors**, which are decorated with 35 endearingly simple panels depicting Old Testament scenes and allegorical figures and animals. Also on view are some precious textiles, including the Byzantine vestments of St Ulrich and Bishop Hartmann, and the artefacts made for the funeral of Emperor Charles V, the most striking being a gilded helmet with a crown on top. Numerous monstrances, chalices, ciboria, reliquaries, altars and other liturgical artefacts illustrate the vitality of Augsburg's goldsmith tradition between the fifteenth and eighteenth centuries. Excavations of the Carolingian Dom of around 800 can also be seen.

Facing the Dom's facade is the **Fronhof**, the former palace of the prince-bishops. Only the tower remains of the medieval building where the Confession of Augsburg, the basic creed of Protestantism, was presented in 1530. The rest was rebuilt in Baroque style, and has served since 1817 as the regional government of Bavarian Swabia; the frescoed staircase and the main Festsaal are freely accessible, except when an official function is taking place.

Further west are the **Heilig-Kreuz-Kirchen**, another of the paired Catholic and Protestant churches, each with its own distinctive interpretation of the Welsche Haube. Originally an Augustinian collegiate foundation, the Gothic Catholic church contains an altarpiece of *The Assumption* by Rubens, but the seventeenth-century Protestant building alongside is the one which really catches the eye, not least because of the startlingly asymmetrical groundplan that resulted from the need to build the facade directly along the line of the street. It contains a large number of paintings, including a small panel of *The Baptism of Christ* by Tintoretto and several canvases by Johann Heinrich Schönfeld, notably the iconographically unusual *Christ Preaching from a Boat*.

North of the Dom, at Frauentorstr. 30, is the **Mozarthaus** (Tues–Sun 10am–5pm; €1.50), which documents the lives of Leopold and Wolfgang Amadeus and contains some of the original furnishings. This modest little house was the birthplace of Leopold, who moved to Salzburg long before his famous son was born. Notorious even in his day as a Svengali figure, he is now recognized as a highly competent composer in his own right, whose works include one of the best trumpet concertos ever written and two effective comic pieces, *A Musical Sleigh Ride* and the *Toy Symphony*. Guarding the far northern end of the Altstadt is the **Wertachbrucker Tor**, a fourteenth-century gateway to which Elias Holl appended two storeys, a pyramidal roof and a lantern.

Outside the Altstadt

Just outside the confines of the Altstadt is the **Synagoge** (Tues–Fri 9am–4pm, Sun 10am–5pm; €1.50) at Halderstr. 8, a few minutes' walk east of the Hauptbahnhof. This imposing Jugendstil complex, grouped round an open courtyard, was built during World War I as the main place of worship for what was one of Germany's largest and most liberal Jewish communities. Nowadays, the tiny orthodox sect that remains uses only the small prayer hall; the domed main temple (which you can only view from the gallery) and ancillary buildings (which house a surprisingly rich treasury) now serve as a museum of Swabian and Bavarian Jewish culture.

Beyond the southwestern fringe of the Altstadt, housed in the Industrie und Handelskammer at Stettenstr. 1–3, is the **Lettl-Atrium** or **Museum für Surreale Kunst** (Mon–Sat 8am–5pm, Sun 11am–5pm; free). This contains well over a hundred canvases by the Augsburg Surrealist **Wolfgang Lettl**, whose work provides a refreshing corrective to the idea that Germans lack a sense of humour.

Eating, drinking and entertainment

In the food and drink field, Augsburg's main strengths are a wide range of restaurants offering hearty traditional fare, plus a large number of student pubs. In addition to the places listed below, and those in the hotels on pp.223–24, it's worth knowing about the market and meat halls off Annastrasse, where there are several Imbiss stands which are the best bet for on-your-feet snacks. The city has a surprising dearth of nightclubs, but is well-endowed with live music and theatrical venues.

Restaurants

Bräustüberl Zum Thorbräu Wertachbrucker-Tor-Str. 9. The tap of the Thorbräu brewery alongside, serving Swabian and Bavarian cuisine.

Bräustüble Zur Goldenen Gans Weite Gasse 11. The beer hall and garden of the eponymous brewery, which is located alongside. At lunchtime, it is transformed into a vegetarian specialist, with hot and cold buffet tables.Closed Sun.

Caruso Karlstr. 9. Good, reasonably priced Italian restaurant.

Die Ecke Elias-Holl-Platz 2. Famous old restaurant in the shadow of the Rathaus; among the most expensive, but also one of the most prestigious in the city.
Drei Königinnen Meister-Veits-Gässchen 32. The Gasthaus and beer garden of the Augusta brewery, with a nicely varied menu; it also hosts regular literary and artistic events.
Fondaco Jacobo Maximilianstr. 38. The cellar restaurant of the Fuggerhäuser has recently been given a makeover, and now has a menu with an Italian flavour. Evenings only (though the courtyard is open at lunchtimes when the weather is fine), closed Sun & Mon.
Fuggerei-Stube Jakoberstr. 26. The "local" of the Fuggerei, serving some of the best food in town. Closed Mon.
Kaiser-Augustus-Weinstuben Frauentorstr. 51. Historic wine cellar-cum-restaurant with summer terrace. Evenings only, closed Sun.
Welser-Kuche Maximilianstr. 83 ⓣ08 21/9 61 10. Extremely gimmicky, but nonetheless a true original, this restaurant does nothing but Renaissance-style banquets using recipes from the cookery book of Philippine Welser. Meals start at 8pm and last for 3 hours; reservations essential.
Wirtshaus am Lech Leipziger Str. 50, Lechhausen. Traditional tavern with beer garden serving really excellent Swabian cooking. It's situated just over the Lechbrücke, and can be reached by tram #1.
Zum Weissen Hasen Unter dem Bogen 4. The city centre Gaststätte of Hasenbräu, one of the big local breweries, offering cheap lunchtime specials.
Zur Alten Feuerwache Zeughausplatz 4. Another good choice for local cuisine, in the historic setting of the Zeughaus itself; there's also a beer garden. Closed Sun evening.

Bars and cafés

Café Dichtl Maximilianstr. 18. A modern variant on the theme of a traditional café.
Café Stadler Bahnhofstr. 30. Another good choice, complete with winter garden, for *Kaffee und Kuchen* – and conveniently placed to while away the time waiting for a train. Closed Sun.
Caféhaus Eber Philippine-Welser-Str. 6. Elegant coffee house which in summer sets up outside tables on Rathausplatz.
Charly-Bräu Ulmer Str. 43, Oberhausen. Hausbrauerei with a predominantly young clientele, located near the Oberhausen S-Bahn station. It makes an amber-coloured *Weizen* and a very dark *Braunbier*.
Courage Jakoberstr. 7. Trendy Bertolt Brecht theme bar.
Feinkost Kahn Annastr. 16. Café cum daytime restaurant attached to Augsburg's most mouthwatering delicatessen shop. It does good-value set lunches. Closed Sun.
Kappeneck Kappeneck 30. Friendly, youthful café-bar with a wide range of drinks and snacks.
Kerosin Gögginger Str. 26–28. Popular live music bar. Tues–Sat 9pm–1am.
König von Flandern Karolinenstr. 12. Basement Hausbrauerei producing very mild-tasting light and dark beers plus a *Doppelbock* called *Alligator*. Also does meals, including cheap daily specials. On Sun, it's only open in the evening.
Sputnik Stettenstr. 32. The leading late-nighter; open 9pm till 3am, 4am at weekends.
Striese Kirchgasse 1. A student favourite, sometimes featuring theatre and live music.
Thorbräukeller Heilig-Kreuz-Str. 20. Beer garden and Kneipe of the brewery of the same name. Evenings only.

Augsburg's festivals

The main local **festival** is Plärrer, which is rather like a smaller version of Munich's Oktoberfest, except that it takes place twice annually, lasting for a fortnight on each occasion. The spring version, the Frühjahrsplärrer, begins on the Sunday after Easter; its autumn counterpart, the Herbstplärrer, takes place on the last week in August and the first in September. Other annual events are the Jakober Kirchweih at the end of July and beginning of August; the Friedensfest (Peace Festival) on August 8; the Mozartsommer in late August and early September; and the Christkindlesmarkt, whose opening on November 23 is marked by a colourful pageant, and which features live Christmas music each subsequent weekend.

Nightclubs

Circus Ludwigstr. 36. The most popular of the city's discos. Sun–Thurs 9pm–3am, Fri 9pm–5am, Sat 9pm–4am.

Rockfabrik Riedinger Str. 24. A meeting-place for heavy rock fans, located north of the city centre on bus route #26 from Königsplatz. Mon–Wed 8pm–3am, Thurs 9pm–3am, Fri 9pm–4am, Sat 9pm–5am.

Spectrum-Club Ulmer Str. 234. Disco, party and live music venue. Thurs & Fri from 9pm, Sat & Sun from 8pm.

Classical music and theatre

Freilichtbühne Am Roten Tor 5 ⓣ08 21/08 21/3 24 49 00, ⓦwww.theater.augsburg.de. This mounts its open-air season of plays – with Brecht now featuring regularly – in June and July.

Kleiner Goldener Saal Jesuitengasse 12 ⓣ08 21/32 44 91 69). A Baroque hall, formerly part of a Jesuit seminary, which makes a highly suitable venue for small-scale classical music concerts.

Kongresshalle Göppinger Str. 10 ⓣ08 21/3 24 23 48. The usual venue forlarge-scale choral and orchestral concerts, including those of the Philharmonisches Orchester Augsburg.

Mozarthaus Frauentorstr. 30 ⓣ08 21/3 24 38 44. Presents a regular season of chamber, instrumental and song recitals.

Puppenkiste Spitalgasse 15 ⓣ08 21/45 03 45 40, ⓦwww.augsburger-puppenkiste.de. This marionette theatre, which presents shows for both kids and adults, is Augsburg's most famous cultural venue and consequently tickets are often hard to come by.

Theater Augsburg Kennedyplatz 1 ⓣ08 21/32 49 00., ⓦwww.theater.augsburg.de The main municipal stage for opera, dance and drama.

The Allgäu

The southwesternmost part of Bavaria is known as the **Allgäu**, and is almost as well-known for its cheeses – the finest produced in Germany – as for its magnificent scenery and famous monuments.

Ottobeuren

The small health resort of **OTTOBEUREN**, some 65km southwest of Augsburg, clusters around the **Reichsabtei**, which stands on a gentle incline above the rest of the village. This still-functioning Benedictine abbey founded in 764 is one of the most imposing and grandiose monasteries north of the Alps. Its patron Charlemagne gave the abbot important rights, elevating him to the status of a prince of the Holy Roman Empire.

Architecturally the abbey has undergone many changes since its foundation. The present Baroque **Basilika** was created, after several false starts by other architects, by the Munich master Johann Michael Fischer in the eighteenth century. It's huge: physical details such as the 90-metre nave and 60-metre transept hardly convey the bombastic impression you get on entering. The wealth of altars, frescoes, paintings and stuccoed embellishments needs time to be appreciated fully, and yet there's nothing busy about the whole effect. Among the many treasures, a twelfth-century Romanesque crucifix is the most precious and the three **organs**, considered among the most beautiful instruments in the world. At least one of them can be heard at the recitals held at 4pm every Saturday between February and November.

Apart from the church, there's also the **Museum der Benediktinerabtei** (daily 10am–noon & 2–5pm; €2), which is housed in a part of the abbot's palace. Highlights are the amazingly delicate seventeenth- and eighteenth-century inlaid furniture pieces and the beautiful Baroque library, which looks more like a ballroom than a place for contemplation, so rich is the decor of

The Romantic Road

Glibly named, but with many beautiful spots along it, the **Romantic Road** (Romantische Strasse) runs for 350km between Würzburg (see p.204) and Füssen. The road gets its name from the fact that it passes gently rolling countryside, which is never very dramatic but instead pleasantly unspoilt and tranquil. If pushed for time, taking the Europabus along the whole or part of the route is a good way to get a quick impression; both Eurailpasses are valid, while InterRail and EuroDomino holders are entitled to a discount, but note that services run just once a day in each direction, and only during the summer. One snag is that stops are very short, which means that you only get a superficial impression unless you break your journey for a day or trust to the infrequent local buses. (Many places on the route are not served by rail.) It's essential to detour from the main drag to get a full impression of the area and to escape the tourists – exploring the regions alongside becomes much more rewarding with your own transport. A bike is an especially appropriate means of transport, as there's a waymarked cycling route, the *Radroute Romantische Strasse*, which utilizes a mixture of pre-existing and specially laid tracks, plus some minor roads. There's a fully comprehensive guide to this: *Germany's Romantic Road* by Gordon McLachlan (Cicerone Press).

For the first section of the Road after Würzburg – the Baden-Württemberg towns of Bad Mergentheim, Weikersheim and Creglingen – see pp.361–365. The stages after that, including Rothenburg, Dinkelsbühl, Nördlingen and Augsburg are described on pp.211–231. For the next stretch, along the Lech valley via Landsberg and Steingaden and the Wieskirche see pp.113–115. The southernmost staging posts are Schwangau and Füssen

marble pillars and frescoed ceiling. Note also the theatre, which was an important element of arts teaching in any eighteenth-century Benedictine monastery.

Ottobeuren is not on a rail line, but has a regular **bus** link with Memmingen, a junction on the Munich–Lindau and Ulm–Oberstdorf lines, 11km to the northwest. The **tourist office** is in the Kurverwaltung, Marktplatz 14 (May–Sept Mon–Thurs 9am–noon & 2–5pm, Fri 9am–noon & 2–4pm, Sat 10am–noon; rest of year Mon–Fri only; ⓣ0 83 32/92 19 50, ⓦwww.ottobeuren.de). There's a **youth hostel** at Kaltenbrunnweg 11 (ⓣ0 83 32/3 68; €12.70), along with plenty of **rooms** in private houses (❷–❸). **Hotels** include *Gasthof Mohren*, Marktplatz 1 (ⓣ0 83 32/9 21 30; ❺); *Hirsch*, Marktplatz 12 (ⓣ0 83 32/79 90, ⓦwww.hotel-hirsch.de; ❺); and *Am Mühlbach*, Luitpoldstr. 57 (ⓣ0 83 32/9 20 50, ⓦwww.hotel-am-muehlbach.de; ❻). *Hirsch* also has the village's best **restaurant**, and is the main tap of the local brewery.

Füssen

FÜSSEN, the southern terminus of the Romantic Road (see box above), lies in a beautiful setting close to the Austrian border between the **Forggensee** reservoir and the **Ammer** mountains. Although used by most visitors merely as a jumping-off point for the two royal castles situated some 4km to the southeast, it's of far more than passing interest. Dominating the Lech valley from a position high above the Altstadt is the **Hohes Schloss**, which assumed its present late Gothic appearance at the turn of the sixteenth century, when the old fortress was rebuilt as a summer residence of the Augsburg prince-bishops. In an ingenious cost-saving device, the inner courtyard is adorned with illusionistic paintings showing elaborate door and window frames and oriels. Part of the north wing houses a branch of the **Bayerische Staatsgalerie** (April–Oct Tues–Sun 11am–4pm; Nov–March Tues–Sun 2–4pm; €2). Paintings by fifteenth- and sixteenth-century south German masters and nineteenth-century Munich artists are on view, but the chief attraction is the **Rittersaal**, which has a magnificent coffered vault.

Below the Schloss is the former **Kloster St Mang**, named in honour of the eighth-century "Apostle of the Allgäu". The present complex is almost entirely Baroque, but below the church, nowadays designated the **Stadtpfarrkirche**, is a Carolingian crypt containing the grave of the saint. This is only accessible on Sunday mornings, or by occasional guided tours, the times for which are posted in the porch. The monastic buildings house the **Museum der Stadt Füssen** (April–Oct Tues–Sun 11am–4pm; Nov–March Tues–Sun 2–4pm; €2.50), though the exhibits are overshadowed by the splendid Baroque interiors themselves, including the sumptuous **Festsaal**, which is still regularly used for concerts; the domed colloquium; and the oval refectory, which has an aperture in its ceiling looking up into the library above. Also of special note is the **Annakapelle**, the original monastic church, which was converted to serve as a funerary chapel and has a remarkable early seventeenth-century mural of *The Dance of Death*.

Practicalities

Füssen's dead-end **Bahnhof** is linked directly with Munich and Augsburg, with services departing on alternate hours. From outside, **buses** marked "Königsschlösser" leave at regular intervals for the castles. A couple of minutes' walk to the east, at Kaiser-Maximilian-Platz 1, is the **tourist office** (June–Aug Mon–Fri 8am–noon & 2–6pm, Sat 9.30am–12.30pm, Sun 10am–noon; Oct–May Mon–Fri 8am–noon & 2–6pm, Sat 10am–noon; ⓣ0 83 62/9 38 50, ⓦwww.fuessen.de). There are plenty of **guesthouses** and **hotels** in town, including *Elisabeth*, Augustenstr. 10 (ⓣ0 83 62/62 75; ❸); *Zum Hechten*, Ritterstr. 6 (ⓣ0 83 62/9 16 00, ⓦwww.hotel-hechten.com; ❹); the American-owned *Suzannes* (ⓣ08362/384 85, ⓦwww.suzannes.de; ❺); *Hirsch*, Kaiser-Maximilian-Platz 7 (ⓣ0 83 62/9 39 80, ⓦwww.hotelhirsch.de; ❺–❼); and *Sonne*, Reichenstr. 37 (ⓣ0 83 62/90 80, ⓦwww.hotel-sonne.de; ❻). The **youth hostel** is at the western edge of town at Mariahilferstr. 5 (ⓣ0 83 62/77 54; €13.70, while there's a **campsite** (ⓣ0 83 62/91 77 10, ⓦwww.camping-hopfensee.de) by the Hopfensee to the north. Füssen's best **restaurants** include that in the aforementioned *Zum Hechten* plus *Zum Schwanen*, Brotmarkt 4, and *Pulverturm* in the *Kurhaus* at the eastern edge of the town centre.

Schwangau

SCHWANGAU, 3km northeast of Füssen, to which it's connected by a frequent bus service, combines the roles of a traditional agricultural community and health resort. Its name literally means "Swan Country", and the presence of a sizeable colony of these aloof birds has cast a spell on rulers of the area down the centuries. As the decoration of their fantasy castles testifies, the nineteenth-century Bavarian kings Maximilian II and his son Ludwig II were obsessed by the swan motif and the medieval Grail legends associated with it.

The only historical monument of note in Schwangau itself is the Baroque **Wallfahrtskirche St Coloman**, which is set in isolation in the meadows north of town. Dedicated to an eleventh-century Irish martyr, it was designed and decorated by Johann Schmutzer. On the second Sunday of October, it's the setting for one of Germany's most picturesque and moving religious festivals, the **Colomansfest**. This features around three hundred horses and some beautifully decorated carriages, which process from the town centre to the surroundings of the church, where an open-air mass is held. The horses are then ridden round the church three times for good luck, after which beer and food, the essential accompaniments to any Bavarian festival, are dispensed from the nearby tents.

Hohenschwangau

Within the Schwangau muncipality is the village of **HOHENSCHWANGAU**, 2km to the southeast. Consisting in the main of hotels, guesthouses, restaurants, snack bars and souvenir shops, not to mention five enormous car parks, it's the most rampantly commercialized place in the whole of Germany – though it's only fair to add that it's set in close proximity to some of the most spectacular scenery the country has to offer. To escape from the worst of the crowds, it's well worth taking a stroll along the footpaths encircling the two beautiful lakes which lie directly to the east. In summer, you can swim or sail in the larger lake, the **Alpsee**, whereas the **Schwansee** (literally, "Swan Lake") is a strict nature reserve surrounded by an English-style park offering wonderful framed vistas of the two royal castles.

The smaller of these, the golden yellow **Schloss Hohenschwangau** (guided tours daily: April–Sept 8.39am–5pm; Nov–March 10am–4pm; €8 or €15 combined ticket with Schloss Neuschwanstein), rises directly above the Alpsee; note that there's free access to its lovely terraced garden, which commands wonderful views. Built in mock-Tudor style in the 1830s for Crown Prince Maximilian to replace a ruined feudal fortress, the Schloss still belongs to the Wittelsbach family, and feels like a lived-in private residence, crammed full of gifts from grateful subjects and fellow rulers. Several rooms are decorated with heroic **fresco cycles** illustrating German history and legends (including that of Lohengrin, the Swan Knight) painted from cartoons by Moritz von Schwind. In the **Hohenstaufensaal** is a square piano where Wagner would entertain **King Ludwig II** with themes from operas in progress. The latter's main contribution to the castle was to have the **ceiling** of his bedroom changed from a daytime to a night sky which could be illuminated by concealed spotlights.

Ludwig's own personal fantasy, the grey granite **Schloss Neuschwanstein** (guided tours daily: April–Sept 9am–6pm; Oct–March 10am–4pm; €8; Ⓦ www.neuschwanstein.de), is a steep twenty-minute walk from the village. The ultimate story-book castle and Germany's most ubiquitous tourist icon, Neuschwanstein has become famous the world over through posters, cards and Disney films, not to mention the innumerable theme park castles directly inspired by it. Begun in 1869 but never finished, it was intended as a tribute to medieval German chivalry and to Wagner, who had evoked this past so intoxicatingly in his vast music dramas; and as a symbol of Ludwig's belief in himself as a divinely chosen king. Plans were drawn by the theatre designer Christian Jank, working in close collaboration with the king; professional architects were used only for supervising the actual construction. It undoubtedly looks far better from a distance than close up or inside. The architecture and decoration draw freely from different historical styles: Byzantine for the **Thronsaal**, Romanesque for the private apartments, Gothic for the showpiece **Sängersaal**.

A path behind Neuschwanstein leads to the **Marienbrücke**, a steel bridge that is a major feat of nineteenth-century engineering; it traverses the Poellat gorge, with its rushing waterfall. Continuing uphill by the steep marked footpath for about an hour, you reach the most celebrated vantage point over Neuschwanstein, in which the castle appears head-on from above, framed by the Alpsee, the Schwansee, the Ammergebirge and the Tyrolean Alps. The trail continues onwards to the top of the **Tegelberg** (1720m), a hike which normally takes a further two hours. This commands panoramas stretching as far as Munich on a clear day, and can also be reached by **cable car** (€9 single, €15 return; Ⓦwww.tegelbergbahn.de).

Practicalities

Schwangau's **tourist office** is in the Kurverwaltung, Münchener Str. 2 (Mon–Fri 7.30am–12.30pm & 1.30–5pm; Ⓣ0 83 62/8 19 80, Ⓦwww.schwangau.de). There's a reasonable supply of **private rooms** (❷–❸), as well as a few similarly inexpensive **pensions**. Among the **hotels** are *Gasthof Hanselewirt*, Mitteldorf 13 (Ⓣ0 83 62/82 37, Ⓦwww.hanselewirt.de; ❸–❺); *Weinbauer*, Füssener Str. 3 (Ⓣ0 83 62/98 60, Ⓦwww.hotel-weinbauer.de; ❹–❻); and *Gasthof Zur Post*, Münchener Str. 5 (Ⓣ0 83 62/9 82 18; ❺), all of which have good, reasonably priced **restaurants**.

If you'd prefer to be based in Hohenschwangau, there are several **pensions**, including *Romantic Pension Neuschwanstein*, Pfleger-Rothut-Weg 2 (Ⓣ0 83 62/8 11 02, Ⓦwww.albrecht-neuschwanstein.de; ❷); and *Weiher*, Hofwiesenweg 11 (Ⓣ0 83 62/8 11 61; ❸). Alternatively, you can stay in style at one of the classy **hotels**, such as *Meier*, Schwangauer Str. 37 (Ⓣ0 83 62/8 11 52, Ⓦwww.alpenhotel-allgaeu.de; ❺); *Müller*, Alpseestr. 16 (Ⓣ0 83 62/8 19 90, Ⓦwww.hotel-mueller.de; ❼–❾); or *Schlosshotel Lisl und Jägerhaus*, Neuschwansteinstr. 1–3 (Ⓣ0 83 62/88 70, Ⓦwww.lisl.de; ❽–❾). Each of these has a top-notch **restaurant**; more basic fare is available at the *Schlosswirtschaft* just below Neuschwanstein. The only ready way of seeing any of Schloss Neuschwanstein at leisure is to attend one of the **concerts** in the *Sängersaal*; these are held over a week in mid- to late September, and tickets can be ordered in advance from the tourist office. In 2000, the Musical Theater Neuschwanstein (Ⓣ0 18 05/58 39 44, Ⓦwww.ludwigmusical.com) was inaugurated with a **musical** about the life of Ludwig II.

Lindau

At their most westerly point the Alps descend to the waters of the **Bodensee** and the tiny island town of **LINDAU**, which is nowadays linked to the mainland by a road bridge and rail causeway. It's the starting point of the **German Alpine Road** (Deutsche Alpenstrasse), a tourist route that runs the length of the German Alps, terminating 250km away in Berchtesgaden. In the Middle Ages, Lindau was a bustling trading post and city-state, and rich merchants built grand gabled houses on town squares that have a distinct Italian flavour. The half-timbered buildings lean over like stacks of dominoes, and narrow streets like Zitronengasse lead to quiet nooks and crannies.

At the southern end of the island is the **Hafen** (harbour), which, with its hazy views across the lake to the Alps, is the most popular spot in town. Its narrow entrance is guarded by two tall pillars, one a lighthouse, the other bearing the defiant Lion of Bavaria. The previous lighthouse, the **Mangturm** (variable opening hours; €1), stands in the middle of the sheltered port and was originally part of the medieval fortifications. As soon as the summer sun comes out, the harbour promenade fills with coffee tables, giving a Mediterranean feel to the bustling waterfront. Several **ferries** operate on the lake (for full information, see box on p.291). All sorts of boats, canoes and windsurfers can be rented from the yacht marina east of the harbour.

On Reichsplatz, in the centre of the island, stands the Gothic **Altes Rathaus**; unfortunately the elaborate murals make it seem overdressed in comparison with the buildings around it. From here, you can walk west along Maximilianstrasse, before turning north to see the **Diebsturm** (Brigands' Tower), the other surviving part of the fortifications. Alongside, Romanesque **St Peter**, now a war memorial, is the sole church in Lindau still in its medieval state. Hans Holbein the Elder's faded Passion cycle in the apse is his only surviving fresco.

The most stylish building in Lindau is the **Haus zum Cavazzen** (April–Oct Tues–Fri & Sun 11am–5pm, Sat 2–5pm; €2) on Marktplatz towards the eastern end of the island, whose three-storey Baroque facade is painted in subtle sandy-red tones, and which contains one of the most attractive local history museums of any town in Bavaria. There's an intriguing collection of seventeenth-century family trees painted on wooden panels that open up like a photo-album, to reveal little portraits and dates for each member, plus paintings of the same period, known as *Spottbilder*, mocking Luther. On the second and third floors are fine displays of furniture, ranging from items from the workshops of Lindau's former artisan guilds to beautifully inlaid Biedermeier furniture.

Practicalities

The **Hauptbahnhof** is at the southwestern corner of the island, right beside the harbour. Just across from the entrance, at Ludwigstr. 68, is the **tourist office** (April to mid-June & mid-Sept to Oct Mon–Fri 9am–noon & 2–6pm, Sat 10am–2pm; May to mid-Sept Mon–Fri 9am–6pm, Sat & Sun 10am–2pm; Nov–March Mon–Fri 9am–noon & 2–5pm; ⓣ0 83 82/26 00 30, ⓦwww.lindau-tourismus.de).

Among the **guesthouses** and **pensions** on the island are *Lädine*, In der Grub 25 (ⓣ0 83 82/53 26; ❸); and *Seerose*, Auf der Mauer 3 (ⓣ0 83 82/2 41 20, ⓦwww.seerose-lindau.de; ❺). The many medium-range **hotels** include *Gasthof Inselgraben*, Hintere Metzgergasse 4–6 (ⓣ0 83 82/54 81, ⓦwww.inselgraben.de; ❺); *Alte Post*, Fischergasse 3 (ⓣ0 83 82/94 39 85, ⓦwww.alte-post-lindau.de; ❻); and *Insel-Hotel*, Maximilianstr. 42 (ⓣ0 83 82/50 17, ⓦwww.insel-hotel-lindau.de; ❻). Along Seepromenade are the four swankiest hotels, the most exclusive being *Bayerischer Hof* (ⓣ0 83 82/91 50, ⓦwww.bayerischerhof-lindau.de; ❽–❾). There are plenty of **rooms** in private houses (❷–❸), but most are on the mainland. The **youth hostel** is at Herbergsweg 11 (ⓣ0 83 82/9 67 10; €17.20) on mainland Lindau; take bus #1, #3 or #6 from the Hauptbahnhof. By the Austrian border at Fraunhoferstr. 20 (ⓣ0 83 82/7 22 36) is the **campsite**, *Park-Camping Lindau am See* (ⓣ0 83 82/7 22 36, ⓦwww.park-camping.de). Inevitably, the leading **restaurants** are in the waterfront hotels, but there are plenty of excellent and far less expensive alternatives: *Zum Sünfzen*, Maximilianstr. 1, *Weinstube Frey*, Maximilianstr. 15, and the restaurant in *Alte Post* are all eminently recommendable. Even cheaper restaurants, plus a few bars, can be found in the suitably named In der Grub, a block north of Maximilianstrasse.

Travel details

Munich to: Augsburg (every 20min; 30min); Berchtesgaden (hourly; 2hr 45min); Cologne (hourly; 5hr 20min); Eichstätt (hourly; 1hr); Frankfurt (frequent; 4hr); Garmisch-Partenkirchen (hourly; 1hr 15min); Hamburg (hourly; 8hr); Ingolstadt (frequent; 45min); Landshut (frequent; 1hr); Lindau (hourly; 2hr 30min); Nürnberg (hourly; 1hr); Oberammergau (hourly; 1hr 45min); Prien (hourly; 1hr); Regensburg (hourly; 2hr); Stuttgart (hourly; 2hr 15min); Ulm (hourly; 1hr 15min); Würzburg (hourly; 2hr 20min).

Nürnberg to: Ansbach (every 30min; 45min); Augsburg (hourly; 1hr); Bamberg (every 30min; 45min); Bayreuth (every 30min; 1hr 10min); Coburg (hourly; 1hr 35min); Frankfurt (hourly; 2hr); Passau (hourly; 2hr 20min).

Würzburg to: Aschaffenburg (hourly; 1hr); Cologne (hourly; 3hr 40min); Frankfurt (hourly; 1hr 20min); Rothenburg (hourly; 45min); Schweinfurt (hourly; 30min); Stuttgart (hourly; 2hr).

Baden-Württemberg

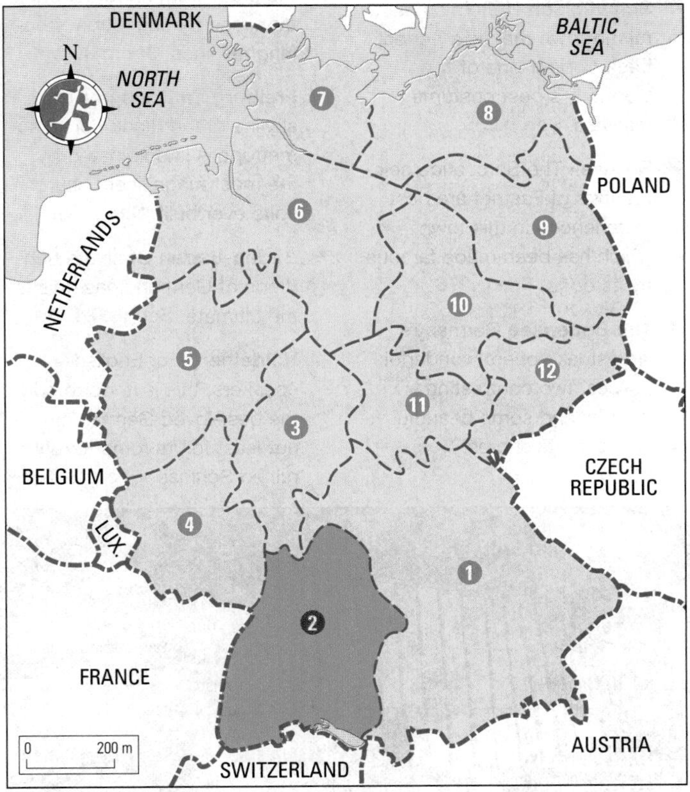

CHAPTER 2

Highlights

* **Stuttgart** The state capital is a spacious, green city with a distinguished tradition in the performing arts. See p.243
* **Maulbronn** The best-preserved medieval monastery north of the Alps. See p.256
* **Schwäbisch Hall** This beautiful old town makes a perfect backdrop for one of Germany's best costume festivals. See p.259
* **Rottweil** The Shrovetide celebrations of Fastnet are best experienced in this town, which has been made famous by its dogs. See p.276
* **The Bodensee** Germany's largest lake offers wonderful cruises, two contrasting islands, and some beautiful towns on its shores. See p.290
* **The Baroque gardens** Mainau, Schwetzingen and Weikersheim are three of Germany's most wonderful gardens. See p.299, p.341 & p.363
* **The Black Forest** By far the largest and most famous of the great German forest tracts, traversed by some truly stunning rail lines. See p.301
* **Freiburg im Breisgau** The skyline of the Black Forest's metropolis is dominated by the most magnificent church spire ever built. See p.302
* **Baden-Baden** Of all the hundreds of German spas, this is the ultimate. See p.324
* **Heidelberg** For English-speakers, this is undoubtedly the best-loved German city, not least for its romantically ruined Schloss. See p.347

△ Neue Staatsgalerie, Stuttgart

Baden-Württemberg

Baden-Württemberg only came into existence in 1952 as a result of the merger, approved by plebiscite, of three relatively small provinces established by the American and French occupying forces. Theodor Heuss, the first Federal president, saw it as "the model of German possibilities", and it hasn't disappointed, maintaining its ranking as the most prosperous part of the country. Being weak in natural resources, the area has had to rely on ingenuity to provide a spur to its industrial development, and ever since the motorcar was invented here in the late nineteenth century, it has been at the forefront of the world technology scene.

Ethnically, culturally and historically, the Land has two separate roots. **Baden**, the western part of the province, has been predominantly Catholic since the incorporation of the Breisgau region in the early nineteenth century, and its people are generally seen as being of a relaxed, almost carefree disposition. Their neighbours in **Württemberg** (or **Swabia**, as the locals still prefer to call it), on the other hand, are renowned for being hard-working, thrifty and house-proud, values instilled in them since the Reformation they embraced so openly. This stark division, however, has been much modified by the extensive influx of refugees from the Eastern Territories after World War II: along with their descendants, they now account for about a quarter of the total population.

For variety of scenery, Baden-Württemberg is rivalled only by Bavaria. The western and southern boundaries of the province are defined by the River Rhine and its bulge into Germany's largest lake, the **Bodensee**. Immediately beyond lies the **Black Forest**, one of Europe's main holiday areas. Here rises another of the continent's principal waterways, the **Danube**, which later forms a grandly impressive gorge at the foot of the **Swabian Jura**, the range in which the **Neckar** begins its increasingly sedate northerly course. At the eastern end of the province there's an even gentler valley, that of the **Tauber**.

Each of Baden-Württemberg's three largest cities – **Stuttgart**, **Mannheim** and **Karlsruhe** – was formerly a state capital (of Württemberg, the Palatinate and Baden respectively). All were extensively damaged in World War II and none could be called beautiful, though all have excellent museums and Stuttgart offers a wide variety of nightlife. Unfortunately, the historic centres of **Freiburg im Breisgau** and **Ulm** were also bombed, but both their Münsters, which rank among Germany's greatest buildings, were spared. Other than this, Baden-Württemberg's lack of a heavy industrial base meant that it escaped the war relatively lightly. Germany's two most famous university cities, **Heidelberg** and **Tübingen**, were hardly touched, enabling the former to maintain its cherished role as the most romantic place in the entire country.

Almost equally enticing is the wealth of towns which stand as period pieces of different epochs. **Bad Wimpfen** and **Schwäbisch Hall** each preserve the

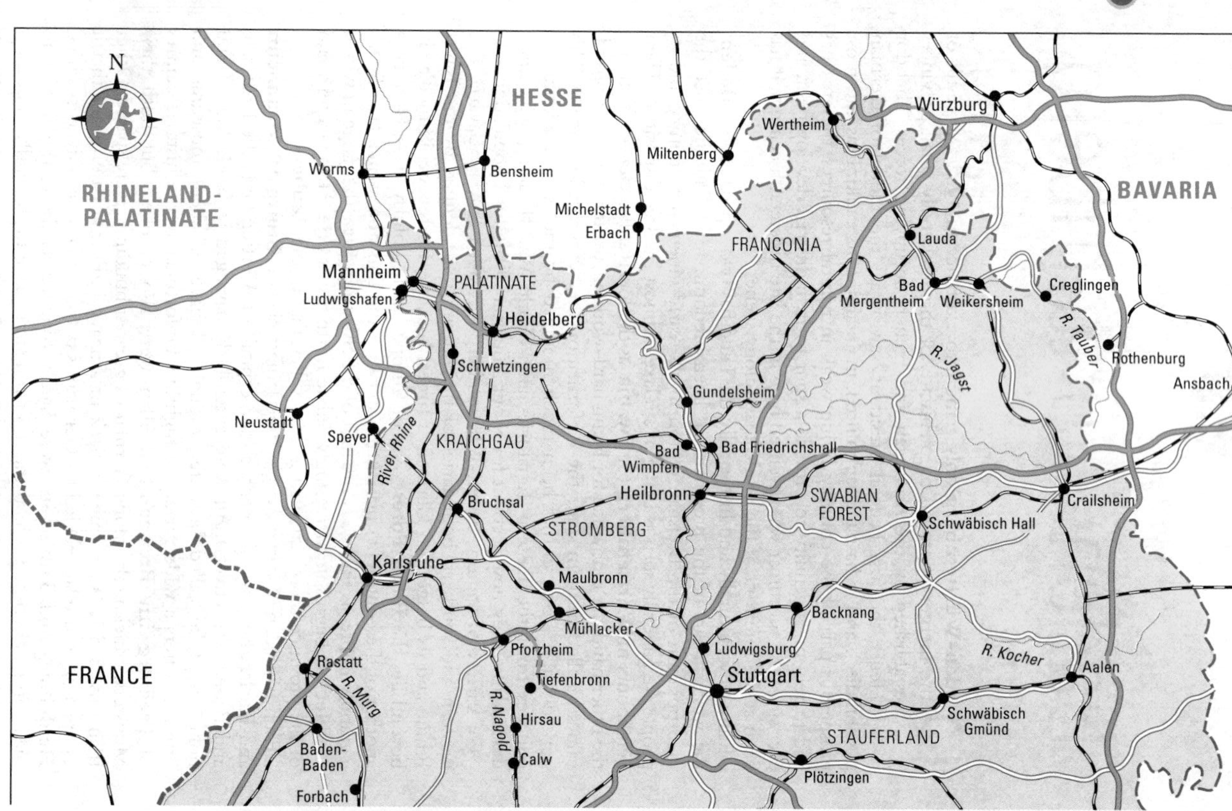
N
HESSE
Würzburg
Wertheim
Miltenberg
BAVARIA
Worms
Bensheim
RHINELAND-PALATINATE
Michelstadt
Erbach
FRANCONIA
Lauda
Mannheim
Ludwigshafen
PALATINATE
Heidelberg
Bad Mergentheim
Weikersheim
Creglingen
R. Tauber
Rothenburg
Ansbach
Schwetzingen
R. Jagst
Gundelsheim
Neustadt
Speyer
River Rhine
KRAICHGAU
Bad Wimpfen
Bad Friedrichshall
Heilbronn
SWABIAN FOREST
Crailsheim
Bruchsal
STROMBERG
Schwäbisch Hall
Karlsruhe
Maulbronn
Backnang
Mühlacker
Pforzheim
Ludwigsburg
R. Kocher
Aalen
Rastatt
FRANCE
R. Murg
Tiefenbronn
Stuttgart
R. Nagold
Hirsau
Schwäbisch Gmünd
STAUFERLAND
Baden-Baden
Calw
Plötzingen
Forbach

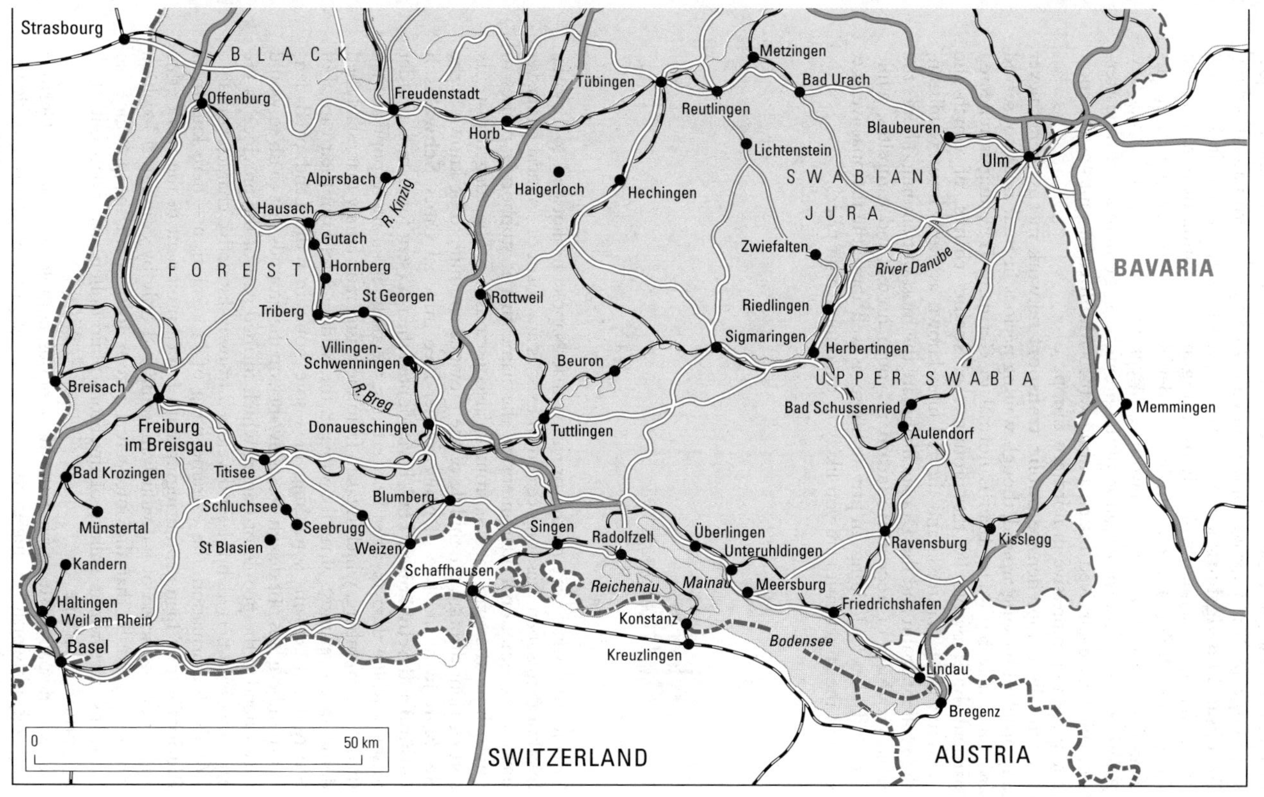
Strasbourg
BLACK
FOREST
Offenburg
Freudenstadt
Horb
Tübingen
Metzingen
Bad Urach
Reutlingen
Blaubeuren
Ulm
Lichtenstein
SWABIAN
JURA
Alpirsbach
R. Kinzig
Haigerloch
Hechingen
Hausach
Gutach
Hornberg
Zwiefalten
River Danube
BAVARIA
St Georgen
Triberg
Rottweil
Riedlingen
Sigmaringen
Herbertingen
Villingen-Schwenningen
Beuron
UPPER SWABIA
Breisach
R. Breg
Bad Schussenried
Memmingen
Freiburg im Breisgau
Donaueschingen
Tuttlingen
Aulendorf
Bad Krozingen
Titisee
Blumberg
Schluchsee
Münstertal
Seebrugg
St Blasien
Weizen
Singen
Radolfzell
Überlingen
Unteruhldingen
Ravensburg
Kisslegg
Kandern
Schaffhausen
Reichenau
Mainau
Meersburg
Haltingen
Weil am Rhein
Friedrichshafen
Konstanz
Basel
Bodensee
Kreuzlingen
Lindau
Bregenz
0
50 km
SWITZERLAND
AUSTRIA

form and appearance of the Middle Ages, whereas **Rottweil** has medieval survivals amid streets which bridge the gap between Renaissance and Baroque, and **Haigerloch** is a varied confection enhanced by a superb natural setting. **Bruchsal**, **Ludwigsburg** and **Rastatt** are proud courtly towns in the full-blown Baroque manner, while **Schwetzingen** is a creation of pure Rococo fantasy and **Baden-Baden** remains wonderfully evocative of its nineteenth-century halcyon years as the favourite playground of European aristocracy. Another special historical feature of the province is the number of monasteries which have survived intact, among which **Maulbronn** ranks as the most complete and impressive in northern Europe.

A typically comprehensive **public transport** network means there's never any problem moving around, though waiting periods in rural areas not served by trains may be longer than is normal in Germany. Travelling is rendered particularly enjoyable by the profusion of **scenic routes**, of which the Schwarzwald-Hochstrasse and the rail lines known as the Schwarzwaldbahn, the Höllentalbahn and the Donautalbahn are the most outstanding. There's the usual provision of **accommodation** in youth hostels and campsites, while the availability of lodgings in private houses is well above the national average. Only in the larger cities are you likely to encounter high prices.

Swabia

Save for the small part of the province that Napoleon allocated to Bavaria, **Swabia** (Schwaben) has long ceased to exist as any form of political entity, yet such is the emotional attachment to the name that it stubbornly refuses to vanish from the map, far less from local consciousness. The rugged plateaux cutting right through the middle of the province continue to be known as the **Swabian Jura**, and two of many former Free Imperial Cities, **Schwäbisch Gmünd** and **Schwäbisch Hall**, have adopted their present forenames in order to show where their loyalties lie. Certainly, the name is far more popular than that of Württemberg, which is taken from the aristocratic family that established dominance over most of rural Swabia in the Middle Ages from their capital of **Stuttgart**. It remains something of a sore point that the Land of Baden-Württemberg was not designated as Swabia, on the grounds that to do so would have offended the people of Baden, which formed part of the province in the early medieval period, but later developed its own distinctive characteristics.

At the Reformation, the extreme wing of Protestantism – here known as **Pietism** – took firm root, bringing with it a commitment to the work ethic and a burning sense of individualism, tempered only by communal loyalties. There's no doubt that the intellectual rigour fostered in the province has led to its nurturing a gallery of inventors, philosophers and poets out of all proportion to its size.

If you despair of mastering the horrendous complexities of the German language, it's worth bearing in mind that the ingenious Swabians have developed a partial solution to the problem, put to everyday use in their own **dialect**. By adding -le to most nouns, they don't have to worry about genders (which immediately become neuter), while they omit the cumbersome ge- prefix from past participles and regularize the declension of verbs. The local **cuisine** is no less distinctive, with noodles as ubiquitous as in Italian or Chinese cooking. Nearly every savoury dish comes with either *Spätzle*, a shredded pasta made from eggs and flour, or *Maultaschen*, which, with the exception of the sauces used to cover it, is broadly similar to ravioli. Equally popular are *Flädle* (pancakes) which turn up in both soups and desserts.

Stuttgart

STUTTGART breathes modern-day success. Düsseldorf and Hamburg may have more millionaires, but Baden-Württemberg's capital has the highest general standard of prosperity of any city in Germany, or, indeed, in Europe. Beaming out imperiously from its lofty station above the city centre is the local trademark, the three-pointed white star of Daimler-Benz – or Daimler-Chrysler as the corporation is now known, following its transatlantic tie-up. As Stuttgart is also home to Porsche and the almost equally celebrated electronics giant Robert Bosch, it has a secure place at the forefront of the global hi-tech industrial scene.

For all Stuttgart's present self-confidence, it was initially slow to develop. Founded around 950 as a stud farm (*Stutengarten* – hence the city's name), it only became a town in the fourteenth century, and lay in the shadow of its more venerable neighbours right up to the early nineteenth century, when

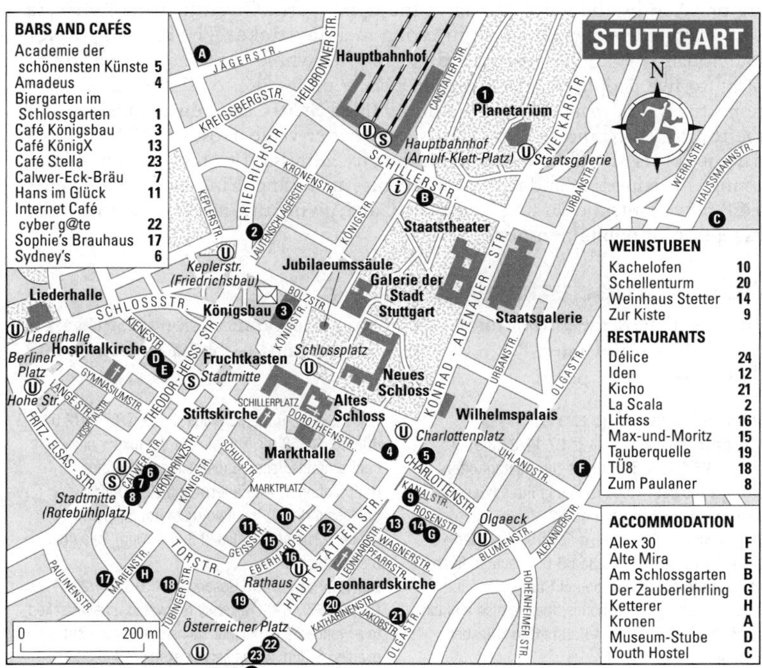

Napoleon raised Württemberg to the status of a kingdom and placed the former Free Imperial Cities under its control. Though Stuttgart's standing as a royal capital was to last for only a century, the city has never looked back.

From the point of view of conventional sights, Stuttgart has relatively little to offer. On the other hand, it has a range of superb **museums** to appeal to all tastes, and a varied cultural and nightlife scene. It also has an enviable **setting** in a hollow surrounded by hills, which enables the cultivation of vineyards within a stone's throw of the centre, and the liberal endowment of parks and gardens successfully softens what would otherwise be a drab and unappealing cityscape.

Arrival and information

The **Hauptbahnhof** – an impressive example of railway architecture, built during the Weimar Republic – is plumb in the centre of the city. Immediately behind is the **bus station**. S-Bahn #2 and #3 offer a regular twenty-minute service from 5am to midnight between the Hauptbahnhof's underground terminal and the **airport** (Ⓣ07 11/9 48 33 88, Ⓦwww.stuttgart-airport.de) in the far south of the city. Across the road from the Hauptbahnhof at Königstr. 1a is the **tourist office**, *i-Punkt* (Mon–Fri 9am–8pm, Sat 9am–6pm, Sun 11am/1pm–6pm; Ⓣ07 11/2 22 82 40, Ⓦwww.stuttgart-tourist.de) which has a free booking service for accommodation (Ⓣ07 11/2 22 82 33).

The integrated **public transport** network, run by VVS (Ⓦwww.vvs.de), covers nearby towns as well as the Stuttgart metropolitan area and enables you to switch between buses, trams, U-Bahns, mainline and S-Bahn trains and a rack railway. Note that all trams and U-Bahns travel both above and below ground; the former are older vehicles, and stop at the lower sections of underground station platforms, whereas their newer counterparts, whose numbers are prefaced by the letter U, halt at the upper parts. Given that the sights are very scattered, it may be worth investing in a **day ticket**. The current cost for individuals is €4.80 for the city, €9.80 for the whole circuit; for mini-groups of up to five people travelling together, these prices rise to €7.80 and €12.50 respectively. For many visitors the drolly titled **StuttCard plus**, available from the tourist office and some hotels, is even better value. Costing €14 for three days, it covers all public transport in the city, admission to most museums and a range of reductions and numerous freebies, including drinks and food. There's a €8.50 variant, known simply as **StuttCard**, giving the same benefits with the exception of public transport.

Accommodation

To some extent, the astronomical cost of rented accommodation in Stuttgart is reflected in **hotel** rates. However, there are bargains to be had, often with a decent location.

Hotels and pensions

Alte Mira Büchsenstr. 24 Ⓣ07 11/2 22 95 02, Ⓕ2 22 95 03 29. This Croat-run Gasthof offers some of the best-value rooms in the city centre, as well as a decent restaurant. ❺

Alter Fritz am Killesberg Feuerbacher Weg 101 Ⓣ07 11/13 56 50, Ⓕ1 35 65 65. Located in the north of the city, this is one of Stuttgart's more characterful upmarket hotels; there's also an innovative restaurant. Take U-Bahn #6 to Killesberg, then bus #43 or #50. ❻

Am Schlossgarten Schillerstr. 23 Ⓣ07 11/2 02 60, Ⓕ2 02 68 88. The pick of the luxury city-centre hotels, located just across from the Hauptbahnhof, with a terrace facing Oberer Schlossgarten. It has two restaurants, one of which, *Zirbelstube* (closed Sun & Mon), has gourmet status. ❾

Der Zauberlehrling Rosenstr. 38 Ⓣ07 11/23 77 77 00, Ⓕ2 87 77 75. Recently renovated hotel attached to a wonderful traditional Weinstube (closed Sat evening & Sun) which serves exquisite food. ❾

Ketterer Marienstr. 3 ⓣ07 11/2 03 90, ⓦwww.ketterer.bestwestern.de. City centre business hotel in a relatively quiet street; has a very reasonably priced restaurant in the form of a traditional beer hall. ❼–❾

Krehl's Linde Obere Waiblinger Str. 113, Bad Cannstatt ⓣ07 11/52 75 67, ⓦwww.krehlslinde.de. Located just to the southeast of the Kurpark, this hotel, which has been run by the same family since 1875, boasts a really outstanding restaurant (closed Sun & Mon). ❻–❽

Kronen Kronenstr. 48 ⓣ 07 11/2 25 10, ⓦwww.vch.de. High-class city-centre hotel, some of whose rooms have balconies. It serves a marvellous breakfast buffet, but no other meals. ❽–❾

Lamm Karl-Schurz-Str. 7 ⓣ07 11/2 62 23 54, ⓕ2 62 23 74. This hotel is handily located for the complex of parks and swimming pools to the east of the city centre. Take U-Bahn #1, #2 or #14 to Mineralbäder. ❹

Museum-Stube Hospitalstr. 9 ⓣ 07 11/29 68 10, ⓕ1 20 43 59. Run by a Slovenian/Croat family, this Gasthof has decent, quiet rooms which are marginally cheaper than those of *Alte Mira*, which is just a few doors away. Also serves inexpensive meals. ❸–❺

Wörtz zur Weinsteige Hohenheimer Str. 30 ⓣ07 11/2 36 70 00, ⓦwww.hotel-woertz.de. Popular hotel at the southeastern end of the city centre; take U-Bahn #5, #6 or #7 to Dobelstrasse. It has a garden terrace and a prestigious wine restaurant (closed Sun & Mon). ❻–❽

Youth hostels and campsites

Alex 30 Alexanderstr. 30 ⓣ07 11/8 38 89 50, ⓦwww.alex30-hostel.de. New privately-run hostel which aims to offer hotel-type standards; its facilities include an Internet café and a beer garden. Singles €19–29, doubles €48, triples €56, optional breakfast €3.

Cannstatter Wasen Mercedesstr. 40, Bad Cannstatt ⓣ07 11/55 66 96, ⓕ55 74 54. This year-round campsite is on the bank of the River Neckar.

IYHF Jugendherberge Haussmannstr. 27 ⓣ07 11/24 15 83. Stuttgart's official youth hostel is only about a fifteen-minute walk east of the Hauptbahnhof. €14.20/16.90

Jugendgästehaus Stuttgart Richard-Wagner-Str. 2–4a ⓣ07 11/2 48 97 30, ⓕ24 89 73 18. This place is intended for travellers aged between 16 and 27. Beds in dorms cost €19; there are also singles at €29. Take tram #15 to Budenbad.

The City

One consequence of having been a late developer is that Stuttgart has one of the most manageable centres of any large German city. The exact opposite is true of the suburbs, where many of the leading attractions are scattered, though everything is readily accessible by the excellent integrated municipal transport network.

Schlossplatz

Königstrasse leads straight from the Hauptbahnhof past the modern Dom (a strong contender for the title of the dullest cathedral in Europe) to **Schlossplatz**. The vast open space here comes as a welcome relief after the hectic bustle of the neighbouring streets, but it does mean that it's the favourite spot of the tramps and alcoholics who form a noticeable sub-class amid the prosperity. On the eastern side of the square is the colossal Baroque **Neues Schloss**, now used for various state purposes by the government of Baden-Württemberg, and out of bounds to visitors except for the cellars which contain the **Römisches Lapidarium** (Sun 10am–noon & 2–5pm; free), a collection of stone fragments from Roman times. Particularly impressive are the surviving parts of a massive Jupitersäule erected around 200 AD in a settlement near Heilbronn. Opposite is the **Königsbau**, lined with shops all along its 135-metre facade and built in the late Neoclassical style much favoured in the city. Another example of this is the **Jubiläumssäule**, erected in the centre of Schlossplatz to commemorate the twenty-fifth anniversary of the accession of King Wilhelm I of Württemberg.

On the north side of the square lies the **Kunstgebäude**. As well as hosting the temporary exhibitions of the Württembergischer Kunstverein, it has long been home to the **Galerie der Stadt Stuttgart** (Tues & Thurs–Sun 11am–6pm, Wed 11am–8pm; free), though in autumn 2004 the latter is due to move to the striking new cube-shaped building diagonally across the square. It owns some seminal works by **Otto Dix**, notably the luridly coloured *Metropolis* triptych, which perfectly conjures up the Weimar Republic's false sense of values and its smoky, decadent nightclub scene. The three leading Stuttgart painters of the twentieth century – Adolf Hölzel, Oskar Schlemmer and Willi Baumeister – are also well represented in the gallery's holdings.

The Altes Schloss

At the southern end of Schlossplatz is the **Altes Schloss**. A fortress was first built on this site in the tenth century to protect the stud farm; one wing survives of the fourteenth-century moated castle which succeeded it. In the 1550s, the rest of the building was replaced by a resplendent Renaissance palace with a majestic triple-tiered courtyard, designed by Aberlin Tretsch. This forms the perfect setting for nominally priced concerts of classical music put on there throughout the summer. The **Schlosskapelle** has a disputed claim to be regarded as the earliest-ever example of Protestant religious architecture, and its interior was specially designed in accordance with the tenets of the new faith, with an emphasis on preaching rather than the sacraments. It's a simple rectangular hall with galleries on three sides, and the elevated pulpit is given the same prominence as the altar.

Much of the Schloss, which was badly damaged in the war, is given over to the **Württemburgisches Landesmuseum** (Tues 10am–1pm, Wed–Sun 10am–5pm; €2.60; Ⓦwww.landesmuseum-stuttgart.de). It's one of the most richly varied museums in the country, and a particular highlight is the **Kunstkammer** of the House of Württemberg, displayed in one of the corner towers. The first floor has small bronze sculptures of predominantly Italian origin, while the second is laid out in the manner of a Renaissance curio cabinet, with the star exhibit being a beautiful set of Gothic playing cards. On the top storey are the nineteenth-century crown jewels, including a necklace with the 22-carat Harlequin diamond, and a Russian-made gold service.

Elsewhere, much of the display space is given over to **archeology**, much of it excavated locally. A tiny head of a lion carved from the ivory of a mammoth is some 30,000 years old, and thus one of the oldest sculptures in existence. One room is devoted to the truly spectacular contents of the grave of the Celtic prince of Hochdorf, including the surviving parts of a chariot, a gilded drinking horn and various pieces of jewellery. Also of special note are the highly distinctive wooden objects discovered in an Alemannian cemetery.

There's also a large and important collection of Swabian devotional **wood sculptures**, arranged thematically rather than chronologically, thus offering inviting comparisons. Many of these are in a folk idiom, though others, such as the graceful Talheim Altar by an anonymous Ulm master and the Passion cycle for the original Münster in Zwiefalten by Jörg Syrlin the Younger, reveal a profound sense of pathos. The top floor is devoted to **decorative arts** and **scientific instruments**. Of particular note are a stunning third-century cameo of Jupiter known as the Stuttgarter Stein (Stuttgart Stone), a wonderful array of clocks, Philipp Matthäus Hahn's Weltmachine (World Machine) of the 1760s, and the so-called Württemberg sewing box of Czarina Feodorowna.

Schillerplatz and the Stiftskirche

To the west, the Altes Schloss overlooks **Schillerplatz**, Stuttgart's sole example of an old-world square. A pensive statue of Schiller himself by Bertel

Thorwaldsen presides in the middle. Also here are three more Renaissance buildings – the **Prinzenbau**, the **Alte Kanzlei** (Old Chancellery) and the gabled **Fruchtkasten** (Granary; same hours and ticket as Landesmuseum). Behind its facade, the last-named preserves its original fourteenth-century core; this has now been converted to house the Landesmuseum's collection of historical musical instruments. At the southwest corner of the square is the Jugendstil **Markthalle**, an ideal place for putting a picnic together.

Directly opposite is the **Stiftskirche**. Its present form is due to the prolific late fifteenth-century Stuttgart architect Aberlin Jerg, whose special skill, shown here to good effect, lay in welding old and new parts of buildings into a coherent whole. The western tower, an octagon on a square base, is Jerg's own work; unfortunately, the planned openwork steeple was never built. Inside the church, the choir is lined with one of the most important pieces of German Renaissance sculpture, an **ancestral gallery** of the counts and dukes of Württemberg. Each of the eleven swarthy figures is brilliantly characterized – a considerable feat of imagination on the part of the sculptor, Sem Schlör. Look out also for the gilded late Gothic pulpit, and the relief of *Christ Sheltering Humanity*.

The eastern boundary

A large modern boulevard, Konrad-Adenauer-Strasse, forms the eastern boundary of the city centre. At the southern end is the **Leonhardskirche**, another church reworked by Aberlin Jerg. Its chancel houses the funerary monument to the celebrated Renaissance humanist and Hebrew scholar, Johannes Reuchlin. Just to the northeast lies the **Bohnenviertel** (Bean Quarter), whose name derives from the vegetable gardens kept by the artisans who formerly lived there. Nowadays, it is home to many of the city's famous Weinstuben (see p.252). Further north is the Neoclassical **Wilhelmspalais**, which was used by the last kings of Württemberg as their main residence and is now the main municipal archive and library.

Across the road, at the back of the Neues Schloss, lies the **Akadamiegarten**. This forms a southerly extension of the **Schlossgarten**, which stretches for 4km all the way to the banks of the Neckar. On the right is the straggling complex of the **Staatstheater** (see p.254) and, further on, close to the Hauptbahnhof, you'll find the **Carl-Zeiss-Planetarium** (sessions Tues & Thurs 10am & 3pm, Wed & Fri 10am, 3pm & 8pm, Sat & Sun 2pm, 4pm & 6pm; €5), whose projection equipment, made by Carl Zeiss, the famous Stuttgart optics company, ranks among the most modern in Europe.

The Staatsgalerie

Facing the Staatstheater from the other side of Konrad-Adenauer-Strasse is the **Staatsgalerie** (Tues, Wed & Fri–Sun 10am–6pm, Thurs 10am–9pm, first Sat in month 10am–midnight; €4.50, free Wed; ⓦwww.staatsgalerie.de). It's not often that an art gallery ranks as one of the most imposing buildings in a major city, but this is an exception. James Stirling, the most highly regarded British architect of his day, was commissioned to build an extension to the stolid Neoclassical home of the city's magnificent collection of paintings, which was no longer big enough to accommodate the ever-growing acquisition of modern works. The result, completed in 1984, is an original masterpiece.

The displays begin upstairs in the old building. Of the medieval works, the earliest and most important is a **Bohemian School** altarpiece made in 1385 for a chapel on the outskirts of Stuttgart. You'll either see the inner part, in which Good King Wenceslas is flanked by St Vitus and Emperor Sigismund, or else the biblical scenes on the wings; the position is changed every fortnight. Among many examples of the fifteenth-century Swabian School, those by the Ulm painters **Bartolomäus Zeitblom** and the **Master of the Sterzing Altar** stand out, particularly the latter's courtly *Journey of the Magi.* The most startling work in the gallery is the huge, violently expressive *Herrenberg Altar* by **Jerg Ratgeb**, a man who knew all about violence himself in his other calling as a radical political leader. His reputation rests almost entirely on this single work, which cleverly compresses the Passion scenes into four panels and has an unusual reverse side, showing the apostles going out to preach the Word to all the corners of the earth. In 2002, the most important old German masters from the Fürstenberg-Sammlingen in Donaueschingen were placed in the gallery on indefinite loan. These include **Hans Holbein the Elder**'s *Grey Passion*, an expressive cycle of twelve pictures formerly in St-Ulrich-und-Afra in Augsburg, and a group of works by the enigmatic **Master of Messkirch**, one of Dürer's most distinctive followers.

The Italian section begins with two wonderfully stylized panels of *The Apocalypse* by a mid-fourteenth-century **Neapolitan** master, and continues with some excellent examples of the Venetian Renaissance, including works by Bellini, Carpaccio and Tintoretto. However, the gems of the display are several sketches by **Tiepolo**, notably a superbly compressed study for the central section of the great staircase fresco in Würzburg's Residenz. **Memling**'s sensual *Bathsheba at her Toilet* kicks off the Low Countries section. The rare Mannerist **Joachim Wtewael** is represented by an animated cycle of portraits of *The Four Evangelists* and by an enamel-like *Adoration of the Shepherds.* There are two masterpieces by **Michael Sweerts**, another long-forgotten artist who has recently come to the fore: the pendants *Taste* and *Sight*, each characterized by an allegorical figure of a child. **Rembrandt** also treated the theme of sight in the tender *Tobit Healing his Father's Blindness*. It forms a sort of unofficial counterpart to the horrific *Blinding of Samson* in Frankfurt, which was painted the same year. One of his earliest works, *St Paul in Prison*, is also on show, along with important examples of Hals, Rubens and Ter Brugghen.

The biggest surprise of the gallery is a whole room devoted to **Edward Burne-Jones**'s cycle of *The Legend of Perseus*. Commissioned by Arthur Balfour, the future British prime minister, this constitutes one of the finest achievements of the Pre-Raphaelite movement. Three of the eight scenes were never completed, but the full-scale cartoons shown here make ample substitutes. Other nineteenth-century highpoints are *Bohemian Landscape* and *The Cross in the Woods* by **Friedrich**, an impressive group of works by a local Neoclassical sculptor, **Johann Heinrich Dannecker**, and a decent cross-section of French Impressionism.

The modern extension features the seven vibrant figures made by **Oskar Schlemmer** for the kaleidoscopic *Triadschen Ballett* in 1922. There are also monumental bronzes by **Matisse**, while examples of many of the century's leading sculptors can be found in the sculpture court downstairs or scattered throughout the galleries. A wooden group entitled *The Bathers* constitutes one of the main items in what's one of the two best **Picasso** collections in Germany. **Modigliani** is represented by *Portrait of Chaim Soutine* (the Russian-born painter) and *Reclining Nude*. The entire progress of German art in the twentieth century is copiously traced: particularly outstanding are **Kirchner**'s *Friedrichstrasse Berlin*, **Marc**'s *Horses*, **Dix**'s *Matchstick Seller* and **Beckmann**'s *Ascension* and *Self-Portrait with Red Scarf*. Avant-garde works occupy the end halls, while important temporary exhibitions are regularly featured downstairs.

The western quarters

The streets in the grid-plan western half of the city centre are given over almost entirely to shopping. Almost the only building of note is the **Hospitalkirche**, which is a rare example of Aberlin Jerg being allowed to design his own building from scratch. Unfortunately only the chancel has survived intact; it houses a monumental *Crucifixion* by the Heilbronn sculptor Hans Seyfer.

Further west, on Hegelplatz at the opposite end of the Stadtgarten, is the **Linden-Museum** (Tues & Thurs–Sun 10am–5pm, Wed 10am–8pm; €3; Ⓦwww.lindenmuseum.de). This well-presented ethnology museum has displays covering the full gamut of non-European cultures, with Peru, Melanesia, Benin and the Congo being particularly well represented. A full-scale reproduction of an Islamic bazaar, using many original exhibits, is one of the most eye-catching features.

The Rosensteinpark

The **Rosensteinpark** at the far end of the Schlossgarten is reached by U-Bahn #1, #2 or #14 to Mineralbäder. At the bottom end of the park is an artificial lake; a little way up the hill you'll find the ritzy **Schloss Rosenstein** (Tues–Fri 9am–5pm, Sat & Sun 10am–6pm; €3; Ⓦwww.naturkundemuseum-bw.de), the former country house of the Württemberg kings, complete with rose garden, fountains and heroic statues. The interior now houses a natural history museum. Although this is fairly conventional in scope, the same cannot be said for the related collection in the modern **Museum am Löwentor** (same times and ticket) at the western end of the park, which has a magnificent display of dinosaur skeletons and fossils, including many recent finds from ongoing excavations in the Swabian Jura.

Just to the south of the Rosensteinpark are two large mineral baths. Overlooking the Neckar, at Am Leuzebad 2-6, is the venerable **Leuze** (daily 6am–9pm); a little to the southeast, at Am Schwanenplatz 9, is **Berg** (Mon–Fri 6am–7.30pm, Sat 6am–8.30pm, Sun 6am–12.30pm). Prices at both start at €6.40 for a two-hour swim.

Bad Cannstatt

Immediately beyond the Rosensteinpark lies the old spa town of **BAD CANNSTATT**, whose favourable situation at a bend in the river meant that it initially outstripped Stuttgart. It gradually declined in importance and was incorporated into its erstwhile rival in 1905.

Bad Cannstatt's major attraction is the superbly landscaped **Wilhelma** (daily: May–Aug 8.15am–6pm; rest of year closing time gradually reduces to 4pm; €9.40, kids €6.50, or €4.70 and €3.20 respectively Nov–Feb and after 4pm; Ⓦwww.wilhlema.de), which stretches northeastwards from the adjoining Rosensteinpark. Originally laid out as a Moorish garden in the mid-nineteenth century for King Wilhelm I, it's nowadays a combined botanical garden and zoo which adds a decidely exotic element to the cityscape. Despite losses to wartime bombs, some of the whimsical mock-Moorish pavilions still stand, and are surrounded by gardens which uncannily evoke those of Granada. Other botanical features include the largest magnolia grove in Europe, four thousand orchids and a large variety of azaleas and camelias. With around nine thousand animals, the zoo ranks among the most diverse in the country.

On the opposite side of the Neckar from Wilhelma is the jetty for the **cruises** along the Neckar run by Neckar Käpt'n (Ⓣ54 99 70 60, Ⓦwww.neckar-kaeptn.de). These include an hour-long round trip (€6.50), a somewhat longer voyage through the local locks (€10), a two-hour tour of the harbour (€10), and various all-day options (up to €22 single, €26 return).

Bad Cannstatt is otherwise best known as the home of a huge beer festival (see p.254), and as the main sports and recreation area of the Stuttgart conurbation. However, it also preserves some of the faded elegance of a once-fashionable spa, and a great deal of self-confident late nineteenth- and early twentieth-century architecture remains in the town centre on the right bank of the Neckar, which can be reached directly from Stuttgart Hauptbahnhof by mainline train, or S-Bahn #1, #2 and #3. There are a few older buildings, too, such as the **Stadtkirche**, another Aberlin Jerg confection, retaining parts of earlier Romanesque and Gothic structures. The **Kurpark**, with its mineral-water springs and shady willow paths, is the most restful spot in Stuttgart. At its western edge is the third of Stuttgart's large bathing complexes, the **MineralBad Cannstatt** (Mon–Fri 9am–9.30pm, Sat 9am–9pm, Sun 9am–5pm; prices start at €6.50 for a two-hour swim).

Just south of the park at Taubenheimstr. 13 is the **Gottlieb-Daimler-Gedächtnisstätte** (Tues–Sun 10am–4pm; free). In 1882, Daimler, who was consumed by the dream of developing a new means of mechanical propulsion, gave up his highly successful corporate career, acquired a villa in Cannstatt (destroyed during the war), and carried out his top-secret experiments in an expanded version of its greenhouse, which somehow managed to escape the bombs. This humble, unpromising setting was where Daimler toiled away in obscurity for four years, aided only by his protégé Wilhelm Maybach. In their quest to create a light, fast-moving internal combustion engine which could power a moving vehicle, Daimler and Maybach invented the motorbike by 1885; the following year, the motorboat and four-wheeled motorcar had been added to their achievements. A year later, they established a factory in the town.

The Mercedes-Benz-Museum

By an extraordinary coincidence, another German, **Carl Benz**, invented a motorcar in the same year as Daimler, though neither was aware of the other's work. Both went on to run highly successful factories producing their inventions; these were united in 1926 (long after Daimler's death and Benz's retirement) and are now based at **Untertürkheim**, immediately south of Bad Cannstatt. In 1986, the **Mercedes-Benz-Museum** (Tues–Sun 9am–5pm; free; Ⓦwww.mercedes-benz.com) was set up to celebrate the centenary of the inventions. Unless you positively rue the day the car was invented, this museum is an absolute must. Even entering here is an experience – take S-Bahn #1 to Gottlieb-Daimler-Stadion, then walk straight ahead at the exit to the works entrance, or else go by bus #56 to Martin-Schrenk-Weg. In accordance with the company's obsession about industrial espionage, you then have to wait for a special sealed minibus to take you through the Daimler-Chrysler factory complex to the museum doors which are opened only in conjunction with these arrivals.

Over seventy **historical vehicles** are on display, all with their bodywork restored to pristine condition. The earliest exhibit is the Daimler Reitwagen of 1885, the first-ever motorbike, which was capable of 12kph. Benz's patent Motorwagen (a tricycle whose engine and bodywork are both his own design) from January the following year just beats the Daimler-Maybach Motorkusche (which was fitted into a four-wheeled horse-carriage) for the title of the world's first car. Both used one-cylinder engines and had a maximum speed of 16kph. The Daimler company's first Mercedes dates from 1902. This Spanish-sounding name was borrowed from the daughter of the firm's principal foreign agent, Emil Jellinek; it proved so successful a trademark that it replaced the recently deceased founder's name on all products.

The exhibits also include a fire engine, a motorboat, an aeroplane and a bus, but it's the **luxury cars** that steal the show – look out for the elite handmade Grand Mercedes models of the 1930s, including one used by the Japanese royal family, the official *300d* limousine of Konrad Adenauer, and the first of the "Popemobiles", the Landaulet of Paul VI. Equally impressive are the space-age vehicles specially designed for **world record attempts**; these look so futuristic it's hard to believe they were made nearly seventy years ago. In 1938, the W125 achieved 437.7kph on the Frankfurt–Darmstadt Autobahn, still the fastest speed ever registered on a public road. The T80 was designed for travel at 600kph – but World War II killed off this project, which was never subsequently revived.

The Porsche-Museum

Based right beside the Bahnhof of the northern suburb of **Neuwirtshaus** (served by S-Bahn line #6), the **Porsche-Museum** (Mon–Fri 9am–4pm, Sat & Sun 9am–5pm; free) at Porschestr. 42 displays some fifty vehicles, illustrating all the company's models from the *356 Roadster* of 1948 to those currently in production. The Bohemian-born **Ferdinand Porsche** had already had a brilliant career when he set up in Stuttgart after World War II. As Austrian director of Daimler-Benz, he was responsible for the design of the handsome if underpowered *Pullman* saloons, and led the technical team involved with the world record attempts. His services had also been acquired by Hitler for the creation of the original Volkswagen, which was at the opposite end of the market from the vehicles Porsche concentrated on in his own enterprise.

The southern suburbs

Marienplatz, which lies just south of the centre on the route of U-Bahn #1 and #14, is the starting-point for a true curiosity of Stuttgart's public transport system, the **Zahnradbahn** or rack railway, popularly known as Zacke. Inaugurated in 1884, it climbs steeply to the suburb of Degerloch, and is a much-used local facility, one for which only a short journey ticket (*Kurzstrecke*) is required.

In the hills due south of the city centre, reached by U-Bahn #7 or tram #15 (the latter takes far longer, but offers a scenic woodland route), is the 217-metre-high **Fernsehturm** (daily 9am–11pm; €3 including ascent by lift). Completed in 1956, this was the first such television tower ever built and has been much imitated round the world, most of all in Germany itself, where it often became a civic obsession to acquire such an amenity. The **view** from the observation platform is much the best Stuttgart can offer, stretching over the Swabian Jura to the Black Forest and the Odenwald, with the Alps visible on clear days.

Schloss Solitude

On a ridge in the hills to the west of the city centre, reached by bus #92, sits the appropriately named **Schloss Solitude** (April–Oct Tues–Sat 9am–noon & 1.30–5pm, Sun 9am–5pm; Nov–March Tues–Sun 10am–noon & 1.30–4pm; €3; Ⓦwww.schloesser-und-gaerten.de). This exquisite oval pleasure palace, built in the 1760s, served for a couple of decades as the main summer residence of the Württemberg court. It ranks as the masterpiece of Pierre Louis Philippe de la Guêpière, one of the prime movers behind the introduction of the Louis XVI style (which marks the transition from Rococo to Neoclassicism) into Germany. A bonus here is that you're free to wander at leisure round its marbled and panelled apartments, which range from the grand festive hall, the

Weisser Saal, to intimate chambers such as the **Marmorsaal** and the **Palmenzimmer**. The Kavaliersbau, one of the paired crescent-shaped buildings to the rear of the Schloss, contains the recently restored **Schlosskirche** and a high-class restaurant.

Eating and drinking

Stuttgart's expensive reputation thankfully doesn't entirely extend to food and drink; though fancy restaurants abound, there are also any number of places offering traditional Swabian dishes at low cost, as well as plenty of ethnic eateries.

Local **wines** are almost equally divided between *Riesling* (white) and *Trollinger* (red) varieties. Demand for these within Stuttgart itself is often so high that they can't be obtained elsewhere. They can be sampled all year round in the city's many **Weinstuben**, cosy, homely establishments which are as well known for their solid cooking as for wine. Note that they're usually open evenings only and are all closed on Sundays. Rather harder to track down are the **Besenwirtschaften**, which are temporary wine bar-restaurants set up for one or two weeks each year by local vintners for the sampling of the latest vintages. To find out which ones are open, ask at the tourist office, consult the local press or simply look out for signs in the vine-growing areas.

A wide variety of **beers** is produced in Stuttgart as well. Under its own label, Dinkelacker produces a classic *CD-Pils*, plus a *Märzen*. It now owns Schwaben-Bräu, whose *Meister-Pils* has a far more bitter taste, as well as the former Sannwald brewery, whose name lives on in light and dark varieties of *Weizen*. The Hofbräu's *Herren-Pils* is gentler and sweeter, and geared towards palates weaned on wine rather than beer.

Weinstuben

Kachelofen Eberhardstr. 10. The preferred haunt of the local bigwigs and in-crowd. Open Mon–Sat 5pm–1am.

Klösterle Marktstr. 71, Bad Cannstatt. A great favourite of the spa town, occupying a beautiful half-timbered medieval beguinage. Open Mon–Fri 5pm–midnight.

Schellenturm Weberstr. 72. Housed in the only surviving tower of the Stadtbefestigung, with an appropriately cosy atmosphere. Open Mon–Sat 5pm–midnight.

Stuttgarter Stäffele Buschlestr. 2a/b. In addition to unusually long opening hours, this Weststadt Weinstube (near the Feurersee S-bahn station) has something of a museum character, with a cabinet of 250 wine rarities and a collection of corkscrews. Open Mon–Fri 11am–1am, Sat & Sun 6pm–1am.

Vetter Bopserstr. 18. In summer this spills over into the square outside. Open Mon–Sat 5pm–1am.

Weinhaus Stetter Rosenstr. 32. Offers the largest choice of wines: some six hundred in all. The meals are extraordinarily good value. Open Mon–Fri 3–11pm, Sat 10am–3pm.

Zur Kiste Kanalstr. 2. The most famous of Stuttgart's Weinstuben, so it's fairly pricey and prone to get very crowded. Open Mon–Fri 5pm–midnight, Sat 11.30am–3.30pm.

Other restaurants

Alt Cannstatt Königsplatz 1, Bad Cannstatt. Excellent traditional restaurant in the elegant setting of the spa town's Kursaal, with a large beer garden outside. Closed Mon.

Datscha Aachener Str. 23, Bad Cannstatt. Both Russian and Georgian dishes are on the menu in this restaurant, whch is tastefully furnished with antiques. Evenings only, closed Mon.

Délice Hauptstätter Str. 61. The leading gourmet restaurant in the city centre, housed in a cellar and featuring modern art exhibitions. Open Mon–Fri, evenings only.

Dinkelacker Tübinger Str. 48. The Gaststätte of the eponymous brewery, decked out in rustic style. Closed Sun.

Fernsehturm Jahnstr. 120. There are two high-class restaurants in the TV tower: *Weber's Gourmet* at the top is very expensive and usually has to be booked far in advance (☎07 11/24 89 96 10); *Primafila* at the foot is far more affordable.

Iden Schwabenzentrum, Eberhardstr. 1. The most interesting of the city's vegetarian restaurants, one where you pay for everything by weight. Open Mon–Fri 11am–8.30pm, Sat 10.30am–5pm.

Kicho Jakobstr. 19. Japanese restaurant and sushi bar.

La Scala Friedrichstr. 41. One of many fine Italian restaurants in Stuttgart. Closed Sun.
Litfass Eberhardstr. 37. Serves both Swabian and Turkish dishes; very popular with students.
Max-und-Moritz Geissstr. 3. Pizzeria with a wood-fired oven; it's particularly popular with students.
Speisemeisterei Am Schloss Hohenheim. Located in the far south of the city, this is generally regarded as Stuttgart's best restaurant. Very expensive; reservations advisable (☎ 07 11/4 56 00 37). Open Tues–Sat 7–10.30pm, Sun noon–2pm.
Tauberquelle Torstr. 19. Fine Swabian Gaststätte with beer garden. Evenings only, closed Sun.
TÜ8 Tübinger Str. 8. A complex of three restaurants that are hugely popular with the young crowd. *O'Mäxle* serves Swabian fare and brews its own *Pils* and *Weizen*; *Spaghetissimo* serves Italian cuisine, *Hacienda* Tex-Mex dishes.
Zum Paulaner Calwer Str. 45. A Bavarian Bierkeller may seem an anomaly in Stuttgart, but this has been in existence since 1879 and includes Swabian dishes on its menu.

Bars and cafés

Academie der schönensten Künste Charlottenstr. 5. Trendy artists' café with regular exhibitions. Has good wine list, serves full meals and has the benefit of a courtyard garden. Closed Sat & Sun evenings.
Amadeus Charlottenplatz 17. Situated in the former orphanage, this serves bistro-style dishes and has space for seven hundred in its beer gardens.
Biergarten im Schlossgarten Canstatter Str. 18. A large beer garden serving hearty traditional cooking is set up in the Schlossgarten every summer.
Café Königsbau Königstr. 28. One of the best places in Stuttgart for *Kaffee und Kuchen*.
Café KönigX Esslinger Str. 22. A traditional café with modern touches, such as the inclusion of wholefood dishes on its menu.
Café Stella Hauptstätter Str. 57. Popular café-bar that makes a good choice for breakfast or for late-night drinking.
Calwer-Eck-Bräu Calwer Str. 31. Hausbrauerei which makes a variety of organic beers and serves good-value meals.
Hans im Glück Geissstr. 8. Cocktail bar which also serves bistro food.
Internet Café cyber g@te Hauptstätter Str. 43. A convenient place for surfing the Net. Open Mon–Thurs & Sun noon–10pm, Fri & Sat noon–11pm.
Jenseitz-Schwulencafé Bebelstr. 25. Stuttgart's main gay café; predominantly male, and prone to become very crowded.
Merlin Augustenstr. 72. Alternative café and arts centre which serves vegetarian food and organically produced beers, wines and fruit juices.
Sophie's Brauhaus Marienstr. 28. This Haubsbrauerei brews light, dark, unfiltered and *Weizen* beers, and also has a full menu.
Sydney's Calwer Str. 31. Australian theme bar directly underneath *Calwer-Eck-Bräu*.
Teehaus Hohenheimer Str. 119. Located in the Weissenburgpark, this is predictably popular during hot summer days.

Entertainment

Local prosperity helps fund a highbrow cultural scene which is arguably richer and more diverse than that of any other city of comparable size in Europe. There's also a lively nightlife which takes place in various pockets throughout the city. The tourist office produces a monthly programme of events, *Stuttgarter Monatsspiegel*, for €2; two other useful listings magazines are *Prinz* (€1) and *Lift* (€2.50).

Nightclubs and live music

Classic Rock Café Eberhardstr. 22. Plays both live and recorded rock music. German, American and vegetarian food are all available. Open daily from 5pm until 2 or 4am.
Jazzothek Rogers Kiste Hauptstätter Str. 35. Jazz bar featuring live music every evening Mon–Thurs & Sun.
Laboratorium Wagenburgstr. 147. Live music and cabaret venue that's been a favourite with Stuttgart's alternative set for the past two decades. Take bus #40.
Perkins Park Stresemannstr. 39. Stuttgart's most popular disco, particularly with those in their 20s and 30s. Open Wed & Thurs 9pm–4am, Fri & Sat 9pm–5am, Sun 7pm–2am.
Röhre Wagenburgtunnel, Willy-Brandt-Str. 2/1. The celebrated "tunnel" nightclub occupies what was originally designed as a new rail line. Live bands play everything from jazz to punk; it's also a disco (Thurs–Sun 11pm–5am) patronized mainly by the most fashion-conscious locals.

Stuttgart's festivals

The main annual event is the sixteen-day **Cannstatter Volksfest**, held in the last week in September and the first in October. Founded in 1818 by King Wilhelm I of Württemberg, it's the second biggest beer festival in the world. In fact, most of the features are direct imitations of the larger Oktoberfest in Munich, although the beers on tap are Swabian. A more fundamental difference is that whereas Oktoberfest is relentlessly Bavarian, this festival has a wider outlook, with one recurrent feature being the Französische Dorf, a group of French-style brasseries.

If wine is your tipple, the **Stuttgarter Weindorf**, held in the city centre from the last Friday in August until the first Sunday in September, has over three hundred varieties available for tasting. Another big wine festival is the **Fellbacher Herbst**, held on the second weekend of October in Fellbach, which adjoins Bad Cannstatt to the east. The **Weihnachtsmarkt**, beginning in late November, has existed since the seventeenth century and is thus one of the oldest in the country, but the harlequins and tightrope walkers have unfortunately long gone, to be replaced by the standard offerings. Other notable events are the **Frühlingsfest**, lasting for a fortnight in late April/early May, and a **Sommerfest** in mid-August.

Classical music

The five halls of the Liederhalle, Berliner Platz 1-3 (Ⓣ07 11/2 02 77 10, Ⓦwww.liederhalle-stuttgart.de) serve for concerts of all kinds. There are two full-sized symphony **orchestras**: the Stuttgarter Philharmoniker and the SWR Radio-Sinfonieorchester; the latter's chief conductor is Britain's Sir Roger Norrington. There's also the Staatsorchester Stuttgart, whose primary function is to play for the opera and ballet, plus a chamber-sized body, the Stuttgarter Kammerorchester (Ⓦwww.stuttgarter-kammerorchester.de), which is currently directed by the American Dennis Russell Davies. The smaller halls often feature performances by the local Melos-Quartett, one of Europe's finest string quartets. Stuttgart is, after Leipzig, the main centre for research into Bach performance practice, so any concerts by Helmut Rilling's Bach Collegium (Ⓦwww.bachakademie.de) are worth looking out for. The city has more top-class **choirs** than anywhere else in Germany, the most celebrated being the Hymnus Chorknaben. Free concerts are often held in the churches – the Stiftskirche has a series at 7pm during the winter months. An annual international Musikfest features a different theme every year.

Theatres

Stuttgart's leading highbrow venue is the **Staatstheater**, Oberer Schlossgarten 6 (Ⓣ07 11/20 20 90, Ⓦwww.staatstheater.de), a complex of three separate houses, with the resident **ballet** and **opera** companies alternating in the Grosses Haus. The former is one of the most famous in the world, with the great tradition established in the 1960s by the South African-born John Cranko. In recent years, the opera company has risen to a similarly prestigious level; indeed, many critics rate it the best in Germany at the moment. **Plays** are performed in the Kleines Haus, while the James Stirling-designed Kammertheater is equipped with a moveable stage and seating, and puts on more experimental work. The city's other theatres include:

FITS Figuren Theater Eberhardstr. 61D Ⓣ07 11/24 15 41, Ⓦwww.figurentheater-stuttgart.de. A great place to take kids, this is the home of several puppet companies.

Friedrichsbau-Varieté Friedrichstr. 24 Ⓣ07 11/22 57 00. Stuttgart's spectacular new variety theatre.

Makal-City-Theater Marienstr. 12 Ⓣ07 11/62 62

08, ⓦ www.makal-city-theater.de). Mime is the predominant fare here.

Stella Erlebnis-Center Plieninger Str. 100, Plieningen ⓣ 07 11/2 22 82 43 or 5 44 44, ⓦ www.erlebniscenter.de. Europe's biggest entertainment centre is based around two theatres for blockbuster musicals. Also on site are no fewer than nineteen theme restaurants (including a Hausbrauerei, *Schlossturm*), plus a casino, a fitness centre and a cinema complex.

Ludwigsburg

The creation of **LUDWIGSBURG** began in 1697, when French troops destroyed an isolated hunting lodge of the House of Württemberg which lay some 15km north of Stuttgart. Desiring to replace his loss with something grander, Duke Eberhard Ludwig hit on the idea of a planned town (named, needless to say, in his own honour); by 1709, he had decided to make this his main residence and the duchy's new capital. To entice people to come to live there, he provided free land and building materials, plus exemption from taxes for fifteen years – an offer which duly found plenty of takers.

In contrast to Mannheim and Karlsruhe, the Schloss is not the epicentre of the Ludwigsburg plan; that distinction belongs to the outsized **Marktplatz**, which has churches for both the Catholic and Protestant faiths facing each other across the square. One of Ludwigsburg's main claims to fame is that it has nurtured rather more than its fair share of literary celebrities, and an obelisk in **Holzmarkt** immediately to the north commemorates four nineteenth-century writers who were born in the town – the Romantic poets Eduard Mörike and Justinus Kerner, and the realist philosophers Friedrich Theodor Vischer and David Friedrich Strauss. Schiller went to school in the town, while the revolutionary writer Friedrich Schubart did a six-year stint as organist of the Protestant church.

Ludwigsburg's complex of palaces and parks lies to the east of the town centre. The Baroque **Residenzchloss** (guided tours in German mid-March to mid-Oct daily 9am–noon & 1–5pm; mid-Oct to mid-March Mon–Fri at 10.30am, 11.45am, 1.30pm & 3pm, Sat & Sun 10am–noon & 1–4pm; guided tours in English Mon–Sat at 1.30pm, Sun 11am, 1.30pm & 3.15pm; €4 or €10 joint ticket with the Schlosspark and Schloss Favorite; ⓦ www.schloss-ludwigsburg.de) took thirty years to build under the direction of a whole team of architects, and was only completed in the year of the patron's death. By then, funds had completely dried up and much of the lavish interior decoration was put in place by his successors, who preferred to live in Stuttgart. There are 452 rooms in all, grouped in eighteen separate buildings arranged round three courtyards; some sixty of these are included in the compulsory tour, which normally lasts upwards of ninety minutes. Among the highlights are two chapels, the sumptuous **Schlosskapelle** and the somewhat stern **Ordenskapelle**, and the exquisite **Schlosstheater**, the first theatre in the world to be equipped with a revolving stage. The most opulent of the many large reception rooms is the throne room or **Ordenshalle**, which nowadays is a venue for the concerts which take place throughout the summer festival season. In the rooms adjacent to the Schlosstheater, but visited independently, is the **Theatermuseum** (daily: mid-March to early Nov 9am–5pm; rest of year 10am–4pm; free), which includes a mock-up of its stage mechanism.

The **Schlosspark**, otherwise known as **Blühendes Barock** (daily mid-March to early Nov 7.30am–8.30pm; €6.50, €3.50 after 5.30pm), has several distinct parts. To the front and rear of the Schloss, the formal Baroque sections have been recreated from old plans. To the east are upper and lower gardens laid out in a more naturalistic style, incorporating a range of attractions including an outlook tower, a rose garden, a rhododendron garden, a Japanese garden, a Sicilian garden, an aviary, a collection of historic fairground objects and a small vineyard with a rustic vintner's house. The entrance ticket also gives admission to the **Märchengarten** (daily 9am–6pm), a kitsch playground with huge model giants, witches and other fairy-tale figures, complete with sound effects.

Another good destination for a stroll is the Wildpark immediately to the north, in which stands **Schloss Favorite** (guided tours mid-March to mid-Oct daily 10am–12.30pm & 1.30–5pm; mid-Oct to mid-March Tues–Sun 10am–noon & 1.30–4pm; €2.50), which was built as a resting place for Ludwig and his cronies on their hunting trips. It has an appropriately playful-looking exterior, with little corner towers and prominent side pavilions. However, only one of the interiors survives in its original Baroque state; the others were partially or completely remodelled in mock-Pompeian style in the late eighteenth century. The third and last of Ludwig's palaces, **Seeschloss Monrepos**, is a thirty-minute walk away. This has a tranquil lakeside setting which is perfect for a picnic, but the building itself is in private hands and is normally closed to the public. Within the grounds is the town's top luxury hotel (see below).

Practicalities

Ludwigsburg's **Bahnhof**, which is linked to Stuttgart by S-Bahn #4 and #5 as well as mainline trains, is a short walk west of the town centre. The **tourist office** (Mon–Fri 9am–6pm, Sat 9am–2pm; ⓣ0 71 41/9 10 22 52, ⓦwww.ludwigsburg.de) is at Wilhelmstr. 10. Tickets for the Ludwigsburger Schlossfestspiele, the music and theatre **festival** held over three and a half months in the summer, are available from the box office at Marstallstr. 5 (ⓣ0 71 41/9 39 60, ⓦwww.schlossfestspiele.de).

There are **hotels** in all price categories. At the budget end of the scale are *Kepler*, Keplerstr. 2 (ⓣ0 71 41/92 83 08; ❸), *Kronen-Stuben*, Kronenstr. 2 (ⓣ0 71 41/9 62 50; ❹), and *Pfauter*, Stresemannstr. 25 (ⓣ0 71 41/9 50 60 10, ⓦwww.hotel-pfauter.de; ❺). Pick of the upmarket options are *Favorit*, Gartenstr. 18 (ⓣ0 71 41/97 67 70; ❻), *Nestor*, Stuttgarter Str. 35 (ⓣ0 71 41/96 70, ⓦwww.nestor-hotels.de; ❽), and *Schlosshotel Monrepos*, Domäne Monrepos 22 (ⓣ0 71 41/30 20, ⓦwww.schlosshotel-monrepos.de; ❽). The **youth hostel** is at Gemsenbergstr. 21 (ⓣ0 71 41/5 15 64; €14.20/16.90); take bus #422 from the Bahnhof to the Schlösslesfeld terminus.

Ludwigsburg has several good, inexpensive places to **eat** and **drink**, including two Hausbrauereien: *Sudhaus*, Bahnhofstr. 17, and *Zum Rossknecht*, Am Rathausplatz 21. *Württemberger Hof*, Bismarckstr. 24, offers a comprehensive vegetarian menu, alongside standard Swabian fare, while *Post-Cantz*, Eberhardstr. 6, is renowned for its home-made Maultaschen and other local specialities cooked in a historic steam oven. The last two hotels mentioned above both have excellent restaurants which are a good deal less expensive than the town's leading gourmet citadel, *Alte Sonne*, Bei der Katholische Kirche 3.

Maulbronn

MAULBRONN, whose famous Cistercian Kloster is the best-preserved medieval monastery north of the Alps (a World Heritage Site since 1993), lies in the heart of the fertile Stromberg region. In 1557, just a couple of decades after the last monks had left, a Protestant school was established under the protection of the Dukes of Württemberg. As a result, Maulbronn never suffered as a target for iconoclasts and revolutionaries, and stands today as a complete monastic complex giving a unique insight into a way of life which exercised such enormous power and influence throughout the medieval period. A wonderfully evocative description of the monastery (thinly disguised as Mariabronn) in its heyday can be found in the picaresque novel *Narziss and Goldmund* by Hermann Hesse, one of the school's most famous old boys.

The Kloster

A characterless modern town has grown up on the slopes above the walled precincts of the **Kloster** (March–Oct daily 9am–5.30pm; Nov–Feb Tues–Sun 9.30am–5pm; €4.50; ⓦ www.schloesser-und-gaerten.de), which was founded in 1147 in what was then the isolated valley of the River Salzach. This was exactly the sort of location favoured by the reforming Cistercian order, whose rule stressed both spirituality and the importance of manual labour. According to legend, the site was chosen when the monks stopped to water their mules – hence the name Maulbronn, meaning "Mule Well".

Entry to the complex is through the Romanesque **Klostertor**. Immediately to the right is a ruined chapel, in which early Masses were said; facing it is the priest's house, now converted into the **Klostermuseum** (April–Oct daily 9.30am–noon & 2–5pm; free). Beyond here, you pass into the spacious main **Klosterhof**, the first part of which is taken up by a jumble of predominantly late Gothic half-timbered buildings. These served as the storerooms and workshops, which were the province of the lay brothers of the monastery. They're now put to a variety of uses: the forge has been converted into a restaurant; the stables serve as the Rathaus. The stone-built mill, the oldest of the buildings, is linked to the passageway along the ramparts, at the end of which is the thirteenth-century **Haspelturm** (Witches' Tower).

Johannes Faust and the Faust legend

Surprisingly little is known about the real-life Johannes Faust, though he seems to have been a celebrity in his day and the leading intellectuals of the time took him seriously, while regarding his practices as wholly evil. Unlike other leading practitioners of the occult, such as Nostradamus and Paracelsus, Faust left no tangible legacy, and his name would certainly have passed into oblivion had it not been for an unknown author who in 1587 published the *Faustbuch*, a pot-boiling collection of tales allegedly told by the magician, who had died nearly half a century before; this quickly became a best seller, despite the crudity of the text. It was the English playwright Christopher Marlowe who, just a few years afterwards, first realized the dramatic possibilities of the story, endowing the hero with a tragic dignity.

Ever since, the Faust legend – with its themes of absolute knowledge, absolute power and the relationship between the two – has ranked as one of the great subjects of the European literary tradition, one capable of a vast variety of interpretations and a convenient backdrop for the discussion of all kinds of issues. Lessing provided a happy ending, a lead followed by Goethe, whose vast two-part drama is the unchallenged summit of all German literature. It took him the best part of sixty years to write; in it, he explored the entire European cultural heritage. Nowadays, the Faust themes are equally relevant, and Thomas Mann provided an appropriately updated version of the story in his novel of 1950, thus following in the footsteps of his son Klaus, whose *Mephisto*, a *roman à clef* about the Third Reich, was banned in Germany for several decades.

At the southeast corner is the **Faustturm**, so called from having been the residence of the original Dr Faust (see box p.257), whose claim to be able to manufacture gold gained him employment for a time by an unscrupulous abbot who was willing to try anything to bolster the monastery's sagging finances. Within the corresponding corner to the north, the Dukes of Württemberg built a Renaissance **Jagdschloss** with fairy-tale corner turrets; it now forms the girls' section of the school they founded.

Facing the Klosterhof is the core of the monastery. The **Klosterkirche** was the first part to be built; it's in the severe, unadorned style laid down in the tenets of the order, with no tower and no decoration. Later generations were less enthusiastic about asceticism; in order to enliven their church they replaced the wooden roof with a lofty net vault, added a row of chapels with elaborate traceried windows to the south side and commissioned works of art. The fathers reserved the eastern part of the church for their own exclusive use, confining the lay brothers to the nave by the erection of a stone screen; members of the public weren't allowed into the church at all. Instead, a **porch** (or "Paradise"), enabling visitors to look in on the services, was built onto the facade of the church in 1220. This seems to be the earliest building in Germany to show awareness of the new Gothic style pioneered in France.

The same anonymous mason then began building the **cloister**, completing the southern wing plus the **monks' refectory** on the opposite side. Appropriately, the refectory is a masterpiece; it was the Cistercian custom to make the dining hall particularly splendid and luminous, in order to draw thoughts away from the frugality of the meals. The rest of the cloister, including the graceful **chapter house** on the east side, dates from around a century later; the use of elaborate tracery is the first visible sign of the dilution of the early Cistercian ideal of austerity. As a culmination, a striking polygonal **well-house** was added to house the fountain where the monks washed before each meal. Buildings continued to be added periodically – the long, narrow **parlatorium** (the room where conversations were held) beside the chapter house was built by a lay brother at the end of the fifteenth century, while the cloister was given a picturesque half-timbered upper storey soon after.

In the early sixteenth century, as the original Cistercian ideal of plain and unadorned architecture held ever less appeal, the most violently expressive of German artists, **Jerg Ratgeb**, was commissioned to execute a series of **fresco cycles**. He made a series of preliminary red-chalk drawings, which can still be seen; these include the depiction of the legend of the monastery's foundation in the well-house, and a number of allegorical subjects (incorporating a stern self-portrait) in the refectory. Completion of the project was interrupted by the Reformation when the painter abandoned art in favour of politics, serving as "War Councillor" and "Chancellor" of the Peasants' War in 1525. The failure of this rebellion led to Ratgeb's arrest; he was quartered in the Markt in Pforzheim a decade before his erstwhile patrons became very different casualties of the Reformation.

Practicalities

Maulbronn is slightly tricky to reach by public transport. One way is to come by **bus** from Mühlacker, which is a regular stop for trains between Stuttgart and Karlsruhe. Alternatively, there's a station, **Maulbronn West**, on the branch rail line to Bruchsal, from where connecting buses cover the remaining 4km to the Kloster. The **tourist office** (Mon & Thurs 8am–noon & 1–5.30pm, Tues & Wed 8am–noon & 1–4.30pm, Fri 8am–1.30pm, Sat & Sun 11am–5pm;

ⓣ0 70 43/10 30, ⓦwww.maulbronn.de) is in the Rathaus, Klosterhof 31. There are a few **private rooms** (❷) plus a couple of **hotels**: *Birkenhof*, Birkenplatz 1 (ⓣ0 70 43/67 63, ⓦwww.maulbronn-birkenhof.de; ❺), and *Klosterpost*, Frankfurter Str. 2 (ⓣ0 70 43/10 80, ⓦww.hotel-klosterpost.de; ❻). Both have good **restaurants**; the excellent but expensive *Klosterkeller*, Klosterhof 32, is the obvious alternative.

Schwäbisch Hall

SCHWÄBISCH HALL, which lies some 50km northeast of Stuttgart, was an important centre of minting, making the silver Häller (or Heller), the smallest unit of currency used in the Holy Roman Empire. Ultimately, the coin's name derives from the industry on which the local economy was originally based: Hall means "Place of Salt". Excavations show that the salt springs attracted Celtic tribes to establish a permanent settlement here; following the medieval revival, they served as the keystone of local prosperity, only going into decline in the nineteenth century with discoveries of richer deposits elsewhere. Little damaged in World War II, the medieval townscape survives largely intact, complete with tantalizing insights into the social and political preoccupations of the time.

Arrival, information and accommodation

Schwäbisch Hall's **Bahnhof**, which lies on a branch line from Heilbronn, is on the western bank of the Kocher; it's a ten-minute walk to the centre straight ahead via Bahnhofstrasse, then over the river. Trains continue along the valley to **Bahnhof Hessental**, a junction on the main Stuttgart–Nürnberg line, which is 3km southeast of the Altstadt by road. The **bus station** is by the bank of the Kocher at the northern fringe of the town centre. From the eastern edge of the Altstadt, buses #1 and #4 run to Bahnhof Hessental via the incorporated village of Hessental, which lies 1km north of its station. The **tourist office** (May–Sept Mon–Fri 9am–6pm, Sat & Sun 10am–3pm; Oct–April Mon–Fri 9am–5pm; ⓣ07 91/75 12 46, ⓦwww.schwaebischhall.de) is in the Markplatz at Am Markt 9.

Both the town centre and Hessental offer a good choice of **hotels**. The **youth hostel** is at Langenfelderweg 5 (ⓣ07 91/4 0 50; €14.20/16.90); from the rear of Marktplatz, follow Crailsheimer Strasse (the ring road) in an easterly direction, then turn left into Blutsteige. South of town, at Steinbacher See, is the **campsite** (ⓣ07 91/29 84, ⓦwww.camping-hohenlohe2000.de); take bus #4.

Hotels

Blauer Bock Lange Str. 51-53 ⓣ07 91/8 94 62, ⓕ85 61 15. Gasthof in a Baroque building on the west side of the Kocher. It offers four well-appointed bedrooms and one of the town's top restaurants (closed Mon), which is well known for its freshwater fish dishes and has a summertime beer garden. ❺

Der Adelshof Am Markt 12–13 ⓣ07 91/7 58 90, ⓦwww.hotel-adelshof.de. Although this hotel is in a prominent historical building, the facilities are modern and include a fitness centre with sauna and solarium. It incorporates the *Ratskeller* restaurant (closed Sun & Mon evenings). ❽

Die Krone Wirtsgasse 1, Hessental ⓣ07 91/9 40 30, ⓦwww.hotel-diekrone.de. A member of the Ringhotel group, this hotel occupies a group of buildings, including a splendid Baroque palace. It has a fine restaurant and good bathing facilities, including steam baths. ❻

Goldener Adler Am Markt 11 ⓣ07 91/61 68, ⓦwww.goldener-adler-sha.de. This graceful half-timbered building with a beautiful two-storey oriel has been an inn since the sixteenth century; the front rooms offer a grandstand view of the theatrical events and festivals enacted outside. It has a reasonably priced restaurant serving local specialities. ❻–❽

Hirsch Sulzdorfer Str. 14, Hessental ⓣ07 91/9 39 02 20, ⓕ93 90 22 11. A traditional family-run Gasthof offering remarkably good-value accommodation and meals. Unusually, the en-suite rooms cost only slightly more than those without facilities. ❸

Hohenlohe Weilertor 14 ⓣ07 91/7 58 70, ⓦwww.hotel-hohenlohe.de. The town's most expensive address, another member of the Ringhotel group, is a large complex of red-roofed buildings on the west bank of the Kocher. Its facilities include a large thermal swimming pool, a sauna, a terrace and a panoramic restaurant. ❼–❾

Krone Klosterstr. 1 ⓣ & ⓕ07 91/60 22. Moderately priced Gasthof just to the rear of Marktplatz. ❹

Wolf Karl-Kurz-Str. 2, Hessental ⓣ07 91/93 06 60, ⓦwww.flairhotel-wolf.de. This half-timbered building closed to Bahnhof Hessental offers good-quality accommodation, but is primarily known for its gourmet *Eisenbahn* restaurant (closed Sat lunchtime & Mon), the best and most expensive in Schwäbisch Hall. ❺

The Town

The Altstadt occupies a hilly site on the east side of the sedate River Kocher. There's a medieval suburb on the west bank, while the most important historic monument, the Klosterburg Gross Comburg, is one of several notable attractions in the outskirts.

Marktplatz

The steeply sloping **Marktplatz** at the heart of the Altstadt is lined by a series of handsome buildings which form an encyclopedia of German architecture. Its present character was largely determined during the late medieval period, at a time when the rampantly successful bourgeoisie had ousted the aristocracy from control of the council, forcing many of the latter to leave town. As a symbol of the self-confident spirit, it was decided to build a spectacular new church, to be approached by a monumental flight of 42 (now 54) steps. The dramatic possibilities of this backdrop were immediately evident, and the space was used for jousting and tournaments. Since 1926, the Marktplatz has been put to use every summer as a hugely impressive **open-air theatre** (see p.263).

The late Gothic **Stadtkirche St Michael** has a nave in the hall church style with slender pillars and wide vaults, contrasting with the much higher choir, which was only completed in 1525, the year that the authorities of Hall decided to go over to Protestantism. Luther's youthful protégé **Johannes Brenz** – a far more tolerant figure than most of the leading lights of the time – came from Heidelberg to be the new preacher. His portrait can be seen on one of the epitaphs in the nave. Another particularly interesting memorial tablet is in the fourth chapel from the left in the ambulatory; this was made for his own tomb by the sixteenth-century artist and calligrapher Thomas Schweicker, who, as the self-portrait shows, painted with his feet, having been born without hands or arms. The most striking work of art, however, is Michel Erhart's impassioned *Crucifixion*, placed above the Netherlandish Passion retable at the high altar. For the best aerial view of the town, climb the **tower** (March to mid-Nov Mon 2–5pm, Tues–Sat 9am–noon & 2–5pm, Sun 11am–noon & 2–5pm; mid-Nov to Feb Tues–Sun 11am–noon & 2–3pm; €1), a survivor of the previous Romanesque church.

Another embellishment to the square, erected at the same time as the Münster's chancel, is the **Fischbrunnen**, showing St Michael in the company of two other warriors against evil, Samson and St George. Rather bizarrely, the structure also incorporates the pillory, still preserving the manacles which bound the wrong-doers. The north side of the square is lined with a picturesque jumble of buildings, including what are now two of the best hotels in town (see p.259). Opposite is a series of houses which traditionally belonged to various religious and charitable bodies. The west side of the square seems to be jinxed – the church which formerly stood there was destroyed by fire in the eighteenth century, to be replaced by the **Rathaus**, which was in turn a rare casualty of the last war. However, it's been successfully restored, its ritzy curved facade and stately belfry giving it the look of a sumptuous Baroque palace.

The rest of the centre

South of Marktplatz run a series of alleys – Untere Herrngasse, Obere Herrngasse and Pfarrgasse – which are all lined with superb old buildings often linked to one another by stairways. They all lead to the **Stadtbefestigung**, which survives in part all round the town, unfortunately shorn of most of the towers which were demolished after Hall was incorporated into Württemberg in the Napoleonic era. Rising high above the weakest part of the defensive system is the massive **Neubau** (New Building), which, in spite of its name, dates back to the time of the Reformation. It served as an arsenal and granary, and is now a concert hall.

The other dominant building at this side of town is the eight-storey **Keckenburg**, a tower-house from the Staufer period. Together with a series of now interconnected historic buildings nearby, it contains the **Hällisch-Fränkisches Museum** (Tues & Thurs–Sun 10am–5pm, Wed 10am–8pm; €2), which features displays on local archeology, history, industry, geology, crafts and sacred sculpture. Among the highlights is a roomful of works by **Leonhard Kern**, a local man who was one of the most accomplished German sculptors of the late Renaissance period. He specialized in highly refined, small-scale figures, the serene *St Sebastian* and the enigmatic *Cannibal* being two characteristic examples of his art. There's also an important collection of painted **marksmen's shields**, all authentically pocked with bullet holes; around eighty of these date back to the eighteenth century. The new annexe in the **Stadtmühle**, an old mill by the riverside, houses sections on the nineteenth century onwards, including a collection of sketches by the panorama painter Louis Braun and a display on Schwäbisch Hall's theatres. It also has a good display on local Jewish life, including the complete interior furnishings of a synagogue of the 1730s which formerly stood in the incorporated village of Unterlimpurg.

The banks of the Kocher are lined with weeping willows and a picturesque group of stone and wooden bridges reaching out to three islets. From the largest of these, **Unterwöhrd**, is the classic **view** of the Altstadt, which can be seen rising majestically in tiers. The left bank, which had its own set of walls and towers, was the artisans' district; it clusters around **St Katharina**, a Gothic church with gorgeous fourteenth-century stained-glass windows. At the northern end is a reproduction of the oldest of the bridges, **Henkersbrücke** (Hangman's Bridge), named after the house on it, in which the holder of the least coveted municipal office was forced to live.

The left bank has recently gained a prominent new landmark in the **Kunsthalle Würth** (daily 10am–6pm; free; ⓦwww.art.wuerth.com), an audacious reinforced concrete building by the Danish architect Henning Larsen. Its terrace commands a wonderful view of the Altstadt, and is also home to *Black Crowd*, a striking sculptural group of twenty headless figures by Magdalena Abakanowicz. The displays inside are subject to change, but are dominated by twentieth-century art; pride of the particularly fine Expressionist collection is

Munch's *The Vampire*. There's also a small Kunstkammer of Renaissance and Baroque objets d'art and sculptures, including examples of Riemenschneider and Kern.

The northern part of the Altstadt presents another characterful old quarter, beginning at the **Säumarkt** (Pig Market), a couple of minutes' walk due north of Marktplatz, which features the Neoclassical guardhouse of the Württemberg army and a sixteenth-century weigh-house, behind which is the late seventeenth-century tannery, whose arcades were used for drying skins until 1972. Leading off the square is Gelbinger Gasse, the longest and arguably the finest street in Hall, whose buildings cover the full gamut of styles from Gothic to Jugendstil.

Comburg

Perched magisterially on its hill a couple of kilometres south of the centre of Hall via the banks of the Kocher is the awesome **Klosterburg Gross Comburg**. In 1079 this collegiate foundation was endowed by the count of Comburg, Burkhard II, who, as a cripple, felt unable to perform the normal aristocratic duties and decided to retire to a monastic life. Much of the original Romanesque architecture survives intact, including the mighty ring wall with its defensive towers. The extensive additions to the complex made down the years included the progressive strengthening of the entrance, and you now pass through the Baroque Bastion and the Renaissance Zwingertor before arriving at the Romanesque **Michaelstor**, guarding a twelve-metre-long tunnel which served as the last line of defence. As the Baroque monastic buildings are now used as a college, there's normally unrestricted entry to the courtyard. Here you can see another Romanesque survival, the hexagonal **Ebehardskapelle**, which is ornamented with a graceful dwarf gallery. Its function is disputed, but it probably served as an ossuary.

The **Klosterkirche** (April–Oct Tues–Fri 10am–noon & 2–5pm, Sat & Sun 2–5pm; €2.70) retains the three imperious towers of the first church, but was otherwise rebuilt in the Würzburg Baroque style. Although the exterior retains much of the austerity of its predecessor, the interior, with its gleaming white stuccowork, comes in complete contrast. It still preserves, however, two stunning twelfth-century treasures made in the monastery's once-celebrated workshop: an enormous golden wheel-shaped **chandelier** (which is even larger and more impressive than those in Aachen and Hildesheim, the only others to have survived) and the gilded beaten-copper **antependium** (altar front), which has engravings of Christ surrounded by his disciples. A number of masterly tombs, including that of the founder, can be seen in the **chapter house**, which still preserves its Romanesque form.

Wackershofen

Some 5km northwest of the centre of Hall is the incorporated village of **WACKERSHOFEN**, which has been made a train stop in order to improve visitor access to the **Hohenloher Freilandmuseum** (late March to April & Oct to early Nov Tues–Sun 10am–5pm; May & Sept Tues–Sun 9am–6pm; June–Aug daily 9am–6pm; €5; ⓦ www.wackershofen.de). This brings together redundant rural buildings from throughout the north of Baden-Württemberg, including the Tauber valley and the eastern Jura but concentrating on the Hohenlohe region. Ceramics, furniture-making and textiles are among the crafts demonstrated, while there's a Backofenfest on the last weekend in September. A historic inn, *Roter Ochsen*, is among the reconstructed buildings, providing a handy stopping-off point for lunch.

Eating and drinking

The leading **restaurants** are to be found in the hotels, but there are many other less expensive places to eat and drink.

Café Ableitner Bahnhofstr. 5–7. Old-world café with a summer garden commanding a wonderful view over the Kocher to the Altstadt.
Café am Markt Am Markt 9–10. Another good *Kaffee und Kuchen* establishment, offering the choice between imbibing in the handsome Baroque interior, or sitting outside on the square.
Salzwerk Schulgasse 4. Brasserie which serves breakfast from 9am, typical Swabian cooking at lunchtime and in the evenings. Closed Sun.
Schuhbäck Untere Herrngasse 1–3. Gaststätte serving inexpensive local dishes. Closed Tues.
Waldhorn Untere Herrngasse 14. Italian restaurant with a wood-fired pizza oven in a prominent building at the top of the town.
Würth Im Weiler 8–10. Weinstube with beer garden; also serves full meals.
Zum Alten Brauhaus Mauerstr. 17. The main tap of the Haller Löwenbrauerei, which makes a range of beers, including a fine *Zwickelbier*. Also serves both German and Balkan cuisine.

Entertainment and festivals

Schwäbisch Hall has a strong **theatre** tradition, with pride of place taken by the Freilichtspiele, the open-air season on Marktplatz. This runs from late May to mid-August, and usually features a play by Shakespeare, a European classic and a modern work. Performances start at 8.30pm, but the scramble for the best seats begins as early as 6pm. Since 2000, the town has had a second, very different open-air stage, the wooden Haller-Globe-Theater on Unterwöhrd, a reproduction of Shakespeare's original Globe. Tickets for both venues can be purchased from the special counter in the tourist office (ⓣ07 91/75 16 00), and cost €5 (€7.50 on Fri & Sat) for standing room, €12.50–32.50 for seats. The town also has a prestigious Marionettentheater, which is near the left-bank quay at Im Lindbach 9 (ⓣ07 91/4 85 36, ⓦwww.gerhards-marionettentheater.de); it uses both historical and modern puppets and has shows for both children and adults.

The local salt heritage is celebrated each Whit weekend in one of Baden-Württemberg's most famous **festivals**, the Kuchen- und Brunnenfest der Haller Salzsieder (Cake and Fountain Festival of the Salt-Simmerers of Hall). This commemorates the occasion when the salt workers quenched a fire at the Stadtmühle. It features dancing and music on the Grasbödele (one of the islets) by the simmerers in their red, black and white historical costumes, as well as a realistic simulation of the blaze. Additionally, historical tableaux are re-enacted on Marktplatz, and there are processions through the streets of the Altstadt.

Schwäbisch Gmünd

SCHWÄBISCH GMÜND is 45km south of Schwäbisch Hall, and a similar distance east of Stuttgart on an almost dead straight rail line. The town lies in the heart of the **Stauferland**, a countryside of castle-crowned conical hills, gentle slopes, lush meadows and juniper heathland. It's named after its former feudal overlords, the Hohenstaufen dynasty, who were among the dominant forces of early medieval Germany and Italy. Gmünd was founded by the first of the Hohenstaufen emperors, Conrad III, but after the family died out it became a Free Imperial City. Known in the Middle Ages for the luxury goods produced by its goldsmiths, silversmiths, jewellers, glass-blowers and watchmakers, today it's a lively provincial town with a compact Altstadt dominated by one of Germany's seminal churches.

The Town

Around 1310, the citizens began the construction of the **Heiligkreuzmünster** as the centrepiece of their town. Some time later, Heinrich Parler arrived from Cologne and took charge of operations; he was later aided by his son Peter, who was soon after called to Prague, where he developed into one of the most brilliant and imaginative architects Europe ever produced. The **Parler style** – of which this church is recognized as the prototype – soon usurped France's long-standing architectural leadership and made its mark on a host of cities throughout central Europe. In spite of the lack of a tower, the Münster, whose exterior bristles with highly elaborate pinnacles, gables and gargoyles, floats high above the town. Its five entrance **portals** introduce the characteristic Parler sculpture, which aimed at a far greater sense of realism than had hitherto been in vogue. The figures are short and stocky, and are often placed in dramatic relationships to each other; they have lifelike facial expressions and wear contemporary dress, with heavy horizontal drapery folds.

However, there's no doubt that it's the **interior** which is the real show-stopper; it was the first hall church to be erected in southern Germany, and triumphantly gives the lie to the theory that this form of building is inherently dull and unvaried. Standing just inside the main western entrance, you're confronted by the majestic spectacle of 22 huge **rounded pillars** marching towards the choir. They support a coloured vault which grows ever richer, moving from a fanciful pattern of ribs in the nave to a rich tapestry of network and star shapes in the chancel. The ring of side chapels, cleverly placed between the buttresses so that their presence is not immediately apparent from outside, contains a wealth of late Gothic altarpieces, notably a *Tree of Jesse* in the baptistry. Above the seats of the Renaissance stalls stand animated figures of the apostles (on the left) and Old Testament prophets; a peculiarity is that each figure is carved twice and placed back-to-back, so that it faces the ambulatory as well as the choir.

The rest of the town

The original parish church, the octagonal-towered **Johanniskirche** (May–Oct Tues–Fri 10am–noon & 2–4pm, Sat 2–4pm, Sun 10am–noon & 2–4pm; €0.50) on the central Bocksgasse, is overshadowed by the Münster but is nevertheless a highly unusual building. It dates from the very end of the Romanesque period in the mid-thirteenth century and is extravagantly adorned all round its exterior with delicate reliefs of fantastic animals, fables, hunting scenes, flowers and foliage. The interior has nineteenth-century pastel murals and also serves as a repository for original lapidary fragments from the Münster and elsewhere.

Facing the west end of the Johanniskirche is the **Prediger**, a former Dominican priory which has been converted into a cultural centre, including the **Predigermuseum** (Tues, Wed & Fri 2–5pm, Thurs 2–7pm, Sat & Sun 11am–5pm; free). This contains good collections of medieval and Baroque sculpture, in addition to examples of the town's expertise in jewellery-making (the most notable being a fifteenth-century cross) and the usual local history displays. On the opposite side of the Johanniskirche, the **Marktplatz**, now largely Baroque in character, has several cheerful mansions and a rather saccharine fountain bearing a double-sided statue of the Madonna and Child.

However, there are also a number of half-timbered houses from earlier periods, notably the **Amtshaus Spital** at the far end. A bit further east are four of the five remaining towers of the fourteenth-century city wall, with the highest of the group, the **Königsturm**, a short walk to the south.

Behind the Hauptbahnhof, there's a wonderful wooded uphill walk along Taubentalstrasse, past shrines dating as far back as the fifteenth century and a life-sized Calvary to the dark, secret **St-Salvator-Kapelle** at the top. This former hermit's cave and its adjoining stone-walled rooms are bedecked with candles, icons, statues and other religious paraphernalia.

Practicalities

Schwäbisch Gmünd's **Hauptbahnhof** is just to the northwest of the centre, which is reached by following Uferstrasse straight ahead, before turning into Bocksgasse. The **tourist office** (Mon–Fri 9am–5.30pm, Sat 9am–noon; ⓣ0 71 71/6 03 42 50, ⓦwww.schwaebisch-gmuend.de) is in the half-timbered former Kornhaus at Kornhausstr. 14.

Among the centrally placed **hotels**, the cheapest is *Gasthof Weisser Ochsen*, Parlerstr. 47 (ⓣ0 71 71/28 12; ❷). More upmarket choices include *Einhorn*, Rinderbacher Gasse 10 (ⓣ0 71 71/6 30 23; ❺), *Patrizier*, Kornhausstr. 25 (ⓣ0 71 71/92 70 30, ⓦwww.hotel-patrizier.de; ❻), and *Das Pelikan*, Türlensteg 9 (ⓣ0 71 71/35 90, ⓦwww.hotel-pelikan.de; ❼).

All the hotels listed above have good **restaurants**, though there are plenty of recommendable alternatives. Best for traditional Swabian fare is the historic *Fuggerei*, Münstergasse 2, though it's on the expensive side. *Kübele*, Engelgasse 2, is a good, less pricey alternative; it's also the main tap for the local Aloisle beers, which are made with the soft spring water of the Swabian Jura. Also very fine is the *Stadtgarten* restaurant in the park between the Hauptbahnhof and the centre, which has dining rooms in two adjacent buildings – a miniature Rococo palace and the Stadthalle, the town's main concert venue. Gmünd has some superb **cafés** including *Margrit*, Johannisplatz 10, which has delicious cakes, the long-established *Zieher*, Marktgässle 3, and *Spielplatz* at Münsterplatz 12, which often features exhibitions of contemporary international artists.

On the second Saturday in June, the Schwabenalter **festival** celebrates those who have passed their 40th birthday – the watershed year for the acquisition of true wisdom, according to Swabian custom. The following Saturday is devoted to 50-year-olds, the next to 60-year-olds, and so on. Otherwise, Fastnet is the main event, reaching a climax on Shrove Tuesday.

Tübingen

"We have a town on our campus," runs a local saying in **TÜBINGEN**. No irony is intended – the **university** dominates the life of this city to an extent unparalleled even in Germany's other world-famous centres of learning, such as Heidelberg, Marburg and Göttingen. Over half the population of 70,000 is in some way connected with the university, and the current size of the town is due entirely to the twentieth-century boom in higher education.

Tübingen's **setting**, on the gentle slopes above the willow-lined banks of the Neckar, some 50km upstream of Stuttgart, immediately sets the tone of the place. Upstream, the river follows a turbulent course, but here it's serene and placid, the perfect backdrop for the unhurried and unworldly groves of academe. With its students punting on the river on a balmy summer evening, the town is often described as a German counterpart of Oxford or Cambridge. Study is a very serious business here, however, with no nostalgic wallowings in ancient traditions – other than the small and discredited duelling fraternities (*Verbindungen*). High jinks by the students are kept firmly in check and the prevailing atmosphere is of peace and quiet and of scholarly contemplation.

Arrival, information and accommodation

The **Hauptbahnhof** and **bus station** are side by side, just five minutes' walk from the Altstadt – turn right and follow Karlstrasse straight ahead. En route, at An der Neckarbrücke, is the **tourist office** (May–Sept Mon–Fri 9am–7pm, Sat 9am–5pm, Sun 2–5pm; rest of year closed Sun; ⓣ0 70 71/9 13 60, ⓦwww.tuebingen-info.de) which has has details of **private rooms** (❷–❸). There are **hotels** in all categories, though they are quite thin on the ground in the centre. The **youth hostel** is on the bank of the Neckar, a short walk to the right on the far side of the bridge at Gartenstr. 22/2 (ⓣ0 70 71/2 30 02; €15.90/18.60). To reach the **campsite**, also with a riverside setting, at Rappenberghalde (ⓣ & ⓕ0 70 71/4 31 45), it's quicker to turn left from the Hauptbahnhof, and cross at Alleenbrücke.

Hotels and guesthouses

Am Schloss Burgsteige 18 ⓣ0 70 71/9 29 40, ⓦwww.hotelamschloss.de. Characterful hotel in a half-timbered building immediately below Schloss Hohentübingen. Around thirty different kinds of *Maultaschen* are among the many different Swabian specialities on the menu of its restaurant *Mauganeschtle*. ❻

An der Steinlach Johannesweg 14 ⓣ0 70 71/9 37 40, ⓕ93 74 99. Small guesthouse in the south of town, a 10 min walk from the Hauptbahnhof. ❸

Barbarina Wilhelmstr. 94 ⓣ0 70 71/2 60 48, ⓕ55 08 39. Fine middle-range hotel in the north-east of town, reached by bus #1, #2, #6 or #7. It also has a good restuarant, though this is open Mon–Fri evenings only. ❹–❻

Hospiz Neckarhalde 2 ⓣ0 70 71/92 40, ⓕ92 42 00. Medium-priced hotel in an imposing old building right in the heart of the Altstadt, with a good restaurant (Mon–Fri only). ❻

IB Gästehaus (Sprachinstitut Tübingen) Eugenstr. 71 ⓣ0 70 71/9 35 40, ⓕ3 84 57. This modern languages centre has a guesthouse geared mainly towards students taking their courses, but normally has rooms available for other visitors. ❹

Krone Uhlandstr. 1 ⓣ0 70 71/1 33 10, ⓦwww.krone-tuebingen.de. Tübingen's top hotel, situated just south of Eberhardsbrücke, has been in existence for well over a century, and remains strongly traditional. It has a similarly high-class restaurant. ❼

Kürner Weizsäckerstr. 1 ⓣ0 70 71/2 27 35, ⓦwww.hotel-kuerner.de. Moderately priced hotel with restaurant in the northeastern quarters; take bus #1, #4 or #7. ❹

Landhotel Hirsch Schönbuchstr. 28, Bebenhausen ⓣ0 70 71/6 80 27, ⓦwww.landhotel-hirsch-bebenhausen.de. Country house-style hotel and restaurant, reached by bus #826 or #828. ❼

The Town

The Altstadt, having been spared the ravages of war, is a visual treat, a mixture of brightly painted half-timbered and gabled houses ranging from the fifteenth to the eighteenth century, grouped into twisting and plunging alleys. There are few truly outstanding buildings, but the whole ensemble is much more than the sum of its parts. Two large squares – **Holzmarkt** and the **Markt** – provide a setting for communal activities. The best **view** is from the Eberhardsbrücke over the Neckar, which embraces the Altstadt, the waterfront and the Platanenallee, the celebrated promenade along the man-made island in the river. **Rowing boats** and **punts** can be rented at Neckarbrücke. Throughout the summer, a number of companies offer **piloted punting** trips from the quayside beside the Hölderlinturm; these cost around €5 per person and leave as soon as there are enough passengers.

Holzmarkt

Dominating Holzmarkt is the **Stiftskirche St Georg**, an outwardly gaunt late Gothic church erected at the end of the fifteenth century, with a contrastingly stunning interior. Under the extravagant stellar vault of the nave, the pulpit is adorned with reliefs of the Madonna and the Four Doctors of the Church, and crowned by a tapering canopy. A triple-arched rood screen sheltering a painted retable by Hans Schäufelein, a pupil of Dürer, leads to the **chancel** (Easter–June, Sept & Oct Fri–Sun 11.30am–5pm; July & Aug daily 11.30am–5pm; €1). Here an outstanding series of stained-glass lancet windows, dating from the same period as the church's construction, cast their reflections on the pantheon of the House of Württemberg. In 1342 this family bought Tübingen, then no more than a village, from the local grandee; on the promotion of their territory to a duchy in 1495, they made the town their second residence. The thirteen **tombs** show the development of Swabian sculpture in the Gothic and Renaissance periods; finest is that of Countess Mechthild, made in the workshop of Hans Multscher of Ulm. Look out, also, for the monument to Duke Eberhard the Bearded, founder of the university. The **tower** (same hours and ticket) can be ascended for a view over the red roofs of Tübingen to the Neckar and the Swabian Jura.

Also on the square are the **Georgsbrunnen**, a fountain with a statue of St George, and the Buchhandlung Heckenhauer, where Hermann Hesse spent a four-year apprenticeship as a bookbinder and bookseller at the end of the nineteenth century, having dropped out of formal education.

On the far corner of Holzmarkt, which doubles as part of Munzgasse, is the original home of the university, the **Alte Aula**, rebuilt in Baroque style for celebrations marking the 300th anniversary of its foundation. Also here, at no. 15, is **Cottahaus**, the former headquarters of the famous company, now based in Stuttgart, which represented the high point of Tübingen's publishing tradition, begun soon after the foundation of the university. The **Studentenkarzer** (Students' Prison) at no. 20 in the same street is older than the one in Heidelberg and has more artistic graffiti, but unfortunately isn't so accessible (guided tours April–Oct Sat, Sun & holidays at 2pm; €1).

The Hölderlinturm and Evangelisches Stift

Overlooking the banks of the Neckar on Bursagasse, the street immediately below Holzmarkt, is the **Hölderlinturm** (Tues–Fri 10am–noon & 3–5pm, Sat & Sun 2–5pm; €1.50). Originally part of the medieval fortifications, it's now named after one of Tübingen's most famous alumni, **Friedrich Hölderlin**, who lived here in the care of a carpenter's family, hopelessly but harmlessly insane, from 1807 until his death 36 years later. There's a collection of memorabilia of the poet, largely ignored in his lifetime, but now regarded as one of the greatest Germany ever produced. Just before the onset of his madness, he produced his most striking work, grandiose apocalyptic visions couched in complex language and original imagery, showing the anguished state of his own existence – "A son of earth I seem, born to love and suffer."

At the end of Bursagasse is the **Evangelisches Stift**, a Protestant seminary established in a former Augustinian monastery in 1547 as the theological faculty of the university. The great astronomer Johannes Kepler studied here at the end of the sixteenth century, and Hölderlin, who never managed to find the

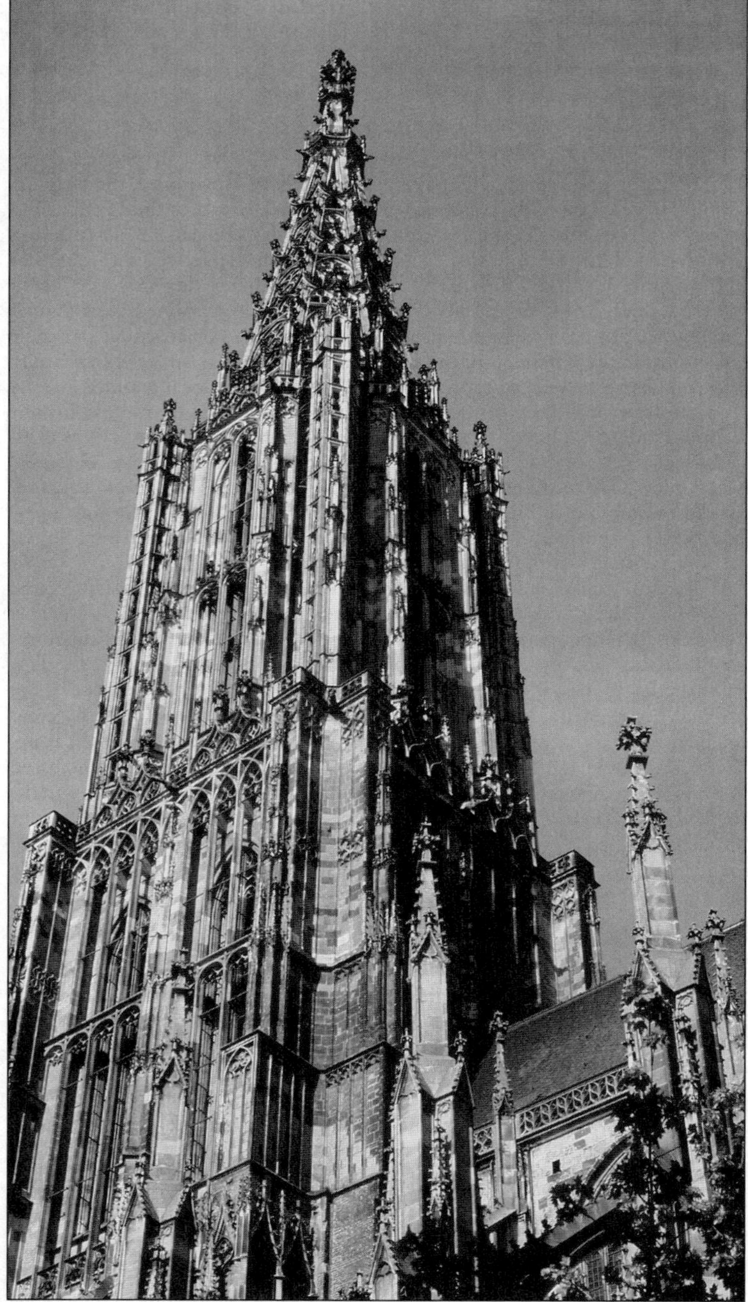

△ Münster tower, Ulm

sense of belief to accompany his essentially religious outlook, was another of its students; he was joined by his classmates, Hegel and Schelling, subsequently the dominant figures of German philosophy. From here you can continue down Neckarhalde; at no. 24 is the birthplace of **Christoph Uhland**, the lyric poet and chronicler of old German legends.

The Markt, the Schloss and around

The **Markt**, heart of old Tübingen, is just a short walk uphill from the Stift. It preserves many of its Renaissance mansions, along with a fountain dedicated to Neptune, around which markets are held on Mondays, Wednesdays and Fridays. The **Rathaus**, originally fifteenth century but much altered down the years, is covered with historical frescoes, though these are hardly more than a hundred years old; other eye-catching features are the pulpit-like balcony for public announcements and the gabled pediment housing an astronomical clock made in 1511.

Burgsteige, one of the oldest and most handsome streets in town, climbs steeply from the corner of the Markt to **Schloss Hohentübingen**, the Renaissance successor to the original eleventh-century feudal castle. Entry is via a superb **gateway** in the form of a triumphal arch, made in 1604. It's adorned with the arms of the House of Württemberg and the riband of the Order of the Garter; the latter had recently been bestowed on Duke Friedrich by Queen Elizabeth I. A second, less ornate doorway leads to the heavily restored courtyard, which still needs time to mellow. One wing of this is given over to the **Universitätsmuseum** (Wed–Sun 10am–5/6pm; €2). One of the largest university museums in the world, it features important archeology displays, notably from the Ice Age and ancient Egypt, as well as the collections of the history and ethnology departments. Weekend guided tours around the Schloss **prison**, and the **cellars** with a vat capable of holding 85,000 litres, have been available in the past, but are currently suspended, hopefully only temporarily.

The northwestern part of town, immediately below the Schloss, has traditionally been reserved for the non-academic community, particularly the *Gogen* or vine-growers who are renowned for their rich fund of earthy humour. Here are some of the city's oldest and most spectacular half-timbered buildings, such as the municipal **Kornhaus** (Tues–Fri 3–6pm, Sat & Sun 11am–6pm; free) on the alley of the same name, which now contains the local history museum, and the **Fruchtschranne**, the storehouse for the yields of the ducal orchards, on Bachgasse.

The northeastern quarters

The quarter to the northeast of the Markt is once more dominated by the university. Down Collegiumsgasse is the **Wilhelmstift**, built in the late sixteenth century as the Collegium Illustre, an academy for members of the Protestant nobility, but since 1817 the site of the Catholic seminary. This building became the focus of worldwide media attention in the early 1970s when its leading theologian, the Swiss **Hans Küng**, published a series of articles and books attacking cherished doctrines, notably papal infallibility. The upshot was that he was stripped of his sacral offices, but he has remained in Tübingen as a professor (now with emeritus status), a celebrity, an ecumenical leader – and a Catholic. Crossing Lange Gasse and continuing along Metzgergasse, you come to the **Nonnenhaus**, most photogenic of the half-timbered houses, with its outside stairway and *Sprachhaus*.

Just outside the northeastern boundary of the old town is the **Botanischer Garten** (Mon–Fri 7.30am–4.45pm, Sat & Sun 8am–4.45pm; free), complete with arboretum and hothouses, located, along with most of the modern buildings of the university, a kilometre or so north by the ring road. The gardens serve as a reminder that botany has long been one of Tübingen's strong subjects. One of the leading lights in the academic life of the sixteenth century, Leonhard Fuchs (after whom the fuchsia is named), published an exhaustive and practical encyclopedia on plants and their medicinal properties. To the east, at Philosophenweg 76, the **Kunsthalle** (Tues 10am–8pm, Wed–Sun 10am–6pm, Ⓦwww.kunsthalle-tuebingen.de; variable charges) has no permanent collection, but hosts tempting art exhibitions, sometimes of international standing.

Bebenhausen

Immediately to the north of the built-up area of Tübingen are the former hunting grounds of the dukes and kings of Württemberg, now re-stocked with deer and designated as the **Naturpark Schönbuch**. The main road to Stuttgart cuts right through this protected landscape, but its 150 square kilometres are virtually uninhabited. Within the park is the village of **BEBENHAUSEN**, just 5km north of the centre of Tübingen, of which it's now officially a part. It can be reached by bus #826 or #828, but it's far more fun to sample the park's scenery on foot. There's a choice of **trails** – you can either follow the course of the Goldersbach, parallel to the main road, or else set out from the Botanical Gardens in Tübingen and continue via Heuberger Tor and the path beside the Bettelbach.

In 1190, a group of Cistercian monks arrived in Bebenhausen, taking over from a Premonstratensian congregation which had settled there just a decade before. The **Abtei** (Tues–Fri 9am–noon & 2–6pm, Sat & Sun 9am–6pm; €2.50) is set in a walled enclosure with many half-timbered outbuildings matching those in the village; the main complex presents a cross-section of medieval European architecture. That the buildings survive in remarkably complete condition is due to the fact that they were converted into a (now defunct) Protestant seminary after the Reformation.

The best place to begin a tour is the **Abteikirche**. Built in the Transitional style between Romanesque and Gothic characteristic of the Cistercians, it was completed in 1228, but modernized a century later with the addition of the huge, airy east window, still with the original stained glass in between the tracery. At the beginning of the fifteenth century an eccentric crown-shaped tower topped with a miniature openwork steeple was built over the crossing. Unfortunately, the nave was truncated to a third of its original size after the suppression of the monastery, so the dimensions are now more those of a chapel.

A suite of rooms – the chapter house, parlatorium and lay brothers' hall – was built along the east walk of the present **cloister** in a pure early Gothic style after work had finished on the church. In the middle of the fourteenth century, the **summer refectory** was added to the southern side. Not only is this Bebenhausen's great glory, it's one of the finest Gothic buildings in Germany, a dining room like no other. Three central pillars stand like palm trees sprouting out their branches to form a vault of consummate grace and precision, which is painted with motifs of plants and birds. Later, the outer walls of the cloister were built, including a pretty **well-house**. This isn't quite symmetrical, as the mason himself realized, playfully confessing his guilt by adding a corbel of a fool holding up a mirror to show him where he had gone wrong.

Also in the monastery grounds is the **Jagdschloss** (guided tours Tues–Fri at 9am, 10am, 11am, 2pm, 3pm, 4pm & 5pm, Sat & Sun at 10am, 11am, 2pm,

3pm, 4pm & 5pm; €3; Ⓦwww.schloesser-und-gaerten.de) of the Württemberg kings. This was adapted from the monastery's former guesthouse and is luxuriantly furnished in nineteenth-century style, with many souvenirs of the chase. The building later did improbable service as a parliament, being the headquarters of the Land of South Württemberg-Hohenzollern (Südwürttemberg-Hohenzollern), which was set up by the French in 1945, but merged into the more viable province of Baden-Württemberg seven years later.

Eating, drinking and entertainment

Predictably, Tübingen is awash with student **bars**, **cafés** and **discos**, and also has plenty of good **restaurants.** The traditional fare of **plays** and **concerts** is presented at the Landestheater, Eberhardstr. 6 (Ⓣ0 70 71/1 59 20, Ⓦwww.landestheater-tuebingen.de).

Restaurants

Forelle Kronenstr. 8. *Gemütlich* old Weinstube in a listed nineteenth-century building, serving good fish and game specialities. Closed Sun.

Krumme Brücke Kornhausstr. 17. Tiny restaurant with kitsch decor and a varied menu including plenty of inexpensive Swabian dishes and vegetarian options. Closed Mon.

Museum Wilhelmstr. 3. Well-regarded restaurant at the corner of Alter Botanischer Garten; it's fairly pricey, but does good-value business lunches.

Ratskeller Haaggasse 4. Cellar restaurant whose speciality is giant pancakes. Evenings only.

Rosenau Rosenau 15. Expensive gourmet restaurant on the heights above the northern end of town, close to the Botanischer Garten. Closed Mon.

Waldhorn Schönbuchstr. 49, Bebenhausen. An even more prestigious restaurant, generally agreed to be the best in Tübingen. Serves both international cuisine and traditional local dishes. Closed Mon & Tues.

Wurstküche Am Lustnauer Tor 8. Cosy restaurant serving good Swabian fare.

Bars and cafés

Café Lieb Karlstr. 6. Traditional coffee house serving the best cakes in town.

Marktschenke Am Markt 11. Lively student bar with jukebox.

Neckarmüller Gartenstr. 4. Hausbrauerei with a big beer garden on the north bank of the Neckar by Eberhardsbrücke. Makes light and dark *Weizen* beers; also serves full meals, including bargain lunches and a decent vegetarian selection.

Neckartor Neckargasse 22. Modern-style bistro serving good breakfasts and snacks.

Piccolo Sole d'Oro Metzgergasse 39. Italian café which is one of the places to be seen. In summer you can sit outside on the so-called "Plaza Tübingen".

Discos and live music pubs

Cinderella Düsseldorfer Str. 4. Big disco which plays chart and techno; particularly popular with younger punters. Open Wed–Sat.

Foyer an der Blauen Brücken Friedrichstr. 12. Student disco in former French army cafeteria. Fri & Sat only.

Jazzkeller Haaggasse 15/2. Discos on Mon, Thurs & Sat, live jazz or blues Wed.

Zentrum Zoo Schleifmühleweg 86. Hugely popular live music pub with beer garden which features regular disco sessions.

The Swabian Jura

The **Swabian Jura** (Schwäbische Alb) is the name given to the series of limestone plateaux forming the watershed between the valleys of the rivers Rhine, Neckar and Danube. It's a harsh, craggy landscape, with poor soils and a severe climate, though its appearance has mellowed thanks to the plantation of forests. Geological faults have meant that individual mountains have become detached from the main mass; these formed ideal natural defensive fortresses for feudal overlords, and many are still crowned by castles. The Jura has few towns and even less in the way of major sights; the area is primarily of note for its **hiking** possibilities. As usual in Germany, marked trails cross the countryside, and the views on offer have a majestic sweep, even if they're often rather monotonous. It's an area rich in **flora**, with thistles, daphnes, anemones and lady's slippers being particularly prominent. Highlights of the region are the beautiful little town of **Haigerloch**, the old ducal capital of **Bad Urach**, the relaxing resort of **Zwiefalten** and the fantasy castles outside **Lichtenstein** and **Hechingen**.

The following section describes the western and central parts of the Jura. For the southern and eastern border (which has much the grandest scenery of all), see pp.279–82. **Public transport** in the area is slightly complicated. The rail lines tend to run parallel to each other, involving circuitous connections, while some of the bus companies are entirely in private hands.

Bad Urach

BAD URACH, some 30km east of Tübingen, is linked to Reutlingen, an industrial town on the main Stuttgart–Tübingen rail route, by the Ermstalbahn, a branch line re-instated a few years ago after a quarter-century gap. It's primarily a health resort and has a typical spa quarter at the western end of town. Nevertheless, the town centre has many half-timbered houses (otherwise a rarity in the Jura), including an impressive sixteenth-century group on **Marktplatz**, which also boasts a late Gothic fountain with a statue of St Christopher.

In 1442, when the county of Württemberg was partitioned, Urach became one of the two capitals and a new **Residenzschloss** (Tues–Sun 9am–noon & 1–4/5pm; €3; Ⓦwww.schloesser-und-gaerten.de), an unusually large-scale example of half-timbering, was built. The most impressive rooms are the Gothic **Türnitz** on the ground floor, and the **Goldener Saal** upstairs. Both were originally built by Eberhard the Bearded, who was born in the town and later reunited Württemberg as a duchy, but were sumptuously transformed at the end of the Renaissance epoch. Also on view is an impressive collection of Baroque sleighs formerly exhibited in the Landesmuseum in Stuttgart. Likewise associated with Eberhard is the **Stiftskirche** opposite, erected in late Gothic style by his court architect, Peter von Koblenz; the octagonal tower was, however, only completed in the nineteenth century.

Just to the west of town is the **Uracher Wasserfall**, set in beautiful secluded surroundings. Further into the hills are more waterfalls, a nature reserve and the ruined **Burg Hohenurach**, the original feudal castle, which is freely accessible at all times and commands a magnificent panoramic view over the town and the Jura. Continuing westwards, towards the tiny village of Glems, the scenery gets more and more luxuriant, brimming with wild flowers and foliage.

Practicalities

Bad Urach's unmanned dead-end **Bahnhof** is directly opposite the Residenzschloss; trains also stop at the **Kurgebiet-Wasserfall** halt at the western end of town. The **tourist office** is in the Kurverwaltung, Bei den Thermen 4 (Mon–Fri 9–11.45am & 2–4.45pm, Sat 9am–11.45am; Ⓣ0 71 25/9 43 20, Ⓦwww.badurach.de); brochures can also be picked up from the Rathaus on Marktplatz during working hours. There are around a dozen **private houses** (❶–❸) with rooms to let. Comparable rates are available at a number of **hotels**, including *Gasthof Weberbleiche,* Weberbleiche 11 (Ⓣ0 71 25/46 88 52; ❸) and *Gasthof Wilder Mann*, Pfählerstr. 7 (Ⓣ0 71 25/88 68; ❸), which has its own small brewery, Quenzer, attached. More upmarket are *Buck*, Neue Str. 5–7 (Ⓣ0 71 25/9 49 40, Ⓦwww.hotel-buck.de; ❺), *Frank Vier Jahreszeiten*, which occupies a splendid timber-framed building at Stuttgarter

Str. 5 (Ⓣ0 71 25/9 43 40, Ⓦwww.flairhotel-vierjahreszeiten.de; ❻), and the spa hotel *Graf Eberhard*, Bei den Thermen 2 (Ⓣ0 71 25/14 80, Ⓦwww.hotel-graf-eberhard.de; ❼). The **youth hostel** is at Burgstr. 45 (Ⓣ0 71 25/80 25; €13.20/15.90) by the trailheads at the western side of town. Bad Urach has many elegant **cafés**, while there are classy **restaurants** in each of the last three hotels, more homely ones in the others.

Lichtenstein

LICHTENSTEIN is the designation given to a federation of villages 12km south of Reutlingen and 10km east of Tübingen. The name is taken from the **Schloss** (guided tours Feb, March & Nov Sat, Sun & holidays 9am–noon & 1–5pm; April–Oct Mon–Sat 9am–noon & 1–5pm, Sun 9am–5.30pm; €4), set on a high, narrow peak, and familiar through its appearance on the covers of all the tourist brochures to the region. Like many other castles in the area, it's a Romantic fantasy, erected in the 1840s as a replacement for one demolished in 1802. In the rebuilding, the architects were strongly influenced by the imaginary descriptions of its predecessor contained in the historical novel *Lichtenstein*, which was published in 1826. This was written by a remarkable author, Wilhelm Hauff, who died at the age of 25 but bequeathed a very considerable output, including many fairy stories which are still popular in Germany today. Inside the Schloss there's an excellent collection of arms and armour, while the chapel has Gothic stained-glass windows and a beautiful fifteenth-century altarpiece. It's a good thirty minutes' walk from Lichtenstein to the castle, but worth doing for the fantastic views across the Jura.

Zwiefalten

Continuing southeast, the peaceful health resort of **ZWIEFALTEN** lies in a valley at the edge of the Swabian Jura, just a few kilometres north of the Danube. Its name, meaning "duplicate waters", refers to the two streams which converge at this point. In the late eleventh century, a daughter church of Hirsau was established here. The huge Romanesque monastic complex survived until 1738 when, in preparation for its change in status to an Imperial Abbey, and in accordance with the passion for all things Baroque, it was demolished to make way for an entirely new set of buildings. This arrangement lasted for only a few decades. After the Napoleonic suppression, the church was given to the local Catholic parish and the outbuildings were converted into an asylum – a situation which persists to this day.

The **Münster**, the former monastic church, is a worthy rival to the great pilgrimage churches of Bavaria. Its highly original design, largely the work of **Johann Michael Fischer**, is already apparent from the outside, with its identical white towers and their green onion domes. Standing by the entrance grille, your eye is drawn down the enormous length of the church, yet is also diverted to the wavy lines of the side chapels; to the grey and rose marble columns with their gold-leaf capitals which shine like jewels against the pristine white walls; to the huge vault paintings glorifying the Virgin; and to the confessionals shaped like fantastic grottoes. At the far end, a statue of the fiery prophet Ezekiel set in an elaborate baldachin with depictions of the coming fall of Babylon faces the **pulpit**, whose base illustrates his visions of sin and death, while the sounding board depicts the triumphant power of the cross. The monks' choir is the most extravagantly sumptuous part of all, featuring a virtuoso set of walnut **stalls**, adorned with gilded limewood reliefs illustrating the life of the Virgin. Note that the entrance grille is generally closed between

11am and 1pm during the summer and all day through the week in winter, leaving only the sweeping initial view.

Following the Ach, one of Zwiefalten's rivers, for a couple of kilometres north of town, brings you to the **Friedrichshöhle** (or **Wimsener Höhle**), where it disappears underground. This is the only subterranean river in Germany which is readily accessible to the public; it's possible to penetrate a short way along the crystal-clear waters into the cave by **boat** (April–Oct daily 9am–5.30pm; €2.70) before the passage becomes too narrow.

Practicalities

The **tourist office** (Mon, Wed & Fri 8am–noon, Tues 8am–noon & 2–4pm, Thurs 8am–noon & 2–6pm; ⓣ0 73 73/20 50, ⓦwww.zwiefalten.de) is in the Rathaus, Marktplatz 3. In addition to **private rooms**, there's a largish **pension**, *Münsterblick*, Gustav-Werner-Str. 1 (ⓣ0 73 73/3 69; ❸), and a couple of good-value **hotels**: *Gasthof zum Hirsch*, Hauptstr. 2 (ⓣ0 73 73/3 18; ❸), and *Gasthof Zur Post*, Hauptstr. 44 (ⓣ0 73 73/3 02; ❸). The last-named has the best **restaurant** in town; the tap of the local brewery, *Klosterbräu-Gaststätte*, Hauptstr. 24, is a good alternative. From Zwiefalten, it's only 13km to Riedlingen on the Danube and regular buses run there, connecting with the trains of the Donautalbahn (see pp.279–82).

Hechingen

The market town of **HECHINGEN** lies on and around a hill some 20km southwest of Tübingen on the rail line which travels across the western Jura, eventually linking up with the Donautalbahn. The main reason for visiting is to see the fabulous Romantic **Burg Hohenzollern** (daily: mid-March to Oct 9am–5.30pm; Nov to mid-March 10am–4.30pm; €2.50 or €5 including a guided tour of the interior; ⓦwww.burg-hohenzollern.de) which rears high above Hechingen some 4km south on the most prominent of all the isolated rocks of the Swabian Jura. From afar, the fortress, girded with intact battlements and bristling with a varied assortment of soaring towers, looks like the perfect incarnation of a vast medieval castle. Close up, however, it's soon apparent that the present complex is almost entirely a Romantic dreamland. It was commissioned by the most heritage-conscious of the Hohenzollern clan, King Friedrich Wilhelm IV, and built by August Stüler, a pupil of the great Schinkel. Only the fifteenth-century **St-Michael-Kapelle** survives from the previous fortress; it has been retained for the use of the Roman Catholic branch of the family and preserves beautiful Gothic stained-glass windows, along with Romanesque reliefs from its own predecessor.

Practicalities

There's no hostel or campsite in the vicinity of Hechingen, but the town has several **hotels**, including *Gasthof Mohren*, Schlossstr. 18 (ⓣ0 74 71/9 86 80; ❷), *Gasthof Bären*, Gutleuthausstr. 3 (ⓣ0 74 71/24 14; ❸), and *Klaiber*, Obertorplatz 11 (ⓣ0 74 71/22 57, ⓦwww.hotel-klaiber.de; ❻), the last of which has the best **restaurant** in town. **Tourist information** is available from the Rathahus, Marktplatz 1 (ⓣ0 74 71/94 01 14, ⓦwww.hechingen.de), during office hours.

Haigerloch

Unchallenged star of the western part of the Swabian Jura is **HAIGERLOCH**. Buses run from Hechingen, which is 17km east, and from Tübingen via Rottenburg, but the rail line is now used only for occasional steam-train jaunts in the summer months. One of the most outstanding small towns in Germany, Haigerloch's isolation means it's considerably less self-conscious than most of its rivals. Here there's a perfect blend of landscape and architecture, with an unorthodox setting, on rocks high above an S-bend on the River Eyach, playing a crucial role. The surrounding countryside is at its most luxuriant in May and June, when the **lilac** is in full, riotous bloom, but it's hard to be disappointed by the picture at whatever time of year you come.

The northern side of the river is dominated by the **Schloss**, a photogenic jumble of mostly Renaissance buildings which replaced a medieval fortress. Until a few years ago, it was in the possession of the Hohenzollern family, who were probably based in Haigerloch in the eleventh century. Nowadays, the Schloss serves as a hotel and arts centre. The **Schlosskirche**, lower down the hill, has an outwardly Gothic appearance, in spite of being built at the turn of the seventeenth century. The interior was given the full Rococo treatment 150 years later, with the addition of elaborate altars, frescoes and stuccowork. It's also worth walking eastwards through the woods from the Schloss courtyard; after a few minutes, you come to the **Kapf**, a belvedere with a large cross which commands a superb view over both parts of Haigerloch.

Underneath the Schloss's rock is the **Atomkeller-Museum** (May–Sept Mon–Sat 10am–noon & 2–5pm, Sun 10am–5pm; March, April, Oct & Nov same times Sat & Sun only; €1). Here, in March and April 1945, a distinguished group of German scientists carried out a series of experiments in nuclear fission. Throughout the war, the Allies had trembled at the prospect that Germany would be first to develop atomic weapons; thankfully, Hitler never took the project very seriously, while Himmler, who was nominally in charge of the scientists, constantly diverted the researchers into absurd pet projects of his own. When the Americans captured Haigerloch on April 23, they made a point of rounding up the scientists; the reactor was dismantled and shipped to the US in order to help with the successful testing of the atomic bomb just three months later.

Ironically, the American victory in this particular race owed a lot to Albert Einstein, who, as a Jew, had been forced to leave Germany in 1933. Haigerloch itself had been something of a Jewish stronghold until 1941. The **ghetto** can be seen at the western edge of the upper town; the synagogue and the rabbi's house still survive, though neither is used for its original purpose. There's also a Jewish cemetery, which (most unusually) is located well inside the municipal boundaries.

Further up is the pilgrimage church of **St Anna**, erected in the 1750s by the Swiss architect Tiberius Moosbrugger as an integrated ensemble with the monumental garden enclosure and the facing curate's house. The interior of the church has a sense of spaciousness out of all proportion to its small size and is filled with examples of Rococo workmanship of the highest class.

Outside the church is a belvedere offering the opposite panorama to that from the Kapf. Another fine view can be had from the **Römerturm** (April–Oct Sat & Sun 9am–6pm, variably on other days; €0.50) which dominates the centre of town. In spite of its name, it's of Romanesque, not Roman origin, and formed part of the citadel of the counts of Zollern. The nineteenth-century Protestant **Pfarrkirche** contains a meticulous copy of Leonardo da Vinci's *Last Supper*.

Practicalities

The **tourist office** (Mon–Wed & Fri 8am–noon, Thurs 8am–noon & 4–6pm; Ⓣ0 74 74/6 97 27, Ⓦwww.haigerloch.de) is in the Rathaus at Oberstadtstr.

11. Haigerloch, like so many places in the Jura, has no hostel or campsite. There are, however, a couple of moderately priced **hotels**: *Gasthof Römer*, Oberstadtstr. 41 (ⓣ0 74 74/10 15; ❸), and *Krone*, Oberstadtstr. 47 (ⓣ0 74 74/9 54 40, ⓦwww.krone-haigerloch.de; ❺). At the opposite end of the scale, there are two special places to stay: the seventeenth-century *Schwanen*, Marktplatz 5 (ⓣ0 74 74/9 54 60, ⓦwww.schwanen-haigerloch.de; ❻), and the aforementioned *Gastschloss Haigerloch* in the Schloss (ⓣ0 74 74/69 30, ⓦwww.schloss-haigerloch.de; ❻–❽). All these hotels have **restaurants**; that of *Schwanen* is a true gourmet paradise renowned throughout southern Germany. The chimney of the Schlossbräu brewery on the banks of the Eyach is the only sign of industry for miles around. An adventurous range of **beers** is made here – *Pils*, three varieties of *Weizen* and *Spezial*. The best place to sample these is its own *Gaststätte Schlössle*, Hechinger Str. 9, which also does good meals at reasonable prices.

Rottweil

ROTTWEIL is perhaps best-known for the stocky **Rottweiler** dog, originally bred here and once used by local butchers to pull their carts. However, this unhurried provincial market town is itself well worth a visit, having changed very little since the seventeenth century. Lying between the Black Forest and the Swabian Jura, it's way off the beaten tourist track, with nothing of interest nearby and no overwhelming set-piece of its own to draw the crowds, yet the town is a visual marvel. Its isolation spared it from the ravages of modern warfare resulting in a range of well-preserved **old houses**. Add to this a dramatic **setting**, one of the most impressive arrays of sculpture in Germany and a rich tradition of festivals, and you have what deserves to be considered one of the most enticing small towns in the country.

The Town

Rottweil developed from the Roman settlement of Arae Flaviae established on a strategically secure spur high above the River Neckar. The restricted area meant that the buildings were packed tightly together over the centuries, with no room for expansion. The town is approached via the **Hochbrücke**, which spans a deep gully. The site of Arae Flaviae lies just over 1km to the left down Königstrasse, and Roman baths have been excavated at the corner of what is now the cemetery.

Hochbrücktorstrasse and the Kapellenkirche

Immediately over the bridge, and named after the tower which once guarded it, is **Hochbrücktorstrasse**, Rottweil's north–south axis. At the head of the street is the **Georgsbrunnen**, one of the town's four Renaissance fountains; beyond are some of the finest of the brilliantly colourful old houses characteristic of Rottweil. These are mostly late Renaissance or Baroque in style, and are adorned with three-sided oriel windows, sometimes reaching up several storeys. Each balcony tries to outdo its neighbour in the profusion of carvings. These often illustrate the coat of arms of the original family or the emblem of the guild to which they belonged; others bear the imperial eagle, proud symbol of a Free Imperial City (a status this little town held for nearly six centuries). At the end of Hochbrücktorstrasse is the slender red sandstone **Marktbrunnen**, the most elaborate of the town's fountains. Built in tiers like

The Rottweil Fastnet

Rottweil is at its most animated during the Carnival season, and its **Fastnet celebrations** – which are fifteenth-century in origin and very different from those in the Rhineland – are arguably Baden-Württemberg's top popular festival. The action begins on the evening of the Thursday before Carnival Sunday (variable date Feb/March) with the *Schmotzige*, in which groups perform satirical revues of the previous year's events. On the Sunday, the mayor hands over control of the town for the duration of the festival, and the afternoon features a procession in which children are given the most prominent roles. The high point comes at 8am sharp the following morning with the *Narrensprung* (Parade of Fools), which is repeated on Shrove Tuesday at both 8am and 2pm. This features a cast of colourfully dressed characters in wooden masks. Their names are untranslatable; among them are the friendly Gschell, who represents the promise of summer, the fiery Biss and the vampire-like Federahannes, who both appear to symbolize the winter months, and Fransenkleid, a haughty aristocratic woman.

a wedding cake, it's decorated with delicate statuettes made after woodcuts by Hans Burgkmair, and is crowned by a figure of a Swiss soldier, in commemoration of the "perpetual bond" between Rottweil and the Confederation of Switzerland.

Standing in a cramped square just behind is the **Kapellenkirche**, Gothic successor to an old pilgrimage chapel. It was begun in the early fourteenth century as a miniature version of the Münster in Freiburg, but money ran out with only the square lower part of the tower completed. Some 150 years later, the duke of Württemberg's architect, Aberlin Jerg, added a double octagonal storey to the tower, providing Rottweil with the dominant central monument it needed. The church's outstanding **sculptural decoration** is by several identifiable masters, with the mystical and gentle style of the so-called "Marienmeister" perfectly contrasting with the lively narrative approach of his successor, the "Christusmeister". These works have been replaced *in situ* by copies; the originals are now in the Lorenzkapelle (see p.278).

Hauptstrasse

From the northern side of the church, you pass into the resplendent main street, **Hauptstrasse**, which runs uphill by constantly changing gradients. It's lined by an even more impressive group of houses than those on the perpendicular Hochbrücktorstrasse. The oldest of these, no. 62, dates back to the thirteenth century, while the next two buildings, including the historic inn **Haus zum Sternen**, are in late Gothic style. To see the backs of these houses, whose half-timbering is uncharacteristic of Rottweil, go down to the massive viaduct, a notable piece of nineteenth-century engineering which carries the road out of town high over the valley. From here, there's also a sweeping view over the Swabian Jura.

In the upper half of Hauptstrasse, at no. 20, is the **Stadtmuseum** (Tues–Sat 10am–noon & 2–5pm, Sun 10am–noon; €0.50), whose star exhibit is the extraordinary **Pürschgerichtskarte** of 1564 – a *tour de force* of detail – proving how little Rottweil's overall appearance has altered. An adjoining room is devoted to the town's **Fastnet** celebrations (see box above), with wooden masks of the principal characters and a painstakingly executed cardboard cut-out of the *Narrensprung* – which makes an acceptable substitute if you don't manage to see the real thing.

Directly across the street, the **Apostelbrunnen**, with its figures of SS Peter, James and John, has been re-erected in front of the **Altes Rathaus**, whose simple Gothic architecture gives the street a rare touch of sobriety.

The top of Hauptstrasse is closed by the formidable **Schwarzes Tor** (Black Tower). Its lower section, with its rough masonry, dates back to 1230; the upper storeys were added around 1600 as a prison. Continuing uphill, you come to the **Hochturm** via the alley of the same name. This also belongs to the Staufian period and is a watchtower guarding Rottweil's vulnerable western flank, the only one to lack a natural defensive barrier. In the late eighteenth century, an octagon was added to the top to serve as a look-out gallery; it commands a superb view of the town and surrounding countryside. A plaque on the door tells you which family currently holds the key; otherwise, ask for it at the tourist office.

The rest of the town

Rathausgasse leads from the Rathaus to Münsterplatz, and the **Heilig-Kreuz-Münster**, a late Gothic basilica with a tall tower. Its most important furnishing is an anguished *Crucifixion* at the high altar, an early work by Veit Stoss. Proceeding down Bruderschaftsgasse at the eastern side of the Münster, you pass the **Dominikanerkirche**, a Gothic church with a sumptuous Baroque interior, and the last of the Renaissance fountains, the **Christophorusbrunnen**, with a relief of the city's coat of arms as well as a statue of St Christopher carrying the Christ Child.

Further north is the gleaming modern building of the **Dominikaner-museum** (Tues–Sun 10am–1pm & 2–5pm; €1.50), a joint venture between the town and the Land of Baden-Württemberg in order that the former's remarkable collection of Swabian wood sculpture could be exhibited in its entirety. The museum also contains important excavations from the Roman settlement of Arae Flaviae, dominated by the second-century **Orpheus mosaic**. Made of some 570,000 coloured stones, this shows the god playing his lyre to the enchantment of the birds and beasts around him – among them a dog, who is doubtless an early Rottweiler.

At the end of Lorenzgasse is the **Lorenzkapelle** (Tues–Sun 2–5pm; €0.50), a late Gothic funerary chapel which is devoted to an array of **stone sculpture**. Pride of place here is given to the original carvings from the Kapellenkirche, including two reliefs by the "Marienmeister": *The Opening of the Book* symbolizes Knowledge, while the tender *Betrothal of the Knight* is an allegory of the marriage of Jesus to the Christian soul. A humorous figure, the *Weckenmännle*, probably served as the basis of the pulpit: it's thought to be a self-portrait of Anton Pilgram, who later became master mason at the Dom in Vienna. Outside the Lorenzkapelle is the **Pulverturm** (Powder Tower), one of the remaining vestiges of the fortifications.

Practicalities

Rottweil lies on the main rail line between Stuttgart and Tuttlingen; it can also be reached from various points in the Black Forest via the junction of Horb, 35km north. Arriving at the **Bahnhof**, turn right and walk straight uphill to the Hochbrücke. The **tourist office** (April–Sept Mon–Fri 9.30am–5.30pm, Sat 9.30am–12.30pm; Oct–March Mon–Fri 9.30am–12.30pm & 2–5pm; ⓣ07 41/49 42 80, ⓦwww.rottweil.de) is in the Altes Rathaus, Hauptstr. 21. All **festivals** stand in the shadow of Fastnet (see box p.277), but other folklore events include the week-long Volksfest in mid-August and the Stadtfest on the second weekend in September.

There's a large concentration of central **hotels**, including *Gasthof Goldenes Rad*, Hauptstr. 38 (☎07 41/74 12; ❸), *Lamm*, Hauptstr. 45 (☎07 41/4 50 15; ❹), *Bären*, Hochmaurenstr. 1 (☎07 41/17 46 00, Ⓦwww.baeren-rottweil.de; ❺), *Parkhotel*, Königstr. 21 (☎07 41/5 34 30, Ⓦwww.parkhotel-rottweil.de; ❻), *Johanniterbad*, Johannsergasse 12 (☎07 41/53 07 00, Ⓦwww.johanniterbad.de; ❻), and the aforementioned *Haus zum Sternen*, Hauptstr. 60 (☎07 41/5 33 00, Ⓦwww.romantikhotels.com/rottweil; ❻). Each of the hotels has a recommendable **restaurant**; that in *Haus zum Sternen* is particularly good, with plenty of vegetarian options. However, the best place to eat is *Villa Duttenhofer*, Königstr. 1, which has an expensive restaurant, *L'Etoile* (evenings only), and a reasonably priced Weinstube. There's also a wide choice of genteel cafés around the town centre.

The Upper Danube valley

For much of its course through Germany, the **Danube** gives little hint of the great river it is to become. Most of the famous landscapes with which it's associated lie in the Balkans, yet there's a short stretch early in its course which is equal to anything downstream. Known as the **Bergland Junge Donau** ("mountain country of the young Danube"), this begins just beyond Donaueschingen and continues as far as Sigmaringen. The **rail** line to Ulm, the Donautalbahn, closely follows the mazy path of the river and ranks as one of the finest **scenic routes** in the country. There are services every couple of hours or so; the only snag is that there are relatively few stops.

The river valley forms the centrepiece of the **Naturpark Obere Donau**, which stretches northwards to the Heuberg, the highest range of the Swabian Jura; about half the area is forest, though a large amount is used for farming. It's superb country for **hiking**, particularly above the valley, where there are any number of belvederes offering wonderful views of the river's meandering course. If you've an interest in **flora**, note that springtime sees the countryside awash with snowdrops, narcissi and daphnes, while orchids and the tall Turk's-cap lily blossom at the end of the season. Autumn is if anything even more beautiful; the white limestone rocks of the valley are perfectly offset by the golden tones of the trees and shrubs lower down. Plenty of inexpensive accommodation makes the region ideal for a break away from the crowds.

Beuron and around

BEURON lies right in the heart of the Junge Donau at the point where the scenery is at its most dramatic, about 15km beyond Tuttlingen, where there's a junction between the Donautalbahn and the rail line between Stuttgart and Switzerland. It's immediately obvious that religion has loomed large in this place – one of the tall, seemingly impenetrable rocks on the opposite bank of the Danube is crowned by a large cross.

The village itself, laid out on a terrace above the river, nestles round the enormous **Kloster**. Completely rebuilt in the Baroque period, its size belies the fact that very few monks (sometimes no more than fifteen) ever actually lived there. Architecturally, the late seventeenth-century monastic buildings by Franz Beer are superior to the **Klosterkirche**, which dates from forty years later. By south German standards, it's fairly restrained, though the nave vaults are decorated with colourful frescoes; the legend of the monastery's foundation is sandwiched between scenes from the lives of its patron saints, Martin and

Augustine. Sixty years after the Napoleonic suppression, the Kloster was taken over by a Benedictine congregation which played a leading role in the revitalization of European monasticism. They pioneered a simple style of architecture based on early Christian and Romanesque models; an example of this is the **Frauenkapelle** which they added to the north side of their own church to house a miracle-working fifteenth-century Swabian sculpture of the *Pietà*. Even more significant was their revival of the use of **Gregorian chant**, and the present-day monks remain among the world's leading executants of this stark, ethereally beautiful music, which can be heard at their main services (High Mass Mon–Sat 11.15am, Sun 10am; Vespers Mon–Sat 6pm, Sun 3pm).

Hikes around Beuron

Among the many wonderful **hikes** which can be made around Beuron, two stand out. Back in the direction of Tuttlingen (but reached via the Holzbrücke, at the opposite side of town from the Bahnhof), you come after 6km to **Knopfmacherfelsen**, the finest of all the belvederes overlooking this stretch of the Danube. To the east, a similar distance away, is **Burg Wildenstein**, a feudal castle-stronghold dating back to the eleventh century in a stunningly precarious location overlooking the Danube; part of it now houses a **youth hostel** (ⓣ0 74 66/4 11; €14.20/16.90).

Practicalities

Tourist information is available during office hours from Beuron's Rathaus (ⓣ0 74 66/2 14, ⓦwww.beuron.de). Here you can also obtain a list of private houses with **rooms** to let (❶–❷). Otherwise, the cheapest place to stay is the pilgrims' guesthouse *Maria Trost*, Edith-Stein-Weg 1 (ⓣ0 74 66/4 83, ⓦwww.mariatrost.de; ❸), opposite the Kloster at Wolterstr. 9; the only **hotel** as such is *Pelikan*, Abteistr. 12 (ⓣ0 74 66/4 06; ❹). The **campsite** (ⓣ0 75 79/5 59) is in the incorporated village of Hausen im Tal to the north.

Sigmaringen

Just beyond Hausen is the last stretch of high cliffs; between Thiergarten and Gutenstein, they are replaced by jagged rock needles. Thereafter the landscape is tamer, though there are exceptions, notably at **SIGMARINGEN**, next stop on the train line to Ulm, 20km from Beuron. This pint-sized princely capital came into the hands of the Hohenzollern dynasty in 1535, having at one time belonged to their rivals, the Habsburgs. The branch of the family who lived here remained Catholic and supplied the last ill-fated kings of Romania. They were very much junior relations of their Berlin cousins, but provided a useful south German foothold for the Prussians during their predatory takeover of the country in the nineteenth century.

The little town is completely dominated by its photogenic **Schloss** (guided tours daily Feb–April & Nov 9.30am–4.30pm, May–Oct 9am–4.45pm, €4; ⓦwww.hohenzollern.com). This is essentially a product of the final phase of the Romantic movement, a sort of Swabian counterpart to "Mad" Ludwig's castles in Bavaria, which moves abruptly from one pastiche style to another. Only the towers remain from the medieval fortress, which was sacked in the Thirty Years War, then ravaged by fire in 1893. The **Waffenhalle**, with over 3000 pieces of arms and armour, is one of the best private collections in Europe; it's also a reminder of just how much the Hohenzollerns' rise to national leadership owed to their militarism. A dream-like neo-Gothic hall contains a good collection of south German paintings and sculptures of the fifteenth and sixteenth centuries, including works by the so-called **Master of Sigmaringen**, who was actually two people: the brothers Hans and Jacob Strüb. The entry ticket also covers admission to the **Kutschenmuseum**, a collection of historic coaches housed in the former stables.

Beside the Schloss is the Rococo **Johanniskirche**, containing the shrine of St Fidelio, a local man who became the first Capuchin martyr when he was murdered in 1622 by the fiercely Calvinist inhabitants of the Grisons region of Switzerland. In the town itself, there's nothing much to see, other than the usual array of half-timbered houses, mostly dating from the Baroque period.

Practicalities

The **tourist office** (May–Sept Mon 9.30am–1pm, Tues–Fri 9.30am–1pm & 2–5pm, Sat 10am–noon; Oct–April Mon–Wed 8.30am–noon & 2–4pm, Thurs 8.30am–noon & 2–6pm, Fri 8.30am–noon; ⓣ0 75 71/10 62 23, ⓦwww.sigmaringen.de) is at Schwabstr. 1, between the **Bahnhof** and the Schloss. There's a **pension**, *Eichamt*, Donaustr. 15 (ⓣ0 75 71/1 35 49, ⓦwww.eichamt-gmxhome.de; ❹), plus several **hotels**: *Traube*, Fürst-Wilhelm-Str. 19 (ⓣ0 75 71/6 45 10, ⓦwww.hotel-traube-sigmaringen.de; ❹), *Jägerhof*, Wentelstr. 4 (ⓣ0 75 71/20 21, ⓦwww.jaegerhof-sigmaringen.de; ❺), and *Fürstenhof*, Zeppelinstr. 14 (ⓣ0 75 71/7 20 60, ⓦwww.fuerstenhof-sig.de; ❻), the last of which has the leading **restaurant** in town. The **youth hostel** is at Hohenzollernstr. 31 (ⓣ0 75 71/1 32 77; €13.20/15.90) on the northeastern side of town, while the **campsite** is by the Danube at Georg-Zimmer-Str. 6 (ⓣ0 75 71/5 04 11, ⓦwww.campingplatz-sigmaringen.de). Sigmaringen's main **festivals** are Fastnet and the Donaufest; the latter is held at the end of July and features a small-scale version of the fishermen's jousts made famous in Ulm.

Blaubeuren

Between the next two train stops, Mengen and Riedlingen, there's an extensive stretch of marshland on the right bank of the Danube, frequented by many species of waterfowl. After Ehingen, the Donautalbahn leaves the Danube and loops towards Ulm via **BLAUBEUREN**, which lies in a wonderful amphitheatre-like setting at the edge of the Swabian Jura. With its mix of natural and artistic attractions, this ranks as one of the most enticing places in the region and a good choice as a **hiking** base. The rocky hills above not only afford marvellous views over the red roofs of the spaciously laid-out little town and the wilder landscape beyond; they also offer constant surprises, such as labyrinths, caves, grottoes and ruined castles.

At the opposite end of town from the Bahnhof is the **Blautopf**, a shady pool formed during the glacial period; it's the source of the River Blau, the Danube tributary from which the town derives its name. In spite of its small size, the Blautopf is 20m deep, and its waters have a constant temperature of 9°C. The best time to see it is on a sunny but showery day. In bright weather, the pool is a deep rich blue, but the rain turns this successively to a lighter shade, then green, then a yellowish brown. Alongside is the **Hammerschmiede** (Palm Sunday to Oct 31 daily 9am–6pm; rest of year Sat & Sun 11am–4pm; closed Dec; €1), a remarkable piece of industrial archeology. Built in the mid-eighteenth century as a water-mill, it was converted into a smithy at the beginning of the following century, before doing service as a mechanical workshop up until 1956, when it was finally retired – though the clanking machinery is still in full working order.

To the side of the Blautopf is the extensive complex of the former **Kloster**. Just 25 years after it had been completely rebuilt in late Gothic style, Württemberg went over to the Reformation; the monastery was disbanded and the buildings were put to use as a Protestant school. As in Maulbronn, with whose seminary Blaubeuren is now united, there's a remarkably complete picture of a monastic community, with a series of picturesque half-timbered workshops lining the courtyard. You can wander around the cloister with its abutting lavabo and chapter house with tombs of the patrons.

The **Klosterkirche** (Jan & Feb Sat & Sun; 11am–4pm; March to Palm Sunday, Nov & Dec Mon–Fri 2–4pm, Sat & Sun 11am–4pm; Palm Sunday to Oct 31 daily 9am–6pm; €1.50) ingeniously preserves the tower of its Romanesque predecessor as a barrier separating the monks' choir from the nave. Only the former is kept open: it bristles with flamboyant works of art, among which the **high altar** – the only one of its kind to have escaped the iconoclasts – stands out. It's a co-operative work by at least two major Ulm studios – that of the sculptor **Michel Erhart** and his son **Gregor**, and of the painter **Bartholomäus Zeitblom**, who was assisted by **Bernhard Strigel** and at least one other pupil. When closed, it illustrates the Passion; the first opening shows scenes from the life of St John the Evangelist, patron of the Kloster. The carved heart of the retable has figures of the Virgin and Saints flanked by reliefs of *The Adoration of the Shepherds* and *The Adoration of the Magi*. Originally, this part was only shown on the major feast days of the Church calendar. Nowadays, it can be seen any time a tour group is passing through, though the only guaranteed times are Sundays at 2.30pm and 3.30pm.

Also within the monastery walls is another survivor which is unique of its kind, the **Badhaus** (April–Oct Tues–Fri 10am–4pm, Sat & Sun 10am–5pm; €1), which was added to the amenities in 1510. It now houses the local museum, but the main interest is in the building itself – on the ground floor, you can see the baths and heating system, while upstairs is a room decorated with hunting frescoes. The archeological part of the collection is housed in the **Spital** (same times and ticket), the most imposing of the half-timbered houses in the town centre.

Practicalities

Tourist information is available at the Rathaus, Karlstr. 2 (Ⓣ0 73 44/13 17, Ⓦwww.blaubeuren.de), during office hours. The **youth hostel** is at Auf dem Rucken 69 (Ⓣ0 73 44/64 44; €14.20/16.90) on a hill at the eastern side of town, between the **Bahnhof** and the Blautopf. There are also several **hotels**, including *Löwen*, Marktstr. 1 (Ⓣ0 73 44/9 66 60, Ⓦwww.hotel-loewen-blaubeuren.de; ❺), *Ochsen*, Marktstr. 4 (Ⓣ0 73 44/62 65; ❺), and *Adler*, Karlstr. 8 (Ⓣ0 73 44/50 27, Ⓦwww.adler-blaubeuren.de; ❺). All of these have good **restaurants**.

Ulm

Right on the border with Bavaria, **ULM** lies on the Danube, 18km downstream from Blaubeuren, and 85km southeast of Stuttgart. The city is famous for having the highest church spire in the world, and for being the birthplace of one of the all-time giants of science, **Albert Einstein**. Regrettably, some perseverance is now necessary for enjoyment of Ulm; a single air raid at the end of 1944 caused one of the worst devastations suffered by any German city, wiping out the vast majority of the historic centre. Much of this had to be rebuilt quickly. Try not to let this put you off; many of the finest streets escaped

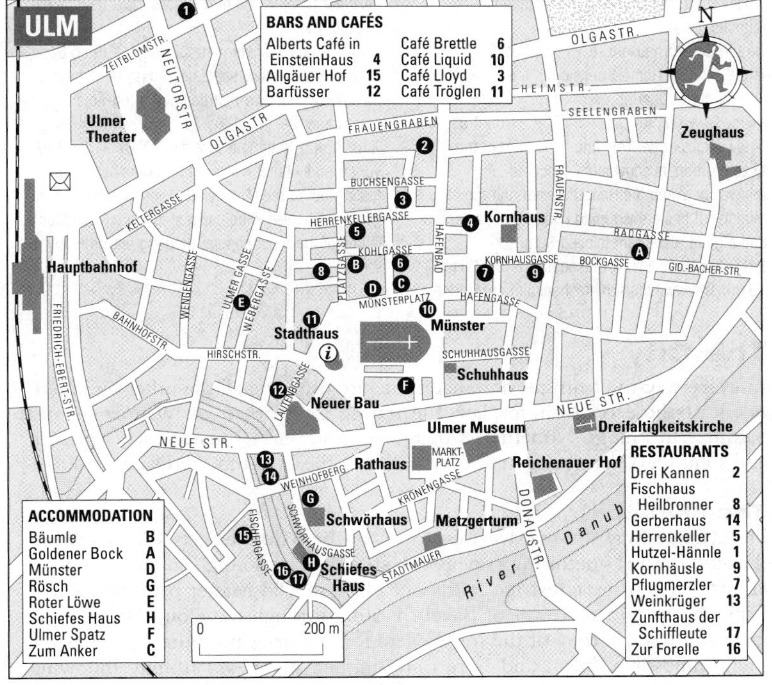

lightly and many painstaking restoration projects have been undertaken in recent years. Moreover, only superficial damage was inflicted on Ulm's magnificent centrepiece, the **Münster**.

Arrival, information and accommodation

Ulm's **Hauptbahnhof** lies to the west of the town centre; an unprepossessing shopping precinct leads straight to Münsterplatz. The **tourist office** (Mon–Fri 9am–6pm, Sat 9am–1pm; ⓣ07 31/1 61 28 30, ⓦwww.tourismus.ulm.de) is housed in the Stadthaus, an audacious modern building by the American architect Richard Meier at Münsterplatz 50. From May to mid-October there are fifty-minute **motorboat trips** (ⓣ07 31/6 27 51) east along the Danube every afternoon; these depart from the Metzgerturm and cost €6.50.

There's a good choice of **hotels** right in the city centre, while the **youth hostel** is 4km southwest of the centre at Grimmelfinger Weg 45 (ⓣ07 31/38 44 55; €14.20/16.90); take S-Bahn #1 to Ehinger Tor, then bus #4 or #8 to Schulzentrum.

Hotels

Bäumle Kohlgasse 6 ⓣ07 31/6 22 87, ⓦwww.baeumle.ulm.de. One of the few hotels in an old building, and one that is excellent value at the price. Its restaurant (Mon–Fri evenings only) occupies two fine rooms which have preserved their late nineteenth-century decoration. ❸–❻

Goldener Bock Bockgasse 25 ⓣ07 31/92 03 40, ⓦwww.hotel-goldener-bock.de. Good middle-range hotel in the east of the Altstadt whose restaurant is one of the very best in the city. ❺

Münster Münsterplatz 14 ⓣ & ⓕ07 31/6 41 62. Functional yet perfectly adequate budget hotel, whose front rooms have a grandstand view of the Münster. ❸

Rösch Schwörhausgasse 18 ⓣ07 31/6 57 18, ⓕ6 02 25 84. Homely pension in the Fischerviertel Quarter. ❹

Roter Löwe Ulmer Gasse 8 ⓣ07 31/6 20 31, ⓦwww.akzent.de. This fine hotel, part of the Akzent group, is conveniently located midway between the Hauptbahnhof and the Münster. It has a swimming pool, sauna, solarium and a good restaurant (closed Sun). ❻

Schiefes Haus Schwörhausgasse 6 ⓣ07 31/96 79 30, ⓦwww.hotelschiefeshausulm.de. Modern designer hotel in one of the city's most famous old houses. ❽

Ulmer Spatz Münsterplatz 27 ⓣ07 31/6 80 81, ⓦwww.hotel-ulmer-spatz.de. Classy hotel by the Münster with its own garden and a top-notch restaurant. ❻

Zum Anker Rabengasse 2 ⓣ & ⓕ07 31/6 32 97. Very friendly hotel whose front rooms have a fantastic view of the Münster. Its lively and absolutely genuine Spanish wine bar-restaurant (closed Mon) is one of the most popular meeting places in town. ❸–❻

The City

In every way, the Münster dominates the city, dwarfing all the other buildings, not least those on Münsterplatz, the setting for markets on Wednesday and Saturday mornings. Nonetheless there are atmospheric quarters to the north and south between the natural boundaries of the hills and the Danube.

The Münster

From miles away, the massive west tower of the **Münster** acts as a beacon to the city. The 161-metre-high openwork **steeple** soars so high above everything else it seems to be a real-life fulfilment of those Old Master paintings which depict an imaginary Tower of Babel shooting through the clouds. In fact, the spire and upper storey of the tower were for centuries no more than a seemingly impossible dream and were only finished in 1890, faithfully following drawings made four hundred years before. A fair amount of puff is needed to climb the 768 steps to the **platform** (daily July & Aug 8am–7pm; times reduce seasonally to 9am–4pm; €3), but you're rewarded with a stupendous panoramic **view** which stretches over the city and the Danube to the Swabian Jura and Black Forest, with the Swiss Alps visible on a clear day. On the final stage, there's also the rare opportunity to see the filigree architecture of an openwork spire at close quarters.

There are no fewer than five superbly carved **portals** to the Münster; that under the tower is appropriately the grandest. Above the doorway are depictions of the Book of Genesis, while the pillars have masterly statues of saints in the "Soft Style" of **Master Hartmann**, the first Ulm sculptor known by name. The ensemble is completed by a poignant *Man of Sorrows* (now replaced by a copy; the original can be seen inside), an early work by **Hans Multscher**, the founding father of the remarkable group of late Gothic and early Renaissance German sculptors.

The sense of massive space in the **interior** is as overwhelming as the tower's great height; the impression is aided by the simplicity of the design, which comprises a wide nave of five aisles culminating in a single chancel, with no intervening transept. The best time to come is on a bright morning, when the sun's rays filter through the stained-glass windows onto the magnificent set of **choir stalls**: "a bold oaken outburst of three-dimensional humanism" was how Patrick Leigh Fermor described them. Made between 1469 and 1474 under the direction of two local men, **Jörg Syrlin the Elder** and **Michel Erhart**, they celebrate the achievements of the antique as well as of the Christian world – with women, for once, given the same recognition as men. The sheer profusion and originality of the carvings is remarkable, and the vibrant life-sized busts are particularly outstanding.

The building of the Münster

Work on the Münster began in the last quarter of the fourteenth century under the direction of the most famous master mason of the day, **Heinrich Parler**, and was continued by his descendants. Credit for its ultimate appearance, however, must go to the head of the succeeding dynasty, **Ulrich von Ensingen**, who altered the plans to make the church wider and loftier, and designed the lower part of the great tower. Despite the Münster's huge size, it was built as, and remains, no more than a parish church. An expression of a vain civic pride, its capacity of 20,000 was more than twice the population of the city, then one of the largest in Germany. At the end of the fifteenth century, when the structure was substantially complete, the architect **Matthäus Böblinger** made a drawing (which can be seen in the Ulmer Museum) for the completion of the tower, reaching to a height that had never previously been attempted. When he tried to build it, however, cracks appeared in the masonry and he fled in disgrace. As his successor's main problem was to repair the existing building, no more work was done on the tower, and the project was abandoned altogether when the city formally adopted the Reformation in 1530. It was only when the Romantic movement re-awakened interest in the Middle Ages that steps were taken to finish it.

Ulm's obsession with the steeple motif can be seen in the huge canopy covering the **font**, and in the sounding board added to the **pulpit** which includes, high up above the column capitals, a second pulpit inaccessible to a human preacher – a symbol that the sermon was really delivered by the Holy Ghost. It's seen even more spectacularly in the slender, tapering **tabernacle**, a structure of gossamer delicacy for all its towering height. In spite of its figurines of popes and bishops, this somehow survived the iconoclasm which denuded the Münster following the introduction of the Reformation. Over the triumphal arch leading to the chancel is a colossal crowded **fresco** of *The Last Judgement*, placed so that every member of the congregation could see it. As an antidote to the massiveness of the Münster, the **Besserer-Kapelle** to the right of the chancel is a small family chapel still retaining its beautifully drawn and coloured fifteenth-century stained-glass windows.

The Rathaus, Marktplatz and around

That other self-conscious symbol of civic pride, the **Rathaus**, is situated just a block away from the Münster across Neue Strasse, the central arterial road. Even in a country as rich in picturesque town halls as Germany, there's none quite so photogenic as this disparate jumble of buildings, which has been restored to a pristine approximation of how it looked in 1540. In this year, the northern front was rebuilt in the Renaissance style and equipped with an arcaded passageway; the local painter **Martin Schaffner** then covered the exterior walls with a series of brilliantly coloured **frescoes** of religious subjects, plus allegories of the Vices and Virtues. On the southern side of the building he painted battle scenes, along with a barge (symbolizing Ulm's dependence on the Danube), plus the coats of arms of the city's trading partners. Between the windows here are polychrome statues of six of the Electors, carved the previous century by Master Hartmann. Even more luxuriant is the eastern facade, with figures by Multscher of Charlemagne, the kings of Hungary and Bohemia, and two pages; there's also an elaborate astronomical clock made in 1520. Inside is a replica of the equipment used in 1811 by **Albrecht Berblinger**, "The Tailor of Ulm", in an ill-fated attempt to fly across the Danube; widely regarded in his own day as an eccentric fool, he's since been elevated to the status of a local hero. In 1944, the

Rathaus formed an appropriately grand backdrop for the notorious state funeral of Field Marshal Erwin Rommel, who accepted this consolation prize, along with a draught of poison, rather than face trial and certain public execution for his alleged involvement in the July Plot against Hitler.

To the rear of the Rathaus is **Marktplatz**, which preserves a few old houses but is dominated by the brightly coloured **Fischkasten** (Fish Crate), finest of the many old fountains in the city. Made during the late fifteenth century in the workshop of Syrlin the Elder, it features statues of three saints attired as knights, bearing the coats of arms of city and empire. In Taubenplätzle, just off the eastern end of the square, is the bronze **Delphinbrunnen**; a century younger, it was formerly part of a water-tower.

Behind stands a Renaissance mansion which, together with a modern extension, houses the **Ulmer Museum** (Tues, Wed & Fri–Sun 11am–5pm, Thurs until 8pm; €2.50, free Fri; Ⓦ www.museum.ulm.de). On the ground floor are choice examples of the city's artistic heritage; the **original figures** from the Rathaus and several of the fountains have been moved here. Alongside further works by Multscher and Erhart are carvings by **Daniel Mauch**, whose Italianate style represents the last flourish of Ulm's great sculptural tradition. The city's heritage in painting is far less rich, but Schaffner's *Eitel Besserer* (a descendant of the family who endowed the chapel in the Münster) is a masterpiece of Renaissance portraiture, and there are several works by an influential master of the previous generation, **Bartholomäus Zeitblom**. Highlight of the archeology department is the weird *Statuette of a Woman with the Head of a Lioness*, which dates back to 30,000 BC. Upstairs, Ulm's history is extensively documented, with an illuminating section on the construction of the Münster.

Westwards down Neue Strasse is the vast bulk of the **Neuer Bau**, a municipal warehouse built in the sixteenth century; its pentagonal courtyard contains a graceful staircase tower and a fountain with a statue of Hildegard, one of Charlemagne's wives. Turning left into Sattlergasse, you come to Weinhof, whose main building is the early seventeenth-century **Schwörhaus** (Oath House). Each year, the mayor addresses the citizens from the balcony, taking an oath according to the constitution of 1397 by which he must be "the same man to rich and poor alike in all common and honourable matters without discrimination or reservation". This was an advanced statement for its time, and is often taken as evidence that medieval Ulm was a democratic state. In fact, what the document signified was a passing of power from the patrician class to the guilds, who established an inbuilt majority for themselves on the council.

The old residential quarters

One of the most interesting features of Ulm is the way the old patterns of settlement can still be clearly discerned. Between the Schwörhaus and the Danube is the celebrated **Fischerviertel** (Fishermen's Quarter), with its quaint scenes of half-timbered houses, waterways, courtyards and tiny bridges. This was actually the area where the artisan classes lived – the island on the Blau and the streets alongside were inhabited by tanners and millers, while on Fischergasse you can see a boatman's house at no. 18, a baker's at no. 22 and a fisherman's at no. 23. Look out for the **Schiefes Haus** (Crooked House), a hefty half-timbered building from about 1500 standing beside a remnant of the twelfth-century fortifications; it takes its name from its pronounced tilt over the river, into whose bed it's fastened by stilts. Another picturesque vista is on Fischerplätzle, which looks towards Häuslesbrücke and boasts the late fifteenth-century **Zunfthaus** (the fishermen's guildhall) and the seventeenth-century **Schönes Haus**, adorned with a scene of shipping on the Danube.

From here, you can walk high above the Danube along the medieval ramparts, now laid out as a shady promenade with a view over the backs of the Fischerviertel. Parallel with the Rathaus is the most impressive surviving gate, the **Metzgerturm** (Butchers' Tower), locally dubbed "The Leaning Tower of Ulm" because it slants a good 2m from the vertical. Beyond Herdbrücke is the patrician **Reichenauer Hof**, while Grünen Hof just to the north has the oldest intact buildings in Ulm – the Romanesque **Nikolauskapelle** (whose interior has Gothic frescoes), and a stone house of similar date. Nearby is the **Dreifaltigkeitskirche**, a plain Lutheran preaching house in the late Renaissance style, incorporating the Gothic chancel of the monastery which previously stood on the site. Only the older part of the building is now used as a church, the remainder having been converted into an ecumenical and cultural centre which often hosts worthwhile exhibitions. For a really superb **view** of Ulm, with the Münster rearing high up behind the houses of the Fischerviertel, cross over to the quays of Neue-Ulm, the city's southern extension, which is actually in neighbouring Bavaria.

The merchants and craftsmen of medieval Ulm tended to live in the streets north of Neue Strasse. These aren't nearly so well preserved, but some fine buildings remain. Just behind the Münster's east end is the sixteenth-century **Schuhhaus**, the guildhall of the shoemakers; it's now used for art exhibitions. Beyond is the Judenhof, the former ghetto; no. 10 seems to pre-date the pogrom of 1499. The streets immediately north of the Münster contain rows of simple houses once inhabited by skilled craft workers, along with several stores, finest of which is the **Kornhaus**, which was built as a panic measure at the end of the sixteenth century in the belief that there would soon be a famine. Look out also for Herrenkellergasse 12, whose turret served as an observation post for fathers trying to keep an eye on the evening jaunts of their eligible daughters.

Further north on Frauengrabben and Seelengrabben are terraces of soldiers' houses from the early seventeenth century, beyond which is the **Zeughaus**, with its monumental Renaissance gateway.

Wiblingen

WIBLINGEN, 5km south of central Ulm and reached by bus #3 or #8, is now a large dormitory suburb but for centuries was no more than a hamlet clustered round the Benedictine **Abtei**. The present extensive complex was erected in a leisurely fashion throughout the eighteenth century. Only twenty years after completion, the abbey was secularized; the monastic quarters are now used by Ulm's university.

Left of the entrance is the **Bibliothek** (April–Oct Tues–Sun 10am–noon & 2–5pm; Nov–March Sat & Sun 2–4pm; €2.50), lavishly adorned with stuccowork of shells, leaves and putti, columns painted pink and blue to resemble marble, large allegorical statues representing the Virtues and a colossal ceiling fresco glorifying wisdom, with subjects from the Bible and pagan mythology freely mixed together. The **Basilika St Martin**, which is later in date, shows a shift from Rococo self-indulgence towards the solemnity of Neoclassicism. On the flattened domes are masterly, highly theatrical trompe l'oeil frescoes by **Januarius Zick**, with a foreshortened *Last Supper* and a cycle illustrating *The Legend of the Cross*.

Eating, drinking and entertainment

Ulm has a wide range of good places to eat and drink, with the Fischerviertel and the streets north of the Münster both ideal areas for a pub crawl. There's also a decent choice of good entertainment.

Restaurants

Drei Kannen Hafenbad 31/1. Traditional Gaststätte housed in an old Brauhaus with an adjoining Renaissance loggia and beer garden. Though it no longer brews its own beer, *Drei-Kannen-Spezial* is still made under licence and only served here. Closed Mon.

Fischhaus Heilbronner Rebengasse 8. Daytime restaurant attached to a fishmonger's shop. Closed from 1.30pm on Sat, all day Sun & Mon.

Gerberhaus Weinhofberg 9. Reasonably priced choice for high-quality Swabian fare. On Fri it's only open in the evening.

Herrenkeller Herrenkellergasse 4. Gaststätte with a pedigree dating back to the seventeenth century, serving both Swabian and Bavarian dishes. Closed Sun.

Hutzel-Hännle Zeitblomstr. 21. Ulm's leading vegetarian restaurant draws on a wide range of international cuisines for inspiration. Closed Wed; open evenings only on Sat.

Kornhäusle Kornhausgasse 8. Small place specializing in salads and crêpes.

Pflugmerzler Pfluggasse 6. High-quality restaurant offering regional cuisine. Closed Sat evening & Sun.

Weinkrüger Weinhofberg 7. Excellent wine bar-cum-restaurant.

Zunfthaus der Schiffleute Fischergasse 31. The old fishermen's guildhall, decked out as a cosy restaurant offering an excellent range of Swabian cuisine.

Zur Forelle Fischergasse 25 ⓣ07 31/6 39 24. Arguably the best restaurant in Ulm, particularly for fish and game dishes. Limited capacity, so booking is advisable.

Bars and cafés

Alberts Café in EinsteinHaus Kornhausplatz 5. Minimalist Internet café.

Allgäuer Hof Fischergasse 12. With its large circle bar, this resembles a traditional British pub. The kitchen offers over forty different kinds of sweet and savoury pancakes, and the usual hearty German fare is available as well.

Barfüsser Lautenberg 1. Hausbrauerei serving its own light, dark and *Weizen* beers plus a good range of food.

Café Brettle Rabengasse 10. Lively student bar.

Café Liquid Münsterplatz 90. Café-bar in a strikingly modern pavilion overlooking the Münster, with outside seating in summer.

Café Lloyd Herrenkellergasse 25. *Szene* café-bar.

Café Tröglen Münsterplatz 5. Established in 1811, this is the most venerable of the several excellent traditional cafés grouped around the Münster. Closed Sun.

Entertainment

In 1641, Ulm became the first city in Germany to establish a permanent civic **theatre**; its modern successor, the Ulmer Theater, Olgastr. 73 (ⓣ07 31/1 61 44 44. ⓦwww.theater.ulm.de), presents drama, opera, operetta, musicals and ballet. **Concert** tickets are available from the Stadthaus, Münsterplatz 50 (ⓣ07 31/1 61 77 00 or 1 61 77 21, ⓦwww.stadthaus.ulm.de), itself a venue for some of the more intimate events, though orchestral and large-scale spectaculars are held at the Congress Centrum, Basteistr. 40 (ⓣ07 31/92 29 90). Choral music is performed in the Münster every other Saturday, while the five-manual organ can be heard daily between 11.30am and noon from Easter to September. There's jazz most evenings at Sauschsdall, Prittwitzstr. 36 (ⓣ07 31/9 26 61 46), and there are live rock bands and alternative film programmes at Charivari, Stuttgarter Str. 13 (ⓣ07 31/1 61 54 42).

The main annual **popular festival** is Schwörmontag on the penultimate Monday of July; this begins at 11am in the Weinhof with the mayor's taking of the oath, and continues in the afternoon with a barge procession down the Danube. On the preceding Saturday evening there's the Lichterserenade, with thousands of illuminations. Each June, the Stadtfest is held in Münsterplatz. However, the most spectacular local tradition, Fischerstechen (Fishermen's Jousting), a colourful tournament with boats in place of horses, is only held at four-year intervals (next in July 2004). Prior to the competitions, there are processions and dances in the streets.

Bad Schussenried

In the heart of Upper Swabia, the triangular-shaped area of rich farmland to the south of the Danube, is a group of health resorts, each specializing in mud bath (*Moorheilbad*) cures, and lying on both of the area's two tourist routes, the Baroque Road (Barockstrasse) and the Spa Road (Bäderstrasse). The most attractive of these spas is **BAD SCHUSSENRIED**, which lies some 60km southwest of Ulm on the rail line to the Bodensee; alternatively, it can be reached by bus from Riedlingen in the Danube valley. Ultra-modern clinics now form a large part of its overall appearance, though the Baroque buildings of the huge former Premonstratensian **Kloster** at the northeastern edge of town retain their pre-eminence. This complex was designed by Dominikus Zimmermann, but built by various other architects.

The monastic church, now the **Pfarrkirche St Magnus**, is rather plain on the outside, save for the single tower with its distinctive onion dome. Its interior, set beneath Januarius Zick's **ceiling frescoes** of scenes from the life of St Norbert, the order's founder, is far more arresting. Highlight of the furnishings is the set of **choir stalls** (€0.50 donation requested), whose backs have limewood reliefs providing a complete illustrated Bible. However, the church is rather overshadowed by the **Bibliotheksaal** (April–Oct daily 10am–noon and 2–5pm; Nov–March Mon–Fri 2–4pm, Sat & Sun 10.30am–noon & 2–4pm; €2.50) in the former conventual buildings; it's a masterly balance of colour, light and shade, with the white porcelain statues contrasting with the pink marble columns and the ethereally blue bookcases with their trompe l'oeil volumes. The ceiling fresco, appropriately enough, is a glorification of Wisdom in both heavenly and earthly guises.

Some 5km northeast of Bad Schussenried, and well connected by bus, is **STEINHAUSEN**, which has always been an integral part of the town. The settlement clusters around the **Wallfahrtskirche**, a building of the highest artistic importance, being generally accepted as the earliest church in the full-blown Rococo style, where architecture, painting and decorations are all fused into an indivisible whole. This unity was made possible by the close collaboration between the **Zimmermann brothers**: Dominikus as architect, Johann Baptist as painter. The church consists of a large nave and a tiny chancel, both oval in shape; pristine white pillars, which look as if they're made of china, shoot up to the vault, whose **fresco**, an evocation of Heaven in limpid pastel colours, seems to be a continuation of the architecture. No less remarkable is the **stuccowork**, with its superbly crafted depictions of the animal, bird and plant kingdoms. The main **pilgrimages** are on Good Friday and on the day of the patron saints, Peter and Paul (29 June).

Another incorporated village, Kürnbach, which is 1.5km south of Bad Schussenried, is home to the **Freilichtmuseum** (April & Oct Tues–Sat 10am –5pm, Sun 11am–5pm; May–Sept Tues–Sat 9am–6pm, Sun 11am–6pm; €2). This brings together redundant rural buildings from the surrounding area, though the centrepiece, a large seventeeth-century farmhouse, is original to the spot.

Practicalities

Bad Schussenried's **Bahnhof** is immediately in front of the Freilichtmuseum, and connected to the town centre by regular buses. However, on Sundays and holidays throughout the summer, trains run along the small branch line, the Schussenbahn, to the Kloster. The **tourist office** (Mon–Fri 9am–noon & 2–4.30pm; ⓣ0 75 83/94 01 71, ⓦwww.badschussenried.de) is in the

Kurverwaltung, Klosterhof 1. There are numerous houses with **rooms** to let (❶–❸); the main concentrations are at the southern end of the main part of town, on Welfenstrasse, Blasius-Erler-Weg and Mozartstrasse. Of the surprisingly few **hotels**, the cheapest is *Landgasthof Linde* at Zum Schussenspring 20 in Steinhausen (Ⓣ0 75 83/23 81, Ⓦwww.zur-linde-steinhausen.de; ❸). In Bad Schussenried itself, choice is between *Barbara*, Schulstr. 9 (Ⓣ0 75 83/2 65 03, Ⓦwww.hotel-barbara.com; ❹) and *Amerika*, Zeppelinstr.13 (Ⓣ0 75 83/9 42 50, Ⓦwww.hotel-amerika.de; ❺). *Landgasthof Linde* and *Amerika* both have good **restaurants**, though the best place to eat is probably *Zur Barockkirche*, Dorfstr. 6 in Steinhausen. Also worth a visit is the *Schussenrieder Erlebnisbrauerei* at Wilhelm-Schussen-Str. 12; apart from being the tap of the Schussenrieder brewery, it has a large beer garden, a huge collection of historic tankards and other beer-related curiosities, and a puppet and marionette theatre.

The Bodensee

The **Bodensee** (also know as Lake Constance, or the Schwäbisches Meer – the "Swabian Sea") is in reality an enormous bulge in the River Rhine, which enters it from the Austrian side to the east and leaves it again on the Swiss border to the west. It's the largest lake in Germany, 14km across at its widest point and about 65km long, and one of the country's most popular holiday destinations. Its main, eastern part is known as the Obersee; the northern of the western forks is the Überlinger See, while its southern counterpart is divided into the Untersee, the Gnadensee and the Zeller See. Thanks to its balmy, dry climate the Bodensee has developed into the nearest the country comes to having a Riviera, though thankfully the shorelines have been preserved from high-rise developments. **Meersburg** and **Überlingen** on the northern side are two of Germany's most picturesque towns; across the water are **Konstanz**, the most cosmopolitan centre in this whole region, and the contrasting islands of **Mainau** and **Reichenau**.

The north shore

Of the three countries bordering the Bodensee, Germany has the lion's share of the shoreline, including the entire northern side. Although the warm climate means that the sweeping views across to the Alps are often lost in haze, this is nevertheless one of the most beautiful parts of Germany. A **corniche road** – served for the length of the Baden-Württemberg stretch by bus #7395 – runs all the way along the shore from the eastern end at Lindau (see p.235). This is far preferable to the rail line, which deviates inland, though the ferries (see box p.291) offer the best means of seeing the lake.

Friedrichshafen

Situated at the widest part of the Bodensee, 22km west of Lindau and 19km south of Ravensburg, **FRIEDRICHSHAFEN** is best known for its

Boat trips on the Bodensee

By far the largest operator of **passenger ships** on the lake is the DB-affiliated Bodensee-Schiffsbetriebe (BSB; Ⓦwww.bsb-online.com) whose main offices are: Seestr. 23, Friedrichshafen (Ⓣ0 75 41/9 23 83 89); Hafenstr. 6, Konstanz (Ⓣ0 75 31/28 13 89); and Schützingerweg 2, Lindau (Ⓣ0 83 82/94 44 16). Fares are very reasonable, being calculated at similar rates to other forms of public transport, and various combination passes, which cover local buses and trains as well as the boats, are available. Bikes can be taken on board without extra charge. Frequency of services is very seasonal, but free current timetables are available at all the harbours, and are also posted on the company website. Excursion cruises are run in summer, though these offer few advantages over the main scheduled routes, which are:

- Friedrichshafen–Romanshorn (Switzerland). The only car ferry operated by the company.
- Kreuzlingen (Switzerland)– Konstanz–Reichenau–Schaffhausen (Switzerland). The most scenic of the routes, continuing along the Rhine and terminating at the Rheinfall.
- Konstanz-Reichenau–Radolfzell
- Konstanz–Meersburg–Friedrichshafen–Lindau–Bregenz (Austria).
- Konstanz–Meersburg–Mainau–Unteruhldingen–Überlingen.

Perhaps the most useful crossing of all, however, is the **car ferry** across the very heart of the lake between Konstanz and Meersburg. Run by the Stadtwerk Konstanz (Ⓣ0 75 31/80 36 66, Ⓦwww.faehre.konstanz.de), it operates throughout the day and night, with frequencies ranging from fifteen minutes to one hour. In addition, various smaller companies offer excursions on the lake. The most luxurious are those in the steamship *Hohentwiel* (Ⓣ0 55 74/7 57 24, Ⓦwww.hohentwiel.com), which was built in 1913 for the use of the royal family of Württemberg.

distinguished place in aviation history. In 1900, it was the scene for the first tests of the gas-powered rigid airship with a cigar-trussed frame developed by Count Ferdinand von Zeppelin. Thereafter, it became both the manufacturing and launch base of these strange, silent machines, capable of going at no more than 35kph, which were used both for long-distance travel and for World War I bombing missions. Although no more Zeppelin flights were undertaken after the *Hindenburg* went up in flames in 1937, Friedrichshafen has maintained its aircraft manufacturing tradition courtesy of Dornier, whose planes were extensively deployed in the Blitz. Despite being the only industrial blot on the lake, the town manages a decidedly curious double existence, taking full advantage of its setting to serve as a rather flashy resort.

The western part of the waterfront has been laid out as an attractive promenade with gardens. At the far end is the Baroque onion-towered **Schlosskirche**, built at the very end of the seventeenth century by Christian Thumb. Its monastic buildings were converted into a palace for the kings of Württemberg in the nineteenth century and are still in the hands of their descendants.

At the opposite end of the town centre, in part of the Bauhaus-style Hafenbahnhof at Seestr. 22, is the **Zeppelin-Museum** (May, June & Oct Tues–Sun 10am–6pm; July–Sept daily 10am–6pm; Nov–April Tues–Sun 10am–5pm; €6). This contains a number of original aircraft, a reconstruction of a section of the *Hindenburg* (which can be boarded for inspection) and fascinating archive film (English soundtrack available) of the Zeppelins. There's also an art gallery, dominated by the works of the folksy school of painters based in the Bodensee in the fifteenth century. Diagonally opposite, at the end of the pier, is the new **Aussichtsturm** (free access at all times), which commands wonderful views over the town and the lake.

Practicalities

Friedrichshafen's **airport** (Ⓣ0 75 41/75 41, Ⓦwww.fly-away.de), which has daily Ryanair flights to London Stansted, is just 4km northeast of the town centre. Directly outside is its own station, Friedrichshafen-Flughafen, which lies on the line linking Ulm with Friedrichshafen's **Stadtbahnhof**, a junction close to the promenade. Some trains continue the short distance onwards to the dead-end Hafenbahnhof. The **tourist office** (May–Sept Mon–Fri 8am–noon & 2–5pm; Oct–April Mon–Thurs 8am–noon & 2–5pm, Fri 8am–1pm; Ⓣ0 75 41/3 00 10, Ⓦwww.friedrichshafen.de) is just across from the Stadtbahnhof at Bahnhofplatz 2.

In addition to numerous **private rooms** (❶–❸), there's an inexpensive **pension**, *Wurster*, Georgstr. 14 (Ⓣ0 75 41/72 69 40; ❹). **Hotels** include *Ailinger Hof*, Ailinger Str. 49 (Ⓣ0 75 41/2 27 88, Ⓦwww.ailinger-hof.de; ❹), *City-Krone*, Schamstr. 7 (Ⓣ0 75 41/70 50, Ⓦwww.hotel-city-krone.de; ❼–❾), and *Buchhorner Hof*, Friedrichstr. 33 (Ⓣ0 75 41/20 50, Ⓦwww.buchhorn.de; ❼–❾). The **youth hostel** is in the eastern part of town at Lindauer Str. 3 (Ⓣ0 75 41/7 24 04; €15.90/18.60); opposite, at Lindauer Str. 20, is the *Dimmler* **campsite** (Ⓣ0 75 41/7 34 21). Another campsite (Ⓣ0 75 41/4 20 59) can be found in the incorporated village of Fischbach to the west of town. The leading **restaurants** are those in the last two hotels mentioned above and the classy *Kurgartenrestaurant* in the Graf-Zeppelin-Haus, Olgastr. 20, which has a terrace overlooking the lake.

Meersburg

MEERSBURG, which clings to a steeply sloping site 16km from Friedrichshafen, is one of those places which perfectly fits the tourist-board image of Romantic Germany. It therefore usually swarms with an uncomfortably large number of day-trippers, but it's an atmospheric and picturesque little town well worth braving the hordes to see.

Arriving by the corniche road, which at this point passes high above the Bodensee, you enter the historic quarter via the dignified **Obertor**. It's then just a short walk down to the riotously picturesque **Marktplatz**, where three streets converge. Steigstrasse, lined on both sides with half-timbered houses, then plummets towards the lake; its west side, with a sloping ramp giving access to the houses, is particularly eye-catching. The **Seepromenade** along the shoreline is the most popular rendezvous point; it's lined with cafés and restaurants, many specializing in fresh fish from the lake.

All over town are tantalizing glimpses of the **Altes Schloss** (daily: March–Oct 9am–6.30pm, Nov–Feb 10am–6pm; €5.50, €7.50 with ascent of the tour in guided groups; Ⓦwww.burg-meersburg.de), whose round corner towers and gabled central block produce a distinctive silhouette. Founded by the Merovingian King Dagobert, it boasts of being the oldest surviving castle in Germany, a claim substantiated by the discovery that some sections of the masonry do actually appear to date back as far as the seventh century. For most of its history, it was a seat of the prince-bishops of Konstanz, who extensively rebuilt it throughout the medieval period, making it their main residence when they were bundled out of their city at the Reformation; since secularization, it has been in private ownership. Germany's greatest woman poet, **Annette von Droste-Hülshoff**, came to live here during the 1840s as guest of the then-owner, her brother-in-law, Baron von Lassberg. Her rooms, whose period furnishings are in stark contrast to the austerity of the medieval chambers, are still as they were in her day, and many of her most famous poems are exhibited on the walls.

The **Neues Schloss** (April–Oct daily 10am–1pm & 2–6pm; €4; ⓦwww.schloesser-und-gaerten.de) above was built under the direction of Balthasar Neumann in the mid-eighteenth century, when the prince-bishops decided they warranted a more comfortable and modern residence. It now houses a cultural centre and local museum, which includes displays on the aircraft entrepreneur Claude Dornier and the fifteenth-century Cologne painter Stefan Lochner, who is thought to have been a native of the town. There's a wonderful view over the Bodensee from the gardens in front; an even better one can be had from the belvedere known as the **Känzele** a short walk to the east.

Practicalities

The **harbour** for BSB ships is at the eastern end of Seepromenade; the terminal for the **car ferry** to Konstanz is some 700m west. **Buses** stop near the latter, as well as near the Obertor; Meersburg is not on the rail line. The **tourist office** (May–Sept Mon–Fri 9am–6.30pm, Sat 10am–2pm; Oct–April Mon–Fri 9am–noon & 2–4.30pm; ⓣ0 75 32/43 11 10, ⓦwww.meersburg.de) is at Kirchstr. 4 at the top of the town.

There is no youth hostel or campsite, but plenty of **private rooms** (➊–➌) and small **guesthouses**, such as *Diana*, Schützenstr. 3a (ⓣ0 75 32/10 01; ➍), and *Am Hafen*, Spitalgasse 3–4 (ⓣ0 75 32/70 69, ⓦwww.amhafen.de.vu; ➍). Among a host of enticing **hotels** are the two historic inns on Marktplatz: the seventeenth-century *Gasthof Zum Bären* at no. 11 (ⓣ0 75 32/4 32 20; ➏) and the fifteenth-century *Löwen* at no. 2 (ⓣ0 75 32/4 30 40, ⓦwww.hotel-loewen-meersburg.de; ➏). Pick of the lakeside hotels are *Seehotel Off*, Uferpromenade 51 (ⓣ0 75 32/4 47 40, ⓦwww.hotel.off.mbo.de; ➏–➑), and *Residenz am See*, Uferpromenade 11 (ⓣ0 75 32/8 00 40, ⓦwww.romantikhotels.com/meersburg; ➑–➒), which boasts a rose garden as well as a terrace. All these hotels have excellent **restaurants**. Less expensive food is served at the many Weinstuben, such as *Im Truben*, Steigstr. 6, *Alemannen-Torkel*, Steigstr. 18, and *Winzerstube zum Becher*, Höllgasse 4. The local **vintages** can be both sampled and bought at the *Winzerverein*, Unterstadtstr. 11.

Unteruhldingen and Birnau

Next resort along the lake, 7km away, is Uhldingen-Mühlhofen, a federation of several previously separate villages. Shoreside **UNTERUHLDINGEN** has the most unusual open-air museum in Germany, the **Pfahlbauten** (guided tours daily: April–Sept 8am–6pm; Oct daily 9am–5pm; March & Nov Sat & Sun 9am–5pm; €5.50; ⓦwww.pfahlbauten.de), featuring conjectural re-creations of Stone and Iron Age dwellings, remains of which were found here, built on huge wooden stilts driven into the bed of the lake.

About twenty minutes' walk uphill is the Cistercian **Basilika Birnau**, whose wonderful, isolated setting above the vineyards is now marred by the proximity of the main road. Built in just four years, it's a collaboration by three of the finest Rococo artists – the architect Peter Thumb, the fresco painter Gottfried Bernard Göz and the sculptor Josef Anton Feichtmayr. The dazzling interior is a paean of praise to the Virgin Mary; its illusionistic tricks reach a climax in the cupola which incorporates a mirror to enhance its effects. Look out for the famous statuette known as the *Honigschlecker* (a cherub sucking the finger that has just been inside a bee's nest); it's placed beside an altar dedicated to St Bernard of Clairvaux, in honour of the claim that his words were as sweet as honey.

Überlingen

A further 5km on, the former Free Imperial City of **ÜBERLINGEN**, nowadays a specialist health resort, rises gently above the lake. For sheer good looks and polished appearance, it has few rivals in all of Germany: with its magnificent public buildings of a distinctive pale green stonework, picturesque alleys of half-timbered houses, glorious lakeward vistas and luxuriant gardens, it seems almost indecently favoured for a place whose population has never numbered more than a few thousand.

Dominating the town is the **Münster**, a huge Gothic structure which was constructed over a period of two hundred years. Its two towers make a fascinating pairing. The tall square clock tower to the south, which provides a landmark visible from far off, was specially heightened to serve as a watchtower, and crowned with an octagonal Renaissance lantern. In contrast, its stumpy northern counterpart which houses the huge *Osanna* bell, nestles under a steeply pitched wooden roof which looks as though it should belong on a barn rather than a church. The sobriety of the rest of the exterior sharply contrasts with the majestic interior, whose intricately vaulted nave of five aisles, built in the second half of the sixteenth century, shows the by-then-archaic Gothic style bowing out with a bang. Also marking the end of an era is the tiered main **altarpiece**, carved by Jörg Zürn in the early seventeenth century, which was the last of the great series of wooden retables illustrating biblical stories adorning so many German churches; soon after, these were completely supplanted by more florid Baroque altars. Zürn also made the graceful tabernacle alongside, while he or members of his family carved four of the altars which adorn each of the fourteen nave chapels.

Across Münsterplatz, and backing onto Hofstatt, the market square, is the **Rathaus** (Mon–Fri 9am–noon & 2–4.30pm, Sat 9am–noon; free). Its first-floor **Ratsaal**, complete with panelled walls, projecting arches and a ribbed ceiling, is a masterpiece of late fifteenth-century design.

Climbing up either Krummebergstrasse or Luitzengasse on the northern side of Münsterplatz brings you to the **Reichlin-von-Meldegg-Haus** (Tues–Sat 9am–12.30pm & 2–5pm, Sun 10am–3pm; €2), another late fifteenth-century building, named after the wealthy doctor whose home it was. The interiors include a chapel and an ornate Rococo **Festsaal**, but most of the space is taken up by a surprisingly good **Städtisches Museum**, including the largest collection of dolls' houses in Germany, ranging from Renaissance to Jugendstil. From the balcony at the end of the gardens is the best **view** in Überlingen, showing the town etched out against the background of the Bodensee and Swiss Alps.

Above the northwest side of Münsterplatz is the **Franziskanerkirche**, with a spare, gaunt exterior typical of the mendicant orders. Its interior, however, was given the full Baroque treatment. More striking than the church is the late Gothic **Franziskanertor**, the northern entrance to the town. This is one of seven surviving gateways and towers of the **Stadtmauer**, which has now been laid out as a shady promenade. The waterfront is dominated by the Neoclassical **Greth**, crowned with a huge slanting roof. Just to the west is the gabled Gothic **Zeughaus**, while at the end of the promenade are the **Kurpark** and a plush new bathing complex, the **Bodensee-Therme** (daily 10am–10pm; Ⓦ www.bodenseetherme.de; prices start at €5.50 for a 2hr swim).

Practicalities

Überlingen's **Bahnhof**, recently renamed Überlingen-Therme, lies at the extreme western end of town; there's now also an unmanned stop, Überlingen-Mitte, just beyond the southern boundary of the Altstadt. Alongside the latter is the **bus station**. The **tourist office** (April & Oct Mon–Fri 9am–1pm & 2–6pm; May–Sept Mon–Fri 9am–6pm, Sat & Sun 10am–1pm; Nov–March Mon–Fri 9am–1pm & 2–5pm; Ⓣ0 75 51/99 11 22, Ⓦwww.ueberlingen.de) is housed in the Greth, Landungsplatz 14.

Among the numerous **pensions** are *Klosterhof*, Christophstr. 17 (Ⓣ0 75 51/35 82; ❹), and *Kussberger*, Goldbacher Str. 6 (Ⓣ0 75 51/57 49; ❹). **Hotels** are mostly pricey by Bodensee standards, being geared to the lucrative spa market. The two best lakeside addresses are *Bad-Hotel*, Christophstr. 2 (Ⓣ0 75 51/83 70, Ⓦwww.bad-hotel-ueberlingen.de; ❻–❽), and *Seegarten*, Seepromenade 7 (Ⓣ0 75 51/91 88 90; ❻–❽). However, the finest views are from the town's most prestigious establishment, *Parkhotel St Leonhard*, which is set in its own park at Obere-St-Leonhard-Str. 71 (Ⓣ0 75 51/80 81 00, Ⓦwww.parkhotel-sankt-leonhard.de; ❽). There's a large modern **youth hostel** at the eastern end of the waterside at Alte Nussdorfer Str. 26 (Ⓣ0 75 51/42 04; €15.30/18). Further along the lake, in the incorporated village of Nussdorf, are a couple of **campsites**: *Nell* (Ⓣ0 75 51/42 54, Ⓦwww.camping-nell.de) and *Luft* (Ⓣ0 75 51/6 15 57, Ⓦwww.camping-luft.de). Each of the listed hotels has a recommendable **restaurant**; less pricey alternatives include *Zur Krone*, Münsterstr. 10, and *Spitalkeller im Steinhaus*, Steinhausgasse 1.

Of the town's **festivals**, the most important is the Schwedenprozession, commemorating this Catholic town's successful defence of its independence against the Swedes in the Thirty Years War. This is performed twice annually: on the Sunday after May 16, and on the second Sunday in July. Fastnacht is also a big annual event and bizarrely features Bengali costumes.

Konstanz (Constance)

By any standards, **KONSTANZ** has a remarkable geographical position. It's split in two by the Rhine, which re-emerges here from the Obersee (the main part of the Bodensee) as a channel for a brief stretch, before forming the Untersee, the arm from which it finally re-emerges as a river. The Altstadt is a tiny enclave on the otherwise Swiss side of the lake, a fact which was of inestimable benefit during the war when the Allies desisted from bombing it for fear of hitting neutral Switzerland. Curiously enough, the latter is one country to which Konstanz has never belonged: probably founded by the Romans, it has been a prince-bishopric and a Swabian Free Imperial City, then Austrian, before finally being allocated to Baden. Between 1414 and 1418, when the conclave (or Council of Konstanz) met here to resolve the Great Schism – eventually managing to replace the three competing popes with one – the city was the nerve-centre of European power politics. Nowadays, it contents itself with more modest roles as a resort town, frontier post and seat of a new university whose students help to give it a relaxed yet lively air all year round.

Arrival, information and accommodation

The **Deutscher Bahnhof**, the terminus of the line from the Black Forest, is close to the Bodensee waterfront; immediately south is its Swiss counterpart, the **Schweizer Bahnhof**. Outside the stations are various stands for

buses servicing both the urban area and destinations beyond. Also here, at Bahnhofplatz 13, is the **tourist office** (April–Oct Mon–Fri 9am–6.30pm, Sat 9am–4pm, Sun 10am–1pm; Nov–March Mon–Fri 9.30am–12.30pm & 2–6pm; Ⓣ0 75 31/13 30 30, Ⓦwww.konstanz.de). For information on **boat trips**, see the box on p.291. Note that the car ferry to Meersburg is in the northern suburb of Staad; all other services leave from the harbour behind the Bahnhof. The main annual **festival** is the Seenachtsfest in August, with a spectacular display of fireworks over the Bodensee. Classical music concerts, the Konstanzer Internationale Musiktage, are held throughout the summer.

There are private **rooms** (❶–❹) all over town. The **youth hostel** is at Zur Allmannshöhe 18 (Ⓣ0 75 31/3 22 60; €15.90/19.60); take bus #4 from the Bahnhof to Jugendherberge, or bus #1 to Allmannsdorf-Post. Among the numerous **campsites** in the vicinity is *Klausehorn* (Ⓣ0 75 31/63 72) in the incorporated fishing village of Dingelsdorf, which can also be reached by bus #4. Many of the more central **hotels** are in historic buildings and therefore somewhat expensive, though arguably worth it for the atmosphere.

Hotels and pensions

Barbarossa Obermarkt 8–12 Ⓣ0 75 31/2 20 21, Ⓦwww.barbarossa-hotel.com. Fine middle-range hotel and restaurant in the heart of the Altstadt. ❻

Graf Wiesenstr. 2 Ⓣ0 75 31/1 28 68 90, Ⓕ12 86 89 14. Inexpensive pension just round the corner from the stations, offering rooms with and without facilities. ❹

Graf Zeppelin Am Stephansplatz 15 Ⓣ0 75 31/2 37 80, Ⓦwww.zeppelin.mdo.de. A somewhat old-fashioned, archetypally German hotel and restaurant, conveniently located near the Münster. ❹–❻

Gretel Zollenstr. 6–8 Ⓣ0 75 31/2 32 83, Ⓦwww.hotel-gretel.de. Altstadt pension run in tandem with a Weinstube, *Zum Guten Hirten*. ❹–❻

Inselhotel Auf der Insel Ⓣ0 75 31/12 50, Ⓦwww.konstanz-steigenberger.de. Konstanz's most prestigious hotel is a notable historic landmark in its own right, and offers wonderful views over the Bodensee. It has two restaurants, *Dominikanerstube* being a bit less pricey than the showpiece *Seerestaurant*. ❾

Schiff am See William-Graf-Platz 2, Staad Ⓣ0 75 31/3 10 41, Ⓦwww.ringhotel-schiff.de. This fine waterfront hotel is handy for the car ferry. It also has a good restaurant (closed Mon & lunchtime Tues). ❼

Seehotel Silber Seestr. 25 Ⓣ0 75 31/9 96 69 90, Ⓕ99 66 99 33. Located in a Jugendstil villa with a lakeside terrace, this is best-known for its gourmet restaurant, generally considered the best in Konstanz. ❾

Seeschau Zur Schiffslände 11, Dingelsdorf Ⓣ0 75 31/51 90, Ⓦwww.gasthaus-seeschau.de. Lakeside Gasthaus in the far north of the urban area; take bus #4. ❹

The Town

Nearly everything of interest in Konstanz lies in the Altstadt, which stretches from the southern bank of the Rhine to the very abrupt border with Switzerland about 1km to the south, though there are a couple of attractions in the suburb of Petershausen on the north side of the river.

The Münster

The famous conclave met in the **Münster**, suitably set on the highest point of the Altstadt. Begun as a Romanesque pillared basilica – whose outline is still obvious – building continued for six hundred years, so there are marked differences in style, particularly in the interior: the aisles and their chapels are Gothic, while the organ-case and gallery were built during the Renaissance, and the original ceiling was replaced by a vaulted Baroque one. The spot on which the theological reformer Jan Hus, the first Czech rector of Prague University, is said to have stood during his trial is marked in the central aisle, by the twenty-fourth row. Despite having been guaranteed a safe return passage by the conclave, he was condemned as a heretic and handed over to the secular authorities to be burnt at the stake.

Of the furnishings, the most remarkable are the vigorously carved fifteenth-century **choir stalls** designed by Nicolaus Gerhaert von Leyden, and the broadly contemporary and equally ornate **Schnegg**, a staircase in the northern transept. From here you descend to the **Konradikapelle**, named in honour of St Konrad, a tenth-century bishop of Konstanz, who is commemorated by a Gothic funerary slab and a golden shrine. The saint would probably still recognize the tiny **crypt** further on, the oldest surviving part of the building, whose walls are hung with remarkable gilded enamel medallions. Beyond are the Gothic cloisters, off which are several imposing chambers, notably the rotunda known as the Mauritiuskapelle, which houses a magnificent late thirteenth-century **Holy Sepulchre**, inspired by the original in Jerusalem. Next door is the Sylvesterkapelle, with a complete cycle of fifteenth-century frescoes of the life of Christ.

The **tower** (previously mid-April to mid-Oct Mon–Sat 10am–5pm, Sun 1–5pm; €1, but closed in 2003 for restoration) commands a fine view of the town and the Bodensee. Its central lantern and openwork spire are nineteenth-century additions to the massive Gothic facade, whose three sections were, unusually, all of similar height, giving it a decidedly forbidding and unecclesiastical look.

Münsterplatz, the Niederburg and Petershausen

On Münsterplatz are a number of fine old mansions, including the **Haus zur Katz**, a fifteenth-century guildhouse which is the earliest example of rusticated stonework in Germany, and the **Haus zur Kunkel** (Tues–Fri 10am–noon & 2–4pm, Sat 10am–noon; free), formerly the residence of the sacristan. Behind the latter's Baroque exterior lurk some original thirteenth-century rooms, one of which features some beautiful early Gothic frescoes showing linen weavers at work; a sign tells you at which door to ring in order to see them.

Also on the square is the brashly modernist facade of the **Kulturzentrum am Münster**, which contains the **Städtische Wessenberg-Galerie** (Tues–Fri 10am–6pm, Sat & Sun 10am–5pm; €3). In addition to enticing temporary exhibitions, this displays art of the Bodensee region from the past two centuries. In recent years, there have been occasional showings of part of its long-overlooked but remarkable collection of drawings – including sheets by Dürer, Rembrandt, Watteau and Menzel, among many others – bequeathed just under a century ago by a Danish-born banker, Wilhelm Brandes.

Between Münsterplatz and the Rhine is the best-preserved part of town, the **Niederburg**, a quarter of twisting little alleys lined by old houses. Overlooking the river are two fragments of the fortifications – the **Pulverturm** and the **Rheintorturm**. The latter, by the modern Rheinbrücke which carries the main road and rail line into the heart of Konstanz, is particularly impressive; it dates back to the late twelfth century and preserves some scanty frescoes.

Across the bridge is **Petershausen**, whose most prominent historic monument is the former convent on Benediktinerplatz which now houses the **Archäologisches Landesmuseum** (Tues–Sun 10am–6pm; €3; Ⓦwww.konstanz.alm-bw.de), with displays ranging from the Stone Age to the nineteenth century. Particular highlights are the second-century bronze treasures – six busts of deities, three sea leopards and two lion's-head door knockers – from the Roman town of Lopodunum, and the oldest surviving Bodensee ship, a six-hundred-year-old trading vessel. Nearby Seestrasse, Peterhausen's riverside waterfront, is a promenade of grandiosely elegant villas, one of which contains the **Casino**, a particular magnet to the Swiss.

At the southeast corner of the Rheinbrücke is the exclusive **Inselhotel**, occupying the old Dominican priory. Its cellars were used to imprison Hus, and it was also the birthplace of Ferdinand von Zeppelin, a statue to whom can be seen overlooking the main **harbour** – a bustle of colourful sails in the summer – just to the south. Behind it is the **Konzilgebäude**, a fourteenth-century storehouse with a prominent hipped roof. It owes its name to the disputed contention that it was the scene of the election of Pope Martin V, the event that brought the Great Schism to an end; nowadays it has been restored to serve as a festival hall and a restaurant.

The rest of the centre

Konstanz's two market squares, Fischmarkt and Marktstätte, are respectively west and southwest of the Konzilgebäude. South of the latter, along the street of the same name, is the **Rosgartenmuseum** (Tues–Fri 10am–6pm, Sat & Sun 10am–5pm; €3), whose displays of local history and culture are housed in the former guildhall of the butchers, grocers and apothecaries. It has recently reopened after many years of closure, and utilises the very latest display techniques. These have enabled the original of one of the great treasures of its medieval section – Ulrich Richtental's richly illustrated *Chronicle of the Council of Konstanz* – to be placed on permanent view. Paradoxically, its Historisches Saal, with neo-Gothic display cabinets containing archeological finds, is under a preservation order and has therefore been left as it was when the museum was founded in 1875. At the end of Rosgartenstrasse is the **Dreifaltigkeitskirche**, the church of the old Augustinian monastery. It was frescoed during the time of the conclave with scenes from the history of the order, plus portraits of various contemporary personalities, among them Emperor Sigismund.

Returning to Marktstätte, Kanzleistrasse leads west past the Renaissance **Rathaus**, whose facade was jollied up by the addition of Romantic murals. At the end of the street is **Obermarkt**, which is lined with more colourful mansions; here, in 1417, the Hohenzollerns were invested with control over the Margraviate of Brandenburg, a crucial step in their drive, achieved four and a half centuries later, to unite the German nation under their control.

To the south, at Hussenstr. 64, is the **Hus-Museum** (June–Sept Tues–Sun 10am–12.30pm & 1.30–5pm; Oct–May Tues–Sun 10am–noon & 2–4pm; free) where the reformer stayed on his arrival in Konstanz. Apart from his importance as a religious thinker, Hus had a major influence on the Czech sense of nationhood and almost single-handedly established his country's national literature. A few paces further on is the **Schnetztor**, a fourteenth-century fortified gateway with an outer courtyard.

Eating and drinking

Konstanz is awash with good places to eat and drink, with plenty of alternatives to the excellent hotel restaurants mentioned on p.296.

Brauhaus Johann Albrecht Konradigasse 2. Hausbrauerei which brews light, dark and *Weizen* beers and serves inexpensive meals.

Bürgerstuben Bahnhofplatz 7. Café-restaurant with a predominantly Italian menu, including good pizzas, plus moderately-priced Bodensee fish specialities.

Casino-Restaurant Seestr. 21. A high-class, fairly expensive restaurant with panorama terrace. Evenings only.

Hafenhalle Hafenstr. 10. Although the menu here has the expected fish dishes, game features as well. In summer, there's the bonus of a large beer garden with fine lakeside views.

Konzil-Gaststätten Hafenstr. 2. The restaurant in the historic Konzilgebäude is reasonably priced considering its quality, and has the benefit of a terrace overlooking the harbour.
Rosgartencafé Rosgartenstr. 9. Good traditional café.
St Stephanskeller St-Stephans-Platz 43. This wine bar-restaurant has a full menu Tues–Sat, a more limited selection of bistro dishes Sun & Mon. The set lunches are particularly good value.
Staader Fährhaus Fischerstr. 30, Staad. One of the town's most creative restaurants, with a strong line in local fish dishes. Closed Tues and open evenings only on Wed.

The Bodensee islands

There are only two islands of any size in the Bodensee, and, notwithstanding the fact that both put their rich soils to good use, they could hardly be more different: **Mainau** is an exotic, scented floral isle which seems to have been wafted up from the Mediterranean, while **Reichenau**, which is mostly given over to the cultivation of fruit and vegetables, retains its three ancient monasteries as vivid reminders of its status as one of the cradles of German civilization. Ironically enough, the easiest way to reach either of the islands is by bus (causeways having been constructed to link them to the mainland), though it's obviously far more atmospheric to arrive by boat.

Mainau

Mainau (Easter to late Oct daily 7am–8pm, €10.50, €5.50 after 4pm, free after 7pm; rest of year daily 9am–6pm, €5.50; Ⓦwww.mainau.de), which lies in the Überlinger See, possesses an aura of immense grandeur, thanks to the riotous colours of the flowers and shrubs which bedeck it, and the exhilarating long-distance views over the lake across to the opposite shore, which are particularly spectacular at sunset. It's like a little tropical paradise – or it would be were it not for the relentless presence of thousands of visitors every day for at least six months of the year. With this in mind, try to come as early as possible: the crowds start to build up by mid-morning. Local bus #4 from the centre of Konstanz stops at the end of the causeway at the western approach to Mainau; ferries between Meersburg and Unteruhldingen call at the landing stage at the opposite side of the island.

For over five hundred years Mainau belonged to the Teutonic Knights, and the **Schloss** at the highest point of the island is a typical example of the Baroque architecture they favoured during the time they were based in Bad Mergentheim. It's now the residence of the island's flamboyant Swedish owner, Count Lennart Bernadotte, a descendant of the grand dukes of Baden who took possession of Mainau in the nineteenth century. Most of the interior is out of bounds to the public, though one hall is used for exhibitions, and the **Schlosskapelle**, with its frothy ceiling paintings and elaborate woodwork, is generally accessible.

The carefully manicured gardens, which occupy almost every available part of the island, are what everyone comes to see. A combination of the freak microclimate and the utilization of scientific techniques means that at least part of the garden is in bloom for half of the year; a unique feature is the presence of three-dimensional **floral sculptures**, which were specially created as diversions for the youngest visitors. **Spring** is the most delightful season here, with a big display of orchids in the Palmenhaus, along with an array of tulips, hyacinths, narcissi and primroses outside; azaleas and rhododendrons appear later. **Summer** sees the rose walk at its best, while palm trees, bananas, lemons and oranges also ripen then. **Autumn** features a dahlia show, after which the colour disappears, leaving only the year-round greenery of the cedars, sequoias and cypresses until the cycle starts again. A recent addition to the facilities is the **Schmetterlingshaus** (Butterfly House; daily: Easter to late Oct 10am–8pm; late Oct to Easter 11am–5pm), which has the largest collection of butterflies in the country.

As well as various snack bars, there are a couple of **restaurants**: the *Comturey-Keller*, which offers set lunch menus, and the classy *Schwedenschenke,* located uphill by the Schloss. Note that, although you can stay on past the official closing time, you have to be off the island by midnight.

Reichenau

Reichenau, whose shores are lapped by the Untersee, the Gnadensee and the Zeller See, lies 8km west of Konstanz, and has a history almost as venerable as the city itself. Monastic life was established here in 724, and three monasteries, which all survive, were in place by the end of the ninth century. Many of the early abbots also held high positions in the Holy Roman Empire, and the island was a famous centre of scholarship, literature and painting, with the two arts combined in the great local speciality of manuscript illumination. However, by the twelfth century the monasteries were already in decline, and there was no more than a token monastic presence for several hundred years before the dissolution in 1803. Nowadays, two-thirds of the island's area is devoted to market gardens, giving it a character not dissimilar to the tulip-growing regions of Holland. Very quiet and sedate, it's a popular holiday resort with pensioners and families, who rent apartments around its coast. In 2000, the island was placed on UNESCO's World Heritage List.

Just 4.5km long and 1.5km wide, the layout of Reichenau is easy to grasp. There are three villages, each centred on a monastery. First up is **OBERZELL**, with the church of **St Georg**, the only one of the trio not completely reconstructed at a later date. The dignified Romanesque entrance hall was the sole significant addition made to the original, one of the most complete examples of Carolingian architecture to have survived anywhere in Europe. Inside is a wonderful set of Ottonian **frescoes**, which are about a century younger than the building and show the same style as the famed Reichenau miniatures, albeit on a monumental scale. The eight main scenes, whose colours remain remarkably vivid, illustrate the miracles of Christ – subjects which were mostly eschewed by later artists.

Little more than 1km further on is **MITTELZELL**, whose large **Münster** is the mother-church of Reichenau. Its present form, apart from the Gothic chancel, dates from the very beginning of the eleventh century and is an impressive sight, particularly when viewed from across the garden on its northern side. The **Schatzkammer** (May–Sept Mon–Sat 11am–noon & 3–4pm; €1) on the northern side of the chancel contains many choice items. These include the *Smaragd*, an Oriental glass floor donated by Charlemagne; a poignant Romanesque crucifix from St Georg; a fourteenth-century ciborium incorporating a fifth-century ivory pyx; and five beautiful reliquary-shrines. In the monastic buildings behind the church is the **Winzerkeller**, where wines from Reichenau – which has Germany's most southerly vineyards – can be purchased.

Towards the far end of the island is **NIEDERZELL**, with the twin-towered twelfth-century Romanesque church of **St-Peter-und-Paul**. This is the least distinctive of the three and is further marred by a fair amount of frivolous Baroque interior decoration, but a fresco of *The Last Judgement*, the final expression of the Reichenau school of painting, can be seen in the apse.

Practicalities

Ferries between Konstanz and the Swiss city of Schaffhausen call at Reichenau. The island is also linked to Konstanz by bus #7372, and has a **Bahnhof** on the rail line to the Black Forest, though this is on the mainland, some 3km from Oberzell. Between the two is the Wollmatinger Ried, a protected landscape of reedy marshes, isles and flowery meadows inhabited by a rich variety of birdlife. Reichenau's swish new **tourist office** (May–Sept Mon–Fri 8.30am–12.30pm & 1.30–6pm, Sat 9am–noon; Oct–April Mon–Fri 8.30am–noon & 2–5pm; ⓣ0 75 34/9 20 70, ⓦwww.reichenau.de) is at Pirminstr. 145 in Mittelzell, a stone's throw uphill from the Münster.

The *Sandseele* **campsite** (ⓣ0 75 34/73 84, ⓦwww.sandseele.de) is on the shore in Niederzell. There are around a dozen **private houses** (❷–❸) with rooms to let, plus several **pensions**, including *Hobelbänkle*, Rosendornweg 5 (ⓣ0 75 34/13 83; ❹), and *Keller*, Am Vögelisberg 13 (ⓣ0 75 34/92 10 21, ⓦwww.pension-keller-reichenau.de; ❹–❻). Among the five **hotels** are two highly prestigious lakeside establishments: *Strandhotel Löchnerhaus*, An der Schiffslände 12 (ⓣ0 75 34/80 30, ⓦwww.strandhotel-reichenau.mdo.de; ❻–❽), and *Seeschau*, An der Schiffslände 8 (ⓣ0 75 34/2 57, ⓦwww.seeschau.mdo.de; ❼–❾). Their **restaurants** are among the best in the Bodensee area. A good alternative is *Zum Alten Mesmer*, opposite the Münster at Burgstr. 9, which has been run by the same family for over a century. Vegetarians are well catered for by the huge self-service cold buffet offered by *Reichenauer Salatstuben*, Untere Rheinstr. 21. The distinctive local traditional dress is worn for the big religious **festivals**, notably the Markusfest (April 25) and the Heilig-Blut-Fest (one week after Whit Monday).

The Black Forest region

Even in a country where woodland is so widespread as to exert a grip over such varied aspects of national life as folklore, literature and leisure activities, the **Black Forest** (Schwarzwald) stands out as a place with its own special mystique. Stretching 170km north to south, and up to 60km east to west, it's by far the largest German forest – and the most beautiful. Geographically speaking, it's a massif in its own right, but forms a pair with the broadly similar French Vosges on the opposite side of the Rhine valley, which demarcates the borders with both France and Switzerland. The name of the forest comes from the dark, densely packed fir trees on the upper slopes; oaks and beeches are characteristic of the lower ranges. With its houses sheltering beneath massive sloping straw roofs, its famous gateau, its cuckoo clocks and its colourful, often outrageous traditional dress, the Black Forest ranks second only to Bavaria as the font of stereotyped images of the country.

Even as late as the 1920s, much of this area was a rarely penetrated wilderness, forming a refuge for everything from boars to bandits. Romantics were drawn here by the wild beauty of watery gorges, dank valleys and exhilarating mountain views. Nowadays, most of the villages have been opened up as spa and health resorts, full of shops selling tacky souvenirs, while the old trails have become manicured gravel paths smoothed down for ramblers and strollers. Yet, for all that – and in spite of fears about the potentially disastrous effects of *Waldsterben* (dying forest syndrome), which may have affected as many as half the trees – it remains a landscape of unique character, and by no means all the modernizations are drawbacks.

Accommodation, for example, is plentiful and generally excellent value. **Rail** fans will find several of the most spectacular lines in Europe, some of them brilliant feats of engineering. Note, though, that the trains tend to stick closely to the valleys,that **bus services** are much reduced outside the tourist season, and that **walking** is undoubtedly the most satisfying way to get around.

Most of the Black Forest is associated with the Margraviate (later Grand Duchy) of **Baden**, whose old capital of **Baden-Baden** – once the ultimate playground of the mega-rich – is at the northern fringe of the forest, in a fertile orchard and vineyard-growing area. This was later usurped by custom-built **Karlsruhe**, which is technically outside the Black Forest but best visited in conjunction with it. The only city actually surrounded by the forest is **Freiburg im Breisgau**, one of the most distinctive and enticing in the country. Nestling in the far southwestern corner of Germany, it lies just 30km from the French border and the gateway town of **Breisach**.

Freiburg im Breisgau

FREIBURG IM BREISGAU, "capital" of the Black Forest, basks in a laid-back atmosphere which seems completely un-German. As the seat of a university since 1457, it has an animated, youthful presence which, unlike so many other academic centres, is kept up all year round, with the help of a varied programme of festivals. Furthermore, the sun shines here more often, and there are more vineyards within the municipal area than in any other city in the country.

Freiburg's singularity is often attributed to the fact that it's really an Austrian city. Between 1368 and 1805, when it was allocated to the buffer state of Baden, it was almost continuously under the protection of the House of Habsburg. It's often claimed that the Austrians brought a touch of humanity to the German character, and that it was their eventual exclusion from the country's affairs which led to the triumph of militarism. The persistence here of the relaxed multicultural climate that was traditionally characteristic of Austria suggests that there's a grain of truth in this cliché.

Freiburg makes the most obvious base for visiting the Black Forest, with fast and frequent public transport connections to all the famous beauty spots. In its own right, it warrants a couple of days' exploration at least, and is renowned for its excellent mix of lively bars and restaurants. Even if you're only passing through, you should make a point of visiting Freiburg's lovely **Münster**. Although the city was extensively destroyed in a single air raid in 1944, no modern building has been allowed to challenge the supremacy of its magisterial tower, which the doyen of art historians, Jacob Burckhardt, described as "the greatest in Christendom".

Arrival, information and accommodation

Freiburg's **Hauptbahnhof**, with the **bus station** on its southern side, is about ten minutes' walk from Münsterplatz. The **tourist office** is en route at Rotteckring 14 (May–Oct Mon–Fri 9.30am–8pm, Sat 9.30am–5pm, Sun 10am–noon; Nov–April Mon–Fri 9.30am–6pm, Sat 9.30am–2pm, Sun 10am–noon; ⓣ07 61/3 88 18 80, ⓦwww.freiburg.de). Outside is an electronic noticeboard equipped with a phone telling you which places have vacancies, though this is not an exhaustive service. The city has a wide range of **hotels**; those in the centre are almost exclusively in the middle and upper ranges, albeit generally good value for what they offer. Further afield are some good budget alternatives, as well as plenty of **private houses** (❷–❹), a **youth hostel** and several **campsites**. If you're staying far out, it makes sense to invest in a rover ticket on the **public transport** system. Prices for 24 hours are €4.60 for the city, €9.20 for the whole circuit; these rise to €6.50 and €13 respectively for two people travelling together.

Hotels and pensions

Colombi Am Colombi-Park ⓣ07 61/2 10 60, ⓦwww.colombi.de. The city's leading hotel, well located at the western edge of the Altstadt and boasting all the luxuries including a swimming pool, steam baths, a sauna, solarium, fitness centre and a renowned gourmet restaurant. ❾

Dionysos Hirschstr. 2 ⓣ07 61/2 93 53, ⓕ2 91 38. Greek-run hotel and ethnic restaurant in the south of the city, halfway towards Schauinsland; take tram #4. ❸

Haus Gisela Am Vogelbach 27 ⓣ07 61/8 24 72, ⓦwww.hausgisela.com. Homely, good-value pension in the northwestern suburbs, reached by bus #10. ❸

Markgräfler Hof Gerberau 22 ⓣ07 61/3 25 40, ⓦwww.markgraeflerhof.de. Occupies a fine fifteenth-century town palace. Its restaurant (closed Sun & Mon), one of the best in town, has a truly amazing wine list. ❼

Oberkirchs Weinstuben Münsterplatz 22 ⓣ07 61/2 02 68 68, ⓕ2 02 68 69. Has an ideal location overlooking the Münster, and one of the city's best wine bar-restaurants (closed Sun). ❽

Rappen Münsterplatz 13 ⓣ07 61/3 13 53, ⓦwww.hotelrappen.de. Another hotel with many rooms overlooking the Münster; also has an excellent restaurant and a cosy Weinstube. ❺–❼

Schemmer Eschholzstr. 63 ⓣ07 61/20 74 90, ⓕ2 07 49 50. The lowest-priced central hotel, just south of the Hauptbahnhof on the opposite side of the tracks from the Altstadt. ❸

Schwarzwälder Hof Herrenstr. 43 ⓣ07 61/3 80 30, ⓦwww.hotel-schwarzwaelder-hof.de. Hotel-cum-Weinstube in the heart of the Altstadt. ❺

Waldheim Schauinslandstr. 20 ⓣ07 61/29 04 94. Budget hotel in the south of the city en route to Schauinsland; take tram #4. ❸

Zum Roten Bären Oberlinden 12 ⓣ07 61/38 78 70, ⓦwww.roter-baeren.de. Germany's longest-functioning inn, now part of the Ringhotel group, is in a house dated 1120. Nonetheless it offers everything that would be expected of a comfortable modern hotel, including a fine if expensive restaurant (closed Sun pm & Mon). ❽

Youth hostel and campsites

Hirzberg Kartäuserstr. 99 ⓣ07 61/3 50 54, ⓦwww.freiburg-camping.de. Campsite situated near the youth hostel on the eastern outskirts of the city. Open all year.

IYHF Jugendherberge Karthäuserstr. 151 ⓣ07 61/6 76 56. Freiburg's youth hostel is at the extreme eastern end of the city, ideally placed for walks in the hills or along the banks of the River Dreisam. Take tram #1 to Römerhof. €15.90/18.60.

Mösle-Park ⓣ07 61/7 29 38, ⓦwww.freiburg-freizeit.de. Situated south of the houses on the opposite side of the river and reached by tram #1. Open mid-March to late Oct.

Tunisee ⓣ07 66/5 22 49, ⓦwww.touridat.de/camping/tunisee-freiburg. An enormous site way to the north of the centre in the village of Hochdorf.

The City

As usual, most of what you'll want to see is in the Altstadt, and even here the main sights are concentrated on Münsterplatz and in the museum quarter to the south. However, it's also well worth venturing into the nearby hills for some wonderful views over the city and the Black Forest.

The Münster

Crafted out of a dark red sandstone quarried in one of the surrounding hills, the **Münster** (or **Dom**) is so magnificent and overpowering that it puts the rest of the city in the shade. Not the least remarkable fact about it is that, though it rivals any of the great European cathedrals, it was built as a mere parish church. No funds from the well-lined coffers of the ecclesiastical top brass were forthcoming for its construction – the costs were met entirely from the pockets of local citizens, to whom it was the ultimate symbol of municipal pride. In 1827, the Münster's artistic standing was given due recognition when it became the seat of the Upper Rhenish archbishopric.

Work on the present building began in about 1200, to replace a much simpler church dating from the time of the town's foundation eighty years before. The **transepts** were built first, in the picturesque late Romanesque style then still popular in Germany. However, there was an abrupt change when the masons became aware of the structural advantages of Gothic, which the French had already mastered. At first, the same masons began building in this unfamiliar idiom; later, one of the architects of Strasbourg cathedral took over. He created a masterly **nave**, resplendent with flying buttresses, gargoyles and statues, already diverging from French models.

Further originality is evident in the west **porch**, begun around 1270. The figures, which still bear traces of colouring, are much the most important German

Freiburg's drains

A peculiarity of Freiburg is the continuous visible presence throughout the old part of the city of its **sewage system**, known as the *Bächle*. These are rivulets, fed by the River Dreisam, which run in deep gullies, serving as a trap for the unwary pedestrian or motorist. Formerly used for watering animals and as a sure precaution against the fire hazard which accounted for so many medieval towns, they have their purpose even today, helping to keep the city cool.

works of their time. A sweetly carved *Madonna and Child* guards the door; above, the tympanum illustrates the entire New Testament. On the end walls, the Wise and Foolish Virgins confront each other, while deliberately shrouded on the west wall (at the point where the natural light is weakest) are the most striking figures: Satan as Prince of Darkness, beguilingly disguised as a youthful knight, and Sensuality, who has toads and serpents writhing on her back.

The single **tower** (March–Nov Mon–Sat 9.30am–5pm, Sun 1–5pm; €1.50) above the porch was a unique design for its time, but was subsequently much imitated, most notably at Ulm. Though it seems to be an organic unity, it wasn't planned as a whole. The square plan of the lower storeys supports a soaring octagon, bearing animated statues of prophets and angels, which forms the stage above the bells. From the platform, you're rewarded with a fine panorama over the city and the Black Forest. However, the best view is of the lace-like tracery of the **openwork spire**, which rounds off the tower with a bravura flourish. The first of its kind, it was inspired by the mysticism of the time and symbolizes the human soul stretching out to receive divine knowledge. Many similar spires were planned for subsequent German churches, though most remained unbuilt until the nineteenth century. Exceptions are the two miniature versions which were immediately placed on Freiburg's own **Hahnentürme** (Cock Towers).

For the **chancel**, begun in the mid-fourteenth century (about 25 years after the completion of the spire), the authorities again struck lucky with their choice of architect, a man named Johannes of the famous Parler dynasty. His regular geometric layout marked a major advance on French models, and his two **portals**, particularly the northern one dedicated to the Creation, are adorned with superbly expressive sculptures – look out for the unusual depiction of God resting on the seventh day.

Inside, the transept is lit by luminous **stained-glass** windows of the early thirteenth century. Most of those in the nave date from a hundred years later and were donated by the local trades and guilds, who incorporated their coats of arms. Other items to look out for are a delicate late thirteenth-century *Madonna* on the west wall, a poignant fourteenth-century *Holy Sepulchre* in the south aisle, and the pulpit, an archaic Gothic work of the mid-sixteenth century with depictions of Freiburg personalities of the day. At the entrance to the chancel is a fine *Adoration of the Magi* by the leading local woodcarver of the late Gothic period, Hans Wydyz. This artist sometimes collaborated with the mercurial **Hans Baldung**, Dürer's most talented follower, whose high altar triptych of *The Coronation of the Virgin* – arguably his masterpiece – can be glimpsed from this point.

To see the chancel, and to get a better view of the Baldung triptych, you may have to take a **guided tour** (Mon–Fri at 11am & 2.30pm; €2). In the Universitätskapelle, there are two wings of a curious **Holbein** retable. The portraits of the donor family are by Hans the Elder, but the main scenes of *The Nativity* and *Epiphany* are youthful works by his son, whose superior gifts are already in evidence. A *Rest on the Flight into Egypt* in the Kaiserkapelle has sculptures by Wydyz and a painted background by Baldung, who also designed many of the stained-glass windows in the chapels, though some of these have been replaced by copies. Hans Sixt von Staufen, another talented local sculptor of the time, carved the *Madonna of Mercy* in the Locherer Kapelle. In the Villinger Kapelle is a rare relic of the first Münster, a silver crucifix.

Münsterplatz

Until the war, the spacious **Münsterplatz** formed a fitting setting for the great church in its midst. However, the north side was flattened by bombs (which miraculously hardly touched the Münster itself) and only the late fifteenth-century **Kornhaus**, the municipal granary, has been rebuilt. The rest of the square has survived in much better shape and hosts an excellent daily market. There are also a couple of pretty fountains directly in front of the Münster – the **Georgsbrunnen** and the **Fischbrunnen** – along with three tall columns that bear statues of the local patron saints.

The south side of the square is dominated by the blood-red **Kaufhaus**, a sixteenth-century merchants' hall; its arcaded facade bears four statues by Sixt von Staufen of members of the House of Habsburg. On either side of the Kaufhaus are handsome Baroque palaces. To the west is the **Haus zum Ritter**, which was once the archbishop's palace but is now the Münster's song school. The **Wentzingerhaus** (Tues–Fri 9.30am–5pm, Sat & Sun 10.30am–5pm; €2 joint ticket with Augustinermuseum; Ⓦwww.msg-freiburg.de) to the east is named after the sculptor Christian Wentzinger who built it as his own residence. It features a resplendent Rococo staircase, complete with frescoed ceiling, while the back courtyard shelters huge allegorical statues of the Four Seasons by Wentzinger himself. The rest of the house is given over to displays on the history of Freiburg. Münsterplatz is closed on the far side by the canons' residences and the former **Hauptwache** (Guard House). The latter is now home to the Haus der Badischen Weine, where local vintages can be sampled and bought.

South of Münsterplatz

Following the main channel of the *Bächle* southwards, you come to the **Schwabentor**, one of two surviving towers of the medieval fortifications. On Oberlinden, just in front, is **Zum Roten Bären**, which is said to be Germany's oldest inn – a function it has held since 1311, although the building itself is two centuries older. The parallel **Konviktstrasse** has won conservation prizes for the restoration of its old houses.

Just to the west is Salzstrasse, which is lined with Baroque and Neoclassical mansions. Also here is the **Augustinermuseum** (Tues–Sun 10am–5pm; €2 joint ticket with Wentzingerhaus; Ⓦwww.augustinermuseum.de), which takes its name from the former monastery whose buildings it occupies. One of the most pleasing smaller collections in Germany, it makes an essential supplement to a visit to the Münster, containing as it does many works of art, such as gargoyles, statues and stained glass, which have been replaced *in situ* by copies to prevent further erosion. Also on show are examples of the religious art of the Upper Rhine, along with folklore displays on the Black Forest. There are also a few top-class old masters. Three panels of a Passion altar, including the central *Crucifixion*, constitute the most important surviving paintings by the great but mysterious draughtsman known as **Master of the Housebook**. *The Miracle of the Snow* by **Grünewald** is one of the wings of the altarpiece now in Stuppach: it depicts Pope Liberius laying the foundation stone of Santa Maria

Views of the city

It's well worth climbing one of the hills surrounding the city for the wonderful views they offer. The **Schlossberg** immediately to the east of the city centre is easily reached by a path from the Schwabentor. An alternative way up is by the **cable car** (€1.75 single, €3 return) from the Stadtgarten at the northeastern edge of the Altstadt. This summit also has the benefit of including close-range views of the Münster. For photography, it's best to come in the morning. Far higher, and thus with more spectacular panoramas, is the **Schauinsland** (1284m), still within the city boundaries but a good 15km southeast, reached by tram #4 to Günterstal, then bus #21. A series of marked nature trails comb the area, which is still inhabited by chamois, or you can ascend in fifteen minutes by **cable car** (€6.60 single, €10.20 return; Ⓦ www.bergwelt-schauinsland.de).

Maggiore in Rome, following a miraculous fall of snow on Midsummer's Day. As well as his stained glass, **Baldung** is represented by three typically unorthodox paintings, notably a *Cupid in Flight*, while there's a brightly coloured *Risen Christ* by **Cranach**.

South of here, on Marienstrasse, is the **Museum für Neue Kunst** (Tues–Sun 10am–5pm; €2; Ⓦ www.mnk-freiburg.de). Though it can't rival the richness of the parent collection, it does have a good cross-section of twentieth-century German painting. Beside it stands the Baroque **Adelhauserkirche**, retaining important works of art from its predecessor, notably a fourteenth-century crucifix. The former convent buildings now house the **Museum für Naturkunde** (Tues–Sun 10am–5pm; €2), which has a dazzling display of gems, and the **Museum für Völkerkunde** (same hours and ticket), with exhibits drawn from non-European cultures. From here, follow Fischerau, the former fishermen's street, and you come to the other surviving thirteenth-century tower, the **Martinstor**, which now stands in the middle of Freiburg's central axis, Kaiser-Joseph-Strasse.

The western quarters

Immediately west of here is the **Uni-Viertel** (university quarter), the liveliest part of the city during term-time and the best place to check out Freiburg's nightlife (see p.308). Alongside the inevitable modern buildings are several interesting older structures, including two Rococo mansions and a large Jugendstil lecture hall. On Bertoldstrasse, to the north, are the **Universitätskirche**, formerly the church of a Jesuit college, and the Baroque **Alte Universität.**

The **Neues Rathaus**, formed out of two separate Renaissance houses, one of which has an oriel adorned with a noble relief of *The Lady and the Unicorn*, was an earlier home of the university. It forms part of a shady chestnut tree-lined square whose other buildings include the **Altes Rathaus**, itself a fusion of several older buildings, and the plain Gothic Franciscan friary church of **St Martin**. A few minutes' walk to the west, in the Columbipark opposite the tourist office, is the **Columbischlössle**, a nineteenth-century villa built for a Spanish countess, which served after the war as parliament for the short-lived Land of South Baden (Südbaden). It now houses the **Museum für Ur- und Frühgeschichte** (Tues–Sun 10am–5pm; free, but donation requested), which has important archeological collections on the Black Forest region, particularly from the times of the Alemanni and the Franks; the treasury items in the basement are particularly worth seeing.

In the alley behind St Martin is the cheerful late Gothic facade of the **Haus zum Wallfisch**. For two years, this was the home of the great humanist **Desiderius Erasmus**, the most conciliatory and sympathetic of the leading figures of the Reformation period, who was forced to flee from his residence in Basel in the light of the turbulent religious struggles there. A late fifteenth-century palace nearby, on the main Kaiser-Joseph-Strasse, is known as the **Baseler Hof** as it served for nearly a century as the residence of the exiled cathedral chapter of the Swiss city.

Eating, drinking and entertainment

Freiburg is a wonderful place for food and drink, with **restaurants** and **bars** to cater for all tastes and pockets, the liveliest concentration clustered around the Uni-Viertel. Many of the leading restaurants are in the hotels (see pp.303–04); for snacks, the Markthalle, Kaiser-Joseph-Str. 237, is the best place to go. The city has a similarly eclectic choice of other entertainments.

Restaurants

Ganter Münsterplatz 18–20. Freiburg's largest brewery has recently re-established a city-centre Gaststätte after a long absence. There's a wide-ranging menu, as well as an unusual range of beers – a *Pils*, an unfiltered *Urtrunk* and a *Doppelbock* called *Wodan*.

Greiffenegg-Schlössle Schlossbergring 3. A good terrace restaurant, accessible by elevator.

Kleiner Meyerhof Rathausgasse 27. Small and select south German restaurant with good-value set lunches.

Klösterle Dreikönigstr. 8 ☎07 61/7 57 84. Small, highly regarded French restaurant southeast of the Altstadt, on the opposite side of the Dreisam; it specializes in organically raised beef and has a wide selection of Burgundy wines. Reservations necessary. Open Tues–Sat evenings only.

Milano Schusterstr. 7. Bargain-priced trattoria and ice cream parlour.

Salatstuben Löwenstr. 1. Vegetarian restaurant with self-service salad bars. In the past, it has been a daytime operation only, but is experimenting with evening opening Thurs–Sat. Closed Sun.

Schlossbergrestaurant Dattler Am Schlossberg 1. First choice for alfresco eating, with a terrace on top of the Schlossberg commanding a superb view of Freiburg and the Kaiserstuhl. Closed Tues.

Tessiner Stuben Bertoldstr. 17. Restaurant-cum-wine bar, complete with garden. Closed Sun.

Wolfshöhle Konviktstr. 8. One of the best Italian restaurants in the country. Closed Sun.

Zur Traube Schusterstr. 17. Quieter alternative to the wine bars on nearby Münsterplatz. Closed Mon lunchtime & Sun.

Bars, cafés and café-bars

Altstadt-Café Gerberau 12. This café specialises in wholemeal cakes.

Café Atlantik Schwabentorring 7. Run-down music pub serving very cheap food in the evenings.

Café Heinmetz Kaiser-Joseph-Str. 193. A fine traditional café, best-known for its home-made pralines and champagne truffles.

Café Journal Universitätsstr. 3. Popular if fairly expensive student hangout.

Feierling Gerberau 46. In addition to the fruity *Inselhopf* and *Inselweisse* beer brewed on the premises, imaginative meals are served, and in summer the large garden across the street is opened up.

Kleines Freiburger Brauhaus Moltkestr. 27. The smallest of the city's three Hausbrauereien produces an excellent *Roggenbier*.

Kornhaus Café Münsterplatz 11. *Kaffee und Kuchen* establishment in the historic setting of the Kornhaus.

Martins Bräu Martinsgässle 1. Hausbrauerei which makes dark, light and *Weizen* beers and also has a short but eclectic menu.

Schlappen Löwenstr. 2. Long-established but still very hip student pub.

Uni-Café Niemensstr. 7. The trendiest café with the Freiburg in-crowd; serves a wide selection of coffees and has good snacks.

Nightclubs

Agar Löwenstr. 8. This operates a different theme each evening (eg soul, the 80s, the 90s). Tues & Thurs 10pm–3am, Fri & Sat 11pm–4am, Sun 10pm–2am.

Exit Kaiser-Joseph-Str. 248. One of Freiburg's most popular clubs, with a predominantly young clientele.

Liquid Lounge Universitätsstr. 3. Tiny nightclub. Open Tues–Thurs 11pm–4pm, Sat & Sun 11pm–6am.

Freiburg's festivals

The **Fastnet** celebrations are among the best in Baden-Württemberg; there are burning ceremonies on the evening of Shrove Tuesday, as well as parades of jesters the day before. Both the **Frühlingsfest** in May and the **Herbstsfest** in October last for ten days, and include spectacular fairground amusements. In late June and early July, the two-week **Internationales Zeltmusikfest** features all varieties of music, performed under canvas. Later in the month, five days are given over to a wine market known as the **Weintagen**. Mid-August has the nine-day-long **Weinkost**, a sampling session for wines produced in the Freiburg region.

Theatre and concert venues

Jazzhaus Schnewlinstr. 1 ⓣ07 61/3 49 73, ⓦwww.jazzhaus.de. Freiburg now ranks as one of the leading German cities for jazz, thanks to this venue which has concerts every evening at 8.30pm.

Konzerthaus Konrad-Adenauer-Platz 1 ⓣ07 61/8 85 81 30, ⓦwww.konzerthaus-freiburg.de. State-of-the-art concert venue, with a large hall, the Grosser Saal, and a more intimate space, the Runder Saal. It regularly features performances by the renowned radio orchestra, the SWR Sinfonieorchester (ⓦwww.swr-freiburg.de), as well as by the Freiburger Philharmonisches Orchester and the period-instrument Freiburger Barockorchester (ⓦwww.barockorchester.de).

Theater Freiburg Bertoldstr. 46 ⓣ07 61/2 01 28 53, ⓦwww.theaterfreiburg.de. The city's main theatre venue featuring drama, dance and opera; there are three auditoria plus the Theatercafé where late-night cabaret and variety shows are held.

Breisach

BREISACH, whose historic heart is perched high above the Rhine on a promontory about 30km west of Freiburg, is an archetypal frontier post in what has been one of the most heavily disputed parts of Europe. Even if the river is now firmly established as a natural border and the town regarded as being indisputably German, the turbulent legacy of its past is still clearly visible. Breisach stands in the shadow of the **Kaiserstuhl**, an isolated volcanic mass in which Frederick Barbarossa, who died on his way to the Holy Land, is said to rest, waiting for his second coming – hence its name, which means "Emperor's Seat".

The Town

The lower town (Unterstadt) by the Rhine is modern – all the sights are located in the spacious, half-deserted upper town (Oberstadt), which is surrounded by the **Stadtbefestigung**, dating from the thirteenth century. The ramparts visible today bear the unmistakable stamp of the greatest of all military engineers, the Frenchman Sébastien Vauban, who was also responsible for laying out the town of Neuf Brisach on the opposite bank. Indeed, the monumental **Rheintor** at the northwest end of Breisach itself is as purely French a building as can be seen in Germany. Yet, just above it, the gabled medieval **Kapftor** could hardly be more German in feel, and the same applies to the earlier **Hagenbachtor** on the brow of the hill further south. Just beyond this is one of Breisach's many belvederes, offering grandstand views of France.

The Münster

Looming high above all else is the **Münster**. From outside, it's no beauty, fashioned out of rough, diffuse stonework, and truncated on the southern side in order to squeeze into an irregular, constricted space. It was originally built in the late Romanesque period on the foundations of a Roman fortress; the nave, transept and the two "Cock" towers survive from this time. The upper parts of the southern tower were re-fashioned in Gothic style in the early fourteenth century, a period which also saw the construction of a new chancel (under which is an open crypt – apparently the only one of its kind in the world) and the stumpy facade, whose tympanum illustrates the life of the Münster's patron, St Stephen. At the end of the fifteenth century, it was decided to commission new decorations for the interior of the Münster rather than rebuild it; as a result, it came to acquire one of the most impressive arrays of **works of art** of any church in Germany, all created at the transitional point between Gothic and Renaissance.

Filling the three walls of the west end is a huge **fresco cycle** of *The Last Judgement*, sadly very faded, by **Martin Schongauer**, the father-figure of the golden age of German art. Contemporary with the frescoes is the filigree **rood screen**. In the chapel beside it is a silver **shrine** containing the relics of the early martyr-saints Gervase and Protase, which were swiped from Milan at the same time as those of the Three Magi (which were taken to Cologne), and allegedly arrived in Breisach by miraculous means, whereupon they became the joint patrons of the town. The reliefs on the lid include an illustration of this journey, complete with a depiction of fifteenth-century Breisach.

The main **retable**, *The Coronation of the Virgin* is an astonishing piece of wholly eccentric yet hyper-skilled woodcarving. It may be late Gothic, but the entwined mass of cherubs, the swirling hair and drapery folds of the figures are uncannily anticipatory of the Baroque style of over a century later. Many attempts have been made to unmask the identity of the mysterious sculptor, known as **Master HL** after his cryptic signature, but to no conclusive effect. The sinuous upper part of the retable is by a more orthodox carver, but is still remarkable for the fact that it's actually higher than the ceiling, a trick achieved by means of a subtle slant.

Practicalities

Breisach's **Bahnhof** is at the southern end of town. The **tourist office** (May–Oct Mon–Fri 9am–5pm, Sat 10am–1pm, Sun 1–4pm; Nov–April Mon–Fri 9.30am–12.30pm & 1.30–5pm, Sat 10am–1pm; Ⓣ0 76 67/94 01 55, Ⓦwww.breisach.de) is at Marktplatz 16. Among the **hotels** are *Gasthof Bayrischer Hof*, Neutorstr. 25 (Ⓣ0 76 67/83 37 67, Ⓦwww.bayerischer-hof-breisach.de; ❸), *Kapuzinergarten*, Kapuzinergasse 26 (Ⓣ0 76 67/9 30 00, Ⓦwww.kapuzinergarten.de; ❹–❼), *Kaiserstühler Hof*, Richard-Müller-Str. 2 (Ⓣ0 76 67/8 30 60, Ⓦwww.kaiserstuehler-hof.de; ❻–❽), and *Am Münster*, Münsterbergstr. 23 (Ⓣ0 76 67/83 80, Ⓦwww.hotelammuenster.de ❼). All of these have good **restaurants**. The spanking-new **youth hostel** is by the river at Rheinuferstr. 12 (Ⓣ0 76 67/76 65; €15.30/18). Alternatively, there's a **campsite**, *Münsterblick* (Ⓣ0 76 67/9 39 30), in the village of Hochstetten 2km south.

The southern Black Forest

The southern part of the Black Forest is a highland region bordered to the west and south by the **River Rhine**, which also forms the frontiers with France and Switzerland. Its landscape of forested hills is especially fine around the peaks of the **Belchen** (1414m) and the **Feldberg** (1493m). Though hardly mountains in the Alpine sense, they offer vast panoramic views, reaching as far as the Swiss Alps and the western Rhine valley on clear days. Travel along the fringes of this area is easy and efficient by train; the interior, on the other hand, sometimes involves circuitous connections by infrequent bus services.

Münstertal and Belchen

MÜNSTERAL, the terminus of a branch railway from Freiburg, is a scattered community stretching all along the lush pastoral valley of the same name, which lies immediately below the north side of the Belchen. It's made up of several distinct hamlets and villages, as well as isolated farms with the steeply pitched shingle roofs characteristic of the Black Forest.

In the seventh century, Irish missionaries came to Christianize the Breisgau region, and the most famous, Saint Trudpert, was murdered in 643 after only three years of missionary work. The **Kloster St Trudpert**, which lies 1.5km up the valley from the Bahnhof, was founded in his memory by Benedictines around the turn of the ninth century, and remains the visual focus of the whole valley to this day. In 1918 it was taken over by the Josephschwestern order of nuns, and has served as their general headquarters since 1970. They extended the largely Baroque complex, notably by the addition of a large domed church clearly modelled on St Blasien (see p.313). Like most of the buildings, this can only be seen from outside, but the former **Klosterkirche** is now in parish use and freely accessible. It still preserves much of its Gothic outline, but was remodelled internally in the late seventeenth and early eighteenth centuries by a number of architects and decorators, notably Peter Thumb. White stuccowork predominates, with only the ceiling frescoes and side altars adding discreet colour. There is also an outstanding example of Romanesque craftsmanship in the niello **processional cross**, which dates back to the late twelfth century. Below and to the east of the church is the only other part of the complex open to the public, the **Brunnenkapelle** (or **Trudpertskapelle**), which was built on the site of the saint's martyrdom. It's the focal point of the big annual **pilgrimage**, which takes place on the Sunday after April 26.

Bus #291, which usually operates three times a day in each direction, runs from Bahnhof Münstertal past the Kloster and all the way up the valley, before ascending to the foothills of the **Belchen**, where it terminates. From here a **cable car** (€4 single, €5 return; ⓦwww.belchen-seilbahn.de) takes you to the summit. A trail round the top of the mountain, which takes around half-an-hour to walk, offers a changing series of long-range **views** in all directions.

The Münsterstal **tourist office** (May–Sept Mon–Fri 8.30am–12.30pm & 2–5.30pm, Sat 10am–noon; Oct–April Mon–Fri 8.30am–12.30pm & 2–5pm; ⓣ0 76 36/7 07 30, ⓦwww.muenstertal.de) is in the Rathaus, midway between the Bahnhof and the Kloster at Wasen 47. There are numerous **private houses** (❶–❷) all over the valley with rooms to let, as well as some enticing **hotels**, including *Café Sonne*, Krumlinden 44 (ⓣ0 76 36/3 19, ⓦwww.sonne-muenstertal.de; ❹), *Adler-Stube*, Münster 59 (ⓣ0 76 36/2 34, ⓦwww.adler-stube.de; ❻), and *Landgasthaus Zur Linde*, an inn with a 350-year-old tradition located a short distance up the valley from the Münster at Krumlinden 13 (ⓣ0 76 36/4 47, ⓦwww.landgasthaus.de; ❻). The last two of these have fine **restaurants**; another good place to eat is the daytime-only *Kreuz* in the Kloster grounds.

The Höllental, Feldberg and the lakes

The most atmospheric approach to the Feldberg region is by train from Freiburg. For the first leg of this, you pass through the narrow and formerly

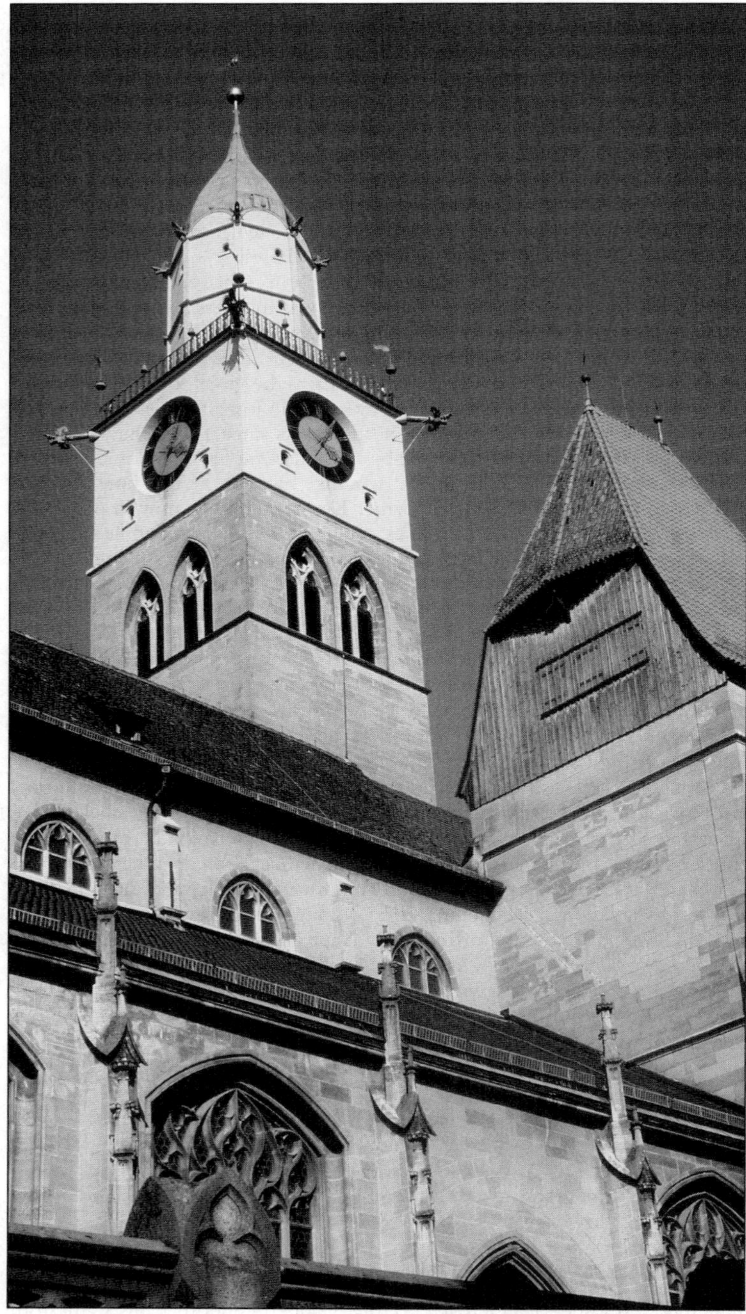

△ Münster towers, Überlinger

almost inaccessible **Höllental** (Hell Valley) gorge, which lies between Himmelreich and Hinterzarten. The track was first laid in 1887 by Robert Gerwig, who had earlier constructed the Schwarzwaldbahn (see p.318), and was an amazing technical achievement for the time, using a network of tunnels and viaducts. To appreciate both the scenery and the engineering, however, you really need to get out and walk along the footpath on the gorge's northern side; it takes about four hours to make a one-way trip.

TITISEE, the next stop after Hinterzarten, lies on the glacial lake of the same name, which is encircled by a footpath. It's a highly commercialized and inordinately popular summer resort, particularly with holidaymakers around retirement age. There's a huge range of accommodation possibilities, from small **guesthouses** (❷–❸) to such luxury **hotels** as *Parkhotel Waldeck*, Parkstr. 4–6 (ⓣ0 75 61/80 90, ⓦwww.parkhotelwaldeck.de; ❻–❽), and *Seehotel Wiesler*, Strandstr. 5 (ⓣ0 76 51/9 80 90, ⓦwww.seehotel-wiesler.de; ❼).

From Titisee, trains crawl uphill to **FELDBERG**, a federation of several constituent villages named after the Black Forest's highest mountain. One of these, **BÄRENTAL**, has Germany's highest mainline station, and is also well-endowed with **hotels**, which include *Waldhotel Zum Falken*, Feldbergstr. 1 (ⓣ0 76 55/93 35 00, ⓦwww.hotel-zum-falken.de; ❺); and *Adler*, Feldbergstr. 4 (ⓣ0 76 55/2 30, ⓦwww.adler-felberg.de; ❻). Buses run east to **FELDBERG-ORT**, which lies directly below the Feldberg itself. There's now a link by **cable car** (€4.70 single, €6 return) to the summit, as an alternative to the footpaths, one of which goes up via the **youth hostel** at Passhöhe 14 (ⓣ0 76 76/2 21; €14.20/16.90).

Trains descend from Bärental to **SCHLUCHSEE**, situated on the glacial lake of the same name, before terminating a couple of kilometres further on at the incorporated hamlet of **SEEBRUGG**, which has a decent beach with sailing and windsurfing facilities. Motorized boats aren't allowed on the lake, which makes for clean and pleasant swimming. There's a **youth hostel** at Im Wolfsgrund 28 in Schluchsee (ⓣ0 76 56/3 29; €14.20/16.90), plus a **campsite** (ⓣ0 76 56/77 39) and numerous **hotels**, the most prestigious being *Parkhotel Flora*, Sonnhalde 22 (ⓣ0 76 56/9 74 20, ⓦwww.parkhotel-flora.de; ❻–❽), and *Park Auerhahn*, Voderaha 4 (ⓣ0 76 56/9 74 50, ⓦwww.auerhahn.net; ❾). Seebrugg also has a hostel, at Haus 9 (ⓣ0 76 56/4 94; €14.20/16.90).

St Blasien

From Seebrugg's Bahnhof, there's a regular bus service south to the health resort of **ST BLASIEN**, which is centred on a monastery founded by Benedictine monks around the same time as St Trudpert. Burnt down a number of times, the **Klosterkirche** was given its present shape in 1768, when the local prince-abbot hired the Frenchman Michel d'Ixnard to design one of Germany's grandest classically inspired buildings. The great dome, carried by twenty Corinthian pillars, was modelled on St Peter's in Rome. Inside, the rotunda is a blaze of shining white marble. Regular classical **concerts**, often featuring performers of international quality, are held in the church from late June to early September, normally on Tuesdays and Saturdays at 8.15pm. A prestigious Jesuit-run school now occupies the monastic buildings.

The **tourist office** (Mon–Fri 9am–noon & 2–5pm, Sat 10am–noon; ⓣ0 76 72/4 14 30, ⓦwww.st-blasien.de) is at Am Kurgarten 1–3. There are plenty of **private rooms** (❷–❸), plus a good choice of **hotels**. These include *Café Kurgarten*, Fürstabt-Gebert-Str. 12 (ⓣ0 76 72/5 27; ❷–❹), *Dom*, Hauptstr. 4

(Ⓣ0 76 72/3 71 or 46 86, Ⓦwww.dom-hotel-st-blasien.de; ❹–❻), *Klosterhof*, Am Kurgarten 9 (Ⓣ0 76 72/5 23, Ⓦwww.hotel-klosterhof.com; ❺), and *Kehrwieder*, which occupies an imposing Jugendstil building high above town at Bützbergstr. 2 (Ⓣ0 76 72/5 06, Ⓦwww.hotel-kehrwieder.de; ❺). The last three of these all have good **restaurants**.

2 Blumberg and the Wutach valley

Towards the eastern edge of the southern Black Forest is a particularly beautiful valley, that of the **River Wutach**. The best base for exporing this is the town of **BLUMBERG**, which is most easily reached by the regular buses from Donaueschingen (see p.316), some of which continue onwards to the Swiss city of Schaffhausen.

Blumberg, or more precisely the Bahnhof in the incorporated village of Zollhaus, is the departure point for a truly amazing rail line, the **Wutachtalbahn** (Ⓦwww.wutachtalbahn.de or www.sauschwaenzlebahn.de), which is popularly known as the **Sauschwänzlebahn** ("Piggy's Tail Railway") because of the mazy course it pursues in its 25-kilometre-long journey to Weizen, which is less than 10km away as the crow flies. This is actually the surviving middle section of a strategic railway built in the late 1880s as a means of moving German troops to the front in an anticipated future war against France without having to pass through Swiss territory. It features numerous horseshoe curves, a bridge, three large viaducts and five tunnels, including the only spiral tunnel in Germany. Excursion services, almost invariably pulled by steam engines, run every Saturday and Sunday from May to mid-October, and variably on Wednesdays to Fridays as well (€10 single, €13 return).

The **Eisenbahnmuseum** (opened in conjunction with all arrivals and departures; free) within Bahnhof Zollhaus documents the history of the railway. Since 1999, the station has also been home to another remarkable technical monument, the elevated signal box on steel supports known as the **Reiterstellwerk**. An exact contemporary of the Sauschwänzlebahn and the last surviving example of its kind, it originally stood in Konstanz, where it bestrode one of the platforms. One more railway-related attraction is a 19-kilometre-long **marked footpath** known as the Eisenbahn Lehrpfad, which follows the Wutachtalbahn's course. Along the way are several good vantage points for photography. One of these is the *Vier-Bahnen-Blick* (Four Railways View) near Epfenhofen, a village which is virtually encircled by the first of the extravagant curves.

Just before the terminus at Weizen, the train crosses over the River Wutach, offering a very brief but tantalising glimpse of one of its loveliest stretches, the **Wutachflühen**. However, the most celebrated part of the valley is the gorge known as the **Wutachslucht**, the so-called "Grand Canyon" of the Black Forest, which lies to the west of Blumberg, and is best entered from the B315 road between the towns of Bonndorf and Löffingen. It's a popular hiking destination, with three main trails whose total length amounts to 35km.

Blumberg's **tourist office** (Mon & Wed 8.30am–noon, Tues 8.30am–noon & 2–4pm, Thurs 8.30am–noon & 2–6pm, Fri 8.30am–1pm; Ⓣ0 77 02/5 10, Ⓦww.stadt-blumberg.de) is at Hauptstr. 97. There's one **hotel** in the town centre: *Gasthof Hirschen*, Hauptstr. 72 (Ⓣ0 77 02/26 57, Ⓦwww.hirschen-blumberg.de; ❹–❻). Two other establishments lie just south of Bahnhof Zollhaus: *Taverna Korfu Adler Post*, Schaffhauser Str. 23 (Ⓣ0 77 02/41 97 86; ❸), and *Kranz*, Schaffhauser Str. 11 (Ⓣ0 77 02/4 30 86, Ⓦwww

.hotel-kranz-blumberg.de; ❺). All of these have **restaurants**, though the most popular place to eat is *Gasthaus Zum Stellwerk*, by the bus stop immediately opposite the station entrance.

Weil am Rhein

Just 8km north of the Swiss city of Basel on the main rail line to Freiburg is the small industrial town of **WEIL AM RHEIN**, whose name is indelibly associated with Vitra, one of the leading players in contemporary international design. The company headquarters are on the other side of the border, but it has a large production base in a green belt site in the north of Weil, reached from the town centre by buses #12, #15 and #55. There's a major visitor attraction here in the **Vitra Design Museum** (Tues–Sun 11am–6pm; €5.50; Ⓦwww.design-museum.de), which presents its diverse holdings of industrially produced furniture and other design objects of the past two centuries in a series of changing exhibitions. However, in many ways the building itself is the main draw – it's a startlingly audacious construction by the Californian-based Frank O. Gehry, clearly anticipating his later commission for the Guggenheim Museum in Bilbao, which catapulted him to the status of the world's most fêted contemporary architect. **Guided tours** (Tues–Sun at noon & 2pm; €7, or €11 joint ticket with the museum) of the rest of the site take in factory buildings by Nicholas Grimshaw and Alvaro Siza; the conference pavilion by Tadao Ando; and the fire station by Zaha Hadid. These depart from the museum entrance, last around two hours and are in German only.

A further 1.5km north is the incorporated wine village of Haltingen, terminus of one more of the Black Forest's celebrated railways, the **Kandertalbahn** (€4 single, €7 return; Ⓦwww.kandertalbahn.de). This 13-kilometre-long line along the valley of the River Kander to the health resort of Kandern is now serviced solely by excursion steam trains; these usually run every Sunday from May to October, with occasional extra departures at other times.

The centre of Weil is well-equipped with **hotels**; among the best are the sixteenth-century *Zur Krone*, Hauptstr. 58 (Ⓣ0 76 21/7 11 64, Ⓦwww.kroneweil.de; ❺), *Schwanen*, Hauptstr. 121 (Ⓣ0 76 21/7 10 47, Ⓦwww.schwanen-weil.de; ❻), and *Adler*, Hauptstr. 139 (Ⓣ0 76 21/9 82 30, Ⓦwww.adler-weil.de; ❼). There are also a couple of enticing alternatives in Haltingen: *Rebstock*, Grosse Gasse 30 (Ⓣ0 76 21/96 49 60, Ⓦwww.rebstock-haltingen.de; ❻), and *Zur Krone*, Burgunderstr. 21 (Ⓣ0 76 21/6 22 03, Ⓦwww.krone-haltingen.de; ❼). All of these have fine **restaurants**, with *Adler* being of gourmet status.

The central Black Forest

The central part of the Black Forest is the one most enshrined in popular imagination. This is the land of cuckoo clocks, of huge balconied farmsteads with hipped roofs, and of some of the world's most outrageous headgear: the *Schäppelkrone*, a "crown" made from hundreds of coloured glass beads and ribbons, and the *Bollenhut*, the woollen pom-pom hat whose colour indicates the wearer's marital status (red for unmarried, black for married). As a result, it's hardly surprising that this is the part of the forest which has gone in most for the tourist hard-sell, and is consequently the most spoiled, with a surfeit of tacky souvenir shops as well as an abundance of accommodation, and a highly developed network of trains and buses. Nonetheless, it's easy enough to escape from the organized tour groups, while the good communications make travel by public transport a pain-free experience.

Donaueschingen

Gateway to the central Black Forest is the rail junction of **DONAUESCHINGEN,** which lies some 50km northwest of the Bodensee on the windswept Baar plateau. Both its name and fame are due to its status as the official source of one of the world's most celebrated rivers, the **Danube** (Donau), though it's also of note as a well-preserved example of a tinpot princely capital. Initially, the harsh climate militated against its growth – it was no more than a hamlet until the 1720s when Prince Joseph Wilhelm Ernst of the **Fürstenberg** dynasty descended from his feudal castle in the hills above to begin the planning of a new courtly town.

Immediately south of the town centre is the **Schlosspark**, where a grandiose early nineteenth century fountain has been erected around the **Donauquelle**, a very unassuming spring credited as being the source of the Danube. The **Schloss** (guided tours April–Sept daily at 1pm, 2.30pm & 3.30pm; €10; Ⓦwww.fuerstenberg-kultur.de) is actually a fairly unassuming Baroque building at the far end of its park; much of the interior was modernized in *belle époque* style at the end of the nineteenth century. Its trappings are typical: Brussels tapestries, assorted objets d'art and family portraits. Among the portraits, there's one surprise – *Max Egon* was painted by the English artist Graham Sutherland. The sitter kept up the family tradition of musical patronage (Mozart and Liszt had both been guests) by establishing a **festival** now known as the Donaueschinger Musiktage. Held each October in the modern Donauhalle at the western end of town, this focuses on the work of contemporary composers. Many of the twentieth century's leading musicians – including Stravinsky, Hindemith, Boulez and Stockhausen – had works premiered there.

The main family treasures, known as the **Fürstenberg-Sammlungen** (Tues–Sat 10am–1pm & 2–5pm, Sun 10am–5pm; €5; Ⓦwww.fuerstenberg-kultur.de), are housed in a building on Karlsplatz, a Baroque square situated over the main road directly behind the Schloss. Here various zoological and mineralogical collections are set out in the old-fashioned manner of cabinets of curiosities. There's also a room devoted to the history of the Fürstenbergs, complete with their ceremonial coach and sleighs. On loan to the museum is the Pisces-Collection, which consists of around 170 works by 21 different international artists of the 1980s and 1990s.

On a terrace to the side of the Schloss is the twin-towered **Johanniskirche**, whose restrained Baroque style is reminiscent of the churches then being built in Bohemia, rather than elsewhere in southern Germany. In the nave there's a wooden *Madonna* by the eccentric **Master HL** which predates the building by over two hundred years.

Other than these obvious attractions, all closely grouped together, Donaueschingen doesn't have much in the way of sights. However, several streets are good examples of period pieces. An example is **Josefstrasse**, which is lined by stately Baroque and Neoclassical mansions. The outbuildings of the court are found on Haldenstrasse; the library here possesses one of the three original thirteenth-century manuscript versions of *The Nibelungenlied*. Though this street is now tucked away between the town centre and the Brigach, it's easily located by the chimneys of the **Fürstenberg-Brauerei**, one of the most famous breweries in Germany. In its present form it dates back to 1705, but the family's initial beer-making rights were granted in the thirteenth century.

Practicalities

Donaueschingen's **Bahnhof** is southwest of the town centre, west of the Schlosspark. The **tourist office** (Mon–Fri 8am–noon & 2–5/6pm, Sat 9am–noon; ⓣ07 71/85 72 21, ⓦwww.donaueschingen.de) is at Karlstr. 58. Here you can pick up a list of **private houses** (❶–❷) with rooms to let. Among the town's hotels are *Zum Hirschen*, Herdstr. 5 (ⓣ07 71/8 98 55 80, ⓦwww.hotel-zum-hirschen.de; ❹), *Linde*, Karlstr. 18 (ⓣ07 71/8 31 80, ⓦwww.hotel-linde-donaueschingen.de; ❺), and *Zur Sonne*, Karlstr. 38 (ⓣ07 71/8 31 30; ❻). Though there's no hostel, an HI card will bring a reduction at the *Naturfreundehaus*, Am Wolterdinger Str. 72 (ⓣ07 71/29 85; ❷), which has individual rooms rather than dorms. The **campsite** (ⓣ07 71/55 11, ⓦwww.riedsee-camping.de) is 8km away on the banks of the Riedsee. All the hotels mentioned above have good **restaurants**, though the obvious place to sample the products of the local brewery (whose *Pils* is one of Germany's best) is its *Bräustüble*, which is housed in a pink Baroque palace on Postplatz.

Villingen-Schwenningen

Created as recently as 1972, the double town of **VILLINGEN-SCHWENNINGEN**, some 15km north of Donaueschingen, is a decidedly curious union, as its two constituent parts belonged for centuries to different countries: Villingen, on the very fringe of the Black Forest, was Austrian before being allocated by Napoleon to Baden, while Schwenningen, set on the Baar plateau, was part of Württemberg. Villingen, much the more attractive of the two, really comes to life during the Shrovetide celebrations of **Fastnet**, which rival those of Rottweil (see box on p.277) as the best in southern Germany.

At other times, Villingen is a busy enough market town, its pristine houses set behind the medieval **Stadtmauer**, of which several sections, including three towers and three impressive gates, survive. The huge **Münster** provides a central focus, particularly the two tall flamboyant towers of the late Gothic chancel, which was tacked on to the Romanesque nave when its predecessor burned down. Unfortunately the interior was completely redecorated – none too successfully – in the eighteenth century, but compensation comes in the variety of colourful mansions which form Münsterplatz. These include the Romanesque **Rabenscheuer** to the north and the gabled Gothic **Altes Rathaus** to the west. Also worth a visit is the **Franziskaner-Museum** (Tues–Sat 10am–noon & 1–5pm, Sun 1–5pm; €2.50) at Rietstr. 39 in the former Franciscan friary on the western edge of the Altstadt, which has comprehensive collections of material on the prehistory, archeology, folklore, crafts and sacred art of the Black Forest.

Villingen's **Bahnhof** is just east of the Altstadt, on the opposite side of the River Brigach. The **tourist office** (Mon & Wed–Fri 9am–5.30pm, Tues 9am–7pm, Sat 9.30am–12.30pm, Sun 1–3pm; ⓣ0 77 21/82 23 40, ⓦwww.villingen-schwenningen.de) is at Niedere Str. 88. There's a reasonable supply of **private rooms** (❶–❸) in the town. The **youth hostel** in the very north of Villingen at St Georgener Str. 36 (ⓣ0 77 21/5 41 49; €13.20/15.90). Among the **hotels**, the most central are *Gasthaus Zum Schlachthof*, Schlachthausstr. 11 (ⓣ07721/9 82 90, ⓦwww.pro-gast-hotels.de; ❹), and *Bären*, Bärengasse 2 (ⓣ0 77 21/5 55 41, ⓦwww.pro-gast-hotels.de; ❻). A good choice for **eating** is the *Ratskeller* in the Oberes Tor, which also has a beer garden.

The Schwarzwaldbahn

Villingen is the terminus for one of the most spectacular rail lines in Europe, the **Schwarzwaldbahn** to Offenburg in the Rhine valley. Laid out between 1863 and 1873, this line successively follows the valleys of the Brigach, Gutach and Kinzig rivers, cutting through what had hitherto been impenetrable countryside, and was intended as a major prestige project by the Grand Duchy of Baden, which was always keen to present itself at the forefront of German progressiveness. It was built by the nation's most celebrated railway engineer, Robert Gerwig, who later went on to construct the St Gotthard route over the Alps, as well as another Black Forest line, the Höllentalbahn. The nature of the terrain posed technical problems which had never previously been tackled, notably the need to climb a gradient of 448m in the short distance of 11km. To achieve this, Gerwig built 36 tunnels through the mountains, plus a series of daring hairpin bends. Two of these – the narrow, deep and rocky stages between St Georgen and Triberg, and between Triberg and Hornberg – involve the rail line virtually doubling back on itself to traverse the gradient.

Triberg

Heart of the central part of the Black Forest is the little town of **TRIBERG**, which lies at an altitude of 1000m, 25km northwest of Villingen. It's a renowned health resort, with the forest acting as a dust filter, ensuring particularly pure air. Some of the most imposing scenery in the region is nearby, and Triberg itself makes a good base for a day or two's relaxation. Prime attraction is the **Gutacher Wasserfall** at the top end of town. At 162m, it ranks as the highest waterfall in Germany and is undeniably impressive, even though it plunges in seven separate stages instead of a single dramatic dive. Unfortunately, in a reverse of the normal German penchant for unrestricted access to nature, it's sealed off, with a €1.50 levy for admission.

The **Schwarzwald-Museum** (April to mid-Nov daily 10am–5pm; mid-Nov to March Tues–Sun 10am–5pm; €3.50; Ⓦwww.schwarzwaldmuseum.de) on Wallfahrtstrasse offers fascinating insights into the rural culture of the Black Forest as it was – and, to some extent, still is. There's a fine group of woodcarvings by the rustic local artist Karl Josef Fortwängler, who depicted the thick-set country bumpkins of the area in an idiosyncratic yet highly sympathetic manner. In addition, there's a large model of the Schwarzwaldbahn, while music boxes, clocks and examples of the traditional dress for carnivals and everyday wear complete the display. Further up the hill is the Baroque **Wallfahrtskirche St Maria in den Tannen**, whose painting of *The Virgin of the Pines* draws pilgrims for its allegedly miraculous qualities.

Arriving at Triberg's **Bahnhof** is a strange experience. As there's nothing but cliffs on either side of the narrow tracks it's easy to understand the derivation of the town's name, a corruption of "three mountains", after the peaks which surround it. It's a fifteen-minute walk uphill to the centre. The **tourist office** (May–Sept Mon–Fri 8am–noon & 2–5pm, Sat 10am–noon; Oct–April Mon–Fri only; Ⓣ0 77 22/95 32 30, Ⓦwww.triberg.de) is in the Kurverwaltung, Luisenstr. 10. **Hotels** include *Zum Bären*, Hauptstr. 10 (Ⓣ0 77 22/44 93; ❸), *Central,* Hauptstr. 64 (Ⓣ0 77 22/43 60, Ⓦwww.triberg-hotel-central.com; ❹), and *Ketterer,* Friedrichstr. 7–11 (Ⓣ0 77 22/86 05 80, Ⓦwww.hotel-ketterer.de; ❹), all of which have restaurants. Top of the range is *Parkhotel Wehrle,* Garbanstr. 24 (Ⓣ0 77 22/8 60 20; ❼–❾), which is set in its own park, and has a gourmet restaurant, *Ochsenstube*, plus the more affordable

Alte Schmiede. The **youth hostel** is high in the hills at Rohrbacher Str. 35 (Ⓣ0 77 22/41 10; €14.20 /16.90); a bus will take you as far as the waterfall and then it's a very steep twenty-minute climb.

The Gutach valley

The **Gutach valley** north of Triberg is best known as the home of the traditional *Bollenhut* hat. At **HORNBERG**, the Schwarzwaldbahn emerges into a light and airy landscape again and traverses a huge viaduct. There's a fine view of the ensemble of town and rail line from the ruined Burg set high on a hill to the west.

A few kilometres north is the town of **GUTACH** itself, outside which is the **Schwarzwälder Freilichtmuseum** (late March–early Nov daily 9am–6pm; €4.50; Ⓦwww.vogtsbauernhof.org), a collection of buildings from the region. Centrepiece is what's probably the most famous house in the Black Forest, the late sixteenth-century **Vogtsbauernhof**. With its huge sloping roof and tiered facade, it's an outstanding example of the characteristic vernacular building style of the region. This was the original farmhouse on the site, whereas the various other exhibits have been moved in from other locations. There are four more farmsteads, along with a wooden chapel and all kinds of workshops – smithies, granaries, a bakehouse, a distillery and various types of mills. Displays on the folklore and lifestyle of the region are also featured, and there are demonstrations of old crafts.

Alpirsbach

The next stop along the rail line, Hausach, is the junction of the Schwarzwaldbahn with the Kinzigtalbahn; this is also the place where the Gutach merges with the **Kinzig**. The most notable destination in the latter's valley is **ALPIRSBACH**, some 30km upstream from the confluence, which clusters around the former **Kloster**. Begun in the late twelfth century, the **Klosterkirche**, which is now a Protestant parish church, preserves much of the simple, pure Romanesque form characteristic of the style of building championed at Hirsau (see p.322). The east end is especially notable – later Gothic masons ingeniously perched the chancel above the existing storey. Only one tower was built, however, and this was not finished until the Renaissance period, when it received an unusual gabled top. **Guided tours** (mid-March to Oct Mon–Sat 9.30am–5.30pm, Sun 11am–5.30pm; Nov to mid-March Thurs, Sat & Sun 1.30–3pm; €2.50, Ⓦwww.schloesser-und-gaerten.de) are run round the monastic buildings and the late Gothic cloisters which are often used for open-air concerts in summer. The new **Klostermuseum** (same hours and ticket) displays clothes and other objects belonging to pupils who studied at the Kloster's school in the sixteenth century. Alongside, at Martkplatz 1, is the former monastic brewery, the **Klosterbräu** (guided tours Easter to mid-Sept Sat & Sun at 3pm, on other days according to demand; €3; Ⓦwww.alpirsbacher.de), which makes a wide variety of excellent beers. Handsome half-timbered buildings, most notably the **Rathaus**, decorate the centre of Alpirsbach.

Alpirsbach's **Bahnhof** is at the southern edge of the town centre. The **tourist office** (Mon–Fri 9am–noon & 2–6pm, Sat 9am–noon; Ⓣ0 74 44/9 51 62 81, Ⓦwww.alpirsbach.de) is in the Kurverwaltung, Hauptstr. 20. There are plenty of reasonably priced **pensions** (❶–❸); a **youth hostel** high on the Sulzberg at Reinerzauer Steige 80 (Ⓣ0 74 44/24 77; €14.20/ 16.90); and a **campsite** at Grenzenbühler Weg 18 (Ⓣ0 74 44/63 13, Ⓦwww.camping-alpirsbach.de) in the incorporated village of Ehlenbogen to the north. **Hotels** include *Rössle*, Aischbachstr. 5 (Ⓣ0 74 44/22 81, Ⓦwww.roessle-alpirsbach.de; ❹), *Gasthof Waldhorn,* Kreuzgasse 4 (Ⓣ0 74 44/9 51 10, Ⓦwww.alpirsbach.com/waldhorn; ❹), and *Schwanen-Post*, Marktstr. 5 (Ⓣ0 74 44/22 05, Ⓦwww.schwanen-post.de; ❺).

The northern Black Forest

To non-Germans, the northern stretch of the Black Forest, most of which belonged to Württemberg rather than Baden, is the least familiar part. Yet here are some of the most imposing landscapes – the forest really does look at its blackest and is cut by several deep, dark valleys which provide the strongest possible contrast to the long panoramic views from the hills. There are three main **touring routes**, each offering a widely varying choice of scenery: the Black Forest Highway, the Black Forest Valley Road and the circuitous Black Forest Spa Road. Walking or cycling are the best ways of **getting around**, but superb scenic rail lines, closely hugging the river valleys, enable all of the second and part of the third of these routes to be followed by even the most sedentary. Buses fill in the gaps, though the frequency of these varies considerably according to season, often drying up altogether in the winter months.

Freudenstadt

The hub of the transport system of the northern Black Forest is **FREUDENSTADT**, situated at high altitude on a plateau bordered by the rivers Murg and Kinzig. It was founded in 1599 by Duke Friedrich I, who charged an Italian-trained architect, Heinrich Schickhardt, with designing Württemberg's first planned town, one earmarked to become its "secret" capital. It was duly laid out in the form of a vast Roman camp centred on a spaciously grandiose central square. Despite its name, which means "town of joy", Freudenstadt has been dogged by ill-luck: it was devastated by epidemic and fire within 35 years of its birth, and quickly lost all importance. Two weeks before the end of World War II, all but a couple of streets were destroyed in an attack by French forces. Within five years, however, it had been completely rebuilt to the old plans – a stunning achievement, even by the standards of German postwar reconstruction.

The **Marktplatz** must have seemed extraordinary when it was first built; it's an impressive sight even to the modern eye which is far more attuned to the large-scale, and it still ranks as much the biggest square in Germany. Although the Schloss which was intended for the middle of the square was never built, there are two important public buildings, the **Rathaus** and the **Stadtkirche**, at diagonally opposite ends. The latter is particularly intriguing, built in an L-shape so that the men and women of the congregation could be segregated. Indeed, the arrangement meant they could not even see each other – the better to keep their minds on the sermon. The church houses a magnificent polychrome wooden **lectern** made around 1150, which bears large statues of the Four Evangelists and their symbols. It's unique of its kind and one of the most important pieces of Romanesque church furniture to have survived. Along with the **font**, made half a century earlier and adorned with carvings of symbolical animals, it presumably came from one of the Black Forest monasteries.

Practicalities

There are two train stations: the **Stadtbahnhof**, on the Murgtalbahn, is just a few minutes' walk north of Marktplatz and has the **bus terminus** just outside, whereas the **Hauptbahnhof** is at the eastern edge of town, at a much lower altitude. The **tourist office** (April–Oct Mon–Fri 9am–6pm, Sat & Sun 10am–2pm; Nov–March Mon–Fri 10am–5pm, Sat 10am–1pm, Sun 11am–1pm; ⓣ0 74 41/86 47 30, ⓦwww.freudenstadt.de) is at Marktplatz 64.

Hotels and **pensions** are scattered all over town; for the lowest rates, try the concentration on Lauterbadstrasse. For something a bit more upmarket there's *Adler*, Forstr. 15–17 (ⓣ0 74 41/9 15 20, ⓦwww.adler-fds.de; ❹), *Jägerstüble*, Marktplatz 12 (ⓣ0 74 41/23 87, ⓦwww.jaegerstueble-fds.de; ❺), *Zum Warteck*, Stuttgarter Str. 14 (ⓣ0 74 41/9 19 20, ⓦwww.warteck-freudenstadt.de; ❺), and *Bären*, Lange Str. 33 (ⓣ0 74 41/27 29, ⓦwww.hotel-baeren-freudenstadt.de; ❻). Alternatively, the **youth hostel** is at Eugen-Nägele-Str. 69 (ⓣ0 74 41/77 20; €14.20/16.90), not far from the Stadtbahnhof, while the **campsite**, *Langenwald* (ⓣ0 74 41/28 62), is 3km to the west. All the hotels listed above have recommendable **restaurants**: *Jägerstüble* is perhaps the best value, while *Zum Warteck* scores for quality.

The Black Forest Highway

The **Black Forest Highway** (Schwarzwald–Hochstrasse), linking Freudenstadt with Baden-Baden, is one of Germany's most famous roads. In summer, buses run daily in each direction along this 60km stretch, which has no villages to speak of. However, there are plenty of **hotels**, many with spa facilities and nearly all on the expensive side. One of the most reasonably priced is *Berghotel Mummelsee* on the shore of the tiny Mummelsee (ⓣ0 78 2/9 92 86, ⓦwww.berghotel-mummelsee.de; ❻). In addition, there's a single **youth hostel**, *Zuflucht* (ⓣ0 78 04/6 11; €14.20/16.90), located at a particularly scenic point just off the main road 19km north of Freudenstadt. It makes an excellent base for hiking in summer and for skiing in winter. Walking along the accompanying trail is really much the best way to see the area, which is pocked with belvederes offering vast panoramas towards the Rhine and the French Vosges.

Just beyond the hostel is the **Buhlbachsee**, the first of several tiny natural lakes along the highway. Before this, however, is a by-road leading west to Oppenau which joins with another fine scenic road running north to the valley of **ALLERHEILIGEN**, rejoining the Hochstrasse at Ruhestein. Allerheiligen has the ruins of a former Premonstratensian **Kloster**, the first Gothic building in southwest Germany, probably built by the same team of masons as Strasbourg Cathedral. There's also an impressively curling stepped **waterfall** and a good restaurant, the *Klosterhof*, which makes its own fruit wines and liqueurs.

East of Ruhestein is the **Wildsee**, but the most celebrated of the lakes is the **Mummelsee** a further 8km north. It stands at the foot of the Hornigsrinde (1164m), the highest point in the northern Black Forest, offering a particularly outstanding view. The Mummelsee itself, now a popular boating centre, is allegedly haunted by water-sprites and by the luckless King Ulmon, who was condemned by a sorceress to live for a thousand years, in spite of his continuous pleas to be released to join his friends in the afterlife. This legend has proved a potent inspiration for many German writers and formed the subject of one of Eduard Mörike's most evocative poems. It's often necessary to change buses here, particularly out of season when there are no through services.

The Murg valley

The **Murg valley** north of Freudenstadt is the second stage of the Black Forest Valley Road (Schwarzwald–Tälerstrasse). This is the only one of the three scenic routes which doesn't officially begin at Freudenstadt, its first stretch being the Kinzig valley from Alpirsbach.

What is arguably the most scenic of all the region's rail lines, the 60km **Murgtalbahn line** to Rastatt, follows a parallel course to the road. Though never more than a modest stretch of water, the River Murg cleaves an impressively grand valley in its downward journey towards its confluence with the Rhine.

All the little towns along the Murg have impressive settings, and make good bases for exploring an underrated part of the Black Forest. Particularly worthy of mention is **FORBACH**, about halfway along the line, which has a wonderful sixteenth-century single-span covered wooden bridge, the largest of its type in Europe. West of town is some fine countryside, with the artifical **Schwarzenbach Stausee**, a watersports centre, and the tiny **Herrenwieser See**; bus #246 runs directly to the former, and continues on to the Mummelsee (see p.321) at weekends. There's a **youth hostel** just to the north of Forbach at Birket 1 (ⓣ0 72 28/24 27; €13.20/15.90) and another at Haus no. 33 in the incorporated village of Herrenwies (ⓣ0 72 26/2 57, ⓕ13 18; €16.90/14.50), which also has a **campsite** (ⓣ0 72 26/4 11, ⓦwww.herrenwies.de). Forbach itself has plenty of **private rooms** and **pensions** (❶–❸). Right beside the town's famous bridge are two contrasting **hotels**, both with restaurants: *Gasthof Zum Löwen*, Hauptstr. 9 (ⓣ0 72 26/22 29; ❷), is a real bargain, particularly as all rooms have balconies and rustic Black Forest furniture; *Goldener Hirsch*, Hauptstr. 2 (ⓣ0 72 26/22 18; ❻), is a luxury establishment with good bathing facilites.

Calw and the Nagold valley

Much the most impressive stretch of the Black Forest Spa Road (Schwarzwald–Bäderstrasse) is the wonderfully dark, secret **Nagold valley**. The Nagoldtalbahn, which runs most of the way alongside it, begins at the rail junction of Horb, which has connections to Stuttgart, Tübingen and Rottweil, but there's also a branch line to Freudenstadt which links up 6km further north, at Eutingen.

"The most beautiful town of all that I know," was how Hermann Hesse described **CALW**, the old textile centre which is the focal point of this valley. The eulogy needn't be taken too seriously – his judgement was more than a little bit coloured by the fact that he happened to have been born and bred there, though he eventually went into exile in Switzerland. Fans of Hesse's novels will certainly want to come here to see his birthplace at Marktplatz 30, now designated the **Hermann-Hesse-Museum** (Tues, Wed & Fri–Sun 11am–5pm, Thurs 11am–7pm; €5), and containing memorabilia of the writer. Calw also boasts an impressive array of half-timbered houses, mostly dating from the late seventeenth and early eighteenth centuries, just after a fire had destroyed the medieval town. One of the few older monuments is the **Nikolausbrücke** from around 1400, which incorporates a picturesque little votive chapel. Hesse, true to form, considered the bridge and the square on its west bank to form an assemblage superior to the Piazza del Duomo in Florence.

HIRSAU, 2km downstream, is now a small health resort and officially part of Calw, but actually has a far longer history. Its Benedictine **Kloster**, indeed, was once the most powerful monastery in Germany, serving as mother-house to a host of dependent congregations and initiating a highly influential reform movement whose main effect was to free religious houses from the clutches of secular patrons, placing them instead under the direct control of the pope. The simple, original monastic church is tucked away in amongst a number of much later buildings, not far from the bridge over the Nagold. A ninth-century Carolingian structure, it was rebuilt in the mid-eleventh century, and now serves as the Catholic parish church of **St Aurelius**. To the rear is the **Klostermuseum** (April–Oct Tues–Sun 2–5pm; Nov–March Sat & Sun 2–5pm; €1.50), which contains local finds plus documentation. The eleventh-century monastic complex, built in warm red sandstone, was directly modelled on the most famous and powerful European monastery of the day – that of Cluny in Burgundy – on sloping ground above the west bank of the Nagold. Almost completely destroyed by the French in the War of the Palatinate Succession, only the **Eulenturm** (Owl Tower), originally one of a pair, survives from this epoch. However, there are also fragments from later building periods, notably the late fifteenth-century **cloisters**, the early sixteenth-century **Marienkapelle** (now restored to serve as the Protestant church), and the Renaissance **Jagdschloss** of the dukes of Württemberg, who expelled the monks after the Reformation, taking over the land as pleasure and hunting grounds.

Practicalities

Calw's **tourist office** is at Marktbrücke (May–Sept Mon–Fri 9am–12.30pm & 2–5pm, Sat 9.30am–12.30pm; Oct–April Mon–Fri only; ⓣ0 70 51/96 88 10, ⓦwww.calw.de). There are three **hotels** in the centre of Calw: *Alte Post*, Bahnhofstr. 1 (ⓣ0 70 51/21 96; ❸), *Ratsstube*, Marktplatz 12 (ⓣ0 70 51/9 20 50; ❹), and *Rössle*, Hermann-Hesse-Platz 2 (ⓣ0 70 51/7 90 00, ⓦwww.roessle-calw.de; ❺). Slightly more upmarket is *Kloster Hirsau*, Wildbadstr. 2 (ⓣ0 70 51/9 67 40, ⓦwww.hotel-kloster-hirsau.de; ❻) in Hirsau. Each of these, with the exception of the first-named, has a **restaurant.** The *Schwarzwaldblick* **campsite** is located high above town at Weidenheige 54/1 (ⓣ0 70 51/1 28 45, ⓦwww.camping-schwarzwald-blick.de); alternatives can be found in the outlying villages of Stammheim (ⓣ0 70 51/48 44, ⓦwww.camp-obermuehle.de) and Altburg (ⓣ0 70 51/5 07 88, ⓕ51419).

Tiefenbronn

TIEFENBRONN, an unassuming-looking village situated at the extreme edge of the Black Forest in the peaceful valley of the River Würm, 12km southeast of the rail junction of Pforzheim (to which it is linked by bus #666), has two claims to fame. First, it's a renowned gastronomic centre: people come from Stuttgart and beyond in order to eat at the *Ochsen-Post*, Franz-Josef-Gall-Str. 13 (ⓣ0 72 34/9 54 50, ⓦwww.ochsen-post.de; ❻), a **hotel** in a seventeenth-century timber-framed building. The main restaurant, one of the best in southern Germany, is expensive, but the *Bauernstuben*, open evenings only, is more affordable.

The other reason to visit is the fourteenth-century Gothic church of **St Maria Magdalena**. Architecturally, it's very ordinary indeed, yet it contains a magnificent array of works of art which put to shame those in most cathedrals. Jewel-like **stained-glass windows**, made in Strasbourg around 1370, illuminate the choir, and there are fifteenth-century **murals** throughout the church, including a depiction of the Last Judgment, a frieze of coats of arms and portraits of the family who provided the endowments. The high altar tells the story of the Passion and has panels of the Nativity on the reverse.

However, this is outclassed by the **altar** dedicated to the local patron saint, which is housed in the southern aisle. One of the most beautiful of all European Gothic paintings, it bears a curious inscription: "Weep, Art, weep and lament loudly, nobody nowadays wants you, so alas, 1432. Lucas Moser, painter of Wyl, master of this work, pray God for him." Nothing is known about the embittered **Lucas Moser**, whose style seems oddly modern for its day. The first German painting to try a realistic approach, including a sense of perspective, it still has all the grace and delicacy characteristic of the earlier Soft Style. It shows Mary Magdalene washing Christ's feet, her miraculous journey in a ship without sail or rudder to Marseille, her stay there and her last Communion in the cathedral of Aix-en-Provence.

Baden-Baden

It is an inane town, full of sham, and petty fraud, and snobbery, but the baths are good ... I had had twinges of rheumatism unceasingly during three years, but the last one departed after a fortnight's bathing there, and I have never had one since. I fully believe I left my rheumatism in Baden-Baden. Baden-Baden is welcome to it. It was little, but it was all I had to give. I would have preferred to leave something that was catching, but it was not in my power.

Mark Twain, *A Tramp Abroad*

Mark Twain's ambivalent reactions to **BADEN-BADEN** – he actually seems to have revelled in the snob aspect, delighting in the fact that the little old woman he sat behind in church and had decided to foster, turned out to be the Empress of Germany – mirror the contrasting reactions of late nineteenth-century visitors to this town, then the glittering rendezvous of the wealthy and famous.

In the twentieth century, the idle rich classes who made Baden-Baden the "summer capital of Europe" were almost entirely wiped out. The Bolshevik Revolution accounted for the Russian landowners, while World War II took care of their counterparts in Prussia and the Balkans. Yet, if Baden-Baden isn't quite what it was, it has still maintained its image remarkably well; like Bath in England, it has a sense of style that no other spa in the country can quite match. This is in large measure thanks to the German infatuation with the concept of the spa cure, which is underpinned by an incredibly lenient health insurance system. Buoyed by the postwar economic prosperity, people flock here to enjoy a taste of a lifestyle their parents could only have dreamed about. It remains a place you're likely to either love or hate, but is somewhere which definitely should be experienced at first hand.

Arrival, information and accommodation

The **Bahnhof**, on the fast Freiburg to Karlsruhe line, is in the suburb of Oos, 4km northwest of the centre, which is reached by bus #201, #205 or #216. There's a link from the Bahnhof (Mon–Fri only) by buses #205 and #234 to the **airport** (Ⓣ0 72 21/66 20 00, Ⓦwww.badenairpark) to the west of town, which is used by Ryanair – under the designation Karlsruhe-Baden – for flights from London Stansted. As Baden-Baden's sights are scattered, it's well worth investing in a 24-hour ticket on the **public transport** network. This costs €4 for Baden-Baden or €9 for the whole region including Karlsruhe and covers up to two adults and two children travelling together. The **tourist**

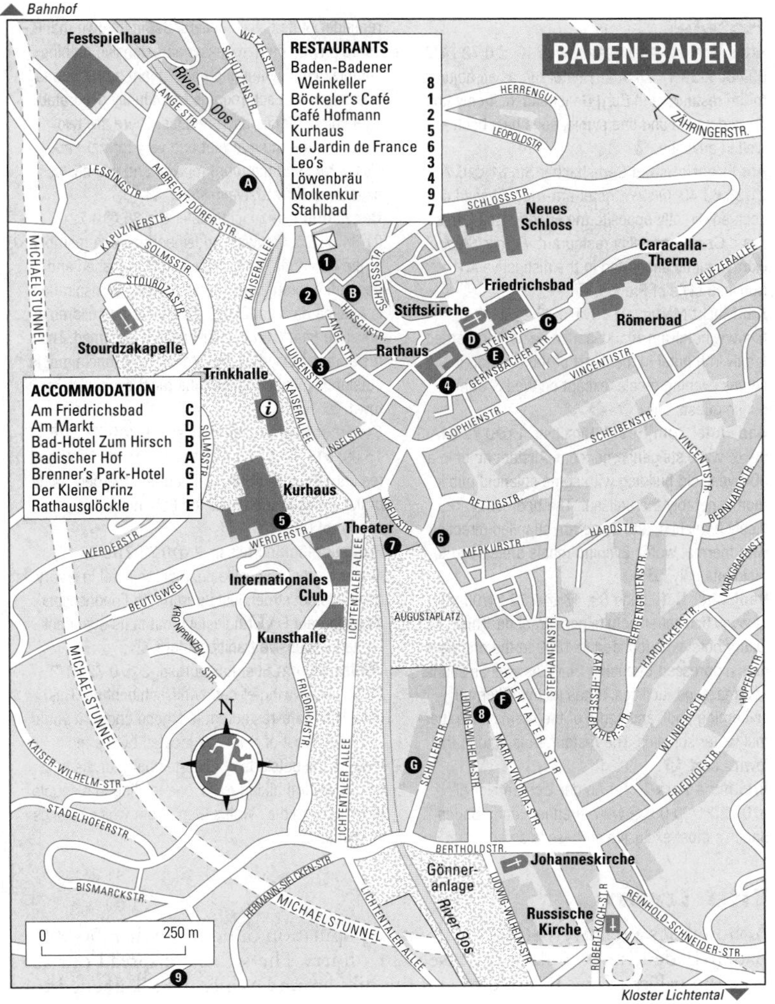

office is in the Trinkhalle, Kaiserallee 11 (Mon–Sat 10am–5pm, Sun 2–5pm; ⓣ0 72 21/27 52 00, ⓦwww.baden-baden.de).

Baden-Baden has **hotels** to suit every pocket, from the plain and serviceable to the super-luxury establishments frequented by aristocrats and oil sheikhs. There are a fair number of **private rooms** (❷–❹); the tourist office has a list but is unlikely to help with bookings. The **youth hostel** is between the Bahnhof and the centre at Hardbergstr. 34 (ⓣ0 72 21/5 22 23; €14.20/16.90); take bus #201, #205 or #216 to Grosse-Dollen-Strasse, from where the way is signposted. **Camping** presents more of a problem, with no sites in the immediate vicinity. Nearest is in a large pleasure park named Oberbruch (ⓣ0 72 23/2 31 94) in the outskirts of Bühl, 10km southwest and three stops away by slow train.

Hotels

Altes Schloss Alter Schlossweg 10 ⓣ0 72 21/2 69 48, ⓕ39 17 75. A tiny hotel run as an adjunct to the restaurant in Burg Hohenbaden. It only has three doubles and one single, so is best booked well in advance. ❹

Am Friedrichsbad Gernsbacher Str. 31 ⓣ0 72 21/38 63 40, ⓦwww.hotel-am-friedrichsbad.de. Located directly opposite the Friedrichsbad, this has a Czech speciality restaurant, *Prager Stuben*, extravagantly decorated in the distinctive Art Nouveau style of Prague. ❻

Am Markt Marktplatz 18 ⓣ0 72 21/2 70 40, ⓦwww.hotel-am-markt-baden.de. Well-regarded family-run hotel in the heart of the Altstadt. It serves evening meals (except on Wed & Sun) to house guests only. ❹–❻

Bad-Hotel Zum Hirsch Hirschstr. 1 ⓣ0 72 21/93 90, ⓦwww.steigenberger.com. Altstadt hotel in a 300-year-old building with some splendid public rooms, notably the Ballsaal. The bedrooms are nicely furnished, and some are supplied directly with thermal water. Evening meals are served to residents only. ❽

Badischer Hof Lange Str. 47 ⓣ0 72 21/93 40, ⓦwww.badischer-hof.steigenberger.de. This luxury hotel was founded in 1809 in the premises of a suppressed Capuchin friary. As well as sauna and massage facilities, it has its own thermal swimming pool, and some of the rooms have thermal water supplies. The restaurant is among the town's best. ❾

Brenner's Park-Hotel An der Lichtentaler Allee ⓣ0 72 21/90 00, ⓦwww.brenners.com. Baden-Baden's most exclusive address is an enduring reminder of its halcyon years. Set in its own manicured private park, it boasts an extensive bathing complex with swimming pool, steam baths, sauna and solarium. Each room is individually decorated with chintz fabrics and antiques. There are two restaurants – the gourmet and very formal *Park-Restaurant* and the more relaxed and slightly less expensive *Schwarzwald-Stube.* ❾

Der Kleine Prinz Lichtentaler Str. 36 ⓣ0 72 21/34 66 00, ⓦwww.derkleineprinz.de. A member of the Romantik group, exquisitely furnished and decorated throughout; a chief source of inspiration is Antoine de Saint Exupéry's illustrated children's novel *Le Petit Prince,* after which it is named. The restaurant (closed all day Mon & Tues lunchtime) is outstanding, albeit among the most expensive in town. ❽–❾

Goldener Stern Ooser Haupstr. 16 ⓣ0 72 21/6 15 09, ⓕ5 43 23. An archetypal German hotel and restaurant (closed Sun) which offers the best value of the concentration near the Bahnhof in the suburb of Oos. ❹

Rathausglöckle Steinstr. 7 ⓣ0 72 21/9 06 10, ⓦwww.rathausgloeckle.de. Historic hotel in a very quiet Altstadt street, just up from the Friedrichsbad. Its restaurant is worth seeking out in its own right for its inexpensive traditional fare. ❺

Wolfsschlucht Ebersteinburgstr. 2 ⓣ0 72 21/2 23 82, ⓦwww.hotel-cafe-wolfsschlucht.de. This hotel with café-restaurant is a good choice if you'd like to stay out of town. It's located by the main road on the outskirts of Ebersteinburg, at the junction of several hiking trails, one leading in a couple of minutes to the "Wolf's Glen" from which it takes its name. ❹

The Town

Although it's a relatively small town with a population of no more than 50,000, Baden-Baden is not a place to be seen in a hurry. The sights are spread out all over the valley of the River Oos and the hills around, while time is needed to bask in the varied spa attractions.

The Kurhaus

Baden-Baden's rise to international fame only came about as a result of Napoleon's creation of the buffer state of Baden in 1806, 35 years after it had lost its role as ducal capital to Karlsruhe. The grand dukes promoted their ancestors' old seat as a resort and began embellishing it with handsome new buildings, many designed by the Neoclassical architect Friedrich Weinbrenner. He built the **Kurhaus** in the 1820s as the focal point of the new spa quarter on the west side of the Oos. The **Casino** (ⓦwww.casino-baden-baden.de) formed an integral part of the facilities from the beginning, though it only took off with the arrival from Paris in 1836 of the flamboyant impresario **Jacques Bénazet**, Le Roi de Bade. With gambling outlawed in France, he devoted all his energies to building up Baden-Baden as the gambling capital of

The naming of Baden-Baden

The division of the Margraviate of Baden into Catholic and Protestant lines in 1525 is the source of the town's curious double-barrelled name. The Protestants moved to Durlach and founded the House of Baden-Durlach; the Catholic branch therefore became known as the House of Baden-Baden, following the usual practice, on the division of a state, of modifying the original name by adding that of its capital. Although this is also what the town itself has commonly been called ever since, the name was only officially adopted in 1931, more out of snobbery than anything else, in order to distinguish it from lesser spa towns named Baden in Austria and Switzerland.

Europe. Bénazet's son Edouard, Le Duc de Zéro, added an opulent suite of gaming rooms to the Kurhaus, employing the same team of designers as had worked on the Paris Opéra; they married the contemporary style of the *belle époque* to the extravagant type of decor found at Versailles. Highlight is the **Wintergarten**, with its glass cupola, Chinese vases and pure gold roulette table, which is used only on Saturdays or for special guests. Almost equally striking is the **Roter Saal**, covered from top to bottom in red silk damask from Lyon, and with a glorious marbled fireplace and raised oval ceiling.

The easiest way to see these is to take a **guided tour** (daily: April–Sept 9.30am–11.45; Oct–March 10am–11.45; €4). However, it's far more fun to go when the action is on. A **day-ticket** costs €3, with no obligation to participate. Formal dress (ie any kind of jacket and tie for men, skirt or dress for women) is a precondition of entry; access is officially forbidden to residents of Baden-Baden, anyone under 21 and students. Roulette is played daily from 2pm to 2am (until 3am on Saturday), black jack from 5pm to 1am Monday to Thursday, from 4pm to 1am Friday and Sunday, and from 4pm to 2am on Saturday, while baccarat is for the real night owls, running daily from 3pm to 6am. Minimum stake is €2.50; maximum is €25,000 – though this limit is waived for baccarat.

Around Lichtentaler Allee

South of the Kurhaus runs Baden-Baden's most important thoroughfare, the **Lichtentaler Allee**. This was originally lined with oaks, but was transformed at the instigation of Edouard Bénazet into a landscape in the English style, with the addition of exotic trees and shrubs. It requires little effort of the imagination to visualize the procession of aristocratic carriages along this route; at Kettenbrücke, at the far end, an attempt was made on the life of Kaiser Wilhelm I in 1861.

First of the buildings on Lichtentaler Allee is the Parisian-style **Theater** which opened in 1862 with the premiere of Berlioz's opera *Béatrice et Bénédict*. Next in line comes the **Internationaler Club**, built by Weinbrenner for a Swedish princess but now the headquarters of the big flat races which are held in Iffezheim, 12km northwest of Baden-Baden. There's a meeting in May, and a *Grosse Woche* in late August, which is the most important in the German calendar and now ranks as the high point of the Baden-Baden season. Further along is the **Kunsthalle** (Tues & Thurs–Sun 11am–6pm, Wed 11am–8pm; €4; Ⓦwww.kunsthalle-baden-baden.de), which has no permanent collection but regularly hosts major loan exhibitions of modern art.

Immediately north of the Kurhaus, the **Trinkhalle** (Pump Room) was built by a follower of Weinbrenner, Heinrich Hübsch. Its arcades shelter fourteen large frescoes by the Romantic painter Jakob Götzenberger, illustrating legends about the town and the nearby countryside. Different varieties of spring water are dispensed from a modern mosaic fountain inside. It also houses the tourist office along with a reading room and café.

The Michaelsberg, which rises behind the spa quarter, is named after the last Romanian Boyar of Moldavia, Michael Stourdza, who settled in Baden-Baden after he had been expelled from his homeland. In 1863, his teenage son was murdered in Paris; as a memorial, he commissioned the **Stourdzakapelle** to be built on the hill. Construction of this domed chapel, the most distinguished of the three nineteenth-century churches in Baden-Baden built for expatriate communities, was entrusted to the aged Leo von Klenze who had created so much of nineteenth-century Munich, but he died before it was complete. It's normally kept locked, but the priest, who lives in the house alongside, will open it on request.

The Altstadt

Little remains of the old town of Baden-Baden, which was almost completely destroyed in a single day in 1689, the result of a fire started by French troops. However, halfway up the Florintinerberg is the Marktplatz, where you'll find the **Rathaus**, formerly a Jesuit college, but partially remodelled by Weinbrenner to serve as the original casino.

Opposite is the **Stiftskirche**, a Gothic hall church whose tower is an amalgam of the Romanesque lower storeys of the first church, a Gothic octagon and a Baroque cap. It may seem unexpected that Baden-Baden possesses one of the all-time masterpieces of European sculpture, but the Stiftkirche's 5.4-metre-high sandstone Crucifixion, depicting Christ as a noble giant triumphant over his suffering, certainly warrants such a rating. Carved in 1467, it stood for nearly five centuries in the Alter Friedhof, before being moved inside for conservation reasons. The work is signed by **Nicolaus Gerhaert von Leyden**, a mysterious, peripatetic sculptor of Dutch origin who pioneered a realist approach to art which was to have a profound influence on the German carvers of the next generation. The tabernacle was made about twenty years later by a mason who had clearly come under Gerhaert's spell, while there are also several impressive **tombs** of the Margraves of Baden lining the chancel; particularly eye-catching is the Rococo monument to "Türkenlouis" (see also p.330 and p.335), replete with depictions of his trophies.

From Marktplatz you can climb the steep steps to the **Neues Schloss** whose terrace commands the best view over Baden-Baden, a dramatic mixture of rooftops, church spires and the Black Forest surroundings. The site served as the seat of the Margraves of Baden from 1437, and of the Catholic line of Baden-Baden when the House divided in 1525. Until a few years ago, the main block was still a residence of the Zähringen family, but they have moved out and auctioned off many of the furnishings, some of which were acquired by the Landesmuseum in Karlsruhe. One of the wings contains the archeology and toy departments of the **Stadtgeschichtliche Sammlungen** (Tues–Thurs noon–5pm, Fri–Sun 11am–5pm; €2.50).

The baths

Hidden underneath the Stiftskirche are the remains of the Roman imperial baths; the more modest **Römerbad** (daily 11am–5pm; €2; Ⓦwww.badruinen.de) just to the east on Römerplatz was probably for the use of soldiers. Above the ruins is what must rank as one of the most magnificent bathing halls in the world, the **Friedrichsbad** (Mon–Sat 9am–10pm, Sun noon–8pm; €21, or €29 with massage treatment; Ⓦwww.carasana.de). Begun in 1869, it's as grandly sumptuous as a Renaissance palace. This elaborateness is at least partly due to the fact that, as Kaiser Wilhlem I outlawed gambling while the building was still under construction, the medicinal springs became even more crucial to local prosperity than they had been before. The red and white sandstone facade is crowned with sea-green cupolas, while inside the pools are surrounded by pillars, arches and classical-style tiles, giving a truly exotic atmosphere. Speciality of the house is a "Roman-Irish Bath", which consists of a two-hour programme of showers, hot air and steam baths, soap and brush massage, thermal bathing and a half-hour snooze in a specially designed rest room. The entire treatment is undertaken in the nude, with mixed bathing every day except Monday and Thursday when men and women are kept segregated in different sections.

The **Caracalla Therme** (daily 8am–10pm; €11 for 2hr, €13 for 3hr, €15 for 4hr; Ⓦwww.carasana.de) on the same square is a vast complex, completed in 1985, as a replacement for the former Augustabad. There are seven pools, both indoors and out, which are all at different temperatures, along with a sauna, solarium and massage facility. In reality, it's no more than an upmarket swimming hall with thermal water springs, though it makes an ideal complement to the Friedrichsbad. Its humbler status is reflected in the considerably cheaper prices.

The Südstadt and Lichtental

The Südstadt, immediately south of the Florintinerberg, was traditionally the home of foreigners. Just off Bertholdsplatz is the onion-domed **Russische Kirche** (March–Dec daily 10am–1pm & 2–6pm; €1), while the neo-Gothic **Johanneskirche** on Bertholdstrasse was the place where Mark Twain had his encounter with the empress. Beyond the church is the **Gönneranlagen**, a fine park with pergolas, fountains and a rose garden.

Further south is the incorporated village of **LICHTENTAL**, which can be reached by bus #201. The tranquil thirteenth-century **Kloster** is still occupied by Cistercian nuns, who keep up a long tradition of handicrafts, and also make several fiery liqueurs, which can be bought at their shop. There are two Gothic chapels: the larger one is used for services, while the other, the **Fürstenkapelle** (guided tours Tues–Sun at 3pm, closed first Sun in month; €1.50), served as the pantheon of the Margraves of Baden prior to the Stiftskirche. Particularly outstanding is the tomb of the foundress Irmengard, carved by a Strasbourg mason in the mid-fourteenth century.

Just down the road from here, at Maximilianstr. 85, is the **Brahms-Haus** (Mon, Wed & Fri 3–5pm, Sun 10am–1pm; €1.50), a tiny attic crammed with memorabilia, left exactly as when the great composer lived in it periodically during the years 1865 to 1874. This was the time when Brahms, ever conscious of his mantle as Beethoven's successor, was struggling to establish himself as a symphonist, only publishing his first, tormented essay in this form after he had passed his 40th birthday. Its elegaic successor was largely written during a later visit to Lichtental, while part of the massive *Ein Deutsches Requiem*, his most important choral work, was also composed here.

Other suburbs

The original castle of the Margraves, **Burg Hohenbaden** (Tues–Sun 10am–10pm; free), is situated on the wooded slopes of the Battert, some 3km from the Neues Schloss, from which it's reached via Alter Schlossweg; alternatively, bus #215 goes there from the town centre. At one time, it boasted over a hundred rooms but is now a ruin, albeit still very much worth visiting for the sake of the sweeping views; there's also a good and reasonably priced restaurant and a small hotel (see p.326). To the east, on the same bus route, lies the wine-growing village of **EBERSTEINBURG**, likewise dominated by a ruined fortress of the local rulers. Further south and reached from Ebersteinburg by footpath (about 30min walk), or from the Bahnhof or centre by bus #205, is the **Merkur**, at 668m the highest hill in the Baden-Baden range. There's a choice of trails along it, or you can ascend to the summit by an unusually steep rack rail line (daily 10am–10pm; €2.50 single, €3.50 return). To obtain much of a view, you then need to climb the Jugendstil **Aussichtsturm**.

Eating and drinking

Most of the best restaurants in Baden-Baden are in the hotels (see p.326), though there are plenty of other enticing places to eat and drink.

Baden-Badener Weinkeller Maria-Viktoria-Str. 2. Small wine bar-restaurant just south of the town centre. Evenings only, closed Sun & Mon.
Böckeler's Café Lange Str. 40–42. Traditional café with a wonderful selection of cakes and sweets; also does light meals.
Café Hofmann Lange Str. 39. Another fine *Kaffee und Kuchen* establishment on the main shopping street.
Eckberg Eckhöfe 12. Baden-Baden's only Weingut, situated in the northern part of Lichtental, has an adjoining wine bar where you can sample its products. Full meals are also served. Open Wed & Thurs 3–10pm, Fri & Sat 3–11pm, Sun noon–10pm.
Kurhaus Kaiserallee 1. Predictably classy restaurant attached to the Casino.
Le Jardin de France Lichtentaler Str. 13. Smart designer-style restaurant with a courtyard terrace serving gourmet French cuisine. Closed all day Mon & Tues lunchtime.
Leo's Luisenstr. 10. Trendy café-bar and, as such, something of a rarity in Baden-Baden.
Löwenbräu Gernsbacher Str. 9. This is like a little piece of Munich successfully transplanted to alien surroundings; it serves typically solid and inexpensive Bavarian fare, and is fronted by a small beer garden.
Molkenkur Quettigstr. 19. Baden-Baden's oldest Gaststätte occupies a timber-framed building characteristic of the Black Forest region. It has a beer garden and specializes in local dishes. Closed Tues.
Stahlbad Augustaplatz 2. An extremely elegant and expensive restaurant with garden terrace. In both cuisine and decor it rivals any of the hotel restaurants. Closed Mon.

Entertainment

Baden-Baden maintains a prestigious highbrow cultural scene, which since 1998 has been centred on the Festspielhaus, Beim Alten Bahnhof 2 (Ⓣ0 72 21/3 01 31 01, Ⓦwww.festspielhaus.de), Europe's second largest **opera house**, a brash modernist structure built onto the plush neo-Renaissance station which had lacked a proper function since the closure of the branch line to Oos. This attracts a starry roster of visiting international artists for its ambitious opera, ballet and concert programmes. The town can also claim to be the smallest in the world to have two distinguished **symphony orchestras**, namely the SWR Sinfonieorchester (Ⓦwww.swr-freiburg.de), which is now shared with Freiburg, and the Baden-Badener Philharmonie (Ⓦwww.philharmonie.baden-baden.de), whose usual performing venue is the Kurhaus. Tickets for its concerts there, and for the **drama** at the nearby Theater on Goetheplatz (Ⓦwww.theater-baden-baden.de), can be had from the box office in the Trinkhalle (Ⓣ0 72 21/93 27 00).

Rastatt

In 1698, Margrave Ludwig, nicknamed "Türkenlouis" on account of his victories over the Turks, decided to shift his seat from Baden-Baden to **RASTATT**, then an insignificant village 15km to the north, just before the point where the River Murg flows into the Rhine. This move was partly precipitated by the dilapidated condition of the Neues Schloss after the War of the Palatinate Succession. However, it was also influenced by the courtly culture of the time, which had decided that hilltop fortresses were redundant and should be replaced by planned palatial towns on the model of Versailles.

Rastatt's town centre was planned in conjunction with its great Schloss but only finished in the mid-eighteenth century. Centrepiece is the elliptical Marktplatz, with several fountains, the **Rathaus** and the **Stadtkirche St Alexander**, the last-named already showing Neoclassical influence. Between here and the Schloss are a number of handsome courtiers' houses. One of these, Herrenstr. 11, houses the **Heimatmuseum** (previously Wed, Fri & Sun 10am–noon & 3–5pm; free, but closed in 2003 for restoration), which traces the history of the town and includes displays of medieval art and souvenirs of Türkenlouis.

The massive red sandstone **Schloss** (guided tours Tues–Sun 10am–4/5pm; €4 or €6 combined ticket with Schloss Favorite; Ⓦwww.schloesser-und-gaerten.de) was built in just ten years to plans by an Italian architect, Domenico Rossi. It's approached via a spacious U-shaped courtyard, guarded by a balustrade with writhing Baroque statues, while the central wing is topped by a glistening figure of Jupiter, dubbed the Goldener Mann. In addition to the recently restored main reception rooms upstairs you can visit the **Wehrgeschichtliches Museum** (Tues–Sun 9.30am–5pm; €3; Ⓦwww.wgm-rastatt.de) and the **Freiheitsmuseum** (Tues–Sun 9.30am–5pm; free; Ⓦwww.freiheitsmuseum-rastatt.de) on the ground floor. The former shows weapons, uniforms and other military memorabilia from medieval times to the present day, while the latter traces the history of German liberalism – a slender theme. Rastatt was chosen as the venue for this museum because it was the last stronghold of the rebels in the revolutions of 1848–49, one of the few occasions when the authoritarian nature of German society was seriously challenged. In the north wing of the building, entered from Lyzeumstrasse, is the sumptuous **Schlosskirche**; it's generally kept locked but a notice will tell you where to get the key.

The most imposing part of the Schlossgarten is now unfortunately cut off by an arterial road to the south, though at least it does leave a peaceful corner at the edge of town. Here is the graceful **Einsiedelner Kapelle**, a miniaturized version of the great Swiss church of the same name. Türkenlouis' widow, Margravine Augusta Sibylla, went on pilgrimage there to pray for her son Ludwig Georg, who, at the age of six, was still unable to speak; needless to say, her faith worked the trick. Later, the **Pagodenburg** was made as a play-house for the prince and his brother. This was modelled on its counterpart in Nymphenburg on the outskirts of Munich; like the chapel, it was built by the new court architect, Johann Michael Ludwig Rohrer. Behind is the Jugendstil **Wasserturm**, now a café.

Some 5km from the centre of Rastatt, on the way to Baden-Baden, is **Schloss Favorite** (guided tours Tues–Sun 10am–4/5pm; €4.50; Ⓦwww.schloesser-und-gaerten.de), the summer residence of Augusta Sibylla in her years as regent. Here, J.M.L. Rohrer attempted to create the smaller-scale opulence characteristic of the Central European courts which the margravine preferred to the French-inspired grandeur favoured by her husband. Some of the interiors are riotously ornate, notably the **Spiegelkabinett** with its 330 mirrors, and the **Florentiner Zimmer,** lavishly adorned with coloured marbles, stucco, rare woods and semi-precious stones.

Practicalities

Rastatt's **Bahnhof** is at the eastern end of town; here the scenic Murgtalbahn from Freudenstadt connects with the express line down the Rhine. The **tourist office** (Mon–Thurs 8.30am–noon & 12.45–4.30pm, Fri 8am–noon & 12.45–3pm; ⓣ0 72 22/97 24 62, ⓦwww.rastatt.de) is in the Schloss, Herrenstr. 18. Reasonably priced **hotels** include *Löwen*, Kaiserstr. 9 (ⓣ0 72 22/3 45 56; ❸), and *Gasthof Kehler Hof*, Kehler Str. 43 (ⓣ0 72 22/3 29 38; ❸). For something more upmarket, try *Zum Schiff*, Poststr. 2 (ⓣ0 72 22/77 20, ⓦwww.hotel-zum-schiff-rastatt.de; ❺), *Zum Engel*, Kaiserstr. 65 (ⓣ0 72 22/7 79 80, ⓦwww.hotel-engel-rastatt.de; ❻), or *Schwert*, in a Baroque mansion at Herrenstr. 3a (ⓣ0 72 22/76 80, ⓦwww.hotel-schwert.de; ❼). Among the best **restaurants** are those in the aforementioned *Zum Engel*, *Sigi's* in *Hotel Schwert*, and *Zum Storchennest*, Karlstr. 24.

Karlsruhe

KARLSRUHE, which lies some 25km northeast of Rastatt, is the baby of German cities. It didn't exist at all until 1715, when **Carl Wilhelm**, Margrave of Baden-Durlach, began the construction of a retreat at the edge of the Hardter Wald. There he could escape from a wife who bored him, in order to pursue his cultural interests – and to enjoy the company of several mistresses. The planned town which subsequently grew up around the palace was given an appropriate appellation – "Carl's Rest". Initially modest in size, its growth was stimulated by its establishment as the capital of the reunited state of Baden in 1771 and by the subsequent elevation of its rulers to the title of grand dukes under Napoleon's reorganization of the European political map. Karlsruhe flourished throughout the nineteenth century, enjoying what was, by German standards, a remarkably liberal atmosphere and becoming a major centre for both science and art. In 1945, however, it finally lost its status as a regional capital; Baden was divided between the American and French occupation zones, and Stuttgart made the obvious choice as seat of government for the former's province, which went under the name of Württemberg-Baden. As if by way of compensation, Karlsruhe was chosen as the home of the two highest courts of the Federal Republic.

The fan town

Looking at a map or an aerial photograph, Karlsruhe appears as an extraordinarily handsome city, thanks to its striking fan-shaped plan. As in an earlier purpose-built princely town, Mannheim, the hub of the system is the Schloss, here placed in isolation to the extreme north. Again this building is U-shaped, but thereafter the geometric patterns become far more imaginative and complex. The Schloss gardens are circular, with the outer half left in a natural state, while the inner is closed by a crescent of regular buildings; this forms a triangle with the Schloss which takes up exactly a quarter of the grounds. From here radiate nine dead-straight avenues (representing each of the Muses); the central axis, Karl-Friedrich-Strasse, runs in a vertical line from the palace's central pavilion, while the two end ones shoot outwards at angles of 45° from the wings, with the others placed at regular intervals in between.

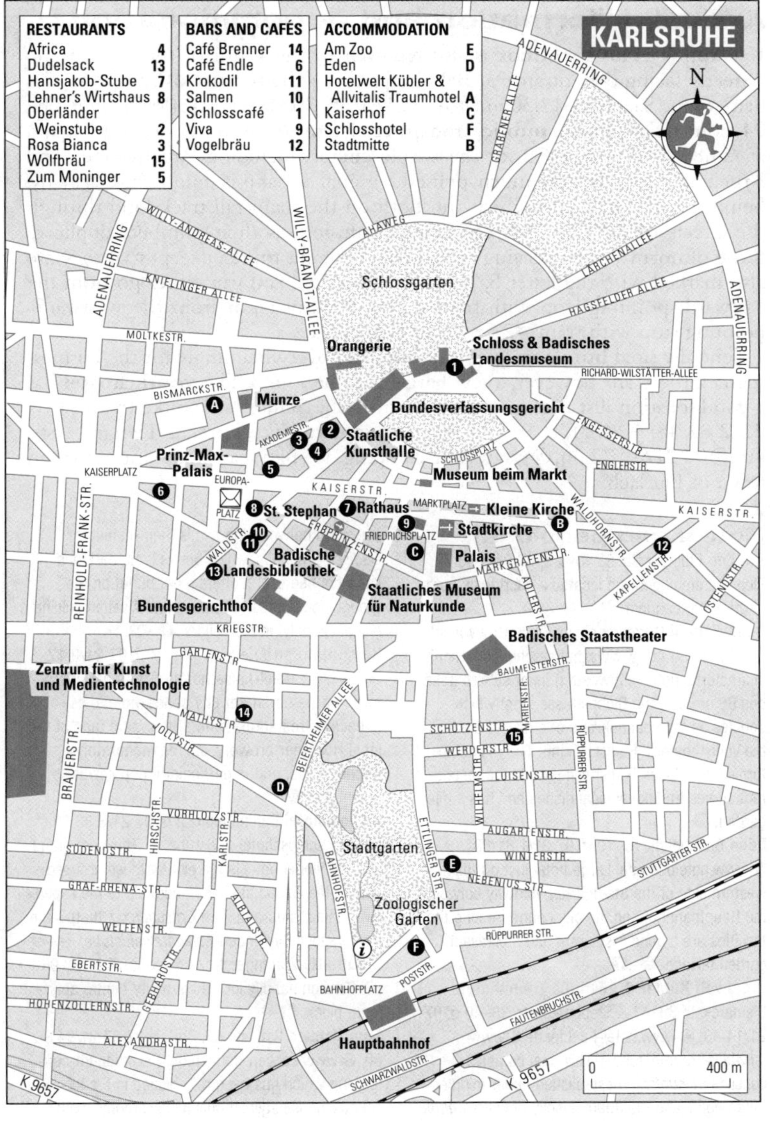

As a standard large industrial city, Karlsruhe is by no means the central target of anyone's travels, but it nonetheless has much to offer – to discerning eggheads at least. The city's own propaganda baldly proclaims that it occupies fifth place in the hierarchy of the country's cultural centres. Whether or not this self-estimation is accurate, the **museums** (which are among the oldest public collections in Germany) are undeniably top class, the **Kunsthalle** alone being sufficient reason to justify a visit.

Arrival, information and accommodation

Karlsruhe's **Hauptbahnhof** is situated well to the south of the city centre. Directly facing the entrance at Bahnhofplatz 6 is the **tourist office** (Mon–Fri 9am–6pm, Sat 9am–12.30pm; ⓣ07 21/3 55 30, ⓦwww.karlsruhe.de). The 24-hour ticket on the **public transport** system (ⓦwww.kvv.de) is a bargain at €4.80 for the city, €9 for the whole circuit (including Baden-Baden and Bruchsal). Note that the much-praised regional S-Bahn is unique in Germany, being serviced by trams which run both on the main rail tracks and through the streets of the city. This can cause confusion, as their numbers duplicate those of normal trams serving completely different routes, except that they are also marked with the letter S. To reach the centre, you can either go from the eastwards-pointing stop with tram #3 to Marktplatz, or from the westward-pointing stop with tram #2 or #4 to Europaplatz.

Centrally sited **hotels** are plentiful, but cater overwhelmingly for the business market; there are, however, a few bargains to be found. The **youth hostel** has a good location just five minutes' walk from the Schloss at Moltkestr. 2b (ⓣ07 21/2 82 48; €14.20/16.90). There's a **campsite**, *Turmbergblick*, Tiengerer Str. 40 (ⓣ07 21/49 72 36, ⓦwww.azur-camping.de), 5km east in the incorporated town of Durlach.

Hotels and pensions

Am Zoo Ettlinger Str. 33 ⓣ & ⓕ07 21/3 36 78. Pleasant small pension located a short walk north of the Hauptbahnhof. ❹

Beim Schupi Durmersheimer Str, 6, Grünwinkel ⓣ07 21/5 59 40, ⓦwww.beim-schupi.de. Highly characterful hotel in a western inner suburb (take bus 60 or 62 to the Blohnstrasse stop) which doubles as the headquarters of a dialect theatre, the Volkstheater d'Badisch Bühn. The rooms are furnished in Black Forest style, while the restaurant serves traditional local dishes and has a beer garden. ❻

Eden Bahnhofstr. 15–19 ⓣ07 21/1 81 80, ⓦwww.hoteleden.de. Large hotel just off the western side of the Stadtgarten, midway between the Hauptbahnhof and the city centre. Among the facilities are a good restaurant and a pleasant garden terrace. ❺–❼

Hotelwelt Kübler & Allvitalis Traumhotel Bismarckstr. 39–43 & Stephanienstr. 38–40 ⓣ07 21/14 40, ⓦwww.hotel-kuebler.de & www.allvitalis-traumhotel.de). This dual complex consists of *Kübler*, an established upper middle-range hotel, and the utterly wacky new *Traumhotel* (Dream Hotel), which consists of a series of luxuriantly furnished apartments in the style of different countries from around the globe. In the courtyard between the two is their restaurant, *Badisch Brauhaus*, which brews light, dark and seasonal beers, and offers a hot buffet on the ground floor, upmarket Baden and Alsatian cuisine (evenings only) in the cellars. ❻–❾.

Kaiserhof Karl-Friedrich-Str. 12 ⓣ07 21/9 17 00, ⓦwww.hotel-kaiserhof.de. The most characterful of the upmarket city centre hotels. Its capacious restaurant, one of the main taps of the local Hoepfner brewery, serves moderately priced meals, and is particularly popular at lunchtime. ❻

Schlosshotel Bahnhofplatz 2 ⓣ07 21/3 83 20, ⓦwww.schlosshotel-karlsruhe.de. This very grand and traditional hotel is the pick of those grouped around the Hauptbahnhof. In addition to the expensive main restaurant, *Zum Grossherzog*, there's the more reasonably priced *Schwarzwaldstube*. ❼–❾

Stadtmitte Zähringerstr. 72 ⓣ & ⓕ07 21/38 96 37. Pension handily located in a city-centre apartment block. ❹

Zum Ochsen Prinzstr. 64, Durlach ⓣ07 21/94 38 60, ⓦwww.ochsen-durlach.de. Seventeenth-century inn which has been refurbished in French country-house style. It only has six rooms, so is best booked well in advance. The gourmet restaurant, which continues the Gallic theme, is generally considered to be the best in Karlsruhe. ❾

The City

At ground level, the streets of the fan-shaped plan are rather less impressive than on a map, largely due to the fact that most of the original buildings have been supplanted by undistinguished successors, something for which war damage is partly, but by no means entirely, responsible. Nonetheless, outstanding architecture survives – including some of the finest **Neoclassical buildings** in Germany – though the Kunsthalle and the Landesmuseum are undoubtedly the city's prime attractions.

The Schloss and Schlosspark

Although the oldest surviving building, the **Schloss**, which is set in the extensive English-style **Schlosspark**, is actually the second on the site, built in the French-influenced Baroque style of the 1750s. Sadly, it was completely gutted in the last war; the interior was later modernized to house the **Badisches Landesmuseum** (Tues–Thurs 10am–5pm Fri–Sun 10am–6pm; €4; Ⓦwww.landesmuseum.de). To the left of the entrance is the **archeology** section. Highlights are the ivory treasure from the Assyrian city of Arslan Tash, a relief of two horsemen from Nineveh, a Sicilian statuette of the goddess Nike and a carving of a gift bringer from Xerxes' palace in Persepolis. Further on are some impressive pieces of Roman sculpture, notably *Hanging Marsyas* from a villa near Rome, *Mithras Killing the Bull*, which came from near Heidelberg, and a relief of two underwater gods from a settlement not far from Karlsruhe. In the corresponding wing to the right of the entrance is the medieval and Renaissance section, which includes four stunningly bold stained-glass windows designed by **Baldung** for the Carthusian monastery in Freiburg and a polychrome limewood *Madonna and Child* by **Riemenschneider**.

Upstairs is a re-creation of the Schloss's **Thronsaal** and the crown jewels of the Grand Duchy of Baden. However, these are completely overshadowed by the **Turkish booty** (*Türkenbeute*), captured by the Margrave Ludwig of Baden-Baden in his seventeenth-century campaigns against the Turks. Unique in western Europe, this includes embroidery, illuminated books, cutlery, jewellery, leather, woodwork, saddles and weapons of all types. From this floor, a staircase leads up to the balcony of the **tower**, the only public place from which the city's famous fan shape can be seen to proper effect.

In a building immediately to the left of the Schloss is housed the highest judicial authority in the country, the **Bundesverfassungsgericht** (Federal Constitutional Court). It is, in theory, an essential bulwark against the rise of any would-be Hitler, whose accession to power was greatly facilitated by the excessively liberal constitution of the Weimar Republic, which gave full rights to groups pledged to its destruction. The German "Basic Law" has been made much tougher; all political parties must now pledge themselves to the democratic process, or else be outlawed by this court.

The Staatliche Kunsthalle

At Hans-Thoma-Str. 2, on the left side of the circular road round the Schlosspark, is the **Staatliche Kunsthalle** (Tues–Fri 10am–5pm, Sat & Sun 10am–6pm; €4; Ⓦwww.kunsthalle-karlsruhe.de), housed in the mid-nineteenth century Kunstakademie. The magnificent collection of old masters on the first floor is reached via a monumental staircase adorned with a huge fresco by **Moritz von Schwind**, *The Consecration of Freiburg Münster*. Focal point of the gallery is one of the world's greatest pictures, *The Crucifixion* by **Grünewald**. The last and most powerful of his four surviving versions of this scene, it conveys an almost unbearable feeling of tragic intensity. One of the most baffling aspects of Grünewald's art is its inconsistency, and *The Fall of Jesus*, which came from the same altarpiece, has far less emotional impact. Two small monochrome pictures, *St Elizabeth* and *St Lucy*, give a good idea of his early style.

A tiny *Christ with Symbols of the Passion* is a recently discovered **Dürer**; there's also a painted version of his famous woodcut *Knight, Death and the Devil* which has been attributed to various different followers. Other German paintings to look out for are **Burgkmair**'s *Portrait of Sebastian Brant* (the satirist), **Cranach**'s *Frederick the Wise Adoring the Virgin and Child* and several works by **Baldung**, among which is *Margrave Christoph I of Baden in Adoration*; Moritz von Schwind included a cameo of the artist painting this work in the stairway fresco. Among the gallery's rarities is *The Raising of Lazarus*, the sole extant painting by **Wendel Dietterlin**, author of a book of fantastical Mannerist engravings which was immensely influential with late sixteenth-century architects and decorators.

The representation of Flemish, Dutch and French painting is equally good. *St Jerome in the Desert* by **Patinir** is one of the few paintings definitely from the hand of this elusive Antwerp master of landscapes with fantastic rock formations. There are also important examples by three other rare painters – **Lucas van Leyden**'s *St Andrew*, **Wtewael**'s *Chicken Inspection* and **Sweerts**' *Roman Wrestling Match*. A recently acquired *Crucifixion* by the great German-born Dutch Mannerist **Hendrick Goltzius** is of special note for being documented as the very first oil painting executed by the artist, who, at the age of 42, abandoned his career as an internationally celebrated engraver and draughtsman. **Rembrandt** is represented by a middle-period oval *Self-Portrait*, while there are several examples of **Rubens**. One of **Claude**'s largest canvases, *Adoration of the Golden Calf*, is the star of the seventeenth-century French section, which also includes a diptych of *The Annunciation*, perhaps the only surviving painting by the great Mannerist engraver **Jacques Bellange**, and canvases by Poussin, Le Brun and the Le Nain brothers. From the following century are four still lifes by **Chardin** and an exquisite pastel, *Karoline Luise of Hesse-Darmstadt as a Child*, by the Swiss **Liotard**.

A notable array of nineteenth-century German painting is dominated by the work of **Hans Thoma**, who was director of this gallery for twenty years. He was accomplished at both landscape and portraiture but had an unfortunate tendency to drift into sentimentality. **Menzel** and **Feuerbach** are represented by important works, but the gem of this section is **Friedrich**'s tiny *Rocky Reef by a Beach*.

The **Orangerie** (same hours and ticket) next door houses paintings by many of the established names of twentieth-century European art, along with a cross-section of nineteenth-century French movements, ranging from Delacroix and Courbet to the Impressionists and their followers. There's a good representation of the Blauer Reiter group, notably a couple of fine animal paintings by **Marc**. Another Expressionist masterpiece is **Kokoschka**'s *View of Mont Blanc from Chamonix*, while **Beckmann**'s *Transport of the Sphynxes* is an allegorical canvas alluding to France's liberation from Nazism.

The rest of the city centre

Few buildings from the same generation as the Schloss remain; an exception is the sole place of worship the town then possessed, the **Kleine Kirche** (Little Church) on the main horizontal street, Kaiserstrasse. The next phase of the building of Karlsruhe only occurred with Baden's promotion to an independent Grand Duchy. During the following 25 years, a remarkable local architect, **Friedrich Weinbrenner**, completely transformed the city into a worthy capital. As a young man, he had travelled to Rome; having assimilated the style of the ancient world, he employed its grand style in the creation of the great public buildings required by a modern city. Between the Schloss and the start of the central axis, he laid out the rectangular Marktplatz, at the far end of which is an austere red sandstone **Pyramid** containing the grave of Carl

Wilhelm. The western side of the square is dominated by the long pink range of the **Rathaus**. Opposite, the Corinthian facade of the **Stadtkirche**, nowadays the seat of Baden's Protestant bishop, looks like an updated version of a Roman temple. Its present interior is modern and functional, the dignified galleried original having been a casualty of wartime bombs.

Just off the northern side of the square at Karl-Friedrich-Str. 6 is the **Museum beim Markt** (Tues–Thur 11am–5pm, Fri–Sun 10am–6pm; same ticket as for Landesmuseum; Ⓦwww.landesmuseum.de). It's devoted to the applied and industrial arts of the twentieth century, featuring a good Art Nouveau/Jugendstil section, as well as works by members of the Bauhaus and other big names in international design.

Immediately south of Marktplatz is a small circus, Rondellplatz. It contains the **Palais** (now a bank), whose forms are almost identical to those of the Stadtkirche. In the centre of the square rises an **Obelisk** in honour of Grand Duke Carl, celebrating his granting of a constitution to the citizens of Baden. West along Erbprinzstrasse is the original late Neoclassical home of the Grand Ducal collections, which nowadays contains the **Staatliches Museum für Naturkunde** (Tues–Fri 9.30am–5pm, Sat & Sun 10am–6pm; €2.50; Ⓦwww.naturkundemuseum-bw.de). In addition to a large array of stuffed animals it has an aquarium and an outstanding prehistoric section. The last-named features the only reasonably complete skeleton of a hipparion (a forerunner of the horse) yet discovered; a number of fossils from Messel (see p.394); and others from Peru, including a finback whale which is six to seven million years old. Alongside is the **Badische Landesbibliothek** (Mon–Wed & Fri 8am–6pm, Thurs 8am–8pm, Sat 9.30am–12.30pm; free; Ⓦwww.blb-karlsruhe.de), which displays its treasures – including many wonderful medieval illuminated manuscripts – in a series of temporary exhibitions.

Further evidence of the enlightened, tolerant nature of the young state of Baden is provided by the Catholic church of **St Stephan** directly opposite the Landesbibliothek. This was built by Weinbrenner, himself a Protestant, at the same time as he was working on the Stadtkirche for members of his own faith. The main body of the church is circular while the portico is Doric, the whole being a conscious re-interpretation of the Pantheon in Rome. Down Ritterstrasse is a heavy late nineteenth-century palace formerly used by the heir to the Grand Duchy; it now houses the second most important law court in Germany, the **Bundesgerichthof** (Federal Supreme Court). This is where the most important postwar criminal trials have been held, including those of several of the Baader-Meinhof gang.

Karlsruhe's third Federal institution is the **Münze** (Mint) on Stephanienstrasse just to the west of the Kunsthalle. Weinbrenner's last building, this is still serving its original purpose, albeit on a much larger scale. Just down Karlstrasse is the **Prinz-Max-Palais**, a stolid Wilhelmine mansion now named after one of its former owners, who served a heady five-week stint in the autumn of 1918 as last chancellor of the Second Reich. In that time, he democratized the constitution, dismissed the military dictator Erich Ludendorff, began peace negotiations and announced the abdication of the Kaiser before the latter had consented; whereupon he himself resigned and vanished from the national stage. The top floor of the building now contains the **Stadtmuseum** (Tues, Wed, Fri & Sun 10am–6pm, Thurs 10am–7pm, Sat 2–6pm; free), with maps and prints, plus a model of how the city looked in 1834, when it was at its most splendid. Also exhibited is the *Draisienne*, first exhibited in Paris in 1818 by the Karlsruhe inventor **Karl von Drais**: decide for yourself whether or not it deserves its disputed title as the world's first bicycle.

Outside the centre

In the past few years, Karlsruhe has suddenly become a major metropolis of modern art, thanks to the establishment of the **Zentrum für Kunst und Medientechnologie** (**ZKM**) in a former armaments factory on Lorenzstrasse in the southwest of the city, which can be reached by tram #6. Billed as the world's largest cultural factory, this contains several institutes plus three museums. The **Medienmuseum** (Wed 10am–8pm, Thurs & Fri 10am–6pm, Sat & Sun 11am–6pm; €5.10, €7.70 combined ticket with Museum für Neue Kunst, €9.70 for all three museums; Ⓦwww.zkm.de) is the first-ever museum of interactive art, and is decidated to demonstarting the creative possibilities of new technologies, whether in film, software or cyberspace. Displayed around two spectacular top-lit halls, the **Museum für Neue Kunst** (Wed 10am–8pm, Thurs–Sun 10am-6pm; €4.10; Ⓦwww.mnk.zkm.de) draws on several of Baden-Württemberg's private collections of European and American art from the 1960s onwards. Particular strengths are Pop Art, Abstract Expressionism, Arte Povera, Conceptualism and the work of fêted contemporary German painters such as Richter, Polke and Baselitz. The **Städtische Galerie Karlsruhe** (same hours as Museum für Neue Kunst; €2.60) displays the municipally-owned collection of German art since 1945, and charts the progress of the local artistic scene since the founding of the Kunstakademie in 1854.

DURLACH, 5km east of the city centre, can be reached by train, or by tram #1 or #2. It was the original seat of the local margraves, and is hence described as the "mother town" of Karlsruhe, of which it now forms a part, while retaining its own quiet atmosphere.The focal point of Durlach is **Schloss Karlsburg**, an unfinished Baroque rebuild of the Gothic-Renaissance castle destroyed by the French in the War of the Palatinate Succession. Part of it now houses the **Pfinzgaumuseum und Karpatendeutsches Museum** (Tues 4–7pm, Wed 10am–noon, Sat 2–5pm, Sun 10am–5pm; free), the former focusing on Karlsruhe's hinterland, the latter on the folklore of the German communities in the Carpathians. A short walk to the east is the lower station of Germany's oldest functioning **rack railway**, the Turmbergbahn, which ascends to the summit of the Turmberg (mid-May to late Sept daily 10am–6/7pm, reducing gradually to weekends only in winter; €0.75 each way).

Eating, drinking and entertainment

Karlsruhe has many fine restaurants in addition to those in the hotels (see p.334). For a university city, it's surprisingly quiet come the evening, though a few pockets – notably around Ludwigsplatz – do spring to life.

Restaurants

Africa Kaiserpassage 22. Has a varied menu of North African food, and sometimes features live music. Closed Mon.

Dudelsack Waldstr. 79. Gourmet restaurant which is well known for its game and fish dishes. It has a pleasant terrace courtyard.

Hansjakob-Stube Ständehausstr. 4. Cellar restaurant offering excellent Baden and French cuisine, including game and its own smoked fish Closed Sun evening & Wed.

Lehner's Wirtshaus Karlstr. 21. What was previously a very traditional Gaststätte of the Hoepfner brewery has been given a makeover, with the clear aim of attracting a younger clientele. However, it still offers the old favourites, with very cheap dishes available at lunchtime.

Oberländer Weinstube Akademiestr. 7. Karlsruhe's oldest wine bar-restaurant has a truly *gemütlich* interior and garden courtyard. It serves some of the best meals in the town centre, and has over 800 vintages to choose from. Closed Sun & Mon.

Rosa Bianca Akademiestr. 23. Small, extremely popular Italian restaurant in a two-hundred year-old house. It does good-value set lunches on weekdays. On Sat, it's only open in the evening; closed Sun.

Schützenhaus Jean-Ritzert-Str. 8, Durlach. Good Gaststätte with beer garden on top of the Turmberg. Closed Mon & Tues.

Wolfbräu Marienstr. 38. The Wirtshaus of the eponymous late nineteenth-century brewery to the rear, whose wide portfolio of beers belies its small size. Inexpensive specials are available at lunchtime.

Zum Moninger Kaiserstr. 142. Grand neo-Gothic Gaststätte and beer garden of the Moninger brewery. It serves German and Italianate dishes, and has a special game menu.

Bars and cafés

Café Brenner Karlstr. 61a. Fine traditional coffee house, with a pedigree dating back to 1896. Closed Tues.

Café Endle Kaiserstr. 241a. A truly original café, which makes superb cakes, some in the shape of ice-creams – which it also produces in summer.

Krokodil Waldstr. 63. Café-bar which offers a good selection of salads and sometimes features live music.

Salmen Waldstr. 55. Animated café-bar much patronized by students; absinth now features on the drinks list.

Schlosscafé Schlossplatz 10. Located in the east wing of the Schloss, this has a pleasant garden terrace. It serves Mediterranean-influenced cuisine as well as *Kaffee und Kuchen.*

Viva Rathaus-Passage, Lammstr. 7a. Vegetarian café in a shopping arcade. Open Mon–Fri 11am–9.30pm, Sat 9am–5.30pm.

Vogelbräu Kapellenstr. 50. Hausbrauerei with beer garden, serving a cloudy unfiltered *Pils* as well as a monthly special brew and inexpensive meals and snacks.

Entertainment

The main **theatre** is the Badisches Staatstheater, Baumeisterstr. 11 (Ⓣ07 21/3 55 74 50, Ⓦwww.staatstheater.karlsruhe.de) which presents opera, operetta, musicals, ballet and concerts in its main auditorium, plays in the smaller hall. Marotte Figurentheater, Kaiserallee 11 (Ⓣ07 21/84 15 55, Ⓦwww.marotte-figurentheater.de) has puppet shows. Other concerts are held at the Stadthalle, Festplatz 4 (Ⓣ07 21/3 72 00), while **live jazz** is performed at Jubez, Am Kronenplatz (Ⓣ07 21/93 51 93, Ⓦwww.jubez.de). In June of even-numbered years, Karlsruhe hosts the Internationales Trachten-und-Folklorefest, a colourful **festival** featuring folk groups from all over Europe and beyond.

Northern Baden-Württemberg

The northern part of Baden-Württemberg consists of various territories which were only incorporated into the Grand Duchy of Baden and the Kingdom of Württemberg as a result of the Napoleonic redistribution of the map of Europe, and whose very different history and geography mean that they're best considered separately.

The fertile **Kraichgau** region, between the Rhine and the Neckar north of Karlsruhe, was particularly associated with the prince-bishops of Speyer, who established their resplendent new palatial headquarters at **Bruchsal** in the eighteenth century. Further north is the heart of the **Palatinate** (Pfalz or Kurpfalz), which was ruled by the Count Palatine of the Rhineland, the most senior official in the Holy Roman Empire and one of the seven Electors. The name of the old state lives on in the Land of Rhineland-Palatinate, but its original boundaries were very different. For five hundred years its capital was **Heidelberg** – a huge favourite with visitors, and a place which definitely warrants several days' stay. The planned town of **Mannheim**, now Baden-Württemberg's second city, was built as the new Palatine capital in the early eighteenth century, with **Schwetzingen** and its fantastical gardens used by the court in the summer months. Down the Neckar from Heidelberg is the well-preserved medieval town of **Bad Wimpfen**, for centuries a Free Imperial City.

Like Swabia, **Franconia** (Franken) was one of the five great provinces of medieval Germany. Under Napoleon, nearly all of this was incorporated into Bavaria, but the northwestern part – consisting of the **Hohenlohe** plain and part of the **Tauber valley** – was split off and used to beef up both Baden and Württemberg. This includes a section of the famous **Romantic Road**, which mostly lies in Bavaria.

Bruchsal

The resplendent Baroque **Schloss** at **BRUCHSAL** is no ordinary palace; indeed, it's a complete courtly town, comprising over fifty different buildings, which stands as an oasis in the midst of the ugly modern community which now surrounds it.

Construction work began in 1720 by order of the newly enthroned prince-bishop of Speyer, Cardinal Hugo Damian von Schönborn, who had fallen out with the local burghers and so decided to move his seat across the Rhine to what was then no more than a hamlet in the heart of the Kraichgau region. Several talented architects were recruited to carry out the work, and the great **Balthasar Neumann** was occasionally seconded from his employment at Würzburg to supply the bravura touches needed to lift the project into the artistic first division. The Schloss complex, whose cheerful yellow, red and white buildings have been restored to pristine condition following devastation in an air raid at the end of the war, stands on Schönbornstrasse, which leads north to Heidelberg. Along the eastern side of the street are a series of offices, with the chancellery centre-stage; an army of lackeys lived in the large edifice to the south. At the northern end of the street is the **Damianstor**, while a smaller triumphal arch gives access to the main courtyard. To the left is the **Hofkirche**, whose haughty onion-domed belfry towers over all the other buildings; the interior has unfortunately been modernized. On the opposite side is the **Kammerflügel**, where prestigious international **concerts** are often held.

The great reception rooms are all in the central Corps de Logis, now the **Schlossmuseum** (Tues–Sun 9.30am–5pm; €3.50; Ⓦwww.schloesser-und-gaerten.de). Facing you on entry is Neumann's ingenious monumental **staircase**. The lower section is laid out as a dark grotto, covered with antique-style frescoes; you then ascend via walls richly covered with stucco to the airily bright oval landing. Here a brilliant trompe l'oeil fresco – an integral part of the overall design – apparently reaches the height of the dome, extending a perspective into the open heavens. Painted by **Januarius Zick**, the most accomplished German decorative artist of the day, it eulogizes the history of the Speyer diocese. Neumann and Zick also collaborated on the two rooms off the staircase.

It's definitely worth paying the extra money to visit the **Museum Mechanischer Musikinstrumente** (guided tours Tues–Sun 9.30am–5pm; €4, or €5 including Schloss admission), which has been installed in some of the vacant rooms. Short demonstrations are given on a cross-section of the two hundred-odd exhibits, which were regarded as scientific miracles in their own time. Earliest of these are the musical clocks which were much in favour in eighteenth-century courts such as Bruchsal itself, and for which even the greatest composers were forced to prostitute their talents – Haydn wrote a delightful set of miniatures, while Mozart created several profound masterpieces, which have to be played on a full-sized organ for maximum effect. From the early twentieth century are examples of the piano-roll system pioneered by the German *Firma Welte*, which enables the accurate play-back of performances by famous pianists. This technique was later ambitiously adapted for the organ, and there's a marvellous instrument here which was formerly used to entertain guests in the *Hotel Excelsior* in Berlin.

Practicalities

Bruchsal's **Bahnhof** is a junction on the rail lines linking Stuttgart, Karlsruhe and Heidelberg. To reach the Schloss from there, turn left and continue straight on; you'll reach the gardens within a few minutes. Alternatively, S-Bahn #31 has a request stop at the Schlossgarten. The **tourist office** (Mon & Tues 8am–2pm, Wed–Fri 10am–1pm & 2–6pm, Sat 9am–noon; ⓣ0 72 51/7 27 71, ⓦwww.bruchsal.de) is in the huge modern shopping centre called Bürgerzentrum at Am Alten Schloss 2. **Hotels** include *Gasthof Graf Kuno*, Württemberger Str. 97 (ⓣ0 72 51/20 13; ❸), *Ratskeller*, Kaiserstr. 68 (ⓣ0 72 51/7 12 30, ⓦwww.ratskeller-bruchsal.de; ❻), *Brauhaus Wallhall*, Kübelmarkt 8 (ⓣ0 72 51/7 21 30; ❻), and *Scheffelhöhe*, Adolf-Bieringer-Str. 20 (ⓣ0 72 51/80 20, ⓦwww.scheffelhoehe.de; ❼). All the hotels listed above, except *Ratskeller*, have **restaurants**; another good place to eat is *Zum Bären*, within the Schloss complex at Schönbornstr. 28, which has the benefit of a beer garden.

Schwetzingen

Another courtly town, **SCHWETZINGEN**, lies on the rail line between Karlsruhe and Mannheim, some 12km west of Heidelberg. It was of very minor significance until the 1740s, when the **Jagdschloss** (guided tours April–Oct Tues–Fri 11am–4pm, Sat & Sun 11am–5pm; €6.50; Nov–March Fri at 2pm, Sat & Sun 11am–3pm; €5; ⓦwww.schloesser-und-gaerten.de) was constructed as a summer residence for Elector Palatine Carl Theodor by the Heidelberg architect Johann Adam Breunig.

The building itself is low-key; it's the **Schlossgarten** (daily: March & Oct 9am–6pm; April–Sept 8am–8pm; Nov–Feb 9am–5pm; €4, or €2.50 Nov–Feb, but included in Jagdschloss entrance) to the rear which gets all the praise and all the visitors. A supreme triumph of the art of landscaping and of the Rococo style, representing a highly original escape into a world of pure fantasy, it took some thirty years to lay out. The whimsical garden buildings aimed at capturing the atmosphere of various far-off civilizations – a fascination with the exotic which marks out Schwetzingen as one of the precursors of the budding Romantic movement. Late spring sees the gardens at their best – the lilac, ivy and chestnut trees are a riot of colour in May, while the linden trees are at their most fragrant during June.

The **Schlosstheater** (accessible in 2003 only for performances, though regular guided tours may be reinstated in the future) was added to the main building by **Nicolas de Pigage**, an ingenious architect from Lorraine who arrived in Schwetzingen in 1750 and spent much of the next three decades constructing its garden buildings. In an individual confection, mixing Rococo with Neoclassicism, Pigage built a triple-tiered auditorium in the shape of a lyre, facing a deep stage harbouring complicated machinery underneath. It was originally intended for the performance of French comedies, and Voltaire, a personal friend of the Elector, was a regular visitor. With its grand dimensions, long vistas, straight avenues and symmetrical layout, the French-style **formal garden** is very much a product of the Age of Reason. It's richly endowed with fountains (which play daily in summer), mock-antique urns and a host of statues.

Just west of here is the **Tempel Apollos**, which served as an open-air auditorium. A sunken garden with sphinxes leads to an artificial mound crowned by a temple in the style of classical Rome, housing a statue of the god. This is the first in a row of buildings by Pigage; alongside is one of his finest works, the **Badhaus**. Its nine rooms (currently closed for restoration) are adorned with rosewood panellings, sculptures, landscape paintings and Chinese tapestries and silks. The marble bath repeats the elliptical shape of the central drawing room; its water pipes are artistically decorated, and the chamber itself adorned with mirrors and jewels. Next to the Badhaus is an arbour with a fountain of water-spouting birds; it's nicknamed "The End of the World" because of the trompe l'oeil perspective, which terminates in a painted diorama. Crossing the moat and continuing northwards, you come to the **Tempel der Botanik**, supposedly representing the trunk of an oak tree, and the **Römischer Wasserweg**, a spectacular fake of a fort and aqueduct, deliberately built as an ivy-covered ruin to enhance its illusory effect. Beyond here are the outer reaches of the park, laid out in the contrastingly untamed style of an English garden. By following the path traversing this section, you can return to the main part of the park via the humpbacked **Chinesische Brücke**.

Pigage's remaining buildings are at the opposite end of the park. The **Tempel Merkurs** is reached via either of the paths along the side of the artificial lake. Originally, this monument was intended to be redolent of ancient Egypt, but ended up as a pastiche of the clifftop ruin of a European Romanesque castle, anachronistically adorned with scenes of the myth of Mercury. From here, there's a spectacular vista over a pond to the pink cupola and minarets of the **Moschee** or Mosque, the most original structure in the gardens and the last to be built. It's a unique translation of oriental forms into the language of eighteenth-century European architecture. Returning in the direction of the circular section of the garden, you come to the sixteen-columned **Tempel Minervas**, which goes back to the favourite source of inspiration, classical Rome. The goddess of wisdom is seated inside; she also appears in a frieze above the entrance, poring over a plan of the gardens of Schwetzingen, to which she gives her seal of approval.

Practicalities

Schwetzingen's **Bahnhof** is five minutes' walk from the Schlossgarten down

Carl-Theodor-Strasse. **Buses** to and from Heidelberg stop on Schlossplatz; services run every half-hour for most of the day. The **tourist office** (April–Sept Mon–Fri 9am–6pm, Sat & Sun 10am–3pm; Oct–March Mon–Fri 9am–6pm, Sat 10am–1pm; ⓣ0 62 02/94 58 75, ⓦwww.schwetzingen.de) is at Dreikönigstr. 3, a stone's throw from Schlossplatz. Although there's no particular reason for staying in Schwetzingen, it makes a good alternative base if Heidelberg is booked solid. Among the **hotels** are *Mama Rosa*, Dreikönigstr. 8 (ⓣ0 62 02/45 35; ❻), *Goldener Löwe*, Schlossstr. 4 (ⓣ0 62 02/2 80 90; ❼), *Adler-Post*, Schlossstr. 3 (ⓣ0 62 02/2 77 70, ⓦwww.adler-post.de; ❼), and *Zum Erbprinzen*, Karlsruher Str. 1 (ⓣ0 62 02/9 32 70, ⓦwww.hotelzumerbprinzen.de; ❼–❾).

Asparagus (Spargel) has been cultivated in Schwetzingen for more than three centuries; in season (April–June) it can be sampled in any of the town's **restaurants**, including those in the hotels listed above, and in the Hausbrauerei, *Brauhaus Zum Ritter*, Schlossplatz 1. Each May and early June, the Schlosstheater is the setting for an international **music festival**, the Schwetzinger Festspiele (ⓦwww.schwetzinger.festspiele.de), which often focuses on the works of Gluck. Another festival in September is devoted mainly to Mozart; there are also regular musical and theatrical performances of all kinds throughout the year.

Mannheim

MANNHEIM was formerly considered one of the most beautiful cities in Germany. Writing in 1826, William Hazlitt called it "a splendid town, both from its admirable buildings and the glossy neatness of the houses. They are too fine to live in, and seem only made to be looked at." A mere stripling among German cities, it was founded in 1606 as a fortress at the strategically important intersection of the rivers Rhine and Neckar. Its meteoric rise to prominence came with the return of the Counts Palatine to Catholicism; unable to establish a satisfactory relationship with the burghers of Heidelberg, Carl Philipp decided in 1720 to make Mannheim the main seat of his court. A daringly original **planned town** was laid out, which served as capital of the Palatinate for the next 57 years, becoming one of Europe's most celebrated centres of the performing arts. The nineteenth century saw heavy industrialization, centred on the harbour trade and shipbuilding, though its most prestigious feature was the automobile factory established by Carl Benz, who demonstrated his first vehicle here in 1886. Alas, the continued prominence of industry, coupled with heavy damage in the last war, means that the city's former glory has long since vanished. However, the highly esteemed **grid-plan** still survives.

The chessboard town

The construction of Mannheim was based on a **chessboard layout** on the strip of land between the Rhine and Neckar. Streets to the west of the central axis are designated A to K, moving northwards; proceeding in the same direction, those to the east are L to U. The street number indicates proximity to the axis, so that D7, for example, is to the far west, whereas R7 is at the extreme east. Obviously, each house then bears a second number, which indicates its position on the square. At first the system can be confusing, particularly when you arrive at the Hauptbahnhof, as the nearby blocks are of widely varying sizes. However, once you get the hang of it, there's really no other European city which is so simple to find your way around.

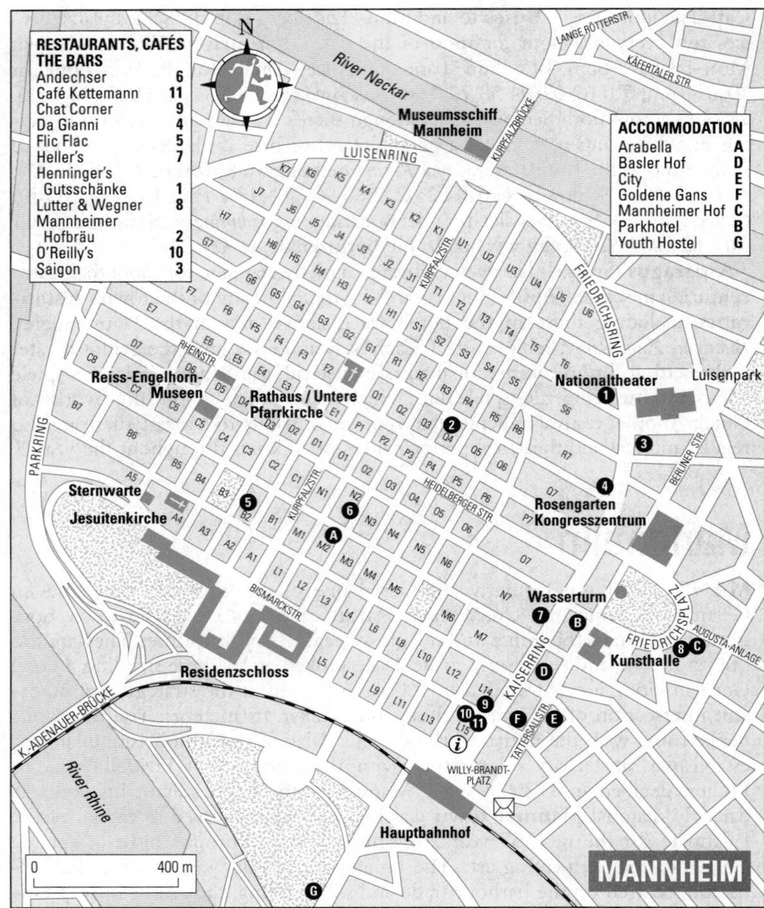

Arrival, information and accommodation

Mannheim's **Hauptbahnhof** is just beyond the southeastern edge of the grid. The **tourist office** (Mon–Fri 9am–7pm, Sat 9am–noon; ⓣ06 21/10 10 11, ⓦwww.tourist-mannheim.de) is diagonally opposite at Willy-Brandt-Platz 3.

Hotels are overwhelmingly geared to the expense-account market, but there are a few budget choices as well. The **youth hostel** is at Rheinpromenade 21 (ⓣ06 21/82 27 18; €13.20/15.90); take the underground passageway at the back entrance of the Hauptbahnhof, then turn left; it's only a few minutes' walk away. **Camping** is possible (April–Sept only) on the banks of either of the city's two great rivers. The larger and cheaper site is at Neuostheim (ⓣ06 21/41 68 40) on the Neckar to the east; the other is to the south on Strandbad in Neckarau (ⓣ06 21/85 62 40); in spite of its name, it's located on a bend of the Rhine.

Hotels and pensions

Arabella M2, 12 ⓣ06 21/2 30 50, ⓕ1 56 45 27. The cheapest rooms in the city centre are in this apartment-block pension. ❷.

Basler Hof Tattersallstr. 27 ⓣ06 21/2 88 16, ⓕ15 32 92. One of several reasonably priced hotels on the street, a couple of minutes' walk north of the Hauptbahnhof. The rooms without facilities are particularly good value, not least on account of the huge buffet breakfasts. ❹–❻

City Tattersallstr. 20–24 ⓣ06 21/40 80 08, ⓦwww.city-hotel-mannheim.de. The basic rooms are a bit more expensive than in the neighbouring hotels; those with facilities are around the same price. ❹

Goldene Gans Tattersallstr. 19 ⓣ06 21/10 52 77 or 42 20 20, ⓕ4 22 02 60. Good value Gasthaus with Weinstube (closed Sun) which includes wonderful buffet breakfasts in the price of a room. ❹–❼

Mannheimer Hof Augusta-Anlage 4 ⓣ06 21/4 00 50, ⓦwww.mannheim.steigenberger.com. Classy hotel with restaurant, part of the Steigenberger chain, at the eastern edge of the city centre. ❼–❾

Parkhotel Friedrichsplatz 2 ⓣ06 21/1 58 80, ⓦwww.maritim.de. Now part of the Maritim chain, this deluxe century-old grand hotel with restaurant is nonetheless a place of real character. ❾

Zum Ochsen Hauptstr. 70, Feudenheim ⓣ06 21/79 95 50, ⓦwww.ochsen-mannheim.de. This seventeenth-century Gasthof, the oldest in Mannheim, is situated north of the Neckar, 5km east of the city centre, near the terminus of tram #2. Its restaurant is among the best in the city for solid German fare, and it also has a shady beer garden. ❻

The City

The pivot of the planned town is the horseshoe-shaped **Residenzschloss**, the most massive Baroque palace ever built in Germany. Soon after its completion, it became an expensive white elephant, as the court transferred to Munich when Carl Theodor inherited the Bavarian Electorate. The dignified exterior is heavily indebted to Palladianism; the interior was far more sumptuous, including rich stuccowork and ceiling frescoes by the Asam brothers. These were obliterated by wartime bombs; afterwards, the building was put to functional use to house the university, with only the outside restored in full.

However, as a real labour of love, the **Schlosskirche** (daily 9am–5pm) at the end of the western wing, plus the main reception rooms, nowadays designated the **Schlossmuseum** (guided tours April–Oct Tues–Sun 10am–1pm & 2–5pm; Nov–March same hours Sat & Sun only; €2.50; ⓦwww.schloesser-und-gaerten.de) were re-created from old photographs. The success of this project is highly debatable, but at least the **Rittersaal**, reached via a monumental staircase, provides an effective concert hall, which is particularly appropriate as the Mannheim court's greatest achievements were in the field of music. Its orchestra, which pioneered the mellow tones of the clarinet, was regarded in the eighteenth century as the best in the world, while the symphony was developed here into the chief form of instrumental music.

On A5, just to the west of the Residenzschloss, is the **Jesuitenkirche**, deliberately constructed as the largest church in town to symbolize the Palatinate court's return to Catholicism; the grandiose facade and the central dome are the most striking features. Immediately to its rear is the **Sternwarte**, an observatory tower now used by artists.

Just to the north on C5 is the **Zeughaus**, erected in the penultimate year of Mannheim's period as Palatine capital. It normally houses the collections of Dutch and Flemish cabinet pictures, decorative arts and local history of the **Reiss-Engelhorn-Museen** (Tues–Sun 11am–6pm; €2.10; ⓦwww.reiss-engelhorn-museen.de), but is likely to be closed until 2007 for reconstruction work. In the meantime, the most important section of the museums, the archeology department, remains on view in the new building on the square directly in front of the Zeughaus. This originated as the Elector's private cabinet of antiquities, and ranges from the Stone Age to the early medieval period.

Also here are ethnological displays from Africa, the Islamic countries, India, China and Japan. There are usually important international loan exhibitions once or twice a year.

The **Marktplatz**, which occupies the square G1, is the scene of markets on Tuesday, Thursday and Saturday mornings. In the centre rises a large monument presented by Carl Theodor; originally representing the four elements, it was reworked into an allegorical composition in praise of Mannheim by the son of the original sculptor. On the south side of the square is a curious Siamese twin of a building, erected just before Mannheim became the seat of the court. Sharing a central tower, the eastern part serves as the **Rathaus**, while the western is the **Untere Pfarrkirche**; their physical union is supposed to symbolize the concord between Justice and Piety, between secular and sacred authority.

Outside the central grid

The other main square, the Jugendstil **Friedrichsplatz**, is due east from here, just outside the central grid. It was laid out around the **Wasserturm**, which is some fifteen years older, and is the main example of a style which left a considerable mark all over the city. Another fine Jugendstil building is the **Kunsthalle** (Tues–Sun 11am–6pm; €2.10, €7 during temporary exhibitions; Ⓦwww.kunsthalle-mannheim.de) on Moltkestrasse, the next street to the south. This contains one of the best collections of nineteenth- and twentieth-century painting and sculpture in Germany, and is now the city's most obvious single draw. Highlight of the collection is one of the great masterpieces of Impressionism, **Manet**'s *Execution of Emperor Maximilian of Mexico*, the largest and most complete of the four versions he painted of this subject. Other notable works in the same room are **Cézanne**'s *Pipe Smoker*, and still lifes by Renoir and Van Gogh. The German section was brutally pruned in the Nazi purges against "degenerate art", but there's a room devoted to Romanticism, including several important examples of **Feuerbach**. *Portrait of the Writer Max Herrmann-Neisse* is one of **George Grosz**'s best canvases, while there's an outstanding array of modern German sculpture, with **Barlach** and **Lehmbruck** strongly represented, along with a host of avant-garde works. Major temporary exhibitions are frequently held in the gallery.

At the northernmost end of the grid-plan the central axis road continues over the Neckar by the Kurpfälzbrücke. Moored close to the bridge is the 1920s passenger steamer *Mainz*, now designated the **Museumsschiff Mannheim** (Tues–Sun 10am–4pm; €1). Nearby is the departure point for **harbour cruises** (Easter & June–Aug; 40min trip €3.50; 90min voyage along the Neckar €6.50).

Eastwards along the river is the city's playground, the **Luisenpark** (daily 9am–dusk; €4, Nov–Feb €3). This boasts various flower gardens, hothouses, an aquarium, a menagerie of farmyard animals and waterfowl, an open-air stadium for concerts, a gondola course and a watersports centre. There's also the TV tower or **Fernmeldeturm** (daily 10am–11pm; €3.50 including ascent by elevator), which offers a sweeping view of the region.

Just south of the park on Wilhelm-Varnholt-Platz is the **Planetarium** (showings Tues, Thurs & Fri 10am–noon & 2–4pm, Wed 2–4pm & 5–7pm, Sat & Sun 12.30–4.30pm; €5.30). Nearby, at Museumsstr. 1, the **Landesmuseum für Technik und Arbeit** (Tues, Thurs & Fri 9am–5pm, Wed 9am–8pm, Sat 10am–5pm, Sun 10am–6pm, Ⓦwww.landesmuseum-mannheim.de; €3), houses a spectacular collection of historic machinery, including a steam locomotive which transports visitors through the grounds.

Eating, drinking and entertainment

Although Mannheim has no obvious concentration of good places to eat and drink, there's a varied assortment of recommendable establishments scattered throughout the city. The city also has a vibrant theatre tradition.

Restaurants

Andechser N2, 10. Serves traditional Bavarian fare and beers from the monastic brewery of Andechs in Upper Bavaria.
Augusta Giovanni Augusta-Anlage 40. Moderately priced Italian restaurant.
Da Gianni R7, 34. One of Germany's most highly regarded Italian restaurants, the cooking showing *nouvelle* touches; predictably, it's very expensive. Closed Mon.
Eichbaum Käfertaler Str. 168. Located just north of the Neckar, this is the Gaststätte of the brewery of the same name, the largest in Mannheim. Its *Weizen* beers, both light and dark, are its most highly regarded products. Take tram #2 or #7 to Bibienastrasse.
Heller's N7, 13. Specialist vegetarian restaurant. Open Mon–Fri 11am–8pm, Sat 11am–4.30pm, Sun 11.30am–3pm.
Henninger's Gutsschänke T6, 28. Excellent and fairly priced wine bar-restaurant. Open daily from 5pm.
Lutter & Wegner Friedrichsplatz 12. Pricey wine bar-restaurant with an international menu.
Martin Lange Rötterstr. 53. This restaurant to the north of the Neckar, reached by tram #4 or #5 to Lange Rötterstrasse, is best known for its fish dishes, though it has a varied menu, including vegetarian options. Closed Sat lunchtime & Wed.
Saigon Goethestr. 4. Highly regarded Vietnamese restaurant, with a much more select menu than usual, including some vegetarian specialities. Evenings only, except Sun, when it's also open for lunch.
Skyline Hans-Reschke-Ufer 2. Panorama restaurant in the Fernmeldeturm.

Bars and cafés

Café Kettemann Willy-Brandt-Platz 11. Arguably the pick of the traditional cafés.
Chat Corner L14, 16–17. The long opening hours make this a convenient place for Internet access. Open daily 9am–3am.
Flic Flac B2, 12. Arty pub which features regular exhibitions and live music.
Mannheimer Hofbräu Q4, 6–8. Located on the site of Mannheim's first brewery, this beer hall has its own range of around a dozen different beers, though these are not made on the premises or even in Mannheim. Also serves full meals, including bargain lunches.
O'Reilly's L15, 7–9. Genuine Irish pub, sometimes with live music.

Theatre and concerts

The main **theatre** is the Nationaltheater on Goetheplatz (Ⓣ06 21/1 68 01 50, Ⓦwww.mannheim.nationaltheater.de), the successor to the now-destroyed building near the Schloss which was associated with Schiller's youthful Sturm und Drang phase. Performances of plays, opera, ballet and musicals are presented, along with special shows for kids. **Concerts** are held at Kongresszentrum Rosengarten on Friedrichsplatz (Ⓣ06 21/4 10 63 03).

Heidelberg

When the Romantic movement discovered **HEIDELBERG** in the late eighteenth century, the city was very much a fallen star. Capital of the Palatinate for five hundred years, it had never fully recovered from two sackings at the hands of French troops in the previous century, and its rulers had abandoned their magnificent, crumbling Schloss in favour of the creature comforts of their new palace in

Mannheim. Yet this wistful feeling of decay only enhanced the charms of the city, majestically set on both banks of the swift-flowing River Neckar between two ranges of wooded hills – a real-life fulfilment of the ideal German landscape, and a site known to be one of the earliest inhabited places in the world. To many of the rushed Grand-Tour-of-Europe coach parties of today, Heidelberg *is* Germany, the only place in the country they see – or, perhaps, want to see.

For English-speaking visitors, the distinguished roll-call of predecessors gives Heidelberg special claims on the attention. Earliest of these was the Scots-born princess, **Elizabeth Stuart**, daughter of the first monarch of Great Britain, James VI and I. She arrived in 1613 as the 17-year-old bride of the Elector Palatine and presided over a spectacular court life for five years, before leaving for Prague and her ill-fated spell as the "Winter Queen". Heidelberg's greatest painter is also Britain's greatest: **J.M.W. Turner** first came to the city in 1836, and, in a series of oils and watercolours, captured its changing moods and magical plays of light in his own inimitable way. Among Americans, **Mark Twain** deserves pride of place: he began the hilarious travels round Europe recounted in *A Tramp Abroad* in Heidelberg in 1878, and his descriptions of the city have never been surpassed. By this time, Heidelberg was already a popular sojourn for Americans visiting Europe, though the numbers were a trickle in comparison with today. After World War II (in which, significantly, the city was spared from aerial bombardment), Heidelberg was chosen as the headquarters of the US Army in Europe, with the soldiers housed in the purpose-built Patrick Henry Village, to the south.

Heidelberg is best avoided in high summer: the students, who make such an essential contribution to the life of the city, clear out then and are replaced by hordes of tourists. Surprisingly, it's possible to cover all the essential sights fairly quickly, but you should certainly plan on staying for several days, in order to soak up the city's atmosphere.

Heidelberg viewpoints

It's the long-range views which have made Heidelberg so famous, and the city is a ready-made subject for picture-postcard **photography**; with its hilly setting, there are plenty of angles to choose from. If you take the trouble to go to the same vantage point at different times of day, you'll see the reason for Heidelberg's hold on painters: the red sandstone buildings change their hue with the movement of the sun, and the shafts of light make magical effects as they illuminate and cast into shadow different parts of the scene. "One thinks Heidelberg by day the last possibility of the beautiful," wrote Mark Twain, "but when he sees Heidelberg by night, a fallen Milky Way… he requires time to consider upon the verdict."

The best-known view is from the northern quays of the Neckar, where there's a full-frontal panorama of the Altstadt nestling snugly below the Schloss, itself sharply etched against the background of the wooded Königstuhl. The spectacle from street level is surpassed by climbing up the slopes of the Heiligenberg via the celebrated **Philosophenweg** (Philosopher's Walk), so called because of the stimulus it offered to the meditation of Heidelberg thinkers. It is best experienced late in the day, as the sun sets on the Schloss. A closer-range view of the Schloss and the Altstadt can be enjoyed from the tower of the Heiliggeistkirche (see p.353). For a completely different perspective, take the late nineteenth-century **funicular** (€4 single, €6 return) from Kornmarkt to the *Molkenkur* hotel, which has a panorama terrace. Here you transfer to a second, slightly younger funicular, which continues up to the **Königstuhl**. This is crowned by the **Fernsehturm** (Television Tower; March–Oct daily 10am–6/7pm; €1), which commands a sweeping view over the Neckar valley and Odenwald.

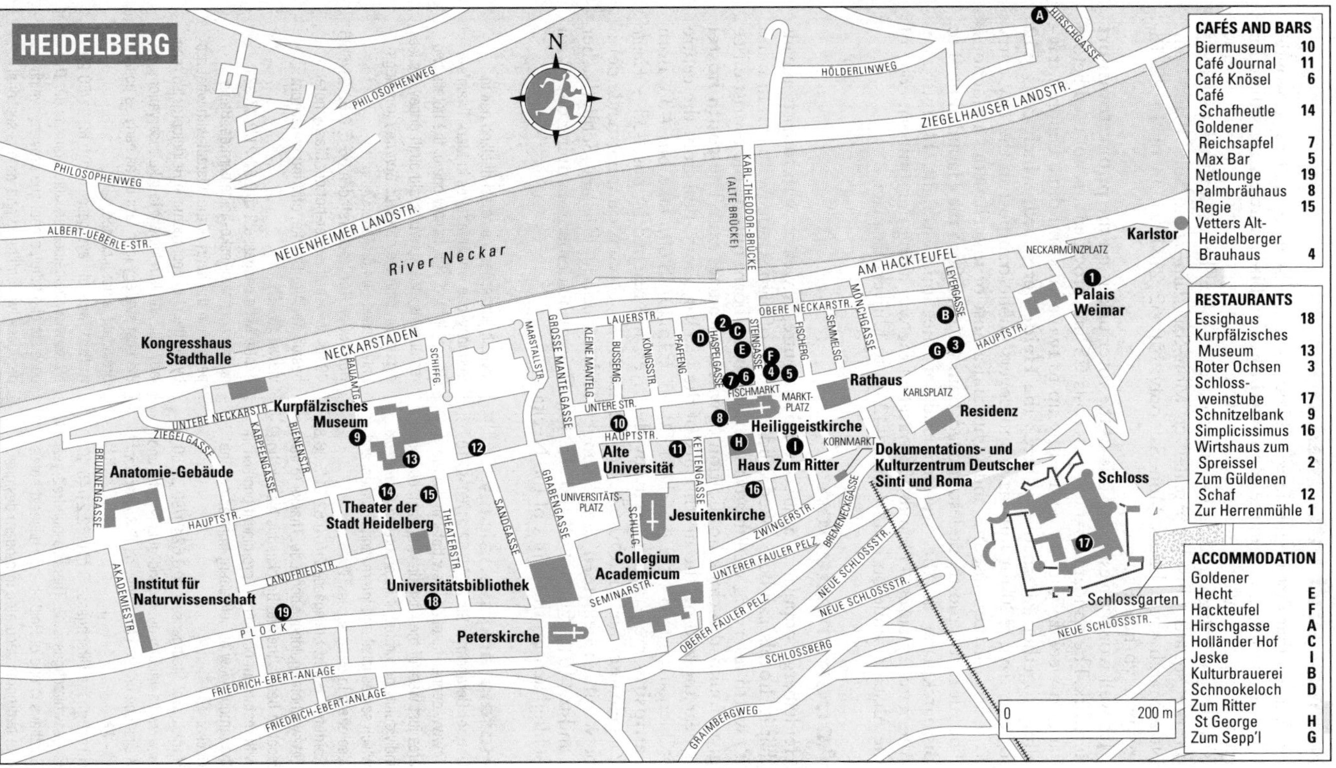
HEIDELBERG
N
CAFÉS AND BARS
Biermuseum 10
Café Journal 11
Café Knösel 6
Café Schafheutle 14
Goldener Reichsapfel 7
Max Bar 5
Netlounge 19
Palmbräuhaus 8
Regie 15
Vetters Alt-Heidelberger Brauhaus 4
RESTAURANTS
Essighaus 18
Kurpfälzisches Museum 13
Roter Ochsen 3
Schlossweinstube 17
Schnitzelbank 9
Simplicissimus 16
Wirtshaus zum Spreissel 2
Zum Güldenen Schaf 12
Zur Herrenmühle 1
ACCOMMODATION
Goldener Hecht E
Hackteufel F
Hirschgasse A
Holländer Hof C
Jeske I
Kulturbrauerei B
Schnookeloch D
Zum Ritter St George H
Zum Sepp'l G
0 200 m
River Neckar
Karl-Theodor-Brücke (Alte Brücke)
Kongresshaus Stadthalle
Kurpfälzisches Museum
Anatomie-Gebäude
Theater der Stadt Heidelberg
Institut für Naturwissenschaft
Universitätsbibliothek
Peterskirche
Collegium Academicum
Jesuitenkirche
Alte Universität
Heiliggeistkirche
Haus Zum Ritter
Rathaus
Residenz
Dokumentations- und Kulturzentrum Deutscher Sinti und Roma
Schloss
Schlossgarten
Palais Weimar
Karlstor
Philosophenweg
Albert-Ueberle-Str.
Neuenheimer Landstr.
Ziegelhauser Landstr.
Hölderlinweg
Hirschgasse
Neckarstaden
Untere Neckarstr.
Ziegelgasse
Brunnengasse
Akademiestr.
Hauptstr.
Karpfengasse
Bienenstr.
Bauamtg.
Schiffg.
Marstallstr.
Grosse Mantelgasse
Kleine Manteig.
Bussemg.
Königsstr.
Pfaffeng.
Lauerstr.
Haspelgasse
Steingasse
Fischerg.
Semmelsg.
Mönchgasse
Obere Neckarstr.
Am Hackteufel
Leyergasse
Neckarmünzplatz
Karlsplatz
Fischmarkt
Marktplatz
Kornmarkt
Untere Str.
Kettengasse
Universitätsplatz
Schulg.
Grabengasse
Sandgasse
Theaterstr.
Landfriedstr.
Plöck
Seminarstr.
Zwingerstr.
Bremeneckgasse
Unterer Fauler Pelz
Oberer Fauler Pelz
Neue Schlossstr.
Schlossberg
Graimbergweg
Friedrich-Ebert-Anlage
Hauptbahnhof & Post Office

Arrival and information

Be warned that first impressions of Heidelberg are likely to make you wonder what all the fuss is about: the **Hauptbahnhof** and **bus station** are situated in an anonymous quarter some 1.5km west of the centre, with a dreary avenue, Kurfürsten-Anlage, leading towards town. The often harassed **tourist office** is on the square outside (April–Oct Mon–Sat 9am–7pm, Sun 10am–6pm; Nov–March same hours Mon–Sat only; ⓣ0 62 21/1 94 33 or 14 22 18, ⓦwww.cvb-heidelberg.de).

It's well worth investing in one of the rover tickets on the **public transport** network. The standard 24-hour pass costs €5 and, provided it is not used before 9am on weekdays, it can be used by up to two adults and three children travelling together. Alternatively, there's the **HeidelbergCard**, which costs €12 for two days, €20 for four days, and covers public transport in the city, entry to nearly all the museums and sights and a host of miscellaneous reductions. The Altstadt is mostly pedestrianized; tram #1 runs from the Hauptbahnhof to Bismarckplatz, at the western end of the long, straight Hauptstrasse. Alternatively, buses #11 and #33 travel all the way along the southern edge of the Altstadt, while buses #41 and #42 go to Universitätsplatz.

Accommodation

Heidelberg's popularity as a convention centre, as well as with tourists, means that its **hotels** can be booked solid even out of high season. With this in mind it's worth reserving well in advance, though the board outside the tourist office gives round-the-clock notification of where vacancies exist. The **youth hostel** is near the zoo on the north bank of the Neckar, about 4km from the centre at Tiergartenstr. 5 (ⓣ0 62 21/41 20 66; €15.90/18.60); take bus #33. Both **campsites** are east of the city by the river, and reached by bus #35 – *Haide* Ziegelhäuser Str. 91 (ⓣ0 62 21/0 62 23/21 11, ⓦwww.camping-haide.de) is between Ziegelhausen and Kleingemünd; *Heidelberg Camping* Schlierbacher Landstr. 151 (ⓣ0 62 21/80 25 06, ⓦwww.heidelberg-camping.de) is in Schlierbach on the banks of the Neckar.

Hotels and pensions

Denner Bergheimer Str. 8 ⓣ0 62 21/60 45 10, ⓦwww.denner-hotel.de. New hotel in the lively area just west of the Altstadt, with each bedroom individually decorated. It incorporates *Café Gecko*, which serves local and international dishes, and also offers Internet access. ❻

Goldener Hecht Steingasse 2 ⓣ0 62 21/5 36 80, ⓦwww.hotel-goldener-hecht.de. Thanks to its location beside the Alte Brücke, this historic hotel with restaurant occupies a prominent position in the famous view of Heidelberg from across the Neckar. ❻–❽

Hackteufel Steingasse 7 ⓣ0 62 21/90 53 80, ⓦwww.hackteufel.de. A good-quality hotel and Weinstube on the same alley as *Goldener Hecht*. ❻–❽

Hirschgasse Hirschgasse 3 ⓣ0 62 21/45 40, ⓦwww.hirschgasse.de. This five-hundred-year-old Gasthaus is one of Heidelberg's poshest hotels, with bedrooms decorated in modern designer style. It possesses the oldest duelling hall in Germany, one which features in Mark Twain's *A Tramp Abroad*. This is now one of the hotel's two restaurants, *Mensurstube*; although pricey, it's less expensive than the other, *Le Gourmet* (evenings only, closed Sun & Mon). ❾

Holländer Hof Neckarstaden 66 ⓣ0 62 21/6 05 00, ⓦwww.hollaender-hof.de. Classy hotel beside the Alte Brücke, offering waterfront views. ❻–❽

Jeske Mittelbadgasse 2 ⓣ0 62 21/2 37 33, ⓦwww.pension-jeske-heidelberg.de. Basic pension in the heart of the Altstadt with what are by far the cheapest rooms in Heidelberg. It's regularly full, and is reluctant to take reservations, so the best strategy is to turn up as early as possible. Breakfast is not included. ❸

Kulturbrauerei Leyergasse 6 ⓣ0 62 21/50 29 80, ⓦwww.heidelberger-kulturbrauerei.de. This consists of a hotel, a boutique brewery which produces two unfiltered and various seasonal beers, a restaurant housed in a splendid old hall, a beer garden, a jazz bar and an art gallery. ❻

Molkenkur Klingenteichstr. 31 ⓣ0 62 21/65 40 80, ⓦwww.molkenkur.de. Stands on the site of the original Schloss, high above its successor, and is directly accessible by the funicular. The terrace commands a grandstand view of the city; there's also a fine restaurant. ❻

Schmitt Blumenstr. 54 ⓣ0 62 21/2 72 96, ⓦwww.hotel-schmitt-heidelberg.de. A decent budget hotel, one of a number located between the Hauptbahnhof and the Altstadt. ❺

Schnookeloch Haspelgasse 8 ⓣ0 62 21/13 80 80, ⓦwww.schnookeloch.de. Heidelberg's oldest surviving inn, dating back to 1407. Its tavern (closed Mon), which has a beer garden, is one of those which has long been associated with the student corps, and is covered throughout with graffiti. ❻–❽

Zum Ritter St George Hauptstr. 178 ⓣ0 62 21/13 50, ⓦwww.ritter-heidelberg.de. Heidelberg's most magnificent mansion is now home to one of its most attractive hotels, a member of the Romantik group. It has a recommendable though fairly expensive restaurant. ❾

Zum Sepp'l Hauptstr. 213 ⓣ0 62 21/1 43 30, ⓦwww.zum-seppl.de. A luxury eight-roomed hotel has been established in this, the oldest of the famous Heidelberg taverns, one which has been used by the student corps continuously since 1634. It commodious dining room, decked out with bric-a-brac, is among the city's most celebrated tourist sights, and serves moderately priced meals. ❾

The Schloss

Centrepiece of all the famous views of Heidelberg is the **Schloss**. A series of disparate, yet consistently magnificent buildings of various dates, it somehow hasn't been diminished by its ruined condition; if anything, it has actually grown in stature. Enough remains (with the help of the plentiful pictorial records which exist) to give a clear idea of what it looked like in its prime, yet a new dimension has been added by the destruction, which reveals otherwise hidden architectural secrets and magnifies its relationship with the surrounding landscape.

The history of the Schloss

The Schloss originally dates back to the first quarter of the thirteenth century. It was then that the title of **Count Palatine**, one of the great imperial offices of state, and one carrying the rank of an Elector, was bestowed on a Wittelsbach, Duke Ludwig of Bavaria, whose family retained the office right to the end of the Holy Roman Empire. The earliest significant portions of what can be seen today date from the following century, as the castle evolved into a sturdy medieval fortress capable of withstanding the most powerful siege weapons of the day. In the sixteenth century, the inner courtyard of the Schloss began to be embellished with sumptuous palatial buildings, as its role as a princely residence became increasingly important; this gathered momentum mid-century when the Electors converted to Protestantism and began the construction of the most splendid **Renaissance buildings** in Germany.

Lutheranism was later jettisoned in favour of Calvinism, and the **Heidelberg Catechism** of 1562 remains the basic creed for many Reformed churches. This took on an increasingly militant aspect when Elizabeth Stuart's youthful husband, **Friedrich V**, became nominal leader of the Calvinist League, which aimed to establish the irreversible supremacy of Protestantism in Germany and to topple the Habsburgs from their position of pre-eminence in the country's affairs. Friedrich's ham-fisted attempt was not only a personal disaster (he was defeated, exiled and stripped of his titles), but also led to the Thirty Years War, which devastated the country. However, it was French designs on the Palatinate in 1689 which led to the destruction of Heidelberg and its Schloss; although their claim on the territory was eventually withdrawn, the Electorship passed to a Catholic branch of the family. Unable to establish a rapport with the locals, they moved their seat; the planned rebuilding of the Schloss never occurred, and Heidelberg was left to vegetate.

The Schloss can be reached by the funicular from Kornmarkt (€2 single, €3.50 return), but it's more fun to walk up via the Burgweg: that way, you can make a complete circuit of the exterior before entering. At the northwest corner is the sixteenth-century **Dicker Turm** (Fat Tower), now a semicircular shell, its outer wall, along with its top, having been blasted away. Behind the northern fortifications you get a glimpse of the Renaissance buildings and pass the **Zeughaus**, before coming to the **Redoute**, built just a few years before the Schloss was destroyed. Behind it stands the **Glockenturm** (Bell Tower), originally a single-storey defence tower, to which six residential levels were later added.

Further along the eastern side is the protruding **Apothekerturm**, an old defensive tower which was later converted into the apothecary's residential quarters. Between it and the Glockenturm is a superb oriel window, part of a now-vanished banqueting hall. At the southeastern corner you'll find the most romantic of the ruins, the **Pulver Turm** (Powder Tower), now generally know as the **Gesprengter Turm** (Blown-up Tower). Originally a gunpowder store, it was destroyed by miners who tunnelled underneath and blew it up from the centre. This left a clean break in the now-overgrown masonry; the collapsed section still lies intact in the moat, leaving a clear view into the chambers of the interior, with their once-elegant central column supports.

From here, it's best to proceed to the western side of the Schloss, an artificial plateau formerly used as a gun battery but converted by Friedrich V into a pleasure garden. At its entrance is the graceful Roman-inspired **Elizabethpforte**, a gateway said to have been erected in a single night in 1615 as a surprise for the princess; the sober **Englischer Bau** adjoining the Dicker Turm was also built in her honour. At the western end of the garden is the semicircular **Rondell**, commanding a view over the rooftops of the city.

The **Schlosshof** (daily 8am–5.30pm; €2.50, but free access outside these hours; guided tours of apartments daily April–Oct 9am–4/5pm; check on noticeboard for times of departures in English; €3.50; Ⓦwww.schloesser-und-gaerten.de) is reached by a series of sixteenth-century defensive structures – the Brückenhaus, the bridge itself and the severe **Thorturm** (Gate Tower), the only part of the Schloss not blown up. Immediately to the left of the entrance is the Gothic **Ruprechtsbau**, where you can see two restored chambers, one with an elaborate chimneypiece. After the ruined library comes the **Frauenzimmerbau**, where the women of the court resided; its colossal ground-floor hall has been restored as a venue for concerts. Looking anti-clockwise from the entrance gate, you first of all see the Gothic **Brunnenhaus** (Well House), a loggia with a graceful star vault. Its marble columns were brought here from Charlemagne's palace, and had previously adorned a Roman building. This is followed by a series of functional buildings – the **Kaserne** (Barracks) and the **Oekonomiebau**, which housed offices and workshops; part of it has been converted to house the *Schlossweinstube* (see p.356).

What really catches your eye in the courtyard, however, is the group of Renaissance palaces on the north and east sides. Next to the Oekonomiebau is the mid-sixteenth-century **Ottheinrichsbau**, now just a shell but preserving its vigorous horizontal facade. The magnificent sculptural decoration has successive tiers of allegorical figures representing Strength, the Christian Virtues and the Planetary Deities. In the basement is the **Deutsches Apothekenmuseum** (daily 10am–5.30pm; included in Schlosshof entrance; Ⓦwww.deutsches-apothekenmuseum.de), an offbeat but worthwhile collection. Among the displays are several complete Baroque and Rococo workshops, an early seventeenth-century travelling pharmacy and a herbarium. You can also descend to the bowels of the Apothekerturm, which has been rigged out with a furnace and distilling apparatus in an attempt to re-create its old appearance.

The triple loggia of the earlier **Saalbau** forms a link to the celebrated late sixteenth-century **Friedrichsbau** built by Alsatian architect Johannes Schoch. A series of bucolic, larger-than-life statues is a pantheon of the House of Wittelsbach, beginning with Charlemagne (the alleged founder of the dynasty) and continuing right up to the ruling Elector. Those now on view are copies, but the originals can be seen inside, along with a number of restored rooms which have been decked out in period style. On the ground floor is the intact **Schlosskapelle**, which, in total contrast to the facade, harks back to the Gothic period; not surprisingly, in view of the photo opportunities outside, it's now a popular venue for weddings.

The **Fassbau** is reached down a passageway in front of the Schlosshof. It contains the celebrated **Grosses Fass** (Great Vat), said to be the largest wine barrel in the world with a capacity of over 50,000 gallons; this is crowned with a platform that did service as a dance floor. Made in the late eighteenth century, the vat is the third in a spectacular line; though a folly and long out of service, it's reputed to have been filled on at least one occasion, when there was a particularly good grape harvest in the Palatinate (whose Elector was entitled to claim a tithe). Facing the entrance, as a ploy to elicit a gasp from visitors when they turn the corner and see the real thing, is the so-called **Kleines Fass** (Little Vat), itself of ample proportions.

The Altstadt

Heidelberg's Altstadt is a largely pedestrianized area between the Schloss and the Neckar, bisected by an unusually long main street, Hauptstrasse. In comparison with the Schloss, its monuments can seem prosaic: although the old layout of the medieval city survives, the French devastation means that nearly all the buildings are eighteenth century or later, and are excessively sober in style. To many people, these are familiar from the Hollywood version of *The Student Prince* by the Hungarian-American composer Sigmund Romberg.

Marktplatz and the eastern Altstadt

The finest surviving buildings in the Altstadt are grouped on Marktplatz, where markets are held on Wednesdays and Saturdays. In the middle is the Gothic red sandstone **Heiliggeistkirche**, founded just after the university at the end of the fourteenth century. Its lofty **tower** (Mon–Sat 11am–5pm, Sun 1–5pm; €0.50), capped by a Baroque dome, is one of the city's most prominent landmarks, and offers wonderful views in all directions. Note the tiny shopping booths between the buttresses, a feature ever since the church was built – this was a common practice in medieval times but has been frowned upon for so long that examples are now rare. The interior is light, airy and uncluttered, but was not always so, as the church was built to house the mausoleum of the Palatinate Electors. Only one tomb now remains – that of Ruprecht III, who became King of Germany in 1400, and his wife, Elizabeth von Hohenzollern. Furthermore, the triforium gallery once housed one of the great libraries of the world, the *Bibliotheca Palatina*; this was confiscated by Field Marshal Johann Tilly as war booty and presented to the pope. Some items were returned in the nineteenth century, but the finest books remain in the Vatican.

Facing the church is the only mansion to survive the seventeenth-century devastation of the town, the **Haus zum Ritter**, so called from the statue of St

George dressed as a knight which crowns the pediment. Built for a Huguenot refugee cloth merchant, it was clearly modelled on the Ottheinrichsbau in the Schloss to which, with its extravagant decoration of caryatids, scrollwork and fancy gables, it stands as a worthy competitor. Now an expensive hotel and restaurant, it completely outclasses its Baroque neighbours, among which is the **Rathaus** on the eastern side of the square.

On Bremeckgasse, a short walk south of Marktplatz, the **Dokumentations- und Kulturzentrum Deutscher Sinti und Roma** (Tues, Wed & Fri 10am–4.30pm, Thurs 10am–8pm, Sat & Sun 11am–4pm; free; Ⓦwww.sinti-und-roma.de) is a belated act of atonement for the often overlooked atrocities committed by the Third Reich against Europe's Gypsy communities. A permanent exhibition documents the deportations and mass murders that were carried out, which resulted, it is estimated, in around 500,000 deaths – a total that was only a fraction of that of the Jews, but on a comparable scale in proportionate terms. Temporary displays illustrate the culture of the two main German-based Gypsy peoples, the Sinti and the Roma.

East of Marktplatz, the imposing Baroque **Residenz** of the Baden grand dukes, which now houses the German Academy of Sciences and Letters, can be seen on Karlspatz. Beyond, at Hauptstr. 235, is the **Palais Weimar**, now containing the **Völkerkunde-Museum** (Wed–Sat 2–6pm, Sun 11–6pm; €3), which has a wonderul group of artefacts from Asmat in western New Guinea, as well as good African collections. At the end of the street is the Neoclassical **Karlstor**, a triumphal arch in honour of Elector Carl Theodor, designed by his court architect, Nicolas de Pigage. However, the most important structure this great artistic patron gave to his ancestors' capital is the **Alte Brücke** downstream. Dating from the 1780s, it's at least the fifth on this site. In the last war, it suffered the inevitable fate of being blown up but has been painstakingly rebuilt, including its fairy-tale gateway.

The university quarter

Much of the western half of the Altstadt is occupied by buildings of the **University**, officially known as the **Ruperto-Carola**, in honour of its two founders. It was established in 1386 by the Elector Ruprecht I: this makes it the oldest in what is now Germany, though German-speaking universities had preceded it in Prague and Vienna. Having fallen into decline in the eighteenth century, it was revived in 1803 by Grand Duke Karl Friedrich as the first state university of Baden.

One side of Universitätsplatz, the Altstadt's second main square, is occupied by the **Alte Universität** (April–Oct Tues–Sun 10am–4pm; Nov–March Tues–Fri 10am–2pm; €2.50); like so many of the city's buildings, it dates back to the first quarter of the eighteenth century, and was designed by the local architect Johann Adam Breunig. The admission ticket gives access to a small museum documenting the university's history, and to the **Alte Aula**, the grand late nineteenth-century graduation hall on the first floor. It is also valid for the most celebrated university building, the former **Studentenkarzer** (Student Prison), on Augustinergasse to the rear. Between 1712 and 1914, this was used to detain students (a sizeable proportion, by all accounts) who had been convicted of an offence. Every available square centimetre of the walls of the otherwise spartan cells is covered with graffiti, with a black silhouette self-portrait of the prisoner the most popular motif.

The **Universitätsbibliothek** (Mon–Sat 10am–6pm; free; Ⓦwww.uni-hd.de) is down Grabengasse to the south of Universitätsplatz, with the entrance for temporary exhibitions round the corner on Plöck. In summer, there's generally a display centred on the treasures of the collection. Outstanding is the fourteenth-century *Codex Manesse*; apart from containing 137 beautiful miniatures, it ranks as the most important collection of Middle High German poetry. Opposite is the Gothic **Peterskirche**, which is now the university church, as well as a regular venue for vocal and choral concerts.

The **Jesuitenkirche**, tucked away just to the east of Universitätsplatz on Schulgasse, is in the sombre, classically inspired style favoured by this evangelizing order, who came here with the intention of recapturing Heidelberg for Catholicism, a mission which doesn't seem to have been particularly successful. Housed in its gallery and the adjoining monastery is a rather moderate **Museum für Sakralkunst** (June–Oct Tues–Sat 10am–5pm, Sun 1–5pm; Nov–May Sat & Sun same hours only; €1.50).

Following Plöck in a westerly direction, you come to the former **Institut für Naturwissenchaften** at the junction with Akadamiestrasse. Heidelberg's most famous scientist, **Robert Wilhelm Bunsen**, was based there for four decades. His name is familiar to school pupils all over the world for popularizing that staple gadget of the laboratory, the "Bunsen burner"; he was also the first to separate the colours of the spectrum.

The curious traditions of Heidelberg University

Of the many traditions associated with the university, the oddest was the fact that, until the twentieth century, its students were not subject to civil jurisdiction. When a **crime** or breach of the peace was committed, the offender had to be dealt with by the university authorities. Moreover, when found guilty, the student did not need to serve his punishment immediately; he could do so at his leisure. Nor was there any stigma attached to imprisonment – indeed, it was seen as an essential component of the university experience. Nobody knows how this system came into being, but it presumably dates back to the times when most alumni were aristocratic and subject to the mores of *noblesse oblige*.

A second Heidelberg tradition – this time one which spread throughout Germany – was the **Mensur**, or fencing match. Students were divided into confraternities (*Verbindungen*) according to the region of their birth; the members wore a distinguishing cap and were forbidden from socializing with those belonging to other groups. At least three (in practice, far more) duels were held on two days of every week. Each bout lasted for fifteen minutes, excluding stoppages, unless it became dangerous to proceed; if the outcome was inconclusive, it had to be re-staged at a later date. The combatants wore goggles and every vital organ was padded, so that the risk of death was minimal. They were placed at arm's length from each other and fought by moving their wrists alone; to flinch or to step back were the ultimate disgraces. Wounds were frequent, particularly on the top of the head and left cheek; these were treated immediately by a surgeon or medical student. What was really bizarre was that the wounds became highly prized badges of courage; for optimum prestige, salt was rubbed into them, leaving scars which would remain for life. The anachronistic ideal of chivalry encapsulated in the *Mensur* staggers on to this day among right-wing toffs, while its effects can still be seen on elderly professorial brows.

Another tradition associated with the fencing corps was the **Kneipe**, a stag party where competition was confined within the group. The idea was to down as many mugs of beer as possible in a given space of time; the winner became the *Bierkönig*. As the rules were concerned solely with emptying the contents of the glass down the throat, and not about retaining the alcohol in the system, those who didn't mind the discomfort of consistently spewing up were able to accomplish prodigious totals of close to one hundred pints in an evening. Several taverns which were the scene of these bouts still exist (see pp.350–51 & p.356).

The Kurpfälzisches Museum

Housed in the **Palais Morass** at Hauptstr. 97, an early eighteenth-century mansion built for a law professor, is the **Kurpfälzisches Museum** (Tues–Sun 10am–6pm; €2.50). The archeology department in the modern extension to the rear includes a cast of the jawbone of *Homo heidelbergiensis* (the original is owned by the university); this is estimated to come from the inter-glacial period 500,000 years ago, making it one of the oldest human bones ever discovered. There are also rooms devoted to excavations from the Roman and Merovingian periods. On the first floor of the Palais Morass itself is a section devoted to the history of the Palatinate. The intact Schloss can be seen in a large documentary picture from the early seventeenth century; it also turns up in the background of Jan Brueghel's exquisite *Allegory of Summer*. There are also sensitive portraits of Elizabeth and her family by the Honthorst brothers, dating from her exile in Holland when she was extolled as "The Queen of Hearts" by a generation of gallants. The museum's prize possession is the limewood *Altar of the Twelve Apostles* by **Tilman Riemenschneider**, which was masked under a thick coat of polychrome for centuries, but has been returned to its original unpainted state.

Eating, drinking and entertainment

Hauptstrasse and the adjacent side-streets are jammed with places of entertainment to suit all tastes; there's no better place for a pub crawl in all of Germany. The much-trumpeted **student taverns** (see also the "Hotels" section on pp.350–51) are a must; they're perfectly genuine and are still patronized by the leftovers of the old fraternities, even if parties of tourists now make up the bulk of the clientele, particularly in summer. They're sights in themselves, with their faded photos and daguerreotypes, their trophies, swords, pads, helmets and miscellaneous paraphernalia.

To find out **what's on** in town, consult the monthly *Heidelberg aktuell* (Ⓦwww.heidelberg-aktuell.de; €0.50)

Restaurants

Da Mario Rohrbacher Str. 3. The best Italian restaurant in the city, situated just west of the Altstadt.

Essighaus Plöck 97. Inexpensive Gaststätte serving traditional German food; also has a small beer garden. On Mon, it's only open in the evening.

Kalimera Römerstr. 26. Good Greek restaurant, with a tiny sheltered garden to the rear, in the residential area east of the Hauptbahnhof.

Kurpfälzisches Museum Hauptstr. 97. This wine bar is situated in the museum courtyard and serves excellent food.

Roter Ochsen Hauptstr. 217. This rivals *Zum Sepp'l* (see p.351) for the right to be regarded as the most famous of Heidelberg's historic student taverns, and is on the itinerary of practically every tourist to the city. Its U-shaped interior has been patronized by the confraternities since it was built at the beginning of the eighteenth century and serves good, reasonably priced food. Closed Sun.

Schlossweinstube Im Schlosshof. Classy and expensive wine bar-restaurant in the Schloss. Evenings only, closed Wed.

Schnizelbank Bauamtsgasse 7. Another of the historic student taverns, and the only one where the drinking emphasis is on wine (with one vintage always available on draught) rather than beer. Evenings only, except at weekends.

Simplicissimus Ingrimstr. 16 Ⓣ0 62 21/18 33 36. High-class French restaurant. Very small, so reservations are obligatory. Evenings only, closed Tues.

Waves Kurfürsten-Anlage 9. Vegetarian restaurant located between the Altstadt and the Hauptbahnhof, with a wide selection of dishes. Mon–Wed & Sat 11.30am–4pm, Thurs & Fri 11.30am–9pm.

Wirtshaus zum Spreissel Neckarstaden 66. Serves huge portions of traditional Baden, Alsatian and Swiss cuisine.

Zum Güldenen Schaf Hauptstr. 115. Historic restaurant which serves both regional and international dishes and has a pleasant garden.

Zur Herrenmühle Hauptstr. 239 ☎0 62 21/1 29 09. Heidelberg's best restaurant, occupying a fine seventeenth-century building with an inner courtyard. The cooking is innovative and therefore expensive; it's advisable to book in advance. Open Tues–Sat, evenings only.

Cafés and bars

Biermuseum Hauptstr. 143. This has the largest selection of beers in Heidelberg, with 101 varieties to choose from, ten of them on draught.
Café Journal Hauptstr. 162. Best of the bistro-type cafés which are all the rage among present-day Heidelberg students. Has a wide selection of newspapers, and makes a good choice for breakfast.
Café Knösel Haspelgasse 20. Heidelberg's oldest and most elegant café; its speciality is the *Heidelberger Studentenkuss* (Heidelberg Student Kiss), a dark chocolate filled with praline and nougat. Full meals also available. Closed Mon.
Café Schafheutle Hauptstr. 94. Another old-world café, with its own garden; it's celebrated for its marzipan fancies. Closed Sun.
Goldener Reichsapfel Untere Str. 35. Popular student bar, one of several on the street.
Hemingway's Fahrtgasse 1. Student café-bar in the west of the Altstadt, with a front garden overlooking the Neckar.
Max Bar Marktplatz 5. French-style bistro that puts tables out onto the square in summer.
Netlounge Plock 75–77. Internet café with very reasonable rates. Open Mon–Fri 9am–11pm, Sat & Sun 11am–11pm.
Palmbräuhaus Hauptstr. 185. A modern re-creation of palm court days, with resident pianist.
Regie Theaterstr. 2. Offers over two hundred different cocktails.
Vetters Alt-Heidelberger Brauhaus Steingasse 9. Hausbrauerei which makes *Pils*, *Weizen* and an extremely powerful *Bock*; also does good-value meals.
Zum Schwarzen Walfisch Bahnhofstr. 27. *Szene* café-bar, which makes a good choice for breakfast.

Clubs and live-music pubs

Cave 54 Krämergasse 2. Normally a nostalgic-style disco, but has live jazz on Tues, jam sessions on Sun.
Fischerstübchen Obere Neckarstr. 2. The favourite club of the local students. Open Thurs–Sat.
Mata Hari Oberbadgasse 10. Gay men's club. Open Tues–Sun 9pm–3am.
Schwimmbad Musik-Club Tiergartenstr. 13. Has regular live gigs and discos Wed–Sat.
Ziegler Bergheimer Str. 1b. Varied late-night spot, featuring a programme of jazz and rock concerts, cabaret and theatre.
Zigarillo Bergheimer Str. 147. Crowded club housed in an old factory.

Entertainment and festivals

Classical music concerts are held in the modern Kongresshaus Stadthalle (☎0 62 21/80 90 80) overlooking the Neckar. The Heidelberger Kammerorchester (Ⓦwww.heidelbergerkammerorchester.de) is a Mozartean-sized band of good standing, even if its programmes tend to be conservative. Both the Philharmonisches Orchester Heidelberg (Ⓦwww.heidelberger-philharmoniker.de) and the Heidelberger Sinfoniker (Ⓦwww.heidelberger-sinfoniker.de) are full-sized symphony orchestras. At the main **theatre**, the Theater der Stadt Heidelberg, Theaterstr. 4 (☎0 62 21/58 20 00), there's a varied mixture of plays, opera, operetta, and performances by an experimental corps de ballet. The Kulturbahnhof Karlstor, Am Karlstorbahnhof 1 (☎0 62 21/97 89 14, Ⓦwww.karlstorbahnhof.de), is a cultural centre with theatre, cinema and café.

Heidelberg's most spectacular **festivals** are those using the Schloss as a backdrop. On the first Saturdays of June and September, and the second in July, there are firework displays and historical pageants; these attract horrendously large crowds, but are highly enjoyable all the same. From late June until early August, there are open-air concerts and opera performances (inevitably, *The Student Prince* is included) in the Schlosshof at 8pm on most evenings (☎0 62 21/58 20 00, Ⓦwww.schlossfestspiele-heidelberg.de for tickets and information); in bad weather, they're transferred indoors. Throughout the year, various **fairs** are held on Karlsplatz, including Heidelberger Frühling (late March/early April, Ⓦwww.heidelberger-fruehling.de) and Heidelberger Herbst (late Sept). The climax of **Carnival** (variable Feb/March) is the Rose Monday parade; there's another procession through the streets on the third Sunday before Easter.

Neckar cruises leave from the quay beside the Stadthalle mid-May to mid-Sept, run by Rhein-Neckar-Fahrgastschifffahrt (Ⓣ0 62 21/2 01 81, Ⓦwww.rnf-schifffahrt.de) and Personenschifffahrt Hornung (Ⓣ0 62 21/48 00 64). A forty-minute local journey costs €3.50; the round trip to Neckarsteinach €9.50.

Bad Wimpfen and around

BAD WIMPFEN, a pocket-sized town built high above a bend in the Neckar on one of the rail lines linking Heidelberg with Heilbronn, is a real visual treat, preserving a wonderful array of monuments as testament to its richly varied history. The site has been inhabited since prehistoric times; Romans, Frankish kings and the bishops of Worms were later rulers, prior to its choice, from around 1200, as a favourite **residence of the Staufian emperors**. Some 150 years later Wimpfen was made a Free Imperial City, an independence it retained, courtesy of the lucrative salt trade, until the advent of Napoleon, who allocated it to the Grand Duchy of Hesse-Darmstadt. After World War II, many locals hoped the town would become a detached southern enclave of the new Land of Hesse, but the American authorities placed it in an administrative district of Baden. Seven years later, it voted to switch allegiance to the other half of the new combined province of Baden-Württemberg, and has been part of the Heilbronn district ever since.

The **skyline** is immediately impressive and one of the most dramatic in Germany: it's best seen from the right bank of the Neckar, where the imperious towers, illuminated by night, give it the appearance of a miniature medieval Manhattan. Bad Wimpfen has two very distinct historic quarters. The upper town, **Wimpfen am Berg**, was originally built within the ruins of the Staufian palace and has the lion's share of the historic sights, though it is the lower town, **Wimpfen in Tal**, which possesses the dominant surviving monument, the Ritterstift.

Wimpfen am Berg

Hauptstrasse is the central street of the cobblestoned Wimpfen am Berg. About a third of the way up is the **Schwibbogen Tor**, which formerly gave access to the **Kaiserpfalz** (Imperial Palace). Substantial portions of the palace remain to this day, ranking among the most important of the relatively few surviving examples of Romanesque civil architecture in Europe. The austere riverside wall, which had the advantage of a formidable natural barrier behind, survives largely intact. At its southern end, it's guarded by the **Nürnberger Türmchen** and the **Roter Turm**, a gaunt box-like structure which was the last line of defence. From here, there's a fine view over the town and valley.

Further along is the **Pfalzkapelle** (April to mid-Oct Tues–Sun 10am–noon & 2–4.30pm; €1), now containing a small collection of religious art. The gallery was reserved for the emperor who could, if necessary, make a quick getaway through a passage to the haven of the Roter Turm. Adjoining the chapel is the sole surviving part of the **Palast** itself – a weather-worn but still elegant row of arcades, each of whose paired columns is carved in a different manner.

Also from the Staufian epoch is the large **Steinhaus** (Stone House), which stands out among the later buildings, most of which are half-timbered. Originally the home of the castle commandant, it was modernized in the sixteenth century by the addition of Gothic gables. It's currently fitted out as the **Museum des Mittelalters** (April to mid-Oct Tues–Sun 10am–noon & 2–4.30pm; €1.50), with exhibits from prehistoric times to the period of the Staufian emperors. Diagonally opposite is the symbol of Wimpfen and the most potent reminder of its days of power and glory, the **Blauer Turm** (Blue Tower; April to mid-Oct Tues–Sun 10am–6pm; €1), which can be ascended for a fine view over the town and the Neckar valley. At noon on Sundays from April to September, the resounding strains of a trumpeter playing chorales from the top can be heard throughout the streets. On Obere Turmgasse just to the south is the town's most imposing half-timbered mansion, the **Bürgermeister-Elsässer-Haus**; it has a sixteenth-century core, though the large oriel window was only added until 1717.

The lower parts of the twin towers of the **Stadtkirche** are the last main features of the Romanesque part of Wimpfen's skyline; the rest of the building is a late Gothic hall church. Its interior boasts a spectacular cellular vault, and contains some notable furnishings, including a fifteenth-century *Christ on the Cross* with moving parts and human hair, and two early sixteenth-century retables. Behind the church is a large and emotional Crucifixion group similar to the one its sculptor, Hans Backoffen, made for his own tomb in Mainz. Close by is the **Wormser Hof**, part of which is also Staufian; it was the residence of the administrator in the service of the Bishop of Worms, with a barn to store the tithe of agricultural produce he collected.

It's worth sauntering round the streets of the old town, which curve and plunge their way past half-timbered houses, Baroque mansions and quiet squares with Renaissance fountains. Among the many surprising vistas, that from the **Adlerbrunnen** (Eagle Fountain) at the junction of Hauptstrasse and Salzgasse is particularly fine. The best-preserved street is **Klostergasse**, one of whose mansions still preserves what was once a characteristic feature – an exterior gallery which served as a bath house. Down Bollwerkgasse is the **Bollwerk** or artillery bastion, built in the sixteenth century to designs by Dürer, no less. Nearby, the monumental half-timbered fifteenth-century **Spital** on Hauptstrasse has been restored to house the **Reichstädtisches Museum** (Tues–Sun: Easter–Oct 10am–5pm; rest of year 10am–noon & 2–5pm; €1.50). This takes up the story of Wimpfen from the Middle Ages through to the nineteenth century; the original interiors themselves justify a visit.

Wimpfen in Tal

The lower town, known as Wimpfen in Tal, is built round the great **Ritterstift St Peter** which, after a break of five centuries, was repopulated in 1947 by Benedictine monks who had fled from Grüssau in Silesia, which had become the Polish town of Krzeszów. Try and catch a service to hear their wonderful Gregorian chant.

The fortress-like facade of the **Stiftskirche**, with a huge porch and a pair of octagonal towers, dates from the tenth century; the rest of the building is a masterly French-inspired Gothic design. This is generally attributed to the near-legendary mason **Erwin von Steinbach**, who built part of Strasbourg Cathedral. Superb original sculptures can be seen on the south doorway and inside the chancel; the latter group includes the then recently deceased St Francis of Assisi. Also of note are some original stained-glass windows, a set of humorously carved choir stalls, and a poignant fifteenth-century terracotta *Pietà*. Access to the **cloister**, which has sections in each of the three phases of the Gothic style, is only allowed to groups who have booked in advance, but you can tag along with one of these (which are frequent during the summer, if not at other times) if you ask at the shop.

Practicalities

Bad Wimpfen still preserves its original **Bahnhof**, a rustic little building of 1868 at Carl-Ulrich-Str. 1 by the river in the lower part of town. The **tourist office** (Easter–Oct Mon–Fri 9am–7pm, Sat & Sun 10am–noon & 2–4pm; rest of year Mon–Fri 9am–1pm & 2–5pm; ⓣ0 70 63/9 72 00, ⓦwww.badwimpfen.org) is housed inside. Turn right outside to reach Hauptstrasse, or follow the main road to the left for ten minutes to reach Wimpfen in Tal. **Neckar cruises**, which run both upstream and down throughout the summer months, depart from the jetty beside the Neckarbrücke.

There are around a dozen private houses – scattered all over town – offering **rooms** (❶–❷). Wimpfen am Berg has one **pension**, *Zur Traube*, Hauptstr. 1 (ⓣ0 70 63/93 43 43, ⓦwww.herberge-zur-traube.de; ❺), plus several **hotels**. These include *Grüner Baum,* Hauptstr. 84 (ⓣ0 70 63/2 94; ❺), *Weinmann*, Marktplatz 3 (ⓣ0 70 63/85 82, ⓦwww.hotelweinmann.de), and *Sonne*, which occupies a lovely half-timbered building at Hauptstr. 87 (ⓣ0 70 63/2 45 or 96 11 60, ⓦwww.sonne-wimpfen.de; ❻). There are also two spa hotels, both with good bathing facilities, in the Kurgebiet at the northern end of town: *Am Kurpark*, Kirschenweg 16 (ⓣ0 70 63/9 77 70, ⓦwww.amkurpark.de; ❻); and *Am Rosengarten*, Osterbergstr. 16 (ⓣ0 70 63/99 10, ⓦwww.hotel-rosengarten.de; ❻).

The leading **restaurants** are those attached to the hotels *Rosengarten* and *Sonne*; the latter is run in tandem with *Weinstube Feyerabend*, Hauptstr. 87. *Zum Kräuterweible*, Marktrain 5, is popular with locals for its chicken dishes; *Hohenstaufenpfalz*, Hauptstr. 34, is a long-established Gasthaus specializing in Swabian fare; *Dobel's*, Hauptstr. 61, serves over thirty different types of Maultaschen; while *Alt-Wimpfener Stuben* in the Bahnhof offers fish and vegetarian specialities plus a beer garden.

Wimpfen in Tal is the scene of one of Germany's oldest **popular festivals**: it's claimed the week-long Talmarkt (straddling the months of June and July) in honour of SS Peter and Paul has been celebrated every year since 965. Nowadays, the end is marked by a spectacular fireworks display. Two more fairs dating back to the Middle Ages are held in the centre of Wimpfen am Berg – the Zunftmarkt for handicrafts at the end of August and the Weihnachtsmarkt in December, which is a cut above the imitative versions found in practically every German town. Fasching also has a long tradition here; highlights are the Sunday parade and the evening celebrations on Ash Wednesday.

Burg Guttenberg

Burg Guttenberg (daily: March & Nov noon–5pm; April–Oct 9am–6pm, ⓦwww.burg-guttenberg.de; €4), the best-known of the many castles in the

Neckar valley region, lies 8km north of Wimpfen am Berg and can be reached by buses bound for Neckarmühlbach, which can be picked up at the stop beside the Bollwerk. Impressively set on a hill, the fortress dates back to the Staufian epoch, but has been much altered; it became the seat of the barons of Gemmingen in 1449 and remains in the possession of their descendants. The principal defensive features are an impressive curtain wall and the tall narrow keep. Inside, the main curiosity is the **Holzbibliothek**, a herbarium in which the flowers, fruit and leaves of nearly all the different local trees are stored in 93 wooden containers arranged to look like books. There's also an impressive tin-figure diorama of the Battle of Wimpfen, an early skirmish of the Thirty Years War.

However, the castle's main claim to fame is as the seat of the **Deutsche Greifenwarte**, Europe's largest station for **birds of prey**. Each day of the season (March & Nov at 3pm, April–Oct at 11am & 3pm; €8, or €11 including admission to the Burg), there's an exhilarating demonstration of several of the birds (usually including eagles and vultures) in free flight. Yet this is by no means just for show – there has been a highly successful programme for breeding endangered species, and an average of fifty birds per year are released back into the wild. There's also a good restaurant, the *Burgschenke*, set on a terrace commanding an extensive view over the valley.

The Tauber valley

At the extreme northeastern corner of Baden-Württemberg, the gentle **River Tauber** cuts through a lush, verdant landscape of undulating hills, often dotted with vineyards, which stands in sharp contrast to the rugged contours of the neighbouring Swabian Jura. It manages to preserve an agreeable atmosphere of rustic peace and quiet, at least outside those towns which are staging posts on the famous tourist route known as the **Romantic Road** (see p.232), which closely follows the entire length of the Tauber valley, with the exception of its northernmost stretch. Bad Mergentheim, Weikersheim and Creglingen all lie on the route, and the first two are on the same rail line, the Taubertalbahn.

Bad Mergentheim

BAD MERGENTHEIM is one of the most celebrated spas in the country. Judging from the evidence of excavations, which have led to the uncovering of a Celtic well, the presence of hot salt springs at this point was known to Bronze Age tribes. However, they lay forgotten for over two millennia, until their rediscovery in 1826 by a shepherd who noticed his flock crowding round a trickle of water close to the north bank of the Tauber. Three years later, the first hotel opened and the town has never looked back. The timing of the finding of the springs was fortuitous, as seventeen years before Mergentheim had lost the prestigious role it had held since 1525 – as seat of the **Order of Teutonic Knights** (see box on p.362). Even if you normally find spas a turn-off, it's worth coming to see the old part of town, on which the Knights left a characteristic stamp. This is sharply differentiated from the cure facilities, and situated on the opposite side of the river.

The town centre

The whole of the eastern part of town is taken up by a gargantuan complex of buildings, most of it now used as offices. The Teutonic Knights originally

The Teutonic Knights

Originally founded as a hospitaller community in Palestine in 1190, the **Order of Teutonic Knights** (Deutschritterorden) quickly took on a religious and military character and increasingly turned its attention towards the Christianization of the Balts, the last heathen peoples of Europe. By the early fourteenth century the Knights had exterminated the Prussians, appropriating their name and controlling a powerful Baltic state from their fortress-headquarters at Marienburg (nowadays the Polish town of Malbork). They repopulated the territories with German peasants, and grew rich from the grain trade. Prosperity bred complacency, and in 1410, in the largest battle of the European Middle Ages, the Knights were defeated at Grunwald by the Poles and Lithuanians. As a result of the Thirteen Years War of 1454–66, in which the German settlers joined the alliance against them, they had to cede half their lands and re-establish themselves at Königsberg in East Prussia.

In 1525, the Grand Master Albrecht von Hohenzollern converted to Protestantism and turned the territory into a secular duchy. Those of the Order still loyal to Catholicism moved to Mergentheim. Although broken as a military force, the order retained great prestige, and its Grand Master belonged among the highest ranks of the German nobility. Mergentheim remained the Knights' base until they were disbanded by order of Napoleon in 1809; however, the order was reconstituted in Vienna 25 years later, where it remains active as a charitable body.

established themselves in the former Hohenlohe castle, which was expanded and rebuilt to form the enormous **Deutschordensschloss**. In accordance with the tenets of the order, the architecture is severely ascetic, with only the occasional touch of frivolity, as in the bright orange **Torbau** which forms the main entrance. At the corner of the main courtyard is the handsome Rococo **Schlosskirche**, in part the work of the two greatest German architects of the day – Balthasar Neumann designed the twin towers, and François Cuvilliés provided plans for the white stuccoed interior, whose vault is covered by a huge fresco glorifying the Holy Cross.

Opposite the facade of the church is the main range of the Schloss, approached by two Renaissance **staircases**: the northern one has an ingenious corkscrew shape and leads up to the **Deutschordensmuseum** (Tues–Sun 10am–5pm; €3.50; Ⓦwww.deutschordensmuseum.de). Apart from the Neoclassical **Kapitelsaal**, the rooms are surprisingly unostentatious and are used for displays on the history of the order, including valuable treasury items and portraits of all the Mergentheim Grand Masters.

The **Schlosspark** beyond, laid out in the English style, forms a south-bank counterpart to the **Kuranlage** opposite. Despite the presence of the railway line, which divides it horizontally, the latter is a beautifully manicured spa park, whose **Wandelhalle** (Pump Room) is a glass palace built in 1935 in a style which echoes both colonial architecture and the geometricity of the Bauhaus.

The spacious central Markt is divided in two by the step-gabled sixteenth-century **Rathaus**; the arms of the Grand Master who built it are borne by the hero Roland in the fountain in front. A colourful array of houses of various dates erected by vassals of the order lines the rest of the square. Immediately to the north of the square is the Gothic **Stadtkirche,** which was founded by another order of Crusaders, that of St John of Jerusalem. Beside it is the **Spital**, with a tiny Rococo chapel. South of Marktplatz is the **Marienkirche**, a former Dominican priory church. On the north wall of its nave is a magnificent Renaissance funerary monument to Grand Master Walter von Cronburg by Hans Vischer of Nürnberg. The chapel opposite has fourteenth-century frescoes of mystical scenes.

The outskirts

Now officially part of Bad Mergentheim, the village of **STUPPACH**, 8km southwest and served by occasional buses, possesses one of the supreme masterpieces of German Renaissance painting, **Grünewald**'s *St Mary of the Snows*, in its otherwise unremarkable Pfarrkirche (daily: March & April 10am–5pm; May–Oct 9am–5.30pm; Nov–Feb 11am–4pm; €1). This is part of a triptych, one wing of which also survives and can be seen in the Augustinermuseum in Freiburg.

In the Katzenwald (Cats' Forest) 5km southeast of Bad Mergentheim on the main road to Crailsheim is the **Wildpark** (mid-March to early Nov daily 9am–6pm; rest of year Sat & Sun 9am–5pm; €7.50, kids €4.50; ⓦwww.wildtierpark.de), the largest zoo in Europe where animals are kept in conditions close to their natural habitats. The best time to visit is in the afternoon, when there are successive feeding sessions, culminating in that of the pack of thirty wolves, which emerges and disperses with lightning speed.

Practicalities

Bad Mergentheim's **Bahnhof** is conveniently situated between the medieval and spa parts of the town, on the same side of the Tauber as the former. The pavilion at Markt 3 contains the **tourist office** (Mon–Fri 9am–noon & 2.30–5pm, Sat 9am–noon; ⓣ0 79 31/5 71 31, ⓦwww.bad-mergentheim.de).

There are plenty of **private rooms** and small **pensions** (❷–❸). The cheapest **hotel** is *Gasthof Zum Wilden Mann*, Reichengässle 6 (ⓣ0 79 31/76 38; ❸). Good middle-range options are *Deutschmeister*, Ochsengasse 7 (ⓣ0 79 31/96 20; ❹–❻), *Alte Münze,* Münzgasse 10 (ⓣ0 79 31/56 60, ⓦwww.hotel-deutschmeister.de; ❺), and *Bundschu,* Cronbergstr. 15 (ⓣ0 79 31/93 30, ⓦwww.hotel-bundschu.de; ❻). Top of the range is *Victoria,* Poststr. 2–4 (ⓣ0 79 31/59 30, ⓦwww.viktoria-hotel.de; ❼), which has a gourmet **restaurant**, *Zirbelstuben,* along with a more affordable Weinstube. All the other hotels listed above, except *Alte Münze*, also have restaurants. There's a **youth hostel** at Erlenbachtalstr. 44 (ⓣ0 79 31/63 73; €14.20/16.90) in the outlying village of Igersheim (which has its own Bahnhof) to the northeast. The **campsite** is 2km south of town at Willinger Tal (ⓣ0 79 31/21 77). Bad Mergentheim's main **festival** is the Stadtfest in late June.

Weikersheim

WEIKERSHEIM, 11km due east of Bad Mergentheim, is the ancestral seat of the **House of Hohenlohe**, which first came to local prominence in the twelfth century. It subsequently split into various branches, which ruled for centuries over tiny tracts of territory between the Free Imperial Cities of Schwäbisch Hall, Heilbronn and Rothenburg ob der Tauber.

In 1586, when Count Ludwig II re-established Weikersheim as the family's main residence, he decided to replace the old moated castle with a magnificent new Renaissance **Schloss** (guided tours daily: April–Oct 9am–6pm; Nov–March 10am–noon & 1.30–4.30pm; €4.50; ⓦwww.schloesser-und-gaerten.de). The Dutch architect Georg Robin chose a daringly original ground plan based on an equilateral triangle. Only one wing of this, characterized by six magnificent scrollwork gables, was built, as the Hohenlohes turned their money and attention to supporting the Protestant cause in the Thirty Years War. In the early eighteenth century the complex was completed in the Baroque style, though still retaining some parts of the medieval fortress. Unquestionably the highlight of the reception rooms is the **Rittersaal**, the most sumptuous banqueting hall ever built in Germany, whose decorations are a hymn of praise to the dynasty and its preoccupations. The huge coffered ceiling is painted with depictions of the glories of the hunt, the entrance doorway is carved with a scene of a battle against the Turks, and the colossal chimneypiece is adorned with a complicated allegory which illustrates the family motto, "God gives Luck". Flanking the fireplace are the reclining stucco figures of Count Ludwig and his wife, sister of William the Silent, above which are their respective family trees. Even more eye-catching are the life-sized stuccos of deer parading along the main walls, joined by an elephant, a beast the craftsmen had clearly never seen.

The **Schlossgarten**, which is contemporary with the later parts of the Schloss, is exceptionally well preserved. On the terrace immediately behind the palace is a series of sixteen caricature statues of members of the court, the only surviving set of the many inspired by the engravings of the Lorraine artist Jacques Callot. In the central pond is a representation of *Hercules Fighting the Hydra*: like many other petty German princes, the Hohenlohes fondly saw analogies between themselves and the great hero. Further evidence of their megalomania comes with the **Orangerie** at the end of the garden, which provides a theatrical backdrop to the Tauber valley beyond. Among the figures represented are the emperors of ancient Assyria, Persia, Greece and Rome whom they imagined to be their spiritual ancestors.

One of the swaggering arcaded buildings fronting the main entrance to the Schloss now houses the **Gutskellerei** (Mon–Fri 8am–5pm, Sat 9am–5pm, Sun 11am–5pm), where local vintages can be sampled and bought. Beyond, the planned central **Marktplatz** was laid out at the beginning of the eighteenth century as a processional way linking the Schloss with the **Stadtkirche**, which contains tombs of members of the Hohenlohe family.

Practicalities

Weikersheim's **Bahnhof** is just a few minutes' walk northeast of Marktplatz. The **tourist office** (Mon–Fri 9am–5.30pm; ⓣ0 79 34/1 02 55, ⓦwww.weikersheim.de) is at Marktplatz 7. If you want to stay, there are a fair number of **private rooms** (❶–❸). The lowest-priced **hotel**, *Gasthof Krone*, Hauptstr. 14 (ⓣ0 79 34/83 14; ❹), is an excellent bargain. Alternatives include *Grüner Hof*, Marktplatz 10 (ⓣ0 79 34/2 52; ❺), *Deutschherren-Stuben*, Marktplatz 9 (ⓣ0 79 34/83 76; ⓦwww.deutschherren-stuben.de ❺), and *Laurentius*, Marktplatz 5 (ⓣ0 79 34/70 07, ⓦwww.hotel-laurentius.de; ❻). There's a **youth hostel** on the bank of the Tauber at Im Heiligen Wöhr 1 (ⓣ0 79 34/70 25; €14.20/16.90). Each of the hotels listed above has a **restaurant**; *Krone* is the best value; *Laurentius* has the most ambitious standards.

Creglingen

CREGLINGEN, 13km upstream from Weikersheim, and on the border with Bavaria, is an old-world village with half-timbered houses. Some of these are built directly over the former ramparts; another, the

Römschlössle, has the dimensions of a Renaissance palace and now serves as a conference centre. After Creglingen, the Romantic Road crosses into Bavaria, the next stops being Detwang and Rothenburg ob der Tauber (see p.216 and p.211).

The village's renown is based on the isolated **Herrgottskirche** (April–Oct daily 9.15am–5.30pm; Nov–March Tues–Sun 10am–noon & 2–4pm; €1.50), a Gothic pilgrimage chapel founded in the fourteenth century after a ploughman had dug up a miraculous holy wafer in a nearby field. If you're travelling by Europabus, a stop is made here; otherwise the quickest and most pleasant way to come from Creglingen is via the path running alongside the brook named after the church.

The Herrgottskirche is architecturally unremarkable but houses the magnificent limewood altar of *The Assumption*, carved by **Tilman Riemenschneider** in about 1510. Set in a filigree shrine specially constructed in order to catch the day's changing light effects, the main scene ranks as the artist's masterpiece. The four reliefs of the life of the Virgin are of markedly lower quality and are presumably not the work of the master, who employed as many as twenty assistants in order to fulfil the flood of commissions which came his way. However, Riemenschneider certainly made the exquisite predella scenes of *The Epiphany* and *Christ Among the Doctors*; the calm, pensive central figure in the group of scholars is probably a self-portrait. A couple of decades after the retable was made, the chapel was given over to the Lutherans; its excellent state of preservation is due to the fact that, as the main scene was anathema to Protestant doctrine, it was closed off and not reopened until the nineteenth century.

Practicalities

Creglingen is no longer on a rail line; **buses** to Weikersheim and Rothenburg leave from the terminal on the town-centre side of the Tauber. The **tourist office** (Mon–Fri 9am–5pm; Ⓣ0 79 33/6 31, Ⓦwww.creglingen.de) is by the roadside on the main route out of town to the north, at An der Romantischen Str. 14. In the town proper there's a **guesthouse**, *Gästehaus Herrgottstal*, Herrgottstal 13 (Ⓣ0 79 33/5 18, Ⓦwww.gaestehaus-herrgottstal.de; ❸), plus two **hotels**: *Gasthof Grüner Baum*, Torstr. 20 (Ⓣ0 79 33/6 18; ❸), and *Gasthof Krone*, Hauptstr. 12 (Ⓣ0 79 33/5 58, Ⓦwww.krone-creglingen.de; ❹). All of these have **restaurants**. Additionally, there are a few **private rooms** (❶–❸) and also a number of **farmhouses** offering bargain deals, the wackiest being the *Heuhotel Stahl* (Ⓣ0 79 33/3 78, Ⓦwww.ferienpension-heuhotel.de; ❸) in the incorporated hamlet of Weidenhof to the northeast, where there's the option of sleeping on hay in the loft for €20, evening meal included. Beside the Münstersee some 3km away is a **campsite** (Ⓣ0 79 33/3 21), while there's a **youth hostel** on a hillside at the eastern end of Creglingen itself at Erdbacher Str. 30 (Ⓣ0 79 33/3 36; €14.20/16.90).

Travel details

Trains

Heidelberg to: Bad Wimpfen (hourly; 50min); Bonn (hourly; 2hr 20min); Bruchsal (every 30min; 20min); Cologne (hourly; 2hr 25min); Mainz (hourly; 1hr 5min); Mannheim (frequent; 10min).
Karlsruhe to: Baden-Baden (every 20min; 20min); Freiburg (every 30min; 1hr); Freudenstadt (hourly; 2hr); Mannheim (frequent; 30min); Schwetzingen (every 30min; 40min).
Stuttgart to: Cologne (hourly; 3hr 45min); Donaueschingen (hourly; 2hr); Esslingen (every 30min; 10min); Frankfurt (hourly; 2hr 5min); Freiburg (hourly; 2hr 45min); Hamburg (8 daily; 6hr 45min); Hannover (9 daily; 5hr 30min); Heidelberg (hourly; 1hr 10min); Karlsruhe (every 30min; 1hr 10min); Konstanz (hourly; 2hr 40min); Ludwigsburg (frequent; 10min); Mainz (hourly; 2hr); Mannheim (hourly; 1hr 30min); Rottweil (hourly; 1hr 30min); Schwäbisch Gmünd (every 30min; 40min); Schwäbisch Hall (hourly; 1hr); Tübingen (every 30min; 1hr); Ulm (every 20min; 1hr).
Ulm to: Blaubeuren (hourly; 10min); Heidelberg (hourly; 2hr 15min); Mainz (hourly; 3hr 5min); Mannheim (hourly; 2hr 25min).

3

Hesse

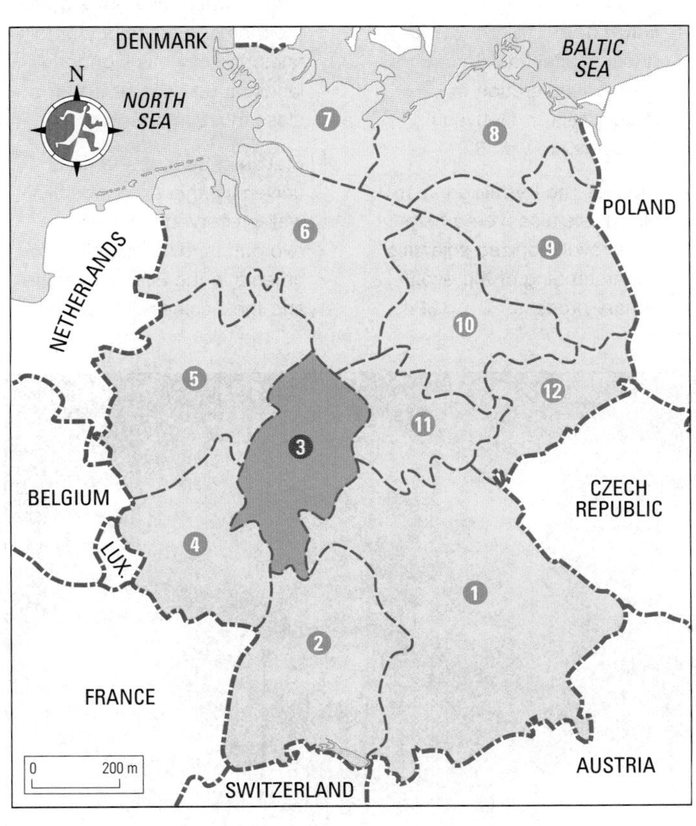
DENMARK
BALTIC SEA
N
NORTH SEA
7
8
POLAND
6
9
NETHERLANDS
10
5
12
3
11
BELGIUM
CZECH REPUBLIC
4
LUX.
1
2
FRANCE
0
200 m
AUSTRIA
SWITZERLAND

CHAPTER 3

Highlights

✱ **Frankfurt am Main** If best-known as one of the world's leading financial centres, this city has plenty of tourist attractions, not least the museums and apple-wine taverns of the Sachsenhausen district. See p.371

✱ **Darmstadt** This grand old ducal capital has Germany's main concentration of Jugendstil (Art Nouveau) buildings. See p.387

✱ **Messel** The 49-million-year-old fossils discovered here have revolutionized scientific understanding of the evolutionary process. See p.394

✱ **The Rheingau** A famous wine-producing area, with splendid Rhenish landscapes and picturesque small towns. See p.399

✱ **Kassel** Briefly a royal capital, and the home of the Brothers Grimm when they put together their famous anthology of folk tales, the city has wonderful landscaped gardens and top class museums. See p.410

✱ **Marburg** Seat of a famous university, this exceptionally well-preserved town boasts two outstanding historic monuments in the Elisabethkirche and the Schloss. See p.421

△ Ernst-Ludwig-Haus, Darmstadt

3

Hesse

Occupying the geographical centre of Germany and manifesting elements of both north and south German culture, **Hesse** (Hessen) claims to be the very heart of the nation. Although one of the parts of the country least visited by foreigners, it's also, paradoxically, one which has created preconceived images of Germany more than any other. This is because of the worldwide familiarity of the folk tales collected by the most famous Hessians, the **Brothers Grimm**, which are set in the darkly forested highlands, feudal castles and half-timbered towns so characteristic of the province.

Modern Hesse – flung together by the Americans as an administrative unit after World War II – represents an approximate revival of a territory founded in 1248 as an offshoot of Thuringia. It reached the height of its power and influence during the Reformation, when its ruler, Landgrave Philip the Magnanimous (Philipp der Grossmütige), was the undisputed champion of **political Protestantism**. On his death in 1567, however, Hesse was divided into four separate states. Within a short period, they had crystallized into two – Hesse-Kassel and Hesse-Darmstadt – and these formed the main basis of the region's division until modern times, though there were many other later fragmentations. In the nineteenth century, the local princes attempted to play Prussia and Austria off against each other. Hesse-Kassel, hitherto regarded as the senior province, backed the wrong side and was absorbed by the expanding Kingdom of Prussia in 1866. The wilier rulers of Hesse-Darmstadt were able to remain as independent Grand Dukes, and in this capacity joined the Second Reich five years later.

Today Hesse is one of the most prosperous of the German Länder, focused on the American-style dynamism of **Frankfurt**. Although traditional heavy industry still exists around the confluence of the Rhine and the Main, it's the serious money generated by banking and modern communications-related industries in Frankfurt which provides the region's real economic base. The two former capitals, **Kassel** and **Darmstadt**, are likewise industrial. Both suffered heavily in the war, though both are worth visiting for the sake of their many reminders of past periods of artistic patronage. Otherwise, apart from occasional light industrial pockets, most of Hesse's inhabitants live from farming or tourism. By far the most beautiful city is modest-sized **Marburg**, Hesse's first capital and home to one of Germany's most prestigious universities; in conjunction with the other towns of the **Lahn valley**, it's a great place to spend a few days. The same can be said of the Baroque city of **Fulda**, still a major episcopal centre. From a tourist point of view, the most popular part of Hesse is the **Rheingau**, a scenic stretch on the right bank of the Rhine, west of the Land capital **Wiesbaden**, a money-oriented playground and gambling centre.

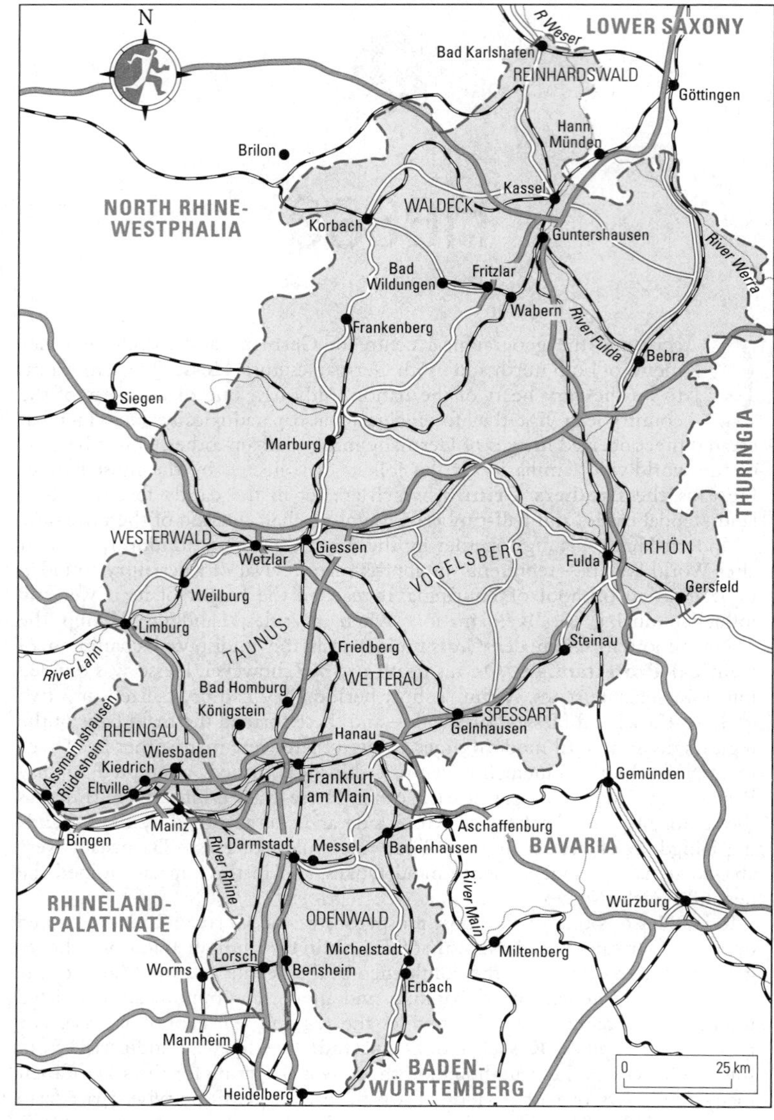

Hesse is very accessible: Frankfurt has the busiest international airport in continental Europe and has fast **rail** and **road** connections with the rest of Germany. **Accommodation** in the major cities is pricier than the national average, whereas the rural areas offer some of the best bargains in the country.

Frankfurt am Main

Straddled across the River Main not long before it converges with the Rhine, **FRANKFURT AM MAIN** is the capital city Germany has never actually had, having been cheated on more than one occasion of the role to which its history and central geographical position would seem to entitle it. Yet that hasn't stopped it becoming the economic powerhouse of the country, a cut-throat financial centre which is home to hundreds of banks, including the Bundesbank and, since 1998, the European Central Bank (Europäische Zentralbank). It's a modern international city, with nearly 30 percent of its residents – the highest proportion in Germany – being of foreign citizenship. Frankfurt is a major communications and transport centre, and consequently gives many travellers their first taste of the country. It's a place with a surprising amount to offer and it's worth spending a couple of days here rather than treating it as a mere transit point.

Over half the city, including almost all of the centre, was destroyed during the war and the rebuilders decided to follow a policy of innovation rather than restoration. The result is a skyline that smacks more of New York than the Federal Republic: it has nine of the ten tallest skyscrapers in the country and its most commonly-used nickname is "Mainhattan". It's also a surprisingly civilized metropolis which spends more per year on the arts than any other city in Europe, and whose inhabitants like nothing better than to spend an evening knocking back a few jugs of the local apple wine in the open-air taverns of the **Sachsenhausen** suburb.

Frankfurt has an energetic nightlife and is a thriving recreational centre for the whole of Hesse, with a good selection of theatres and galleries, and an even better range of museums, mostly concentrated along the south bank of the River Main. It comes across as a confident and tolerant city, and in the **Bockenheim** district there's a healthy "alternative" scene.

Arrival and accommodation

Frankfurt **airport** (ⓣ0 69/69 00, ⓦwww.frankfurt-airport.de) is one of the world's busiest, and is a major point of entry into Germany from abroad. There are regular rail departures from the airport **Bahnhof** to most of Germany's major cities. Trains leave approximately once every ten minutes for Frankfurt's **Hauptbahnhof** (journey time 11min), from where there are even more comprehensive services. On the south side of the Hauptbahnhof is the **bus station**, from where there are plentiful international links, as well as regular services to the misleadingly named **Frankfurt-Hahn airport** (see p.450).

The regional **public transport** company (RMV, ⓦwww.rmv.de) is responsible for bus, tram, S-Bahn and U-Bahn services. A curiosity of the Frankfurt system is that single tickets are more expensive between 6–9am and 4–6.30pm Mondays to Fridays. A day ticket costs €4.60 (€7.10 including the airport), though it's usually better to invest in the **Frankfurt Card** (€7.50 for one day, €11 for two days), which includes half-price entry to virtually all the city's museums; bear in mind that most of these are **free** on Wednesdays. An alternative to the latter is the two-day **Museumsufer Ticket**, which excludes

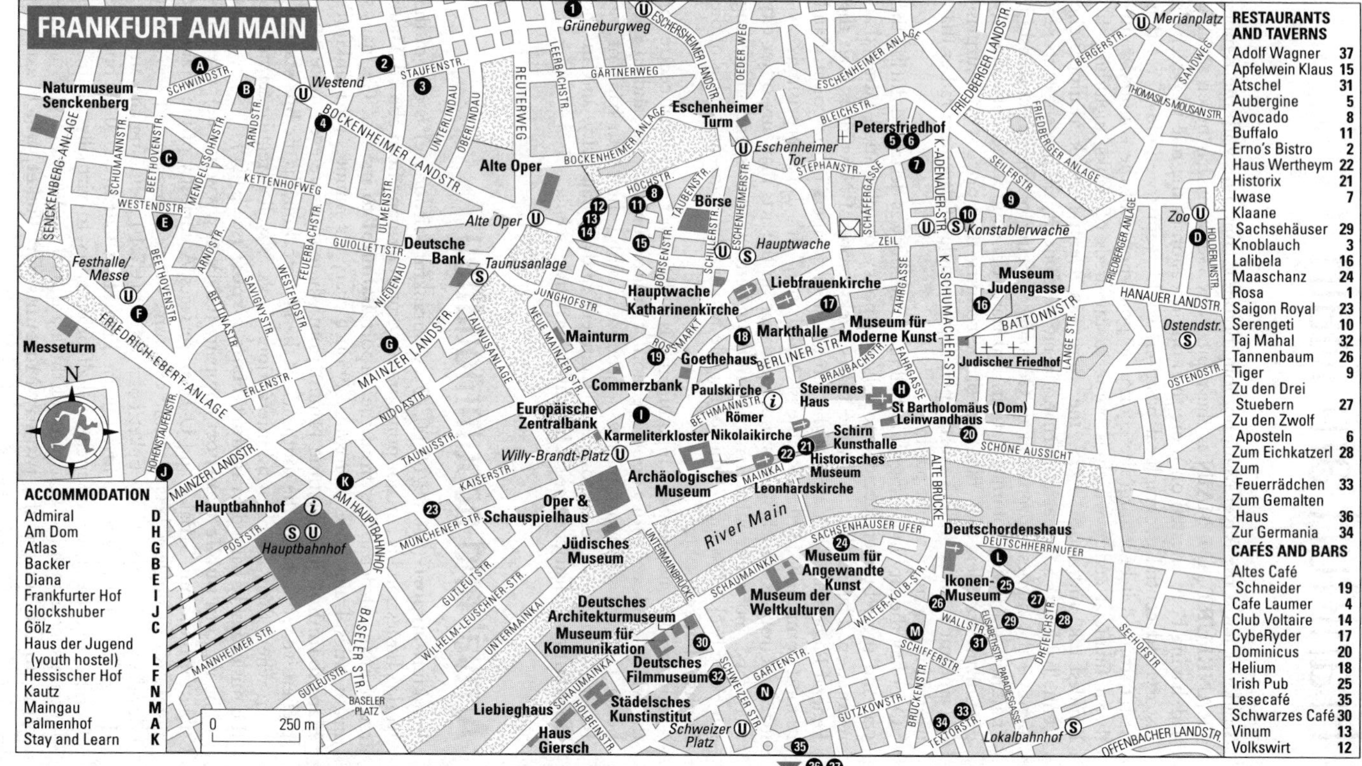
FRANKFURT AM MAIN
RESTAURANTS AND TAVERNS
Adolf Wagner 37
Apfelwein Klaus 15
Atschel 31
Aubergine 5
Avocado 8
Buffalo 11
Erno's Bistro 2
Haus Wertheym 22
Historix 21
Iwase 7
Klaane Sachsehäuser 29
Knoblauch 3
Lalibela 16
Maaschanz 24
Rosa 1
Saigon Royal 23
Serengeti 10
Taj Mahal 32
Tannenbaum 26
Tiger 9
Zu den Drei Stuebern 27
Zu den Zwolf Aposteln 6
Zum Eichkatzerl 28
Zum Feuerrädchen 33
Zum Gemalten Haus 36
Zur Germania 34
CAFÉS AND BARS
Altes Café Schneider 19
Cafe Laumer 4
Club Voltaire 14
CybeRyder 17
Dominicus 20
Helium 18
Irish Pub 25
Lesecafé 35
Schwarzes Café 30
Vinum 13
Volkswirt 12
ACCOMMODATION
Admiral D
Am Dom H
Atlas G
Backer B
Diana E
Frankfurter Hof I
Glockshuber J
Gölz C
Haus der Jugend (youth hostel) L
Hessischer Hof F
Kautz N
Maingau M
Palmenhof A
Stay and Learn K
Naturmuseum Senckenberg
Messeturm
Festhalle/Messe
Westend
Grüneburgweg
Alte Oper
Deutsche Bank
Taunusanlage
Eschenheimer Turm
Eschenheimer Tor
Börse
Petersfriedhof
Hauptwache
Konstablerwache
Liebfrauenkirche
Katharinenkirche
Mainturm
Markthalle
Museum für Moderne Kunst
Museum Judengasse
Judischer Friedhof
Goethehaus
Commerzbank
Paulskirche
Römer
Steinernes Haus
St Bartholomäus (Dom)
Leinwandhaus
Europäische Zentralbank
Karmeliterkloster
Nikolaikirche
Schirn Kunsthalle
Historisches Museum
Willy-Brandt-Platz
Archäologisches Museum
Leonhardskirche
Oper & Schauspielhaus
Hauptbahnhof
Jüdisches Museum
River Main
Museum für Angewandte Kunst
Deutschordenshaus
Ikonen-Museum
Museum der Weltkulturen
Deutsches Architekturmuseum
Museum für Kommunikation
Deutsches Filmmuseum
Städelsches Kunstinstitut
Liebieghaus
Haus Giersch
Schweizer Platz
Lokalbahnhof
Zoo
Merianplatz
Ostendstr.
BOCKENHEIMER LANDSTR.
MAINZER LANDSTR.
FRIEDRICH-EBERT-ANLAGE
SENCKENBERG-ANLAGE
REUTERWEG
ZEIL
BERLINER STR.
K.-SCHUMACHER-STR.
K.-ADENAUER-STR.
HANAUER LANDSTR.
FRIEDBERGER LANDSTR.
ESCHERSHEIMER LANDSTR.
BASELER STR.
AM HAUPTBAHNHOF
KAISERSTR.
MÜNCHENER STR.
SCHAUMAINKAI
SACHSENHÄUSER UFER
ALTE BRÜCKE
SCHÖNE AUSSICHT
UNTERMAINBRÜCKE
UNTERMAINKAI
SCHWEIZER STR.
OFFENBACHER LANDSTR.
N
0 250 m

public transport but covers the full costs of museum entry, and is priced at €8 for individuals, €15 for families.

From the Hauptbahnhof, tram #11 goes right through the heart of the historic city centre; it takes about fifteen minutes to walk the same distance. One of the **tourist offices** is in the entrance hall of the Hauptbahnhof (Mon–Fri 8am–9pm, Sat & Sun 9am–6pm; ⓣ0 69/21 23 88 49 ⓦwww.frankfurt-tourismus.de); the other is in the heart of the city at Römerberg 27 (Mon–Fri 9.30am–5.30pm, Sat & Sun 10am–4pm; ⓣ0 69/21 23 87 08).

Accommodation

Accommodation is generally pricey, thanks to the expense-account business people who come for the various *Messen* (trade fairs). During the most important of these, such as the Book Fair at the end of September/beginning of October, normal rates are heavily marked up – often by 100 percent – and it is essential to reserve well in advance. To do this via the tourist office, contact the administrative headquarters at Kaiserstr. 56 (ⓣ0 69/21 23 08 08). Long-stay lets of apartments can be arranged via one of the **Mitwohnzentralen**: City, An der Staufenmauer 3 (ⓣ0 69/1 94 30, ⓦwww.city-mitwohnzentrale.de); Homecompany, Berger Str. 27 (ⓣ0 69/1 94 45, ⓦwww.homecompany.de); and Mainhattan, Fürstenberger Str. 145 (ⓣ0 69/5 97 55 61, ⓦwww.mitwohnzentrale-mainhattan.de).

Frankfurt's **youth hostel** (Haus der Jugend) is at Deutschherrnufer 12, Sachsenhausen (ⓣ0 69/6 10 01 50; €14.50/17.60) and reached by taking bus #46 from the Hauptbahnhof. There's also a privately run hostel, *Stay & Learn*, run in conjunction with a language school, almost directly opposite the Hauptbahnhof at Kaiserstr. 74 (ⓣ0 69/25 39/52, ⓦww.room-frankfurt.de; dorm beds €20, singles €35–45, doubles €50–60). You can **camp** in the northern suburb of Heddernheim at Campingplatz Heddernheim, An der Sandelmühle 35 (ⓣ0 69/57 03 32); take U-Bahn #1, #2 or #3.

Hotels and pensions

Predictably, budget hotels and pensions are scant, especially in the city centre. If you don't mind the sleazy environs, most of the few reasonably priced hotels cluster around the Hauptbahnhof. There's also a clutch in the more enticing location of the Westend district by the University. Expensive business-class hotels, on the other hand, are thick on the ground, and there's unlikely to be a problem finding a room outside the times of the major trade fairs.

Admiral Hölderlinstr. 25 ⓣ0 69/44 80 21, ⓦwww.hoteladmiral.de. For Frankfurt this is a good, reasonably priced hotel, located beside the Zoo, a short distance east of the Altstadt. ❻–❽

Am Dom Kannengiessergasse 3 ⓣ 0 69/1 38 10 30, ⓕ28 32 37. Scores for its location in a quiet Altstadt alley, with the museums and nightspots of Sachsenhausen only a short walk away over the Alte Brücke. ❻–❾

Atlas Zimmerweg 1 ⓣ0 69/72 39 46, ⓕ72 39 46. Small, homely hotel in an apartment block within easy walking distance of the Hauptbahnhof, yet away from the sleazier streets. ❹

Backer Mendelssohnstr. 92 ⓣ & ⓕ0 69/74 79 92. An excellent budget choice, this no-frills but well-maintained pension is located just round the corner from the U-Bahn Westend station. ❸

Diana Westendstr. 83 ⓣ0 69/74 70 07, ⓕ74 70 79. Very pleasant Westend hotel on a quiet residential street. ❻

Frankfurter Hof Am Kaiserplatz ⓣ0 69/2 15 02, ⓦwww.frankfurter-hof.steigenberger.de. This is the grandest of Frankfurt's grand hotels, occupying a palatial edifice from the time of the Second Reich. Of its restaurants, *Français* (closed Sat lunchtime, Sun & Mon) is a gourmet paradise ranking among the most prestigious in the country, while *Oscar's* has traditional German fare at more reasonable prices. ❾

Glockshuber Mainzer Landstr. 120 Ⓣ0 69/74 26 28, Ⓕ74 26 29. Pleasant budget hotel on the top floors of a tenement just north of the Hauptbahnhof, away from the sleazier streets. ❹

Gölz Beethovenstr. 44 Ⓣ0 69/74 67 35, Ⓦwww.hotel-goelz.de. A good Westend pension, situated in a grand old villa near the university. ❺

Hessischer Hof Friedrich-Ebert-Anlage 40 Ⓣ0 69/7 54 00, Ⓦwww.hessischer-hof.de. Super-luxury hotel directly opposite the Messe buildings. It's beautifully furnished throughout, with a valuable porcelain collection in the restaurant. ❾

Kautz Gartenstr. 17 Ⓣ0 69/61 80 61, Ⓦwww.hotelkautz.de. One of surprisingly few options in Sachsenhausen, this is run in conjunction with a wine merchant's shop which imports quality vintages from around the world. ❻–❽

Maingau Schifferstr. 38–40 Ⓣ0 69/60 91 40, Ⓦwww.maingau.de. The pick of the Sachsenhausen hotels, with the bonus of a fine restaurant. ❻–❽

Palmenhof Bockenheimer Landstr. 89–91 Ⓣ 0 69/7 53 00 60, Ⓦwww.palmenhof.com. One of Frankfurt's most characterful hotels, a family-run concern in a tastefully furnished late nineteenth-century building near the Palmengarten. Its restaurant, *L'Artichoc* (closed Sat & Sun), serves top-class European fare. ❽–❾

The City

Most of central Frankfurt can be covered on foot; almost all the main sights lie within the bounds of the old city walls, which have been turned into a stretch of narrow parkland describing an approximate semicircle around the city centre. From here it's an easy matter to cross the Main into Sachsenhausen, where most of the museums are conveniently located along the southern river bank.

The Altstadt

Until it was devastated in two massive air raids in 1944, Frankfurt had the largest and most complete Altstadt of any important German city. After the war, the most significant monuments were carefully restored; other parts were hastily rebuilt in a modern manner. Even so, large gaps remained until the 1970s, when, after much debate, they were filled with a mixture of pastiche medieval buildings and ultra-modern public commissions.

The Römerberg

As good a point as any to begin your explorations is the **Römerberg**, the historical and, roughly speaking, geographical centre of the city. Charlemagne built his fort on this low hill, on the site of earlier Roman and Alemannic settlements, to protect the ford which gave Frankfurt its name – Frankonovurd (Ford of the Franks). Throughout the Middle Ages the Römerberg was Frankfurt's focal point, serving as market place, fairground, and – less frequently – for the celebrations associated with an Imperial coronation. At the start of the last century the Römerberg was still the heart of the city, an essentially medieval quarter ringed by half-timbered houses built by the rich merchants and bankers who had made Frankfurt one of Germany's richest centres – its "secret capital", according to Goethe.

At the western end of the Römerberg is the **Römer** itself, which maintains its historic function as the Rathaus. Its distinctive Gothic facade, with triple-stepped gables, was more or less all that remained after the war, but the building has been restored with consummate skill. Its two upper storeys house the **Kaisersaal** (daily 10am–1pm & 2–5pm; €1.50), the former imperial coronation hall, which contains 52 bombastic nineteenth-century portraits of the German emperors. The building fronts Römerplatz, the market square, with the Mannerist **Gerechtigkeitsbrunnen** (Justice Fountain) in the middle.

Facing the Römer, a row of seven half-timbered houses was built in the late 1970s using original plans and traditional construction methods.

On the southern side of Römerplatz stands the Gothic **Nikolaikirche**, originally the court chapel, now a Protestant parish church. It's a highly distinctive and lovingly restored little building, built on a virtually square ground plan. Opposite is the **Steinernes Haus** (Tues–Sun 11am–7pm; variable charges; Ⓦwww.fkv.de), a postwar reconstruction of one of the few stone-built houses of the Frankfurt Altstadt. It now serves as an exhibition space for the contemporary art shows of the Frankfurter Kunstverein.

Off the northern side of Römerplatz is the Neoclassical **Paulskirche** (daily 10am–5pm; free), built in the late eighteenth century as a Lutheran preaching hall. However, it was soon taken over for secular purposes, and it was here that the ill-fated German National Assembly met during the revolutionary upheavals of 1848–49. The church still functions as a meeting hall and looks totally unecclesiastical inside. On the northern wall there's a monument to the victims of the Nazis.

Around the Römerberg

East of Römerplatz is the most controversial of the inner-city developments. At its core is the **Schirn Kunsthalle** (Tues & Sun 11am–7pm, Wed–Sat 11am–10pm; variable charges; Ⓦwww.schirn-kunsthalle.de), a cultural centre consisting of a glass tunnel and a rotunda. Initially, it regularly attracted prestigious temporary exhibitions of archeology, old master paintings and modern art. However, in recent years, it has struggled to maintain such exalted standards, its reputation having been tarnished by the theft in 1993 of three paintings, including two Turners from London's Tate Gallery which were not recovered until nine years later. The centre also houses the **Struwwelpeter-Museum** (Tues–Sun 11am–5pm; free), which has displays of international editions of the eponymous children's classic, and documentary material on its creator, the nineteenth-century physician, psychiatrist and liberal politician, Heinrich Hoffmann. Locals have dubbed the Schirn the "Federal Bowling Alley", or, in their more fanciful moments, "Murder at the Cathedral", due to its proximity to the Dom. Nevertheless, it represents a brave attempt to re-create a sense of the Römerberg as the centre of Frankfurt. Running roughly parallel with it, and bounded to the south by Saalgasse, is a row of gabled townhouses which, though essentially modern in design and construction, echo the medieval past of the Römerberg.

Beyond is the **Historischer Garten**, where the foundations of some of the Roman, Carolingian and medieval buildings which previously occupied the site have been laid bare to form a little park. Diagonally opposite is the Gothic **Leinwandhaus** (Tues, Thurs & Fri 11am–6pm, Wed 11am–8pm, Sat & Sun 11am–5pm; Ⓦwww.ffi-frankfurt.de; variable charges). Formerly a cloth hall, it now hosts the highly prestigious photography exhibitions of the Fotografie Forum international. Just to the north, in Domstrasse, looms the **Museum für Moderne Kunst** (Tues & Thurs–Sun 10am–5pm, Wed 10am–8pm; €5, free Wed; Ⓦwww.mmk-frankfurt.de), looking like a hi-tech slice of cake. This has attracted a fair amount of criticism on the grounds that the collection is unworthy of its setting, though it does include some ambitious installations plus examples of such famous postwar artists as Beuys, Warhol and Lichtenstein.

The Dom

The most significant building in the Altstadt is the red sandstone church of **St Bartholomäus**, popularly if inaccurately referred to as the **Dom**, a courtesy title granted it by virtue of the fact that, being the venue for the election and coronation of the Holy Roman Emperors, it was far more important than most cathedrals. In essence, it's a Gothic hall church built in the thirteenth and fourteenth centuries. The two **portals** – and particularly that on the south side, which retains most of its original sculptures – are the finest features from this period. However, the outstanding part of the Dom is its 95-metre **tower** (previously April–Oct 9am–1pm & 2.30–6pm; €1.50, but closed in 2003 for restoration), added in the early fifteenth century by the brilliantly idiosyncratic municipal architect **Madern Gerthener**, whose quirky genius left a profound mark on the city. The pinnacled summit is one of the most original creations of German Gothic and is a clear attempt to re-think earlier spires, such as those of Freiburg's Münster, in a more modern idiom. Before the construction of the modern skyscrapers, the tower was the tallest structure in the city, and even today, strict planning rules are enforced to preserve its dominance over the Altstadt, of which there's a marvellous **view** from the top.

The treasures of the spacious, light-filled interior include a monumental Crucifixion group on the west wall by the Mainz sculptor Hans Backoffen; the poignant fifteenth-century Maria-Schlaf-Altar in the north transept chapel; the polychromed fourteenth-century tombstones directly opposite; and an intricately carved set of choir stalls of the same period. To the right of the choir is the relatively simple and unadorned **Wahlkapelle**, where the seven Electors used to make their final choice as to who would become emperor. Housed in the cloister is the **Dommuseum** (Tues–Fri 10am–5pm, Sat & Sun 11am–5pm; €2), which contains treasury items and historic ecclesiastical garments, plus precious artefacts such as jewellery unearthed a few years ago from royal Merovingian graves during restoration work.

The southern Altstadt

Immediately south of Römerberg is the **Saalhof**, an amalgam of several architecturally diverse Imperial buildings which also incorporates the Rententurm, one of the few surviving towers from the old city defences, and a Romanesque chapel, the **Saalkapelle**. The complex and its modern extensions house the excellent **Historisches Museum** (Tues, Thurs & Sun 10am–5pm, Wed 4–8pm, Fri 10am–2pm, Sat 1–5pm; Ⓦ www.historisches-museum.frankfurt.de; €4, free Wed). One gallery is devoted to medieval and Renaissance artworks which formerly adorned the city's churches; these include the *St Anne Altar* by the so-called **Master of Frankfurt**; the *St Thomas Altar*, a co-operative venture which includes grisailles of *St Cyriac* and *St Lawrence* by **Grünewald**; and a *Baptism of Christ* triptych by **Baldung**. Upstairs, look out for the magnificent coloured woodcut, exhibited with part of the original block, showing a bird's-eye view of Frankfurt as it was during the siege of 1552; it's the masterpiece of one of the city's finest artists, **Conrad Faber von Kreuznach**. There's also an intriguing section on the seventeenth-century **Merian family**, who were responsible for the detailed topographic engravings of German cities which are such a ubiquitous feature of museums all over the country. Frankfurt's greatest painter, **Adam Elsheimer**, is represented by a tiny panel of *Tobias and the Angel*, displayed alongside a strong showing of the city's many highly accomplished still-life specialists. Another section of the museum offers belated homage to **Anne Frank**, the young Frankfurt-born Jewish girl, who died at Belsen but who gained posthumous international fame through her intensely moving diaries.

A short distance to the west is the **Leonhardskirche**, originally a pilgrimage station on the well-trodden route to Santiago de Compostela in northern Spain. Surviving from this Romanesque church are the octagonal east towers and two beautiful portals, but the latter are now indoors as a Gothic aisle was built over them. At the end of this is the **Salvatorchörlein**, a chapel whose amazing pendant vault was considered the great sight of Frankfurt in the early days of tourism. The replacement chancel, built by Madern Gerthener, preserves most of its luminous stained-glass windows; to the side is a magnificent gilded altar from Antwerp.

A little to the northwest, entered from Münzgasse, is the **Karmeliterkloster** (Mon–Fri 8.30am–5pm, Sat & Sun 10am–5pm; Ⓦwww.stadtgeschichte-ffm.de; free), a secularized late Gothic friary. It now houses temporary exhibitions on the history of the city, though it's the marvellously idiosyncratic murals by the sixteenth-century painter and revolutionary leader **Jerg Ratgeb** which provide the main reason for a visit. Although badly damaged in the war, they have been painstakingly restored: their faded condition is due largely to their having been executed in tempera. The cycle in the cloisters forms a complete illustrated Bible; that in the refectory narrates the lives of the prophets Elijah and Elisha and the mission and martyrdom of Carmelite friars in the Holy Land.

The complex also contains the **Archäologisches Museum** (Tues & Thurs–Sun 10am–5pm, Wed 10am–8pm; Ⓦwww.archaeologischesmuseum.frankfurt.de; €4, free Wed), which has a separate entrance on Karmelitergasse. This features archeological finds from the Near East and Classical Greece and Rome, but is mainly dedicated to material excavated locally. In the transept of the former church are finds from a wide variety of prehistoric sites, the most notable being the contents of an Iron Age warrior's grave. The nave is entirely devoted to the Roman period, with stone monuments, glass, ceramics, weapons and jewellery, much of it dug up in the settlement of Nida, which lies within the present-day boundaries of Frankfurt. Finally, the chapel alongside has rich hoards of valuables from Alemannic and Frankish graves, plus early medieval artefacts found underneath the city centre.

Further west, at Untermainkai 14–15, is the **Jüdisches Museum** (same hours; Ⓦwww.juedischesmuseum.de; €2.50, free Sat), which recounts the history of Frankfurt's once powerful and wealthy Jewish community, the largest in Germany after that of Berlin.

The northern Altstadt

A few minutes' walk north of the Karmeliterkloster, at Grosser Hirschgraben 23, is the **Goethehaus und Goethe-Museum** (April–Sept Mon–Fri 9am–6pm, Sat & Sun 10am–4pm; Oct–March Mon–Fri 9am–4pm, Sat & Sun 10am–4pm; Ⓦwww.goethehaus-frankfurt.de; €5), the interior of which has been immaculately restored after being completely burned out during the war. This is where Goethe was born and raised, and the house has been made to look as much as possible like it did when he lived here. There are a few original objects which survived the war, while the well-stocked library has some autograph examples of his writings.

The **Katharinenkirche**, a little further along on Kleiner Hirschgraben, is where Goethe was baptized and confirmed. Opposite is the **Hauptwache**, an eighteenth-century Baroque building which used to be Frankfurt's biggest police station. These days it's a pricey city-centre café, while the station of the same name is a junction on nearly all of Frankfurt's S- and U-Bahn lines.

Nearby on the Liebfrauenberg stands the **Liebfrauenkirche**, a fifteenth-century church now belonging to a Capuchin friary. Look inside for the unusual Baroque altar, a huge alabaster and gilt affair which sits well in the dusky pink sandstone interior. Even finer is the original south doorway, now only visible from the inside; its gorgeous and still brightly coloured tympanum of *The Adoration of the Magi* is a masterpiece of the "Soft Style", and is thought to be the work of Madern Gerthener.

The **Markthalle** just behind the church is a hive of activity and sells the best fresh fruit and veg in town as well as fresh imported produce from Turkey. To the north, **Zeil** is one of Germany's most expensive and exclusive shopping streets, though the area around **Konstablerwache** has become notorious for its drugs pedlars: one downside of Frankfurt's prosperity is that it has become the undisputed drugs capital of Germany.

A little to the northwest of the Hauptwache is the **Börse**, Germany's stock exchange. Appropriately enough two of the most expensive shopping streets in the city are just around the corner. **Goethestrasse** sells highly priced jewellery and designer clothes, while **Grosse Bockenheimer Strasse**, known to the natives as *Fressgasse* (Guzzle Lane), is home to upmarket delicatessens and smart restaurants.

Both of these streets lead into Opernplatz, home of the grandiose **Alte Oper**, built in 1880 in imitation of, and as a rival to, the opera houses of Paris and Dresden. The present structure is the result of years of work to restore the damage of 1945 – the vestibule and first-floor café, all fake marble and colonnades, recapture something of the late nineteenth-century ambience. With its excellent acoustics, the Alte Oper is often used as a congress hall as well as playing host to classical musicians and stars of stage and screen. Oddly enough you won't see much opera here, apart from the occasional production which doesn't need elaborate staging.

Around the Altstadt

It's worth taking a walk through the **Taunusanlage** and the **Gallusanlage**, two narrow stretches of parkland running into each other that begin south of Opernplatz and curve round to the Main, following the line of the old city wall. With the Alte Oper to the north, the Hauptbahnhof to the west, the Römerberg to the southeast and all around you the ultra-modern high-rise office buildings which give the city its distinctive skyline, it's a great place to capture a view of the city. Unfortunately this area is a favourite hangout of the city's junkies, and it's best to steer clear of the area at night.

A much more pleasant stroll from Opernplatz is in the opposite direction through the **Bockenheimer Anlage** and past a small lake to the **Nebbienisches Gartenhäuschen**, a playful little villa built in 1810 by a local publisher to mark his third marriage. At the end of the Bockenheimer Anlage rises the **Eschenheimer Turm**, the highest defensive tower in Germany. There were once 42 towers ringing the city and this is the most imposing of the fifteenth-century survivors; its fantastical shape, peppered with oriels and turrets and looking like it was designed in the Hollywood dream factory, marks it out as the handiwork of the ever-resourceful Madern Gerthener. Look out for the nine holes in the shape of a figure 9 on the weather vane which, according to legend, were shot into it by a local poacher.

Nearby in Stephanstrasse is the **Petersfriedhof**, which for years was Frankfurt's most fashionable cemetery. In the adjacent school courtyard you can see the grave of Goethe's mother, "Frau Aja". About ten minutes' walk to the south, just off Fahrgasse, is a surviving stretch of the **Staufenmauer**, the twelfth-century city wall which was the grand daddy of all Frankfurt's subsequent defences. Just beyond here, a left turn into Berliner Strasse leads to

Battonstrasse and the **Jüdischer Friedhof**, which was in use from 1462 to 1828 and contains the Rothschild family vault. Immediately to the west is the **Museum Judengasse** (same hours as the Archäologisches Museum; €1.50, free Sat), where you can see the excavated foundations of five seventeenth-century Jewish houses, two ritual baths (one of which partially dates back to the Middle Ages) and a part of the sewage system.

Sachsenhausen

If you want to visit Frankfurt's finest museums, or have a laid-back evening out, then head for **Sachsenhausen** on the south bank of the Main, which is linked to the city centre by a series of bridges, including two for pedestrian use only. Although it has been part of Frankfurt since 1318, this city-within-a-city retains a distinctive atmosphere. It's best known as the "apple wine quarter", in honour of its most famous product, which is served in practically every bar in the area, and it's here that you'll find Frankfurt's most civilized nightlife (see pp.383–86).

The heart of the quarter

The Alte Brücke, the road bridge at the eastern end of the Altstadt, leads across the Main to the **Deutschordenshaus**, a triple-winged eighteenth-century building formerly belonging to the Teutonic Knights, whose Baroque facade cunningly hides a Gothic church. A section of the conventual buildings has been adapted to house the **Ikonen-Museum** (Tues & Thurs–Sun 10am–1pm & 1.30–5pm, Wed 10am–1pm & 1.30–8pm; Ⓦwww.ikonenmuseum.frankfurt.de; €1, but included on Museum für Angewandte Kunst ticket – see below – free Wed), a collection of icons concentrating on the eighteenth and nineteenth centuries. Overlooking the river just a couple of minutes' walk away is the **Kuhhirtenturm** (Cowherds' Tower): built in 1490 as part of the Sachsenhausen fortifications, it looks like an elongated fortified barn.

Most people go to Sachsenhausen to eat, drink and be merry in the restaurants and bars of **Alt-Sachsenhausen**, the network of streets around Affentorplatz to the south. The main attractions are the apple wine houses – recognized by the *Fichtekränzi* (pine wreath) hanging outside – where drinkers sit at long wooden benches in an atmosphere that makes it easy to get into conversation (see p.384).

At the southernmost end of the quarter looms the 120-metre **Henninger Turm** (Mon–Sat 3–11pm, Sun 11am–11pm; €3) of the eponymous Frankfurt brewery. The entrance fee includes ascent by lift to the observation platform, which commands a fine view over Frankfurt. There are also a couple of top-notch restaurants, which are pricey, though not unreasonably so.

Along Museumsufer

Between the Eiserner Steg and the Friedensbrücke to the west is Schaumainkai, popularly known as the **Museumsufer**, as the best museums in Frankfurt, seven in all, are straddled along its bank. First up, at no. 15, is the **Museum für Angewandte Kunst** (Tues & Thurs–Sun 10am–5pm, Wed 10am–8pm, Ⓦwww.mak.frankfurt.de; €5, free Wed), which has one of the largest and best collections of applied art in Germany. It's housed in a discreetly innovative building designed by the American architect Richard Meier, all sloping ramps in place of stairs and glassless internal windows framing *objets d'art*. The museum is divided into four sections: European, featuring furniture, glassware and ceramics; Islamic, with some fine carpets; Far Eastern, with lots of jade and lacquer work plus a liberal sprinkling of porcelain and sculptures; and finally a section devoted to books and writing. In a nineteenth-century villa at no. 29, the **Museum der Weltkulturen** (Tues, Thurs, Fri & Sun 10am–5pm, Wed 10am–8pm, Sat 2–8pm; Ⓦwww.mdw.frankfurt.de; €3.60, free Wed) is a recently revamped ethnographical museum celebrating the diversity of world cultures. A few doors along at no. 37 is its offshoot, **Galerie 37** (same times and ticket), whose stated aim is to bring before a European audience the work of unfamiliar artists from other continents.

The **Deutsches Filmmuseum** (Tues, Thurs, Fri & Sun 10am–5pm, Wed 10am–8pm, Sat 2–8pm; Ⓦwww.deutsches-filmmuseum.de; €2.50, free Wed) at no. 41 is Germany's biggest and best on the subject, featuring a huge collection detailing the development of films and the film industry. A distinctly "hands-on" approach encourages visitors to get to grips with the various film-related items on display, which range from early bioscopes to modern movie cameras. On a larger scale, there's a reconstruction of the *Grand Café* in Paris where the Lumière brothers showed the first-ever public film, and of a Frankfurt cinema from 1912. There's also a good collection of film posters and an extensive section on film music. Not surprisingly the museum has its own cinema (€5.50).

A passage leads from the Filmmuseum café to the **Deutsches Architekturmuseum** (Tues & Thurs–Sun 10am–5pm, Wed 10am–8pm; Ⓦwww.dam-online.de; €5, free Wed) at no. 43, installed in a self-consciously avant-garde conversion of a nineteenth-century villa. The high point of the interior, which has been gutted and restyled in dazzling white, is the "house within a house", which dominates the museum like an oversized doll's house. Most of the space is given over to changing exhibitions on architectural themes, though the top floor has a permanent display of miniature theatre sets presenting a potted history of world architecture.

More conventional in layout is the **Museum für Kommunikation** (Tues–Fri 9am–5pm, Sat & Sun 11am–7pm, Ⓦwww.museumsstiftung.de; free) at no. 53, which is devoted to postal and telecommunications history. The transport section features a postal coach of the 1890s and a post bus of 1925, while Frankfurt's claim to be the birthplace of the telephone is set out in an exhibition on Philipp Reis, who disputes with Alexander Graham Bell the right to be regarded as the inventor of the first prototype. The displays are enlivened by a number of thematically appropriate artworks, including Dalí's *Lobster Telephone* and an amusing installation entitled *TribuT* by Jean Luc Cornec.

The Städelsches Kunstinstitut

Very much the star of the Museumsufer, the **Städelsches Kunstinstitut** or **Städel** (Tues & Fri–Sun 10am–5pm, Wed & Thurs 10am–8pm; Ⓦwww.staedelmuseum.de; €6, free Wed) at no. 63 ranks as one of the most comprehensive art galleries in Europe. Unlike its Munich and Berlin counterparts, it is not rooted in a royal collection – it was founded in the early nineteenth century by a local banker as an art college, with an assembly of old masters from which students could learn.

Chronologically, the layout begins on the top floor. Highlights of the German section include a naive but surpassingly beautiful *Garden of Paradise* by an unknown Middle Rhenish master of the early fifteenth century; the squeamish *Martyrdom of the Twelve Apostles* by the normally placid **Lochner**; *The Resurrection* by **Master of the Housebook**; and *Job on his Dungheap* by **Dürer**. **Holbein the Elder**'s large *Passion Altar*, painted for the city's Dominican friary, is one of his finest but most gruesome works. **Cranach**'s *The Holy Kinship*, which incorporates portraits of some of the leading personalities of the day, is another major altarpiece from the eve of the Reformation. The idiosyncratic art of **Baldung** is represented by *Two Weather Witches*, while in **Altdorfer**'s opulent *Adoration of the Magi* the artist typically indulges his love of rich and elaborate detail. The outstanding *Portrait of Simon George of Cornwall* by **Holbein the Younger** is particularly intriguing for the fact that the subject was clean-shaven when the sittings began; the artist had to carry out a skilful modification in order to show the beard his patron subsequently grew.

One of the main strengths of the gallery is its wealth of paintings from the early Netherlandish School, dominated by the gem of the whole collection, **Jan van Eyck**'s *Lucca Madonna*, which shows his legendary precision at its finest. The first great painter of the School, now generally identified as **Robert Campin** but labelled here as the Master of Flémalle, is represented by several works, while his pupil **Rogier van der Weyden** features with a magnificent *Virgin and Child with SS Peter, John the Baptist, Cosmas and Damian*. There are also superbly observed male portraits by Memling and Massys, and one of **Bosch**'s earliest known works, *Christ Presented to the People*; though restrained by his standards, it already shows his penchant for caricature and facial distortions. The Madonna and Child, a frequent subject in the Netherlandish section, also dominates the Italian, where the outstanding treatment is the ethereal image by **Fra Angelico**. Versions by Verrocchio, Moretto da Brescia, Perugino, Bellini, Cima and Carpaccio make fascinating comparisons. Other highlights here are an *Annunciation* by **Carlo Crivelli**, *St Mark* by **Mantegna**, *An Ideal Female Portrait* by **Botticelli** and **Pontormo**'s *Lady with Lap-Dog*.

Pride of place among seventeenth-century paintings goes to Frankfurt's own **Adam Elsheimer**. The largest work ever painted by this master of the small-scale is the *Altarpiece of the Cross*, the seven panels of which have been patiently accumulated over the years. Also here are *The Great Flood* – a miracle of compression – and *The Dream of Joseph*. Poussin, Claude and Rubens, all admirers of Elsheimer, are on display in the next section, which also includes the most purely Baroque work in **Rembrandt**'s entire output, the violent *Blinding of Samson* – a striking contrast with the quiet dignity of his very early *David Playing the Harp before Saul*. There's a gloriously luminous **Vermeer**, *The Geographer*, and examples of most of the lesser artists of seventeenth-century Holland. Representation of the early eighteenth century is sparser, but there are two scenes from a *Horrors of War* series by **Goya**, the frothy *Isle of Cythera* by **Watteau**, and examples of Tiepolo, Canaletto and Chardin.

Paintings from the late eighteenth century onwards occupy the first floor. Of the big French names, **Courbet** (a *View of Frankfurt*), **Degas** and **Monet** are the ones to look out for. However, German artists predominate. *Goethe in the Roman Campagna* by **Johann Heinrich Tischbein** is the most celebrated of the many Romantic portrayals of the writer. The Nazarene Brotherhood figures strongly, notably with paintings by **Philip Veit**, once director of the Städel. If this isn't to your taste, you might prefer the realism of **Wilhelm Leibl**, whose *Unlikely Couple* is an update of a favourite Renaissance theme – mercenary love.

Until the days of the Third Reich, the Städel had perhaps the finest array of modern painting in Germany. However, over 500 paintings were removed in the measures against "degenerate art", and the collection has never recovered, although it now has the benefit of being able to display loans from local industrialists and financial institutions. German highlights include

Liebermann's *Amsterdam Orphanage Courtyard*, **Beckmann**'s *The Synagogue*, **Dix**'s unflattering *The Artist's Family*, **Ernst**'s spooky *Nature in Morning Light* and **Kirchner**'s *Nude Wearing a Hat*; the most notable foreign paintings are **Matisse**'s *Still Life* and **Picasso**'s *Portrait of Fernance Olivier*. Some avant-garde works, including several huge canvases by **Anselm Kiefer**, are also on view.

The Liebieghaus and the Haus Giersch

Next in line is the **Liebieghaus** (Tues & Thurs–Sun 10am–5pm, Wed 10am–8pm; Ⓦwww.liebieghaus.de; €2.50, free Wed) at no. 71. The villa which houses it can easily be identified by the bits and pieces of statuary on display in the garden, including *Ariadne on the Panther* by Johann Heinrich Dannecker. The collection is a step-by-step guide to the history of sculpture, and as such is the most important in the country. Sumerian, Egyptian, Greek, Roman and Coptic examples give a comprehensive overview of the Classical world. German works predictably predominate in the later periods; look out in particular for the late fifteenth- and early sixteenth-century golden period, featuring important carvings by Nicolaus Gerhaert, Hans Multscher and Tilman Riemenschneider. There's also an illuminating section on Baroque altarpieces.

The final institution on Museumsufer is the **Haus Giersch** or **Museum Regionaler Kunst** (Tues–Fri noon–7pm, Sat & Sun 11am–5pm; Ⓦwww.haus-giersch.de; €4) at no. 83. This hosts temporary displays only, on the art of the Rhine-Main region. Some of these are of broader appeal than others, though in its short lifetime the museum, which has concentrated on the nineteenth and early twentieth centuries, has already done much to re-establish the reputations of several once fashionable but now neglected artists.

Westend and Bockenheim

Frankfurt's financial district, the **Westend**, developed as home to the commercial class during the nineteenth century. Until the Nazis came to power many of the wealthier members of Frankfurt's Jewish community (the second largest in Germany) lived here – for example huge swathes of land between Bockenheimer Landstrasse and Reuterweg were owned by the Rothschild family until the city bought them out in 1938, for a "bargain" price. In the 1960s the property speculators moved in, forcing people out of their homes so the old buildings could be converted into offices or the sites used for skyscrapers. A rash of house occupations and squattings ensued, but caused only temporary delays to the process of redevelopment. The most impressive of the high-rise buildings which now dominate the Frankfurt skyline are the sleek **Deutsche Bank**, a little to the west of the Alte Oper, and the graceful **Messeturm** by the German-American Helmut Jahn, which provides a suitably dominant landmark for the vast complex of trade fair buildings north of the Hauptbahnhof. It's just two metres and one storey lower than the tallest of the skyscrapers, the 239m **Commerzbank** tower, which stands just west of the Goethehaus. Immediately to its north is the **Mainturm**, the only one of the towers generally accessible to the public, thanks to its panorama restaurant on the 53rd floor.

Westend has its own stretch of greenery along its northern fringe. Starting from the east, there's the **Grüneburgpark**, a nineteenth-century English-style park which these days is popular with joggers and weekend footballers. Next is the **Botanischer Garten**, a good place to go for a walk as it has a sort of cultivated wildness to it. At the western end of the green belt is the wonderful **Palmengarten** (daily: Feb–Oct 9am–6pm; Nov–Jan 9am–4pm; €5), where it's easy enough to while away several hours. The subtropical palms which give the garden its name can be seen in the majestic Palmenhaus, which was erected in 1869, while a host of tropical plants are grouped according to region in the Tropicarum, a complex of interconnected greenhouses. However, the attractions are by no means all indoors: there are separate manicured gardens for roses, rhododendrons, summer flowers, cacti, and many others. The water garden, with its colourful whirling jets, adds a lighter note.

Bockenheimer Landstrasse, once Frankfurt's millionaires' row, leads from Westend to **Bockenheim**, a predominantly working-class district which since the 1960s has been turned into the centre of Frankfurt's alternative scene by a big influx of students and arty types. The area also has a large *Gastarbeiter* population and has a similar flavour to Berlin's Kreuzberg. Leipziger Strasse is the main shopping drag (on U-Bahn lines #6 and #7) and there are plenty of good bars and restaurants around (see pp.385–86).

The university complex is at the southeastern edge of Bockenheim, which partly accounts for its popularity with students. In the vicinity, at Senckenberganlage 25, is the **Naturmuseum Senckenberg** (Mon, Tues, Thurs & Fri 9am–5pm, Wed 9am–8pm, Sat & Sun 9am–6pm, ⓦwww.senckenberg.uni-frankfurt.de; €3.50), one of the most important natural history museums in Europe. On the ground floor is a remarkable paleontology collection with an awe-inspiring array of dinosaur skeletons, including the only reasonably complete example of the *Edmontosaurus* yet discovered. One room is devoted to some of the spectacular fossils discovered at the shale pit of Messel (see p.394), whose excavation is in the hands of scientists from the museum's research institute. Another shows skeletons of animals, such as elephants, sabre-toothed tigers, hippopotamuses and rhinoceroses, which inhabited the Rhine-Main region half a million years ago. The section on human evolution features the oldest and best-preserved skeleton of *Australopithecus afarensis*, a proto-human which still has many characteristics of an ape. On the upstairs floors, compendious collections of stuffed animals, birds, fishes and insects can be seen.

Eating, drinking and nightlife

Not surprisingly, given its status as one of Germany's main urban centres, Frankfurt has a wealth of gastronomic possibilities. Thanks largely to the trade fair business, gourmet restaurants are thick on the ground, while the diverse international make-up of the local population is mirrored in an unusually wide choice of ethnic eateries. The city is situated close to several famous wine-producing regions, and is itself an important beer centre, with two well-known labels in Binding and Henninger, which have recently come under the same ownership. However, the city's favourite beverage is apple wine (Apfelwein; known as *Ebbelwei* or *Ebbelwoi* in the local dialect), a cider variant best sampled in the specialist taverns in Sachsenhausen.

Apple wine taverns

The apple wine tavern (Apfelweinwirtschaft) is as distinctive a Frankfurt institution as the Bierkeller is of Munich, or the Weinstube of Stuttgart. Although l the best-known establishments are concentrated in Sachsenhausen, re dotted all over the city. They're strongly traditional, a fact reflected urprisingly restricted opening hours many choose to operate. In addi- the apple wine, they invariably offer hearty local cuisine, usually at very ite prices.

Adolf Wagner Schweizer Str. 71, Sachsenhausen. One of the best of the taverns, with a lively clientele ranging from young to middle-aged. Frequently packed out. Open daily from 11am.

Apfelwein Klaus Meisengasse 10. The most celebrated apple wine tavern in the city centre, with a tradition dating back to 1914. Open Mon–Sat from 11am.

Atschel Wallstr. 7, Sachsenhausen. This offers a more extensive menu than many of its counterparts, and has a garden at the back. Open daily from 5pm.

Historix Saalgasse 19. The Historisches Museum's very own tavern boasts a collection of apple wine memorabilia, and has the benefit of a capacious garden.

Klaane Sachsehäuser Neuer Wall 11, Sachsenhausen. A family place favoured by native Sachsenhauseners which has been run since 1886 by five generations of the same family. Open from 4pm; closed Sun.

Zu den Drei Stuebern Dreieichstr. 28, Sachsenhausen. Mainly patronized by locals; has a small bar-room and pleasant terrace at the rear. Open Tues–Fri only from 3.30pm.

Zum Eichkatzerl Dreieichstr. 29, Sachsenhausen. An excellent traditional tavern which is particularly popular on account of its low-priced food. Open from 4pm, closed Mon.

Zum Feuerrädchen Textorstr. 24, Sachsenhausen. One of several traditional taverns on the street. Open from 3pm on weekdays, 11am at weekends, closed Mon.

Zum Gemalten Haus Schweizer Str. 67, Sachsenhausen. A bit kitschy with its oil-painted facade and stained-glass windows, yet quite intimate and lively, with long rows of tables outside. Open Wed–Sun from 10am.

Zur Germania Textorstr. 16, Sachsenhausen. Another of the recommendable taverns on this street; nearly always crowded. Open daily 4pm–midnight.

Restaurants

Many of the restaurants in the city centre are fast-food joints or credit-card rip-offs for unwary lunching business people, but you will find some of the best Thai, Mexican, Greek and Italian food here too. Other districts with good concentrations of restaurants are Sachsenhausen, Westend, Bockenheim and Bornheim, the inner suburb due north of the Altstadt. When there's a trade fair on, advance bookings are virtually mandatory, and most restaurants are open on the day or days they're normally closed.

Apple wine

There's a theory that Europe has a cider belt separating the areas producing wine and beer, and that Frankfurt is the hub of this. This seems tenuous at best, as the apple wine tradition here is historically a relatively recent one, having started in 1750. Made by the same process used in the production of ordinary wine, apple wine is bought in blue-grey stone jugs called *Bembel* and drunk from a *Schobbeglas*. There are four types: *Süsser*, sweet and fresh from the presses in autumn, and relatively weak; *Rauscher*, which will blow your head off if you don't treat it with respect; *Heller*, which is clear and smooth; and the hazy and golden *Altar*. Those in the know order *Handkäs mit Musik* (cheese served with onions and vinaigrette) or *Rippchen mit Kraut* (smoked pork chop with *Sauerkraut*) as a culinary accompaniment to their *Ebbelwei*.

If you're feeling in the mood for a bit of tourist tack, the *Ebbelwei-Express*, an old-time tram with on-board apple wine and Bretzels plies a circular route round the city centre on summer weekends.

Al Arischa Leipziger Str. 108, Bockenheim. A small family-run Lebanese place serving lamb and vegetarian dishes at reasonable prices. Evenings only, closed Sun.
Aubergine Alte Gasse 14. Good French food, good service, reasonable prices (by central Frankfurt standards). Open evenings only on Sat, closed Sun.
Avocado Hochstr. 27. Fine bistro fare, complemented by a carefully selected wine list. Closed all day Sun & Mon lunchtime.
Ban Thai Leipziger Str. 26, Bockenheim. Good, reasonably priced Thai restaurant, which also has a cheap Imbiss section.
Bistrot 77 Ziegelhüttenweg 1–3, Sachsenhausen ⓣ0 69/ 61 40 40. French restaurant with strong lines in game and fish. Has an outstanding selection of French wines, including some from the family's own vineyard in Alsace. Closed Sun; booking essential.
Buffalo Kaiserhofstr. 18. City-centre steakhouse, much favoured by the American community. Also does good enchiladas and tacos. Closed Sun.
Erno's Bistro Liebigstr. 15 ⓣ0 69/72 19 97. Sublime mix of French and German cuisine that regularly wins top awards in the international dining guides. Closed Sat & Sun. Expensive; book in advance.
Golfo di Napoli Leipziger Str. 16. Pricey Italian, popular with the Westend young professionals, but the food and atmosphere are good. Closed Sun.
Haus Wertheym Fahrtor 1. A medieval Gaststätte on the Römerberg with *Bockbier*, traditional food and a friendly atmosphere. Closed Tues.
Isoletta Feldbergstr. 31. One of the more affordable Italian restaurants, popular with the nearby ad agency types during the day.
Iwase Vilbeler Str. 31. Reasonably priced Japanese, with seating at the counter or the few tables. Closed Mon.
Knoblauch Staufenstr. 39. Friendly, intimate little place where everything comes liberally laced with garlic. Closed Sat & Sun.
Lalibela Klingerstr. 2. An Ethiopian restaurant with finger eating only, low prices and plenty of vegetarian options. Closed Mon.
Maaschanz Färberstr. 75 ⓣ0 69/62 28 86. Small, congenial restaurant specializing in French cuisine, notably fish dishes, at affordable prices. Evenings only; closed Mon. Book ahead.
Nibelungenschänke Nibelungenallee 55, Bornheim. Typical Greek food at reasonable prices. The clientele is young and the place is usually open until 1am. Take U-Bahn #5 to Nibelungenallee.
Rosa Grüneburgweg 25. The walls hung with pictures of pigs lend an element of kitsch, but the food is excellent. Evenings only, closed Sun & Mon.
Saigon Royal Kaiserstr. 67. This Vietnamese restaurant, which is conveniently close to the Hauptbahnhof, offers good-value set lunches.
Serengeti Porzellanhofstr. 10. Eritrean-run restaurant with a variety of African dishes including crocodile, springbok and ostrich and tasty vegetarian options. Bargain lunches but evenings only on Sun.
Taj Mahal Schweizer Str. 28. Popular Pakistani-run restaurant which has won an award as the city's best curry house. It offers bargain lunch dishes on weekdays.
Tiger Heiligkreuzgasse 20 ⓣ0 69/92 00 22 25. The restaurant attached to the Tigerpalast variety theatre presents some of the most creative and expensive cooking in Frankfurt. Evenings only; closed Mon. Reservations advisable.
Wolkenbruch Rotlintstr. 47, Bornheim. No-smoking vegetarian restaurant serving everything from tofu burgers to wholemeal pizzas.

Bars, cafés and café-bars

Sachsenhausen, with its cobbled streets and lively atmosphere, has many modern alternatives to its famous apple wine taverns. As home to a large student population, Bockenheim has plenty of youthful, inexpensive cafés. In the city centre, there are a few gems which are well worth seeking out in preference to the many overcrowded and overpriced alternatives.

Altes Café Schneider Kaiserstr. 12. This traditional café is one of the best places in town for *Kaffee und Küchen.*
Café Laumer Bockenheimer Landstr. 67. One of Frankfurt's oldest cafés, halfway up the Westend's main thoroughfare, now enjoying a new lease of life with a young arty clientele.
Club Voltaire Kleine Hochstr. 5. An eclectic clientele in one of Frankfurt's best-established meeting places. Also serves good bistro-type food at moderate prices.
CybeRyder Töngesgasse 31. Frankfurt's longest-established internet café. Open Mon–Thurs 10am–11pm, Fri & Sat 9am–midnight, Sun 11am–11pm.
Dominicus Brückhofstr. 1. A vaulted cellar establishment which draws a young crowd, particularly when there's live music on. Evenings only, closed Sun.
Harvey's Bornheimer Landstr. 64, Bornheim. Slick, high-ceilinged colonnaded bar which in the

evening hosts a mainly gay and lesbian crowd. Excellent breakfasts and daily specials.

Helium Bleidenstr. 7. Trendy bar which stays open late and serves night-time snacks. Daily 11am–4am.

Irish Pub Kleine Rittergasse 11–13, Sachsenhausen. Frankfurt's original Irish pub, established in 1971 and still one of the best in the country, with regular live music sessions.

Lesecafé Diesterwegstr. 7, Sachsenhausen. Popular with would-be intellectuals, you can read as you eat and drink. Select a book from the next-door bookshop, or just admire the art on the walls.

Plazz Kirchplatz 8, Bockenheim. Fun café offering a full repertoire of international breakfasts, including German, French, Italian and Russian. Attracts a mixed crowd.

Schwarzes Café Schweizer Str. 14, Sachsenhausen. This café has a distinctive black and mirrored decor which attracts a hip clientele. Closed Sat lunchtime & Sun.

Stattcafé Grempstr. 21, Bockenheim. Good breakfasts and an emphasis on healthy eating in an informal atmosphere. Popular with the Bockenheim arty crowd, it features displays by local artists on the walls.

Tannenbaum Brückenstr. 19, Sachsenhausen. Friendly English pub-style place with beer garden and tasty food.

Vinum Kleine Hochstr. 9. Popular traditional cellar wine bar, founded in 1863 and specializing in vintages from the Rheingau. Arrive early to secure a table. Evenings only; closed Sun (also Sat in summer).

Volkswirt Kleine Hochstr. 9. Located directly above *Vinum*, this has a pleasant summer garden at the front.

Zu den Zwölf Aposteln Rosenberger Str. 1. Frankfurt's first Hausbrauerei, producing organically brewed light and dark beers. The ground floor restaurant serves Balkan cuisine.

Nightclubs and live music

Not surprisingly Frankfurt's nightlife is pretty eclectic, and there's a wide range of live music on offer. The local club scene is heavily dance music-oriented, with most venues serving up house/techno beats for predominantly young crowds. Places tend to stay open until 4am during the week and 5am or 6am at weekends. Entry starts at about €5. For details of events, the best magazines are *Prinz* (Ⓦwww.prinz.de; €1) and *Journal Frankfurt* (Ⓦwww.journal-frankfurt.de; €2). Free magazines such as *Fritz* and *Strandgut*, which cover other towns in central Hesse as well, are also useful.

Batschkapp Maybachstr. 24 Ⓣ0 69/95218410, Ⓦwww.batschkapp.de. Live music or fairly up-to-the-minute DJ dance sounds. Daily 9pm–1am. Take S-Bahn #6 to Eschersheim.

Blue Angel Brönnerstr. 17. Popular gay dance bar. Open daily from 11pm.

Brotfabrik Bachmannstr. 2–4 Ⓣ0 69/7 89 55 13, Ⓦwww.brotfabrik.de. Innovative venue featuring live and recorded world music particularly salsa, African and Asian. Also has a café and a Spanish restaurant. U-Bahn #6 to Fischstein or U-Bahn #7 to Grosse Nelkenstrasse.

Cooky's Am Salzhaus 4. Frankfurt's best-known and most popular disco. Dance music and chart stuff draws in a youthful crowd. On Mon there are usually live bands. Daily 10pm–4/6am.

Jazzhaus Kleine Bockenheimer Str. 12. Half-timbered house on Frankfurt's *Jazzgasse* (Jazz Alley), where many leading jazzers cut their musical teeth.

Jazzkeller Kleine Bockenheimer Str. 18. Atmospheric cellar which is Frankfurt's premier jazz venue. Open 9pm–3am; closed Mon.

Sinkkasten Brönnerstr. 5 Ⓣ0 69/280335, Ⓦwww.sinkkasten-frankfurt.de. This place has everything – pool room, cabaret stage, disco and concert hall where they put on everything from jazz to avant-garde and indie stuff. Daily 9pm–2am.

Culture

Frankfurt has a predictably lively performing arts scene, with a wide range of choice in both music and theatre, and an established tradition of productions in English.

Alte Oper Opernplatz Ⓣ0 69/1 34 04 00, Ⓦwww.alteoper.de. There are three halls here, of which the largest is used for orchestral concerts (the Radio-Sinfonie-Orchester-Frankfurt is the pick of the local bands), while the other two host chamber, instrumental and vocal recitals.

English Theater Kaiserstr. 52 Ⓣ0 69/24 23 16 20, Ⓦwww.englishtheater-frankfurt.de. Flourishing

company which performs only in English.
Gallus-Theater Kleyerstr. 15 ⓣ0 69/75 80 60 20, ⓦwww.gallustheater.de. *Gastarbeiter* theatre which is arguably the country's most distinguished cultural institution of the immigrant community.
Oper Willy-Brandt-Platz ⓣ0 69/1 34 04 00, ⓦwww.oper-frankfurt.de & www.ballett-frankfurt.de. Presents top-class performances of opera and ballet. The latter company has been directed since 1984 by the American choreographer William Forsythe, and has an unashamedly avant-garde repertoire.
schauspielfrankfurt Willy-Brandt-Platz ⓣ0 69/1 34 04 00, ⓦwww.schauspielfrankfurt.de. The main civic theatre, offering drama old and new.
Theater am Turm Eschenheimer Landstr. 2 ⓣ0 69/21 23 72 88, ⓦwww.schauspielfrankfurt.de. Also known as Das TAT or the Bockenheimer Depot, this spartan performance space is used for the more experimental productions of the Oper and the schauspielfrankfurt.
Tigerpalast Heiligkreuzgasse 16–20 ⓣ0 69/9 20 02 20, ⓦwww.tigerpalast.com. The place to come for good old-fashioned variety shows.

Listings

Bike rental Per Pedale, Leipziger Str. 4, Bockenheim ⓣ0 69/70 76 91 10.
Book Fair Held annually in Sept/Oct at the Messe Frankfurt to the northwest of the Hauptbahnhof, this is the largest book fair in the world. On the last day you can often pick up great bargains from the English and American stalls.
Bookstore British Bookshop, Börsenstr. 17 ⓣ0 69/28 04 92.
Consulates Australian, Grüneburgweg 58-62 ⓣ0 69/90 55 80; British, Bockenheimer Landstr. 42 ⓣ0 69/1 70 00 20; US, Siesmayerstr. 21 ⓣ0 69/7 53 50.
Doctor ⓣ0 69/1 92 42.
Festivals Main folklore events are the Waldchestag at Whit weekend and the Mainfest in early August.
Pharmacy ⓣ0 69/1 92 92 for details of late-opening pharmacies.
Post offices The main post office with poste restante is at Goetheplatz 2–4 (Mon–Fri 9.30am–8pm, Sat 9.30am–4pm); the longest hours are kept by the branch on the first floor of the Hauptbahnhof (Mon–Fri 6.30am–9pm, Sat & Sun 11am–6pm).

Southern Hesse

The southern part of Hesse includes the wooded heights of the **Odenwald** at the extreme tip of the province and the famous vine-growing **Rheingau** on the east bank of the Rhine. Although there are several outstanding small towns in the area, there are only two cities: the staid spa of **Wiesbaden** and the former ducal residence of **Darmstadt**, which is a place with more than a few surprises in store.

Darmstadt

A cursory inspection of **DARMSTADT**, some 30km south of Frankfurt, at the end of S-Bahn line #3, is unlikely to leave you with much of an impression. The only way it apparently differs from any other prosperous German city rebuilt after the war is in the survival of the planned Neoclassical layout, with broad streets and spacious squares. Don't be discouraged, though; Darmstadt has a rich cultural heritage, traces of which have survived both the bombs and the planners.

During the second half of the eighteenth century the *Darmstädter Kreis* (Darmstadt Circle) flourished under the protection of Landgravine Karoline, numbering among its members Goethe, Martin Wieland and Johann Herder. The playwright Georg Büchner spent much of his short life in the city and wrote his great drama *Danton's Death* here in 1834, while under police observation for suspected revolutionary activities. It was at the turn of the last century, however, that the arts flourished most freely in Darmstadt when Grand Duke Ernst Ludwig (a grandson of Queen Victoria) supported the first and finest flowering of **Jugendstil**, the German form of Art Nouveau. The surviving monuments of this period are the most lasting and visible symbol of the city's support for artistic innovation.

Arrival, information and accommodation

If you arrive at the **Hauptbahnhof**, which is about 1km west of the city centre, you'll immediately get your first taste of the local Jugendstil heritage, as

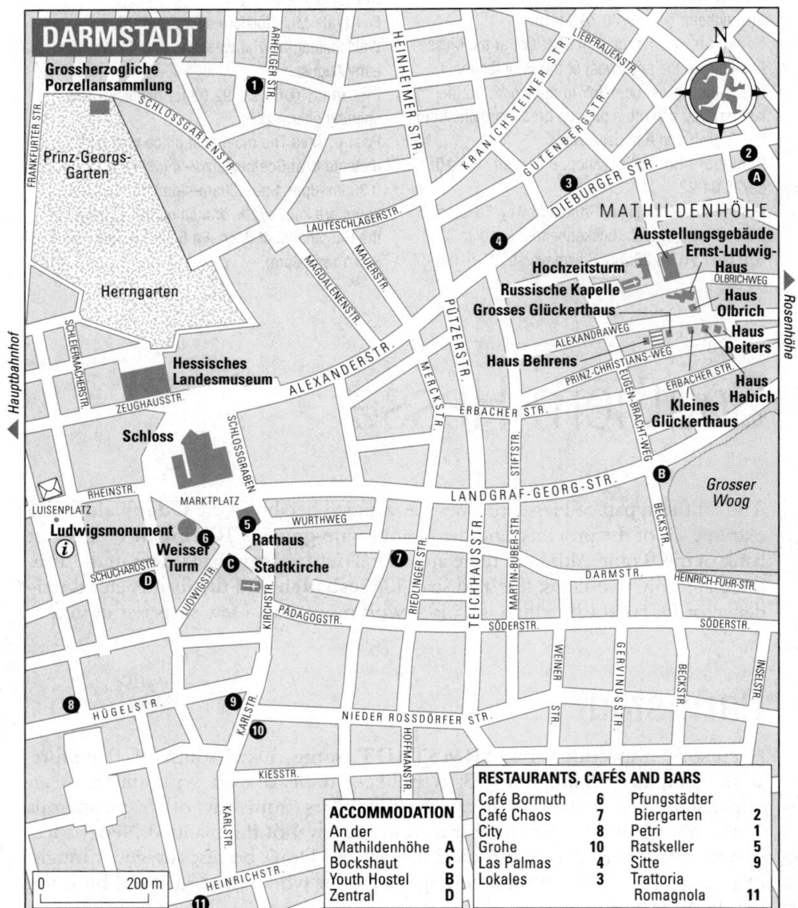

the station was a key part of the style's second phase in the second decade of the century. Buses #D and #H and tram #3 go by different routes to the city centre. The **tourist office** (Mon–Fri 9.30am–7pm, Sat 9.30am–4pm; ⓣ0 61 51/13 27 81, ⓦwww.info.darmstadt.de) is at Luisenplatz 5.

As for **accommodation**, the cheapest hotels are out in the suburbs, while the city centre has plenty of mid- and upper-range options. Darmstadt's **youth hostel** is at Landgraf-Georg-Str. 119 (ⓣ0 61 51/4 52 93; €18/20.70), right beside the open-air swimming pool at the Grosser Woog lake and also handily placed for visiting the Jugendstil buildings on Mathildenhöhe; take bus #D to Woog/Beckstrasse.

Hotels

An der Mathildenhöhe Spessartring 53 ⓣ0 61 51/4 80 46, ⓦwww.hotel-mathildenhoehe.de. This hotel is on the eastern side of the eponymous hill, ideally placed for visiting the city's Jugendstil heritage. ❻

Bockshaut Kirchstr. 7–9 ⓣ0 61 51/9 96 70, ⓦwww.bockshaut.de. Good old-fashioned German inn with a convenient position in the very heart of the city and alfresco eating in the inner courtyard in summer. ❼

Hornung Mornewegstr. 43 ⓣ0 61 51/92 66, ⓕ89 18 92. Located a couple of minutes' walk from the Hauptbahnhof, on the way to the city centre. ❺

Prinz Heinrich Bleichstr. 48 ⓣ0 61 51/8 13 70, ⓦwww.hotel-prinz-heinrich.de. On the western edge of the centre, with tasteful furnishings and a high-quality restaurant. ❻

Waldfriede Friedrich-Naumann-Str. 8, Eberstadt ⓣ0 61 51/5 26 19, ⓦwww.hotel-waldfriede.de. Occupies a large old villa in the northern part of an incorporated town which lies due south of Darmstadt proper. Take tram #1, #7 or #8 to Carl-Ulrich-Strasse: it lies one block to the south. ❺

Zentral Schuhardstr. 6 ⓣ0 61 51/2 64 11, ⓕ2 68 58. As central as its name suggests, located on a pedestrianized shopping street just off the east side of Luisenplatz. ❺

Zum Weingarten Hagenstr. 18, Eberstadt ⓣ0 61 51/5 22 61, ⓕ5 32 47. Darmstadt's best-value hotel is very traditional establishment on a quiet suburban street; rooms with and without private facilities are available. Its restaurant (closed Thurs) occupies two fine old chambers lit by stained-glass windows, and is serviced by its in-house butcher. Take tram #1, #6, #7 or #8 to Wartehalle, then walk two blocks north. ❸

The City

Between 1567 and 1918, the city was capital of Hesse-Darmstadt, a Landgraviate which was promoted to a Grand Duchy, with control over a large chunk of the Rhineland, during the Napoleonic period. The subsequent flurry of building activity to create a worthy capital meant that Darmstadt had its fair share of grand streets and squares, but most were destroyed on the night of September 11, 1944 when it was hit by 300,000 incendiary bombs and 700 high explosive bombs. The resulting fire-storm, deliberately created following the tried and tested Hamburg pattern, killed 12,000 people. Darmstadt made a remarkably quick recovery in the cultural arena, but most of its historic quarter was gone forever.

The centre

At the centre of modern Darmstadt sprawls **Luisenplatz**, a windswept shopping plaza crisscrossed by tram and bus lines and notable only for the **Ludwigsmonument** (April–Sept first Sat of month 10am–4pm; €1) or "Der Lange Lui", a 33-metre-high column crowned by a statue of Grand Duke Ludwig I. From here, Rheinstrasse leads east to Ernst-Ludwig-Platz, on which stands the **Weisser Turm** (April–Oct Wed 4–8pm, Sat 11am–6pm; €1), a fifteenth-century defensive tower which was later restyled in fashionable Baroque. Beyond is the spacious triangular Marktplatz, on whose southern side stands the gabled Renaissance **Rathaus**. Round the corner, the much-altered fourteenth-century **Stadtkirche** is mainly of note for the colossal Renaissance funerary monument to Landgrave Georg I and his wife Magdalena zur Lippe.

On the north side of Marktplatz is the **Schloss**, an extensive complex which developed gradually over seven hundred years. Reduced to a shell in the 1944 bombing raid, it has been diligently restored. The Baroque Neuschloss houses a library and the town archive, while the predominantly Renaissance Altschloss is home to a technical university and the **Schlossmuseum** (guided tours Mon–Thurs 10am–1pm & 2–5pm, Sat & Sun 10am–1pm; Ⓦwww.schlossmuseum-darmstadt.de; €2.50). Basically this is another German local history museum, but for the past 150 years has been home to **Hans Holbein the Younger**'s *Madonna of Jacob Meyer*, painted in 1526, one of the supreme masterpieces of Renaissance painting. It's particularly intriguing in being the last Catholic altarpiece by any of the great German masters of the period, all of whom (including Holbein himself) became Protestant. In 2004 the painting was loaned to the Städelsches Kunstinstitut in Frankfurt (see p.380). When it returns to Darmstadt in 2006, it is likely that it will be displayed in the Hessisches Landesmuseum (see below).

The Hessisches Landesmuseum

Slightly to the north of the Schloss is the **Hessisches Landesmuseum** (Tues & Thurs–Sat 10am–5pm, Wed 10am–8pm, Sun 11am–5pm; Ⓦwww.hlmd.de; €2.50, free Wed 3–8pm, 4–5pm other days), one of the best general museums in the country. Though there's a small **archeology** section, featuring a life-size sandstone sculpture of a Celtic warrior of the fifth century BC, an impressive Roman floor mosaic and jewellery from Frankish graves, most of the ground floor is given over to **applied art**. The medieval section is outstanding, highlights being a beautiful pair of tenth- or eleventh-century brooches found under the Dom in Mainz, and several masterly twelfth-century reliquaries from Cologne, including the domed *Darmstädter Kuppelreliquar*. In the basement, there's a glittering array of stained glass, notably a complete set from the Ritterstiftskirche in Bad Wimpfen, and a fragmentary ninth-century *Head of a Saint* from Kloster Lorsch. There's also an excellent Art Nouveau/Jugendstil section which sets Darmstadt's contribution in an international perspective. The first floor is devoted to **natural history**, and is dominated by a display of fossils found at the redundant open-cast shale pit at Messel in the outskirts of the city (see p.394).

However, the Landesmuseum's main claim to fame is as a picture gallery. In the ground floor's east wing is an outstanding collection of German Primitives, going back as far as a mid-thirteenth-century altar-table from Worms. **Lochner**'s gorgeous *Presentation in the Temple* shows the Cologne School at its mid-fifteenth-century peak, while the **Master of St Bartholomew**'s *Madonna and Child with SS Adrian and Augustine* belongs to the final flowering of this movement a couple of generations later. Mid-Rhenish painters closely followed Cologne's lead, and two of the finest products of this region are the works from which the **Master of the Ortenberg Altar** and the **Master of the Darmstadt Passion** derive their names. Several pictures by **Cranach** dominate the Renaissance section, including one of his greatest canvases, *Cardinal Albrecht von Brandenburg as St Jerome*.

Among the old masters on the second floor, the most important is the enigmatic *Magpie on the Gallows*, one of **Pieter Bruegel the Elder**'s last works. Highlights from the seventeenth century include pieces by Rubens, Domenichino and Domenico Feti, and a touching *Lamentation over the Dead Christ* by **Louis Le Nain**. A number of canvases by the Swiss **Arnold Böcklin** dominate the Romantic section, which also includes *Iphigenia*, one of

Feuerbach's finest works. The rest of the floor is designated the **Beuys-Block** and contains some 300 works by the iconoclastic sculptor **Joseph Beuys**, the largest collection of his work in existence. The German avant-garde gets precedence in the galleries of the new extension, though many of the country's best-known twentieth-century artists, such as Corinth, Kirchner, Beckmann and Dix, are also represented.

The Herrngarten

Just behind the Landesmuseum is the **Herrngarten**, a spacious English-style park which contains the tomb of Landgravine Karoline and a Jugendstil monument to Goethe. At the northeastern end is the **Prinz-Georgs-Garten**, a formal Rococo garden. Its pavilion, the Prinz-Georg-Palais, houses the **Grossherzogliche Porzellansammlung** (Mon–Thurs 10am–1pm & 2–5pm, Sat & Sun 10am–1pm; Ⓦwww.porzellanmuseum-darmstadt.de; €2.50), an extensive porcelain museum featuring examples from the local Kelsterbach factory, other leading German centres, and major pieces from England and Russia.

Mathildenhöhe

Mathildenhöhe (Ⓦwww.mathildenhoehe.info.de), a unique artists' colony on the eastern edge of the city centre, is a living monument to Jugendstil. It's only a fifteen-minute walk along Erich-Ollenhauer-Promenade from just behind the Schloss; alternatively, take bus #F to Lucasweg. At the centre of the complex stands a building which fits in well with the Jugendstil buildings but pre-dates the colony itself – the **Russische Kapelle** (daily April–Sept 9am–6pm; Oct–March 9.30am–5pm; €0.75). This heavily ornamented Russian Orthodox chapel crowned by two gilded domes was built in 1898 at the behest of the last tsar of Russia, Nicholas II, who often spent the summer in Darmstadt with his Hessian wife.

Work on the Mathildenhöhe colony began in 1901 with the construction of the **Ernst-Ludwig-Haus**, designed by the Viennese architect Joseph Maria Olbrich for the *Dokument Deutscher Kunst 1901*, an exhibition whose aim was to encapsulate all aspects of the Jugendstil movement. Approached via a broad flight of steps, the building has something of the mausoleum about it, with its imposing portal flanked by monumental figures of Adam and Eve carved by Ludwig Habig. The **Museum Künstlerkolonie Darmstadt** (Tues–Sun 10am–5pm; €2.50) now occupies the interior, showing products made by the colony – ranging from stained-glass windows to furniture, jewellery, silverware and porcelain. These are grouped in sections corresponding to the four great exhibitions held during the life of the colony.

To complement the Ernst-Ludwig-Haus, Olbrich built seven houses as artists' residences immediately below on Alexandraweg and Mathildenhöhweg, also in 1901. Five survive in reasonably authentic shape: they vary in style and all have unique and intricate design features which differentiate them from each other. Directly below the Ernst-Ludwig-Haus is the **Haus Olbrich**, a villa with a slightly subverted appearance where the architect spent the last years of his life. Directly facing it is the **Haus Habich**, which is almost Cubist in style, while further south is the smallest of the group, **Haus Deiters**, a striking re-interpretation of the English cottage style. Immediately west of Haus Habich are the **Kleines Glückerthaus**, which has an angular southern European look, and the **Grosses Glückerthaus**, which best represents the ethos of the original project. Next door to the latter is the **Haus Behrens**, designed by the Hamburg architect Peter Behrens, also in 1901. Its brick-framed white facade and red-tiled roof inject an element of Hanseatic sobriety into the colony, in deliberate contrast with Olbrich's more playful Mediterranean efforts. Only the door, decorated with swirling bronze appliqué work and flanked by rippling turquoise columns, has much in common with the neighbouring houses. Unfortunately, opportunities for viewing any of the interiors are far more limited than they were a few years ago. However, on the first Sunday of each month during the summer there are usually guided tours of the colony which include access to Haus Deiters and/or the Grosses Glückerthaus; ask at the tourist office or the Museum Künstlerkolonie Darmstadt for exact details.

In 1908 work on the huge and gleaming **Austellungsgebäude** (Exhibition Hall; Tues–Sun 10am–6pm; variable entrance charge) at the top of Mathildenhöhe was completed. It's still in use, and the first-floor café is equipped with Jugendstil furnishings. Look out for the Olbrich-designed mosaic in the roof of the pavilion halfway up the entrance steps. Next to the Austellungsgebäude rises the **Hochzeitsturm** (Wedding Tower; March–Oct Tues–Sun 10am–6pm, €1.50), a 48-metre-high brick tower with a distinctive roof which, when seen head-on, looks like a hand facing palm outwards. It was presented to Grand Duke Ernst Ludwig and his bride by the city three years after their 1905 wedding and has become so popular that it's now Darmstadt's official emblem. A lift takes visitors to the top, though it's worth walking back down in order to glance into the two ornate reception rooms in the tower.

To the west is the **Platanenhain**, a formal garden of clipped plane trees first laid out in the 1830s, though its present appearance is a legacy of the colony's last exhibition in 1914, when it was adorned with symbolic sculptures and reliefs of the stages of life by Bernhard Hoetger. For the same exhibition, Albin Müller, who had taken over the leadership of the colony on Olbrich's death in 1908, designed the **Lilienbecken**, the fountain and basin immediately south of the Platanenhain, as well as the **Schwanentempel**, a garden pavilion beside the Russische Kapelle.

Rosenhöhe

Because most of the Mathildenhöhe buildings are now used by various design institutes and cultural organizations, Darmstadt's practising artists have moved to the nearby **Rosenhöhe** area. This is reached in about ten minutes from the Haus Olbrich by following Alexandraweg, turning right into Fiedlerweg, left into Seitersweg and then crossing the rail bridge. During the late 1960s a new artists' colony was established here in the **Rosenhöhe-Park**, whose original purpose was to provide a last resting place for members of the ruling family of Hesse-Darmstadt. At the entrance to the park is the **Löwentor**, a gate comprising six Jugendstil lions standing on top of decorative brick pillars. Nearby is the **Ostbahnhof**, built in the style of a Russian country station at the request of Tsar Nicholas II.

Eating, drinking and nightlife

Darmstadt's nightlife is somewhat fragmented. Many of the best **restaurants** are in the hotels (see p.389), while there's also a good cluster of places to eat and drink just west of the Herrngarten. Most of the **apple wine** places are to the east of the same park; this area is where many of the students live, and makes a good starting point for a pub crawl. There's also a wide range of **music** and **theatre** venues.

Restaurants

Braustüb'l Goebelstr. 7–10. Offering a good range of local fare, this is the main restaurant of the Darmstädter brewery, located right alongside. It makes no fewer than ten different styles of beer, five of which can be sampled for €3.30.
City Wilhelminenstr. 31. The city centre branch of the above has slightly lower prices, particularly at lunchtime, when it offers good-value set menus.
Las Palmas Dieburger Str. 22. Good, inexpensive Spanish restaurant; also serves German food.
Lokales Dieburger Str. 50. Specializes in cheap, mouth-watering Italian pizzas.
Oberwaldhaus Dieburger Str. 257. This picturesque large house in the woods at the eastern edge of the city might have come straight out of a German fairy tale. A popular weekend excursion destination, it offers a moderately-priced menu of German and Balkan dishes and has a large beer garden. Take bus #F.
Orangerie Bessunger Str. 44. Stylish designer restaurant, occupying the former hothouse of the Baroque Orangerie, in a fine park of the same era; it's 1.5km south of Luisenplatz, on the route of tram #3. The predominantly Italianate cuisine ranks among the city's best. Closed Mon.
Ratskeller Marktplatz 8. Located on the ground floor of the Rathaus, rather than the usual cellars. It has its own Hausbrauerei, which makes light, dark and *Weizen* beers, plus a seasonal *Bock*.
Sitte Karlstr. 15. The main Gaststätte of the local Pfungstädter brewery.
Trattoria Romagnola Heinrichstr. 29. This offers all the classics of Italian cuisine. Closed Sat lunchtime & Sun.

Bars, cafés and café-bars

Bembelsche Irenenstr. 1. One of several apple wine taverns, in this case with a small front garden.
Café Bormuth Marktplatz 5. The city's best traditional café, well-known for its home-made pralines and biscuits.
Café Chaos Mühlstr. 36. Popular café-bar which also serves good pizzas and light meals.
Grohe Nieder-Ramstädter Str. 1. Small Kneipe with beer garden alongside the tiny brewery of the same name, which makes a *Vollbier* and a *Bock*.
Kulturcafé Hermannstr. 7. Vegetarian café with garden terrace whose name reflects its former status as a cultural centre. Open Tues–Fri 9.30am–7pm, Sat & Sun 10am–6pm. It's located directly opposite the Freiberger Platz stop of tram #3.
Pfungstädter Biergarten Dieburger Str. 97. Beer garden worth checking out if the weather's good.
Petri Ahrheilger Str. 50. Favourite haunt of hip youngsters, complete with beer garden. Evenings only.
Sumpf Kasinostr. 105. Studenty pub which does fairly cheap snacks.

Live music pubs, clubs and discos

Comedy Hall Heidelberger Str. 131. Pub attached to a popular performance venue which is best-known for the adult puppet shows of Kikeriki (see below).
Goldene Krone Schustergasse 18. An amazing warren of a place, with several bars, games rooms and stages presenting live acts ranging from cabaret to various kinds of music. Entry is €2.50.
Jagdhofkeller Bessunger Str. 84. Jazz bar featuring live sessions Wed–Sun at 9pm.
Studentenkeller Im Schlosshof. Enduringly popular student meeting place, situated in the Schloss courtyard. Open daily from 9pm.
Tanzclub Huckebein Heidelberger Str. 89a. Currently the city's hippest disco.

Culture

The main venue for **drama**, **opera** and formal **concerts** is the Hessisches Staatstheater on Georg-Büchner-Platz (Ⓣ0 61 51/29 38 38, Ⓦwww.staatstheater-darmstadt.de), which maintains Darmstadt's reputation for artistic innovation with three-quarters of its performances per season likely to be new productions. Kikeriki presents **puppet** shows for children at Bessunger Str. 88 (Ⓣ0 61 51/6 55 93), and for adults just around the corner at the aforementioned Comedy Hall. Local **festivals** include the Frühlingfest in March or April, the Heinerfest for five days in early July, and the Herbstfest in late September.

The Odenwald region

The **Odenwald** is a large upland forest area – which is designated as the Naturpark Bergstrasse-Odenwald – occupying almost all of the southernmost part of Hesse and stretching into both Bavaria and Baden-Württemberg. The hilly countryside at its heart, which is serviced by a branch rail line from Darmstadt, is punctuated by postcard-pretty half-timbered towns where traditional craft industries continue to flourish. The misleadingly named **Bergstrasse** (Mountain Road) runs along the eastern fringe of the Odenwald. To the Romans – who called it the Strata Montana – it was a major military road, but nowadays it is a tourist route linking Darmstadt and Heidelberg, as well as a small but high-quality wine-producing area. Spring starts here earlier than anywhere else in Germany, and the best time to visit is in late March or early April, when the fruit trees that line it all suddenly come into bloom. At the northern edge of the Odenwald region, practically on Darmstadt's doorstep, Messel is one of the most scientifically and (pre)historically significant sites in the whole of Germany.

Messel

MESSEL, which likes to style itself the "Pompei of Paleontology", lies beyond the eastern boundary of Darmstadt, on the rail line to Aschaffenburg. It's a village in two distinct parts, separated by an area of open countryside: to the north, Messel proper is a sleepy half-timbered village absolutely typical of rural Hesse, while **Grube Messel**, the area around the Bahnhof, grew up as an adjunct to the huge redundant **shale pit** – which measures 1km by 700m, and is 70m deep – from which it takes its name. In 1900, just sixteen years after mining began, the pit was already responsible for 40 percent of Germany's crude oil. Together with the on-site carbonisation furnaces, which produced petrol, diesel, highly refined paraffin and pure carbon used in paint manufacture, it remained an important industrial enterprise until it gradually succumbed to competition from petroleum mining. The furnaces were shut down in 1962; mining ended nine years later, though the vast slag heap continues to be a source for tennis courts and cinder running tracks.

Fossils from the Eocene Period of 49 million years ago, when the pit was a lake surrounded by a tropical forest, were first discovered around the time that mining began. However, it is only since the site lost its industrial function that systematic scientific excavations have been undertaken. The fossils, which are extraordinarily well-preserved, are of particular interest for showing animals at an early stage in their evolutionary process. Some, notably the horses, hardly resemble their modern-day counterparts, being no bigger than large dogs; others, such as the bats and crocodiles, are far more obvious ancestors. Such is the importance of the findings that the pit has gained inclusion on UNESCO's World Heritage List – the only natural wonder in Germany to be so honoured. Excavation work is still ongoing; a grandstand view of this, and the pit itself, can be had from the **observation platform**, which is freely accessible at all times, and reached by going 1km southwards along the main road from the Bahnhof, turning left down the signposted side road, then following the marked footpath. The only way the public can actually enter the pit is by booking one of the **guided tours** run by the Museumsverein Messel, Kohlweg 15 (Ⓣ0 61 59/2 56) well in advance.

Some of the fossils excavated at Messel are displayed in the Hessisches Landesmuseum in Darmstadt (see p.390), the Naturmuseum Senckenberg in

Frankfurt (see p.383), and the Staatliches Museum für Naturkunde in Karlsruhe (see p.337). Others can be seen in a half-timbered former school building in the centre of the village at Langgasse 2 which is now designated the **Fossilien- und Heimatmuseum** (May–Oct Tues–Sat 2–5pm, Sun 10am–noon & 2–4pm; Nov–April Sat 2–4pm, Sun 10am–noon & 2–4pm; free).

Lorsch

The undoubted highlight of the Bergstrasse is **LORSCH**, which lies on the small branch railway linking nearby Bensheim (on the eastern of the two main Darmstadt–Mannheim lines) with the Rhenish city of Worms. Once again, the centre is half-timbered, but everything is completely overshadowed by the former Benedictine **Kloster** (free access at all times; guided tours of the interiors Tues–Sun 10am–5pm; Ⓦwww.kloster-lorsch.de; €3), another UNESCO-listed World Heritage Site. Founded in 764, the monastery was once among the most powerful in Germany, its abbot ranking as a secular prince answerable directly to the emperor. The extraordinary **Torhalle** (or **Königshalle**), which probably dates back to the ninth century, is the best-preserved monument to have survived from the Carolingian period. Its outline was clearly inspired by Roman triumphal arches, while the patterned stonework, arranged in the manner of a mosaic, is of outstanding quality. Inside, the upper storey, which functioned as a chapel, has a lively series of fourteenth-century frescoes. The only other intact part of the monastery is the austere mid-twelfth-century **Vorkirche** which, despite its dimensions, was no more than the narthex of the main church, of which nothing other than the foundations can be seen. Included in the entrance ticket is admission to the **Museumszentrum**, which features displays on folklore, local history and the tobacco industry.

Lorsch's **tourist office** (Mon–Thurs 9am–noon & 2–4pm, Fri 9am–noon; Ⓣ0 62 51/59 67 50, Ⓦwww.lorsch.de) is in the finest of the half-timbered buildings, the Rathaus, Marktplatz 1. The town's **hotels** include *Jäger*, Bahnhofstr. 79 (Ⓣ0 62 51/5 22 44; ④) and *Gasthof Schillereck*, Schillerstr. 27 (Ⓣ0 62 51/5 23 01; ⑤). Both of these have **restaurants**, but the best place to eat is the renowned and expensive *Zum Schwannen*, Nibelungenstr. 52.

Wiesbaden

WIESBADEN, 40km west of Frankfurt, is the modern capital of Hesse, a role bestowed on it by the American occupying forces, in large part because – in contrast to all its possible rivals – it came through World War II virtually unscathed. Historically speaking, it does not even belong to the province and – its Roman origins notwithstanding – is very much a late developer. Indeed, it still had little more than two thousand inhabitants when, under the Napoleonic reforms, it became capital of Nassau, which was reunified and raised to the status of a duchy.

Strolling through the centre – complete with its grandiloquent Historicist architecture – it's not difficult to imagine how the city must have looked during its glory days as a nineteenth-century *Kurstadt*, when the aristocracy of Europe flocked to take the waters at the numerous thermal spas and to gamble away their fortunes in the famous casino. Today the Russian nobles who were once the main patrons have been replaced by wealthy Arabs and tanned, *nouveau-riche* Germans, and Wiesbaden bears little resemblance to any other major German city.

Arrival, information and accommodation

Wiesbaden's **Hauptbahnhof** is about fifteen minutes' walk south of the city centre, which can be reached by bus #1 or #8. The **tourist office** (Mon–Fri 9am–6pm, Sat 9am–3pm; ⓣ06 11/1 72 97 80, ⓦwww.tourist.wiesbaden.de) is at Marktstr. 6. **Hotels** in the city are predictably pricey, but if you're prepared to splash out a bit, there are some excellent upmarket choices. Most of the budget options are out in the suburbs; the **youth hostel** is at Blücherstr. 66 (ⓣ06 11/4 86 57; €19), best reached by bus #14 from the Hauptbahnhof.

Hotels

Ambrosius Alfred-Schumann-Str. 9, Schierstein ⓣ06 11/2 23 24, ⓕ2 04 72 41. A rare budget option in an incorporated village which is a train stop between Biebrich and Eltville. ❸

Bären Bärenstr. 3 ⓣ06 11/30 10 21, ⓦwww.baeren-hotel.de. One of the least outrageously priced of the upmarket hotels in the city centre, notwithstanding the fact that it has its own thermal baths. It also has a restaurant serving French cuisine. ❼

Domäne Mechtildshausen An der Airbase, Erbenheim ⓣ06 11/73 74 60, ⓕ73 74 79. Wiesbaden's most unexpected hotel is an organic farm 4km southeast of the city centre. Its highly creative restaurant (closed Sun evening & Mon) is a popular excursion destination with locals. Take bus #5 to its terminus. ❽

Hansa Bahnhofstr. 23 ⓣ06 11/90 12 40, ⓦwww.hansa.bestwestern.de. This classy hotel is conveniently located between the Hauptbahnhof and the centre. It has a good, reasonably-priced restaurant, *Warsteiner Stube* (closed Sat lunchtime & Sun). ❻

Landhaus Diedert Am Kloster Klarenthal 9 ⓣ06 11/1 84 66 00, ⓦwww.landhaus-diedert.de. Country house-style hotel with gourmet restaurant 5km northwest of the city centre. Take bus #12 or #14. ❼

Meuser Stettiner Str. 13, Biebrich ⓣ06 11/6 93 60, ⓕ69 36 88. Pleasant yet inexpensive hotel in Wiesbaden's most attractive suburb, a short walk north of the Rheinufer terminus of buses #3 and #4. ❹

Nassauer Hof Kaiser-Friedrich-Platz 3 ⓣ06 11/13 30, ⓦwww.nassauer-hof.de. This is not only Wiesbaden's grandest hotel, but also among the most renowned and expensive in Germany, boasting every conceivable luxury, thermal baths included. Its principal restaurant, *Ente*, is no less celebrated, while the *Orangerie* is a leading exponent of *neue deutsche Küche*. ❾

Oranien Platter Str. 2 ⓣ06 11/1 88 20, ⓦwww.hotel-oranien.de. Excellent, fully modernized nineteenth-century hotel with restaurant in the pedestrian zone. ❽–❾

The city centre

At the heart of Wiesbaden is the **Kurhaus**. Completed in 1906 in a Neoclassical style which would have been fashionable a hundred years previously, it's the self-conscious symbol of a city where appearances are everything. The building also houses the casino or **Spielbank** (daily 3pm–3am), which opened in 1949. However, gambling first started in earnest in 1771 and Wiesbaden's original casino was the inspiration for "Roulettenburg", in Dostoyevsky's novel *The Gambler*. Gambling was suspended between 1872 and 1949 as a result of a ban imposed by Kaiser Wilhelm I after his son, Crown Prince Friedrich III, had formed an "unsuitable" attachment to a woman gambler. The **Kurhauskolonnade** to the north, the longest pillared hall in Europe, contains the slot machine section of the casino complex and a space for exhibitions. Opposite, the **Theaterkolonnade**, with its luxury boutiques, forms a front to the lavish neo-Rococo **Hessisches Staatstheater**, which was built at the end of the nineteenth century by Viennese architects. To the rear of the Kurhaus is the **Kurpark**, an English-style park. From there you can walk up into the wooded slopes of the Taunus, which rise to the north of the city.

Wilhelmstrasse, the main shopping street, runs past the Kurhaus into Friedrich-Ebert-Strasse and is full of expensive antique shops and glitzy designer stores. On Schlossplatz stands the **Stadtschloss**, built in the 1840s as the town residence of the Nassau dukes. Nowadays, it's the Hesse state parliament. Facing the Stadtschloss is the seventeenth-century **Altes Rathaus**, the oldest building in the city. In front of it, on Marktplatz, where markets are held on Wednesdays and Saturdays, there's a small fountain topped by a playful-looking lion, one of the symbols of the city. The brick **Marktkirche** (Tues, Fri & Sat 10.30am–12.30pm, Wed 10.30am–noon, Thurs 3.30–5.30pm), which bristles with towers, steeples and turrets, bears the hallmarks of the pervasive influence of the English Gothic Revival style.

A few minutes' walk to the northwest, at Langgasse 38–40, is the most atmospheric and expensive of the city's thermal baths, the mock-Roman **Kaiser-Friedrich-Bad** (Mon–Thurs, Sat & Sun 10am–10pm, Fri 10am–midnight; Tues women only, rest of the week mixed; €17.50), which dates back to 1913. The entry ticket is valid for four hours and includes a full Roman-Irish steam bath plus the use of the solarium. On Kranzplatz, not much more than a stone's throw to the north, is the **Kochbrunnen**, which has no fewer than fifteen different hot springs. You can sample the sulphuric-tasting waters at the taps in the little Neoclassical temple. Despite their much-vaunted healing properties, the recommended maximum intake is one litre per day.

Many of the finest of the grand villas so characteristic of Wiesbaden can be seen in the streets immediately south of the Kurhaus. Particularly notable is the **Villa Clementine** at the head of Frankfurter Strasse. Nowadays a cultural centre, it was the scene in 1888 of the abduction of Crown Prince Alexander of Serbia, who was forceably repatriated by his captors. Alongside is the mid-nineteenth-century Anglican church of **St Augustine of Canterbury**, which is still in regular use, thanks to the continued presence of a sizeable American community. Just to the south, at the top end of Friedrich-Ebert-Allee, is the **Museum Wiesbaden** (Tues 10am–8pm, Wed–Fri 10am–4pm, Sat & Sun 10am–5pm, Ⓦwww.museum-wiesbaden.de; €2.50). This possesses a large number of paintings by the Russian artist Alexej Jawlensky – a member of the Expressionist *Der Blaue Reiter* group who was a Wiesbaden resident for the last two decades of his life – and extensive collections of locally-excavated Roman and early medieval antiquities.

The outskirts

On the northern edge of Wiesbaden looms the **Neroberg**, a 245-metre Taunus foothill commanding good views of the city. To get there take bus #1 to Nerotal and from there ascend by the water-powered funicular railway, the **Nerobergbahn** (April & Sept Wed & Sat noon–7pm, Sun 10am–7pm; May–Aug daily 9.30am–8pm; Oct Wed Sat & Sun noon–6pm; €1.30 single, €1.80 return), whose technology has remained unchanged since its inauguration in 1888. On the summit stand the Neoclassical **Neroberg-Tempel** and the **Opelbad** (May–Sept daily 7am–8pm; €6), a Bauhaus-style open-air swimming pool. A short distance downhill is the **Russische Kapelle** (April–Oct daily 10am–5pm; Nov–March Sat noon–3pm, Sun 10am–4pm; €0.60), a nineteenth-century Russian-style chapel instantly recognizeable by its five gilded cupolas. It was built as a mausoleum for the Russian-born Duchess Elisabeth of Nassau, who died in childbirth at the age of nineteen. Nearby is the **Russischer Friedhof**, with the elaborate tombs of many Russian aristocrats and soldiers.

It's also worth making a trip south to the incorporated town of **BIEBRICH** on the Rhine, which can be reached by bus #3 or #4. Its Baroque **Schloss**, the original Wiesbaden home of one of the lines of the Nassau dynasty, has a restrained elegance which puts the showy city centre to shame. Though the building itself is used for state functions and only open to the public for the occasional concert or guided tour, you can stroll in the fine park. Biebrich is also the first embarkation point after Mainz for **cruises** down the Rhine (for more details on these, see p.449).

Eating, drinking and entertainment

Predictably enough, **eating** and **drinking** in Wiesbaden can be an expensive business. There are plenty of upmarket restaurants (see also "Accommodation" section on p.396), but good cheaper places (including several run as adjuncts to food shops) do exist and there are some excellent centrally located pubs too.

Restaurants

Centro Italia Wörthstr. 18. One of several notable Italian restaurants, distinguished by its range of Sicilian wines and speciality dishes. Closed Tues.

Der Stephan Armenruhstr. 6, Biebrich. A successful transplant of a Bavarian Bierkeller, serving good food (particularly fish dishes) and having the obligatory beer garden. Closed Sat.

Feinkost Feickert Wilhelmstr. 10. This elegant delicatessen has a bistro-restaurant open during shopping hours.

Frickel Marktstr. 26. Daytime restaurant attached to a high-class fishmonger's shop that has been in existence since 1899. There's another branch at Moritzstr. 3.

Käfer's Kurhausplatz 1. One of the best of Wiesbaden's upmarket restaurants, located in the Kurhaus. The cooking has a German accent, even though the decor is reminiscent of a Parisian bistro.

Rheingold Saalgasse 30. This is reckoned to be *the* place in Wiesbaden for *gutbürgerliche Küche*. Evenings only.

Salat Inn Schützenhofstr. 3. Vegetarian and wholefood restaurant on a terrace above its own shop. It has a huge selection of dishes which you pay for by weight. Open Mon–Fri 9am–7.30pm, Sat 9am–4pm.

Sir Winston Churchill Taunusstr. 23. Long-established restaurant-cum-bistro-cum-café which starts serving breakfast at 8.30am and remains open till 4am. It aims to combine high culinary standards with the atmosphere and style of a British club.

Trüffel Marktstr. 9. Located in one of the city's best delicatessens, this serves Italianate bistro food and is a lunchtime favourite with shoppers and office workers. Closed Sat evening and all day Sun.

Zum Dortmunder Langgasse 34. Excellent traditional Gaststätte serving hearty cuisine and Dortmund beers.

Bars and cafés

Café Maldaner Marktstr. 34. Elegant coffee house in the heart of the shopping district.

C/O Moritzstr. 52. An alternative bar with a good atmosphere which also serves cheap meals.

Die Klappe Nerostr. 20. Trendy café-bar with beer garden.

Irish Pub Michelsberg 15. One of the better and more original of the new wave of Irish pubs which have sprung up all over Germany. There's often live music, and it's generally packed out by mid-evening.

Park-Café Wilhelmstr. 36. Extremely chic nightspot patronized by the beautiful set. Open Wed–Sun 9pm–4am.

Sächsische Konditorei Langgasse 43. The café is an adjunct to the shop, which makes what are reckoned to be the best cakes and sweets in Wiesbaden.

Schloss Biebrich Rheingaustr. 140, Biebrich. The café in the basement of the central rotunda is the only part of the building regularly open to the public. It serves light meals and has outdoor seating on the terrace in summer.

Sherry & Port Adolfsallee 11. The name of this bar, which combines English and Irish influences, is due to the large selection of sherries and ports on offer. Live jazz, folk and classical music sessions take place several times a week, and it serves dishes inspired by cuisines from all around the world.

Culture

The Hessisches Staatstheater on Kurhausplatz (ⓣ06 11/3 23 25, ⓦwww.staatstheater-wiesbaden.de) is the principal cultural venue; it presents **opera**, **operetta** and **ballet** in the plush main auditorium, **drama** on the two smaller, plainer stages. Classical **concerts** take place in the ornate Friedrich-von-Thiersch-Saal (ⓣ06 11/1 72 99 30) in the Kurhaus. The main **cabaret** venues are Pariser Hoftheater, Spiegelgasse 9 (ⓣ06 11/30 06 07) and Hinterhaus, Karlsruher Str. 15 (ⓣ06 11/37 95 48). The Internationales Maifestspiel throughout May is Wiesbaden's most important cultural **festival**, while the top popular event is the Theatrium, a huge street fair on Wilhelmstrasse at a weekend in early June.

The Rheingau

The Hessian side of the Rhine, running from Wiesbaden to the border with Rhineland-Palatinate at Lorchhausen, is known as the **Rheingau**. Sheltered from the elements by the gentle slopes of the Taunus, the region has developed into one of Germany's foremost wine-producing districts, and its vineyards, ruined castles and drowsy little villages make it a favourite destination for coach parties and package tourists. Road B42, running from Wiesbaden to the Rhineland-Palatinate border and taking in all the little wine villages, has been designated the **Rheingauer-Riesling Route**, a special-interest stretch for wine fans, enabling them to stop off and do a spot of tasting and buying. Classical music buffs should make a point of visiting during the three months in summer when the Rheingau-Musik-Festival takes place, as it features of dozens of concerts by international musicians of the highest rank. Though some performances are in Wiesbaden, the vast majority take place in the region's smaller towns and villages.

Eltville

The first stop out of Wiesbaden, just beyond its suburbs, is **ELTVILLE**, which lies on the main rail line north, and has plenty of bus connections into the surrounding countryside. It's famous for its sparkling wines, for its 20,000 rose bushes which burst into a riot of colour in summer, and for being the place where the urbane conman Felix Krull, hero of Thomas Mann's comic novel (see p.1046), spent his youth. Overlooking the Rhine is the ruined **Burg** of the Archbishop-Electors of Mainz, now a shady promenade with rose garden. There are plenty of cute half-timbered houses, plus a Gothic **Pfarrkirche** with a fifteenth-century fresco of *The Last Judgment* and a font made in the workshop of the Mainz sculptor Hans Backoffen.

However, Eltville is above all a place for **eating** and, especially, **drinking**. Many of its **Weingüte** can be visited and most serve food as well as wines. *Koegler*, at Kirchgasse 5, is of special note: it occupies the fifteenth-century Bechtermünzhof, the home and printing workshop of Gutenberg in his final years. Others to head for are *Diefenhardt'sches Weingut*, Hauptstr. 11, and *Krone*, Platz von Montrichard 3. There are also plenty of **wine bar-restaurants** where you can sample the local vintages – the best are *Weinhaus Weinpumpe*, Rheingauer Str. 3, and *Gelbes Haus*, Burgplatz 3. The town also has its own Hausbrauerei, *Kleines Eltviller Brauhaus*, Schwalbacher Str. 41–43, with an adjoining beer garden.

Eltville's **Bahnhof** is at the northern end of the town centre, while the **tourist office** (Mon–Fri 9.30am–noon & 2–5pm; ⓣ0 61 23/9 09 80, ⓦwww.eltville.de) is at Schmittstr. 2. Accommodation is in rather short supply,

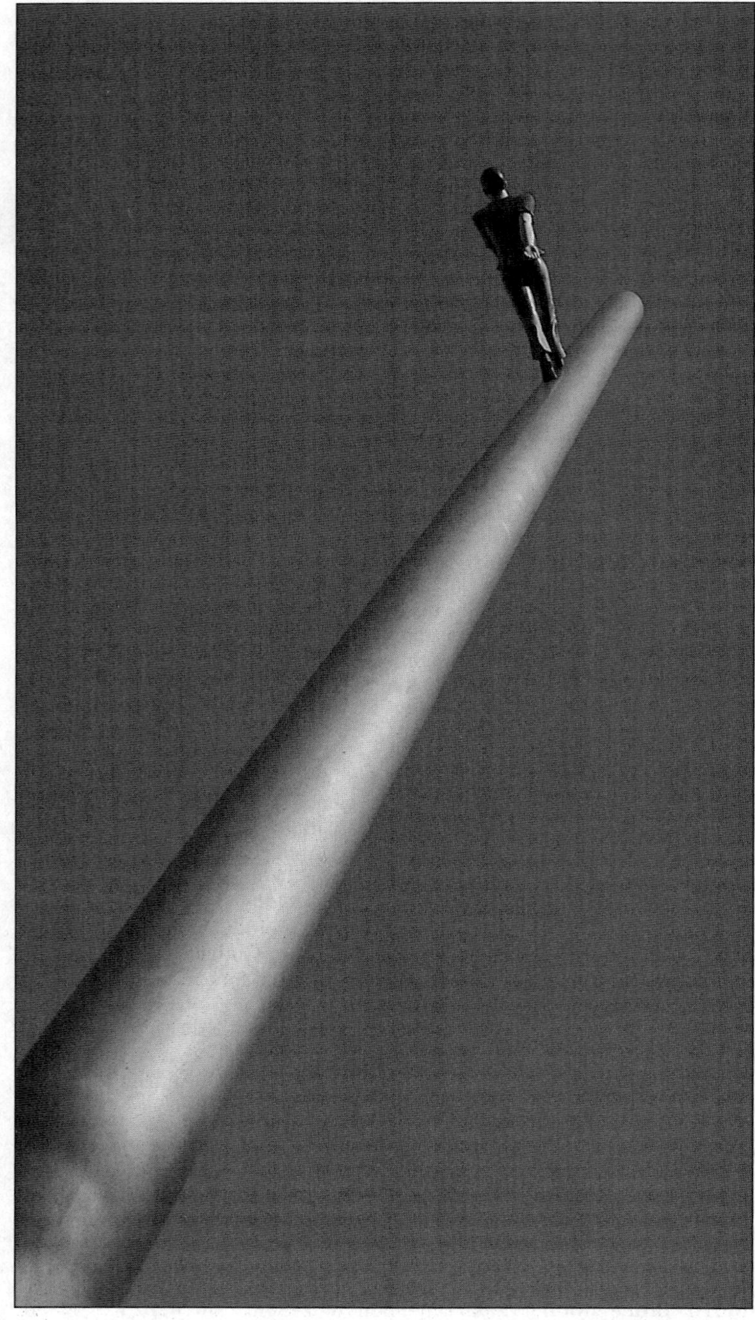

△ *Man Walking to the Sky* sculpture, Kassel

with only a few **private rooms** (❷–❸) and **hotels**; the latter include *Café Glockenhof*, Marktstr. 3 (ⓣ0 61 23/6 11 41, ⓦwww.hotelglockenhof.de; ❻); *Parkhotel Sonnenberg*, Friedrichstr. 65 (ⓣ0 61 23/6 05 50, ⓦwww.parkhotel-sonnenberg.de; ❻); and *Frankenbach-Mainzer Hof*, Wilhelmstr. 13 (ⓣ0 61 23/90 40, ⓦwww.hotel-frankenbach-mainzer-hof.de; ❻). The big local **festival** is the Biedermeier- und Sektfest over five days in early July.

Kiedrich

From Eltville, it's only a 3km bus journey inland to **KIEDRICH**, a wine-growing village of half-timbered houses. Dominating it from the north is **Burg Scharfenstein**, a ruin since the seventeenth century, which commands a fine view over the region. In the centre of town is a walled close containing two imposing late Gothic churches. The smaller of these, the fifteenth-century **St Michaelskapelle**, has a tall lantern turret crowned with an openwork spire, an indication of its function as a funerary chapel. There are actually two chapels, the lower serving as the ossuary. Its counterpart above, which is generally kept open, is light and airy, with a graceful altar recess (or *Chörlein*) and an elaborate candelabra bearing a double-sided sculpture of the Madonna and Child. The external pulpit was used to address the epilepsy sufferers who once flocked to Kiedrich on pilgrimage.

Although it preserves parts of its predecessor, the **Pfarrkirche St Valentin** (March–Oct Mon–Sat 10.30am–12.30pm, Sun 2.30–4pm; Nov–Feb Sat 10.30am–12.30pm, Sun 2.30–4pm) is likewise predominantly fifteenth-century in date. Entry is via the main portal, which has an exquisite "Soft Style" polychromed **tympanum** with a combined scene of the Annunciation and Coronation of the Virgin. The interior is an extraordinary evocation of the Middle Ages, preserving as it does virtually all the original furnishings including the rood screen, pulpit, tabernacle, altars, choir stalls and the pews with their remarkable carved and painted vine motifs and Gothic script. Even more precious are the *Kiedrich Madonna*, a gorgeous fourteenth-century statue showing strong French influence, and what is claimed as the oldest largely intact church **organ** in the world still in working order. The latter, which preserves about eighty percent of its original pipework from around 1500, can be heard every Sunday morning at 9.30am, along with the local **choir**, the Chorbuben, who since 1333 have practised a unique form of singing Gregorian chant in Germanic dialect. Immediately after the service, their illuminated missals can be viewed in the parish house opposite.

Kiedrich has one large **pension**, *Ankermühle*, Eltviller Str. 6 (ⓣ0 61 23/9 05 70; ❻), and a couple of **hotels**, both with **restaurants**: *Zum Scharfenstein*, Oberstr. 5 (ⓣ0 61 23/9 05 60; ❺); and *Nassauer Hof*, Bingerpfortenstr. 17 (ⓣ0 61 23/24 76; ❻). Also recommended, whether for a meal or a glass of wine, are *Schloss Groenesteyn*, Oberstr. 36 and *Winzerhaus*, Kammstr. 3.

Kloster Eberbach

Several buses per day continue 5km westwards from Kiedrich to **Kloster Eberbach** (daily: April–Oct 10am–6pm; Nov–March 11am–5pm; ⓦwww.kloster-eberbach.de; €3.50), one of the best-preserved medieval monasteries in Germany. It's situated at the lower end of the valley of the Kisselbach directly below the Taunus – exactly the sort of secluded setting favoured by the Cistercian order, who founded it in 1135. The Romanesque **Klosterkirche** is grandiosely austere, and devoid of decoration save for a few aristocratic tombs, the most notable being that in the chancel of a fourteenth-century Archbishop of Mainz, Gerlach von Nassau. Behind the church are the leafy cloisters, surrounded by the former living quarters of the monks. The upstairs **dormitory** is an immense vaulted room divided into two aisles, with a slight incline in its floor-level to make it seem even longer than it actually is. Built in the 1240s, it ranks among the supreme masterpieces of early Gothic architecture. Below it is the **Fraternei**, another impressive hall, which formerly contained the monastic workshops. In the **lay brothers' refectory** the huge wine presses once used by the monks are on display; some date back to the seventeenth century.

Wine production continued after the dissolution of the monastery in 1803, and the outbuildings are now used to press, ferment and store the produce of the Eberbacher Steinberg, the former monastic vineyard. Tasting sessions for groups are held in the **Hospital**, a magnificent Transitional-style building which is the only medieval monastic infirmary anywhere in Europe to have survived in its original form. Otherwise, you can buy the products at the shop, or drink them in the **restaurant** of the *Gästehaus Kloster Eberbach* (ⓣ0 67 23/9930, ⓦwww.klostereberbach.com; ❼), an upmarket **hotel** which has been established in the monastery.

Rüdesheim

RÜDESHEIM, which is 17km down the Rhine from Eltville, claims the dubious distinction of being the most visited town in the region, attracting over three million sightseers a year. It's a favourite stopping-off point for coach parties and Rhine cruises as it conforms pretty well to the general conception of what a typical Rhine town should look like – all crooked narrow streets, half-timbered houses and souvenir shops, sloping down gently from the wooded hills and terraced vineyards above.

The big local attraction is the **Drosselgasse**, a street comprised entirely of taverns offering "traditional" German entertainment, which is crowded all day long with tourists being ripped off. The twelfth-century **Brömserburg**, a squat and angular fortress a few minutes' walk to the west, now houses the **Weinmuseum** (March–Nov daily 9am–6pm; ⓦwww.rheingauer-weinmuseum.de; €3). It contains 21 old presses and a vast collection of wine vessels, including some fine examples of vases that were used to store and transport wine from Roman times through to the Middle Ages. There's the bonus of a marvellous view over the town and the Rhine from the top of the keep.

The twelfth-century defensive tower called the **Boosenburg** just to the north and the circular late Gothic **Adlerturm** at the eastern end of the waterfront are further reminders of an era when this stretch of the Rhine was a turbulent and contested area. Lining Oberstrasse to the east of the Boosenburg are a number of nobles' houses, notably the **Brömserhof**, which has a picturesque half-timbered tower. It now houses **Siegfried's Mechanisches Musikkabinett** (guided tours March to mid-Dec daily 10am–6pm; €5), one of the largest collections of mechanical musical instruments in the country. Just off the central Marktplatz is another fine mansion, the **Klunkardshof**, which has a particularly well-preserved half-timbered facade.

The much-restored **Pfarrkirche Eibingen** at the extreme northeastern edge of Rüdesheim was formerly part of a convent established by the great mystic, poet and composer **Hildegard of Bingen** (see pp.449–50). In the early years of the twentieth century, a new, considerably larger **Abtei St Hildegard** was built in neo-Romanesque style on the heights above. Wines from its vineyard, plus a couple of powerful spirits, can be purchased at its shop.

The main road just west of the abbey continues up to the **Niederwalddenkmal**, a bombastic statue of Germania built to mark the unification of Germany in 1871. This immense monument 225m above the town can be reached more directly by foot or by **gondola** (Ⓦwww.seilbahn-ruedesheim.de; €4 single, €6 return) over the vineyards which swarm up the slopes behind Rüdesheim. Lower down, by one of the footpaths to Assmannshausen, are the undeniably romantic ruins of the thirteenth-century **Burg Ehrenfels**. This one-time toll castle was used in conjunction with the Mäuseturm, a tower built on a mid-river island by the Archbishops of Mainz to control traffic on the Rhine.

Practicalities

Ferries dock right by the town centre, whereas the **Bahnhof** lies a short distance further west. The **tourist office** (May–Sept Mon–Fri 8.30am–6.30pm, Sat & Sun 11am–5pm; rest of year Mon–Fri only; Ⓣ0 67 22/1 94 33, Ⓦwww.ruedesheim.de) is east of the town centre at Geisenheimer Str. 22.

There are plenty of **private rooms** (❷–❹) and **hotels**, but they tend to be booked up during the high summer. A couple of inexpensive possibilities are *Weinstube zur Lindenau*, Löhrstr. 10 (Ⓣ0 67 22/33 27; ❹) and *Gasthof Zur Guten Quelle*, Katharinenstr. 3 (Ⓣ0 67 22/27 57, Ⓦwww.saengerlust-ruedesheim.de; ❹–❻). More luxurious options include *Felsenkeller*, Oberstr. 39–41 (Ⓣ0 67 22/9 42 50, Ⓦwww.ruedesheim-rhein.com; ❻); *Zum Bären*, Schmidtstr. 31 (Ⓣ0 67 22/10 91, Ⓦwww.zumbaeren.de; ❻); *Central*, Kirchstr. 6 (Ⓣ0 67 22/91 20, Ⓦwww.centralhotel.net; ❻–❽); and *Rüdesheimer Schloss*, Steingasse 10 (Ⓣ0 67 22/9 05 00, Ⓦwww.ruedesheimer-schloss.com; ❻–❽). The local **youth hostel** is set amidst the vines, a long walk from the town, at Am Kreuzberg (Ⓣ0 67 22/27 11; €15/17). There are two **campsites** in Rüdesheim: *Campingplatz am Rhein* (Ⓣ0 67 22/25 28 or 25 82, Ⓦwww.campingplatz-ruedesheim.de) on Kastanienallee and *Ponyland* (Ⓣ0 67 22/25 18) near the Niederwalddenkmal.

All the hotels listed above have **restaurants**. Many of the **Weingüte** have a Vinothek where their vintages can be sampled: they include *Jakob Christ*, Grabenstr. 17; *Georg Breuer*, Grabenstr. 8; *Fendel*, Marienthalerstr. 46; and *Dr Heinrich Nägler*, Friedrichstr. 22. At the beginning of July there's a firework display and in mid-August Rüdesheim has its *Weinfest*. During the latter it seems like all of those three million visitors have hit town at once and accommodation is impossible to find unless booked a very long time in advance.

Assmannshausen

Just out of Rüdesheim proper, the Rhine suddenly bends through ninety degrees to flow more or less south–north, and there follows a treacherous stretch of rapids called the **Binger Loch**. After 5km (one stop on the train or an enticing hour-long walk along the marked footpath) you arrive at **ASSMANNSHAUSEN**, a smaller and less touristy version of Rüdesheim, of which it now forms a part. In the terraced vineyards round about some of Germany's best red wines are produced from Spätburgunder grapes. A chairlift (€4 single, €6 return) runs up to **Jagdschloss Niederwald**, an eighteenth-century hunting lodge turned hotel (Ⓣ0 67 22/10 04, Ⓦwww.niederwald.de; ❽) near the Niederwalddenkmal, and commanding similarly good views of the Rhine.

Milberg, Am Rathaus 2 (Ⓣ0 67 22/29 45; ❹) is a centrally located **pension**. The sixteenth-century *Krone*, Rheinuferstr. 10 (Ⓣ0 67 22/40 30,

ⓦwww.hotel-krone.com; ❽–❾), ranks among the most exclusive **hotels** in the whole of the Rhineland, with a **restaurant** renowned for its fish and game specialities – and a remarkable wine list.

Central and northern Hesse

The attractions of central and northern Hesse are diverse. To the west is the valley of the Lahn, a Rhine tributary, on whose banks stand **Marburg**, home of one of Germany's most famous universities, **Wetzlar**, with its distinguished legal and literary traditions, the Residenzstadt of **Weilburg** and the small cathedral city of **Limburg**. Further south is the wooded Taunus, with the famous spa of **Bad Homburg**. Eastwards is the **Spessart**, another forested highland range, with the well-preserved medieval town of **Gelnhausen**, and the childhood home of the Brothers Grimm, **Steinau an der Strasse**. Between the volcanic Vogelsberg and the Rhön lies **Fulda**, one of Germany's leading episcopal centres. The far north of Hesse is dominated by **Kassel**, which may have one of the dullest city centres in Germany, but which boasts wonderful parks and fabulous art treasures. Nearby are the half-timbered town of **Fritzlar** and the elegant spa of **Bad Wildungen**.

Bad Homburg vor der Höhe

S-Bahn #5 links Frankfurt with **BAD HOMBURG**, which is situated in the southern foothills of the Taunus, a hilly forest area bordered on three sides by the rivers Rhine, Main and Lahn. Following nearly two centuries as capital of the tiny state of Hesse-Homburg, it was annexed by Prussia in 1866 and quickly established itself as the favourite summer retreat of the Kaisers. It's very much a place of two faces: the historic centre, with its market-town air, is built on a steeply pitched hill, while the somnolent spa quarter – which ranks second only to Baden-Baden's as the classiest in Germany – is laid out on the low ground to the north.

The Town

At the very top of the town, set in an extensive landscaped park, is the **Schloss** (guided tours Tues–Sun: March–Oct 9am–5pm; Nov–Feb 10am–4pm; ⓦwww.schloesser-hessen.de; €3.50). The predominantly Baroque exterior of the palace is largely due to Friedrich II: his **bust**, a masterly portrait by the Berlin sculptor Andreas Schlüter, stands in the entrance hall, while his famous wooden leg, known as the "Silver Leg" because of its silver joints, is one of the highlights of the tour. For the most part the interiors are nineteenth-century and reflect the taste of the Empress Augusta: among the adornments she ordered is one of the world's first telephone kiosks.

A second guided tour, run on Sundays only (on the hour 11am–3pm; €3.50) goes round the **Englischer Flügel** (or **Elisabethenflügel**), which is named in honour of Princess Elizabeth, daughter of King George III of Great Britain, who married Landgrave Friedrich VI in 1818. She was a talented amateur artist, and many of her own creations, including some striking works in lacquer, are displayed throughout her apartments. This tour also takes in the galleried **Schlosskirche**, which contains the burial vault of the House of Hesse-Homburg. The tall **Weisser Turm** (White Tower; March–Oct Mon 9am–3.30pm, Tues–Sun 9am–4pm; Nov–Feb daily 9am–3pm; €0.50) in the Schloss courtyard is the only reminder of the previous medieval castle. It can be ascended for an extensive panorama over the Taunus.

Opposite the Schloss, at the corner of Löwenstrasse and Dorotheenstrasse, is the **Sinclair-Haus** (Tues–Fri 3–7pm, Sat & Sun 10am–5pm; free), a Baroque mansion named after a prominent Homburg courtier. It's used for temporary art exhibitions, a mixture of ephemera and international blockbusters. Across the road is the **Erlöserkirche** (Church of the Redeemer), an extravagant Historicist building funded by Kaiser Wilhelm II.

The **Kurpark** is a huge and beautiful landscaped park designed by Peter Joseph Lenné. Along its main axis of Brunnenallee are no fewer than seven mineral springs, the most prestigious being the **Elisabethenquelle**, over which stands a handsome Neoclassical pavilion. At the heart of the park is the stolidly Wilhelmine building of the **Kaiser-Wilhelm-Bad**, which is still the main centre for therapeutic cures. Alongside, the **Spielbank** (daily 2.30pm–3am; day ticket €2.50) is the oldest casino in the world, founded in 1841 by the Frenchman François Blanc, who decamped to Monte Carlo when gambling was outlawed throughout Germany in 1872. It's essential to be respectably dressed in order to gain admission; minimum stakes are €2 for roulette, and €10 for poker and blackjack.

Further east are the two main bathing complexes. The **Taunus-Therme** (Mon, Tues, Thurs & Sun 9am–11pm, Wed, Fri & Sat 9am–midnight; €12.50 for 2hr, €24 for the whole day, rising to €14.50 and €26 at weekends) occupies a Japanese-style building with garden, and includes a Roman-Irish steam bath and a Finnish sauna among its facilities. Its more conventional neighbour, the **Seedammbad** (previously Mon 2–9pm, Tues–Fri 7am–9pm, Sat & Sun 8.30am–8pm; €3 for a 2hr swim, €7.50 for a sauna, but currently closed for repairs) likewise has indoor and outdoor sections. Also worth seeking out are a couple of exotic little turn-of-the century buildings: the **Russische Kirche** at the southern end of the park and the **Siamesischer Tempel** at the north-western corner, which was donated to the spa by one well-satisfied partaker of the waters, the King of Siam.

Practicalities

Bad Homburg's **Bahnhof** is on the south side of town. The **tourist office** (Mon–Fri 8.30am–7pm, Sat 9am–1pm; ⓣ0 61 72/17 81 10, ⓦwww.bad-homburg.de) is in the Kurhaus building in the heart of the town centre at Louisenstr. 58.

There's a huge range of accommodation to suit all pockets, including a **youth hostel** opposite the Schlosspark at Mühlweg 17 (ⓣ0 61 72/2 39 50; €21.10/23.80) and plenty of **private rooms** (❷–❹). Several of the **hotels** are surprisingly reasonable, particularly *Johannisberg*, Thomasstr. 5 (ⓣ0 61 72/2 13 15; ❸); and *Haus Fischer am Park*, Landgrafenstr. 12 (ⓣ0 61 72/86 79 27; ❹). *Villa Kisseleff*, Kisseleffstr. 19 (ⓣ0 61 72/90 22 90; ❻–❽) is a good medium-range choice, while a couple of the less outrageously priced upmarket options are *Haus Dalheim*, Elisabethenstr. 42 (ⓣ0 61 72/67 73 50; ❻–❽) and the Jugendstil *Villa* *am Kurpark*, Kaiser-Friedrich-Promenade 57 (ⓣ0 61 72/1 80 00; ❼–❾). At the very top of the range is *Steigenberger Bad Homburg*, Kaiser-Friedrich-Promenade 69–75 (ⓣ0 61 72/18 10, ⓦwww.bad-homburg.steigenberger.com; ❽–❾), an Art Deco-style glass palace offering every conceivable luxury.

There's an equally wide variety of places to **eat** and **drink**, quite apart from the hotel restaurants. These include a vegetarian place, *Kartoffelküche*, Audenstr. 4 and a Hausbrauerei, *Graf Zeppelin*, Zeppelinstr. 11. *Schreinerei Pfeiffer*, Audenstr. 6, has Hessian specialities, while *Isoletta*, Louisenstr. 80, is a good and not too expensive Italian. *Sänger's*, Kaiser-Friedrich-Promenade 85, is a gourmet restaurant with a national reputation.

Antidotes to the peace and quiet of the spa quarter are provided by Germany's oldest **dance-bar**, the *Tennis Bar* (Tues–Thurs 9pm–4am, Fri & Sat 9pm–5.45am, Sun 3pm–4am) at Kisseleffstr. 20, and by *Gambrinus* in the Fürstenbahnhof, the former royal terminal beside the Bahnhof, which has a **disco** or live music each evening. The Kulturzentrum Englische Kirche in the deconsecrated Anglican Christ Church on Ferdinandplatz (ⓣ0 61 72/10 03 10) presents a varied programme of **cabaret**, **jazz** and **classical** music. Bad Homburg's churches host an international **organ** festival, Fugato, in the second half of September.

The Spessart

The **Spessart**, which is divided between Hesse and Bavaria, forms Germany's largest continuous upland forest area. Most of it has been dedicated a *Naturpark*, though strung along the valley of the River Kinzig, which separates it from the Vogelsberg, are a number of towns, the most notable being **Gelnhausen**, a long-time Free Imperial City, and **Steinau**, of Brothers Grimm fame.

Gelnhausen

GELNHAUSEN lies 40km east of Frankfurt on the fast road and rail routes to Fulda, and is also the starting point for a branch rail line along the western fringe of the Vogelsberg. One of the most atmospheric and picturesque small towns in Germany, it was a city-state for most of its history and exudes a grandeur which belies the fact that its population has never numbered more than a few thousand. It likes to call itself Barbarossastadt, a reference to its foundation in the twelfth century by **Frederick Barbarossa**, the emperor who was primarily responsible for moulding the feudal structure of the Holy Roman Empire. However, it's equally proud of being the birthplace of the seventeenth-century writer **Johann Jacob Christoffel von Grimmelshausen**, whose semi-autobiographical *Simplicissimus* is the first great German novel and one of the leading tragi-comedies of European literature.

The ruins of Barbarossa's palace, the **Kaiserpfalz** (Tues–Sun 10am–4/5pm; ⓦwww.schloesser-hessen.de; €1.80), stand in what was formerly an island in the Kinzig, midway between the Bahnhof and the Altstadt, which clings to the steep hillside above. Substantial sections of the red sandstone masonry survive, including parts of the gateway, the tower and the chapel, though the most notable feature is a wall of the royal residence itself, featuring arcades adorned with beautifully carved Romanesque capitals. Above the palace portal is an enigmatic grotesque sculpture of a man, traditionally presumed to depict the red-bearded emperor himself.

The upper town is centred on two market squares, Untermarkt and Obermarkt, but the main feature of the skyline is the **Marienkirche** between them. Although built at various stages, it's a magnificent structure which graphically illustrates the transition from Romanesque to Gothic. Especially worthy of note are the four **towers**, which form an irresistibly photogenic ensemble, and the elaborately decorated interior of the chancel. This features a **rood screen** bearing highly expressive sculptures illustrating the Last Judgment, a gleaming set of stained-glass windows, and a carved and painted high altar. In the vestry are two precious fifteenth-century tapestries, which the caretaker will show for a small donation. Immediately below the church, and nowadays serving as its hall, is the **Romanisches Haus**, which was built for the officials of Barbarossa's court.

Half-timbered buildings are otherwise predominant in the upper town, with the **Rathaus** on Obermarkt ranking as the most imposing. On Brentanostrasse, just west of Untermarkt, the **Synagoge**, now a cultural centre, retains some of its original Baroque decoration and furnishings, notably the Torah shrine. Much of the **Stadtbefestigung** enclosing the town also survives, including the picturesque **Hexenturm** on the southeast side, where supposed witches were imprisoned. It's well worth continuing uphill from here to the **Halbmondturm**, which commands a breathtaking view over the town and the valley.

Practicalities

Gelnhausen's **tourist office** (Mon–Fri 8am–noon & 2–4.30pm, Sat 9am–noon & 2–4.30pm, Sun 2–4.30pm; ⓣ0 60 51/83 03 00, ⓦwww.gelnhausen.de) is at Obermarkt 24. Within the historic centre are five **hotels**: *Schelm von Bergen*, Obermarkt 22 (ⓣ0 60 51/27 55, ⓦwww.schelm-von-bergen.de; ❸); *Zur Burgschänke*, Burgstr. 19 (ⓣ0 60 51/29 15; ❺); *Grimmelshausen*, Schmidtgasse 12 (ⓣ0 60 51/9 24 20; ❺); *Burg-Mühle*, Burgstr. 2 (ⓣ0 60 51/8 20 50; ❺); and *Stadt-Schänke*, Fürstenhofstr. 1 (ⓣ0 60 51/1 60 51; ❻). Each of the hotels, except *Grimmelshausen*, has a **restaurant**; another good choice for a meal is the historic tavern *Zum Löwen*, Langgasse 28, which also has the benefit of a beer garden.

Steinau an der Strasse

The little half-timbered town of **STEINAU**, some 25km northeast of Gelnhausen on the main transport routes to Fulda, was the childhood home of the Brothers Grimm (see box on p.416), a connection resulting in a considerable volume of tourism these days. Focal point of the town is a large Renaissance **Schloss** (Tues–Thurs, Sat & Sun 10am–4/5pm; ⓦwww.schloesser-hessen.de; €3.50), which contains period furnishings plus extensive documentation on the work of the brothers. There's more on the Grimms in the nearby **Amtshaus** (daily mid-March to mid-Dec 2–5pm; €1.50) at Brüder-Grimm-Str. 80, where they lived during the period of their father's service as the local magistrate. **Puppet performances** of some of their most famous stories are regularly performed at the Marionettentheater in the Schloss' former stables at Am Kumpen 4 (ⓣ0 66 63/2 45).

Steinau's **Bahnhof** is at the northwestern fringe of town, a 15-minute walk from the centre. The **tourist office** is in the Rathaus, Brüder-Grimm-Str. 47 (Mon–Thurs 8.30am–noon & 1.30–4pm, Fri 8.30am–noon; ⓣ0 66 63/9 63 10, ⓦwww.steinau.de). There are several **hotels**, including *Burgmannenhaus*, Brüder-Grimm-Str. 49 (ⓣ0 66 63/9 64 00; ❸–❺); *Landgasthof Grüner Baum*, Leipziger Str. 45 (ⓣ0 66 63/97 40; ❹); and *Gasthaus Weisses Ross*, Brüder-Grimm-Str. 48 (ⓣ0 66 63/58 04; ❹).

Fulda

Lying in a narrow valley between the Vogelsberg and the Rhön, **FULDA** was best known throughout the Cold War as the weak point in NATO's front line (the so-called "Fulda Gap") through which the massed tanks of the Warsaw Pact were supposedly most likely to pour into Western Europe. With that dubious threat now gone, the city can concentrate once more on its role as a major episcopal centre, the venue for the annual meetings of both the Catholic Bishops' Conference and the German Protestant Convention. Church affairs have dominated Fulda's history. Its roots go back to the eighth century when a small town grew up around the abbey founded by Saint Boniface, a monk sent from England to convert the Germans. After his martyrdom in 754, Fulda became a pilgrimage site, and over the years its abbey grew into one of the most important monasteries in Germany. It was here that a couple of monks transcribed the *Lay of Hildebrand*, one of the first recorded pieces of German literature. For centuries, the abbots doubled as secular princes, and on their promotion to the rank of bishops they transformed their seat into a Baroque vision of golden towers and crosses.

Arrival, information and accommodation

Fulda's **Hauptbahnhof** is at the northeastern end of the town centre. The **tourist office** (Mon–Fri 8.30am–6pm, Sat 9.30am–4pm, Sun 10am–2pm; ⓣ06 61/1 02 18 13, ⓦwww.tourismus-fulda.de) is at Bonifatiusplatz 1. The main venue for **cultural** events is the Schlosstheater, Schlossstr. 5 (ⓣ06 61/1 02 14 83).

Fulda is quite well off for **hotels** in all price categories. There's a **youth hostel** at the southwestern edge of town at Schirrmannstr. 31 (ⓣ06 61/7 33 89; €16/18.70); the easiest way there is by bus #12 to Stadion.

Hotels and pensions

Brauhaus Wiesenmühle Wiesenmühlenstr. 13 ⓣ06 61/92 86 80, ⓦwww.wiesenmuehle.de. Occupying a converted fourteenth-century mill, this place has an upmarket restaurant plus a hugely popular bar and beer garden serving a range of inexpensive food. The Hausbrauerei brews a wide variety of seasonally appropriate beers. ❻

Goldener Karpfen Simpliziusbrunnen 1 ⓣ06 61/8 68 00, ⓦwww.hotel-goldener-karpfen.com. Now a member of the Romantik group, and equipped with plenty of mod cons such as a sauna and solarium, this has long been Fulda's top hotel: Goethe was once a patron, writing much of the *Ost-West Divan* here. It has a distinguished wine bar-restaurant. ❽–❾

Hodes Peterstor 14 ⓣ06 61/7 28 62, ⓕ24 11 79. Bargain-price pension at the edge of the Altstadt. ❸

Kurfürst Schlossstr. 2 ⓣ06 61/8 33 90, ⓦwww.kurfuerst-fulda.de. Hotel and restaurant occupying an eighteenth-century palace opposite the Stadtschloss. ❽

Wenzel Heinrichstr. 38–40 ⓣ06 61/7 53 35, ⓕ7 53 36. Homely pension, conveniently close to the Hauptbahnhof. ❸

Zum Bratwurstglöckle Am Stockhaus 10–12 ⓣ06 61/7 28 75, ⓕ24 09 13. Located in the heart of the Altstadt, this is the epitome of a traditional Gasthof. Since the 1930s, its butcher's shop has been well-known locally for its horsemeat, which features extensively (but not exclusively) on the restaurant menu. ❸

Zum Kronhof Am Kronhof 2 ⓣ & ⓕ06 61/7 41 47. Gasthof just to the rear of the Dom, offering some of the cheapest rooms in town. ❸

Zum Ritter Kanalstr. 18–20 ⓣ06 61/25 08 00, ⓦwww.hotel-ritter.de. Grand nineteenth-century hotel modernized a few years back to a very high standard. Its restaurant is quite reasonably priced. ❻–❽

The City

Fulda's imposing **Dom**, on the western edge of the town centre, is a classic early Baroque structure by Johann Dientzenhofer, the most accomplished member of a dynasty of architects, and is totally unlike any other German cathedral. The glory of the spacious and stuccoed interior is the high altar, depicting the Assumption of the Madonna in full-blown gilded splendour and flanked by six marble columns. Behind is a small and austere chapel where the monks used to assemble for prayer. St Boniface's tomb is in the crypt beneath the high altar – it's incorporated into a sepulchral black marble altar with carved reliefs depicting the saint's martyrdom and his resurrection on Judgment Day.

The **Dommuseum** (April–Oct Tues–Sat 10am–5.30pm, Sun 12.30–5.30pm; Nov, Dec, Feb & March Tues–Sat 10am–12.30pm & 1.30–4pm, Sun 12.30–4pm; €2.50) occupies the Dechanei (deanery) adjoining the northern transept. It contains Boniface's relics, which include his sword, his head and the book with which he vainly tried to fend off his murderers. There's also an impressive collection of ecclesiastical vestments, while the most important painting is Cranach's *Christ and the Woman Taken in Adultery*.

Next to the Dom is the Romanesque **Michaelskirche** (daily: April–Oct 10am–6pm; Nov, Dec, Feb & March 2–4pm), built in the shape of a Greek cross as a copy of the Church of the Holy Sepulchre in Jerusalem. It's among the very few significant buildings to have survived the wholesale conversion of Fulda to the Baroque. In comparison to the mighty Dom it's quite inconspicuous, but in some ways is more impressive than its larger neighbour, incorporating as it does the rotunda of an earlier church. Although this has been much altered, two of its eight columns date back to 822. Inside, look out for the fourteenth-century **stone tablet** in the Baroque chapel built onto the northern transept: it illustrates the Passion in an unusual graphic code for the benefit of the illiterate of the time.

Across from the Dom stands the former episcopal palace, the cream-coloured **Stadtschloss** (Mon–Thurs, Sat & Sun 10am–6pm, Fri 2–6pm; €2). Again the work of Johann Dientzenhofer, it's a huge building with several wings which has housed the municipal offices ever since it was acquired by the city last century. The most imposing chambers are the small **Spiegelsaal** (Mirror Room) and the main **Daalbergsaal**, which is painted with a quirky representation of the Four Seasons, with winter in the guise of a harlequin. There are also extensive displays of locally produced porcelain. The **tower** (same times; €0.25) can be ascended (at 10.30am & 2pm, 2pm only on Fri; €0.25) for a view over the city.

It's well worth taking a stroll in the **Schlossgarten**, a geometrical ornamental park which leads to the **Orangerie**, the best-looking of Fulda's secular Baroque buildings, nowadays a café. Inside, look out for the *Sauerkrautbild*, a ceiling painting showing Greek deities eating the favourite German meal of sausages with pickled cabbage. The **Floravase** in front of the Orangerie, named after the floral goddess whose statue crowns it, is a masterpiece of the art of garden sculpture. Opposite the Schlossgarten are two more Baroque showpieces, the **Paulustor**, an ornamental gateway, and the **Hauptwache**, the former guard house.

In the heart of the pedestrianized shopping district, reached from the Hauptwache via Friedrichstrasse, is the **Stadtpfarrkirche**, which pretty much conforms to Fulda house style, and the **Altes Rathaus**, which breaks the mould by having a half-timbered facade. Just to the south is the Jesuit Alte Stadtschule, now housing the **Vonderau-Museum** (Tues–Sun 10am–6pm; €2), a collection covering archeology, natural history, and the arts. Among the exhibits is the *Fuldamag*, a locally produced three-wheeled car which was once a familiar sight on the streets of Britain as well as Germany. A short distance to the west is the **Abtei St Maria**, a seventeenth-century convent built in an archaic Gothic style. It's still active, and indeed is a flourishing centre of contemporary religious art. Finally, on Heinrich-von-Bibra-Platz, the eastern continuation of Schloss-Strasse, the **Hessische Landesbibliothek** (Mon & Fri 10am–noon, Tues–Thurs

10am–noon & 2–4pm; free) has a permanent exhibition featuring a Gutenberg Bible and some beautiful illuminated manuscripts.

Outside the centre

The **Petersberg**, a four-hundred-metre-high hill about 4km to the east of the centre and reached by bus #3, commands wonderful views of Fulda itself and across to the Vogelsberg and Rhön. The hill is crowned by the **Peterskirche** (previously April–Dec Tues–Sun 10–11.30am & 2.30–4pm; Feb & March Tues–Sun 2.30–4pm, but closed in 2003 for restoration), the most significant of the four monastic churches grouped round the town in the symbolic shape of a cross. Its **crypt**, the burial place of Saint Lioba, a kinswoman of Saint Boniface, survives from the first building on the spot, and has precious if rather ghostly ninth-century frescoes. The main part of the church was rebuilt in the fifteenth century but preserves six outstanding **Romanesque reliefs** on and around its triumphal arch. On the western bank of the River Fulda, much closer to town, is the **Andreaskirche**, a former monastic church which has some more or less intact tenth- or eleventh-century frescoes in the crypt; these are currently the subject of a painstaking restoration programme.

Further delights await at **Schloss Fasanerie** (guided tours April–Oct Tues–Sun 10am–5pm; ⓦwww.schloss-fasanerie.de; €5), about 6km southwest of the centre, and some fifteen minutes' walk beyond the Engelhelms terminus of bus #3. It was built at enormous expense in the eighteenth century as a hunting lodge and summer residence for the local Prince-bishops. However, its original Baroque character was modified after it came into the possession of the Electors of Hesse-Kassel, with several of the main reception rooms refurbished to suit their penchant for the Neoclassical style. A stud farm occupies the subsidiary buildings, while the landscaped **Schlosspark** features Chinese and Japanese pavilions.

Eating and drinking

Some of the best places to eat and drink are in the hotels (see p.408), but there's a wide variety of other options.

Café Thiele Mittelstr. 2. Perhaps the pick of several good traditional cafés in the town centre.
Da Mario Bonifatiusplatz 2. Moderately priced Italian restaurant in the Hauptwache, serving tasty pizzas made in a wood-fired oven.
Dachsbau Pfandhausstr. 7–9. Upwardly mobile types gravitate here to sample what's arguably the most creative cooking in Fulda. Closed Mon.
Felsenkeller Leipziger Str. 12. Gaststätte of the Hochstift brewery, which is located alongside. It makes a fine dark beer, *Schwarzer Hahn*, as well as a *Pils*.
Löhertor Gerberstr. 9. A large complex which has several bars and restaurants plus a disco and cinema.
Schoppenkeller Paulustor 6. Weinkeller with a very mixed clientele and quiet atmosphere. Closed Mon.
Waidesgrund Esperantostr. 10. Vegetarian and wholefood restaurant, situated just to the rear of the Hauptbahnhof. Closed Mon.
Wirtshaus Zum Schwarzen Hahn Friedrichstr. 18. Decked out with nostalgic bric a brac, this serves a range of regional specialities from all over Germany.

Kassel

Although nowadays chiefly famous for the *documenta*, the huge modern art exhibition which takes place there once every five years (next held June 16–Sept 29 2007), **KASSEL** is basically an industrial city. Its big armaments industry ensured four-fifths destruction of its centre during the war, and

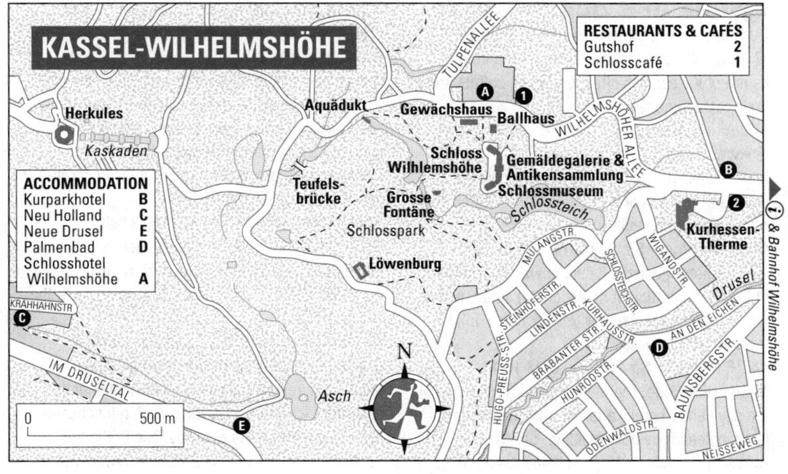

consequently most of the buildings here are functional products of the 1950s. Despite the unenticing appearance of most of the centre, the city is one of the greenest in Germany, primarily due to the enormous **Wilhelmshöhe** park. It also preserves plenty of reminders of its period of glory, which began in the late seventeenth century with the arrival of Huguenots expelled from France, continued throughout the following century with the acquisition of all the trappings of a capital city, and culminated in the years 1806–13, when it was the royal seat of the Kingdom of Westphalia.

Arrival, information and accommodation

Kassel has two main train stations. Express services, including ICE trains, tend to use the gleamingly modern **Bahnhof Wilhelmshöhe**, which is about 1km east of the Wilhelmshöhe park. The increasingly overshadowed **Hauptbahnhof**, 2.5km away at the northern edge of the city centre, is a dead end. To reverse its descent into seediness, it has been revamped as the Kulturbahnhof (see p.417). There are **tourist offices** in the Rathaus, Obere Königstr. 8 (Mon–Fri 9am–6pm, Sat 9am–2pm; ⓣ05 61/7 07 71 64, ⓦwww.kassel.de) and in Bahnhof Wilhelmshöhe (Mon–Fri 9am–1pm & 2–6pm, Sat 9am–1pm; ⓣ05 61/3 40 54).

Given the spread-out nature of the city, it's worth investing in the €5 **public transport** ticket, which covers any 24-hour period, or the entire weekend. An alternative to this is the **KasselCard**, which additionally gives reduced entry to the museums and other attractions; for one person, it costs €7 for one day, €10 for three days, or €15 and €19 for the same periods for up to four people travelling together.

It's probably best to base yourself in Wilhelmshöhe, which has a wide variety of **hotels** – the budget end of the market is particularly well served here. Those in the city centre itself are mostly geared towards expense-account travellers. Kassel's **youth hostel** is a fifteen-minute walk west of the Hauptbahnhof at Schenkendorfstr. 18 (ⓣ05 61/77 64 55; €18/20.70, and there are **camping** facilities (March–Oct only) at *Fulda-Camp*, on the banks of the Fulda just south of Karlsaue at Giesenallee 7 (ⓣ05 61/ 2 24 33, ⓦwww.fulda-camp.de).

Hotels and guesthouses

Deutscher Hof Lutherstr. 3–5 ⓣ05 61/9 18 00, ⓦwww.deutscher-hof.de. Located right in the centre of Kassel, this offers breakfast buffets and a good restaurant. ❺

Elfbuchen Habichtswald ⓣ05 61/96 97 60, ⓦwww.waldhotel-elfbuchen-kassel.de. Country house hotel with café-restaurant in a peaceful woodland setting north of the Herkules. It has been run by the same family since 1879. ❼

Gude Frankfurter Str. 299 ⓣ05 61/4 80 50, ⓦwww.hotel-gude.de. By some way the classiest of the concentration of hotels on the street, with a highly regarded restaurant, *Pfeffermühle*. Take tram #5, #6 or #9. ❼

Kö 78 Kölnische Str. 78 ⓣ05 61/7 16 14, ⓦwww.koe78.de. The most obviously attractive of the city centre hotels, a family-run concern in a late nineteenth-century building. ❺–❼

Kurfürst Wilhelm I Wilhelmshöher Allee 257, Wilhelmshöhe ⓣ05 61/3 18 70, ⓦwww.kurfuerst.bestwestern.de. This very traditional hotel is right outside Bahnhof Wilhelmshöhe. Its restaurant, *Tavolo*, serves high-class Italian cuisine. ❼

Kurparkhotel Wilhelmshöher Allee 336, Wilhelmshöhe ⓣ05 61/3 18 90, ⓦwww.kurpark-hotel-kassel.de. One of the city's best hotels, with a fine restaurant and a health centre complete with swimming pool, sauna and solarium. It's on the route of tram #1. ❼

Neu Holland Hüttenbergstr. 6, Wilhelmshöhe ⓣ05 61/3 32 29, ⓕ31 58 29. Small guesthouse and beer garden (closed Tues) at the extreme western edge of Kassel, a short distance south of the Herkules; take bus #43 from the Druseltal terminus of tram #3. ❺

Neue Drusel Im Druseltal 42, Wilhelmshöhe ⓣ05 61/3 08 00, ⓦwww.hotel-neuedrusel.de. Medium-range hotel with café-restaurant at the edge of the Habichtswald, not far from a path leading up to the Herkules. ❺

Palmenbad Kurhausstr. 27, Wilhelmshöhe ⓣ & ⓕ05 61/3 26 91. A recommendable budget hotel in the residential part of Wilhelmshöhe; its restaurant (closed Sun evening & Mon lunchtime) has a good line in game dishes. The Brabanter Strasse stop of tram #3 is a stone's throw away. ❸

Schlosshotel Wilhelmshöhe Schlosspark 8, Wilhelmshöhe ⓣ05 61/3 08 80, ⓦwww.schlosshotel.com. Luxurious modern hotel immediately north of the Schloss. The facilities include a high-class restaurant, a casino, a swimming pool, sauna and solarium. ❼–❾

Wilhelmshöhe

It was Landgrave Carl, the same ruler who invited the Huguenots to settle in Kassel, who began the laying-out of the **Wilhelmshöhe**, a huge upland forest park which is the largest urban example of its kind in Europe. Situated at the western edge of the city, and reached by tram #1, it remains its most enduring permanent attraction. Although originally intended as a formal garden in the Italian Baroque manner, it was modified by Carl's successors in line with the eighteenth-century preference for the English approach to landscaping, with a predominantly "natural" appearance mingled with an assortment of hidden follies.

Bus #23 runs through the heart of the park, travelling between the Wilhelmshöhe terminus of tram #1 and the Brabanter Strasse stop of tram #3. From the Druseltal terminus of the last-named, bus #43 travels uphill to the Herkules via the main road on the park's western fringe.

The Schloss and the Gemäldegalerie Alte Meister

Curiously enough, the gargantuan **Schloss Wilhelmshöhe** was something of an afterthought, only begun in the 1780s. One of the finest Neoclassical buildings in Germany, it was designed and partly built by Simon-Louis du Ry, the last and most distinguished of a dynasty of local architects of Huguenot extraction. Its **Weissensteinflügel** is now designated the **Schlossmuseum** (guided tours Tues–Sun 10am–4/5pm; ⓦwww.schloesser-hessen.de; €3.50), and is decked out with opulent furniture, glassware, porcelain and other *objets d'art*, many from the time when Napoleon's brother Jérôme held court here as king of the puppet state of Westphalia.

On the ground floor of the central block of the Schloss is the **Antikensammlung** (Tues–Sun 10am–5pm; Ⓦwww.museum-kassel.de; €3.50 combined day ticket for all museums with this web address, free Fri), a collection of Egyptian, Greek, Etruscan and Roman antiquities. Its prize possession is the **Kassel Apollo**, a Roman copy of a lost bronze by the great Greek sculptor Phidias. In the basement, a fascinating display on "modern" reinterpretations of the classical tradition includes a series of cork models of the monuments of ancient Rome made in the eighteenth century by Antonio Chichi.

The rest of the building is occupied by the **Gemäldegalerie Alte Meister** (Old Masters Picture Gallery; Ⓦwww.museum-kassel.de; same times and ticket as the Antikensammlung), which originated in the collection of Landgrave Carl's successor Wilhelm VIII, whose spell as Governor of Breda and Maastricht fuelled a passion for the painting of the Dutch Golden Age. He accumulated what remains one of the world's finest collections of this period, supplemented by seventeenth-century paintings from elsewhere in Europe.

Most of the prize works are displayed on the third floor. There are a dozen masterpieces by **Rembrandt**, most notably the profoundly touching *Jacob Blessing his Grandchildren*. This rarely depicted subject shows the patriarch choosing to bless Joseph's second son Ephraim first, on the grounds he was destined for greater things – namely, to be the ancestor of the Gentiles. Rembrandt accordingly showed Ephraim as a fair-haired Aryan-type, in contrast to the dark features of the first-born, Manasseh. From roughly the same period comes one of his greatest portraits, *Nicolaes Bruyningh*, vividly conveying the sitter's animated personality. Two paintings from a decade earlier are unique in Rembrandt's oeuvre. *Winter Landscape* is his only nature study executed in bright colours, while the intimate *Holy Family with the Curtain* presents the scene in the manner of a tiny theatre set. *Profile of Saskia* is a demonstration of the young artist's virtuosity, with his first wife, gorgeously decked out in velvet and jewellery, depicted as an icon of idealized womanhood.

Hals' *Man in a Slouch Hat* is a late work, clearly showing the influence of Rembrandt married to his own talent for caricature, which can be seen more plainly in the earlier *Merry Toper*. **Ter Brugghen**'s *Flute Player* and *Recorder Player* make for striking pendants, not least because the difference in social class between the two players echoes their different instruments. In spite of Landgrave Wilhelm's strict Calvinism, which drew him to the Dutch School above all others, he assembled a magnificent group of Flemish paintings of the same period. There are some choice canvases by **Rubens**, notably *The Crowning of the Hero*, *The Madonna as a Refuge for Sinners*, the highly unflattering *Nicolas de Respaigne as a Pilgrim to Jerusalem*, and a beautiful nocturnal *Flight into Egypt*. **Van Dyck** is represented by portraits drawn from all phases of his career, while the examples of **Jordaens** show his taste for the exotic on a large scale. More paintings from seventeenth-century Holland, including over twenty canvases by **Philips Wouwerman**, can be seen on the second floor, along with sixteenth- and eighteenth-century works from the same country.

In the first floor galleries are some notable fifteenth- and sixteenth-century German paintings. Highlights include **Cranach**'s early *Resurrection Triptych*, **Dürer**'s *Elsbeth Tucher*, **Baldung**'s *Hercules and Antaeus*, an impassioned *Crucifixion*, set in a Danube landscape, by **Altdorfer**, and a painted table top of *The Creation of the World* by **Martin Schaffner**. A group of Italian Renaissance pictures is dominated by a magnificent full-length *Portrait of a Nobleman* by **Titian**, and the enigmatic *Leda and her Children* by a mysterious painter named **Giampetrino**, who based his composition on a drawing by Leonardo da Vinci. However, once again it was the seventeenth-century artists who most appealed to the Hessian taste, and there are some spectacular examples of Italian Baroque, finest of which is **Preti**'s *Feast of Herod*. From Spain come outstanding canvases by **Murillo** and **Ribera**, while **Poussin**'s *Cupid's Victory over Pan* represents French art of the same period. **Schönfeld**'s *The Great Flood* is one of the finest of all seventeenth-century German paintings, while the effervescent *Game of Morra* by the brilliant but short-lived **Johann Liss** is strikingly anticipatory of the Rococo style of a century later. In the side wing of this floor are some fascinating documentary paintings, notably the gargantuan *Menagerie of Landgrave Karl* by **Johann Melchior Roos**.

The rest of the park

Immediately to the north of the Schloss is the **Ballhaus** (April–Oct Tues–Sun 10am–5pm; €3.50 combined day ticket; Ⓦwww.museum-kassel.de) a neat little Neoclassical building which King Jérôme, Napoleon's brother, had built as a theatre in 1808 to plans by the young Leo von Klenze, who went on to design so much of Munich. Twenty years later it was turned into a ballroom with rich mock-Pompeian decoration and is nowadays used for temporary exhibitions. Alongside is the **Gewächshaus** (first day of Advent to May 1 daily 10am–5pm; €1.80), an impressive steel and glass hothouse built in 1822. On the other side of the lake is the **Löwenburg** (guided tours Tues–Sun 10am–4/5pm; Ⓦwww.schloesser-hessen.de; €3.50), built in the late eighteenth century as a medieval-style ruin, complete with artificial portcullis and drawbridge, and decked out inside with genuinely historic arms and armour. Among the 21 other follies scattered throughout the park are a huge aqueduct and the Teufelsbrücke (Devil's Bridge).

The **Bergpark**, the original Baroque ornamental garden, features a 250-metre-long, 885-tiered cascade. It's overlooked by the famous **Herkules** (mid-March to mid-Nov Tues–Sun 10am–5pm; Ⓦwww.schloesser-hessen.de; €1.80), which might look like an eighteenth-century Michelin Man, but which commands a sweeping panoramic view, as well as being a source of great pride to the burghers of Kassel, who have made it the symbol of their town. The statue, by the Italian Giovanni Francesco Guerniero, lounges on top of a bizarre pyramidal structure, which is in turn set into a purely decorative castle called the **Oktogon**. At 2.30pm on Wednesdays, Sundays and holidays in summer, the floodgates at the foot of Herkules are opened and water pours down the cascade and over a series of obstacles, culminating about an hour later in a 52-metre-high jet of water spurting from the **Grosse Fontäne** in front of the Schloss.

Finally, at the park's eastern entrance, at Wilhelmshöher Allee 361, the Japanese-style **Kurhessen-Therme** (Mon, Tues, Thurs & Sun 9am–11pm, Wed, Fri & Sat 9am–midnight; €11 for 90min or €24 for the day) is an ultra-modern, open-plan spa complex complete with indoor and outdoor thermal pools, saunas, jacuzzis, a cinema and restaurant.

The city centre

Kassel's half-timbered Altstadt has all but completely disappeared, while only a few isolated monuments remain from the Oberneustadt, the Baroque suburb of the Huguenots; these are now marooned among the postwar buildings of the business district which has engulfed the city centre. Nonetheless, there are several **museums** in this area well worth taking the trouble to see.

The Hessisches Landesmuseum

Starting from the west, the **Hessisches Landesmuseum** (Tues–Sun 10am–5pm; €3.50 combined day ticket, free Fri; Ⓦwww.museum-kassel.de) on

Brüder-Grimm-Platz contains several collections. By far the most important is that of applied arts and sculpture, entitled **SchatzKunst 800 bis 1800**. The circuit begins with a display of fifteenth-century **German sculpture**, among which the outstanding works are a sweetly rendered *Madonna and Child* from Kaub, a contrastingly anguished *Pietà* from Kloster Eberbach, and a *Man of Sorrows* by Hans Multscher. These are followed by a stunning array of **treasury items** of the same period: the *Wilkomm* of the Counts of Daun, one of the earliest ceramics ever produced in Germany; the magnificent griffin-borne silver-gilt *Wilkomm* of the Counts of Katzenelnbogen; the *Erde von Indien* (Earth of India), a Chinese porcelain bowl with a base, surround and lid by a Rhenish goldsmith; and the swords of Landgrave Wilhelm I and Boabdil, the last Moorish ruler of Granada.

Dominating the Renaissance section are four large **alabaster wall reliefs**, executed by Elias Godefroy Dupré and assistants, which formerly adorned Philip the Magnanimous' now vanished Schloss in the centre of Kassel. From the same building are the surviving parts of a **portrait gallery** that was unique for its time, containing as it did likenesses of over 130 contemporary European monarchs and nobles – among them Queen Elizabeth I of England. There are also many beautiful artefacts commissioned by Landgrave Moritz the Learned, notably his own four-poster bed. The most striking **Baroque** items are the bust of Landgrave Carl accompanied by two Virtues and two lions by Gabriel Grupello; the Kassel *Dance of Death* from the 1630s; a colourful enamel tea service from Augsburg which is an early manifestation of the then new craze for hot drinks; and the silk morning dress of Princess Louise Dorothea of Brandenburg-Prussia.

Twentieth-century items are housed in the adjacent **Torwache**, a Neoclassical guard house which was the home of the Brothers Grimm from 1814 until 1822. Back in the main building, the **archeology** department on the ground floor has displays on the pre- and early history of Hesse. Upstairs is the **Deutsches Tapetenmuseum** (German Wallpaper Museum), which adopts a generous interpretation of the word to cover all kinds of hangings, with exhibits from all eras and continents

Other museums on Brüder-Grimm-Platz and Schöne Aussicht

Directly across the street from the Hessisches Landesmuseum is the **Murhardsche Bibliothek**, whose most valuable books are displayed under conditions of the strictest security in the basement **Schatzkammer** (Mon, Wed & Fri 2–5pm; free). Its treasures include the ninth-century *Hildebrandtlied*, which features the earliest written occurrence of the word *Deutsch*; also on view are a Gutenberg Bible and some beautiful illuminated manuscripts.

Only a couple of minutes' walk to the southeast, the **Neue Galerie** (Tues–Sun 10am–5pm; Ⓦwww.museum-kassel.de; €3.50 combined day ticket, free Fri) at Schöne Aussicht 1 takes up the history of art where the Schloss Wilhelmshöhe collection leaves off. It contains a large number of works by the Tischbeins – in particular Johann Heinrich the Elder, the Kassel-based member of the dynasty – and by the members of the Willingshausen artists' colony, the first such in Germany. There's also a room devoted to the omnipresent Joseph Beuys.

Next door is **Schloss Bellevue**, a rare survivor of the Huguenots' Oberneustadt. Designed by Paul du Ry as an astronomical observatory, but later converted into a grand town house, it now contains the **Brüder-Grimm-Museum** (daily 10am–5pm; Ⓦwww.grimm-museum.de; €1.50). A model of its kind, with helpful translations into English, this documents the

The Brothers Grimm

One of the great inseparable partnerships, **Jacob Grimm** (1785–1863) and **Wilhelm Grimm** (1786–1859) were of an impeccable Hessian background. Born in Hanau, they were brought up in Steinau and educated in Marburg, before moving to Kassel, where they worked principally as court librarians. It was at Kassel that they put together their collection of tales, which they first published in 1812 under the title *Kinder- und Hausmärchen*. This was primarily a work of scholarship; the stories were all of folk origin and were taken straight down from oral sources. The book went through many editions, culminating in the definitive version of 1857, which contained two hundred tales. In the process, the desire of Jacob (the more gifted scholar of the two) to preserve the original unadorned version of the stories underwent increasing modification at the hands of Wilhelm, who had superior literary talents and favoured a certain amount of stylization and embroidering of the folk idiom.

The collection made the brothers celebrities, and such characters as Cinderella, Rumpelstiltskin, Hansel and Gretel, Snow White and Little Red Riding Hood became familiar to children all over the world. Yet this popular success did not interfere with their dedication to serious scholarship, particularly in their later years as professors at Göttingen (where they were expelled for their liberal views) and Berlin. In 1854, they began to compile *Das Deutsche Wörterbuch* – the German equivalent of the Oxford English Dictionary – a task taken up by several subsequent generations of scholars and finally completed in 1961.

lives and times of the famous fairy tale collectors and philologists (see box above) in a vivid and imaginative manner. Their own annotated manuscript version of the *Fairy Tales* takes pride of place among the displays of their publications, while the various personal artefacts, plus their appearances in many of the delightful watercolour paintings by their lesser-known younger brother, Ludwig Emil, add a very human dimension to the presentation.

Friedrichsplatz and around

Along Frankfurter Strasse is the vast open space of Friedrichsplatz, on which stands the oldest purpose-built museum building in Europe, the **Museum Fredericianum** (variable times and prices; Ⓦwww.fridericianum-kassel.de), designed by Simon-Louis du Ry before he began work on Schloss Wilhelmshöhe. Nowadays, it's used for temporary exhibitions, and is also the headquarters of the *documenta* (Ⓦwww.documenta.de), a retrospective of contemporary art inaugurated in 1955 which has become a multi-media event embracing everything from painting to video art. In effect, the whole city has become its venue, and many of the spectacular sculptures you see dotted throughout Kassel are leftovers from *documenta* events of previous years. One of the best-known of these is the **Rahmenbau** at the opposite end of the square, which frames the views down to the Orangerie and beyond.

Across from the museum, at Steinweg 2, is the **Ottoneum**, constructed in the first decade of the seventeenth century as the first permanent theatre in Germany. Today it is home to the **Naturkundemuseum** (Tues–Sun 10am–5pm; €1.50), itself one of the oldest natural history collections in Europe. Among its curiosities are the sixteenth-century Ratzenberger Herbarium; the eighteenth-century Schildbach'sche Holzbibliothek, whose boxes are made from the wood of different trees and contain a leaf, fruit and flower from each; and the Goethe-Elefant, a stuffed elephant on which Goethe carried out pioneering research.

Oberste Gasse and Mittelgasse both lead from here to the **Martinskirche**. Like all the churches in the city centre, this was devastated during the war, and it has been rebuilt in a compromise style which makes no attempt to restore it to its original form. However, it's worth a quick visit to take a look at the huge Renaissance memorial to Landgrave Philip the Magnanimous, champion of Luther and founder of Marburg University.

At the northern end of the city centre, the Hauptbahnhof, in its new guise as the **Kulturbahnhof**, has become an essential part of the tourist trail, not least becuase of Jonathan Borofsky's wonderfully comic (and, if seen from the right angle, startlingly trompe l'oeil) *Man Walking to the Sky*, the most famous work from the 1992 *documenta*, which has been re-erected in front of the main entrance. Within the station building is the **Caricatura** (Tues–Fri 2–8pm, Sat & Sun noon–8pm; variable charge), the first gallery in Germany solely devoted to comic and satirical art.

The Karlsaue

The southeastern edge of the city centre, by the banks of the River Fulda, is taken up by another large Baroque park, the **Karlsaue**. In it stands the aforementioned **Orangerie**, a long, orange-coloured Baroque palace, which now houses the **Museum für Astronomie und Technikgeschichte** (Tues–Sun 10am–5pm; Ⓦ www.museum-kassel.de; €3.50 combined day ticket, free Fri). This contains a valuable collection of historic scientific instruments, notably those used in the then revolutionary observatory set up in the former Schloss in 1560 by Landgrave Wilhelm IV. There's also a **Planetarium** (introductory shows Tues & Sat at 2pm, Wed, Fri & Sun at 3pm, Thurs at 2pm & 8pm; €1 supplement). Alongside is the recently restored **Marmorbad** (guided tours Tues–Sun 11am–4/5pm; Ⓦ www.schloesser-hessen.de; €3.50), an ornate bathing hall adorned with mythological statues and reliefs by the French sculptor Pierre Etienne Monnot. At the far southern end of the Karlsaue is the **Blumeninsel Siebenbergen** (daily April to early Oct 10am–7pm; €1.80), a lovely island strewn with flowers, trees, and exotic plants and shrubs.

Eating, drinking and entertainment

As with everything else in Kassel, the best places to eat and drink are scattered throughout the city. See also the hotels section on p.412 for some of the leading restaurants.

Restaurants

Boccaccio Querallee 36. Though prices are low and the decor decidedly minimalist, this serves some of the best Italian food in the city.

El Mesón Oberste Gasse 2–8. Spanish restaurant with good food and wines, occupying part of the medieval Elisabeth-Hospital. Evenings only, except at weekends.

Enoteca Osteria Jordanstr. 11. Upmarket Italian wine bar-restaurant. Evenings only, closed Sun.

Gutshof Wilhelmshöher Allee 347a, Wilhelmshöhe. High-quality Gaststätte with beer garden, in a rustic building alongside the Kurhessen-Therme.

Montenegro Bürgermeister-Brunner-Str. 6. Long-established Balkan restaurant; as its name suggests, it specialises in Montenegran (rather than the usual Croatian) food and wines.

Odysseus Mergellstr. 33, Kirchditmold. Long-established Greek restaurant in a half-timbered house with summertime courtyard. Take tram # 8 to Teichstrasse.

Park Schönfeld Bosestr. 13. Classy restaurant in an eighteenth-century Schloss near the Botanischer Garten in the south of the city. Take tram #5, #6, or #9, or bus #50. Closed Sun.

Ratskeller Obere Königsstr. 8. Typically reliable purveyor of *gutbürgerliche Küche*.

Tigris Oberste Gasse 9. What is claimed as Europe's very first Iraqi restaurant serves traditional Mesopotamian fare, such as *Kadma*, a puffy bread stuffed with a choice of fillings, many of them vegetarian. Closed Mon; Tues–Thurs open evenings only.

Bars and café-bars

Barranquilla Friedrich-Ebert-Str. 14. Latin-American dance bar which gets very crowded on Fri and Sat, yet is quiet at other times.

Come In Königs-Galerie 2. This internet café, which serves snacks and light meals and spills out in summer onto Friedrichplatz below, is found on the upper floor of the city centre's most prestigious shopping mall.

FES Karthäuserstr. 17. A favourite meeting place with the younger crowd.

Gleis 1 Bahnhofsplatz 1. Popular bar within the revamped Kulturbahnhof. Closed Sat lunchtime & Sun.

Irish Pub Bürgermeister-Brunner-Str. 1. Features live music each evening, often with visiting foreign musicians. Open daily from 8pm.

Lohmann Königstor 8. A long-standing Kassel institution; the bar itself is very small, but it has a summertime beer garden.

Mr Jones Goethestr. 31. One of Kassel's hippest spots, a place to be seen in; it serves good food, including late breakfasts and full meals.

Schlosscafé Alte Hauptwache, Schlosspark Wilhelmshöhe. This traditional café in the old guard house is the best place to break for a light meal or a snack when visiting the Wilhelmshöhe park.

Festivals and entertainment

There are several worthwhile **festivals** in addition to the *documenta*. The Zissel in early August is a folklore event centred on the River Fulda, with processions, jousting and live music. On the first Saturday of September, the Lichtfest sees Wilhelmshöhe lit by a fireworks display and thousands of torchlights, with a large fair held earlier in the day. The beginning of November marks the Kasseler Musiktage, one of Europe's oldest festivals of classical music.

Cruises on the Fulda are run by Rehbein, Weserstr. 5 (Ⓣ05 61/1 85 05, Ⓦwww.fahrgastschiff.com) and Söllner, Die Schlagd (Ⓣ05 61/77 46 70, Ⓦwww.personnenschiffahrt.com). Most **concerts** are held in the Stadthalle, Friedrich-Ebert-Str. 152 (Ⓣ05 61/7 88 20). The main **theatre** is the Hessisches Staatstheater, Friedrichsplatz 15 (Ⓣ05 61/1 09 42 22, Ⓦwww.staatstheater-kassel.de), which features **opera** as well as **drama**.

Fritzlar

Some 30km southwest of Kassel, the market town of **FRITZLAR** presents one of the best-preserved medieval cityscapes in Germany. Built on a gentle slope on the north bank of the River Eder, Fritzlar's historic core is enclosed by the thirteenth-century **Stadtmauer**. This was actually built as a protection against the predatory designs of the Landgraves of Hesse when the town belonged to the Mainz Electorate; the fabric remains substantially intact, with nine watchtowers and five bastions, though these are in varying states of repair. The wall encloses the Altstadt, with a separate extension around the tiny riverside Neustadt. A fine view of the ensemble can be had from the **Alte Brücke**, which you cross when approaching the town from the Bahnhof. An even better view is from the top of the **Grauer Turm**, the largest surviving watchtower in Germany, guarding the western entrance to the Altstadt. Though it doesn't have set opening times, there's generally a guardian on duty in summer; otherwise the key can be obtained from the tourist office (see p.419).

Built at the securest point of the town's defences, the **Dom** has always been Fritzlar's principal building. The present building, a successor to one founded by the Englishman St Boniface, was begun in the picturesque late Romanesque style of the Rhineland. From this period belongs the mighty west end, with its twin towers and graceful "paradise" porch, though most of the rest of the church was constructed in the Gothic style.

The **Dommuseum und Domschatz** (May–Oct Sun & Mon 2–5pm, Tues–Sat 10am–noon & 2–5pm; Nov–April Sun–Thurs 2–4pm, Fri & Sat 10am–noon & 2–4pm; €2.50) occupies the buildings around the cloisters. There are some stunning treasury items, notably the reliquary of St Boniface, the jewelled cross of Emperor Heinrich IV, and the oldest monstrance in Germany, dating back to 1320. Also included in the entrance ticket is admission to the two **crypts**, the larger of which contains the fourteenth-century tomb of St Wigbert, Fritzlar's first abbot, featuring an imaginary statue of him clasping a model of his church. Upstairs are the **Bibliothek**, with a valuable collection of printed books and manuscripts, and the festive **Musikzimmer**, whose walls are decorated with a lively cycle of fourteenth-century frescoes.

Directly opposite the Dom is the **Rathaus**, one of the oldest town halls in Germany still used as such. Originally, it was in the style characteristic of Fritzlar's secular buildings – with a lower storey of stone and an upper one of half-timbering – but the latter was replaced in the nineteenth century with a tiled mansard roof. A block further north is **Marktplatz**, on which stand some of the finest half-timbered mansions in town, the most imposing being a fifteenth-century guildhall, the **Gildehaus der Michaelsbruderschaft**, on the eastern side. In the middle of the square is the Renaissance **Rolandsbrunnen**, a rather more modest counterpart to the statues of the legendary hero found in the Hanseatic towns of the German coast.

On Burggraben west of Marktplatz is the most impressive of Fritzlar's half-timbered buildings, the **Hochzeitshaus**, built in the late sixteenth century to host weddings and civic receptions. Together with the patrician residence next door, it contains the unusually engrossing **Regionalmuseum** (March–Dec Tues, Thurs & Sun 10am–noon & 3–5pm, Sat 10am–noon; Ⓦwww.regionalmuseum-fritzlar.de; €1.50), which, in addition to the standard displays on archeology, history and folklore, has some nicely offbeat sections, including a collection of the painted roof tiles which are characteristic of the area, and a roomful of unusual inventions, many (including a sort of aerial bicycle) the brainchildren of a talented but totally eccentric local engineer.

Outside the perimeters of the Altstadt, there are only a couple of set piece attractions. The Neustadt clusters around the **Ursulinenkloster**, a still-inhabited fourteenth-century convent whose church can be visited. It's also worth following Fraumünsterstrasse for about 1km east of the town centre to the **Fraumünster**, Fritzlar's oldest building, which stands in a walled garden just north of the Eder. Its stone walls date back to the Carolingian period, while the upper part adopts the Gothic half-timbering so typical of the town's mansions; inside is a cycle of Romanesque frescoes.

Practicalities

Fritzlar's **Bahnhof** is southeast of the centre, whereas the **bus station** is just outside the Stadtmauer, at the top end of Kasseler Strasse. If travelling by train, note that it's often necessary to change at Wabern, 6km to the east, which lies on the main Kassel–Marburg line. The **tourist office** (Mon 10am–6pm, Tues–Thurs 10am–5pm, Fri 10am–4pm, Sat & Sun 10am–noon; Ⓣ0 56 22/98 86 43, Ⓦwww.fritzlar.de) is next door to the Rathaus at Zwischen den Krämer 5. There are four centrally-sited **hotels**, all with **restaurants**: *Zur Post*, Giessener Str. 25 (Ⓣ0 56 22/22 63; ❹); *Zur Spitze*, Marktplatz 25 (Ⓣ0 56 22/18 22; ❺); the Greek-run *Kreta*, Neustädter Str. 9 (Ⓣ0 56 22/65 30; ❹); and *Kaiserpfalz*, Giessener Str. 22 (Ⓣ0 56 22/99 37 70; ❺).

Festivals include a Rhenish-style Karneval which reaches its climax on Rose Monday (variable date Feb/March); the Pferdemarkt, a four-day-long horse fair beginning on the second Thursday in July; and the Stadtfest and Mittelalterisches Fest, held in alternate years on the third weekend of August.

Bad Wildungen

BAD WILDUNGEN, which was formed from the union of two previously separate communities, is set in wooded countryside just 10km west of Fritzlar. It's undoubtedly the most enticing destination in the **Waldeck** (or Waldecker Land), which is now an administrative region of Hesse, but which was for more than seven centuries an independent territory within the German empire, firstly as a county, then as a principality.

The present-day centre of Bad Wildungen, formerly the town of Niederwildungen, was originally a fortified settlement tightly packed on a small hill. Its skyline is dominated by the **Stadtkirche** (daily April–Sept 10.30am–noon & 2–5pm; Oct–March 2–4pm), whose **winged altar** by the Westphalian **Conrad von Soest** ranks among the loveliest and best preserved of fifteenth-century German paintings, and one of the supreme masterpieces of the courtly International Gothic style. The thirteen panels narrate the life of Jesus in a markedly individual way, and are full of (often humorous) anecdotal detail, including the first representation of spectacles in Northern European art. Likewise in the chancel are two swaggering Baroque **memorial monuments** to rulers of the House of Waldeck.

Immediately west of the centre is **Brunnenallee**, the spa quarter's main promenade. It terminates at the palatial **Fürstenhof**, an extremely self-confident Jugendstil building which has, throughout its history, maintained its position as the town's top sanatorium. Beyond is the **Kurpark**, a landscaped park merging seamlessly with the wooded hills above, with the **Wandelhalle**, a late Neoclassical pump room, at its far end.

On a much higher hill north of the centre is the former town of Altwildungen, dominated by one of the secondary residences of the Waldeck princes, **Schloss Friedrichstein** (Tues–Sun 10am–1pm & 2–5pm; Ⓦwww.museum-kassel.de; €2.50). A Baroque rebuild of the original medieval castle, it's now a museum of hunting and weapons, including booty captured in the seventeenth- and eighteenth-century wars against the Turks, though is equally of note for the wonderful view it commands over the surrounding countryside.

Practicalities

Bad Wildungen's **Bahnhof** lies at the eastern end of town, a ten-minute walk from the centre. It's now a dead-end for passenger services, except on summer Sundays, when excursion services are run along the otherwise disused line to Hemfurth, which lies just 1km south of the Edertalsperre, a prime target of the Dambusters operation in World War II. One of the **tourist offices** is in the Kurverwaltung, just beyond the end of Brunnenallee at Langemarckstr. 2 (Mon–Fri 8.30am–4.30pm, Sat 9am–noon; Ⓣ0 56 21/9 65 59 20, Ⓦwww.bad-wildungen.de); the other is in the Rathaus, Am Markt 1 (Mon–Wed 8am–4pm, Thurs 8am–6pm, Fri 8am–12.30pm, Sat 10am–noon; Ⓣ0 56 21/70 13 20).

Both places can book **private rooms** (❶–❸), of which there's an abundant supply. There are also plenty of good-value **guesthouses** and **hotels**, often in atmospheric old villas in the spa quarter. Look particularly on Hufelandstrasse, a block south of Langemarckstrasse, where you'll find *Villa Hügel* at no. 17 (Ⓣ0 56 21/25 14; ❷); *Daheim* at no. 14 (Ⓣ0 56 21/27 16; ❸); and *Villa Heilquelle* at no. 15 (Ⓣ0 56 21/23 92, Ⓦwww.villa-heilquelle.de; ❹). The two top hotels are *Quellenhof*, Brunnenallee 54 (Ⓣ0 56 21/80 70, Ⓦwww.treff-hotels.de; ❼) and *Maritim Badehotel*, Dr-Marc-Str. 4 (Ⓣ0 56 21/79 99, Ⓦwww.maritim.de; ❼).

There are plenty of **cafés** and **restaurants** all along Brunnenallee, though the best place for a meal, other than the two luxury hotels mentioned above, is the *Neues Kurhaus* in the Kurpark.

Marburg

The cradle of Hesse and its original capital, **MARBURG** clusters up the slopes of the Lahn valley some 80km southwest of Kassel in a maze of narrow streets and medieval buildings. There are distinctive lower and upper towns, dominated respectively by two of Germany's greatest buildings, the Elisabethkirche and the Schloss. However, the whole ensemble is in many ways the most remarkable feature, as the town has been touched by war less than almost any other city in the country.

Marburg was one of the major pilgrimage centres of northern Europe on account of its patron **St Elisabeth** – a thirteenth-century Hungarian-born princess who had devoted herself to the poor – until the cult was abolished by her descendant, **Landgrave Philip the Magnanimous**, at the time of the Reformation. In 1527 he established the university, the first in the world to be subject to the new Protestant faith. Nowadays, nearly a quarter of the population is in some way associated with the university, and the presence of 15,000 students gives it a relaxed and lively atmosphere. Marburg has good rail and road links with Frankfurt, Kassel and Koblenz, and is worth going out of your way to visit.

Arrival, information and accommodation

Marburg's **Hauptbahnhof** is on the right bank of the Lahn at the northern end of town, just five minutes' walk from the Elisabethkirche. The **tourist office** (Mon–Fri 9am–6pm, April–Sept also Sat 10am–2pm; Ⓣ0 64 21/9 91 20, Ⓦwww.marburg.de) is at Am Pilgrimstein 26.

There's a surprising lack of **hotels** with a convenient location and it might be a good idea to enquire at the tourist office about places in outlying villages if you're after a budget deal. The **youth hostel** is at Jahnstr. 1 (Ⓣ0 64 21/2 34 61; €18), a little to the southeast of the Altstadt; the *Lahnaue* **campsite** (Ⓣ0 64 21/2 13 31) is a bit further down the river at Trojedamm 47.

Hotels and guesthouses

Europäischer Hof Elisabethstr. 12 Ⓣ0 64 21/69 60, Ⓦwww.europaeischer-hof-marburg.de. This hotel, which has been in existence since 1834, has rooms of varying degrees of luxury and offers a good breakfast buffet. The restaurant, *Atelier*, has a predominantly Italianate menu. ❻–❾

Hesse-Stübche Untergasse 10 Ⓣ0 64 21/2 58 87, Ⓕ16 29 47. Typically German hotel with pub-restaurant in the heart of the upper town. ❻

Müller Deutschhausstr. 29 Ⓣ0 64 21/6 56 59. Good-value guesthouse in the lower town, close to the Elisabethkirche. ❹

Schneider Gladenbacher Weg 37 Ⓣ0 64 21/3 42 36, Ⓕ35 03 52. Inexpensive pension in the far southwestern part of town. ❷

Tusculum Gutenbergerstr. 25 Ⓣ0 64 21/2 27 78, Ⓦwww.tusculum.de. Hotel located just south of the upper town, with brightly painted rooms. ❺

Vila Vita Rosenstr. 18-28 Ⓣ0 64 21/6 00 50, Ⓦwww.vilavitahotels.com. Marburg's classiest hotel, a modern building beautifully furnished with antiques and with a gourmet restaurant and fitness centre. ❾

Waldecker Hof Bahnhofstr. 23 Ⓣ0 64 21/6 00 90, Ⓦwww.waldecker-hof-marburg.de. The facilities at this hotel, which is conveniently close to the Hauptbahnhof, include a swimming pool, sauna, solarium and fitness room. ❻

Zur Sonne Markt 14 ⓣ0 64 21/1 71 90, ⓕ17 19 40. This pretty half-timbered building, a Gasthaus since the sixteenth century, is the most atmospheric place to stay in Marburg. It also has a superb restaurant. ❻

The lower town

Although much of it is now taken up with functional modern buildings of the university and by a business and shopping district, the kernel of the lower town (Unterstadt) survives from the thirteenth century. It was then the property of the **Order of Teutonic Knights** (see p.362). Given their bellicosity, it's all the more ironic that they showed such dedication to St Elisabeth, whose life could hardly have presented a greater contrast. Never a lover of the high lifestyle which had been her lot since birth, she donned the grey habit of a Franciscan nun on becoming widowed at the age of twenty, and devoted the rest of her life to the hospital she founded in Marburg, where she died of exhaustion four years later.

The Elisabethkirche

No sooner had Elisabeth gained papal recognition as a saint in 1235, than the Teutonic Knights began the construction of the **Elisabethkirche** (April–Sept Mon–Sat 9am–6pm, Sun 12.30–6pm; Oct Mon–Sat 9am–5pm, Sun 12.30–5pm; Nov–March Mon–Sat 10am–4pm, Sun 12.30–4pm; ⓦwww.elisabethkirche.de; €1.50 for admission to the chancel) on the site of her hospice, encasing her tomb in the process. The first purely Gothic building on German soil, it's also one of the most original and most beautiful, with the hall church format (which necessitated heavy wall buttresses), and the trefoil or "clover leaf" plan for the east end adapted to the new style of architecture for the first time. The twin **towers**, with their relentless upward movement and tall pointed steeples, are also very Germanic and noticeably different from their more varied and elaborate French counterparts.

Inside, the church is full of statues and frescoes, mainly celebrating Elisabeth's piety. Curiously enough, her cult underwent a major revival just before the Reformation, and five magnificent winged **altars** were created by the local master carver Ludwig Juppe and the painter Johann von der Leyten. On the right as you enter is one of these, the *Elisabeth-Altar*, which vividly relates the saint's life. In an alcove to the other side is the tomb of **Paul von Hindenburg**, the *Reichspresident* who appointed Hitler Chancellor in 1933. His body was brought to this decidedly unsuitable location after the war by the Americans. At the opposite end of this aisle, a curvaceous **statue of Elisabeth** from about 1470 depicts her in a pose she would have despised – as a richly robed, crowned princess clutching a model of her church.

Just around the corner is the **Elisabeth-Chor**, as the northern part of the clover leaf plan is known. Its centrepiece is the towering **mausoleum** containing her coffin in its original location. Look out for the reliefs on the pedestal, which show her being mourned by beggars and cripples instead of the kings and bishops who normally occupied such a position. Among the **altars**, pride of place goes to that dedicated to the Virgin, in which Juppe skilfully incorporated a much-venerated older sculpture of *The Pietà* into the predella. A number of **murals** illustrating the saint's life, long covered up and only rediscovered last century, can also be seen.

The main choir, or **Hochchor**, still preserves its original thirteenth-century adornments – a curious high altar shaped like the narthex of a church, a complete set of stalls and stained-glass windows. Some of the windows have been mutilated, although an engagingly stylized series illustrating the Crucifixion remain. On the north side, the former sacristy now contains the church's most spectacular treasure, the resplendent mid-thirteenth-century **golden shrine** which contained the relics of Elisabeth until Philip the Magnanimous had them re-interred. Elisabeth's life is illustrated yet again on the reliefs on the lid.

Finally, the **Landgrafen-Chor**, the southern arm of the trefoil plan, serves as the **pantheon** of the rulers of Hesse. The first tomb in the eastern row is to Elisabeth's brother-in-law Conrad, while the fourth, artistically the finest of the group, commemorates Heinrich I, the first Landgrave of Hesse. The only alabaster intruder among the stone tombs is Philip the Magnanimous' father Wilhelm II, who is gruesomely depicted as a decaying corpse.

The rest of the quarter

Grouped around the Elisabethkirche are several other buildings formerly belonging to the Teutonic Knights. Forming a sort of close around the church's east end are the thirteenth-century **Brüderhaus** and **Herrenhaus**, the fifteenth-century **Deutschordenhaus** and the sixteenth-century **Kornspeicher**. All are now used by the University: the Kornspeicher, formerly a corn store and bakehouse, now houses the **Mineralogisches Museum** (Wed 10am–1pm & 3–6pm, Thurs & Fri 10am–1pm, Sat & Sun 11am–3pm; free), which is more interesting than it sounds, with a glittering array of precious stones. Up a little hill to the west of the Elisabethkirche is the **Michaelskapelle**, a funerary chapel for the Knights and pilgrims to the shrine. St Elisabeth herself was buried in its peaceful little cemetery once the ban on her cult had been imposed.

Following Deutschhausstrasse southeastwards, then turning right into Biegenstrasse, at no. 11 you'll find the **Universitätsmuseum für Bildende Kunst** (Tues–Sun 11am–1pm & 2–5pm; free), which has a Lucas Cranach the Elder portrait of Luther, a Klee, a Kandinsky and a Picasso, and works by German artists, notably the local painter Karl Bantzer.

The upper town

Other than its one supreme monument, the most remarkable feature of the upper town (Oberstadt) is its atmospheric appearance, with plunging streets, steep stairways, narrow alleys, secluded corners and surprising vistas. The most enticing way up is to follow the **Steinweg**, an old stepped street hemmed in by half-timbered buildings, from the Elisabethkirche.

Marktplatz and around

Heart of the Altstadt is the **Marktplatz**, with its St-Georg-Brunnen and a line-up of golden half-timbered houses. During term-time the square is the focal point of Marburg's nightlife, but out of term it's very peaceful except for the twice-weekly markets. Here you might see older women in the traditional costumes still sometimes worn in the area, a hangover from the days when Protestant and Catholic had to be able to tell each other apart – the Protestants wore black, dark brown, blue or green, while the Catholics wore bright colours with plaited hair. The **Rathaus** is a sixteenth-century Gothic building with a gabled Renaissance staircase tower featuring another statue of Elisabeth by Ludwig Juppe, holding the arms of the Landgraves of Hesse. The heraldic symbol is supposed to be a lion, but the sculptor mischievously made it look like a monkey.

South of the Markt is the **Kilianskirche**, Marburg's oldest church, but one which has been secularized since the sixteenth century. In the Nazi period it was appropriated for use as the local SS headquarters, and was also the final place to which Marburg's Jews were taken before deportation. Nowadays, it's the head office of the German Green Cross. Further south is the **Alte Universität**, which took over a Gothic Dominican friary, of which only the church (Tues–Sun 9am–5pm) now remains. The rest of the complex was rebuilt in a grandiose neo-Romanesque style, with the centrepiece being the **Aula**, a ceremonial hall adorned with frescoes depicting the history of the city.

Nicolaistrasse leads west from Marktplatz to the thirteenth-century **Marienkirche**, from whose terrace there's a good view out over Marburg and the Lahn. Just past here is a stairway called the Ludwig-Bickell-Treppe which provides the shortest route up to the top of the town. Alternatively, you can ascend the slower way to the northeast via the Renaissance **Kanzlei**, which now houses another University collection, the **Religionskundliche Sammlung** (Mon–Fri 10am–1pm; free), with material on the history of religions.

The Schloss

Towering above Marburg at a height of 102m above the Lahn is the **Schloss** (April–Oct Tues–Sun 10am–6pm; Nov–March Tues–Sun 11am–5pm; €1.50). There has been a castle on this site as far back as the twelfth century, but the present structure was begun by order of Sophie of Brabant, daughter of St Elisabeth, to serve as the seat of the Landgraves of the new state of Hesse. Marburg lost its role as capital to Kassel at the beginning of the fourteenth century, but before then a substantial portion of the present Schloss had been built. This included the south wing, at the end of which is the **Schlosskapelle**. Inside, the lurid rose-coloured interior is quite striking; some original murals and part of the mosaic pavement also survive.

From the same period is the **Saalbau** on the northern side. This is notable for illustrating that this Schloss was primarily a residential palace, as opposed to the then standard fortified castle. Although the magnificent great hall, the largest structure of its kind in Germany, is known as the **Rittersaal**, it actually had no military function, instead being a venue for feasts and receptions. The most famous of these was the **Marburg Colloquy** of 1529, when Philip the Magnanimous failed to unite Protestantism.

The hall's two spectacular Renaissance inlaid-wood doorways are among the many additions and embellishments made to the Schloss during the fifteenth and sixteenth centuries, when Marburg periodically regained its position as capital of all or part of Hesse. At the eastern side of the complex, the **Wilhelmsbau**, linked to the main courtyard by a covered bridge, was the last significant part to be built. It now contains the miscellaneous archeology, applied art and local history displays of the **Museum für Kulturgeschichte**. From the terrace outside there's a wonderful aerial **view** over the Elisabethkirche and the lower town.

Eating and drinking

There's no shortage of places for eating and drinking in this student-dominated town. The best bars are among the half-timbered buildings on Hirschberg, the street leading off from the Markt, and on Untergasse.

Alter Ritter Steinweg 44. Classy restaurant which offers reasonably-priced lunches and set dinners.
Café Barfuss Barfüsserstr. 33. Café-bar which serves a good selection of food, including its own pizza variant, *Fetizzo*.
Das Kleine Restaurant Barfüssertor 25. Intimate little place serving some of the best cuisine in town. Pricey. Closed Mon.
Hinkelstein Markt 18. Cellar tavern with occasional live music, popular with students.
Kalimera Lingelgasse 13a. Greek taverna with riverside garden, featuring a good choice of vegetarian options on its menu.
Milano Biegenstr. 19. Highly regarded upmarket Italian restaurant.
Piscator Stadthalle, Biegenstr. 15. A good traditional German restaurant and a worthy rival to *Zur Sonne* (see p.422).
Quodlibet Am Grün 37. Good bar with billiard tables.
Roter Stern Am Grün 28. Housed in a bookshop, this is where Marburg's coolest crowd hang out. Well known for its superb Nicaraguan coffee.
Weinlädele Schlosstreppe 1. A cosy wine bar in a half-timbered building. Evenings only.

Entertainment

It's always worth checking up on **events** held on the Schlosspark's open-air stage. Otherwise, the principal highbrow **drama** and **concert** venue is the *Stadthalle*, Biegenstr. 15 (ⓣ0 64 21/2 56 08); *KFZ*, Schulstr. 6 (ⓣ0 64 21/1 38 98) is an alternative cultural centre featuring all kinds of live music, theatre and cabaret. The only **nightclub** as such is *Kult-Lager*, in the south of town at Terminstr. 9. Marburg's main **festival** is the bucolic Marktfrühschoppen on the first Sunday in July, while the Elisabethmarkt in mid-October is another good time to visit. **Boats** can be rented from Bootsverleih, Auf dem Wehr (ⓣ0 64 21/2 68 64).

The lower Lahn valley

The lower valley of the **River Lahn** forms a natural boundary dividing the upland forest areas of the Taunus and the Westerwald. Most of it lies within Hesse, but a small downstream stretch, shortly before it flows into the Rhine just south of Koblenz, is in Rhineland-Palatinate. A series of historic towns, each conveniently separated by intervals of approximately 20km, punctuate the Hessian section. Exploration is made easy by the road and rail line which closely follow the river for all but its uppermost stretch.

Wetzlar

The long-time city-state of **WETZLAR**, some 45km downstream from Marburg, occupies a hallowed place in the annals of German literature (see box p.426), which in turn was a consequence of its role from 1693 to 1803 as seat of the Reichskammergericht, the highest civil court of the Holy Roman Empire. These days it's a light industrial town, and is centred on a well-preserved Altstadt of half-timbered, grey-roofed houses precipitously clinging to the hillside above the Lahn.

Of the many steeply plunging squares in Wetzlar's Altstadt, the largest is Domplatz, named after the so-called **Dom**, a former collegiate church used for both Catholic and Protestant worship. It offers a fascinating insight into medieval building practices, as the Romanesque structure was demolished piece by piece to make way for a Gothic hall design. However, money ran out before completion, with the result that the old north tower and main entrance (the Heathens' Portal) still survive, the latter marooned behind its partly completed successor. The Gothic **south tower**, later capped with a Baroque belfry, is the symbol of the town and its most prominent landmark.

Just off the south side of Domplatz is the small Fischmarkt, on which stands the former **Rathaus**, later the seat of the Reichskammergericht, and now a café. Following Pfaffengasse uphill from Domplatz brings you to the **Hof des Deutschen Ritterordens** (Court of the Teutonic Knights). Within the courtyard is the **Lottehaus** (Tues–Sun 10am–1pm & 2–5pm; €1.50, or €4 combined ticket for all the town's museums), the house where Lotte Buff (see p.426) lived with her parents and siblings. A must for Goethe aficionados, it has been turned into a small museum containing period furniture, pictures and books – with lots of first editions and translations of *Werther*. Next door is the **Stadt- und Industriemuseum** (same times and conditions), which details Wetzlar's history as a Free Imperial City and the development of its iron and optical industries. It was here that Oskar Barnack pioneered today's standard 35mm camera, and the town is home to Leitz, a leading camera manufacturer.

The Sorrows of Young Werther

While working at the Reichskammergericht as a legal clerk, **Goethe** fell in love with Lotte Buff, the fiancée of a close friend. His response to this awkward situation was to run away from it. However, when another friend there, Karl Wilhelm Jerusalem, committed suicide over an unrequited love affair, he was inspired to fuse the two episodes by writing an epistolary novella, *The Sorrows of Young Werther*. It was an immediate sensation; before his twenty-fifth birthday, Goethe had become the most celebrated literary figure in Europe, inspiring a Romantic reaction against the Age of Reason and creating a continent-wide phenomenon of young men wearing blue coats and yellow breeches, suffering from melancholy and contemplating suicide.

At the southeastern corner of the Altstadt, reached via the picturesque squares of Kornmarkt and Eisenmarkt, are three more small museums each well worth a visit. The pick of these is the **Sammlung Dr Irmgard von Lemmers-Danforth** (same times and conditions as the Lottehaus) at Kornblumengasse 1, which has a really lovely collection of Renaissance and Baroque furniture and decorative art from all over Europe, displayed in a handsome town mansion. A few paces away, at Hofstatt 19, is the **Reichskammergerichtsmuseum** (same times and conditions), detailing the history of the institution that brought Wetzlar its fame. Finally, just to the south at Schillerplatz 5 is the half-timbered **Jerusalemhaus** (same times and conditions), which has been restored to give a period feel of the time when it was the home of the lovelorn youth who was the inspiration for Goethe's Werther.

Practicalities

Wetzlar's **Bahnhof** is about 1km north of the Altstadt and on the opposite side of the Lahn. The **tourist office** is at Domplatz 8 (Mon–Fri 9am–1pm & 2–4.30pm, Sat 10am–noon; ⓣ0 64 41/9 93 38, ⓦwww.wetzlar.de).

Hotels with a central location include *Domblick*, Langgasse 64 (ⓣ0 64 41/9 01 60, ⓦwww.domblick.de; ❺); *Wetzlarer Hof*, Obertorstr. 3 (ⓣ0 64 41/90 80, ⓦwww.wetzlarerhof.de; ❻); *Bürgerhof*, Konrad-Adenauer-Promenade 20 (ⓣ0 64 41/90 30, ⓦwww.buergerhof-wetzlar.com; ❻); and *Mercure*, Bergstr. 41 (ⓣ0 64 41/41 70, ⓦwww.mercure.com; ❻). There are cheaper alternatives in the outlying villages and the tourist office can help with these. Wetzlar's **youth hostel** is in a lovely secluded setting southeast of the Altstadt at Richard-Schirrmann-Str. 3 (ⓣ0 64 41/7 10 68; €18.50/21.20); take bus #12 to Sturzkopf. There are two local **campsites** – the first of these, *Niedergirmes*, is north of the Bahnhof (ⓣ0 64 41/3 41 03); the other is at *Dutenhofener See* (ⓣ06 41/2 32 20), about halfway to Giessen, near the Bahnhof Wetzlar-Ost.

The last three hotels listed above all have excellent **restaurants**. Otherwise, try *Zur Domtreppe*, Domplatz 5, which has a secluded beer garden, or head north of the Altstadt to *Häusler's*, Garbenheimer Str. 18, the evenings-only Gaststätte of the local Euler brewery.

Weilburg

What **WEILBURG** lacks in size, it makes up for in visual appeal. Standing on a promontory surrounded on three sides by the River Lahn, its compact centre is grouped around the elegant sixteenth-century **Schloss** (guided tours Tues–Sun 10am–4/5pm; ⓦwww.schloesser-hessen.de; €3.50) which, together with its outbuildings and grounds, almost forms a town in itself. Once the residence of an offshoot line of the House of Nassau, the Schloss has a particularly beautiful central courtyard, offering an almost rustic interpretation of the Renaissance style. In the eighteenth century, the complex was greatly expanded by the addition of the **Marstall** (stables) on the northern side, and by the laying out of the **Schlossgarten** as a series of terraces leading down to the Lahn. Within the latter is the curvaceous **Obere Orangerie** (same hours as Schloss; €1), which is used for temporary exhibitions of *objets d'art*, and the **Untere Orangerie**, now a café-restaurant. Alongside is the **Schlosskirche**, one of the finest Baroque churches in Hesse – its elaborate pillared altar, decorated with cherubs and sunbursts, has an almost Rococo feel to it.

Directly opposite the main entrance to the Schloss is the **Bergbau- und Stadtmuseum** (April–Oct Tues–Sun 10am–noon & 2–5pm; Nov–March Mon–Fri 10am–noon & 2–5pm; €3), whose main attraction is the Tiefe Stollen, a full-sized mock-up of a local mine. Upstairs, there's an early nineteenth-century pharmacy and the Weilburger Herbarium of 1842, which is still in its original display cabinets. In the middle of the adjacent Marktplatz is a heavily ornamented Renaissance fountain, the **Neptunbrunnen**.

North of the Schloss, the Lahn is crossed by the five-arched **Steinerne Brücke**, first erected in the 1760s. On either side of the peninsula, you can see the two entrances to the **Schiffstunnel**, the only such construction in Germany, which was dug in the middle of the nineteenth century to save ships from having to sail all the way round the town. It cuts underneath the **Kalvarienberg**, a hill with an unfinished sixteenth-century attempt at re-creating the Holy Places of Jerusalem.

Practicalities

Weilburg's **Bahnhof** is beside the Lahn, on the opposite bank from the Schloss. The **tourist office** (Mon–Fri 9am–noon & 2–4.30pm, Sat 10am–noon; ⓣ0 64 71/76 71 or 3 14 67, ⓦwww.weilburg.de) is south of the Schloss at Mauerstr. 6.

Among the **hotels**, the most convenient are *Am Schiffstunnel,* Ahäuser Weg 4 (ⓣ0 64 71/6 18 72, ⓦwww.hotel-am-schiffstunnel.de; ❹); *Weilburg*, Frankfurter Str. 27 (ⓣ0 64 71/9 12 90, ⓦwww.hotel-weilburg.de; ❺); *Villa im Park*, Frankfurter Str. 12 (ⓣ0 64 71/9 38 30; ❻); and *Schlosshotel*, which occupies the Marstall, Langgasse 25 (ⓣ0 64 71/3 90 96, ⓦwww.schlosshotel-weilburg.de; ❽). There's a riverside **campsite** (ⓣ0 64 71/76 20), but the **youth hostel** is a long walk from town, above the outlying village of Odersbach, 4km to the west, at Am Steinbühl (ⓣ0 64 71/71 16; €16.50).

Weilburg has an abundance of good places to **eat** and **drink**. Predictably, the *Schlosshotel* has the best and most expensive restaurant. *Weilburger Hof,* Schwannengasse 14, is another good choice for traditional German dishes; *La Lucia*, Marktplatz 10, is a fine Italian restaurant; while *Zur Turmschmiede* on Turmgasse has a shady beer garden.

Limburg an der Lahn

The little episcopal city of **LIMBURG**, which lies hard by the Land border, and some 50km north of Wiesbaden, is beautifully situated on a rocky spur on the south bank of the Lahn. Compact enough to be seen in a short time, it's deservedly a popular destination with day-trippers from the Rhineland.

Limburg's **Dom** is built right at the top of the town and might at first sight appear to be a sacred counterpart to the fantasy castles erected all over Germany in the Romantic period. In fact, it's a perfectly genuine church from the first half of the thirteenth century, with an orange, white and yellow colour scheme and an exotic roofline comprising seven towers and spires. In essence the Dom belongs to the last phase of Romanesque, and, despite using some elements of the newly emerging Gothic style, it seems that the builders were unaware of the structural advantages of pointed arches and rib vaults, using them merely for novelty value and decorative effects. Just before the church was consecrated, it was endowed with a series of naive but vigorous **frescoes**, most of which survive; look out in particular for the striking depiction of Samson in the south transept. Two other furnishings from the same period can also be seen – the elaborate stone **font** in a south aisle chapel, and the **tomb** of the founder, Conrad Kurzbold, in the northern transept.

To the rear of the Dom, the **Schloss** of the local lords is another very picturesque jumble of buildings now used to house offices and the municipal archives. Down Domstrasse is the **Diözesanmuseum** (mid-March to mid-Nov Tues–Sat 10am–1pm & 2–5pm, Sun 11am–5pm; €1). This contains some stunning treasury items, notably the **Staurothek**, a Byzantine reliquary in the shape of a cross, which was brought back from the Crusades by a local knight; the jewelled **staff of St Peter**, made by a tenth-century goldsmith from Trier; and the eleventh-century lead **reliquary** from the high altar of the previous church on the site of the Dom.

The venerable houses of the Altstadt at the foot of the hill are predominantly half-timbered, with the cluster around **Fischmarkt** ranking among the oldest in the country. Here also is the **Historisches Rathaus**, which served as the town hall for exactly six centuries. To end your visit, cross over the **Alte Lahnbrücke**, a fourteenth-century bridge which preserves its original defensive tower. From here, or better still the opposite bank, you're rewarded with a wonderful **view** of the skyline.

Practicalities

Limburg's **Bahnhof** is just south of the Altstadt. The **tourist office** (April–Oct Mon–Fri 8am–12.30pm & 2–6pm, Sat 10am–noon; Nov–March Mon–Thurs 8am–12.30pm & 2–5pm, Fri 8am–12.30pm; ⓣ0 64 31/61 66, ⓦwww.limburg.de) is just minutes' walk to the north at Hospitalstr. 2.

There's one inexpensive central **guesthouse**, *Zum Weissen Ross*, Westerwaldstr. 2 (ⓣ0 64 31/87 76; ❹). Around the Bahnhof are several **hotels**, including *Martin*, Holzheimer Str. 2 (ⓣ0 64 31/4 10 01 or 9 48 40, ⓦwww.hotel-martin.de; ❺); *Huss*, Bahnhofsplatz 3 (ⓣ0 64 31/9 33 50, ⓦwww.telehotel.de/huss-limburg; ❻); and *Zimmermann*, Blumenröder Str. 1 (ⓣ0 64 31/46 11; ❻–❽). Altstadt establishments include *Nassauer Hof*, Brückenstr. 1 (ⓣ0 64 31/99 60; ❼); and *Dom-Hotel*, Grabenstr. 57 (ⓣ0 64 31/90 10, ⓦwww.domhotel.net; ❼). There's a **youth hostel** at the extreme southern edge of town at Auf dem Guckucksberg (ⓣ0 64 31/4 14 93; €16/18.70); take bus #3. The **campsite** (ⓣ0 64 31/2 26 10) is at Schleusenweg 16, at the northern end of town.

Both *Nassauer Hof* and *Dom-Hotel* have excellent **restaurants**; otherwise the best place to eat in Limburg is *St Georgsstube* in the Stadthalle, Hospitalstr. 4.

Travel details

Trains

Frankfurt to: Bremen (hourly; 4hr 20min); Cologne (hourly; 2hr 20min); Darmstadt (every 20min; 30min); Fulda (every 30min; 1hr); Hannover (hourly; 3hr 15min); Kassel (every 30min; 2hr); Koblenz (hourly; 1hr 40min); Marburg (every 30min; 1hr); Trier (hourly; 2hr 45min); Wiesbaden (every 30min; 30min).

Kassel to: Fulda (hourly; 40min); Marburg (hourly; 1hr).

Wiesbaden to: Rüdesheim (hourly; 35min).

Rhineland-Palatinate and Saarland

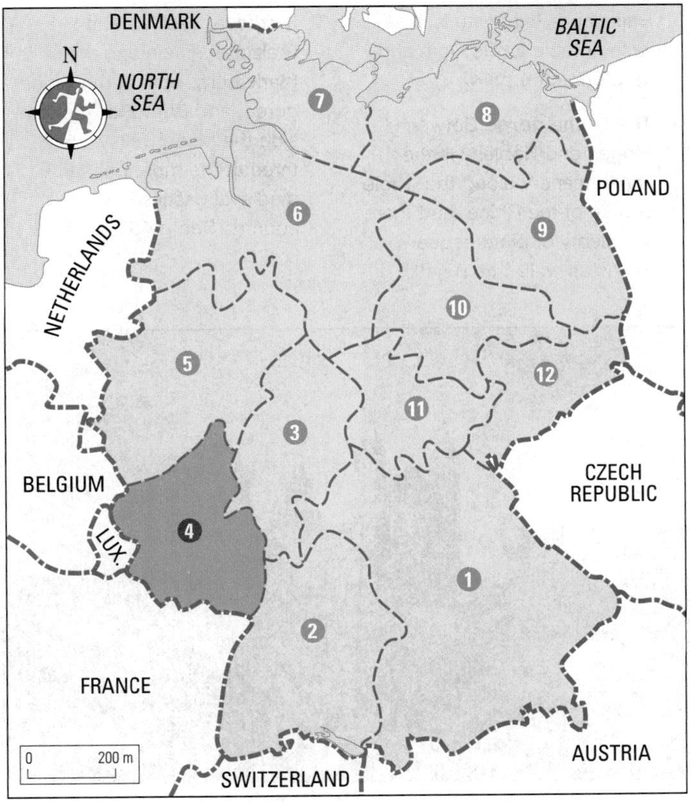

CHAPTER 4 Highlights

* **Speyer** One of Germany's most impressive small cities, with a magnificent Dom and a distinguished gastronomic tradition. See p.433
* **Worms** The home of the *Nibelungenlied* and Liebfraumilch has another fine Dom. See p.437
* **Mainz** The state capital of Rhineland-Palatinate is likewise notable for its Dom and its wines. See p.442
* **The Rhine gorge** Between Bingen and Koblenz is the finest scenery along the whole course of the Rhine, and there are plenty of picturesque towns as well. See p.449
* **Trier** Germany's oldest city has the finest Roman monuments to be found north of the Alps. See p.465
* **The Mosel Wine Road** Germany's most characteristic wines are produced along the banks of the Mosel, which also has its fair share of pretty old towns. See p.473
* **Medieval castles** The Pfalzgrafenstein and the Marksburg, both in the Rhine gorge, and Burg Eltz, just outside the Mosel valley, are three of the most beautiful medieval castles in the country. See p.452, p.455 & p.478

△ The Dom, Worms

Rhineland-Palatinate and Saarland

Of all the German Länder, the **Rhineland-Palatinate** (Rheinland-Pfalz) is the one most overlaid by legend. The **River Rhine** is seen here at its majestic best, and there's hardly a town, castle or rock along this stretch which hasn't made a distinctive contribution to its mythology. This is the land of the national epic, the *Nibelungenlied*, an extraordinary tale of heroism, chicanery, dynastic rivalry, vengeance and obsession, which bites deep into the German soul. It's also the land of the deceptively alluring Lorelei, of the robber barons who presided over tiny fiefs from lofty fortresses, and of the merchant traders who used the natural advantages of the river to bring the country to the forefront of European prosperity.

Nowadays, the Rhine's once treacherous waters have been tamed, enabling pleasure cruisers to run its length, past a wonderful landscape of rocks, vines, white-painted towns and ruined castles. Everything conforms perfectly to the image of Germany promoted by the tourist office; visitors swarm in, and people living off the trade do very nicely. Although the **Rhine gorge** is the bit most people want to write home about, the rest of the Land has plenty to offer. The **Mosel valley**, running all the way from France to its confluence with the Rhine at **Koblenz**, scores highly for scenic beauty and is not quite as over-subscribed and spoilt. Further north, the valley of the **River Ahr**, which flows into the Rhine near **Remagen**, rivals both of the larger rivers for spectacular scenery.

Industry exists merely in isolated pockets, and **Mainz**, the state's capital and chief city, only just ranks among the forty largest in Germany. Its monuments, together with those of the two other Imperial cathedral cities of **Worms** (the font of Germany's once-rich Jewish culture) and **Speyer**, are of major importance, though the number one destination from the point of view of sights is **Trier**, which preserves the finest buildings of classical antiquity this side of the Alps.

Trier's Roman survivals are a potent reminder of the area's illustrious **history**. The Rhine itself marked the effective limit of Roman power, and from that period onward the settlements along its western bank dominated national development. Throughout the duration of the Holy Roman Empire, the importance of this area within Germany can be gauged by the fact that two of the seven Electors were the Archbishops of Mainz and Trier, while another was the *Pfalzgraf*, or Count Palatine of the Rhine. This has provided the present Land, an artificial postwar construct, with its name, though the heart of his territory lay in the north of what is now Baden-Württemberg. Like the

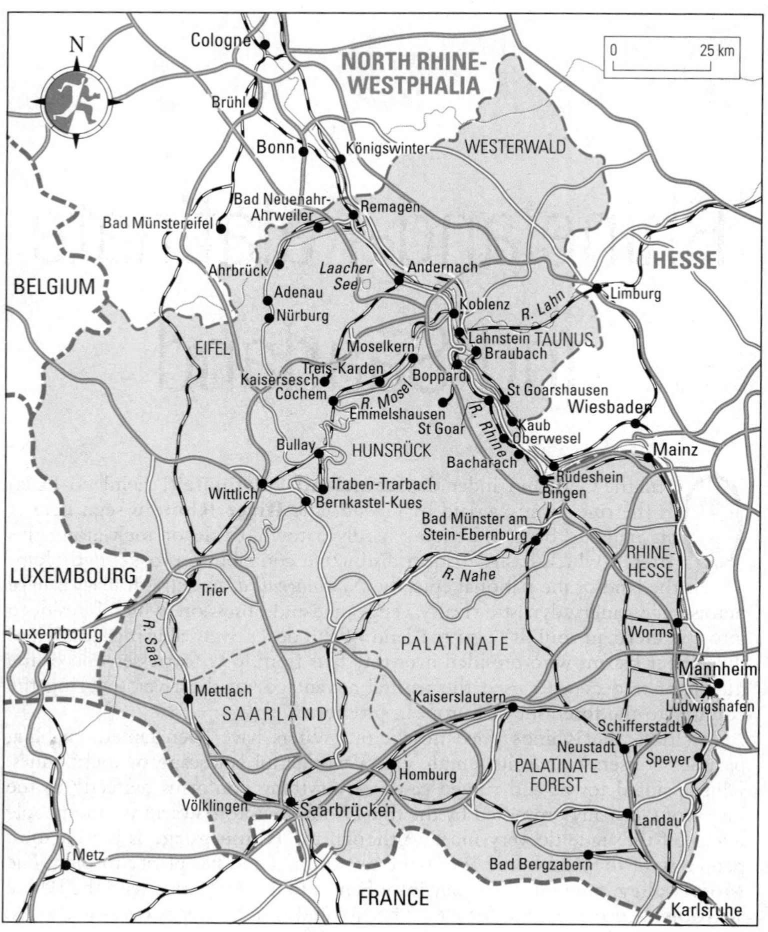

Romans, the French have often regarded the Rhine as the natural limit of their power, and their designs on the region – ranging from the destructive War of the Palatinate Succession launched in 1689, via the Napoleonic grand design, to the ham-fisted attempts to foster an independent state there after World War I – have had a profound impact on European history.

Adjoining Rhineland-Palatinate to the southwest is the miniature province of the **Saarland**. Long disputed between Germany and France because of its natural mineral wealth, it's predominantly an industrial region. From a tourist point of view, it's the least rewarding of all the German Länder, though it does have a few beauty spots, and a vibrant capital in **Saarbrücken**.

As far as **getting around** is concerned, this is one part of Germany where having your own wheels can be of benefit, as there are a few enticing destinations which are only sporadically served by the otherwise excellent public transport network. Despite their associations with over-organized tour groups, the pleasure **steamers** which glide down the great rivers throughout the summer are certainly worth sampling, as they offer – admittedly at a price – far better views and a pleasanter atmosphere than the buses and trains which ply the same routes. **Accommodation**, whether in hotels, youth hostels or campsites, is plentiful, but is best reserved in advance during the high season in the most popular areas.

The Rhine Valley

Inevitably, the **Rhine** itself, and the towns along its banks, are the Land's main tourist draws. Spaced out along the western bank in the southern half of the province are three of Germany's most venerable cities – **Speyer**, **Worms** and **Mainz** – which have all, at one time or another, played a key role in the country's history, the most potent reminder of their status being the mighty Romanesque Dom dominating each city. Beyond Mainz, the Rhine bends westwards and continues its hitherto stately but unspectacular journey. Suddenly, there's a dramatic change – the river widens and swings back to a northerly course, threatening the low banks on either side, while long wooded islands block the view ahead.

This marks the entry to the spectacular **gorge**, which, though it's only a small part of the river's total length of 1320km, is the Rhine of popular imagination. The combination of the treacherous waters, whirlpools and rocky banks lining the sharp twists of the river poses a severe test of navigational skill. Nowadays, this has been considerably eased by the digging of channels to control the movement of the river, but it has inevitably thrown up legends of shipwrecks, sirens and mermaids. The lure of the castles of the medieval robber barons, such postcard-pretty towns as **Braubach**, **Oberwesel**, **St Goar** and **Boppard**, the raw elemental beauty of the landscape itself and the famous wines made from the vines which somehow cling to the lower slopes make for one of Europe's major tourist magnets. Yet the pleasure steamers are still greatly outnumbered by the long, narrow commercial barges, a reminder of the crucial role the river has played in the German economy down the centuries.

Speyer

SPEYER, the smallest and most beautiful of the Rhineland-Palatinate's triumvirate of Imperial cathedral cities, lies in the far southeast of the province. It has regular direct rail links with both Mannheim and Karlsruhe in Baden-Württemberg, though it is on a relatively minor line: to reach other points in Rhineland-Palatinate, it is often necessary to change trains at either Schifferstadt or the sprawling industrial city of Ludwigshafen. In 1990, Speyer celebrated the 2000th anniversary of its foundation as a Roman infantry camp and it's one of the few Rhenish towns to have come through World War II unscathed. Even though its role was once much grander, it stands today as an archetypal episcopal and market town, lively enough never to seem staid, yet not to the extent of spoiling its atmosphere of restrained dignity.

Speyer is a great culinary city with a really marvellous choice of restaurants. It also claims to have invented the Brezel, the crispy salted bread which is such a German favourite, and the main local **festival**, the Brezelfest, is held on the second weekend of July.

Arrival, information and accommodation

Speyer's **Hauptbahnhof** and **bus station** are about ten minutes' walk north-west of the centre, but some buses continue down Bahnhofstrasse to the Altpörtel. The **tourist office** is at Maximilianstr. 11 (April–Oct Mon–Fri 9am–5pm, Sat 10am–3pm, Sun 10am–2pm; Nov–March Mon–Fri 9am–5pm, Sat 10am–noon; ⓣ0 62 32/14 23 92, ⓦwww.speyer.de).

There's a good choice of hotels in the heart of Speyer, some in attractive old buildings. The **youth hostel** is at Geibstr. 5 (ⓣ0 62 32/6 15 97; €16.60/21.80), on the banks of the Rhine a little south of the centre.

Hotels

Domhof Im Bauhof 3 ⓣ0 62 32/1 32 90, ⓦwww.domhof.de. Stylishly designed new hotel in an old courtyard building just in front of the Dom. ❼

Goldener Engel Mühlturmstr. 1a ⓣ0 62 32/1 32 60, ⓕ13 26 95. A modern designer touch has been applied to this historic hotel at the western edge of the city centre, creating a wonderfully distinctive environment. ❻

Graf's Löwengarten Schwerdstr. 14 ⓣ0 62 32/62 70, ⓦwww.graf-hotel.de. Fine middle-range hotel just to the south-west of the city centre. Its wine bar-restaurant (evenings only, closed Sat & Sun) serves both local and international dishes. ❻

Grüne Au Grüner Winkel 28 ⓣ0 62 32/7 21 96, ⓕ29 28 99. Rustic-looking, ivy-covered Gasthof in the north of the city centre. ❸

Kutscherhaus Fischmarkt 5a ⓣ0 62 32/7 05 92, ⓦwww.kutscherhaus-speyer.de. Half-timbered old coaching inn with a top-notch restaurant (closed Wed) and a huge beer garden. ❺

Schlosser Maximilianstr. 10 ⓣ0 62 32/7 64 33. Small budget hotel run in tandem with a café on Speyer's main street. ❹

Trutzpfaff Webergasse 5 ⓣ0 62 32/29 25 29, ⓕ29 26 15. Has a central but quiet location, and an excellent Weinstube (closed Mon) which serves specialities of the Palatinate and vegetarian dishes. ❺

The City

The city itself is easily seen on foot as it has never grown very large; the focal point, as it always has been, is the Dom.

The Dom

Speyer rocketed to a prominent position in the second quarter of the eleventh century, when the Salian dynasty of emperors chose it, alongside Goslar, as their favourite seat. They ordered the construction of a huge new **Dom** (or **Kaiserdom**) as their burial place. This regal building, in the purest Romanesque style, has dominated Speyer ever since; indeed, when it was finished, it was the largest church in the West. At the turn of the twelfth century it was partially rebuilt, notably with the erection of a new stone vault which was far higher than any ever previously attempted. The **towers** were also added, as were the **dwarf galleries** round the exterior which were to become such an essential feature of Rhineland churches. It's easy enough to distinguish the two building phases, as the smooth ashlar of the embellishments contrasts with the rough-hewn stonework of the original. The Dom was badly damaged by French troops in 1689, when Speyer was almost entirely destroyed; half the nave was left in ruins, but it was later brilliantly restored. Only the **westwork**, a romanticized nineteenth-century replacement for the one destroyed by the French, is a let-down, having taken its inspiration from the decorative late

Romanesque style of Worms rather than the austere purity which is the hallmark of the rest of the building.

The interior has been all but stripped of furnishings in order to focus attention on its awesome proportions. Its great glory is the **crypt**: although the earliest part to be built, it remains the largest in Germany, and is justifiably claimed as the most beautiful in the world. With its alternately coloured sandstone pillars and slabbed marble floor, it has an almost Middle Eastern quality. It's divided into three connecting spaces and contains the coffins of four emperors and four kings, among them Rudolf von Habsburg (the first of the dynasty to gain the German throne), who is depicted in a magnificently carved sepulchral slab displayed on the west wall of the burial vault.

In the nineteenth century, an English-style park, the **Domgarten**, was laid out around the Dom, meaning that there's an uninterrupted view of the great building from all sides. Particularly fetching is that from the **Heidentürmchen** (Heathens' Tower) to the east, one of the rare surviving sections of the medieval city wall; this formerly overlooked the Rhine, but the river has since been diverted to the east. Occupying the centre of the former cloisters on the south side is the sixteenth-century shrine of *Christ on the Mount of Olives*; however, the sculptures are pastiches of the originals, the sole survivors of which are kept under the northwest tower.

The Historisches Museum der Pfalz

Diagonally across Domplatz, housed in a triple-towered mock-medieval palace, built in the early twentieth century, is the **Historisches Museum der Pfalz** (Tues–Sun 10am–6pm; €7; Ⓦwww.museum.speyer.de). Highlights of the outstanding archeology department are the so-called Golden Hat of Schifferstadt, a gold-plated Bronze Age cone named after the nearby town where it was found, and the contents of a Celtic prince's grave excavated in Bad Dürkheim. The Roman section includes the *terra sigillate* vessels from Rheinzabern, the largest surviving pieces of pottery of the period from north of the Alps, and a Mithras altar from Neustadt which was dedicated in 325, not long before the introduction of Christianity. Lapidary fragments from churches and Jewish buildings illustrate the medieval history of the region, while the paintings of the Speyer artists Anselm Feuerbach and Hans Purrmann dominate the section devoted to the modern Palatinate.

The building houses two other collections, both covered by the same ticket. In the **Weinmuseum**, every conceivable wine-related object is featured, including several historic presses and what is claimed to be the oldest bottle of grape wine in the world, dating from around 300 AD. The **Domschatzkammer** contains a wonderful array of treasures, the earliest being the Phrygian Omphaloschale from the sixth or seventh century BC, which is still used on special occasions. Other highlights are the burial crowns of four Salian monarchs; a Romanesque holy water vessel from Mainz; the robe and shoes of King Philipp of Swabia; and the jewelled Gothic staff of Bishop Johannes von Dalberg.

The rest of the city

Across Grosse Pfaffengasse, on the northern side of the museum, lies the enclosed heart of the former Jewish quarter, which can be entered from Judengasse. The east wall of the **Synagoge** still stands, but the main surviving monument is the **Judenbad** (April–Oct daily 10am–noon & 2–5pm; €1), a twelfth-century ritual bath-house for women. Seemingly built by the same masons who had recently completed the Dom, it's the oldest and best-preserved example in Germany and a poignant reminder of a vanished culture.

On the northern side of the Dom are the fourteenth-century **Sonnenbrücke**, Speyer's only remaining old bridge, and the **Wirtschaft zum Halbmond**, a seventeenth-century half-timbered inn with a strange polygonal oriel window. On the other side of Hasenpfulstrasse is the **Kloster St Magdalena**, a Carmelite convent whose church has a tastefully understated Baroque interior. The now-canonized Jewish-born philosopher Edith Stein, whom the Nazis gassed at Auschwitz, was a nun here from 1923 to 1931.

Following Grosse Himmelsgasse from the Dom brings you to the **Dreifaltigkeitskirche**, a Protestant example of the many Baroque buildings built in Speyer after the devastation of 1689. It boasts elaborate double galleries, and a painted wooden ceiling illustrating events from the Bible. Further west, along Korngasse, is **St Ludwig**, the church of a thirteenth-century Dominican priory. It contains the only surviving medieval altar front in the Palatinate and the winged late Gothic Bossweiler Altar.

Speyer's main street, **Maximilianstrasse**, forms a dead-straight processional way right across the heart of the city to the Dom, widening towards the end to form a spacious square. Among the colourful Baroque and Rococo buildings which line it are the **Rathaus** (whose interior can usually be visited during normal working hours) and the **Alte Münze**, the former mint. Closing off the western end of the street is the **Altpörtel** (April–Oct Mon–Fri 10am–noon & 2–4pm, Sat & Sun 10am–5pm; €1), a craggy thirteenth-century gateway which is the only other surviving part of the city walls. A graceful arcaded gallery was built on top in the early sixteenth century, while the steep hip roof which finishes it off was added a couple of hundred years later. From the top, there's a wonderful **view** over Speyer and the Palatinate.

Down Gilgenstrasse and across Bartholomäus-Weltz-Platz is the **Gedächtniskirche der Reformation** (or **Retscherkirche**), a heavy neo-Gothic church built at the turn of the twentieth century in honour of the 1529 Diet of Speyer, at which supporters of Luther made their formal protest against the Edict of Worms, thus gaining the name "Protestants" for the first time. A large statue of the reformer dominates the porch; the interior blazes with a complete set of stained-glass windows. A few minutes' walk east at Allerheiligenstr. 9 is the **Feuerbachhaus** (Mon–Fri 4–6pm, Sun 11am–1pm; donation expected), the birthplace of the Romantic painter Anselm Feuerbach, who is chiefly remembered for his sweeping Italianate canvases of mythological scenes. The house is now a wine bar, but upstairs is an exhibition of his paintings and drawings.

South of the Altstadt is the extensive complex of the **Technik Museum Speyer** (daily 9am–6pm; €10.50; Ⓦwww.technik-museum.de). The main exhibition hall, the Liller Halle, is a protected industrial monument built in 1913. It now contains a collection of historic cars, aeroplanes, submarines, trains, fire engines and musical instruments, with the star piece being Antonus AN22, the largest propelled aeroplane in the world. A second building, the Wilhelmsbau (open from 11am), has been decked out in evocation of life at the turn of the twentieth century, with furniture, mechanical musical instruments, uniforms, weapons and 2500 puppets. Also on site are two IMAX cinemas (€7.50, or €15 combined ticket with museum entrance).

Eating and drinking

Few small German cities offer such a variety of places to eat and drink, with the excellent hotel restaurants mentioned above rivalled by several other establishments.

Altpörtel-Café Postplatz 2. Café with rooftop garden in the shadow of the eponymous gateway.
Anglerstubb Zum Binsfeld 6a. Fish speciality restaurant which does its own smoking. Closed Mon.
Backmulde Karmeliterstr. 11. Very classy restaurant offering innovative Mediterranean-style cooking. Closed Sun & Mon.
Café Hindenburg Maximilianstr. 91. Popular traditional coffee house, halfway along the city's main street.
Café Schumacher Wormser Str. 23. This long-established family-run concern is another recommendable choice for *Kaffee und Kuchen* or a light meal. Closed Mon.
Domhof-Brauerei Grosse Himmelgasse 6. Hausbrauerei run in association with the nearby hotel of the same name. It brews light, dark and *Weizen* beers, serves Palatinate speciality dishes and has a large garden.
Maximilian Korngasse 15. Extremely trendy bistro-cum-café, a good choice for breakfast or a snack.
Pfalzgraf Gilgenstr. 26b. Fine traditional and quite moderately priced Gaststätte. Closed Wed evening & Thurs.
Wirtschaft zum Alten Engel Mühlturmstr. 1a. Highly atmospheric restaurant in a vaulted cellar decked out with antique furniture. The food is outstanding, and includes Alsatian as well as local dishes. Evenings only, closed Sun.
Zum Domnapf Domplatz 1. Historic Gasthaus named after the old stone trough in front of the Dom. Its four dining rooms are all tastefully furnished; the food is of a high standard, the fish dishes especially, and the set lunch is a particular bargain. Closed Sun evening & Mon.

Worms

A rich web of fact and myth has been spun around **WORMS**, which lies on the left bank of the Rhine some 50km downstream from Speyer. Originally settled by Celtic tribes and then by the Romans, the city became the heart of the short-lived fifth-century Burgundian kingdom described in the *Nibelungenlied* (see box below). It was a favoured seat of various subsequent royal dynasties, the scene of the weddings of both Charlemagne and Frederick Barbarossa and of the Concordat of 1122 which settled the power struggle between the papacy and the empire. In the Middle Ages Worms achieved great prosperity and was for a while a venue for sittings of the Imperial parliament or **Diet**, most famously that of 1521 at which Luther was declared an outlaw. Unfortunately, much of its magnificence was destroyed in successive wars against the French, but several outstanding

The Nibelungenlied – Germany's national epic

Written at the end of the twelfth century, the **Nibelungenlied** describes the fall and virtual genocide of the Burgundian nation at the hands of King Etzel (Attila) the Hun. This was the culmination of the long vengeance planned by Etzel's wife, the Burgundian princess Kriemhild, in retribution for the murder of her first husband Siegfried, the famed dragon-slayer. The saga is actually a brilliant fusion, with a great deal of imaginative embroidering, of two quite separate episodes in Worms' colourful early history. The Burgundians, originally allies of the declining Roman Empire, settled in Worms in 413, but were driven out by Attila in 436 shortly after they had established their independence from Rome. At the turn of the seventh century, Worms was the residence of the Visigoth princess Brunichildis (the inspiration for Kriemhild's rival Brunnhild), one of two sisters who married kings of different parts of the Merovingian Empire; a subsequent quarrel led to a fratricidal war which claimed the lives of all four leading participants. The great nineteenth-century epic that is **Wagner's** *Ring Cycle* covers similar ground to the *Nibelungenlied*, but is, somewhat ironically, based for the most part on the Nordic versions of the same legends.

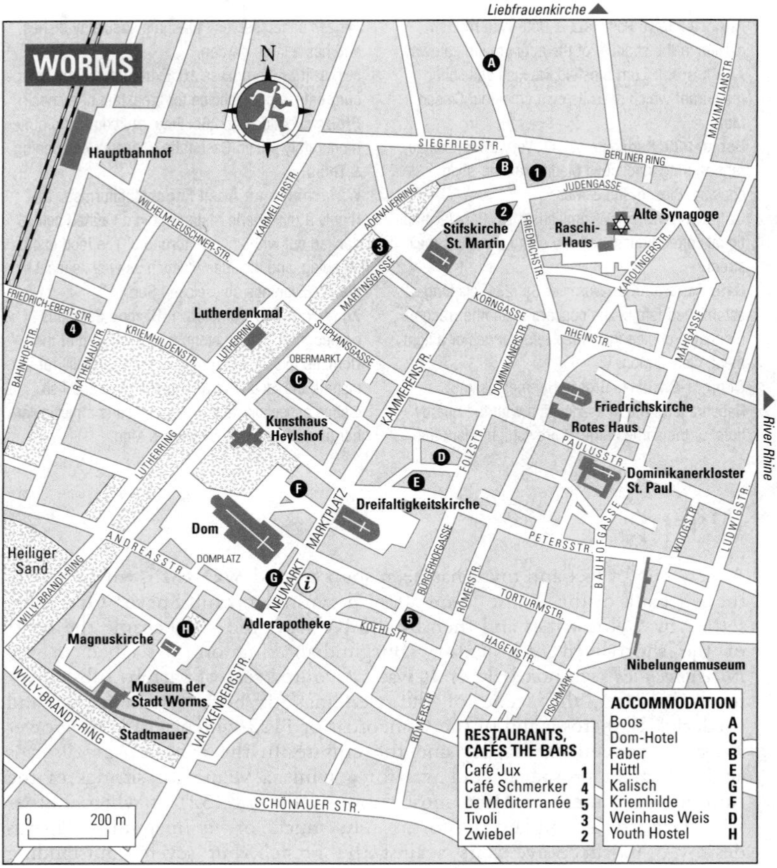

WORMS

RESTAURANTS, CAFÉS THE BARS	
Café Jux	1
Café Schmerker	4
Le Mediterranée	5
Tivoli	3
Zwiebel	2

ACCOMMODATION	
Boos	A
Dom-Hotel	C
Faber	B
Hüttl	E
Kalisch	G
Kriemhilde	F
Weinhaus Weis	D
Youth Hostel	H

monuments remain in the midst of the functional modern city centre which has grown up since World War II. As Worms was formerly home to a large **Jewish community**, earning the nickname "Little Jerusalem", it's appropriate that it preserves the most important reminders to be found in Germany of this once-rich heritage.

Arrival, information and accommodation

Worms' **Hauptbahnhof**, on the main line between Mainz and Mannheim, is northwest of the Altstadt. The **tourist office** is at Neumarkt 14 (April–Sept Mon–Fri 9am–6pm, Sat 10am–3pm; Oct–March Mon–Fri 9am–6pm; ⓣ0 62 41/2 50 45, ⓦwww.worms.de). For nine days in late August and early September, the city celebrates the Backfischfest, a wine **festival** where fried fish is the culinary speciality.

Worms is quite well off for **hotels**; most are reasonably priced for what they offer, but those in the city centre can get oversubscribed. There's a **youth hostel** handily located between the Dom and the Andreasstift at Dechaneigasse 1 (ⓣ0 62 41/2 57 80; €16.60/21.80).

Hotels

Asgard Gutleutstr. 4 ⓣ0 62 41/8 60 80, ⓦwww.asgard-hotel.de. Classy hotel in the southern part of the city. It serves good breakfast buffets, but no other meals. ❻

Boos Mainzer Str. 5 ⓣ0 62 41/94 76 39, ⓕ94 76 38. Budget hotel with restaurant, located a short walk north of the centre. ❹

Dom-Hotel Obermarkt 10 ⓣ0 62 41/90 70, ⓦwww.dom-hotel.de. Typical modern business-class hotel with restaurant. ❻

Faber Martinspforte 7 ⓣ0 62 41/92 09 00, ⓕ92 09 09. Good medium-range hotel with restaurant (closed Mon lunchtime & Wed) at the northern edge of the Altstadt. ❺

Hüttl Petersstr. 5–7 ⓣ0 62 41/9 05 90, ⓕ90 59 43. Pleasant, centrally sited hotel with an adjoining restaurant, *Marktstübchen*. ❹

Kalisch Neumarkt 9 ⓣ0 62 41/2 76 66, ⓕ2 50 73. Moderately priced hotel whose back rooms directly face the Dom's east choir. ❺

Kriemhilde Hofgasse 2–4 ⓣ0 62 41/9 11 50, ⓕ9 11 53 10. Good-value hotel and restaurant (closed Sat) in a quiet location immediately north of the Dom. ❺

Weinhaus Weis Färbergasse 19 ⓣ0 62 41/2 35 00, ⓕ26 71 40. This small, no-frills hotel attached to a wine bar (closed Sun) on an alley just east of the Dom charges the lowest rates in the city centre. ❸

The City

Given the present size of the city, the Altstadt is surprisingly extensive. The main Jewish monuments are at opposite ends, with the Dom providing the expected centrepiece. There are also a few places worth visiting outside the centre, noteably the famous Liebfraumilch vineyards.

The Dom

Foremost among the survivors of Worms' bygone days of glory are the seven city-centre churches, not one of them built later than 1744. By far the largest and most imposing is the **Dom** (or **Kaiserdom**), a huge twelfth-century building which dominates the skyline even from a distance. From outside, it's highly distinctive in appearance, with its two domed choirs and four corner towers; it also displays great unity, with only a few Gothic additions having been made to the original late Romanesque structure.

The **east choir**, the first part to be built, was the prototype for what was to become a distinctive trick of the local school of architecture – although the exterior walls are straight, they are rounded inside. Peering out from the arcades are statues of lions devouring their prey, their terrifying looks apparently intended to frighten off the devil; look out also for the enigmatic figure of a workman (thought to be a self-portrait of the master mason) with a monkey on his shoulder. Even more decorative is the **west choir**, the culmination of the building programme half a century later; with its rose windows, zigzag arcades and rich mouldings it ranks among the most imposing examples of all Romanesque architecture.

On the north side of the nave is the **Kaiserportal**, according to the *Nibelungenlied* the site where Kriemhild and her sister-in-law Brunnhild had a quarrel about who had the right to enter the building first; this led to the murder of Siegfried and the eventual collapse of the Burgundian nation. These days, however, it's the richly decorated Gothic **Südportal** – a veritable Bible in stone – which is the main entrance. Most unusually, the sculptures from its Romanesque predecessor weren't wasted, being placed on the wall immediately indoors.

Balthasar Neumann's huge Baroque **high altar** is an extravaganza in gilded wood and marble, featuring awe-inspired statues of SS Peter and Paul with two angels pointing at the Madonna and Child, who seem to be coming straight towards you. Otherwise the Dom is relatively spartan, no more so than in the dark and eerie **crypt**, the last resting place of five generations of the Salian dynasty, whose eight plain sarcophagi sit in oppressive silence. Off the south aisle is the **Niklauskapelle**, an elegant Gothic chapel divided down the middle by pillars, in the manner of a monastic refectory; it contains a font and a relief of three virgin martyrs. In the north aisle are five large late Gothic **tympana** (a Tree of Jesse and four scenes from the life of Christ) which formerly adorned the now-demolished cloister.

The western city centre

From the Dom, Dechaneigasse leads south to the **Magnuskirche**, the first church in this part of Germany to go over to Protestantism. It dates back to Carolingian times but has been repeatedly extended and altered. Across the square stands the former **Andreasstift**, now housing the **Museum der Stadt Worms** (Tues–Sun 10am–5pm; €2). The Romanesque church forms an appropriate setting for a display of medieval sacred art; the collegiate buildings contain Roman and Frankish antiquities, an unexpected collection of Coptic textiles, plus the Lutherzimmer, which details the events of the 1521 Diet and includes some of Luther's original writings. Just behind the Andreasstift is a surviving section of the **Stadtmauer**, with the still-intact **Andreastor**.

A modern ring road parallels the course of the wall. At its extreme southwest corner is the **Heiliger Sand**, the oldest Jewish cemetery in Europe and the most visible reminder, in its leafy tranquillity, of the influential Jewish community of Worms. The **tombstones**, which have many beautiful inscriptions and carvings, date back as far as 1076. For reasons which have never been explained, they do not have the customary orientation to Jerusalem, the sole exception being that of the martyr Rabbi Meir von Rothenburg at the lowest point of the grounds. Although it's a miracle that the cemetery survived the Third Reich, its situation outside the old walls, and the neglected appearance of the twisted and sunken tombstones, are not as sinister as they appear. Jewish tradition believed that contact with the dead, who should be allowed to rest in peace, caused impurity; hence they themselves chose to locate their cemetery at the opposite end of town from where they lived and to eschew the Gentile fashion for tending graves. The absence of tombstones later than 1940 likewise has nothing to do with Nazi depredations: by 1911, the cemetery had become so full that a new burial ground was created elsewhere, with only long-established families allowed to use the Heiliger Sand.

On the north side of the Dom, just up Lutherring from the Heiliger Sand, is the **Heylshofgarten**, occupying the site of the now-vanished Imperial palace. In April 1521 this was the scene of the Diet at which Luther refused to renounce his views; he was forced to go into exile and the Reformation was set in motion. Within the park is the **Kunsthaus Heylshof** (May–Sept Tues–Sun 11am–5pm; Oct–April Tues–Sat 2–4pm, Sun 11am–4pm; €2.50), a foundation established by the leading family in Worms' nineteenth-century leather trade. Their exquisite collection of fine and applied arts includes a colourful array of medieval stained glass; a tender *Madonna and Child* by Rubens, along with several of his modellos; a large number of seventeenth-century Dutch cabinet pictures; and a statue of *Adam* by the sixteenth-century Worms sculptor Conrad Meit, one of the few German artists to adopt the full-blooded Italian Renaissance style.

Across the Lutherring directly opposite is the nineteenth-century **Lutherdenkmal**, the largest-ever monument in honour of the Reformation. The bronze figure of Luther is flanked by Frederick the Wise of Saxony and Philip the Magnanimous of Hesse, the two powerful princes whose support made the Reformation a practical reality; behind stand the two scholars,

Johannes Reuchlin and Philipp Melanchthon. The remaining male figures are the main precursors of Protestantism – Petrus Waldus, John Wycliffe, Jan Hus and Girolamo Savonarola; the seated women represent the first German cities to adopt the new faith.

The eastern city centre

On the eastern side of the Dom on Neumarkt is the **Adlerapotheke**, a Baroque town house and pharmacy which is one of the few surviving examples of the Baroque architecture which blossomed in Worms following its destruction in the War of the Palatinate Succession. Also from this period is the nearby **Dreifaltigkeitskirche**, but, although it preserves its handsome frontage, the interior was modernized after being burnt out in World War II. North along Kammerer Strasse is the Romanesque **Stiftskirche St Martin**, whose red sandstone walls have recently been stripped of their whitewash. Saint Martin was supposedly once imprisoned in a dungeon underneath this church.

Just east of here is the old Jewish quarter, centred on Judengasse. The **Alte Synagoge** (daily April–Oct 10am–12.30pm & 1.30–5pm; Nov–March 10am–noon & 2–4pm; free) was reduced to ruins on *Kristallnacht* and further damaged by World War II bombing, but was rebuilt using the old stones and rededicated in 1961; it's occasionally used for worship, mostly by the American army's Jewish personnel. The main part of the synagogue was built in 1174–75 in a late Romanesque style, probably by the same masons as were then working on the Dom, and was for the use of men only. An extension for the use of women, featuring the new pointed arch, was added in 1212, at right-angles to the existing structure. Adjoining the synagogue is the Talmudic teaching room known as the **Raschi-Kapelle**, while in the precincts is the underground **Mikwe** or ritual bath house (both same times; free). In the **Raschi-Haus**, a former school, meeting house and dance hall, is the **Jüdisches Museum** (Tues–Sun 10am–12.30pm & 1.30–5pm; €1.50), with an extensive collection detailing the history of the Jews of Worms.

Further along Judengasse is another well-preserved section of the city wall, with the **Raschiturm** and the **Friesenspitze**. South of here, Karolingerstrasse leads to the junction of Rheinstrasse and Römerstrasse, on which is the dignified Lutheran Baroque **Friedrichskirche**. Beside it stands the **Rotes Haus**, the only surviving Renaissance town house in Worms. A couple of minutes' walk southwest brings you to the **Dominikanerkloster St Paul**, which has a rough sandstone Romanesque church. Although the present nave was rebuilt in the Baroque era, the building as a whole, and in particular the chancel and triple-towered westwork, is self-evidently a miniaturized version of the Dom. The exotic-looking dome appears to have been based on Crusaders' descriptions of Middle Eastern architecture. Other surviving parts of the city walls, including the **Burgerturm**, the **Torturm** and **Lutherpförtchen**, are located just to the east. Together with the relatively discreet modern extension, they now contain the **Nibelungenmuseum** (Tues–Thurs, Sat & Sun 10am–5pm, Fri 10am–10pm; €5.50; Ⓦwww.nibelungenmuseum.de), a hi-tech multimedia presentation on the great literary epic.

Outside the centre

Because the centre lies about a kilometre inland, visitors to Worms often fail to realize that the city is actually on the banks of the Rhine. It's well worth walking along Rheinstrasse to the **Torturm**, a massive gateway which straddles the **Nibelungenbrücke** over the river. This Historicist extravaganza was built as recently as 1900, but coming into town by the B46 road gives the impression of entering some mysterious medieval world. Below the gateway, the bronze **Hagenstandbild** illustrates the scene from the *Nibelungenlied* when the villainous Hagen hurls the cursed treasure of the Nibelungen into the Rhine just after he has murdered Siegfried.

Just ten minutes' walk from the centre in the northern suburbs is the Gothic **Liebfrauenkirche**. The church, of cathedral-like dimensions, with multicoloured stonework and fantastical towers, is set in the **vineyards** from which *Liebfraumilch*, which was first produced here, takes its name. The wine's reputation has been tarnished by the sickly sweet versions that are hugely popular abroad, particularly in the UK. At its best, however, it is a product that fully justifies its official status as a quality wine: *Blue Nun* and *Madonna* are the best-known labels.

Eating and drinking

From a gastronomic point of view, Worms does not match Mainz or Speyer. Nonetheless, there's a wide choice of places to eat and drink.

Café Jux Judengasse 3. Trendy café-bar with beer garden.
Café Schmerker Wilhelm-Leuschner-Str. 9. Worms' most elegant café and cake shop, whose speciality is known as *Wormser Nibelungenschätze*.
Hagenbräu Am Rhein 3. Hausbrauerei directly overlooking the Rhine; it brews light, dark and various seasonal beers and serves full meals.
Kolb's Biergarten Am Rhein 1. Cosy Gaststätte with beer garden located right alongside the above, serving the products of Mannheim's Eichbaum brewery.
Le Mediterranée Kranzbühlerstr. 1. The best and priciest restaurant in the city centre, the cooking showing both French and Italian touches. Closed Tues.
O'Shea Rheinstr. 54. An absolutely genuine Irish pub, housed in a grand Romantic-era building between the centre and the Rheinbrücke. Evenings only, with live music on Fri & Sat.
Tivoli Adenauer-Ring 4. First-rate and not too expensive Italian restaurant. Closed Mon.
Zwiebel Kämmererstr. 77. There's a bar on the ground floor, an internet café upstairs. Evenings only.

Mainz

"The capital of our dear Fatherland" was how Goethe styled **MAINZ**, though this 2000-year-old city, situated by the confluence of the Rhine and Main, 40km north of Worms, has never officially held such a position. Mainz's importance developed in the mid-eighth century, thanks to the Englishman Saint Boniface, who raised it to the main centre of the Church north of the Alps. Later, the local archbishop came to be one of the most powerful princes in the Holy Roman Empire, holding Electoral rank and having the official title of Archchancellor, in addition to his ecclesiastical role as Primate of Germany. Further kudos was gained courtesy of Mainz's greatest son, the inventor **Johannes Gutenberg** (see p.445), whose revolutionary developments in the art of printing made a colossal impact on European civilization. Since the Napoleonic period – which saw Mainz for a time become the French city of Mayence – it has never managed to recover its former status, while its strategic location inevitably made it a prime target of World War II bombers. Nonetheless, it's now Land capital of the Rhineland-Palatinate and is an agreeable mixture of old and new.

Arrival, information and accommodation

Mainz's **Hauptbahnhof** is situated just beyond the northwestern edge of the Altstadt. The **tourist office** (Mon–Fri 9am–6pm, Sat 10am–3pm; ⓣ0 61

31/28 62 10, ⓦwww.info-mainz.de) is in the Brückenturm am Rathaus at the corner of Rheinstrasse. Rhine **cruises** depart from in front of the Rathaus (March–Oct only). You'll also find the K-D Linie offices here (ⓣ0 61 31/2 45 11, ⓦwww.k-d.com).

Mainz is a relatively expensive city for accommodation. There's a handy concentration of **hotels** around the Hauptbahnhof, but this is the most unsalubrious part of the city, and it's far pleasanter to stay in the Altstadt. Detailed information on all the city's hotels can be found on the tourist office website. The **youth hostel** (ⓣ0 61 31/8 53 32; €16.60/21.80) is situated 2km east of the centre at Otto-Brunfels-Schneise 4 in the wooded heights of Am Fort Weisenau; catch bus #61 or #62.

Hotels

Austria Kaiserstr. 20 ⓣ0 16 31/27 02 70, ⓕ27 02 71 10. Modern and recommendable hotel with a conveniently central location. 6

Cityhotel Neubrunnenhof Grosse Bleiche 26 ⓣ0 16 31/23 22 37, ⓦwww.cityhotel-neubrunnenhof.de. This hotel has an excellent city-centre location, a stone's throw from the Landesmuseum. 6

Favorite Parkhotel Karl-Weiser-Str. 1 ⓣ0 16 31/8 01 50, ⓦwww. favorite-mainz.de. The most attractive of the city's luxury hotels, with a pleasant setting at the edge of the Stadtpark, just to the south of the Altstadt. It has an extensive bathing complex, a fine upmarket restaurant (closed Sun evening & Mon) and a beer garden. 9

Hof Ehrenfels Grebenstr. 5–7 ⓣ0 16 31/9 71 23 40, ⓦwww. hof-ehrenfels.de. Small hotel with

Weinstube (evenings only) in an atmospheric Altstadt location. ❻

Schwan Liebfrauenplatz 7 ⓣ0 16 31/14 49 20, ⓦwww.mainz-hotel-schwan.de. This newish venture in a sixteenth-century building is an adjunct to Mainz's oldest wine bar, the *Alt-Deutsche-Weinstube* (evenings only), a popular establishment serving inexpensive daily dishes; *Specht*, the city's oldest Gaststätte (closed Mon lunchtime), which is right alongside at Rotekopfgasse 2, is under the same management. During the daytime, entry is usually via the back of the building. ❼

Stadt Coblenz Rheinstr. 49 ⓣ&ⓕ0 16 31/6 29 04 44. Hotel in a grand Baroque building which also houses a wine bar, *Weinhaus Wilhelmi*, and a cocktail bar, *Havana*. The location would be excellent were it not for the fact that the front rooms are subject to heavy traffic noise for all but a few hours of the day. ❹

Terminus Alicenstr. 4 ⓣ0 16 31/22 98 76, ⓦwww.hotel-terminus-mainz.de. Moderately priced hotel diagonally opposite the Hauptbahnhof. ❺

Weinhaus Rebstock Leichhofstr. 5 ⓣ0 16 31/23 03 17, ⓕ23 03 18. Occupying an old half-timbered building directly overlooking the Dom, this hotel is run in tandem with a wine bar-restaurant (evenings only, closed Sun & Mon). ❹

The City

Modern Mainz stretches over both sides of the Rhine, but the Altstadt, with all the important sights as well as the best bars and restaurants, is on the western bank. In line with the city's historic importance it occupies a considerable area, though the Dom provides a ready reference point.

The Dom

Rearing high above all the other buildings in the centre of Mainz are the six towers of the massive red sandstone **Dom** (or **Kaiserdom**). A few years ago it celebrated its thousandth anniversary, though little remains from this epoch other than the ground plan, some of the lower masonry and the bronze doors by the north entrance. Most of what can be seen today is twelfth-century Romanesque.

One of the Dom's most singular features – which is a deliberate ploy to emphasize its mass – is that it's completely surrounded by buildings, stuck right up against its walls. The present picturesque group of houses dates from the eighteenth century, but the **St-Gothard-Kapelle**, two storeys high and of a contrasting grey stone, is from the first half of the twelfth century. Once the archbishops' own chapel, it's now the area set aside for private prayer and is entered from the north transept. The Dom's status as an Imperial cathedral, with a special area required for the emperor as well as the clergy, is apparent in the **choirs** at both ends of the building, each flanked by one large and two small towers. What's perhaps less immediately obvious, but a further emphasis of its historical importance, is that it follows the precedent of St Peter's in Rome in being orientated from east to west, the reverse of normal.

The solemn and spacious **interior** for the most part preserves its architectural purity. Above the nave's arcades is a cycle of murals of the life of Christ. Painted in the gentle Nazarene style – which aimed at recapturing the freshness and faith of medieval painting – they're a far more successful adornment than most such well-meaning nineteenth-century attempts at "improving" old churches. However, the interior is remarkable above all for serving as a very superior cemetery for the archbishops. These men were no shrinking violets, commissioning grandiose monuments to themselves which adorn the piers of the nave, forming an unrivalled panorama of funerary sculpture from the thirteenth to nineteenth centuries.

Among the finest is the poignant late fifteenth-century **monument to Adalbert of Saxony**, third from the end on the north side; its youthful subject died before his consecration and is thus not shown in ecclesiastical robes. The same anonymous sculptor made the touching **Holy Sepulchre** in the Magnuskapelle. From early the following century are the most grandiose of all the tombs, those carved by **Hans Backoffen**, one of the outstanding crop of German sculptors of the period, whose work can be seen throughout the city centre. His masterpiece is the **monument to Uriel von Gemmingen**, on the last but one pillar of the north side of the nave; two others by him are directly opposite.

The **Bischöfliches Dom- und Diözesanmuseum** (Tues–Sat 10am–5pm, Sun 11am–5pm; free), laid out in rooms opening off the cloisters, houses the greatest sculptures of all. These are fragments from the demolished rood screen, created around 1240 by the anonymous mason – one of the supreme artistic geniuses of the Middle Ages – known as the **Master of Naumburg** from his later work in the eastern German cathedral of that name. In his carvings here, such as the scenes of the Elect and the Damned, and above all in the *Head with Bandeau*, his uncanny realism and characterization are far in advance of any other sculpture of the time. The adjoining **Domschatzkammer** (same hours; €3) houses, in addition to treasury items, a collection of late Gothic **tapestries**, which look wonderfully fresh following their recent restoration. In addition to seven mid-fifteenth-century courtly scenes of maidens, wild men and fabulous beasts, there's an early sixteenth-century *Tree of Jesse*, and two heraldic designs showing the arms of Cardinal Albrecht von Brandenburg.

The central squares

The spacious central **Markt** alongside the Dom is the scene of markets on Tuesday, Friday and Saturday mornings. Here also is the riotously colourful **Marktbrunnen**, the finest of Mainz's many fountains. A joyful Renaissance concoction, adorned with putti and topped by a statue of the Virgin and Child, it was made in the workshop of Hans Backoffen.

Adjoining the Markt to the east is Liebfrauenplatz, which has been a vast open space since the church from which it took its name was pulled down during the Napoleonic Wars. On the north side of the square is the resplendent pink Renaissance facade of the **Haus zum Römischen Kaiser**, which houses the offices of the **Gutenberg Museum** (Tues–Sat 9am–5pm, Sun 11am–3pm; €3; Ⓦwww.gutenberg.de); the actual displays are in a modern extension behind. The illegitimate son of canon of Mainz, Johannes Gutenberg (1400–68) pioneered the development of moveable type to enable the mass production of books that achieved the beauty and standard of copyists without the hard labour involved. His inventions were tremendously significant, but owing to short-sighted creditors, he became destitute, and had to rely on charitable handouts. The museum is a fitting tribute to the great inventor, making amends for the abysmal treatment he received from the authorities in his own day. Until 1978, Mainz had only the second volume of Gutenberg's most famous work, the **42-line Bible**. Made in the 1450s, it's a gravely beautiful production employing magisterial Gothic lettering. The city then managed to repatriate from America the last of the forty-odd surviving complete versions still in private hands, and this has pride of place in the strong room on the second floor. The basement contains a mock-up of Gutenberg's workshop and printing machines of later dates; elsewhere there are displays of printed books from all around the world.

Across Schöfferstrasse from the Dom is Gutenbergplatz, with the red sandstone **Staatstheater Mainz** and the **Gutenberg-Denkmal**, which bears a statue of the inventor by the Danish Neoclassical sculptor, Bertel Thorwaldsen.

The central streets

Despite war damage, the centre of Mainz, especially around the Dom, contains many fine old streets and squares lined with examples of vernacular building ranging from half-timbered Gothic to Rococo. North of the Dom, the magnificent **Knebelscher Hof** is reminiscent of the Weser Renaissance style of northern Germany, while Kirschgarten and Augustinerstrasse to the south are particularly well preserved. Just off the end of the latter is the sumptuous church of **St Ignaz**, marking the transition from Rococo to Neoclassicism. Outside, a monumental *Crucifixion* group by Hans Backoffen stands over the sculptor's own tomb, which is even more imposing than those he had made for the archbishops. This marks the end of the historic quarter – beyond are the rare survivors of the sleazy red-light district that flourished until a few years ago. The former Markthalle on Holzhofstrasse a little further on is home to the **Museum für Antike Schiffahrt** (Tues–Sun 10am–6pm; free). Here you can watch ongoing restoration work on six Roman warships found under the city some years ago, and also see full-sized conjectural reconstructions.

Ludwigstrasse leads west from the Dom to Schillerplatz and Schillerstrasse, which are lined with impressive Renaissance and Baroque palaces, now offices. Here too is the elaborate modern **Fastnachtsbrunnen**, honouring the annual Carnival festivities, whose celebration here ranks for spectacle second only to Cologne's. Up the hill by Gaustrasse is the fourteenth-century Gothic church of **St Stephan** (daily 10am–noon & 2–5pm). Although a pleasant enough building with a pretty cloister, it's chiefly remarkable for its impressive postwar windows. In 1976, the parish priest persuaded **Marc Chagall**, the great Russian Jewish artist long resident in France, to make a series of stained-glass windows. The theme chosen was reconciliation, symbolizing that between France and Germany, Christian and Jew. There are nine windows in all, luminously brilliant in their colouring and quite astonishingly vibrant for an artist in his nineties; they were finished in November 1984, just a few months before Chagall's death.

Along the Rhine

Most of Mainz's remaining monuments of interest are situated in close proximity to the **Rhine**. The quayside is dominated by the stark black and white lines of the 1970s **Rathaus** by Arne Jacobsen – another impressive modern addition to the city's heritage. Across the road is the so-called **Eiserner Turm** (Iron Tower), once part of the medieval fortifications, now a commercial art gallery; the other surviving city gate, the **Holzturm** (Wooden Tower), is south down Rheinstrasse.

Northwards up the same street is the Baroque **Zeughaus**, behind which is its gabled Renaissance predecessor as the Electoral arsenal, the **Sautanz**; both buildings have been adopted to house the Staatskanzlei. The Zeughaus is also linked to the handsome sandstone **Deutschhaus**, which was built in the 1730s as a commandery of the Teutonic Knights, and since 1951 has been the seat of the Landtag or state parliament. Opposite the entrance, a copy of the **Jupitersäule** – whose original is in the Landesmuseum (see p.447) – has been set up. The nearby church of **St Peter** has a Rococo interior more characteristic of Bavaria than the Rhineland.

On the opposite side of Grosse Bleiche is the **Schloss**, the enormous former palace of the Archbishop-Electors, a superbly swaggering late Renaissance building with a Baroque extension. The once-famous interiors were completely destroyed in the war; in their place is the **Römisch-Germanisches Museum** (Tues–Sun 10am–6pm; free), a rather confusing collection in which copies of famous antiquities mingle with original pieces.

The Landesmuseum Mainz

The **Landesmuseum Mainz** (Tues 10am–8pm, Wed–Sun 10am–5pm; €3, free Sat; Ⓦwww.landesmuseum-mainz.de) occupies the old Imperial stables directly down Grosse Bleiche from the Schloss. Its outstanding **archeology** department has some important Celtic items, including a dog made from coloured glass, but is principally renowned for its Roman antiquities. The largest of these are displayed in a hall dominated by the dismantled original parts of the Jupitersäule, the most important Roman triumphal column in Germany, and a triple-arched triumphal gate. In the **medieval** section, there are some fabulous treasures, notably a tenth-century ivory Madonna from Trier and an eleventh-century fibula in the shape of an eagle which once belonged to a German empress. The next hall displays spectacular fragments from demolished buildings, including the Liebfrauenkirche and the fourteenth-century trading hall or Kaufhaus; the latter is one of only two German secular facades of the era to have survived intact. There are also several sculptures, notably the *Madonna of the Vines*, by an unknown early fifteenth-century local master with a distinctively florid style. The **Baroque** section which follows also has some impressive lapidary remains, as well as figures and sculptural models from the collection of the Electoral court sculptor, Johann Pfaff.

In the gallery at the southeast end of the ground floor are the most important German paintings. They include a cycle of nine canvases of the *Life of the Virgin* from the studio or circle of the mysterious, highly original fifteenth-century Middle Rhenish draughtsman known as **Master of the Housebook**. Also of note are copies of Dürer's celebrated pendants *Adam* and *Eve* by his pupil **Baldung**, *St Jerome* by **Cranach**, and an altar wing of *SS Andrew and Columba* by the **Master of St Bartholomew**, whose companion is in London's National Gallery. Works by an international cast of seventeenth-century artists, including Van Dyck, Jordaens, Guercino and Claude, can be seen in the adjoining rooms and their counterparts upstairs. The upper floors house a variety of other displays, including Jewish liturgical treasures saved from a short-lived prewar museum, ceramics, Expressionist and modern paintings, Jugendstil art (particularly glass) and local history.

Eating, drinking and nightlife

Mainz is unashamedly a **wine** city, boasting more vineyards within its boundaries than any other German municipality. If you fancy a wine crawl, there's an abundance of traditional **Weinstuben** on Liebfrauenplatz, Grebenstrasse, Augustinerstrasse, Kartäuserstrasse and Jakobsbergstrasse; see the hotels section on pp.443–44 for additional recommendations. Some offer full menus, others only a limited choice of snacks and hot dishes, though these are always chosen for their compatibility with the wines served. **Nightlife** is especially lively due to the large number of students in the city.

Weinstuben

Geberts Weinstuben Frauenlobstr. 94. Family-run restaurant close to the Rhine to the north of the city centre with excellent German cooking and a great choice of wines. Closed all day Sat & Sun lunchtime.

Haus des Deutschen Weines Gutenbergplatz 3. High quality and moderately priced restaurant with a huge range of wines from all over Germany.

Löschs Weinstube Jakobsbergstr. 9. Tiny Weinstube which has a short menu, though the portions are generous and the prices low. Daily from 4pm.

Weinhaus Schreiner Rheinstr. 38. Best of the *Weinstuben* for top-notch food at reasonable prices. Open Mon–Fri from 5pm, Sat from 3pm, closed Sun.

Weinhaus Zum Spiegel Cnr of Heiliggrabgasse and Leichhofstrasse. One of the quieter options, occupying a fine old half-timbered house. Closed Sun.

Weinstube Michel Jakobsbergstr. 8. Small establishment offering a wide selection of wines from its own vineyards. Open Mon–Sat from 4pm, closed Sun.

Other restaurants

al Cortile Kartäuserstr. 14. The twelfth-century Kartäuser Hof, Mainz's oldest inn, has been given a new lease of life as an Italian restaurant equipped with a wood-fired pizza oven.
Augustinerkeller Augustinerstr. 26. Something of a cross between a Weinstube and a Bierkeller, and very popular with business visitors and tourists.
Drei Lilien Ballplatz 2 ⓣ0 61 31/22 50 68. Highly rated citadel of French *nouvelle cuisine*; very expensive, though set meals are available. Reservations recommended.
Heiliggeist Rentengasse 2. The beautiful vaulted chambers of the thirteenth-century hospital now house a bistro with an international menu.
Incontro Augustinerstr. 57. Good Italian restaurant in the heart of the Altstadt.
Zum Goldstein Kartäuserstr. 3. Housed in a former brewery, so it's appropriate that it has the best beer garden in the city.
Zum Salvator Grosse Langgasse 4. Excellent Bavarian-style restaurant, an outstation of Munich's Paulaner brewery.
Zur Kanzel Grebenstr. 4–6. Well-regarded Altstadt restaurant serving high-class, fairly pricey meals. Evenings only except Sat, when it's open for lunch; closed Sun.

Cafés and bars

Café dell arte Badergasse 18–22. Pleasant, modish café-bar on a quiet Altstadt street.
Caveau Schillerstr. 11. Entered from the park to the rear, this friendly pub attached to the Institut Francais has live music on Tues and discos at the weekend.
Cuban Bar Kötherhofstr. 2. Has the widest choice of cocktails – more than a hundred in all. Also serves Cuban and Mexican food.
Dom-Café Am Markt 12–14. The oldest and best of the traditional cafés, occupying one of the Baroque pavilions built onto the Dom.
Eisgrub-Bräu Weissliliengasse 1a. Hausbrauerei serving its own light and dark unfiltered beers. As well as full meals it does very good-value buffet breakfasts (9am–noon) and hot and cold lunches (12.15–4pm).
Irish Pub Weissliliengasse 5. Always crowded, with live music every evening. Open daily from 5pm.
Kamin Kapuzinerstr. 8. Has a big open chimney in the middle, and features an unusually wide choice of drinks, including no fewer than 40 malt whiskies, plus nine beers on draught.
Networld Neutorstr. 2. Internet and computer games café with fast connections and printing facilities. Open daily 1pm–1am.
Pieter van Amstel An der Theodor-Heuss-Brücke, Kastel. Bar in a three-masted sailing ship moored to the right bank of the Rhine, offering a great view of the city-centre skyline.
Pomp Grosse Bleiche 29. A favourite haunt of the in-crowd.

Nightclubs

Jazzid Malakoff-Center, Rheinstr. 4. New jazz club with a wide variety of music styles.
KUZ Dagobertstr. 20b. Concert and theatre venue with a disco on Wed and at weekends.
L'Escalier Am Winterhafen 19. Popular chart music disco.
Red Cat Emmerich-Josef-Str. 13. Very much the in-venue at the moment, with music ranging from jazz to rock.
Terminus Industriestr. 13, Mombach. Sparsely decorated warehouse, attracting clubbers from miles around.

Entertainment and festivals

The main **theatre** venue is the Staatstheater Mainz (ⓣ0 61 31/2 85 12 22, ⓦwww.staatstheater-mainz.de) on Gutenbergplatz, which stages both opera and drama. A cultural centre, *Frankfurter Hof*, Augustinerstr. 55 (ⓣ0 61 31/22 04 38, ⓦwww.frankfurter-hof-mainz-online.de), is also worth checking out for music, dance and theatre. On the **classical music** front, look out for concerts by the Mainzer Kammerorchester (ⓦwww.mainzer-kammerorchester.de), whose Mozart performances are particularly renowned.

Other than Carnival (here known *as Fastnacht* and using a far more intelligible dialect than in Cologne), the principal **popular festivals** are the Johannisnacht in mid-June, which includes fishermen's jousts and firework displays; and the Weinmarkt jamboree on the last weekend in August and the first in September.

The Rhine from Bingen to Koblenz

The first stretch of the Rhine gorge, from Bingen to the confluence with the Mosel, is undoubtedly the finest, lined with cute half-timbered towns and an extensive range of castles in various states of repair. In high season, this means a flood of organized tour parties, particularly from the UK, this being the one part of Germany the British have really taken to their hearts. If you must do this part of the Rhine in summer and are on a tight budget, then try and book your accommodation well in advance, or be prepared to commute from elsewhere. In addition to the hotels mentioned in the text, there's a reasonable – if not especially extensive – provision of **private rooms** (❶–❹), bookable via the appropriate local tourist office. Bearing in mind that the true identity of the region has been sacrificed to hard sell, you could do worse than take the **train** through this stretch and admire the best feature – the scenery – in comfort, but it's undeniably more fun to go by **boat**. Although there are no bridges between Bingen and Koblenz, fairly frequent ferry links for passengers enable you to hop from one side of the river to the other without too much difficulty.

Bingen

Despite its imposing setting at the point where the Nahe joins the Rhine, **BINGEN** is generally regarded as something of a poor relation of Rüdesheim on the latter's opposite bank. Nonetheless, its star has been in the ascendant of late because of the burgeoning interest in one of the great female figures of the European Middle Ages, **Abbess Hildegard of Bingen** (1098–1179). Placed in a convent at the age of eight, Hildegard became abbess in 1136 and was the only medieval woman known to have undertaken preaching tours. She wrote visionary depictions of the relationship between God and the world, produced a tract on natural sciences and the art of healing and also wrote songs, canticles

Boat trips along the Rhine

The imperious white vessels of the **K-D Linie** (Rheinwerft, Koblenz; ⓣ02 61/3 10 30, ⓦwww.k-d.com; see also listings in Mainz, Bonn and Cologne) have several sailings each way during the June to September high season; the services thereafter progressively run down, and stop altogether at the end of October, to resume in a skeleton format at Easter or the beginning of April, whichever is the earlier. Prices are far from cheap (Bingen to Koblenz costs €23.20; Mainz to St Goar €26.40). However, day returns are available for only slightly more (€24.50 and €30.50 respectively in the case of the two examples quoted), and you travel free of charge if you can prove that it's your birthday. Eurail is valid, while other rail passes should bring a discount. In addition, a number of smaller companies offer much cheaper sailings along shorter stretches.

Ferry companies and routes

Bingen-Rüdesheimer Fährgastschiffahrt Rheinkai 10, Bingen ⓣ0 67 21/1 41 40, ⓦwww.bingen-ruedesheimer.com; Bingen–St. Goar.
Hebel Linie Rheinallee 35, Boppard ⓣ0 67 42/24 20, ⓦwww.boppard.com/Hebel-Linie; Boppard–Koblenz–Kobern–Gondorf.
Hölzenbein Rheinzollstr. 4, Koblenz ⓣ02 61/3 77 44; Koblenz–Bingen.
Merkelbach Emster Str. 57, Koblenz ⓣ02 61/7 68 10; Koblenz–Braubach.
Rheinschiffahrt Goar ⓣ0 67 71/26 20; St Goarshausen–St Goar.

and the earliest-known morality play. Her canonization was never completed, but she is still widely admired for her music and her holistic writings.

The extensive programme of events marking the 900th anniversary of Hildegard's birth brought a permanent memorial in the form of a wide-ranging display on her life and career in the **Historisches Museum am Strom** (Tues–Sun 10am–5pm; €3), which occupies a converted electricity station towards the western end of the town waterfront. Although presented in an informative manner, it suffers from a lack of any tangible objects associated with Hildegard herself. However, it has obtained on loan from the Diözesanmuseum in Mainz two exquisite carvings of wild vines and hops by the Master of Naumburg, which are the earliest botanically accurate representations in western art and postdate Hildegard by only a few decades. The museum also has a major archeological exhibit, a collection of 66 **surgical instruments** (many of them remarkably similar to those used nowadays) of a Roman army doctor of the second century AD, who was probably based at the fort in Bingen. It includes a complete set of implements for performing operations on the skull, as well as no fewer than thirteen scalpels.

The main historic monument in the town centre is the **Basilika St Martin** overlooking the Nahe, which is actually two churches in one: the original building, an early fifteenth-century collegiate church, and the **Barbarabau**, a double-aisled extension tacked on later the same century to serve for parish use. Additionally, an eleventh-century **crypt** survives from a previous church on the site. In the main church, the side altars have beautiful statues of Saints Barbara and Catherine which are contemporary with the architecture, while the pulpit and ciborium are Baroque, the high altar unashamedly avant-garde. The Barbarabau houses a touching Gothic relief of *The Lamentation* and a colourful Mannerist triptych of scenes from the life of the Virgin.

Towering high above Bingen is **Burg Klopp**, a former castle of the Archbishop-Electors of Mainz. The original fortress was destroyed in 1689 and the ruins were blown up in 1711, so that what can be seen today is very largely a nineteenth-century replica. Housed within the tower, which commands a marvellous view over the Rhine to the Taunus, is the **Heimatmuseum** (April–Oct Tues–Sun 9am–noon & 2–5pm; €0.50), which contains more local finds from the Roman era. Another good vantage point is the **Rupertsberg** above Bingerbrück, the suburb on the opposite side of the Nahe. This is the site of the **Kloster** where Hildegard was abbess, but unfortunately only the cellars plus scanty remains of the church still survive. Although rarely accessible to visitors, the town's best-known monument is the **Mäuseturm**, a former customs tower on an island in the Rhine immediately north of Bingerbrück in which, according to grisly legend, Archbishop Hatto of Mainz was devoured alive by mice after having burned all the local beggars during a famine.

Practicalities

Bingen's **Hauptbahnhof** adjoins the huge rail yards in Bingerbrück; the **Stadtbahnhof** is at the southern edge of the town centre. From outside the latter is the stop from where regular scheduled buses begin the ninety-minute journey to **Hahn airport** (Ⓣ0 65 43/50 92 00, Ⓦwww.hahn-airport.de), a former military base deep in the Hunsrück which has experienced a mushroom growth in the past few years. Under the misleading designation of Frankfurt-Hahn, it's used by Ryanair, and has various special bus links with Frankfurt and other cities. A little further along, at Rheinkai 21, is the **tourist office** (April–Nov Mon–Fri 9am–6pm, Sat 9am–12.30pm; Dec–March Mon–Fri 9am–4pm; Ⓣ0 67 21/18 42 05, Ⓦwww.bingen.de). A good range of **hotels** includes *Römerhof*, Rupertsberg 10 (Ⓣ0 67 21/3 22 48; ❹); *Café Köppel*, Kapuzinerstr. 12 (Ⓣ0 67 21/1 47 70; ❹); *Krone*, Rheinkai 19–20 (Ⓣ0 67 21/1 70 16; ❹); *Martinskeller*, Martinstr. 1 (Ⓣ0 67 21/1 34 75; ❻); and *Rheinhotel*, Hindenburganlage 1 (Ⓣ0 67 21/79 60; ❻–❽). There's a **youth hostel** at Herterstr. 51 (Ⓣ0 67 21/3 21 63) in Bingerbrück, but it's currently closed for repairs and not due to reopen until April 2005. The **campsite** (May–Oct only; Ⓣ0 67 21/1 71 60) is near the Hindenburgbrücke in the incorporated village of Kempten to the south. Bingen's leading **restaurants** are those in the last three hotels listed above, plus *Brunnenkeller*, Vorstadt 60. Adjoining the last-named, at Vorstadt 58, is *Brunnenstübschen*, a cosy little Weinstube; another good place to drink local vintages is *Weinhaus Zum Alten Rathaus*, Rathausstr. 28.

Bacharach

BACHARACH, 10km downstream, was called Baccaracum by the Romans after an altar stone to Bacchus which once stood in the Rhine. This was blown up in 1850 to ease navigation of the river, but parts of the old town wall are still intact and there are plenty of half-timbered houses, particularly around Marktplatz and in Blücherstrasse. The thirteenth-century **Peterskirche** on Marktplatz has both late Romanesque and early Gothic features, and is one of the few medieval churches in Germany with an interior of four tiers. Above rises **Burg Stahleck**, a chunky-looking castle, dating back at least as far as the twelfth century, which was once a seat of the Counts Palatine of the Rhine. It still preserves its keep, battlements and a residential tract. From the overgrown and half-timbered Posthof square there's a good view of the **Wernerkapelle**, the red sandstone frame of a ruined Gothic chapel.

The **tourist office** (April–Oct Mon–Fri 9am–5pm, Sat 10am–4pm; Nov–March Mon–Fri 9am–noon; Ⓣ0 67 43/91 93 03, Ⓦwww.bacharach.de) is at Oberstr. 45. A wide choice of **hotels** includes *Im Malerwinkel*, Blücherstr. 41–45 (Ⓣ0 67 43/12 39; ❷–❺); *Gelber Hof*, Blücherstr. 26 (Ⓣ0 67 43/91 01 00; ❸); *Altkölnischer Hof*, Blücherstr. 2 (Ⓣ0 67 43/13 39; ❹–❼); and *Parkhotel*, Marktstr. 8 (Ⓣ0 67 43/14 22; ❺–❼). All except the first of these have **restaurants**. The **youth hostel** is in Burg Stahleck (Ⓣ0 67 43/12 66; €15.10/18.40), while the **campsite** is at Strandbadweg (Ⓣ0 67 43/17 52).

Kaub

KAUB, a few kilometres north on the opposite bank of the Rhine, was another stronghold of the Counts Palatine, who in 1277 purchased **Burg Gutenfels** above the town, together with the right to levy tolls on passing ships. The present castle is a late nineteenth-century rebuild of the original, and nowadays functions as a hotel (see p.452). Though you can't even enter the grounds unless you're a guest, it's worth following the footpath round the back, which leads to a vantage point offering a magnificent view over the Rhine.

It was at Kaub that Field Marshal Blücher, the Prussian commander who saved the day with his late arrival at the battle of Waterloo, crossed the Rhine during an earlier campaign against Napoleon by ordering the construction of a spectacular pontoon bridge. He's commemorated in the **Blüchermuseum** (April–Oct Tues–Sun 10am–noon & 2–4pm; Nov–March Tues–Sat 10am–noon, Sun 10am–noon & 2–4pm; €2) at Metzgergasse 6, the Baroque town house he used as his headquarters. The rooms are decorated in grand Empire style and are full of military memorabilia from the Napoleonic Wars and old Prussia.

From Kaub's waterfront promenade you get a great view of one of the most famous symbols of the Rhineland, the **Pfalzgrafenstein** or **Pfalz** (April–Sept Tues–Sun 10am–1pm & 2–6pm; Oct, Nov & Jan–April Tues–Sun 10am–1pm & 2–5pm; €2 plus €1.50 for the ferry; note that access is suspended when the river's water level is high; Ⓦwww.burgen-rlp.de). Construction of this white-walled toll fortress, which stands on an islet in the river like a permanently moored ship, was begun in 1326 by order of the Count Palatine Ludwig the Bavarian. Brought up to date in the seventeenth century by the provision of gun emplacements and look-out oriels, the Pfalzgrafenstein continued to serve as a toll-levying station until 1867.

Kaub's **tourist office** (Mon–Fri 8am–noon; Ⓣ0 67 74/2 22, Ⓦwww.tal-der-loreley.de) is in the Rathaus, Metzgergasse 26. The cheapest of several reasonably priced **hotels** are *Weinhaus Bahles*, Bahnstr. 10 (Ⓣ0 67 74/2 58; ❷); and *Deutsches Haus*, Schulstr. (Ⓣ0 67 74/2 66; ❸), which also has a good restaurant. Top of the range in every sense is *Burg Gutenfels* (Ⓣ0 67 74/2 20, Ⓦwww.rhinecastles.com; ❾). There are **camping** facilities at *Am Elsleinband* on Blücherstrasse (Ⓣ0 67 74/5 60).

Oberwesel

OBERWESEL, back on the left bank just to the north, possesses the finest extant fortifications in the Rhineland, a three-kilometre-long **Stadtmauer** which still preserves 16 of its towers from an original total of 21. Unfortunately, the section guarding the riverfront is marred by the proximity of the railway, which runs directly alongside, but the whole ensemble is nonetheless impressive, not least at the hilly northwestern edge, where the fortified church of **St Martin** (popularly known, for obvious reasons, as the "white church") forms an integral part of the municipal defences. At the opposite end of town is a huge fortress, the **Schönburg**, which is now a ruin but still imposing. Below it stands the Gothic **Liebfrauenkirche** (which the locals call the "red church", after the huge red sandstone blocks used to build it). In its airy interior, look out for the St Nicholas altar, on which the saint is shown helping three knights who have been sentenced to death for crimes they didn't commit, saving three sisters who have been forced into prostitution by their father, and protecting passengers on board a ship.

The **tourist office** (Mon–Fri 9am–1pm & 2–6pm; July–Sept Sat 10am–noon; Ⓣ0 67 44/15 21, Ⓦwww.oberwesel.de) is at Rathausstr. 3. There are a couple of **hotels** right alongside: *Weinhaus Weiler*, Marktplatz 4 (Ⓣ0 67 44/70 03, Ⓦwww.weinhaus-weiler.com; ❹); and *Römerkrug*, Marktplatz 1 (Ⓣ0 67 44/70 91; ❹). The best place and most expensive place to stay in town is *Auf Schönburg* (Ⓣ0 67 44/9 39 30, Ⓦww.hotel-schoenburg.com; ❽–❾) within the castle complex. All three of these have recommendable **restaurants**. There's a **campsite** (Ⓣ0 67 44/2 45) just off the B9 road to the north of town, while the **youth hostel** is by the castle at Auf dem Schönberg (Ⓣ0 67 44/9 33 30; €16.60/21.80).

The Lorelei and St Goarshausen

Next stop is **ST GOARSHAUSEN**, which trails along the eastern bank of the Rhine for a couple of kilometres. Just before the entrance to the town is the **Lorelei** (or **Loreley**), the famous outcrop of rock where, according to legend, a blonde woman used to sit combing her hair while she lured passing sailors to watery graves with her eerily compelling song. There's a naff statue at the water's edge to commemorate the legend. The rock itself has been over-hyped – it's impressive, but no more so than dozens of other cliffs in the Rhine gorge. However, there are outstanding views from the top, which, in accordance with a project undertaken in connection with EXPO 2000, has recently been made the focal point of a landscape park. In tandem with this, a brand new multi-media visitor centre, the **Besucherzentrum Loreley** (daily April–Oct 10am–6pm; Nov–March 11am–5pm; €3; Ⓦwww.loreley-touristik.de) has been built. This offers information on a range of topics, including the Lorelei legend and the literature it has inspired, as well as local geology, flora and fauna, Rhine tourism and shipping, and the Rhenish wine industry. Also up here are the *Loreley Freilichtbühne*, an **open-air stage** that is frequently used for rock concerts, and a **campsite**, *Auf der Loreley* (Ⓣ0 67 71/86 26 97, Ⓦwww.loreley-campingplatz.de).

Above St Goarshausen itself is **Burg Katz** (Cat Castle), the fourteenth-century fortress of the Counts of Katzenelnbogen. It was built to rival another castle a few kilometres downstream, which belonged to the Archbishops of Trier and earned the inevitable nickname **Burg Maus** (Mouse Castle) because of its relative puniness. This is now an eagle and falcon station, giving displays of bird flight (March–Oct Mon–Sat at 11am & 2.30pm, Sun 11am, 2.30pm & 4.30pm; €6.50; Ⓦwww.burg-maus.de).

There's an inexpensive **guesthouse**, *Winzerschänke*, on the way from St Goarshausen to the Lorelei at Forstbachstr. 38 (Ⓣ0 67 71/3 37; ❷). **Hotels** include *Deutsches Haus*, Wellmicher Str. 7 (Ⓣ0 67 71/26 17; ❸); *Colonius*, Am Rheinufer (Ⓣ0 67 71/26 04, Ⓦwww.hotel-colonius.de; ❸–❺); and *Pohl's Rheinhotel Adler*, Bahnhofstr. 6 (Ⓣ0 67 71/26 13; ❻). The *Weinwoche* is during the second and third weeks in September, and there are other **wine festivals** at the end of September and during the third weekend in October.

St Goar

A ferry will take you back across to the west bank of the Rhine and **ST GOAR**, which is slightly prettier and more touristy than its counterpart. Looming above town is the enormous **Burg Rheinfels** (daily April–Sept 9am–6pm; Oct 9am–5pm; Ⓦwww.burgen-rlp.de; €3) which, until the French blew it up in 1797, was one of the most powerful fortresses on the Rhine. It was founded in 1245 by Count Dieter von Katzenelnbogen, who wanted to look after his Rhine toll-collecting racket, and just ten years later withstood a 9000-man siege by soldiers of the Alliance of Rhenish Towns. During the sixteenth and seventeenth centuries the Landgraves of Hesse extended what was already a formidable castle into an enormous fortification complex which was to prove virtually impregnable: it was the only Rhineland castle that the French were unable to take during the War of the Palatinate Succession. In 1796 the castle surrendered to the troops of Napoleon without a shot being fired, and over the next three years the French did their best to demolish it. Today, the medieval outline can still be seen and you can walk through the underground passages of the later battlements. Models in the **Heimatmuseum** (April–Sept 9.30am–noon & 1–5pm; admission included in Burg entrance fee), which is housed in a rebuilt section, show how the place looked before it was destroyed.

St Goar's **tourist office** is at Heerstr. 86 (May–Sept Mon–Fri 8am–12.30pm & 2–5pm, Sat 9.30am–noon; Oct–April Mon–Fri 8am–12.30pm & 2–4.30pm; Ⓣ0 67 41/3 83, Ⓦwww.st-goar.de). There are plenty of **hotels** in the town centre, including *Germania*, Heerstr. 47 (Ⓣ0 67 41/16 10; ❸); *Zur Post*, Bahnhofstr. 3 (Ⓣ0 67 41/3 39, Ⓦwww.hotelzurpost-online.de; ❸); and *Zum*

Goldenen Löwen, Heerstr. 82 (ⓣ0 67 41/16 74; ❸–❻). If you want to splash out, try the *Schlosshotel* in the Burg Rheinfels complex (ⓣ0 67 41/80 20, ⓦwww.schlosshotel-rheinfels.de; ❼). All of these hotels also have **restaurants**. The **youth hostel** is just north of the town centre at Bismarckweg 17 (ⓣ0 67 41/3 88; €11.80). Of the two **campsites**, *Friedenau* is west of town at Gründelbachstr. 103 (ⓣ0 67 41/3 68), while *Loreleyblick* is directly across the Rhine from the Loreley at An der Loreley 29–39 (ⓣ0 67 41/20 66, ⓦwww.camping-loreleyblick.de).

Boppard

At **BOPPARD**, 14km downstream from St Goar, the Rhine gorge starts to level out and the valley landscape becomes a gentler one of rounded, vine-covered slopes. The town benefits enormously from an unspoiled and relatively quiet Rhine promenade running along its entire length, having forced the rail authorities to lay the tracks on the opposite side of the centre, instead of their customary position by the river.

Boppard's dominant building is the late Romanesque **Severuskirche** on Marktplatz. A twin-towered structure, brightly painted in white and yellow, it was built during the thirteenth century to house the remains of Saint Severus, Bishop of Ravenna. Contemporary with the church are the wall paintings illustrating the life of the saint, and the poignant triumphal cross. The squat Gothic **Karmelitenkirche**, near the Rhine quay, has elaborate fifteenth-century choir stalls, a couple of seventeenth-century altars and various tombs of local bigwigs. At the east entrance is a recess which houses the fourteenth-century *Traubenmadonna*. Traditionally, local vine growers place the first ripe bunch of grapes of the year by the statue and leave it there until it withers away.

At the end of Kirchgasse, which is just off Oberstrasse (Boppard's main street), are the remains of the Roman **Stadtmauer**, which has weathered the years remarkably well. Four watchtowers survive of the 28 which guarded the military camp of Baudobirga, laid out in the fourth century, on the site of present-day Boppard. Remains of more recent fortifications can be seen at the end of Binger Gasse. The **Binger Tor** was built during the Middle Ages and has survived more or less intact, bar the odd bit of crumbling here and there. Between Burgplatz and Rheinallee is the **Alte Burg**, a castle and residence built by the Archbishops of Trier to consolidate their grip in the area. The central keep, with its apertures for the pouring of boiling oil, molten lead and the like, was built around 1327, while the more civilized-looking wings were added during the seventeenth century. These days the building houses the **Museum der Stadt Boppard** (April–Oct Tues–Sun 10am–noon & 2–5pm; free). Part of this is devoted to Michael Thonet, a son of Boppard, who, during the early nineteenth century, perfected the technique of laminating wood and earned himself a fortune for his highly distinctive furniture, of which there is a fine collection on display.

At the northern end of town, a **chairlift** (€4 single, €6 return) ascends to the belvedere known as **Vierseenblick** (Four Lakes View) because the only parts of the Rhine which are visible are four seemingly separate stretches of water. A short waymarked walk away is another viewpoint, the **Rheinschleife**, which commands a magnificent panorama over the Rhine's most spectacular bend.

Practicalities

Boppard's **Bahnhof** is a few minutes' walk to the northwest of the town centre. This is a terminus of the **Hunsrückbahn**, Germany's steepest standard-gauge line, which passes through five tunnels and over two viaducts in the spectacular ascent to Buchholz, climbing 300m in 8km. It then continues for just one more stop, terminating at Emmelshausen. The **tourist office** is in the Rathaus on Marktplatz (April–Sept Mon–Fri 8am–5.30pm, Sat 9am–noon; Oct–March Mon–Fri 8am–4pm; ⓣ0 67 42/38 88, ⓦwww.boppard.de). There are several inexpensive **hotels** in the town centre, the most recommendable being the Anglo-German *Ohm Patt*, Steinstr. 30 (ⓣ0 67 42/23 66; ❸); and *Weinhaus Sonnenhof*, Kirchgasse 8 (ⓣ0 67 42/32 23, ⓦwww.hotel-weinhaus-sonnenhof.de; ❸–❺), which also has a good restaurant. Of the more upmarket waterfront hotels, best value is the German-American *Günther*, Rheinallee 40 (ⓣ0 67 42/8 90 90, ⓦwww.hotelguenther.de; ❹–❻), many of whose rooms have balconies offering grandstand views of the river. Top of the range is *Bellevue Rheinhotel*, Rheinallee 41 (ⓣ0 67 42/10 20, ⓦwww.bellevue-boppard.de; ❼–❾), which has the two leading **restaurants** in town. There are **camping** facilities at *Sonneck* (ⓣ0 67 42/21 21), just north of town on the B9 right next to the Rhine.

Braubach

On the right bank of the Rhine 12km downstream from Boppard is **BRAUBACH**. It's a typical Rhenish village with several **hotels**, including *Weinhaus Wieghardt*, Marktplatz 7 (ⓣ0 26 27/2 42; ❹) and the outstanding *Zum Weissen Schwanen*, Brunnenstr 4 (ⓣ0 26 27/98 20, ⓦwww.zum-weissen-schwanen.de; ❻), a seventeenth-century Weinhaus with an attached fourteenth-century mill; note that the restaurant is open evenings only.

Set in the hills a good half-hour's walk above the town, the **Marksburg** (guided tours daily Easter–Oct 10am–5pm; Nov–Easter 11am–4pm; €4.50; ⓦwww.marksburg.de) is the only medieval castle on this stretch of the Rhine, other than the Pfalzgrafenstein, to escape destruction by the French. Being an absolutely genuine original, it looks far more impressive than the often heavy-handed nineteenth-century reconstructions elsewhere in the valley. Most of the fortress, including the turreted sandstone keep, was built between the twelfth and fourteenth centuries with a few additional defensive features added in the seventeenth century. Inside there's a big collection of weapons from the Middle Ages, including some extremely unpleasant instruments of torture. The Marksburg preserves its chapel, kitchen, wine cellars and armoury, and also has the only medieval botanic garden in Germany.

Koblenz

It's appropriate that the name of **KOBLENZ** derives from the Latin word for confluence, as it was the Romans who first recognized the favourable properties of the site at the point where the Mosel flows into the Rhine, establishing a settlement there in 14 AD. Nowadays, the town has become one of Germany's major tourist centres, profiting from its ready access to the two great river valleys and the hill ranges beyond. Koblenz itself polarizes opinion – some enjoy its relaxed, rather faded charm; others find it smug and boring. The connection with tourism actually has deep roots, as it was in Koblenz in 1823 that **Karl Baedeker** began publishing his famous series of guidebooks which aimed at saving travellers from having to depend on unreliable and extortionate local tour guides for information.

Arrival, information and accommodation

The **Hauptbahnhof** and **bus station** are side by side, to the southwest of the Altstadt. Between them, on Bahnhofplatz, is the **tourist office** (May–Sept Mon–Fri 9am–7pm, Sat & Sun 10am–7pm; Oct Mon–Fri 9am–6pm, Sat & Sun 10am–6pm; Nov–April Mon–Fri 9am–6pm, Sat & Sun 10am–2pm; ⓣ02 61/3 13 04, ⓦwww.koblenz.de). There's another branch in the Rathaus (same times, but open Nov–March until 6pm on Sat; ⓣ02 61/13 09 20) on Jesuitenplatz. The **ferry** to Ehrenbreitstein departs from Konrad-Adenauer-Ufer; its Mosel counterpart runs in summer only from the pier west of Deutsches Eck.

Koblenz offers a huge choice of accommodation, with **hotels** in every category, most of them competitively priced in terms of what they offer. The **youth hostel** (ⓣ02 61/97 28 70; €15.10/18.40) in Festung Ehrenbreitstein – buses #7, #8, #9 and #10 go closest – must rate as one of the most enticing in Germany. There's a **campsite** at Lützel, directly opposite Deutsches Eck (April to mid-Oct; ⓣ02 61/8 27 19).

Hotels and pensions

Brenner Rizzastr. 20–22 ⓣ02 61/91 57 80, ⓦwww.hotel-brenner.de. Elegant, beautifully furnished hotel with garden, located between the Hauptbahnhof and the Altstadt. ❼

Diehl's Am Pfaffendorfer Tor 10, Ehrenbreitstein ⓣ02 61/9 70 70, ⓦwww.diehls-hotel.de. Koblenz's leading hotel is right by the Rhine, and commands wonderful views. Its facilities include thermal baths, a sauna and solarium, and there's a first-rate restaurant, *Rheinterrasse*. ❼

Im Stüffje Hohenzollernstr. 5 ⓣ02 61/91 52 20, ⓦwww.handicap-hotel.de. A fine mid-range hotel with restaurant (Mon–Fri only), just round the corner from Brenner. ❻

Jan van Werth Van-Werth-Str. 9 ⓣ02 61/3 65 00, ⓕ3 65 06. Good-value hotel between the Hauptbahnhof and Altstadt. ❹

Kleiner Riesen Kaiserin-Augusta-Anlagen 18 ⓣ02 61/30 34 60, ⓕ16 07 25. Fine traditional hotel on the right-bank waterfront. ❻

Kornpforte Kornpfortstr. 11 ⓣ02 61/3 11 74, ⓕ3 11 76. Medium-range hotel with *Weinstube* in the heart of the Altstadt. ❺

Sessellift Obertal 22, Ehrenbreitstein ⓣ02 61/7 52 56. One of a number of inexpensive options in the right-bank suburb. Its restaurant has Indian and Italian menus, as it has chefs of both these nationalities. ❸

The town centre

The place to begin a tour of Koblenz is the **Deutsches Eck**, where the Mosel flows into the Rhine. In 1897, a colossal equestrian monument in the heroic taste of the time was erected here to Kaiser Wilhelm I. It was destroyed in World War II, but the base, itself a pompous structure with over a hundred steps, was rebuilt and piously dedicated to the unification of Germany. After much soul-searching, a copy of the statue was re-erected in 1993 in belated celebration of the achievement of this.

Close by is the largely twelfth-century Romanesque collegiate foundation of **St Kastor**, whose imposing facade has twin towers with characteristic "bishop's mitre" roofs. Inside, look out for the elaborate **keystones** of the Gothic vault, especially the one showing the Virgin and baby Jesus in a boat. Also of note are a fifteenth-century *Madonna and Child* in the south aisle, and the elaborate **wall tombs** of the Trier archbishops Kuno and Werner von Falkenstein in the chancel. There's a good view of the church from the floral garden of the adjacent **Deutschherrenhaus**, which now contains the **Ludwig-Museum** (Tues–Sat 10.30am–5pm, Sun 11am–6pm; €2.50), an important collection of (predominantly French) modern art.

The Rhine bank is today largely given over to tourist facilities; the curious old crane, the **Rheinkran**, now a restaurant, overlooks the waterfront. Only a few monuments of Koblenz's Altstadt, which borders on the Mosel, remain; they're rather over-restored in the romantic image of old Germany, with the exterior walls painted in bright colours, but are undeniably picturesque. By the riverside is the **Deutscher Kaiser**, a sixteenth-century tower house which also is now a restaurant. To the rear is Florinsmarkt, with the Romanesque-Gothic **St Florin**, now a Protestant parish church, the **Schöffenhaus**, a pretty little orange building with corner turrets, and the **Altes Kaufhaus**. This last building now houses the **Mittelrhein-Museum** (Tues–Sat 10.30am–5pm, Sun 11am–6pm; €4; Ⓦwww.mittelrhein-museum.de), a fairly miscellaneous collection of paintings, sculptures and antiquities. There are a few Gothic and Renaissance works, including an *Adoration of the Magi* by the Augsburg painter **Jörg Breu** which unashamedly plagiarizes a portrait by his fellow-citizen, Holbein the Elder, for the figure of one of the kings. Upstairs are many works by one of Germany's most accomplished Rococo painters, **Januarius Zick**, who eventually settled in Koblenz.

Further along the Mosel bank is the **Alte Burg**, altered to a Renaissance palace and now housing the municipal library, but originally constructed to defend the fourteenth-century **Balduinbrücke**. Turning away from the river, you come to **Münzplatz**, which still preserves the mint master's house. Also in the square is the mansion birthplace of the wily Habsburg statesman **Clemens von Metternich**, high priest of the theory (which was to dominate nineteenth-century politics) that the key to a peaceful Europe lay in maintaining a balance of power among the main states. His peak of influence came during his dominant hosting role at the Congress ofVienna in 1815, which laid down the structure of post-Napoleonic Europe; ironically, his native town was given to Prussia – arch-rival of his adopted Austria – as a result.

Down the pedestrian precinct at the intersection of Löhrstrasse and Markstrasse there's a fine grouping of four houses, each with ornamental oriel windows. Left from here is another large square, Plan, behind which are the exotic Baroque onion-shaped spires of the **Liebfrauenkirche**, a handsome if diffuse church with a galleried Romanesque nave and a Gothic chancel. Just beyond stands the **Rathaus**, incongruously housed in a cavernous former Jesuit college.

In the late eighteenth century, Koblenz was expanded to the south in the form of a planned Neoclassical town. The Archbishop-Electors of Trier moved their court here, centred on the huge **Schloss**; three years after its completion, the Elector fled in the wake of Napoleon's advance, never to return. The buildings were gutted during the last war and now serve as offices. A more lasting memento of the period is the stately **Theater** fronted by an obelisk on Deinhardplatz.

The outskirts

Across the Rhine lies **EHRENBREITSTEIN**, with the original **Residenz** of the Electors, designed by Balthasar Neumann. Looming high above is the vast **Festung** (mid-March to mid-Nov daily 9am–5pm, €1.10, €3.10 including Landesmuseum). One of the largest fortresses in the world, this has an impressive set of defences which the Prussians painstakingly and quite needlessly rebuilt over a ten-year period after Koblenz passed into their hands. Commanding memorable panoramic views of the city and its two great rivers, the Festung is now home to the youth hostel and the **Landesmuseum Koblenz** (open from 9.30am). The latter contains displays on the local wine trade and other industries, but the star exhibit is the punningly named *Vogel Greif* (bird of prey), a **cannon** made for a sixteenth-century Archbishop-Elector of Trier, Richard von Greiffenklau. In season, there's an expensive **chairlift**

(€4.20 single, €5.80 return) to the Festung; otherwise, follow the main road along the shore of the Rhine until you come to a path which snakes upwards.

At Koblenz's southernmost extremity, reachable by bus #650, is **Schloss Stolzenfels** (Tues–Sun: Easter–Sept Tues–Sun 9am–6pm; Oct, Nov & Jan–March Tues–Sun 10am–noon & 2–4pm; €2.50; Ⓦwww.burgen-rlp.de), a Romantic-era fantasy designed by Karl Friedrich Schinkel to replace a thirteenth-century Burg which had gone up in smoke in 1688. The great Prussian architect let his imagination run riot, drawing inspiration not only from the old fortresses of the Rhineland – as evidenced by the main **Rittersaal** with its suits of armour and medieval weaponry – but from a variety of other historical sources, notably the Moorish palaces of Andalucia.

Eating and drinking

If not one of the Rhineland's more renowned gastronomic centres, Koblenz still has a decent choice of places to eat and drink.

Altes Brauhaus Brauhausgasse 4. The Altstadt tap of Koblenz's own Königsbacher brewery, one of the few major beer producers in Rhineland-Palatinate. It makes a bitter-tasting *Pils* and a dark beer.

Café Baumann Löhrstr. 93. Traditional coffee house with an excellent selection of cakes.

Irish Pub Burgstr. 7. Has all the main Irish beers on tap, and features live music on Mon and Wed evenings.

Loup de Meer Neustadt 12. Small and expensive speciality fish restaurant with an open kitchen, located just to the west of the Schloss. Closed Sun, also Sat Oct–April; evenings only May–Sept.

Rüüan Thai Florinspfaffengasse 7. This is reckoned to be one of the very best Thai restaurants in Germany. Evenings only.

Salatgarten Gymnasialstr. 14. Self-service vegetarian and wholefood restaurant. Closed Sun.

Weindorf Julius-Wegeler-Str. 2. A complex of four wine taverns, grouped together in the form of a village square. Although very tourist-orientated, it's a good place to sample the local *Riesling* and *Müller-Thurgau* vintages, and to eat typically Rhenish dishes. Closed all Nov.

Winninger Weinstube Rheinzollstr. 4. Fine old Weinstube with a terrace overlooking the Rhine. Open Tues–Sun from 4pm.

Entertainment

The principal **cultural** venue is the aforementioned Theater der Stadt Koblenz on Deinhardplatz (Ⓣ02 61/1 29 28 40, Ⓦwww.theater-koblenz.de), whose programme of plays, opera and other events put those of many larger cities to shame. Koblenz also boasts one of Germany's rare specialist **comedy** venues in Blaue Biwel, Entenpful 9 (Ⓣ02 61/3 55 77); English-language acts are featured occasionally. The two main **festivals** are Carnival and Der Rhein in Flammen; the latter takes place on the second Saturday in August, and features fireworks and bonfires.

The Rhine from Andernach to Remagen

Soon after leaving Koblenz, the Rhine gorge opens out, cutting between the ranges of the Eifel and Westerwald. If this stretch doesn't quite match the grandeur of the preceding section, it's impressive nonetheless and well worth following by either boat or train. With exceptions, it also has the benefit of being less touristy.

Andernach

ANDERNACH, which lies 16km down the Rhine from Koblenz, can trace its history back further than almost any other German town. It celebrated its two-thousandth anniversary in 1988, commemorating the foundation of a Roman base for the campaigns against the tribes on the eastern side of the Rhine. Subsequently Andernach became a Franconian royal seat, before passing to the control of the Archbishop-Electors of Cologne, serving as the southern border of their territory until the Napoleonic invasion. Nowadays, it's an odd hybrid, having a fair amount of industry, yet taking advantage of its situation and monuments to double as a holiday resort.

If you're travelling along the Rhine by boat, it's definitely worth breaking your journey for a couple of hours in order to walk round the thirteenth-century **Stadtmauer**, which was laid out on the Roman foundations. The walls survive largely intact, making a solid back for many later buildings, including a well-concealed row of houses. Extra defence on the southern stretch was provided by the **Burg**, the most important town castle in the Rhineland. Blown up by French troops in 1688, a fair amount has nevertheless survived, notably the later embellishments such as the **Pulverturm** and residential palace wing.

Round to the north, overlooking the river, is the **Rheintor**, whose inner gate has weather-worn statues illustrating the best-known local legend, that of the Andernacher Bäckerjungen (baker boys of Andernach), who saved the town from occupation by letting loose their bees on the invading army. The most picturesque feature of Andernach's fortifications, however, is the fifteenth-century **Runder Turm** overlooking the Rhine on the northern side of town, whose octagonal upper storeys give it an exotic, oddly Moorish air. Thankfully, the French siege guns failed to penetrate its thick walls, but the enormous dent they made can still be seen clearly. Continuing down the river bank, there's the remarkable sixteenth-century **Alter Kran**, a crane whose original wooden mechanism remained in service into the twentieth century and is still in full working order.

Just to the west of the Runder Turm, the tall twin facade towers of the **Pfarrkirche Maria Himmelfahrt** rise majestically above the rest of the skyline. For the most part, it's an archetypal late Romanesque basilica with a pronounced Rhenish accent, though the northeastern belfry is in fact a survivor of the previous church on the site.

Andernach's main axis, Hochstrasse, runs from here to the Burg. About halfway down is the **Altes Rathaus**, occupying the site of the former ghetto; a Jewish bath was discovered underneath a few years ago. On the adjacent Läufstrasse is the Gothic **Christuskirche**, a former Minorite friary church with a curiously lopsided interior. A little further down the street is the **Haus von der Leyen**, a Renaissance patrician mansion that now houses the **Stadtmuseum** (Tues–Fri 10am–noon & 2–5pm, Sat & Sun 2–5pm; €1). Lack of space means that only a small collection of antiquities is permanently on display, but the changing exhibitions (prominently featured on posters outside) are often surprisingly good.

Practicalities

Andernach's **Bahnhof** is on Kurfürstendamm; to reach the centre, walk straight ahead, then turn right under the rail bridge. **Buses** operate from Am Stadtgraben, the western range of the Stadtmauer. The **tourist office** (May–Sept Mon–Fri 8am–6pm, Sat 9am–1pm; Oct–April Mon–Fri 9am–5pm; ⓣ0 26 32/29 84 20, ⓦwww.andernach.net) is at Läufstr. 4. In summer, the town is a popular overnight stop with tour coach operators; hence there are plenty of **hotels**, but many of these are often fully booked and charge independent travellers inflated prices. Nonetheless, there are plenty of places worth trying, including *Andernacher Hof*, right beside the Bahnhof at Breite Str. 83 (Ⓣ0 26 32/4 31 75; ❸); *Villa am Rhein*, Konrad-Adenauer-Allee 3 (Ⓣ0 26 32/9 27 40, Ⓦwww.villa-am-rhein.de; ❺); *Alte Kanzlei*, Steinweg 30 (Ⓣ0 26 32/9 66 60, Ⓦwww.alte-kanzlei.de; ❻); and *Fischer*, Am Helmwartsturm 4–6 (Ⓣ0 26 32/9 63 40, Ⓦwww.hotel-fischer.net; ❼). All of these have **restaurants**; *Alte Kanzlei* offers a particularly attractive ambience in its vaulted cellar and garden courtyard. Andernach hosts a number of **festivals**, including the *Bäckerjungenfest* (early July); *Die Tausenden Lichten* (The Thousand Lights), featuring fireworks and illuminations (first weekend in September); and, of course, Carnival.

Remagen

REMAGEN, 25km downstream from Andernach, is a town famous for a **bridge** which – apart from its support towers – no longer exists. The towers on the Remagen side have been converted into the **Friedensmuseum** (daily March–Oct 10am–5/6pm; €3.50; Ⓦwww.bruecke-remagen.de), which chroncles the story of the bridge (see box below) by means of old photographs.

In the centre of town, the dominant building is the curious church of **St Peter und Paul**. At the turn of the twentieth century, it was decided that the original Romanesque-Gothic church was no longer sufficiently big for the town's expanding population; accordingly, a new church, imitating the style of the old but on a much larger scale, was tacked on to it at right angles. More directly appealing is the enigmatic **Pfarrhoftor**, a double gateway forming the entrance to the parish close. It's covered with carvings made by a Romanesque sculptor of limited technique but fertile imagination.

High above Remagen stands the mid-nineteenth-century **Apollinariskirche**, goal of a popular ten-day pilgrimage at the end of July. The church was built in tandem with the completion of the Dom in Cologne, and is a miniature version of it. Inside, the walls are covered with frescoes of the lives of Christ, the Virgin and Saint Apollinaris.

With its central location, Remagen is undoubtedly the best base for this part of the Rhine, and there's a **campsite**, *Goldene Meile* (Ⓣ0 26 42/2 22 22), right beside the river. **Hotels** include *Fassbender*, Marktstr. 78 (Ⓣ0 26 42/2 34 72; ❸); *Pinger Old Inn*, Geschwister-Scholl-Str. 8 (Ⓣ0 26 42/9 38 40; ❺); and *Vita*, Alte Str. 42–46 (Ⓣ0 26 42/20 70; ❻). There are also a number of **private houses** (❷–❸). For a full list, contact the **tourist office**, Kirchstr. 6 (Mon–Thurs 8.30am–noon & 2–4pm, Fri 8.30am–noon; Ⓣ0 26 42/2 01 87, Ⓦwww.remagen.de).

The bridge at Remagen

Remagen's bridge was built during World War I to aid the movement of troops and supplies to the Western Front. On March 7, 1945, an advance regiment of the US Armoured Division reached this point, to find that the bridge – unlike all the others along the Rhine, Germany's most crucial natural defensive barrier – was still intact. The token Nazi force who had been left to guard it was quickly routed, enabling the Americans to establish a base on the opposite bank. Eisenhower declared the bridge to be "worth its weight in gold", while Hitler ordered the execution of four officers for their carelessness in failing to blow the bridge up. In retrospect, the importance of the Remagen episode seems exaggerated, as crossings were made by the Allies further up the Rhine the following week. Moreover, the bridge itself collapsed ten days later due to overloading, killing 28 American soldiers. However, it was symbolically a telling blow and has remained a popular subject for books, as well as being the basis for the classic film, starring George Segal and Robert Vaughn.

ROLANDSECK, a further 6km north, has now been absorbed by Remagen. The train station building is now designated the **Künstlerbahnhof** (Tues–Sun 10am–5pm; €3), and houses a notable collection of works by Hans Arp, along with changing exhibitions of contemporary art. More sculptures by Arp and by Henry Moore can be seen for free on the lawn outside.

One of the most famous Rhine legends is closely associated with the vicinity of Rolandseck. In the middle of the Rhine, just beyond the village, is the island of **Nonnenwerth**, occupied by a former convent. On hearing news of the death of Roland (Charlemagne's nephew) in an ambush in northern Spain, his betrothed is alleged to have come here, taking her final vows the moment before the hero, miraculously recovered from his wounds, arrived to claim her. Stricken by grief, he built the **Rolandsbogen** fortress on the hill above in order to catch occasional glimpses of her. Whatever the veracity of the story, it's well worth climbing up to the ruin, which commands one of the most extensive views of this part of the Rhine, with Bonn and the Siebengebirge (see p.500 and p.507) immediately to the north.

West of the Rhine

Outside the Rhine valley, the Land's principal attraction is one of the great river's main tributaries, the **Mosel**. Better known in English under its French name, Moselle, this rises in the foothills of the Vosges in France. In its German stretch, it flows between the **Eifel** and **Hunsrück** massifs, entering the Rhine at Koblenz. It's famous for its **wines**, which are widely exported, and have come to be regarded internationally as the most characteristic of the distinctive German style, and vineyards crowd the south-facing slopes, with more rugged terrain elsewhere. The combination of wine and scenery, plus castles and history, attracts a lot of visitors and in high season hordes of organized tour groups descend on the most popular destinations, such as **Cochem** and **Bernkastel-Kues**. However, there are still a few corners which have managed to fend off coach-trip attacks and retain some of the atmosphere which so impressed the Romans, on the edge of whose world the Mosel valley was. They've left their mark all along the valley, particularly in **Trier**, which has some of the best-preserved remains of Classical antiquity in northern Europe.

On the opposite side of the Hunsrück is another Rhine tributary, the **Nahe**, which is likewise a wine-producing area, albeit on a much smaller scale. Its most dramatic landscape can be found around the town of **Bad Münster am Stein-Ebernburg**. One more Rhine tributary, the **Ahr** in the far north of the Land, is another producer of quality wines, as well as the main tourist magnet in the Eifel range.

The Eifel

The **Eifel**, which forms the northwestern part of Rhineland-Palatinate and stretches beyond into North Rhine-Westphalia, is a gentle area of wooded hills and bare heathland, dotted with volcanic lakes and intersected by quiet, unspoiled valleys. By far the most magnificent scenery is in the **Ahr valley**, a real Brothers Grimm landscape of idyllic little towns, ruined castles, forests and vineyards. Most unusually for Germany, the vineyards are known primarily for their red wines and, because of the relatively low yield, are not easily obtainable outside the region. The Ahr is best explored by taking the branch railway, the Ahrtalbahn, from Remagen; at first the valley seems flat and nondescript but gradually vineyards start to crowd up to the rail line and the sides of the valley become steeper. Elsewhere in the Eifel are two very contrasting setpiece attractions – the **Nürburgring** race track and the abbey of **Maria Laach**.

Bad Neuenahr-Ahrweiler

The main resort in the Ahr valley is **BAD NEUENAHR-AHRWEILER**, even although it lies some distance east of the grand landscapes, at a point when the river has been reduced to little more than a stream as it flows towards its confluence with the Rhine. Originally, its two constituent parts, which came together in 1969, were completely separate communities: Ahrweiler is a walled medieval town, Bad Neuenahr a health resort whose main buildings date from the late nineteenth and early twentieth centuries. However, the area between them is now continuously built up, and it's no longer easy to tell where one begins and the other ends.

Bad Adenauer's compact spa quarter is on the south side of the Ahr; indeed, one side of the **Kurhaus** is set directly above the river. The eastern part of the building contains the **Spielbank** (daily from 2pm; minimum stake €2.50), Germany's largest casino. Directly opposite is the massive **Kurhotel**, now run by Steigenberger (see p.463). This is directly linked to the elegant **Thermal-Badehaus** round the corner on Kurgartenstrasse, which is now a full modernized health and fitness centre known as **Sinfonie der Sinne** (Mon–Fri 7.30am–7pm, Sat 9am–4pm, Sun 10am–2pm; massages from €16; Ⓦwww.sinfonie-der-sinne.de). Across the street is the main entrance to the well-tended **Kurpark**, beyond which lies the riverside **Dahliengarten**. The latest addition to the facilities is the **Ahrthermen** (daily 9am–11pm; prices start at €9.20 for a two-hour swim), a large bathing complex a few paces to the southeast of the Spielbank.

The kernel of Ahrweiler, which is 3km west on the north side of the Ahr, dates back to the Middle Ages and seems wildly archaic with its narrow streets and half-timbered buildings. It's ringed by the **Stadtmauer**, which was built between the thirteenth and fifteenth centuries by the Archbishop-Electors of Cologne, and is still more or less intact. Four gateways survive, including the Niedertor on the east side. This leads into Niederhutstrasse, which has plenty of tacky souvenir shops, along with delicatessens and wine merchants. The street terminates at the broad Marktplatz, on the northern side of which is the thirteenth-century **Pfarrkirche St Laurentius**, whose main external feature is its single octagonal tower. Inside are fourteenth- and fifteenth-century frescoes and modern stained-glass windows, some of which have an almost Expressionist feel to them. At Altenbaustr. 3, just off the western end of Marktplatz, in a three-storey tower house which was originally built in the thirteenth century but partially remodelled in Baroque style, is the **Museum der Stadt** (March–Dec Wed–Sun 10am–5pm; €1.50). It contains objects relating to the town and the Ahr valley area, including some fine medieval sculptures – notably a large polychromed relief of *The Way to Calvary* which formerly adorned the southern gateway, the Ahrtor – and a section on local wine production methods through the centuries.

From the western gateway, the Obertor, Walporzheimer Strasse leads southwest to the **AhrWeinForum** (Mon–Fri 8am–noon & 1–6pm, Sat & Sun 10am–noon & 1–5pm), where the local vintages can be sampled and bought. A few minutes' walk to the northwest, on the opposite side of the rail tracks, the startling new building of the **Museum Roemervilla** (Tues–Fri 10am–6pm, Sat & Sun 10am–5pm; €3.60) can be seen on the brow of the hill above. This protects the excavations of a huge Roman villa discovered in 1980 which is the only one of its size and scale north of the Alps, and directly comparable with those in Pompei and Herculaneum. On the southern side of town, surrounded by vineyards, is the most prominent local landmark, the huge **Ursulinenkloster Kalvarienberg**. Housing a convent and girls' school, it received its present silhouette, which resembles that of a French château, in the nineteenth century, though it preserves a plain and severe Gothic church with a fifteenth-century *Crucifixion* group in its chancel.

Practicalities

Bad Neuenahr's **Bahnhof** is a few minutes' walk to the northeast of the spa quarter. Its Ahrweiler counterpart is of little use to most visitors, lying well to the northeast of the Altstadt, but there's also an unmanned train stop, **Ahrweiler Markt**, just a few paces beyond the northern gateway to the Altstadt, the Adenbachtor. There are **tourist offices** in both parts of town: Bad Neuenahr's is opposite the Spielbank at Felix-Rütten-Str. 2 (late March to mid-Nov Mon–Fri 9am–6pm, Sat & Sun 10am–2pm; rest of year Mon–Fri 9am–5pm, Sat 10am–1pm; ⓣ0 26 41/9 77 30, ⓦwww.wohlstein365.de); Ahrweiler's at Markt 21 (late March to mid-Nov Mon–Fri 9.30am–5pm, Sat & Sun 10am–3pm; rest of year Mon–Fri 9.30am–5pm, Sat 10am–1pm; same contact details).

There's a fair provision of **private rooms** (❶–❸) and also many **pensions**. In Ahrweiler, the latter include *Zur Erholung*, Schützenstr. 74 (ⓣ0 26 41/3 49 36; ❷); and *Ippendorf*, Wolfgasse 7 (ⓣ0 26 41/3 49 41; ❷); in Bad Neuenahr there's the somewhat larger *Höper*, Kreuzstr. 40 (ⓣ0 26 41/2 85 66; ❸). Among the huge range of **hotels** in Bad Neuenahr are *Zum Ahrtal*, Sebastianstr. 68 (ⓣ0 26 41/2 69 69, ⓦwww.hotel-ahrtal.de; ❹); *Fürstenberg*, Mittelstr. 4–6 (ⓣ0 26 41/9 40 70, ⓦwww.hotel-fuerstenberg.de; ❻), which incorporates the *Beethovenhaus*, where the great composer took his holidays; *Griffels Goldener Anker*, Mittelstr. 14 (ⓣ0 26 41/80 40, ⓦwww.griffelsgoldeneranker.de; ❻–❽); and *Steigenberger*, Kurgartenstr. 1 (ⓣ0 26 41/94 10, ⓦwww.bad-neuenahr.steigenberger.de; ❾). The best address in Ahrweiler is *Hohenzollern*, high above the Museum Roemervilla at Am Silberberg 50 (ⓣ0 26 41/93 70, ⓦwww.hotelhohenzollern.com; ❼). The **youth hostel** is on the south bank of the river midway between the two centres at St-Pius-Str. 7 (ⓣ0 26 41/3 49 24; €16.60/21.80), while the **campsite** is on the way to the Ursulinenkloster at Kalvarienbergstr. 1 (ⓣ0 26 41/3 56 84). All the hotels listed above have recommendable **restaurants**, though there are plenty of enticing alternatives, particularly in the centre of Ahrweiler. *Prüner Hof*, Markt 12, is of gourmet status, yet does good-value set lunches; *Eifelstube*, Ahrhutstr. 26, is equally fine. *Deutscher Hof*, Johannes-Müller-Str. 1, is a Weinstube in one of the town's most notable half-timbered buildings, while *Franz Poels*, Ahrhutstr. 13, serves vintages from its own Weingut.

Nürburg and the Nürburgring

From the Ahrtalbahn's terminus at Ahrbrück, buses run south to Adenau, then on to the tiny health resort of **NÜRBURG**. This takes it name from the **Nürburg**

(Tues–Sun 9am–1pm & 2–5/6pm, closed Dec; €2; Ⓦwww.burgen-rlp.de), which stands on one of the highest peaks in the Eifel range (678m). It was originally the site of a Roman fort, but the ruins you see today are of a twelfth-century castle destroyed by French soldiers after a long siege in 1690. There are numerous **pensions** (❸–❹) and a few **hotels**, including *Am Tiergarten*, Kirchweg 4 (Ⓣ0 26 91/9 22 00, Ⓦwww.am-tiergarten.de; ❹–❻); and *Zur Burg*, Burgstr. 4 (Ⓣ0 26 91/75 75, Ⓦwww.nuerburgring-hotel.de; ❺).

Easily reached from the village is the famous race track, the **Nürburgring** (Ⓦwww.nuerburgring.de). This is in two parts, much the larger being the northern loop, which was laid out between 1925 and 1927. For decades it was regarded as the ultimate test in Grand Prix motor racing; not only is it an exceptionally long circuit, travelling some 23km through the forested High Eifel, it incorporates a fearsomely fast two-kilometre-long straight as well as numerous hills and bends. Jackie Stewart dubbed it "the green hell" and, following Niki Lauda's near-fatal crash in 1976, it was decided that it was too dangerous for Formula 1 races. Ever since, the German Grand Prix has been held at Hockenheim near Heidelberg. However, a new five-kilometre-long southern loop was opened in 1984, and this has since been used for both the Luxembourg and European Grand Prix. If you're travelling by car or motorbike you can take a spin round the northern loop yourself, at whatever speed you like and with no formalities other than paying the fee of €14 per lap (to check the opening times, which are subject to wide variation, phone ahead (Ⓣ0 26 91/30 20) or consult the website. For €85 a professional racing driver will chauffeur a maximum of three passengers round this circuit in the so-called Ringtaxi. This usually has to be booked many months in advance (Ⓣ0 26 91/30 21 78), as demand is high and the number of trips per day strictly limited.

Alongside the track is the **Erlebniswelt** (daily 10am–6pm; €10, €7.50 after 4.30pm). The first of the four halls features both historic and present-day racing vehicles, the others a variety of motoring-related entertainments including simulators which enable you to take part in a Grand Prix race and test your reactions to a crash. There's also an upmarket **hotel** with restaurant run by Dorint (Ⓣ0 26 91/30 90, Ⓦwww.dorint.de; ❼–❾).

Maria Laach

By far the most outstanding historical monument in the Eifel is the Benedictine **Abtei Maria Laach** (Ⓦwww.maria-laach.de), which lies in an isolated setting of forests, meadows and fields. Its name is derived from the adjacent **Laacher See**, which was formed by a volcanic cave-in, and which still has a raw primeval feel to it. Bus #6032 links Maria Laach with the nearest train station at Niedermendig, while bus #6031 runs there from Andernach.

The **Abteikirche** ranks as the most beautiful of all the great Romanesque churches of the Rhineland. Its sense of unity is all the more remarkable in that, although begun at the end of the eleventh century, it was not finished until well into the thirteenth century. One of its most distinctive features is its stonework – for the most part it's constructed from the local yellow-brown tufa, but dark basalt was used for architectural highlighting. Each end of the church is girded with an arrangement of three towers, presenting as varied and striking a silhouette as the Middle Ages ever produced.

Even more remarkable is the last part to be built, the **Paradise**, a courtyard placed in front of the building, enclosing the western choir. Apparently intended as a symbol of the innocence of the Garden of Eden, it's unique in Christian architecture, being suggestive of Islamic places of worship, an impression strengthened by the addition of the burbling Lions' Fountain in the middle. The capitals, showing a fabulous bestiary, were carved with a gossamer delicacy by a mason dubbed the Samson Master, who is also known to have worked at Andernach and Bonn.

After all this, the pure Romanesque sobriety of the interior comes as a surprise. However, the early Gothic **baldachin** at the high altar is again reminiscent of the art of Islam and is quite unlike any other such object in Europe. To see the **crypt**, the earliest part of the building, you have to join one of the regular guided tours (donation expected) conducted by the monks. It's worth catching one of the services to hear the Gregorian chant. Vespers are at 5.30pm, and finish in time to catch the last bus.

The monastery has its own **hotel**, the *Seehotel Maria Laach* (Ⓣ0 26 52/58 40; ❼–❾), which has an excellent restaurant, and there's a simple cafeteria alongside. You can also **camp** (Ⓣ0 26 36/24 85) on the shore of the Laacher See.

Trier

"Trier existed 1300 years before Rome" exclaims the inscription on one of the city's historic buildings. In fact, this is a piece of hyperbole: although **TRIER** is the oldest city in Germany, it was actually founded by the Romans themselves in about 16 BC. Once the capital of the Western Empire, with some splendid buildings to prove it, Trier was also an important early centre of Christianity and it while he was living here that Emperor Constantine was converted. Despite a period of decline when Constantinople became the imperial capital, Trier managed to retain political clout throughout the Middle Ages and beyond, its archbishop ranking as one of the seven Electors. Nowadays, Trier has the less exalted role of regional centre for the upper Mosel valley, its relaxed air a world away from the status it formerly held. Despite a turbulent history, an amazing amount of the city's past has been preserved: it presents a veritable encyclopedia of European architectural styles, with pride of place going to the most impressive group of **Roman monuments** north of the Alps.

Arrival, information and accommodation

The **Hauptbahnhof** is northeast of the centre, and it's about ten minutes' walk along Theodor-Heuss-Allee to the main entry-point to the Altstadt. Here, at An der Porta Nigra, is the **tourist office** (Jan–March Mon–Fri 9am–5pm, Sat 9am–3pm; April–Oct Mon–Sat 9am–6pm, Sun 10am–3pm; Nov & Dec Mon–Sat 9am–6pm, Sun 9am–1pm; Ⓣ06 51/97 80 80, Ⓦwww.trier.de). **Mosel cruises** operate from Zurlaubener Ufer in both directions; in addition to the longer voyages (see box on p.474), one-hour (€7) and two-hour (€10) round trips are offered by Gebrüder Kolb (Ⓣ06 51/2 66 66, Ⓦwww.kolb-mosel.com).

Trier has plenty of **accommodation** to suit all tastes and pockets. Although many of these are in the centre, some of the most enticing choices are in the outskirts.

Hotels

Alte Villa Saarstr. 133 Ⓣ06 51/93 81 20, Ⓦwww.hotelaltevilla.de. Baroque villa, only converted into a hotel a few years back, in the southern part of the centre. It has a high-quality restaurant, and a pleasant garden terrace. ❻

Blesius-Garten Olewiger Str. 135, Olewig Ⓣ06 51/3 60 60, Ⓦwww.blesius-garten.de. Capacious hotel in the eighteenth-century premises of a former wine-producing estate. The facilities include mineral baths, sauna, solarium, and a shady terrace with trees and a spring water fountain. The restaurant offers a predominantly French menu, a distinguished wine list and the products of its Hausbrauerei, Trier's only brewery. ❻

Casa Chiara Engelstr. 8 ⓣ06 51/27 07 30, ⓕ2 78 81. Fine modern hotel in a quiet street close to the Portra Nigra. It serves large buffet breakfasts, but no other meals. ❻

Maximin Ruwerer Str. 12, Ruwer ⓣ & ⓕ06 51/5 25 77. Very inexpensive, old-fashioned hotel with bar-restaurant in a northern suburb, a couple of kilometres beyond the Altstadt. ❷

Villa Hügel Bernhardstr. 14 ⓣ06 51/3 30 66, ⓦwww.hotel-villa-huegel.de. Occupies a 1914 villa set in a park above the Kaiserthermen. It has a sauna, swimming pool and a terrace with a panoramic view over the city. ❻–❽

Warsberger Hof Dietrichstr. 42 ⓣ06 51/97 52 50, ⓦwww.warsberger-hof.de. Just off the Hauptmarkt and part of the Kolpinghaus complex, this offers cell-like but perfectly adequate rooms. ❸

Weinhaus Becker Olewiger Str. 206, Olewig ⓣ06 51/93 80 80, ⓦwww.weinhaus-becker.de. Another of the Weinhäuser in this wine-producing suburb. There are often opportunities for cellar visits and wine tasting. ❻

Weinhaus Haag Am Stockplatz 1 ⓣ06 51/97 57 50, ⓦwww.hotel-weinhaus-haag.de. Budget hotel, centrally located in a pleasant square between the Porta Nigra and the Hauptmarkt, with a decent pizzeria, *Portofino*, on the ground floor. ❹–❻

Wirtshaus Zur Glocke Glockenstr. 12 ⓣ06 51/7 31 09. Traditional inn right in the heart of the Altstadt. The rooms are unmodernized and inexpensive; the restaurant serves gargantuan portions of hearty food. ❷

Zum Christophel Simeonstr. 1 ⓣ06 51/7 40 41, ⓦwww.zumschristophel.de. An old-fashioned hotel right beside the Porta Nigra with an excellent restaurant specializing in game and lamb dishes. ❻

Youth hostels and campsites

Jugendgästehaus An der Jugendherberge 4 ⓣ06 51/14 66 20, ⓕ1 46 62 30. Trier's official youth hostel is situated on the bank of the Mosel, near the lower station of the cable car. €16.60/21.80.

Kolpinghaus Jugendhotel Dietrichstr. 42 ⓣ06 51 /97 52 59, ⓦwww.warsberger-hof.de. The dormitory part of this complex costs from €13.50 per bed.

Trier-City Luxemburger Str. 81 ⓣ06 51/8 69 21, ⓕ8 30 79. Campsite situated on the western bank of the Mosel.

URANUS ⓣ&ⓕ0 65 01/8 38 78. This is a ship which is moored in the Mosel between April and Oct; €12.50 for a dorm bed.

The City

Despite being relatively small in modern terms, some of Trier's sights are fairly far out, and there is plenty to keep you occupied for a few days. However, if time is limited, it's still worth stopping as there is a handy concentration of things to see in the centre.

The Porta Nigra and Simeonstift

The Black Gate or **Porta Nigra** (daily 9am–5/6pm; €2.10, or €6.20 combined ticket for all Trier's Roman monuments) retains its historic function as the main entry point to the old city. By far the most imposing Roman building in northern Europe, it's also the biggest and best-preserved city gate of the Classical period anywhere in the world and dates from the end of the second century. The massive sandstone blocks are held together by iron rods set in lead, and it has been weathered black by the passage of time (hence the name, bestowed in medieval times). Towering above the surrounding streets and buildings, it's an awesome symbol of Roman architectural skill and military might. Would-be attackers were trapped between inner and outer gates, enabling defenders to pour boiling oil and molten lead down from above; the gateway served its purpose well and was never breached.

The Porta Nigra owes its survival to the fact that, during the eleventh century, Saint Simeon, a Greek hermit who was a friend of the powerful Archbishop Poppo, chose the gloomy ground floor of the east tower as a refuge from the world. After his death in 1035 the Porta Nigra was transformed into the **Simeonstiftkirche**, a church in his honour. Various further additions were

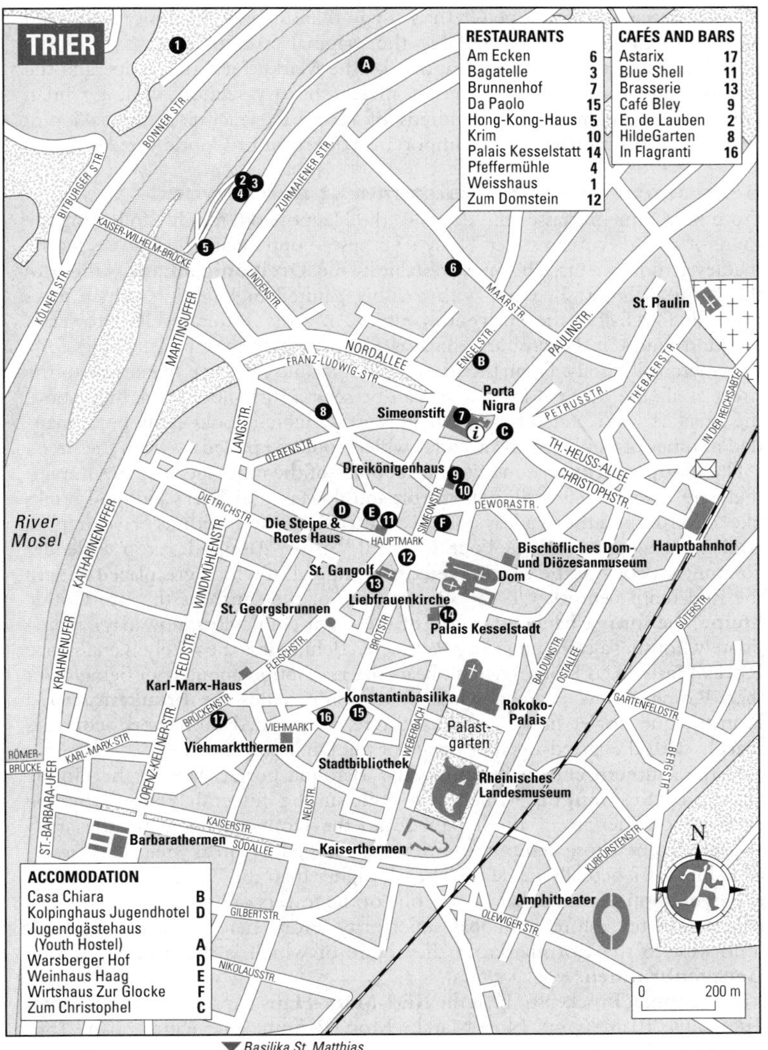

made, but in 1804 Napoleon ordered their removal, so that only the twelfth-century Romanesque choir and some slightly frivolous Rococo carvings remain from the post-Roman period.

Adjoining the western side is the **Simeonstift**, the collegiate foundation attached to the church. Its cloister, the **Brunnenhof**, is the oldest double cloister in Germany, and unusual in that the main walk is on the upper floor, which is supported by massive arcades below. Today the ground floor houses a restaurant (see p.472), with the **Städtisches Museum** (March–Oct daily 9am–5pm; Nov–Feb Tues–Fri 9am–5pm, Sat & Sun 9am–3pm; €2.60; Ⓦ www.museum-trier.de) above. This version of the inescapable

Heimatmuseum is vastly better than usual, thanks to an anarchic layout and some outstanding exhibits, notably the original sculptures of some of the prominent structures on the Hauptmarkt: the Marktkreuz, the Steipe and the Petrusbrunnen. Also here is a good ancient history section, with Egyptian grave masks and paintings, hundreds of Roman terracotta lamps, a lot of Greco-Roman statuary and an important collection of Coptic textiles.

Simeonstrasse, the Hauptmarkt and beyond

From here, Simeonstrasse runs down to the Hauptmarkt, roughly following the route of an old Roman street. Today it's a busy shopping area, but boasts several medieval monuments. The most notable is the **Dreikönigenhaus** (House of the Magi), whitewashed but with garishly painted highlighting, which dates from the first half of the thirteenth century. An early Gothic dwelling tower of the kind found in Regensburg, this was a secure home in uncertain times for a rich merchant family. Then, the ground floor would not have opened onto the street at all: the original front door can be seen at first-floor level, high above the street. It was reached by a wooden staircase which could easily be dismantled in times of trouble, or by a ladder which could be pulled up from the street.

The **Hauptmarkt** remains a real focal point of the city, especially in summer: there are always a few stalls selling fruit and flowers, and Trier's kids and punks like to loll around the brightly coloured **Petrusbrunnen**, with its ornate replica Renaissance figures of the Four Cardinal Virtues. Alongside, atop a slender column, is a copy of the **Marktkreuz**, the original of which was placed here in the mid-tenth century. On the western side of the square is the late Gothic **Steipe**, the former banqueting hall of the town councillors, nowadays appropriately housing a café and pricey Ratskeller. Behind it is the stately Renaissance **Rotes Haus** (Red House), which bears the inscription about Trier being older than Rome. A few paces down Dietrichstrasse stands the **Frankenturm**, a Romanesque tower-house whose austere, unadorned stonework contrasts sharply with the tarted-up appearance of the Dreikönigenhaus.

At the southern end of Hauptmarkt a Baroque portal leads to the Gothic church of **St Gangolf**, which was built in the fifteenth century by the burghers of Trier in an attempt to outdo the Dom and wind up the archbishops, from whose temporal power they hoped to break free. The tower, added in 1507, actually made the church higher than the Dom, which angered the archbishop so much that he had one of the towers of his cathedral specially heightened to restore episcopal superiority. From here Fleischstrasse leads southwest to the Kornmarkt, in the centre of which is the ornate Baroque **Georgenbrunnen**.

Further on, at Brückenstr. 10, is the **Karl-Marx-Haus** (April–Oct Mon 1–6pm, Tues–Sun 10am–6pm; Nov–March Mon 2–5pm, Tues–Sun 10am–1pm & 3–6pm; €2). In this archetypally bourgeois Baroque mansion the famous revolutionary theoretician and economist was born in 1818 to parents of Jewish extraction: his father was a respected lawyer who had converted to Protestantism, his mother a Dutchwoman who never mastered the German language. Unfortunately the displays here neglect the human angle, concentrating instead on detailed expositions of Marx's political theory. The museum is run by the SPD – something of an irony, as Marx did his best to scupper the party in its early days.

The Domfreihof

Up Sternstrasse from the Hauptmarkt is the **Domfreihof** (Cathedral quarter), which has a history as illustrious as that of Trier itself. Saint Helena, the mother of Constantine, supposedly donated the site of her palace for the creation of an immense double church, which was begun in 330 AD. It was one of the quartet of great churches founded more or less simultaneously by the emperor as the showpieces of the new imperial religion, the others being Old St Peter's in Rome, the Holy Sepulchre in Jerusalem and the Church of the Nativity in Bethlehem.

Some of the basilica's masonry survives in the present quadruple-towered **Dom**, which was started in 1030, though not finished until a couple of centuries later. However, the most tangible reminders of the original church are two granite pillars: one, the **Domstein**, can be seen in front of the southern portal, the other in the courtyard between the Dom and the Liebfrauenkirche. Save for the extension made to the southern tower to make it higher than St Gangolf, the Dom's austerely impressive facade has changed little since the eleventh century. Inside, there's an incredible sense of space, much enhanced by the ribbed vaulting of the ceiling. The most eye-catching items, such as the pulpit and the densely peopled All Saints' Altar on the third pillar on the south side of the nave, were carved by **Hans Ruprecht Hoffmann**, an inventive local sculptor who was also responsible for the Petrusbrunnen on Hauptmarkt. The Dom's most important relic is the **Seamless Robe**, supposedly the garment worn by Christ when he was crucified: only rarely displayed for veneration, it's kept in the raised **Heiltumskammer** at the east end, whose over-the-top Baroque decoration adds a rare jarring note. Also upstairs is the **Schatzkammer** (April–Oct Mon–Sat 10am–4.45pm, Sun 2–4.45pm; Nov–March Mon–Sat 11am–3.45pm, Sun 2–3.45pm; €1). This has examples of local goldsmiths' work, notably a bizarre tenth-century portable altar to hold a relic of the sandal of St Andrew.

From the airy **cloisters** you get a wonderful view of the ensemble of the Dom and the adjoining **Liebfrauenkirche**. The latter occupies the site of the southern section of Constantine's great double church, and thus continues the original idea of there being two separate places of worship in the complex. Begun in 1235, it was only the second church to be built in Germany in the Gothic style, of which it's a wonderfully pure example. The ground plan is highly original, taking the form of a rotunda with a cross superimposed on it; the vault is supported by twelve pillars representing each of the Apostles. Now darkened by the insertion of modern stained-glass windows, the interior contains the Baroque marble tomb of the warlike Karl von Metternich.

Facing the north side of the Dom on Windstrasse is the **Bischöfliches Dom- und Diözesanmuseum** (April–Oct Mon–Sat 9am–5pm, Sun 1–5pm; Nov–March Tues–Sat 9am–1pm & 2–5pm, Sun 1–5pm; €2). The most important exhibit is the fourth-century **ceiling painting** from the palace which preceded the Dom. Also of special note is the ninth-century **fresco** from the vanished Carolingian church of St Maximin, although it has worn its years less successfully. Upstairs is an important collection of **sculptures**, including most of the original statues from the facade of the Liebfrauenkirche, fragments of the Dom's rood screen and the refined **monument to Archbishop Jakob von Sierck** by Nicolaus Gerhaert von Leyden.

The Konstantinbasilika and the Palastgarten

From the Liebfrauenkirche, Liebfrauenstrasse leads past the ritzy Baroque Palais Kesselstadt to the **Konstantinbasilika** or **Aula Palatina** (April–Oct Mon–Sat 10am–6pm, Sun noon–6pm; Nov–March Tues–Sat noon–1pm & 3–4pm, Sun noon–1pm; free) on Konstantinplatz. This huge brick structure, once Constantine's throne hall, dates back to 310 AD, and is the most impressive of Trier's Roman remains after the Porta Nigra. Its dimensions are awe-inspiring: although 30m high and 75m long, it's completely self-supporting. Now the

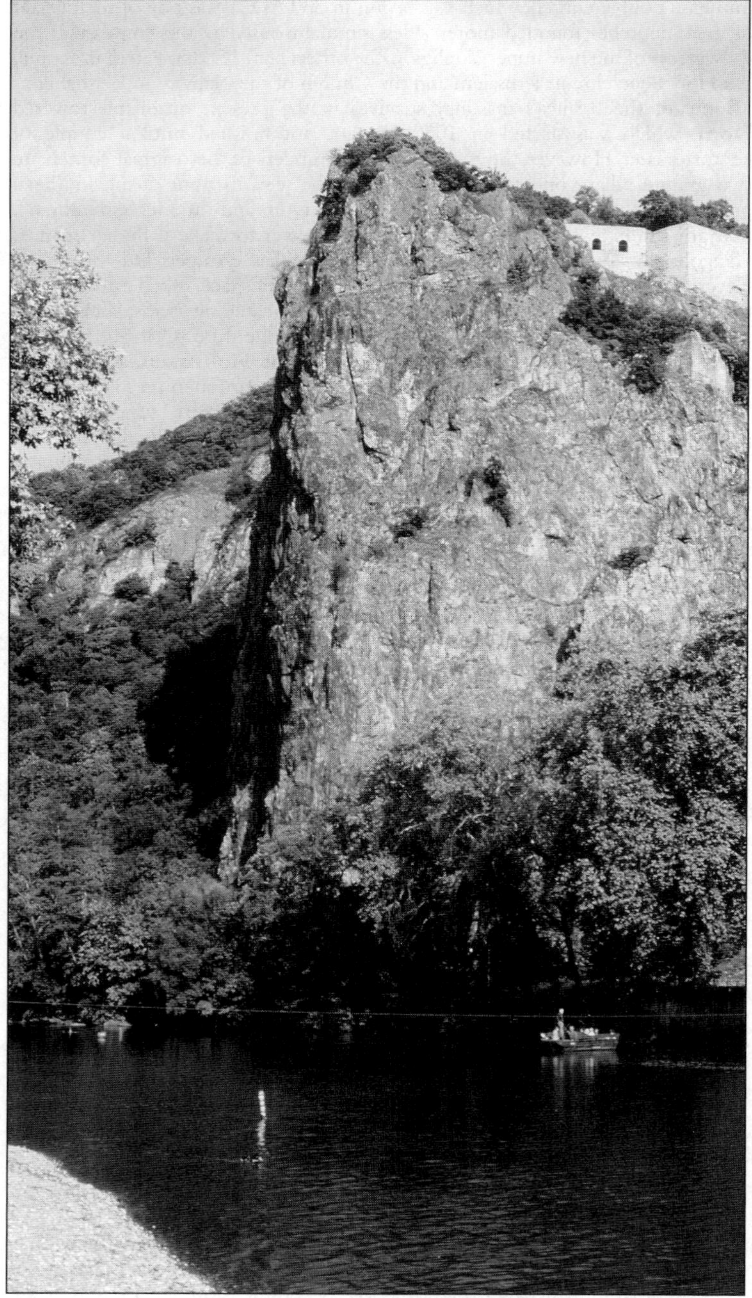

△ The Rheingrafenstein, Bad Münster am Stein – Ebernburg

Protestant Kirche Zum Erlöser (Church of the Redeemer) and comparatively spartan, in Roman times it was richly decorated in accordance with its (albeit short-lived) role as seat of the Roman Empire. At 3pm on most days in summer, there are guided visits to the excavations below.

Next door is the seventieth-century **Kurfürstliches Schloss**, once the residence of the Archbishop-Electors but now, more mundanely, a local government office. It's rather overshadowed by the adjoining **Rokoko-Palais der Kurfürsten**, which was built in 1756 for an archbishop who felt that the old Schloss wasn't good enough for him. Although it took some knocks over the next two hundred years, particularly in World War II, the facade survives and now sits in shockingly pink glory overlooking the **Palastgarten**, which is populated by Rococo statues.

At the southern end of the garden is the **Rheinisches Landesmuseum** (Tues–Fri 9.30am–5pm, Sat & Sun 10.30am–5pm; €5.50; Ⓦwww.landesmuseum-trier.de), which houses a fantastic collection of Roman relics – one of the best outside Italy. The prize exhibit, kept in the entrance hall, is the **Neumagener Weinschiff**, a stone sculpture found at Neumagen-Dhron in the Mosel valley, depicting a wine ship complete with crew. The following rooms have superb mosaics – among which the third-century **Rennführer Mosaik**, showing the charioteer Polydus and his four horses, stands out. The **Igeler Säule**, the magnificent 23-metre-high column in the courtyard, however, is only a copy: the original can be seen in the centre of the incorporated village of Igel, 8km up the Mosel. An important recent addition to the collections is a hoard of **gold coins** unearthed in 1993, the largest ever found in the Roman Empire. Trier's illustrious post-Roman history is illustrated in the following rooms by jewellery and weapons from Merovingian graves, and by sculptural and architectural fragments from the early Middle Ages.

A couple of minutes' walk to the west at Weberbach 25 is the **Schatzkammer der Stadtbibliothek** (previously Easter–Oct Mon–Fri 10am–5pm, but currently closed for repairs; free). Here are two of the world's most beautiful books: the ninth-century *Ada Evangelistary* with an antique cameo of Constantine on the cover, and the tenth-century *Codex Egberti*, which was partly illuminated in Trier by the man regarded as the first great German painter, the Master of the Registrum Gregorii.

The Roman baths and the Amphitheater

Behind the Landesmuseum are the **Kaiserthermen** (daily 9am–5/6pm; €2.10 or €6.20 combined ticket for all Trier's Roman monuments), the imperial baths built in the reign of Constantine. Although they haven't survived intact, the scale of what was once one of the largest bathing complexes in the Roman world is still apparent. Today only the ruined **Caldarium** (hot bath), with its distinctive strips of brick among the stonework, is visible above ground. The extensive underground heating system has also survived, and you can walk among the service channels and passages. By the Middle Ages local lords had turned the baths into a castle, which was incorporated into the **Stadtmauer**, surviving sections of which can still be seen nearby.

An earlier ruined set of Roman baths, the **Barbarathermen** (daily 9am–5/6pm; €2.10), lie at the opposite end of Südallee from the Kaiserthermen. Built in the second century, only the subterranean sections retain their original shape, a seemingly endless maze of passages, channels and chambers. A yet older bathing complex, the **Viehmarktthermen** (Tues–Sun 9am–5pm; €2.10) in the south of the Altstadt, was excavated in the 1990s, and has now been placed under a protective glass building.

From the Kaiserthermen the route to the **Amphitheater** (daily 9am–5/6pm; €2.10) is well signposted. It was built into the slopes of the Petrisberg above the city in around 100 AD and is the oldest of the surviving Roman buildings in Trier. The structure has been exposed in most of its original glory, and you can sense the grandeur of the original, which had a seating capacity of 20,000. It's still possible to see some of the arched cage rooms where the animals were kept and take a look under the arena itself, which is partly supported by timber blocks and has an elaborate – and still functioning – drainage system cut into its base.

Outside the centre

The hills around Trier provide many marvellous panoramic views of the city and the Mosel valley. Easiest of access is the **Weisshaus**, which has a currently out-of-action cable car link with **Zurlaubener Ufer**, a picturesque quayside lined with old fishermen's houses, many now converted into bars and restaurants.

Two contrasting churches are within easy walking distance of the centre. On the southern edge of town, about fifteen minutes' walk down Saarstrasse from Südallee, is the **Basilika St Matthias**. In 1127 Crusaders brought back from the Holy Land relics of St Matthias (the apostle who replaced Judas Iscariot); this huge church was then built on the site of an existing one to provide sufficient space for the pilgrims who came here to venerate the only one of Jesus' followers to be buried north of the Alps. The whitewashed facade is startling, the original Romanesque modified by the addition of Baroque and Neoclassical features to create a truly sumptuous fricassee. The tomb of Saint Matthias is found at the intersection of the nave and transept; those of the first two bishops of Trier, SS Eucharius and Valerius, to whom the previous church was dedicated, are in two Roman sarcophagi in the crypt.

At the other end of town is **St Paulin**, designed by Balthasar Neumann. From the outside it looks quite restrained, sober even, but the interior is an all-singing, all-dancing Rococo extravaganza of colour and light. The eye is assaulted by the complex ceiling frescoes and the ornate pillars, dripping with cherubs and scrollwork. It's all just as Neumann intended: his idea was that entering a church should be like entering heaven. Look out for the carvings on the high altar and the choir stalls by Ferdinand Tiez, which are some of the best Rococo decoration in the Rhineland-Palatinate.

Eating and drinking

Alongside several high-class traditional **restaurants** are plenty of central **bars** where you can get good and inexpensive food, thanks to the presence of a large and hungry student population. There are also numerous opportunities for wine tasting, if you want to sample the full range of the superb local vintages.

Restaurants

Am Ecken Maarstr. 45. This neighbourhood Gaststätte is a big favourite with locals for its reasonably priced regional fare. Closed Sat & Sun.

Bagatelle Zurlaubener Ufer 78. Although overshadowed by the neighbouring *Pfeffermühle*, this is nevertheless one of the best restaurants in Trier, particularly for *neue deutsche Küche*.

Brunnenhof Im Simeonstift. Prone to be mobbed by tourists, but the food is of good quality, with the bonus of being able to sit outside in the historic cloister in fine weather.

Da Paolo Neustr. 17. A reasonably priced pizzeria with a wood-fired oven.

Hong-Kong-Haus Georg-Schmitt-Platz 2. The best of the city's Chinese restaurants. Closed Tues.

Krim Glockenstr. 6–7. Serves Mediterranean-style cuisine, including plenty of fish and seafood dishes. Breakfasts are also available, and there are bargain lunch dishes.

Wine tasting

Five or six different wine estates (Weingüte) within the city boundaries (most of them in the incorporated village of Olewig, which is east of the Amphitheater, and reached by bus #6) are normally open (daily 10am–6pm) for a week at a time on a rotational basis throughout the year. At these, you can sample four wines for €4.50, six for €6.50 or eight for €8.50; check with the tourist office which one is open during your stay. Two of Germany's most celebrated wine cellars are in Trier's Altstadt. The Reichsgraf von Kesselstatt Weinkeller, Liebfrauenstr. 10, occupies a total of 4300 square metres under the city. Alongside its prestigious restaurant, *Palais Kesselstatt* (see below), it has an informal bar or Gutsstube, open until late in the evening, where wines from open bottles can be sampled in measures of 0.1 litre upwards. Bischöfliche Weingüter, a grouping of four estates of ecclesiastical origin, have their central cellar at Gervasiusstr. 1 (Mon–Fri 9am–5pm), part of which dates back to the sixteenth century. The wines are well-known for their elegance and bouquet; nearly all are *Riesling*, and over half are dry or medium-dry.

Palais Kesselstatt Liebfrauenstr. 10 ⓣ06 51/4 02 04. Trier's most famous and upmarket restaurant, housed in a magnificent Baroque palace, and serving high-quality wines from its own Reichsgraf von Kesselstatt estates. Advance booking recommended; closed Sun & Mon.

Pfeffermühle Zurlaubener Ufer 76 ⓣ06 51/2 61 33. Another celebrated, very intimate restaurant, serving French *haute cuisine*. Reservations usually necessary; closed all day Sun & Mon lunchtime.

Weisshaus Weisshaus 1. Located right by the cable-car terminus with a wonderful view of Trier, though the food alone is worth the journey. Closed Mon.

Zum Domstein Hauptmarkt 5. Trier's most innovative restaurant, offering adventurous vegetarian cuisine in addition to the standard *gutbürgerliche Küche*, while Roman-style dishes are served in the cellar. Bargain menus at lunchtime.

Bars and cafés

Astarix Karl-Marx-Str. 11. Big, relaxed student bar serving an eclectic range of mountainous piles of cheap grub. Note that the entrance is to the rear, or via the passageway from the street.

Blue Shell Stockstr. 5. One of a row of trendy café-bars.

Brasserie Fleischstr. 12. Housed in a handsome Baroque mansion with an attached winter garden, this is the Trier outpost of the Bitburger brewery in the Eifel, the largest and best-known beer producer in such a wine stronghold.

Café Bley Simeonstr. 19. Elegant traditional café in the Dreikönigenhaus.

En de Lauben Zurlaubener Ufer 77. A pleasant traditional tavern, with good cider as well as wines. It has a garden pavilion overlooking the river, equipped with a heating system which enables it to be kept open all year round.

HildeGarten Deutschherrenstr. 12. Vegetarian and wholefood self-service café. Open Mon–Fri 11.30am–3pm, with fish dishes on Tues & Fri.

InFlagranti Viehmarkt 13. One of the most popular student haunts; also serves light meals.

The Mosel Wine Road

From Trier you can follow the **Mosel Wine Road** (Mosel Weinstrasse) by bus or car to the river's confluence with the Rhine at Koblenz. The Mosel meanders past innumerable wine villages and towns in a series of tortuous curves, the slopes of its valley covered with vineyards. This journey can also be accomplished by rail, but the line leaves the valley for substantial stretches and goes through relatively nondescript countryside, whereas the B53 road criss-crosses the Mosel and misses none of the splendid scenery along the route. An even more enticing way to travel, whether for all or just part of the way, is by **boat** – see the box on p.474 for details.

Boat trips along the Mosel

Between May and early October, you can travel the length of the River Mosel from Trier to Koblenz, or just make short local trips; Eurail passes allow you to travel on the K-D Linie steamers without charge, while other rail passes bring reductions.

Ferry companies and routes

Hölzenbein Rheinzollstr. 4, Koblenz ⓣ02 61/3 77 44; Cochem–Koblenz.

Gebrüder Kolb Briedern ⓣ0 26 73/15 15, ⓦwww.kolb-mosel.de; Trier–Treis–Karden.

Hans Michelis Goldbachstr. 52, Bernkastel-Kues ⓣ0 65 31/68 97 or 82 22, ⓦwww.mosel-schiffstouristik.de; Bernkastel-Kues–Traben–Trarbach.

K-D Linie Rheinwerft, Koblenz ⓣ02 61/3 10 30, ⓦwww.k-d.com; Cochem–Koblenz.

Bernkastel-Kues

Like many towns in the Mosel valley, **BERNKASTEL-KUES**, which is 50km downstream from Trier, was originally two completely separate communities facing each other across the river. It attracts its fair share of coach-tripping tourists and can get pretty busy in summer, but is well worth a visit, both for its sights and its wines.

In Bernkastel, on the south side of the Mosel, the main attraction is the half-timbered, sloping **Marktplatz**, which really does live up to tourist brochure hyperbole, with a stately coffee-and-cream-coloured Renaissance **Rathaus** as the focal point. Next door is the **Spitzhäuschen**, an absurdly narrow half-timbered building with a steep grey slate-pitched roof, which now houses a tiny Weinstube. In the middle of the vineyards above Bernkastel stands **Burg Landshut**, a thirteenth-century castle which went up in flames in 1693 and has been a ruin ever since, but from which you get panoramic views of the town and around.

In Kues, on the other side of the river, the bank is lined with the houses and villas of nineteenth-century vineyard owners. Alongside the bridge is the Gothic **St Nikolaus-Hospital** (Sun–Fri 10am–6pm, Sat 10am–3pm; free; guided tours, subject to a minimum of five visitors, Tues at 10.30am, Fri at 3pm; €4; ⓦwww.cusanus.de), also known as the **Cusanusstift**, a poorhouse founded by the town's most famous son, the fifteenth-century theologian and philosopher Nikolaus Cusanus, who pursued a highly successful ecclesiastical career, latterly as a cardinal and vicar-general in Rome. The buildings were constructed to house 33 destitute old men – a symbolic figure representing each year of Christ's life – and have maintained the same function ever since. In the heavily ornate **Kapelle** there's a vivid mid-fifteenth century *Crucifixion* triptych by the Cologne narrative painter known as the Master of the Life of the Virgin. On the pavement in front is a memorial brass to Cusanus, though only his heart is buried below. His sister's finely carved tomb can be seen on the south wall, directly facing a fresco of *The Last Judgment*. The **Bibliothek**, which contains 314 ninth- to fifteenth-century manuscripts collected by Cusanus, is considered one of the most valuable private libraries in the world, but is only accessible on the twice-weekly guided tours. Also within the complex is the **Mosel-Weinmuseum** (mid-April to Oct Tues–Sun 10am–5pm; Nov to mid-April Tues–Sun 2–5pm; €2), which features a large collection of wine presses, vessels and other related objects. There's also a Vinothek where local wines can be sampled and bought.

Practicalities

Bernkastel-Kues is one of the most unexpected gaps on the German rail network, the former branch line having been torn up and replaced by a cycle track. To reach it from either Trier or Koblenz, take a train as far as Wittlich, from where a connecting **bus** service covers the remaining 16km. The **tourist office** (May–Oct Mon–Sat 8.30am–12.30pm & 1–5pm; Nov–April Mon–Fri 8.30am–12.30pm & 1–5pm; ⓣ0 65 31/40 23, ⓦwww.bernkastel-kues.de) is at Am Gestade 5 in Bernkastel.

There are dozens of **guesthouses** and **hotels**, but the town can still get full up because of the volume of summer traffic. A particularly enticing selection on the Bernkastel side includes *Kapuzinerstübchen*, Römerstr. 35 (ⓣ0 65 31/23 53; ❸); *Römischer Kaiser*, Markt 29 (ⓣ0 65 31/9 68 60; ❹); *Binz*, Am Markt 1 (ⓣ0 65 31/22 25, ⓦwww.hotel-binz.com; ❺); *Doctor-Weinstuben*, in a seventeenth-century house with inner courtyard at Hebegasse 5 (ⓣ0 65 31/60 81 or 9 66 50, ⓦwww.doctor-weinstuben.de; ❻); and *Zur Post*, Gestade 17 (ⓣ0 65 31/9 67 00, ⓦwww.hotel-zur-post-bernkastel.de; ❻). In Kues try *Weinhaus St Maximilian*, Saarallee 12 (ⓣ0 65 31/9 65 00; ❹); or *Drei Könige*, Bahnhofstr. 1 (ⓣ0 65 31/20 35, ⓦwww.hoteldreikoenige.de; ❻). There's a **youth hostel** uphill from Burg Landshut at Jugendherbergstr. 1 (ⓣ0 65 31/23 95; €12.60), and a **campsite** at Am Hafen 2 (ⓣ0 65 31/82 00) in Kues.

Not surprisingly, there are dozens of **cafés** and **restaurants** in Bernkastel-Kues and the general rule is that the ones in the quieter streets are less likely to be full of tourists being ripped off. All the Bernkastel hotels listed above can also be recommended as places to eat and drink, while the *Ratskeller*, Am Markt, and *Rotisserie Royale*, Burgstr. 19, are also particularly good. During the first weekend in September the biggest **wine festival** on the Mosel takes place here, when consumption of gallons of the most famous local vintage, *Bernkasteler Doctor*, brings plenty of life to the streets.

Traben-Trarbach

Another double town, **TRABEN-TRARBACH**, is 24km downstream from Bernkastel-Kues, though only a fraction of that distance away as the crow flies. It was once a prime strategic site, as the ruined fortresses high above the banks of the river testify. On the Trarbach side, the medieval **Schloss Grevenburg**, now reduced to a couple of walls, was blown up in 1697 in accordance with the terms of a recently signed peace treaty. In 1734 **Mont Royal**, built just 44 years previously by the celebrated French military architect Sebastian Vauban, suffered similar treatment.

In both parts of the double town, half-timbered houses rub shoulders with more substantial upper-middle-class villas from the nineteenth century. There are also numerous Jugendstil buildings, many of them by the Berlin architect Bruno Möhring. His most visible creation is the **Brückentor**, a monumental gateway on the Trarbach side of the connecting bridge. He was also responsible for **Haus Huesgen**, Am Bahnhof 20, and **Haus Breucker**, An der Mosel 7, both on the river bank in Traben.

Traben's **Bahnhof**, actually no more than a shelter, is the terminus of a branch railway which runs right along the side of the Mosel, connecting with the main Trier–Koblenz line at Bullay. The **tourist office** is nearby at Bahnstr. 22 (July–Oct Mon–Fri 9am–5pm, Sat 11am–3pm; Nov–June Mon–Fri 9am–noon & 2–4pm; ⓣ0 65 41/8 39 80, ⓦwww.traben-trarbach.de). In Traben the accommodation options include a **guesthouse**, *Germania*, Kirchstr. 101 (ⓣ0 65 41/93 98; ❷); and **hotels** such as *Krone*, An der Mosel 93 (ⓣ0 65 41/8 38 70, ⓦwww.krone-hotel-traben.de; ❺); *Oase Moselschlösschen*, Neue Rathausstr. 12–16 (ⓣ0 65 41/83 20, ⓦwww.moselschloesschen.de; ❺–❼); and *Bellevue*, in a large Möhring-designed building at Am Moselufer (ⓣ0 65 41/70 30,

Ⓦwww.bellevue-hotel.de; ❻–❽). There is less choice in Trarbach: the best address is *Moseltor*, Moselstr. 1 (Ⓣ0 65 41/65 51, Ⓦwww.moseltor.de; ❻). The **youth hostel** is at Hirtenpfad 6 (Ⓣ0 65 41/92 78, Ⓕ37 59; €15.90/21.20), about fifteen minutes' walk from the Bahnhof on the same side of the river. Also in Traben are **camping** facilities at Rissbacher Str. 165 (Ⓣ0 65 41/31 11), while there's another site 2km down the road at Wedenhofstr. 25 (Ⓣ0 65 41/91 74) in the incorporated village of Wolf. All the hotels listed above have recommendable **restaurants**, with that in *Krone* being particularly renowned. Another atmospheric place to eat and drink is *Storcke Stütz* at Brückenstr. 4 in Trarbach, which occupies medieval cellars, serves its own vintages, and presents tasty local dishes.

Cochem

The next town of any size is **COCHEM**, which lies 55km downstream from Traben-Trarbach, and on the main Trier–Koblenz rail line. It's a place which has sold its soul to tourism and should be avoided like the plague in summer. The main attraction is the **Reichsburg** (daily mid-March to Oct 31 9am–5pm; €4; Ⓦwww.reichsburg-cochem.de), one of the Rhineland-Palatinate's most famous replica castles. If it weren't a Romantic-era pastiche (the eleventh- to fourteenth-century original went up in smoke in 1689, assisted by enthusiastic French soldiers), the castle, which dominates the town with its cluster of towers and implacable walls, would be very impressive. Inside, it has been decorated in mock medieval style, though there are some fine pieces of genuine Renaissance furniture. **Falconry** demonstrations are given daily at 11am, 1pm & 3.30pm (€2).

Cochem has a half-timbered **Marktplatz** with a sober Baroque **Rathaus**. Behind stands the **Martinskirche**, with a tower that looks like a Rococo soldier's helmet. It's a postwar rebuild of an original which dated back to the ninth century, and the modernized interior is only of note for the fifteenth-century reliquary of St Martin, a gift from Emperor Maximilian I. Parts of the **Stadtmauer** are also still intact, including three chunky city gates. From one of them, **Enderttor**, it's a short walk west to the valley station of the **chairlift** (daily 9am–6pm; €4 single, €5.50 return) to the **Pinnerkreuz** hill, which offers the best view of the town and its environs.

The town centre bridge goes over the Mosel to the suburb of Cond. Directly overlooking the waterfront, at Stadionstr. 1–3, is an early twentieth-century villa which is now home to an eighteenth-century mustard mill known as the **Historische Senfmühle** (guided tours daily at 11am, 2pm, 3pm & 4pm; €2; Ⓦwww.senfmuhle.net). Its seven different products – one made to a fifteenth-century monastic recipe – can be sampled and purchased in the adjoining shop. Directly below is one of Cochem's many wine cellars, the **Wein- und Sektkellerei Hieronomi** (guided tours Easter to early Nov Mon–Fri at 11am & 3pm, Sat & Sun at 11am, 3pm & 5pm; €5). The visit ends with the sampling of a selection of wines, and also includes a bottle to take away.

Practicalities

Cochem's **Bahnhof** is at the northern end of town. The **tourist office** (April–Oct Mon–Thurs 9am–5pm, Fri 9am–6pm; May–Aug also Sat 9am–5pm; July & Aug also Sun 10am–noon; Nov–March Mon–Fri 9am–1pm & 2–5pm; Ⓣ0 26 71/6 00 40, Ⓦwww.cochem.de) is at Endertplatz 1. Accommodation is plentiful, and includes some **private rooms** (❷–❸), but can get booked out at the height of the season. Among about a score of **pensions** are *Hendriks*, Jahnstr. 8 (Ⓣ0 26 71/91 73 61, Ⓦwww.pension-hendriks.de; ❸); and *Café Becker*, Oberbachstr. 20–22 (Ⓣ0 26 71/72 24; ❸). An even larger number of **hotels** includes *Am Hafen*, Uferstr. 4, Cond (Ⓣ0 26 71/9 77 20, Ⓦwww.hotel-am-hafen.de; ❺–❼); *Karl Müller*, Moselpromenade 9 (Ⓣ0 26 71/1 33 33, Ⓦwww.hotel-karl-mueller.de; ❻); and *Lohspeicher*, Obergasse 1 (Ⓣ0 26 71/39 76, Ⓦwww.lohspeicher.de; ❻). All of these have good **restaurants**, with the palm going to the last-named, which is of gourmet status. There's a **youth hostel** at Klottener Str. 9 (Ⓣ0 26 71/86 33, Ⓕ85 68; €16.60/21.80) on the south side of the Mosel. The most convenient of the local **campsites** is *Freizeitzentrum*, Klottener Str. 17 (Ⓣ0 26 71/44 09).

Treis-Karden

From Cochem it's just 11km by road or rail to the little double town of **TREIS-KARDEN**, though this is a whole world away in atmosphere, normally being completely devoid of coach party hordes. The dominant landmark in Karden, on the north side of the Mosel, is the **Stiftskirche St Kastor**, which was under construction for over three hundred years, marking the full transition from Romanesque to Gothic. Although of modest dimensions, its simple white lines make it one of the most visually appealing churches of the Mosel region. The furnishings include a fine Baroque organ and a small but beautiful early fifteenth-century terracotta high altar of the Adoration of the Magi. Beside the church is a thirteenth-century tithe barn, which has been converted to house the **Stiftsmuseum** (Wed–Fri 2–5pm, Sat & Sun 10am–noon & 2–5pm; €3). This displays Roman and Celtic archeological finds plus a collection of sacred art, including a series of Gothic panel paintings of saints which formerly adorned the chancel of the Stiftskirche.

The **Bahnhof** is in Karden, where the **tourist office** (Mon–Fri 9am–noon & 2–4/5pm; May–Oct Sat 9am–noon; Ⓣ0 26 72/61 37, Ⓦwww.treis-karden.de) can be found at Hauptstr. 27. Most of the **hotels** are also in this part of town: they include *Am Stiftstor*, Hauptstr. 17 (Ⓣ0 26 72/13 63, Ⓦwww.hotel-stiftstor.de; ❹); *Brauer*, Moselstr. 26 (Ⓣ0 26 72/12 11; ❹); and *Schlosshotel Petry*, St-Castor-Str. 80 (Ⓣ0 26 72/93 40; ❺–❼). All have fine **restaurants**, and *Am Stiftstor* also offers the opportunity to sample the wines from its own estate.

Moselkern and Burg Eltz

MOSELKERN, a further 8km downstream (two stops away by slow train), is an even more somnolent wine-producing village whose **Bahnhof** still preserves its original Romantic-era form. On its main street, Oberstrasse, is the oldest **Rathaus** in the Mosel valley, a graceful half-timbered building of 1535. A few paces away, in front of the **Pfarrkirche**, is a Merovingian cross from around 700, the oldest yet discovered north of the Alps, though the one here is only a copy, the original having been moved to the Rheinisches Landesmuseum in Bonn for safekeeping. There's a wide choice of good-value accommodation, including a **campsite**, *Zur Burg Eltz* (Ⓣ0 26 72/73 81); several **guesthouses**, including *Heinrichs*, Oberstr. 49 (Ⓣ0 26 72/25 34; ❷); and a couple of **hotels** – *Rebstock*, Oberstr. 30 (Ⓣ0 26 72/87 60; ❷) and *Anker Pitt*, Moselstr. 15–16 (Ⓣ0 26 72/13 03; ❹). The last-named has a fine **restaurant**; an alternative is *Weinschänke Weckbecker*, Oberstr. 28, which also serves wines from its own estates.

Moselkern is the nearest village to **Burg Eltz** (guided tours daily April–Oct 9.30am–5.30pm; €6; Ⓦwww.burg-eltz.de), one of only three intact medieval fortresses in the Rhineland-Palatinate (the others are the Pfalzgrafenstein and the Marksburg – see p.452 and p.455). Although this unquestionably ranks among Germany's greatest and most dramatic sights, it's also one of the hardest to reach. The only way to approach it by road is from the village of Münstermaifeld to the north, but no buses ply this route, and private vehicles have to be left at a car park nearly 1km from the castle (though a taxi is available for those unable to manage the steep walk). There are marked footpaths from both Moselkern and Karden: the former is much shorter, gentler and shadier, taking around 45 minutes. Despite the relative difficulty of getting there, the place is prone to be swamped by tourists, and it's advisable to visit early, or during the early or late part of the season.

Burg Eltz seems to rise vertically straight out of the woods of the Elzbach valley and bristles with conical towers. It goes back at least as far as the twelfth century, developing over the next four hundred years as a defensive home for the various branches of the Eltz family, who managed to live there peaceably for a couple of hundred years until a run-in with Balduin, the Elector of Trier. This resulted in a two-year siege, during which the now totally ruinous **Burg Trutzeltz** was built by Balduin directly in front in order to lob rocks at the castle. After Burg Eltz fell the Eltz family were allowed to remain in possession as vassals of Balduin and peace returned. Most of what you see today was built during the fifteenth century: inside the walls are a number of residential towers crammed together round an inner courtyard, which escaped destruction by the French in 1689 only because a member of the Eltz family happened to be an officer in the French army.

The **interior** of the castle is more or less as it was during medieval times, complete with original furnishings, wall hangings and paintings. Particularly impressive is the **Rübenacher Untersaal**, with sixteenth-century Flemish tapestries of unlikely-looking exotic animals and plants, and a number of panel paintings, including Cranach's *Madonna with Grapes*. The **Schatzkammer** (€2.50 extra), the only part of the interior which can be visited at leisure, contains family mementoes, glass, porcelain, weapons and armour, but is primarily of note for some superb examples of German Renaissance gold- and silverware, including a clockwork drinking vessel in the shape of the goddess Diana and a comical piece showing a personification of Gluttony being pushed in a barrel by Bacchus, representing Drunkenness.

Bad Münster am Stein-Ebernburg

As the Nahe flows towards the confluence at Bingen, the river becomes broad and grand, assuming a truly spectacular aspect around the little town bearing the somewhat clumsy name of **BAD MÜNSTER AM STEIN-EBERNBURG**. Indeed, this landscape, a favourite subject with painters of the Romantic era, was once so famous that it was regarded as an obligatory stop on a Grand Tour of Europe. While it remains a popular destination with the Germans themselves, it has been all but forgotten by almost everyone else – though it is undoubtedly one of the country's most unusual and impressive beauty spots. Bad Münster am Stein-Ebernburg itself only came into existence in 1969, and a curiosity of their pre-twentieth-century history is that, despite many changes of ownership, the two constituent villages always belonged to different states.

No more than a cluster of houses until it was developed as a resort in the second half of the nineteenth century, Bad Münster is bordered on three sides by a loop of the Nahe, and faces the **Rheingrafenstein**, a dramatic cluster of red porphyry cliffs rising almost directly from the river. On top of one of these, at a height of 136m, is **Burg Rheingrafenstein**, the feudal seat of the Lords of Stein, later the Rheingrafen or Counts of the Rhine. Despite its seemingly impregnable position, the castle was captured and blown up by the French in 1689, and has remained a ruin ever since. To the rear is a 245m cliff, on top of which is an observation platform commanding a superb view of the town and the valley. There is a **chained ferry** (daily May–Aug 8am–8pm, reducing gradually in the off-season to 9am–6pm; €0.75 single) from Bad Münster to the foot of the Rheingrafenstein, from where a path snakes up to the Burg and beyond. Boats are available for hire at the same jetty.

The **Kurpark**, which stretches almost as far as the waterfront, is a peaceful spot, enhanced by its whimsical spa buildings. These look particularly quaint when viewed from the north, where they appear dwarfed by the backdrop of the Rheingrafenstein. On either side of the manicured gardens are the **Salinen**, graduation towers which have existed since the first half of the eighteenth century, and are still used by guests for the original purpose of inhaling purified air. The **Kurverwaltung** at the southwestern corner is an eighteenth-century half-timbered building which was the administration office of the original salt industry, while the **Kurmittelhaus** alongside is an ingenious early twentieth-century structure which marries traditional timber frame architecture with Jugendstil design. Inside the latter is a pump room with fountains dispensing the local mineral waters, and a sunken former bathing hall.

The **Ebernburg**, the large fortress from which the left-bank part of the town takes its name, lies on top of a vineyard-clad hill on the opposite side of the Alsenz, a Nahe tributary, from the Rheingrafenstein. Thirteenth-century by origin, it has been rebuilt on many occasions, and now serves as a family holiday home run under the auspices of the Protestant churches. Back across the Nahe, at the extreme northwestern edge of town, is the sheer-faced porphyry massif known as the **Rotenfels** (literally, "red cliffs"). A footpath runs along the top, offering yet more wonderful panoramic views.

Practicalities

The **Bahnhof**, a junction with direct connections to Bingen, Mainz and Saarbrücken as well as south through the Palatinate, lies towards the northeastern end of Bad Münster. A few minutes' walk to the southwest, at Berliner Str. 60, is the **tourist office** (Mon–Fri 8.30am–noon & 2–5pm, Sat 10am–noon; ⓣ0 67 08/39 93, ⓦwww.bad-muenster-am-stein.de). Bad Münster has plenty of **guesthouses** and **pensions**, including *Thomas*, Kurhausstr. 9 (ⓣ0 67 08/6 30 00, ⓦwww.gaestehaus-thomas.de; ❸); and *Rheingrafenblick*, Kapitän-Lorenz-Ufer 16 (ⓣ0 67 08/14 16; ❸). There are also several fine **hotels**: *Haus Lorenz*, Kapitän-Lorenz-Ufer 18 (ⓣ0 67 08/18 41; ❹); *Naheschlösschen*, Berliner Str. 69 (ⓣ0 67 08/66 10 31, ⓦwww.naheschloesschen.de; ❺); *Am Kurpark*, Kurhausstr. 19 (ⓣ0 67 08/62 90 00; ❺); and *Krone*, Berliner Str. 73–75 (ⓣ0 67 08/8 40, ⓦwww.hotel-krone-nahe.de; ❻). All of these have **restaurants**, though the last two are for residents only. In Ebernburg, there are a couple of hotels run in tandem with **wine estates**: *Landhaus Rapp*, Schlossgartenstr. 100 (ⓣ0 67 08/23 12; ❸); and *Weinhotel Schneider*, Gartenweg 2 (ⓣ0 67 08/20 43; ❹). At both of these there are wine gardens where the vintages can be sampled.

Saarland

The **Saarland**, named after the River Saar which cuts through its length, is the poorest of the western German Länder, traditionally a big coal-mining area which is now suffering from a bad case of post-industrial malaise. It was for long a political football; much of it belonged to France up until 1815, and there were repeated wrangles about its ownership during the first six decades of the twentieth century. After World War I the Saarland passed into League of Nations control, which effectively meant that the French took over, with the right to exploit local mines in compensation for damage done to their own mining industry during the war. In the January 1935 plebiscite ninety percent of Saarlanders voted for union with Nazi Germany. After World War II the Saar once again found itself in limbo, nominally autonomous but with the French government pushing for economic union. In November 1952 the population voted against reunion with Germany, but by January 1957 the increasing prosperity of the Federal Republic had convinced the Saarlanders that their future lay there, and they thus rejoined the fold – much to the chagrin of the French government.

The Land is modestly endowed in terms of tourist attractions, though it does have a surprising amount of pleasant gently rolling wooded countryside. Moreover, the satanic-looking mills of the industrial era which dominate many of the townscapes are now regarded as valuable parts of the heritage, particularly as this is one of the few parts of Western Europe where they have not already been demolished en masse. The French have left a small linguistic legacy in the shape of the greeting *Salü* which replaces the normal *Guten Tag* here. There's also been a marked French influence on local **cuisine**, traditionally a poor man's fare based on innumerable potato variations, such as *Hooriche* (rissoles).

Saarbrücken

The Land capital **SAARBRÜCKEN** is a sizeable and predominantly modern industrial city which has generally been given a bad press. However, it is very much on the ascendant at the moment, its historical role as a melting-pot of German and French culture making it ideally placed to profit from the European Union's moves towards ever closer integration. It also has its fair share of visitor attractions, including a fine setting on a broad bend of the River Saar, a large array of handsome Baroque public buildings from its eighteenth-century heyday as the Residenzstadt of one of the Nassau principalities, some good museums, a lively nightlife and – thanks in no small measure to the French connection – a distinguished culinary tradition.

Arrival, information and accommodation

Saarbrücken's **Hauptbahnhof** is at the northern end of the city centre. The **tourist office** (Mon–Fri 9am–6pm, Sat 10am–4pm; ⓣ06 81/93 80 90, ⓦwww.die-region-saarbruecken.de) is directly opposite, in the front part of the SaarGalerie shopping centre, Reichsstr. 1. Saar **cruises** (€8 for a two-hour trip) are run from the landing stage on Berliner Promenade by Saarbrücker Personenschiffahrt (ⓣ06 81/3 40 84, ⓦwww.saarbruecker-personenschiffahrt.de).

Hotels are mainly geared to business visitors, and correspondingly expensive, though there are some reasonably priced options. The **youth hostel** is at Meerwiesertalweg 31 (☎06 81/3 30 40; €16.60/21.80), on the northeastern edge of town; take bus #19, #49 or #50 (note that these do not run at weekends) to the Prinzenweiher stop. There are two **campsites**: *Saarbrücken* (March–Oct only) is at Am Spicherer Berg (☎06 81/5 17 80), near the Deutsch-Französischer Garten on the Franco-German border and reached by bus #42; *Burbach*, which is open all year round, is by the Saar on Mettlacher Strasse (☎06 81/79 29 21) in the eponymous western suburb, served by buses #10, #17, #38 and #39.

Hotels

Am Triller Trillerweg 57 ☎06 81/58 00 00, Ⓦwww.hotel-am-triller.de. Designer hotel in the historic part of town; the facilities include a swimming pool, sauna, solarium, fitness room and garden. There's also a restaurant, *Galerie Marianne*, and a bistro-bar, *Palü*. 8–9

Atlantic Ursulinenstr. 59 ☎06 81/37 92 10, Ⓦwww.hotel-atlantic.de. Good, moderately priced hotel, a short walk east of the Hauptbahnhof. 5

Im Fuchs Kappenstr. 12 ☎06 81/93 65 50, Ⓦwww.hotel-im-fuchs.de. This small hotel with restaurant is located in the lively nightlife quarter of St Johann. 6

La Résidence Faktoreistr. 2 ☎06 81/3 88 20, Ⓦwww.la-residence.net. High-class hotel, midway between the Hauptbahnhof and the River Saar. It also has a fine restaurant, *Casablanca* (closed Sat lunch & Sun). 7

Madeleine Cecilienstr. 5 ☎06 81/32228, Ⓦwww.hotel-madeleine.de. Mid-range hotel located directly opposite the Rathaus. 5

Schlosskrug Schmollerstr. 14 ☎06 81/3 6735, Ⓕ37 50 22. Situated at the eastern edge of St Johann, this hotel with restaurant is the nearest Saarbrücken has to a budget option. 4

Stadt Hamburg Bahnhofstr. 71–73 ☎06 81/3 46 92, Ⓕ3 7 43 30. Pleasant hotel on the upper floors of a building on the main pedestrianised shopping street, which means it's quiet at night. The room prices are very reasonable, and include a sizeable buffet breakfast. 5

Victor's Residenz Deutschmühlental ☎06 81/58 82 10, Ⓦwww.victors.de. A French-style grand hotel alongside the Spielbank in the west of the city, not far from the border, and reached by bus #11 or #30. It offers a choice of individually-decorated suites and has a fitness centre with sauna, solarium and massage. Local fare is served in the rustic *Victor's Stube*, Gallic cuisine in *Victor's Restaurant*, which is decked out in the style of a Paris brasserie. 7–9

The City

The city is bisected by the Saar, with the original town, now known as **Alt-Saarbrücken**, on the left side of the bend in the river. Directly opposite is **St Johann**, a former fishing village which is now the main gastronomic and nightlife district. Immediately to its north, stretching towards the Hauptbahnhof, is the modern city centre, a largely pedestrianized area of shops and offices. Of the suburbs, the most noteable from a historic point of view is the once separate town of **St Arnual** to the south.

Alt-Saarbrücken

The focal point of Alt-Saarbrücken is the sloping **Schlossplatz**, which was designed in a classically inspired Baroque idiom by **Friedrich Joachim Stengel**, the prolific court architect to the House of Nassau-Saarbrücken. Badly damaged in World War II, the **Schloss** at the top end of the square was remodelled in the early 1980s by Gottfried Böhm, who replaced the original central pavilion with an unashamedly avant-garde glass and steel structure which is guaranteed to startle the first-time viewer. The Schloss has long lost all its historic interiors, but the basement, together with Böhm's annexe on the east side, contains the **Historisches Museum** (Tues, Wed, Fri & Sun 10am–6pm, Thurs 10am–8pm, Sat noon–8pm; €2.50; Ⓦwww.historisches-museum.org), which has permanent exhibitions on Saarland under the Third Reich and in the uncertain times of the immediate postwar period, as well as temporary displays.

By far the most important of the three museums on the square is the **Museum für Vor- und Frühgeschichte** (Tues–Sat 9am–5pm, Sun 10am–6pm; free; Ⓦwww.vorgeschichte.de), which occupies the former parliament building on the west side. This contains a wide range of local archeological finds, the most notable being a major discovery of the Celtic period, the intact contents of a princess's grave from around 400 BC, which includes some beautiful jewellery and drinking vessels. On the south side of the square, the top floor of the **Altes Rathaus** houses the **Abenteuermuseum** (Tues & Wed 9am–1pm, Thurs & Fri 3–7pm, first Sat of month 10am–2pm; €2), which is devoted in roughly equal parts to the lives and cultures of "primitive" peoples and to the ego of its founder Heinz Rox-Schulz, who has spent most of his life travelling to far-flung corners of the world collecting and filming. Bizarre items from the collection include a 2000-year-old Peruvian mummy and some shrunken heads. Between Schlossplatz and the river is the fifteenth-century **Schlosskirche**, a Gothic church which is normally kept locked, though it is a regular venue for concerts. Inside are some tombs of the local counts.

From here head down Schlossstrasse and turn right into Eisenbahnstrasse. On the right is the plain white **Friedenskirche** (Peace Church) by Stengel, which is now used by Old Catholic and Russian Orthodox congregations. The former face eastwards to worship, and a single small crucifix is their altar's only adornment; the latter face west to their colourful iconostasis. Across the road is **Ludwigsplatz**, a masterly piece of late Baroque town planning, based on the French concept of a monumental *Place Royale*, which ranks as Stengel's greatest achievement. Its sides are lined with handsome urban palaces; that which closes it off to the west originally had the combined functions of poorhouse, orphanage, workhouse and prison. In the middle of the square stands the **Ludwigskirche** (Tues 3–5pm, Wed 10am–noon & 4–5.30pm, Sat 4–6pm, Sun 11am–noon), a highly original design with an unconventional tower placed over the opposite end of the building from the facade. The exterior, with its rich sculptural decoration, is unusually sumptuous for a Protestant church. In contrast, the gleaming white interior, whose four internal galleries were only reinstated a few years ago following war damage, is a classic example of Lutheran Baroque, not least in the tiered assemblage of altar table, pulpit and organ.

St Johann and the city centre

The pedestrianized **Alte Brücke**, which dates back to the sixteenth century but has been much altered since, crosses the Saar from the bank alongside the Schlosskirche. Just over the other side, the angular **Staatstheater**, a typical example of the kind of architectural thinking that went on in the Third Reich, can be seen to the right. Saarstrasse leads east to **St Johanner Markt**, an elongated old-world square with some elegant eighteenth-century houses and a Baroque fountain, all designed by Stengel. A block further east is the **Basilika St Johann**, another fine church by Stengel, this time in full Catholic pomp, with elaborate confessionals, balconies and high altar.

The **Saarland Museum** (Tues & Thurs–Sun 10am–6pm, Wed 10am–10pm; €6; Ⓦwww.saarlandmuseum.de) occupies two buildings at the southern end of St Johann. A short distance beyond the Staatstheater, at Bismarckstr. 11–19, is the **Moderne Galerie**, which contains art from the late nineteenth century until the present day. In the first hall, an excellent representation of the three leading German Impressionists, **Liebermann**, **Corinth** and **Slevogt**, is juxtaposed with a smaller group of works by their French counterparts, including

Monet, Renoir and Sisley. The gallery owns the most important collection of works by **Albert Weisgerber**, an Expressionist who was one of many artistic talents to perish on the battlefields of Flanders during World War I. Though relatively little-known, the works here, notably *Absalom* and *David and Goliath*, which both manage to convey a vivid sense of movement, show him to have been a highly original spirit. Other Expressionist masterpieces on view include *Bathers in a Room* by **Kirchner** and *The Blue Horse* by **Marc**. There are also important paintings by Nolde, Jawlensky, Ernst, Dix and Beckmann, and sculptures by Barlach and Lehmbruck. Opposite, at Karlstr. 1, is the **Alte Sammlung**, which covers fine and applied art of earlier periods. Its main strength is a collection of medieval sculpture from not only the Saarland, but neighbouring Luxembourg and Lorraine as well. Appropriately enough, the highlight of the small array of old master paintings is a *Classical Landscape* by **Claude Lorraine**.

At the northern end of St Johann is the massive Historicist **Rathaus**, built in the last years of the nineteenth century by Georg von Hauberisser, who is best known for designing its equally pretentious Munich counterpart. A more aesthetically pleasing architectural curiosity is the **Bergwerksdirektion** (Mining Administration Headquarters) at the corner of Bahnhofstrasse and Reichsstrasse near the northern end of the large pedestrian precinct which forms Saarbrücken's commercial heart. Built in 1880, it resembles Schinkel's buildings of half-a-century before, which makes it seem all the odder that it was co-designed by the young Walter Gropius, founder of the revolutionary Bauhaus movement.

St Arnual

St Arnual, which can be reached by buses #26, #36 and #46, still preserves a village-like atmosphere, and seems a world away from downtown Saarbrücken, though it is in fact only 3km distant. Just off its market square, St Arnualer Markt, stands the Gothic **Stiftskirche**, nowadays the Protestant parish church. It was the favoured burial place of the House of Nassau-Saarbrücken, and contains several dozen tombs of family members. The most imposing is that in the middle of the choir to Elisabeth of Lorraine. A pioneering translator of French literature into German, she is depicted in the widow's outfit she wore on assuming the role of regent following the death of her husband in 1429. Most of the later memorials are placed upright against the walls; many are executed in a somewhat folksy version of the Renaissance style and still preserve their bright polychromy.

Eating, drinking and entertainment

Saarbrücken is one of Germany's leading gourmet cities, with many highly cosmopolitan restaurants, and has a vibrant nightlife scene, thanks to the presence of a sizeable student population. A concentration of recommendable establishments is clustered on and around St Johanner Markt, though others can be found all over town, with some of the best restaurants being in the hotels (see p.481).

The Staatstheater, Tbilisser Platz 1 (Ⓣ06 81/3 32 04, Ⓦwww.theater-saarbruecken.de) is the main **cultural** venue, presenting opera, operetta, dance, drama and concerts. One unusual event is the Perspectives du Théâtre **festival** of young French theatre, held every May, which usually throws up a few avant-garde offerings. There's also the Max-Ophüls-Preis film festival held every January.

Restaurants

Bitburger Residenz Dudweilerstr. 56. Well-regarded brasserie named after the Bitburger brewery in the Eifel, whose beer is available on draught. Closed Sat lunchtime.
Hashimoto Cecilienstr. 7. Quality Japanese restaurant which serves good-value set lunches. On Sat, it's only open in the evening; closed Mon.
Kuntze's Handelshof Wilhelm-Heinrich-Str. 17. One of Saarbrücken's leading gourmet addresses, serving both French and German cuisine. Closed Sat lunchtime & Sun evening.
Michelangelo Rathausplatz 6. Italian restaurant decorated with pastiches of the heroic frescoes of the great Renaissance master.
Ratskeller Rathausplatz 1. This is something of a cross between the normal German municipal cellar restaurant and a French brasserie.
tierlieb Cecilienstr. 12. By German standards, this is an unconventional vegetarian restaurant, having a bistro-style ambience instead of the usual minimalism, and being open in the evenings, though it also serves lunch Mon–Fri.
Weinhaus Hauck St Johanner Markt 7. Wine bar-cum-wine merchant, with a large choice of local and international vintages and bistro-style food to match.
Zum Stiefel Am Stiefel 2. This eighteenth-century Gasthaus is the flagship of the Bruch brewery, and has a menu with a good choice of local specialities. Closed Sun lunchtime.

Bars and cafés

Big Ben Försterstr. 17. The heart of the local gay scene (both men and women).
Ein-und-Fünfzig (51) Am Schlossplatz. Trendy café with outside tables on Schlossplatz; it also serves light, Mediterranean-type cuisine.
Fürst Ludwig Ludwigsplatz 13. Incongruously sharing a building with a police station, this small Kneipe sets up outdoor tables on Ludwigsplatz in summer. It offers a good range of salads, pasta and pancakes.
Kulturcafé St Johanner Markt 24. Café attached to the Stadtgalerie; in the summer, there's a choice of sitting outside or surrounded by the artworks upstairs.
Schubert Sulzbachstr. 2. Multiple award-winning coffee house, particularly renowned for its hand-made liqueur chocolates, *Perlen der Saar*.
Stiefelbräu Cnr of Am Stiefel and Fröschengasse. Hausbrauerei which makes light and dark beers and serves cheaper and more basic meals than its sister restaurant next door.

Völklingen and Mettlach

Beyond Saarbrücken, the two most notable destinations in the Saarland are **Völklingen** and **Mettlach**, each of which offers a major piece of industrial heritage. Within the boundaries of the latter is the Land's finest scenery, a particularly beautiful stretch of the River Saar.

Völklingen

Few places can have experienced such dramatic swings of fortune in recent decades as the Saarland's third largest town, **VÖLKLINGEN**, which lies just 14km down the Saar from Saarbrücken. In the 1960s it was a thriving industrial community to which thousands of workers commuted every day. By the mid-1970s its heavy industry had gone into irreversible decline, and the town had become an economic blackspot. Yet twenty years later, it was propelled to the status of something that would have seemed totally implausible only a short time before – a tourist attraction of international stature.

This last development is a result of UNESCO's decision to include its redundant iron works, the **Alte Völklinger Hütte** (daily: late March to Oct 10am–7pm, rest of year indoor sections only 10am–6pm; €7.50, free Tues after 2pm; Ⓦwww.voelklinger-huette.org), on the highly prestigious World Heritage List. This is frequently referred to as a "cathedral of the Industrial Age", though the description does not even begin to suggest the awesome size and extent of the buildings on the 60-hectare complex, the only one of its type anywhere in the world to survive intact. Founded in 1873, the works were taken over by the Röchling family eight years later, and remained in their hands until they were closed down in 1986, just two decades after the workface had peaked at 17,000. By the entrance is the **Gasgebläsehaus**, whose ground floor regularly hosts international photography exhibitions. The first-floor hall, now in regular service as a somewhat improbable concert venue, contains six huge gas compressors, all dating from just before World War I, which remained in operation right up until the day of closure. However, the most imposing feature of the works is the **Hochofengruppe**, a row of six huge blast furnaces erected between 1882 and 1916. Coke was transported to them by the **Hängebahn**, a remarkable technical monument in its own right, using systems derived from both funiculars and hanging railways. Ironically, it was the presence of such technologically advanced features that was responsible for the ultimate demise of the Völklingen works, as it was less adaptable to modernisation than competitors with more primitive equipment. Among the various exhibitions in the administration buildings, a photographic documentation on the life of the workers deals very honestly with the health problems that were endemic throughout the history of the works, due to the employees' constant exposure to heat, dust and dirt. It is small wonder that local emotions were mixed when production finally ceased.

Völklingen's **Bahnhof** is on the opposite side of the tracks from the ironworks. The **tourist office** (Mon–Fri 9.30am–4.30pm, Sat & Sun 9.30am–12.30pm & 1–4.30pm; Ⓣ0 68 98/2 11 00, Ⓦwww.voelklingen.de) is right alongside, in the late nineteenth-century Alter Bahnhof, Rathausstr. 57. Although there's no real reason to stay the night, the town has a few **hotels**, including *Heidstock*, Gerhardstr. 124 (Ⓣ0 68 98/85 26 54; ❸); and *Parkhotel Gengenbach*, Kuhlweinstr. 70 (Ⓣ0 68 98/91 47 00; ❼). The latter's *Orangerie* is Völklingen's best and most expensive **restaurant**; the bistro in the aforementioned Alter Bahnhof is a good and much cheaper alternative.

Mettlach

Another 40m along the Saar is **METTLACH**, which ranks as one of Saarland's prettier towns, despite being a virtual fiefdom of the ceramics and interior design firm Villeroy & Boch, whose specialist factories dominate the townscape. The massive Baroque **Benediktinerabtei** overlooking the waterfront, which had fallen victim to the Napoleonic suppression, was taken over by Jean-François Boch in 1809 to serve as the new headquarters of his family firm, founded in Lorraine back in 1748. This merged with the rival Villeroy works in 1836, and is still in the hands of the descendants – a situation which has no parallel in any other major European industrial enterprise. Part of the abbey complex is given over to a newly revamped visitors' centre or **Erlebniszentrum** (Mon–Fri 9am–6pm, Sat & Sun 9.30am–4pm; €2.50; Ⓦwww.villeroy-boch.com). This is in three parts: Keravision, a film about the company; a series of tableaux about its products; and the Keramikmuseum, which offers a chronological presentation of its historical collection.

On the western side of the Benediktinerabtei is a park in which can be seen one of the company's most spectacular recent productions, the **Living Planet Square**. Designed by the ceramic artist Stefan Szczesny for EXPO 2000, it features a dozen tile pictures illustrating the continents of the world in the manner of a giant jigsaw puzzle. Alongside is the so-called **Alter Turm**, an octagonal chapel erected at the very end of the tenth century as a mausoleum for the town's founder, St Lutwinus, who had been Bishop of Trier at the turn of the eighth century. Some valuable treasures associated with him – a seventh-century bowl and bishops' ring, and a thirteenth-century triptych-reliquary – can be seen in the **Pfarrkirche St Liutwin**, a pretentious Historicist church high above the town centre on Freiherr-von-Stein-Strasse.

From the town's jetty, several competing companies, among them Mettlacher Personenschiffahrt (Ⓣ0 68 64/8 02 20), run **cruises** (€7.50 round trip) every day between March and October to the Saarland's best-known beauty spot, the **Saarschleife** (Saar Bend), a colossal loop in the river, between which is a thickly wooded peninsula. However, this is not really seen at its best from water level; the famous view which features in all the tourist brochures is an aerial one from the **Cloef** belvedere. This is at the edge of the little health resort of **ORSCHOLZ**, which lies 6km northwest of Mettlach, of which it now forms a part.

Bus #6309 runs between Mettlach and Orscholz from the former's **Bahnhof**, which is a short walk northeast of the town centre. The **tourist office** (Mon–Fri 8.30am–4.30pm; Ⓣ0 68 64/83 84, Ⓦwww.tourist-info.mettlach.de) at Freiherr-von-Stein-Str. 64 has a list of **private rooms** (❶–❸). Reasonably priced **hotels** in Mettlach itself include *Zur Post*, a stone's throw from the rear of the Bahnhof at Heinertstr. 17 (Ⓣ0 68 64/5 57, Ⓦwww.hotel-post-mettlach.de; ❸), and *Saarblick*, Freiherr-von-Stein-Str. 14 (Ⓣ0 68 64/5 83, Ⓦwww.hotel-saarpark.de; ❸). More upmarket options are *Zum Schwan*, Freiherr-von-Stein-Str. 34a (Ⓣ0 68 64/72 79, Ⓦwww.hotel-schwan-mettlach.de; ❺); and *Saarpark*, Bahnhofstr. 31 (Ⓣ0 68 64/92 00, Ⓦwww.hotel-saarpark.de; ❼). In Orscholz, the best place to stay is *Zur Saarschleife*, Cloefstr. 44 (Ⓣ0 68 64/17 90, Ⓦwww.hotel-saarschleife.de; ❻). There's a **youth hostel** at Herbergstr. 1 (Ⓣ0 68 68/27 0, Ⓕ0 68 68/5 56; €16.60/21.80), in the incorporated village of Dreisbach to the west. All the hotels listed have **restaurants**, though there are a couple of enticing alternatives. *Abtei-Bräu*, Bahnhofstr. 32, is a Hausbrauerei with a large garden which makes an unfiltered beer and serves Saarland specialities. *Schloss Ziegelberg*, high above the northern edge of town, was built in the 1870s in the style of a French Renaissance chateau as the home of the Boch family, and is now a gourmet restaurant with a strong line in fish dishes.

Travel details

Trains

Koblenz to: Andernach (hourly; 15min); Bingen (hourly; 45min); Boppard (hourly; 15min); Cologne (hourly; 1hr 30min); Rüdesheim (hourly; 1hr); Saarbrücken (8 daily; 2hr 25min); Trier (hourly; 1hr 20min).

Mainz to: Bonn (hourly; 2hr 15min); Cologne (hourly; 2hr 30min); Frankfurt (frequent; 30min); Idar-Oberstein (hourly; 1hr 20min); Karlsruhe (hourly; 1hr 5min); Koblenz (frequent; 1hr); Saarbrücken (8 daily; 2hr 30min); Worms (every 30min; 40min).

Saarbrücken to: Cologne (5 daily; 3hr 30min); Koblenz (8 daily; 2hr 25min); Trier (hourly; 1hr 5min).

5

North Rhine-Westphalia

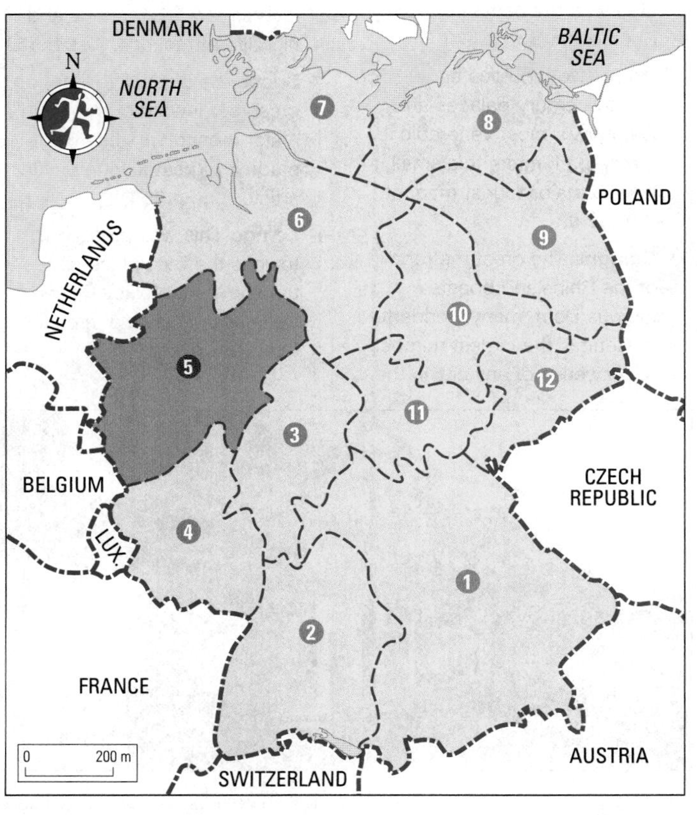

CHAPTER 5

Highlights

* **Aachen** The capital of Charlemagne's great empire preserves one of the world's most spectacular arrays of treasures in its Dom and Schatzkammer. See p.493
* **Bonn** The secondary seat of the German government boasts a fine setting on the Rhine, and is indelibly associated with the name of Beethoven. See p.500
* **Brühl** Two fabulous eighteenth-century palaces and Germany's most venerable theme park make this small town a major tourist magnet. See p.509
* **Cologne** The great metropolis of the Rhineland boasts a famous Dom, many wonderful museums, the largest number of breweries of any city in the world and spectacular Shrovetide celebrations. See p.510
* **Wuppertal** This city's hanging railway or Schwebebahn is a public transport system unlike any other on the planet. See p.533
* **Münster** This lively university and episcopal city offers a diverse range of cultural and nightlife attractions. See p.553
* **Soest** The distinctive lime green stonework of this town's major monuments has long made it a great favourite with artists. See p.563
* **Lemgo** This well-preserved town is the best place to see the somewhat folksy Weser Renaissance style of architecture. See p.572

△ The Schwebebahn, Wuppertal, with a historical vehicle

5

North Rhine-Westphalia

North Rhine-Westphalia (Nordrhein-Westfalen) is only the fourth largest of the Länder in terms of area, but has, with seventeen million inhabitants, by far the largest population. As its double-barrelled name suggests, it's historically two distinct provinces whose separateness dates back to the very beginnings of German history, the North Rhine having belonged to the Franks, while Westphalia marked the beginning of Saxon territory. With the industrialization process in the nineteenth century, any lingering distinction between the two provinces – both of which had been absorbed by the expansionist Kingdom of Prussia – became hopelessly blurred with the mushroom growth of a vast built-up area around the mineral-rich valley of the River Ruhr. This formed a clearly recognizable unit, yet was divided almost exactly in half by the traditional boundaries. After World War II, it was decided to preserve the economic integrity of the **Ruhrgebiet**, as the area came to be known, by creating a single new Land out of the two old provinces.

Of the 38 German cities registering a population of over 200,000, ten are in North Rhine and a further six in Westphalia. Many begin just as another ends, and the Ruhrgebiet is joined to a string of other cities stretching right to the southern border with Rhineland-Palatinate, making up the most densely populated area in Europe. In this conurbation, **Cologne** is by far the most outstanding city, managing to preserve much of the atmosphere and splendours of its long centuries as a free state, at times the most powerful in Germany. The Land's other city of top-class historical interest is **Aachen**, the original capital of the Holy Roman Empire. Next in line comes **Münster**, which would presumably be capital of Westphalia, if such a division still existed. As it is, the Land government meets in self-consciously cosmopolitan **Düsseldorf**, which inspires admiration and revulsion in roughly equal measure. At the southern end of the Land is **Bonn**, capital of the West German state for its forty-year existence, and still one of the national seats of government. Never suited for the role it was so casually given in 1949, it's a place all too easily maligned.

In spite of the stranglehold heavy industry has traditionally held over North Rhine-Westphalia, much of the landscape is rural, with agriculture, forestry and tourism making key contributions to the economy. There are also some

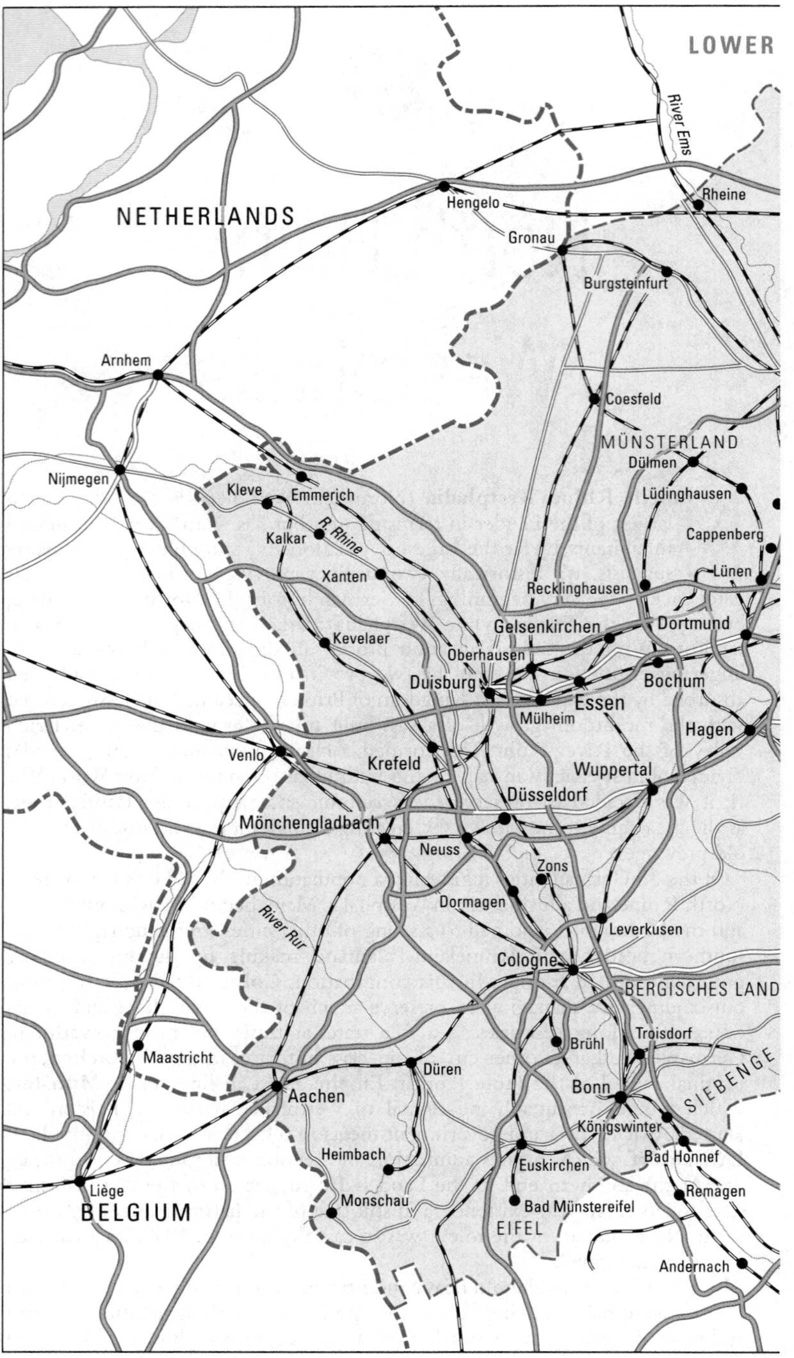
LOWER
River Ems
NETHERLANDS
Hengelo
Rheine
Gronau
Burgsteinfurt
Arnhem
Coesfeld
MÜNSTERLAND
Nijmegen
Dülmen
Kleve
Emmerich
Lüdinghausen
R. Rhine
Kalkar
Cappenberg
Xanten
Lünen
Recklinghausen
Gelsenkirchen
Dortmund
Kevelaer
Oberhausen
Duisburg
Bochum
Essen
Mülheim
Hagen
Venlo
Krefeld
Wuppertal
Düsseldorf
Mönchengladbach
Neuss
Zons
Dormagen
River Rur
Leverkusen
Cologne
BERGISCHES LAND
Troisdorf
Brühl
Maastricht
Düren
SIEBENGE
Bonn
Aachen
Königswinter
Heimbach
Euskirchen
Bad Honnef
Liège
Monschau
Remagen
Bad Münstereifel
BELGIUM
EIFEL
Andernach

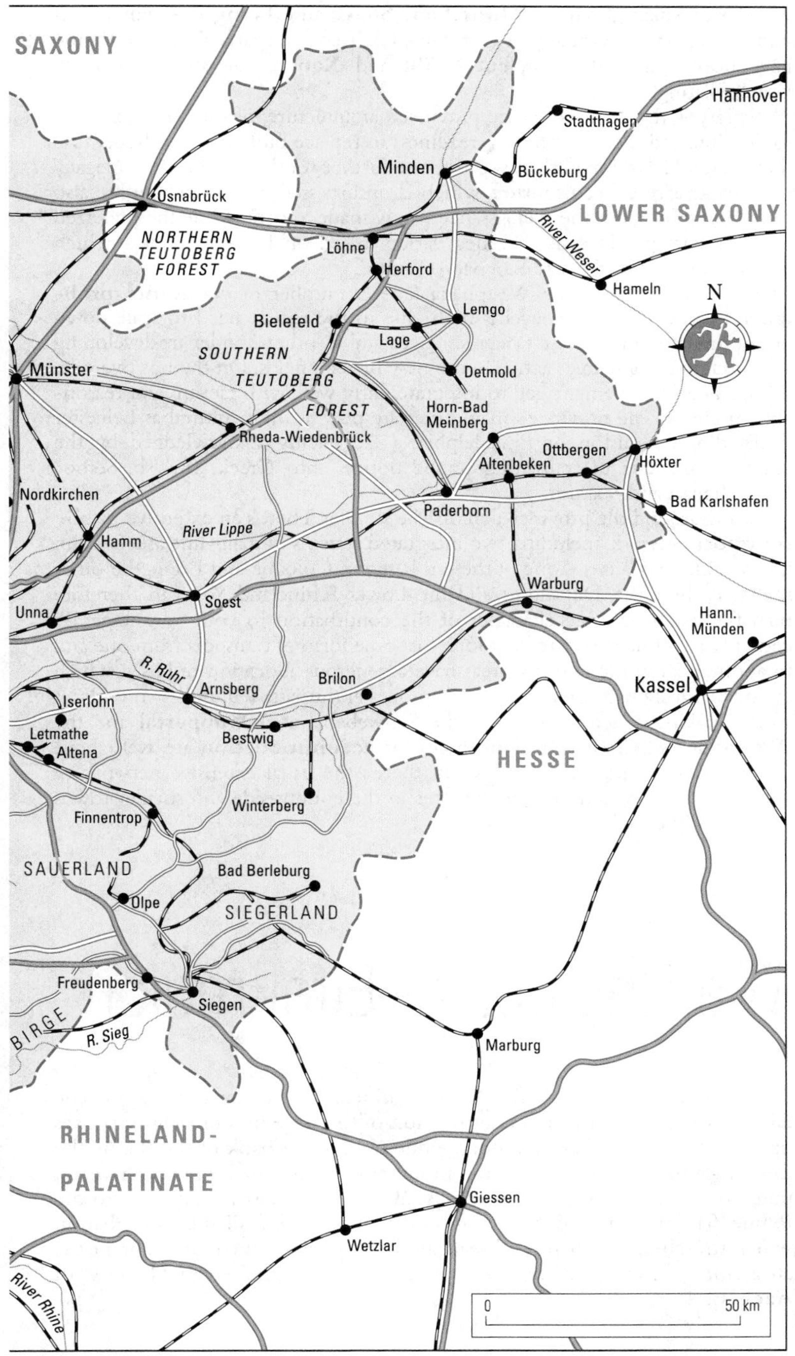

5

NORTH RHINE-WESTPHALIA

wonderful small towns – **Monschau**, **Soest** and **Lemgo** – which can stand comparison with any in Germany. Their counterparts along the Rhine have been scarred by war, but **Brühl** and **Xanten** are still particularly worth visiting.

Sobriety is the keynote of the province's architecture; new styles were slow to develop, and there was far less readiness to replace buildings simply because they were old-fashioned than was the case further south. There is thus a legacy of **Romanesque architecture** which is unsurpassed in Europe. Gothic also took strong root, but the Renaissance barely made a mark, while the preferred form of Baroque was the dignified variety based on Roman models, which didn't lend itself to flowery Rococo offshoots.

Currently, North Rhine-Westphalia faces a number of **economic problems**. Its unemployment level is high, due to the recent need to scale down heavy industry, and it hasn't been as successful as other Länder in developing and attracting companies active in the new hi-tech fields. On the positive side, the *Gastarbeiter* have managed to integrate fairly well, with racism kept reasonably in check. The province's main cities are now as multicultural as Leicester or Bradford, Houston or Philadelphia, a fact tacitly acknowledged by the common practice of translating public notices into Greek, Turkish, Serbo-Croat, Italian and Spanish.

Getting around the province couldn't be simpler. There's an extensive **public transport** network, including two integrated systems of main-line and S-Bahn trains, trams and buses – one of these is based in Cologne and Bonn, the other in the Ruhrgebiet, Düsseldorf and the Lower Rhineland. You can therefore turn the claustrophobic character of the conurbation to your advantage: it's certainly never necessary to wait long for some form of transport from one city to another. Even the country areas have a generous allocation of buses, which are often hardly used by the locals. Transport enthusiasts will find two oddities worth making a detour to see – the Schwebebahn in **Wuppertal** and the Wasserstrassenkreuz in **Minden**. Prices for **accommodation** are well above the national average in the cities, but there's the usual extensive network of youth hostels and campsites, while rates in the countryside and smaller towns are generally excellent value.

The Rhineland–Eifel region

The southwestern part of the North Rhineland is an upland region. The **Eifel range**, which forms a continuation of the Ardennes in Belgium, takes up the lion's share of this territory, while on the east bank of the Rhine the **Siebengebirge** are the last of the mountain ranges which give the river so much of its characteristic grandeur. At **Bonn**, the landscape adjacent to the Rhine flattens out, and here begins the enormous built-up conurbation which stretches, with hardly a break, all the way up to Dortmund. The prime attraction of this area, however, is undoubtedly the venerable city of **Aachen**.

Aachen

"In Aachen I saw all kinds of priceless treasures, the like of which no man has seen rarer," wrote Dürer following a visit there in 1560. His enthusiasm can still be echoed; **AACHEN** possesses fabulous riches fit to be compared with those of Istanbul or Venice, as UNESCO duly recognized by choosing the magnificent Dom – which has since been superbly restored for its 1200th anniversary celebrations in 2000 – as one of the dozen global wonders which comprised the very first list of World Heritage Sites.

Now a frontier post – the municipal area includes stretches of border with both Belgium and the Netherlands – Aachen has metamorphosed from a far grander role. In the late eighth and early ninth centuries the city was seen as the successor to ancient Rome, the hub of the great Frankish empire of **Charlemagne** (Karl der Grosse) which comprised pretty well all of present-day Germany, France, the Benelux, Austria and Switzerland, as well as much of Italy and part of northern Spain. In 794, after 26 years of almost constant campaigning, Charlemagne established Aachen as the main seat of his court. The choice was made partly for strategic reasons, but also because of the presence of hot springs, over which the Romans had first built thermal baths.

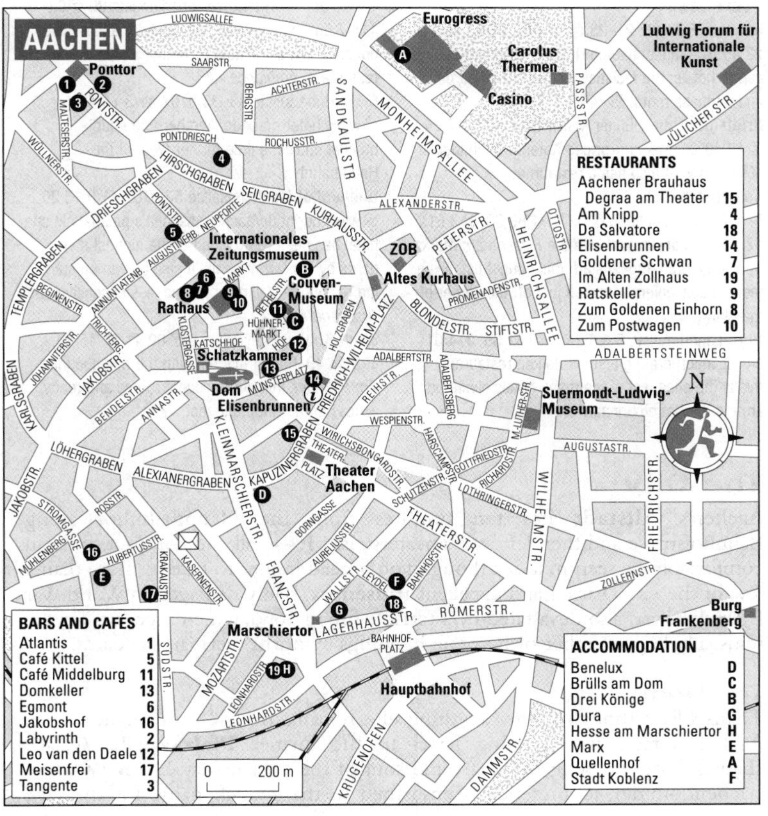

Exercising in these waters was one of the emperor's favourite pastimes, and his contemporaries rated him a swimmer without peer. The **spa** has continually given the city prestige and visitors, but its political power was short-lived, lasting only a generation after Charlemagne's death.

Arrival, information and accommodation

Aachen's **Hauptbahnhof** is just south of the city centre. Some buses stop outside, but others – including those to Monschau – leave from the **bus station** at the corner of Peterstrasse and Kurhausstrasse. The **tourist office** (Mon–Fri 9am–6pm, Sat 9am–2pm; ⓣ02 41/1 80 29 60, ⓦwww.aachen-tourist.de) occupies the Atrium Elisenbrunnen (one of the pavilions of a Schinkel-designed building centred on the main public drinking fountain) on Friedrich-Wilhelm-Platz.

There's a large concentration of **hotels** near the Hauptbahnhof, but most of the genuine budget options are a long way out. The **youth hostel** is also out of the centre, situated on a little hill in a suburban park to the southwest, at Maria-Theresia Allee 260 (ⓣ02 41/71 10 10; €20.90/23.60); take bus #2 direction Preuswald from the Elisenbrunnen and alight at Brüsseler Ring or Ronheide.

Hotels

Benelux Franzstr. 21–23 ⓣ02 41/2 23 43, ⓕ2 23 45. The most characterful of the upmarket city-centre hotels; the facilities include a roof garden and a fitness room. ❻–❽

Brülls am Dom Hühner Markt ⓣ02 41/3 17 04, ⓕ40 43 26. Medium-priced hotel in the handiest of locations; it also has a restaurant, *Couvenstube*. ❼

Drei Könige Büchel 5 ⓣ02 41/4 83 93, ⓕ3 61 52. Run in conjunction with the *Pizzeria am Markt* by a truly international staff, this budget establishment is conveniently located just off the corner of the Markt. ❹

Dura Lagerhausstr. 5 ⓣ02 41/40 31 35, ⓕ4 01 84 50. Incorporating a small Balkan restaurant, this is the cheapest of the many hotels clustered around the Hauptbahnhof. ❸

Hesse am Marschiertor Friedlandstr. 20 ⓣ02 41/47 05 40, ⓦwww.hotelhesse.de. Good-value option which also has a recommendable Italian restaurant, *Ambience*. ❺

Marx Hubertusstr. 33–35 ⓣ02 41/3 75 41, ⓦwww.hotel-marx.de. Another fine middle-bracket choice, a little further west of the Hauptbahnhof. ❹–❻

Quellenhof Monheimsallee 52 ⓣ02 41/9 13 20, ⓦwww.dorint.de/aachen. Aachen's palatial old spa hotel has been refurbished to the highest standards by the Dorint chain. It also has an outstanding restaurant, *Lakmé*, plus the less expensive *La Brasserie*. ❾.

Stadt Koblenz Leydelstr. 2 ⓣ02 41/47 45 80, ⓕ3 54 49. Run in tandem with the neighbouring *Am Bahnhof*, this offers decent rooms and ready access to the Hauptbahnhof. ❹

The City

Aachen's **Altstadt** lies ten minutes from the Hauptbahnhof along Bahnhofstrasse and then left into Theaterstrasse. It's small and compact, and can comfortably be seen in a day, though you'll need longer to take in more than a few of the city's varied and excellent **museums**. Badly damaged in World War II, Aachen was also devastated by a terrible fire in 1656, which accounts for the unusually large number of Baroque buildings by north German standards.

The Dom

Thankfully, although hardly anything else remains from Charlemagne's time, Aachen retains its crowning jewel in the former **Pfalzkapelle** (palace chapel). Now forming the heart and soul of the present-day **Dom** (ⓦwww.aachendom.de), its presence is enshrined in the French name for the city,

Aix-la-Chapelle. A ninth-century monk-chronicler, Notker the Stammerer, relates how skilled workmen were brought from many lands in order that this edifice should surpass any previously erected, and concluded that it was "built by human hands, yet with the inspiration of God". Charlemagne's courtier Einhard, who must have watched the building's construction, attributed its splendour to the emperor's religious devotion, and fills in details of the decoration – "gold and silver, with lamps, and with lattices and doors of solid bronze". He also explained that marble columns were brought from as far as Ravenna, on whose basilica of San Vitale the chapel was largely modelled.

Even after such descriptions, you can't help being overwhelmed by its extraordinary symmetry, height and grandeur. Designed by **Odo von Metz**, it's an eight-sided dome, surrounded by a sixteen-sided ambulatory, above which is a two-tiered gallery with eight arcades of columns; the number eight is significant, representing perfection and harmony. The circumference of the octagon is 144 Carolingian feet – the cardinal number of the heavenly Jerusalem – and that of the outer polygon exactly twice that: an impeccable concord and order intended to symbolize Heaven. As a result of the cult of Charlemagne (he was canonized by an anti-pope in 1165) and the possession of the so-called Great Aachen Relics (allegedly the swaddling clothes and loincloth of Christ, the gown of the Virgin and the garb of St John the Baptist), pilgrims poured into the city in such numbers that the building needed to be expanded. An airily high and narrow **Gothic chancel** was therefore added, modelled on the Ste-Chapelle in Paris. Its original stained glass has been lost, but the replacements at least give the right effect. Also from this period is a series of two-storey chapels encircling the octagon. The one specially endowed for the use of Hungarian pilgrims was later replaced by an Italianate Baroque design, as successive generations sought to leave their mark on the Dom; another important addition was the western **tower**, which was under construction for several centuries.

Some of the original furnishings survive: in the vestibule alone you can see the bronze doors with lions' heads mentioned by Einhard, along with a pine cone which seems to have been a waterspout and an antique she-wolf. These are rather overshadowed by the costly embellishments with which Charlemagne's successors enhanced the Dom, making it positively drip with treasure. Adorning the main altar is the **Pala d'Oro**, an early eleventh-century altar front with ten embossed scenes of the Passion. Behind, and of similar date, is the **ambo**, a pulpit like no other, fashioned from gold-plated copper adorned with precious stones, reliefs of the Evangelists and ancient Egyptian ivories of profane subjects. Suspended from the dome by means of a mighty iron chain is the enormous twelfth-century **chandelier** given by Frederick Barbarossa. Regrettably, its weight quickly caused the mosaics to crack; those to be seen today are a nineteenth-century attempt at re-creating the effect of the originals. The gilded **shrine of Charlemagne** at the end of the chancel was finished in 1215, having been fifty years in the making. It contains the remains of the saint, who is depicted on the front, and also serves as a glorification of the Holy Roman Empire he founded, with portraits of his successors along the sides, instead of the normal biblical personages. Likewise in the chancel is the **shrine of St Mary**, which was made to house the Great Aachen Relics, but not started until the companion-piece to Charlemagne had at last been finished – a revealing illustration of how important his cult had become. Charlemagne's status is further emphasized by the early fifteenth-century statue of him on the pier behind his shrine, the only outsider in a cycle of the Virgin and Apostles.

In the gallery is the **imperial throne**, a marble chair with a wooden seat approached by six steps, in the manner of that in Solomon's temple; from here the emperor had a grandstand view of all that was happening below. The most recent scientific examination has all but conclusively confirmed the traditional belief that it did indeed belong to Charlemagne. In order to see the throne (with an added bonus of a different perspective on the Dom and its furnishings) and enter the chancel you've no choice but to join a **guided tour**. These cost €2 and leave from the Schatzkammer, which has its own entrance on Klostergasse; there are at least a couple a day, with hourly departures at the height of the season.

The Schatzkammer

The **Schatzkammer** (Mon 10am–1pm, Tues, Wed & Fri–Sun 10am–6pm, Thurs 10am–9pm; €2.50), housed in chambers off the cloisters, is as much an essential sight as the Dom. Quite simply, it's the richest treasury in northern Europe, a dazzling feast for the eyes and an unashamed glorification of the wealth and power of the Church Triumphant. Prominent among its treasures is the greatest of all processional crucifixes, the late tenth-century **Lothar cross**, studded with jewels and bearing an antique cameo of the Emperor Augustus; the Crucifixion is modestly engraved on the reverse. From the beginning of the following century come a **holy-water vessel**, carved from an elephant's tusk, and a **golden book cover** with an ivory of the Madonna and Child, which was made as an accessory to the Pala d'Oro in the decoration of the altar. The only items dating from the time of Charlemagne are a damaged **ivory diptych** and the Byzantine **Quadriga cloth**; the latter was used as his burial shroud, while the large **Roman sarcophagus** carved with a scene of the rape of Proserpine served as his improbable coffin from his death until his canonization.

Other priceless textiles include two associated with the coronation of Emperor Charles IV in 1349: the **Griffin cloth** and the so-called **Cappa Leonis**. Among many superb fourteenth-century **reliquaries**, note the idealized portrait head of Charlemagne and the two shaped like Gothic chapels. Gifts from such devotees as Margaret of York and Louis of Hungary show the international extent of the Aachen cult. The astonishing vibrancy of the local goldsmith tradition down the centuries is proved by the sixteenth-century work of **Hans von Reutlingen**, which stands comparison with any of the older masterpieces.

The Rathaus

Charlemagne's palace once extended across the Katschhof, now lined with ugly modern buildings, to the site of the present **Rathaus** (daily 10am–1pm & 2–5pm; €1.50). Fronting the Markt, which boasts the finest of the medieval houses left in the city, its facade is lined with the figures of fifty Holy Roman emperors – 31 of them crowned in Aachen. Above the entrance, Charlemagne shares a niche with Christ and Pope Leo III, who conducted his coronation ceremony in Rome on Christmas Day 800. Built in the fourteenth century on the palace foundations, and incorporating two of its **towers**, the Rathaus is a mix of attempts to restore its original Gothic form with the inevitable Baroque changes of later years. The finest feature of the interior is the much-restored **Kaisersaal**. Here the *Karlspreis* (Charlemagne Prize) is awarded annually to the citizen who is deemed to have made the largest contribution to European unity. A cycle of frescoes by the Düsseldorf artist Alfred Rethel gives a Romantic portrayal of scenes from Charlemagne's life, but your attention is more likely to be drawn by the crown jewels, dazzlingly displayed at one end. These are only reproductions, however; the originals have been kept in Vienna since the early nineteenth century, when they were commandeered by the Habsburgs for their new role as emperors of Austria.

The rest of the centre

Southeast of the Markt is another square, the Hühner Markt, where livestock was formerly sold. Here stands the **Couven-Museum** (Tues–Fri 10am–5pm, Sat & Sun 11am–5pm; €3; Ⓦwww.couven-museum.de), an elegant merchant-class home which has been named after a father-and-son team of architects who designed many of the city's Baroque buildings. It has been fitted out with mid-eighteenth- to mid-nineteenth-century furnishings gathered from houses of the Aachen-Liège region, giving an idea of the stylish if frivolous priorities of the local bourgeoisie. Look out for the complete pharmacy, a lavishly decorated first-floor living room with carved chimneypiece and the huge Advent crib in the attic. Before the construction of modern facilities, the hub of Aachen's spa life was the **Altes Kurhaus**, an ornate late eighteenth-century building by the younger Couven, situated east of the Markt at Komphausbadstr. 19.

In a house on Pontstrasse, which leads north of the Markt, **Paul Julius von Reuter** established his famous news agency, using carrier pigeons to circulate the reports. To commemorate this, the **Internationales Zeitungsmuseum** (Tues–Fri 9.30am–1pm; free; Ⓦwww.izm.de), with a collection of some 120,000 newspapers, has been established at no. 13 in the same street. An exhibition room has been set up to show by means of original editions how the press (German- and English-language examples dominate) reacted to great stories, from the 1848 revolutions via the two world wars to contemporary conflicts. At the end of Pontstrasse – which functions as the hub of the student nightlife scene – is the **Ponttor**, an awesome early fourteenth-century gateway which was formerly the strongest part of the city's fortification system. Of the ten other gates, the only survivor is the **Marschiertor** just to the west of the Hauptbahnhof.

At the eastern edge of the centre, at Wilhelmstr. 18, is the **Suermondt-Ludwig-Museum** (Tues & Thurs–Sun noon–6pm, Wed noon–9pm; €3, or €5 combined ticket with Burg Frankeburg, the Couven-Museum and the Ludwig Forum; Ⓦwww.suermondt-ludwig-museum.de). It has an excellent collection of northern European medieval sculpture, with an extensive array of Pietàs, Madonnas and Passions; these are almost exclusively anonymous and predominantly folksy in style, though some, such as the large Lower Rhenish *St Peter Altar*, achieve a rather more developed artistic sense. Also of special note are the Baroque fancies of **Dietrich von Rath**, the city's last important goldsmith, and the sculptures and stained glass by **Ewald Mataré**, an Aachen artist best known for his role in creating new works for German cathedrals and churches in the period of their restoration following war damage. There are also a number of old masters, including notable works by Joos van Cleve, Cranach, Van Dyck, Ribera and Zurbarán.

The suburbs

One of Aachen's two spa quarters is centred on **Monheimsallee** to the north-east of the Altstadt. It's best known for its **Casino** (Mon–Thurs & Sun 3pm–2am, Fri & Sat 3pm–3am; minimum stake €2.50 at the cheapest roulette table), housed in a Neoclassical building with a glitteringly modernized interior.

Note that the management want only the better class of visitor, with full evening dress the normal attire. Due east through the well-tended **Kurgarten** is the city's new showpiece bathing complex, the **Carolus Thermen** (daily 9am–11pm; prices start at €9 for 2hr 30min, or €17 with sauna).

Just south of the quarter, housed in a Bauhaus-style former umbrella factory building at Jülicher Str. 97–109, is the **Ludwig Forum für Internationale Kunst** (Tues–Sun noon–6pm; €3). This is one of Germany's most vibrant centres for contemporary visual arts and while what's on display at any one time is obviously a lottery; all the big names of modern American painting and sculpture, including Roy Lichtenstein, Andy Warhol, Chuck Close and Duane Hanson, are well represented. Soviet and Eastern European art is another strength, with two large installations by the Ukrainian **Igor Kopytianskij** being particularly eye-catching. Also worth seeking out is a papier-mâché piece by a German-American sculptor, **Thomas Lanigan-Schmidt**, *A Rite of Passage – the Leprechaun*, which took eleven years to make; displayed alongside is his even more spectacular *Iconostasis*. **Jörg Immendorff**'s *Brandenburg Gate* is the highlight of an extensive representation of the German avant-garde.

About fifteen minutes' walk east of the Hauptbahnhof, at Bismarckstr. 68, is a moated medieval castle, **Burg Frankenberg** (Tues–Thurs 9am–noon, Sun 11am–2pm; €1; Ⓦwww.burgfrankenberg.de). The interior has been restored to house the local history museum; though mainly of parochial appeal, this has interesting models which attempt to re-create the likely original form of Charlemagne's palace. Ceramic products from Aachen are displayed in the tower. On the opposite side of the rail tracks is the suburb of **Burtscheid**, the second spa quarter, which has a distinctive skyline, thanks to a handsome pair of churches built on its heights by the elder Couven. Again, it features thermal bathing facilities and sedate areas of parkland.

Eating, drinking and nightlife

Many of the best places to eat and drink are found in and around the Markt, while the most animated district is the student quarter, centred on Pontstrasse. Popular **clubs** include *Aoxomoxoa*, Reihstr. 15; *B9*, Blondelstr. 9; and the all-night *Club Voltaire*, Friedrichstr. 9.

Restaurants

Aachener Brauhaus Degraa am Theater Kapuzinergraben 4. The name of Aachen's now-defunct brewery lives on in this Gaststätte, which serves up huge portions of traditional fare, including bargain lunches Mon–Fri, in its wonderfully evocative galleried interior. By the entrance is a stand-up Kneipe, which claims to be the smallest bar in Europe.

Am Knipp Bergdriesch 3. Finely appointed beer and wine restaurant, with a tradition dating back to 1698. Evenings only, closed Tues.

Da Salvatore Bahnhofplatz 5. High-class but not unduly expensive Italian restaurant, whose menu features plenty of Sardinian specialities. Closed Wed.

Elisenbrunnen Friedrich-Wilhelm-Platz 14. Offers first-class traditional German cooking in the elegant surroundings of one of the city's finest buildings.

Goldener Schwan Markt 37. Typical Gaststätte occupying a fine old mansion with a Gothic facade.

Im Alten Zollhaus Friedlandstr. 22–24. Cosy Gaststätte with a tradition dating back to 1876; the drinks list includes its own spirits. Open evenings only at the weekend.

Ratskeller Markt 40. Housed in the Rathaus cellars, this features more innovative cooking than in most of its German counterparts.

Zum Goldenen Einhorn Markt 33. Has an enormous and inexpensive menu with Italian and Greek cuisine as well as German, the speciality being thin fillets of veal with a huge choice of sauces. Closed Mon.

Zum Postwagen Krämerstr. 2. Unquestionably Aachen's most famous Gaststätte, and a sight in itself, both for its cheerful Baroque exterior tacked onto the Rathaus and the cramped and irregular rooms within.

Bars and cafés

Atlantis Pontstr. 147–9. Attached to the cinema of the same name, this popular student pub was decorated by two Berlin artists in an evocation of the lost continent.

Café Kittel Pontstr. 39. Trendy café-bar with beer garden.

Café Middelburg Rethelstr. 6. Traditional café which serves excellent cakes.

Domkeller Hof 1. A genuine local, in spite of its location just off the Markt; always full, though it expands to the terrace outside in summer.

Egmont Pontstr. 1. French-style bistro featuring a range of live music including jazz, chansons, soul and funk as well as karaoke sessions.

Jakobshof Stromgasse 31. Very trendy bar featuring live jazz and cabaret; also does full meals. Closed Mon.

Labyrinth Pontstr. 156. Labyrinthine student bar with huge tables and minimalist decor. Serves Greek-style food.

Leo van den Daele Büchel 18. Historic wood-panelled café-cum-Weinstube with exquisite furnishings. Renowned for its huge rice cakes, it's also the best place to sample *Printen*, a spiced gingerbread which is the city's main claim to culinary fame.

Meisenfrei Boxgraben 72. This café-bar has a bewildering choice of games to entertain you.

Tangente Pontstr. 141. An elegant daytime café with terrace which transforms itself into a lively bar frequented by Aachen's younger residents at night.

Entertainment and festivals

The Eurogress centre next to the Casino at Monheimsallee 48 (Ⓣ02 41/9 13 10, Ⓦwww.eurogress-aachen.de) is where both rock and classical **concerts** are held. Either **drama** or **opera** is performed most evenings at the Theater Aachen on Theaterplatz (Ⓣ02 41/4 78 42 44, Ⓦwww.theater-aachen.de). The main **festivals** are Karneval, which is celebrated here with typical Rhenish enthusiasm; the Karlspreis (Ⓦwww.karlspreis.de) in May; and the Europamarkt der Kunsthandwerker, a handicrafts fair held on the first weekend of September. CHIO (Ⓦwww.chioaachen.de), an international jumping and riding tournament in late June or early July, is the main sporting event.

Monschau

The German section of the Eifel massif is divided by the Land boundary between North Rhine-Westphalia and Rhineland-Palatinate; the former's share consists mainly of the Hohes Venn, an extensive plateau of impervious rocks which stretches into Belgium. Variation in the scenery is provided by the River Rur, which cuts a deep, winding valley, and by the vegetation of gorse, broom and cotton grass. No cities have ever developed, but the well-preserved small town of **MONSCHAU**, some 30km south of Aachen, ranks among the finest in Germany. It's only accessible by road, with slow but fairly frequent bus services; most of the Eifel rail lines have closed because of the high cost of maintenance and low usage levels.

Monschau's main attraction is its dramatic setting deep in the Rur valley, with ruined fortresses – the **Burg** and the **Haller** (both with unrestricted access) – crowning two of the hills above. These offer some of the many superb **views** to be had in the area; others can be enjoyed from a belvedere just off the main road to Aachen, or from the commanding heights of the continuation of this road in the direction of Nideggen. The Burg, much the larger of the ruins, is the building from which Monschau developed. Its keep and gateway are Romanesque originals; the ring wall and parapets date from a strengthening of the defences in the fourteenth century, while the large **Eselsturm** (Asses' Tower), originally built in the same period, was modified a couple of hundred years later, when the central **Palast** was added.

The lower part of Monschau is an almost completely preserved historic townscape, dominated by the magnificent **multistorey mansions** lining the Rur, whose slate roofs are sometimes pierced by two tiers of dormer windows. Though half-timbering is used extensively, these houses aren't as old as they might appear – they date from Monschau's main period of prosperity, centred on cloth production, which followed the Thirty Years War. The most imposing of all, the **Rotes Haus** (Red House; guided tours Easter to end Nov Tues–Sun 10am–4pm; €2.50) at Laufenstr. 10, adds a rare splash of colour to the town, which is otherwise so monochromatic that it seems to grow organically out of the landscape. Built by a merchant in the 1750s as a combined factory, office and house, it features a Rococo staircase with an elaborate iron railing, and is fully furnished in the same style. The **Troistorff Haus** on the same street, which is now used as municipal offices, is smaller, but has a fancier exterior and another fine stairway.

A number of old enterprises still using historic equipment operate in Monschau, and some can be visited. These include a nineteenth-century brewery, the **Felsenkeller-Brauerei** (guided tours Easter to end Oct Tues 2–6pm, Wed–Sun 11am–6pm; rest of year same times Sat & Sun only; €2; Ⓦwww.brauerei-museum.de), in the southwest of town at St-Vither-Str. 22–28. It is named after its rock-hewn cellars, and its speciality is *Monschauer Zwickelbier*, a dark, cloudy, bottom-fermented beer rich in vitamin B.

Practicalities

Monschau's **tourist office** (Easter–Oct Mon–Fri 10am–5pm, Sat & Sun 10am–3pm; rest of year Mon–Fri only; Ⓣ0 24 72/33 00, Ⓦwww.monschau.de) is at Stadtstr. 1 beside the main bridge. **Hotels** are numerous and almost always good value. Right in the centre are *Eifeler Hof*, Stadtstr. 10 (Ⓣ0 24 72/50 46; ❸), *Burghotel*, Laufenstr. 1 (Ⓣ0 24 72/23 32; ❸), *Alt Montjoie*, Stadtstr. 18 (Ⓣ0 24 72/32 89, Ⓦwww.alt-montjoie.de; ❸), and *Royal*, Stadtstr. 4–6 (Ⓣ0 24 72/9 87 70, Ⓦwww.hotelroyal.de; ❸–❺). High above the town and commanding a wonderful view is *Hubertusklause*, Bergstr. 45 (Ⓣ0 24 72/80 36 50 36; ❺). There are two **youth hostels**, one located in the Palast, Auf dem Schloss 4 (Ⓣ0 24 72/23 14; €13.80/16.50), and the other at Hargardsgasse 5 in Hargard (Ⓣ0 24 72/21 80; €13.30/15.90), some 3km away. **Private houses** (❷–❸) with rooms to let can be found on Kirchstrasse, Laufenstrasse and Oberer Mühlenberg. There's a **campsite** at Perlenau on the B399 road (Ⓣ0 24 72/41 36, Ⓦwww.monschau-perlenau.de). Among the **restaurants** which crowd the town centre *Alte Herrlichkeit*, Stadtstr. 7, and *Remise*, Stadtstr. 14, are particularly outstanding; that in the aforementioned *Hubertusklause* is also very fine.

Bonn

The name of **BONN** is indissolubly associated with the West German state, having served as its capital from the time the country was set up in 1949 until the unification of 1990, when Berlin was restored to its former role as Bundeshauptstadt (Federal Capital City). A year later, Bonn's tantalizingly narrow defeat in the bitter battle to retain its role as the main seat of government and parliament dealt an even more telling blow to the supreme self-confidence it had acquired. In some ways, this was no more than it deserved, as it was the most unlikely and unloved of European capitals: just "A Small

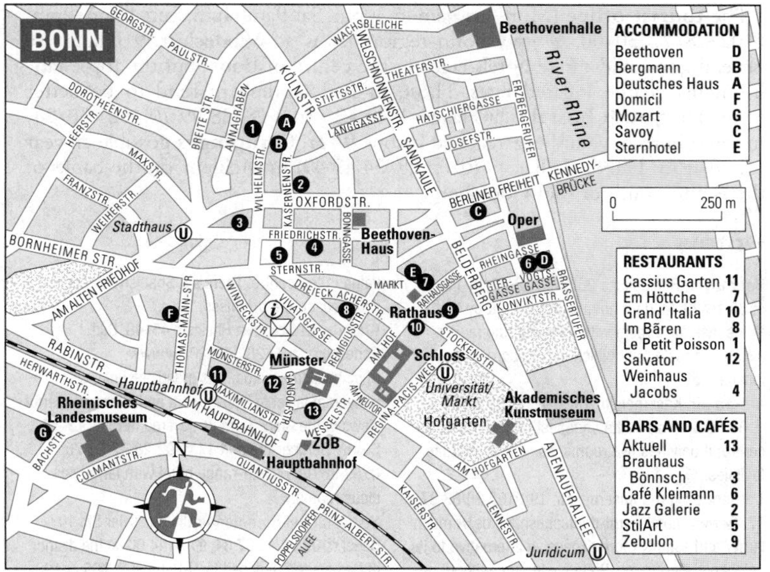

Town in Germany" according to the title of John le Carré's spy thriller, or "The Federal Village" in the condescending eyes of the inhabitants of grander German cities. Yet Bonn subsequently confounded its critics by its stubborn refusal to lapse back into provinciality: in response to widespread fears about the dangers of Berlin becoming too dominant, it secured for itself, under the designation of Bundesstadt (Federal City), the status of a secondary governmental seat. Accordingly, seven federal ministries (including, significantly, defence and education), plus numerous other public bodies, will continue to have their headquarters there. Its official role aside, Bonn is a notable historic town, chiefly renowned, prior to its elevation as capital, as the birthplace of **Ludwig van Beethoven**.

Arrival, information and accommodation

The **Hauptbahnhof** lies plumb in the middle of the city, the central pedestrian area opening out immediately before it. To the right is the **bus station**, whose local services, along with the trams (which become the U-Bahn in the city centre), form part of a system integrated with that of Cologne. As the attractions are well spaced out, it's advisable to invest in one of the many runabout tickets on the integrated **public transport** network run by VRS (Ⓦwww.vrsinfo.de). A 24-hour pass for the whole city costs €5.30; there's also a €7.50 mini-group ticket for up to five people travelling together as well as a three-day individual pass for €13.50, or €26.50 including Cologne. An enticing alternative to these is the **Bonn Regio WelcomeCard**, which includes entrance to the city's museums. The 24-hour version of this is priced at €9 for individuals, €18 for families or up to three adults; for 72 hours these prices rise to €19 and €38 respectively. Also shared with Cologne is the **airport** (Ⓣ0 22 03/40 40 01, Ⓦwww.airport-cgn.de), which is linked with Bonn's Hauptbahnhof by bus #670 at least every thirty minutes.

The **tourist office** (Mon–Fri 9am–6.30pm, Sat 9am–4pm, Sun 10am–2pm; Ⓣ02 28/77 50 00, Ⓦwww.bonn-region.de) is at Windeckstr. 9. There are several good mid-range hotels right in the centre of Bonn, but the top establishments charge inflated rates. Those in Bad Godesberg tend to be better value. The **youth hostel** is at Haager Weg 42 (Ⓣ02 28/28 99 70; €21.30/24) in the suburb of Venusberg, reached by bus #621. **Camping** is possible all year round at Im Frankenkeller 49 (Ⓣ02 28/34 49 49) in Mehlem, on the banks of the Rhine south of Bad Godesberg.

Hotels

Beethoven Rheingasse 26 Ⓣ02 28/63 14 11, Ⓕ69 16 29. Modern hotel situated right by the Rhine; ask for a room with a view of the river. It also has a restaurant which serves bargain set lunches. ❻

Bergmann Kasernenstr. 13 Ⓣ02 28/63 38 91, Ⓕ63 50 57. This is the cheapest option in the city centre; it only has five rooms, none with en-suite facilities. ❹

Deutsches Haus Kasernenstr. 19 Ⓣ02 28/63 37 77, Ⓦwww.hotel-garni-deutscheshaus.de. A much larger and slightly more expensive alternative to its neighbour, *Bergmann*. Rooms with and without private facilities are available. ❹–❻

Domicil Thomas-Mann-Str. 24–26 Ⓣ02 08/72 90 90, Ⓦwww.bestwestern.de. Well-appointed designer hotel. ❾.

Mozart Mozartstr. 1 Ⓣ02 28/65 90 71, Ⓕ65 90 75. On a quiet corner a few minutes' walk southwest of the Hauptbahnhof, this is among the best value in the centre. There's a Spanish restaurant, *Amadeo*, on the premises. ❹–❻.

Rheinhotel Dreesen Rheinstr. 45–49, Bad Godesberg Ⓣ02 28/8 20 20, Ⓦwww.rheinhoteldreesen.de. This grandiose hotel with restaurant is set in its own park and offers wonderful views of the Rhine from its covered terrace. ❽–❾.

Savoy Berliner Freiheit 17 Ⓣ02 28/72 59 70, Ⓕ69 68 99. Middle-range hotel with large, spacious rooms. ❻

Schlosshotel Kommende Oberkasseler Str. 10, Beuel Ⓣ02 28/44 07 34, Ⓕ44 44 00. In the district of Ramersdorf (reached by U-Bahn #62, #66 or #68), this occupies a neo-Gothic Schloss of the Teutonic Knights, with beautiful furniture and antiques. It also has a top-notch Italian restaurant. ❻

Sternhotel Markt 8 Ⓣ02 28/7 26 70, Ⓦwww.sternhotel-bonn.de. A member of the Akzent group, this fine old hotel has an ideal location in the heart of the Altstadt. ❻–❽

The City

Present-day Bonn is actually a federation of a host of formerly separate communities on both banks of the Rhine. The main attractions are far more spread out than in many much larger German cities, meaning that it isn't a place easily appreciated in a hurry.

The Altstadt

The small Altstadt is now predominantly a pedestrianized shopping area centred on two spacious squares. That to the south is named after the huge Romanesque **Münster**, whose central octagonal tower with its soaring spire is the city's most prominent landmark. Inside, it's airy and pleasing, the sensitive proportions reinforcing the feel of massive space. Below the chancel is a fine crypt, while there's an impressively severe and monumental **cloister** adjoining the southern side. The pink Rococo **Rathaus** adds a touch of colour to the other square, the Markt, which still hosts a market each weekday.

A couple of minutes' walk north of here, at Bonngasse 20, is the **Beethoven-Haus** (Mon–Sat 10am–5/6pm, Sun 11am–4pm; €4; Ⓦwww.beethoven-haus-bonn.de). This is one of the few old buildings in the centre to have escaped wartime devastation, and together with the more imposing house next door it contains an unfussy and intelligently presented museum dedicated to the great composer. Beethoven served his musical apprenticeship at the electoral court of his home town, but left it for good at the age of 22, though this hasn't deterred Bonn from zealously building up the best collection of memorabilia of its favourite son. There's a bunch of uncomfortable portraits of the tormented genius (who was a reluctant sitter), along with manuscripts and correspondence. The three instruments with which he was associated as a professional performer are shown in the form of the console of the destroyed organ on which he played as a youth, his last piano and his viola. Most poignant of all are the ear-trumpets which a friend made specially in order to combat his advancing deafness.

The Altstadt's second dominant building is the Baroque **Schloss**, an enormously long construction which was formerly the seat of the Archbishop-Electors of Cologne and is now used by the university. To the south, the Schloss is bounded by the open spaces of the Hofgarten, at whose far end is the **Akademisches Kunstmuseum** (Mon–Wed, Fri & Sun 10am–1pm, Thurs 10am–1pm & 4–6pm; €1.50; ⓦwww.antikensammlung.uni-bonn.de), housed in a Neoclassical pavilion designed by Schinkel. This has an eerie collection of casts of famous antique sculptures, originally made for the benefit of art students.

The Rheinisches Landesmuseum

Despite the advent of a brand-new museum quarter, the pick of Bonn's collections is still the **Rheinisches Landesmuseum** (Tues, Thurs & Sat 10am–6pm, Wed & Fri 10am–9pm, Sun 11am–6pm; €6.50) at Colmantstr. 14–16 behind the Hauptbahnhof. Star exhibit is the **skull of Neanderthal Man**, found in a valley near Düsseldorf, and calculated to be some 60,000 years old. Highlights of the important Roman department are the tomb of Marcus Caelius, a set of arcades from Aachen and a mosaic dedicated to the sun. The medieval section includes the anguished sculpture known as the *Roettgen Pietà* and some lovely examples of the fifteenth-century Cologne School of painters, notably the delicate *Deposition* and *St Sebastian* by an anonymous artist who has been named **Master of the Bonn Diptych** as a result, and five panels by the painter known as **Master of the St Ursula Legend** after the dispersed series from which these came. Among later German paintings, a rare work by **Elsheimer**, *The Three Marys at the Sepulchre*, stands out.

Poppelsdorf and Kreuzberg

Also branching out from the Schloss is the kilometre-long avenue of chestnut trees which leads to **Poppelsdorf**, now a suburb of the city, where the Frenchman **Robert de Cotte**, who had undertaken modifications to the Schloss, was commissioned to build a second Electoral residence. The resulting **Schloss Poppelsdorf** follows an ingenious trompe l'oeil design, its circular courtyard concealed within a rectangular ground plan. Again, the palace is now occupied by university departments, the grounds serving as the **Botanischer Garten** (April–Sept Mon–Fri 9am–6pm, Sun 9am–1pm; Oct–March Mon–Fri 9am–4pm; free). For a sociological as well as architectural stroll, wander in the **Südstadt**, the streets immediately to the east, such as Schloss-Strasse, Kurfürstenstrasse, Argelanderstrasse and Bismarckstrasse. These represent a remarkably complete picture of late nineteenth- and early twentieth-century town planning for the better-off sections of the middle classes.

To the other side of Schloss Poppelsdorf at Sebastianstr. 182 is the **Robert-Schumann-Haus** (Mon & Fri 10am–noon & 4–7pm, Wed & Thurs 10am–noon & 3–6pm; free), containing a collection of memorabilia of the Romantic composer. In spite of a blissful marriage to the pianist Clara Wieck, who inspired so many of his yearning, passionate song settings and virtuoso piano pieces, Schumann had a history of psychological instability, culminating in a complete mental breakdown and attempted suicide when he threw himself into the Rhine. At his own request, he spent the last two years of his life in Bonn confined to the sanatorium adjoining his house.

Continuing south from Poppelsdorf, a road leads uphill to the isolated pilgrimage church of **Kreuzberg**. The original seventeenth-century chapel was given the full Rococo treatment a hundred years later, including the addition of the Holy Steps, an imitation in the lavishly ornate style of Balthasar Neumann of those now in Rome on which Christ allegedly ascended to receive Pilate's judgement.

The Regierungsviertel

Bonn's **Regierungsviertel** (government quarter) can be reached either by following Reuterstrasse from Poppelsdorf, or by taking Adenauerallee from the Hofgarten: the distance is about the same (around 20min walk). Saddled with its "temporary status", it was not custom-built, but utilized a series of existing structures. Ironically enough, work had just started on new buildings when the sudden fall of Communism in East Germany in 1989 shook the city out of its complacent assumption that it was going to be a long-term capital.

Both the **Villa Hammerschmidt** and the **Palais Schaumburg** are pompous Empire buildings from the nineteenth century, once private dwellings of the mega-rich and later the official residences of the Federal President and Chancellor respectively. Further south, the **Bundeshaus** complex is in the Bauhaus style of the 1930s. More enticing than the buildings is the wonderful **view** over the Rhine and the Siebengebirge on the opposite bank.

Planned as a fitting cultural accompaniment to the government quarter, the **Museumsmeile** (Museum Mile) on its western edge only came to fruition after national unification had been achieved, by which time it already seemed an anachronism. Of the four institutions along its route, only the **Alexander-Koenig-Museum** (Tues and Thurs–Sun 10am–6pm, Wed 10am–9pm; €3; Ⓦwww.museumkoenig.uni-bonn.de) at Adenauerallee 160 existed prior to 1992. One of the best natural history collections in the country, its displays are laid out on four floors with a true Germanic thoroughness. Next in line, at no. 250 on the same boulevard, is the **Haus der Geschichte der Bundesrepublik Deutschland** (Tues–Sun 9am–7pm; free; Ⓦwww.hdg.de), which traces the political, cultural, social and economic history of the Federal Republic. To non-Germans, its emphases might seem ephemeral, though the presentations are greatly enlivened by the extensive use of archive film, including John F. Kennedy's famous "Ich bin ein Berliner" speech.

At the head of Friedrich-Ebert-Allee, the continuation of Adenauerallee, is the **Kunstmuseum** (Tues & Thurs–Sun 10am–6pm, Wed 10am–9pm; €5, or €10 combined ticket with Kunst- und Ausstellungshalle), which contains the municipal gallery of modern art. Its main strength lies in its representation of the Expressionists, and in particular the brilliant **August Macke**, who spent part of his brief life in the city. The upper floor is devoted to the avant-garde, notably Joseph Beuys, Sigmar Polke and Anselm Kiefer. To the rear is the most attention-seeking of the three new museums, the **Kunst- und Ausstellungshalle der Bundesrepublik Deutschland** (Tues & Wed 10am–9pm, Thurs–Sun 10am–7pm; €6.50; Ⓦwww.kah-bonn.de), a space-age arts centre which can host up to five temporary exhibitions at one time.

Already it has staged several blockbuster shows, including an ongoing series of loans from the great museums of the world.

Bad Godesberg

When Bonn was officially expanded in 1969, it gobbled up a string of small villages, giving it a foothold on the eastern bank of the Rhine for the first time. It also annexed the old spa town of **BAD GODESBERG** (reached by U-Bahn #66 or main-line train) to the south, stretching its boundaries to the Land border. Bad Godesberg's character had already made it a favoured location for many of the diplomatic missions, who found its grandiose Empire-style villas just the sort of headquarters they were looking for. The town is also a famed conference centre, and has hosted at least two momentous events: the series of meetings between Chamberlain and Hitler in 1938, which paved the way for the Munich Agreement by which "peace in our time" was bought at Czechoslovakia's expense; and the 1959 conference of the Social Democrats, when the party, bidding to end a period of three decades in opposition, disavowed its earlier connections with Marxism, class warfare and anticlericalism, and became part of the postwar consensus rooted in acceptance of the idea of a "social market economy".

Rearing high over the town is the **Godesburg**, the most northerly of the great series of castles crowning promontories above the Rhine, built in the thirteenth and fourteenth centuries by the archbishops of Cologne and blown up in 1583. The cylindrical **keep** is still intact and can be ascended (April–Oct Wed–Sun 10am–6pm; €1) for a panoramic **view**, including a distant glimpse of Cologne and the Siebengebirge. Views, indeed, are Bad Godesberg's major attraction; you'll find plenty more if you saunter down the **Rheinufer**, the promenade along the river bank. Otherwise, there are two spa parks in the town centre, separated by fashionable buildings, prominent among which is the late eighteenth-century **Redoute**, formerly the ballroom of the Electors, now a prestigious function suite.

Schwarzrheindorf

The only one of Bonn's outer villages worth making a special detour to see is **SCHWARZRHEINDORF**, on the right bank of the Rhine to the extreme north, reached by bus #550 or #640. It boasts a relatively little-known but outstanding monument in the **Doppelkirche**, a former manorial church. Built in the mid-twelfth century, this offers an intriguing insight into the social and religious preoccupations of the medieval world. The exterior cleverly disguises the fact that it encases two separate chapels, the upper reserved for the lord, the lower for the use of the labourers. Apart from its architectural idiosyncrasies, the church has rare Romanesque **fresco** cycles. Turning on the light by the door reveals *The Vision of Ezekiel*, *The Transfiguration* and *The Crucifixion*, while upstairs the great visions of *The Apocalypse* were painted for their lordships' contemplation.

Eating, drinking and nightlife

Bonn has a fairly eclectic range of places to eat. Most of the best bars are conveniently located in the Altstadt and the Südstadt.

Restaurants

Cassius Garten Maximilianstr. 28d. Offers a mouth-watering choice of vegetarian food, which you pay for by weight. Closed Sun.

Em Höttche Markt 4. Good traditional Gaststätte which, in a previous incarnation, was patronized by the young Beethoven.

Grand' Italia Bischofsplatz 1. The best of the city's many Italian restaurants.
Im Bären Acherstr. 1–3. Excellent Gaststätte owned by the local Kurfürsten brewery, which brews a *Kölsch* known as *Maximilian*.
Le Petit Poisson Wilhelmstr. 23a. Expensive but very highly rated French restaurant. Evenings only, closed Sun & Mon.
Philoxenia Clemens-August-Str. 34. Located near the Botanischer Garten, this is one of Germany's few specifically Cypriot restaurants; it also features dishes from other Mediterranean countries.
Redüttchen Kurfürstenallee 1, Bad Godesberg. *Gemütlich* little restaurant in the former gardener's house beside the Redoute.
Salvator In der Sürst 5–7. A Bavarian-style beer hall-restaurant, operated by Munich's Paulaner brewery.
Weinhaus Jacobs Friedrichstr. 18. Evenings-only wine bar-restaurant, which has been on the go since 1845. It offers a good choice of vintages from all over Germany. Closed Sun.
Zur Lindenwirtin Aennchen Aennchenplatz 2, Bad Godesberg. Historic student tavern with garden terrace, restored as an upmarket restaurant.

Bars and cafés

Aktuell Gerhard-von-Are-Str. 8. Best known as the favoured haunt of journalists, a profession represented in Bonn in force. On Sun, it's only open in the evening.
Brauhaus Bönnsch Sterntorbrücke 4. Hausbrauerei producing a distinctive blond ale known as *Bönnsch*, which is served in a curious horn-shaped glass. Also does good-value meals.
Café Kleimann Rheingasse 16–18. Excellent traditional café. Closed Mon.
Jazz Galerie Oxfordstr. 24. Features live jazz sessions most evenings and a weekly jam session.
StilArt Friedensplatz 12. Exquisitely furnished café attached to a crafts shop. Closed Sun.
Zebulon Stockenstr. 19. A big favourite with arts students, particularly for breakfast.
Zur Kerze Königstr. 25. Subtitled *Künstlerkeller* (Artists' Cellar), this popular Südstadt bar. Bristling with alcoves and partitions, it's frequented by a mixed age range, and serves excellent (if fairly pricey) Italianate dishes. Open daily 7pm–5am.

Entertainment

Although not a national leader in any cultural field, Bonn offers a range of entertainment, with classical music – and in particular peformances of works by Beethoven – featuring strongly. There's a festival dominated by his music, the Internationales Beethovenfest (Ⓦwww.beethovenfest.de), every September and October. The monthly *De Schnüss* (€2), available from newsagents, gives full listings of what's on.

Beethovenhalle Wachsbleiche 26 ⓣ02 28/7 22 20, Ⓦwww.beethovenhalle.de. Bonn's principal concert hall, regularly featuring its own house orchestra, the Orchester der Beethovenhalle (Ⓦwww.beethoven-orchester.de).
Kammermusiksaal Bonngasse 24–26 ⓣ02 28/9 81 75 15, Ⓦwww.beethoven-haus-bonn.de. Adjoining the Beethoven-Haus, this small hall is used for chamber, instrumental and vocal recitals.
Oper Am Boeslagerhof 1 ⓣ02 28/77 80 08, Ⓦwww.theaterbonn.bgp.de. Hosts not only opera, but also dance and drama.

Listings

Bookstores There's a wide selection in and around Am Hof (behind the Schloss).
Embassies and consulates Britain, Argelanderstr. 108a ⓣ02 28/9 16 70; Canada, Friedrich-Wilhelm-Str. 18 ⓣ02 28/96 80; Ireland, Godesberger Allee 119, Bad Godesberg ⓣ02 28/95 92 90; US, Deichmanns Aue 29, Bad Godesberg ⓣ02 28/33 91.
Markets Daily on the Markt; every third Sat of the month, there's a flea market on Rheinaue.
Post office The main post office is at Münsterplatz 17 with a post restante service.
Rhine cruises These depart from Brassertufer just south of Kennedybrücke: K-D Linie ⓣ02 28/63 21 34, Ⓦwww.k-d.com; Bonner Personenschiffahrt ⓣ02 28/63 63 63, Ⓦwww.b-p-s.de.

The Siebengebirge

The **Siebengebirge** (Seven Mountains), on the eastern bank of the Rhine just before the Land boundary with Rhineland-Palatinate, rank among the river's most suggestively grand stretches, steeped in the lore of legend and literature. According to one story, the mountains were created by seven giants clearing the dirt from their shovels. They're also sometimes regarded – though there are other claimants – as the site of the most famous of the Grimms' fairy-tales, *Snow White and the Seven Dwarfs*.

Despite the name, there are around thirty summits in this extinct volcanic range, which stretches for about 15km north to south and 5km east to west. From Bonn, six of the main peaks can be seen; the number seven, with its traditional mystical significance, applies only to those visible from a point further north. Of the group, **Drachenfels** (321m), **Wolkenburg** (325m) and **Lohrberg** (435m) are all of a mineral called trachyte; **Petersberg** (331m), **Nonnenstromberg** (336m) and **Grosser Ölberg** (461m) are of basalt, a later formation; while **Löwenburg** (455m) is of dolerite. For centuries, stone from these mountains was quarried to construct the great buildings of the Rhineland, notably the Dom in Cologne; this quarrying was brought to an end in 1889, when the whole area was designated as the first protected landscape in Germany. The Siebengebirge are covered with thick woods, which means that views are very restricted most of the time, though all the more spectacular when you do reach a belvedere. This wasn't always so; old prints show the upper parts of the peaks free of trees, and generally crowned with a fortress.

Königswinter

Although the Siebengebirge make an easy day-outing from Bonn, to which they're connected by U-Bahn #66, the best base for exploring them is the holiday resort of **KÖNIGSWINTER**, which has a relaxed, somewhat dated air. It offers a wide variety of **hotels**, including *Wenzel*, Hauptstr. 457 (Ⓣ0 22 23/2 18 61; ③–⑤), *Siebengebirge*, Hauptstr. 342 (Ⓣ0 22 23/2 13 59; ⑤), *Jesuiter Hof*, Hauptstr. 458 (Ⓣ0 22 23/2 26 50; ⑤), *Rheinhotel Loreley*, Rheinallee 12 (Ⓣ0 22 23/92 50, Ⓦwww.hotelloreley.de; ⑥), and *Maritim*, Rheinallee 3 (Ⓣ0 22 23/70 70, Ⓦwww.maritim.de; ⑧–⑨). The last of these has the best and most expensive **restaurant** in town. There are also several enticing old Weinhäuser: one is the aforementioned *Jesuiter Hof*, which serves wines from its own estate; another is *Altes Fährhaus*, Rheinallee 4.

Königswinter's mainline **Bahnhof** lies at the northern end of town; the U-Bahn trams run along the waterfront. The **tourist office** (Mon 10am–5pm, Tues–Fri 9am–5pm, Sat 10am–1pm; Ⓣ0 22 23/91 77 11, Ⓦwww.koenigswinter.de or www.siebengebirge.com) is at Drachenfelsstr. 11. It's worth trying to time your visit to coincide with one of the numerous **festivals**, the most spectacular of which is Der Rhein in Flammen, a display of fireworks and illuminations held on the first Saturday in May; a week later, the cutting of the first crop of asparagus is celebrated. The main wine festival, the Winzerfest, takes place on the first weekend in October.

The mountains

Although the lowest of the mountains, **Drachenfels**, situated immediately behind Königswinter, is by far the most interesting, unfortunately it's also the most-climbed mountain in Europe, heavily tourist-oriented and even more heavily exploited. The **Drachenfelsbahn** (Ⓦwww.drachenfelsbahn-koenigswinter.de), a **rack rail** line built in 1883 using a system pioneered in Switzerland, is an ingenious piece of engineering, rising 220m over a total length of 1.5km. However, the fare (€6.50 single, €8 return) is a bit of a rip-off, the more so as the footpath is paved and makes for a steep but easy ascent. About a third of the way up is the **Nibelungenhalle** (mid-March to mid-Nov daily 10am–6pm; rest of year Sat & Sun 10.30am–4pm; €3), a Jugendstil temple of honour to Richard Wagner, built in 1913 to commemorate the centenary of his birth. Along the walls of the interior of the rotunda is a cycle of twelve large Symbolist paintings illustrating scenes from *The Ring* by the academic artist Hermann Hendrich. The same ticket gives admission to the adjacent **Drachenhöhle**, which contains a thirteen-metre-long stone sculpture of the fearsome monster supposedly slain there by the hero Siegfried. By immediately immersing himself in its warm blood he gained a horny skin which would have rendered him invincible had a falling leaf not left a spot as vulnerable as Achilles' heel. From this legend comes the name of the wine, *Drachenblut* (dragon's blood), made from the grapes cultivated on these slopes, the most northerly vineyard in western Germany. Alongside the cave, and likewise included in the entrance fee, is a small zoo of live reptiles.

A short distance uphill is **Schloss Drachenburg** (guided tours April–Oct Tues–Sun 11am–6pm; €2, or €0.50 for entrance to the park only; Ⓦwww.schloss-drachenburg.de), which is a good example of the nineteenth-century German love of macabre Gothic fantasy. From the terrace there's a really spectacular **view**, though there's an even wider panorama from the Romanesque **Burg**, a ruin since the Thirty Years War, at the summit of the mountain. Apart from being able to trace the Rhine's path both upstream and down, you can see over the Eifel to the west, and get a different perspective on the Siebengebirge themselves; on an even half-decent day, the spires of Cologne can also be distinguished.

A series of well-marked hiking trails enables you to choose your own route round the rest of the range. **Petersberg** is probably the best known; its summit is occupied by a grandiose luxury **hotel**, *Gästehaus Petersberg* (Ⓣ0 22 33/7 40, Ⓦwww.gaestehaus-petersberg.com; ➒), which was Chamberlain's base for his ill-fated talks with Hitler in Bad Godesberg. **Löwenburg** is allegedly haunted by a wild huntsman, doomed to an eternal chase as punishment for his cruelty when alive. **Grosser Ölberg** is the most enticing after Drachenfels, commanding the next best views. Although furthest from the Rhine of all the peaks, it has the advantage of being the highest, and of including panoramas over the Taunus to the east.

Kloster Heisterbach

From Grosser Ölberg, it's only a short descent to the area's sole great monument, the ruins of the early thirteenth-century Cistercian **Kloster Heisterbach**, which can also be reached by bus #520 or #521 from Königswinter. Like so many of this order's foundations, it was built in the Transitional style between Romanesque and Gothic. Heisterbach was pulled down at the beginning of the nineteenth century following the Napoleonic suppression, but the apse and its ambulatory were spared when the explosives failed to ignite. This tiny fragment had an impact on the Romantic imagination out of all proportion to its size; depictions of lonely, overgrown and crumbling abbeys set in wooded valleys, often illuminated by moonlight, became one of the favourite subjects of the movement's painters. Nowadays, the eighteenth-century monastic buildings are occupied by a convent of Augustinian nuns, who have built a modern church. They also run a café-restaurant, specializing in a huge choice of irresistible home-made gateaux.

Brühl

Midway between Bonn and Cologne, set inland from the Rhine, lies **BRÜHL**, a town which developed from a castle founded by the Archbishop-Electors in the thirteenth century. In the eighteenth century, it was transformed into a splendid Residenzstadt by **Clemens August**, a member of the Bavarian Wittelsbach dynasty, who was a prolific accumulator of aristocratic titles and territories, gaining four prince-bishoprics in addition to the Cologne Electorate, and also becoming Grand Master of the Teutonic Knights. He showed no piety whatsoever, living a life of unashamedly pampered luxury and gaining a reputation as a womanizer – he was summoned to Rome by the pope to explain the presence of two particularly beautiful singers at his court, and his death came after he had danced the night away rather too energetically.

The Town

Clemens August's two palaces – which are both on the UNESCO World Heritage list – lie at opposite ends of the Schlosspark, which stretches south-east of the pedestrianized town centre. **Schloss Augustusburg** (guided tours Feb–Nov Tues–Sun 9am–noon & 1.30–4pm; €4; ⓦwww.schlossbruehl.de) is a direct replacement for the medieval moated castle destroyed by French troops in 1689. Initially the design was in dignified Baroque by Johann Conrad Schlaun, but the project was later entrusted to **François Cuvilliés**, who eliminated all features reminiscent of a fortress and transformed it into a pleasure palace which is like a little piece of Bavaria wafted northwards. As the final *pièce de résistance*, the greatest architect of the day, **Balthasar Neumann**, was recruited to draw up plans for the ceremonial **staircase** – a fricassee of marble and stucco, crowned by a fresco by Carlo Carlone glorifying the Virtues. The decorative scheme of this and the following **Wachenhalle** (Hall of Guards) and **Musikzimmer** (Music Room), which are almost equally sumptuous, is a complicated series of allegories in honour of the Wittelsbach dynasty. Facing the Schloss are the **Schlossgarten** and the **Jardin Secret**, two splendid French-style formal gardens seen at their best in the full bloom of summer.

Adjoining the west front of the Schloss is the **Orangerie**; now housing a café-restaurant and an exhibition room, it forms a processional way to **St Maria zu den Engeln**. This was originally a Franciscan friary church, built in the simplest form of Gothic, but its interior was greatly pepped up for its new function as court chapel by the insertion of a lavish **high altar** – taking up the entire chancel – designed by Neumann. Facing the north wing of the Schloss, at Bahnhofstr. 21, is the villa where the Dadaist and Surrealist painter Max Ernst was born. It now houses the **Max-Ernst-Kabinett** (Mon–Thurs & Sun 10am–5pm; €2), which contains a few early oil paintings, though the bulk of the material is graphic work, displayed in a changing series of exhibitions. Work is underway on converting a nearby Neoclassical building, the Benediktusheim, into a much larger museum in Ernst's honour; this is due to open in 2004 (check ⓦwww.maxernstmuseum.de for the latest information).

Some 2km east through the Schloss grounds is the **Jagdschloss Falkenlust** (Feb–Nov Tues–Fri 9am–12.30pm & 1.30–5pm, Sat & Sun 10am–6pm; €3; ⓦwww.schlossbruehl.de), Clemens August's base for his favourite hobby of falconry. Designed once again by Cuvilliés, it's intimate in scale, and this time you're allowed to explore it at leisure. In the oval main Salon is a series of portraits of the Wittelsbachs in their hunting attire, but the most impressive rooms are the smallest – the **Lacquerkabinett**, reflecting the contemporary taste for chinoiserie, and the **Spiegelkabinett** directly above. Outside is the tiny **Kapelle**, a folly in imitation of a hermitage.

Brühl's heritage of palaces and gardens is not the reason it attracts two million visitors annually; for that it can thank **Phantasialand** (daily April–Oct 9am–6pm, also weekends in Advent; adults €24.50, or €37 for a ticket valid on two consecutive days, children under 1m free; Ⓦwww.phantasialand.de), the first amusement park in Europe to rival Disneyland in the United States. Laid out on the site of an open-cast mine at the extreme southern end of town, by the junction of the main roads to Trier and Aachen, it can be reached by a regular bus service from the Bahnhof. Attractions range from re-creations of prewar Berlin, a Wild West town and China of a thousand years ago, through rides on a Viking ship, an overhead monorail, the world's largest roller-coaster and a mock-up of outer space. Be warned that even the park's owners admit that there are an uncomfortably large number of visitors on Sundays and throughout July and August.

Practicalities

Brühl's **Bahnhof** lies on the opposite side of the Schloss from the town centre. The **tourist office** (May–Oct Mon–Fri 9am–7pm, Sat 9am–4pm, Sun 1–5pm; Nov–April Mon–Fri 9am–7pm, Sat 9am–1pm; Ⓣ0 22 32/7 93 45, Ⓦwww.bruehl.de) is at Uhlstr. 3. There are a fair number of **hotels**, including *Rheinischer Hof*, Euskirchner Str. 123 (Ⓣ0 22 32/93 30 10; ❹), *Brühler Hof*, Uhlstr. 30 (Ⓣ0 22 32/41 01 32; ❻), *Ramada-Treff*, Römerstr. 1 (Ⓣ0 22 32/20 40, Ⓦwww.ramada-treff.de; ❽), and *Phantasia*, a new fantasy hotel in mock-Chinese Imperial style within Phantasialand (Ⓣ0 22 32/3 66 66, Ⓦwww.phantasialand.de; ❼). Places to **eat** include *Brühler Schlosskeller*, Kölnstr. 74, and the aforementioned *Orangerie*, Schlossstr. 6, which functions as a café in the afternoon and a restaurant serving cross-Mediterranean cuisine in the evening. **Concerts** by top international musicians in the Schloss (Ⓦwww.schlossfest.de) are the main cultural attraction, while October sees a **festival** of international puppet theatre.

Cologne (Köln)

Although now in the political shadow of the neighbouring upstarts of Bonn and Düsseldorf, **COLOGNE** stands as a colossus in the vast urban sprawl of the Rhine-Ruhr conurbation, and is currently Germany's fourth largest city, with a population which crept over the million mark in the 1990s. The huge Gothic **Dom** is the country's most visited monument, while its assemblage of Roman remains and medieval buildings is unsurpassed and the museums bettered only by those in Berlin, Dresden and Munich. Cologne also ranks high as a **beer** centre: despite some recent amalgamations and takeovers it still has more breweries than any other city in the world, all of which produce the distinctive *Kölsch*. Also of special note is one of Europe's most important popular celebrations, the annual **Karneval** in early spring.

Originally founded in 33 BC, Cologne quickly gained importance. It was the birthplace of Julia Agrippa, wife of Emperor Claudius, who in 50 AD raised it to the status of a colony (hence its name) with full rights as a **Roman city**. Subsequent development owed much to ecclesiastical affairs – a bishopric was founded in the fourth century and SS Severin, Gereon and Ursula were all martyred in the city; churches were soon dedicated to each and built over their graves. The **cult of Saint Ursula** was especially popular, being associated with the alleged death of her 11,000 virgin companions (the true figure was probably a more realistic eleven). In the twelfth century, Cologne forcibly acquired the relics of the Three Magi from Milan, thus increasing its standing as one of the greatest centres of **pilgrimage** in northern Europe.

Medieval Cologne, a Free Imperial City with 150 churches, became enormously prosperous because of its strategic situation on the Rhine at the intersection of trade routes. The largest city in Germany, it was one of the great European centres of learning and boasted a distinctive school of painters. Decline inevitably set in, but something of a comeback was made in the eighteenth century with a recipe imported from Italy, which involved distilling flower blossoms in almost pure alcohol. Although originally meant as an aphrodisiac, this was to achieve worldwide fame as a toilet water under the euphemism by which customers ordered it – water from Cologne, or *eau de Cologne*.

The modern city has reclaimed its old role as a major trade and business centre, and has also become Germany's radio and television metropolis. As a welcome contrast to the class-consciousness and frantic status-seeking of its neighbours, it has an openness about it similar to that of the city-states of Hamburg and Bremen. To this is added a general atmosphere of fun and irreverence more characteristic of the Mediterranean than Germany.

Arrival, information and accommodation

Cologne's **Hauptbahnhof** is right in the centre of the city, immediately below the Dom. **Bahnhof Deutz**, on the opposite side of the Rhine, is also a major station, not least because it is situated right alongside the trade fair buildings. Directly by the rear exit of the Hauptbahnhof is the **bus station**. From there, bus #170 runs five times an hour throughout most of the day via Bahnhof Deutz to the **airport** (Ⓣ0 22 03/40 40 01, Ⓦwww.airport-cgn.de), which is shared with Bonn; the journey takes around twenty minutes.

The **tourist office** is at Unter Fettenhennen 19, directly in front of the Dom (Mon–Sat 9am–9/10pm, Sun 10am–6pm; Ⓣ02 21/1 94 33 or 22 13 04 00, Ⓦwww.koelntourismus.de or www.stadt-koeln.de). This is also a good place to try for a hotel room; a booking fee is charged, but last-minute deals at huge savings over normal prices are often available. Cologne's **public transport** system is shared with Bonn, and is likewise part of the VRS network (Ⓦwww.vrsinfo.de); it uses a mixture of buses and trams, with the latter becoming the U-Bahn in and around the centre. Single ticket prices are high, making it better to invest in a pass: those valid for 24 hours cost €5.30 for individuals, €7.50 for up to five people travelling together; there's also a three-day version of the former for €13.50. Another option is the **Köln WelcomeCard**, which includes entrance to all the municipally-owned museums plus reduced

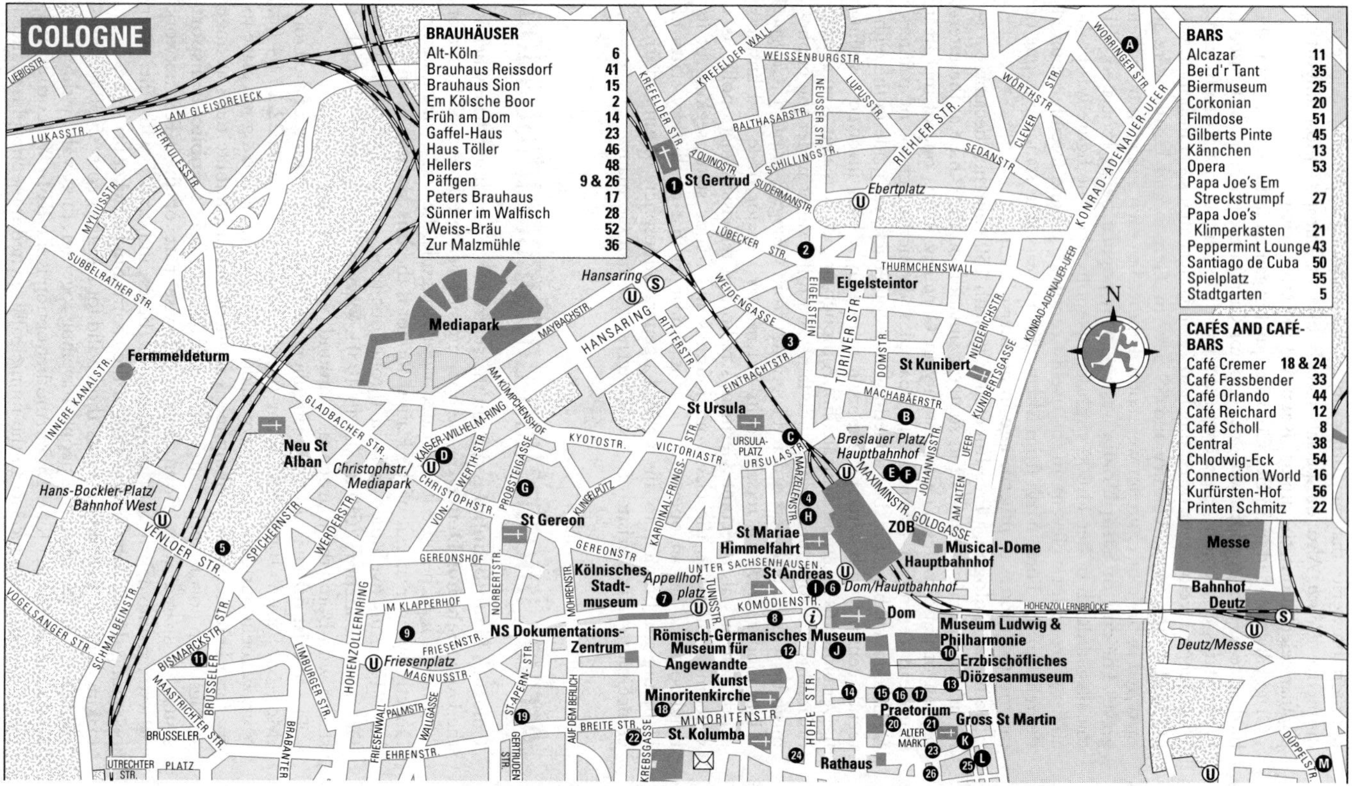
COLOGNE
BRAUHÄUSER
Alt-Köln 6
Brauhaus Reissdorf 41
Brauhaus Sion 15
Em Kölsche Boor 2
Früh am Dom 14
Gaffel-Haus 23
Haus Töller 46
Hellers 48
Päffgen 9 & 26
Peters Brauhaus 17
Sünner im Walfisch 28
Weiss-Bräu 52
Zur Malzmühle 36
BARS
Alcazar 11
Bei d'r Tant 35
Biermuseum 25
Corkonian 20
Filmdose 51
Gilberts Pinte 45
Kännchen 13
Opera 53
Papa Joe's Em Streckstrumpf 27
Papa Joe's Klimperkasten 21
Peppermint Lounge 43
Santiago de Cuba 50
Spielplatz 55
Stadtgarten 5
CAFÉS AND CAFÉ-BARS
Café Cremer 18 & 24
Café Fassbender 33
Café Orlando 44
Café Reichard 12
Café Scholl 8
Central 38
Chlodwig-Eck 54
Connection World 16
Kurfürsten-Hof 56
Printen Schmitz 22
N
St Gertrud
Ebertplatz
Eigelsteintor
Hansaring
Mediapark
Fermmeldeturm
St Kunibert
St Ursula
Breslauer Platz/ Hauptbahnhof
Neu St Alban
Christophstr./ Mediapark
Hans-Bockler-Platz/ Bahnhof West
St Gereon
St Mariae Himmelfahrt
ZOB
Musical-Dome
Hauptbahnhof
Messe
Bahnhof Deutz
Deutz/Messe
Kölnisches Stadt-museum
Appellhof-platz
St Andreas
Dom/Hauptbahnhof
Dom
NS Dokumentations-Zentrum
Römisch-Germanisches Museum
Museum für Angewandte Kunst
Museum Ludwig & Philharmonie
Erzbischöfliches Diözesanmuseum
Minoritenkirche
Praetorium
Gross St Martin
St. Kolumba
Rathaus
Friesenplatz
HOHENZOLLERNBRÜCKE
KONRAD-ADENAUER-UFER
WORRINGER STR.
RIEHLER STR.
NEUSSER STR.
KREFELDER STR.
TURINER STR.
EIGELSTEIN
HANSARING
VENLOER STR.
HOHENZOLLERNRING
KOMÖDIENSTR.
HOHE STR.
MINORITENSTR.
BREITE STR.

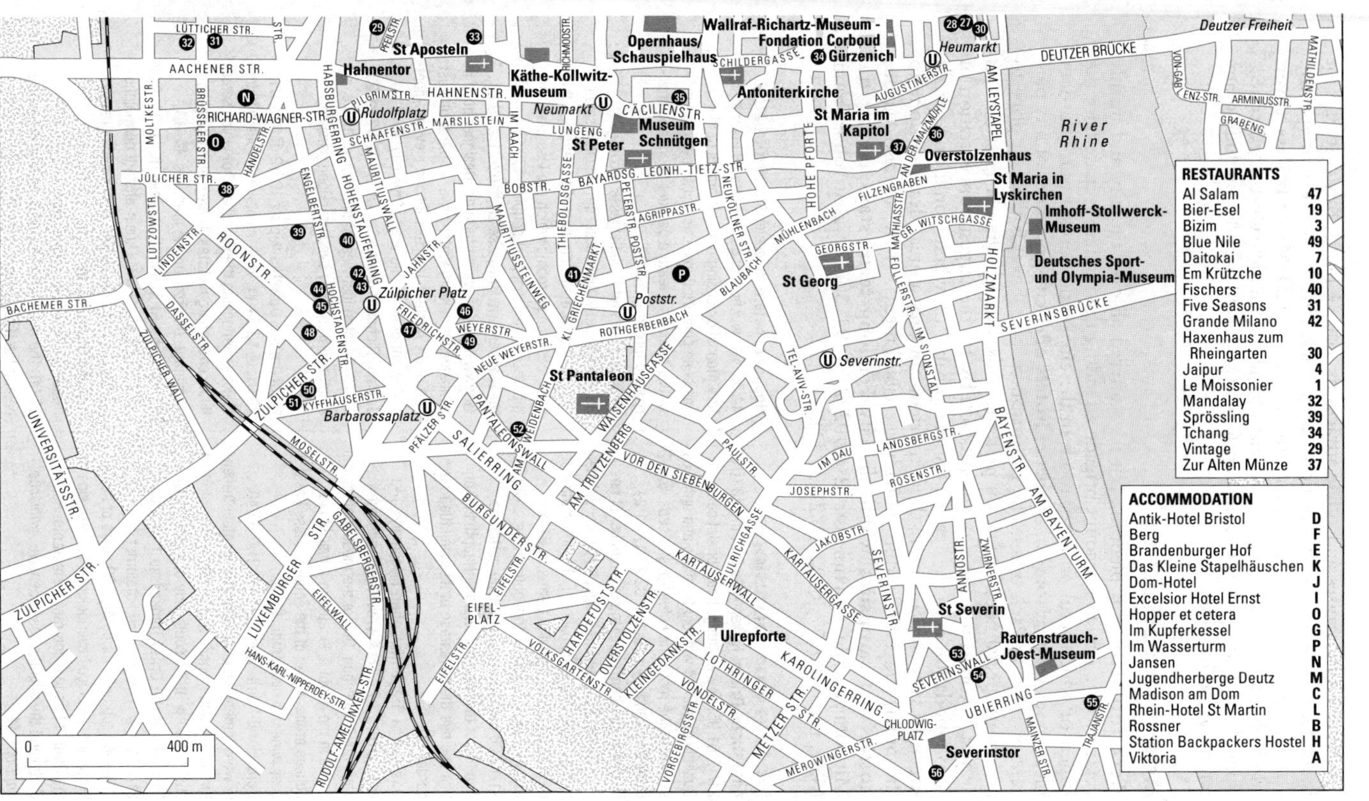
RESTAURANTS
Al Salam 47
Bier-Esel 19
Bizim 3
Blue Nile 49
Daitokai 7
Em Krützche 10
Fischers 40
Five Seasons 31
Grande Milano 42
Haxenhaus zum Rheingarten 30
Jaipur 4
Le Moissonier 1
Mandalay 32
Sprössling 39
Tchang 34
Vintage 29
Zur Alten Münze 37
ACCOMMODATION
Antik-Hotel Bristol D
Berg F
Brandenburger Hof E
Das Kleine Stapelhäuschen K
Dom-Hotel J
Excelsior Hotel Ernst I
Hopper et cetera O
Im Kupferkessel G
Im Wasserturm P
Jansen N
Jugendherberge Deutz M
Madison am Dom C
Rhein-Hotel St Martin L
Rossner B
Station Backpackers Hostel H
Viktoria A
River Rhine
Deutzer Freiheit
DEUTZER BRÜCKE
SEVERINSBRÜCKE
Heumarkt
Neumarkt
Rudolfplatz
Zülpicher Platz
Barbarossaplatz
Poststr.
Severinstr.
Wallraf-Richartz-Museum - Fondation Corboud
Gürzenich
Opernhaus/ Schauspielhaus
Käthe-Kollwitz-Museum
St Aposteln
Hahnentor
Antoniterkirche
St Maria im Kapitol
Overstolzenhaus
St Maria in Lyskirchen
Imhoff-Stollwerck-Museum
Deutsches Sport- und Olympia-Museum
Museum Schnütgen
St Peter
St Georg
St Pantaleon
St Severin
Rautenstrauch-Joest-Museum
Severinstor
Ulrepforte
0
400 m

fares for Rhine cruises and other attractions. For 24 hours, this costs €9 for individuals, €18 for families or up to three adults; for 72 hours the respective charges are €19 and €38. Alternatively, the €10.20 **MuseumPass** covers admission costs on two consecutive days to all the municipally-owned collections (identified by the Web address (w)www.museenkoeln.de), including any temporary exhibitions.

Accommodation

Accommodation is plentiful, but it's scattered all over the city and mainly geared to the expense-account brigade attending the numerous trade fairs, the largest of which result in every room in the city being booked out. This does mean, however, that some of the better **hotels** offer cut-price rates of fifty percent or more at slack times. The tourist office (see above) is the best place to ask about special rates, but if you prefer to look yourself, the cheapest options lie just beyond the fringes of the Altstadt. By far the largest concentration of accommodation is to the rear of the Hauptbahnhof, where you'll find several streets of very similar hotels, though prices can vary a great deal from one to the other, and even within individual establishments. There are also various **hostels** and **campsites** within the city. For **long-term stays**, contact the Mitwohnzentrale, Maximenstr. 2 ((t)02 21/1 94 30), or Zeitwohnagentur März, Lindenstr. 77 ((t)02 21/21 05 11).

Hotels and pensions

Antik-Hotel Bristol Kaiser-Wilhelm-Ring 48 (t)02 21/12 01 95, (w)www.antik-hotel-bristol.com. Quaintly appointed with old furniture and antiques; several of the rooms have four-poster beds. 6–9

Berg Brandenburger Str. 6 (t)02 21/12 11 24, (w)www.hotel-berg.com. One of a number of no-frills yet perfectly decent budget hotels immediately to the rear of the Hauptbahnhof; the firm mattresses on the beds are unusual in Germany. 3–7

Brandenburger Hof Brandenburger Str. 2–4 (t)02 21/12 28 89, (w)www.brandenburgerhof.de. Another of the hotels behind the Hauptbahnhof; this one has the advantage of its own little rear garden. 4–7

Das Kleine Stapelhäuschen Fischmarkt 1–3 (t)02 21/2 72 77 77, (w)www.koeln-altstadt.de/stapelhaeuschen. One of the most characterful hotels in the Altstadt, located in a pair of old houses at the corner of the square. It also has a cosy wine bar-restaurant. 5–7.

Dom-Hotel Domkloster 2a (t)02 21/2 02 40, (w)www.lemeridien.com. Splendid nineteenth-century luxury hotel whose restaurant terrace offers a stunning view of the south side of the Dom. 9

Excelsior Hotel Ernst Trankgasse 1–5 (t)02 21/27 01, (w)www.excelsiorhotelernst.de. Cologne's top hotel for all the 130 years of its existence; ideally placed overlooking the north side of the Dom. It has two gourmet restaurants: *Hanse-Stube* and the slightly less expensive *Ambiance am Dom*. 9

Hopper et cetera Brüsseler Str. 26 (t)02 21/92 44 00, (w)www.hopper.de. The late nineteenth-century monastic building of the Brothers of Mercy has been converted into this stylish designer hotel, whose bedrooms feature parquet floors and cherrywood furniture. 7–9.

Im Kupferkessel Probsteigasse 6 (t)02 21/13 53 38, (w)www.im-kupferkessel.de. Pleasant small hotel in the northwestern part of the Altstadt. It has some cosy single rooms which are less than half the price of the cheapest doubles. 5–7

Im Wasserturm Kaygasse 2a (t)02 21/2 00 80, (w)www.hotel-im-wasserturm.de. Designer hotel in a nineteenth-century water-tower in the southeast part of the Altstadt. Its glass-topped eleventh-floor restaurant offers a fine view of the city. 9

Jansen Richard-Wagner-Str. 18 (t)&(f) 02 21/25 18 75. Situated just west of the Altstadt, this is a small and frequently oversubscribed pension. 4–6

Madison am Dom Ursulaplatz 10-12 (t)02 21/13 29 91, (f)12 54 11. Well-maintained modern hotel directly overlooking the Hauptbahnhof which sometimes offers bargain rates. There's also an Italian restaurant, *Da Enzo*, on the premises. 5–9.

Rhein-Hotel St Martin Frankenwerft 31–33 (t)02 21/2 57 79 55, (w)www.koeln-altstadt.de/rheinhotel. Good-value hotel whose front rooms directly face the Rhine. 5–7

Rossner Jakordenstr. 19 (t)02 21/12 27 03, (f)12 27 00. The homeliest and best value of the hotels behind the Hauptbahnhof. 3–5

St Georg Rolandstr. 61 ⓣ02 21/9 37 02 00, ⓦwww.gaestehaus-st-georg.de. A small guesthouse to the south of the Ring, run by the Boy Scout offices. It incorporates *Bi Pis Bistro*, which has a left-wing clientele and regular cultural events, such as poetry readings. ④–⑦

Viktoria Worringer Str. 23 ⓣ02 21/9 73 17 20, ⓦwww.hotel-viktoria.com). Fine century-old hotel, situated close to the Rhine just north of the Altstadt. ⑦–⑨

Youth hostels

Jugendgästehaus Riehl An der Schanz 14 ⓣ02 21/76 70 81. Located in the northern suburb of Riehl, this youth guesthouse has modern spacious rooms with lockers and a bar. Take U-Bahn #16 to Boltensternstrasse. €19.40.

Jugendherberge Deutz Siegesstr. 5a ⓣ02 21/81 47 11. The more central of the city's hostels, about a 15-min walk from the centre over the Hohenzollernbrücke, or just two blocks south of Bahnhof Deutz. €18.90/21.60.

Station Backpackers Hostel Marzellenstr. 44–48 (ⓣ02 21/9 12 53 01, ⓦwww.hostel-cologne.de). Privately-owned hostel whose facilities include a laundry and Internet access. Dorm beds from €15, singles €27, doubles €40.

Campsites

Berger Uferstr. 53a, Rodenkirchen ⓣ02 21/39 22 11. Located in a right bank suburb by the Rodenkirchener Brücke and reached by U-Bahn #16 to Rodenkirchen, then bus #130.

Städtischer Familienzeltplatz Weidenweg, Poll ⓣ02 21/83 19 66. In a suburb to the south of Deutz, this convenient campsite is reached by U-Bahn #16 to Rodenkirchen, after which it's just a short walk across the Rodenkirchener Brücke. Open May to early Oct.

Waldbad Peter-Baum-Weg, Dünnwald ⓣ02 21/60 33 15. Located in an extreme northeastern suburb.

The City

The best-known attractions of Cologne – the Dom and the main museums – are grouped conveniently together, with some of the traditional beer halls close by. Although many visitors venture no further, it would be a pity not to see a bit more of the medieval **Altstadt**, which occupies an enormous area. Among the buildings to have survived are twelve Romanesque churches, much the finest collection anywhere. It's also well worth venturing a bit further afield. Indeed, the best introduction to the city is to cross over to the right-bank suburb of Deutz – or at least to go some distance across either the Hohenzollernbrücke or the Deutzer Brücke – for the classic **view**, with the tall houses of the burghers lining the banks of the Rhine (crossed by no fewer than eight bridges within the city boundaries), and the chunky Romanesque tower of Gross St Martin providing an ideal counterfoil to the soaring openwork steeples of the Dom.

The Altstadt

In the Middle Ages, Cologne rivalled Paris for the right to be regarded as the premier city on the continent, and this helps to explain the size of its Altstadt, which is on a far larger scale than any other in Germany. It suffered grievous damage in the last war, and many fine old buildings were lost or left as ruins. Much of what can be seen today is modern: the historic monuments are scattered among the main shopping streets, several business districts, and plenty of new housing, though at least this means that it's a lively place throughout the daytime and beyond. The **twelve Romanesque churches** – which range in date from the tenth to the thirteenth century – form one of the most coherent groups in a single architectural style to be found in any European city, and four of their number (St Gereon, St Maria im Kapitol, Gross St Martin and St Aposteln) are artistically outstanding. There are also several notable **museums**, some very traditional, others thoroughly modern.

Inevitably, however, it's the Dom which remains the principal landmark – and the main tourist draw.

The Dom

One of the most massive Gothic buildings ever constructed, the **Dom** (Ⓦwww.koelner-dom.de) dominates the city in every sense. Its size reflects its power and status as "queen and mother of all German churches", whose archbishop was one of the seven Electors of the Holy Roman Empire. Today, pollution has made it hard to distinguish between the medieval and nineteenth-century parts of the Dom, and the facade, of which you get a great uninterrupted view from the square in front, has an overwhelming, crushing power. Originally, the **spires** were, at 157m, the tallest structures in the world, but they were soon dwarfed by the Eiffel Tower and are no longer even the highest in Cologne. All the same, you need a fair bit of energy to climb up to the observation platform of the **south tower** (daily 9am–4/5/6pm; €2, or €5 combined ticket with Schatzkammer) for a fine **panorama** over the city and the Rhine.

Enter by the west door and your eye is immediately drawn down the great length of the building to the high altar with the Romanesque **shrine to the Magi**, which illustrates the history of the world as described in the Bible, with Epiphany given due prominence. Also within the chancel is an unparalleled set of furnishings contemporary with the architecture – choir stalls, painted wooden panels, vibrant statues of Christ, the Virgin and the Apostles, and a delicate altar front. To penetrate beyond the barrier for a marginally better view of all of these, you have to take one of the **guided tours** which leave from the main portal. English-language tours (€3.50) start at 10.30am and 2.30pm every day except Sunday, when they take place in the afternoon only.

At the entrance to the north side of the ambulatory is the ninth-century **Gero crucifix**, the most important monumental sculpture of its period. The

The history of the Dom

The history of the present Dom is an odd one, for, although the foundation stone was laid in 1248, work was only completed in 1880. Most of what can be seen today was put up in two concentrated periods of activity separated by five centuries, yet in an almost identical architectural style. The impetus for the creation of a new cathedral came with the arrival of the alleged relics of the Magi and the subsequent increase in pilgrims. A spectacular **shrine** was commissioned to house the relics, begun in 1181 by **Nicholas of Verdun**, the greatest goldsmith of the day, and finished in 1220 by local craftsmen. What was then needed was a fitting palace to house this memorial to the kings. It was decided to adopt the ethereal new Gothic style of architecture for the cathedral, rather than the late Romanesque style still in vogue in the Rhineland, but to surpass earlier French models in size and splendour.

The chancel, designed by **Master Gerhard**, was completed in 1322, but thereafter the sheer ambitiousness of the plans began to take its toll. In 1560, the project was abandoned, with only the south tower and the lower parts of the nave and facade having been built. That might have been the end of the story, had it not been for the impact of the Romantic movement in the early nineteenth century, which led to a campaign for the completion of the cathedral, boosted by the discovery of two pieces of parchment which showed the medieval builders' designs for the facade. From 1842, in a remarkable act of homage from one age to another, the work was carried out in a style that would have been completely familiar to the original masons.

corresponding chapel to the south has the greatest achievement of the fifteenth-century Cologne School of painters, the *Adoration of the Magi* triptych by **Stefan Lochner**. His refined, idealized style finds a perfect outlet in this truly gorgeous scene; the wings feature two of the Cologne martyrs, SS Ursula and Gereon, with their companions. Look out also for an elaborate sixteenth-century carved retable from Antwerp in the south transept, a colossal wooden *St Christopher* nearby, and (at the intersection of the north transept and the nave aisle) the fourteenth-century *Clares Altar*.

Stained-glass windows are essential components of a Gothic cathedral, and Cologne has a marvellously varied assemblage. The oldest, dating from 1260, is in the axis chapel of the ambulatory and is a "Bible" window, pairing New Testament scenes with a parallel from the Old Testament; another is two chapels to the south. In a wholly different, far more monumental style is the late Gothic glass on the north side of the nave, designed by some of the leading local painters. These in turn contrast well with the brilliantly coloured nineteenth-century Bavarian windows opposite, a gift from King Ludwig I towards the Dom's completion. Around the time of the festivals of Whitsun and Corpus Christi each year, eight huge **tapestries** of *The Triumph of the Eucharist*, woven from designs by **Rubens** (whose childhood was spent in Cologne), are displayed in the nave.

The Domschatzkammer and the Erzbischöfliches Diözesanmuseum

In celebration of the millennium, the full richness of the **Domschatzkammer** (daily 10am–6pm; €4) was presented to the public for the first time ever in its new home in the medieval cellars under the Dom; the entrance is outside the north transept. The Heiltiumskammer beside the ticket office houses the most venerated objects, ranging from the ivory **staff of St Peter** (which was actually carved in Rome in the fourth century) to the spectacular Baroque **shrine** – made during the Thirty Years' War – containing the relics of the martyred thirteenth-century Cologne bishop St Engelbert. On the floor below are some magnificent medieval treasures, including a **crozier** made to celebrate the consecration of the chancel, a fifteenth-century **ceremonial sword** symbolizing the status of the local archbishops as Electors of the Holy Roman Empire, and an early sixteenth-century gilded bronze **epitaph** to a former provost of the Dom, Jakob von Croy. There are also some lovely Baroque pieces, notably a locally made gilded and jewelled **monstrance** with a double crown; this was grievously damaged during a theft in 1975, but restored to its original state after nine years of patient restoration. The original wooden core of the shrine to the Magi is exhibited in an alcove; the chamber alongside displays changing selections from the Dom's library. In the basement are many of the **original figures** from the portal of the south tower, the only one dating from the medieval building period. Carved by members of the Parler family and their associates, they have been replaced *in situ* by faithful copies. Alongside are jewellery and other artefacts from two princely graves of the Frankish era. A roomful of textiles is dominated by the **Capella Clementina**, a costly set of 44 liturgical vestments woven in Paris for the notorious Elector Clemens August to wear at his brother's coronation as Emperor Charles VII.

Just outside the Dom, at Roncalliplatz 2, is the **Erzbischöfliches Diözesanmuseum** (daily except Thurs 11am–6pm; free; Ⓦwww.kolumba.de). This is due to move to much larger premises (by St Kolumba, see p.524) in the near future; in the meantime, it is only able to show selections drawn from its holdings. A beautiful **Lochner**, *Madonna of the Violets*, normally forms the centrepiece of the displays; there's also a small *Nativity* by the same artist. Other highlights include: an eleventh-century crucifix which bizarrely uses an antique lapis lazuli of a woman as the head; a recently acquired ivory crucifix of enormous poignancy from the following century; the St Severin Medallion, with a portrait of the saint; and two priceless textiles – a sixth-century Syrian silk illustrating a hunt, discovered in the shrine of Saint Kunibert, and a Byzantine cloth embroidered with lions. The museum has collected a great deal of modern art in recent years, and more of this will be on view in the new building.

The Römisch-Germanisches Museum

Germany's most important collection of indigenous archeological finds, the **Römisch-Germanisches Museum** (Tues–Sun 10am–5pm; €3.60; Ⓦwww.museenkoeln.de) at Roncalliplatz 4 is specially constructed around the star exhibit, the **Dionysos Mosaic**, excavated here in 1941. The finest work of its kind in northern Europe, it adorned the dining room of a patrician villa of about 200 AD. The mosaic is made from over a million pieces of limestone, ceramics and glass, covering an area of some 70 square metres, and depicts the inebriated Bacchus surrounded by Cupid, Pan, dancers, satyrs and vignettes of the delights of the table. Its astonishing state of preservation is due to the protective covering it received from the burnt-out remains of the building falling on it when sacked by a Germanic tribe in the fourth century. The other main item is the **tomb of Poblicius**, a veteran who had served in the Fifth Legion. Dating from about 40 AD, this is an even more recent discovery. It stands about 15m high and has been re-erected beside the mosaic, although considerably more restoration has been necessary.

Otherwise, the museum is arranged thematically. The collection of **glass** is reckoned to be unsurpassed anywhere in the world. Among the early pieces is a tiny idealized portrait of Augustus Caesar made in 27 BC. From the second century, the Cologne workshops developed their own distinctive forms, with coloured serpentine threads used for decorative effects. This style culminated around 330 AD in the *diatreta* glass, decorated with a delicate network design. Perhaps of more general appeal is the dazzling array of **jewellery** on the first floor, most of which was found in Frankish graves. Also of special note are the fragments of the city's northern gateway, the Philosophers Mosaic of 260 AD and a spectacular array of over a thousand terracotta lamps.

The Museum Ludwig

Immediately to the east, at Bischofgartenstr. 1, is a large 1980s building housing the city's main concert hall, the Philharmonie, and the modern art holdings of the **Museum Ludwig** (Tues 10am–8pm, Wed–Fri 10am–6pm, Sat & Sun 11am–6pm; €5.10; Ⓦwww.museenkoeln.de). This features a notable American section, including a large display of Pop Art which includes such favourite **Andy Warhol** subjects as Brillo boxes, Pepsi Cola and tins of Campbell's Tomato Juice, as well as examples of Tom Wesselmann and Roy Lichtenstein. **Claes Oldenburg** is represented by *The Street*, which occupies a whole room. The many other eye-catching sculptures include the uncanny fibreglass creations of the Realists and **Ed Kienholz**'s *Portable War Memorial*, a devastating satire on his country's cultural values.

Among German works, there's a fine batch by **Kirchner**, notably a group portrait of *Die Brücke*; around it hang examples of these very painters. **Max Ernst** provided a similar memento of the Surrealists, including co-opted dead members, Raphael and Dostoyevsky. By the same artist is an iconoclastic ringing of the changes on the theme of the *Madonna and Child*; the furious mother administers a sound thrashing on the infant's buttocks while Ernst and friends look on. **Beckmann, Nolde** and **Kokoschka** are all strongly represented; look out for the latter's *View of Cologne*. There are three superb portraits by **Dix**, including one of himself, and a number of sculptures in various media by **Barlach**. Two rooms are devoted to **Picasso**, with sculptures and ceramics as well as paintings from most phases of his career. In contrast, there's only a single spectacular **Dalí**, *Perpignan Station*. Beside it hangs one of the most famous Surrealist canvases, *Presence of Mind* by **Magritte**. An impressive array of Russian paintings includes a large **Chagall**, *Moses Destroying the Tablets of the Law*.

A second museum in the premises, the **Agfa-Foto-Historama**, shows old photographic equipment and a changing selection of prints from the vast holdings of the famous company, whose headquarters are in nearby Leverkusen.

From Gross St Martin to the Rathaus

A short walk south of the Museum Ludwig is **Gross St Martin**, a former monastic church that was for long occupied by Benedictines from Scotland and Ireland. For nearly six hundred years its **tower**, surrounded by four turrets, was the dominant feature of the Cologne skyline, not being usurped by the Dom's spires until the late nineteenth century. The rest of the building seems rather truncated for such a splendid adornment, although the interior has been returned to its simple original form.

Just beyond is the Alter Markt, one of three large squares in the heart of the city. From here, you can see the irregular octagonal tower of the **Rathaus** (normally Mon–Thurs 7.30am–4.45pm, Fri 7.30am–2pm; free), a building which is a real jumble of styles, yet with marvellous features. Its core is fourteenth-century Gothic; the following century the tower was added in a more flamboyant idiom, while in the 1570s a graceful loggia, a rare example of Renaissance architecture in the Rhineland, was provided as a frontispiece. Highlights of the interior include the **Hansa-Saal** from the first building period, and the tower rooms with doorways of inlaid woods.

In front of the entrance to the Rathaus is a glass pyramid sheltering the **Mikwe**, a Jewish ritual bath house dating from about 1160, the only remnant of the ghetto which was razed soon after the expulsion order of 1424. It's officially open on weekends from 11am to 3pm, but from Monday to Friday you can ask for the key during office hours at the porter's desk in the Rathaus. More subterranean sights can be seen just a short distance away in the form of the foundations of the **Praetorium** (Tues–Fri 10am–4pm, Sat & Sun 11am–4pm; €1.50), the Roman governor's palace, and the **Römischer Kanal** (same times and ticket), a surprisingly elegant vaulted sewer some 100m long. The entrance to both of these is on Kleine Budengasse.

The Wallraf-Richartz-Museum - Fondation Corboud

Diagonally opposite the Rathaus is the strikingly angular building, inaugurated in 2001, of the **Wallraf-Richartz-Museum – Fondation Corboud** (Tues 10am–8pm, Wed–Fri 10am–6pm, Sat & Sun 11am–6pm; €5.10; Ⓦwww.museenkoeln.de). The Wallraf-Richartz collection of old masters begins on the first floor with the unique holdings of the fifteenth-century **Cologne School** (see p.1021), and it's worth looking out for the many intriguing backdrop depictions of the medieval city, often featuring the unfinished Dom. **Stefan Lochner** is the most admired artist of the school, and his *Last Judgement* is a major work, enormously inventive in its detail, gentle and

Karneval

While there's no doubt that Cologne is worth visiting at any season, by far the best time to come is during the Shrovetide celebrations of **Karneval** (Ⓦwww.karneval.de). This is celebrated with a verve normally associated with Mediterranean countries, and is a useful corrective to the common misapprehension that the Germans are an excessively serious and respectful people. For the *drei tollen Tage* ("three crazy days"– the Thursday, Sunday and Monday before Shrove Tuesday), life in the city comes to a complete stop and everyone, from punks to grannies, dons make-up and costume, taking to the streets as clown, fool, harlequin or historical personality.

The present highly organized festival dates back to 1823, but its true origins are considerably older. In part it derives from a pagan exorcism of evil spirits in the transition from one season to another, and in part from a Christian tradition of periods of fasting, which were invariably preceded by counterbalancing periods of merriment. This latter factor governs the timetable of the festival, which has moveable dates; the climax occurs in the week preceding Ash Wednesday, immediately before the stringencies of Lent. However, the Karneval season actually begins as early as "the eleventh of the eleventh", ie November 11, a date which was seen as having a foolish significance. From then on, Cologne holds both costume balls and *Sitzungen* (sessions); at the latter, speeches are made in rhyming couplets in the local *Kölsch* dialect (incomprehensible to outsiders, but fairly close to Dutch).

The festivities

The real celebrations begin with **Weiberfastnacht** on the Thursday prior to the seventh Sunday before Easter. A ceremony in the Alter Markt, starting at 10am, leads to the official inauguration of the festival with the handing over of the keys of the city by the mayor at 11.11am precisely to Prinz Claus III, who assumes command for the "three crazy days". Whereas in other cities he's aided by a princess, in Cologne he has two companions, the peasant Bauer Knut and the virgin Jungfrau Karla, who is played by a man and is emphatically not his betrothed. The fun can then begin in earnest; in repentance for the chauvinism of earlier centuries, this particular day is now given over to the supremacy of women, who are allowed to take the liberties of their choice. At 3pm there's the first of the great **processions**, beginning at Severinstor, based on the **legend of Jan and Griet**. The former was Jan von Werth, a seventeenth-century cavalry officer who saved the city from ruin in the Thirty Years War. Griet was the Cologne girl who had spurned him, prompting him to assume a military career; they were not to meet again until she, as an ageing spinster, saw him enter the city as a general at the head of his troops. In the evening, the great series of **costume balls** begins, the most prestigious being those in the Gürzenich.

fantastic in its view. More typical of his style is the exquisite *Madonna of the Rose Bower*, his artistic swansong. From the preceding generation, the **Master of St Veronica** is the most accomplished painter, represented here by two contrasting versions of the *Crucifixion*, one as delicately refined as an illuminated manuscript, the other with monumental figures. The most detailed vignettes of Cologne are by the **Master of the Glorification of the Virgin**, but the gems of the whole display are arguably the two triptychs made for the Carthusians by the **Master of St Bartholomew**, who represented the final flowering of the school at the beginning of the sixteenth century. His figures are executed as if in imitation of sculpture and have a haunting, mystical quality. These are displayed in the company of other large-scale Cologne altarpieces in the central chamber, which has been given a symbolic cruciform shape. Also on view on this floor are a small **Dürer**, *Fifer and Drummer*, several typical examples of

However, there are plenty of spontaneous bouts of singing, dancing and boisterous conviviality in the streets and taverns as an authentic alternative.

For the next two days, the city returns to relative normality during daylight hours, although fancy dress is still much in evidence, and on the Saturday morning there's the **Funkenbiwack**, featuring the Rote und Blaue Funken (Red and Blue Sparks), men dressed up in eighteenth-century military outfits; they disobey every order – a symbol of Cologne's long tradition of anti-militarism. The celebrations come to a climax with the two big costumed processions with floats; on Sunday the **Schull-un Veedleszög**, largely featuring children, forms a prelude to the more spectacular **Rosenmontagzug** (Rose Monday Parade). The latter is unquestionably the highlight of the celebrations, a riot of colour featuring over seven thousand people, half of them musicians, and three hundred horses. Its first part is a pageant on the history of the city; then comes the satirical section in which local, national and international politicians appear in effigy; finally there's a gala in honour of the Cologne Karneval, with the spectacular retinues of the peasant, the virgin and the prince bringing up the rear. It's all done with a proper sense of Germanic thoroughness, taking all of four hours to pass by. After this, the festival runs down; there are numerous smaller parades in the suburbs on Shrove Tuesday, while the restaurants offer special fish menus on Ash Wednesday.

Karneval practicalities

Although the city gets jam-packed with visitors during Karneval, many are day-trippers and there's no problem finding **accommodation**. A greater difficulty comes in deciding **where to stand** during the processions; if you want the backdrop of the Dom, make sure you come several hours before they start (12.30pm on Sun, noon on Mon) and choose a position on the elevated terrace. Alternatively, go somewhere towards the beginning or end of the route (the tourist office provides free maps), where the crowds are thinner. You could consider renting one of the grandstand **seats**, positioned all along the course of the route; these are expensive for the Rose Monday Parade, but good value on the Sunday. Remember to keep well wrapped up; even when the weather is sunny, it's likely to be cold. Don't expect to do anything else during the "three crazy days"; all the museums and most of the shops are closed, and even the Dom's doors are firmly locked except for the occasional service. Above all, join in the fun; it isn't essential to get dressed up (though it helps), and don't hesitate to follow the crowds, usually congregated round a big drum – it's the impromptu events as much as the setpieces which make this such a great festival. Note that there's a special deal allowing unlimited travel on the public transport network between Weiberfastnacht and Shrove Tuesday.

Cranach; and some Flemish and Italian Primitives, notably a *Madonna and Child* by **Simone Martini**.

On the second floor, the most important German work is the small *Martyrdom of St Stephen* by **Elsheimer**. A good selection of **Rubens**' varied output includes two impressively large-scale canvases: *Juno and Argus* and *The Stigmatization of St Francis*. The latter was painted for the Capuchins of Cologne and makes for a fascinating comparison with *St Francis in the Porzincula Chapel* by the Spaniard **Murillo**, another of the great masters of the Counter-Reformation. A rich representation of seventeenth-century Dutch artists includes masterpieces by Hals, Ter Brugghen and Ruisdael, as well as what is probably the very last of **Rembrandt**'s great series of self-portraits, in which he depicted himself in the guise of a laughing philosopher (or perhaps the satirical painter Zeuxis) from ancient Greece.

The third floor is devoted to the nineteenth century, and includes several examples of **Friedrich** and a large collection of the local artist **Wilhelm Leibl**, leader of the Realist movement, which are hung in juxtaposition with those of his French counterpart **Courbet**. A decent section on **French Impressionism** has been enormously enhanced by the permanent loan of the collection formed by the Swiss businessman Gérard Corboud and his wife Marisol, a native of Cologne. This comprises nearly 200 Impressionist, Neo-Impressionist and Pointillist paintings, whose common theme is colour in all its brilliance. Although famous artists such as Monet and Cézanne are represented, the most memorable works are by their lesser-known compatriots, such as Gustave Caillebotte, Maximilien Luce, Paul Signac and Henri Le Sidanier. Unfortunately, space constraints mean that it is usually only possible to keep a small selection on display.

The rest of the eastern Altstadt

The Wallraf-Richartz-Museum – Fondation Corboud is built right up against the burnt-out church of **Alt St Alban**, which has been left as a war memorial. It in turn adjoins the **Gürzenich**, a much-rebuilt Gothic festive hall, best known as the home of the Karneval balls. A little further south is the tower which is all that survives of **Klein St Martin**.

Behind is **St Maria im Kapitol**, which is not seen to advantage from outside as it was built in a severe convent style and is now hemmed in by modern houses; however, it possesses a majestic interior complete with a full circuit for processions around the aisles. Originally constructed in the eleventh century, it pioneered the trefoil or clover-leaf chancel that became a staple feature of the churches of the Rhineland for the next two hundred years. Look out for the **wooden doors**, contemporary with the architecture and among the most precious works of their kind, depicting Christ's Nativity, Teachings and Passion. The church has a magnificent monumental Renaissance **rood screen**, while the **cloisters**, unusually placed adjoining the facade, are the only ones left in Cologne.

Continuing in a southerly direction, Rheingasse leads to the **Overstolzenhaus**, the finest mansion in the city, a step-gabled patrician home contemporary with the later Romanesque churches. A short walk from here is the sailors' church of **St Maria in Lyskirchen**, which contains several fine works of art, notably the *Beautiful Madonna* of about 1420. The vaults are covered with thirteenth-century frescoes of scenes from the Old and New Testaments and lives of saints, which are seen to best effect by climbing the stairs to the gallery.

From the nearby Rhine promenade, a little bridge crosses over the Rheinauhafen to the picturesque jumble of old and new buildings housing the **Imhoff-Stollwerck-Museum** (Tues–Fri 10am–6pm, Sat & Sun 11am-7pm; €5.50; Ⓦwww.schockoladenmuseum.de). This is an unashamed advert for the eponymous company, which, despite having come close to going out of business on more than one occasion, is now firmly established as one of the world's top ten chocolate manufacturers. With that proviso aside, the museum is a model of its kind, with a miniature working factory – complete with a chocolate fountain from which samples are dispensed – on the ground floor, and well-presented historical sections upstairs. The latter include a large number of vessels from the Central American cultures which first developed chocolate some three thousand years ago, as well as beautiful examples of the porcelain for drinking chocolate which were fashionable in eighteenth-century Europe. Chocoholics are presented with all sorts of temptations in the shop and in the café, which offers more than a dozen different chocolate-based beverages.

Of more dubious merit is the **Deutsches Sport- und Olympia-Museum** (Tues–Fri 10am–6pm, Sat & Sun 11am–7pm; €4; Ⓦwww.sportmuseum

-koeln.de) alongside. This aims to illustrate the entire history of sport, but inevitably ends up with a heavy German bias. There are mementoes of many of the country's sporting heroes, such as the car Michael Schumacher drove when he won his first Formula One world championship, and tennis rackets wielded by Boris Becker and Steffi Graf. Among several interactive attractions are a boxing ring with punchbags, a cycle wind tunnel, and a mini-football pitch on the rooftop, which is promoted as Cologne's highest sports field.

Returning via St Maria in Lyskirchen, head up Grosse Witschgasse and Georgstrasse to **St Georg**, an eleventh-century pillared basilica which resembles early Christian churches. The westwork, added the following century, looks squat and stumpy from without, but is impressively spacious inside.

The southern Altstadt

Immediately south of St Georg is the **St Severin** quarter, which formed an extension to the original Altstadt. The church from which it takes its name is classified among the twelve surviving Romanesque foundations in Cologne, though only the twin-towered apse and part of the transept remain from that time, the rest being late Gothic. Now it's mainly of interest to archeology buffs, on account of the **Roman-Frankish graveyard** which has been found directly underneath; this can be visited on guided tours (Mon & Fri 4pm; €1). Just beyond the church is the **Severinstor**, part of the medieval fortifications which were largely demolished last century when the Ring was built. A short walk to the east, at Ubierring 45 (but due to relocate to the new cultural centre on Neumarkt in 2006), is the **Rautenstrauch-Joest-Museum** (Tues–Fri 10am–4pm, Sat & Sun 11am–4pm; €2.60; Ⓦwww.museenkoeln.de). The particular strengths of this large ethnological museum are Indo-China (notably some outstanding Khmer sculptures) and Pre-Columbian America; West Africa, the Pacific and Indonesia are also well represented. Following the ring road in a northwesterly direction is the **Ulrepforte**, another turreted gateway.

The western Altstadt

Further along Sachsenring, a right turn along Waisenhausgasse brings you to **St Pantaleon**, the oldest surviving church in the city, dating from the end of the tenth century. It's chiefly notable for its massive westwork with vestibule. Inside, there's an airy Flamboyant Gothic rood screen, crowned by a seventeenth-century organ in a Rococo case. Northwards via Poststrasse and Peterstrasse is **St Peter**, a Gothic church whose otherwise spare and austere interior houses a bravura high altar of *The Martyrdom of St Peter* by **Rubens**. The Josef-Haubricht-Kunsthalle, which formerly stood to the west, at the corner of Neumarkt, has been demolished, and the site is being developed as a new cultural centre which will house a variety of institutions, including the Rautenstrauch-Joest Museum.

It will also provide a much-needed extension for the **Museum Schnütgen** (Tues–Fri 10am–5pm, Sat & Sun 11am–5pm; €2.60; Ⓦwww.museenkoeln.de), which occupies the Romanesque convent church of **St Cäcilien** immediately north of St Peter. This is one of the world's most important collections of medieval religious art (except paintings), and inevitably has a strong Rhenish emphasis. There are some wonderful **ivories**, notably a diptych which belonged to Charlemagne and the comb of St Heribert. Major pieces of **Romanesque sculpture** include the church's own tympanum, carved in a heavily antique style; the wooden crucifix from St Georg; the mysterious *Siegburg Madonna*; the enamel and bronze altarpiece of St Ursula; and a cylindrical reliquary made of rock crystal, gold and jewels. From the **Gothic** period the museum's most important possessions are some of the original carvings from the Dom's altar front, a polychrome console bust of a woman carved by a member of the Parler family, and contrasting Calvary groups made in Kalkar and the neighbouring Netherlands.

Across the road and down Antongasse is the tiny Gothic **Antoniterkirche**, now a Protestant parish church, best known for housing one of the most famous of twentieth-century sculptures, **Barlach**'s *Memorial Angel*. This is a cast made from the plaster of the original, which was created for the 700th anniversary of the Dom in Güstrow but destroyed in the perverse Nazi measures against "degenerate art". Around the church is the main shopping centre; the streets follow the same plan as their Roman predecessors, but almost all the buildings are modern.

Up Herzogstrasse are the ruins of the Gothic **St Kolumba**, which wasn't restored after the war; instead Gottfried Böhm inserted a minute chapel within the shell in 1950. The new Erzbischöfliches Diözesanmuseum is being built alongside. A block further north is another Gothic church, the severe **Minoritenkirche**. It contains the tomb of John Duns Scotus, the Scots-born theologian who was the leading intellectual in early fourteenth-century Cologne. Ironically, he's the origin of the word "dunce": his defences of traditional religious orthodoxies so enraged his radical fellow countrymen at the time of the Reformation that they used his name as a personification of stupidity. Alongside the church is the **Museum für Angewandte Kunst** (Tues & Thurs–Sun 11am–5pm, Wed 11am–8pm; €3.60; Ⓦ www.museenkoeln.de), a comprehensive array of applied art from the Middle Ages to the present day. The Art Nouveau/Jugendstil section is particularly impressive, though the incongruous highlight of the museum is an exquisite little panel of *The Nativity* by **Memling**.

Housed in a bank at Neumarkt 18, a short distance west of the Antoniterkirche, is the **Käthe-Kollwitz-Museum** (Tues–Fri 10am–6pm, Sat & Sun 11am–6pm; €2.50; Ⓦ www.kollwitz.de). It has a large display of graphics and a few sculptures by Käthe Kollwitz, one of the leading female artists of the twentieth century. Her preference for black-and-white media helps give her work an enormous pathos, evident in her variation on the *Mother and Child* theme, and her denunciations of the follies and sufferings of war.

The far end of Neumarkt is dominated by the majestic early thirteenth-century apse of **St Aposteln** (Holy Apostles – an unusual dedication outside the Orthodox world). This is an archetypal Rhenish basilica with all the characteristic features – clover-leaf chancel with dwarf-gallery, central octagon with turrets and, above all, the great western tower with its "bishop's mitre" roof. Despite its apparently homogeneous design, building actually began in the eleventh century; the interior is surprisingly plain. Nearby is another of the city gates, the **Hahnentor**, which resembles a castle's barbican.

The northern Altstadt

Due north of St Aposteln is **St Gereon**, the most idiosyncratic of the twelve Romanesque churches and a truly great building. Its kernel was an oval-shaped fourth-century chapel; in the eleventh and twelfth centuries a crypt, chancel and twin towers were added. Then, in the early thirteenth century, the Roman masonry was harnessed to form the basis of a magnificent four-storey decagon with ribbed dome vault, a work which has no parallel in European architecture. At this time, the adjoining baptistry was also built and adorned with frescoes. The decagon's interior seems more graceful and less massive than from outside; its modern stained glass is a controversial addition. In the crypt the original mosaic floor with Old Testament scenes is perserved.

From here, you can return towards the Dom, passing a fragment of Roman wall and the **Zeughaus**, which houses the **Kölnisches Stadtmuseum** (Tues

10am–8pm, Wed–Sun 10am–5pm; €3.60; Ⓦwww.museenkoeln.de). This focuses on the history of local trade and industry, along with sections on Karneval and eau de Cologne. Some good models show the city's building development. A stone's throw to the south at Appellhofplatz 23–25, is the former Gestapo prison or El-De-Haus, which now contains the **NS Dokumentations-Zentrum** (Tues–Fri 10am–4pm, Sat & Sun 11am–4pm; €3.60; Ⓦwww.museenkoeln.de). The basement cells where opponents of the Nazis were tortured and murdered can be visited; upstairs are documentary photographic displays (in German only) on Cologne during the Third Reich.

Just to the east of the Zeughaus is **St Andreas**, which has a stately Romanesque nave preceded by a mighty westwork, an octagonal lantern tower and a Gothic chancel. Inside is the **Maccabeus shrine**, a piece of early sixteenth-century craftsmanship, doubtless inspired by the Dom's shrine to the Magi. Another casket contains the relics of St Albertus Magnus, the thirteenth-century scholar who was the star teacher at Cologne's renowned Dominican College; his pupils there included St Thomas Aquinas, later to develop into the greatest philosopher of his time and arguably of the entire medieval period. A short way along Marzellenstrasse is the pink exterior of **St Mariae Himmelfahrt**, a seventeenth-century Jesuit foundation and Cologne's only Baroque church of note. Its galleried interior, which surprisingly employs the long-out-of-favour Gothic pointed arch, is lavishly decorated – unusually for the Rhineland, where Bavarian excesses never caught on.

A bit further down the same street, turn left into Ursulaplatz, where **St Ursula**, with its prominent sturdy tower, still retains some Romanesque features, along with Gothic and Baroque accretions. Try to get hold of the sexton, who will show you the **Goldene Kammer** (normally Mon, Tues, Thurs & Fri 10am–1pm & 2–3pm, Wed & Sat 9am–1pm & 2–5pm, Sun 2–5pm; €1), an ornate Baroque chamber gruesomely lined with human bones arranged in geometric patterns around the reliquaries. From here, the **Eigelsteintor**, another impressive survival of the medieval fortifications, is reached via the street of the same name. Dagobertstrasse then leads east to **St Kunibert**, the final fling of the Romanesque in the early thirteenth century, completed just as work began on the Dom. It was also the last church to be restored following war damage, with the nave and massive westwork having only been joined up a few years back. Inside, note the stained-glass windows in the apse, which are contemporary with the architecture. On the piers of the transept are the two dramatic polychrome figures of an *Annunciation* group, an important piece of Gothic carving by **Conrad Kuyn**, master mason at the Dom in the early fifteenth century.

Outside the centre

If you want to stray beyond the confines of the Altstadt, Cologne's suburbs offer a wide choice of **parks** and some of the most exciting **modern architecture** in Germany. In every way, the dominant building outside the centre is the **Fernmeldeturm** (telecommunications tower; daily 10am–10pm; €2.50, including ascent by elevator to the viewing platform), in the Stadtgarten west of the Ring. At 243m it's considerably higher than the Dom, and it's definitely worth going up for the breathtaking views over the city and the Rhine. Just to the east, within the Stadtgarten, is **Neu St Alban**, one of several highly praised modern churches in Cologne.

Proceeding along the outskirts of the Ring in a clockwise direction, you come to the **Meidapark**, a series of striking new buildings grouped around a large pond. No. 7 houses the **Stiftung Kultur der Stadtsparkasse Köln**

(2–7pm, closed Wed; €4.50; Ⓦwww.sk-kultur.de). This mounts major temporary displays of international photography, and often exhibits selections from the archive of Germany's most revered photographer, **August Sander** (1876–1964), who spent most of his long career in Cologne. Best-known for his portfolio of portraits, *People of the Twentieth Century*, Sander was also a chronicler of nature, landscape and architecture, and made a valuable record of his adopted city before, during and after World War II.

On Krefelder Strasse, on the opposite side of the rail tracks from the Mediapark, is **St Gertrud**, easily recognizable from its amazing tapering tower. It's the work of **Gottfried Böhm**, whose father **Dominikus** was a pioneer of radical church design in the inter-war period. An example of the latter's 1930s Expressionism is **St Engelbert**, a centrally planned building of eight identical concrete shells, located further north, very near the Jugendgästehaus on Riehler Gürtel.

Further round towards the Rhine are two of the city's best-loved areas of greenery - the **Flora- und Botanischer Garten** (daily 8am–9pm or dusk; free) and the **Zoo** (daily 9am–5/6pm; €10, €7 on Mon & Tues–Fri after 4pm; Ⓦwww.zoo-koeln.de). These are linked by the gondolas of the **Rheinseilbahn** (April–Oct daily 10am–6pm; €3.80 single, €5.50 return; Ⓦwww.koelner-seilbahn.de) to the **Rheinpark** in Deutz on the opposite side of the Rhine; en route are marvellous aerial views. The Rheinpark – a legacy of large garden shows – is itself a popular recreation ground; its focal point is the **Tanzbrunnen** (Dance Fountain), round which concerts are held in summer.

From the Hahnentor, Aachener Strasse runs in a dead-straight line westwards to the outer suburbs. Just beyond the Ring, a short walk down Universitätstrasse brings you to the **Museum für Ostasiatische Kunst** (Tues, Wed & Fri–Sun 11am–5pm, Thurs 11am–8pm; €3.60; Ⓦwww.museenkoeln.de). Devoted to the arts of China, Japan and Korea, this is yet another of Cologne's collections which has been given specially designed modern premises, appropriately enough by a Japanese architect and with a traditional Japanese garden. It's arranged thematically, with leaflets in English available on each topic.

Further along Aachener Strasse at no. 1328, in the suburb of Weiden, is the city's final important Roman monument, the **Grabkammer** (Tues–Thurs 10am–1pm, Fri 10am–5pm, Sat & Sun 1–5pm; €1), a second-century burial chamber. It contains marble busts of a couple and a young woman which are contemporary with the building, and a sarcophagus from the following century with carvings of the seasons.

Weiden lies about halfway along the route to **BRAUWEILER**, reached by regular bus services from the Hauptbahnhof. The village clusters around the **Abteikirche**, built as a Benedictine monastery in the twelfth and thirteenth centuries. There are no fewer than six towers, and inside the pillars of the nave are capped by sensual figurative capitals. The serene stone retable in the south apse is one of the masterpieces of German Romanesque sculpture, depicting St Nicholas, the church's patron, in a gathering around the Madonna and Child.

Eating and drinking

The gastronomy of Cologne is as distinctive and distinguished as that of any German city, with plenty of **local food specialities** in addition to the renowned *Kölsch* beer. With over three thousand restaurants, bars and cafés crammed into a relatively small area, there's certainly no shortage of choice, with the chic and trendy often standing cheek by jowl with the staid and traditional.

Kölsch

Kölsch beer is as much a piece of the local life of Cologne as the Dom or Karneval, and may only be produced in the breweries located in and around the city. It's clear, light, highly fermented and aromatically bitter, with a strong accentuation of hops. Invariably, it's served with a substantial head in a tall, thin glass (*Stange)* which holds only a fifth of a litre. This gives it a rather effete image among macho beer drinkers from elsewhere in Germany who tend to revile it, in contrast to the almost religious reverence it's accorded in Cologne.

Brauhäuser

The great Cologne institutions for both eating and drinking are the **Brauhäuser** (or *Weetschaften*, as they're known in the local dialect). Most of these brewery-owned beer halls date from the turn of the twentieth century, though they claim a much longer pedigree; a few of them still brew their *Kölsch* in-house, though most have moved production to larger premises elsewhere in the city. Whilst smaller than their Munich counterparts, they have similarly cavernous interiors with sparse decor. They're staffed by horribly matey *Köbes*, who all year round keep up the Karneval tradition of making insulting and corny jokes. These beer halls are often overrun with visiting businessmen and tourists, but they're definitely worth sampling as they offer some of the best-value food in the city, specializing in the local cuisine. Don't be misled by the dialect, however – *Halve Hahn* is not the half-chicken its name suggests but a rye roll with cheese, while *Kölsche Kaviar* is less of a bargain than it appears when you realize it's a cold black pudding, again with rye bread.

Alt-Köln Trankgasse 7–9. This is a real one-off, its picturesque folly of an interior featuring a whole series of wooden alcoves and galleries which together represent a Romantic vision of a complex of old German taverns. The food is as good as the beer (from the Gilden brewery), and very reasonably priced for a place which gets an outsized share of tourists.

Brauhaus Reissdorf Kleiner Griechenmarkt 40. The main tap of the strongly traditional Reissdorf brewery is a true neighbourhood local, situated as it is in a residential part of the Altstadt.

Brauhaus Sion Unter Taschenmacher 5. Though close to the Dom, the side-street location means that locals rather than visitors form the bulk of the clientele here. It serves generous portions of *gutbürgerliche Küche*; its *Kölsch* is notable for its strong bouquet and dry finish.

Dom Brauhaus Altenburger Str. 157. Situated at the far end of the Südstadt (take U-Bahn #16 to Schönhauser Strasse), but definitely worth a special trip. As well as the beer garden and tavern, reconstructed to resemble those in the city centre, there's the added attraction of Cologne's Brauerei-Musuem (currently only open to tour groups).

Em Kölsche Boor Eigelstein 121-3. This atmospheric old Brauhaus, which dates back to 1760, is currently one of Gaffel's outlets.

Früh am Dom Am Hof 12–14. The most visited of the Brauhäuser, partly because of its wonderful location opposite the Dom, partly because of its excellent food, and above all because of the prestige of its delicately fruity *Cölner Hofbrau*, a classic *Kölsch*.

Gaffel-Haus Alter Markt 20. Gaffel's *Kölsch* is the driest and bitterest in Cologne; the food here is pretty good too.

Haus Töller Weyerstr. 96. Undoubtedly the cosiest of the Brauhäuser, occupying a fourteenth-century house that was one of the first in Cologne to be built of stone. Meals are good value; the beer is from Sion. Evenings only, closed Sun.

Hellers Roonstr. 33. Modern Hausbrauerei which brews a *Weissbier*, a *Bock*, a *Doppelbock* called *No.33*, and a *Kölsch*. Evenings only.

Päffgen Friesenstr. 64. This traditional Hausbrauerei in the northwest Altstadt is the smallest brewery in Cologne, producing a *Kölsch* with a pleasingly hoppy finish. Also has a more centrally located branch at Heumarkt 62.

Peters Brauhaus Mühlengasse 1. Though it looks as old as any of its competitors, this is a fairly recent addition, housed in the palatial premises of the long-defunct *Brauhaus Zum Kranz*.

Sünner im Walfisch Salzgasse 13. Another relative newcomer, though it belongs to the oldest family-run brewery in the city. It occupies a beautiful half-timbered seventeenth-century house moved here from its original location. From Mon to Thurs it's open evenings only.

Weiss-Bräu Am Weidenbach 24. This was the first of Cologne's new-generation Hausbrauereien, established in a long-redundant brewery. It introduced locally produced *Weissbier* to the city, and also makes a *Kölsch* and a dark beer.

Zur Malzmühle Heumarkt 6. A traditional Hausbrauerei, one whose name is reflected in the distinctly malty taste of its *Malzmühlenkölsch* and low-alcohol *Koch'sches Malzbier*.

Restaurants

Central Cologne has restaurants serving cuisines from all around the world, including a few surprises.

Al Salam Hohenstaufenring 22. Formal restaurant serving a wide range of Arab dishes to the accompaniment of Lebanese wines. Evenings only, except Sun, when it is only open for brunch.

Bier-Esel Breite Str. 114. This Gaststätte with winter garden is well-known locally for its mussels; the *Kölsch* comes from the Sünner brewery.

Bizim Weidengasse 47. Turkish restaurants are now among the most ubiquitous features of German cities, but this, which is in the far north of the Altstadt, is one of very few to aspire to *haute cuisine* status, and is correspondingly expensive. Closed Sun & Mon.

Blue Nile Weyerstr. 71. This inexpensive but good-quality Ethiopian restaurant incongruously preserves the decor of the traditional Cologne tavern it has supplanted.

Daitokai Kattenbug 2. Highly rated Japanese restaurant. Closed all day Mon & Tues lunchtime; reasonably priced set lunches are available other days.

Em Krützche Am Frankenturm 1–3. Historic Gasthaus with quayside garden which is probably Cologne's best traditional restaurant, renowned for its game and fish specialities. Closed Mon.

Fischers Hohenstaufenring 53. A truly creative restaurant whose weekday set lunches are quite exceptional value; set dinners are also available, but are more than twice the price. Closed Sat lunchtime and all day Sun.

Five Seasons Brüsseler Str. 54. Vegetarian restaurant with winter garden attached to a cookery school. It offers good-value set lunches.

Grande Milano Hohenstaufenring 37. Arguably the best of a wide choice of Italian restaurants. It also has a moderately priced bistro, *Pinot di Pinot*. Closed Sun.

Haxenhaus zum Rheingarten Frankenwerft 19. Located right on the Rhine promenade, this specializes in pork and lamb knuckles and metre-long sausages.

Jaipur Marzellenstr. 50–56. Well-regarded, fairly upmarket Indian restaurant.

Le Moissonier Krefelder Str. 25. Fine and authentically French restaurant located just north of the Hansaring S-Bahn station, decked out with mirrors like a Parisian brasserie. Closed Sun & Mon.

Mandalay Brüsseler Str. 53. Offers a rare chance to sample the little-known but delicious cuisine of Burma, which, logically enough, stands somewhere between that of India and China. Closed Tues.

Sprössling Mozartstr. 9. Good all-round veggie and wholefood specialist which stays open until late and has a courtyard garden. Closed Tues; set lunches are available other days (brunch on Sun).

Tchang Grosse Sandkaul 19. Perhaps the pick of Cologne's abundant supply of Chinese restaurants, offering the usual bargain lunches.

Vintage Pfeilstr. 31–35. Restaurant attached to a wine shop which has over nine hundred vintages from all over the world to choose from. The cuisine is also suitably international.

Zur Alten Münze Corner of Heumarkt and Piectrudengasse. Croatian speciality restaurant in the vaulted medieval cellars of a former mint.

Bars

There are plenty of good drinking establishments in the Altstadt, particularly in the area around Gross St Martin. However, the liveliest places at night are to be found in the streets immediately beyond the Ring – both to the west (the so-called Belgisches Viertel and Quartier Lateng) and south (the Südstadt).

Alcazar Bismarckstr. 39a. Snug and candlelit, with tasty if fairly pricey menu and a somewhat older clientele.
Bei d'r Tant Cäcilienstr. 28. This cosy little place with a circular bar looks much like a British pub, but serves traditional German food, including bargain set lunches, and *Kölsch* from Gaffel.
Biermuseum Buttermarkt 39. A favourite haunt with tourists and correspondingly pricey; there are usually around twenty beers on tap, an even wider choice in bottles.
Corkonian Alter Markt 49. Large Irish pub serving Guinness and Kilkenny, often featuring live Irish music. Packed out, especially at weekends.
Filmdose Zülpicher Str. 39. One of the most original fun pubs in Cologne when busy (particularly at weekends). It has a tiny stage for cabaret and also shows films in English.
Gilberts Pinte Engelbertstr. 1. Notorious student dive, home to numerous *Stammtische*, but with plenty of atmosphere.
Kännchen Am Bollwerk 13. Tiny traditional pub with a riverside terrace. Its *Kölsch* comes from the Gilden brewery.
Opera Alteburger Str. 1. Garishly-coloured bar which attracts very young punters, particularly at weekends.
Papa Joe's Em Streckstrumpf Buttermarkt 37. Germany's oldest jazz bar, this is a cosier, smaller, equally good version of *Klimperkasten*. Invariably it's standing-room only, with music beginning at 8.30pm and special Sun sessions at 11am.
Papa Joe's Klimperkasten Alter Markt 50. The deservedly popular place to go for traditional live jazz, which is belted out to an appreciative audience from 8pm onwards; an automatic tuba-accordion of the 1920s is pressed into service during the intermissions. Drinks are expensive, though this does not deter a young clientele at weekends; businessmen are prominent at other times.
Peppermint Lounge Hohenstauffenring 23. One of the most popular late-nighters, springing into action around midnight; also good for a late breakfast.
Santiago de Cuba Zülpicher Str. 25. Has a long list of cocktails and also serves Latin American dishes.
Spielplatz Ubierring 58. More in the style of a beer hall, with a lot more character than some of its newer counterparts.
Stadtgarten Venloer Str. 40. Home of the Kölner Jazzhaus Initiative, so most of the jazz is modern and experimental. It also serves good food, while in summer the park is used as a beer garden.

Cafés and café-bars

Cologne has a good choice of both traditional cafés and modern café-bars.

Café Cremer Brückenstr. 1–3. An enduringly favourite rendezvous point with city-centre shoppers. There's another branch at Breite Str. 48-50.
Café Fassbender Bazaar de Cologne, Mittelstrasse. The location in a big central shopping precinct may seem unpromising, but this café enjoys a high reputation for its pralines and other handmade chocolates.
Café Orlando Engelbertstr. 9. Quiet café offering breakfast and health food; it has 1950s decor with an old jukebox.
Café Reichard Untere Fettenhennen 11. Cologne's best-known bastion of *Kaffee und Kuchen*, an elegant salon profiting from its situation hard by the Dom.
Café Scholl Komödienstr. 17. Small traditional café that has been in business since 1890.
Central Jülicher Str. 1. Stylish café which is one of the best places for breakfast; it has a good selection of newspapers and outside tables when the weather is fine.
Chlodwig-Eck Annostr. 1. Very trendy Südstadt café-bar.
Connection World Becher Gasse 5.Handily located Internet café. Open Mon–Fri 10am–11pm, Sat 11am–11pm, Sun 3–11pm.
Kurfürsten-Hof Kurfürstenstr. 1. Südstadt café-bar offering salads, sandwiches and hot specials.
Printen Schmitz Breite Str. 87. Coffee house with a pedigree dating back to 1842. It has a wonderful range of gingerbread, cakes and home-made chocolates.

Entertainment

The tourist office publishes a comprehensive monthly programme, detailing important forthcoming events, *Köln-Monatsvorschau*, (€1); commercial listings magazines include *Stadt Revue* (€2), *Prinz* (€1) and the free *Live!*. Advance **tickets** for most events can be purchased from KölnTicket on Roncalliplatz (ⓣ02 21/28 01, ⓦwww.koelnticket.de).

Clubs and live music

Nightclubs can be found throughout the Altstadt and the streets beyond the Ring, though the main venues for large-scale events are out in the suburbs (see also "Bars").

Alter Wartesaal Johannisstr. 11. The elegant former waiting room of the Hauptbahnhof is a die-hard of the Cologne nightlife scene. It serves full meals and plays music ranging from Europop to Gothic.
E-Werk Schanzenstr. 37, Mülheim ⓣ02 21/96 27 90. Converted power station used for live rock concerts; also has house nights on Fri & Sat.
Kauri Auf dem Rothenberg 11. Altstadt cellar bar with good selection of jazz, funk and blues; free entry but drinks are extortionate.
Kölnarena Willy-Brandt-Platz 1, Deutz ⓣ02 21/28 10, ⓦwww.koelnarena.de. The main venue for big-name bands on tour.
Petit Prince Hohenzollernring 90. Mainstream club with different nights devoted to different sorts of music, including jazz, salsa and reggae.
Prime Club Luxemburger Str. 40. Nightclub with a healthy mixture of dance music and chart stuff; also a popular live venue. Students' evening is on Wed.

Classical music and theatre

Cologne offers the usual wide range of theatrical and musical experiences. There are two **symphony orchestras** – the Gürzenich-Orchester Kölner Phiharmoniker (ⓦwww.guerzenich-orchester.de) and the WDR Sinfonieorchester (ⓦwww.wdr.de/radio/orchester), the latter being attached to the national radio, whose headquarters are in Cologne. The radio studios were one of the pioneering centres of electronic music, being particularly associated with the work of Cologne resident Karlheinz Stockhausen. Other **musical ensembles** based in the city include Cantus Cölln, a small group renowned for its interpretations of early vocal music; Musica Antiqua Köln (ⓦwww.musica-antiqua-koeln.de), Germany's best-known performers on period instruments, which they play in an unashamedly astringent manner; and the chamber orchestra Concerto Köln (ⓦwww.concerto-koeln.de). There are any number of free concerts in the churches; these are all listed in a monthly programme which you can pick up in the venues themselves.

Venues

Funkhaus Wallrafplatz ⓣ02 21/28 01, ⓦwww.wdr.de. The radio studios host regular broadcast concerts by the WDR Sinfonieorchester and smaller ensembles.
Musical-Dome Goldgasse 1 ⓣ02 21/5 77 90, ⓦwww.musical-dome-koeln.de. One of the recent prominent additions to the Cologne skyline, this is an appropriately brash venue for blockbuster musicals.
Opernhaus Offenbachplatz ⓣ02 21/22 12 84 00, ⓦwww.buehnenkoeln.de. Cologne's opera house presents high-quality performances of works from the Baroque period to the present day.
Philharmonie Bischofsgartenstr. 1 ⓣ02 21/28 01, ⓦwww.koelner-philharmonie.de. Modern concert hall in the same building as the Museum Ludwig. Both local orchestras regularly perform there, as do soloists and chamber groups.
Puppenspiele der Stadt Köln Eisenmarkt 2–4 ⓣ02 21/2 58 12 01. This celebrated marionette theatre has been on the go since 1802, but be warned that the unintelligible *Kölsch* dialect is used in its performances.
Schauspielhaus Offenbachplatz ⓣ02 21/22 12 84 00, ⓦwww.buehnenkoeln.de. The flagship municipal theatre. Schlosserei is part of the same complex, but has a more experimental programme.

Listings

Bookstores The streets circling Neumarkt have a dense concentration of bookstores. Walter König, Ehrenstr. 4, is Germany's pre-eminent specialist on books on the arts; next door to the main shop is its Büchermarkt, which stocks a huge range of cut-price titles, including many in English. Gleumes, Hohenstaufenring 45, is a specialist guidebook and map retailer.
Cultural institutes Amerikahaus, Apostelnkloster 13–15 ⓣ02 21/20 90 10; British Council, Hahnenstr. 6 ⓣ02 21/20 64 40.
Doctor ⓣ02 21/1 92 92.
Festivals Everything else inevitably stands in the shade of Karneval (see box pp.520–21). However, the Corpus Christi celebrations (variable date in May or June) are also impressive, featuring a barge procession along the Rhine, and another from the Dom through the streets of the Altstadt.
Markets The large squares in the Altstadt provide a fitting setting for frequent markets; there is a weekly one all day Fri in Alter Markt, and a flea market in the same location every third Sat. Special occasions are: the flower market in Alter Markt on weekends in late April and early May; the junk market in Neumarkt in mid-May and again in mid-Sept; the Weinwoche (actually nearer a fortnight) in Neumarkt in late May/early June; and the Weihnachtsmarkt in both locations throughout Advent.
Pharmacist ⓣ02 21/1 15 00 for information on late-opening pharmacies.
Post office The main office with poste restante is at Breite Str. 6–62 (Mon–Fri 8am–8pm, Sat 8am–4pm).
Rhine cruises K-D Linie, Frankenwerft 15 (ⓣ02 21/2 08 83 18 or 2 58 30 11, ⓦwww.k-d.com); Kölntourist-Personenschiffahrt at Konrad-Adenauer-Ufer (ⓣ02 21/12 16 00, ⓦwww.koelntourist.com); Dampfschiffahrt Colonia, Lintgasse 18-20 (ⓣ02 21/2 57 42 25). Prices start at €5 for a 45min round trip.
Shopping The pedestrian section of the Altstadt is the city's main shopping street. Eau de Cologne (*Kölner Wasser*) can be bought in innumerable stores. About twenty companies make the product: Farina, founded in 1709 and with headquarters on Gülichplatz, is one of the original manufacturers; another firm with a long pedigree is Mülhens, whose best-known product, 4711, takes its name from the number on the shop in Glockengasse.
Sports The main outdoor ground is at Aachener Strasse in the western suburb of Müngersdorf; FC Köln play here, and there's an international athletics meeting in Aug or early Sept. An ice rink and swimming stadium are at Lentstr. 30 in Riehl, and a huge Sporthalle for indoor events is at Mülheimer Strasse in Deutz.

The Lower Rhineland

The **Lower Rhineland** (Niederrhein) is the name given to the predominantly flat area north of Cologne; the great river thereafter offers no more dramatic scenery. Industrialization, though significant, is held in check most of the way up to **Düsseldorf**. Immediately beyond, however, begins the Ruhrgebiet, the most developed industrial region in the world. Although most of this forms part of Westphalia, the westernmost cities, **Duisburg** and **Essen**, belong to the North Rhine region, as does **Wuppertal** to the southeast. After this, there's a dramatic change to a countryside very close in spirit to nearby Holland. There are no more cities, but a number of small historic towns, the most notable of which are **Xanten** and **Kalkar**.

North from Cologne

Immediately north of Cologne, making for easy excursions from the city, are some exciting destinations. On the left bank of the Rhine are the medieval customs post of **Zons** and the monastery of **Knechtsteden**. On the right bank, the area known as the Bergisches Land is punctuated by the bleak manufacturing towns that put Germany at the forefront of industrial development in the nineteenth century. It retains much green countryside, however, now designated a *Naturpark*, and shelters a magnificent former monastic church, **Kloster Altenberg**.

Zons

The curious village of **ZONS** lies 25km downstream from Cologne. It's now part of the municipality of Dormagen, an industrial town of no interest in itself, and is some 3km east of the latter's Bahnhof, to which it's connected by regular bus services (#875 and #882). In 1372 the Archbishop of Cologne, Friedrich von Saarwerden, decided to levy taxes on the profitable shipping route through his domain, and began the building of a walled town on the site of his predecessors' long-destroyed castle. For all Zons' history of bad luck – it's repeatedly been ravaged by fires and floods down the centuries – the original **Stadtbefestigung** remains largely intact. It ranks as one of the most important surviving examples of a medieval defensive system in Germany, though it now requires a bit of imagination to visualize the original setting, as silting means it's now some way back from the Rhine.

The best views are obtained by walking around the outside of the circuit. Beginning at the bus stop, turn right and you come to the **Mühlenturm**, the upper section of which was converted into a windmill early in its history. From here, continue along the south side of the town, which has a double wall, the outer having been added for protection against flooding. At the corner are the ruins of **Schloss Friedestrom**, including the gateway, the chunky keep and a courtyard which forms a fitting setting for open-air theatre and pageants (every Sun afternoon mid-June to mid-Sept; also other random days). The eastern wall has two cylindrical defensive towers, along with an octagonal watchtower; at its far corner is the **Rheinturm**, the medieval entrance to the town and the place where customs dues were collected. Three watching posts pierce the northern wall, which terminates in the battlemented **Krötschenturm**. In the town centre there's one more tower, the round **Juddeturm**, which served as both prison and look-out. Around the Rheinturm are the few old houses which have survived the natural disasters; everything else is Baroque or later. The handsome **Herrenhaus** contains the **Kreismuseum** (Tues–Fri 2–6pm, Sat & Sun 10am–12.30pm & 2–5pm; €2), which mounts temporary exhibitions alongside its own collection of Jugendstil art.

Practicalities

Zons' **tourist office** (Mon–Fri 9am–1pm & 2–4pm, Sun 2–4pm; ⓣ0 21 33/37 72, ⓦwww.zons.de) is at Schlossstr. 37. **Hotels** include *Schloss Destille*, Mauerstr. 26a (ⓣ0 21 33/4 76 58, ⓦwww.schloss-destille.de; ❹–❻); *Zum Feldtor*, Schlossstr. 40 (ⓣ0 21 33/2 45 90, ⓦwww.zum-feldtor.de; ❺); and *Schloss Friedestrom*, Parkstr. 2 (ⓣ0 21 33/50 30, ⓦwww.friedestrom.de; ❼). All of these have **restaurants**, and there are plenty of other places in town where you can have a full meal or a snack. There are two **campsites** at Stürzelberg 1km to the north: *Strandterrasse* (ⓣ0 21 06/7 17 17) and *Pitt-Jupp* (ⓣ0 21 06/4 22 10). Throughout the summer, regular daily **boat trips** (ⓣ0 21 06/4 21 49 or 4 23 49) run to Benrath; there are also very occasional sailings to Cologne.

Around Zons: Kloster Knechtsteden

Also within the municipality of Dormagen is the Romanesque **Kloster Knechtsteden**, built in the austere style favoured by its Premonstratensian founders, but enlivened by a central octagon flanked by twin towers. It stands in an isolated setting 3km west of the Bahnhof, connected by a frequent bus service (#876). As in the great imperial cathedrals, there's a choir at both ends of the building; the eastern one is a late Gothic replacement, while that to the west is adorned with mid-twelfth century **frescoes** showing *Christ as Pantocrator*, surrounded by angels and the Evangelical symbols, with portraits of the Apostles below. Just outside the monastery gates is the *Klosterhof*, a **restaurant** with beer garden with its own specially-made dark brew, *Knechtstedener Schwarze*.

Kloster Altenberg

Set in isolation in a wooded valley of the River Dhün about 15km northeast of Cologne is **Kloster Altenberg** (ⓦ www.altenberger-dom.de), popularly known as the **Bergischer Dom**; it can be reached from the city centre by taking U-Bahn #16 to Wiener Platz, then bus #434. In spite of its nickname, it's not a cathedral but a monastery built by the Cistercians, whose rule prescribed secluded settings of this kind. What makes the present building, begun in 1255, particularly interesting is that it's contemporary with, and of similar stature to, the Dom in Cologne, only this time it was completed in just over a hundred years. In accordance with the austere Cistercian tradition there's no tower and little in the way of decoration. Nevertheless, it's still enormously photogenic, seeming to blend effortlessly into the landscape; the best view is from the hill to the east, where you see the choir with its corona of chapels (the earliest and finest feature) to best advantage.

Few buildings so perfectly encompass the basic tenets of the Gothic style: there are no grand gestures; everything is spacious, bright and harmonious, a visible manifestation of the order's quest for spiritual tranquillity. The chancel has wonderful original silvery-grey **stained-glass windows** which have geometric motifs only. This same type of glass, but with floral shapes, fills the big lights of the north transept, beaming down on the tombs of the counts (later dukes) of Berg. Relaxation of the normal Cistercian rejection of representational subjects is confined to the giant facade window, the largest in Germany: it depicts *The Heavenly Jerusalem* in predominantly golden tones, a particularly memorable sight when illuminated by the setting sun. On Sundays, Altenberg acts as a magnet for urban dwellers seeking their weekly retreat; a curiosity is that both Catholic and Protestant services are held. This was a condition laid down by the Prussian King Friedrich Wilhelm IV when he arranged for the church's repair and return to worship, after a period of disuse and decay following the Napoleonic suppression.

Wuppertal

WUPPERTAL stands at the northernmost end of the Bergisches Land group of industrial towns, and some 30km east of Düsseldorf. The overriding justification for a detour is to see its genuinely unique public transport system, the **Schwebebahn** (hanging rail line; see box on p.134). Wuppertal didn't exist as such when the line was built between 1898 and 1900 to link the various towns strung along the valley of the River Wupper. These communities united in 1929, yet still preserve distinct identities.

The Schwebebahn

The **Schwebebahn** (Ⓦwww.schwebebahn-wtal.de), Wuppertal's creaking monorail line, is suspended on high by a steel structure supported by 472 triangular girders. Between fifteen of its nineteen stations, it runs directly above the river, then passes over the main thoroughfares of Sonnborn and Oberwinkel to the west, leaving them permanently dank. It's well worth travelling along the whole route for a complete picture of the city; the Werther Brücke station, which preserves its original Jugendstil decoration, is a sight in itself. The sleek orange and blue cars are fourth generation; at weekends in summer, one of the original models is run. This is the only gimmick associated with a genuine local facility which is both fast (it's immune from delays) and efficient (services run every few minutes). The brainchild of **Carl Eugen Langen**, who failed to interest Berlin and Munich in his idea, the Schwebebahn gained the reputation of being the safest public transport system ever devised: for nearly a century, it never had a serious accident, never mind a fatality. Tragically, that proud record came to an abrupt end in 1999, when a car which had not been properly re-assembled after maintenance work plunged into the river, killing three passengers instantly. The accident caused massive dismay locally, but has made the authorities all the more determined to avoid even a single accident during the Schwebebahn's second century of operation.

The centre of **ELBERFELD**, one of the two main constituent towns, is a vast pedestrian shopping precinct. At Poststrasse 11, look out for the watchmaker's shop whose incredible display is trumped by its own **Uhrenmuseum** (Mon–Fri 4–6pm, Sat 11am–2pm; €2.50). Here you can see over a thousand weird and wonderful timepieces, ranging from the earliest watch made in Germany to an eighteenth-century London fancy with an elephant and a rotating Chinese emperor's court.

Round the corner, at Turmhof 8, is the neo-Renaissance bulk of the former Rathaus, now containing the **Von-der-Heydt-Museum** (Tues, Wed & Fri–Sun 11am–6pm, Thurs 11am–8pm; €1; Ⓦwww.von-der-heydt-museum.de), one of the country's finest galleries of nineteenth- and twentieth-century art. Centrepiece of the display is a group of some two dozen canvases by a local man, **Hans von Marées**, whose pronounced intellectual approach, marked Italianate influence and preference for a dark palette combine to make him one of Germany's most distinctive painters. Other artists particularly well represented are **Carl Spitzweg** (with five wonderfully humorous Biedermeier vignettes), **Max Beckmann** (notably self-portraits as a clown and as a World War I Red Cross worker), Paula Modersohn-Becker and Alexej Jawlensky, while individual highlights include **Kirchner**'s *Women in the Street*, **Dix**'s satirical *An die Schönheit* and **Schlemmer**'s *Twelve Figures in an Interior*. A good cross-section of French Impressionism is headed by a study for **Manet**'s seminal *Déjeuner sur l'Herbe*.

At Engelsstrasse in **BARMEN**, the other main constituent town, is a collection of more marginal interest, the **Museum für Frühindustrialisierung** (Museum of Early Industry; Tues–Sun 10am–1pm & 3–5pm; €1.50). In front stands the **Engels-Haus** (same times and ticket), an elegant late eighteenth-century building which belonged to a family of textile entrepreneurs. It now serves as a memorial to their celebrated black sheep **Friedrich Engels**, who was born nearby. As a young man, he was sent to England to work at the sister factory of Ermen & Engels in Manchester; there he became fascinated by the plight of the urban proletariat, and on his return to Barmen in 1845 wrote his celebrated *The Condition of the Working Class in England*. Soon afterwards, he began collaborating with Karl Marx, returning to work as a capitalist in Manchester in order to provide funds for their joint revolutionary writings. Though very much the junior partner in these, Engels always had a large input on matters concerning nationalities, diplomacy, the military and business practices – even in the books such as *Das Kapital* in which Marx appears as sole author.

Practicalities

Wuppertal's **tourist office** (Mon–Fri 9am–6pm, Sat 9am–1pm; ⓣ02 02/1 94 33, ⓦwww.wuppertal.de) is just across from the **Hauptbahnhof** in Elberfeld at Am Döppersberg. **Hotels** are scattered all over the city. Barmen has a number of reasonably priced establishments, including *Wittenstein*, Wittensteinstr. 223 (ⓣ02 02/25 55 60, ⓦwww.a-econ.de; ❸–❺), and *City*, Fischertal 21 (ⓣ02 02/59 50 78; ❺). Those in Elberfeld tend to be on the expensive side; options there include *Astor*, Schlossbleiche 4–6 (ⓣ02 02/45 05 11, ⓦwww.astor-wuppertal.de; ❻), and *Central*, Poststr. 4 (ⓣ02 02/45 01 31, ⓦwww.central.bestwestern.de; ❼). The **youth hostel** is at Obere Lichtenplatzer Str. 70 (ⓣ02 02/55 23 72; €14.60/17.30), a few minutes' walk to the south of Barmen's Bahnhof.

Reasonably priced places to **eat** and **drink** can be found all over the city, especially in the large pedestrian precinct in the centre of Elberfeld, though the best traditional restaurant is probably *Zum Futterplatz*, south of Barmen's Bahnhof at Obere Lichtenplatzer Str. 102. The Schauspielhaus, near the tourist office at Bundesallee 260 (ⓣ02 02/5 69 44 44, ⓦwww.wuppertaler-buehnen.de), presents plays and operas, but is best known for Pina Bausch's Tanztheater (ⓦwww.pina-bausch.de), by some way Germany's leading **modern dance** company.

Düsseldorf

DÜSSELDORF disputes with Hamburg and Stuttgart the right to be regarded as Germany's richest city, and in many ways is the paragon of the postwar face of the Federal Republic – orderly, prosperous and self-confident. Few places can have a name so inappropriate to their present status: the "village on the Düssel" is now a thriving Land capital of 600,000 inhabitants on both banks of the Rhine, crossed here by no fewer than six bridges. Since the war, it has developed a cosmopolitan and strangely un-European character. Never as industrialized as its neighbours in the Ruhr, Düsseldorf has concentrated on its role as the region's financial and administrative centre, its skyline punctuated by the skyscrapers of innumerable multinational giants.

The extent to which you'll like or loathe Düsseldorf depends very much on your reaction to the way it has sold its soul to the corporate dream. The city likes to think of itself as Germany's leading fashion centre, and if **luxury shops** are your scene, there are none more stylish between Paris and Berlin. Even for a short visit, it's an expensive option, but there's no doubt that the **nightlife**, at least, is one of the most varied and enjoyable in the country.

Arrival, information and accommodation

The **Hauptbahnhof** is situated in the southeast part of the city centre; from here, the shopping streets begin to fan out. S-Bahn trains #7 and #21 leave at twenty-minute intervals for the **airport** (ⓣ02 11/42 10, ⓦwww.duesseldorf-airport.de) to the north. As most of Düsseldorf's attractions are

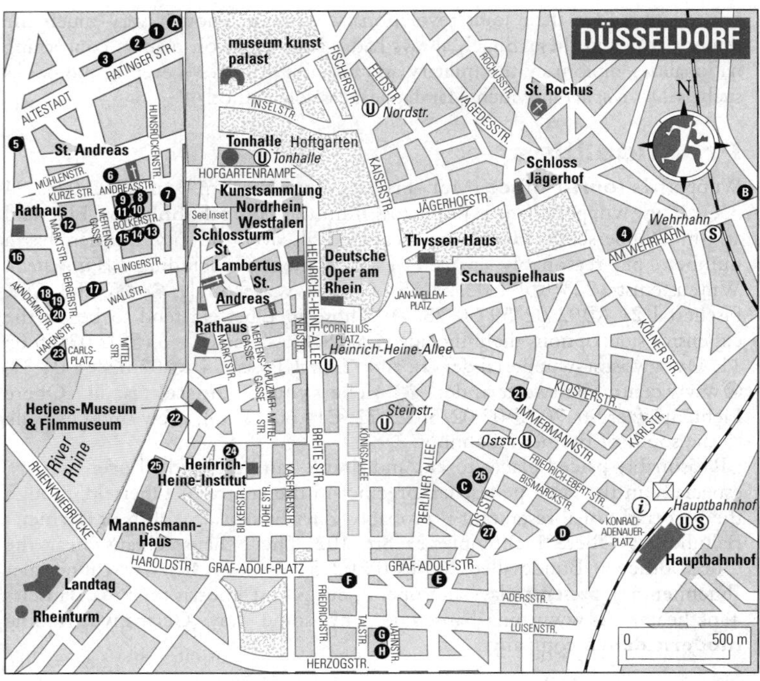

BRAUEREIGASTSTÄTTEN		OTHER RESTAURANTS		BARS AND CAFÉ-BARS				ACCOMMODATION	
Diebels Fasskeller	12	Daitokai	7	Café Alte Bastion	22	Schnabelewopski	13	Am Füchschen	A
Ferdinand Schumacher	26	Eremitage	21	Café Bernstein	27	Weisser Bär	15	Amsterdam	C
Frankenheim	4	Fischhaus	19	Dr Jazz	17	Zum Goldenen		Bristol	F
Im Füchschen	1	Muschelhaus		Front Page	25	Einhorn	2	CVJM	D
Im Goldenen Kessel	11	Benders Marie	8	g@rden	16			Diana	H
Im Goldenen Ring	5	Tante Anna	6	Irish Pub	10			Haus Hillesheim	G
Zum Schiffchen	23	Zum Csikos	9	Marktwirtschaft	24			Manhattan	E
Zum Schlüssel	14			Miles Smiles	20			Windsor	B
Zum Uerige	18			Ratinger Hof	3				

within walking distance of each other, the €6.55 24-hour ticket on the integrated **public transport** system run by Rheinbahn (Ⓦwww.rheinbahn.de) – which is part of the larger VRR (Ⓦwww.vrr.de) network covering the Rhine-Ruhr conurbation – is really only of use if travelling in a group (it covers up to five people) or visiting the outlying suburbs. A better alternative is the **WelcomeCard**, which covers public transport and gives reduced entry to museums and other attractions. For individuals, this costs €9 for 24 hours, €14 for 48 hours and €19 for 72 hours; for families or up to three adults travelling together, these charges are doubled. Rhine cruises, run by K-D Linie (Ⓣ02 11/3 23 92 63), depart from Schlossufer. The **tourist office** (Mon–Fri 10am–6pm, Sat 10am–2pm; Ⓣ02 11/17 20 20, Ⓦwww.duesseldorf-tourismus.de) is at Immermannstr. 65b.

Hotels are overwhelmingly geared to the business traveller, and prices are far above the national norm, even in the suburbs. Several of the least expensive options are in Friedrichstadt, the old suburb immediately south of the city centre, though the main concentration is in the business district between the Hauptbahnhof and the Altstadt. The **youth hostel** is the first building over the

Rheinkniebrücke, at Düsseldorfer Str. 1 in Oberkassel (Ⓣ02 11/57 73 10; €20.70/23.40), and can be reached from the Hauptbahnhof by bus #835. Likewise on the left bank of the Rhine is the **campsite** (April–Sept only) at Niederkasseler Deich 305, Oberlörick (Ⓣ02 11/59 14 01); take U-Bahn #70, #74, #75, #76 or #77 to Belsenplatz, then bus #828.

Hotels

Am Füchschen Ratinger Str. 32 Ⓣ02 11/86 79 60, Ⓕ8 67 96 61. Small hotel in an Altstadt street which is well known for its bars and restaurants. ❻–❾.

Amsterdam Stresemannstr. 20 Ⓣ02 11/8 40 58, Ⓕ8 40 50. Good medium-priced city-centre choice. ❹–❾.

Bristol Adersstr. 8 Ⓣ02 11/37 07 50, Ⓕ37 37 54. Surprisingly reasonable considering its location in the very north of Friedrichstadt, just south of the prestigious Königsallee. ❹–❻.

CVJM Graf-Adolf-Str.102 Ⓣ02 11/17 28 50, Ⓦwww.cvjm-duesseldorf.de. Refurbished YMCA-run hotel whose bedrooms are mostly grouped around an inner courtyard and are therefore well sheltered from street noise. ❻–❾

Diana Jahnstr. 31 Ⓣ02 11/37 50 71, Ⓦwww.hoteldiana.de. Popular, moderately priced hotel in a quiet Friedrichstadt street. ❹–❼

Haus Hillesheim Jahnstr. 19 Ⓣ02 11/38 68 60, Ⓦwww.hotel-hillesheim.de. Pleasant Friedrichstadt hotel that has been in existence since 1894. It has a quaintly furnished bar open to residents only. ❸–❼

Manhattan Graf-Adolf-Str. 39 Ⓣ02 11/6 02 22 50, Ⓕ6 02 22 51 10. Reasonably priced hotel popular with young travellers. ❸–❺

Windsor Grafenberger Allee 36 Ⓣ02 11/91 46 80, Ⓦwww.windsor-hotel.de. The elegant furnishings mark this out as one of Düsseldorf's most appealing hotels. ❽–❾

The city centre

The **Altstadt**, close to the Rhine, reflects the meaning of Düsseldorf's name in its modest proportions. Never one of Germany's great cities from an architectural point of view, it's chiefly renowned today for its remarkable range of places of entertainment. Immediately to the east is a planned **green belt**, created by French landscape gardeners in the eighteenth and nineteenth centuries when Düsseldorf was a seat of the Electors Palatine, who succeeded the defunct line of the Dukes of Berg, the city's founders.

The Altstadt

Over two hundred restaurants, beer halls, wine cellars, bistros, snack bars, jazz centres and discos are crammed into the small area of the Altstadt, which pulsates with activity day and night. This fact tends to overshadow the historical sights, but two very contrasting churches do catch the eye. **St Lambertus**, a fourteenth-century brick building in the hall church style, is easily recognizable because of its tall twisted spire, now ousted from its former physical and spiritual dominance over the city by the huge corporate skyscrapers. Inside, there's a graceful Gothic tabernacle, a fifteenth-century *Pietà*, and the spectacular late sixteenth-century marble and alabaster tomb of Duke Wilhelm V.

A short walk to the east is **St Andreas**, a Jesuit foundation of 1629 which is one of the chief reminders of the period when Düsseldorf was the seat of the Electors Palatine. Its galleried interior is ornately decorated with stucco; the **Mausoleum** (Mon–Fri 3–5.30pm) to the rear contains the surprisingly simple tin coffins of the Electors. The most famous and genuinely popular of these rulers was Johann Wilhelm II, better known as **Jan Wellem**, who ruled from 1679 to 1716. He's commemorated in the huge open area named after him in the heart of the city, and by a masterly equestrian statue (the work of his Italian court sculptor Gabriel de Grupello), erected during his own lifetime outside the Renaissance **Rathaus**. In the square immediately to the north is the

Schlossturm, the only remnant of the old fortifications; it has been restored to house the **Schiffahrtmuseum** (Tues–Sun 11am–6pm; €3), a small display of Rhineland navigation.

At Schulstr. 4, towards the southern end of the Altstadt, the former Palais Nesselrode now houses the **Hetjens-Museum** (Tues & Thurs–Sat 11am–5pm, Wed 11am–9pm; €3), which boasts of being the only one in Germany entirely devoted to the art of ceramics. The exhibits range over eight thousand years of history, and come from all over the world. International highlights include Mesopotamian grave objects from 3500 BC, painted vases from ancient Greece, figures from China's Tang dynasty period and a spectacular seventeenth-century Islamic cupola from Multan in Pakistan. There are also fine examples from most of the German porcelain manufactories; the largest collection of Rhenish stoneware in existence; and an exquisite Art Nouveau/Jugendstil section. The new extension is shared with the **Filmmuseum** (same times; €3), which operates the Black Box (€5), the city's most adventurous cinema. Nearby, at Bilkerstr. 14, is the **Heinrich-Heine-Institut** (Tues–Fri & Sun 11am–5pm, Sat 1–5pm; €2), a museum and research centre devoted to the great nineteenth-century poet who is Düsseldorf's favourite son.

Overlooking the Rhine at the extreme southern end of the Altstadt is Peter Behrens' **Mannesmann-Gebäude**, a distinguished example of corporate architecture from the first decade of the twentieth century, but now dwarfed by the **Mannesmann-Haus**, the skyscraper which pioneered the postwar identification of Düsseldorf's appearance with the power of multinational companies. The quayside alongside is also named after the company, which lost its independence in 2000, when it succumbed to a hostile takeover – the first ever mounted in German business history – by the British mobile phone giant Vodafone. Just to the south is Düsseldorf's highest building, the **Rheinturm** (Mon–Fri 11am–11.30pm, Sat & Sun 10am–11.30pm; €3), a radio tower built between 1979 and 1982. You can ascend by high-speed lift to its observation platform for an absolutely stunning view over the city and the Rhine. Alongside is the **Landtag**, a building completed in 1988 as the new home of the state parliament of North Rhine-Westphalia. Beyond is the old commercial harbour, which has recently been re-developed by a number of internationally celebrated architects - including Frank O. Gehry and David Chipperfield – as the **Media-Hafen**.

The museum quarter

Housed in an ultra-modern gallery in Grabbeplatz just north of St Andreas is the **Kunstsammlung Nordrhein–Westfalen** (Tues–Thurs, Sat & Sun 10am–6pm, Fri 10am–8pm; €2.50, or €6 when there's a loan exhibition; Ⓦwww.kunstsammlung.de). The genesis of this collection was a remarkable act of postwar contrition by the authorities. **Paul Klee**, the abstract painter, was a professor at the Düsseldorf Kunstakademie from 1930 until dismissed in the Nazi purges of 1933. In atonement for this, around ninety of his works were purchased from a private American source in 1960; shortly afterwards, a rapid acquisitions policy, of twentieth-century art only, was adopted. The Klee collection remains the obvious draw, although only about two-thirds of the works are on show at any one time. Even if you aren't attracted to this painter, there are many other highlights, such as one of **Picasso**'s most famous representational works, *Two Sitting Women*, **Léger**'s large *Adam and Eve*, **Kirchner**'s *Negro Dance*, **Modigliani**'s *Diego Rivera* and self-portraits by **Kokoschka** and **Chagall**. Already the collection resembles a who's who of modern art, and it continues to grow.

The **museum kunst palast** (Tues–Sun 11am–6pm; €7; Ⓦwww.museum-kunst-palast.de), directly north of the Altstadt at Ehrenhof 5, has the mission of presenting art in a new and challenging way. A large part of the display area is given over to temporary exhibitions, with an emphasis on blockbuster shows which juxtapose Western art with that of other cultures. In the rest of the building, the former Kunstmuseum has been revamped as the **Künstlermuseum**, and hung in an unconventional thematic manner. Traditionalists will be infuriated by the abandonment of any sort of chronology, though many illuminating cross-references emerge. One example is the contrast between the documentary approach of the great nineteenth-century painter Menzel and that of the contemporary Düsseldorf photographers Thomas Struth and Andreas Gursky, who have gained international fame and fortune for their starkly realist takes on modern life. In terms of overall quality the collection is rather patchy, and a large **Rubens** altarpiece of *The Assumption* puts almost all the other old masters completely in the shade. Among the few paintings not wholly outclassed are *Venus and Adonis* by the same painter, a *St Jerome* attributed to **Ribera** and *St Francis in Meditation* by **Zurbarán**. There's extensive representation of the once-lionised nineteenth-century landscape and historical painters of the **Düsseldorf Kunstakademie**, whose work is slowly coming back into fashion after a long period in the critical doldrums. Also on view is a series of powerful lithographs by **Otto Pankok** called *The Passion*, though in fact Christ's whole life is depicted. Their gloomy, highly charged emotionalism, with hateful mobs and angst-ridden victims, directly reflects the contemporary horrors of the Holocaust. On a very different note, there's a sparkling **glass** section on the ground floor, dominated by Art Nouveau and Art Deco pieces from Germany, France and America.

The Königsallee and Hofgarten

The city's main thoroughfare, the **Königsallee**, laid out at the beginning of the nineteenth century, was the culmination of the transformation of Düsseldorf by the Electors Palatine into a city of parks, ponds and canals. It's one of Germany's most famous streets and is chic rather than beautiful; down one side are banks and offices, with expensive stores, representing all the trendiest names in international designer-made goods, lining the other. Only the late Jugendstil **Kaufhaus** by the Viennese Joseph Maria Olbrich has any merits as a building, though it has suffered from an interior modernization. Diagonally opposite its rear entrance is **Wilhelm-Marx-Haus** erected in the 1920s, the earliest visible expression of Düsseldorf's infatuation with the New World.

The largest of the parks is the **Hofgarten**, shaped like a great stiletto-heeled shoe, and now incongruously cut in several places by busy streets. Towering over it is the **Thyssen-Haus**, by far the most arresting of the corporate structures which so altered the city skyline in the 1950s, offering a fascinating play of light on its three huge silvery-green slabs. Beside it, the daring white curves of the **Schauspielhaus**, built in 1970, provide an effective counterpoint, as well as a reminder that, in this city, the public structures stand very much in the shadow of big business.

At the far end of the Hofgarten is **Schloss Jägerhof**, a Baroque palace which sustained severe damage in the last war. Its interior decorations have been refitted as the **Goethe-Museum** (Tues–Fri & Sun 11am–5pm, Sat 1–5pm; €2; Ⓦ www.goethe-museum-kippenberg-stiftung.de), reckoned to be the best collection of memorabilia of the great poet and playwright after those in Frankfurt and Weimar. Unless you're an avid fan, the contents will seem fairly mundane, though it's worth glancing over the section on works of art inspired by his most celebrated drama, *Faust*. Just to the north of the Schloss is the city's finest modern church, **St Rochus**. Outside, it resembles a giant beehive; the interior is deliberately dark, in an attempt to re-create the old mysteries of religion.

Benrath

Of the towns which have been swallowed up by Düsseldorf, by far the most interesting is **BENRATH** to the south, best reached by S-Bahn #6. The **Schloss** (guided tours Tues & Thurs–Sun 10am–5pm, Wed 10am–8pm; €3.50; ⓦwww.schloss-benrath.de) and its park were commissioned by Elector Carl Theodor in the mid-eighteenth century; the unusual harmony of the whole complex is due to the fact that the architect, the French-born **Nicholas de Pigage**, was also a landscape gardener. Its main block, in a style hovering between Rococo and Neoclassical, represents a very clever piece of trompe l'oeil construction – for all its seemingly small size, it contains eighty rooms. The tours take in the sumptuous reception and garden rooms on the ground floor, as well as some of the private apartments upstairs.

Eating, drinking and nightlife

Walking through the Altstadt – "the longest bar in Europe" according to the tourist office – is an enjoyable activity in itself, especially on summer days when it's even more crowded than usual and virtually every bar and restaurant offers the opportunity for imbibing alfresco. This small quarter contains a large percentage of the city's most recommendable eateries, though there are, of course, plenty of alternatives elsewhere. Düsseldorf's multicultural make-up ensures a wide choice of ethnic cuisines; the best places for traditional local fare are the Brauereigaststätten, the restaurants cum beer halls of the local breweries, several of which still maintain the time-honoured tradition of brewing in-house. Their most popular product by far is the highly distinctive **Alt**, which is dark in colour and tending towards sweetness in some varieties, caused by the higher quantity of malt used than in lagers.

Brauereigaststätten

Diebels Fasskeller Bolkerstr. 14–16. The main Düsseldorf outlet of Diebels, the largest producer of *Alt*, which is actually situated well outside the city, in the small town of Issum.

Ferdinand Schumacher Oststr. 123. Although located in the modern business district, this Hausbrauerei dates back to the 1870s. It makes a delicate, fruity *Alt* and offers full meals.

Frankenheim Wielandstr. 17. Another very traditional Brauereigaststätte, though the production of its tangy *Alt* has moved from the site to more modern premises across the Rhine in Neuss.

Im Füchschen Ratinger Str. 28. Hausbrauerei producing a relatively bitter *Alt*, plus a wheat beer called *Silberfüchschen*. It also serves filling and inexpensive meals.

Im Goldenen Kessel Bolkerstr. 44. Altstadt flagship of the Schumacher brewery, renowned for its reasonably priced food.

Im Goldenen Ring Burgplatz 21. Fine traditional Gaststätte of the Schlösser brewery, which produces the sweetest-tasting *Alt*. It serves excellent food, including good-value set meals.

Zum Schiffchen Hafenstr. 5. The Altstadt Gaststätte of the Frankenheim brewery offers slightly more upmarket cuisine than its competitors, and is therefore a little pricier, though it does reasonably priced set lunches. Closed Sun.

Zum Schlüssel Bolkerstr. 45. Hausbrauerei, founded in 1850, which produces a fairly malty *Alt*. High-quality local dishes are served in its cavernous and well-patronized interior.

Zum Uerige Berger Str. 1. This nineteenth-century Hausbrauerei, one of the most famous in Germany, produces the ultimate in *Alt* beer, plus a good *Weizen*. It's primarily a drinking pub, though snacks are available from the sausage kitchen on the premises.

Other restaurants

Daitokai Mutter-Ey-Str. 1. As Düsseldorf is the main European outpost of Japanese commerce, it's not surprising that the city is well endowed with Japanese restaurants, of which this is one of the very best.

Ermitage Oststr. 63. Russian speciality restaurant, serving bargain lunches on weekdays.

Fischhaus Berger Str. 3. Hugely popular fish restaurant.

Muschelhaus Benders Marie Andreasstr. 13. As its name suggests, this is a specialist in mussels,

Düsseldorf's festivals

It's worth trying to time your visit to coincide with one of Düsseldorf's three main **popular festivals**. The **Karneval** celebrations (seven weeks before Easter) are ranked third in Germany, although those in nearby Cologne are the best of all. The celebrations are supposed to signify the end of winter; its beginning is heralded by the **Martinsfest** on November 10, marked by an enormous procession of lantern-bearing children. In late July, the **Grosses Schützenfest** (Riflemen's Meeting) is an eight-day festival along the banks of the Rhine. Simultaneously, there's a huge funfair (claimed to be the largest of its type in the world) offering gut-churning rides on the Ferris wheel, the big dipper and other machines. The most celebrated local tradition is **cartwheeling** by local lads in the streets of the Altstadt. This is in honour of an urchin who saved the day when a wheel came loose on the popular Elector Palatine Jan Wellem's wedding coach, but the reason it survives is the less romantic one of extorting money from tourists. In spite of serving as an unofficial symbol of the city, you're unlikely to see any demonstrations out of season.

though other seafood and fish dishes are also served. From Mon-Thurs it's only open in the evening.

Tante Anna Andreasstr. 2. Historic wine bar-restaurant in a converted sixteenth-century chapel. There are 150 vintages to choose from. Closed Sun.

Zum Csikos Andreasstr. 9. Highly rated but pricey Hungarian restaurant. Evenings only.

Bars, café-bars and clubs

Café Alte Bastion Rathausufer 12. This genteel quayside café is a good place for *Kaffee und Kuchen.*

Café Bernstein Oststr. 158. Stylish place for a nightcap, patronized by a distinctive Düsseldorf group – monied student couples.

Dr Jazz Flingerstr. 11. Jazz hangout, with different bands each evening.

Front Page Mannesmann-Ufer 9. Cosy piano bar.

g@rden Rathausufer 8. Internet café-bar, one of several modish hangouts along the waterfront.

Irish Pub Hunsrückenstr. 13. Genuine reminder of traditional Hibernia, owned and staffed by expatriats. Such is the current German mania for all things Irish that it now has several competitors, one of them just three doors away.

Marktwirtschaft Bernrather Str. 7. This serves good breakfasts and set lunches, while in the evening it's a favourite haunt of the well-heeled youth of Düsseldorf.

Miles Smiles Akademiestr. 6. Jazz bar which doubles as an Italian trattoria.

Ratinger Hof Ratinger Str. 10. Germany's first and most notorious punk bar lives on, frequented by diehards of the cult and blasting out ear-splitting music.

Sassafras Düsseldorfer Str. 90, Oberkassel. Left-bank café-bar with a youthful and unpretentious clientele.

Schnabelewopski Bolkerstr. 53. Literary café-bar housed in Heine's birthplace.

Tor 3 Ronsdorfer Str. 143, Bilk (ⓣ02 11/4 91 59 90, ⓦwww.tor3.com. Düsseldorf's leading club is a huge barn of a place in the south of the city. It has few concessions to comfort, but its customers are young, friendly and out to enjoy themselves with a vengeance.

Weisser Bär Bolkerstr. 33. Popular pub with raucous music frequented by a curious mixture of young Düsseldorfers and young tourists, and staffed by relics of the '68 generation.

ZAKK Fichtenstr. 40, Oberbilk. A bar with a difference, drawing visitors from neighbouring cities to its exhibitions, video showings and other arty events. It's reached by tram #706 or #716 to Fichtenstrasse.

Zum Goldenen Einhorn Ratinger Str. 18. An enduringly popular spot with the youth of the city, especially in summer when it opens its leafy little beer garden.

Entertainment

Düsseldorf has a strong tradition in **classical music**, even if present standards are short of the nineteenth-century heydays when both Mendelssohn and Schumann did stints in charge of the city's musical affairs. It also offers a wide range of **theatrical** entertainments. To find out what's on, consult the listings magazines *Prinz* (€1) or the free *Coolibri*.

Deutsche Oper am Rhein Heinrich-Heine-Allee 16a ⓣ02 11/8 90 82 11, ⓦwww.deutsche-oper-am-rhein.de. The city's opera house, run in tandem with its Duisburg namesake.

Kom(m)ödchen Kay-und-Lore-Lorentz-Platz ⓣ02 11/32 94 43, ⓦwww.kommoedchen.de. This theatre with the bizarrely spelt name is one of Germany's best-known venues for political cabaret and satire.

Marionettentheater Bilkerstr. 7 ⓣ02 11/32 84 32, ⓦwww.marionettentheater-duesseldorf.de. Housed in the Baroque Palais Wittgenstein, this well-regarded marionette theatre stages opera performances as well as the expected children's shows.

Philipshalle Siegburger Str. 15, Overbilk ⓣ02 11/8 99 36 79, ⓦwww.philipshalle.de. This huge hall hosts large-scale spectaculars, including pop concerts.

Schauspielhaus Gustav-Grundgens-Platz 1 ⓣ02 11/36 99 11, ⓦwww.duesseldorfer-schauspielhaus.de. One of Düsseldorf's most imposing modern buildings, this is the city's principal dramatic stage.

tanzhaus nrw Erkrather Str. 30 ⓣ02 11/17 27 00, ⓦwww.tanzhaus-nrw.de. A new, custom-designed venue for dance, featuring ethnic groups from around the world as well as contemporary ballet-inspired work.

Tonhalle Hofgartenufer ⓣ02 11/8 99 61 23, ⓦwww.tonhalle-duesseldorf.de. This converted planetarium is the main concert hall, featuring regular performances by the Dusseldorfer Symphoniker (ⓦwww.duesseldorfer-symphoniker.de).

Duisburg

With **DUISBURG**, separated from Düsseldorf by just a few kilometres of open countryside, the Ruhrgebiet begins with a vengeance. Until the early nineteenth century, this small walled town of about five thousand inhabitants had changed little since the great geographer **Gerhard Mercator** worked there in the sixteenth century. The Industrial Revolution saw it expand out of all recognition thanks to its key location at the point where the Ruhr enters the Rhine. It still ranks as the world's largest inland port, but recent years have seen a movement towards a modern economy, with most of the heavy industrial enterprises closed down, and the city now boasts a fine roster of museums.

The City

Central Duisburg is bounded to the north by the **Innenhafen**, whose redundant industrial buildings have, in the course of the past decade, been given new leases of life as offices, flats and cultural institutions. A former mill and warehouse on Johannes-Corputius-Platz have been converted to contain the **Kultur- und Stadthistorisches Museum** (Tues–Thurs & Sat 10am–5pm, Fri 10am–2pm, Sun 10am–6pm; €3; ⓦwww.stadtmuseum-duisburg.de), housing the usual archeology and local history exhibits alongside an outstanding (German-only) display on the work of **Gerhard Mercator**, born in Flanders of German stock, who settled in Duisburg in 1552 and remained there until his death 42 years later. His most enduring legacy is the Mercator projection, still in use in a modified form today in both sea and air transport. It enabled maps to be drawn accurately on a flat surface and meant sailors could steer a course by plotting straight lines, instead of continually resorting to the compass. He was a prolific cartographer – several of his maps are shown – and it's from one of his collections that the term "atlas" has passed into use. The most eye-catching items here are the terrestrial globe of 1541 and its celestial counterpart of ten years later, works of art as much as science, whose beauty can be attributed to Mercator's early training in Antwerp as an engraver.

The geographer is buried in the **Salvatorkirche**, a large Gothic church just a couple of minutes' walk to the southeast, which is one of the few reminders of the medieval town. Further east along the waterfront, towards the end of the

Innenhafen, are several other recently renovated warehouses. One of these, at Philosophenweg 55, houses the **Museum Küppersmühle** (Wed 2–6pm, Thurs 11am–6pm, Sat & Sun 11am–6pm; €6; Ⓦwww.museum-kueppersmuehle.de), the city's new forum for contemporary art. It exhibits more than twenty works by Georg Baselitz, plus examples of other leading German painters such as Sigmar Polke and Anselm Kiefer, and also mounts temporary thematic displays of international art in all sorts of different media.

This forms a fitting complement to the long-established **Wilhelm-Lehmbruck-Museum** (Tues–Sat 11am–5pm, Sun 10am–6pm; €4; Ⓦwww.lehmbruckmuseum.de), Germany's premier collection of twentieth-century sculpture, which is situated in the Immanuel-Kant-Park at the southern end of the city centre. Its centrepiece is the legacy of the sculptor **Lehmbruck** himself, who was born to a Duisburg mining family and committed suicide in 1919 at the age of 38. There are many examples here of his classically beautiful portrait busts, but it's his more ambitious compositions of elongated, writhing figures, such as *The Fallen One* (*Der Gestürzte*), *Mother and Child*, *Kneeling Woman* (*Kniende*) and *The Brooder* (*Sinnende*), which make a more lasting impression. Works by many of the most prestigious international sculptors of the twentieth century – Rodin, Barlach, Giacometti, Henry Moore, Archipenko, Marini, Lipchitz, Arp and Naum Gabo – are also on view. An attractive feature is the way artists chiefly famous as painters are represented by their much rarer sculptures – the Fauvist **Derain** abandons his usual bright palette in *The Twin*; the Surrealists **Dalí** and **Magritte** provide two of the most memorable pieces in *Head of Dante* and *L'Avenir des Statues*; while their colleague **Max Ernst**'s *Un Ami Empressé* and *Objet Mobile* are shown alongside two of his canvases. The most spectacular exhibits include **Joseph Beuys**' *End of the Twentieth Century* and **Duane Hanson**'s *Vietnam War Piece*, a devastating attack on the folly of the conflict, with a horrifyingly real depiction of five American soldiers dead and dying in the mud. In contrast, there's the light-hearted *Das Märchenrelief* by **Jean Tinguely**, which needs to be set in motion for full effect; ask an attendant.

Practicalities

The **Hauptbahnhof** is at the eastern end of the city centre. Turning right from the exit brings you to the beginning of Königstrasse, the main shopping street, where the **tourist office** (Mon–Fri 9am–6pm, Sat 10am–1pm; Ⓣ02 03/28 54 40, Ⓦwww.duisburg-information.de) occupies the pavilion at no. 86. **Harbour cruises** are run from April to October by DHG, Harry-Epstein-Platz 10 (Ⓣ02 03/6 04 44 39, Ⓦwww.dvv.de/dhg), and cost €6.50 for one hour, €8.50 for two. The two main departure points are the Schwanentor near the Salvatorkirche (11am, 1pm & 3pm), and the Schifferbörse in the heart of the docklands at Ruhrort (12.15pm & 2.15pm).

There are a few reasonably priced **hotels** in the immediate vicinity of the Hauptbahnhof: *Zum Alten Fritz* is immediately to the rear at Klöcknerstr. 10 (Ⓣ02 03/35 14 86; ❸–❺); *Mamma Leone* is directly in front at Kremerstr. 21 (Ⓣ02 03/28 54 92 00; ❺); while *Haus am Kantpark* is just to the west at Gallenkampstr. 6 (Ⓣ02 03/28 28 90; ❺). Pick of the luxury options is *Duisburger Hof*, in the heart of the city at Neckarstr. 2 (Ⓣ02 03/3 00 70, Ⓦwww.steigenberger,de; ❾). One of the **youth hostels** is at Kalkweg 148 (Ⓣ02 03/72 41 64; €14.20/16.90) in the suburb of Wedau; take bus #934 or #944. Another has recently opened at Lösorter Str. 133 (Ⓣ02 03/41 79 00; €21.10/23.80) in the Landschaftpark Nord (a recreation area on the site of a

△ Half-timbered houses on the Rivr Rur, Monschau

former ironworks); it's in the suburb of Meiderich, which can be reached by S-Bahn.

The city's best **restaurants** are *La Provence*, Hohe Str. 29, plus that in the aforementioned *Duisburger Hof*. For more moderately priced fare, try one of the Hausbrauereien: *Brauhaus Schlacht 4/8*, which occupies a converted bank at Düsseldorfer Str. 21, or *Webster*, just north of Immanuel-Kant-Park at Dellplatz 13. Elsewhere, the obvious beer to sample is the locally produced *König Pils*, made in the largest brewery in Germany still in private hands; its own city centre outlet is *König-City*, Düsseldorfer Str. 4. **Concerts** by the Duisburger Philharmoniker (Ⓦwww.duisburger-philharmoniker.de) feature alongside **opera** and **drama** at the Theater der Stadt Duisburg, Neckarstr. 1 (Ⓣ02 03/3 00 91 00, Ⓦwww.theater-duisburg.de & www.deutsche-oper-am-rhein.de).

Essen

Although its population has plummeted in recent years, **ESSEN** remains the largest city of the Ruhrgebiet, and the sixth in Germany. For centuries it was a small town under the control of its convent's abbesses, but it sprang to prominence as the steel metropolis in the nineteenth-century industrialization process, being effectively run by the most powerful of all Germany's commercial dynasties, the **Krupp** family. Essen is proud of its heritage, boasting northern Europe's oldest parish church, largest synagogue and tallest town hall, and it's one Ruhr city that definitely merits a day or more of anybody's time.

Arrival, information and accommodation

Essen's **Hauptbahnhof** is situated bang in the city centre, only a couple of blocks south of the Münster. The **tourist office** (Mon–Fri 9am–5.30pm, Sat 10am–1pm; Ⓣ02 01/8 87 20 41, Ⓦwww.essen.de) is at Am Hauptbahnhof 2. Given the size of the city, a 24-hour ticket on the **public transport** network run by VRR (Ⓦwww.vrr.de) can be a good investment as it doesn't take many journeys to cover the €6.55 price, particularly as it can be used by up to five people travelling together.

The **youth hostel** (Ⓣ02 01/49 11 63; €18/20.70) is in Werden, at Pastoratsberg 2, a long way from the centre, but in a delightful location in the woods. To reach it, take the road passing uphill directly in front of the abbey, and carry straight on; it lies well above the houses. Also in Werden, but on the opposite side of the river near the S-Bahn station, is one of the **campsites** (Ⓣ02 01/49 29 78). The other is on the south shore of the Baldeneysee in Fischlaken (Ⓣ02 01/40 20 07).

Hotels

Europa Hindenburgstr. 35 Ⓣ02 01/23 20 41, Ⓦwww.hotel-europa-essen.de. Mid-range hotel in the southwest of the city centre. ❺–❼

Kessing Hachestr. 30 Ⓣ02 01/23 99 88, Ⓕ23 02 89. Moderately priced hotel in a handy location just west of the Hauptbahnhof. ❺

Lindenhof Logenstr. 18 Ⓣ02 01/23 30 31, Ⓕ23 43 08. Budget place on the west side of the centre. ❹

Mövenpick Am Hauptbahnhof 2 Ⓣ02 01/1 70 80, Ⓦwww.moevenpick-essen.com. Fine old station hotel which was given a thorough refurbishment when it was taken over by the Swiss chain a few years back. Its restaurant is quite reasonably priced. ❼–❾

Parkhaus Hügel Freiherr-vom-Stein-Str. 209 Ⓣ02 01/47 10 91, Ⓦwww.parkhaus-huegel.de. Located right by Villa Hügel and boasting one of the very best restaurants in Essen. ❻

Schloss Hugenpoet August-Thyssen-Str. 51 Ⓣ02 01/0 20 54 or 1 20 40, Ⓦwww.hugenpoet.de. This is, without doubt, the best place to stay in Essen, a magnificent *Wasserschloss* in the suburb of Kettwig immediately south of Werden, 11km from the city centre. Its restaurant has an extensive wine list. ⑨

Zum Deutschen Haus Kastanienallee 16 ⓣ02 01/23 29 89, ⓕ23 06 92. Situated in the northern part of the centre, this has some of the least expensive rooms in the city. ④

The city centre

The centre of Essen consists largely of an enormous shopping precinct. At the northeastern end are the **Rathaus**, a dull 1970s skyscraper, and the domed **Alte Synagoge** (Tues–Sun 10am–6pm; free), a neo-Moorish monstrosity from the early twentieth century, which now houses a documentary centre on the suffering of the Jews under the Nazis.

In this setting, the **Münster** (or **Dom**) seems rather incongruous. A ninth-century foundation, it functioned as a collegiate church for aristocratic women until the Reformation. Since 1958, it has been the cathedral of a diocese centred on the Ruhr. The west end is an eccentric tripartite eleventh-century structure apparently modelled on the Dom at Aachen; the rest of what must have been a magnificent building was destroyed by fire and replaced by a Gothic hall church. A stupendous collection of **treasures** by Ottonian craftsmen nonetheless makes the Münster a place of outstanding interest. Most prominent of these is the **Golden Madonna** of 965, the first known work of its kind. Housed in its own locked chapel beside the entrance to the crypt, it's highly venerated. Also in the church is a large seven-branched candelabrum from about 1000. All the other star pieces are in the **Schatzkammer** (Tues–Sat 10am–5pm, Sun 12.30–5pm; €2.50; ⓦwww.domschatz.info), housed in rooms off the south transept. Here are four dazzling **processional crosses** of the tenth and eleventh centuries; a gospel book cover with scenes carved in ivory; the crown Otto III wore as a child; and many other priceless items. Joined to the front of the Münster by means of an atrium is the **Johanniskirche**, a miniature Gothic baptismal church containing a double-sided altarpiece by Barthel Bruyn; whether you see the Christmas or Easter scenes depends on the time of year.

The main museum complex is at Goethestr. 41; to reach it, take Kruppstrasse westwards at the back of the Hauptbahnhof, turn left at Bismarckplatz into Bismarckstrasse and continue straight ahead. Here are two separate collections – the **Ruhrlandmuseum** and the **Museum Folkwang** (Tues, Wed & Fri–Sun 10am–6pm, Thurs 10am–9pm; combined ticket €5; ⓦwww.ruhrlandmuseum.de & ⓦwww.museum-folkwang.de). The former has the usual local displays, with geology on the ground floor, customs, folklore and industries upstairs. Far more enticing is the Folkwang Museum, one of Germany's top galleries of nineteenth- and twentieth-century art. Two rooms are devoted to the French Impressionists and their followers, including versions of **Monet**'s favourite subjects, *Rouen Cathedral* and *Water Lilies*; an outstanding **Manet** *Fauré as Hamlet*; and four good examples each of **Gauguin** and **van Gogh**. In the German section, two works by **Friedrich** stand out among the Romantics, while there are examples of all the main figures of the twentieth century, with **Nolde**, **Rohlfs** and **Kirchner** being particularly well represented; Kirchner's *Three Women in the Street* ranks as one of the key paintings in the development of the Expressionist movement.

The outskirts

In the south of Essen, a large green belt begins with the **Gruga-Park** (daily April–Sept 8am–midnight; Oct–March 9am–dusk; €2), which incorporates the Botanischer Garten and large recreation areas. Beyond are extensive forests on both sides of the **Baldeneysee**, a long, narrow reservoir formed out of the River Ruhr. It's a popular leisure centre in summer, with watersports and walking trails.

By the S-Bahn station Hügel are the grounds of the **Villa Hügel** (Tues–Sun 10am–6pm; €1; Ⓦwww.villahuegel.de), built for the **Krupp** family between 1868 and 1872, and serving as their home until 1945. The idyllic setting gives little clue to the significance of the family, who personify many of the tragedies of modern German history, their genius for both engineering and organization being channelled into the most destructive of ends; during the Second World War, Gustav Krupp and his son Alfried made extensive use of concentration camp labour to produce weapons for the Nazis, and were later sentenced as war criminals at Nürnberg (though they were subsequently released). In the smaller of the houses there's a PR-type presentation of the achievements of the corporation (which in 1997 merged with its longtime bitter rival, Thyssen); upstairs, the family history of the Krupps is described, with the darker episodes carefully glossed over. Every year or so there's a blockbuster international **loan exhibition** on a major artistic theme.

South of Hügel and connected by S-Bahn lies **WERDEN**, officially a suburb of Essen but still preserving its small-town atmosphere. It's built round the **Abteikirche St Liudger**, one of the last of the great series of Romanesque basilicas in the Rhineland, dating from the end of the twelfth century. The exterior is especially impressive, with its massive westwork and central octagon, while an oddity is that the crypt, where St Liudger is buried, is an extension of the chancel, rather than being its lower storey. In a building behind the church is the **Schatzkammer** (Tues–Sun 10am–noon & 3–5pm; €2) containing many precious items, such as a fifth-century pyx, a ninth-century chalice, a bronze Romanesque crucifix and fragments of the saint's sarcophagus. Along Heckstrasse is the **Luciuskirche**, a daughter church of the abbey, but an even older building which is claimed as the earliest parish church in northern Europe still in existence. It's been restored to its original and simple tenth-century form.

In the north of Essen, reached by tram #108, is the **Zeche Zollverein**, a redundant mine which is a recent and somewhat improbable addition to the UNESCO World Heritage list. When it opened in 1932, it was the largest and most modern colliery in the world, and it is also claimed as the most beautiful, as its buildings were strongly influenced by the design principles of the Bauhaus school of architecture. Production ceased in 1986, and over the past few years the site has been developed as a tourist attraction and recreational complex. The **Besucherzentrum** (daily 10am–5/7pm; Ⓦwww.zollverein-foundation.de & Ⓦwww.zollverein-touristik.de) offers various **guided tours**. By far the most popular is that round the heart of the mine, **Schacht XII** (normally Mon–Fri at 11am, 2pm & 4pm, Sat & Sun at 11am, 1pm, 2pm, 3pm & 4pm; €6). Another on-site attraction is the **Design Zentrum Nordrhein-Westfalen** (Tues–Thurs 11am-6pm, Fri–Sun 11am–8pm; variable charge) in the former boiler house, which was remodelled for its new role by Lord (Norman) Foster.

Eating, drinking and entertainment

Many of the city's best **restaurants** are in the luxury hotels, but there are a few others worth seeking out.

Bahnhof Süd Rellinghauser Str. 175. Located south of the city centre, this is a favourite with the student crowd. Has a beer garden in the summer and a reasonably priced menu.

Brauhaus Graf Beust Kastanienallee 95. One of a small chain of Hausbrauereien in the Ruhrgebiet. Its standard products are the blond *Gruben Gold* and *Mulvany's*, an Irish-style stout, but it brews other beers seasonally and also offers wholesome German fare.

Kockshusen Pilgrimsteig 51, Rellinghausen. Located in a southeastern suburb, this outstanding restaurant occupies a half-timbered building from the seventeenth century, and has a garden terrace.

La Grappa Italian restaurant with a good choice of fish dishes, as well as some vegetarian options.

Rüttenscheider Hausbrauerei Girardetstr. 2, Rüttenscheid. Another boutique brewery with restaurant, situated in the *Girardetshaus*, not far from the Gruga Park.

Zodiac Witteringstr. 41, Rüttenscheid. Vegetarian specialist with an eclectic range of international fare. Evenings only, closed Thurs.

Entertainment

Aalto-Theater Rolandstr. 10 ⓣ02 01/8 12 22 00, ⓦwww.theater-essen.de. Named in honour of Alvar Aalto, the great Finnish architect who designed it, this is Essen's opera and dance stage.

Grillo-Theater Theaterplatz ⓣ02 01/8 12 22 00, ⓦwww.theater-essen.de. The principal municipally-run dramatic stage.

Grugahalle Norbertstr. 2 ⓣ02 01/7 24 42 90, ⓦwww.grugahalle.de. Large hall used for pop concerts and other large-scale events.

Saalbau Huyssenallee 53 ⓣ02 01/22 78 73 or 24 70 40, ⓦwww.theater-essen.de. The main concert hall, featuring a regular series of performances by the Essener Philharmonie.

Zeche Carl Wilhelm-Nieswandt-Allee 100 ⓣ02 01/8 34 44 10, ⓦwww.zechecarl.de. This former mine has live music or discos two or three times per week.

Xanten

XANTEN, set just back from the Rhine some 40km downstream from Duisburg, is one of the oldest settlements in Germany. In about 100 AD Colonia Ulpia Traiana was founded as a residential town (the only one in the Rhineland other than Cologne) in succession to the nearby garrison of Vetera, centre of operations for the campaign to subdue the eastern Germanic tribes. It in turn was abandoned with the collapse of the empire, and followed by a new community built immediately to the south around the graves of Christians martyred in the fourth century during the last wave of purges. The graves were popularly but implausibly believed to contain St Victor and members of the Thebian Legion; the name given to the town is a contraction of the Latin *Ad Sanctos Martyres* (To the Holy Martyrs). Writing at the end of the twelfth century, the anonymous poet of *The Nibelungenlied*, describing semi-mythical events centuries earlier, characterizes Xanten as "great", "splendid" and "far-famed", the birthplace and court of the invincible hero Siegfried, Lord of the Netherlands, Norway and the mysterious Nibelungland, home of the fantastic gold treasure of the Rhine which was to form the basis of the very different version of the legend unfolded in Wagner's epic *Ring* cycle 700 years later.

Xanten is something of a Peter Pan, its current population of 16,000 little more than the probable size of the Roman town. It kept its medieval aspect until the last war, when it was badly bombed. Modern Xanten has successfully risen from the debris to appear once more as one of Germany's neatest country towns, the recipient of several prestigious conservation prizes.

The Town

The **Stadtbefestigung** survives in part, still defining the town's perimeter on the north and east sides. It's pierced by several towers, many of which have been converted into luxury flats, including the grandest of the group, the **Klever Tor**, whose double gateway formed the northwest entrance to the town. Just up Nordwall, the next tower underwent a more radical conversion in the eighteenth century, being reshaped to form a windmill. Immediately facing it is Brückstrasse, best preserved of the old streets.

Between here and the Markt is the **Propsteikirche St Viktor**, popularly known as the **Dom**, though it's only the seat of a suffragan bishop. It lies cocooned in its own close or "Immunity", so named from its status as a haven from external laws and taxes. From afar, the massive facade dominates the town; it was the only part of the Romanesque church spared when a sober Gothic replacement was put up in the late thirteenth century. Subsequent builders tampered with it right up until 1525, by which time the towers had been heightened considerably. On the exterior of the chancel is a polychrome fifteenth-century statue to the Dom's patron saint, St Victor. The five-aisled **interior** gives a rare opportunity of sampling the genuine, cluttered feel of a medieval church, thanks to the extraordinary range of objects it has preserved – expressive pier statues of saints, a rood screen, choir stalls, a hanging *Double Madonna*, stained-glass windows and a crowd of altars. Particularly notable are the four carved and painted late Gothic winged **retables** in the aisles, one from Antwerp and three from nearby Kalkar; finest is that on the south side, with scenes from the life of the Virgin springing from a pyrotechnic *Tree of Jesse* by Henrik Douverman. The same sculptor made the reliquary busts for the high altar, which also incorporates the twelfth-century shrine of St Victor.

At the southwest corner of the close is the **Regionalmuseum** (Tues–Fri 9/10am–5pm, Sat & Sun 11am–6pm; €3, or €7 combined ticket with Archäologischer Park and Grosse Thermen), which has extensive archeology and local history collections, although the most important finds from local excavations are housed in its parent museum, the Rheinisches Landesmuseum in Bonn. In the past, the museum has housed items from the Dom's **Schatzkammer**, whose treasures include the *Achillespyxis*, a sixth-century pyx from Syria; the *Embriachi-Kästchen*, a fourteenth-century Venetian casket crowned a century later with a locally-made crucifix; and many superb textiles, such as the twelfth-century chasuble of St Bernard of Clairvaux and the fourteenth-century *Almosentasche*, a French creation woven from costly gold thread. Over the past few years, the entire contents of the Schatzkammer have been exhibited in many other towns and cities, with the aim of raising funds for a new home.

From the close, you can pass out into the **Markt**, which is something of a hotchpotch of styles, with houses ranging from Gothic to Rococo. Running northwestwards from the square is **Karthaus**, a street named after the former Charterhouse whose Baroque facade is its dominant feature.

Along Rheinstrasse and across the main road is the site of Colonia Ulpia Traiana, now the **Archäologischer Park** (daily: March–Nov 9am–6pm; Dec–Feb 10am–4pm; €5.50). Unlike many Roman towns in northern Europe, it was never built upon. That it subsequently disappeared is due to the fact that its stones were ideal building materials for later constructions, including the Dom. In the 1970s a proposal was made to develop the area into a recreation zone, but in return for sparing the site the authorities insisted that the excavations be given populist appeal. Thus, instead of merely uncovering ground plans, full-blooded conjectural reproductions of the main buildings of the town were attempted. The result is controversial to say the least, and purists will be horrified by the Disneyland touches. However, if you normally find archeological sites hamstrung by scholarly timidity, this will come as a revelation, giving a graphic picture of the true size and scale of a Roman town. Eventually, the aim is to go as far as re-creating the original riverside setting, which has now completely disappeared; at the moment, the **walls** with their massive fortifications, notably the **Hafentor** (Harbour Gate) at the very far end of the park, form the most impressive feature. Just inside the main entrance, an **inn** has been reconstructed; here the presentation goes outrageously over the top with toga-clad waiters serving the sort of meals it's alleged the Romans would have eaten. The **amphitheatre**, which is partly original, is now a venue for open-air theatrical performances; the **temple**, on the other hand, has been rebuilt only as a ruin.

Just west of the park are the **Grosse Thermen** (same times and ticket), a bathing complex thought to have been built on the personal orders of Emperor Hadrian. The excavated ruins have been covered by a protective glass building whose appearance mirrors the likely form of the original building.

Practicalities

Xanten's **Bahnhof**, terminus of a branch line from Duisburg, is only a few minutes' walk from the town centre via either Hagenbuschstrasse or Bahnhofstrasse. The **tourist office** (April–Sept Mon–Fri 9am–6pm, Sat & Sun 10am–4pm; Oct–March Mon–Fri 10am–5pm, Sat & Sun 10am–2pm; ⓣ0 28 01/9 83 00, ⓦwww.xanten.de) is at Kurfürstenstr. 9. There are around a dozen **private houses** (❷–❸) – some central, others in a more rural location – offering rooms to let. The least expensive of the **hotels**, all centrally situated, is *Galerie an de Marspoort*, Marsstr. 78 (ⓣ0 28 01/10 57, ⓦwww.hotel-an-de-marspoort; ❹), which doubles as an artists' gallery and café. Alternatives are *Nibelungen Hof*, Niederstr. 1 (ⓣ0 28 01/7 80, ⓦwww.hotel-nibelungenhof.de; ❻); *Neumaier*, Orkstr. 19–21 (ⓣ0 28 01/7 15 70, ⓦwww.minexa.de; ❻); *Hövelmann*, Markt 31–33 (ⓣ0 28 01/40 81; ❻); and the historic and luxurious *Van Bebber*, Klever Str. 12 (ⓣ0 28 01/66 23, ⓦwww.ccl-hotels.com; ❼). The best **restaurants** are in the last two hotels; there's also an inexpensive Balkan eatery, *Dalmatien*, at Markt 20. The town also has several good **cafés**, such as *Stadtcafé*, Markt 36–38, and *Café de Fries*, Kurfürstenstr. 8.

Kalkar (Calcar)

The little market town of **KALKAR** (originally spelt "Calcar" but the letter c was deemed too French), some 12km beyond Xanten, was built on a sandbank completely surrounded by an arm of the Rhine, but heavy silting has meant that it's now well inland. Its central **Markt** lost much of its character to wartime bombs, but some old houses have been restored to provide fitting company for the **Rathaus**, a brick building with a prominent octagonal turret. Behind, a step-gabled merchant's residence, connected by a modern extension to the oldest house in the town, contains the **Stadtmuseum** (Tues–Sun 10am–1pm & 2–5pm; €1). This has an excellent collection of manuscripts and charters, along with the work of painters, most notably the Expressionist **Heinrich Nauen**, who lived in the town.

None of this prepares you for the splendours of **St Nicolai** (April–Oct Mon–Fri 10am–noon & 2–6pm, Sat 10am–noon & 2–4.45pm, Sun 2–4.45pm; Nov–March daily 2–4.45pm; €1), built to the side of the Markt at the same time as the Rathaus. From the outside, it looks quite ordinary – a plain fifteenth-century brick building, enlivened only by its tall tower. The gleaming white interior is another matter altogether, bristling with such an astonishing array of **works of art** that it's now designated a "church-museum". It seems odd that what has never been more than a parish church in a town which has never been very large could have garnered such riches, but medieval Kalkar became wealthy through a cloth industry that used locally produced wool. The rich burghers showed their appreciation for this bounty by funding a school of woodcarving which flourished continuously for about a century from 1450, producing one great altarpiece after another, to illustrate the lives of Christ and the saints for the enlightenment of a largely illiterate congregation. Fifteen large retables and numerous other statues and paintings originally embellished the church; some were sold in the nineteenth century, but all the important pieces remain *in situ*.

It's worth taking time to examine the myriad details to be found in the big showpieces as all display an amazing level of technical virtuosity. **Henrik Douverman**, who made the *Altar of the Seven Sorrows of the Virgin* in the south apse, the *Double Madonna Candelabrum* in the middle of the nave and the superbly expressive *St Mary Magdalene* in the north aisle, has long been recognized as a highly individual artist, one who proved the continuing vitality of late Gothic forms well into the sixteenth century. However, many of his little-known predecessors, who were forced to submerge their artistic personalities in co-operative ventures, showed equal skill, nowhere more than in the crowded main *Passion Altar*, begun by the founder of the school, **Master Arnt**, and continued by **Ludwig Jupan**. These carvers were also responsible respectively for the *St George Altar* and the *Altar to the Virgin* fronting the entrance to the chancel. Painted panels were added to many of the retables to fill out the story; particularly fine are the colourful scenes on **Jan Joest**'s *Passion Altar*, which features a topographically accurate depiction of Kalkar's Markt as the backdrop to *The Raising of Lazarus*.

Practicalities

Kalkar has lost its rail link, but **buses** between Xanten and Kleve (which run hourly Mon–Fri, spasmodically on Sat and not at all on Sun) stop on the Markt. Though there's no **tourist office** as such, leaflets can be picked up at the Stadtverwaltung, Markt 20 (ⓣ0 28 24/13 11 20, ⓦwww.kalkar.de) during normal working hours. There are three **hotels**, all bang in the centre: *Seydlitz*, Markt 25 (ⓣ0 28 24/97 15 97; ❺), *Stil(l)leben*, Wallstr. 10 (ⓣ0 28 24/97 15 97, ⓦwww.hotel-stillleben.de; ❺), and *Siekmann*, Kesselstr. 32 (ⓣ0 28 24/9 24 50; ❺). The best **restaurants** are the one in *Siekmann* and the excellent but pricey *Ratskeller*, Markt 20. There's also a pleasant **café-bar** in an old windmill, *Kalkarer Mühle*, just to the rear of the Stadtmuseum on Mühlensteg. Just north of Kalkar there's a **campsite** (ⓣ0 28 24/66 13) at the **Wisseler See**, a natural lake which is a watersports centre.

Westphalia

Westphalia (Westfalen) is named after one of the three main Saxon tribes, and by the early Middle Ages the term came to be used for all of Saxony west of the River Weser. Despite this long tradition as a definable part of Germany, it's never really been governed as a unit, and the boundaries have often been changed dramatically. The short-lived Kingdom of Westphalia, established by Napoleon for his brother Jérôme, consisted mostly of Hesse, while the present political division of the country has seen parts of the historic province transferred to Lower Saxony. Apart from the cities in the **Ruhrgebiet** which are traditionally Westphalian (notably **Dortmund**), there are three distinct constituent parts – the fertile **Münsterland** plain to the north; the predominantly rural **Sauerland** and Siegerland to the south; and the depression to the east bounded by the vast stretch of the **Teutoburg Forest**. The last-named incorporates what was formerly one of the smallest states of the German Reich, the **Principality of Lippe**, which has two notable historic towns in **Detmold** and **Lemgo**. Elsewhere, **Münster** is the epitome of middle-class prosperity and is, like **Paderborn**, an important episcopal centre. However, it's the much smaller town of **Soest** which rivals Lemgo for the right to be regarded as the most beautiful in the province.

According to its tourist board, Westphalia is associated with "the solid and substantial things in life". In architecture, the characteristic features are moated castles, lofty hall churches and half-timbered farm buildings. Gastronomically, it's famous for hams, spit roasts, beer, schnapps and, above all, rye bread. It's an archetypal German province and a favourite holiday destination with the Germans themselves.

Münster

MÜNSTER, which served as capital of the Prussian province of Westphalia, is one of the most varied and enticing of the cities spread across the flat north German plain. It has an unusually rich architectural heritage, including examples of all the main styles from Romanesque to Baroque. Industry has been confined to the peripheries, and the chic shops crowding the centre are an unabashed celebration of the affluent consumerism enjoyed by a population which is overwhelmingly middle-class. The university is among the largest in Germany, and one consequence of this is that the city has come firmly under the rule of the bicycle. However, the dominant influence on Münster has been the Church, its very name – the equivalent of the English word "minster" – deriving from the evangelizing monastery of **St Liudger**, who was consecrated bishop in 805 as part of Charlemagne's policy of converting the Saxon tribes to Christianity. Except for the years 1534–35 when it was taken over by the fanatical Anabaptist sect, it has remained intensely loyal to Roman Catholicism, even during the Third Reich, when the city's bishop, **Clemens August von Galen**, was one of the regime's most courageous and persistent opponents. In 1936, he organized a popular revolt which overturned an edict to remove crucifixes from school buildings – an apparently trivial incident, but one of the few occasions the Nazis gave in to domestic opponents. This defiance counted for nothing with the Allied bombing missions, which administered particularly brutal treatment on Münster, but the city recovered well, adopting a much praised rebuilding programme.

Arrival, information and accommodation

The **Hauptbahnhof** is directly to the east of the city centre. **Bus** services both within the city and to other places in the province leave from the string of stops on both sides of Bahnhofstrasse. The **tourist office** (Mon–Fri 9am–6pm, Sat 9am–1pm; ⓣ02 51/4 92 27 10, ⓦwww.muenster.de) is at Klemensstr. 9.

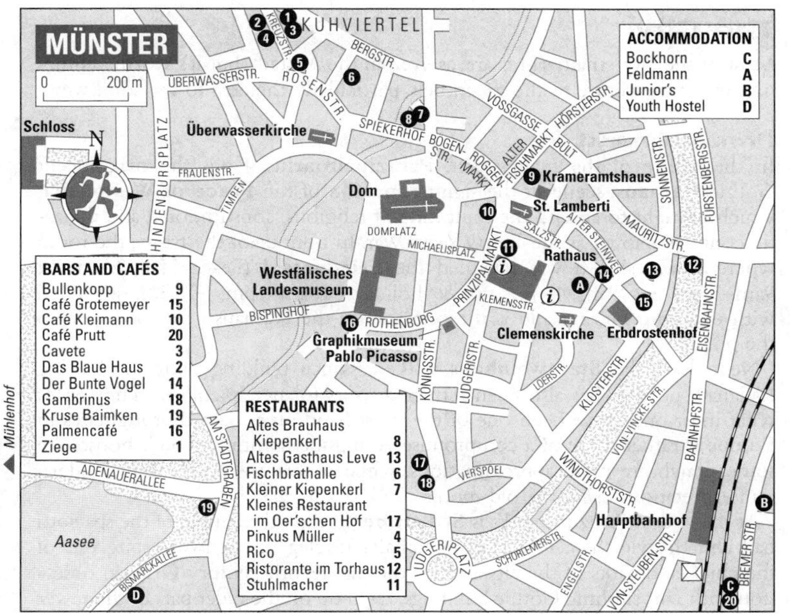

Münster has some splendid middle- and upper-range hotels, but relatively few inexpensive options. The **youth hostel** is in a good location by the right bank of the Aasee at Bismarckallee 31 (ⓣ02 51/53 02 80 or 5 30 28 12; €21.20/23.80); take bus #10 or #34 to Hoppendamm. **Camping** is possible in the northeastern suburb of Handorf at Dorbaumstr. 35 (ⓣ02 51/32 93 12; closed mid-Oct to mid-March).

Hotels

Bockhorn Bremer Str. 24 ⓣ02 51/6 55 10, ⓕ6 74 31 61. Somewhat old-fashioned budget hotel, offering rooms with and without attached bathroom, conveniently situated immediately to the rear of the Hauptbahnhof. ④–⑥

Feldmann An der Clemenskirche 14 ⓣ02 51/41 44 90, ⓦwww.feldmann-muenster.de. Quality hotel at the eastern end of the Altstadt. It also has a fine restaurant (closed Sun & Mon). ⑤–⑦

Haus von Guten Hirten Mauritz Lindenweg 61, St Mauritz ⓣ02 51/3 78 70, ⓕ37 45 49. Church-run guesthouse offering some of the cheapest rooms in Münster. Situated in an inner suburb 2km east of the Hauptbahnhof; take bus #14 to Mauritz-Friedhof. ④

Hof zur Linde Handorfer Werseufer 1, Handorf ⓣ02 51/3 27 50, ⓦwww.hof-zur-linde.de. Classy hotel, part of the Romantik group, in a seventeeth-century farmhouse 7km northeast of the centre; take bus #10 to Kirschgarten. It also has a top-class if rather pricey restaurant. ⑧

Junior's Schillerstr. 27 ⓣ02 51/66 11 66, ⓕ6 76 81. Situated right behind the Hauptbahnhof, this recently refurbished hotel has a *Pilsstube* offering reasonably priced meals. ⑤

Schloss Wilkinghege Steinfurter Str. 374 ⓣ02 51/14 42 70, ⓦwww.schloss-wilkinghege.de. Münster's top hotel, complete with gourmet restaurant, occupies a sixteenth-century *Wasserschloss* in a landscaped park just off the B54 at the northwestern edge of the city; take bus #1 to Wilkinghege. ⑧–⑨

Wienburg Kanalstr 237 ⓣ02 51/2 01 28 00, ⓦwww.wienburg.de. Located in a park 2km north of the Altstadt, reached by bus #9 or #17, this has a renowned restaurant (closed Mon). ⑥

Windsor Warendorfer Str. 177 ⓣ02 51/13 13 30, ⓦwww.hotelwindsor.de. Located east of the centre, reached by bus #2 or #10 to Danziger Freiheit. It has a high-class Italian restaurant, *Il Cuchiaio d'Argento* (closed Sat lunch & Mon). ⑥

The City

Most of the city's main sights are, as ever, in the Altstadt, but it's worth venturing out of the centre to the green belt, particularly the area to the southwest.

Prinzipalmarkt

In the centre of the main street, **Prinzipalmarkt**, stands the magnificent Gothic **Rathaus**, scene of the signing in 1648 of the **Peace of Westphalia**, which brought to an end the multitude of religious, constitutional and dynastic conflicts known as the Thirty Years' War. In honour of the treaty, the room where it was signed was renamed the **Friedensaal** (Peace Hall; Mon–Fri 9am–5pm, Sat 9am–4pm, Sun & holidays 10am–1pm; €1.50); it's filled with exquisite carving and is the one part of the Rathaus generally open to the public.

Next door, the **Stadtweinhaus**, a Renaissance building with an abutting Italianate portico, has also been returned to its former splendour. The rest of what must once have been one of the most handsome main thoroughfares in Europe is rather more of a compromise. Alongside faithfully rebuilt houses are some which are mere approximations, while others are deliberately modern reinterpretations using the old motifs.

At the end of Prinzipalmarkt is **St Lamberti**, a good example of the spacious hall-church style characteristic of Westphalia. Its elegant openwork spire, one of the chief landmarks of the city, reflects the nineteenth-century German obsession with embellishing Gothic buildings. High up on the older part of the tower hang three wrought-iron cages; in them were displayed the bodies of the Anabaptist leader **Jan van Leyden** and his two principal lieutenants, following the crushing of their "Reich" by the prince-bishop's army in 1535. Apart from insisting on adult baptism, this sect believed in the common ownership of property and in heeding the biblical injunction to be fruitful and multiply – the leader himself took no fewer than sixteen wives. The iconoclastic tendencies of the Anabaptists led them to destroy the beautiful sculptural decoration which were key features of the city's medieval churches; one of the rare examples left *in situ* is the elaborate *Tree of Jesse* over St Lamberti's south doorway. Facing the church's apse on Alter Steinweg is the **Krameramtshaus**, a late sixteenth-century building in the Dutch style which is the oldest guildhall to have survived; nowadays it serves as the main public library.

Domplatz

Almost any point on the vast **Domplatz**, on which markets are held on Wednesdays and Saturdays, offers a superb view of the huge thirteenth-century **Dom**, built in less than forty years in a style bridging the transition from Romanesque to Gothic. The only entrance is via the **porch** (or "Paradise"), which is adorned on the inside with statues of Christ and the Apostles dating from the very beginning of the building period; the pier figure of St Paul, the Dom's patron, is from three hundred years later, the first of several subsequent additions to make up a full programme worthy of a Gate of Heaven, to which such doorways aspired.

The Dom's **interior** is highly unusual, the nave having just two bays of massive span. It's jam-packed with sculptural memorials and other works of art. What really catches your eye is the **astronomical clock**, made in the 1530s, in the southern arm of the ambulatory. Based on the most precise mathematical calculations available at the time, it shows the orbit of the planets and the movement of the fixed stars, as well as fulfilling the normal function of charting the course of the sun and the moon; the lowest section is a calendar. The leading Münster painter of the day, **Ludger tom Ring the Elder**, decorated the clock with the Evangelical symbols, delicate scenes of the Labours of the Months and a gallery of entranced spectators. At noon, you can hear the carillon and see the emergence of the Magi to pay tribute to the infant Christ.

At the far end of the cloisters the **Domkammer** (Tues–Sun 11am–4pm; €1) houses the treasury. Pride of place goes to the eleventh-century gold reliquary of St Paul, studded with jewels a couple of hundred years later; other outstanding pieces are the thirteenth-century processional cross and fourteen bust-reliquaries of the prophets.

The Westfälisches Landesmuseum

The Domplatz, which also contains several Baroque mansions, serves as the city's museum centre. The **Westfälisches Landesmuseum** (Tues–Sun 10am–6pm; €2.60) houses works of art of mostly Westphalian origin, but is of far more than parochial significance. On the ground floor is a really outstanding collection of **medieval sculpture**, including the original statues from the Überwasserkirche (see below). The massive group of *Christ's Entry into Jerusalem* originally adorned the upper part of the Dom's facade, destroyed in the war, and is the work of **Hinrik Brabender**, one of the most individual of the remarkable group of late Gothic German sculptors. Likewise by him is a series of Passion scenes made for the Domplatz; despite their weary appearance – the Anabaptists smashed them only a few years after they were made – the wonderful dignity and characterization of the figures can still be appreciated. Altogether different is the art of his son **Johann Brabender**, who was fully Renaissance in style and happiest on a small scale, as in sensitive and delicate works such as *Calvary* from the Dom's rood screen and *Adam and Eve* from the Paradise. Also on view are some prime examples of early Westphalian painting, beginning with the "Soft Style" of **Conrad von Soest** and the **Master of Warendorf** in the early fifteenth century. From the next generation is **Johann Koerbecke**, whose masterpiece, the *Marienfeld Altar*, contains background depictions of Münster.

The Renaissance and Baroque section on the floor above contains a wide-ranging array of paintings by members of the local **tom Ring** family. Apart from the portraits for which they are best known, there are religious works by Hermann and pioneering still lifes by Ludger the Younger. Displayed alongside are some magnificent pieces of furniture, notably the **Wrangelschrank**, a cupboard made in mid-sixteenth-century Augsburg, which has carved reliefs of antique battles on the outside, gorgeous intarsia scenes inside. A locally-made silver-gilt **goblet** in the shape of a ship is the highlight of the decorative arts section. Among the seventeenth-century paintings are three fine portraits by **Wilhelm Heimbach**, a deaf-mute who served for a time as court artist to the Münster prince-bishops, and some important Dutch works, including *St Sebastian* by **Goltzius** and four panels of *The Evangelists* by **Ter Brugghen**. On the second floor is a large collection of Expressionist paintings, with a good cross-section of the work of **August Macke**; the large *Paradise* was painted jointly with **Franz Marc** for his own studio.

The rest of the Altstadt

A short distance to the west of the Dom stands the **Liebfrauenkirche**, usually known as the **Überwasserkirche** (Church by the Water) since it stands beside the Aa, Münster's tiny river. Like St Lamberti, it's a fourteenth-century hall church, with a floridly decorated tower. Its superb sculptures proved particularly repugnant to the Anabaptists, who smashed and buried them; some 350 years later, they were dramatically rediscovered but were considered too fragile to return to their original location.

From here, Frauenstrasse leads to Schlossplatz with the resplendent eighteenth-century **Schloss** of the prince-bishops, its two side wings reaching out like embracing arms. The front facing the **Botanischer Garten** (daily 7.30am–5pm; free) is quite different, but the interior was completely destroyed in the war, and has been modernized for use by the university. Its architect, **Johann Conrad Schlaun**, was almost single-handedly responsible for making Münster the capital of north German Baroque, which was far more restrained than its southern counterpart. There are two other notable buildings by him at the opposite end of the city centre, reached from the Rathaus by following Klemensstrasse. The **Erbdrostenhof**, a nobleman's mansion, again shows his talent for the grand manner and has survived in better shape than the Schloss. Immediately opposite, the circular **Clemenskirche**, a former hospital church, presents a clever solution to the problem of building in a restricted space, and is richly decorated with a huge ceiling fresco glorifying the patron saint.

A couple of blocks further west, at the top end of Königsstrasse, two old town houses have been adapted to house the **Graphikmuseum Pablo Picasso** (Tues–Fri 11am–6pm, Sat & Sun 10am–6pm, €4.50; Ⓦ www.graphikmuseum-picasso-muenster.de). The first museum in Germany specifically devoted to the Spanish master, it contains the only complete collection of his lithographs, some eight hundred works in all. Thematic selections from this are shown in rotation; the rest of the display area is given over to temporary exhibitions on other aspects of the art of Picasso and his contemporaries.

Outside the centre

Heading southwest from the centre, the sausage-shaped **Aasee**, some 6km in circumference, is the most popular recreation area in the city, particularly at the weekend when the yachts and motorboats of prosperous locals crowd the water. At the lower end of the left bank, reached by bus #14, is the **Mühlenhof** (mid-March to Oct daily 10am–6pm; Nov to mid-March Mon–Sat 1–4.30pm, Sun 11am–4.30pm; €3), one of Germany's longest-established open-air museums. On a fine day, it's worth a plod round the twenty or so agricultural buildings from the province which have been re-erected here, the centrepieces being a trestle windmill of 1748 and an early seventeenth-century millhouse, fitted out with authentic furnishings. A short walk south is the **Westfälisches Museum für Naturkunde** (Tues–Sun 9am–6pm; €2.60), which is best-known for its collection of fossils. Some of the fishes and aquatic plants date back several hundred million years, to an age when Westphalia lay in the tropics, but the most spectacular find, a **giant ammonite**, is a comparative stripling at eighty million years of age.

Some 5km northwest of the city centre, reached by bus #5, is **Haus Rüschhaus** (guided tours March, April & Nov to mid-Dec Tues–Sun 11am–1pm & 2–4pm; May–Oct Tues–Sun 10am–1pm & 2.30–5.30pm; €3), which Johann Conrad Schlaun designed and built from 1745 to 1748 as a summer house for himself. It's quite an eccentric little construction, mostly homely in feel, but with touches of Baroque swagger, as in the sloping roofline and the sweeping facade which in fact fronts a fully practical barn, integrated into the house as was the norm in traditional local farmsteads. Germany's leading woman author of the nineteenth-century, **Annette von Droste-Hülshoff** (1797–1848), lived here for twenty years from 1826, during which time she produced much of her finest work.

Best known for her charming poetic vignettes of nature, the writer spent the first three decades of her life in the original seat of her aristocratic family, **Haus Hülshoff** (daily Feb to mid-Dec 9.30am–6pm; €3). Buses #563 and #564 go there from Münster's Hauptbahnhof, or you can walk from Rüschhaus in about half an hour by continuing straight ahead and turning left down the footpath just past the highway junction; don't follow the road, which adds a considerable distance to the journey. Set in an attractive park, this castle is a classic example of the Renaissance *Wasserburg* design. The outer barrier (*Vorburg*) is a severe, low-lying building with square corner towers; the inner building (*Hauptburg*) is an airy L-shaped dwelling in the Dutch style, with a suite of six rooms authentically furnished in the early nineteenth-century style familiar to the poet, plus an appended neo-Gothic chapel.

Eating, drinking and nightlife

One of Münster's greatest attractions is its wonderful choice of **bars**, **cafés** and **restaurants**. The most obvious place to begin is around the Prinzipalmarkt, but an equally notable nightlife area is the **Kuhviertel** just beyond the Überwasserkirche; this is usually described as the Latin quarter, but students no longer predominate. Look out for the amazing range of **beers** – *Pils*, *Alt*, *Hefeweizen*, *Malz*, *Leicht*, *Spezial* and the strong *Jubiläumsbier* – made by *Pinkus Müller*; although small, and the only one left in Münster, it's among the most highly regarded of all German breweries. *Alt*, whether from Pinkus or imported from Düsseldorf, is Münster's most popular drink and can be mixed with syrup (*mit Schuss*) or with a punch of fresh raspberries and peaches (*Altbierbowle*). Popular **nightclubs** include *Cascade*, Berliner Platz 23, and *Elephant*, Roggenmarkt 15.

Restaurants

Altes Brauhaus Kiepenkerl Spiekerhof 45. Named after the statue of the pedlar outside, this has a ground-floor restaurant cum beer hall and an elegant upstairs café. Closed Tues.

Altes Gasthaus Leve Alter Steinweg 37. This distinguished old restaurant, which has an elegant tiled interior, boasts of a tradition dating back to 1607. Closed Mon.

Fischbrathalle Schlaunstr. 8. Seemingly belonging to a vanished age, this inexpensive lunchtime fish restaurant has been run by the same family since it was founded in 1926. Open Mon–Fri 11am–3pm, Sat 11am–2.30pm.

Kleiner Kiepenkerl Spiekerhof 47. The food here is if anything superior to that served in its larger sister restaurant alongside. Closed Mon.

Kleines Restaurant im Oer'schen Hof Königstr. 42. Expensive restaurant serving top-notch French cuisine and fish specialities. Closed Sun & Mon.

Pinkus Müller Kreuzstr. 4–10. The brewery offers both a restaurant, *Altbierüche*, and a bar, *Biergalerie*. The former, which is decked out in traditional style, fills up heavily from mid-evening – notably with members of the American community. Not the cheapest, but arguably the best place in town for a traditional Westphalian meal. Closed Sun.

Rico Rosenplatz 7. Vegetarian self-service restaurant, with a wide range of hot and cold dishes. Open Mon–Sat 11.30am–4.30pm.

Ristorante in Torhaus Mauritzstr. 27. Italian restaurant with a strong line in fish dishes, named after the Neoclassical guardhouse it occupies. Evenings only, closed Mon.

Stuhlmacher Prinzipalmarkt 6. The city's most celebrated Gaststätte, with a strongly traditional menu. It has a wide selection of beers, including one brewed in Bavaria for its exclusive use.

Villa Medici Ostmarkstr. 15. Located to the east of the Altstadt (a 10min walk), this rivals *Il Cuchiaio d'Argento* (see p.553) for the right to be regarded as Münster's best Italian restaurant. Closed Sun & Mon.

Bars, cafés and café-bars

Bullenkopp Alter Fischmarkt 24. Traditional Kneipe still preserving its original late nineteenth-century appearance. Closed Sun.

Café Grotemeyer Salzstr. 24. Elegant traditional coffee house, founded in 1850 and well-known for its marzipans.

Café Kleimann Prinzipalmarkt 48. Occupying one of the finest of the old guild houses, this is another good choice for *Kaffee und Kuchen*. Closed Sun.

Café Prutt Bremer Str. 32. Vegetarian and wholefood specialist, situated just behind the Hauptbahnhof. Unusually for such institutions it stays open until late, and has its own little beer garden.

Cavete Kreuzstr. 38. Popular bar with a young crowd, loud music and a selection of inexpensive pastas and puddings. Open daily 7pm–1am.

Das Blaue Haus Kreuzstr. 16. A direct competitor of *Cavete* in every respect, with the same opening hours.

Der Bunte Vogel Alter Steinweg 41. Another beer hall, though a bit trendier than usual.

Gambrinus Königsstr. 34. Lively pub which does good-value schnitzels cooked in a score of different ways.

Kruse Baimken Am Staatgraben 52. Located by the north bank of the Aasee, this is the place to come on a fine evening, when you may find close on a thousand people, including many of the beautiful set, relaxing in its beer garden.

Palmencafé Aegidiimarkt 1. Offers the best selection of teas in town. Closed Sun.

Ziege Kreuzstr. 33. The smallest pub in Münster, with a truly *gemütlich* interior. Open Tues–Sun 8pm–1am.

Festivals and entertainment

The main **festival**, known as Send, is a fair held for five days at a stretch three times annually (March, June & Oct) in the Hindenburgplatz in front of the Schloss. Karneval is also celebrated, if not with the same gusto as in the Rhineland, while the Lambertusfest, beginning on September 17, is a festival for children. Münster's main **theatre** venue is the Städtische Bühnen, Neubrückenstr. 63 (Ⓣ02 51/41 46 71 00, Ⓦwww.theater.muenster.org); **concerts** by the Symphonieorchester der Stadt Münster are also held there. Charivari, Körnerstr. 3 (Ⓣ02 51/52 15 00), features puppet shows, while large-scale events are hosted by the Halle Münsterland, to the south of the centre at Albertsloher Weg 32 (Ⓣ02 51/6 60 01 12).

Münsterland

Münsterland is the name given to the large tract of Westphalia stretching from the Rhine to the Teutoburg Forest, bounded by the Netherlands and Lower Saxony to the north, and by the Ruhrgebiet to the south. Its rich soils are agriculturally highly productive, and it remains predominantly rural, with over fifty **historic castles** surrounded by tracts of water (known as *Wasserburgen*), the nearest the country comes to rivalling the French Loire châteaux. The vast majority of these remain private dwellings, and are generally still in the hands of old aristocratic families, though a few are now publicly owned.

Lüdinghausen

There's a choice of bus or train from Münster to **LÜDINGHAUSEN**, 30km south; the buses are better, as the rail route is circuitous and the Bahnhof is a long way out. The moated castle named after the town itself has been too messed about down the years to be of much interest, but **Burg Vischering** at the northern boundary is an archetypal *Wasserburg*, as well as the only one wholly given over to tourism, being designated the **Münsterland-Museum** (Tues–Sun 10am–12.30pm & 1.30–4.30/5.30pm; €2). Its *Hauptburg*, horseshoe in shape, with a singular octagonal tower in the centre of the courtyard, was beautified around 1620 by the addition of an abutting Renaissance section with an elegant oriel window. Directly facing this are the spreading branches of a trumpet tree, the most remarkable of several rare species planted in the grounds. As is normal, the interiors are plain by comparison, but the **Rittersaal** with wooden beamed ceiling has been restored to good effect. There's an exhibition on life in the medieval castles of the region; other folklore displays, this time on the farms and the towns, are to be found in the *Vorburg*.

Nordkirchen

If you've only a day to spare on the castles, the best way to spend it is by combining a visit to Lüdinghausen and **NORDKIRCHEN**, 8km southeast. This redbrick giant is by far the largest and most spectacular **Schloss** of the group, a manifestation of the fantastic wealth of the **Plettenberg** dynasty of prince-bishops, who decided to replace their old fortress with a palace in the French manner. Every tourist brochure refers to it as the "Westphalian Versailles", a nickname it has had since its conception in 1703, when it referred to the older and much smaller palace at Versailles, on which Nordkirchen was directly modelled. The complex is on one island only (instead of the two normally required for a *Wasserburg*), and exhibits all the sense of order characteristic of the Age of Reason. It's almost completely symmetrical and is specially designed to produce a spectacular main vista, an effect achieved by breaking up the main block into sections and preceding them with long, narrow pavilions. Behind, there's a formal garden with Baroque sculptures. Nowadays, Nordkirchen belongs to the Land government, which has adapted it as a college for financial studies; consequently there's free access at all times, and what you can see from outside definitely justifies a visit. Official opportunities for viewing the **interior** aren't generous (guided tours May–Sept Sun 11am–6pm; Oct–April Sun 2–4pm; €2). However, there are many private visits on weekdays throughout the summer, with which you're allowed to tag along; consult the list posted in the porter's office or, better still, phone ahead (mornings only; ⓣ0 25 96/93 34 02). The rooms are less grandiose than might be imagined from outside, but have the full pomp of the Baroque in their rich stuccowork, ceiling paintings, wood panelling and plentiful furnishings. Note that there are no **buses** out of Nordkirchen on Sundays, and that the nearest station, on a line with a very restricted weekend service, is at Cappel, 5km east.

Cappenberg

CAPPENBERG, 12km south of Nordkirchen, stands just outside the industrial town of Lünen, which marks the beginning of the Ruhrgebiet. There has been a **Schloss** here since the ninth century; the present building is Baroque, and now hosts temporary exhibitions of various kinds. Far more significant is the **Stiftskirche** directly in front, founded by the brothers Gottfried and Otto von Cappenberg in atonement for the part they had played in helping Lothair of Saxony sack the city of Münster in 1121, destroying most of the Dom in the process. Their confessor, St Norbert, suggested that a fit form of repentance would be the establishment of a German headquarters for the Premonstratensian order he had recently founded in France. The plain architecture favoured by these monks, Romanesque with later Gothic additions, gives no hint of the riches within, which include two of the supreme masterpieces of German medieval art. Displayed in a safe in the south transept is the stunning **head-reliquary of Frederick Barbarossa**, the oldest surviving portrait of a German emperor made from life. Actually intended to contain a relic of St John the Evangelist, it's probably the work of an Aachen goldsmith of about 1160. In the choir is the early fourteenth-century **founders' memorial**, depicting them as rather jolly youths with virtually identical features clasping a model of the church. At around the same time, a tomb was made for the now-canonized Gottfried; it's now in the south transept. Other important works of art are the polychrome Romanesque triumphal cross and the elaborately carved Gothic stalls with their imaginative misericords.

Dortmund

At the far eastern end of the Ruhrgebiet is **DORTMUND**. Its name immediately brings **beer** to mind – it was first granted brewing rights in 1293, and even jealous rivals are forced to admit it's the national drink's number one city. In all, six million hectolitres are produced annually, a total surpassed in world terms only by Milwaukee. Much of it is for export, which has led to the word being used to categorize certain types of beer. Although many old labels live on, the number of breweries has declined markedly in recent years – the venerable Kronen acquired both Thier and Stifts, then was itself taken over by DAB. As a result, all production is now concentrated in the hands of just two conglomerates, the aforementioned DAB and Union, the latter's name reflecting its late nineteenth-century origins as a union of several breweries. Union's huge U logo is still one of the city centre's most prominent landmarks, though the building on which it stands has been converted into shops and flats, with operations transferred to a modern plant in the suburbs.

Alone among Ruhr cities, Dortmund was important in the Middle Ages when it was a Free Imperial City and an active member of the Hanseatic League. This helps give it a rounded and distinctive character which all its neighbours somehow lack. Provided you're prepared to overlook the obvious limitations of a place where wartime bombs wreaked horrendous damage and where heavy industry is prominent, it's an interesting and enjoyable city in which to spend a day or two.

Arrival, information and accommodation

Dortmund's **Hauptbahnhof** is immediately beyond the northern end of the Altstadt. Directly opposite, at Königswall 20, is the **tourist office** (Mon–Fri 9am–6pm, Sat 9am–1pm; ⓣ02 31/5 02 56 66, ⓦwww.dortmund-tourismus.de). The **youth hostel** has a conveniently central location at

Silberstr. 24–26 (☎02 31/14 00 74; €21.20/23.80), and there's a **campsite** at Syburger Dorfstr. 69 (☎02 31/77 43 74) not far from the casino, the Spielbank Hohensburg; take bus #444.

Hotels

Carlton Lütge-Brückstr. 5–7 ☎02 31/52 80 30, Ⓕ55 38 42. Functional but fully acceptable budget hotel just a short walk from the Hauptbahnhof. ④–⑥

Cläre-Fritz Reinoldstr. 6 ☎ & Ⓕ02 31/57 15 23. Small pension facing the Reinoldikirche. ④

hotellennhof Menglinghauser Str. 20 ☎02 31/75 81 90, Ⓦwww.hotellennhof.de. This modern designer hotel in a traditionally-designed half-timbered building in the far south of the city has the official patronage of the Boroussia Dortmund football club. It also has a high-class restaurant, *lennis.* ⑥–⑨

Königshof Königswall 4–6 ☎02 31/5 70 41, Ⓦwww.hotel-koenigshof.de. The most conveniently located of the mid-range hotels. ⑥

Holiday Inn Dortmund-City Olpe 2 ☎02 31/54 32 00, Ⓦwww.eventhotels.com. This is one of the best upmarket choices, not least because it has as a well-regarded restaurant offering budget menus. ⑦–⑨

Mercure Grand Hotel Lindemannstr. 88 ☎02 31/9 11 30, Ⓦwww.accorhotels.com. Dortmund's most prestigious hotel is located in the south of the city, directly opposite the main congress centre, the Westfallenhallen. It also has a high-quality restaurant, which offers good-value lunchtime buffets. ⑦–⑨

Stiftshof Stiftstr. 5 ☎02 31/52 47 01, Ⓕ52 47 02. A reasonably priced hotel in a good central location. ④

The City

The inner ring road, whose sections all bear the suffix "wall", follows the line of the vanished thirteenth-century fortifications and thus defines the perimeter of the medieval city. Only a fraction of this area was left standing after the war, and not a single secular building from the Hansa days remains. The four civic churches, however, survived the onslaught in a battered condition, and a painstaking restoration programme which lasted into the 1980s has returned them to their former state. Although they're now marooned in a modern shopping centre, the layout of the old streets and squares has been followed.

The churches

Directly facing the Hauptbahnhof is the **Petrikirche** (Tues–Fri noon–5pm, Sat 11am–4pm), boasting a colossal **Antwerp altar** from around 1520, which opens out to show expressively carved scenes of the Passion and Legend of the Cross, featuring no fewer than 633 separate figures. These can be seen between autumn and Whit; during the summer they're hidden behind the more modest painted section narrating the earlier part of Christ's life. A short walk down the central axis of Westenhellweg is the **Propsteikirche**, the one church retained by the Catholics when Dortmund embraced the Reformation. On the high altar is a colourful and crowded triptych from about 1490 by the Westphalian painter **Derick Baegert**, aided by his son **Jan**. Straddling the scenes of *The Holy Kinship*, *The Crucifixion* and *The Adoration of the Magi* is a view of a medieval town proudly girt with numerous towers and spires – the earliest-known depiction of Dortmund, and a poignant memorial to its long-lost splendours.

Continuing across Hansastrasse, Ostenhellweg leads to a large square overshadowed by the **Reinoldikirche**, which is named after the city's patron; he was stoned to death in Cologne, whereupon his coffin is supposed to have rolled all the way to Dortmund under its own steam. He's depicted as a young knight in a superb fourteenth-century wooden statue guarding the entrance to the chancel; the corresponding but later figure of a richly attired emperor is almost certainly Charlemagne. Unfortunately the choir area is fenced off, so you can only admire its abundant furnishings at a distance.

Immediately opposite is the **Marienkirche** (Tues–Fri 10am–noon & 2–4pm, Sat 10am–1pm), the oldest of the churches, with a nave which is still largely Romanesque. Its two masterpieces of International Gothic painting are the city's finest works of art. The high altar triptych dates from around 1420 and is by **Conrad von Soest**, a Dortmund citizen in spite of his name, and as endearing a painter as Germany ever produced. These panels of *The Nativity*, *The Dormition of the Virgin* and *The Adoration of the Magi* show the uniquely graceful and delicate "Soft Style" at its greatest, even though all were truncated in order to fit into a Baroque altar. The inner wings of *The Annunciation* and *The Coronation of the Virgin* have suffered such heavy paint loss that they're generally kept under cover, although the caretaker will open them if you ask. In the nave, the *Berswordt Altar*, a Crucifixion triptych, is about 25 years earlier, but has survived in much better shape. See also the late Gothic stalls – their irreverent carvings include, appropriately enough, a man downing a mug of beer.

The museums

The **Museum für Kunst und Kulturgeschichte** (Museum of Art and Cultural History; Tues, Wed, Fri & Sun 10am–6pm, Thurs 10am–8pm, Sat noon–6pm; €2; Ⓦwww.museendortmund.de) at Hansastr. 3 occupies an Art Deco building of the 1920s which was formerly a savings bank. Its highlight is a series of reassembled **interiors** – an eighteenth-century Westphalian pharmacy, the *Fliesensaal* (Tiled Room) with hunting scenes in Delft tiles, and a panelled music room from a bourgeois residence in Bremen. The most important of the rooms is *Der Raum als Gesamtkunstwerk* (The Room as a Complete Work of Art) by the Jugendstil architect-designer Joseph Maria Olbrich, in which every detail has been thought out in relation to its effect on the whole. Among the notable paintings is a stunning, sombre **Friedrich**, *Night on the Sea*. The archeology display is dominated by the *Dortmunder Goldschatz*, a hoard of fourth- and fifth-century gold coins found locally.

On the inner ring road is the **Museum am Ostwall** (Tues, Wed, Fri & Sun 10am–6pm, Thurs 10am–8pm, Sat noon–6pm; €2; Ⓦwww.museendortmund.de), devoted to the municipal collection of modern art, with changing exhibitions on the ground floor. Upstairs is a comprehensive display of Expressionism, dominated by what's arguably **August Macke**'s masterpiece, *Grosser Zoologischer Garten*, which experiments with the new Cubist forms in an anachronistic triptych format. Experimental sculpture includes several works by **Jospeh Beuys**, but the most eye-catching is **Wolf Vostell**'s *Thermo-Elektronischer Kaugummi* of 1970. Occupying a whole gallery, this has 13,000 forks and spoons grouped behind two barbed wire fences, and features 5000 pieces of chewing gum.

The **Mahn- und Gedenkstätte Steinwache** (Tues–Sun 10am–5pm; free), a short walk north of the Hauptbahnhof at Steinstr. 50, is housed in a building formerly used as a prison by the Gestapo. Between 1933 and 1945, thirty thousand opponents of the Nazi regime were detained here. Using original documents, photographs, personal effects and taped interviews, the exhibition comprehensively documents the rise of National Socialism, the resistance to it, and the brutal persecution of its opponents. Some of the rooms have been returned to their former state as prison cells, giving an added edge to the overall atmosphere.

Eating, drinking and entertainment

Inevitably, the **beer halls** are the focus for eating and drinking, and the city centre is ideal for a pub crawl. There's no need to move very far to sample the products of all the different breweries and the Markt makes the obvious place to begin.

Bass Münsterstr. 95. Jazz bar a short walk north of the centre, with regular live performances. Also serves food, including many vegetarian options, and has a small beer garden. Closed Sat & Sun.
Brauhaus Kronen am Markt Betenstr. 1. Kronen have had an uninterrupted presence on this spot since 1430, an even longer pedigree than the *Hofbräuhaus* in Munich. It currently has a Hausbrauerei which produces a dark beer and *Wenkers Utrüb*, a blond ale top-fermented with plenty of yeast sediment left in.
Brinkhoffs No. 1 Alter Markt. A flagship Gaststätte for the giant Union brewery, named after its premier product. Union's beers are generally milder, sweeter and maltier than those of the DAB group.
Café Hemmer Ostenhellweg 62. If hardly typical for Dortmund, this genteel salon is a good place for the archetypally German fare of *Kaffee und Kuchen*.
FZW Neuer Graben 167. *Szene* bar to the south of the centre, an easy walk away, with regular discos and live rock.
Holzknecht Hohe Str. 5. Offers Swabian as well as Westphalian dishes, and Stifts beer.
Hövels Hausbrauerei Hoher Wall 5. An offshoot of the Thier brewery, the main product line here is the deceptively named *Bitterbier*, a malty bronze-coloured brew; various seasonal beers are also produced. There's the bonus of a beer garden, while the food on offer is among the best in the city.
La Table Hohensyburgstr. 200, Syburg. The casino's restaurant is a renowned gourmet address, generally regarded as by far the best in the city. Evenings only.
Pfefferkorn Hoher Wall 38. Fine old Gaststätte of the Union brewery.
Zum Alten Markt Alter Markt 3. Traditional Westphalian cooking and the full range of Thier beers, which include a very dry *Pils* as well as a typical *Export*.

Entertainment

The spanking new Konzerthaus, Brückstr. 21 (Ⓣ02 31/22 69 62 00, Ⓦwww.konzerthaus-dortmund.de) is the venue for **concerts** by the Philharmonisches Orchester Dortmund, as well as visiting orchestras and soloists. **Opera** is performed at the Opernhaus at Platz der Alten Synagoge (Ⓣ02 31/16 30 41, Ⓦwww.theaterdo.de), while **drama** is staged at the Schauspielhaus and its Studio on Hiltropwall (Ⓣ02 31/5 02 72 22, Ⓦwww.theaterdo.de). The huge Westfalenhalle (Ⓣ02 31/1 20 46 66) south-west of the centre is used for **sports** and big shows such as **jazz** and **pop concerts**. Live Station, Am Hauptbahnhof (Ⓣ02 31/16 17 83) presents **discos** and live music from Fridays to Sundays.

Soest

SOEST, some 50km east of Dortmund, was a city of similar importance in the era of the Hanseatic League. Nowadays it's a whole world away in spirit, ranking as one of Germany's most delightful towns, yet it could so easily have been incorporated into the Ruhr conurbation. This proximity to the industrial heartland led to Soest being heavily bombed during the war, but restoration has been so deft that the scars have healed completely and there's scarcely a street within the fortifications which doesn't live up to the tourist board image of Romantic Germany. All the main buildings were constructed from a local sandstone whose deep lime greens bestow a distinctive character on the town and are well offset against the many red-roofed and whitewashed half-timbered houses. The play of light on these surfaces produces such magical effects it's little wonder that Soest has nurtured more than its fair share of German artists.

The Town

The town has never expanded much beyond its **Stadtmauer**, which survives minus its battlements, and it preserves a medieval air and layout, with a varied group of churches and secular buildings.

Rising majestically above the northern part of the Altstadt are the twin spires of the Gothic **Wiesenkirche** (Our Lady of the Meadows). This is a key building in German architectural history, when the favoured but problematic hall-church design finally acquired an elegance to match any other style of building. Although only a parish church, it's a cathedral in miniature, with an interior nothing short of stupendous. Slender unadorned piers thrust effortlessly up to the lofty vault, and the walls seem to be made of nothing but dazzlingly brilliant **stained glass**. These were inserted over a period ranging from just after the church's construction in the fourteenth century to the early sixteenth century, when money ran out before the south side could be glazed. The masterpiece of this assemblage, placed over the north portal, is from the final period, showing *The Last Supper* with a Westphalian menu of beer, ham and rye bread. Also of note are three large triptychs; that in the right-hand apse chapel was painted by **Heinrich Aldegraver**, a resident of Soest and one of Dürer's most accomplished followers.

On higher ground to the rear stands the **Hohnekirche** (Our Lady on the Hill). The same Protestant congregation owns both this and the Wiesenkirche, taking refuge in the cosier surroundings of this squat, box-like structure for the winter months. It's a Romanesque attempt of about a century earlier at creating a hall church. The rather plain result was, however, greatly enlivened by a sumptuous fresco decoration, much of which has survived. Also here are a couple of fine works of art in the *Passion* altar by the late fifteenth-century Westphalian painter known as the Master of Liesborn, and the remarkable **Scheibenkreuz**, a four-metre-high triumphal cross from about 1200, adorned with delicate reliefs of the life of Christ.

The heart of the city is soon reached from here by returning to Wiesenstrasse, then continuing via an old water mill up Am Seel. Dominating the skyline is the noble tower of **St Patrokli**, generally (if inaccurately) referred to as the **Dom**. This forms part of a resplendent Romanesque westwork, which is so grandiose a frontage that the rest of the building comes as an anticlimax, though it preserves a fine cycle of eleventh-century murals in the north transept apse.

Only a few yards in front stands the **Petrikirche**, towering over the square of the same name which also has the **Rathaus**, the only significant Baroque addition to the city. Again with a westwork as its most notable feature, the Petrikirche is Romanesque with the addition of a Gothic chancel. On the third piers of the nave are two *Crucifixion* frescoes attributed to **Conrad von Soest**, a major figure of the fifteenth century, and one of the few early German masters known by name. An important painting which may also be by this artist, *St Nicholas Enthroned with SS Catherine, Barbara and the two Johns*, occupies the altar of the tiny Romanesque **Nicolaikapelle**, situated behind the east end of St Patrokli. In spite of an unprepossessing exterior, the inside of the chapel is a real gem, another variation on the hall-church theme, with rounded column shafts dividing the space into two equal aisles. It's generally locked (officially open 11am–noon on Tues, Wed, Fri & Sun); if so, ask for the key at the **Wilhelm-Morgner-Haus**, the local cultural centre based in a modern building directly in front (Tues–Sat 10am–noon & 3–5pm, Sun 10.30am–12.30pm; free). This is named after Soest's own Expressionist painter, whose short career overlapped with the presence in the city of two of the movement's leading lights, Christian Rohlfs and Emil Nolde. A number of Morgner's canvases can be seen on the first floor, revealing a versatile talent which was to end at the age of 26 on a Flanders battlefield. Also on view is a selection of Aldegraver's engravings, his favourite and most effective medium.

From here, follow Ulricher Strasse south, turning left into Burghofstrasse, and you'll come to a complex of buildings, including a rare Romanesque house and the **Burghof** (Tues–Sat 10am–noon & 3–5pm, Sun 11am–1pm; €2), a sixteenth-century mansion now housing the local history museum. The main feature is the **Festsaal** on the ground floor, whose walls are covered with white stuccowork; the biblical subjects are original, the battle scenes and emperors skilful modern pastiches. Another small museum is housed in the **Osthofentor** (April–Sept Tues–Sat 2–4pm, Sun 11am–1pm; Oct–March Wed 2–4pm, Sun 11am–1pm; same ticket as Burghof), a stately Renaissance gateway which once formed the northeast entrance to the town, and a rare surviving adornment of the Stadtmauer. The display here is mostly concerned with medieval warfare; what looks like a spectacular modern sculpture in the attic turns out to be a fancy arrangement of 25,000 crossbow bolts.

Practicalities

Both the **Hauptbahnhof** and the **bus station** are located just outside the northern stretch of the Stadtmauer. The **tourist office** (Mon–Fri 8.30am–12.30pm & 2–4.30pm, Sat 10am–1pm; ⓣ0 29 21/10 33 23, ⓦwww.soest.de) is at Am Seel 5. Soest is at its liveliest during the five-day-long Allerheiligenkirmes, which is claimed as the biggest town centre **fair** in Europe; beginning on the Wednesday after All Saints' Day (Nov 1), it features a massive fairground, a horse market, and fireworks displays. Other local festivals include the Bördetag on a weekend in May and the Gauklertag on a Saturday in September.

Within the Altstadt is a broad range of **hotels**, of which the best budget choices are *Braustübl*, Thomästr. 53 (ⓣ0 29 21/41 66; ❸), and *Gasthof Drei Kronen*, Jakobistr. 37–39 (ⓣ0 29 21/1 36 65; ❹). More upmarket places include *Im Wilden Mann*, Markt 11 (ⓣ0 29 21/1 50 71, ⓦwww.im-wilden-mann.de; ❺), *Stadt Soest*, Brüderstr. 50 (ⓣ0 29 21/3 62 20, ⓦwww.hotel-stadt-soest.de; ❻), and the wonderful old *Pilgrim-Haus*, Jakobistr. 75 (ⓣ0 29 21/18 28, ⓦwww.pilgrimhaus.de; ❻), Westphalia's oldest inn with an uninterrupted tradition dating back to the fourteenth century. The **youth hostel** is just outside the southern section of the Stadtmauer at Kaiser-Friedrich-Platz 2 (ⓣ0 29 21/1 62 83; €13/15.70).

One consequence of the relentless flow of day-trippers from the Ruhr each weekend is an enormous choice of **restaurants** – over a hundred in all. Among the best are those in the last three hotels mentioned above. Alternatively, *Kanter*, which occupies the oldest house in Westphalia at Höggenstr. 1, serves Italian cuisine; *Biermanns*, Thomästr. 47, offers very expensive international dishes in designer premises; and *Am Kattenturm*, Dasselwall 1, is of similar quality and more reasonably priced. *Brauhaus Zwiebel*, Ulrichstr. 24, is a Hausbrauerei producing both light and dark beers. Many traditional **cafés**, such as *Café Fromme*, Markt 1, and *Café am Dom*, Am Vreithof 2, provide a relaxed atmosphere for *Kaffee und Kuchen*; while *Haus Sauerland*, Filzenstr. 4, is a café-restaurant which has been run by the same family for two centuries.

The food you should on no account miss is Soest's own contribution to culinary history, the famed **Pumpernickel**, a strongly flavoured rye bread popular throughout Germany at breakfast time. For the genuine article, go to *Wilhelm Haverland*; its factory at Markt 6 has been in operation since 1799, and you can choose from several different recipes in its side-street shop behind.

The Sauerland

The **Sauerland** stretches from the eastern edge of the Ruhrgebeit across to the border with Hesse. It's rural, upland country, supposedly containing a thousand mountains; nowadays it serves as an obvious holiday and recreation area for the teeming millions who live in the nearby cities of the Rhine-Ruhr conurbation. The Sauerland's attractions are quintessentially German – above all, it's good hiking country, with nearly 12,000km of marked footpaths, and four nature parks fall wholly or largely within its boundaries. Dotted with rivers and artificial lakes, it's also one of the country's main centres for **angling** and **activity holidays**, such as surfing, rowing, canoeing, sailing and hang-gliding, while riding in covered wagons Wild-West style has also been made into a regional speciality. Much of the Sauerland is of a surprisingly Alpine character for a place so far north, and **winter sports** help to keep its tourist trade going all year round. The soft local spring water is a crucial ingredient in Sauerland **beers**. Warsteiner's *Pils*, dubbed "the queen of beers" for its delicate taste, is Germany's best-selling brew, and is also heavily promoted abroad. Sauerland water, moreover, plays a key role in the economy of the Ruhrgebeit, and the great **dams** of the region are key features of the German inland waterway system.

A short bus ride south of Soest is a ten-kilometre-long artificial lake, the **Möhnesee**. The northern bank has been developed as a holiday resort area for angling and watersports, and **cruises** depart from Günne, Delecke and Körbecke from April to October. Between these first two villages is the famous dam which, though not the largest, was the prime target of the "Dambusters" (see box), due to its proximity to the industrial centres. Controlling the flow of the River Heve into the River Ruhr, it's 650m long and 40m high; when it was breached, 134 million tonnes of water gushed out into the countryside. Now long repaired, it's one of four footbridges interspersed at fairly regular intervals allowing walkers to cross over to the opposite bank of the lake. This has been left in its natural state and a southerly arm, the **Hevesee**, is a protected area for birdlife.

The obvious star among the Sauerland towns is **ALTENA**, 40km southeast of Dortmund. It has a superb setting deep in the valley of the River Lenne, high

The Dambusters

The importance of the Ruhr dams to the economy of the Third Reich was highlighted by the famous "**Dambusters**" episode of World War II (told in Paul Brickhill's book and in the popular film which, however, wasn't shot on location). At the time, these massive concrete structures would hardly have been grazed by existing explosives. In order to penetrate them, the inventor **Barnes Wallis** developed enormous ten-ton bombs which skipped across the water surface like a pebble, sinking behind the defensive nets and lodging themselves against the weakest point of the dams' walls. These "**bouncing bombs**" were dropped with devastating effect by the Lancasters of 617 Squadron, commanded by Wing Commander Guy Gibson, on May 17, 1943. Such havoc was caused by the ensuing flooding, which destroyed 123 factories, 25 bridges and 30 square kilometres of arable land, that it was estimated to have taken the equivalent of several months' work by 100,000 men to repair the damage – a telling blow to the whole Nazi war effort and a major propaganda coup. This, at any rate, is how the evidence has traditionally been presented. Latest research suggests that the claims were exaggerated, and that the Möhne dam, far from being wrecked, was eventually repaired. Fifty-six members of 617 Squadron were killed in the raid. "If only I'd known," Barnes Wallis said when he discovered the RAF losses, "I'd never have started this."

above which is the massive **Burg** (Tues–Fri 9.30am–5pm, Sat & Sun 11am–6pm; €5; Ⓦ www.burg-altena.maerkischer-kreis.de), one of the largest medieval castles in Germany. Built between the twelfth and sixteenth centuries, the complex consists of a central keep protected by an outer bailey and no fewer than three consecutive gateways. The world's first **youth hostel**, with its dorm of wooden bunks standing in triple tiers, has been converted into one of several museums in the Burg. Elsewhere, several rooms have been restored in period style. Highlights include the **Stadthalle** by the entrance, with its carved Renaissance chimneypiece; the **Grosser Saal**, with a notable collection of pewter; and the **Burgkapelle**, adorned with retables from Antwerp and Cologne and a graceful fifteenth-century *Madonna and Child* made from Bamberg sandstone.

In the far south of the Sauerland is the **Naturpark Rothaargebirge** (Red-Haired Mountains), a range covered with conifers and deciduous woods. Best-known as winter-sports country, its main resort is **WINTERBERG**, the terminus of a branch railway from Bestwig, on the main Wuppertal to Kassel line. As well as the pistes, Winterberg has an indoor skating rink, and bobsleigh and toboggan runs, while international dog-sleigh races are held each January. The town stands at the foot of the **Kahler Asten**, which at 841m is the highest peak in the Sauerland; it's covered with snow for about a third of the year, and the average winter temperature is freezing point. On the summit is an observation platform (€1), which commands a huge panorama of the district.

Paderborn

The cathedral and market city of **PADERBORN** lies some 55km northeast of Soest, just before the north German plain gives way to the Teutoburg Forest. It's a characterful place, with a variety of archeological and artistic attractions to add to the geological curiosity from which it derives its name, meaning "source of the Pader". This, the country's shortest river at a mere 4km in length, rises in a park, the Paderquellgebiet, in the heart of the city. It's formed by the surfacing of more than two hundred warm springs, which pour out over 5000 litres of water per second.

The City

The **Paderquellgebiet**, right in the centre of the city, is an idyllic spot and makes the obvious place to begin any tour, offering as it does the best view of the city's two main churches – the twin-towered **Kloster Abdinghof** in the foreground, with the massive single steeple of the Dom rearing up behind.

During postwar rebuilding of the city, the foundations of the **Carolingische Kaiserpfalz**, the site of Charlemagne's momentous meeting with Pope Leo III in 799 which led to the foundation of the Holy Roman Empire, were discovered just to the north of the Dom; they had been hidden from view since a fire destroyed the building in the year 1000. Soon it became the most exciting archeological site in the country, and was excavated in the 1960s, revealing the ground plan of a sizeable complex which included a king's hall, a church, a monastery and courtyards. Also unearthed was an open-air throne, now under cover beneath the Dom's north portal; you can see it by peering in through the protective glass. To the rear was found the replacement **Ottonische Kaiserpfalz** (Tues–Sun 10am–6pm; €2.50), dating from immediately after the 1000 fire and itself desecrated by another fire in 1165. This time the controversial decision was taken to go beyond a routine excavation, and to try and re-create its original form in as scholarly a manner as possible. In 1976 the palace made its belated reappearance, its pristine stonework making an odd contrast with the venerable status of the design. It now houses the regional archeology museum, but interest centres on the structure itself, as no original palaces from this epoch survive. The vestibule lies through a subsidiary building; to the right is the two-storey Ikenbergkapelle, while to the left is the great hall, which takes up the lion's share of the complex. Standing on its own near the entrance is the only authentic remnant of the palaces, the tiny **Bartholomäuskapelle**. As the very first hall church erected in Germany, it can claim to be the initiator of what was to become the pre-eminent national architectural form. Despite a glum exterior, it's very dapper inside, a classically inspired design of three aisles of rounded pillars crowned with flowery Corinthian capitals.

In preparation for Pope Leo's visit, Charlemagne ordered the construction of a no-expense-spared church which was almost immediately raised to the status of a cathedral; ever since, the city's history has been dominated by its ecclesiastical role. The present **Dom** is a cavernous thirteenth-century Gothic hall church whose tower, slit by numerous little windows, is a remnant of its Romanesque predecessor. It's entered by the southern **porch** (or "Paradise") whose portal is adorned with French-style figures. More refined carvings from a now vanished doorway can be seen on either side of the transept window; look out for the cartoon-like fables – a boar blowing a horn, a hare playing the fiddle, a crane removing a bone from a wolf's throat, and a fox dressed as a scholar to receive his diploma. Inside, the Dom resembles a museum of seventeenth-century heroic sculpture to the glory of the Prince-bishops, much of it by one of Germany's few Mannerists, **Heinrich Gröninger**. His masterpiece, almost facing you on entry, is the grandiose **monument to Dietrich von Fürstenberg**, complete with depictions of the buildings this bishop commissioned to transform the face of the city. The Dom's most enduring attraction returns to the animal theme and comes in the form of a puzzle, which you should try to work out in advance. Follow the signs marked *Hasenfenster* into the cloister garden; the tracery of one of the windows is the emblem of Paderborn, and a mason's trick which was celebrated in its day. This shows three hares running around in a circle, but, although each clearly has two ears of his own, it has only been necessary to carve one per creature.

The south side of the Dom faces the open space of the vast Markt, lined with tall Baroque houses and the Romanesque **Gaukirche**. In this setting, the lead-plated glass palace which houses a couple of shops, a café and the brashly modernist **Erzbischöflisches Diözesanmuseum** (Tues–Sun 10am–6pm; €2.50; Ⓦ www.dioezesanmuseum-paderborn.de) creates a strident impact, the more so as it masks some of the wonderful views of the Dom. In the museum basement, the **Schatzkammer**'s most valuable pieces are two inlaid reliquary cabinets, made for the Dom and the Adinghof in about 1100, and the Baroque shrine of Paderborn's patron, St Liborius. Upstairs, pride of place is rightly given to the *Imad Madonna*, a hierarchic mid-eleventh-century wooden statue named after its bishop donor.

The remaining Altstadt sights can be covered by means of a short circular walk. Following Schildern at the southwest corner of the Markt, you come to the city's most handsome building, the **Rathaus**, bedecked with arcades, gables and oriel windows, and fronted by a zappy facade. Erected in the early seventeenth century in the Weser Renaissance style, it was modelled on the patrician **Heisingsches Haus** just down the street. Up the hill from here is the **Jesuitenkolleg** from the end of the same century, whose church, like the one in Cologne, has a vast galleried interior with anachronistic Gothic pointed arches.

Further along Kamp is the sober **Dalheimer Hof** by the Westphalian Baroque architect, Johann Conrad Schlaun. Back downhill along Kasseler Strasse is the Romanesque **Busdorfkirche**, whose main joy is its tiny cloister. A couple of minutes' walk down Heierstrasse, then left into Thisaut, is Hathumarstrasse, with the oldest remaining half-timbered house, **Adam-und-Eva-Haus** (Tues–Sun 10am–6pm; free). This now houses the local museum, whose most eye-catching exhibits are a couple of exquisite drawings of the city by Schlaun, and a display of engravings by **Heinrich Aldegraver**, a native of Paderborn who was one of Dürer's most faithful followers. From here, the Dom is back in view and only a few minutes' walk away.

Paderborn's newest major attraction is the **Heinz-Nixdorf-Museumsforum** (Tues–Fri 9am–6pm, Sat & Sun 10am–6pm; €4; Ⓦwww.hnf.de), northwest of the centre at Fürstenallee 7 (reached by bus #11). It's the largest computer museum in the world, and traces the entire history of information technology from ancient times right up to the present day.

Practicalities

Paderborn's **Hauptbahnhof** is southwest of the centre, which is reached by turning right at the exit and continuing straight ahead. Buses #400 and #460 provide at least an hourly service to the **airport** (Ⓣ0 29 55/7 70, Ⓦwww.flughafen-paderborn-lippstadt.de), which lies west of the city and has a regular link with Air Berlin to London Stansted. The **tourist office** is at Marienplatz 2a (Mon–Fri 9.30am–6pm, Sat 9.30am–2pm; Ⓣ0 52 51/88 29 80, Ⓦwww.paderborn.de).

Centrally sited **hotels** include *Haus Irma*, Bachstr. 9 (Ⓣ0 52 51/2 33 42; ❸), *Krawinkel*, Karlstr. 33 (Ⓣ0 52 51/2 36 63; ❸), *Cherusker Hof*, Detmolder Str. 1 (Ⓣ0 52 51/5 55 34, Ⓦwww.cherusker-hof.de; ❺), *Galerie Abdinghof*, Bachstr. 1a (Ⓣ0 52 51/1 22 40, Ⓦwww.galerie-hotel.de; ❻), and *Arosa*, Westernmauer 38 (Ⓣ0 52 51/12 80, Ⓦwww.arosa.bestwestern.de; ❽–❾). For once, the **youth hostel** is conveniently sited just a few minutes' walk from the main attractions at Meinwerkstr. 16 (Ⓣ0 52 51/2 20 55; €13/15.70), the continuation of Heierstrasse. The two **campsites** are both in the northern outreaches of the city – *Am Waldsee* at Husarenstr. 130 (Ⓣ0 52 51/73 72) and *Stauterrassen* at Auf der Thune 14 (Ⓣ0 52 51/45 04).

Among the best **restaurants** in the centre is that in the *Arosa* hotel; the *Ratskeller* in the Rathaus offers both Westphalian dishes and *neue deutsche Küche*. Concerts, musicals, dance, opera and jazz are performed at the ultra-modern PaderHalle, Heiersmauer 45–51 (Ⓣ0 52 51/2 50 01). The main **popular festivals** occur in July, including a Schützenfest on the second weekend. There's also a beer week in October.

Detmold and the Southern Teutoburg Forest

Some 30km northeast of Paderborn is **DETMOLD**, the capital of the former Lippe principality, which makes the obvious base for seeing the varied attractions of the southern part of the **Teutoburg Forest** (Teutoburger Wald). If you're understandably baffled by the competing claims of Germany's innumerable forests, then this is one with a difference, adding extra natural, historical and artistic delights to the usual woodland trails.

The Town

An old jingle, quoted ad infinitum in tourist brochures and on billboards all over town, describes Detmold as *eine wunderschöne Stadt* (a wonderful town). That ranks as something of an exaggeration, but it's an agreeable place nonetheless, with a far more laid-back approach to life than is usual in Germany. Lange Strasse, the Altstadt's main thoroughfare, and the streets around, such as Bruchstrasse, Schülerstrasse, Krumme Strasse and Exterstrasse, are lined with large **half-timbered houses**, interspersed with self-confident stone buildings of the Wilhelmine epoch. However, easily the most attractive street is the venerable and smaller-scale Adolfstrasse, running parallel to and east of Lange Strasse.

North of the Markt is a green area centred on the **Residenzschloss** (guided tours daily: April–Oct at 10am, 11am, noon, 2pm, 3pm, 4pm & 5pm; Nov–March at 10am, 11am, noon, 2pm, 3pm & 4pm; €3.50; Ⓦwww.schloss-detmold.de), which is surrounded by water on three sides. The keep of the medieval fortress was incorporated into the present Renaissance structure, which was progressively shorn of its defensive features down the years. It remains in the possession of the descendants of the counts (later princes) of Lippe who built it. The interior was transformed in the eighteenth and nineteenth centuries according to the tastes of the time, but the most valuable adornment is a superb set of seventeenth-century Brussels tapestries of *The Life of Alexander the Great*, woven from cartoons made by the great French artist Charles Le Brun.

From here, the **Lippisches Landesmuseum** (Tues–Fri 10am–6pm, Sat & Sun 11am–6pm; €3; Ⓦwww.lippisches-landesmuseum.de) is reached down Ameide, to the rear of the Schloss. It's housed in two buildings, with natural history in one, archeology, local history and folklore in the other. The second building has a number of reconstituted period rooms, and displays on the history of fashion and on local agriculture, incorporating a rebuilt tithe barn and granary.

The Landesmuseum makes a good prelude to the spectacular **Westfälisches Freilichtmuseum** (April–Oct Tues–Sun 9am–6pm; €5), the most important open-air museum in Germany, which is being laid out at the southern side of the town; to reach it, go in a straight line down the Allee, the continuation of Lange Strasse. When complete (which will not be for several years yet) it will comprise 168 redundant original buildings from rural Westphalia; currently just over a hundred are in place. These are grouped together according to region, thus giving a clear picture of the different construction styles. Apart from farmsteads and workshops of diverse kinds, you can see water mills and windmills, humble privys, wayside chapels and a complete school. The whole way of life associated with these buildings is preserved as well – thus the traditional crafts of weaving, spinning, pottery, milling and forging are demonstrated, farmyard animals are reared, and the gardens are planted to give a practical yield of vegetables. Reasonably priced lunches are available at the eighteenth-century inn *Zum Wilden Mann* on the main street of the Paderborn village, less substantial fare at *Tiergartenkrug* near the Tecklenburg and Minden group of houses.

Practicalities

Detmold's **Bahnhof** is situated next to the **bus station**, just a short walk from the centre of town: turn left along Bahnhofstrasse, then right into Paulinenstrasse and you'll reach the historic area down to the left. The **tourist office** (April–Oct Mon–Fri 10am–6pm, Sat 11am–2pm; Nov–March Mon–Thurs 10am–4pm, Fri 10am–2pm; Ⓣ0 52 31/97 73 28, Ⓦwww.detmold.de) is in the Rathaus, Markt 5.

There are plenty of **private rooms** and small **pensions** (❶–❸) in the surrounding area (most of which are only practical if you've got your own transport), but only a couple in Detmold itself. The cheapest **hotel** in town is *Brechmann*, Bahnhofstr. 9 (ⓣ0 52 31/2 56 55; ❹). In the middle range there's *Nadler*, Grabbestr. 4 (ⓣ0 52 31/9 24 60, ⓦwww.hotel-nadler.de; ❺), whose *Café Stuck* serves good bistro-type meals. There are three excellent upmarket choices in *Detmolder Hof*, Lange Str. 19 (ⓣ0 52 31/9 91 20, ⓦwww.ringhotels.de; ❻), *Lippischer Hof*, Willy-Brandt-Platz 1 (ⓣ0 52 31/93 60, ⓦwww.hotellippischerhof.de; ❻), and *Residenz*, Paulinenstr. 19 (ⓣ0 52 31/93 70, ⓦwww.residenz-detmold.bestwestern.de; ❻–❽). All of these have top-notch **restaurants**, though they're rivalled by *Speisekeller im Rosental* in the Stadthalle, Schlossplatz 7. The **youth hostel** is at Schirrmannstr. 49 (ⓣ0 52 31/2 47 39; €13/15.70) right on the edge of town; from Paulinenstrasse, turn right into Freilingrathstrasse, then left into Brahmsstrasse, and follow its continuation, Schützenberg, to the end. A varied programme of **drama**, **music** and **dance** is presented at the Landestheater, Theaterplatz 1 (ⓣ0 52 31/9 74 60, ⓦwww.landestheater-detmold.de).

Around Detmold

Four of the top sights of the **Teutoburg Forest** are within 10km of Detmold; at a push, it's possible to see them all in a day, following a southerly route. Unless you've got your own transport, however, a fair amount of walking is necessary.

The Hermannsdenkmal

Firstly, there's what can be regarded as Germany's equivalent of the Statue of Liberty, the **Hermannsdenkmal** (daily: April–Oct 9am–6.30pm; Nov–March 9.30am–4pm; €1; ⓦwww.hermannsdenkmal.de), situated on the **Grotenburg**, 3km southwest of the town; two buses go out daily (mid-May to mid-Sept only), or it can be reached on foot (20–30min) by gently ascending paths from the suburb of Hiddesen. The monument commemorates **Arminius** (or "Hermann"), a warrior prince of the Cherusci tribe who inflicted a crushing defeat on the Roman army in 9 AD, using techniques akin to modern guerilla warfare. To the Romantic movement, he was regarded (rather fancifully) as the first man with the vision of a united Germany, which was at long last to be achieved. Although the monument was sited as near as possible to what was thought to be the scene of his famous victory, this is now known to have taken place elsewhere. The completion of the project was entirely due to the single-minded dedication of the architect-sculptor **Ernst von Bandel**, who worked at it on and off from 1838 to 1875, according to the availability of funds. Resting on a colonnaded base, the monument is crowned with an idealized vision in copper of the hero brandishing his sword on high; the total height to the tip of the sword is 53m, and the figure weighs 76,865kg. From the platform there's a fine **view** over the whole range of the Teutoburg Forest.

The Vogel- und Blumenpark and the Adlerwarte

Following Denkmalstrasse you descend in less than 2km to the first of two ornithological treats, the **Vogel- und Blumenpark** (Bird and Flower Park; daily mid-March to Oct 9am–6pm; €4; ⓦwww.vogelpark-heiligenkirchen.de). This has over two thousand species of bird from all over the world, from miniature hens hardly bigger than insects to the large South American nandu. Particularly impressive is the collection of parrots and cockatoos, sufficiently domesticated to be left uncaged.

From here, you can follow the footpath to the right and continue in a straight line to the **Adlerwarte** (Eagle Watch; daily: March to mid-Nov 9.30am–5.30pm; mid-Nov to Feb 10am–4pm; €5; Ⓦ www.adlerwarte-berlebeck.de) in Berlebeck. This eyrie, commanding a fine panorama over the forest, serves as a breeding station and clinic for birds of prey, with around ninety of these magnificent creatures kept here permanently. Displayed on chains or in cages are all kinds of eagles – imperial, golden, prairie, sea, bald, martial, and the enormous and rare harpy – as well as falcons, hawks, kites, buzzards, vultures, condors, griffons and various breeds of owls. The site was specially chosen because of its suitability for **free flight**, and throughout the season there are daily demonstrations (March, April & Oct to mid-Nov at 11am & 3pm; May–Sept at 11am, 3pm & 4.30pm).

The Externsteine

The **Externsteine**, a further 3km south (just before the town of Horn-Bad Meinberg), is a jagged clump of sandstone rocks set by an artificial lake, a striking contrast to the wooded landscape to be found all around. It's one of Germany's most evocative sites, an enigmatic mixture of natural and man-made features, whose precise origin and significance has teased and baffled generations of scholars. Bus #782 passes nearby; a €1 charge is levied when the caretaker is on duty, but access is always free in the evening.

Adorning the bulky rock at the far right is a magnificent large **twelfth-century relief** of *The Descent from the Cross*, which was carved on the spot, making it quite unlike any other known sculpture of the period. Although Romanesque in style, it's imbued with the hierarchical Byzantine spirit, one of the few German works of art – illuminated manuscripts apart – so influenced. Some limbs have been lost, but its state of preservation is otherwise remarkable. Directly below is a worn carving, probably representing Adam and Eve entwined around the serpent. To the side is a series of caves, now closed off; one of these bears an inscription saying it was consecrated as a chapel in 1115. There's also a stairway leading up to a viewing platform at the top. The next rock, fronted by an open-air pulpit, retains its natural peak, below which is a roofless chapel with a circular window exactly aligned to catch the sunrise on the summer solstice. It's too upright to accommodate a staircase, but you can ascend from the top of the stumpy rock to the left by means of a little bridge bent like a bow; from the ground it looks precarious, but it is totally secure. The fourth rock, bearing a plaque depicting the coat of arms of the counts of Lippe, is again crowned with apparent danger, in this case a large stone which seems ready to fall down, but which is actually fastened with iron hooks, following the repeated failure of attempts to dislodge it.

Many are convinced that the Externsteine served as a centre of pagan worship; others maintain that the site's religious origins go back no further than the twelfth century, and that it's a re-creation of the Holy Places of Jerusalem, inspired by Crusaders' tales. What's known for sure is that it was an anchorite hermitage throughout medieval times, and that it then passed to the local counts, serving successively as a fortress, a pleasure palace and a prison, undergoing many alterations in the process, before being restored to its present form – assumed to be the original – early in the nineteenth century.

Lemgo

With its surprising vistas and architectural groupings, and the myriad delicate details on its buildings, **LEMGO**, which lies 12km north of Detmold, would be a strong contender in any competition to find the prettiest town in northern

Germany, especially as it has escaped the ravages both of war and of mass tourism. Many of the buildings from its sixteenth-century Hanseatic heyday survive, and are now immaculately cared for, with the merchant class which built them from the profits of foreign trade now replaced by a mixture of retailers, wealthy commuters (over half the population works elsewhere) and public bodies.

The Town

Breite Strasse, the main axis linking the southern part of town with the central Markt, is one of Lemgo's finest thoroughfares, dominated by the spectacular **Hexenbürgermeisterhaus** (Witches' Burgomaster House) at no. 19. The facade, with its elegantly tapering gables, its *Fall of Man* over the doorway and its two quite different oriel windows (something of a Lemgo speciality) adorned with the Seven Cardinal Virtues, ranks as one of the supreme masterpieces of the Weser Renaissance style. It was built in 1571, three years after the completion of the rest of the house, by a local man, **Hermann Wulf**. Originally commissioned by a merchant family, the house's present curious name derives from an occupant in a later, more mordant period, the notorious **Hermann Cothmann**. He was burgomaster of Lemgo at the height of the hysterical campaign against supposed witches between 1666 and 1681, apparently sentencing some ninety women to death. Inside, the **Städtisches Museum** (previously Tues–Sun 10am–12.30pm & 1.30–5pm, but closed since 1999 for restoration) appropriately includes a display of gruesome instruments of torture, as well as an exhibition on a more enlightened Lemgo citizen of the same period, **Engelbert Kämpfer**. A pioneering traveller in Russia, Persia, Java and Japan, Kämpfer had de luxe accounts of his journeys printed and published in his native town, which was then a leading centre of book production.

Just off Breite Strasse down Stiftstrasse is the **Marienkirche**, the Gothic hall church of a convent which was suppressed when Lemgo went over to the Reformation. It has one of the richest musical traditions in Germany and there's a small international festival in the first week of June. The choir is celebrated, the **swallow's nest organ** even more so. Built between 1587 and 1613, initially by a Dutchman, and then by two brothers from Hamburg, the latter is rated amongst the sweetest-sounding instruments in Europe. If you aren't lucky enough to hear it, the woodwork is still an artistic treasure in its own right, although sadly stripped of its original bright polychromy. Also from the Renaissance era is the **font**, the work of a local sculptor, **Georg Crossmann**, with unashamedly sensual figures of the Four Christian Virtues. Behind it are statues of the nobleman Otto Zur Lippe and his wife, masterpieces of late fourteenth-century funerary art.

The Markt and around

Beyond the end of Breite Strasse, past a fine series of gabled houses, you reach the **Wippermannsches Haus**, the only one of the great merchant buildings in the extravagant late Gothic style. Just a few paces away is the **Markt**, lined with a wealth of superb structures from the fourteenth century onwards. The **Rathaus** complex on the east side represents the changing building fashions in its photogenic jumble of arcades, pinnacles and gables. Its northern corner, the old **Apothekenerker**, is still used as a pharmacy, and has a magnificent oriel window. The gossamer carvings, again the work of Crossmann, include a frieze of ten famous scientists, while the columns of the upper windows show the Five Senses.

The south side of the square is fronted by the early seventeenth-century **Ballhaus**; beside it is the sixteenth-century **Zeughaus**, whose rear wall is painted in psychedelic zigzags. The stately Renaissance edifices on the west side are flanked by two prize-winning Modernist buildings from the 1970s imbued with motifs from Lemgo's past. If this is arguably too stridently self-confident, there can be no complaints about the northern frontage of the square, which also forms part of Lemgo's central axis, Mittelstrasse. Appropriately, this is the street most evocative of the Hansa; half-timbering was used extensively, and some of the mansions have nicknames deriving from their decoration, such as **Planetenhaus** (House of the Planets) and **Sonnenuhrhaus** (Sundial House). The buildings to the right also have handsome backs, forming part of the close of the Gothic **Nikolaikirche**, whose twin towers were later varied by the addition of contrasting lead spires. Its interior, a characteristic hall design, has an assortment of works of art of various periods and styles, including another early Renaissance font by Crossmann.

The Junkerhaus and Schloss Brake

Continuing to the end of Mittelstrasse, then straight ahead down Bismarckstrasse to Hamelner Strasse, brings you to the remarkable **Junkerhaus**, which is under long-term restoration, though there is limited access (Sun 3–4.30pm; €1). It's the obsessive single-handed creation of a totally eccentric local architect, painter and sculptor, **Karl Junker**, who was determined to bequeath his own vision of a dream house as a modern counterpart to the sixteenth-century mansions he knew so well. From the outside, it looks like the witch's cottage from *Hansel and Gretel*, while the interior is spookier than anything Hammer House of Horror ever produced; the sinuous woodcarvings are the stuff of nightmarish fantasies.

Returning down Hamelner Strasse, a sharp left into Pagenhelle before the start of Bismarckstrasse takes you to **Schloss Brake**, a moated Renaissance palace of the counts of Lippe, whose striking six-storey tower has a secret stairway leading to the most private apartments. The Schloss now houses the **Weserrenaissancemuseum** (Tues–Sun 10am–6pm; €3; Ⓦwww.wrm-lemgo.de), which has extensive collections of Renaissance paintings, sculptures, furniture and *objets d'art*. Of particular note are the canvases of *Lazarus Before the Rich Man's House* and *Christ Driving the Traders from the Temple* by the great architectural theorist **Hans Vredeman de Vries**; the ostensible subjects are mere foregrounds to spectacularly detailed perspective views. In the grounds are two old mills, the **Schlossmühle** and the **Ölmühle** (Sat 2–5pm, Sun noon–5pm; free), together with the miller's house, now fitted out as the **Mühlenmuseum** (Tues–Sun 10am–12.30pm & 2–5pm; free).

Practicalities

Lemgo's **Bahnhof**, the dead-end of a short branch line, is just to the south of the Altstadt; **buses** operate from the bays in front. The **tourist office** is just off the Markt at Kramerstr. 1 (Mon–Fri 9am–5pm, Sat 9am–1pm; Ⓣ0 52 61/9 88 70, Ⓦwww.lemgo.de or www.lemgo-marketing.de).

Centrally located **hotels** include *Hansa*, Breite Str. 14 (Ⓣ0 52 61/9 40 50, Ⓦwww.hansa-hotel.de; ❺), *Lemgoer Hof*, Detmolder Weg 14 (Ⓣ0 52 61/9 76 70, Ⓦwww.lemgoer-hof.de; ❻), and *Schlosshotel Stadtpalais*, Papenstr. 24 (Ⓣ0 52 61/9 49 90; ❻). Further out are several budget options, including *Gasthof Zum Landsknecht*, Herforder Str. 177 (Ⓣ0 52 61/6 82 64; ❷), and *Zum Ilsetal*, Sommerhäuschenweg 45 (Ⓣ0 52 61/51 77; ❹). The **campsite** *Alte Hansestadt Lemgo* (Ⓣ0 52 61/1 48 58, Ⓕ18 83 24) has a riverside setting at Regentorstr. 106 between Schloss Brake and the Altstadt. Among a wide choice of **restaurants**, that in the aforementioned *Schlosshotel Stadtpalais* and the cosy *Zur Neustadt*, Breite Str. 40, stand out.

Minden

The one-time prince-bishopric of **MINDEN** lies in the far northeast of Westphalia, close to the border with Lower Saxony. Its strategic location, at an easily fordable point of the River Weser, has meant that military affairs have dominated its history: the old ramparts were converted into a full-blown fortress by the Swedes during the Thirty Years' War; it was the scene of a decisive battle in 1759 in which the British and Prussians defeated the French; and, during the Napoleonic Wars, it was equipped with the latest defensive systems as a leading Prussian frontier town, a role it retained until the unification of Germany in 1871. Unable to expand and industrialize because of its role as a fortress, the city kept its historic appearance until the last war, when its strategic importance inevitably led to severe aerial bombardment.

The City

The Altstadt is dominated by the **Dom** (ⓦwww.dom-minden.de), whose massive westwork, with two subsidiary towers stuck like glue to the main belfry, is in the severest form of Romanesque. The main body of the building, however, is a hall church, erected in the late thirteenth century in a pure early Gothic style; this has a light and airy feel, thanks to the huge windows decorated with highly elaborate tracery. On the south transept wall is a frieze of Apostles, the remnant of a former Romanesque rood screen; from the same period is the bronze *Minden Crucifix*, the Dom's most important work of art. However, the one currently displayed here is a copy; the original is in the **Schatzkammer** (Tues, Thurs, Sat & Sun 10am–noon, Wed & Fri 3–5pm; free) in the Haus am Dom opposite. Among many other valuable items, note the gilded twelfth-century reliquary of St Peter.

Just beyond lies the Markt, whose north side is taken up by the **Rathaus**. Its lower storey, featuring an arcaded passageway, is contemporary with the Dom; the upper part is late Renaissance. Continuing up the steps from here takes you to the best-preserved part of the Altstadt, centred on Martinikirchhof. On this square are two survivors of the Prussian garrison buildings, the **Körnermagazin**, where weapons were stored, and the **Martinihaus**, which served as the bakery. Also here is the **Schwedenschänke**, used by the Swedish troops as their refectory during the Thirty Years' War. **St Martini** itself is the pick of Minden's gaunt and blackened parish churches, with a dignified interior housing notable furnishings – late Gothic stalls, Renaissance pulpit and wrought-iron font – and a magnificent organ, partly dating back to the sixteenth century.

Just off the square on Brüderstrasse is the **Alte Münze**, formerly the house of the master of the mint; today, it's a Greek restaurant. A rare example of Romanesque civil architecture, it owes its survival to the fact that it was subsequently embellished according to the tastes of the time (with a stepped gable in the Gothic period, and an oriel window in the Renaissance). Mansions in the characteristic Weser Renaissance style are dotted all over the quarter – the finest are on Bäckerstrasse, Am Scharn and Papenmarkt. The densest concentration, however, is on Ritterstrasse, where five houses have been adapted to contain the **Mindener Museum** (Tues–Sun 11am–5pm; €1.50). Displayed in two courtyards are fragments of sculptural decoration from buildings such as these; see in particular a wonderful *Story of Samson*. Upstairs, along with the usual folklore displays, there's a room devoted to the **Battle of Minden**, a turning point in the Seven Years' War. Its outcome was to a large extent determined by the British infantry's successful assault on the French cavalry – the first time such a rash role reversal had ever been attempted.

Minden's favourable geographical position led to its development as the hub of the German inland water transport system, and it's from this function that its main present-day attraction derives. To the northern part of the city is the **Wasserstrassenkreuz** (Waterway Junction; Ⓦwww.wsa-minden.de), which is unique in Europe. The most eye-catching feature is the surrealistic **Kanalbrücke** (Canal Bridge), a 375-metre-long aquatic flyover built between 1911 and 1914. This allows the **Mittellandkanal** – which stretches right across north Germany, linking the Rhine with the Elbe – to pass directly over the Weser. The volume of traffic was such that a second structure was added in 1998. The heart of the system is the fortress-like **Schachtschleuse** (Great Lock), which shifts 12,000 cubic metres of water while transferring ships from canal to river or vice versa in just seven minutes. Alongside is the exhibition hall (April–Oct Mon–Sat 9am–5pm, Sun 9am–6pm; €1), which explains the layout and working of the Wasserstrassenkreuz by means of models and diagrams. A series of paths enable you to explore the area on foot, but it's far more fun to take a **cruise**. Run by the Mindener Fahrgastschiffahrt (Ⓣ05 71/6 48 08 00, Ⓦwww.mifa.com), these leave from the jetty immediately opposite the Schachtschleuse. There's a choice of fifty- and ninety-minute trips, costing €5 and €7 respectively. The former departs six times daily in the high season (mid-May to mid-Sept), and three times a day for the six weeks before and after these dates. Though the longer cruise is the more enticing, taking in a short stretch of the Weser as well as the harbour, it only runs once daily (Mon–Sat at 2pm in low season, 3pm in high season, Sun at 10.15am throughout the season). Longer stretches up and down the Weser can also be sailed from here.

Practicalities

Minden's **Hauptbahnhof** is on the right side of the Weser; its situation, a good twenty minutes' walk from town, is explained by the fact that it was built as part of the Prussian fortifications, and has three small forts grouped in a semi-circle around it. The **tourist office** (Mon–Fri 8am–1pm & 2–5pm, Sat 9am–1pm; Ⓣ05 71/8 29 06 59, Ⓦwww.minden.de) is at Domstr. 2. There are only a handful of conveniently located **hotels**. These include *Wappenkrug*, Marienstr. 121 (Ⓣ05 71/4 52 92; ❸), *Altes Gasthaus Grotehof*, Wettinerallee 14 (Ⓣ05 71/5 04 50, Ⓦwww.grotehof.de; ❺), *Stadthotel Kronprinz*, Friedrich-Wilhelm-Str. 1–3 (Ⓣ05 71/93 40 80; ❻), and *Silke*, Fischerglacis 21 (Ⓣ05 71/82 80 70, Ⓦwww.hotel-silke.de; ❻). Other cheaper options tend to be far out – such as *Grashoff*, Bremer Str. 83 (Ⓣ05 71/4 18 34; ❸), in the suburb of Todtenhausen, site of the Battle of Minden. Among the best places to **eat** and **drink** are the *Ratskeller*, Markt 1, the vegetarian *Vita Table*, Hahler Str. 14a, and the fish specialist *Zum Fishbäcker*, Obermarktstr. 34.

Travel details

Trains

Cologne to: Aachen (every 20min; 45min); Bonn (frequent; 20min); Dortmund (frequent; 1hr 10min); Duisburg (frequent; 40min); Düsseldorf (frequent; 25min); Essen (frequent; 50min); Hannover (frequent; 2hr 50min); Münster (frequent; 1hr 45min); Soest (hourly; 2hr 20min); Wuppertal (hourly; 30min).
Dortmund to: Aachen (hourly; 1hr 50min); Düsseldorf (frequent; 50min); Essen (frequent; 25min); Hannover (hourly; 2hr); Minden (hourly; 1hr 15min); Münster (hourly; 30min).
Düsseldorf to: Duisburg (frequent; 15min); Essen (frequent; 30min); Münster (frequent; 1hr 30min); Soest (4 daily; 1hr 20min); Wuppertal (every 30min; 40min).
Münster to: Bremen (frequent; 1hr 15min); Essen (frequent; 55min); Osnabrück (frequent; 25min); Wuppertal (hourly; 1hr 25min).

6

Bremen and Lower Saxony

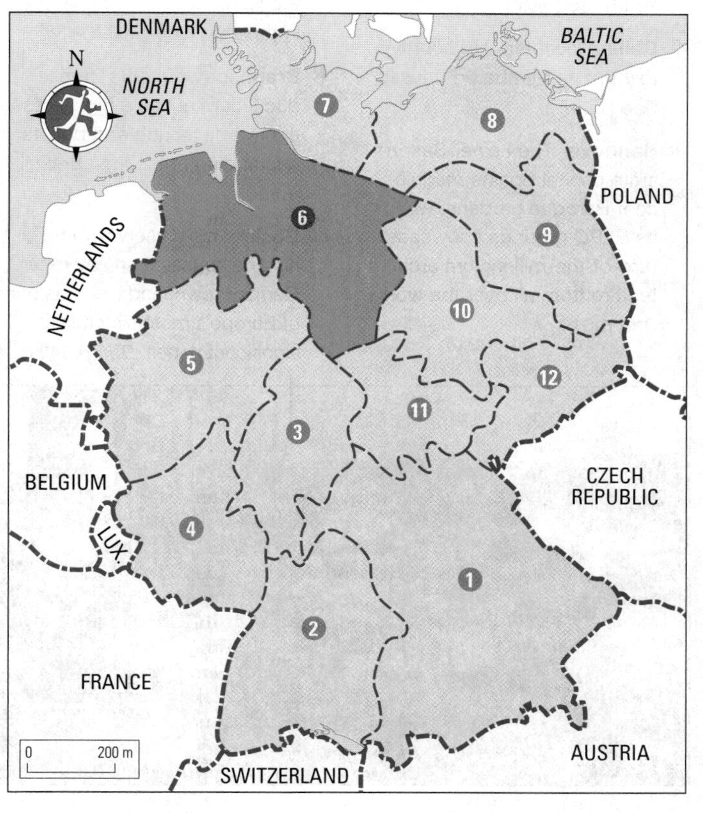

CHAPTER 6

Highlights

* **Bremen** This proud city-state offers several spectacular new attractions in addition to a fine legacy of historic sights. See p.582

* **Lüneburg** The best-preserved of Germany's old brickwork cities gives its name to the famous heathland to the south. See p.601

* **Celle** A beautiful old courtly town of half-timbered houses. See p.607

* **Hannover** The Lower Saxon state capital boasts magnificent Baroque gardens, while its EXPO grounds showcase turn-of-the-millennium architecture from all over the world. See p.610

* **Hameln** A pretty town with a picturesque setting on the River Weser, which will forever be associated with the Pied Piper legend. See p.622

* **Hildesheim** The wonderful legacy of the first great flourishing of Northern Europe's first indigenous artistic style, the Romanesque, can be seen in this city. See p.627

* **Braunschweig** This former ducal capital has a highly distinctive cityscape and boasts oustanding museums. See p.633

* **Goslar** This preserves more historic houses than any other German town, and also has one of Europe's most historically significant mines. See p.642

△ View of Lüneburg from the Wasserturm

6

Bremen and Lower Saxony

The Land of **Lower Saxony** (Niedersachsen) only came into being in 1946, courtesy of the British military authorities. In forging this new province, the former **Kingdom of Hannover** – which had shared its ruler with Britain between 1714 and 1837, but which had later been subsumed into Prussia – was used as a basis. To it were added the two separate ex-duchies of **Braunschweig** and **Oldenburg**, plus the minute but hitherto seemingly indestructible principality of **Schaumburg-Lippe**. In spite of this diverse patchwork, the Land has strong historical antecedents, forming the approximate area inhabited by the Saxon tribes during the Roman period and the Dark Ages. In accordance with the general north–south divide, the Reformation took strong root in most of Lower Saxony.

Geographically, Lower Saxony is highly diverse. It contains much of Germany's sparse provision of **coastline** and **islands**, behind which stretches a flat landscape, at times below sea level. Further south is the monotonous stretch of the North German Plain, but this gives way to the **Lüneburg Heath** to the east, and to highland countryside further south, in the shape of the hilly region around the **River Weser** and the gentle wooded slopes of the **Harz** mountains. Although it is the most extensive Land after Bavaria, it has a very low population density. None of its cities is as big as the old Hanseatic port of **Bremen**, an enclave within the province, but a Land in its own right, in continuation of its age-long tradition as a free state. Otherwise, there are just two cities with a population of over 200,000: the state capital, **Hannover**, which only came to prominence in the seventeenth century and is to be visited more for its museums and magnificent gardens than for its monuments; and the altogether more venerable **Braunschweig**, which still preserves considerable reminders of its halcyon period at the end of the twelfth century.

The province's smaller towns and cities present a fascinating contrast. **Hildesheim**, with its grandiloquent Romanesque architecture (revolutionary in its day, and of enormous influence throughout Europe), is the most outstanding from an artistic point of view. Nowhere is the mercantile heyday of the Hansa more vividly evoked than in **Lüneburg**, with its masterly brick Gothic showpieces. **Wolfenbüttel** is an early example of a planned town, and, with **Celle** and **Bückeburg**, is among the few places in Germany to be strongly marked by Italian-inspired Renaissance and Mannerist styles. Very

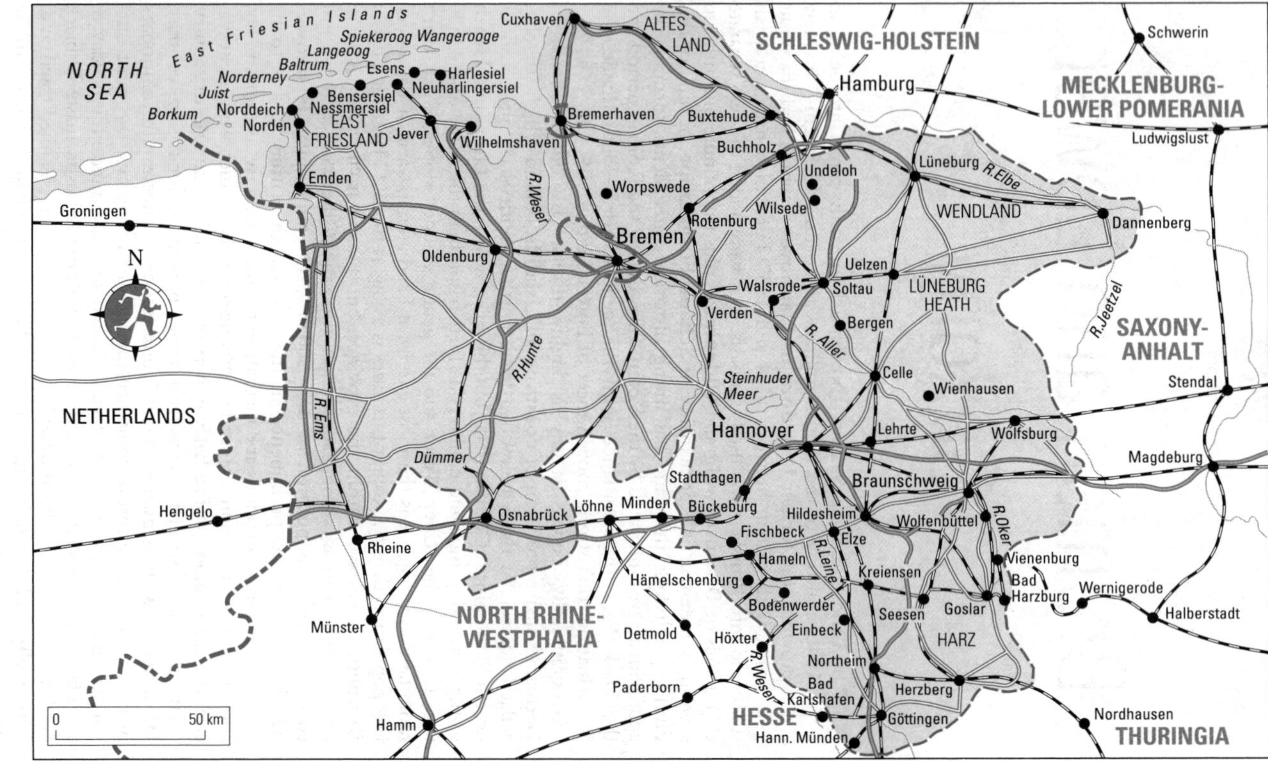
NORTH SEA
East Friesian Islands
Borkum
Juist
Norderney
Baltrum
Langeoog
Spiekeroog
Wangerooge
Cuxhaven
ALTES LAND
SCHLESWIG-HOLSTEIN
Schwerin
Hamburg
MECKLENBURG-LOWER POMERANIA
Ludwigslust
Esens
Harlesiel
Neuharlingersiel
Bensersiel
Nessmersiel
Norddeich
Norden
EAST FRIESLAND
Jever
Wilhelmshaven
Bremerhaven
Buxtehude
Buchholz
Undeloh
Lüneburg
R.Elbe
WENDLAND
Dannenberg
Emden
Groningen
R.Weser
Worpswede
Wilsede
Rotenburg
Bremen
Oldenburg
Uelzen
Walsrode
Soltau
LÜNEBURG HEATH
Verden
Bergen
R. Aller
R.Jeetzel
SAXONY-ANHALT
N
R.Hunte
Steinhuder Meer
Celle
Wienhausen
Stendal
NETHERLANDS
R. Ems
Hannover
Lehrte
Wolfsburg
Dümmer
Magdeburg
Stadthagen
Braunschweig
Hengelo
Osnabrück
Löhne
Minden
Bückeburg
Hildesheim
Wolfenbüttel
R.Oker
Fischbeck
Elze
Rheine
Hameln
R.Leine
Vienenburg
Kreiensen
Hämelschenburg
Bad Harzburg
Wernigerode
Bodenwerder
Seesen
Goslar
Halberstadt
Münster
NORTH RHINE-WESTPHALIA
Detmold
Einbeck
Höxter
HARZ
Northeim
R. Weser
Paderborn
Bad Karlshafen
Herzberg
Nordhausen
0
50 km
Hamm
HESSE
Göttingen
Hann. Münden
THURINGIA

different is the exuberantly ornate architecture of the archaic Weser Renaissance style, which reached its peak in and around the Pied Piper's stamping ground of **Hameln**. A mining town quite unlike any other in the world can be seen at **Goslar**, while **Göttingen** boasts one of Germany's most famous universities, and thus the liveliest nightlife in the province. **Einbeck**, home of *Bockbier*, is a reminder of the strength of the brewing tradition in these parts, and beer aficionados will find themselves spoilt for choice.

Getting around is seldom a problem, thanks to the usual efficient network of buses and trains. The only possible exceptions to this rule are in the Lüneburg Heath (in much of which there's a ban on fuelled transport) and in travelling to and from the islands off the coast, where ferry prices are relatively expensive.

Bremen and western Lower Saxony

Throughout much of its past **Bremen** was governed not by the nobility, but by its merchants, as a free city state – a sharp contrast to the hundreds of German principalities, some tiny, that were run by feudal barons right into the nineteenth century. Those centuries of self-government and economic power have marked the character of the city and its inhabitants. There's a certain air of self-assuredness, superiority even, and pride in their political independence that marks out the Bremen people – a hangover that's inextricably linked to the town's **Hanseatic** past. Bremen still governs itself (and its deep-water harbour of **Bremerhaven**, 60km to the north) as the **smallest state in the Federal Republic**. It's the country's oldest and second largest port too, safe from the North Sea on the banks of the River Weser. Imports of commodities from far-flung destinations – cotton, coffee, tobacco, tropical fruits and cereals – coupled with the export trade in wool and wood have been the foundation of Bremen's status as one of Germany's most prosperous cities.

The hinterland is entirely within Lower Saxony, and the city makes the obvious jumping-off point for exploring the western part of this province. This incorporates the area known as **East Friesia** (Ostfriesland), whose inhabitants have, over the centuries, resolutely avoided complete absorption by their German neighbours, retaining their own language and cultural identity. The **islands** off the coast, with their long sandy beaches, have, for the past century and a half, been immensely popular holiday resorts with the Germans themselves. However, they are among the parts of the country least visited by foreign nationals, not least because they are singularly ill-suited to modern-day tourists who want and expect to cover a lot of ground in a short time, and are frustrated by the ferries' dependency on weather and the tides, not to mention the lack of connecting services from one island to another. There is, nonetheless, a fine historic Friesian town in **Jever**, which is nowadays best-known for its bitter-tasting beer. Elsewhere in the western part of Lower Saxony, the main attractions are two cities: the former ducal seat of **Oldenburg** and the old episcopal centre of **Osnabrück**, which is also a major rail junction.

Bremen

Of the cluster of north German cities, it's **BREMEN** which is the most manageable. Though a city, it has an atmosphere reminiscent of an English country town, lacking the commercial buzz of Hamburg, and the ugly redevelopment of Hannover. In one or two days you can get a good impression of the place: the former fortifications where a windmill still stands, almost in the centre of town; the Altstadt, with its impressive showpiece public buildings; the Schnoorviertel, crammed with the former homes of fisherfolk; the bold, mural-painted backs of houses near the river; and the elegant nineteenth-century villas around the Bürgerpark.

In the eighth century the Emperor Charlemagne dispatched the Anglo-Saxon Willehad to the Weser to convert the Saxons there to Christianity. Seven years later a bishop of Bremen was appointed, and in 789 the first church was built where the Dom stands today. Two hundred years on, the city was granted free market status, giving independent merchants the same **trading rights** as those working on behalf of the Crown, a vital step for Bremen's economic expansion. By the eleventh century the city had also become an important centre for the Church, and over the centuries civic and ecclesiastical interests struggled for dominance. In 1358 Bremen joined the Hanseatic League, but the power of its prince-archbishops was not finally broken until the Reformation, when the city opted for Protestantism. Having survived a virtual cessation of trade during the Thirty Years' War, it became a Free Imperial City in 1646.

Although a latecomer to the role of a city-state, Bremen was one of just four which preserved their independence after Napoleon dismantled the old structures of the Holy Roman Empire. This status was renewed in 1949 when Bremen, together with its deep-water port of Bremerhaven, was declared a Land of the Federal Republic of Germany. Since then, it's had a reputation for being the most politically radical part of the country, with the SPD having held power without a break. One of their most significant acts was the establishment of a university, which has set up an alternative, multi-disciplinary curriculum in opposition to the normal conservative, highly specialized bent of the country's higher education system.

Arrival, information and accommodation

The **Hauptbahnhof** is just to the north of the city centre. In a pavilion immediately outside on Bahnhofsplatz is the **tourist office** (Mon–Wed 9.30am–6.30pm, Thurs & Fri 9.30am–8pm, Sat & Sun 9.30am–4pm; ⓣ04 21/30 80 00 or 0 180 05/10 10 30, ⓦwww.bremen-tourism.de); there's a second, smaller branch at Liebfrauenkirchhof (same hours). The **airport** (ⓣ04 21/5 59 50, ⓦwww.airport-bremen.de), which is 6km south of the city centre, is linked to the Hauptbahnhof by tram #6. A day ticket on the **public transport** network costs €4.60, but it's usually better value to invest in the the **ErlebnisCARD**, available from the tourist offices. This covers all public transport plus a wide range of reductions in entry prices; for one adult plus one child it costs €6 for one day, €8.50 for two days; for up to five people travel-

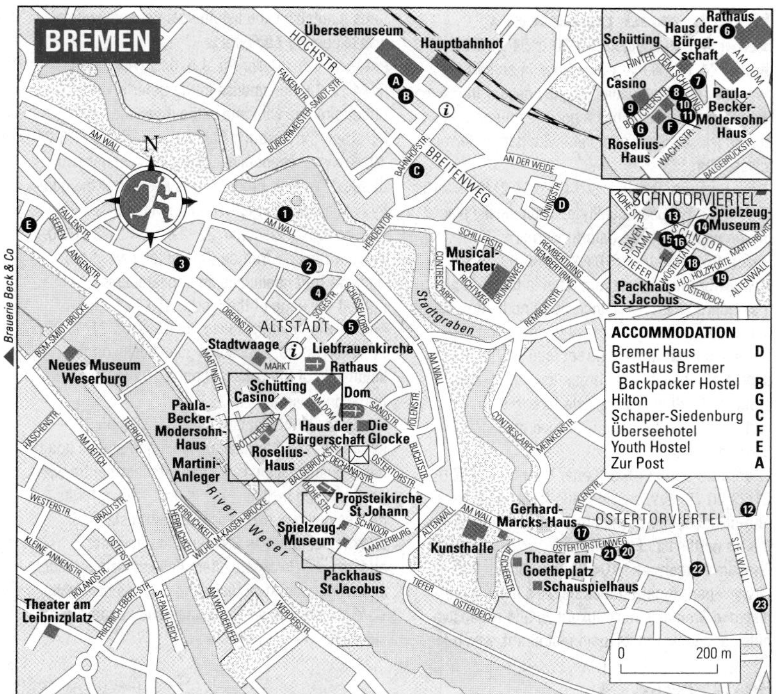

BARS & CAFES				**RESTAURANTS**			
Bistro Brasil	21	Kaffeemühle	1	Alte Gilde	3	Knurrhahn	5
Café Engel	17	Piano	12	Amstfischerhaus	15	Ratskeller	6
Café Knigge	4	Schnoor Teestübschen	18	Beck's in'n Snoor	16	Schröters	14
Café Stecker	2	Schüttinger	10	Flett	9	Souterrain	23
Café Tolke	13	Spitzen Gebel	7	Friesenhof	11		
Hegarty's	20			Kleiner Olymp	19		
lift	22			Kleiner Ratskeller	8		

ling together these prices rise to €12 and €18 respectively. Bremen is flat and therefore ideal for exploring by **bike**, which you can rent from the Fahrradstation opposite the tourist office. It charges €8 per day, with a €30 deposit on each bike.

The densest and most convenient cluster of **hotels** in the centre of town is near the Hauptbahnhof; not surprisingly, these are expensive. Budget accommodation is spread out all over the suburbs. Bremen's **youth hostel** is very well located in the western part of the Altstadt at Kalkstr. 6 (ⓣ04 21/17 13 69; €17.50/20.20), reached by tram #1 or #8 to Am Brill, but is expected to be closed for refurbishment until August 2004. The privately-owned *GastHaus Bremer Backpacker Hostel* is little more than a stone's throw from the Hauptbahnhof at Emil-Waldmann-Str. 5–6 (ⓣ04 21/2 23 80 57, ⓦwww.bremer-backpacker-hostel.de; dorm beds €16, singles €27, doubles €44, triples €60, quads €72). There's a good central **campsite**, *Internationaler Campingplatz Freier Hansestadt Bremen*, Am Stadtwaldsee 1 (ⓣ04 21/21 20 02, ⓦwww.campingplatz-bremen.de), on the north side of the Bürgerpark close to the university; bus #28 stops nearby.

Hotels and pensions

Bremer Haus Löningstr. 16–20 ⓣ04 21/3 29 40, ⓕ3 29 44 11. Middle-range hotel in an early twentieth-century building slightly east of the Hauptbahnhof. It also has a good restaurant, *Löning* (closed Sun), complete with garden terrace (closed Sun). ❻

Haus Bremen Verdener Str. 47 ⓣ04 21/94 94 10, ⓕ9 49 41 10. Good-quality pension ideally placed for the nightlife of the Ostertorviertel. ❺

Hilton Böttcherstr. 2 ⓣ04 21/3 69 60, ⓦwww.bremen.hilton.com. This is far from being a standard chain hotel, incorporating as it does one of the wonderful fantasy buildings on Bremen's most famous street (see p.586). It serves a Swedish-style breakfast buffet, and presents Mediterranean-style fare in its main restaurant, *L'Oliva*, Japanese food in *Captain Sushi*. ❼–❾

Landhaus Louisenthal Leher Heerstr. 105 ⓣ04 21/23 20 76, ⓦwww.landhaus-louisenthal.de. Attractive country house hotel with restaurant in the far northeast of the city. ❻

Park Im Bürgerpark ⓣ04 21/3 40 80, ⓦwww.park-hotel-bremen.de. This is by some distance Bremen's most luxurious and expensive hotel. In addition to its main restaurant, which features a notable wine list, there's the somewhat less expensive *La Fontana*. ❾

Peterswerder Celler Str. 4 ⓣ04 21/44 71 01, ⓕ44 72 02. Guesthouse in the Ostertorviertel, offering rooms with and without facilities. ❹

Schaper-Siedenburg Bahnhofstr. 8 ⓣ04 21/3 08 70, ⓦwww.schapersiedenburg.de. A member of the Best Western group, this is another of the quality hotels close to the Hauptbahnhof. ❻

Überseehotel Wachtstr. 27–29 ⓣ04 21/3 60 10, ⓦwww.ramada-treff.de. This hotel, part of the Ramada Treff chain, has an unbeatable location right at the edge of the Markt. ❼

Walter Buntentorsteinweg 86–88 ⓣ04 21/55 80 27, ⓕ55 80 29. Functional guesthouse on the south side of the Weser, about a 10min walk from the Schnoorviertel. ❸

Zur Post Bahnhofsplatz 11 ⓣ04 21/3 05 90, ⓦwww.bestwestern.com. This grand station hotel has a beauty salon as well as a fitness centre with good bathing facilities, but is best-known for its diverse culinary expertise. Its main restaurant, *L'Orchidée*, ranks as Bremen's top gourmet address; *La Dolce Vita* offers Italian cuisine; *Wabch* is an American-style diner and cocktail bar; while *Café Hauptmeier* serves homemade pastries and cakes. ❼–❾

The City

Although more than half a million people live here, Bremen doesn't give the impression of being a large city – partly because the main area of historical interest is the compact **Altstadt** on the Weser's northeast bank. The former fortification that surrounded it, the **Wall**, is now an area of green park, with a zigzagging moat forming a curve around the perimeter of the old city. To the east, the **Ostertorviertel** (known as *das Viertel* – "the Quarter") was the first part of the city to be built outside those city walls, and is today the liveliest part of town, the area to head for at night. North of the Hauptbahnhof, the **Bürgerpark** and **Schwachhausen** areas are worthy of a stroll for their many streets of villas, each discreetly advertising Bremen's fin-de-siècle wealth. The Bürgerpark is twice the size of London's Hyde Park, and apart from being beautiful in itself, contains old wartime bunkers too sturdy to be blown up, which have been decorated by local artists and now sport political murals.

The Markt

The central **Markt** is dominated by the **Rathaus** (guided tours Mon–Sat at 11am, noon, 3pm & 4pm, Sun at 11am & noon; €4), whose highly ornate **facade** – rich in mouldings, life-size figures and bas-reliefs, and with the undersides of its large rounded arches set with enormous "jewels" – is in Weser Renaissance style. It was added to the original Gothic structure between 1609 and 1612, two hundred years after the latter was first built. One of the most splendid of north Germany's buildings, it fortunately survived World War II undamaged. Inside, Bremen's civic pride is manifested in some splendidly decorated chambers, notably the main upstairs hall, the **Obere Saal**, and the small **Güldenkammer**, which has extravagantly carved Renaissance woodwork and allegorical paintings. Downstairs, the inevitable **Ratskeller** (guided tours, departing from the tourist office at Liebfrauenkirchhof, late April to early Oct Fri at 4pm; €8 including a glass of wine; see also p.590) ranks as one of the most distinguished in the country, not least because of its cellar of over six hundred German vintages, some of which are stored in the eighteenth-century barrels which double as partitions. Bottles of these wines can also be bought from the shop to the rear of the Rathaus at Schoppensteel 1.

On the left as you face the Rathaus is a ten-metre-high stone statue of **Roland**, nephew of Charlemagne, who brandishes the sword of justice and carries a shield bearing the inscription (in the *Plattdeutsch* dialect): "Freedom do I give you openly". Erected by the burghers in 1404 as a symbol of Bremen's independence from its archbishop, he's the city's traditional protector; as long as Roland stands, they say, Bremen will remain free. Roland's pointy kneecaps were used as a medieval measurement-check by local housewives: the distance between the two is the exact length of one *Elle*, by which cloth was sold. In 1989 he was de-Nazified when a time-capsule placed there in 1938, and containing documents from the time of the Third Reich, was removed. Poor Roland now spends his time staring at the much-disputed modern facade of the **Haus der Bürgerschaft** (Parliament Building), one of the ugliest edifices ever to disgrace a German town centre.

A happier postwar addition to the square is the bronze group of the **Bremer Stadtmusikanten** (Bremen Town Band) by the local sculptor, Gerhard Marcks. Rising like a pyramid, it shows a cock standing on a cat standing on a dog standing on a donkey, and is an illustration of an old folk tale retold by the **Brothers Grimm**. In fact, this is the town band that never was: en route to

△ Böttcherstrasse, Bremen

the city, the animals arranged themselves in the way depicted and started to make music. In so doing, they frightened a group of robbers away from their hideout and took over the house for themselves, remaining there ever after.

Surviving buildings from Bremen's Hanseatic heyday are rare, but include the restored patrician houses lining much of the rest of the Marktplatz, and the **Schütting**, the ritzy, sixteenth-century Flemish-inspired mansion with contrasting gables, which was where the guild of merchants convened. Round the corner on Langenstrasse is the equally imposing step-gabled **Stadtwaage**, the municipal office for weights and measures. Unser Lieben Frauen Kirchhof, the small square immediately northwest of the Rathaus, serves as a flower market. It takes its name from the **Liebfrauenkirche**, a hall church with contrasting Romanesque and Gothic towers and a number of built-in booths around its walls.

The Dom

On the opposite side of the Rathaus stands the **Dom** (ⓦwww.stpetridom.de), formerly the seat of one of medieval Germany's archbishops, but a Protestant church since the Reformation. Its brooding interior preserves its Romanesque arcades, but is otherwise predominantly Gothic in appearance. There are **crypts** at both ends of the building, one intended for the use of the emperor, the other for the archbishop. That to the west – which contains some notable works of art, including an eleventh-century *Enthroned Christ* and a magnificent thirteenth-century bronze **font** – had to be truncated when the huge twin-towered facade was erected in the thirteenth century. Its eastern counterpart preserves its harmonious original form, including a series of delicately carved capitals. The early sixteenth-century **organ gallery** is adorned with statues, including Charlemagne and Willehad, by the Münster sculptor Hinrik Brabender. From a century later comes the Mannerist **pulpit**, with its elaborate sounding board. Many finely carved **epitaphs** can be seen throughout the building.

Just inside the main doorway is the stairway to the south **tower** (May–Oct Mon–Fri 10am–5pm, Sat 10am–1.30pm, Sun 2–5pm; Nov–April Mon–Fri 11am–4pm, Sat 10am–1.30pm, Sun 2–5pm; €1), which can be ascended for a view over the Markt and the city. At the southeastern corner of the church is the entry to the **Dommuseum** (same hours; €2), which features a large panel of *The Man of Sorrows* by Cranach and two specially dimmed rooms containing ecclesiastical vestments and other treasures found in the graves of the medieval archbishops. Entered from outside is the **Bleikeller** (Easter Sat to Nov 1 Mon–Fri 10am–5pm, Sat 10am–2pm, Sun noon–5pm; €1.40), where lead for the roofing was stored. It contains eight mummies, whose bodies are perfectly preserved due to the lack of air. For three centuries, these have been popular if macabre attractions for visitors to the city, though mystery still surrounds the identities of some of the figures – one of whom was supposedly an English countess – and why exactly they were buried there. However, some are known to have been Swedish officers during the Thirty Years' War, while one was a pauper put there for experimental purposes in the eighteenth century, after the discovery of the other mummified bodies. Also on display are lapidary fragments from the Dom, including two impressive late Gothic tympana which adorned the now-demolished cloister.

Böttcherstrasse

Off the south side of Marktplatz is **Böttcherstrasse** (ⓦwww.zumboettcherstrasse.de) or Coopers' Street, a strange street which combines elements of neo-Gothic, Jugendstil, Expressionism and sheer fantasy. Once a humble alleyway in which barrel-makers lived and worked, it was transformed between 1923 and 1931 by the Bremen magnate **Ludwig Roselius**, who made much of his fortune from *Kaffee Hag*, the first-ever decaffeinated coffee. He commissioned local avant-garde artists, most notably **Bernhard Hoetger**, to effect the change. During the Nazi era, the whole street was to be demolished because it was considered corrupt art, but the charismatic Roselius persuaded the authorities to let it stand as a warning example, so to speak, of all that was considered bad in the arts.

The northern gateway to the street is guarded by a gilded relief of *The Bringer of Light* by Hoetger. A short way down, at no. 6, is the only old house, a fourteenth-century step-gabled building with a sixteenth-century facade, that's now known as the **Roselius-Haus** (Tues–Sun 11am–6pm; €5). This contains Roselius' collection of late medieval and early Renaissance art, the star pieces being a small *Man of Sorrows* by Cranach and a relief of *The Lamentation* by Riemenschneider. There is also an intriguing *Still Life* plus a couple of portraits by Gottfried Kneller, who later pursued a highly successful career at the British royal court. On permanent loan to the museum is the **treasury** of the Companie der Schwarzer Häupter, a charitable body, now based in Bremen, established by unmarried members of the German mercantile community in Rīga. In addition to some valuable documents, including their own statute book of 1416, this features some outstanding pieces of gold- and silverware from the sixteenth to the twentieth centuries. Highlights include a late Gothic reliquary of St George, Renaissance welcome cups made in Rīga and Lübeck, and two spectacular Baroque pieces from Augsburg – a tankard with the mounted figure of St Maurice and a salver illustrating the Fall of Phaeton. In the interconnected **Paula-Becker-Modersohn-Haus** (same hours and ticket) are a number of paintings by the eponymous artist, who lived and worked in the nearby village of Worpswede (see p.592).

At no. 3–5 on the street is the **Casino** (daily 5pm–3am), which offers a choice of roulette, blackjack, poker and gaming machines, with introductory films in German and English. Opposite, at no. 2, is a building which is now incorporated into the **Hilton Hotel**; it preserves some amazing decor, including a spectacular spiral staircase. Elsewhere on the street are boutiques, craft workshops, restaurants and the **Glockenspiel**, a carillon of Meissen porcelain bells in a revolving tower with ten wooden panels illustrating the history of transatlantic navigation and flight. It chimes hourly between noon and 6pm daily from May to December; at noon, 3pm and 6pm during the other months, except during frosty spells.

The pedestrian tunnel at the end of Böttcherstrasse leads to Martini-Anleger, the departure point for **harbour cruises**. These cost €8, and depart daily at 11.45am, 1.30pm and 3.15pm in March and October; at 11.45am, 1.30pm, 3.15pm and 4.45pm from April to September; and at 1.30pm and 3.15pm on Saturdays and Sundays only between November and February.

The Schnoorviertel

Tucked away between the Dom and the river is a small, extraordinarily well-preserved area of medieval fisherfolks' houses known as the **Schnoorviertel** (Ⓦ www.derschnoor.de). Dating from the fifteenth century, this is Bremen's oldest surviving quarter. It's worth a wander through the small streets, which have a toytown feel and are far too narrow for modern traffic to pass. Predictably, in being preserved the area has been prettified and now houses pricey specialist shops selling antiques, crafts and toys, as well as many restaurants, cafés and bars plus several theatres (see pp.590–91) Thankfully, it still manages to be a residential area too.

At the western edge of the quarter is the fourteenth-century **Propsteikirche St Johann**, a fine example of Gothic brickwork, whose towerless shape is a reflection of its original function as a Franciscan friary church. The house at Schnoor 24 contains the **Spielzeugmuseum** (April–Dec Mon–Sat 11am–6.30pm, Sun 11am–6pm; €1.50), a collection of historic toys. That at Wüste Stätte 5 is known as the **Hochzeitshaus** (Marriage House), and has its origins in the custom that couples from the surroundings of Bremen who got married in the city had to spend one night there. It's now a three-roomed "hotel" which can be hired by honeymooning couples – or anyone else for that matter. At no. 10 on the same alley is the **Packhaus St Jacobus**, the only historic warehouse in the city centre to have survived in its original form. It was restored in conjunction with EXPO 2000 and now contains the **ZeitRaum** (daily: April–Oct 10.30am–8pm; Nov–March 11am–6pm; €6; Ⓦwww.zeitraum-packhaus.de), an interactive permanent exhibition, using the very latest computer technology, on Bremen's history.

The Kunsthalle

Just east of the Schnoorviertel at Am Wall 207 is the **Kunsthalle** (Tues 10am–9pm, Wed–Sun 10am–5pm; €5; Ⓦwww.kunsthalle-bremen.de), one of the oldest municipal art galleries in Germany. The ground floor is mostly given over to changing displays of modern art, but also contains a Jugendstil room containing valuable collections of graphic art. Most of the outstanding group of watercolours by **Dürer** were for long thought to have been destroyed in the war, but were actually confiscated by the Soviets as war booty; negotiations for their return are still ongoing. Meanwhile a small panel of *St Onofrio* by this artist can be seen in the first room upstairs, along with **Altdorfer**'s earliest surviving work, *The Nativity*, and several examples of **Cranach**. The adjacent galleries contain Dutch and Flemish paintings: *Noli Me Tangere* is a successful co-operative composition between **Rubens** (who painted the figures) and **Jan Brueghel** (who did everything else); there's also a striking full-length *Duke Wolfgang Wilhelm of Pfalz-Neuburg* by **van Dyck**, and a *Portrait of a Man* by **Rembrandt** or a member of his immediate circle. In the small cabinet rooms to the side are works by earlier European masters, notably Italians, of which the most important are *Madonna and Child* by **Masolino** (one of very few works by this artist to have left Italy) and *A Doctor* by **Moroni**.

However, the gallery's main draw is its superb array of nineteenth-century and early twentieth-century painting. Among the French School, there are five canvases by **Delacroix**, including *King Rodrigo*. A room is devoted to the Nabis: the most impressive works here are *Homage to Cézanne* by **Maurice Denis** and **Vuillard**'s designs for the decoration of the former Champs Elysées Theatre. Other highlights are an important early **Monet**, *Camille*, and **Manet**'s *The Poet Zacharie Astruc*. Pick of the German works are **Beckmann**'s *Apache Dance* and *Self-Portrait with Saxophone*, **Kirchner**'s *Street Scene by Night,* and a comprehensive representation of the Worpswede colony, with some forty examples of **Paula Modersohn-Becker** on view around the landing.

Next door to the Kunsthalle is the **Gerhard-Marcks-Haus** (Tues–Sun 10am–6pm; €3.50; Ⓦwww.marcks.de) which contains sculptures, drawings and watercolours by the artist. Apart from the monument to the Bremen Town Band, Marcks is best known for the bronze doors and other works of art he made for a number of German cathedrals and churches to replace those lost in the war.

Out of the centre

Among several important museums outside the historic centre is the **Neues Museum Weserburg** (Tues–Fri 10am–6pm, Sat & Sun 11am–6pm; €5;

Ⓦwww.nmwb.de), which occupies a group of converted warehouses on the peninsula formed by the two arms of the Weser due west of the Altstadt. Devoted to art from the 1960s onwards, it features extensive displays of most of the big guns, such as Warhol, Kienholz, Beuys, Fontana and Serra.

A short distance downstream, on the south bank of the Weser, is Germany's most internationally famous brewery, **Brauerei Beck & Co** (guided tours: in German Tues–Sat 10am–5pm, Sun 10am–3pm; in English same days at 1.30pm; €3; Ⓦwww.becks.de). The visit takes in the brewhouse, where the brewmasters can be seen at work; the stables, with horses and wagons; the museum and cinema; and the lounge, where a glass of beer is served at no extra charge. Although Bremen's brewers' guild, founded in 1489, is the oldest in the country, Beck is a comparative newcomer, having been founded in 1873. The ubiquitous *Premium Pilsener*, an amber-coloured brew in a green bottle or can, is made primarily for export, and sold in over 100 different countries. Products bearing the *Haake-Beck* label are of superior quality and aimed at the home market; they include both a filtered and an unfiltered *Pils* (the latter known as *Kräusen*), as well as a dark beer.

Directly opposite the Hauptbahnhof at Bahnhofsplatz 13, the **Übersee-Museum** (Tues, Wed & Fri–Sun 10am–6pm, Thurs 10am–9pm; €5; Ⓦwww.uebersee-museum.de) celebrates Bremen's maritime tradition in a huge display of ethnographical objects from all the different countries with which local merchants traded. A recent addition to the city's ever-growing roster of museums is the **Universum Science Centre** (Mon, Tues, Thurs & Fri 9am–6pm, Wed 9am–9pm, Sat & Sun 10am–7pm; €10; Ⓦwww.usc-bremen.de), which occupies custom-built premises between Bürgerpark and the university, reached by taking tram #6 to Wiener Strasse. It's very much a hands-on experience, offering as it does more than 250 interactive exhibits.

Another newish attraction is the visitor centre of **Astrium** (guided tours Fri at 5pm, Sat at 11am, 1pm & 3pm, Sun at 11.30am; €16.50), the headquarters of the German aeronautics and space administration. Beginning at the tourist office counter at the airport, the two-hour tour covers the exhibition hangar and part of the ISS International Space Station that is being assembled there, including demonstrations on how experiments in space are carried out by ground control. In 2004, the space theme will be given a much larger presence with the opening of the **Space Park** by the riverside in the northwest of the city. This huge and ambitious theme park will be based around the Space Centre, offering simulated space travel and other special effects; there will also be a multiplex cinema, shopping malls, restaurants and a platform for open-air events.

The **Focke-Museum** or **Bremer Landesmuseum** (Tues 10am–9pm, Wed–Sun 10am–5pm; €3.50; Ⓦwww.focke-museum.de) is unfortunately rather a long way northeast of the centre at Schwachhauser-Heerstr. 240, though it's easily reached by tram #4. Laid out in an imaginative and informative manner, this traces the history of Bremen and its port, and has a collection of decorative arts. Among the most important exhibits are the original statues of Charlemagne and the seven Electors from the Rathaus facade. If you're out this way, it's well worth continuing to the nearby **Rhododendronpark** (daily 7.30am–sunset) which, in May and June, is ablaze with some 680 different species of wild rhododendrons and azaleas, plus another 1000 or so cultivated varieties. In the middle of the park is the new **botanika** (daily 9am–6pm; €9; Ⓦwww.botanika.net), which incorporates a discovery centre, authentic reconstructions of the natural habitats of wild rhododendrons in the Himalayas and Borneo, and a Japanese garden with cultivated rhododendrons.

Eating and drinking

In the gastronomic field, Bremen is renowned for its fish (particularly eel) specialities, best sampled in the *gemütlich* old restaurants of the Altstadt and Schnoorviertel. The city also has an excellently varied range of bars and cafés. For drinking and nightlife, the place to head for is the Ostertorviertel, in particular along Ostertorsteinweg and in the short yard called Auf den Höfen, near the junction of Humboldtstrasse and Am Dobben.

Restaurants

Alte Gilde Ansgaritorstr. 24. In the vaulted cellar of a seventeenth-century house, this is a good place for full meals, whether fish or otherwise. Closed Sun.
Amtsfischerhaus Schnoor 31. Fish speciality restaurant in the heart of the Schnoorviertel.
Beck's in'n Snoor Schnoor 34–36. Fine Gaststätte of the eponymous brewery.
Flett Böttcherstr. 3. In one of the fantasy houses in Bremen's most famous street (it has an impressive ceiling painted with floral motifs and walls covered with posters and photos), this is another leading choice for fresh seafood dishes.
Friesenhof Hinter dem Schütting 12. Excellent restaurant serving Friesian specialities.
Gerken Feldstr. 77. Popular Gaststätte in the Ostertorviertel.
Kleiner Olymp Hinter der Holzpforte 20. Another Schnoorviertel Gaststätte with a fish-based menu; it also has a good choice of beers, including the specially made *Schnoor-Bräu*, which is not available elsewhere.
Kleiner Ratskeller Hinter dem Schütting 11. Offers solid, reasonably priced *gutbürgerliche Küche* along with one of the widest ranges of beer in town.
Knurrhahn Schüsselkorb 32. One of the best and most inexpensive places for fresh fish. Open Mon–Wed 11am–7pm, Thurs & Fri 11am–8pm, Sat 11am–6pm.
Ratskeller Am Markt 1. The most celebrated example of a great national institution, this offers a wide range of dishes which are fairly pricey, though not exorbitantly so. It has an extraordinary wine list of around 650 vintages, all of them German and some extremely rare.
Schröters Schnoor 13. Gourmet restaurant in the heart of the Schnoorviertel.
Souterrain Sielwall 50. Good, basic pizza place on the main vertical axis of the Ostertorviertel.

Bars and cafés

Bistro Brasil Ostertorsteinweg 83. Open all night, with a tropical atmosphere – at its best in the early hours of the morning.
Brommy Hemelinger Str. 7. One of the liveliest and most popular hangouts of the Ostertorviertel.
Café Engel Ostertorsteinweg 31. Occupies a former pharmacy, whose furnishings it still preserves. If has good breakfasts and inexpensive daily specials, and pleasant outdoor seating in summer.
Café Knigge Sögestr. 44. Bremen's best (and best-known) traditional café, founded back in 1880.
Café Stecker Knochenhauerstr. 14. Along with the *Knigge*, another highly recommendable place for *Kaffee und Kuchen.*
Café Tölke Schnoor 23a. Serves a good range of teas, coffees and homemade cakes.
Hegarty's Ostertorsteinweg 80. Large Irish pub which serves good grub and often features live music.
lift Weberstr. 18. Internet café in a quiet Ostertorviertel side street. Open daily except Tues 3pm to midnight or later.
Kaffeemühle Am Wall 212. Café in an old windmill; also serves full meals.
Leierkasten Pagentorner Heimweg 13. Tucked away between Staderstrasse and Friedrich-Karl-Strasse, this excellent pub has the bonus of a leafy beer garden.
Piano Fehrfeld 64. Bustling bar in the Ostertorviertel which serves Mediterranean-style dishes.
Schnoor Teestübschen Hinter der Holzpforte 4. The ground-floor shop sells a huge variety of teas, which can be sampled in the cosy little café upstairs.
Schüttinger Hinter den Schütting 12–13. The only Hausbrauerei in the city centre; it makes a malty dark beer, a *Pils* and various seasonal brews, serves good-value meals and is frequently packed out at weekends.
Spitzen Gebel Hinter den Schütting 1. Tiny Kneipe directly opposite the entrance to Böttcherstrasse.

Entertainment

The best source of nightlife information is the tourist office, which is the city's main ticket-booking agency, and also publishes a free monthly **listings magazine**, *bremer umschau*. Also of use are two commercial magazines: *Prinz* (€1, ⓦwww.prinz.de) and *Bremer* (€2.50, ⓦwww.bremer.de). Bremen has a distinguished theatre tradition, and offers live performances of all kinds of music. The leading folklore **festivals** are the Eiswette on Jan 6 (Epiphany), and the Freimarkt (or Ischa Freimaak) which begins with a procession in mid-Oct and lasts for 17 days.

Nightclubs

Aladin/Tivoli Hannoversche Str. 9-11, Hemelingen. Has discos Wed & Sat from 10pm, live rock and blues at sundry other times.

Modernes Neustadtwall 28. A cinema during the week and a disco at weekends, playing half-hour snatches of all sorts of mainstream music; also has live rock, blues, soul and musical cabaret. Always busy and gets very hot, though there are periodic 5min breaks when the ceiling is opened for ventilation.

Sinatra's Dancing Rembertiring 18. Presents all sorts of dance music, from foxtrots to the latest chart sounds.

Stubu Rembertiring 21. Has discos every evening from 9pm.

Music and theatre

In addition to the venues listed below, concerts and solo recitals frequently take place in Bremen's churches, most frequently in the Dom, which has a regular Thursday series at 7pm.

Die Glocke Domsheide ⓣ04 21/33 66 99, ⓦwww.glocke.de. Bremen's fine old concert hall regularly hosts concerts by both of the city's orchestras. Of these, the Bremer Philharmoniker (ⓦwww.bremerphilharmoniker.de) is a full-sized symphony orchestra, while the Deutsche Kammerphilharmonie (ⓦwww.kammerphilharmonie.com) is an excellent chamber body with plenty of young musicians.

Musical-Theater Bremen Richtweg 7–13 ⓣ04 21/3 65 33 33, ⓦwww.bremertheater.com. New venue for Broadway-style musicals.

Schauspielhaus Ostersorsteinweg 57a ⓣ04 21/3 65 33 33, ⓦwww.bremertheater.com. The city's principal mainstream dramatic stage.

Schlachthof Findorffstr. 51 ⓣ04 21/37 77 50, ⓦwww.schlachthof-bremen.de. This converted slaughterhouse is now a cultural centre hosting world music events, as well as theatre and cabaret.

Stadthalle Bürgerweide ⓣ04 21/3 50 53 30, ⓦwww.stadthalle-bremen.de. The municipal hall behind the Hauptbahnhof is used for large-scale spectaculars and concerts by well-known pop soloists and bands.

Theater am Goetheplatz Goetheplatz ⓣ04 21/3 65 33 33, ⓦwww.bremertheater.com. Bremen's most prestigious stage offers a mixed programme of operas, operettas and ballet. For the duration of the restoration of the building, performances are being held at the Musical-Theater.

Theater am Leibnizplatz Am Leibnitzplatz ⓣ04 21/50 03 33, ⓦwww.shakespeare-company.com. The home of the bremer shakespeare company, the only theatre troupe in Germany to have ten of Shakespeare's plays in rep at any one time.

Theatrium Puppentheater im Packhaus Wüste Stätte 11 ⓣ04 21/32 68 13, ⓦwww.theatrium-puppentheater.de. A specially fitted puppet theatre, with shows for both adults and children.

Around Bremen

If you're staying in Bremen and want a trip out, the most obvious places to head for are the port of **Bremerhaven**, the former artists' colony of **Worpswede**, and the old city of **Verden**, which is also a worthwhile stopoff en route to Hannover or the Lüneburg Heath.

Bremerhaven

Founded in 1827 as the deep-water harbour of Bremen, which lies 60km to the south, **BREMERHAVEN** is the Federal Republic's busiest fishing port. The pride of the town is the **Deutsches Schiffahrtsmuseum** (German Museum of Navigation; April-Oct daily 10am-6pm; Nov-March Tues–Sun 10am–6pm; €4; Ⓦwww.dsm.de) on Hans-Scharoun-Platz by the Alter Hafen, which lies between the modern commercial and fishing harbours. This traces the history of German sailing from prehistoric times to the present, and the star exhibit is a fourteenth-century Hanseatic log which was dredged up from the port of Bremen. Outside in the harbour are several museum-shops, including a wartime U-boat, the **Wilhelm Bauer** (April–Oct daily 10am-6pm; €2), the only one of its kind still in existence.

The other main attractions are in the immediate vicinity. Just to the south are the **Kunsthalle** (Tues–Fri 2–6pm, Sat & Sun 11am–1pm; €2), which mounts temporary exhibitions, principally of modern art, and the **Radarturm** (Radar Tower; April–Sept Tues–Sun 10am–1pm & 2–6pm; Oct–March Sun 10am–1pm & 2–5pm only; €2), which commands a fine view over the harbours. To the north is the **Zoo am Meer** (previously daily 8am–5/7pm; €2), which is due to reopen in 2004 after an extensive period of refurbishment. It has an aquarium plus a number of animals with an aquatic connection.

Bremerhaven's **Hauptbahnhof** is at the eastern end of town, about 15 minutes' walk from the Alter Hafen. There are two **tourist offices**: at Van-Ronzelen-Str. 2 (May–Oct Mon-Wed 8am–4.30pm, Thurs 8am-4pm, Fri 8am-3.30pm; Ⓣ04 71/9 46 46 10, Ⓦwww.bremerhaven-tourism.de) and in the Columbus-Center, opposite the Schiffahrtsmuseum (Mon–Wed 9.30am-6pm, Thurs 9.30am-8pm, Fri 9.30am–7pm, Sat 9.30am–4pm; Ⓣ04 71/41 41 41). Ask at either of these about **private rooms** (❷–❸). There are plenty of **hotels**; those with a central location include *Elbinger Platz*, Georgstr. 2 (Ⓣ04 71/92 44 30; ❸); *Geestemünde*, Am Klint 20 (Ⓣ0471/2 88 00; ❹); *Comfort*, Am Schaufenster 7 (Ⓣ04 71/9 32 00, Ⓦwww.comfort-hotel-bremerhaven.de; ❻); and *Haverkamp*, Prager Str. 34 (Ⓣ04 71/4 83 30, Ⓦwww.hotel-haverkamp.de; ❻-❽). The **youth hostel** is at Gaussstr. 54–56 (Ⓣ04 71/98 20 80; €15.40/18.10); take bus #502 or #509 to Gesundheitsamt. Pick of the town's fish speciality **restaurants** is *Natusch*, Am Fischbahnhof 1. Worthy rivals are *Strandhalle*, at the Seebäderkaje by the northern end of Hermann-Heinrich-Meier-Strasse, and *Seute Deern*, a triple-masted barque in the Alter Hafen. Near the latter, at Van-Ronzelen-Str. 18, is *Koggen-Bräu*, a *Hausbrauerei*. Various harbour, river and sea **cruises** are available daily throughout the summer for around €6.50; there are also sailings to Helgoland (see p.706).

Worpswede

About 25km north of Bremen in the **Teufelsmoor** (the forbiddingly named "Devil's peat bog") is the intriguing village of **WORPSWEDE**. Back in the 1880s this was a simple farming village, where the inhabitants scraped together a living. The artists Fritz Mackensen and Otto Modersohn came here then, and over the next ten or so years Worpswede developed into an artists' colony, a movement run on roughly similar lines to the Pre-Raphaelites. The famous poet Rainer Maria Rilke was closely associated with them, as was his wife, Clara Westhoff. It was **Paula Becker**, who subsequently married Modersohn, who became the most significant of the set – her powerful, depressing pictures depicting the grim realities of peasant life, poverty and death stand out from the pretty, though comparatively facile, impressionistic scenes of the others.

Work by the first generation of Worpswede artists can be seen in a number of locations, notably the two main galleries in the heart of the village, the **Kunsthalle** (daily 10am–5/6pm; €2.50) at Bergstr. 17 and the **Grosse Kunstschau** (same hours; €2.50) round the corner at Lindenallee 3. The latter is among Worpswede's most significant buildings, one of several Expressionist masterpieces by Bernhard Hoetger. However, you're by no means limited to seeing the work of long-dead artists: the colony tradition is maintained to this day, and it's possible to visit – and, of course, to buy from – the workshops of a number of contemporary craftsmen.

Practicalities

Worpswede can be reached by bus #140 from Bremen's Hauptbahnhof; alternatively, there are infrequent boat services in summer. The **tourist office** (Mon–Fri 9am–1pm & 2–6pm, Sat & Sun 10am–2/4pm; Ⓣ0 47 92/95 01 21, Ⓦwww.worpswede.de) at Bergstr. 13 has details of **private rooms** (❶–❸) and small **pensions** (❷–❺). Of the latter, the most intriguing is the *Haus im Schluh* (Ⓣ0 47 92/95 00 61; ❺), run by the descendants of Worpswede artist Heinrich Vogeler, whose work is on display here. One of the town's highly distinctive stock of **hotels**, *Buchenhof*, Ostendorfer Str. 16 (Ⓣ0 47 92/9 33 90, Ⓦwww.hotel-buchenhof.de; ❻), occupies the Jugendstil villa of another member of the colony, Hans von Ende. Other options are *Gasthof Zur Post*, Ostersoder Str. 11 (Ⓣ0 47 92/2 20; ❷); *Haar*, Hembergstr. 13 (Ⓣ0 47 92/9 32 50; ❹); *Am Kunstcentrum*, Hans-am-Ende-Weg 4 (Ⓣ0 47 92/94 00; ❻); *Waldhotel*, Hintern Berg 24 (Ⓣ0 47 92/9 31 80; ❻); and *Der Eichenhof*, Ostendorfer Str. 13 (Ⓣ0 47 92/26 76, Ⓦwww.der-eichenhof.de; ❽–❾). There's a **youth hostel** a few minutes' walk west of the centre at Hammeweg 2 (Ⓣ0 47 92/13 60; €15/17.70).

Among an enticing array of **cafés** (which generally also serve full meals), *Kaffee Worpswede*, Lindenallee 1, housed in striking custom-designed premises by Hoetger, stands out, as does *Kaffeehaus Niedersachsen*, Am Thiergarten 2, which has original Worpswede furniture. The best **restaurants** are *Worpsweder Landhaus*, Findorffstr. 2, and those in the hotels *Am Kunstcentrum* and *Der Eichenhof*.

Verden

The former episcopal seat of **VERDEN**, some 28km southeast of Bremen on the main rail line to Hannover, nowadays christens itself Reiterstadt in honour of its status as Germany's equestrian capital, the setting for seven **horse markets** each year, of which those in mid-April and mid-October, with their attendant festivals, are the most important.

The compact Altstadt lies on the right bank of the River Aller. Much of it is now a bland pedestrianized shopping precinct, but towards the end of the latter is the impressive Gothic **Dom**. This imparts a surprising sense of unity, given that it was constructed over an unusually protracted period, and even then retains the tower and cloister of its Romanesque predecessor. The late thirteenth-century chancel is one of the earliest essays in the distinctively German hall-church style; although not finished until two hundred years later, the nave and transept dovetail perfectly with it.

In the shadow of the Dom is the Romanesque **Andreaskirche**, whose great treasure is the brass funerary slab – the oldest known example of its kind – of its founder Bishop Yso. Just north of the Dom at Untere Str. 13 is the **Domherrenhaus**, a timber-framed building from the early eighteenth century, which now houses the **Historisches Museum** (Tues–Sun 10am–1pm & 3–5pm; €2). Alongside the expected archeology, folklore, handicraft and local history displays is a wooden spear which is believed to be the oldest hunting weapon ever discovered. The main building in the northern half of the Altstadt is the **Johanniskirche** on Ritterstrasse, a Romanesque brick basilica transformed into a Gothic hall church in the fifteenth century. It has well-restored cycles of medieval wall and ceiling frescoes and notable furnishings, including a relief of *The Last Judgment*.

On Holzmarkt, just to the east of the Altstadt, the former barracks have been converted to serve as the home of the **Deutsches Pferdemuseum** (Tues–Sun 10am–5pm; €3; Ⓦwww.dpm-verden.de), a rather serious institution with a huge collection of equine artefacts and a valuable library of books on the same theme.

Practicalities

Verden's **Hauptbahnhof** is situated east of the Altstadt. Between the two, at Holzmarkt 15, is the **tourist office** (May–Oct Mon–Fri 8.30am–6pm, Sat 10am–1pm; Nov–April Mon–Fri 8.30am–5pm; Ⓣ0 42 31/80 71 80, Ⓦwww.verden.de). The Niedersachsenhalle, scene of all the **equestrian events**, is situated in a park on the opposite side of the Hauptbahnhof from the town centre. In the suburb of Eitze, at the southeastern extremity of town, are a couple of budget **hotels**: *Der Oelfkenhof*, Im Dicken Ort 17 (Ⓣ0 42 31/6 29 63, Ⓦwww.oelkenhof.de; ❸); and *Eitzer Hof*, Walsroder Str. 42 (Ⓣ0 42 31/6 30 04; ❸). Those with a more central location are far pricier; they include *Haag's Hotel Niedersachsenhof*, Lindhooper Str. 97 (Ⓣ0 42 31/66 60, Ⓦwww.niedersachsenhof-verden.de; ❺–❼); and *Höltje*, Obere Str. 13 (Ⓣ04231/89 20, Ⓦwww.hotelholtje.de; ❼). The **youth hostel** is situated to the rear of the Niedersachsenhalle at Saumurplatz 1 (Ⓣ0 42 31/6 11 63; €16.10/18.80). There are fine **restaurants** in each of the last two hotels, but the top gourmet address is *Pades*, Grüne Str. 15. Cheaper places to eat and drink include *Am Rathaus*, Grosse Str. 46, *Domstein*, Lugenstein 11–13, and the fish specialist cum delicatessen *Bremer*, Grosse Str. 70.

Oldenburg

OLDENBURG, a junction on the two rail lines between Bremen and the North Sea ports, has enjoyed an eventful history. Having fallen under Danish rule for a century, it made a spectacular comeback in 1773 as the seat of the independent duchy of Oldenburg-Holstein-Gottorp, which kept its place on the map (latterly as a grand duchy and then as a free state) until it fell victim to Hitler's centralization policies. Nowadays the capital of the Weser-Ems region, it's a busy inland port, market and shopping centre which usually teems with people from the neighbouring countryside. Although it was only minimally damaged in World War II, Oldenburg looks surprisingly modern, almost all its older buildings having been swept away in a huge fire in 1676.

The City

Much of the moated Altstadt is a pedestrian precinct, with the main sights clustered together at the extreme southern end. Of these, the most important is the **Schloss**, an irregular horseshoe-shaped building begun in the early seventeenth century in a plain Renaissance style, but subsequently altered and enlarged. It now contains the **Landesmuseum für Kunst und Kulturgeschichte** (Tues, Wed & Fri 9am–5pm, Thurs 9am–8pm, Sat & Sun 10am–5pm; €2; Ⓦwww.landesmuseum-oldenburg.de), whose lure is a large collection of paintings and *objets d'art* set in period interiors. Particularly notable is the extensive array of the work of **Johann Heinrich Wilhelm Tischbein**, a friend of Goethe and the most accomplished member of one of Germany's best-known artistic dynasties. Duke Peter Friedrich Ludwig, an astute patron of the arts, brought him to the Oldenburg court in 1804, and he remained there for the last twenty-five years of his life. The large canvases, such as *Of Naked Men* and *Hector's Farewell to Andromache*, show his talent for the grand manner, but what really steals the show is the *Idyllen-Zyklus*, a cycle of 44 little mythological and pastoral scenes and landscapes, tree, bird and animal studies.

On the opposite side of Schlosswall is the **Schlossgarten**, originally a dairy and market garden for the court, but later remodelled into an English-style park. Nowadays, it also boasts hothouses, a rose garden and extensive patches of rhododendrons, and makes a good place to picnic or relax. Just across the moat on the corner of Elisabethstrasse and the Damm is a branch of the Landesmuseum, the **Augusteum** (same hours and ticket). It houses the modern parts of the collection: most of the leading Expressionists are represented, while there are plenty of works by Franz Radzwill and other German Surrealists. Round the corner at Damm 40–44, the **Museum für Natur und Mensch** (Tues–Thurs 9am–5pm, Fri 9am–3pm, Sat & Sun 10am–5pm; €2; Ⓦwww.naturundmensch.de) features natural history displays laid out in the manner of nineteenth-century curio cabinets. There are also archeological finds from prehistoric times to the early Middle Ages, the most eye-catching being the 2400-year-old corpses found in Lower Saxon peat bogs.

A couple of minutes' walk north of the Schloss, the Markt is dominated by the **Lambertikirche**, whose brick Gothic exterior has repeatedly been rebuilt, giving it an incongruously modern sheen. Its interior was completely transformed in the 1790s by order of Duke Peter Friedrich Ludwig into a Neoclassical rotunda based on the Pantheon in Rome. The overall effect is astonishing – rather like a Wedgwood vase turned inside out. Alongside are the **Altes Rathaus**, a Historicist fantasy borrowing freely from the vocabulary of the Gothic and Renaissance, and the early sixteenth-century **Haus Degode**, the oldest surviving house in the city.

Practicalities

It's easy to get disorientated when arriving at the **Hauptbahnhof**, which is about fifteen minutes' walk northeast of the Altstadt. Following Bahnhofstrasse straight ahead, then turning left into Gottorpstrasse will take you in the direction of the Schloss. The **tourist office** (Mon–Fri 10am–6pm, Sat 10am–2pm; Ⓣ04 41/3 61 61 30, Ⓦwww.oldenburg-tourist.de) is at the extreme northwest corner of the Altstadt at Wallstr. 14.

The best budget **hotels** are *Harmonie*, southeast of the Schloss at Dragonerstr. 59 (Ⓣ04 41/2 77 04; ❸); and *Hegeler*, north of the Altstadt at Donnerschweer Str. 27 (Ⓣ04 41/8 75 61; ❹). More central options include *Posthalter*, Mottenstr. 13 (Ⓣ04 41/21 90 80; ❺); *Antares*, Am Staugraben 8 (Ⓣ04 41/9 22 50, Ⓦwww.antares-hotel.info; ❻); and *Wieting*, Damm 29 (Ⓣ04 41/9 24 05, Ⓦwww.hotel-wieting.de). The tourist office also has details of a few **private rooms** (❷–❸), while the **youth hostel** is about ten minutes' walk north of the Altstadt at Alexanderstr. 65 (Ⓣ04 41/8 71 35; €15/17.70).

There are **restaurants** to suit all tastes. *Seewolf*, Alexanderstr. 41, specializes in fish dishes; the *Fürsten- und Jugendstilsaal* in the Hauptbahnhof serves *gutbürgerliche Küche* in surprisingly elegant surroundings; *Steffmann*, Kurwickstr. 23, is a typical Gaststätte; *Le Journal*, Wallstr. 13, is an upmarket French-style bistro; while *Die Stube*, Achternstr. 63, caters for vegetarians. *Leutbecher*, Schlossplatz 18, is the pick of the traditional **cafés**. There are plenty of **bars** along Kurwickstrasse; a good alternative is *Ulenspiegel*, Burgstr. 12.

Oldenburg has plenty of **festivals**, including the Hafenfest on the weekend after Whitsun, the Altstadtfest on the last weekend in August, and the Kramermarkt for ten days in late September and early October. The main **theatre** is the Staatstheater, Theaterstr. 28 (Ⓣ04 41/2 22 51 11, Ⓦwww.oldenburg.staatstheater.de), while **concerts** are held at the Weser-Ems-Halle, Europaplatz 12 (Ⓣ04 41/8 00 30, Ⓦwww.weser-ems-halle.de).

Jever

Situated some 60km northwest of Oldenburg, modest little **JEVER** is the most attractive town in Friesia. For more than four centuries the capital of a minute aristocratic territory, it reached its apogee in the sixteenth century under the last of its noble rulers, the energetic and gifted **Fräulein Maria**, who gave it municipal rights, had the fortifications built, founded a school, and commissioned several splendid works of art. Later, through marriage and conquest, Jever came under Russian, Dutch and French control, but it never developed into a place of significance, and remains something of a backwater to this day.

Jever's dominant monument is the rather magnificent pink **Schloss** (March to mid-Jan Tues–Sun 10am–6pm; July & Aug daily 10am–6pm; €2.50; Ⓦwww.schlossmuseum.de). Begun in the fifteenth century as a fortified castle, it was transformed by Fräulein Maria into a Renaissance palace. Highlight of the interior is the carved oak ceiling of the **Audienzsaal**, the work of the great Antwerp artist Cornelis Floris. Between May and September, it's possible to go up the **tower** (€0.50 extra) for a fine view over the skyline and the Schlosspark.

The town centre to the north is laid out round two squares. Neuer Markt is dominated by the **Stadtkirche**, which has been burned down and rebuilt at least nine times in its nine-hundred-year history. It last had a fire in 1959, when over half of the church was destroyed and replaced with a contemporary design. The enormous **funerary monument** by Floris that Fräulein Maria commissioned in honour of her father, Edo Wiemkem the Younger, somehow survived, and can be seen in the remains of the Baroque church, which is now integrated into the new building. A work of architecture as much as sculpture, it's particularly remarkable for the extraordinary variety of materials used – wood, marble, sandstone and clay.

A few blocks further north, at Elisabethufer 17, is the distinctive silhouette of the **Friesisches Brauhaus zu Jever** (guided tours Mon–Fri throughout the day, Sat & Sun mornings only; book in advance by calling Ⓣ0 44 61/1 37 11, or ask in the shop; €6.50; Ⓦwww.jever.de), which is claimed as the most modern brewery in Germany. Its *Pils* enjoys cult status as the bitterest-tasting beer made in the country. Other products are the low-alcohol, low-calorie *Light* and the drolly named *Fun*, which is alcohol-free. The price of the tour includes not only a visit to the production lines and the museum, but also a presentation glass, which can be filled up twice, with a *Brezel* to ward off any hunger pangs.

Practicalities

Jever's **Bahnhof** is situated some distance southwest of the centre. The **tourist office** (May–Sept Mon–Fri 10am–6pm, Sat 10am–2pm; Oct–April Mon–Fri 9am–5pm, Sat 9am–noon; ⓣ0 44 61/7 10 10, ⓦwww.stadt-jever.de) is at Alter Markt 18. Ask here about **private rooms** (❶–❸), which are in reasonable supply, both in the town itself and in the surrounding countryside.

There are several budget **hotels**: *Schwarzer Adler*, Alter Markt 3 (ⓣ0 44 61/9 16 60 22; ❸); *Weisses Haus*, Bahnhofstr. 20 (ⓣ0 44 61/68 39; ❸); and *Stöber*, Hohnholzstr. 10 (ⓣ0 44 61/55 80; ❹). The classiest hotel in town is *Friesen*, to the south of the centre at Harlinger Weg 1 (ⓣ0 44 61/93 40, ⓦwww.jever-hotel.de; ❻). There's a **youth hostel** (April–Oct only), centrally sited at Mooshüttenweg 12 (ⓣ0 44 61/35 90; €12.70/15.40).

Among the **restaurants**, the historic *Haus der Getreuen* deserves special mention; it's the Gaststätte of the brewery, situated across from it at Schlachstr. 1. Also very fine, albeit somewhat pricier, is *Alte Apotheke*, Apothekerstr. 1, while *Friesische Brasserie*, Kattrepel 2a, is a fish and mussel specialist. Main **festivals** are the Kiewittmarkt, a spring market usually held at the end of March, and the Altstadtfest in mid-August.

Osnabrück

OSNABRÜCK, a major rail junction, lies close to the Land border, 105km south of Oldenburg. Geographically and historically, it really belongs to Westphalia, and it has many parallels with Münster (see pp.552–58), which is just 55km further south. Both owe their foundation to Charlemagne, and in the Middle Ages both were ruled by a prince-bishop, and were important trading centres. Subsequently, they shared the hosting of the long negotiations – regarded as the birth of modern diplomatic practices – which led to the signing of the **Peace of Westphalia** in 1648, bringing the Thirty Years' War to an end. One curious agreement resulting from these talks was that Osnabrück was to be ruled in future by a Catholic and a Protestant bishop in turn. When the bishopric was secularized under Napoleon, the Hanoverians annexed its territories. Accordingly Osnabrück joined the rest of Hannover in the new province of Lower Saxony after World War II.

Arrival, information and accommodation

Osnabrück's **Hauptbahnhof** is ten minutes' walk southeast of the city centre, which is reached by following Möserstrasse straight ahead, then crossing the River Hase. **Bahnhof Hasetor**, which is serviced by northbound stopping trains, is just beyond the northern boundaries of the Altstadt. The **tourist office** (Mon–Fri 9.30am–6pm, Sat 10am–4pm; ⓣ05 41/3 23 22 02, ⓦwww.osnabrueck.de) is just off the Markt at Krahnstr. 58. A varied **cultural** programme is mounted at the Theater Osnabrück, a fine Jugendstil building at Domhof 10–11 (ⓣ05 41/3 22 33 14, ⓦwww.theater.osnabrueck.de).

Osnabrück has a good choice of **hotels** in all price categories. There's a **youth hostel** to the south of town at Iburger Str. 183a (ⓣ05 41/5 42 84; €15.40/18.10); take bus #62, #463, #464 or #465, and alight at Kinderhospital. A privately run alternative, *Penthouse Backpackers*, has a much more cnetral location at Möserstr. 19 (ⓣ05 41/6 00 96 06, ⓦwww.penthousebp.com; dorm beds €13, doubles €30–35). The *Niedersachsenhof* **campsite** (ⓣ05 41/7 72 26) is in the northeast of the city at Nordstr. 109.

Hotels

Dom-Hotel Kleine Domsfreiheit 5 ⓣ05 41/2 15 54, ⓦwww.dom-hotel-osnabrueck.de. Recommendable hotel right in the heart of the city. It also has a fine restaurant, though this is open Mon–Thurs evenings only. ❻

Hohenzollern Heinrich-Heine-Str. 17 ⓣ05 41/3 31 70, ⓦwww.adventahotels.com. Business-class hotel with café-restaurant, located directly opposite the Hauptbahnhof. ❻

Jägerheim Johannistorwall 19a ⓣ05 41/2 16 35. Located on the southern inner ring road, this has the cheapest rooms in the city centre. It's attached to a fish restaurant, *Casa Lopez* (evenings only, except at weekends). ❸

Kulmbacher Hof Schlosswall 65–67 ⓣ05 41/3 57 00, ⓦwww.kulmbacher-hof.de. Another good middle-range hotel with restaurant on the southwestern section of the inner ring road. ❻

Nord-Hotel Hansastr. 31 ⓣ05 41/6 41 33, ⓕ6 41 22. Very good value hotel a short distance northwest of Bahnhof Hasetor. Its restaurant serves huge portions at amazingly low prices, especially at lunchtime. ❸

Walhalla Bierstr. 24 ⓣ05 41/3 49 10, ⓦwww.hotel-walhalla.de. Despite occupying a seventeenth-century timber-framed house, this is a modern hotel with all the amenities including sauna and solarium. Its restaurant is among the best in the city. ❼

Welp Natruper Str. 227 ⓣ05 41/91 30 70, ⓕ9 13 07 34. Good medium-priced hotel with restaurant located just to the northwest of the Altstadt. ❺

The City

Much of the city is modern. Heavy damage was caused by bombing in World War II, and restoration has been less successful than in Münster. Some highly characterful streets and squares do remain, but it's a pity that more thought wasn't given to the planning of the bland shopping areas with which they're now intermingled.

The Dom

The **Dom** has a spacious setting in the middle of its own square in the heart of the city. Built in fits and starts between the twelfth and sixteenth centuries, its facade **towers** are a fascinating combination – the late Gothic one on the southern side is almost twice the width of its Romanesque neighbour. Inside, the Dom presents a pleasingly sober, predominantly Gothic appearance. Among a number of notable works of art, the early thirteenth-century bronze **font** and the exactly contemporary polychrome wood **triumphal cross** are outstanding. The latter's name is something of a misnomer, as Christ is here depicted as a pathetic, suffering, all-too-human figure. Wonderful gilded wrought-iron gates guard the entrance to the ambulatory, at the end of which is the *Margarethenaltar*, a limewood retable by the sculptor who also carved the *Madonna of the Rosary* in the transept. The identity of this emotional artist, who was still working in the late Gothic style well into the sixteenth century, remains elusive: he's known simply as the **Master of Osnabrück**.

Further works by this carver can be seen in the **Domschatzkammer und Diözesanmuseum** (Tues–Fri 10am–1pm & 3–5pm, Sat & Sun 11am–2pm; €1.50), housed in rooms above the cloister. The most eye-catching item here, however, is the gilded *Kapitelkreuz*, a **crucifix** made in the early eleventh century and studded with two pontifical rings, a couple of Roman cameos and a variety of coloured gems. The early seventeenth-century **confessional**, from a nearby convent, was made in the wake of the Tridentine reforms and is the earliest example in northern Europe of what was to become a very familiar structure.

The Markt

Just beyond the Dom is the other main square, the triangular-shaped **Markt**. Its colourful step-gabled mansions are modelled on the merchant houses of the Hanseatic ports, while in the centre there's a fountain which gushes with beer whenever there's a festival on. On the northern side of the square is the Gothic **Marienkirche**, which takes the hall-church design to its logical conclusion by omitting the transept. Inside are a fourteenth-century triumphal cross, a sixteenth-century **Passion altar** from Antwerp and numerous tombs – including that of Justus Möser, whose researches into Westphalian folklore in the eighteenth century were to serve as a trail-blazer for the Romantic movement. Normally the **tower** can be climbed on Sundays (11.30am–1pm; €1) for a view of the city, though in 2003 visits were suspended because of restoration work. In the Stadtsbibliothek opposite is the **Erich-Maria-Remarque-Friedenszentrum** (Tues–Fri 10am–1pm & 3–5pm, Sat & Sun 10am–1pm; free), a documentary record of the career of the local author Erich Maria Remarque, whose novel *All Quiet on the Western Front* is the enduring German classic of World War I literature.

Closing the end of the Markt is the early sixteenth-century **Rathaus** (Mon–Fri 8am–6pm, Sat & Sun 10am–4pm; free), from whose steps the Peace of Westphalia was proclaimed. The present stairway dates from the nineteenth century, as do the large statues of German emperors, among which Kaiser Wilhelm I is lined up alongside his medieval predecessors. Inside, the wood-panelled **Friedenssaal** features generally glum portraits of the representatives of Sweden and the Protestant German principalities, who deliberated here while their Catholic counterparts met in Münster. The **Schatzkammer** opposite contains valuable documents and treasury items. Star piece is the magnificent fourteenth-century *Kaiserpokal*, a **goblet** adorned with coloured glass and figurines.

The rest of the city

Facing the rear of the Rathaus on Bierstrasse is the pretty half-timbered frontage of Osnabrück's most famous inn, **Walhalla**, which features extensively in Erich Maria Remarque's *The Black Obelisk*, a novel describing the traumatic hyper-inflation of 1923. Most of Osnabrück's surviving **old houses** are nearby – on Marienstrasse, Hegerstrasse, Grosser Gildewartare, Krahnstrasse and Bierstrasse itself. The first three form a pedestrian precinct, where antique shops and bistros vie with each other for prominence. At the end of Bierstrasse is the former **Dominikanerkirche** (Tues–Fri 11am–6pm, Sat & Sun 10am–6pm; €3), now a cultural centre which regularly features temporary exhibitions of contemporary art. It also contains a weather-worn late Gothic statue of Charlemagne, the only survivor of the original cycle from the Rathaus facade. Beyond here, several fragments of the city wall can be seen round the ring road, including the Neoclassical **Heger Tor**, celebrating the victory at Waterloo.

Diagonally opposite is the **Kulturgeschichtliches Museum** (Tues–Fri 11am–6pm, Sat & Sun 10am–6pm; €4). Dominating the archeology section are the spectacular Roman finds from nearby Kaltkriese, which is now known to be the site of their defeat by the Cherusci under Arminius in AD 9. The medieval section displays some notable sculptures, including the original figures from the *Brautportal* of the Marienkirche. A new extension, the **Felix-Nussbaum-Haus** (same times and ticket), was built by Daniel Libeskind, the architect of the much-praised Jüdisches Museum in Berlin, in order that the large holdings of works by the local Jewish artist **Felix Nussbaum** could at last be displayed in their entirety. It's an extraordinary, highly symbolic structure, without an exterior entrance, and with unconventional exhibition rooms, including sloping passageways, which deliberately leave the visitor disorientated. There could surely be no more appropriate setting for the poignant paintings of Nussbaum, an associate of the *Neue Sachlichkeit* art movement, who was murdered at Auschwitz, aged forty, in 1944. Alongside the main museum building is the Neoclassical **Villa Schlikker**, which is being converted to house displays on the everyday life of the twentieth century. One further historic house, the **Dreikonenhaus** (same hours and ticket) at Marienstr. 5 in the Altstadt, is also used as an annexe by the museum. It contains textiles – including a remarkably well-preserved cashmere shawl of 1830 – and displays on local history and industry.

Southwards along Heger-Tor-Wall is the tall tower of the **Katharinenkirche**, a church broader than it is long. In the big square behind is Osnabrück's most original building, the **Leidenhof**. The sixteenth-century merchant owners converted their original fourteenth-century stone house into a miniature palace by the addition of a staircase tower and a new wing, whose facade resembles a gigantic cardboard cut-out. What really catches the attention, however, are the zigzags painted on the two Renaissance additions, making them look strangely modernistic. Opposite, set in its own fine park, is the huge yellow **Schloss** of the prince-bishops. Built in Italianate Baroque style, it nowadays houses part of the university.

Eating and drinking

Osnabrück is a lively city come the evening, and is well endowed with places to eat and drink. See the "Hotels" section (p.598) for more recommendations.

Alte Gaststätte Holling Hasestr. 53. Nowadays more a pub than a restaurant, though it does light meals. Evenings only except Sat, when it's open lunchtime.

Café am Markt Markt 26. Good choice for *Kaffee und Kuchen*, in the handiest of locations.

Filmkneipe 81/2 Hasestr. 71. Trendy bar attached to a cinema. Games can be hired, and there are changing monthly art exhibitions.

Grüner Jäger An der Katharinenkirche 1. Hugely popular student Kneipe with minimalist decor and a glass-roofed beer garden.

Joducus Weinstube Kommenderiestr. 116. Excellent wine bar-restaurant attached to a wine merchant's shop.

Pfannkuchenhaus Lotter Str. 22. Specializes in wholemeal and buckwheat pancakes; also serves salads and pasta dishes. Evenings only except Sun, closed Mon.

Rampendahl Hasestr. 35. Hausbrauerei which produces light and dark beer and a *Korn*. Also does full meals, including cheap set lunches.

Eastern Lower Saxony

In the east of Lower Saxony, the landscape transforms itself from coastal plain to the rolling **Lüneburg Heath** (Lüneburger Heide), which contains the contrasting towns of **Lüneburg** and **Celle**, as well as several nature reserves. Further south is the most heavily populated part of the Land, with the state capital of **Hannover**, the second city, **Braunschweig**, and the old ducal seat of **Wolfenbüttel**. Continuing in a southerly direction, you soon come to more elevated countryside: there are fine rolling landscapes around **Hameln** in the valley of the River Weser, beyond which is the former princely capital of **Bückeburg**. **Hildesheim** stands in the foothills leading to the wooded slopes of the **Harz** mountain range; this was long a famous mining area, thanks to rich deposits of gold, silver and other less precious minerals, but these have, in the course of the past century, become exhausted. At the edge of the mountains, the old imperial city of **Goslar** is the area's main draw. Nothing else within the Lower Saxon section of the Harz is of comparable quality, but just beyond the range are a number of impressive old half-timbered towns, such as **Einbeck** and **Hann. Münden**. As a complete contrast to these, there's the university city of **Göttingen**, which boasts the most exciting atmosphere of any town between Hannover and Frankfurt.

Lüneburg

Of all the many medieval trading cities built by the Germans on and near the Baltic coast between Hamburg and Rīga, only **LÜNEBURG** has survived virtually unscathed. It was all but ignored by the World War II bombing missions which destroyed so much of northern Germany, having by then declined into economic insignificance. Yet in the Middle Ages the city was immensely wealthy, profiting from the fact that it was (literally) built on **salt** – then a rare and essential commodity, almost worth its weight in gold. At its peak, the Lüneburg saltworks had two thousand employees, which probably made it the largest commercial enterprise in Europe. The city's magnificent brick buildings were funded from exports of the salt to Scandinavia, Burgundy, Poland and Russia, and the other trading links which ensued. Gabled facades, from Gothic to Baroque, still line the streets of the centre. Many have a pronounced tilt, as a result of subsidence caused by disused mines – the salt deposits haven't been worked since 1980, leaving the saline springs of the spa quarter as the only active reminder of a tradition dating back to the tenth century.

Arrival, information and accommodation

Lüneburg's **Hauptbahnhof** has two terminals facing each other across Bahnhofsplatz. The quickest way to reach the centre is to go north along Lüner Weg, then turn left into Lünertorstrasse; this brings you to the Wasserviertel. Alternatively, turn right at the southern end of Bahnhofsplatz into Altenbrückertorstrasse, which takes you straight to Am Sande. Under the front arches of the Rathaus, Am Markt, is the municipal **tourist office** (May–Oct Mon–Fri 9am–6pm, Sat & Sun 9am–4pm; Nov–April Mon–Fri 9am–5pm, Sat 9am–2pm; Ⓣ0 41 31/2 07 66 20, Ⓦwww.lueneburg.de).

Regular **cruises** on the River Ilmenau depart from the Wasserviertel; the office is at Im Wendischen Dorfe 3 (Ⓣ0 41 31/3 10 16). All kinds of **cultural** events are mounted at the Theater Lüneburg, An der Reeperbahn 3 (Ⓣ0 41 31/75 20, Ⓦwww.theater-lueneburg.de). The main **festivals** are the *Bachwoche* in June, devoted to music by J.S. Bach, and the *Stadtfest* in July.

There's a **youth hostel** at Saltauer Str. 133 (Ⓣ0 41 31/4 18 64; €13.80/16.50) well to the south of town, best reached by taking bus #11 to the Scharnhorststrasse stop. The **campsite**, *Rote Schleuse* (Ⓣ0 41 31/79 15 00), is by the banks of the River Ilmenau even further south; catch a bus towards Deutschevern. Lüneburg has a reasonable number of **private rooms** (❷–❹); contact the tourist office for a list.

Hotels

Alt-Lüneburger-Kutscherstube Heiligengeiststr. 44 Ⓣ0 41 31/44 11 34, Ⓦwww.hotel-kutscherstube.de. Small former coaching inn in the heart of the Altstadt; the hotel and restaurant are now separately run. ❺

Bergström Bei der Lüner Mühle Ⓣ0 41 31/30 80, Ⓦwww.moevenpick-lueneburg.com. Lüneburg's best hotel is beautifully situated in the Wasserviertel, and has both old and modern sections: the luxury suites are in a Gothic water tower. There's also an excellent if pricey restaurant. ❻–❾

Bremer Hof Lüner Str. 12–13 ⓣ0 41 31/22 40, ⓦwww.bremer-hof.de. Characterful hotel in a former merchant's home. It has a good and not over-expensive restaurant whose menu features dishes of the distinctive sheep of the Lüneburg Heath. ❼

Das Stadthaus Am Sande 25 ⓣ0 41 31/4 44 38, ⓦwww.das-stadthaus.de. Situated directly opposite St Johannis, this hotel has been in business since 1880, and has recently been given a thorough modernisation. ❺

Parkhotel Uelzener Str. 27 ⓣ0 41 31/4 11 25, ⓦwww.parkhotel.eulink.net. Occupies a villa in a quiet location near the Salztherme. ❺

Scheffler Bardowicker Str. 7 ⓣ0 41 31/2 00 80, ⓦwww.hotel-scheffler.de. Long-established hotel and restaurant in a seventeenth-century half-timbered house just off the Markt. ❻

Zum Heidkrug Am Berge 5 ⓣ0 41 31/2 41 60, ⓦwww.zumheidkrug.de. Small hotel in a brick Gothic mansion, run as an adjunct to the town's leading Italian restaurant. ❺

The Town

Today, Lüneburg is far from being the museum piece it might appear. Its population almost doubled in 1945 as a result of an influx of refugees from the confiscated Eastern Territories, and it has again become a lively regional centre.

The Markt

The **Markt** is the focus of the town's commercial life, particularly on Wednesdays and Saturdays, when markets are held. In the middle of the square is the sixteenth-century **Lunabrunnen**, a bronze fountain with a statuette of the moon goddess Luna, after whom Lüneburg is supposedly named.

The grandiose **Rathaus** (guided tours daily 10am–5pm; €3.70) occupies the west side of the Markt. Its Baroque facade is a mere frontispiece to the largest and most impressive medieval town hall in Germany. The **Grosser Ratssaal**, the old council chamber, is the most famous part. Originally from the fourteenth century, it was embellished a hundred years later with richly traceried windows bearing stained-glass portraits of nine great heroes. Another century later, it received its impressive wall and ceiling decoration, which included a scene of *The Last Judgment* in honour of its new function as the court of justice. Other highlights include the tiny **Körkammer** where the burgomasters (four of whom are depicted in the windows) were elected, and the **Fürstensaal**, the former dance hall, with its fifteenth-century candelabra made from stags' antlers, and seventeenth-century portraits of the local dukes. However, the finest room of all is the **Grosse Ratsstube**, which ranks as one of Germany's most important Renaissance interiors thanks to the pyrotechnic woodwork – benches, panelling and, most notably, the doorways – carved by Albert von Soest. At the end of the tour, you're allowed to linger over the municipal silverware, by far the finest collection in Germany. Unfortunately, what you see here are only replicas: the originals are now in the Kunstgewerbemuseum in Berlin.

Am Sande and around

Lüneburg's largest square is the elongated **Am Sande**, whose name reflects the fact that it was laid out on a sandy marsh. It lies almost due south of the Markt, and is reached along the partly pedestrianized Bäckerstrasse. On the way, take a peek inside the late sixteenth-century **Rathsapotheke**, whose orderly interior forms a perfect complement to the elaborate gable and portal outside. Am Sande itself has the finest group of burghers' mansions in town, illustrating the seemingly inexhaustible variations the local builders worked on the theme of the brick gable. The **Schwarzes Haus** (Black House) – so called from the colour of its glazed brickwork – is particularly impressive. Situated on the west side of the square, it was formerly an inn and brewery, and is now the seat of the local chamber of commerce.

The opposite end of Am Sande is closed off by the impressively large brick church of **St Johannis**. This was begun in the thirteenth century, but the tall tower (which leans a couple of metres out of true) was only erected in the early fifteenth century. The **organ** is celebrated – the case and some of the pipework are early eighteenth-century, but it incorporates much of its mid-sixteenth-century predecessor, one of the oldest instruments in the country. It can be heard briefly each Friday at 5.30pm; from July to October, longer recitals are given on Tuesdays at 8pm. Equally precious is the **high altar**, a co-operative work by several fifteenth-century artists from Hamburg and Lübeck. Its reverse side, illustrating the lives of Saints John the Baptist, Cecilia, George and Ursula, was painted by Hinrik Funhof with a delicacy worthy of comparison with the great Flemish masters of the period. Two other notable retables are housed in the chapels to either side; look out also for the *Madonna and Child* candelabrum in the north aisle, which has a marked similarity to those in the Rathaus.

A few paces to the south is the **Wasserturm** (April–Oct daily 10am–6pm; Nov–March Tues–Sun 10am–5pm; €3.30; Ⓦ www.wasserturm.net), which was built in neo-Gothic style in the first decade of the twentieth century on the remains of the medieval fortifications. It can be ascended for a marvellous panoramic view over the town and the Lüneburg Heath beyond.

The museums

From the rear of St Johannis, follow the River Ilmenau south for a couple of minutes, and cross over by Wandrahmstrasse, on which stand an old mill and the **Museum für das Fürstentum Lüneburg** (Tues–Fri 10am–4pm, Sat & Sun 11am–5pm; €3; Ⓦ www.museumlueneburg.de). This features a good collection of medieval artefacts, including the tomb of a local duke, along with the predictable folklore and local history displays. The most intriguing exhibit is a copy of the once-famous thirteenth-century map of the world from the nearby convent of Ebstorf, the original of which was destroyed in a bomb raid on Hannover.

Just off the western end of Am Sande, at Heiligengeiststr. 39, the **Kronen-Brauerei-Museum** (Tues–Sun 1–4.30pm; free) has been set up in the former premises of what was, until the advent of a new-generation Hausbrauerei next door, the only brewery left out of the eighty the town once had. A free English leaflet guides you round the four floors of equipment, enabling you to see every stage of the traditional beer-making process. The historic lobby and staircase of the front house are also open to view, and there's a permanent exhibition of old drinking vessels. You can end your tour in suitable style by enjoying the products of the modern brewery – the smooth *Lüneburger Pils* and the very dry *Moravia Pils* – in the beer hall, complete with garden.

Immediately to the rear, at Ritterstr. 10, is the **Ostpreussisches Landesmuseum** (Tues–Sun 10am–5pm; €3; Ⓦ www.ostpreussisches landesmuseum.de), which owes its existence to Lüneburg's large influx of refugees from the Baltic state of East Prussia, which in prewar years was the most far-flung part of Germany. In 1945, it was divided horizontally along the middle, with the southerly half allocated to Poland, while the remainder, including the capital city of Königsberg (which was renamed Kaliningrad), was made a province of Russia. The museum illustrates East Prussian history from the German viewpoint, in the process showing why bitterness at the Russian annexation remains so acute.

The rest of the Altstadt

At the edge of the Altstadt, several minutes' walk west of the Ostpreussisches Landesmuseum, is the site of the old saltworks. The surviving installations have been turned into the **Deutsches Salzmuseum** (Mon–Fri 9/10am–5pm, Sat & Sun 10am–5pm; €4; Ⓦwww.salzmuseum.de), which tells you everything you are ever likely to want to know about the extraction, history, geology and economics of salt. In addition, you get to see the city's sole surviving saltpan, which is put into production each day in summer at 3pm. Continuing southwards, you come to the **Kurzentrum**, a modern spa complex set in an extensive park. The **Salztherme** (Mon–Sat 10am–11pm, Sun 8am–9pm), a thermal bathing complex, forms the centrepiece (€7.20 for 2 hours, €9.80 for 4 hours, €11.30 for a day ticket).

In the opposite direction from the Salzmuseum is **St Michael**, another brick Gothic hall church, and the original home of the celebrated *Goldene Tafel* treasures, which are now divided between the Kestner-Museum and Landesgalerie in Hannover (see p.615). It stands on J.S.-Bach-Platz, which is so named because the great composer was a pupil at the school established in the monastic buildings after secularization. From here, you can ascend **Kalkberg**, the low-lying hill to the west for a fine long-range view over Lüneburg and its surroundings. The best route back to the Markt is via Auf dem Meere, a street lined with old craftsmen's houses.

North from the Markt along Bardowicker Strasse is the fifteenth-century parish church of **St Nicolai**, where the sailors and artisans used to worship; its tower is a neo-Gothic replacement of the original. The exterior is somewhat overshadowed by the vertiginous, star-vaulted interior. In the ambulatory, the oldest view of Lüneburg, painted in 1465, can be seen. The old port or **Wasserviertel** lies just to the east along Lüner Strasse. With its peaceful riverside setting, trees, bridges, mills and other imperious buildings, it's the most evocative spot in town, creating a picture about as far removed from a modern-day harbour as it is possible to imagine. Formerly a herring warehouse, the **Altes Kaufhaus** had to be rebuilt after a fire in 1959, but still has its cheery Baroque facade. Opposite is the **Alte Krane** (old crane), which received its present form in the 1790s, though it dates back at least as far as the fourteenth century.

Kloster Lüne

Kloster Lüne (guided tours April 1–Oct 15 Tues–Sat at 10.30am, 2.30pm & 5pm, Sun at 11.30am, 2.30pm & 5pm; €2.50, or €3.50 combined ticket with the Textilmuseum; Ⓦwww.kloster-luene.de) lies 2km northeast of the Wasserviertel. The present complex dates largely from the late fourteenth and early fifteenth centuries, though the half-timbered outbuildings were added later. It became a Protestant convent at the Reformation, and has remained so to this day. Among the highlights of the tour are the church, with its intricately carved sixteenth-century altar and seventeenth-century organ; the frescoed winter refectory; the simple pre-Reformation cells, and their painted Baroque equivalents from a few centuries later. The **Textilmuseum** (Tues–Sun 10.30am–12.30pm & 2.30–5pm; €2.50) displays under ultra-modern lighting conditions an astonishing collection of textiles, most of which were probably woven in the convent. Especially notable are the white embroideries from the thirteenth and fourteenth centuries, and the three huge, colourful tapestries from the early years of the sixteenth.

Eating and drinking

Some of the best restaurants are in the hotels, but there are plenty of other enticing places to eat and drink.

Camus Am Sande 30. Does breakfasts until well into the afternoon, as well as pizzas cooked in a wood oven, meats grilled on lava stones, and various vegetarian and bistro-type dishes.
Kloster-Krug Am Domänenhof 1. Gaststätte in a sixteenth-century timber-framed building directly opposite Kloster Lüne.
Kronen-Brauhaus Heiligengeiststr. 39. The beer hall-cum-restaurant of the local brewery, offering typical North German cuisine.
Le Petit Am Stintmarkt 7. One of a row of lively waterfront pubs which are particularly attractive in summer, when tables are placed outside.
Mälzer Heiligengeiststr. 43. This Hausbrauerei has thrown down the gauntlet to its venerable next-door neighbour. It makes light and dark beers and a seasonal Weizen, and offers a full menu including all-you-can-eat lunch buffets.
Markt-Café Bardowicker Str. 2. Good traditional coffee house, founded in 1846, with a pleasant back garden.
Ratskeller Am Markt 1. In the cellars of the Rathaus, fairly pricey but with a more imaginative menu than most of its counterparts in other German cities.
The Internet Café (TIC) Am Sande 10. The most convenient place in town for surfing the net. Open daily 10am–midnight.

The Lüneburg Heath

Partly wooded, but mainly uncultivated open heathland, the **Lüneburg Heath** (Lüneburger Heide) between Lüneburg and Celle is grazed by large flocks of *Heidschnucken*, goaty-sheep descended from the Corsican mouflon. In late August the heather erupts in deep purple swathes, adding a mass of colour to the heath's otherwise subtle palette. Picturesque villages, with timber-and-brick houses and churches, are also dotted around, forming an idyllic backdrop for festivals, the annual coronation of the queen of the heath, and shepherds who still wear their traditional green outfits. It was here, on May 4, 1945, that Field Marshal Montgomery received the unconditional German surrender. British troops still exercise on the heath, though their presence has been much reduced in recent years. This is one part of Germany where a car or bike is a distinct advantage, as public transport to and within the area is fiddly, serving the northern part of the heath from Lüneburg, the southern from Celle.

The Naturschutzpark Lüneburger Heide

The **Naturschutzpark Lüneburger Heide** is a 200-square-kilometre nature reserve in the northwest of the region, where the heathland and villages are least changed. Motor traffic is forbidden in much of this park, but there are networks of footpaths and cycle paths (renting a bike is easy in most towns) and horse-riding is another possibility. Bees buzz over the heather, and the local honey is renowned – as are the potatoes, oddly enough. Places to stay (mostly at low rates) abound, so you can normally rely on finding **accommodation** as you go, particularly as most towns have a tourist office.

Buses run from Soltau (a junction of several railway lines, including one from Hannover and another from Uelzen on the main line between Lüneburg and Celle) to **UNDELOH**, an attractive village in the heart of the park which boasts a half-timbered church dating back to the twelfth century. In addition to some two dozen pensions and private houses with rooms to let, there are a couple of fine **hotels**: *Witte's*, Zum Loh 2 (Ⓣ0 41 89/81 33 60, Ⓦwww.ringhotels.de; ❺); and *Heiderose*, Wilseder Str. 13 (Ⓣ0 41 89/3 11; Ⓦwww.hotel-heiderose.de; ❻).

From Undeloh, you can walk or cycle 4km south to ultra-quaint **WILSEDE**, along a road closed to all forms of motorised traffic. An old farmhouse, **Dat Ole Huss** (May–Oct daily 10am–4pm; €1.50), has been opened as a museum illustrating the rural ways of the past. You can also climb up northern Germany's highest hill, the 169-metre **Wilseder Berg**, for all-round views of the heath.

Walsrode

The most popular destination in the Lüneburg Heath is **WALSRODE**, which lies on the direct rail line between Soltau and Hannover; it can be reached from Verden by bus, cycle path or by the very occasional excursion trains run on a privately owned rail line formerly used for the transportation of potash. The town itself is of scant appeal, but 3km north of the centre is the **Vogelpark Walsrode** (daily March–Oct 9am–7pm; Nov–Feb 10am–4pm; €12; Ⓦwww.vogelpark-walsrode.de), with over 5000 indigenous and exotic birds representing some of the 850 different species on view in a beautifully manicured park which is the largest of its type in the world. There's a choice of three café-restaurants, and there's also a **hotel**, *Luisenhöhe* (Ⓣ0 51 61/9 86 20; ❻).

Bergen

On the main road between Soltau and Celle is **BERGEN**, which has the misfortune to have its name immortalized in the name of one of the most infamous Nazi concentration camps, the **Konzentratsionslager Bergen-Belsen** (daily 9am–6pm; Ⓦwww.bergenbelsen.de; free), though this lies some 6km southwest of the town. Some 50,000 people died there, many as a result of starvation and disease (this was the fate of the young diarist Anne Frank), or by the personal whim of the notorious camp commandant, Josef Kramer, the "Beast of Belsen". When the camp was liberated some 13,000 unburied bodies were found lying in heaps; many of the 30,000 were on the point of death and thousands died within hours or days of being liberated since the British couldn't cope with such overwhelming numbers of dying and diseased people. The film made of the camp's liberation, which can be seen in the documentation centre, still appals: a number of Germans, who were forced to watch it and realize the extent of the atrocities that had been carried out in their name, subsequently committed suicide. In Britain the film was shown in every cinema in the country, revealing the horror of the "Final Solution" to the public for the first time. The camp buildings themselves were destroyed at the end of the war by the British, for fear of a typhus outbreak, but the mass graves remain, and a visit to the site of such horror is deeply disturbing.

By **car**, the camp is 22km northwest of Celle on the B3; turn left when you reach Bergen. It's also reachable by turning off the main E4 route between Hannover and Hamburg at the Soltau-Süd junction. There are up to five direct **buses** a day from Celle, though only two – both in the late afternoon – in the opposite direction.

Wienhausen

At the extreme southeastern edge of the Lüneburg Heath, some 10km from Celle, to which it's connected by fairly regular buses, lies **WIENHAUSEN**, a village of half-timbered houses clustered around a remarkable **Kloster** (guided tours April to mid-Oct Tues–Sat at 10am, 11am, 2pm, 3pm, 4pm & 5pm, Sun at noon, 1pm, 2pm, 3pm, 4pm & 5pm; €3.50; Ⓦwww.wienhausen.de). Founded in 1231 by Agnes von Meissen, daughter-in-law of Henry the Lion, the convent became Protestant at the Reformation, and is still in use today. The severity of the brick buildings stands in contrast to the walls of the **nuns' chancel**, which are covered with a heavily restored cycle of fourteenth-century **frescoes** illustrating the life of Christ and the legend of the Holy Cross, along with secular subjects. In the centre of the chancel is a wooden **Holy Sepulchre**, complete with a figure of the dead Christ, which dates from the late thirteenth century.

The Kloster's most valuable treasures are its **tapestries**. Woven by the nuns in the fourteenth and fifteenth centuries, they rank among the greatest ever made. Also on view are some intriguing excavations, which include the implements used to weave the tapestries, and the spectacles worn by their creators. For conservation reasons, the display has traditionally only been open to the public for two weeks around Whitsun each year, in conjunction with a shorter version of the normal guided tour (€6). However, in 2003 the tapestry exhibition was also made accessible by a self-guided audio tour between June and September (Tues–Sat 10am–6pm, Sun noon–6pm; combined ticket €6), and it is to be hoped that this arrangement will continue in future years.

Celle

Despite being roughly the same size, having a closely connected history, and lying no more than 90km apart at opposite ends of the Lüneburg Heath, **CELLE** and Lüneburg seem to have come from different worlds. Celle has none of the massive brickwork public buildings which define the skyline of the Hanseatic trading cities of the north. For long a ducal Residenzstadt, it marks the transition to the timber-framed buildings so characteristic of central Germany. Like Lüneburg, it has been spared from serious war damage, and its centre retains whole streets of intact historic houses.

Arrival, information and accommodation

Celle's **Hauptbahnhof** is ten minutes' walk west of the town centre along Bahnhofstrasse. The **tourist office** (mid-May to mid-Oct Mon–Fri 9am–7/8pm, Sat 9am–4pm, Sun 11am–2pm; rest of year Mon–Fri 9am–5pm, Sat 10am–1pm; ⓣ0 51 41/12 12, ⓦwww.region-celle.de) is in the Altes Rathaus, Markt 14–16.

Celle has a particularly exciting range of **hotels**, many in wonderful old buildings. Alternatively, there's a **youth hostel** at Weghausstr. 2 (ⓣ0 51 41/5 32 08; €13.80/16.50); turn left on leaving the Hauptbahnhof and continue straight ahead for about 2km, or take bus #3. The **campsite**, *Silbersee* (ⓣ0 51 41/3 12 23), is in Vorwerk, a suburb at the northern end of town, close to the terminus of bus #6.

Hotels

Am Landgestüt Landgestütstr. 1 ⓣ0 51 41/21 72 19, ⓕ2 39 77. Although the cheapest hotel in Celle, this is a very pleasant place to stay, and has a decent location in a whitewashed house on a quiet street opposite the Landgestüt. ④

Café Rössli Neue Str. 25 ⓣ0 51 41/68 26, ⓕ2 49 27. Reasonably priced hotel attached to an Altstadt coffee house. ⑤–⑦

Celler Hof Stechbahn 11 ⓣ0 51 41/2 0 11 40, ⓦwww.residenzhotels.de. Modernized Baroque palace in the handiest of settings directly across from the Schloss. ⑥–⑨

Fürstenhof Hannoversche Str. 55–56 ⓣ0 51 41/20 10, ⓦwww.fuerstenhof.de. Celle's most prestigious hotel occupies a seventeenth-century nobleman's palace a short distance south of the Altstadt. Its main restaurant, *Endtenfang*, is one of the best (and most expensive) in northern Germany; *Palio*, which serves Italian cuisine, and *Le Bistro*, which offers French country cooking, are altogether more affordable. ⑨

St Georg St-Georg-Str. 25–27 ⓣ0 51 41/21 05 10, ⓦwww.hotel-st-georg.de. Again in a seventeenth-century building, this time a half-timbered house at the eastern edge of the centre. ⑥–⑧

Schifferkrug Speicherstr. 9 ⓣ0 51 41/37 47 76, ⓦwww.schifferkrug-celle.de. Medium-priced hotel with a particularly fine restaurant, midway between the Hauptbahnhof and the Schloss. ❺

Utspann Im Kreise 13 ⓣ0 51 41/9 27 20, ⓦwww.utspann.de. Yet another restored half-timbered house, this time in the old Jewish quarter, with a good wine bar-restaurant. ❼–❾

The Town

The Schloss dominates the town, much as it has always done, and the streets of the Altstadt, which lies to the east, run towards it with a gesture of subservience. These contain Celle's other outstanding feature, an array of 480 **half-timbered buildings**, many of which have been adapted successfully to commercial use.

The Schloss

Originally built in the late thirteenth century, the **Schloss** (guided tours April–Oct Tues–Sun at 10am, 11am, noon, 1pm, 2pm & 3pm; Nov–March Tues–Sun at 11am & 3pm; €3) became the main residence of the Dukes of Braunschweig-Lüneburg in 1371, when the independently minded burghers of Lüneburg flexed their collective muscle and chucked out their feudal overlords. In 1530, the building was completely rebuilt in the Renaissance style and the present whitewashed exterior, with its idiosyncratic corner towers, decorative gable and lofty, confined courtyard, dates almost entirely from this period.

Sole survivor of the medieval castle, and the highlight of the tour, is the **Schlosskapelle**, which was cleverly incorporated into the southeastern tower facing the town, its pointed Gothic windows being the only giveaway as to its presence there. Its architectural simplicity was obscured in the second half of the sixteenth century by an integrated programme of Mannerist decoration that's still stunningly fresh and vibrant. The cycle of 76 paintings, commissioned from the Antwerp artist **Marten de Vos** (once an assistant to Tintoretto in Venice), forms a complete illustrated Bible, in accordance with the new Protestant doctrines. The two galleries are adorned with portrait sculptures of Old and New Testament figures, and wacky pendants of varying shapes and sizes hang from the vault. Both the pulpit, with beautiful reliefs of the Passion, and the organ, with painted shutters, are intrinsic parts of the scheme.

Early in the eighteenth century the Duchy of Lüneburg was reunited with Hannover (which had split off the previous century) when Sophie Dorothea, daughter of the last Duke of Lüneburg, married the future George I of Britain. Thereafter, Celle was no more than the second-string German residence of the Hanoverian dynasty, and a place where those who had fallen from grace could readily be dumped. In the 1770s the Schloss became home for a few years to an exiled queen, Caroline Mathilde of Denmark, who was banished following an indiscretion with a courtier. Her suite of rooms, the **Caroline-Mathilde-Räume** (Tues–Sun 10am–5pm; €2.50 including Bomann-Museum), contains a museum of the history of the Kingdom of Hannover.

An especially pleasant way to sneak a look inside other parts of the Schloss is to go to a performance at the **Schlosstheater** – dating back to 1674, it's the oldest one in Germany to have a resident company. Concerts and plays are performed throughout the year, except during July and August. Tickets and information are available from the special counter in the tourist office (ⓣ0 51 41/1 27 13, ⓦwww.schlosstheater-celle.de). Although some of the guided tours of the Schloss do include a visit to the handsome Baroque auditorium, this is entirely dependent on whether or not it is being used for rehearsals at the time.

The Altstadt

Every street in the Altstadt is a visual treat, and well worth including in a gentle stroll. The place to begin is Stechbahn (formerly a yard used for tournaments) which runs from the centre of Schlossplatz. Opposite the early sixteenth-century court pharmacy, the **Löwenapothek**, is the Gothic **Stadtkirche**, whose **tower** (April–Oct Tues–Sat 10–11.45am & 2–4.45pm; €1), which was added as recently as 1913, commands the best view of the town. A trumpeter plays a chorale from here at 6.30am and 6.30pm every day. The interior of the church was transformed in the late seventeenth century by the addition of the Italianate stuccowork and painted galleries, another complete illustrated Bible. A whole series of elaborate Gothic, Renaissance and Baroque **tombs** of the local dukes line the walls of the chancel. Behind the Stadtkirche is the **Rathaus**, whose fourteenth-century *Ratskeller* is the oldest restaurant in northern Germany. Most of the building, however, is in the carefree Weser Renaissance style, and is distinguished by two beautifully contrasted oriel windows: one at street level, the other an extension of a gable.

The most outstanding half-timbered house in Celle is the **Hoppener-Haus** at the corner of Rundestrasse and Poststrasse. Built for a courtier in 1532, it's richly carved with allegorical figures, monsters, scrollwork and scenes of rural life. The oldest dated house, at Am Heiligen Kreuz 26, states that it was built in 1526, though Neue Str. 32 (originally fifteenth-century but with a Renaissance oriel) has the best claim to be regarded as the most venerable house in town. Look out for the corner of Nordwall and Bergstrasse, where someone built their home on top of a piece of the original city wall. Among later Baroque stone buildings is the **Stechinellihaus** on Grosser Plan, named after an influential Italian architect and courtier who lived in a house on this site.

The **Bomann-Museum** (Tues–Sun 10am–5pm; €2.50 including Caroline-Mathilde-Räume; Ⓦwww.boumann-museum.de), in a grandiose Jugendstil building at the corner of Schlossplatz and Stechbahn, is above average for a local collection. Its displays on regional trades, history and folklore feature several reconstructed farmhouses and (in the courtyard) a half-timbered house fully furnished in the Biedermeier style. Alongside is the new **Kunstmuseum** (Tues–Sun 10am–5pm; €2.50), which is devoted to contemporary painting, sculpture and luminous art. It's billed as the first 24-hour art museum in the world, as the objects on the ground floor are permanently illuminated, and hence clearly visible from outside at all hours of the day and night.

The rest of the town

Just outside the eastern edge of the Altstadt is the old ghetto, though the colourful Baroque half-timbered houses themselves hardly offer any clue to the area's former status. Within one of these houses, Im Kreise 24, is the **Synagoge** (Tues–Thurs 3–5pm, Fri 9–11am, Sun 11am–1pm). Its decoration was destroyed on *Kristallnacht*, but, most unusually, it wasn't burned down. After the war it was well restored, and it stands today as one of the very few historic Jewish temples left in Germany.

Not far from here, bounding the southern side of the Altstadt, is the **Französischer Garten** (French Garden), which was laid out in the seventeenth century and later adapted in the informal English manner. Beyond is the **Ludwigskirche**, a Neoclassical church built by local architects in close imitation of the style of Karl Friedrich Schinkel, who did so much to define the appearance of Berlin. The interior is a gem – a miniature, updated version of the columned basilicas of the Romans.

To the south, down Breite Strasse, is the **Niedersächsisches Landgestüt** (Lower Saxon Stud Farm), which was founded by King George II in 1735. It can be visited outside the season, when the 250 or so stallions are put out to stud (mid-July to mid-Feb Mon–Fri 8.30am–noon & 1–3.30pm; free; ⓦwww.landgestuetcelle.de), but the best time to come is during the big autumn **festival**, the highlight of Celle's social calendar. Held on the last two Sundays in September and the first in October, plus the Wednesday preceding these, each programme (€25) lasts for three hours, and features a parade of the stallions, as well as a quadrille performed by coaches and ten.

Eating and drinking

As well as the restaurants in the hotels above, there are plenty of other good places to eat and drink in Celle.

Bier-Akademie Weisser Wall 6. Traditional beer hall-cum-restaurant, with summer garden.
Café Interpool Bahnhofstr. 14. Drolly-named café-bar with pool tables and internet access. Open daily 5pm–2/4am.
Café Kraatz Piltzergasse 4–5. One of several good cafés in the Altstadt, particularly recommended for its cakes.
Café Kraemer Stechbahn 7. Another fine coffee house, in a half-timbered building opposite the Stadtkirche.
Congress Union Thaerplatz 1. Classy, municipally owned restaurant in a custom-built Jugendstil building with a winter garden. It offers bargain lunchtime menus and a mouth-watering cold table. Closed Sun & Mon.
Hannen-Fass Am Heiligen Kreuz 5. Normally the liveliest of the Altstadt pubs, with the bonus of a front beer garden.
Ratskeller Markt 14. Famous old cellar restaurant, among the best of its ilk in Germany. It's also among the priciest, though its set lunches are good value.
Weinkeller Postmeister von Hinüber Zöllnerstr. 25. Very classy wine bar-restaurant, offering a wide choice of vintages and a menu which changes every week. Closed Sun & Mon.

Hannover (Hanover)

HANNOVER, which lies some 50km southwest of Celle, was something of a late developer, only coming to the fore in the second half of the seventeenth century. Subsequently, it had the benefit of a long special relationship with Britain, thanks to a quirk of fate which resulted in its ruling dynasty inheriting the British throne in 1714, and from 1814 to 1866 it was also a **royal capital city** in its own right. This status was suddenly lost when it fell victim to the expansionist policies of Prussia, and it was reduced to a marginal role until 1946, when it returned to prominence as capital of the new Land of Lower Saxony. Hannover's reputation as a dynamic, thrusting business centre was given a major boost when it was chosen to host **EXPO 2000**, the first World Exposition ever held in Germany, and the city hopes to profit from the legacy of this for many years to come.

Hannover suffers from the fact that it does not fit most people's perception of what a major historical metropolis should be like. It lacks a dominant architectural landmark, such as a great cathedral, castle or palace, and does not even have an obvious main thoroughfare or a grand public square. What it does have are really magnificent **gardens**: those at Herrenhausen rank among the most impressive in Europe, preserving their spectacular original Baroque features almost intact. They now have a fitting modern complement in the EXPO site, which seems sure to become an important permanent tourist attraction. As the city also has a number of first-class **museums** and a vibrant cultural scene, it well warrants a visit of a couple of days at least.

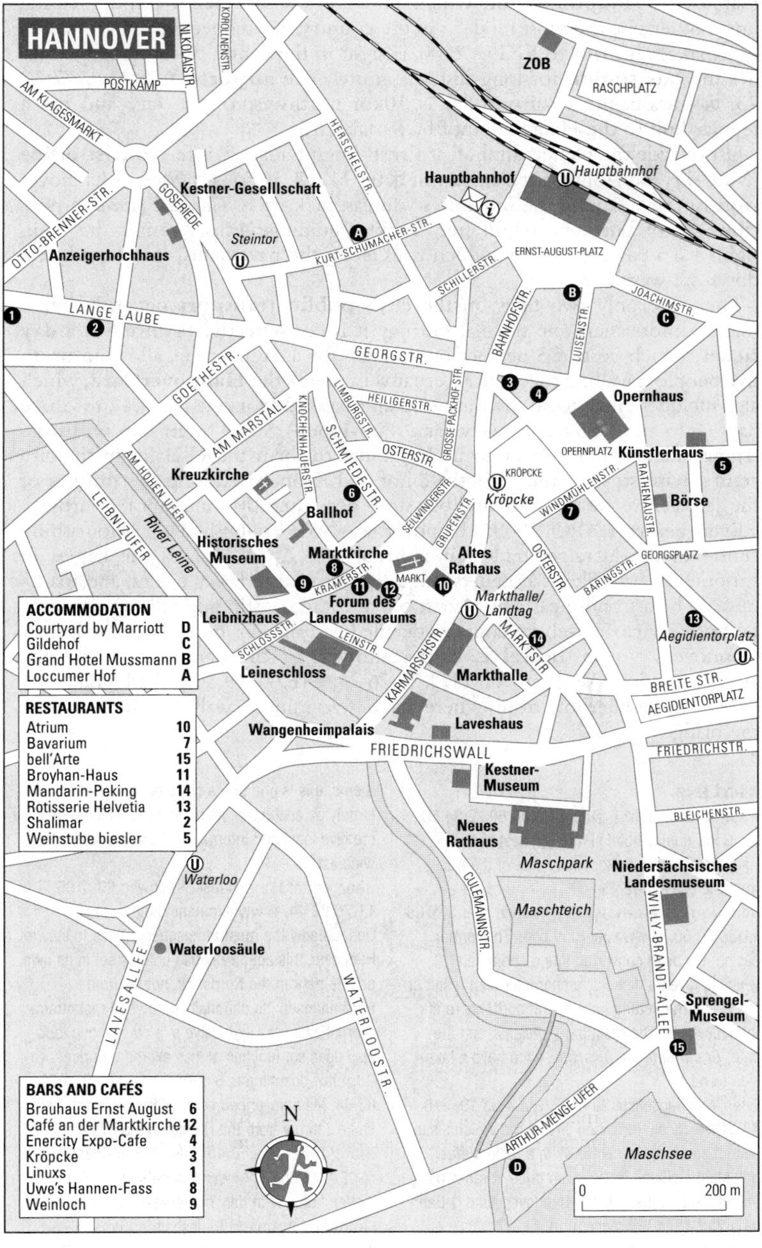

HANNOVER

ACCOMMODATION	
Courtyard by Marriott	D
Gildehof	C
Grand Hotel Mussmann	B
Loccumer Hof	A

RESTAURANTS	
Atrium	10
Bavarium	7
bell'Arte	15
Broyhan-Haus	11
Mandarin-Peking	14
Rotisserie Helvetia	13
Shalimar	2
Weinstube biesler	5

BARS AND CAFÉS	
Brauhaus Ernst August	6
Café an der Marktkirche	12
Enercity Expo-Cafe	4
Kröpcke	3
Linuxs	1
Uwe's Hannen-Fass	8
Weinloch	9

NIKOLAISTR.
KOROLINENSTR.
POSTKAMP
AM KLAGESMARKT
ZOB
RASCHPLATZ
HERSCHELSTR.
Hauptbahnhof
Hauptbahnhof
Kestner-Gesellschaft
GOSERIEDE
OTTO-BRENNER-STR.
Anzeigerhochhaus
Steintor
KURT-SCHUMACHER-STR.
ERNST-AUGUST-PLATZ
SCHILLERSTR.
JOACHIMSTR.
BAHNHOFSTR.
LUISENSTR.
LANGE LAUBE
GEORGSTR.
GOETHESTR.
HEILIGERSTR.
GROSSE PACKHOF STR.
Opernhaus
AM MARSTALL
KNOCHENHAUERSTR.
LIMBURGSTR.
SCHMIEDESTR.
OSTERSTR.
OPERNPLATZ
Künstlerhaus
KRÖPCKE
Kröpcke
AM HOHEN UFER
Kreuzkirche
WINDMÜHLENSTR.
RATHENAUSTR.
Börse
LEIBNIZUFER
River Leine
Ballhof
SEILWINDERSTR.
GRUPENSTR.
Historisches Museum
Marktkirche
Altes Rathaus
OSTERSTR.
GEORGSPLATZ
KRAMERSTR.
MARKT
BARINGSTR.
Forum des Landesmuseums
Markthalle/ Landtag
Leibnizhaus
SCHLOSSSTR.
LEINSTR.
MARKTSTR.
Aegidientorplatz
KARMARSCHSTR.
Leineschloss
Markthalle
BREITE STR.
AEGIDIENTORPLATZ
Laveshaus
Wangenheimpalais
FRIEDRICHSWALL
FRIEDRICHSTR.
Kestner-Museum
BLEICHENSTR.
Neues Rathaus
Maschpark
Niedersächsisches Landesmuseum
Waterloo
CULEMANNSTR.
Maschteich
WILLY-BRANDT-ALLEE
Waterloosäule
LAVESALLEE
WATERLOOSTR.
Sprengel-Museum
ARTHUR-MENGE-UFER
N
Maschsee
0 200 m

Arrival, information and accommodation

Hannover's **Hauptbahnhof**, which preserves its nineteenth-century facade but is otherwise the most modern in the country, having been given an expensive makeover prior to EXPO 2000, is right in the centre of town; to the rear lies the **bus station** for long-distance routes. The **airport** (Ⓣ05 11/9 77 12 23, Ⓦwww.hannover-airport.de) is 10km northwest of the city and has a regular link to the Hauptbahnhof by S-Bahn #5.

Just outside the Hauptbahnhof, at Ernst-August-Platz 2, is the **tourist office** (Mon–Fri 9am–6pm, Sat 9am–2pm; Ⓣ05 11/12 34 51 11, Ⓦwww.hannover-tourism.de). Among the brochures you can pick up is *The Red Thread*, a horribly chatty but very useful free booklet guiding visitors round the main sights via a painted red line which runs along the pavements, across roads and down subways.

There are only two fares on the city's **public transport** network, but if making more than one normal journey it is cost-effective to invest in a **day ticket**, which costs €3 per person and €6 for a mini-group, allowing up to five people travelling together. Alternatively, there's the **HannoverCard**, which also includes entry to all the museums and costs €8 for one day, €12 for three days (€15 and €25 respectively for a mini-group). Some trams stop on Ernst-August-Platz, while others go underground to form the U-Bahn in the city centre, with stops at the Hauptbahnhof and Kröpcke. Among the features of the city centre are the tram and bus stops decorated by contemporary artists.

Even before EXPO 2000, Hannover was well established as a flourishing centre of the lucrative trade fair industry (the April *Messe* is the largest in Europe). As a result, its hoteliers can afford to charge fancy prices, and mark-ups can be astronomical. The tourist office charges a stinging €8 for its room-finding service. Its website contains detailed descriptions of many of the hotels. Hannover's **youth hostel** is 2km southwest of the centre at Ferdinand-Wilhelm-Fricke-Weg 1 (Ⓣ05 11/1 31 76 74; €16.60/19.30); take U-Bahn #3 or #7 to Fischerhof, from where it's a five-minute walk to the left over the bridge.

Hotels

Atlanta Hinüberstr. 1 Ⓣ05 11/3 38 60, Ⓕ34 59 28. Good-quality hotel just to the east of the Hauptbahnhof, on the opposite side of the tracks from the city centre. 6–9

Courtyard by Marriott Arthur-Menge-Ufer 3 Ⓣ05 11/36 60 00, Ⓦwww.marriott.com. The former casino has been converted into a chain hotel, which is given a distinctive character as a result of the wonderful setting right by the north shore of the Maschsee. The restaurant, *Julian's*, and the café, *Grand Café am Maschee*, each have a lake-side terrace. 8

Eden Waldhausenstr. 30 Ⓣ05 11/84 83 10, Ⓕ8 48 31 44. Nicely furnished villa in the Waldhausen district south of the centre. With a good buffet breakfast included in the room price, it ranks as one of the best bargains in Hannover. Take U-Bahn #1, #2 or #8 to Döhrener Turm. 4–6

Feuchers Lila Kranz Berliner Allee 33 Ⓣ05 11/85 89 21, Ⓕ85 43 83. Although it has only five rooms, this is one of the city's best-known hotels, largely on account of its restaurant, which offers creative local and international cooking and a huge wine list. 6–8

Georgenhof Herrenhaüser Kirchweg 20 Ⓣ05 11/70 22 44, Ⓦwww.romantikhotels.com. Undoubtedly the most atmospheric place to stay in Hannover, this country house hotel is set in its own private park in the Nordstadt, not far from Herrenhausen. Its nationally renowned restaurant, *Stern*, has a very expensive a la carte menu, but also does set lunches at less exorbitant prices. 7

Gildehof Joachimstr. 6 Ⓣ05 11/36 36 80, Ⓕ30 66 44. Medium-priced hotel with restaurant, just a stone's throw from the Hauptbahnhof. 4–6

Grand Hotel Mussman Ernst-August-Platz 7 Ⓣ05 11/3 65 60, Ⓦwww.grandhotel.de. Fine old station hotel, with fully modernised rooms. 8–9

Landhaus Ammann Hildesheimer Str. 185, Waldenhausen Ⓣ05 11/83 08 18, Ⓕ8 43 77 49. Set in its own grounds just east of the Maschsee, and reached by U-Bahn #1, #2 or #8 to Döhrener Turm, this is another hotel in the country house style, and again has a renowned gourmet restaurant. 8–9

Loccumer Hof Kurt-Schumacher-Str. 16 ⓣ05 11/1 26 40, ⓦwww.loccumerhof.de. Classy establishment with equally good restaurant, conveniently close to the Hauptbahnhof. 7

Reverey Aegidiendamm 8 ⓣ&ⓕ05 11/88 37 11. Medium-priced hotel just beyond the southeastern fringe of the Altstadt, handy for the Maschpark and the museums. 6

The City

Hannover had to reconstruct itself after being badly damaged by World War II bombing. The northern part of the city centre is a vast shopping area of mostly pedestrianized streets and arcades. Further south is the modest-sized **Altstadt**, beyond which lie the inner ring road, the best museums and an attractive green belt. To the northwest lie the royal gardens of **Herrenhausen** (as Höringhusen came to be known). In the outer suburbs there's an important new attraction in the **EXPO-Gelände**.

Around the Hauptbahnhof

The view on arrival at the Hauptbahnhof, to the north of the centre, isn't exactly prepossessing, with a bland pedestrian precinct stretching ahead. Underneath runs the **Passarelle**; mostly under cover, but with sections in the open air, it's meant to be a sort of subterranean bazaar-cum-piazza. While the prime sites at the flashy end are occupied by expensive shops, towards the station it predictably becomes seedier.

Standing at Hannover's most popular rendezvous, the **Café Kröpcke**, slap bang in the middle of the precinct, the most imposing building in view is the **Opernhaus**, a proud Neoclassical design which is arguably the finest of the city's showpiece buildings by the court architect Georg Ludwig Friedrich Laves. On Sophienstrasse, the yellow- and red-brick **Künstlerhaus**, originally a museum, is now a lively arts centre, while the neo-Renaissance **Ständehaus**, built as a guildhall, houses the state treasury department. The **Börse** on Rathenaustrasse actually imitates the Tudor style – proof that British influence continued long after the end of the monarchical link.

If you're keen on twentieth-century architecture, make a detour along Georgstrasse to Goseriede to see the **Anzeigerhochhaus**. This newspaper office, made of brick-clad reinforced concrete and topped with a green copper dome, is an example of the 1920s Expressionism of Fritz Höger. Even if it's hardly the skyscraper it purports to be, and is less dramatic than the same architect's Chilehaus in Hamburg, it's nonetheless an arresting, balanced and well thought-out design. The dome now houses the city's most adventurous cinema. A little further up the same street, the **Kestner-Gesellschaft** (Mon–Wed & Fri–Sun 10am–7pm, Thurs 10am–9pm; variable entrance charges) mounts important temporary exhibitions, principally of contemporary art, in a converted swimming pool.

The Altstadt

A few minutes' walk south of the Anzeigerhochhaus are a few streets of rebuilt **half-timbered houses**. These convey something of the impression of the medieval town, which had already been much altered before the devastation of World War II. Its form is easier to imagine if you've seen nearby Celle, which is preserved almost intact. The first major building in their midst is the fourteenth-century **Kreuzkirche** where there's a *Passion Triptych* by Cranach at the high altar. One of the chapels is used by the local Serbian community, and is decorated with icons – a stark contrast with the Protestant sobriety of the rest of the church.

On Am Hohen Ufer to the south is the **Beginenturm**, the last surviving remnant of the city walls. It has been incorporated in the fabric of the modern building housing the **Historisches Museum** (Tues 10am–8pm, Wed–Fri 10am–4pm, Sat & Sun 10am–6pm; €2.50, free Fri), one of Germany's most imaginative local history museums. On the ground floor to the left are the four **state coaches** of the House of Hannover. These are still family property – even the gold carriage, adorned with Rococo paintings and carvings, which was made in London in 1783 and used for state openings of the Westminster parliament. Upstairs, there's a telling contrast to these limousines in the form of the *Hanomag*, a tiny two-seater convertible developed in 1928 as a sort of trial run for the Volkswagen Beetle.

Just across the road is the **Ballhof**, a seventeenth-century half-timbered sports hall which is now the main repertory theatre. On nearby Holzmarkt (not its original location) the **Leibnizhaus** has been re-erected following its total destruction in the war. This magnificent Renaissance mansion was the home of **Gottfried Wilhelm Leibniz.** A historian by profession, Leibniz was active in a vast range of intellectual fields: he developed Pascal's calculating machine, arrived independently at the theory of differential calculus at the same time as Newton, charted the origins and migrations of mankind, and made enormous contributions to the disciplines of jurisprudence, philosophy, theology, geology and linguistics.

The Altstadt's dominant building is the fourteenth-century **Marktkirche**, one of the most southerly of the series of brick hall churches characteristic of the Baltic lands. Its bulky tower, terminating in a spire of unusual design, has long been the emblem of the city. Originally, it was meant to be much higher, but an old chronicle reports that it was finished off quickly because "the masons had become tired and sick in the purse". The unadorned interior walls are now closer to how the building originally looked than has been the case for some three hundred years. There's a noble carved **Passion retable**, made around 1500, at the high altar; miraculously, the fourteenth- and fifteenth-century stained glass in the east windows has survived, and was cleaned and restored a few years back.

Directly opposite is the high-gabled fifteenth-century **Altes Rathaus**, whose elaborate brickwork is enlivened with colourful glazed tiles. On the west side of the square is the **Forum des Landesmuseums** (Tues, Wed & Fri–Sun 10am–5pm, Thurs 10am–7pm; €4, or €5 combined ticket with Landesmuseum; Ⓦwww.nlmh.de). Otherwise known as the Georg-von-Cölln-Haus, this five-storey nineteenth-century building, which uses iron as a key component in the construction, is the city's main venue for temporary exhibitions.

Friedrichswall and around

The line of the former city wall is now occupied by the inner ring road, forever seething with traffic. On Friederikenplatz stands the **Leineschloss**, which is now the Land parliament. Its dignified porticos, modelled on the temples of ancient Greece, were added by Laves, who carried out a thorough transformation of the original structure. Immediately to the east, two more buildings by him – the **Wangenheim-Palais** and the **Laveshaus** – stand side by side; the latter was his own home. Down Lavesallee is yet another of his works, the **Waterloosäule**, a triumphal column commemorating the part played by the Hanoverian troops in the final defeat of Napoleon.

Opposite the Laveshaus is the **Kestner-Museum** (Tues & Thurs–Sun 11am–6pm, Wed 11am–8pm; €1.50, free Fri; ⓦwww.kestner-museum.de). This compact decorative arts museum is named after its founder August Kestner, a Hanoverian diplomat in Rome. He was the son of Charlotte Buff, Goethe's first love and a central character in his novella *The Sufferings of Young Werther*. On the first floor, the medieval collection features treasures and textiles from Lower Saxon convents. Outstanding are surviving items from the *Goldene Tafel* of St Michael in Lüneburg, and the magnificent gilded bronze head-reliquary of an unknown saint, made around 1200 for Stift Fischbeck. The remaining galleries have an eclectic array of exhibits, ranging from Renaissance bronzes through eighteenth-century porcelain to a luxuriant selection of Art Nouveau *objets d'art* from America as well as Europe. Upstairs are examples of the ancient Greek, Etruscan, Roman and Cypriot civilizations, along with a more comprehensive Egyptian collection.

Next door is the **Neues Rathaus**, a gargantuan early twentieth-century Art Deco-cum-neo-Gothic fantasy, which is held into its marshy foundations by over 6000 piles of beechwood. It's definitely worth a peek inside; there are occasional guided tours but you can just wander round, up and down the spiral staircases. The **dome** (April–Oct daily 10am–12.45pm & 1.30–4.45pm; €1.50) offers the best views of the city, though the main attraction is the lift which takes you up – it follows an inclined path and is apparently one of only two in Europe like this. Look out for the models of Hannover at various stages of its history; the one of the bombed wartime city is a shocking record of the damage it suffered.

Directly behind the Neues Rathaus is the **Maschpark**, with a small artificial lake. Further on is a much larger man-made lake, the **Maschsee**, which serves as the locals' main playground, with the north bank turned into a huge beer garden in summer. You can saunter down its tree-lined promenades, rent a rowing boat or canoe, or take a cruise on a pleasure steamer; the last-named are run by *üstra-Reisen* (ⓣ05 11/70 09 50, ⓦwww.uestra-reisen.de) and cost €6 for a round trip.

The Niedersächsisches Landesmuseum

The **Niedersächsisches Landesmuseum** (Tues, Wed & Fri–Sun 10am–5pm, Thurs 10am–7pm; €4; ⓦwww.nlmh.de) occupies stolid-looking premises facing the east side of the Maschpark. Its main draw is the Landesgalerie on the second floor, which has an excellent collection of paintings from the Middle Ages to the early twentieth century. On the left are two rooms of Primitives, of which the most notable is a *Passion Altar* by the first German artist known by name, **Master Bertram**. Most of the other works are by his anonymous Saxon contemporaries and include the retables from which the **Master of the Golden Table** and the **Master of the Barfüsser Altar** get their pseudonyms. Another highlight is the *SS Peter and Paul Altar* by the Hildesheim artist dubbed **Master of the Lambertikirche**; in a triumph of museum politics, all fourteen panels of this were reassembled here in 2000, having previously been split among six different German collections. In the following rooms, the star painting is an exquisite *Portrait of Philipp Melanchthon* by **Hans Holbein the Younger**, displayed alongside its lid, which is one of the few surviving examples of Holbein's skill as a decorative artist. Hanging beside it is a lurid *Luther on his Deathbed* by **Cranach**, and a small *Christ Carrying the Cross* attributed to **Dürer**. A decent display of Italian Renaissance work includes pictures by Botticelli, Raphael, Pontormo and Bronzino.

The large *Bacchus and Venus* by the Antwerp Mannerist **Bartholomeus Spranger** is an allegory illustrating an old proverb: "Wine and women bring two sorrows to life". It's one of the most imposing paintings created in the erotic style cultivated at the turn of the seventeenth century at the court of Emperor Rudolf II in Prague – and in the tiny neighbouring principality of Schaumburg-Lippe. Pick of the seventeenth-century Flemish paintings are **Rubens**' *Madonna and Child*, **Van Dyck**'s *A Gentleman of Santander, The Governor of Antwerp*, and *Men Bathing by Moonlight* by **Michael Sweerts**; the last, characteristically for the artist, is a highly original subject, with wonderful luminous effects. There's a good cross-section of the Dutch school, including one of **Rembrandt**'s rare excursions into nature painting, *Landscape with the Baptism of the Eunuch*, another masterly exposition of light and shade. Also of special note is *A Woman in Profile* by his most talented pupil, the short-lived **Carel Fabritius**.

A comprehensive array of the varied styles practised in nineteenth-century Germany includes a set of four small canvases illustrating *The Times of Day* by **Friedrich**; **Leibl**'s haunting *Peasant Girl*; several humorous paintings by Spitzweg; and numerous examples of the Impressionists Liebermann, Corinth and Slevogt. A specially dimmed room shows the giant cartoons made by the members of the **Nazarene Brotherhood** for the decoration of the Casa Bartholdy in Rome.

On the first floor of the museum, the **archeology** department has as its showpiece the bodies of prehistoric men preserved naturally in the peat bogs of Lower Saxony. The varied contents of several excavated graves are another highlight, as is an array of Bronze Age jewellery. On the same floor is a **natural history** section with a wide variety of stuffed animals and a full-scale reconstruction of a dinosaur. Downstairs there's an **aquarium** with live fish from round the world and the **ethnography** department, with artefacts from Indonesia, Cameroon, Peru and the native tribes of North America.

The Sprengel-Museum

Further down the road, on Kurt-Schwitters-Platz, is the **Sprengel-Museum** (Tues 10am–8pm, Wed–Sun 10am–6pm; €3.50; Ⓦ www.sprengel-museum.de). Named after the chocolate magnate Bernhard Sprengel, whose gift of his private collection formed the basis of the museum, this ranks as one of the most exciting places in Germany in which to see modern art. Much of the display space is given over to changing exhibitions of photography, graphics and various experimental art forms, but there's also a first-rate permanent display of modern painting and sculpture.

Centrepiece of the museum is a huge range of the work of one of the twentieth century's most controversial and influential artists, Hannover's own **Kurt Schwitters**. His pleasing early landscapes and still lifes come as a surprise if you're only familiar with the famous Dadaist collages. The artist coined the term *Merz* to describe these, and set himself the target of creating a *Merzbau*, a work of art which would fill a house. Both completed versions of this were destroyed in the Nazi measures against "degenerate art", but an accurate reconstruction can be seen here.

Other highlights of the museum include a cross-section of **Picasso**'s work; complete rooms devoted to **Klee** and **Arp**; sculptures by Barlach and Henri Laurens; an updated *Prodigal Son* by **Beckmann**, along with self-portraits painted forty years apart; Surrealist paintings by Magritte, Tanguy and Ernst; and a huge range of Expressionists, with Munch, Nolde, Kirchner and Kokoschka all well represented.

The Welfengarten and the Georgengarten

There are four separate gardens which collectively make up the Herrenhäusen complex. The least remarkable of these, the **Welfengarten**, lies closest to the city centre, and is reached by proceeding northwards along Nienburger Strasse. It's dominated by the huge neo-Gothic pile of the **Welfenpalais**, now occupied by the university. To the left, the dead-straight avenue of lime trees named Herrenhäuser Allee cuts through the **Georgengarten**. This is a *jardin anglais* of the type beloved by the Romantics, featuring trees arranged in an apparently natural setting, and an artificial lake, crossed by two graceful little bridges designed by Laves.

Also within this park is the Neoclassical **Georgenpalais**, home of the **Wilhelm-Busch-Museum** (Tues–Sat 10am–5pm, Sun 10am–6pm; €4; Ⓦwww.wilhelm-busch-museum.de). The temporary exhibitions on the ground floor centre on the work of artists who have made a significant contribution to satirical expression – Daumier, Doré and Cruickshank have all been featured in recent years, as well as contemporary cartoonists. Upstairs, there's a permanent display on **Wilhelm Busch**, who lived and worked in Hannover in the nineteenth century. He was a capable painter of landscapes and genre scenes, but gained worldwide popularity through his illustrated books, notably *Max and Moritz*. In these, he invented what has become a stock vocabulary for strip-cartoonists, using patterns of oscillation to express movement, and conventional signs to depict each emotion.

The Grosser Garten

The Georgengarten was created as a foil to the magnificence of the formal **Grosser Garten** (daily 9am–4.30/8pm; €4, free in winter; Ⓦwww.herrenhaeuser-gaerten.de) beyond. This is justifiably the city's pride and joy, and can be reached directly from the centre by U-Bahn #4 or #5. It's best to time your visit to coincide with the playing of the **fountains** (late March to early Oct Mon–Fri 11am–noon & 3–4pm, Sat & Sun 11am–noon & 3–5pm) or when the **illuminations** are switched on (Wed–Sun at dusk). Credit for the splendour of the layout goes to the Electress Sophie, who called them "my life", and her gardener, the Frenchman Martin Charbonnier, who transformed the modest garden into a spectacular showpiece which drew on elements of the French, Italian and Dutch traditions. Sadly the royal palace was totally destroyed by Allied bombing in the war, but the **Galerie**, a festive hall adorned with frothy frescoes of Virgil's *Aeneid*, and the **Orangerie** have survived.

Just inside the entrance gate is one of the most striking features, the **Gartentheater**. Temporary structures for music and drama were commonplace within royal gardens, but this one was permanent, featuring an auditorium in the form of an amphitheatre. The hornbeam hedges cleverly doubled as scenery and changing rooms, while a series of gilded statues on pedestals served as stage props. Plays by Molière and Racine, and music by Handel formed the staple repertoire of this theatre in its early days, and are still performed during the summer season (Ⓦwww.festwochen-herrenhausen.de). Immediately to the west is the **Grosses Parterre**, whose eight sections are planted with geometric arrangements of flowers and shrubs. In front stands the Italianate **Grosse Kaskade**, belonging to the original garden, plus a sundial and the **Historische Grotte**. The last of these was stripped bare back in the eighteenth century, but, in one of the myriad EXPO-associated projects carried out in and around Hannover, the French artist Niki de Saint Phalle was commissioned to provide a new decorative scheme. The only woman ever to be granted the freedom of Hannover died in 2002 with the work still incomplete, but it was finished off the following year by her assistants, using the detailed plans she had left.

Behind the Grosses Parterre is a modern embellishment: eight small plots have been laid out to illustrate different styles of landscape gardening down the centuries. Particularly notable is the **Renaissancegarten**, which reproduces a section of the now-vanished Hortus Palatinus in Heidelberg. East of here is the secluded **Boskettgarten**, used by courtiers for intrigues and romantic encounters. The rear section of the Grosser Garten consists of a series of radiating avenues bounded by hedges and trees, each ending at a fountain. As a centrepiece, there's the **Grosse Fontäne**, whose 82m water jet is the highest of any garden fountain in Europe.

The Berggarten and the Fürstenhaus

Across Herrenhäuser Strasse to the north of the Grosser Garten is the **Berggarten** (same hours and ticket as the Grosser Garten; €2 in winter), set up to tend rare and exotic plants. Its collection of orchids was considered the finest in Europe, and many are still cultivated in its hothouses. Behind these are a rock garden, a pergola garden and an iris garden; the last-named is in full bloom in April and May. Even more glorious is the central "Paradise" of rhododendrons. At the far end of the Berggarten stands the **Mausoleum** of the House of Hannover, a late work by Laves in the sternest Neoclassical manner. A graphic illustration of how the architect's style had developed is provided by the domed **Bibliothekspavilion** at the entrance, which he designed thirty years earlier in a carefree idiom still showing echoes of the Baroque. Alongside is the latest addition to the facilities, the EXPO-associated **Regenwaldhaus** (Mon–Thurs 10am–7pm, Fri & Sat 10am–10pm; €8.50, €4.50 after 6.30pm on Fri & Sat; Ⓦwww.regenwaldhaus.de). This presents a miniaturised recreation of the Brazilian rain forest, complete with over 6000 plants, a waterfall, and exotic birds and animals.

Some compensation for the loss of the royal palace is provided by a number of courtly buildings to be found to the west along Herrenhäuser Strasse. The so-called **Fürstenhaus** (Tues–Sun 10am–5/6pm; €3) has been adapted as a sort of museum of the House of Hannover. There's one striking room entirely covered by a panorama of a hunt, and some fine portraits, including likenesses of King George III and Queen Sophie Charlotte by both Thomas Gainsborough and Johann Zoffany.

The EXPO-Gelände

The **EXPO-Gelände**, where the World Exposition was held in 2000, lies in the far southeastern outskirts of Hannover. U-Bahn #6 and #16 go to the east entrance, #8 and #18 to the north entrance, though the latter is usually only open when there's a trade fair on. To anyone who visited when EXPO was in full swing, what remains on site must inevitably seem a rather sad and ghostly reminder of the big event. Many of the pavilions – which were required to employ ecological construction techniques and re-usable materials – were removed soon after EXPO closed, while others were left in a semi- abandoned state. However, new roles are gradually being found for the buildings that remain, and the EXPO-Gelände has assumed a key position in the business and cultural life of Hannover; it also serves as a permanent showcase of international turn-of-the-millennium architecture.

The central square, **EXPO-Plaza**, is by far the best-preserved part of the grounds. Its buildings include the former German pavilion, an inward-curving transparent glass construction; the Preussag Arena, which is now used for concerts and sporting events; Planet M, which has metamorphosed from a media centre into an office building; and the Europa-Haus, originally the EU pavilion, part of which is now home to the **Exposeeum** (Sun 11am–4pm; €1; Ⓦwww.exposeeum.de), a museum commemorating EXPO 2000.

Many other reminders of EXPO can be seen in the adjacent **Ostgelände**. While it remains to be seen whether any of the Hannover buildings will assume the same iconic status as previous World Fair showpieces – such as the Eiffel Tower in Paris and the Atomium in Brussels – one possible candidate is Deutsche Post's **Postbox**, which at 46.5m in height is by far the largest post box in the world, complete with an observation platform offering a grandstand view of the grounds. Another very striking yellow building, the Lithuanian pavilion – which is in the shape of the tail of an aeroplane – has been retained by the country which built it as a trade centre. The British pavilion also remains *in situ*, and is now used for film production. One very popular survivor is the pavilion of the Netherlands, which gained the nickname of the "Eco-Sandwich" because of the re-creations of five very different Dutch landscapes on each of its levels. It has been given a new lease of life as a forum for renewable energy.

Eating, drinking and nightlife

There's a huge choice of places to eat and drink, with the Altstadt and the streets around being the liveliest area at night. Most of the gourmet restaurants are attached to hotels (see pp.612–13). For a daytime **snack** or a quick lunch, head for the Markthalle on Karmarschstrasse, where the stallholders sell a host of different kinds of ethnic cooking. Hannover's **beer** tradition continues unabated: Gilde, the best-known local brewery, has operated uninterruptedly since 1546; its main rival is Herrenhausen. The city also has a predictably wide range of musical and theatrical venues.

Restaurants

Atrium Schmiedestr. 3. Hannover here offers a modern re-interpretation of the traditional Ratskeller, with tables in the splendid main hallway of the Altes Rathaus and an international menu.

Bavarium Windmühlenstr. 3. Tucked away on an unassuming side street is this authentically Bavarian beer hall and garden, serving Löwenbräu beers and typically hearty cuisine.

bell'Arte Kurt-Schwitters-Platz 1. The restaurant attached to the Sprengel-Museum remains open until late in the evening. It has a terrace overlooking the Maschee, and has a predominantly Italianate menu.

Broyhan-Haus Kramerstr. 24. Three-storey Gaststätte in the heart of the Altstadt, complete with historic cellars. It's named in honour of the sixteenth-century Hannover brewer who is credited with the invention of export beer.

Carmel-Wintergarten Berliner Allee 34. Evenings-only kosher Jewish restaurant, just to the east of the centre.

Hiller Blumenstr. 3. Founded in 1955, this is Germany's oldest continually functioning vegetarian and wholefood restaurant. It's located on the eastern edge of the city centre, and serves inexpensive set lunches. Closed Sun.

Mandarin-Peking Marktstr. 45. The city's best Chinese restaurant, with the usual bargain menus at lunchtime.

Mexcal in der Roneburg Königsworther Str. 27. A decidedly unusual combination of a Mexican restaurant and a Hausbrauerei, located just to the west of the city centre.

Rotisserie Helvetia Georgsplatz 11. Top-notch Swiss speciality restaurant; it's a little on the pricey side, but not excessively so, and has bargain lunch dishes Mon–Sat.

Shalimar Lange Laube 13. Good-quality Indian restaurant with an authentic tandoori oven. It offers inexpensive lunch specials.

Weinstube biesler Sophienstr. 4. Wine bar-restaurant, offering a good selection of vintages from throughout Germany and beyond, with food to match.

Bars and cafés

Brauhaus Ernst August Schmiedestr. 13. Hausbrauerei occupying the site of the original Broyhan brewery. One of the most popular spots in town, it serves reasonably priced meals and an excellent unfiltered *Pils*.

Café an der Marktkirche Am Markte 9. A good choice for *Kaffee und Kuchen*. Closed Sun.

enercity Expo-Café Ständehausstr. 6. This looks as though it will be a permanent city-centre legacy of EXPO 2000. It offers a huge variety of coffees and often features live music in the evening.
Kröpcke Georgstr. 35. This famous café, now run by Mövenpick, is a real Hannover institution, one of its main landmarks. It has several different sections, including the vegetarian *Grün Schnabel*.
Linuxs Lange Laube 27. Internet café on the western edge of the centre. Open Mon–Fri 9am–8pm, Sat 11am–10pm.
Uwe's Hannen-Fass Knochenhauerstr. 36. Hugely popular Altstadt student bar which offers mountainous piles of cheap pub grub.
Weinloch Burgstr. 33. Liveliest of the several good pubs to be found in this street in the heart of the Altstadt.

Nightclubs and live music venues

Faust Zur Bettfedernfabrik 3, Linden. This former factory building by the River Leine is one of Hannover's major nightlife venues, with live music, parties, festivals and other events. There's also a beer garden and café-bar. Take U-Bahn #10 to Glocksee.
Jazz-Club Lindener Berge 39. The main jazz venue, with regular sessions on Mon & Fri.
Osho Raschplatz 7L. Bhagwan-run disco, patronised mainly by teenagers and twenty-somethings, in the "Bermuda Triangle" to the rear of the Hauptbahnhof.
Palo Palo Raschplatz 8a. Small disco which plays funk and soul daily from 10pm.
Pavillon Lister Meile 4. This multi-functional cultural centre in an old shopping mall is Hannover's main world music venue, with an annual festival, *Masala*. It also incorporates *Mezzo*, which is said to be the city's most patronised café.
UJZ Glocksee Glockseestr. 35. A one-time squat having a new lease of life as a youth culture centre, with live music, discos and theatre. Take U-Bahn #10 to Glocksee.

Festivals, classical music and theatre

Hannover's Schützenfest, held over ten days in late June/early July, is the most spectacular of the many **marksmen's festivals** held in northern Germany. It features processions with floats, fireworks and a considerable intake of alcohol, notably the *Lüttje-Lage*, in which you drink simultaneously from 2 glasses – one containing beer, the other schnapps – placed one inside the other. Many of the best **classical music** performances are to be heard in the Protestant churches; these are listed in a bi-monthly leaflet. The Knabenchor Hannover (Hannover Boys' Choir) is currently at least as good as its famous Viennese counterpart; in spite of the name it generally performs with adult male voices as well. There's also a female equivalent, the Mädchenchor Hannover. Choice in **theatre** is predictably wide-ranging.

Funkhaus des NDR Rudolf von Bennigsen Ufer 22 ⓣ05 11/98 80, ⓦwww.ndr.de. Classical concerts are often held at the radio studios overlooking the Maschsee.
Opernhaus Opernplatz 1 ⓣ05 11/99 99 11 11, ⓦwww.staatstheater-hannover.de. In this Neoclassical masterpiece there are alternating opera and ballet performances, as well as occasional concerts by the Niedersächsisches Staatsorchester.
Schauspielhaus Prinzenstr. 9 ⓣ05 11/99 99 22 22, ⓦwww.staatstheater-hannover.de. This uncompromisingly modern building is the city's main dramatic stage.
Tanztheater im Hof Lister Meile 33 ⓣ05 11/3 48 09 95. Small specialist venue for modern dance.

Bückeburg

The tiny principality of Schaumburg-Lippe (formerly Holstein-Schaumburg) was one of the great survivors of imperial Germany. By skilful diplomacy it managed to avoid being swallowed up by unwelcome suitors, and kept its place on the map until 1946, when it was incorporated into Lower Saxony. At the turn of the seventeenth century, the then hamlet of **BÜCKEBURG** – which now lies on the Hannover–Osnabrück rail line, just 8km east of the

Westphalian town of Minden – was chosen as the new capital, and it remains the seat of the former ruling family.

Set in its own extensive grounds at the edge of the town centre, the **Schloss** (guided tours daily 9.30am–5/6pm; €4.50; ⓦwww.schloss-bueckeburg.de) was originally a fourteenth-century tower house. It was transformed into a splendid Renaissance palace in the mid-sixteenth century, though one wing had to be rebuilt a couple of hundred years later following its destruction in a fire. Inside, the apartments are eclectic, to say the least, passing in quick succession from a grandiose Wilhelmine banqueting chamber with a huge Venetian-style fresco, through an intimate Rococo smoking room, to a Renaissance hall hung with superb Brussels tapestries. The **Schlosskapelle**, which was originally Gothic, was adapted in the Mannerist period for Protestant worship. As if to give the lie to the belief that the new faith was inimical to worldly beauty, it was decorated in the most extravagant manner possible. The walls are covered with frescoes, and there's a complete set of gilded and carved furnishings. In the same period, the even more sumptuous **Goldener Saal** was built as a secular counterpart. Its doorway, rising to the full height of the room, is flanked by huge statues of Mars and Flora, with Mercury floating above in the company of cherubs and goddesses.

Also within the Schlosspark is a sombre neo-Romanesque **Mausoleum** (daily April–Oct 10am–5pm; €2.50), whose dome has what's apparently the largest mosaic in Germany. On the bridge over the moat which separates the park from the town proper are two writhing **bronzes**, *Venus and Adonis* and *The Rape of Prosperine*, both the work of Adrian de Vries.

The brothers Hans and Ebbert Wulf of Hildesheim, who had carried out the decoration of the Schlosskapelle and Goldener Saal, were afterwards commissioned to build Bückeburg's other focal building, the **Stadtkirche** (mid-April to mid-Oct Mon–Fri 10.30am–noon & 3–5pm, Sat 3–5pm; mid-Oct to mid-April Thurs & Sat 2–4pm), which lies at the top of the main Lange Strasse. This competes with Wolfenbüttel for the title of first full-scale Protestant church ever to be built. It's much the more unified building of the two, and is a real masterpiece of design, notwithstanding the Latin inscription running across the facade which declares that it is: "An Example of Piety, not of Architecture". Apart from its facade the exterior is a glum affair, but the **interior** is stunning. Massive Corinthian pillars shoot right up to the vault, and your eye is drawn to the gleaming gold case of the massive organ at the far end, at which Johann Christoph Friedrich Bach, son of J.S., presided for 45 years. In adapting the old hall-church formula to the Protestant emphasis on preaching, brightly painted galleries were added all round, and the **pulpit**, whose base is lined with gold-plated reliefs of the life of Christ, was placed in the centre. Even more impressive is Adrian de Vries' **font**, where the Holy Ghost, hooked up by wires, hovers above the Baptism of Christ.

Housed in a half-timbered house with a jarring modern extension on Sablé Platz, the pedestrian area between Lange Strasse and Bahnhofstrasse, is the **Hubschraubermuseum** (Helicopter Museum; daily 9am–5pm; €4; ⓦwww.hubschraubermuseum.de), apparently the only one of its kind in the world. A reminder of the proximity of the German and British military bases, it incorporates an educational display on vertical flight technique, and is well labelled in English. Following a section on the history of man's attempts to fly, there are dozens of original machines, representing all the famous names in helicopter design.

Practicalities

Bückeburg's **Bahnhof** lies at the northern end of town; it's a straight ten-minute walk down Bahnhofstrasse to the Schloss. The **tourist office**

(Mon–Fri 8am–12.30pm & 2–5pm, Sat 9–11am; ⓣ0 57 22/20 61 80, ⓦwww.bueckeburg.de) is at Marktplatz 4. There are five **hotels** in the town centre: *Brauhaus*, Braustr. 1 (ⓣ0 57 22/9 67 70, ⓦwww.brauhaus-bueckeburg.de; ❺); *Altstadtkeller*, Tempelerstr. 1 (ⓣ0 57 22/64 40; ❺); *Bemfert*, Brauhausstr. 8 (ⓣ0 57 22/47 21, ⓦwww.hotel-bemfert.de; ❺); *Am Schlosstor*, Lange Str. 33 (ⓣ0 57 22/9 59 90; ❻); and *Ambiente*, Herminenstr. 11 (ⓣ0 57 22/96 70; ❻–❾). The last-named has the best **restaurant** in town; cheaper alternatives are the *Ratskeller* in the Rathaus directly opposite the Schloss gates and the seventeenth-century *Zur Falle*, Lange Str. 13.

Hameln (Hamelin)

"A pleasanter spot you never spied" was how Robert Browning characterized the venerable town of **HAMELN**, situated on the River Weser 45km southwest of Hannover. His verse rendition of the **legend of the Pied Piper** has made the place one of the best-known towns in Germany as far as English-speaking people are concerned – and earned him the eternal gratitude of the local tourist board.

Inevitably, the Pied Piper legend – perhaps the most endurably fascinating of Germany's rich store of folktales – always looms large, which makes Hameln an ideal outing if you have kids. However, there are more serious attractions as well. Along with nearby Lemgo (see p.572), it's the best place to see the distinctive **Weser Renaissance** style, a form of civil architecture which typically features large projecting bay windows, richly decorated gables ornamented with pyramids and scrollwork, ornamental fillets with coats of arms and inscriptions, and lavish grotesque carvings, many of which are appropriately dubbed *Neidköpfe* – envious "neighbours' heads".

The Pied Piper legend

The **Pied Piper legend** was first chronicled in 1384, the exact centenary of when the event allegedly took place. A mysterious stranger dressed in a multicoloured coat appeared in Hameln and offered to rid the town of its plague of rats and mice. Upon promise of payment, he played on his pipe and lured the vermin to the Weser, where they all drowned. The ungrateful burghers reneged on the reward and sent the rat-catcher packing. He returned one Sunday morning when the adults were at church, dressed in a weird yellow and red huntsman's costume. This time it was the town's 130 children who answered the magnetic strains of his pipe, and they followed the stranger out of town and out of sight, apparently disappearing into a cavern, never to be seen again. The only children who were saved were a cripple and a deaf-mute.

Many **interpretations**, none of them conclusive, have been placed on this story. It may symbolize the plague epidemics that were a fact of life in medieval Europe – the term "children" of a town was often used in old chronicles as a synonym for "citizens". Alternatively, it's possible the piper was actually a land agent charged with finding settlers – the Count of Schaumburg had a plantation in Moravia, while there are communities in Transylvania which claim descent from the children of Hameln. Another plausible theory is that the events were linked to the disastrous Children's Crusade of 1212, when youngsters from all over Europe joined in an attempt to conquer the Holy Land from the Infidel by peace – something their seniors had failed to do by force. One of the two main leaders was a boy from Cologne called Nicolas, and it's quite likely that there were recruits to the cause from Hameln.

Arrival, information and accommodation

Hameln's **Bahnhof** is situated well to the east of the centre, which is reached via Bahnhofstrasse and Deisterstrasse. The **tourist office** (April Mon–Fri 9am–6pm, Sat & Sun 9.30am–1pm; May–Sept Mon–Fri 9am–6.30pm, Sat 9.30am–4pm, Sun 9.30am–1pm; Oct–March Mon–Fri 9am–6pm, Sat 9.30am–1pm; ⓣ0 51 51/95 78 23, ⓦwww.hameln.de) is at Deisterallee 1, just before the entrance to the Altstadt.

During the tourist season, it's better to spend the night in Hameln; that way you can see the town before or after the day-trippers have come and gone, though there are surprisingly few **hotels**, and they're not particularly cheap. The **youth hostel** is well placed about five minutes' walk north of the Altstadt at Fischbecker Str. 33 (ⓣ0 51 51/34 25; €14/16.70), at the point where the Hamel (no more than a stream) flows into the Weser. On the latter's western bank is the **campsite** at Uferstr. 80 (ⓣ0 51 51/6 11 67), which is open all year round. There are a number of private houses, including some in the Altstadt, with **rooms** to let (❷–❸). Some of the hotels occupy fine old buildings.

Hotels

Alte Post Hummerstr. 23 ⓣ&ⓕ0 51 51/4 34 44. Gasthof in a three-hundred-year-old half-timbered house. Its restaurant serves inexpensive meals. ❹

An der Altstadt Diensterallee 16 ⓣ0 51 51/4 02 40, ⓦwww.hotel-hameln.de. Fine old hotel which was modernized a few years back. ❺

Christinenhof Alte Marktstr. 18 ⓣ0 51 51/9 50 80, ⓦwww.christinenhof-hameln.de. Upmarket hotel in an old half-timbered building with sauna and swimming pool. ❼

City Neue Marktstr. 9 ⓣ0 51 51/72 61, ⓕ4 59 74. Budget hotel on a quiet Altstadt street. ❹

Jugendstil Wettorstr. 18 ⓣ0 51 51/9 55 80, ⓦwww.hotel-jugendstil.de. Part of the Akzent chain, this occupies a huge terraced house in the Jugendstil quarter of the city immediately north of the Altstadt. ❻

Stadt Hameln Münsterwall 2 ⓣ0 51 51/90 10, ⓦwww.hotel-stadthameln.de. The town's leading hotel, a palatial building with a modern extension. It has two restaurants, one on the terrace overlooking the river. ❼

Zur Krone Osterstr. 30 ⓣ0 51 51/90 70, ⓦwww.hotelzurkrone.de. Another upmarket hotel and restaurant, this time in a renovated half-timbered mansion on the main street. ❻

The Town

For centuries Hameln was no more than a small milling and market town, which lay within a heavily fortified circular **Stadtmauer**. In the wake of the Thirty Years' War, its potential for growth was stunted by the strengthening of its defences by the Hanoverians, to the extent that it acquired the nickname of "the Gibraltar of the North". Napoleon ordered the demolition of the fortress so that the town could expand.

The only surviving sections of the Stadtmauer are two isolated medieval towers at the north end of town – the **Pulverturm** and the **Haspelmathsturm** – and the **Garnisonkirche**, now deconsecrated and used as a savings bank. It guards the entrance to **Osterstrasse**, the town's central axis – and one of Germany's finest streets. Facing the Garnisonkirche on the left is the **Rattenfängerhaus** (Rat-Catcher's House). Built for a local councillor at the beginning of the seventeenth century, its name is due solely to an inscription on the side wall documenting the legend. Its facade is one of the most original in Hameln, the delicacy of its ornamental details (which include plenty of "envious heads") standing in deliberate contrast to the massiveness of the overall design. The interior is only marginally less impressive; it now houses a restaurant (see p.625). Further up the street to the right is the

Leisthaus, built about fifteen years earlier for a merchant by the local mason Cord Tönnies. The statue of Lucretia in a niche above the oriel window offers a profane contrast to the figures of the Seven Christian Virtues on the frieze below, a juxtaposition of sacred and secular that is typical of the German Renaissance. In this case inspiration was obviously provided by the carvings on the timber supports of the sixteenth-century **Stiftsherrnhaus** next door, which feature the planetary deities along with the Apostles and other biblical personages.

The rest of the Stiftsherrnhaus, along with all of the Leisthaus, is given over to the **Museum Hameln** (Tues–Sun 10am–4.30pm; €3). Among the collection of religious art on the first floor, the most striking items are a set of statues of the Apostles which formerly stood on the rood screen of the Münster, and the *Siebenlingsstein*. The latter commemorates another Hameln legend, that of the birth of septuplets to a local family in 1600. Though the parents and elder siblings are shown praying at the foot of a crucifix, there was again no happy ending, as all the babies died soon afterwards.

At the end of Osterstrasse is the huge **Hochzeithaus** (Wedding House), a festival hall erected in the early seventeenth century, whose main features are its high end gables and elaborate dormer windows, under each of which there is a doorway, which formerly led into a shop. On the side facing the Markt, a **carillon** has been installed. At 1.05pm, 3.35pm and 5.35pm each day, its figures enact the Piper's two visits to Hameln. Opposite is one of the most magnificent houses, the **Dempterhaus**, which was built a few years earlier for the burgomaster after whom it is named. The **Marktkirche** rather detracts from the scene; it was Hameln's only major loss to wartime air raids, and has been poorly rebuilt with smooth stones which clash with the remains of the original masonry.

Among many fine buildings on Bäckerstrasse, which begins off the left-hand side of the Markt, two stand out. The Gothic **Löwenapotheke**, still in use as a pharmacy, illustrates that the Weser Renaissance style sprang from quite plain origins – the basic form is similar, but there's almost no decoration, apart from the hexagonal star on the gable, which was intended to ward off evil spirits. Further along is the **Rattenkrug**, built by Cord Tönnies a couple of decades before the broadly similar Leisthaus. Originally the home of a burgomaster, it has long served as a Gaststätte.

Halfway down Wendenstrasse, a fine narrow street opposite the Löwenapotheke, is the **Lückingsches Haus**, whose profuse carvings mark it out as the best example of the revival of half-timbering which occurred in the mid-seventeenth century. Also worth seeing is Alte Marktstrasse, which joins Bäckerstrasse by the Rattenkrug. Its most notable building is **Kurie Jerusalem**, a large half-timbered store from about 1500 which was long derelict, but has been magnificently restored as a play-centre (where kids can be left if you want to go sightseeing without them in tow). Further down stands the **Redenhof**, the only remaining nobleman's mansion in Hameln. Dating from the mid-sixteenth century, it's surprisingly plain in comparison with the contemporary houses of the prosperous burgher families.

At the end of Bäckerstrasse, overlooking the Weser, is the **Münster**, successor to a Benedictine monastery founded around 800. It's something of a mix of styles – the eleventh-century crypt and the squat octagonal lantern tower survive from a Romanesque basilica which was converted into a Gothic hall church from the thirteenth century onwards, the austere belfry only being added some two hundred years later. Inside, the raised chancel is the most striking feature.

Eating, drinking and entertainment

Hameln is not a major gastronomic centre: it has few high quality restaurants other than those in the last two hotels listed on p.623. Where it does score is in the range of highly distinctive eateries geared primarily to day-trippers and in many cases housed in premises which are sightseeing attractions in their own right. The Pied Piper legend is enacted in a **historical costume play** held in the town centre at noon every Sunday from mid-May to mid-September; performances last thirty minutes and are free. **Cruises** on the Weser (bear in mind that strong currents mean the upstream journeys are painfully slow) are run by Oberweser Dampfschiffahrt (Ⓣ0 51 51/93 99 99, Ⓦwww.weserschiffahrt.de), with departures from the jetty by the Münster; prices start at €4 for an hour-long round trip.

Restaurants and cafés

Kaffeestuben Wendenstr. 9. Coffee house in an old bakery. A good choice for *Kaffee und Kuchen*; also does light meals.
Kartoffelhaus Kupferschmiedstr. 13. Potato-based dishes predominate in this restaurant in the Bürgerhaus, one of Hameln's most ornate timber-framed houses.
Klütturm Auf dem Klütberg. One of the town's very best restaurants, commanding a powerful view over the Weser valley from its hilltop position to the southwest.
Museums-Café Osterstr. 8. Traditional café in the Stiftsherrnhaus, with outside tables in summer. Inevitably its speciality is called *Rattenfängertorte*.
Paulaner Bäckerstr. 16. A Gaststätte of the celebrated Munich brewery is the current occupant of the Rattenkrug.
Pfannekuchen Hummenstr. 12. There are some 40 different pancakes – sweet and savoury, flour- or potato-based – on the menu in this cosy little restaurant in this delightful half-timbered house.
Rattenfängerhaus Osterstr. 28. The cuisine here is predominantly *gutbürgerliche Küche*, though there are plenty of ice-cream based dishes if you don't want a full meal.

The Weser country around Hameln

As a supplement to a visit to Hameln, it's well worth taking in some of the nearby sights in the Weser country. Two destinations in particular stand out; both are easy to reach, and needn't take up too much time. **Fischbeck** has an intriguing collegiate foundation, while **Bodenwerder** was the home town of Baron Münchhausen.

Fischbeck

Situated 8km north of Hameln and connected by buses #20, #25 and #26 (passenger trains no longer stop there), **FISCHBECK** is dominated by its **Stift** (guided tours Easter to mid-Oct Tues & Fri 9am–11am & 2–4pm, Wed, Thurs, Sat & Sun 2–4pm, Ⓦwww.stift-fischbeck.de; €2.50). This women's collegiate church was founded in 955, and has preserved an unbroken tradition ever since, having turned Protestant in the mid-sixteenth century. Today, five elderly canonesses keep up its charitable work, only taking their vows once they have retired from a professional career; their tasks include showing visitors round the complex. It's best to phone ahead first (Ⓣ0 51 52/86 03), or check at Hameln's tourist office, to ensure admission; a tour in English can be arranged.

The **Stiftskirche** was built in the twelfth and early thirteenth centuries as a columned basilica. A drastic restoration a century ago removed most of the Baroque accretions, but some additions remain – such as the wooden balconies from where the canonesses, in true aristocratic manner, observe the services. Architecturally the finest part of the Stift is the **crypt**, whose capitals are all carved in a different manner. The **cloister** is a Gothic structure, with the houses of the canonesses on its upper storey.

Fischbeck has several outstanding works of art, but there's only a copy of the most famous, a gilded head-reliquary of a saint; the original is now in the Kestner-Museum in Hannover (see p.615). Earlier this century, the long-lost polychrome wood **statue of the foundress Helmburg** was discovered and placed in the chancel. Made around 1300, it's an imaginary, idealized portrait, showing her as a young woman, instead of the elderly widow she was when she founded the Stift, a story illustrated in a late sixteenth-century **tapestry** in the south transept. On a wooden beam high above the end of the nave is a thirteenth-century **triumphal cross**, while beside the pulpit there's an extraordinary wooden **seated Man of Sorrows** – carved around 1500, it radiates enormous pathos. According to legend, it was made for the Stift by an itinerant craftsman in gratitude for having been cured there of the plague.

Bodenwerder

BODENWERDER, 25km downstream from Hameln, is a good choice of destination if you want to take a short cruise on the Weser; it can also be reached by bus #520. Its name is synonymous with **Baron Münchhausen**, the King of Liars, who is one of Germany's most famous literary characters. Münchhausen's mansion, now the **Rathaus** (daily April–Oct 10am–noon & 2–5pm; €1), plus the two adjacent buildings, contain a museum in his honour. Among the exhibits is the pistol with which he claimed to have shot down his charger from a church steeple. Outside is a fountain illustrating one of Münchhausen's most famous exploits (one that has always defeated the film-makers) – stopping to water his prize Lithuanian horse, he found that the liquid was pouring out of its body, the rear end having been shot off in battle. On the first Sunday of each month between May and September, some of Münchhausen's exploits are re-enacted.

Baron Münchhausen

The real-life **Karl Friedrich Hieronymous von Münchhausen** was an eighteenth-century soldier of fortune who fought for the Russians against the Turks, before retiring to his ancestral seat, where he regaled credulous listeners with monstrously boastful tales of his adventures. These came to the attention of **Rudolph Erich Raspe**, himself a real rogue, who embroidered the stories further and published them under the Baron's name in Britain. For all his failings, Raspe was highly talented – he had been a protégé of Leibniz in his native Hannover – and the book is stylishly written, perfectly capturing the understated manner of a boring old raconteur launching every few minutes into yet another totally implausible anecdote. The Baron's numerous adventures included stranger travels than even Gulliver's – he made two trips to the moon (one of them unintentional), a journey all the way through the earth's crust, and a voyage through a sea of milk to an island of cheese. In less far-flung parts, he shot a stag with a full-sized cherry tree between its antlers (thus obtaining haunch and sauce at the same time), served as a human cannonball in the war against the Turks, and single-handedly saved Gibraltar from falling into Spanish hands by tossing the enemy's 300 pieces of artillery into the sea. For all its spectacular special effects, Terry Gilliam's 1988 movie, *The Adventures of Baron Münchhausen*, is a leaden creation which flopped at the box office. Far more successful from an artistic point of view is the Goebbels-financed film of the same name – an incredibly futuristic wartime fantasy made in the UFA studios in Babelsberg.

The **tourist office** (Mon–Fri 9am–12.30pm & 2.30–6pm, Sat 9am–noon; ⓣ0 55 33/4 05 41, ⓦwww.bodenwerder.de) is in the First Reisebüro, Weserstr. 3. If you want to stay, there's an abundant range of **pensions** and **private rooms** (❶–❸); a **youth hostel** in the hills to the east of town on Richard-Schirrmann-Weg (ⓣ0 55 33/26 85; €14/16.70); and a **campsite** at An der Himmelspforte (ⓣ0 55 33/49 38). There are also three fine **hotels**: *Königszinne*, Linser Str. 12 (ⓣ0 55 33/9 72 40; ❺); *Deutsches Haus*, Münchhausenplatz 4 (ⓣ0 55 33/40 07 80, ⓦwww.hotel-deutsches-haus-bodenwerder.de; ❺); and *Goldener Anker*, Weserstr. 13 (ⓣ0 55 33/40 07 30, ⓦwww.goldeneranker.com). All of these have good **restaurants**, though they face strong competition from *Münchhausen Stube*, Grosse Str. 5.

Hildesheim

HILDESHEIM, which lies 30km southeast of Hannover, stands unrivalled as Lower Saxony's premier city of art. Some of the finest buildings in all of Germany are to be found here, and its importance to European culture can hardly be exaggerated. During the eleventh-century Ottonian period, the **Romanesque style** – emerging hesitantly elsewhere – achieved a state of perfection here, not only in architecture, but in sculpture and painting as well. Five hundred years later, the city was adorned with a multitude of

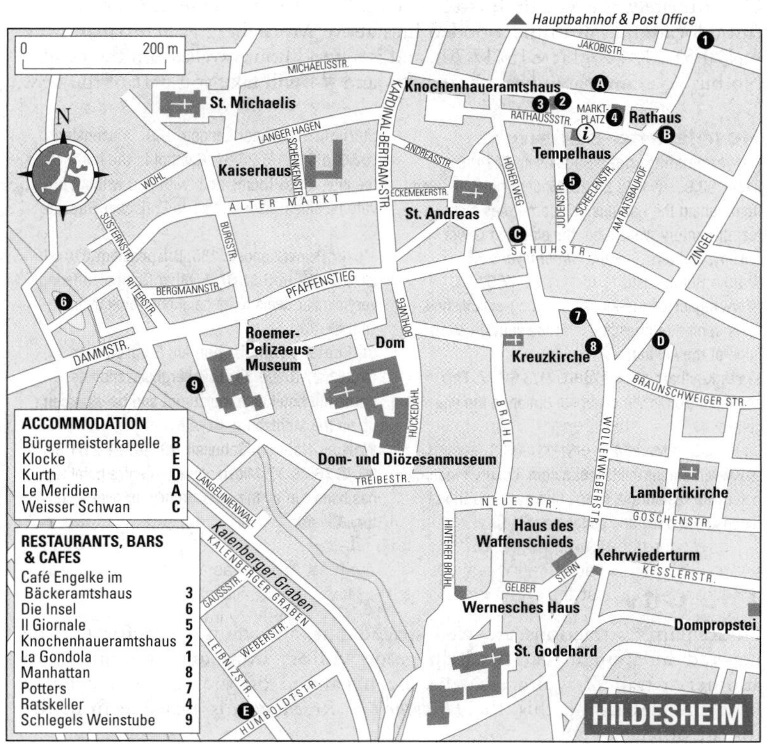

half-timbered buildings whose sheer artistry far surpassed those of any other German city.

Because of this legacy, prewar guides used to consider Hildesheim as one of the "must" cities of Germany. Just a month before the German surrender in 1945, however, Hildesheim was bombed and the consequent fire, fuelled by the wooden buildings, caused damage which even some exemplary restoration cannot disguise, and left the surviving monuments marooned among typically bland, functional modern developments. For decades, the city was a shadow of its former self, until it made an astonishing comeback in the 1980s. Fortified by commercial prosperity, the local council made the bold decision to re-create what had hitherto been regarded as irretrievably lost. A fillip was given by UNESCO's decision to include the two main churches, both of which had been shattered in the war, on its World Heritage List.

Arrival, information and accommodation

Hildesheim's **Hauptbahnhof** is at the northern end of the city; the best way to reach the centre is to follow Bernwardstrasse, then Almstrasse, but be warned that these characterless shopping precincts make rather an inauspicious introduction. The **tourist office** (Mon–Fri 9am–6.30pm, Sat 9.30am–3.30pm; ⓣ0 51 21/1 79 80, ⓦwww.hildesheim.de) is in the Tempelhaus, Rathausstr. 18–20.

Hildesheim isn't well off for budget **hotels**, at least in the centre, though there's plenty of choice in the middle and upper ranges. The nearest **campsite** is way to the east of town, by the B6 at Derneburg (ⓣ0 50 62/5 65, ⓕ87 85). Unfortunately, the **youth hostel** isn't much more convenient; it occupies a rustic location high in the wooded hills above Moritzberg at Schirrmannweg 4 (ⓣ0 51 21/4 27 17; €15/17.70), and is a good hour's walk from the centre. No bus goes anywhere near, though #1 and #4 will take you part of the way.

Hotels and pensions

Bürgermeisterkapelle Rathausstr. 8 ⓣ0 51 21/17 92 90, ⓕ1 79 29 99. Modern hotel situated right behind the Rathaus. It incorporates a sixteenth-century Weinstube, the oldest in Lower Saxony, and a restaurant, *Strohmeyer's*. ❻

Klocke Humboldstr. 11 ⓣ0 51 21/17 92 13, ⓦwww.gaestehaus-klocke.de. Long-established, fairly upmarket guesthouse at the southwestern edge of the Altstadt. ❻

Kurth Küsthardtstr. 4 ⓣ0 51 21/3 62 72. This small pension is the cheapest option in the city centre. ❹

Le Meridien Markt 4 ⓣ0 51 21/30 00, ⓦwww.meridien-hildesheim.com. Luxury modern hotel with restaurant, sauna and gym in a trio of reconstructed historic buildings. ❼–❾

Marheineke Peiner Landstr. 189, Drispenstedt ⓣ&ⓕ0 51 21/5 26 67. Gasthof in the north of the city; it has rooms both with and without private facilities. Take bus #1 to Ehrlacher Strasse. ❸–❻

Meyer Peiner Landstr. 185, Drispenstedt ⓣ0 51 21/5 31 79, ⓕ5 31 07. Another Gasthof, offering very similar deals to its neighbour directly opposite. ❹–❻

Parkhotel Berghölzchen Am Berghölzchen 1 ⓣ0 51 21/97 90, ⓦwww.berghoelzchen.de. Upmarket hotel with restaurant and beer garden up on the Moritzberg. ❻–❾

Weisser Schwan Schuhstr. 29 ⓣ0 51 21/1 67 80, ⓕ16 78 90. Mid-range city-centre hotel which has been run by the same family for over a century. ❺–❼

The City

Hildesheim's attractions are well spaced out, and cannot comfortably be covered in a single day. To help guide visitors from one monument to another, a trail of white roses has been painted on the streets; a detailed brochure describing this, the *Hildesheimer Rosenroute*, is available from the tourist office.

Marktplatz

In 1983 work began on resurrecting the picturesque jumble of buildings around the central **Marktplatz**, which has now re-emerged, following its almost complete destruction in the war, as Germany's most imposing market square. Only two of the buildings are original: the early Gothic **Rathaus** at the eastern end, which was only partially destroyed and hurriedly rebuilt, and the fifteenth-century **Tempelhaus** at the southeast corner, which somehow remained intact while all its neighbours collapsed. The most likely explanation for the latter's puzzling name and distinctive shape is that it was inspired by a Crusader's description of buildings he had seen in the Holy Land. Some softening of the rather spare, flat textures occurred with the addition of a late sixteenth-century oriel window bearing carvings of the Prodigal Son. Nowadays, the building houses a bookstore and the offices of the *Hildesheimer Allgemeine Zeitung*, the longest continually running daily newspaper in Germany. The Renaissance **Wedekindhaus** next door, the Baroque **Lüntzelhaus** and the part-Gothic, part-Baroque **Rolandstift** were restored by the local savings bank to serve as its headquarters. Directly opposite, the mid-seventeenth-century inn known as the **Stadtschänke**, along with the aptly named **Rokokohaus** and the early sixteenth-century **Wollenwebergildehaus** (Wool Weavers' Guild House), were rebuilt to serve collectively as a luxury hotel. The council themselves paid for a copy of the Renaissance **Marktbrunnen**, which is topped by a figure of a knight and has the municipal arms depicted on the basin.

As the culmination of the restoration project, the small **Bäckeramtshaus** (Bakers' Guildhall) of 1800 and the colossal early sixteenth-century **Knochenhaueramtshaus** (Butchers' Guildhall) on the west side of the square were re-created from scratch. The latter had earned for itself the title of "the most beautiful half-timbered house in the world", a title few would dispute on seeing its highly distinctive architecture and seemingly inexhaustible range of carvings on Christian, pagan and humorous subjects. Part of it now houses a restaurant, while the upper storeys contain the local history displays of the **Stadtgeschichtliches Museum** (Tues–Sun 10am–6pm; Ⓦ www.rpmuseum.de/stadtgeschichte; €1.50).

St Michaelis

Hildesheim's supreme building, the mould-breaking church of **St Michaelis** (Ⓦ www.st-michaelis-hildesheim.de), is about ten minutes' walk west of the Marktplatz, reached via Michaelisstrasse. Perched on a little hill and girded with six towers, it's not too fanciful to see it as a depiction of the heavenly Jerusalem. Originally part of a Benedictine monastery, St Michaelis' was very much a personal creation of **Bishop Bernward**. A confidant of Emperor Otto II and tutor to Otto III, this well-travelled, erudite man ruled the see of Hildesheim between 993 and 1022, and did much to foster the art and architecture of the city.

The nave forms the centrepiece of St Michaelis' meticulously thought-out design. An important innovation was the move away from the columned basilica of the Romans to a new system, subsequently known as the **Lower Saxon style**, whereby each bay is demarcated by a hefty square pillar, between which are placed two columns. These are topped by another new device, the cubiform capital, from which spring the arches, coloured in alternate white and red to impart a sense of rhythmic movement. The height of the roof is exactly twice the length of each bay of the nave. Shortly after Bernward was canonized in 1192, substantial embellishments were made in order that it should be a worthy resting place for his relics. Seven capitals were carved for the nave, and in the west transept a **choir screen** was erected; only part of this remains, yet its stucco carvings rank among the masterpieces of German sculpture.

An even more spectacular addition was the **ceiling**, which is one of only two Romanesque painted wooden ceilings to have survived. Fortunately, it had been removed for safety during World War II, and its fresh state of preservation is remarkable – three-quarters of its 1300 separate oak panels are original. Executed in the style of contemporary illuminated manuscripts, its programme is based on the imagery of the tree, a decision prompted by the fact that the church's most sacred relic was a piece of the Holy Cross. In the first main scene, Adam and Eve are shown beside the Tree of Knowledge. Next comes the sleeping Jesse, from whose loins springs the rod which passes through descendants such as David and Solomon before arriving at the Virgin Mary and Christ himself.

St Bernward's body is interred in a stone sarcophagus in the ground-level **crypt** at the western end of the building. This necessitated a rebuilding to accommodate a raised chancel, which impaired the previously perfect architectural unity of the church. The Catholics were allowed to retain the crypt when St Michaelis became Protestant at the Reformation. It's only open for Mass, but you can peek in by opening the door to the left of the choir screen. Another later addition was the Gothic **cloister** to the north of the church, of which only one wing survives.

The Dom

The **Dom**, which is set in its own close and reached via Burgstrasse, is architecturally a poor relation of St Michaelis, but its hauntingly romantic cloister and superb art treasures convinced UNESCO that it was an equally important piece of cultural heritage. The exterior is largely a fake, with prominent Gothic side chapels and a Romanesque facade and towers that are a modern guess at how the building might have looked before it was completely transformed in the Baroque epoch. Inside, the architecture has been restored to its original eleventh-century layout, a close adaptation of the forms pioneered at the great monastery fifty years before.

One of St Bernward's particular enthusiasms was the art of bronze-casting, and he established a foundry which was to flourish for centuries. Its first major product was a pair of **processional doors**, originally made for St Michael's, but moved a few years later to the Dom's main entrance, where they were installed on the inside. They tell the story of Adam and Eve on the left-hand side, and of Christ on the right. Soon afterwards, the craftsmen made the **triumphal column**, now in the southern transept. Rather more obviously inspired by Roman victory monuments, this illustrates the lives of Jesus and St John the Baptist in a manner akin to strip cartoons. Around 1065, the huge **wheel-shaped chandelier** was suspended from the vault of the nave. Mantled with alternate towers and gateways, it's yet another representation of the heavenly Jerusalem and was to serve as the prototype for the even more ornate candelabra in Aachen and Gross Comburg. In the baptismal chapel is the **font**; made in 1225, it rests on personifications of the four sacred rivers, while the basin and lid illustrate various biblical stories, mostly with a watery theme.

Most unusually, the **cloister** (April–Oct Mon–Sat 9.30am–5pm, Sun noon–5pm; €0.50) is built onto the transepts, forming a protective shield round the apse, on which grows the **thousand-year-old rosebush**, to which the legend of Hildesheim's foundation is inextricably tied. In 815, Ludwig the Pious, a son of Charlemagne, hung the royal chapel's relics of the Virgin on the tree while he was out hunting near Hildwins Heim. When he tried to remove them, they would not budge; taking this to be divine instruction, he decided to endow the mother church of a new diocese on the very spot. Whether this is really the original bush is disputed, but it's certainly many centuries old, and does seem to lead a charmed life – it burst into flower not long after the air-raid which had flattened most of the Dom itself, and has blossomed every year since. In the centre of the cloister garden is the **St-Annen-Kapelle**, a beautiful fourteenth-century miniaturization of a Gothic cathedral, with a set of gargoyles spouting from its walls. The sumptuous Renaissance **rood screen**, which fenced off the Dom's chancel until 1945, can be seen in the Antoniuskapelle off the cloister's southern walk.

On the south side of the Dom is the **Dom- und Diözesanmuseum** (Tues–Sat 10am–5pm, Sun noon–5pm; €3.50; Ⓦwww.dommuseum-hildesheim.de), one of the richest ecclesiastical treasuries in Germany. Among the highlights are several works dating from the time of St Bernward – the Golden Madonna (actually wooden but covered with gold leaf), a pair of candlesticks, and two crucifixes named after the bishop himself. Equally imposing are various twelfth-century pieces – the cross of Henry the Lion, the shrine of St Godehard, three shield-shaped crucifixes and a set of enamel plates. The head-reliquary of St Bernward dates from the turn of the following century, while the eagle-lectern was made around the same time as the font. Although it has no real connection with the bishop, the so-called chalice of St Bernward is an outstanding piece of goldsmith's work from around 1400.

The rest of the central Altstadt

Adjoining the north side of the Dom's close is the old Franciscan friary, which, together with its new extension, now contains the **Roemer-Pelizaeus Museum** (daily 10am–6pm; €6; Ⓦwww.rpmuseum.de). Refreshingly different from the standard provincial museum, this hosts an international **loan exhibition** on a major archeological or historical topic each year. The collection of **Egyptian antiquities**, which is now exhibited in its entirety in a beautifully lit display, is one of the best in Europe and set attendance records for a touring show from Germany when it was shown in several North American cities at the end of the millennium. Its most famous exhibit is the white limestone funerary monument of Hem-iunu from 2530 BC. Other outstanding sculptures include statuettes of Amenophis III and Teje (parents of Akhenaton), a statue of the fearsome half-man, half-jackal Anubis (the god of death) and the reliefs from the tomb of Seschemnefer IV. The museum's other main strengths include a comprehensive collection of Chinese porcelain and a varied array of exhibits from the Peru of the Incas.

On Alter Markt, a short walk to the northeast, the heavily Italianate facade of Hildesheim's most celebrated Renaissance mansion, the **Kaiserhaus**, was re-erected a few years ago. Named after the statues and medallions of Roman emperors which adorn it, the facade has been placed in front of the headquarters of the **Hornemann-Institut** (Ⓦwww.hornemann-institut.de), the scientific service centre of the Society for the Preservation and Conservation of World Cultural Heritage. Itself named in honour of one of Hildesheim's most famous sons, the pioneering Africa explorer Friedrich Konrad Hornemann, the institute mounts a programme of temporary exhibitions on global heritage themes in the Roemer-Pelizaeus Museum and elsewhere.

A little further to the east is the church of **St Andreas**. Within its exhilaratingly lofty Gothic interior, Luther's friend Johannes Bugenhagen converted the city to the Reformation. The church itself actually gained from the air raids – it was rebuilt according to the ambitious schemes of the original masons, which had never previously been fully put into effect. On the other hand, this hardly makes up for the almost complete loss of the square round the church, formerly regarded as a worthy rival to Marktplatz. For a fine view over the city, climb up the tall **tower** (April–Oct Mon–Sat 11am–4pm, Sun noon–4pm; €1.50).

The southern Altstadt

The southern part of Hildesheim was largely spared from war damage, and presents several streets of half-timbered houses as a reminder of what the whole of the old city once looked like. At the top end of Brühl, the nearest of these streets to the centre, the one surviving secular building from the time of St Bernward can be seen. Originally a fortified reception hall-cum-law court, it was converted into a collegiate foundation known as the **Kreuzkirche** in the late eleventh century, and now forms part of the otherwise Baroque parish church of the same name, making a truly odd combination. To the west of the southern section of Brühl runs the parallel Hinterer Brühl, an almost completely preserved old street. Look out for the early seventeenth-century **Wernersches Haus**, with its allegorical depictions of the Virtues and Vices, and representations of historical personalities.

At the end of the street is **St Godehard**, a former Benedictine monastery church built in the mid-twelfth century to commemorate the recent canonization of the man who had succeeded St Bernward as Bishop of Hildesheim. Unusually well preserved, it boasts a pair of round towers on its facade, with a larger version of these over the transept. There is a delicate stucco relief over the north doorway showing Christ between St Godehard (holding a model of the church) and St Epiphanus. The interior proves the durability of the style pioneered at St Michaelis, the only advance being the rich carvings on the capitals. The star piece of the church's **treasury** is a magnificent early twelfth-century psalter illuminated at the sister English monastery of St Albans. To see this, it is normally necessary to ask at the sexton's house in the cloister on the south side of the church.

East of St Godehard is another fine old street, Gelber Stern, among whose buildings is the mid-sixteenth-century **Haus des Waffenschieds**, the guild house of the armourers, decorated with carvings of the tools of the trade. At the end of the road, Lappenberg, which runs perpendicular to the south, has a complete row of craftsmen's homes. Nearby stands the **Kehrwiederturm**, the only surviving example of the gates which once surrounded the inner city. To the east is Kesslerstrasse, arguably the most imposing of the old streets, lined with impressive Renaissance and Baroque mansions. The largest and finest of these is the **Dompropstei** (Deanery) at no. 57, set in its own spacious yard. Just north of here is the **Lambertikirche**, which contains a lovely early fifteenth-century Soft Style retable painted by an unknown local master.

The suburbs

Another well-preserved old quarter is the **Moritzberg**, on a hill to the west of the city centre, and reached along Dammstrasse, Bergsteinweg and Bergstrasse. It's grouped round yet another Romanesque church, **St Mauritius**. Although dating from the second half of the eleventh century, this favoured the traditional format of a columned basilica, which is still evident despite the fact that the interior is now cloaked with Baroque decoration. The crypt and cloister, however, have been preserved in their original state. Unfortunately, there isn't much of a view from these heights; for that you have to go to the **Galgenberg**, at the opposite end of the city.

Eating, drinking and entertainment

Other than around Marktplatz, there's no obvious concentration of good places to eat and drink in Hildesheim, but there are plenty of possibilities dotted around the city which are well worth seeking out.

Restaurants

Die Insel Dammstr. 30. Named after its "island" setting among the canals at the western end of the Altstadt, this is a good choice for both full meals and *Kaffee und Kuchen*.

Knochenhaueramtshaus Markt 7. The magnificent butchers' guildhall has eateries on four of its levels, offering everything from snacks to high-class cuisine.

Krehla Moritzstr. 9. Up on the Moritzberg, this Weinstube with garden is a Hildesheim institution, having been run by the same family since 1853. Best known for its seven kinds of homemade fruit wines, it also serves inexpensive meals. Evenings only, closed Tues.

Kupferschmiede Am Steinberg 6, Ochtersum ⓣ0 51 21/26 30 25. In a secluded forest setting 5km south of the Altstadt, this is one of the most famous restaurants in northern Germany, offering both *nouvelle cuisine* and hearty German fare. One for a splurge, although the set menus are far from extortionate. Closed Sun & Mon; reservations recommended.

La Gondola Ostertorpassage, Osterstr. 41–44. Depsite its unprepossessing location in a shopping centre, this serves the best Italian food and wines in town.

Ratskeller Markt 1. Far less expensive than its counterparts in most other cities (there are cheap daily specials at lunchtimes), yet it can rival them in quality. Closed Mon.

Schlegels Weinstube Am Steine 4–6. Cosy, highly atmospheric little wine bar-restaurant in a half-timbered sixteenth-century building directly opposite the Roemer-Pelizaeus Museum. Evenings only; closed Sun.

Vier Linden Alfelder Str. 55b. Part of a cultural centre which puts on cabaret and concerts, this has one of the most creative menus in Hildesheim, with plenty of vegetarian and wholefood dishes. Open Wed–Sun evenings only.

Bars and cafés

Café Engelke im Bäckeramtshaus Markt 8. Appropriately, the rebuilt bakers' guildhall houses a fine old-style café.

Hildesheimer Brauhaus Speicherstr. 9. Just a short walk from the Hauptbahnhof, this evenings-only Hausbrauerei produces an organically brewed Pils; it also has a full menu and often features live music.

Il Giornale Judenstr. 3–4. Internet café which also serves pizzas, salads, ice creams and daily specials. Closed Sun.

Manhattan Wollenweberstr. 78. Hildesheim is well-known for its cocktail bars, and this is reckoned to be the coolest of the lot, with around 200 different cocktails to choose from. Tues–Sun 9pm–4/5am.

Potters Friesenstr. 17–18. Another very chic cocktail bar, one in which fresh fruit juices regularly feature among the mixes. Daily 6/7pm-2am, until 5am at weekends.

Spanier Immengarten 5. Hildesheim's longest-established student Kneipe, offering a wide range of beers and inexpensive main courses. Open 8pm–2/3am, closed Sun.

Entertainment

Jazz fans should head for Hildesheim at Whit weekend, when the Jazz-Time festival presents the whole gamut of styles, both in formal concerts and impromptu open-air events. The regular year-round venue for live jazz is Bischofsmühle, Dammstr. 32. All kinds of **music** are featured along with **drama** in the varied programmes of the Stadttheater, Theaterstrasse 6 (ⓣ0 51 21/3 31 64, ⓦwww.stadttheater-hildesheim.de); there are also regular recitals and concerts in the Protestant churches. The main **popular festivals** are the Frühlingsfest for nine days in March, the Weinfest for a week in mid-May, and the ubiquitous Schützenfest in mid-June.

Braunschweig (Brunswick)

Today **BRAUNSCHWEIG**, which lies 65km southeast of Hannover and 50km northeast of Hildesheim, is the epicentre of the most heavily industrialized part of Lower Saxony, but it preserves plenty of reminders of the far grander role it once played. During the twelfth century it was the chosen residence of **Henry the Lion** (Heinrich der Löwe), one of the most powerful princes in Europe, who commissioned innumerable monuments and works

of art to grace his capital. Over the next few centuries the city became increasingly important as a commercial centre; its trade connections stretched into Russia, Scandinavia, Flanders and England, and the consequent wealth was put to use creating buildings worthy of the city's power and status. In the mid-eighteenth century Braunschweig had yet another brilliant period. The first technical university in the world, the Collegium Carolinum, was established here in 1745. When the local dukes took up residence again the following decade, having been absent for over three hundred years, their wonderful art treasures were put on public display and the city became a flourishing cultural centre.

Arrival, information and accommodation

Braunschweig's **Hauptbahnhof** is some distance to the southeast of the centre. It's quite a walk, so it's best to take tram #1, #2 or #5 to the "island" at the heart of the city. The main **tourist office** is at Vor der Burg 1 (May–Sept Mon–Fri 9.30am–6pm, Sat 10am–2pm, Sun 10am–12.30pm; rest of year closed Sun; ⓣ05 32/27 35 50, ⓦwww.braunschweig.de). The 24hr **public transport tickets** are good value: within the city, they cost €4 for individuals, €6.80 for up to five people travelling together; these prices rise to €5.50 and €9.20 respectively if Wolfenbüttel and the surrounding area are included as well.

Braunschweig has a good range of **hotels** to suit all budgets, with several enticing upmarket options. The **youth hostel** is at Salzdahlumer Str. 170 (ⓣ05 3226 43 20; €14/16) to the south of the city, reached by bus #11 or #19 to Krankenhaus, and has a few double rooms in addition to dormitories.

Hotels

Café am Park Wolfenbütteler Str. 67 ⓣ05 32/7 30 79, ⓦwww.hotel-cafeampark.de. Very pleasant hotel and café at the eastern edge of the Bürgerpark, about a 10min walk west of the Hauptbahnhof. Rooms with and without facilities are available. ④–⑥

Deutsches Haus Ruhfäutchenplatz 1 ⓣ05 32/1 20 00, ⓦwww.ringhotel-braunschweig.de. Fine old traditional hotel at the corner of Burgplatz, to which it is linked by a picturesque "Bridge of Sighs". Its restaurant, *Zum Burglöwen*, is good and reasonably priced. ⑦

Friedrich Am Magnitor 5 ⓣ05 32/4 17 28, ⓕ2 40 77 43. Long-established Gasthof in the Magniviertel. It only has a few rooms, and is better-known for its wine bar-restaurant, which has a huge vat with a capacity for storing 10,000 litres of wine. ②

Haus zur Hanse Güldenstr. 7 ⓣ05 32/24 39 00, ⓦwww.haus-zur-hanse.de. This hotel, which occupies a large half-timbered building, has one of the city's best restaurants, offering French-style cuisine as well as traditional German fare. ⑥

Simoné Celler Str. 111 ⓣ05 32/57 78 98, ⓕ57 43 13. Budget hotel a short distance to the north-west of the Altstadt, not far from the terminus of tram #1. ③–⑤

Stadthotel Magnitor Am Magnitor 1 ⓣ05 32/4 71 30, ⓦwww.stadthotel-magni.de. Modern designer hotel in a fifteenth-century timber-framed building that was originally a storehouse. Its restaurant features both moderately priced and expensive dishes. ⑥–⑧

Stadtpalais Hinter Liebfrauen 1a ⓣ05 32/24 10 24, ⓦwww.palais-braunschweig.bestwestern.de. Another designer hotel, this time in the whitewashed late eighteenth-century former orphanage. ⑦

The City

The historic heart of the city is still completely surrounded by water – a man-made system based on the two arms of the River Oker – and contains several distinct medieval districts, which were formerly governed separately. Each of these quarters was centred on a market square and usually had its own parish church. Severe bomb damage in World War II means that the old buildings are now interspersed with plenty of ugly modern shops and offices, but it's still possible to visualize the medieval layout.

Burgplatz

To look at the city in chronological order, the **Burgplatz** in the middle of the "island" is the place to start. It's full of memories of Henry the Lion, who was at the peak of his power at the time the square was laid out. In 1166, he commissioned the **Burglöwe** (Lion Monument) to form its centrepiece. Perched high on a pedestal, this bronze statue, which was originally gilded, was the first freestanding sculptural monument to be made since the days of the Romans. Even though it has been replaced twice, the lion still stands as a potent reminder of the long centuries of power enjoyed by the Welfs.

In 1173 the **Dom** was begun, and was substantially complete before the end of the century. Its craggy, fortress-like external appearance (which seems to be another symbol of the power of the Welfs) is the prototype of a distinctive Braunschweig style, which was followed in all the other medieval churches of the city. Another feature copied throughout the city was the later insertion of a Gothic bell-gable between the two towers, which further increases the sense of the facade's massiveness. The interior is far lighter in feel. This is partly due to the well-preserved Romanesque **frescoes**, dating from around 1220, which were hidden behind plaster for centuries. The portraits of saints in the nave, executed with the finesse of manuscript miniatures, are particularly fine. An even more crucial addition was the opening out of the north side of the Dom in the mid-fifteenth century by masons who seem to have been familiar with English Tudor architecture; the two new aisles are separated by a row of writhing **columns** which twist in alternate directions. On the end wall is the sole survivor of the previous cathedral which stood on this site, a Byzantine-inspired wooden **Crucifixion** signed by a certain Master Imerward. At the entrance to the choir a seven-branched **candelabrum**, donated by the founder, springs from a base of four crouching lions. In front is the limestone **tomb** of Henry the Lion and his second wife Matilda, daughter of Henry II of England. Memorials to other members of the Welf dynasty are housed in the crypt.

Facing the Dom is Henry's castle, **Burg Dankwarderode** (Tues & Thurs–Sun 10am–5pm, Wed 1–8pm; €2.50 joint day ticket with Herzog-Anton-Ulrich-Museum; Ⓦwww.musem-braunschweig.de). Named in honour of the semi-mythical ninth-century founder of the city, it was constructed at the same time as the Dom. Its unusually complete appearance is mainly due to a nineteenth-century restoration, which follows the original form far more faithfully than most projects inspired by the Romantic reverence for the Middle Ages. From 10 to 11am (2.30–4pm on Wed) the showpiece **Rittersaal** on the first floor can be seen; for the remainder of the opening hours it is the museum of medieval art and artefacts on the ground floor which is on view. The star attraction of the latter is the **original Burglöwe**. Other highlights include an eighth- or ninth-century walrus-tooth casket, the eleventh-century arm-reliquary of St Blasius (patron of the Dom), and the cloak of Otto IV, son of Henry the Lion – and the only Welf to become Holy Roman Emperor.

The Burgplatz used to be a courtyard in its truest sense – the houses that stood around its edge belonged to the courtiers. Two half-timbered sixteenth-century successors to these survive – the **Von Veltheimsches Haus** and the **Huneborstelsches Haus** – and nowadays serve as the headquarters of the local chamber of commerce. The Neoclassical mansion in the opposite corner of the square was originally a publishing house, but now accommodates the **Braunschweigisches Landesmuseum** (Tues, Wed & Fri–Sun 10am–5pm, Thurs 10am–8pm; €1.50, or €2.50 combined ticket with Jüdisches Museum and the Abteilung Ur- und Frühgeschichte in Wolfenbüttel; Ⓦwww.landesmuseum-bs.de). This contains local history displays on the Braunschweig region; in the entrance hall is the second version of the Burglöwe.

Altstadtmarkt

The other significant cluster of Braunschweig's past is found in and around the **Altstadtmarkt** to the west. A corner of this is taken up by the former **Rathaus** (Tues–Fri & Sun 10am–1pm & 2–5pm; free), which ranks as one of the most beautiful and original secular buildings in Germany. Consisting of two wings arranged in an L-shape, its present form dates back to the early fifteenth century, when the open upper arcades, with their flowing tracery and statues of the Welfs, were added. A museum of local history has recently been installed inside, the highlight of which is a collection of Baroque silverware. On the first floor, the festive hall, the Grosse Dornse, can be viewed from behind glass, but not entered. The graceful lead **Marienbrunnen** in the middle of the square was made around the same time; it's topped by a shrine-like structure with the Virgin and Child and the four Evangelists.

Opposite stands the **Gewandhaus** (Drapers' Hall), its grandeur reflecting the importance of the medieval tailors. The facade is a Dutch-influenced

Renaissance composition of extraordinary elaborateness, whose gable, shaped like an equilateral triangle, is crowned by a figure of Justice. Alongside is the half-timbered seventeenth-century **Zollhaus**, once used by customs officials and the military. Also on the square is the Baroque **Stechinellihaus**, designed by the Italian court architect after whom it's named, who was also responsible for many buildings in Celle.

St Martini, originally a twelfth-century basilica, stands at the far end of Altstadtmarkt. The finest and earliest of Braunschweig's parish churches, it follows a pattern repeated elsewhere – it was initially modelled on the Dom, but was later altered internally to form a spacious hall. It also gained some fine sculptures in the fourteenth century, notably the group of the Wise and Foolish Virgins on the north doorway. Another addition is the Gothic chapel dedicated to St Anne, housing a Renaissance pulpit that shows St Martin dividing his coat in order to clothe a beggar.

The other historic quarters

North of Burgplatz, reached via Casparistrasse or Bohlweg, is the old district of Hagen, centred on Hagenmarkt. Its fountain bears a nineteenth-century statue of Henry the Lion carrying a model of the church of **St Katharinen**, which he also founded. Closely modelled on the Dom, St Katharinen's interior was later transformed into a spacious Gothic hall church. The same is true of **St Andreas** further to the west, which was the parish church of the Neustadt district. Its south **tower** (May–Sept Mon, Wed & Fri 9am–noon & 2–4pm, Tues & Thurs 2–4pm, Sat 10am–noon; €1) can be ascended for a view over the city. Across from this church is the **Liberei**, a fifteenth-century library building which is the only example of Gothic brick architecture in the city. Further west, on Bäckerklimt, is the bronze **Eulenspiegelbrunnen**, commemorating the legendary jester Till Eulenspiegel. The owls and monkeys on the fountain represent the shapes into which he would work dough as an apprentice in a nearby bakery. The shop itself was bombed in 1944, but similar breads remain a local speciality to this day.

Raised above the old city on a slight hillock at its southern edge stands the former Benedictine monastery of **St Ägidien**, which incorporates the only church in Braunschweig built in a pure Gothic style. Its handsome pulpit retains the original late Gothic reliefs by Hans Witten, a sculptor who was the equal of the more famous Riemenschneider and Stoss, but whose reputation suffers from the fact that most of his work is in remote Saxon towns. The monastic buildings now house the **Jüdisches Museum** (Tues & Thurs–Sun 10am–5pm, Wed 10am–8pm; €1.50; Ⓦwww.landesmuseum-bs.de), which vividly illustrates German Jewish culture down the centuries. There's even a full-scale reconstruction, complete with all the original fittings, of a Baroque synagogue dismantled last century.

Braunschweig's other significant district is the Altewiek a few blocks further north. This is now usually known as the Magniviertel after the church of **St Magni** which forms its core. The few half-timbered streets in the city which completely escaped destruction in the air raids are found around here, and the semicircular group immediately behind the church and the blind alley called Herrendorftwerte, just to the east, are particularly evocative. These now have to compete for attention with an almost unbelievably wacky new landmark in the **James-Rizz-Haus**, a garishly coloured apartment block decorated with all sorts of encrustations. The Magniviertel is also one of the liveliest areas at night, with a host of pubs and restaurants.

The Herzog-Anton-Ulrich-Museum

North of the Magniviertel, on Museumstrasse, is the **Herzog-Anton-Ulrich-Museum** (Tues & Thurs–Sun 10am–5pm, Wed 1–8pm; €2.50 joint day ticket with Burg Dankwarderode; Ⓦwww.museum-braunschweig.de). It's particularly intriguing in that it reflects the personal artistic tastes of the duke after whom it's named, who was responsible for building it up some three hundred years ago. The collection was opened to the public in 1754, thus making it the first museum in Germany.

In the second-floor picture gallery, pride of place goes to the Dutch school, and in particular to one of **Rembrandt**'s most psychologically acute works, *A Family Group*. It was painted at the very end of his life, and shows his style at its most advanced and daring, with its loose brushwork supplemented by extensive use of the palette knife, its heavy chiaroscuro effects, and the informal arrangement of its subjects. Rembrandt's very personal vision of biblical stories is represented here by a tender nocturne of *The Risen Christ Appearing to Mary Magdalene*. The dramatic *Landscape with Thunderstorm*, bathed in warm golden hues, shows yet another side of his diverse genius.

Vermeer's *Girl with the Wineglass* displays a level of technical virtuosity fully equal to, but very different from, Rembrandt's. Probably executed with the help of a camera obscura, it captures the three-dimensional space of the interior to uncanny effect. Two other highlights of the Dutch collection include a subtly delicate late fifteenth-century portable altar known as the *Braunschweig Diptych*; and a sharply observed *Self-Portrait* by the country's leading sixteenth-century artist, **Lucas van Leyden**. Among Flemish works of the same period are several examples of **Rubens**, a fine **van Dyck** and a fetching **Teniers**, *The Alchemist's Workshop*.

The most important of the German works on view in the gallery is the *Portrait of Cyriacus Kale* by **Holbein the Younger**. It was painted in London, where the Braunschweig-born sitter worked at the Hansa trading headquarters, as the inscription states. A strong representation of **Cranach** includes a lively workshop cycle of *The Labours of Hercules*, and a *Hercules and Omphale*. The latter is by Cranach's hand alone, as is the *Portrait of Albrecht von Brandenburg-Ansbach*, which depicts the cross-eyed Hohenzollern who had been Grand Master of the Teutonic Knights. By the time this picture was painted, Albrecht had converted to Protestantism, secularized his Order's holdings and thereby became Duke of Prussia – events which were crucial in his family's ultimately successful drive to win leadership of the German nation. A delicate *Morning Landscape* by the short-lived **Elsheimer** rounds off this section.

Duke Anton Ulrich's taste in Italian painting seems to have been confined to the sixteenth-century Venetians and the bombastic artists of the Baroque. The most fascinating work is what's labelled a *Self-Portrait* by the mysterious father figure of Venice's Renaissance, **Giorgione**. One of the few surviving paintings widely accepted as genuine, it's probably a cut-down version of a *David with the Head of Goliath*. Important examples of the later Venetian Renaissance include works by Veronese, Tintoretto and Palma il Vecchio.

In the **decorative arts** section on the top floor Italy features rather more extensively, with a notable array of bronzes and porcelain, plus a valuable onyx vase from Mantua. Other particular strengths are Chinese lacquerwork, Limoges enamels, and jewellery, ceramics and furniture from all over Europe.

Eating, drinking and entertainment

In addition to the excellent hotel restaurants mentioned above, Braunschweig has plenty of good places to eat and drink. There's a good concentration of these in the Altstadt, and another in the Uni-Viertel just to the north.

Restaurants

Brodocz Stephanstr. 1. Rather formal vegetarian and wholefood restaurant (it also serves fish dishes) in a pretty half-timbered courtyard. It offers bargain menus at lunchtime. Closed Sun in winter.

Gewandhaus Altstadtmarkt 1. High quality restaurant in the Gothic cellars of the Gewandhaus. The menu includes several dishes in a dark sauce known as *Mumme*, named after a famous malt beer which was exported to England until the eighteenth century. Closed Sun.

Mutter Habenicht Papensteig 3. This candlelit Gaststätte with beer garden has been going strong since 1870. Closed Sun.

Rialto Wendenring 1–4. Italian restaurant just to the north of the city centre whose evening menu includes a selection of fresh fish displayed on a trolley. There's live music at weekends.

Schalander Stobenstr. 12. Serves very moderately priced *gutbürgerliche Küche*; the lunchtime dishes are quite incredibly cheap.

Stadtpark Jasperallee 42. This late nineteenth-century half-timbered Gaststätte in the Stadtpark features both Swabian and local dishes, including freshly-caught carp; it also has the city's largest beer garden. Closed Mon.

Tricolore Güldenstr. 77. Occupying a fine historic house, this offers modern Italian cuisine and a good selection of Sicilian wines. There are inexpensive set lunches Mon–Fri.

Welfenstübli Jüddenstr. 3. Cosy old Gastsätte, now run by Mövenpick.

Cafés and bars

Anders Am Magnitor 7. Trendy bar in the Magniviertel.

Bassgeige Bäckerklint 11. Bar which holds regular live jazz sessions.

Café L'Emigré Rosenhagen 3. French-style café.

Café Voigt Friedrich-Wilhelm-Platz 6. The pick of the traditional cafés.

Die Schüssel Konstantin-Uhde-Str. 4. Student Kneipe with beer garden; it has live jazz on Thurs, jam sessions on Fri.

Leonhard Leonhardstr. 2. This bar has a beer garden directly alongside a peaceful stretch of the River Oker.

Schadt's Höhe 28. Hausbrauerei which makes a *Pils* and a *Weizen* plus a seasonal *Märzen*; also serves full meals.

Zum Löwen Waisenhausdamm 13. A larger offshot of the above, housed in the same historic building as the *Stadtpalais* hotel.

Entertainment

Braunschweig has a strong **theatre** tradition; in the now demolished building on Hagenmarkt the first part of Goethe's *Faust* received its premiere in 1829. The building was replaced a few decades later by the Staatstheater (Ⓣ05 32/1 23 45 67, Ⓦwww.staatstheater-braunschweig.de) at Am Theater (between Museumpark and Theaterpark), which remains the leading venue for opera and drama. **Concerts** of all kinds are held at the modern Stadthalle on Leonhardplatz (Ⓣ05 32/7 07 70, Ⓦwww.stadthalle-braunschweig.de), not far from the Hauptbahnhof. The main folklore **festival** is a medieval market held on Burgplatz at Whitsun.

Wolfenbüttel

Reached in just a few minutes from Braunschweig via the first state-owned rail line in Germany (opened in 1838), **WOLFENBÜTTEL** is a place which deserves to be far better known. One of the Welf duchies had its seat there from 1432 to 1754, and even today it preserves much of the layout and atmosphere of a ducal Residenzstadt. When the local dukes moved back to Braunschweig, Wolfenbüttel seems to have fallen into a deep slumber. It came through World

War II unscathed, and no fewer than 600 historic half-timbered houses survive, as well as plenty of large public buildings.

The Town

Wolfenbüttel is the earliest example in Germany of a **planned town** – in fact, it evolved from several consecutive plans, all of whose outlines are still visible. At the western end is the spacious **Schlossplatz** with the main ducal showpieces, while beyond lies the **Alte Heinrichstadt**, the original centre. The subsequent planned suburbs lie further east.

Schlossplatz

On the western side of Schlossplatz is the huge, dazzlingly white **Schloss** (Tues–Sun 10am–5pm; €3). Apart from the moat and some re-used masonry, nothing remains of the medieval moated fortress, the present structure being a conflation of Renaissance and Baroque. The most distinguished feature is the Renaissance **tower**, whose unusual design includes a gabled clockface on each side. It was built in the early seventeenth century by **Paul Francke**, who was responsible for many of the buildings in the first phases of the planning of Wolfenbüttel. This apart, the exterior of the Schloss dates from a century later and was designed by the highly inventive **Hermann Korb**. The upper arcades of the Palladian-style inner **courtyard** were originally open, following normal Italian practice; however, they were filled in soon after, when the incompatibility of open arcades and northern weather became apparent. Round the back of the Schloss, a troupe of English actors under Thomas Sackville established themselves as the first permanent theatre company in Germany in 1590. This ushered in a golden era for the performing arts in Wolfenbüttel, but the opera house built there the following century has unfortunately not survived. The surprisingly modest **state apartments** give a good impression of how the dukes lived.

On the north side of Schlossplatz is the **Zeughaus**, again by Francke. Its cheerful crimson exterior, decorated with richly carved gables, hardly suggests its original function as an arsenal, whose cavernous lower floor once housed the biggest and most powerful cannons in Germany. Immediately behind is the grandest of Wolfenbüttel's half-timbered buildings, a huge mid-seventeenth-century storehouse.

Nowadays, the Zeughaus hosts temporary exhibitions from the pride of the town, the **Herzog-August-Bibliothek** (Tues–Sun 10am–5pm; €3, including entry to the Lessinghaus; Ⓦ www.hab.de), whose headquarters are in the nineteenth-century pseudo-*palazzo* diagonally opposite. The Dukes of Braunschweig-Wolfenbüttel were true bibliophiles and by the mid-seventeenth century the scholarly August the Younger had built up the largest library in Europe, consisting of 130,000 volumes, all catalogued by himself. Several rooms of the main library have been laid out as a museum, with changing selections from its holdings of rare books, as well as other specialities such as Renaissance maps and globes and twentieth-century artists' sketchbooks. A strongroom holds a display on the library's greatest treasure, the **Gospel book of Henry the Lion**, but unfortunately the initial intention to put on permanent public display the original manuscript itself has not been honoured, though it is occasionally exhibited, usually in the month of September. Arguably the most sumptuous manuscript produced in the Renaissance period, it set a world-record price for a work of art when it was bought for £10 million in 1983, and this remains, in real terms, the highest sum ever paid for a book.

The **Lessinghaus** (same hours and ticket) in front of the Bibliothek was the official residence of the librarian. A triple-winged summer house, it was finished just three years before the dukes decided to abandon Wolfenbüttel as a residence. Its present name comes from the second famous holder of the librarian's post, the hugely influential playwright **Gotthold Ephraim Lessing**, who spent the last eleven years of his life there; a collection of memorabilia pays tribute to him. The main work from his Wolfenbüttel years is *Nathan the Wise*, a piece particularly interesting in the light of subsequent German history – its wholly admirable hero is a Jew modelled on the famous philosopher Moses Mendelssohn.

Alte Heinrichstadt

East of Schlossplatz is the original late sixteenth-century planned town, the **Alte Heinrichstadt**. One of its focal points is the **Stadtmarkt**, a square lined with half-timbered buildings, in the centre of which is a bronze statue of Duke August the Younger, depicted leading his horse rather than riding it.

Off the north side of the square, on the street named after it, is the **Kanzlei** (Chancellery). Though somewhat messed about, it's notable as being the only surviving building by the Dutchman Hans Vredeman de Vries, the leading architectural theoretician of the Northern European Renaissance. The Kanzlei now houses the Braunschweigisches Landesmuseum's archeology department, the **Abteilung Ur- und Frühgeschichte** (Tues–Fri & Sun 10am–5pm; €1.50, €2.50 combined ticket with the two associated museums in Braunschweig; Ⓦwww.landesmuseum-bs.de). Almost all the other streets around here are worth walking along; look out for **Klein-Venedig** (Little Venice), so named because it fronts a canal.

As a climax to the Alte Heinrichstadt, the **Hauptkirche** (Tues–Sat 10am–noon & 2–4pm) was begun in 1608 by Paul Francke. Notwithstanding the dedication to Beatae Mariae Virginis, it was not only Lutheran from the outset, but was the first parish church to be built specifically for the Protestant faith (although Bückeburg's Stadtkirche, started three years later, was actually finished first). It's an extraordinary confection, mixing late Gothic, Renaissance and Mannerism, while the main portal – designed like a triumphal arch with statues of two of the dukes ensconced between Moses and Aaron below, and Christ at the summit – has all the swagger of the emergent Baroque style. On the long sides of the building are profusely decorated gables, while on the facade and in the vestibule are hundreds of delicately carved reliefs of animals and demons. The church's light and spacious interior doubles as the ducal pantheon. There's also a painted epitaph in the form of an *Allegory of the Old and New Testaments* by Hans Vredemann de Vries, complete with a detailed background view of Jerusalem. Regular recitals are held on the early Baroque organ, first presided over by the composer **Michael Praetorius**, who is buried below. He's best known for his beguiling arrangements of over three hundred foot-tapping dance melodies, collectively known as *Terpsichore*.

The rest of the town

East of the Hauptkirche is the **Neue Heinrichstadt**, centred on the Holzmarkt; for the most part, its buildings faithfully follow the style of the earlier part of town. In the early eighteenth century, Hermann Korb finished off the square in an ingenious fashion by inserting the oval **Trinitatiskirche** (Tues 11am–1pm, Wed 11am–1pm & 2–4pm, Thurs 3–5pm, Sat 11am–4pm) between the two redundant gateways at the far end, transforming the latter into a pair of towers for the church in the process.

Further east, across the Oker, a huge new town of manufacturing workshops called the **Juliusstadt** was once planned. However, it never got beyond a couple of streets. Instead, the far more modest craftsmen's suburb of **Auguststadt** was laid out at the opposite end of Wolfenbüttel, to the west of the Schloss. Its houses are remarkably similar to those in the "better" part of town, and the half-timbered **Johanniskirche**, set beside its detached belfry in a shady green, brings a touch of rusticity to the quarter.

Practicalities

Wolfenbüttel's **Bahnhof** is immediately south of the historic centre, on the opposite side of the River Oker. The **tourist office** (May–Sept Mon–Fri 9am–5pm, Sat & Sun 11am–2pm; Oct–April same hours Mon–Fri only; Ⓣ0 53 31/8 62 80, Ⓦwww.wolfenbuettel-tourismus.de) is at Stadtmarkt 7.

Many of the **hotels** occupy interesting old buildings. North of the Altstadt the half-timbered *Forsthaus*, Neuer Weg 5 (Ⓣ0 53 31/7 17 11, Ⓦwww.hotel-forsthaus-wf.de; ❸) was for 30 years the holiday home of the cartoonist Wilhelm Busch. *Gasthof Kaltes Tal*, to the rear of the Bahnhof at Goslarsche Str. 56 (Ⓣ0 53 31/4 38 28; ❸), is an inn first documented in the seventeenth century. *Kronprinz*, Bahnhofstr. 12 (Ⓣ0 53 31/12 65, Ⓦwww.hotel-kronprinz-wolfenbuettel.de; ❹) has an inner courtyard and a winter garden, while *Gasthof Altes Haus*, Enge Str. 25 (Ⓣ0 53 31/13 62; ❺) and *Bayrischer Hof*, Brauergildenstr. 5 (Ⓣ0 53 31/50 78, Ⓦwww.bayrischer-hof-wf.de; ❺) both occupy timber-framed buildings in the Altstadt. The most luxurious hotel is the modern *Parkhotel Altes Kaffeehaus* just beyond the southeastern fringe of the centre at Harztorwall 18 (Ⓣ0 53 31/88 80, Ⓦwww.parkhotel-wolfenbuettel.de; ❻–❽). There's an unofficial **youth hostel** at Jägerstr. 17 (Ⓣ0 53 31/2 71 89, Ⓦwww.jgh.wf-net.de; €13.50/16.50).

The best **restaurants** are in the hotels listed above, especially the *Historisches Weingrotte* in the *Parkhotel Altes Kaffeehaus*, a reconstruction of the once celebrated but long destroyed *Türkisches Kaffeehaus* of 1838. Main **festivals** are the open-air Theaterfest in June/July and the Altstadtfest in late August.

Goslar

The stereotype of a mining town immediately conjures up images of rows of grim identikit terraced houses paying obeisance to the gargantuan, satanic-looking machinery in whose shadow they lie. **GOSLAR**, which stands in an imposing location at the northern edge of the Harz, could not be more different. Admittedly, the mining here was always of a very superior nature – silver was discovered in the nearby six-hundred-metre-high **Rammelsberg** in the tenth century, and the town immediately prospered, soon becoming the "treasure chest of the Holy Roman Empire", and a favourite royal seat. As a Free Imperial City in the later Middle Ages, Goslar, though never very large, ranked as one of the most prosperous communities in Europe, with lead and zinc now added to the list of ready-to-hand mineral deposits. Despite two fires sweeping through the streets in 1800, much survives as a reminder of this heady epoch. The presence of a POW hospital during World War II helped to spare it from Allied bombing, ensuring that the entire town now enjoys the status of a protected monument. With just cause too, as Goslar claims to have more **old houses** (over 1500, with 168 dating from before 1550) than any other town in Germany.

Arrival, information and accommodation

Goslar's **Bahnhof** and **bus station** are at the northern edge of the Altstadt. It's only about ten minutes' walk to Marktplatz, where you'll find the municipal **tourist office** at no. 7 (May–Oct Mon–Fri 9.15am–6pm, Sat 9.30am–4pm, Sun 9.30am–2pm; Nov–April Mon–Fri 9.15am–5pm, Sat 9.30am–2pm; ⓣ0 53 21/7 80 60, ⓦwww.goslarinfo.de). The €9 MuseumSpass gives admissions to the main monuments and sights in the Altstadt.

There are around two dozen private houses (❶–❸) with **rooms** to rent; a full list is available from the tourist office. If travelling in a group and intending to stay for at least three days, it can be an even better deal to rent a **holiday home**; most atmospheric are the luxury apartments in *Burg im Zwinger*, Thomasstr. 2 (ⓣ0 53 21/4 10 88 or 8 51 35, ⓦwww.zwinger.de; ❸). The **youth hostel**, Rammelsberger Str. 25 (ⓣ0 53 21/2 22 40; €14/16.70), is at

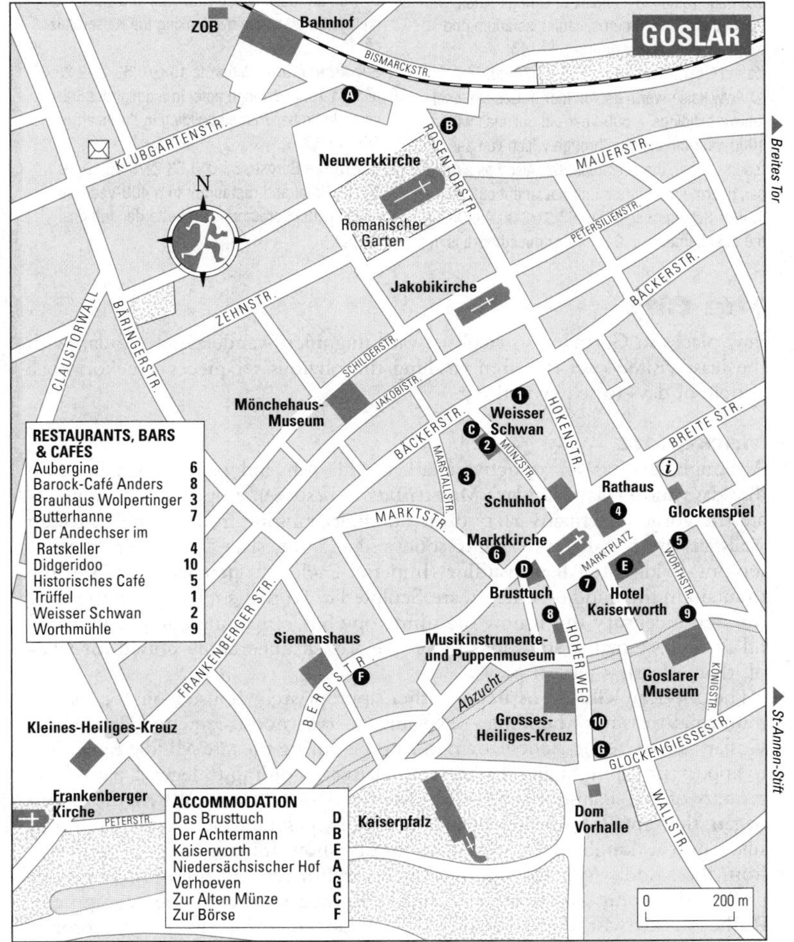

the foot of the mine, not too far from the centre, but a long trek from the Bahnhof. Nearest **campsite** is the well-equipped *Sennhütte*, Clausthaler Str. 28 (ⓣ0 53 21/2 24 98), in the Gose valley, along the B241 in the direction of Clausthal-Zellerfeld. Goslar is amply endowed with **hotels** and **guesthouses**, many of them in historic buildings.

Hotels and guesthouses

Das Brusttuch Hoher Weg 1 ⓣ3 46 00, ⓦwww.treff-hotels de. Treff chain hotel in a famous sixteenth-century patrician mansion with salacious carvings on its facade. It has a restaurant and a Weinstube, and includes large breakfast buffets in the room price. ❼–❾

Der Achtermann Rosentorstr. 20 ⓣ0 53 21/7 00 00, ⓦwww.der-achtermann.de. Goslar's most prestigious hotel, diagonally opposite the Bahnhof, is a huge rambling complex of various dates, with thermal and steam baths, sauna, solarium and romantic old-style restaurant. ❼–❾

Kaiserworth Markt 3 ⓣ0 53 21/70 90, ⓦwww.kaiserworth.de. Another of Goslar's best-known buildings, a 500-year-old guildhall with a 1000-year-old cistern, through which you pass to reach the bar, the *Dukatenkeller*. Also has a wine bar, gourmet restaurant and pavement café. ❼–❾

Möller Schieferweg 6 ⓣ0 53 21/2 30 98. One of the best bargains in Goslar, this guesthouse is in a large Jugendstil villa few minutes' walk west of the Bahnhof. The buffet breakfasts, with lots of homemade goodies, are remarkable. ❸

Niedersächsischer Hof Klubgartenstr. 1–2 ⓣ0 53 21/31 60, ⓦwww.alemannia-hotels.de. Grand old station hotel, which underwent a thorough modernisation just a few years ago; many of the bedrooms have balconies. There's a good restaurant and a bistro, *Pieper's*. ❼–❾

Verhoeven Hoher Weg 12 ⓣ0 53 21/2 38 12, ⓕ4 66 53. Guesthouse with café in a slate and half-timbered house overlooking the Kaiserpfalz. ❸

Zur Alten Münze Münzstr. 10 ⓣ0 53 21/2 25 46, ⓕ1 84 16. Mid-range hotel in a delightful 500-year-old timber-framed building in the heart of the Altstadt. ❺

Zur Börse Bergstr. 53 ⓣ0 53 21/3 45 10, ⓕ1 84 37. Hotel and restaurant in a 400-year-old house with characteristic rosette decorations. ❹–❻

The City

Few places in Germany so richly reward unguided wandering as Goslar, with the least visited corners often rivalling the obvious set pieces. Reckon on a couple of days to see everything.

Marktplatz

Although it hosts an attractive market with fish and pastry specialities on Tuesdays and Fridays, Goslar's **Marktplatz** is best seen empty to fully appreciate the gorgeous visual variety of its buildings, ranging from creamy-textured walls, via pretty half-timbering to sober red and grey slate. The rather comical-looking gold-plated **Reichsadler** (Imperial Eagle) sits perched on top of the fountain in the middle of the square. Sculpted in Romanesque style in the early thirteenth century, this is now the third copy, but, remaining completely faithful to the original, it still looks more like a cock uncertainly poised for take-off than a fearless bird of prey.

The modern **Glockenspiel** – rather appropriately housed on top of the municipal treasurer's building – explains (at 9am, noon, 3pm and 6pm), how Goslar rose to be the richest town in Europe during the late Middle Ages. First to appear are a knight and his horse; the latter, according to legend, pawed the ground of the Rammelsberg, and uncovered silver traces. When the boom began, the emperors moved in, and Otto I is presented here with a lump of silver by the knight. The remaining groups show miners hacking their way from the Middle Ages through to the nineteenth century, finishing with their present-day counterparts proudly displaying their state-of-the-art equipment. Rather a sad twist, then, that due to depletion of the various ores, Europe's oldest mine – which had nearly three thousand employees – closed down for good in 1988.

Across the square is the **Rathaus** (guided tours daily 11am–4pm; €2), whose **Huldigungssaal** (Hall of Homage) ranks as one of the best-preserved secular interiors of the Middle Ages. The name is rather misleading, as homage was actually paid in the great hall where the admission desk is now situated. Its gold-starred, marine-blue panelled ceiling dates from the original construction of the building in the latter half of the fifteenth century; the chandeliers, carved from antlers and carrying figures of the emperors, were transported from the Dom a few decades later. The Huldigungssaal itself was the assembly hall of the city council from 1500 onwards and later used for the town's archives. Its richly decorated panels, painted by an unknown artist over 400 years ago, show scenes from the life of Christ and portraits of various citizens of Goslar. Several valuable relics are hidden in altar niches and closets behind the panelling. Among them are a precious gold and silver tankard from the fifteenth century, elaborately embellished with mining and hunting scenes, and a facsimile of the **Goslarer Evangeliar** (Goslar Evangelistary), a thirteenth-century manuscript with exquisite Byzantine-inspired Romanesque miniature paintings. The **original Reichsadler** is also on view.

Opposite is the **Hotel Kaiserworth**, previously the guild house of tailors and cloth-makers. Here Baroque and Gothic tumble down on top of Renaissance arches, while the frontage bears eight statues of German emperors, with a corbel depicting a naked man excreting a gold coin thrown in for good measure. Just behind the Rathaus is the **Marktkirche**, dedicated to the Roman martyrs Saints Cosmas and Damian, patrons of the medical profession. The architecture, a mix of Romanesque and Gothic, with rough-hewn masonry, is typical of Goslar. Inside, look out for the cycle of stained-glass windows illustrating the saints' lives, and the bronze baptismal **font** created by a local artist, Magnus Karsten, in 1573: just about every major biblical event is represented on it in magnificent detail. It is hoped that the northern of the twin towers will be made accessible to the public in the near future, thereby giving a vantage point that the town currently lacks.

The southwestern quarters

Goslar's **half-timbered** beauty begins in earnest in the streets behind the Marktkirche. The styles to look out for are Gothic, Renaissance and Baroque, many homes having two and sometimes all of these: Gothic pointed arches are transformed into three-stepped inlays, usually dull red, gold and olive green in colour; sombrely brilliant rosettes cartwheel across the rafters of the Renaissance houses, while gaudily coloured Baroque devils lie like flattened gargoyles bereft of their power in their prisons of beam.

The oldest houses lie in the Bergstrasse and Schreiberstrasse areas; the **Siemenshaus** (Tues & Thurs 9am–noon; free), which was built by a forefather of what is today one of Europe's largest suppliers of medical equipment, electrical appliances and armaments parts, is conveniently situated on the corner of both. Further down Schreiberstrasse, classic Gothic brick houses abound, the style exemplified by the early sixteenth century embodied at no. 10, with its lavishly decorated chimney passing through the two single-roomed storeys. From here, turn left into Frankenberger Strasse and continue down to Frankenberg Plan, on which stands the **Kleines-Heiliges-Kreuz**, set in spacious gardens where the old folk who retire there – and dozens of chickens – can amble about at their leisure.

Through the archway to the right, you can walk up to the **Frankenberger Kirche**, once the church favoured by miners for their weddings, which is situated in tranquil solitude on the little hill above. Built during the twelfth century as a Romanesque basilica, the later Gothic additions form part of the town's western ramparts. The gigantic Baroque carved wooden passion altar verges on pastiche and could easily dominate the place until you begin to take in a few other details. Towards the back of the church, two fierce lions stand facing each other to absorb the evil believed to have come from the west. Some faint thirteenth-century frescoes compete in vain for attention against an overcharged Baroque pulpit, and there's a strange *Triumphal Cross*, with a deathly-white Christ macabrely topped with a wig of the artist's own hair, a device used frequently in the Harz area.

On Peterstrasse immediately to the east are some of the most intriguing of the town's houses: the **Kuhhaus** (Cow House) at no. 27 is named after its previous function, while the **Kürbishaus** (Pumpkin House) at no. 23 is named after its shape. In the **Klauskapelle** to the right and the **Schmiedhaus** (Blacksmith's House) opposite, the miners would respectively pray and collect their sharpened tools before beginning their daily trek up to the Rammelsberg.

The Kaiserpfalz

Dominating a spacious park at the southern end of the Altstadt is the **Kaiserpfalz** (daily 10am–4/5pm; €4.50). By far the largest and most important Romanesque royal palace to have survived anywhere in Europe, its exterior is still a potent symbol of the power and wealth enjoyed by Germany's medieval rulers. Built at the beginning of the eleventh century to be home to a succession of greedy emperors enticed by the riches hidden in the Rammelsberg behind it, the Kaiserpfalz continued to flourish for nearly 300 years, hosting important Imperial Diets and benefiting from Goslar's proximity to the crossroads of the two major trade routes of the Middle Ages – from Flanders to Magdeburg, and from Lübeck to Venice. A fire which gutted the palace in 1289 and a decline of interest around the same time by the emperors kept the building in a state of disrepair over the next few centuries, humbling it even to the point where it was used as a barn and stables during the seventeenth century. Kaiser Wilhelm I came to the rescue in 1868, paying for its reconstruction.

By present-day standards, the building seems over-restored. This is particularly true of the interior, where the vast **Reichsaal**, whose enormous arched window openings must have given birth to many a draughty Diet during the palace's heyday, was covered, floor to ceiling, with Romantic paintings. Various emperors are depicted being valiant (in battle), pious (distributing riches to the poor), conquering the earth and being blessed by heaven. On the southern side of the hall is the early twelfth-century **Ulrichskapelle**. This chapel, the most authentic part of the complex, is an ingenious piece of design: the ground plan is a Greek cross, but the upper storeys are shaped as a Byzantine-style octagon. In the centre stands the tomb of Emperor Heinrich III, though it contains only his heart: the rest of his body lies in Speyer.

Behind the palace, the *Goslar Warrior* by **Henry Moore** lies reclining with his shield on his toe; this is a legacy of the first of the annual prizes awarded by the city to a famous modern artist. Beyond it a pretty semi-walled rose garden, dotted about with firs and shady spreading trees, leads down to a small bridge, the Abzucht stream, and a stone-walled tower.

Hoher Weg

On the opposite side of the Kaiserpfalz, facing the Hoher Weg, the enormous car park stretching below you was once the site of the eleventh-century **Dom** – more accurately, the **Stiftskirche St Simeon und Judas** – pulled down in 1822 due to lack of funds for restoration. Only the **Vorhalle** with its facade of stucco statues survived. Behind the protective glass door is the original part-bronze **imperial throne**; it was used symbolically at the opening assembly of the Second Reich in Berlin in 1871. Other relics from the church are housed in the Goslarer Museum (see p.648). The Dom's stones are now embedded in any number of houses, having been sold at the time of demolition to townsfolk who subsequently built their homes with them.

Directly in front of the Dom, Hoher Weg leads down to the **Grosses-Heiliges-Kreuz** (daily 11am–4/5pm; free) at no. 7, one of the oldest hospices in Germany, dating back to 1254. Following its restoration a few years ago, it has been given a new lease of life as a handicrafts centre. The magnificent main hall hosts several markets a year, and a number of small shops have been set up in the ground-floor cells. Further down the street is the **Musikinstrumente- und Puppenmuseum** (daily 11am–5pm; €3). On the first floor, an eclectic array of musical instruments from around the world features such oddities as a combined violin and trumpet, a cello with a keyboard, and a sub-contrabass lute. What is thought to be the oldest musical instrument in Germany, a hurdy-gurdy from around 1500, is also on view. The second floor has a collection of rare old dolls.

Goslar's most famous mansion, the sixteenth-century **Brusttuch**, lies at the bottom of Hoher Weg, almost opposite the Marktkirche. It's an outstanding example of the "Wild Man" style, whose theme of "natural" unbridled sexuality was a great favourite with German artists and craftsmen of the period. The beams of the top storey are crammed with satirical carvings of figures from medieval life, folklore, religion and mythology: mischievous cherubs firing arrows at angels, dignified ladies perched on top of goats, and a carelessly suggestive dairymaid churning the butter and squeezing her buttocks at the same time. Facing it across Marktstrasse is the **Bäckergildehaus** (Bakers' Guild House), a far more sober, yet equally imposing, example of half-timbering.

The northern quarters

Immediately north of the Marktkirche is the **Schuhhof**, the site of the former shoemakers' guildhall and market. Fires over the centuries have ravaged one part of the square, but the surviving side has three- and four-storey half-timbered houses from the seventeenth century. Münzstrasse on its western side contains more architectural beauties, including a seventeenth-century coaching inn, the **Weisser Schwan** at no. 11, where the **Zinnfigurenmuseum** (Tin Figure Museum; daily 10am–5pm; €3.50) depicts in miniature scenes from the history of Goslar and the Roman Empire.

At the end of the street, turn into Jakobistrasse, where, at no. 15, a Renaissance craftsman's house has been the subject of one of the most polished and professional pieces of restoration in Goslar. The **Mönchehaus Museum** (Tues–Sat 10am–5pm, Sun 10am–1pm; €3) lies just beyond, at the corner with Mönchestrasse. A black and white half-timbered sixteenth-century building, it's the curious home to Goslar's permanent modern art exhibition, featuring works by recipients of the city's annual prize. The contrast works amazingly well indoors, with de Koonings, Tinguelys and Vasarelys hanging amidst the oak beams. The effectiveness of the huge metal sculptures parked in the garden is more debatable, but it's good to see something in Goslar with an experimental touch.

On the square at the eastern end of Jakobistrasse is the Catholic parish church, the **Jakobikirche**. Only the west wing remains from the original Romanesque structure, which was rebuilt in Gothic style. Inside, there's a moving *Pietà* by the great but elusive early sixteenth-century sculptor, Hans Witten. North along Rosentorstrasse, the **Neuwerkkirche** (Mon–Fri 10am–noon & 2.30–4.30pm, Sat & Sun 2.30–4.30pm) stands in a peaceful garden. It was built as a Cistercian convent church during the late twelfth and early thirteenth centuries; the most striking exterior features are the two polygonal towers, and the delicate late Romanesque carvings on the apse. Inside, there are works of art dating back to the period of construction, notably the choir screen and some rather clumsily retouched frescoes. The curious **stone handles** high up on the pillars of the nave are unique in the history of architecture and have a didactic purpose: those on the south have grotesque carvings and represent the temptations of the devil; the wreaths on the north symbolize the eternity for which the soul should strive. On the south side of the church is the **Romanischer Garten**, a recreation, based on the writings of Hildegard of Bingen, among others, of a conventual garden of the period.

The Abzucht and the Stadtbefestigung

From Marktplatz, south along Worthstrasse, a fairly successful attempt at an artists' quarter has been constructed along and around the banks of the **Abzucht**, the tiny stream that passes through the southern part of Goslar. On the corner of Abzuchtstrasse and Königstrasse is the **Goslarer Museum** (Tues–Sun 10am–4/5pm; €3). This contains the usual local history displays, including a section on mining in the Rammelsberg. However, the collection is taken out of the ordinary by some superb treasures from the Dom, including a couple of stained-glass windows and the exotic *Krodoaltar* – which looks more as if it were fashioned deep in the heart of Africa than in eleventh-century Europe. The original **Goslarer Evangeliar** is also on view, though only the cover can be seen. Other highlights are the late Gothic *Bergkanne*, the ceremonial tankard of the miners, and the seventeenth-century laboratory of the **Ratsapotheke**.

The Abzucht bubbles along the cobbles to occasionally bump into one of the handful of rickety water mills still remaining of an original twenty-five; follow the red stones in the middle of the pathways to find the sites of the former mills, now replaced by houses. Look out for the **St-Annen-Stift** (Mon–Thurs 10am–noon & 2–4/5pm, Fri & Sat 10am–1pm; knock at the door for entrance; free), a hospice dating from 1488, which is the oldest half-timbered building in Goslar. Inside, you can view the chapel with its medieval woodwork and seventeenth-century wall paintings.

From here, it's a short walk down St Annenhöhe to see the best-preserved parts of the **Stadtbefestigung**. It takes about two hours to walk the complete circuit, which is interspersed with many stretches of greenery. If pressed for time, go down Zingerwall to see the **Zwinger** (daily: March 10am–4pm; April to mid-Nov 10am–5pm; €2), an ivy-covered, thick-walled tower once used by the town's artillery. It commands a fine view over Goslar and the Harz; there's also a display of medieval weapons and a restaurant. The most imposing part of the town's fortifications is the bulky ensemble of the **Breites Tor** at the north-easternmost corner, the sight of which alone must have been enough to scare off any would-be invaders.

The Rammelsberg

The **Rammelsberg**, the mountain which provided the city with its wealth, is connected with the town centre by bus #C. Since mining ceased, it has gradually been transformed into a major tourist attraction, and to see everything that is now accessible to the public takes up a large chunk of the day. Visits begin in the **Bergbaumuseum** (daily 9am–6pm; €5.50, or €8.50 including any one of the guided tours, €13.50 for two, €18.50 for all three; Ⓦwww.rammelsberg.de), which explains the historical background to the operations. In the hall-like changing room, you don a miner's overalls and helmet before descending into the bowels of the earth. Each of the three separate tours on offer lasts between 60 and 75 minutes. The first is a walk through the tunnels to see some of the old machinery, including the giant water wheels; the second is a ride on the underground railway to the part of the mine that was the last to be exploited; while the third covers the equipment used for ore processing.

Eating and drinking

Goslar's food and drink scene is geared to the fact that many of the town's visitors are taking a relaxing holiday – hence the presence of so many cafés. Many of the best restaurants are in the hotels (see p.644).

Aubergine Marktstr. 4. This has a Turkish owner/chef, though the menu ranges over a whole gamut of Mediterranean cuisines.

Barock-Café Anders Hoher Weg 4. Best place in town for *Kaffee und Kuchen*; there's a Baroque room upstairs and a garden at the back with a leafy vista of the Harz.

Brauhaus Wolpertinger Marstallstr. 1. This Hausbrauerei, serving one dark and two light beers, revived Goslar's medieval brewing tradition after a long gap. It also serves full meals, and is one of several bars and restaurants grouped round a courtyard which has become the liveliest spot in town.

Butterhanne Marktkirchhof 3. Located in a sixteenth-century hatmaker's shop, this café-restaurant specializes in home-made cakes and dishes using fresh game from the Harz.

Der Andechser im Ratskeller Markt 1. Goslar's Ratskeller has been revamped as a Bavarian-style restaurant with beer from the monastic brewery of Andechs.

Digeridoo Hoher Weg 13. Australian theme bar and restaurant serving kangaroo steaks and *Foster*'s lager. It's hugely popular with the locals.

Historisches Café Markt 4. Another good choice for those with a sweet tooth, particularly when the weather is good and you can sit outside on the square.

Trüffel Bäckerstr. 106. The long menu here features plenty of inventive vegetarian dishes.

Weisser Schwan Münzstr. 11. Part of this famous old inn is given over to a Balkan grillroom that's a cut above the German norm.

Worthmühle Worthstr. 4. Does excellent hot provincial cooking at very low prices. It's also the main town centre outlet for *Gose*, a fruity brew named after Goslar (though it's also associated with Leipzig) which is similar to the Belgian *Gueze*. Production of this was revived a decade ago, after a gap of over a century and a half, at a tiny brewery in the incorporated village of Oker.

Einbeck

EINBECK, which lies just to the west of the Harz range, some 50km from Goslar, is something of a mecca for **beer** lovers, being the original home and the most authentic producer of Germany's famous strong brew. Originally, this was called *Einpökisches Bier*, but later became known as *Bockbier* after a corruption of the town's name. In the Middle Ages, Einback had no fewer than seven hundred breweries, virtually all of them tiny part-time operations run within the household. Nowadays, only the Einbecker brewery is left: it produces both light (*Hell*) and dark (*Dunkel*) varieties of *Bockbier*, as well as the special brown *Maibock*, available only in springtime. All of these have a smooth, dry and highly satisfying flavour.

The town is almost equally well known for its **half-timbered houses**, characteristically painted in yellow, red, green and black – around 120 survive from the sixteenth century alone. Many of the houses where beer was brewed can still be identified: two clues to look for are double doorways (one of which was used for rolling the barrels through), and dense groupings of dormer-like ventilation openings in the attic, where the raw ingredients were stored.

The hub of life in Einbeck is the **Marktplatz**, which is surrounded by well-kept and obviously genuine sixteenth-century houses. Look out for the **Brodhaus** and the **Ratsapotheke,** which stand next door to each other like two superannuated old men opposite the **Ratswaage** (Weigh House) and the vaguely sinister-looking **Rathaus**. The Rathaus could well have served as a model for the witch's house in the Hansel and Gretel story, thanks to three low conical spires which sprout out of the stairwell and the two sharply contrasted oriel windows. Dominating the square from its central position is the **Marktkirche**, a box-like Gothic hall church with a striking red sandstone Baroque facade.

Immediately to the west lies **Tiedexer Strasse**, the most impressive street in town, with a gloriously picturesque ensemble of half-timbered houses. However, the finest house of all is no. 13 in **Marktstrasse**, whose whole facade is covered with intricate allegorical carvings, drawing on Christian and Classical themes. Another handsome street, Steinweg, leads north to another red sandstone Gothic church, the **Stiftskirche St Alexandri** (Mon–Fri 10am–noon). Its set of choir stalls, bearing the date of 1288, is the oldest in Germany, though the main treasure is a magnificent Romanesque chandelier. At Steinweg 11, a fine patrician mansion has been adapted to contain the local history collections of the **Städtisches Museum** (April–Sept Tues–Fri 10am–noon & 3–5pm, Sat & Sun 11am–4pm; Oct–March Tues–Fri 10am–noon & 3–5pm, Sat & Sun 1–4pm; €1.50). The ticket also gives admission to the **Fahrradmuseum** (same times), a short walk south of Marktplatz at Pupenstr. 1–3, a collection of bikes which has everything from the wooden-wheeled boneshakers of 1817 to the very latest racers. It's also worth taking a walk round the surviving sections of the **Stadtmauer**; much of the fortification network is intact and you can stroll along the massive earthworks which were constructed to increase the protection afforded by the wall itself.

Practicalities

Einbeck's **Bahnhof** is 4km from the centre in the castle-crowned village of Salzderhelden. **Buses** have replaced the former branch rail line into the town, but beware that these do not necessarily connect with the arrival and departure of trains. The **tourist office** is in the Rathaus (May–Oct Mon–Fri 9am–5.30pm, Sat 10.30am–3pm, Sun 2–4pm; Nov–April Mon–Thurs 9am–1pm & 2.30–5pm, Fri 9am–12.30pm; Ⓣ0 55 61/91 61 21, Ⓦwww.einbeck-online.de), Marktplatz 6.

Of the **hotels** with a central location, the most reasonably priced are *Zur Stadt Einbeck*, Benser Str. 27 (Ⓣ0 55 61/40 86; ④) and *Haus Joanna*, Bürgermeisterwall 8 (Ⓣ0 55 61/9 33 50; ⑤). For a bit more luxury, try *Der Schwan*, Tiedexer Str. 1 (Ⓣ0 55 61/46 09, Ⓦwww.schwan-einbeck.de; ⑥); or *Gildehof*, Marktplatz 3 (Ⓣ0 55 61/7 23 22, Ⓦwww.hotel-gilde-hof.de; ⑥). These also have two of the best **restaurants** in town – the former is the more expensive and is open evenings only – and are good places to sample the local beers. An alternative is *Zum Brodhaus*, which occupies a wonderful fourteenth-century building at

Marktplatz 13. There are also several elegant **cafés**, including the exquisitely furnished *Antik Café*, Tiedexer Str. 42–44.

Göttingen

GÖTTINGEN is positively metropolitan in contrast to the surrounding area. It owes its exciting, buzzing atmosphere to its **university**. Founded in 1737 by King George II of Great Britain, in his capacity as Elector of Hannover, it quickly gained a reputation as a free-thinking, liberal institution whose whole culture was totally different from the authoritarian tradition of Germany's older seats of learning. The roll-call of distinguished teachers includes the Romantic balladeer Gottfried August Bürger, the Brothers Grimm, the inventor and philosopher Georg Christoph Lichtenberg (whose *Book of Apohorisms*, available in Penguin Classics, is a storehouse of worldly wisdom), the physicist Carl-Friedrich Gauss, and the chemist Friedrich Wöhler. Since 1945, the town has been the headquarters of the fifty separate high-powered scientific research units of the Max-Planck-Institut, named in honour of the discoverer of quantum theory, who passed his last years there. Its student population (30,000 out of a total populace of 130,000), have made sure that the **nightlife** here almost has a big-city feel to it. In fact, a lot of students come to Göttingen after studying in Berlin, and they seem to have brought some of the latter's pace with them. Things quieten down a little outside term time – but there's usually something going on.

Arrival, information and accommodation

Göttingen's **Hauptbahnhof**, a major rail junction, lies just to the west of the centre, which is reached by going straight ahead via the underpass, then along Goetheallee. The **tourist office** (April–Oct Mon–Fri 9.30am–6pm, Sat & Sun 10am–4pm; Nov–March Mon–Fri 9.30am–1pm & 2–6pm, Sat 10am–1pm; ⓣ05 51/49 98 00, ⓦwww.goettingen-tourismus.de) is on the first floor of the Altes Rathaus.

The **youth hostel** is 3km east of the centre at Habichtsweg 2 (ⓣ05 51/5 76 22; €15/17.70); take bus #6 or #9 from Kornmarkt. Göttingen's centrally sited **hotels** tend to be on the pricey side, but there are plenty of bargains a bit further out.

Hotels

Berliner Hof Weender Landstr. 43 ⓣ05 51/38 33 20, ⓦwww.berlinerhof.de. Moderately priced hotel, handily placed for the university. ❹

Central Jüdenstr. 12 ⓣ05 51/5 71 57, ⓦwww.hotel-central.com. The only hotel in the heart of the Altstadt. ❻–❽

Gebhards Goetheallee 22–23 ⓣ05 51/4 96 80, ⓦwww.romantikhotels.com/goettingen. Göttingen's leading hotel occupies a renovated eighteenth-century palace just across from the Hauptbahnhof on the way to the centre. It also has a fine restaurant, *Georgia-Augusta-Stuben*. ❽–❾

Kasseler Hof Rosdorfer Weg 26 ⓣ05 51/7 20 81, ⓦwww.kasseler-hof.de. Mid-range hotel a short distance southwest of the Altstadt. ❻

Landgasthaus Lockemann Im Beecke 1, Herberhausen ⓣ05 51/20 90 20, ⓕ2 09 02 50. Offering very good value by Göttingen standards, this country house style hotel with restaurant (closed Mon) is in an eastern suburb, reached by bus #10. ❸

Onkel Toms Hütte Am Gewende 10–11 ⓣ05 51/70 71 10, ⓕ7 70 00 34. Very pleasant hotel with restaurant and beer garden in the southern outskirts, reached by bus #5 or #6. ❺

Stadt Hannover Goetheallee 21 ⓣ05 51/54 79 60, ⓦwww.hotelstadthannover.de. Good quality hotel, run by the same family since 1919, right alongside *Gebhards*. ❻

The Town

Most of Göttingen's sights are in the small Altstadt, particularly in and around the Markt. The famous university is spread out all over the town, though its most imposing buildings are found in the eastern part of the Altstadt, and around the green belt encircling the former fortifications.

The central Markt is dominated by the **Altes Rathaus**, a massive sandstone structure which has an almost Venetian feel to it, quite at odds with the half-timbered buildings nearby. Most of what you can see today dates back to the fourteenth and fifteenth centuries, when Göttingen was at the height of its commercial prosperity, but it was never completely finished, as resources had to be diverted to constructing the municipal fortifications. The only way of seeing much of the building is by taking a **guided tour** (Sun at 3pm; free). At other times, unless there's an exhibition on, you'll have to be content with viewing the medieval-looking frescoes and coats of arms painted on the inner walls; these are only a little over one hundred years old, having been commissioned by the authorities during the restoration of the building in the 1880s. When the weather is good the *Rathskeller* takes over part of the Markt and you can have a drink or a meal while looking at the **Gänseliesel**, "the most kissed girl in the world", a bronze statue of a goose-girl erected at the beginning of last century, to whom, according to tradition, the students must give a few smackers when they pass their finals.

Behind the Altes Rathaus is the **Johanniskirche** (daily May–Oct 11am–noon), a twin-towered fourteenth-century Gothic church. Theological students are allowed free accommodation in one of the **towers**, but they have to endure the sound of the bells from the other tower and miserable living conditions (no running water or WC), as well as granting admission on Saturdays between 2pm and 4pm to anyone wanting to climb up for a view of the town (though this facility is currently suspended because of restoration work). Behind the church is the medieval **Johannesviertel**, more or less a slum district until the 1970s, when the city finally got round to tarting it up. At the point where Johanniskirchhof runs into Paulinerstrasse is the former **Paulinerkirche**, which was built in the early fourteenth century by Dominican friars. In 1529 it was the scene of the first Lutheran church service in Göttingen. Used as the provisional home of the university when it first opened, the building now houses part of its library.

Following the pedestrianized main street, Weender Strasse, north from the Markt brings you to the **Jakobikirche**, another Gothic church, dominated this time by a single octagonal **tower** (May–Oct daily 11am–5pm; €1), which was designed by an associate of the famous Parler dynasty of masons. The **winged altar**, which bears the date of 1402, is a masterpiece of German Gothic art, though nothing is known about the artists who created it. When closed, it shows eight scenes from the life of the church's patron, St James; the first opening (the one most often on view) has sixteen beautifully coloured and detailed scenes of the life of Christ, while the second opening has gilded carvings of the Coronation of the Virgin and sixteen saints. From Judenstrasse at the back of the church, turn right into Ritterplan, where the only aristocratic mansion left in the town has been refurbished to house the **Städtisches Museum** (Tues–Fri 10am–5pm, Sat & Sun 10am–5pm; €1.50), which has a good collection of religious art and plenty of examples of locally produced glass and porcelain.

Finest of all the University buildings is the Neoclassical **Aula** on Wilhelmsplatz, a couple of blocks south of the Städtisches Museum and a similar distance east of the Markt; this graduation hall was built to celebrate the centenary of the university's foundation. Many of the departments have their own museum; unfortunately, these tend to be open only one day a week, or by appointment. One definitely worth trying to catch is the **Völkerkundliche Sammlung**, Theaterplatz 15 (Sun 10am–1pm; €2.50), which includes part of the famous collection assembled by Captain Cook in the South Seas and a bizarre array of four hundred fertility symbols and mother-god effigies.

Anybody who knows anything about German history won't be able to resist the **Bismarckhäuschen** (Tues 10am–1pm, Thurs & Sat 3–5pm; free), a small tower on the southern edge of the town centre which forms part of the old city wall. In 1833 this was home to the seventeen-year-old **Otto von Bismarck**, then a student in the city. The man who later became the "Iron Chancellor" and who finally realized, by a mixture of brute force and astute politicking, the long-established ideal of a united Germany, was forced to live here, having been banned from the city centre for drunkenness and "misbehaviour of various kinds".

North along Angerstrasse is the **Marienkirche**, which stands on what used to be the boundary between the Altstadt and the so-called Neustadt, built as a rival town outside the original city walls by a local nobleman in an attempt to challenge the increasingly powerful burghers. The citizens' response to this threat was an astute one. They waited until the nobleman went bankrupt and then bought the Neustadt from him, incorporating it into Göttingen itself. The church looks quite unecclesiastical, as its bell tower used to be one of the gateways to the Neustadt, and the street still passes through an archway cut through it.

Eating, drinking and entertainment

Above all, Göttingen is a city where you can enjoy yourself. There are dozens of cafés, bars and restaurants which, thanks to the large student contingent, tend to be high on atmosphere and low in cost. Among them are several historic student taverns.

Restaurants

Fellini Groner-Tor-Str. 28. Recommended pizzeria with back garden.

Gauss am Theater Obere Karspüle 22. Rivals the *Georgia-Augusta-Stuben* (see p.651) as the most distinguished restaurant in town. Evenings only, closed Sun.

Junkerschänke Barfüsserstr. 5. Another of Göttingen's best restaurants, housed in a beautiful fifteenth-century half-timbered building; rather pricey, but worth it. Closed Mon.

Kleiner Ratskeller Judenstr. 30. Dating back to 1738, this is the oldest of Göttingen's student taverns. Evenings only, closed Sun.

Naturell Lange-Geismar-Str. 40. Inventive vegetarian and wholefood restaurant. Open Mon–Fri 10am–6pm, Sat 10am–3pm.

Pfannkuchenhaus Speckstr 10. A student favourite with a huge variety of filing and inexpensive sweet and savoury pancakes.

Rathskeller Markt 9. Notwithstanding the anachronistic spelling, Göttingen's town hall restaurant is archetypal, with food to rival any in Germany.

Zum Schwarzen Bären Kurze Str. 12. Romantic Gaststätte dating back to the sixteenth century, complete with stained-glass windows and cosy little alcoves; the food is first class and fairly reasonable in price. Closed Sun evening & Mon.

Zum Szültenbürger Prinzenstr. 7. Another celebrated student tavern, with basic dishes such as *Schmalzbrot* as an alternative to full meals.

Bars and cafés

Blue Note Wilhelmsplatz 3. Slightly upmarket jazz/blues bar underneath the Mensa. It seems to be particularly favoured by medical and law students.

Cron & Lanz Weender Str. 25. Celebrated traditional café with roof terrace; it makes wonderful cakes, chocolate and marzipan.

KAZ-Keller Hospitalstr 6. Trendy pub with beer garden; also does light meals.
Nörgelbuff Groner Str. 23. Favourite haunt of the more bohemian members of the student community; features occasional live music and theatre.
Teehaus Klunje Lange-Geismar-Str. 34. Attached to a tea merchant's shop, this has the best selection of teas in town.
Zum Altdeutschen (ADe!) Prinzenstr. 16. Göttingen's most famous student tavern was a bastion of tradition until quite recently, but has been given a radical makeover and is now a trendy bar.

Entertainment

Göttingen's main **cultural** venues are the Deutsches Theater, Theaterplatz 11 (Ⓣ05 51/49 69 11, Ⓦwww.dt-goettingen.de), and the Stadthalle, Albaniplatz 2 (Ⓣ05 51/4 97 00 20), which face each other across Theaterplatz. Each June, Göttingen celebrates the music of Handel in the **Händelfest**, one of Europe's best and most adventurous celebrations of the work of a single composer; many long-forgotten masterpieces have been dusted down here and successfully brought back into the repertoire.

Hann. Münden

Playing the time-honoured game of listing the Seven Wonders of the World, the great German traveller-scholar Alexander von Humboldt – who had seen a fair bit of the globe for himself – listed **HANN. MÜNDEN** as ranking among the seven most beautifully sited towns. Even if this judgement seems tinged by excessive patriotism, there can be no doubt about the charm of the setting, below thickly wooded hills at the point where the **River Weser** is formed by the merging of the **Fulda** and **Werra**. The town's odd name, by the way, is the official contraction of "Hannoversch Münden", the name it assumed when it was part of the Kingdom of Hannover.

Hann. Münden has more than seven hundred **half-timbered houses**. Separated by some six centuries of history, they completely dominate the face of the town, and their main attraction lies in the effect of the overall ensemble – individually, they're less impressive than their counterparts elsewhere. Look out, however, for no. 34 on the main street, Lange Strasse. This was the home of the town's most celebrated citizen, **Johann Andreas Eisenbart**, an eighteenth-century doctor whose controversial medical techniques to do operations, such as the removal of cataracts, gained him a reputation as a miracle-worker. A statue of him stands outside, while his life is the subject of an open-air costume play (€2.50) held each Sunday at 11.15am between mid-July and the end of August.

Curiously enough, Hann. Münden's few set pieces are all of a more solid stone construction. The most impressive of these is the **Rathaus.** This dates back in part to the fourteenth century, but the side facing the Markt was rebuilt at the turn of the seventeenth century in the cheerful Weser Renaissance style by Georg Crossmann, the creator of many similar buildings in Lemgo. The facade is masterly, with the ornate gables, resplendent doorway and the obligatory two-storey oriel window all competing for pre-eminence. During working hours, the interior, including the elaborate main **Festsaal**, is freely accessible. Across Kirchplatz is **St Blasius** (May–Sept Mon–Fri 11am–12.30pm & 2–5pm, Sat 11am–12.30pm, Sun 2–5pm), an unusual-looking Gothic hall church with a hexagonal tower and a very steeply pitched roof of red slate. It contains a couple of masterpieces of late fourteenth-century bronzework in the font and the door of the sacrament niche.

The other major monument is the **Schloss** (Wed–Fri 10am–noon & 2.30–5pm, Sat 10am–noon & 2.30–4.30pm, Sun 10am–12.30pm; €1), an L-shaped Renaissance palace overlooking the Werra from which one branch or other of the Welf family ruled the town for most of its history. It now houses the standard local history displays, but of more interest are the fresco cycles dating from soon after the time of the building's construction, among the few in Germany from this period. However, these can only be seen on group guided tours, bookable at the tourist office.

Behind the Schloss is the **Werrabrücke**, a bridge which dates back at least as far as the fourteenth century. From here, you can cross over to **Doktorwerder**, an island with a sculpture garden. Of the other islands around the confluence, the largest is **Unterer Tanzwerder**, a popular recreation area. Here also are the landing stage for cruise boats, a swing bridge over the Fulda, and the **Weserstein**, a stone marking the birth of the great river at the point where, according to the rather trite inscription, "the Fulda and Werra kiss". Encircling the town centre are several towers, the remnants of the dismantled medieval **Stadtmauer**.

To appreciate the beauty of Hann. Münden's setting, and the harmonious layout of the town with its sea of red roofs, you really need to see it from above. One possibility is to cross over the Werrabrücke and follow the signs up to the **Weserliedanlage** belvedere. For a really magnificent bird's-eye view, at its best in the late afternoon or evening, cross the Fulda by the Pionierbrücke, and climb up to the nineteenth-century tower known as the **Tillyschanze** (April–Oct daily 9am–8pm; Nov–March Mon 11am–1pm, Tues–Sun 11am–8pm; €1).

Practicalities

Hann. Münden lies on the express rail line between Göttingen and Kassel, 35km from the former, 23km from the latter; the **Bahnhof** is a few minutes' walk east of the town centre. The **tourist office** (May–Sept Mon–Fri 8am–5.30pm, Sat 10.30am–3pm, Sun 11am–3pm; Oct–April Mon–Thurs 9am–1pm & 2–4pm, Fri 9am–1pm; ⓣ0 55 41/7 53 13, ⓦwww.hann.muenden.de) is in the Rathaus.

In addition to an abundant supply of **private rooms** (❶–❸), there's a trio of cheapish centrally sited **hotels**: *Gasthaus im Anker*, Bremer Schlagd 18 (ⓣ0 55 41/49 23; ❸); *Aegidienhof*, Aegidienstr. 7–9 (ⓣ0 55 41/9 86 40, ⓦwww.fahrrad-hotel.de; ❹); and *Rathausschänke*, Ziegelstr. 12 (ⓣ0 55 41/88 66, ⓦwww.hotel-rathausschaenke.de; ❹-❻). There are also more upmarket options in *Schlosschänke*, Vor den Burg 3–5 (ⓣ0 55 41/7 09 40; ❻); and *Alter Packhof*, Bremer Schlagd 10–14 (ⓣ0 55 41/9 88 90; ❼). Two enticing alternatives lie high above town on the left bank of the Fulda: *Schmucker Jäger*, Wilhelmshäuser Str. 45 (ⓣ0 55 41/9 81 00; ❹); and *Berghotel Eberburg*, Tillyschanzenweg 14 (ⓣ0 55 41/50 88, ⓦwww.berghotel-eberburg.de; ❻). The **youth hostel** is way to the north of town at Prof-Oelkers-Str. 10 (ⓣ0 55 41/88 53; €13.80/16.50), while the **campsite**, *Grüner Insel*, is on the island of Oberer Tanzwerder (ⓣ0 55 41/1 22 57). Excellent **restaurants** can be found in the hotels *Schlosschänke*, *Schmucker Jäger* and *Eberburg*; the *Waldgaststätte* below the Tillyschanze is another good place to eat. In summer, several companies run both long and short **river cruises** from Unterer Tanzwerder. For example, Rehbein-Linie (ⓣ0 55

41/7 31 09, Ⓦ www.schifffahrtslinie-rehbein.de) offers several trips daily except Mondays along the three rivers (€5.50 for 1hr 15min, €6.50 for 1hr 45min), and three return journeys per week to Kassel (€11 each way).

Travel details

Trains

Bremen to: Bremerhaven (hourly; 50min); Hannover (every 30min; 1hr); Oldenburg (every 30min; 35min); Osnabrück (hourly; 2hr).
Hannover to: Braunschweig (every 30min; 50min); Bremen (hourly; 1hr); Celle (every 20min; 25min); Einbeck (hourly; 1hr); Goslar (hourly; 1hr 20min); Göttingen (every 20min; 1hr); Hameln (hourly; 50min); Hann. Münden (hourly; 2hr); Hildesheim (every 20min; 25min); Lüneburg (every 30min; 1hr 20min), Wolfenbüttel (every 30min; 1hr 10min).

7

Hamburg and Schleswig-Holstein

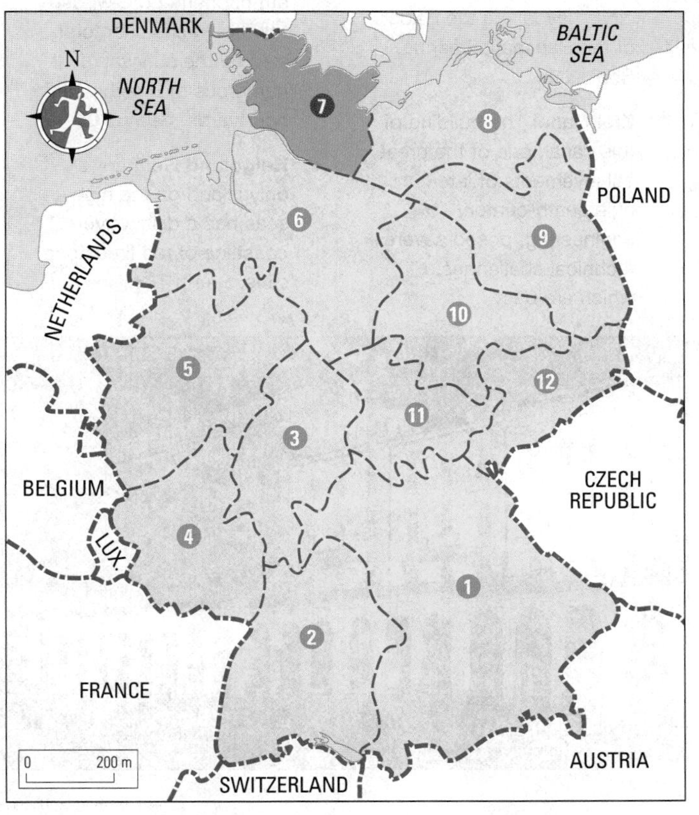

CHAPTER 7 Highlights

* **Hamburg** The nation's second city is notable for its massive port, its lakeside centre, its museums, its tradition in the performing arts – and its steamy nightlife. See p.661
* **Lübeck** A magnificent heritage of medieval brickwork buildings evokes the city's heyday as the leader of the Hanseatic League. See p.680
* **Kiel Canal** The building of this canal, one of the great achievements of late nineteenth-century engineering, posed severe technical challenges, which are best appreciated in the town of Rendsburg. See p.696
* **Schleswig** This ancient town preserves spectacular reminders from the eras of the early Germanic tribes and the Vikings. See p.696
* **Flensburg** A highly atmospheric port, whose town centre is characterized by the survival of numerous old merchants' courtyards. See p.700
* **Helgoland** Germany's only island on the high seas has a distinctive coastline of red limestone cliffs. See p.706

△ The Alsterarkarden, Hamburg

Hamburg and Schleswig-Holstein

Jutting up between the Baltic and North Sea, and stretching as far as the Danish border, **Schleswig-Holstein** is the northernmost of Germany's Länder. It's far removed from the stereotyped image of the country – there are no mountains, cute fairy-tale towns or back-slapping dances, and a Bavarian would surely feel less at home than someone from Britain. Both geographically and culturally, Schleswig-Holstein might seem to belong more naturally to Scandinavia. Indeed, for most of its history it was quasi-independent, suspended nebulously between Germany and Denmark.

As the name suggests, Schleswig-Holstein was originally two separate territories, divided horizontally by the River Eider. The duchy of Schleswig was a fief of the Danish Crown, whereas Holstein was a county of the Holy Roman Empire. However, in 1386 the two came together under the same ruler, and in 1459 the king of Denmark was accepted as the perpetual overlord, even though this meant that the predominantly German-speaking Holstein had dual loyalties. Subsequently, the united duchy was partitioned among different branches of its ruling family, blurring the division between the two original component parts. This arrangement lasted until the nineteenth century when, under the impact of the nationalist fervour gripping Europe, both Denmark and the emerging German nation set their sights on absorbing at least "their" part of the territory. Because of the threat it posed to international peace and security, the so-called **Schleswig-Holstein Question** was a major preoccupation of chancelleries throughout the continent. The exasperation felt about finding a solution was summed up in 1864 by the British Prime Minister Lord Palmerston, who declared: "Schleswig-Holstein's history is so complicated that only three people have ever understood it. One of them, Prince Albert, is already dead. Another is myself, but I have already forgotten it all again. And the third is a Danish statesman, and it drove him mad."

The same year, the arch-manipulator of European power politics, the Prussian Chancellor **Otto von Bismarck**, solved the problem by his tried and trusted method of brute force. Precipitated into action by an ill-judged attempt to integrate Schleswig into Denmark, he formed an alliance with Austria which wrested the whole of the united duchy from all vestiges of Danish control, then picked an argument with his erstwhile ally to ensure it passed to Prussia and thence into the Second Reich established soon after. Following German defeat

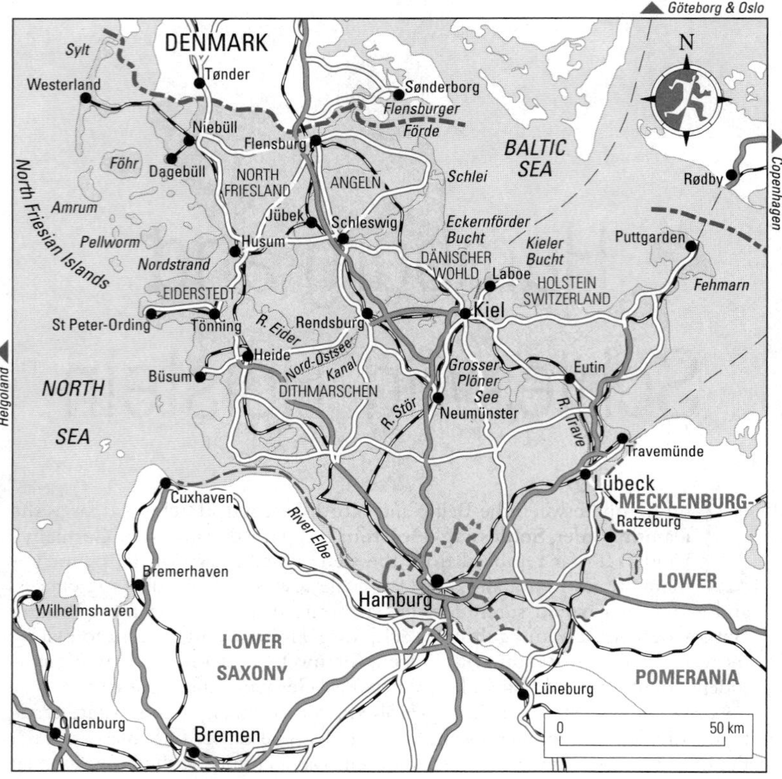

in World War I, the victorious Allies held a plebiscite in Schleswig, which resulted in its northern half being returned to Denmark. These borders remain in force to this day.

A rare lasting legacy of the Third Reich has been the incorporation of **Lübeck** – a proud city-state for the previous seven centuries – into Schleswig-Holstein. One of only two places in the Land large enough to be regarded a city, its legacy of buildings from its heyday as Germany's premier mercantile port constitutes one of the country's most magnificent and distinctive monumental ensembles. In this, and many other respects, it totally overshadows the slightly larger city of **Kiel**, the somewhat surprising choice as capital of the modern Land and the starting point of the famous canal which bears its name. Stripped of its historic role as a seat of government, the lovely old town of **Schleswig**, which first came to prominence under the Vikings, has sunk into blissful obscurity. On the other hand, the bustling port of **Flensburg**, hard by the Danish border, has made a spectacularly successful adaptation of its well-preserved centre to modern needs.

North Friesland, Schleswig-Holstein's northwestern corner, has a reputation as Germany's bleakest region – a landscape of marshes and bogs whose few trees are contorted into strange shapes by the constant onshore winds, and which has to be protected by a network of dykes from the constant danger of encroachment by the North Sea. However, it's also one of the nation's favourite holiday areas, thanks to the archipelago off its coast, which features mile upon mile of beaches and a surprising amount of summer sunshine; indeed **Sylt**, the largest of the islands, is normally the sunniest place in the country. The much gentler **Baltic coast**, characterized by a series of long, narrow inlets or fjords, is also popular with German holidaymakers. A car or bike would be a definite asset for **travel** in the rural areas, though public transport links between the main centres are as comprehensive as elsewhere in Germany.

Hamburg, a Land in its own right, exists like an enclave in the south of the state. Firmly established as the nation's second city, its name is synonymous with the prostitution and sleaze of the infamous Reeperbahn. That's as much as many people care to know about the place, but it actually has plenty to offer – an extraordinary verdant setting among lakes, a sparkling nightlife, a vibrant cultural scene and a city centre made up of enjoyable, easily explorable, neighbourhoods.

Hamburg

The River Elbe marks the southern border of Schleswig-Holstein, and 120km inland stands the port of **HAMBURG**. It originally formed part of Holstein, and only officially became a city-state in 1770, though it had been this in a de facto sense since 1459, as the Danish kings, who then became the nominal overlords, never attempted to exercise any control over the independently minded burghers of this great trading metropolis. Its official designation of "Freie und Hansestadt" (Free and Hanseatic City) is borne to this day.

Hamburg was often attacked during World War II, as it was on the flightpath for bombers flying from England on the North Sea route into central Germany. On July 28, 1943 it became the first city to suffer a **firestorm**, when the combination of high explosives and incendiary bombs turned 21 square kilometres of the centre into one huge conflagration, with winds the speed of hurricanes uprooting trees and sucking people into the inferno. On that night, over 42,000 civilians were killed.

Hamburg recovered quickly in the postwar years, and although its reputation is tainted by lurid tales of the **red-light area**, that's only a small part of what the city is about. It's a stylish media centre, a huge modern seaport, a scene of radical protest, and home of the latest generation of a long-standing merchant class. In spite of the vast proportions of the municipal area, only one third is actually built up. The rest is made up of **parks**, **lakes** or tree-lined **canals**, and the city boasts that it has more **bridges** than Venice.

Arrival, information and city transport

Hamburg's huge **Hauptbahnhof** lies at the eastern edge of the city centre. Many express trains also stop at **Bahnhof Dammtor**, which is just beyond the northern end of the centre, while **Bahnhof Altona** in the west of the city and

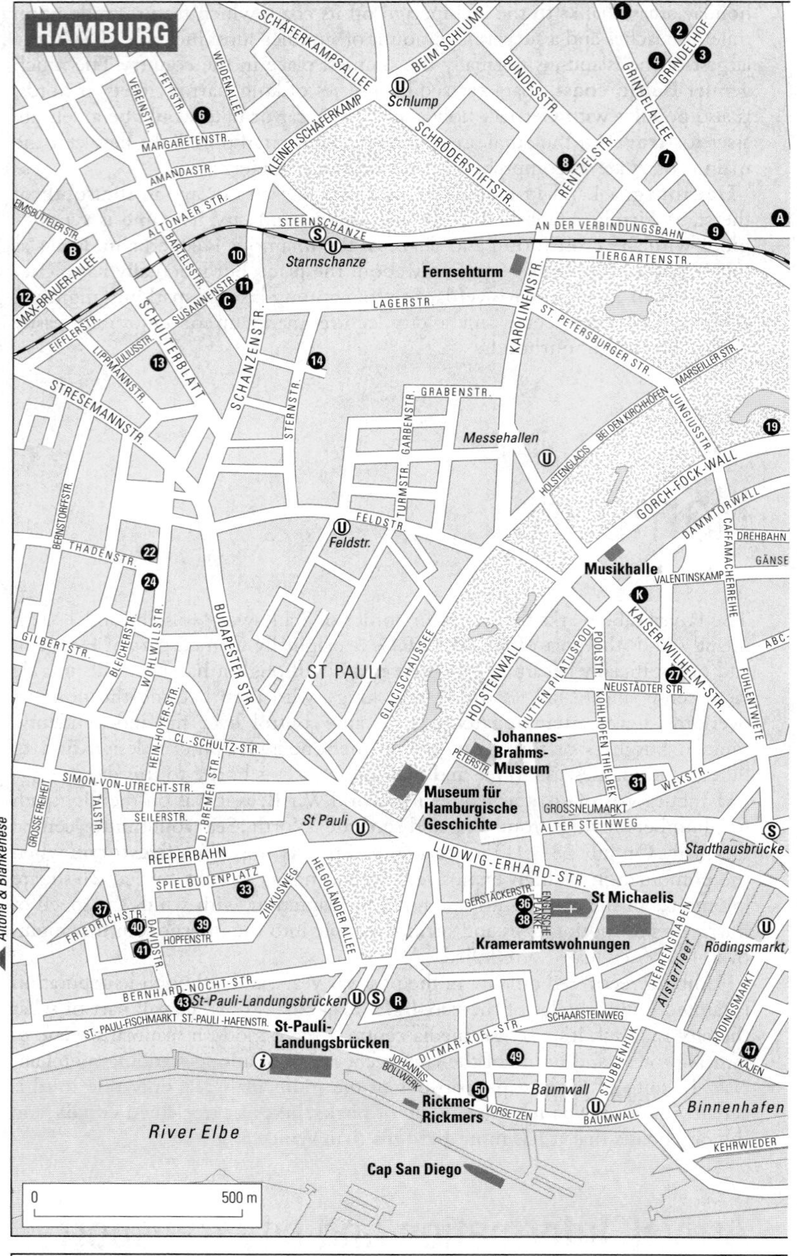

RESTAURANTS: GERMAN CUISINE

Alt Hamburger Aalspeicher	48	Das Kontor	44	Old Commercial Room	38
Anno 1750	42	Deichgraf	45	Ratsweinkeller	32
Brahmskeller	5	Fischküche	47	Vienna	6
		Franziskaner	21	Weinkeller Cremon	46

RESTAURANTS: OTHER CUISINES

Arkadasch	2	Den Danske		Matsumi	20	Petit Delice	28
A Varinha	49	Hereford	34	New York Deli	29	Sagres	50
Balutschi	7	Hindukusch	4	Pasadena	26	San Michele	36
Cuneo	41	Le Plat du Jour	35	Peking Enten Haus	8	Suryel	24

Bahnhof Harburg in the south are the starting or finishing point for many more services than the Hauptbahnhof itself. The **bus station** (ZOB), which has a wide range of international as well as local routes, is just to the southeast of the Hauptbahnhof, between Adenauerallee and Kurt-Schumacher-Allee.

Ferries dock at **St Pauli Landungsbrücken** further to the east, which has a combined S- and U-Bahn station attached. The **airport** (Ⓣ0 40/5 07 50, Ⓦwww.ham.airport.de) is in the north of the city, and linked at ten-minute intervals by an express bus to the S- and U-Bahn station of Ohlsdorf; there's also a more expensive direct connection to the Hauptbahnhof with the privately run Jasper buses.

Hamburg's **tourist office** (Ⓣ0 40/30 05 13 00 or 30 05 13 51, Ⓦwww.hamburg-tourism.de) operates three branches. There's one by the Kirchenalle exit in the Hauptbahnhof (daily 7am–10pm); another between bridges 4 and 5 of the St Pauli-Landungsbrücken (daily: April–Sept 10am–7pm; Oct–March 10am–5.30pm); and a third in terminal 4 of the airport (daily 6am–11pm).

Public transport around the city is quick and efficient by the integrated network of buses and S- and U-Bahn trains run by HVV (Ⓦwww.hvv.de). A **day ticket** costs €5.25 (€4.45 after 9am) and can be used by one adult accompanied by up to three children under 14; the group version of this, covering five people of any age, is only valid after 9am and priced at €7.40. However, it's usually much better value to buy a **HamburgCARD**, which also gives free entry to the municipally owned museums (or reduced entry to their special exhibitions) and substantial reductions on a number of other attractions, including lake and harbour cruises. Current prices are €7 for a day ticket (which can be used from 6pm the day before) and €14.50 for a three-day ticket (valid from the first day until midnight on the last). Tickets for families, or for up to five people travelling together, cost €13 for one day, €23 for three days. A slightly cheaper variant, known as the **Power-Pass**, is available for those under 30; it costs €6.70 for the first day, then is renewable for up to six days for a daily supplement of €3.

Accommodation

Despite the wide choice of accommodation, it can be difficult to find somewhere affordable if you don't want to use the youth hostels or campsites. It's true that there are plenty of cheapish hotels in the St Georg quarter, next to the Hauptbahnhof, but in Bremer Reihe and the adjacent streets the unsuspecting will as likely as not end up in a brothel: it's impossible to tell them apart from "normal" hotels. To avoid this happening, choose one of those described below, or one which features on the much longer approved list published by the tourist office. For long-term stays in furnished or unfurnished apartments or shared flats, contact one of the Mitwohnzentralen: HomeCompany, Schulterblatt 112, Schanzenviertel (Ⓣ0 40/1 94 45), or Die Mitwohnzentrale, Lobuschstr. 22, Altona (Ⓣ0 40/1 94 30).

Hotels and pensions

Amsterdam Moorweidenstr. 34 Ⓣ0 40/4 41 11 10, Ⓦwww.hotelamsterdam.de. One of several mid-range hotels in the Dammtorpalais, a huge redbrick building at the southern end of the Univiertel. ❻

Annenhof Lange Reihe 23 Ⓣ0 40/24 34 26, Ⓦwww.hotel-annenhof.de. A good-value hotel in a sturdy old tenement building to the east of the Hauptbahnhof, well away from any sleaziness. ❹

Baseler Hof Esplanade 11 Ⓣ0 40/35 90 60, Ⓕ35 90 69 18, Ⓦww.baselerhof.hamburg.vch.de. Very highly regarded hotel with a location equally handy for the city centre, the Univiertel and the Alster lakes. Its restaurant, *Kleinhuis*, offers bargain lunches. ❼

Bei der Esplanade Colonnaden 45 ⓣ0 40/35 50 11 70, ⓦwww.hotel-bei-der-esplanade.com. This hotel has a convenient location in the shopping area, just west of the Binnenalster. ❺

Frauenhotel Hanseatin Dragonerstall 11 ⓣ0 40/34 13 45, ⓦwww.hotel-hanseatin.de. Women-only hotel just west of the city centre, near the Gänsemarkt U-Bahn. It incorporates the *Frauencafé endlich.* ❼

Fürst Bismarck Kirchenallee 49 ⓣ0 40/2 80 10 91, ⓦwww.fuerstbismarck.de. One of a clutch of hotels directly facing the main entrance to the Hauptbahnhof. ❻

Kempinski Hotel Atlantic An der Alster 72-79 ⓣ0 40/2 88 80, ⓦwww.kempinski.atlantic.de. Opened in 1909, this imperious grand hotel with a wonderful setting overlooking the Aussenalster was intended for passengers of transatlantic ocean liners, and its whitewashed architecture readily evokes the golden age of the great cruise ships. It has a wide range of facilities, including swimming pool, sauna, solarium, massage, garden terrace and two restaurants. ❾

Kronprinz Kirchenallee 46 ⓣ0 40/24 32 58, ⓦwww.kronprinz-hamburg.de. Renowned for its restaurant, the top-notch *Schifferbörse*, though the accommodation is also of a good standard. ❻

Lilienhof Ernst-Merck-Str. 4 ⓣ0 40/24 10 87, ⓦwww.hotel-lilienhof.de. Decent if somewhat functional modern hotel by the Hauptbahnhof. ❹–❻

Nord Bremer Reihe 22 ⓣ & ⓕ0 40/28 05 17 33. Despite some very dubious neighbours, this hotel is respectable, and reasonably priced. ❹

Raffles Vier Jahreszeiten Neuer Jungfernstieg 9–14 ⓣ0 40/3 49 40, ⓦwww.raffles.com. This luxury hotel beside the Binnenalster – in business for a century – is elegantly furnished with antiques, while some rooms overlook the lake. *Haerlin* (closed Sat lunch, Sun & Mon) is its most upmarket restaurant, though there are also the more reasonably priced *Jahreszeiten Grill* and *Doc Cheng's* (closed Sun evening & Mon), the latter with a mixed European and Asian menu. ❾

Sarah Petersen Lange Reihe 50 ⓣ0 40/24 98 26. ⓦwww.galerie-hotel-sarah-petersen.de. Small hotel in a nineteenth-century building, named after the artist who runs it. It has a certain celebrity status, so advance booking is advisable. ❺–❽

Steens Holzdamm 43 ⓣ0 40/24 46 42, ⓕ2 80 35 93. Charmingly located hotel in a quiet, pretty corner of St Georg. ❻

Terminus Steindamm 5 ⓣ0 40/2 80 31 44, ⓕ24 15 18. Conveniently close to the Hauptbahnhof, and a regular choice for foreign budget travellers. ❸–❺

Wedina Gurlittstr. 23 ⓣ0 40/2 80 89 00, ⓕ2 80 38 94. On the southeastern edge of the Aussenalster, this nicely renovated hotel with a garden and swimming pool is one of the pleasantest places to stay in central Hamburg. ❻

Youth hostels

Backpacker Hostel Instant Sleep Max-Brauer-Allee 277 ⓣ0 40/43 18 23 10, ⓦwww.instantsleep.de. Independent hostel in the lively Schanzenviertel, with cooking and laundry facilities, and Internet access. Take S-Bahn #3 or #21 or U-Bahn #3 to Sternschanz. Dorm beds €16, singles €26, doubles €42, triples €57; plus a one-off €2 bed linen charge.

Jugendgästehaus Horner Rennbahn Rennbahnstr. 100 ⓣ0 40/6 51 16 71. Slightly the more appealing of the two official hostels, situated in an airy modern building next to the horse-race track in the eastern suburb of Horn (and peaceful enough when there isn't a race on). Take U-Bahn #3 to Horner Rennbahn. €18.50/21.20.

Jugendherberge auf dem Stintfang Alfred-Wegener-Weg 5 ⓣ0 40/31 34 88. Official hostel with an excellent location, perched on a steep incline above the port, boasting panoramic maritime views. Take S-Bahn #1, #2 or #3 or U-Bahn #3 to Landungsbrücken. €18.50/21.20.

Schanzenstern Bartelsstr. 12 ⓣ0 40/4 39 84 41, ⓦwww.schanzenstern.de. Independent hostel in the Schanzenviertel, with a wholefood restaurant serving organically produced drinks. Dorm beds from €17, singles €35, doubles €50, triples €60, quads €73; optional breakfast €4.

Campsites

Buchholz Kieler Str. 374 ⓣ0 40/5 40 45 32, ⓦwww.campingplatz-buchholz.de. Year-round campsite located in a northern suburb, a short walk from the Zoo. Take U-Bahn #2 to Hagenbecks Tierpark or S-Bahn #3 or #21 to Stellingen.

Schnelsen-Nord Wunderbrunnen 2 ⓣ0 40/5 59 42 25, ⓦwww.campingplatz-hamburg.de. In the far north of the city; open March–Oct. Take U-Bahn #2 to Niendorf Markt, then bus #291.

The City

Central Hamburg, consisting of the **Altstadt** and the **Neustadt**, is bordered by broad roads which trace the original city's fortifications. It has a semicircular shape, with its base facing the River Elbe and the massive **port**. To the north-east are the glamorous **Alster lakes**, lined by some of the poshest quarters in town. West of the centre lie the districts of **St Pauli** and **Altona**, and just north of these the **Schanzenviertel** and **Univiertel**, which together form the heartland of Hamburg's nightlife. Finally, there are some well-known **outer suburbs** worth visiting, chiefly Blankenese, Oevelgönne and Neuengamme.

Most of the centre of Hamburg was consumed in the Great Fire of 1842: the flames ran out of control for several days, which is why there are few surviving buildings from before that period. Add to that the British "Operation Gomorrah" in 1943, when half of the city was destroyed by bombs, and it's a wonder there's anything over sixty years old left to see at all. As it is, there are a great many nineteenth- and early twentieth-century buildings remaining, tucked in between prize-winning modern developments, and hidden within this central area are the sole surviving seventeenth-century houses of the city.

The Altstadt

Hamburg's original **Altstadt** is separated from the Neustadt, the "new" quarters established to the west towards the end of the twelfth century, by the slanting Alsterfleet canal. Most maps no longer record the division, since the two districts have melted into one, but it remains a useful one for visitors to the city.

The historic core

The oldest part of Hamburg is around the ruined tower of **St Nikolai**, formerly one of Germany's finest neo-Gothic churches. Designed by Sir George Gilbert Scott, it was flattened by his countrymen about a hundred years later, and its blackened stump stands as an anti-war memorial. Close by, and nowadays surrounded by modern office buildings, is the **Trostbrücke**, which connected the Altstadt with the Neustadt. The two statues on the bridge are of St Ansgar, Hamburg's first archbishop, and Count Adolf III, founder of the Neustadt and instigator of the imperial decree which gave Hamburg the right to tax-free import of goods and transport of passengers from the sea to its port, 120km inland along the River Elbe.

Following the canal south, crossing the busy Ost-West-Strasse at Holzbrücke you'll find the remaining eighteenth-century merchant homes, with their grand facades facing the street and the red-brick, gabled backs facing the canal, where goods were directly hoicked into the merchant's attic store rooms. The most famous examples are the row of houses along **Deichstrasse**, which is also where the Great Fire broke out. Seven rooms within no. 37, which is now designated the **Alt-Hamburg Bürgerhaus**, have been decked out with period furnishings, each of a different style or era. All of these can be rented for dinners or functions, and although the building is not a regular tourist sight it's usually possible to take a peek inside. The best place to see the crooked backs of the Deichstrasse houses is from the Hohe Brücke to the east. Further along the canal front is the Gothic church of **St Katharinen**, which was badly damaged in the war but sympathetically restored. Its tower, like those of the four other historic churches, remains a prominent feature of the skyline.

The eastern Altstadt

Northeast along the Dovenfleet, directly opposite Messberg U-Bahn station, is the remarkable **Chilehaus**. Built with the traditional red bricks of north German architecture, this unconventional office block ranks as one of the most original works of the early 1920s. It was designed by the Expressionist architect Fritz Höger, who aimed to mirror Hamburg's ocean-going liners: the staggered balconies represent the various decks, while the sharp eastern corner is reminiscent of a ship's bow. The name, incidentally, has nothing to do with the building but recalls the country in which the architect originally made his fortune.

Due north, on the opposite side of the busy Steinstrasse, is **St Jakobi**. Inside are three beautiful carved and painted Gothic **retables**: the high altar was donated by the coopers, that in the apse of the first aisle by the fishermen, while the one in the apse of the second aisle was a gift of the St Luke guild of painters to Hamburg's medieval Dom, which was pulled down in 1805. The last-named features delicately coloured panels by the leading local artist of the late fifteenth century, Hinrik Bornemann, though he died before the work was completed. Also in the church are some striking epitaphs, and an intriguing documentary painting showing the Hamburg skyline as it looked in the seventeenth century. However, the best-known adornment is the **organ** by the seventeenth-century master Arp Schnitger, which ranks among the greatest instruments ever made and is still in frequent use. Every Thursday at noon, there's a short recital followed by a free guided tour and demonstration of the organ, while between July and early September there's a regular concert series on Tuesdays at 8pm.

Directly behind St Jakobi lies **Mönckebergstrasse**, the old town's main shopping street, while just to the west is **St Petri**, the oldest of the city's churches, which is believed to have originated as an eleventh-century chapel. Destroyed in the Great Fire and then again in 1943, it nevertheless retains much of its nineteenth-century neo-Gothic architecture and boasts Hamburg's oldest surviving piece of craftwork, the fourteenth-century bronze **door-knocker** on the central western portal.

Around the Rathaus

A stone's throw from St Petri, the **Rathaus** (guided tours in English hourly Mon–Thurs 10.15am–3.15pm, Fri–Sun 10.15am–1.15pm; in German every 30min Mon–Thurs 10am–3pm, Fri–Sun 10am–1pm; €1.50) sits heavily in all the boastful splendour of the German neo-Renaissance, with statues of the city's patron saints and maritime images lined up alongside each other along its cornice. The home of the city-state's parliament has 647 rooms – a total, it is proudly pointed out, that exceeds that of Buckingham Palace.

Directly to the north, on the same side of the teeming Rathausmarkt, is the **Bucerius Kunst Forum** (daily 11am–7pm; €4; Ⓦwww.buceriuskunstforum.de). This has no permanent display, but every year presents a themed exhibition in each of its four chosen subject categories – the ancient cultures of the Mediterranean, the art of the Silk Road, European old master paintings, and classic modern art. Round the back of the Rathaus on Adolphsplatz is the restored Neoclassical **Börse**, Germany's first stock market (founded in 1558) and still Hamburg's financial heart.

The Neustadt

Hamburg's Neustadt is a "new town" only in the relative sense – although founded 378 years after the Altstadt, it celebrated its 800th birthday back in 1988.

Around Jungfernstieg

On the opposite side of Alsterfleet from Rathausmarkt are the elegant **Alsterarkarden**, with their expensive stores. Beyond is the **Binnenalster**, which is the petite forerunner of the larger Aussenalster lake beyond. The promenade along its southern bank is known as **Jungfernstieg**, after the young women who used to stroll there. Neuer Jungfernstieg, the promenade along the western bank, is lined with the splendid houses of the city's bankers and businessmen, as well as Hamburg's best address: the **Raffles Vier Jahreszeiten**, which boasts of being one of the leading hotels in the world, and charges accordingly. The least expensive way to sample it is to go for a coffee in its lovely Biedermeier café, *Conti*.

If you're tempted by any of the **boat trips** offered along the Jungfernstieg, the best is undoubtedly the two-hour Kanal-Fahrt (daily: late March to late April & late Sept to late Oct at 9.45am, 12.45pm & 3.45pm; late April to late Sept at 9.45am, 11.45am, 12.45pm, 2.45pm, 3.45pm & 5.45pm; €12). This tour will take you round both the Alster lakes, and also along the River Alster itself, passing many of the city's finest villas and sailing clubs, and presenting a view of Hamburg otherwise impossible to see.

The Hanseviertel

The streets spreading out behind the Jungfernstieg, towards the Gänsemarkt and down Neuer Wall, Grosse Bleichen and ABC-Strasse, are collectively known as the **Hanseviertel**, an area of offices and the city's flashest shopping arcades. Heading southwest you enter a more residential area on the other side of Kaiser-Wilhelm-Strasse. Nearby **Peterstrasse** is one of Hamburg's most beautiful streets, whose restored eighteenth-century town houses are built in traditional red-brick style. In one of these is located the **Johannes-Brahms-Museum** (Tues & Thurs 10am–1pm, first Sun of month 11am–2pm; €2), Peterstr. 39, which has documentation on the life and work of the composer, who was born in Hamburg and spent many unsuccessful years here.

Immediately to the west is Holstenwall, which marks the boundary between the Neustadt and St Pauli. At no. 24 the **Museum für Hamburgische Geschichte** (Tues–Sat 10am–5pm, Sun 10am–6pm; €7.50; Ⓦwww.hamburgmuseum.de) presents Hamburg's history in an exceptionally informative and entertaining manner, with almost all labels translated into English. On the ground floor are displays on the twentieth century, plus the entire history of the arts, fashion and the sciences in the city. The star exhibit is an early eighteenth-century model offering an idealized reconstruction of Solomon's Temple in Jerusalem. A chronological presentation on the first floor begins with a few precious **medieval** survivals, such as part of the Dom's thirteenth-century rood screen; the mid-fifteenth-century sarcophagus of Adolf IV of Schauenburg; and an early fifteenth-century parapet slab of St George, a distinguished example of an art form peculiar to the region. The Baroque section includes a spectacular **scale model**, made in advance of its construction in 1720, of the East Indianman Wappen von Hamburg III, a veritable floating palace. On the second floor are a number of intact **interiors** from grand Hamburg houses, including that at Deichstr. 55, with a series of mid-seventeenth-century paintings of Old Testament scenes made after engravings by Matthäus Merian, and the drawing room from the house where the poet Klopstock spent the last three decades of his life. Under the painted and stuccoed ceiling from Katharinenstr. 9 are displayed some notable canvases, including a *Quodlibet* by the seventeenth-century trompe l'oeil master, Cornelius Gijsbrechts, who later became the royal court painter in Copenhagen. Also on this floor is Europe's largest **model railway**, a miniaturization of the area between Mamburg's Hauptbahnhof and Bahnhof Harburg; this is demonstrated at 11am, noon, 2pm and 3pm, and also at 4pm on Sundays only.

St Michaelis and the Krameramtswohnungen

A few minutes' walk to the southeast stands Hamburg's city symbol and finest church, **St Michaelis**. Seated on a small hillock, its copper-plated tower is visible from most parts of the city. The church was originally built between 1649 and 1661, but has burned down no fewer than three times since then, though full interior restoration means you can still marvel at its superb northern Baroque elegance. Inside is a typically Lutheran design, which directs the congregation's eyes not to the altar, but to the pulpit. The best bird's-eye view of the city is from the tower's 82-metre-high **look-out platform** (mid-March to Sept Mon–Sat 9am–6pm, Sun 11am–6pm; Oct to mid-March Mon–Sat 10am–5pm, Sun 11am–5pm; €2.50). The **vaults** (same times; €1.25, or €3 inclusive ticket with tower) meanwhile contain both the grave of the composer Carl Philipp Emanuel Bach, son of J.S. and pioneer of the symphonic form, and an exhibition about the history of the church. There is also a **multimedia show**, *Multivision Hamburg* (Thurs–Sun at 12.30pm, 2.30pm & 3.30pm; €2.50; combined ticket for all three €4.50). If your German is up to it, this is an accessible introduction to the city's history and development.

Round the corner from St Michaelis, at Krayenkamp 10, the **Krameramtswohnungen** (Tues–Sun 10am–5pm; €1) is the last remaining backyard of seventeenth-century housing in the city. They were built as retirement homes for the widows of storekeepers, who were forbidden to carry on their husbands' trade after their death, and the houses were in use as late as the early 1960s. Now, all except the one preserved as a museum, have been turned into trinket shops or art galleries.

The port: from Fischmarkt to Speicherstadt

The best place and time to begin an exploration of Hamburg's harbour is the **Fischmarkt**, not far from St Pauli Landungsbrücken, early on a Sunday morning. Between 5am and 10am (7–10am Oct-March), the former fishmarket hall and a large part of the surrounding waterfront are given over to a weekly circus of shopping and selling, where you can buy anything from live ducks to tacky souvenirs. The bars and Imbiss stands are filled with shoppers and late-night survivors alike, all tucking in to the sounds of early morning jazz, while stallholders bellow out their sales pitches. By 10am, the market is supposed to end, in accordance with an old law that was to ensure trade didn't compete with Sunday church services. In fact, it lingers on for a good hour more, but many of the most colourful traders have sold out by then.

Back down by the **Landungsbrücken**, many bridges lead to the floating pontoon, where there are plenty of boats offering hour-long **harbour tours** (*Hafenrundfahrten*) for €9 (tours in English go from Brücke 1 between March and November daily at noon). Make sure you go on one of the small ferries and not the large double-decker, since only the small ones take in the canals of the Speicherstadt as well as the port itself.

The distinctive green-hulled **Rickmer Rickmers** (daily 10am–6pm; €3) is moored opposite the S-Bahn station. Built in 1896, this three-masted ocean-going barque had a history of international sailing before it was impounded by the British in 1916. A little to the east, at Überseebrücke, lies the **Cap San**

Diego (daily 10am–6pm; €4), a typical 1960s freighter, which you can also walk all over, gaining a vivid impression of the sailors' living and working conditions.

A brisk fifteen minutes' walk further along the waterfront will take you to the separate world of the **Speicherstadt**. The world's largest self-contained warehouse complex, complete with canals and cobblestone streets, it was built between 1885 and 1910 in the traditional red-brick style. Goods can be stored here over many years tax-free, until the merchant thinks he'll get the best price. With sacks of coffee piled high, thousands of oriental carpets in rolls, and the scent of teas and spices wafting out of open doors, men can be seen heaving goods by the traditional hooks used a hundred years ago. All the buildings are under protection, so there are no lifts or other machinery to assist present-day workers. The Speicherstadt contains several museums, notably the **Speicherstadtmuseum** (Tues–Sun 10am–5pm; €2.50) at St Annenufer 2, which has exhibits on the working life of the old warehouse quarter.

The museum quarter

Hamburg's museums are scattered all over the city, but the two which are of world-class importance – the **Kunsthalle** and the **Museum für Kunst und Gewerbe** – are to be found on either side of the Hauptbahnhof. Nearby are several temporary exhibition venues, the most important being the **Deichtorhallen** (Tues–Sun 11am–6pm; variable charges; Ⓦwww.deichtorhallen.de) on Deichtorstrasse to the south. These wrought-iron and glass structures, which formerly served as the fruit and veg market halls, were restored some years ago as an important addition to the municipally owned stock of art galleries.

The Kunsthalle

Immediately north of the Hauptbahnhof on Glockengiesserwall are three interconnected buildings housing the renowned **Kunsthalle** (Tues, Wed & Fri–Sun 10am–6pm, Thurs 10am–9pm; €7.50; Ⓦwww.hamburger-kunsthalle.de). Its collection of paintings and sculpture ranges from medieval to contemporary, and is often augmented by special exhibitions. A pillared hall at the back of the original nineteenth-century building houses *Café Liebermann*, Hamburg's grandest **café**, and it's well worth scheduling a stop there for *Kaffee und Kuchen* or a light lunch. Starting upstairs to the right with the earliest works, the collection is arranged in a broadly chronological fashion.

Two rooms are entirely devoted to three retables by **Master Bertram**, the country's first painter identifiable by name, who worked for most of his life in Hamburg. His masterpiece is the huge folding altar, mixing paintings and sculpture, which was made for the city's church of St Petri. The panel showing *The Creation of the Birds and Beasts* is outstanding; the characterization of each creature is delightfully fresh, but a prophetic warning note is struck – already the polecat has attacked a sheep. In the next room is part of the dismembered *St Thomas à Becket Altar* by Bertram's successor, **Master Francke**. Painted for the league of merchants who traded with England, it's in a very different style – the figures are more monumental, the structure tauter, the mood more emotional. The most interesting work here from the Renaissance period is **Cranach**'s *The Three Electors of Saxony*. This uses the religious format of the triptych, with a continuous landscape background, in order to show the deceased, Frederick the Wise and John the Fearless, alongside the then ruler, John Frederick the Magnanimous.

The Flemish section includes a mature religious masterpiece by **van Dyck**, *The Adoration of the Shepherds*. Most of the specialist painters of seventeenth-century Holland are represented, but they're rather overshadowed by two examples of **Rembrandt**. *The Presentation in the Temple* is one of his earliest surviving works: he was only 21 when he painted it, yet there's no sign of immaturity or lack of confidence. From five years later, when Rembrandt was established as a fashionable society portraitist, comes *Maurits Huyghens*. Highlights among the display of seventeenth- and eighteenth-century European painting are: **Claude**'s *Dido and Aeneas at Carthage*; a pair of **Tiepolos**, *The Agony in the Garden* and *The Crowning with Thorns*; **Bellotto**'s *Ideal View with Palace Steps*; **Goya**'s *Don Tómas Pérez Estala*; and *The Creation of Eve* by the eccentric Swiss artist **Heinrich Füssli**, whose sensationalism makes a fascinating contrast with the paintings of Bertram from four hundred years earlier. There is one outstanding sculpture from this period – a bust of a cardinal by **Bernini**.

The nineteenth-century German section is one of the museum's main strengths. Of a dozen works by **Caspar David Friedrich**, three rank among his most haunting and original creations. *Wanderer above the Mists* shows an isolated figure with his back to the viewer, contemplating an eternity of sky and clouds; overpowering and intimate at the same time, it stresses the awesome, unfathomable power of the natural world. This same theme is present to even greater effect in *Eismeer*; inspired by the voyages of polar exploration, which were then beginning, it depicts a ship half-submerged against a cracked iceberg. It also has political significance, since the picture symbolizes lost hopes after the 1848 Revolution. In contrast, *The First Snow of Winter* imparts a dimension of grandeur to a quite ordinary landscape scene. Another German artist with a distinctive vision of the world was the short-lived **Philipp Otto Runge**, most of whose best work can be seen here. His most arresting images are portraits of children (usually his own). Chubby-cheeked, over life-size and bursting with energy, they're placed at eye level to face the viewer head-on. Very different, but equally effective, is the realist approach of **Wilhelm Leibl**. *Three Women at Church*, with its phenomenal detail, super-smooth texture and uncanny evocation of the rapt concentration of the subjects, is rightly considered his masterpiece.

The German Impressionists, **Max Liebermann** and **Lovis Corinth**, are each allocated a room, while there's a choice collection of their French counterparts, including a version of **Manet**'s *Fauré as Hamlet* which is less finished but livelier than the one in Essen. Among the Expressionists, look out for two masterpieces by **Munch**: *Girls at the Seaside* and *Girls on the Bridge*. The twentieth-century section includes a number of works by the Surrealist **Richard Oelze**; other highlights are **Otto Dix**'s *Der Krieg* triptych, a powerful anti-war statement, and **Paul Klee**'s translucent *Goldfish*, an abstract composition with a rare sense of poetry.

Connected to the two older buildings by an underground passageway is the shining modernist cube of the **Galerie der Gegenwart** (Gallery of Contemporary Art; same times and ticket), which is devoted to art from the 1960s to the present, with much of the display space given over to installations. A large collection of American Pop Art, including examples by Andy Warhol, Robert Rauschenberg, Claes Oldenburg, George Segal, Tom Wesselmann, Larry Rivers and Jim Dine, can be seen in the basement alongside works by their German contemporaries, such as Joseph Beuys. The first floor features young German artists; recent art from America, beginning with Bruce Nauman, can be found on the second; while the top floor is host to some of the established contemporary stars of the German art world, including Georg Baselitz, Gerhard Richter, Sigmar Polke and Markus Lüpertz.

The Museum für Kunst und Gewerbe

On Steintorplatz, facing the southern side of the Hauptbahnhof, is the **Museum für Kunst und Gewerbe** (Museum of Arts and Crafts; Tues, Wed & Fri–Sun 10am–6pm, Thurs 10am–9pm; €8.20; Ⓦ www.mkg-hamburg.de). The European displays are arranged chronologically, and begin to the left of the entrance with an important **medieval** section. Among its most notable treasures are a twelfth-century bronze reliquary chest by one of the craftsmen who made the famous bronze doors of the church of San Zeno in the Italian city of Verona; a gilded and bejewelled silver reliquary of St George attributed to the late fifteenth-century Lübeck master Bernt Notke; carvings of the *Madonna and Child* by two of the great German sculptors of the late Gothic period, Nicolaus Gerhaert von Leyden and Tilman Riemenschneider; and a magnificent Easter embroidery woven at the beginning of the sixteenth century by the nuns of Kloster Lüne in Lüneburg (displayed in odd-numbered years only for conservation reasons).

The **Renaissance** section which follows contains bronzes by Peter Vischer the Younger and Hubert Gerhard; a spectacular inlaid doorway from the now-destroyed Schloss of the dukes of Prussia in Königsberg; and many notable examples of the work of German goldsmiths and silversmiths, including the ceremonial *Wilkomm* of Hamburg's coopers' guild. Many more luxury items can be seen in the **Baroque** department, which features some outstanding pieces made in Augsburg, including a very early example of an enamel tea set and a toilet service commissioned by the Mecklenburg court. The **nineteenth-century** displays which complete the ground floor circuit include several interiors from Hamburg mansions, one of them a curious little chamber modelled on a ship's cabin.

On the first two floors of the glass extension which has been discreetly built in one of the courtyards is one of the world's finest collections of **historic keyboard instruments**, including many items of real beauty. Some of the instruments are demonstrated every Saturday at 3pm and Sunday at 4pm. The first floor of the main museum building has a wonderful **Art Nouveau/Jugendstil** section featuring several intact interiors, including two rooms purchased from the Paris World Exhibition of 1900 plus others designed by Henry van de Velde and Josef Hoffmann. Further highlights are a complete set of furniture made for a house in Hagen by Hamburg's own Peter Behrens; a tapestry of *The Adoration of the Magi* by William Morris and Edward Burne-Jones; and a stained-glass window by Charles Rennie Mackintosh. Also on the first floor are displays of modern crafts and design; of antiquities from Egypt, Greece and Rome; of the art of the Islamic world; and of the decorative arts of East Asia. The last-named includes a **Japanese tea house**, where ceremonies are occasionally held. A far more regular culinary attraction on the same floor is the museum's **café-restaurant**, *Destille*, which is decorated in the style of a Hamburg Gaststube of the turn of the twentieth century, and offers a superb Scandinavian-style cold table. The second floor is largely devoted to **photography**, and regularly features special exhibitions.

The inner suburbs

Hamburg's inner suburbs present very contrasting pictures. Around the **Aussenalster** lake are several exclusive villa districts which are home to some of the large number of seriously wealthy people in the city. The western curve of the city centre's traditional edge is made up of the four quarters of **Univiertel**, **Schanzenviertel**, **St Pauli** and **Altona**, which incorporate traditional working-class areas and collectively form the main stomping ground for night-time revellers of all kinds.

Around the Aussenalster

The large **Aussenalster** lake is one of the defining features of Hamburg. Whether with ice-skating in winter or sailing and boating in summer, it's always a busy place, and all around the shoreline there are operators renting out boats to visitors. Walking round its perimeter takes about three hours, and the route leads past many of the city's finest villas, clubs and consulates.

The eastern shore presents a well-heeled facade for most of its length. However, immediately beyond its southern end are the sleazy streets of **St Georg**, the quarter best known for its budget hotels and brothels, though its dominant landmark is the huge redbrick **Dom** on Danziger Strasse, which was built in the 1890s on the model of its counterpart in Bremen. In 1995, it became the seat of the revived Roman Catholic archbishopic of Hamburg, which had been defunct since the Reformation.

On the western shore, the districts of **Rotherbaum** and **Harvestehude** are two of the most exclusive residential parts of Hamburg, and if you enjoy nineteenth-century and Jugendstil architecture, it's worth exploring here, especially along Harvestehuder Weg and the side streets branching off Klosterstern. Around Pöseldorfer Weg and Milchstrasse, parallel with Harvestehuder Weg, is a fashionable area known locally as **Pöseldorf**, where media types hang out in posey cafés and expensive restaurants. Further west, at Rothenbaumchaussee 64, is the **Museum für Völkerkunde** (Tues, Wed & Fri–Sun 10am–6pm, Thurs 10am–9pm; €6; Ⓦwww.voelkerkundemuseum.com), where the city's maritime associations with Africa, the South Pacific, the Americas and Russia are on display. It provides a particularly refreshing look at the various regions' present-day societies, studying the effects of tourism on the Pacific, for example, rather than presenting the culture as a mere exotic curiosity.

Univiertel and Schanzenviertel

On the opposite side of Rothenbaumchaussee lies the **Univiertel**, or university quarter. The streets of most interest are **Grindelhof** and **Rentzelstrasse**, where you'll find the largest variety of reasonably priced restaurants and café-bars and the city's most popular "alternative" cinema, the *Abaton* (see p.677). On Lagerstrasse, just to the southwest of the Univiertel, is Hamburg's tallest building, the 280-metre-high **Fernsehturm**. Its observation platform commands sweeping panoramic views in all directions, and also claims to offer the most spectacular bungee jump in the world, but the tower is not currently accessible to the public.

Further west lies the **Schanzenviertel.** One of its main streets, **Schulterblatt** (near the Sternschanze S- and U-Bahn stop), is home to several popular student Kneipen, as well as excellent cheap restaurants. A very different atmosphere prevails around here, not so much trendy as relaxed and unpretentious. **Schanzenstrasse**, which splits away from Schulterblatt, is also worth checking out, and for all bar and café listings, see pp.677–78.

St Pauli

St Pauli, defined by the River Elbe, the Holstenstrasse towards Altona and the rail tracks to the north, was originally home to Hamburg's sea-related trades and crafts. The **Reeperbahn**, nowadays an infamous red light district, was where the rope-makers once lived; and the Grosse and Kleine Freiheit (Big Freedom and Little Freedom) are streets so-named not because of the live sex shows you see there today, but because in medieval times craftsmen were free to practise their trade here. To a large extent, St Pauli is still a working-class, residential area, with the sex industry confined to the very small area of the Reeperbahn and short streets running off either side, especially those leading towards the port. Lately, St Pauli has been infiltrated by a new set of after-dark revellers, since many bars and clubs have been taken over by avant-garde theatre operators and entrepreneurs.

Altona

Heading west, **Altona**, which was only incorporated into Hamburg in 1937, follows directly on from St Pauli. Like its neighbour, it has its share of river, partly lined with industrial fish-processing plants but also featuring the leafy environs of the **Palmaille** and **Elbchaussee**, grand avenues of nineteenth-century villas. Its western border is roughly defined by Fischersallee, while to the north it spreads almost as far as Fruchtallee. Although much of Altona is unremarkable for the visitor, it has had an interesting history. Originally a Danish settlement on the edges of German Hamburg, it has always been a haven of free-thinkers and religious tolerance, and as maritime trade brought more and more foreigners to the area, many chose to settle in Altona. Consequently, you'll find many Portuguese restaurants near the harbour, and plenty of Turkish, Greek and Arabic kebab shops and takeaway kiosks around Bahnhof Altona, especially along Ottenser Hauptstrasse. To find out more about the quarter's history, and in particular its Dutch heritage, the **Altonaer Museum** (Tues–Sun 11am–6pm; €6), just south of the Bahnhof at Museumstr. 23, has displays on the entire region, concentrating on trades such as boat-building, farming, fishing and the many different crafts associated with ships and the sea.

Traditionally, Altona was not much more upmarket than St Pauli, but developers have slowly been moving in on the beautiful, decaying nineteenth-century buildings, and certain areas are rapidly becoming rather chic. One such street is the **Friedensallee**, still unremarkable at its northwestern end but with ritzy, neon-lit stores and sophisticated restaurants and bars along the short stretch beginning near Bahnhof Altona.

The outer suburbs

West along the Elbe from Altona is the former fishing village of **Ovelgönne**, whose tiny but beautiful houses now fetch massive prices. Around twenty carefully restored working vessels, ranging from nineteenth-century wooden fishing trawlers and double-masted freighters to early twentieth-century fire brigade boats, are moored in the **Museumshafen**. This is a private museum, run by enthusiasts, who willingly show visitors around.

A short distance to the west, in the district of Othmarschen, is the **Jenischpark**, whose northern reaches – not far from the Klein Flottbek S-Bahn station (lines #1 and #11) – contain two worthwhile museums. The **Jenisch-Haus** (Tues–Sun 11am–6pm; €4, or €5 combined ticket with Ernst-Barlach-Haus) is a fine old villa with exhibits illustrating the bourgeois culture of the Elbe region from the sixteenth to the nineteenth century. Alongside, the **Ernst-Barlach-Haus** (same hours; €4; Ⓦ www.barlach-haus.de) contains some 130 sculptures – including two dozen wooden figures or groups – by the great Expressionist Ernst Barlach. Important temporary exhibitions of early twentieth-century art are regularly featured as well.

Two stops further on by S-Bahn is **Blankenese**, another one-time fishing village, situated on a small yet steep hill, a great rarity in this flat part of Germany. Villas have been squeezed tightly alongside the older houses, and steep roads and stairway paths wind in among them. It's very picturesque, and down by the beach of beautiful white sand, refined cafés and restaurants cater to your every need. Nearby, there's also a fragrant park of ancient trees, now home to many deer; the woods conceal many cafés as well.

Bergedorf, on the other side of Hamburg, towards its eastern edge, is reached by S-Bahn #2 or #21. Its thirteenth-century redbrick **Schloss** (Tues–Thurs, Sat & Sun 10am–5pm; €2.50; Ⓦwww.schloss-bergedorf.de) was situated on an important medieval trade route, and its role was primarily as a tax-collecting point rather than a noble residence. Inside is a local museum, which concentrates on regional folklore and costumes, as well as traditional rural arts and crafts. The Nazi concentration camp of **KZ-Gedenkstätte Neuengamme** (Tues–Fri 10am–5pm, Sat & Sun 10am–5/6pm; free), which can be reached from Bergedorf by bus #227, is now a political education centre. It has an exhibition of photos and documents that re-creates the horrors of the past and records the story of resistance. Hamburg's other concentration camp was at Fuhlsbüttel (near the airport), and some 50,000 people, including over 6000 Hamburg Jews, died in these two locations.

Finally, **Hagenbecks Tierpark** (daily 9am–6pm or dusk; €12.50, children €7.50) in the north of the city (take U-Bahn #2 to the station of the same name) is generally regarded as one of the world's leading zoos. It pioneered the modern practice of simulating the animals' natural habitat, rather than keeping them caged up, and currently has 56 different compounds, which are collectively home to around 2500 creatures.

Eating and drinking

When it comes to choosing where to eat and drink in Hamburg, it's worth looking further afield than the city centre, as the choice and variety is greater, and the prices lower, in the nearby **Univiertel** and **Schanzenviertel**. For Imbiss-type food, the stalls in the St Georg area near the Hauptbahnhof offer cheap snacks, as do those in the Reeperbahn in St Pauli. The most famous fast food of them all, the **hamburger**, is not especially popular in its "home" town – invented in the mid-nineteenth century and introduced to America by German immigrants, the popular snack takes its name from the city.

Restaurants

Traditional Hamburg Gaststätten, including many specializing in **fish dishes**, can be found throughout the city. There are two **local specialities** to try. *Aalsuppe*, generally made with plums and mixed vegetables as well as eels, is one of the most outstanding soups you'll encounter in Germany. *Labskaus*, a traditional sailor's dish, is more controversial, not to say indigestible; it's a hash which typically contains pickled corned beef, herring, beetroot, mashed potato, onions and gherkins, all topped with a fried egg. The city also has an amazingly diverse range of **ethnic cuisines**, including a large number of Portugese restaurants (which are seldom encountered elsewhere in Germany) and some other rarities.

German cuisine

Ahrberg Strandweg 33, Blankenese. Located down by the river, this ranks among the city's best German/fish restaurants, with carp a speciality.
Alt Hamburger Aalspeicher Deichstr. 43. One of the best places to sample *Aalsuppe*. It's not cheap, but is always excellent. Try to avoid the place during lunch hour when hordes of businessmen descend.
Anno 1750 Ost-West-Str. 47. Eighteenth-century Gaststätte on the ground floor of the Gröninger Haus. Closed Sat lunchtime & Sun.
Brahmskeller Mittelweg 24, Rotherbaum. Traditional beer and wine restaurant with a strong line in game and duck dishes.
Das Kontor Deichstr. 32. Serves high-quality German cuisine, and has a good selection of organically produced wines from around the world.
Deichgraf Deichstr. 23. Elegantly furnished restaurant with an upmarket menu of traditional and international dishes. Closed Sat lunchtime & Sun.
Fischerhaus St-Pauli-Fischmarkt 14, St Pauli. Offers no-nonsense fish dishes down by the Fischmarkt, not necessarily at cheap prices.
Fischküche Kajen 12. Serves some of the best fish dishes in the city, and has a different business lunch menu every weekday. Closed Sat lunchtime & Sun.
Franziskaner Grosse Theaterstr. 9. A Bavarian-style beer hall and garden, a real rarity in these northerly climes. Closed Sun.
Landhaus Scherrer Elbchaussee 130, Altona ⓣ0 40/8 80 13 25. Located in the Othmarschen district in the west of Altona, this very expensive restaurant has long been considered Hamburg's premier gourmet address, raising traditional German cooking to unexpected levels of excellence. Reservations advisable; closed Sun.
Old Commercial Room Englische Planke 10. Touristy restaurant facing St Michaelis which has the decor and ambience of an English club but serves very traditional Hanseatic cuisine. Its guest book reads like an international who's who.
Ratsweinkeller Grosse Johanisstr. 2. Hamburg's version of the inevitable town-hall cellar restaurant is posher – and better – than most. Closed Sun.
Vienna Fettstr. 2. Small bistro serving good-quality modern German cooking.
Weinkeller Cremon Cremon 33–34. Wine bar-restaurant with bargain lunchtime menus.

Other cuisines

Arkadasch Grindelhof 17. Offers a large choice of Turkish dishes at very affordable prices.
A Varinha Karpfangerstr. 16. Excellent, reasonably priced Portuguese restaurant, with portions often big enough for two.
Balutschi Grindelallee 33. Pakistani food in authentic surroundings; leave your shoes at the door before sitting on the floor at one of the low tables.
Cuneo Davidstr. 11. Long-established Italian, particularly good for pasta dishes. Evenings only, closed Sun.
Den Danske Hereford Schopenstehl 32. Danish grill in a handsome old Baroque house. On Sat & Sun it's open evenings only.
Hindukusch Grindelhof 15. Afghan restaurant with plenty of vegetarian options.
Le Canard Elbchaussee 139, Altona ⓣ0 40/8 80 50 57. Located directly across the street from *Landhaus Scherrer*, this is one of Hamburg's very best restaurants, with some quite moderately priced options at lunchtime. Reservations advisable; closed Sun.
Le Plat du Jour Dornbusch 4. Excellent French restaurant; it's pretty pricey, though the set dinners are reasonable value.
Matsumi Colonnaden 96. Japanese restaurant with sushi and sashimi bars. Closed Sun.
Medded Bahrenfelder Chaussee 140. Egyptian food that's a bargain at the price. Evenings only.
New York Deli Levantehaus, Mönckebergstr. 7. Plenty of American visitors seem to find their way to this daytime diner, on the upper floor of a shopping centre, to gorge themselves on hero sandwiches, hamburgers, bagels and *Ben & Jerry* ice cream.
Pasadena Kirchenallee 19. The location alongside the Hauptbahnhof looks unpromising, but it serves decent Tex-Mex cooking.
Petit Delice Grosse Bleichen 21. Small restaurant in the classy Galleria shopping arcade, offering creative cooking and a well-chosen wine list.
Peking Enten Haus Rentzelstr. 48. As the name suggests, the house speciality is Peking duck: the poultry served is specially reared, and is prepared by chefs from the Chinese capital. Evenings only, except Sun, when it's also open for lunch.
Sagres Vorsetzen 42. One of the many eating houses around the harbour, this is a homely place, popular with Portuguese dock workers – which means giant portions.
Saliba Leverkusenstr. 54, Altona. Well-regarded, fairly pricey Syrian restaurant. Closed Sat lunchtime & Sun.
San Michele Englische Planke 8. Classic Italian restaurant in the shadow of St Michaelis – the food is pricey but very good.

Shalimar Dillstr. 16. Arguably the city's best Indian restaurant, specializing in Mughal cuisine. Evenings only.
Suryel Thadenstr. 1. Good all-round veggie specialist, with bargain lunches Mon-Fri.
Tibet Harkorstieg 4, Altona. Tibetan restaurant with a wide-ranging menu, including vegetarian dishes. Evenings only, closed Mon.
Tre Fontane Mundsburger Damm 45. Cosy and well-priced Italian.

Bars

Hamburg's **bars** regularly move in and out of favour, but the following make up the heart of the city's nightlife. These days it centres around the St Pauli area and many places don't open before 10pm. Popular student bars, which are drinking haunts as well as good for cheap meals, can be found in the **Univiertel** and the **Schanzenviertel**. In the former, Grindelhof, Rentzelstrasse and Grindelallee are particularly good streets to explore.

Abaton Grindelhof 14a. Usually teeming with students, this serves bistro-type food and has an innovative cinema attached.
Bambus Brüderstr. 15. Long-established bar, with nearly five hundred different cocktails to choose from.
Blaue Nacht Gerhardstr. 16, St Pauli. This is the one that started the trend into St Pauli in the mid-1980s. Its popularity is waning, but it's not dead yet.
Christiansen Pinnasberg 60, St Pauli. The drinks list here features some five hundred spirits, including over a hundred whiskies.
Down Under Grindelallee 1. Australian theme bar.
Eisenstein Friedensallee 9, Altona. Situated in an old factory, bare stone walls and a high ceiling are the setting for people to show just how important they are, or at least how good they are at looking like it. The pizzas are excellent.
Erika's Eck Sternstr. 98. The favoured haunt of late-night drinkers who work in the nearby slaughterhouse. Open 1am–2pm, during which time it serves one of the best breakfasts in the city.
Filmhauskneipe Friedensallee 7, Altona. The interior is plain, with simple wooden tables and chairs comfortable enough for a whole night's drinking. The food is good, though the atmosphere gets very smoky.
Frank und Frei Schanzenstr. 93. A big, slow-paced favourite with students.
Gröninger Braukeller Ost-West-Str. 47. This Hausbrauerei in the cavernous cellars of the Gröninger Haus brews an amber-coloured Pils and a wheat bear; it also serves full meals.
Kurhaus Beim Grünen Jäger 1. Tiny bar that is currently one the hottest spots of the Hamburg *Szene.*
Luxor Max-Brauer-Allee 251. Something of a hybrid between a bar and a restaurant, with good cocktails and international cuisine showing Asian influences.
Mary Lou's Hans-Albers-Platz 3, St Pauli. Red lighting notwithstanding, a hangout favoured by the new set of St Pauli.
Molotow Spielbudenplatz 5, St Pauli. Post-punk background music is played in this increasingly popular haunt.
Oma's Apotheke Schanzenstr. 87. Another student favourite, with rustic-style decor and a good, wide-ranging menu.
Prinzenbar Kastanienallee 20. Stuccoed angles and chandeliers are the setting for drinking, with good soul sounds as well as occasional live shows.

Gay Hamburg

Not surprisingly, Hamburg has a lively **gay scene**. Other than talking to people in bars and cafés, the best way to find out what's on is from the city's free gay magazine *hinnerk*, which is available in most gay bars. Good starting points for **men** are *Café Gnosa* (see "Cafés and café-bars"); and the current favourite rendezvous, *Baluga Bar*, Lincolnstr. 6, St Pauli.

For **women**, the best place to find out what's on and where to go around town is probably the *Frauenbuchladen*, Bismarckstr. 98 (☎0 40/4 20 47 48), which also runs a café. Other women's cafés, not necessarily exclusively lesbian, are *Frauenkneipe*, Stresemannstr. 60, and *Frauencafé endlich*, which is now part of the *Frauenhotel Hanseatin* on Dragonerstall (see p.665). At these, you can pick up a copy of the local lesbian magazine, *Escape*.

Cafés and café-bars

Cafés and **café-bars** tend to reflect the area they are in: those in St Georg are somewhat bohemian, the Univiertel and Schanzenviertel more studenty, and Altona with a mixed, unpretentious clientele. Note that three of the museums (the Museum für Hamburgische Geschichte, the Kunsthalle and the Museum für Kunst und Gewerbe) have cafés that are well worth a visit in their own right.

Amphore Hafenstr. 140, St Pauli. *Szene* café-bar.

Café Backwahn Grindelallee 148. Café offering a choice of set breakfasts.

Café Gnosa Lange Reihe 93. Lovely 1930s café with good food; it's popular with the gay community but attracts a straight crowd too.

Café Koppel Koppel 66. Best known for its delicious wholemeal chocolate cake; it also serves a good range of vegetarian dishes, and has a summer garden.

Café Schöne Aussichten Gorch-Fock-Wall 1. Situated in the middle of the park, this is an excellent summertime place, with a tree-shaded terrace.

Café Stenzel Schulterblatt 61. A traditional *Kaffee und Kuchen* establishment in the heart of the district.

Café Urlaub Lange Reihe 63. Serves good breakfasts, plus salads and baguettes at other times.

Die Rösterei Levantehaus, Mönckebergstr. 7. A wide range of freshly ground coffees are served in this shopping-centre café.

Geel Haus Koppel 76. Evenings-only café-bar, sometimes with live jazz.

Gestern & Heute Kaiser-Wilhelm-Str. 55. Legendary for the variety of its breakfasts, this place is open around the clock.

Max und Consorten Spadenteich 7. Situated on a deceptively pretty square, whose trees shade daytime prostitutes.

Maybach Heussweg 66, Altona. On the northern edges of the quarter, this has a beer garden too, a rarity in these parts.

Strandperle Am Schulberg, Ovelgönne. Situated by the beach, this is a favourite summertime hangout with the in-crowd.

Witthüs Elbchaussee 499a, Blankenese. Idyllic manor house which functions as a café in the afternoons (and on Sun morning), a nouvelle cuisine restaurant in the evenings.

Arts, nightlife and entertainment

Hamburg is renowned for its **clubs**, boasts just about the best jazz scene in Germany, and attracts a good range of visiting international bands to a variety of **live music** venues. The city also has a high reputation for its opera, ballet, orchestral, choral and organ music. There are three full-sized **orchestras** – the Philharmonisches Staatsorchester, whose primary function is to play for the opera and ballet; the Hamburger Symphoniker (ⓦwww.hamburgersymphoniker.de); and the NDR-Sinfonie-Orchester (ⓦwww.ndrsinfonieorchester.de). The last-named, the house orchestra of the locally based radio station, gained a cult international following for its concerts and recordings under the baton of the late Günter Wand, an autocratic maestro of the old school; its current conductor one of Germany's most distinguished pianists, Christoph Eschenbach. There's also a chamber orchestra, the Hamburger Camerata (ⓦwww.hamburgercamerata.com). In addition to the venues listed below, it's always worth looking out for concerts and recitals in the city's **churches**, especially St Jakobi. More than any other city in the country, Hamburg has caught the national craze for British and American **musicals**, which are translated into German and performed for years on end in the same (often custom-built) venue. However, there's also a long and distinguished tradition of serious **drama**, while traditional **variety** also has a strong hold.

To find **what's on**, consult the magazines *Szene Hamburg* (€2.50; ⓦwww.szene-hamburg.de) or *Prinz* (€1; ⓦwww.prinz.de), or the more abbreviated listings in the tourist office's free *Hamburg Führer*. **Festivals** are by no means a Hamburg speciality, but the Übersee Tag on May 7 celebrates the founding of the port in 1189. A funfair, the Dom, is held on the Heiligengeistfeld, close to the St Pauli U-Bahn station, with separate spring, summer and autumn sessions.

Clubs

Angie's Nightclub Spielbudenplatz 27–28, St Pauli. One of the best-known clubs in Germany, and a favourite celebrity haunt. Wed–Sat from 10pm.
Grünspan Grosse Freiheit 58, St Pauli. Long-established late-closing hard rock joint. Fri & Sat 10pm–7am.
Kaiserkeller Grosse Freiheit 36, St Pauli. Part of *Grosse Freiheit 36* (see below), and one of the city's largest clubs. Daily 9pm–4am.
Kontor Altstädter Str. 1. Altstadt club particularly favoured by young locals. Thurs–Sat from 10pm.
Madhouse Hans-Albers-Platz 15a, St Pauli. Much the liveliest of the city's clubs on weekdays. Open Tues, Thurs, Fri & Sat from 11pm.

Live music venues

Birdland Gärtnerstr. 122, Eimsbüttel ⓣ040/40 52 77, ⓦwww.jazzclub-birdland.de. Prestigious jazz venue; the music varies from avant-garde experimentation to trad Dixieland.
Cotton Club Alter Steinweg 10, St Pauli ⓣ040/34 38 79, ⓦwww.cotton-club-hamburg.de. Traditional jazz club, with live music Mon–Sat at 8.30pm.
Docks Spielbudenplatz 19, St Pauli. Worth checking out, but the acoustics here are dodgy, and it can get very stuffy.
Fabrik Barnerstr. 36, Altona ⓣ040/39 10 70, ⓦwww.fabrik.de. One of the longest-enduring live music venues in Hamburg, this place is always worth a visit.
Grosse Freiheit 36 Grosse Freiheit 36, St Pauli ⓣ040/31 77 78 11, ⓦwww.grossefreiheit36.de. The city's main venue for rock/contemporary live music, with big-name bands mostly playing at weekends.
Logo Grindelallee 5. Mainly English and American underground bands.
Werkstatt 3 Nernstweg 32, Altona ⓣ040/39 21 91, ⓦwww.werkstatt3.de. This is a centre for alternative projects, which often acts as a stage for world music acts. Fri and Sat evenings are global dance nights.

Classical music venues

Allee Theater Max-Brauer-Allee 76 ⓣ0 40/38 29 59, ⓦwww.alleetheater.de. The home of the Hamburger Kammeroper, staging a wide range of operas, with a particular emphasis on rarities. The performances, regardless of the original language, are in German.
Hamburgische Staatsoper Dammtorstr. 28 ⓣ0 40/35 68 68, ⓦwww.hamburgische-staatsoper.de. This has long ranked among the top ten opera houses in the world, even if it has strong competition for supremacy within Germany from Munich and Stuttgart. The ballet company attached to the house, run by the American John Neumeier, enjoys a particularly high reputation.
Hochschule für Musik und Theater Harvestehuder Weg 12, Rotherbaum ⓣ0 40/42 84 80, ⓦwww.musikhochschule-hamburg.de. Hamburg's music academy features regular concerts and recitals by established professional orchestras and soloists as well as students.
Musikhalle Johannes-Brahms-Platz ⓣ0 40/34 69 20, ⓦwww.musikhalle-hamburg.de. Two concert halls, the larger used for symphonic concerts by the three local orchestras, among others, the smaller for chamber, vocal and instrumental music.

Theatre

Deutsches Schauspielhaus Kirchenallee 39 ⓣ0 40/24 87 13, ⓦwww.schauspielhaus.de. This is one of Germany's leading dramatic theatres, the successor to the Nationaltheater, one of whose first employees was the great eighteenth-century playwright and critic Gotthold Ephraim Lessing.
English Theatre of Hamburg Lerchenfeld 14 ⓣ0 40/2 27 70 89, ⓦwww.englishtheatre.de. Performs predominantly light fare, such as comedies and thrillers, in English.
Musicaltheater Norderelbstr. 6, St Pauli ⓣ0 40/30 05 11 50. Tent-like theatre for musicals alongside the St Pauli Landungsbrücken.
Operettenhaus Spielbudenplatz 1, St Pauli ⓣ0 40/30 05 13 50. Theoretically this is a specialist operetta theatre, but it is monopolized by musicals.
St-Pauli-Theater Spielbudenplatz 29, St Pauli ⓣ0 40/47 11 06 66, ⓦwww.st-pauil-theater.de. Hosts musicals by British and American touring companies.
Schmidt Spielbudenplatz 24, St Pauli ⓣ0 40/30 05 14 00. Cabaret and variety venue.
Thalia-Theater Alstertor ⓣ0 40/32 81 44 44, ⓦwww.thalia-theater.de. Intimate galleried theatre, founded in 1834, with a high reputation and a wide-ranging programme.

Listings

American Express Ballindamm 39 ⓣ0 40/30 39 38 11.
Consulates Canada, Ballindamm 35 ⓣ0 40/4 60 02 70; Republic of Ireland, Feldbrunnenstr. 43 ⓣ0 40/44 18 62 13; New Zealand, Domstr. 19 ⓣ0 40/4 42 55 50; UK, Harvestehuder Weg 8a ⓣ0 40/4 48 03 20; US, Alsterufer 27 ⓣ0 40/4 11 17 11 00.
Cultural Institute British Council, Rothenbaumchaussee 34 ⓣ0 40/44 60 57.
Doctor ⓣ0 40/22 80 22.
Post office For the main post office with poste restante facilities, take the Kirchenallee exit out of the Hauptbahnhof.
Sports Hamburger SV, one of Germany's best football teams, play in the Volksparkstadion in Altona. Sailing regattas are frequently held on the Aussenalster and there are various international events, such as a tennis championship in late May, and an equestrian event in early June.
Swimming The beautiful baths at Bismarckbad in Altona are the city's most luxurious, and have women-only days. For outdoor swimming the smaller lakes around Hamburg (such as the Grossensee, Mönchsteich and Bredenbeker Teich) are the best, but getting to them by public transport is tricky.
Taxis Call ⓣ21 12 11, 22 11 22 or 66 66 66.

Schleswig-Holstein

A land between two seas, **Schleswig-Holstein** is chiefly an agricultural region, with large areas of forest and moorland. There's little heavy industry, and only two major cities. **Kiel**, destroyed in the war and drably rebuilt, is the capital of the Land and seat of its only fully fledged university. For most of its history, it has lain in the shadow of **Lübeck**, once northern Europe's leading merchant city and the undoubted highlight of a visit to the province. Of the other towns, **Flensburg** is another highly atmospheric trading port, **Husum** is an attractive old fishing harbour, while **Schleswig**, the province's historic capital, is incongruously rich in treasures for a place so small.

Schleswig-Holstein has two very contrasting coastlines: the gently lapped and undulating **Baltic shore** and the flat, windblown **North Sea coast**, off which lie the **North Friesian islands**, providing a relaxing, if uneventful, break from the mainland. Hot tea and stiff alcohol are the traditional means of making the long, cold and dark winters pass. In summer, though, the landscape vibrates with blues and greens, the corn dotted with poppies and cornflowers, the fields burning with the bright yellow of rapeseed. It's beautiful countryside to meander through by any means, most perfectly by cycling, and along the coast frequent local boat services provide enjoyable alternatives.

Lübeck

Between the thirteenth and fifteenth centuries, **LÜBECK** was one of Europe's richest cities, thanks to its leadership of the Hanseatic League, the trading alliance which controlled the highly lucrative routes along the Baltic. Although it has long been overshadowed by the North Sea harbours of Hamburg and Bremen, the city proudly displays the magnificent architectural wealth of its

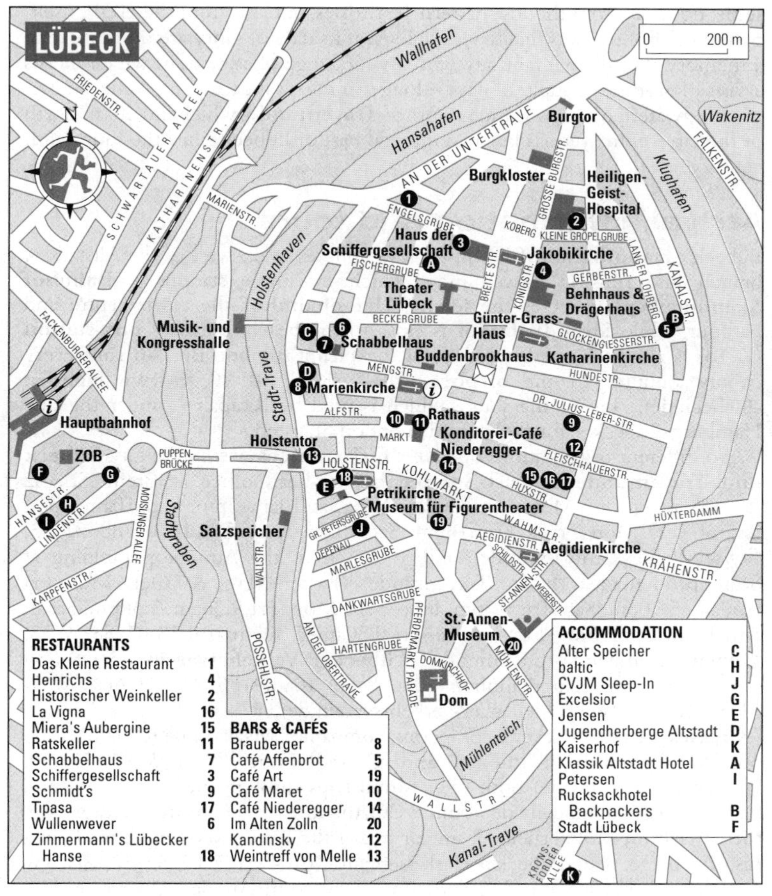

mercantile heyday – Germany's oldest town hall still in use, beautiful merchants' houses, fine redbrick Gothic churches, and quaint old charitable institutions – many of which employ a highly decorative form of brickwork. Indeed, Lübeck's leadership in the artistic sphere was as pronounced as it was in commerce, influencing the appearance of cities along the entire length of the northern European coast, from Amsterdam to Tallinn. The importance of Lübeck's heritage was given official recognition in 1987 by UNESCO's decision to place its entire Altstadt on the list of the world's most significant monuments – the first place in northern Europe to be so honoured. This award was not only a tribute to the past, but also to the skill and efficacy of modern German restoration techniques: the city was severely bombed in World War II, with a quarter of the centre completely destroyed, but the little surviving evidence of this has mostly been left as a deliberate reminder.

In the Cold War years, Lübeck was the only important city to be sited alongside the notorious barbed-wire frontier. Paradoxically, this stimulated a revival in its fortunes after a long period of decline. Nearly 100,000 refugees came to settle, not only from the lost Eastern Territories, but also from the GDR itself, before the frontier was finally sealed. Even if its days of glory are no more than a memory, it's still a vibrant city with a wide range of attractions which merits a visit of at least a couple of days – longer if you want to spend some time in the deepwater port cum seaside resort of **Travemünde**, which lies 20km north of the city centre, yet has been an integral part of Lübeck since the fourteenth century.

Arrival, information and tours

Lübeck's **Hauptbahnhof** lies just a few minutes' walk west of the Altstadt. A branch line runs to Travemünde, which has three stations – **Bahnhof Skandinavienkai** serves the ferries, **Hafenbahnhof** the town centre and harbour, while **Strandbahnhof** is close to the beach. Lübeck's **bus station** (ZOB) is almost immediately east of the Hauptbahnhof. Bus #6 runs every twenty minutes to the **airport** (Ⓣ04 51/58 30 10, Ⓦwww.flughafen-luebeck.de), 7km to the south, which is used by Ryanair – under the title Hamburg-Lübeck – for flights from London Stansted.

Two different organisations operate **tourist offices** within the city. **Lübeck und Travemünde Tourist-Service** has its head office at Breite Str. 62 (June–Sept & Dec Mon–Fri 9.30am–7pm, Sat 10am–3pm, Sun 10am–2pm; rest of year Mon–Fri 9.30am–6pm, Sat 10am–3pm; Ⓣ0 18 05/88 22 33, Ⓦwww.luebeck-tourismus.de), and a branch in the Aqua Top building at Strandpromenade 1b in Travemünde (Easter–May & Oct Mon–Fri 9.30am–5.30pm, Sat 10am–3pm; June–Sept Mon–Fri 9.30am–5.30pm, Sat & Sun 10am–5pm; Nov–Easter Mon–Fri 9.30am–5.30pm; Ⓣ0 18 05/88 22 33, Ⓦwww.travemuende-tourismus.de). **Lübecker Verkehrsverein** operates an office inside the Hauptbahnhof (Mon–Sat 9/10am–1pm & 2/3–6pm; Ⓣ04 51/86 46 75, Ⓦwww.luebecker-verkehrsverein.de).

Cruises are run by several competing companies. Maak-Linie (Ⓣ04 51/7 06 38 59, Ⓦwww.maak-linie.de) and Quandt-Linie (Ⓣ04 51/7 77 99, Ⓦwww.quandt-linie.de) both offer round trips through the city's canals and harbour (year-round daily departures; €6); the former departs from Untertrave, the latter from Moltebrücke. A similar trip at the same price can be made in a historic barge with Lübecker Barkassenfahrt (Ⓣ04 51/7 07 82 22, Ⓦwww.luebecker-barkassenfahrt.de), departing daily from An der Obertrave 15a. KuFra Schiffahrtslinien (Ⓣ04 51/2 80 16 35, Ⓦwww.koenemannschiffahrt.de) sails between Untertrave and Travemünde (€7 single, €12 return). Wakenitzschiffahrt Quandt (Ⓣ04 51/79 38 85, Ⓦwww.wakenitz-schiffahrt-quandt.de; €7 one way, €11 return) and Personenschiffahrt Reinhold Maiworm (Ⓣ04 51/3 54 55, Ⓦwww.maiworm-schiffahrt.de; €8 one way, €14 return) both run trips from Moltekbrücke along the River Wakenitz to Rothenhusen on the Ratzeburger See, where you can connect with a service to Ratzeburg. See p.691 for more details of the complete journey to Ratzeburg.

Accommodation

Lübeck is a good place for budget travellers, with a wide choice of **hostel** accommodation. **Hotels** are clustered mainly around the Hauptbahnhof or within the Altstadt; there are also some enticing options in Travemünde. Although only a few **rooms** are available in private houses (❷–❹), it's worth asking one of the tourist offices about these, as some have enticing locations in the Altstadt.

Hotels and pensions

Alter Speicher Beckergrube 91–93 ⓣ04 51/7 10 45, ⓦwww.hotel-alter-speicher.de. A converted warehouse in the Altstadt fitted out with all the mod cons. ❻

baltic Hansestr. 11 ⓣ04 51/8 55 75, ⓦwww.baltic-hotel.de. One of several inexpensive hotels immediately to the rear of the bus station. Small basic singles cost less than half the price of the doubles. ❹

Deutscher Kaiser Vorderreihe 52, Travemünde ⓣ0 45 02/84 20, ⓦwww.deutscher-kaiser-travemuende.de. Fine, very traditional waterfront hotel with restaurant. ❻

Excelsior Hansestr. 3 ⓣ04 51/8 80 90, ⓦwww.hotel-excelsior-luebeck.de. Capacious hotel by the bus station, with large breakfast buffets a definite plus. ❻

Jensen Obertrave 4–5 ⓣ04 51/70 24 90, ⓦwww.hotel-jensen.de. Occupies a modernized old mansion with a waterside view. It also has a good fish restaurant, *Yachtzimmer*. ❻

Kaiserhof Kronsforder Allee 11–13 ⓣ04 51/70 33 01, ⓦwww.kaiserhof-luebeck.de. Nicely furnished upmarket hotel located in a pair of former patrician mansions just to the south of the Altstadt. ❻–❽

Klassik Altstadt Hotel Fischergrube 52 ⓣ04 51/70 29 80, ⓦwww.klassik-hotel.com. Elegant hotel in Neoclassical premises in the heart of the Altstadt. It serves good breakfast buffets, but no other meals. ❺–❼

Maritim Strandhotel Trelleborgallee 2, Travemünde ⓣ0 45 02/8 90, ⓦwww.maritim.de. Tower-block hotel dominating the beach front, offering wonderful views from its upper storeys. It also has a good if pricey restaurant. ❼–❾

Petersen Hansestr. 11a ⓣ04 51/8 45 19, ⓕ86 45 92. Budget hotel by the bus station, offering a choice of rooms with and without private bathroom. ❹

Siemer Mecklenburger Landstr. 36, Travemünde ⓣ0 45 02/24 08. Travemünde's cheapest rooms are in this pension in Priwall on the south side of the Trave, which can be reached by ferry from the centre of the resort. ❹

Stadt Lübeck Am Bahnhof 21 ⓣ04 51/8 38 83, ⓦwww.stadt-luebeck-hotel.de. Somewhat old-fashioned hotel whose location directly opposite the Hauptbahnhof is much quieter than might be expected. ❺

Strandperle Kaiserallee 10, Travemünde ⓣ0 45 02/30 89 89, ⓕ86 60 18. Good-value mid-range hotel by the beach; it has a fine restaurant serving Italian and international dishes. ❻

Campsite and youth hostels

Campingplatz Schönböcken Steinrader Damm 12 ⓣ04 51/89 30 30. Lübeck's campsite is in a western suburb, reached by bus #7.

CVJM Sleep-In Grosse Petersgrube 11 ⓣ04 51/7 19 20, ⓦwww.cvjm-luebeck.de. A YMCA hostel in a renovated historic house in the middle of the Altstadt, offering the cheapest accommodation in the city. Dorm beds €10, singles €23, doubles €30, optional breakfast €4.

Jugendherberge Altstadt Mengstr. 33 ⓣ04 51/7 02 03 99. This official youth hostel has an excellent Altstadt location. €16.10/18.80.

Jugendherberge Vor den Burgtor Am Gertrudenkirchhof 4 ⓣ04 51/3 34 33. Located just outside the Altstadt: go through the Burgtor, then bear left for about 200m. €15.10/17.80.

Jugendherberge Travemünde Mecklenburger Landstr. 69, Travemünde ⓣ0 45 02/25 76. Located by the beach on the Priwall side of the Trave, reached by ferry from the resort centre. There are also several campsites in the immediate vicinity. Closed mid-Oct to March. €12.50/15.20.

Rucksackhotel Backpackers Kanalstr. 70 ⓣ04 51/70 68 92, ⓕ7 07 34 29). A privately owned canalside hostel. Dorm beds from €13, doubles €34.

The City

All the historic sights are in the **Altstadt**, an egg-shaped island still surrounded by the water defences of the Trave and the city moat. Its streets, while not conforming to a pre-arranged plan, are nevertheless arranged symmetrically, so it's easy to find your way around. For a general view of the magnificent skyline, walk northeast from the Hauptbahnhof to the Marienbrücke: better still, take one of the cruises round the harbour area.

The Holstentor, the Petrikirche and around

Entry to Lübeck was once through, but is now along the side of, the **Holstentor** (Holstein Gate; Tues–Sun 10am–4/5pm; €4), whose two sturdy circular towers with turret roofs, joined by a gabled centre section, form the city's emblem. Built in 1477, it leans rather horrifyingly these days, but that shouldn't put you off calling in at its small historical museum, which provides a useful introduction to the city and Hanseatic history. On the waterfront to the right of the Holstentor is a row of lovely old gabled buildings, the **Salzspeicher** (salt warehouses). They were built in the sixteenth and seventeenth centuries to store precious salt, extracted in Lüneburg and destined for Scandinavia.

Straight ahead over the bridge and up Holstenstrasse, the first church on the right is the Gothic **Petrikirche**, one of the many buildings to suffer during the massive Allied bombing of March 29, 1942. It no longer functions as a place of worship; instead, the whitewashed, five-aisled interior is put to use for concerts and changing exhibitions of contemporary art. A lift goes to the top of the **tower** (March–Dec daily 10am–4/7pm; €2), and Lübeck's centre is compact enough for this to be very useful for getting to grips with the layout of the city.

In the shadow of the church, at Kolk 16, is the **Museum für Puppentheater** (daily 10am–6pm; €3), which claims to be the world's largest collection of puppet theatre material, with examples from all over Europe, Asia and Africa. Special matinees for children (€4) are staged daily (except Mondays) at 3pm in the **Marionettentheater** (Ⓣ04 51/7 00 60, Ⓦwww.fritzfey.de) on the block to the south; performances for adults are held on Fridays and Saturdays at 7.30pm (€6.50–9.50). The next street along, **Grosse Petersgrube**, ranks as one of the finest in the city, with an impressive array of mansions showing all the different vernacular styles from Gothic to Neoclassical.

The Rathaus

Across Holstenstrasse from the Petrikirche is the Markt, two sides of which are occupied by the imposing **Rathaus**, which illustrates Lübeck's characteristic brickwork – with alternating rows of red unglazed and black glazed bricks – at its most inventive. The north wing, which dates from the mid-thirteenth century, has a high superstructure with spire-topped turrets and two huge holes to lessen wind resistance; its side facing the Markt was further enlivened by the addition of a Renaissance loggia made of white-coloured stone from the city's old trading partner, the Swedish island of Gotland. At the turn of the fourteenth century, the east wing, with an arcade leading to Breite Strasse behind, was added. Its extension, the **Neue Gemach**, was begun around 1440 and is the finest part of all, providing a highly refined variation on the earlier theme of windbreaks and corner turrets, with the bonus of coats of arms embedded in the brickwork. On the Breite Strasse side, it was further embellished with an extremely elaborate stone staircase in the Dutch Renaissance style and an oriel window.

Guided tours (Mon–Fri at 11am, noon & 3pm; €2) go round some of the interiors, though it has to be said that these don't quite match what you see from outside. The most notable rooms are the late Baroque **Audienzsaal**, with its allegorical paintings and Renaissance doorway, and the neo-Gothic **Bürgerschaftssal**. Leaving by the north side, you get a good view of the original thirteenth-century building, and can also see the **Kanzleigebäude**, the chancellery building tacked on in the fifteenth century.

The Marienkirche

Rearing up behind the north wing of the Rathaus is the city's largest and finest church, the **Marienkirche**. The two buildings were intended to be seen as a coherent architectural group, as the Marienkirche was where the city's richest citizens worshipped – and they planned from the outset that it should overshadow the bishops' Dom. Built at a leisurely pace between the early thirteenth and mid-fourteenth centuries, it's a tall, soaring building in the French Gothic style – but in brick, rather than stone, which gives it a very different and authentically German appearance. Its twin square **towers** are topped by spires to a height of 185m, while the nave is supported by flying buttresses that rise from the verdigris roofs of the side aisles. The church was severely damaged in the 1942 bombings and, although subsequently restored, the bells in the southern tower chapel were left smashed on the ground, the way they fell during the bombing. The war damage was actually a mixed blessing: the spires were destroyed, and both organs and much fine woodwork were lost, but on the other hand, original Gothic **wall paintings** which had been covered for centuries were revealed – indeed the entire interior was laid bare for a restoration to its original simplicity.

Today the interior is very light, with a feeling of great loftiness. The fifteenth-century high altar, in front of which is a pretty fourteenth-century font, is of modest dimensions, but a number of impressive **works of art**, dating from the late fifteenth and early sixteenth centuries, can be seen in the ambulatory. These include a life-size carving of St John the Evangelist (unfortunately only partly restorable after war damage), a series of powerful Passion reliefs by the Münster sculptor Hinrik Brabender and a beautiful locally made gilded tabernacle. In the axial chapel is a magnificent carved and painted altar from Antwerp in a gilded wood frame, depicting the life of the Virgin Mary, while in the Alenkapelle, the chapel adjoining the northern transept, is a grave slab of a merchant cast by Lübeck's greatest artist, Bernt Notke. Before leaving, have a look inside the **Briefkapelle** at the southwestern end of the nave, a masterly miniature church which is used by the congregation during the winter.

Mengstrasse and Breite Strasse

On the north side of the Marienkirche is **Mengstrasse**, which is lined with an impressive row of patrician houses. At no. 4 is the Baroque **Buddenbrookhaus** (daily 10am–5/6pm; €6, or €8 combined ticket with Günter-Grass-Haus; ⓦwww.buddenbrookhaus.de), which was where the famous literary brothers Heinrich and Thomas Mann grew up. It's now a memorial museum in their honour, named after the latter's youthful novel of mercantile life in the city. Further up the street, nos. 48 and 50 are together designated the **Schabbelhaus**. It's now one of several restaurants in the city that are regarded as sightseeing attractions in their own right, crammed as it is with antiques. A few doors down at no.64 is the oldest of the city's wine merchants, **Weinhandel Carl Tesdorpf** (Mon–Fri 9am–6pm, Sat 9am–2pm), founded in 1678. It is best known for its own-brand *Sekt* and for a high-quality French red wine that goes under the name of *Lübecker Rotspon*.

Facing the Rathaus across Breite Strasse is the **Konditorei-Café Niederegger** (Mon–Fri 9am–7pm, Sat 9am–6pm, Sun 10am–6pm; ⓦwww.niederegger.de), whose marzipan is internationally renowned. This is the oddest hangover from the city's trading heyday: the confection was first produced in Lübeck in the Middle Ages from fine almonds imported from Italy. The Niederegger family perfected the art in 1806, and the mind-boggling range on sale in the shop is the result of the uninterrupted continuation of the business. On the second floor is a display on the history of marzipan, complete with some "sculptures". At the opposite, northern end of Breite Strasse are two impressive Renaissance halls – the **Haus der Kaufmannschaft**, the offices of the local chamber of commerce, and the **Haus der Schiffergesellschaft**, the former sea captains' guild house. The latter is another of the city's best-known restaurants, and is decked out inside with all sorts of seagoing paraphernalia; predictably, it's on the programme of every tour group.

Across the street stands the **Jakobikirche**, traditionally the parish church of the seafaring community. In comparison with the Marienkirche, it's modest in scale, the only obvious point of similarity being the Gothic wall paintings on its square pillars. Nonetheless, it's rich in works of art, the finest being the **Brömbse Altar** in one of the south aisle chapels, which features a carving of *The Crucifixion* by Hinrik Brabender and delicate little Flemish-style paintings. The carved oak **organ lofts** are also impressive; a beautifully worked spiral staircase leads up to the large Baroque organ in the west gallery, though its smaller counterpart in the transept, dating back in part to the fifteenth century, is the more precious instrument of the two.

Grosse Burgstrasse and Königstrasse

Guarding the extreme northern end of the Altstadt is the formidable-looking **Burgtor**, a square tower topped by a bell-shaped roof. The side buildings of the gateway were originally used for stabling the horses of people arriving in the city at this point. On Hinter der Burg just to the south is the **Burgkloster** (Tues–Sun 10am–4/5pm; €3), a thirteenth-century Dominican priory which served after secularisation as a poor house, then as a court and prison, and is now a cultural centre. It's Lübeck's main venue for temporary artistic exhibitions, but also has a couple of permanent displays. One is a photographic record of Jewish life in the city, the other an account of the city's mercantile and monetary history, centred on the Lübecker Münzschatz, a horde of 24,000 coins from 84 different locations, which was buried in the first half of the sixteenth century and not discovered until 1984.

Following Grosse Burgstrasse back towards the city centre, you come to the thirteenth-century **Heiligen-Geist-Hospital** (Tues–Sun 10am–4/5pm; free), one of the earliest and best-preserved hospices of the medieval period, whose rhythmic facade is characterized by its gables and tall pepperpot turrets. Inside, the vaulted chapel is richly decorated with frescoes, retables and a Gothic rood screen bearing delicate paintings telling the story of St Elizabeth.

Königstrasse, the southern continuation of Grosse Burgstrasse, is dominated by stately mansions of the Baroque period and later. The **Gemeinnützige Gesellschaft** at no. 5 was another charitable institution; some of its elegant interiors are now used as a restaurant (see p.690). Two patrician homes, the **Drägerhaus** at no. 9 and the **Behnhaus** at no. 11, have been combined to form the **Museum für Kunst und Kulturgeschichte** (Museum for Art and Cultural History; Tues–Sun 10am–4/5pm; €3, free first Fri of the month). It's surprising to see how large these houses are inside, compared with the narrow street frontage; tax was once paid on a building's width rather than its overall size, which led to houses being built long and narrow. The Drägerhaus has impressive interiors with original nineteenth-century furniture, clocks, porcelain and other *objets d'art*. A gallery of nineteenth- and early twentieth-century paintings occupies the Behnhaus. This includes a room devoted to Lübeck's own **Johann Friedrich Overbeck**, founder and guiding light of the influential Nazarene Brotherhood (see p.1031). There's also a lovely *Coastal Landscape by Evening Light* by Friedrich, and fine examples of the Expressionists Kirchner and Munch.

At the corner of the next block is the **Katharinenkirche** (April–Sept Tues–Sun 10am–1pm & 2–5pm; free), formerly the church of a Franciscan

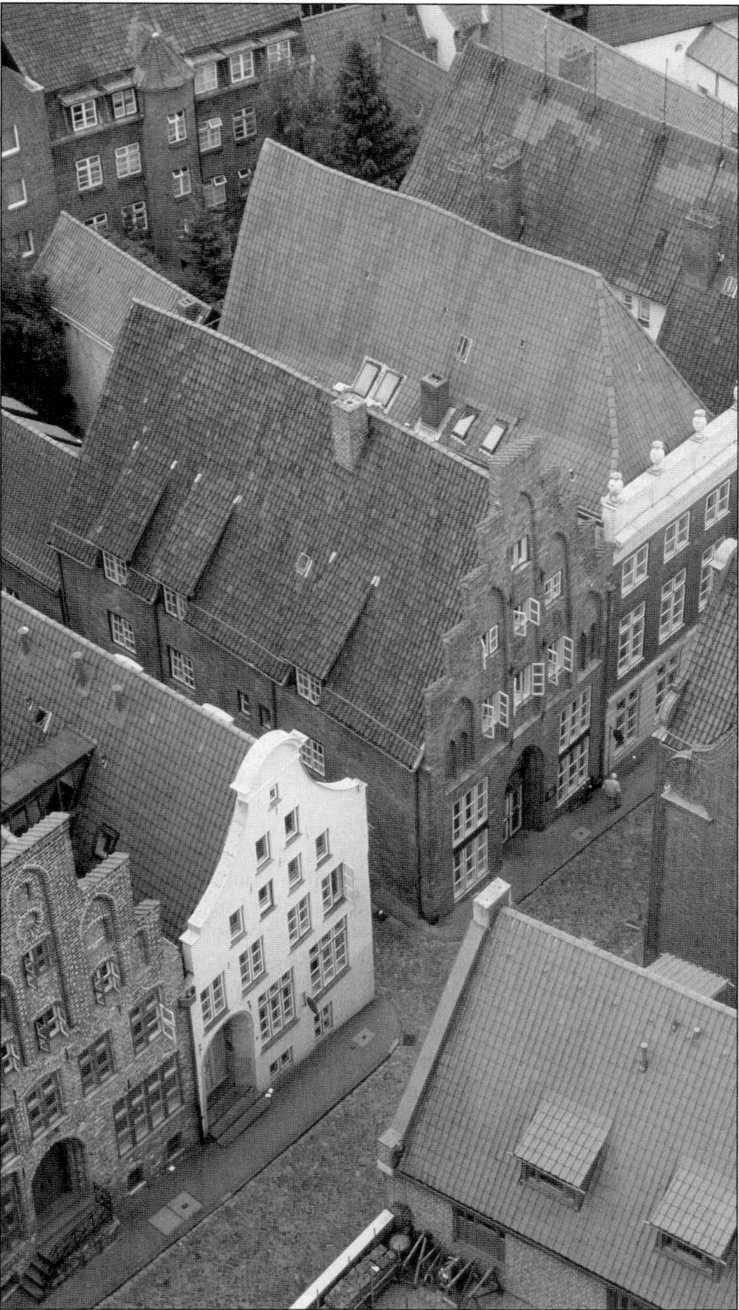

△ Gabled houses seen from above, Lübeck

convent – the city's only monastic foundation from the days of the Hansa to have survived intact. In the niches of the facade are nine life-sized figures, the first three on the left (*Woman in the Wind*, *The Beggar* and *The Singer)* by **Ernst Barlach**: he was commissioned to make the series in the early 1930s, but these were all he had completed by 1932, when his work was banned by the Nazis. The other six were added after the war by **Gerhard Marcks**: you can have a closer look at them in Schloss Gottorf in Schleswig, where another set of terracotta castings from the same moulds is exhibited. Inside, the main peculiarity is the two-storey chancel, the lower of which functioned as a crypt, even though it's at ground level. On the west wall is a large altarpiece of *The Raising of Lazarus* by **Tintoretto**, brought from Venice by a Lübeck merchant. Nearby stands a cast of Bernt Notke's masterpiece, a spectacular group of *St George and the Dragon*, the original of which is in Stockholm.

The eastern quarters

At Glockengiesser Strasse 21, to the side of the Katharinenkirche, the **Günter-Grass-Haus** (Tues–Sun 10am–5/6pm; €3.50; Ⓦ www.guenter-grass-haus.de) commemorates the work of Günter Grass, the most recent German winner of the Nobel Prize for Literature. Ironically enough, he is a native of Danzig (now Gdańsk), the city which ousted Lübeck from its pre-eminent position in the Hanseatic League in the late fifteenth century. Grass has devoted a large part of his time to the visual arts, and the museum has a complete collection of his engravings, and also displays some of his sculptures.

Also on this street, you can step through what appear to be doors in the wall into two of Lübeck's finest courtyards, whose small almshouses were built by seventeenth-century benefactors. The **Füchtings-Hof** at no. 23 was built for the widows of sea captains and merchants; the slightly earlier **Glandorps-Gang** and **Glandorps-Hof** further down at no. 39 were intended for the widows of craftsmen. Another attractive example is the **Haasenhof**, a couple of blocks to the south at Dr-Julius-Leber-Str. 37. At the junction of this street with Königstrasse is the **Löwen-Apotheke**, the oldest remaining house in the city. Two groups of Gothic almshouses can be seen in streets further south – **Von-Höveln-Gang** at Wahmstr. 73–77 and **Dornes-Hof** at Schlumacher Str. 19.

Presiding over the quiet, village-like streets of the southeastern quarter (an area into which few tourists venture) is the handsome single tower of the **Aegidienkirche** (Tues–Sat 10.30am–4pm), Lübeck's smallest parish church, whose congregation was made up of craftsmen, smallholders and the less affluent merchants. There was a strong musical tradition here, and the early Baroque organ rivals any in Lübeck. What really catches the eye, however, is the richly decorated Renaissance **choir gallery** which shuts off the chancel from the nave. A Protestant variant on the old Catholic idea of the rood screen, its very positioning emphasizes the importance of music in Lutheran worship, while its paintings interpret biblical stories in line with the doctrines of the new faith.

Round the corner, the **St-Annen-Museum** (Tues–Sun 10am–4/5pm; €3, free first Fri of the month) is housed in the surviving parts of the late Gothic St-Annen-Kloster, an Augustinian convent which burned down in the nineteenth century. It has a first-rate collection reflecting domestic, civic and religious art and history from the thirteenth to the eighteenth century. The star piece is the magnificent *Passion Triptych* which **Memling** painted for the Dom. There's also a room full of retables commissioned by the various guilds for their chapels; the finest, predictably enough, is that made for the artists' own Guild of St Luke, which has attractive paintings illustrating the life of their patron by the leading Lübeck master of the late fifteenth century, **Hermen Rode**. The courtyard, surrounded by very Dutch-looking buildings, is one of the most restful spots in the city; its garden contains many imposing monumental Baroque statues, including the original figures from the Puppenbrücke, the bridge leading from the Hauptbahnhof to the Holstentor.

The Dom

At the extreme southern end of the Altstadt is the only surviving monument commissioned by Henry the Lion, who founded the port of Lübeck in 1159: the huge brick-built **Dom** (Ⓦwww.domzuluebeck.de). It was completed in 1230, with its two 120-metre towers, as a Romanesque basilica. A couple of decades later, the pure early Gothic porch or "Paradise" was added on the south side to serve as the main entrance. Soon after, work began on replacing the original chancel with a spacious Gothic hall. The whitewashed interior is dominated by an enormous **triumphal cross**, the first important work of **Bernt Notke**, who was a celebrity throughout the Baltic lands in the late fifteenth and early sixteenth centuries. Probably a painter as well as a sculptor, he specialized in the grandiose, making highly original works to adorn churches in Denmark, Sweden and Estonia. This one is a complicated allegory on the salvation offered by the Cross, which rests on an elaborate beamed structure bearing marvellously expressive figures of saints and angels. Notke was also responsible for the carvings on the **rood screen** behind, to which an astronomical clock was appended in the seventeenth century. Among the Dom's numerous other adornments, look out for the ornate Renaissance pulpit in the main nave, the fifteenth-century *Müllerkrone* candelabrum in the north aisle, the winged retables in the transept, and, in the chancel, the memorials to bishops and noblemen, which range from simple Gothic tombs to commemorative chapels in the swankiest Baroque.

Travemünde

Despite having been part of Lübeck for nearly seven centuries, **TRAVEMÜNDE** is so far from the city centre that it seems like a separate town. Its initial importance was as an outer harbour, and the fishing and shipping quays retain their dominant positions. However, Travemünde has also become a rather glamorous seaside resort. Go there in winter and you might find the odd playful seal on the fine sandy beach. In summer, though, it is hardly the place to go to get away from it all. The beach is packed full of busy *Strandkörbe* (hooded basket-seats rented out like deck chairs to keep off the breeze), sailing boats and windsurfers ply the water, and the fashionable **Casino** makes fat profits (not least on its terrace, *the* place to sit for cool drinks and ice cream). By the southern end is a large indoor bathing complex, **Aqua Top** (daily 10am–9pm). From the beach it's odd to watch large ships apparently sailing right onto land, whereas they are actually entering the mouth of the Trave. If you walk northwards up the beach, it eventually peters out and is replaced by cliffs, the **Brodtener Ufer**. This is the place to get a rare view of the Baltic from above sea level.

Eating and drinking

You'll pass many of Lübeck's most prestigious **restaurants** on a tour around the Altstadt and though all are pricey, less expensive menus are often available at lunchtimes. However, the city also has plenty of cheaper alternatives, many of them of comparable quality. In addition, there's a varied selection of **cafés and bars** to choose from.

Restaurants

Das Kleine Restaurant An der Untertrave 39. The menu here includes a ten-course gourmet set dinner for €33. Evenings only, closed Sun.

Heinrichs Königstr. 5–7. Classy restaurant in the Gemeinnützige Gesellschaft, which has beautifully furnished interiors plus a garden terrace. Closed Sun evening.

Historischer Weinkeller Koberg 8. Wine bar-cum-restaurant in the cellars of the Heiligen-Geist-Hospital. Its offshoot, *Kartoffelkeller*, at the same address, serves potato-based dishes. Closed Tues.

La Vigna Hüxstr. 69. Italian delicatessen and restaurant, with a fine selection of Sardinian wines. Closed Sun.

Miera's Aubergine Hüxstr. 57. Large general delicatessen shop with attached restaurant (evenings only, closed Sun & Mon) and bistro (closed Sun). It also has a wine bar (closed Sun) a couple of doors down the street.

Ratskeller Markt 13. Among the best of its ilk, with hearty *gutbürgerliche Küche*, some vegetarian options, and a good wine list.

Schabbelhaus Mengstr. 48–52. Upmarket restaurant in a sixteenth-century merchant's house with courtyard, serving Italian and international dishes. Closed Sun.

Schiffergesellschaft Breite Str. 2. Famous old seaman's tavern, often overrun by tour groups, but it serves excellent food and is not unduly expensive. Closed Mon.

Schmidt's Dr-Julius-Leber-Str. 60–62. Inexpensive restaurant in the heart of the student quarter, with an eclectic menu of salads, pasta, pizzas, tandoori and vegetarian dishes. Evenings only.

Tipasa Schlumacher Str. 14. A great student favourite, featuring a large, ever-changing and reasonably priced menu of bistro-type dishes, plus wonderful pizzas and bread.

Wullenwever Beckergrube 71 ⓣ04 51/70 43 33. Occupying a sixteenth-century mansion, this is currently Lübeck's most prestigious gourmet address, with fish and duck dishes the main specialities. Evenings only, closed Sun & Mon. Reservations advisable.

Zimmermann's Lübecker Hanse Kolk 3–7. Housed in a beautiful old building by the Petrikirche, this excellent if pricey restaurant features French cuisine as well as German dishes. Mon–Fri only, except in Nov & Dec, when it's also open Sat.

Bars and cafés

Brauberger Alfstr. 36. Hausbrauerei serving low-cost meals and its own unfiltered beer. Evenings only, closed Sun.

Café Affenbrot Im Werkhof, Kanalstr. 70. Vegetarian café with summer terrace and winter garden; it serves changing daily lunchtime specials and organically produced beer and wine.

Café Art Kapitelstr. 4-8. Café-bar, with a large summer garden, which serves breakfasts until 3pm and offers free Internet access.

Café Maret Markt 17. Traditional café claiming a pedigree dating back to 1786.

Café Niederegger Breite Str. 89. The celebrated marzipan shop has an elegant backroom café, plus a first-floor dining room; there's a wide choice of breakfasts, plus good-value set lunches. Another branch is at Vorderreihe 56, Travemünde.

Im Alten Zolln Mühlenstr. 93. The most atmospheric of the city's traditional Kneipen; it also does full meals and sometimes has live music.

Kandinsky Fleischhauerstr. 89. Trendy café-bar that often features live music of various kinds.

Weintreff von Melle Holstentorpassage, Holstenstr. 20. Small bar run by a long-established wine merchant who imports red wines from all over the world.

Music, theatre and festivals

No German city is better known for its **organ recitals** – a tradition dating back to the early seventeenth century, when the Danish composer Diderik Buxtehude became one of the first musicians to achieve fame as a virtuoso solo instrumentalist, drawing huge crowds to his improvisatory recitals at the Marienkirche (see p.684). The Marienkirche's two modern organs (one of which is the biggest mechanical musical instrument in the world) are used alternately for recitals each Saturday at 6.30pm, while one or other of the Jakobikirche's historic organs is played on Saturdays at 5pm. For details of these, and other musical events in Lübeck's churches, log on to ⓦwww.kirchenmusik-luebeck.de.

Concerts by the Philharmonisches Orchester der Hansestadt Lübeck are held at the Musik- und Kongresshalle, Willy-Brandt-Allee 10 (ⓣ04 51/7 90

44 00). Other classical music can be heard at the Musikhochschule, Grosse Petersgrube 17–29 (Ⓣ04 51/1 50 51 05, Ⓦwww.mh-luebeck.de). The Theater Lübeck, Beckergrube 10–14 (Ⓣ04 51/7 45 52, Ⓦwww.theater.luebeck.de) stages **opera** in its Grosses Haus, **drama** in the Kammerspeile. Among the many **clubs**, the most enduringly popular are *Body and Soul*, which is housed in a boat moored at Kanalstr. 78, and *Queen's Club*, in a huge converted factory at Falkenstr. 45. For **live jazz**, go to *Dr Jazz*, An der Untertrave 1.

Lübeck's main **festivals** are Markt Anno Dazumal, an old-time fair held in the Rathausmarkt for 10 days in May; a two-week Volksfest in mid-July; and the Altstadtfest on the second weekend in Sept (even-numbered years only). The Advent celebrations are a cut above the norm, thanks to the setting of the Kunsthandwerker-Weihnachtsmarkt in the Heiligen-Geist-Hospital, and the fairyland displays of the Weichnachtsmärchenwald outside the Marienkirche.

Ratzeburg

The idyllic town of **RATZEBURG** lies 23km from Lübeck, towards the southern end of the **Ratzeburger See**, the largest of the forty or so lakes punctuating the wooded countryside through which the notorious border with the GDR used to run. Its picturesque if vulnerable-looking Altstadt is built on a small island linked by causeways to the modern suburbs on either bank.

Towards the northern tip of the Altstadt is the **Dom** which, like Lübeck's, was founded by Henry the Lion. The main external features of this Romanesque brick basilica are its massive west tower and porticoed southern porch. Inside, the triumphal cross and choir stalls remain from the original furnishings. Gothic additions include the pew used by the Dukes of Saxony and the stone **Passion altar** in the chancel, an outstanding example of the Westphalian Soft Style. The Renaissance pulpit, with its elaborate sounding board, is the most prominent of the post-Reformation embellishments. Also within the Dom are many tomb slabs to local bishops and dukes.

Back towards the commercial centre, the **A. Paul-Weber-Museum**, Domhof 5 (Tues–Sun 10am–1pm & 2–5pm; €1.50; Ⓦwww.weber-museum.de), displays the work of a satirical artist best known for his attacks on the Nazis. A few doors down at Domhof 12 is the **Kreismuseum** (Tues–Sun 10am–1pm & 2–5pm; €1.50), which has displays on the archaeology and history of the town and surrounding district. A few minutes' walk further south, the **Ernst-Barlach-Haus** (mid-March to Nov Tues–Sun 10am–noon & 2-5pm; €3), on Barlachplatz to the rear of the Markt, commemorates an even more celebrated artistic opponent of the Third Reich. Barlach spent part of his youth in this house, which now contains examples of his wonderful Expressionist carvings and graphic work. It's also worth crossing over to the eastern side of the lake to ascend the **Aussichtsturm** (May–Sept Tues–Sun 10am–5pm; €1), which commands fine views.

Cruises on the lake are run by Schiffahrt Ratzeburger See, Schlosswiese 6 (Ⓣ0 45 41/79 00, Ⓦwww.schiffahrt-ratzeburg.de). A round trip costs €8, but it's well worth sticking to the water all the way from Ratzeburg to Lübeck (€10 one-way, day return €15.50). This is a combination ticket: the leg between Ratzeburg and Rothenhusen at the northern end of the lake is with

Schiffahrt Ratzeburger See, the stage along the River Wakenitz is with Wakenitz Schiffahrt Quandt (see p.682). Because of the proximity of the border, this voyage was impossible throughout the four decades of German division, and the impenetrability of the area meant that it remained marvellously unspoiled. Even if not exactly the "Amazon of the North" it is billed in publicity material, the beautiful swampy forest landscape is now a protected nature reserve inhabited by herons, cormorants and kingfishers.

Practicalities

Ratzeburg's **Bahnhof**, on the line between Lübeck and Lüneburg, lies at the extreme western fringe of town. If time is of the essence, it's better to make the 25-kilometre journey from Lübeck by **bus**, as this takes you right into the Altstadt. The **tourist office** (May–Sept Mon–Thurs 9am–5pm, Fri 9am–6pm, Sat & Sun 10am–4pm; Oct–April Mon–Fri 9am–5pm; ⓣ0 45 41/80 00 81, ⓦwww.ratzeburg.de) is just to the west of the Altstadt at Schlosswiese 7. You can book **private rooms** (❶–❸) here, or the other local budget option is the **youth hostel** at Fischerstr. 20 (ⓣ0 45 41/37 07; €13.50/16.20), which has the benefit of an Altstadt setting with lakeward views. Also within the Altstadt are several **hotels**, including *Seegarten*, Theaterplatz 5 (ⓣ0 45 41/73 77; ❹), *Wittler's*, Grosse Kreuzstr. 11 (ⓣ0 45 41/32 04, ⓦwww.wittlers-hotel.de; ❻), and *Der Seehof*, Lüneburger Damm 1–3 (ⓣ0 45 41/86 01 00, ⓦwww.derseehof.de; ❻–❽). Alternatively, *Haus Betzinger*, Dermin 2a (ⓣ0 45 41/8 34 30; ❸) is a small **pension** on the west side of town. The terrace **restaurant** at *Der Seehof* is the best and most expensive place to eat in town; *Wittler's* is another good choice, as is the sixteenth-century *Askanier-Keller*, Töpferstr. 1, which serves local specialities.

Kiel

The naval port of **KIEL**, Schleswig-Holstein's capital, lies some 90km northwest of Lübeck at the head of the Kieler Förde, a typical Baltic coast fjord (though nothing like as dramatic as the Norwegian variety). Long overshadowed by Lübeck, the city's fortunes soared with the opening in 1895 of what is still the world's biggest and busiest man-made shipping lane. This is always known in English as the **Kiel Canal**, though its German title of Nord-Ostsee-Kanal is a more accurate designation of its status as the link between the North Sea and the Baltic. In 1918, it was a mutiny by the sailors of Kiel that sparked off the German Revolution, leading to the abdication of the Kaiser and the birth of the Weimar Republic. As the main **U-boat centre** in World War II, it was a prime target for Allied bombing missions, and much of it subsequently had to be rebuilt from scratch. Consequently, there's not much point in looking for charm amid its sober 1950s three- and four-storey blocks: from a sightseeing point of view, Kiel is one of Germany's least rewarding cities. Nonetheless, it attracts hordes of visitors in the last full week of June for the Kieler Woche (ⓦwww.kieler-woche.de), Germany's premier annual **regatta**.

Arrival, information and accommodation

Kiel's **Hauptbahnhof** and **bus station** are located together at the southern end of the central shopping area. The **tourist office** (Mon–Fri 9am–6pm, Sat

9am–1pm; ⓣ04 31/67 91 00, ⓦwww.kiel-tourist.de) is a short walk away at Andreas-Gayk-Str. 31. In summer, there are regular **cruises** round the harbour, across the Kieler Förde, and down the Kiel Canal. **Ferries** also run to various Danish destinations, as well as to Oslo and Göteborg.

Hotels in all categories are scattered throughout the city, but bear in mind that **accommodation** of any kind is very difficult to come by during the Kieler Woche. Kiel's **youth hostel** is at Johannesstr. 1 (ⓣ04 31/73 14 88; €15.10/17.80) in the suburb of Gaarden on the right bank of the Kieler Förde; take bus #11 or #12 or walk over via the pedestrian bridge.

Hotels

Berliner Hof Ringstr. 6 ⓣ04 31/6 63 40, ⓦwww.berlinerhof-kiel.de. Good medium-range hotel just west of the Hauptbahnhof. 6

Kieler Yacht-Club Hindenburgufer 70 ⓣ04 31/8 81 30, ⓦwww.kieleryachtclub.de. This yachting enthusiasts' haunt occupies a lovely waterside setting only a short distance north of the city centre, with wonderful views over the Kieler Bucht. It also has a well-regarded restaurant. 7–9

Parkhotel Kieler Kaufmann Niemannsweg 102 ⓣ04 31/8 81 10, ⓦwww.kieler-kaufmann.de. This has a pleasant park setting just north of the city centre, and also boasts a fine restaurant. 8–9

Rendsburger Hof Rendsburger Landstr. 363, Russee ⓣ04 31/69 01 31, ⓕ69 17 41. Budget hotel in a suburban setting 2km southwest of the centre. 3

Runge Elisabethstr. 16, Gaarden ⓣ04 31/73 33 96, ⓦwww.hotel-runge.de. Located in a right-bank suburb, this good-value hotel offers a choice of rooms with and without facilities. 5

Schweriner Hof Königsweg 13 ⓣ04 31/6 14 16 or 6 26 78, ⓕ67 41 34. The cheapest hotel with a central location; it incorporates a daytime café, *Presseclub*. 4–6

Steigenberger Conti-Hansa Schlossgarten 7 ⓣ04 31/5 11 54 44, ⓦwww.kiel.steigenberger.de. Kiel's most luxurious hotel has an ideal location at the northern fringe of the centre. Its restaurant, *Jakob*, is among the best in the city. 9

Waffenschmiede Friedrich-Voss-Ufer 4, Holtenau ⓣ04 31/36 96 90, ⓦwww.hotel-waffenschmiede.de. Good-value hotel directly overlooking the north side of the Kiel Canal, just to the west of the Schleusen. The restaurant is moderately priced and has a garden terrace. 6

The City

Central Kiel's dominant building is the huge Jugendstil **Rathaus** (guided tours May–Sept Wed & Sun at 9.30am & 10.30am; €1) on Rathausstrasse, whose tower commands an extensive panorama of the city and its fjord. A few minutes' walk to the northeast is the Alter Markt, on which stands the **Nikolaikirche**, a Gothic church partially restored and modernized following war damage. Inside are a few notable furnishings, such as a fourteenth-century font and a fifteenth-century altar and triumphal cross, while outside stands an imposing sculpture by Barlach, *Der Geistkämpfer* (literally, "The Fighter for the Spirit").

A few paces away, at Dänische Str. 19, the Warleberger Hof, one of the few surviving old mansions, now houses the **Stadtmuseum** (mid-April to mid-Oct daily 10am–6pm; rest of year Tues–Sun 10am–5pm; free), with changing exhibitions on the city's history. A little further along, set in gardens overlooking the promenade, the exceedingly modest **Schloss** contains the **Stiftung Pommern** (Tues–Fri 10am–5pm, Sat & Sun 2–6pm; €1), a collection of paintings by seventeenth-century Dutch masters as well as examples of German art from Romanticism to Impressionism.

The old fish market hall just opposite at Wall 65 has been adapted as the **Schiffahrtsmuseum** (mid-April to mid-Oct daily 10am–6pm; rest of year Tues–Sun 10am–5pm; free), documenting local maritime history. During the summer months, you can also look round the three sailing craft moored outside – the steamship *Bussard*, the lifeboat *Hindenburg* and the fireship *Kiel*. A few minutes' walk further north, at Düsternbrooker Weg 1, is the **Kunsthalle** (Tues & Thurs–Sun 10am–6pm, Wed 10am–8pm; €5; Ⓦwww.kunsthalle-kiel.de), which has a large array of predominantly modern art plus a collection of classical antiquities. At no. 20 on the same street, the **Aquarium im Institut für Meereskunde** (daily April–Sept 9am–7pm; Oct–March 9am–5pm; €1.60; Ⓦwww.aquarium-kiel.de) is home to seals and large aquaria of Baltic fish.

The **Schleusen** (locks) at the eastern end of the Kiel Canal are among the most interesting parts of the waterway; to reach them, take bus #11 from the bus station to the terminus at Wik. There are raised platforms on both banks; to cross over to the northern side, walk west for a few minutes to catch one of the regular free ferries.

At Molfsee, 6km southwest of the centre (take bus #500 or #504), is the **Schleswig-Holsteinisches Freilichtmuseum** (April–June & mid-Sept to Oct Tues–Sun 9am–6pm; July to mid-Sept daily 9am–6pm; Nov–March Sun & holidays 11am–4pm in fine weather only; €4.50; Ⓦwww.freilichtmuseum-sh.de). Here around thirty sixteenth- to nineteenth-century farmsteads and barns from throughout Schleswig-Holstein have been reassembled in regional groups to give a comprehensive picture of rural life down the ages. A pottery, bakery, four mills, a forge and a dairy are all worked in the old ways, and their products are on sale. Many of the houses have tiny cabin beds in which whole families used to sleep: in winter they slept sitting up and huddled together against the cold.

Eating, drinking and entertainment

Many of the best **restaurants** are in the hotels, but Kiel has a reasonable range of other places to eat and drink. The main cultural venues are the Opernhaus, Rathausplatz 4 (Ⓣ04 31/9 50 95, Ⓦwww.theater-kiel.de), where **opera and ballet** are performed, and the Schauspielhaus, Holtenauer Str. 103 (Ⓣ04 31/9 50 95, Ⓦwww.theater-kiel.de), which is principally used for straight **drama**.

Cafés and restaurants

Dratenhof Hamburger Landstr. 99, Molfsee. This converted eighteenth-century farmhouse by the Freilichtmuseum serves excellent, fairly priced food. Closed Sun evening & Mon.

Friesenhof Fleethörn 9. Located in the Rathaus, this is the ubiquitous Ratskeller masquerading under another name.

Im Schloss Wall 80. This is generally regarded as Kiel's leading restaurant, and is expensive, though not excessively so. Closed Sat evening & Mon lunchtime (all day Sun & Mon in July & Aug).

Klosterbrauerei Alter Markt 9. Hausbrauerei which produces an unfiltered dark beer and a Bock; also serves inexpensive meals.

Oblomow Hansastr. 82. A longstanding student favourite, which does good cheap food.

Seeburg Düsternbrooker Weg 2. Café-restaurant handy for the museums, with the bonus of a view over the fjord.

Zauberlehrling Lutherstr. 24. This has a good vegetarian menu, though it also caters for carnivores.

Laboe, Eutin and Rendsburg

Within easy reach of Kiel are a wide variety of enticing destinations making good full or half-day trips; some of them are also possible stopovers on the way to or from Lübeck, Flensburg or Schleswig. Places to head for include the beach resort of **Laboe**, the former ducal residence of **Eutin** and **Rendsburg**, where the most interesting features of the Kiel Canal can be seen.

Laboe

The Kieler Förde has a number of fine beaches, none better than that at **LABOE**, a popular resort some 18km from the city, reachable in well under an hour either by bus #100 or #101 or by one of the regular ferries which ply the inlet in summer. The waterfront is dominated by the celebrated 85-metre **Marine-Ehrenmal** (daily 9.30am–4/6pm; €2.80), a memorial to sailors of all nationalities who died in the two world wars. Part of this now contains the **U-Boot-Museum** (€2.10 supplement), which tells you all you're likely to want to know about German submarines. The ticket also covers admission to U-Boot 995, which is moored alongside.

Laboe has plenty of **pensions** (❷–❸), plus an excellent **hotel**, *Seeterrassen*, at Strandstr. 86 (Ⓣ0 43 43/60 70, Ⓦwww.seeterrassen-laboe.de; ❺). Full information about accommodation is available from the **tourist office** (May–Sept Mon–Fri 10am–noon & 1–4pm, Sat & Sun 10am–3.30pm; April & Oct daily 10am–2pm; Nov–March Mon–Fri 10am–2pm; Ⓣ0 43 43/42 75 53, Ⓦwww.laboe.de) at Strandstr. 25.

Eutin

EUTIN, which lies to style itself "Rosenstadt" (the town of roses), lies almost exactly midway along the road and rail lines linking Lübeck and Kiel, about 45km from either. It's the most attractive of the many *Kurorte* in Holstein Switzerland, an area which contains no mountains and so presumably owes its nickname to the presence of a multiplicity of lakes, some 140 in all.

The town's focal point is the **Schloss** (guided tours March–Oct Tues–Sun at 10am, 11am, noon, 2pm, 3pm & 4pm; €2.50), which is set in a fine park with both French and English sections. It has its origins in a fortified castle of the Lübeck prince-bishops, who were forbidden to reside within the boundaries of the city-state itself; later, it became one of the residences of the Holstein-Gottorf-Oldenburg dukes, and was rebuilt in the Baroque period. Inside the apartments, decorated in late Baroque, Regency and Neoclassical styles, is a series of large **ship models** donated by Czar Peter the Great of Russia and a collection of portraits by Goethe's friend **Johann Heinrich Wilhelm Tischbein**, who resided in Eutin as court painter for 21 years. The former Marstall (stables) now house the **Ostholstein-Museum** (April–Sept Tues, Wed & Fri–Sun 10am–1pm & 2–5pm, Thurs 10am–1pm & 2–7pm; Oct–Jan & March Tues & Wed 3–5pm, Thurs–Sun 10am–noon & 3–5pm; €1.50), primarily devoted to evoking the town's golden era in the early nineteenth century, yet also displaying memorabilia relating to **Carl Maria von Weber**, the founding father of musical Romanticism, who was born in Eutin in 1786. Weber's compositions are the mainstay of the **Eutiner Festspiele** (Ⓦwww.eutiner-festspiele.de), a festival held in the Schloss in July and August.

Eutin's **Bahnhof** is at the western edge of the Altstadt. The **tourist office** (Jan–March Mon–Fri 9am–5pm; April to mid-May & mid-Sept to Dec Mon–Fri 9am–6pm, Sat 10am–1pm; mid-May to mid-Sept Mon–Sat 9am–6pm, Sat & Sun 10am–3pm; Ⓣ0 45 21/7 09 70, Ⓦwww.eutin-tourismus.de) is at Markt 19. There are some very pleasant **hotels** in the town and its surroundings, including *Voss-Haus*, which occupies a beautiful eighteenth-century building at Vossplatz 6 (Ⓣ0 45 21/4 01 60, Ⓦwww.vosshauseutin.de; ❻), *Ferienhaus Uklei*, by the Kellersee, 5km north of the centre at Eutiner Str. 7 in the incorporated village of Sielbeck (Ⓣ0 45 21/24 58, Ⓦwww.ferienhaus-uklei.de; ❺), and *Am See – Der Redderkrug*, 3km northeast of town at Am Redderkrug 5 (Ⓣ0 45 21/22 32, Ⓦwww.redderkrug.de; ❻). There's also a

youth hostel overlooking the town, at Jahnhöhe 6 (Ⓣ0 45 21/21 09; €13.50/16.20).

All of the three hotels listed above have good **restaurants**. Other enticing places to eat are *Brauhaus Eutin*, a Hausbrauerei at Markt 11; *Schlossterrassen*, which occupies the former ducal riding hall in the Marstall; and *L'Etoile*, Lübecker Landstr. 36, one of Schleswig-Holstein's foremost gourmet addresses, which runs a moderately priced bistro as an adjunct.

Rendsburg

One of the two rail lines linking Kiel with Flensburg first travels westwards for 35km to the garrison town of **RENDSBURG**. It's well worth going here for the ride alone, the last part of which is one of the most spectacular in Germany, as the rail line has to perform some extraordinary gymnastics in order to cope with crossing the Kiel Canal high enough for shipping to pass underneath, yet get back to ground level again for the Bahnhof at the southeastern edge of the town centre, only a few hundred metres ahead. The solution is ingenious – having traversed the bridge, the **Schwebefähre Hochbrücke**, the train descends via a gently sloping loop, which circles for a good 2km all the way round the inner suburb of Scheleife. Bizarrely, this trip offers one of the best views of Rendsburg: when there's a train approaching in the opposite direction, the effect is positively surreal. Other impressive feats of transport engineering in town are the four-lane road tunnel taking road traffic beneath the canal, and Europe's longest **escalator**, which takes pedestrians down to it.

The main historic buildings are clustered together around the Altstädter Markt, a few minutes' walk north of the Bahnhof. Here the timber-framed sixteenth-century **Altes Rathaus** is notable for the archway cut through it, allowing the street to pass underneath. Nearby is the brick **Marienkirche**, which dates back to the thirteenth century and is the oldest building in town.

In the opposite direction from the Bahnhof, at Prinzessinstr. 8, the handsome nineteenth-century **Synagoge** (Tues–Sun noon–5pm; €3) has been restored to house a museum of Jewish life and culture. Just to the west is the spacious Paradeplatz, on which stands the late seventeenth-century **Christuskirche**, which was specially designed so that the garrison's entire contingent of two thousand men could all attend services at the same time.

Rendsburg's **tourist office** (Mon–Fri 10am–5pm, Sat 10am–1pm; Ⓣ0 43 31/2 11 20, Ⓦwww.rendsburg.de) is in the Altes Rathaus. There are plenty of **hotels**, such as *Deutsche Eiche*, Herrenstr. 12 (Ⓣ0 43 31/5 80 20, Ⓦwww.hotel-deutscheeiche.de; ❺); *Tüxen*, Lancasterstr. 44 (Ⓣ0 43 31/2 70 99, Ⓦwww.tuexen-hotel.de; ❺); *Hansen*, Bismarckstr. 26 (Ⓣ0 43 31/5 90 00, Ⓦwww.hotelhansen.de; ❺); and *Pelli-Hof*, a fine eighteenth-century mansion at Materialhofstr. 1 (Ⓣ0 43 31/2 22 16, Ⓦwww.pelli-hof.de; ❻). The **youth hostel** is 1km west of the Altstadt at Rotenhöfer Weg 48 (Ⓣ0 43 31/7 12 05; €13.50/16.20). Most of the best **restaurants** are in the aforementioned hotels, but a cheaper alternative is *Niewarker* on Paradeplatz, a Hausbrauerei that makes both a bottom-fermented light beer and a top-fermented dark beer.

Schleswig

Though well off the tourist track, **SCHLESWIG**, 25km north of Rendsburg, is worth going far out of your way to see. Nowadays an administrative centre with a sleepy pace, it dozes gently on the banks of a beautiful fjord, the Schlei, and could easily trick you into thinking that nothing had ever happened there. It did, though – for three centuries from after around 800 the **Vikings**, whose trade routes stretched from the Black Sea to Greenland, had their main northern European trading centre here, the shortest crossing point between the Baltic and North Sea. Following their demise, the town was re-established on the opposite side of the Schlei. This subsequently became a Danish royal residence, and then, after the partition of Schleswig-Holstein in 1544, the seat of one of its lines, the House of Gottorf. This illustrious history has bequeathed a marvellous legacy of monuments, making Schleswig one of the most outstanding small towns in all of Germany.

Arrival, information and accommodation

Schleswig's **Bahnhof** is over 1km south of Schloss Gottorf, and about 3km from the centre. Local buses #1 and #2 run from there via Schloss Gottorf to the **bus station**, which is located just to the north of the Altstadt. A couple of minutes' walk south of here, at Plessenstr. 7, is the **tourist office** (May–Sept Mon–Fri 9.30am–5.30pm, Sat 9.30am–noon; Oct–April Mon–Thurs 10am–4pm, Fri 10am–1pm; ⓣ0 46 21/98 16 16, ⓦwww.schleswig.de). **Bikes** and **boats** can both be rented at the Stadthafen during the summer months, when various companies also run **cruises** on the Schlei.

Schleswig offers a good choice of **hotels**. The **youth hostel** is at Spielkoppel 1 (ⓣ0 46 21/2 38 93; €13.50/16.20): from the Bahnhof, take a bus as far as the Landestheater (ie before the bus station), then walk up the steps known as the Lollfusstreppe. There's a **campsite** (ⓣ0 46 21/3 24 50) at Haddeby, near the Wikinger Museum.

Hotels

Dom-Hotel Domziegelhof 6 ⓣ0 46 21/97 77 67, ⓕ2 38 36. Moderately priced hotel with restaurant, just to the west of the Altstadt. ❹

Gottorfer Hof Gottorfstr. 7 ⓣ0 46 21/9 39 90, ⓦwww.gottorferhof.de. Hotel with restaurant located by the entrance to Schloss Gottorf. ❹

Olschewski Hafenstr. 40 ⓣ0 46 21/2 55 77, ⓦwww.hotelolschewski.de.vu. Small hotel overlooking the Schlei at the edge of the Altstadt, attached to the best restaurant in town. ❻

Schleiblick Hafengang 4 ⓣ & ⓕ0 46 21/2 34 68. The most atmospheric of the cheaper hotels, located in an old fishermen's house in the Altstadt. To book, it may be necessary to go to the *Friesenstube* restaurant, Fischbrückstr. 15 (at the end of the same street). ❺

Strandhalle Strandweg 2 ⓣ0 46 21/90 90, ⓦwww.hotel-strandhalle.de. This hotel with restaurant is located alongside its own yachting marina just to the west of the Altstadt. ❻

Waldschlösschen Kolonnenweg 152 ⓣ0 46 21/38 30, ⓦwww.hotel-waldschloesschen.de. Schleswig's best hotel lies 2km southwest of the centre in a rustic woodland setting where the Dukes of Gottorf used to go hunting. It has a swimming pool, whirlpool, steam baths, saunas and an excellent restaurant, *Adam Olearius*. ❼

Zum Stadtfeld Stadtfeld 2a ⓣ0 46 21/2 39 47. Located to the north of the bus station, this bargain hotel is run as an adjunct to a Gaststätte. ❸

The Town

Despite a present-day population that barely tops the 25,000 mark, Schleswig possesses a sense of grandeur to match its past, not least in the way it sprawls over a large area. Its attractions are well spread out, meaning that it's a place not easily seen in a hurry, but all the sights are served by city buses.

The Dom

Schleswig's skyline, best viewed from across the Schlei, is dominated by the **Dom** (ⓦwww.schleswigerdom.de), and in particular its oversized late nineteenth-century tower, which, close up, looks even more modern than it is, due to a re-facing of its brickwork in the 1950s. The main body of the building is essentially a Gothic hall church, though the imposing south portal and the transepts are Romanesque. Inside, the vaults of the latter, plus the triumphal arch of the choir, are covered with precious thirteenth-century **frescoes**, the most notable being *The Saviour of the Rainbow*. On the south wall is another of the Dom's early adornments, a lovely polychromed **retable** to the Three Magi, carved around 1400.

However, your attention is most likely to be drawn to the twelve-metre-high **Bordesholm altar** in the choir, one of Europe's most astonishing pieces of woodcarving. Carved from oak between 1514 and 1521, and originally commissioned for the Augustinian Kloster of Bordesholm south of Kiel, it shows some 400 figures on a background so delicate it resembles filigree. The Passion scenes appear to be based on woodcuts by Dürer, and are certainly the closest sculptural equivalent to the work of Germany's most famous artist. Yet the creator of this long-celebrated masterpiece, one **Hans Brüggemann** of Husum, remains a shadowy figure about whom little else is known, though one of his earlier works is the remarkable elongated **statue of St Christopher** by the transept entrance. Legend has it that the jealous monks of Bordesholm fed him with a potion which caused him to go blind, ensuring that he could never create an altar to rival their own.

In the northern ambulatory is the magnificent **tomb of King Friederick I**, carved in the 1550s by the Antwerp sculptor-architect **Cornelis Floris**. Its pure Renaissance style, with classically inspired Virtues and mourning angels bearing the reclining effigy of the deceased monarch, shows how tastes changed in the generation after Brüggemann. Nearby hangs the **Kilmannseck altar**, an elaborate Baroque epitaph with an allegorical painting by the local painter **Jürgen Ovens**, a student of Rembrandt and the only German artist to take up the style of the great Dutch master. He was also responsible for *The Blue Madonna* on the pillar of the end bay of the nave.

The rest of the Altstadt and Holm

Everything else in the Altstadt stands very much in the shade of the Dom. There are plenty of grand mansions of various dates, but the only other setpiece attraction is the **Graukloster** on Rathausmarkt immediately to the east. This former Franciscan friary is the unlikely-looking headquarters of the local administration, and is linked to the **Rathaus** proper, a plain Neoclassical structure. You're free to wander around during working hours; at weekends, only the ground floor of the cloister is left open.

A couple of minutes' walk beyond the eastern end of the Altstadt is the formerly separate fishing village of **Holm**, whose name (meaning "surrounded by water") reflects the fact that it was an island until 1935. These days, there are only some twenty fishermen still eking a living from the eel and herring catches of the Schlei, instead of the three hundred or so in Holm's heyday. Nonetheless, the quarter preserves the appearance of a tightly knit community. The immaculately tended circular **Friedhof** (cemetery), with a rustic nineteenth-century chapel as its bull's-eye, provides the unexpected centrepiece. The houses around it are notable for their two-piece doorways (the so-called "chatting doors") and for their bay windows, which give views in three directions.

At the eastern edge of Holm is the fascinating **Adeliges St-Johannis-Kloster**, a one-time Benedictine convent which has been a Protestant collegiate foundation since the Reformation. The canonesses, who only come here on retirement from their normal careers, live in the splendid Baroque houses grouped round the courtyard. Call at the home of the prioress at no. 8, or, better still, phone in advance (Ⓣ0 46 21/2 42 36), for a **guided tour** (€2) of the church, cloister and refectory.

Schloss Gottorf

On a little moated island in the Bergsee, a lake close to the head of the Schlei, about 1.5km west of the Altstadt, stands **Schloss Gottorf** (April–Oct daily 10am–6pm; Nov–March Tues–Fri 10am–4pm, Sat & Sun 10am–5pm; €5; Ⓦwww.schloss-gottorf.de), whose regal façade ranks as one of the finest achievements of northern European Renaissance architecture. Together with its dependencies, it's home to the **Schleswig-Holsteinisches Landesmuseum**. Note that the entrance ticket gives admission to several separate collections, which in total warrant at least half a day, and that it's best to avoid Mondays, when only some parts are open.

At the entrance, the **Königshalle**, a stately Gothic hall, houses Gothic paintings and sculptures, though the finest pieces are in the small rooms beyond. These include a gorgeous *Nativity* by the Lübeck painter **Hermen Rode** and a small *Retable of the Holy Kinship* by Brüggemann; the latter postdates the Bordesholm altar, thereby suggesting that the story of the sculptor's blinding is a myth. Important later paintings are *Frederick the Wise* by **Cranach** and a wonderfully luminous *Cain and Abel* by **Johann Liss**. Passing through the re-erected interior of a seventeenth-century Weinstube from Lübeck, you come to a suite of rooms decorated in Baroque style, of which the finest, the **Blauer Saal** (Blue Room), makes an elegant backdrop for a number of canvases by Ovens. Beyond is the **Schlosskirche**, a perfectly preserved Renaissance gem complete with painted gallery, an ornate ducal oratory and a still-functioning sixteenth-century organ. Adjoining this is the most spectacular chamber of all, the main festive hall, known as the **Hirschsaal** because of the life-sized, startlingly realistic polychromed stuccos of deer on the walls. Finally, there's a first-class **folklore collection** upstairs, complete with a series of reconstructed interiors from rural houses.

On the west side of the Schloss, the contents of the modern **Nydamhalle** illustrate the pre- and early history of the region, and are themselves sufficient reason for a visit to Schleswig. The major treasure is the huge **Nydamboot**, an oak rowing boat from around 350 AD. This is the single most important object to have survived from the era of the Germanic tribes who eventually came to form the German nation. There are other impressive sailing craft on show as well, including one from Roman times. Another highlight is the grisly display of *Moorleichen*, **peat-bog corpses** reckoned to be around two thousand years old. Most shocking are the facial expressions, ranging from the beatific look of one who seems to have died in peace, to the utter anguish of another, whose fate can only be imagined.

The **Kreuzstall**, a cross-shaped stables building on the other side of the Schloss, is home to a fine array of twentieth-century German art. On the ground floor, particular works to look out for are the second set of castings of the figures on the facade of the Katharinenkirche in Lübeck by **Gerhard Marcks** and the cartoons by **Kokoschka** for the destroyed mosaic he made for St Nikolai in Hamburg. Many of the other big names, such as Kirchner, Nolde, Macke, Rohlfs and Barlach are also well represented. Upstairs are more modern pieces, of which the most eye-catching is the brightly coloured set of 33 scenes by **Hap Grieshaber** illustrating Thomas Mann's biblical epic, *Joseph and his Brothers.*

The inclusive ticket also gives admission to the **Reithalle**, the riding hall immediately east of the Kreuzstall, where temporary exhibitions are held, and the **Kutschensammlung**, a collection of old coaches kept in the building behind the Nydamhalle. A display on local crafts and industries, the **Volkskundliche Sammlung**, has been relocated from another of the Schloss outbuildings to a former Prussian army storehouse about 1km to the northeast on Hesterberg.

Haithabu

Haithabu, the site of the original Viking settlement, is about 4km from the Altstadt by road. It can be reached by any bus going in the direction of Kiel, but in summer there's the far more atmospheric option of reaching it by a small boat across the Schlei which leaves the Stadthafen just south of the Dom. The earthwork ramparts of the otherwise vanished town have survived, and the extensive excavations yielded by the site are now kept in the **Wikinger Museum** (April–Oct daily 9am–5pm; Nov–March Tues–Sun 10am–4pm; €3), a bold modern design constructed, Viking-fashion, like a series of upturned boats. The main discovery has been a longship, now partially reconstructed to its original state and exhibited alongside models illustrating how it was built. Elsewhere, there are informative displays (English translations are available) on all aspects of Viking life; look out in particular for some wonderful jewellery and for the runic stones, one of which is engraved with a lurid orange script.

Eating, drinking and entertainment

Many of the best **restaurants** are found in the hotels, though there are several other enticing possibilities. The **folklore** tradition of Holm continues in the Holmer Beliebung held two weeks after Whitsun and featuring processions, music, and a ball in which the minuet and fandango are performed; another big annual event is the Twiebakken-Regatta in late August. An ambitious **cultural** programme, including opera, concerts and drama, is mounted at the Landestheater, Lollfuss 53 (ⓣ0 46 21/2 59 89, ⓦwww.sh-landestheater.de).

Cafes and restaurants

Asgaard Königstr. 27. The restaurant of Schleswig's only brewery, which is located on site. It has a high reputation for its dry, fruity premier product, known simply as *Asgaard*, as well as its Pils and *Weizen*.

Holm Café Süderholmstr. 15. Cosy little daytime café in Holm, serving homemade cakes and a good selection of teas and coffees.

Panorama Plessenstr. 15. The varied menu includes pizzas baked in a wood-fired oven, as well as noodle, vegetarian and fish dishes. There are inexpensive daily specials at lunchtime.

Ringelnatz Fischbrückstr. 3. Good-value food, teas and beer, available in a series of intimate little rooms, each quite different from the other.

Schleimöwe Süderholmstr. 8. Fish speciality restaurant in Holm, offering dishes prepared from seasonal catches in the Schlei.

Senatorenkroog Rathausmarkt 9–10. Founded back in 1884, this serves fairly upmarket *gutbürgerliche Küche*.

Stadt Flensburg Lollfuss 102. Handily located near Schloss Gottorf, this intimate restaurant occupies a house built in 1699 and presents both local and international dishes. Closed Wed.

Flensburg

There's a quite astonishing contrast in feel between Schleswig and its larger near neighbour **FLENSBURG**, a bustling commercial port and border town just over 30km to the north. Once the richest mercantile city under the Danish Crown, Flensburg has continued to prosper in spite of having lost much of its hinterland to Denmark in the wake of the 1920 plebiscite, when it opted to remain part of Germany. Standing at the head of the gentle Flensburger Förde, the town has expanded from its original waterside location up into the hills on either side of the inlet. Until the 1980s, it looked rather scruffy, but its Altstadt, which was surprisingly little touched by war, has gradually been restored to pristine shape as a result of an imaginative urban regeneration programme.

The Town

Flensburg's pride and joy is its central axis, a pedestrian precinct successively known as Holm, Grosse Strasse and Norderstrasse, which stretches for well over a kilometre along the entire length of the Altstadt from the Südermarkt to the Nordertor. Along its length are a series of **Höfe**, former merchants' courtyards (see box, which have no counterpart anywhere else in Germany. They are illuminating documents of social history, as well as the main contributory factor to the town's indubitably distinctive appearance.

The Südermarkt, on which **markets** are held on Wednesdays and Saturdays, is dominated by the **Nikolaikirche**, whose massive late sixteenth-century steeple, a very tardy example of Gothic, had to be reconstructed in the nineteenth century following fire damage. Inside, the most important adornment is the Renaissance **organ**, the largest in Schleswig-Holstein, which preserves its original case, a loving piece of craftsmanship by the sculptor Heinrich Ringerinck, who probably made the pulpit as well.

Proceeding up Holm, look out for nos. 19–21, a courtyard dating back to the sixteenth century, and for house no. 10 opposite, which has a well-restored facade. At the back of no. 24 on Grosse Strasse is the **Westindienspeicher** (West Indies Warehouse), a late eighteenth-century "skyscraper" which stands as a reminder of the importance of the rum and sugar trade to the local economy. Now restored, it serves as offices and apartments. On the left-hand side further up Grosse Strasse, the fourteenth-century **Heiliggeistkirche** has been the main place of worship of the local Danish-speaking community since 1588.

Just beyond is Nordermarkt, on which stands the **Neptunbrunnen**, which gushes out the famous spring water used for rum-making. Also here is the **Marienkirche**, a Gothic hall church with impressive frescoes from about 1400 in its northern aisle and a fine set of Renaissance furnishings – altar, pulpit and font. Alongside are the **Schrangen**, covered arcades where traders' stalls have stood since the sixteenth century. Kompagniestrasse goes down to the right to the **Kompagnietor**, the former mariners' guildhall, where a plaque reveals something of the northern mercantile philosophy that behaving justly will, with the help of God, always bring large profits.

The Flensburg Höfe

Most of Flensburg's courtyards are laid out according to a clear pattern. Facing the main street is the showpiece home of the merchant, with his offices often incorporated as well. The two side wings typically have the stables and workshops where the imported raw materials were turned into finished products, while the far end is normally closed off by a large warehouse building with an entrance gateway and crane. For obvious reasons of convenience, most of these back directly onto the harbour, which is only one block to the east. Therefore, the western side of Flensburg's main axis was left to those of lesser means and was populated mainly by craftsmen, whose modest houses stand in stark contrast to the courtyards directly opposite.

Continuing onwards, the **Künstlerhof** at Norderstr. 22 is a courtyard of half-timbered houses which have been restored as artists' studios. The central axis terminates at the **Nordertor**, a step-gabled Renaissance gateway which has become the symbol of the town. It bears the coats of arms of both Flensburg and King Christian IV of Denmark. Facing the harbour at Schiffbrücke 39, only a couple of minutes' walk from Nordertor, a warehouse has been adapted to contain the **Schiffahrts- und Rum-Museum** (Tues–Sun 10am–4/5pm; €3.50 combined ticket with Städtisches Museum), devoted to the history of the port and its trade, and including a section on the local rum business; around sixty different varieties are currently produced in Flensburg.

Returning to Norderstrasse, the stone stairway known as the Marientreppe leads up 150 steps to the **Schlosswall**, the site of the former castle, from where there's a good view across the harbour to the opposite side of town. Also on the heights, a bit further south on Lutherplatz, and reached via Rathausstrasse from the junction of Grosse Strasse and Holm, is the vast neo-Renaissance bulk of the **Städtisches Museum** (same times and ticket at Schiffahrt- und Rum-Museum). Its displays include some fine medieval artefacts, a series of interiors from rural farmsteads, and a collection of watercolours by Emil Nolde.

Finally, it's worth crossing eastwards from Südermarkt to reach the oldest part of the town, grouped round the **Johanniskirche**, a rustic little twelfth-century church. Viewed from inside, the building almost seems to sag under the weight of its wacky sixteenth-century vault, which is covered with what is, for the most part, a decidedly unecclesiastical decorative fresco scheme.

Practicalities

Flensburg's **Hauptbahnhof** is about fifteen minutes' walk due south of the centre; the **bus station** is south of the harbour, on the opposite side of the busy Süderhofenden from the Altstadt. **Boat trips** are run by Förde-Reederei, Norderhofenden 20 (Ⓣ04 61/86 40). The **tourist office** (Mon–Sat 9am–6.30pm; Ⓣ04 61/9 09 09 20, Ⓦwww.flensburg-tourist.de) is housed in a converted warehouse at Speicherlinie 40, in the heart of the Altstadt.

There are plenty of **private rooms** (❷–❸) on offer, plus an inexpensive **pension**, *Ziesemer*, right beside the bus station at Wilhelmstr. 2 (Ⓣ04 61/2 51 64; ❸). **Hotels** include: *Handwerkerhaus*, Augustastr. 2 (Ⓣ04 61/14 48 00; ❹); *Am Wasserturm*, Blasberg 13 (Ⓣ04 61/3 15 06 00; ❻); *Am Rathaus*, Rote Str. 32–34 (Ⓣ04 61/1 73 33 35, Ⓦwww.hotel-am-rathaus.com; ❻); *Flensburger Hof*, Süderhofenden 38 (Ⓣ04 61/14 19 90, Ⓦwww.hotel-flensburger-hof.com; ❻); and the top-of-the-range *Mercure*, Norderhofenden 6–9 (Ⓣ04 61/8 41 10, Ⓦwww.mercure.com; ❼). Well to the northeast of town, reached by Glücksburg-bound buses, is the **youth hostel**, Fichtestr. 16 (Ⓣ04 61/3 77 42; €13.50/16.20).

The Altstadt has a nicely varied selection of places to **eat and drink**. *Hansens*, Schiffbrücke 16, is a Hausbrauerei brewing its own *Pils* and *Alt*. This marks a bold challenge to the renowned *Pilsener* of the Flensburger brewery, which holds sway in most of the other bars and restaurants – and whose distinctive flip-top bottles have helped make it something of a cult drink elsewhere in Germany, notably Berlin. *Fischerklause*, Schiffbrücke 6, and *Piet Henningsen*, Schiffbrücke 20, are both fish specialists, while *Das Kleine Restaurant*, Grosse Str. 73, has a varied menu including good pastas and salads. *Borgerforeningen*, Holm 17, serves what are arguably the best meals of all.

Drama, opera and concerts by the Schleswig-Holsteinisches Sinfonieorchester all feature on the programme of the Landestheater, Nordergraben 2–6 (Ⓣ04 61/2 33 88, Ⓦwww.sh-landestheater.de).

Niebüll

A one-horse town in Schleswig-Holstein's farthest-flung northwest corner isn't top of anyone's list of places to visit, but **NIEBÜLL**, which lies in the bleak North Friesian landscape 40km west of Flensburg, has its attractions, notably two terrific museums dedicated to artists who fell foul of the Third Reich – Emil Nolde and, less famously, Richard Haizmann. It's also the gateway to the North Friesan Islands, with the mainland beyond Niebüll linked to the largest island, Sylt (see below), by a causeway.

The **Richard-Haizmann-Museum** (Tues–Fri 11am–4.30pm, Sat 10am–noon, Sun 2–5pm; €1.50) in the Rathaus on Rathausplatz is dedicated to the artist's sculpture, pottery and pictures. Haizmann was exiled to Schleswig-Holstein in what was termed "inner emigration" following the banning of his work by the Nazis. Some of it had been displayed in the famous 1930s Berlin exhibition of so-called degenerate art and was subsequently destroyed. Haizmann's work bears the influence of oriental and African art, and is beautifully displayed in a museum created by the curator and the artist's widow, who struggled for many years to open a museum, achieving her ambition only days before her death. Elsewhere in the town centre, the only place of interest is the **Friesisches Heimatmuseum** (June–Sept daily 2–4pm; €1) at Osterweg 76, an old farmhouse decked out in seventeenth-century style.

The **Nolde-Museum** (Tues–Sun: March–Oct 10am–6pm, Nov 10am–5pm; €4; Ⓦwww.nolde-stiftung.de) stands alone in the countryside at Seebüll, 5km from the town centre, in the house and gallery that Emil Nolde built in the 1950s, once his work could be acknowledged again. A novel by postwar author Siegfried Lenz, *The German Lesson*, has as a main character an artist, painting in secret during the war, who was based on Nolde. The museum can be very full in summer, but if you are there on a quiet day you may have the luxury of enjoying Nolde's vibrant colours on your own. His Expressionistic paintings have some brutal themes; the brilliant flower and landscape series are simpler, but powerful nonetheless. A bus runs out to the museum from Niebüll, and the way is clearly signposted if you are travelling by car or bike.

Although plenty of **trains** pass through on the Hamburg–Sylt line, the cross-country route to Flensburg is serviced only by **buses**. Niebüll's **tourist office** (Mon, Wed & Fri 8am–noon, Tues 8am–noon & 2–4pm, Thurs 8am–noon & 2–6pm; Ⓣ0 46 61/60 10, Ⓦwww.niebuell.de) is in the Rathaus, at Hauptstr. 44. In addition to **private rooms** (❷–❸), there's a **pension**, *Insel*, Gotteskoogstr. 4 (Ⓣ0 46 61/21 45, Ⓦwww.inselpension.de; ❹). **Hotels** include *Morgenstern*, Deezbüller Str. 70 (Ⓣ0 46 61/42 04; ❹); *Zur Alten Schmiede*, Hauptstr. 27 (Ⓣ0 46 61/9 61 50; ❹); and *Bossen*, Hauptstr. 15 (Ⓣ0 46 61/60 80 01; ❺). There's also a **youth hostel** at Deezbülldeich 2 (Ⓣ0 46 61/87 62; €13.50/16.20).

Sylt

Scattered off the North Sea coast of Schleswig-Holstein are the storm-battered **North Friesian islands**, which, until recently, were home to a small population of fisherfolk and farmers eking out a fragile existence. Nowadays, tourism is by far the biggest source of income, particularly in **Sylt**, a highly developed holiday area which is completely different from the other homely islands of

Föhr and Amrum. Sylt is a big favourite among moneyed Germans and the island is heavily populated during the major holidays (including Christmas and Easter), when prices for both eating out and accommodation can be high. Indeed, such is the demand for accommodation that unless you have booked a couple of months in advance – regardless of when you visit – you could be unlucky.

Around the island

The island is shaped rather like a T on its side, and runs north to south for about 40km in a narrow strip under 1km wide. In addition to an ample supply of sandy beaches, there are dunes and small cliffs. **WESTERLAND**, the main town, is on the west side of the stalk. It's the terminus of the railway across the causeway (onto which cars have to be loaded beforehand) and is also the hub for the island's bus services. A chic and glamorous resort, its social life is centred on the Casino on Andreas-Nilsen-Strasse.

North of Westerland is **KAMPEN**, an exclusive enclave of around 650 inhabitants. Formerly a place of inspiration for the writers Thomas Mann and Carl Zuckmayer and the painter Emil Nolde, its tiny streets are today packed with antique stores, gourmet restaurants and expensive clothes stores. It's doubtful whether such a large amount of luxury is spread so thick on so small an area anywhere else in Germany. Further north is Sylt's most famous stretch of beach, **Buhne 16**, a haven for naked (but gold-dripping) sun worshippers. After sunset the place to be is *Gogärtchen* on the strip known as "Whiskystrasse". Beyond lies **LIST**, which has Germany's largest expanse of sand dune around it.

Practicalities

Accommodation is best found through Westerland's **tourist office** (Mon–Sat 9am–6pm, Sun 10am–6pm, reduced hours out of season; Ⓣ01 80/5 00 99 80, Ⓦwww.westerland.de) at Strandstr. 35. The town is particularly well endowed with upmarket **hotels**, ranging from the small *Jörg Müller*, Süderstr. 8 (Ⓣ0 46 51/2 77 88, Ⓦwww.hotel-joerg-mueller.de; ❾); via the medium-sized *Atlantic*, Johann-Möller-Str. 30 (Ⓣ0 46 51/9 88 00, Ⓦwww.sylt-atlantic.de; ❾); to the resort's most prestigious address, the capacious *Stadt Hamburg*, Strandstr. 2 (Ⓣ0 46 51/85 80, Ⓦwww.relaischateaux.com/stadthamburg; ❾).

A good choice for traditional German food in Westerland is *Alte Friesenstube*, Gaadt 4, which is housed in one of the oldest buildings on the island. The hotel **restaurants** are more upmarket (*Jörg Müller* is of true gourmet stature) though the *Stadt Hamburg* has a reasonably priced bistro in addition to its expensive main dining room.

One of the island's three **youth hostels** is in the dunes to the south of Westerland at Fischerweg 36-40 (Ⓣ0 46 51/8 35 78 25; €15/17.70). Another has an isolated setting outside List (Ⓣ0 46 51/87 03 97; €15/17.70); the third is at Friesenplatz 2 (Ⓣ0 46 51/88 02 94; €15/17.70) in Hörnum at the southern tip of the island.

Husum

HUSUM, 40km south of Niebüll and 35km west of Schleswig, is by far the most attractive town in North Friesland. Its character is defined by the small harbour right in the centre, which has given welcome shelter to generations of fishermen returning from the perils of the North Sea. A mixture of small-scale grandeur and workaday simplicity, the town's name is indelibly associated with that of **Theodor Storm**, a nineteenth-century novelist, poet and civil activist who gave Husum its rather unfair title *Die graue Stadt am Meer* ("the grey town by the sea").

The main axis of the town centre is the broad **Grossstrasse**, which opens out into the Markt. Both of these are lined with large houses, mainly eighteenth- and nineteenth-century (though there are one or two beautiful seventeenth-century gabled buildings reminiscent of Lübeck), most of which have stores on the ground floor. Here too is the step-gabled fourteenth-century **Herrenhaus**, the oldest building in town, albeit with sandstone pillars and a doorway added in the seventeenth and eighteenth centuries. On the north side of the square stands the seventeenth-century **Rathaus**.

Turning northwards from here, you come to the Schlossgang, a narrow walkway leading to the **Schloss vor Husum** (April–Oct Tues–Sun 11am–5pm; €2.50), whose curious name (Schloss before Husum) is explained by the fact that it originally lay outside the boundaries of the town. Over to the left, the **Torhaus**, the former gatehouse, is actually more attractive than the main building. It has retained some ornate Renaissance features, whereas the Schloss itself, built at the same time, underwent extensive later modifications, giving it a Baroque interior with fine sandstone and alabaster fireplaces. The **Schlosspark**, which contains a memorial to Theodor Storm, turns into a great sea of mauve crocuses in spring. These were originally planted in the Middle Ages by monks who had a monastery on the site.

About 100m south of Grossstrasse is the **Schiffbrücke**, an inner harbour busy with fishing boats; it's also the place where the ferry takes shelter in winter. One famous catch landed here is *Husumer Krabben* – not crabs, confusingly, but tasty little brown shrimps. They're found in abundance on local menus, especially in the form of *Husumer Krabbensuppe*, a soup that often comes topped with whipped cream. In summer, there's a shrimp stall on Hafenstrasse, towards the outer harbour, selling the freshly boiled catch.

Up Wasserreihe, the narrow street to the right, is the **Theodor-Storm-Haus** (April–Oct Mon & Sun 2–5pm, Tues–Fri 10am–5pm, Sat 11am–5pm; Nov–March Tues, Thurs & Sat 2–5pm; €2; ⓦwww.storm-gesellschaft.de), the home of the writer between 1866 and 1880, when he was at the height of his career. It's chiefly of interest to his fans, though as the rooms still have their original furnishings the house is worth seeing as an example of nineteenth-century middle-class life. Storm's wood-panelled study, where he produced about twenty of his novels, has a display of correspondence with the Russian novelist Turgenev and other literary figures.

At the southern end of the town centre, in the Nissenhaus at Herzog-Adolf-Str. 25, is the **Nordfriesisches Museum** (April–Oct daily 10am–5pm; Nov–March Tues–Fri & Sun 10am–4pm; €2.50; ⓦwww.nissenhaus.de), founded in the early 1930s by local-boy-made-good Ludwig Nissen, who amassed a fortune in the United States. It's especially good on the geological background of the area, flood control and town history.

Practicalities

Both the **Bahnhof** and the **bus station** are just a short walk from the town centre, which is reached via Herzog-Adolf-Strasse. The **tourist office** (June to mid-Sept Mon–Fri 9am–6pm, Sat 10am–1pm; rest of year Mon–Thurs

9am–noon & 2–4pm, Fri 9am–noon & 2–3pm; ⓣ0 48 41/8 98 70, ⓦwww.husum.de) is in the Altes Rathaus, Grossstr. 27.

In addition to **private rooms** (❶–❸), there's a good range of hotels in every category. At the lower end are *Rödekrog*, Wilhelmstr. 10 (ⓣ0 48 41/37 71; ❸), and *Wohlert*, Markt 30 (ⓣ0 48 41/22 29; ❹). In the medium range, *Zur Grauen Stadt am Meer*, overlooking the harbour at Schiffbrücke 8–9 (ⓣ0 48 41/8 93 20, ⓦwww.husum.net/grauestadt; ❻), is a lovely place, with an excellent restaurant serving local fish specialities. Alternatives in this category are *Osterkrug*, Osterende 56 (ⓣ0 48 41/28 85, ⓦwww.osterkrug.de; ❻), also with a fine restaurant; and *Theodor Storm*, Neustadt 60 (ⓣ0 48 41/8 96 60, ⓦwww.theodor-storm-hotel.de; ❻), which has a restaurant serving hot and cold buffets every day, plus its own Hausbrauerei. Top of the range is *Altes Gymnasium*, which occupies a historic school building at Süderstr. 6 (ⓣ0 48 41/83 30, ⓦwww.altes-gymnasium.de; ❽–❾) and has wonderful bathing facilities plus two prestigious restaurants, *Wintergarten* and *Eucken*. Husum's **youth hostel** is at the far northwestern end of town at Schöbuller Str. 34 (ⓣ0 48 41/27 14; €14.50/17.20), while the **campsite** is right by the beach to the west of the centre at Dockkoog (ⓣ0 48 41/6 19 11, ⓦwww.husum-camping.de). The best **restaurants** are in the hotels; a good alternative is *Dragseth's Gasthof* at Zingel 11, a sixteenth-century house with a small gallery and teashop, offering a selection of food including vegetarian dishes.

Helgoland (Heligoland)

There are no fewer than seventeen possible starting-points for a trip to Germany's most isolated corner, the red limestone island of **Helgoland**, which is about a square kilometre in area and stands isolated in the North Sea, 70km from the mouth of the Elbe. From the west coast of Schleswig-Holstein, there are sailings from Husum, among others; alternative places to catch a boat include Hamburg, Bremen, Bremerhaven and the Lower Saxon ports of Cuxhaven and Wilhelmshaven. Between April and October, there are daily **departures** from many of these harbours, but the frequency of service falls sharply during the winter months, when the only regular service is from Cuxhaven. Period returns cost €28–38, day trips €26–32; the snag with the latter is that they only allow three or four hours on the island – roughly the same time as it takes to get there. However, Reederei Warrings (ⓣ9 44 64/9 49 50, ⓦwww.reederei-warrings.de) runs a daily summer catamaran service from Bremen (€50 return) at 8am, with the MS Speedy. This always halts in Bremerhaven (€42 return), and on the days designated for the direct passage (not all sailings from Bremerhaven are direct) it only takes ninety minutes to reach Helgoland from here, allowing a halt of five-and-a-half-hours before the return journey. On other days, the timetabled halt is just three hours, and the journey itself correspondingly longer.

Once an important naval base and coaling station, Helgoland was long occupied by the British, and only came into German hands in 1890, when it was swapped for Zanzibar. Bombarded during World War II, its inhabitants were forcibly evacuated in 1947, and the remaining fortifications were blown up. For five years it served as a bombing target for the RAF, until finally returned to Germany in 1952. Reconstruction began immediately and Helgoland has become a popular holiday resort with all the usual facilities, plus the added advantage of **duty-free** status, which, due to a legal loophole, still exists here, despite its abolition throughout the EU. This is undoubtedly the main reason it attracts so many visitors, though the presence of dramatic craggy **cliffs** mean that it is scenically far superior to any of Germany's other North Sea islands. There's also a setpiece attraction in the **Aquarium Biologische Anstalt** (April–Sept Mon–Fri 10am–5pm, Sat & Sun 1–4pm; €2.60) on Kurpromenade, which is devoted to the fish and plant life of the North Sea.

If you decide you would like to stay over, it would be advisable to contact the **tourist office** (May–Sept Mon–Fri 9am–5pm, Sat & Sun 11.30am–5pm, reduced hours out of season; ⓣ0 47 25/81 37 11, ⓦwww.helgoland.de) at Lung Wai 28 in advance to arrange accommodation. Alternatively, you could book directly with the **youth hostel** (ⓣ0 47 25/3 41; €14/16.70), which is open from April to October and situated only a shortish walk from the harbour, or with one of the **hotels**. There are several classy establishments, usually with fine fish and seafood **restaurants** attached; these include *Helgoland-Schwan*, Am Südstrand 16 (ⓣ0 47 25/8 15 30, ⓦwww.helgoland-schwan.de; ❻); *Seehotel*, Lung Wai 23 (ⓣ0 47 25/8 13 10; ❻); and *Atoll*, Lung Wai 27 (ⓣ0 47 25/80 00, ⓦwww.atoll.de; ❼–❾).

Travel details

Trains

Hamburg to: Flensburg (every 2hr; 1hr 45min); Husum (hourly; 2hr); Kiel (hourly; 1hr 15min); Lübeck (hourly; 40min); Rendsburg (every 2hr; 1hr 10min); Schleswig (every 2hr; 1hr 30min).

Kiel to: Eutin (hourly; 35min); Flensburg (hourly; 1hr 10min); Husum (hourly; 1hr 30min); Lübeck (hourly; 1hr 10min); Rendsburg (hourly; 30min); Schleswig (hourly; 50min).

8

Mecklenburg-Lower Pomerania

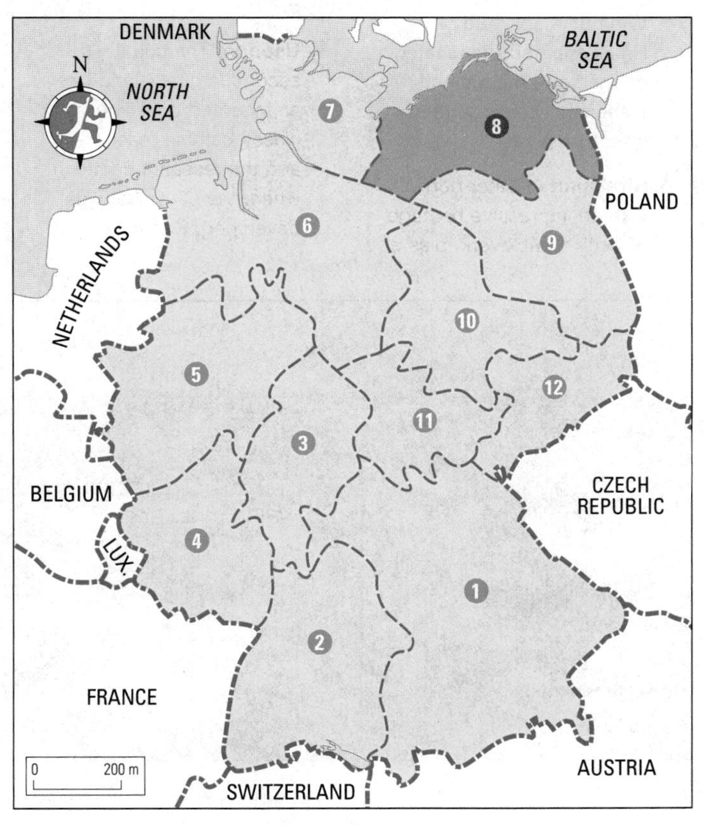

CHAPTER 8

Highlights

* **Schwerin** The state capital is a lakeside city with grand nineteenth-century buildings and a proud cultural tradition. See p.713
* **Güstrow** Another old courtly town, with a fine setting in the heart of the Mecklenburg Lake District. See p.719
* **Wismar** A splendid old Hanseatic port, dominated by medieval monuments of a seemingly exaggerated size. See p.720
* **Stralsund** Another port with an impressive heritage of Gothic brickwork, plus a causeway link to Rügen. See p.728
* **Rügen** Dramatic chalk cliffs, windswept headlands, a planned town, fine beaches and a narrow-gauge railway are just some of the attractions of Germany's biggest and most beautiful island. See p.731
* **Usedom** The country's second largest island has an indented coastline, classy bathing resorts – and the research centre where the V2 rocket was developed. See p.741

△ View over Stralsund towards Rügen

8

Mecklenburg-Lower Pomerania

Mecklenburg-Lower Pomerania (Mecklenburg-Vorpommern) is eastern Germany's maritime province. The tideless Baltic Sea laps at the 370-km-long coastline, while the rivers Elbe and Oder form natural borders to the west and east; to the south is a spacious lakeland which is the most thinly populated part of Germany. The Land is something of a compromise creation, most of its territory once belonging to two separate grand duchies; the remainder is the German rump (not deemed to be viable as a Land in its own right) of the ancient and much-disputed province of Pomerania, the greater part of which was ceded to Poland in 1945.

From **Wismar**, the incongruously large-scale medieval town at the western end of the province, the coastal landscape gradually changes from flat indented shores to the windswept dunes behind **Rostock**, the chief port and largest city. Further east, within the surviving German part of Pomerania, is **Stralsund**, whose grand Hanseatic buildings look across a narrow channel to **Rügen**, Germany's largest island, characterized by battered headlands and chalky cliffs rising steeply from the sea. Beyond here, the coast curves southeastwards via the university city of **Greifswald**, the sandy island of **Usedom** and the Polish border. During the summer the coast is overrun by holidaymakers, but for the rest of the year the region returns to a peaceful emptiness.

Inland, the great **Mecklenburg Lake Plateau** tilts gently south, with few major towns disturbing the rural landscape. This, eastern Germany's granary, is a real backwater and has changed relatively little since debt-enslaved peasants worked the land for their aristocratic masters. The GDR era left a surprisingly small mark around here, mainly manifesting itself in the shape of ugly apartment buildings next to villages. The Land capital and former ducal residence of **Schwerin** in the northwest is a grand, predominantly nineteenth-century city which seems disproportionately sophisticated and elegant in such a rustic region. Not far southwest lies **Ludwigslust**, a fascinating planned town which was temporarily the Schwerin dukes' main seat in the eighteenth century. A little further northeast, picturesque **Güstrow**, another former ducal seat, makes an ideal base for exploring the lakes. **Neubrandenburg**, at the eastern edge of the lake district, retains a spectacular medieval defensive system, while nearby **Neustrelitz** is a Baroque town specially built to serve as capital of the smaller of the two Mecklenburg duchies.

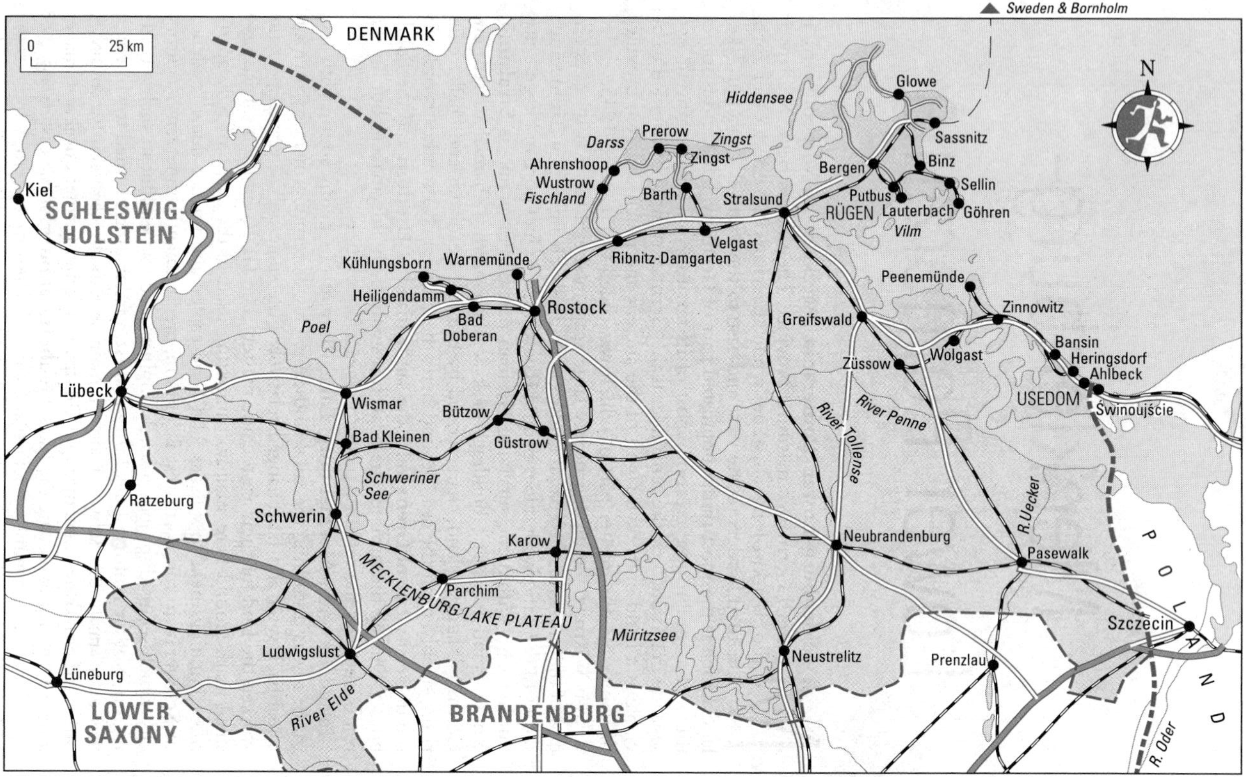

Sweden & Bornholm
DENMARK
0 25 km
N
Kiel
SCHLESWIG-HOLSTEIN
Hiddensee
Glowe
Sassnitz
Binz
Sellin
Göhren
Bergen
Putbus
Lauterbach
RÜGEN
Vilm
Darss
Prerow
Zingst
Zingst
Ahrenshoop
Wustrow
Fischland
Barth
Stralsund
Velgast
Ribnitz-Damgarten
Kühlungsborn
Warnemünde
Heiligendamm
Bad Doberan
Rostock
Poel
Peenemünde
Zinnowitz
Greifswald
Bansin
Heringsdorf
Ahlbeck
Wolgast
Züssow
USEDOM
Świnoujście
Lübeck
Wismar
Bützow
Bad Kleinen
Güstrow
River Penne
River Tollense
Schweriner See
Ratzeburg
Schwerin
R. Uecker
Karow
Neubrandenburg
Pasewalk
POLAND
MECKLENBURG LAKE PLATEAU
Parchim
Szczecin
Müritzsee
Ludwigslust
Neustrelitz
Prenzlau
Lüneburg
LOWER SAXONY
River Elde
BRANDENBURG
R. Oder

Schwerin

SCHWERIN, situated amid a chain of lakes 65km east of Lübeck, was the winner of the tussle to become capital of Mecklenburg-Lower Pomerania. Revelling in its role, it has become one of the ex-GDR's most go-ahead cities, and is undoubtedly among the most rewarding to visit, helped enormously by the fact that it is relatively unencumbered with Communist-era eyesores. Founded in 1160 by Henry the Lion, Schwerin is the oldest town in the province, though little remains of its early heritage. Its glory period began in 1837, when Grand Duke Paul Friedrich of Mecklenburg-Schwerin decided to demote Ludwigslust to a secondary residence and to reinstate his dynasty's original base as the main seat of his court. This led to the creation of a monumental nineteenth-century city with a vibrant cultural life, which has been of significance ever since.

Arrival, information and accommodation

Schwerin's **Hauptbahnhof** is in the Paulusstadt, a ten-minute walk from the Altstadt where you'll find the **tourist office**, at Am Markt 10 (April–Sept Mon–Fri 9am–7pm, Sat & Sun 10am–6pm; Nov–March Mon–Fri 10am–6pm, Sat & Sun 10am–4pm; ⓣ03 85/5 92 52 12, ⓦwww.schwerin-tourist.de). There are plenty of **hotels** in town, including several highly imaginative conversions of old buildings, and it's also worth considering staying in the suburbs, where there are a number of enticing establishments in attractive surroundings. Otherwise, **private rooms** (❷–❸) are available via the tourist office. The **youth hostel** is in a lakeside setting at Waldschulweg 3 (ⓣ03 85/3 26 00 06; €14.50/17.50); it's near the terminus of bus #14, though a pleasanter means of access is to take the ferry to the jetty at Zippendorf (see "The Schweriner See", p.716), from where it's only a few minutes' walk northwards. Along the banks of the Schweriner See are a number of **campsites**, the most convenient being *Seehof* (ⓣ03 85/51 25 40; bus #8) in the village of the same name just north of the city.

Hotels

Alt Schweriner Schankstuben Schlachtermarkt 9 ⓣ03 85/59 25 30, ⓦwww.alt-schweriner-schankstuben.de. Traditional Altstadt hotel with wine bar-restaurant. ❺.

Altstadthotel Ritters Reichshof Grunthalplatz 15–17 ⓣ & ⓕ03 85/56 57 98. Pleasant, recently refurbished and reasonably priced hotel in a late nineteenth-century building immediately opposite the Hauptbahnhof. ❹

An den Linden Franz-Mehring-Str. 26 ⓣ03 85/51 20 84, ⓕ51 22 81. Fine medium-range hotel in a late Neoclassical building; its facilities include a sauna and a winter garden. ❻

Niederländischer Hof Karl-Marx-Str. 12–13 ⓣ03 85/59 11 00, ⓦwww.niederlaendischer-hof.de. A grand hotel and restaurant on the west side of the Pfaffenteich, stylishly furnished throughout. ❼

Seehotel Frankenhorst Frankenhorst 5, Wickendorf ⓣ03 85/55 50 71, ⓦwww.erlebnis-schwerin.de. Located in a lovely landscaped park at the northern tip of the Ziegelsee, in the far north of the city. The restaurant, *Bootshaus*, has a winter garden and terrace overlooking the lake. ❼

Strand-Hotel Am Strand 13, Zippendorf ⓣ03 85/20 83 80, ⓕ2 00 22 02. Hotel with café-restaurant named after the small beach it overlooks. ❹

Wöhler Puschkinstr. 26 ⓣ03 85/55 58 30, ⓦwww.woehler-weinhaus.de. Historic hotel with wine bar-restaurant. ❻

Zur Guten Quelle Schusterstr. 12 ⓣ03 85/56 59 85, ⓕ56 59 85. Small hotel with restaurant in a half-timbered building in the heart of the city. ❺

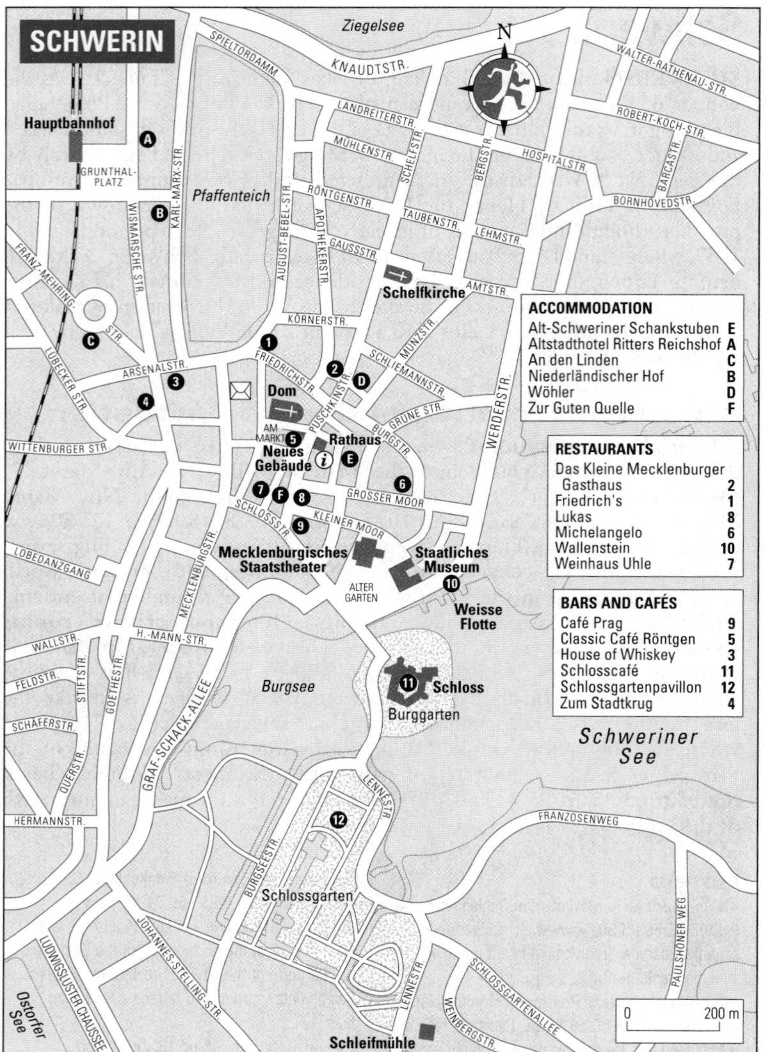

The City

Water is an omnipresent feature of Schwerin: the city is built around no fewer than ten lakes (the largest being the **Schweriner See** to the east), while the constituent parts of the centre – the **Altstadt**, the Baroque **Schelfstadt**, and the nineteenth-century **Paulusstadt** – each border a different side of the pond known as the **Pfaffenteich**. Although there's a concentration of sights in the city centre, you'll need to stay at least two days to cover everything, as there are several worthwhile attractions on the outskirts.

The centre

The only significant medieval building left in Schwerin is the **Dom**, whose massive bulk rises high above the rest of the centre. It was one of four cathedrals founded by Henry the Lion, but, unlike the others, was completely rebuilt a century later in Gothic style. The **tower** (Mon–Fri 11am–noon & 2–3pm, Sat 11am–noon & 2–4pm, Sun noon–3pm; €1) gives a fine view over the city. Inside, the most remarkable furnishing is the gilded fifteenth-century **triumphal cross**, a work of enormous poignancy and pathos brought here after the war from the destroyed Marienkirche in Wismar. It rather overshadows the beautiful but undersized **high altar** below, carved later the same century in a Lübeck workshop. In the north transept are some splendid brasses in honour of fourteenth-century bishops, while a varied range of **funerary monuments** to aristocrats can be seen in the ambulatory and its chapels. Particularly outstanding are those to Helena von der Pfalz by the great Nürnberg bronze-founder Peter Vischer, and to Duke Christopher of Mecklenburg and his consort Elizabeth of Sweden.

To the rear of the Dom is the **Markt**, the hub of the city's commercial life. On its eastern side, the mock-Tudor facade of the **Rathaus** is typical of the city's nineteenth-century architecture. The altogether grander **Neues Gebäude** on the north side, an imperious Neoclassical building with a columned portico, is now a café. Most of the rest of the Altstadt is a pedestrianized shopping centre with a fair number of surviving half-timbered houses.

The far more atmospheric **Schelfstadt** immediately to the northeast was founded at the beginning of the eighteenth century but not integrated into Schwerin until well over a hundred years later; it has street after street of old houses, and is a good place for strolling at leisure. At the heart of the quarter is the **Schelfkirche**, a Baroque parish church with a strikingly emphatic cruciform design, including entrance portals on each wing. Across the Pfaffenteich are the straight-laced buildings of the **Paulusstadt**, the most notable being the huge **Arsenal**, which again mimics the architectural tastes of Tudor England.

The Staatliches Museum

On the spacious square named Alter Garten, southeast of the Markt, stands the stern Neoclassical premises of Schwerin's pride and joy, the **Staatliches Museum** (Tues 10am–8pm, Wed–Sun 10am–5/6pm; €3, or €6 including temporary exhibitions; Ⓦwww.museum-schwerin.de). One of Germany's most engaging art galleries, it's informed by the tastes of the local ducal family which was responsible for most of the acquisitions. The displays on the main floor begin with a section on early German painting, including official portraits by **Cranach** of Luther and his wife Katharina von Bora and of King Ferdinand, the brother and successor of Emperor Charles V. However, most of the rest of the floor space is given over to a marvellous array of works illustrating the full diversity of the art of seventeenth-century Holland. **Hals** is represented by an enchanting pair of roundels of laughing boys, while there are several examples of the highly polished genre scenes of Rembrandt's collaborator **Gerrit Dou**, plus a rare masterpiece, *The Guard*, by his most talented pupil, the short-lived **Carel Fabritius**. Another painter who died very young, the animal specialist **Paulus Potter**, is represented by some of his best works, notably *The Milkmaid*. **Ter Brugghen**'s *St Peter Liberated from Prison* ranks as one of the finest examples of Dutch Tenebrism. One gallery is devoted to still-life specialists, including a number of canvases by the Haarlem artist **Jan de Heem**. Equally fascinating are the compositions of the little-known **Otto**

Marseus van Schrick, which typically feature reptiles or butterflies among the flowers and fruit.

There's also a fine array of seventeenth-century Flemish painting, including two examples of **Rubens** – *Lot and His Daughters* and *Pan and Syrinx*, the latter being a colloboration with **Jan Breughel**. The museum has copious holdings of the works of **Jean-Baptiste Oudry**, court painter to King Louis XV of France; these include several of his familiar hunting scenes and trophies, though the keenly observed animal studies, such as *The Antelope* and *The Leopard*, make a more lasting impression. There's also a magnificent full-length portrait of a British queen, the former Princess Charlotte of Mecklenburg-Strelitz, by **Gainsborough**. The nineteenth-century section includes a *Winter Landscape* by **Friedrich** and canvases by Liebermann, Corinth and Franz von Stuck. A large group of works by the Frenchman **Marcel Duchamp** forms the centrepiece of the displays of twentieth-century art; another highlight is the roomful of sculptures by **Barlach**.

The Schloss and its gardens

A few paces south of the museum, a bridge leads over to Schwerin's vast neo-Renaissance **Schloss** (Tues–Sun 10am–5/6pm; €4; Ⓦwww.schloss-schwerin.de), which occupies the site of Henry the Lion's original castle, an island in the Schweriner See. Gloriously over the top, it was modelled on the famous château of Chambord in France's Loire valley. Plans were originally drawn up by the Dresden architect Gottfried Semper, though only the main tower was built according to his plans. The rest is the work of two pupils of Schinkel, Georg Adolph Demmler and Friedrich August Stüler, who between them were responsible for most of Schwerin's showpiece nineteenth-century buildings. A rare survivor of the previous building is the Renaissance nave of the **Schlosskapelle**; the pulpit and alabaster reliefs inside likewise date from the sixteenth century. On the first floor, highlights are the wood-panelled **Speisezimmer** and the circular **Teezimmer** next door, with its ornate white stuccowork. Upstairs, the **Ahnengalerie** is hung with (mostly imaginary) portraits of all the Mecklenburg dukes, while the gilded **Thronsaal**, like the Schloss itself, is of a scale and splendour more appropriate for a powerful kingdom than a tiny duchy. There's also a gallery devoted to local painters, of whom the most notable are **Carl Malchin**, with his evocative nineteenth-century landscapes, and **Erich Venzmer**, who specialized in stark views of sodden Mecklenburg flatlands. Other parts of the building are used by the state parliament of Mecklenburg-Lower Pomerania.

The remainder of the island is occupied by the **Burggarten**, a fine example of nineteenth-century landscape gardening. It makes a fascinating comparison with the much larger **Schlossgarten** to the south, which is in the formal Baroque style, and features a set of statues (now replaced by copies) of Classical gods by the great sculptor of Baroque Dresden, Balthasar Permoser. At the far end, about fifteen minutes' walk from the Schloss, is the **Schleifmühle** (April–Nov Fri–Sun 10am–5pm; €2), a half-timbered water mill, the only one of its kind in Europe still in full working order. It dates back to 1705 but was rebuilt fifty years later for grinding down the precious stones needed to make the furnishings for the Mecklenburg palaces. The actual process, which is painfully slow but highly effective, is demonstrated to visitors.

The Schweriner See

No trip to Schwerin is complete without a cruise on the **Schweriner See**: this is *the* way of seeing the city's skyline to best effect. One-hour **boat trips**, run by Weisse Flotte Schwerin (daily April–Oct; €7; Ⓣ03 85/55 77 70,

Ⓦ www.weisse-flotte-schwerin.de), depart from the jetty on the north side of the Schloss, leaving every half an hour at the height of summer. A good alternative is the ferry service which runs back and forth from May to October down the lake to the beach at **Zippendorf** (€3) and the idyllic island nature reserve of **Kaninchenwerder** (€5).

Set back from the lake at Crivitzer Landstr. 13 in the suburb of Muess, a twenty-minute walk east of Zippendorf, is the **Mecklenburgisches Volkskundemuseum** (May–Oct Tues–Sun 10am–6pm; €2), an open-air museum featuring eighteenth- and nineteenth-century buildings brought here from all over rural Mecklenburg.

Eating, drinking and entertainment

The centre of Schwerin is well endowed with good **cafés** and **restaurants**, while the city has kept up a distinguished tradition in the performing arts since the nineteenth century. Drama, opera and concerts are staged in the main **theatre**, the Neoclassical Mecklenburgisches Staatstheater, opposite the Staatliches Museum at Alter Garten (Ⓣ 03 85/5 30 01 23, Ⓦ www.theater-schwerin.de). In summer, the courtyard of the Schloss is used for the open-air performances of the Schlossfestspiele.

Restaurants

Das Kleine Mecklenburger Gasthaus Puschkinstr. 37. Serves high-quality local dishes at reasonable prices.

Lukas Grosser Moor 5. The main fish specialist.

Friedrich's Friedrichstr. 2. Pleasant restaurant in a villa at the southeastern edge of the Pfaffenteich.

Michelangelo Grosser Moor 36. The city's leading Italian restaurant.

Wallenstein Werderstr. 140. This café-restaurant with terrace is located right alongside the jetty of the Weisse Flotte cruise boats, and offers good lakeside views.

Weinhaus Uhle Schusterstr. 15. A superemely elegant wine bar housed in fine Rococo premises; it's attached to a wine merchant's shop which has been in business since 1751.

Cafés and bars

Café Prag Schlossstr. 17. As its name suggests, this is a café in the Central European style. As well as cakes and pastries, it also serves light meals.

Classic Café Röntgen Neues Gebäude, Markt. Although a newcomer, this is a very traditional café, located in the Neues Gebäude, with outside seating in summer.

House of Whiskey Arsenalstr. 14. This evenings-only bar has over 100 kinds of Scottish and Irish whisk(e)y, as well as eight beers on tap; it also serves snacks and meals, and often features live music.

Schlosscafé Lennéstr. 1. Good place for *Kaffee und Kuchen*, located in the Schloss itself.

Schlossgartenpavillon Am Kreuzkanal. Café in the grounds of the Schloss.

Zum Stadtkrug Wismarsche Str. 126. This Hausbrauerei brews light and dark beers, and serves hearty traditional fare.

Ludwigslust

LUDWIGSLUST, 35km south of Schwerin, was founded in 1756 on the site of a hunting lodge as the residence of the local dukes, remaining as such until 1837, when the court moved back to the original capital. In accordance with the taste of the time, it's a planned town with a generous complement of green spaces, and – as it remains almost completely intact – it makes a fascinating contrast with Neustrelitz, its direct counterpart in the other former Mecklenburg duchy. The story of the construction of Ludwigslust is dogged by a yawning gap between the ambition of its rulers and the finances available to them. This meant that all kinds of cost-cutting measures were adopted, the most immediately obvious being the use of plain, ordinary bricks for the construction of almost all the buildings.

The outsized **Schloss** (Tues–Sun 10am–5/6pm; €3; ⓦwww.schloss-ludwigslust.de) in the heart of the town provides the clearest evidence of the crafty measures taken to skimp on money. Outwardly, it looks very imposing indeed, its show frontage revealing the first stirrings of Neoclassicism while retaining the full pomp of late Baroque. However, the resplendent stonework is a facade in both senses of the word, masking the brickwork from which the palace is actually built. An even cleverer trick is played in the **Goldener Saal**, the main reception hall of the interior. Glittering with mirrors and gilt, and adorned with golden vases, columns and figures of cherubs, it makes a stunning setting for concerts. Almost everything, however, is fashioned from a form of papier-mâché known as *Ludwigsluster Carton*, which was specially developed here to produce such trompe l'oeil effects. The rest of the interior, which served as the home of the deposed ducal family until 1945, has recently been restored and refurnished in period style. A particular highlight is a group of animal and hunting paintings by Jean-Baptiste Oudry, from the collection of the Staatliches Museum in Schwerin.

To the north and west stretches the enormous **Schlosspark**, a masterly exercise in English-style landscaping by the ubiquitous Peter Joseph Lenné. Its varied delights include a canal, fountains, cascades, a beautiful stone bridge, two Neoclassical mausolea, a neo-Gothic chapel, a grotto, and a bizarre funeral monument to a horse.

South of the Schloss is a large oval-shaped green, down the sides of which are the modest little cottages built for the estate workers. More greenery separates the axial road from the second main focal point of the town, the **Stadtkirche** (Tues-Sat 11am-3/4pm, Sun 11am-noon & 3-4pm). Designed, like the Schloss and most of the rest of Ludwigslust, by the local architect Johann Joachim Busch, it ranks as one of the most distinctive and unexpected Protestant churches in Germany. The monumental facade is like a great classical Roman temple, though the rest of the exterior is completely plain. Inside, everything is pure theatre, from the ornate ducal loft at one end to the vast mural of *The Adoration of the Shepherds* at the other. In the latter, the church's organ, most of which is hidden from view, appears to be played by one of the angels in the heavenly apparition above.

Practicalities

Ludwigslust's **Bahnhof**, which is on the main line between Schwerin and Stendal in Saxony-Anhalt, lies at the far northern end of town, a fifteen-minute walk from the centre. The **tourist office** (Mon–Fri 10am–12.30pm & 1.30–4pm; ⓣ0 38 74/5 26 25, ⓦwww.stadtludwigslust.de) is at Schlossstr. 36. Here you can book **private rooms** (❷–❸), which are in reasonable supply and noticeably cheaper than in Schwerin. There are also several small **pensions**, including *Schwarzenberg*, Am Seminargarten 4 (ⓣ0 38 74/2 24 38; ❸). Between the Bahnhof and the centre are three good **hotels**: *Landhaus Knöfel*, Kanalstr. 19 (ⓣ0 38 74/2 20 15, ⓦwww.landhaus-knoefel.m-vp.de; ❹); *Stadt Hamburg*, Letzte Str. 4–6 (ⓣ0 38 74/41 50, ⓦwww.hotel-stadt-hamburg-lulust.de; ❹); and *Erbprinz*, Schweriner Str. 38 (ⓣ0 38 74/2 50 40, ⓦwww.hotel-erbprinz.m-vp.de; ❻). In the heart of town, occupying a ritzy mansion at Schlossstr. 15, *Landhotel de Weimar* (ⓣ0 38 74/41 80, ⓦwww.landhotel-de-weimar.de; ❻) is the best and most expensive of the lot. All of these hotels have recommendable **restaurants**.

Güstrow

About 60km northeast of Schwerin lies **GÜSTROW**, formerly the capital of one of the Mecklenburg duchies, which was for a short time ruled by the mercurial and inscrutable military genius Alfred von Wallenstein, supreme commander of the imperial forces in the Thirty Years' War. When the ruling house died out in 1695, however, the town was reduced to the status of a second-string residence of the dukes of Mecklenburg-Schwerin, and has remained pretty provincial ever since, a fact that enabled it to escape the attentions of wartime bombers. Before the war it was the home and workplace of **Ernst Barlach**, the greatest German sculptor of the twentieth century, and it retains important collections of his work. Güstrow's other highlight is the gorgeous surrounding countryside, with easy access to lakes such as the Inselsee and Sumpfsee on the outskirts of the town, and the much larger Krakower See to the south.

The Town

The largely pedestrianized **Altstadt** is still the heart of the modern town. Its predominantly eighteenth- and nineteenth-century buildings retain many original features such as brass shop signs and elaborately carved doors. In the central Markt, the secular and the sacred, in the shape of the Baroque **Rathaus** and Gothic **Pfarrkirche**, are given equal billing. The church contains a marvellous array of furnishings, dominated by a magnificent early sixteenth-century high altar made in Brussels. When open, it shows delicately carved and polychromed oak scenes of the Passion by the sculptor Jan Borman; when closed, the brightly coloured paintings of the life of the Virgin by Barent van Orley, court painter to the Habsburgs, are on view.

A couple of blocks away, at the southern end of the Altstadt, is the huge sixteenth-century **Schloss** (Tues–Sun 9am–5pm; €3; Ⓦwww.schloss-guestrow.de). From the outside, it's one of the most impressive Renaissance palaces anywhere in Germany, providing a classic example of how Italianate forms could be ever so subtly modelled to suit more northerly climes. Unfortunately, it fell into disrepair on the demise of the local duchy, and was only regularly used again in 1811 when Napoleon's troops set up a field hospital here on their way to Russia. The Nazis transformed it into a prison, destroying much of what was left of the furniture and decor. Nonetheless, some fine original interiors remain, notably in the south wing. It also has on long-term loan from the Staatliches Museum in Schwerin a number of German, Italian, Dutch and Flemish paintings of the sixteenth and seventeenth centuries, the most memorable being *The Unicorn* by the Antwerp artist Marten de Vos.

Unassumingly located at the southwestern corner of the Altstadt is the **Dom** (Ⓦwww.dom-guestrow.de), another brick Gothic church which was first a collegiate foundation, then the court chapel, rather than the cathedral its name would suggest. The architecture is almost totally overshadowed by some extraordinary furnishings, which include a gilded high altar by the fifteenth-century Hamburg carver Hinrik Bornemann, and a vibrant series of apostles on the pillars of the nave by the sixteenth-century Lübeck sculptor, Claus Berg. Even more arresting are the Renaissance **funerary monuments** in the choir by the Dutchman Philipp Brandin. Look out in particular for the two largest – to the Dom's founder Heinrich Borwins II, and to the sculptor's patron Duke Ulrich with his two wives – each of which has an elaborate armorial background. In the northern aisle of the nave are three **Barlach sculptures**, including the famous

Flying Angel, which is suspended above an ornate Renaissance grille. The original of this, a memorial to the dead of World War I, was melted down in 1938 as part of the Nazi measures against "degenerate art". Fortunately, a cast had previously been taken, enabling the work to be re-created after the war.

The stature of Ernst Barlach continues to rise, and few would now dispute his right to be regarded among the twentieth century's most significant artists. His bronzes and woodcarvings, borrowing techniques from the medieval and Renaissance German masters, show a warm humanity and a haunting sense of pathos; he also carried his Expressionism over into other media, being a fine graphic artist and an accomplished playwright. There are two museums in Güstrow devoted to him; between them they contain the largest collection of his work in existence. The museum in the **Gertrudenkapelle** (March–Oct Tues–Sun 10am–5pm; Nov–Feb Tues–Sun 11am–4pm; €3, or €5.50 combined ticket with Atelierhaus; Ⓦwww.barlach-stiftung.de) is the obvious destination, particularly if you're pressed for time, as it contains original versions of many of his finest works. It's in a little Gothic chapel set in its own grounds, just over the ring road from the northwestern side of the Altstadt. Barlach's house and workshop, the **Atelierhaus** (same hours; €3, Ⓦwww.barlach-stiftung.de), lies in the narrow strip of land between the Inselsee and the wooded Heidberg, about 4km south of the Altstadt (bus #4). Here you can see the sculptures left unfinished at his death in 1938, along with casts of his other work in a variety of different media.

Practicalities

Güstrow's **Bahnhof**, which has regular services on the lines to Schwerin, Rostock and Neubrandenburg, is five minutes' walk from the northern end of the Altstadt. The **tourist office** is at Domstr. 9 (May–Sept Mon–Fri 9am–6pm, Sat & Sun 9.30am–1pm; rest of year closed Sun; Ⓣ0 38 43/68 10 23, Ⓦwww.guestrow-tourismus.de).

Plenty of **private rooms** (❶–❸) can be booked at the tourist office, while the **youth hostel** is by the Inselsee at Schabernack 70 (Ⓣ0 38 43/84 00 44; €16/19); take bus #204 or #252 to the Schabernack/Inselsee stop. There's a centrally sited **pension**, *Villa Camenz*, Lange Stege 13 (Ⓣ0 38 43/2 45 50, Ⓦwww.villa-camenz.de; ❸), plus several **hotels**: *Rubis*, Schweriner Str. 89 (Ⓣ0 38 43/6 93 80; ❺); *Stadt Güstrow*, Pferdemarkt 58 (Ⓣ0 38 43/78 00; ❺); *Am Güstrower Schloss*, Schlossberg 1 (Ⓣ0 38 43/76 70, Ⓦwww.schlosshotel-guestrow.de; ❻); and *Altstadt*, Baustr. 8–10 (Ⓣ0 38 43/4 65 50, Ⓦwww.nordik-hotels.de; ❻). All these hotels, with the exception of the last-named, have **restaurants**, and they rank among the best in town, though strong competition comes from *Barlach-Stuben*, Plauer Str. 7, which features typical Mecklenburg dishes. Reliable alternatives include the *Ratskeller*, Markt 10, and *Marktkrug*, Markt 14. The best place for *Kaffee und Kuchen* is the long-established *Café Küpper*, Domstr. 15.

Festivals include the Stadtfest in June, the Schlossfest in July, and the Inselseefest on the first weekend of August. The main year-round **cultural** venue is the Ernst-Barlach-Theater on Franz-Parr-Platz (Ⓣ0 38 43/68 41 46).

Wismar

History has not always been kind to **WISMAR**, the first Hanseatic city east of Lübeck, the dominant force in the great trading alliance. It was a rich and influential port during the League's golden age, but after it was taken over by the Swedes in 1648, Wismar was regarded as a vital defensive bulwark against Denmark and turned into a strong fortress. In 1803, it was mortgaged to the Duke of Mecklenburg-Schwerin on a hundred-year lease, but not reclaimed. It has remained a modest-sized town ever since, the monumentality of the Hanseatic buildings in its Altstadt completely out of scale with its modern status. Badly neglected in the GDR epoch, Wismar now takes tourism very seriously indeed, and its beautiful centre deservedly draws plenty of day-trippers from Hamburg, Lübeck and the Baltic resorts.

The Altstadt

The **Altstadt**, set back from the sheltered bay of the Wismarbucht, was quite badly damaged during World War II, though its sense of faded grandeur was, if anything, increased by the fact that key monuments were left as ruins. Since the *Wende*, however, ambitious restoration projects have been initiated, and within a few years the town should look in immaculate shape once more.

The hundred-square-metre **Marktplatz**, one of the largest in Germany, has regained its commercial function since the fall of Communism. Showpiece of the square, though sometimes rather obscured by all the stalls, is the **Wasserkunst**, a domed wrought-iron pavilion in the Dutch Renaissance style which shelters the municipal well, the town's only source of drinking water until 1897. Opposite is a mansion misleadingly known as the **Alter Schwede**: the oldest surviving house in town, dating back to 1380, it's a fine example of the brick Gothic architecture typical of the Baltic. In contrast to the gabled east and south sides of the square, the northern end is dominated by the slate-blue of the Neoclassical **Rathaus**.

Standing forlorn in the middle of the Marienkirchhof, the next square to the west, is the disembodied tower of the **Marienkirche**, the rest of which was destroyed in the war; sadly, this seems to be the one building accepted as being past meaningful restoration. At the square's southeastern corner is the **Archdiakonat**, a fine example of black and red brickwork from the fifteenth century. Kellerstrasse leads west to Wismar's most distinctive building, the **Fürstenhof**, a mid-sixteenth-century palace constructed in a Baltic adaptation of the Italian Renaissance style. It's adorned with beautiful friezes: the lower is of limestone and depicts the Trojan War on the street facade, the story of the Prodigal Son on the courtyard side; the upper is of terracotta and has portrait medallions of personalities of the day intermingled with heroes of the classical world. The magnificent portal bears the coat of arms of the Mecklenburg dukes.

Beyond is the hefty torso of the **Georgenkirche**, Wismar's largest church, a highly decorative example of Gothic brickwork which, in the days of the Hansa, was the place of worship of the craftsmen and tradesfolk. Left as a roofless shell in 1945, it's currently the subject of the town's most ambitious restoration project, scheduled to take several more years. On Lübsche Strasse, a block north of Marktplatz, the **Heiligen-Geist-Spital** (daily 10am–4pm; free), ranks second to Lübeck's as the best-preserved old hospital in Germany. Originally fifteenth-century Gothic, it was partially remodelled a couple of hundred years after in late Renaissance style. The most notable feature from the latter period is the painted wooden ceiling of the church, whose medallions illustrate Old Testament scenes. Look out also for some notable older furnishings, including a pair of processional candelabra and a regal stone group of the Adoration of the Magi.

Further north, the Altstadt is bisected by the **Grube**, the oldest landscaped canal in any German city, which is lined with recently restored buildings. On its southern bank, alongside Schweinsbrücke, the **Schabbellhaus** (May–Oct Tues–Sun 10am–6pm; Nov–April Tues–Sun 10am–5pm; €2, free Fri; Ⓦwww.schabbellhaus.de) is a ritzy mansion in the Dutch Renaissance style, built as the home and workplace of a local brewer and town councillor. It now contains an excellent museum on the history of Wismar, whose most notable exhibit is a gory section on medieval torture, showcasing two shrivelled human hands preserved in a bowl. These came from a murder victim and were used to confront the perpetrator in court – an accusing finger from the grave, so to speak, successfully used to extract a confession. Other, more aesthetic, highlights are the bronze doorknocker from the Georgenkirche, the drinking horn of the wool weavers' guild and the original figures from the Wasserkunst. A small archeology department features the so-called Wismar Horn from 1200 BC.

Directly opposite stands the **Nikolaikirche**, the only one of the three brick Gothic churches to remain intact in 1945. As with Marktplatz, its monumental proportions seem highly exaggerated for this small town: indeed, its dizzying 37-metre-high interior makes it the tallest church in the whole of the former GDR. The lofty sense of space conveyed is undoubtedly the most memorable feature, though there are a few fine works of art, notably in the chapel beside the sacristy, which has a fourteenth-century bronze font and the fifteenth-century retable of the mariners' guild. Just to the northwest is the **Wassertor**, the only one of the five medieval gateways to have survived. It guarded the entrance to the harbour, the **Alter Hafen**, which these days still buzzes with fishing boats.

Practicalities

Wismar lies on the Wismarbucht, a Baltic bay 32km north of Schwerin. The **Hauptbahnhof** is just outside the northeastern confines of the Altstadt, with the **tourist office** (daily 9am–6pm; Ⓣ0 38 41/2 51 30 25, Ⓦwww.wismar.de) located in the Stadthaus, at Am Markt 11. **Private rooms** (❷–❸) are available, and there's a **youth hostel** at Juri-Gagarin-Ring 30a (Ⓣ0 38 41/3 26 80; €16/18.70); take bus #C or #D to the Frauenklinik stop. Among several small **pensions**, the most convenient is *Am Wassertor*, Lohberg 1, (Ⓣ0 38 41/20 02 21, Ⓦwww.seelord.de; ❹). There are several centrally located medium- and upper-range **hotels**, including *Altes Brauhaus*, Lübsche Str. 33 (Ⓣ0 38 41/21 14 16; ❺); *Reingard*, Weberstr. 18 (Ⓣ0 38 41/28 49 72; ❻); *Alter Speicher*, Bohrstr. 12 (Ⓣ0 38 41/21 17 46, Ⓦwww.hotel-alter-speicher.de; ❻); and *Stadt Hamburg*, Am Markt 24–25 (Ⓣ0 38 41/23 90, Ⓦwww.wismar.steigenberger.de; ❼). All of these hotels have excellent **restaurants**, as does *Am Wassertor* pension, which is actually an adjunct to the fish specialist *Seelord*. Other places to eat and drink include *Alter Schwede*, Am Markt 22, which offers Swedish as well as German cuisine; the historic *Zum Weinberg*, Hinter dem Rathaus 3; and the fish restaurant *Seehase*, Altböterstr. 6. A good choice for *Kaffee und Kuchen* is *Caféhaus 15*, Lübsche Str. 15, while *Brauhaus am Lohberg*, Kleine Hohe Str.15, is a Hausbrauerei.

Bad Doberan and the beach resorts

Between Wismar and Rostock lie a number of holiday resorts, which have recently reclaimed the prestigious status they held before the GDR brought them firmly downmarket. Prominent among these, and an excellent touring base for the whole region, is the spa town of **Bad Doberan**, 50km northeast of Wismar and 17km west of Rostock. It now forms a joint municipality with nearby **Heiligendamm**, the oldest seaside resort in Germany, while just to the west is an even bigger beachcomber's paradise, **Kühlungsborn**. An added attraction is that the three towns are linked by one of eastern Germany's celebrated narrow-gauge rail lines.

Bad Doberan

BAD DOBERAN, the one-time summer residence of the Grand Dukes of Mecklenburg-Schwerin, began life as an adjunct to one of the country's most powerful Cistercian monasteries. Of this, the **Münster** (Ⓦwww.doberanermuenster.de), the former monastic church, still survives at the eastern edge of the centre. It incorporates a fragment of the original Romanesque building, but is otherwise a peerless example of the brick Gothic architecture characteristic of the Baltic lands. Although the graceful pillars and vaulting provide the most imposing features of the interior, there are a number of impressive adornments, including the winged fourteenth-century high altar and the tall tabernacle. Just to the northeast of the church is a curious octagonal structure in a similar style; known as the **Beinhaus**, it used to serve as an ossuary.

To the west, the **Kamp**, formerly a common, was transformed into an English-style park when Doberan came into favour with the Schwerin court. On the east side of August-Bebel-Strasse, which bisects the park from north to south, are a number of grand Empire buildings from the same period, among them the ducal **Palais**, which has been converted into a hotel (see below). Amid the greenery to the west are two whimsical garden pavilions in the Chinese style: the smaller **Roter Pavillon** is a commercial art gallery, while the larger **Weisser Pavillon** is a café. Northwest of here lies **Goethestrasse**, a street of eighteenth- and nineteenth-century mansions. The **Molli**, the narrow-gauge railway linking Bad Doberan with the two coastal resorts (hourly service in summer, reduced out of season; one-way ticket €3; Ⓦwww.molli-bahn.de), begins its fifteen-kilometre journey by running right along the middle of this street before chugging through a forest nature reserve towards the nearby beaches.

Bad Doberan's **Bahnhof** is located at the southern end of the town centre. The **tourist office** (May–Sept Mon–Fri 9am–6pm, Sat 9.30am–1pm; Oct–April Mon–Fri 9am–4pm; Ⓣ03 82 03/6 21 54, Ⓦwww.bad-doberan.de) at Alexandrinenplatz 2 has plenty of **private rooms** (❶–❸) on its books. The **youth hostel** is on the western side of town at Am Tempelberg (Ⓣ03 82 03/6 24 39; €12.50/15.50). There are also several **pensions**, including *Am Fuchsberg*, Am Fuchsberg 7 (Ⓣ03 82 03/6 34 74, Ⓦwww.pensionamfuchsberg.de; ❹), but only two **hotels**, *City*, Alesandrinenplatz 4 (Ⓣ03 82 03/74 74 00; ❺), and *Friedrich-Franz Palais*, August-Bebel-Str. 2 (Ⓣ03 82 03/6 30 36, Ⓦwww.friedrich-franz-palais.de; ❼). The latter has the best **restaurant** in town, though the *Ratskeller*, Am Kamp 3, is a reliable and cheaper alternative.

Heiligendamm and Kühlungsborn

The first main stop on the narrow-gauge railway is **HEILIGENDAMM**, a grand remnant of Germany's aristocratic past. Founded in 1793 by Duke Friedrich Franz I, this was the first place in Germany where the well-heeled came to enjoy the newly fashionable pastime of swimming in the sea.

Throughout the GDR period, its palatial white buildings served as holiday homes for manual workers. However, over the past few years the former Kurhaus and five adjacent historic structures at the heart of the resort have been lavishly renovated as the *Kempinski Grand* (Ⓣ03 82 03/74 00, Ⓦwww.kempinski-heiligendamm.de; ❾), now one of the most exclusive **hotels** on the entire Baltic coast.

For a bit more life and bustle, continue to the Molli's terminus of **KÜHLUNGSBORN**, one of the Baltic's largest holiday resorts. Here there are dozens of **hotels**, particularly along the seafront. Many are in elegant Wilhelmine and Jugendstil buildings; among the most attractive are *Poseidon*, Hermannstr. 6 (Ⓣ03 82 93/71 82; ❺); *Villa Patricia*, Ostseeallee 2 (Ⓣ03 82 93/85 40, Ⓦwww.all-in-all.com/patricia; ❻); *Westfalia*, Ostseeallee 17 (Ⓣ03 82 93/1 21 95, Ⓦwww.westfalia-kuehlungsborn.de; ❼); and *Neptun*, Strandstr. 37 (Ⓣ03 82 93/6 30; ❼). The **youth hostel** is at Dünenstr. 4 (Ⓣ03 82 93/1 72 70; €14.50/17.50). Further information about accommodation can be had from the **tourist office**, Ostseeallee. 19 (Ⓣ03 82 93/84 90, Ⓦwww.kuehlungsborn.de).

Rostock

ROSTOCK, the German Baltic's main port and Mecklenburg-Lower Pomerania's largest city, is situated on the broad estuary of the River Warnow. It presents an intriguing architectural mix – medieval and 1950s architecture in the centre, nineteenth-century villas in the inner suburb of Steintor-Vorstadt, quaint fishermen's houses and grand hotels in the seaside suburb of Warnemünde, and modern housing estates elsewhere. The city has had a tough time coming to terms with the consequences of German unification, which brought to a speedy end its postwar role as the shipbuilding metropolis of the Communist bloc, resulting in mass unemployment.

Arrival, information and accommodation

Rostock's **Hauptbahnhof** is situated well to the south of the Altstadt, but from its underground terminal trams #2, #5 and #6 run to the city centre. **Ferries** (plus catamarans and jetfoils) dock at the **Überseehafen** on the right bank of the Warnow by the S-Bahn terminus Seehafen-Nord, and at the **Fährhafen** beside Warnemünde's Bahnhof. There are international services to and from Trelleborg in Sweden, Gedser in Denmark, Helsinki in Finland and Tallinn in Estonia. Harbour **cruises** are run by several competing companies from Alter Strom in Warnemünde and from the Stadthafen on the west side of the city centre.

The main **tourist office** (Mon–Fri 10am–6pm, Sat & Sun 10am–3pm; Ⓣ03 81/1 94 33 or 3 81 22 22, Ⓦwww.rostock.de) is at Neuer Markt 3. There's another in Warnemünde at Am Strom 59 (May–Aug Mon–Fri 10am–7pm, Sat & Sun 10am–4pm; Sept–April Mon–Fri 10am–6pm, Sat & Sun 11am–4pm; Ⓣ03 81/03 81/54 80 00). Both sell the **RostockCard** (€8, valid 48hr), which covers all public transportation costs within the city boundaries and gives discounts at museums, leisure facilities and restaurants.

Accommodation in **private homes** (❶–❹) is plentiful in Warnemünde and the coastal villages between Rostock and Bad Doberan, but the tourist office also has some city-centre rooms on its books. There's a **youth hostel** in a moored former merchant navy vessel, the *Traditionsschiff* (Ⓣ03 81/6 70 03 20;

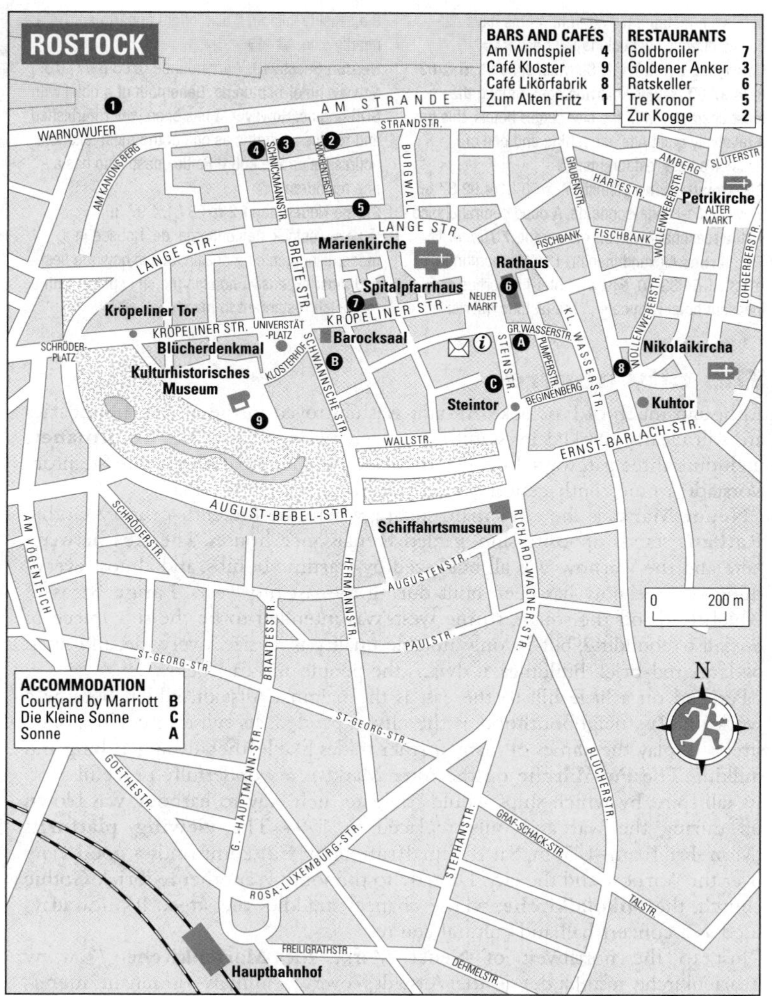

€17/20), in the suburb of Schmarl; take the S-Bahn to Lütten-Klein, from where it's a twenty-minute walk. Another is at Parkstr. 46 (ⓣ03 81/54 81 70; €19.50/23.50) in Warnemünde. Most **hotels** in the city centre are geared to business visitors and priced accordingly, so it's Warnemünde, which has plenty of seaside pensions, that is an altogether happier hunting ground for anyone on a budget.

Hotels and pensions

Alabama Alexandrinenstr. 80, Warnemünde ⓣ03 81/54 82 50, ⓕ5 48 25 33. Run in tandem with a Wirtshaus, this is one of a number of moderately priced pensions in picturesque old houses in the heart of Warnemünde. ❹

Am Alten Strom Am Strom 60, Warnemünde ⓣ03 81/54 82 30, ⓦwww.hotel-am-alten-strom.de. Large hotel with restaurant, located by the old harbour. ❻

Bellevue Seestr. 8, Warnemünde ⓣ03 81/5 43 33, ⓕ5 43 34 44. Good old-fashioned seaside hotel with restaurant. The front rooms have balconies directly overlooking the beach. ❻

Courtyard by Marriott Schwaansche Str. 6 ⓣ03 81/4 97 00, ⓦwww.marriott.com. Among the most characterful of the city-centre hotels, this has a relatively quiet Altstadt setting and one of Rostock's best restaurants. ❻

Die Kleine Sonne Steinstr. 7 ⓣ03 81/4 92 37 06, ⓦwww.die-kleine-sonne.de. A good central choice with a reasonably priced restaurant, *7 Türme*. ❻

Fischerhus Alexandrinenstr. 124, Warnemünde ⓣ03 81/54 83 10, ⓦwww.hotel-fischerhus.de. Pleasant hotel with café in the historic quarter of the seaside village. It also offers appartments in a nearby villa. ❻–❽

Neptun Seestr. 19, Warnemünde ⓣ03 81/77 70, ⓦwww.hotel-neptun.de. Behemoth of a hotel with GDR origins. However, it has been well refurbished and retains its status as one of the most luxurious addresses on the entire Baltic coast. Also has a fine restaurant. ❾

Sonne Neuer Markt 2 ⓣ03 81/4 97 30, ⓦwww.rostock.steigenberger.de. Housed in a modernised gabled mansion, this is now the best and most expensive hotel in the city centre, with a top-notch restaurant to match. ❽–❾

The city centre

Although much of Rostock's Altstadt was destroyed in the war, its boundaries are still clearly marked by significant surviving sections of the **Stadtmauer**, including three gateways. Between here and the Hauptbahnhof is the Steintor-Vorstadt, a nineteenth-century inner suburb of residential villas.

Neuer Markt is the city's main square, where the fifteenth-century Gothic **Rathaus** stands opposite slim, gabled Renaissance houses. The area between here and the Warnow was all but razed by wartime bombs, and almost everything you see now has been built during the last fifty years. **Lange Strasse**, which leads off the square to the west, was intended to be the showpiece of Socialist rebuilding, but its only notable quality is its size: overwide, and lined by large red-brick buildings, it dwarfs the people and cars below.

Perched on a little hill to the east is the original Altstadt, which became a working-class neighbourhood as the city expanded. Its twisting cobblestoned streets display the names of many former trades like leather-dyeing, fishing and milking. The **Petrikirche** on the Alter Markt is a wonderfully peaceful spot. Its tall spire, by which ships would navigate their way to harbour, was blown off during the war and only replaced in 1994. The **viewing platform** (Mon–Fri 10am–4/5pm, Sat & Sun 10am–5pm; €2) commands a good view over the Warnow and the city. Directly to the south is another redbrick Gothic church, the **Nikolaikirche**, whose chancel straddles the street. It's nowadays used as a concert hall and cultural centre.

Just to the northwest of Neuer Markt, the **Marienkirche** (ⓦwww.marienkirche-rostock.de) is the Altstadt's overwhelmingly dominant monument. It was intended to rival its counterpart in Lübeck, but the nave collapsed, leaving only two bays extant, and a long hall transept had to be added to stabilize the structure. The result is a building of strange yet striking proportions, whose prize feature is its **astronomical clock**, the only one of its kind left in Europe. Originally made in 1472, it's been running continuously since 1643, when it was modernized in accordance with the latest scientific knowledge. Its upper clockface is divided into 24 hours, as well as rings showing monthly star signs and the work associated with each one. The lower, older face consists of thirteen concentric circles showing time and planetary movements.

Kröpeliner Strasse cuts through the pedestrianized heart of the city to the west of Neuer Markt. Look out for the **Spitalpfarrhaus** at no. 82, the finest brick gabled Gothic house remaining in the city; formerly belonging to the medieval hospital, it's now the public library. Beyond lies **Universitätsplatz**, where people loll around the Brunnen der Lebensfreude (Fountain of

Happiness). Around here are the main buildings of the university, founded in 1419, the first in northern Germany. Although nothing remains from this period – most of the structures are examples of the varied but heavy-handed Historicist tastes of the nineteenth century – there's a fine **Barocksaal** on the east side of the square, which is regularly used as a concert hall. Across from it is the **Blücherdenkmal**, erected in 1819 immediately after the death of the city's most illustrious son, the Prussian Field Marshal Gebhard Leberecht von Blücher. Both the statue and the bas-reliefs were carved by the great Berlin Neoclassical sculptor Johann Gottfried Schadow; the latter depict Blücher's most important victories, among them Waterloo.

Just to the west of Universitätsplatz is the **Kloster zum Heiligen Kreuz**, a former Cistercian monastery whose Gothic interiors now house the **Kulturhistorisches Museum** (Tues–Sun 10am–6pm; €3 combined ticket with all the city's other museums). Its ground-floor exhibits include fourteenth- and fifteenth-century religious artefacts and retables and eighteenth-century travelling trunks. On the first floor are works from both before and after World War II from the artists' colony in nearby Ahrenshoop. The second floor covers paintings of the late nineteenth- and early twentieth-century period, during which Ahrenshoop was first "discovered".

At the end of Kröpeliner Strasse stands the **Kröpeliner Tor** (Tues–Sun 10am–6pm; €3), the most impressive of the city's gateways. Its lower part dates back to the late thirteenth century, while the more elegant upper storey was added around 1400. Inside is the local history museum. From here, you walk southeastwards through the landscaped Wallangen, laid out alongside a well-preserved segment of the medieval walls. Between here and the **Steintor** is a rose garden, while immediately to the east of the latter is another surviving section of wall, including the **Kuhtor**, the oldest of the gates.

A couple of minutes' walk south of the Steintor, at August-Bebel-Str. 1, the **Schiffahrtsmuseum** (Tues–Sun 10am–5pm; €3) is mainly concerned with the region's seafaring history. It contains collections of model boats and sailing craft from the days of the Hanseatic League to the battleships of Kaiser Wilhelm II.

Warnemünde

WARNEMÜNDE, now Rostock's seaside suburb but still preserving the distinctive feel of a separate town, is best reached by S-Bahn. Unlike the rest of the city, it has profited enormously from the demise of the GDR, and has undergone a spectacular visual transformation, with many of its villas returned to their nineteenth-century splendour. On either side of the picturesque old harbour, **Alter Strom**, small fishermen's houses stand sideways to the sea to avoid biting winds, and along the seafront a boulevard stretches for about a kilometre, with cafés on one side and a white sandy beach on the other. It's not exactly St Tropez – the ugly **Hotel Neptun**, a five-star monstrosity built to obtain hard currency from westerners, disfigures the far end of the seafront – but it's still one of the country's favourite holiday spots. For a view over the harbour, climb up the hundred-year-old **Leuchtturm** (May–Sept daily 10am–7pm; €1.50). To see what the old fishermen's homes looked like inside, visit the **Heimatmuseum** at Alexandrinenstr. 30–31 (Tues–Sun 10am–6pm; €3).

Eating, drinking and entertainment

As you'd expect, Rostock's main strength in the food and drink field lies in the many **fish restaurants**, though there are plenty of other establishments as well, including good restaurants inside many of the hotels. The main **cultural** venue is the Volkstheater, Doberaner Str. 134/5 (Ⓣ03 81/47 00, Ⓦwww.volkstheater-rostock.de), which puts on a varied programme of drama, opera and ballet, plus orchestral concerts by the Norddeutsche Philharmonie. Local **festivals** tend to be dominated by the nautical theme and include the Warnemünder Woche (Ⓦwww.warnemuender-woche.com) in early July and the Hanse Sail (Ⓦwww.hansesail.com) in early August.

Restaurants

Braukeller Doberaner Str. 27. Located to the west of the Altstadt, this Bierkeller is the main tap of the Rostocker brewery alongside (nowadays a subsidiary of the famous Beck's of Bremen).

Fischerklause Am Strom 123, Warnemünde. Speciality fish restaurant located right by the harbour where the catch is landed.

Gartenlaube Anastasiastr. 24, Warnemünde. One of the city's best and most inventive restaurants.

Goldbroiler Kröpeliner Str. 81. A hardy survivor from GDR days, offering *Kaffee und Kuchen* as well as full meals.

Goldener Anker Strandstr. 35. Has a wide-ranging menu of fish and other dishes, and a summertime terrace overlooking the river.

Il Ristorante Am Strom 107, Warnemünde. Excellent but pricey Italian restaurant overlooking the harbour. Evenings only.

Ratskeller Neuer Markt 1. Typically reliable choice for *gutbürgerliche Küche*.

Tre Kronor Lange Str. 11. This curious two-storey pavilion to the rear of the main boulevard houses a Swedish restaurant.

Zur Kogge Wokrenterstr. 27. Historic seamen's tavern that's cosy in an obvious, tourist-catering, sort of way.

Zur Troika Alte Warnemünder Chaussee 42. Russian speciality restaurant.

Bars and cafés

Am Windspiel Schnickmannstr. 7. Hip hangout which puts on regular art exhibitions.

Café Kloster Klosterhof 6. Pleasant café in one of the courtyard buildings of the Kloster zum Heiligen Kreuz.

Café Likörfabrik Grubenstr. 1. Located in an old distillery, this café has a small but good selection of cakes.

Zum Alten Fritz Warnowufer 65. Hausbrauerei which makes unflitered light and dark beers and also serves inexpensive meals, including weekday bargain lunches.

Stralsund

Pomerania's westernmost city is **STRALSUND**, which lies 70km along the coast from Rostock. It's far more provincial than its neighbour, but is also far more attractive, and is undoubtedly one of the best places to stay along the coast, particularly as it's possible to make day-trips to the holiday island of Rügen (see p.731), to which it's linked by a causeway carrying both road and rail traffic. First impressions of the city don't flatter, as it's ringed by horrid concrete suburbs, but the Altstadt, despite four decades of neglect under the GDR, is wonderfully evocative of its past, preserving a wealth of outstanding buildings. In particular, there remains a fine legacy of Gothic architecture from its Hanseatic days, and Baroque from the two centuries of Swedish rule. Life in Stralsund has always been tied closely to the fisheries trade: the German Baltic's main fishing fleet is based here, and the local shipyard specializes in building trawlers and the enormous fish-processing ships that work the North and South Atlantic. These activities help to ensure that the town is in no danger of turning into a museum piece.

Arrival, information and accommodation

From the **Hauptbahnhof**, the Tribseer Damm traverses the isthmus leading directly into the Altstadt. The **tourist office** is at Alter Markt 9 (May–Sept

Mon–Fri 9am–7pm, Sat 9am–2pm, Sun 10am–2pm; Oct–April Mon–Fri 10am–5pm, Sat 10am–2pm; ⓣ0 38 31/2 46 90, ⓦwww.stralsund.de). Weisse Flotte, Fährstr. 16 (ⓣ0 38 31/26 81 38, ⓦwww.weisse-flotte.com), runs regular **ferry services** across to Altefähr on Rügen; the same company offers **harbour cruises** several times daily from May to September (€6). In summer, Reederei Hiddensee (ⓣ0 38 31/2 68 10, ⓦwww.frs.de/hiddensee) runs three services per day to Hiddensee.

Plenty of **private rooms** (❷–❸) are available at the tourist office, but these tend to be booked out well in advance in mid-summer. There are two **youth hostels** – one has an ideal position in a half-timbered building with a courtyard at Am Kütertor 1 (ⓣ0 38 31/29 21 60; €14.50/17.50), the other is 8km from the Altstadt in the seaside suburb of Devin at Strandstr. 21 (ⓣ0 38 31/49 02 89; €14.50€17.50); take bus #3. The medium-priced range of the **hotel** market is very well served, but there are only a few **pensions** to cater for the budget end.

Hotels and pensions

Im Grünen Rostocker Chaussee 28a ⓣ0 38 31/49 48 68, ⓕ44 57 26. Capacious pension offering some of the most reasonably priced rooms in town. The drawback is its suburban location, 3km southwest of the centre. ❹

Klabautermann Am Querkanal 2 ⓣ0 38 31/29 36 28, ⓕ28 06 12. Small hotel with Kneipe directly overlooking the harbour. ❹

Norddeutscher Hof Neuer Markt 22 ⓣ0 38 31/29 31 61, ⓦwww.nd-hof.de. Pleasant hotel in a historic building in the very heart of the Altstadt. ❺

Regenbogen Richtenberger Chaussee 2a ⓣ & ⓕ0 38 31/49 76 74. A rare budget pension, situated in the Tribseer Vorstadt, a 10min walk west of the Hauptbahnhof. ❸

Royal Am Bahnhof Tribseer Damm 4 ⓣ0 38 31/29 52 68, ⓦwww.royal-hotel.de. Palatial station hotel with a very reasonably priced restaurant, *Esprit*. ❻

Stralsund Heinrich-Heine-Ring 105 ⓣ0 38 31/36 70 or 39 03 30, ⓕ36 71 11. Located in the Kneiper Vorstadt, 2km north of the centre. Its restaurant, *Herwig's*, is among the best in Stralsund. ❺

Zur Post Tribseer Str. 22 ⓣ0 38 31/20 05 00, ⓦwww.hotel-zur-post-stralsund.de. Very pleasant and traditional hotel and restaurant just off Neuer Markt. ❼

The Altstadt

The **Altstadt** stands on what is almost an island, with the sea and two natural ponds – the **Frankenteich** and the **Kneiper Teich** – forming a kind of moat. The skyline, framed by the towers of the great brick Gothic churches, is best seen from the southern shore of the willow-lined Frankenteich.

Crossing the isthmus via Tribseer Damm, Tribseer Strasse leads to Neuer Markt, one of the two town squares. Here stands Stralsund's largest church, the late fourteenth-century **Marienkirche**. It's a good idea to start your tour by ascending the original medieval wooden staircase of its single **tower** (July & Aug Mon–Sat 9am–6pm, Sun 11.30am–6pm; rest of year Mon–Sat 10am–4/5pm, Sun 11.30am–4/5pm; €1), as from the top there's a marvellous view of the medieval town, as well as of Rügen a couple of hundred metres across the straits. The scrubbed interior of the church is notable for its vertiginous elevation; the most spectacular vaults are in the narthex, which are fashioned into a dazzling variety of star shapes. Of the many Baroque adornments, pride of place goes to the **organ**, one of the most celebrated in the country, which was made by the Lübeck master, Friedrich Stellwagen, in the 1650s. During the summer months, it can normally be heard at 11am each day, except on Thursdays, when there's a full-scale recital at 8pm on alternate weeks.

On Mönchstrasse just north of Neuer Markt, the **Katharinenkloster**, the former Dominican priory, has been converted to contain the city's two main museums. The church itself contains what has long been the most popular sightseeing attraction in the whole of the former GDR, the **Deutsches Museum für Meereskunde und Fischerei** (daily: June–Sept 9am–6pm; Oct–May 10am–5pm; €8; Ⓦwww.meeresmuseum.de). Much loved by kids, but also a serious scientific institute, it focuses on all aspects of life under the sea. On the ground floor is an aquarium full of tropical fish, while the upper floors focus on evolution and on the fishing trade. The most spectacular exhibit is the skeleton of a finback whale washed up on Rügen in 1825. Next door, occupying the conventual buildings, is the **Kulturhistorisches Museum** (Tues–Sun 10am–5pm; €3, or €5 including the two branch museums), whose medieval artefacts are beautifully displayed in a series of elegant Gothic halls. Unfortunately, only facsimiles are on view of the glittering hoard of tenth-century treasure dug up on the nearby island of Hiddensee. Another highlight is the wonderful collection of eighteenth- and nineteenth-century dolls' houses and other children's toys. The six-hundred-year-old house at no.38 on the same street has been designated as the **Museumshaus** (same hours), and decked out with a series of period interiors. On Böttcherstrasse immediately to the south, the museum has another branch in a splendidly grand old warehouse or **Speicher** (same hours); this is devoted to the folklore, costumes and lifestyle of the rural communities of the Baltic coast. At the end of this street is the **Jacobikirche**, the youngest of the three brick Gothic parish churches; it's no longer used for worship and isn't generally open for visits. From here, follow Jacobiturmstrasse north to **Badenstrasse**, Stralsund's finest street, lined with mansions ranging in style from Gothic to Neoclassical.

Towards the northern end of the Altstadt is the **Alter Markt**, the original main square, one clearly modelled on its Lübeck counterpart. The focal point is the **Rathaus**, whose showpiece late fourteenth-century facade, crafted from delicately glazed bricks and bristling with fantastical gables, ranks as one of the greatest masterpieces of Gothic civil architecture. Very different in style is the Baroque southern portal on Ossenreyerstrasse, which bears the royal coat of arms of Sweden. Another important legacy of Stralsund's era as a Swedish town is the **Commandanten-Hus** at no. 14 on Alter Markt, the mansion of the local governor. It stands in stark contrast to the city's finest Gothic house, the **Wulflamhaus** at no. 5, named after the mayor who commissioned it as his residence.

Behind the Rathaus is the **Nikolaikirche**, which was built virtually in tandem with it. In design, above all in its twin towers (one of which is now capped by a Baroque helmet and spire), it's clearly modelled on the Marienkirche in Lübeck, which pioneered the Hanseatic format of pairing the main civic church with the town hall. Inside are a number of outstanding furnishings, including two **high altars** – the one in the choir itself is a carved Passion retable made around 1500, while that in front of the screen is a frilly Baroque creation designed by the great Berlin sculptor, Andreas Schlüter. The **astronomical clock** in the ambulatory is dated 1394 and is thus one of the oldest in Europe. However, the most intriguing adornment is the **Novgorod stall** in the southern aisle, named after the Russian city that was the easternmost outpost of the Hanseatic League. Its reliefs depict Russians hunting for animal skins, and taking honey and wax from bees, products which they then sell to a German merchant.

To the north and west of the Alter Markt are **Fährstrasse**, **Schillstrasse** and **Mühlenstrasse**, which together contain many of Stralsund's finest medieval town houses. Mühlenstr. 3 is particularly worth seeking out: as it's now an exhibition hall, you can go inside and see the interior of this typical Hanseatic trader's residence. There are no partitioning walls, only three open-plan levels, which were used as combined living and storage quarters. At the southern end of the same street is the **Kütertor**, one of two surviving city gates. From here, it's worth following the course of the old fortifications, passing along the shore of the Kneiper Teich, then continuing via the **Kneiper Tor** to the **Johanniskloster** (early May to mid-Oct Tues–Sun 10am–6pm; €1.50). Although this former Franciscan friary was badly damaged in the war, some parts still survive, including the remarkable **Räucherboden** (Smoking Floor) and the Baroque **Bibliothek** (Library). The ruined church serves as an occasional open-air theatre.

Eating, drinking and entertainment

Many of the fine old buildings in Stralsund's Altstadt now house **restaurants**, or you can eat well in the hotels listed above. The main **cultural** venue is the Theater Stralsund on Olaf-Palme-Platz (Ⓣ0 38 31/2 64 60, Ⓦwww.theater-vorpommern). Stralsund's **festivals** include the Stralsunder Segelwoche (July), a regatta round Rügen and Hiddensee; and the Wallensteintage (several days around July 24), a commemoration of the city's successful defence during the Thirty Years' War against the siege mounted by the Imperial forces of Alfred von Wallenstein.

Cafés and restaurants

Café am Markt Alter Markt 12. Good traditional coffee house.

Hansekeller Mönchstr. 48. Cellar restaurant offering reasonably priced local dishes.

m@trix Wasserstr. 89. Internet café and ice-cream parlour overlooking the harbour. Open daily 2am–10pm/midnight.

Nur Fisch Heilgeiststr. 92. Inexpensive fish specialist, open daytime only (until 6pm, Thurs until 7pm, Sat until 4pm), closed Sun.

Torschliesserhaus Am Kütertor 1. Trendy bar next door to the youth hostel which does bistro-type food.

Zum Alten Fritz Greifswalder Chaussee 84-5. This is the parent of a small chain of Hausbrauereien in the northern half of the former GDR. It produces a Zwickelbier and various seasonal brews, and serves full meals.

Zur Kogge Tribseer Str. 26. Traditional Gaststätte on the ground floor and a bar-disco in the basement.

Rügen

Rügen is Germany's largest island and has been a favourite summer destination since bathing first became fashionable during the nineteenth century. Its long sandy beaches and airy forests make it ideal for a family vacation and even in GDR days it drew over a million visitors a year. Since then, many of the crumbling old villas and faded hotels have undergone expensive refurbishments as the islanders have striven to re-establish Rügen at the upper end of the holiday market. The island splits into four distinct areas: **South Rügen** with the best, and most heavily populated stretches of beach; **Jasmund** with its forested national park and chalk cliffs overlooking the Baltic; windswept **Wittow** in the north; and **West Rügen**, a gentle landscape of farmland and woods. The last-named is generally taken to embrace the island of **Hiddensee**, an isolated strip of land a few kilometres offshore with a landscape of surprising contrasts and an idyllic, car-free atmosphere.

Rügen's highlights include the lighthouses of **Kap Arkona** at the northeastern corner of Wittow and, nearby, the secluded fishing village of **Vitt**. Jasmund's celebrated white cliffs of **Stubbenkammer** have become Rügen's unofficial symbol, partly because of the romanticized paintings of Caspar David Friedrich. Running back from the coast here is the forested pocket of **Stubnitz**, where easy walking routes criss-cross a woodland landscape more

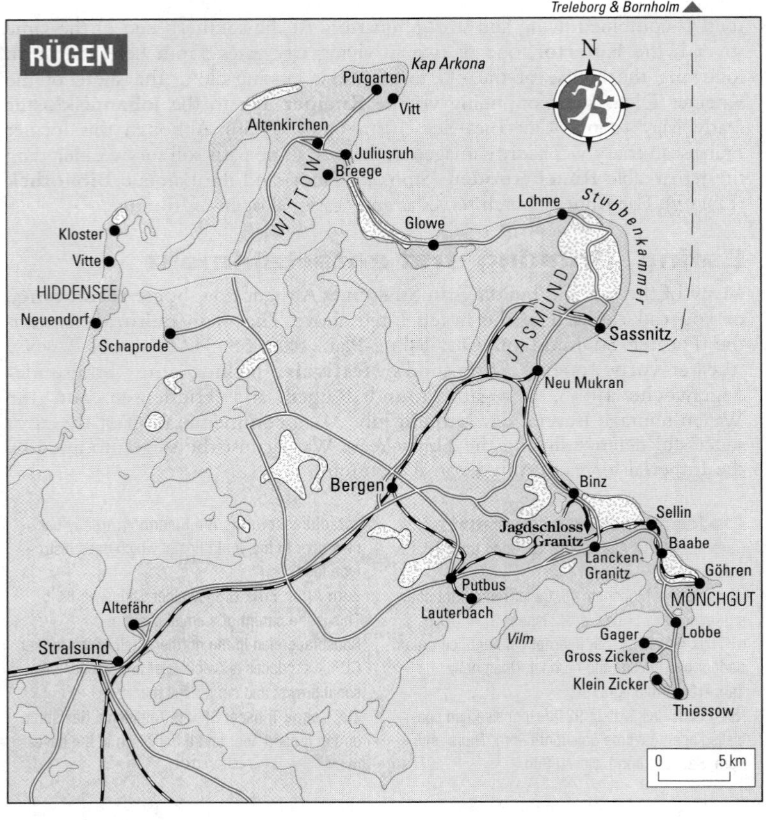

reminiscent of Europe's centre than its northern coast. Among the island's towns, the most attractive are in South Rügen: **Binz** is an archetypal Baltic resort with tree-lined boulevards and grandiose villas, many of which are now in use as hotels, while **Putbus** is, in effect, a giant Neoclassical folly built during the early 1800s to the greater glory of a local prince. **Sassnitz** in Jasmund is a bustling port offering ferry services to Sweden and the Danish island of Bornholm.

Rügen is linked to Stralsund by a **causeway** (opened five times daily to let ships pass through) which takes both road and rail traffic. The quickest approach is by **train** – there are very frequent services on the line from Stralsund to Sassnitz, a fair number of which originate in Berlin or even further afield. There's a regular local **bus** link between Stralsund and Altefähr on Rügen's southern coast, a route also served by ferries, which leave at approximately two-hour intervals. Island **transport links** are fairly good, with various branch rail lines leading from the main line on the eastern half of the island, and bus services to more out-of-the-way destinations. Travelling around the island is considerably easier if you have your own car; cycling is a possibility but Rügen is hilly and roads are often potholed or cobbled. **Accommodation** is virtually unobtainable during the months of July and August without advance booking, and you should certainly consider visiting off-season. Rügen is particularly atmospheric and empty in winter when the Baltic often freezes over.

Putbus

The little town of **PUTBUS**, built as a planned Neoclassical Residenzstadt by local grandee Prince Wilhelm Malte during the early nineteenth century, lies 8km southeast of Bergen, the island's somewhat nondescript capital. With its attractive layout and architecture, based on plans originally drawn up by Karl Friedrich Schinkel, it's the artistic and cultural hub of Rügen. At its heart is the **Circus**, a large roundel with a plain pillar commemorating the founding of the town. Alleestrasse runs southwest from the Circus past the **Theater** (Ⓣ03 83 01/80 80, Ⓦwww.theater-putbus.de), the only one on Rügen, whose flamboyant exterior is bedecked with an exaggerated portico and pseudo-classical friezes showing poets, lyre-players and assorted muses. Next to it is the **Marktplatz**, ringed by stolid nineteenth-century buildings, with a monument at its centre commemorating Prussia's military triumphs over Austria, Denmark and France.

On the other side of Alleestrasse, the **Schlosspark** is bisected from north to south by the chestnut-tree-lined Kastanienallee. The Schloss itself was demolished in 1962, just before a visit to the area by Walter Ulbricht, the then GDR leader. Allegedly, the local party bosses hoped to score points with the SED top brass by eradicating this symbol of the feudal past. Fortunately some fine-looking ancillary buildings remain, and the leafy lanes of the park and the banks of the **Schwanenteich**, a small lake with adjacent ruined stables, make for good strolling. At the western end is the **Christuskirche**, which has been the parish church for the past century, but was built fifty years before as the dining room, games room and ballroom for visitors on recuperative holidays. Towards the eastern end of the park (just off Kastanienallee) is the **Orangerie**, once a winter refuge for exotic plants from the park, and now housing exhibition rooms.

Some 3km southeast of Putbus, but still within its municipality, is the small fishing and sailing port of **LAUTERBACH**. It's the terminus of the branch rail line from Bergen, and is also served by buses from the Circus. Lauterbach was chosen as the site of Wilhelm Malte's very own purpose-built resort, and his opulent colonnaded Neoclassical **Badehaus** still stands on the eastern outskirts. The large wooded park behind it is the beginning of a pleasant coastal walking route. Lauterbach is the starting point for boat trips around the island of **Vilm**, which was inaccessible to the public during the GDR period. Then, its designation as a nature reserve served mainly to camouflage its role as an exclusive holiday island for the SED hierarchy. Vilm was opened to the public after the *Wende* but then closed again, since it was felt that indigenous rare animal and plant species were being harmed by the renewed tourist traffic. Access was then reinstated, albeit on a strictly limited basis, and most cruises simply circumnavigate the island. To find out about whether there's any possibility of making a landing, contact Fahrgastreederei Lenz, Alleestr. 9 (Ⓣ03 83 01/6 18 96, Ⓦwww.ruegen-schifffahrt.de/lenz.php) in Putbus.

Practicalities

Putbus's **Bahnhof** is at the eastern edge of town, downhill from the Circus. As well as being on a branch line from Bergen, which continues on to Lauterbach, it's the western terminus of **Rasender Roland**, a narrow-gauge steam railway that runs to Göhren via the main resorts on Rügen's southeastern coast (summer 4 trains daily; services reduced out of season; whole one-way journey €8, family ticket €16; Ⓦwww.rasender-roland.de). The **tourist office** is at

August-Bebel-Str. 1 (July & Aug Mon–Fri 8am–noon & 1–6pm; rest of year Mon & Wed–Fri 8am–noon & 1–4pm, Tues 8am–noon & 1–6pm; ⓣ03 83 01/4 31, ⓦwww.putbus.de).

Although there are a fair number of **private rooms** (❷–❸) in Putbus, the only **hotel** in the main part of town is *Koos*, Bahnhofstr. 7 (ⓣ03 83 01/2 78, ⓦwww.hotel-auf-ruegen.de; ❺). There are, however, several possibilities in Lauterbach, including *Hafenhotel Viktoria*, Dorfstr. 1 (ⓣ03 83 01/64 60; ❺); and *Am Bodden*, Chausseestr. 10 (ⓣ03 83 01/80 00, ⓦwww.am-bodden.de; ❺). For **eating** and **drinking**, the *Rosencafé*, Bahnhofstr. 1, serves Italianate dishes, while the *Kurhaus* at the western end of Alleestrasse has a good German menu. Another possibility is the *Jägerhütte*, just beyond the Tierpark in the Schlosspark, which specializes in game.

Binz

In common with the rest of the Baltic coast, Rügen's main beach resorts preface their names with the official designation Ostseebad. Biggest of these is **BINZ**, which lies 14km east of Putbus by road or the narrow-gauge rail line. It's been in business since the days of the Kaisers and retains much of its nineteenth-century atmosphere. The town's tree-shaded streets are lined by solid mansions with wrought-iron balconies and fancy gables. These houses were originally built as holiday residences for wealthy families; most were confiscated by the GDR government for use as workers' rest homes but have since been sold off and converted into luxury hotels and apartments.

At the end of Hauptstrasse, the main shopping street, is Binz's apparently endless sandy **beach**, scattered with *Strandkörbe*. Nearby stands the impeccably grand **Kurhaus**, whose terrace looks out over the Baltic. The beach stretches north for about 10km to the cranes of Neu Mukran, while in the opposite direction it curves southeast for a kilometre or so before disappearing at the foot of tree-covered cliffs. At the southern end of the beach a sewage-polluted stream flows into the sea; from here, a path leads through the cliff-top woods to the headland viewpoints of **Silvitzer Ort** and **Granitzer Ort**.

Jagdschloss Granitz (May–Oct daily 9am–6pm; Nov–April Tues–Sun 10am–4pm; €3), another Wilhelm Malte folly, built on top of the 107-metre Tempelberg, lies within the municipality of Binz; the easiest means of access is to take the narrow-gauge rail line to Haltepunkt Jagdschloss. Again designed by Schinkel, it's in the heavily romanticized neo-Gothic style the great architect favoured for his fantasy castles. Within, a vertiginous cast-iron staircase leads up the viewing tower to a prospect of Binz and the Jasmunder Bodden freshwater lake to the west, and the island of Vilm. The Jagdschloss also houses a small hunting museum, plus portraits of Malte's ancestors.

Practicalities

Binz's **Bahnhof**, north of the centre, is the terminus of the branch railway up the coast which connects with the main line between Bergen and Sassnitz. Southeast of the centre is **Bahnhof Binz-Ost**, which is used only by Rasender Roland. The **tourist office** is in the Kurverwaltung, Heinrich-Heine-Str. 7 (Jan–March, Nov & Dec Mon–Fri 9am–4pm; April, May, Sept & Oct Mon–Fri 9am–6pm, Sat 10am–1pm; June–Aug Mon–Fri 9am–8pm, Sat 10am–1pm & 2–5pm, Sun 2–5pm; ⓣ03 83 93/3 06 75, ⓦwww.binz.de). Town-centre **hotels** include *Vineta*, Hauptstr. 20 (ⓣ03 83 93/3 90, ⓦwww.hotel-vineta-binz.de; ❻), and *Central,* Hauptstr. 13 (ⓣ03 83 93/34 60; ❻). There are more options down by the seafront, with *Villa Schwanebeck*, Margaretenstr. 18 (ⓣ03 83 93/20

13, Ⓦwww.villa-schwanenbeck.de; ❻), and *Binzer Hof*, Lottumstr. 15 (Ⓣ03 83 93/23 26, Ⓦwww.hotel-binzer-hof.de; ❻), both just a block away from the beach. Directly on the Strandpromenade are most of the top addresses, including *Villa Salve* at no. 41 (Ⓣ038393/22 23, Ⓦwww.ruegen-schewe.de; ❽); *Strandhotel Lissek* at no. 33 (Ⓣ03 83 93/38 10, Ⓦwww.strandhotel-lissek.de; ❽); and *Arkona Strandhotel* at no. 59 (Ⓣ03 83 93/5 70, Ⓦwww.arkona-ruegen.de; ❽–❾). The **youth hostel** is at Strandpromenade 35 (Ⓣ03 83 93/3 25 97; €18.50/22.50), while the **campsite** is in the north of town at Proaer Chaussee 30 (Ⓣ03 83 93/3 26 24). Alternatives to the excellent **restaurants** in all the hotels listed above are the fish specialist *Poseidon*, Lottumstr. 1; *Dünenhaus*, Strandpromenade 23, which has a pleasant terrace; and *Strandhalle*, Strandpromenade 5.

Göhren and the Mönchgut peninsula

Rügen's southeastern extremity is the **Mönchgut**, a jagged, three-pronged peninsula of gentle hills, sheltered bays and sandy beaches. Straddling an exposed headland on its eastern coast is the windswept little resort of **GÖHREN**. Just offshore is the **Buskam**, a glacier-deposited rock, once used as an altar by the Slav inhabitants of the island. The name is derived from the old Slavonic *bogis kamien*, meaning "God's Stone", and it's the biggest of Rügen's many *Findlinge* – rocks left by the passage of Ice-Age glaciers. At the junction of Strandstrasse and Poststrasse is the **Heimatmuseum** (April, May, Sept & Oct daily 10am–5pm; June–Aug daily 10am–6pm; Nov–March Mon–Fri 10am–4pm; €3, or €10 combined ticket for all the village's museums; Ⓦwww.moenchguter-museen-ruegen.de), a mildly diverting display of folk costumes and material about the development of tourism and other local industries. A few doors down the same street is the **Museumshof** (same times; €3), essentially an old barn crammed with agricultural implements. There's another museum, the **Rookhus** (April, May, Sept & Oct daily 11am–2pm; June–Aug daily 11am–5pm; €3), a seventeenth-century fishing cottage, on the road to Lobbe. Just out of town, off the main road in the dunes of the southern beach, is the **Museumsschiff Luise** (April, May, Sept & Oct daily 1–5pm; June–Aug daily 11am–5pm; €3), an old beached freighter.

Göhren's **Bahnhof**, a terminus of the Rasender Roland narrow-gauge line, is close to the seafront. The **tourist office** is at Schulstr. 8 (May–Sept daily 9am–7pm; Oct–April Mon–Sat 10am–5pm; Ⓣ03 83 08/2 59 10, Ⓦwww.goehren.de). In addition to **private rooms** (❷–❸), there are numerous **hotels**, inlcuding *Albatros*, Ulmenallee 5 (Ⓣ03 83 08/54 30; ❻); *Waldhotel*, Waldstr. 7 (Ⓣ038308/5 05 00; ❼); and *Nordperd*, Nordperdstr. 11 (Ⓣ03 83 08/70; ❼). The **campsite** (April–Oct; Ⓣ03 83 08/21 22) is hidden away in the woods, a stone's throw from the sea, just northeast of the Bahnhof; with a capacity of four thousand, it's the largest on the island but can still get overrun in high season. Inexpensive alternatives to the hotel **restaurants** are *Kaiser's Hofkneipe*, Waldstr. 11, and the fish restaurant *Zur Muschel Bar* on Strandweg.

Jasmund

Rügen's most striking scenery is to be found in **Jasmund**, an area of undulating woods and fields jutting out into the Baltic on the island's northeastern shore. The only town of any size is the large port of **SASSNITZ**, the terminus of Rügen's main rail line. Before World War II, it was the most popular seaside resort in Rügen and tourism is slowly regaining its prominent role. **Ferries** run regularly from Sassnitz to the Danish island of Bornholm and the

Swedish port of Trelleborg, and there are also **cruises** up the coast, giving a sea view of the famous cliffs to the north. The **tourist office** at Hauptstr. 27 (April–Oct Mon–Fri 9am–7pm, Sat & Sun 10am–2pm; Nov–March Mon–Fri 9am–5pm, Sat 10am–2pm; Ⓣ03 83 92/6 69 45, Ⓦwww.sassnitz.de) offers the usual booking service for **private rooms** (❷–❸), while **hotels** include *Waterkant*, Walterstr. 3 (Ⓣ03 83 92/5 08 44, Ⓦwww.hotel-waterkant.de; ❻); *Villa Aegir*, Mittelstr. 5 (Ⓣ03 83 92/30 20, Ⓦwww.villa-aegir.de; ❻); and *Gastmahl des Meeres*, Strandpromenade 2 (Ⓣ03 83 92/5 17 01; ❻). The last-named incorporates one of the many **fish restaurants** on the waterfront; a good alternative is the neighbouring *Zur Mole*.

The area's real attraction is the **Nationalpark Jasmund** (Ⓦwww.nationalpark-jasmund.de), containing both the famous **Stubbenkammer** chalk cliffs of the coast and the surrounding **Stubnitz** forest. The direct road to Stubbenkammer is a pleasant hilly route through the woods, served by regular buses. Alternatively, you can follow the coastal path from the northern end of Sassnitz (allow at least 3hr). Mostly it's a cliff-top walk, but occasionally the route dips down into steep-sided stream valleys. *Waldhalle*, a Gaststätte a few kilometres beyond the edge of Sassnitz, is a handy place to interrupt your journey. Adjacent is the **Wissower Klinken**, first of the really large chalk blocks, best appreciated from the cliff-top viewpoint on the **Ernst-Moritz-Arndt-Sicht**, just to the north.

The path continues for several kilometres to the **Kleine Stubbenkammer** with the best views of the mighty **Königstuhl**, a vast pinnacle of chalk standing free from the main cliff face. Königstuhl means "king's seat", and legend has it that in days of yore whoever could climb the seaward side of the 117-metre cliff would become king of Rügen and occupy a stone throne at the top. These days the place swarms with visitors, most of whom choose an easier means of access via the narrow footbridge (€1) from the car park at the head of the road from Sassnitz. The view from the Königstuhl is splendid though you may have to fight for space by the rail at the summit. In summer, the lines of parked cars along the approach road usually stretch back for several kilometres and the army of day-trippers is served by a Gaststätte, a couple of Imbiss stands and souvenir shops. From the Königstuhl footbridge a precipitous path meanders down to the beach, which stinks and is strewn with seaweed. The last couple of metres are descended by ladder.

Shortly before the Königstuhl, a track branches off into the forest from the main road. A path leads from this junction to the mysterious **Herthasee**, a dark lily-bedecked pool hidden in the woods, said to have been the bathing place of the Germanic goddess Hertha, who rewarded the efforts of local farmers with rich harvests. According to the tale, after bathing Hertha would drown her mortal servants, and their spirits gather on the shore each night. North of the Herthasee is the **Herthaburg,** a small hill with a large stone block nearby, which is thought to have served Rügen's early Slav inhabitants as a sacrificial altar.

Wittow

Wittow is Rügen's northern extremity, wind-battered and sparsely populated. The area has some decent beaches but these tend to be more exposed than those elsewhere on the island. Fish figures highly on local menus and is well worth sampling.

Towards the northern end of Wittow, and reachable by bus from various points on Rügen, is **PUTGARTEN**, from where the lighthouses of **Kap Arkona** are clearly visible. Just north of the village is a large parking lot for visitors to the cape; here also is the **tourist office** (daily 10/11am–5/7pm; ⓣ03 83 91/41 90), which can help find **private rooms** (❷–❸) in the area. The **Neuer Leuchtturm** (New Lighthouse), dating from the turn of the twentieth century and looking very business-like with its orange and black stripes, is the first to assert itself. Moving closer, the **Alter Leuchtturm** (Old Lighthouse), designed by Schinkel in 1826, doesn't really look much like a lighthouse at all, but this three-storey red-brick building, with its inset windows and verdigris-dusted dome, does justice to its creator.

The small fishing port of **VITT** lies hidden in the trees about 1km southeast of Putgarten at the end of a rudimentary concrete road. This is out of bounds to visitors' cars, so the best approach is to walk from Kap Arkona, though multi-seated horse-drawn carriages run to and from Putgarten. At the village entrance is the small thatched **Dorfkapelle** with an octagonal ground plan (the hand of Schinkel once again). The interior is almost bare with only naive wall paintings of fishing-village life as decoration. From the chapel a path leads down into a small valley and to the village itself, a cluster of well-preserved and unspoiled thatched cottages. Vitt survives almost unchanged since the nineteenth century, seemingly oblivious to the tourists who flock here to wonder at its unique atmosphere, which owes much to the absence of cars, supermarkets and other facets of modern life. Its **beach** is stony and not particularly attractive, but it's quiet, the water is fairly clean and there's not a *Strandkorb* in sight.

Vitt's justly famous *Gasthof zum Goldenen Anker* is one of the best **restaurants** around, serving up wonderful fish and seafood dishes (particularly eel). Inside it's intimate and a model of *gemütlichkeit,* while outside you can sit on benches in good weather. The chances of finding somewhere **to stay** in Vitt are practically nil, at least in summer. There are no pensions or hotels, and what few rooms do exist are privately rented, usually to long-standing regular visitors, but you could try your luck at the small craft shop at Vitt no. 8, which may be able to find accommodation. **Rowing boats** can be rented from the small harbour or you can let a local sea dog do the work for you in a motorboat.

Hiddensee

Hiddensee, a sixteen-kilometre-long finger of land that stands like a barrage between Rügen and the Baltic, experiences a heavy volume of visitors, but with a little leg-work or pedalling it's not difficult to escape the crowds. Most of the 1300 inhabitants – whose numbers swell considerably in summer – are concentrated in the villages of **Kloster**, **Vitte** and **Neuendorf**. Kloster is easily the most appealing of the trio, and the best way to explore the rest of the island is by renting a bike (around €6 per day). Most visitors come to Hiddensee as day-trippers, and the relatively small number of available beds means that it's effectively impossible to find somewhere to stay during July and August without a reservation made far in advance.

Ferries to the island are run by Reederei Hiddensee, Diek 4, Vitte (ⓣ03 83 00/2 10, ⓦwww.frs.de/hiddensee). The nearest port of access is Schaprode on the west coast of Rügen, from where there are several daily sailings throughout the year; these cost €12.10 return to Neuendorf, €14.20 return to Vitte or Neuendorf. In summer, there are normally three daily sailings from Stralsund (€15.50 return to Neuendorf, €16 to Vitte or Neuendorf).

Kloster

Hiddensee's most popular destination is the little village of **KLOSTER**, which straddles the northern end of the island. It's incredibly unspoilt, and is at its best when the daytime crowds have disappeared. There's easy access from the village to the west coast of the island, which basically forms an eight-kilometre-long beach.

From the small harbour, where ferries from the mainland dock, a lane leads into the village. A left turn at the pond leads along Hauptstrasse, the nearest thing there is to a main street. To the north is the **Inselkirche** (Island Church), in whose graveyard **Gerhart Hauptmann** (1862–1946) is buried. Hauptmann, one of the many writers and artists who moved to Rügen in the nineteenth century, belonged to the Naturalist movement of the 1880s, and his dramas focused mainly on the lives and struggles of ordinary people. The realism of his most famous play *Vor Sonnenaufgang* (Before Sunrise), a "social drama" dealing with the human impact of industrialization, caused a sensation at its premiere, and though his earlier works remain his most famous Hauptmann's influence on modern German drama has been extensive. Signposts point the way to the **Gerhart-Hauptmann-Haus** (daily: April–Oct 10am–5pm; Nov–March 11am–4pm; €2), which the writer bought with the money he received from winning the Nobel Prize for Literature. It's also known more picturesquely as *Haus Seedorn* and is packed with photos, manuscripts and theatre posters, though some of the rooms have been left as they were when the playwright lived and worked in them.

The **beach**, protected by blocks of rock, can be windswept and wave-battered, but on a good day it's perfect, and if you're willing to walk you can soon leave your fellow visitors behind. To the north the beach rounds a headland, continuing for several kilometres at the base of the steepish cliffs of the Dornbusch.

The most obvious **accommodation** possibilities in Kloster are *Haus Wieseneck*, Kirchweg 18 (ⓣ03 83 00/316, ⓦwww.wieseneck.de; ❸), and *Hitthim*, Hafenweg 8 (ⓣ03 83 00/66 60, ⓦwww.hitthim.de/hitthim; ❻), which also has a good fish restaurant.

The Dornbusch

The gentle hills of the **Dornbusch** area to the north of Kloster are the most appealing part of the Hiddensee and dominated by a lighthouse that warns ships of the island's presence. It's a good region to explore by bike: take the road north to the minuscule hamlet of **GRIEBEN** and *Zum Enddorn* (ⓣ03 83 00/4 60, ⓦwww.hitthim.de/enddorn; ❺), a hotel with a restaurant and beer garden. From the "main" road – in reality a crudely concreted track – there are a couple of turnings in the direction of the **Leuchtturm**, reached after a steep climb, but worth the effort for the excellent views of the island. Adjacent to the lighthouse is a military installation and signs warn of the risk of being shot if you approach. Skirting the edge of the nearby woods leads to a clearing and *Zum Klausner* (ⓣ03 83 00/2 15; ❹), one of the island's best eating and drinking places with outside tables during summer. In addition to its own double rooms, it also has rustic-looking twin-bedded bungalows for rent. From here a steep path leads back down into Kloster.

Vitte and Neuendorf

A kilometre or so south of Kloster is **VITTE**, Hiddensee's biggest settlement and a kind of island capital. The **tourist office** (for the whole island) is at Norderende 162 (July & Aug Mon–Fri 8am–5pm, Sat & Sun 10am–noon; rest of year Mon–Fri 8am–5pm; ⓣ03 83 00/6 42 26, ⓦwww.insel-hiddensee.de). There are several **hotels**, including *Godewind*, Süderende 53 (ⓣ03 83 00/66 00, ⓦwww.hitthim.de/godewind; ❹–❼); *Zum Hiddenseer*, Wiesenweg 22 (ⓣ03 83 00/4 19; ❺); and *Post Hiddensee*,

Wiesenweg 26 (☎03 83 00/64 30; ❻). *Zum Hiddenseer* has the best **restaurant** on the island.

South of Vitte is the **Dünenheide**, an area of heathland which is at its best in August when the abundant heather blooms purple. A road leads across it via the *Heiderose*, In den Dünen 127 (☎03 83 00/6 30; ❻-❽), a pleasant **hotel** with restaurant; it also has holiday bungalows for rent.

Southernmost of the island's three villages is **NEUENDORF**, a quiet little place which makes a good starting point for wandering the **Gellen**, a tapering spit of ever-shifting sand dunes jutting out south towards the mainland. On the western shore, just south of Neuendorf, is a bathing beach, though on the Gellen itself you're restricted to marked paths as the whole area is a nature reserve. *Am Meer* (☎03 83 00/2 01; f), a GDR-era luxury **hotel** with a swanky restaurant, is the only accommodation option. An alternative place for drinks and light snacks is the *Strandcafé*.

Greifswald

GREIFSWALD, the final member of the province's quartet of old Hanseatic trading cities, lies 30km south of Stralsund on the fast rail line to Berlin. Founded in the thirteenth century by the Cistercian monks of Kloster Eldena, it became the seat of a university in 1456, and retains a distinct academic atmosphere to this day. In contrast to its Hanseatic neighbours, the Altstadt of Greifswald lies 3km inland from the Baltic. Both in terms of individual monuments and overall appearance, it seems rather small-scale in comparison with the others. However, substantial parts of the **Stadtbefestigung**, which ringed the original town, survive intact and the area around them has been transformed into a shady promenade.

The City

Greifswald's skyline was immortalized in a number of paintings by the town's favourite son, the Romantic artist Caspar David Friedrich. The dominant building, then as now, is the **Dom**, a typical example of Gothic brickwork, which lies close to the middle of the Altstadt. Its most remarkable feature is the mighty **tower** (May–Sept Mon–Fri 11am–3pm, Sat 10am–2pm, Sun 11.30am–12.30pm; €2), whose four turrets, octagonal upper storeys and onion-domed Baroque spire combine to produce a memorable silhouette. A medieval wooden staircase leads to the viewing platform, which commands a fine panorama over the Altstadt to the Baltic. The Dom's interior was given a romanticized neo-Gothic remodelling in the nineteenth century, with most of the walls covered with a coat of whitewash. However, a precious series of **frescoes**, painted around 1400 in the manner of manuscript illuminations, still adorns some of the south side chapels.

Diagonally opposite the west front of the Dom are the buildings of the **Ernst-Moritz-Arendt-Universität**, whose main block is a fine example of the dignified Baroque so characteristic of northern Germany. Its **Aula** is a fittingly splendid graduation hall, but unfortunately neither this nor other parts of the complex – such as the graffiti-covered student prison, which is reminiscent of its renowned counterpart in Heidelberg – are regular tourist sights, so it's pot luck whether you find anything open.

A couple of minutes' walk to the east of the Dom is the **Markt**, a bustling square lined with a variety of well-restored buildings. Principal among these is the **Rathaus**, originally Gothic, but nowadays with a rather composite appearance as the result of various alterations. On Brüggstrasse just to the north, the **Marienkirche** is the town's oldest surviving church, unmissable with its distinctive square tower. It lacks a chancel, a fact which gives it striking dimensions, both inside and out. Look out for the humorous frescoes in the entrance hall, and for the Renaissance pulpit with its portraits of the reformers Luther, Melanchthon and Bugenhagen.

When complete, the new **Pommersches Landesmuseum** (Tues–Sun 10am–6pm; €3; Ⓦwww.pommersches-landesmuseum.de) will occupy a group of historic buildings in the vicinity of the Markt. The first part of the project, the **Gemäldegalerie** in the late Neoclassical **Quistorp-Gebäude**, contains a couple of oils plus a number of drawings by Caspar David Friedrich, as well as paintings by Hals, Runge, Van Gogh and Liebermann, among others. The museum headquarters, together with the archeology, history and folklore displays, will be housed in the **Graues Kloster**, the former Franciscan friary. If all goes to plan, it will open some time in 2004.

Greifswald's most famous sights are not in the centre, but in two incorporated villages by the River Ryck (which also forms the northern boundary of the Altstadt), just before it disgorges itself into the Baltic. They can be reached by bus #40 from the Hauptbahnhof or from Wolgaster Strasse immediately beyond the eastern boundary of the Altstadt. **WIECK** is a fishing village of the active rather than tourist variety, as the smell of herring wafting from the harbour testifies. The river is traversed here by the photogenic **Klappbrücke**, a pristinely restored Dutch-style wooden drawbridge, and on the northern side you can take a stroll along Dorfstrasse, where there are a number of old fishermen's cottages. A few minutes' walk south of Wieck is **ELDENA**, whose ruined **Kloster**, directly facing Wolgaster Strasse, was

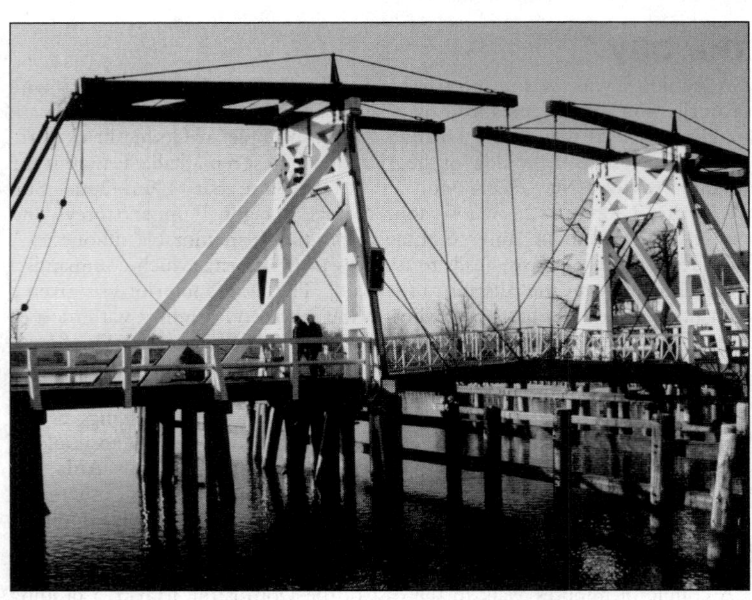

△ The Klappbrücke at Wieck, Greifswald

home to a wealthy Cistercian congregation. It was a favourite subject of Caspar David Friedrich, and thus became at least the indirect inspiration for the vogue depictions of lonely, overgrown and crumbling monasteries in secluded settings produced by so many painters of the Romantic movement. Founded in the twelfth century by Danish monks, the Kloster was destroyed by Swedish soldiers, who carted off most of its bricks as building material. Only skeletal remains survive, but the arched doorways and empty windows of the ruin are undeniably romantic, and, more prosaically, make a good spot for a picnic.

Practicalities

Greifswald's **Hauptbahnhof** lies immediately below the southwestern corner of the Stadtbefestigung, only a few minutes' walk from the Dom. The **tourist office** is in the arcades of the Rathaus, Am Markt (Mon–Fri 10am–5/6pm; Ⓣ0 38 34/52 13 80, Ⓦwww.greifswald.de). There are a fair number of **private rooms** (❶–❸) available, while the **youth hostel** has a conveniently central location at Pestalozzistr. 11–12 (Ⓣ0 38 34/5 16 90; €17.50/21.50). In Wieck there's an inexpensive **pension**, *Schipp in*, Am Hafen 3 (Ⓣ0 38 34/84 00 26; ❸), plus several **hotels**, including the historic *Zur Fähre*, Fährweg 2 (Ⓣ0 38 34/84 00 49; ❹); *Maria*, Dorfstr. 45 (Ⓣ0 38 34/84 14 26, Ⓦwww.hotel-maria.de; ❺); and *Ryckhotel*, Rosenstr. 17b (Ⓣ0 38 34/8 33 00, Ⓦwww.ryck-hotel.de; ❻). Among the options in town are *Alter Speicher*, Rossmühlenstr. 25 (Ⓣ0 38 34/7 77 00, Ⓦwww.alter-speicher.de; ❻); *Am Dom*, Lange Str. 44 (Ⓣ0 38 34/7 97 50; ❻); and *Kronprinz*, Lange Str. 22 (Ⓣ0 38 34/79 00, Ⓦwww.hotelkronprinz.de; ❻). All these hotels have **restaurants**; other good choices are *Zur Hütte*, Am Markt 12, which does everything from *Kaffee und Kuchen* to light meals, and *Zum Alten Fritz*, Am Markt 13, a Hausbrauerei with beer garden.

Usedom

Usedom, Germany's second largest island, has some fine beaches but is very much in the shadow of Rügen as a Baltic holiday destination, lacking the latter's variety of landscape. Fifty kilometres in length and at times only a kilometre wide, the island has a random shape, like the pattern of spilled liquid, and is separated from the mainland by the Peene Strom, which, though little more than a narrow channel for most of its length, expands suddenly and takes a big bite out of the southern shore as the **Achter Wasser** bay. At its eastern end Usedom is abruptly cut off by the border with Poland, leaving a tiny sliver of its area, including the port of **Świnoujście** (formerly German Swinemünde), in Polish hands.

Before the war Usedom was the haunt of Europe's rich and its resorts ranked among Germany's most fashionable. In the GDR period, it catered primarily to working-class holidaymakers, but since the *Wende* it has gradually moved upmarket again, with many of the grand old Wilhelmine hotels having undergone expensive refurbishments. Much fine Baltic shorefront architecture, and some of the ambience that drew the prewar glitterati, can be experienced in the trio of resorts – **Bansin**, **Heringsdorf** and **Ahlbeck** – which are virtually contiguous and collectively called the "Kaiserbäder", though each retains a distinct identity. Further west is the island's only historic site of note, the rocket research station of **Peenemünde**. As everywhere on the Baltic coast, there's little chance of being able to find a room in July or August without booking in advance. Usedom is fairly flat and thus well suited to cycling, although the volume of car traffic in summer is heavy. It is also well served by public transport, with the railway, the **Usedomer Bäderbahn**, running from the mainland over a new bridge across the Peene Strom and along the entire length of the island to the Polish border. There are also buses serving the main destinations.

Peenemünde

At the extreme northwestern tip of Usedom, at the end of a branch rail line, lies **PEENEMÜNDE**, a former restricted-access military village, which is a world away in spirit from the nearby beach resorts. The army arrived in 1936 to build the research centre at which the long-range liquid-fuel rocket known as the V2 was developed under Werner von Braun, and successfully launched in October 1942. The following August, the base suffered massive damage in an RAF raid, but the V2 was eventually put into production and first used in an attack on London in September 1944. After the war, the base was taken over by the Red Army, later passing to the GDR's Volksarmee, and remained operational until 1990. The **Historisch-Technisches Informationszentrum** (Tues–Sun 9am–4/6pm; €3; Ⓦwww.peenemuende.de), housed in the control bunker of the research station's redbrick power station, documents the base's wartime role, somewhat disingeuously advertising itself as the "Birthplace of Space Travel" – a claim founded on von Braun's subsequent career in the United States as chief designer of the Apollo rocket that put man on the moon, and on the fact that the October 1942 launch was the first time a flying object had left the earth's atmosphere.

Bansin

BANSIN, the westernmost of the Kaiserbäder, is very much a family holiday destination with an excellent, but inevitably crowded, sandy beach. There's otherwise not much to detain you, though Seestrasse, the town's main drag, running from station to beach, is lined by impressive turn-of-the-century houses in brilliant white with wrought-iron balconies. The street terminates at a small square with a clock, which marks the main entrance to the beach.

The **tourist office** (April–Oct Mon–Fri 9am–5/6pm, Sat & Sun 10am–1/3pm; Nov–March Mon–Fri 9am–4pm, Sat & Sun 10am–noon/1pm; Ⓣ03 83 78/4 70 50, Ⓦwww.bansin.de) is in the Haus des Gastes on Strandpromenade. As well as **private rooms** (❶–❸), there are plenty of **hotels**, including *Villa Ingeborg*, Bergstr. 25–26 (Ⓣ03 83 78/2 92 47; ❹); *Admiral*, Strandpromenade 36 (Ⓣ0 38 78/6 60; ❼); *Zur Post*, Seestr. 5 (Ⓣ03 83 78/5 60, Ⓦww.hotel-zur-post-usedom.de; ❼); and *Strandhotel Atlantic*, Strandpromenade 18 (Ⓣ03 83 78/6 05; ❽). The **restaurants** of these hotels are the best places for full meals.

Heringsdorf

The most attractive of the Kaiserbäder triumvirate is **HERINGSDORF**, which retains something of its pre-war atmosphere to complement its near-impeccable looks. Described by Baedeker as "the most fashionable of the Baltic sea-bathing places", Heringsdorf is the oldest resort on Usedom and at one time attracted aristocratic and wealthy holidaymakers from all over Europe, despite its rather unprepossessing name – "Herring Village" – a leftover from its origins as a small fishing port.

Its central square, **Platz des Friedens**, is disfigured by an enormous residential/shopping complex, but elsewhere the town's architecture is mostly in the familiar Baltic-resort style of abundant white facades and attractive balconies. The **Seebrücke** is the longest in Germany, its imposing dimensions being a direct tribute to its celebrated predecessor, which was demolished by the Communists. Heading west, the **Strandpromenade**, decked out with well-regimented flowerbeds, leads past the **Kunstpavillon**, an odd structure looking like a futurist bandstand enclosed by glass, that plays host to temporary art exhibitions.

At the western end of Strandpromenade, a sharp left into Strandstrasse, followed by a right turn, leads you into Maxim-Gorki-Strasse. Here, at no. 13, is the **Maxim-Gorki-Gedenkstätte** (daily 9am–noon & 1–4pm; €1), a small museum devoted to Maxim Gorky and the time he spent in Heringsdorf in 1922. It's housed in the former *Pension Irmgard*, where the author stayed, a period in which he wrote the autobiographical volume *My Universities*. Returning to Platz des Friedens via Badstrasse and Kulmstrasse offers a chance to appreciate Heringsdorf at its best; quiet leafy streets straggle up a hill, flanked by small villas with flaking facades set in little gardens.

The **tourist office** (April–Oct Mon–Fri 9am–5/6pm, Sat & Sun 10am–1/3pm; Nov–March Mon–Fri 9am–4pm, Sat & Sun 10am–noon; ⓣ03 83 78/24 51, ⓦwww.heringsdorf-usedom.de) is at Kulmstr. 33. There are plenty of **private rooms** (❶–❸); the other budget option is Usedom's sole **youth hostel**, which is in a half-timbered house at Puschkinstr. 7–9 (ⓣ03 83 78/2 23 25; €17.50/21.50). Most **hotels** are of high quality and consequently expensive; among the most attractive are *Wald und See*, Rudolf-Breitscheid-Str. 8 (ⓣ03 83 78/3 14 16, ⓦwww.hotel-waldundsee.de; ❻); *Pommerscher Hof*, Seestr. 41 (ⓣ0 3 83 78/6 10; ❼); *Strandhotel Ostseeblick*, Kulmstr. 28 (ⓣ03 83 78/5 40, ⓦwww.all-in-all.com/strandhotel-ostseeblick; ❼); and *Oasis*, Puschkinstr. 10 (ⓣ03 83 78/26 50, ⓦwww.hotel-oasis.de; ❼–❾). All these hotels have **restaurants**; other possibilities for eating and drinking are *Zur Klause*, Strandstr. 6, which does a reasonable selection of inexpensive dishes, and *Terrassencafé*, Kulmstr. 29, which has a good sea view.

Ahlbeck

AHLBECK is another good-looking town with some ornate villas and grand hotels, and there's a pleasant promenade and sandy beach. Its **Seebrücke**, which is graced with four corner towers, is by far the most picturesque on the island. At the far eastern end of town is the border with Poland, around which is an informal market with plenty of inexpensive goods on offer from Polish traders.

The **tourist office** is at Dünenstr. 45 (April–Oct Mon–Fri 9am–5/6pm, Sat & Sun 10am–1/3pm; Nov–March Mon–Fri 9am–4pm, Sat & Sun 10am–noon; ⓣ03 83 78/2 44 97, ⓦwww.ahlbeck.de). There's the usual supply of **private rooms** (❶–❸) and plenty of **hotels**, particularly at the upper end of the market. Among the best are *Seeperle*, Dünenstr. 38 (ⓣ03 83 78/25 50, ⓦwww.seeperle-ahlbeck.kaiserbaeder.de; ❻); *Ostseehotel*, Dünenstr. 41 (ⓣ03 83 78/6 00; ❼); *Villa Auguste Viktoria*, Bismarckstr. 1 (ⓣ03 83 78/24 10, ⓦwww.auguste-viktoria.de; ❼); *Strandhotel*, Dünenstr. 19 (ⓣ0 38 78/5 20, ⓦwww.strandhotelahlbeck.de; ❼); *Ostende*, Dünenstr. 24 (ⓣ03 83 78/5 10, ⓦwww.hotel-ostende.de; ❼); and *Ahlbecker Hof*, Dünenstr. 47 (ⓣ03 83 78/6 20; ❽-❾). All of these have fine **restaurants**.

Neubrandenburg

At the eastern end of the Mecklenburg lake district, about 75km southeast of Güstrow and 100km south of Stralsund, is **NEUBRANDENBURG**, an important rail junction, especially for routes into Poland. Like so many places in the former GDR, it offers the dichotomy of historic monuments of the highest class co-existing with the most painful of eyesores. As the main sights can be seen in a few hours, it's best viewed as a stopoff en route to or from the Baltic coast or the lakes to the west.

Neubrandenburg was founded in 1248 by Margrave Johann I of Brandenburg (hence its name), but was incorporated into Mecklenburg early the following century. From this period dates the extraordinary 2.5-kilometre-long **Stadtmauer** – one of the most impressive municipal fortification systems anywhere in Europe – encircling the Altstadt. Miraculously, it came through World War II virtually intact, though the rest of the town was almost completely destroyed. Subsequently, the Altstadt was filled with the concrete architecture beloved of the GDR regime, with the fifteen-storey **Haus der Kultur und Bildung** (House of Culture and Education) placed smack in the middle. Its one saving grace is the view from the **platform** (daily 10am–5.45pm; €1) at the top, which can be reached by lift.

To appreciate the Stadtmauer to the full, you need to walk round it twice – once on the inside, once on the outside. It's pierced by four colossal gateways, whose patterned brickwork is of a scale or delicacy more in keeping with a great civic church or town hall than a defensive system. Earliest of these is the **Friedländer Tor**, the northeastern entrance to the town, which has inner and outer gateways linked by a stretch of fortified wall, plus a semi-circular tower, known as the Zinger, as a first line of defence. Today it's a café and commercial art gallery. Only slightly less formidable-looking is the **Treptower Tor** (Tues–Sun 10am–5pm; €1) on the western side of town, which now houses the local archeology museum. The most elaborately decorative brickwork of all is found on the southern gateway, the **Stargarder Tor**, whose inner face is adorned with nine enigmatic, highly stylized female figures. Eight more statues in the same vein can be seen on the **Neues Tor** to the east, which is distinguished by enormous finger-shaped gables. Another curiosity of Neubrandenburg is the presence of 26 (out of an original total of 56) half-timbered houses, known as **Wiekhäuser**, which are conversions of the bastions built directly onto the Stadtmauer. Not surprisingly, they're the most sought-after properties in town; several are now craft shops.

Two large brick Gothic churches are the only set-piece attractions within the walls. The modest architecture of the **Johanniskirche** at the northern end of the Altstadt is a reflection of its original function as a Franciscan friary: the church itself is now a Protestant parish, while the refectory is used as local government offices. Altogether grander is the **Marienkirche** a few minutes' walk to the south, which forms a clear ecclesiastical counterpart to the four gateways. Grievously damaged in the war, it has recently been restored and is now a concert hall.

Practicalities

Neubrandenburg's **Bahnhof** is just beyond the northern confines of the Altstadt, separated from it only by the width of Friedrich-Engels-Ring, which follows the perimeter of the Stadtmauer. The **tourist office** (Mon–Fri

9am–6pm, Sat 10am–2pm; Ⓣ03 95/1 94 33, Ⓦwww.neubrandenburg.de), which is in a glass pavilion on Turmstrasse, directly opposite the Kaufhof, can arrange **private rooms** (❷–❸). A fair number of **hotels** can be found just outside the perimeters of the Stadtmauer. These include *Jahnke*, Rostocker Str. 12 (Ⓣ03 95/58 17 00; ❹); *Weinert*, Ziegelbergstr. 23 (Ⓣ03 95/58 12 30, Ⓦwww.hotel-weinert.de; ❹); and *St Georg*, St Georg 6 (Ⓣ03 95/5 44 37 88, Ⓦwww.hotel-sankt-georg.de; ❺). The top-of-the-range *Radisson SAS* is in the heart of town at Treptower Str. 1 (Ⓣ03 95/5 58 60, Ⓦwww.radissonsas.com; ❼). Both *St Georg* and *Radisson SAS* have good **restaurants**, and the former also has a beer garden. Quality meals are also served at *Fritz Reuter,* at Friedländer Str. 2a in the Altstadt, while other restaurants with a cosy atmosphere are *Wiekhaus 45* and *Mudder-Schulten-Stuben*, both on 4-Ringstrasse, and *Zur Lohmühle*, Am Stargarder Tor 4, a converted mill with a wine and beer garden. The Marienkirche (Ⓣ03 95/5 59 51 77, Ⓦwww.konzertkirche-nb.de) is the main venue for **concerts**, including those by the town's own symphony orchestra, the Neubrandenburger Philharmonie (Ⓦwww.philharmonie-online.de).

Neustrelitz

About 35km south of Neubrandenburg by road or rail is the odd town of **NEUSTRELITZ**, which was founded in 1732 as the custom-built capital of Mecklenburg-Strelitz, the smaller of the two duchies into which Mecklenburg was divided in 1701. It's a fascinating example of a planned Residenzstadt built to a strict geometric plan around a small hunting lodge transformed into a grand ducal palace. Streets of sober Baroque buildings radiate out from a central square to striking effect, and the town slopes down towards the tree-lined shores of the Zierker See. Though it initially prospered from its position on trade routes between the coast and Berlin, it never rose above sleepy backwater status, as the absence of significant post-eighteenth-century development testifies. It was allowed to decay in the GDR period, and has struggled in recent years to come to terms with post-unification realities. Nonetheless, it benefits from its setting between the two constituent parts of the **Nationalpark Müritz**, which was established to protect a section of the Mecklenburg Lake District particularly rich in flora (especially orchids) and bird life. Much the larger of the two parts lies immediately west of town, and stretches all the way to the eastern bank of the Müritzsee.

The focal point of Neustrelitz itself is the central **Markt**, which is a perfect square measuring 120 metres on each side. For several years after the *Wende*, a huge Soviet war memorial stood in the grassy area in the middle. Although it has now been removed, the square has not yet followed the normal eastern German pattern of being reclaimed for commerce. The one set piece remaining is the Baroque **Stadtkirche**, which was built according to plans drawn up by a doctor in the service of one of the local dukes.

From the Markt, the streets radiate outwards in eight directions. Head down Schlossstrasse to the **Schlosspark**, a lakeside ornamental garden laid out in the English style by the great Berlin landscape gardener, Peter Joseph Lenné. The Schloss itself was destroyed in 1945 and no traces now remain, though its **Orangerie**, built in 1755 as a winter home for plants, still survives. Its previously bare interior was transformed in the 1840s by two more leading lights of the Berlin art world – the architect Karl Friedrich Schinkel and the sculptor

Christian Daniel Rauch. Together they created three highly ornate interiors for festive purposes, each dominated by a particular colour scheme and decorated in a pseudo-Pompeiian style.

Schinkel's very personal and visionary neo-Gothic manner was the inspiration for the architecture of the nearby **Schlosskirche**, though he was not involved in the actual construction. At the northwestern end of the Schlosspark, just past the small Neoclassical **Tempel**, the **Zierker See** begins. Its shores are wonderful for strolling; you can also **rent boats**, and there are **cruises** during the summer months.

Practicalities

Neustrelitz's **Bahnhof** is only about ten minutes' walk from the Markt along Strelitzer Strasse. The **tourist office** is at Markt 1 (April & Oct Mon–Fri 9am–noon & 1–4.30pm; May–Sept Mon–Fri 9am–5pm, Sat & Sun 10am–1.30pm; Nov–March Mon–Thurs 9am–noon & 1–-4.30pm, Fri 9am–1pm; ⓣ0 39 81/25 31 19, ⓦwww.neustrelitz.de). Chances are that you won't want to stay overnight, but there are plenty of **private rooms** (❷–❸) available, plus several **hotels,** which are better value than normal by eastern German standards. These include *Haegert*, Zierker Str. 44 (ⓣ0 39 81/2 00 31 56; ❹); *Pinus*, Ernst-Moritz-Arndt-Str. 55 (ⓣ0 39 81/44 53 50; ❹); *Schlossgarten*, Tiergartenstr. 15 (ⓣ0 39 81/24 50 00, ⓦwww.hotel-schlossgarten.de; ❻); and *Park Hotel Fasanerie*, Karbe-Wagner-Str. 59 (ⓣ0 39 81/44 36 00, ⓦwww.parkhotel-neustrelitz.de; ❻). Each of these, except *Pinus*, has a **restaurant**. An alternative place for a meal is the *Inselgaststätte Helgoland*, on an islet linked to the shore by a footbridge; it's near the town's harbour area, just north of the Schlosspark. The Neoclassical Landestheater Neustrelitz, Friedrich-Ludwig-Jahn-Str. 14 (ⓣ0 39 81/27 70, ⓦwww.landestheater-mecklenburg.de), is the main venue for both **drama** and **music**.

Travel details

Trains

Neubrandenburg to: Berlin (10 daily; 2hr 10min); Güstrow (8 daily; 2hr); Neustrelitz (17 daily; 45min); Stralsund (10 daily; 1hr 50min).
Rostock to: Bad Doberan (16 daily; 25min); Berlin (12 daily; 3hr); Güstrow (frequent; 40min); Magdeburg (9 daily; 4hr); Neubrandenburg (13 daily; 2hr 30min); Neustrelitz (13 daily; 2hr); Sassnitz (15 daily; 1hr); Schwerin (12 daily; 1hr 15min); Stralsund (15 daily; 1hr 20min); Wismar (11 daily; 1hr 45min).
Schwerin to: Berlin (7 daily; 3hr); Güstrow (12 daily; 1hr); Ludwigslust (hourly; 30min); Magdeburg (6 daily; 3hr); Rostock (15 daily; 2hr 30min); Wismar (11 daily; 1hr).
Stralsund to: Berlin (17 daily; 4hr 30min); Greifswald (frequent; 25 min); Neubrandenburg (10 daily; 1hr 50min); Neustrelitz (7 daily; 2hr 30min); Rostock (15 daily; 1hr 20min); Sassnitz (10 daily; 1hr 10min).

9

Berlin and Brandenburg

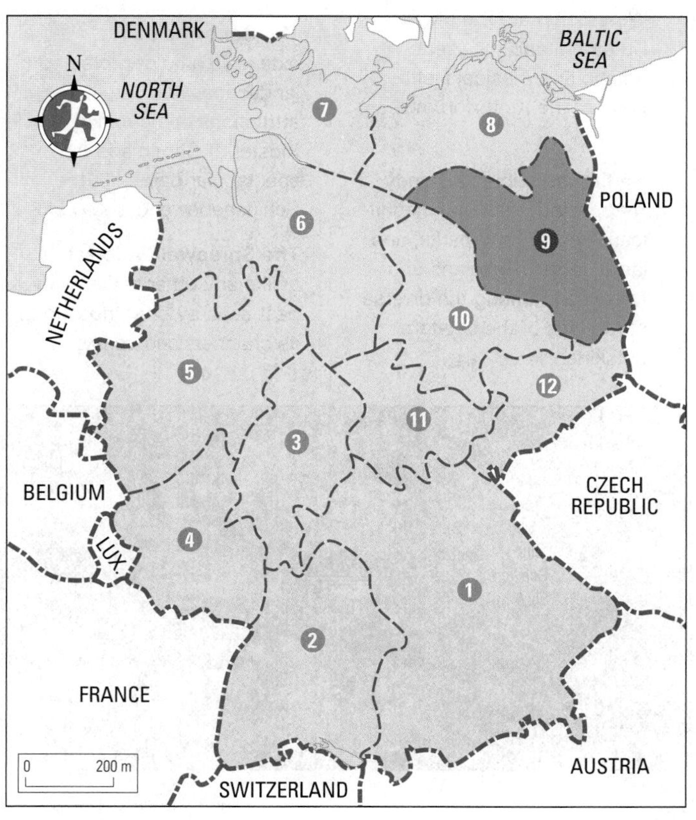

CHAPTER 9

Highlights

✱ **Berlin: the eastern centre** The heart of the former GDR capital includes the iconic Brandenburger Tor, the famous boulevard of Unter den Linden and the fabulous archeological collections on Museumsinsel. See p.758

✱ **Berlin: the western centre** In the centre of the former West Berlin are the ritzy Ku'damm and the great artistic and musical institutions of the Kulturforum. See p.773

✱ **Berlin: the suburbs** Trendy "happening" districts, magnificent palaces and parks, and large tracts of lakeland and forests are among the diverse attractions of the capital's outskirts. See p.781

✱ **Potsdam** Once the great pride of the Prussian kingdom, this garden city is a wonderful fusion of nature and art. See p.802

✱ **Brandenburg** A venerable city with fine medieval monuments and a lovely setting on a series of islands in the River Havel. See p.814

✱ **The Schorfheide** An extensive area of protected landscape, with setpiece attractions in the ruined Kloster of Chorin and the spectacular barge-lift, the Schiffshebewerk. See p.818

✱ **The Spreewald** A forest unlike any other in Germany, best seen by boat trips along its channels and canals. See p.820

△ Brandenburger Tor (Brandenburg Gate), Berlin

9

Berlin and Brandenburg

Berlin is something of a weather-vane of modern European history, yet its rise to national prominence was a long and slow process. Founded in the thirteenth century, it is little more than a third of the age of Cologne or Augusburg. It did not achieve the early growth and economic development of other medieval foundations, such as Hamburg, Lübeck, Frankfurt or Nürnberg; it was not even the capital of a substantial feudal duchy, as were Munich and Stuttgart. Instead, it belatedly became the capital of **Brandenburg**, a marshland territory at the very eastern extremity of the Holy Roman Empire. This province was founded as a margraviate, or frontier district, by **Albert the Bear** (Albrecht der Bär) in 1157 from land bequeathed to him by Pribislav-Heinrich, a Slav king who had converted to Christianity.

In 1411, Brandenburg was made a hereditary possession of the **Hohenzollern** family, and four years later the margraviate was raised to the status of an Electorate of the Holy Roman Empire. However, for all the dynasty's lofty ambitions, Berlin remained little more than a village until the seventeenth century. The first important step towards a grander role came in 1618, when Elector Johann Sigismund inherited the Baltic duchy of **Prussia**, and merged it with his family's heartlands to form the new state of Brandenburg-Prussia, which quickly established itself as an expansionist miltary force on the European stage. Named after the exterminated tribe that had inhabited it in the early Middle Ages, Prussia lay outside the Holy Roman Empire and thus was not subject to any of its rules. In 1701, Elector Friedrich III circumvented one of the most important of these – the ban on the assumption of royal status – by crowning himself King Friedrich I of Prussia. Thereafter, the Hohenzollern state, although still centred on Berlin, went under the misleading designation of Prussia. It became ever more predatory in its policy of territorial acquisition, eventually stretching all the way west to the Rhineland.

When the Prussians finally forged a unified Germany for the first time ever in 1871, Berlin was the only possible choice for the new role of **national capital**. Hitler intended to take this a stage further by transforming it into a world capital named Germania. Instead, the city found itself **partitioned** among the victors after World War II, and quickly became a microcosm of the

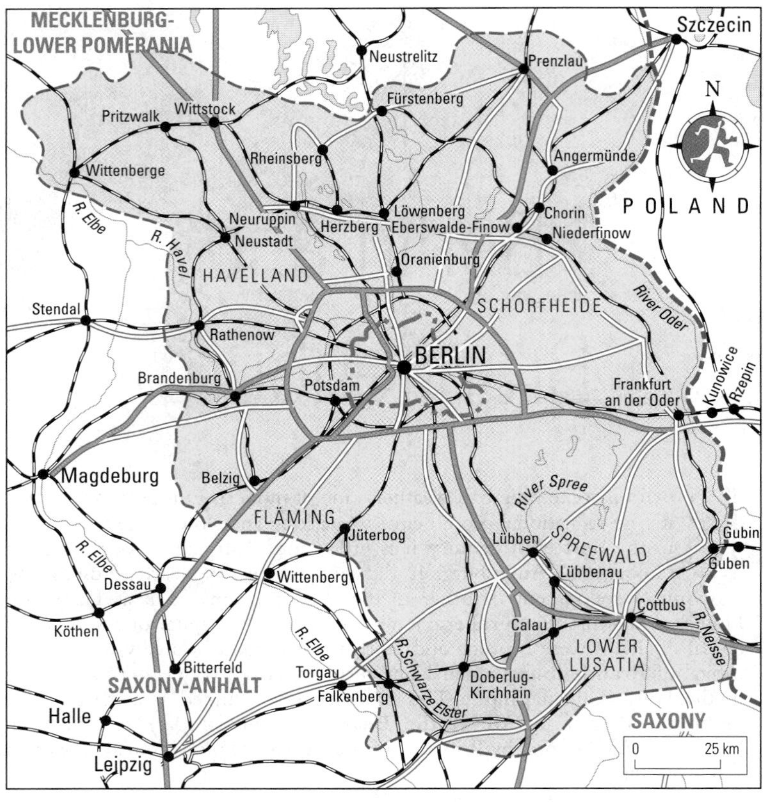

Cold War era. While the Soviet-occupied eastern sector – which included the historic city centre – duly became the capital of the rump state that was the GDR, the larger part of the city was left as the stranded enclave of West Berlin, a place with an ambiguous status (it was never formally merged into the Federal Republic) propped up by vast outside subsidies, with a declining population only kept in check by an influx of immigrants (principally from Turkey), draught dodgers and seekers of alternative lifestyles. From 1961, the two parts of the city were physically separated by the **Berlin Wall**, the first frontier in history built to keep its own citizens in, rather than an invader out.

After the Wall fell in 1989, Berlin's status as capital of Germany (which it had never officially lost) was reconfirmed. However, it faced determined opposition from Bonn in its desire to re-establish itself as the national **seat of government**. Although Berlin eventually emerged triumphant from this argument, it was decided to keep several key ministries and other public bodies in Bonn. This was a calculated measure designed to ensure that Berlin – with its deeply tainted historical record – does not become too dominant within Germany. Thus the vast rebuilding and re-development that the city is currently undergoing is something of a delicate balance. There is a clear need to increase the population (which had fallen by more than a million from its prewar level), and to create a city that is a worthy capital of Europe's most powerful nation, yet at the same time to ensure that it does not become a direct German counterpart of London or Paris.

One unintended consequence of Berlin's postwar division is that it has belatedly become a city-state, with the rest of the old Brandenburg margraviate now an entirely separate Land of the Federal Republic. Though there were hopes that the two Länder would eventually merge, that now seems a distant prospect at best, having been flatly rejected by the latter in a referendum. **Potsdam**, Brandenburg's present-day capital, forms a virtually seemless whole with Berlin, and its wonderful palaces and parks easily outdo those of its larger neighbour. Elsewhere in the province are time-warped towns, most notably **Brandenburg** itself, and a highly distinctive scenic area, the water-strewn **Spreewald**.

Berlin

The division of **BERLIN** into zones of occupation in 1945, although seemingly arbitrary, followed existing local government boundaries, and the dual profile which emerged was by no means solely a product of the Cold War. In his famous interwar collection of short stories, *Goodbye to Berlin*, Christopher Isherwood wrote:

> **Berlin is a city with two centres – the cluster of expensive hotels, bars, cinemas, shops around the Memorial Church, a sparkling nucleus of light, like a sham diamond, in the shabby twilight of the town; and the self-conscious civic centre of buildings around the Unter den Linden, carefully arranged.**

The latter, the political and cultural core of the Imperial German capital, duly became the heart of East Berlin and of the GDR, while the former quickly adapted itself to the makeshift role of city centre of the stranded enclave that was West Berlin. Because of the decades of division, the reunited city found itself with two of almost everything, but the rationalization process has already reduced the duplication quite markedly, and will eliminate it almost entirely over the course of the next decade.

Although never a conventionally beautiful city, Berlin has much fine architecture, as well as an extraordinary spread of **museums** which collectively rank among the very richest on the planet. It also has a wide range of **bars** and **restaurants**, a vibrant **nightlife** and strong traditions in the **performing arts**. Because it occupies a vast geographical area, one interrupted by a plethora of parks, forests and lakes, Berlin is not a place that is appreciated easily or quickly.

Arrival and information

Berlin has three international **airports** (all ⓣ01 80/5 00 01 86, ⓦwww.berlin-airport.de). Most scheduled and charter flights arrive at **Tegel**, in the north of the city, from where buses #X9 and #109 run every five to fifteen minutes to Bahnhof Zoo, while JetExpressBus TXL goes to Unter den Linden. Alternatively, take bus #109 to Jakob-Kaiser-Platz or bus #128 to Walter

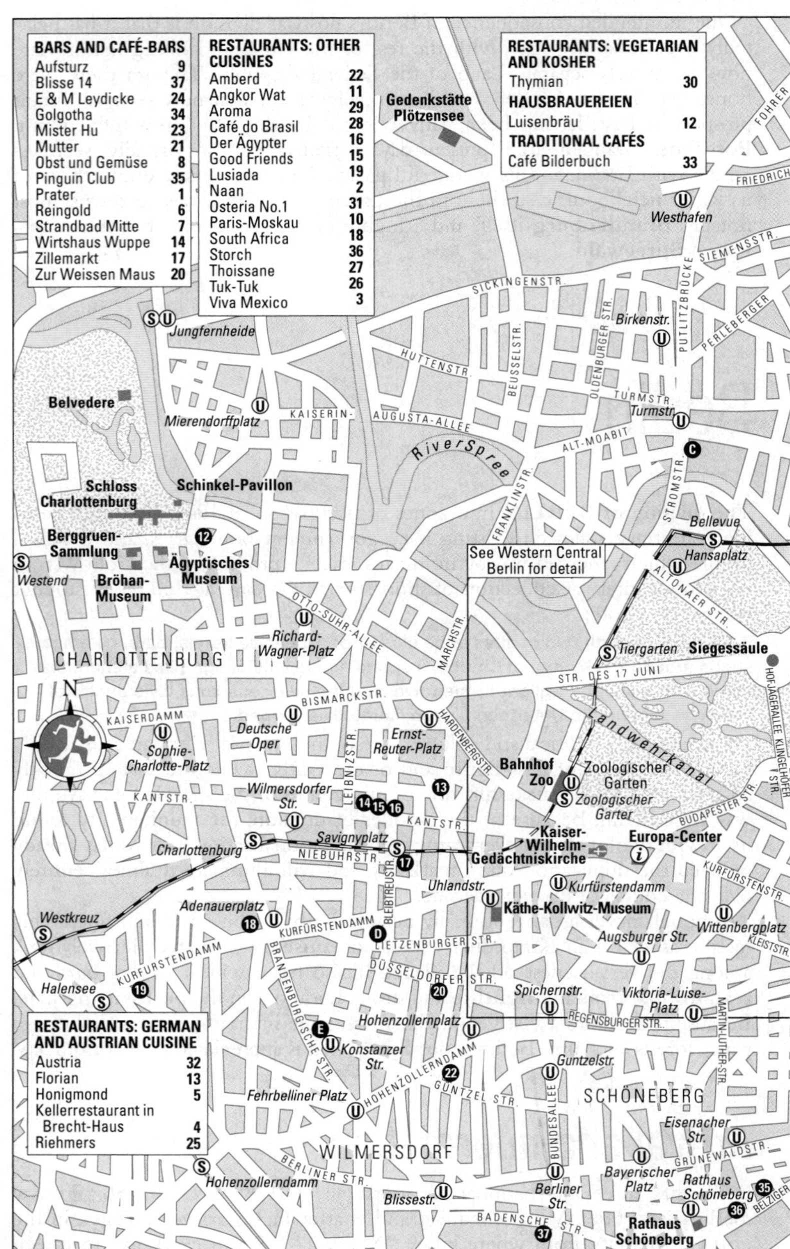

BARS AND CAFÉ-BARS
Aufsturz 9
Blisse 14 37
E & M Leydicke 24
Golgotha 34
Mister Hu 23
Mutter 21
Obst und Gemüse 8
Pinguin Club 35
Prater 1
Reingold 6
Strandbad Mitte 7
Wirtshaus Wuppe 14
Zillemarkt 17
Zur Weissen Maus 20
RESTAURANTS: OTHER CUISINES
Amberd 22
Angkor Wat 11
Aroma 29
Café do Brasil 28
Der Ägypter 16
Good Friends 15
Lusiada 19
Naan 2
Osteria No.1 31
Paris-Moskau 10
South Africa 18
Storch 36
Thoissane 27
Tuk-Tuk 26
Viva Mexico 3
RESTAURANTS: VEGETARIAN AND KOSHER
Thymian 30
HAUSBRAUEREIEN
Luisenbräu 12
TRADITIONAL CAFÉS
Café Bilderbuch 33
RESTAURANTS: GERMAN AND AUSTRIAN CUISINE
Austria 32
Florian 13
Honigmond 5
Kellerrestaurant in Brecht-Haus 4
Riehmers 25
See Western Central Berlin for detail
Gedenkstätte Plötzensee
Jungfernheide
Westhafen
Belvedere
Mierendorffplatz
Schloss Charlottenburg
Schinkel-Pavillon
Berggruen-Sammlung
Ägyptisches Museum
Bröhan-Museum
Westend
Richard-Wagner-Platz
CHARLOTTENBURG
Deutsche Oper
Ernst-Reuter-Platz
Sophie-Charlotte-Platz
Wilmersdorfer Str.
Savignyplatz
Charlottenburg
Westkreuz
Adenauerplatz
Halensee
Bahnhof Zoo
Zoologischer Garten
Kaiser-Wilhelm-Gedächtniskirche
Europa-Center
Tiergarten
Siegessäule
Bellevue
Hansaplatz
Birkenstr.
Turmstr.
Uhlandstr.
Kurfürstendamm
Käthe-Kollwitz-Museum
Augsburger Str.
Wittenbergplatz
Spichernstr.
Viktoria-Luise-Platz
Hohenzollernplatz
Konstanzer Str.
Fehrbelliner Platz
Guntzelstr.
SCHÖNEBERG
WILMERSDORF
Eisenacher Str.
Bayerischer Platz
Rathaus Schöneberg
Hohenzollerndamm
Berliner Str.
Blissestr.
River Spree
Landwehrkanal
SICKINGENSTR.
HUTTENSTR.
KAISERIN-AUGUSTA-ALLEE
ALT-MOABIT
TURMSTR.
BEUSSELSTR.
OLDENBURGER STR.
PUTLITZBRÜCKE
PERLEBERGER
SIEMENSSTR.
FRIEDRICH
FÖHRER
FRANKLINSTR.
STROMSTR.
ALTONAER STR.
OTTO-SUHR-ALLEE
MARCHSTR.
STR. DES 17 JUNI
BISMARCKSTR.
HARDENBERGSTR.
KAISERDAMM
KANTSTR.
LEIBNIZSTR.
NIEBUHRSTR.
BLEIBTREUSTR.
KURFÜRSTENDAMM
LIETZENBURGER STR.
DÜSSELDORFER STR.
BRANDENBURGISCHE STR.
HOHENZOLLERNDAMM
GÜNTZEL STR.
BUNDESALLEE
REGENSBURGER STR.
MARTIN-LUTHER-STR.
GRUNEWALDSTR.
BERLINER STR.
BADENSCHE STR.
BUDAPESTER STR.
KURFÜRSTENSTR.
KLEISTSTR.
HOFJÄGERALLEE
KLINGELHÖFER STR.
BELZIGER

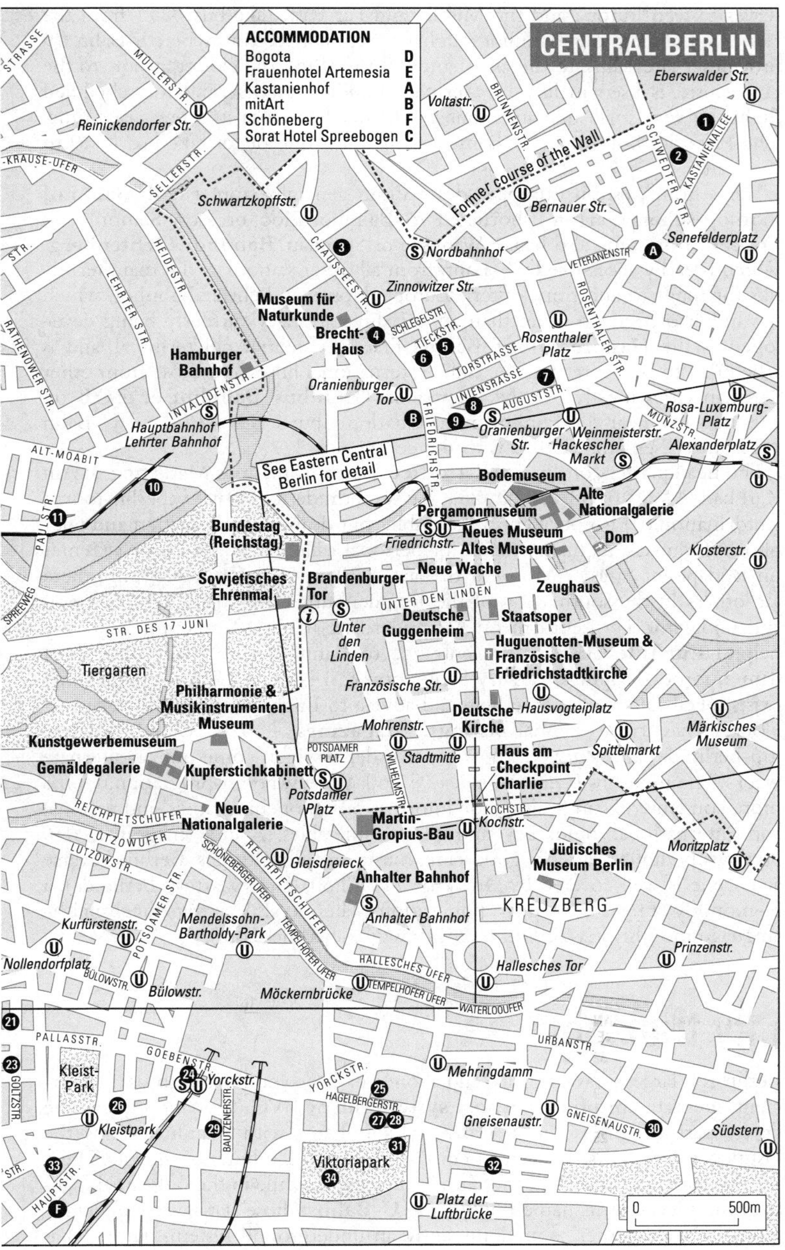
CENTRAL BERLIN
ACCOMMODATION
Bogota D
Frauenhotel Artemesia E
Kastanienhof A
mitArt B
Schöneberg F
Sorat Hotel Spreebogen C
Former course of the Wall
See Eastern Central Berlin for detail
Museum für Naturkunde
Brecht-Haus
Hamburger Bahnhof
Hauptbahnhof Lehrter Bahnhof
Bodemuseum
Pergamonmuseum
Alte Nationalgalerie
Neues Museum
Altes Museum
Dom
Bundestag (Reichstag)
Sowjetisches Ehrenmal
Brandenburger Tor
Neue Wache
Zeughaus
Deutsche Guggenheim
Staatsoper
Huguenotten-Museum & Französische Friedrichstadtkirche
Tiergarten
Philharmonie & Musikinstrumenten-Museum
Kunstgewerbemuseum
Gemäldegalerie
Kupferstichkabinett
Neue Nationalgalerie
Deutsche Kirche
Haus am Checkpoint Charlie
Martin-Gropius-Bau
Jüdisches Museum Berlin
Anhalter Bahnhof
KREUZBERG
Mendelssohn-Bartholdy-Park
Kleist-Park
Viktoriapark
Märkisches Museum
0 500m

Schreiber Platz and transfer to the U-Bahn system. Berlin's second airport, **Schönefeld**, lies just beyond the southeastern edge of the city, and mainly serves eastern Europe and the Middle and Far East. Take bus #171 from the terminal building to S-Bahnhof Flughafen Schönefeld, from where S-Bahn #9 provides a direct link to the city centre. **Tempelhof**, the closest airport to the city centre, is used mainly by German domestic carriers and for scheduled flights by very small operators, but is scheduled to close in a few years time. The Platz der Luftbrücke U-Bahn station is just outside, or take bus #119 to the centre.

Trains from western European destinations generally stop at both **Bahnhof Zoologischer Garten** (shortened to Bahnhof Zoo or Zoo Station) and **Ostbahnhof**; some also halt at Wannsee or Spandau. **Bahnhof Lichtenberg**, which is easily accessible by S-Bahn from all other stations, is the main terminus for trains to and from eastern Europe. However, Lehrter Bahnhof, which has hitherto been no more than an S-Bahn station, is currently being developed as the **Hauptbahnhof**, Berlin's first-ever central rail terminal, and is scheduled to be operational in 2005. International buses and those from other German cities mostly use the **Zentraler Omnibus Bahnhof** or **ZOB** on Masurenallee near the Funkturm, in Charlottenburg. Bus #149 and U-Bahn #2 from Kaiserdamm link it with the centre.

The headquarters of the **tourist office**, Berlin Tourismus Marketing, at Am Karlsbad 11 (Ⓣ0 30/25 00 25, Ⓦwww.btm.de or Ⓦwww.berlin-tourist-information.de) is not open to the public, but deals with all written and telephone enquiries. Its main branch for personal callers is in the Europa-Center on Budapester Strasse (Mon–Sat 8.30am–8.30pm, Sun 10am–6.30pm); there are others in the south wing of the Brandenburger Tor (daily 9.30am–6pm) and under the Fernsehturm on Alexanderplatz (daily 10am–6pm). The very helpful **EurAide** office at the entrance to Bahnhof Zoo (daily: June–Sept 8am–noon & 1–6pm; Oct–May 8am–noon & 1–4.30pm; Ⓦwww.euraide.de) exists specifically to dispense help and advice to English-speaking travellers.

Berlin has two essential **listings magazines** – *Tip* (€2.50, Ⓦwww.tip-berlin.de) and *Zitty* (€2, Ⓦwww.zitty.de) – which come out on alternate weeks. The monthly *Berlin Programm* (€1.60, Ⓦwww.berlin-programm.de) has more condensed listings, alongside information on opening times, and national and international train, bus and plane timetables. A free magazine, *030* (Ⓦwww.berlin030.de), has good club, music and film listings. Berlin's diverse arts scene is well covered by *Artery Berlin* (€2.50, Ⓦwww.artery-berlin.de), a bi-monthly English/German publication. There's also a general English-language monthly, *Ex-Berliner* (€2, Ⓦwww.ex-berliner.com).

City transport

Berlin is a large, sprawling city, and sooner or later you'll need to use its efficient integrated **public transport system** run by BVG (Ⓦwww.bvg.de). The fastest part of this is the **S-Bahn**, which shares with mainline trains the distinctive elevated tracks which cut right through the heart of the city. There are also some underground stretches in the centre, while in the outskirts it runs at ground level. As its name implies, the **U-Bahn**, whose stations are generally much closer together, is predominantly an underground system, but also has stretches of both elevated and ground-level track. Free coloured **maps** of Berlin's **Schnellbahnnetz** (the entire network of S-Bahn, U-Bahn and mainline trains) can be picked up from the cubicle outside Bahnhof Zoo, and from the kiosks on station platforms. **Buses** cover most of the areas that cannot be reached by train, while #100 and #200, which run between Bahnhof Zoo and Alexanderplatz, are particularly useful for sightseeing. Eastern Berlin's **tram** network survives from prewar days, and has been extensively modernized in the last few years.

Tickets are valid on all forms of transport within the system, including regional mainline trains, and can be bought from the orange-coloured machines at the entrances to all U- and S-Bahn stations, and from kiosks at the larger stations. The network is divided into three tariff zones (A, B and C), which are colour coded on maps. Paying for single journeys can be an expensive business, and it's usually better to invest in a **day ticket** (*Tageskarte*), costing €5.60 for zones A and B, €5.70 for B and C, or €6 for all three zones. You can also buy a **seven-day ticket** (*Sieben-Tage-Karte*) for €23.40–29, depending on the zones, or a **monthly ticket** (*Monatskarte*) for €72.50–82.50. A **premium monthly ticket** (*Monatskarte Premium*), costing €67.30–83.40, allows unlimited travel for one accompanying adult plus up to three children after 8pm, all day Saturday and Sunday and on public holidays. Note that, although monthly tickets offer considerable savings, their validity commences on the first of each month, not on the date of purchase. Another option, available from tourist offices and hotels as well as ticket kiosks, is the **Berlin WelcomeCard**, which costs €19 for three days, giving unlimited travel across the system for an adult and up to three children, plus reduced entry to many museums and attractions.

Accommodation

Berlin offers a wide variety of **accommodation** of all types, located all over the city. Finding a hotel room, in particular, is a bit easier than it used to be, particularly in the middle and upper ranges, but it's still advisable to book well in advance, particularly during trade shows or for special events such as the Love Parade (early July), the Berlin Marathon (first Sunday in October) and the Internationales Filmfestspiele (February).

Moderate and budget **hotels and pensions** are found in much greater numbers in the west than in the east. Even if it is not so well endowed as it was before unification, the area around Kurfürstendamm and Savignyplatz remains a fruitful hunting ground for reasonably priced rooms. Berlin's three DJH **youth hostels**, which all require HI membership, are used extensively by school and sporting parties, and are frequently full so it's always advisable to phone ahead. However, there's also an ever-growing number of more informal, **privately run hostels**, which tend to dispense with the traditional surcharge for older guests, lockouts and curfews. None of Berlin's **campsites** is close to the centre, though all are inexpensive. Finally, several **bed-and-breakfast agencies** offer private rooms at moderate prices, while the long-stay specialists, the **Mitwohnzentralen**, can almost always locate a suitable room or apartment (generally for a minimum stay of a week) at reasonably short notice.

Hotels and pensions

Altberlin am Potsdamer Platz Potsdamer Str. 67, Tiergarten ⓣ0 30/2 61 29 99, ⓦwww.altberlin-hotel.de. Large pension just a few minutes' walk from the Tiergarten museums, refurbished a few years ago with *fin-de-siècle* trappings to match the architecture. ❻–❾

Am Anhalter Bahnhof Stresemannstr. 36, Kreuzberg ⓣ0 30/2 51 03 42, ⓦwww.hotel-anhalter-bahnhof.de. A good location south of Potsdamer Platz and the Kulturforum, but don't expect peace and quiet, as the hotel faces a major thoroughfare. ⑤–⑦

art'otel Berlin Mitte Wallstr. 70–73, Mitte ⓣ0 30/24 06 20, ⓦwww.artotel.de/berlin. Prestigious designer hotel, partly in a historic mansion, partly in a modern extension. It has two restaurants – the expensive *Im Ermelerhaus* (evenings only, closed Sun & Mon) and the quite moderately priced *Raabe-Diele*. ⑧–⑨

Bogota Schlüterstr. 45, Charlottenburg ⓣ0 30/8 81 50 01, ⓕ88 33 58 87. Pleasant large hotel in a nineteenth-century building, offering a choice of rooms of varying degrees of luxury. ⑤–⑦

Brandenburger Hof Eislebener Str. 14, Wilmersdorf ⓣ0 30/21 40 50, ⓦwww.relaischateaux.com. This occupies a grand Wilhelmine palace with Bauhaus interior decoration. One of its restaurants, *Die Quadriga* (weekday evenings only) ranks among Berlin's top gourmet addresses. ⑨

Brauhaus in Spandau Neuendorfer Str. 1, Spandau ⓣ0 30/3 53 90 70, ⓦwww.brauhaus-spandau.de. A charming small hotel in Spandau, at the far western edge of the city. Its Hausbrauerei brews a Pils and various seasonal brews; moderately priced meals are served in the beer garden and restaurant (closed Mon lunchtime). ⑥

Columbus Meinekestr. 5, Charlottenburg ⓣ&ⓕ0 30/8 81 50 61. Quiet and comfortable pension in a tenement just off the Ku'damm. ④–⑥

Frauenhotel Artemisia Brandenburgische Str. 18, Wilmersdorf ⓣ0 30/8 73 89 05, ⓦwww.frauenhotel-berlin.de. A popular women-only hotel, with a roof garden and exhibitions. Fills up quickly, so book well in advance. ⑥

Funk Fasanenstr. 69, Charlottenburg ⓣ0 30/8 82 71 93, ⓦwww.hotel-pensionfunk.de. Approached via a marble stairway with antique lift, this pension just off Ku'damm still preserves many of the period features from when it was the home of Danish silent movie star Asta Nielsen. It has some basic rooms, as well as more luxurious ones, which are all individually furnished. ④–⑥

Imperator Meinekestr. 5, Charlottenburg ⓣ0 30/8 81 41 81, ⓕ8 85 19 19. Good value, intimate hotel, situated in the same building as *Columbus*. Rooms are spacious and stylishly decorated. ⑤–⑦

Kastanienhof Kastanienallee 65–66, Mitte ⓣ0 30/44 30 50, ⓦwww.hotel-kastanienhof-berlin.de. Offers well-appointed rooms at reasonable prices, and is handy for the nightlife of nearby Prenzlauer Berg. ⑥–⑧

Kempinski Hotel Bristol Kurfürstendamm 27, Charlottenburg ⓣ0 30/88 43 40, ⓦwww.kempinskiberlin.de. For many years this ranked as the city's most famous luxury hotel, and, despite being challenged by a host of newcomers, still ranks among the very best. It has two prestigious restaurants – the very expensive *Kempinski Grill* (closed Mon) and the more reasonably priced *Kempinski-Eck*. ⑨

Korfu II Rankestr. 35, Charlottenburg ⓣ0 30/2 12 47 90, ⓦwww.hp-korfu.de. Occupying three floors of a tenement immediately opposite the Kaiser-Wilhelm-Gedächtniskirche, this offers no-frills but well-maintained rooms, free Internet access, and a discount on first-night bookings made after 6pm. ③–⑤

Luisenhof Köpenicker Str. 92, Mitte ⓣ0 30/2 41 59 06, ⓦwww.luisenhof.de. This nineteenth-century coaching company building has been converted into a very tastefully appointed hotel and restaurant. ⑨

Meineke Meinekestr. 10, Charlottenburg ⓣ0 30/8 89 21 20, ⓦwww.hotel-meineke-berlin.de. Old-fashioned, typical Berlin hotel, with an amiable atmosphere, a minute's walk from the Ku'damm. ⑥

mitArt Friedrichstr. 127, Mitte ⓣ0 30/28 39 04 30, ⓕ28 39 04 32. Originally a pension for artists, this is handy for the nightlife of the Schanzenviertel. A wholefood breakfast is included in the room price. ⑤

Park Inn Alexanderplatz 8, Mitte ⓣ0 30/2 38 90, ⓦwww.rezidorparkinn.com. A big, ugly block dominating Alexanderplatz, but its 1000 en-suite rooms are pleasant enough in a bland way, with unbeatable views over the city. It also has a decent restaurant. ⑦–⑨

Schöneberg Hauptstr. 135, Schöneberg ⓣ0 30/7 80 96 60, ⓦwww.hotel-schoeneberg.de. Pleasant hotel bordering leafy surburban Friedenau to the south of the city centre. There are some no-smoking rooms. ⑥

Sorat Hotel Spreebogen Alt-Moabit 99, Tiergarten ⓣ0 30/39 92 00, ⓦwww.sorat-hotels.com. A gleaming hotel directly overlooking the Spree, offering very high standards. It also has a fine if expensive restaurant (closed Sun evenings). ⑨

Sylter Hof Kurfürstenstr. 116, Schöneberg ⓣ0 30/2 12 00, ⓦwww.sylterhof-berlin.de. Large, well-appointed hotel close to Wittenbergplatz and the Ku'damm. It also has a good restaurant (closed Sun). ⑦

Unter den Linden Unter den Linden 14, Mitte ⓣ0 30/23 81 10, ⓦwww.hotel-unter-den-linden.de. A survivor of the GDR era, this simply furnished but comfortable mid-range hotel is at the junction of Friedrichstrasse and Unter den Linden. ⑥

Mitwohnzentralen and Bed and Breakfast

Bed & Breakfast in Berlin Ahlbecker Str. 3, Prenzlauer Berg ⓣ0 30/44 05 05 82, ⓦwww.bed-and-breakfast-berlin.de. Single and double rooms starting at about €28 and €44 per night respectively. Mon–Fri 9am–6pm.

bed & breakfast privatzimmervermittlung Mehringdamm 66, Kreuzberg ⓣ0 30/78 91 39 71, ⓦwww.bed-and-breakfast.de. Part of a national chain, offering rooms ranging from simple to luxurious. Mon–Fri 10am–6pm.

Fine + Mine Neue Schönhauser Str. 20, Mitte ⓣ0 30/2 35 51 20, ⓦwww.fineandmine.de. International agent offering long- and short-term rooms and apartments. English spoken. Mon–Fri 10am–6pm.

Home Company Joachimstaler Str. 17, Charlottenburg ⓣ0 30/1 94 45, ⓦwww.berlin.homecompany.de. A long-established agency with lots of listings. Mon–Fri 9am–6pm, Sat 11am–2pm.

Wohnagentur am Mehringdamm Mehringdamm 66, Kreuzberg ⓣ0 30/7 86 20 03, ⓦwww.wohnung-berlin.de. Has a particularly good selection of rooms and apartments in Kreuzberg and Schöneberg. Mon–Fri 10am–6pm.

Zimmervermittlung Dentler ⓣ0 30/5 66 55 51 11, ⓦwww.zimmervermittlung24.com. Rooms for short-term stays all over the city, starting from about €30, without breakfast. Mon–Fri 8am–6pm.

Youth hostels

Circus Hostel Rosa-Luxemburg-Str. 39-41, Mitte; and Weinbergsweg 1a, Mitte ⓣ0 30/28 39 14 33, ⓦwww.circus-berlin.de. Both the original hostel and its larger offshoot are located within easy reach of the attractions of the east. For the former, take U-Bahn #2 to Rosa-Luxemburg-Strasse; for the latter, U-Bahn #8 to Rosenthaler Platz. Dorm beds €15, singles €32, doubles €48; breakfast not included.

Globetrotter Hostel Odyssee Grünberger Str. 23, Friedrichshain ⓣ0 30/29 00 00 81, ⓦwww.globetrotterhostel.de. Hard by the emerging scene in Friedrichshain, this has imaginatively decorated rooms and a young staff; the website also has links to several other Berlin hostels. Take bus #240 from the Ostbahnhof to the Grünberger Strasse stop; alternatively, the Frankfurter Tor station (U-Bahn #5) is just a short walk away. Dorm beds from €13, singles €35, doubles €45–52.

Heart of Gold Johannisstr. 11, Mitte ⓣ0 30/29 00 33 00, ⓦwww.heartofgold-hostel.de. Well located, both for the historic sights and the Schanzenviertel nightlife, this is Berlin's wackiest hostel, constructed around the theme of a spaceship. Dorm beds €14, doubles €48–56, triples €60.

Jugendherberge am Wannsee Badeweg 1, Zehlendorf ⓣ0 30/8 03 20 35. This DJH hostel is very pleasantly located, with plenty of woodland walks on hand near the beaches of the Wannsee lakes, but it's far from the city centre. Take S-Bahn #1 or #7 to Nikolassee. €18.50/21.20.

Jugendherberge Berlin-International Kluckstr. 3, Tiergarten ⓣ0 30/2 61 10 97. This is the most conveniently located of the DJH hostels, just a few minutes' walk from the Kulturforum and Potsdamer Platz. Take U-Bahn #1 to Kurfürstenstrasse, or bus #129 to the Gedenkstätte Deutscher Widerstand stop. €17/19.70.

Jugendherberge Ernst Reuter, Hermsdorfer Damm 48–50, Reinickendorf ⓣ0 30/4 04 16 10. Situated in the distant northern outskirts, this is the least popular of the DJH hostels and therefore least likely to fill up in summer, despite being by far the smallest. Take U-Bahn #6 to Alt-Tegel, then bus #125 towards Frohnau. €15/17.70.

Lette'm Sleep 7 Lettestr. 7, Prenzlauer Berg ⓣ0 30/44 73 36 23, ⓦwww.backpackers.de. Spare but comfortable rooms just steps away from the nightlife of Prenzlauer Berg; take U-Bahn #2 to Eberswalder Strasse. Dorm beds €13–18, doubles €44. Breakfast not included.

Campsites

Am Krossinsee Wernsdorfer Str. 38, Köpenick ⓣ0 30/6 75 86 87, ⓕ6 75 91 50. The only site in the erstwhile GDR, pleasantly located in the woods and with easy access to local lakes. There are also bungalows for rent. Take S-Bahn #8 to Grünau, then tram #68 to Schmöckwitz, then bus #463.

Gatow Kladower Damm 207–213, Spandau ⓣ0 30/3 65 43 40, ⓕ36 80 84 92. Not far from the long-established Kladow site. Take U-Bahn #7 to Rathaus Spandau, then bus #134 or #X34 to Flugplatz Gatow.

International Jugendcamp Ziekowstrasse 161, Reinickendorf ⓣ0 30/4 33 86 40. Basic facilites only open to those aged between 14 and 26; a sleeping mat and blanket are provided. Take U-Bahn #6 to Alt-Tegel then bus #222 (direction Alt-Lübars) to Titusweg. Open late June or early July until end of Aug.

Kladow Krampnitzer Weg 111–117, Spandau ⓣ0 30/3 65 27 97, ⓕ3 65 12 54. Friendly campsite on the western side of Lake Havel, with the best facilities of all the campsites, including a free crèche, plus bar, restaurant and shop. Take U-Bahn #7 to Rathaus Spandau, followed by bus #134 to Alt-Kladow, and finally bus #234, alighting when it swings off Krampnitzer Weg; the site is then a short walk to the west.

The eastern centre

Berlin's historic heart is the **Mitte** district, which the Hohenzollern rulers developed into the showpiece centre of their capital. Throughout the life of the GDR, it enacted a similar role, though this was one for which it was decidedly ill-suited, not only from a practical point of view – it protruded so far to the west that it was bounded on three sides by sectors held by the British and Americans – but also because of the ever-present imperialistic and militaristic associations. The Communist authorities never really came to grips with this conundrum. They demolished some key buildings which were seen as embarrassments, notably the huge royal palace, the Stadtschloss, but restored and redeployed others; they also tried to give parts of the district a "socialist" face by erecting grand new public buildings as well as identikit apartment blocks and huge offices for the state bureaucracy. A great deal of restoration work on the historic buildings has been carried out since the *Wende*, but the debate about how far this should go still rages on. There is a vocal lobby in favour of re-creating as much as possible of the imperial legacy, and erasing the visual reminders of the GDR, and an equally determined body of opinion determined to retain the present mix.

The central axis

Since the fall of the Wall, the broad boulevard of **Unter den Linden** ("Beneath the Lime Trees") has been restored to its position as the city's main east-west artery. Originally a bridal path linking the Stadtschloss with the hunting grounds of the Tiergarten, it was beautified after the Thirty Years' War by the planting of lime and walnut trees. These were axed by the Nazis to allow room for processions, but replanted by the Communists. The street is closed off at its western end by **Pariser Platz**, a square that was the most exclusive address in the city in the 1930s. Devastated by bombs in World War II, it was left as a closed-off wasteland during the GDR era, but has since been the subject of a highly exclusive redevelopment programme.

The Brandenburger Tor

The **Brandenburger Tor** (Brandenburg Gate) at the far end of Pariser Platz is so dense with meaning and historical significance that it is the obvious place to begin a tour of Berlin. Built as a city gate-cum-triumphal arch between 1788 and 1791, it was designed by Carl Gotthard Langhans on the model of the Propylaea, the entrance to the Acropolis, thereby symbolizing Berlin's self-image as a modern Athens. Guarding as it did the city's grandest thoroughfare, the gate became the backdrop for many epic events. It was where Prussian troops celebrated their great victories of 1815 and 1871, which saw the demise of Napoleon and the belated achievement of Germany unity. Nazi Storm Troopers held torch-lit marches there to celebrate Hitler's assumption of power in 1933, while on August 13, 1961 it was the first place to be sealed off as construction work on the Berlin Wall began. Inaccessible to the general public for 28 years, it was the scene of the first euphoric chipping-away at the hated frontier on November 9, 1989, and of the gargantuan celebrations on the last day of the same year and on October 3 the following year, when the two Germanies were united. These events were captured on film and broadcast to a huge international audience, with the result that the Brandenburger Tor is now one of the world's most famous monuments.

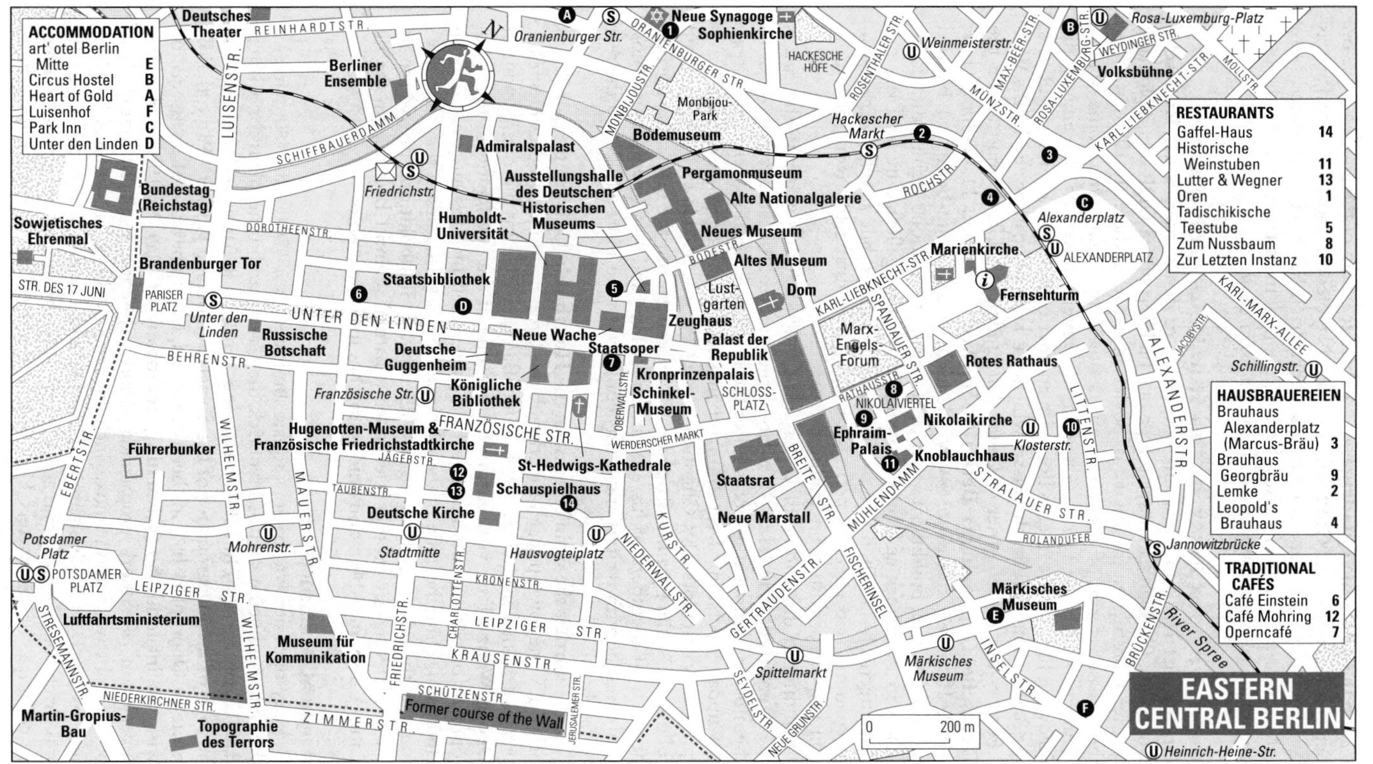

EASTERN CENTRAL BERLIN
ACCOMMODATION
art' otel Berlin Mitte E
Circus Hostel B
Heart of Gold A
Luisenhof F
Park Inn C
Unter den Linden D
RESTAURANTS
Gaffel-Haus 14
Historische Weinstuben 11
Lutter & Wegner 13
Oren 1
Tadschikische Teestube 5
Zum Nussbaum 8
Zur Letzten Instanz 10
HAUSBRAUEREIEN
Brauhaus Alexanderplatz (Marcus-Bräu) 3
Brauhaus Georgbräu 9
Lemke 2
Leopold's Brauhaus 4
TRADITIONAL CAFÉS
Café Einstein 6
Café Mohring 12
Operncafé 7
Deutsches Theater
Berliner Ensemble
Admiralspalast
Bundestag (Reichstag)
Sowjetisches Ehrenmal
Brandenburger Tor
Humboldt-Universität
Ausstellungshalle des Deutschen Historischen Museums
Staatsbibliothek
Neue Wache
Zeughaus
Staatsoper
Deutsche Guggenheim
Königliche Bibliothek
Russische Botschaft
Hugenotten-Museum & Französische Friedrichstadtkirche
St-Hedwigs-Kathedrale
Schauspielhaus
Deutsche Kirche
Führerbunker
Luftfahrtsministerium
Museum für Kommunikation
Martin-Gropius-Bau
Topographie des Terrors
Former course of the Wall
Neue Synagoge
Sophienkirche
Monbijou-Park
Bodemuseum
Pergamonmuseum
Alte Nationalgalerie
Neues Museum
Altes Museum
Lustgarten
Dom
Palast der Republik
Kronprinzenpalais
Schinkel-Museum
Schlossplatz
Marx-Engels-Forum
Marienkirche
Fernsehturm
Rotes Rathaus
Nikolaiviertel
Nikolaikirche
Ephraim-Palais
Knoblauchhaus
Staatsrat
Neue Marstall
Märkisches Museum
Volksbühne
Hackesche Höfe
Hackescher Markt
Alexanderplatz
Rosa-Luxemburg-Platz
Oranienburger Str.
Weinmeisterstr.
Friedrichstr.
Unter den Linden
Französische Str.
Stadtmitte
Hausvogteiplatz
Mohrenstr.
Potsdamer Platz
Spittelmarkt
Klosterstr.
Schillingstr.
Jannowitzbrücke
Heinrich-Heine-Str.
River Spree
Unter den Linden
Karl-Marx-Allee
Alexanderstr.
Leipziger Str.
Friedrichstr.
Wilhelmstr.
Pariser Platz
Str. des 17 Juni
0 200 m

Atop the gate is the **Quadriga**, a huge bronze group of the goddess Nike on her chariot by Johann Gottfried Schadow. Napoleon removed this to Paris as war booty in 1806. On its return, Karl Friedrich Schinkel transformed Nike into a personification of Victory, bearing the new military decoration, the Iron Cross, and wearing a wreath with the Prussian eagle.

From Pariser Platz to the Humboldt-Universität

On the first block of the south side of Unter den Linden is the **Russische Botschaft** (Russian Embassy), the pivotal building of the GDR-era diplomatic quarter. Constructed for the use of Soviet diplomats in the early 1950s, it mixes the debased form of Neoclassicism favoured by Stalin with some Cubist elements, which are most evident in the lantern tower. At the end of the following block is the intersection with another of Berlin's most important axes, the 3.5km-long **Friedrichstrasse**, which was formerly partitioned by the Wall.

Further on, at the corner of Unter den Linden and Charlottenstrasse, is the **Deutsche Guggenheim Berlin** (Mon–Wed & Fri–Sun 11am–8pm, Thurs 11am–10pm; €3, free Mon; ⓦ www.deutsche-guggenheim-berlin.de). Housed in a former bank building, it's a far cry from the institution's architectural landmarks in New York and Bilbao, though its modest galleries are well laid out and effectively lit. There are no permanent displays, but a rolling exhibition programme (separated by periods of closure) featuring the work of leading contemporary artists from around the world.

Standing in the middle of Unter den Linden a little further to the east is the **Denkmal Friedrich II**, a large mid-nineteenth-century memorial to the most influential and successful of the Prussian kings, Frederick the Great. An updated version of the bronze equestrian monuments of classical antiquity, it was sculpted by Christian Daniel Rauch, Schadow's most talented follower. On the pyramid-shaped base are scenes from the monarch's life and portraits of members of his entourage: soldiers and statesmen feature most prominently, with writers and artists confined to the short end below the rear of the horse.

To the north is the main building of the **Humboldt-Universität**, which was originally the town palace of Frederick the Great's younger brother Heinrich. It was designed in a classically inspired Baroque style by the court architect **Georg Wenzeslaus von Knobelsdorff**, one of the key figures in the development of both Berlin and Potsdam, and erected by the Dutchman Johann Boumann. On either side of the entrance are marble statues of the university's founder, the educational reformer Wilhelm von Humboldt, and his even more influential younger brother Alexander, a natural scientist best known for his Latin American explorations and researches into the cosmos.

August-Bebel-Platz

Directly opposite is a spacious square, built between 1741 and 1780, which is the only completed part of Frederick the Great's ambitious plans for a latter-day Roman forum. The GDR authorities renamed it **August-Bebel-Platz** in honour of the joint founder of the Social Democratic Workers' Party; the old name of Opernplatz has not been reinstated, largely because of its association with the infamous **book-burning ceremony** of May 10, 1933. Under the supervision of Hitler's propaganda minister, Joseph Goebbels, thousands of publications went up in smoke, including the works of "un-German" authors such as Erich Maria Remarque, Heinrich and Thomas Mann, Stefan Zweig and Erich Kästner (who was an eye-witness to the event), along with volumes by countless foreign writers, H.G. Wells and Ernest Hemingway among them.

The most fitting comment on this episode was made with accidental foresight by the poet Heinrich Heine during the previous century: "Where they start by burning books, they'll end by burning people." An intriguing memorial to the book-burning incorporates these words on a plaque: go to the middle of the square and look through the glass pane set in the ground.

Opernplatz took its name from the **Staatsoper** on the east side, whose porticoed facade faces Unter den Linden. Knobelsdorff used Palladio's famous Villa Rotonda near Vicenza as his model, giving the structure four separate projections. As a freestanding theatre, rather than a part of a complex, it was a revolutionary design for its day. Another unusual feature was that the stalls of the auditorium could be raised and the space used for balls and receptions. Although it has been damaged by fire and bombs and subject to internal modifications, it remains a magnificent performance space.

Knobelsdorff also drew up the plans for **St-Hedwigs-Kathedrale** (Ⓦwww.hedwigs-kathedrale.de) on the south side of the square. This was the first permanent place of worship for Berlin's Roman Catholic minority, whose numbers had swelled as a result of Prussia's annexation of most of the erstwhile Austrian province of Silesia, and hard-nosed political calculations were behind the decision of Frederick the Great – an agnostic member of a staunchly Protestant dynasty – to sponsor its construction. According to tradition, the king wanted the church to be in the shape of an upturned teacup with handle. However, it is more likely that he was having his own private joke by choosing the pagan Roman Pantheon as a model, particularly as its centralized plan is totally unsuited to the Catholic liturgy. Badly damaged in World War II, the building was belatedly restored with a modernized interior.

On the western side of the square is the **Königliche Bibliothek**, a former royal library known colloquially as the **Kommode** ("chest of drawers") because of its curvaceous Baroque facade. Its design was a plagiarization of an unbuilt plan made half-a-century earlier by Fischer von Erlach for an extension to the Hofburg in Vienna. As such, it was another conscious piece of one-upsmanship on the Austrians, and in particular on Frederick's bitter rival, Empress Maria Theresia. Its contents were transferred shortly before World War I to the new Staatsbibliothek on the opposite side of Unter den Linden, and it is now used by the university.

The eastern end of Unter den Linden

Immediately east of the Staatsoper are four statues by Christian Daniel Rauch to the Prussian heroes of the Napoleonic Wars: Gerhard von Scharnhorst is on Unter den Linden itself, August von Gneisenau, Gebhard von Blucher and Ludwig Yorck von Wartenburg are on the lawn behind. Beyond is the **Kronprinzenpalais**, a Baroque palace that was once the Berlin residence of the Prussian crown princes. There are future plans for it to serve as a national portrait gallery, which will make it the first such insitution outside the English-speaking world.

Another key element in the ambitious plans for the re-ordering of Berlin's state-owned museums over the next decade (see also the box below) is the vacant plot alongside the Kronprinzenpalais, which was formerly occupied by the strikingly angular **Bauakademie**, the masterpiece of **Karl Friedrich Schinkel**, the nineteenth-century architect who gave Berlin its distinctive Neoclassical stamp. Damaged in the war but eminently restorable, this was razed by the Communists and replaced by the ugly Aussenministerium (Foreign Ministry), which was in turn bulldozed in 1995. A small section of the Bauakademie has since been recreated on site, and at some point in the next

△ *Dying Warriors* by Andrew Schlüter in the Zeughaus courtyard, Berlin

decade the whole building is likely to make a phoenix-like return to serve as an architectural museum.

Diagonally opposite the Kronprinzenpalais is one of Schinkel's most famous surviving buildings, the **Neue Wache**. It was built between 1816 and 1818 to serve both as a guardhouse and a memorial to the Prussian casualties of the Napoleonic Wars, and the architecture mirrors both functions, having the plan of a Roman fort, with the addition of a Doric portico to impart a sense of spirituality. In 1931 it was converted into a memorial to the military dead of World War I, and rededicated in 1957 to the "Victims of Fascism and Militarism". Since 1993, it has been the official national memorial to "Victims of War and Tyranny".

Just east of the Neue Wache is one of Berlin's greatest buildings, the old arsenal or **Zeughaus**, whose size and majesty reflect the dominant role played by militarism in the rise and expansion of Brandenburg-Prussia. The state's predilection for warfare goes some way to explain why this Baroque masterpiece was built by outsiders: it was begun in 1695 by the Dutchman Johann Arnold Nering, who was succeeded three years later by a partnership of Jean de Bodt, a Huguenot refugee from France, and Andreas Schlüter, a native of the city-state of Danzig (now Gdańsk). Adorning the ground floor of the exterior are 76 keystones of military trophies carved in the workshop of de Bodt and Schlüter. The attic decoration, consisting of huge groups of Mars and Minerva with their entourages, plus a further 44 trophies, is the work of another Huguenot, Guillaume Hulot. For all their splendour, these sculptures are eclipsed by those of the **Schlüterhof**, the wonderfully harmonious inner courtyard. Here Schlüter carved the 22 keystones known as the *Dying Warriors*, a deeply moving and highly individualistic pictorial record of death. In a highly controversial move inspired by the success of his Louvre pyramid in Paris, the Chinese-American architect Ieoh Ming Pei was commissioned to cover the Schlüterhof with a glass roof, and this is due to open to the public in 2004.

By the end of the same year, the long-awaited **Deutsches Historisches Museum** (Ⓦwww.dhm.de), illustrating the entire history of the German nation, should be installed in the Zeughaus. Pei also designed the triangular-shaped **Austellungshalle des Deutschen Historischen Museums** (daily 10am–6pm; €2) to the rear for the institution's temporary exhibitions. Architecturally, it's notable for its huge protruding glass-walled stairway.

The southern districts

Friedrichswerder, the first Baroque extension to the medieval city of Berlin, lay to the southeast of Unter den Linden. Another Baroque suburb, the much larger Friedrichstadt, was later laid out to a grid pattern immediately to the east.

Friedrichswerder

Nothing remains of the original settlement of Friedrichswerder, but its name lives on in the **Friedrichswerdersche Kirche**, which was built by Schinkel to face its market square, Werderscher Markt. Although nowadays an open space, the area was then a dense and irregular network of streets, and the great architect decided that a church in a medieval idiom would dovetail far better with these surroundings than one in the Neoclassical style he favoured for most of his Berlin commissions. Because of the restricted site, he eventually settled on a design modelled on the chapels of the Oxbridge colleges, though the twin towers, each of two identical superimposed cubes, are in his own very personal vein. The deconsecrated church is now designated the

The Staatliche Museen Berlin

Despite heavy wartime losses, the state-run museums of Berlin, the **Staatliche Museen Berlin Stiftung Preussischer Kulturbesitz**, rival those of London and Paris (which are concentrated in a far smaller number of much larger institutions) for the right to be regarded as the finest and most wide-ranging in the world. During the decades of German division, their treasures were split between East and West Berlin, and the task of putting them back together again is a massive task, which is unlikely to be completed before 2010. Until then, whole collections are liable to be closed for several years at a time – though they are not necessarily entirely inaccessible to the public, as selections are sometimes displayed in other museums in the group, or are sent abroad as touring exhibitions.

For the forseeable future, the museums will be spread among four main locations – Museumsinsel, the Tiergarten Kulturforum, Charlottenburg and Dahlem. In the longer term, it is hoped that most will be concentrated in Museumsinsel and the area around, with a key role being given to the Stadtschloss, if it is indeed rebuilt. A **day-ticket** (€6) is valid for all the state museums (which can be identified in the text by the website address Ⓦwww.smb.spk-berlin.de), while entry to all the museums is free on the first Sunday of each month. There's a **three-day ticket** known as SchauLust (€10), which gives access to most of Berlin's other museums as well.

Schinkel-Museum (Tues–Sun 10am–6pm; €3; Ⓦwww.smb.spk-berlin.de), whose interior gallery displays documents and plans from throughout Schinkel's career. The main body of the church houses works by the leading Neoclassical sculptors of Berlin, notably Schadow, Rauch and Christian Friedrich Tieck.

Gendarmenmarkt

Friedrichstadt was centred on **Gendarmenmarkt**, the most imposing square in Berlin. It was first laid out in the late seventeenth century, but only given its showpiece character a hundred years later, when Frederick the Great decided to turn it into a monumental public square on the model of the Piazza del Popolo in Rome.

Dominating the square are two churches, which at first sight seem identical, but are actually very different. On the north side is the **Französische Friedrichstadtkirche** (Ⓦwww.franzoesischer-dom-berlin.de), which was built at the very beginning of the eighteenth century for the influential Huguenot community, whose descendants still worship there. One of their number, military engineer Jean Louis Cayart, was entrusted with the design, which he modelled on the destroyed "mother church" of the Huguenots at Charenton in the Paris outskirts. In 1780, Frederick the Great commissioned one of his favourite architects, Carl von Gontard, to build an extension to the plain and severe original building. This grandiose domed edifice, known as the **Turmbau**, is crowned by a cupola and fronted by three great pedimented porticos, which are profusely decorated with sculptures made from designs provided by two artists who successively served as directors of Berlin's academy, Daniel Nikolaus Chodowiecki and Christian Bernard Rode. It completely dwarfs the actual church, and the curious dual structure has popularly if inaccurately been known as the Französischer Dom (French Cathedral) ever since. Within the Turmbau is the **Huguenotten-Museum** (Tues–Sat noon–5pm, Sun 11am–5pm; €2), which details the history of the Huguenots in France and Brandenburg. A longish spiral stairway leads to the **viewing**

platform (daily 9am–7pm; €2) below the tower, which offers good views over the surrounding construction sites.

At the southern end of the square is the **Deutsche Kirche**, otherwise known as the Deutscher Dom, which served the German and Swiss citizens of Friedrichstadt of both Lutheran and Calvinist persuasions. The church itself was built to a more elaborate design than its neighbour, but Gontard's Turmbau is an almost identical twin, differing only in the subjects of its sculptural programme. Nothing remains of the original interior, which is now used to house a permanent exhibition, **Fragen an die Deutsche Geschichte** (Questions on German History; Tues 10am–10pm, Wed–Sun 10am–6pm; free). This contains some good archive footage, but the German-only text suffers from the common fault of trying to smooth over the most calamitous events in the nation's not-so-distant past.

Between the two churches is the **Schauspielhaus**, which Schinkel built as a replacement for Langhans' fire-damaged Nationaltheater, whose Doric portico, approached by a broad flight of steps, was incorporated into the new design. Schinkel himself designed the pediment reliefs, while the bronze sculptural group of Apollo in his chariot on the roof of the building was made by Rauch. A month after its opening, the playhouse premiered Weber's *Der Freischütz*, which is nowadays generally considered the first opera of the Romantic era. Since 1984, the building has been used as a concert hall rather than a theatre, as is generally known as the **Konzerthaus Berlin** (see p.799). Outside stands the **Schillerdenkmal**, an elaborate commemorative monument, unveiled in 1871, to the Enlightenment-era poet and playwright Friedrich Schiller.

Leipziger Strasse and Potsdamer Platz

From Gendarmenmarkt, Charlottenstrasse continues south to **Leipziger Strasse**, once a main shopping street running from Alexanderplatz to Potsdamer Platz. Towards the western end of the street, at the junction with Mauerstrasse, is the former Imperial postal ministry, now the home of the **Museum für Kommunikation** (Tues–Fri 9am–5pm, Sat & Sun 11am–7pm; free; Ⓦwww.mspt.de). Its exhibits include a complete set of German stamps from 1849 to the present day, as well as equipment ranging from a prototype of the telephone to the latest computer hardware.

At the next junction to the west, Leipziger Strasse bisects Wilhelmstrasse, which was formerly the heart of the government quarter. Here can be found one of the most prominent surviving buildings of the Third Reich, the **Luftfahrtministerium** (Air Ministry). Its head, Hermann Göring, rashly promised Berliners that not a single bomb would fall on the city during the war, declaring that, should his confidence prove misplaced, he would change his name to the Jewish one of Meyer. In the GDR era, the building served as the Haus der Ministerien (House of Ministries), and afterwards became the headquarters of the Treuhandanstalt, the agency responsible for the privatization of the state-owned enterprises. In its latest incarnation, it houses the Bundesministerium der Finanzen (Federal Finance Ministry).

Beyond, Leipziger Strasse runs into **Potsdamer Platz**, once the heart of Berlin and a prewar hub of the city's transport and nightlife. It was made desolate by wartime bombing, and for fifty years after the war remained wasteland: the Berlin Wall wrapped around it, ensuring that it would remain undeveloped. However, the dismantling of the Wall produced one of Europe's most valuable lots, and the square has been transformed in recent years by the building of large commercial complexes (see p.780).

East of Potsdamer Platz, and just above An der Kolonnade, is the site of the **Führerbunker**, where Hitler spent his last days, issuing meaningless orders as the Battle of Berlin raged above. On April 30, 1945, he shot himself, and his body was hurriedly burned by loyal officers.

Fischerinsel and Museumsinsel

Immediately east of Unter den Linden is a large island in the Spree. This was the site of the fishing village of Cölln, which was first documented in 1237 – seven years before the earliest mention of Berlin, which was originally confined to the east bank of the river. Although the two communities built a joint town hall in 1307, they did not formally merge until 1432. Cölln's name subsequently fell into disuse, though the larger part of the island is known as **Fischerinsel** (Fishermen's Island) in its honour. The peninsula at the northern end, once a swampy marsh, is called **Museumsinsel** (Museum Island), as it is entirely given over to a group of publicly owned museums housed in palatial premises.

Schlossplatz and the Lustgarten

At the eastern end of Unter den Linden, the Spree is spanned by the Schinkel-designed **Schlossbrücke**, whose eight flanking marble groups each depict a goddess of war accompanied by a mythological hero. The bridge leads to **Schlossplatz**, formerly the site of the **Stadtschloss**, the old imperial palace, razed by the Communist authorities in 1950–51, despite having been Berlin's pivotal landmark for centuries. Two decades later, the vacant space was occupied by the **Palast der Republik**, which housed a number of different institutions, including the *Volkskammer*, the GDR's rubber-stamp parliament. Irreverently dubbed *Ballast der Republik*, this huge angular building with its bronzed, reflecting windows was completed in less than a thousand days, and was a source of great pride to the Honecker regime. The hundreds of lamps hanging from the ceiling of the main foyer gave rise to its other nickname, *Erichs Lampenladen* – "Erich's lamp shop". Shortly before unification an asbestos hazard was discovered in the building, and it was closed indefinitely. Today it still stands forlorn and empty, an unmissable reminder of the old GDR and an embarrassment to the new Germany. Its demolition would be necessary were the Stadtschloss to be rebuilt, as now seems quite likely, despite widespread public concern about the astronomical cost of such an ambitious undertaking.

The one significant surviving portion of the Stadtschloss is the Baroque portal incorporated in the 1960s **Staatsrat** on the south side of the square. Its preservation had nothing to do with its artistic qualities, but with the fact that its balcony was the place where Karl Liebknecht proclaimed the establishment of the German Socialist Republic in 1918. Immediately to the east of the Staatsrat is the **Neue Marstall**, a derivative late nineteenth-century construction built to house the hundreds of royal coaches and horses. Nowadays, it is used for exhibitions, especially those related to large public projects.

Immediately north of Schlossplatz is the **Lustgarten**, which since 1999 has reverted to its original function as a garden, having served a variety of functions in the interim, such as being a parade ground for the Prussian army and the setting for some of the Nazis' most infamous propaganda exercises. At its far northern end is the **Granitschale**, which was made in 1830 from a single Ice Age granite block. Formerly considered one of the wonders of Berlin, it is now perpetually vandalized and popularly referred to as the "soup bowl".

On the eastern side of the Lustgarten stands the hulking pile of the **Dom** (daily 9am–5/8pm; €5; Ⓦwww.berliner-dom.de), which was built in a pompous Historicist style at the turn of the twentieth century as a replacement for its much smaller predecessor, a Baroque building remodelled by Schinkel. Ever since it was built, it has attracted widespread scorn, though it's worth going inside to see the several magnificent **tombs** of the Hohenzollern dynasty: that of the Elector Johann Cicero was cast in one of the great foundries of the Renaissance era, the Vischer workshop in Nürnberg; those of King Friedrich I and Queen Sophie Charlotte were both designed by Schlüter. The candelabra and the screen with figures of the apostles at the high altar are the work of Schinkel. An aerial view of the vast central space can be obtained from the balcony at the top of the **Kaiserliches Treppenhaus**, a marble staircase at the southwest corner of the building. From there, you can ascend to the walkway round the exterior of the **cupola**, which offers fine panoramas over the city.

The Altes Museum and the Neues Museum

Museumsinsel is deemed to begin at the **Altes Museum** (Tues–Sun 10am–6pm; €6; Ⓦwww.smb.spk-berlin.de), which faces the northern end of the Lustgarten. It's arguably Schinkel's most impressive surviving work, and is the most extreme example of his classicizing manner, though its carefully calculated architectonic relationship to the previous Dom and the Stadtschloss is now irretrievably lost. Externally, the main feature is the **portico** of eighteen Ionic columns, which gives the impression that the building is of one storey rather than two. Inside, the central **rotunda**, with its elaborate coffered vault, offers a modernized variant of the Pantheon in Rome, and has been returned to its original function as a showcase for Classical sculptures.

Part of the **Antikensammlung**, a collection of Greek and Roman antiquities, is exhibited in the ground-floor rooms around the rotunda. This has the finest collection of **Attic vases** in the world, the star piece being the so-called Berlin Amphora, which dates from around 490 BC and came from Vulci in Etruria. It also has a distinguished array of Greek sculpture, ranging from Cycladic figures of 2200 BC to first-century clay statuettes found in the excavations of Priene in Asia Minor. Of special note is one of the few surviving life-sized bronzes of the antique era, the third-century BC *Praying Boy* from Rhodes. There are also two treasury chambers, devoted to gold and silver artefacts respectively. The former includes a Scythian horde of around 800 BC excavated at Vetterfelde in southeastern Brandenburg; the latter is dominated by the **Hildesheim Silver**, a trove of seventy magnificent pieces from the first century BC and the first century AD named after the Lower Saxon city where they were found.

As Berlin's collections grew too large for the Altes Museum, Schinkel's pupil August Stüler was commissioned to build the **Neues Museum** (Ⓦwww.smb.spk-berlin.de) immediately to its rear. This was almost totally destroyed in World War II, and left as a ruin by the GDR authorities, but is now being rebuilt to plans by the London architect David Chipperfield. When complete (around 2008), it will once again house Berlin's famous Ägyptisches Museum, plus another archeological collection – likewise currently on display in Charlottenburg – the Museum für Vor- und Frühgeschichte.

The Pergamonmuseum

Immediately to the north of the Neues Museum is the **Pergamonmuseum** (Tues, Wed & Fri–Sun 10am–6pm, Thurs 10am–10pm; €6; Ⓦwww.smb.spk-berlin.de), a massive inter-war structure in the style of a Babylonian temple. It was specially designed in order to display to best effect what are undoubtedly some of the most spectacular exhibits to be found in any museum anywhere in the world – a series of huge architectural showpieces unearthed by German archaeologists from various ancient civilizations.

The museum is divided into three sections, the best-known being the large-scale exhibits of the **Antikensammlung**. These are centred on a hall containing the structure which gives the museum its name, the **Pergamon Altar**, which formerly stood on the acropolis of the eponymous town in Asia Minor, the present-day Bergama in Turkey. Dating from 180 to 160 BC, it ranks as the supreme masterpiece of late Hellenistic art. In the centre of the hall is a conjectural full-scale reconstruction of the altar, while around the walls are the originals of its reliefs. The main **frieze**, the second largest monumental sculpture to have survived from ancient Greece, vividly depicts the battle between the giants and the gods, whose victory was achieved with the help of the mortal Hercules, father of Telephus, founder of Pergamon. Telephus' life is told in a smaller frieze in somewhat lower relief from a subsidiary altar. In the room to the north are more Greek architectural fragments, including the Temple of Athena from Pergamon, which predates the altar by a century. Dominating the Roman room to the south is the colossal Market Gate of Miletus; the Orpheus Mosaic comes from the same city.

The **Vorderasiatisches Museum**, also on the main floor, is laid out around the spectacular reconstruction, based on original excavated materials, of parts of the fabulous **Palace of King Nebuchadnezzar II of Babylon**, dating from around 600 BC. Although the constructions look awesome, they are miniaturizations of the originals: the **Processional Way**, with its parade of lions set between geometric borders and rosette friezes, was six times longer and six times broader, while the **Ishtar Gate**, with its symbolic bulls and dragons, was not only taller but also no more than a front to a much larger structure. Parts of the facade of the **Throne Room**, which shows lions below highly stylized depictions of palm trees, are also on view. The smaller rooms contain many impressive artefacts excavated at other sites in the Near East, notably the Sumerian city of Uruk, the Assyrian courts of Nineveh and Nimrud, and King Darius of Persia's royal palace at Susa.

Pride of place in the **Museum für Islamisches Kunst** on the first floor goes to the exquisitely carved facade of an eighth-century caliph's palace from Mschatta in present-day Jordan, which was presented to Kaiser Wilhelm II by the Sultan of Turkey. Other highlights are the prayer niches from two thirteenth-century mosques, and a room with mixed Arab and Western decoration from the seventeenth-century house of a Christian merchant of Aleppo in Syria. There are also many small-scale exhibits from all over the Islamic world, including miniature paintings, carpets, ceramics, leatherwork, and wooden and ivory carvings.

The Bodemuseum

At the northeastern tip of Museumsinsel is the **Bodemuseum** (Ⓦwww.smb.spk-berlin.de), housed in an intimidating, triangular-shaped neo-Baroque building. Before the war it was known as the Kaiser-Friedrich-Museum and contained the city's magnificent holdings of old master paintings; in the GDR era it was re-named in honour of a former director of the Berlin museums, Wilhlem Bode, and displayed the rumps of several divided collections. It is presently closed (probably until 2006) for structural repairs. When it reopens, it will house the re-united **Skulpturensammlung**, an excellent collection of sculpture particularly strong in the work of German masters of the fifteenth and sixteenth centuries, including major figures such as Nicolaus Gerhaert, Michel Erhart, Hans Multscher and Tilman Riemenschneider. In the meantime, a selection of this is on view in the Gemäldegalerie (see p.776). Also finding a home here will be the **Museum für Spätantike und Byzantische Kunst**, which has a wonderful range of artefacts from the pre-medieval eastern Mediterranean, including some notable sculptures from Constantinople and a monumental sixth-century mosaic from Ravenna.

The Alte Nationalgalerie

Just to the north of the Neues Museum is the **Alte Nationalgalerie** (Tues, Wed & Fri–Sun 10am–6pm, Thurs 10am–10pm; €6; Ⓦwww.smb.spk-berlin.de), likewise the work of Stüler, who offered a somewhat exaggerated re-interpretation of a Corinthian temple. Recently restored, it is now devoted exclusively to nineteenth-century art, with a strong emphasis on Germany. Most of the permanent collection is displayed on the top floor, with one gallery highlighting the works of **Caspar David Friedrich**, all of which express a powerful elemental and religious approach to landscape, particularly *Morning in the Riesengebirge* and *The Watzmann*. Comparably memorable are the visionary compositions of **Karl Friedrich Schinkel**, even although he was never more than an occasional painter. His works here are punctilliously drawn Gothic fantasies, often with sea settings: *Gothic Church on a Seaside Bluff* is the most moodily dramatic. There are fascinating paintings by **Johann Erdmann Hummel** – who was a professor of perspective and optics – showing the grinding, turning and installation of the Granitschale. Look out, too, for the topographical works of **Eduard Gaertner**, which provide an accurate record of Berlin's appearance in the early nineteenth century. Also of particular note is *The Story of Joseph*, an intact co-operative venture by the members of the **Nazarene Brotherhood**, which was painted for the house of the German consul in Rome. *The Rose* and *The Adventures of the Painter Joseph Binder* are archetypal examples of the highly colourful, detailed and very romanticized art of **Moritz von Schwind**.

In the first-floor galleries are around fifty works by the Berlin artist **Adolph Menzel**: these range from an exquisite early interior, *The Balcony Room*, via detailed historical scenes of the life and times of Frederick the Great, to *The Ironworks*, a seminal documentary record of the dawn of the Industrial Age. There are also a few paintings by French Impressionists and Post-Impressionists, including examples of Monet, Degas and Van Gogh, and more copious representation of their German counterparts, Max Liebermann and Lovis Corinth.

The medieval centre

The original settlement of Berlin lay on the east side of the Spree, immediately opposite Cölln. A few medieval buildings still stand as a reminder of the city's early life, but although some remain prominent landmarks they are engulfed by later surroundings, this being a part of the city that still bears strong visible evidence of the Communist years.

From Schlossplatz to Alexanderplatz

Karl-Liebknecht-Strasse, linking Schlossplatz with Alexanderplatz, is in effect an eastern continuation of Unter den Linden. On its south side is the **Marx-Engels-Forum**, a small park with a lumpen bronze representation of the founders of Communism at its heart. Beyond, on the other side of Spandauer

Strasse, is a large open space on which stands the **Neptunbrunnen**, a large late nineteenth-century fountain showing the sea god surrounded by creatures from his kingdom. Across Rathausstrasse to the southeast, the **Rotes Rathaus** has been the seat of the united Berlin city government since October 1991. It's a grand Historicist building of the 1860s, influenced by Italian, Flemish and North German medieval architecture. A terracotta frieze above the ground-floor windows illustrates the history of the city in 36 panels.

To the north of Neptunbrunnen is medieval Berlin's most significant surviving building, the **Marienkirche** (Ⓦwww.marienkirche.de). It's a typical example of a Gothic hall church, begun in the mid-thirteenth century, but extensively rebuilt following a fire in 1380. The tower dates from the following century, except for the upper storeys, which were added at the end of the eighteenth century by Langhans. In the porch is a **frieze** of the Dance of Death, painted by an unknown artist soon after the plague of of 1484. Among the notable furnishings in the main body of the church are a fifteenth-century bronze **font** resting on dragons; the **tomb** of Field Marshal Otto Christoph von Sparr, which was executed by the Antwerp sculptor Artus Quellinus while the subject was still alive; and the magnificent **pulpit** by Schlüter, which is exceptionally ornate by Protestant standards. The **organ** by the Baroque master Joachim Wagner is both visually and tonally splendid; recitals are normally given at 4.30pm on Saturdays.

Along with every other building in the vicinity, the Marienkirche is overshadowed by the gigantic, 365-metre-high TV tower, or **Fernsehturm** (daily: March–Oct 9am–1am; Nov–Feb 10am–midnight; €6.50; Ⓦwww.berlinerfernsehturm.de), the second highest structure in Europe, which dominates the eastern Berlin skyline. There's a tremendous **view** (40km on a rare clear day, although the summit is often shrouded in cloud) from the observation platform, which is reached by a very fast lift. Immediately above is the *Tele-Café*, which revolves on its own axis twice an hour. When the sun shines on the globe of the tower, the reflected light forms a cross visible even in western Berlin, much to the chagrin of the old GDR authorities and amusement of the locals, who dubbed it the "Pope's Revenge", or, in a sarcastic reference to the then dictator Walter Ulbricht, "St Walter".

To the east is the open space of **Alexanderplatz**, popularly known as "Alex". It acquired its present name after the Russian tsar Alexander I visited Berlin in 1805, and was made famous beyond the city by Alfred Döblin's epic novel of low life in the Weimar era, *Berlin Alexanderplatz*. This windswept pedestrianized plaza has figured prominently in city upheavals ever since revolutionaries set up barricades here in 1848. Memorably, it was the focal point of the million-strong city-wide **demonstration** of November 4, 1989, when hundreds of thousands of people crammed into the square to hear opposition leaders speak. Five days later, the Wall was breached. Alexanderplatz remains an unmistakable product of the old East Germany, having been remodelled as the showpiece centre of a modern "Socialist" capital city. The only older structures to have survived are the labyrinthine S- and U-Bahn station, and the angular **Berolinahaus** and **Alexanderhaus**, at nos.1 and 2 on the square, which are both late works by Peter Behrens, the one-time Jugendstil architect who latterly concentrated on industrial and commercial design, strongly influencing the founders of the Bauhaus.

The Nikolaiviertel and Am Köllnischen Park

Slightly to the southwest of the Rotes Rathaus lies the **Nikolaiviertel**, a showpiece GDR development carried out in the run-up to Berlin's 750th anniversary celebrations of 1987. Not only did this restore the main monuments of Berlin's oldest quarter, complete with its medieval layout, it also re-erected there replicas of historic buildings from elsewhere in the city which didn't make it through to the postwar era, such as *Zum Nussbaum* (see p.793), a convincing enough re-creation of a celebrated sixteenth-century *Wirtshaus,* as well as stylized buildings not based on anything in particular, but striving for an "old Berlin" feel.

At the centre of it all is the Gothic **Nikolaikirche** (Tues–Sun 10am–6pm; €1.50, or €5 combined ticket with Knoblauchhaus and Ephraim-Palais, free Wed; Ⓦwww.stadtmuseum.de), a deconsecrated brickwork hall church now given over to temporary exhibitions. Among the furnishings are Schlüter's monument to the court goldsmith Daniel Mannlich, which can be seen above a mock doorway on the west wall. Nearby, at Poststr. 23, is the Rococo **Knoblauchhaus** (Tues–Sun 10am–6pm; €1.50, free Wed; Ⓦwww.stadtmuseum.de), one of only four houses from the prewar Nikolaiviertel to have survived. At the end of the street, facing Mühlendamm, is the rebuilt **Ephraim-Palais** (Tues–Sun 10am–6pm; €3, free Wed; Ⓦwww.stadtmuseum.de), a rather more splendid Rococo mansion built for Frederick the Great's court jeweller and mint master, Nathan Veitel Heine Ephraim. It contains displays of Berlin artworks of the period.

South of the Spree is the former suburb of Neukölln am Wasser, nowadays known as Am Köllnischen Park. Its dominant monument is the **Märkisches Museum** (Tues–Sun 10am–6pm; €4; Ⓦwww.stadtmuseum.de), an early twentieth-century building in the style of a medieval monastery. The displays are devoted to the history of Berlin and the province of Brandenburg from prehistoric times to the present day. Among the highlights are a beautiful Gothic sculpture known as the *Spandau Madonna*; the horse's head from Schadow's original casting of the Quadriga on the Brandenburger Tor; and the Panorama, a late nineteenth-century rotating drum, which shows a series of fascinating 3-D photos of old Berlin.

The northern quarters

North of Unter den Linden lies **Dorotheenstadt**, another of Berlin's Baroque quarters, which postdates Friedrichswerder but predates Friedrichstadt. It was later joined by several other inner suburbs, full of fascinating corners which nevertheless lie off the well-worn tourist track.

From **Bahnhof Friedrichstrasse**, a 1920s terminal that was once the most important border crossing between East and West Berlin, Friedrichstrasse itself runs north across the River Spree over the wrought-iron **Weidendammbrücke**. Immediately to the left on Bertolt-Brecht-Platz is the late nineteenth-century building of the **Berliner Ensemble**, Berlin's "Brecht theatre", complete with a statue of the playwright himself in front.

A little way further north is Oranienburger Tor, beyond which is the **Dorotheenstädtische Friedhof** (daily: April–Sept 8am–7pm; Oct–March 8am–4pm), eastern Berlin's VIP cemetery. Here are the graves of, among others, Brecht and his actress wife Helene Weigel, the architect Schinkel, the sculptors Schadow and Rauch, the philosophers Hegel and Fichte, the novelist Heinrich Mann and the Dadaist artist John Heartfield. Just beyond the cemetery, at Chausseestr. 125, is the **Brecht-Haus** (guided tours Tues, Wed & Fri 10am–noon, Thurs 10am–noon & 5pm–7pm, Sat 9.30am–2pm, Sun 11am–6pm; €3; Ⓦwww.adk.de), a two-storey tenement flat where the poet and playwright lived for the last three years of his life. The most unexpected feature is the large collection of English-language crime novels, which he liked to read in the original.

Continuing northwestwards along Chausseestrasse, a left turn into Invalidenstrasse leads to the **Museum für Naturkunde** (Tues–Fri 9.30am–5pm, Sat & Sun 10am–6pm; €3.50; Ⓦwww.naturkundemuseum-berlin.de) at no.43. In the top-lit central hall are five reasonably complete 150-million-year-old dinosaur skeletons unearthed during a palaeontological expedition of 1909–13 to German East Africa (present-day Tanzania); these include the *Brachiosaurus brancai*, the largest and most spectacular yet discovered. The museum also has a fine collection of minerals, including a number of meteorites, and some charming 1920s dioramas, the first to be made outside the United States.

Since the *Wende*, **Oranienburger Strasse**, which runs southeast from Oranienburger Tor, has become the heart of a major bar/café-crawling strip full of stylish watering holes. The revitalization of the street began with **Tacheles** (Ⓦwww.tacheles.de), a group of young international artists who took over a spectacularly ruined building on the southern side of the street, just beyond the Oranienburger Tor junction, in early 1990. The exterior is usually festooned with works-in-progress, and the building has become home and workplace to an ever-changing band of painters, sculptors, kindred spirits and hangers-on.

The presence of the grand **Neue Synagoge** (Mon–Thurs & Sun 10am–6pm, Fri 10am–2pm; €3; Ⓦwww.cjudaicum.de) halfway down Oranienburger Strasse is a reminder that this area was, before the war, Berlin's main Jewish quarter. Designed by two prominent non-Jewish architects, Eduard Knoblauch and August Stüler, in an exotic idiom combining Moorish and Byzantine elements, the synagogue was inaugurated in the presence of Bismarck in 1866. Partially burned on *Kristallnacht* and further damaged by bombing during World War II, it stood derelict for many years, a silent reminder of the savagery of Nazi rule. On November 9, 1988, the fiftieth anniversary of *Kristallnacht*, work began on restoration of the facade and the reconstruction of the gilded dome, and this was completed seven years later, though it was decided not to re-create the main body of the temple, whose groundplan is marked out in the rear garden. The front rooms now serve as the **Centrum Judaicum**, a Jewish cultural centre.

At the eastern end of Oranienburger Strasse, turn left into Grosse Hamburger Strasse, where on the immediate right is the **Alter Jüdischer Friedhof**, Berlin's oldest Jewish cemetery, established in 1672. Most of the headstones were smashed by the Nazis and the space was subsequently grassed over, though a monument to Moses Mendelssohn, the Enligthenment-era philosopher and grandfather of composer Felix, was re-erected after the war. Alongside is the site of the first Jewish old people's home to be founded in the city. The Nazis used this as a detention centre, and 55,000 Jews were held here before being shipped off to the camps. A memorial tablet (on which people, following Jewish practice for gravesite visits, have placed pebbles) and a sculpted group of haggard-looking figures representing deportees mark the spot where the home stood.

Continuing along the street, past turn-of-the-century neo-Baroque apartment buildings with shrapnel-pitted facades, brings you to the entrance gateway of the **Sophienkirche**. Built at the beginning of the eighteenth century, this closely resembles Wren's London churches, though the tower is modelled on Schlüter design for the Münzturm of the Stadtschloss, which collapsed due to weak foundations. It was the only central Berlin church to survive the war more or less undamaged.

The western centre

The centre of the artificially created city of West Berlin, a pocket of capitalism kept alive by interested parties in the heart of Soviet-occupied territory, consisted of the district of **Tiergarten**, which takes its name from the former hunting grounds at its core, as well as part of the sprawling district of **Charlottenburg**, which was a separate municipality until 1920 and therefore had a clearly-defined town centre. Since losing its *raison d'être* with the reunification of the city, some of the lustre has worn off the old western centre. However, it remains home to a world-class cultural complex, the **Kulturforum**, while in the evening the area awakens into a nightlife that ranks among the best in Europe.

The commercial heart

If you come to Berlin by train, or on the bus from Tegel airport, chances are you'll arrive at **Bahnhof Zoologischer Garten** (Zoo Station). Despite the lack of a large lobby or grand portal, it's an atmospheric place to end a journey, its elevated glass-covered platforms conjuring up memories of the steam trains which called there when it was built in the run-up to the 1936 Olympics. In recent years, it has been smarted up quite a bit and although there's still a retinue of urban casualties permanently posted by the entrance it has changed markedly from a decade ago, when it was a marketplace for heroin dealing and child prostitution.

Step out east from Bahnhof Zoo and you're in the centre of the west end's maelstrom of bright lights, traffic and high-rise buildings. Another block south is the eastern end of **Kurfürstendamm** (universally known as the **Ku'damm**), a 3.5-kilometre strip of ritzy shops, cinemas, bars and cafés that homes in on the centre like the spoke of a broken wheel.

The major landmark here is the **Kaiser-Wilhelm-Gedächtniskirche** (Kaiser Wilhelm Memorial Church; Ⓦwww.gedaechtniskirche.com), built at the end of the nineteenth century and destroyed by British bombing in November 1943. Left as a ruin, it's a strangely effective memorial, the crumbling tower providing a hint of the old city. The narthex or **Gedenkhalle** (Mon–Sat 10am–4pm; free) features a mosaic of Hohenzollern rulers, as well as a small exhibit showing wartime destruction and a "before and after" model of the city centre. Adjacent, a 1960s concrete and glass chapel contains the tender, sad *Stalingrad Madonna*, while at the back the blue glass campanile from the same period has gained the nickname of the "Lipstick" or the "Soul-Silo": its base contains a shop selling Third World gifts. The area around the church is a magnet for vendors, caricaturists, and street musicians.

Breitscheidplatz marks the beginning of Tauentzienstrasse, with the **Europa-Center**, a huge shopping centre that contains the main tourist office, on its northern side. There's nothing much of interest in this rather generic mall, which was built in the 1960s as a capitalist showcase for West Berlin, topped by a huge, rotating Mercedes-Benz symbol. Further down Tauentzienstrasse, and claiming to be the largest store on the continent, is the **KaDeWe**, an abbreviation of Kaufhaus Des Westens – "the Department Store of the West". It's an impressive statement of the city's standard of living, and the sixth-floor food hall is a mouthwatering inducement to sample the many exotic snacks sold there.

There's little to do on Ku'damm other than spend money, and there's only one cultural attraction in the vicinity, the **Käthe-Kollwitz-Museum**

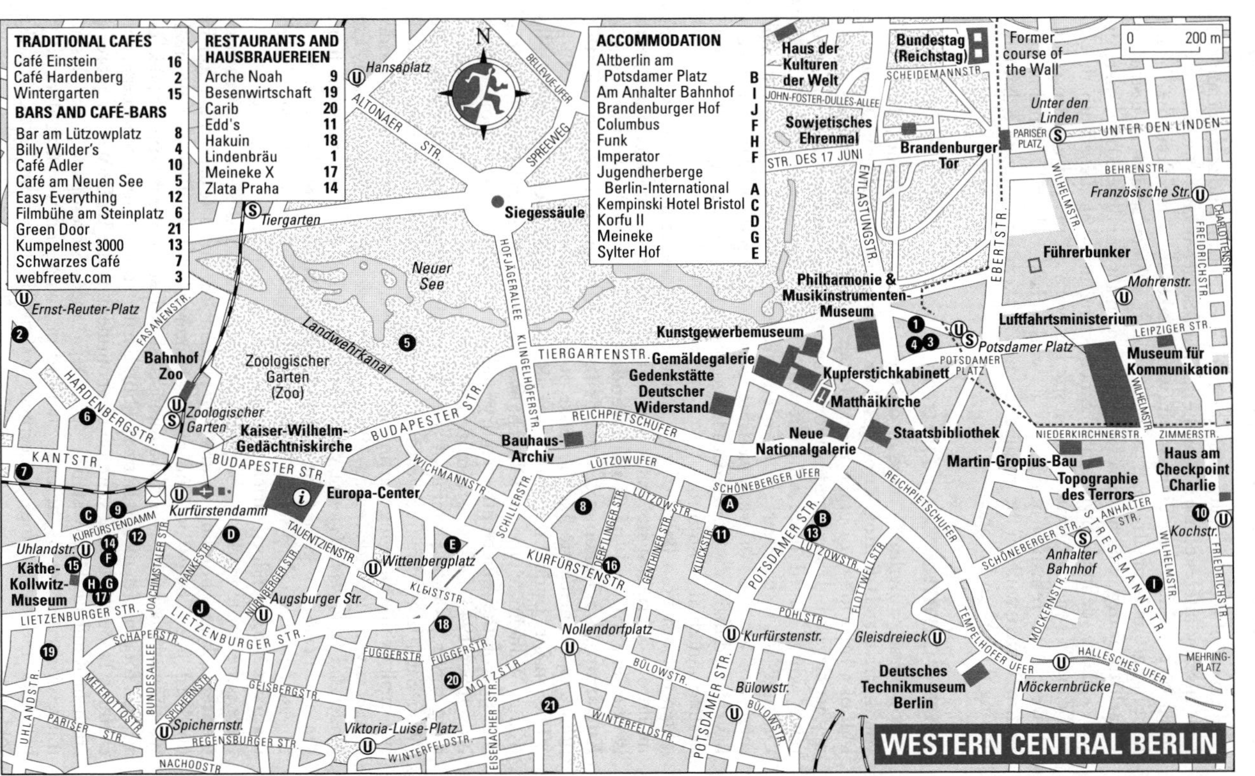
WESTERN CENTRAL BERLIN
TRADITIONAL CAFÉS
Café Einstein 16
Café Hardenberg 2
Wintergarten 15
BARS AND CAFÉ-BARS
Bar am Lützowplatz 8
Billy Wilder's 4
Café Adler 10
Café am Neuen See 5
Easy Everything 12
Filmbühe am Steinplatz 6
Green Door 21
Kumpelnest 3000 13
Schwarzes Café 7
webfreetv.com 3
RESTAURANTS AND HAUSBRAUEREIEN
Arche Noah 9
Besenwirtschaft 19
Carib 20
Edd's 11
Hakuin 18
Lindenbräu 1
Meineke X 17
Zlata Praha 14
ACCOMMODATION
Altberlin am Potsdamer Platz B
Am Anhalter Bahnhof I
Brandenburger Hof J
Columbus F
Funk H
Imperator F
Jugendherberge Berlin-International A
Kempinski Hotel Bristol C
Korfu II D
Meineke G
Sylter Hof E
0 200 m
Former course of the Wall
N
Haus der Kulturen der Welt
Bundestag (Reichstag)
Sowjetisches Ehrenmal
Brandenburger Tor
Unter den Linden
Siegessäule
Tiergarten
Ernst-Reuter-Platz
Hansaplatz
Neuer See
Landwehrkanal
Zoologischer Garten (Zoo)
Bahnhof Zoo
Zoologischer Garten
Kaiser-Wilhelm-Gedächtniskirche
Europa-Center
Kurfürstendamm
Uhlandstr.
Käthe-Kollwitz-Museum
Wittenbergplatz
Augsburger Str.
Nollendorfplatz
Kurfürstenstr.
Bülowstr.
Gleisdreieck
Viktoria-Luise-Platz
Spichernstr.
Bauhaus-Archiv
Philharmonie & Musikinstrumenten-Museum
Kunstgewerbemuseum
Gemäldegalerie
Gedenkstätte Deutscher Widerstand
Kupferstichkabinett
Matthäikirche
Neue Nationalgalerie
Staatsbibliothek
Potsdamer Platz
Führerbunker
Mohrenstr.
Französische Str.
Luftfahrtsministerium
Museum für Kommunikation
Martin-Gropius-Bau
Topographie des Terrors
Haus am Checkpoint Charlie
Kochstr.
Anhalter Bahnhof
Möckernbrücke
Deutsches Technikmuseum Berlin
MEHRING-PLATZ
UNTER DEN LINDEN
BEHRENSTR.
WILHELMSTR.
FRIEDRICHSTR.
CHARLOTTENSTR.
LEIPZIGER STR.
EBERTSTR.
SCHEIDEMANNSTR.
JOHN-FOSTER-DULLES-ALLEE
STR. DES 17 JUNI
ENTLASTUNGSTR.
ALTONAER STR.
BELLEVUE-UFER
SPREEWEG
HOFJÄGERALLEE
KLINGELHÖFERSTR.
TIERGARTENSTR.
REICHPIETSCHUFER
LÜTZOWUFER
BUDAPESTER STR.
HARDENBERGSTR.
FASANENSTR.
KANTSTR.
KURFÜRSTENDAMM
JOACHIMSTALER STR.
RANKESTR.
TAUENTZIENSTR.
NÜRNBERGER STR.
LIETZENBURGER STR.
SCHAPERSTR.
BUNDESALLEE
MEIEROTTOSTR.
UHLANDSTR.
PARISER STR.
SPICHERNSTR.
REGENSBURGER STR.
NACHODSTR.
GEISBERGSTR.
FUGGERSTR.
MOTZSTR.
EISENACHER STR.
WINTERFELDSTR.
KLEISTSTR.
WICHMANNSTR.
SCHILLERSTR.
KURFÜRSTENSTR.
DERFLINGER STR.
GENTHINER STR.
KLUCKSTR.
LÜTZOWSTR.
SCHÖNEBERGER UFER
POTSDAMER STR.
PÜHLSTR.
BÜLOWSTR.
FLOTTWELLSTR.
TEMPELHOFER UFER
MÖCKERNSTR.
SCHÖNEBERGER STR.
STRESEMANNSTR.
ANHALTER STR.
HALLESCHES UFER
NIEDERKIRCHNERSTR.
ZIMMERSTR.
PARISER PLATZ
POTSDAMER PLATZ

(11am–6pm, closed Tues; €5; Ⓦ www.kaethe-kollwitz.de) at Fasanenstr. 24. The drawings and prints of Käthe Kollwitz are among the most moving works from the first half of the twentieth century. Born in 1867, she lived for almost all her life in Prenzlauer Berg in the eastern part of Berlin, where her work evolved a radical left-wing perspective. Following the death of her son in World War I, her woodcuts, lithographs and prints became explicitly pacifist, often dwelling on the theme of mother and child. When her grandson was killed in World War II her work became even sadder and more poignant. The museum's comprehensive collection of her work makes it possible to trace its development, culminating in the tragic sculptures on the top floor.

By the time you reach **Adenauerplatz**, the slick showrooms of the Ku'damm have died out and the bars become affordable: although the clientele tends to consist of loud and brash teenagers, it's not a bad starting point for a bar crawl. Best of all for eating, drinking and nightlife, though, is the squashed rectangle of streets south and west of Bahnhof Zoo, roughly bordered by Kantstrasse, Hardenbergstrasse and Leibnizstrasse, and centred on **Savignyplatz**.

The Zoologischer Garten and the Tiergarten

Back in the centre, the **Zoologischer Garten** (daily 9am–5/6.30pm; €9, or €14 combined ticket with Aquarium, children €4.50 & €7 respectively; Ⓦ www.zoo-berlin.de) was laid out in the 1840s at the southern end of the Tiergarten. It is beautifully landscaped with trees and flowers, and offers many framed views of the landmarks of the city centre. For the most part, the animals are kept out of cages and allowed to roam freely in re-creations of their natural habitats, though some spend part of their time in the whimsical garden pavilions – the elephants in a mock-Burmese pagoda, the antelopes in an imitation mosque, the zebras in a pseudo Arab fort.

The **Tiergarten** proper was landscaped into an English-style park by Peter Lenné in the 1830s. It was destroyed during the Battle of Berlin in 1945 – though so successful has its replanting been that these days it's hard to tell it's not original. You can wander through the park, tracing the course of the **Landwehrkanal**, an inland waterway off the River Spree. Near the Corneliusbrücke, a small, odd sculpture commemorates the radical leader **Rosa Luxemburg**, co-founder of the short-lived Socialist Republic of 1918, whose body was dumped in the canal at this point by the militia group who had kidnapped her. **Karl Liebknecht**, her co-conspirator, was gunned down while "attempting to escape" and thrown into a nearby lake, the Neuer See.

The broad avenue cutting through the Tiergarten is the **Strasse des 17 Juni**, whose name commemorates the day in 1953 when workers in East Berlin rose in revolt against the occupying Soviet powers, demanding free elections, the removal of all borders separating the two Germanys, and the release of political prisoners. Soviet forces were quickly mobilized, and between two and four hundred people died; the authorities also ordered the execution of twenty-one East Berliners and eighteen Soviet soldiers – for "moral capitulation to the demonstrators".

At the centre of the avenue is the **Siegessäule** (April–Oct Mon–Fri 9.30am–6pm, Sat & Sun 9.30am–7pm; Nov–March Mon–Fri 10am–5pm, Sat & Sun 10am–5.30pm; €1), a column commemorating Prussia's military victories over Denmark, Austria and France in the period 1864–71. In 1938 the column was shifted to this spot on Hitler's orders from what is today the Platz der Republik. Though the boulevard approaches exaggerate its size, it's still an eye-catching monument: 67m high and topped with a colossal gilded winged statue of Victory that symbolically faces France. The viewing platform, approached via a spiral stairway of 285 steps, offers good distant views. At the base of the column are mosaics illustrating the main consequence of the victories, namely the unification of the German peoples into one nation for the first time ever.

Strasse des 17 Juni terminates at the Brandenburger Tor; a little further north, albeit still on the western side of the former wall, is the former **Reichstag**, which is nowadays officially known as the **Bundestag**. This late nineteenth-century parliament building, inscribed with the words *Dem Deutschen Volke* ("To the German People"), has witnessed many dramatic events. In November 1918 the German Republic was declared from its balcony by the Social Democrat Philipp Scheidemann, while Karl Liebknecht was proclaiming a Socialist Republic down the road from the Stadtschloss. The Reichstag was seriously damaged by fire in 1933, an event Hitler used as a pretext for his seizure of power. For decades, the building stood as a symbol of national unity hard by the border that underlined its division, and was belatedly restored in a simplified form to host occasional plenary sessions of parliament. In 1990, the new all-German parliament held its first session there, and when Berlin was later confirmed as the national capital and main seat of government, preparations began on equipping it for a resumption of its former role, which it duly assumed in 1999. During the intervening period, the interior was completely gutted and refashioned, and a new glass **dome** was placed on top. Designed by British architect Lord (Norman) Foster, the dome, controversial when proposed, has proven a huge popular success. A circular ramp winds up the glass cupola to a **viewing deck** (daily 8am–10pm; free) that offers a stunning view of the city; beware that there are often very long queues for admission.

By the riverbank at the northeastern corner of the Reichstag is one of several small cemeteries close to the Berlin Wall commemorating those, many of them unknown, who died trying to escape. Southwest of the Reichstag is the **Sowjetisches Ehrenmal** (Soviet War Memorial) to the Red Army troops who died in the Battle of Berlin. Built from the marble of Hitler's destroyed Berlin HQ, the Reichskanzlei, it's flanked by two tanks that were supposedly the first to reach the city.

The Kulturforum

Immediately west of Potsdamer Platz is the **Kulturforum**, a group of museums and other cultural institutions that could easily fill several days of your time. It's almost entirely a postwar development: the only older building is Stüler's **Matthäikirche**, though even that has a modernized interior. The **tower** (Tues–Sun noon–6pm; €1) commands a fine general view over Berlin, and in particular over the brand new buildings of Potsdamer Platz.

The Gemäldegalerie

The jewel of the complex is the **Gemäldegalerie** (Picture Gallery; Tues, Wed & Fri 10am–6pm, Thurs 10am–10pm; €6; Ⓦ www.smb.spk-berlin.de), one of the world's most comprehensive collections of old masters. Originally housed in the prewar Kaiser-Friedrich-Museum, the paintings were stashed in various locations for safekeeping during the war years. The lion's share of the collection was held in the west, and was eventually displayed in less than ideal conditions at Dahlem; only the surviving rump held in the Soviet sector (the rest of which perished in a fire after the war had ended) returned to its renamed former home. The current premises were opened in 1998, but even so many fine paintings have had to be banished to a densely hung study section in the basement in order that the reunited collection can be displayed in full. It is therefore likely that part of the collection will move back to the Bodemuseum when it reopens, and there is a longer-term plan to build a new and much larger gallery in the vicinity of Museumsinsel.

Arranged in chronological order, and subdivided geographically, the displays begin on the north side of the building with German works of the Middle Ages and Renaissance. Highlights include the large *Wurzach Altar* of 1437, made in the workshop of the great Ulm sculptor **Hans Multscher**; its exaggerated gestures and facial distortions mark it out as a distant precursor of Expressionism. An interesting contrast is offered by the far more subtle *Solomon before the Queen of Sheba*, painted in the same year by **Konrad Witz**, while the exquisite *Nativity* by **Martin Schongauer** is the most important surviving panel by the father-figure of the German Renaissance.

Of the brilliant generation which followed, **Altdorfer** is represented by several canvases – *Allegory of Beggary Sitting on the Train of Pride* is the most individualistic – which show his love of lush landscapes and exotic architecture. His works are hung alongside those of **Dürer**, by whom there are some penetrating portraits, notably of two future mayors of Nürnberg – *Hieronymous Holzschuher* and *Jacob Muffel*. Among an impressive group of works by Dürer's eccentric pupil **Hans Baldung** is an exotic *Adoration of the Magi* triptych. **Holbein the Younger** is represented by five superbly observed portraits, the most celebrated being *The Danzig Merchant Georg Gisze*, with a still-life background that's a real tour-de-force of artistic virtuosity. Notable among the many examples of **Cranach** are his tongue-in-cheek *The Fountain of Youth*, and his free reinterpretation of Bosch's famous triptych *The Garden of Earthly Delights*.

In the Netherlandish section, **Jan van Eyck**'s beautifully lit *Madonna in the Church* is crammed with architectural detail, with the Virgin lifted in the perspective for gentle emphasis. **Petrus Christus** is thought to have been a pupil of van Eyck, and certainly knew his work, as *The Virgin and Child with St Barbara and a Carthusian Monk* reveals: in the background are tiny Flemish houses and street scenes, the artist carefully locating the event in his native Bruges. **Dieric Bouts**' figures tend to be rather formalized, but his *Christ in the House of Simon the Pharisee* is filled with gesture, expression and carefully drawn detail. **Rogier van der Weyden** developed the Eyckian technique to a warmer, much more emotional treatment of religious subjects, and the figures in his *Middelburg Altar* reveal a delicacy of poise and an approachable humanity that was to greatly influence German painting in the fifteenth century. *Etienne Chevalier with St Stephen*, a rare panel by the great French illuminator **Jehan Fouquet**, makes for a fascinating comparison with the Flemish works; it depicts the Treasurer of France accompanied by his patron saint.

The Dutchman **Albert van Ouwater** was another influential artist, although *The Raising of Lazarus* is his only complete work to have survived; it's a daring picture, the richly dressed merchants on the right contrasting strongly with the simplicity of the Holy Family on the left. **Geertgen tot Sint Jans** was Ouwater's pupil, but his *St John the Baptist* is quite different from his master's painting – the saint sits almost comically impassive against a rich backdrop of intricately constructed landscape. Among the gallery's most prized possessions are two of the few surviving altarpieces by **Hugo van der Goes**. *The Adoration of the Magi* has a superbly drawn realism that marks a new development in Netherlandish art, carrying precision over into a large-scale work with a deftly executed, complex perspective; *The Adoration of the Shepherds* (painted when the artist was in the first throes of madness) displays an exalted sense of religious fervour, especially in the dramatic device of Old Testament prophets drawing back a curtain to unveil the scene. *St John the Evangelist on Patmos* is a typically unconventional composition by **Hieronymus Bosch**, while **Pieter Bruegel the Elder**'s *Netherlandish Proverbs* is an amusing, if hard-to-grasp, depiction of over a hundred sixteenth-century maxims.

The final rooms in this wing are devoted to seventeenth-century Flemish and Dutch paintings, beginning with the fleshy canvases of **Rubens** – whose *Child with a Bird*, a portrait of his nephew, gives a rare glimpse of a more intimate vein – and several grand portraits of Genoese nobility by **Van Dyck**. *Kitchen Scene with View of the Last Supper* by **Joachim Wtewael** is a virtuoso example of Dutch Mannerism, while **Frans Hals** is represented by several portraits, among which the satirical *Malle Babbe* stands out. In total contrast are two enchantingly luminous examples of the very distinctive art of **Vermeer**: *Woman with a Pearl Necklace* and *Man and Woman Drinking Wine*.

Formerly, Berlin boasted of owning 25 paintings of **Rembrandt** – the largest collection in the world – but the exhaustive research carried out on the painter in recent years has reduced this figure markedly. Controversy still surrounds the authorship of some of the canvases, but one that has been conclusively proved to be a member of the studio is the most famous picture here, *The Man in the Golden Helmet*, though this does little to detract from the elegance and power of the portrait. Works definitely by the master himself include the luxuriantly Baroque *Rape of Prosperine*; *The Mennonite Preacher Anslo and his Wife*, one of the finest achievements of his middle period; and two visionary late masterpieces – *Jacob Wrestling with the Angel* and *Moses Destroying the Tables of the Law*.

The galleries on the southern side are largely devoted to Italian paintings, with the Florentine School figuring strongly. Of the early works, pride of place is taken by **Giotto**'s largest surviving panel, *The Dormition of the Virgin*. **Fra Angelico**'s *The Last Judgment* is a radiant Dantesque vision, while *The Adoration in the Forest* by his pupil **Fra Filippo Lippi** is a mystical image of unusual grace and beauty, rightly one of the most admired paintings of the period. A gorgeously coloured tondo of *The Adoration of the Magi* is one of the tantalisingly few surviving panels by **Domenico Veneziano**. Finest of several **Botticelli** masterpieces is a large altarpiece, *The Madonna and Child Enthroned with the two St Johns*. From elsewhere in Italy are examples of Mantegna, Bellini, Raphael, Titian and **Correggio**, whose playfully suggestive *Leda with the Swan* so offended an eighteenth-century religious fanatic that he hacked it to pieces.

In the following rooms, paintings by seventeenth-century Italian masters are hung alongside works by their Latin contemporaries. Particularly celebrated are **Caravaggio**'s *Cupid Victorious*, heavy with symbolism and homoeroticism, and **Poussin**'s *Self-Portrait*, one of only two purely figurative works in his entire ouevre. The displays end with eighteenth-century paintings from all over Europe, including canvases by Tiepolo and Canaletto, and three Watteaus which once belonged to Frederick the Great. There is also a surprisingly good representation of British portraiture, including characteristic examples of Gainsborough, Reynolds, Lawrence and Raeburn.

The Kupferstichkabinett and the Kunstgewerbemuseum

Two further collections of European art can be found in buildings interlinked with the Gemäldegalerie. The **Kupferstichkabinett** (Engraving Cabinet; Tues–Fri 10am–6pm, Sat & Sun 11am–6pm; €3; ⓦ www.smb.spk-berlin.de), holds an extensive array of manuscripts, prints, drawings, watercolours and engravings, selections from which are shown to the public in a series of temporary exhibitions. Its most famous possessions are 84 exquisite drawings by Botticelli illustrating scenes from Dante's *Divine Comedy*.

The **Kunstgewerbemuseum** (Museum of Applied Arts; Tues–Fri 10am–6pm, Sat & Sun 11am–6pm; €3; ⓦ www.smb.spk-berlin.de) is an encyclopedic collection, whose displays begin with the medieval section on the ground floor. Some of the earliest items come from the Westphalian town of Enger; these include an eighth-century purse-shaped reliquary that belonged to Duke Widikund, leader of the Saxon resistance to Charlemagne. There are dazzling groups of treasures from the Dom in Braunschweig (including a crucifix, a reliquary and a book cover, all donated by the Welf family) and from the Münster in the Swiss city of Basel. In the following rooms are many magnificent examples of Renaissance silverware, notably the 32-piece set made for ceremonial municipal use in Lüneburg. At the entrance to the top floor are the surviving parts of the Pommersche Kunstschrank, an ebony cabinet of curious formerly in the Stadtschloss; the following galleries illustrate changing artistic tastes from Rococo to Jugendstil and Art Deco. In the basement is a small assembly of Bauhaus furniture, glittering contemporary jewellery, and a display on the evolution of product design.

The Scharoun buildings

Opposite the Kunstgewerbemuseum is the **Philharmonie**, home of the Berliner Philharmoniker (Berlin Philharmonic), which has for long enjoyed an unmatched reputation in the musical world, being distinguished for its richness and precision of tone, and its supreme artistic discipline. The distinctive gold-plated building, an irregular pentagon with a tent-shaped roof, was designed in the early 1960s by Hans Scharoun, who was also responsible for the general plan of the Kulturforum. Its interior arrangement is unconventional, with terraced seating around a central orchestral podium, yet this ensures that every member of the audience enjoys a clear view as well as excellent acoustics. Just over two decades later, the **Kammermusiksaal**, a venue for smaller-scale groups, was added alongside. Again, the design is Scharoun's, though it was built by his pupil Edgar Wisniewski.

The same architectural team was also responsible for the **Musikinstrumenten-Museum** (Tues–Fri 9am–5pm, Sat & Sun 10am–5pm; €3, free first Sun of month; ⓦ www.sim.spk-berlin.de) on the north side of the Philharmonie. This has a fine collection of historic musical instruments, including some pretty Rococo musical clocks and two full-sized organs – one from early nineteenth-century England, the other a "Mighty Wurlitzer". Recordings of appropriate short pieces of music have been made on many of the instruments, and these can be heard via the headphones placed throughout the museum. There are also regular live performances at 11am on Sundays.

Across Potsdamer Strasse is the **Staatsbibliothek** (Mon–Fri 10am–8pm, Sat 10am–7pm; free), which has over three and a half million books, occasional exhibitions, a small concert hall, a reasonable café and a wide selection of foreign-language newspapers. The library was used as an important backdrop in Wim Wenders' poetic film elegy to the city, *Wings of Desire*.

Potsdamer Platz

From the Staatsbibliothek, Potsdamer Strasse curves round to the new developments on **Potsdamer Platz**. On its southern side, the **Daimler-Benz-Areal**, designed by Renzo Piano, includes several restaurants, a stage theatre, a movie multiplex, a 3D big-screen movie theatre, and the obligatory shopping mall. Opposite, Helmut Jahn's **Sony-Center** – several glass-sheathed buildings grouped around a capacious, tented circular courtyard – has the same touristy pull as its neighbour, but also includes a setpiece attraction in the **Filmmuseum Berlin** (Tues, Wed & Fri–Sun 10am–6pm, Thurs 10am–8pm; €6; Ⓦwww.filmmuseum-berlin.de). This contains an excellent presentation on the history of the movies, concentrating on the German film industry, and also has a large collection of Marlene Dietrich artefacts.

The Neue Nationalgalerie

At the southern end of the Kulturforum is the **Neue Nationalgalerie** (Tues, Wed & Fri 10am–6pm, Thurs 10am–10pm, Sat & Sun 11am–6pm; €6; Ⓦwww.smb.spk-berlin.de), a black-rimmed glass box that seems almost suspended above the ground, its clarity of line and detail having all the intelligent simplicity of the Parthenon. Designed by Mies van der Rohe in 1965, the ground-floor section is used for temporary exhibits, often of contemporary art, while the underground galleries contain paintings from the beginning of the twentieth century onwards. There's a notable array of paintings by the Expressionist Brücke group, including **Kirchner**'s *Potsdamer Platz* of 1914, though it might as well be in another country instead of just down the road. Another work with a Berlin setting is **Grosz**'s *The Pillars of Society*, a savage attack on the hypocrisy endemic in the power structures of the Weimar Republic. Cubism is represented by examples of **Braque**, **Gris** and **Picasso** (though the last-named is seen in greater number and to better effect in the Berggruen-Sammlung in Charlottenburg). There are also works by, among others, Klee, Dix, Beckmann and Feininger.

Paintings and sculpures of more recent decades are exhibited in the Neue Nationalgalerie's annexe, the **Hamburger Bahnhof** (Tues–Fri 10am–6pm, Sat & Sun 11am–6pm; €6; Ⓦwww.smb.spk-berlin.de) housed in a former railway station in the northern district of Moabit, one of the early working-class suburbs of the city.

The Bendlerblock and the Bauhaus-Archiv

On Stauffenbergstrasse, a block west of the Kulturforum proper, is the **Bendlerblock**, a huge building where the one nearly successful attempt on Hitler's life, the Bomb Plot of July 1944, was hatched, and where the conspirators were subsequently executed. The rooms on the second floor have been designated the **Gedenkstätte Deutscher Widerstand** (Memorial to the German Resistance; Mon–Wed & Fri 9am–6pm, Thurs 9am–8pm, Sat & Sun 10am–6pm; free; Ⓦwww.gdw-berlin.de), and contain a fascinating documentary record on the many groups and individuals who actively opposed the Third Reich, despite the risk of death or imprisonment that was the automatic consequence. It thus serves as a useful corrective to the oft-expressed view that all Germans were Nazis, though it does little to help explain why the opposition was uncoordinated and ineffective, or why so many prominent anti-Nazis – including Count Claus Schenk von Stauffenberg, the hero of the Bomb Plot – were initially prepared to serve Hitler quite loyally.

Further west, occupying a quayside setting at the junction of Klingelhöferstrasse and Von-der-Heydt-Strasse, is the **Bauhaus-Archiv** (daily

10am–5pm, closed Tues; €4; Ⓦwww.bauhaus.de). The building was designed in 1964 by Walter Gropius, the first director of the Bauhaus, and was originally conceived for a hilly site in the Hessian city of Darmstadt. However, this project failed to come to fruition, and it was not until seven years later (by which time Gropius was already dead) that a modified version could be built on this flat location. Unless displaced by a temporary display, the exhibition halls inside display some of the classics of Bauhaus design, such as Marcel Breuer's tubular steel chair, Marianne Brant's tea and coffee set, and László Moholy-Nagy's *Light-Space Modulator*. There are also paintings by Klee, Kandinsky, Feininger and Schlemmer.

The suburbs

Berlin's suburbs are nothing if not diverse. In the former West Berlin, they range from densely populated inner-city districts such as **Kreuzberg** and **Schöneberg**, both of which have been through a self-consciously trendy period, to the vast rural landscapes of the **Grunewald** and the **Havel lakes**. From a historic point of view, **Schloss Charlottenburg** is the main highlight, and its park is a wonderful place to spend a lazy afternoon. In its immediate vicinity are some important public museums; yet another group can be found in the academic quarter of **Dahlem**. While **Plötzensee** offers one of the most chilling reminders of the brutality of the Third Reich, the **Olympiastadion** is one of the few monuments of that era still regarded with a certain amount of affection – largely because the Games for which it was built did not entirely go according to script.

Rebuilding has significantly changed the face of the suburbs of the former East Berlin. **Prenzlauer Berg**, a part working-class, part bohemian district that fans out northeast of the city centre, has long been a centre of "alternative" culture and lifestyle and is home to some of the best cafés, bars and nightlife in the entire city. **Friedrichshain**, immediately to the east of the centre, features some fascinating examples of GDR architecture, and is nowadays the new frontier for the city's clubbers and bar hoppers. To the southeast is **Treptow** and its massive Soviet war memorial; further out is **Köpenick**, which retains a village-like atmosphere.

Kreuzberg

Kreuzberg, which lies south of Mitte, is famed for its large immigrant community and self-styled "alternative" inhabitants, nightlife and goings on. Effectively there are two Kreuzbergs: the west, the area bounded by Friedrichstrasse, Viktoriapark and Südstern, is a richer, fancier, more sedate area than its neighbour to the east. The latter is sometimes referred to as **SO 36** after its old postal code and is a "happening" quarter of raucous nightspots frequented by punks and old hippies.

Western Kreuzberg

Southeast of Potsdamer Platz is the **Martin-Gropius-Bau** (10am–8pm, closed Tues; variable charges; Ⓦwww.gropiusbau.de). Designed in 1877 by Martin Gropius, a pupil of Schinkel and the uncle of Walter, the building was, until its destruction in the war, home of the Kunstgewerbemuseum. In recent years it has been rebuilt and refurbished, and now hosts major temporary exhibitions of archeology, architecture and photography. Alongside is the **Topograpie des**

Terrors (Tues–Sun 10am–6pm; free; Ⓦwww.topographie.de), an outdoor exhibition in a grassy field where once stood the Reich Security offices, including the headquarters of the Gestapo and SS. A numbered series of noticeboards with photographs and English texts indicate the sites of the most important Nazi buildings in the area. It was here that Himmler planned the Final Solution, the deportation and genocide of European Jews.

From here it's a ten-minute walk down Wilhelmstrasse, then along Kochstrasse, to the site of **Checkpoint Charlie**, one of the most famous names associated with Cold War-era Berlin. This allied military post on the corner of Friedrichstrasse marked the border between East and West Berlin until July 1990, when it was removed. While it stood it was one of Berlin's more celebrated landmarks and the building lent its name informally to the adjacent GDR border crossing (official title *Grenzübergang Friedrichstrasse*), which, with its dramatic "YOU ARE NOW LEAVING THE AMERICAN SECTOR" sign (a replica of which can still be seen) and unsmiling border guards, used to be the archetypal movie-style Iron Curtain crossing.

Tangible evidence of the trauma the Wall caused is still on hand at the **Haus am Checkpoint Charlie** (daily 9am–10pm; €7.50; Ⓦwww.mauermuseum.de). Here the history of the Wall is told through photographs of escape tunnels and with the homemade aircraft and converted cars by which people attempted, succeeded, and sometimes tragically failed to break through the border. Films document the stories of some of the approximately 230 people murdered by the East German border guards, and there's a section on human rights behind the Iron Curtain and elsewhere, but it's a somewhat dated collection, and not the harrowing experience some visitors seem to expect.

A brisk twenty-minute walk southeast from here, through streets levelled during wartime bombing, takes you to the **Jüdisches Museum Berlin** (Mon 10am–10pm, Tues–Sun 10am–8pm; €5; Ⓦwww.jmberlin.de) at Lindenstr. 14. This is housed in a stunning "deconstructivist" building by Daniel Libeskind which is shaped like a compressed lightening bolt, sheathed in polished metallic facing, with windows – mere thin angular lines – that trace geometric patterns on the exterior. Inside, an empty and inaccessible diagonal shaft, signifying loss and emptiness, cuts through the building. Three long intersecting corridors, each symbolic of an element of the Jewish experience comprise the basement – the "axis of continuity", leading to the exhibition space; an "axis of exile," which leads outside to a garden of steles; and an "axis of the Holocaust", which leads to the dimly lit and completely empty tower. The displays are divided into thirteen different sections, covering the entire history and culture of German-speaking Jewry. Art works, ceremonial artefacts and everyday objects complement the documentary material.

A fifteen-minute walk south from the Martin-Gropius-Bau, down Stresemannstrasse and Möckenstrasse, is the **Deutsche Technikmuseum Berlin** (Tues–Fri 9am–5.30pm, Sat & Sun 10am–6pm; €3; Ⓦwww.dtmb.de) at Trebbiner Str.9. This is one of the city's most entertaining museums and a children's and button-pushers' delight. The technology section has plenty of experiments, antiquated machinery and computers to play with, alongside some elegant old cars and planes. Meanwhile, the polished steam trains and carriages of the transport section have been brought to rest in the former goods depot of the old Anhalter Bahnhof.

It's another half an hour's walk south from here (down Grossbeerenstrasse) to **Viktoriapark** (the "Kreuzberg", as it's popularly known), a relaxed ramble of trees and green space on the slopes of a hill, with a pretty brook running down the middle. Atop the hill is the **Kreuzberg** itself, the monument from which the district takes its name. More correctly known as the **Befreiungsdenkmal** (Liberation Memorial), this huge neo-Gothic cast-iron spire, crowned with Prussia's highest military honour, the Iron Cross, is the only completed part of Schinkel's ambitious scheme for a series of monuments to commemorate the victory over Napoleon.

Eastern Kreuzberg

Despite its reputation as a hotbed of radical protest and alternative lifestyles (a leftover from the days when West Germany's disaffected youth came to Berlin, since those living in the city were exempt from military service), you don't need any interest in revolution or city machinations to enjoy **eastern Kreuzberg** (U-Bahn line #1 to Kottbusser Tor or Schlesisches Tor). The nightlife here is among the city's wildest and it's an enjoyable area to wander through by day, stopping off at one of the innumerable Turkish snack bars for a kebab, breakfasting on a 9am vodka-and-beer special at a café, or just taking in the feel of the place – which is much like an Istanbul market in an eastern bloc housing development. Kreuzberg's main strip is **Oranienstrasse** which, from Moritzplatz eastwards, is lined with café-bars, art galleries and clothes shops, and in a way forms an "alternative" Kurfürstendamm. South of the Landwehrkanal is the **Südstern**, which has a convenient U-Bahn station and another clutch of café-bars, while nearby Gneisenaustrasse has some good restaurants. However, by this point the distinctive flavour of eastern Kreuzberg has gone, and things are a lot tamer.

Schöneberg

Schöneberg, immediately to the west of Kreuzberg, is a largely residential area with little in the way of conventional sights, but it has important reminders of the city's Anglo-American connections. From the middle of Potsdamer Strasse, it's a short detour west along Bülowstrasse to **Nollendorfplatz**, which, on its southern side, has the proto-Deco **Metropol-Theater**. Maassenstrasse then leads on to Nollendorfstrasse, where at no. 17 stands the building in which **Christopher Isherwood** lived during his years in prewar Berlin, a time that was to be elegantly recounted in perhaps the most famous collection of stories about the city ever written – *Goodbye to Berlin*.

Schöneberg has since been reborn as a fancy, even chic neighbourhood; the would-be Isherwoods of the moment hang out in Kreuzberg or Prenzlauer Berg. At night, this part of Schöneberg, particularly the area around **Winterfeldtplatz**, is good for eating and especially drinking: tidily bohemian, less sniffy than Savignyplatz and much more middle-of-the-road than eastern Kreuzberg. On Wednesday and Saturday mornings the square holds an excellent **market**.

The **Rathaus Schöneberg** on Martin-Luther-Strasse (U-Bahn #4) was the seat of the West Berlin parliament and senate after the last war, and it was outside here in 1963 that **John F. Kennedy** made his celebrated "Ich bin ein Berliner" speech on the Cold War political situation, just a few months after the Cuban missile crisis. What the president hadn't realized as he read from his phonetically written text was that by mistakingly including the word ein he had actually said "I am a small doughnut", since *Berliner* is the German name for a jam doughnut. More recently, the **Bundeskanzler-Willy-Brandt-Stiftung** (daily 10am–6pm; free; ⓦwww.willy-brandt.de) has been established inside the building, featuring a permanent exhibition focusing on the freedom campaigning undertaken by former Berlin mayor and German Chancellor Willy Brandt.

Charlottenburg: the Schloss and museums

The district of **Charlottenburg** stretches north and west of the city centre, reaching as far south as the forests of the Grunewald. The most significant attraction here, one that needs half a day at least to cover, is the **Schloss Charlottenburg and museum complex** on Spandauer Damm. The nearest U-Bahn stations – Richard-Wagner-Platz on the #7 line and Sophie-Charlotte-Platz on the #2 line – are five to ten minutes away by foot; a more direct means of access is by buses #X21, #X26, #109, #110 and #145.

Schloss Charlottenburg

Schloss Charlottenburg (Tues–Fri 9am–5pm, Sat & Sun 10am–5pm; separate tickets priced individually below, combined ticket for Knobelsdorff-Flügel, Schinkel-Pavillon, Belvedere and Mausoleum €7; Ⓦwww.spsg.de) comes as a surprise after the unrelieved modernity of the city streets. Commissioned as a country house by the future Queen Sophie Charlotte in 1695 (who also gave her name to the district), the Schloss was expanded and added to throughout the eighteenth and early nineteenth centuries to provide a summer residence for the Prussian kings. Approaching through the main courtyard, you're confronted with Andreas Schlüter's **Denkmal des Grossen Kurfürsten**, an equestrian statue of Friedrich Wilhelm, the Great Elector, cast as a single piece in 1700. It's in superb condition, despite (or perhaps because of) spending the war years sunk at the bottom of the Tegeler See for safekeeping.

Immediately behind is the entrance to the oldest part of the Schloss, now known as the **Nering-Eosanderbau** (lower floor €8, upper floor €2) in honour of the two architects (the Dutchman Johann Arnold Nering and the Swede Johann Eosander von Göthe) who designed it. The ground floor, containing the main state apartments, can only be seen on a German-language guided tour. Highlights are the **Porzellan-Zimmer**, which is packed to the ceiling with china, and the **Schlosskapelle**, which is exceptionally extravagant for a Protestant chapel, and includes a portrait of Sophie Charlotte as the Virgin ascending to heaven. The upper floor has a suite of rooms refurbished in the nineteenth century for King Friedrich Wilhelm IV, but is mainly of note for the Hohenzollern family collections of porcelain and silver, plus miscellaneous heirlooms, of which the oldest are the Florentine Renaissance sword and scabbard of Margrave Albrecht III Achilles. Also on view are the **regalia** used at the 1701 ceremony where Elector Friedrich III crowned himself King Friedrich I, so raising Prussia to the rank of a kingdom. The two crowns and the imperial seal were specially made for the event, where they were used in conjunction with a sixteenth-century sword and a seventeenth-century orb and sceptre.

Frederick the Great's eastern extension to the Schloss is known as the **Knobelsdorff-Flügel** (€5), again in honour of its architect. Six rooms on the garden side have been restored to their original appearance, and are hung with portraits by Frederick's court painter **Antoine Pesne**: the vivacious *La Barberina*, which immortalizes an Italian dancer, stands out from the others. On the front part of the ground floor are the quarters of Friedrich Wilhelm III; here can be seen **Jacques Louis David**'s famous heroic image *of Napoleon Crossing the Alps*, which Blücher took as war booty from Paris following his victory over the French dictator at Waterloo. The eastern section of the upper floor contains the main reception rooms – the **Weisser Saal**, whose ceiling paintings have been replaced by witty contemporary pastiches; and the

Goldene Galerie, which ranks among Knobelsdorff's finest interiors. The small chambers beyond contain part of Frederick's personal collection of French paintings. These include several masterpieces by **Watteau**, notably *The Embarcation for Cythera*, a delicate Rococo frippery tinged with sympathy and sadness, and *The Shop Sign*, an astonishingly original mixture of reality and illusion, which the dying artist painted in eight mornings for an art dealer friend.

The final addition to the main structure of the Schloss was Carl Gotthard Langhans' Neoclassical **Theaterbau** at the far western end. Its modernized interior now contains the **Museum für Vor- und Frühgeschichte** (Museum of Pre- and Early History; Tues–Fri 10am–5pm, Sat & Sun 11am–5pm; €3; Ⓦ www.smb.spk-berlin.de), a miscellaneous collection of archeological finds from both the Berlin area and abroad. A spectacular recent acquisition is a Bronze Age golden hat, which was probably a priestly headdress. Some artefacts from the Schliemann excavations of Troy are on view, though the most precious items (some represented here in reproductions) are in Moscow, having been carted away in 1945 as spoils of war. Delicate negotiations for the return of the Schliemann treasures continue, and the hope is they will be back in Berlin by the time this collection moves to the Neues Museum on Museumsinsel in 2008.

The Schlossgarten

The **Schlossgarten** is a mixture of different elements of landscaping styles. Closest to the Schloss is a formal Baroque garden; the rest was transformed by Lenné into an English-style landscaped park in which water plays a key role, the Spree being complemented by a series of ponds and canals spanned by graceful little bridges. Just a few metres away from the northeastern corner of the Schloss is the **Schinkel-Pavillon** (Tues–Sun 10am–5pm; €2; Ⓦ www.spsg.de), which was built as a Neapolitan-style retreat for Friedrich Wilhelm III. Schinkel designed the interior down to the minutest detail, and some of his drawings and paintings are on display, as are topographical canvases by Gaertner, including views of Paris and Moscow as well as the remarkable hexagonal *Panorama from the Friedrichswerdersche Kirche*.

Much deeper into the gardens, on the north side of the carp pond, is the **Belvedere** (April–Oct Tues–Sun 10am–5pm; Nov–March Tues–Fri noon–4pm, Sat & Sun noon–5pm; €2; Ⓦ www.spsg.de), built by Langhans as a combined outlook tower, teahouse and chamber music venue. It now houses a historical display of Berlin-made porcelain. On the western side of the gardens a long tree-lined avenue leads to the hushed and shadowy **Mausoleum** (April–Oct Tues–Sun 10am–5pm; €1; Ⓦ www.spsg.de), where Friedrich Wilhelm III is buried, his sarcophagus, carved by Christian Daniel Rauch, making him seem a good deal younger than his seventy years. Friedrich Wilhelm had commissioned the mausoleum to be built thirty years earlier for his wife, Queen Luise, whose own delicate sarcophagus, likewise by Rauch, depicts her not dead but sleeping. Later burials here include Kaiser Wilhelm I, looking every inch a Prussian king.

The Charlottenburg museums

Facing the Schloss across Spandauer Damm are two domed barracks built by Stüler in the 1850s for the royal guard. The eastern of these is currently home to the **Ägyptisches Museum** (Tues–Sun 10am–6pm; €6; Ⓦ www.smb.spk-berlin.de), which displays the fruits of innumerable German excavations in Egypt from the early part of the twentieth century. The museum's pride and joy is the **bust of Nefertiti** on the first floor, a treasure that has become a symbol for the city as a cultural capital. There's no questioning its beauty – the queen has a perfect bone structure and gracefully sculpted lips – and the history of the piece is equally interesting. Created around 1350 BC, the bust probably never left the studio of the sculptor Thutmosis in Akhetaten, acting as a model for other portraits of the queen (its use as a model explains why the left eye was never drawn in). When the city was abandoned, the bust remained behind in the studio, to be discovered some 3000 years later in 1912. Elsewhere in the museum, atmospheric lighting focuses attention on the exhibits, which are of a uniformly high standard. Look out for the astonishingly modern-looking **Green Man** of the Ptolemaic period, and the **Kalabsha Monumental Gate**, given to the museum by the Egyptian government in 1973.

The corresponding building directly opposite contains the **Berggruen-Sammlung** (Tues–Sun 11am–6pm; €6; Ⓦwww.smb.spk-berlin.de), whose large array of paintings by Picasso was initially placed on loan by the private collector Heinz Berggruen but later acquired for the city at a knock-down price. There are works from all periods of Picasso's career, plus rooms devoted to Matisse and Klee, and canvases by Cézanne and Van Gogh.

Just to the south is the **Bröhan-Museum** (Tues–Sun 10am–6pm; €4; Ⓦwww.broehan-museum.de), which is devoted exclusively to the Jugendstil and Art Deco movements. The walls are hung with paintings of the Berlin Secession, notably the luxuriant landscapes of Karl Hagenmeister; many of the other artworks – ceramics, furniture, glass, tapestries, ivories, gold- and silverware – are grouped together as simulated interiors of the period.

Northern and western Charlottenburg

In the far north of Charlottenburg, by the border with Wedding, is the place where the Nazis brought dissidents and political opponents for imprisonment and execution. Nowadays known as the **Gedenkstatte Plötzensee** (daily 9am–5pm; free; Ⓦwww.gedenkstaette-ploetzensee.de), it can be reached directly by bus #123 from Tiergarten S-Bahn station. The former prison buildings have been refurbished as a juvenile detention centre, while the memorial is in the buildings where over 2500 people were hanged or guillotined between 1933 and 1945. Following the July Bomb Plot, 89 of the 200 people condemned were executed here in the space of a few days. Hitler ordered the hangings to be carried out with piano wire, so that the victims would slowly strangle rather than die from broken necks, and spent his evenings watching movie footage of the executions. Today the execution chamber has been restored to its wartime condition: on occasion, victims were hanged eight at a time, and the hanging beam, complete with hooks, still stands. Though decked with wreaths and flowers, the atmosphere in the chamber is chilling, and in a further reminder of Nazi atrocities an urn in the courtyard contains soil from each of the concentration camps.

Westwards from Schloss Charlottenburg is the **Funkturm** (Mon 11am–9pm, Tues–Sun 10am–11pm; €3.50), a skeletal transmission mast built in 1928 and inspired by the Eiffel Tower; to reach it, take U-Bahn #2 to Kaiserdamm, then travel one stop south on bus #204, or catch bus #149 from Bahnhof Zoo. Between 1941 and 1945 it transmitted the world's first regular TV service (one of the lesser-known achievements of Joseph Goebbels), which could only be received in Berlin. Today the Funkturm continues to be used for police and taxi frequencies, while the mast remains popular for the toe-curling views from its 126-metre-high observation platform.

The 1936 Olympics

Hitler used the international attention the **1936 Olympics** attracted to show the "New Order" in Germany in the best possible light. The huge pseudo-Neoclassical Olympic stadium was a deliberate rejection of the modernist architecture then prevalent elsewhere. Anti-Semitic propaganda and posters were suppressed in the city, German half-Jewish athletes were allowed to compete, and when the Olympic flame was relayed from Athens, the newsreels and the world saw the road lined with thousands wearing swastikas and waving Nazi flags. To the outside world, it seemed that the new Germany was rich, content and firmly behind the *Führer*.

Though the Games themselves were stage-managed with considerable brilliance – a fact recorded in Leni Riefenstahl's poetic and frighteningly beautiful film of the events, *Olympia* – not everything went according to official National Socialist doctrine. Black American athletes did supremely well in the games, **Jesse Owens** alone winning four gold medals, disproving the Nazi theory that blacks were "subhuman" and the Aryan race all-powerful. But eventually Germany won the most gold, silver and bronze medals (there's a memorial at the western end of the stadium), and the Games were deemed a great success.

Three stops to the west by U-Bahn #2 is the largest Nazi-era building in the city, the **Olympiastadion**, which was purpose-built for the 1936 Olympic Games (see feature above); it's currently being prepared for the football World Cup in 2006 during which it will host the final (renovation work is set to finish summer 2004). If you cut south and west around the stadium, down the road named after Jesse Owens, and take a right onto Passenheimer Strasse, you reach the bell tower or **Glockenturm** (April–Oct daily 9am–6pm; Nov–March Sat & Sun only 10am–4pm; €2.50). Rebuilt after wartime damage, it's chiefly interesting for the stupendous view it gives, not only over the stadium but also north to the natural amphitheatre that forms the Waldbühne, an open-air concert site, and across the beginnings of the Grunewald to the south. Also easy to spot is the **Teufelsberg** (Devil's Mountain), a massive artificial mound topped with a fairytale castle that used to be a US signals and radar base. It's popular as a place for weekend kite flying, and for skiing and tobogganing in winter.

Spandau

Spandau, situated at the confluence of the Spree and Havel, about 10km northwest of the city centre (take U-Bahn #7 or mainline train), is Berlin's oldest district – it was granted a town charter in 1232, and preserved its municipal independence until 1920. Its name immediately brings to mind the name of its jail's most famous – indeed in later years only – prisoner, **Rudolf Hess**, Hitler's former deputy, who flew to Scotland in 1941 on a bizarre peace mission, and who hanged himself there in 1989.

The jail, 4km away from the centre on Wilhelmstrasse, was demolished to make way for a supermarket for the British armed forces, and the chief reason to come to Spandau is to visit the **Zitadelle** (Tues–Fri 9am–5pm, Sat & Sun 10am–5pm; €2.50; Ⓦwww.zitadelle-spandau.net), a fort established in the twelfth century and greatly strengthened in the second half of the sixteenth-century, when it was equipped with high-walled bastions on the Italian model which were believed to be impregnable. From the round **Juliusturm**, the only surviving part of the original castle, there's a good view over the complex and the surrounding countryside.

Spandau's Altstadt, which occupies a small island at the confluence of the rivers, is centred on the **Nikolaikirche**, a typical example of Gothic brickwork. At the quiet north end of the island is a well-restored medieval street, **Kolk**. Nearby, at Neuendorfer Str. 1, is the **Brauhaus in Spandau**, a nineteenth-century brewery with attached beer garden, restaurant and hotel (see p.756). It's also possible in the summer months to catch **boats** from Spandau to Tegel, Wannsee and elsewhere.

Dahlem

Dahlem, which is served by U-Bahn #1, lies to the southwest of central Berlin in the district of Zehlendorf. It's a neat village-like enclave that feels a world away from the technoflash city centre. Mostly residential, it's home to the Freie Universität (Free University), the better-off bourgeoisie and a large museum complex, the **Staatlichen Museen Dahlem** (Tues–Fri 10am–6pm, Sat & Sun 10am–6pm; €6; Ⓦwww.smb.spk-berlin.de), which has entrances on Arminallee and Lansstrasse.

The largest of the three museums housed here is now known as the **Ethnologisches Museum**. When founded in 1873, it was a pioneering institution for the study of the cultures of non-European peoples, and its early acquisitions, mostly from the German colonies, brought so-called "Primitive" art to the attention of a Western audience, and later had a profound impact on the country's own Expressionist movement. Its **African** section is of special note, including magnificent sculptures from two of the continent's greatest artistic centres, the Nigerian cities of Ife and Benin. The twelfth- to fifteenth-century terracotta heads from the former are the only examples to be seen outside Nigeria; the more widely disseminated tradition of the latter is represented by some wonderfully characterized portrait heads of the fifteenth century, and elaborate plaques from the following two centuries. The **Oceanic** department vividly evokes the island societies of the South Seas in a display of sailing craft, a complete clubhouse building, several totem polls, and an array of masks and cult objects. What the museum itself styles the **North American Indian** department was put back on public view a few years ago after a half-century gap, complete with artefacts looted by the Red Army and only recently returned. Other sections of the museum are devoted to Ancient America, East Asia, South Asia and musical ethnology.

The name of the **Museum für Indische Kunst** is something of a misnomer, as it includes objects from China, Nepal, Tibet, Burma, Thailand, Cambodia, Indonesia and Afghanistan as well as the Indian sub-continent. Particularly outstanding are the **Buddhist cave paintings** from the famous Silk Road; dating from the fifth to the eleventh centuries, they were excavated by German archaeologists in several expeditions just before World War I. The **Museum für Ostasiatische Kunst** concentrates on the art and calligraphy of China and Japan, but here the objects are displayed in rotation, most being too fragile for permanent display.

The Grunewald, Havel and Wannsee

Few people associate Berlin with walks through dense woodland or swimming from crowded beaches, though that's just what the **Grunewald** has to offer. It consists of 32 square kilometres of mixed woodland between the suburbs of Dahlem and Wilmersdorf, and the **Havel lakes** to the west. Seventy percent of the Grunewald was cut down in the postwar years for badly needed fuel, and subsequent replanting has replaced pine and birch with oak and ash.

One possible starting point is the **Jagdschloss Grunewald** (mid-May to mid-Oct daily 10am–5pm, rest of year Sat & Sun guided tours only at 11am, 1pm & 3pm; €2; Ⓦ www.spsg.de), reached by taking S-Bahn #7 to Grunewald and then walking to the southeast through the forest. The royal hunting lodge was built in Renaissance style in the sixteenth century by Caspar Theyss, who was also responsible for the Stadtschloss. Inside are several paintings by Cranach, as well as a fascinating series of portraits commissioned by the House of Orange of the first twelve Roman emperors. Each of these was entrusted to a different artist: for example, Rubens was responsible for *Julius Caesar*, Ter Brugghen for *Claudius*.

Just southeast of the Jagdschloss, the **Brücke-Museum** (Mon & Wed–Sun 11am–5pm; €4; Ⓦ www.bruecke-museum.de) at Bussardsteig 9 houses a collection of works by the Expressionist artistic group known as *Die Brücke* (The Bridge), who worked in Dresden and Berlin from 1905 to 1913. There is a generous representation of each of the five regular members (Kirchner, Heckel, Schmidt-Rottluff, Pechstein and Müller), as well as of Nolde, who was only affiliated for a brief period.

An alternative approach to the Grunewald, and to the start of a strip of beaches, is to take S-Bahn #1 or #7 to Nikolassee, from where it's a ten-minute walk to **Strandbad Wannsee**, a kilometre-long strip of pale sand that's the largest inland beach in Europe, and one which is packed as soon as the sun comes out. From here it's easy to wander into the forests. Travel one station further on the S-Bahn, to Wannsee, and you can catch one of several **ferries**, either across the lake to Kladow on the F#10 (your S-Bahn ticket is valid, otherwise €2), south to Potsdam, or north to Spandau by other seasonal (or private) services.

Another possible destination is the **Pfaueninsel** (Peacock Island; daily: April & Oct 9am–5pm; May–Sept 8am–6pm; Nov–Feb 10am–4pm; ferry €1; Ⓦ www.spsg.de), whose **Schloss** (April–Oct Tues–Sun 10am–5pm; €3) – a folly in the form of a ruined medieval castle – was built for the mistress of King Friedrich Wilhelm II. Inside, almost all the original decoration and furniture still survives; particularly intriguing is the **Tahitikabinett** in the northern tower, which is painted to resemble the interior of a bamboo hut. Equally enjoyable are the **gardens**, which were landscaped by Lenné so as to provide as many surprising vistas as possible. No cars are allowed on the island (nor, incidentally, are dogs, ghetto-blasters or smoking), which has been designated a conservation zone and is home to a flock of peacocks. To get here, take bus #216 or #316 from Wannsee S-Bahn station to Nikolskoe, from where it's a two-minute ferry crossing to the island.

Prenzlauer Berg

The old working-class district of **Prenzlauer Berg** radiates out from the city centre in a network of tenement-lined cobbled streets, and has for all intents and purposes usurped Kreuzberg's role as home of the Berlin *Szene*. In GDR days it was a uniquely vibrant and exciting corner of East Berlin, home to large numbers of artists and young people who chose to live here on the edge of established GDR society (literally as well as figuratively – the western boundary of Prenzlauer Berg was marked by the Berlin Wall). Since 1989 countless bars, restaurants and boutiques have opened, particularly in the streets around Kollwitzplatz, thriving partly because the area's original inhabitants have been joined by an influx of people (often students) drawn from the west. The forces of gentrification are on the move, but the area still preserves a sense of freshness and energy. The quickest way to get there is to take the U-Bahn #2 to either Eberswalder Strasse or Schönhauser Allee. For a more atmospheric approach, take tram #1 from Hackescher Markt, which, going up Prenzlauer Allee, is the most direct route to the Kollwitzplatz area, or trams #13 or #53, which will take you through some of eastern Berlin's lesser known backstreets.

Schönhauser Allee is Prenzlauer Berg's main drag and cuts through Senefelder Platz. A stone's throw from here, at Schönhauser Allee 23–25, is the **Jüdischer Friedhof** (Mon–Thurs 10am–4pm, Fri 10am–1pm), which contains over twenty thousand Jewish graves. In 1943, most of the gravestones were smashed, but today many of the stones have been restored and repositioned, and a memorial stone near the cemetery entrance entreats visitors: "You stand here in silence, but when you turn away do not remain silent." Immediately to the north, on Sredzkistrasse, is the **Schultheiss-Brauerei**, an 1890s brewery built in the pseudo-Byzantine style much favoured by Berlin's architects at that time. Its grounds have been transformed into the **KulturBrauerei**, a cultural centre with an alternative slant.

Beyond the junction of Schönhauser Allee, Danziger Strasse, Kastanienallee and Eberswalder Strasse, **Schönhauser Allee** assumes its true identity as an old-fashioned shopping street with cobbles and narrow shop facades. Just to the southeast of Schönhauser Allee U-Bahn station, at the intersection of Stargarder Strasse and Greifenhagener Strasse, is the **Gethsemenekirche**, which was an important focal point for reformist activities during the summer 1989 exodus from the GDR.

The other eastern districts

Spreading out east from the city centre, **Friedrichshain** is mainly residential in the north, but given over to extensive goods yards and moribund industry around the Ostbahnhof and down towards the River Spree in the south. The district's longest-established attractions are the Stalinist architecture of **Karl-Marx-Allee**, and the **Volkspark Friedrichshain**, resting place of the victims of the 1848 revolution. Since 1989, these have been augmented by the **East Side Gallery**, a surviving stretch of Wall that has been transformed into a unique open-air art gallery. Running along Mühlenstrasse, between the Ostbahnhof and the Oberbaumbrücke in the south of the district, it has been daubed with various political/satirical images, some imaginative, some trite and some impenetrable. Take U-Bahn #1 to Schlesisches Tor and walk across the Oberbaumbrücke for the best approach.

In the neighbouring district of **Lichtenberg** are the former headquarters of the *Stasi*, the huge parasitical ministry that was GDR's all-pervasive secret police. Part of the complex, (Ruschestr. 103, Haus 1), is now designated the **Forschungs- und Gedenkstätte Normannenstrasse** (Normannenstrasse Research and Memorial Centre; Tues–Fri 11am–6pm, Sat & Sun 2–6pm; €3; Ⓦ www.stasimuseum.de). This incorporates the polished stained wood offices of Erich Mielke, the GDR's all-too-real Big Brother, as well as displays of the surveillance apparatus used by the *Stasi* to monitor real or imagined opponents of the regime.

To the south is **Treptow**, whose sole setpiece attraction is the huge and sobering **Sowjetisches Ehrenmal**, Berlin's main Soviet war memorial. Standing in the Treptower Park, a well-known interwar assembly point for revolutionary workers about to embark on demonstrations, it commemorates the Soviet soldiers killed during the Battle of Berlin in April and May 1945, and is the burial place of 5000 of the Soviet Union's estimated 305,000 battle casualties. To get there, take the S-Bahn to Treptower Park: from there it's just a few hundred metres to the memorial's arched entrance on the south side of Puschkinallee. A little way to the south of the entrance is a sculpture of a grieving woman representing the Motherland, to the left of which a broad concourse slopes upwards towards a viewing point flanked by two vast triangles of red granite, fashioned from stone bought from Sweden by the Nazis to furnish Berlin with projected victory monuments. From the viewing point the vista is dominated by a vast symbolic statue, a typically Soviet piece of gigantism fashioned out of marble from Hitler's Chancellery. Over 11m high and set on top of a hill, it shows an idealized Russian soldier clutching a saved child and resting his sword on a shattered swastika. Inside the plinth is a memorial crypt with a mosaic in true Socialist Realism style, showing Soviet citizens honouring the dead. In the long sunken park area which leads up to the statue are the mass graves of the Red Army troops, lined by sculpted frescos of stylized scenes from the Great Patriotic War.

Köpenick is one of eastern Berlin's more pleasant *Bezirke*, located on the banks of the River Spree towards the southeast edge of the city, and easily reached by S-Bahn #3. At the southern end of its Altstadt, a footbridge leads to the Schlossinsel, an island at the confluence of the Spree and the Dahme, on which stands the **Schloss**, which was built in the late seventeenth century for the Great Elector Friedrich Wilhelm. For the past few years the building has been undergoing refurbishment in order that it can once again house part of the **Kunstgewerbemuseum** (Ⓦwww.smb.spk-berlin.de), and is due to reopen some time in 2004. This will display interior decorations from the sixteenth to eighteenth centuries, including the most important surviving furnishing from the Stadtschloss – the Berlin Silver Buffet, which was made by Augsburg silversmiths to designs by Andreas Schlüter.

Eating and drinking

Eating and drinking in Berlin is still pretty good value, though it's best to steer clear of the obvious tourist strips, like Unter den Linden and Kurfürstendamm, where standards tend to be lower and prices higher. The city's cosmopolitan nature means that it has **restaurants** offering a whole gamut of cuisines from around the globe. Indeed, ethnic eateries – many of which serve full meals for under €7.50 – are at least as ubiquitous as traditional German Gaststätten. The cheapest places for a meal are the **Mensas** of the Technische Universität (on Ernst-Reuter-Platz and at Hardenbergstr. 34), but these are officially for student-card holders only. Otherwise, there are **snack bars** – Turkish fast-food stands, Italian pizzerias, or Chinese and Thai takeaways – on just about every street corner.

Nowhere is more than a stone's throw from a **bar** in the western part of the city, ranging from lugubrious beer-swilling holes to slick, upscale hangouts for Berlin's night people. Most stay open later than elsewhere in Germany: it's quite feasible to drink around the clock here, the result of a law that requires bars to close only for an hour a day for cleaning. It's worth bearing in mind that many are excellent (and inexpensive) choices for food, especially breakfast, which may be served till afternoon – or later.

Restaurants

The more established restaurants are in the west, but in the last few years the eastern districts of the city (particularly Mitte and Prenzlauer Berg) have

Berliner Weisse

The city's most distinctive drink is *Berliner Weisse*, a top-fermented, very pale-coloured wheat **beer** with a low alcohol content (usually around 2.5 percent). It has an acidic taste when drunk neat, but it's normally pepped up with a shot of fruity syrup, or *Schuss*, and served in a large bowl-shaped glass as a summer refresher. Ask for it *mit grün* and you get a dash of woodruff, creating a greeny brew with a strong herby taste; *mit rot* is a raspberry-flavoured kiddy drink that works wonders at breakfast time. The city's two large **breweries**, Kindl and Scultheiss, both make *Berliner Weisse*, in addition to their own version of *Pils*. A broader portfolio of beers is available from an ex-GDR brewery, Berliner Bürgerbräu, whose products include a dark *Bock* and an even darker *Schwarzbier*.

experienced a restaurant boom. Generally speaking, these eastern establishments cater to a young crowd and emphasize nouvelle and ethnic menus.

German and Austrian

Austria Bergmannstr. 30, Kreuzberg. Generous portions of excellent Austrian food are served in dark rustic surroundings. Evenings only.

Besenwirtschaft Uhlandstr. 159, Wilmersdorf. This brings a touch of southern Germany to the capital – the food and the wines are from Württemberg, the beers from Bavaria. Evenings only.

Florian Grolmanstr. 52, Charlottenburg. A leading light of the *neue deutsche Küche* movement, this is as much a place to be seen as to eat in. The food, similar to French nouvelle cuisine, is light, flavourful – and expensive. Evenings only.

Gaffel-Haus Taubenstr. 26, Mitte. A successful transplant of a Cologne Brauhaus, serving Rhenish cuisine and *Kölsch* beer.

Gugelhof Knaackstr. 37, Prenzlauer Berg. Serves inventive and beautifully presented German, French and Alsatian food.

Henne Leuschnerdamm 25, Kreuzberg ⓣ0 30/6 14 77 30. Pub-style restaurant with the best chicken in Berlin. The interior here is original – it hasn't been changed, the owners claim, since 1905. Open Tues–Sun from 7pm; reservations essential.

Historische Weinstuben Poststr. 23, Mitte. A reasonable little wine bar-restaurant in the basement of the Knoblauchhaus in the Nikolaiviertel.

Honigmond Borsigstr. 28, Mitte. Understated and tastefully appointed dining rooms serving well prepared fresh cuisine, both traditional and modern.

Jolesch Muskauer Str. 1, Kreuzberg. Noisy, smoky and very popular Austrian restaurant, particularly renowned for its desserts.

Kellerrestaurant im Brecht-Haus Chausseestr. 125, Mitte. Atmospheric restaurant, decorated with Brecht memorabilia, including models of his stage sets, in the basement of the poet's old house. Serves Viennese specialities from recipes supposedly dreamed up by his wife Helene Weigel.

Luise Königin-Luise-Str. 40–42, Zehlendorf. A handy place to repair for a meal when visiting the Dahlem museums, this has a pleasant beer garden and is a big favourite with students from the nearby Freie Universität.

Lutter & Wegner Charlottenstr. 56, Mitte. A Berlin institution that has been in existence for nearly two centuries (the writer E.T.A. Hoffmann was a patron in its early years), this serves top-notch German and Austrian cuisine and has a wine list of around a thousand different vintages.

Meineke X Meinekestr. 10, Charlottenburg. A traditional Berlin restaurant that has hardly changed in decades.

November Husemannstrasse 15, Prenzlauer Berg. Has imaginative daily specials and the best weekend brunch in Prenzlauer Berg.

Offenbach-Stuben Stubbenkammerstr. 8, Prenzlauer Berg ⓣ0 30/4 45 85 02. A near-legend even in GDR days and one of the best places in Prenzlauer Berg, with all kinds of unexpected specialities on the menu. Theatrical decor and intimate seating niches great for late-night conversation. Evenings only; booking essential.

Restauration 1900 Husemannstr. 1, Prenzlauer Berg. A Prenzlauer Berg culinary highlight, serving traditional German dishes that spring a few surprises.

Riehmers Hagelberger Str. 9, Kreuzberg. Husband-and-wife-run restaurant with a comfortable ambience and outstanding food and service. In summer, there's outdoor seating in the historic Riehmer's Hofgarten. Evenings only, except Sun, when it's open for lunch; closed Mon.

Weltrestaurant Markthalle Pücklerstr. 34, Kreuzberg. Spacious restaurant with long communal tables offering German food in hearty portions.
Wirtshaus Schildhorn Str. am Schildhorn 4a, Grunewald. Housed in an attractive old Wirtshaus on the edge of the Havelsee, this is an ideal spot if you've spent the day exploring the forest and lakes. In winter, it's only open Fri evening, Sat & Sun.
Zum Nussbaum Am Nussbaum 3, Mitte. A convincing copy of a destroyed prewar Wirtshaus once patronized by the artists Heinrich Zille and Otto Nagel. It serves typically hearty Berlin fare.
Zur Letzten Instanz Waisenstr. 14–16, Mitte. One of the city's oldest Gaststätten, with a wonderfully evocative interior, complete with tiled oven, and a beer garden. Reasonably priced traditional dishes all have legal-themed names, a reminder of the days when people used to drop in on their way to the nearby courthouse.

Other cuisines

Amberd Uhlandstr. 67, Wilmersdorf. An outstanding Armenian restaurant, specializing in marinated meats grilled on lava stones. Evenings only, closed Mon.
Angkor Wat Paulstr. 22, Tiergarten. Wonderful, subtle Cambodian food that is often surprising and always pleasing. Evenings only.
Aroma Hochkirchstr. 8, Schöneberg ☎0 30/7 82 58 21. Inexpensive, yet well-above-average, Italian restaurant with photo gallery and Italian films on Tues nights. On weekdays, it's open evenings only; bookings advisable after 8pm.
Café do Brasil Mehringdamm 72, Kreuzberg. Inexpensive Brazilian restaurant, which also serves some Mexican dishes. Open daily from 4pm.
Carib Motzstr. 31, Schöneberg. Offers moderately priced Caribbean cuisine and friendly service from the Jamaican owner. Evenings only.
Chez Maurice Botzowstr. 39, Prenzlauer Berg ☎0 30/4 25 05 06. A little out of the way but worth the trip for the totally authentic food and theatrics of the eponymous French chef. Service can be slow; reservations recommended. Closed Sun & Mon lunch.
Chopin Wilhelmplatz 4, Zehlendorf. Located in the old village centre of Wannsee, this serves traditional Silesian cooking, with dishes from both the Polish and German traditions.
Der Ägypter Kantstr. 26, Charlottenburg. This Egyptian restaurant, run in tandem with a jewellery shop, is an adventurous alternative to the safe bets around Savignyplatz. It serves spicy, filling meals, including good vegetarian selections.
Edd's Lutzowstr. 81, Schöneberg. Huge portions of superbly cooked fresh Thai food make this a very popular place. Evenings only, except Sun, when it opens at 2pm; closed Mon.
Good Friends Kantstr. 30, Charlottenburg. A long-established Cantonese restaurant with a strong line in roast duck dishes.
Lusiada Kurfürstendamm 132a, Charlottenburg. Boisterous, moderately priced Portugese place renowned for its fish dishes.
Merhaba Hasenheide 39, Kreuzberg. Highly rated Turkish restaurant that's usually packed with locals. A selection of the starters here can be more interesting than a main course.
Naan Oderberger Str. 49, Prenzlauer Berg. Authentic and inexpensive Indian, a favourite of the local art and student crowd.
Osteria No. 1 Kreuzbergstr. 71, Kreuzberg ☎0 30/7 86 91 62. Classy, inexpensive and therefore highly popular Italian *osteria* run by a collective. Booking essential.
Paris-Moskau Alt-Moabit 141, Tiergarten ☎0 30/3 94 20 81. Gourmet international dishes and fine wines are served in the intimate interior of a late nineteenth-century half-timbered building. Evenings only; reservations advisable.
Pasternak Knaackstr. 24, Prenzlauer Berg. Authentic, intimate Russian restaurant in the thick of the bustling local *Szene*. In winter, it's only open in the evening.
South Africa Kurfürstendamm 72, Charlottenburg. Crocodile, ostrich, antelope and zebra are all on the menu here, and there's a good selection of Cape wines. Open daily from 3pm.
Storch Wartburgstr. 54, Schöneberg. Rustic eatery serving cuisine from the Alsace region in what was once – they claim – a brothel. The excellent, reasonably priced food is served at long communal tables, so don't come for an intimate chat. Evenings only.
Tadschikische Teestube Palais am Festungsgraben 1, Mitte. Housed in an eighteenth-century palace, this is a convincing re-creation of a Tadzhik tea room, where you take off your shoes on entry, then recline or sit on cushions placed around the floor. Speciality teas, plus Russian and Tadzhik meals available. Open Mon–Fri 5pm–midnight, Sat & Sun 3pm–midnight.
Thiossane Hagelberger Str. 46, Kreuzberg. West African restaurant-cum-cultural-centre. The cuisine is predominantly that of Gambia and Senegal, with fish and vegetarian dishes featuring strongly. Evenings only.
Tuk-Tuk Grossgörschenstr. 2, Schöneberg. Amiable Indonesian restaurant. It's advisable to enquire about the heat of your dish before ordering.
Viva Mexico Chausseestr. 36, Mitte. A real rarity this side of the Atlantic – a Mexican restaurant

that is actually run by a Mexican family. The food is very reasonably priced and absolutely authentic; if you take a table at the front you can watch your meal being prepared. On Sun, it's only open in the evening.

Zlata Praha Meinekestr. 4, Charlottenburg. Moderately priced yet high-quality Czech restaurant, with the original *Budweiser Budvar* on tap.

Vegetarian and kosher

Abendmahl Muskauer Str. 9, Kreuzberg. A magnificent restaurant with excellent food (especially the soups – try the *Kürbis* or pumpkin), a busy but congenial atmosphere, and reasonable prices. Evenings only.

Arche Noah Fasanenstr. 79, Charlottenburg. Fine kosher restaurant in the Jüdisches Gemeindehaus.

Hakuin Martin-Luther-Str. 1, Schöneberg. Excellent Japanese vegetarian-macrobiotic place, run by a Buddhist order, featuring tofu and tempura dishes, often complemented by a seaweed salad. Evenings only, except Sun, when it's open for lunch; closed Mon.

Oren Oranienburger Str. 28, Mitte. Next door to the Neue Synagoge, offering light vegetarian (and kosher-esque) dishes in a stylish interior.

Thymian Gneisenaustr. 57, Kreuzberg. Serves an inventive menu of international vegetarian and fish dishes.

Hausbrauereien

Berlin has supplanted Munich from the leading role in the national enthusiasm for new-generation **Hausbrauereien**, where beer is brewed in the bar-cum-restaurant where it is served. In addition to those listed below, one other can be found in the hotels section on p.756.

Alter Fritz Karolinenstr. 12, Reinickendorf. A popular excursion destination in the north of the city, this is set in a huge and leafy beer garden. Its speciality is a malty, copper-coloured beer; it also brews a *Bock* and a *Weizen*.

Brauhaus Alexanderplatz (Marcus-Bräu) Münzstr. 1–3, Mitte. A small place which brews both filtered and unflitered versions of *Pils*, plus a dark beer, *Preussen Dunkel*. Its short but eclectic menu includes both British and American versions of fish and chips, plus standard German fare.

Brauhaus Georgbräu Spreeufer 4, Mitte. This riverside Hausbrauerei in the historic heart of the city makes light and dark beers and its own powerful *Korn*; it also has a menu of hearty old-style Berlin cuisine.

Brauhaus in Rixdorf Glasower Str. 27, Neukölln. Berlin's closest relative to the British village pub, this is crammed full of knick-knacks and beer-related paraphernalia.

Lemke S-Bahn arch 143 by Hackescher Markt, Mitte. Always has three varieties of the house beer on tap: *Export*, *Bock*, and *Festbier*. Serves, incongruously, Japanese as well as German cuisine.

Leopold's Brauhaus Karl-Liebknecht-Str. 13, Mitte. Despite its unpromising location in a modern shopping centre, this makes a good attempt at re-creating the ambience of a Bavarian beer hall. It makes an excellent *Zwickelbier* as well as various season brews, and has a good menu, particularly of poultry dishes.

Lindenbräu Sony Center, Bellevuestr. 3–5, Tiergarten. Housed in one of Berlin's most imposing new buildings, this brews a fine *Hefeweizen* and serves filling Bavarian fare.

Luisenbräu Luisenplatz 1, Charlottenburg. Large, bustling Hausbrauerei directly opposite Schloss Charlottenburg. You can watch the light and dark beers being brewed; they're served in 0.2 litre glasses to ensure maximum freshness. The food is inexpensive, particularly at lunchtime, when there are changing daily specials; live music is performed several evenings per week.

Traditional cafés

Berlin is well endowed with elegant old-world cafés serving delicious *Kaffee und Kuchen* in an unhurried environment.

Café Bilderbuch Akazienstr. 28, Schöneberg. Classy yet cosy Viennese-style Kaffeehaus with delicious spiked coffee drinks. Various kinds of live music (with dancing Thurs 7–8.30pm & Sun 4–7pm) are performed several times a week in the back room.

Café Einstein Kurfürstenstr. 58, Tiergarten. Housed in an old villa with a fine garden, this is as close as you'll get to the ambience of a prewar Berlin Kaffeehaus. International newspapers are available, and breakfast is served 10am–2pm.

There's also a branch at Unter den Linden 42, Mitte.

Café Hardenberg Hardenbergstr. 10, Charlottenburg. Large, old-fashioned café with excellent, cheap food that draws in local students.

Café Möhring Charlottenstr. 55, Mitte. This offers a changing daily selection of two dozen cakes, plus a range of main courses, ice creams and fresh fruit cocktails.

Operncafé Opernpalais, Unter den Linden 5, Mitte. Located in a former royal palace, this café successfully evokes the atmosphere of Imperial Berlin. Coffee and amazing cakes make it a recommended place for a break from sightseeing.

Wintergarten Fasanenstr. 23, Charlottenburg. Occupying a handsome villa in a quiet garden, this is part of the Literaturhaus, an institution devoted to poetry readings and other bookish events. Breakfast is served from 10am.

Bars and café-bars

Berlin's bar and café-bar scene is focused on a number of distinct areas. The **Scheunenviertel** in the north of Mitte and the inner-city district of **Prenzlauer Berg** boast the city's most eclectic possibilities. **Friedrichshain**, a district characterized by working-class neighborhoods and former squats, offers refuge to those disenchanted with increasingly chi-chi Prenzlauer Berg or Mitte. Meanwhile, the institutionalized anarchy of **Kreuzberg** – for so long the area to be after hours – is starting to feel slightly shopworn, though it would be quite easy to spend a few weeks bar-crawling here before you even began to exhaust the possibilities. Adjacent **Schöneberg** tends to be a little smarter and a little more sedate; you'll find a scattering of slick cafés alongside corner Kneipen, but none of the extremities of its neighbour.

Ankerklause Maybachufer 1, Kreuzberg. A sleepy, nautically themed pub overlooking a canal has been transformed into a hip bar playing techno and easy listening. Usually packed by 11pm.

Astro Bar Simon-Dach-Str. 40, Friedrichshain. With its Seventies sci-fi trappings and DJs most nights a week, this is spearheading Friedrichshain's campaign to be the next boho borough.

Aufsturz Oranienburger Str. 67, Mitte. Not as hip as some of the local hangouts but comes into its own on those occasional broiling summer days, thanks to outdoor seating on the shady side of the street. An additional attraction is the extensive range of bottled beers, taking in everything from erstwhile GDR premium beer *Radeberger Pils* to cherry-flavoured Belgian arcana.

Bar am Lützowplatz Lützowplatz 7, Tiergarten. Distinguished in having the longest bar in the city, this also has Berlin's best selection of whiskies (63) and a superb range of moderately priced cocktails.

Bierhimmel Oranienstr. 183, Kreuzberg. Candlelit bar with a cosy 1950s cocktail lounge (open Wed–Sun from 10pm) out back. Great atmosphere, and a second home to many locals.

Billy Wilder's Potsdamer Str. 2, Tiergarten. Situated alongside the Filmmuseum, this extremely trendy, fast-service café-bar has walls lined with photos of Billy Wilder and stills from his films.

Blisse 14 Blissestr. 14, Wilmersdorf. Café-bar designed especially, but not exclusively, for disabled people. A good meeting place.

Café Adler Friedrichstr. 206, Kreuzberg. Small café whose popularity comes from the fact that it is next to the site of the Checkpoint Charlie border crossing. Serves breakfasts and meals.

Café am Neuen See Lichtensteinallee 1, Tiergarten. Upmarket venue in a beautiful lakeside setting in the Tiergarten park. Serves Italian food and has pleasant summer outdoor seating.

Café Anita Wronski Knaackstr. 26–28, Prenzlauer Berg. This smart Wasserturm café-bar is an excellent place to start local wanderings, though it can get very crowded. Good breakfasts 10am–3pm.

Easy Everything Kurfürstendamm 224, Charlottenburg. Internet café with a convenient location. Open daily 6.30am–2am.

E & M Leydicke Mansteinstr. 4, Schöneberg. Claims to be the oldest Kneipe in western Berlin, and has been run by the same family for well over a century. It's best known for its homemade fruit wines.

Filmbühne am Steinplatz Corner of Hardenbergstr. and Steinplatz. One of the least pretentious and most original of Berlin's café-bars, most of it contained within a cleverly designed conservatory. Breakfast is served from 10am.

Golgotha Dudenstr. 48–64, Kreuzberg. Enormous, hugely popular open-air café and summer-only disco, perched near the top of Kreuzberg's hill in the Viktoriapark. Breakfast served 11am–3pm.

Green Door Winterfeldtstr. 50, Schöneberg. Somewhat snooty cocktail bar, attracting a well-dressed crowd of young professionals and party goers. Once you're past the pretension, though, the place can be fun, and they mix an awfully good cocktail.

Kumpelnest 3000 Lützowstr. 23, Tiergarten. Carpeted walls and a mock-Baroque effect attract a rough-and-ready crew of thirtysomethings to this erstwhile brothel. Gets going around 2am. Fine fun, and the best place in the area. Normally standing room only.

Mister Hu Goltzstr. 39, Schöneberg. Cool blue cocktail bar with a great offering of drinks and some of the city's best bartenders.

Mutter Hohenstaufenstr. 4, Schöneberg. Large café and bar with indirect lighting and loud music. Quite popular and usually crowded. Sushi available.

Obst und Gemüse Oranienburger Str. 48, Mitte. Always crowded, always chaotic, in many ways this is the quintessential Scheunenviertel bar, although it is past its hipness zenith. You can wait a while to get served but, as the place attracts a lot of tourists, at least you'll be waiting in company.

Pinguin Club Wartburgstr. 54, Schöneberg. Tiny and cheerful bar with 1950s and 1960s America supplying its theme and background music.

Prater Kastanienallee 7–9, Prenzlauer Berg. A traditional beer garden, built in the nineteenth century and renovated a few years ago. In summer you can swig beer, feast on *Bratwurst*, *Eisbein* or other native food, and listen to German rock from the 1970s. A true Berlin experience.

Reingold Novalisstr. 11, Mitte. Sophisticated Art Deco cocktail lounge with a clientele in its twenties and thirties.

Schwarzes Café Kantstr. 148, Charlottenburg. The best young, chic hangout on the street, with a relaxed atmosphere, good music and food (including all-day breakfast). Dated perhaps, but still a classic. Open round the clock, except Tues, when it's open 8am–8pm.

Strandbad Mitte Kleine Hamburger Str. 16, Mitte. At the end of a small street off the beaten tourist track, this inviting café and bar makes a good retreat when it all becomes too much. Excellent breakfasts served 9am–4pm.

Supamolly Jessnerstr. 41, Friedrichshain. A holdover from Friedrichshain's turbulent squatter days shortly after the fall of the Wall, this cheap bar is still popular with the alternative set.

Gay Berlin

With the notable exception of the Nazi years, Berlin has a long record of tolerating an open and energetic gay scene. As far back as the 1920s, Christopher Isherwood and W.H. Auden were drawn to the city, where, in sharp contrast to the oppressiveness of London, there was a gay community that did not live in fear of harassment and legal persecution.

The most concentrated area of gay **men's bars** is to be found in precisely the area they lived, around Wittenbergplatz and Nollendorfplatz in the district of Schöneberg. *Tom's Bar*, Motzstr. 19, a dark and sweaty cruising bar with a large back room is the most popular gay hangout in the area – possibly in the whole of Berlin. Further south in the same district is *Anderes Ufer*, Hauptstr. 157, which opened at the tail end of the gay movement heyday in the late 1970s and is still going strong, featuring regular art and photography exhibitions. It attracts a mixed gay and lesbian crowd, as does *Roses*, Oranienstr. 187, Kreuzberg. The best-known gay place in the east is *Schoppenstube*, Schönhauser Allee 44, Prenzlauer Berg; this has a pleasant wine bar upstairs, and a steamy cruisers' haven downstairs. In Friedrichshain, *Die Busche*, Mühlenstr. 11–12, is a club which has survived from the East Berlin gay scene. For more extensive listings, pick up a free copy of either *Siegessäule* or *Serjei*, available from most bars.

Many of Berlin's **women-only bars** have a strong lesbian following, though straight women are welcome everywhere. In Schöneberg, *Begine*, Potsdamer Str. 139, is a stylishly decorated bar-bistro and gallery, which serves inexpensive food and hosts films, readings and concerts. *Café Seidenfaden* at Dircksenstr. 47 in Mitte is an alcohol-free café, open only until 9pm, while *Offenbar*, Schreinerstr. 5, is a lesbian hangout in Friedrichshain.

webfreetv.com Potsdamer Str. 2, Tiergarten. Internet café on the street front of the Sony Center. Open Mon–Fri 10am–7pm, Sat & Sun 11am–7pm.

Wirtshaus Wuppke Schlüterstr. 21, Charlottenburg. Old-fashioned Kneipe without the sleaze.

Würgeengel Dresdener Str. 122, Kreuzberg. Named after the Buñuel film *El angel exterminator* and next to the Babylon movie theater, this is a popular hangout for cineastes.

Zillemarkt Bleibtreustr. 48a, Charlottenburg. Wonderful if shabby bar that attempts a *fin-de-siècle* feel. Unpretentious and fun, and a good place to start Savignyplatz explorations – it's by the S-Bahn station. Breakfast 10am–4pm.

Zur Weissen Maus Ludwigkirchplatz 12, Charlottenburg. Chic 1920s-style bar with reproductions of Otto Dix and Max Beckmann reflected in the mass of mirrors. Popular with older artists and has good, if expensive, cocktails. Opens around 10pm.

Music, nightlife and entertainment

Berlin has long had a reputation for being a global leader in the performing arts – and for having some of the best (and steamiest) nightlife on the planet. It still maintains a dominant position in the field of **classical music**, thanks to its peerless orchestra, the Berliner Philharmoniker. However, vanishing subsidies have cast a shadow over the other **orchestras**, **opera houses** and **theatres** in the city, which, as a legacy of the decades of division, currently has a surplus of instutitions. Some rationalization is inevitable in the coming years, though it's likely that all the big names will survive. If the tradition in cabaret and variety is not what it once was, it is firmly at the forefront of the German **club** scene, largely through the impact of the many manic dance places set up in abandoned buildings on or around the former no-go area of the East-West border strip. There's also a wide range of more traditional clubs, ranging from slick hangouts for the trendy to raucous punk dives.

To find out exactly **what's on**, look in the local listings magazines (see p.754) or on the innumerable flyposters about town. Advance bookings for most events can be made at **ticket offices** such as Hekticket (Ⓦwww.hekticket.de), which has branches at Hardenbergstr. 29d, Charlottenburg (Ⓣ0 30/2 30 99 30) and Karl-Liebknecht-Str. 12, Mitte (Ⓣ0 30/24 31 24 31), but note that they charge a hefty commission.

Clubs

Berlin's clubs are smaller, cheaper and less exclusive than their counterparts in London or New York – and fewer in number. You don't need much nous to work out that the places along the Ku'damm are tourist rip-offs: the real all-night sweats take place in the newer **dance-music clubs** that have opened up, mainly in the former East Berlin, where glitz is out and raving is in. Don't bother turning up until midnight at the earliest, since few places get going much before then. Admission is often free – when you do pay, it shouldn't be much more than €8. Some of the ravey places have strict door policies, but if you look the part you'll probably get in.

Casino Mühlenstr. 26–30, Friedrichshain Ⓣ0 30/29 00 97 99, Ⓦwww.casino-bln.com. Techno club which sometimes plays other music styles, including rock.

Knaack-Klub Greifswalder Str. 224, Prenzlauer Berg Ⓣ0 30/44 27 60, Ⓦwww.knack-berlin.de. Rock (David Byrne to Nirvana) in the cellar and dance on the first floor of a big old club building in a Prenzlauer Berg courtyard, drawing a young, mainly east Berlin crowd.

Kurvenstar Kleine Präsidentenstr. 3, Mitte Ⓣ0 30/24 72 31 15, Ⓦwww.kurvenstar.de. Beautifully decorated retro Seventies club with a front bar and dancefloor at the back. Caters now to a young, not very gregarious hip hop crowd on Wed and Sat, although other nights feature drum 'n' bass or triphop.

Soda Knaackstr. 97, Prenzlauer Berg. Eclectic club-cum-literary salon-cum-restaurant in the Kulturbrauerei complex. On Fri, there's a GDR rock disco in the neighbouring *Alte Kantine*.

WMF Karl-Marx-Allee 34, Friedrichshain Ⓣ0 30/2 88 78 89 10, Ⓦwww.wmfclub.de. Legendary post-Wall club now at its sixth location, still worth checking out if you're into any flavour of house.

Live music

You should book well in advance for major **rock and pop** gigs at the larger venues – though invariably you can't buy tickets from the venues themselves, but need to go to a ticket office. Berlin also offers a good range of live **jazz** venues, and is an important centre of the burgeoning **world music** movement. It's worth remembering that, in addition to the places listed below, many bars and cafés put on live music.

Rock and pop

Columbiahalle Columbiadamm 13–21, Tempelhof Ⓣ0 30/6 98 09 80, Ⓦwww.columbiahalle.de. Located right across the street from the Tempelhof airport, this hosts crowd-pleasing international acts.

Eierschale Zenner Alt-Treptow 14–17, Treptow Ⓣ0 30/5 33 73 70. A large and popular beer garden by the shore of the River Spree, playing 1950s and 1960s rock and roll and other summery music.

Tacheles Oranienburger Str. 53–56, Mitte Ⓣ0 30/2 81 61 19, Ⓦwww.tacheles.de. The performers are likely to be pretty eclectic, ranging from guitar bands to industrial noise merchants. Concerts start at around 10pm.

Tempodrom Möckernstr. 10, Kreuzberg Ⓣ0 30/69 53 38 85, Ⓦwww.tempodrom-berlin.de. Tent venue hosting mid-level rock and world music acts.

Tränenpalast Reichstagsufer 17, Mitte Ⓣ0 30/2 38 62 11, Ⓦwww.traenenpalast.de. A former waiting room at the border between east and west is now a medium-sized hall featuring rock, soul and jazz.

Waldbühne Glockenturmstrasse, Charlottenburg Ⓣ0 30/3 04 06 76. Open-air spot in a natural amphitheatre near the Olympiastadion that features movies, bands, classical concerts, and other entertainments. Great fun on summer evenings, but arrive early as it often gets crowded.

Jazz and world music

b-flat Rosenthaler Str. 13, Mitte Ⓣ0 30/2 80 63 49, Ⓦwww.b-flat-berlin.de. Small jazz club with live groups on weekends and a serious audience – don't talk during sets. Open from 10pm.

Flöz Nassauische Str. 37, Wilmersdorf Ⓣ0 30/8 61 10 00. Basement club that's the meeting point for Berlin's jazz musicians and a testing ground for the city's new bands. Also offers occasional salsa and cabaret.

Haus der Kulturen der Welt John-Foster-Dulles-Allee 10, Tiergarten Ⓣ0 30/39 78 71 75, Ⓦwww.hkw.de. The city's number one venue for world music.

Pfefferberg Schönhauser Allee 176, Prenzlauer Berg Ⓣ0 30/44 38 31 10. A converted East Berlin industrial space offering world-music-themed concerts and club nights.

Podewil Klosterstr. 68–70, Mitte Ⓣ0 30/24 74 97 77, Ⓦwww.podewil.de. Avant garde jazz, world music and occasional classical concerts. Less lively than some other venues but dedicated to the music.

Quasimodo Kantstr. 12a, Charlottenburg Ⓣ0 30/3 12 80 86, Ⓦwww.quasimodo.de. Berlin's best jazz spot, with nightly programmes starting at 10pm. A high-quality mix of international (usually American) stars and up-and-coming names. Small, with a good atmosphere. Often free on weekdays.

Classical music

For centuries, Berlin's standing in the musical world lagged well behind that of other major German cities such as Leipzig, Dresden, Munich and Hamburg. That situation began to change with the foundation in 1882 of the Berliner Philharmonisches Orchester or **Berliner Philharmoniker** (Berlin Philharmonic Orchestra; Ⓦwww.berliner-philharmoniker.de), which established a position of global pre-eminence in the field of large-scale orchestral music under its principal conductor Hans von Bülow and his successors Arthur Nikitsch, Wilhelm Fürtwängler, Herbert von Karajan, Claudio Abbado and the current incumbent, Englishman Sir Simon Rattle. Of the other full-sized symphony orchestras based in the city, the oldest is the **Rundfunk-Sinfonieorchester Berlin** (Ⓦwww.rso-berlin.com), which is currently directed by Marek Janowski; being attached to the local radio station, it tends to have a more adventurous repertoire than its rivals. The **Deutsches Sinfonie Orchester** (Ⓦwww.dso-berlin.de) built up a formidable reputation under the Russian-born pianist-conductor Vladimir Ashkenazy, who has been succeeded by the American Kent Nagano. East Berlin's old orchestra, the **Berliner Sinfonie-Orchester** (Ⓦwww.berlinersinfonieorchester.de) has survived the traumas of unification and now has as its principal conductor the Israeli Eliahu Inbal. The city also has numerous smaller orchestras, usually specializing in music of a particular period: they include the Akademie für Alte Musik Berlin (Ⓦwww.akamus.de), the Berliner Bach-Akademie (Ⓦwww.berlinerbachakademie.de), the Kammerorchester Berlin (Ⓦwww.koberlin.de) and the Neues Berliner Kammerorchester (Ⓦwww.nbko.de).

As a legacy of the decades of division, Berlin still operates three **opera houses**, which is probably one more than it needs. Although none has yet come close to demise, the first steps towards rationalization have been taken with the merger of the ballet companies formerly attached to each house into one ensemble, **Berliner Ballett**. The city is home to several highly distinguished **choirs**, two of the finest being those attached to the Protestant and Catholic cathedrals, the Dom and St-Hedwigs-Kathedrale, where their liturgical contributions are supplemented by regular concerts.

In addition to the main venues listed below, concerts and recitals are regularly held in the city's churches and other historic buildings, while the Musikinstrumenten-Museum (see p.779) hosts a weekly series at 11am on Sundays.

Venues

Deutsche Oper Berlin Bismarckstr. 35, Charlottenburg Ⓣ0 30/3 43 84 01, Ⓦwww.deutscheoperberlin.de. This is a modern building, which was built to give West Berlin the opera house it would otherwise have lacked, and has an established tradition of attracting star international singers and conductors, with Christian Thielemann the current musical director.

Komische Oper Behrenstr. 55-57, Mitte; box office at Unter den Linden 41, Mitte Ⓣ0 30/47 99 74 00, Ⓦwww.komische-oper-berlin.de. In contrast to its two rivals, this is a repertory company which eschews expensive jet-set soloists; tickets therefore cost around half the price. The Viennese-style neo-Baroque interior stages a wider range of operas than its name would suggest, being suitable for all but the grandest examples of the genre.

Konzerthaus Berlin (Schauspielhaus) Gendarmenmarkt, Mitte Ⓣ0 30/2 03 09 21 01, Ⓦwww.konzerthaus.de. Although the acoustics of the Grosser Saal – which hosts regular concerts by the Berliner Sinfonie-Orchester, among others – are not absolutely ideal, the architectural splendour of the converted playhouse by Schinkel more than makes amends. On the top floor of the southern wing is the delectable little Kammermusiksaal, Schinkel's original concert hall, which is used for vocal, instrumental and chamber recitals.

Philharmonie Matthäikirchstr. 1, Tiergarten Ⓣ0 30/25 48 89 99, Ⓦww.berliner-philharmoniker.de. The custom-built home of the Berliner Philharmoniker was specially designed to give the best possible acoustic effects. Tickets for the orchestra's concerts are not as hard to come by as is often supposed, as the same programme is often performed on three consecutive evenings. Concerts by visiting orchestras take place frequently, while the adjoining Kammermusiksaal, a versatile venue in the round, is used by soloists and smaller groups, including contemporary music specialists.

Staatsoper Unter den Linden 5–7, Mitte Ⓣ0 30/20 35 45 55, Ⓦww.staatsoper-berlin.de. This is undoubtedly one of the most beautiful opera houses in the world. It has a distinguished performing tradition: among the predecessors of the present musical director, the Israeli pianist-conductor Daniel Barenboim, were the composers Giacomo Meyerbeer and Richard Strauss. Be warned, however, that the cheapest seats in the main auditorium have only a partial view of the stage. Chamber operas, predominantly of the Baroque era, and concerts by the house orchestra, the Staatskapelle Berlin, usually take place in the Apollo-Saal.

Theatre

Although their standing within Germany remains high, Berlin's **theatres** face a tough task living up to the heady golden eras of the not so distant past: throughout the first three decades of the twentieth century, the city's theatrical life enjoyed an unparalleled international reputation under the inspired tutelage of Max Reinhardt, while in the immediate aftermath of World War II the celebrity status of Bertolt Brecht ensured that theatre played a prominent role in the cultural life of the GDR capital. Sadly, Berlin's legendary **cabaret scene** is now little more than a memory, but some establishments gamely strive to keep alive the tradition of political satire, while in recent years old-style variety shows have made something of a comeback in the city (as elsewhere in Germany).

Venues

Berliner Ensemble Bertolt-Brecht-Platz 1, Mitte ⓣ0 30/28 40 81 55, ⓦwww.berliner-ensemble.de. Now privatized, Brecht's old theatre (like the man himself) polarizes opinion, with many now regarding it as a cultural dinosaur. Brecht still forms the staple fare here, though the productions are a little livelier and less reverential than in GDR days.

Deutsches Theater Schumannnstr. 13a, Mitte ⓣ0 30/28 44 12 21, ⓦwww.deutschestheater.de. Good, solid productions taking in everything from Schiller to Mamet make this one of Berlin's best dramatic stages.

Freunde der Italienischen Oper Fidicinstr. 40, Kreuzberg ⓣ0 30/6 91 12 11, ⓦwww.freunde-der-italienischen-oper.de. Tiny courtyard theatre specializing in fringe productions performed in English.

Friedrichstadtpalast Friedrichstr. 107, Mitte ⓣ0 30/23 26 23 26, ⓦwww.friedrichstadtpalast.de. Big flashy variety theatre with leggy chorus girls, but the real stuff is to be found in their small café-theatre.

Schaubühne am Lehniner Platz Kurfürstendamm 153, Wilmersdorf ⓣ0 30/89 00 23, ⓦww.schaubuehne.de. Erich Mendelsohn's Expressionist-style cinema of the 1920s was converted into a state-of-the-art theatre half-a-century later for Peter Stein's brilliant theatrical troupe. The current directorship stages a mixed programme of classics, experimental pieces and modern dance.

Stella Musical Theater Marlene-Dietrich-Platz 1, Tiergarten ⓣ0 18 05/44 44. New venue for blockbuster musicals.

Theater des Westens Kantstr. 12, Charlottenburg ⓣ0 18 05/44 44, ⓦwww.theater-des-westens.de. Housed in a beautiful *fin-de-siècle* building, this features classic musicals, operettas, and the odd Broadway-type show.

Wintergarten Variete Potsdamer Str. 96, Tiergarten ⓣ0 30/23 08 82 30, ⓦwww.wintergarten-variete.de. A glitzy attempt to re-create the Berlin of the 1920s, with acts from all over the world – cabaret, musicians, dance, mime, etc.

Zaubertheater Igor Jedlin Roscherstr. 7, Charlottenburg ⓣ0 30/3 23 37 77, ⓦwww.zaubertheater.de. Jedlin's long-established one-man magic shows usually take place Thurs–Sun at 3.30pm for children, Thurs–Sat at 8pm for adults.

Listings

Bike rental Fahrradstation, with branches at Bahnhof Friedrichstrasse neighbourhood ⓣ0 30/20 45 45 00; Bergmannstr 9, Kreuzberg ⓣ0 30/2 15 15 66; and Auguststr 29a, Mitte ⓣ0 30/28 59 56 61. Prices start at €10 per day.

Bookstores The best selections of English-language paperbacks and books on the city can be found at the British Book Shop, Mauerstr. 83–84, Mitte, and Kiepert, Hardenbergstr. 4–5, Charlottenburg.
Cultural Centre British Council, Hackescher Markt 1, Mitte ⓣ30 30/3 11 09 90; ⓦwww.britcoun.de.
Dentist ⓣ0 30/89 00 43 33.
Disabled travel Movado, Langhansstr. 64, Weissensee ⓣ0 30/4 71 51 45, ⓦwww.movado.de, has a great wealth of information on hotels and restaurants that are wheelchair accessible, city tours for disabled travellers and transportation services.
Doctor ⓣ0 30/31 00 31.
Embassies Australia, Wallstr. 76, Mitte ⓣ0 30/8 80 08 80, ⓦwww.australian-embassy.de; Britain, Wilhelmstr. 70/71, Mitte ⓣ0 30/20 45 70, ⓦwww.britischebotschaft.de; Canada, Friedrichstr. 95, Mitte ⓣ0 30/20 31 20, ⓦwww.kanada.de; Ireland, Friedrichstr. 200, Mitte ⓣ0 30/22 07 20, ⓦwww.botschaft-irland.de; New Zealand, Friedrichstr. 60, Mitte ⓣ0 30/20 62 10, ⓦwww.nzembassy.com; US, Neustadtische Kirchstr. 4–5, Mitte ⓣ0 30/8 30 50, visa section, Clayallee 170, Zehlendorf ⓣ0 30/8 32 92 33, ⓦwww.usembassy.de.
Festivals Big annual events include the third largest film festival in the world, the Internationales Filmfestspiele (ⓦwww.berlinale.de) in February; and the Love Parade (ⓦwww.loveparade.de), a big techno and party event in early July.
Pharmacies Apotheke im Bahnhof Zoo ⓣ0 30/31 50 33 61 (Mon–Fri 7.30am–8pm, Sat 8.30am–4pm). When it's closed, check the list on the door of this, or any other *Apotheke*, for the nearest place open.
Post office Bahnhof Friedrichstrasse, Mitte (Mon–Fri 6am–10pm); Joachimstaler Str. 7, Charlottenburg (Mon–Sat 8am–midnight, Sun 10am–midnight).
Sports The Olympiastadion, Olympischer Platz 3, Charlottenburg ⓣ 30 06 34 30, is the main venue for spectator sports, including the home matches of the city's only top-flight football team, Hertha Berlin.
Taxis Ranks are found outside KaDeWe; on Savignyplatz; by Bahnhof Zoo; at the northern entrance to Bahnhof Friedrichstrasse station; the entrance to Alexanderplatz S-Bahn station; and in front of the nearby *Park Inn Hotel*. To book, call ⓣ 0 30/21 01 01 or 0 30/26 10 26.

Brandenburg

Brandenburg is geographically the largest of Germany's five new Länder, though it has a very low population density, largely because it is now shorn of Berlin, its epicentre and traditional capital. Its landscape consists in the main of undulating farmland and sandy forests which are unexceptional but by no means unattractive. In lieu of Berlin, the old royal residence of **Potsdam** on its outskirts has taken over as Land capital, and its outstanding group of Baroque palaces is the province's prime draw. West of here lies the long-overshadowed city of **Brandenburg an der Havel** which, despite the ravages of war and pollution, preserves an important medieval heritage. The only other major towns, **Frankfurt an der Oder** and **Cottbus**, are similarly scarred, though the latter has the good fortune to lie close to the province's one area of outstanding natural beauty, the water-strewn **Spreewald**, which is still inhabited by the Sorbs, Germany's only indigenous Slav minority. To the north of Berlin, within easy reach of the capital by day trips, are **Oranienburg**, where one of the most notorious of the concentration camps on German soil is to be found, and the wooded lakeland known as the **Schorfheide**.

Potsdam

"The first fine day should be devoted to Potsdam, without which a complete impression of Berlin can scarcely be obtained," intoned the prewar *Baedeker*, a nod to the fact that **POTSDAM**, although not officially part of Berlin, was the natural completion of the Hohenzollern capital, forming an almost seamless extension of its western suburbs. Although founded as far back as 993, Potsdam was of little significance until 1660, when Friedrich Wilhelm, the Great Elector, decided to built a new residence there. His successors – most notably Frederick the Great, who made it the main seat of his court – oversaw a stunning triumph of man over nature, whereby the swampy marshland of the Havel and its lakes was gradually transformed into the proudest adornment of the Prussian kingdom, a glorious planned townscape replete with palaces, parks and gardens. It was precisely because Potsdam was such a national showpiece that the "Big Three" of the United States, the United Kingdom and the Soviet Union held their victorious conference there after World War II, showing the Germans in the most unambiguous way possible that they had been totally and utterly defeated, thus eliminating any possibility of a repetition of the "stab in the back" legend which had quickly gained currency after World War I.

Potsdam's **Altstadt** – notwithstanding grievous losses in the war and the hamfisted attempt by the GDR regime to give parts of it a "socialist" makeover – is a fine example of a Baroque and Neoclassical town, even if it is overshadowed by the nearby parks. Of these, the wondrous **Park Sanssouci** is rightly the most famous and visited, but there are two other splendid areas of landscaped greenery in the **Neuer Garten** and **Park Babelsberg**. Nor is Potsdam resting on its laurels with regard to its distinctive heritage. The bi-annual national garden show, the **Bundesgartenschau** (held here in 2001) has bequeathed a legacy of new gardens, squares and promenades to the city, while the **Filmpark Babelsberg** presents the city's cinematic past within a modern theme park.

Arrival, information and accommodation

Potsdam's **Hauptbahnhof**, just a short walk across Lange Brücke from the town centre, is linked to Berlin's Bahnhof Zoo and Bahnhof Friedrichstrasse by S-Bahn #7 and mainline trains. Alternatively, bus #116 from S-Bahnhof Wannsee will deposit you on the Potsdam side of the Glienicker Brücke, from where tram #93 runs to the central Platz der Einheit. **Cruises** on the Havel and its lakes are run by Weisse Flotte (Ⓣ03 31/2 75 92 10, Ⓦwww.schiffahrt-in-potsdam.de), departing from Lange Brücke. The standard three-hour round trip costs €10.

Just south of Platz der Einheit, at Friedrich-Ebert-Str. 5, is the **tourist office** (April–Oct Mon–Fri 9am–8pm, Sat 9am–6pm, Sun 9am–4pm; Nov–March Mon–Fri 10am–6pm, Sat 10am–4pm, Sun 10am–2pm; Ⓣ03 31/27 55 80, Ⓦwww.potsdamtourismus.de). Another useful source of information is the visitor centre of the **Stiftung Preussische Schlösser und Gärten Berlin-Brandenburg**, at the northern edge of Park Sanssouci at An der Historischen Mühle (daily: April–Oct 8.30am–5pm; Nov–March 9am–4pm; Ⓣ03 31/9 69 42 02, Ⓦwww.spsg.de). A day's **admission ticket** for all the monuments other than Schloss Sanssouci costs €12 for individuals; the equivalent version for families is valid for a month and costs €20. The premium version of these tickets, which includes Schloss Sanssouci, costs €15 for individuals and can be used on two

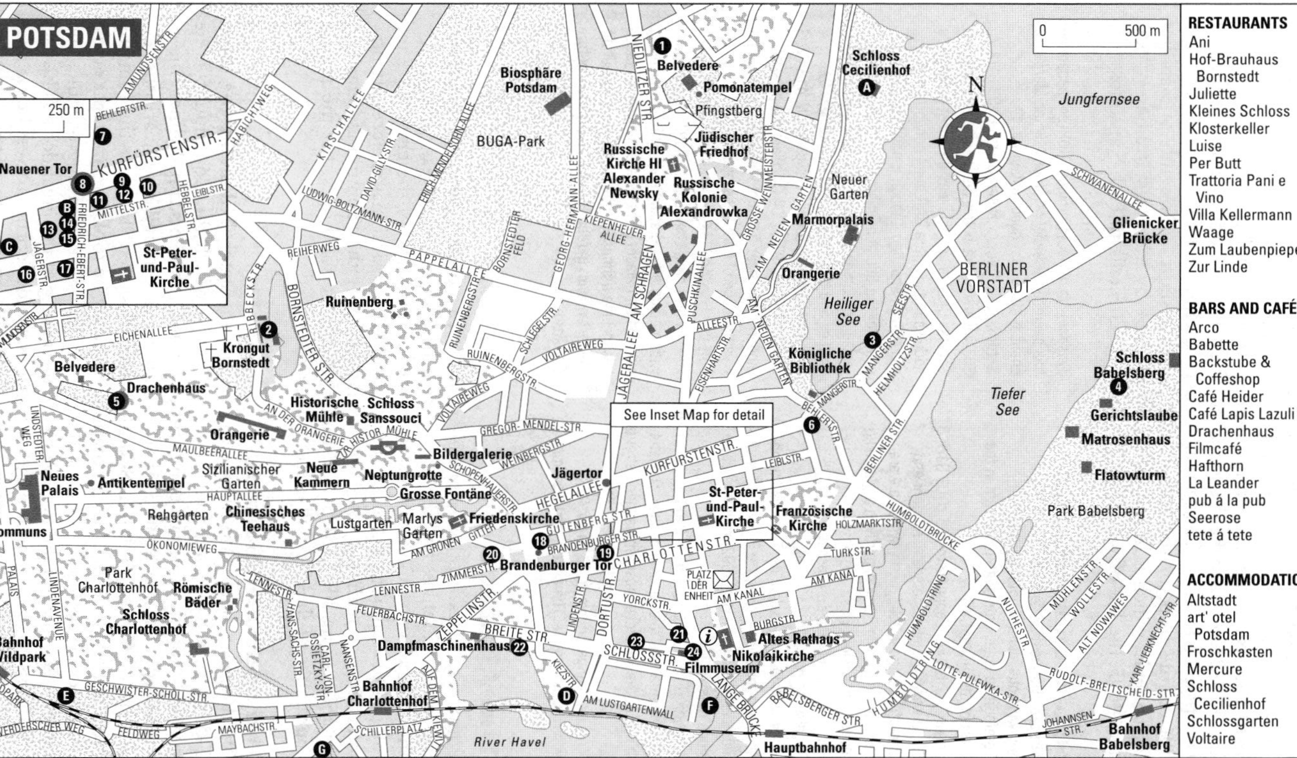
POTSDAM
0 500 m
0 250 m
RESTAURANTS
Ani 6
Hof-Brauhaus Bornstedt 2
Juliette 13
Kleines Schloss 4
Klosterkeller 17
Luise 20
Per Butt 16
Trattoria Pani e Vino 7
Villa Kellermann 3
Waage 21
Zum Laubenpieper 1
Zur Linde 19
BARS AND CAFÉS
Arco 8
Babette 18
Backstube & Coffeshop 15
Café Heider 11
Café Lapis Lazuli 10
Drachenhaus 5
Filmcafé 24
Hafthorn 14
La Leander 9
pub á la pub 23
Seerose 22
tete á tete 12
ACCOMMODATION
Altstadt C
art' otel Potsdam G
Froschkasten D
Mercure F
Schloss Cecilienhof A
Schlossgarten E
Voltaire B
See Inset Map for detail
Nauener Tor
St-Peter-und-Paul-Kirche
Belvedere
Pomonatempel
Pfingstberg
Jüdischer Friedhof
Russische Kirche Hl Alexander Newsky
Russische Kolonie Alexandrowka
Biosphäre Potsdam
BUGA-Park
Schloss Cecilienhof
Neuer Garten
Marmorpalais
Orangerie
Heiliger See
Königliche Bibliothek
Jungfernsee
Glienicker Brücke
BERLINER VORSTADT
Tiefer See
Schloss Babelsberg
Gerichtslaube
Matrosenhaus
Flatowturm
Park Babelsberg
Krongut Bornstedt
Ruinenberg
Drachenhaus
Historische Mühle
Schloss Sanssouci
Orangerie
Bildergalerie
Neue Kammern
Neptungrotte
Grosse Fontäne
Jägertor
Sizilianischer Garten
Neues Palais
Antikentempel
Communs
Rehgarten
Chinesisches Teehaus
Lustgarten
Marlys Garten
Friedenskirche
Französische Kirche
Brandenburger Tor
Park Charlottenhof
Römische Bäder
Schloss Charlottenhof
Bahnhof Wildpark
Dampfmaschinenhaus
Bahnhof Charlottenhof
Altes Rathaus
Nikolaikirche
Filmmuseum
Hauptbahnhof
Bahnhof Babelsberg
River Havel
Telegrafenberg & Einsteinturm

consecutive days; the family version, again valid for a month, is €25.50. All tickets are available from either the tourist office or from participating monuments.

Private rooms (❷–❹) can be booked via the tourist office. A new official **youth hostel** is due to open in summer 2004 at Schulstr. 9 (ⓣ03 31/2 64 95 20; €19/21.70) in Babelsberg, not far from the S-Bahn station. The nearest **campsite**, *Sanssouci-Gaisberg*, is at An der Pirschheide 1 (ⓣ & ⓕ0 33 27/5 56 80) on the bank of the Templiner See; it's a short walk south of Bahnhof Pirschheide, which is linked to the town centre by tram #94 and buses #631 and #695, the last of which goes via the Maulbeeralle in Park Sanssouci.

Hotels and pensions

Altstadt Dortusstr. 8 ⓣ03 31/28 49 90, ⓦwww.hotel.altstadt-hotel-potsdam.de. Comfortable small hotel with restaurant in the heart of the Altstadt. ❺

art'otel potsdam Zeppelinstr. 136 ⓣ03 31/9 81 50, ⓦwww.artotel.de/potsdam. A bright and colourful designer hotel, partly within a warehouse building by Ludwig Persius, partly in a gleaming modern extension. ❼

Filmhotel Lili Marleen Grossbeerenstr. 75, Babelsberg ⓣ03 31/74 32 00, ⓦwww.filmhotel.potsdam.de. This is a theme hotel and restaurant, aimed at cinema fans visiting the nearby Filmpark. Bus #692 from the centre stops outside. ❺

Froschkasten Kiezstr. 3-4 ⓣ & ⓕ03 31/29 13 15. Pension attached to a recommendable Gaststätte in one of the Altstadt's most atmospheric streets. ❺

Mercure Lange Brücke ⓣ03 31/27 22, ⓦwww.mercure.de. The once notorious *Stadt Potsdam*, an all-too-prominent GDR-era behemoth, has been successfully revamped by the Mercure chain. It also has a good restaurant. ❻

Schloss Cecilienhof Neuer Garten ⓣ03 31/3 70 50, ⓦwww.relaxa-hotels.de. Housed in a wing of Schloss Cecilienhof, this was the most prestigious address of the entire GDR hotel network, and is still of high standing, though it now has several rivals for the title of best hotel in Potsdam. Its restaurant serves both hearty Brandenburg specialities and high-quality lighter fare. ❽–❾

Schlossgarten Geschwister-Scholl-Str. 41a ⓣ03 31/97 17 00, ⓕ97 17 04 04. Plain but pleasant modern hotel near Bahnhof Wildpark, at the south-western edge of Park Sanssouci. ❻

Voltaire Friedrich-Ebert-Str. 88 ⓣ03 31/2 31 70, ⓦwww.nh-hotels.com. Luxury hotel, decked out with modern artworks, in Palais Brühl, a splendid old Altstadt palace, and a new extension. Its facilities include a fitness centre, a gourmet restaurant, *Hofgarten*, with garden terrace, and a lively pub, *Bar Karree*. ❽–❾

The Altstadt

Potsdam's **Altstadt** is unfortunately shorn of two of its most important buildings, the Stadtschloss and the Garnisonkirche, which were damaged in the war and erased by the Communists as unwanted reminders of the city's royal and militaristic traditions. Baroque, Rococo and Neoclassical masterpieces are now intermingled with ugly high-rise buildings from the Communist era. This situation seems likely to persist, though there are still hopes that the prewar appearance of the city will eventually be re-created.

The southern Altstadt

On the main square, Am Alten Markt, stands the stately **Nikolaikirche** (Mon 2–5pm, Tues–Sat 10am–5pm, Sun noon–5pm), which the Communists were unable to displace from its dominant position on the Potsdam skyline. One of the indisputably great churches of the nineteenth century, it is the aritistic testimony of **Karl Friedrich Schinkel**, who designed not only the building itself, but every detail of its decoration. Ironically, he took no part in the actual construction, which was entrusted to his disciples Friedrich August Stüler and Ludwig Persius, and did not live to see the raising of the great dome. This was one of his most audacious projects, the four slender corner towers being necessary to counteract the otherwise unsustainable pressure the dome exerts on the body of the church. It is as impressive from inside as from out, being adorned with fourteen statues of Old Testament figures and gigantic paintings of the four major prophets: Isiah, Jeremiah, Ezekhiel and Daniel.

In front of the church is the **Obelisk** by Georg Wenzeslaus von Knobelsdorff. Alongside, a reproduction of the **Fortunaportal**, an elaborate gateway to the vanished Stadtschloss, has recently been erected as a taster for a possible reconstruction of the entire building. The eastern side of the square is dominated by the **Altes Rathaus** by another of Frederick the Great's favourite architects, the Dutchman Johann Boumann, who used an unbuilt design by the last great master of the Italian Renaissance, Andrea Palladio. Until 1875 the circular tower, on top of which a gilded Atlas bears the world on his shoulders, served as the town jail. The Rathaus lost its municipal function in 1885, and was taken over by a bank. In the GDR era it became an arts centre, a role it retains.

To the south is the **Freudschaftsinsel**, a leafy Havel island with a number of gardens, the most recent of which, specially planted for the Bundesgartenschau, is the only one in Germany specifically devoted to herbaceous perennials. West of Am Alten Markt are Yorckstrasse and Wilhelm-Staab-Strasse, which both boast a number of fine **Baroque houses**. Am Neuen Markt, just to the south of Yorckstrasse, also has a couple of good-looking survivors, including, on the west side (behind the *Waage* restaurant), some improbably grand (but decrepit) eighteenth-century coaching stables with an entrance in the form of a triumphal arch. At Am Neuen Markt 1 is the **Kabinetthaus**, a small mansion that was the birthplace of Friedrich Wilhelm II, the only member of the Hohenzollern family actually born in Potsdam.

A little further south, at Schlossstr. 1, is the former Marstall or royal stables, which now houses the **Filmmuseum** (Tues–Sun 10am–6pm; €2, or €5 including special exhibits; Ⓦ www.filmmuseum-potsdam.de). Drawing on material from the UFA studios in nearby Babelsberg (later DEFA, the GDR state film company), the museum presents both a technical and artistic history of German film from 1895 to 1980. There's a vaguely hands-on feel, with a few visitor-operated Bioscopes and numerous screens playing clips. The museum **cinema** (€4.50) is the best in Potsdam.

From here it's worth making a quick detour down **Kiezstrasse**, where a number of eighteenth-century Rococo houses have been beautifully restored. In the midst of the high-rises to the west is the **Dampfmaschinenhaus** (guided tours mid-May to mid-Oct Sat & Sun 10am–5pm; €3; Ⓦ www.spsg.de), the most imaginative pump-house in Germany. The architect, Ludwig Persius, designed it to resemble a mosque, with the chimney taking the form of a minaret. However, it is no Romantic-era folly: it belatedly solved the problem of the supply of water to Park Sanssouci, at last enabling the Grosse Fonatäne to function effectively.

The northern Altstadt

North of Am Alten Markt are two more large squares. The first of these is the Platz der Einheit, dominated by the neo-Baroque mass of the **Postamt**. Immediately to the north, a plaque marks the site of the **Synagoge**, which was wrecked on *Kristallnacht* and later demolished. Beyond is Bassinplatz, at the southeastern corner of which is the oval **Französische Kirche**, which was erected in the 1750s by Boumann to plans by Knobelsdorff for the Huguenot community. Dating from just over a century later, the much larger **St Peter und Paul** was the first major church to be built for Roman Catholic worship in this staunchly Protestant town.

To the west of here, on and around **Brandenburger Strasse**, Potsdam's pedestrianized main shopping street, are many ornate Baroque houses, which were built, with slight variations in detail to avoid monotony, for tradespeople in the then rapidly expanding town. At the end of the street is the **Brandenburger Tor**, one of three surviving gateways from the 1730s fortifications system. Four decades after it was built, it was transformed by Carl von Gontard into a triumphal arch, adorned with Rococo carvings which give it a playful character wholly lacking in its Berlin namesake. The only one of the gates to have survived in something like its original form is the **Jägertor** (Hunter's Gate), at the end of Lindenstrasse to the northeast, which is surmounted by a sculpture of a stag succumbing to a pack of baying hounds. Further east along Hegelallee is the **Nauener Tor**, which was rebuilt in the 1750s as the first German essay in the English Gothic style, which had brought the long unfashioned pointed arch back into favour.

Between here and Bassinplatz is the **Holländisches Viertel** (Dutch quarter), the earliest of several settlements in Potsdam established for specific immigrant communities. It was Boumann's first major Prussian commission, and he adhered closely to the vernacular architecture of his native Amsterdam, using brick instead of stone, and building elbaorately gabled houses, numbering 134 in all, arranged in terraces. Unfortunately, relatively few Dutch settlers took up the invitation to settle there, and many of those who did returned home when the promised employment dried up. A number of excellent restored examples can be found along **Mittelstrasse**, particularly at the junction with Benkertstrasse. Mittelstrasse has been gentrified to a large extent, with a number of trendy shops and cafés.

Park Sanssouci

Park Sanssouci, Frederick the Great's fabled retreat, stretches out for two kilometres west of the Altstadt, and its gardens and palaces are what draw most visitors to the town. In 1744 Frederick, who had no great love for his capital, Berlin, or his queen, Elizabeth Christine, ordered the construction of a residence where he could live "without cares" – or *sans souci* in the French spoken at court. Huge teams of craftsmen, led by the finest German architects, sculptors, painters, decorators and landscape gardeners of the day, were employed to turn the king's whims into reality. The plan adopted was an original one, abandoning the traditional Baroque format of a grandiose palace as the park's centrepiece. Instead, there are numerous buildings: the earliest of these are modest in scale, though Frederick himself later initiated the trend towards adding larger structures that was also favoured by the most artistically minded of his successors, Friedrich Wilhelm IV. The park is at its most stunning in autumn, when it erupts into a blaze of colour worthy of New England, but spring, when the trees are in leaf and the flowers in bloom, is also delightful. These days the park is all too often overrun by tourists; to avoid the crowds, visit on a weekday, preferably outside summer.

The eastern park

The main entrance to the park is the **Obeliskpforte** by Knobelsdorff at the eastern end, which features two clusters of pillars flanked by statues of the goddesses Flora and Pomona by Friedrich Christian Glume. It is named after the nearby **Obelisk**, which is covered with Egyptian-style hieroglyphs, though these are purely decorative, predating the first modern deciphering of the ancient script.

Just to the south is the Italianate **Friedenskirche** (Peace Church; mid-May to mid-Oct daily 10am–6pm), which was built to plans by Persius to commemorate Sanssouci's centenary. With its 39-metre campanile and lakeside setting, it conjures up the southern European atmosphere that Friedrich Wilhelm IV was striving to create when he ordered the construction of the church using the San Clemente basilica in Rome as a model. The shape and measurements of the building were predetermined by the magnificent apse mosaic which the king had acquired from Murano in the Venetian lagoon. With the exception of the damaged example owned by Berlin's Bodemuseum, this is the only intact Byzantine mosaic to be found north of the Alps. Adjoining the church is a domed Hohenzollern mausoleum containing the tombs of Friedrich Wilhelm IV, Friedrich III and their wives.

Immediately west of the Friedenskirche is **Marlys Garten**, a kitchen garden transformed by Lenné into a *jardin anglais*. On the opposite side of Hauptallee, the avenue running straight through the middle of the park, is the playful Rococo **Neptungrotte**, Knobelsdorff's last work. Further along the main axis is the **Grosse Fontäne**, a huge water jet in a circular basin. It's surrounded by statues of mythological figures, some of which – notably the figures of Venus and Mercury by the Frenchman Jean Baptiste Pigalle – rank among the great masterpieces of garden sculpture. Immediately to the north is a tiered vineyard, one of the most northerly in Europe, known as the **Weinbergterrassen**. In 1991, the uppermost level of this was the setting for a midnight ceremony attended by many prominent national figures, at which Frederick the Great was finally laid to rest in his favoured place alongside his greyhounds. Deeming this an unsuitable grave for a king, his heirs had interred him in the now-demolished Garnisonkirche, from where his coffin was spirited away at the end of World War II to his ancestral seat of Burg Hohenzollern near the Swabian town of Hechingen. On the same terrace is an ornate trellis pavilion sheltering the statue of a deity.

Schloss Sanssouci

Schloss Sanssouci (guided tours Tues–Sun 9am–4/5pm; €8; Ⓦ www.spsg.de) is a relatively modest single-storey palace whose fragility has led to the imposition of strict quotas on the number of visitors allowed on any one day. It's therefore advisable to arrive as early as possible to secure a ticket: if desired, the actual visit can be postponed until a set time later on. The building was constructed by Knobelsdorff from drawings by Frederick the Great himself, who had very clear ideas as to what he wanted. Externally, the main feature is the garden front, which has a truly festive air, with a protruding domed central section and a superb series of 36 caryatids, each individually characterized, by Friedrich Christian Glume. The entrance facade, which is fronted by a colonnaded *cour d'honneur*, commands a fine view up to the Ruinenberg, a hall crowned with mock classical ruins and the reservoir supplying the park's fountains.

All but one of the Schloss' dozen rooms are included on the tour; they are decorated in archetypal Rococo style, with coloured marble, stuccowork, gilded wood, ceiling frescoes, specially-made furniture and both real and imitation antique statues. There are also many French paintings of the period, including several canvases by Watteau. The most impressive chamber is the central **Marmorsaal**, which is fashioned with marble from the famous quarries of Carrara. Also of special note is the **Konzertzimmer**, with its murals by Antoine Pesne illustrating Ovid's *Metamorphoses*; this was where Frederick staged his musical soirées, at which he himself often played the flute. His other favourite haunt was the tiny circular **Bibliothek**.

The Schloss was little used between the time of Frederick the Great's death and the accession of Friedrich Wilhelm IV. However, the latter commissioned an appropriately modest-looking western extension, known as the **Damenflügel** (mid-May to mid-Oct Sat & Sun 10am–5pm; €2, Ⓦwww.spsg.de) for the use of ladies-in-waiting and kitchen staff.

The Bildergalerie and the Neue Kammern

On the eastern side of Schloss Sanssouci, overlooking the ornamental Holländischer Garten (Dutch Garden), is the **Bildergalerie** (Picture Gallery; mid-May to mid-Oct Tues–Sun 10am–5pm; €3; Ⓦwww.spsg.de), a restrained Baroque design of 1755 by Johann Gottfried Büring. Generally considered to be the first building in mainland Europe to be erected specifically as a museum, it contains a single festive hall with a cabinet at the far end for the smaller works. All the paintings are hung closely together in the traditional but now unfashionable manner. The most celebrated work is Caravaggio's *Incredulity of St Thomas*; there's also a wonderful *Supper at Emmaus* by his most talented Dutch follower, Ter Brugghen. Rubens and Van Dyck are both well represented: the most important canvases by the former are *St Jerome in his Study* and *The Four Evangelists*; by the latter are portraits of members of the British court and a couple of mythological works, *Venus in Vulcan's Workshop* and *Rinaldo and Armida*.

On the opposite side of the Schloss, steps lead down to a very similar-looking building known as the **Neue Kammern** (early April to mid-May Sat & Sun 10am–5pm; mid-May to mid-Oct Tues–Sun 10am–5pm; €3; Ⓦwww.spsg.de). Originally an orangery, it was transformed in the 1770s into a plush guesthouse for visiting dignitaries. The interiors are slightly less grand than those of the Schloss and include the Ovidgalerie, with reliefs illustrating scenes from Ovid's *Elegies*, and the oval Bankettsaal. Below the Neue Kammern is a peaceful rose garden, to the west of which is the **Sizilianischer Garten** (Sicilian Garden), which Lenné laid out according to the formal patterns of the Italian Renaissance.

The northern park

There are several notable buildings on the northern side of Maulbeerallee (Mulberry Alley), a road open to traffic which cuts right through Park Sanssouci. Easternmost is the **Historische Mühle** (April-Oct daily 10am–6pm; Nov–March Sat & Sun 10am–4pm; €2), an old windmill damaged in the 1945 air raid on the town but restored to working order as part of the 1993 celebrations of Potsdam's millennium. Further west is the **Orangerie** (mid-May to mid-Oct Tues–Sun 10am–5pm; €3; Ⓦwww.spsg.de), a bombastic 1850s building by Persius and Stüler whose dimensions – the facade is 330m long – are wholly at odds with the original conception of the park. The western wing is still used as a refuge for tropical plants in winter, and during the summer it's possible to ascend its **tower**. In the central block is the **Raphaelsaal**, whose walls are hung with specially commissioned nineteenth-century copies of paintings thought to be by Raphael. These include some of his most familiar masterpieces, but also works now known to be by his master Perugino, or by pupils such as Giulio Romano.

From the western wing of the Orangerie, the arrow-straight Krimlindenallee, lined with lime trees, leads up towards the Rococo **Belvedere** by Georg Christian Unger, the last of the park pavilions to be built under Frederick the Great. A couple of hundred metres short of the Belvedere, a path branches off left towads the **Drachenhaus**, which Gontard modelled on the Chinese pagoda in London's Kew Gardens. Today there's a genteel café inside, an ideal point to interrupt your wanderings.

The Neues Palais

At the far western end of Park Sanssouci is the **Neues Palais** (9am–4/5pm, closed Fri; €6; Ⓦwww.spsg.de), built between 1763 and 1769 to celebrate the end of the Seven Years' War, which had seen Prussia oust Austria from its centuries-long role as the dominant power in German affairs. The scale of the three-storey palace, which marked a radical departure from the intimate single-level buildings that had previously been constructed in the park, was intended as a deliberate triumphalist statement. Büring drew up the original plans, but was replaced early in the construction process by Gontard. A huge team of craftsmen was recruited to carve the rich programme of statuary adorning the balustrade and gardens. The most striking external feature, however, is the massive windowless central dome over the central block.

Inside, the **Grottensaal** makes for a startling introduction: its walls are encrusted with marble, shells, fossils, precious stones, glass and corals, all dimly lit to enhance the sense of mystery. Alongside, the **Marmorgalerie**, which is modelled on the halls of mirrors characteristic of the French royal palaces, has walls and floor of white marble and red jasper and ceiling frescoes of morning noon, and evening by Christian Bernard Rode. One of the bedrooms contains a documentary painting by Menzel, *The Coronation of Wilhelm I*, which illustrates in magnificent detail an event which took place at Königsberg in 1861. Upstairs, directly above the Grottensal, is the **Marmorsaal**, the principal festive hall. The adjacent **Obergalerie**, which corresponds to the Marmorgalerie below, is hung with canvases by seventeenth-century Italian painters, including Giudo Reni and Artemesia Gentileschi. In the southern wing are Frederick's apartments and the **Schlosstheater**, a delectable Rococo auditorium where the king enjoyed Italian opera and French plays. A francophile to the point of near mania, Frederick believed that the Germans were philistines incapable of producing great art. It was said that he'd "rather a horse sang him an aria, than allow a German in his opera".

Facing the front entrance of the Neues Palais are the **Communs**, a couple of porticoed and domed structures linked by a curved colonnade. They look grandiose, but they merely housed serving and maintenance staff, and blocked off what would otherwise have been an unsightly view of the marshland beyond. Two small temples lie just east of the palace's garden front, on either side of Hauptallee. The **Antikentempel** is a domed rotunda, built to house Frederick the Great's collection of antiquities but later converted to serve as the last resting place of a number of Hohenzollerns, including the Empress Auguste Victoria, and Hermine, the woman Wilhelm II married in exile, who came to be known as the "last Empress". The circular **Freundschaftstempel** is a memorial to Frederick's sister, Margravine Wilhelmine of Brandenburg-Bayreuth, one of the few women for whom the great misogynist showed the slightest affection.

The Rehgarten and Park Charlottenhof

Ökonomieweg leads eastwards through the **Rehgarten** (Deer Garden), the former court hunting ground, to Sanssouci's kitschiest yet most endearing pavilion, the **Chinesisches Teehaus** (mid-May to mid-Oct Tues–Sun 10am–5pm; €1; Ⓦwww.spsg.de). Built by Büring in the 1750s, it was based on descriptions provided by contemporary visitors to China. Eerily lifelife statues of Oriental figures drinking tea and coffee and playing musical instruments are grouped around the exterior, while inside, the main hall and the adjoining cabinets are used to display Chinese and Meissen porcelain.

South of Ökonomieweg is **Park Charlottenhof**, which now forms a seemless whole with the much larger Park Sanssouci, though it was originally a separate estate. This was acquired by the future Friedrich Wilhelm IV, and transformed by Lenné into a *jardin anglais* of lawns, hillocks and artificial stretches of water. Schinkel was commissioned to design two buildings for the park. Of these, the **Römische Bäder** (mid-May to mid-Oct Tues–Sun 10am–5pm; €2 or €5 combined ticket with Schloss Charlottenhof; Ⓦwww.spsg.de), which was actually built by Persius, consists of a tea pavilion, a Renaissance-style villa, and a suite of rooms in the manner of a Roman house, including the bathroom from which the whole building takes its name. Further south is **Schloss Charlottenhof** (same times; Ⓦwww.spsg.de), a Neoclassical villa which is clearly modelled on its Roman predecessors, yet never resorts to slavish imitation.

The northern quarters

Potsdam has several rewarding corners that lie well off the beaten tourist track of the Altstadt and Sanssouci, and the quarters **north of the Altstadt** are particularly well endowed with often surprising sights.

Alexandrowka

About ten minutes' walk north of the Nauener Tor is **Alexandrowka**, the only surviving example of the once common Russian military villages, and the only one built outside Russia. Its origins lie in the capture of 500 czarist soldiers by the Prussians in 1812, from whom 62 were selected to form a choir to entertain their captors. These men remained in Prussian service after the erstwhile enemies became allies. By 1825, only a dozen of the singers were still alive, and it was decided to reward them with a permanent home in Potsdam that would remind them of their native land. The settlement was laid out along two avenues in the form of a St Andrew's cross, with the homes of the twelve singers placed along the axes, and the residence of the Prussian overseer in the middle. The houses, with their distinctive balconies and ornamental gables, give the appearance of genuine Russian log cabins, but in reality they are half-timbered with wooden facing. Each has at least one nameplate in Cyrillic script, showing the name of the first occupant. When that is all that is shown, the house remains in the hands of a direct descendant of one of the choristers; those which have been re-let also show the name of the present tenant.

As an adjunct to Alexandrowka, the **Russische Kirche Hl Alexander Newsky** was built on the wooded Kapellenberg immediately above. The plans for its construction were drawn up at the St Petersburg court, and it has an archetypally Russian appearance, with a central onion-domed tower surrounded by four smaller domes. Inside, the iconostasis has some icons painted in Russia at the same time as construction work was underway, as well as others of later date. The church has remianed in constant use by the émigré community, which nowadays mostly consists of Belarussians.

The Pfingstberg

Immediately to the north of the Kapellenberg is the wooded **Pfingstberg**, at the foot of which is the walled **Jüdischer Friedhof** (Jewish cemetery). Only organized visits are possible, every Sunday at 10am – enquire at the tourist office in town for details. The cemetery was given by the town to Potsdam's growing Jewish population in 1763; until then they had had to bury their dead in Berlin. As recently as 1933 the Jewish community of Potsdam numbered several hundred, of whom just two returned after the war.

At the top of the hill is the **Belvedere** (April–Oct daily 10am–4pm; Nov–March Sat & Sun 10am–4pm; €3.50), a vast and improbable-looking Italianate folly designed to provide sweeping views over Potsdam, the Havel and its lakes. The small building just to the southeast is the **Pomonatempel** (April–Oct Sat & Sun 3–6pm; donation requested), Schinkel's first-ever finished building, constructed in 1800 when he was a nineteen-year-old student..

Immediately west of the Pfingtberg is the **BUGA-Park** (daily 5am–11pm; €1), where the Bundesgartenschau was held. Its main attraction, right by the entrance, is the **Biosphäre Potsdam** (daily 9am–8pm; €9.50; Ⓦwww.biosphaere-potsdam.de), which features some 20,000 tropical plants, orchids and trees, including a palm grove and a mangrove swamp.

The Neuer Garten

On the opposite side of the Pfingstberg is another large park complex, the **Neuer Garten**, which was laid out from 1786 onwards by order of Friedrich Wilhlem II, the immediate successor of Frederick the Great. As an antidote to the geometric formality of Sanssouci, it marked the Potsdam debut of the naturalistic English style of landscape gardening.

Near the northernmost tip of the park, and reachable from the town centre by bus #694, is **Schloss Cecilienhof** (April–Oct Tues–Sun 9am–5pm; Nov–March Tues–Sun 10am–12.30pm & 1–5pm; €5; Ⓦwww.spsg.de), which looks like a mock-Tudor mansion transplanted from England. Building work on this, the last palace to be commissioned by the Hohenzollerns, began in 1913 and was completed in 1917, the war apparently having done nothing to change the owners' architectural tastes. Cecilienhof would only rate a mention in passing, were it not for the fact that it was the setting for the **Potsdam Conference** of July 17 to August 2, 1945. This confirmed the decisions made earlier that year at Yalta about the postwar European order, and formally set the limit of German territory at the Oder-Neisse Line, thereby confiscating well over 100,000 square kilometres of the prewar Reich. The **Konferenzsaal**, where the Allied delegates worked out the details of the division of Europe at a huge round table specially made in Moscow, still looks much as it did in 1945. Much the same can be said of the chambers used by the delegates: the Soviets had the music room and parlour, the Americans the smoking and living rooms, the British the library and reading room.

Further south, directly beside the Heiliger See, is the **Marmorpalais** (Marble Palace; April–Oct Tues–Sun 10am–5pm; Nov–March Sat & Sun 10am–12.30pm & 1–5pm; €3; Ⓦwww.spsg.de), which is actually mainly built of brick. The central pavilion, with its graceful belvedere on top, was built by Gontard and Langhans in a hybrid Rococo and Neoclassical style. In addition to many notable furnishings, including a distinguished Wedgwood collection, it has some highly individual interiors, notably the Grottensaal and the upstairs Konzertsaal and Orientalisches Kabinett, the last of which mimicks the appearance of the tents used by the Turks in their seventeenth-century campaigns against Christian Europe. The palace's wings were only completed in the 1840s, and their interior decoration consequently reflects quite different artistic tastes.

Further on, the **Holländisches Etablissement**, Potsdam's second Dutch-style settlement, was built for the palace's servants, on the model of the distinctive almshouses of Holland. Behind them is the **Orangerie** by Langhans, whose facade, in a curious juxtaposition of Egyptian and Greek motifs, features a sphinx seated on a portico of Doric columns. The same architect built the **Königliche Bibliothek** (Royal Library) at the southern tip of the Heiliger See. This time it is Neoclassical and neo-Gothic elements that are mixed in an usual design of two single-room storeys, with the upper surrounded by a viewing platform.

Berliner Vorstadt

On the opposite shore of the Heiliger See to the Neuer Garten is the **Berliner Vorstadt**, formerly an elegant Potsdam suburb, whose crumbling villas were given over to various party and social institutions under the SED regime. Here, too, were numerous Imperial army barracks, housing elite units like the Garde du Corps and Hussars, which until the summer of 1994 were in Russian hands. At the end of Berliner Strasse, leading back to Berlin, is the **Glienicker Brücke**, the famous spy-swap bridge which inspired many a Cold War film scene. Here, in 1962, U-2 pilot Gary Powers was traded for a Soviet agent, while in 1986 Jewish dissident Anatoly Scharansky was freed into the West in an early manifestation of Gorbachev's *glasnost*.

The southern quarters

On the opposite side of the Havel from Potsdam's Altstadt are several more suburbs, including the formerly separate town of Babelsberg.

Teltower Vorstadt

Directly facing the Altstadt is the hilly suburb known as the **Teltower Vorstadt**. Crossing over by the Lange Brücke from Potsdam, it's hard not to notice a square tower rising up out of the trees atop the Brauhausberg above. This is the former local SED headquarters or **Kreml** (Kremlin), to give it its local nickname. Originally built as a military college at the turn of the twentieth century, it later served as a state archive building.

Albert-Einstein-Strasse leads up the western side of the Brauhausberg to the **Telegrafenberg**. This was the site chosen in 1832 for a telegraph station, one of a whole network positioned between Berlin and Koblenz to relay messages by means of mechanical signals. Three decades years later, other scientific institues were set up on the hill, notably the **Astrophysicalisches Observatorium**, a triple-domed observatory built of bricks interspersed with ceramic tiles.

A path leads onwards to the nearby **Einsteinturm**, a twenty-metre-high observatory tower, which is the product of a chance meeting between the architect Erich Mendelsohn and the astrophysicist Erwin Finlay-Freundlich, who wanted to commission a structure where he could test Einstein's theory of relativity by means of practical experiments. The resultant building, the most famous architectural product of the Expressionist movement, looks like an element from a Dalí dreamscape and seems astonishingly futuristic for something erected as long ago as 1920. Although the initial tests carried out there were inconclusive and regarded as a failure, scientific work continues there today with research into the sun's magnetic field.

Babelsberg

East of the Teltower Vorstadt is **BABELSBERG**. Just north of the S-Bahn station of the same name is another intriguing example of town planning, the settlement of **Nowawes**, which was established by Frederick the Great in 1750 as a home for Protestant weavers and spinners fleeing religious persecution in Bohemia. It was shortly afterwards extended to accommodate craftsmen from southern Germany and Switzerland who came to work on the Neues Palais. Unfortunately, none of the original single-storey semi-detached houses around the triangular-shaped **Weberplatz** survives in an absolutely authentic shape, though many give a fair impression of how they once looked. Rather better preserved is the rustic double-galleried **Friedrichskirche** in the centre of Friedrichsplatz.

North of Nowawes is Potsdam's third major landscape garden, the often-overlooked **Park Babelsberg**, which is also easily accessible from the Berlin side of the Glienicker Brücke. Its focal point is **Schloss Babelsberg** (April–Oct Tues–Sun 10am–5pm, Nov–March Sat & Sun 10am–4pm; €3; Ⓦwww.spsg.de), a neo-Gothic architectural extravaganza built by Schinkel and Persius for the future Kaiser Wilhelm I. Their main source of inspiration was the recent extension to England's Windsor Castle, and the contrast in style with the same duo's Nikolaikirche, which was under construction at the same time, could hardly be starker. Inside, the most striking rooms are the two-storey Tanzsaal inside the great octagon; the Teesalon, with its star-shaped ceiling; and the Bibliothek, with its distinctively English fan vault. A couple of nineteenth-century architectural oddities lurk in the park: the **Flatowturm** (April to mid-Oct Sat & Sun 10am–5pm; €2), an improbable-looking neo-Gothic guesthouse and lookout tower, and the **Matrosenhaus**, a gabled house built for the crews of the royal boats. The park is also home to the Gothic **Gerichtslaube**, Berlin's original town hall and lawcourt, which was brought here in 1872 after being displaced by the Rotes Rathaus.

At the eastern end of Babelsberg, reached by buses #690 and #692, is the **Filmpark Babelsberg** (mid-March to early Nov daily 10am–6pm; €15; Ⓦwww.filmpark.de), a huge complex of 430,000 square metres entered from Grossbeerenstrasse. Production began here in 1912, though its halcyon years coincided with those of the Weimar Republic. Under the name of UFA, it rivalled Hollywood as a centre of cinematic innovation, producing over a thousand films. These included Robert Wiene's Expressionist masterpiece *Das Kabinett des Dr Caligari* ("The Cabinet of Dr Caligari"), Fritz Lang's *Metropolis* and *Der Blaue Engel* ("The Blue Angel") starring the young Marlene Dietrich. During the Third Reich, the studios were taken over by Goebbels' Ministry of Propaganda, whose most notorious production was *Jud Süss*, which corrupted Lion Feuchtwanger's pro-Jewish novel into an anti-Semitic tirade. Against all the odds, the war years produced a masterpiece in the special effect-laden colour epic *Münchhausen*, which was scripted by Erich Kästner, who wrote under a pseudonym in order to circumvent the Nazi ban on him as a supposedly subversive writer. Renamed DEFA, the studios were the heavily subsidized centre of the East German film industry, which produced some fine children's films, such as *Little Muck*, but which didn't last much longer than the GDR itself. Since the *Wende*, Babelsberg has reinvented itself as a film theme park, and visitors can wander through the costume and props departments and watch technicians going through the motions of shooting film scenes for their benefit. In addition, there are carnival-type rides, several featuring cartoon characters familiar to German children, and animal shows. It's also possible to visit the hangar-like studio where Fritz Lang is believed to have filmed *Metropolis* and admire a reproduction of his futuristic set. It takes several hours to see round the whole site, which makes a good day-trip in itself.

Eating, drinking and entertainment

Potsdam has a good array of places to eat and drink. Some of the best **restaurants** are located in the hotels (see p.804), though otherwise the most convenient concentration of establishments is along Brandenburger Strasse, but it pays to go a little further afield.

Potsdam's main venue for **drama and opera** is the Hans-Otto-Theater, Zimmerstr. 10 (Ⓣ03 31/9 81 18, Ⓦwww.hot.potsdam.de), though smaller-scale opera performances (and occasional concerts) are usually staged at the Schlosstheater in the Neues Palais (Ⓦwww.potsdamerhofkonzerte.de). The Waschhaus, Schiffbauergasse 1 (Ⓣ03 31/2 71 56 26; Ⓦwww.waschhaus.de) is a large complex with **live music**, parties, galleries and an open-air cinema. It's just off Berliner Strasse on the way into town from the Glienicker Brücke. At the same address is Fabrik (Ⓣ03 31/2 80 03 14), a theatre for **contemporary dance** and new music.

Restaurants

Ani Kurfürstenstr. 34. Armenian speciality restaurant. On weekdays, it's only open in the evening.

Hof Brauhaus Bornstedt Ribbeckstr. 6–7. Forms part of the recently restored Krongut Bornstedt, a nineteenth-century working estate built in an Italianate style. It brews a black beer called *Büffel*, distils several spirits and has an enticing menu of moderately priced local fare.

Juliette Jägerstr. 39. High quality and very expensive French restaurant.

Kleines Schloss Park Babelsberg. A traditionally minded daytime restaurant with a lakeside setting. Closed Mon.

Klosterkeller Friedrich-Ebert-Str. 94. Historic restaurant, founded in 1734, serving archetypal German fare.

Luise Luisenplatz 6. Serving mid-priced German and continental food in casual surroundings, this is the perfect place to eat before tackling Sanssouci, just up the road.

Per Butt Gutenbergstr. 25. High-quality if somewhat pricey fish restaurant. Closed Mon.

Trattoria Pane e Vino Friedrich-Ebert-Str. 35. Wonderfully simple but tasty Italian food – mostly pasta dishes and salads – is served up at this combined restaurant and deli.

Villa Kellermann Mangerstr. 34. Potsdam's best Italian restaurant occupies a villa on the eastern bank of the Heiliger See.

Waage Am Neuen Markt 12. Serves inventive dishes with local ingredients, though it's a little on the pricey side. Closed Mon.

Zum Laubenpieper Am Pfingstberg 25. Rustic restaurant offering huge servings of traditional German food. Its hilltop beer garden is open during the summer.

Zur Linde Lindenstr. 50. Personable and relaxing restaurant with typical German food.

Bars and cafés

Arco Corner of Friedrich-Ebert-Str. and Kurfürstenstr. Occupying the east wing of the Nauener Tor, this small café, which has outdoor seating is summer, serves excellent continental food.

Babette Brandenburger Str. 71. Pleasant little café and cocktail bar.

Backstube & Coffeshop Friedrich-Ebert-Str. 92. Home bakery-cum-Internet café.

Café Heider Friedrich-Ebert-Str. 29. Founded in 1878, this is a recommendable choice for *Kaffee und Kuchen*.

Café Lapis Lazuli Benkertstr. 21. Hippie-ish café with old wooden tables and candles. Light snacks only are served.

Drachenhaus Maulbeerallee. A pleasant, genteel little café in Park Sanssouci, housed in a pagoda-style building once used by royal vintners. You can also eat well here.

Filmcafé Schlossstr. 1. Occupying the east wing of the Filmmuseum, this serves dishes from around the world and stays open until midnight. Closed Mon.

Hafthorn Friedrich-Ebert-Str. 90. Large and lively Kneipe offering Swabian specialities at low prices.

La Leander Benkertstr. 1. In the Holländisches Viertel, a dark and relaxing café with a short menu.

pub à la pub Breite Str. 1. A student hangout in a classic GDR concrete building. adorned with a Socialist Realist mosaic.

Seerose Breite Str. 24. Housed in a bizarre-looking modern building, this popular bar offers good views across the Neustädter Havelbucht.

tete á tete Mittelstr. 33. This has the best selection of teas in town.

Brandenburg an der Havel

BRANDENBURG, the city from which the province takes its name, lies on the main Berlin–Hannover rail line just over 30km west of Potsdam. For all its illustrious past – it was founded by the Slavs in the sixth century, made the seat of a precarious missionary German bishopric in the tenth century, before becoming the capital of the margraviate established by Albert the Bear in 1157 – its more recent history has been a catalogue of misfortunes. These began when the Nazis chose it as the site of a concentration camp (where the murder count included 10,000 victims of a compulsory euthanasia programme for the mentally handicapped) and continued with severe wartime damage followed by postwar transformation into a steel metropolis that suffered from some of the worst air pollution in Europe. Since the *Wende*, Brandenburg has been cleaned up and can once more be appreciated as a place with a great deal to offer, including some magnificent examples of north German brick architecture and a beautiful natural setting at a point where the broad course of the Havel fashions a wondrous lake-strewn landscape.

The City

Brandenburg's historic centre is divided into three distinct parts – the **Dominsel**, the **Altstadt** and the **Neustadt** – each of which is situated on its own island in the Havel.

The Neustadt

The **Neustadt** is new only in a relative sense, having been founded as the commercial quarter at the end of the twelfth century, a generation after the previously Slav Altstadt had been re-established as a German town. Despite conspicuous gaps left by the war, its narrow streets retain much of their old feel. Guarding its southern side is the cylindrical **Steintor** (Tues–Fri 9am–5pm, Sat & Sun 10am–5pm; €3), one of four surviving gateways out of the ten the two settlements once possessed. There's a small museum inside showing special exhibitions on the city's history. East of here is the **Paulikloster**, a thirteenth-century Dominican priory left in ruins during World War II, though some reconstruction work has been carried out since the *Wende*.

Right in the middle of the island is the Neustädtischer Markt, now returned to its age-old role as a market square. It's dominated by the **Katharinenkirche**, a Gothic pile from the turn of the fifteenth century. Outside, the walls are crammed with spouting gargoyles and frilly gables tacked on for purely decorative effect, with the varied colouring and positioning of the bricks helping to transform the surface effects yet further. The fantastical interior design tends to overshadow the church's treasures, which include a finely carved fifteenth-century altar and a fourteenth-century stained-glass window in the choir, which was fortuitously removed from the Paulikloster in 1942.

The Altstadt

Hauptstrasse runs northwestwards over the Havel into the **Altstadt**, which occupies only a small portion of a much larger island. Immediately over the river is the **Johanniskirche**, another brick Gothic church still remaining in the burnt-out state it was left in at the end of the war. Further along, at Hauptstr. 96, is the **Freyhaus** (Tues–Fri 9am–5pm, Sat & Sun 10am–5pm; €3), a Baroque mansion which now houses the district museum. This array of local ephemera is more interesting than you might expect, particularly the displays on the archeology of the Havelland, the graphic art section and a fascinating toy collection.

At the end of Ritterstrasse, the continuation of Hauptstrasse, Plauer Strasse leads north to the Altstädtischer Markt, over which looms the fourteenth-century **Altstädtisches Rathaus**, whose facade is topped with an unusual stepped gable. In front of it stands a mighty five-metre-high **statue of Roland**, medieval symbol of Brandenburg's status as a market town.

Continuing northwards, you come to the parish church of the Altstadt, the **Gotthardtkirche**. Its facade is in the austere Romanesque style of the Premonstratensian monks, but behind it stands a light and airy Gothic hall church erected in the fifteenth century. Inside, look out for the thirteenth-century font and the lovely Burgundian tapestry showing the hunting of the unicorn. On the square facing the church is the **Schulhaus**, a half-timbered former school building from the sixteenth century.

The Dominsel

The **Dominsel**, the smallest of the three islands on which the historic quarters of Brandenburg are built, escaped the worst of the bombing and is by far the most visually pleasing part of town. From the Gotthardtkirche, you have to approach it circuitously via yet another island, occupied mainly by sports fields, to the north; there's a more direct approach along Mühlendamm from the Neustädtischer Markt. Taking the latter approach, the first monument you come to is the **Petrikapelle**, a thirteenth-century chapel given a spectacular interior transformation three hundred years later, with the addition of the intricate late Gothic cellular vault resting on hexagonal pillars.

The **Dom** was begun around 1165 as a Romanesque basilica, and slowly converted to Gothic in the fourteenth and fifteenth centuries, though many parts of the old structure were retained, notably the arcades of the nave. The most atmospheric part is the **crypt**, which houses the poignant original **triumphal cross**, supplanted *in situ* by a more monumental Gothic group. Even more eye-catching are the **capitals**, whose carvings of fabulous beasts and eerie half-human creatures show the vivid flights of imagination of which the medieval mind was capable. A contrastingly sombre note is struck by a series of metal plates, each accompanied by an appropriate biblical quotation, commemorating local clergymen murdered by the Nazis. In the south transept is a beautifully carved and painted **Bohemian altar** from around 1375, whose radiantly joyous saints mark a refreshing change from the anguished figures normally found in religious art. This was originally the high altar, but it was displaced in favour of a large retable brought from a suppressed monastery after the Reformation. In front of the latter stands a delicately modelled fourteenth-century **font**, with scenes from the childhood of Christ on its basin, and more fantastic animals on the base. On the north side of the choir, look out for the appropriately named **Bunte Kapelle** (Painted Chapel), another survivor from the Romanesque period. Joachim Wagner's **organ** is a magnificent Baroque instrument, and is regularly used for recitals.

The **Dommuseum** (Mon–Fri 10am–4pm, Sat 10am–5pm, Sun 11am–5pm; €3) occupies the conventual buildings of the Premonstratensian collegiate foundation which moved here from the Gotthardtkirche. There's a superb array of medieval textiles, including a *Hungertuch* of 1290, made to cover the altar during Lent. Even finer is the collection of manuscripts, of which the star piece is the **Brandenburg Evangelistary**, a sumptuous late Romanesque gospel book adorned with colourful miniatures. The original is displayed with one page open; a facsimile of the whole book is kept for examination at leisure.

Practicalities

Brandenburg's **Hauptbahnhof** lies to the south of the historic quarters, five minutes' walk from Neustadt. The **tourist office** (May–Sept Mon–Fri

8.30am–7pm, Sat & Sun 10am–3pm; Oct–April Mon–Fri 10am–6pm, Sat 10am–2pm; ⓣ0 33 81/58 58 58, ⓦwww.stadt-brandenburg.de, www.fvv-brandenburg.de) is at Steinstr. 66–67 in the Neustadt. **Cruises**, which depart from the Altstadt side of the river, are run by Nordstern Reederei, Neuendorfer Str. 70 (ⓣ0 33 81/22 69 60, ⓦwww.nordstern-reederei.de), and Reederei Röding, Neuendorfer Str. 86 (ⓣ0 33 81/52 23 31, ⓦwww.fgs-havelfee.de); prices start at €5 for a ninety-minute round trip, though longer options are available.

As usual, the tourist office can arrange **private rooms** (❶–❸), while among the **pensions** are some with a central location, such as *Zum Birnbaum*, Mittelstr. 1 (ⓣ0 33 81/5 27 50; ❹); *Engel*, Grosse Gartenstr. 37 (ⓣ0 33 81/20 03 93; ❹); and *Gerono*, Magdeburger Str. 12 (ⓣ0 33 81/3 40 90; ❹). There are only a few **hotels** within the city: *City*, Grosse Gartenstr. 2 (ⓣ0 33 81/52 26 92; ❹); *Axxon*, Magdeburger Landstr. 288 (ⓣ0 33 81/32 10, ⓦwww.axxon-hotel.de; ❻); *Am St Gotthard*, Mühlentorstr. 56 (ⓣ0 33 81/5 29 00; ❻); and *Sorat*, Altstädtischer Markt 1 (ⓣ0 33 81/59 70, ⓦwww.sorat-hotels.com; ❼). The most convenient of the **campsites** by the lakes around the city is *Seecamp Malge* (ⓣ0 33 81/66 31 34) on the Breitlingsee, which also has bungalows for rent.

All the hotels listed above have recommendable **restaurants**. Alternatives include *Kartoffelkäfer*, Steinstr. 56, whose menu is centred on potato dishes; the fish specialist *An der Dominsel*, Neustädtischer Fischerstr. 14; and the popular excursion destination *Bismarck Terrassen*, Bergstr. 20, which commands a fine view of the city and serves really excellent local cuisine. *Domcafé*, Burghof 11, is a good choice for *Kaffee und Kuchen*.

Oranienburg

About 20km northwest of Berlin at the terminus of S-Bahn #1 is **ORANIENBURG**, a drab-looking place set apart from dozens of other towns around the capital by a monument that recalls the grimmest chapter in German history – the Konzentrationslager Sachsenhausen. The concentration camp, now officially known as the **Gedenkstätte und Museum Sachsenhausen** (daily: April–Sept 8.30am–6pm; Oct–March 8.30am–4.30pm, exhibitions Tues–Sun only; free) is in the northern suburb of Sachsenhausen, reached from S-Bahnhof Oranienburg by bus #273 or on foot after a twenty-minute walk.

A tree-lined road leads to a museum devoted to the history of the camp and special exhibitions. Just north of here is **Turm A**, the gatehouse entrance to the camp proper with a stretch of the original electrified camp fence running either side of it. Beyond is the **Apellplatz** or parade ground, where the prisoners were gathered for roll call and often kept standing for hours on end or forced to witness executions on the camp **gallows**. Behind the gallows, in four semicircular rows, were the **barrack buildings**, originally intended to hold 130 prisoners in cramped conditions but each filled by the end of the war with up to 500 men. Only two remain: one now houses a museum (dating from the GDR period), while the other is a memorial hall where documentaries are regularly shown. The positions of the other barracks are marked with granite blocks. Beyond them is an open space leading to the stylized camp **memorial**.

Many of the victims commemorated by the memorial died nearby at **Station Z**, where the Germans turned the process of executing Soviet prisoners of war into an almost industrial one, dispatching tens of thousands of men with shots to the back of the neck. At the opposite side of the camp are two surviving barrack blocks used to house **Jewish inmates**, with a special exhibition devoted to their sufferings. In 1992, these barracks were set on fire by young right-wing radicals, and the burnt walls remaining have been incorporated into the exhibit. Just beyond here are **cells** where prominent prisoners, mainly workers' leaders and patriots from the occupied countries, were held in isolation, usually pending execution. One of the inmates best known to posterity is the anti-Nazi cleric, **Pastor Martin Niemöller**, who was one of the few to survive incarceration here. At the northeast end of the camp is an exhibition devoted to the history of the camp after 1945, when it was used by the Soviets, intially for Nazis and former army officers, later for large numbers of Social Democrats who had protested about the forced merger of their party with the Communists.

The Schorfheide

The largest area of protected landscape anywhere in Germany is the **Schorfheide** to the northeast of Berlin, which occupies a total of almost 1300 square kilometres. Nearly half of this is forest; there are also some 250 lakes, plus moorland, wetland and farmland. Although the Schorfheide is distinctive enough to have gained inclusion on the UNESCO list of World Biosphere Reserves, it's better known for its set-piece attractions, which include the magnificent ruined monastery at **Chorin** and what is surely the most visually impressive technical monument in the country, the barge-lift, or Schiffshebewerk, at **Niederfinow**. When travelling between the two it's necessary to change at Eberswalde-Finow, a rather nondescript industrial town 50km from the capital.

Chorin

Some 60km from Berlin, on the main rail line to the Polish city of Szczecin, is the tiny village of **CHORIN**. Alight at Bahnhof Kloster Chorin, the first of the two train stations, to see the evocatively ruined Cistercian **Kloster** (daily: April–Oct 9am–7pm; Nov–March 9am–4pm; €3; Ⓦwww.kloster-chorin.com), set in a secluded setting in the middle of the woods by a small lake, the Amtssee. To reach it, walk all the way through the village, bearing right, then follow the forest path. Established in 1273, the monastery was constructed over the following sixty years, and is an example of Gothic brick architecture at its most daringly inventive. In the nineteenth century, Schinkel carried out major structural repairs on the long-abandoned complex, then in danger of collapse. Both the church and the monastic quarters are substantially intact, though the former now gapingly opens out directly onto the cloister – helping create a much expanded auditorium for the **concerts** which are regularly held throughout the summer. Architecturally, the finest feature is the highly idiosyncratic **facade**, the last part of the church to be built. A dazzling exercise in patterned brickwork, it contrasts sharply but effectively with the solemn grandeur of the structure behind. Also of special note are the gabled **brewery** by the entrance and the **kitchen** to its rear.

There are two **hotels** near the Kloster: *Neue Klosterschänke*, Neue Klosterallee 12 (Ⓣ03 33 66/53 10, Ⓦwww.neue-klosterschaenke.de; ④); and *Haus Chorin*, Neue Klosterallee 10 (Ⓣ03 33 66/5 00, Ⓦwww.chorin.de; ⑤). Both of these have **restaurants**; an alternative for meals is *Alte Klosterschänke*, Am Amt 9.

Niederfinow and the Schiffshebewerk

Around 10km east of the Eberswalde rail junction, in the municipality of **NIEDERFINOW**, is one of the area's more unexpected sights, the Schiffshebewerk, a barge-lift of titanic proportions on the Havel–Oder canal. It can be reached by bus from Niederfinow's Bahnhof, although it's a pleasant enough walk of only a couple of kilometres: cross the bridge near the station and head north. By far the most atmospheric approach, however, is by boat – regular **cruises** from the harbour at Niederfinow (€6) are run during the summer months by Personenschiffart Schiffshebewerk (ⓣ03 33 69/7 52 69).

The **Schiffshebewerk** (ⓦwww.schiffshebewerk.de) is used to transport barges from the western upland section of the canal down into the Oder valley and vice versa. It was opened in 1934, replacing an antiquated system of locks, and at the time of its construction was the largest structure of its kind in the world: 94m long, 27m wide and an amazing 60m high. Subsequently it became an important staging post on the canal network linking Germany and Poland, reducing the time taken to lower and raise vessels from several painstaking hours to about fifteen minutes. The lift is basically an enormous steel trough capable of accommodating a thousand-tonne barge, raised and lowered by an electric-powered system of counterweights, within a casing of steel girders. For a closer look at how it works, go up the steps on the western side of the road. These will bring you to the upper canal level and a **walkway** (March & Oct Mon–Fri 9am–4pm, Sat & Sun 9am–5pm; April–Sept daily daily 9am–6pm; Nov–Feb daily 9am–4pm; €1) that runs around the outside of the barge-lift.

The structure attracts its fair share of visitors and there's a large car park with souvenir shop and Imbiss stands in the shadow of its massive girders. If you want something more substantial to eat or drink, head back along the main road towards the Bahnhof, where there are a couple of Gaststätten and a plush modern **hotel**, *Am Schiffshebewerk* (ⓣ03 33 62/7 00 99, ⓦwww.hotel-schiffshebewerk; ❺).

Frankfurt an der Oder

Some 90km east of Berlin lies the border town of **FRANKFURT AN DER ODER**. Like so many communities along the course of the River Oder, it was split in two in 1945, with the Altstadt on the west bank remaining in German hands, while the east bank suburb became the Polish town of Slubice. As Frankfurt was almost totally destroyed during the war, it's mainly of interest as a stopover point on journeys to and from Poland. Nonetheless, it's a place with a long and distinguished history, dating back to the thirteenth century, when German merchants founded a settlement and built a wooden bridge over the Oder. Subsequently, the town developed as an important trade centre and was also home to a prestigious university, the Viadrina, which was founded in 1506 and revived in 1991 after nearly two centuries of closure.

Today the **Marktplatz** remains the focal point of the Altstadt. On its southern side is the **Marienkirche**, the biggest of all Germany's brick Gothic hall churches. Reduced to a roofless ruin during the war, and left forlorn throughout the GDR epoch, the roof has now been restored and the enormous interior is used for temporary exhibitions. Directly opposite, forming a deliberate juxtaposition of the sacred and secular, the **Rathaus** presents another exercise in virtuoso brickwork, and ranks among the most impressive town halls in Germany. Between Marktplatz and the river is the **Kleist-Museum**

(Tues–Sun 10am–5pm; €3), devoted to the life and works of the town's favourite son, the dramatist and short story writer **Heinrich von Kleist** (1777–1811). Despite his early death in a bizarre suicide pact with a woman dying of cancer, Kleist bequeathed an astonishingly varied body of literature, which speaks more forcefully to the modern reader than that of any other great German writer of his time. For displays on the archeology and history of Frankfurt and the surrounding region, head then to the **Museum Viadrina** (Tues–Sun 11am–5pm; €3; Ⓦwww.museum-viadrina.de), C.-P.-E.-Bach-Str. 11, a grandiose Prussian Junker house.

Further north, beyond the bridge to Poland, is the town's main concert hall, the **Konzerthalle C.P.E. Bach** (Ⓦwww.konzerthalle-bach.de). The building, an intact Gothic hall church, is named in honour of Carl Philipp Emmanuel Bach – son of J.S. and one of the most bizarrely idiosyncratic composers in musical history – who spent part of his life in the town. Finally, at the southern end of the Altstadt, the curious two-storey **Gertraudkirche** (Mon–Fri 8am–4:30pm) contains the treasures formerly kept in the Marienkirche, including two outstanding fourteenth-century pieces: a tall candelabra and a font adorned with 44 reliefs of Old and New Testament scenes.

Practicalities

Frankfurt's **Hauptbahnhof**, itself a border crossing point, occupies an elevated position about ten minutes' walk southwest of the Altstadt. The **tourist office** (Mon–Fri 10am–6pm, Sat 10am–12.30pm; Ⓣ03 35/32 52 16, Ⓦwww.frankfurt-oder-tourist.de) lies just west of Marktplatz at Karl-Marx-Str. 8a. **Private rooms** (❷–❸) can be booked there; in addition the town has several **pensions**, including *Am Kleistpark*, Humboldstr. 14 (Ⓣ03 35/2 38 40; ❹), and *Graham's*, August-Bebel-Str. 11 (Ⓣ03 35/4 33 54 29; ❹). There are three **hotels** in the town centre: *Gallus*, Fürstenwalder Str. 47 (Ⓣ03 35/5 61 50; ❹); *Zur Alten Oder*, Fischerstr. 32 (Ⓣ03 35/55 62 20, Ⓦwww.zuraltenoder.de; ❺); and *City Park*, Lindenstr.12 (Ⓣ03 35/5 53 20; ❻). The best **restaurant** in town is the *Ratskeller* in the historic cellars of the Rathaus, Marktplatz 2, which includes vegetarian dishes on its menu. There's also a restaurant, *Turm 24*, atop the town's lone skyscraper at Logenstr. 8, which, although a bit pricey, affords wonderful views of the surrounding greenery.

The Spreewald

The **Spreewald**, a unique forest area bisected by the River Spree, 100km southeast of Berlin, is by far the most beautiful landscape in the Land of Brandenburg, although its atmosphere can be marred by the sheer volume of visitors. It falls into two parts: the **Unterspreewald** and **Oberspreewald**, north and south of the town of Lübben respectively. Although the Unterspreewald, east of Schlepzig, is pleasant enough, the real attraction is the Oberspreewald, a 500-square-kilometre area of deciduous woodland. The woods, which are broken up in places by land given over to market gardening – the cucumbers produced here are renowned – are watered by three hundred channels (fed by the River Spree) known as *Fliesse*, and criss-crossed by man-made canals, creating an environment that Theodor Fontane described as "Venice as it might have been 1500 years ago".

Most of the local populace are Slavic **Sorbs** (also known as **Wends**; see box opposite) with their own language and traditions, and Sorbish street signs add more than a hint of exotica to an already unusual region. Unfortunately, the Spreewald was discovered a long time ago and tourists flock here in unbelievable numbers during the summer, overrunning the local Gaststätten and block-booking seats on the **punts** that ferry visitors around the area (motorized craft are banned), charging on average €3 per hour for trips which can last from anything between ninety minutes and ten hours. Nevertheless, the Spreewald really does live up to tourist-brochure hyperbole. **Walking** is just as good a way of getting around as taking a punt, but it's essential to get hold of the local *Wanderkarte*, as it's all too easy to get lost or disorientated. The provision of **accommodation** has mushroomed since the *Wende*, but if visiting in summer it's still advisable to book in advance.

Lübben (Lubin)

LÜBBEN, which is easily reached by rail from Berlin, is the first major town in the Spreewald and from its harbour it's possible to take punt trips into both the Unter- and Oberspreewald. The town also has a sixteenth-century church, the **Paul-Gerhardt-Kirche**, which is named in honour of the religious poet buried there, and a **Schloss**. Within the latter is the **tourist office** (April–Oct daily 10am–6pm; Nov–March Mon–Fri 10am–4pm; ⓣ0 35 46/30 90, ⓦwww.luebben.de), at Ernst-von-Houwald-Damm 15, where you can book **private rooms** (❷–❸). There are also several small **pensions**, the most convenient being *Am Markt*, Hauptstr. 5 (ⓣ0 35 46/32 72; ❸); while **hotels** include *Spreeblick*, Gübbener Str. 53 (ⓣ0 35 46/23 20, ⓦwww.spreeblick.de; ❺); *Spreeufer*, Hinter der Mauer 4 (ⓣ0 35 46/2 72 60, ⓦwww.hotels-in-spreewald.de; ❺) and *Stephanshof*, Lehnigksberger Weg 1 (ⓣ0 35 46/2 72 10, ⓦwww.hotel-stepahnshof.de; ❺). The **youth hostel** is at the southern edge of town at Zum Wendenfürsten 8 (ⓣ0 35 46/30 46; €11.50/14.10), while the **campsite** is across the Spree from the Schloss at Am Burglehn (ⓣ0 35 46/70 53, ⓦwww.spreewald-camping-luebben.de). All the hotels mentioned above have good **restaurants**, though the best place to eat is the *Schloss-Restaurant*, Ernst-von-Houwald-Damm 14.

The Sorbs

A West Slav tribe whose language resembles both Czech and Slovak, the **Sorbs** have lived throughout their history in the province known as **Lusatia** (Lausitz), which still maintains a tenuous position on maps of Germany. In the fifteenth century it was divided into Upper Lusatia (Oberlausitz) and Lower Lusatia (Niederlausitz): the former is now in Saxony; the latter (of which the Spreewald forms the northern part) is in Brandenburg. As many as 100,000 Sorbs still live throughout the region. There were nationalist stirrings in the nineteenth century, leading in 1912 to the formation of the *Domowina* (a word equivalent to the German *Heimat* or "homeland", a cultural and political organization which is still the main vehicle for Sorbist aspirations.

They were particularly persecuted under the Nazis when Göring proposed expelling them to turn the Spreewald into a gigantic game park stocked with elk and bison. Things improved under the GDR, when the Sorbs were allowed a degree of cultural autonomy, with their language given equal status with German. However, they were mercilessly exploited for tourist purposes: their vivid costumes and popular **festivals** added a much-needed dash of colour to that grey puritanical land. The latter include the Vogelhochzeit (Marriage of the Birds) on January 25, Carnival, horseback Easter processions and, on April 30, the Hexenbrennen, a variant of the witches' Walpurgisnacht.

Lübbenau (Lubnjow)

Perhaps a better starting point for exploring the Oberspreewald is the slightly larger town of **LÜBBENAU**, a 15km train journey southeast of Lübben. It gets incredibly crowded, though, giving the impression that all of the one million visitors who come here each year are passing through at once. Lübbenau's origins are also Slavonic, and it was defended by a wooden wall, later destroyed by the Germans who built a castle here. The original castle was in turn replaced by the Neoclassical **Schloss** visible today, which was built just after the Napoleonic Wars by Count Lynar. The Lynar family owned much of the area until 1945, after which their castle became a school; they returned to claim their seat after the *Wende*, converting it into a hotel (see below). At the **Spreewaldmuseum** at Topfmarkt 12 (April to mid-Sept Tues–Sun 10am–6pm; mid-Sept to Oct Tues–Sun 10am–5pm; €3; Ⓦwww.spreewald-web.de/museum) are comprehensive displays on the history of the town and area.

Punt trips run from either of the **harbours**, the Grosser Hafen and Kleiner Hafen. It's best to be there as early as possible (preferably by 8am) as there are very heavy crowds throughout the tourist season. The **tourist office** at Ehm-Welk-Str. 15 (March–Oct Mon–Fri 9am–6pm, Sat & Sun 10am–6pm; Nov–Feb Mon–Fri 9am–4pm; Ⓣ0 35 42/36 68, Ⓦwww.luebbenau-spreewald.de) can book **private rooms** (❷–❸). Among many **pensions** are *Höhn*, Dammstr. 38 (Ⓣ0 35 42/4 57 22; ❸); and *Lübbenauer Hof*, Ehm-Welk-Str. 20 (Ⓣ0 35 42/8 31 62; ❺). There are also three upmarket **hotels**: *Turm*, Nach Stottof 1 (Ⓣ0 35 42/8 75 80; ❻); *Spreewaldeck*, Dammstr. 31 (Ⓣ0 35 42/8 90 10, Ⓦwww.spreewaldeck.de; ❻); and *Schloss Lübbenau*, Schlossbezirk 6 (Ⓣ0 35 42/87 30, Ⓦwww.schloss-luebbenau.de; ❼). All of these have fine **restaurants**, though a good alternative is the often packed riverside *Zum grünen Strand der Spree*.

Lehde (Ledy)

One way to escape the crowds is to walk from Lübbenau (rather than take a punt) to the incorporated village of **LEHDE**, which will take about thirty minutes. Until 1931 the village could only be reached by water transport or by crossing the ice of the frozen channels in winter. Lehde's **Freilandmuseum** (daily: April to mid-Sept 10am–6pm; mid-Sept to Oct 10am–5pm; €3; Ⓦwww.spreewald-web.de/museum) is packed with information about the area's history and customs. Farmhouses typical of the region have been brought here from other parts of the Spreewald and you can see how they were constructed: the foundations were built on large stones which in turn rested on timber poles driven deep into the marshy ground. Inside, examples of furniture (look out for the large beds designed to accommodate a whole family) and household objects offer an impression of how the Sorbish populace lived during the last century.

If you don't mind paying much more than you would for similar facilities in Lübbenau, Lehde has a couple of **pensions**: *Hirschwinkel* (Ⓣ0 35 42/89 99 50; ❺) and *Quappenschänke* (Ⓣ0 35 42/89 99 60; ❺). *Café Venedig* is a good place to **eat**.

Cottbus (Chośebuz)

At the southern end of the Spreewald stands **COTTBUS**, formerly the capital of one of the three *Bezirke* into which Brandenburg was divided in GDR days. It has a long industrial tradition, the twin pillars of the local economy being the textile industry, established by Dutch settlers in the Middle Ages and later developed by Huguenot refugees, and coal mining, which was the chief cause of the city's rapid growth in the nineteenth century. Because of this pedigree, Cottbus was seen by the Communists as something of a role model for the rest of the country, though its mixture of crumbling old tenements and Stalinist-style apartment buildings was not one that many others found attractive. Since the *Wende*, however, the city has done much to make itself more appealing, and has added a new dimension to its existence by becoming the seat of a technical university.

The heart of Cottbus is the **Altmarkt**, whose impressive series of Baroque mansions dates from immediately after one of the many disastrous fires that have ravaged the town. The **Brandenburgisches Apothekenmuseum** at no. 24 (guided tours Tues–Fri 11am & 2pm, Sat & Sun 2pm & 3pm; €2) has functioned continuously as a pharmacy since 1573 and contains a number of historic interiors. A block to the south, at Mühlenstr. 12, is the **Wendisches Museum** (Tues–Fri 8.30am–6pm, Sat & Sun 2–6pm; €2), which features extensive displays on the history and culture of the Sorbs. Just north of Altmarkt is the Gothic **Klosterkirche**, though a later Gothic church, the **Oberkirche**, northeast of the Altmarkt, commands more appeal. Its high altar, fashioned in marble, wood, alabaster and sandstone, is a hymn of late Renaissance extravagance.

Between here and the Spree is the **Münzturm**, where the town's first coins were minted. It's one of three towers surviving from the old fortifications: the others are the **Lindenpforte**, through which the path from the Stadtpromenade to the Altstadt leads, and the **Spremberger Turm**, at the far end of Spremberger Strasse, which goes south from the Altmarkt.

Cottbus' star attraction, however, is **Schloss Branitz** (April–Oct daily 10am–6pm; Nov-March Tues–Sun 11am–5pm; €3.50; Ⓦwww.pueckler-museum.de) at the southeastern edge of town. This was the custom-built seat of one of the great characters of nineteenth-century Germany, Prince Hermann von Pückler-Muskau, who was the worthy successor to Lenné as landscape gardener to the Prussian court, as well as a writer, world traveller, and landowning aristocrat in his own right. The Schloss itself, designed by the Dresden architect Gottfried Semper in a tardy Baroque idiom, contains displays on the life of the prince. Directly opposite is the **Marstall** (April–Oct daily 10am–12.30pm & 1–6pm; €2), a grandiose stables building in English Gothic Revival style which now contains a collection of historic racing cars. Pückler-Muskau was himself responsible for the design of the wonderful **Schlosspark**, which features a whimsical series of buildings, including a pergola and a curious series of mock-Egyptian pyramids, one of which serves as his own mausoleum.

Practicalities

Cottbus' **Hauptbahnhof** is situated well to the southwest of the centre in a particularly unsalubrious neighbourhood, so it's worth taking tram #1 to Stadtpromenade, then walking east along Marktstrasse to the Altmarkt. The **tourist office** (Mon–Fri 9am–6pm, Sat 9am–1pm; Ⓣ03 55/7 54 20, Ⓦwww.cottbus.de) is in the Stadthalle, Berliner Platz 6.

As an overnight stop, Cottbus is less enticing than the smaller towns of the Spreewald, but plenty of **private rooms** (❷–❸) can be booked via the tourist office. There are also a number of **pensions**, with *Harzbecher*, Beuchstr. 22 (Ⓣ03 55/2 58 49; ❷), being conveniently central, while *Café Pücklerstube*,

Menzelstr. 4 (Ⓣ03 55/71 57 31; ❹), is close to the Schlosspark. Among the many **hotels** are *Zur Sonne*, Taubenstr. 7–8 (Ⓣ03 55/3 81 88 01; ❹); *Ostrow*, Wassenstr. 4 (Ⓣ03 55/78 00 80, Ⓦwww.hotel-ostrow.de; ❺); and *Sorat*, Schlossplatz 2 (Ⓣ03 55/7 84 40, Ⓦwww.sorat-hotels.com; ❼). There's also a **youth hostel**, occupying an old half-timbered house at Klosterplatz 2 (Ⓣ03 55/2 25 58; €11.50/14.10).

The choice of **restaurants** and **cafés** is also good. *Wendisches Café*, August-Bebel-Str. 82, serves Sorb dishes; *Lipa*, Wendenstr. 1, does regional specialities; *Paulaner Bräu*, Sandower Str. 57, is a Bavarian-style beer hall; while *Café Altmarkt*, Altmarkt 10, is good for either *Kaffee und Kuchen* or a full meal. **Nightlife** possibilities include *Stadtwächter*, a cosy tavern in an old watchman's house attached to the Stadtmauer at Mauerstr. 1; *Molle*, Stadtpromenade 10, with nine different beers on tap; and *Clou Nachtbar*, Oberkirchplatz 10, a bar with a dance floor. The Jugendstil Staatstheater Cottbus, Schillerplatz 1 (Ⓣ03 55/7 82 40, Ⓦwww.staatstheater-cottbus.de) presents a varied programme of **theatre** and **music**.

Travel details

Berlin-Zoologischer Garten or Ostbahnhof to: Brandenburg (frequent; 1hr); Chorin (hourly; 1hr); Cottbus (hourly; 1hr 45min); Dessau (15 daily; 2hr); Dresden (every two hours; 2hr 10min); Frankurt an der Oder (hourly; 50min); Hamburg (hourly; 2hr 40min); Hannover (hourly; 2hr 50min); Leipzig (hourly; 2hr 20min); Lübben (hourly; 1hr); Lübbenau (hourly; 1hr 10min); Munich (15 daily; 7hr 20min); Potsdam (frequent; 30min).

10

Saxony-Anhalt

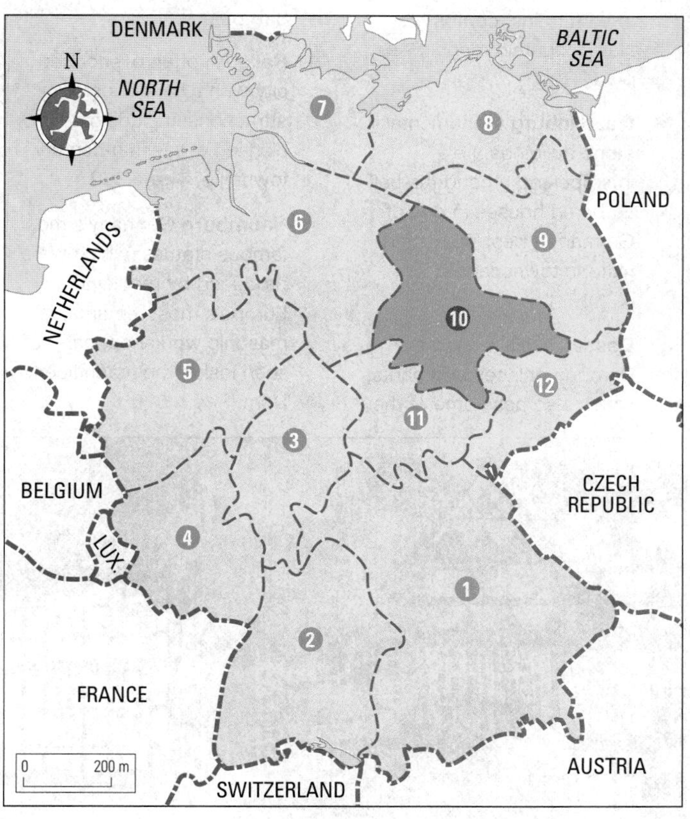

10 SAXONY-ANHALT

CHAPTER 10 **Highlights**

* **Magdeburg** The state capital has an imposing Dom and a fine setting on the River Elbe. See p.829

* **The Harz's narrow-gauge railways** Europe's largest network of narrow-gauge railways, mostly still plied by stream trains, combs the Harz mountain range. See p.844

* **Quedlinburg** Monumental stone buildings are interspersed among the half-timbered houses in one of Germany's best-preserved historic townscapes. See p.848

* **Dessau** A city ringed by Baroque palaces and parks, which also has some of the finest legacies of the Bauhaus movement. See p.859

* **Wittenberg** The small town where the Reformation was launched preserves important reminders of this crucial period of European history. See p.865

* **Halle** An often overlooked city with a varied roster of attractions, including a planned eighteenth-century township. See p.868

* **Naumburg** Germany's most famous statues, which were produced by medieval Europe's most remarkable masonic workshop, can be seen inside the magnificent Dom. See p.876

△ Half-timbered houses, Quedlinburg

10

Saxony-Anhalt

After the fall of the GDR, there was much talk about the reinstatement of the five "historic" Länder in the east. In the case of **Saxony-Anhalt** (Sachsen-Anhalt), the description was a complete misnomer: the province had first come into existence, courtesy of the Soviet military authorities, in 1947. Five years later it was abolished in line with the GDR's policy of concentrating power in the centre. Despite its dubious pedigree, there was genuine popular demand that this somewhat artificial Land should be revived, and it has duly taken its place on the new political map of the country.

The "**Saxony**" in the Land's title is a throwback to the old Prussian province of that name. It came into existence after the 1815 Congress of Vienna forced the Kingdom of Saxony to cede about half of its territories as a punishment for having supported Napoleon. These were then united with a number of secularized bishoprics Prussia had acquired after the Thirty Years War. **Anhalt** was a duchy founded by descendants of Albert the Bear, the first Margrave of Brandenburg. For centuries it was splintered into a number of petty principalities; these finally reunited in 1863, and the province served as a constituent state of Germany up to World War II.

Given its diverse make-up, it's hardly surprising that Saxony-Anhalt is the most varied of the new German Länder. The northernmost tract is the **Altmark**, the first piece of Slav territory taken over by the Germans in the great drive to the east they launched in the early medieval period. It's a varied landscape, with stretches of heath and sandy marshes in addition to farmland. The **River Elbe** defines its eastern border; the same river washes the **Börde**, the plain to the south. This has some of Germany's richest and most productive soils, and the otherwise monotonous agricultural countryside is punctuated by **Magdeburg**, the state capital and one of only two major cities in the Land.

Continuing southwards, the **Harz**, Germany's northernmost mountain chain, is approached via gentle foothills. Thickly covered with forests, the Harz proper is by far the best-known part of the Land. The home of the Walpurgisnacht legend, it's archetypally German in character, containing some outstanding scenery plus a clutch of well-preserved old towns. Beyond here, eastern Germany's largest area of heavy industry can be found in and around **Halle**, the Land's largest city, and **Dessau**, the historical capital of Anhalt. Further up the valley of the **Saale**, at the southern end of the province, the scenery becomes more rustic and the towns smaller.

Because the early history of the territories which make up Saxony-Anhalt is closely associated with missionary activity directed at heathen Slavs, the Land is unusually rich in medieval cathedrals and monasteries. The archbishops' Dom

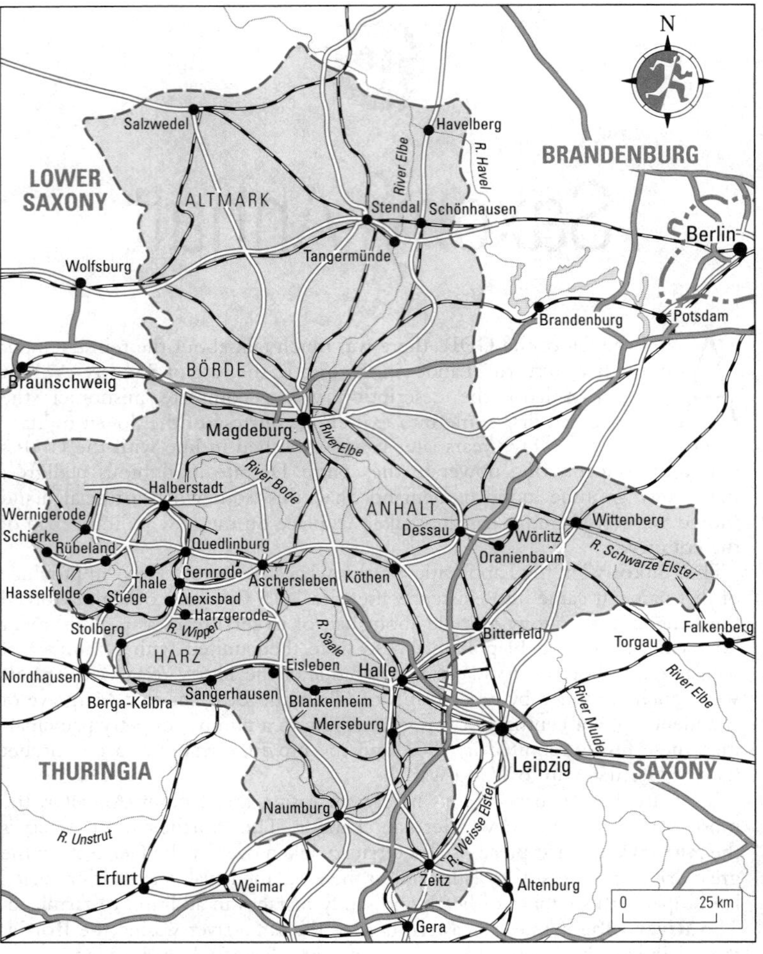

in Magdeburg ranks among the finest in all of Germany, yet its counterparts (all demoted to parish churches centuries ago) in **Halberstadt**, **Havelberg**, **Merseburg** and especially **Naumburg** are worthy rivals. For all the impact these had on the history of Germany, their influence pales beside that of **Wittenberg**, the little university town from where Martin Luther launched the Protestant Reformation. Two other modest-sized places, **Quedlinburg** and **Tangermünde**, had short spells as the capital of Germany; each retains a striking medieval appearance, and respectively has some of the best half-timbered and brick architecture to be found in the country.

Travel throughout the region presents few problems. The transport network itself is one of the main draws of the Harz, which retains the most comprehensive network of **narrow-gauge steam rail lines** to be found anywhere in Europe. The popularity of this with foreigners in GDR days is one reason the tourist facilities are so much better here than anywhere else in the Land.

Northern Saxony-Anhalt

The highlights of northern Saxony-Anhalt are thinly spread. In the Börde, **Magdeburg** is the only destination of note; as well as its Dom, it boasts a range of historical and technical monuments. The Altmark's chief town, **Stendal**, has reclaimed its role as a bustling market centre, though its monuments are rather overshadowed by those of nearby **Tangermünde**, which, but for a twist of fate, might have developed into a great metropolis. East of the Altmark lies a thin strip of land around the confluence of the Elbe and the Havel that was controversially allocated to Saxony-Anhalt rather than to Brandenburg; this includes the outstanding yet little-known town of **Havelberg**.

Magdeburg

Thanks to its pivotal position on the key communications network between Berlin and Hannover, **MAGDEBURG** received strong West German backing in its acrimonious tussle with Halle for the status of capital of Saxony-Anhalt just before unification. This support proved crucial; had Magdeburg lost out, it would have been one more reverse in what had been a long run of bad luck. Its first calamity came in the Thirty Years War: during the Catholic siege and occupation of 1631, over two-thirds of the population perished, and the city was burnt to the ground. It made a spectacular recovery after the Peace of Westphalia, but the grandiose Baroque centre which then emerged suffered a similar fate to its medieval predecessor in the Anglo-American air raids of 1945.

Under Communism, Magdeburg had the reputation of being the greyest of grey cities. The surviving historic monuments in the centre – with the partial exception of the imperious Dom, the largest church in eastern Germany – were engulfed by new buildings in the brutalist style favoured by the Stalinist regime. The antiquated infrastructure of heavy industry was retained with no thought for the environment or for the future. However, post-unification, the city, buoyed by its new role as a regional capital, underwent an astonishingly swift transformation, developing a vibrant get-up-and-go atmosphere wholly at odds with its recent past. The worst Communist eyesores have been demolished; the more palatable "wedding cake" buildings of the same period have been given colourful makeovers and the surviving Baroque mansions and grand Wilhelmine tenements gradually restored.

Arrival, information and accommodation

Magdeburg's **Hauptbahnhof** is situated just a few minutes' walk west of the city centre. There are also several suburban stations on the small S-Bahn network which can be useful if you're staying far out or intending to visit some of the outlying sights. The **tourist office** (May–Sept Mon–Fri 10am–7pm, Sat 10am–4pm; Oct–April Mon–Fri 10am–6pm, Sat 10am–1pm; ⓣ03 91/5 40 49 00, ⓦwww.magdeburg-tourist.de) is at Ernst-Reuter-Allee 12.

A large number of **hotels** have opened since the *Wende*; the majority cater to business people and are priced accordingly. However, there are some bargains to be had, and in addition plenty of **private rooms** (❷–❸) can be booked via

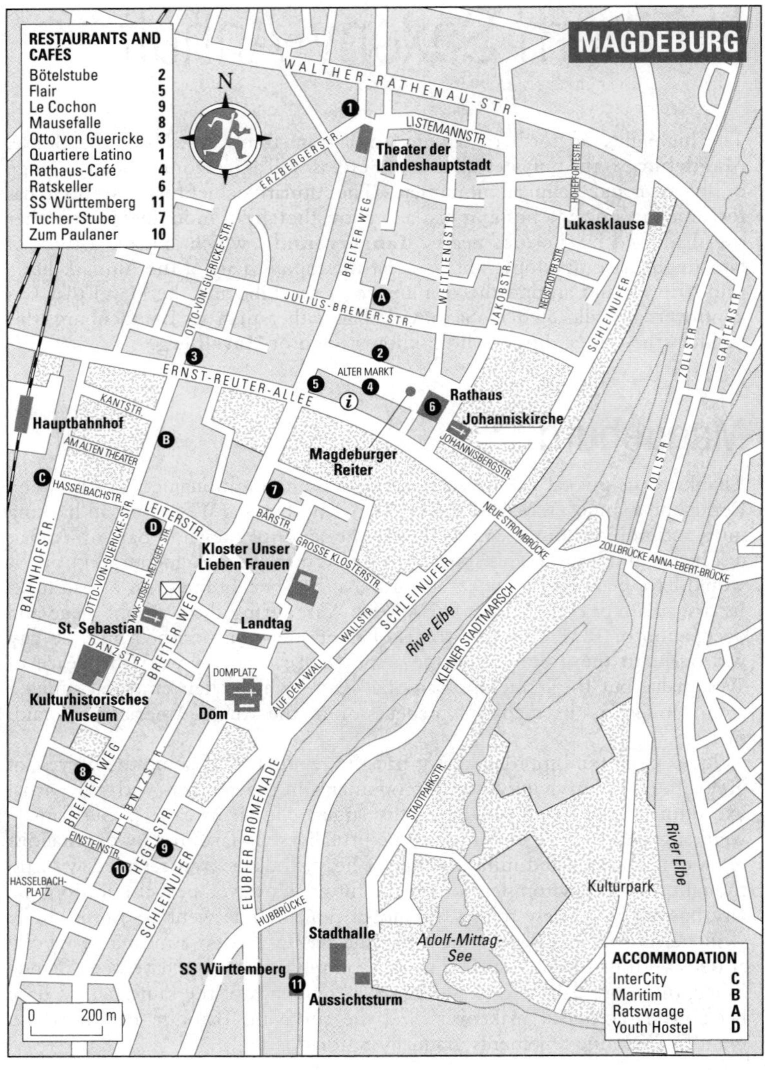

the tourist office's special number (Ⓣ03 91/5 40 49 04). The **youth hostel** is just a short walk from the Hauptbahnhof at Leiterstr. 10 (Ⓣ03 91/5 32 10 10; €18/20.70). There's a **campsite** (Ⓣ03 91/50 32 44) on the banks of the Barleber See at the extreme northern end of the city; take the S-Bahn to the station of the same name.

Hotels and pensions

Alt Prester Alt Prester 102, Prester Ⓣ03 91 /8 19 30, Ⓕ8 19 31 18. Excellent mid-range hotel located in a southeastern suburb abouth 5km from the Aldstadt on the right bank of the Elbe. Its inexpensive restaurant with beer garden is a popular excursion destination with locals. ❻

Geheimer Rat von G. Goethestr. 38 ⓣ03 91/7 38 03, ⓦwww.geheimer-rat-von-g.de. High-quality hotel, a member of the Best Western group, about 1km west of the Altstadt. Its restaurant serves bistro-style evening meals to residents only. ❻

InterCity Bahnhofstr. 69 ⓣ03 91/5 96 20, ⓦwww.intercityhotel.de. Large business-class hotel with restaurant directly opposite the Hauptbahnhof. ❼

Maritim Otto-von-Guericke-Str. 87 ⓣ03 91/5 94 90, ⓦwww.maritim.de. Gleaming modern hotel whose facilities include a restaurant, *Sinfonie*, and a swimming pool. ❾

Parkhotel Herrenkrug Herrenkrugstr. 194 ⓣ03 91/85 08 00, ⓦwww.herrenkrug.de. Magdeburg's most prestigious hotel occupies a mansion located in an Elbe-side park designed by the doyen of German landscape gardeners, Peter Joseph Lenné. Its two restaurants, *Eiskeller* (evenings only, closed Sun & Mon) and *Die Saison* (which has original Jugendstil decor), are among the very best in the city. ❽

Ratswaage Ratswaageplatz 1–4 ⓣ03 91/5 92 60, ⓦwww.ratswaage.de. Luxury modern hotel with restaurant, part of the Upstalboom chain, located on the square immediately north of Alter Markt. ❻–❽

Residenz Joop Jean-Burger-Str. 16 ⓣ03 91/6 26 20, ⓦwww.residenzjoop.de. One of the city's most attractive hotels, occupying a nineteenth-century villa, about ten minutes' walk southwest of the Dom, on the opposite side of the rail tracks. ❼

Zum Jahnring Jahnring 3 ⓣ & ⓕ03 91/5 44 07 98. Small guesthouse in a villa just beyond the southern boundaries of the Altstadt. ❸

The City

The Dom overshadows everything else in Magdeburg, but there's a variety of other sights well worth seeking out. These are scattered all over the city, with an attractive group on and around the banks of the Elbe.

The Dom

Through all Magdeburg's tribulations, the **Dom** has somehow managed to survive with little damage to its fabric. The present building is the immediate successor to the monastic foundation which Emperor Otto the Great raised in 962 to be the seat of a prince-archbishop. It's one of the country's most impressive cathedrals, its lofty Gothic architecture complemented by a truly dazzling array of **sculpture** spanning an entire millennium. There's also the bonus of a picturesquely landscaped setting above the Elbe and, as the Dom stands in isolation, there are several wonderful vantage points. One is from the vast **Domplatz**, two sides of which are lined with dignified Baroque buildings which have been refurbished to house the Land parliament and ministries. Even more spectacular is the view from the Dom's own south-side **cloister**, one wing of which is a survivor of Otto's original monastery.

Construction of the present Dom began in the early thirteenth century with the building of the ambulatory and its chapels in a primitive Gothic style still showing Romanesque influence. Soon after, the masons who had built the Swabian monastery of Maulbronn took over the construction of the main part of the chancel, introducing more refined and progressive architectural forms. They in turn were succeeded by architects who built the transepts and nave in the High Gothic manner of the great French cathedrals, doubling the length of the bays to create an impression of space, and designing large traceried windows which flood the building with light. With the addition of the north transept **porch** (or Paradise) in the mid-fourteenth century, the body of the Dom was substantially complete. However, work on the facade, whose distinctive **towers**, with their spire-crowned octagonal turrets, are such a feature of the city's skyline, wasn't concluded until 1520. Later that century, the prince-archbishop was ousted in favour of a Protestant bishop, as Magdeburg became one of the stoutest promoters of the Reformation.

The ambulatory, whose capitals are inventively carved with depictions of fabulous beasts, luxuriant foliage and contorted human heads, contains a number of notable **tombs**. Oldest of these are the bronze monuments to two twelfth-century archbishops. There's also a touching stone memorial to a fourteenth-century successor to these, Otto of Hesse, the great-grandson of St Elisabeth, and a highly elaborate Flamboyant Gothic cenotaph belatedly honouring Empress Edith, wife of Otto the Great.

This contrasts with the plain, box-like tomb of the emperor himself, which sits in solemn grandeur in the middle of the choir. Also surviving from his original cathedral are the **Easter candlestick** in front of the high altar and the beautiful coloured **marble columns** from Ravenna, which were reused to support the statues of saints placed high up between the piers of the tribune gallery. These figures, together with the unique little scenes in the niches below, belong to the period in the mid-thirteenth century when the Magdeburg workshop, along with its counterparts in Bamberg and Naumburg, was producing some of the greatest sculpture of the Middle Ages. The most arresting figure made here is the **statue of St Maurice**, placed on a pedestal on the south side of the choir; although now truncated, the masterly originality of what was probably the first representation of a black African in Western art is still very apparent. Only marginally less fine are the companion figure of St Catherine, the Dom's other patron, directly opposite, and the Annunciation group on the pillar behind. The fourteenth-century oak **choir stalls** and the fifteenth-century **rood screen** illustrate the way the Gothic style evolved over the following two hundred years.

A more substantial production of the earlier Magdeburg sculptors is the inner **portal** of the Paradise, which features superbly dramatic portrayals of the Wise and Foolish Virgins, and the enlightened Church and blindfolded Synagogue, along with a tympanum of the Death of the Virgin. Just indoors, in the northern transept, is a masterpiece of twentieth-century sculpture, the haunting **Monument to the Victims of World War I** by Ernst Barlach. It forms a surprisingly effective counterfoil to the idealized beauty of the late thirteenth-century Madonna and Child – once believed to have miracle-working powers – in the other transept.

The most intriguing feature of the nave is the freestanding **sixteen-sided chapel**, whose original function is an enigma. It contains thirteenth-century statues of a seated royal couple, leading to speculation that it's another memorial to Otto the Great and Edith, though it's more likely to be an allegorical representation of Christ as ruler of the world, with the Church as his bride. Behind it is the most significant adornment of the Protestant era, the elaborate alabaster Renaissance **pulpit** by the Thuringian sculptor Christoph Kapup. At the far end of the nave is the oldest furnishing, a porphyry **font** which belonged to Otto's cathedral, but which is thought to have originated in ancient Egypt or Assyria. Finally, under the western porch is the **Ernstkapelle**, a memorial chapel to Archbishop Ernst of Saxony, whose decision to honour himself in such a way has meant that the Dom's main entrance has been blocked up for the past five centuries, an act of megalomania partially mitigated by the sheer magnificence of the tomb, cast by the great Nürnberg bronze-founder, Peter Vischer the Elder. The chapel contains two other notable examples of late Gothic art: a seven-branched candelabrum and an alabaster statue, this time intact, of St Maurice.

The rest of the city centre

A couple of minutes' walk west of the Dom, at Otto-von-Guericke-Str. 68–73, is the **Kulturhistorisches Museum** (Tues–Sun 10am–5pm; €2; Ⓦwww.khm-magdeburg.de). This suffered heavy losses in World War II – partly, it now seems, as a result of Soviet looting. Only since the turn of the millennium have the first steps been taken towards restoring the building and its collections to their rightful position of importance. The star possession is the original of the **Magdeburg Rider** (*Magdeburger Reiter*), a secular product of the mid-thirteenth-century Dom workshop, which disputes with its Bamberg counterpart the right to be regarded as the first equestrian statue since classical antiquity. This time, it's quite likely that the mounted figure is an idealized portrait of Otto the Great, accompanied by two maidens. The paintings section contains works by Cranach and Friedrich, the decorative arts department is dominated by locally-made silverware, while some notable Flemish tapestries are the highlight of the textiles collection.

Immediately north of the museum is the former monastic church of **St Sebastian**, itself a cathedral nowadays, being the seat of the local Catholic bishop. Outwardly unprepossessing, it has a light late Gothic interior, with slender, twisting columns.

Magdeburg's oldest surviving building, the **Kloster Unser Lieben Frauen** (Tues–Sun 10am–6pm; €2; Ⓦwww.kunstmuseum-magdeburg.de), lies just beyond the northern end of Domplatz. Badly damaged during the war, this severe-looking former Premonstratensian monastery has been patiently restored to serve as a museum and cultural centre. The **Klosterkirche**, now the city's main concert hall, has a highly unusual interior, the original Romanesque forms having been clad with Gothic overlay and vaulting at around the same time as work began on the Dom. However, the most impressive part of the monastery is the **cloister**, and in particular its picturesque well chapel, nicknamed the *Tonsur*. Housed in the conventual buildings is a nationally owned collection of **small sculptures** (closes at 5pm), divided into a medieval section of mostly anonymous devotional works and a more extensive gallery of modern pieces, with examples of Rodin, Barlach and Lehmbruck, plus examples of the Socialist Realism fostered by the GDR state.

Ten minutes' walk to the north, the **Alter Markt** has regained, since the fall of Communism, its former role as the hub of day-to-day trading activity, with markets every day except Sunday. Sadly, the square itself is a shadow of its former self, with only the Baroque **Rathaus** restored to its prewar state. A recently gilded bronze replica of the Magdeburg Rider has been set up under the Baroque canopy which once housed the original. There is also a memorial to Otto von Guericke (see below), while the Gothic **Johanniskirche** rears up behind. Burnt out in 1945, the shell of this hall church was made into a war memorial, but the post-unification fever for overturning decisions made in the Communist epoch led to it being rebuilt.

Along the River Elbe

From 1680, when it was incorporated into Brandenburg-Prussia, until just before World War I, Magdeburg was one of the most strongly fortified cities in Germany. Fragments of the Prussian-built fortress system or **Festungsanlagen** can be seen all along the banks of the Elbe; the most impressive bits are those incorporating parts of the medieval city walls, which include the two towers immediately to the rear of the Dom and the section north of the Johanniskirche. The latter terminates at the **Lukasklause** (Tues–Sun 10am–5pm; free; Ⓦwww.uni-magdeburg.de), a brick-built fifteenth-century tower now housing a special display on the inventions of **Otto von Guericke**, inventor of the "Magdeburg hemispheres" that first demonstrated the power of the vacuum in the seventeenth century.

For a better perspective on these, it's well worth crossing over to the **Kulturpark Rotehorn**, a large park laid out in the 1920s between two branches of the Elbe, utilizing a smaller central arm as a boating area. Overlooking the main course of the Elbe towards the southern end of the park, across from the striking **Pferdetor** (a row of columns topped by stylized sculptures of horses), is the Bauhaus-influenced **Aussichtsturm** (Tues–Sun 10am–6pm; €1), which you can ascend by lift for a fine panoramic view. By the river is the **SS Württemberg** (Tues–Fri 10am–4pm, Sat & Sun 10am–5pm; free), a paddle steamer built at the beginning of the twentieth century, which has been preserved as a reminder of the sort of vessels used at the time Elbe shipping was at its peak; it also houses a decent restaurant. Immediately north is the city's most remarkable industrial monument, the **Hubbrücke**. This was built in the 1840s as a rail bridge on the line to Potsdam and was equipped with a turning central mechanism to allow ships to pass through. Some fifty years later, it was converted into a lift bridge, before being transformed to its present appearance in the 1930s.

To the northeast, on the right bank of the Elbe, is the **Elbauenpark** (Tues–Sun 10am–6pm; €2.60; Ⓦwww.elbauenpark.de), a permanent legacy of the big garden show of 1999. The admission ticket includes entry to the **Fetterlingshaus** (Butterfly House) and the **Jahrtausendtrum** (Millennium Tower). The latter is a remarkable slanting, tapering construction claimed as the only one of its type in the world, and was designed with the intention of being a major modern landmark for the city.

Eating and drinking

Even if Magdeburg still lags well behind comparable western German cities in the gastronomic field, it's relatively well off by ex-GDR standards. Many of Magdeburg's best restaurants are in the hotels (see pp.830–31).

Bötelstube Alter Markt 11. Gaststätte serving traditional and inexpensive Czech and German fare.
Damm-Mühle Alt Prester 1, Prester. Cosy restaurant on three floors of a converted mill in the southeast of the city. Closed Mon.
Flair Breiter Weg 20. Popular café-bar in the heart of the commercial district.
Le Cochon Hegelstr. 39. French-style bistro, one of several new eateries in the government quarter.
Mausefalle Breiter Weg 224. Student pub serving salads, pasta and steaks grilled on lava stones.
Otto von Guericke Otto-von-Guericke-Str. 104. Pleasant city-centre Gaststätte with beer garden.
Quartiere Latino Erzbergerstr. 1. Italian restaurant much favoured by audiences attending performances at the Theater des Landeshaupstadt opposite.
Rathaus-Café Markt 4. A good choice for either *Kaffee und Kuchen* or full meals.
Ratskeller Alter Markt 13. Historic restaurant under the Rathaus, with similar standards and prices to its western counterparts. Closed Mon.
SS Württemberg Heinrich-Heine-Platz. Restaurant located in Magdeburg's museum ship. Evenings only, except at weekends; closed Tues.
Tucher-Stube Breiter Weg 19. This offers Franconian cuisine and beer from the eponymous Nürnberg brewery.
Zum Paulaner Einsteinstr. 13b. Eastern outpost of the eponymous Munich brewery, serving typically hearty food and with the obligatory beer garden.

Entertainment

Elbe **cruises** are run by Weisse Flotte (Ⓣ03 91/5 43 39 26, Ⓦwww.weisseflotte-magdeburg.de) from the Petriförder landing stage near the Lukasklause. The main **theatre**, with a varied programme of drama, opera, operetta and ballet, is the Theater der Landeshauptstadt, Universitätsplatz 13 (Ⓣ03 91/5 40 64 64, Ⓦwww.theater-magdeburg.de); it's also the venue for **concerts** by the

Magdeburgische Philharmonie while the Kloster Unser Lieben Frauen (Ⓣ03 91/5 40 24 33) is used by smaller ensembles, and for vocal and choral music. In March, the legacy of the most prolific composer of all time, the Magdeburg-born **Georg Philipp Telemann**, is celebrated in a **festival** (Ⓦwww.telemann.org). In his lifetime, Telemann was considered at least the equal of his great contemporaries, Bach and Handel. His reputation in Germany is still only slightly below theirs though he is under-appreciated elsewhere.

Stendal

STENDAL, which lies 60km north of Magdeburg, is an important rail junction on the main route to the Baltic with the second-string line between Berlin and Hannover. It has maintained its historic role as the main town of the Altmark, and, despite its modest size, is positively cosmopolitan in comparison with the rest of this rural backwater.

The Altstadt comprises a surprisingly large proportion of the present-day town and retains two medieval gateways. The **Tangermünder Tor**, on Bahnhofstrasse in the southern Altstadt, has a stone lower storey dating back to the town's thirteenth-century origins; the upper part, with its characteristically fancy brickwork, is from a hundred years later. Just across the street, occupying the former Katharinenkloster, is the **Altmärkisches Museum** (Tues & Sat 1–5pm, Wed, Thurs & Fri 10am–noon & 2–5pm, Sun 11am–6pm; €2.50), which documents the history of Stendal and the Altmark region, and includes a collection of medieval religious art.

Set, in the manner of many an English cathedral, in splendid isolation in the spacious green to the west of here is the **Stiftskirche St Nikolaus**, popularly if inaccurately known as the **Dom**. It's the largest of the town's medieval churches – which display a remarkable degree of similarity with one another, reducing the favoured north German format of the brick hall church to the barest essentials, with fortress-like towers and a minimum of surface decoration. A rare touch of extravagance, however, was allowed in the north transept, with its elaborate gable and bricks patterned into a false rose window and six-sided stars. Pride of the interior is one of the most impressive sets of **stained-glass windows** in Germany – 23 in all, each dating from the fifty-year period in the middle of the fifteenth century when the church itself was erected. The twelve windows in the choir use sombre colours in a deliberate attempt to create a mystical atmosphere in the holiest part of the building; those in the nave and transepts, in contrast, sparkle like jewels. Of similar vintage are the **choir stalls**, whose misericords are vivid illustrations of the humour of the day. Also of special note are the **reliefs** of the life of Christ on the back of the rood screen, masterly Romanesque carvings retained from the church which previously stood on the spot.

From the north side of the Dom, follow Am Dom to the east, then turn right into Hallstrasse, which eventually leads to the central **Markt**. Guarding the picturesquely gabled Renaissance **Rathaus** is a weather-worn statue of Roland, almost as big as its celebrated counterpart in Bremen. However, it's only a replica of the sixteenth-century original, which was destroyed by a hurricane in 1972. Rising up behind the Rathaus is the main parish church, the **Marienkirche**, whose similarities with the Dom even extend to having Romanesque carvings adorning the Gothic rood screen. However, the main treasure is the painstakingly reconstructed sixteenth-century **astronomical**

clock. It's set underneath the organ gallery, whose frieze of paintings of the life of Christ, along with part of the instrument itself, are from the same epoch.

Breite Strasse leads north from here to the oldest quarter of town, which is dominated by the **Jacobikirche**. This church has another magnificent array of stained glass in the chancel; this time some of the windows date back to the fourteenth century. At the end of Breite Strasse, Altes Dorf leads west to the symbol of the city, the **Uenglinger Tor** (May–Sept Sat & Sun 10am–noon & 3–5pm; €1). Incredible as it seems, this lovingly crafted masterpiece of fifteenth-century patterned brickwork was built for a purely defensive role. Nowadays it provides something of an obstacle for traffic – as well as the best view of the town.

Just south of here, at Winckelmannstr. 36, the **Winckelmann-Museum** (Tues–Sun 10am–noon & 1–5pm; €2.50) has been set up in the half-timbered house where Johann Joachim Winckelmann, connoisseur and art historian, the son of the local shoemaker, was born in 1717. The rooms are devoted to displays on the life and work of the man whose writings, based on exhaustive research during a twelve-year stay in Rome, set the study of archeology and art history on a rigorous scientific footing and provided the most potent stimulus for the great flowering of German classicism in Weimar.

Practicalities

Stendal's **Hauptbahnhof** is situated just beyond the southern edge of the Altstadt. The **tourist office** (May–Sept Mon–Fri 8.30am–noon & 12.30–5pm, Sat 9.30am–3pm; rest of year Mon–Fri only; ⓣ0 39 31/65 11 90, ⓦwww.stendal.de) is in the Rathaus, Markt 1. There's a reasonable provision of **private rooms** (❷–❸). **Hotels** with a central location are *Am Uenglinger Tor*, Moltkestr. 17 (ⓣ0 39 31/68 48 01, ⓦwww.hotelstendal.de; ❹), *Postamt* 3, Hallstr. 64 (ⓣ0 39 31/71 56 47; ❺), *Altstadt*, Breite Str. 60 (ⓣ0 39 31/6 98 90, ⓦwww.altstadt-hotel-stendal.de; ❻), and *Am Bahnhof*, Bahnhofstr. 30 (ⓣ0 39 31/71 55 48; ❻). Both of the last two hotels have **restaurants**; other good places to eat are the *Ratskeller*, in the vaulted former merchants' hall under the Rathaus, and *Altstadt-Bierstube*, Mittelstr. 6.

Tangermünde

Towns languishing in centuries-long decay are a common enough feature of the Mediterranean lands, but are a rarity in Germany. **TANGERMÜNDE**, which lies at the confluence of the rivers Tanger and Havel 10km southeast of Stendal, is an exception – and a truly spectacular exception at that. When Charles IV, King of Bohemia and the most astute and successful Holy Roman Emperor of the later medieval period, acquired the Margraviate of Brandenburg in 1373, he chose this prosperous market town, a midway point on the trade routes between the Baltic and central Europe, as the second-string royal residence to Prague. Tangermünde's planned development into a national capital received a setback with the emperor's death five years later, though it continued to prosper for another hundred years, whereupon its star rapidly waned. At the beginning of the twentieth century, it became the Altmark's only industrial centre other than Stendal. The GDR regime's ideology kept it in a time warp, its skyline presenting an endearing juxtaposition of magnificent but crumbling medieval brick buildings and outdated factories.

The Town

Tangermünde's **Stadtmauer** is one of the most complete and impressive municipal defences to have survived in Germany. The north side, the first you see if you arrive in town by public transport, has been laid out as a park and is relatively unforbidding, save for the bleak cylindrical **Schrotturm** which guards the northwestern corner. Altogether more arresting is the **Neustädter Tor** on the west side. Its elaborately patterned tower is a stylistic twin of the Uenglinger Tor in Stendal and was the work of the same builders; in addition, there's a sturdy barbican, adorned with coats of arms.

The defences were particularly strong along the harbour side, in case of attack from the river. To see them to best advantage, it's well worth crossing over to the rustic pathway laid out on the opposite bank. Towards the far end of this section is another fine gateway, the **Elbtor**. The part-brick, part-timber extension suspended above its archway on the side facing the town was the home of the watchman. Subsequent expansion of the town has partially obscured the eastern side of the walls, though the oldest gateway, the **Hünendorfer Tor**, survives as a marker at the opposite end of Lange Strasse from the Neustädter Tor.

Charles IV's **Burg** was built overlooking the Elbe just outside the confines of the Stadtmauer. It was successively occupied by the Danes and the imperial forces during the Thirty Years War, and was all but destroyed in 1640 during an ultimately successful siege by the Swedes. At the beginning of the twentieth century, the ruins were made into a shady public park, to which there's free access at all times. In addition to the main gateway and two very picturesque towers, the **Amtshaus**, erected in the early years of the eighteenth century by order of King Friedrich I of Prussia, still survives. This has recently been converted into a hotel (*Schloss Tangermünde* – see p.838).

Set in its own close just to the east of the Hünendorfer Tor is the fourteenth-century **Stephanskirche**, whose mighty westwork looks more like a fortress than any of the far more decorative towers of the fortification system. Most of the rest of the exterior is equally austere, though there are occasional deft touches, such as the patterned double doorway. The hall interior, with its graceful pillars, is altogether lighter in feel. After its conversion to Protestant worship, it gained a number of intriguing adornments, including a Baroque altar which has an unusual depiction of Christ in the guise of the Lion of Judea. The early seventeenth-century **organ** is by one of the greatest-ever masters of the craft, the Hamburg builder Hans Scherer. It's especially valuable for being his only instrument to have survived relatively intact. Recitals are normally held at 4.30pm on Saturdays from mid-May to late October.

Tangermünde's other set piece is the **Rathaus**, which was built on the central Markt in the 1430s, the period when the town was at its commercial peak. Its fantastical eastern facade, bristling with pinnacles and gables, and pierced by ornate open and false rose windows, is one of the great achievements of secular Gothic architecture. The vaulted basement is given over to the **Stadtgeschichtliches Museum** (Feb–Nov Tues–Sun 10am–5pm; €1), a small local history collection. You can also see the two upstairs halls, the **Festsaal** and the **Standesamt**, upon request.

Close to the harbour, the streets are cobblestoned and still medieval in aspect. In the centre, on the other hand, are large numbers of **half-timbered houses** from the seventeenth and eighteenth centuries, some with elaborate doorways. The reason for this new building activity was that much of Tangermünde was destroyed by fire in 1617. A woman by the name of Grete Minde was made the scapegoat and burned as a witch. Over 250 years later, she became the eponymous heroine of a novel by Theodor Fontane, who used the incident to write one of his many powerful indictments of the moral injustices suffered by women.

Practicalities

Tangermünde's **Bahnhof**, which is a couple of blocks north of the Altstadt, is the terminus of a branch line from Stendal. The **tourist office** (April–Oct Mon–Fri 10am–6pm, Sat & Sun 11am–4pm; Nov–March Mon–Fri 10am–5pm, Sat & Sun 1–4pm; ⓣ03 93 22/37 10, ⓦwww.tangermuende.de) is at Marktstr. 13. Here you can book **private rooms** (❶–❷), of which the town has a reasonable number.

There are also several **pensions**, including *Am Schrotturm*, Lindenstr. 5 (ⓣ03 93 22/9 76 50; ❷), *Zur Guten Stube*, Luisenstr. 38 (ⓣ03 93 22/7 35 40; ❸), and *Zur Altstadt*, Lange Str. 40 (ⓣ03 93 22/25 18 or 9 85 00; ❸). Likewise on Lange Strasse are three **hotels**: *Alte Brauerei* at no. 34 (ⓣ03 93 22/4 41 45, ⓦwww.hotel-alte-brauerei-de; ❹), *Stars Inn* at no. 47 (ⓣ03 93 22/98 70; ❺), and *Schwarzer Adler* at no. 52 (ⓣ03 93 22/23 91, ⓦwww.schwarzer-adler-tangermuende.de; ❻). The town's top address is *Schloss Tangermünde*, Amt 1 (ⓣ03 93 22/73 73, ⓦwww.schloss-tangermuende.de; ❻). The best **restaurants** are in the last two hotels. Other possibilities are *Neustädter Platz*, Stendaler Str. 60, *Zur Post*, Lange Str. 4, and *Störtebeker*, a ship moored outside the Burg. *Reederei Kaiser*, Goethestr. 21 (ⓣ03 93 22/36 54) runs a variety of **cruises**, mostly short round trips (€7.50), but also weekly sailings to both Magdeburg and Havelberg.

Havelberg

HAVELBERG, which lies just shy of the confluence of the Havel with the Elbe some 35km northeast of Stendal, is another medieval gem as yet barely touched by overzealous restoration, or by the invasion of foreign visitors. Founded in 968 by Otto the Great as a missionary bishopric, in what was then heathen Slav territory, it proved impossible to defend and was abandoned for nearly a century and a half before being resettled by Premonstratensian monks. The town subsequently became a fishing port, even managing to establish a monopoly on fish sales on the Hamburg–Berlin trading route. When it fell to Brandenburg-Prussia after the Thirty Years War, it was developed into a major shipbuilding centre.

Dominating the town from its hillside location above the north bank of the Havel, the **Dom** is no more than a Protestant parish church nowadays. The lower part of its gaunt, fortress-like **westwork** probably belongs to the original Ottonian cathedral, which the Premonstratensians restored and expanded in the twelfth century. This building in turn was ravaged by fire a hundred years later. The subsequent reconstruction features Gothic vaulting and false arcades superimposed on the Romanesque framework. Also from this period are the monumental triumphal cross, the choir stalls and the three large column-shaped candelabra. However, the most imposing work of art is the fourteenth-century **choir screen**, which ranks among the masterpieces of monumental German sculpture. In the manner of a poor man's Bible, it bears statues of saints and twenty large reliefs illustrating the Passion of Christ, carved by a workshop familiar with both the Soft Style of Prague and the more realistic Netherlandish masters. Contemporary with the screen are two **stained-glass windows** at the end of the northern aisle, unusual grisailles with depictions of vine, acorn and ivy leaves.

Adjoining the south side of the Dom is a complex of part-Romanesque, part-Gothic brick monastic buildings. The upper storeys now contain the **Prignitz-Museum** (April–Sept Tues–Sun 10am–noon & 1–6pm; Oct–March Wed–Sun 10am–noon & 1–5pm; Ⓦwww.prignitz-museum.de; €2), which details the history of Havelberg and the vicinity from prehistoric times to the nineteenth century.

At the foot of the Dom's hill is the **Annenkapelle**, a small octagonal Gothic brick chapel with a strikingly pointed roof. From here, the Steintorbrücke leads to the compact little **Altstadt**, which occupies an island in the Havel; an alternative approach is by the Dombrücke, directly below the Dom. Crooked old houses once occupied by fisher folk and farmers line the banks of the river; even today, smallholdings and market gardening are clearly in evidence. The main attraction of the Altstadt is its constantly changing range of watery panoramic views. However, it's well worth walking all round the tightly packed little streets. Look out for the late fourteenth-century **Beguinenhaus**, whose portal has a lintel of *The Crucifixion* carved in a similar style to the Dom's choir screen. Towering above the rest of the island is the Gothic **Stadtkirche St Laurentius**, whose vivid ceiling frescoes were discovered when the wooden vaulting which had concealed them for over a century was removed.

Practicalities

Havelberg is no longer on a rail line, but there's a reasonable **bus** link with Stendal via Tangermünde; the best place to alight or embark is at the stop by the Annenkapelle. The **tourist office** (April–Sept Mon–Fri 9am–6pm, Sat & Sun 1–5pm; Oct–March Mon–Fri 9am–5pm, Sat 1–5pm; Ⓣ03 93 87/7 90 91 or 1 94 33, Ⓦwww.havelberg.de) is on the waterfront, at Uferstr. 1. In addition to **private rooms** (❶–❷), there are a few small **pensions**, including *Elb-Havel*, Genthiner Str. 5 (Ⓣ03 93 87/8 93 79, Ⓦwww.elb-havel-pension.de; ❸). However, the only **hotels** are *Lichthaus*, Lange Str. 22 (Ⓣ03 93 87/8 88 70, Ⓦwww.lichthaus-knopf.de; ❹) and *Am Schmokenberg*, Schönberger Weg 6 (Ⓣ03 93 87/8 91 77; ❹). The town's best **restaurants** are the one in *Am Schmokenberg*, plus *Güldene Pfanne*, Lehmkule 2, and the *Ratskeller*, Markt 1.

On the first weekend in September, Havelberg takes on a wholly different appearance with the arrival of over 100,000 visitors – most of whom end up camping or sleeping in their cars – for the Pferdemarkt, one of the biggest **festivals** in the former GDR. As its name suggests, it was originally a horse market, but now spawns a flea market in which anything and everything is bought and sold, a handicrafts bazaar, a giant funfair, sports events, dancing and beer tents.

The Harz region

The **Harz** mountains were formerly divided right through the middle by the notorious barbed wire frontier separating the two German states. The eastern side always had the best of the scenery, several gorgeous unspoiled old towns and an extensive network of **narrow-gauge steam rail lines**. Since unification, it has become one of the most desirable areas in the east in which to travel.

The old cathedral city of **Halberstadt** makes an impressive introduction to the region, with its Gothic Dom and carefully restored houses. Further west, **Wernigerode** is the starting point of the Harzquerbahn, the longest of the narrow-gauge rail lines; from here you can reach the peak of the **Brocken**, rendezvous of the witches on Walpurgisnacht. Scenically, the finest landscapes are to be found in the **Bode valley**, particularly around **Thale**, a great base for hiking. In the eastern foothills, **Quedlinburg** has been designated a World Heritage Sight on account of its range of half-timbered houses, and the nearby health resort of **Gernrode** has one of Germany's most distincive churches. Further east, **Eisleben** is a key attraction on the Luther trail, being both his place of birth and death.

Halberstadt

Set in the gentle foothills of the Harz, about 55km southwest of Magdeburg, **HALBERSTADT** is one of the oldest cities in eastern Germany, having been established as a bishopric by Charlemagne at the turn of the ninth century. It was also considered one of the most beautiful, until it was devastated by an Anglo-American air raid in the closing days of World War II. The Communists restored some showpieces, but demolished the ruins of others which interfered with the creation of a new Stalinist-style commercial centre. Unification has heralded a face-lift: Halberstadt was one of five cities granted special government funds for restoration, and has used this for an extensive programme of cleaning its old buildings, and for erecting copies of key landmarks lost in the war.

Arrival, information and accommodation

Halberstadt's **Hauptbahnhof** is situated well to the east of the centre, take tram #1 or #2 as the walk is boring. There are also a couple of suburban stations, including one for Spiegelsberge. The **bus station** is about midway between the Hauptbahnhof and the Markt, while the **tourist office** is at Hinter den Rathause 6 (May–Oct Mon–Fri 9am–6pm, Sat 10am–2pm, Sun 10am–1pm; Nov–April Mon–Fri 9am–6pm, Sat 10am–1pm; ⓣ0 39 41/55 18 15, ⓦwww.halberstadt.de).

There's now a reasonable choice of **hotels** and **pensions**, thanks to the opening of a number of new establishments. Otherwise, you should be able to find a **private room** (❷–❸) via the tourist office. The **campsite**, *Camping am See*, is on the right bank of the Halberstädter See at the north-eastern edge of the city at Warmholzberg 70 (ⓣ0 39 41/60 93 08, ⓦwww.camping-am-see.de).

Hotels and pensions

Abtshof Abtshof 27a ⓣ0 39 41/6 88 30, ⓦwww.abtshof-halberstadt.de. This new guest-house in a half-timbered Altstadt house offers excellent value. ❺

Am Grudenberg Grudenberg 10 ⓣ0 39 41/6 91 20, ⓦwww.hotel-grudenberg.de. Another fairly recent venture, this hotel is again in a half-timbered building, and includes a sauna and fitness room among its facilities. ❹–❺

Antares Sternstr. 6 ⓣ0 39 41/60 02 50, ⓦwww.hotel-antares.de. New, custom-built business-class hotel with restaurant (closed Sun evening) in the west of town. ❺

Halberstädter Hof Trillgasse 10 ⓣ0 39 41/2 70 80, ⓦwww.hotel-halberstaedter-hof.de. High-class hotel and restaurant in a renovated half-timbered building. ❻

Heine Kehrstr. 1 ⓣ0 39 41/3 14 00, ⓦwww.hotel-heine.de. Newish hotel, with restaurant and Hausbrauerei, located close to the Hauptbahnhof. ❼

Jagdschloss In den Spiegelsbergen ⓣ0 39 41/56 88 88. The hunting lodge in the Spiegelsberge is home to a small hotel and a long-established restaurant. ❹

Parkhotel Unter den Linden Klamrothstr. 2 ⓣ0 39 41/60 00 77, ⓦwww.pudl.de. Occupying a villa built according to the principles of the British Arts and Crafts movement, this was, until recently, unchallenged as Halberstadt's top hotel. It remains among the best in town – and the same is true of its restaurant. ❻

The City

Most of Halberstadt's prime attractions are grouped together on the spacious elliptical **Domplatz**. It suffered as much from bomb damage as the rest of the city, but monopolized the postwar restoration funds and ranks among the country's most impressive squares. Below it is the lower town whose half-timbered houses are gradually reappearing in pristine shape after restoration. Another attractive corner is the **Spiegelsberge** hill range at the extreme southern edge of the city.

The Dom and Domschatz

Halberstadt's **Dom** is the only one in Germany to conform to the pure Gothic forms established in the great French cathedrals. The only exception to this is the facade. Its lower storeys were built in the early thirteenth century by the same team of masons engaged on the archbishop's Dom in Magdeburg, while the current look of the towers is the result of a neo-Gothic remodelling at the very end of the nineteenth century. There was a long lull before work on the main body of the building got under way, and the whole project took the better part of three hundred years to complete.

Placed proudly atop its rood screen is the Dom's greatest work of art, a late Romanesque wooden **triumphal cross**. Elsewhere, the pillars are adorned with unusually characterful **statues** of saints and biblical figures, the most eye-catching being the unashamedly sensual pair of Adam and Eve in the transept. The ensemble of **stained-glass windows** in the choir and the ambulatory is among the most complete in the country. The earliest and finest are the five large lancets in the apsidal Marienkapelle, which date from 1330. Also of special note is the one in the south ambulatory illustrating the life of Charlemagne, the Dom's original founder.

One of the richest treasuries in Germany, the **Domschatz** (guided tours April–Oct Tues–Fri at 10am, 11.30am, 2pm & 3.30pm, Sat at 10am, noon & 2pm, Sun at 11.30am & 2.30pm; Nov–March Tues–Fri at 11.30am & 2.30pm, Sat & Sun at 11.30am, 1pm & 2.30pm; donation expected) is housed in the cloister and its dependencies; entrance is via the doorway on the southeast side. The most valuable items are the textiles, and in particular three twelfth-century **tapestries** which are among the oldest in existence. One tells the story of the patriarch Abraham, another is dedicated to the Apostles, while the third shows Charlemagne with philosophers of classical antiquity. From the same period are two outstanding pieces of **woodcarving** – *The Seated Madonna*, which was probably made in the same workshop as the great triumphal cross, and a cupboard painted with a depiction of *The Visitation*. The **treasury** items include the fourth-century *Consular Diptych* from Rome and the Byzantine *Weihbrotschale*, a magnificent gilded silver dish for consecrated bread which was brought here by a crusader. Also included on the tour is a visit to the **Kapitelsaal**, the only surviving part of the Romanesque Dom.

The Domplatz

The two long sides of Domplatz are lined with the **Kurien**, the houses of the members of the Dom chapter. Oldest of these is the **Dompropstei**, the elegant Renaissance mansion in the middle of the south side, which marries two very disparate styles in its Italianate arcaded lower storey and archetypally German half-timbered upperwork.

A similar architectural mix is found in the **Gleimhaus** (Mon–Fri 9am–4/5pm, Sat & Sun 10am–4pm; €2.50 including admissions to the Städtisches Museum, the Heineanum and the Schraube Museum) at the far northeast corner of the square. It was the home of the eighteenth-century poet **Johann Wilhelm Ludwig Gleim**, who served as secretary to the Dom for 56 years, and has been preserved as one of the earliest – and best – literary museums in the country. A prolific letter-writer, he maintained contact with almost all the great and good in the German society of his day. To celebrate his range of contacts, he hit upon the idea of creating a **Freundschaftstempel** (Temple of Friendship), commissioning 150 portraits, which are hung throughout the first-floor rooms.

Next door, the stately Baroque **Domdechanei** is now a medical school. The slightly more modest palace next to it houses the **Städtisches Museum** (Tues–Fri 9am–5pm, Sat & Sun 10am–5/6pm; same ticket as the Gleimhaus), which documents the history of the town, including material on the buildings lost in the bombings. However, the exhibits in the main building are overshadowed by those in the garden extension, the **Heineanum** (same hours and ticket). Greeting you on entry are two spectacular dinosaur skeletons, thought to be up to 220 million years old, found during excavations in the town. The rest of the collection is devoted to ornithology, with stuffed birds of the Harz region on the ground floor and an international display upstairs.

Forming a counterbalance to the Dom at the western end of Domplatz is the Romanesque **Liebfrauenkirche**, formerly an Augustinian collegiate church. The main feature of the exterior is the roofline, with the two octagonal towers with pointed spires at the east end forming a contrast with the pair of "bishops' mitres" on the facade. Inside are two more products of the school of sculptors active here in the early thirteenth century. Suspended on high is another **triumphal cross**, with a youthful-looking Christ in a strikingly classical pose. Even more impressive is the **choir screen**, a rare work in stucco which still preserves its original polychromy; it features realistic portraits of Christ, the Virgin and the Apostles, plus decorative friezes carved with a gossamer sense of delicacy. Look out also for the **Barbarakapelle**, whose walls are covered with a cycle of late fourteenth-century frescoes.

Set in an idiosyncratic position in front of the church, the Gothic **cloister** (Mon–Fri 9am–4pm; free) has been made into a small open-air museum, with decorative fragments from some of the many half-timbered houses destroyed in 1945. Adjoining it to the south is the **Petershof**, the massive former bishops' palace, entered via a handsome Renaissance portal.

The rest of the centre

The **lower town** (Unterstadt) on the north side of Domplatz has a confusingly mazy layout, with some of the streets following quasi-circular routes. This quarter, which has most of the surviving **half-timbered houses**, fell into shocking disrepair in the 1970s, eventually taking on the appearance of a ghost town as the inhabitants were evacuated to ugly new apartment buildings nearby. Soon after the revolution, private citizens began buying up the properties, and many have been turned into dream homes. A few showpieces had previously been restored by the GDR state, prominent among them being the mansion at Voigtei 48. Its courtyard wing, now the **Schraube Museum** (Tues–Sun 10am–4pm; same ticket as the Gleimhaus), formerly the home of a wealthy burgher family, was bequeathed to the city as a time capsule of life at the turn of the twentieth century.

Another half-timbered building well worth seeking out is the **Johanniskirche**, which lies in a peaceful garden just off Westendorf, the busy street immediately to the south of Domplatz. This rustic-looking church, built for a Protestant congregation at the end of the Thirty Years War, has a disarmingly artless appearance from the outside, with its barn-like roof and stumpy detached belfry. Inside, however, it's surprisingly dapper, the coffered ceiling, galleries and pulpit all finely carved in late Renaissance style.

To the east of Domplatz lies the **Markt**. The ruined buildings on this square, including the Gothic **Rathaus**, were bulldozed after the war in favour of a windswept piazza which had no apparent function until open-air markets returned after the fall of Communism. In 1998, after a building period lasting just sixteen months, the Markt became a fully fledged square once again, complete with a reproduction of the demolished Rathaus. The sole original building is the severe Gothic **Martinikirche**, which was the local rallying point during the *Wende* of 1989 – an appropriate choice, as it had been built by the citizens as a deliberate statement of civic pride in opposition to the prince-bishops' Dom across the road. Indeed, the two towers, linked by a lookout gallery, were a key part of the city's defences, with the huge fifteenth-century **statue of Roland** underneath as a good luck charm. The church's furnishings include an elaborate Renaissance **pulpit** and an early fourteenth-century bronze **font** resting on symbolic representations of the four rivers of Paradise and adorned with brightly coloured scenes from the life of Jesus.

The Spiegelsberge

At the southern edge of the city, reached by tram #2 or stopping train, is the range of hills known as the **Spiegelsberge**. Following a visit to the famous gardens of Wörlitz, the poet Gleim had the idea of creating something similar in Halberstadt. The result was the construction here of a number of follies which, while falling short of their great model, nevertheless make for a pleasing diversion. Centrepiece of the complex is the **Jagdschloss**, now a hotel and restaurant (see p.841). Ask to see inside the cellars, whose Renaissance doorway and great vat – the second largest in Germany – were brought here from the former country house of the defunct bishopric. Other attractions include a mausoleum, a grotto, a memorial column and the **Belvedere**, an observation tower (free access) built against a romanticized rocky backdrop, which commands a fine distant view of the city.

Eating and drinking

Alt Halberstadt Voigtei 17–19. Café-restaurant with beer garden offering local speciality dishes. Closed Mon.
Alt Westendorfer Hanse Haus Westendorf 16. Large complex of eateries including a bistro, a café, a beer bar and a cellar restaurant which offers "medieval" dishes.
Am Kühlinger Tor Kühlingerstr. 24. Good traditional Gaststätte.
Galerie Café 1580 Lichtengraben 15. Recommendable place for *Kaffee und Kuchen*, with the bonus of exhibitions of contemporary art on the walls.
Kreuzgang Domplatz 5. The eclectic menu here includes plenty of vegetarian dishes.
Museumscafé Domplatz 36. Pleasant café with garden which offers inexpensive light meals.

Wernigerode and around

Known as "the colourful town in the Harz" because of the kaleidoscopic paintwork on its half-timbered buildings, **WERNIGERODE** has by far the most animated atmosphere to be found in the region. In part, this is due to the fact that it's no stranger to international tourism – in GDR days, it was the only place in the Harz where Westerners were encouraged to stay. This led to an influx of steam-train buffs from all over the world, who came to ride the Harzquerbahn, the longest and most scenic **narrow-gauge rail line** in the country (see box below). Wernigerode is its northern terminus, and the sight of antiquated locomotives puffing their way through the streets before beginning their ascent into the mountains remains the most enduring image of a town plentifully endowed with picturesque corners.

The Harz's narrow-gauge railways

A great way to see the countryside of the Harz and visit some out-of-the-way places is to take a ride on its historic narrow-gauge rail network. Covering over 130km, it's the longest of its type in Germany and carries one million passengers a year on a fleet of steam and diesel locomotives.

The network consists of three lines – the **Harzquerbahn**, **Brockenbahn** and **Selketalbahn** – all run by Harzer Schmalspurbahnen (Harz Narrow-Gauge Railways; ⓦwww.hsb-wr.de). From Wernigerode, it costs €8 single, €14 return for the full Harzquerbahn route to Nordhausen; €10 single, €18 return to Gernrode, including the entire main stretch of the Selketalbahn; and €14 single, €22 return to the Brocken. A better alternative to the last-named is a €24 ticket which allows one further journey anywhere else on the network. Additionally, various **passes** for unlimited travel are available. For adults, these cost €35 for three days, €40 for four days, €50 for five days; children are charged half-price. Also available is a €60 **day ticket**, which can be used by two adults and up to four children.

The Harzquerbahn

One of Europe's most memorable rail lines, the **Harzquerbahn** travels the 60.5km between Wernigerode and Nordhausen in Thuringia. Up to five trains per day make the complete trip; many others cover shorter stretches. Most of the locomotives used are steam trains built in the 1950s, but diesels, to the horror of purists, were introduced in 1988.

The first stop, Westerntor, is located just outside the eponymous medieval gateway at the western end of the Altstadt; it's a handy place to pick up the train if you don't want to trail down to the Hauptbahnhof. After leaving Wernigerode, the train makes an exhilarating climb – maintaining an almost constant one in thirty gradient – to its highest point at **Drei Annen Hohne**. Here is the junction with the Brockenbahn; it's also the place to alight if you want to follow the 10km trail up the other main mountain in the area, the Hohneklippen (908m). The line then descends to the villages of **Elend** and **Sorge**, whose names ("Misery" and "Sorrow") seemed particularly appropriate in GDR days, when they found themselves right up against the notorious frontier between the two Germanys. Indeed, the train used to travel within a few metres of the electrified barbed wire on this stretch, and guards kept a wary eye on passengers' behaviour. Only the markings on the trees now indicate where the border used to be. After climbing again to the little resort of **Benneckenstein**, the train begins its rapid descent to Nordhausen,

The town

The town clusters along the valleys of the Holtemme and Zillerbach, with the Altstadt lying just to the east of their confluence. From the streets of the Altstadt, the striking silhouette of the Schloss, perched high on a hill at the southern end of town, can often be seen looming in the background. Immediately beyond the Schloss, the thickly wooded slopes of the Harz mountains begin to unfold, and even within the boundaries of the town there are marked walking trails which give a good idea of the characteristic scenery and vegetation of the range.

Wernigerode's pride and joy is the **Rathaus** on Marktplatz, a building of stridently pictorial qualities that could only belong in Germany. The bright-orange facade, with sharply pointed lead steeples sprouting from resplendent double-storey oriels, represents the final phase of Gothic in the mid-sixteenth century.

crossing into Thuringia just before the junction with the Selketalbahn at **Eisfelder Talmühle**.

The Brockenbahn

From Drei Annen Hohen, the **Brockenbahn** – which was put back into operation in 1992, having been mothballed for most of the GDR era – takes fifty minutes to travel the winding 19km-route up to the peak of the legendary **Brocken** (see p.847). In the process, it climbs 582m – no mean achievement, considering that the trains are not equipped with gears. The terminus, the Brockenbahnhof, lies at 1125m, and is thus the highest narrow-gauge station in Germany. While this trip – which offers wonderful panoramic views of the Nationalpark Hochharz (Upper Harz National Park) en route – is worth making at any time of year, it's particularly atmospheric in winter, when the upper ranges of the mountains are blanketed with snow.

The Selketalbahn

The **Selketalbahn,** named after the peaceful valley of the **River Selke**, runs the 35km between **Gernrode** (see p.854) and **Stiege**. Built in 1887, the line is plied by a number of antique locomotives, among them a *Mallet* of 1897, the oldest still-functioning train in Germany; as with the Harzquerbahn, (relatively) modern diesels have been introduced as well.

After leaving Gernrode the route goes through secluded lakes and wooded countryside to reach the Selke at Mägdesprung, 10km to the south. A couple of stops further on is **Alexisbad**, a curious little resort whose spa buildings are an illustration of the Romantic movement's infatuation with chinoiserie. From here there's a three-kilometre branch line (served by four trains a day) to **Harzgerode**. For several decades this town was the capital of a minute principality of the House of Anhalt – hence the late Renaissance Schloss, which, with the half-timbered Rathaus and the slate-towered Marienkirche, gives the place an air of grandeur wholly inconsistent with its size.

Three trains a day go all the way to **Stiege**, where the link with the Harzquerbahn, 8km away at Eisfelder Tamühle, was reinstated in 1984. Here you can choose between continuing on the two through trains to the Harzquerbahn's southern terminus at Nordhausen; going as far as Eisfelder Talmühle, then changing to the service north to Wernigerode; taking the five-kilometre-long branch line to Hasselfelde; or returning with the train to its shed in Gernrode.

On the western side of the Markt is the **Gothisches Haus**, another richly decorated building, originally the home of a wealthy fifteenth-century burgher family. Since the middle of the nineteenth century, it has been a restaurant, and latterly a hotel as well. At no. 5 on Klintgasse is the **Teichmühle**, a seventeenth-century mill popularly known, for obvious reasons, as "The Leaning House of Wernigerode". The Neoclassical mansion at no. 10 on the same street houses the **Harzmuseum** (Mon–Sat 10am–5pm; €2), which features displays on the town's half-timbered houses and their construction, as well as on the history, geology, flora, fauna and industries of the Harz region.

Just south of here is the **Silvestrikirche**, the parish church of the Altstadt. Far more remarkable than the church itself is its peaceful close, the **Oberkirchhof**, which is lined with a beautiful and varied group of houses that range from two to four hundred years old. Particularly outstanding is no. 13, the **Gadenstedtsches Haus**, a late Gothic half-timbered construction to which was added a spectacularly protruding upper-storey oriel in High Renaissance style.

On **Kochstrasse**, at the southernmost end of the Altstadt, can be seen the more modest dwellings of the local craftsmen. Notwithstanding its three storeys, no. 43 is the smallest house in town. Its "main" level, consists of a single room with a floor space of just 10 square metres. Another street worth seeking out is **Hinterstrasse**, a block north of the Markt, which has the oldest houses in town, some of which date back to the 1400s.

Much the most imposing street, however, is **Breite Strasse**, the pedestrianized main shopping thoroughfare leading east from the Markt. Despite some losses in a 1944 air raid, it preserves an almost uninterrupted array of high-quality vernacular architecture. Oldest house is the late sixteenth-century merchant's residence at no. 4, which was given an improbable but effective Jugendstil interior refit as a Viennese-style café. Even more eye-catching is the **Krummelsches Haus** at no. 72, whose half-timbering is all but obscured by the exuberant Baroque carvings which cover almost all its facade. At no. 95 is the **Krell'sche Schmiede** (Wed–Sat 10am–4pm; €2.50; Ⓦwww.schmiedemuseum-wernigerode.de), decorated with horseshoes to indicate its function as a smithy, an uninterrupted tradition dating back over three hundred years.

The **Schloss** (May–Oct daily 10am–6pm; Nov–April Tues–Fri 10am–4pm, Sat & Sun 10am–6pm; €4.50; Ⓦwww.schloss-wernigerode.de), a Romantic fantasy which almost completely replaced the original fortress, was the brainchild of Count Otto of Stolberg-Wernigerode, one of Bismarck's closest cronies. Although the architecture is pseudo-Gothic and Renaissance in style, there's nothing fake about the furnishings, which include valuable pieces ranging from the thirteenth to the nineteenth centuries, many of them brought from the former count's first-string residence of Stolberg. Especially notable are two works in the **Schlosskapelle** – an embroidery dedicated to St Mary Magdalene woven around 1250 and the late fifteenth-century retable carved by Ulrich Mair. The other big attraction is the **view** over Wernigerode and the Harz from the ramparts.

Practicalities

Wernigerode's **Hauptbahnhof** – which, in addition to being the terminus of the Harzquerbahn, has mainline services to Magdeburg via Halberstadt – lies about fifteen minutes' walk north of the town centre. Alongside is the **bus station**. The **tourist office** (Mon–Fri 9am–5/6pm, Sat & Sun 10am–3pm; Ⓣ0 39 43/63 30 35, Ⓕ0 39 43/63 20 40, Ⓦwww.wernigerode-tourismus.de)

is at Nicolaiplatz 1. There's the usual **private room** (①–②) booking service, though this has competition from the *Zimmervermittlung* agency at Breite Str. 70 (daily 10am–8pm; Ⓣ0 39 43/60 60 00, Ⓕ0 39 43/60 61 61, Ⓦwww.t-online.de/home/schlossbahn).

Among many good-value **pensions** are *Oberbeck*, Hilleborchstr. 4 (Ⓣ0 39 43/63 26 62; ③), *Zur Neuen Quelle*, Friedrichstr. 129 (Ⓣ0 39 43/63 27 25; ③), *Hasseröder Hof*, Amtsfeldstr. 33a (Ⓣ0 39 43/63 25 06, Ⓦwww.hasseroeder-hof.de; ④), and *Altstadt-Café*, Grüne Str. 48 (Ⓣ0 39 43/60 10 19 or 63 27 83, Ⓦwww.pension-gellert.de; ④). There's a wide choice of **hotels**, mostly in grand half-timbered buildings, including *Zur Tanne*, Breite Str. 57–59 (Ⓣ0 39 43/63 25 54; ③–⑤), *Schossblick*, Burgstr. 58 (Ⓣ0 39 43/63 20 04; ⑤), *Zur Post*, Marktstr. 17 (Ⓣ0 39 43/6 90 40, Ⓦwww.hotel-zur-post-wernigerode.de; ⑥), *Weisser Hirsch*, Am Markt 5 (Ⓣ0 39 43/60 20 20, Ⓦwww.hotel-weisser-hirsch.de; ⑥–⑧), and *Gothisches Haus*, Am Markt 2 (Ⓣ0 39 43/67 50, Ⓦwww.tc-hotels.net; ⑧–⑨). The local **youth hostel** is at Am Eichberg 5 (Ⓣ0 39 43/60 61 76; €15/17.70) in the incorporated village of Hasseröde.

All the recommended hotels have **restaurants**, though they face strong competition from the *Ratskeller* under the Rathaus, which is as good as any in eastern Germany. *Café Wien*, Breite Str. 4, is the obvious place to go for ice cream or coffee; *Krummmelsches Haus*, Breite Str. 72, is a café with a somewhat wider menu. Wernigerode's *Hasseröder* **beer** ranks high by eastern standards; its premium product is called *Pilsator*. The town has a number of **festivals**, including the Weintage towards the end of May, the Rathausfest in late June and the Schützenfest in mid-July.

The Brocken

Southwest of Wernigerode is the celebrated peak of the **Brocken** (1142m), meeting place of the witches on **Walpurgisnacht** (April 30), an event vividly described in the first part of Goethe's *Faust*. The legend seems to have arisen at least partly as a result of the so-called "spectre of Brocken" – when the sun is low, it casts magnified silhouettes from the peak onto clouds hanging around the lower neighbouring mountains. Walpurgisnacht is somewhat oddly named after St Walburga, an eighth-century English-born missionary whose name is evoked as a protection against evil spirits; however, it seems she gained this role through her name having been confused with that of Waldborg, the pagan goddess of fertility.

Throughout the entire history of the GDR, the Brocken's mystique was increased by the fact that it was a restricted military area used for border surveillance activities, with Westerners forbidden to come anywhere near it. Such is its impact on the German consciousness, however, that it was made accessible to walkers within a month of the fall of the Berlin Wall. Soon afterwards work began on restoring the Brockenbahn, a **narrow-gauge railway** (see box, pp.844–45) branching off from the Harzquerbahn, and the full length of this, from Drei Annen Hohne to the summit of the mountain, was put back in operation. Near the terminus, a curious domed building, nicknamed the Moschee (Mosque), houses the **Brockenmuseum** (daily 9.30am–5.30pm; €4; Ⓦwww.brockenmuseum.de), and has displays on the geology, history and legends of the peak. Alongside is *Der Brockenwirt* (Ⓣ03 94 55/1 20, Ⓦwww.brockenherberge.de; ④), a **hotel** with restaurant.

Of the many other paths up the mountain, the most atmospheric is that from Torfhaus in Lower Saxony, which offers the best views of the peak. Another favourite hiking base is **SCHIERKE** which has a station on the Brockenbahn line, and which can also be reached from Wernigerode in about forty minutes by bus. This resort village has a **youth hostel** at Brockenstr. 48 (Ⓣ03 94 55/5 10 66; €15/17.70), and is amply endowed with **private rooms** and **pensions** (❶–❸). There are also several **hotels**, including *König*, Kirchberg 15 (Ⓣ03 94 55/3 83 or 5 10 56, Ⓦwww.harz-hotel-koenig.de; ❸), *Brockenscheideck*, Brockenstr. 49 (Ⓣ03 94 55/5 10 37, Ⓦwww.harz-hotel-brockenscheideck.de; ❺), and *Waldschlösschen*, Hermann-Löns-Weg 1 (Ⓣ03 94 55/86 70, Ⓦwww.waldschloesschen-schierke.de; ❻). A full accommodation list is available from the **tourist office** (daily 8.30am–4.30pm; Ⓣ03 94 55/3 10, Ⓦwww.schierke-am-brocken.de) at Brockenstr.10.

Quedlinburg

QUEDLINBURG, 14km southeast of Halberstadt, is one of the most remarkable places in all of Germany – over 1600 of its buildings are listed as being of historic interest, and the entire town has been declared a World Heritage Site by UNESCO. Although the big set pieces are all hewn out of a whitish sandstone which has taken on a grey patina, the town's character is defined by the **half-timbered houses** which line almost all its streets. The full diversity of this quintessentially German architectural form is on view, with examples ranging from the fourteenth to the nineteenth century. Thankfully, the GDR authorities saw Quedlinburg as a great national asset. The factories the state's dogma deemed essential were confined to the outskirts and have caused only a modest degree of pollution. This has helped to ensure that Quedlinburg is the ideal combination of a genuine, living community in a stunning visual setting, which has avoided the fate – suffered by so many of its western German counterparts – of becoming over-reliant on tourism.

Quedlinburg owes its distinctive silhouette to the buildings on the **Burgberg**, the larger of the two hills at the southern end of town. In the early part of the tenth century this became the headquarters of the German nation when the expansionist drive to the east was begun by the Saxon king, **Henry the Fowler** (Heinrich der Vogler). He built a palace here, which on several occasions hosted meetings of the Imperial Diet. On his death in 936, his widow **Mathilde** established a collegiate foundation for aristocratic women, which survived until the Napoleonic suppression. Its abbesses effectively controlled the town which grew up in the valley below. When it attempted to assert municipal independence by joining the Hanseatic League in the fifteenth century, the abbesses succeeded in re-establishing ecclesiastical dominance – hence the reason Quedlinburg never developed into a major city.

Arrival, information and accommodation

Quedlinburg's **Bahnhof** and **bus station** are side by side to the east of town. The Neustadt lies just over the Bode, while the Altstadt is a ten-minute walk away straight ahead along Bahnhofstrasse, then left into August-Wolf-Strasse. However, the most atmospheric approach to the town is to follow the Bode upstream towards the Burgberg; many picturesque panoramic views open up en route. The **tourist office** (April–Sept Mon–Fri 9am–7pm, Sat 10am–4pm, Sun 10am–3pm; Oct–March Mon–Fri 9.30am–6pm, Sat 10am–2pm; Ⓣ0 39 46/90 56 24, Ⓦwww.quedlinburg.de or www.quedlinburg-info.de) is at Markt 2.

The **youth hostel** has a central location at Nuendorf 28 (ⓣ0 39 46/81 17 03; €13.50/17.20). There's a plentiful supply of **private rooms** (❶–❸) on the books of the tourist office, which also rents out two of the town's medieval towers as holiday homes. A good stock of **hotels** includes many in fine old buildings.

Hotels and pensions

Am Brühl Billungstr. 11 ⓣ0 39 46/9 61 80, ⓦwww.hotelambruehl.de. Classy hotel in a historic building that was formerly a barn, then a spirits factory. Appropriately, a home-made liqueur, *Harzgeist*, can be ordered in its Weinstube (closed Sun), one of the best restaurants in town. ❻

Am Dippeplatz Breite Str. 16 ⓣ0 39 46/77 14 11, ⓕ70 50 22. Moderately priced hotel in the heart of town. ❹

Engelhardt Weberstr. 24 ⓣ0 39 46/70 54 07, ⓕ91 57 48. Good-value pension in a large Neoclassical villa at the edge of the town centre. ❸

Schlossmühle Kaiser-Otto-Str. 28 ⓣ0 39 46/78 70, ⓦwww.schlossmuehle.de. Quedlinburg's leading hotel occupies a grandiose old mill, and boasts two restaurants, a bar, library and fitness centre. ❻

Theophano Markt 13–14 ⓣ0 39 46/9 63 00, ⓦwww.hoteltheophano.de. Offers an absolutely ideal location, nicely furnished rooms and a fine vaulted Weinkeller which serves some of the best food in Quedlinburg. ❻

Zum Bär Markt 8–9 ⓣ0 39 46/77 70, ⓦwww.zumbaer.de. This eighteenth-century inn was for long the top address in town, and was the only place Westerners were allowed to stay in GDR days. It then suffered a huge slump in its reputation because of its *Stasi* connections, but has made a successful comeback. ❻

Zur Goldenen Sonne Steinweg 10–11 ⓣ0 39 46/9 62 50, ⓦwww.hotel-qlb.de. Occupies a magnificent example of Baroque half-timbering, complete with oriel window and saddle roof. The restaurant serves reasonably priced specialities of the Harz. ❺

The Town

The original medieval layout of the town is preserved intact: the River Bode divides the Altstadt, the merchants' quarter on the right bank, from the Neustadt, where the smallholders lived, while at the southern end of the former are the two hills where monastic life was centred.

The Burgberg

The present **Schloss** complex on the Burgberg is predominantly Renaissance, though the plain exterior walls below the frilly gables are evidence of the original defensive function. Access from the town is via the **Torbau**, a much-modified medieval gateway, beyond which are a number of half-timbered service buildings and a terrace with a sweeping view.

Apart from the Stiftskirche, the two main buildings on the courtyard are the **Residenzbau**, the palace of the abbesses, and the L-shaped **Wohntrakt**, which contained the apartments of the other canonesses, the kitchen, bakery, pharmacy and workshops. The former now contains the **Schlossmuseum** (Mon, Tues & Thurs–Sun 10am–5pm, Wed 10am–8pm; €2.50), a rambling, old-fashioned display which ranges through Ice Age fossils, a hoard of Bronze Age treasure and a comprehensive array of medieval instruments of torture, to regional costumes and sections on the history of the town. However, the main attraction is being able to wander through the building itself, whose rooms are surprisingly modest – even in the elegantly furnished Baroque extension which replaced a redundant part of the fortifications.

The **Stiftskirche St Servatius** (Tues–Sat 10am–4/6pm, Sun noon–4/6pm; €3) is the eleventh- and twelfth-century successor to Mathilde's original church. Apart from the twin towers, which are nineteenth-century pastiches, and the Gothic apse, it's a very pure example of Romanesque architecture. The

capitals, together with the friezes above, provide the only decoration; carved with supreme delicacy by Lombard craftsmen, they show animal, plant and geometric motifs. Another fine group is in the **crypt** (closed for restoration in 2003), the last resting place of Henry and Mathilde. Their plain sarcophagi are overshadowed by those of the abbesses, which are placed upright against the south wall, a position which helps endow the life-size effigies with a Byzantine sense of hierarchy.

In the northern transept is the fabulous **Schatzkammer**. The glittering twelfth-century **reliquary** of the church's patron, St Servatius, is outstanding, with its vibrant ivory carvings of the Apostles and its encrusted diamonds and enamels. The gilded **casket** dedicated to St Catherine, though more orthodox, is equally beautiful. Another highlight is an early thirteenth-century **bridal chest**, decorated with 31 different coats of arms, which rank as the earliest surviving heraldic symbols in Germany. Of the items pilfered by an American soldier and only returned in 1993, the finest are two Gospel books and the so-called **comb of Heinrich I**, an elaborate ivory creation perhaps dating back as far as the seventh century. Housed in the transept opposite is the church's most valuable treasure, the oldest **tapestry** north of the Alps; woven around 1200, it shows the marriage of Mercury to Philology, the Queen of Knowledge.

The Altstadt

At no. 12 on Schlossberg, the street of half-timbered houses below the Schloss, is the **Klopstockhaus** (Tues–Sun 10am–5pm; €2), the boyhood home of the eighteenth-century poet **Friedrich Gottlieb Klopstock**. Founder of the classicizing tendency in German literature, Klopstock self-consciously regarded himself as a Christian Homer, devoting much of his life to the composition of a huge twenty-part epic, *The Messiah*. Though his reputation is somewhat in eclipse, his verses have gained a wide audience through Mahler's settings, notably in the *Resurrection Symphony*. The museum also contains memorabilia of two other influential Quedlinburgers of the same epoch: **Dorothea Christiana Erxleben**, the first German woman to gain the title of doctor, in 1754, and **Johann Christoph GuthsMuths**, the founding father of school gymnastics – and thus the unwitting begetter of the somewhat sinister role sport has played in German society, from Prussian militarism via the Nazis to the GDR.

To the rear of here, in a heavy *fin-de-siècle* building at Finkenherd 5a, is the **Lyonel-Feininger-Galerie** (Tues–Sun 10am–5/6pm; €3), devoted to the German-American Cubist, a key member of staff of the Bauhaus during its Weimar and Dessau periods. A large selection of his woodcuts, engravings, lithographs, drawings and watercolours are on display in specially dimmed galleries; there are also a few oil paintings, including an early *Self-Portrait*.

A couple of minutes' walk northwest of here, on the bank of an arm of the Bode at Wordgasse 3, is the **Fachwerkmuseum Ständerbau** (Mon–Wed & Fri–Sun 10am–5pm; €2). The building itself, which probably dates from the early fourteenth century, is the earliest surviving timber-framed house in Germany and a good 150 years older than any other in Quedlinburg. Inside, the displays illustrate how the different styles of half-timbering evolved. Immediately to the north is the **Blasiikirche**, a strange combination of an octagonal Baroque church and a massive Romanesque tower. Long derelict, the elegant interior, with its theatre-like box galleries, has recently been restored and made accessible to the public.

The spacious triangular **Markt**, just a few paces to the east, was the subject in the 1970s of the sort of thorough restoration programme characteristic of western Germany. The buildings are a varied mix – no. 5 and nos. 13/14 were the sixteenth-century guild houses of the weavers and tanners respectively. The music school at no. 2 occupies a large Baroque palace, while the Neoclassical *Zum Bär* is a celebrated hotel. At the far end stands the **Rathaus** (guided tours daily at 1.30pm; €2), most of which, including the graceful portal, is Renaissance.

To the rear of the Rathaus, and set in an unusual semicircular close, is the **Marktkirche St Benedikti**. Its fortress-like facade shows the transition from Romanesque to early Gothic; the rest of the structure was rebuilt at the end of the Gothic period. Entrance is via the Kalandskapelle on the north side, whose walls are hung with Renaissance memorials to local dignitaries. The main body of the church is of particular interest for the furnishings dating from after its conversion to Protestant worship, in particular the Mannerist wooden pulpit and the sober Baroque high altar. A more effusive form of Baroque was employed in the burial chapel of the Gebhardt family, which stands outside the church.

Breite Strasse, the long street leading north from here, has some superb half-timbered buildings, notably no. 33, which is Gothic, and no. 39, the Renaissance **Gildehaus zur Rose**, which is generally regarded as the most beautiful house in Quedlinburg. East of here, at Klink 11, is the **Freihaus**, another outstanding Renaissance mansion of almost palatial dimensions.

The rest of the town

Across the Bode from the Freihaus is Steinweg, the main east–west axis of the Neustadt, with the best examples of half-timbering to be found in the quarter. Particularly notable are the Baroque **Zur Goldenen Sonne** at no. 11, which has been immaculately restored and returned to its historic role as a hotel (see p.849), and the late Renaissance **Zur Börse** at no. 23, which boasts an ingenious corner oriel. Due south of here, on Hinter der Mauer, are the best-preserved fragments of the **Stadtmauer**, including a couple of watchtowers.

The **Nikolaikirche**, the Gothic parish church of the Neustadt, is principally of note for its wonderful setting in the middle of a close of truly monumental grandeur. Outwardly, the two towers, one somewhat broader than the other, tend to overwhelm the rest of the building, an impression confirmed by the squat appearance of the hall interior, whose most notable furnishings are the elaborately Baroque high altar and pulpit and a touchingly naive statue of St Godehard.

The **Münzenberg**, the hill just to the west of the Burgberg, was formerly crowned by a convent founded in Quedlinburg's tenth-century heyday. This was dissolved at the Reformation, whereupon a community of artisans, minstrels and travelling folk settled here, reusing its stones in the construction of their modest little houses. Even now, the quarter has an engagingly quiet, run-down feeling, and the view of the Burgberg from here alone justifies the trek up.

In the valley to the south, a large cemetery has grown up around the **Wippertikirche** (guided tours daily May–Oct, usually at 11am; €3), a former monastic church whose simple architecture rather resembles that of a barn – which is exactly the function it performed throughout most of the nineteenth century. Its crypt dates back to the tenth century and is the only surviving monument from Quedlinburg's period as the German capital, while the Romanesque north portal, with its exquisite columns and weather-worn carvings, was brought here from the destroyed convent on the Münzenberg.

Eating and drinking

Am Finkenherd Schlossberg 15. Good traditional coffee house.
Boulevard-Café Markt 1. Another option for *Kaffee und Kuchen*, particularly recommendable in summer, when tables are placed out on the square.
Brauhaus Lüdde Blasiistr. 14. This was one of the first home-brew pubs to open in the former GDR. It makes a *Pils* and an *Alt* as well as various seasonal beers, and also serves full meals.
Münzenberger Klause Pölle 22. Fine traditional Gaststätte. Closed Thurs.
Ratskeller Markt 1. Offers really splendid *gutbürgerliche Küche*, and as such is a worthy rival to any of the hotel restaurants. Closed Wed.
Schlosskrug Schlossberg 1. Restaurant with a handy location in the Schloss complex. Closed Mon, and at 8pm on other days.
Word-Haus Im Wasserwinkel 4. Occupying an example of nineteenth-century half-timbering, this serves regional specialities and has a good wine list.
Zur Roland Breite Str. 2–8. Café-restaurant occupying no fewer than seven historic houses.

The Bode valley

Before reaching Quedlinburg, the **River Bode** travels a mazy route right through the Harz mountains. Not only is it, at 169km, the longest river in the range, it also offers by far the most beautiful scenery the region has to offer. Seen at its best – under the menacingly dramatic skies the uncertain climate so often brings – it's easy to understand why such a rich store of supernatural folklore has grown up in association. The Bode has stirred the imagination of the literati to an extent unmatched by any other beauty spot in the country: Goethe, Herder, Klopstock, Eichendorff, Heine and Fontane all sang its praises.

Thale and around

German unification meant that **THALE**, which lies right on the edge of the Harz 10km southwest of Quedlinburg, was forced to look to tourism for its future. Its ironworks – the bedrock of the local economy for over five hundred years – have been reduced to a relatively minor operation. The town itself is of scant interest, the only monument of note being the **Wendhusenturm**, a tower house (perhaps dating back as far as the tenth century) in the old quarter north of the Bode. However, the surroundings are marvellous; with 150km of marked trails in the vicinity, Thale is unquestionably one of the best **hiking** bases in eastern Germany. Nor should the unenergetic be put off: the best of the scenery starts to unfold just beyond the Friedenspark, the park across from the Bahnhof, terminus of a branch line from Quedlinburg.

Guarding the southern entrance to Thale are two rocky crags, both known to have been sites of pagan worship and commanding superb views over the valley and beyond. On the right bank, 454m above the valley, is the vertiginous **Hexentanzplatz** (Witches' Dancing Place), so named because it was where the local witches supposedly had their initial rendezvous on Walpurgisnacht (see p.847), before flying off to the main celebration on the Brocken. The lazy way to reach it is by **cable car** (€3 single, €4.50 return; Ⓦwww.seilbahnen-thale.de); the station for this is on the opposite side of the Bode, just over the bridge at the end of Friedenspark. There's also a road up from the southeastern end of Thale, plus several pathways, quickest and most convenient being the steps of the Hexenstiege, which lead to the belvedere via the **Harzer Bergtheater** (Ⓣ0 39 47/23 24, Ⓦwww.harzer-bergtheater.de), a fine natural amphitheatre where plays are staged regularly during the summer months.

Alongside is the **Walpurgishalle** (April–Oct daily 9am–5pm; €1.50), an exhibition hall with displays on the Walpurgisnacht legend.

Directly across the river, at a height of 437m, is the **Rosstrappe** (Horse's Clip-Clops). There were once plans to make a direct transport link with the Hexentanzplatz, but instead a **chair lift** was built just north of the valley terminus of the cable car (€2 single, €3 return; Ⓦwww.seilbahnen-thale.de). Alternative ways up are the looping main road from the centre of Thale, and a walking trail, the Präsidentenweg. From the plateau-like summit, you can descend to a curious group of rocks poised directly above the river; here can be seen a natural indentation closely resembling that of a horse's hoof. According to legend, this was made by the mighty steed being ridden by a princess called Brunnhilde, who was being chased through the Harz by a lustful knight by name of Bodo. Coming to this point, she spurred her mount on to make a successful leap across to Hexentanzplatz. Bodo, however, plunged into the chasm, where he was turned into a hound, compelled forever to guard the crown of Brunnhilde which had fallen into the river in her wake.

Up the valley

The classic walk from Thale is the 10km route along a path (identified by signs marked with blue triangles) that closely follows the course of the Bode. Contrary to what you'd expect, the views from the valley floor surpass those from the heights. If you don't want to walk the whole way, the best of the scenery can be seen in the first 3km, around the **Teufelsbrücke** (Devil's Bridge), from where you can make a detour up to the Rosstrappe via a belvedere-punctuated trail named the Schurre. Beyond the Teufelsbrücke, the main path climbs high above the river, affording wonderful views back to the Rosstrappe and of the spectacular **Bodekessel** below, a gorge in which steep granite cliffs rise directly from the foaming waters with their angry whirlpools. You then descend to a more placid landscape, which is chiefly notable for its richly varied flora and fauna. Orchids, daphnes, Turk's-cap lilies and hart's-tongues are among the plants here. Some of the trees are hundreds of years old, while the large numbers of waterfowl make this stretch a magnet for bird-watchers. **TRESEBURG**, the terminus of the walk, is a scattered resort village of grand houses picturesquely spaced out along the banks of the Bode, with a very ruinous castle crowning the hill above (buses are available for the return to Thale).

Practicalities

Thale's **tourist office** (May–Oct Mon–Fri 9am–5pm, Sat & Sun 9am–3pm; Nov–April Mon–Fri 9am–5pm; Ⓣ0 39 47/25 97, Ⓕ0 39 47/22 77, Ⓦwww.thale.de) is in the pavilion directly facing the Bahnhof at Rathausstr. 1. Here you can get a list of **private houses** (❶–❷) with rooms to rent. **Pensions** include *Kleiner Ritter*, Markt 2 (Ⓣ0 39 47/25 70; ❷), *Schröder*, Karl-Marx-Str. 10 (Ⓣ0 39 47/23 92; ❹), and *Am Steinbach*, Poststr. 9 (Ⓣ0 39 47/93 50; ❹). There are **hotels**, both with restaurants, on the summits of the two mountains: *Berghotel Rosstrappe* (Ⓣ0 39 47/30 11, Ⓦwww.rosstrappe-thale.de; ❺) and *Berghotel Hexentanzplatz* (Ⓣ0 39 47/47 30; ❺). The **youth hostel** (Ⓣ0 39 47/28 81; €13.50/16.20) occupies an ideal position for a hiking centre, on the right bank of the Bode just beyond the Hexenstiege.

Rübeland

Some 15km due west of Thale is **RÜBELAND**, another old iron-smelting town, which clusters round a remarkable group of stalactite caves. Oldest of these, formed some 600,000 years ago, is the **Baumannshöhle** (guided tours daily: Feb–June, Sept & Oct 9.30am–5pm; July & Aug 9.30am–6pm; Nov–Jan 9am–3.30pm; €5, or €8 combined ticket with the Hermannshöhle, though out of season the caves are usually only open on alternate days; Ⓦwww.ruebeland.com). It was once inhabited by prehistoric bears – some of whose skeletons, between 20,000 and 40,000 years old, are on display – and, much later, by Stone Age people. If anything, the stalactite formations are even finer in the only other cave open to the public, the triple-tiered **Hermannshöhle** (same hours and prices; Ⓦwww.ruebeland.com), which lies directly opposite. Rübeland can be reached by regular **buses** from Thale and the other villages of the Bode valley. It also lies on a branch rail line from Halberstadt; the **Bahnhof** is right beside the entrance to the Baumannshöhle.

Gernrode

The recuperative health resort of **GERNRODE**, situated 9km south of Quedlinburg on the fringe of the Harz mountains, clusters round one of Germany's oldest and most remarkable churches. For the most part it's a sleepy little place – except around the Bahnhof to the north of the town proper, where the shed and freight yards of the Selketalbahn (see box, pp.844–45), the oldest **narrow-gauge steam rail line** in the region, stand directly opposite the main line.

Gernrode's history goes back to the mid-tenth century, when a women's collegiate church, the **Stiftskirche St Cyriakus**, was founded. This is substantially the same building as the one which can be seen today, with the exception of the west choir and towers and the double-storey cloister, all of which were added a couple of hundred years later. By far the best preserved of any church of its date, it exhibits most of the characteristics associated with Romanesque, the first original architectural style indigenous to northern Europe. The nave's triforium gallery was the first ever built north of the Alps, and suggests a certain Byzantine influence – a connection explained by the fact that the dowager Empress Theophanu, a native of Greece, was then living in Quedlinburg. Another innovation pioneered at Gernrode – alternating columns and pillars – became a hallmark of churches throughout the Saxon lands.

In the southern aisle stands a **Holy Sepulchre**, the oldest German reproduction of Christ's tomb in Jerusalem, which probably dates back to the late eleventh century. Unfortunately, it's somewhat mutilated, but the high quality of its carvings can still be seen on two of its sides, one showing Jesus appearing to Mary Magdalene after the Resurrection, the other with a wonderfully delicate frieze – a sort of carved version of an illuminated manuscript – featuring prophets, fantastic animals, foliage and a decorative border. Other highlights of the interior are the retouched frescoes in the east choir, the twelfth-century font and the late-Gothic monument in honour of Margrave Gero.

Practicalities

The survival of the steam rail line ensured a steady stream of foreign visitors in GDR days, but they were forced to stay elsewhere, and tourist facilities are still underdeveloped in comparison with other parts of the Harz. However, there are a fair number of **private rooms** (❶–❷) plus a single **hotel**, *Gasthof zum*

Bären, Marktstr. 21 (Ⓣ03 94 85/54 50, Ⓦwww.gasthof-zum-baeren.de; ❹), which also has a restaurant. There are also several **pensions** in the outskirts of town: in a rustic setting 2km north of the centre is *Bückemühle*, Am Bückeberg 3 (Ⓣ03 94 85/4 19, Ⓦwww.bueckemuehle.de; ❸), which is attached to a fresh-water fish speciality restaurant. Gernrode's **tourist office** (Mon–Fri 9am–4pm; Ⓣ03 94 85/43 54, Ⓦwww.gernrode.de) is on Suderoder Strasse.

Eisleben

Mansfelder Land, the Landkreis encompassing the eastern foothills of the Harz, takes its name from Mansfeld, a small county that survived as a constituent state of the Holy Roman Empire until 1780, when it was subsumed into Saxony. While not its historic capital, **EISLEBEN**, which lies midway along the rail line from Berga-Kelbra to Halle, has always been its principal town, and is the administrative centre of the present-day district. Since 1946, its official name has been Lutherstadt Eisleben, in honour of its indelible association with **Martin Luther**, the man whose impact on German society and culture has arguably been more profound and long-lasting than that of any other individual. The scourge of the papacy and the Holy Roman Empire, the founder of Protestantism and – almost as a by-product – of modern written German, was born there in 1483 to parents who had been brought up on humble peasant farms in Thuringia. Although his family moved to the nearby town of Mansfeld the following year, Eisleben remained a place for which Luther retained a special affection, and it was where he spent the last few weeks of his life, dying there in 1546. These connections led to the town becoming a pioneer of heritage tourism long before the concept was invented; indeed, the first steps to ensure the preservation of its Luther memorials were taken as far back as 1689, in the wake of a fire which caused widespread destruction.

The Town

Despite never growing very large, Eisleben preserves a sizeable historic core, consisting not only of the usual Altstadt, which dates back to the tenth century, but also three suburbs, all founded in the twelfth century, plus an early sixteenth-century Neustadt which was for long a separate town in its own right.

The Petriviertel

Martin Luther was born to Magarete and Hans Luder (the reformer himself altered the surname) in a half-timbered house on Lange Strasse (nowadays Lutherstrasse) in Eisleben's southern suburb, the Petriviertel. Opened to the public in 1693 as the first memorial museum in Germany, it now goes under the name of **Luthers Geburtshaus** (Luther's Birth House; April–Oct daily 10am–6pm; Nov–March Tues–Fri 10am–4pm, Sat & Sun noon–4pm; €2/3 combined ticket with Luthers Sterbehaus). In preparation for the opening, the main room on the first floor was transformed into a festive hall, the **Schöner Saal**, which is decorated with a large ceiling painting of an angel, full-length portraits of Luther, his close colleague Philipp Melanchthon and the Electors of Saxony, and a statue of a swan, one of the metaphorical symbols associated with the Reformation. A medieval kitchen can be seen on the ground floor, though this was probably used by the landlord rather than the Luders. There are also various books and works of art from the time of Luther's childhood, including a German-language Bible with coloured woodcuts which was printed in Nürnberg the year he was born. Across the courtyard, and included in the entry price, is an early nineteenth-century school for the poor, the **Lutherarmenschule**, displaying minerals and fossils from the Harz region, plus the presses used by the Eisleben-born Friedrich Koenig, whose printing works, founded in 1818, is still in business today.

Just a few steps south of the house is **St Peter und Paul** (Mon–Fri 10am–noon & 2–4pm, Sat 11am–4pm, Sun 11am–1pm), the parish church of the Petriviertel, and the place where Luther was baptized. Architecturally, it's a somewhat gaunt Gothic hall church, but it contains two beautiful Gothic **retables**, the one at the high altar being in honour of St Anne, the miners' patron saint. On the walls are four imposing examples of an art form which flourished during the early Protestant period, the **painted epitaph**. That to the Heidelberg family is of particular note, as it features a distant view of Eisleben, with Luther and his associates conversing in the middle ground, as the backdrop to an allegorical depiction of the doctrine of Redemption and portraits of eighteen members of the clan.

The Altstadt

The heart of Eisleben's Altstadt is the sloping **Markt**, which is lined with relatively plain Renaissance and Baroque burghers' mansions. In the middle of the square is the **Lutherdenkmal**, a Romantic-era statue of Luther on a plinth adorned with bas-reliefs of scenes from his life.

Directly above the square is **St Andreas** (Mon–Fri 10am–noon & 2–4pm, Sat 11am–4pm, Sun 11am–1pm), another somewhat stern-looking Gothic hall church, albeit one with a distinctive silhouette, with the slender pair of octagonal towers over the facade offset by their massive single counterpart on the north side. The **pulpit**, still preserved in its original early sixteenth-century form, has gained independent renown as the place from which Luther preached his last four sermons. It was formerly draped with a fine stumpwork **embroidery**, which is now displayed in a glass case on the south wall. Despite its modest dimesions, the **high altar** – and in particular the reverse side, whose delicate panels were painted in a Nürnberg workshop – is a distinguished example of late Gothic art. The church served as the mausoleum of the House of Mansfeld, and contains several notable **funerary monuments**, the most splendid being the bronze and sandstone tomb of Count Hoyer VI in the north apse, carved in full Renaissance pomp by Hans Schlegel of Halle. In 1817, in celebration of the three hundredth anniversary of the Reformation, the **busts** of Luther and Melanchthon were commissioned from the great Berlin Neoclassical sculptor Johann Gottfried Schadow, who used contemporary painted portraits by Cranach as his models.

On the south side of Andreaskirchplatz, the square around the church, is the **Luther Sterbehaus** (Luther Death House; April–Oct daily 9am–5pm; Nov–March Tues–Fri 10am–4pm, Sat & Sun noon–4pm; €2), where the reformer spent his last weeks; he was drawn back to the town of his birth to settle some disputes concerning his family's business interests. The wood-panelled front-facing rooms have been restored to their original, wonderfully evocative, late Gothic appearance. Luther did not die in the room with the bed, as might be supposed, but in the adjacent chamber, where his death mask and the original wooden pall for his coffin can be seen. The perpendicular courtyard wing contains a display on the history of the

Reformation, including a beaker which is thought to have belonged to Luther, and the gilded Communion cup he presumably used at St Andreas. The building opposite, for which the same ticket is valid, is home to the **Regionalgeschichtliches Museum**, an entertaining array of artefacts associated with the Mansfeld region, ranging from a Bronze Age boat to a 90-piece dinner set painted with local views made in the nineteenth century at Berlin's royal porcelain factory.

The Neustadt

Adjoining the Altstadt to the west is the Neustadt, which was built to house the families who worked in the mines on which the town's prosperity rested for 800 years. This tradition is commemorated by a polychromed statue of an Eisleben miner, popularly known as **Kamerad Martin**, in the heart of the quarter.

Uphill is **St Annen**, which was built in the second decade of the sixteenth century to serve both the Neustadt parishioners and a small eremitical community of Luther's own order, the Augustinians, whose members lived in the picturesque row of gabled houses alongside. (The present occupants take it in turns to open the church to visitors: if shut, a notice tells you which doorbell to ring for admission.) In 1523, with only the chancel in place, the church became the first in Mansfeld county to embrace Protestantism. Impetus towards completing the building came in 1585 from the widowed Countess Margarete, who commissioned the remarkable **Steinbilder-Bibel** from the Münster sculptor Hans Uttendrup. A work with no obvious parallel anywhere in Europe, this consists of a set of 39 sandstone reliefs, arranged in the format of a poor man's Bible, placed in front of the choir stalls. With the exception of the first two scenes of the Passion, and the four Evangelical symbols at the end, they illustrate the Old Testament only. However, the New Testament is given due prominence in the slightly later polychromed stuccowork **pulpit** alongside, in which a jolly sense of humour is apparent. The church's nave is a classic example of the Lutheran Renaissance style, being a spacious hall designed primarily for preaching. It boasts a spectacular coffered **ceiling**, whose central section features paintings of the Trinity and the Apostles.

Practicalities

Eisleben's **Bahnhof** is in the southeastern part of town; the quickest way to the centre is to go sharp left along Bahnhofsring, then right into Bahnhofstrasse. The **tourist office** (Mon & Wed–Fri 10am–5pm, Tues 10am–6pm, Sat 9am–noon; ⓣ0 34 75/60 21 24, ⓦwww.stadt-lutherstadt-eisleben.de) is at Bahnhofstr. 36. In September the town hosts the largest **popular festival** in Saxony-Anhalt, the Eisleber Wiesenmarkt (ⓦwww.wiesenmarkt.de).

As well as a reasonable supply of **private rooms** (❷–❸), there a few **pensions**, the most convenient being *Huber*, Bucherstr. 2 (ⓣ0 34 75/6 54 63; ❸) and *Morgenstern*, Hallesche Str. 18 (ⓣ0 34 75/60 28 22; ❸). Among the **hotels** are *Parkhotel*, Bahnhofstr. 12 (ⓣ0 34 75/9 27 30; ❸), *Alter Simpel*, Glockenstr. 7 (ⓣ0 34 75/69 65 07; ❹), and *Mansfelder Hof*, Hallesche Str. 33 (ⓣ0 34 75/66 90; ❺). The last of these has the town's leading **restaurant**. Another good place to eat and drink is *Brauhaus Zum Reformator*, Friedensstr. 12, a *Hausbrauerei* which makes light and dark beers, bakes bread, smokes eels and serves "medieval" dishes as well as the normal traditional fare.

Southeastern Saxony-Anhalt

The main tourist draws in the south of Saxony-Anhalt are found in the basin of the Elbe and one of its major tributaries, the Saale. **Köthen**, a former princely capital, has a fine selection of museums including a collection of Bach memorabilia. Nearby **Dessau**, despite being devastated in the war, has a wonderful heritage of Bauhaus architecture; it's also the hub of an eighteenth-century scheme of landscaped gardens which reached its climax at nearby **Wörlitz**. Not far from here is **Wittenberg**, the unlikely-looking university town which was the main setting for the Reformation. **Halle** is of note as a major city which still evokes the nation's vanished prewar existence; nearby **Merseburg** preserves reminders of its time as a missionary bishopric, though its Dom is overshadowed by that of **Naumburg** further up the Saale.

Köthen

KÖTHEN, the former capital of one of the Anhalt principalities, lies midway between Magdeburg and Halle, at the northern end of the notorious industrial region centred on the latter city. This led to severe pollution problems during the GDR era, but it has been cleaned up over the past decade. The town holds an honoured place in musical history as a result of **Johann Sebastian Bach**'s period of service as court *Kapellmeister* from 1717 to 1723, and an equally distinguished position in the field of ornithology as the home town of the German Audubon, **Johann Friedrich Naumann**, whose work is commemorated in a gem of a museum.

At the northeastern end of the town centre is a typically outsized **Schloss**. Its southern wing, the **Ludwigsbau**, was built in Renaissance style at the turn of the seventeenth century, when the principality of Anhalt-Köthen was first established. Now designated the **Historisches Museum** (Tues–Fri 10am–5pm, Sat & Sun 10am–1pm & 2–5pm; €2), its interiors include two which are regularly used for concerts: the **Schlosskapelle**, which has a splendid Baroque organ, albeit one postdating Bach's stay, and the Neoclassical throne room, the **Spiegelsaal**. The museum also houses the **Bach-Gedenkstätte**, a large collection of memorabilia of the great composer, whose Köthen years occupy a special place in his career. As his patron, Prince Leopold, was a Calvinist, Bach was freed from his usual obligation to produce a continuous stream of church music. Inspired by the virtuosity of the eighteen-strong court orchestra, he wrote a host of instrumental masterpieces, including the *Brandenburg Concertos*, the first part of *The Well-Tempered Clavier*, and the extraordinary works for solo violin and cello.

Across the courtyard, the Neoclassical **Ferdinandsbau**, erected by the last ruler of Anhalt-Köthen, houses the **Naumann-Museum** (Tues–Fri 9am–5pm, Sat & Sun 10am–1pm & 2–5pm; €1.50). A series of Biedermeier display cabinets contain the collection of stuffed birds instituted by the great nineteenth-century ornithologist, one of the pioneers of taxidermy and author of a definitive thirteen-volume study of the bird life of Germany. Naumann was a highly talented artist who made all the illustrations for his publications, and the highlight of the museum is a display of original watercolours that served as the basis for these.

The three town-centre churches make for a fascinating contrast. On Springstrasse, to the west of the Schloss, is the Neoclassical **Marienkirche**, which Duke Ferdinand erected to mark his conversion to Catholicism. Just to the west, on Stiftstrasse, is **St Agnus**, a plain Baroque building that was built at the behest of Prince Leopold's mother, Princess Gisela Agnes, for her fellow Lutherans. Bach was a member of this church, whose most notable adornments are an altarpiece of *The Last Supper* by Cranach the Younger in which the disciples flanking Christ bear the features of Luther and Melanchthon, and a portrait of the foundress in mourning gear attributed to Antoine Pesne, court painter to Frederick the Great. Much the largest and oldest of the churches is the gaunt Gothic **Jakobskirche**, which dominates the central Marktplatz. Its sparsely adorned interior is a testament to the long era when Calvinism held sway in the town.

Practicalities

Köthen's **Bahnhof**, an important junction offering good connections to Magdeburg, Halle and Dessau, is about ten minutes' walk east of the centre. The **tourist office** (May–Sept Mon–Fri 9am–12.30pm & 1–5pm, Sat 9am–1pm; Oct–April Mon–Fri only; ⓣ0 34 96/21 62 17, ⓦwww.koethen-anhalt.de) is housed in a tower that survives from the medieval fortifications, the Hallesches Turm at Hallesche Str. 10. As well as a few **private rooms** (❷), there are numerous **pensions** such as *Der Keller*, Lange Str. 51 (ⓣ0 34 96/21 47 19; ❸), *Zum Rüdesheimer*, Friedrich-Ebert-Str. 48 (ⓣ0 34 96/21 30 26; ❸), and *Zur Schlachteplatte*, Lindenstr. 1 (ⓣ0 34 96/21 24 98; ❹). There are also three **hotels**: *Stadt Köthen*, Friedrich-Ebert-Str. 22 (ⓣ0 34 96/55 61 06; ❸), *Am Hubertus* on Fasanerieallee (ⓣ0 34 96/57 40; ❺), and *Anhalt*, Ludwigstr. 53 (ⓣ0 34 96/55 00 10, ⓦwww.hotelanhalt.de; ❺). Each of these pensions and hotels has a **restaurant**, with the last two ranking as the best in town. A **festival** of Bach's music, the Köthener Bachfesttage (ⓦwww.bach-in-koethen.de) is held in September.

Dessau

DESSAU, the historic capital of Anhalt, lies 20km northeast of Köthen and 60km southeast of Magdeburg. It suffered from horrendous wartime damage followed by drab Stalinist rebuilding, and in the GDR era was generally considered to be one of the bleakest and most soulless cities in the country. However, it had previously maintained a highly distinguished cultural tradition, and this legacy has enabled it to stage a remarkable revival, which has been crowned by the granting of two separate multiple entries on UNESCO's World Heritage List. One of these is for the **Gartenreich** (Garden Kingdom), a series of Baroque parks and palaces laid out all around the city and the surrounding countryside. The other listing commemorates the **Bauhaus**, the most influential architecture and design movement of the twentieth century, which was based in Dessau during its most exciting and innovative period between 1925 and 1932.

The City

There are plenty of delights to be found amid the prefabricated concrete jungles – but this requires time and patience given that they are very scattered. Curiously the city centre is fairly low on sights, but there are important clusters of Bauhaus buildings in both the northern and southern quarters, plus several lovely areas of greenery.

The Bauhausgebäude and the Meisterhäuser

The **Bauhausgebäude** (guided tours Feb 16 to Oct 31 Mon–Fri at 11am & 2pm, Sat & Sun at 11am, 2pm & 4pm; Nov 1 to Feb 15 daily at 11am & 2pm; €4; Ⓦwww.bauhaus-dessau.de), one of the seminal buildings of the twentieth century, stands just west of the Hauptbahnhof on Gropiusallee, and can be reached in about five minutes from the rear exit via Schwabestrasse and Bauhausstrasse. A striking-looking structure even today, it was a sensation when the Bauhaus director, **Walter Gropius**, designed it in 1925 as the new custom-built headquarters for the school on its move here from Weimar (see p.891). Built according to the very latest methods around a steel and concrete skeleton with much use of light-admitting glass, it was the forerunner of architectural styles that would not come into their own until the 1950s and 1960s. There are actually three interconnected structures – one with the classrooms, a second with the workshops, the third the student residence. Following a comprehensive restoration programme in the 1970s (the Bauhausgebäude was damaged in World War II and not properly restored), an art and design college was re-established here. The workshop wing – whose starkly Cubist appearance has inspired countless buildings around the world – houses the **Bauhausmuseum** (Tues–Sun 10am–5/6pm; €4). This contains an enormous collection of furniture, ceramics, graphics and photographs detailing the work done here, with background information about the Germany of the 1920s.

Ten minutes' walk north of the Bauhausgebäude itself, at the beginning of Ebertallee, are the **Meisterhäuser**, a collection of five houses (two others were destroyed in the war) built for the senior staff of the school. Gropius, who was again responsible for the design, lived in the first house in the scheme, which was later occupied in turn by the subsequent directors, Hannes Meyer and Mies van der Rohe; the others were the homes of Moholy-Nagy, Feininger, Muche, Schlemmer, Kandinsky and Klee. These angular buildings were revolutionary for 1926, though the passing of years and familiarity with styles of architecture derived from Gropius and others lessens their impact today. Following their restoration a few years ago, the interiors of the **Kandinskyhaus** and the **Kleehaus** (both Tues–Sun 10am–5/6pm; €5; Ⓦwww.meisterhaeuser.de) have been made accessible to the public. The **Feiningerhaus** (same times and ticket) is now home to the **Kurt-Weill-Zentrum**, a display on the work of the Dessau-born composer. Best known for *The Threepenny Opera* and other collaborations with Bertolt Brecht, Weill was one of the twentieth century's most versatile and distinctive musicians, with a legacy ranging from symphonies to Broadway musicals.

About fifteen minutes' walk north of here, overlooking a horseshoe bend in the Elbe, is the **Kornhaus**, a restaurant-cum-dance hall by Carl Fieger, one of Gropius's assistants. With the fine views over the river from its terrace, it makes a good spot for a relaxing break from sightseeing.

△ Cantilevered balconies on the Bauhausgebäude, Dessau

The Georgium and the city centre

Immediately to the northwest of the Hauptbahnhof is the **Georgium**, the most accessible of the eighteenth-century parks to be found in and around the city. At its heart stands the modest-sized and graceful Neoclassical **Schloss Georgium** (Tues–Sun 10am–5pm; €3) by Friedrich Wilhelm von Erdmannsdorff, who is best known for his work at nearby Wörlitz. The collection of old masters inside includes works by Cranach, Rubens, Hals and Dou; there are also a large number of official portraits of members of the ruling house, many by J.F.A. Tischbein. It's worth walking through the shady park itself, which is dotted with pools and artificial ruins. At its eastern end, just across Georgenallee, is the **Lehrpark**, planted with 125 different kinds of tree and home to numerous semi-captive small animals.

The few surviving old buildings in the Altstadt are the **Stadtbibliothek**, which lies just north of Schlossplatz, and, on the square itself, the *fin-de-siècle* **Rathaus** and the **Marienkirche**. Although the last of these, the most southerly of the brick Gothic churches so characteristic of northern Germany, was badly damaged in the war and left as a ruin throughout the entire GDR era, it has now been rebuilt. Its **tower** (April–Oct Sat & Sun 10am–5pm; €2) contains a small local history display and can be climbed for a view over the city. However, the **Schloss** itself is probably too far gone for any kind of meaningful restoration: the fragment known as the Johannbau is all that remains of what must once have been a splendid Renaissance palace.

A few minutes' walk west of here, on August-Bebel-Platz, is Gropius's **Arbeitsamt**, an employment office designed at the end of the 1920s, nowadays a health centre. The building consists of a semicircular hall, well lit by glass skylights, joined to a two-storey administration building. It was built to achieve maximum efficiency, serving job-seekers as quickly as possible – something that was to become an urgent necessity after the start of the Depression in 1929.

The outskirts

A few kilometres south of town, reached by tram #1 from the Hauptbahnhof or the centre to Damaschkestrasse, is the suburb of **Törten**, a purpose-built settlement designed under the direction of Gropius to provide decent living conditions for Dessau's working-class population. The earliest buildings include the large **Konsumgebäude** in the middle of the scheme and the rows of houses along Kleinring, Mittelring and Doppelreihe; a second phase, constructed to designs by Hannes Meyer, added the **Laubenganghäuser**, the monumental apartment buildings on Peterholzstrasse. Unfortunately, the Bauhaus buildings are now somewhat engulfed by later developments. Nevertheless, fans of the school should definitely come out here to see two of its finest products – the austere, appropriately named **Stahlhaus** (Steel House; Tues–Sun 10am–5/6pm; free) by Georg Muche, and the futuristic **Haus Fieger**, built by Carl Fieger as his own home. Both are among the detached houses standing in their own gardens at the southern end of Südstrasse.

In the outer fringes of Dessau are two more palace-park complexes. The older of these is **Schloss Mosigkau** (guided tours Tues–Sun: April & Oct 10am–5pm; May–Sept 10am–6pm; €4.50; Ⓦwww.gartenreich.com) in the western suburb of the same name, which can be reached by bus #D or #L or mainline train. Designed by Georg von Knobelsdorff, court architect to Frederick the Great, it contains a fine array of *objets d'art* and seventeenth-century Dutch and Flemish paintings, including works by Rubens and Jordaens and Van Dyck's *Portrait of Wilhelm II of Oranien-Nassau*.

Schloss Luisium (guided tours Tues–Sun: April & Oct 10am–5pm; May–Sept 10am–6pm; €4.50; Ⓦwww.gartenreich.com), set in an English-style park with fake ruins, grottoes and sculpture at the northeastern extremity of the city near the terminus of bus #G, is another small Neoclassical summer palace by Erdmannsdorff. The ground-floor **Festsaal** is adorned with reliefs, stucco and paintings; the upper chambers are contrastingly intimate in character.

Practicalities

Dessau's **Hauptbahnhof** lies immediately west of the Altstadt. The **tourist office** (April–Oct Mon–Fri 9am–6pm, Sat 9am–1pm; Nov–March Mon–Fri 9am–5pm, Sat 10am–1pm; Ⓣ03 40/2 04 14 42, Ⓦwww.dessau.de) is at Zerbster Str. 2c. Here you can buy the **DessauCard**, which costs €8 for three days, and covers local transportation costs plus entry to many of the sights. A varied **cultural** programme, encompassing opera, musicals, dance, drama and concerts by the Anhaltische Philharmonie, is performed at the Anhaltisches Theater, Friedensplatz 1a (Ⓣ03 40/2 51 10, Ⓦwww.anhaltisches-theater.de).

There's a reasonable provision of **private rooms** (❷–❸). Alternatively, there are several **pensions**, including *An der Sieben Säulen*, Ebertallee 66 (Ⓣ03 40/61 96 20; ❸), *Bürgerhaus*, Mendelssohnstr. 43 (Ⓣ03 40/2 20 45 28; ❹), *Süd*, Heidestr. 181 (Ⓣ03 40/8 82 51 84, Ⓦwww.pension-sued.de; ❹), and *City*, Ackerstr. 3a (Ⓣ03 40/8 82 30 76, Ⓦwww.city-pension-dessau.de; ❹). The only central **hotels** are *NH*, Zerbster Str. 29 (Ⓣ03 40/2 51 40, Ⓦwww.nh-hotels.com; ❺), and *Fürst Leopold* on Friedensplatz (Ⓣ03 40/2 51 50, Ⓦwww.hotel-fuerst-leopold.de; ❽), which is decked out in Bauhaus style. An enticing alternative to these is *Zum Kleinen Prinzen*, Erich-Weinert-Str. 16 (Ⓣ03 40/51 70 71, Ⓦwww.kleinerprinz.de; ❺) in Mosigkau. Dessau also has a **youth hostel** at Waldkaterweg 11 (Ⓣ03 40/61 94 52; €11.50/14.20); take bus #K from the Hauptbahnhof for four stops. The **campsite** is at An der Adria 1 (Ⓣ03 40/2 16 09 45) in the eastern lakeside suburb of Mildensee, reached by bus #B or #G.

There are recommendable **restaurants** in each of the three hotels listed above. Good alternatives for a full sit-down meal are the *Ratskeller* in the Rathaus, Zerbster Str. 4, and *Jägerklause*, just south of Törten at Alte Leipziger Str. 76, which specializes in game dishes. The aforementioned *Kornhaus*, Kornhausstr. 146, is the obvious destination when visiting the Bauhaus buildings. In the Bauhausgebäude itself, there's a **café** serving coffee, cakes and snacks; while the *Teehäuschen* in the Stadtpark at the western edge of the city centre is a tea house which also serves full meals.

Wörlitz

WÖRLITZ, which lies 18km east of Dessau, seems a world away in spirit: there's no sign of industrial blight here, just a quiet rural village destined to prosper as one of eastern Germany's greatest tourist magnets. For that, it can thank Leopold Friedrich Franz of Anhalt-Dessau, an enlightened despot who commissioned Friedrich Wilhelm von Erdmannsdorff, Anhalt's court architect, to upgrade his family's old hunting seat into the crowning showpiece of the principality's Gartenreich. In the village itself are a number of buildings by Erdmannsdorff, including the central Markt with the Rathaus, a brewery and a farm.

The **Schlosspark** seems to grow seamlessly out of the village, an embryonic relationship inspired by the then revolutionary intention that the public should be free to enjoy the park at all times – hence the lack of entrance barriers. Its layout, with carefully planned axes and perspectives, was strongly influenced by the spirit of the Age of Reason and the theoretical writings of Rousseau and Winckelmann. It's a very conscious act of homage to England, then in the first throes of the Industrial Revolution, which had made a great impression on both Prince Leopold and Erdmannsdorff when they travelled there together. In particular, it copies the very English idea of a country house with a working estate, a concept then completely foreign to Germany, where the aristocracy retained a far greater degree of feudalistic political power and hence generally resided in urban palaces, creating gardens for purely private recreational use.

To further emphasize the narrowing of the gap between rulers and ruled, the pristine white **Schloss** (guided tours Tues–Sun: April & Oct 10am–5pm; May–Sept 10am–6pm; €4.50, or €8 combined ticket with the Gotisches Haus; Ⓦwww.gartenreich.com) was built right beside the village, at the edge rather than the middle of the park. Strongly influenced by the neo-Palladian stately homes of England, it marked the German debut of full-blooded Neoclassicism. Inside, there's none of the bombast normally found in German palaces; instead, everything is on an intimate scale. There are a number of impressive antique statues, the most important being the *Amazon of Wörlitz*, a Roman copy of a lost Greek original. Pick of a choice group of old master paintings is Rubens' *Alexander the Great Crowning Roxana*.

To the rear of the Schloss is the elliptical **Wörlitzer See**, the largest of the park's four lakes, which are interconnected by means of canals. It's overlooked by the circular **Synagoge**, which, in a sad reversal of the original ideals of Wörlitz, had its interior burnt out on *Kristallnacht*. To reach the main gardens you have to take a ferry over the lake from here, but you can avoid the expense by making a detour east to the least visited but perhaps the most attractive part of the park. At the **Grotto der Egeria**, which stands opposite the **Stein**, an island with a number of fake Roman ruins, the path swings north, passing over a miniature version of the Industrial Revolution's symbol, the Iron Bridge in Shropshire, to the lakeside **Pantheon**, a mini-version of its great Roman counterpart.

West of here, on the northern shore of the Wörlitzer See, the central **Schochs Garten** is dotted with mock-classical statues, urns and sarcophagi, plus temples to Flora and Venus. The wider Historicist sympathies marking the beginnings of Romanticism are shown by the inexhaustible types of **bridges** – chain, swing, stepped, floating and arched being just some of the varieties. An even clearer indication of this trend comes with the second of the palaces, the **Gotisches Haus** (guided tours as for Schloss; €4.50; Ⓦwww.gartenreich.com), which presents a somewhat squat, dreamlike vision of the long-neglected Gothic style. The interior furnishings cunningly mix the genuine and the pastiche; among the former are a roomful of paintings by Cranach. At the southernmost end of the park are a number of islands. Largest of these is **Neumarks Garten**, which features a labyrinth, a pergola, a library and an exhibition building.

Practicalities

To see Wörlitz properly, you really need the best part of a day: it takes several hours just to walk round the entire length of the park – and there are surprises in even the most far-flung corners. If possible, avoid weekends and holidays, when an uncomfortably large number of people throng the immediate vicinity of the Schloss. Unfortunately, the most atmospheric way to approach the village – on the Wörlitzer Eisenbahn, a **train** which leaves from its own station just north of Dessau's Hauptbahnhof – is only possible on Wednesdays, Saturdays and Sundays between Easter and October; historic locomotives are sometimes used. Otherwise, there's a very regular **bus** link with Dessau and a somewhat less frequent one with Wittenberg.

The **tourist office** (Feb Mon–Fri 9am–4pm, Sat & Sun 11am–3pm; March–Oct daily 9am–6pm; Nov–Jan Mon–Fri 9am–4pm; ⓣ03 49 05/2 02 16, ⓦwww.woerlitz-information.de) is at Förstergasse 26. There are numerous **private houses** (❶–❷) in the village with rooms to rent, as well as some small **pensions**, including *Am Park*, Markt 12 (ⓣ03 49 05/2 02 82; ❸). Additionally, there are three very fine **hotels**: *Parkhotel*, Erdmannsdorffstr. 62 (ⓣ03 49 05/2 03 22, ⓦwww.parkhotel-woerlitz.de; ❻), *Wörlitzer Hof*, Markt 96 (ⓣ03 49 05/41 10, ⓦwww.woerlitzer-hof.de; ❻–❽), and *Zum Stein*, Erdmannsdorffstr. 228 (ⓣ03 49 05/5 00, ⓦwww.hotel-zumstein.de; ❼). All of these have **restaurants** and beer gardens.

Wittenberg

It's seems hard to believe such a small and unassuming town as **WITTENBERG**, which lies 35km east of Dessau on the main Berlin–Halle rail line, played a pivotal role in the history of Europe. Although the capital of Electoral Saxony, it stretched for no more than 1.5km along a sandbank on the north side of the Elbe and had a population of just 2500 at the time when **Martin Luther** formulated his 95 theses (see box) attacking the corrupt trade in indulgences and so launched the Protestant Reformation.

Nowadays bearing the official designation of Lutherstadt Wittenberg, the town shows few signs of the usual GDR-era neglect. This is because a comprehensive restoration programme was carried out in 1983 to mark the five-hundredth anniversary of Luther's birth, an event preceded by a stealthy political rehabilitation of the reformer, hitherto regarded as a great historical villain for his opposition to the Peasants' War of 1525. Further restoration work has been carried out in recent years, in part because of the increased volume of tourism which has ensued since Wittenberg was given a a joint UNESCO World Heritage listing with Eisleben in 1997.

The town

All Wittenberg's historic sights are within the confines of the Altstadt. Although the university at which Luther taught was shut down in 1815 and incorporated into that of Halle, there has been a renewal of academic life revolving around a theology faculty which is a leading centre of Protestant thought.

Collegienstrasse

At the eastern end of Wittenberg's main street, Collegienstrasse, is the **Luthereiche**, an oak planted on the exact spot where, in December 1520, Luther burned the papal bull threatening him with excommunication if he failed to retract his views.

About halfway down the street, at no. 54, is the **Augusteum**, the former medical faculty building of the university. On the southern side of its courtyard stands the **Lutherhalle** (April–Sept Tues–Sun 9am–6pm; Oct–March Tues–Sun 10am–5pm; €5, or €6 combined ticket with Melanchtonhaus;

Luther's 95 theses

Luther, then an Augustinian monk, came to give philosophy lectures in 1508 at Wittenberg's university, settling permanently in the town three years later, whereupon he was appointed to the chair of biblical studies and quickly established a reputation as its star teacher. The subsequent course of the Reform movement was directed by Luther and his associates from Wittenberg, earning it the nickname of "the Protestant Rome".

The issue which finally triggered the Reformation was the trade in **indulgences**, a blatantly corrupt practice used by the Church for raising revenues. Their purchase enabled the buyer to gain some form of remission of sin. Many of the great medieval cathedrals were largely funded from this racket; ironically enough, Wittenberg's university was itself financially dependent on cash raised from indulgences sold at the Schlosskirche on All Saints' Day each year.

Luther's theses were conceived in reaction against the campaign mounted in 1517 by the most renowned and skilful indulgence salesman, the Dominican friar **Johann Tetzel**. One of the main beneficiaries was the luxury-loving Pope Leo X, who required extra money for the rebuilding of St Peter's in Rome. Luther was incensed on two counts – from a political point of view he saw his beloved Germany being bled dry by Italian popes; and from the perspective of a devout monk he regarded the whole trade as outright blasphemy. In formulating his theses, he mounted an audacious attack on both these fronts; by pinning them to the door of the Schlosskirche, he was following the accepted practice for initiating a scholarly dispute. The matter at first seemed a monkish quarrel, bound up in the long-running rivalry between the Augustinians and Dominicans, and Tetzel retaliated by formulating 122 antitheses. However, Luther's theses were translated into German, and gained immediate and powerful popular support. He broadened his attack on indulgences to a more general repudiation of the religious and political status quo. Within a couple of years, Luther was regarded as the veritable champion of the nation - the "German Hercules".

Ⓦwww.martinluther.de), which was originally the Augustinian monastery that Luther entered on arriving in Wittenberg. When this was dissolved at the beginning of the Reformation, part of it was made into a hall of residence for students, while the rest was given to Luther as a home for himself and his family. Entry to the latter is via the ornate **Katharinenportal**, a birthday gift to Luther from his wife, the former Cistercian nun Katharina von Bora, in 1540. Of the interiors, particularly intriguing is the **Lutherstube**, a grand hall with a coffered wooden ceiling and Renaissance tiled oven. The Lutherhalle contains the world's most important collection of objects related to the history of Reformation. These include the originals of Luther's own desk and the pulpit from which he normally preached, as well as first editions of his books. There's also an illuminating section on Reformation art, dominated by examples of the propaganda work executed by a member of Luther's immediate circle, **Lucas Cranach the Elder**; his celebrated didactic painting illustrating *The Commandments* is of special note.

A couple of doors down from the Lutherhaus at Collegienstr. 60 is the **Melanchthonhaus** (same hours; €5), a Renaissance mansion with a gable that resembles fingers rising above an outstretched palm. It was the home of Luther's closest lieutenant and the greatest scholar of the Reformation period, **Philipp Schwarzerd** - who is generally known as **Melanchthon** - from 1536 until his death in 1560. Melanchthon came to Wittenberg as professor of Greek in 1519, when aged just 21, and soon found himself caught up in the dramatic events which had begun there two years previously. Though he lacked Luther's self-assuredness, he possessed a sharper intellect and was primarily responsible for the precise articulation of the new Protestant doctrines: the Augsburg Confession, the definitive statement of the Lutheran faith, is chiefly his work. The displays, which have been revamped using modern presentation techniques, commemorate his life and career.

Marktplatz

Collegienstrasse terminates at the **Marktplatz**, on which stand memorials to the two great Reformers. The **Lutherdenkmal** was erected in 1821, with a statue by the great Berlin Neoclassical sculptor Johann Gottfried Schadow topped with a cage-like canopy designed by Schinkel. The similarly styled **Melanchthondenmal** was not added until 1860.

Prominent among the imposing Renaissance buildings lining the square is the former **Rathaus**, an august gabled edifice with a richly decorated portal adorned with allegorical figures. Also on the square is the **Cranachhaus**, the home of the great painter. Cranach had an astonishingly successful career in Wittenberg, not only as a prolific artist who ran a picture workshop, but also as a local businessman and politician, who was for several years the mayor of the town.

Rising high above the row of houses at the eastern end of Marktplatz is the **Stadtkirche St Marien**. This twin-towered Gothic church is Wittenberg's oldest surviving building; the choir dates back to around 1300, though work on the rest went on until 1470, while the distinctive octagonal turrets were only added after the Reformation. Luther, who often preached in the church, was married there in 1525, while each of his six children were baptized in the magnificent late Gothic **font**, which was made by Hermann Vischer, founder of the renowned Nürnberg dynasty of bronze-casters. The church's walls are hung with a splendid series of carved and painted **epitaphs**, the finest being that to Lucas Cranach the Younger. However, the most eye-catching decorative feature is the large and complex **Reformation altar** by Cranach the Elder. In the central scene of *The Last Supper*, Luther is shown as the disciple receiving the cup; in the predella he preaches on the theme of the crucified Christ; while other leading figures of the Reformation, including Melanchthon and Elector Frederick the Wise, are featured on the wings.

The Schlosskirche and the Residenzschloss

Schlossstrasse leads west from Marktplatz to the far end of the Altstadt, and the **Schlosskirche**, which is late Gothic by origin, but extensively remodelled in the nineteenth century. The famous wooden **doors** where Luther nailed his theses on October 31, 1517 were destroyed during the Seven Years' War; their heavy bronze replacements were installed in 1858 to commemorate the 375th anniversary of Luther's birth, and have the Latin texts of the 95 theses inscribed on them. More or less opposite the doorway of the church are the simple tombs of Luther and Melanchthon. The rest of the interior is a riot of statues, reliefs, portraits and epitaphs of local worthies. Look out for the bronze epitaph to Frederick the Wise, and the pair of large alabaster statues of the same Elector and his heir, John the Steadfast. You can also ascend the **tower** (Mon–Fri 2–4pm, Sat & Sun 10am–noon & 2–4pm; €1) for a view over the town.

The Schlosskirche forms part of the **Residenzschloss**, though this once-resplendent Renaissance palace is but a shadow of its former self, having been repeatedly ravaged by fire and war. These days, it houses a youth hostel, reached via an unusual exterior staircase in the western wing. The same wing is also home to the **Museum für Natur- und Völkerkunde** (Tues–Sun 9am–5pm; €1), which has natural history and ethnography collections.

Practicalities

Wittenberg's **Hauptbahnhof** is a few minutes' walk east of the Altstadt; some westward-bound slow trains also stop at **Bahnhof Elbtor**, just south of the Markt. The **tourist office** is at Schlossplatz 2 (March–Oct Mon–Fri 9am–6pm, Sat 10am–3pm, Sun 11am–4pm; Nov–Feb Mon–Fri 10am–4pm, Sat 10am–2pm, Sun 11am–3pm; ⓣ0 34 91/49 86 10, ⓦwww.wittenberg.de).

In addition to the **youth hostel**, with its enticing location in the Residenzschloss (ⓣ 0 34 91/40 32 55; €11.50/€14.20), there are plenty of **private rooms** (❷–❸) for rent. Budget rates are also available at a number of **pensions**, some of which are in the Altstadt, including *Central*, Mittelstr. 20 (ⓣ0 34 91/41 15 72; ❸); and *Zur Elbe*, Elbstr. 4a (ⓣ0 34 91/41 90 24; ❸). Wittenberg also has a good choice of **hotels**. Those with a central location are *Acron*, Am Hauptbahnhof 3 (ⓣ0 34 91/4 33 20; ❹); *Am Schwanenteich*, Töpferstr. 1 (ⓣ0 34 91/41 10 34; ❹); *Art*, Puschkinstr. 15 (ⓣ0 34 91/46 73 10 ❺); and *Stadtpalais*, Collegienstr. 56 (ⓣ0 34 91/42 50, ⓦwww.bestwestern.de; ❼). There are also a couple of enticing options in the outskirts: *Klabautermann*, 3km west of the centre at Dessauer Str. 93 (ⓣ0 34 91/66 21 49; ❹); and *Grüne Tanne*, 2km northwest at Am Teich 1 (ⓣ0 34 91/62 90; ❹). The last three hotels listed above have good **restaurants**, with *Klabautermann* being well-known for its fish specialities. Other options include the swanky *Schlosskeller*, Schlossplatz 1; and the gimmicky *Schlossfreiheit*, which offers Reformation-era dishes, at Coswiger Str. 24 just off the Markt.

Halle

When the Land of Saxony-Anhalt was created in 1947, the old market town and salt-producing centre of **HALLE** was chosen as capital. It recommended itself to the authorities on account of its position at the heart of one of eastern Germany's largest industrial belts and its distinguished Socialist pedigree. Communist favour, however, proved a severe disadvantage when it competed with Magdeburg to become capital of the resurrected Land in 1990. In compensation, it became the Land's largest city by the incorporation of Halle-Neustadt (the most important new town built during the GDR period) on the opposite side of the Saale, and still holds this status, despite suffering heavy depopulation over the past decade. Relatively little damaged in World War II, Halle ranks, along with Erfurt, as the German city most reminiscent of its prewar self. It has been racked by pollution, but still preserves a nicely varied roster of sights.

Arrival, information and accommodation

Halle's **Hauptbahnhof** is just beyond the southeastern edge of the city centre. From there, a pedestrian underpass leads under Riebeckplatz, a monumental Stalinist-style square-cum-highway intersection, to Leipziger Strasse, the main shopping street. Leipzig-Halle **airport** (ⓣ03 41/2 24 11 55, ⓦwww.leipzig-halle-airport.de) has its own Bahnhof on the rail line linking the two cities. The **tourist office** (Mon–Fri 10am–6pm, Sat 10am–2pm; ⓣ03 45/2 02

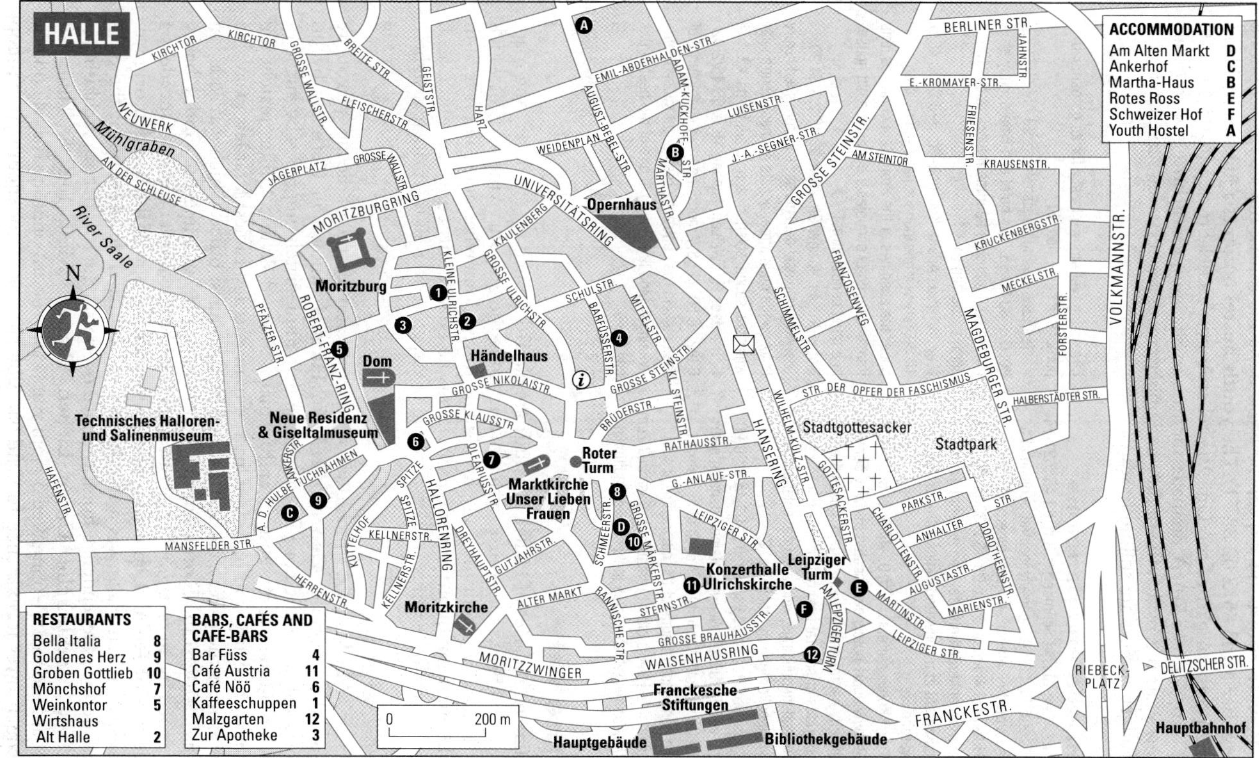
HALLE
ACCOMMODATION
Am Alten Markt D
Ankerhof C
Martha-Haus B
Rotes Ross E
Schweizer Hof F
Youth Hostel A
RESTAURANTS
Bella Italia 8
Goldenes Herz 9
Groben Gottlieb 10
Mönchshof 7
Weinkontor 5
Wirtshaus Alt Halle 2
BARS, CAFÉS AND CAFÉ-BARS
Bar Füss 4
Café Austria 11
Café Nöö 6
Kaffeeschuppen 1
Malzgarten 12
Zur Apotheke 3
0 200 m
N
Moritzburg
Dom
Händelhaus
Opernhaus
Neue Residenz & Giseltalmuseum
Technisches Halloren- und Salinenmuseum
Roter Turm
Marktkirche Unser Lieben Frauen
Moritzkirche
Konzerthalle Ulrichskirche
Leipziger Turm
Stadtgottesacker
Stadtpark
Franckesche Stiftungen
Hauptgebäude
Bibliothekgebäude
Hauptbahnhof
River Saale
Mühlgraben
RIEBECK-PLATZ
VOLKMANNSTR.
MAGDEBURGER STR.
HANSERING
UNIVERSITÄTSRING
MORITZBURGRING
ROBERT-FRANZ-RING
HALLORENRING
MORITZZWINGER
WAISENHAUSRING
FRANCKESTR.
GROSSE STEINSTR.
DELITZSCHER STR.
BERLINER STR.
MANSFELDER STR.

33 40, ⓦwww.halle-tourist.de) is in a shopping centre, the StadtCenter Rolltreppe, Grosse Ulrichstr. 60.

Private rooms (❷–❹) can be booked via the tourist office's special phone number (ⓣ03 45/2 02 83 71). The **youth hostel** occupies a Jugendstil villa in the northern part of the Uni–Viertel at August-Bebel-Str. 48a (ⓣ03 45/2 02 47 16; €13/15.70). A dramatic increase in the number of **hotels** in the past few years means that the middle and upper ranges are very well served, whereas budget choices are still quite scarce.

Hotels and pensions

Am Alten Markt Schmeerstr. 3 ⓣ03 45/5 21 14 11, ⓕ5 23 29 56. Centrally located pension in a renovated nineteenth-century tenement. ❹

Ankerhof Ankerstr. 2a ⓣ03 45/2 32 32 00, ⓦwww.ankerhofhotel.de. Fine new hotel and restaurant in a converted nineteenth-century warehouse. ❺

Apart Kohlschütterstr. 5 ⓣ03 45/5 29 50, ⓦwww.apart-hotels.de. Located midway between the city centre and Giebichenstein, this is the most luxurious of several new hotels set up in Jugendstil buildings, with a sauna, solarium and whirlpool among the facilities. ❹–❻

Dessauer Hof Paracelsusstr. 9 ⓣ03 45/2 90 90 28, ⓕ2 90 90 20. Well-maintained pension near the Jugendstil Wasserturm (reached by tram #1) at the northeastern edge of the city centre. It's an adjunct to Halle's oldest restaurant, *Gasthaus Zum Tagelöhner*, which serves inexpensive traditional fare, being well-known locally for its gargantuan portions of spare ribs. ❸

Kaffeehaus Sasse Geiststr. 22 ⓣ03 45/23 33 80, ⓕ2 83 63 55. This hotel and café occupy a renovated Jugendstil apartment block about 1km north of the centre. ❺

Martha-Haus Adam–Kuckhoff-Str. 5–8 ⓣ03 45/5 10 80, ⓦwww.marthahaus.halle.vch.de. Run under the auspices of the Protestant churches, this immaculate hotel occupies a handsome old house in a quiet central street. ❻

Rotes Ross Leipziger Str. 76 ⓣ03 45/2 3 34 30, ⓦwww.kempinski.de. This stylishly furnished luxury hotel on the main street boasts a fitness centre with whirlpool, sauna, solarium and steam baths. ❾

Schweizer Hof Waisenhausring 15 ⓣ03 45/2 02 6392, ⓕ50 30 68. Among the most characterful of the hotels in the centre. Its restaurant (closed Sun evening & Mon lunchtime) is one of the best in the city. ❺

The City

The boundaries of Halle's **Altstadt** are clearly defined by the inner ring road, which follows the course of the fortifications, the only surviving parts of which are some fragments of wall plus a single tower. Somewhat unusually, several of the most important historic monuments lie outside this compact central area, and it really requires at least a couple of days to cover all the principal sights.

Marktplatz

Halle's **Marktplatz**, which is surveyed by a pensive statue of the city's favourite son, the composer **George Frideric Handel** (known in Germany by his original name of Georg Friedrich Händel), immediately impresses by virtue of its monumental dimensions and its many-towered skyline. Unfortunately, the square's beauty is impaired by mass of tram rails and cables. A far less excusable eyesore is the gallery, recently vacated by the tourist office, which was added in the 1970s to the **Roter Turm** (Red Tower), a freestanding late Gothic belfry topped by an engagingly fantastical spire with little corner turrets. Outside is a **statue of Roland**, an eighteenth-century stone copy of the wooden original, erected when Halle was a member of the Hansa as an assertion of the city's desire for independence from its feudal overlords, the Magdeburg archbishops.

The **Marktkirche Unser Lieben Frauen** (Mon, Tues & Thurs–Sat 10am–noon & 3–6pm, Wed 3–6pm, Sun 11am–noon) opposite is a real oddity, which owes its existence to Cardinal Albrecht von Brandenburg, Archbishop of Magdeburg and Mainz, who planned to turn Halle into a showpiece

Catholic city to spearhead a counter-attack on the Wittenberg-led Reformation. Originally, the **Hausmannstürme** (Watchman's Towers) to the east, which can be ascended (Mon–Sat at 3.30pm; €2.50) for a view over the city, and the **Blaue Türme** (Blue Towers) to the west, belonged to two different Romanesque churches. These were demolished in 1529 and the two pairs of towers linked up by a brand-new hall church in the Flamboyant Gothic style. An unknown follower of Cranach, dubbed the Master of Annaberg, painted its **high altar**, which immodestly features a large portrait of Cardinal Albrecht flanked by SS Mary Magdalene, John the Evangelist and Catherine; he also turns up at the far right of the predella in the group of saints adoring the Madonna and Child. A few years after the Marktkirche was completed, Halle adopted the Reformation; the church was then converted to Protestant use. A later adornment was the tiny Baroque **organ**, on which Handel received lessons; it can be heard on Tuesdays and Thursdays at 4pm.

The northern Altstadt

Immediately north of Marktplatz is a maze of evocative old streets, some still showing the familiar signs of GDR-era neglect. At Grosse Nikolaistr. 5 is the **Händelhaus** (Mon–Wed & Fri–Sun 9am–5.30pm, Thurs 9am–7pm; €2.60, free Thurs; Ⓦwww.haendelhaus.de), the large Baroque mansion where the great composer was born. It contains extensive documentation on his life and times, and you can listen on headphones to many of Handel's most famous works.

A couple of minutes' walk west of the Händelhaus is the **Dom** (June–Oct Mon–Sat 2–4pm). This was built as the church of a Dominican priory, and the basic structure employs the simple, unadorned forms favoured by the preaching orders. Its present eccentric appearance, however, is largely due to a remodelling commissioned by Cardinal Albrecht, who took it over to serve as his court church. A curious gabled upper storey in brick, one of the earliest Renaissance constructions in central Germany, was tacked onto the old building; the entrance portal and interior staircase are also in this style. Most of the lavish interior decorations have been dispersed (notably to Schloss Johannisburg in Aschaffenburg – see pp.201–02), though seventeen over-life-sized **statues of saints** by Peter Schroh remain *in situ*. A later Baroque transformation, carried out after the Dom became a Protestant parish church, brought the high altar and the organ, at which Handel presided as a teenager.

On the south side of the Dom is the **Neue Residenz**, a Tuscan-style *palazzo* which the cardinal hoped to develop into the Catholic answer to Wittenberg University, but which, in a neat twist of fate, is used by the institution now known as the Martin-Luther-Universität Halle-Wittenberg. Part of the building is given over to the **Geiseltalmuseum** (Mon–Fri 9am–noon & 1–5pm, 2nd & 4th Sat & Sun of month 9am–1pm; free; Ⓦwww.geologie.uni-halle.de), a fascinating collection of fossils, reckoned to be fifty million years old, found perfectly preserved in the brown coal region of the Geisel valley just south of the city.

A couple of blocks north of the Dom is the **Moritzburg**, constructed as a citadel against the rebellious burghers by Archbishop Ernst at the end of the fifteenth century, but converted into a palace a generation later under Cardinal Albrecht. A satirical cabaret and a student club occupy the east tower, while the former palace chapel, the **Magdalenenkapelle**, has been taken over by a Calvinist congregation. The rest of the complex is home to the **Staatliche Galerie** (Tues 11am–8.30pm, Wed–Sun 10am–6pm; €5, free Tues; Ⓦwww.moritzburg.halle.de). In the vaulted cellars is a good decorative arts section, the most notable pieces being statues from demolished buildings. Two spectacular Mannerist chambers – the courtroom and the festive hall – from a demolished building, the Talamt, have been reconstructed inside the recently restored south wing. Elsewhere, the emphasis is on painting and sculpture of the nineteenth and twentieth centuries: Klimt, Kirchner, Marc, Munch, Beckmann and Barlach are among those represented. There are also striking Cubist paintings by **Feininger** of Halle's Dom and Marktkirche, with the former's unusual silhouette providing the artist with what he himself admitted to be one of his biggest challenges.

The southern Altstadt

From the Marktplatz, Schmeerstrasse leads to the **Alter Markt**, the elongated original square with the **Eselbrunnen** (Donkey Fountain) in the centre, which was used for markets until supplanted by its much larger successor. **Rannische Strasse**, which leads south from the intersection of Schmeerstrasse and Alter Markt, boasts a superb array of Renaissance, Baroque and Rococo mansions, among which nos. 10, 17, 20 and 21 are particularly outstanding.

Beyond the western end of Alter Markt is the fifteenth-century **Moritzkirche**, the Catholic parish church. From outside, it presents an austere picture, an appearance accentuated by the fact that it's built directly onto one of the surviving sections of the medieval walls. The hall interior, in contrast, is light and spacious, with elaborate star and network vaults and limpid sculptures by Conrad von Einbeck, the church's master mason; these include a poignant *Man of Sorrows* and a sharply characterized *Bust of a Man*, traditionally assumed to be a self-portrait.

The Franckesche Stiftungen

Immediately south of the Altstadt, across the ugly ring road, is Halle's most singular sight, the vast complex of buildings – forming what is in effect a complete township – known as the **Franckesche Stiftungen** (Ⓦwww.francke-halle.de). The greatest single legacy of the evangelical Pietist movement, it's named in honour of its founder, **August Hermann Francke**, who came to Halle in 1692 to serve both as Professor of Greek and Oriental Languages and as pastor of the rundown parish of Glaucha. On Easter Day 1695, an anonymous donation placed in his church poor box inspired Francke to set up a school for needy children. Three years later, he established an orphanage as well, and in due course his foundation spawned several educational institutions, a prestigious public library and a number of workshops. Living quarters were also built, and by the time of Francke's death in 1727, his "town within a town" had a population of almost 3000. New buildings were added right up until 1914, but the foundation was dissolved by the Communists in 1946. Although taken over by the university, the complex was thereafter allowed to fall into a state of semi-dereliction, and was in a perilous state by the time of the *Wende*. In 1991, however, the foundation was reconstituted, and is active once again in the social and educational spheres.

Although reconstruction work on the complex will take many years, the **Hauptgebäude** (Tues–Sun 10am–5pm; €3), a huge U-shaped structure in the plainest possible Baroque style, has already been beautifully restored. On the ground floor are an exhibition on the life of Francke and the **Cansteinsche Bibelkabinett**, a chronological display of the products of the foundation's printing workshop, which for more than two centuries was the principal Bible press in the German-speaking world. The attic contains the truly astonishing **Kunst- und Naturalienkammer**, an eighteenth-century variant on the princely cabinet of curiosities, though in this case the objects were intended not for amusement, but for pedagogic instruction. Exhibited in the centre of the room are the largest pieces: a model of the geocentric world system, flanked by globes of the earth and the heavens; an apothecary's table, with individual compartments for each drug; and models of buildings and a sailing ship. The colourful display cabinets around the walls contain an amazingly disparate array of items, including stuffed animals, preserved plants, shells, stones, weapons, coins, masks, clothes, paintings, sculptures, religious objects, mechanical models and ethnographic artefacts from around the world.

Francke's library, established in 1698, was opened to the public ten years later, and grew so quickly as a result of donations and bequests that a separate structure to house it, the **Bibliothekgebäude**, was built immediately east of the Hauptgebäude in the 1720s. The oldest secular library building in Germany, it still preserves its historic core, the so-called **Kulisse Bibliothek** (Tues–Sun 10am–noon & 2–4pm; €1) on the first floor. This name literally means "Scenery Library", as the bookshelves, which are closed off by a graceful wooden gate, are arranged in the manner of a theatre set.

Elsewhere in the city

Francke, in common with many of the most notable figures from Halle's past, is buried in the **Stadtgottesacker**, which lies just to the northeast of the Altstadt, beyond the sole surviving tower of the fortifications, the **Leipziger Turm**. Founded by Cardinal Albrecht, the cemetery was converted by Nickel Hoffmann into a grand galleried necropolis in the manner of the Campo Santo in Pisa. It is the only one of its type in Germany.

Likewise just beyond the confines of the Altstadt is the old saltworks, now the **Technisches Halloren- und Salinenmuseum** (Tues–Sun 10am–5pm; €2), which is set on an island formed by two arms of the Saale. It can be reached on foot in about ten minutes from either the Moritzkirche or the Neue Residenz, with the tall brick chimney which rises above the half-timbered buildings providing a useful pointer. If you come on a Sunday, you can see the last surviving saltpan being used to produce an excellent coarse-grained salt – which is on sale at the shop. At other times, you'll have to be content with seeing the machinery and the associated historical documentation.

To the north of the city centre, at Richard-Wagner-Str. 9, is the **Landesmuseum für Vorgeschichte** (Tues 9am–7.30pm, Wed–Fri 9am–5pm, Sat & Sun 10am–6pm; €1; Ⓦwww.archsla.de), a major but long neglected archeology museum which in 2003 began the slow process of putting its collections back on view in a modern guise. The first part to go on display was the Paleolithic section, which features the skeletons of a 220,000-year-old mammoth and a 120,000-year-old bull elephant killed by hunters, as well as some exceptionally well-preserved tools. During the course of the next few years, more of the museum's treasures should become accessible. These include some spectacular recent excavations, notably the three hundred luxury items – some of Roman provenance, others Germanic in origin – found in a prince's grave at Gommern.

To get to the museum, it's best to take tram #7, which continues on to **Burg Giebichenstein** (also served by tram #8 from the centre). There are actually two castles here, both of which were destroyed in the Thirty Years War. The lower, or **Unterburg**, was first constructed in the tenth century under King Henry the Fowler, although the oldest surviving portions are mid-fifteenth-century. It was rebuilt in the Baroque period, and now serves as a school of arts and crafts. The fourteenth-century **Oberburg** (April–Oct Tues–Fri 9am–6pm,

Sat & Sun 9am–6.30pm; €2), perched on the cliff above, has been left in an appropriately ruinous and overgrown state, but it's worth climbing for the sake of the sweeping view over the Saale valley.

Eating, drinking and entertainment

Halle has developed into one of the best places in the former GDR for **food** and **drink** (see "Hotels and pensions", p.870, for further recommendations) and has by far the liveliest nightlife in Saxony-Anhalt.

Restaurants

Bella Italia Markt 2. The cellars of Halle's Rathaus are occupied by this hugely popular Italian restaurant, rather than the usual *Ratskeller*. In summer, it sets up tables on the square.

Goldenes Herz Mansfelder Str. 57. Bohemian speciality restaurant. Closed Sun evening.

Groben Gottlieb Grosse Märkerstr. 20. Very traditional Gaststätte on a quiet side street close to the Markt.

Mönchshof Talamtstr. 6. Directly overlooking the Marktkirche, this is among Halle's best restaurants, yet is very moderately priced, particularly at lunchtime, when there is a bargain menu. Closed Sun evening.

Quinoa Ludwigstr. 37. Vegan and vegetarian restaurant, about 1km south of the Altstadt.

Weinkontor Robert-Franz-Ring 21. Very classy wine bar-restaurant, offering high-quality cuisine plus over 200 different vintages. Evenings only.

Wirtshaus Alt Halle Kleine Ulrichstr. 32–33. Cosy Gaststätte in a sixteenth-century timber-framed building which offers many local specialities. Evenings only, closed Fri.

Zum Mohr Burgstr. 72. Historic inn below Burg Giebichenstein; it serves fine traditional dishes and has a summer beer garden.

Bars, cafés and café-bars

Bar Füss Barfüsserstr. 15. Pleasant Kneipe in a newly renovated half-timbered building with inner courtyard.

Café Austria Kleiner Berlin 2. This relatively recent venture aims to recreate the ambience of a Viennese coffee house.

Café Nöö Grosse Klausstr. 11. Café-bar much patronized by the alternative set; it serves light meals and sometimes features live music.

Kaffeeschuppen Kleine Ulrichstr. 11. *Szene* café-bar whose clientele includes artists, students and foreign construction workers.

Malzgarten Grosse Brauhausstr. 6. Large beer garden alongside the Stadtmauer, with a wood-fired grill for cooking steaks and sausages.

Objekt 5 Seebener Str. 5. Student bar in the north of the city, reached by tram #3 or #10, with live music and other artistic events.

Zur Apotheke Mühlberg 4a. Popular theme bar, decked out with all sorts of pharmaceutical paraphenalia.

Entertainment

The main **theatre** venues are the Opernhaus, Universitätsring 24 (Ⓣ03 54/2 02 64 58, Ⓦwww.opernhaus-halle.de), which features opera and dance; the Steintor Varieté, Am Steintor 10 (Ⓣ03 45/2 97 70 10, Ⓦwww.steintor.de), one of Germany's oldest variety theatres, founded back in 1884. There's also a Puppentheater at Universitätsplatz (Ⓣ03 45/68 88 70, Ⓦwww.puppentheater-halle.de) and a satirical cabaret. **Concerts** by the Philharmonisches Staatsorchester Halle (Ⓦwww.philharmonie-halle.de) are normally held in the new Georg-Friedrich-Händel-Halle, Salzgrafenplatz 1 (Ⓣ03 45/2 92 90); smaller ensembles often play at the Händelhaus (Ⓣ03 45/50 09 00, Ⓦwww.haendelhaus.de); while the Konzerthalle Ulrichskirche, a deconsecrated Gothic church at Kleine Brauhausstr. 26 (Ⓣ03 45/2 21 30 21) is generally favoured for choral music. One of the trendiest **nightspots** is the Studentenclub Turm in the Moritzburg (free admission with student ID).

Festivals include the Händel-Festspiele (Ⓦwww.haendelfestspiele.halle.de) in June, featuring the music of Handel, the Lanternenfest on the last weekend of August, and the Drachenfest in October. **Cruises** on the Saale, run by Reederei Riedel (Ⓣ03 45/2 83 20 70), depart daily in summer from the landing stage immediately below Burg Giebichenstein.

Merseburg

MERSEBURG, the most venerable of the towns in the region, was a favourite royal seat in the tenth century but is now a virtual satellite of Halle. It has the misfortune to be sandwiched between two giant chemical plants, Buna-Werke and Leuna-Werke; these are nowadays operating at a very reduced capacity, but their incessant burning of lignite throughout the GDR period left the historic monuments badly scarred. Nonetheless, the upper town still retains its arresting medieval skyline, which is seen to best advantage from the bridge spanning the Saale.

Set high above the river, the **Dom** (Mon–Sat 9am–4/6pm, Sun noon–4/6pm; €4) was founded as a missionary bishopric in the early eleventh century, though only the crypt survives from this time. Of the thirteenth-century Transitional-style rebuilding there remain the choir, transepts and westwork, whose pair of octagonal towers contrasts well with their cylindrical counterparts at the east end. A Flamboyant Gothic hall nave was substituted in the sixteenth century. The most eye-catching furnishings are the **funerary monuments**. Look out in particular for the hauntingly hierarchical bronze memorial in the choir to the eleventh-century royal pretender Rudolf of Swabia, and the Renaissance epitaph in the north transept, cast by Hermann Vischer of Nürnberg, to Bishop Thilo von Trotha. A chapel in the cloisters houses the mid-thirteenth-century memorial to the Knight Hermann von Hagen, carved with a sense of characterization clearly inspired by the famous workshop of nearby Naumburg.

Adjoining the north side of the Dom is the stately **Schloss**, originally the residence of the prince-bishops, later of the secular dukes. Its wings range in style from Flamboyant Gothic to Baroque, though Renaissance predominates, with the superb portal and oriel being the most distinguishing features. The peace of the courtyard is constantly disturbed by the squawkings of the caged **raven**, the latest in a line dating back to the late fifteenth century. Its presence is explained by the fact that, when Bishop Thilo von Trotha's most precious ring was stolen, an innocent man was charged with the crime, tried and executed. After his death, the missing ring was found in a raven's nest, whereupon the guilty bird was imprisoned in a cage for the rest of its life, with its sin ever after being visited on a member of the same species. Most of the Schloss is used as offices, but a small part contains the **Kulturhistorisches Museum** (Tues–Sun: April–Sept 10am–6pm; Oct–March 9am–5pm; €2), with the standard archeology and local history displays.

Practicalities

Merseburg's **Bahnhof** lies at the western edge of the town centre. The **tourist office** (Mon–Fri 9am–1pm & 2–6pm, Sat 9am–3pm; Ⓣ0 34 61/21 41 70, Ⓦwww.merseburg.de) is at Burgstr. 5. There are several budget **pensions** on the opposite side of the Bahnhof from the centre, including *Leisner*, Klobikauer Str. 58 (Ⓣ0 34 61/21 06 95; ③), *Elisa*, August-Bebel-Str. 23 (Ⓣ0 34 61/20 24

35; ❸), and *Am Park*, Gutenbergstr. 18 (Ⓣ0 34 61/21 54 72; ❸). Centrally sited **hotels** include *C'est la Vie*, König-Heinrich-Str. 47–49 (Ⓣ0 34 61/20 44 20; ❺), *Ritters Weinstuben*, Grosse Ritterstr. 22 (Ⓣ0 34 61/3 36 60, Ⓦwww.rittersweinstuben.de; ❺), and *Radisson SAS*, Oberalenburg 4 (Ⓣ0 34 61/4 52 00, Ⓦwww.radissonsas.com; ❼). The best **restaurants** are in the last two hotels; otherwise there's the *Ratskeller*, Ölgrube 1.

Naumburg

Before the war, **NAUMBURG**, which is set on heights overlooking the Saale valley 20km upstream from Merseburg, was considered one of Germany's most beautiful and distinctive towns, thanks mainly to its peerless Dom, which shows medieval architecture and sculpture at their highest peak. Although it suffered minimal bomb damage, Naumburg fell off tourist itineraries in the GDR period and became the headquarters of a large Soviet garrison. Since the *Wende* the town has made giant steps in scraping off the grime which had smothered its buildings and is well on the way to reappearing at its best.

The Town

Naumburg was founded at the beginning of the eleventh century by Margrave Ekkehardt of Meissen. Originally a fortress, it soon afterwards became the seat of a prince-bishopric transferred from nearby Zeitz. By the beginning of the thirteenth century, the town had prospered as a market centre, and it was decided to replace the original cathedral with a spectacular new structure – the present Dom. This has dominated the skyline ever since, leaving everything else in its shadow, though most of the Altstadt is quietly attractive.

The Dom

Naumburg's **Dom** (Mon–Sat 9am–4/5/6pm, Sun noon–4/5/6pm; €4) is among the country's greatest buildings, above all for its wondrous sculptural decoration. Yet, although it was built as one of Germany's showpiece cathedrals, with choirs at both ends of the building to emphasize its imperial status and a monastery-like range of ancillary buildings, it's been no more than a Protestant parish church since 1564, when the bishopric was suppressed following the reign of the first and last Lutheran incumbent.

Because the Dom was built at a time of rapidly changing architectural tastes, it exhibits a variety of different yet compatible styles – despite having been substantially completed in the relatively short period of fifty years. The original masons began by erecting the **east choir**, complete with its almost oriental-looking **towers**, according to florid late Romanesque principles; the cupolas added in the Baroque period further add to the exotic appearance. The transepts and the nave are Transitional in approach, whereas the marvellously harmonious **west choir**, with its polygonal apse (a replica of which was added to the east choir the following century), adopts the pure High Gothic of the great French cathedrals. Nonetheless, its towers help give it a distinctively German accent, though only the northern one dates back to this time. Its stylistic twin was added, in accordance with the original plans, at the end of the nineteenth century, as a result of the Romantic movement's frenzied enthusiasm for all things Gothic which inspired the belated completion of so many important German churches.

Pride of the interior is the assemblage of sculptures in the west choir, which rank among the all-time masterpieces of the art. They were carved by a workshop led by the so-called **Master of Naumburg**, by far the most idiosyncratic and original of all the masons who created the great European cathedrals: his ideas and techniques were at least 150 years ahead of their time, anticipating both the Renaissance and the Reformation. Though it's reasonable to suppose that he was a German, he was trained in France, after which he worked at the Dom in Mainz, where a few carvings by him can still be seen.

The polychrome **rood screen**, illustrating the Passion, is unlike anything previously found in religious art. Each of the life-sized figures of the crucified Christ, the Virgin and St John radiates an enormous sense of suffering and pathos – but recognizably human, not other-worldly. On the upper frieze, the small scenes unfold like a great drama, with plenty of anecdotal detail and a wonderfully rhythmic sense of movement imparted in the gestures and groupings of the figures. Sadly, the last two of these were destroyed by fire, and replaced by Baroque pastiches, whose feebleness serves to emphasize the Master's genius. Plants, flowers and fruits are featured on a second frieze, and on the capitals and keystones; carved with a matchless sensitivity, these are, apart from their fragmentary counterparts in Mainz, the earliest botanically accurate depictions in Western art.

Very different from the rood screen, but recognizably the product of the same humanistic mind, are the twelve large **statues of the founders**, again still preserving much of their original colouring, which are placed on pedestals within the west choir. The granting of such prominent positions of honour to lay personages was, to say the least, unusual, but what is even more remarkable, given that they were long dead, is that each is given a highly distinctive and noble characterization. Particularly outstanding are the imperiously serene couple **Ekkehard II and Uta**, who stand together on the first pillar on the north side of the apse; they've become the most famous statues in the country, symbolizing the Germans' own romantic view of their chivalrous medieval past.

Inevitably, the east choir is overshadowed by the west, though it's equally well preserved. It also has a **rood screen** – this is the only medieval church in Europe to have two – in this case a simple Romanesque structure adorned with a cycle of retouched frescoes. Ascending to the intimate **high choir**, with its elaborate late Gothic stalls, its fourteenth-century high altar and its gleaming stained-glass windows, is like eavesdropping on the past, as it can hardly have changed in centuries. Here also are two more works from the celebrated sculptural workshop – the statue of a deacon and the tomb of Bishop Dietrich II.

The rest of the town

Steinweg and its continuation Herrenstrasse – each of which has its fair share of fine houses – lead eastwards from the Dom to the central **Markt**. Dominating the square is the **Rathaus**, late Gothic by origin but remodelled in Renaissance style in the sixteenth century, when it received the huge curved gables which clearly served as a model for other mansions in the city. The Mannerist portal, a later addition, strikes a supremely self-confident note, but the building's most endearing feature is the polychrome capital at the northeastern corner, showing two dogs fighting over a bone – this symbolizes the conflict between the ruling prince-bishops and the increasingly self-confident burghers.

At no. 18 on the square is **Hohe Lilie**, a late Gothic mansion incorporating a Romanesque tower house which is of the same vintage as the Dom. It has been restored as the new home of the **Stadtmuseum** (daily 10am–5pm; €2; Ⓦwww.museumnaumburg.de), an entertaining local history display whose star exhibit is the *Ratstrinkhorn*, the elegant late fourteenth-century municipal **drinking horn**. Also of note is the house's own **Prunkstube**, with its pair of console figures bearing the date 1526. Of the other houses on the Markt, the most imposing are the **Schlösschen** at no. 6, which was built for the one Protestant bishop, and the **Alte Residenz** at no. 7, three houses knocked together to serve as the temporary palace for Duke Moritz of Saxony while he waited for Schloss Moritzburg outside Dresden to be completed.

Rising behind the south side of the Markt is the curiously elongated **Stadtkirche St Wenzel**, which was the burghers' answer to the prince-bishop's Dom. In the Baroque period, this late Gothic church was given an interior face-lift, including the provision of an **organ** by Zacharias Hildebrand, a pupil of the great Silbermann. It was highly praised by Bach, and its qualities can be heard in the short recitals (€2) held at noon on Wednesdays, Saturdays and Sundays between May and October. Also of note are two paintings by **Cranach** – *The Adoration of the Magi* and *Christ Blessing Children*. The single **tower** (April–Oct daily 10am–5pm; €1.50), which was deliberately built higher than those of the Dom, commands a magnificent panorama over the city and the Saale valley.

More fine mansions can be seen on Jacobstrasse, which leads eastwards from the Markt. Also well worth seeing is the **Marientor** (daily 10am–4.30pm; €0.50) at the northeastern edge of the inner ring road. This double gateway, one of the best preserved in the country, is the only significant reminder of the fifteenth-century fortifications which, on this evidence, must have presented a formidable obstacle to would-be invaders. In summer, the courtyard is used as a puppet theatre. At the southeastern edge of the Altstadt, at Weingarten 18, is the **Nietzsche-Haus** (Tues–Fri 2–5pm, Sat & Sun 10am–4pm; €1.50; Ⓦwww.museumnaumburg.de), the philosopher's home throughout his childhood and youth. Nietzsche was one of the GDR's all-time bogeymen, and it was not until well after the *Wende* that the house was restored to serve as a memorial museum.

Practicalities

Naumburg's **Hauptbahnhof**, which has good rail links with Halle, Leipzig and Weimar, is below and northwest of the historic centre, which is reached by heading along Bahnhofstrasse, then up Bergstrasse. Established in 1892, the town's **tram network** (Ⓦwww.ringbahn-naumburg.de) was for long the only one in the world to use a circular route, and is still the only example of this type in Germany. Part of the circuit is now used for tourist purposes, and plied by historic vehicles of different vintages. The **tourist office** (March–Oct Mon–Fri 9am–6pm, Sat 10am–4pm, Sun 9am–2pm; Nov–Feb Mon–Fri 9am–1pm & 2–5pm; Ⓣ0 34 45/20 16 14, Ⓦwww.naumburg-tourismus.de) is at Markt 6.

In addition to **private rooms** (❶–❸), there are a number of small **pensions**: among them *Wenzelsblick*, Fischstr. 23 (Ⓣ0 34 45/20 16 90; ❷), *Hentschel*, Lindenhof 16 (Ⓣ0 34 45/20 12 30; ❸), and *Caféhaus Kattler*, Lindenring 36–37 (Ⓣ0 34 45/20 28 23; ❹). There's also a good range of **hotels**: *Deutscher Hof*, Franz-Ludwig-Rasch-Str. 10 (Ⓣ0 34 45/70 27 34; ❹), *Zum Alten Krug*, Lindenring 44 (Ⓣ0 34 45/20 04 06; ❹), *St Marien*, Marienstr. 12 (Ⓣ0 34 45/2 35 40; ❹), *St Wenzel*, Friedrich-Nietzsche-Str. 21 (Ⓣ0 34 45/7 17 90, Ⓦwww.sankt-wenzel.de; ❹), *Zur Alten Schmiede*, Lindenring 36 (Ⓣ0 34 45/2

43 60, Ⓦwww.hotel-zur-alten-schmiede.de; ④), and *Stadt Aachen*, Markt 11 (Ⓣ0 34 45/24 70, Ⓦwww.hotel-stadt-aachen.de; ⑥). The **youth hostel** is way to the south of the centre at Am Tennisplatz 9 (Ⓣ0 34 45/70 34 22; €13/15.70).

With the exception of *St Marien*, all the hotels listed above have **restaurants**, with *Carolus Magnus* in *Stadt Aachen* perhaps having the edge over the others. However, it faces strong competition from the *Ratskeller* in the Rathaus, Markt 1, and *Domklause*, Herrenstr. 8. The main local **festivals** are the Kirschfest (Cherry Festival) on the last weekend in June and the Weinfest at the end of August.

Travel details

Trains

Dessau to: Köthen (frequent; 30min); Wittenberg (frequent; 30min).
Halberstadt to: Quedlinburg (frequent; 30min); Thale (frequent; 45min); Wernigerode (frequent; 40min).
Halle to: Dessau (frequent; 45min); Eisleben (hourly; 40min); Halberstadt (8 daily; 1hr 45min); Merseburg (frequent; 15min); Naumburg (12 daily; 30min); Wittenberg (frequent; 45min).
Magdeburg to: Dessau (frequent; 1hr 45min); Halberstadt (hourly; 1hr 15min); Halle (frequent; 1hr 30min); Köthen (frequent; 1hr); Stendal (frequent; 1hr).

11

Thuringia

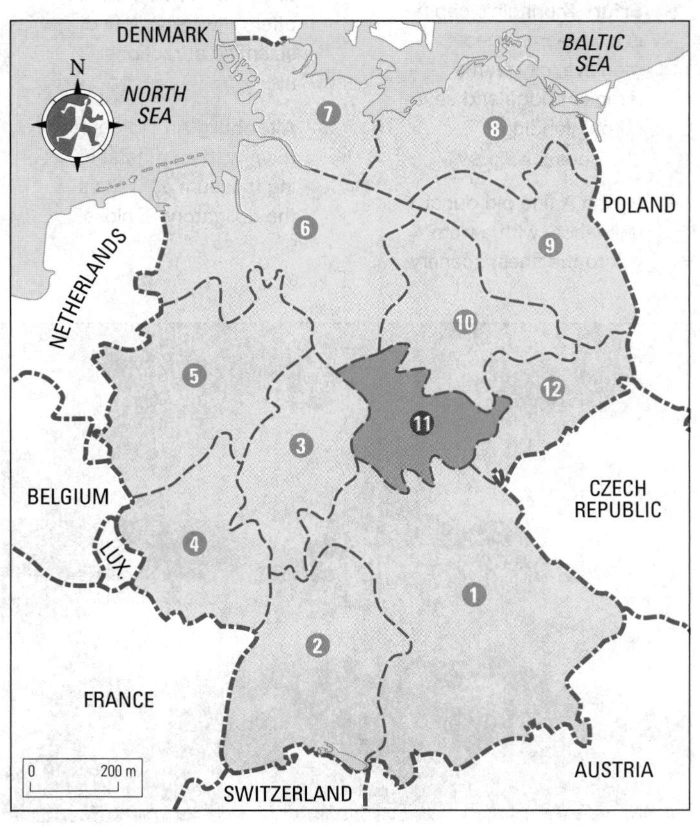

CHAPTER 11 Highlights

* **Weimar** This town, which has a grandeur out of all proportion to its size, holds a special place in the German national conciousness through its literary associations. See p.885

* **Erfurt** Thuringia's capital is a well-preserved medieval city with a famous bridge and several outstanding churches. See p.894

* **Gotha** A fine old ducal residence, with a tram link to the finest scenery of the Thuringian Forest. See p.901

* **Eisenach** The town of the Wartburg, Germany's most famous medieval castle. See p.908

* **Jena** Home of a celebrated university, the city offers a wide variety of scientific attractions. See p.917

* **Altenburg** An old courtly town with an outstanding museum as well as the obligatory Schloss. See p.925

△ The Wartburg, Eisenach

11

Thuringia

Of all the Länder, east or west, it's **Thuringia** (Thüringen) which comes nearest to encapsulating the nation's soul – and to providing an insight into the Germany of old, which elsewhere has largely been swept away by one or other of the dramatic events of the twentieth century. In many ways, it stands apart from the other eastern provinces – for one thing, it has been German since the Dark Ages, rather than land won from Slavs; for another, it suffers relatively little from industrial blight, thanks to being predominantly rural in character, with a vast forest accounting for a considerable proportion of its area.

Despite having been one of the five original provinces of early medieval Germany, Thuringia became defunct as a political entity in the thirteenth century. Most of it fell to the powerful **House of Wettin**, who amalgamated it with their Saxon holdings; smaller tracts were held by the dynasties of **Schwarzburg** and **Reuss**. In the sixteenth century, the Wettin possessions began to fragment into a series of tiny duchies (identified in English by the prefix "Saxe-"), while Schwarzburg and Reuss were also partitioned. Despite many subsequent amalgamations, there were still eight separate Thuringian principalities among the 25 states which came together to form the Second Reich in 1871. It took German defeat in World War I to bring this feudalistic situation to an end: the aristocracy was forced to follow the Kaiser's lead in resigning political power and Thuringia made a phoenix-like return to the map, having managed to preserve a definite regional identity throughout this long history of political fragmentation.

The most visible expression of Thuringia's past is the unparalleled number of **castles** and **palaces**, many of which turned what would otherwise have been villages into proud capital cities. Yet these are not always empty expressions of the vanity of petty princes – some of the courts were vibrant cultural centres which have made an impact on the nation out of all proportion to their size. Indeed, **Weimar** was the main driving force behind the German Enlightenment, and its overall contribution to the country's development far surpasses that of most of its major cities. Nearby **Jena** has maintained a strong academic tradition, particularly in the sciences, while **Eisenach**, which likewise belonged to the same duchy for a considerable period, has also made a huge mark on the national consciousness.

The capital of modern Thuringia is **Erfurt**. Although its population is less than a quarter of a million, it's by far the largest city in the province and a place very different from the former courtly towns, the well-preserved historic core evoking its past as a major episcopal centre. Walled **Mühlhausen** is, if anything, even more suggestive of the Middle Ages, while **Schmalkalden** offers plenty of reminders of its heyday during the Renaissance and Reformation. In

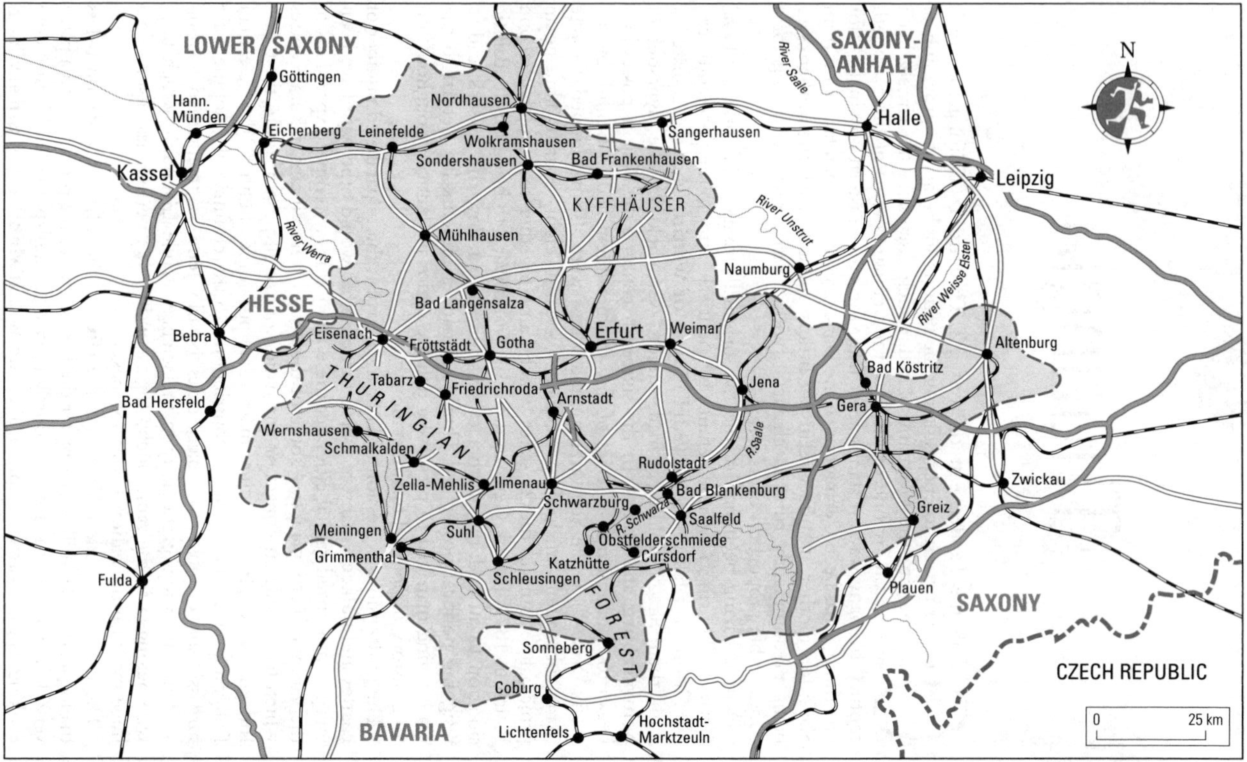

LOWER SAXONY
SAXONY-ANHALT
N
Göttingen
Hann. Münden
Nordhausen
Halle
Eichenberg
Leinefelde
Wolkramshausen
Sangerhausen
Kassel
Sondershausen
Bad Frankenhausen
Leipzig
KYFFHÄUSER
River Saale
River Unstrut
River Werra
Mühlhausen
Naumburg
HESSE
Bad Langensalza
River Weisse Elster
Bebra
Eisenach
Fröttstädt
Gotha
Erfurt
Weimar
Altenburg
Tabarz
Friedrichroda
Bad Köstritz
Jena
THURINGIAN
Arnstadt
Gera
Bad Hersfeld
Wernshausen
Schmalkalden
R.Saale
Rudolstadt
Zella-Mehlis
Ilmenau
Bad Blankenburg
Zwickau
Schwarzburg
R. Schwarza
Saalfeld
Greiz
Meiningen
Suhl
Obstfelderschmiede
Grimmenthal
Katzhütte
Cursdorf
Fulda
Schleusingen
FOREST
Plauen
SAXONY
Sonneberg
Coburg
CZECH REPUBLIC
Lichtenfels
Hochstadt-Marktzeuln
BAVARIA
0
25 km

contrast, **Gera**, the province's second city, has shrugged off its past as a Residenzstadt to become a bustling modern community. Of the other princely capitals, **Altenburg** and **Gotha** have (in common with Weimar, Jena and Eisenach) become medium-sized towns, whereas all the others – **Arnstadt**, **Meiningen**, **Sonderhausen**, **Bad Frankenhausen**, **Greiz**, **Rudolfstadt** and **Saalfeld** – remain engagingly provincial. In terms of scenery, the attractions are fairly low-key, though the **Thuringian Forest** has its fair share of beauty spots, as does the valley of the **Saale** at its far end, while at the far north of the province are the **Kyffhäuser**, a miniature mountain chain.

Travel in Thuringia is rendered particularly easy by the small distances separating most of the major attractions. Indeed it is possible to cover much of the province from a single centrally sited base, such as Weimar, Erfurt or Gotha.

Weimar

If Heidelberg is the German city foreigners are most prone to drool over, then **WEIMAR** is the one the Germans themselves hold dearest. Despite its modest size, its role in the development of national culture is unmatched. Above all, it was here that the German Enlightenment had its most brilliant flowering, when it was home to the writers Friedrich Schiller, Johann Gottfried Herder, Christoph-Martin Wieland and, most significantly, **Johann Wolfgang von Goethe** (see box on p.890), whose name is commemorated all over the town. Prior to this, Weimar's roll call of famous citizens had included Lucas Cranach and J.S. Bach; it would later number Franz Liszt, Richard Strauss, Friedrich Nietzsche and the architects and designers of the Bauhaus school. Later, the name of Weimar became synonymous with the republic established after defeat in World War I, which marked the birth of German democracy. Its inglorious failure, culminating fifteen years later with the Nazis gaining power by largely legal means, brought a sad twist to the town's cultural reputation, as it was the birthplace of the Hitler Youth movement and the site of Buchenwald, one of the most notorious concentration camps.

Arrival, information and accommodation

Weimar's **Hauptbahnhof** is well to the north of the main sights. The **tourist office** (April–Oct Mon–Fri 9.30am–6pm, Sat & Sun 9.30am–3pm; Nov–March Mon–Fri 10am–6pm, Sat & Sun 10am–2pm; ⓣ0 36 43/2 40 00 or 1 94 33, ⓦwww.weimar.de) is in the Stadthaus at Markt 10. Other useful **information offices** are those of the Konzentrationslager Buchenwald at Markt 5 (Mon–Fri 10am–12.30pm & 1–5pm, Sat 10am–3pm, Sun 10am–2pm; ⓣ0 36 43/43 02 00, ⓦwww.buchenwald.de), and of the Stiftung Weimarer Klassik und Kunstsammlungen (which administers Thuringia's literary sites and Weimar's art collections) at Frauentorstr. 3 (April–Oct Mon–Fri 10am–5.30pm, Sat 9am–noon & 1–4pm; Nov–March Mon–Fri 9am–4pm; ⓣ0 36 43/54 51 02, ⓦwww.swkk.de). It is well worth investing in the **Weimar Card** (available from the tourist office), which gives unlimited travel on the town's buses as well as admission to most (though not all) of the museums and sights; it costs €10 for three consecutive days and an extra €5 for a three-day extension to this.

You can book **private rooms** (❶–❸) at the tourist office. The plentiful provision of these is a real boon, given that there's a shortage of budget **hotels** (although there are now plenty of options in the middle and upper ranges). Weimar also has no fewer than four DJH/HI **youth hostels**.

Schloss Tiefurt
WEIMAR
Hauptbahnhof
0 200 m
N
SCHOPENHAUER STR.
CARL-AUGUST-ALLEE
BRENNERSTR.
MEYERSTR.
SCHLACHTHOFSTR.
FRIEDRICH-EBERT-STR.
CARL-VON-OSSIETZKY-STR.
ERNST-THÄLMANN-STR.
DÖLLSTADTSTR.
ROHRSTR.
BERTUCHSTR.
EDUARD-ROSENTHAL-STR.
ACCOMMODATION
Alt Weimar G
Amalienhof H
Elephant F
InterCity B
Jugendherberge Am Poseckschen Garten I
Jugendherberge Germania C
Russischer Hof E
Savina D
Thüringen A
RESTAURANTS AND CAFÉS
Bratwurstglöck'l 1
Crêperie du Palais 5
Der Kaukasische Kreiderkreis 2
Eckermann 9
Felsenkeller 12
Frauentor 8
Gastmahl des Meeres 3
Ratskeller 6
Residenz-Café 4
Sommers Weinstuben 11
Theater-Café 7
Zum Weissen Schwan 10
Neues Museum
JENAERSTR.
FRIEDENSSTR.
JAKOBSTR.
KARL-LIEBKNECHT-STR.
Jakobskirche
Weimarhallenpark
SCHWANSEESTR.
GRABEN
GOETHEPLATZ
COUDRAYSTR.
Kirms-Krackow-Haus
Stadtkirche
HERDERPLATZ
Schloss
SCHLOSSGASSE
BURGPLATZ
GELEITSTR.
HEINRICH-HEINE-STR.
Bauhaus-Museum
Buchenwald Information
THEATERPLATZ
Wittumspalais
Stadthaus
GRÜNER MARKT
Rathaus
MARKT
Cranachhaus
Deutsches Nationaltheater
Schillerhaus
ERFURTER STR.
SCHILLERSTR.
Rotes Schloss
River Ilm
FRAUENTORSTR.
Bachstube
Stiftung Weimarer Klassik und Kunstsammlungen
PLATZ DER DEMOKRATIE
Grünes Schloss
Gelbes Schloss
Fürstenhaus
FRAUENPLAN
STEUBENSTR.
Haus Stein
Park an der Ilm
ACKERWAND
SCHUBERTSTR.
Goethewohnhaus und Nationalmuseum
AM HORN
LISZTSTR.
PRELLERSTR.
Goethes Gartenhaus
Museum für Ur- und Frühgeschichte Thüringens
TRIERER STR.
MARIENSTR.
THOMAS-MÜNTZER-STR.
Park an der Ilm
CRANACHSTR.
Liszthaus
AM POSECKSCHEN GARTEN
HUMBOLDTSTR.
AMALIENSTR.
Musterhaus am Horn
GUTENBERGSTR.
Alter Friedhof
BELVEDERER ALLEE
WINDMÜHLENSTR.
Mausoleum
RUDOLF-BREITSCHEID-STR.
Hochschule für Architektur und Bauwesen
Russische Kirche
Nietzsche-Archiv
WILHELM-KÜLZ-STR.
BERKAER STR.
Römisches Haus
Schloss Belvedere

Hotels and pensions

Alt Weimar Prellerstr. 2 ⓣ0 36 43/8 61 90, ⓦwww.alt-weimar.de. Characterful hotel and restaurant at the southern edge of the centre. ❻

Amalienhof Amalienstr. 2 ⓣ0 36 43/54 90, ⓦwww.vch.de/amalienhof. Church-affiliated hotel occupying an Enlightenment-era palace. ❻

Dorotheenhof Dorotheenhof 1, Schöndorf ⓣ0 36 43/45 90, ⓦwww.dorotheenhof.com. Located 4km north of the centre on the route of bus #7, this hotel with restaurant was formerly the manor house of a cavalry officer, and is set in its own park. ❼

Elephant Markt 19 ⓣ0 36 43/80 20, ⓦwww.arabellasheraton.com. Weimar's most famous hotel dates back to 1696, but the interior is predominantly Art Deco. It has a gourmet restaurant, *Anna Amalia* (evenings only except at weekends), plus the surprisingly affordable *Elephantenkeller* (closed Sun evening). ❾

InterCity Carl-August-Allee 17 ⓣ0 36 43/23 40, ⓦwww.intercityhotel-weimar.de. Modernized mid-nineteenth-century hotel, complete with winter garden restaurant, directly opposite the Hauptbahnhof. ❻

Russischer Hof Goetheplatz 2 ⓣ0 36 43/77 40, ⓦwww.deraghotels.de. A grand, beautifully furnished hotel with restaurant with a tradition dating back to 1805. ❼–❾

Savina Meyerstr. 60 ⓣ0 36 43/8 66 90, ⓦwww.pension-savina.de. Large pension situated a few minutes' walk south of the Hauptbahnhof. ❹–❻

Thüringen Brennerstr. 42 ⓣ0 36 43/90 36 75, ⓦwww.hotel-thueringen-weimar.de. Medium-price hotel and restaurant diagonally opposite the Hauptbahnhof. ❺

Youth Hostels

Am Ettersberg Ettersberg-Siedlung ⓣ0 36 43/42 11 11. Rustic hostel in the Prinzenschneise nature reserve north of the city, a five-minute walk from the Obelisk stop on the route of bus #6. Advance bookings should be made via the *Maxim Gorki* hostel. €17.50/20.50.

Am Poseckschen Garten Humboldtstr. 17 ⓣ0 36 43/85 07 92. The most central of the hostels, located close to the Alter Friedhof; take bus #6 to Cranachstrasse. €16.50/19.50.

Germania Carl-August-Allee 13 ⓣ0 36 43/85 04 90. Located just a few paces south of the Hauptbahnhof. €16.50/19.50.

Maxim Gorki Zum Wilden Graben 12 ⓣ0 36 43/85 07 50. This lies 5km south of the centre, reached by bus #8 to Rainer-Marie-Rilke-Strasse. €17.50/20.50.

The Town

If you aren't interested in its literary and artistic associations, Weimar can seem a provincial sort of place. But its great merit is that it uncannily preserves both the appearance and atmosphere of its heyday as the most influential of the hundreds of capitals of pint-sized independent states which once littered the map of Germany. A rather tatty place in GDR days, it underwent a frantic programme of restoration in preparation for 1999, when it celebrated the 250th anniversary of Goethe's birth and served as European City of Culture.

The Schloss

Set by the River Ilm at the eastern edge of the town centre, Weimar's **Schloss** (Tues–Sun: April–Oct 10am–6pm; Nov–March 10am–4.30pm; €4.50; ⓦwww.swkk.de) is of a size more appropriate for ruling a great empire than a duchy whose population never rose much above 100,000. The complex is mostly in the Neoclassical style typical of the town: only the tall tower and the portal at the southwest corner remain of the original Renaissance palace of John Frederick the Magnanimous of Saxony, who established Weimar as the capital of his truncated duchy in 1547, following the loss of Wittenberg in the Schmalkaldic Wars.

On the ground floor there are notable collections of Thuringian medieval sculpture, fifteenth- to nineteenth-century Russian icons, and old master paintings. The last of these is dominated by important examples of the **Cranach** family, who followed the erstwhile Elector here from Wittenberg. Pick of the works by Lucas the Elder are *Luther as Junker Jörg* (showing him in the disguise he adopted when in hiding at the Wartburg), *John Frederick the Magnanimous and Sybille von Cleve* (a pair of official bridal portraits), *Samson and the Lion*, and the erotically suggestive *Age of Silver*, illustrating the favourite Renaissance theme of a battle between "wild men". Other highlights are **Dürer**'s *Hans and Elspeth Tucher* (a pair of portraits of a prominent Nürnberg patrician couple), and a typically idiosyncratic canvas by his pupil **Baldung**, *The Sacrifice of Marcus Civitius*.

On the first floor, some fine original interiors can be seen, the most imposing being the huge main **Festsaal** and the **Grosse Galerie**. There are also memorial chambers devoted to each of the four great Weimar poets; these are decorated with murals illustrating their main works. Also here are seventeenth-century Dutch still lifes and German painting from the Age of Enlightenment to the present day: look out for **Friedrich**'s haunting *Tomb of Hutten*, **Runge**'s touching *Portrait of Louise Perthes*, and **Moritz von Schwind**'s colourful *Seven Ravens*. The second floor displays works by painters of the Weimar School, including a good selection of canvases by **Christian Rohlfs**, among which *The Ilm Bridge at Buchfart* stands out.

Herderplatz, Jakobstrasse and beyond

Just west of the Schloss on Herderplatz is the **Stadtkirche St Peter und Paul** (April–Oct Mon–Sat 10am–noon & 2–4pm, Sun 11am–noon & 2–3pm; Nov–March daily 11am–noon & 2–3pm), a much-remodelled Gothic church usually known as the **Herderkirche** in honour of the poet, folklorist and literary theorist who was its chief pastor for three decades. Inside, the eye is drawn to the large **triptych** at the high altar, which is usually described as the artistic swan song of the elder Cranach, but was almost certainly painted as a memorial by his son, as it features the aged painter and his friend Luther as the main spectators at a Crucifixion scene arranged as a propaganda statement of the new Protestant doctrine of salvation. On the wings, John Frederick can be seen in the company of his wife and children. Also in the choir are a number of elaborate **tombstones**, including that of the elder Cranach and members of the ducal family; Herder is commemorated by a plain tablet under the organ loft.

Up Jakobsstrasse at the northeast corner of the square is the **Kirms-Krackow-Haus** (Tues–Sun: April–Oct 9am–6pm; Nov–March 10am–4pm; €2; Ⓦwww.swkk.de). This mansion, now a literary centre with a regular programme of events, belonged to a rich bourgeois family and preserves a suite of rooms furnished according to early nineteenth-century taste. Its courtyard of wooden galleries is particularly characteristic of the domestic architecture favoured in Weimar's glory days.

Further up the street is the **Jakobskirche**, a plain Baroque church with a Neoclassical interior. In 1806, it was the scene of the wedding of Goethe to Christiane Vulpius, with whom he had been living for eighteen years in a relationship that had scandalized many influential figures in Weimar society. Christiane lies buried in the peaceful cemetery surrounding the church, as does Cranach, whose original tombstone has been replaced here by a copy.

Further north on Carl-August-Allee, the long-derelict Grossherzogliches Museum has been renovated to house the **Neues Museum** (Tues–Sun: April–Oct 10am–6pm; Nov–March 10am–4.30pm; €3; Ⓦwww.swkk.de). This displays changing selections from the international avant-garde collection of Paul Maenz, who for two decades ran a highly successful commercial gallery in Cologne. A strong American showing includes examples of Carl Andre, Donald Judd, Dan Flavin and Sol LeWitt; another feature is the Italian section, in which Giulio Paolini and Piero Manzoni are particularly well represented.

The Markt and the Platz der Demokratie

South of Herderplatz is the **Markt**, lined by an unusually disparate jumble of buildings. Most eye-catching is the green-and-white gabled **Stadthaus** on the eastern side. Beside it is the **Cranachhaus**, where the artist spent his final years; directly opposite stands the neo-Gothic **Rathaus**. On the south side is the **Hotel Elephant**, the setting for all but the last chapter of Thomas Mann's novel about the town in Goethe's day, *Lotte in Weimar*. The historic inn was much favoured by Hitler, and it was just about the only place Westerners were allowed to stay during the GDR period, when it swarmed with *Stasi* agents; subsequently it has reclaimed its former position as one of Germany's leading hotels (see p.887). Adjoining it are two more old hostelries and the **Bachstube**, where the composer lived during his years as leader of the court orchestra and organist from 1708 to 1717. This ended with a month-long imprisonment, following his fury at being passed over for the musical directorship, whereupon he left for a new position at the much smaller court of Köthen.

Beyond is an even larger square, the **Platz der Demokratie**, lined by a colourful series of palaces, over which an equestrian statue of Grand Duke Carl August presides. On the north side is the **Rotes Schloss** (Red Palace), a Renaissance building with Neoclassical additions, while to the south the grand Baroque **Fürstenhaus** is where Goethe was received on his arrival in Weimar. It now houses the Liszt-Hochschule, a prestigious academy of music. The east side of the square is closed by the **Grünes Schloss** (Green Palace). The finest of the group, it contains the **Herzogin-Anna-Amalia-Bibliothek** (April–Oct Mon–Sat 11am–12.30pm; tickets on sale from 10.30am and numbers limited to 80 per day; €2; Ⓦwww.swkk.de). One of the most important collections of German literature in the world, it has an exquisite central **Rokokosaal**. Beside it stands the more modest **Gelbes Schloss** (Yellow Palace), while further south is the **Haus Stein**, the former ducal stables, which the stablemaster, Baron Friedrich von Stein, converted into a house. His wife Charlotte was Goethe's first great Weimar love, notwithstanding the fact that she was seven years the poet's senior and the mother of seven children.

Schillerstrasse, Theaterplatz and Frauenplan

Schillerstrasse snakes away from the southwest corner of the Markt to the **Schillerhaus** (daily except Tues: April–Oct 9am–6pm; Nov–March 9am–4pm; €3.50; Ⓦwww.swkk.de), the home of Friedrich Schiller for the last three years of his life, following his resignation of his academic chair at Jena. Here he wrote his last two dramas on great historical personalities, *The Maid of Orleans* (the story of Joan of Arc) and *William Tell*; and the rooms are furnished as he knew them. The modern extension behind contains the **Schillermuseum** (same times and ticket), with extensive documentation on his life and work.

Beyond lies **Theaterplatz**, in the centre of which is a large monument to Goethe and Schiller. The **Deutsches Nationaltheater** on the west side of the square was founded and directed by Goethe, though the present building, for all its stern Neoclassical appearance, is a pastiche: the facade from the beginning of the twentieth century, the rest from a rebuilding necessitated by its almost complete destruction in World War II. Apart from having seen the premieres of many of the greatest plays in the German language, the theatre was also the venue for the National Assembly's sittings in 1919 and saw the adoption of the constitution of the Weimar Republic.

Opposite is the **Wittumspalais** (Tues–Sun: April–Oct 9am–6pm; Nov–March 9am–4pm; €3.50; Ⓦwww.swkk.de), a large Baroque palace built as the retirement home of Regentess Anna Amalia, Weimar's great patron of the arts. Even as a dowager duchess, she continued to play a leading role in the town's intellectual life, organizing "Round Table" sessions here at which Goethe presided each Friday. The interiors are among the finest in Weimar, with the main **Festsaal** a design based on Goethe's ideas. There's also a large array of mementos of Christoph-Martin Wieland, now a rather neglected figure, but then regarded as the leading theoretician of the Enlightenment, as well as a major poet and philosopher.

Also on the square is the Kunsthalle, which has been converted to house the **Bauhaus-Museum** (Tues–Sun: April–Oct 10am–6pm; Nov–March 10am–4.30pm; €4; Ⓦ www.swkk.de). The main gallery displays works produced by artists of the Bauhaus during its early years in Weimar. One of the two small rooms is devoted to its forerunner, the Belgian Art Nouveau architect Henry van de Velde's Kunstgewerbeschule, founded in 1900 in an attempt to revive Weimar as a major artistic centre. The other room documents the successor to the Bauhaus, Otto Bartning's Staatliche Bauhochschule.

On Frauenplan south of the Markt is the excellent **Goethewohnhaus und Nationalmuseum** (Tues–Sun: April–Oct 9am–6pm; Nov–March 9am–4pm; €6; Ⓦ www.swkk.de). As its name suggests, it's in two parts. The more rewarding of these is the large Baroque mansion where the titan of German literature resided for some fifty years until his death in 1832. It's been preserved exactly as he knew it, and still has a lived-in feel to it, particularly the study with the desk where he sat dictating works to his secretary (he only composed poems with his own hand), and the little chamber where he died. In the adjoining museum the full range and versatility of his achievement is chronicled with typically Teutonic attention to detail.

The Südstadt

Most of the remaining sights are found in the **Südstadt**, the southern part of town. From the Goethewohnhaus, continue down Marienstrasse to the **Liszthaus** (Tues–Sun: April–Oct 9am–1pm & 2–6pm; Nov–March

Johann Wolfgang von Goethe (1748–1832)

Often regarded as the last of the great universal geniuses, **Johann Wolfgang von Goethe** produced a vast and diverse literary output – ranging from lyric to philosophic poetry, via comic and tragic dramas, to novels, short stories, travelogues, artistic criticism and scientific tracts – even though he was never truly a full-time writer. Despite his youth, he had already gained a European-wide literary reputation before his appointment to the Weimar court, thanks largely to the epistolary novel *The Sorrows of Young Werther*. His first decade in Weimar furnished him with a broad range of practical experience which he would later put to full use, but it left him little time for writing. By undertaking a long Italian sojourn in 1786, his creative spark was rekindled, though the play *Torquato Tasso* is a thinly veiled exposition of the frustration he felt at having to operate in the environment of a small court. His major prose work, *Wilhelm Meister*, is a cycle of six novels written over a period of five decades which, in common with much of his output, is a close reflection of his own personal development. A similarly protracted process attended the writing of his supreme masterpiece, the two-part drama *Faust*, completed just before his death, which symbolically examines the nature of Western man, his errors and ultimate salvation. The reverence accorded Goethe in Germany, and the academic industry which has grown up around him, is almost as extensive as that surrounding Shakespeare in the English-speaking world.

10am–1pm & 2–4pm; €2; Ⓦwww.swkk.de), the garden house of the great Austro-Hungarian composer Franz Liszt. His move to Weimar in 1848, where he spent eleven years as director of the local orchestra and opera company, marked a sea change in his career away from his earlier preoccupation with barnstorming virtuoso piano music towards richly scored programmatic orchestral pieces – the most ambitious being the Goethe-inspired *Faust Symphony* – which in turn cast a strong spell over his son-in-law, Richard Wagner. Despite leaving in a huff over the town's narrow-minded tastes, he returned in 1869, staying at this house for each of the remaining seventeen summers of his life.

A couple of minutes' walk to the west down Geschwister-Scholl-Strasse is Henry van de Velde's custom-built home for the Kunstgewerbeschule, the **Hochschule für Architektur und Bauwesen**. In 1919, Walter Gropius established the original **Bauhaus** in this college. However, it only remained here for six years before its move, prompted by hostility from reactionary elements in the town, to the more liberal climate at Dessau. The building still functions as an art college (one raised in 1993 to university status), and isn't a regular tourist sight, though you're free to wander in and look at any exhibitions that may be on.

Further to the west, at Amalienstr. 6, is the **Museum für Ur- und Frühgeschichte Thüringens** (Museum of Ancient and Early Thuringian History; Mon–Fri 9am–5pm, Sat & Sun 10am–5pm; €3.10; Ⓦwww.tlad.de), which charts the history and prehistory of Thuringia from the Stone Age to the tribes of the early medieval period. Highlights include Bronze Age jewellery from Schwarza, imaginatively displayed on reconstructed period dresses; the contents of a Germanic princess's grave unearthed at Hassleben; and the spectacular hoard of jewellery from the time of the fifth-century Thuringian kingdom found at nearby Ossmanstedt.

Immediately south of here is the **Alter Friedhof** (Old Cemetery), complete with a poignant array of carved tombstones and the Neoclassical **Fürstengruft** (Princes' Tomb) (daily: April–Oct 9am–1pm & 2–6pm; Nov–March 9am–1pm & 2–4pm; €2; Ⓦwww.swkk.de). Originally, this was intended for the Grand Ducal family, but it now has the tombs of Goethe and Schiller as well, following Carl August's decision that he wanted to be buried beside the two brightest stars of his court – though this necessitated reinterring the latter's corpse. Built onto the rear of the Mausoleum is the tiny **Russische Kirche** (Mon & Wed–Sun: April–Oct 9am–4.45pm; Nov–March 10am–3.45pm; free), built for the Grand Duchess Maria Pavlova, daughter-in-law of Carl August, who insisted on remaining loyal to the Orthodox faith of the Russian royal family to which she belonged.

Further to the southwest, at Humboldtstr. 36, is the Villa Silberblick, where the philosopher Friedrich Nietzsche, by then mentally ill, spent the last three years of his life. His sister commissioned Henry van de Velde to remodel the ground floor as a memorial and study centre, the **Nietzsche-Archiv** (Tues–Sun: April–Oct 1–6pm; Nov–March 1–4pm; €2; Ⓦwww.swkk.de). This has now re-opened, having been closed by the GDR authorities, who used the villa as an official guesthouse.

The Park an der Ilm

The **Park an der Ilm** is a large English-style park, complete with ruined follies, a statue of Shakespeare and a cemetery for Soviet soldiers killed in World War II, stretching southwards on both sides of the Ilm from the Schloss to the southern edge of town. At the western fringe of the park, close to the

Liszthaus, a stairway leads down to the **Parkhöhle Weimar** (Tues–Sun: April–Oct 9am–noon & 1–6pm; Nov–March 10am–noon & 1–4pm; €3; Ⓦwww.swkk.de). As their appearance indicates, these subterranean chambers have had an eventful history: originally used by the court as an ice cellar, they later became the focus of scientific interest, on account of the minerals and prehistoric fossils discovered there, and in World War II served as an air-raid shelter.

Almost due east, though on the opposite bank, is **Goethes Gartenhaus** (Tues–Sun: April–Oct 9am–6pm; Nov–March 10am–4pm; €3; Ⓦwww.swkk.de), where the writer stayed when he first came to Weimar; later, it served as his summer retreat. A few years ago, it was the subject of a drastic and highly controversial restoration, which has led to the banishment of all the furniture which had been acquired since Goethe's time, leaving the interiors looking very bare. Further south and back on the west side of the Ilm is the Neoclassical ducal summer house, known as the **Römisches Haus** (same hours; €2; Ⓦwww.swkk.de), whose ground-floor apartments are adorned with mock-Pompeiian murals. In the basement is a (German-only) documentary exhibition on the history of the park.

Overlooking the east side of the Park an der Ilm is one of Weimar's most exclusive streets, Am Horn. Among its many grand villas is one seemingly incongrous intruder, the **Musterhaus am Horn** (Wed, Sat & Sun 10am–5/6pm; €2) at no. 61. This was designed by Georg Muche for the first Bauhaus exhibition in 1923, and was intended to be the prototype for a complete garden city, but ended up as the only true Bauhaus building ever erected in the movement's birthplace. Belately recognized as a classic of twentieth-century architecture, it has gained inclusion on UNESCO's World Heritage List.

The outskirts

Another villa worth visiting is Henry van de Velde's own custom-built home, the **Haus Hohe Pappeln** (House Under the Tall Poplars; Tues–Sun: April–Oct 1–6pm; Nov–March 1–4pm; €2; Ⓦwww.swkk.de) at Belvederer Allee 58 in the incorporated village of Ehringsdorf; it can be reached by bus #1 or #12 to Papiergraben. Designed in the shape of an upturned boat, the upper floor and attic were intended as living quarters, and remain as such today, with the ground floor used for changing exhibitions.

Bus #12 continues onwards to the extreme south of town and the full-blown summer palace, **Schloss Belvedere** (April–Oct Tues–Sun 10am–6pm; €3.50; Ⓦwww.swkk.de). Its light and airy Rococo style and its collections of porcelain form a refreshing contrast to the Neoclassical solemnity of so much of the town. The **Orangerie** contains a dozen historic coaches which served the Weimar court, while the surroundings were transformed under Goethe's supervision into another English-style park.

Schloss Tiefurt (Tues–Sun: April–Oct 9am–6pm; Nov–March 10am–4pm; €3; Ⓦwww.swkk.de), situated northeast of the town centre and reached by bus #3 or #4, is a far more modest palace, more like a small manor house in fact. It was created for the Dowager Duchess Anna Amalia, who transferred her "Round Table" meetings here during the summer months. Again, there's a fine park with plenty of small follies and retreats.

The **Gedenkstätte Buchenwald** (May–Sept Tues–Sun 9.45am–6pm; Oct–April Tues–Sun 8.45am–5pm; free; Ⓦwww.buchenwald.de) is to the north of Weimar on the Ettersberg heights, and can be reached by bus #6, which runs hourly from the Hauptbahnhof. Over 240,000 prisoners were incarcerated in this concentration camp, with 56,000 dying here from starvation, torture and disease, but despite the high number of deaths – averaging 200 a day – Buchenwald was never an extermination camp. Among the prisoners killed here was the interwar leader of the German Communist Party, **Ernst Thälmann**. This gave the place a special significance for the GDR authorities, but the official state propaganda was tarnished by the discovery in 1990 of mass graves in the nearby woods, which provided conclusive proof that the Soviets used the camp after the war to round up and eliminate former Nazis and other political opponents. A documentary centre on the history of the camp has been set up in the former storehouse. The crematorium, disinfection chambers and prisoners' canteen are the other main buildings which may be visited.

Eating and drinking

Many of Weimar's best **restaurants** are in the hotels (see p.887), though there are plenty of good alternatives.

Bratwurstglöck'l Carl-August-Allee 17a. Just a stone's throw from the Hauptbahnhof, this delightful little half-timbered Gasthaus with front beer garden has been in existence since 1870.

Crêperie du Palais Am Palais 1. Serves not only crêpes, but other Gallic dishes, as well as wines and cider.

Der Kaukasische Kreiderkreis Rollplatz 12. Offers a rare chance to sample the cuisine of Georgia, with dishes prepared by a former chef to the Georgian government.

Eckermann Brauhausstr. 13. A genuine Hungarian restaurant, specializing in fiery, freshly made goulashes, with a good selection of wines as accompaniments.

Felsenkeller Humboldtstr. 37. Thuringia's first Hausbrauerei, set among the villas of the Südstadt, brews light and dark beers known as *Deinhardt* and also serves reasonably priced meals.

Frauentor Schillerstr. 2. Serves both *Kaffee und Kuchen* and bistro-type meals.

Gastmahl des Meeres Herderplatz 16. Fish speciality restaurant with a garden shaded by chestnut trees to the rear.

Ratskeller Markt 10. Typically German cellar restaurant, though it's opposite rather than underneath the Rathaus.

Residenz-Café Grüner Markt 4. Weimar's oldest offee house founded in 1839. It's a particularly good choice for breakfast.

Sommers Weinstuben Humboldtstr. 2. Wine bar-cum-restaurant which has been run by the same family, save for a short interregnum during the GDR period, for five generations. It's decked out in nineteenth-century style and has a small garden to the rear. Evenings only, closed Sun.

Theater-Café Theaterplatz 1a. Offers late breakfasts, vegetarian and other dishes, with regular live music sessions.

Zum Weissen Schwan Frauentorstr. 23. Historic Gasthaus whose praises were sung by Goethe. It's still among the best in town, with the game dishes particularly recommendable.

Entertainment

Weimar's main **theatre** venue is the Deutsches Nationaltheater, Theaterplatz 2 (ⓣ0 36 43/75 53 34, ⓦwww.nationaltheater-weimar.de), which regularly stages plays by Goethe and Schiller among others, as well as opera. Puppet shows, cabaret and dance all feature on the programme of the Theater im Gewölbe in the cellars of the Cranachhaus, Markt 11-12 (ⓣ0 36 43/77 73 77). **Concerts** are held at the gleamingly modern congress centrum neue wemarhalle, UNESCO-Platz 1 (ⓣ0 36 43/81 00, ⓦwww.weimarhalle.de). The liveliest **nightspot** is the *Studentenklub Kasseturm*, Goetheplatz 1, which is no longer exclusively for students. **Festivals** include the Thüringer Bachwochen (ⓦwww.bach-wochen.de), which is shared with several other Thuringian towns over several weeks around Easter, the Lisztage in October and the Zwiebelmarkt (Onion Market) on the second weekend of October.

Erfurt

Of all Germany's major cities, it's the Thuringian capital of **ERFURT**, which lies 20km west of Weimar, that's most redolent of its prewar self. Although it lost several important monuments in the air raids of 1944 and 1945, the damage to the overall historic fabric was relatively slight, while the many streets of stately *fin-de-siècle* shops were saved by the Communist interregnum from the developers who would have demolished them had the city lain on the other side of the Iron Curtain.

In 1970, Erfurt was the scene of the meeting between West German Chancellor Willy Brandt and East German Premier Willi Stoph which marked the beginning of the former's **Ostpolitik** and the end of the GDR's status as an international pariah. During the *Wende*, the city again provided a national lead by being the first place where the *Stasi* offices were stormed, thus preventing the destruction of incriminating files. Erfurt celebrated its 1250th birthday in 1992 with a year-long programme of events. The culmination was the re-establishment of the **university**, which was founded in 1392; it was once one of the largest and most prestigious in northern Europe, numbering Martin Luther among its graduates, but had been dormant since the Prussians suppressed it in 1816.

Arrival, information and accommodation

Erfurt's **Hauptbahnhof** is situated at the southeastern corner of the city centre. The **tourist office** (Mon–Fri 9am–6/7pm, Sat 9am–6pm, Sun 10am–4pm; ⓣ03 61/6 64 00, ⓦwww.erfurt-tourist-info.de) is at Benediktsplatz 1. Here you can buy the **Erfurt Card** (€7 for 24hr, €14 for 72hr), which covers travel on the local trams and buses, plus entry to all the municipally owned museums and sights.

The **youth hostel** is at Hochheimer Str. 12 (ⓣ03 61/5 62 67 05), southwest of the centre; take tram #5 to the Steigerstrasse terminus. **Private rooms** (❷–❸) can be booked in advance via the tourist office's special number (ⓣ03 61/6 64 01 10). **Hotels** are overwhelmingly geared toward the upper and middle range of the market, though the scarcity of inexpensive options is compensated for by the presence of numerous small **pensions**.

Hotels and pensions

Excelsior Bahnhofstr. 35 ⓣ03 61/5 67 00, ⓦwww.excelsior.bestwestern.de. Upmarket modern hotel behind a Jugendstil facade on the way from the Hauptbahnhof to the city centre. It has recently opened a restaurant, *Zum Bürgerhof*, which features an open kitchen. ❼–❾

Gartenstadt Binderslebener Landstr. 212 ⓣ03 61/2 10 45 12 or 2 25 60 50, ⓦwww.hotel-gartenstadt.de. Excellent middle-range hotel and restaurant not far from the ega grounds (see p.899), reached by tram #1. It has a sauna and solarium and serves good buffet breakfasts. ❺

Haus zum Pfauen Marbacher Gasse 12–13 ⓣ03 61/2 11 11 00. Characterful old inn in the Altstadt. In its courtyard is what is claimed to be the world's smallest brewery, which makes light (*Pfauenbräu*) and dark (*Der Schluntz*) beers to a recipe of 1587. ❸

Kalunov Stadtweg 22 ⓣ03 61/4 22 21 39, ⓦwww.erfurt-pensionen.de/kalunov. Pension in a large house in the southern inner suburbs. Take tram #3 or #6 to Sozialversicherungszentrum: it's then a short walk to the east. ❸

Nikolai Augustinerstr. 30 ⓣ03 61/59 81 70, ⓦwww.hotel-nikolai-erfurt.com. Fine mid-range hotel by the River Gera at the northern end of the Altstadt. It has a good restaurant (evenings only, except at weekends) with garden terrace. ❻

Scheel Paulinzeller Weg 23 ⓣ03 61/41 38 38, ⓦwww.erfurt-pensionen.de/scheel. Homely pension in a quiet street in the southern suburbs; there are several alternatives in the near neighbourhood. Take tram #3 or #6 to Blücherstrasse, from where it's a couple of minutes' walk to the west. ❸

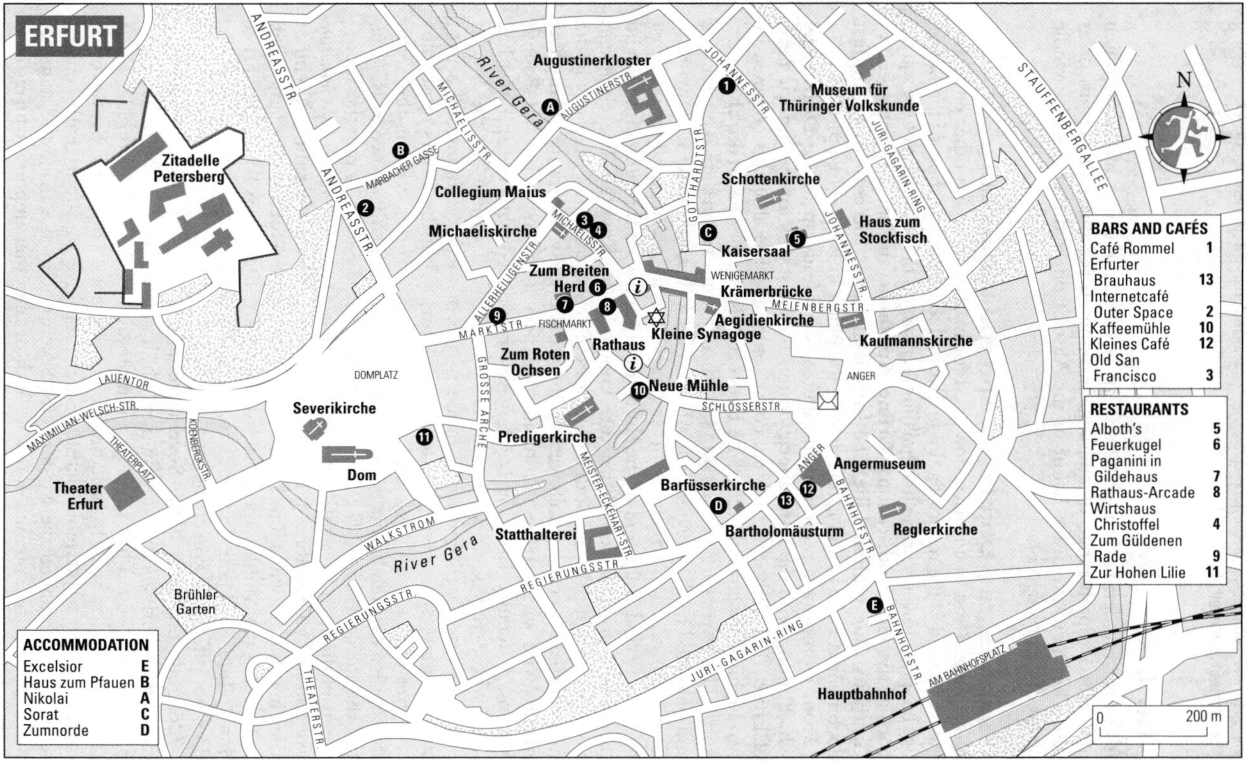

ERFURT

Zitadelle Petersberg
Augustinerkloster
Museum für Thüringer Volkskunde
Collegium Maius
Michaeliskirche
Schottenkirche
Haus zum Stockfisch
Kaisersaal
Zum Breiten Herd
Krämerbrücke
Aegidienkirche
Kleine Synagoge
Kaufmannskirche
Rathaus
Zum Roten Ochsen
Neue Mühle
Severikirche
Dom
Predigerkirche
Angermuseum
Barfüsserkirche
Bartholomäusturm
Reglerkirche
Statthalterei
Theater Erfurt
Brühler Garten
Hauptbahnhof

ANDREASSTR.
MICHAELISSTR.
MARBACHER GASSE
River Gera
AUGUSTINERSTR.
JOHANNESSTR.
GOTTHARDTSTR.
JURI-GAGARIN-RING
STAUFFENBERGALLEE
WENIGEMARKT
MEIENBERGSTR.
ALLERHEILIGENSTR.
MARKTSTR.
FISCHMARKT
DOMPLATZ
ANGER
SCHLÖSSERSTR.
LAUENTOR
MAXIMILIAN-WELSCH-STR.
THEATERPLATZ
KOENBERGKSTR.
GROSSE ARCHE
MEISTER-ECKEHART-STR.
BAHNHOFSTR.
WALKSTROM
REGIERUNGSSTR.
THEATERSTR.
AM BAHNHOFSPLATZ
N
0 200 m

ACCOMMODATION	
Excelsior	E
Haus zum Pfauen	B
Nikolai	A
Sorat	C
Zumnorde	D

BARS AND CAFÉS	
Café Rommel	1
Erfurter Brauhaus	13
Internetcafé Outer Space	2
Kaffeemühle	10
Kleines Café	12
Old San Francisco	3

RESTAURANTS	
Alboth's	5
Feuerkugel	6
Paganini in Gildehaus	7
Rathaus-Arcade	8
Wirtshaus Christoffel	4
Zum Güldenen Rade	9
Zur Hohen Lilie	11

Sorat Gotthardstr. 27 ⓣ03 61/6 74 00, ⓦwww.sorat-hotels.com. New designer hotel built alongside, and incorporating, the historic *Zum Alten Schwan* restaurant. ❼–❾

Zumnorde Anger 50 ⓣ03 61/5 68 00, ⓕ5 68 04 00. Classy hotel with spacious bedrooms, a restaurant, bar and roof terrace. ❼–❾

The City

It's worth wandering through almost any street in the centre of Erfurt, which preserves a superb range of buildings evoking all the different periods of its past. The open, expansive layout of the Altstadt offers the bonus of a whole range of surprising vistas.

Domplatz, the Domhügel and the Petersberg

Domplatz, a vast open space, now used for markets, fairs and other entertainments, formed as the result of a fire in 1813 which destroyed most of the houses on the spot. However, some fine buildings remain on the south side of the square, notably the eighteenth-century **Grüne Apotheke** and the sixteenth-century **Gasthaus Zur Hohen Lilie**. The latter is the direct successor to an inn first documented in 1341 and is thus among the oldest in Europe (see p.900).

From Domplatz, a monumental flight of steps leads up to the **Domhügel** which, along with the **Petersberg**, dominates the skyline of the historic heart of Erfurt. Formerly the city's episcopal centre, the Domhügel is crowned by two highly distinctive churches, the **Dom** and the smaller **Severikirche** to the north. The lower parts of the Dom's north and south **towers** are Romanesque and belonged to the previous church on the site, but otherwise it's a masterly Gothic construction which uses its sloping site to full advantage. From the first building period at the end of the thirteenth century are the central tower, and the massive, fortress-like substructure known as the **Kavaten**. The choir and transepts, in a pure High Gothic style, were perched on top of the latter in the mid-fourteenth century, followed by the flamboyantly decorative **triangular porch** with vivid statues illustrating the parable of the Wise and Foolish Virgins. A century later, the building was completed with the spacious hall nave, whose very German appearance is in marked contrast to the French influence manifested elsewhere. Inside is one of the most impressive sets of **stained-glass windows** to be found in Germany, but the Dom's most valuable treasures are the two mid-twelfth-century masterpieces in the south transept – a **candelabrum** in the shape of a man, popularly known as *Wolfram*, and the stucco **altar** of *The Enthroned Madonna with Saints*. Among the adornments of the nave are a small altar of *The Madonna and Child with SS Catherine and Barbara* by **Cranach**, and the **tomb** of the supposedly bigamous Count of Gleichen and his wives. The central tower houses the **Gloriosa**, the largest bell cast during the Middle Ages. Guided tours (July–Oct Thurs 9am–1pm, Fri & Sun 1–4pm, Sat 11am–4pm; €2) are run to the bell chamber, but note that it does not offer a view over the city.

Alongside the Dom is the **Severikirche**, whose distinctive triple-towered east end, sheltering a disarmingly small choir, acts as a perfect foil to its neighbour. The five-aisled hall nave has an impressively lofty feeling considering its relatively modest size. It contains the monumental **tomb of St Severus**, carved out of a soft pink sandstone by a sensitive mid-fourteenth-century sculptor, now dubbed the Master of St Severus, who also made the statue of the saint over the entrance doorway. Both of the other important furnishings – **the alabaster relief** of *St Michael* on the south wall, and the **font** with its spectacular fifteen-metre-high canopy – date from the year 1467.

Behind the Domhügel is a much larger hill, the **Petersberg**, which lies off the well-worn tourist trail. It was likewise once a centre of religious life, as the site of a Benedictine abbey, the **Peterskirche**, which five times hosted the imperial Reichstag in the days of Emperor Frederick Barbarossa. The church still survives, now cocooned within the **Zitadelle**, one of the finest surviving examples of Baroque military architecture anywhere in Europe. As a bonus, there's a wonderful view over the city, with the spires on the Domhügel in the foreground.

Marktstrasse and Fischmarkt

Marktstrasse, which leads eastwards from Domplatz, was once on the trade route that linked Frankfurt and Leipzig with the Russian city of Novgorod. These days, it seems a tad narrow for a major thoroughfare. It's worth making detours off it south down Grosse Arche, and north along Allerheiligenstrasse. At no. 11 on the latter is one of the city's finest houses, **Zum Roten Stern**, the late Gothic home, complete with oriel window, of one of the city's many distinguished printers.

Given that it was trade and commerce which made Erfurt rich in the Middle Ages, the central **Fischmarkt** is of unassuming dimensions. The statue of Roland in the middle was built as a symbol of defiance against the feudal overlords, the archbishop-electors of Mainz, though Erfurt never managed to gain the status of a Free Imperial City. On the north side of the square is a showy Renaissance mansion, **Zum Breiten Herd**, which rivals the less demonstrative, more classically balanced **Zum Roten Ochsen** (Wed & Fri–Sun 11am–6pm, Thurs 11am–10pm; €2.50; Ⓦwww.kunsthalle-erfurt.de) on the west side for the title of best building on the square. The latter is now a gallery, often featuring major temporary exhibitions of modern art.

Directly opposite is the bulky nineteenth-century **Rathaus**, which is primarily of note for the heroically Romantic fresco cycles inside, depicting scenes from the lives of legendary and historical figures with a Thuringian connection. To its rear, on Stadtmünze, is the **Kleine Synagoge** (Tues–Sun 11am–6pm; free), a small Neoclassical building of 1840 which ranks as the oldest undamaged Jewish temple left in Germany. It has been restored to house a permanent exhibition on Erfurt's Jews.

The Krämerbrücke and Michaelisstrasse

Just east of Fischmarkt is Erfurt's most singular sight, the **Krämerbrücke**, which adds a welcome dash of colour to a city which, for all its grandeur, can appear rather monochrome. Walking along, you have the illusion of entering a narrow medieval alley; the fact that this is actually a bridge lined with shops in the manner of the Ponte Vecchio in Florence is concealed at street level and only becomes obvious if you go down to the banks of the River Gera. The Krämerbrücke is known to have existed in the early twelfth century, but the history of the present structure begins with the stone rebuilding of 1325. In the Middle Ages, there were over sixty little shops on it, mostly associated with the trade in silk, spices, sugar and paper; their larger half-timbered replacements currently number 32 and contain a mixture of boutiques, antique dealers and commercial art galleries. House no. 31, the **Haus der Stiftungen** (daily 10am–6pm; free) has been painstakingly restored to the way it was at the time it was built in the 1570s. The far end of the Krämerbrücke is framed by the **Aegidienkirche**, a small upstairs church used by a German Methodist congregation. Its **tower** (variable opening times; €1.50) commands a marvellous view over the city.

Shortly before the western end of the Krämerbrücke, the **Michaelisstrasse** – the heart of the old University quarter, but now one of the quietest parts of the city – stretches northwards. Just off it is Waagegasse, a picturesque alley lined with sixteenth- and seventeenth-century storehouses. At the junction with Allerheiligenstrasse is the **Michaeliskirche**, an early Gothic church which was the main place of worship of the academic community. Its great treasure – visually as well as sonically – is the **organ**, built by Ludwig Comenius in the 1650s, and recently restored to pristine condition. On Thursday evenings in July and August, it can be heard in recitals given by an international cast of university-based organists. Also of note is the Renaissance **high altar**, which doubles as a memorial to a local councillor. The **Dreifaltigkeitskapelle**, added at the turn of the sixteenth century, boasts a prominent oriel window, an embellishment rarely found in ecclesiastical architecture, while the galleried courtyard is one of the most peaceful spots in Erfurt.

Across the street is the imposing Flamboyant Gothic portal of the **Collegium Majus**; the rest of this, the main university building, was a casualty of World War II bombs and is only now being reconstructed. Its outstanding collection of old manuscripts, the **Amploniana**, survived and is currently kept in the nineteenth-century science library behind.

East of the River Gera

Across the river is the **Augustinerkloster** (guided tours April–Oct Mon–Sat at 10am, 11am, noon, 2pm, 3pm & 4pm, Sun at 11am; Nov–March Tues–Sat at 10am, noon & 2pm, Sun at 11am; €3.50; Ⓦ www.augustinerkloster.de), the monastery where Luther lived between 1505 and 1511, first as a novice, then as a monk and priest. The complex, which has been in Protestant hands since the Reformation, was badly damaged in the war and has only been partially restored. A visit to a reconstruction of Luther's cell forms part of the tour, which also includes the cloister and the typically austere church. The latter is enlivened by some of Erfurt's most beautiful stained-glass windows, including one depicting the life of the order's founder, St Augustine.

A few blocks to the south, not far from the eastern end of Krämerbrücke, is the **Schottenkirche** (Scottish Church), so called from the nationality of the monks who lived here in the Middle Ages. The Baroque facade masks a simple pillar basilica which is one of the few Romanesque buildings left in Erfurt.

To the east is the north–south Johannesstrasse, the longest street in the Altstadt, lined with some of its most impressive Renaissance mansions. Particularly striking is the **Haus zum Stockfisch** at no. 169, which has a rusticated facade reminiscent of an Italian *palazzo*, with a carving of a dried cod above the door which gives the house its name. The interior now contains the local history displays of the **Stadtmuseum** (Tues–Sun 10am–6pm; €1.50). Further east, the Juri-Gagarin-Ring marks the boundary of the medieval city. Across it, at no. 140a, is the sixteenth-century hospital, now housing the **Museum für Thüringer Volkskunde** (Tues–Sun 10am–6pm; €1.50), a folklore collection focusing on the province's traditional lifestyles (re-created in a number of interiors), festivals, costumes, crafts and industries.

Anger and around

Johannesstrasse terminates at the **Kaufmannskirche** (Merchants' Church), with a memorial to Luther outside. This also marks the beginning of **Anger**, which starts off as a square but continues westwards as one of the main shopping streets, lined with the most opulent mansions in the city. It's worth making a short detour down Bahnhofstrasse to see the **Reglerkirche**, another former

Augustinian collegiate church, whose high altar is the best of the large carved and painted retables which were an Erfurt speciality in the fifteenth century.

Straddling Bahnhofstrasse and Anger is an ornate Baroque palace built as a weigh house and repository. It's now the **Angermuseum** (Tues–Sun 10am–6pm; €1.50; Ⓦ www.angermuseum.de), an excellent collection of fine and decorative arts. The highlight is the medieval section, which features the painted shields which formerly adorned the ceiling of the demolished fourteenth-century Rathaus, and several works – a *Crucifixion*, a *Pietà* and a *St Michael* – by the Master of St Severus. From the Renaissance period are paintings by Cranach and Baldung, while the usual range of nineteenth- and twentieth-century German paintings is supplemented by a chamber frescoed by the Expressionist Erich Heckel.

Further down Anger, you pass the **Bartholomäusturm**, the only surviving part of the court church of the counts of Gleichen. At the far end of the street, there's a fork; the northern branch, Regierungsstrasse, leads to the **Statthalterei**, a magnificent Baroque palace built by Maximilian von Welsch, court architect to the archbishops of Mainz, to serve as the headquarters of the city's government. A room on the first floor was the scene in 1808 of one of history's famous meetings – that between Goethe and Napoleon, who conversed knowledgeably about the former's plays.

The Barfüsserkirche and the Predigerkirche

Just north of here is the **Barfüsserkirche** (April–Oct Tues–Sun 10am–1pm & 2–6pm; €1), a vast, austere Franciscan friary church which was the most serious casualty of World War II bombs. Its nave has been left as a shell, but the choir has been restored to house a small branch of the Angermuseum's medieval collection. The stained-glass windows, which include a depiction of the life of St Francis, have been restored to their original position; some of them date back to the early thirteenth century.

On the other side of the river is the **Predigerkirche**, formerly the Dominican priory but since the Reformation the city's main Protestant church. Its exterior takes plainness to an extreme, but the interior is a masterpiece of spacial harmony in the purest Gothic style, and has preserved its layout and furnishings intact. The church was constructed in the thirteenth century when Master Eckhart, Germany's most celebrated mystic, was a friar there; he later became prior and vicar of Thuringia, in spite of holding pantheistic beliefs which many regarded as heresy. On the **rood screen** is a beautiful mid-fourteenth-century group of *The Annunciation*; the niches of the **choir screen** behind shelter a *Madonna and Child* and a painted *Calvary* from the same period. Elsewhere in the church are many elaborate epitaphs, a fifteenth-century carved and painted high altar and some lovely thirteenth-century stained glass made up of floral motifs.

To the rear of the church at Schlösserstr. 25a is the **Neue Mühle** (guided tours hourly Tues–Sun 10am–6pm; €1.50), the last still-functioning water mill in the city.

Cyriaksburg

For the past three decades, the ample grounds of the **Cyriaksburg** (daily: April–Oct 8am–8pm; Nov–March 8am–6pm; €3.60; Ⓦ www.ega-erfurt.com), a castle southwest of the city centre at the terminus of tram #2, have been given over to the **Internationale Gartenbauausstellung** (commonly known as ega), a vast garden show. It's best visited in spring, when the vast plantations of flowers are in full bloom. However, there are plenty of other attractions, notably the **Gartenbaumuseum** (Tues–Sun 10am–4/6pm; Ⓦwww.gartenbaumuseum.de; included in entrance ticket) in the Cyriaksburg itself, which traces the history of gardening. There are also several restaurants, exhibition halls, a look-out tower and hothouses displaying orchids, cacti and other tropical plants.

Eating and drinking

Restaurants

Alboth's Futterstr. 15. Located in part of an elegant eighteenth-century building known as the Kaisersaal (Imperial Hall) because it hosted the 1808 meeting of Napoleon and Czar Alexander I, this is currently Erfurt's best and most expensive restaurant. Open Tues–Sat, evenings only.

Feuerkugel Michaelisstr. 3–4. Very popular restaurant with back garden serving tasty Thuringian dishes, including several made to old recipes. Closed Mon.

Paganini in Gildehaus Fischmarkt 13. An upmarket Italian restaurant now occupies the ground floor of Zum Breiten Herd and its neo-Renaissance extension, the Gildehaus.

Rathaus-Arcade Fischmarkt 1. Smart new restaurant in the ground floor of the Rathaus.

Wirtshaus Christoffel Michaelisstr. 41. This "medieval" theme restaurant is one of a number of lively new ventures in the old university district.

Zum Güldenen Rade Marktstr. 50. Located in an old tobacco mill, this offers a wide-ranging menu, Köstritzer beer and a back garden with chestnut trees.

Zur Hohen Lilie Domplatz 31. Erfurt's oldest Gasthaus (see p.896) has returned in a new guise. The ground-floor restaurant specializing in local cuisine is open daily, the cellars only at weekends.

Bars and cafés

Café Rommel Johannesstr. 34. Very traditional café, founded in 1912 and still preserving its original Viennese-style decor. It has a garden to the rear. Closed Mon.

Erfurter Brauhaus Anger 21. Hausbrauerei which makes light, dark and various seasonal beers, and also serves hearty local cuisine.

Internetcafé Outer Space Andreasstr. 23. As well as being an Internet café, this is a favourite hang-out of local DJs. Open Mon–Thurs 2–10pm, Fri 2pm–midnight, Sat 3pm–midnight, Sun 3–10pm.

Kaffeemühle Schlösserstr. 25a. Café-bar in the Neue Mühle, with riverside garden. Open till late (1am on Fri & Sat), closed Mon.

Kleines Café Anger 19–20. Tucked away down a shopping alley, this has been going strong for over half a century, and makes really mouth-watering cakes. It's also a good choice for breakfast.

Old San Francisco Michaelisstr. 40. One of several American theme bars that have sprouted up in Erfurt in recent years, this is decked out with paraphenalia of San Francisco of the 1950s and 60s. It serves both American and German food.

Waldhaus Rhodaer Chaussee 12. This Hausbrauerei, which makes a *Pils* and a *Spezial*, and has both a winter garden and a summer beer garden, is one of a number of enticing destinations in Erfurt's green belt. Take bus #60.

Entertainment

Erfurt's principal **festival**, the Kramerbrückenfest, is held in the latter part of June and features a medieval market and all kinds of music. The city is one of those hosting the Thüringer Bachwochen around Easter (see p.893), while in July the steps leading up to the Dom are put to full operatic use in the Domstufenfestspiele (Ⓦwww.domstufen.de).

Theatre and concert venues

Kaisersaal Futterstr. 15 Ⓣ03 61/5 68 81 23).Though this still sometimes serves its original purpose as a ballroom, it is also used for concerts of all kinds of music.

Theater Erfurt Theaterplatz Ⓣ03 61/2 23 31 55, Ⓦwww.theater-erfurt.de. Erfurt's state-of-the-art showpiece stage opened in 2003. Its main priority is opera, though the consequent marginalization of drama – which previously had a separate civic theatre of its own – has caused controversy.

Waidspeicher Domplatz 18 Ⓣ03 61/5 98 29 12, Ⓦwww.waidspeicher.de. Hosts the puppet shows of the Puppentheater.

Clubs and live music

Centrum Anger 7. Plays a variety of music (hip-hop, techno, pop and rock) several evenings per week from 9pm.

Jazzkeller Fischmarkt 13–16. The city's premier jazz venue, with live music Thurs & Fri at 8.30pm.

Museumskeller Juri-Gagarin-Ring 140a. Features live bands Fri & Sat at 10.30pm, and the rest of the time is a hip-hop club.

Studentenclub Engelsburg Allerheiligenstr. 20. The liveliest dance club in the city, with events most evenings.

Gotha and around

GOTHA, which lies 25km west of Erfurt, is a handsome market town and main gateway to the popular holiday area of the Thuringian Forest. In the English-speaking world, it is indelibly associated with the **House of Saxe-Coburg-Gotha**, the name of the British royal family until they changed it to Windsor for patriotic reasons at the outbreak of World War I. The end of the war saw the dissolution of this united duchy, with the citizens of Coburg plumping for union with Bavaria rather than joining all the region's other petty states in the revived province of Thuringia. Gotha also holds an honoured place in the pantheon of the German left, as it was here in 1875 that the Socialist Workers' Party of Germany – renamed the **Social Democratic Party** fifteen years later, and still one of the country's main political forces – was formed.

The Town

Almost the whole of the southern half of central Gotha is taken up by the **Schlosspark**, whose spacious effect is slightly marred by being divided by two main thoroughfares – through the middle by Parkallee, and down the eastern fringe by Friedrichstrasse. After the park, the rest of Gotha is for the most part an anticlimax, though the Hauptmarkt is a highly original square.

Schloss Friedenstein

Schloss Friedenstein, which lies towards the northwestern end of the Schlosspark, is a U-shaped palace with massive square corner towers, built in sober early Baroque style. Its historical apartments and art collections are together designated the **Schlossmuseum** (Tues–Sun 10am–4/5pm; €4). Despite the plain exterior, it's highly elaborate inside, forming a visual encyclopedia of changing tastes in interior design, ranging from the heavy Baroque stuccowork of the main **Festsaal** to the **Dichter-Zimmer** (Poets' Chamber), adorned with Romantic landscapes, including **Friedrich**'s *Cross in the Mountains*, a variant of one of his favourite themes. The **Kunstkammer** is a typical princely curio cabinet, whose dazzling if slightly frivolous treasures include a gilded elephant by the great Dresden goldsmith Dinglinger.

The picture gallery's star attraction is the hauntingly enigmatic *Pair of Lovers*, the most important of the few surviving paintings by the mysterious Rhenish draughtsman dubbed the **Master of the Housebook**. No less striking are the little boxwood figures of *Adam and Eve* by **Conrad Meit**, which rank among the greatest carvings of the German Renaissance. A marvellous group of works by **Cranach** includes several known to be by the master's own hand, rather than the more usual products of his workshop. *The Adoration of the Magi* is the masterpiece of his middle period, while a rare self-portrait of the artist can be seen at the far left corner of *Judith at the Table of Holofernes*, a story continued in the companion *Death of Holofernes*. A diptych of *The Fall and Salvation of Man* is a complicated tract illustrating the theological teachings of Melanchthon. Another, albeit far less sophisticated work inspired by the new Protestant doctrines, is a folding altar painted by **Heinrich Füllmaurer** with 157 scenes full of anecdotal details on German life of the day. There's also an array of paintings from the Low Countries; look out for a brilliant pair of **Rubens** sketches for the ceiling of the Jesuit church in Antwerp.

The southwest tower of the Schloss contains the **Ekhof-Theater** (same hours as the Schlossmuseum; €2), a perfectly preserved Baroque gem, which is still in regular use. It's named in honour of Conrad Ekhof, a theatrical reformer who between 1774 and 1778 directed here the first company in Germany staffed by fully professional actors. Upstairs is the **Museum für Regionalgeschichte und Volkskunde** (same hours and ticket as Schlossmuseum), with the usual local history and folklore displays.

The **Schlosskirche** (April–Sept Tues–Sat 9am–4pm) is tucked away in the eastern part of the north wing, with no clue as to its presence from outside. Its interior is a fine example of courtly Lutheran Baroque: at the east end, the altar, pulpit and organ are all piled on top of one another; while the ceiling is covered with stuccowork and allegorical paintings, the one in the nave being a glorification of the wise regime of the House of Saxe-Gotha.

The rest of the town

Facing the Schloss across Parkallee is a heavy neo-Renaissance pile built to house the Kunstkammer, but now containing the **Museum der Natur** (Tues–Sun 10am–5pm; €2). This contains displays on the flora and fauna of the Thuringian Forest – including creatures such as the wolf and the lynx now extinct there. In addition, there's a section on the Thüringer Waldbahn, the forest tramway (see p.903). Elsewhere in the southern half of the Schlosspark are a large boating lake and the **Dorischer Tempel**, designed by Friedrich Wilhelm von Erdmannsdorff, creator of the gardens of Wörlitz. East of Schloss Friedenstein is the so-called **Teeschlösschen**, a folly, long used as a kindergarten, built in imitation of an English church. Beyond are the two pavilions of the **Orangerie**, one of which is a library, the other a café.

The **Hauptmarkt** is built on a pronounced incline, which sweeps majestically up to Schloss Friedenstein. Standing in splendid isolation in the middle is the Renaissance **Rathaus**, whose **tower** (daily 10am–4pm; €1) can be ascended for a view over the town. Also on the square are a Baroque fountain and a number of colourful houses, among them the **Lucas-Cranach-Haus** at the top end, which is known to have belonged to the painter, though the facade is much later. From here, Lucas-Cranach-Strasse leads to the Rococo **Frankenbergsches Gartenhaus**, which stands in its own pretty courtyard down a little alley.

Practicalities

Gotha's **Hauptbahnhof** is at the southern end of town; trams #1, #2 and #4 will all take you in the direction of the centre. The **tourist office** (Mon–Fri 9am–6pm, Sat & Sun 10am–2pm; Nov–March closed Sun; ⓣ0 36 21/22 21 38, ⓦwww.gotha.de) is at Hauptmarkt 2. As ever, it can book **private rooms** (❷–❸).

The **youth hostel** is handily located just east of the Schlosspark and north of the Hauptbahnhof at Mozartstr. 1 (ⓣ0 36 21/5 40 08; €12.50/15.50). There are also plenty of conveniently located **pensions**, including *Am Schloss*, Bergallee 3a (ⓣ0 36 21/85 32 06; ❷), *Gaa*, Kleine Fahnenstr. 6 (ⓣ0 36 21/75 58 90,

Ⓦ www.pension-gaa.de; ❸), *Café Suzette*, Bebelstr. 8 (Ⓣ 0 36 21/85 67 55; ❹), and the much larger *Regina*, Schwabhäuser Str. 4 (Ⓣ 0 36 21/40 80 20, Ⓦ www.pension-regina.de; ❹). Among several good medium-priced **hotels** are *St Gambrin*, Schwabhäuser Str. 47 (Ⓣ 0 36 21/3 36 00; ❺), which also has a fish speciality restaurant (*Da Bruno*), and *Waldbahn*, Bahnhofstr. 16 (Ⓣ 0 36 21/23 40, Ⓦ www.waldbahn-hotel.de; ❺), whose amenities include a sauna, solarium, beer garden and reasonably priced restaurant. At the top of the range is *Am Schlosspark*, Lindenauallee 20 (Ⓣ 0 36 21/44 20, Ⓦ www.hotel-am-schlosspark.de; ❼), which features Roman-style baths and two classy restaurants.

Other good **restaurants** are the *Pagenhaus* in the Schloss, the historic *Weinschänke*, Gartenstr. 28, and *König-Sahl*, Brühl 7, an evenings-only Hausbrauerei which makes light and dark beers and serves full meals. There are several excellent traditional **cafés**: close to the Hauptbahnhof is *Café Suzette* (see pension above), while in the centre are *Loesche*, Buttermarkt 6, and *Junghans*, Hauptmarkt 42.

Around Gotha: the Thuringian Forest

Just 20km southwest of Gotha, the area centred on **FRIEDRICHRODA** makes an excellent place for some serious hiking in the **Thuringian Forest**. The best approach is by the **forest tramway**, the Thüringer Waldbahn (tram #4; Ⓦ www.waldbahn-gotha.de), which runs from Gotha Hauptbahnhof to Friedrichroda, before veering westwards to its terminus at the neighbouring resort of Tabarz. It's painfully slow – the 23-kilometre journey often takes more than an hour – but it's the easiest way to see the scenery in comfort. On leaving Friedrichroda, the Waldbahn stops outside the forest's most important natural curiosity, the **Marienglashöhle** (guided tours daily 9am–4/5pm; €4). This is the largest crystalline cave in Europe, complete with underwater lake; its name comes from the fact that, in times past, its products were used for making jewels to adorn statues of the Virgin Mary.

By far the most popular **hike** in the area is the ascent of the Thuringian Forest's third highest and best-known peak, the **Grosser Inselberg** (916m), which lies just to the southwest of Tabarz. The summit itself is disfigured by an ugly TV tower and a number of other buildings, but in compensation there's a truly sweeping view. Taking the Friedrichroda to Brotterode bus to the Grenzwiese stop leaves only a short walk up. The same place marks the convergence of several other trails; among these is the 168-kilometre-long **Rennsteig**, one of Germany's oldest and finest long-distance wilderness footpaths (see box below).

The Rennsteig

The 168-kilometre-long **Rennsteig** cuts right through the heart of the Thuringian Forest, from Hörschel, west of Eisenach, all the way to Blankenstein by the border with the Czech Republic. In the Dark Ages, it served as the frontier between the Thuringians and the Franks; later, it was used to demarcate the limits of the province's petty principalities; and in the nineteenth century, it was laid out as a marked footpath, identified by signs bearing a large R. Five or six days is the normal time needed for the complete walk. Hostels, campsites and refuges lie directly on the trail, though there are also plenty of resorts on the way – Brotterode, Oberhof, Neustadt, Neuhaus and Steinbach – which make obvious places for an overnight stop. If you don't want to do the complete route, plenty of small sections make for satisfying walks in their own right.

Arnstadt

First documented in 704, **ARNSTADT**, which lies just beyond the fringes of the Thuringian Forest, 18km southwest of Erfurt, has the best claim to be regarded as the oldest town in eastern Germany. Its well-preserved historic centre of narrow alleys and half-timbered houses evokes the sort of timeless provincial air that has all but vanished from the western Länder and may not last for much longer here; it also has the advantage of being surrounded by a typically Germanic landscape of woods and hills.

Arnstadt's layout is characteristic of the feudal pattern of Thuringia with the princely palace occupying a green area, now known as the Stadtpark, at the edge of the town centre. The tower and a few other scanty fragments are all that remain of the sixteenth-century **Schloss Neideck**, the original seat of the House of Schwarzburg-Arnstadt. Before it fell into disrepair, a second palace, the **Neues Palais** (May–Sept Tues–Sun 9.30am–6pm; Oct–April Tues–Sun 10am–4pm; €3), was built to the south in the early eighteenth century. Its main attraction is **Mon Plaisir**, a collection of over 400 dolls arranged into 82 scenes, depicting the life of all social classes of the day. Far from being intended as playthings for children, these scenes were commissioned over half a century by Princess Augusta Dorothea as a serious artistic enterprise. As well as the figures, the clothes, utensils and furniture are all precisely crafted, and constitute a valuable documentary source on social conditions in the period. The palace is also renowned for its seventeenth- and eighteenth-century porcelain, some of which is ingeniously displayed on gilded tables in the **Spiegelkabinett**.

A few minutes' walk to the west is the Markt, where the Renaissance **Rathaus** springs a surprise in its uncompromising imitation of Dutch-style architecture. The church opposite was once known as the Neue Kirche. In 1703, the eighteen-year-old J.S. Bach gained his first major professional appointment as organist here; as a result, it's now officially called the **Bachkirche**, and the organ on which he played still survives. Unfortunately, the Arnstadt congregation failed to appreciate his genius as either a composer or performer and, stung by criticism of his revolutionary improvisatory playing style, he left four years later for Mühlhausen.

Beyond the far end of the Markt is the **Liebfrauenkirche**, whose architecture, and in particular the two magnificent west towers, is loosely based on the Dom in Naumburg. The chapel on the north side of the choir served as the mausoleum of the counts of Schwarzburg and contains the beautiful double **tomb** of Günther XXV and his wife Elisabeth, thought to have been carved in the famous workshop of Peter Parler in Prague. Also of note are the **stained-glass windows** in the nave aisles, and the **high altar** of *The Coronation of the Virgin*, a fine example of fifteenth-century Thuringian woodcarving. Alongside the church is one of the town's oldest half-timbered houses, the **Alte Mühle**, which began life as the corn mill of a convent.

Practicalities

Arnstadt's **Hauptbahnhof** is situated at the northern end of town, while the **tourist office** (Mon–Fri 10am–6pm, Sat 10am–1pm; ⓣ0 36 28/60 20 49, ⓦwww.arnstadt.de) is at Markt. 3. The best times to visit are during the **musical festivals**, the Bachtage at the end of March and the Orgelsommer in June and July. As well as the **private rooms** (❶–❸), which can be booked at the tourist office, there are **hotels** to suit most pockets. At the budget end of the scale are *Goldene Sonne*, Ried 3 (ⓣ0 36 28/60 27 76, ⓦwww.goldene-sonne-arnstadt.de; ❸–❺); *Riedschenke*, Vor dem Riedtor 6 (ⓣ0 36 28/60 23 74; ❹); and *Goldene Henne*, Ried 14 (ⓣ0 36 28/58 95 60, ⓦwww.henne-arnstadt.de; ❹). More upmarket choices include *Brauhaushotel*, Brauhausstr. 3 (ⓣ0 36 28/60 74 00, ⓦwww.arnstadt-stadtbrauerei.de; ❺); *Krone*, Am Bahnhof 8 (ⓣ0 36 28/7 70 60, ⓦwww.krone-2000.de; ❺); and *Anders*, Gehrener Str. 22 (ⓣ0 36 28/74 53, ⓦwww.hotel-anders.de; ❺).

There are fine **restaurants** in each of the last two hotels, while the *Brauhaushotel* is part of a complex centred on the Stadtbrauerei, which brews a distinctive black *Weizen* (it is claimed that *Hefeweizen* was invented in Arnstadt in 1617) and serves excellent food. It has a covered winter garden and a

The Goethe trail

The famous footpath, **Auf Goethes Spuren** (In Goethe's Footsteps), takes in a number of places connected with the poet in the course of an 18.5 km route from the old glass-making and porcelain-producing town of **ILMENAU**, some 20km south of Arnstadt. While primarily of interest to literary buffs, it also offers an excellent overview of the scenery of the Thuringian Forest, and along the route are several excellent country Gaststätten offering wholesome German cooking. The terrain is fairly demanding; allowing for regular sightseeing stops, it's likely to take up a full day. It's very well signposted by means of a G monogram copied from Goethe's own handwriting.

The starting point for the walk is Ilmenau's **Amtshaus** (daily: May–Oct 9am–noon & 1–4.30pm; Nov–April 10am–noon & 1–4pm; €1), at the top end of the Markt, which houses a small museum containing mementos of Goethe, who lived and worked there during his sorties to the town. From the Markt, the route travels westwards to the village of Manebach, from where it ascends to the celebrated **Kickelhahn** (861m), which can also be reached directly by a much shorter path from the southern end of Ilmenau. On this mountain are an outlook tower, which commands an extensive panorama over Ilmenau and the Thuringian Forest, and a replica of the long-destroyed **Goethehäuschen**, the little wooden hideaway, where the poet composed one of his most quoted poems, *The Wayfarer's Night Song II*. About fifteen minutes' walk further along the route is the **Jagdhaus Gabelbach** (March & Oct Wed–Sun 11am–3pm; April–Oct Tues–Sun 9am–5pm; €2; ⓦwww.swkk.de), a hunting lodge containing a museum devoted to Goethe's studies in natural history. From here, the trail continues south to its terminus at the village of **STÜTZERBACH**, where the **Gundelachsches Haus** (same times; €2; ⓦwww.swkk.de) preserves rooms where Goethe stayed and worked, and also features displays on the local glass industry.

Ilmenau practicalities

Ilmenau is connected by a direct rail link to Arnstadt, and has two stations – the **Hauptbahnhof** is east of the town centre and marginally closer to the Markt than the **Bad-Bahnhof** to the south. The latter is more useful if you want to take the direct trail to the Kickelhahn. It's also closer to the **tourist office** (Mon–Fri 9am–6pm, Sat 9am–noon; ⓣ0 36 77/20 23 58, ⓦwww.ilmenau.de), which is just over the Ilm at Lindenstr. 12.

You can book **private rooms** (❶–❸) at the tourist office. There are also a few small **pensions**, including *Melanie*, just south of the Bad-Bahnhof at Heinrich-Heine-Str. 3 (ⓣ0 36 77/67 01 45; ❸). The one budget **hotel**, *Zum Elephant*, is right in the heart of town at Marktstr. 16 (ⓣ0 36 77/20 24 41; ❸); the **youth hostel** is in the southeastern part of town at Am Stollen 49 (ⓣ0 36 77/88 46 81; €15/18).

summer beer garden, while alongside are *Schalander*, a live music and cabaret cellar, and the Stadthalle (Ⓣ0 36 28/60 77 06), where concerts and large-scale events take place.

Meiningen

On the banks of the River Werra at the extreme southwestern corner of the Thuringian Forest lies **MEININGEN**, an old ducal capital with a very distinctive tradition in the performing arts. In the latter half of the nineteenth century, under the enterprising rule of Duke Georg II, it became one of Germany's leading centres for both theatre and music, with a resident orchestra, the Meininger Hofkapelle, which was among the most celebrated in the world, and one of the first to undertake global concert tours. Today Meiningen is a purely provincial town with a population of little more than 25,000, but it's an agreeable place with beautiful surroundings and an interesting Schloss, and warrants a stay of a day or two.

The Town

Meiningen's dominant building is **Schloss Elisabethenburg** (Tues–Sun 10am–4.45/6pm; €3 or €5 combined ticket with Reiterhalle; Ⓦwww.meiningermuseen.de), which stands in its own park at the northern end of the Altstadt, this combined area being separated from the rest of the town by a narrow canal system linked to the Werra. The Schloss was built in the late seventeenth century, immediately after the foundation of the duchy of Saxe-Meiningen, and is in the plainest possible Baroque style; indeed its geometric austerity seems strangely anticipatory of the Bauhaus, with the red-and-white colour scheme providing one of the few surface distractions. However, its ground plan is highly unusual, featuring an enclosed courtyard as a result of the addition of the so-called **Rundbau** (Round Building) to the orthodox palace format. Most of the **interiors** were remodelled according to the historicist tastes of Duke Georg, and evoke the whole gamut of European architectural styles. They house three separate permanent exhibitions. That devoted to the fine arts includes notable examples of Gothic wood sculpture, plus an eclectic display of old masters whose star piece is *Lot and his Daughters* by Ribera. There are also displays on the Hofkapelle's **music directors**, who included Hans von Bülow – one of the first virtuoso conductors – and the composers Richard Strauss and Max Reger.

Most of the **Theatermuseum** has been moved to the former riding hall, the **Reiterhalle** (same hours; €2.50; Ⓦwww.meiningermuseen.de), which features some spectacular stage sets plus a number of sketches for costume designs by Duke Georg himself. On the top storey of the Schloss's central tower is the ornate **Hessensaal**; one of the few original interiors to have survived, it now houses a daytime café, the *Turmcafé*. The only other Baroque interior which can be visited is the former **Schlosskirche** in the southern wing, which has been converted, albeit with the retention of all its furnishings, into a concert hall.

Just across from the entrance to the Schloss, at Burggasse 22, is one of the town's finest half-timbered constructions, the **Baumbachhaus** (same times and ticket as the Schloss; Ⓦwww.meiningermuseen.de). This houses a small museum on literary figures who have stayed in or near the town, among them Schiller and Jean Paul; the latter was the most popular and influential German novelist of the late eighteenth and early nineteenth centuries.

A few minutes' walk south, in the very heart of the Altstadt, is the spacious rectangular Markt. It's dominated by the **Stadtkirche St Marien** whose eccentrically fantastical twin spires help create a memorable silhouette. Although by origin late Gothic, the church's present appearance, both inside and out, is yet another manifestation of the artistic tastes of Duke Georg.

East of the Altstadt is Bernhardstrasse, a stately boulevard lined with several imposing buildings, notably the **Meininger Theater** (ⓣ0 36 93/45 12 22, ⓦwww.das-meininger-theater.de). Despite its uncompromising Neoclassicism, above all in the porticoed facade, it only dates from the first decade of the twentieth century, and is a replacement for its fire-damaged predecessor. It retains the services of a full-sized orchestra, now rechristened the Orchester des Meininger Theaters, and presents ambitious programmes of music, opera, ballet and drama. Behind is the town's second important park, the **Englischer Garten**.

Practicalities

Meiningen's **Bahnhof** directly overlooks the Englischer Garten, and is just a few minutes' walk from the centre. The **tourist office** (April–Oct Mon–Fri 9am–6pm, Sat 10am–3pm; Nov–March Mon–Fri 9am–5pm; ⓣ0 36 93/4 46 50, ⓦwww.meiningen.de) at Markt 14 performs the usual booking service for **private rooms** and small **pensions** (❷–❹), which are fairly numerous.

Town-centre **hotels** include *An der Kapelle*, Anton-Ulrich-Str. 19 (ⓣ0 36 93/4 49 20; ❹), *Schlundhaus*, Schlundgasse 4 (ⓣ0 36 93/81 38 38, ⓦwww.meininger-hotels-mit-flair.de; ❻), and *Sächsischer Hof*, Georgstr. 1 (ⓣ0 36 93/45 70, ⓦwww.romantikhotels.com; ❽). However, the most enticing place to stay has to be *Schloss Landsberg*, a medieval castle rebuilt in the nineteenth century in neo-Gothic style; it's situated 4km northwest of the centre at Landsberger Str. 150 (ⓣ0 36 93/4 40 90, ⓦwww.meininger-hotels-mit-flair.de; ❼). The best places to **eat** and **drink** are the hotels (all those listed have recommendable restaurants), or there's the *Schlossstube* in the Rundbau of the Schloss, which offers Hungarian as well as traditional German dishes.

Schmalkalden

SCHMALKALDEN, a bustling market town 25km northeast of Meiningen, is associated above all with the Reformation, in which it played a key role. In 1531, it was the setting for the formation of the Schmalkaldic League, an alliance of Protestant princes and Free Imperial Cities determined to protect their independence against the renewed threat of a reimposition of centralized political and religious authority posed by Emperor Charles V. The Schmalkaldic Wars, which broke out just after Luther's death in 1546, led to a disastrous defeat for the Protestants and the occupation of Wittenberg, but they staged such a spirited recovery that by 1555 their aim of a decentralized Germany with each state free to choose its own religion had been enshrined in the Peace of Augsburg.

Schmalkalden's main square, the Altmarkt, is dominated by the **Stadtkirche St Georg** (May–Oct Mon–Sat 10am–noon & 2–4pm), a late Gothic hall church whose clock face shows Death claiming a young girl. Among the many notable old houses are the half-timbered **Lutherhaus** on Luthermarkt (formerly the potters' market), where the reformer stayed during his visits to the town; the **Heiliggrabesbehausung**, a huge sixteenth-century tenement on Weidebrunner Gasse; and the **Hessenhof** on Neumarkt.

Standing proudly on its hill at the eastern end of town is the whitewashed **Schloss Wilhelmsburg** (Tues–Sun: Feb–Oct 9am–5pm; Nov–Jan 10am–4pm; €3.50), built in the 1580s as a summer residence and hunting seat for the landgraves of Hesse-Kassel, who had recently won complete control of the town. One of the best-preserved Renaissance palaces in Germany, its interior now houses exhibits outlining the town's complicated history, but these are overshadowed by the reception rooms themselves, most of which have elaborate coffered ceilings and huge decorative wall paintings. Particularly outstanding is the **Riesensaal** (Hall of Giants), with Landgrave Wilhelm intruding among the portraits of Old Testament and mythological heroes.

However, the most striking and significant part of the building is the **Schlosskirche**, the earliest surviving church to adhere faithfully to the design tenets of Protestantism. Taking up most of one wing, the only clue to its presence from outside is the small tower. Inside, each of the three tiers has, grouped vertically one above the other, the three essential props of Protestant worship: the plain marble **altar table**, here resting on the four Evangelical symbols, the **pulpit**, whose basin is carved with a depiction of Pentecost and the **organ**, which has wooden pipes and is adorned with painted shutters. The organ is still in fine working order, and is regularly used for recitals.

Practicalities

Schmalkalden's **Bahnhof** is a short walk west of the town centre. The **tourist office** (April–Oct Mon–Fri 9am–1pm & 2–5pm, Sat 10am–1pm & 2–5pm; Nov–March Mon–Fri 9am–1pm & 2–5pm, Sat 10am–1pm; Ⓣ0 36 83/40 31 82, Ⓦwww.schmalkalden.de) is at Mohrengasse 1a. Plenty of **private rooms** (❶–❸) can be booked there. In the town centre there are two **hotels**: *Teichhotel*, Teichstr. 21 (Ⓣ0 36 83/40 26 61, Ⓦwww.teichhotel.de; ❹), and *Stadthotel Patrizier*, Weidebrunner Gasse 9 (Ⓣ0 36 83/60 45 14, Ⓦwww.stadthotel-patrizier.de; ❺). There are a couple of enticing alternatives in the outskirts: *Jägerklause*, Pfaffenbach 45 (Ⓣ0 36 83/60 01 43; ❹), and *Henneberger Haus*, Notstr. 33 (Ⓣ0 36 83/6 50 00; ❻). All these have good **restaurants**, though they're rivalled by the *Ratskeller*, Altmarkt 2.

Eisenach

EISENACH, 35km northwest of Schmalkalden and 28km west of Gotha, grew up as an appendage to the **Wartburg**, the original seat of the landgraves of Thuringia, which overlooks it from the fringe of the Thuringian Forest to the south. Though foreigners may prefer the fantasy creations of King Ludwig II of Bavaria, the Wartburg's rich historical associations make it the castle the Germans themselves most treasure, and its proximity to the hated postwar border has made it something of a symbol of the united nation.

Arrival, information and accommodation

Eisenach's **Hauptbahnhof** lies just beyond the eastern boundaries of the Altstadt. The **tourist office** (Mon 10am–6pm, Tues–Fri 9am–6pm, Sat & Sun 10am–2pm; Ⓣ0 36 91/7 92 30 or 1 94 33, Ⓦwww.eisenach-tourist.de) is at Markt 2. There is also a separate information centre for the Wartburg in the town centre at Schlossberg 2 (Mon–Fri 9am–5pm, April–Oct also Sat 9am–4pm; Ⓣ0 36 91/7 70 72). The main **festivals** are the folkloric

Sommergewinn on the Saturday three weeks before Easter, and the concerts of the Thüringer Bachwochen (see p.893). A varied **cultural programme** is presented all year round at the Thüringer Landestheater, Theaterplatz 4–7 (ⓣ0 36 91/25 62 19, ⓦwww.thueringerlandestheater.de).

Eisenach's **youth hostel** is at Mariental 24 (ⓣ0 36 91/74 32 59; €15/18), on a road which branches off Wartburger Allee. There is the usual supply of **private rooms** (❶–❸) bookable via the tourist office. The town also has a wide range of **hotels** and **pensions**, including many in fine old buildings.

Hotels and pensions

Am Bachhaus Marienstr. 7 ⓣ0 36 91/2 04 70, ⓕ2 04 71 33. Refurbished town-centre hotel with restaurant and *Musikkeller*, the latter decked out with elaborate murals. ❹

Auf der Wartburg ⓣ0 36 91/79 70, ⓦwww.wartburghotel.de. Luxury hotel with restaurant in the Wartburg itself. ❾

Burgfried Marienstr. 60 ⓣ0 36 91/21 42 21, ⓦwww.flairhotel.com. Good old-fashioned hotel, in a large villa at the southern edge of the centre. ❹–❻

Kaiserhof Wartburgallee 2 ⓣ0 36 91/21 35 13, ⓦwww.bestwestern.de. The top hotel in the town centre; it has two restaurants – the *Weinrestaurant Turmschänke* is archetypically Thuringian, whereas *Der Zwinger* is in the style of a Bavarian Bierkeller. ❻

Schlosshotel Markt 20 ⓣ0 36 91/21 42 60, ⓕ21 42 59. New hotel in the converted buildings of the former Franziskanerkloster; also has a good wine bar-restaurant. ❻

Storchenturm Georgenstr. 43 ⓣ0 36 91/21 52 50, ⓕ73 32 65. New Gasthof tucked away in a courtyard behind its street address, with plain but exceptionally good-value rooms and a restaurant in a renovated barn. ❸

Villa Anna Fritz-Koch-Str. 12 ⓣ0 36 91/2 39 50, ⓕ23 95 30. Charming small hotel in a Jugendstil villa with tasteful modern furnishings in the southern part of town. ❹–❻

Villa Kesselring Hainweg 32 ⓣ0 36 91/73 20 49, ⓦwww.wartburgkreis-info.de. Pension in an extravagant Romantic-era villa in a very quiet setting just south of the centre, near one of the paths up to the Wartburg. ❸

The Town

For all its modest size, Eisenach is so rich in monuments and museums that it warrants an unhurried visit. It's best to proceed systematically southwards, perhaps leaving the Wartburg, the undoubted climax, for a second day.

The fortifications and the Markt

From the Hauptbahnhof, it's only a couple of minutes' walk along Bahnhofstrasse to the **Nikolaitor**, a massive gateway erected in the second half of the twelfth century. Above its arch are two sculptures, one presumed to be of Ludwig I, founder of the Ludowingian dynasty which first ruled Thuringia, the other the province's heraldic lion. A few decades later, the **Nikolaikirche** was built directly onto the Nikolaitor to serve both as a parish church and as a convent for Benedictine nuns. One other significant section of the **Stadtmauer**, including a couple of towers, survives; it can be seen at the northern end of town, just beyond Jakobsplan.

Heading diagonally across Karlsplatz brings you to Karlstrasse, leading to the bright orange **Rathaus**, many times rebuilt, which faces onto the Markt. On the north side of the square is the **Stadtschloss** (Tues–Sun 10am–5pm; €2.60) a compact Rococo palace begun in 1741 as the second residence of the newly united House of Saxe-Weimar-Eisenach. Its elegant interiors now house a museum of Thuringian decorative arts.

In the middle of the Markt stands the **Georgenkirche**, cathedral of the Protestant diocese of Thuringia. It is the late Gothic successor to the church where Landgrave Ludwig IV married the Hungarian princess now known as St Elisabeth (see also pp.421–23) in 1221, and where Luther, whose mother was a native of the town, sang as a choirboy. Soon after its construction, it was adapted to the needs of Protestant worship, notably by the erection of the tiered galleries. J.S. Bach was baptized here in 1685, and the church maintained its reputation as a place of destiny by being a key meeting place of opposition groups in the *Wende* of 1989. On the walls are a number of fourteenth-century carved epitaphs commemorating the Ludowingian rulers. Outside is the mid-sixteenth-century **Marktbrunnen**, showing the church's patron, St George, in his familiar dragon-slayer role.

The Thüringer Museum, the Lutherhaus and the Bachhaus

Just off the eastern side of the Markt is the **Predigerkirche**, built in the simple and austere Gothic style favoured by the Dominicans whose priory church it was. For the past century it has been home to the **Thüringer Museum** (Tues–Sun 9am–5pm; €2.60), an outstanding collection of wood sculpture, an art form in which Thuringia excelled throughout the Middle Ages. Highlights include a twelfth-century *St John the Evangelist* of enormous tragic pathos and several large winged altars made in Erfurt and Saalfield immediately prior to the Reformation, but the most intriguing exhibit is the thirteenth-century **statue of Heinrich Raspe**, carved under the realist influence of the Naumburg School. As the crown on his head indicates, Raspe, the brother-in-law of St Elisabeth, usurped the German throne, though he was subsequently accorded the status of an "anti-king". He was also the last Landgrave of Thuringia, his death without issue leading to a war which saw the end of the province as a unit.

Off the southwestern corner of the Markt is Lutherplatz, on which stands the **Lutherhaus** (daily 9/10am–5pm; €2.50; ⓦwww.lutherhaus-eisenach.de), in actual fact the home of the Cotta family, with whom Luther boarded as a schoolboy. The present house, predominantly a half-timbered structure of the sixteenth and eighteenth centuries, encloses the original, which preserves the two rooms used by the famous lodger. Inside are displays on his two periods in Eisenach, plus a large collection of Reformation books and other archive material.

A few minutes' walk south of the Lutherhaus is Frauenplan, with the **Bachhaus** (daily 10am–6pm; €4; ⓦwww.bachhaus.de), a large Baroque house presumed to be the birthplace of J.S. Bach. Inside, an attempt has been made at re-creating the sort of bourgeois interiors typical of the composer's childhood. There's also extensive documention on his career and a valuable collection of historical musical instruments. To round off the visit, it's worth waiting for one of the demonstrations given by a member of staff, who puts a harpsichord, clavichord and chamber organ through their paces in performances of short pieces by Bach.

Elsewhere in the centre

Just east of the Bachhaus is Marienstrasse, where at no. 45 is the **Goldener Löwe** (Mon–Fri 9am–4pm; free), the former inn where August Bebel and Wilhelm Liebknecht set up their revolutionary socialist party in 1869, only to amalgamate it with its more moderate rival six years later in Gotha. At the end of Marienstrasse, Reuterweg leads west to the **Reutervilla** (Tues–Sun 10am–5pm; €3), home of the nineteenth-century Low German writer Fritz Reuter, and still furnished as he knew it. Of more general appeal is the huge array of Wagner memorabilia, including his death mask. These were bought to commemorate the composer's sojourn in Eisenach, where he came to find inspiration for his opera *Tannhäuser*, which is set in and around the Wartburg.

Housed in temporary premises in the savings bank building at Rennbahn 6–8, a short walk west of the Hauptbahnhof on the opposite side of the tracks from the town centre, is the **Automobilbaumuseum** (Tues–Sun 10am–5pm; €2). This collection of historic vehicles celebrates Eisenach's tradition, dating back to 1898, as a leading centre of the German car industry. Exhibits include a 1920s Dixi, capable of the then mind-boggling speed of 60km per hour; this was renamed the BMW 3/15, the first BMW car, when the Bavarian company bought Dixi in 1928. Also on display are different versions of the Wartburg, flagship of GDR car production and a quality motor unlike the ridiculous Trabant.

The Wartburg

From the Reutervilla, it's a steep thirty-minute ramble through the woods to the **Wartburg** (daily March–Oct 8.30am–8pm; Nov–Feb 9am–5pm; €3.50; Ⓦwww.wartburg-eisenach.de) – a far more atmospheric approach than the circuitous main road. Alternatively, the castle can be reached from the Hauptbahnhof by bus #10 or #13. If at all possible, avoid visiting at weekends or holiday periods, when the crowds can be unbearable.

Given its richly varied history, it's perhaps appropriate that the Wartburg is a melange of several different epochs, unfolding like a great picture book of German architecture. The oldest and most imposing part is the late twelfth-century **Palas** at the left-hand end of the second courtyard, one of Europe's few surviving examples of a Romanesque palace. A number of structures – including the **Torhalle** between the courtyards, the cross-crowned **Bergfried**, or keep and the **Neue Kemenate** adjoining the Palas – were added in Romantic style in the nineteenth century, when the whole castle was given a thorough, albeit over-enthusiastic, restoration. The entrance ticket entitles you to climb the **Südturm**, from where there's a good view over the complex and the dense tracts of the Thuringian Forest beyond.

To see the interiors of the Palas, you have to take a **guided tour** (March–Oct 8.30am–5pm; Nov–Feb 9am–3.30pm; additional €2.50). In all the Palas has around two hundred carved **capitals**, a third of them original, highly stylized masterpieces of late Romanesque carving. The finest are those on the central columns which are a distinguishing feature of most of the rooms, including the fourteenth-century **Burgkapelle**. To the modern eye, it's a matter of regret

The history of the Wartburg

The Wartburg was founded by Count Ludwig I in 1067. His descendants, promoted to the status of Landgraves, presided over a cultured court, patronizing some of the greatest Minnesänger (German troubadours), including Wolfram von Eschenbach, who wrote part of his epic *Parzifal* here, and Walter von der Vogelweide, the finest lyric poet of the day. The most significant event in the Wartburg's history began in May 1521 when **Martin Luther**, having been declared an outlaw by the Diet of Worms, was kidnapped by order of Elector Frederick the Wise and taken to this safe haven. During his ten-month stay, the hitherto tonsured and clean-shaven monk disguised himself under a head of hair and beard, passing as a minor landowner by name of Junker Jörg (Farmer George). In a frenzy of activity, he translated the New Testament from Erasmus's Greek into the vernacular language spoken by the people of his day, so creating the foundations of modern written German. In 1817 the Wartburg was the rallying place of the **Burschenschaften**, idealistically minded students protesting at the continued division of Germany, even after the Congress of Vienna, into a host of tinpot principalities.

that there are so many Romantic embellishments, though these are often beautiful works in their own right, notably the three fresco cycles by **Moritz von Schwind** illustrating the life of St Elisabeth, the Minnesänger contest and the history of the castle. Rather more over the top are the Jugendstil mosaics in the saint's bedroom, and the colossal coffered vault of the main **Festsaal**, where the Burschenschaften met.

The museum in the Neue Kemenate is largely devoted to artefacts from around the time of the Reformation, including paintings, sculptures, weapons, furniture and tapestries. Among several works by **Cranach**, look out for the pendants of *Hans and Margarete Luther*, the parents of the great reformer.

From here, you cross the courtyard to the beamed interior of the Wehrgang (sentry walk), which leads round to the **Lutherstube**, the simple wood-panelled room where the German translation of the Bible was made. In the glass case is a copy of the original *Lutherbibel*, while on the walls hang portraits of Luther and Melanchthon, plus an engraving of Luther as *Junker Jörg*, all by Cranach. There was once a blot on the wall by the stove which, according to tradition, was made when Luther threw an inkpot at an apparition of the Devil, but souvenir hunters chipped away at it so much that there's now nothing but a hole going right through to the bare masonry.

Eating and drinking

Many of the best restaurants and cafés are in the hotels listed on p.909, but there are plenty of others elsewhere.

Alt Eisenach Karlstr. 51. Offers Thuringian specialities plus *Kaffee und Kuchen*.
Brunnenkeller Markt 10. Restaurant in cellars formerly used by the local court.
Café Moritz Bahnhofstr. 7. Long-established café, complete with summer terrace.
Lackner Johannisstr. 22. Another traditional café, good for breakfast though it also does full meals.
Residenzkeller corner of Esplanade and Markt. Cosy little restaurant with a shady beer garden. Evenings only, except at weekends.
Rheinischer Hof Clemensstr. 15. Inexpensive Gaststätte to the rear of the Hauptbahnhof.

Mühlhausen

Even within Thuringia, there are few places which conjure up the past so vividly as **MÜHLHAUSEN**, some 35km northeast of Eisenach, which dates back at least as far as Charlemagne. Its historic core has almost completely intact medieval walls, inside which is a maze of alleys lined with half-timbered houses and six Gothic churches, with a further four standing just outside the fortifications. As a Free Imperial City throughout the Middle Ages, Mühlhausen was a rare island of independence in this part of the country, which explains why it became the headquarters of the ill-fated **Peasants' War** of 1525, led by the town's firebrand pastor, **Thomas Müntzer**. Hoping to lead a crusade against the ungodly (he was as vitriolic about Luther as about Catholicism), Müntzer allied his cause with that of the peasants already in revolt against their feudal masters. The rebellion was condemmed by Luther and crushed by the princely armies at Frankenhausen; Müntzer himself was captured, tortured and finally executed. To the GDR authorities, this was the first great social revolution in German history; accordingly, Müntzer – who in reality was a somewhat sinister father-figure to all the myriad forms of sectarian Protestantism which retain such an influence to this day – became one of the state's supreme heroes, regarded as a Moses-like precursor of Marx. In 1975, to mark the 450th anniversary of the event, the town was officially renamed "Thomas-Müntzer-Stadt-Mühlhausen", and two of the churches were made over as memorials to him. Although the latter have survived the post-*Wende* re-evaluations, the town's forename has been discarded.

The Town

The best introduction to Mühlhausen is to walk all the way round the outside of the 2.7-kilometre-long **Stadtmauer**, which still preserves six towers and two gateways. It's at its most impressive around the main western entrance, the **Inneres Frauentor**. Here a small section has been opened to the public, enabling you to go along part of the sentry walk and ascend the **Rabenturm** (April–Oct Tues–Sun 11am–5pm; €3).

On Holzstrasse, the northern of the two streets leading to the centre, you pass the thirteenth-century **Hospital** and a number of fine houses. Herrenstrasse to the south also has fine buildings, though the parish house at the far end is a replacement of the one where Müntzer lived, which was destroyed by fire.

Both streets terminate at the **Marienkirche** (Tues–Sun 10am–5pm; €3), where Müntzer served as pastor during the three fateful months he lived in Mühlhausen. The church itself has a distinctive triple-towered **facade** in which the massive Flamboyant Gothic central tower, crowned with a bravura nineteenth-century steeple, is flanked by its two modest counterparts, one late Romanesque, the other early Gothic. No less idiosyncratic is the **south portal**: although some of its original statuary – carved by the Parler school of Prague – was destroyed as a result of the iconoclasm fomented by Müntzer, the balcony with the peering figures of Emperor Charles IV, Empress Elisabeth and two courtiers survives intact. Inside, the most impressive feature is the soaring architecture of the five-aisled hall nave with its elaborate vault. The furnishings include the grand white **Ratsstuhl**, where councillors sat during services.

Following Ratsstrasse south from here brings you to the **Rathaus** complex, which dates back to about 1300 but which grew in size to such an extent down the centuries that it straddles the street, with the two parts linked by a covered passageway. In the **Ratsstube**, adorned with Gothic wall paintings, Müntzer held his daily *Ewig Rat* (Perpetual Council). The **Archiv** (Mon–Thurs 11am–noon & 1–3pm, Fri 11am–noon; €2), with its complete set of Renaissance furniture and documents pertaining to Mühlhausen's period as a city-state, is also of special note.

A couple of blocks south on Kornmarkt is the **Barfüsserkirche** (Tues–Sun 10am–5pm; €3), a barn-like former Franciscan friary church given over to a museum on the Peasants' War. Further south on Johann-Sebastian-Platz is the **Divi-Blasii-Kirche**, a former church of the Teutonic Knights, whose place in musical history is assured as a result of the year Bach spent there as organist following his departure from Arnstadt. Despite the shortness of his tenure, he drew up the specification for a new organ, a much-prized instrument still reguarly used for recitals. The twin towers are a good illustration of the way late Romanesque passed seamlessly into Gothic. The rest of the building is, like the Marienkirche, a fourteenth-century hall church.

Practicalities

Mühlhausen's **Bahnhof** is three blocks beyond the easternmost part of the Stadtmauer. The **tourist office** (Mon–Fri 9am–5pm; May–Oct also Sat 10am–noon; ⓣ0 36 01/45 23 21, ⓦwww.muehlhausen.de) is at Ratsstr. 20.

Mühlhausen was one of the few places in the GDR which kept up much of a tradition in **festivals**, of which the most important is the *Kirmes*, a fair held at the end of August.

As usual, the tourist office can book **private rooms** (❶–❸). The **youth hostel** is in the outskirts of town at Auf den Tonberg 1 (Ⓣ0 36 01/81 33 18; €12.50/15.50); take bus #5 or #6 to Blobach. There are many **pensions**, some of them centrally located, such as *Höfler*, Kuttelgasse 23 (Ⓣ0 36 01/4 46 99 09; ❸), and *Adam's*, Allerheiligengasse 2 (Ⓣ0 36 01/44 24 18; ❹). **Hotels** include *Gasthof Bundschuh*, Jüdenstr. 43 (Ⓣ0 36 01/88 91 72; ❹), *Ammerscher Bahnhof*, Ammerstr. 83–85 (Ⓣ0 36 01/87 31 32; ❺), *Mirage*, Karl-Marx-Str. 9 (Ⓣ0 36 01/43 90, Ⓦwww.mirage-hotel.de; ❺), *An der Stadtmauer*, Breitenstr. 5 (Ⓣ0 36 01/4 65 00; ❻), and *Brauhaus Zum Löwen*, Kornmarkt 3 (Ⓣ0 36 01/47 10, Ⓦwww.brauhaus-zum-loewen.de; ❻). The last two of these have particularly good **restaurants**, with *Brauhaus Zum Löwen* offering the advantage of its own freshly brewed beer. It is not the only Hausbrauerei in town, competition coming from *Thüringer Brauhaus*, Johanisstr. 26.

Nordhausen

NORDHAUSEN lies just to the south of the Harz mountains, at the fringe of the fertile plain known as the Goldene Aue (Golden Meadow), about 45km northeast of Mühlhausen. It's predominantly an industrial town, best known for its production of spirits (a mouth-burning *Korn* has been made here since the early sixteenth century) and tobacco (especially *Kautabak*, or "chewing tobacco"). Unfortunately, this rather overshadows its historical role as a former Free Imperial City, the more so as a large number of monuments were destroyed in 1945, during the severest bombing raid carried out on any Thuringian town. Nonetheless, there are a few sights well worth stopping to see if you happen to find yourself here – Nordhausen is the southern terminus of the narrow-gauge steam rail line through the Harz, the Harzquerbahn (see box on p.844–45).

The **Stadtmauer** was among the monuments damaged in the war, though 1.5km of the circuit still remain. Following the wall northwards, you can see the **Finkenburg**, one of the oldest and finest of the few half-timbered houses spared by the bombs, at An der Wassertreppe. East of here is the Markt, whose late Renaissance **Rathaus** was rebuilt from wartime ruins. Further up, the skyline is dominated by the so-called **Dom**, more correctly the **Kloster zum Heiligen Kreuz**, the successor to a nunnery founded in 963. The present church is an architectural jumble of Romanesque, early and late Gothic. The more modest **Blasiikirche** just to the east exhibits a similar architectural mix.

In 1943, a subsidiary concentration camp of Buchenwald, under the name of **Dora**, was set up at the foot of the Kohnstein at the northernmost fringe of Nordhausen. The following year, renamed **Mittelbau**, it became a full-blown camp in its own right. Some 60,000 prisoners from twenty-one countries were interned here, engaged on the secret production of V1 and V2 missiles, working underground in a network of tunnels and caverns. Nearly a third of them died here; in their honour, the site has been turned into a memorial, the **Gedenkstätte Mittelbau-Dora** (daily 10am–4/6pm; free; Ⓦwww.dora.de), with documentary displays on the conditions they suffered. The easiest way to get here is to take the Harzquerbahn to Krimderode, then follow the main road round to the west.

Practicalities

Nordhausen's **Hauptbahnhof** lies south of the Altstadt, on the opposite side of the River Zorge; the Harzquerbahn's terminus, misleadingly designated Nordhausen-Nord, is just across Bahnhofsplatz. The **tourist office** (Mon–Fri 8am–6.30pm, Sat & Sun 9am–3.30pm; ⓣ03631/629151, ⓦwww.nordhausen.de) at Bahnhofstr. 3a can book **private rooms** (❶–❸). The town has few **hotels**, the best being *Avena*, Hallesche Str. 13 (ⓣ0 36 31/60 20 60; ❺), and *Handelshof*, Bahnhofstr. 13 (ⓣ0 36 31/62 50; ❻). There's also a **youth hostel** at Parkallee 2 (ⓣ0 36 31/90 23 91; €14.50/17.50) near the Stadtpark; take bus #6 to Altentor. Nordhausen doesn't score highly for **eating** and **drinking**, but try *Café Altstadt*, Kranichstr. 19, or the *Ratskeller*, Markt 15. The main local **festival** is the Rolandfest on the second weekend in June.

Sondershausen

SONDERSHAUSEN, which lies 20km south of Nordhausen in a pretty setting in the valley cut by the River Wipper between two groups of wooded hills, the Hainleite and the Windleite, is a place which deserves to be far better known. Formerly the capital of the county of Schwarzburg, and later of the principality of Schwarzburg-Sondershausen, its main attraction is as one of the courtly towns so characteristic of Thuringia. However, it's far less soporific than most of its counterparts. The huge winding tower (now preserved as a technical monument) which greets you on arrival at the Hauptbahnhof is a reminder that Sondershausen has for centuries been a major centre of potash production, while the historic heart of the town has regained its former role as a market and trading centre.

A typically oversized **Schloss** (April–Sept Tues–Sun 10am–4/5pm; €3) is Sondershausen's overwhelmingly dominant building. It can be approached from the west via its rustic park, or from the Markt by the monumental steps to the side of the Neoclassical guardhouse, the Alte Wache. The north wing dates back to the sixteenth century, while the seventeenth century saw the beginning of a massive extension programme, including the addition of a Baroque tower and south wing. A late Rococo palace, subsequently modified in Neoclassical style, was then added at an angle of 45 degrees to the original, creating an almost triangular courtyard. The wonderfully eclectic interior graphically conjures up the real-life fantasy world of a petty German court. In the original palace is the most individual chamber, the Mannerist **Wendelstein**, which boasts a dazzlingly brilliant stucco vault showing the Elements, the Seasons, the Virtues, putti and mythological characters. The main reception room is the Baroque **Riesensaal** (Giants' Hall), so called from the sixteen over-life-sized statues of classical deities; it also boasts a superb coffered vault with ornate stucco trophies and paintings illustrating Ovid's *Metamorphoses*. In its Rococo counterpart, the turquoise **Festsaal**, the antique theme is continued with the story of Jupiter and Calypso. Two other highlights are the **Liebhabertheater** (Conoisseurs' Theatre), a Biedermeier gem which is one of the smallest theatres in Germany, and the gilded **state coach**.

In the park west of the Schloss is the **Karussel** or **Achteckiges Haus**, a tall, eccentric-looking octagon with interior galleries and a fresco of *The Triumph of Venus*. Built at the beginning of the eighteenth century to serve as the main venue for court entertainments, it's occasionally used for concerts by the Loh-Orchester.

Practicalities

Sondershausen's **Hauptbahnhof** is about fifteen minutes' walk west of the centre; the Haltepunkt Sondershausen-Süd below the Hainleite is actually slightly nearer the Markt and the Schloss. The **tourist office** (Mon–Fri 9am–12.30pm & 1.30–5pm, Sat 9–11am/noon; ⓣ0 36 32/78 81 11, ⓦwww.sondershausen.de) is in the Alte Wache, Markt 9.

In addition to a **youth hostel**, which has a conveniently central location at Güntherstr. 26–27 (ⓣ0 36 32/60 11 93; €10.50/13.50), there are plenty of **private rooms** (❶–❸) for rent from the tourist office. Alternatively, there are a few **pensions**, including *Zur Sonne*, Conrad-Röntgen-Str. 11 (ⓣ0 36 32/60 24 86; ❷), *Schweizer Haus*, Im Loh 1a (ⓣ0 36 32/60 11 11; ❸), and *Haus Waldheim*, Erfurter Str. 29 (ⓣ0 36 32/75 87 79, ⓦwww.pension-waldheim.de; ❺). However, there is currently just one **hotel**, *Thüringer Hof*, Hauptstr. 30–32 (ⓣ0 36 32/65 60, ⓦwww.thueringerhof.com; ❺). The best **restaurants** are the one in *Thüringer Hof*, the *Ratskeller*, Markt 7, and the *Schlossrestaurant* in the Schloss.

The Kyffhäuser

The **Kyffhäuser**, a small group of wooded sandstone mountains, form a virtual southern continuation of the Harz, which they closely resemble – except for the fact that they're virtually uninhabited. Despite their modest dimensions – they occupy less than 60 square kilometres, while the peaks are all under 500m – they have a grandeur that belies their actual size. In addition, they hold a special place in the national consciousness, being the seat of one of the great imperial castles of early medieval Germany and the place where, according to legend, Emperor Frederick Barbarossa (the country's real-life counterpart of King Arthur) lies slumbering, awaiting his second coming. For the GDR state, the Kyffhäuser had the additional allure of being where the first German revolution, the Peasants' War of 1525, came to its untimely end.

Bad Frankenhausen

The gateway to the Kyffhäuser, and the obvious base for a visit, is the small spa town of **BAD FRANKENHAUSEN**, which lies at their southern edge, 20km east of Sondershausen, just below the **Schlachtberg** (Battle Hill) where Thomas Müntzer's peasant army was routed by vastly superior forces loyal to the nation's rulers.

In the late sixteenth century, Frankenhausen became the capital of one of the four counties into which Schwarzburg was divided, an event which necessitated the building of the modest little **Schloss** (Tues–Sun 10am–5pm; €2.50) at the southern end of the Altstadt. It's now a museum devoted to the Kyffhäuser region, with displays on its flora, fauna, archeology, history, arts and crafts, with the highlight being a diorama of the battle of 1525. Just north of the Schloss is the Markt, with a Neoclassical Rathaus; from here, Kräme, a pedestrianized shopping street, leads to **Anger**, the spacious main square, which boasts a few half-timbered houses. Uphill lies the best-preserved section of the thirteenth-century fortification system, centred on the impressive **Hausmannsturm**.

Much further up, crowning the top of the Schlachtberg, is the white rotunda housing the **Bauernkriegs-Panorama** (guided tours April–June, Sept & Oct Tues–Sun 10am–6pm; July & Aug Mon 1–6pm, Tues–Sun 10am–6pm; Nov–March Tues–Sun 10am–5pm; €5; ⓦwww.panorama-museum.de).

Claimed as the largest painting in the world, this huge, vividly coloured panoramic picture of the battle was unveiled in 1989 to celebrate Müntzer's 500th anniversary, and the 40th birthday of the GDR. Over 70 percent of the painting is by the Liepzig professor **Werner Tübke**, with much of the rest being detail provided by specialists. Both politically and artistically the end result is controversial, though neither critical derision nor the relatively high entrance fee deters the crowds who flock here.

Practicalities

Bad Frankenhausen's **Bahnhof** is immediately south of the Altstadt. The **tourist office** (May–Sept Mon–Fri 9am–6pm, Sat 10am–3pm, Sun 10am–noon; Oct–April Mon–Fri 9am–5pm, Sat 10am–noon, ⓣ03 46 71/7 17 16, ⓦwww.bad-frankenhausen.de) is at Anger 10. You can book a **private room** (❶–❸) here, though they're easy enough to find on your own by looking for the *Zimmer frei* signs. For a bit more luxury, there are several **hotels**, notably *Alte Hämmenlei*, Bornstr. 33 (ⓣ03 46 71/51 20, ⓦwww.alte-hammenlei.de; ❹), *Thüringer Hof*, Am Anger 15 (ⓣ03 46 71/5 10 10, ⓦwww.thueringer-hof.com; ❹), *Reichental*, Rottleber Str. 4 (ⓣ03 46 71/6 80, ⓦwww.hotelreichental.de; ❻), and *Residenz Frankenburg*, Am Schlachtberg 3 (ⓣ03 46 71/7 50, ⓦwww.residenz-frankenhausen.de; ❻). All of these also have good, reasonably priced **restaurants**.

The mountains

The Kyffhäuser are combed with marked walking trails, and it's easy enough to devise your own circular routes. Easiest hike is to the **Barbarossahöhle** (guided tours April–Oct daily 10am–5pm; Nov–March Tues–Sun 10am–4pm; €6; ⓦwww.cavern-barbarossa.com), 5km to the west and just north of Rottleben, the next stop on the rail line to Sondershausen. Discovered during mining operations in the nineteenth century – whereupon it immediately became coupled to the Barbarossa legend – this is, with a total length of 800m, one of Europe's largest gypsum caves, featuring some amazing vaults and tiny lakes with crystal-clear waters. For the more energetic, there's a ten-kilometre path from Bad Frankenhausen which travels right through the heart of the Kyffhäuser to its highest summit, the **Kulpenberg** (477m).

A few kilometres east of here, and linked by a direct trail to Bad Frankenhausen, is the **Kyffhäuserdenkmal** (daily: May–Sept 9am–7pm; Oct–April 10am–5pm; €3). This historicist monstrosity, which commands another sweeping view over the region, was erected at the end of the nineteenth century in honour of the recently deceased Kaiser Wilhelm I, the first emperor of the Second Reich and thus the man seen as something of a reincarnation of Frederick Barbarossa, an early champion of German unity. In order to build it, a substantial portion of the surviving fragments of the upper fortress of the famous Romanesque **Reichsburg**, one of the strongholds of the Hohenstaufen emperors, had to be demolished – an act of vandalism uncharacteristic of the time. Thankfully, the ruins of the lower fortress, including a well some 176m deep, survive to give an idea of the scale and appearance of the original.

Jena

JENA, which is just 20km southeast of Weimar, lies at the point where the Saale valley is at its grandest, surrounded by red sandstone and chalk hills, which have a climate mild enough for the growing of vines. The **university** is among the most famous in Germany; founded in 1558 with the help of Melanchthon, it was closely associated with the great flowering of Classicism in Weimar, to which Jena then belonged, following its own short-lived period as capital of an independent duchy. In the nineteenth century, it played a leading role in scientific research, and had strong links with the world-renowned optics company, the Carl-Zeiss-Stiftung, whose works are still a prominent feature of the skyline.

Sadly, the city was exceptionally badly bombed in World War II and still bears the scars of this. Nevertheless, there's still plenty to see – particularly if you are at all of a scientific bent – while the atmosphere is the liveliest, and the choice in eating, drinking and nightlife as good as any in Thuringia.

Arrival, information and accommodation

Jena has two main train stations. The **Saalbahnhof** in the north of the city is on the express Berlin–Munich line, with local services northwards to Naumburg and southwards to Rudolstadt and Saalfeld. The **Westbahnhof** to the southwest of the centre is on the line linking Erfurt and Weimar with Gera. Many of the trains to and from the Saalbahnhof stop at the **Paradiesbahnhof**, which is at the southern fringe of the centre; slightly to the north of here is the **bus station**.

The **tourist office** (Mon–Fri 9am–6pm, Sat 9am–2pm; ⓣ0 36 41/80 64 04, ⓦwww.jena.de) is at Johannisstr. 23. **Private rooms** (❷–❸) can be booked, as usual, through them. The **youth hostel** is at Am Herrenberge 3 (ⓣ0 36 41/68 72 30; €16.50/19.50) in the suburb of Lichtenhain southwest of the centre, reached by bus #10, #13 or #40. **Hotels** and **pensions** are scattered all over the city, with something to suit all pockets.

Hotels and pensions

Esplanade Carl-Zeiss-Platz 4 ⓣ0 36 41/80 00, ⓦwww.jena.steigenberger.de. Jena's most prestigious hotel, part of the exclusive Goethe-Galerie shopping centre. Its restaurant *Rotunda* occupies a hexagonal tower with a panorama terrace. ❻–❾

Jembo Park Rudolstädter Str. 93, Göschwitz ⓣ0 36 41/68 50, ⓦwww.jembo.de. Thuringia's first motel, located on the B88 just a short distance north of Bahnhof Göschwitz, 4km south of the centre. Has bungalows as well as hotel rooms, a restaurant and an English-style pub. ❺

Jenaer Hof Bachstr. 24 ⓣ0 36 41/44 38 55, ⓕ44 38 66. Small hotel with café in a Jugendstil building right in the city centre. ❹

Papiermühle Erfurter Str. 102 ⓣ0 36 41/4 59 80, ⓕ45 98 45. An old paper mill on the west side of the city has been converted to house this combined hotel, restaurant and *Bockbier* brewery. ❺

Schwarzer Bär Lutherplatz 2 ⓣ0 36 41/40 60, ⓦwww.schwarzer-baer-jena.de. Hotel with a tradition dating back some 500 years at the northwestern corner of the Altstadt, not far from the Saalbahnhof. Its restaurant is very reasonably priced. ❺

Zur Noll Oberlauengasse 19 ⓣ0 36 41/44 15 66, ⓦwww.zur-noll.de. Gasthof in the very heart of the Altstadt, with restaurant, beer garden and exhibition gallery. Often hosts different types of live music. ❺

Zur Schweiz Quergasse 15 ⓣ0 36 41/5 20 50, ⓕ5 20 51 11. Another good central Gasthof, with a particularly recommendable restaurant and a beer garden. ❺

Zur Weintraube Rudolstädter Str. 70, Winzerla ⓣ0 36 41/60 57 70, ⓦwww.weintraube-jena.de. Eighteenth-century inn on the B88, 3km south of the centre. Its excellent, moderately priced restaurant offers many Thuringian specialities. Recently, it has started brewing its own light and dark *Glockenbräu* beers, using a fifteenth-century recipe. ❻

The City

Given its size, Jena's attractions are fairly spread out. However, most of what you're likely to want to see is concentrated in a few easily assimilated areas and can be covered comfortably on foot.

Eichplatz, the Markt and around

Dominating the centre of Jena from the middle of the spacious Eichplatz, dwarfing even the Carl Zeiss buildings just to the west, is the **Universitätshochhaus**, a 120-metre-high cylindrical tower inaugurated in 1972. Though by no means the worst example of the GDR school of brutalist architecture, it's distinctly unloved locally: irreverent students were quick to dub it *Phallus Jenensis*, and this has since passed into the cruder vernacular form of *Jenaer Pimmel* (Jena's Willie). The demise of the GDR inevitably led to calls for its demolition, but instead it has been the subject of a massive cleaning and reconstruction programme.

In order to build the tower, many of the surviving historical buildings on Eichplatz and the streets around had to be razed, and it was only as a result of a protest campaign that the original university, the **Collegium Jenense**, which stands just to the south on Collegienstrasse, was spared. Originally a Dominican priory, it's a marvellously ramshackle array of bits and pieces from various epochs, which evoke the cloistered tranquillity of academe. The most arresting feature is the bravura Renaissance carving in the courtyard of the coat of arms of the Ernestine line of the House of Wettin, the university's original patrons. Just east of the Collegium is the ruined **Anatometurm**, one of the three towers surviving from the fourteenth-century fortification system.

Separating Eichplatz from the much smaller Markt is the **Rathaus**, a simple Gothic structure crowned with a miniature Baroque belfry housing the *Schnapphans*, a mechanism which strikes the hours. In the middle of the square stands the **Hannfried-Denkmal**, a memorial bearing the nickname given locally to the university's founder, John Frederick the Magnanimous.

Such few old houses as Jena possesses can be found mostly on the Markt itself and in the two alleys, Oberlauengasse and Unterlauengasse, immediately to the east. The finest of these, at Markt 7, is now the **Stadtmuseum Göhre** (Tues, Wed & Fri–Sun 10am–5pm, Thurs 2–10pm; €3). It contains displays on local arts and crafts, wine-making, religious art, the so-called "Seven Wonders of Jena" and the history of the university (including a reproduction of the Studentenkarzer or prison with its characteristic graffiti). There's also a reconstruction of a nineteenth-century café if you need a bit of light refreshment.

Despite its name, Unterm Markt, which stretches to the west, is a street rather than a square. At no. 12a is the large Baroque mansion which was formerly the home of Johann Gottlieb Fichte, one of a host of renowned philosophers (Hegel, Schelling, the Schlegels and the Humboldts were others) based in Jena during the Romantic period. Now designated the **Romantikerhaus** (Tues–Sun 10am–1pm & 2–5pm; €3), it's decked out with period furnishings, and also has a small art gallery.

Behind the Markt rises the Gothic **Stadtkirche St Michael**. Outside, the main features are the Brautportal (Bridal Doorway) on the south side, and the remarkable street passageway under the chancel, the best-known of the "Seven Wonders", the more so as there's not the slightest hint of its presence in the brightly painted hall interior, whose light and lofty feel is achieved by means of slender pillars which shoot directly up to the vault. The church's most celebrated treasure is the original bronze **tombstone of Luther** – with a full-length portrait cast from designs provided by Cranach – on the north wall. It was brought here for safekeeping because of the threat of desecration from the imperial forces occupying Wittenberg, but was never returned.

From the Stadtkirche, Johanniskirche leads west along the northern side of Eichplatz; no. 12, the **Haus zur Rosen**, is a Baroque mansion whose cellars contain a renowned student club. At the end of the street is the **Johannistor**, the only gateway remaining from the city's fortifications; just to the north is the most impressive of the surviving towers, the battlemented **Pulverturm**.

The fringes of the city centre

Across Goetheallee is the **Botanischer Garten** (daily 9am–5/6pm; €2), which was first created for growing medicinal herbs; it was then turned into a pleasure park before assuming its current function, which is primarily one of scientific research. The **Inspektorhaus** on the street side was designed by Goethe and was his favourite residence during his many sojourns in Jena, which he found to be a more amenable working environment than Weimar. Here he completed many of his literary projects; he also undertook a great deal of scientific research and produced the rather odd work he himself considered his masterpiece, *The Theory of Colours*. Part of the building is now designated the **Goethe-Gedenkstätte** (April–Oct Wed–Sun 11am–3pm; €1) and contains memorabilia of his stays there.

On the eastern fringe of the garden is the domed **Zeiss-Planetarium** (Ⓦwww.planetarium-jena.de), which, when it was built in 1925, was the first such structure in the world. Now as then, it utilizes the technology of the Carl Zeiss works. There are several sessions (Tues-Sun; €5), including occasional showings in English for groups to which it is possible to tack on.

The factory buildings of the **Carl-Zeiss-Stiftung**, mostly dating from the first two decades of the twentieth century, stand immediately to the west of Eichplatz; among them is a tower which is claimed as Germany's earliest skyscraper. **Carl Zeiss** was a mechanic who established himself in Jena in 1846, and attempted to develop microscopes of improved optical performance. Having failed to make the desired progress within twenty years, he formed what proved to be a spectacularly fruitful partnership with the physicist **Ernst Abbe**. Their company soon became the world leader in the field of optics, and has maintained this position ever since. The **Optisches Museum** (Tues–Fri 10am–4.30pm, Sat 11am–5pm; €5) on Carl-Zeiss-Platz is in two parts. In the first, there's a re-creation of the 1866 workshop of Zeiss and Abbe; the second contains a huge collection of historic spectacles, microscopes, telescopes and other instruments. Outside stands the imposing **Ernst-Abbe-Denkmal**, a shrine-like memorial by Henry van de Velde, inside which are four bronze reliefs of working-class life by Constantin Meunier.

A few minutes' walk to the south is Ernst-Haeckel-Strasse, where, at the corner with Berggasse, is the **Ernst-Haeckel-Haus** (guided tours Tues–Fri at 8.30am, 10am, 11.30am, 2pm & 3.30pm; €2). Haeckel, the leading Continental protagonist of Darwin's theories of evolution, dominated intellectual life at Jena around the turn of last century. He was also a talented artist, and his watercolour landscapes are the highlight of the displays in the villa where he lived. Just to the south, at Am Paradiesbahnhof, is the **Phyletisches Museum** (daily 9am–4pm; €2), which Haeckel founded in 1907. It's a natural history collection with a difference, concentrating on how each species developed.

For a time Haeckel lived in the house at Schillergässchen 2, which is now known as **Schillers Gartenhaus** (April–Oct Tues–Sun 11am–3pm; Nov–March Tues–Sat 11am–3pm; €1) in honour of a previous occupant, the poet and dramatist **Friedrich Schiller**, after whom the university is now named. As professor of history, he lived in Jena for ten years, the longest he spent in any one place. The conditions in which he worked have been lovingly re-created; particularly evocative is the upstairs room in the garden pavilion, his favourite work place.

Eating, drinking and nightlife

Undoubtedly one of the prime attractions of Jena is its wide variety of places to eat, drink and socialize; indeed, within the former GDR it offers a better choice than almost anywhere outside Leipzig and Dresden.

Restaurants, bars and cafés

Alt Jena Markt 9. Upmarket wine bar, offering nearly a hundred different vintages, plus a good range of food, including plenty of fish dishes.
Fiddler's Green Sophienstr 10. The local Irish pub, often with live music. Daily 5pm–1am.
Fuchsturm Turmgasse 26. Traditional Gaststätte in a tower on top of the Hausberg, a hill on the west side of the Saale. Closes 10pm during the week, midnight on Sat, 7pm on Sun.
Grüne Tanne Karl-Liebknecht-Str. 1. Historic Gasthaus with a courtyard beer garden, serving hearty yet inexpensive traditional cuisine. Evenings only, closed Sun & Mon.
Marktmühle Saalstr. 23. Bar with a good selection of whiskies, plus Irish and English beers.
Rosenkeller Johannisstr. 13. By far the most popular student club, set in cavernous cellars. Often features live music; even out of term, it has an animated atmosphere. Free admission with student ID, otherwise you'll have to pay around €2 to get in.
Talschänke Pennickental 44, Wöllnitz. Hausbrauerei in an incorporated village on the east bank of the Saale, south of the city centre. It brews a mild *Weissbier* and serves freshly-caught trout.
Zum Roten Hirsch, Holzmarkt 10. Offers cheap but decent food, with a fast lunchtime service.

Gera

Thuringia's second largest city is **GERA**, which lies 45km east of Jena in the hilly countryside of the Weisse Elster valley. For nearly four centuries it was the capital of one of Germany's smallest states, the junior of the two Reuss principalities (see p.923). However, it's totally different from the province's other courtly residences, being predominantly an industrial town, with a long tradition in the production of textiles and musical instruments. Indeed, during the Second Reich it was one of the richest places in Germany, and the multitude of industrialists' villas which can still be seen in its inner suburbs is a reminder of this heady epoch. Despite extensive wartime damage, it's a surprisingly agreeable place, generally recognized as being the one and only town in the GDR where postwar planning was carried out with sensitivity and good taste. The result is a lively city which offers a balanced mixture of old and new.

The City

At the heart of the compact Altstadt is the **Markt**, whose good looks compensate for its modest dimensions. In the centre burbles the **Simsonbrunnen**, showing the Old Testament hero Samson wrestling with the lion; this is a modern replica of the water-worn late seventeenth-century original. The whitewashed Renaissance **Rathaus**, the town's finest building, stands proudly to the northeastern corner. Designed by Nicol Gromann, the Saxon court architect, it boasts a dignified off-centre octagonal tower and a riotously decorative portal with busts, grotesque figures, inscriptions and brightly painted coats of arms. A similar style can be seen on the oriel of the **Stadt-Apotheke** at the opposite end of the square; apart from heraldic motifs, its carvings show the Apostles and the Four Seasons. Kleine Kirchstrasse leads to a vast open square, Zentraler Platz, whose handsome red Baroque palace standing in splendid isolation was once the town orphanage. Nowadays it houses the local history displays of the **Stadtmuseum** (closed for restoration at time of writing, due to reopen in 2004; Ⓦwww.gera-hoehler.de).

Uphill from the Markt, Grosse Kirchstrasse – which is lined with a number of fine mansions, now mostly shops – leads to the **Salvatorkirche**, a large Baroque church with Jugendstil furnishings perched at the top of a monumental stairway. On its northern side stands the **Schreiberhaus**, the late seventeenth-century mansion of a rich merchant. It is now the **Museum für Naturkunde** (Tues–Sun 10am–5pm; €2.50), with displays on the natural history and geology of the Gera region, including the skeleton of a prehistoric rhinoceros. The interior itself is at least as good a reason for a visit, however. At the back of the house is the entrance to the town's most unusual attraction, the **Geraer Höhle** (guided tours Mon–Fri at 11am & 3pm, Sat at 11am, 2pm & 3pm, Sun at 10am, 11am, 2pm & 3pm; €2.50 or €3.50 combined ticket with Museum für Naturkunde; Ⓦwww.gera-hoehler.de), a network of caverns and tunnels used in the seventeenth and eighteenth centuries as workshops, and as a place where home-brewed beer could mature in cool conditions.

About fifteen minutes' walk to the northwest of the Altstadt is the Küchengarten, a pleasant park at whose far end stands the Rococo **Orangerie** (Tues 1–8pm, Wed–Fri 10am–5pm, Sat & Sun 10am–6pm; €2.50). Inside is a collection of paintings and sculptures from the Middle Ages to the present day. Mohrenplatz, just to the west over the Weisse Elster, is the finest square in Gera after the Markt, and is dominated by the Romanesque-Gothic **Marienkirche**. At no. 4 on the square is the **Otto-Dix-Haus** (Tues–Fri 10am–5pm, Sat & Sun 10am–6pm; €2.50 or €3.50 combined ticket with Orangerie), birthplace of one of the most highly regarded German artists of the twentieth century, the leading light of the Neue Sachlichkeit movement. In addition to a huge number of drawings and graphics, displayed in rotation, there are a couple of dozen canvases, the pick of which is *St Christopher*, an allegorical work inspired by the emigration from Germany under the Nazis.

Schlossbergstrasse leads up from Mohrenplatz to the site of **Schloss Osterstein**, now occupied by a terrace café-restaurant. The huge Baroque palace of the Reuss princes which stood there was damaged by bombs in the last days of the war and subsequently razed by the Communists – an action which marred the city's otherwise exemplary preservation record during the GDR era. However, the restored Romanesque **tower** survives, and on the afternoons of summer weekends and holidays it may be ascended (€1) for a view over the town.

Practicalities

Gera's **Hauptbahnhof** is northwest of the Altstadt, immediately in front of the Küchengarten. The **tourist office** (Mon–Fri 9am–8pm, Sat 9am–2pm; Ⓣ03 65/61 93 01, Ⓦwww.gera.de) is just a short walk away at Ernst-Toller-Str. 14. There is a good selection of **hotels** in town. At the budget end of the scale is the huge *Am Galgenberg*, Laasener Str. 108 (Ⓣ03 65/8 37 26 77; ❹). The best mid-range establishments are *An der Elster*, Südstr. 12 (Ⓣ03 65/7 10 61 61; ❺) and *Galerie*, Leibnizstr. 21 (Ⓣ03 65/2 01 50; ❺); the latter is in the western suburb of Untermhaus and – as its name implies – incorporates an art gallery.

Pick of the upmarket options is *Regent Gera*, Schülerstr. 22 (Ⓣ03 65/9 18 10, Ⓦwww.bestwestern.de; ❻).

Among the **restaurants** *Trakia*, Altenburger Str. 16, offers a rare chance to sample Bulgarian cuisine, while *Royal*, Sorge 19, presents high-quality French cooking. *Paulaner Keller*, Clara-Zetkin-Str. 14, represents the burgeoning Bavarian influence, *Riebeck's Braustüb'l*, Braustr. 2, is the tap of Gera's own brewery, *Köstritzer Schwarzbierhaus*, Humboldtstr.7, is the city's main outlet for the rich, smooth, coal-black beer produced in the little spa town of Bad Köstritz, 8km to the north. It's Germany's best-selling dark beer, with a near-mythical status akin to that enjoyed by *Guinness* in the English-speaking world.

The main venue for **drama** and **concerts** is the Theater Gera (Ⓣ03 65/8 27 91 01, Ⓦwww.theater.altenburg.gera.de), immediately to the rear of the Hauptbahnhof at Küchengartenallee 2. There's also a Puppentheater on Gustav-Henning-Platz (Ⓣ03 65/2 47 07, Ⓦwww.theater.altenburg.gera.de), and a satirical cabaret, Fettnäppchen, in the cellars of the Rathaus (Ⓣ03 65/2 37 31).

Greiz

GREIZ, 30km up the Weisse Elster valley from Gera, was the capital of the senior of the two Reuss principalities (the smallest of the 25 states which formed the Second German Reich). Since 1875, the two old Reuss capitals have been linked by the Elstertalbahn, a railway which continues on to the Saxon town of Plauen. This beautiful line passes through terrain that posed severe challenges to the engineers, the most difficult being the 270-metre-long tunnel which had to be cut through the Schlossberg, the hill overlooking the centre of Greiz. The town itself has been dogged by ill-luck: it has repeatedly been destroyed by fire down the ages, and is suffering notably from post-GDR blight, which has seen the end of its 500-year-old textile tradition. Yet it's an attractive place nonetheless, with a glorious natural setting and a fine ensemble of buildings from the late eighteenth to the early twentieth century.

The Town

By far the oldest surviving building is the **Oberes Schloss** (guided tours April–Oct Mon–Fri at 10am & 2pm, Sat & Sun at 10am, 2pm & 4pm; €1.50) atop the Schlossberg. This dates at least as far back as the thirteenth-century, and was the residence of Heinrich II of Plauen, who in 1306 founded the dynasty and county of Reuss, a name derived from his marriage to a Russian princess. Relatively little medieval masonry survives, the complex being a jumble of Renaissance, Baroque and Rococo buildings. Since the nineteenth century, many of these have been used as houses, though the residents are now gradually moving out. The highlights of the tour are the elaborately stuccoed reception rooms and the sweeping view from the top of the seventeenth-century **Schlossturm**.

A group of monumental Neoclassical buildings dominate the town centre's waterfront. The most prominent is the **Unteres Schloss**, a direct replacement for its predecessor, which was destroyed in the most serious of Greiz's fires, that of 1802. It now houses a music academy, various municipal offices, a café and two museums. Of these, the **Heimatmuseum** (daily except Fri 10am–12.30pm & 1–5pm; €1) occupies a suite of Beidermeier rooms overlooking the river, including the externally prominent winter garden. It contains the expected local history displays, including a lovingly crafted model of the town as it was in 1899. Across the courtyard, the **Schauwerkstatt** (same times; €1) documents Greiz's textile tradition, featuring a number of historic looms as well as others which were recently still in service.

Adjoining the Unteres Schloss, and likewise rebuilt after the great fire, is the former court church, now the **Stadtkirche St Marien**. Its galleried interior contains the tomb of the most celebrated of the Reuss rulers, the military hero Heinrich VI, who died in combat against the Turks at the Battle of Zenta in 1697. Other notable buildings from the same period are the former guard-house, the **Alte Wache**, to the rear, and the former **Lyzeum**, now the public library, to the side. The Neoclassical ensemble is completed by the huge **Gymnasium** to the east. Otherwise, the town centre is characterized by the presence of a large number of **Jugendstil houses**, which were erected in the wake of two fires in the first decade of the twentieth century. The best examples are to be seen on Thomasstrasse and Burgstrasse, with the most eye-catching being that at the corner of the latter and Marktstrasse, which has a facade mosaic of a goldsmith at work.

On the opposite side of the Oberes Schloss from the town centre is the town's greatest joy, the **Greizer Park**. Originally a kitchen garden, then a formal Rococo garden, it was extended and transformed into a Romantic-era landscape park in the English style, assuming its definite appearance as late as the 1870s. It's a wonderful place for a stroll, with its long and often unexpected vistas, and its spectacular array of imported trees and shrubs, including some not found elsewhere in Europe, which erupt into a riot of colour in autumn. There are also several picturesque garden buildings, including the late eighteenth-century **Rotunde** at the eastern edge, which was built to house the princely porcelain collections but was later converted into a chapel and then a war memorial, and the half-timbered **Schwanenhaus** on the islet in the large artificial lake. From here, there's a sweeping view upwards to two popular vantage points – the **Weisses Kreuz** (White Cross) and the **Pulverturm** (Powder Tower).

At the southern end of the Greizer Park is the **Sommerpalais** (Tues–Sun 10am–4/5pm; €1), a French-inspired building in an early Neoclassical style still showing lingering Rococo influence. It was begun in 1779 as a summer pleasure palace for the ruling family, which had gained promotion to princely status the previous year. The extravagantly stuccoed **Gartensaal** on the ground floor is used for temporary exhibitions, including the Triennale, the tri-annual (next in June–Oct 2006) national festival of caricatures, cartoons and satiric art. In the handsome suite of reception rooms on the first floor are a selection of books and engravings from the foundation established by the Reuss family after its abdication from power. This includes a valuable library of French Enlightenment works, still displayed in the original bookcases, plus a collection of eighteenth-century **British political cartoons**, the only one of its type on the Continent. Amassed by Princess Elizabeth, the future Landgravine of Hesse-Homburg (see pp.404–05), who bequeathed it to her niece, Princess Caroline of Reuss, the latter features examples of the work of Thomas Rowlandson and James Gillray, among others. Exhibitions from the holdings of **Satiricum**, the satirical art collection somewhat improbably established by the GDR – a regime which offered a host of ready-made targets for cartoonists – are staged on the top floor.

Practicalities

Greiz's **Bahnhof** lies just to the southwest of the town centre. The **tourist office** (Mon–Wed & Fri 9am–6pm, Thurs 9am–7pm, Sat 9am–1pm; ⓣ0 36

61/68 98 15, Ⓦwww.greiz.de) is in the Unteres Schloss on Burgplatz. There's a very good-value **pension** with restaurant, *Krug zum Grünen Kranz*, right beside the Greizer Park at Parkgasse 7 (Ⓣ0 36 61/67 28 88, Ⓦwww.krug-zum-gruenen-kranz.de; ❸); plus a budget riverside **hotel**, *Haus Friedensbrücke*, Carolinenstr. 1–3 (Ⓣ0 36 61/22 21; ❸). The sole upmarket address is *Schlossberg*, Marienstr. 1–5 (Ⓣ0 36 61/62 21 23, Ⓦwww.schlossberghotel-greiz.de; ❺). Greiz's **youth hostel** is high above the town at Amselstieg 12 (Ⓣ0 36 61/21 76; €12.50/15.50).

Among the places to **eat** and **drink** are the taps of the two local breweries, *Grüne Linde*, Grüne Linde 2, and *Feldschlösschen*, Feldschlösschenstr. 4. However, they're now somewhat overshadowed by *Zapfwerk I/3*, due west of the Greizer Park at Zeulenrodaer Str. 6, an evenings-only entertainment complex which claims to have the largest number of beers on draught (80 in all, with half from Germany, half from the rest of the world) of any hostelry in Europe.

Altenburg

ALTENBURG, 40km northeast of Gera, dubs itself Skatstadt in honour of the fact that Skat, Germany's most popular card game, has both its main production centre and governing headquarters here. Its name is relatively little-known abroad, though it's one of the most worthwhile of Thuringia's old courtly towns. Lying in the easternmost part of the Land, close to the borders with both Saxony and Saxony-Anhalt, Altenburg makes an excellent base for forays into three provinces; alternatively, it can be used as a stopover if travelling on the main rail route south from Leipzig.

The vast hilltop **Schloss** complex, which features just about every European architectural style, has to be entered from the southern end of its park. Despite its long spell as a ducal residence, it still preserves part of its medieval defences, among which the round tower known as the **Flasche**, built into the northern walls, dates back as far as the eleventh century. Nearby is a freestanding tower of uncertain vintage, the **Hausmannsturm** (Tues–Sun 10am–5pm; €1), which can be ascended for a fine view over the Schloss and the town.

Across the courtyard, in the centre of which is a Mannerist fountain to Neptune, lies the main palace block, now designated the **Schloss- und Spielkarten Museum** (same times; €3). Predictably, the main emphasis is on the history of playing cards throughout the last five centuries, Skat in particular. Other highlights are a display of medieval weapons, the collections of oriental and Meissen porcelain amassed by the nineteenth-century statesman Bernhard von Lindenau, and a new presentation on what is claimed as Germany's first kidnapping – the abduction here in 1455 of the two sons of Elector Frederick the Wise. From the museum, **guided tours** are run round the state apartments of the Schloss. They're a surprising mixture: the **Goldsaal** is elegantly Baroque, while the main **Festsaal** is a nineteenth-century historicist extravaganza in red, white and gold, with frothy ceiling frescoes by the Munich Romantic artist Karl Mossdorf depicting stories from Apuleius' *The Golden Ass*. It's occasionally used for concerts, as is the more intimate **Bachsaal**, an early twentieth-century pastiche of its fire-destroyed Renaissance predecessor.

Included in the tour is a visit to the sumptuous **Schlosskirche**. This is otherwise only open for services and for the summer weekend recitals on the eighteenth-century **organ**. The church itself is predominantly late Gothic, with a magnificent star vault. However, the general appearance owes much to a mid-seventeenth-century interior transformation, which added the ducal loft at the west end, the galleries with their statues of saints and Old Testament figures, and the theatrical high altar.

The rusticated neo-Renaissance *palazzo* containing the **Lindenau-Museum** (Tues–Sun 10am–6pm; €4; ⓦwww.lindenau-museum.de) can be seen facing you from the Schlosspark at the far end of Wettinerstrasse. Its cosmopolitan displays, originating in the private collections of Bernhard von Lindenau, are a world away from those normally found in small German towns. On the ground floor, an important group of Greek and Roman vases are kept in one wing, changing selections of modern art in the other. Upstairs, the old masters department includes choice examples of Gothic and Renaissance paintings from Florence and Siena. Small panels from dispersed polyptychs predominate – look out for a rare pair by **Masaccio** of *The Agony in the Garden* and *St Jerome in the Desert,* and for **Fra Angelico**'s exquisite *Three Dominicans* and *St Francis' Trial by Fire*. Of the larger works, the star pieces are *Catherina Sforza as St Catherine* by **Botticelli**, *St Helena* and the *Blessed Filippo Benizzi* by **Perugino**, and a tondo of *The Holy Family* by **Beccafumi**. A diptych of *The Madonna and Child and St John the Baptist* has recently been identified as being by the great fifteenth-century Provençal artist **Enguerrand Quarton**, by whom only a handful of works survive.

The townscape south of the Schloss is dominated by the **Rote Spitze** (Red Points), the two brick towers of a twelfth-century Augustinian collegiate church. To the west, across the busy Wallstrasse, lies the old merchant quarter, centred on two squares. Much the larger of these, the Weibermarkt, has become the modern commercial heart of town. It's overlooked by the handsome Renaissance **Rathaus**, with its dignified portal and showpiece corner oriel. Further north is the Alter Markt, with the Baroque **Seckendorff'sche Palais** and a turn-of-the-century fountain that honours the game of Skat. Just off the square is the main parish church, the **Bartholmäikirche**, whose kernel is Gothic, but whose most notable features are the tapering octagonal Renaissance tower and the graceful little Romanesque crypt.

Practicalities

Altenburg's **Hauptbahnhof** is in the northern part of town. Buses run to and from there to connect with flights to the **airstrip** (ⓣ0 34 47/59 00, ⓦwww.flugplatz-altenburg.de), which is used by Ryanair – under the grand title of Leipzig-Altenburg airport – for flights from London Stansted. The **tourist office** (Mon–Fri 9.30am–6pm, Sat 9.30am–noon; ⓣ0 34 47/59 41 74, ⓦwww.stadt-altenburg.de) is at Moritzstr. 21, with the entrance on Kornmarkt.

Private rooms (❷–❸) are in plentiful supply; there are also several **pensions**, including *Treppengasse*, Treppengasse 5 (ⓣ0 34 47/31 35 49; ❸). Among a good cross-section of **hotels** are *Altenburger Hof*, Schmöllnsche Landstr. 8 (ⓣ0 34 47/58 40, ⓦwww.altenburger-hof.de; ❸–❻), *Parkhotel*, August-Bebel-Str. 16–17 (ⓣ0 34 47/58 30, ⓦwww.parkhotel-altenburg.de; ❹–❻), *Am Rossplan*, Rossplan 8 (ⓣ0 34 47/5 66 10; ❺), and *Astor*, Bahnhofstr. 4 (ⓣ0 34 47/58 70, ⓦwww.astor-altenburg.de; ❻). Each of these has a **restaurant**. Other good places to eat are the *Ratskeller* in the Rathaus, Markt 1, and *Die Villa*, Friedrich-Ebert-Str. 14. Altenburg manages to maintain an ambitious **cultural** programme centred on the Landestheater, Theaterplatz 19 (ⓣ0 34

47/58 51 61, Ⓦwww.theater.altenburg.gera.de). In 2005, the town will host a **festival** (Ⓦwww.prinzenraub.de) commemorating the 550th anniversary of the abduction of the princes from the Schloss.

Rudolstadt and the Schwarza valley

Some 40km upstream from Jena is **RUDOLSTADT**, set in a picturesque stretch of wooded and hilly countryside, near the point where the Saale is joined by the **River Schwarza**, which cuts a particularly beautiful valley to the southwest. For three and a half centuries it was the capital of the county, later principality, of Schwarzburg-Rudolstadt, then, for the decade before its abolition after World War I, of the united province of Schwarzburg, and it still preserves both the authentic appearance and the languid atmosphere of a rural county town.

The Town

Perched high on a hill above Rudolstadt is the vast bulk of **Schloss Heidecksburg** (Tues–Sun 10am–5/6pm; €4; Ⓦwww.heidecksburg.de). The previous Renaissance Schloss was so badly damaged by fire in 1735 that Friedrich Anton, who also wanted to celebrate his earlier promotion from count to a fully fledged prince of the Holy Roman Empire, decided to commission an extravagant new building in the Dresden Rococo style. In lieu of the great Pöppelmann, who was too ill to accept, the plans were drawn up by the most talented Dresden architect of the next generation, Johann Christoph Knöffel, while the work was completed by another native of that city, Gottfried Heinrich Krohne.

The former **Schlosskapelle** in the west wing has been stripped of all religious connotations and now houses a collection of porcelain, much of it of local manufacture. This is the departure point for the **guided tours** round the ornate state apartments. Highlights are the galleried main **Festsaal**, with its huge ceiling fresco of Mount Olympus, the gorgeous **Spiegelkabinett**, with its striking inlaid floor and mock oriental touches and the highly original **Bänderzimmer**, whose medallion portraits give a foretaste of the forthcoming Neoclassical style. At the end of the tour, you're free to wander round the art gallery at leisure – the star piece is Friedrich's brooding *Morning Mist in the Mountains*. The north wing of the Schloss, which still preserves the brightly painted double Renaissance portal with statues of the Virtues, now houses the **Schlossmuseum**. On the ground floor is an outstanding arsenal, containing weapons from the fifteenth to the nineteenth centuries. The upstairs displays on local history are more prosaic, but include the **Schwarzenburger Willkomm**, a fine piece of late sixteenth-century goldsmithery.

In the Altstadt, the main building is the **Stadtkirche St Andreas** at its eastern end, which in its own way evokes the local courtly tradition as vividly as the Schloss itself. By origin an unexceptional Gothic hall church, it was progressively beautified down the years to create the present sumptuous effect. From the Renaissance period are the fantastical portal with its fake door knockers and resplendent coat of arms, and the monumental marble and alabaster epitaph to the Schönefeld family on the end wall of the nave. A burst of creative activity after the Thirty Years War brought a host of Baroque embellishments, including the eccentric sculptures of angels suspended from the vault, plus the princes' loft and burial chamber, the pulpit and the organ.

Rudolstadt's only other notable sight is the **Volkskundemuseum Thüringer Bauernhäuser** (March–Oct Wed–Sun 9am–noon & 1–4/5pm; €2) in the Stadtpark to the east of the centre. One of Germany's oldest open-air museums, this brings together two redundant farmhouses from the region, complete with their furnishings. The larger, standing alongside its original barn, dates back to the 1660s; the other, which is a few decades younger, houses a complete village apothecary's shop.

Practicalities

Rudolstadt's **Bahnhof** lies between the Altstadt and the Stadtpark. The **tourist office** (Mon–Fri 9am–6pm, Sat 9am–noon; ⓣ0 36 72/42 45 43, ⓦwww.rudolstadt.de) is at Marktstr. 57; there's the usual booking service for **private rooms** (❶–❸). The **youth hostel** has a central location at Schillerstr. 50 (ⓣ0 36 72/31 36 10; €14/17. There are only a few **hotels**, including *Schwarzperle*, Schwarzburger Str. 31 (ⓣ0 36 72/35 31 20; ❸), *Zur Pilsener Schenke*, Mörlaer Str. 8 (ⓣ0 36 72/42 23 43; ❹), *Thüringer Hof*, Bahnhofsgasse 3 (ⓣ0 36 72/41 24 22; ⓦwww.thueringer-hof-rudolstadt.de; ❹), and *Adler*, Markt 17 (ⓣ0 36 72/44 03, ⓦwww.adler-rudolstadt.de; ❻). Overlooking Rudolstadt, some 3km to the southeast, is the *Panoramahotel Marienturm*, Marienturm 1 (ⓣ0 36 72/4 32 70, ⓦwww.hotel-marienturm.de; ❻). The best **restaurants** are in the last three hotels. Rudolstadt's main **festival** is the Tanz- und Folkfest, a folk music and dance event of international standing held in July.

The Schwarza valley

Southwest of Rudolfstadt, the **Schwarza valley** is at its most imposing in the ten-kilometre canyon between Bad Blankenburg and Schwarzburg, the original seat of the princely dynasty. This stretch also has an exceptionally rich indigenous flora, including Turk's-cap lilies, columbines, akelei and liverworts. Although there's a road linking the two towns, you really need to follow the footpath, which is liberally endowed with belvederes, to appreciate the landscape to the full. The wonderfully scenic **rail line**, the Schwarzatalbahn from Rudolstadt (part of the regular DB network with regular daily services), does not follow the Schwarza at this point, instead travelling along its tributary, the Rottenbach, to the town of the same name, a junction on the line to Arnstadt. From Schwarzburg, however, it hugs the bank of the Schwarza all the way along the remaining 20km of its route to the terminus at Katzhütte.

About halfway along this last stage is **OBSTFELDERSCHMIEDE**, the valley station of one of Germany's great transport curiosities, the Oberweissbacher Bergbahn. This is the world's steepest **cable rail line** on which normal carriages can run. It ascends 323m in the 1.4-kilometre-long track to **LICHTENHAIN**, a journey which takes eighteen minutes. At the summit, passengers transfer to a tiny diesel train, which takes a further eight minutes to cover the journey through meadows to **CURSDORF**, a pretty resort village of slate-faced houses.

Saalfeld

The old mining town of **SAALFELD**, 10km south of Rudolstadt, marks the transition between the middle and upper parts of the Saale valley. Beyond lie

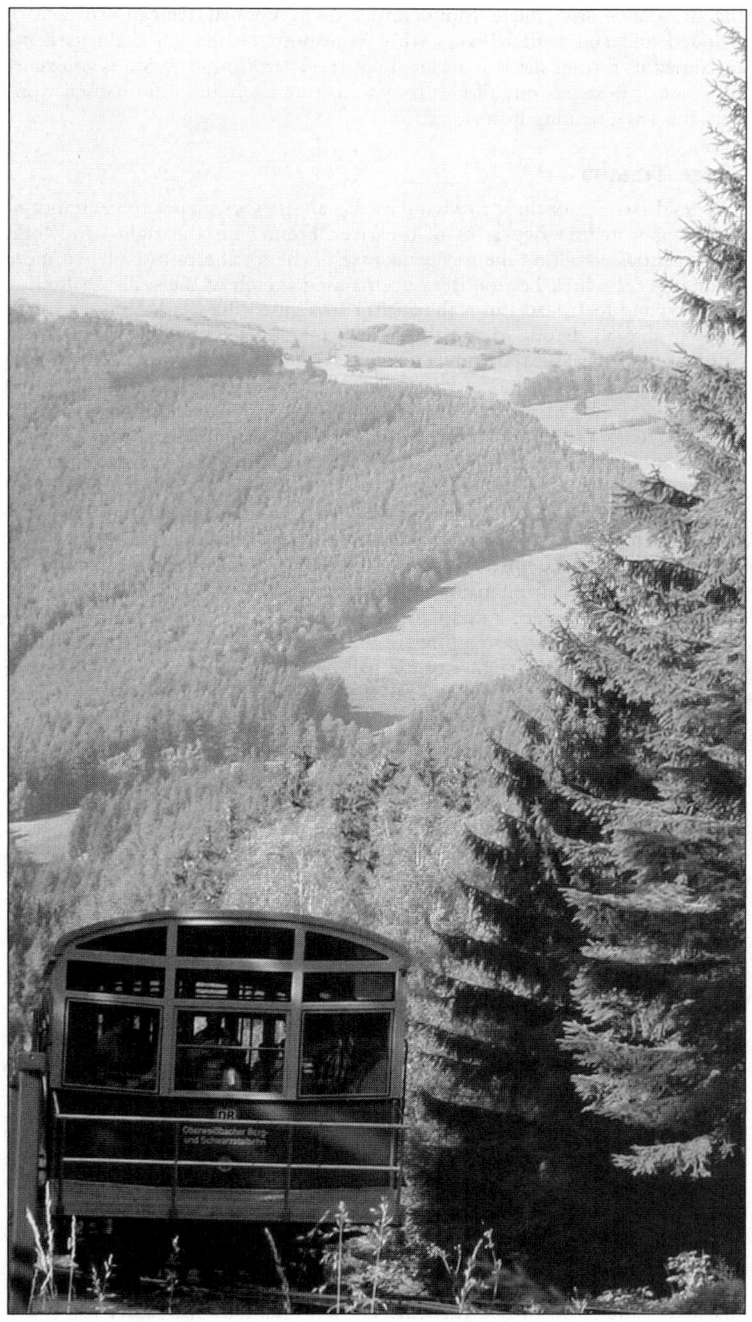

△ The Oberweissbacher Bergbahn, Obstfelderschmiede

the Schiefergebirge (Slate Mountains), now a popular recreational area of wooded hills and artificial lakes with watersports facilities. Saalfeld itself has reclaimed its former status as a tourist resort – apart from its value as an excursion base, it possesses one of Germany's most strangely beautiful natural wonders and has a striking historic centre.

The Town

The **Saaltor**, one of three surviving medieval gateways, guards the entrance to the town from the two arms of the river. From here, the right-hand fork, Puschkinstrasse, follows the former course of the fortifications past two more gates, beyond which lies the largest remaining stretch of the walls. Saalstrasse, the left-hand fork, leads from the Saaltor straight to the Markt, but it's worth making a small detour to the south up Am Hügel to see the Renaissance **Schlösschen Kitzerstein** (now the music school), with its stylized, Dutch-looking gable, and the ruins of the **Hoher Schwarm**, a feudal castle of the type characteristic of the Saale. At the southeastern corner of the Markt is the pristine white **Rathaus**. It's a quintessential building of the German Renaissance with its lingering Gothic feel, its protruding stairwell, its prominent gables and its two strongly contrasted oriel windows. Opposite is the partially Romanesque **Marktapotheke**, which dates back to the town's twelfth-century origins, though it's been altered repeatedly down the centuries.

Towering above the northern side of the Markt, and fronting Blankenburger Strasse, the pedestrianized main shopping street, is the Gothic **Johanniskirche**. Its exterior is richly decorated with late fourteenth-century sculptures of the Parler school; the west portal tympanum of *The Last Judgement* is particularly fine. The most startling feature of the hall interior is the bright red colouring of the vault – a symbolical reference to the blood of Christ. It reaches its climax in the elaborate network design in the chancel, which is painted with a vision of the path to Heaven. Up Brudergasse is the former Franciscan friary, now housing the **Stadtmuseum** (Tues–Sun 10am–5pm; €2), a good-quality regional collection featuring displays on mining, folklore and arts and crafts, the highlight being examples of the local Gothic school of woodcarvers.

Between 1680 and 1735, Saalfeld was capital of the duchy of Saxe-Saalfeld, which was then assumed into Saxe-Coburg. The inevitable legacy of this period is a large Baroque **Schloss**, situated a few minutes' walk north of the confines of the Altstadt along Schlossstrasse, then right into Schlossberg. It's now used by the municipality as offices, but you can wander in and have a look round, particularly at the showpiece staircase. Ask to see the ornate **Schlosskapelle**, which is regularly used for concerts in summer; extravagantly decorated with stuccowork and trompe l'oeil frescoes, its unorthodox design features an irregular octagon within a rectangular ground plan.

The **Feengrotten** (Fairy Grottoes; guided tours March–Oct daily 9am–5pm; Nov Sat & Sun 10am–3.30pm; Dec–Feb daily 10am–3.30pm; €5; Ⓦwww.feengrotten.de), Saalfeld's chief attraction, lie about 1.5km southwest of the town centre, and can be reached by bus #B. Geologically formed 400 million years ago, the present astonishing appearance of this site is the result of a fluke caused by the interaction of natural and human forces. From the mid-sixteenth century, there was a mine here, which was exploited for its alum slate and vitriol until the 1840s. In 1910, waters rich in mineral resources were found pouring out of the abandoned mine. An investigation of its interior revealed that oxidization had turned the galleries into a natural drip-water cave, with stalactites and stalagmites formed from iron phosphate, and the walls cloaked in an astonishing kaleidoscope of colours. Artificial lighting further enhances the effect, seen at its best in the Märchendom (fairy-tale cathedral), also known as the Gralburg (Holy Grail castle) because of its uncanny resemblance to a Wagnerian theatre set.

Practicalities

Saalfeld's **Hauptbahnhof** lies on the east bank of the Saale. The **tourist office** (Mon–Fri 9am–6pm, Sat 10am–2pm; ⓣ0 36 71/3 39 50, ⓦwww.saalfeld.de) is at Markt 6. There are plenty of **private rooms** (❶–❸) available. A wide choice of **hotels** in the town centre includes *Weltrich*, Saalstr. 44 (ⓣ0 36 71/27 32; ❸), *Am Hohen Schwarm*, Schwarmgasse 18 (ⓣ0 36 71/28 84, ⓦwww.schwarmhotel.de; ❹–❻), *Tanne*, Saalstr. 35 (ⓣ0 36 71/82 60, ⓦwww.hotel-tanne-shakarnez.de; ❺), and *Anker*, Markt 25–26 (ⓣ0 36 71/59 90, ⓦwww.hotel-anker-saalfeld.de; ❻). A good-value alternative in the outskirts is *Asterra*, high above the town to the east at Sperberhölzchen 34 (ⓣ0 36 71/51 74 40; ❹), whose **restaurant** serves innovative local specialities. The best places to eat, however, are the *Ratskeller*, Markt 1, and *Zum Güldenen Gans*, a historic cellar restaurant in the *Anker* hotel.

Travel details

Trains

Erfurt to: Arnstadt (frequent; 25min); Eisenach (frequent; 1hr); Gera (11 daily; 2hr); Gotha (frequent; 30min); Jena (frequent; 45min); Meiningen (14 daily; 2hr 30min); Mühlhausen (11 daily; 1hr); Nordhausen (10 daily; 1hr 30min); Sondershausen (10 daily; 1hr 30min/2hr); Weimar (frequent; 15min).

Gera to: Saalfeld (frequent; 1hr 15min/2hr); Greiz (hourly; 40min).

Gotha to: Friedrichroda (frequent; 35min); Mühlhausen (frequent; 1hr).

Jena to: Gera (frequent; 1hr); Rudolstadt (frequent; 1hr); Saalfeld (frequent; 1hr 20min); Weimar (frequent; 30min).

Travel details

12

Saxony

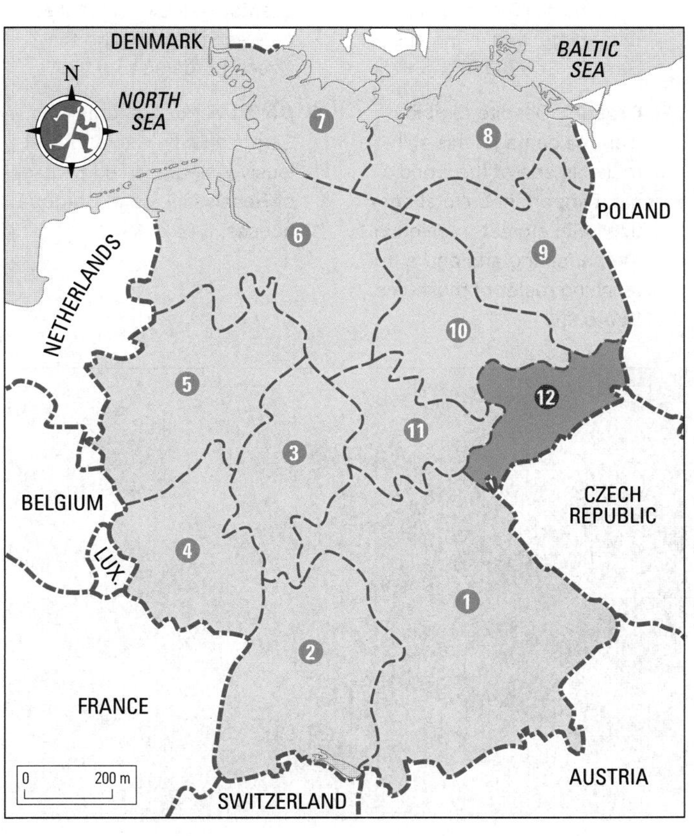
DENMARK
N
NORTH SEA
BALTIC SEA
7
8
POLAND
6
9
NETHERLANDS
10
5
12
11
3
BELGIUM
CZECH REPUBLIC
4
LUX.
1
2
FRANCE
0
200 m
AUSTRIA
SWITZERLAND

CHAPTER 12 Highlights

✱ **Leipzig** The great trade fair city which led the peaceful overthrow of the GDR regime has since profited from an extensive and still ongoing makeover. See p.937

✱ **The narrow gauge steam railways** Some amazing old rail lines still function in the Erzgebirge, and in the east of Saxony. See p.956 & p.975

✱ **Dresden** Despite terrible wartime damage, this still ranks as one of the world's most important cultural centres, with a great tradition in the perfoming arts and a truly stunning roster of museums. See p.959

✱ **Meissen** As well as being the home of Europe's first and most famous porcelain, this beautiful town has has a dramatic setting above the River Elbe. See p.975

✱ **Saxon Switzerland** Wonderfully rocky landscapes characterize the Elbe valley between Dresden and the Czech border. See p.979

✱ **Görlitz** A true Central European city, with a marvellously well-preserved heritage of Renaissance and Baroque houses. See p.984

△ The River Elbe, Saxon Switzerland

12

Saxony

Saxony (Sachsen) is the most enigmatic of Germany's Länder. Its identity appears very secure and well defined, yet it has only the most nebulous connection with the tribes and territories after which it's named. Seemingly so archetypally German, it occupies land which originally belonged to the Slavs, while much of its scenery has more in common with the neighbouring Czech Republic than anywhere in Germany, and many of its towns bear the distinctive central European hallmark of a diversity of cultural influences. Other than Berlin, all three of the ex-GDR's largest cities are here, yet the Land is politically by far the most right-wing in all of Germany. Whereas at least two of the major cities have slotted into the new economic framework without too much disruption, other parts of Saxony seem to belong to a bygone age, trying to maintain the same industries that have supported them for centuries. The list of contradictions seems endless.

Like Thuringia, Saxony's history is closely tied to that of the **Wettin** family, whose original early medieval power base was as **Margraves of Meissen**, charged with securing the Holy Roman Empire's eastern frontier and pushing it deeper into Slav territory to the east and south. The name of "Saxony" only came to be associated with the territory when it became the heartland of the **Albertine** line of the dynasty, which usurped the rival **Ernestine** line from the prized Electorate in the Holy Roman Empire in 1547 and thereafter built up a strong, centralized state. Descendants gained the crown of Poland on three separate occasions, but failed to make it a hereditary possession. Compensation came in 1806, when Napoleon proclaimed Saxony a **kingdom** in its own right; a heavy price had to be paid for this nine years later, when Prussia made huge territorial annexations, although the royal status was retained until 1918.

Dresden, the capital since the foundation of the Albertine line in 1485, is nowadays chiefly associated with the terrible Anglo-American bomb raid of 1945 which obliterated one of Europe's greatest artistic and cultural centres. Its remarkable comeback has gathered pace since the *Wende*, the ultimate aim being to return it to its former appearance. The similarly sized city of **Leipzig** has been able to bask in the glory of having provided the leadership of the revolution which overthrew Communist rule. **Chemnitz**, the third major city, is a place only the most dedicated of travellers will include on their itinerary, but is of special interest for the remarkable insights it offers into the preoccupations of the GDR period and is the jumping-off point for the great Schloss complex at **Augustburg**. The one other place large enough to be regarded as a city is **Zwickau**, whose attraction of a well-preserved centre is overshadowed by a reputation as home of the infamous Trabi car.

Of the smaller towns, the undoubted star is **Meissen**, the original political heart of the region, and the place where the first European porcelain was

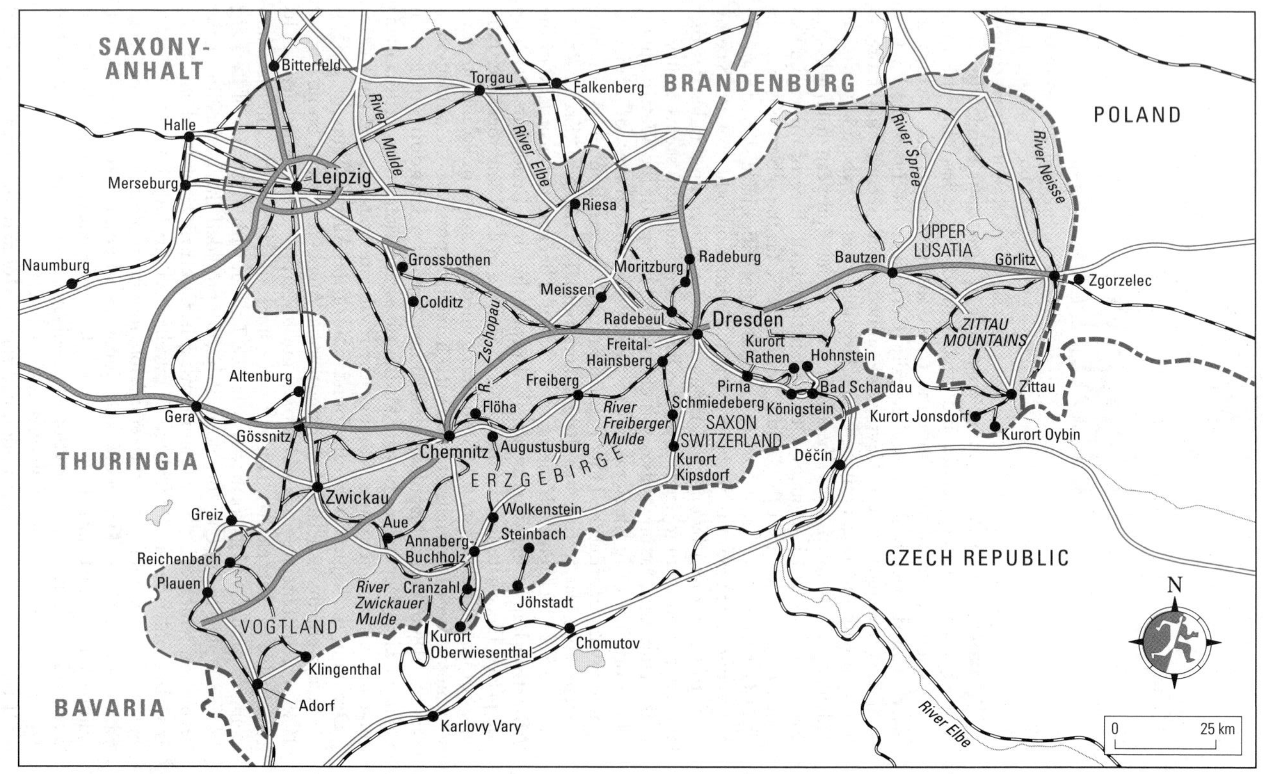
SAXONY-
ANHALT
BRANDENBURG
POLAND
THURINGIA
BAVARIA
CZECH REPUBLIC
Bitterfeld
Torgau
Falkenberg
Halle
Merseburg
Leipzig
River Mulde
River Elbe
Riesa
River Spree
River Neisse
UPPER
LUSATIA
Naumburg
Grossbothen
Moritzburg
Radeburg
Bautzen
Görlitz
Zgorzelec
Meissen
Colditz
Radebeul
Dresden
Zschopau
R.
ZITTAU
MOUNTAINS
Freital-
Hainsberg
Kurort
Rathen
Hohnstein
Altenburg
Freiberg
Pirna
Bad Schandau
Zittau
Gera
Flöha
River
Freiberger
Mulde
Schmiedeberg
Königstein
Kurort Jonsdorf
Kurort Oybin
Gössnitz
Chemnitz
Augustusburg
SAXON
SWITZERLAND
Děčín
Kurort
Kipsdorf
ERZGEBIRGE
Zwickau
Wolkenstein
Greiz
Aue
Steinbach
Annaberg-
Buchholz
Reichenbach
Plauen
River
Zwickauer
Mulde
Cranzahl
Jöhstadt
VOGTLAND
Kurort
Oberwiesenthal
Chomutov
Klingenthal
Adorf
Karlovy Vary
River Elbe
N
0
25 km

manufactured. **Freiberg** and **Annaberg-Buchholz** are the most notable of the mining towns which reached the height of their prosperity in the sixteenth century, a period commemorated in the dazzlingly rich interiors of their churches. **Bautzen** is the main cultural centre of the Sorbs, the Slav people who have remained in the area throughout a millennium of German rule, while **Görlitz** is another place with a richly diverse historical tradition. The little town of **Colditz** brings back the most vivid memories of the war era. **Saxon Switzerland**, the rocky and wooded countryside round the Elbe south of Dresden, is deservedly the best-known scenic part of the Land.

Travel throughout the area presents few problems; a comprehensive rail network includes numerous **narrow-gauge** lines (some only recently put back into operation) on which steam trains regularly run. One of these offers a particularly atmospheric way of reaching the famous Schloss in **Moritzburg**.

Leipzig

Pictures from **LEIPZIG** filled the world's television screens in the autumn of 1989, as the GDR's second city assumed leadership of the *Wende*, the peaceful revolution that toppled the Communist dictatorship and ushered in the elections which led to national unification a year later. Having traditionally been one of Germany's most dynamic cities, it was perhaps inevitable that Leipzig was the place where the frustration of GDR citizens about their postwar lot reached breaking point. Its **trade fairs** (the only ones in Europe with an uninterrupted tradition dating back to the Middle Ages) remained of importance during the Communist interregnum: for all the difficulties the authorities had in squaring these with their ideology, the lure of promoting and developing the GDR as the economic success story of Eastern Europe, with Leipzig as its commercial heart, proved too difficult to resist. This did mean, however, that the city never suffered the sense of isolation from outside influences experienced by so many places behind the Iron Curtain.

In Goethe's *Faust*, Leipzig is described as "Little Paris". That was always an exaggeration – it has never been considered one of Germany's more visually appealing cities – and the analogy seemed very far-fetched indeed during the Communist era, when a legacy of eyesores and pollution was added to the destruction wrought by wartime bombs. However, large advances have been made in the past decade. The general appearance of the centre has changed, almost out of recognition, by a combination of restoration work (which has allowed many architectural gems to re-emerge from the grime that had obscured them), demolition and new building, while the state-of-the-art trade-fair site opened in 1996 in the northern suburb of Wiederitzsch should ensure the city's future economic prosperity. Through all the upheavals of the past century, one factor that has remained constant is Leipzig's importance as a cultural centre, particularly in the field of **music**, where the great tradition of Bach, Mendelssohn, Schumann and Wagner is jealously maintained.

Arrival, information and accommodation

Leipzig's vast **Hauptbahnhof** is at the northeastern end of the Ring (ring road), which encircles the Altstadt; by the eastern side is the **bus station**. Some local trains, particularly from Zwickau, use the **Bayerischer Bahnhof**, which is a few minutes' walk south of the Ring. The **airport** (ⓣ03 41/2 24 11 55, ⓦwww.leipzig-halle-airport.de), the most important in the former GDR, is

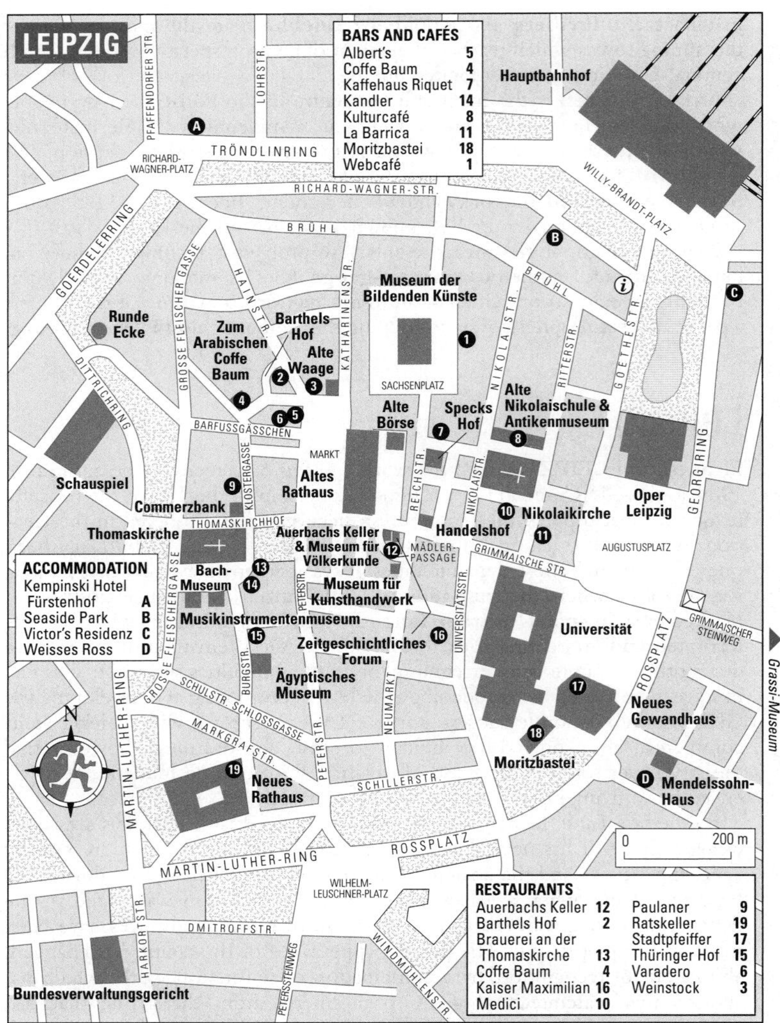

shared with Halle, and now has its own Bahnhof on the rail line linking the two cities.

Directly opposite the Hauptbahnhof, at Richard-Wagner-Str. 1, is the **tourist office** (Mon–Fri 9am–7pm, Sat 9am–4pm, Sun 9am–2pm; ⓣ03 41/7 10 42 60, ⓦwww.leipzig.de). It's well worth investing in the **Leipzig Card**, which covers all public transport in the city, and gives reduced entry prices to the museums. For individuals, it costs €5.90 for a day, €11.50 for three days; for families of two adults and up to three children of 14 or under, there's a three-day card for €19.

Leipzig is exceptionally well endowed with **hotels** geared to expense-account travellers and priced accordingly; these are scattered all over the city, with only a minority in the centre. There's also a much smaller provision of accommodation in small hotels and **pensions**, which are likewise spread over the entire urban area. **Private rooms** (❸–❹) can be booked via the tourist office (Ⓣ03 41/7 10 42 55 for advance reservations); many of these are in Communist-era apartment blocks in the city centre, which at least means that they are convenient, though the trade fair business results in prices being higher than might be expected for the facilities on offer. Alternative **hostel** options are the official Jugendherberge Leipzig-Centrum (Volksgartenstr. 24, Schönefeld; Ⓣ03 41/2 45 70 11; €18.50/21.20.), take tram #17, #27 or #31 to Löbauer Strasse; and the privately run **Hostel Sleepy Lion** (Käthe-Kollwitz-Str. 3, Lindenau; Ⓣ03 41/9 93 94 80, Ⓦwww.hostel-leipzig.de; dorm beds €14, singles €24, doubles €36.50) in the west of the city – take tram #1, #2 or #8. Leipzig's **campsite**, Campingplatz am Auensee (Ⓣ03 41/4 65 16 00, Ⓕ4 65 16 17), is at Gustav-Esche-Str. 5, Wahren, 5km northwest of the centre and reached by tram #10 or #28; it also has bungalows for rent.

Hotels and pensions

Accento Tauchaer Str. 260, Portitz Ⓣ03 41/9 26 20, Ⓦwww.accento-hotel.de. Leipzig's first – and, as yet, only – hotel in the modern designer style, located 6km northeast of the city centre, very close to the A14. It also has a fine restaurant (evenings only). ❺–❼

Galerie Hotel Leipziger Hof Hedwigstr. 1–3 Ⓣ03 41/6 97 40, Ⓦwww.leipziger-hof.de. Situated just over 1km east of the Hauptbahnhof, this hotel is given a distinctive character by the presence throughout of art works, some by established names, others by unknowns. It also has a restaurant with beer garden. ❻

Im Sachsenpark Walter-Köhn-Str. 3, Wiederitzsch Ⓣ03 41/5 25 20, Ⓦwww.sachsenparkhotel.de. Modern business hotel with restaurant situated right alongside the new trade fair grounds in the north of the city, by the terminus of trams #16 and #21. ❻–❾

Kempinski Hotel Fürstenhof Tröndlinring 8 Ⓣ03 41/14 00, Ⓦwww.kempinski.com. Leipzig's top address is a late eighteenth-century patrician palace transformed internally when it became a hotel a century later. Long dormant, it was restored at enormous expense by the *Kempinski* chain, with the addition of modern facilities, including a fitness centre. There's also a top-notch restaurant. ❼–❾

Merseburger Hof Merseburger Str. 107, Lindenau Ⓣ03 41/4 77 44 62, Ⓦwww.merseburger-hof.de. Located in a western suburb, reached by S-Bahn or by tram #5, #13 or #15. Its facilities include a fitness centre and a restaurant with beer garden. ❻

Prima Dresdner Str. 82 Ⓣ03 41/6 88 34 81. A medium-sized pension directly on the main east-bound road, about 2km from the Ring; take tram #2, #4, #6 or #20 to Reudnitz Strassenbahnhof. ❷

Ratskeller Plagwitz Weissenfelser Str. 10, Plagwitz Ⓣ03 41/48 75 80, Ⓕ48 75 82 01. Fine traditional hotel and restaurant in an eastern suburb which can be reached by S-Bahn or tram #2. ❺

Seaside Park Richard-Wagner-Str. 7 Ⓣ03 41/9 85 20, Ⓦwww.seaside-hotels.de. The new name of this Art Deco hotel directly facing the Hauptbahnhof may be incongruous, but it has been refurbished to a high standard and is a very convenient place to stay. There's a recommendable restaurant (evenings only, closed Sun) on the premises. ❼–❽

Victor's Residenz Georgiring 13 Ⓣ03 41/6 86 60, Ⓦwww.victors.de. Another of the clutch of grand hotels around the Hauptbahnhof; it has likewise undergone a makeover and has a good restaurant. ❻–❾

Weisses Ross Auguste-Schmidt-Str. 20 Ⓣ03 41/9 60 59 51. Small budget hotel just south of the Ring run in conjunction with a traditional Gaststätte which is open weekdays only. ❸

The City

Leipzig is easy to get to grips with: the historic buildings lie mostly within the Altstadt, whose boundaries are defined by the Ring, or just outside. The only sights beyond immediate walking distance are conveniently grouped near to each other southeast of the centre.

The Hauptbahnhof, Ring, Nikolaikirche and Alte Nikolaischule

The **Hauptbahnhof** is a masterpiece of early twentieth-century rail architecture and deserves to be considered one of the main sights of Leipzig – especially now that the sad decline it fell into during the GDR days has been reversed by a thorough restoration and the addition of an underground shopping mall. It's the largest dead-end passenger station in the world and covers a site formerly occupied by four small terminals. A curiosity is that it has two entrance halls and two levels, as until centralization was introduced under the Third Reich, the Prussian and Saxon authorities each ran their own half of the station as a separate concern. The top-lit **Wartessal** is by far the grandest waiting room in the country.

Now busy with a far heavier volume of traffic than it had in GDR days, the **Ring** is familiar from news footage as the place where the famous Monday demonstrations against totalitarian abuses of power took place. It's therefore particularly appropriate that the **Runde Ecke** (daily 10–6pm; free; Ⓦwww.runde-ecke-leipzig.de), the former *Stasi* headquarters building at Dittrichring 24, now contains a permanent exhibition on the organization entitled *Macht und Banalität* (Power and Banality). As well as documentary material, you can see examples of the different types of surveillance equipment used, as well as massive piles of confiscated mail.

Following Nikolaistrasse (the street immediately facing the Hauptbahnhof's entrance) due southwards brings you to the **Nikolaikirche** (Ⓦwww.nikolaikirche-leipzig.de), one of the two main civic churches, and one which has gained an honoured place in the national consciousness. Not only was it the local key rallying point during the *Wende*, but the Monday meetings and prayers which had been held there since 1982 entitle it to be considered as the true fountainhead of the revolution. Although a sombre medieval structure from outside, the church's interior is a real eye-opener, thanks to an audacious late eighteenth-century transformation which flirts between Rococo and Neoclassical. The double-galleried nave is particularly striking: its coffered vault is supported by fluted Corinthian columns with capitals sprouting out in the shape of palm trees.

Opposite the church is its former school, the **Alte Nikolaischule**. It's now used by the University, with one floor given over to the **Antikenmuseum** (Tues–Thurs, Sat & Sun noon–5pm; €2; Ⓦwww.uni-leipzig.de), an important collection of classical antiquities only returned to public view a few years ago after several decades of closure. The main highlights are a fine array of Attic vases and the so-called *Leipzig Alexander*, a marble head of Alexander the Great carved in Roman-occupied Egypt around 150 BC.

The heart of the Altstadt

A couple of blocks to the west of the Nikolaikirche is the open space of the Markt, whose eastern side is entirely occupied by the city's finest building, the **Altes Rathaus** (Tues–Sun 10am–6pm; €2.50, free first Sun in month). Designed by **Hieronymous Lotter**, who also served as the mayor of the city, it's in the grandest German Renaissance style, with elaborate gables, an asymmetrical clock tower and the longest inscription to be found on any building in the world. The ground floor retains its traditional function as a covered walkway with shops; the upper storeys, long abandoned as the town hall, now house the local history museum. However, the main reason for going in is to see the 53-metre-long **Festsaal** on the first floor, with its ornate chimneypieces and haughty full-length portraits of the local mayors and Saxon Electors. Also on view is the only likeness of J.S. Bach painted during his lifetime.

△ The Altes Rathaus, Leipzig

On the north side of the Markt is another handsome public building by Lotter, the old weigh house or **Alte Waage**; only its sundial-crowned facade was restored following its destruction in the war. A survivor of the Baroque period is **Barthels Hof**, just off the west side of the square. This is the sole extant example of the courtyards where trading used to take place – a distinctive feature is that it also opens out onto Kleine Fischergasse behind, in order that carriages bearing goods for sale did not have to turn. As the trade fair grew in the early years of the twentieth century, many historic buildings nearby were demolished to make way for the functional modern structures which now predominate, a fate the Altes Rathaus escaped through the casting vote of the mayor. Another survivor is the **Alte Börse** (Old Exchange), the joyous little Baroque building immediately to its rear.

A further distinctive legacy of Leipzig's commercial tradition is the presence of a number of covered shopping malls, of which the largest is the partially modernized **Specks Hof**, entered from Reichstrasse, a block to the east of the Markt. A better-preserved example is the **Mädler-Passage** at the head of Grimmaische Strasse, just off the Markt's southeastern corner. Tucked away underneath its boutiques is **Auerbachs Keller** (Ⓦwww.auerbachs-keller-leipzig.de), a tavern founded in 1525 which is the setting for the famous scene in Goethe's *Faust* when Mephistopheles tricks the local topers with optical illusions before vanishing into the air on a barrel. This, along with other scenes from the play, is depicted in the murals now adorning the cellar. Next door to the Mädler-Passage is the new **Zeitgeschichtliches Forum Leipzig** (Tues–Fri 9am–6pm, Sat & Sun 10am–6pm; free; Ⓦwww.hdg.de), which contains a permanent documentary exhibition, complete with archive film material, on the history and everyday life of the GDR era, with a special emphasis on resistance to the regime. There are also temporary exhibitions on a broad range of historical themes.

Following Barfussgässchen off the western side of the Markt brings you to Kleine Fleischergasse and Leipzig's other celebrated refreshment house, the cheerful Baroque **Zum Arabischen Coffe Baum** (Ⓦwww.coffe-baum.de). Leipzig was one of the main centres of the craze for coffee which followed the Turkish invasion of central Europe in the late seventeenth century, a theme satirized by Bach in the *Coffee Cantata*. Above the doorway is a delightful relief showing a small cherub proffering a cup to a Turk reclining under a coffee tree. In addition to a series of restaurants and cafés (see p.946 & p.947), the building houses the **Museum Coffe Baum** (daily 11am–7pm; free), whose second-floor entrance is guarded by an early eighteenth-century polychromed statue of the "coffee god". Its fifteen rooms illustrate the history of coffee culture in Europe, with a particular emphasis on Saxony. On display are works of art inspired by the beverage, as well as all kinds of coffee-making equipment and coffee sets, including some beautiful examples of Meissen porcelain.

The Museum der Bildenden Künste

Since 1998, the **Handelshof** (an early twentieth-century trade fair hall) at Grimmaische Str. 1 has been the temporary home of the **Museum der Bildenden Künste** (Tues & Thurs–Sun 10am–6pm, Wed 1–8pm; €2.50), an eclectic collection of paintings and sculptures from the Middle Ages to the present day, which was previously housed in the building now known as the Bundesverwaltungsgericht (see p.943), its original premises having been lost to wartime bombs. The museum has some fine early German works, notably a *Man of Sorrows* by Hamburg's **Master Francke** and an erotic allegory, *The Magic of Love*, by an unknown Lower Rhenish painter. There are also a few outstanding Netherlandish panels of the same period, among which *The Visitation* by **Rogier van der Weyden** and *The Institution of the Rosary*, attributed to the very rare **Geertgen tot Sint Jans**, stand out. German painting of the Renaissance is dominated by several examples of **Cranach**, among which *Nymph at the Well* is outstanding, and **Baldung**, whose *Seven Ages of Woman* is one of his most inspired compositions. Highlights of a broad range of seventeenth-century works from across Europe are *The Mulatto* by **Hals**, *The Miracle of St Walburga* by **Rubens** and *The Annunciation* by **Murillo**. From a strong display of Romantic painting, *The Steps of Life* by **Friedrich**, the marvellously comic *The Knight Kuno von Falkenstein* by **Moritz von Schwind**, and the celebrated *Isle of the Dead* by **Böcklin** stand out. There are also many works by the versatile Leipzig artist **Max Klinger**, who was equally proficient at painting, engraving and sculpture, and who is increasingly being seen as a figure of some stature.

A new museum is currently under construction on Sachsenplatz, immediately north of the Markt; it should transform this square, one of the worst eyesores of the Communist era, and also provide much-needed extra display space for the collection. However, the work has been beset by problems and is running well behind schedule; the expected opening date is now October 2004. If current plans are implemented, the first floor will be devoted to Klinger, Jugendstil and classic modern art; the second floor to old masters, with three terraces for sculptures and installations; and the third floor to German and French art from the late eighteenth century to the present day (including, significantly, a section on the GDR period).

The Thomaskirche and the southwestern quarter

A short distance southwest of the Markt is the **Thomaskirche** (Ⓦwww.thomaskirche.org), the senior of the two big civic churches, and the place where **Johann Sebastian Bach** served as *Kantor* for the last 27 years of his life, composing a vast body of choral works for use in its services. Originally part of an Augustinian monastery, the church is predominantly Gothic but has been repeatedly altered down the centuries. Its single **tower** can normally be ascended in summer (Sat 11am–2pm & 4.15–6pm, Sun 2–6pm; €2) for a view over the city. The main features of the interior are the galleries added by Hieronymous Lotter, in line with the Protestant emphasis on preaching, the Gothic winged altarpiece, the Renaissance font, and the many elaborate epitaphs. However, the most remarkable feature of the church is its musical tradition, and its **choir**, the Thomanerchor, which Bach once directed, can usually be heard on Fridays at 6pm, Saturdays at 3pm and at the Sunday service at 9.30am.

Outside the southern entrance to the church is the **Bach-Denkmal**. Across from it, at Thomaskirchhof 16, the **Bosehaus** contains a small concert hall, a satirical cabaret and the **Bach-Museum** (daily 10am–5pm; €3; Ⓦwww.bach-leipzig.de), which has an extensive show of mementos of the great composer, along with a collection of musical instruments of his time. Facing the opposite side of the church is the **Commerzbank**, the most imposing of Leipzig's historic bank buildings, not least for its huge gold figures, which positively glitter when the sun is shining. Almost due south of the Thomaskirche is Burgplatz, on which stands the **Neues Rathaus**. This Historicist monstrosity from the turn of the twentieth century employs elements of just about every European architectural style, even incorporating a "Bridge of Sighs" to link the main building to its extension.

South across the Ring is Georgi-Dimitroff-Platz and the bulky neo-Renaissance palace of justice now known as the **Bundesverwaltungsgericht**

(Federal Administrative Court). Before the war, it was the German supreme court, and the opulent main courtroom and its ancillary chambers on the first floor were the setting for the famous trial on the Reichstag fire – the event which served as a pretext for the Nazis' clampdown on the activities of their political opponents. During the trial, one of those accused of starting the fire, Georgi Dimitroff, the Bulgarian head of the Communist International, completely outwitted Hermann Göring, the chief prosecutor. This was celebrated with relish in GDR days, when the building served as a museum. However, its return to judicial use in 2002 means that it is no longer a regular tourist sight.

Augustusplatz and the University quarter

East of the Markt is a vast square, returned to its old name of Augustusplatz, which serves as the main focus of both academic and musical life in the city. On its northern side is the **Oper Leipzig**, whose sombre pseudo-Neoclassical form recalls the architecture of the Third Reich, though it was actually built under Communism. Very different is the **Neues Gewandhaus** opposite, an avant-garde building inaugurated in 1981 as the new home of the famous Gewandhausorchester, the oldest and largest orchestra in the world.

Rising high up from the centre of the square is the 34-storey **Universitätshochhaus**, begun in 1968 as a prestige project of the then dictator of the GDR, Walter Ulbricht, a native of Leipzig. In order to build this new home for the university, which was founded back in 1409, a number of historic buildings were demolished, including the Universitätskirche. Only a Schinkel-designed gateway on the west side remains, looking hopelessly forlorn against the skyscraper, which is shaped to resemble an open book. A few years ago, it seemed to be a potential candidate for demolition, but was instead given a thorough restoration. A lift whizzes straight up to the panorama restaurant on the 29th floor, from where a stairway leads up a further two storeys to the **observation platform** (daily 11am–11pm; €1.50), which commands a breathtaking view over the city and surrounding countryside. The **Moritzbastei** to the rear, another Lotter creation, is the only surviving part of the fortifications, and has found a new lease of life as what is claimed to be Europe's largest student club. To the west, in temporary premises at Burgstr. 21, the **Ägyptisches Museum** (Tues–Sat 1–5pm, Sun 10am–1pm; €2; Ⓦ www.uni-leipzig.de) has a surprisingly good collection of Egyptian antiquities from nineteenth-century excavations by university archeologists.

Just across the Ring from the Moritzbastei, the late Neoclassical tenement building at Goldschmidtstr. 12 contains the **Mendelssohn-Haus** (daily 10am–6pm; €2.50; Ⓦ www.mendelssohn-stiftung.de), the flat where Felix Mendelssohn Bartholdy spent the last two years of his short life, dying there in 1847. He lived in Leipzig for twelve years in all and, in addition to his compositional activities, he directed the Gewandhausorchester, founded the Conservatory, and revived the long-forgotten music of his great predecessor J.S. Bach. The apartments are furnished in the Biedermeier style the composer would have known: indeed, his work room is an accurate reconstruction based on a contemporary watercolour. Elsewhere, a number of watercolours by Mendelssohn himself, who was a talented amateur painter, can be seen. There are also some original documents and possessions, including the wood and leather trunk with a view of *Ye George Inn* presented to him during his triumphant British tour of 1840; a piano he is known to have played is also on display.

The Grassi-Museum

On Täubchenweg, a short walk to the northeast, is the **Grassi-Museum**, a vast Bauhaus complex. Badly damaged during the war, it remained in partial use until 2001, when it was closed for restoration work that is scheduled to be completed by late 2004. In the interim, the three separate museums contained within are showing selections of their holdings in temporary premises. The **Musikinstrumentenmuseum** (Tues–Sat 10am–5pm, Sun 10am–1pm; €2.50; ⓦwww.uni-leipzig.de), the university's collection of historical musical instruments, is installed alongside the Bach-Museum at Thomaskirchhof 20. In the Mädlerpassage, in rooms directly above Auerbachs Keller, is the **Museum für Völkerkunde** (Tues–Fri 10am–6pm, Sat & Sun 10am–5pm; €2; ⓦwww.mv-grassimuseum.de). Its ethnology displays range across Russia and the other states of the former Soviet Union, Africa (including a distinguished group of bronze sculptures from the Nigerian city of Benin), Persia, China, India, Australia and the South Seas. Just around the corner, at Neumarkt 20, is the temporary home of the **Museum für Kunsthandwerk** (Tues & Thurs–Sun 10am–6pm, Wed 10am–8pm; €4; ⓦwww.grassimuseum.de), one of Europe's finest collections of decorative arts. Highlights include several Renaissance goldsmiths' pieces from the municipal treasure, the *Leipziger Ratsschatz*; the ivory, bronze, copper and wood *Triumph of the Cross* by the Dresden Baroque sculptor Balthasar Permoser; the gem cabinet from the Stadtbibliothek; and a group of sketches for Meissen chinoiserie.

South of the centre

Rail buffs should make the trek south of the Altstadt to see the **Bayerischer Bahnhof**, the oldest functioning train station in Europe. The grand Neoclassical structure erected in the 1840s was virtually flattened during World War II, and just a handful of services still run from here, suggesting it's kept open principally for the sake of preserving its record. However, it now has a new role as the home of the Hausbrauerei (see p.946) which produces a modern version of the historic *Leipziger Gose*, a fruity, acidic brew similar in character to the Belgian *Gueuze* – though in German terms it's technically not a beer, as it contains spices banned under the *Reinheitsgebot* (see p.43).

A few other worthwhile sights lie south of here on the route of tram #21; they can also be reached by tram #15 from elsewhere. On Deutscher Platz is the **Deutsche Bücherei**, the largest German-language library in the world. Part of it is given over to the **Deutsches Buch- und Schriftmuseum** (Mon–Sat 9am–4pm; free; ⓦwww.ddb.de), which traces the history of books during the past 5000 years. Just to the east is the **Russische Gedächtniskirche St Alexij**, a striking pastiche of the churches of Novgorod, decorated inside with original eighteenth-century icons. It was built in 1913 to commemorate the 22,000 Russian soldiers who died in the **Battle of the Nations** a hundred years previously.

The actual site of this conflict, in which the Russians combined with the Prussians, Austrians and Swedes to defeat Napoleon, lies just to the south, on the opposite side of the old trade fair site. Subsequently, the French dictator was banished to exile in Elba. A colossal and tasteless monument, known as the **Völkerschlachtdenkmal** (daily April–Oct 10am–6pm; Nov–March 10am–4pm; €3; ⓦwww.voelkerschlachtdenkmal.de), was erected to commemorate the centenary of the victory. It can be ascended for an extensive if unexciting view over the city and the flat countryside around, and is increasingly in use as a cultural venue (see p.947). The **Forum 1813** (same times; €2) alongside contains several hundred artefacts associated with the battle. These include the personal effects of the most famous casualty, the Polish marshal Prince Józef Poniatowski: his defeat and death meant that hopes for the revival of Poland's independence, lost in 1795, were laid to rest, not to be renewed for another century. There is also a large diorama of the Battle of Probstheida which took place a few days later, completing Napoleon's defeat.

Eating and drinking

Leipzig rivals and indeed surpasses most western German cities in its choices for eating and drinking, offering a wide range of traditional German taverns, ethnic restaurants, cafés and bars. Many of the best places are conveniently close to the Markt; there are also some particularly recommendable establishments in the northern suburb of Gohlis.

Restaurants

Apels Garten Kolonnadenstr. 2. Located just to the west of the Altstadt, this is one of the very best restaurants in Leipzig, though it is quite moderately priced. Featured on the menu are several dishes made according to recipes from the *Leipziger Kochbuch* of 1706. Closed Sun from 3pm.

Auerbachs Keller Mädler-Passage, Grimmaische Str. 2–4. This restaurant's fame makes it a must, and the food served is of high quality. Except when there's a fair on, there's seldom any problem getting a table in either the cavernous main cellar, the *Grosser Keller* (which serves beers from the out-of-town Krostitz brewery) or in the smaller and more upmarket *Historische Weinstuben* (evenings only, closed Sun) on the other side of the stairway.

Avocado Karl-Liebknecht-Str. 79. Leipzig's main vegetarian specialist, situated in an up-and-coming area just south of the Altstadt.

Barthels Hof Hainstr. 1. Restaurant and wine bar in a celebrated Renaissance courtyard. The house specialities are the *Eintopf* dishes, which are available as either starters or main courses.

Bayerischer Bahnhof Bayerischer Platz 1. An offshoot of *Gosenschenke Ohne Bedenken* (see opposite), this Hausbrauerei is the place where *Leipziger Gose* is now brewed.

Brauerei an der Thomaskirche Thomaskirchhof 3–5. A somewhat unexpected combination of an Italian restaurant, serving moderately-priced pizzas, pasta and other typical food, and a Hausbrauerei which brews light, dark and various seasonal beers.

Coffe Baum Kleine Fleischergasse 4. On the ground floor are three cosy little dining rooms serving rustic local fare and beers from the Krostitz brewery; these include the *Schumannzimmer*, which is named after one-time regular, the composer Robert Schumann. Directly above is *Lusatia* (evenings only), which presents somewhat more expensive and upscale cuisine.

Gohliser Schlösschen Menckestr. 23, Gohlis. This beautiful little late Baroque palace, the only building of its type in Leipzig, houses a restaurant serving French and Saxon dishes plus a café. Closed Sun & Mon evenings.

Gosenschenke Ohne Bedenken Menckestr. 5, Gohlis. Just down the road from the above, this late nineteenth-century Gaststätte is decked out in period style and has a spacious beer garden to the rear. It serves hearty meals and was responsible for reviving production of *Gose*.

Hopfenspeicher Oststr. 38, Reudnitz. The Gaststätte and beer garden of the Reudnitzer brewery, Leipzig's largest, with a larger than usual product range for the former GDR. Open from 11am at weekends, 3pm on weekdays.

Kaiser Maximilian Neumarkt 9. Fairly pricey restaurant serving a variety of Mediterranean cuisines.

Kaiser Napoleon Prager Str. 233. Long defunct, this historic Gasthaus has been revived as a Hausbrauerei cum theme restaurant, offering typical dishes from each of the different countries which participated in the Battle of the Nations.

Medici Nikolaikirchhof 5. Leipzig's leading Italian restaurant, presenting upmarket cuisine in very formal surroundings. Closed Sun.

Paulaner Klostergasse 3. The city centre Gaststätte of the eponymous Munich brewery offers both Bavarian and Saxon dishes and has firmly established itself as one of Leipzig's most popular eateries.

Ratskeller Lotterstr. 1. Typically reliable cellar restaurant in the Neues Rathaus; because of its situation well away from the Markt, it's less than usually prone to be full of tourists. Closed Sun evening.

Stadtpfeiffer Augustusplatz 8. Highly rated, rather pricey restaurant of the Neues Gewandhaus, serving an international menu. Closed Sun in July & Aug.

Thüringer Hof Burgstr. 19. Leipzig's oldest surviving Gaststätte, with a pedigree dating back to

1454. It has a rambling layout of rooms and a glass-covered inner courtyard, and is the best-value choice in the Altstadt for a hearty German meal.

Varadero Barfussgässchen 8. Popular and genuine Cuban restaurant, a hardy survivor of the GDR era, specializing in grills and cocktails. On Mon, it's only open in the evening.

Weinstock Markt 7. Mirror-lined wine bar cum bistro, whose set lunch is exceptionally good value.

Cafés and bars

Albert's Markt 2. Lively café-bar which serves tapas snacks.

Coffe Baum Kleine Fleischergasse 4. There are two new cafés on the second floor of this famous old coffee house: one French in style, the other Viennese. A third is decked out in the Arabian manner, but has a purely decorative function.

Kaffeehaus Riquet Schumachergässchen 1. Viennese-style coffee house and wine cellar in a wacky Jugendstil shop building.

Kandler Thomaskirchhof 11. This has a huge range of teas, which are stored in large jars, and home-made pralines.

Kulturcafé Nikolaikirchhof 1. Offers breakfast from 10am, organic wines, beers from the Reudnitzer brewery, and regular live music sessions in the evening.

La Barrica Ritterstr. 4. This award-winning Spanish speciality delicatessen and wine merchant incorporates an eat-in section offering wines by the glass and hot daily specials in addition to the cold fare on general sale.

Moritzbastei Universitätstr. 9. Complex of student clubs, bars and a disco which offers a choice of live entertainment most evenings.

Webcafé Reichsstr. 18. The most convenient internet café. Open Mon–Sat 10am–10pm, Sun 2–8pm.

Culture

Leipzig occupies a hallowed place in the musical world, and hosts performances of the highest standards in several different genres all year round – a remarkable achievement for a city of its size. It also has a strong theatrical tradition, not least in the field of cabaret. Full listings of **what's on** can be found in the free magazine *Fritz*.

Classical music

The **Thomaskirche** (see p.943) continues to play a very prominent role in Leipzig's musical life, with regular organ recitals and choral concerts (by the Thomanerchor and others), to which there's often free admission. As in Bach's lifetime, the **Nikolaikirche** (see p.940) is an important secondary venue for performances of sacred music. In the **orchestral** field, the Gewandhausorchester, which is renowned for the clean, beautifully balanced sound it produces, remains one of the world's best, the tradition of Felix Mendelssohn, Arthur Nikisch, Wilhelm Furtwängler and Bruno Walter having been maintained by Kurt Masur (who also played a key role in the *Wende*) and current music director, Herbert Blomstedt. The local radio orchestra, the MDR-Sinfonieorchester, is also of good standing, while the associated MDR-Chor and MDR-Kinderchor are among Europe's best large mixed-voiced and children's **choirs** respectively.

Bosehaus Thomaskirchhof 16 ⓣ03 41/96 44 10, ⓦwww.bach-leipzig.de. The hall here is used primarily for performances of Baroque music.

Mendelssohn-Haus Goldschmidtstr. 12 ⓣ03 41/1 27 02 94, ⓦwww.mendelssohn-stiftung.de. In honour of a tradition established by Mendelssohn himself, recitals of chamber music or lieder are held every Sun at 11am.

Neues Gewandhaus Augustusplatz 8 ⓣ03 41/1 27 00, ⓦwww.gewandhaus.de. In addition to the main concert hall, the home of the Gewandhausorchester, there's also a smaller room, the Mendelssohn-Saal, for chamber, instrumental and vocal music.

Oper Leipzig Augustusplatz 12 ⓣ03 41/1 26 12 61, ⓦwww.oper-leipzig.de. Presents a varied programme of opera and ballet, including a generous number of contemporary works.

Völkerschlachtdenkmal Prager Str. 210 ⓣ03 41/8 78 04 71, ⓦwww.voelkerschlachtdenkmal.de. A venue of true curiosity value, whose own choir performs regular concerts under quite extraordinary acoustic conditions: the echo lasts up to twenty seconds.

Theatre

Haus Dreilinden Dreilindenstr. 30 ⓣ03 41/12 61 19, ⓦwww.oper-leipzig.de. Specialist venue for musicals and musical comedies.

Puppentheater Sterntaler Talstr. 30 ⓣ03 41/9 61 54 35, ⓦwww.sterntaler.de.vu. Leipzig's puppet theatre.

Schauspiel Bosestr. 1 ⓣ03 41/1 26 81 68, ⓦwww.schauspiel-leipzig.de. The main municipally-run stage for dramatic fare.

Festivals

Leipzig now has a wide variety of festivals throughout the year. The twice yearly Honky Tonk (in May and late October or early November) is billed as Europe's largest **bar festival**, with around 100 different acts performing in nearly as many different venues. The Markt is the setting for various **markets**, notably the nine-day-long Ostermesse at Easter. Of the annual **cultural** events, the ten-day Bachfest (ⓦwww.bach-leipzig.de) centred on Ascension Day (variable date in May/June) celebrates the music of J.S. Bach; the Leipziger Kulturwochen in the first half of October offers a varied programme of concerts; the Lachmesse (ⓦwww.lachmesse.de) in mid-October is a festival of humour and satire; while the Dokfest in mid-November features documentaries and short films.

Colditz

Mention the name of **COLDITZ** to most Germans and you're likely to be met with a blank stare. This is the one place in the country that, because of **Oflag IVC**, the wartime maximum security camp for prisoners of war, is far better known abroad than at home. The main reason for this is that the GDR regime, embarrassed about the fact that the camp had been on their territory and unable to make any pro-Communist propaganda out of it (as they could with the concentration camps, where many of their own number had been incarcerated), chose to suppress its very existence. No references to it could be found in the official English-language guide to the country, while the 64-page German booklet on the town gave it just one paragraph. Although a fair number of English-speaking visitors used to travel the 48km south from Leipzig out of curiosity, they were unable to visit the site of the camp, which reverted to its prewar status as a psychiatric hospital, while Colditz itself went back to being a sleepy rural community. Since the *Wende*, there has been a positive encouragement of visitors and a willingness to make a dispassionate examination of the past.

On its own merits, Colditz is a surprisingly pretty town in attractive surroundings: add in the wartime connection and it's easy to see why the potential for tourism is very real. The streets, laid out on a ramshackle old pattern, are full of historic half-timbered houses, while the main **Markt** is a highly distinctive sloping cobblestoned square. At the top stands a handsome gabled **Rathaus** in the ebullient style of the German Renaissance.

From the foot of Marktplatz, there's a great view of the huge **Schloss** (guided tours daily 10am–5pm; €5; ⓦwww.colditz-4c.com), the former Oflag IVC, which completely dominates the town from its cliff-top site. There's been a fortress here since the eleventh century, which came into the possession of the Wettins, the Saxon ruling house, in 1404. In the middle of the following century, Elector August rebuilt it as a Renaissance palace, though retaining its

Oflag IVC

Schloss Colditz was chosen as the site of **Oflag IVC**, the Third Reich's most secure prisoner-of-war camp, principally because of its geographical position – it was 700km to any border not controlled by the Nazis. The nature of the castle itself, with its secure medieval defences and situation above a small, isolated town, was another factor. **Major Pat Reid**, who wrote a trilogy of books about his Colditz experiences, recorded his initial impression of it as "beautiful, serene, majestic and yet forbidding enough to make our hearts sink into our boots". According to the Nazi authorities, Colditz castle was impossible to escape from, but in all, 31 men performed the feat, aided by the fact that the main qualification for being sentenced to the castle – that of having attempted to escape before – gave the prisoners a rich fund of experience and ingenuity, which they gladly pooled.

In 1941, **Peter Allan** became the first Briton to escape, by hiding in a sack which was taken away in a delivery van; however, on reaching Vienna, he was recaptured and sent back. Following a number of successful getaways by French prisoners, **Airey Neave** (who later led the campaign to make Margaret Thatcher the Conservative Party leader, five years before he was blown up by the IRA) made the first of the eleven British "home-runs" early in 1942, dressed in the uniform of a German officer; Reid was among the others who accomplished the feat that same year. The latter's books are the best source for an insight into life in the camp; for a completely different perspective, see *Colditz – the German Story* by Reinhold Eggers, the official in charge of security.

medieval format of defensive *Vorburg* protecting the main *Hauptburg*. The magnificent armorial decoration above the second gateway shows his own coat of arms, alongside that of his wife. Under Augustus the Strong, the Schloss was used as a hunting lodge, but it was abandoned by later Saxon rulers in favour of more modern palaces. In 1800, it became the local poorhouse, and was later one of Germany's first psychiatric hospitals. It was specially chosen in World War II as the place to house men who had escaped from less secure confinements and subsequently been recaptured, and for *Prominenten*, prisoners who were specially prized because of their high rank or important connections.

Currently, its future is uncertain. The Land government moved out the psychiatric patients and put it up for sale in 1994, hoping to find a foreign buyer prepared to turn it into a hotel or conference centre. They are still looking for outside investment, but have opened a documentary exhibition centre, the **Fluchtmuseum** (same hours and tickets as the tours, otherwise €3) in the old guard house. The exhibits include a large number of photographs taken during World War II plus a fascinating display of some of the ingenious devices the prisoners used in planning their escapes, including a typewriter which could be taken to pieces to prevent its discovery, a razor transformed into a saw and a home-made sewing machine, along with false identification papers and German banknotes. You can also see inside the galleried **Schlosskapelle** and descend to the 44-metre-long **tunnel** which the French prisoners dug over an eight-month period. They intended this to be the means of a mass escape, but it was discovered before it could be used.

The entrance ticket also normally includes the **Städtisches Museum** (same hours, but closed in 2003 for restoration), which occupies a fine Baroque house at Tiergartenstr. 1, just uphill from the church near the entrance to the Schloss. It's a decent local history museum in its own right; the exhibits include the original sculptures from the Schlosskapelle and the Rathaus' eighteenth-century clock.

Practicalities

Colditz lies on the beautiful rail line which runs from Grossbothen along the Zwickauer Mulde valley, but this has recently been supplanted – perhaps permanently – by a **bus** service which, for most visitors, will be less convenient than the alternative direct route from Leipzig. The **tourist office** is at An der Kirche 1 (April–Oct Mon–Fri 9am–5pm, Sat & Sun 10am–4pm; Nov–March Mon–Fri 9am–4pm; ⓣ03 43 81/4 35 19, ⓦwww.colditz.de or www.fremdenverkehrsamt-colditz.de). **Accommodation** options are limited – there's a youth hostel just below the Schloss at Haingasse 42 (ⓣ03 43 81/4 33 35; €13/15.70); a few private rooms (❷–❸); a pension, *Zur Alten Stadtmauer*, Am Graben 5 (ⓣ03 43 81/5 33 63; ❸); and, at the edge of town, a hotel, *Waldhaus*, Lausicker Str. 60 (ⓣ03 43 81/4 33 71; ❸). The best places to **eat** and **drink** are the *Schloss-Café*, Markt 9, and the *Marktstübl*, Markt 20.

Zwickau

ZWICKAU, Saxony's fourth largest city, is a major rail junction and gateway to both the rural areas in the south of the province, the Vogtland and the Erzgebirge (Iron Ore Mountains). It's about 90km south of Leipzig, and can be reached directly by express services via the Thuringian town of Altenburg, though the most atmospheric approach is from the south. Indeed, the journey from Plauen in the Vogtland (a stretch of the Nürnberg–Leipzig line) is one of Germany's most spectacular train rides – the viaducts, and in particular the triple-tiered Göltzschtalbrücke near Mylau, are triumphs of mid-nineteenth-century engineering. For the foreseeable future, Zwickau's name will be irrevocably associated with the Trabant (popularly known as the Trabi), the wretched but now rather celebrated "people's car" of the GDR, which was manufactured here. However, in spite of its industrial tradition, it's an agreeable city of broad parks, with a historic centre which came through World War II almost entirely unscathed.

Zwickau grew up as a market town trading in minerals mined in the Erzgebirge. Its Altstadt occupies a roughly circular area inside the busy inner ring road, Dr-Friedrichs-Ring, with the River Zwickauer Mulde forming a second boundary to the east. Because of earlier wars, only a few monuments from the Middle Ages remain; instead, there's a varied assemblage, with plenty of grand nineteenth- and early twentieth-century offices and stores. Largely pedestrianized, it has developed into a modern commercial city centre on the western German model. Several other worthwhile attractions lie to the north of the centre.

The City

At the southwestern corner of the central Hauptmarkt is the **Robert-Schumann-Haus** (Tues–Fri 10am–5pm, Sat & Sun 1–5pm; €4; ⓦwww.robert-schumann-haus.de), birthplace of German music's purest Romantic spirit. It documents all phases of his career, from his early days as a virtuoso pianist in Leipzig (which were brought to an end after his fingers were damaged in a hand-stretching machine), to his sad final years, during which he was racked by mental instability. There's similarly extensive material on his devoted wife, **Clara Wieck**, who inspired his vast outpourings of passionate, heart-on-sleeve piano pieces and songs. As the leading pianist of her day and an accomplished composer in a style derived from her husband's, she was herself a substantial figure.

In the middle of the south side of the square is the **Rathaus**, whose showy facade masks a medieval structure. Further along is the Renaissance **Gewandhaus**, built in the early sixteenth century as the market hall and guild house of the drapers. Now serving as the town's main theatre, its most notable feature is the amazing five-tiered gable.

Just off the western side of Hauptmarkt is the main civic church, the **Marienkirche** (now designated as the **Dom**, though it's never been a cathedral). Its decorative late Gothic hall-church format, and the profusion of furnishings from the same period, are typical of the Erzgebirge region. Many of the present sumptuous exterior adornments, including the large south porch with its depiction of the Wise and Foolish Virgins, and the now very blackened figures on the buttresses, were only added a century ago in a flush of Romantic over-enthusiasm. The **tower**, whose lead helmet with double cupola is a Baroque embellishment, can be ascended for a view over the Hauptmarkt and the city (Mon–Fri at 3.30pm; €1). Inside, the main adornment is the magnificent **high altar**, made in the Nürnberg workshop of **Michael Wolgemut**, the teacher of Dürer. It can be opened to reveal any of three sections, though only one of these is visible at a time. Normally the carved part, with life-size gilded figures of the Madonna and Child surrounded by eight female saints, is on view, but the cycles of paintings illustrating the Nativity and the Passion are shown during their respective seasons. Also in the chancel is a **Holy Sepulchre**, carved in filigree style in the manner of a Flamboyant Gothic chapel, and adorned with figures of sleeping knights. The other work of art of special note is the *Pietà* in a north aisle chapel, the masterpiece of **Peter Breuer**, a local man who is one of the brilliant group of German sculptors straddling the late Gothic and early Renaissance eras.

Just south of the Marienkirche, on the triangular site formed by the pointed intersection of Domhof and Münzstrasse, is Zwickau's most eccentric building, the **Schiffchen-Haus**, a late fifteenth-century house shaped like the prow of a ship. The Altstadt's remaining sights are all north of the Hauptmarkt. The semicircular Nicolaistrasse loops round via the back of the **Pulverturm** (Powder Tower), the only remaining part of the city walls, to the **Katharinenkirche**, another late Gothic hall church, which formerly belonged to a Benedictine monastery. Inside are a high altar made in Cranach's workshop and a statue of *The Risen Christ* by Breuer. Opposite is the Renaissance **Posthalterei**, which was built as the home of a wealthy cloth manufacturer and merchant. At the extreme northern end of the Altstadt is an even grander Renaissance structure, **Schloss Osterstein**, a former residence of the Electors of Saxony. Alongside is the late fifteenth-century **Kornhaus**, one of the largest and oldest grain stores in the country.

Between the Altstadt and the Hauptbahnhof to the west is the extensive **Stadtpark**, which provides welcome peace in the middle of the city. It's centred on a huge artificial boating lake; other attractions are an open-air theatre, a music pavilion and an aviary, though it's fun enough just to wander through and watch the locals at play. About ten minutes' walk to the north, via Crimmitschauer Strasse, is Lessingstrasse, on which stands the **Städtisches Museum** (Tues–Sun 1–6pm; €2), a rambling, old-fashioned collection in a specially designed domed building from the end of the Jugendstil epoch. Its exhibits range from medieval sculpture, including a triptych and a Crucifixion by Breuer, via displays of locally produced porcelain and official portraits of the Saxon Electors, to the minerals and mining history of the Erzgebirge.

From here, it's just a short walk north to the **Automobilmuseum August Horch** at Walter-Rathenau-Str. 51 (Tues–Thurs 9am–5pm, Sat & Sun 10am–5pm; €3; Ⓦwww.trabant.de), which celebrates Zwickau's role as a leading centre of car production. As the exhibits show, the Trabi was the unworthy and improbable inheritor of a distinguished tradition dating back via the prewar Audi to the Horch factory of 1904. Another ten minutes' walk to the northeast brings you to Leipziger Strasse, the city's north–south arterial road. At no. 182, set in a small park by the Zwickauer Mulde, is **Neue Welt** (New World), a Jugendstil complex built for concerts and dances. Part of it now houses a restaurant; a door on the north side is usually kept open, allowing you to peek in at the ornate main hall.

Practicalities

Zwickau's **Hauptbahnhof** is about fifteen minutes' walk west of the Hauptmarkt. The **tourist office** (Mon–Fri 9am–6.30pm, Sat 10am–4pm; Ⓣ03 75/1 94 33 or 2 72 59 74, Ⓦwww.zwickau.de or www.kultourz.de) is right in the heart of town at Hauptstr. 6, and can arrange **private rooms** (❷–❹). There's a good choice of middle-range **hotels**, including *Park Eckersbach*, northeast of the Altstadt near the terminus of tram #1 at Trillerplatz 1 (Ⓣ03 75/47 55 72, Ⓦwww.telehotel.de/park-eckersbach; ❹–❻); *Merkur*, Bahnhofstr. 58 (Ⓣ03 75/29 42 86, Ⓦwww.merkur-hotel-zwickau.de; ❺); *Achat*, Leipziger Str. 180 (Ⓣ03 75/87 20, Ⓦwww.achat-hotel.de; ❻); and *Airport*, Olzmannstr. 57 (Ⓣ03 75/5 60 20, Ⓦwww.airport-zwickau.bestwestern.de; ❺). Top of the range is *Holiday Inn*, Kornmarkt 9 (Ⓣ03 75/2 79 20, Ⓦwww.holiday-inn-zwickau.de; ❼).

There are **restaurants** in all these hotels except *Merkur*, and they rank among the best in town. *Brauhaus Zwickau*, Peter-Breuer-Str. 14 is a Hausbrauerei located in a terrace of historic priests' houses; it brews a *Weizen*, a *Bock* and both light and dark beers and serves full meals. Other good places to eat and drink are *Zur Grünhainer Kapelle*, Peter-Breuer-Str. 3; the fish specialist *Gastmahl des Meeres*, Marienplatz 1; *Ringkaffee*, Dr-Friedrichs-Ring 21a; and *Drei Schwäne*, Tonstr. 1.

Chemnitz and Augustusburg

When the GDR authorities looked for a place to be renamed in honour of Karl Marx, their choice fell on **CHEMNITZ** (pronounced "Kemnitz"), their fourth largest city, set in the northern foothills of the Erzgebirge, at a pivotal point on the main communications network between Zwickau and Dresden. Thus, between 1953 and 1990, the city became "Karl-Marx-Stadt", with its real name expunged altogether – though the West Germans insisted on retaining it as a suffix. As a city which was rebuilt after the war in a deliberately Soviet-influenced style, Chemnitz has a special curiosity value. In GDR days, its broad boulevards, with their creaking trams and Stalinist-style high-rise offices and tenements, looked and felt quite unnervingly like Russia rather than Germany, and the illusion to some extent persists, despite the heavy volume of traffic. However, from a tourist point of view, such attractions as the city has are completely overshadowed by nearby **Schloss Augustusburg**.

The City

Chemnitz's main north–south axis is Strasse der Nationen. Towards its southern end is the **Versteinerter Wald**, the remains of a petrified forest, with tree stumps reckoned to be 250 million years old. Behind stands the huge pile of the **König-Albert-Museumsbau**, which contains two separate collections. Of these, the **Kunstsammlungen Chemnitz** (Tues–Sun noon–7pm; €2.50; ⓦwww.musehen.de) features a large number of works by the local painter Karl Schmidt-Rottluff, the most abstract member of the Expressionist Die Brücke group, and several galleries of twentieth-century art. The **Museum für Naturkunde** (Tues–Fri 9am–noon & 2–5pm, Sat & Sun 11am–5pm; €2.50; ⓦwww.musehen.de) is mainly of note for its explanatory displays on the Versteinerter Wald.

Turning right at the next junction, previously Karl-Marx-Allee, now Brückenstrasse, you come to the Soviet-made **Karl-Marx-Denkmal**, which consists of a huge bronze head of the founder of Communism and a plaque bearing his famous dictum, "Working men of all countries, unite!", in several languages. After the *Wende*, there were plans to tear this monument down, but it's been decided to retain it as a reminder of the "culture" of the GDR years. Across the road is a park containing the Stadthalle and the **Roter Turm** (Red Tower), a survivor from the medieval city wall.

Further south, the Markt – the only olde-worlde corner of Chemnitz – is once more the scene of market stalls. The whitewashed **Altes Rathaus** is entered via a portal bearing statues of Judith and Lucretia. Behind is the **Hoher Turm** (High Tower) and the turn-of-the-century Neues Rathaus. This incorporates a few Jugendstil features, but a better example of the style is the facade which was added to the Gothic **Jakobikirche** alongside. The house at no. 20, with its frilly Rococo facade, seems something of an anomaly in this city, though all the more welcome for that. South of the centre, at Parkstr. 58, is the **Villa Esche** (Wed & Fri–Sun 10am–6pm; €2.50; ⓦwww.villaesche.de), a Jugendstil building designed by Henry van de Velde. It contains original furnishings by the architect.

At the far northern end of the centre is a park centred on a large artificial lake, the Schlossteich. On the hill above is the **Schlosskirche**, a late Gothic hall church with a stumpy neo-Gothic tower, incorporating some of the masonry from a former twelfth- century monastery. Inside are two masterpieces by **Hans Witten** – a typically idiosyncratic carved group of *Christ at the Column* at the high altar, and the church's original north portal, carved with the help of Franz Maidburg, which now stands against the south wall. This has a tympanum showing the Holy Trinity, along with carvings of the church's founders, Emperor Lothar and Empress Richenza.

A Renaissance **Schloss** for the Electors of Saxony supplanted the former monastic buildings. In commemoration of the five-hundredth anniversary of the birth of Georgius Agricola, Chemnitz's favourite son and four times burgomaster, and an early pioneer in the sciences of mineralogy and metallurgy, it was restored to serve as home to the local history displays of the **Schlossbergmuseum** (Tues–Fri 11am–4/5pm, Sat & Sun 10am–5/6pm; €2.50).

In the far north of Chemnitz, standing in a disarmingly rustic setting in open fields and served by bus #40, is the **Stiftskirche Ebersdorf** (if shut, get the key from the parish house at the back of the close). This was a popular pilgrimage spot in the late Middle Ages, the goal being the beautiful Marienkapelle, the star-vaulted chapel on the south side. The whole interior bristles with works of art, notably of the late Gothic period, including several by Witten – a Crucifixion, statues of an angel and a deacon, and the tomb of Dietrich von Harras, which bears a startlingly realistic effigy of the dead knight.

Practicalities

Chemnitz's **bus station** lies just off the western side of Strasse der Nationen, while the **Hauptbahnhof** is a block to the east. The **tourist office** (Mon–Fri 9am–6pm, Sat 9am–1pm; ⓣ03 71/69 06 80, ⓦwww.chemnitz-tourismus.de) is at Markt 1. There are plenty of **private rooms** (❷–❹) on offer, though many are in distant suburban locations. However, there are now a couple of conveniently sited **pensions**: *SAVO*, Str. der Nationen 37 (ⓣ03 71/44 29 29, ⓦwww.savopension.de; ❸); and *Am Zöllnerplatz*, Mühlenstr. 108 (ⓣ03 71/42 59 86, ⓦwww.pension-zoellnerplatz.de; ❹). **Hotels** with a central location include *Elisenhof*, Mühlenstr. 102 (ⓣ03 71/47 16 90, ⓦwww.hotelelisenhof.de; ❺); *Mercure*, Brückenstr. 19 (ⓣ03 71/68 30, ⓦwww.mercure.com; ❻); *Europa*, Str. der Nationen 56 (ⓣ03 71/68 10, ⓦwww.guennewig.de; ❻); and *Chemnitzer Hof*, which occupies an original Bauhaus building of the 1920s at Theaterplatz 4 (ⓣ03 71/68 40, ⓦwww.guennewig.de; ❼). Chemnitz's **youth hostel** is out in the southeastern suburbs, at Augustusburger Str. 369 (ⓣ03 71/7 13 31; €15.10/17.80) – take an Augustusburg-bound bus, or tram #1 or #6, to Pappelhain and then walk the remaining 1.5km.

Each of the last three hotels listed above has an excellent **restaurant**; another good choice is the *Ratskeller*, Markt 1. Vegetarians should head for *Café Henrie* in the basement of the Umweltzentrum, Henriettenstr. 5.

Chemnitz maintains a lively **cultural** scene, with concerts by the Robert-Schumann-Philharmonie as well as operas at the Opernhaus, Theaterplatz 2 (ⓣ03 71/6 96 96 96, ⓦwww.theater-chemnitz.de), plays at the Schauspielhaus in the Park der Opfer des Faschismus (ⓣ03 71/6 96 97 77, ⓦwww.theater-chemnitz.de), and puppet shows at the Puppentheater, Hartmannstr. 9 (ⓣ03 71/44 64 34, ⓦwww.theater-chemnitz.de).

Augustusburg

The most obvious excursion from Chemnitz is to the village of **AUGUSTUSBURG** 14km to the east. Augustusburg clusters below its cliff-top Renaissance **Schloss** (daily April–Oct daily 9am–6pm Nov–March 10am–5pm; €6.15; ⓦwww.die-sehenswerten-drei.de) combined entry to the Jagtier- und Vogelkundemuseum, Motorradmuseum, Kutschenmuseum and Kerker, otherwise separate tickets required for each section), built as the hunting lodge of the Saxon Electors by the Leipzig architect, Hieronymous Lotter, though its colossal dimensions suggest an altogether grander function.

Guided tours (€2.60) take you to the **Brunnenhaus**, a deep well still preserving its original wooden machinery, the historic apartments of the **Lindenhaus**, and the **Schlosskapelle**, a beautiful galleried Renaissance chapel. The last-named is among the earliest buildings designed specifically for Lutheran worship. It features a tiny historic organ on which recitals are occasionally given, an altarpiece by Cranach the Younger showing the Elector Augustus and his wife with fourteen children, and a pulpit adorned with paintings of scenes from the life of Christ by the same artist.

Other parts of the Schloss can be visited independently. They include the **tower** (€1), which not only commands a fine view, but also houses an art gallery. The **Hasenhaus** (€2.60) contains the **Jagdtier- und Vogelkundemuseum**, which has displays on the animal and bird life of the

Erzgebirge region, but is mainly of note for the rooms themselves, adorned with monumental trompe l'oeil murals, including the humorous depictions of hares in the guise of humans which give the wing its name. Within the Küchenhaus is the **Motorradmuseum** (€2.60), Germany's most impressive museum of bicycles and motorbikes, with a collection ranging from a Laurin-Klement from the end of the nineteenth century, through the many productions of NSU to the latest roadsters. The **Marstall** (€1.50) or stables houses the **Kutschenmuseum**, a collection of historic coaches including those used by the postal services; while the **Kerker** (€1.50) or prison displays historic instruments of punishment and torture. Finally, the **Adler- und Falkenhof** (Easter–Sept Tues–Sun; €5) has a wide variety of birds of prey, some of which take part in the free-flight demonstrations at 11am and 3pm.

To get to Augustusburg, alight at Erdmannsdorf, on the main rail line between Chemnitz and Annaberg-Buchholz; from here the **Drahtseilbahn** (€2.10 single, €3.10 return; Ⓦwww.drahtseilbahn-augustusburg.de), a funicular built in 1911, ascends directly to the Schloss. There's a really top-notch **restaurant**, the *Augustuskeller* (closed Mon) within the Schloss, which also houses a **youth hostel** (Ⓣ03 72 91/2 02 56; €15.90/18.60). The village has several **hotels**, including *Morgensonne*, Morgensternstr. 2 (Ⓣ03 72 91/2 05 08, Ⓦwww.hotel-morgensonne.de; ❹); and *Café Friedrich*, Hans-Planer-Str. 1 (Ⓣ03 72 91/66 66, Ⓦwww.cafe-friedrich.de; ❹). A full accommodation list is available from the **tourist office** (Mon–Fri 9am–noon & 1–5pm, Sat 9am–2pm; Ⓣ03 72 91/3 95 50, Ⓦwww.augustusburg.de) in the Rathaus, Marienberger Str. 24.

Annaberg-Buchholz

In the early sixteenth century, the largest town in Saxony was **ANNABERG**, 30km south of Chemnitz, which grew up alongside the richest silver mines of the Erzgebirge, high above both sides of the Sehma valley and in the lee of the commanding heights of the Pöhlberg. Nowadays the northern half of the double town of Annaberg-Buchholz, it's very provincial in feel, but is the undoubted star of the Erzgebirge, possessing the finest artistic and technical monuments in the region.

Occupying the dominant position in town, the **Stadtkirche St Annen** was erected during the town's short-lived heyday in the first quarter of the sixteenth century. Crafted from rough masonry, the exterior's only feature of note is the tower, shaped like the keep of a castle with an octagonal superstructure; the rest is little more than a shell covering one of Germany's most dazzlingly brilliant interiors. Ribs spring in all directions from the slender columns, forming an intricate star vault adorned with fancy keystones and elaborate little carved figures. The rich and colourful furnishings are contemporary with the architecture. There are two masterpieces by **Hans Witten**, whose reputation has suffered from the fact that most of his work is found in the relative obscurity of the Erzgebirge region. The **Schöne Pforte** (Beautiful Doorway) at the facade end of the northern aisle shows the Holy Trinity adored by the angelic host, with Saints Francis and Clare looking on. Witten's **font** is another extraordinary creation, strangely foreshadowing the productions of Fabergé. Both the **pulpit** and the **gallery** were carved by his colleague Franz Maidburg; the latter forms 100 illustrated Bible scenes. The **high altar**, by the Augsburg sculptor Adolf Daucher, shows the Tree of Jesse,

The narrow-gauge railways of the western Erzgebirge

Two of Saxony's famous narrow-gauge rail lines are in the western part of the Erzgebirge, within easy reach of Annaberg-Buchholz. The **Fichtelbergbahn** (Ⓦwww.bvo.de), otherwise known as the Erzgebirgsbahn, opened in 1897. It was the last such railway to be built in Germany, and has functioned continuously ever since. **CRANZAHL**, on the main line south to the Czech Republic, is the starting point for the 17.4km route to the mountain health resort of **KURORT OBERWIESENTHAL**. The latter's tourist industry was greatly stimulated by the opening of the line, and its grand Alpine-style hotels continue to flourish, particularly in winter, as this is one of the few parts of Germany where snow is virtually guaranteed. In the course of its journey, the train climbs 238 metres, passing through the valleys of the Sehma and Pöhlbach before traversing a 110-metre-long iron viaduct shortly before reaching its terminus.

Until it was closed and dismantled in 1984, the **Pressnitztalbahn** (Ⓦwww.pressnitztalbahn.de) was considered by rail buffs to be the most enjoyable of all eastern Germany's narrow-gauge railways. Beginning at **WOLKENSTEIN**, on the main line north from Annaberg-Buchholz to Flöha, it climbed 293 metres and crossed 52 bridges in the course of its 23km-long journey south along the River Pressnitz to the winter sports resort of **JÖHSTADT** on the Czech border. Since the *Wende*, the final 7.8km of this line have been reinstated, with a new northern terminus at **STEINBACH**. The rest of the route is now a cycle track, and seems likely to remain so.

its cool Renaissance poise standing in contrast to the late Gothic sumptuousness of the other works.

Just across from the Stadtkirche, at Grosse Kirchgasse 16, is the **Erzgebirgsmuseum** (Tues–Sun 10am–5pm; €2.50), which has some fine displays on the folk art of the region. There's also a roomful of medieval sculptures, plus sections on mining and the guilds. In the courtyard is the entrance to the **Schaubergwerk Im Gössner** (guided tours same hours; €3.50, or €5.50 combined ticket), 260 metres of tunnels used by sixteenth-century silver miners.

In the valley below the town is the **Frohnauer Hammer** (guided tours daily 9–11.45am & 1–4pm; €2.50). The visit has three separate parts, beginning with the hammer mill itself, the only one of its kind left in Europe. In the fifteenth century it was a grain mill with four millstones, but was rebuilt at the turn of the seventeenth century for iron and copper production, worked by three huge hammers which each weigh nearly six hundredweight (almost 300kg). After this has been demonstrated, you cross over the road to see another collection of local crafts, before touring the Baroque **Herrenhaus**, the half-timbered mansion of the mill owner.

Practicalities

Annaberg-Buchholz has three train stations, the most useful being the **Unterer Bahnhof**, which lies about ten minutes' walk east of the Frohnauer Hammer, and immediately below the town centre. The **bus station** is at the western end of the upper part of town. Among the centrally sited accommodation options are a **pension**, *Clärchen*, Buchholzer Str. 21 (Ⓣ0 37 33/2 49 55; ❸); and three **hotels**: *Alt Annaberg*, Farbegasse 4 (Ⓣ0 37 33/1 83 10; ❸); *Goldene Sonne*, Adam-Ries-Str. 11 (Ⓣ0 37 33/2 21 83, Ⓦwww.goldene-sonne.de; ❺); and *Wilder Mann*, Markt 13 (Ⓣ0 37 33/14 40, Ⓦwww.hotel-wildermann.de; ❻). Down in the valley, choice is between *Gasthof Zur Schmiede*, Sehmatalstr. 8 (Ⓣ0 37 33/2 30 19, Ⓦwww.gasthof-zur-schmiede.net; ❹) and *Parkhotel*

Waldschlösschen, Waldschlösschenpark 1 (ⓣ0 37 33/6 45 81, ⓦwww.parkhotel-waldschloesschen.de; ❻). As usual, there are plenty of **private rooms** (❶–❸), though these are often inconveniently situated; they can be booked at the **tourist office** (Mon–Fri 10am–6pm, Sat 10am–1pm; ⓣ0 37 33/1 94 33, ⓦwww.annaberg-buchholz.de) in the Rathaus, Markt 1.

The best **restaurants** are in the hotels *Waldschlösschen*, *Goldene Sonne* and *Wilder Mann*; the last-named has a beautiful dining room covered by a sixteenth-century wooden ceiling. Other possibilities are the *Ratskeller* in the Rathaus and the *Frohnauer Hammer* in the Herrenhaus. Annaberg is host to the biggest **festival** in the Erzgebirge, the Rät, which has been going since 1520, and begins on the Saturday after Trinity Sunday (variable date in May/June).

Freiberg

Exactly halfway along the eighty-kilometre-long rail line between Chemnitz and Dresden is **FREIBERG**, whose centre looks, by eastern German standards, startlingly immaculate. Somehow the town came through World War II completely undamaged, and thereafter its long history as a mining community so endeared it to the GDR authorities that they had all the historic buildings cleaned and spruced up in the 1980s. The mining tradition is enshrined in the town's name, "Free Mountain", which is a reference to a twelfth-century imperial decree allowing anyone to come to the area to prospect for minerals and keep all the proceeds. In 1765, the Bergakademie, the world's first college of mining, was founded here; now raised to university status, it's a centre of metallurgical training and research of international repute, imparting a degree of sophistication to what might otherwise now be a very provincial town indeed.

The Town

Freiberg is centred on two market squares, Obermarkt and Untermarkt. From the outside the most remarkable feature is the assemblage of old buildings, but the overall highlight is the interior of the Dom, the town's principal monument.

At the corner of Am Dom and Untermarkt, a number of late Gothic houses have been knocked together to contain the **Stadt- und Bergbaumuseum** (Tues–Sun 10am–5pm; €3), which explains the history of mining in the area in a surprisingly illuminating way, with plenty of large-scale models.

The harmonious-looking main square, the **Obermarkt**, is where local youths loll around the central fountain with its statue of Emperor Otto the Rich, the town's founder. The late Gothic **Rathaus** stands on the east side, with the (for once) separate **Ratskeller**, entered via a handsome Renaissance portal, to the north. Just to the west of Obermarkt, set in its own peaceful close, is the Gothic **Petrikirche**, proud possessor of another Silbermann organ.

The Dom

The **Dom** (guided tours only May–Oct Mon–Sat at 10am, 11am, 2pm, 3pm & 4pm, Sun at 11.30am, 2pm, 3pm & 4pm; Nov–April Mon–Sat at 11am, 2pm & 3pm, Sun at 11.30am; €2; ⓦwww.freiberger-dom.de), as the Marienkirche is officially designated despite never having been a bishop's seat, is outwardly unassuming and doesn't even have a prominent position, being stuck at the back of the lower of the two main squares, the Untermarkt. However, in sheer richness and variety of interior decoration (a legacy of the patronage of the

Saxon Electors, and of the wealth brought by the mines), it's unsurpassed by any of the country's cathedrals.

Two important survivors of the original building, destroyed by fire in the late fifteenth century, were incorporated in the airily light hall church that replaced it. One is the **Goldene Pforte** (Golden Doorway – a reference to its original gilding), which formed the main entrance, but is now placed on the south side. Dating from the 1230s, it's one of the few German counterparts of the great figure portals characteristic of the Gothic cathedrals of France; it's a symbolical vision of a heavenly paradise, centred on a tympanum showing *The Adoration of the Magi*. Similar in date, though still Romanesque in spirit, is the anguished **triumphal cross** group placed high up on a beam above the entrance to the choir. Below it is an early example of a Protestant **high altar**; painted by a follower of Cranach, it incorporates suitably modest-sized figures of a host of local burghers as spectators at the Last Supper.

In the nave, your eye is drawn to the extraordinary writhing, twisting forms of the most precious adornment from the time of the church's construction, the **Tulpenkanzel** (Tulip Pulpit) by **Hans Witten**. Even judged against his own prodigious originality, it's a singular work, being an allegory of the Church as the flower in the garden of God. Resting at the foot is the figure of a local miner in the guise of Daniel in the lion's den, a theme developed in the second pulpit alongside, accordingly known as the **Bergmannskanzel** (Miners' Pulpit), which was made just over a century later. The chancel was transformed to serve as the **mausoleum** of the Albertine line of the House of Wettin. The huge tomb of the Elector Moritz occupies centre stage, though the double memorial to two princesses by Balthasar Permoser, the Baroque sculptor of Dresden, is no less imposing. Another addition from this period is the **ducal loft** on the north side of the nave, designed by the Dresden architect Pöppelmann.

However, the church's most significant Baroque adornments are the two **organs**, both the work of **Gottfried Silbermann**, a friend of Bach and one of the first manufacturers of pianos. The ringing, silvery tones of the larger of these, which many organists regard as the greatest instrument ever made, can be heard (€1 supplement) on the 11.30am Sunday tour and (May–Oct only) the 3pm Wednesday tour, as well as at the longer recitals held each Thursday at 8pm during these same months.

Practicalities

Freiberg's **Hauptbahnhof** is located about fifteen minutes' walk south of Obermarkt, while the **bus station** is about halfway between the two, just before the inner ring road. The **tourist office** (Mon–Fri 9am–5/6pm, Sat 9am–noon; Ⓣ0 37 31/2 36 02, Ⓦwww.freiberg.de) at Burgstr. 1 offers the usual booking service for **private rooms** (❶–❸) and small **pensions** (❸–❹).

Freiberg has a good supply of characterful **hotels**. *Gasthof Brauhof*, Körnerstr. 2 (Ⓣ0 37 31/3 53 30, Ⓦwww.brauhof-freiberg.de; ❹) is a particular bargain; it serves excellent meals and also has a beer garden. *Mauck'sches Gut*, Hornstr. 20 (Ⓣ0 37 31/3 39 78, Ⓦwww.hotel-mauckschesgut.de; ❺) occupies an old farmstead just outside the Altstadt; *Am Obermarkt*, Waisenhausstr. 2 (Ⓣ0 37 31/3 43 61; ❻) has an ideal location plus a fine café and cellar restaurant; *Alekto*, Am Bahnhof 3 (Ⓣ0 37 31/79 40, Ⓦwww.alekto.de; ❻) is a grand station hotel with a distinguished restaurant; while *Silberhof*, Silberhofstr. 1 (Ⓣ0 37 31/2 39 70 or 2 68 80, Ⓦwww.silberhof.de; ❻) occupies a Jugendstil mansion on a quiet inner suburban street and has a fine evenings-only restaurant.

Other good **restaurants** include the *Ratskeller*, Obermarkt 16; *Zum Alten*

Brennmeister, Kesselgasse 30, a specialist in game dishes; and the wine bars *Weinstube St Nikolai*, Kesselgasse 24, and *Weinhaus Blasius*, Burgstr. 26. Also recommended is a long-established **café**, *Hartmann*, Peterstr. 1a. A varied programme of **music** and **drama** is presented at the late eighteenth-century *Mittelsächsisches Theater*, Borngasse 3 (Ⓣ0 37 31/35 82 30, Ⓦwww.mittelsaechsiches-theater.de). The main **festival** is the Bergstadtfest in late June, a celebration of local mining tradition.

Dresden

The name of **DRESDEN** stands alongside Hiroshima as a symbol of the horrendously destructive consequences of modern warfare. What was generally regarded as Germany's most beautiful large city – the "Baroque Florence" – survived World War II largely unscathed until the night of February 13–14, 1945. Then, in a matter of hours, it was reduced to a smouldering heap of ruins in the most savage **saturation bombing** ever mounted by the British and American air forces against civilian targets (see box below). At least 35,000 people died – though the total may have been considerably higher (according to the Soviet estimate, by as much as 100,000), as the city was packed with refugees fleeing from the advancing Red Army. With this background, it's all the more remarkable that Dresden has adapted to the economic framework of the reunited Germany better than anywhere else in the former GDR. Its ambitious reconstruction programme, which aims to restore all the historic buildings left as ruins by the Communists, suffered a severe blow in summer 2002, when horrendous flooding of the River Elbe wreaked havoc throughout the city. Fortunately most of the damage was put right within a year.

The bombing of Dresden

The **bombing of Dresden** has attracted far more criticism of British and American methods during World War II than any other event – even though it was in reality merely the culmination of a deliberately destructive bombing policy, operational since 1940, in which civilian targets and historic buildings were regarded as fair game. However, the sheer extent of the damage, and the fact that thousands of innocent people who were themselves victims of Nazism perished in the raids, put it in a different class from all previous such attacks.

The greatest tragedy of Dresden is that it remains unclear exactly why the raids were carried out at all. The genesis seems to have been a nebulous decision taken in 1944 to carry out a saturation raid on some city (none was specified) which had hitherto not been bombed, as a means of breaking the German resolve once and for all. Although the Soviets specifically requested this tactic, they later distanced themselves from it completely, using it during the Cold War period as a useful propaganda tool against the West (their estimate of 135,000 casualties is now believed to have been a deliberate exaggeration). Winston Churchill, who certainly authorized the attack, also tried to feign ignorance almost immediately afterwards, leaving most of the opprobrium to fall on **Sir Arthur Harris**, the controversial head of Bomber Command. After the war, Harris was denied the peerage which all other service chiefs received, and was shunned by the British establishment, while his forces, who had suffered appalling casualties throughout the war, were refused a campaign medal. The posthumous reassessment of his reputation, culminating in the decision to honour him with a statue in central London, drew widespread official protests from Dresden and other bombed cities.

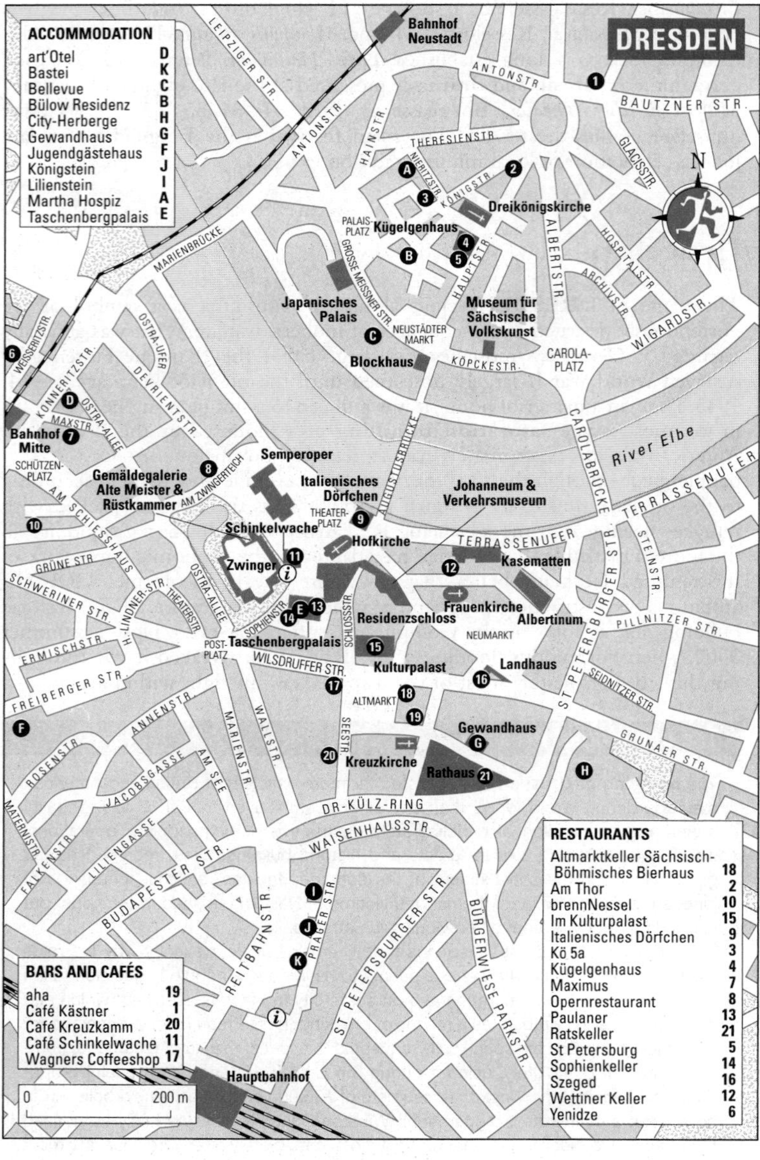

12

SAXONY | Dresden

By origin a Slav fishing village, Dresden stood in the shadow of nearby Meissen until it was made capital of the Albertine line of the House of Wettin in 1485. Its glory period came in the early eighteenth century, under the Elector **Augustus the Strong** (1670–1733), who also held the offices of King of Poland and Grand Duke of Lithuania. Although an exceptionally loathsome figure even by the standards of the Age of Absolutism, as well as an utterly disastrous political operator,

Augustus gathered round him a brilliant group of artists, architects and craftsmen who transformed the city into a great European capital built in a distinctive, highly decorative Baroque style. At the same time, the court collections were organized into outstanding public **museums**. The city built on its already distinguished musical tradition during the Romantic period, becoming one of Europe's leading performance centres, a position it has retained to this day.

Arrival, information and accommodation

Dresden has two major train stations – the **Hauptbahnhof** is south of the Altstadt, while **Bahnhof Neustadt** is at the northwestern corner of the "new town" (which in fact is eighteenth-century) on the opposite bank of the Elbe, and only slightly further away from the main sights, which are grouped close to the river. Between the two, alongside Yenidze, an old cigarette factory built in the shape of a mosque, is the unmanned **Bahnhof Mitte**, but, in spite of its name, it's no more convenient than the others. The **airport** (Ⓣ03 51/8 81 33 60, Ⓦwww.dresden-airport.de), in the far north of the city, is linked to the Hauptbahnhof by an hourly S-Bahn service.

Undoubtedly the most atmospheric way to arrive in Dresden is by **boat**. All services run by Sächsische Dampfschiffahrt, Hertha-Lindner-Str. 10 (Ⓣ03 51/86 60 90, Ⓦwww.saechsische-dampfschiffahrt.de), which operates the world's oldest and largest fleet of paddle steamers, dock at the landing stage at Terrassenufer in the very heart of the city. There are trips downstream to Meissen and upstream to Saxon Switzerland, as well as shorter cruises within the city.

Dresden's **tourist office** (Ⓣ03 51/49 19 20, Ⓦwww.dresden-tourist.de) operates two branches. One is in a pavilion just a couple of minutes' walk from the Hauptbahnhof at Prager Str. 10 (Mon–Fri 9.30am–7pm, Sat 9.30am–4pm); the other is in the Schinkelwache on Theaterplatz (Mon–Fri 10am–6pm, Sat & Sun 10am–4pm). Both sell the **Dresden City-Card**, which costs €18 for 48 hours, and covers public transport costs, entry to the main museums, and sundry discounts; there's also a **Dresden Regio-Card**, costing €29 for 72 hours, which extends the coverage to the surrounding region, including Moritzburg, Meissen, and Saxon Switzerland. Otherwise, a 24-hour public transport ticket within the city costs €4 for individuals, €5 for up to two adults and four children; a day ticket for the state museums (those with the website Ⓦwww.skd-dresden.de) is €10 per person.

Nowhere is the recent revitalization of Dresden more manifest than in the improvement in its stock of **hotels**, which can rival that of any German city, at least in the middle and upper ranges. Any deficiency at the budget end of the market is remedied by small suburban **pensions** and a plentiful supply of **private rooms** (❷–❹), which can be booked at either tourist office (Ⓣ03 51/49 19 22 22 for advance reservations) or the independently run Zentraler Zimmernachweis (Mon–Sat 9am–8pm, Sun 10am–3pm; Ⓣ03 51/4 71 61 21) just inside the entrance to the Hauptbahnhof. Dresden is well equipped with **youth hostels** and also has a campsite.

Hotels and pensions

art' otel Ostra-Allee 33 Ⓣ03 51/4 92 20, Ⓦwww.artotels.de. Trendy modernist venture whose distinctively arty appearance is the joint work of a local painter and a Milanese designer. Its restaurant, *Factory*, serves high-quality Californian-style food. ❻–❾

Bastei Prager Strasse Ⓣ03 51/48 56 66 61, Ⓦwww.ibishotel.com. One of a trio of huge GDR-era concrete boxes (the others are *Königstein* and *Lilienstein*) on this street, all now part of the ibis chain. They're worth trying for their geographical convenience and for the special deals which are often available, though solo travellers get, at best, just a small discount on the price of a double. With over 300 rooms in each hotel, there are usually vacancies. ❹

Bellevue Grosse Meissner Str. 15 ⓣ03 51/80 50, ⓦwww.westin.com. Before the *Wende*, this modern hotel incorporating a Baroque palace was Dresden's flagship address. Despite losing this status, it still offers the advantage of a marvellous Neustadt location right by the Elbe, and has a fine restaurant. ❾

Bülow Residenz Rähnitzgasse 19 ⓣ03 51/8 00 30, ⓦwww.buelow-residenz.de. Exclusive hotel in a renovated Baroque palace in Neustadt with a handsome interior courtyard. Its restaurant, *Caroussel*, currently ranks as Dresden's top gourmet address. ❾

City-Herberge Lingnerallee 3 ⓣ03 51/4 85 99 00, ⓦwww.city-herberge.de. Large modern hotel just east of the Altstadt, which is somewhat institutional in feel but succeeds in its aim of offering modern standards at bargain rates – though the rooms without facilities, while bright and spacious, lack a washbasin. The room price includes a large buffet breakfast. ❸

Gewandhaus Ringstr. 1 ⓣ03 51/4 94 90, ⓦwww.radissonsas.com. Occupying the former cloth hall, this was a medium-range hotel in GDR days, but has been refurbished to five-star standard by the Radisson SAS chain. It has a similarly pricey restaurant. ❽–❾

Martha Hospiz Nieritzstr. 11 ⓣ03 51/8 17 60, ⓦwww.vch.de/marthahospiz.dresden. Century-old church-affiliated Neustadt hotel modernized to a high standard. Its cellar houses the *Kartoffelkeller*, where potato-based dishes predominate. ❻

Schloss Eckberg Bautzener Str. 134, Loschwitz ⓣ03 51/8 09 90, ⓦwww.schloss-eckberg.de. English-style neo-Gothic stately home set in its own lovely park high above the north bank of the Elbe, linked to the centre by tram #11. Its restaurant serves reasonably-priced menus at lunchtime. ❼

Taschenbergpalais Taschenberg 3 ⓣ03 51/4 91 20, ⓦwww.kempinski-dresden.de. This magnificent palace alongside the Residenzschloss was built by Augustus the Strong for one of his mistresses, Countess Kosel. Left as a burnt-out shell for four decades, it was restored according to the original plans by the Kempinski chain and is now easily the best hotel in town, with every conceivable luxury including swimming pool, sauna and solarium. The *Intermezzo* restaurant serves high-calibre Mediterranean cuisine; there are two independently-run eateries in the same building (see p.972). ❾

Zur Pillnitzer Schlossfähre Hosterwitzer Str. 22, Kleinzschachwitz ⓣ03 51/2 00 93 03, ⓦwww.pension-schlossfaehrer.de. Budget pension with café at the extreme southeastern edge of the city, close to the terminus of trams #9 and #14, and the ferry to Schloss Pillnitz from which it takes its name. ❸

Youth hostels and campsites

Campingplatz Mockritz Boderitzer Str. 30, Mockritz ⓣ03 51/4 71 52 50, ⓦwww.camping-dresden.de. Has bungalows to rent as an alternative to pitching a tent. Take bus #76 from the Hauptbahnhof.

CVJM-Jugendschiff Leipziger Str. 15c ⓣ03 51/8 94 58 50, ⓦwww.cvjm-sachsen.de. A YMCA-run hostel on a ship moored on the Neustadt side of the Elbe, in the harbour just north of the bridges. Beds from €23 for those under 18 only; otherwise singles €36.50, doubles €59.

Herbergsschiff Pöppelmann Leipziger Str. 15 ⓣ03 51/03 51/8 40 09 81, ⓕ8 40 09 85. Another hostel-ship, docked immediately to the north of the above. Beds from €14.80.

Jugendgästehaus Maternistr. 22 ⓣ03 51/49 26 20. The DJH youth guest house, by far the largest of the city's hostels, is in a modern tower block just a few minutes' walk southwest of the main Altstadt sights. €18.50/21.20.

Jugendherberge Rudi Arndt Hübnerstr. 11 ⓣ03 51/4 71 06 67. DJH hostel located just to the south of the Hauptbahnhof. €14.80/17.50.

Jugendhotel Die Boofe Hechtstr. 10 ⓣ03 51/8 01 33 61, ⓦwww.boofe.com. A youth hotel-cum-hostel in Neustadt. Singles €29, doubles €44–48, breakfast €4.60 extra.

Mondpalast Louisenstr. 77 ⓣ03 51/5 63 40 50, ⓦwww.mondpalast.de. Another privately-owned Neustadt hostel. Dorm beds from €13.50, singles €29–39, doubles €37–50, breakfast €4.50 extra.

The City

Central Dresden consists of two distinct districts, the **Altstadt** and the **Neustadt**, which lie south and north of the Elbe respectively. The former contains the lion's share of sights, but both have Baroque masterpieces from the city's golden age – as well as plenty of Communist-era concrete buildings. In stark contrast to the centre, some of the **suburbs** of Dresden sustained very little damage in the 1945 air raids. Although off the beaten tourist track, they contain some of the city's most rewarding sights, and are well worth a day of anyone's time.

The southern Altstadt

If you arrive at the Hauptbahnhof, you see the worst of modern Dresden first, as **Prager Strasse**, which leads to the historic part of the city, is an example of Stalinist town planning on the grand scale – a spacious pedestrian precinct containing the standard cocktail of high-rise luxury hotels, public offices, box-like apartments, soulless cafés and restaurants catering mainly for organized tour groups, with a few fountains and statues thrown in for relief. It was here that masses of people congregated in October 1989, hoping to be able to jump aboard the special trains laid on for the East Germans who had sought refuge in the West German embassy in Prague. Ongoing construction work is gradually giving the area a new capitalist face.

At the far end, beyond the inner ring road, is the **Altmarkt**, which was much extended after its wartime destruction; the only building of note which remains is the **Kreuzkirche**, the Protestant cathedral. The present structure mixes a Baroque body with a Neoclassical **tower** (April–Sept Mon, Tues, Thurs & Fri 10am–5.30pm, Wed & Sat 10am–4.30pm, Sun noon–5.30pm; Oct–March Mon–Sat 10am–3.30pm, Sun noon–4.30pm; €1) and a modernized interior impressive in its starkness and loftiness. On Saturdays at 6pm and at the 9.30am Sunday service you can usually hear the church's world-renowned **choir**, the Kreuzchor, which is especially renowned for its performances of the seventeenth-century Dresden composer Heinrich Schütz, father figure of Germany's rich musical tradition.

Behind stands the heavy bulk of the **Rathaus**, built in the early twentieth century in a lumbering Historicist style complete with a **belfry** (April–Oct daily 10am–6pm; €2.50) which rises well above that of the church. Further east is the late eighteenth-century **Gewandhaus**, the old cloth hall, which has been transformed into a hotel. Across the wide Wilsdruffer Strasse from here is the contemporary **Landhaus**, home to the local history collections of the **Stadtmuseum** (10am–6pm, closed Fri; €2.05), which are presented in a far more interesting manner than usual.

The Zwinger

North of Wilsdruffer Strasse lies the palace quarter. At its western end is the great glory of Baroque Dresden, the joyous pleasure palace known as the **Zwinger**, built for festivals and tournaments. It was badly damaged in the war, but quickly rebuilt and has recently been the subject of another major restoration programme. The building was designed by **Matthaeus Daniel Pöppelmann**, one of the most original architects Germany ever produced, and the plan he chose here is appropriately daring: a vast open space with fountains surrounded by a single-storey gallery linking two-storey pavilions, and entered from exuberantly grandiose gateways. The effect is further enhanced by the marvellously expressive decoration by the sculptor **Balthasar Permoser**, though much of this has had to be replaced by copies. Unfortunately, the northern wing was never built because funds ran out.

The main entry to the courtyard is via the **Kronentor**, which guards the moat on the western side; shaped like a triumphal arch, it takes its name from the huge carving of the Polish royal crown which stands on top. An alternative way in is via the **Glockenspielpavillon** at the southwest corner, which has a carillon of forty bells crafted out of Meissen porcelain. At the opposite end of the courtyard is the most beautiful pavilion, the lantern-shaped **Wallpavillon**, astride which rises a heroic figure of Hercules carrying the world on his shoulders. Behind it is the **Nymphenbad**, an elaborate sculptured fountain which ranks as Permoser's most ornate creation.

The Zwinger contains several museums. Beautifully displayed in the south-eastern pavilion, entered from Sophienstrasse, is the **Porzellansammlung** (Tues–Sun 10am–6pm; €5; Ⓦwww.skd-dresden.de). Examples drawn from the two-thousand-year-old history of Chinese porcelain manufacture form a prelude to a wonderful selection of prime products of the eighteenth-century Meissen factory. Of special note are two commissions partly executed by Johann Joachim Kaendler, the greatest ceramic artist of the time: the animals and birds of the menagerie, which were of a mould-breaking size for their time; and items from the now-dispersed 3000-piece Swan Service made for the powerful statesman Count Heinrich von Brühl. A small natural history and geology display, the **Staatliches Naturhistorische Sammlungen** (Tues–Sun 10am–6pm; €3), is housed in the Zwinger's southern gallery. The southwestern pavilion is known as the **Mathematisch-Physikalischer Salon** (Tues–Sun 10am–6pm; €3; Ⓦwww.skd-dresden.de). This is a good deal more interesting than it sounds, with a ground floor devoted to old globes and astronomical instruments, the upper storey to a spectacular array of historic clocks.

The Rüstkammer

The open space on the north side of the Zwinger was filled by the **Semperbau**, which is named in honour of its architect Gottfried Semper, who was responsible for many of the city's finest nineteenth-century buildings. Exhibited in an elegant columned hall on its ground floor is a selection of pieces from the Saxon armoury or **Rüstkammer** (Tues–Sun 10am–6pm; €3; Ⓦwww.skd-dresden.de), which has a really magnificent collection of historic arms and armour from around the world. The focal point of the display is a dazzling Renaissance suit of armour for a man and a horse, adorned with engravings of scenes of the Labour of Hercules and the Trojan War, which was made in Antwerp in the 1560s by Eliseus Libaerts. Other highlights include the sword commissioned by Duke Moritz of Saxony to celebrate his promotion to the rank of Elector; the tournament armour of Elector August; tiny suits of armour made for the children of the court; and various ornate artefacts used in the pageants held in the Zwinger. Augustus the Strong's coronation robes are also on view, as is a horseshoe he is said to have broken with his bare hands. This is one of the reasons given for his nickname, though his sexual prowess – he allegedly sired a child for each day of the year – is often cited as an alternative explanation.

The Gemäldegalerie Alte Meister

The **Gemäldegalerie Alte Meister** (Tues–Sun 10am–6pm; €6; Ⓦwww.skd-dresden.de) is also within the Semperbau, except for the early Netherlandish and German paintings, which are displayed in an interconnected chamber in the Baroque Zwinger. Although it has had relatively few additions made to it in the past century, the collection of old masters built up by the Saxon Electors still ranks among the dozen best in the world.

The Gemäldegalerie contains some of the most familiar of all Italian Renaissance paintings, of which the star is **Raphael**'s *Sistine Madonna*, a wondrous vision of the Virgin and Child among the clouds, adored by Saints

Sixtus (who bears the features of the warrior pope Julius II) and Barbara. Almost equally celebrated is the *Holy Night* by **Correggio**, which interprets one of the most ubiquitous artistic subjects in a completely fresh manner, stressing the nocturnal element ignored by so many other painters. The *Sleeping Venus* by **Giorgione** is one of the most sensual nudes of western art, and among the few paintings almost universally accepted as being by this short-lived father figure of the Venetian Renaissance. It's documented as having been unfinished at the time of his death by plague and was completed by his friend **Titian**, who is represented here by several of his own finest works, including *Young Woman with a Fan* and the deeply psychological *Christ and the Pharisees*. Among several typically resplendent works by **Veronese** is one of his famous banquet scenes, *The Marriage at Cana*, while **Tintoretto** is represented with a diverse group of works, the most memorable being the vividly sketched *St Michael*.

Antonello da Messina's *St Sebastian* is a composition of startling audacity, using an unorthodox low vantage point and incorporating plenty of anecdotal detail in the background, to which the eye is irresistibly drawn. Other Renaissance works to look out for are the sumptuous depiction of *The Annunciation* by the rarely seen Ferrarese painter **Francesco del Cossa**; the disarmingly simple *Portrait of a Boy* by **Pinturicchio**; and the consciously theatrical *Scenes from the Life of St Zenobius* by **Botticelli**. A distinguished group of seventeenth-century Italian pictures includes **Carracci**'s *The Genius of Fame* and **Guercino**'s arresting *Ecstasy of St Francis*. However, the gems are the series of the Parables – including many rarely depicted scenes – which rank as the masterpieces of the short-lived **Domenico Feti**; the wonderfully simple *Parable of the Lost Coin* is particularly memorable. From the eighteenth century, the brilliantly detailed views of Dresden, then at its most resplendent, by the court painter **Bernardo Bellotto** (often known as Canaletto, after his more celebrated uncle) particularly merit attention, not least for the poignance they have acquired since the wartime destruction of the city. Several of his views of Pirna and other parts of Saxon Switzerland are also on show.

Among the German pictures are two masterpieces by **Holbein the Younger** – *Thomas and John Godsalve* presents, in its unusual diagonal poses, a successful solution to the particularly tricky art of the double portrait, while *Le Sieur de Morette* is executed with stunning virtuosity of technique. Very different is the almost abstract style apparent in the pendants *Duke Henry the Pious* and *Duchess Anna of Mecklenburg* by **Cranach**, which are among the earliest full-length portraits ever painted. The same artist's *Martyrdom of St Catherine* was painted for the Schlosskirche in Wittenberg, as was the so-called *Dresden Altarpiece* by **Dürer**, who is also represented by *The Seven Joys of the Virgin* and *Portrait of Bernard von Reesen*. Among later paintings, there's a striking *Rape of Prosperine* by **Josef Heintz**, a Swiss Mannerist who worked at the Imperial court in Prague, and a large number of works by the highly influential Neoclassicist **Anton Raffael Mengs** and other painters of the Dresden school.

The Gemäldegalerie has few early Netherlandish works, but the *Madonna and Child* triptych by **van Eyck**, executed with a miniature-like precision, is unquestionably one of its supreme treasures. Pick of the many works by **Rubens** is *Bathsheba Receiving King David's Letter*, a subject which provided him with an excuse to paint a suggestive portrait of his youthful second wife. **Van Dyck** is represented by one of the variants of his *The Three Children of King Charles I*, and by a superbly characterized *Man in Armour*. The most famous of the **Rembrandt** canvases here is *Self-Portrait with Saskia*, in which he somewhat enigmatically shows himself with his new and clearly not over-joyous wife in the guise of the Prodigal Son carousing in an inn. His interpretation of *The Rape of Ganymede* is also highly unconventional – instead of showing the handsome young boy being carried off to become the cupbearer to the gods by the jealous Jupiter disguised as an eagle, he chose to depict an infant being dragged by his shirt tail, stricken with fear and urinating in desperation. There are two canvases by **Vermeer** – *Girl Reading a Letter* is a typical work, set by a window, and concentrating on the subtle play of light and shade, while the painting known as *The Procuress* is a mysterious composition whose exact meaning is unclear.

Among the French paintings, **Poussin**'s vivacious mythological scenes, such as *The Kingdom of Flora* and *Pan and Syrinx*, make a fascinating contrast with the coolly classical approach favoured by **Claude** in works like *Landscape with Acis and Galatea*. In the eighteenth-century section, **Watteau**'s frilly *Conversation in a Park* stands out. Though the Spanish section is modest, it shows no fall-off in quality, with **El Greco**'s *Christ Healing the Blind* (which actually dates from his Venetian years), **Ribera**'s *St Agnes in Prison* and **Zurbarán**'s *St Bonaventure Kneeling before the Papal Crown* being particularly outstanding. The final room is devoted to pastels, and contains a huge collection of portraits by the Venetian **Rosalba Carriera**, fittingly displayed alongside the work she herself considered the greatest of all pastel paintings, *The Chocolate Girl* by the Swiss **Liotard**.

The Residenzschloss

Across from the Zwinger is the colossal main palace of the Electors and Kings of Saxony, the predominantly Renaissance **Residenzschloss**. This was horribly destroyed in the war, and, although the GDR authorities paid lip service to the idea of restoring it, in practice they did little more than employ two or three workmen to ensure that the ruins, which were kept fenced off, remained upright. The rebuilding programme which has been under way since the *Wende* is a massive task, which will cost an estimated €250 million; the projected completion date is 2006 – the city's 800th anniversary. A good view of the building site, and the city beyond, can be had from the top of the **Hausmannsturm**.

On September 8, 2004, the famous **Grünes Gewölbe** (Green Vault 10am–6pm, closed Thurs; €6; Ⓦwww.skd-dresden.de), one of the richest and most dazzling treasuries in the world, is due to return here from its long-time temporary home, the Albertinum (see p.968), to its original location in the **Spiegelzimmern** (Mirror Rooms), which miraculously survived the bombing but are not currently accessible to the public. However, a number of rooms in the Schloss's **Georgenbau** (10am–6pm, closed Tues; €4; Ⓦwww.skd-dresden.de) have been open to the public for the past few years, and temporary thematic displays, largely drawn from Dresden's own collections, are regularly featured.

The Hofkirche

At the end of this street is the **Hofkirche** (also known as the **Kathedrale**, as it is now the seat of a Roman Catholic bishop), the largest church in Saxony. It was commissioned by Friedrich August II, the only legitimate son of Augustus the Strong, who succeeded him as Elector of Saxony and, after a short interregnum, as King of Poland as well. To emphasize its Catholic allegiance in what was otherwise a staunchly Protestant province, the Italian architect Gaetano Chiaveri was imported to draw up plans. He responded with a highly original design, featuring advancing and receding walls topped by numerous theatrical statues, the whole rounded off with a flourish by an elegant campanile. The gleaming white interior has an elliptical central space surrounded by large chapels. Some of these are normally fenced off; to see them, and the crypt with its tombs of members of the Wettin dynasty, you have to take a **guided tour** (Mon–Wed at 2pm, Fri & Sat at 1pm & 2pm, Sun at 1pm; donation expected).

At the **high altar** is a large canvas of *The Ascension* by Anton Raffael Mengs, who had been appointed court artist in Madrid by the time he finished the work. The side altar of *The Immaculate Conception* and *The Dream of Joseph* are by the same artist. Balthasar Permoser made the wonderfully frilly limewood **pulpit**, which was later given an extravagant canopy; he also made the marble font, and the huge statues of Saints Ambrose and Augustine under the gallery. The immaculately voiced **organ** (on which short recitals are given on Wednesday and Saturday at 11.30am, longer ones on the evenings of the third Thursday of the month) is the artistic testament of the doyen of the craft, Gottfried Silbermann.

Theaterplatz, the Johanneum, the Frauenkirche and the Kasamatten

Facing the Hofkirche across Theaterplatz is the **Italienisches Dörfchen** (Italian Village), whose name recalls that it was the site of the huts of the Italian masons who built the church. Since its immaculate restoration a few years ago, it houses a trio of restaurants (see p.972). Opposite is the plush **Sächsische Staatsoper**, now usually known as the **Semperoper** in honour of its architect. Its tradition is second to none, having seen the premieres of Wagner's *The Flying Dutchman* and *Tannhäuser* and Richard Strauss' *Elektra*, *Salome* and *Der Rosenkavalier*. **Guided tours** (€4.50) of the interior take place throughout the year, except for two months in mid-summer; check the notice board for details. Tickets for performances are hard to come by – the box office for this and other musical events is in the **Schinkelwache**, a sternly Neoclassical guard house designed by Karl Friedrich Schinkel.

Augustusstrasse snakes southeast from the Hofkirche between the **Landtag**, Saxony's parliament building, and the back of the **Johanneum**, the former stables. Along the wall of the latter can be seen a huge turn-of-the-century Meissen porcelain frieze, the *Fürstenzug*, showing a procession of all the ruling members of the Wettin dynasty. On the other side of the complex is the **Lange Gang** (Long Walk), an arcaded late sixteenth-century courtyard in Florentine Renaissance style, and the **Schöne Pforte** (Beautiful Gateway). Part of the building is given over to the **Verkehrsmuseum** (Transport Museum; Tues–Sun 10am–5pm; €3; Ⓦ www.verkehrsmuseum.sachsen.de), with exhibits ranging from trams to aeroplanes.

The entrance to the museum is on Neumarkt, which was formerly dominated by the **Frauenkirche** (Ⓦ www.frauenkirche-dresden.de), a domed church by Georg Bähr, the most talented Dresden Baroque architect after Pöppelmann. One of the finest ever built for Protestant worship, it was designed as both a foil and rival to the Hofkirche. As it was reduced to a heap of rubble in the war with only a fragment of wall left standing, the Communists decided to leave it in this condition as a permanent war memorial. It became the focus for annual peace meetings to mark the anniversary of the wartime bomb raids, and was an important rallying point during the *Wende*. After a fierce controversy, the decision was taken in 1991 to rebuild it completely, and work, thanks in no small part to a successful international fundraising drive, is proceeding at a steady pace – indeed the shell is already complete and it may well be finished before the target date of 2006. The very latest computer technology is being utilised to make this the most faithful reconstruction project ever undertaken: not only are the original stones being re-used, they are actually being put back in their original positions, with little more than ten percent of the total masonry being new. Several **guided tours** (free, but donation expected) are run round the building site every day; the **crypt** is fully operational and a regular concert venue. The area around the church has also been the subject of a massive regeneration project, including the opening of a host of new eateries collectively known as the Kneipenmeile (Bar Mile).

North of Neumarkt, a spacious promenade, the Brühlsche Terrasse, runs along the bank of the Elbe. Here are the **Kasamatten** (guided tours daily 10am–4/5pm; €3.10; Ⓦwww.schloesser-dresden.de), the underground sections of the municipal fortification system, which were built in the mid-sixteenth century according to the most advanced principles of Renaissance military architecture.

The Albertinum

Also on Brühlsche Terrasse is the **Albertinum** (10am–6pm, closed Tues; €4; Ⓦwww.skd-dresden.de), a huge Historicist building which houses many of Dresden's most celebrated art treasures, grouped in several collections.

Taking centre stage, but due to be removed from here in early 2004, is the major part of the **Grünes Gewölbe**. The most fetching works are the extraordinarily elaborate fancies created by the chief jeweller at the court of Augustus the Strong, **Johann Melchior Dinglinger**, a highly original craftsmen who was strongly influenced by Asian art. His first important commission was a gold and enamel **coffee set**, one of the earliest manifestations of the craze for what was, for Europeans, a brand new beverage. After its completion, Dinglinger and his brothers, together with a host of apprentices, worked for the next seven years on a depiction of the **Court of Delhi** on the birthday of the Great Moghul Aurangzeb. This is a real tour de force, featuring 137 gilded and enamelled figures studded with 3000 diamonds, emeralds, rubies and pearls; its glorification of an absolute monarch is a thinly veiled allegory in praise of Augustus the Strong. Many of Dinglinger's smaller pieces were made in collaboration with Balthasar Permoser – the pick of these are the riotously ornate *Bath of Diana* and the *Moor with a Basket of Emeralds*. By Permoser himself are a number of dainty little ivories, notably the *Hottentot Couple*.

Also of special note are the 57 recently restored little grotesques known as the **Perlfiguren**. These are made of misshapen pearls (hence their name) plus gold, enamel and precious stones. Based on the famous engravings of the Lorraine artist Jacques Callot, they were created over a period of several decades by Johann Heinrich Köhler, another of Augustus the Strong's court jewellers, and a Huguenot goldsmith from Berlin, Jean Louis Girardet. Of the nine **jewellery sets** displayed in the final room, those made from sapphires and cornelians are the products of Dinglinger's workshop. All the others are slightly later in date; among them is a set of brilliants with a 41-carat green diamond, the world's largest.

The Albertinum's second main collection is the **Gemäldegalerie Neue Meister**, which features paintings and sculptures from the nineteenth century onwards. It begins with German Romantic paintings, among which the dozen or so canvases by **Friedrich** stand out. These include one of his most famous and haunting works, *The Cross in the Mountains*, a purely secular subject framed to resemble an altarpiece and originally used as such in a private chapel. **Johann Christian Dahl**, a Norwegian who for a while lived in the same Dresden tenement as Friedrich, is also well represented; his nocturnal landscapes are especially atmospheric. The Saxon **Ludwig Richter**, better known as a book illustrator, is shown to be an accomplished talent when working on a larger scale, while the Biedermeier style is seen at its best in the humorous compositions of **Spitzweg**. Realist masterpieces include several striking works by **Menzel**, but the portraits – including **Lenbach**'s *Paul Heyse* (the Nobel Prize-winning writer) and *Wilhelm Busch* (the cartoonist), and **Leibl**'s *Baron von Stauffenberg* – steal the show. Works by most of the French Impressionists and their German contemporaries, including Liebermann and Corinth, precede a section devoted to the Expressionist artists of Die Brücke, the artistic group founded in Dresden. Of the later pictures, look out for two pacifist works in an anachronistic triptych format: *War* by **Otto Dix** and the Bosch-like *The Thousand Year Reich* by **Hans Grundig**, a local artist who spent four years in a concentration camp.

Likewise in the Albertinum, and covered by the same entry ticket, are the **Münzkabinett** with its displays of coins and medallions, and the **Skulpturensammlung**. The latter is particularly strong on the classical period, with Roman copies of lost Greek originals; it also has some fine examples of Mannerist and Baroque sculpture, including works by Giambologna, Adrian de Vries and Balthasar Permoser.

The Neustadt

The Neustadt across the Elbe was a planned Baroque town, and its layout is still obvious, even if few of the original buildings survive. In the centre of the Markt rises the **Goldener Reiter**, a gilded equestrian statue of Augustus the Strong. The only Baroque building to have been rebuilt here is the **Blockhaus**, a guardhouse designed by Zacharias Longuelune, a Frenchman who worked closely with Pöppelmann. Just to the east of the square, on Köpckestrasse, is the seventeenth-century **Jägerhaus**, now housing the **Museum für Sächsische Volkskunst** (Tues–Sun 10am–6pm; €3; Ⓦ www.skd-dresden.de), a collection of folklore objects from throughout Saxony.

The Neustadt's central axis, Hauptstrasse, is a pedestrian precinct lined with a host of restaurants and cafés. It's something of a compromise between the old and the new. Although it in some ways resembles Prager Strasse, a number of Baroque houses have been preserved, among them the **Kügelgenhaus** at no. 13, now decked out with early nineteenth-century furnishings as the **Museum zur Dresdner Frühromantik** (Wed–Sun 10am–6pm; €2). Beyond stands the Neustadt's parish church, the **Dreikönigskirche**, which was designed by Pöppelmann and built by Georg Bähr. Only recently restored following war damage, it is now an ecumenical centre, and the interior of the church, which has been rebuilt in a reduced form, is currently home to the huge carved Renaissance frieze of *The Dance of Death* which formerly adorned a gateway to the Residenzschloss. From the top of the **tower** (Mon–Sat 10am–5pm, Sun noon–5pm; €1) there's a fine view across the Elbe to the Altstadt.

In the park overlooking the river is the most esoteric creation of Dresden Baroque, the **Japanisches Palais**, in which most of the city's leading architects had a hand. It now contains the **Landesmuseum für Vorgeschichte** (Tues–Sun 10am–6pm; €3.50), a turgid archeological museum, and the rather more rewarding **Staatliches Museum für Völkerkunde** (Tues–Sun 10am–6pm; €4), a collection of ethnographic objects from around the globe. There's free access to the courtyard, a fantasy inspired by the eighteenth-century infatuation with chinoiserie.

Another whimsical attraction is **Pfund's Molkerei** at Bautzner Str. 79 at the eastern end of Neustadt. Long derelict, its tiled Jugendstil decoration, a mixture of grotesque motifs and picture-book scenes, has been lovingly restored, and its claim to be regarded as "the most beautiful dairy shop in the world" is surely justified. It sells a marvellous selection of cheeses from around the world, and makes a good spot for lunch – whether in the stand-up section in the shop itself, or in the café-restaurant upstairs (see p.972).

The villa quarters

During Dresden's period as capital of the Kingdom of Saxony, it grew to be Germany's fourth largest city, with a population far in excess of its present-day level. In the process, it spawned a whole series of new suburbs, the most prosperous of which consisted largely of exclusive custom-built **villas** commissioned by the most affluent members of society. Collectively they form an important and distinctive feature of the cityscape; although many have fallen into decay, others have been restored and some now serve as hotels and restaurants.

The densest and most architecturally distinguished group of villas is to be found in **Blasewitz** on the left bank of the Elbe 3km east of the centre; as a result, the entire district has been given the status of a protected monument. To get there, take tram #1 from the Altstadt, or tram #6 from Neustadt. One of Germany's most famous bridges, the so-called **Blaues Wunder** (Blue Wonder) links Blasewitz with **Loschwitz**, a villa suburb on the opposite side of the river. Opened in 1893 after a two-year construction period, this steel suspension bridge was a revolutionary design for its day, and was subsequently much imitated.

In Loschwitz there are two impressive transport curiosities from the time of the Second Reich; it costs €1.50 for a single ticket for either, though they're free with the Dresden Card, and half-price with the 24-hour public transport ticket. Just up from the Blaues Wunder is the valley station of the **Drahtseilbahn**, a funicular railway which runs to the former spa of **Weisser Hirsch**. Instituted in 1895, the funicular was given a thorough overhaul and modernization in preparation for its centenary. A couple of minutes' walk to the south is the rather less orthodox **Bergschwebebahn** (Hanging Mountain Railway), which ascends to Oberloschwitz, the upper part of the quarter. It was put into operation in 1901, and thus postdates its much larger counterpart in Wuppertal, though it was the first of its type in the world built to negotiate a gradient.

At Grundstr. 26, in the valley between the Drahtseilbahn and the Bergschwebebahn, is one of the most spectacular villas, the **Leonhardi-Museum** (Tues–Fri 2–6pm, Sat & Sun 10am–6pm; €1; Ⓦwww.leonhardi-museum.de). This mock-medieval mansion was the home and studio of Edouard Leonhardi, a landscape painter of the late Romantic period who was a professor at the Dresden Academy. Several of his huge, luxuriantly detailed canvases are on view; regular exhibitions of the work of contemporary artists are also featured. A stone's throw south of the Bergschwebebahn station is Loschwitz's parish church, now known as the **Georg-Bähr-Kirche** in honour of its architect. Left as a shell after the war, it has only recently been rebuilt.

Schloss Pillnitz

Schloss Pillnitz, which lies up the Elbe at the extreme edge of the city boundary, is a Pöppelmann creation inspired by the mystique of the Orient. He built two separate summer palaces: the **Wasserpalais** (late April to late Oct 10am–6pm, closed Tues; €3; ⓦwww.skd-dresden.de), directly above the river, contains a museum of applied arts; the **Bergpalais** (late April to late Oct Tues–Sun 10am–6pm; €3; ⓦwww.schloesser-dresden.de) across the courtyard is an almost exact replica, although this time you get to look round the apartments. However, what can be seen inside is of small account in comparison with the exteriors, whose main inspiration seems to have been the palaces of Moghul India, despite the painted Chinese scenes under the eaves. Between the two palaces is a formal garden, while the **Neues Schloss** at the far end is a Neoclassical replacement for its burnt-out Renaissance predecessor, which Pöppelmann retained as the focus of his design. In addition, there's a fine park laid out according to the aristocratic tastes of the time, with sections in both the English and Chinese styles.

Pillnitz can be reached from Blasewitz or Loschwitz by bus #83, or from the city centre by taking tram #1 to the terminus at Kleinzschachwitz, then crossing the Elbe by ferry. More enjoyably, it's a stop on the route of the Sächsische Dampfschiffahrt cruise ships which sail from the Terrassenufer in the heart of the city down into Saxon Switzerland.

Eating and drinking

Dresden's gastronomic scene has changed out of all recognition over the past decade. Although some of the better establishments from the GDR era still remain in business, they're now heavily outnumbered by more recent ventures, which are continuing to spring up all the time. Consequently, there's a wide choice of places to eat and drink in both the Altstadt and the Neustadt, as well as several worthwhile destinations in the suburbs, some of which lie conveniently close to sight-seeing attractions. At night, the liveliest areas are the outer fringes of the Neustadt, and the Uni-Viertel to the south of the Hauptbahnhof.

Restaurants

Altmarktkeller Sächsisch-Böhmisches Bierhaus Altmarkt 4. One of Dresden's golden oldies, the Altmarktkeller has been relaunched as a Bierkeller serving the cuisine and beers of both Saxony and neighbouring Bohemia.

Am Thor Hauptstr. 35. A worthy survivor from GDR days, this small Gaststätte serves tasty food, with changing daily specials, and a small but good selection of draught beers.

Ballhaus und Brauhaus Watzke Kötzschenbroder Str. 1, Mickten. This grand late nineteenth-century building has an upstairs ballroom and a lamplit Hausbrauerei belo, which makes an amber *Spezial*, a *Weizen* and a *Pils*, and serves tasty and inexpensive traditional fare. Its beer garden commands a fine view up the Elbe to the Altstadt, from which it can be reached by tram #4.

brennNessel Schützengasse 18. Dresden's best vegetarian restaurant, presenting creative, freshly prepared dishes. Pending the restoration of its pub-type premises, it is located in the Umweltzentrum to the rear.

Drachen Bautzner Str. 72. Founded in 1919 by the former court butcher to the Saxon kings, and still in the hands of his descendants, this restaurant presents changing seasonal dishes and a fine view of the Elbe, whether from the cosy little *Turmzimmer* or the terrace and beer garden outside. Take tram #11 to Diakonissenkrankenhaus.

Feldschlösschen Stammhaus Budapester Str. 32. The Gaststätte of the brewery, which used to be located alongside, but has moved to new premises in the outskirts: it's best known for a black beer, *Schwarzer Steiger*. Inexpensive *Eintopf* dishes are available Mon–Fri lunchtimes.

Im Kulturpalast Schlossstr. 2. Classy second-floor restaurant, serving both local and international dishes, in the main arts centre.

Italienisches Dörfchen Theaterplatz 3. This historic building with a terrace overlooking the Elbe has a suite of dining rooms plus a terrace directly above the river. *Kurfürstenzimmer*, *Biersaal* and *Weinzimmer* all serve German fare; *Bellotto* presents upscale Italian cuisine; *Caffee* offers *Kaffee und Kuchen*.

Kö 5a Königstr. 5a. *Gutbürgerliche Küche* is served in several tastefully furnished rooms of this restored Baroque building with a pretty inner courtyard.

Kügelgenhaus Hauptstr. 13. Atmospheric restaurant, with a Bierkeller underneath, in a fine Baroque building.

Maximus Maxstr. 5. Art Deco-style café-restaurant with beer garden. It has an international menu, and is open continuously 9am–3am.

Opernrestaurant Theaterplatz 2. Modern, expensive restaurant and bar right beside the opera house. Evenings only, except on Sun, when it's also open for lunch.

Paulaner Taschenberg 3. This Bavarian-style beer hall with front garden occupies part of the Taschenbergpalais and makes an inexpensive alternative to the hotel restaurant in the same building.

Ratskeller Dr-Kulz-Ring 19. Cavernous cellar restaurant decorated in the German Romantic manner, serving typically hearty fare, some to old local recipes. It was badly damaged by the 2002 floods, just two years after an expensive refit, but should now be open again – check ⓦwww.ratskeller-dresden.de for updates.

St Petersburg Hauptstr. 11. The only restaurant in Germany to offer Uzbek cuisine. Russian dishes from the time of the Czars also feature on the menu.

Schillergarten Schillerplatz 9, Blasewitz. Nineteenth-century half-timbered restaurant right beside the Blaues Wunder, with a winter garden directly overlooking the river.

Sophienkeller Taschenberg 3. The rambling cellars of the Taschenbergpalais have been made into a theme restaurant of the era of Augustus the Strong, with a slow-moving carousel for one of the tables. Although gimmicky, it offers excellent food, including (in season) freshly spit-roasted suckling pig.

Szeged Wilsdruffer Str. 4. The local Hungarian restaurant, now with a ground-floor bar. Dishes are prepared with extra hot spices on request.

Waldschlösschen Am Brauhaus 8b. Hausbrauerei with beer garden in the administration building of what was once a full-sized brewery. It makes a *Hefeweizen* as well as light and dark beers, and has an extensive menu. Tram #11 stops outside.

Wettiner Keller Terrassengasse 1. This Weinkeller, which serves wines from Meissen and high-class cuisine, is one of a number of new ventures in the vicinity of the Frauenkirche. Open Tues–Sat, evenings only.

Yenidze Weisseritzstr. 3. Restaurant with a menu of local and international fare in the dome of one of Dresden's most prominent landmarks, the Moorish-style former cigarette factory beside Bahnhof Mitte. It also has a terrace beer garden, which has the bonus of fine views.

Zur Eule Grundstr. 100, Loschwitz. Historic Gasthaus, serving typical Saxon dishes, with a tradition dating back to 1378.

Cafés, bars and café-bars

aha Kreuzstr. 7. Wholefood café attached to a shop selling ethnic goods.

Café B. liebig Liebigstr. 24. Café-bar in the heart of the Uni-Viertel, with a good selection of food and wines.

Café Kästner Alaunstr. 1. Neustadt café-bar named in honour of Erich Kästner, author of the children's classic *Emil and the Detectives*, who was born nearby.

Café Kreuzkamm Am Altmarkt 18. Dresden's best-known coffee house, founded in 1823, has returned to its genteel traditions since the fall of Communism.

Café Schinkelwache Theaterplatz 1. *Kaffee und Kuchen* establishment occupying part of the Altstädter Wache. In summer, when tables are put out on the square, some of Dresden's finest views can be enjoyed while imbibing.

Linie 6 Schaufusssr. 24, Blasewitz. Award-winning theme bar containing a host of paraphernalia associated with tramcars. Its cellar, inevitably named *U6*, hosts late-night cabaret sessions Thurs–Sat. As you'd expect, it lies on the route of tram #6 (and #4 and #10 as well); the nearest stop is Ludwig-Hartmann-Strasse.

Müllers Café Bergstr. 78. A big student favourite, situated right by the entrance to the university campus.

Pfund's Bautzner Str. 79. Although a relatively recent venture, this aims to re-create the appearance and atmosphere of a prewar Dresden coffee house. Some of the items on the menu come from the famous dairy shop downstairs (see p.970).

Planwirtschaft Louisenstr. 20. Has one of Dresden's largest and most popular beer gardens, and is a good choice for breakfast.

Raskolnikoff Böhmische Str. 34. One of the city's trendiest watering holes, offering Russian food and a large selection of vodkas in minimalist surroundings. Evenings only.

Wagners Coffeeshop Altmarkt 25. The most convenient spot for surfing the net; the café is open shopping hours only, but computers are available Mon–Fri 10am–10pm, Sat & Sun 10am–6pm.

Culture and nightlife

Dresden now has quite an adventurous nightlife, though this is still overshadowed by more highbrow cultural offerings, for which the city has a world-class reputation. To find out **what's on**, there's no real need to look further than a couple of free monthly magazines: *Fritz* and *Dresdner Kulturmagazin* (Ⓦwww.dresdner.nu).

Theatre and classical music

Dresden has two international-class symphony **orchestras**, the Staatskapelle Dresden (which also plays for the opera, and is renowned for its silky sound) and the Dresdner Philharmonie, plus an excellent chamber-sized body, the Virtuosi Saxoniae. The last-named is directed by Germany's leading trumpeter, Ludwig Güttler, who has been a key figure in raising money for the restoration of the Frauenkirche. Tickets for the Sächsische Staatsoper and Schauspielhaus are available from the booking office in the Altstädter Wache on Theaterplatz (Ⓣ03 51/49 19 22 33); unsold tickets can be bought at the venue immediately before each performance. It's also well worth checking up on the regular musical events in the city's churches.

Kulturpalast Northern end of Altmarkt Ⓣ03 51/48 66 66, Ⓦwww.konzert-kongress-dresden.de. A large arts centre with a concert hall used for all kinds of music, including a regular series by the Dresdner Philharmonie (Ⓦwww.dresdnerphilharmoniel.de).
Sächsische Staatsoper Theaterplatz 2 Ⓣ03 51/4 91 17 05, Ⓦwww.semperoper.de. One of the city's finest buildings, this stages a wide-ranging operatic programme plus concerts by its house orchestra, the Staatskapelle Dresden.
Schauspielhaus Ostra-Allee 3 Ⓣ03 51/4 91 35 55, Ⓦwww.staatschauspiel-dresden.de. The city's main venue for classical drama.
Staatsoperette Pirnaer Landstr. 131 Ⓣ03 51/2 07 99 29, Ⓦwww.staatsoperette-dresden.de. Dresden's home of operetta and light opera, located in the southeast of the city. Take tram #6, #9, #12 or #14 to Altleuben.

Nightclubs

Bärenzwinger Brühlscher Garten 1. Student club with a varied nightly programme of discos, films, folk music, jazz and dancing.
Dance Factory Bautzner Str. 118. Huge disco and live music stage. Open Thurs–Sun.
Down Town Katharinenstr. 11–13. Club which plays a varied daily mixture of indie, soul, rap and funk. Upstairs is a rock bar, *Groove Station*.
Jazzclub Neue Tonne Königstr. 15. The main jazz venue in the city, with live music on Fri, Sat and Sun at 8.30pm.
Motown Club St-Petersburger-Str. 9. Open as a café-bar during the week, a live music club with international acts at weekends.
Scheune Alaunstr. 36–40. Arts centre in Neustadt with live music, theatre and a cinema. Its café serves Indian food, including plenty of vegetarian dishes, and has a beer garden.
Yenidze Weisseritzstr. 3. Disco in the basement of the former cigarette factory.

Festivals

Dresden's main annual **folklore festival** is the Advent market, here known as the Striezelmarkt (Ⓦwww.striezelmarkt.de). It features a medieval-style market in the courtyard of the Residenzschloss, plus food and handicrafts stalls in the streets and squares of Neustadt. There is copious consumption of *Christstollen*, the German Christmas cake that is now a firm international favourite; the earliest recipe for this dates back to the mid-fifteenth century and is preserved in Dresden's Stadtmuseum. One day of the market is designated the Stollenfest, and features a procession in which a giant *Christstollen* is carried from the

Zwinger to the Altmarkt. In mid-April Dresden hosts a **cinematic** festival, the Filmfest (ⓦwww.filmfest-dresden.de), centred on the celebrated Rundkino on Prager Strasse. A big **jazz** event, the International Dixieland Festival (ⓦwww.dixieland.de), is held each May/June; around the same time, there's a **classical music** festival, the Dresdner Musikfestspiele (ⓦwww.musikfestspiele.com). Soon after the latter ends, there begins a month-long cross-border event, the Sächsisch Böhmisches Musik Festival (ⓦwww.sbmf.de).

Moritzburg

The small village of **MORITZBURG**, 15km north of Dresden, is connected with the Hauptbahnhof by bus #326, but it's far more fun to take the narrow-gauge railway, the Lössnitztalbahn (see box on p.975).

At the edge of Moritzburg is the **Schloss** (May–Sept daily 10am–5.30pm; Nov–March Tues–Sun 10am–4pm; €4.10, €6 combined ticket with the Federzimmer; ⓦwww.schloss-moritzburg.de). It was founded as a hunting lodge in 1542 by Duke Moritz of Saxony, but was almost completely rebuilt in the 1720s for Augustus the Strong using designs provided by Pöppelmann – only the **Schlosskapelle** (an addition of the 1660s), the **corner towers** and foundations were retained. A large artificial lake, fashioned out of several small ponds, was created round the Schloss, giving it an appearance akin to the great French châteaux of the Loire. Like them, the interior doesn't quite match the exterior, though there are some fine rooms, notably the **Audienzsaal** with its grand mythological paintings, the **Zimmer mit Damenbildnissen**, featuring portraits of court beauties (including some of Augustus' mistresses) and the **Speisesaal**, which was used both as a dining room and a theatre and is adorned with a large number of hunting trophies. The **Federzimmer** (same times; €3.50), with Augustus' spectacularly ornate bed, reopened to the public in 2003 after many years of painstaking restoration work.

It's also worth taking a stroll in the vast English-style **Schlosspark**. Towards its western end is the **Fasanenschlösschen**, a small gaming lodge of the 1780s. This previously contained a museum of stuffed birds, but has been under restoration for several years. Nearby, at the side of the lake, are two follies – the **Mole** (pier) and the **Leuchtturm** (lighthouse).

Between the wars, Moritzburg was the main home of the Wettin family, who had recently been stripped of royal status. In 1944, Prince Ernst Heinrich invited the great Berlin sculptress and graphic artist Käthe Kollwitz, whose home had been bombed, to settle at Meissner Str. 7 in the village, and she spent the last year of her life there. Now designated the **Käthe-Kollwitz-Gedenkstätte** (April–Oct Mon–Fri 11am–5pm, Sat & Sun 10am–5pm; Nov–March Tues–Fri noon–4pm, Sat & Sun 11am–4pm; €2; ⓦwww.kollwitz-moritzburg.de), it contains displays of her work.

Practicalities

Moritzburg's **tourist office** (April–Oct daily 10am–6pm; Nov–March Mon–Fri 9am–5pm; ⓣ03 52 07/8 54 10, ⓦwww.moritzburg.de) is at Schlossallee 3b. In addition to **private rooms** (❶–❷), there are a couple of **pensions**: *Alte Posthalterei*, Bahnhofstr. 1 (ⓣ03 52 07/8 11 03; ❸); and *Am Rossmarkt*, Rossmarkt 11 (ⓣ03 52 07/8 11 30, ⓦwww.pension-am-rossmarkt.de; ❸). **Hotels** include *Eisenberger Hof*, Kötzschenbrodaer Str. 8

The narrow-gauge railways of eastern Saxony

Moritzburg lies about halfway along the 16.5km-long **Lössnitztalbahn** (Ⓦwww.traditionsbahn-radebeul.de), otherwise known as the Lössnitzgrundbahn, one of several enticing narrow-gauge lines in eastern Saxony. It starts from the Ostbahnhof at **RADEBEUL**, on the S-Bahn line between Dresden-Neustadt and Meissen, and takes about an hour to cover the 17km to its terminus at **RADEBURG**. No fewer than seventeen bridges are crossed in the course of the journey along the Lössnitz valley, which is mostly a pastoral landscape with fields, meadows and ponds.

The **Weisseritztalbahn** (Ⓦwww.weisseritztalbahn.de), also known as the Osterzgebirgsbahn, likewise takes its name from the river whose valley it follows. Having been in operation since 1883, it's the longest-running narrow-gauge service in Germany. It begins at **FREITAL-HAINSBERG**, on the main line between Dresden and Freiberg. From there, it skirts the eastern edge of the Erzgebirge all the way to its terminus at **KURORT KIPSDORF**, 26km away. This unassuming little health resort has by far the largest narrow-gauge station in Germany, a sight in itself with its eight running lines. However, the highlight of the journey comes 5km before at **SCHMIEDEBERG**, where the train passes high above the village on a stone viaduct.

The city of **ZITTAU**, in the far southeast of Saxony, some 120km from Dresden, is the starting-point for the **Bimmelbahn** (Ⓦwww.zoje.de), which travels from the Hauptbahnhof into the Zittau mountains (Zittauer Gebirge) to the south. It was earmarked for closure a few months before the *Wende*, as a seam of lignite, the GDR's favourite but most environmentally damaging fuel, was discovered in the area, but national unification won it a reprieve. After 9km, there's a fork in the line at Bertsdorf. One part of the train branches 4km southwest to **KURORT JONSDORF**, while the other continues a further 3km south to **KURORT OYBIN**, an enticing destination in its own right. This quiet little health resort is centred on the **Bergkirche**, a perfectly preserved example of Baroque at its most rustic. Towering above the village is **Berg Oybin** (daily May–Aug 9am–6pm; Sept–April 9am–4pm; €2), on which stand a ruined castle and monastery founded by Emperor Charles IV in his capacity as King of Bohemia, and built by masons of the great Parler workshop of Prague, but destroyed by lightning in the sixteenth century. A great deal of the monastic church still survives; given its semi-overgrown appearance and theatrical backdrop, it's hardly surprising that it was a favourite subject with painters of the Romantic movement.

(Ⓣ03 52 07/8 16 73, Ⓦwww.hotel-eisenberger-hof.de; ❻); *Landhaus*, Schlossallee 37 (Ⓣ03 52 07/8 16 02; ❻); and *Churfürstliche Waldschänke*, an eighteenth-century hostelry in a wooded setting off Grosse Fasanenstrasse (Ⓣ03 52 07/86 00, Ⓦwww.churfuerstliche-waldschaenke.de; ❻). All of these have fine **restaurants**.

Meissen

Regular S-Bahn trains take around 45 minutes to cover the 25km between Dresden and **MEISSEN**, although you can also take the slow scenic route by boat down the Elbe. Meissen is associated in most people's minds with "Dresden china", yet the famous porcelain factory is only one of the attractions of this photogenic and unspoiled old city. In total contrast to Dresden, it came through World War II almost unscathed; it suffered quite badly from pollution under the GDR, but is steadily being cleaned up, having been one of five towns selected to receive special Federal restoration grants.

Arrival, information and accommodation

Meissen's **Hauptbahnhof** is on the right bank of the Elbe directly across the river from the city centre. The **tourist office** (Jan Mon–Fri 10am–5pm; Feb, March & Nov Mon–Fri 10am–5pm, Sat 10am–3pm; April–Oct Mon–Fri 9am–6pm, Sat & Sun 10am–4pm; Dec Mon–Fri 10am–5pm, Sat & Sun 10am–3pm; ⓣ0 35 21/4 19 40, ⓦwww.touristinfo-meissen.de or www.meiland.de) is at Markt 3.

Meissen has a decent number of **pensions** and **hotels** in most price categories, as well as **private rooms** (❷–❹) bookable via the tourist office.

Hotels and pensions

Burkhardt Neugasse 29 ⓣ0 35 21/45 81 98, ⓕ45 81 97. Pension with an ideal location in the heart of the Altstadt. ❹

Goldgrund Goldgrund 14 ⓣ0 35 21/4 79 30, ⓦwww.hotel-goldgrund-meissen.de. Fine medium-range hotel with restaurant in a very quiet woodland setting at the southern edge of town, a few minutes' walk from the Staatliche Porzellan-Manufaktur. ❹–❻

Landhaus Nassau Nassauweg 1 ⓣ0 35 21/73 81 60, ⓕ73 81 69. Good-value hotel and restaurant set at the edge of a nature reserve at the extreme eastern edge of town, reached by bus #D. ❸–❺

Mercure Grand Hafenstr. 27–31 ⓣ0 35 21/7 22 50, ⓦwww.mercure.com. Meissen's leading hotel occupies a large Jugendstil villa in a park by the right bank of the Elbe. Its facilities include a fine restaurant, a summer terrace and a whirlpool. ❼

Ross Grossenhainer Str. 9 ⓣ0 35 21/75 10, ⓦwww.minotel.com. Grand, well refurbished late nineteenth-century hotel with restaurant close to the Bahnhof. ❻

Schweizerhaus Rauhentalstr. 1 ⓣ0 35 21/45 71 62, ⓦwww.schweizerhaus-meissen.de. Pension with restaurant in a half-timbered chalet opposite the Staatliche Porzellan-Manufaktur. ❷–❹

Tagungszentrum Domherrenhof Freiheit 10 ⓣ0 35 21/46 09 40, ⓕ46 09 49. A small hotel occupies part of this former canons' residence. Its café-restaurant has a summer terrace which commands a wonderful view over the Altstadt to the Burgberg. ❺

The City

Never having grown into a major city, Meissen is compact and ideal for exploration on foot. Even from afar, its feudal layout is apparent, with the houses of the **Bürgerstadt** clustered in the valley under the **Burgberg**, which is crowned by the buildings of the joint rulers, the margrave and the bishop. The city centre lies on the left bank of the Elbe, but it is from the right bank (where you will arrive if you come by train) that the strategic significance of the site can be appreciated more easily. You're also rewarded with the best of the many breathtaking panoramas the town has to offer.

The Albrechtsburg

Centrepiece of all the views is the commandingly sited **Albrechtsburg** (daily 10am–5/6pm; €3; ⓦwww.albrechtsburg-meissen.de). This isn't the original castle of the Margraves of Meissen, but a late fifteenth-century replacement commissioned by Elector Ernst of Saxony and his brother Duke Albrecht, who jointly ruled the combined Wettin territories. It retains the medieval requirement for a military fortress, but combines this, for the first time in Germany, with the new demands of Renaissance princes for a residential palace. It's the masterpiece of one of the most prolific and accomplished builders of the time, **Arnold von Westfalen**. To appreciate the ingenuity of his design, it really needs to be viewed from afar: that way, you can see how the architect was forced to use the contours of the rocky, sloping site, solving the problem by building in huge blocks of six storeys, the first two essentially being to support the superstructure. While work was under way, the heirs of the two brothers split into two hostile factions, with Meissen becoming the seat of the Albertines, the junior of the two lines. Soon after completion, the court decamped to Dresden, leaving the Albrechtsburg as something of a white elephant. In 1710, it was given a wholly new function as the headquarters of the original porcelain factory, the first in Europe.

As it stands directly above the valley, the Albrechtsburg has to be approached from the rear, where it's guarded by a bridge and gateway leading into a vast courtyard. The under-use of the palace largely explains the somewhat bare feeling of most of its **interior**, which over-enthusiastic nineteenth-century Romantic painters tried to liven up by adding cycles of heroic historical frescoes, with decidedly dubious consequences. Nonetheless, it's worth paying to go inside just to see the truly spectacular, almost crazy, **vaulting**, which was something of a speciality of Arnold von Westfalen. There's a seemingly inexhaustible range of variations, those with deep pyramidal niches between their ribs being the most original. The other highlight of the visit is the ascent of the beautiful **external staircase**, the *Grosser Wendelstein*, the main feature of the castle's courtyard exterior. Housed in the last few rooms on the visitors' circuit is the medieval section of the state sculptural collection, the rest of which is in Dresden.

The Dom

Cocooned within the Albrechtsburg courtyard is the **Dom** (daily: April–Oct 9am–6pm; Nov–March 10am–4pm; €2), along with its subsidiary buildings, such as the bishop's palace and the houses of the canons, most of which have been altered repeatedly down the years. For the most part, the Dom itself is a pure High Gothic structure, begun in the mid-thirteenth century by the same masonic workshop that had built the famous west choir in Naumburg, though the relative decline in quality suggests that its director, the so-called Master of Naumburg, had died in the interim. However, the somewhat eccentric **facade** long remained unfinished: Arnold von Westfalen added the third storey in Flamboyant Gothic style, but the florid openwork **spires**, which soar above the rest of Meissen's skyline, only date from the early 1900s. It's now possible to ascend to the base of one of these (guided tours April–Oct daily at 1pm, 2pm, 3pm & 4pm; €2.50).

Entry to the Dom is via the **Fürstenkapelle**, which was tacked onto the facade in the fifteenth century to serve as a mausoleum for members of the Wettin family. It contains a number of resplendent bronze memorials, sometimes using designs by Dürer and Cranach. The richly sculptured **portal** behind was made the previous century as the main entrance to the Dom; its archway is cleverly used as a frame for the depiction of Christ in Majesty. Just to the right of here is the **Georgenkapelle**, the private memorial chapel of Duke George the Bearded, entered via a strikingly Italianate Renaissance doorway. At the far end of the south nave aisle is the **Achteckbau** (Octagon); it opens directly outside, and contains three fine statues by the Naumburg carvers. The same men were also responsible for the **rood screen**, except for its flamboyant upper storey, added in the sixteenth century as a choir gallery; and for the statues of the founders and patron saints in the choir. The central **stained-glass window**, showing Old and New Testament scenes in pairs, dates back to the thirteenth century, while *The Adoration of the Magi* **triptych** is by an unknown Netherlandish painter of the turn of the sixteenth century. From here you can exit via the **cloister**, off which is the **Magdalenenkapelle**, where the original statues of the south portal have been brought for conservation reasons.

The Bürgerstadt

The Bürgerstadt is laid out as a series of twisting and meandering streets between the Burgberg and the Elbe. More impressive as an ensemble than for any outstanding highlights, it's ideal for an aimless stroll. Centrepiece is the Markt, dominated by the **Rathaus**, in which the dying flickers of Flamboyant Gothic are fused with the new spirit of the Renaissance. At no. 8 on the square is the *Fachgeschaft*, the porcelain factory's shop, which is well worth a visit even if you aren't intending to buy. Next door, at no. 9, the *Küfertheke*, is one of the places where you can try local wines.

On its own small square to the side is the Flamboyant Gothic **Frauenkirche** (daily May–Oct 10am–12.30pm & 1–4pm), whose carillon, with the first bells in the world to be fashioned from porcelain, can be heard six times daily. The pride of the interior is the retable of *The Coronation of the Virgin*, made around 1500, while the **tower** (same hours; €2) commands a superb view over the city and the Elbe. On the terrace above the church is the celebrated **Gasthaus Vincenz Richter**, an old half-timbered tavern which preserves an early eighteenth-century wine press. The wines served here have the reputation of being the best in eastern Germany, though that's less of a claim than it might appear, as the area around is the only significant part of the former GDR with a climate mild enough for growing grapes.

The Staatliche Porzellan-Manufaktur Meissen

The **Staatliche Porzellan-Manufaktur Meissen** (Ⓦwww.meissen.de) lies about 1.5km south of the Markt, and is easiest reached by going down Fleischer Gasse, then continuing straight along Neugasse; it also lies close to the S-Bahn terminus, Meissen–Triebischtal. This is the latest factory to manufacture "Dresden china", whose invention had truly bizarre origins. Augustus the Strong imprisoned the alchemist **Johann Friedrich Böttger** in Festung Königstein in Saxon Switzerland, charging him with what was then believed to be a feasible task, the production of gold. Instead, he invented the first true European porcelain, according to a formula which remains a jealously guarded secret – its products are identified by the trademark of crossed blue swords.

Guided tours (daily 9am–5/6pm; €3) are run round the workshops, enabling you to see all the different stages of the production process. Be aware that this is on the itinerary of just about every tour group visiting eastern Germany and in summer you can be faced with a horrendous wait unless you arrive early. No such problems beset the **Schauhalle** (same hours; €4.50), which in any event is of far more immediate appeal: it contains the largest collection of Meissen porcelain in existence, and shows how the style of the factory has developed from the beginning to the present day. Highlight is the display of the gloriously over-the-top Rococo fripperies created by the most talented artist employed here, **Johann Joachim Kaendler**.

If you're walking between the town centre and the factory, it's worth stopping off at the **Nikolaikirche** (May–Sept Tues–Thurs & Sun 2–4pm), a little Romanesque church set in the Stadtpark. Inside, forming a poignant memorial to the fallen of World War I, are the largest porcelain figures ever made, two groups of mothers with children, each of which is 2.5m high and 300kg in weight.

Eating and drinking

Few ex-GDR towns are as well equipped gastronomically as Meissen, whose wine bar-restaurants represent its main strength in this field.

Bahrmanns Brauereikeller Webergasse 2. Large cellar restaurant, warmed by a huge open fire, in the nineteenth-century premises of a former brewery.
Café Schönitz Neugasse 22. French-style café-bistro which often features live music.
Café Zieger Rote Stufen 5. Traditional coffee house which has been run by the same family for over 150 years. Its speciality is a puff pastry known as the *Meissner Fummel*.
Domkeller Domplatz 9. Meissen's oldest restaurant, with a tradition dating back to 1520. It serves Saxon specialities and has a terrace offering a fine view over the town.
Vincenz Richter An der Frauenkirche 12. This sixteenth-century Weinschänke is one of the essential sights of Meissen. Although the menu is short, the food served is arguably the best in town. Open Tues–Fri 4–11pm, Sat 3pm–midnight, Sun noon–6pm.
Weinprobierestube der Sächsischen Winzergenossenschaft Bennoweg 9. Historic wine restaurant in the northeast of town, offering local dishes served on Meissen porcelain, and regular sampling sessions. Evenings only.
Zur Seemannsruhe Uferstr. 12. Restaurant in a late sixteenth-century house directly on the left bank of the Elbe offering Bohemian cuisine and a variety of fish dishes.

Saxon Switzerland

The area between Dresden and the Czech border 50km south is popularly known as **Saxon Switzerland** (Sächsische Schweiz), though this nickname, first coined by artists of the Romantic movement, is misleading. Now designated the **Nationalpark Sächsische Schweiz**, the landscape, far from looking Swiss, is archetypally Middle European, with the meandering **River Elbe** cutting a grand valley through dense forests interrupted by outcrops of rock welded into truly fantastic shapes. There's no better **hiking** country in all of Germany, and some walking is essential if you want to see the best of the scenery. If pressed for time, the S-Bahn line down the left bank offers a good overview of the region, and, even on a day-trip from Dresden, it should be possible to combine this with a visit to a couple of the main set-piece attractions. A good alternative is to take a **cruise** with the Sächsische Dampfschiffahrt ships: there are two or three departures daily from Dresden throughout the season (see p.961). However, given that there's abundant and inexpensive **accommodation** in all the resorts mentioned below, it would be a pity not to stay for a few days.

Pirna

PIRNA, 17km south of Dresden, is the gateway to Saxon Switzerland. Untouched in World War II, this old market town has been spruced up in line with its new role as a major tourist centre. Set on a hill overlooking the town is **Schloss Sonnenstein**, now mainly used as offices, though it does have a terrace restaurant. The central **Markt** is lined with a variety of handsome mansions, while the Rathaus stands on its own in the middle of the square.

Between the Schloss and the Markt is the **Stadtkirche St Marien**, a Flamboyant Gothic hall church similar to those in the Erzgebirge region, with all interest concentrated inside. Here, it's the stupendous star and network **vaulting** that steals the show – at times the ribs erupt into audacious flights of fancy, notably in the chancel, where they take on the form of a tree trunk. A curiosity of the church's building history is that it was begun at the turn of the sixteenth century as a Catholic parish church, but was appropriated for Protestant use before its completion. This change was immediately given visible expression in the painted decoration which was added to the vault: two of the Evangelists are depicted with the features of Luther and Melanchthon.

The **tourist office** (Mon–Fri 9am–6pm, Sat 9.30am–1pm; ⓣ0 35 01/4 65 70, ⓦwww.touristservice-pirna.de) is at Markt 7. Here you can book **private rooms** (❶–❸) in the town, and in other places in Saxon Switzerland. A wide range of **hotels** includes *Weisse Taube*, Arthur-Thiermann-Str. 58 (ⓣ0 35 01/52 41 20; ❷–❻); *Sächsicher Hof*, Gartenstr. 21 (ⓣ0 35 01/4 47 55 13; ❹); and, both situated in old buildings, *Pirna'scher Hof*, Am Markt 4 (ⓣ0 35 01/4 43 80, ⓦwww.pirnascher-hof.de; ❹); and *Deutsches Haus*, Niedere Burgstr. 1 (ⓣ0 35 01/44 34 40; ❻). There's also a **youth hostel**, situated on the opposite side of the Elbe from the centre in the incorporated village of Copitz at Birkwitzer Str. 51 (ⓣ0 35 01/44 56 01, ⓕ44 56 02; €15.90/18.60). The best **restaurants** are in the last three hotels listed above.

Kurort Rathen and Hohnstein

If visiting Saxon Switzerland on a day-trip, one place you should definitely make for is **KURORT RATHEN**, a small health resort on the east bank of the Elbe, linked by regular ferries to its Bahnhof, which is 12km and three stops on from Pirna. There are ample accommodation possibilities on both sides of the river, including plenty of **private rooms** (❶–❸). The best hotel is *Erbgericht*, Elbufer 5 (ⓣ03 50 34/77 90, ⓦwww.erbgericht-rathen.de; ❻) with a terrace overlooking the river.

High above the village, about thirty minutes' walk away, is the **Bastei** (daily 9am–6pm; €1, free access outside these times). Even the unfortunate siting of the GDR-era *Berghotel* (ⓣ03 50 24/7 04 06, ⓦwww.bastei-berghotel.de; ❻) cannot detract from the grandeur of this natural belvedere of strangely shaped rocks, which is not only astonishing in itself – seemingly fashioned by some great divine sculptor – but also commands really stunning views, both over the Elbe and into the forest. As a bonus, there are the ruins of **Felsenburg Neurathen**, a thirteenth-century castle ingeniously juxtaposed among the rocks. Lower down, the setting has been put to a more peaceful use by the creation of a spectacular open-air theatre.

Another walk well worth making is the hour-long trail along the Knotenweg to **HOHNSTEIN**, the most picturesque of the villages set away from the riverside, with a hilly site which affords a wide range of perspectives. The **Schloss**, itself a fine vantage point, houses a **Historisches Museum** (previously March–Oct daily 9am–5pm; €1, but closed in 2003 for restoration) and an attractive *Naturfreunde* **hostel** (ⓣ03 59 75/8 12 02; €18.90). There are a number of fine Baroque buildings on and around the Markt, notably the **Georg-Bähr-Kirche**, a rustic-looking church named in honour of its architect, one of the key figures of Dresden Baroque.

Königstein

From Rathen, the train follows the loops of the Elbe round to the small country town of **KÖNIGSTEIN**, 6km away. It's of no interest in itself, but the colossal fortress above, **Festung Königstein** (daily: April–Sept 9am–8pm; Oct 9am–6pm; Nov–March 9am–5pm; €4; ⓦwww.festung-koenigstein.de), rivals the Bastei as the most impressive sight in Saxon Switzerland. It takes a steep climb of thirty or forty minutes to reach it, though a tourist "train" has been introduced for the benefit of the better-heeled visitors who now visit the region. Once a virtually impregnable frontier post of the Saxon state, the fortress was continually strengthened right up until the Napoleonic period, so that it forms a virtual encyclopedia of changing defensive techniques. Long before this, it had ceased to have much strategic value, and its main function was as Saxony's most secure prison. Johann Friedrich Böttger, the inventor of Meissen porcelain, was incarcerated here by Augustus the Strong; the same fate later befell the nineteenth-century Socialist leader August Bebel, and a number of prominent anti-Nazis. It also proved a secure home in World War II for the movable art treasures of Dresden. The most remarkable structure is the sixteenth-century **Tiefer Brunnen** (Deep Well), which is 152m deep and took a group of miners from Freiberg six years to dig. Also of note are the cellars, the barracks and the two arsenals, both containing an array of historic weapons. However, there's no doubt that the view – even finer than that from the Bastei – is the prime draw.

To see Königstein itself at reasonably close range, there's a choice of vantage points – the **Pfaffenstein** to the south, or the **Lilienstein** on the opposite side of the Elbe. Ferries run across to the latter from Königstein; it's then a walk of about an hour to the summit.

In town, there are plenty of **private rooms** (❶–❸) bookable via the **tourist office** (April–Oct Mon, Tues, Thurs & Fri 9am–5.30pm, Wed 1–5.30pm, Sat 9am–noon; Nov–March same times, but closed Sat; ⓣ03 50 21/6 82 61, ⓦwww.koenigstein-sachsen.de), just off the central Markt at Schreiberberg 2. There are a couple of small **pensions**: *Schrägers*, Kirchgasse 1 (ⓣ03 50 21/6 83 52, ⓦwww.pension-schraegers.de; ❸); and *Amtshof*, Pirnaer Str. 30 (ⓣ03 50 21/6 85 11; ❹). In the outskirts, there are three **hotels**: *Vogelsberg*, Elbhäuser Weg 20 (ⓣ03 50 21/76 50, ⓦwww.hotel-vogelsberg.de; ❹); *Panoramahotel Lilienstein*, Ebenheit 7 (ⓣ03 50 21/5 30, ⓦwww.hotel-lilienstein.de ❺); and *Lindenhof*, Gohrischer Str. 2 (ⓣ03 50 21/6 82 43, ⓦwww.lindenhof-koenigstein.com; ❻). The **youth hostel** occupies a seventeenth-century half-timbered house directly below the Lilienstein at Am Tempel 39 (ⓣ0 50 21/4 27 60; €15.90/18.60).

Bad Schandau and around

Next stop, a further 5km on, is the spa of **BAD SCHANDAU**, the chief resort of the area and a wonderful base for hikes. It's also the border post, having swallowed up all the villages before the frontier. The best view over the area is from the tall platform tower of the iron lift or **Personenaufzug** (daily 9am–5/6/7pm; €2) which was built at the southern end of town in 1904. Also worth a quick look is the **Johanniskirche** just off the Markt, a Gothic church remodelled in the Baroque period, which contains two notable Renaissance furnishings in the pulpit and the high altar.

From the park in the centre of Bad Schandau, the Kirnitzschtalbahn, one of only two surviving examples of the once-ubiquitous **rural tramways**, creaks along the banks of the River Kirnitzsch to the **Lichtenhainer Wasserfall** 7km northeast. (If driving along this stretch, take extra care, as the tram travels on the main road most of the time, making overtaking extremely hazardous.) From the terminus, where there's a restaurant, it's a gentle uphill signposted walk to the **Kuhstall** (Cow Stall), one of Saxon Switzerland's most picturesque rock groupings and a fine vantage point over the wooded countryside away from the Elbe. Overlooking the river, a couple of hours' walk from here or Bad Schandau, are the **Schrammsteine**, the most extended group of rock formations in the area and a favourite haunt of daredevil climbing enthusiasts.

Bad Schandau's **Bahnhof** is on the west side of the Elbe; regular **ferries** run from there to the town centre on the opposite bank. The **tourist office** (April–Oct Mon–Fri 9am–7pm, Sat & Sun 9am–4pm; Nov–March Mon–Fri 9am–5pm; ⓣ03 50 22/9 00 30 30, ⓦwww.bad-schandau.de) at Markt 12 provides the normal booking service for **private rooms** (❶–❸). There are several homely **pensions**, including *Café Menge*, Badallee 12 (Ⓣ03 50 22/58 30; ❹). The town has many fine **hotels**, such as *Zum Roten Haus*, Marktstr. 10 (Ⓣ03 50 22/4 23 43; ❹); *Elbheim*, Elbufer 11 (Ⓣ03 50 22/4 25 79, Ⓦwww.elbheim.de; ❹); *Lindenhof*, Rudolf-Sendig-Str. 11 (Ⓣ03 50 22/48 90, Ⓦwww.lindenhof-bad-schandau.de; ❻); and *Parkhotel*, Rudolf-Sendig-Str. 12 (Ⓣ03 50 22/5 20, Ⓦwww.parkhotel-bad-schandau.de; ❻). All of these, except *Elbheim*, have **restaurants**. There's a **campsite** at Ostrauer Mühle on the Kirnitzsch (Ⓣ03 50 22/4 27 42, Ⓦwww.ostraue-muehle.de) and a **youth hostel** at Rudi-Hempel-Str. 14 (Ⓣ03 50 22/4 24 08; €16.40/19.10) in the village of Ostrau.

Bautzen (Budyšin)

Some 60km east of Dresden is **BAUTZEN**, the cultural capital of the Sorbs, Germany's only indigenous Slav minority, whose homeland is divided between Upper Lusatia in Saxony and Lower Lusatia in Brandenburg (see p.821). They settled in this area as far back as the sixth century, and have remained ever since; the bilingual signs, and the two official forms of the city's name, impart a touch of exoticism, though in Bautzen itself (as opposed to some of the outlying villages) you're unlikely to hear Sorb spoken in the streets. Bautzen, which celebrated its millennium in 2002, has a magnificent silhouette, dotted with towers of all shapes and sizes. It occupies a compact site high above the still young River Spree, which looks wild and untamed, although it's harnessed to form a reservoir immediately beyond the northern suburbs.

The Town

A good way to begin your tour is by climbing the **Reichenturm** (April–Oct daily 10am–5pm; €1.20), which lies at the top end of Kornmarkt at the eastern edge of the Altstadt. The original defensive tower dates back to the late fifteenth century, and was subsequently adorned with a relief portrait of Bautzen's then overlord, Emperor Rudolf II, ruler of the famously degenerate court at Prague. When an over-large Baroque lantern was added in the early eighteenth century, a pronounced tilt immediately occurred – hence the nickname of "the leaning tower of Bautzen". From the top, you get a good overview of the layout of the town.

The busy pedestrianized **Reichenstrasse**, lined with Baroque houses built after one of the many fires that have ravaged the town throughout its history, leads from the Reichenturm to the **Hauptmarkt**, where markets are held on Tuesdays, Thursdays and Saturdays. This is separated from a second market square, Fleischmarkt, by the **Rathaus**, a classically-inspired Baroque building whose most pleasing feature is the tall tower, Gothic by origin, but neatly remodelled to harmonize with the rest of the structure. Opposite is the **Gewandhaus**, a neo-Renaissance replacement of the old trading hall and weigh house, whose handsome vaulted cellars survive underneath.

Fleischmarkt's top end is closed by the very parochial-looking **Dom**, whose late Gothic architecture reduces the hall church to its simplest format. It's chiefly of note for two peculiarities. First, as can be seen from the outside, but is far more noticeable within, the body of the church is built with a very pronounced curve, possibly symbolic of the body of Christ on the cross, but more likely to be due to the restrictions of the site. The second curiosity is that this is a *Simultankirche*, one used by Protestants and Catholics alike. Immediately the Reformation was introduced, it was divided in two, the Catholics taking the choir and the Protestants the nave, a situation that persists to this day, with only a small iron barrier separating the two congregations. The very different sets of furnishings immediately betray which part you're in; the Catholics have the star piece in the large Crucifixion by Balthasar Permoser, a donation from the sculptor himself. There are limited opportunities for ascending the single **tower** (guided tours June–Sept at 4pm; €1).

To the rear of the Dom is the **Domstift**, a triple-winged Baroque palace entered via a cheerful gateway adorned with statues inspired by Counter-Reformation theology. Inside, the ecclesiastical treasures of the **Domschatzkammer** (Mon–Fri 10am–noon & 1–4pm; free) are on view. All around this area are twisting little alleys of peeling houses which are marvellously evocative of days gone by.

The Reichenturm also makes a good starting point for a walk round the fortifications, of which many portions survive. Immediately to the north is the **Wendischer Turm**, whose name signifies that it presided over the quarter where the Wends (the alternative name for the Sorbs) lived. Long used as a prison, it was saved from demolition through the ingenuity of Gottfried Semper, who incorporated it into the castellated **Kaserne** (barracks) he was commissioned to build on the site. This rather wonderful neo-Gothic fantasy itself became redundant, but has found a new lease of life as municipal offices.

The L-shaped alley known as Gickelsberg leads from here to the **Schülerturm**, beyond which is Am Zwinger, a rustic-looking road leading west past the **Gerberbastei** (now the youth hostel) to the **Nikolaiturm**. Alongside the latter is the **Nikolaikirche**, once the church of the Catholic Sorbs, but a ruin since its destruction in the Thirty Years' War. It's a peaceful spot, now used as a cemetery, commanding a fine view over the Spree.

An even better vantage point is the terrace of **Schloss Ortenburg** further west. The present castle, replacing a much earlier stronghold of the Margraves of Meissen, was erected in the late fifteenth century by order of Matthis Corvinus, King of Hungary and Bohemia, who is depicted seated between crown-bearing angels in the nine-metre-high memorial on the entrance gateway. Later additions include the playful Renaissance gables and the plain Baroque wing now housing the **Sorbisches Museum** (Mon–Thurs 10am–4.30pm, Sat & Sun noon–4.15pm; €1.50), documenting the festivals, costumes and literature of the Sorbs. It's well worth descending to the Spree and crossing the footbridge to a belvedere offering a view of the Schloss and the town.

Following Osterweg southwards, you pass the **Mühlenturm** en route to the **Michaeliskirche**, the parish church of the Sorb Protestants, which forms a picturesque corner in conjunction with the **Alte Wasserkunst** (April–Oct daily 10am–5pm; Nov, Dec, Feb & March daily 10am–4pm; Jan Sat & Sun 10am–4pm; €1.50), a mid-sixteenth-century water tower which was operational until 1963. Inside is a small museum outlining the technical particulars of its machinery, while the viewing platform at the top offers yet another outlook on the valley. On the bank of the Spree below is the **Hexenhäuschen** (Witches' House), the only old fisherman's house to have withstood all the fires which destroyed its counterparts – the belief that the inhabitants must therefore have been possessed of magical powers led to its present nickname. Finally, the wonderful full-frontal view of Bautzen that appears in all the tourist brochures can be seen for real by walking a short distance south to **Friedensbrücke**.

Practicalities

Bautzen's **Hauptbahnhof** is about fifteen minutes' walk south of the Altstadt, which is reached via Bahnhofstrasse and Karl-Marx-Strasse. The **tourist office** (March–Oct Mon–Fri 9am–6pm, Sat & Sun 10am–4pm; Nov–March Mon–Fri 10am–5pm, Sat 10am–2pm; Ⓣ0 35 91/4 20 16, Ⓦwww.bautzen.de) is at Hauptmarkt 1. There's a reasonable number of **private rooms** (❶–❸) on its books. The **youth hostel** is located in an old bastion at Am Zwinger 1 (Ⓣ0 35 91/4 03 47 ; €15.90/18.60). There are several conveniently sited **pensions**, such as *Stadtwall*, Flinzstr. 4a (Ⓣ0 35 91/4 48 41, Ⓦwww.pension-stadtwall.bei.t-online.de; ❸); *Lausitz*, Bahnhofstr. 16 (Ⓣ0 35 91/3 78 10; ❹); and *Spree*, Fischergasse 6 (Ⓣ0 35 91/4 89 60, Ⓦwww.spree-pension.de; ❹). Centrally located **hotels** include *Alte Gerberei*, Uferweg 1 (Ⓣ0 35 91/30 10 11, Ⓦwww.hotel-alte-gerberei.de; ❺); *Schloss-Schänke*, Burgplatz 5 (Ⓣ0 35 91/30 49 90, Ⓦwww.schloss-schaenke.net; ❺); *Holiday Inn*, Wendischer Graben 20 (Ⓣ0 35 91/49 20, Ⓦwww.bautzen.holiday-inn.com; ❺–❼); and *Goldener Adler*, Hauptmarkt 4 (Ⓣ0 35 91/4 86 60, Ⓦwww.goldeneradler.de; ❻).

Each of the hotels listed above has a **restaurant**. For more exotic fare, head to either of the Sorb eateries: *Sorbisches Café*, Postplatz 2, or *Wjelbik*, Kornstr. 7. Another oddity is *Zum Haseneck*, just east of the Reichenturm at Kurt-Pchalek-Str. 1, whose menu largely consists of different sorts of rabbit dishes. *Gastmahl des Meers*, Steinstr. 15a, is a fish specialist, while *Bautzener Brauhaus*, Thomas-Mann-Str. 7, is a Hausbrauerei. The Deutsch-Sorbisches Volkstheater, Seminarstr. 12 (Ⓣ0 35 91/58 40, Ⓦwww.theater-bautzen.de), is the only bilingual **theatre** in the country, with performances in Sorb alternating with German. A folklore group, the Sorbisches National-Ensemble (Ⓦwww.sne-gmbh.com), is also based in the town, and regularly performs there. The main **festival** is the Bautzener Frühling in May.

Görlitz

GÖRLITZ, the largest town of Upper Lusatia and Germany's easternmost point, lies 45km east of Bautzen. One of the consequences of the Oder–Neisse border was that Görlitz found itself divided between two countries – the historic part of the city lies on the west bank and therefore remained German, while the suburbs opposite became the Polish town of Zgorzelec. Perhaps that's an appropriate fate for a true central European city which doesn't easily fit into any nationalist framework. Slav by origin, Görlitz has been dominated by Germans since the thirteenth century, but belonged to Bohemia for much of its history. It fell to Saxony in the Thirty Years' War; following its annexation by Prussia in 1815, it was incorporated into Silesia, and now stands as one of the few reminders of a province that the Germans have finally accepted is lost to them forever.

The Town

Wartime damage to Görlitz, whose ensemble of Renaissance and Baroque houses is unsurpassed in Germany, was minimal. The Communist authorities put the entire city centre under a preservation order; thus, though it has suffered badly from pollution, it is gradually being restored to its original beauty.

Marienplatz at the southern end of the Altstadt is dominated by the **Frauenkirche**, the late Gothic church of the former hospital and poorhouse, whose most notable feature is the double portal topped by an Annunciation group. Close by is the **Karstadt-Warenhaus**, a large Jugendstil department store which survives as an intact period piece, both in its statue-lined exterior, and in its steel-framed galleried interior. Just to the north, the **Dicker Turm** (Fat Tower) is a cylindrical structure of the early fourteenth century, adorned with a prominent sandstone relief of Görlitz's coat of arms and crowned by a graceful Renaissance cupola.

Following either of the alleys to the left, you come to Demianiplatz, the first in a row of three squares at the heart of the town. On the south side is the Neoclassical **Gerhard-Hauptmann-Theater**, which takes its present name from the Nobel Prize-winning Realist writer. His intense early drama *The Weavers*, set against the background of a heroic but inevitably futile mid-nineteenth-century uprising by the Silesian weavers against the mill owners, was a theatrical sensation, gaining its reputation as the first "Socialist" play by having a collective rather than single hero.

The west side of the square is framed by the **Kaisertrutz** (Tues–Thurs, Sat & Sun 10am–5pm, Fri 10am–8pm; €1.50, or €3.50 combined ticket with the Reichenbacher Turm and the Städtisches Museum), a circular double bastion from the middle of last century, encasing its fifteenth-century predecessor. Inside is part of the local museum, including sections on medieval religious art, Upper Lusatian painters of the last two centuries and the history of the city, though the curious building is itself the main attraction. The original formed a defensive pair with the tall **Reichenbacher Turm** (same hours, €1.50) opposite, whose lower storey, culminating in the sentry gallery, dates back to the fourteenth century. The cylindrical upper section was added a hundred years later, and the whole finally topped off with a Baroque turret. A collection of arms and armour is housed inside; you can also climb to the summit for a fine view over the city.

Demianiplatz opens out to the east into the oblong **Obermarkt**, the main market square, which is lined with a colourful array of Baroque houses. At the northeastern corner stands the **Dreifaltigkeitskirche**, formerly the church of a Franciscan friary. Its splendidly musty interior has several fine late Gothic furnishings, including a set of richly carved choir stalls, a touching *Holy Sepulchre* and a carved retable to the Virgin. Underneath the **Mönch** (Monk), as the church's tall, curiously thin-looking tower is popularly known, is the **Kunstbrunnen**, a Renaissance figure bearing the arms of Electoral Saxony. Bruderstrasse, which prolongs the Obermarkt to the east, is lined with some of the town's finest mansions, including the **Schönhof** at no. 8, the work of Wendel Roskopf, the leading local architect of the Renaissance period.

Downhill is the **Untermarkt**, one of Germany's most imposing squares, which is built up in the middle, on the normal central European model. Best of the many mansions are nos. 2–5, late Gothic and early Renaissance, along the south side, which are collectively known as the **Lange Laube**. They belonged to the richest merchants and officials, and characteristically have bright vaulted entrance halls. It's particularly worth peeking into no. 5, whose original murals have survived. Also of special note are the Renaissance **Ratsapotheke** at no. 24, with its elaborate sundial; the **Flüsterbogen** (Whispering Arch) at no. 22; the large **Waage** (Weigh House) in the central block; and the early Baroque **Alte Börse**, the merchant's hall.

The **Städtisches Museum** (Tues–Thurs, Sat & Sun 10am–5pm, Fri 10am–8pm; €2) occupies a Baroque mansion just off the east side of Untermarkt at Neiss-Str. 30. It displays fine and decorative arts from the Renaissance to Biedermeier, along with material on Upper Lusatian folklore, and documentation on **Jakob Böhme**, the city's most distinguished son, the man regarded as both the first true German philosopher and the last of the medieval mystics and alchemists. Alongside at no. 29 is one of Görlitz's most unusual buildings, the **Biblisches Haus**; it dates from about 1570 and is adorned with little reliefs of scenes from the Old and New Testaments – a sure sign that the Reformation had taken root here, as religious depictions had hitherto been banned from secular buildings. Peterstrasse, which leads north from Untermarkt, is another impressive street; take a look inside no. 14, whose amazing stairway seems to defy gravity.

At the end of Peterstrasse is the **Peterskirche**, a five-aisled Flamboyant Gothic hall church with whitewashed exterior walls, a sturdy pair of towers crowned by fantastical nineteenth-century steeples, and a crypt which is itself of church-like dimensions. To the south side, the thirteenth-century **Renthaus** is the oldest house in the city; the terrace beyond preserves remnants of the former walls and commands a view over the Neisse to Poland. A few minutes' walk to the northeast lies the **Nikolaifriedhof**, a hillside cemetery with many elaborate tombstones, including that of Jakob Böhme.

East along Steinweg is Görlitz's most intriguing sight, the **Heiliges Grab** (Mon–Sat 10am–6pm, Sun 11am–6pm; donation expected). The only complete and reasonably authentic medieval reproduction of the Holy Places of Jerusalem, it was built by Georg Emmerich, a rich young citizen of Görlitz. Prevented from marrying the girl of his choice, he went on pilgrimage to the Holy Land, where he made plans of the biblical sites which he commissioned Conrad Pflüger, the architect of the Peterskirche, to build on a site meant to resemble the Garden of Gethsemane. The visit begins with the **Kapelle zum Heiligen Kreuz**, a two-storey chapel whose crypt is named in honour of Adam, the upper part after Golgotha, symbolizing the tradition that Christ was crucified on the site of Adam's grave. Alongside is the tiny **Salbhaus**, behind whose wrought-iron gates is a sculpture of the Virgin Mary lamenting over Jesus' dead body. Finally comes the **Grabkapelle**, which is of special interest as being a far more accurate, if miniaturized, version of the original, than its much-altered counterpart in Jerusalem. It's an elegant building in its own right; particularly outstanding is the turret, a skilful fusion of European and Middle Eastern architecture.

Practicalities

Görlitz's **Hauptbahnhof** lies southwest of the Altstadt; from there, it's only a ten-minute walk straight ahead to Marienplatz. The **tourist office** (Mon–Fri 9am–6.30pm, Sat 10am–4pm, Sun 10am–1pm; Ⓣ0 35 81/4 75 70, Ⓦwww.goerlitz.de or www.touristinfo.goerlitz.de) occupies a handsome Baroque mansion at Obermarkt 29.

There are plenty of **private rooms** (❷–❸) on offer – contact the tourist office. Additionally, there are several inexpensive **pensions**, some with a central location, including *Picobello*, Uferstr. 31 (Ⓣ0 35 81/42 08 50, Ⓦwww.picobello-pension.de; ❷); *Haus Wiesbaden*, Schulstr. 7 (Ⓣ0 35 81/42 08 50, Ⓦwww.pension-haus-wiesbaden.de; ❹); and *Destille*, Nikolaistr. 6 (Ⓣ0 35 81/40 53 02, Ⓦwww.destille-goerlitz.de; ❹). A good spread of **hotels** can likewise be found in the heart of town: *Goldener Engel*, Hugo-Keller-Str. 1 (Ⓣ0 35 81/40 33 37; ❹); *Sorat*, in a Jugendstil mansion at Struvestr. 1 (Ⓣ0 35 81/40 65 77, Ⓦwww.sorat-hotels.com/goerlitz; ❻); and *Tuchmacher*, in a palatial Renaissance house at Peterstr. 8 (Ⓣ0 35 81/4 73 10, Ⓦwww.tuchmacher.de; ❼). In the Südstadt, on the opposite side of the rail tracks from the city centre, there's an enticing alternative in *Zum Grafen Zeppelin,* Jauernicker Str. 15–16 (Ⓣ0 35 81/35 74, Ⓦwww.frenzelhof.de; ❻). Also in this area is the **youth hostel**, which occupies a spectacular Jugendstil villa at Goethestr. 17 (Ⓣ0 35 81/40 65 10; €14.40/17.10).

Restaurants can be found in all the hotels listed above, with *Goldener Strauss* in the *Sorat* being perhaps the pick of the bunch. Also very fine, and very traditional, is the one attached to the *Destille* pension. The main **cultural** venues are the aforementioned Gerhard-Hauptmann-Theater, Demianiplatz 2 (Ⓣ0 35 81/47 47 47, Ⓦwww.theater-goerlitz.de), which puts on a varied programme of drama, ballet, opera and musicals, and the Stadthalle, Am Stadtpark 1 (Ⓣ0 35 81/4 75 00, Ⓦwww.stadthalle.goerlitz.de), where concerts are held. On the last weekend of August the leading local **festival**, the Altstadtfest, is held.

Travel details

Trains

Chemnitz to: Annaberg-Buchholz (10 daily; 2hr); Freiberg (every 30 min; 50min); Zwickau (hourly; 1hr).

Dresden to: Bad Schandau (every 30min; 1hr); Bautzen (hourly; 1hr); Chemnitz (hourly; 1hr 30min); Freiberg (every 30min; 50min); Görlitz (hourly; 2hr); Leipzig (hourly; 2hr); Meissen (every 30 min; 45min); Pirna (every 30min; 30min); Zittau (10 daily; 2hr).

Görlitz to: Bautzen (hourly; 1hr); Zittau (10 daily; 1hr).

Leipzig to: Chemnitz (15 daily; 1hr 30min/2hr); Torgau (frequent; 1hr); Zwickau (hourly; 1hr 30min).

Contexts

Contexts

History

To think of a continuous German history is impossible, since there was no single nation called Germany until 1871, and even then it was not strictly speaking a country, but an empire made up of a number of sovereign states. Nevertheless, a recognizable German culture can be traced through the history of a large and disparate group of territories and traditions.

The beginnings

From around the eighth century BC, the bulk of present-day Germany was inhabited by **Celtic peoples**, who established the first permanent settlements. Warlike, nomadic **Germanic tribes** gradually appeared further north and began pushing their way into the Celtic lands. Their loose structure later made them awkward opponents of the expanding **Roman Empire**, which decided to use the natural boundaries of the rivers Rhine and Danube as the limit of their territory: attempts to push eastwards were finally abandoned after a crushing defeat in the Teutoburg Forest in 9 AD.

A number of towns founded by the Romans – Trier, Regensburg, Augsburg, Mainz and Cologne – were to be the main bases of urban settlement for the next millennium. **Christianity** was introduced under Emperor Constantine, and a bishopric (the first north of the Alps) was established in Trier in 314.

At the beginning of the fifth century Germany was overrun by the Huns, an action which precipitated the indigenous Saxons into invading England. Gradually the **Franks**, who had been based in what is now Belgium, began to assert themselves over the other Germanic peoples, particularly towards the end of the fifth century under King Clovis, who established the **Merovingian** dynasty and built up a powerful Rhenish state. In time, the Merovingians were supplanted by their former henchmen, the **Carolingians**, with the help of papal support. The new dynasty was bent on expansion, and saw the benefits of involving the Church in its plans. Missionaries – the most influential of whom was the English-born St Boniface – were recruited to undertake mass conversion campaigns among rival tribes.

Under **Charlemagne**, who succeeded to the throne in 768, the fortunes of the Franks went from strength to strength. A series of campaigns saw them stretch their power base from the North Sea to Rome, and from the Pyrenees to the River Elbe. In the context of Western Europe, only Britain plus the southern parts of Spain and Italy lay beyond their control. A power-sharing structure for Europe, in which the pope and the king of the Germans would be the dominant forces, was agreed. On Christmas Day 800, Charlemagne was anointed emperor in Rome, giving him the official status of heir to the Caesars. Though the name was only coined much later, this brought into existence the concept of the **Holy Roman Empire of the German Nation**, which was to last for the next thousand years. This gave the German king considerable power over Italian internal affairs, while the Church's influence in matters of state was similarly assured.

When Charlemagne died, however, the empire began to crack because of its very size. In 843, by the **Treaty of Verdun**, it was split into a Germanic Eastern Europe and a Latin Western Europe, thus sharply delineating the French and

Germans for the first time. The first king of the newly formed German eastern empire was **Ludwig the German**. Under his rule the Germanic people became more closely defined, with a specific culture of their own – still with many disparate regions but recognizably made up of the same peoples. When the last of Charlemagne's descendants died in 911, rulership passed to the Saxon King Henry the Fowler, bringing the Carolingian era to an end.

The building of a new empire

In the mid-tenth century the second Saxon monarch, **Otto the Great**, was faced with the problem of the growing power of the hereditary duchies which posed a threat to the unity of the empire. In order to curb this, he strengthened his alliance with the papacy. The Church was given grants of land, coupled with temporal powers of jurisdiction over them, thus creating the basis for subsequent ecclesiastical dominance over much of the country by a large number of prince-bishoprics and imperial monasteries and convents. In 962, he was crowned **Holy Roman Emperor**, firmly establishing himself as the main ruler in the Christian world. In many respects, this marks a second foundation of the curious dichotomy that characterized the Holy Roman Empire; from then on, only kings of Germany could gain the title of Roman Emperor, and it was only the pope who could grant this title.

Following a series of bitter **power struggles** between the papacy and the emperors, imperial interference in Church affairs was severely curtailed. So too was the centralized power of the emperor, as the nobility were released by the pope from their vows of allegiance to any secular authority. They soon made their own demands, the most important of which was that emperors should no longer be hereditary rulers, but elected by a council of princes.

By the twelfth century, most of the powerful **dynasties** which were to dominate German politics at both local and national level for hundreds of years to come had appeared. There was an intense feud between the two most powerful, the **Hohenstaufens** and **Welfs**, which was to continue for centuries, particularly in Italy. The Hohenstaufens, until they died out, managed to keep the upper hand, holding onto the office of Holy Roman Emperor for well over a century. **Frederick Barbarossa**, best known as an enthusiastic crusader in the Holy Land, was their most successful ruler.

By the mid-thirteenth century the nation's boundaries began to be pushed increasingly eastwards, following a policy begun by Otto the Great. Impetus for this came from many sources, being particularly associated with the **Knights of the Teutonic Order**, who turned their attentions towards the Christianization of Eastern Europe. By the early fourteenth century, they had conquered much of the Baltic (notably the area known as Prussia) and repopulated the land with German peasants. Subsequently, they grew rich on their control of the highly profitable grain trade.

The Middle Ages

In the fourteenth century, a number of significant changes were made to the structure of the Holy Roman Empire. The **Golden Bull** of 1356 finally established the method for choosing the monarch. This fixed the electoral college at the traditional number of seven, with three **Electors** drawn from the ecclesiastical sphere (the archbishops of Cologne, Mainz and Trier) and four from different ranks of the nobility (the King of Bohemia, the Duke of Saxony, the Margrave of Brandenburg and the Count Palatine of the Rhine).

From then on, these seven princes were tremendously powerful grandees – they had the right to construct castles, mint their own coinage, impose tolls and act as judges in all disputes, with no right of appeal. Oddly enough, the title of emperor almost invariably went to a candidate outside this group. Increasingly, it was conferred on a member of the **Habsburg** dynasty, who had built up Austria into the most powerful of the German states.

The papacy's residual power over internal German affairs was killed off by the **Great Schism** of 1378–1417, when rival popes held court in Rome and Avignon. By this time, the social structure was undergoing changes that had far-reaching effects. The most important was the growth of **towns** at strategic points and along important trading routes. Initially, these were under patrician control. However, merchants and craftsmen organized themselves into guilds which gradually wrested control of civic life and laid the foundations for a capitalist economy.

Most important towns gained the status of **Free Imperial City**, which meant they were independent city-states, responsible only to the emperor. Their prosperity was greatly enhanced by the ruinous Hundred Years War between France and England, which enabled them to snap up diverted trade to and from the Mediterranean. Though in many ways in competition with each other, the leadership of the towns realized they also had common cause. This led to the foundation of various trading and defence leagues. Of particular importance was the north German **Hanseatic League**, founded in Lübeck, which successfully combated piracy, and led not only to German economic domination of the Baltic and North Sea, but to increased political power as well, with the establishment of German communities in Scandinavia and all along the opposite coast as far as Estonia.

The **bubonic plague** swept across Europe in the fourteenth century, wiping out a quarter of the German population. In all probability, the plague was introduced by merchants returning from Asia, but a different scapegoat had to be found, and the **Jews**, who lived in segregated settlements around the towns, readily fitted the bill. Jews had lived in Europe since the tenth century, but their place had never been an easy one, with their close-knit and separate communities giving rise to popular suspicion and prejudice. Excluded from guilds and trades, they took up the only occupation forbidden to Christians: money-lending – a service that did nothing to endear them to the locals. **Pogroms**, therefore, frequently occurred.

The fifteenth century saw the Habsburgs establish themselves firmly as the driving force in high politics, holding onto the office of Holy Roman Emperor almost continuously from 1432 until its abolition nearly four hundred years later. **Maximilian I** acceded to the title in 1493, and embarked on a policy of making his family the most powerful not just in Germany, but in all of Europe. His own wedding to Mary of Burgundy gained him the Netherlands; a series of astute dynastic marriages involving his relatives led to Spain, Hungary and Bohemia all coming under Habsburg control. However, he antagonized the members of the Swiss Confederation, which broke away from the empire to become a separate state in 1499.

The Reformation and after

In order to cash in on popular fear, the Church demanded money from the faithful to ensure salvation of their souls, and a lucrative trade in **indulgences** was established, whereby people could buy absolution of their sins. Bishops across the land acted as agents, and the papal coffers filled up to finance the building of St Peter's in Rome and many other great sacred buildings. Discontent with the Church was particularly widespread in Germany, given the Church's dual role within society and the fact that territories under the control of religious office-holders tended to be particularly harshly run. Thus it was hardly surprising that it was here that the full-frontal assault on the Church's traditional powers began.

The attack was led by a man of burning religious convictions, the Augustinian monk **Martin Luther**, who had been appointed Professor of Theology at the University of Wittenberg. Believing that the Church was corrupt and had lost its way totally, Luther focused his attentions on the problem of **salvation**, finding in the Bible that Man justifies himself by faith alone. This meant that he could play no part in his own salvation; therefore the trade in indulgences was a total fraud. On the eve of All Saints' Day, 1517, he nailed his **95 theses** to the door of the Schlosskirche in Wittenberg. This was, in fact, the normal way of inviting academic discussion, but it was seen as a deliberately provocative act and is now considered the official **beginning of the Reformation**.

In time Luther widened his attack, denouncing the centralized power of the pope, the privileged position of priests as intercessors between God and the faithful, and the doctrine of transubstantiation, which maintained that the bread and wine used in the sacrament of the Eucharist physically turned into Christ's body and blood.

However, Luther's arguments might have had as little impact as any other scholarly dispute, or led to his immediate execution as a heretic, had not the curious power structure in Germany dealt him an amazing piece of good fortune. The death of Maximilian I in 1519 led to a bizarre **Europe-wide power struggle** for the crown of the Holy Roman Empire. Francis I of France decided to stake a claim for the title, in order to stop the unhealthy concentration of power which would ensue if victory went to the Habsburg candidate, Charles I of Spain. In order to stop this interference from abroad, the pope had to keep the Electors sweet, even suggesting one of their number, Luther's patron Elector Frederick the Wise of Saxony, as a compromise candidate.

After much bribery by the two main contenders, the Spanish king won the election unanimously and took office as Emperor Charles V. However, he immediately became embroiled in a war with France. As a result, the powerful princes of the Holy Roman Empire seized this chance to establish a far greater degree of independence. Many of them saw the religious struggle as a convenient cloak for their ambitions. Luther was excommunicated in 1520, but still had the right, as a citizen of the empire, to have a hearing before an Imperial Diet. This was hastily convened at Worms the following year, and, though Luther was branded an outlaw and his books were ordered to be burned, he was given a safe haven at the Wartburg outside Eisenach, under the protection of Elector Frederick. There he **translated the Bible into German**, thus making it accessible to the common man for the first time; this work is also seen as the foundation stone of the modern German language.

Luther's ideas spread like wildfire throughout society, greatly aided by the fact that books could now be produced cheaply and quickly, thanks to the printing revolution launched by the German inventor **Johannes Gutenberg** during the previous century. They found a ready market among the oppressed classes, who took the attacks on Church authority as invitations to attack authority in general.

This formed one of the causes of the **Peasants' War** of 1524–25, which brought wholesale destruction of monasteries and castles. Poorly armed, organized and led, it was brutally crushed by the princely armies. To the dismay of the rebels, Luther aligned himself on the side of worldly authority, arguing that it was God's will that there should be different strata in society; equality was only for the hereafter. Thus, the Reformation progressed as a revolution controlled from above, setting the tone for German history for centuries to come.

In 1529, the representatives of six principalities and fourteen Free Imperial Cities which supported Luther met at Speyer, where the name **Protestant** came to be used for the first time. The following year, Charles V convened a Diet at Augsburg in an attempt to defuse the growing crisis. However, he was confronted by a closely argued definition of the Reformers' position, thereafter known as the **Confession of Augsburg**, which was drawn up by Luther's lieutenant, the brilliant scholar Philipp Melanchthon. This set the seal not only on the division of the Western Church, but also on the effective division of Germany into a multitude of small states.

So many states had joined the Protestant cause by 1555 that Charles V had to admit defeat, abdicating in order to retire to a Spanish monastery. He was succeeded by his brother Ferdinand, who almost immediately signed the **Peace of Augsburg**, a historic agreement that institutionalized religious tolerance, leaving the decision as to the form of religion practised in each state firmly in the hands of its secular rulers. Though a measure of considerable significance, it was in effect a carve-up between the Catholics and Lutherans at the expense of more radical Protestant groups.

The struggle for religious supremacy

After Luther's death in 1546, the Catholics began to make something of a comeback after the reforms thrashed out at the Council of Trent launched the **Counter-Reformation**. Radical Protestantism was also given a fillip by Melanchthon's shift away from central Lutheran doctrines to more extreme solutions. Inevitably, one of the political goals of Protestantism was to gain control of the imperial electoral college, and oust the Catholic Habsburgs from their long tradition of pre-eminence.

Bavaria's annexation of the predominantly Protestant free city of Donauwörth in 1608 led to the formation of the **Protestant Union**, an armed alliance under the leadership of the Palatinate. The **Catholic League** was set up in opposition by the Bavarians the following year, meaning that there was now a straight division of the country into two hostile camps. Meanwhile, the way central authority in Germany had collapsed was cruelly exposed by the weak 36-year reign of Rudolf II, who chose to govern from

Prague, at the very fringe of the empire. There he presided over a bizarre court filled with astrologers and alchemists, until his growing insanity led to his deposition in 1611.

As it happened, this same city was to see the beginning of the great trial of strength between the two faiths. In 1618, the youthful Count Palatine Friedrich V usurped the crown of Bohemia, which itself was an elected office, thus seemingly ensuring a Protestant majority in the next imperial election. Unfortunately for him, he lost both his titles a year later, and had by then set in train the complicated series of religious and dynastic conflicts commonly known as the **Thirty Years War**.

Much of the German countryside was laid waste, towns were pillaged, and there was mass rape and slaughter, at the end of which the total population of the country may have been reduced by as much as a third. Initially, the Catholic League, commanded by the brutal Johann Tilly, held the upper hand, but first Denmark, then Sweden intervened, fearing for both their independence and their Protestant faith. The Swedes, led by King Gustavus II Adolphus, had their greatest moment of triumph on the European stage, defeating Tilly and overrunning the country, thus rising to the rank of a major power. Spain intervened on behalf of its Habsburg cousins, while Catholic France supported the Protestants, on the grounds that their faith was a lesser evil than the threatened Habsburg hegemony.

From 1643, concerted attempts were made to end the war, with the Catholics meeting in Münster, the Protestants in Osnabrück. The negotiations are generally seen as the beginnings of modern diplomacy; they culminated five years later in the signing of the **Peace of Westphalia**. While the ending of the messy conflicts was a major achievement in itself, for Germany the peace treaty was as disastrous as the war itself; the Holy Roman Empire was killed off in all but name, with the emperor reduced to a figurehead.

Real power was diffused among a **plethora of states**, numbering some three hundred principalities, plus over a thousand other territories, some of them minute – a system which could hardly have been better designed to waste resources and stunt economic and political development. Germany ceased to be a factor of importance on the European stage.

The rise of Prussia

In the course of the late seventeenth and eighteenth centuries, almost all the petty German princes adopted an **absolutist** system of government, based on the divine right of rulers. They spent a vast amount of their revenue building palaces on a scale out of all proportion to their needs, to create at least the visual pretence that they were mighty monarchs. Only a few managed to rise above the general level of mediocrity; one of these was the House of Welf, which made an astonishing comeback after centuries of confinement to its Lower Saxon heartlands. As a result of clever politicking, the **Hanoverian** branch of the family gained the British crown in 1714 and maintained a royal union until 1837.

Within the Holy Roman Empire itself, **Austria** at first maintained her dominance, with the Habsburgs holding on to the imperial title, for what it was worth. The country received a severe jolt when the Turks reached the gates of Vienna in 1683, but after the enemy was beaten back, the way was cleared for

Austria to build up an empire in the Balkans. As German-speaking influence spread eastwards, so the western flank became vulnerable. The **French**, like the Romans before them, saw the Rhine as the natural limit of their territory. They formally annexed Alsace and Strasbourg in 1681, then laid claim to the Palatinate in a series of bloody campaigns between 1688 and 1697.

By then, a new power had arisen in north-eastern Germany in the shape of **Brandenburg-Prussia**. In 1411, the old frontier district of Brandenburg was given to the ambitious **Hohenzollern** family, whose attempts to gain power at the heart of the empire had met with no success. Since 1525, the family had also held the Baltic territory known as Prussia, which lay outside the Holy Roman Empire and thus was not subject to any of its rules. One of these forbade princes from promoting themselves to royal titles: in 1701, Friedrich III defied this with impunity by having himself crowned King of Prussia. The Habsburgs duly turned a blind eye to this in order to gain Hohenzollern support in the **War of the Spanish Succession**, which broke out as a result of rival Austrian and French claimants for the throne of Spain.

Throughout the eighteenth century, Prussia was built up as a strongly centralized state, based in Berlin. There was a tight administrative structure, but it became associated above all with **militarism**. It was a second Sparta, described with some justification as not a state with an army, but an army with a state: at times, two-thirds of national revenue was spent on the military. The other dominant force in society was the **Junker** class, landowners who ran huge estates in which the labourers were treated as little more than serfs.

Prussia's rise to the rank of a major European power was achieved under **Frederick the Great**, who came to the throne in 1740. A Francophile and epitome of the enlightened despot, Frederick softened his country's rough-hewn image by introducing a few liberal reforms at home, and developed a cultured courtly life. However, his main concern was expansion by military force, and he used an old Brandenburg claim on one of the tiny Silesian principalities to extract most of Silesia from Austria. In revenge, the Habsburgs launched the Seven Years War in 1756, thereby hoping to annihilate Prussia as a potential rival; in this, they had the full military backing of the two other great continental powers, France and Russia, whereas Frederick had only the tacit support of Britain and Hannover to fall back on.

Within three years, the highly rated Prussian troops seemed to have overreached themselves. They were given an unexpected reprieve when the Austrians and Russians fell out; new recruits were thrown into the conflict, eventually achieving an incredible turn-around in fortunes, in the process establishing Prussia as a force of the first rank. By annexing much of Poland in the partition of 1772, Frederick achieved his aim of establishing a north German version of Austria.

The Napoleonic period and its aftermath

Ironically, the first steps towards unifying Germany came as a result of the expansionist aims of revolutionary France. By the War of the First Coalition of 1792–97, the left bank of the Rhine fell under French control. However, it was only with the advent of the dictator **Napoleon Bonaparte** that radical changes were made. Following the defeat of Austria in 1802 in the War of the Second Coalition (in which Prussia tactfully remained aloof), he decided to completely reorder the German map, which he rightly saw as anachronistic. All but four of the free cities (Frankfurt, Bremen, Hamburg and Lübeck), and every single one of the ecclesiastical territories, were stripped of their independence, which in many cases went back five or six centuries.

Napoleon created a series of buffer states: Bavaria, Württemberg and Saxony were raised to the rank of kingdoms, while Baden and Hesse-Darmstadt became grand duchies. In 1806, during the War of the Third Coalition, the Holy Roman Empire was officially abolished, with the Habsburgs consoling themselves for suffering yet another defeat by promoting themselves from archdukes to emperors of Austria, deciding thereafter to concentrate their energies on preserving their Balkan lands. Gradually, the German satellite states began to remove economic, religious and servile restrictions, developing into societies which were liberal by German standards.

The same year, Prussia suffered a series of humiliating defeats; Berlin was occupied and the country forced to sign away half its territory and population. Thereafter, it was made to mend its ways: serfdom was abolished, and its cities were allowed to develop their own municipal governments. In the event, Prussia's humiliation was short-lived, and it soared in international prestige as a result of its key role at the **Battle of Waterloo** in 1815, when Napoleon's overambitious plans for the total subjugation of Europe were finally put to rest.

The **Congress of Vienna**, which met the same year to determine the structure of post-Napoleonic Europe, established Prussian dominance in German affairs. Westphalia and the Rhineland were added to its territories, meaning that it now stretched all the way from the French border to the River Memel, interrupted only by a few enclaves. Otherwise, much of the Napoleonic reorganization of the Holy Roman Empire was ratified, with Hannover added to the list of kingdoms. In all 39 independent states were left – still far too many, but a major step forward nonetheless. A German Confederation was established, with each state represented in the Frankfurt-based Diet, which, however, had no effective power.

Towards German unification

Whereas the main political forces in German society in the aftermath of the Congress of Vienna were still staunchly conservative, the accelerating **Industrial Revolution** was resulting in radical economic and social changes. This closely followed the British lead, but profited by learning from the pioneering country's mistakes. The first German railway was established in 1835, and industrial production advanced in leaps and bounds. Thanks to its rich mineral deposits, the dominant centre for industry was the Rhine-Ruhr area, which had recently been allocated to Prussia. In 1834, Prussia's increasingly dominant role within the German nation was underlined by the establishment of a customs union, known as the **Zollverein**.

The Industrial Revolution led to a whole **new social order**, with wage-earning workers and an emergent bourgeoisie. Both groups were quick to agitate for their interests – the workers for better working conditions and the bourgeoisie for political representation. Meanwhile, the large peasantry was still living in abject poverty and under almost feudal conditions, which pressed hard during the failed harvests of the late 1840s. Social unrest was inevitable, and violence erupted both in the countryside and the cities, causing ever more reactionary policies from the landowning elite with the political power.

In 1848, there were uprisings all over Europe. This forced the Prussian king to allow elections to the **National Assembly** in Frankfurt, thereby hoping to nip republican and socialist aspirations in the bud. For the first time, an opportunity was presented to found a liberal tradition in the country, but it was completely muffed. The bourgeois members of the Assembly were much too keen to establish the new-found status of their own social groups to attempt any far-reaching political reforms, and they certainly posed no threat to the existing order. Thus, when armed rebellions broke out in 1849, the National Assembly was exposed as an ineffective talking shop, easily disbanded in the face of the revolutionary emergency. Any steps towards constitutional rule were wiped out by the combined forces of the Prussian army and battalions from other German kingdoms and principalities.

The 1850s saw political stagnation, but the increasing success of the Industrial Revolution meant that the creation of a single internal German market, preferably accompanied by a political union, was of paramount importance. By now, Prussia had manoeuvred itself into a position of such power that it was the only possible agent for enforcing such a change.

In 1862, **King Wilhelm I** chose as his chancellor the career diplomat **Otto von Bismarck**, a member of the Junker class who had already gained a reputation as an operator of rare sharpness. In order to win over the Prussian liberals, Bismarck backed the concept of universal male suffrage. He also played the nationalist card immediately: seeing that the chancellor was bent on creating a united Germany, the liberals muted their opposition and backed his plans for a thorough modernization of the army.

In 1864, Bismarck lured Austria into supporting him in a war against Denmark to recapture the lost duchies of Schleswig and Holstein. Having achieved an easy victory, he then provoked a disagreement over the spoils: the result was the **Seven Weeks War** of 1866, in which the superior Prussian weapons and organization achieved a crushing victory. Not only was Austria forced out of Germany's affairs, but those states which had remained neutral, including Hannover and Hesse-Kassel, were incorporated into Prussia. The German Confederation was dissolved, to be replaced by one covering the north of the country only, which was totally under Prussian domination.

To complete the jigsaw, Bismarck still needed to woo the southern states. His tactic was an original one: to provoke a war against the old enemy, France. In 1870, having carefully prepared the diplomatic ground to ensure that no other power would intervene to support the French, he goaded them by proposing that a Hohenzollern should succeed to the vacant throne of Spain. The French emperor, Napoleon III, managed to force the Prussians to withdraw, but foolishly sent a telegram asking for an apology. Bismarck doctored this to make it seem worse than it was, giving the excuse to begin the **Franco-Prussian War**.

By January 1871, the Prussian field guns had helped chalk up yet another easy victory. A united German empire, which once more included the long-disputed provinces of Alsace and Lorraine, was proclaimed in Versailles. King Wilhelm I of Prussia was the inevitable choice as Kaiser; three other kings were among the rulers who were henceforth subjugated to him. The new empire became known as the Second Reich, in honour of the fact that it had revived the German imperial tradition after a gap of 65 years.

The Second Reich

In his domestic policy for the united Germany, Bismarck indulged in a series of **liberal reforms**. Uniform systems of law, administration and currency were introduced, an imperial bank was set up, restrictions on trade and movement of labour were lifted, and cities were given municipal autonomy.

By such measures, Bismarck aimed to control the opposition parties in the Reichstag and to keep power in the hands of the elite. The darker side of his nature came out in the **Kulturkampf**, which aimed at curbing the power of the Catholic Church, whose power and influence was anathema to the Protestant aristocracy of Prussia. However, this met with spirited opposition, which led to Bismarck making a rare retreat, though not until he had exacted his price: the Catholics were forced to support protectionist agricultural measures, designed to subsidize the large, outdated Junker estates. By then, a formidable new opposition had arisen in the shape of the **Social Democratic Party** (SPD), founded in 1875. In order to take the wind out of its sails, Bismarck introduced a system of welfare benefits for workers, a system belatedly copied in many other industrialized countries.

Bismarck's **foreign policy** involved a complicated set of jugglings. He set up the Dreikaiserbund, an alliance of the three great imperial powers of Germany, Austria and Russia; indulged in a Mediterranean naval alliance with Britain in order to check Russian designs on the Balkans; yet initiated a bit of colonial rivalry with the British.

Bismarck's awesome reputation for political surefootedness meant that Germany's internal and external stability seemed completely safe in his hands. However, Friedrich III, who succeeded his father Wilhelm I in 1888, died after only a few months on the throne. His son, **Wilhelm II**, was a firm believer in the divine right of kings. He was of a generation which did not feel beholden to Bismarck, and strongly disliked the veteran politician. Two years later, he removed the chancellor from office – a move compared to dropping the pilot from a ship – and thereafter relied on a series of ineffective kowtowing men to lead his government.

Britain, which had hitherto been a natural ally of Germany as a result of dynastic ties and mutual suspicion of France, was increasingly seen as the main rival. A notorious telegram sent by the Kaiser in support of the Boers in 1896 signalled the beginning of a severe deterioration in relations between the two countries. This was fuelled by an **arms race**, affecting all of Europe, in which the Krupp armaments factory played a crucial role. Nowhere was the attempt to establish supremacy more evident than in the naval sphere, where the Germans set out to usurp Britain's long period of supremacy, achieving parity by 1909.

By this time, the major powers of Europe were divided into **two nervous alliances**. Bismarck's successors failed to maintain his two-faced foreign policy. As a result, Germany was bound up once more with Austria, whose eastern empire was tottering under the nationalist aspirations of the many ethnic groups contained within it; Italy was a somewhat reluctant partner. Ranged against them were France and Russia, drawn together by mutual fear of the ever-increasing power of the German-speaking countries. Britain, while maintaining its time-honoured policy of trying to preserve an effective balance of power in Europe, was increasingly drawn towards the latter alliance.

World War I

Everybody expected that war would come sooner or later, and master strategies were carefully planned. The Germans developed the **first-strike theory**, which envisaged a quick knock-out blow against both France and Russia, as a prelude to a tougher struggle against the more formidable British. Public opinion in the country was easily won over by the bogus theory that the Fatherland was under threat from the "iron ring" which surrounded it. Even the Social Democrats were persuaded of the necessity and desirability of a war.

The spark which lit the inferno happened to come in **Austria's unwieldy empire**. In 1914, the crown prince, Archduke Franz Ferdinand, was assassinated in Sarajevo by a Bosnian nationalist. Austria sent the independent neighbouring state of Serbia a threatening ultimatum, although no connection between the Serbian government and the conspirators was ever proved. This inevitably provoked the Russians, who had an agreement to protect their fellow Slavs from any threat. The German generals saw this as a golden opportunity to put their first-strike theory into operation. As soon as the Russians mobilized, German troops were sent to attack France. The quickest route was through Belgium, thus violating its neutrality, which was guaranteed by Britain. So fast did events move that the Kaiser sent a telegram ordering withdrawal, but this was ignored. **World War I** was thus under way.

The German High Command believed the French would capitulate within six weeks, the Russians within six months. They were soon proved hopelessly wrong, and found themselves with what they had been most anxious to avoid – a war on two fronts. Even then, they could hardly have anticipated the Armageddon which was unleashed. After rapidly advancing towards Paris, they were forced to retreat at the first Battle of the Marne in September, and dig **trenches** all across northern France and Belgium. This gave rise to a wholly new form of warfare, with casualties quite unlike any that had previously been known. In 1916, an attempt to exhaust the French at the four-month-long Battle of Verdun proved to be self-defeating, and the same year the British proved their continued mastery of the seas at the Battle of Jutland.

As a result of these setbacks, the Kaiser handed over effective military and political power to the dual leadership of Field Marshal **Paul von Hindenburg**, and his quartermaster-general, **Erich Ludendorff**; though the latter was nominally the junior partner, he became the effective dictator of the country. In January 1917, it was decided to introduce unrestricted submarine warfare. This was a complete disaster, its barbarity prompting the United States to enter the war. A reprieve was gained as a result of the revolution in Russia that autumn, which ended the fighting on the eastern front. This allowed the Germans to transfer large numbers of troops to the west, break through the Allied lines in February 1918, and advance deep into France.

The end of the war; failure of the German revolution

The euphoria of this triumph soon faded, however: the German lines became hopelessly over-extended; captured Allied supply dumps showed the German troops how poorly provisioned they were by comparison; many soldiers from the east had acquired Communist views and were agitating against the war; and American troops were at last beginning to arrive in substantial numbers. On August 8, 1918 – the "Black Day of the German Army" – the Allies broke the German offensive and turned it into a rout. Finally convinced that the war was lost, Ludendorff looked about for ways to minimize the High Command's loss of face. He seized on the idea of letting a parliamentary government handle the **peace negotiations**; it would be likely to secure more lenient terms, and would also be a useful scapegoat in the event of a harsh treaty. Furthermore, it would help counteract the far more horrifying alternative of a Bolshevik-style revolution, an only too real prospect once the German people realized the extent to which their leaders had been deceiving them.

Accordingly, he persuaded the Kaiser to appoint the liberal monarchist **Prince Max von Baden** as chancellor. A full parliamentary democracy was proclaimed; the cabinet was drawn from the ranks of the Reichstag, with Social Democrats included for the first time. On October 3, Prince Max sued for peace. Ludendorff, sensing that the Allies were going to drive a hard bargain, subsequently resigned; Hindenburg offered to do likewise, but was allowed to remain at his post.

Towards the end of the month, Admiral Scheer decided to mount a futile last-ditch offensive; his crews mutinied, refusing to lay down their lives so unnecessarily. This revolt spread throughout northern Germany and might well have developed into the full-scale revolution Ludendorff had been conniving to avert, had it not been for the bitter **division of the political left-wing** into three factions.

The SPD had previously split into two separate parties over the war; the pacifist group, the USPD, was now frustrated by the tepid nature of their erstwhile colleagues' socialism, which embraced constitutional monarchy and a bourgeois social order. In turn, their politics were seen as too tame by the Spartakist League, a Marxist group who aimed to follow the example of their Russian mentors by seizing power in Berlin. **Friedrich Ebert**, leader of the SPD, decided to forestall them by calling a general strike to demand the Kaiser's abdication. Prince Max took matters into his own hands by announcing this without the monarch's consent, and then himself resigned in favour of Ebert. Matters were still delicately poised with the news that **Karl Liebknecht** of the Spartakists intended to proclaim the establishment of a socialist republic on November 9.

In order to wrest the initiative, Ebert's lieutenant **Philipp Scheidemann** made an impromptu declaration of a free German Republic from the Reichstag balcony, thus bringing the regime of the Kaisers to an abrupt end. Two days later, an armistice was signed, as Ebert realized that either a collapse of military discipline, or the spread of Bolshevism, would lead to an Allied invasion. As part of his plans, he made a pact with the High Command, which provided him with an army to protect the state against internal left-wing opponents, but at the price of allowing it almost complete autonomy.

This policy paid immediate dividends for him, as the military was used to crush an attempted revolution by the Spartakists in January, a last-ditch attempt at a Communist seizure of power before the elections for the new National Assembly later in the month. The brutal behaviour of the army – Liebknecht and his co-leader Rosa Luxemburg were among those murdered – was to have disastrous long-term consequences for the fledgling republic, which should have made a purging of the anti-democratic and war-crazed officer class one of its most urgent priorities.

The Weimar Republic

The elections confirmed the SPD as the new political leaders of the country, with 38 percent of the vote; as a result, Ebert was made president, with Scheidemann as chancellor. Initially, **Weimar**, the small country town which had seen the most glorious flowering of the German Enlightenment, was chosen as the seat of government in preference to Berlin, which was tinged by its monarchical and militaristic associations.

A **new constitution** was drawn up, hailed as the most liberal and progressive in the world. While on the surface an admirable document, this constitution was hopelessly idealistic for a people so unfamiliar with democratic practice and responsibilities. No attempt was made to outlaw parties hostile to the system; this opened the way for savage attacks on the republic by extremists at both ends of the political spectrum. The use of proportional representation, without any qualifying minimum percentage of the total vote, favoured a plethora of parties promoting sectional interests. This meant that the Weimar governments were all unwieldy coalitions, whose average life was about eight months and which often pursued contradictory policies in different ministries.

Two months before the constitution was ratified in July 1919, Germany had been forced to accede to the **Treaty of Versailles**. In contrast to the Habsburg Empire, which was broken up into a series of successor states, German territorial integrity was largely preserved, but the losses were painful ones – the industrially productive Saarland and Alsace-Lorraine went to France, while the resurrected country of Poland was given Upper Silesia plus a corridor to the sea, which left East Prussia cut off from the rest of the country. All overseas colonies were confiscated, the Rhineland was declared a demilitarized zone, the navy limited to six light battleships, and the army to a hundred thousand men with conscription prohibited. Germany and her allies were found guilty of having started the war and, as a result, were landed with an enormous **reparations bill**, which would have taken over half a century to pay.

In all, this amounted to a pretty stiff settlement, albeit one considerably less harsh than the Germans had recently enforced on the Russians at Brest-Litovsk. So incensed were the military leaders with this humiliating Diktat that they toyed with the idea of resuming hostilities. As this was not a feasible option, they contented themselves with inventing the **"stab in the back" legend**, maintaining that the army, undefeated in the field, had been betrayed by unscrupulous politicians – a preposterous distortion accepted all too easily by gullible sections of the public.

The treaty spelled the beginning of the end for the Social Democratic republic. Scheidemann immediately resigned as chancellor, and, following gains by the two political extremes in the 1920 elections under the new constitution, the party, though still the largest in the Reichstag, withdrew from government altogether, leaving power in the hands of minority administrations drawn from liberal and moderate conservative parties. Right-wing extremism flourished in a series of political murders and attempted putsches, which were barely punished by a judiciary which rivalled the army in its contempt for the republic.

The reparations bill crippled the economy, to the extent that payments began to be withheld. This gave the French the excuse to occupy the Ruhr in 1923; they were met by a policy of passive resistance. As no work was done, galloping **inflation** – the most catastrophic ever known in world history – quickly ensued, causing the ruin of the entire middle class as the currency became utterly worthless. The Weimar Republic seemed irretrievably doomed, but it made an astonishing comeback, largely due to the political skills of the new chancellor, **Gustav Stresemann**. He was an unlikely saviour, an old-fashioned conservative who had begun his career as Ludendorff's mouthpiece in the Reichstag, and whose precise commitment to the republic is still disputed. A supreme pragmatist, he realized the danger of economic collapse and the futility of confrontation with the Allies. Therefore he ended passive resistance and negotiated huge American loans to rebuild the economy. This was so successful that by October 1924 money had regained its former value; (nearly) full employment and general prosperity soon followed.

Although Stresemann's government broke up long before these effects were felt, he subsequently served as foreign minister for six years in a variety of coalitions, achieving **Germany's rehabilitation on the world stage**. By the 1925 Locarno Pact, he gained *rapprochement* with France and guarantees that there could be no further threat of foreign occupation. Reparation payments were scaled down, and further American aid given. It seemed that the republic was set for a secure future, even if the political immaturity of the German people was still apparent, most notably in the presidential election of 1925. This was won by the 78-year-old Hindenburg, a wily operator basking in an undeserved military reputation, vocal exponent of the "stab in the back" legend and an embarrassing reminder of times past.

The rise of Nazism

The **National Socialist German Workers' Party** was founded in 1918 by a locksmith by the name of Anton Drexler, but only gained momentum when he was ousted three years later by **Adolf Hitler**, a failed artist and ex-corporal from Austria. It was a rag-bag group of fanatics and misfits whose views, as the party name suggests, were an odd mixture of the extreme right and left. They modelled their organization on the Communists and the Italian Fascisti, adopting their own uniform and slogans, and developing a private army, the brown-shirted **SA** (*Sturmabteilung*, or "Storm Troopers"). Such limited success as the party enjoyed was at first confined to Bavaria, where a botched attempt at a putsch was made in 1923; following this, Hitler was arrested and convicted of high treason.

The leniency shown by the judiciary to right-wing opponents of the republic – aided by the fact that he had involved Ludendorff in the plot – meant that Hitler only served nine months in prison, during which he set out his ideology and political programme in his autobiography, *Mein Kampf*. This consists of verbose rantings and ravings, drawing from all the nastiest and most reactionary theories of the day, but is an important source, as it sets out unequivocally what Hitler genuinely believed, and was to serve as his blueprint for power.

Racism forms the keynote: the so-called Aryans were the earth's rightful masters, while inferior peoples such as the Slavs were fit only to serve them. All ills could ultimately be laid at the door of the Jews, who were stealthily conspiring for world dominance. The German Volk had been betrayed by socialism, democracy and the traitors who had signed the Versailles Treaty. A new German Reich must be created under the direction of an all-powerful *Führer*, uniting with Austria and gaining living space (*Lebensraum*) to the east; to this end, France had to be subdued and Russia crushed.

Sales of the book – in spite of its ready captive market in the ranks of the party faithful – failed to reach 10,000 in the first year, and declined steadily for the next five. Nazi representation in the Reichstag also decreased from twenty-five in 1924 to just twelve after the 1928 elections, making it the ninth and smallest party, and one widely regarded as something of a joke. Only the extraordinarily mesmeric personality of Hitler held it together; having learnt from past mistakes, he was now determined to gain power by strictly legal means.

Stresemann died in October 1929, exhausted by overwork and by persecution from his former right-wing allies. Three weeks later came the **Wall Street crash** in America, whose repercussions swiftly destroyed the new German order he had created. Wholesale withdrawal of credit – on which the economy was totally dependent – led to another bout of escalating unemployment and inflation, to which there was no ready-made solution, as there had been in 1923. The coalition partners quarrelled over what measures to take; as a result, the SPD, who had only recently returned to government following eight years voluntarily out of office, once more abdicated the responsibility of leadership. A minority government was set up under **Heinrich Brüning** of the Catholic Centrists; frustrated by having to rely on rule by presidential decree, he took a gamble by asking Hindenburg to dissolve the Reichstag.

The elections, held in September 1930, offered a golden opportunity for the political extremes, with their formulas for righting all wrongs. The Nazi rise was meteoric, taking even Hitler by surprise – they gained 6.4 million votes and became the second largest party. This support was overwhelmingly from the disaffected ranks of the unemployed (particularly the young) and the ruined petty bourgeoisie. Though a significant breakthrough, it was far from being a decisive one, and there was still no inevitability about the Nazi triumph, which was only achieved because of the **short-sightedness and greed of the traditional right wing**.

In Hitler, they at last found their Kaiser-substitute, a man who could deliver the broad mass of support they could not otherwise muster and who would return Germany to its traditions of hierarchical authoritarian rule at home and military glory abroad. Leading figures in industry and politics latched onto Hitler and gave him respectability; by acting as his financiers and power brokers, they believed they would be able to control his excesses. Nazi coffers were swelled by contributions from many of the giant corporations, following a lead given some years before by the steel magnate Fritz Thyssen. The army began to abandon its role above party politics, overlooking its earlier aversion to the paramilitary SA.

Hitler offered a clue as to the naivety of these hopes by standing against the revered Hindenburg in the 1932 presidential election, only just managing to secure German citizenship in time to be eligible. The desperate straits into which the republic had fallen were shown by the fact that the ancient soldier, teetering on the verge of senility, was supported by the SPD and all the other democratic parties, who abstained from fielding a candidate of their own in the belief that there was no other way of beating Hitler.

In the event, Hindenburg only just failed to obtain an outright majority on the first ballot, and comfortably won the second, with the Communists trailing a very poor third. Fresh hope was provided by the remarkable success of Chancellor Brüning, still dependent on presidential decree, who was developing into a worthy successor to Stresemann. His sensible economic programme alleviated the worst hardships, and he was on the verge of pulling off a tremendous double success in foreign affairs, with the end of reparations and the return of Germany's right to equality of armaments in sight. An attempt at reforming the outdated pattern of land ownership proved to be Brüning's undoing; the aristocracy howled with rage at this alleged crypto-Bolshevism, and Hindenburg was left with no alternative but to ditch him.

That marked the last attempt to make the republic work; power passed to a small coterie of traditional conservatives close to the president, who would bear the final responsibility for Hitler's assumption of power. The next two chancellors – the bumbling intriguer **Franz von Papen** and the far more astute fixer **General Kurt von Schleicher**, who had elaborate plans for using Hitler and then destroying him – had no taste for democracy, and were content to play courtier-style politics.

Two elections held in 1932 were inconclusive; in the first, following a campaign of mass terror by the SA, the Nazis gained nearly fourteen million votes and became the largest party, but were still well short of a majority. As Hindenburg's hand-picked cabinet failed to secure the support of the Reichstag, new elections had to be called; these saw the Nazis lose two million votes, as the party's true aims and methods became clearer. However, having been toppled by von Schleicher, it was von Papen – a figure seemingly escaped from a comic opera, now centre-stage in one of the world's greatest-ever tragedies – who entered into a disastrous plot with Hitler which brought the end of the republic.

Von Papen persuaded Hindenburg to make Hitler chancellor, with himself as deputy, of a coalition able to command a Reichstag majority. As the Nazis would only be given two other cabinet seats, von Papen assumed that he would retain the real control for himself. Hitler was therefore sworn in on January 30, 1933, having achieved with ease his objective of coming to power by constitutional means.

The Third Reich

Once in power, **Hitler acted swiftly to make his position absolute**; he had no intention of being beholden to anyone, least of all a fool and political amateur such as von Papen. New elections were arranged for March; this time, the Nazis had the advantage of being able to use the full apparatus of the state to back up their campaign of terror. In this, they were greatly aided by the fact that **Hermann Göring**, one of the Nazis in the cabinet, was Prussian minister of the interior and thus in control of the police.

On the night of February 27, the **Reichstag** was burned down; a simple-minded Dutch Communist was arrested for this, though the fire was almost certainly the work of the Nazis themselves. At any rate, it gave them the excuse to force Hindenburg into declaring a state of emergency. Thereafter, opponents could be gagged legally, and Communists persecuted. The Nazis were duly elected with over seventeen million votes, just short of an absolute majority.

An **Enabling Bill** was laid before the Reichstag, which was effectively asked to vote itself out of existence. By the arrest of the Communist deputies and some of the SPD, and with the support of the traditional right, Hitler was only just short of the two-thirds majority he needed to abolish the Weimar Republic quite legally. The SPD salvaged some self-respect by refusing to accede to this, but the Catholic Centrists failed to repeat their act of defiance against Bismarck, meekly supporting the measure in return for minor concessions.

Now officially the country's dictator, Hitler immediately put into effect the remainder of his **policy of coordination** (*Gleichschaltung*), by which society was completely Nazified. With breathtaking speed, every institution surrendered. The Länder were stripped of their powers, making Germany a centralized state for the first time. All political parties except the Nazis were forced to dissolve, and free trade unions were banned. Purges were carried out in the police, judiciary and professions, to ensure that each was in the control of party loyalists.

Many of the vicious features for which Nazism became notorious soon made their appearance. **Jews were ostracized and persecuted**; their businesses were boycotted and they were banned from the professions; two years later, they were stripped of citizenship and forbidden to marry Germans. Fifty or so **concentration camps** were set up for political opponents, who were sadistically tortured and often cold-bloodedly murdered. Conformity was ensured by networks of informers under the control of the secret police, the **Gestapo**. The educational system was perverted in order to indoctrinate the great "truths" of Nazi ideology.

Recognizing the importance of controlling young minds at all times, membership of the **Hitler Youth** and League of Young German Women was made compulsory. Cultural life virtually collapsed, as "degenerate" forms of expression were suppressed. These ranged from virtually all modern art to books and plays with a liberal or socialist slant; it even affected music, as the performance of works by composers with Jewish blood was outlawed. Soon the main threat to the regime lay within the Nazi Party itself, with the original socialist wing, backed by the SA, pressing for a second revolution.

On June 30, 1934, the "**Night of the Long Knives**", hundreds of potential Nazi opponents were assassinated, notably the leading left-winger Gregor Strasser and the SA chief Ernst Röhm. The SA was stripped of its powers and put under the control of **Heinrich Himmler**'s black-shirted **SS** (*Schutzstaffel*), originally no more than Hitler's bodyguard. This measure also had the benefit of laying to rest the one remaining threat, that of intervention by the army; with their potential usurpers out of the way, they quickly came to terms with Nazism. When Hindenburg died a few weeks later, Hitler combined the offices of president and chancellor into that of an all-powerful *Führer*, a measure he had ratified by a plebiscite in which he was endorsed by 90 percent of those eligible to vote.

The genuine **popular support** Hitler enjoyed is one of the most striking and disturbing features of what became known as the Third Reich, the successor to the empires of Charlemagne and Bismarck. Although many of the most talented people, especially in the arts and sciences, fled the country, and many others tenaciously defied it from within, the level of opposition was negligible.

However, there's no doubt that the economic policies Hitler pursued were popular on both sides of industry. Full employment was restored and, although industrial and agricultural workers were effectively reduced to the status of serfs, there was no question of starvation or total financial ruin. Business leaders were pleased for a different reason – when it came to profits, the totalitarian state stopped short of its normal all-embracing function.

One by one, the terms of Versailles were breached – reparation payments were stopped, the formerly secret rearmament was stepped up and made open, with conscription reintroduced; the Rhineland was reoccupied; and Austria was forced into becoming part of the Reich. The German-speaking people in the Sudetenland part of Czechoslovakia, who had never previously been a source of discontent, were used as an excuse to begin the policy of *Lebensraum*; the matter escalated into an international crisis in 1938, in which the British and French made a humiliating climb-down by an agreement signed at Munich, in which they sacrificed Czech territorial integrity for what they believed would be world peace.

Hitler was encouraged by this show of weakness to launch one of his most cherished ambitions the following year – the elimination of Poland. It's probable he believed there would be a similar collapse of will by the western powers, the more so as he first pulled off the spectacular coup of signing a non-aggression pact with his ultimate enemy, the Soviet Union, thus ensuring there would not be a war on two fronts. However, this was a miscalculation; two days after the invasion began on September 1, Britain and France, realizing that the earlier promises of an end to German expansion in Eastern Europe were a sham, decided to honour their treaty obligations. Thus **World War II** began.

World War II

At first, the war went well for the Nazis, aided by the fact that Germany was the only country properly prepared, by reason of the massive arms build-up that it had semi-secretly been instigating since 1930. Poland was routed and the Low Countries soon fell, leading to the British evacuation from Dunkirk in May 1940. Within a month, France had signed an armistice, and a puppet government was installed. A quick invasion would probably then have accounted for Britain, but Hitler delayed in favour of an aerial bombardment in which the Luftwaffe was repulsed by the RAF. Rather than prolong this approach, German sights turned eastwards again. The Balkans were subdued, and in June 1941 plans were hatched for the largest military operation in history – the invasion of the Soviet Union. This period also marks the beginnings of the worst **concentration camps**, in which Nazi racial theories were put fully into practice. Inmates from the conquered territories were used as slave labour, and horrendous experiments in the name of Nazi "science" were carried out, followed by an attempt at the "final solution" of the Jewish "problem". Over six million (about a third of the population of world Jewry) perished as a result; a similar number of other "undesirable" peoples were massacred in addition.

On December 7, 1941 Hitler's Japanese allies (courted in the hope they would attack the USSR from the east) attacked Pearl Harbor, an action which almost immediately **brought the US into the war**, the very reverse of German intentions. In any event, Nazi Germany had hopelessly overreached itself; defeats in North Africa in 1942 were followed by **the turning-point at Stalingrad** the following year when the Russian winter and the vast size of the country combined, not for the first time, to repulse a foreign invader. German losses rivalled those sustained in World War I, and a crushing blow was dealt to morale, as this ranked as the most disastrous defeat in the country's military history.

From then onwards, the story is one of Nazi retreat on all fronts. A **German resistance movement** sprang up under the leadership of senior army officers. Various attempts were made to assassinate Hitler, and he had several extraordinary escapes, most notably in the carefully hatched plot of July 20, 1944, when a planted bomb killed several people sitting alongside him. Yet, bad luck apart, the conspiratorial groups were handicapped by their excessive concern to secure in advance lenient terms for a defeated but democratic Germany; they also had no firm base of popular support, nor a detailed plan of campaign for what to do once Hitler had been killed.

As it turned out, the country's ultimate collapse was drawn out, and did not occur before nearly all major German cities and innumerable small towns had been ruthlessly bombed. Eventually, the Allies occupied the entire country and on April 30, 1945, marooned in his Berlin bunker, Hitler committed suicide, so bringing the "thousand-year Reich" to an inglorious end.

The division of Germany

The Allied powers, determined not to repeat the mistakes of Versailles, now had to decide **what to do with Germany**. At Potsdam in August, the country was partitioned into four zones of occupation, corresponding to an agreement made earlier in the year at Yalta when the war was still in progress; Berlin was similarly divided. The eastern frontier of Germany was redrawn at the Oder–Neisse line, meaning that East Prussia and most of Pomerania and Silesia passed to Poland, in compensation for territory annexed by the Soviet Union.

Initially, there was a great deal of co-operation amongst the Allies. All the leading Nazis who had survived were brought to **trial in Nürnberg** for war crimes or crimes against humanity, and the civil service was purged of the movement's sympathizers. Relief measures were taken against the terrible famine sweeping the country, refugees from the former Eastern Territories were given help to begin a new life, and the first steps were made towards rebuilding destroyed cities and the shattered economy.

Germany's internal **political life** was relaunched under the leadership of prominent anti-Nazis. The right of the spectrum was occupied by a new and moderate party, the **Christian Democrats** (CDU), in which the Catholic Centrists were joined by Protestants who held similar social views. Left-wing politics were still marred by the legacy of bad blood between the SPD and the Communists. In the Russian zone, the SPD took the lead in forming a new group, the **Socialist Unity Party** (SED), which was intended to be Marxist but not Marxist-Leninist; the Communists only tagged along under Russian pressure after the poor showing of the party in the Austrian elections. This new grouping was not repeated in the other zones.

Inevitably, **strains developed among the Allies**; the zones began to develop in different ways, mirroring the societies of their conquerors. Frustrated by Russian stalling, the Western powers began a currency reform in their zones in 1948, soon extended to West Berlin. This gesture was regarded as highly provocative by the Soviets, who retaliated by cutting off western access to the divided city in the **Berlin Blockade**. Another world war could have ensued, but the beleaguered western zones were saved by the success of **airlifts** bringing essential supplies, forcing the Russians to abandon the blockade within a year.

By this time, two different societies were emerging on German soil: the Russians enforced massive nationalization and collectivization; in contrast, the Western powers allowed even those industrialists most associated with the Nazis, such as Thyssen and the Krupps, to return to their businesses with minimal punishment. Rocked by the independent line taken by Tito in Yugoslavia, the Russians transformed the SED into a Soviet-style party led by a Politburo into which the erstwhile SPD members were trapped, while a Parliamentary Council was set up in the west to draft a new constitution. The logical conclusion of these events – the creation of two rival states – soon followed. In May 1949, the three western zones amalgamated to form the **German Federal Republic**; four months later, the Russians launched their territory as the **German Democratic Republic**.

The Federal Republic

Like the Weimar Republic, the new West German state was founded on **liberal democratic principles**, only this time the constitution was much tighter. The power of the president was sharply reduced, giving him a role not unlike that of the British monarch. A true federal structure was created, in which the Länder were given considerable powers over all areas of policy except defence, foreign affairs and currency control. Proportional representation was retained, but with a 5 percent qualifying minimum, and elections were fixed for every four years. A constitutional court was established to guarantee civil and political liberties, and anti-democratic parties were outlawed.

Konrad Adenauer became the first chancellor following elections in which his Christian Democrats emerged as the largest party, though far short of a majority. Aged 73 and with no experience of national politics – he had been mayor of Cologne until removed by the Nazis – he bore the look of a temporary leader, though as an elder statesman with an untainted past he fitted the precise needs of the time exactly.

In the event, the evening of his career was a prolonged one; he remained in power for fourteen years, during which time he developed an aura of indispensability at home and appeared as a figure of substance abroad. Much of this success was due to the "**Economic Miracle**" masterminded by **Ludwig Erhard**, in which the wrecked economy made a spectacular recovery, with high-quality products fuelling an export boom. An annual growth rate of 8 percent was achieved; within a decade West Germany ranked as the most prosperous major European country. In many ways, this was due simply to disciplined hard work by the bulk of the population, but it was also aided by the fact that a fresh start had to be made. Industry was relaunched with the most modern equipment, and in a sensible atmosphere of partnership between management and just seventeen large trade unions which eliminated the class-based fear and inter-union rivalry which continued to dog other countries. Erhard also promoted the concept of the "social-market economy", giving due emphasis to the development of a welfare state.

In foreign affairs, priority was given to **ending the long era of enmity with France**; the two countries formed the European Coal and Steel Pact in 1951, serving as a prelude to the creation of the European Economic Community six years later. The Federal Republic's integration into the Western alliance was cemented by admission to **NATO**, and the adoption of a hard-nosed attitude towards the Soviet Union and her satellites.

By the **Hallstein Doctrine**, the Federal Republic claimed to be the legitimate voice of all Germany, arguing that it was the only part properly constituted. Not only did it fail to recognize the GDR, it successfully ostracized its neighbour by refusing to establish diplomatic relations with any country who did.

The German Democratic Republic

Meanwhile, the inappropriately styled German Democratic Republic rapidly evolved a **centralized system of government on the Soviet model**. The Christian Democratic and Liberal parties were forcibly subordinated to the SED, and two further bourgeois groups were created from above. Elections were still held, but a single list of candidates was drawn up which the voters had to accept *en bloc*. The only method of protest was to reject it outright, which had to be done publicly, making it a dangerous as well as a futile gesture. Police, education and management of the economy were all put under SED control. Real power was centralized in the hands of party secretary **Walter Ulbricht**, a hard-line Stalinist who had spent almost the entire Nazi period ensconced in the Soviet Union.

At first, the Russians were ambivalent about their rump state. They administered punitive reparations, stripping it of much of its industry and shipping valuable plants and machinery to the Soviet Union; they were worried about the GDR's long-term viability and may even have been prepared to sacrifice it altogether in their own defensive interests. Stalin was on record as saying in 1944, "Communism fits Germany as a saddle fits a cow", and it's doubtful if he was ever particularly keen on a separate GDR. In 1952, he made **an offer to establish a unified and neutral Germany on a democratic basis**, which was rejected out of hand in the West as mere bluff.

The **GDR began life unpromisingly**, exploited by its parent, having no historical or economic rationale, unloved by the vast majority of its populace, thousands of whom emigrated to the West, and seemingly wanted only by its leaders who had had power handed to them on a plate. A second industrial revolution had to be launched, simply to meet reparation commitments; the existing infrastructure included very little heavy industry (which was now developed apace, though more for ideological reasons than out of necessity), and was now deprived of access to its commercial hinterland. The pressure of this caused the first revolt in the Soviet satellite states, a series of **workers' strikes** in 1953, put down by Russian tanks. The following year, reparations were ended and the country began to develop as a key member of the bloc, becoming one of the founder members of the **Warsaw Pact**.

In spite of many problems – access to Western markets was hindered by the lack of a convertible currency, trade with the Soviet Union was conducted on unfavourable terms, and imbalances were caused by the ideological imperative to give massive subsidies to basic necessities – the 1950s saw an **economic recovery** which in its own way was as extraordinary as West Germany's. Once again, the people showed their legendary ability to adapt to any kind of regime; they were in any event now well attuned to totalitarian life. If West Germans felt a sense of superiority in their far more advanced lifestyle, the comparison was hardly a fair one: they had received munificence from their conquerors, not retribution; they had also started with the enormous benefit of being in possession of the Ruhr and other areas of rich natural resources and advanced industry. At the 1958 Party Congress, Ulbricht was rash enough to predict that, within a few years, the country would overtake its neighbour in terms of per capita income, thus proving the inherent superiority of the Communist system.

The Berlin Wall

This optimism proved short-lived, as the late 1950s saw the beginning of a period of **unprecedented West German prosperity and economic expansion**. A shortage of labour meant that workers had to be imported; the unskilled labourers tended to come from Turkey, Greece, Yugoslavia, Italy and Spain. For the better-qualified positions, industry looked to East Germany and a flood of **emigration** started.

Quickly realizing that he could not afford to lose so many professionals, engineers, intellectuals and craftsmen, Ulbricht was forced into drastic action. The loophole was the western sector of Berlin; if it could be sealed off, the problem would disappear. Having failed at a second attempt to make the Allies evacuate the city, Ulbricht persuaded the Soviets of the necessity of constructing the **Berlin Wall**, erected on August 13, 1961. It was immediately patrolled by armed guards under instructions to shoot to kill, and the main boundaries of the country were also greatly strengthened. A visual and moral affront to humanity, it was justified as the "Anti-Fascist Protection Wall", a label it retained until its demolition.

In the Federal Republic, Adenauer was finally forced into retirement in 1963, to be succeeded by Erhard, who proved far less successful as the country's leader than he had been as economic guru. The liberal Free Democrats (FDP), who had served as the CDU's junior coalition partners for all but a short period of the Federal Republic's history, went into opposition in 1966. A "**Grand Coalition**" was established with the SPD, who thus returned to government for the first time since 1930. To rid itself of its tarnished image, the party had undergone a substantial reform (or sell-out, according to many) at its 1959 conference, disavowing its roots in Marxism and class conflict and its traditional anticlericalism, embracing instead the CDU's "social-market economy", but with a stronger emphasis on the social side of the equation.

The chancellor, the CDU's Kurt Georg Kiesinger, was remarkable mainly for being a reformed Nazi – a rather uncomfortable indicator as to how far West Germans were prepared to forget the past. It was hardly surprising that the period of the Grand Coalition saw the first simmerings of disenchantment with the cosy form of consensus politics which had dominated the country's postwar history, with the Communists re-formed as a counterweight to the neo-Nazi NPD; neither party, however, gained much of a following. More serious were the beginnings of what became a persistent feature of West German life, **extra-parliamentary opposition**. This first came to the fore with the 1968 student revolt under Rudi Dutschke. Grievances initially centred on unsatisfactory conditions in the universities but spread to wider discontent with society and the new materialistic culture.

Ostpolitik

A more positive feature of the Grand Coalition was the rise of **Willy Brandt**, the dynamic leader of the SPD, who assumed the foreign affairs portfolio. A former Resistance journalist, he had been mayor of West Berlin throughout the period of crisis leading up to the building of the Wall, and was determined to take a new tack on the problem. His **Ostpolitik** began in earnest, helped by a general thawing of the Cold War, when he became chancellor in 1969, at the head of a SPD–FDP coalition, itself something of a mould-breaker. Treaties were signed with the Soviet Union and Poland in 1970, recognizing the validity of the Oder–Neisse line; West Berlin's special status was guaranteed by the Four Power Agreement the following year; and in 1972 a Basic Treaty was signed between the two Germanys which at last normalized relations.

This stopped short of full diplomatic recognition of the GDR, but the Federal Republic recognized its frontiers and separate existence, abandoning the Hallstein Doctrine. In return, West Germans were allowed to visit family and friends over the border, though movement the other way was confined to pensioners and the disabled. One consequence of Ostpolitik was the **fall of Ulbricht** in 1971; he wanted to drive a harder bargain than suited the Soviets, who were in any case tired of his constant lectures to them on ideological purity. His replacement was **Erich Honecker**, who, although regarded as a comparative liberal, had first come to prominence as construction supremo of the Berlin Wall.

With the mirage of reunification now cleared, the two German societies were able to continue developing in their separate ways. **The GDR began to clarify and modify its image**; in 1974, the country was given yet another new constitution, which omitted previous references to overcoming the division of Germany, and stated the country was "forever and irrevocably" allied with the USSR. The GDR was characterized as a "developed socialist society", in which different divisions existed. This had the twin benefits of justifying both the inequality which was still clearly manifest (though less extreme than in the West) and the continued leadership role of the SED – along with all the attendant privileges for its elite.

To counterbalance this, a "**social contract**" was made with the population, which curbed arbitrary use of police powers, effectively meaning that only active dissidents were persecuted. Honecker cultivated an avuncular image for himself which came as a refreshing change after the austere authoritarianism of his predecessor. **Sports** – or at least those with a high profile in the Olympic Games, such as athletics, swimming and skiing – were increasingly used as the chief means of gaining international prestige, and the results proved stunningly successful, catapulting the country to the dizzy heights of the improbable third "super-power" in these events. **Economic performance** became ever more impressive, and was easily the best in the Soviet bloc; full employment was preserved as much out of necessity as principle. However, in comparison with West Germany the economic mix looked hopelessly outdated, and the average earner was little more than half as well off in real terms, with the gap widening rather than narrowing. As well as all the old problems, there were frequent shortages (often caused by sudden opportunities to sell stocks to gain hard currency) and a lack of consumer goods for which the demand was growing apace.

Boosted by the success of both his Ostpolitik and his welfare programmes, Brandt led his coalition to victory in 1972, with the SPD winning more votes than the CDU for the first time. In view of the reconciliatory nature of his approach to the GDR, it was ironic that Brandt's downfall occurred two years later as a result of the unmasking of one of his closest aides as an East German spy.

Staying on in the influential role as SPD chairman (until 1987, when another scandal, this time over a bizarre choice of a young CDU-sympathizing Greek woman as party spokesperson, caused his retirement), Brandt was succeeded by **Helmut Schmidt**, an able pragmatist who increasingly came to be seen as something of a right-winger, though this was in part due to the nature of the problems he faced. The quadrupling of OPEC oil prices in 1974, and the stagnation in world trade which ensued, posed particular difficulties for the export-led and growth-geared German economy. These were tackled more successfully than in most countries, but **unemployment** became an issue for the first time since Hitler.

Extra-parliamentary opposition had by now taken on a fearsome and anarchic character. In the early 1970s, there had been a spate of kidnappings and armed bank robberies by the Baader-Meinhof gang. These had no sooner been quelled than there arose a far more organized and ruthless offshoot, the **Red Army Faction**, which assassinated a number of public figures. The turning point in the government's campaign against them came with the hijacking of a Lufthansa plane in 1977, and a threat to kill the hostages if the remaining members of the gang were not released from prison.

On personal instructions from Schmidt – on which he was prepared to stake his chancellorship – the aircraft was successfully stormed; within three years, most of the terrorist leaders had been arrested and imprisoned. Peaceful extra-parliamentary opposition proved to have a far more potent significance. This was inspired above all by fears that divided Germany would serve as the stage for a future nuclear war. NATO's 1979 decision to install medium-range American nuclear missiles in West Germany was a particular source of protest, but there was also **increased general concern about the environment**, especially pollution of the beloved forests.

These issues then served as a focus for the many who were dissatisfied with a society which had become over-competitive and too obsessed with consumerism, and out of an amorphous collection of pressure groups active in these areas the **Green Party** was born. Schmidt's backing of the bases alienated the SPD's left wing, but he was still able to lead his coalition to victory in 1980. In this he was aided by the CDU's recurrent leadership problem, which reached its nadir at this point with the fielding of **Franz-Josef Strauss**, who had last held federal office under Adenauer, as chancellor candidate. Longstanding leader of the CSU, the separate and exclusively Bavarian counterpart of the CDU, this blatant careerist and strident right-winger unsurprisingly proved to be a major electoral liability.

The road to reunification

Despite this lifeline, the long period of SPD domination was coming to an end. Schmidt's tough economic policies under the influence of another round of drastic oil price increases further widened the party's divisions, leading the FDP to lose confidence and withdraw from the government in September 1982. The CDU, now revived under **Helmut Kohl**, gambled on a "constructive vote of no confidence" – the only way round the fixed-term parliaments enshrined in the constitution. Having won this, they formed a new government with the FDP and called for fresh elections. Fears that the FDP would fail to surmount the 5 percent threshold (having damaged themselves by their rather dubious stance) proved unfounded, and Kohl was able to continue as before.

Kohl was something of a departure, the first German leader drawn from a generation too young to have Nazi associations of any kind. He remained in power for sixteen years, unexpectedly seeing Germany through its biggest upheaval since World War II. Initially, his government was rather unexciting, cutting back on the state's very modest role in economic intervention, but making **further strides in Ostpolitik**. Since Brandt, this had become low-key, and depended very much on the climate of superpower relations. The new developments were in many cases cynical – massive **interest-free loans** were given to the GDR in return for allowing greater numbers of its citizens to emigrate, and football-style transfer fees were paid for its political prisoners.

Honecker was keen to **set the seal of legitimacy on the GDR** by paying an official visit to the Federal Republic; two attempts were abandoned in the face of Soviet pressure before he finally made it in September 1987. It was the high point of his career and seemed to provide its justification as, amid much publicity, he was received in a way just below that for a head of state. However, by this time his regime was already beginning to be undermined by the new policies of *glasnost* and *perestroika* introduced in the Soviet Union under **Mikhail Gorbachev**, and somewhat desperate attempts were made to insulate GDR citizens from the seemingly inexorable move towards reform in the eastern bloc.

As it transpired, the initial impetus for the astonishing and rapid transformation of Germany (what Germans call *die Wende*), came from outside the country. On May 2, 1989, the Hungarian authorities began taking down the barbed wire along their border with Austria, creating **a hole in the Iron Curtain**. Many East Germans headed there, ostensibly for their holidays, and by August around two hundred were **crossing into Austria** every night; additionally, about twenty thousand GDR refugees were being housed in the West German embassy in Budapest and in Hungarian holiday camps, awaiting their chance for an official emigration to the West. On September 10 the Hungarian government finally **gave the East Germans leave to depart**. Now forbidden to travel to Hungary, would-be GDR refugees instead made for Prague, swamping the West German embassy. On September 30 they too were allowed to leave, the result of a special deal announced by West German foreign minister Hans-Dietrich Genscher.

In the GDR **opposition groups** such as Neues Forum were starting to emerge. Popular unrest came to a head at the **October 7** celebration of the 40th anniversary of the GDR. Guest Mikhail Gorbachev stressed the need for dialogue and openness to new ideas, while Erich Honecker responded with a clichéd speech praising the status quo. A vainglorious official parade of military hardware was followed by angry **demonstrations** which were brutally suppressed by the police. There were also demonstrations in Leipzig and Dresden, and open popular unrest spread across the country over the following weeks despite widespread fears of an armed crackdown by the authorities. The expected violence never materialized and on October 18 Erich Honecker was suddenly replaced by **Egon Krenz**, his long-time heir apparent, a man widely regarded as a neo-Stalinist hardliner.

To everyone's surprise Krenz **expressed a desire for dialogue** with opposition groups. The exodus of GDR citizens continued but there was now a feeling that change might be possible. On November 4 one million people gathered in the centre of East Berlin, in **the biggest anti-Communist demonstration** since the workers' uprising of 1953. Three days later most of the old government resigned and **Hans Modrow**, the former Dresden SED chief, a man regarded as a liberal, was appointed prime minister. By now two hundred thousand East Germans had left the GDR since the start of the year.

The **opening of the Berlin Wall** was announced almost casually. On the evening of Thursday, November 9, Berlin party boss Günter Schabowski told a press conference that East German citizens were free to leave the GDR with valid exit visas which were henceforth to be issued without delay. Events immediately took on a momentum of their own. TV stations broadcast the announcement and citizens began heading for the nearest border crossings. All along the frontier, border guards began letting through the masses, and people on both sides of the city flocked to the Wall. Huge crowds converged on the Brandenburger Tor where an impromptu street party broke out celebrating an event that many Germans had never imagined they would see. Over the days that followed, **East Germans poured across the border**: 2,700,000 exit visas were issued in the first weekend after the Wall was opened, and the two Germanys rediscovered each other at breakneck speed.

On December 1 the East German parliament passed a motion ending the leading role of the SED and **free elections were promised** for the following May. The SED repackaged itself as the supposedly voter-friendly PDS – Partei des Demokratischen Sozialismus or "Democratic Socialist Party". A more significant event for the future of Germany was Chancellor Helmut Kohl's visit to Dresden on December 19 when he declared to cheering crowds that his ultimate goal was a **united Germany**.

Germany since 1990

With the new decade things progressed rapidly. The GDR elections, brought forward to March 18, resulted in a **victory for a right-wing alliance dominated by the CDU** under Lothar de Mazière. This really represented a victory for Chancellor Helmut Kohl, the self-proclaimed champion of reunification.

Almost immediately the new East German government set about dissolving the GDR. An agreement with the West Germans about **economic union** was hammered out and put into effect on July 1. The next step was to work out a formula for political reunification. This was effectively left to Helmut Kohl and Mikhail Gorbachev (who at this stage still had the final say); between them during a July summit in the Caucasus, they worked out a mutually acceptable agreement which was quickly rubber-stamped by the GDR parliament.

October 3, 1990 was the date of **German reunification**, an event which did not see a repeat of earlier celebrations. For many people in the east, dazed by the rapid economic collapse of the GDR and subsequent social dislocation, reunification seemed to offer little, other than the prospect of unemployment and uncertainty. Nonetheless, Kohl remained determinedly upbeat, maintaining that no German would lose out as a result of unification. His opportunistic masterminding of events meant that the SPD was forced into making penny-pinching complaints about costs, thereby inviting the charge that it was not up to dealing with the great historical challenge facing the nation. Now that the two states had formally merged, Kohl's fast-track approach to a fully integrated economy and society offered no more risks than the slower methods advocated by his opponents, and it was therefore no surprise that the **CDU-led coalition scored a landslide victory** in the first united German elections, held in December 1990.

The rosy picture painted by Kohl of the country's economic prospects was not mere optimistic posturing. He rashly calculated that an initial spending spree would be unleashed in the east as a result of the introduction of the

Deutschmark, and that the natural capacity of Germans to work hard, coupled with the fact that a large percentage of women in the former GDR were in gainful employment, would thereafter fuel a major boom which would spread to the west as well.

The essential weakness in this prognosis was that it failed to anticipate the speed and totality of the **collapse of the Soviet Union** in the wake of its satellites. This spelt absolute ruin for whole sectors of the economy of the former GDR, which were suddenly left without markets for their products. Worse, the logistics of central planning meant that entire towns, dependent on a single industry, found themselves facing a desperate future, with half or more of the local population out of work at a single stroke.

Not only did the government's standing plummet in the east, it also nose-dived in the west when vastly unpopular **tax increases** were introduced in 1991 for the specific purpose of funding the unification process. The CDU paid the electoral penalty in the state elections in the Rhineland-Palatinate soon afterwards, losing to the SPD what had always been considered a sure-fire stronghold, the place where Chancellor Kohl had built his original power base. Similar humiliations befell the party in subsequent elections in other Länder.

One of the beneficiaries of the government's discomfiture was the **far right**, which had hitherto failed to make much of an impact on postwar Germany. Playing heavily on the political immaturity of the eastern German Electorate, and on the fears and resentments building up in the west, the far right, in the shape of the outwardly respectable Republican Party, made some unexpectedly strong showings in these local elections, leading many at home and abroad to voice fears that Germany might yet again embrace Nazism.

The far right concentrated on the issues of **unemployment and immigration**, making a direct and largely bogus connection between the two. Violent racist attacks on foreigners, sometimes resulting in deaths, soon became commonplace, particularly in the former GDR, where a number of shocking incidents of mob hatred were captured on film and broadcast round the world. The official response to this was a review of Germany's exceptionally liberal immigration laws, introduced as an atonement for the crimes of the Third Reich, and these were eventually repealed in 1993.

While the government was widely condemned for what looked like a weak-kneed reaction to the problem of racist violence, it was also possible to see its response as a pragmatic one to a situation that was otherwise in danger of getting out of hand, particularly when political refugees from the disintegrating **Yugoslavia** started to arrive in force to swell the ranks of the mainly economic refugees from the former Soviet bloc. It certainly seemed to help put the advance of the far right firmly into reverse, though it failed to touch on a key issue of race relations – the lack of citizenship rights of the large *Gastarbeiter* population, which now includes an entire generation who were born in Germany and have lived their whole lives there.

By 1992, it was clear that the economy was in **recession**. Defeat for the CDU in the fixed-term general elections set for October 1994 looked inevitable, but the SPD's massive lead in the opinion polls was gradually whittled away by its seemingly perennial crisis over its choice of chancellor candidate, while an economic upturn rallied CDU support. Meanwhile, the PDS profited from the renewed sympathy for reformed Communists expressed throughout Eastern Europe. Kohl's biggest worry was the very real prospect that his coalition partners in the FDP would fail to get the 5 percent of votes necessary to gain parliamentary representation – a scenario which would virtually ensure the accession of some form of left-wing coalition.

In the event, the FDP achieved the qualifying minimum with a bit to spare, and the **Kohl government continued in office**, albeit with its majority slashed to just ten seats.

Kohl's fourth term in office was dominated by the drive towards **European Monetary Union**, for which he lobbied energetically in the face of the misgivings of many of Germany's European partners. After announcing that the 1998 election would mark his retirement, he changed his mind and decided to run for an unprecedented fifth term, in the grandiose belief that, having achieved German unification, he was the only living statesman with the necessary clout to pull off the task of delivering full European integration. However, the performance of the domestic economy did not bode well for electoral success: the austerity measures demanded by the need to meet the convergence criteria for EMU exacerbated problems that remained unsolved in the wake of reunification; the Deutschmark was at its lowest for decades, while **unemployment** had reached almost five million – its highest since 1933. It was therefore no surprise that Kohl went down to a comprehensive defeat at the hands of an alliance of the SPD and Greens, bringing the latter into national government for the first time.

The new chancellor, **Gerhard Schröder**, had modelled himself quite closely on Britain's Tony Blair, though in one key area of difference – his reputation as a serial bridegroom – he faced the problem of a question mark against his trustworthiness. Moreover, the corporate style of leadership favoured by the SPD during their years in opposition meant that it was initially unclear who was really in charge of the government – Schröder or the maverick 1990 chancellor-candidate Oskar Lafontaine, who assumed the portfolio of Finance Minister in addition to his duties as party chairman. This issue was, however, soon resolved conclusively in favour of the former, as Lafontaine was ousted from both roles, to be replaced by the chancellor himself in the latter.

Meanwhile the CDU found itself embroiled in a series of financial scandals, with Kohl himself incriminated in allegations of fraudulent fundraising. In the foreign press, these were often presented as the total ruination of his carefully cultivated reputation as one of the seminal figures of German history, though it seems highly unlikely that future historians will judge these misdemeanors so harshly. Nonetheless, the scandals claimed the scalp of his anointed successor, Wolfgang Schäuble, and resulted in the unopposed election of Angela Merkel, a former GDR citizen with only a decade of political experience, as party leader. She was not, however, chosen as the Chancellor-candidate to oppose Schröder in the **2002 elections**: that role was bestowed on the far more battle-hardened Edmund Stoiber of the CSU. In the event, it was a decision that backfired: Stoiber's stolid, very conservative and very Bavarian persona competed at a severe disadvantage against the media-savvy Schröder, and the latter was able to use the catastrophic floods which occurred during the campaign to full advantage, adopting a statesman-like pose which his rival conspicuously failed to match. The governing parties were also able to capitalize on public unease about the increasingly bellicose foreign policy of the United States (which the CDU and CSU were happy to support) by adopting a clearly independent line. Despite the poor performance of the economy under their stewardship – which had made electoral defeat seem a virtual certainty earlier in the year – they pulled off a knife-edge victory and were able to continue as before.

Painting and graphics

Germany's artistic history is marked more by solid and sustained achievement than by the more usual pattern of pre-eminence followed by decline. As in Italy, the fragmentation of the nation into a multitude of tiny states led to the development of many important centres of art, often of a very distinctive character.

The country's geographical position has meant that it has been a melting pot for influences from Italy, France and the Low Countries, although, with several notable exceptions, the work of German painters never managed to gain the same international esteem. This, however, is mainly because the vast majority of German paintings have remained within the German-speaking countries, a consequence of the fact that many of the petty princes were great art collectors, and also because of the Romantic movement, which fostered a sense of awareness of the national heritage. As a result, important **museums** existed all over the country by the mid-nineteenth century.

German **graphic work**, being by its nature intended for dissemination, is perhaps more immediately familiar; the stark contrasts enforced by the media of woodcut, engraving and etching obviously proved temperamentally ideal for the country's artists, whose legacy in these fields far surpasses that of anywhere else in Europe.

The beginnings

German painting has its roots in the ninth-century Carolingian epoch. **Illuminated manuscripts** were created in the scriptoria of the court and the monasteries; these typically featured vibrant figures in flowing draperies, charged with movement and set in elaborate architectural surrounds. This art form was refined and developed in the subsequent Ottonian period, most notably in Trier, which in the late tenth century boasted the first great German artist in an illuminator now dubbed **Master of the Registrum Gregorii**. A number of manuscripts by him have been identified; they show a new, more plastic style based on an understanding of Classical antiquity, solving the problems of space and form which baffled all the other illuminators of the time. He built up a highly influential fund of forms which was imitated in the other great places of book production – Fulda, Hildesheim and Bavaria – although there were also more conservative centres, particularly those on the island of the Reichenau, favouring an expressive linear form.

Fresco cycles were the other chief form of painting, and were often more closely related to the art of the book than might be supposed from the contrasting nature of the two forms. One of the best early examples to have survived is again from Trier; probably dating from the end of the ninth century, it originally adorned the crypt of St Maximin, but has been removed to the Bischöfliches Museum. From the following century, there is an important cycle still *in situ* at St Georg in Oberzell on the Reichenau, along with one in the Andreaskirche in Fulda. Belonging more obviously to international Romanesque currents are the later fresco cycles of the Lower Rhineland and Regensburg. The former – St Gereon in Cologne, Schwarzrheindorf and Knechtsteden – are all influenced by Byzantine concepts of form, style and iconography; regrettably, their quality has been impaired by over-enthusiastic nineteenth-century restorers who indulged in far too much speculative retouching.

Later Romanesque illuminated manuscripts tend to follow rather than develop the Ottonian forms, although there was something of a revival in the late twelfth century, with such de luxe products as the *Gospels of Henry the Lion*, now in Wolfenbüttel. Roughly contemporary is a survival which is unique of its kind, the painted **wooden ceiling** illustrating the *Tree of Jesse* which adorns the vault of St Michaelis in Hildesheim.

The early Gothic period

The earliest Gothic **panel paintings** to have survived in Germany date from around 1300. Throughout the fourteenth century, religious themes retained their monopoly, and the most active workshops were in Cologne and Westphalia. The former was the dominant city of medieval Germany, and maintained its own strong and characteristic traditions right up until the early sixteenth century, assimilating varied foreign influences yet remaining rooted in tradition. Painting there was based on a strict **guild system**, which imposed stiff tests of skill on would-be applicants and even stipulated the quality of materials which had to be employed. Among the most important productions of this school in the fourteenth century were the monumental paintings on the backs of the Dom's stalls, the *Clares Altar*, again in the Dom, and some very ruinous frescoes for the Rathaus which have been attributed to a somewhat legendary figure named **Master Wilhelm**.

The first German artist about whom much information has survived is **Master Bertram** (c.1345–1415), a Westphalian who worked in Hamburg. He seems to have been influenced by the art of Bohemia, which was part of the Holy Roman Empire, and was far in advance of fourteenth-century Germany in terms of the achievements of its painters. Bertram favoured narrative cycles of little panels grouped round pieces of sculpture; his major work is the *St Petri Altar* of 1379, which is now in Hamburg's Kunsthalle, and displays prodigious and original imaginative powers, particularly in the charming scenes of the Creation. From about a decade later is the *Passion Altar* in Hannover, while the *Buxtehude Altar*, again in Hamburg, is from ten years later; both are remarkably consistent in style.

Another Westphalian was the **Master of the Berswordt Altar** (active in the late fourteenth century), named after a triptych still *in situ* in the Marienkirche in Dortmund. The influence of French and Burgundian manuscripts is apparent, and he was an early representative of the courtly and idealized International Gothic style which was to spread all over Europe. In Germany, this is usually referred to as the **Soft Style**, and is found in sculpture as well as painting. Its greatest exponent was **Conrad von Soest** (active c.1394–1422), one of the most immediately appealing of all German painters, who may even have been the son of the previous artist. His panels are refined and beautiful, executed in glowing colours and including a fair amount of amusing anecdotal detail. The late high altar triptych of the Marienkirche in his native Dortmund shows his art at its peak, but is sadly truncated. The triptych in Bad Wildungen, however, has survived in remarkable shape. Another major painter in this style was **Master Francke** (active c.1405–25), who succeeded Bertram in Hamburg and could conceivably have been his pupil; his reputation rests largely on the *St Thomas à Becket Altar* which was commissioned by the local merchants who traded with England. Also active at this time were the **Master of the Virgin of Benediktbeuern** in Bavaria and various artists in Lower Saxony. Most of the surviving examples of the latter are now in the Landesgalerie in Hannover; a notable exception is the high altar of the Jakobikirche in Göttingen.

The fifteenth-century Cologne school

The entire fifteenth century was an outstandingly brilliant artistic period for Cologne. Although the artists mostly remain anonymous, their styles became far more contrasted than in former times, and art historians have been able to group bodies of work under pseudonyms based on the names of their major masterpieces, which are now mostly housed in the city's Wallraf-Richartz-Museum, or in the Alte Pinakothek in Munich. As well as large-scale commissions to adorn the plethora of churches and monasteries, there's increasing evidence of the burgeoning of the merchant class in the number of small altarpieces (obviously intended for private devotion) which have survived. The symbolic depiction of the Madonna and Child in the Garden of Paradise was enduringly popular; another vogue subject (the two were sometimes combined) was the Holy Kinship, depicting the extended family of Christ. First to develop a distinctive style was the **Master of St Veronica** (active c.1400–20), named after *St Veronica with the Sudarium*, now in Munich. The monumental faces in this work, mirrored elsewhere in his output, give evidence of influence from Bohemia, but that he had also understood the lessons of Burgundian miniatures is proved by the crowded *Calvary* in Cologne. His workshop may have been taken over after his death by the **Master of St Lawrence** (active c.1415–30), whose main work is a retable made for the demolished church of St Lorenz, parts of which survive in the museums of Cologne and Nürnberg.

These artists were surpassed by **Stefan Lochner** (c.1400–51), a Swabian who settled in the city and perfectly assimilated its traditions, along with innovations from Flanders. His soft, gentle and painstakingly detailed panels are among the peaks of the entire International Gothic movement, and he appears to have been something of a celebrity, which accounts for his name surviving the oblivion into which his rivals have plunged. His masterpiece is the *Epiphany* triptych now in Cologne's Dom, but originally painted for the Rathaus, which is a far more monumental work than was usual in Cologne. It has been criticized for a failure to characterize the figures, but that is to miss the point – Lochner's art is quite consciously ethereal in spirit. If anything, the later *Presentation in the Temple*, now in Darmstadt, is even more sumptuous, while his last work, *Madonna of the Rose Bower* in Cologne, takes the art of the small altar to a level beyond which it could not progress. Even with gruesome subjects, such as *The Last Judgment* in Cologne and its reverse, *Martyrdoms of the Apostles*, now in Frankfurt, Lochner did not depart from his essential gentleness, always drawing the optimistic lesson from the subject; if that can be counted as a failing, his extraordinary inventive powers amply compensate.

The following generation moved away from static and decorative effects to a lively narrative style, clearly modelled on the great contemporary

Netherlanders. Rogier van der Weyden's late *St Columba* triptych (now in Munich) was painted for a church in Cologne, and must have made an enormous impact, although the more rounded and less emotional style of Dieric Bouts is the obvious source for the leading artist of the group, the **Master of the Life of the Virgin** (active c.1460–85), so named from a cycle of eight panels, seven of which are also now in Munich. He displays all the qualities of a great storyteller, the figures strongly drawn and richly clad, standing out in sharp relief from the background, with plenty of subsidiary anecdotal detail, including exquisite still lifes. This artist's later work includes portraits of merchants, which mark the end of the ecclesiastical monopoly over art. Three other painters closely associated with him are the **Master of the Lyversberg Passion**, the **Master of the St George Legend** and the **Master of the Bonn Diptych**; they may even have shared the same studio. Slightly later is the **Master of the Glorification of the Virgin** (active c.1475–95) who is less overtly Flemish in spirit; his backgrounds include accurate depictions of Cologne and its surrounding countryside.

Among the final generation of Cologne painters, the **Master of the Holy Kinship** (c.1450–1515) takes his name from the most spectacular version ever painted of the favourite Cologne subject, which shows acquaintance with the very latest Flemish innovations; otherwise, he seems to have been more adept on a smaller scale, his larger canvases betraying the use of inexperienced assistants. His contemporary, the **Master of the St Ursula Legend** (active c.1490–1505), developed the narrative tradition in a now dispersed series, partly preserved in the museums of Cologne, Bonn and Nürnberg. This artist displays far more interest in integrating the backgrounds with the action, and his handling of space and perspective shows a sizeable advance, while his technique of rapid brushstrokes is quite different from the smooth layered approach of his predecessors. He influenced the **Master of St Severin** (active c.1490–1510), a prolific and uneven painter, with whom he probably shared a studio.

Ultimately, the Cologne School simply burned itself out, but it did come to a fitting climax with the **Master of the St Bartholomew Altar** (active c.1470–1510), whose highly idiosyncratic compositions display all the sense of freedom and mannerism which so often characterize the final fling of an artistic style. He was trained in Utrecht and may have been Dutch; at first he worked as a manuscript illuminator. His earlier panels are rather hesitant, but by about 1495 he was painting with ever-increasing confidence, using bright, enamel-type colours. Invariably his figures are executed as if in imitation of sculpture, and some of his paintings, such as the eponymous work in Munich and the *Crucifixion* triptych in Cologne, appear as trompe l'oeil versions of carved retables. Even more bizarre are canvases such as the *St Thomas Altar* in Cologne, where the highly realistic figures are made to float quite illogically in space.

Gothic elsewhere in Germany

In the early fifteenth century, Cologne unquestionably held the artistic lead in Germany; a gorgeous *Garden of Paradise* preserved in Frankfurt by an unknown Upper Rhenish master from about 1420 is a clear case of the hegemony this style enjoyed. The equally beautiful *Ortenberg Altar* in Darmstadt, painted the following decade by an anonymous Middle Rhenish artist, is likewise imbued with the idealized forms characteristic of Cologne, though it has a greater sense of monumentality.

As the century wore on, however, it was Swabian painters who pioneered moves towards more realistic forms, and thus paved the way to the Renaissance. First of these was **Lucas Moser**, probably a stained-glass designer by training, whose sole known work is the outside of the triptych still *in situ* in Tiefenbronn, dated 1431. Although the execution is still very soft and beautiful, an attempt is made at diminishing perspectives, while the water in the sea has both ripples and reflections. Very different is the *Wurzach Altar* of six years later, now in Berlin, which was made in the workshop of the great Ulm sculptor **Hans Multscher** (c.1400–67), though it's unresolved as to whether it was executed by the master himself, or by an unknown assistant who specialized in the painting side of the business. The figures in these Passion scenes are made deliberately crude, with exaggerated theatrical gestures, and seem to have been modelled on real-life peasants; they are about as far away from the contemporary work of Lochner as it is possible to get.

A far more refined realist painter was **Konrad Witz** (c.1400–46) of Rottweil, who spent his working life in Switzerland. His surviving legacy consists of about twenty panels taken from three separate retables; Basel and Geneva have the best examples, but others are in Berlin and Nürnberg. In them, he successfully resolved the new realism with traditional forms and grappled with such problems as perspective and movement. His figures have a sculptural quality and are treated as masses, not as means of portrayal; the rich and luminous colours employed are also an important feature. Most enduring of all was his contribution to landscape painting, being the first to introduce topographically accurate views of scenery, as opposed to cities, into his pictures. Witz's influence is discernible in the few surviving works of the **Master of the Darmstadt Passion**, who was active mid-century in the Middle Rhine region. **Friedrich Herlin** (c.1435–1499) of Nördlingen, who painted grave, severe figures, was another to follow his example; he in turn was succeeded by **Bartholomäus Zeitblom** (c.1455–1520) of Ulm.

Among Bavarian painters of this period, **Gabriel Angler** (c.1405–60), previously dubbed the Master of the Tegernsee Altar, was somewhat archaic in style but capable of highly dramatic effects, notably the curious *Crucifixion* in his native Munich, which is set within elaborate Gothic architecture. Also working in this city was the **Master of the Polling Panels** (active c.1434–50), who retained the International Gothic style, whilst injecting it with a dose of realism. In the same period, Nürnberg boasted the **Master of the Imhoff Altar** and the **Master of the Tucher Altar**; the latter's work is characterized by strongly drawn thick-set figures, prominent still lifes, and attempts at perspective. They were succeeded by **Hans Pleydenwurff** (c.1420–72), who showed a thorough knowledge of Netherlandish artists such as Bouts in colour, figure modelling and background cityscapes, often with small subsidiary scenes; he was also a notable portraitist. After his death, his workshop was taken over by **Michael Wolgemut** (1434–1519). **Rueland Frueauf** (c.1440–1507) founded the Danube School of painting in Passau and Salzburg; although few works by him survive, the *Man of Sorrows* in Munich is an arresting masterpiece, achieved by great economy of means. His son of the same name (c.1470–1545) carried on his style.

The late Gothic period also saw something of a revival in Westphalia. In Münster, **Johann Koerbecke** (active 1446–90) gave a more forceful treatment to facial expression than his Cologne contemporaries. A sensitive touch is revealed in the work of the **Master of Liesborn** (active late fifteenth century);

whilst **Derick Baegert** (c.1440–1515) imbued his paintings with a rugged dramatic quality.

Jan Joest of Kalkar (c.1455–1519) submerged himself in the art of the nearby Netherlands; he appears to have had a remarkable career, travelling as far afield as Spain, where he painted a retable for Palencia Cathedral which remains *in situ*. Two north German practitioners of the new Netherlandish-influenced realism were **Hinrik Funhof** (c. 1435–85), whose masterpiece is in St Johannis in Lüneburg, and Lübeck's **Hermen Rode** (active 1485–1504).

The rise of the graphic arts

Gutenberg's printing revolution sounded the death knell for illuminated manuscripts and gave an enormous stimulus to the black-and-white arts, with the traditional woodcut being followed by the new techniques of line engraving and drypoint, which appeared in the 1440s. At first, the forms were dominated by obscure figures from the Mainz area – the two pioneers were the so-called **Master of the Playing Cards**, whose reputation rests on an elaborate card deck, and **Master ES**, whose creations include a fantastic alphabet. Another engraver known only by his initials is **Master LCZ** of Bamberg, by whom some expressive panels also survive. **Israhel van Meckenem** (c.1440–1503), who came from the Lower Rhineland, was the first artist to exploit the new commercial opportunities offered by engravings, flooding the market with plagiarizations of his contemporaries in addition to original work, which includes a cycle of twelve love scenes with contemporary characters, costumes and backgrounds.

Another sizeable body of work is associated with the **Master of the Housebook** (active c.1470–1500). Many attempts have been made to equate him with **Erhard Reuwich**, who executed a series of woodcuts for a book on a journey to the Holy Land. His pseudonym derives from an extraordinary book of drawings in a private collection; it was the manual of a master of munitions at a princely court, and contains elaborate astrological groupings as well as scenes of warfare. Even finer are his delicate drypoints, which depict with both humanity and humour the everyday life of the time, from the fashions and fantasies of the small courts to the earthy pastimes of the peasantry. The draughtsman's technique is also evident in the linear form of his few paintings, which include two retables, one in Mainz, the other dispersed in the museums of Freiburg, Berlin and Frankfurt.

An equally great but very different graphic artist was **Martin Schongauer** (c.1450–91) of Colmar, which was then very much a German city. He has always been a revered figure, as he marks the transition from the late Gothic to the Renaissance, and is thus the founding father of the short but glorious period when the German visual arts reached the highest peaks of their achievement. Over a hundred surviving engravings show his successful fusion of realism and expressionism from northern artists with the exotic interests and technical innovations of space, form and perspective which characterize the Italian Renaissance. They were to serve as a model and an inspiration to the succeeding generation, who increasingly came to realize that the print was an important new democratic art form closely in tune with the spirit of the age, with potential for reaching a far wider public than had ever been possible before. Schongauer's surviving paintings are tantalizingly few but always of very high quality – they include the large *Madonna of the Rose Bush* in his native city, some damaged frescoes of *The Last Judgment* in nearby Breisach, and several little panels of *The Nativity*, the finest of which is in Berlin.

The triumph of the Renaissance

The most dominant personality in the history of German art was **Albrecht Dürer** (1471–1528), who trained under Wolgemut in his native Nürnberg. Dürer was a true man of the Renaissance, gaining a broad range of experiences in antithesis to the painstaking workshop traditions which were the lot of the medieval artist. He undertook travels to Italy, Switzerland, Alsace and the Low Countries, assimilating their traditions, and gained mastery in all artistic media, yet also found time to write and engage in mathematical and scientific research as well as to be involved in the Reformation, ending up excommunicated for Lutheran sympathies. Surprisingly, canvas painting does not always show Dürer at his best – he was at times rather conservative in his earlier religious panels, but increased in confidence with time, as can be seen in his valedictory *Four Apostles* in Munich. His portraits from life, however, are almost uniformly superb, laying bare the soul of the subject in penetrating psychological observations, as in *Jacob Muffel* and *Hieronymus Holzschuher*, both now in Berlin. With the woodcut, Dürer was in a class of his own; while still in his twenties he created an *Apocalypse* series of quite menacing power and profound imagination, which he printed and published himself. This was followed by two *Passion* series, a lovely *Life of the Virgin* and the stupendous *Triumphal Arch* commissioned by the Emperor Maximilian; he also made many memorable engravings, often deeply overlaid with symbolic meaning. Dürer was also the first artist to realize the possibilities of watercolour, executing beautiful landscapes and plant and animal studies. The originals of these are now rarely exhibited for conservation reasons, yet such works as *Young Hare* and *Blades of Grass* rank among the most familiar images in Renaissance art.

Hans Wertinger (c.1465–1533), who worked primarily in Landshut and Freising, was an ambitious and versatile artist who is nowadays remembered principally for his tiny, highly detailed paintings of the months and seasons, which were intended to adorn domestic interiors. In Munich, the Polish-born **Jan Polack** (active c.1480–1519) painted mannered altarpieces featuring emotional figures clad in swirling draperies, along with portraits more obviously imbued with the new Renaissance outlook.

A far more significant artistic centre was Augsburg, a seat of the Habsburg court. **Hans Holbein the Elder** (c.1465–1524) showed increasing Renaissance influence in his prolific output of retables, although he was never entirely able to free himself from the old forms. His brother-in-law **Hans Burgkmair** (1473–1531) was more successful, benefiting from a spell as Schongauer's assistant; he particularly delighted in the most luxuriant Italianate features, which he skilfully synthesized into his altars. This decorative talent was given full rein by Emperor Maximilian I, who commissioned him to supervise the overall programme of the huge series of woodcuts of his *Triumphal Procession*; many of the leading German artists, including Dürer, contributed, although the success of the project was due to the relish shown by Burgkmair. **Jörg Breu** (c.1475–1537) was another fine retable painter resident in the city, while **Bernhard Strigel** (c.1460–1528), who served as court portraitist, developed family groups as an independent art form.

By far the greatest painter Augsburg produced was **Hans Holbein the Younger** (1497/8–1543), but he left while still in his teens, and spent the rest of his career in Switzerland and England. He first settled in Basel (which retains by far the best collection of his paintings), where he was enormously productive in all kinds of media – portraits, altarpieces, decorative schemes of many types (now mostly lost) and woodcuts, including the celebrated *Dance of Death*. One of his masterpieces from this period, and one of the few works by him actually in Germany, is the *Madonna of Burgomaster Mayer* in Darmstadt, which combines sharply characterized portraits and a devotional theme. He subsequently concentrated almost exclusively on portraiture, developing a cool, detached style based on absolute technical mastery, and frequently incorporating amazingly precise still lifes based on the paraphernalia of the sitter's occupation; *The Danzig Merchant Georg Gisze*, now in Berlin, is an outstanding example. On his second visit to England, he became court painter to Henry VIII, and left a haunting series of drawings of that magnificent but tragic circle, though sadly few of the finished paintings have been preserved.

Lucas Cranach the Elder (1472–1553) was the earliest great Saxon painter. The first thirty years of his life are obscure; he is first known as a mature artist playing a dominant role in the Danube School, painting portraits and religious scenes set in lush and suggestively beautiful verdant landscapes. Whereas these works have consistently been admired, Cranach's long second phase at Wittenberg in the service of the Electors of Saxony is far more controversial. He ran the equivalent of a picture factory, often repeating the same subjects ad infinitum with only minor variations; the style is mannered with imperfections in drawing and subjects placed in wholly unrealistic relationships. Yet these were surely deliberate traits by a great humorist and individualist, whose sinuous nudes and erotic mythological scenes added a dimension to German painting which had previously been lacking. He seems to have invented the full-length portrait as a genre, and excelled at characterization. As a personal friend of Luther and Melanchthon, he created the definitive images of the leaders of the Reformation and made propaganda woodcuts on their behalf, but was not averse to accepting traditional commissions from the Catholics as well. His son **Lucas Cranach the Younger** (1515–86) took over the workshop and continued its tradition faithfully, albeit with a coarser style.

Albrecht Altdorfer (c.1480–1538) of Regensburg became the leading master of the Danube School; his luxuriant landscape backgrounds assume even greater significance than with Cranach, and at times the ostensible subject is quite unimportant, as with *St George and the Dragon* in Munich. Fantastic buildings also feature in several of his works, reflecting the fact that he was also a practising architect. When the figures do matter, they are integrated with their surroundings and given highly expressive tendencies, achieved by deliberate anatomical imprecisions and exaggerated gestures. Light is often an important feature, with unnaturally colourful effects; unorthodox aerial perspectives further distinguish his paintings. The largest group of Altdorfer's work, in which all these features appear, is still mostly *in situ* in the Austrian monastery of St Florian. However, his masterpiece is the *Battle of Darius and Alexander* in Munich, commissioned as part of a war series, each by different artists. The actual battle is depicted with all the skill of a miniaturist, yet it is set within a spectacular cosmic perspective in what ranks as one of the most formidable displays of sheer pyrotechnics in the history of painting. His chief follower was **Wolf Huber** (c.1490–1553) of Passau, who was rather more restrained in his effects.

The extreme tendency towards expression in German painting is found in the work of the painter known as **Grünewald**, although his real name was **Mathis Gothardt Neithardt** (c.1470/5–1528), who is almost a direct opposite of Dürer. Fully proficient in the new Renaissance developments of space and perspective, he used them as mere adjuncts to his sense of drama; he was also the only great German artist of his time who seems to have had no interest in the print. Even in an early work such as *The Mocking of Christ* in Munich, Grünewald's emotional power is evident. No artist ever painted Passion scenes with anything like the same harrowing intensity; in the words of the nineteenth-century French novelist Huysmans, "he promptly strikes you dumb with the fearsome nightmare of a Calvary". His huge folding polyptych, the *Isenheim Altar*, represents the majority of his surviving work. Though its panels are of uneven quality, its moods – ranging from a tender *Madonna and Child* to the blazing triumphant glory of *The Resurrection* – are of such variety that it deserves its reputation as the ultimate masterpiece of German painting. Ironically, its Colmar home is now French territory, though Karlsruhe possesses a later and even more overpowering *Crucifixion* panel.

Grünewald's art is so individual and overpowering that he had no successors. However, **Jerg Ratgeb** (c.1480–1526) must have come under his influence as his few works – fresco cycles in Frankfurt and Maulbronn, and the *Herrenberg Altar* in Stuttgart – have an even rawer expressiveness, which might have developed had he not been quartered for his leading role in the Peasants' War.

Of the younger generation of Renaissance artists, by far the most interesting is **Hans Baldung Grien** (1484/5–1545), a flawed genius who studied under Dürer and eventually settled in Strasbourg. Colour and volume play a large part in his pictures, but his fascination with the bizarre is the most obvious recurring element, with moralistic fantasies being among his finest works. Baldung's main religious works are two altars for the Freiburg Münster, but there is no concentration of his output, which is now spread among many museums. The late engravings such as *Wild Horses* and *Bewitched Stable Boy* are quite unlike the work of any other artist, and arguably rank as his greatest achievements.

Hans Suess von Kulmbach (c.1480–1522) and **Hans Leonard Schäuffelein** (c.1483–1539/40) were loyal followers of Dürer's example, but their productions ultimately lack his inspired touch; the specialist engravers, the brothers **Hans Sebald Beham** (1500–50) and **Barthel Beham** (1502–40), and the Westphalian **Heinrich Aldegraver** (1502–60) were arguably more successful at capturing his spirit. A personal expressive sense was added to the Düreresque idiom by the **Master of Messkirch** (active c.1530–45).

The early sixteenth century also saw a mushrooming of talented provincial portraitists who were able to satisfy the ever-increasing demand from the rising middle classes; they often painted religious and mythological subjects as well, but with less success. In Nürnberg, **Georg Pencz** (c.1500–50), possibly another pupil of Dürer, was strongly influenced by Venetian models. Augsburg at this time had **Cristoph Amberger** (c.1500–62), who was more associated with the court, and **Ulrich Apt** (c.1460–1532). **Hans Mielich** (1516–73) dominated artistic life in Munich for several decades, though his panel paintings are rather stiff and formal in comparison with his exquisite manuscript illuminations. The portraits of Frankfurt's **Conrad Faber von Creuznach** (c.1500–53) are particularly felicitous, with the sitters placed against landscapes reminiscent of the Danube School; he also executed a magnificent woodcut of the siege of his home city. **Barthel Bruyn** (1492/3–1555) was the first Cologne painter to break away from two centuries of tradition; in spite of several diverse influences, the city's great heritage seems to have made little impression on his art. In

Münster, **Ludger tom Ring the Elder** (1496–1547) founded a dynasty which specialized in slightly crude portraits and altars for both Protestant and Catholic use. His style was continued by his sons **Hermann tom Ring** (1521–96) and **Ludger tom Ring the Younger** (1522–84); the latter seems to have been the first German artist to treat still life as an independent form.

Mannerism and the early Baroque

Mannerism is already evident in the work of the generation after Dürer, but only appears in a full-blooded way with **Hans von Aachen** (1552–1616), who particularly excelled at sensual mythological subjects, and who played a leading role in the highly distinctive erotic style fostered at the court of Emperor Rudolf II in Prague. **Wendel Dietterlin** (c.1550–99) was a specialist architectural painter, but all his monumental facades and ceilings have been destroyed and only one panel, now in Karlsruhe, still survives, leaving his reputation resting on a book of over two hundred fantastical engravings – some of which hark back to the Gothic, while others are uncannily anticipatory of the High Baroque style to come. **Johann Rottenhammer** (1564–1625) travelled extensively in Italy, before returning to his native Augsburg. He came under the spell of Paolo Veronese's huge decorative works filled with figures; his response was to reduce such compositions onto little copper panels, adding an extra degree of luminosity into the landscapes.

This highly skilled technique was developed by his pupil, **Adam Elsheimer** (1578–1610), who settled in Rome and achieved a remarkable synthesis of diverse influences which gives his works a stature that belies their small size. Elsheimer drew on Altdorfer's heritage in creating a union between the subjects and nature, which Rottenhammer left as rather disparate features. He also seemed to share the earlier master's genius for light effects, and was particularly adept at night scenes and at strong contrasts of brightness and shadow derived from Caravaggio. A slow and deliberate worker, his early death meant that his legacy is numerically modest, but it was to influence such contrasting great successors as Rubens, Rembrandt and Claude. The largest assemblage of his work is the *Altar of the Holy Cross*, whose panels have been painstakingly reassembled over the years in his native Frankfurt; many of his best paintings are in Britain, due to the esteem in which he was held by the aristocrats of the Grand Tour.

Unfortunately, there was no great German successor, although his style was continued with varying success long after his death by **Johann König** (1586–1642). Elsheimer's influence is also evident in the legacy of **Gottfried Wals** (c.1595–1638), best known as the teacher of Claude, but a distinctive artist in his own right, specializing in small copper roundels of landscapes with figures bathed in light.

The other main German painter of the early seventeenth century, **Johann Liss** (1597–1629), was constantly on the move, leaving his native Holstein for the Low Countries and then Italy, absorbing their diverse traditions. One vein of his work, the small arcadian landscapes, reveals the impact of Elsheimer or at least his Roman followers, but his best canvases are far more monumental in scale, swaggering in the full pomp characteristic of the new Baroque age. These religious and mythological scenes, sometimes featuring sumptuous banquets, are executed with fluid brushwork in daringly unorthodox colours.

Liss was also to occupy a premature grave, and it seems as if German painting in the seventeenth century was to be jinxed, in contrast to its richness and diversity in this period over the rest of Europe. The Thirty Years' War, which so exhausted and preoccupied the country, acted as a massive restraint on artistic activity at the time, but was to fuel a long-standing vogue for depictions of battles and genre scenes of military life evidenced in the work of **Matthias Scheits** (c.1630–1700), though these tend to follow the decorative Dutch manner, rather than convey the true horrors the country suffered. An increased religious fervour as a result of the war is mirrored in the emotional cycles of canvases and frescoes by the Catholic convert **Michael Willmann** (1630–1706), the best of which are in the monasteries in Silesia (now part of Poland).

The Moravian-born **Georg Flegel** (1566–1638) was the first German artist to specialize exclusively in still life, initiating a vogue for this genre in his adopted city of Frankfurt. His pupil **Jakob Marell** (1613/4–81) was particularly accomplished at flower painting. Equally precise and detached, the works of the last major Frankfurt master of still life, **Abraham Mignon** (1640–79), are altogether lusher in effect, typically showing ripe fruit and flowers in full bloom. The deaf-mute **Wolfgang Heimbach** (c.1613–78) served for a time as portraitist to the Münster prince-bishops; he also painted small scenes of middle-class life and used nocturnal lighting to good effect. **Carl Andreas Ruthart** (c.1630–73) and **Philipp Peter Roos** (1655–1706) both specialized in painting animals.

Far more versatile than any of these was **Johann Friedrich Schönfeld** (1609–84), whose output is rather uneven due to an excessive number of changes of style in response to the diversity he encountered on his Italian travels. His best paintings are colourful history scenes with elaborate backgrounds, painted under the influence of the classically derived compositions of Poussin which held sway in Rome, but tempered by the more light-hearted Neapolitan approach. **Joachim von Sandrart** (1606–88) is nowadays principally remembered as the pioneering historian of German art, but he had a long and successful peripatetic international career as a portraitist, and was also an accomplished allegorical painter. The only German artist to fall under the spell of Rembrandt was **Jürgen Ovens** (1623–78), who spent part of his career in Amsterdam in the circle of the great Dutch master, before returning to his native Schleswig-Holstein, where he produced portraits and history scenes in his teacher's most Baroque vein.

However, the most significant art works produced in mid-seventeenth-century Germany were the detailed engravings of towns, known as *Topographia Germaniae*, started by **Matthäus Merian the Elder** (1593–1650). The project was continued by his sons **Matthäus Merian the Younger** (1621–87), who was also a notable portraitist, and **Caspar Merian** (1627–86). In due course, the appearances of some two thousand German communities – a unique pictorial record – were preserved for posterity. The brothers' half-sister **Maria Sibylla Merian** (1647–1717) was raised and trained by her step-father Jakob Marell, and followed in his footsteps as a floral specialist, albeit with more of a scientific bent.

Late Baroque, Rococo and Neoclassicism

The best late Baroque German painting is not to be found in any museum, but on the walls of the ornate pilgrimage churches of Bavaria and Baden-Württemberg. These buildings, which aimed at fusing all the visual arts into a coherent synthesis, are among the most original creations in the country. Their rich interior decoration formed an intrinsic part of the architecture from the outset, and was often the work of the same masters.

One of the most accomplished of these was **Cosmas Damian Asam** (1686–1739), who formed a team with his sculptor brother, Egid Quirin Asam. At first they decorated existing churches, such as the Dom in Freising, but later moved on to undertaking the entire programme themselves. They trained in Rome and were for the most part loyal to its dignified High Baroque, rather than to the more frivolous Rococo derivatives favoured by their fellow countrymen. C.D. Asam's ceiling frescoes fall into two separate categories – the trick device of diminishing perspective in the manner of the Italian Jesuit Andrea Pozzo, and a more conventional spatial format of open heavens.

Johann Baptist Zimmerman (1680–1758), in contrast, is fully Rococo; he did not design buildings himself, but enjoyed a particularly close relationship with two of the leading architects of the time: François Cuvilliés, with whom he collaborated on the Munich Residenz and Schloss Nymphenburg; and his own younger brother Dominikus, with whom he worked at Steinhausen and the Wieskirche. Two other major fresco painters were **Johann Georg Bergmüller** (1688–1762) and **Matthäus Günther** (1705–88), who successively directed the Augsburg Academy, one of several founded in the major cities in order to foster a theoretical approach to painting.

By this time, Prussia had arisen as a major power in European affairs, and was by far the dominant German state. Frederick the Great was a major patron of the arts, but he was also a Francophile whose court painter was the Parisian-born **Antoine Pesne** (1683–1757). This artist was commissioned to paint allegorical and mythological decorative schemes for the royal palaces, but his realistic portraits, very much in the French manner of the time with rich colours and subtle lighting effects, were more successful and ultimately highly influential, serving as the model for later Berlin artists. His most important pupil was **Bernhard Rode** (1725–97), who was also involved in the work on the palaces, but who is seen at his best in quietly observed genre scenes. For the last period of his life, he directed the Berlin Academy. Another of this circle was **Daniel Nikolaus Chodowiecki** (1726–1801), although his talent was best suited to vignette etchings, mostly to illustrate books. A later Berlin artist, **Asmus Jakob Carstens** (1754–98) was also at his finest in black and white media, executing large chalk cartoons of Classical subjects.

One of the guiding lights of the movement was **Anton Raffael Mengs** (1728–79), son of the court painter in Dresden, who had ruthlessly prepared him for artistic fame from a very early age. Mengs was to have an amazingly successful career in Germany, Italy and Spain. He was a key theorist and guru of the new Neoclassicism; his works are enormously skilful technically, but emotionally cold. The Swiss-born **Anton Graff** (1736–1835) was also a leading academic portraitist in Dresden. This same city was home to a succession of landscape painters throughout the century, whose work foreshadows the far more arresting compositions of the Romantics; **Johann Alexander Thiele** (1685–1752) was the first and most accomplished of these.

A strict Neoclassical style was adopted at the Kassel Academy under **Johann Heinrich Tischbein** (1722–89). This was modified by his nephews **Johann Friedrich August Tischbein** (1750–1812) and **Johann Heinrich Wilhelm Tischbein** (1751–1829), who introduced the greater warmth found in English and French works of the time, though both remained loyal academicians. The latter's *Goethe in the Campagna* in Frankfurt is the most celebrated work of the dynasty.

Another family of painters had as by far its most accomplished member **Januarius Zick** (1730–97), who turned his back on his academic training. He was a theatrical but effective frescoist in the grand manner, as can be seen in the cycles in Wiblingen and Bruchsal. In contrast, his canvases are often of modest size, achieving an original synthesis of the light effects usually found in Rembrandt's deeply intimate small-scale works with the airy Rococo grace of Watteau.

Romanticism

The Romantic movement, a reaction against the rigidity of Neoclassicism but with the same Roman roots, was particularly strong in Germany; the rich outpourings of music and literature make it one of the supreme high points in the country's cultural history. Although there was not the same depth of talent in painting, the haunting and highly original landscapes of **Caspar David Friedrich** (1774–1840) form a fitting visual counterpart to the works of the great poets and composers of the time. Friedrich created a new spiritual way of looking at scenery: it was always the immensity and majesty of Nature that he sought to convey, often using the technique of enormously long perspectives. Unlike his great predecessor Altdorfer, he did not stress the unity of man and landscape, but rather the unconquerable power of the latter. Where figures are introduced, they are typically seen from the back, contemplating the wonders before them; in the more common absence of humans, the evidence of Man's presence tends to stress his fragility and ephemeral status – as in the famous *Eismeer* in Hamburg, or the many scenes with classical temples and Gothic abbeys – in comparison with the omnipotent changelessness of the surroundings.

The influence of Friedrich's way of looking can sometimes be detected in the canvases of **Karl Friedrich Schinkel** (1781–1841), who was forced by financial considerations to turn to painting, where he abandoned the Neoclassicism of his buildings in favour of vast panoramas and architectural fantasies. **Leo von Klenze** (1794–1864), the other great architect of German Neoclassicism, was likewise a gifted occasional painter, producing romanticized views of the ruins of Greece and Rome. More orthodox followers of Friedrich include **Carl Gustav Carus** (1787–1869) and **Ernst Ferdinand Oehme** (1797–1855).

Philipp Otto Runge (1777–1810) might have developed into Friedrich's figurative counterpart had he lived longer. He had enormously grandiose ideas, aiming to recover the lost harmony of the universe through the symbolism of colours and numbers, and began a project called *The Times of Day*, of four panels over 8m in height, which he aimed to install in a specially designed building in which poetry and music would be performed. That he managed to persuade Goethe to co-operate in this suggests that there was genuine substance to this apparently utopian dream, but it was never executed and only studies survive, leaving Runge's reputation to rest largely on his portraits, particularly the oversized ones depicting children.

Johann Friedrich Overbeck (1789–1869) was another Romantic with original convictions, settling in Rome where he and the short-lived **Franz Pforr** (1788–1812) founded the **Nazarene Brotherhood** of painters who lived like monks in a deconsecrated monastery. They produced two large co-operative fresco cycles: *The Story of Joseph*, now in the Alte Nationalgalerie in Berlin, and another, still *in situ*, of scenes taken from Italian Renaissance literature. These detailed works emphasized theme and content at the expense of form.

Whereas Overbeck remained in Italy, his collaborators **Peter von Cornelius** (1783–1867), **Philipp Veit** (1793–1877), **Julius Schnorr von Carolsfeld** (1794–1872) and **Wilhelm Schadow** (1788–1862) returned to Germany where they pursued careers in the academies. Cornelius had spells in charge of the two most dominant, Düsseldorf and Munich, and aimed to establish a tradition of monumental historical painting to rival the great frescoes of Italy. Although both influential and genuinely popular in its day, this style of painting has, for the past century, attracted nothing but critical scorn, appearing as an empty display of bombastics. It can still be seen all over the country, often desecrating the walls of great medieval buildings; among the better efforts are the cycles by **Alfred Rethel** (1816–59) in the Aachen Rathaus and by the Austrian-born **Moritz von Schwind** (1804–71) in Karlsruhe's Kunsthalle, and the Wartburg near Eisenach. The latter was the most refined illustrator of the Romantic view of the German Middle Ages, whose ethos he captured in numerous beautifully coloured and detailed canvases, such as *The Knight Kuno von Falkenstein* in Leipzig. **Ferdinand Olivier** (1785–1841) painted narrative canvases in the Nazarene style, as well as more conventional Romantic landscapes.

Standing somewhat apart are the expansive, open-ended fresco views painted in Munich by Ludwig I's court artist **Carl Rottmann** (1797–1850). Other Munich artists took the grand academic manner to its most extreme. Prominent among them were **Wilhelm von Kaulbach** (1805–76), a pupil of Cornelius, who produced monumental designs for the decoration of the Neue Pinakothek, and **Karl von Piloty** (1826–86), whose huge, highly theatrical history paintings were intended to evoke patriotic sentiment.

Romanticism in one form or another flourished throughout the nineteenth century. The brothers **Andreas Achenbach** (1815–1910) and **Oswald Achenbach** (1827–1905) continued in Friedrich's manner; the former was particularly successful at evocative northern scenery, whereas the latter added popular scenes to his pictures. **Carl Blechen** (1798–1840) also began in this style, but his later works, following a visit to Paris, became more consciously realist. **Anselm Feuerbach** (1829–80) pursued a heavily Italianate form of Romanticism in his portraits and densely crowded mythological scenes. There is a highly personal mixture of the Neoclassical and Romantic in **Hans von Marées** (1837–87), who achieved his masterpiece in his one commission for monumental frescoes, the Aquarium in Naples. For long out of critical favour, his canvases have recently begun to attract a great deal of interest. The inconsistent **Hans Thoma** (1839–1924) tried many styles in his time; the Romantic views of the Black Forest are by far the most successful.

Other nineteenth-century styles

Although many different trends were current in nineteenth-century German painting, none of them can match the vitality of the best Romantic work. A style which was largely confined to the country and its immediate neighbours from about 1815 to 1848 was Biedermeierstil, a bourgeois-inspired Classicism which drew on the pleasant aspects of living. Its principal exponent was **Carl**

Spitzweg (1808–85), a gentle humourist whose canvases poke fun at the pretentions and hypocrisies of the day, favourite targets being bored soldiers, careless servant girls, lustful monks, lonely widowers, hobby-obsessed bachelors and impecunious poets willing to sacrifice everything for their art. Although nowadays regarded with ever-increasing affection as a quintessentially German artist, Spitzweg was strongly influenced by the French Barbizon School in his landscapes, while his figures are based on the caricatures of their countryman Honoré Daumier.

Franz Krüger (1797–1857) chronicled Berlin life of the time in a more straight-laced vein, particularly in his ceremonial scenes and architectural views; **Eduard Gaertner** (1801–77) executed more felicitous topographical views of Berlin, while the Prussian court painter **Carl Graeb** (1816–84) produced exquisitely detailed little works of the same city and of the palaces and gardens of nearby Potsdam. Though he sometimes worked in the Düsseldorf academic manner, **Georg Friedrich Kersting** (1785–1847) was at his best in small-scale interiors, in which he showed his interest in everyday objects and activities as matters of beauty in their own right. The Dresden artist **Ludwig Richter** (1804–83) was a fine landscape painter, but again his true métier lay in a quite different field, in this case illustrations of legends for children's books. His pupil **Edouard Leonhardi** (1825–1905) specialized in highly detailed, meticulously executed forest scenes.

In contrast to this movement, there was a continued demand for official portraitists; one of the most accomplished was **Franz von Lenbach** (1836–1904), who painted Bismarck eighty times. **Franz Xaver Winterhalter** (1805–73) had the most dazzling career of all, progressing round all the main European courts, leaving behind unremittingly flattering portrayals of smug monarchs.

Standing in total contrast is the versatile **Adolph Menzel** (1815–1905), who complemented his superb technique with meticulous background research on his subject-matter. He painted wonderfully characterized portraits throughout his long life; few of these are in oil, as he preferred to use chalk, pencil, pastel or gouache for portraiture. Among his most hauntingly distinctive compositions are small paintings of unoccupied interiors, but he adopted the grand manner for his history scenes (predominantly of the life of Frederick the Great), which nonetheless eschew the heroic idealized imagery then fashionable in favour of a psychological approach. In the second half of his career, Menzel devoted much of his energy to documenting contemporary life, and his masterpiece, *The Iron Rolling Mill* in the Alte Nationalgalerie in Berlin, was the first painting to offer a detailed and accurate picture of the realities of working life in the Industrial Age.

Germany's other leading Realist was **Wilhelm Leibl** (1844–1900), who aimed to re-create the technical skill of the old masters. To this end he conducted such experiments as reviving tempera to create an enamel-like surface, and painting with the attention to detail of a miniaturist, as in *Three Women in Church* in Hamburg. Much of his finest work was done in the 1870s, when he lived in rural Bavaria, and used peasants as real-life models. **Wilhelm Trübner** (1851–1917) was another practitioner of Realism, one who undertook a broad mix of subjects.

Impressionism was very slow to catch on, and never seems to have suited the German temperament, but three major artists adopted it at some point in their careers. Of these, **Max Liebermann** (1847–1935), originally favoured the sombre colours of the Barbizon School and the Realists, and it was in the latter vein that he executed his many large, highly detailed canvases of life in Dutch orphanages, schools and old peoples' homes. Following his Impressionist phase, he ended his long working life as the most sought-after society portraitist of the Weimar Republic. **Lovis Corinth** (1858–1925) painted an unusually wide range of subjects; his religious and mythological canvases often exude a sense of raw emotional power and menace, yet he also produced sun-filled interior views and highly erotic nudes. Among his most distinctive compositions are the late views of the Walchensee in Bavaria, executed in cold colours; these postdate a stroke which had left his original painting hand paralysed. **Max Slevogt** (1868–1932) was also a book illustrator and, late in life, a painter of monumental frescoes.

Liebermann was the leading figure in the Berlin section of the **Secession movement** which began in the 1890s; this was a reaction by the avant-garde against the stultifying power wielded by the academies. Prominent members of the earlier Munich group were **Fritz von Uhde** (1848–1911), who painted intimate genre scenes and strikingly original re-interpretations of Biblical stories in contemporary dress, and **Franz von Stuck** (1863–1928), an artist of violent mythological scenes, humorous drawings and large-scale decorative work. Based in the artistic backwater of Leipzig, the painter, sculptor and engraver **Max Klinger** (1857–1920) cut a somewhat solitary figure; although his output is very uneven in quality, he was capable, particularly in his graphic work, of real emotional power.

The most successful of several artists' colonies was that at Worpswede near Bremen, which was founded by **Fritz Mackensen** (1866–1953) in 1889. It survives to this day, though much of the best work done there was in its early years, when Mackensen and his friends **Otto Modersohn** (1856–1943), and **Hans am Ende** (1864–1918) produced a stream of canvases illustrating the bleakness of the local landscape and the harshness of life for its inhabitants.

Expressionism

Much as the early part of the nineteenth century saw the dominance of Romanticism in German painting, so the first decades of the twentieth century came under the sway of Expressionism, a new and largely indigenous style, which aimed to root modern painting firmly in the tradition of the old German masters, and to establish it on an equal footing with France, for some time the dominant force in world art. Because of the entrenched power of existing interests, artists found they had to bind themselves into **groups** in order to make an impact; the early history of Expressionism is particularly associated with two of these.

Although its members were younger, **Die Brücke** (The Bridge) was the first to be founded, in 1905. Its initial personnel, **Ernst Ludwig Kirchner** (1880–1938), **Erich Heckel** (1883–1970) and **Karl Schmidt-Rottluff** (1884–1976), were architecture students in Dresden who felt constrained by the inability of their subject to capture the immediate freshness of inspiration. Consequently, they turned to painting, in which none had much experience; they were shortly joined by **Max Pechstein** (1881–1955) and **Otto Müller** (1874–1930). They valued colour as a component in its own right, and later strove to enhance its surface effect as well. Their devotion to the country's artistic heritage was shown in the emphasis they placed on feeling, and on their revival of the woodcut as a valid alternative to oils.

The group moved to Berlin, where they turned away from their original preoccupation with landscapes to the depiction of city life. Kirchner developed into the leader and best artist of the group. *Three Women in the Street*, now in Essen, is a key work; its strong sense of line shows the impact made by the arts of primitive peoples, then being appreciated in Europe for the first time. The group broke up in 1913, and thereafter each artist pursued an independent career. Kirchner turned to decorative design in the 1920s, working on embroideries and tapestries; his later paintings show a stronger sense of abstraction. Heckel's work is closest to Kirchner's, though he was later to add a greater sense of realism to his pictures. Pechstein, at the time regarded as the most important Expressionist of all, has since suffered a slump in reputation; he was the most loyal to naturalistic representation and thus stands furthest removed from the path followed by Schmidt-Rottluff. Gypsy culture features strongly in Müller's work; he seems to have felt a genuine affinity with it, and spent much of the 1920s travelling among Balkan communities.

The second group of artists was **Der Blaue Reiter** (The Blue Rider), a strongly intellectual movement originating in Munich which aimed at uniting all the arts. Its name is taken from its magazine, which appeared only once (in 1912); it was very loosely structured and far more diverse than Die Brücke, with the lead being taken by two contrasting artistic personalities. The Russian-born **Wassily Kandinsky** (1866–1944) was a pioneer of pure abstraction, using fluid and soft forms, but strong and vibrant colours; he was also a noted writer and used words as the starting points for his images. **Franz Marc** (1880–1916), on the other hand, always retained at least a partial form of representation in his compositions. He was devoted to nature, and animals are a recurrent theme in his art; he regarded them as noble and uncorrupted, the complete antithesis to Man. At first they appear detached in the foreground; from 1913, when he adopted more abstract methods, they are more closely integrated with their surroundings. Geometry was always important to Marc, and he favoured prismatic colours, to which he attached a mystical significance. His development was cut short by the outbreak of war, and he died in combat.

This fate also befell an even younger member of the group, **August Macke** (1887–1914). Although Macke was clearly influenced by the new Cubist movement, his works are always representational, and he ranks as the most poetic and gentle of all the Expressionists. The figures are unmistakable; slim and column-like, they glide across the picture surface, taking their Sunday stroll in the park, or indulging in a bit of window-shopping. More often than not, they wear a hat, which serves to distinguish them, as their facial features are never included. Strong colours are used, but they are never strident; they rather add to the happy and relaxed atmosphere.

Paul Klee (1879–1940), born in Switzerland but having German nationality as well, was the fourth main member of the group. He never concerned himself with any of the social, political or psychological problems of the age, but preferred to construct his own abstract language in which he aimed to recapture the mystery and magic of the universe. To this end, he developed a series of fractured and fragmented forms – arcs, forks and bars – which were usually painted black against a coloured background. In the 1920s, when they worked at the Bauhaus, he and Kandinsky formed **Die Blauen Vier** (The Blue Four) as a successor to Der Blaue Reiter.

The other members were **Alexej Jawlensky** (1864–1941), also of Russian birth, who specialized in characterful portrait heads; and **Lyonel Feininger** (1871–1956), who was born and died in New York, but who can be regarded as the most loyal German Cubist, being most notable for his architectural and marine scenes. Russian influence is apparent in the paintings of **Heinrich**

Campendonk (1889–1957), the youngest member of Der Blaue Reiter, although his preferred medium was the woodcut.

A number of Expressionists unattached to either group were active in the Rhine-Ruhr area, where Macke also spent much of his life. Throughout a very long career, **Christian Rohlfs** (1849–1938) tried many different styles; he clearly came under the influence of the Impressionists but never fully adopted their manner. His true artistic personality did not emerge until his Expressionist phase, particularly the architectural paintings he made in Soest and Erfurt, and the very late flower pieces. Rohlfs clearly inspired **Wilhelm Morgner** (1891–1917), another war casualty. **Heinrich Nauen** (1880–1940) was one of several Expressionists who were quite overt about following French leads, in his case Matisse and the Fauves, whose bright colours form an important feature of his hybrid style.

Hans Purrmann (1880–1966) was Matisse's most loyal German disciple, while Fauvism, particularly the Classically-inspired works of Derain, heavily influenced **Carl Hofer** (1878–1955). Primitive art as filtered through Gauguin made a strong impression on **Paula Modersohn-Becker** (1876–1907), the most talented artist of the colony at Worpswede. Whether or not she is really an Expressionist is debatable, as she did not concern herself with drama or emotions, though her favourite *Mother and Child* theme has achieved a certain poignancy as she later died in childbirth.

The most individualistic Expressionist of all, even though he had a spell as a member of Die Brücke, was **Emil Hansen** (1867–1956), generally called **Nolde** after his birthplace. In his depictions of the rugged North Sea coastline that was his home, he can be regarded as the successor to Friedrich. However, there's no sense of romance in Nolde's landscapes, which convey the harsh and forbidding nature of the terrain and its climate, emphasized in the way he captured its special colours and light effects by means of rich, strong and violently contrasting tones. Flowers and garden scenes provide a lighter note, but he also revived the somewhat lost art of religious painting, in which he aimed to recreate something of the intensity of Grünewald, along with the simple devotion he found in primitive art.

Ludwig Meidner (1884–1966) was dubbed the most Expressionist of the Expressionists, as a result of the powerful apocalyptic visions he painted before the war, which stand at the opposite extreme to the primitive trends in the movement. The union of all the arts sought by so many found its best individual manifestation in the work of **Ernst Barlach** (1870–1938). Primarily a sculptor, he was also a talented graphic artist, illustrating his own plays and travel writings. Another sculptor, **Käthe Kollwitz** (1867–1945) achieved great emotional power in her pacifist woodcuts, engravings and lithographs of wartime horrors.

Other twentieth-century movements

Expressionism, in spite of its dominance, does not by any means cover the entire richness of German art in the early part of the twentieth century. The nihilistic Dada movement, which grew up during the war, included **Kurt Schwitters** (1887–1948), who took the concept of non-art to its extreme, experimenting with collages incorporating pieces of torn-up paper before moving on to using rubbish as his basic component. He dubbed his art *Merz* after the letters from one of the pieces of paper he used, and intended his life's work to be a huge composition which would fill a house, but the first two completed versions were destroyed, and his last attempt, in exile in England, was unfinished at his death. **Hannah Höch** (1889–1978) and the Austrian-born **Raoul Hausmann** (1886–1944) were two rather milder Dadaists.

George Grosz (1893–1959) also began in this style, but his later works were more representational. A committed Communist, he was a savage satirist, particularly in his humorous drawings, ruthlessly attacking the corrupt and decadent vested interests of the Weimar Republic. Ironically, he was entranced by America and emigrated there just before the Nazi rise to power. Another prominent Dadaist and left-winger was **John Heartfield** (1891–1968), who adopted an anglicized form of his original name, Helmut Herzfeld, in protest at German xenophobia. Best known as the inventor of the photomontage, which he used to devastating effect to attack the Nazis from his exile in Czechoslovakia and Britain, he settled in the GDR after World War II, where his work, in the service of the state, lost much of its sharpness.

Inevitably, there grew a tendency which stood in polar opposition to Expressionism: **Neue Sachlichkeit** (New Objectivity), a term first used in 1923 to describe trends already apparent. This can be thought of as an updated form of realism, which aimed at depicting subjects in a straightforward and detailed way. Some of Grosz's work belongs to this style, but its finest practitioner was **Otto Dix** (1891–1969), who had been profoundly affected by the war. This formed a persistent subject of his work, although he used it to depict Man's suffering as opposed to any directly political overtone. He aimed to recapture the actual technique of the old masters, and his portraits show larger-than-life characters under a rich sheen of paint. In spite of the overt eroticism of many of his canvases, he was also drawn to the Passion, on which he placed a humanitarian and allegorical interpretation.

The former Dadaist **Christian Schad** (1894–1982) represents a more extreme form of Dix's style, with many explicit scenes drawn from the bohemian world he himself inhabited; **Rudolf Schlichter** (1890–1955) had similar preoccupations. In contrast, there was a romantically inclined wing of this movement, exemplified by **Georg Schrimpf** (1898–1938). The Jewish artist **Felix Nussbaum** (1900–1944), an associate of Neue Sachlichkeit, is best known for his sombre late works depicting the Auschwitz concentration camp where he was murdered.

Max Beckmann (1884–1950) defies classification, lying somewhere between Expressionism and Neue Sachlichkeit. He believed it was the artist's duty to express Man's spiritual condition. To this end, he used the self-portrait as a means of expressing his changing reaction to world events, making himself appear in different guises, whether as clown, convict, king or hero. The symbolism associated with Carnival and the circus is a recurring theme in his work, as are the use of gesture to reveal character and the manipulation of space. To express opposition to the Nazis, he took to the anachronistic format of the triptych.

Max Ernst (1891–1976) was another who began as a Dadaist, producing first collages and then frottages. However, he is best known as one of the leading Surrealist painters, a style he turned to on its foundation in 1924, and for which his early interest in psychology and the creative works of the mentally ill made him most suitable. To what extent he can be considered a German artist is debatable, as he left his native country in 1922, taking first American then French nationality. The most accomplished Surrealist who can definitely be classed as German is **Edgar Ende** (1901–66), whose compositions are directly comparable with those of the Italian Giorgio de Chirico. **Wolfgang Lettl** (b. 1919) keeps the tradition alive in a distinctive manner, in which humour is very much to the fore.

Oskar Schlemmer (1888–1943) was one of the most varied German painters of the century, touched by seemingly every style; he also practised both decorative and functional art. Among the practitioners of abstraction following Kandinsky and Klee, **Willi Baumeister** (1889–1955), **Ernst Wilhelm Nay** (1902–68) and **Alfred Wolfgang Schulze** (1913–51), better known as **Wols**, acquired the greatest reputations.

Apart from Heartfield, leading luminaries of the GDR artistic establishment in its early years included **Otto Nagel** (1894–1967), who had established his reputation before the war as a chronicler of proletarian life in Berlin, and Dresden's **Hans Grundig** (1901–58), whose powerful visionary images show an obvious debt to medieval and Renaissance predecessors. For most of its life, however, the state fostered a particularly sterile form of Socialist Realism as the only acceptable form of artistic activity; artists who rebelled against this, such as **Roger Loewig** (b.1930), faced persecution and eventual expulsion. Few products of the state-sponsored style still survive on public display, except as mere historical curiosities. An exception is the most spectacular commission granted by the regime, the controversial *Panorama* in Bad Frankenhausen in honour of the Peasants' War, painted by Leipzig professor **Werner Tübke** (b. 1929).

In the postwar Federal Republic, avant-garde artistic activity flourished, thanks to generous subsidy levels by all tiers of government. How many of the painters whose work currently lines the walls of the country's many museums of modern art will prove to be of lasting significance remains a moot point. Among those who have gained international standing, **Georg Baselitz** (b.1940) paints figuratively but groups the different components of his works in a deliberately arbitrary way. **Sigmar Polke** (b.1941) can be seen as something of a disciple of Dadaism in the objects he tacks on to his canvases, mirroring his interest in German society's obsession with kitsch. **Anselm Kiefer** (b.1945) has been concerned with the German psyche in its historical context, focusing on gestures, symbols and myths. **Jörg Immendorff** (b.1945) and **Bernd Koberling** (b.1938) have taken an overtly left-wing political stance in their work, with ecological themes also being associated with the latter.

Books

Books with this symbol ★ are particularly recommended.

Travel

Heinrich Heine *Deutschland: A Winter's Tale* (also included in the *Complete Poems*). This magisterial verse travelogue describes Heine's journey from exile in Paris to his family home in Hamburg. It's full of insight into the places he passed through, and contains devastating exposés of mid-nineteenth-century German society. *The Harz Journey* (included in Penguin's *Selected Prose*) is one of the author's *Travel Pictures* – much imitated travelogues featuring inserted poems within the narrative.

Patrick Leigh Fermor *A Time of Gifts*. The author set out to walk from Rotterdam to Constantinople in 1933, travelling along the Rhine and Danube valleys en route. Written up forty years later in luscious, hyper-refined prose, it presents the fresh sense of youthful discovery distilled through considerable subsequent learning and reflection. Prewar Germany is shown suffering from all the schizophrenic influences of the era, yet the country's enduring beauty is also captured.

Claudio Magris *Danube*. Absorbing, searching exploration of the great river and the places along it from the Black Forest to the Black Sea, mixing travelogue with all manner of scholarly diversions; not the easiest of reads, but rewards the effort.

★ **Mark Twain** *A Tramp Abroad*. The early, German-based part of this book, particularly the descriptions of Heidelberg, show Twain in top form, by turns humorous and evocative. There's an over-the-top appendix entitled "The Awful German Language", which mercilessly pillories the over-complexity of "this fearsome tongue".

History

★ **Roland Bainton** *Here I Stand*. The best and liveliest biography of Martin Luther, one of the undisputed titans of European history.

Geoffrey Barraclough *Origins of Modern Germany*. The most easily digestible general introduction to the country's history, tackling the medieval period better than any more specialized book.

Volker Berghahn *Germany and the Approach of War in 1914*. An instructive general picture of Germany before World War I. It chronicles the political, economic and social pressures, and succeeds in giving plausible explanations for the apparently inevitable.

Owen Chadwick *The Reformation*. Traces the German origins of the biggest-ever rupture in the fabric of the Church, and follows its impact on the rest of Europe.

★ **Einhard and Notker the Stammerer** *Two Lives of*

Charlemagne. Einhard was a leading courtier in the service of the founder of the Holy Roman Empire, and provided a beautifully written, all-too-short biography of his master. Written a century later, Notker's book is a series of monkish anecdotes, many no doubt apocryphal, which help flesh out the overall portrait of Charlemagne.

Mary Fulbrook *A Concise History of Germany*. "Concise" is the key word for this general history, whose brevity is simultaneously its strength and its weakness.

Sebastian Haffner *The Rise and Fall of Prussia*. A short study of the legend behind the remarkable state which forged German unity in 1871, yet vanished from the map in 1947.

Friedrich Heer *The Holy Roman Empire*. Comprehensive account of the thousand-year history of the First German Reich.

Golo Mann *The History of Germany Since 1787*. Written by the son of Thomas Mann, this wide-ranging study traces not only the politics but also the intellectual and cultural currents of the period.

Nancy Mitford *Frederick the Great*. Lively biography of the man who brought Prussia to the forefront of German affairs, and to a place among the great powers of Europe.

Detlev Pleukert *The Weimar Republic*. Trenchant dissection of the endlessly fascinating but fundamentally flawed state – until recently the only experiment at a united and democratic German nation – which survived for just fourteen years.

Alexandra Richie *Faust's Metropolis*. The most detailed history of Berlin in English, with the emphasis placed firmly on the momentous events of the twentieth century.

Tacitus *The Germania*. Brilliant series of concise analyses of each of the warlike Germanic tribes, which are often compared favourably with the author's native Rome. Some of the observations about German character are startlingly prophetic.

A.J.P. Taylor *Bismarck: The Man and the Statesman*. The controversial British historian here provides a typically stirring portrait of the ruthless schemer who forged (reluctantly, in the author's view) the nineteenth-century unification of Germany.

★ **Veronica (C.V.) Wedgwood** *The Thirty Years War*. Easily the most accomplished book on the series of conflicts which devastated the country and divided the continent in the first half of the seventeenth century.

Andrew Wheatcroft *The Habsburgs*. Wide-ranging history of the extraordinary dynasty which not only dominated German affairs for several centuries, but controlled much of the rest of Europe as well.

Nazism and World War II

Antony Beevor *Berlin: The Downfall 1945*. A grand, painstakingly researched narrative on the collapse of the Third Reich.

Alan Bullock *Hitler: A Study in Tyranny*. Ever since it was published, this scholarly yet highly readable tome has ranked as the classic single-volume biography of the failed Austrian artist and discharged army corporal whose evil genius fooled a nation and caused the deaths of millions.

Michael Burleigh *The Third Reich: A New History*. A massive book in every way, offering a highly original portrait of Nazism – which the author interprets as an evil political religion – and its impact on the wider world.

Joachim Fest *The Face of the Third Reich*. Mainly of interest for its biographies of the gallery of rogues surrounding the Führer – Göring, Goebbels, Hess, Himmler, Speer et al.

Daniel Jonah Goldhagen *Hitler's Willing Executioners*. This controversial tome, which has attracted praise and derision in almost equal measure, sets out to prove that guilt for the implementation of the Holocaust lies with a far broader constituency than the Nazi elite.

Adolf Hitler *Table Talk*. Hitler in his own words: Martin Bormann, one of his inner circle, recorded the dictator's pronouncements at meetings between 1941 and 1944. The early *Mein Kampf*, a series of rambling, irrational and hysterical outbursts on every subject under the sun, is also of interest, as it genuinely constituted Hitler's blueprint for power.

Ian Kershaw *Hitler*. A recent and well-nigh definitive two-volume biography of Hitler, the first part covering the years up to 1936, the second, the last nine years of his life.

Guido Knopp *Hitler's Holocaust, Hitler's Henchmen, Hitler's Children, Hitler's Women*. A series of thematic books on the Third Reich, written with a general rather than an academic audience in mind.

Gitta Sereny *The German Trauma*. This memoir by the distinguished investigative journalist focuses on the impact made by Nazism on the history of the twentieth century, and includes accounts of her famous interviews with Albert Speer and Leni Riefenstahl.

William Shirer *The Rise and Fall of the Third Reich*. Notwithstanding the inordinate length and excessive journalese, this book by an American journalist stationed in German during the Nazi period is full of insights and is ideal for dipping into, with the help of its exhaustive index.

Hugh Trevor-Roper *The Last Days of Hitler*. A brilliant reconstruction of the closing chapter of the Third Reich, set in the Berlin Bunker. Trevor-Roper subsequently marred his reputation as the doyen of British historians by authenticating the forged *Hitler Diaries*, which have themselves been the subject of several books.

Postwar society and politics

John Ardagh *Germany and the Germans*. The most comprehensive English-language characterization of the country and its people, taking into account its history, politics and psyche, and covering almost every aspect of national life, revised after unification. Its approach is always lively, yet remains scrupulously unbiased.

David Childs *The GDR – Moscow's German Ally*. The best book on the GDR period, fully revised the year before the *Wende*, when the regime still seemed fully secure. Obviously now dated, but still of considerable interest for its detailed descriptions and explanations.

David Childs and Richard Popplewell *The Stasi*. In-depth academic study of the huge parasitical ministry that was the East German secret police.

★ **Timothy Garton Ash** *The File*. Following the opening of the Stasi archives, the author followed up all those who had spied on him, and lays bare the informer society that was the GDR.

Christopher Hilton *The Wall: The People's Story*. Based on an extensive series of first-hand accounts, this charts the impact the Berlin Wall made on everyday life on both sides of the border.

Stuart Parkes *Understanding Contemporary Germany*. Sympathetic examination – with a broadly optimistic conclusion – of the political, economic and social structures of post-unification Germany.

Peter Schneider *The Germany Comedy*. Discussion of the myriad problems caused by unification, with many wry descriptions and observations of the bizarre contradictions and anomalies that ensued.

Günther Wallraff *Lowest of the Low*. In 1983, Wallraff spent two years labouring among Turkish and other immigrant workers, finding out about the underside of German affluence. The book was a political bombshell when it came out, painting a picture of exploitation and malpractice rarely discussed in Germany. Unfortunately, it seems that the author was guilty of fabricating some of the evidence, thus diminishing its long-term impact. *The Undesirable Journalist* is a collection of short but similarly shocking pieces exposing some of the nastier aspects of the country's postwar prosperity.

Alan Watson *The Germans – Who are they now?*. A guide to German identity and the way it is shaping for the future. Each of the eight chapters attempts to provide an answer to one strand of the question posed in the title.

Germany in English-language fiction

Elizabeth von Arnim *Elizabeth and her German Garden, Elizabeth in Rügen*. Although billed as novels, these are effectively autobiographical works by Katherine Mansfield's cousin, an Australian who married a German aristocrat and went to live in his Pomeranian estates.

Sybille Bedford *A Legacy*. Semi-autobiographical novel about two German families – one Berliner, Jewish and mercantile, the other rural, Catholic and aristocratic – improbably united by marriage. Full of sparkling dialogue and richly comic episodes.

Erskine Childers *The Riddle of the Sands*. Set against the background of the Great Naval Race in the run-up to World War I, this is generally regarded as the first modern spy novel. The authentic descriptions of the Friesian islands give it a strong local colour.

Daniel Defoe *Memoirs of a Cavalier*. The first half of this novel is set in the Germany of the Thirty Years' War, and offers vivid descriptions of some of the key battles: indeed the book is so lifelike that Defoe was able to pass it off as a true autobiography of a soldier of fortune.

Thomas de Quincey *Klosterheim*. The only novel by the celebrated opium eater, this spooky Gothic fantasy again uses the backdrop of the Thirty Years' War, but (in contrast to Defoe) is told from the point of view of the Catholic side.

★ **Richard Hughes** *The Fox in the Attic, The Wooden Shepherdess*. The most taciturn of writers, Hughes established an enormous literary reputation on a handful of works, including these first two parts of an unfinished trilogy about an Anglo-German family in the years following World War I. Focusing heavily on the fatal attraction of the Nazis, each mixes fictional episodes with vivid descriptions of real-life events, including Hitler's Beer Hall Putsch and the Night of the Long Knives.

★ **Christopher Isherwood** *Mr Norris Changes Trains, Goodbye to Berlin*. Set in the decadent atmosphere of the Weimar Republic, these stories brilliantly evoke the period and bring to life some classic Berlin characters; they subsequently formed the basis of the films *I Am a Camera* and *Cabaret*.

Jerome K. Jerome *Three Men on the Bummel*. Sequel to the (deservedly) more famous *Three Men in a Boat*, this features the same trio of feckless English travellers taking a cycling holiday through Germany at the turn of the twentieth century. The second half of the book features plenty of entertaining anecdotes, with opinions bandied about on every conceivable subject. *Diary of a Pilgrimage* is an account of the same author's visit to see the Oberammergau Passion Play.

John Le Carré *A Small Town in Germany*. Vintage spy novel set in 1960s Bonn. The then recently built Berlin Wall is the setting for both the beginning and ending of *The Spy Who Came in from the Cold*, Le Carré's best-known Cold War fiction.

Katherine Mansfield *In a German Pension*. One of the author's earliest works, this is a collection of short stories set in early twentieth-century Bavaria. Funny but often acerbic too.

Robert Muller *The World That Summer*. A beautifully written novel based on the author's own experience as a half-Jewish boy growing up in Hamburg during the Third Reich, with all the inevitable conflicts that involved.

★ **Rudolph Erich Raspe** *The Adventures of Baron Münchausen*. The outrageously exaggerated humorous exploits of the real-life Baron Münchhausen were embroidered yet further by Raspe and first published in English. Copies with the classic nineteenth-century engravings of Gustave Doré can often be found in remainder and secondhand shops.

Stephen Spender *The Temple*. Set in Hamburg and the Rhineland during the Weimar Republic years, this makes a fascinating comparison with the closely related works of Isherwood, who is actually one of the main characters. Because of its explicit homosexuality, it could not be published at the time, and remained in draft manuscript until 1988.

Anthony Trollope *Linda Tressel*. One of the Victorian master novelist's shorter full-length works, a powerful psychological study, set against the backdrop of Nürnberg, of the crushing of a young woman's spirit by her bigoted aunt.

German fiction classics

Theodor Fontane *Before the Storm*. Set in Prussia during the period of the Napoleonic Wars, this epic is the greatest German historical novel of the second half of the nineteenth century, dealing with the conflict between patriotism and liberty. The much shorter *Effi Briest* focuses on adultery in the context of the social mores of the age. *Cécile* likewise deals with moral dilemmas and ends tragically, while *Two Novellas* demonstrate the author's mastery of the small-scale.

★ **Johann Wolfgang von Goethe** *The Sorrows of Young Werther*. An early epistolary novella, treating the theme of suicide for the first time ever. *Wilhelm Meister: The Years of Apprenticeship* and *Wilhelm Meister: The Years of Travel* is a huge, episodic and partly autobiographical cycle of novels. *Tales for Transformation* is a series of short stories, showing Goethe's interest in the supernatural.

★ **Johann Jacob Christoffel von Grimmelshausen** *Simplicius Simplicissimus*. This massive, brilliantly witty semi-autobiographical novel is one of the high points of seventeenth-century European literature. Set against the uncertainties of the Thirty Years' War, it charts the adventures of its hero from boyhood to middle age. The lives of two of the subsidiary characters are recounted in the much shorter spin-off novels, *The Life of Courage* and *Tearaway*.

Gerhart Hauptmann *Lineman Thiel and Other Stories*. These three remarkable stories, written towards the end of the nineteenth century, anticipate Freud in their psychological penetration, and the techniques of the cinema in their use of strong visual symbols.

Johann Peter Hebel *The Treasure Chest*. A wonderful collection of moral tales, anecdotes, jokes, reports of murders, disasters and mysteries, all originally written for inclusion in a popular religious almanac.

★ **Ernst Theodor Amadeus Hoffmann** *Tales of Hoffmann*. There are several overlapping selections of short stories and novellas by the schizophrenic master of fantasy and the macabre. Penguin includes *Mademoiselle de Scudéry*, the world's first detective story, while the nightmarish allegory *The Golden Pot* features in the Dover and OUP anthologies. *The Life and Opinions of the Tomcat Murr* is a full-scale novel on the author's favourite theme of two juxtaposed stories, in this case the supposed memoirs of a cat and and a musician clearly modelled on Hoffmann himself.

★ **Heinrich von Kleist** *The Marquise of O and Other Stories*. Like Hoffmann, who was only one year older, Kleist was one of the all-time greats of short story writing. His eight tales range in length from three to one hundred pages, but they're all equally compelling.

Frank G. Ryder (ed.) *German Romantic Stories*. A marvellous anthology which includes three of the classic novellas of German Romanticism: *Memoirs of a Good-for-Nothing* by Joseph von Eichendorff; *Undine* by Friedrich de la Motte Fouqué and *The Strange Story of Peter Schlemihl* by Adelbert von Chamisso.

Jeffrey L. Sammons (ed.) *German Novellas of Realism*. Another fine collection, including two exquisite prose idylls by writers better known as poets: *The Jew's Beech* by Annette von Droste-Hülshoff and *Mozart on the Way to Prague* by Eduard Mörike.

Theodor Storm *The Dykemaster.* Powerful short novel, set against the bleak western coastline of Schleswig-Holstein, about the inventor of a new type of dyke who is demonized by the self-centred community which opposes him. *Hans and Heinz Kirch*, a novella about a father-son conflict in a family of Baltic merchants, is the lead title in an anthology which includes two of the author's finest short stories.

German fiction since 1900

★ **Heinrich Böll** *The Lost Honour of Katharina Blum.* Winner of the Nobel Prize for Literature in 1972, Heinrich Böll is the most popular postwar German novelist – at least with non-Germans. This is the harrowing story of a young woman whose life is ruined by the combined effects of a gutter-press campaign and her accidental involvement with a wanted terrorist. *The Clown* again uses the backdrop of Cologne for a more detailed critique of modern German society. *And Where Were You, Adam?* is set in 1944, chronicling the effect of war and Nazism on ordinary German people.

Bertolt Brecht *Short Stories.* A highly entertaining collection, proving that this side of Brecht's output has been unfairly neglected. In contrast, his single large-scale prose work, *The Threepenny Novel*, a much-expanded version of the *Opera*, is stultifyingly verbose.

Lothar-Günther Buchheim *Das Boot* (*The Boat*). The most famous German novel of World War II is an evocation, based on first-hand experience, of the perilous existence of the U-boat crews who operated in the Atlantic.

Alfred Döblin *Berlin-Alexanderplatz.* A prominent socialist intellectual during the Weimar period, Döblin went into exile shortly after the banning of his books in 1933. *Berlin-Alexanderplatz* is his weightiest and most durable achievement, an unrelenting epic of the city's underclass.

★ **Hans Fallada** *Little Man, What Now?* A once-famous but now unjustly neglected masterpiece, describing with style, humour and tenderness the story of a young couple struggling against the spiralling inflation of the final Weimar years. The German psyche on the eve of the Nazi takeover is captured and distilled far more effectively than in any history book.

★ **Günter Grass** *The Tin Drum.* Grass, the Nobel Laureate of 1999, and one of Germany's best-known postwar personalities, came to prominence with this multi-layered epic, which presents a searing critique, interspersed with elements of fantasy, of German society and politics between 1925 and 1955. Political analysis and fable are also combined in such hefty later novels as *Dog Years*, *The Flounder* and *From the Diary of a Snail*, while the author's comic touch appears in an altogether lighter vein in *Headbirths*, a strong contender for the funniest book ever written by a German.

Hermann Hesse *Narziss and Goldmund.* A beautifully polished novel, set in medieval Germany and narrated in the picaresque vein, about two monks, one a dedicated scholar, the other a wanderer, artist and lover. *Steppenwolf* is a bizarre fantasy about schizophrenia, while

The Glass Bead Game is a monumental utopian novel, set in a future where an elite group develops a game which resolves the world's conflicts.

Georg Heym *The Thief and Other Stories*. These seven Expressionist stories, notable for their rich imagery and relentlessly grim subject matter, comprise the entire prose output of the author, who was already a well-established poet at the time of his death in a skating accident at the age of 25.

Stefan Heym *The King David Report*. Heym was one of the many Marxist writers who chose to settle in the GDR, but he quickly became disillusioned and for decades functioned as a one-man opposition to the regime. This is his best novel, a devastatingly witty send-up of modern totalitarianism by means of a Biblical allegory.

Gert Hofmann *The Parable of the Blind, Our Conquest*. Hofmann was a latecomer to fiction, but quickly established himself among the most original contemporary German writers. The first of these is an imaginative rendering of the story behind Bruegel's enigmatic painting; the other offers a child's-eye view of the aftermath of defeat in World War II.

Ernst Jünger *The Glass Bees, Eumeswill, Aladdin's Problem*. Jünger was the most controversial German writer of the twentieth century, mainly because, although never a Nazi, he was an avowed right-winger who willingly served as a soldier in World War II. His novels belong to the genre of utopian fiction and are multi-layered in approach, offering critiques which can be taken to apply to Germany in particular or modern society in general.

Wolfgang Koeppen *Pigeons on the Grass*. A collage-like novel describing through a score of different characters the events in a single day in an occupied German city after World War II. It's part of an informal trilogy which also includes *Death in Rome*, a ruthless dissection of the various component parts of the German soul as manifested through four members of the same family, each of whom personifies one of its key elements.

Siegfried Lenz *The German Lesson*. A classic German novel about World War II, focusing on the clashes between a father and son, and between duty and personal loyalty. *The Lightship* examines similar themes in a very different setting.

Heinrich Mann *Man of Straw*. The best novel by Thomas Mann's more politically committed elder brother, here analysing the corrupt nature of political and business life under the Second Reich.

Klaus Mann *The Pious Dance, Mephisto*. The erotic novels of Thomas Mann's son were long banned; he now appears as a remarkable individual voice in his own right. His vivid descriptions of the Berlin underworld in the former strongly influenced Isherwood, while *Mephisto* is a striking *roman à clef* about an actor who sells his soul to the Nazi party.

★ **Thomas Mann** *The Magic Mountain*. Generally considered the author's masterpiece, this is a weighty novel of ideas discussing love, death, politics and war through a collection of characters in a Swiss sanatorium, whose sickness mirrors that of European society as a whole. *Buddenbrooks* is the story of a merchant dynasty in the author's native Lübeck; *Confessions of Felix Krull, Confidence Man* is the great comic novel of German literature; *Lotte in Weimar* is a brilliant evocation of Weimar in the era of Goethe; while *Doctor Faustus* updates the Faust legend through the story of a twentieth-century German composer. The novella *Death in Venice* and the anthology *Little Herr Friedemann and Other Stories* show Mann's mastery of the small-scale.

Erich Maria Remarque *All Quiet on the Western Front.* The classic German novel of World War I, focusing on the traumatic impact of the conflict on the life of an ordinary soldier. *Three Comrades* explores the theme of friendship in the uncertain atmosphere of late 1920s Germany.

Herbert Rosendorfer *The Architect of Ruins.* This, the first and best novel of one of Germany's most admired contemporary writers, is an amusing, dreamlike work consisting of a series of stories within stories. *The Night of the Amazons* is a black comedy about Nazi Germany, while *Stephanie* narrates a German housewife's trips back in time to her previous existence as an eighteenth-century Spanish duchess.

Bernhard Schlink *The Reader.* The most widely praised German-language novel of recent years, this is a Holocaust book with a difference, based around the postwar love story of the narrator and an older woman. Written in spare, taut prose, it deals with the great themes of guilt, atonement, redemption, forgiveness and conscience with extraordinary power and economy of means. The same subjects are tackled in *Flights of Love*, a compellingly crafted but somewhat uneven collection of short stories.

Peter Schneider *The Wall Jumper.* A series of vignettes about the Berlin Wall: about those who crossed it (in both directions), and about the two different states of mind it induced. Although billed as fiction, much of it is clearly autobiographical and factual, albeit larded with a few hoaxes.

W.G. Sebald *The Emigrants.* Billed as a work of fiction – notwithstanding the inclusion of numerous old photographs as evidence of its factual basis – this is a haunting lament for the vanished Jewish culture of Germany, illustrated through the lives of four exiles.

★ **Kurt Tucholsky** *Germany? Germany!* A reader drawn from the writings of the sharpest German satirist of the twentieth century. The outrageously witty monologues of the complacent Jewish businessman Herr Wendriner are chillingly prophetic.

Jakob Wassermann *Caspar Hauser.* A masterly exposition of the theme of innocence betrayed, this novel is the finest of the many books inspired by the true story of the famous foundling. *The Maurizius Case* is a weighty novel about the pursuit of justice.

Christa Wolf *A Model Childhood.* The author gained a reputation for literary integrity, despite her loyalty to the GDR. This book is a fictionalized account of her own youth in Bavaria in the 1930s, providing an excellent portrait of a child's confrontation with Nazi ideas and the shattering disillusionment that came from facing the truth as an adult.

Poetry

Anon *Carmina Burana.* A wonderful collection of (originally) dog-Latin songs and poems from the thirteenth-century Alpine lands. In spite of their monastic origin, the texts are often bawdy and erotic. Many were used by

Carl Orff in his choral showpiece named after the manuscript.

Bertolt Brecht *Poems*. Brecht's poems have worn far better than his plays. They sound even more inspired when heard in the musical settings provided by Kurt Weill and the more ideologically inspired Paul Dessau and Hans Eisler. Many recordings are available of these – the best are by Lotte Lenya (Sony), Ute Lemper (Decca) and, in English, Robyn Archer (EMI).

★ **Leonard Forster** (ed.) *The Penguin Book of German Verse*. Best of the anthologies, representing all the big names (and many more) from the eighth century to the present day, with folk songs, ballads and chorales added for good measure.

Johann Wolfgang von Goethe *Selected Poems*, *Selected Verse*, *Epigrams and Poems*. Varied anthologies drawn from Goethe's prodigious output. *Roman Elegies and The Diary* couples two of Goethe's most accessible poetic works.

★ **Heinrich Heine** *Complete Poems*, *Selected Verse*. Heine's works, with their strong rhythms and dramatic, acerbic thrusts, translate far better into English than those of any of his contemporaries; he was also the favourite poet of the great Romantic composers.

Friedrich Hölderlin *Selected Verse*. Hölderlin's poetry, with its classical metres and vivid imagery, is notoriously difficult to translate, but this anthology makes a successful stab at the thankless task. Another selection also includes some of the very different lyric poetry of Eduard Mörike.

Novalis (Georg Philipp von Hardenberg) *Hymns to the Night*. Several translations are available of the great mystic masterpiece of German Romanticism.

Drama

Bertolt Brecht *Plays*. Brecht's short but fruitful collaboration during the Weimar Republic with the composer Kurt Weill – *The Threepenny Opera*, *The Rise and Fall of the City of Mahagonny* and *The Seven Deadly Sins* – show him on top form, though the music is an essential component in these works. Of his other plays, the "parables" – *The Caucasian Chalk Circle* and *The Good Woman of Setzuan* – are generally more successful than those with a more overtly political tone.

★ **Georg Büchner** *Complete Plays*. Büchner died in 1837 at the age of 23. Two of his three plays are masterpieces – *Danton's Death* is a political statement about the French Revolution, while the astonishing unfinished *Woyzeck*, a tragedy based on the life of an insignificant soldier, must be the tersest drama ever written, with not a word wasted in the telling.

★ **Johann Wolfgang von Goethe** *Faust Part One*, *Faust Part Two*. Goethe made the completion of this vast drama – which examines the entire gamut of preoccupations of European civilization – the major task of his life, and he duly finished it just before his death, having worked at it for around sixty years. All his other important works for the stage are collected together in *Early Verse Drama and Prose Plays* and *Verse Plays and Epics*.

Georg Kaiser *Plays Vol. 1*, *Plays Vol. 2*. These contain a selection of the vast output of the leading dramatist of the Expressionist movement, typically using very stark language and stressing ideas at the expense of characterization – the players are typically denoted by their worldly function, rather than their name. Another piece by Kaiser features in *Seven Expressionist Plays* (John Calder/Riverrun), which also contains works by two dramatists better known as artists – Ernst Barlach and Oskar Kokoschka.

Heinrich von Kleist *Five Plays.* Ranges over Kleist's varied output, from German theatre's finest comedy, *The Broken Jug*, to the patriotic drama, *Prince Frederick of Homburg*.

Gotthold Ephraim Lessing *Nathan the Wise, Minna von Barnhelm and Other Plays.* The first of these plays is unusual in German literature in having a Jew as the hero; the second is one of German theatre's earliest examples of middle-class comedy, using contemporary eighteenth-century events as a backdrop.

★ **Friedrich Schiller** *The Robbers, Wallenstein.* This pairs an early *Sturm und Drang* drama (which established Schiller as the leader of that movement) with one of his later historical plays, set against the background of the Thirty Years' War. *William Tell* is the playwright's last work.

Ottmar Weiss and Alois Daisenberger *Oberammergau: A Passion Play.* A complete translation of the classic nineteenth-century text of the play.

Legends and folklore

★ **Anon** *The Nibelungenlied.* Germany's greatest epic was written around 1200 by an unknown Danubian poet; the story varies greatly from Wagner's *Ring*, which draws equally heavily on Nordic sources of the legend. It's here given a highly entertaining prose translation.

Anon *Till Eulenspiegel.* The complete adventures of Germany's most famous folk hero, a roguish jester who fought pomposity in all its many manifestations.

Francis G. Gentry (ed.) *German Medieval Tales.* Includes most of the best-known German legends with a medieval origin, notably the *Historia and Tale of Doctor Johannes Faustus*, which became one of European literature's most fertile sources.

★ **Jakob and Wilhelm Grimm** *Complete Grimm's Tales.* The world's most famous collection of folk tales, meticulously researched by the Brothers Grimm, has stories to appeal to all age ranges. Penguin's selection of the tales has the ingenious idea of rendering some of them in Scots and Irish, thus capturing something of the dialect flavour of the originals, which is otherwise lost in translation.

Jennifer Russ *German Festivals.* Rather a pity it's not a bit longer, but this book provides useful background information on all the main annual folklore celebrations.

Frank G. Ryder (ed.) *German Literary Fairy Tales.* An anthology of elaborate reworkings of folk tales made by Goethe, Novalis, Eichendorff, Mörike, Storm and others.

Lewis Spence *Germany – Myths and Legends.* Narrates the rich store of legends associated with the Rhine, arranged in the form of a journey down the great river.

Gottfried von Strassburg *Tristan*, **Wolfram von Eschenbach** *Parzifal*. Two more epic masterpieces from early thirteenth-century Germany, both based on the Grail legends.

The visual arts

Peter Adam *The Arts of the Third Reich*. Engrossing and well-written account of the officially approved state art of Nazi Germany – a subject that for many years has been ignored or deliberately made inaccessible. Includes over three hundred illustrations, many reproduced for the first time since the war.

Jost Amman *The Book of Trades*. The 114 woodcuts illustrate the trades and crafts practised in early sixteenth-century Germany; each is accompanied by a poem by the most famous Mastersinger, Hans Sachs.

★ **Michael Baxendall** *The Limewood Sculptors of Renaissance Germany*. Examines the work of Tilman Riemenschneider, Veit Stoss, and many other lesser-known artists in their social and political context. A lavish series of photographs accompanies the text.

Wolf-Dieter Dube *The Expressionists*. A general introduction to Germany's most distinctive contribution to twentieth-century art.

★ **Albrecht Dürer** *The Complete Woodcuts, The Complete Etchings, Engravings and Drypoints*. These two books enable you to own, at minimal cost, a complete set of the graphic work of one of the world's greatest-ever masters of the art. The book of woodcuts is particularly recommended.

William Vaughan *German Romantic Painting*. A good introduction to many of Germany's best nineteenth-century artists.

Frank Whiteford *Bauhaus*. Introduction to the twentieth century's most influential art and design movement, tracing its development during its early years in Weimar, Dessau and Berlin.

Guide books

Karl Baedeker *The Rhineland, Northern Germany, Southern Germany, Berlin*. The old Baedekers, all long out of print, are still indispensable classics. They covered a Germany which was considerably more extensive than today, stretching all across Poland into Lithuania and Russia. Look out for the editions dating from the early years of the twentieth century, immensely learned and full of now-untenable opinions. The glossy modern successors to these are not in the same class.

Grant Bourne and Sabine Kröner-Bourne *Walking in the Bavarian Alps*. Gives details of a wide range of hikes in Germany's most spectacular scenic region.

Alan Castle *Walking the River Rhine Trail*. Guide to a long-distance hiking route along the most beautiful stretch of the country's most famous river.

Jack Holland and John Gawthrop *The Rough Guide to Berlin*. Companion volume to the book you're holding, this gives the full lowdown on the sights, culture and nightlife of one of Europe's most exciting cities.

Gordon McLachlan *Berlin* Predominantly a cultural guide, lavishly illustrated with both archive and commissioned photographs. The main text is accompanied by a wide selection of literary excerpts. *Germany's Romantic Road* is a detailed guide, with special reference to walkers and cyclists, to the country's most popular tourist route.

Fleur and Colin Speakman *Walking in the Black Forest*, *King Ludwig Way*, *Walking in the Harz Mountains*. Three guides for specific hikes in Germany.

Language

Language

German

German is a very complex language and you can't hope to master it in a short time. As English was a compulsory subject in the West German school curriculum, many people have some familiarity with it, which eases communication a great deal. English is now compulsory in schools throughout Germany.

Nonetheless, a smattering of German does help, especially in out-of-the-way rural areas, or in the former East, where Russian was more commonly taught in schools. Also, given the long-standing and continued presence of American and British forces who make little effort to integrate into local communities or learn German, people are particularly sensitive to presumptuous English-speakers. On the other hand, most will be delighted to practise their English on you once you've stumbled through your German introduction.

Should you be interested in **studying the language** during your stay, the best places to enrol in are the Goethe-Instituten, which can be found in most major cities. The German Tourist Board or local information offices have all relevant addresses.

Pronunciation

English-speakers find the complexities of German grammar hard to handle, but **pronunciation** isn't as daunting as it might first appear. Individual syllables are generally pronounced as they're printed – the trick is learning how to place the stresses in the notoriously lengthy German words.

Vowels and umlauts

a as in f**a**ther
e as in d**ay** or as in w**e**t
i as in l**ee**k
o as in b**o**ttom or as in r**o**se
u as in b**oo**t
ä is a combination of a and e, sometimes pronounced like **e** in b**e**t (eg Länder) and sometimes like **ai** in p**ai**d (eg spät)
ö is a combination of o and e, like the French eu
ü is a combination of u and e, like tr**ue**, only sharper in sound

Vowel combinations

ai as in **lie**
au as in h**ou**se
äu as in **oi**l
ie as in fr**ee**
ei as in h**ei**ght
eu as in **oi**l

Consonants

Consonants are pronounced as they are written, with no silent letters. The differences from English are:

r is given a dry throaty sound, similar to French

j pronounced similar to an English y
s pronounced similar to, but slightly softer than an English z
v pronounced somewhere between f and v
w pronounced same way as English v
z pronounced ts
The German letter ß, the Scharfes S, sometimes replaces ss in a word: pronunciation is identical.

Consonant combinations

ch is a strong back-of-the-throat sound as in the Scottish loch
sp (at the start of a word) is pronounced shp
st (at the start of a word) is pronounced sht

Gender

German words can be one of three genders: masculine, feminine or neuter. Unfortunately, the designation of these can appear very illogical: for example, a train is masculine, a cat (even a tomcat) is feminine, and a girl is neuter. Each has its own definite article (respectively der, die, das); as with qualifying adjectives, these decline according to the case used.

German words and phrases

ja, nein	yes, no
bitte	please, you're welcome
bitte schön	a more polite form of bitte
danke, danke schön	thank you, thank you very much
wo, wann, warum?	where, when, why?
wieviel?	how much?
hier, da	here, there
geöffnet, offen, auf	all mean "open"
geschlossen, zu	both mean "closed"
da drüben	over there
dieses	this one
jenes	that one
gross, klein	large, small
mehr, weniger	more, less
wenig	a little
viel	a lot
billig, teuer	cheap, expensive
gut, schlecht	good, bad
heiss, kalt	hot, cold
mit, ohne	with, without
rechts	right
links	left
geradeaus	straight ahead
oben	above
unten	below

Greetings and times

Guten Morgen	Good morning
Guten Abend	Good evening
Guten Tag	Good day
Grüss Gott	Good day (in southern Germany)
Gute Nacht	Good night
Wie geht es Ihnen?	How are you? (polite)
Wie geht es dir?	How are you? (informal)
Lass mich in Ruhe	Leave me alone
Hau ab	Get lost
Geh weg	Go away
Auf Wiedersehen	Goodbye
Tschüs	Goodbye (informal)
jetzt, später	now, later
früher	earlier
Heute	today
Gestern	yesterday
Morgen	tomorrow

Vorgestern	the day before yesterday
Übermorgen	the day after tomorrow
Tag	day
Nacht	night
Mittag	midday
Mitternacht	midnight
drei Uhr	three o'clock
viertel nach drei	quarter past three
halb vier	half past three (ie half to four)
viertel vor vier	quarter to four
Woche	week
Wochenende	weekend
Monat	month
Jahr	year
am Vormittag/ vormittags	in the morning
am Nachmittag/ nachmittags	in the afternoon
am Abend/abends	in the evening

Days, months and dates

Montag	Monday
Dienstag	Tuesday
Mittwoch	Wednesday
Donnerstag	Thursday
Freitag	Friday
Samstag	Saturday
Sonnabend	Saturday (in northern Germany)
Sonntag	Sunday
Januar	January
Februar	February
März	March
April	April
Mai	May
Juni	June
Juli	July
August	August
September	September
Oktober	October
November	November
Dezember	December
Frühling	Spring
Sommer	Summer
Herbst	Autumn
Winter	Winter
Ferien	holidays
Feiertag	bank holiday
Montag, der erste April	Monday, the first of April
der zweite April	the second of April
der dritte April	the third of April

Questions and requests

All enquiries should be prefaced with the phrase **Entschuldigen Sie bitte** (Excuse me, please). Note that **Sie** is the polite form of address to be used with everyone except close friends, though young people and students often don't bother with it. The older generation will certainly be offended if you address them with the familiar **Du**, as will all officials.

Sprechen Sie Englisch?	Do you speak English?
Ich spreche kein Deutsch	I don't speak German
Sprechen Sie bitte langsamer	Please speak more slowly
Ich verstehe nicht	I don't understand
Ich verstehe	I understand
Wie sagt man das auf Deutsch?	How do you say that in German?
Können Sie mir sagen wo ... ist?	Can you tell me where... is?
Wo ist...?	Where is...?
Wie komme ich nach ...?	How do I get to (a town)?
Wie komme ich zur/zum...?	How do I get to (a building, place)?
Wieviel kostet das?	How much does that cost?
Wann fährt der nächste Zug?	When does the next train leave?
Um wieviel Uhr?	At what time?
Wieviel Uhr ist es?	What time is it?
Sind die Plätze noch frei?	Are these seats taken?
Die Rechnung bitte	The bill please
Ist der Tisch frei?	Is that table free?
Die Speisekarte bitte	The menu please

Fräulein...!	Waitress...! (for attention)
Herr Ober...!	Waiter...! (for attention)
Haben Sie etwas billigeres?	Have you got something cheaper?
Haben Sie Zimmer frei?	Are there rooms available?
Wo sind die Toiletten bitte?	Where are the toilets?
Ich hätte gern dieses	I'd like that one
Ich hätte gern ein Zimmer für zwei	I'd like a room for two
Ich hätte gern ein Einzelzimmer	I'd like a single room
Hat es Dusche,Bad, Toilette...?	Does it have a shower, bath, toilet...?

Some signs

Damen/Frauen	Women's toilets
Herren/Männer	Men's toilets
Eingang	Entrance
Ausgang	Exit
Ankunft	Arrival
Abfahrt	Departure
Ausstellung	Exhibition
Autobahn	Motorway
Einfahrt	Motorway entrance
Ausfahrt	Motorway exit
Geschwindigkeit Begrenzung	Speed limit
Umleitung	Diversion
Achtung!	Attention!
Vorsicht!	Beware!
Notausgang	Emergency exit
Baustelle	Building works
Ampel	Traffic light
Krankenhaus	Hospital
Polizei	Police
Nicht rauchen	No smoking
Kein Eingang	No entrance
Drücken	Push
Ziehen	Pull
Frei	Vacant
Besetzt	Occupied
Verboten, Untersagt	Prohibited
Zoll	Customs
Kasse	Cash desk
Grenzübergang	Border crossing

Numbers

1	**eins**
2	**zwei, zwo**
3	**drei**
4	**vier**
5	**fünf**
6	**sechs**
7	**sieben**
8	**acht**
9	**neun**
10	**zehn**
11	**elf**
12	**zwölf**
13	**dreizehn**
14	**vierzehn**
15	**fünfzehn**
16	**sechszehn**
17	**siebzehn**
18	**achtzehn**
19	**neunzehn**
20	**zwanzig**
21	**ein-und-zwanzig**
22	**zwei-und-zwanzig**
30	**dreissig**
40	**vierzig**
50	**fünfzig**
60	**sechzig**
70	**siebzig**
80	**achtzig**
90	**neunzig**
100	**hundert**
1000	**tausend**
1999	**neunzehn-hundert-neun-und-neunzig**

Menu reader

Basics

Abendessen	supper, dinner
Belegtes Brot	open sandwich
Bierteig	batter
Brot	bread
Brötchen	bread roll
Butter	butter
Butterbrot	sandwich
Ei	egg
Eintopf	a soup–stew hybrid
Essig	vinegar
Fisch	fish
Fleisch	meat
Frühstück	breakfast
Gabel	fork
Gemüse	vegetables
Glas	glass
Hauptgericht	main course
Honig	honey
Joghurt	yoghurt
Käse	cheese
Löffel	spoon
Marmelade	jam
Maultaschen	form of ravioli
Messer	knife
Mittagessen	lunch
Nachspeise	dessert
Nudeln	noodles
Obst	fruit
Öl	oil
Pfeffer	pepper
Rechnung	bill
Reis	rice
Salz	salt
Senf	mustard
Sosse	sauce
Spätzle	shredded pasta
Speisekarte	menu
Tasse	cup
Teller	plate
Trinkgeld	tip
Vorspeise	starter
Zucker	sugar

Soups and starters

Bohnensuppe	bean soup
Erbsensuppe	pea soup
Flädlesuppe, Pfannkuchensuppe	clear soup with pancake strips
Fleischsalat	sausage salad with onions
Fleischsuppe	clear soup and meat dumplings
Grüner Salat	mixed green salad
Gulaschsuppe	thick soup in imitation of goulash
Gurkensalat	cucumber salad
Hühnersuppe	chicken soup
Lachsbrot	smoked salmon on bread
Leberknödelsuppe	clear soup with liver dumplings
Leberpastete	liver paté
Linsensuppe	lentil soup
Melone mit Schinken	melon and ham
Ochsenschwanzsuppe	oxtail soup
Schnittlauchbrot	chives on bread
Sülze	jellied meat loaf
Suppe	soup
Würzfleisch	supreme of pork
Zwiebelsuppe	onion soup

Meat and poultry

Aufschnitt	mixed slices of cold sausage
Blutwurst	blood sausage, similar in taste to the British black pudding
Bockwurst	chunky boiled sausage
Bratwurst	grilled sausage
Broiler	chicken
Currywurst	sausage served with piquant sauce
Eisbein	boiled knuckle of pig
Ente	duck

Fasan	pheasant
Fleischpflanzerl	meatball (in Bavaria)
Frikadelle	meatball
Froschschenkel	frogs' legs
Gans	goose
Geschnetzeltes	shredded meat, usually served with rice
Gyros	kebab
Hackbraten	mincemeat roast
Hackfleisch	mincemeat
Hähnchen, Hendl, Huhn	chicken
Hase	hare
Herz	heart
Hirn	brains
Hirsch, Reh	venison
Innereien	innards
Jägerschnitzel	cutlet in mushroom sauce
Kanninchen	rabbit
Kassler Rippchen	smoked and pickled pork chops
Kotelett	cutlet
Krautwickerl	cabbage leaves filled with mincemeat
Lamm	lamb
Leber	liver
Leberkäse	baked meatloaf
Lunge	lungs
Nieren	kidneys
Ochsenschwanz	oxtail
Pferdefleich	horsemeat
Rahmschnitzel	cutlet in cream sauce
Rinderroulade	beef olive
Rindfleisch	beef
Sauerbraten	braised pickled beef
Saure Lunge	pickled lungs
Schaschlik	diced meat with piquant sauce
Schinken	ham
Schlachtplatte	mix of cured meats
Schnecke	snail
Schnitzel Natur	uncoated cutlet (usually pork)
Schweinebauch, Wammerl	pork belly
Schweinebraten	roast pork
Schweinefleisch	pork
Schweinehaxe	grilled knuckle of pig
Spanferkel	suckling pig
Speck	bacon
Spiessbraten	Skewered meat
Truthahn	turkey
Weisswurst	white herb sausage
Wiener Schnitzel	thin pork or veal cutlet in breadcumbs
Wild	wild game
Wildschwein	wild boar
Wurst	sausage
Zigeunerschnitzel	cutlet in paprika sauce
Zunge	tongue

Fish

Aal	eel
Forelle	trout
Goldbarsch	redfish
Hecht	pike
Hering, Matjes	herring
Hummer	lobster
Kabeljau	cod
Karpfen	carp
Kaviar	caviar
Krabben	prawns
Lachs	salmon
Makrele	mackerel
Muscheln	mussels
Rotbarsch	rosefish
Sardellen	anchovies
Sardinen	sardines
Schellfisch	haddock
Scholle	plaice
Schwertfish	swordfish
Seezunge	sole
Skampi	scampi
Thunfisch	tuna
Tintenfisch	squid
Zander	pike-perch

Vegetables

Blumenkohl	cauliflower
Bohnen	beans

Bratkartoffeln	sautéed potatoes
Champignons	button mushrooms
Erbsen	peas
Grüne Bohnen	green beans
Gurke	cucumber
Karotten, Möhren	carrots
Kartoffelbrei	mashed potatoes
Kartoffelpuree	creamed potatoes
Kartoffelsalat	potato salad
Knoblauch	garlic
Knödel, Kloss	dumpling
Kopfsalat	lettuce
Lauche	leeks
Maiskolben	corn on the cob
Paprika	green or red peppers
Pellkartoffeln	jacket potatoes
Pilze	mushrooms
Pommes frites	fries
Reibekuchen	potato cake
Rosenkohl	brussels sprouts
Rote Rübe	beetroot
Rotkohl	red cabbage
Rübe	turnip
Salat	salad
Salzkartoffeln	boiled potatoes
Sauerkraut	pickled cabbage
Spargel	asparagus
Tomaten	tomatoes
Weisskohl	white cabbage
Zwiebeln	onions

Fruits

Ananas	pineapple
Apfel	apple
Aprikose	apricot
Banane	banana
Birne	pear
Brombeeren	blackberries
Datteln	dates
Erdbeeren	strawberries
Feigen	figs
Himbeeren	raspberries
Johannisbeeren	redcurrants
Kirschen	cherries
Kompott	stewed fruit or mousse
Mandarine	tangerine
Melone	melon
Obstsalat	fruit salad
Orange	orange
Pampelmuse	grapefruit
Pfirsich	peach
Pflaumen	plums
Rhabarber	rhubarb
Rosinen	raisins
Schwarze Johannisbeeren	blackcurrants
Stachelbeeren	gooseberries
Trauben	grapes
Zitrone	lemon

Cheeses and desserts

Apfelstrudel mit Sahne	apple strudel with fresh cream
Berliner	jam doughnut
Dampfnudel, Germknödel	yeast dumpling, usually served hot with vanilla sauce
Eis	ice cream
Eisbecher	ice-cream sundae
Emmentaler	Swiss Emmental
Gebäck	pastries
Kaiserschmarrn	shredded pancake served with powdered sugar, jam and raisins
Käsekuchen	cheesecake
Käseplatte	mixed selection of cheeses
Keks	biscuit
Krapfen	doughnut
Nüsse	nuts
Nusskuchen	nut cake
Obstkuchen	fruit flan
Pfannkuchen	pancake
Schafskäse	sheep's cheese
Schokolade	chocolate
Schwarzwälder Kirschtorte	Black Forest gateau
Torte	gateau
Weichkäse	cream cheese
Ziegenkäse	goat's cheese

Common terms

art	style of
blau	rare
eingelegte	pickled
frisch	fresh
gebacken	baked
gebraten	fried, roasted
gedämpft	steamed
gefüllt	stuffed
gegrillt	grilled
gekocht	cooked
geräuchert	smoked
gutbürgerliche Küche	traditional German cooking
hausgemacht	home-made
heiss	hot
kalt	cold
neue deutsche Küche	German form of nouvelle cuisine
paniert	coated in breadcrumbs, then fried
schmoren	casseroled, stewed
vom heissen Stein	raw meats you cook yourself on a red-hot stone

Vegetarian terms

Ich bin Vegetarier	I am a vegetarian
Haben Sie etwas ohne Fleisch?	Do you have anything without meat?

Drinks

Apfelsaft	apple juice
Apfelwein	apple wine
Bier	beer
Federweisser	new wine
Glühwein	hot mulled wine
Grog	hot rum
Herrengedeck	cocktail of beer and Sekt
Kaffee	coffee
Kaffee mit Milch	coffee with milk
Kakao	cocoa
Korn	rye spirit
Kräutertee, Pflanzentee	herbal tea
Likör	liqueur
Milch	milk
Milchshake	milk shake
Mineralwasser	mineral water
Orangensaft	orange juice
Roséwein	rosé wine
Rotwein	red wine
Sekt	sparkling wine
Tee	tea
Tomatensaft	tomato juice
Traubensaft	grape juice
Trinkschokolade	drinking chocolate
Wasser	water
Weinbrand	brandy
Weinschorle	spritzer
Weisswein	white wine
Zitronenlimonade	lemonade
Zitronentee	lemon tea

Glossaries

Art and architecture

AISLE part of church to the side of the nave.

AMBULATORY passage round the back of the high altar, in continuation of the aisles.

APSE vaulted termination of the east (altar) end of a church.

ART DECO geometrical style of art and architecture prevalent in 1930s.

ART NOUVEAU sinuous, highly stylized form of architecture and interior design; in Germany, mostly dates from period 1900–15 and is known as Jugendstil.

BALDACHIN canopy over an altar or tomb.

BAROQUE expansive, exuberant architectural style of the seventeenth and early eighteenth centuries, characterized by ornate decoration, complex spatial arrangements and grand vistas. The term is also applied to the sumptuous style of painting of the same period.

BASILICA church in which nave is higher than the aisles.

BAUHAUS plain, functional style of architecture and design, originating in early twentieth- century Germany.

BIEDERMEIERSTIL simple, bourgeois style of painting and decoration practised throughout first half of the nineteenth century.

CAPITAL top of a column, usually sculpted.

CHANCEL part of the church in which altar is placed; normally at east end, though some German churches also have one at the west.

CHOIR part of church in which service is sung, usually beside the altar.

CRYPT underground part of a church.

DIPTYCH carved or painted altarpiece on a pair of panels.

EXPRESSIONISM emotional style of painting, concentrating on line and colour, extensively practised in early twentieth-century Germany; term is also used for related architecture of the same period.

FRESCO mural painting applied to wet plaster, so that colours immediately soak into the wall.

GOTHIC architectural style with an emphasis on verticality, characterized by pointed arch, ribbed vault and flying buttress; introduced to Germany around 1235, surviving in an increasingly decorative form until well into the sixteenth century. The term is also used for paintings of this period.

GRISAILLE painting or stained glass window executed entirely in subdued monochrome.

HALF-TIMBERED style of building in which the walls have a framework of timber interspersed with either bricks or plaster.

HALL CHURCH (*Hallenkirche*) church design much favoured in Germany, in which all vaults are of approximately equal height.

HISTORICIST architectural movement with a strong emphasis on past styles such as the Romanesque, Gothic, Renaissance and Baroque.

LAVABO well-house in a cloister.

MANNERISM deliberately mannered style of late Renaissance art and architecture.

MISERICORD often elaborately carved bracket on the turn-up seat of a choir stall.

MODELLO small version of a large picture, usually painted for the patron's approval.

NAVE main body of a church, generally forming the western part.

NEOCLASSICAL late eighteenth- and early nineteenth-century style of art and architecture returning to classical models as a reaction against Baroque and Rococo excesses.

ORIEL projecting bay window.

PARADISE (*Paradies*) richly sculpted porch forming the entrance to some cathedrals.

POLYPTYCH carved or painted altarpiece on several joined panels.

PREDELLA lowest part of an altarpiece, with scenes much smaller than in main sections.

RENAISSANCE Italian-originated movement in art and architecture, inspired by the rediscovery of classical ideals.

RETABLE altarpiece.

ROCOCO highly florid, light and graceful eighteenth-century style of architecture, painting and interior design, forming the last phase of Baroque.

ROMANESQUE solid architectural style of late tenth to mid-thirteenth centuries, characterized by round-headed arches and a penchant for horizontality and geometrical precision. The term is also used for paintings of this period.

ROMANTICISM late eighteenth and early nineteenth-century movement, particularly strong in Germany, rooted in adulation of the natural world and rediscovery of the achievements of the Middle Ages.

ROOD SCREEN screen dividing nave from chancel (thus separating laity and clergy), originally bearing a rood (crucifix).

SOFT STYLE (*Weicher Stil*) delicate style of painting and sculpture pioneered in fourteenth-century Bohemia, which dominated German art to the mid-fifteenth century.

STUCCO plaster used for decorative effects.

TABERNACLE a freestanding canopy or ornamental recess designed to contain the Holy Sacrament.

TONDO painting or carving in a circular format.

TRANSEPT arm of a cross-shaped church, placed at ninety degrees to nave and chancel.

TRANSITIONAL architectural style between Romanesque and Gothic in which the basic shapes of the older style were modified by the use of such new forms as the pointed arch and ribbed vault.

TRIPTYCH carved or painted altarpiece on three panels.

TROMPE L'OEIL painting designed to fool the viewer into believing the image is three-dimensional.

TYMPANUM sculptured panel above a doorway.

WESER RENAISSANCE archaic, highly elaborate style of secular Renaissance architecture cultivated in and around the Weser valley in Hesse, Lower Saxony and Westphalia.

WESTWORK (*Westwerk*) grandiose frontage found on many German medieval churches, traditionally reserved for the use of the emperor and his retinue.

German terms

ABTEI abbey.

ALTSTADT old part of a city.

AUSKUNFT information.

AUSLÄNDER foreigner; the word has come to be a pejorative term for any non-white non-German.

AUSSTELLUNG exhibition.

AUSWEIS identity document.

BAD spa (before the name of a town), bath.

BAHNHOF station.

BAU building.

BEFESTIGUNG fortification.

BERG mountain, hill.

BERGBAHN funicular.

BIBLIOTHEK library.

BIERGARTEN beer garden.

BIERKELLER beer cellar; beer hall.

BOTSCHAFT embassy.

BRÜCKE bridge.

BRAUEREI, BRAUHAUS brewery.

BRUNNEN fountain, well.

BUNDESKANZLER Federal Chancellor (Prime Minister).

BUNDESRAT Upper House of German Parliament.

BUNDESTAG Lower House of German Parliament.

BURG castle, fortress.

BÜRGERMEISTER mayor.

CAROLINGIAN (*Karolingisch*) dynasty founded by Charles Martel in the early eighth century which ruled Germany until the last quarter of the ninth century. The term is particularly associated with the reign of Charlemagne (768–814).

DENKMAL memorial.

DIET Parliament of Holy Roman Empire.

DOM cathedral.

DONAU River Danube.

DORF village.

EASTERN TERRITORIES (*Ostgebiete*) lands to the east of the Oder–Neisse line, occupied by German-speaking peoples since the Middle Ages, but forcibly evacuated, and allocated to Poland and the Soviet Union after World War II.

EINBAHNSTRASSE one-way street.

ELECTOR (*Kurfürst*) sacred or secular prince with a vote in the elections to choose the Holy Roman Emperor. There were seven for most of the medieval period, with others added later.

EVANGELISCHE KIRCHE federation of Protestant churches, both Lutheran and Reformed.

FACHWERKHAUS half-timbered house.

FAHRSTUHL lift, elevator.

FASCHING name given to Carnival, especially in Bavaria.

FASTNET name given to Carnival, especially in Baden-Württemberg.

FEIERTAG holiday.

FEST festival.

FESTUNG fortress.

FLUGHAFEN airport.

FLUSS river.

FRANCONIA (*Franken*) historical province of central Germany, stretching as far west as Mainz; name later became associated only with the eastern portion of this territory, most of which is now incorporated in Bavaria.

FREE IMPERIAL CITY (*Freiereichstadt*) independent city-state within the Holy Roman Empire.

FREIHERR baron.

FREMDENZIMMER room for short-term let.

FÜRST prince.

FUSSGÄNGERZONE pedestrian area.

GASSE alley.

GASTARBEITER (guest worker) anyone who comes to Germany to work.

GÄSTEHAUS guesthouse.

GASTHAUS pub, inn.

GASTHOF inn.

GASTSTÄTTE restaurant serving traditional German cuisine.

GEDENKSTÄTTE memorial museum.

GEMÄLDE painting.

GEMÜTLICH snug or cosy.

GRAF count.

GRÜNEN, DIE (The Greens) political party formed from environmental and anti-nuclear groups.

HABSBURG the most powerful family in medieval Germany, operating from a base in Austria. They held the office of Holy Roman Emperor almost continuously from 1452 to 1806, and by marriage, war and diplomacy acquired territories all over Europe.

HAFEN harbour, port.

HANSEATIC LEAGUE (*Hansebund*) medieval trading alliance of Baltic and Rhineland cities, numbering about one hundred at its fifteenth-century peak. Slowly died out in the seventeenth century with competition from Baltic nation-states and rise of Brandenburg-Prussia.

HAUPTBAHNHOF main train station in a city.

HAUPTBURG central, residential part of a castle.

HAUPTSTRASSE main street.

HEIDE heath.

HEIMAT (homeland) often given a mystical significance and used emotively in connection with Germans displaced from the Eastern Territories.

HERZOG duke.

HOF court, courtyard, mansion.

HOHENSTAUFEN Swabian dynasty who held office of Holy Roman Emperor from 1138 to 1254.

HOHENZOLLERN dynasty of Swabian origin, who became margrave-Electors of Brandenburg in 1415, and slowly built up their territorial base. In the nineteenth century they ousted the Habsburgs from their pre-eminent place in German affairs, forging the Second Reich in 1871 and serving as its emperors until 1918.

HÖHLE cave.

HOLY ROMAN EMPIRE (*Heiliges Römisches Reich*) title used to describe the First German Reich, established in 800. Despite its weak structure, it survived until 1806, when the ruling Habsburgs, in response to the Napoleonic threat, began building up a more solid empire from their Austrian base.

IMBISS snack bar.

INNENSTADT inner city.

INSEL island.

JAGDSCHLOSS hunting lodge.

JUGENDHERBERGE youth hostel.

JUGENDSTIL German version of Art Nouveau.

JUNKER Prussian landowning class.

KAISER emperor.

KAMMER room, chamber.

KAPELLE chapel.

KARNEVAL term used for Carnival, especially in Rhineland.

KAUFHAUS department store.

KINO cinema.

KIRCHE church.

KLOSTER monastery, convent.

KNEIPE drinking pub.

KÖNIG king.

KREUZGANG cloister.

KRISTALLNACHT Nazi pogrom of November 9/10 1938, when synagogues were burned and Jewish businesses looted.

KUNST art.

KURHAUS assembly rooms in a spa.

KURORT health resort.

KURVERWALTUNG reception building in spa resorts.

LAND (pl. **LÄNDER**) name given to the constituent states of the Federal Republic; first introduced in Weimar Republic.

LANDGRAVE (*Landgraf*) count in charge of a large province.

LEUCHTTURM lighthouse.

MARGRAVE (*Markgraf*) count in charge of a Mark (March; later Margraviate), a frontier district established at the time of Charlemagne.

MARKT market, market square.

MAUER wall.

MEER sea.

MEROVINGIAN Frankish dynasty established by Clovis in 481; ruled until the early eighth century.

MESSE trade fair

MIKWE Jewish ritual bath.

MÜNSTER minster, large church.

NATURPARK area of protected countryside.

NEUES FORUM umbrella group for political opposition organizations within the former GDR.

NEUSTADT New part of the city.

ODER–NEISSE LINE eastern limit of German territory set by victorious Allies in 1945.

OSTPOLITIK West German policy of détente towards the GDR.

OTTONIAN (*Ottonisch*) epoch of Otto I and his two eponymous successors. Term is used in connection with the early Romanesque art forms pioneered in this and the subsequent Salian epoch (mid-tenth to mid-eleventh century).

PALAS, PALAST residential part of a castle.

PALATINATE (*Pfalz*) territory ruled by the Count Palatine, a high-ranking imperial official. The present Land is only the western part of the historical province, whose original centre is now part of Baden-Württemberg.

PFARRKIRCHE parish church.

PLATZ square.

PRINZ prince; since 1918, used in a less grandiose way as a courtesy title for aristocrats in place of the plethora of now-defunct titles.

PRUSSIA (*Preussen*) originally, an eastern Baltic territory (now divided between Poland and the Russian Federation). In 1525 it became a duchy under the control of the Hohenzollerns, who merged it in 1618 with their German possessions to form Brandenburg-Prussia (later shortened to Prussia); this took the lead in forging the unity of Germany, and was thereafter its dominant province. The name was abolished after World War II because of its monarchical and militaristic connotations.

QUITTUNG official receipt.

RASTPLATZ picnic area.

RATHAUS town hall.

RATSKELLER cellars below the Rathaus, almost invariably used as a restaurant serving *gutbürgerliche Küche*.

REICH empire.

REISEBÜRO travel agency.

RESIDENZ palace.

RESIDENZSTADT courtly town.

RITTER Knight.

ROMANTISCHE STRASSE ("Romantic Road") scenic road in Bavaria and Baden-Württemberg, running between Würzburg and Füssen.

RUNDGANG way round.

SAAL hall.

SALIAN dynasty of Holy Roman Emperors, 1024–1125.

SAMMLUNG collection.

SÄULE column.

S-BAHN commuter railway network operating in and around conurbations.

SCHATZKAMMER treasury.

SCHICKIE or **SCHICKIE-MICKIE** yuppie.

SCHLOSS castle, palace (equivalent of French château).

SCHMALSPURBAHN narrow-gauge railway.

SEE lake, sea.

SEEBRÜCKE pier.

SEILBAHN cable car.

SESSELBAHN chair lift.

STADT town, city.

STADTMITTE town or city centre.

STAMMTISCH table in a pub or restaurant reserved for regular customers.

STANDSEILBAHN funicular.

STASI (*Staatssicherheitsdienst*) former "State Security Service" or secret police of the GDR.

STAUFIAN pertaining to the epoch of the Hohenstaufen.

STAUSEE reservoir.

STIFTSKIRCHE collegiate church.

STIFTUNG foundation.

STRAND beach.

STRANDKORB wicker beach chair with hood.

STRASSENBAHN tram.

SWABIA (*Schwaben*) name used for the southwestern part of Germany from the eleventh century onwards; after the ruling Hohenstaufen dynasty died out, it became politically fragmented.

SZENE trendy bar or club.

TAL valley.

TALSPERRE dam.

TANKSTELLE petrol station.

TOR gate, gateway.

TRABI conversational shorthand for the now-famous Trabant, East Germany's two-cylinder, two-stroke car.

TURM tower.

U-BAHN network of underground trains or trams.

VERKEHRSAMT, VERKEHRSVEREIN tourist office.

VIERTEL quarter, district.

VOLK people, folk; given mystical associations by Hitler.

VORBURG outer, defensive part of a castle.

VORSTADT suburb.

WALD forest.

WALDSTERBEN (dying forest syndrome) term used to describe the environmental pollution which has decimated Germany's forests.

WALLFAHRT pilgrimage.

WASSERBURG castle surrounded by a moat.

WECHSEL exchange.

WEIMAR REPUBLIC (*Weimarische Republik*) parliamentary democracy established in 1918 which collapsed with Hitler's assumption of power in 1933.

WEINGUT wine-producing estate.

WEINSTUBE wine bar.

WELF dynastic rivals of Hohenstaufens in Germany and Italy. Descendants became Electors of Hannover, and subsequently kings of Great Britain.

WENDE literally "turning point" – the term used to describe the events of November 1989 and after.

WETTIN dynasty chiefly responsible for pushing Germany's frontiers eastwards from the tenth century, becoming Electors of Saxony in 1423 and ruling the province and the Thuringian principalities until 1918. The Saxe-Coburg line provided monarchs for several countries; renamed as Windsor, one branch is the current British royal family.

WIESE field, meadow.

WILHELMINE (*Wilhelminisch*) pertaining to the epoch of the Second Reich (1871–1918).

WIRTSCHAFT, WIRTSHAUS tavern.

WITTELSBACH dynasty which ruled Bavaria from 1180 to 1918; a branch held the Palatinate Electorate, while the family often held several bishoprics, notably the Archbishop-Electorate of Cologne.

ZAHNRADBAHN rack railway.

ZEITSCHRIFT magazine.

ZEITUNG newspaper.

ZEUGHAUS arsenal.

ZIMMER room.

Acronyms

BRD (Bundesrepublik Deutschlands) official name of West German state (1949–90) and of the unified Germany since 1990.

CDU (Christlich Demokratische Union) Christian Democratic Party.

CSU (Christlich Soziale Union) Bavarian-only counterpart of CDU, generally more right-wing in outlook.

DB (Deutsche Bahn, formerly Deutsche Bundesbahn) national rail company retaining the logo of its West German predecessor under a modified name.

DDR (Deutsche Demokratische Republik) the Communist East German state, 1949–90.

DJH (Deutsches Jugendherbergswerk) German Youth Hostel Association.

FDP (Freie Demokratische Partei) Free Democratic Party.

GDR (German Democratic Republic) English version of DDR.

NSDAP (National Sozialistische Deutsche Arbeiterpartei, "National Socialist German Workers' Party") official name for the Nazis, totalitarian rulers of Germany in the Third Reich, 1933–45.

PDS (Partei des Demokratischen Sozialismus) repackaged former SED.

SED (Sozialistische Einheitspartei Deutschlands) Socialist Unity Party of Germany, the permanent governing party of the GDR, formed in 1946 as a union of the SPD and Communists in the Russian zone of occupation.

SPD (Sozialdemokratische Partei Deutschlands) Social Democratic Party.

ZOB (Zentral-Omnibus-Bahnhof) main bus station.

Rough Guides

advertiser

Rough Guides travel...

UK & Ireland
Britain
Devon & Cornwall
Dublin
Edinburgh
England
Ireland
Lake District
London
London mini guide
London Restaurants
London & SE England, Walks in
Scotland
Scottish Highlands & Islands
Wales

Europe
Algarve
Amsterdam
Andalucía
Austria
Baltic States
Barcelona
Belgium & Luxembourg
Berlin
Brittany & Normandy
Bruges & Ghent
Brussels
Budapest
Bulgaria
Copenhagen
Corfu
Corsica
Costa Brava
Crete
Croatia
Cyprus
Czech & Slovak Republics
Dodecanese & East Aegean
Dordogne & The Lot
Europe
First-Time Europe
Florence
France
Germany
Greece
Greek Islands
Hungary
Ibiza & Formentera
Iceland
Ionian Islands
Italy
Languedoc & Roussillon
Lisbon
The Loire
Madeira
Madrid
Mallorca
Malta & Gozo
Menorca
Moscow
Netherlands
Norway
Paris
Paris Mini Guide
Poland
Portugal
Prague
Provence & the Côte d'Azur
Pyrenees
Romania
Rome
Sardinia
Scandinavia
Sicily
Slovenia
Spain
St Petersburg
Sweden
Switzerland
Tenerife & La Gomera
Turkey
Tuscany & Umbria
Venice & The Veneto
Vienna

Asia
Bali & Lombok
Bangkok
Beijing
Cambodia
China
First-Time Asia
Goa
Hong Kong & Macau
India
Indonesia
Japan
Laos
Malaysia, Singapore & Brunei
Nepal
Philippines
Singapore
South India
Southeast Asia
Thailand
Thailand Beaches & Islands
Tokyo
Vietnam

Australasia
Australia
Gay & Lesbian Australia
Melbourne
New Zealand
Sydney

North America
Alaska
Baltic States
Big Island of Hawaii
Boston
California
Canada
Chicago
Florida
Grand Canyon
Hawaii
Honolulu
Las Vegas
Los Angeles
Maui
Miami & the Florida Keys
Montréal
New England
New Orleans
New York City
New York City Mini Guide
New York Restaurants
Pacific Northwest
Rocky Mountains
San Francisco
San Francisco Restaurants
Seattle
Skiing & Snowboarding in North America
Southwest USA
Toronto
USA
Vancouver
Washington DC
Yosemite

Caribbean & Latin America
Antigua & Barbuda
Argentina
Bahamas
Barbados
Belize
Bolivia
Brazil
Caribbean
Central America
Chile
Costa Rica
Cuba
Dominican Republic
Ecuador
First-Time Latin America
Guatemala
Jamaica
Maya World
Mexico
Peru
St Lucia
South America
Trinidad & Tobago

Rough Guides are available from good bookstores worldwide. New titles are published every month. Check www.roughguides.com for the latest news.

small print and
Index

A Rough Guide to Rough Guides

In the summer of 1981, Mark Ellingham, a recent graduate from Bristol University, was travelling round Greece and couldn't find a guidebook that really met his needs. On the one hand there were the student guides, insistent on saving every last cent, and on the other the heavyweight cultural tomes whose authors seemed to have spent more time in a research library than lounging away the afternoon at a taverna or on the beach.

In a bid to avoid getting a job, Mark and a small group of writers set about creating their own guidebook. It was a guide to Greece that aimed to combine a journalistic approach to description with a thoroughly practical approach to travellers' needs – a guide that would incorporate culture, history and contemporary insights with a critical edge, together with up-to-date, value-for-money listings. Back in London, Mark and the team finished their Rough Guide, as they called it, and talked Routledge into publishing the book.

That first *Rough Guide to Greece*, published in 1982, was a student scheme that became a publishing phenomenon. The immediate success of the book – with numerous reprints and a Thomas Cook prize shortlisting – spawned a series that rapidly covered dozens of destinations. Rough Guides had a ready market among low-budget backpackers, but soon also acquired a much broader and older readership that relished Rough Guides' wit and inquisitiveness as much as their enthusiastic, critical approach. Everyone wants value for money, but not at any price.

Rough Guides soon began supplementing the "rougher" information about hostels and low-budget listings with the kind of detail on restaurants and quality hotels that independent-minded visitors on any budget might expect, whether on business in New York or trekking in Thailand.

These days the guides – distributed worldwide by the Penguin group – offer recommendations from shoestring to luxury and cover more than 200 destinations around the globe, including almost every country in the Americas and Europe, more than half of Africa and most of Asia and Australasia. Our ever-growing team of authors and photographers is spread all over the world, particularly in Europe, the USA and Australia.

In 1994, we published the *Rough Guide to World Music* and *Rough Guide to Classical Music*; and a year later the *Rough Guide to the Internet*. All three books have become benchmark titles in their fields – which encouraged us to expand into other areas of publishing, mainly around popular culture. Rough Guides now publish:

- Travel guides to more than 200 worldwide destinations
- Dictionary phrasebooks to 22 major languages
- History guides ranging from Ireland to Islam
- Maps printed on rip-proof and waterproof Polyart™ paper
- Music guides running the gamut from Opera to Elvis
- Restaurant guides to London, New York and San Francisco
- Reference books on topics as diverse as the Weather and Shakespeare
- Sports guides from Formula 1 to Man Utd
- Pop culture books from *Lord of the Rings* to Cult TV
- World Music CDs in association with World Music Network

Visit **www.roughguides.com** to see our latest publications.

Rough Guide credits

Desk editors: Andy Turner and Alison Murchie
Layout: Umesh Aggarwal
Cartography: Rajesh Mishra, J.P. Mishra, Manish Chandra, Rajesh Chhibber
Picture research: Jj Luck
Proofreaders: Madhulita Mohapatra, Hemant Sareen
Editorial: **London** Martin Dunford, Kate Berens, Helena Smith, Claire Saunders, Geoff Howard, Ruth Blackmore, Gavin Thomas, Polly Thomas, Richard Lim, Lucy Ratcliffe, Clifton Wilkinson, Fran Sandham, Sally Schafer, Alexander Mark Rogers, Karoline Densley, Ella O'Donnell, Andrew Lockett, Joe Staines, Duncan Clark, Peter Buckley, Matthew Milton; **New York** Andrew Rosenberg, Richard Koss, Yuki Takagaki, Hunter Slaton, Chris Barsanti, Thomas Kohnstamm, Steven Horak
Design & Layout: **London** Helen Prior, Dan May, Diana Jarvis; **Delhi** Madhulita Mohapatra, Umesh Aggarwal, Ajay Verma
Production: Julia Bovis, John McKay, Sophie Hewat
Cartography: **London** Maxine Repath, Ed Wright, Katie Lloyd-Jones; **Delhi** Manish Chandra, Rajesh Chhibber, Jai Prakash Mishra, Ashutosh Bharti, Rajesh Mishra, Animesh Pathak
Cover art direction: Louise Boulton
Picture research: Sharon Martins, Mark Thomas, Jj Luck
Online: **New York** Jennifer Gold, Cree Lawson, Suzanne Welles; **Delhi** Manik Chauhan, Amarjyoti Dutta, Narender Kumar
Marketing & Publicity: **London** Richard Trillo, Niki Smith, David Wearn, Chloë Roberts, Demelza Dallow; **New York** Geoff Colquitt, David Wechsler, Megan Kennedy
Finance: Gary Singh
Manager India: Punita Singh
Series editor: Mark Ellingham
PA to Managing Director: Julie Sanderson
Managing Director: Kevin Fitzgerald

Publishing information

This sixth edition published April 2004 by **Rough Guides Ltd**,
80 Strand, London WC2R 0RL.
345 Hudson St, 4th Floor,
New York, NY 10014, USA.
Distributed by the Penguin Group
Penguin Books Ltd,
80 Strand, London WC2R 0RL
Penguin Putnam, Inc.
375 Hudson Street, NY 10014, USA
Penguin Books Australia Ltd,
487 Maroondah Highway, PO Box 257,
Ringwood, Victoria 3134, Australia
Penguin Books Canada Ltd,
10 Alcorn Avenue, Toronto, Ontario,
Canada M4V 1E4
Penguin Books (NZ) Ltd,
182–190 Wairau Road, Auckland 10,
New Zealand
Typeset in Bembo and Helvetica to an original design by Henry Iles.

Printed in Italy by LegoPrint S.p.A

1104pp includes index
A catalogue record for this book is available from the British Library

ISBN 1-84353-293-x

1 3 5 7 9 8 6 4 2

Help us update

We've gone to a lot of effort to ensure that the second edition of **The Rough Guide to Germany** is accurate and up-to-date. However, things change – places get "discovered", opening hours are notoriously fickle, restaurants and rooms raise prices or lower standards. If you feel we've got it wrong or left something out, we'd like to know, and if you can remember the address, the price, the time, the phone number, so much the better.

We'll credit all contributions, and send a copy of the next edition (or any other Rough Guide if you prefer) for the best letters. Everyone who writes to us and isn't already a subscriber will receive a copy of our full-colour thrice-yearly newsletter. Please mark letters: **"Rough Guide to Germany Update"** and send to: Rough Guides, 80 Strand, London WC2R 0RL, or Rough Guides, 4th Floor, 345 Hudson St, New York, NY 10014. Or send an email to **mail@roughguides.com**

Have your questions answered and tell others about your trip at **www.roughguides.atinfopop.com**

Acknowledgements

On this edition, special thanks are due to the Rough Guides' editorial team of Claire Saunders, Alison Murchie and Andy Turner, who have all been a pleasure to work with; to the cartographers Manish Chandra, Rajesh Chhibber, Jai Prakesh Mishra, Ashutosh Bharti, Rajesh Mishra, Animesh Pathak and Katie Lloyd-Jones for a stunning new set of maps; and to Janice and Steve Hopwood, for their boundless hospitality in Munich. Thanks also to Umesh Aggarwal for typesetting; to Jj Luck for picture research; to Jules Brown for last-minute editing; to Madhu Mohapatra for proofreading; and to Vicky Weller, Astrid Ganssen, Dr Stephan v. Paczynski, Helen McLachlan and Ian McLachlan.

Readers' letters

Thanks to all the readers who wrote in with helpful comments and suggestions about the last edition. Apologies to any whose names have been omitted or spelt wrongly.

Brenna B. Aileo, Roger Beadle, John Bonnin, Chris Clayton, Ellen Conway and Peter Close, Wendy Crozier, Susan Dennis-Jones, Margaret Donsbach, Dave Eatom, Michael Field, Stefan Hagel, Carlos Hood, John Johnson, Mike Jory, Jennifer Prestwich, Yizhar Regev, Ilse Rudolf, Pat Ruthven, H.H. Saffery, Robert Sandham, Karen Smith, Kevin Stannard, Haidee Steudler, K. Tan, Neda Ulaby, Anne Vaughan, Tracey Wallman, Mary and Gavin Walmsley, Anita and John Weeks, John Wooliscroft.

Photo credits

Cover credits
Main front picture: Römer © Powerstock
Front top picture: Maypole © Robert Harding
Front lower: Limburg © Getty
Back top picture: Sanssouci Castle © Robert Harding
Back lower picture: Ramsau © Robert Harding

Introduction
Lübeck Altstadt © Steve Raymer/CORBIS
Crocus field and Karwendl Mountains, Upper Bavarian Alps © Edmund Nägele
Gilded sunburst, Park Sanssouci, Potsdam © Brandenburg TMB
Half-timbered houses, Goslar © Bo Zaunders/CORBIS
Street Café © Presse- und Informationsamt des Landes Berlin/J. Gläser
Memorial artwork on the Appellplatz at Dachau concentration camp © Ira Nowinski/CORBIS
Buildings at Dusk, Potsdamer Platz, Berlin © Bryan Reinhart/Masterfile
Gartentheater of the Grosser Garten, Herrenhausen, Hannover © Dave Bartruff/CORBIS
Watzmann peaks, the Berchtesgadener Land © Ric Ergenbright/CORBIS
Passau, view of the Altstadt from the River Inn © GW McLachlan
Kochelsee boathouse in winter © Greogor Schmid/CORBIS
Pergamonmuseum, Berlin © Presse- und Informationsamt des Landes Berlin/C.Bach

Things not to miss
01. Bamberg © Edmund Nägele
02. Park Sanssouci, Potsdam © Peter Wilson
03. Ceiling fresco in the Wieskirche © GW McLachlan
04. Bamberg's Corpus Christi © GW McLachlan
05. Burg Eltz © GW McLachlan
06. *Moor with a Basket of Emeralds*, The Grünes Gewölbe, Dresden © Grünes Gewölbe, Staatliche Kunstsammlungen Dresden
07. Skyline at dawn, Frankfurt am Main © Jeremy Woodhouse/Masterfile
08. Walpurgisnacht, Harz mountains © Harzer Verkehrsverband
09. Wutachtalbahn, southern Black Forest © GW McLachlan
10. Chalk Cliffs of Rügen © Jeremy Woodhouse/Masterfile
11. Memorial to Goethe and Schiller, Weimar © Thüringer Tourismus GmbH
12. Fastnet in Rottweil © GW McLachlan
13. Pfalbauten at Unteruhldigen on the Bodensee © GW McLachlan
14. Bakery and Café in Rathausplatz, Berchtesgaden © Adam Woolfitt/CORBIS
15. Kuchen- und Brunnenfest, Schwäbisch Hall © GW McLachlan
16. A beer garden, Munich © Franz-Marc Frei/CORBIS
17. Hiking on Zugspitze overlooking Alps © Ric Ergenbright/CORBIS
18. View of the Schloss and the Altastadt from the Philosophenweg, Heidelberg © GW McLachlan
19. Christkindlesmarkt, Nürnberg © Nürnberg, Congress & Tourismus Zentrale
20. Vineyard in the Mosel valley © Bo Zaunders/CORBIS
21. The Friedrichsbad in Baden-Baden © Friedrichsbad, Baden-Baden
22. The Residenz, Würzburg © GW McLachlan
23. Charlemagne's throne in the Dom, Aachen © Adam Woolfitt/CORBIS
24. The Murg valley at Forbach, Black Forest © GW McLachlan
25. Aerial view of city centre and River Alster, Hamburg © Edmund Nägele
26. Ekkehard II and Uta, The Dom, Naumburg © Dorling Kindersley
27. Carving on the Stiftsherrnhaus, Hameln – detail © GW McLachlan
28. Marksburg overlooking the River Rhine © Wolfgang Kaehler/CORBIS
29. Oktoberfest © Larry Fisher/Masterfile
30. The Dom and the River Rhine, Cologne © Miles Ertman/Masterfile
31. Bundestag dome in Berlin by Norman Foster © B Morandi/Robert Harding
32. St Michaelis, Hildesheim © Archivo Iconografico, S.A./CORBIS
33. Historische Wurstküche, Regensburg © Historische Wurstküche, Regensburg
34. Porta Nigra, Trier © GW McLachlan
35. Schloss Neuschwanstein, Hohenschwangau © Edmund Nägele

Black and white photos

Plönlein, Rothenburg ob der Tauber © Edmund Nägele (p.58)
Dinkelsbühl © Miles Ertman/Masterfile (p.105)
Augsburg; Zeughaus facade © Adam Woolfitt/CORBIS (p.169)
The Neue Staatsgalerie, Stuttgart © N. Setchfield (p.238)
Tower of the Münster, Ulm © GW McLachlan (p.268)
The Münster, Überlingen © GW McLachlan (p.312)
The Ernst-Ludwig-Haus, Darmstadt © Ulli Emig (p.368)
Man Walking to the Sky sculpture, Kassel © GW McLachlan (p.400)
The Dom, Worms © Worms Tourist Info (p.430)
Bad Münster am Stein-Ebernburg - Rheingrafenstein © GW McLachlan (p.470)
The Schwebebahn, Wuppertal © Peter Bosbach (p.488)
Monschau © GW McLachlan (p.544)
Lüneburg from the Wasserturm © GW McLachlan (p.578)
Böttcherstrasse in Bremen © Lee Snider/CORBIS (p.585)
The Alsterarkaden, Hamburg © GW McLachlan (p.658)
View from above of red-roofed houses in Lübeck © Steve Raymer/CORBIS (p.687)
View from the Marienkirche over Stralsünd towards Rugen © GW McLaclan (p.710)
Wiecker Klappbrücke, in Wieck, Greifswald © Press Office of the Hanseatic City Greifswald (p.740)
Brandenburger Tor (Brandenburg Gate), Berlin © International Stock/Robert Harding (p.748)
Heads of the Dying Warriors by Andreas Schlüter in the courtyard of the Zeughaus © Deutsches Historisches Museum (p.762)
Half-timbered buildings, Quedlinburg © Carmen Redondo/CORBIS (p.826)
Cantilevered balconies, Bauhausgebäude, Dessau © Michael Jenner/Robert Harding (p.861)
The Wartburg, Eisenach © DZT/Eichberger, Eric (p.882)
Oberweissbacher Bergbahn, Obstfelderschmiede © G. Kretzschmar (p.929)
River Elbe, Saxon Switzerland © Wolfgang Kaehler/CORBIS (p.934)
Altes Rathaus, Leipzig © Richard Klune/CORBIS (p.941)

Index

Map entries are in **colour.**

INDEX

C

D

E

F

G

H

I

J

K

L

M

N

O

P

Q

R

S

T